Department for Economic and Social
Information and Policy Analysis
Statistics Division

Département de l'information économique
et sociale et de l'analyse des politiques
Division de statistique

Statistical Yearbook
Forty-first issue

Annuaire statistique
Quarante et unième édition

1994
Data available as of
31 March 1996

Données disponibles
au 31 mars 1996

United Nations / Nations Unies   New York, 1996

Note

The designations employed and the presentation of material in this publication do not imply the expression of any opinion whatsoever on the part of the Secretariat of the United Nations concerning the legal status of any country, territory, city or area or of its authorities, or concerning the delimitation of its frontiers or boundaries.

In general, statistics contained in the present publication are those available to the United Nations Secretariat up to March 1996 and refer to 1994 or earlier. They reflect country nomenclature in use in 1995.

The term "country" as used in this publication also refers, as appropriate, to territories or areas.

The designations "developed" and "developing" are intended for statistical convenience and do not necessarily express a judgment about the stage reached by a particular country or area in the development process.

Symbols of United Nations documents are composed of capital letters combined with figures.

Note

Les appellations employées dans la présente publication et la présentation des données qui y figurent n'impliquent de la part du Secrétariat de l'Organisation des Nations Unies aucune prise de position quant au statut juridique des pays, territoires, villes ou zones ou de leurs autorités, ni quant au tracé de leurs frontières ou limites.

En règle générale, les statistiques contenues dans la présente publication sont celles dont disposait le Secrétariat de l'Organisation des Nations Unies jusqu'à mars 1996 et portent sur la période finissant à 1994. Elles reflètent la nomenclature des pays en vigueur à l'époque.

Le terme "pays", tel qu'il est utilisé ci-après, peut également désigner des territoires ou des zones.

Les appellations "développées" et "en développement" sont employées à des fins exclusivement statistiques et n'expriment pas nécessairement un jugement quant au niveau de développement atteint par tel pays ou telle région.

Les cotes des documents de l'Organisation des Nations Unies se composent de lettres majuscules et de chiffres.

ST/ESA/STAT/SER.S/17

UNITED NATIONS PUBLICATION
Sales No. E/F.96.XVII.1

PUBLICATION DES NATIONS UNIES
Numéro de vente : E/F.96.XVII.1

ISBN 92-1-061167-5
ISSN 0082-8459

Inquiries should be directed to:
SALES SECTION
PUBLISHING DIVISION
UNITED NATIONS
NEW YORK 10017
USA

Adresser toutes demandes de renseignements à la :
SECTION DES VENTES
DIVISION DES PUBLICATIONS
NATIONS UNIES
NEW YORK 10017
USA

e-mail: publications@un.org
Internet: http://www.un.org/Pubs

Preface

This is the forty-first issue of the United Nations *Statistical Yearbook*, prepared by the Statistics Division, Department for Economic and Social Information and Policy Analysis of the United Nations Secretariat, since 1948. The present issue contains series covering, in general, 1984–1993 or 1985–1994, using statistics available to the Statistics Division up to 31 December 1995.

The *Yearbook* is based on data compiled by the Statistics Division from over 40 different international and national sources. These include the United Nations Statistics Division in the fields of national accounts, industry, energy, transport and international trade; the United Nations Statistics Division and Population Division in the field of demographic statistics; and data provided by over 20 offices of the United Nations system and international organizations in other specialized fields.

United Nations agencies and other international organizations which furnished data are listed under "Statistical sources and references" at the end of the *Yearbook*. Acknowledgement is gratefully made to them for this generous cooperation in providing data.

The Statistics Division also publishes the *Monthly Bulletin of Statistics* [25]*, which provides a valuable complement to the *Yearbook* covering current international economic statistics for most countries and areas of the world. Each month, the *Bulletin* also provides quarterly data of world and regional aggregates. Subscribers to the *Monthly Bulletin of Statistics* may also access MBS On-line via the World Wide Web on Internet. MBS On-line allows time-sensitive statistics to reach users much faster than the traditional print publication. Further information on MBS On-line can be accessed at http://www.un.org/Depts/unsd/.

The present issue of the *Yearbook* reflects a phased programme of major changes in its organization and presentation, undertaken in 1990, which until then was relatively unchanged since the first issue, in 1948. This programme of changes was adopted in response to the continuing long-term expansion of international data available and demanded by users, in terms of country and subject-matter coverage and level of detail, and the more recent impact of new electronic data processing technologies on data compilation and typesetting. One result of this process has been to reduce the total number of tables from 140 in the 37th issue to 84 in the present issue. An index is continued in the present issue.

---

* Numbers in brackets refer to numbered entries in the section "Statistical sources and references" at the end of this book.

Préface

La présente édition est la quarante et unième de l'*Annuaire statistique* des Nations Unies, établi depuis 1948 par la Division de statistique du Département de l'information économique et sociale et de l'analyse des politiques du Secrétariat de l'Organisation des Nations Unies. Elle contient des séries qui portent d'une manière générale sur la période 1984-1993 ou 1985-1994 et pour lesquelles ont été utilisées les informations dont disposait la Division de statistique au 31 décembre 1995.

L'*Annuaire* est établi à partir des données que la Division de statistique a recueillies auprès de plus de 40 sources différentes, internationales et nationales. Ces sources sont : la Division de statistique du Secrétariat de l'Organisation des Nations Unies pour ce qui concerne les comptabilités nationales, l'industrie, l'énergie, les transports et le commerce international; la Division de statistique et la Division de la population du Secrétariat de l'Organisation des Nations Unies pour les statistiques démographiques; et plus de 20 bureaux du système des Nations Unies et d'organisations internationales pour les autres domaines spécialisés.

Les institutions spécialisées des Nations Unies et les autres organisations internationales qui ont fourni des données sont énumérées dans la section "Sources et références statistiques" figurant à la fin de l'ouvrage. Les auteurs de l'*Annuaire statistique* les remercient de leur généreuse coopération.

La Division de Statistique publie également le *Bulletin Mensuel de Statistiques* [25]*, qui est un complément intéressant à l'*Annuaire Statistique* qui couvre les statistiques économiques courantes sur la plupart des pays et zones du monde. Chaque mois le *Bulletin* fournit également des données trimestrielles sur des aggrégats significatifs, au niveau du monde et des grandes régions. Les abonnés au *Bulletin Mensuel de Statistiques* ont aussi à leur disposition "BMS en ligne", accessible sur Internet par le "World Wide Web". Grâce à "BMS en ligne" les utilisateurs disposent plus rapidement des données conjonctuelles que par la voie traditionnelle de la publication imprimée. Des informations supplémentaires sur "BMS en ligne" sont disponibles sur http://www.un.org/Depts/unsd/.

La présente édition de l'*Annuaire* tient compte des importantes transformations qui, depuis 1990, ont été apportées par étapes successives à son organisation et à sa présentation, lesquelles étaient restées pratiquement inchangées depuis la première édition parue en 1948. Ces modifications ont été adoptées en réponse à la croissance continue et à long terme des données internationales disponibles et demandées par les utilisateurs, par pays et par sujet, avec une précision toujours plus grande, et compte tenu de

---

* Les chiffres entre crochets se réfèrent aux entrées numérotées dans la liste des sources et références statistiques à la fin de l'ouvrage.

Recognizing the tremendous worldwide growth in recent years in the use of microcomputers and the corresponding interest in obtaining statistics in machine-readable form for further study and analysis by users, the thirty-eighth issue of the *Yearbook* was published for the first time in compact disk (CD-ROM) for IBM-compatible microcomputers, in addition to the traditional book form, followed by the thirty-ninth and forthieth issues in 1994[1] and 1996[2], respectively. The present issue will also be published in CD-ROM in 1997. Ad hoc or standing orders for the *Yearbook* in both hard copy and CD-ROM are available from United Nations Publications sales offices in New York and Geneva. A full list of machine-readable products in statistics available from the United Nations Statistics Division may be obtained on request to the Statistics Division at the United Nations Secretariat, New York. The Division has also prepared an inventory of over 100 international statistical databases with some form of public access, *StatBase Locator on Disk—UNSTAT's Guide to International Computerized Statistical Databases*.[3]

The organization of the *Yearbook*, described in the Introduction below in more detail, consists of four parts. Part One, World and Region Summary, consists of key world and regional aggregates and totals and is essentially unchanged from previous issues. In the remaining parts, the main subjectmatter is mainly presented according to countries or areas, with in some cases world and regions aggregates also shown. Parts two, three and four cover, respectively, population and social topics, national economic activity and international economic relations. The organization of the population and social topics generally follows the arrangement of subjectmatter in the United Nations framework for integration of demographic and social statistics (FSDS) [56]; economic activity is taken up according to the classes of the United Nations International Standard Industrial Classification of All Economic Activities (ISIC) [46]; and tables on international economic relations cover merchandise trade, international tourism (a major factor in international trade in services and balance of payments) and financial transactions including development assistance. Each chapter includes brief technical notes on statistical sources and methods for the tables in that chapter. Complete references to sources and related methodological publications are provided at the end of the *Yearbook* in the section "Statistical sources and references".

Annex I provides complete information on country and area nomenclature, and regional and other groupings used in the *Yearbook*, and annex II on conversion coefficients and factors used in various tables. Other symbols and conventions used in the *Yearbook* are shown in the section "Explanatory notes", preceding the Introduction.

Important changes in the last two issues of the *Yearbook* include extensive revisions to the list of basic commodity

l'impact plus récent des nouvelles techniques informatiques sur la compilation des données et la composition automatique des textes. Ce processus a ainsi permis de ramener le nombre de tableau de 140 dans la trente-septième édition à 84 dans l'édition actuelle. L'index (en anglais seulement) fourni pour la première fois dans l'édition précédente figure également dans celle-ci.

En raison de l'expansion extraordinaire que la micro-informatique a connue ces dernières années et de l'intérêt croissant que suscite la présentation de statistiques sur des supports lisibles en machine et exploitables directement par l'utilisateur, la trente-huitième édition de l'*Annuaire* a été publiée pour la première fois sur disque compact (CD/ROM) pour micro-ordinateurs IBM et compatibles. Les trente-neuvième et quarantième éditions comprenaient également des versions CD-ROM (publiées respectivement en 1994[1] et 1996[2]). La présente édition sera également publiée sur CD/ROM en 1997. Les commandes individuelles et les abonnements à l'*Annuaire statistique* (édition imprimée ou sur CD/ROM) peuvent être adressées aux bureaux de vente des publications des Nations Unies à New York et à Genève. La Division de statistique du Secrétariat de l'Organisation des Nations Unies à New York fournit sur demande la liste complète de produits statistiques disponibles sur supports lisibles en machine. La Division publie également *StatBase Locator on Disk — UNSTAT's Guide to International Computerized Databases*,[3] inventaire de plus de 100 bases de données statistiques internationales accessibles au public.

Le plan de l'*Annuaire*, qui est décrit ci-après de manière plus détaillée dans l'introduction, comprend quatre parties. La première partie, "Aperçu mondial et régional", qui se compose des principaux agrégats et totaux aux niveaux mondial et régional, est reprise presque sans changement des éditions précédentes; les trois autres sont consacrées à la population et aux questions sociales (deuxième partie), à l'activité économique nationale (troisième partie) et aux relations économiques internationales (quatrième partie). L'organisation de la deuxième partie, "Population et questions sociales", suit généralement le plan adopté par l'ONU pour intégrer les statistiques économiques et sociales [56]; dans la troisième partie, l'activité économique est présentée conformément aux catégories adoptées par l'ONU dans la *Classification internationale type, par industrie, de toutes les branches d'activité économique* [46]; les tableaux de la quatrième partie, consacrée aux relations économiques internationales, portent sur le commerce des marchandises, le tourisme international (élément essentiel du secteur international des services et balance des paiements) et les opérations financières, y compris l'aide au développement. Chaque chapitre comprend une brève note technique sur les sources et méthodes statistiques utilisées pour les tableaux du chapitre. On trouvera à la fin de l'*Annuaire*, dans la section "Sources et références statistiques", des références complètes aux sources et publications méthodologiques connexes.

tables in part three, reviewed in consultation with FAO. A substantial number of basic commodities has been deleted and replaced by commodities of more contemporary importance in agriculture and manufacturing. New tables on telecommunications and national accounts have been added to improve and update coverage in these key areas. The complete list of tables added and omitted from the last issue of the *Yearbook* is given in annex III.

Another modification introduced in the last two issues and continued in this *Yearbook* is to exclude tables for which new data are not available but to retain them in the table of contents for publication in a later issue as new data are compiled and published by the collecting agency. However, all of these tables will be retained in the CD-ROM version of the *Yearbook*.

The new format adopted for typesetting tables in the *Yearbook* was developed in cooperation with the Graphic Presentation Unit of the United Nations Secretariat, to meet new challenges and design opportunities offered by microcomputer "desktop publishing" technologies. Since the disappearance in the 1970s of mechanical typesetting, photocomposition techniques and equipment and in turn table design for statistics have become much more flexible. As a result, it is no longer possible to expect data suppliers for the *Yearbook* to follow a standard design format, nor economically feasible to reset the tables, which are provided in a wide variety of tabulation and database formats, except using microcomputer techniques. This issue of the *Yearbook* continues to make extensive use of microcomputer database, spreadsheet and typesetting technologies, and an "open" table design, which is easier to photocompose than enclosed designs using horizontal and vertical rules and boxes common to the mechanical era.

As described more fully in the Introduction below, every attempt has been made to ensure that the series contained in the *Yearbook* are sufficiently comparable to provide a reliable general description of economic and social topics throughout the world. Nevertheless, the reader should carefully consult the footnotes and technical notes for any given table for explanations of general limitations of series presented and specific limitations affecting particular data items. Complete information concerning the definitions and concepts used and limitations of the data are provided in the section "Statistical sources and references" at the end of the *Yearbook*. Readers interested in more detailed figures than those shown in the present publication, and in further information on the full range of internationally assembled statistics in specialized fields, should also consult the specialized publications listed in that section.

L'annexe I donne des renseignements complets sur la nomenclature des pays et des zones et sur la façon dont ceux-ci ont été regroupés pour former les régions et autres entités géographiques utilisées dans l'*Annuaire*; l'annexe II fournit des renseignements sur les coefficients et facteurs de conversion employés dans les différents tableaux. Les divers symboles et conventions utilisés dans l'*Annuaire* sont présentés dans la section "Notes explicatives" qui précède l'introduction.

Entre autres modifications importantes apportées à l'édition précédente de l'*Annuaire*, la liste de produits de base figurant dans la troisième partie a été révisée et largement remaniée en liaison avec la FAO. De nombreux produits ont été supprimés et remplacés par des produits plus d'actualité dans les secteurs agricoles et industriels. De nouveaux tableaux sur les télécommunications et les comptabilités nationales ont été ajoutés afin d'améliorer et d'actualiser la portée des statistiques dans ces secteurs essentiels. La liste complète des tableaux ajoutés et supprimés depuis la dernière édition de l'*Annuaire* figure à l'annexe III.

Autre modification, déjà introduite dans l'édition précédente, les tableaux pour lesquels on ne dispose d'aucune donnée nouvelle ont été omis, mais ils figurent toujours dans la table des matières et seront repris dans une prochaine édition à mesure que des données nouvelles seront dépouillées et publiées par l'office statistique d'origine. Tous les tableaux qui figuraient dans la trente-neuvième édition seront cependant repris dans la quarantième édition publiée sur CD/ROM.

La nouvelle présentation adoptée pour la composition automatique des tableaux de l'*Annuaire* a été mise au point en coopération avec l'Unité de présentation graphique du Secrétariat de l'ONU, afin de satisfaire de nouvelles demandes et d'utiliser les possibilités offertes par les techniques de publication assistée par micro-ordinateur. Depuis la disparition de la composition mécanique dans les années 70, les techniques et le matériel de photocomposition — donc la conception des tableaux statistiques — peuvent varier beaucoup plus librement. En conséquence, il ne faut plus s'attendre à ce que les fournisseurs de données suivent un mode de présentation type et il n'est plus rentable de recomposer les tableaux qui utilisent des présentations et des modèles de bases de données très diverses, sinon en recourant à la micro-informatique. La présente édition de l'*Annuaire* continue à utiliser largement une base de données, un tableur et des techniques de composition empruntés à la micro-informatique, et à adopter un mode de tabulation "ouvert" qui convient mieux à la photocomposition que les modes fermés faisant appel à des lignes horizontales et verticales et à des encadrés, procédé courant à l'époque de la composition mécanique.

Of course much more remains to be done to improve the *Yearbook* in its scope, coverage, timeliness and design, and in its technical notes. The process is inevitably an evolutionary one. Comments on the present *Yearbook* and its future evolution are welcome and should be addressed to the Director, United Nations Statistics Division, New York 10017 USA, or via e-mail to statistics@un.org .

Comme il est précisé ci-après dans l'introduction, aucun effort n'a été épargné afin que les séries figurant dans l'*Annuaire* soient suffisamment comparables pour fournir une description générale fiable de la situation économique et sociale dans le monde entier. Néanmoins, le lecteur devra consulter avec soins les renvois individuels et les notes techniques de chaque tableau pour y trouver l'explication des limites générales imposées aux séries présentées et des limites particulières propres à certains types de données. On trouvera à la fin de l'ouvrage, dans la section "Sources et références statistiques", des renseignements complets concernant les définitions et concepts utilisés et les limites des données. Les lecteurs qui souhaitent avoir des chiffres plus détaillés que ceux figurant dans le présent volume ou qui désirent se procurer des renseignements sur la gamme complète des statistiques qui ont été compilées à l'échelon international dans tel ou tel domaine particulier devraient consulter les publications énumérées dans la section "Sources et références statistiques".

Il reste sans doute beaucoup à faire pour mettre l'*Annuaire* pleinement à jour en ce qui concerne son champ, sa couverture, sa mise à jour et sa conception générale, ainsi que ses notes techniques. Il s'agit là inévitablement d'un processus évolutif. Les observations sur la présente édition de l'*Annuaire* et les modifications suggérées pour l'avenir seront reçues avec intérêt et doivent être adressées au Directeur de la Division de statistique de l'ONU, New York, N.Y. 10017 (États-Unis d'Amérique), ou e-mail à statistics@un.org .

[1]   *Statistical Yearbook, thirty-ninth issue, CD-ROM* (United Nations publication, Sales No. E.95.XVII.5).

[2]   *Statistical Yearbook, fortieth issue, CD-ROM*, (United Nations publication, Sales No. E.96.XVII.7).

[3]   United Nations publication, Sales No. E.94.XVII.8 (issued on one 3 1/2" diskette for IBM-compatible microcomputers).

[1]   *L'Annuaire statistique, la trente-neuvième édition sur CD/ROM* (Publication des Nations Unies, numéro de vente E.95.XVII.5).

[2]   *L'Annuaire statistique, quarantième édition sur CD-ROM* (Publication des Nations Unies, numéro de vente E.96.XVII.7).

[2]   Publication des Nations Unies, numéro de vente E.94.XVII.8 (sur une disquette de 3,5 inches pour micro-ordinateurs IBM et compatibles).

Contents

Preface. iii
Explanatory notes xiv
Introduction 1

Part One
World and Region Summary

I. *World and region summary*
  Tables 1-7 9
  Technical notes 29

Part Two
Population and Social Statistics

II. *Population and human settlements*
  Table 8 35
  Technical notes 47
III. *Education and literacy*
  Tables 9-11 49
  Technical notes 80
IV. *Health and child-bearing; nutrition*
  Tables 12 and 13 83
  Technical notes 98
V. *Culture and communications*
  Tables 14-19 101
  Technical notes 145

Part Three
Economic Activity

VI. *National accounts and industrial production*
  Tables 20-26 149
  Technical notes 226
VII. *Financial statistics*
  Tables 27 and 28 229
  Technical notes 241
VIII. *Labour force*
  Tables 29 and 30 242
  Technical notes 267
IX. *Wages and prices*
  Tables 31-33 269
  Technical notes 302
X. *Agriculture, hunting, forestry and fishing*
  Tables 34-40 305
  Technical notes 386
XI. *Manufacturing*
  A. Food, beverages and tobacco
    Tables 41-44 389
  B. Textile, wearing apparel and
    leather industries
    Tables 45 and 46 438

Table des matières

Préface. iii
Notes explicatives xiv
Introduction 1

Première partie
Aperçu mondial et régional

I. *Aperçu mondial et régional*
  Tableaux 1 à 7 9
  Notes techniques 29

Deuxième partie
Statistiques démographiques et sociales

II. *Population et établissements humains*
  Tableau 8 35
  Notes techniques 47
III. *Instruction et alphabétisation*
  Tableaux 9 à 11 49
  Notes techniques 80
IV. *Santé et maternité; nutrition*
  Tableaux 12 et 13 83
  Notes techniques 98
V. *Culture et communications*
  Tableaux 14 à 19 101
  Notes techniques 145

Troisième partie
Activité économique

VI. *Comptabilités nationales et production industrielle*
  Tableaux 20 à 26 149
  Notes techniques 226
VII. *Statistiques financières*
  Tableaux 27 et 28 229
  Notes techniques 241
VIII. *Main-d'oeuvre*
  Tableaux 29 et 30 242
  Notes techniques 267
IX. *Salaires et prix*
  Tableaux 31 à 33 269
  Notes techniques 302
X. *Agriculture, chasse, forêts et pêche*
  Tableaux 34 à 40 305
  Notes techniques 386
XI. *Industries manufacturières*
  A. Alimentation, boissons et tabac
    Tableaux 41 à 44 389
  B. Textile, habillement et cuir
    Tableaux 45 et 46 438

C. Wood and wood products; paper
    and paper products
    Tables 47 and 48   453
D. Chemicals and related products
    Tables 49-52   465
E. Basic metal industries
    Tables 53 and 54   485
F. Non-metalic mineral products and
    fabricated metal products,
    machinery and equipment
    Tables 55-60   496
    Technical notes   518

XII. *Transport*
      Tables 61-65   523
      Technical notes   590
XIII. *Energy*
       Tables 66 and 67   592
       Technical notes   632
XIV. *Environment*
      Tables 68-70   635
      Technical notes   659
XV. *Intellectual property; science and technology*
     Table 71   663
     Technical notes   669

Part Four
International Economic Relations

XVI. *International merchandise trade*
      Tables 72-75   672
      Technical notes   728
XVII. *International tourism*
       Tables 76-78   733
       Technical notes   773
XVIII. *Balance of payments*
        Table 79   775
        Technical notes   805
XIX. *International finance*
      Tables 80 and 81   807
      Technical notes   830
XX. *Development assistance*
     Tables 82-84   833
     Technical notes   858

     Annexes
I.   Country and area nomenclature,
     regional and other groupings   860
II.   Conversion coefficients and factors   871
III.   Tables added and omitted   874

Statistical sources and references   875
Index (English only)   879

C. Bois et produits dérivés; papier
    et produits dérivés
    Tableaux 47 et 48   453
D. Produits chimiques et apparentés
    Tableaux 49 à 52   465
E. Industries métallurgiques de base
    Tableaux 53 et 54   485
F. Produits minéraux non métalliques
    et fabrications métallurgiques,
    machines et équipements
    Tableaux 55 à 60   496
    Notes techniques   518

XII. *Transports*
      Tableaux 61 à 65   523
      Notes techniques   590
XIII. *Energie*
       Tableaux 66 et 67   592
       Notes techniques   632
XIV. *Environnement*
      Tableaux 68 à 70   635
      Notes techniques   659
XIV. *Propriété intellectuelle; science et technologie*
      Tableau 71   663
      Notes techniques   669

Quatrième partie
Relations économiques internationales

XVI. *Commerce international des marchandises*
      Tableaux 72 à 75   672
      Notes techniques   728
XVII. *Tourisme international*
       Tableaux 76 à 78   733
       Notes techniques   773
XVIII. *Balance des paiements*
        Tableau 79   775
        Notes techniques   805
XIX. *Finances internationales*
      Tableaux 80 et 81   807
      Notes techniques   830
XX. *Aide au développement*
     Tableaux 82 à 84   833
     Notes techniques   858

     Annexes
I.   Nomenclature des pays et zones,
     groupements régionaux et autres
     groupements   860
II.   Coefficients et facteurs de conversion   871
III.   Tableaux ajoutés et supprimés   874

Sources statistiques et références   875

List of tables

Part One
World and Region Summary

Chapter I. *World and region summary*
1. Selected series of world statistics 9
2. Population, rate of increase, birth and death rates, surface area and density .. 12
3. Index numbers of total agricultural and food production 14
4. Index numbers of per capita total agricultural and food production 15
5. Index numbers of industrial production: world and regions 16
6. Production, trade and consumption of commercial energy 24
7. Total exports and imports: index numbers 26

Part Two
Population and Social Statistics

Chapter II. *Population and human settlements*
8. Population by sex, rate of population increase, surface area and density 35
*   Population in urban and rural areas, rates of growth and largest city population (see *Yearbook*, 40th issue, Table 9)

Chapter III. *Education and literacy*
9. Education at the first, second and third levels 49
10. Public expenditure on education at current market prices 62
11. Illiterate population by sex 74

Chapter IV. *Health and child-bearing; nutrition*
12. Selected indicators of life expectancy, child-bearing and mortality 83
13. Estimates of cumulative HIV infections, AIDS cases and HIV/AIDS deaths and number of reported AIDS cases 90
    A. Estimated cumulative HIV infections, AIDS cases and HIV/AIDS deaths to mid 1996 90
    B. Reported and estimated AIDS cases to mid 1996 90

Liste des tableaux

Première partie
Aperçu mondial et régional

Chapitre I. *Aperçu mondial et régional*
1. Séries principales de statistiques mondiales 9
2. Population, taux d'accroissement, taux de natalité et taux de mortalité, superficie et densité 12
3. Indices de la production agricole totale et de la production alimentaire 14
4. Indices de la production agricole totale et de la production alimentaire par habitant 15
5. Indices de la production industrielle: monde et régions 16
6. Production, commerce et consommation d'énergie commerciale 24
7. Exportations et importations totales : indices 26

Deuxième partie
Statistiques démographiques et sociales

Chapitre II. *Population et établissements humains*
8. Population selon le sexe, taux d'accroissement de la population, superficie et densité 35
*   Population urbaine, population rurale, taux d'accroissement et population de la ville la plus peuplée (voir l'*Annuaire*, 40ème édition, Tableau 9)

Chapitre III. *Instruction et alphabétisation*
9. Enseignement des premier, second et troisième degrés 49
10. Dépenses publiques afférentes à l'enseignement aux prix courants du marché 62
11. Population analphabète, selon le sexe 74

Chapitre IV. *Santé et maternité; nutrition*
12. Choix d'indicateurs de l'espérance de vie, de maternité et de la mortalité 83
13. Chiffres estimatifs du nombre cumulé de personnes infectées par le VIH, de cas de SIDA et de décès causés par le VIH ou le SIDA, et nombre de cas déclarés de SIDA . 90

C. Reported AIDS cases 91

* Food supply (see *Yearbook*, 38th issue, Table 22)

Chapter V. *Culture and communications*
14. Daily newspapers 101
15. Non-daily newspapers and periodicals 108
16. Television and radio receivers 116
17. Cinemas: number, seating capacity, annual attendance and box office receipts 124
18. Telefax stations and mobile cellular telephone subscribers 128
19. Telephones 135
* Book production: number of titles by UDC classes (see *Yearbook*, 40th issue, Table 14)
* Book production: number of titles by language of publication (see *Yearbook*, 40th issue, Table 15)

Part Three
Economic Activity

Chapter VI. *National accounts and industrial production*
20. Gross domestic product: total and per capita 149
21. Expenditure on gross domestic product at current prices 167
22. Gross domestic product by kind of economic activity at current prices 177
23. Relationships between the principal national accounting aggregates 187
24. Government final consumption expenditure by function at current prices 195
25. Private final consumption expenditure by type and purpose at current prices 200
26. Index numbers of industrial production 204

Chapter VII. *Financial statistics*
27. Rates of discount of central banks 229
28. Short-term rates 234

Chapter VIII. *Labour force*
29. Employment by industry 242
30. Unemployment 252

Chapter IX. *Wages and prices*
31. Earnings in manufacturing 269

A. Chiffres estimatifs cumulés du nombre de personnes infectées par le VIH, de cas de SIDA et de décès causés par le VIH ou le SIDA jusqu'au milieu de 1996 ... 90
B. Cas de SIDA : nombre de cas déclarés, et chiffres estimatifs jusqu'au milieu de 1996 90
C. Cas de SIDA déclarés 91
* Disponibilités alimentaires (voir l'*Annuaire*, 38ème édition, Tableau 22)

Chapitre V. *Culture et communications*
14. Journaux quotidiens 101
15. Journaux non quotidiens et périodiques ... 108
16. Postes récepteurs de télévision et de radio . 116
17. Cinémas : nombre d'établissements, nombre de sièges, fréquentation annuelle et recettes guichet 124
18. Postes de télécopie et abonnés au téléphone mobile cellulaire 128
19. Téléphones 135
* Production de livres : nombre de titres classés d'après la CDU (voir l'*Annuaire*, 40ème édition, Tableau 14)
* Production de livres : nombre de titres par langue de publication (voir l'*Annuaire*, 40ème édition, Tableau 15)

Troixième partie
Activité économique

Chapitre VI. *Comptabilités nationales et production industrielle*
20. Produit intérieur brut: total et par habitant 149
21. Dépenses imputées au produit intérieur brut aux prix courants 167
22. Produit intérieur brut par genre d'activité economique aux prix courants 177
23. Relations entre les principaux agrégats de comptabilité nationale 187
24. Consommation finale des administrations publiques par fonction aux prix courants .. 195
25. Consommation finale privée par catégorie de dépenses et par fonction aux prix courants 200
26. Indices de la production industrielle 204

Chapitre VII. *Statistiques financières*
27. Taux d'escompte des banques centrales 229
28. Taux à court terme 234

32. Producers prices and wholesale prices 278
33. Consumer price index numbers 287

Chapter X. *Agriculture, hunting, forestry and fishing*
34. Agricultural production (index numbers) .. 305
35. Cereals 312
36. Oil crops, in oil equivalent 320
37. Livestock 328
38. Roundwood 347
39. Fish catches 354
40. Fertilizers (production and consumption) .. 363

Chapter XI. *Manufacturing*
    A. Food, beverages and tobacco
41. Sugar (production and consumption) 389
42. Meat 400
43. Beer 426
44. Cigarettes 432
    B. Textile, wearing apparel
       and leather industries
45. Fabrics (cotton, wool, cellulosic
    and non-cellulosic fibres) 438
46. Leather footwear 448
    C. Wood and wood products;
       paper and paper products
47. Sawnwood 453
48. Paper and paperboard 460
    D. Chemicals and related products
49. Tires 465
50. Cement 468
51. Sulphuric acid 475
52. Soap, washing powders and detergents 479
    E. Basic metal industries
53. Pig-iron and crude steel 485
54. Aluminium 491
    F. Non-metalic mineral products
       and fabricated metal products,
       machinery and equipment
55. Radio and television receivers (production) 496
56. Passenger cars 500
57. Refrigerators for household use 502
58. Washing machines for household use 505
59. Machine tools (drilling/boring machines,
    lathes, milling machines and
    metal-working presses) 508
60. Lorries (trucks) 514

Chapter XII. *Transport*
61. Railways: traffic 523
62. Motor vehicles in use 534
63. Merchant shipping: fleets 550
64. International maritime transport 568
65. Civil aviation 575

Chapitre VIII. *Main-d'oeuvre*
29. Emploi par industrie 242
30. Chômage 252

Chapitre IX. *Salaires et prix*
31. Gains dans les industries manufacturières ... 269
32. Prix à la production et des prix de gros 278
33. Indices des prix à la consommation 287

Chapitre X. *Agriculture, chasse, forêts et pêche*
34. Production agricole (indices) 305
35. Céréales 312
36. Cultures d'huile, en équivalent d'huile 320
37. Cheptel 328
38. Bois rond 347
39. Quantités pêchées 354
40. Engrais (production et consommation) 363

Chapitre XI. *Industries manufacturières*
    A. Alimentation, boissons et tabac
41. Sucre (production et consommation) 389
42. Viande 400
43. Bière 426
44. Cigarettes 432
    B. Textiles, habillement et cuir
45. Tissus (coton, laines, fibres cellulosiques
    et non cellulosiques) 438
46. Chaussures de cuir 448
    C. Bois et produits dérivés; papier
       et produits dérivés
47. Sciages 453
48. Papiers et cartons 460
    D. Produits chimiques et apparentés
49. Pneumatiques: enveloppes 465
50. Ciment 468
51. Acide sulfurique 475
52. Savons, poudres pour lessives et détersifs .. 479
    E. Industries métallurgiques de base
53. Fonte et acier brut 485
54. Aluminium 491
    F. Produits minéraux non métalliques
       et fabrications métallurgiques,
       machines et équipements
55. Radiodiffusion et télévision (production) .. 496
56. Voitures de tourisme 500
57. Réfrigérateurs ménagers 502
58. Machines et appareils à laver, à usage
    domestique 505
59. Machines-outils (perceuses, tours, fraiseuses
    et presses pour le travail des métaux) 508
60. Camions 514

Chapter XIII. *Energy*

66.	Production, trade and consumption of commercial energy	592
67.	Production of selected energy commodities	618

Chapter XIV. *Environment*

68.	Selected indicators of natural resources ...	635
69.	Selected indicators of environmental protection	644
70.	CO$_2$ emissions estimates	651
*	Concentration of suspended particulate matter at selected sites (see *Yearbook*, 39th issue, Table 84)	
*	Global water quality in selected rivers (see *Yearbook*, 39th issue, Table 85)	
*	Surface and land area and land use (see *Yearbook*, 39th issue, Table 86)	

Chapter XV. *Intellectual property; science and technology;*

71.	Patents	663
*	Number of scientists, engineers and technicians in research and experimental development (see *Yearbook*, 40th issue, Table 68)	
*	Expenditure for research and experimental development (see *Yearbook*, 40th issue, Table 69)	

Part Four
International Economic Relations

Chapter XVI. *International merchandise trade*

72.	Total imports and exports	672
73.	World exports by commodity classes and by regions	692
74.	Total imports and exports: index numbers	706
75.	Manufactured goods exports	722

Chapter XVII. *International tourism*

76.	Tourist arrivals by region of origin	733
77.	Tourist arrivals and international tourism receipts	756
78.	International tourism expenditures	765

Chapter XVIII. *Balance of payments*

79.	Summary of balance of payments	775

Chapitre XII. *Transports*

61.	Chemins de fer : trafic	523
62.	Véhicules automobiles en circulation	534
63.	Transports maritimes : flotte marchande ...	550
64.	Transports maritimes internationaux	568
65.	Aviation civile	575

Chapitre XIII. *Energie*

66.	Production, commerce et consommation d'énergie commerciale	592
67.	Production des principaux biens de l'énergie	618

Chapitre XIV. *Environnement*

68.	Choix d'indicateurs concernant certaines ressources naturelles	635
69.	Choix d'indicateurs de la protection de l'environnement	644
70.	Estimations des émissions de CO$_2$	651
*	Concentration de particules en suspension en divers lieux (voir l'*Annuaire*, 39ème édition, Tableau 84)	
*	Qualité générale de l'eau de certains cours d'eau (voir l'*Annuaire*, 39ème édition, Tableau 85)	
*	Superficie totale, superficie des terres et utilisation des terres (voir l'*Annuaire*, 39ème édition, Tableau 86)	

Chapitre XV. *Propriété intellectuelle science et technologie;*

71.	Brevets	663
*	Nombre de scientifiques, d'ingénieurs et de techniciens employés à des travaux de recherche et de développement expérimental (voir l'*Annuaire*, 40ème édition, Tableau 68)	
*.	Dépenses consacrées à la rechercheet au développement expérimental (voir l'*Annuaire*, 40ème édition, Tableau 69)	

Quatrième partie
Relations économiques internationales

Chapitre XVI. *Commerce international des marchandises*

72.	Importations et exportations totales	672
73.	Exportations mondiales par classes de marchandises et par régions	692
74.	Importations et exportations totales: indices	706
75.	Exportations des produits manufacturés ...	722

Chapter XIX. *International finance*
80.   Exchange rates 807
81.   Total external and public/publicly
      guaranteed long-term debt of developing
      countries 823
      A. Total external debt 823
      B. Public and publicly guaranteed
          long-term debt 825

Chapter XX. *Development assistance*
82.   Disbursements to individual recipients
      of bilateral and multilateral official
      development assistance 833
83.   Net official development assistance
      from DAC countries to developing
      countries and multilateral
      organizations 843
84.   Socio-economic development assistance
      through the United Nations system 844
      A. Development grant expenditures 844
      B. Development loan and relief
          expenditures 851

Chapitre XVII. *Tourisme international*
76.   Arrivées de touristes par régions
      de provenance 733
77.   Arrivées de touristes et recettes
      touristiques internationales 756
78.   Dépenses provenant du tourisme
      international 765

Chapitre XVIII. *Balance des paiements*
79.   Résumé des balances des paiements 775

Chapitre XIX. *Finances internationales*
80.   Cours des changes 807
81.   Total de la dette extérieure et dette publique
      extérieure à long terme garantie par l'Etat
      des pays en développement 823
      A. Total de la dette extérieure 823
      B. Dette publique extérieure à long
          terme garantie par l'Etat 825

Chapitre XX. *Aide au développement*
82.   Paiements aux destinataires d'aide publique
      au développement bilatérale et
      multilatérale 833
83.   Aide publique au développement nette de
      pays du CAD aux pays en développement et
      aux organisations multilatérales 843
84.   Assistance en matière de développement
      socio-économique fournie par le système
      des Nations Unies 844
      A. Aide au développement 844
      B. Prêts au développement et secours 851

Explanatory notes

The metric system of weights and measures has been employed throughout the *Statistical Yearbook*. For conversion coefficients and factors, see annex II.

Certain tables contain global aggregates designated variously as "total" or "world". Where a figure represents the summation of the country series shown in the table but is not considered comprehensive for the world, it is labelled "total". Where, however, an aggregate is considered to represent substantially complete world coverage, it is labelled "world". As a rule, allowance has been made in the "world" figures for any gaps that may exist in the country series shown.

In some cases, the comparability of the statistics is affected by geographical changes. As a general rule, the data relate to a given country or area within its present de facto boundaries. Where statistically important, attention is called to changes in territory by means of a footnote. The reader is referred to annex I, concerning country and area nomenclature, where changes in designation are listed.

Numbers in brackets refer to numbered entries in the section "Statistical sources and references" at the end of this book.

In general, statistics presented in the present publication are based on information available to the Statistics Division of the United Nations Secretariat up to 31 March 1996.

Symbols and conventions used in the tables

A point (.) is used to indicate decimals.

A hyphen (-) between years, e.g., 1984-1985, indicates the full period involved, including the beginning and end years; a slash (/) indicates a financial year, school year or crop year, e.g., 1984/85.

"Δ p.a." (change per annum) is used to indicate annual rate of change.

Not applicable or not separately reported	..
Data not available	...
Magnitude zero	-
Magnitude zero or less than half of unit employed	0 or 0.0
Provisional or estimated figure	*
United Nations estimate	x
Marked break in series	#

Details and percentages in tables do not necessarily add to totals because of rounding.

Notes explicatives

Le système métrique de poids et mesures a été utilisé dans tout l'*Annuaire statistique*. On trouvera à l'annexe II les coefficients et facteurs de conversion.

Certains tableaux contiennent des agrégats globaux désignés par la mention "total" ou "monde", selon les cas. Quand un chiffre représente l'addition des chiffres correspondant à chacun des pays qui figurent dans le tableau, mais ne paraît pas recouvrir le monde entier, il porte la mention "total". Si un agrégat semble correspondre au total mondial, ou très peu s'en faut, il porte la mention "monde". En règle générale, les chiffres portant la mention "monde" s'entendent compte tenu des lacunes qui peuvent exister dans la série de pays indiqués.

Dans certains cas, les changements géographiques intervenus influent sur la comparabilité des statistiques. En règle générale, les données renvoient au pays ou zone en question dans ses frontières actuelles effectives. Une note appelle l'attention sur les changements territoriaux, si cela importe du point de vue statistique. Le lecteur est renvoyé à l'annexe A (nomenclature des pays et zones et groupements régionaux) où il trouvera une liste des changements de désignation.

Les chiffres figurant entre crochets se réfèrent aux entrées numérotées dans la liste des sources et références statistiques à la fin de l'ouvrage.

En général, les statistiques qui figurent dans la présente publication sont fondées sur les informations dont disposait la Division de statistique du Secrétariat de l'ONU au 31 mars 1996.

Signes et conventions employés dans les tableaux

Les décimales sont précédées d'un point (.).

Un tiret (-) entre des années, par exemple "1984-1985", indique que la période est embrassée dans sa totalité, y compris la première et la dernière année; une barre oblique (/) renvoie à un exercice financier, à une année scolaire ou à une campagne agricole, par exemple "1984/85".

Le symbole "Δ p.a." signifie qu'il s'agit du taux annuel de variation.

Non applicable ou non communiqué séparément	..
Données non disponibles	...
Néant	-
Valeur nulle ou inférieure à la moitié de la dernière unité retenue	0 ou 0.0
Chiffre provisoire ou estimatif	*
Estimation des Nations Unies	x
Discontinuité notable dans la série	#

Les chiffres étant arrondis, les totaux ne correspondent pas toujours à la somme exacte des éléments ou pourcentages figurant dans les tableaux.

Introduction

This is the forty-first issue of the United Nations *Statistical Yearbook*, prepared by the Statistics Division, Department for Economic and Social Information and Policy Analysis, of the United Nations Secretariat. It contains series covering, in general, 1984-1993 or 1985-1994, based on statistics available to the Statistics Division up to 31 December 1995.

The major purpose of the *Statistical Yearbook* is to provide in a single volume a comprehensive compilation of internationally-available statistics on social and economic conditions and activities in the world, at world, regional and national levels, covering roughly a ten-year period.

Most of the statistics presented in the *Yearbook* are extracted from more detailed, specialized publications prepared by the Statistics Division and by many other international statistical services. Thus, while the specialized publications concentrate on monitoring topics and trends in particular social and economic fields, the *Statistical Yearbook* tables provide data for a more comprehensive, overall description of social and economic structures, conditions, changes and activities. The objective has been to collect, systematize and coordinate the most essential components of comparable statistical information which can give a broad and, to the extent feasible, a consistent picture of social and economic processes at world, regional and national levels.

More specifically, the *Statistical Yearbook* provides systematic information on a wide range of social and economic issues which are of concern in the United Nations system and among the governments and peoples of the world. A particular value of the *Yearbook*, but also its greatest challenge, is that these issues are extensively interrelated. Meaningful social and economic analysis of these issues requires systematization and coordination of the data across many fields. These issues include:
— General economic growth and related economic conditions;
— Economic situation in developing countries and progress towards the objectives adopted for the United Nations development decades;
— Population and urbanization, and their growth and impact;
— Employment, inflation and wages;
— Production of energy and development of new energy sources;
— Expansion of trade;
— Supply of food and alleviation of hunger;
— Financial situation and external payments and receipts;
— Education, training and eradication of illiteracy;
— Improvement in general living conditions;
— Pollution and protection of environment;
— Assistance provided to developing countries for social and economic development purposes.

Introduction

La présente édition est la quarante-et-unième de l'*Annuaire statistique* des Nations Unies, établi par la Division de statistique du Département de l'information économique et sociale et de l'analyse des politiques du Secrétariat de l'Organisation des Nations Unies. Elle contient des séries de données qui portent d'une manière générale sur les années 1984 à 1993 ou 1985 à 1994, et pour lesquelles ont été utilisées les informations dont disposait la Division de statistique au 31 décembre 1995.

L'*Annuaire statistique* a principalement pour objet de présenter en un seul volume un inventaire complet de statistiques disponibles sur le plan international et concernant la situation et les activités sociales et économiques dans le monde, aux échelons mondial, régional et national, pour une période d'environ 10 ans.

Une bonne partie des données qui figurent dans l'*Annuaire* existent sous une forme plus détaillée dans les publications spécialisées établies par la Division de statistique et par bien d'autres services statistiques internationaux. Alors que les publications spécialisées suivent essentiellement l'évolution dans certains domaines socio-économiques précis, l'*Annuaire statistique* présente les données de manière à fournir une description plus globale et exhaustive des structures, conditions, transformations et activités socio-économiques. On a cherché à recueillir, systématiser et coordonner les principaux éléments de renseignements statistiques comparables, de manière à dresser un tableau général et autant que possible cohérent des processus socio-économiques en cours aux échelons mondial, régional et national.

Plus précisément, l'*Annuaire statistique* a pour objet de présenter des renseignements systématiques sur toutes sortes de questions socio-économiques qui sont liées aux préoccupations actuelles du système des Nations Unies ainsi que des gouvernements et des peuples du monde. Le principal avantage de l'*Annuaire* — et aussi la principale difficulté à surmonter — tient à ce que ces questions sont étroitement interdépendantes. Pour en faire une analyse économique et sociale utile, il est essentiel de systématiser et de coordonner les données se rapportant à de nombreux domaines différents. Ces questions sont notamment les suivantes :
— La croissance économique générale et les aspects connexes de l'économie;
— La situation économique dans les pays en développement et les progrès accomplis vers la réalisation des objectifs des décennies des Nations Unies pour le développement;
— La population et l'urbanisation, leur croissance et leur impact;
— L'emploi, l'inflation et les salaires;
— La production d'énergie et la mise en valeur des énergies nouvelles;
— L'expansion des échanges;
— La pollution et la protection de l'environnement;
— Les approvisionnements alimentaires et la lutte contre la faim;

Organization of the *Yearbook*

The contents of the *Statistical Yearbook* are planned to serve a general readership. The *Yearbook* endeavours to provide information for various bodies of the United Nations system as well as for other international organizations, for governments and non-governmental organizations, for national statistical, economic and social policy bodies, for scientific and educational institutions, for libraries and for the public. Data published in the *Statistical Yearbook* are also of interest to companies and enterprises and to agencies engaged in marketing research.

The 84 tables of the *Yearbook* are grouped into four broad parts:
— World and Region Summary (chapter I and tables 1-7);
— Population and Social Statistics (chapters II-V and tables 8-19);
— Economic Activity (chapters VI-XV and tables 20-71);
— International Economic Relations (chapters XVI-XX and tables 72-84).

These four parts present data at two levels of aggregation. The more aggregated information shown in Part One provides an overall picture of development at the world and region levels. More specific and detailed information for analysis concerning individual countries or areas in the three following parts. Each of these is divided into more specific chapters, by topic, and each chapter includes a section, "Technical notes". These notes provide brief descriptions of major statistical concepts, definitions and classifications required for interpretation and analysis of the data. Systematic information on the methodology used for computation of figures can also be found in the publications on methodology of the United Nations and its agencies, listed in the section "Statistical sources and references" at the end of the *Yearbook*. Additional general information on statistical methodology is provided in the section below on "Comparability of statistics" and in the explanatory notes following the Introduction.

More specifically, Part One, World and Region Summary, comprises 7 tables highlighting the principal trends in the world as a whole as well as in regions and in the major economic and social sectors. It contains global totals of important aggregate statistics needed for the analysis of economic growth, the structure of the world economy, major changes in world population, expansion of external merchandise trade, world production and consumption of energy. The global totals are, as a rule, subdivided into major geographical areas.

Part Two, Population and Social Statistics, comprises 12 tables which contain more detailed statistical series on social conditions and levels of living, for example, data on education and cultural activities.

— La situation financière, les paiements extérieurs et les recettes extérieures;
— L'éducation, la formation et l'élimination de l'analphabétisme;
— L'assistance fournie aux pays en développement à des fins socio-économiques.

Présentation de l'*Annuaire*

Le contenu de l'*Annuaire statistique* a été préparé à l'intention de tous les lecteurs intéressés. Les renseignements fournis devraient pouvoir être utilisés par les divers organismes du système des Nations Unies ainsi que par d'autres organisations internationales, par les gouvernements et les organisations non gouvernementales, par les organismes nationaux de statistique et de politique économique et sociale, par les institutions scientifiques et les établissements d'enseignement, les bibliothèques et les particuliers. Les données publiées dans l'*Annuaire statistique* peuvent également intéresser les sociétés et entreprises, et les organismes spécialisés dans les études de marché.

Les 84 tableaux de l'*Annuaire* sont groupés en quatre parties :
— Aperçu mondial et régional (chap. I et tableaux 1 à 7);
— Statistiques démographiques et sociales (chap. II à V et tableaux 8 à 19);
— Activité économique (chap. VI à XV et tableaux 20 à 71);
— Relations économiques internationales (chap. XVI à XX et tableaux 72 à 84).

Ces quatre parties présentent les données à deux niveaux d'agrégation : les valeurs les plus agrégées qui figurent dans la première partie donnent un tableau global du développement à l'échelon mondial et régional, tandis que les trois autres parties contiennent des renseignements plus précis et détaillés qui se prêtent mieux à une analyse par pays ou par zones. Chacune de ces trois parties est divisée en chapitres portant sur des sujets donnés, et chaque chapitre comprend une section intitulée "Notes techniques" où l'on trouve une brève description des principales notions, définitions et classifications statistiques nécessaires pour interpréter et analyser les données. Les méthodes de calcul utilisées sont également décrites de façon systématique dans les publications se référant à la méthodologie des Nations Unies et de leurs organismes, énumérées à la fin de l'*Annuaire* dans la section "Sources et références statistiques". Le lecteur trouvera un complément d'informations générales ci-après dans la section intitulée "Comparabilité des statistiques", ainsi que dans les notes explicatives qui suivent l'introduction.

Plus spécialement, la première partie, intitulée "Aperçu mondial et régional", comprend sept tableaux présentant les principales tendances dans le monde et dans les régions ainsi que dans les principaux secteurs économiques et sociaux. Elle fournit des chiffres mondiaux pour les principaux agrégats

Part Three, Economic Activity, provides data in 25 tables of statistics on national accounts, index numbers of industrial production, interest rates, labour force, wages and prices, transport, energy, environment and intellectual property; and in 27 tables on production in the major branches of the economy (using, in general, the international standard industrial classification, ISIC), namely agriculture, hunting, forestry and fishing; mining and quarrying; manufacturing; and transport and communications. In an innovation in the general approach of the *Yearbook*, consumption data are now being combined with the production data in tables on specific commodities, where feasible.

Part Four, International Economic Relations, comprises 13 tables on international merchandise trade, balance of payments, tourism, finance and development assistance. It focuses on the growth and structure of exports and imports by countries or areas, international tourism, balance of payments and development assistance provided by multilateral and bilateral agencies to individual recipients.

An index (in English only) is provided at the end of the *Yearbook*.

Annexes and regional groupings of countries or areas

The annexes to the *Statistical Yearbook* and the section "Explanatory notes", preceding the Introduction, provide additional essential information on the *Yearbook*'s contents and presentation of data.

Annex I provides information on countries or areas covered in the *Yearbook* tables and on their grouping into geographical regions. The geographical groupings shown in the *Yearbook* are generally based on continental regions unless otherwise indicated. However, strict consistency in this regard is impossible. A wide range of classifications is used for different purposes in the various international agencies and other sources of statistics for the *Yearbook*. These classifications vary in response to administrative and analytical requirements.

Neither is there a common agreement in the United Nations system concerning the terms "developed" and "developing", when referring to the stage of development reached by any given country or area and its corresponding classification in one or the other grouping. Thus, the *Yearbook* refers more generally to "developed" or "developing" regions on the basis of conventional practice. Following this practice, "developed regions" comprises northern America, Europe and the former USSR, Australia, Japan and New Zealand, while all of Africa and the remainder of the Americas, Asia and Oceania comprise the "developing regions". These designations are intended for statistical convenience and do not necessarily express a judgement about the stage reached by a particular country or area in the development process.

statistiques nécessaires pour analyser la croissance économique, la structure de l'économie mondiale, les principaux changements dans la population mondiale, l'expansion du commerce extérieur de marchandises, la production et la consommation mondiales d'énergie. En règle générale, les chiffres mondiaux sont ventilés par grandes régions géographiques.

La deuxième partie, intitulée "Statistiques démographiques et sociales", comporte 12 tableaux où figurent des séries plus détaillées concernant les conditions sociales et les niveaux de vie, notamment des données sur l'éducation et les activités culturelles.

La troisième partie, intitulée "Activité économique", présente en 25 tableaux des statistiques concernant les comptes nationaux, les nombres indices relatifs à la production industrielle, les taux d'intérêt, la population active, les prix et les salaires, le transport, l'énergie, l'environnement, et propriété intellectuelle; et en 27 tableaux des données sur la production des principales branches d'activité économique (en utilisant en général la *Classification internationale type, par industrie, de toutes les branches d'activité économique*) : agriculture, chasse, sylviculture et pêche; mines et carrières; industries manufacturières; transports et communications. Une innovation a été introduite dans la présentation générale de l'*Annuaire* en ce sens que les tableaux traitant de certains produits de base associent autant que possible les données relatives à la consommation aux valeurs concernant la production.

La quatrième partie, intitulée "Relations économiques internationales", comprend 13 tableaux relatifs au commerce international de marchandises, aux balances des paiements, au tourisme, aux finances et à l'aide au développement. Elle est consacrée essentiellement à la croissance et à la structure des exportations et des importations par pays et par zone, au tourisme international, aux balances des paiements et à l'aide au développement fournie aux pays par les organismes multilatéraux et bilatéraux.

Un index (en anglais seulement) figure à la fin de l'*Annuaire*.

Annexes et groupements régionaux des pays et zones

Les annexes à l'*Annuaire statistique* et la section intitulée "Notes explicatives" offrent d'importantes informations complémentaires quant à la teneur et à la présentation des données figurant dans le présent ouvrage.

L'annexe I donne des renseignements sur les pays ou zones couverts par les tableaux de l'*Annuaire* et sur leur regroupement en régions géographiques. Sauf indication contraire, les groupements géographiques figurant dans l'*Annuaire* sont généralement fondés sur les régions continentales, mais une présentation absolument systématique est impossible à cet égard car les diverses institutions internationales et autres sources de statistiques employées pour la confection de l'*Annuaire* emploient, selon l'objet de

Annex II provides detailed information on conversion coeffients and factors used in various tables, and annexe III provides listings of tables added and omitted in the present edition of the *Yearbook*.

Comparability of statistics

One major aim of the *Statistical Yearbook* is to present series which are as nearly comparable accross countries as the available statistics permit. Considerable efforts are also made among the international suppliers of data and by the staff of the *Yearbook* to ensure the compatibility of various series by coordinating time periods, base years, prices chosen for valuation and so on. This is indispensable in relating various bodies of data to each other and to facilitate analysis across different sectors. Thus, for example, relating data on economic output to those on employment makes it possible to derive some trends in the field of productivity; relating data on exports and imports to those on national product allows an evaluation of the relative importance of external trade in different countries and reveals changes in the role of trade over time.

In general, the data presented reflect the methodological recommendations of the United Nations Statistical Commission, issued in various United Nations publications, and of other international bodies concerned with statistics. Publications containing these recommendations and guidelines are listed in the section "Statistical sources and references" at the end of the *Yearbook*. Use of international recommendations not only promotes international comparability of the data but also ensures a degree of compatibility regarding the underlying concepts, definitions and classifications relating to different series. However, much work remains to be done in this area and, for this reason, some tables can serve only as a first source of data, which require further adjustment before being used for more in-depth analytical studies. Although, on the whole, a significant degree of comparability has been achieved in international statistics, there are many limitations, for a variety of reasons.

One common cause of non-comparability of economic data is different valuations of statistical aggregates such as national income, wages and salaries, output of industries and so forth. Conversion of these and similar series originally expressed in national prices into a common currency, for example into United States dollars, through the use of exchange rates is not always satisfactory owing to frequent wide fluctuations in market rates and differences between official rates and rates which would be indicated by unofficial markets or purchasing power parities. For this reason, data on national income in United States dollars which are published in the *Yearbook* are subject to certain distortions and can be used as only a rough approximation of the relative magnitudes involved.

l'exercice, des classifications fort différentes en réponse à diverses exigences d'ordre administratif ou analytique.

Il n'existe pas non plus dans le système des Nations Unies de définition commune des termes "développé" et "en développement" pour décrire le niveau atteint en la matière par un pays ou une zone donnés ni pour les classifier dans l'un ou l'autre de ces groupes. Ainsi, dans l'*Annuaire*, on s'en remet à l'usage pour qualifier les régions de "développées" ou "en développement". Selon cet usage, les régions développées sont le continent américain au nord du Mexique, l'Europe et l'ancienne URSS, l'Australie, le Japon et la Nouvelle-Zélande, alors que toute l'Afrique et le reste des Amériques, l'Asie et l'Océanie constituent les régions en développement. Ces appellations sont utilisées pour plus de commodité dans la présentation des statistiques et n'impliquent pas nécessairement un jugement quant au stade de développement auquel est parvenu tel pays ou telle zone.

L'annexe II fournit des renseignements sur les coefficients et facteurs de conversion employés dans les différents tableaux, et l'annexe III contient les listes de tableaux qui ont été ajoutés ou omis dans la présente édition de l'*Annuaire*.

Comparabilité des statistiques

L'*Annuaire statistique* a principalement pour objet de présenter des statistiques aussi comparables d'un pays à l'autre que les données le permettent. Les sources internationales de données et les auteurs de l'*Annuaire* ont réalisés des efforts considérables pour faire en sorte que les diverses séries soient compatibles en harmonisant les périodes de référence, les années de base, les prix utilisés pour les évaluations, etc. Cette démarche est indispensable si l'on veut rapprocher divers ensembles de données pour faciliter l'analyse intersectorielle de l'économie. Ainsi, en liant les données concernant la production à celles de l'emploi, on parvient à dégager certaines tendances dans le domaine de la productivité; de même, en associant les données concernant les exportations et importations aux valeurs du produit national, on obtient une évaluation de l'importance relative des échanges extérieurs dans différents pays et de l'évolution du rôle joué par le commerce.

De façon générale, les données sont présentées selon les recommandations méthodologiques formulées par la Commission de statistique de l'ONU et par les autres organisations internationales qui s'intéressent aux statistiques. Les titres des publications contenant ces recommandations et lignes directrices figurent à la fin de l'ouvrage dans la section intitulée "Sources et références statistiques". Le respect des recommandations internationales tend non seulement à promouvoir la comparabilité des données à l'échelon international, mais elle assure également une certaine comparabilité entre les concepts, les définitions et classifications utilisés. Mais comme il reste encore beaucoup à faire dans ce domaine, les données présentées dans certains

The use of different kinds of sources for obtaining data is another cause of incomparability. This is true, for example, in the case of employment and unemployment, where data are collected from such non-comparable sources as sample surveys, social insurance statistics and establishment surveys.

Non-comparability of data may also result from differences in the institutional patterns of countries. Certain variations in social and economic organization and institutions may have an impact on the comparability of the data even if the underlying concepts and definitions are identical.

These and other causes of non-comparability of the data are briefly explained in the technical notes to each chapter.

Statistical sources and reliability and timeliness of data

Statistics and indicators have been compiled mainly from official national and international sources, as these are more authoritative and comprehensive, more generally available as time series and more comparable among countries than other sources. In a few cases, official sources are supplemented by other sources and estimates, where these have been subjected to professional scrutiny and debate and are consistent with other independent sources. The comprehensive international data sources used for most of the tables are presented in the list of "Statistical soruces and references" at the end of the *Yearbook*.

Users of international statistics are often concerned about the apparent lack of timeliness in the available data. Unfortunately, most international data are only available with a delay of at least one to three years after the latest year to which they refer. The reasons for the delay are that the data must first be processed by the national statistical services at the country level, then forwarded to the international statistical services and processed again to ensure as much consistency across countries and over time as possible.

tableaux n'ont qu'une valeur indicative et nécessiteront des ajustements plus poussés avant de pouvoir servir à des analyses approfondies. Bien que l'on soit parvenu, dans l'ensemble, à un degré de comparabilité appréciable en matière de statistiques internationales, diverses raisons expliquent que subsistent encore de nombreuses limitations.

Une cause commune de non-comparabilité des données réside dans la diversité des méthodes d'évaluation employées pour comptabiliser des agrégats tels que le revenu national, les salaires et traitements, la production des différentes branches d'activité industrielle, etc. Il n'est pas toujours satisfaisant de ramener la valeur des séries de ce type — exprimée à l'origine en prix nationaux — à une monnaie commune (par exemple le dollar des États-Unis) car les taux de change du marché connaissent fréquemment de fortes fluctuations tandis que les taux officiels ne coïncident pas avec ceux des marchés officieux ni avec les parités réelles de pouvoir d'achat. C'est pourquoi les données relatives au revenu national, qui sont publiées dans l'*Annuaire* en dollars des États-Unis, souffrent de certaines distorsions et ne peuvent servir qu'à donner une idée approximative des ordres de grandeur relatifs.

Le recours à des sources diverses pour la collecte des données est une autre facteur qui limite la comparabilité, en particulier dans les secteurs de l'emploi et du chômage où les statistiques sont obtenues par des moyens aussi peu comparables que les sondages, le dépouillement des registres d'assurances sociales et les enquêtes auprès des entreprises.

Dans certains cas, les données ne sont pas comparables en raison de différences entre les structures institutionnelles des pays. Certaines variations dans l'organisation et les institutions économiques et sociales peuvent affecter la comparabilité des données même si les concepts et définitions sont fondamentalement identiques.

Ces causes de non-comparabilité des données sont parmi celles qui sont brièvement expliquées dans les notes techniques de chaque chapitre.

Origine, fiabilité et actualité des données

Les statistiques et les indicateurs sont fondés essentiellement sur des données provenant de sources officielles nationales et internationales; c'est en effet la meilleure source si l'on veut des données fiables, complètes et comparables et si l'on a besoin de séries chronologiques. Dans quelques cas, les données officielles sont complétées par des informations et des estimations provenant d'autres sources qui ont été examinées par des spécialistes et confirmées par des sources indépendantes. On trouvera à la fin de l'*Annuaire* la liste des "Sources statistiques et références", qui récapitule les sources des données internationales utilisées pour la plupart des tableaux.

Les utilisateurs des statistiques internationales se plaignent souvent du fait que les données disponibles ne sont pas actualisées. Malheureusement, la plupart des données internationales ne sont disponibles qu'avec un délai de deux ou trois ans après la dernière année à laquelle elles se rapportent. S'il en est ainsi, c'est parce que les données sont d'abord traitées par les services statistiques nationaux avant d'être transmises aux services statistiques internationaux, qui les traitent à nouveau pour assurer la plus grande comparabilité possible entre les pays et entre les périodes.

Part One
World and Region Summary

I

World and region summary (tables 1-7)

This part of the *Statistical Yearbook* presents selected aggregate series on principal economic and social topics for the world as a whole and major regions. The topics include population and surface area, agricultural and industrial production, energy, commodity prices, motor vehicles in use, external trade and government financial reserves. More detailed data on individual countries and areas are provided in the subsequent parts of the present *Yearbook*. These comprise Part Two, Population and Social Statistics; Part Three, Economic Activity; and Part Four, International Economic Relations.

Regional totals may contain incomparabilities between series owing to differences in definitions of regions and lack of data for particular regional components. General information on regional groupings is provided in annex I of the *Yearbook*. Supplementary information on regional groupings used in specific series is provided as necessary in table footnotes and in the technical notes at the end of chapter I.

Première partie
Aperçu mondial et régional

I

Aperçu mondial et régional (tableaux 1 à 7)

Cette partie de l'*Annuaire statistique* présente, pour le monde entier et ses principales subdivisions, un choix d'agrégats ayant trait à des questions économiques et sociales essentielles : population et superficie, production agricole et industrielle, énergie, prix des produits de base, véhicules automobiles en circulation, commerce extérieur et réserves financières publiques. Des statistiques plus détaillées pour divers pays ou zones figurent dans les parties ultérieures de l'*Annuaire*, c'est-à-dire dans les deuxième, troisième et quatrième parties intitulées respectivement : population et statistiques sociales, activités économiques et relations économiques internationales.

Les totaux régionaux peuvent présenter des incomparabilités entre les séries en raison de différences dans la définition des régions et de l'absence de données sur tel ou tel élément régional. A l'annexe I de l'*Annuaire*, on trouvera des renseignements généraux sur les groupements régionaux. Des informations complémentaires sur les groupements régionaux pour certaines séries bien précises sont fournies, lorsqu'il y a lieu, dans les notes figurant au bas des tableaux et dans les notes techniques à la fin du chapitre I.

1
Selected series of world statistics
Séries principales de statistiques mondiales
Population, production, external trade and finance
Population, production, commerce extérieur et finances

Series Séries	Unit or base Unité ou base	1986	1987	1988	1989	1990	1991	1992	1993	1994
World population [1] **Population mondiale** [1]	**million**	**4938**	**5024**	**5112**	**5201**	**5292**	**5385**	**5480**	**5572**	**5630**

Agriculture, forestry and fishing production • Production agricole, forestière et de la pêche
Index numbers • Indices

All commodities Tous produits	1979−81	115	116	119	123	126	127	129	129	131
Food Produits alimentaires	1979−81	116	116	118	123	126	127	129	130	132
Crops Culture	1979−81	115	116	116	122	125	124	128	127	130
Cereals Céréales	1979−81	118	114	112	122	127	122	128	124	127
Livestock products Produits de l'élevage	1979−81	115	118	121	123	126	128	128	129	130

Quantities • Quantités

Oilcrops Huile cultures	million t.	65	68	68	72	76	77	79	80	88
Meat Viande	million t.	157	163	169	172	178	182	185	190	198
Roundwood Bois rond	million m³	3268	3343	3401	3459	3506	3397	3405	3416	3440
Fish catches Prises de poissons	million t.	92.8	94.3	98.9	100.1	97.4	97.4	98.8	101.4	...

Industrial production • Production industrielle
Index numbers [2] • Indices [2]

All commodities Tous produits	1980	109.4	113.0	119.3	123.3	122.8	121.8	122.3	122.9	128.6
Mining Mines	1980	89.2	90.5	95.8	100.3	100.1	97.7	101.3	101.4	107.2
Manufacturing Manufactures	1980	112.9	116.9	123.6	127.4	126.5	125.2	124.9	125.3	131.1

Quantities • Quantités

Coal Houille	million t.	3328	3423	3505	3581	3516	3467	3529	3465	3580
Lignite and brown coal [3] Lignite et charbon brun [3]	million t.	1196	1225	1243	1256	1191	1081	1040	995	963
Crude petroleum [4] Petrole brut [4]	million t.	2770	2772	2891	2935	3299	2981	3004	2985	3032
Natural gas Gaz naturel	pétajoules	62541	67202	70426	73078	75003	76697	75782	77611	79687
Pig−iron and ferro−alloys Fonte et ferro−alliages	million t.	500	507	536	544	529	501	500	502	523
Fabrics • Tissus										
Cellulosic and non cellulosic fibres Cellulosiques et non cellulosiques	million m²	20860	20330	21337	22292	23290	21097	21563	20156	20553
Cotton and wool Coton et laines	million m²	92833	84552	94830	103340	88228	97853	97583	100129	...
Leather footwear Chaussures de cuir	million pairs	4455	4194	4556	4493	4488	4132	4037	4134	* 3673
Sulphuric acid Acide sulfurique	million t.	131	134	142	140	135	127	121	111	118
Soap Savons	million t.	22	22	23	24	20	19	20	20	21
Refrigerators Réfrigérateurs	million	45	50	56	55	53	48	50	* 56	* 60
Washing machines Machines et appareils à laver	million	42	45	48	46	45	38	37	* 45	* 47

1

Selected series of world statistics
Population, production, external trade and finance [*cont.*]
Séries principales de statistiques mondiales
Population, production, commerce extérieur et finaces [*suite*]

Series Séries	Unit or base Unité ou base	1986	1987	1988	1989	1990	1991	1992	1993	1994
Machine tools · Machines outils										
Drilling and boring machines										
Perceuses	1000	153	147	156	151	141	158	135	129	116
Lathes										
Tours	1000	161	120	110	150	270	273	310	194	183
Lorries · Camions										
Assembled										
Assemblés	1000	403	412	517	575	673	703	680	698	* 849
Produced										
Fabriqués	1000	11855	12452	13516	12794	11812	10843	11483	11103	* 10692
Aluminium										
Aluminium	1000 t.	18949	19261	20338	20736	21125	18082	18499	18753	* 21184
Cement										
Ciment	million t.	986	1034	1101	1136	1143	1161	1214	1274	* 1354
Electricity [5]	billion									
Electricité [5]	milliard kWh	10055	10587	11117	11483	11788	12017	12115	12325	12681
Fertilizers [6]										
Engrais [6]	million t.	143.5	152.4	152.2	158.3	152.9	147.6	144.2	138.6	131.5
Sugar, raw										
Sucre, brut	million t.	100.0	103.5	104.6	107.2	110.9	112.1	117.6	112.4	110.3
Woodpulp										
Pâte de bois	million t.	141.3	146.9	151.8	156.5	155.1	155.2	151.9	151.2	155.4
Sawnwood										
Sciages	million m³	484	505	508	507	505	370	377	420	413
Motor vehicles · Véhicules automobiles										
Passenger										
Tourisme	million	32.41	32.80	33.84	34.69	34.90	33.52	33.70	30.90	...
Commercial										
Utilitaires	million	12.44	12.90	13.86	13.53	12.44	12.01	12.61	...	...

Transport · Transports

Motor vehicles in use · Véhicules automobiles en service

Passenger cars										
Voitures de tourisme	1000	395129	407959	422240	438525	450596	451928	464514	458489	...
Commercial vehicles										
Véhicules utilitaires	1000	124037	129593	133832	137869	140969	141930	144681	146501	...

External trade · Commerce extérieur

Value, billion US$ · Valeur, milliard $E−U

Imports, c.i.f.										
Importations c.i.f.		2198.1	2559.0	2913.5	3134.6	3547.7	3538.1	3791.4	3720.5	4220.5
Exports, f.o.b.										
Exportations f.o.b.		2129.8	2491.7	2827.9	3022.4	3423.5	3417.9	3654.8	3639.2	4143.8
Quantum: index of exports · Quantum : indice des exportations										
All commodities										
Tous produits	1990	77	82	88	95	100	104	109	114	124
Manufactures										
Produits manufacturés	1990	74	80	93	92	100	105	111	115	130
Unit value: index of exports [7] · Valeur unitaire : indice des exportations [7]										
All commodities										
Tous produits	1990	77	85	90	92	100	98	100	95	99
Manufactures										
Produits manufacturés	1990	77	86	93	92	100	100	103	99	101
Primary commodities: price indexes [78] · Produits de base : indices des prix [78]										
All commodities										
Tous produits	1980	63	66	70	72	79	69	68	62	63
Food										
Produits alimentaires	1980	74	75	87	87	88	85	87	82	87
Non−food: of agricultural origin										
Non alimentaires: d'origine agricole	1980	75	86	100	98	100	93	91	84	95
Minerals										
Minéraux	1980	57	59	59	62	71	59	57	51	49

1
Selected series of world statistics
Population, production, external trade and finance [*cont.*]
Séries principales de statistiques mondiales
Population, production, commerce extérieur et finaces [*suite*]

Series Séries	Unit or base Unité ou base	1986	1987	1988	1989	1990	1991	1992	1993	1994
Finance • Finances										
International reserves minus gold, billion US $ [9] · Réserves internationales moins l'or, milliard $E−U [9]										
All countries										
Tous les pays		419.0	507.8	542.7	591.0	637.7	671.8	693.3	765.1	823.0
Position in IMF										
Disponibilité au FMI		35.3	31.5	28.3	25.5	23.8	25.9	33.9	32.8	31.7
Foreign exchange										
Devise étrangères		364.1	456.1	494.2	545.0	593.6	625.4	646.6	717.7	775.6
SDR (special drawing rights)										
DTS (droits de tirage spéciaux)		19.5	20.2	20.2	20.5	20.4	20.6	12.9	14.6	15.8

Source:
Statistics Division of the United Nations Secretariat (New York),
Food and Agriculture Oganization of the United Nations (Rome),
Motor Vehicle Manufacturers' Association (Detroit) and
International Monetary Fund (Washington, DC).

1 Annual data: mid−year estimates.
2 Excluding Albania, China, Democratic People's Republic of
   Korea, Viet Nam, former Czechoslovakia, former USSR and
   Yugoslavia.
3 Excluding peat for fuel.
4 Excluding natural gas liquids.
5 Electricity (hydro, geothermal, thermal, nuclear) generated by
   establishments for public or private use.
6 Year beginning 1 July.
7 Indexes computed in US dollars.
8 Export price indexes.
9 End of period.

Source:
Division de statistique du Sécretariat des Nations Unies (New York),
Organisation des Nations Unies pour l'alimentation et l'agriculture
(Rome), "Motor Vehicles Manufacturers' Association" (Detroit) et
Fonds monétaire internationale (Washington, DC).

1 Données annuelles : estimations au milieu de l'année.
2 Non compris l'Albanie, la Chine, la République populaire
   démocratique de Corée, le Viet Nam, l'ancienne Tchèchoslovaquie,
   l'ancienne URSS et la Yougoslavie.
3 Non compris la tourbe combustible.
4 Non compris le gaz naturel liquéfié.
5 L'électricité (hydraulique, géothermique, thermique, nucléaire)
   produite par des entreprises d'utilisation publique ou privée.
6 L'année commençant le 1er juillet.
7 Indice calculé en dollars des Etats−Unis.
8 Indice des prix à l'exportation.
9 Fin de la période.

2
Population, rate of increase, birth and death rates, surface area and density
Population, taux d'accroissement, taux de natalité et taux de mortalité, superficie et densité

Macro regions and regions Grandes régions et régions	Mid–year estimates (millions) Estimations au milieu de l'année (millions)								Annual rate of increase Taux d'accrois-sement annuel % 1990–95	Birth rate Taux de natalité (0/000) 1990–95	Death rate Taux de mortalité (0/000) 1990–95	Surface area (km²) Superficie (km²) (000's) 1994	Density[1] Densité[1] 1994
	1950	1960	1970	1975	1980	1985	1990	1994					
World													
Monde	**2520**	**3021**	**3697**	**4077**	**4444**	**4846**	**5285**	**5530**	**1.6**	**25**	**9**	**135641**	**42**
Africa													
Afrique	**224**	**282**	**364**	**414**	**476**	**549**	**633**	**708**	**2.8**	**42**	**14**	**30306**	**23**
Eastern Africa													
Afrique orientale	66	83	110	125	145	168	196	221	3.0	46	16	6356	35
Middle Africa													
Afrique centrale	26	32	40	45	52	61	70	80	3.1	46	15	6613	12
Northern Africa													
Afrique septentrionale	53	67	85	96	110	126	143	157	2.3	31	9	8525	18
Southern Africa													
Afrique méridionale	16	20	25	29	33	38	42	46	2.3	32	9	2675	17
Western Africa													
Afrique occidentale	63	80	104	118	135	156	181	204	3.0	46	16	6138	33
Northern America[2]													
Amérique septentrionale[2]	**166**	**199**	**226**	**239**	**252**	**265**	**278**	**290**	**1.0**	**16**	**9**	**21517**	**13**
Latin America													
Amérique latine	**166**	**217**	**283**	**320**	**358**	**398**	**440**	**474**	**1.8**	**26**	**7**	**20533**	**23**
Caribbean													
Caraïbes	17	20	25	27	29	31	34	35	1.3	24	8	235	150
Central America													
Amérique centrale	37	49	67	78	89	101	113	124	2.2	30	6	2480	50
South America													
Amérique du Sud	112	147	191	214	240	267	293	314	1.7	25	7	17819	18
Asia[3]													
Asie[3]	**1403**	**1703**	**2147**	**2406**	**2642**	**2904**	**3186**	**3403**	**1.6**	**25**	**8**	**31764**	**107**
Eastern Asia													
Asie orientale	671	792	987	1097	1179	1259	1352	1410	1.0	18	7	11762	120
South Central Asia													
Asie central méridionale	499	621	788	886	990	1113	1243	1353	2.1	31	10	10776	126
South Eastern Asia													
Asie méridionale orientale	182	225	287	324	360	401	442	476	1.8	27	8	4495	106
Western Asia[3]													
Asie occidentale[3]	50	66	86	99	113	131	149	164	2.4	32	7	4731	35
Europe[3]													
Europe[3]	**549**	**605**	**656**	**676**	**693**	**706**	**722**	**726**	**0.2**	**12**	**11**	**22986**	**32**
Eastern Europe													
Europe orientale	221	254	276	286	295	303	310	309	−0.1	12	12	18813	16
Northern Europe													
Europe septentrionale	78	82	87	89	90	91	92	93	0.3	14	11	1749	53
Southern Europe													
Europe méridionale	109	118	128	132	138	141	143	144	0.1	11	10	1316	109
Western Europe													
Europe occidentale	141	152	165	169	170	172	176	180	0.6	12	11	1107	163
Oceania[2]													
Océanie[2]	**12.6**	**15.7**	**19.3**	**21.4**	**22.7**	**24.5**	**26.4**	**28.1**	**1.5**	**19**	**8**	**8537**	**3**
Australia and New Zealand													
Australie et Nouvelle Zélande	10.1	12.6	15.4	17.0	17.7	18.9	20.2	21.4	1.4	15	8	7984	3
Melanesia													
Mélanésie	2.1	2.6	3.3	3.7	4.2	4.7	5.2	5.7	2.2	32	9	541	11
Micronesia													
Micronésie	0.2	0.2	0.2	0.3	0.3	0.4	0.4	0.5	2.3	33	6	3	157
Polynesia													
Polynésie	0.2	0.3	0.4	0.4	0.5	0.5	0.5	0.6	1.5	31	6	9	65

2
Population, rate of increase, birth and death rates, surface area and density [*cont.*]
Population, taux d'accroissement, taux de natalité et taux de
mortalité, superficie et densité [*suite*]

Source:
Demographic statistics database of the Statistics Division of
the United Nations Secretariat.

1 Population per square kilometre of surface area. Figures
   are merely the quotients of population divided by surface
   area and are not to be considered as either reflecting
   density in the urban sense or as indicating the supporting
   power of a territory's land and resources.
2 Hawaii, a state of the United States of America, is included
   in Northern America rather than Oceania.
3 The European portion of Turkey is included in Western
   Asia rather than Europe.

Source:
Base de données pour les statistiques demographique du
Bureau de statistique du Secrétariat de l'ONU.

1 Habitants per kilomètre carré. Il s'agit simplement du quotient calculé
   en divisant la population par la superficie et n'est pas considéré
   comme indiquant la densité au sens urbain du mot ni l'effectif de
   population que les terres et les ressources du territoire sont capables
   de nourrir.
2 Hawaii, un Etat des Etats – Unis d'Amérique, est compris en Amérique.
   septentrionale plutôt qu'en Océanie.
3 La partie européenne de la Turquie est comprise en Asie Occidentale
   plutôt qu'en Europe.

3
Index numbers of total agricultural and food production
Indices de la production agricole totale et de la production alimentaire

1979-1981 = 100

Region Région	1985	1986	1987	1988	1989	1990	1991	1992	1993	1994
A. Total agricultural production • Production agricole totale										
World ***Monde***	**114**	**115**	**116**	**119**	**123**	**126**	**127**	**129**	**129**	**131**
Africa Afrique	111	116	116	122	127	128	134	131	136	139
North America Amérique du Nord	108	104	102	97	104	109	109	116	108	123
South America Amérique du sud	115	111	117	123	125	126	130	134	133	139
Asia Asie	123	126	129	135	139	146	150	156	160	165
Europe Europe	108	109	109	109	110	109	110	106	105	102
Oceania Océanie	109	110	109	113	109	112	112	119	121	112
former USSR† ancienne URSS†	109	116	116	117	121	120	106	...	...	...
B. Food production • Production alimentaire										
World ***Monde***	**114**	**116**	**116**	**118**	**123**	**126**	**127**	**129**	**130**	**132**
Africa Afrique	111	116	116	123	128	129	136	133	139	141
North America Amérique du Nord	109	106	103	96	106	109	109	117	108	124
South America Amérique du sud	115	113	118	125	128	129	132	137	137	145
Asia Asie	122	126	128	134	139	146	149	156	161	166
Europe Europe	107	109	109	108	110	109	110	106	106	102
Oceania Océanie	107	108	106	110	108	111	111	119	124	114
former USSR† ancienne URSS†	110	117	118	118	123	122	108	...	...	...

Source:
Food and Agriculture Organization of the United
Nations (Rome).

† For detailed descriptions of data pertaining to
former Czechoslovakia, Germany, SFR Yugoslavia and former
USSR, see Annex I - Country or area nomenclature, regional
and other groupings.

Source:
Organisation des Nations Unies pour l'alimentation et
l'agriculture (Rome).

† Pour les descriptions en détails des données
relatives à l'ancienne Tchécoslovaquie, l'Allemagne, la Rfs
Yougoslavie et l'ancienne URSS, voir l'Annexe I -
Nomenclature des pays ou zones, groupements régionaux et
autres groupements.

4
Index numbers of per capita total agricultural and food production
Indices de la production agricole totale et de la production alimentaire par habitant

1979-1981 = 100

Region Région	1985	1986	1987	1988	1989	1990	1991	1992	1993	1994
A. Per capita total agricultural production • Production agricole totale par habitant										
World Monde	**105**	**104**	**103**	**103**	**105**	**106**	**105**	**105**	**103**	**104**
Africa Afrique	96	98	95	98	98	97	98	93	94	93
North America Amérique du Nord	101	96	93	87	92	95	94	98	90	101
South America Amérique du sud	104	98	102	105	105	104	104	106	103	107
Asia Asie	112	113	113	116	118	121	122	125	127	128
Europe Europe	106	107	107	106	107	106	106	102	101	100
Oceania Océanie	102	101	98	100	95	96	95	99	100	91
former USSR† ancienne URSS†	105	110	109	108	112	110	97	...	...	...
B. Per capita food production • Production alimentaire par habitant										
World Monde	**104**	**104**	**103**	**103**	**105**	**106**	**105**	**105**	**104**	**105**
Africa Afrique	96	98	95	98	99	97	99	95	96	95
North America Amérique du Nord	102	97	94	87	93	96	94	99	91	102
South America Amérique du sud	103	100	102	106	107	105	106	108	106	111
Asia Asie	111	113	112	115	117	121	122	125	127	129
Europe Europe	106	107	106	106	107	106	106	102	101	100
Oceania Océanie	100	99	95	98	95	95	94	99	102	92
former USSR† ancienne URSS†	105	111	111	110	114	112	98	...	...	...

Source:
Food and Agriculture Organization of the United Nations (Rome).

Source:
Organisation des Nations Unies pour l'alimentation et l'agriculture (Rome).

† For detailed descriptions of data pertaining to former Czechoslovakia, Germany, SFR Yugoslavia and former USSR, see Annex I - Country or area nomenclature, regional and other groupings.

† Pour les descriptions en détails des données relatives à l'ancienne Tchécoslovaquie, l'Allemagne, la Rfs Yougoslavie et l'ancienne URSS, voir l'Annexe I - Nomenclature des pays ou zones, groupements régionaux et autres groupements.

5
Index numbers of industrial production: world and regions
Indices de la production industrielle : monde et régions
1980=100

Regions and industry [ISIC] Régions et industrie [CITI]	Weight(%) Pond.(%)	1986	1987	1988	1989	1990	1991	1992	1993	1994
World · Monde										
Total industry [2−4] **Total, industrie [2−4]**	**100.0**	**109**	**113**	**119**	**123**	**123**	**122**	**122**	**123**	**129**
Total mining [2] **Total, industries extractives [2]**	**16.9**	**90**	**90**	**96**	**100**	**100**	**98**	**101**	**101**	**107**
Coal Houille	1.7	109	108	108	109	100	99	96	91	91
Petroleum, gas Pétrole, gaz	12.6	83	84	88	93	94	91	96	97	105
Metal Minerais métalliques	1.4	113	116	128	134	136	137	138	134	133
Total manufacturing [3] **Total, industries manufacturières [3]**	**76.3**	**113**	**117**	**124**	**127**	**126**	**125**	**125**	**125**	**131**
Light industry Industrie légère	26.6	110	114	117	119	118	117	118	119	122
Heavy industry Industrie lourde	49.7	114	119	127	132	131	129	128	129	136
Selected manufacturing **Industries manufacturières déterminées**										
Food, beverages, tobacco Industries alimentaires, boissons, tabac	9.6	113	115	119	120	122	124	126	127	130
Textiles Textiles	3.9	104	107	107	108	103	100	100	99	100
Apparel, leather, footwear Articles d'habillement, cuir et chaussures	3.0	101	102	100	100	95	92	89	88	89
Wood products, furniture Bois, meubles	3.3	107	112	116	118	116	114	115	116	121
Paper, printing, publishing Papier, imprimerie, édition	5.5	119	125	131	134	135	135	136	139	142
Chemicals and related products Produits chimiques et alliés	11.2	117	123	130	134	133	132	136	137	144
Non−metallic mineral products Produits minéraux non métalliques	3.4	102	105	110	114	112	110	109	109	113
Basic metals Métallurgie de base	6.0	96	100	107	109	107	104	101	102	106
Metal products Ouvrages en métaux	29.2	118	123	132	138	138	136	134	133	142
Electricity, gas, water [4] **Électricité, gaz et eau [4]**	**6.5**	**120**	**125**	**130**	**135**	**139**	**144**	**146**	**150**	**155**
A. Developed regions · Régions developpées										
Total industry [2−4] **Total, industrie [2−4]**	**100.0**	**110**	**114**	**120**	**123**	**122**	**120**	**119**	**119**	**124**
Total mining [2] **Total, industries extractives [2]**	**8.8**	**104**	**106**	**107**	**107**	**106**	**107**	**108**	**108**	**113**
Coal Houille	2.0	107	105	105	105	95	93	89	83	81
Petroleum, gas Pétrole, gaz	4.6	102	103	102	99	100	104	107	112	123
Metal Minerais métalliques	1.2	114	119	135	144	148	148	149	145	141
Total manufacturing [3] **Total, industries manufacturières [3]**	**83.7**	**110**	**114**	**121**	**125**	**123**	**120**	**119**	**118**	**124**
Light industry Industrie légère	27.4	107	111	114	115	113	111	111	111	114
Heavy industry Industrie lourde	56.3	112	116	124	129	127	124	123	122	128
Selected manufacturing **Industries manufacturières déterminées**										
Food, beverages, tobacco Industries alimentaires, boissons, tabac	9.5	108	111	114	115	115	116	116	117	119

5

Index numbers of industrial production: world and regions [*cont.*]
Indices de la production industrielle : monde et régions [*suite*]
1980=100

Region and industry [ISIC] Région et industrie [CITI]	Weight(%) Pond.(%)	1986	1987	1988	1989	1990	1991	1992	1993	1994
Textiles										
Textiles	3.6	99	101	101	103	94	90	89	86	86
Apparel, leather, footwear										
Articles d'habillement, cuir et chaussures	3.1	97	96	94	92	86	82	79	77	77
Wood products, furniture										
Bois, meubles	3.7	106	112	115	117	113	110	112	113	117
Paper, printing, publishing										
Papier, imprimerie, édition	6.3	117	123	128	131	132	130	131	133	136
Chemicals and related products										
Produits chimiques et alliés	11.5	113	118	125	129	126	124	126	127	133
Non−metallic mineral products										
Produits minéraux non métalliques	3.6	98	100	106	108	106	101	99	97	100
Basic metals										
Métallurgie de base	6.8	93	96	104	105	102	99	95	94	99
Metal products										
Ouvrages en métaux	34.4	117	121	130	137	135	132	130	128	136
Electricity, gas, water [4]										
Electricité, gaz et eau [4]	**7.5**	**116**	**120**	**124**	**128**	**131**	**135**	**136**	**139**	**142**

North America • Amérique du Nord

	Weight(%) Pond.(%)	1986	1987	1988	1989	1990	1991	1992	1993	1994
Total industry [2−4]										
Total, industrie [2−4]	**100.0**	**111**	**116**	**122**	**123**	**123**	**120**	**125**	**130**	**139**
Total mining [2]										
Total, industries extractives [2]	**12.4**	**90**	**92**	**95**	**94**	**96**	**95**	**94**	**94**	**96**
Coal										
Houille	1.6	109	114	118	122	128	124	122	117	128
Petroleum, gas										
Pétrole, gaz	8.7	82	82	84	81	82	81	81	82	83
Metal										
Minerais métalliques	1.2	107	119	132	138	140	143	146	139	136
Total manufacturing [3]										
Total, industries manufacturières [3]	**79.4**	**115**	**120**	**127**	**129**	**128**	**124**	**130**	**136**	**146**
Light industry										
Industrie légère	24.1	118	124	126	126	125	122	126	130	136
Heavy industry										
Industrie lourde	55.3	114	119	127	130	129	125	131	139	151
Selected manufacturing										
Industries manufacturières déterminées										
Food, beverages, tobacco										
Industries alimentaires, boissons, tabac	7.5	112	115	117	117	118	119	122	123	128
Textiles										
Textiles	2.4	106	112	111	112	108	108	115	122	126
Apparel, leather, footwear										
Articles d'habillement, cuir et chaussures	2.6	94	97	95	92	89	87	89	91	93
Wood products, furniture										
Bois, meubles	3.9	136	145	145	145	141	131	138	144	153
Paper, printing, publishing										
Papier, imprimerie, édition	8.0	126	134	136	137	137	134	136	138	142
Chemicals and related products										
Produits chimiques et alliés	10.6	119	126	132	136	138	136	142	145	154
Non−metallic mineral products										
Produits minéraux non métalliques	2.6	111	113	115	115	112	102	104	105	109
Basic metals										
Métallurgie de base	6.1	85	92	100	99	98	91	94	100	107
Metal products										
Ouvrages en métaux	34.5	118	122	132	136	134	131	138	148	165
Electricity, gas, water [4]										
Electricité, gaz et eau [4]	**8.2**	**107**	**109**	**114**	**118**	**118**	**121**	**121**	**125**	**127**

Europe • Europe

	Weight(%) Pond.(%)	1986	1987	1988	1989	1990	1991	1992	1993	1994
Total industry [2−4]										
Total, industrie [2−4]	**100.0**	**107**	**110**	**115**	**118**	**114**	**111**	**109**	**106**	**110**

5
Index numbers of industrial production: world and regions [*cont.*]
Indices de la production industrielle : monde et régions [*suite*]
1980=100

Regions and industry [ISIC] Régions et industrie [CITI]	Weight(%) Pond.(%)	1986	1987	1988	1989	1990	1991	1992	1993	1994
Total mining [2]										
Total, industries extractives [2]	**7.0**	**114**	**115**	**112**	**110**	**104**	**106**	**109**	**111**	**120**
Coal										
Houille	2.6	101	97	94	93	76	73	68	60	53
Petroleum, gas										
Pétrole, gaz	3.3	132	136	130	126	127	138	148	160	185
Metal										
Minerais métalliques	0.3	84	78	78	80	79	71	67	57	55
Total manufacturing [3]										
Total, industries manufacturières [3]	**86.2**	**106**	**108**	**114**	**118**	**113**	**110**	**107**	**103**	**106**
Light industry										
Industrie légère	30.2	103	106	109	112	108	106	104	102	104
Heavy industry										
Industrie lourde	55.9	107	110	116	121	116	112	108	103	108
Selected manufacturing										
Industries manufacturières déterminées										
Food, beverages, tobacco										
Industries alimentaires, boissons, tabac	10.6	108	110	113	115	114	115	114	114	116
Textiles										
Textiles	4.4	98	99	100	102	90	85	81	76	75
Apparel, leather, footwear										
Articles d'habillement, cuir et chaussures	3.8	98	95	93	92	83	78	73	70	69
Wood products, furniture										
Bois, meubles	3.7	92	96	102	105	102	104	102	101	104
Paper, printing, publishing										
Papier, imprimerie, édition	5.2	110	116	122	127	128	127	126	126	130
Chemicals and related products										
Produits chimiques et alliés	12.7	111	114	122	125	117	115	116	116	120
Non-metallic mineral products										
Produits minéraux non métalliques	4.1	94	96	102	106	103	98	95	92	95
Basic metals										
Métallurgie de base	5.9	96	96	104	105	98	93	88	84	88
Metal products										
Ouvrages en métaux	34.1	110	112	119	125	120	115	110	103	107
Electricity, gas, water [4]										
Electricité, gaz et eau [4]	**6.8**	**119**	**124**	**127**	**130**	**131**	**136**	**138**	**139**	**140**

European Community [+] • Communauté européenne [+]

	Weight(%) Pond.(%)	1986	1987	1988	1989	1990	1991	1992	1993	1994
Total industry [2−4]										
Total, industrie [2−4]	**100.0**	**106**	**108**	**112**	**116**	**113**	**112**	**110**	**106**	**109**
Total mining [2]										
Total, industries extractives [2]	**6.9**	**112**	**111**	**104**	**97**	**90**	**92**	**92**	**93**	**100**
Coal										
Houille	2.7	100	94	91	90	76	72	67	59	51
Petroleum, gas										
Pétrole, gaz	3.2	129	132	119	103	101	108	114	125	147
Metal										
Minerais métalliques	0.2	75	64	65	71	72	70	65	49	47
Total manufacturing [3]										
Total, industries manufacturières [3]	**86.0**	**104**	**106**	**112**	**117**	**113**	**112**	**109**	**104**	**107**
Light industry										
Industrie légère	29.5	102	105	109	112	110	109	108	105	106
Heavy industry										
Industrie lourde	56.5	105	107	114	120	115	113	110	104	107
Selected manufacturing										
Industries manufacturières déterminées										
Food, beverages, tobacco										
Industries alimentaires, boissons, tabac	10.6	108	111	114	117	119	121	121	121	122
Textiles										
Textiles	4.2	98	99	99	101	93	90	86	80	79
Apparel, leather, footwear										
Articles d'habillement, cuir et chaussures	3.9	95	92	89	88	82	77	73	70	68

5
Index numbers of industrial production: world and regions [cont.]
Indices de la production industrielle : monde et régions [suite]
1980=100

Regions and industry [ISIC] Régions et industrie [CITI]	Weight(%) Pond.(%)	1986	1987	1988	1989	1990	1991	1992	1993	1994
Wood products, furniture Bois, meubles	3.4	88	93	99	103	100	102	100	98	99
Paper, printing, publishing Papier, imprimerie, édition	5.0	106	112	119	124	126	126	126	124	126
Chemicals and related products Produits chimiques et alliés	13.0	110	113	120	124	118	117	118	116	120
Non—metallic mineral products Produits minéraux non métalliques	4.2	91	93	99	104	102	99	97	93	96
Basic metals Métallurgie de base	5.9	92	93	101	103	97	94	90	85	90
Metal products Ouvrages en métaux	34.6	107	110	116	124	119	117	112	103	107
Electricity, gas, water [4] **Electricité, gaz et eau [4]**	**7.1**	**118**	**122**	**124**	**128**	**130**	**136**	**136**	**137**	**138**

European Free Trade Association [+]
Association européenne de libre échange [+]

	Weight(%) Pond.(%)	1986	1987	1988	1989	1990	1991	1992	1993	1994
Total industry [2–4] **Total, industrie [2–4]**	**100.0**	**114**	**118**	**123**	**130**	**134**	**134**	**136**	**139**	**151**
Total mining [2] **Total, industries extractives [2]**	**7.6**	**141**	**155**	**169**	**211**	**222**	**244**	**270**	**286**	**321**
Coal Houille	0.1	190	171	122	165	155	165	173	127	137
Petroleum, gas Pétrole, gaz	6.4	146	162	179	229	241	268	298	318	356
Metal Minerais métalliques	0.5	104	106	104	101	99	94	93	95	94
Total manufacturing [3] **Total, industries manufacturières [3]**	**84.0**	**110**	**113**	**118**	**122**	**125**	**123**	**122**	**123**	**133**
Light industry Industrie légère	30.9	105	106	108	110	112	110	108	108	113
Heavy industry Industrie lourde	53.1	114	117	123	128	133	130	130	132	145
Selected manufacturing **Industries manufacturières déterminées**										
Food, beverages, tobacco Industries alimentaires, boissons, tabac	10.4	106	107	109	112	115	118	117	119	124
Textiles Textiles	2.7	93	91	91	90	91	87	84	78	82
Apparel, leather, footwear Articles d'habillement, cuir et chaussures	2.9	92	86	79	74	72	69	62	57	55
Wood products, furniture Bois, meubles	6.9	97	100	103	109	112	107	104	104	112
Paper, printing, publishing Papier, imprimerie, édition	11.4	120	127	132	134	135	133	134	137	146
Chemicals and related products Produits chimiques et alliés	9.8	119	126	136	144	147	145	148	154	168
Non—metallic mineral products Produits minéraux non métalliques	3.5	104	109	109	112	118	112	109	104	109
Basic metals Métallurgie de base	5.0	108	111	120	122	120	115	116	117	128
Metal products Ouvrages en métaux	30.4	114	114	120	125	132	129	127	128	142
Electricity, gas, water [4] **Electricité, gaz et eau [4]**	**8.4**	**125**	**136**	**139**	**142**	**147**	**151**	**156**	**163**	**169**

B. Developing regions · Régions en voie de développement

	Weight(%) Pond.(%)	1986	1987	1988	1989	1990	1991	1992	1993	1994
Total industry [2–4] **Total, industrie [2–4]**	**100.0**	**106**	**110**	**117**	**123**	**127**	**128**	**134**	**138**	**146**
Total mining [2] **Total, industries extractives [2]**	**48.4**	**80**	**80**	**88**	**95**	**96**	**91**	**97**	**96**	**103**
Coal Houille	0.4	149	157	163	175	181	203	226	247	256

5
Index numbers of industrial production: world and regions [*cont.*]
Indices de la production industrielle : monde et régions [*suite*]
1980=100

Regions and industry [ISIC] Régions et industrie [CITI]	Weight(%) Pond.(%)	1986	1987	1988	1989	1990	1991	1992	1993	1994
Petroleum, gas Pétrole, gaz	43.7	75	76	83	91	91	86	91	91	98
Metal Minerais métalliques	2.6	111	109	116	116	116	118	120	114	119
Total manufacturing [3] **Total, industries manufacturières [3]**	**47.8**	**128**	**136**	**142**	**146**	**153**	**158**	**164**	**171**	**180**
Light industry Industrie légère	23.1	124	128	132	136	140	145	148	153	159
Heavy industry Industrie lourde	24.7	132	144	151	156	165	171	178	188	200
Selected manufacturing **Industries manufacturières déterminées**										
Food, beverages, tobacco Industries alimentaires, boissons, tabac	10.3	129	131	136	141	146	152	157	162	168
Textiles Textiles	4.7	120	125	123	124	127	130	132	136	140
Apparel, leather, footwear Articles d'habillement, cuir et chaussures	2.3	121	127	131	136	136	137	137	140	144
Wood products, furniture Bois, meubles	1.8	113	117	122	126	132	138	142	145	153
Paper, printing, publishing Papier, imprimerie, édition	2.3	142	152	158	163	172	180	187	198	204
Chemicals and related products Produits chimiques et alliés	9.7	136	147	155	158	165	167	177	185	195
Non–metallic mineral products Produits minéraux non métalliques	2.8	118	127	130	138	142	150	157	165	174
Basic metals Métallurgie de base	3.0	125	136	139	143	149	151	154	166	174
Metal products Ouvrages en métaux	9.7	134	147	157	162	175	186	192	204	218
Electricity, gas, water [4] **Electricité, gaz et eau [4]**	**3.8**	**150**	**163**	**176**	**188**	**201**	**214**	**225**	**239**	**255**

Latin America and Caribbean · Amérique latine et Caraïbes

Total industry [2–4] **Total, industrie [2–4]**	**100.0**	**109**	**112**	**113**	**114**	**115**	**117**	**118**	**121**	**126**
Total mining [2] **Total, industries extractives [2]**	**16.8**	**114**	**113**	**119**	**121**	**125**	**124**	**125**	**125**	**129**
Coal Houille	0.2	142	141	171	164	156	154	134	128	126
Petroleum, gas Pétrole, gaz	12.0	114	112	118	119	123	122	123	124	127
Metal Minerais métalliques	3.4	120	120	126	132	136	140	146	148	155
Total manufacturing [3] **Total, industries manufacturières [3]**	**77.9**	**106**	**110**	**109**	**110**	**109**	**112**	**113**	**115**	**121**
Light industry Industrie légère	36.8	110	111	111	112	114	117	118	119	122
Heavy industry Industrie lourde	41.1	103	108	107	108	105	107	107	112	120
Selected manufacturing **Industries manufacturières déterminées**										
Food, beverages, tobacco Industries alimentaires, boissons, tabac	18.2	113	114	114	116	120	123	125	124	126
Textiles Textiles	5.2	102	102	100	99	96	98	96	96	97
Apparel, leather, footwear Articles d'habillement, cuir et chaussures	3.7	98	94	93	95	91	90	90	93	94
Wood products, furniture Bois, meubles	3.0	102	104	104	104	107	117	122	122	134
Paper, printing, publishing Papier, imprimerie, édition	4.4	133	139	142	141	145	152	153	160	162

5
Index numbers of industrial production: world and regions [*cont.*]
Indices de la production industrielle : monde et régions [*suite*]
1980=100

Region g and industry [ISIC] Région g et industrie [CITI]	Weight(%) Pond.(%)	1986	1987	1988	1989	1990	1991	1992	1993	1994
Chemicals and related products										
Produits chimiques et alliés	14.0	114	120	118	118	119	121	122	124	131
Non—metallic mineral products										
Produits minéraux non métalliques	4.8	94	101	97	98	94	97	98	102	106
Basic metals										
Métallurgie de base	5.6	101	107	107	110	106	104	105	110	116
Metal products										
Ouvrages en métaux	17.2	97	100	99	100	95	98	96	103	114
Electricity, gas, water [4]										
Electricité, gaz et eau [4]	**5.3**	**137**	**147**	**157**	**163**	**168**	**176**	**178**	**186**	**193**

Asia • Asie

Total industry [2—4]										
Total, industrie [2—4]	**100.0**	**112**	**118**	**130**	**138**	**144**	**146**	**147**	**148**	**156**
Total mining [2]										
Total, industries extractives [2]	**32.5**	**73**	**75**	**85**	**94**	**92**	**84**	**92**	**92**	**102**
Coal										
Houille	0.5	131	132	130	140	142	160	181	198	205
Petroleum, gas										
Pétrole, gaz	30.0	70	71	80	90	87	78	86	85	96
Metal										
Minerais métalliques	0.7	83	85	91	97	91	89	87	78	79
Total manufacturing [3]										
Total, industries manufacturières [3]	**61.7**	**131**	**138**	**151**	**159**	**170**	**175**	**172**	**173**	**178**
Light industry										
Industrie légère	20.4	118	122	129	133	138	142	145	147	151
Heavy industry										
Industrie lourde	41.3	137	146	162	172	185	192	186	186	192
Selected manufacturing										
Industries manufacturières déterminées										
Food, beverages, tobacco										
Industries alimentaires, boissons, tabac	6.6	126	131	140	145	151	157	162	166	172
Textiles										
Textiles	4.2	114	119	118	120	124	125	127	128	132
Apparel, leather, footwear										
Articles d'habillement, cuir et chaussures	1.7	128	141	144	148	149	152	152	152	157
Wood products, furniture										
Bois, meubles	2.1	94	99	103	105	109	109	108	108	108
Paper, printing, publishing [1]										
Papier, imprimerie, édition [1]	4.0	126	136	145	156	165	170	171	173	178
Chemicals and related products										
Produits chimiques et alliés	9.5	132	142	155	161	171	174	182	188	197
Non—metallic mineral products										
Produits minéraux non métalliques	2.9	114	120	130	138	147	154	156	159	166
Basic metals										
Métallurgie de base	6.8	107	112	121	124	131	134	127	129	131
Metal products										
Ouvrages en métaux	22.7	151	161	182	195	210	220	208	204	211
Electricity, gas, water [4]										
Electricité, gaz et eau [4]	**5.8**	**133**	**141**	**151**	**160**	**174**	**184**	**193**	**200**	**215**

Oceania [2] • Océanie [2]

Total industry [2—4]										
Total, industrie [2—4]	**100.0**	**121**	**128**	**140**	**144**	**146**	**147**	**151**	**158**	**162**
Total mining [2]										
Total, industries extractives [2]	**15.9**	**202**	**215**	**259**	**292**	**315**	**331**	**338**	**336**	**342**
Coal										
Houille	4.7	173	165	181	187	196	210	209	210	222
Petroleum, gas										
Pétrole, gaz	2.5	139	142	138	166	171	177	181	188	207
Metal										
Minerais métalliques	7.3	251	282	363	418	458	482	495	488	486

5

Index numbers of industrial production: world and regions [*cont.*]

Indices de la production industrielle : monde et régions [*suite*]

1980=100

Region ꬶ and industry [ISIC] Région ꬶ et industrie [CITI]	Weight(%) Pond.(%)	1986	1987	1988	1989	1990	1991	1992	1993	1994
Total manufacturing [3] **Total, industries manufacturières [3]**	**73.2**	**103**	**108**	**115**	**113**	**110**	**108**	**112**	**121**	**126**
Light industry Industrie légère	31.9	104	109	114	110	108	106	109	117	120
Heavy industry Industrie lourde	41.3	102	108	115	115	113	110	114	125	130
Selected manufacturing **Industries manufacturières déterminées**										
Food, beverages, tobacco Industries alimentaires, boissons, tabac	13.7	104	109	111	112	114	117	126	136	144
Textiles Textiles	2.8	112	111	113	108	109	113	101	85	78
Apparel, leather, footwear Articles d'habillement, cuir et chaussures	3.1	107	108	111	99	92	86	88	92	93
Wood products, furniture Bois, meubles	4.2	101	113	118	106	96	93	88	92	90
Paper, printing, publishing Papier, imprimerie, édition	6.8	116	124	133	125	121	116	111	127	130
Chemicals and related products Produits chimiques et alliés	8.8	99	103	112	110	112	108	112	124	125
Non-metallic mineral products Produits minéraux non métalliques	3.5	104	108	117	114	102	96	105	116	122
Basic metals Métallurgie de base	8.3	106	110	116	128	132	133	133	141	144
Metal products Ouvrages en métaux	21.3	96	103	111	108	103	98	105	117	123
Electricity, gas, water [4] **Electricité, gaz et eau [4]**	**10.9**	**131**	**136**	**143**	**149**	**152**	**155**	**158**	**160**	**162**

Source:
Industrial statistics database of the Statistics Division
of the United Nations Secretariat.

+   For Member States of this grouping, see Annex I —
    Other groupings.

ꬶ   All series exclude Albania, China, Democratic
    People's Republic of Korea, Viet Nam, former Czechoslovakia,
    former USSR and Yugoslavia. Series for "Developed regions"
    include North America (Canada and the United States), Europe
    (excluding former Czechoslovakia and the European countries
    of the former USSR), Australia, Israel, Japan, New Zealand
    and South Africa. Series for "Developing regions" exclude
    Australia, Israel, Japan, New Zealand, South Africa and the Asian
    countries of the former USSR.

1   Excluding printing and publishing.
2   Including Australia and New Zealand.

Source :
Base de données de statistiques industrielles de la Division de statistique
du Secrétariat de l'ONU.

+   Les Etats membres de ce groupement, voir annexe I —
    Autres groupements.

ꬶ   Aucune série ne comprend l'Albanie, la Chine,
    la République populaire démocratique de Corée, Viet Nam,
    l'ancienne Tchécoslovaquie, l'ancienne URSS et la Yougoslavie.
    Les "régions developpées" comprennent l'Amérique du nord
    (le Canada et les Etats-Unis), l'Europe (non compris l'ancienne
    Tchécoslovaquie et les pays européens de l'ancienne URSS),
    l'Australie, Israël, le Japon, la Nouvelle-Zélande et l'Afrique du sud.
    Les séries pour les "Régions en voie de développement" excluent
    l'Australie, Israël, le Japon, la Nouvelle-Zélande, l'Afrique du sud
    et les pays asiatiques de l'ancienne URSS.

1   Non compris l'imprimerie et l'édition.
2   Y compris l'Australie et la Nouvelle-Zélande.

Table 6 follows overleaf
Le tableau 6 est présenté au verso

6
Production, trade and consumption of commercial energy
Production, commerce et consommation d'énergie commerciale
Thousand metric tons of coal equivalent and kilograms per capita
Milliers de tonnes métriques d'équivalent houille et kilogrammes par habitant

| Regions | Year | Primary energy production – Production d'energie primaire | | | | | Changes in stocks Variations des stocks | Imports Importations | Exports Exportations |
		Total Totale	Solids Solides	Liquids Liquides	Gas Gaz	Electricity Electricité			
World	1991	11 444 484	3 170 143	4 567 227	2 616 970	1 090 145	59 593	3 569 970	3 512 907
	1992	11 493 654	3 204 302	4 593 034	2 585 749	1 110 569	46 786	4 147 663	4 078 453
	1993	11 494 743	3 120 866	4 583 003	2 648 146	1 142 729	36 449	4 203 754	4 121 728
	1994	11 893 443	3 330 835	4 666 316	2 719 022	1 177 269	71 624	4 221 833	4 232 859
Africa	1991	739 200	142 767	485 853	99 936	10 644	1 599	70 076	491 896
	1992	733 690	139 919	484 157	98 976	10 639	−3 105	73 204	488 387
	1993	732 121	145 381	474 028	103 073	9 639	−3 893	75 773	476 466
	1994	732 327	146 096	468 581	107 056	10 594	−2 760	80 118	470 362
America, North	1991	2 998 549	806 924	982 558	844 630	364 437	10 530	761 757	473 007
	1992	3 009 953	800 638	974 208	871 064	364 043	−14 304	800 901	482 373
	1993	2 972 565	748 099	958 265	894 657	371 544	4 877	874 913	464 803
	1994	3 236 232	945 519	961 865	939 485	389 363	45 965	916 678	484 886
America, South	1991	493 041	30 680	331 722	81 270	49 369	3 107	84 321	221 643
	1992	500 850	28 029	341 430	81 219	50 172	1 979	87 058	221 807
	1993	527 276	28 811	360 134	84 373	53 957	125	96 591	244 492
	1994	561 383	30 764	383 158	90 923	56 537	−1 309	101 198	263 040
Asia	1991	3 270 390	1 117 517	1 657 646	314 831	180 396	35 596	1 092 226	1 335 731
	1992	3 740 223	1 262 102	1 825 123	463 384	189 614	30 894	1 289 110	1 587 405
	1993	3 859 803	1 292 608	1 871 548	487 891	207 756	32 896	1 324 260	1 646 831
	1994	4 016 714	1 357 630	1 926 956	513 966	218 162	17 051	1 359 273	1 663 946
Europe	1991	1 485 727	487 561	319 480	308 734	369 953	8 541	1 528 460	582 838
	1992	3 261 907	814 057	922 991	1 036 177	488 682	31 915	1 865 892	1 165 872
	1993	3 153 371	744 997	874 077	1 041 301	492 996	5 594	1 794 297	1 148 937
	1994	3 085 530	677 309	883 089	1 029 018	496 113	17 880	1 725 590	1 200 668
Oceania	1991	239 911	150 721	49 260	32 245	7 685	219	28 543	122 294
	1992	247 032	159 558	45 124	34 929	7 421	−593	31 396	132 608
	1993	249 606	160 970	44 950	36 850	6 837	−3 149	37 818	140 200
	1994	261 258	173 518	42 668	38 573	6 500	−5 202	38 875	149 956
former USSR †	1991	2 217 666	433 974	740 707	935 323	107 661	..	4 484	285 499
	1992	...	...	...	...	...	..	...	...
	1993	...	...	...	...	...	..	...	...
	1994	...	...	...	...	...	..	...	...

Source:
Energy statistics database of the Statistics Division of the
United Nations Secretariat.

† For detailed descriptions of data pertaining to
former Czechoslovakia, Germany, SFR Yugoslavia and former
USSR, see annex I − Country or area nomenclature, regional
and other groupings.

Source:
Base de données pour les statistiques énergétiques de la Division
de statistique du Secrétariat de l'ONU.

† Pour les descriptions en détails des données relatives
à l'ancienne Tchécoslovaquie, l'Allemagne, la Rfs
Yougoslavie et l'ancienne URSS, voir l'Annexe I −
Nomenclature des pays ou zones, groupements régionaux et
autres groupements.

| Bunkers – Soutes | | | Consumption – Consommation | | | | | | | |
Air Avion	Sea Maritime	Unallocated Nondistribué	Per capita Par habitant	Total Totale	Solids Solides	Liquids Liquides	Gas Gaz	Electricity Electricité	Année	Régions
58 179	138 456	306 644	2 028	10 938 675	3 183 918	4 048 125	2 615 889	1 090 742	1991	*Monde*
62 252	165 285	358 124	1 996	10 930 417	3 223 261	3 996 185	2 600 514	1 110 456	1992	
66 284	146 406	324 289	1 978	11 003 340	3 173 494	4 051 546	2 635 427	1 142 872	1993	
69 504	148 715	334 572	1 993	11 258 003	3 355 435	4 053 983	2 671 437	1 177 147	1994	
3 157	5 254	19 855	442	287 513	103 872	119 457	53 594	10 590	1991	Afrique
3 230	5 078	29 915	423	283 390	101 192	121 773	50 027	10 398	1992	
3 390	5 070	29 709	431	297 152	107 184	125 565	55 080	9 322	1993	
3 508	5 278	26 948	436	309 110	107 959	127 159	63 692	10 300	1994	
1 942	32 911	26 527	7 469	3 215 389	701 802	1 304 552	844 295	364 741	1991	Amérique du Nord
2 009	33 298	30 377	7 505	3 277 100	707 744	1 323 131	881 885	364 339	1992	
1 880	31 386	28 268	7 488	3 316 264	684 748	1 364 357	895 572	371 587	1993	
2 067	32 289	37 844	7 906	3 549 859	841 670	1 390 106	928 717	389 365	1994	
1 383	3 961	18 436	1 102	328 833	25 665	172 884	81 017	49 268	1991	Amérique du Sud
1 341	3 762	24 392	1 102	334 626	26 126	177 323	81 176	50 001	1992	
1 452	3 955	22 399	1 137	351 444	26 327	187 432	83 895	53 791	1993	
1 720	4 164	22 606	1 184	372 359	27 844	197 275	90 944	56 296	1994	
17 197	43 498	162 618	867	2 767 976	1 269 657	995 073	322 872	180 373	1991	Asie
19 115	46 996	186 219	953	3 158 705	1 385 005	1 133 674	449 417	190 609	1992	
19 818	50 322	176 038	967	3 258 159	1 425 881	1 163 187	460 378	208 713	1993	
20 501	52 750	167 899	1 009	3 453 839	1 506 431	1 211 140	516 835	219 433	1994	
31 094	51 101	17 301	4 626	2 323 312	613 169	863 219	474 124	372 800	1991	Europe
32 962	74 390	98 389	5 138	3 724 270	942 961	1 183 312	1 110 309	487 688	1992	
35 957	53 808	78 661	4 997	3 624 711	870 720	1 149 222	1 112 147	492 622	1993	
37 857	52 074	88 936	4 700	3 413 705	807 594	1 068 334	1 042 525	495 252	1994	
3 406	1 637	−7 446	5 525	148 346	57 790	56 307	26 564	7 685	1991	Océanie
3 594	1 668	−11 167	5 585	152 318	60 233	56 964	27 700	7 421	1992	
3 788	1 772	−10 787	5 618	155 602	58 634	61 776	28 356	6 837	1993	
3 851	2 066	−9 662	5 658	159 124	63 938	59 963	28 724	6 500	1994	
..	...	69 353	6 415	1 867 297	411 963	536 625	813 424	105 286	1991	ancienne URSS †
..	...	...	...	...	...	...	...	...	1992	
..	...	...	...	...	...	...	...	...	1993	
..	...	...	...	...	...	...	...	...	1994	

7

Total exports and imports: index numbers
Exportations et importations totales: indices
Quantum, unit value and terms of trade (1990 = 100)
Quantum, valeur unitaire et termes de l'échange (1990 =100)

Regions[1] Régions[1]	1985	1986	1987	1988	1989	1990	1991	1992	1993	1994
A. Exports • Exportations										
Quantum indices[2]• Indices du quantum[2]										
Total	74	77	82	88	95	100	104	109	114	127
Developed economies **Econ. développées**	78	79	82	88	95	100	102	106	108	118
North America Amérique du Nord	69	71	77	89	95	100	106	114	119	132
Europe **Europe**	78	80	83	88	96	100	101	104	106	116
EC+ CE+	79	80	83	88	96	100	102	105	107	118
EFTA AELE	76	79	82	87	95	100	100	102	104	111
Africa[3] Afrique[3]	64	66	61	62	68	100	100	99	102	106
Asia Asie	87	87	88	91	95	100	102	103	102	104
Oceania Océanie	83	82	89	90	94	100	115	121	125	137
Developing economies **Econ. en dévelop.**	63	72	81	87	94	100	110	120	129	156
America Amérique	85	89	92	87	99	100	107	116	126	151
Europe[4] Europe[4]	100	100	105	100	104	100	...	...	...	...
Africa Afrique	73	85	80	81	86	100	104	102	111	106
Asia **Asie**	56	66	78	88	93	100	112	122	137	165
Middle East Moyen-Orient	64	79	88	104	104	100	102	96	102	130
Other Asia Autres pays d'Asie	54	63	75	86	93	100	114	128	142	172
Unit value indices in US dollars[5]• Indices de la valeur unitaire en dollars E-U[5]										
Total	73	77	85	91	92	100	98	100	95	97
Developed economies **Econ. développées**	67	76	86	91	91	100	99	101	95	98
North America Amérique du Nord	88	87	89	96	99	100	99	98	98	98
Europe **Europe**	60	72	84	88	87	100	97	100	90	93
EC+ CE+	60	72	84	88	87	100	97	100	90	93
EFTA AELE	64	72	84	86	84	100	97	97	89	93
Africa[3] Afrique[3]	62	71	87	90	94	100	99	101	97	100
Asia Asie	70	83	91	101	101	100	107	114	123	133

7
Total exports and imports: index numbers
Quantum, unit value and terms of trade (1990 = 100) [cont.]
Exportations et importations totales: indices
Quantum, valeur unitaire et termes de l'échange (1990 =100) [suite]

Regions[1] Régions[1]	1985	1986	1987	1988	1989	1990	1991	1992	1993	1994
Oceania Océanie	71	70	78	95	99	100	91	89	87	89
Developing economies **Econ. en dévelop.**	**96**	**78**	**84**	**88**	**92**	**100**	**96**	**97**	**95**	**95**
America Amérique	93	74	80	96	93	100	91	86	83	93
Europe[4] Europe[4]	74	72	76	88	90	100	...	...	...	...
Africa Afrique	107	72	83	81	87	100	92	92	81	86
Asia **Asie**	**95**	**81**	**86**	**88**	**93**	**100**	**98**	**100**	**99**	**96**
Middle East Moyen-Orient	127	83	83	71	81	100	90	94	88	87
Other Asia Autres pays d'Asie	86	80	87	93	96	100	100	101	101	98

B. Imports • Importations
Quantum indices[2] • Indices du quantum[2]

	1985	1986	1987	1988	1989	1990	1991	1992	1993	1994
Total	**73**	**78**	**84**	**91**	**98**	**100**	**106**	**113**	**114**	**130**
Developed economies **Econ. développées**	**75**	**81**	**86**	**92**	**98**	**100**	**104**	**108**	**108**	**120**
North America Amérique du Nord	86	93	97	102	101	100	99	108	119	136
Europe **Europe**	**72**	**77**	**83**	**89**	**98**	**100**	**106**	**109**	**104**	**113**
EC+ CE+	72	77	83	89	98	100	107	111	105	114
EFTA AELE	78	86	90	93	97	100	98	90	90	100
Africa[3] Afrique[3]	80	85	84	100	100	100	99	102	105	126
Asia Asie	63	69	76	87	93	100	103	103	108	121
Oceania Océanie	81	79	79	86	104	100	105	113	108	121
Developing economies **Econ. en dévelop.**	**66**	**71**	**75**	**87**	**95**	**100**	**113**	**130**	**135**	**162**
Europe[4] Europe[4]	78	84	86	78	87	100	...	...	...	...

Unit value indices in US dollars[5] • Indices de la valeur unitaire en dollars E-U[5]

	1985	1986	1987	1988	1989	1990	1991	1992	1993	1994
Total	**76**	**78**	**85**	**90**	**91**	**100**	**98**	**99**	**93**	**95**
Developed economies **Econ. développées**	**73**	**76**	**84**	**89**	**91**	**100**	**98**	**99**	**92**	**94**
North America Amérique du Nord	83	80	85	89	97	100	99	98	97	97
Europe **Europe**	**67**	**74**	**84**	**88**	**88**	**100**	**98**	**99**	**89**	**92**
EC+ CE+	67	74	84	88	88	100	98	99	89	92

7
Total exports and imports: index numbers
Quantum, unit value and terms of trade (1990 = 100) [cont.]
Exportations et importations totales: indices
Quantum, valeur unitaire et termes de l'échange (1990 =100) [suite]

Regions[1] Régions[1]	1985	1986	1987	1988	1989	1990	1991	1992	1993	1994
EFTA AELE	61	74	85	89	87	100	97	100	92	94
Africa[3] Afrique[3]	70	76	91	94	92	100	103	105	99	100
Asia Asie	87	78	84	91	95	100	98	97	96	97
Oceania Océanie	77	80	89	98	96	100	101	99	98	104
Developing economies[6] Econ. en dévelop.[6]	88	83	88	92	93	100	98	98	95	99
Europe[4] Europe[4]	82	74	78	89	90	100	...	...	...	...

C. Terms of trade[7] • Termes de l'échange[7]

	1985	1986	1987	1988	1989	1990	1991	1992	1993	1994
Developed economies Econ. développées	91	100	101	103	100	100	100	102	104	104
North America Amérique du Nord	106	109	105	107	102	100	100	100	101	101
Europe Europe	90	98	100	100	99	100	99	101	101	101
EC+ CE+	89	98	100	100	99	100	99	101	101	101
EFTA AELE	105	98	100	97	97	100	100	96	97	98
Africa[3] Afrique[3]	89	94	95	95	102	100	96	96	98	99
Asia Asie	80	107	108	111	106	100	109	117	128	136
Oceania Océanie	93	88	88	96	104	100	91	90	88	85
Developing economies Econ. en dévelop.	108	95	95	96	99	100	98	99	100	96
Europe[4] Europe[4]	90	97	98	99	99	100	...	...	...	...

Source:
Trade statistics database of the Statistics Division of the
United Nations Secretariat.
+   For Member States of this grouping, see
    Annex I - Other groupings.

1 For the composition of the regions see table 74.

2 Quantum indices are derived from value data and unit value
   indices. They are base period weighted.

3 South African Customs Union.
4 Socialist Federal Republic of Yugoslavia only.

5 Regional aggregates are current period weighted.

6 Indices, except those for Europe, are based on estimates
   prepared by the International Monetary Fund.

7 Unit value index of exports divided by unit value index of
   imports.

Source:
Base de données pour les statistiques du commerce extérieur
de la Division de statistique du Secrétariat de l'ONU.
+   Les Etats membres de ce groupement, voir
    annexe I - Autres groupements.

1 Pour la composition des régions, voir le tableau 74 du
   présent numéro.
2 Les indices du quantum sont calculés à partir des chiffres
   de la valeur et des indices de la valeur unitaire. Ils sont
   à coéfficients de pondération correspondant à la période en
   base.
3 L'Union Douanière d'Afrique Méridionale.
4 La République fédérative socialiste de Yougoslavie
   seulement.
5 Les totaux régionaux sont à coéfficients de pondération
   correspondant à la période en cours.
6 Le calcul des indices, sauf ceux pour l'Europe, sont basés
   sur les estimations preparées par le Fonds monétaire
   international.
7 Indices de la valeur unitaire des exportations divisé par
   l'indice de la valeur unitaire des importations.

Technical notes, tables 1-7

Table 1: These series of world aggregates on population and production have been compiled from statistical publications of the United Nations and the specialized agencies.[2, 4, 5, 6, 8, 13, 22, 23, 25] Reference should be made to these sources for details of compilation and coverage.

Table 2 presents for the world and regions estimates of population size, rates of population increase, crude birth and death rates, surface area and population density. Unless otherwise specified all figures are estimates of the order of magnitude and are subject to a substantial margin of error.

All population estimates and rates presented in this table were prepared by the Population Division of the United Nations Secretariat and published in *World Population Prospects 1994*.[27]

The average annual percentage rates of population growth were calculated by the Population Division of the United Nations Secretariat, using an exponential rate of increase formula.

Crude birth and crude death rates are expressed in terms of the average annual number of births and deaths respectively, per 1,000 mid-year population. These rates are estimated.

Surface area totals were obtained by summing the figures for individual countries or areas.

Density is the number of persons in the 1994 total population per square kilometre of total surface area.

The scheme of regionalization used for the purpose of making these estimates is presented in annex I. Although some continental totals are given, and all can be derived, the basic scheme presents eight macro regions that are so drawn as to obtain greater homogeneity in sizes of population, types of demographic circumstances and accuracy of demographic statistics.

Tables 3-4: The index numbers in table 3 refer to agricultural production, which is defined to include both crop and livestock products. Seeds and feed are excluded. The index numbers of food refer to commodities which are considered edible and contain nutrients. Coffee, tea and other inedible commodities are excluded.

The index numbers of agricultural output and food production in table 3 are calculated by the Laspeyres formula with the base year period 1979-1981. The latter is provided in order to diminish the impact of annual fluctuations in agricultural output during base years on the indices for the period. Production quantities of each commodity are weighted by 1979-1981 average national producer prices and summed for each year. The index numbers are based on production data for a calendar year. As in the past, the series include a large number of estimates made by FAO in cases where figures are not available from official country sources.

Notes techniques, tableaux 1-7

Tableau 1 : Ces séries d'agrégats mondiaux sur la population et la production ont été établies à partir de publications statistiques des Nations Unies et d'institutions spécialisées [2, 4, 5, 6, 8, 13, 22, 23, 25]. On doit se référer à ces sources pour tous renseignements détaillés sur les méthodes de calcul et la portée des statistiques.

Le *Tableau 2* présente les estimations mondiales et régionales de la population, des taux d'accroissement de la population, des taux bruts de natalité et de mortalité, de la superficie et de la densité de population. Sauf indication contraire, tous les chiffres sont des estimations de l'ordre de grandeur et comportent une assez grande marge d'erreur.

Toutes les estimations de la population et tous les taux présentés dans ce tableau ont été établis par la Division de la population du Secrétariat des Nations Unies et publiés dans "World Population Prospects 1994" [27].

Les pourcentages annuels moyens de l'accroissement de la population ont été calculés par la Division de la population du Secrétariat des Nations Unies, sur la base d'une formule de taux d'accroissement exponentiel.

Les taux bruts de natalité et de mortalité sont exprimés, respectivement, sur la base du nombre annuel moyen de naissances et de décès par tranche de 1.000 habitants en milieu d'année. Ces taux sont estimatifs.

On a déterminé les superficies totales en additionnant les chiffres correspondant aux différents pays ou régions.

La densité est le nombre de personnes de la population totale de 1994 par kilomètre carré de la superficie totale.

Le schéma de régionalisation utilisé aux fins de l'établissement de ces estimations est présenté à l'Annexe I. Bien que les totaux de certains continents soient donnés et que tous puissent être déterminés, le schéma de base présente huit grandes régions qui sont établies de manière à obtenir une plus grande homogénéité en ce qui concerne l'ampleur des populations, les types de conditions démographiques et la précisions des statistiques démographiques.

Tableaux 3-4 : Les indices du Tableau 3 se rapportent à la production agricole, qui est définie comme comprenant à la fois les produits de l'agriculture et de l'élevage. Les semences et les aliments pour les animaux sont exclus de cette définition. Les indices de la production alimentaire se rapportent aux produits considérés comme comestibles et contenant des éléments nutritifs. Le café, le thé et les produits non comestibles sont exclus.

Les indices de la production agricole et de la production alimentaire présentés au Tableau 3 sont calculés selon la formule de Laspeyres avec les années 1979-1981 comme période de référence, cela afin de limiter l'incidence, sur les indices correspondant à la période considérée, des fluctuations annuelles de la production agricole enregistrée pendant les années de référence. Les chiffres de production de chaque produit sont pondérés par les prix nationaux moyens à la production pour la période 1979-81 et additionnés pour chaque année. Les indices sont fondés sur les données de production

Index numbers for the world and regions are computed in a similar way to the country index numbers except that, instead of using different commodity prices for each country group, "international commodity prices" derived from the Gheary-Khamis formula are used for all country groupings. This method assigns a single "price" to each commodity.

The indexes in table 4 are calculated as a ratio between the index numbers of total agricultural and food production in table 3 described above and the corresponding index numbers of population.

For further information on the series presented in these tables, see the production yearbook published by FAO.[8]

Table 5: The indices of industrial production are classified according to divisions, major groups or combinations of major groups of the International Standard Industrial Classification of All Economic Activities (ISIC) for mining, manufacturing and electricity, gas and water.[46] The indices indicate trends in value added in constant US dollars. The measure of value added used is the national accounts concept, which is defined as the gross value of output less the cost of materials, supplies, fuels and electricity consumed and services received.

Each series is compiled by use of the Laspeyres formula, that is, the indices are baseweighted arithmetic means. The weight base year is 1980 and value added, generally at factor values, is used in weighting.

For most countries the estimates of value added used as weights are derived from the results of national industrial censuses or similar inquiries relating to 1980. These data, in current national currency are adjusted to the ISIC where necessary and are subsequently converted into US dollars. In the case of some of the countries in transition, value added estimates are computed separately for the major cost components, i.e. compensation of employees, operating surplus and consumption of fixed capital, based on the official data provided by national statistical authorities. Estimates thus obtained are adjusted to the ISIC and then converted into US dollars.

The elementary series used in compiling indices for the ISIC major groups are, in general, indices for the corresponding ISIC category, or its sub-divisions, compiled by national statistical authorities. Adjustments are made, when necessary, to align the national industrial classification with the ISIC.

Within each of the ISIC categories (major divisions, divisions, major groups or combinations of major groups) shown in the tables, the indices for the country aggregations (regions of economic groupings) are calculated directly from the country data. The indices for the *World*, however, are calculated from the aggregated indices for the groupings of developed and developing regions.

de l'année. Comme dans le passé, les séries comprennent un grand nombre d'estimations établies par la FAO lorsqu'elle n'avait pu obtenir de chiffres de sources officielles dans les pays eux-mêmes.

Les indices pour le monde et les régions sont calculés de la même façon que les indices par pays, mais au lieu d'appliquer des prix différents aux produits de base pour chaque groupe de pays, on a utilisé des "prix internationaux" établis d'après la formule de Gheary-Khamis pour tous les groupes de pays. Cette méthode attribue un seul "prix" à chaque produit de base.

Les indices du Tableau 4 sont calculés comme ratio entre les indices de la production alimentaire et de la production agricole totale du Tableau 3 décrits ci-dessus et les indices de population correspondants.

Pour tout renseignement complémentaire sur les séries présentées dans ces tableaux, voir l'Annuaire publié par la FAO [8].

Tableau 5 : Les indices de la production industrielle sont classés par catégorie, classe ou groupement de classes de la Classification internationale type, par industrie, de toutes les branches d'activité économique (CITI) et portent sur les industries extractives et manufacturières et les industries de l'électricité, du gaz et de l'eau [46]. Ces indices mesurent les variations de la valeur ajoutée en dollars constants des Etats-Unis. La mesure de la valeur ajoutée utilisée est celle de la comptabilité nationale, qui se définit comme la valeur brute de la production moins le coût des matières premières et des fournitures, des combustibles et de l'électricité consommés ainsi que des services reçus.

Chaque série d'indices est calculée à l'aide de la formule de Laspeyres, c'est-à-dire sous forme de moyennes arithmé-tiques pondérées. L'année de base pour la pondération est 1980 et la valeur ajoutée utilisée dans la pondération est généralement calculée au coût des facteurs.

Pour la plupart des pays, les estimations de la valeur ajoutée qui sont utilisées comme coefficients de pondération sont tirées des résultats des recensements industriels nationaux ou enquêtes analogues concernant l'année 1980. Ces données, en monnaie nationale courante, sont ajustées s'il y a lieu aux normes de la CITI et ultérieurement converties en dollars des Etats-Unis. Dans le cas de certains pays en période transition, les estimations de la valeur ajoutée sont calculées séparément pour les principaux éléments de coût, à savoir la rémunération des salariés, l'excédant net d'exploitation et la consommation de capital fixe, sur la base des données officielles fournies par les statistiques nationaux. Les estimations ainsi obtenues sont ajustées aux normes de la CITI, puis converties en dollars des Etats-Unis.

Les séries élémentaires utilisées dans le calcul des indices pour les classes de la CITI sont en générale les indices de la catégorie correspondante de la CITI, ou de ses subdivisions, calculés par les services statistiques nationaux. Des ajustements sont effectués s'il y a lieu pour aligner la classification industrielle nationale sur la CITI.

Table 6: For description of the series in table 6, see technical notes to table 66 of chapter XIII.

Table 7: For description of the series in table 7, see technical notes to chapter XVI. The composition of the regions is presented in table 74.

A l'intérieur de chacune des subdivisions de la CITI (branches, catégories, classes ou combinaisons de classes) indiquées dans les tableaux, les indices relatifs aux assemblages de pays (régions géographiques ou groupements économiques) sont calculés directement à partir des données des pays. Toutefois, les indices concernant le *Monde* sont calculés à partir des indices agrégés applicables aux groupements de régions développées et de régions en développement.

Tableau 6 : On trouvera une description de la série de statistiques du Tableau 6 dans les Notes techniques du Tableau 66 du Chapitre XIII.

Tableau 7 : On trouvera une description de la série de statistiques du Tableau 7 dans les notes techniques du Chapitre XVI. La composition des régions est présentée au Tableau 74.

Part Two
Population and Social Statistics

II
Population and human settlements (table 8)
III
Education and literacy (tables 9-11)
IV
Health and child-bearing; nutrition (tables 12 and 13)
V
Culture and communications (tables 14-19)

Part Two of the *Yearbook* presents statistical series on a wide range of population and social topics for all countries or areas of the world for which data are available. These include population and population growth, surface area and density; education at first, second and third levels; life expectancy, child bearing and mortality; AIDS cases; newspapers, television and radio, telefax stations and telephones.

Deuxième partie
Population et statistiques sociales

II
Population et établissements humains (tableau 8)
III
Education et alphabétisation (tableaux 9 à 11)
IV
Santé et maternité; nutrition (tableaux 12 et 13)
V
Culture et communications (tableaux 14 à 19)

La deuxième partie de l'*Annuaire* présente, pour tous les pays ou zones du monde pour lesquels des données sont disponibles, des séries statistiques intéressant une large gamme de questions démographiques et sociales : population et croissance démographique, superficie et densité; enseignement des premier, second et troisième degrés; espérance de vie, maternité et mortalité; cas de SIDA; journaux, télévision et radio, postes de télécopie et téléphones.

8
Population by sex, rate of population increase, surface area and density
Population selon le sexe, taux d'accroissement de la population, superficie et densité

Country or area Pays ou zone	Latest Census Dernier recensement Date	Both sexes Les deux sexes	Male Masculin	Female Féminin	Midyear estimates (thousands) Estimations au milieu de l'année (milliers) 1990	1994	Type[1] 1994	Annual rate of increase Taux d'accrois- sement annuel % 1990-94	Surface area (km²) Superficie (km²) 1994	Density Densité 1994[2]
Africa · Afrique										
Algeria[3] Algérie[3]	20−III−87	23 033 942	...	...	25 012	x27 325	A7 c1	2.2	2 381 741	11
Angola[4] Angola[4]	15−XII−70	5 646 166	2 943 974	2 702 192	10 020	x10 674	A24c1	1.6	1 246 700	9
Benin Bénin	15−II−92	4 915 555	2 390 336	2 525 219	4 739	*5 387	A15c3	3.2	112 622	48
Botswana Botswana	21−VIII−91	1 326 796	634 400	692 396	1 300	x1 443	A3 c1	2.6	581 730	2
British Indian Territory[5] Territoire britannique de l'océan indien[5]	(6)	(6)	(6)	(6)	x2	x2	D29d	0.0	78	26
Burkina Faso Burkina Faso	10−XII−85	7 964 705	3 833 237	4 131 468	9 001	*9 889	A9 c3	2.4	274 000	36
Burundi Burundi	16−VIII−90	5 139 073	2 473 599	2 665 474	5 458	*6 134	A15c3	2.9	27 834	220
Cameroon Cameroun	IV−87	*10 493 655	...	...	x11 526	x12 871	A7 c3	2.8	475 442	27
Cape Verde Cap−Vert	23−VI−90	341 491	161 494	179 997	341	x381	A4 c1	2.7	4 033	94
Central African Republic République centrafricaine	8−XII−88	2 463 616	1 210 734	1 252 882	x2 927	x3 235	A6 c3	2.5	622 984	5
Chad Tchad	8−IV−93	*6 158 992	*2 950 415	*3 208 577	5 687	*6 214	B31c3	2.2	1 284 000	5
Comoros Comores	15−IX−91	*446 817 [7]	*221 152 [7]	*225 665 [7]	x543	x630	A14c3	3.7	2 235	282
Congo Congo	22−XII−84	1 843 421	...	...	x2 232	x2 516	A10c3	3.0	342 000	7
Côte d'Ivoire Côte d'Ivoire	1−III−88	10 815 694	5 527 343	5 288 351	11 717	*13 695	A6 c3	3.9	322 463	42
Djibouti Djibouti	1960−61	81 200	...	...	x517	x566	A34d	2.3	23 200	24
Egypt Egypte	17−XI−86	48 254 238	24 709 274	23 544 964	52 691	*57 851	A8 c1	2.3	1 001 449	58
Equatorial Guinea[8] Guinée équatoriale[8]	4−VII−83	300 000	144 760	155 240	348	x389	A11c3	2.8	28 051	14
Eritrea Erythrée	9−V−84	2 748 304	1 374 452	1 373 852	x3 082	x3 437	A10c3	2.7	117 600	29
Ethiopia Ethiopie	9−V−84	39 868 572	20 062 490	19 806 082	48 360	*54 938	A10c3	3.2	1 104 300	50
Gabon Gabon	31−VII−93	*1 011 710	*498 710	*513 000	x1 146	x1 283	A34c3	2.8	267 668	5
Gambia Gambie	13−IV−93	*1 025 867	*514 530	*511 337	x923	x1 081	A11c1	4.0	11 295	96
Ghana Ghana	11−III−84	12 296 081	6 063 848	6 232 233	x15 020	x16 944	A10c1	3.0	238 533	71
Guinea Guinée	4−II−83	4 533 240	...	...	x5 755	x6 501	A11c3	3.0	245 857	26
Guinea−Bissau Guinée−Bissau	1−XII−91	983 367	476 210	507 157	x964	x1 050	A3 c1	2.1	36 125	29
Kenya Kenya	24−VIII−89	21 443 636	10 628 368	10 815 268	24032 [10]	*29 292	A5 c2	(11)	580 367	50
Lesotho Lesotho	12−IV−86	*1 447 000	...	...	x1 792	x1 996	A8 c3	2.7	30 355	66
Liberia Libéria	1−II−84	2 101 628	...	...	2 407	*2 700	A10c3	2.9	111 369	24
Libyan Arab Jamahiriya Jamahiriya arabe libyenne	31−VII−84	3 642 576	1 953 757	1 688 819	4 151 [10]	*4 899	A20c3	(11)	1 759 540	3

8
Population by sex, rate of population increase, surface area and density [cont.]
Population selon le sexe, taux d'accroissement de la population,
superficie et densité [suite]

Country or area Pays ou zone	Latest Census Dernier recensement Date	Both sexes Les deux sexes	Male Masculin	Female Féminin	Midyear estimates (thousands) Estimations au milieu de l'année (milliers) 1990	1994	Type[1] 1994	Annual rate of increase Taux d'accrois- sement annuel % 1990–94	Surface area (km²) Superficie (km²) 1994	Density Densité 1994[2]
Madagascar Madagascar	1–VIII–93	*12 092 157	*5 991 171	*6 100 986	11 197	x14303 [10]	A20c3	([11])	587 041	24
Malawi Malawi	1–IX–87	7 988 507	3 867 136	4 121 371	8 289	*9 461	A7 c3	3.3	118 484	80
Mali Mali	1–IV–87	7 696 348 [3]	3 760 711 [3]	3 935 637 [3]	10 8 156 [10]	x10 462	A7 c3	([11])	1 240 192	8
Mauritania Mauritanie	5–IV–88	1 864 236 [12]	923 175 [12]	941 061 [12]	x2 003	*2 211	A6 c3	2.5	1 025 520	2
Mauritius Maurice	1–VII–90	1 056 660	527 760	528 900	1 059	x1 104	A4 b1	1.0	2 040	541
Island of Mauritius Ile Maurice	1–VII–90	1 022 456	510 676	511 780	1 025	...		..	1 865	...
Rodrigues Rodrigues	1–VII–90	34 204	17 084	17 120	34	...		..	104	...
Others[13] Autres[13]	30–VI–72	366	272	94	...	...		..	71	...
Morocco Maroc	3–IX–82	20 419 555	...	...	24 487	*26 590	A12c2	2.1	446 550	60
Mozambique[9] Mozambique[9] .	1–VIII–80	11 673 725	5 670 484	6 003 241	14 151	*16 614	A14c1	4.0	801 590	21
Namibia Namibie	21–X–91	1 409 920	686 327	723 593	x1 349	x1 500	A3 c3	2.7	824 292	2
Niger Niger	20–V–88	7 248 100	3 590 070	3 658 030	x7 731	x8 846	A6 c3	3.4	1 267 000	7
Nigeria Nigéria	26–XI–91	*88 514 501	*44 544 531	*43 969 970	x96 154	x108 467	A31c2	3.0	923 768	117
Reunion[3] Réunion[3]	15–III–90	597 828	294 256	303 572	601	x644	A4 b3	1.7	2 510	257
Rwanda Rwanda	15–VIII–91	*7 142 755	...	...	7 181	x7 750	A3 c3	1.9	26 338	294
St. Helena ex. dep. Sainte–Hélène sans dép.	22–II–87	5 644	2 769	2 875	6	7	A7 b3	0.6	122	54
Ascension Ascension	31–XII–78	849	608	241	...	...	..	...	88	...
Tristan da Cunha Tristan da Cunha	22–II–87	296	139	157	...	...	..	...	...	...
Sao Tome and Principe Sao Tomé–et–Principe	4–VIII–91	116 998	57 837	59 161	115	*125	A13c1	2.0	964	129
Senegal Sénégal	27–V–88	6 896 808	3 353 599	3 543 209	7 504	x8 102	A6 c3	1.9	196 722	41
Seychelles Seychelles	17–VIII–87	68 598	34 125	34 473	70	*74	A7 b2	1.5	455	162
Sierra Leone[9] Sierra Leone[9]	15–XII–85	3 515 812	1 746 055	1 769 757	x3 999	x4 402	A9 c1	2.4	71 740	61
Somalia Somalie	1986–87	*7 114 431	*3 741 664	*3 372 767	x8 677	x9 077	A19c3	1.1	637 657	14
South Africa Afrique du Sud	7–III–91	30986 920 [14]	15 479 528 [14]	15 507 392 [14]	x37 066	*40 436	A3 c1	2.2	1 221 037	33
Sudan Soudan	15–IV–93	*24 940 683	*12 518 638	*12 422 045	25 752	*28 947	A11c3	2.9	2 505 813	12
Swaziland Swaziland	25–VIII–86	681 059	321 579	359 480	768	x832	A8 c1	2.0	17 364	48
Togo Togo	22–XI–81	2 703 250	...	...	x3 531	*3 928	A13c1	2.7	56 785	69
Tunisia Tunisie	20–IV–94	*8 785 364	*4 447 341	*4 338 023	8 074	x8 733	A10c1	2.0	163 610	53
Uganda Ouganda	12–I–91	16 671 705	8 185 747	8 485 958	x17 949	x20 621	A14c1	3.5	241 038	86
United Rep. of Tanzania Rép.–Unie de Tanzanie	28–VIII–88	23 174 336	11 327 511	11 846 825	25 635	x28 846	A6 c3	3.0	883 749	33

8
Population by sex, rate of population increase, surface area and density [*cont.*]
Population selon le sexe, taux d'accroissement de la population,
superficie et densité [*suite*]

Country or area Pays ou zone	Latest Census Dernier recensement Date	Both sexes Les deux sexes	Male Masculin	Female Féminin	Midyear estimates (thousands) Estimations au milieu de l'année (milliers) 1990	1994	Type[1] 1994	Annual rate of increase Taux d'accrois- sement annuel % 1990-94	Surface area (km²) Superficie (km²) 1994	Density Densité 1994[2]
Tanganyika Tanganyika	28–VIII–88	22 533 758	11 012 647	11 521 111	24 972	...	..	...	881 289	...
Zanzibar Zanzibar	28–VIII–88	640 578	314 864	325 714	663	...	..	...	2 460	...
Western Sahara[15] Sahara occidental[15]	31–XII–70	76 425	43 981	32 444	x230	x272	A24c1	4.2	266 000	1
Zaire Zaïre	1–VII–84	29 916 800	14 543 800	15 373 000	35 562	x42 552	A10c3	4.5	2 344 858	18
Zambia Zambie	20–VIII–90	7 818 447	3 843 364	3 975 083	8 073	x9 196	A14c1	3.3	752 618	12
Zimbabwe Zimbabwe	18–VIII–92	10 412 548	5 083 537	5 329 011	9 369	*11 150	A2 c1	4.4	390 757	29
America, North · Amérique du Nord										
Anguilla Anguilla	10–IV–84	6 987	3 428	3 559	x7	x8	A10b1	3.3	96	83
Antigua and Barbuda Antigua–et–Barbuda	28–V–91	62 922	...	...	x64	x65	A3 b1	0.4	442	147
Aruba[3] Aruba[3]	6–X–91	66 687	32 821	33 866	x67	x69	A3 b1	0.7	193	358
Bahamas Bahamas	1–V–90	255 095	124 992	130 103	255	x272	A4 b1	1.6	13 878	20
Barbados Barbade	2–V–90	*257 082	...	...	257	x261	A4 b1	0.3	430	607
Belize Belize	12–V–91	189 774	96 289	93 485	189	*211	A3 c1	2.8	22 696	9
Bermuda Bermudes	20–V–91	74 837	...	...	61 [16]	x63 [16]	A3 b1	1.0	53	1 189
British Virgin Islands Iles Vierges britanniques	12–V–91	17 809	...	...	x16	x18	A3 b1	2.9	153	118
Canada[3] Canada[3]	4–VI–91	27 296 859	...	...	26 584	*29 248	A3 b1	2.4	9 970 610	3
Cayman Islands[3] Iles Caïmanes[3]	15–X–89	25 355	12 372	12 983	26	x30	A5 c1	3.6	264	114
Costa Rica[3] Costa Rica[3]	10–VI–84	2 416 809	1 208 216	1 208 593	2 805	*3 071	A10b2	2.3	51 100	60
Cuba Cuba	11–IX–81	9 723 605	4 914 873	4 808 732	10 625	x10 960	A13b1	0.8	110 861	99
Dominica Dominique	12–V–91	71 794	35 927	35 867	x71	x71	A3 b1	0.0	751	95
Dominican Republic Rép. dominicaine	12–XII–81	5 545 741	2 793 884	2 751 857	7 170	*7 760	A13c1	2.0	48 734	159
El Salvador El Salvador	27–IX–92	5 047 925	2 423 004	2 624 921	x5 172	x5 641	A23b1	2.2	21 041	268
Greenland[3] Groenland[3]	26–X–76	49 630	26 856	22 774	56	*55	A18a1	-0.1	2 175 600	–
Grenada[17] Grenade[17]	30–IV–81	89 088	42 943	46 145	x91	x92	A13b1	0.3	344	267
Guadeloupe[3][18] Guadeloupe[3][18]	15–III–90	387 034	...	...	x385	x421	A4 b1	2.2	1 705	247
Guatemala[9] Guatemala[9]	26–III–81	6 054 227	3 015 826	3 038 401	9 198	*10 322	A13b2	2.9	108 889	95
Haiti[3] Haïti[3]	30–VIII–82	5 053 792	2 448 370	2 605 422	6 486	*7 041	A12c3	2.1	27 750	254
Honduras Honduras	V–88	4 248 561	2 110 106	2 138 455	5 105	*5 770	A20c1	3.1	112 088	51
Jamaica Jamaïque	7–IV–91	*2 366 067	...	...	2 415	*2 496	A3 b1	0.8	10 990	227
Martinique[3] Martinique[3]	15–III–90	359 579	173 878	185 701	362	x375	A4 b1	0.9	1 102	340

8

Population by sex, rate of population increase, surface area and density [*cont.*]

Population selon le sexe, taux d'accroissement de la population, superficie et densité [*suite*]

Country or area Pays ou zone	Latest Census Dernier recensement Date	Both sexes Les deux sexes	Male Masculin	Female Féminin	Midyear estimates (thousands) Estimations au milieu de l'année (milliers) 1990	1994	Type[1] 1994	Annual rate of increase Taux d'accroissement annuel % 1990–94	Surface area (km²) Superficie (km²) 1994	Density Densité 1994[2]
Mexico[3] Mexique[3]	12−III−90	81 140 922	39 878 536	41 262 386	86 154	*93 008	A4 c1	1.9	1 958 201	47
Montserrat Montserrat	12−V−80	11 932	...	...	x11	x11	A14b1	0.0	102	108
Netherlands Antilles[3 9 19] Antilles néerlandaises[3 9 19]	27−I−92	189 474	90 707	98 767	190	x197	A2 c1	0.9	800	246
Nicaragua[3] Nicaragua[3]	20−IV−71	1 877 952	921 543	956 409	3 871	*4 401	A23b3	3.2	130 000	34
Panama Panama	13−V−90	2 329 329	1 178 790	1 150 539	2 398	*2 583	A4 c1	1.9	75 517	34
Puerto Rico[3 20] Porto Rico[3 20]	1−IV−90	3 522 039	...	...	3 528	x3 646	A4 b1	0.8	8 897	410
Saint Kitts and Nevis Saint−Kitts−et−Nevis	12−V−80	44 224	...	...	x42	x41	A14b1	−0.6	261	157
Saint Lucia Sainte−Lucie	12−V−91	135 685	65 988	69 697	x133	x141	A3 b1	1.5	622	227
St. Pierre and Miquelon Saint−Pierre et Miquelon	9−III−82	6 037	2 981	3 056	x6	x6	A12d	0.0	242	25
St. Vincent and Grenadines[21] St.−Vincent−et−Grenadines[21]	12−V−91	106 499	53 165	53 334	x107	x111	A3 b1	0.9	388	286
Trinidad and Tobago Trinité−et−Tobago	2−V−90	1 234 388	618 050	616 338	1 227	*1 257	A4 b1	0.6	5 130	245
Turks and Caicos Islands Iles Turques et Caïques	31−V−90	12 350	6 289	6 061	x12	x14	A4 d	3.9	430	33
United States[22] Etats−Unis[22]	1−IV−90	248 709 873	121 239 418	127 470 455	249 911	*260 651	A4 b1	1.1	9 363 520	28
United States Virgin[3 20] Iles Vierges américaines[3 20]	1−IV−90	101 809	49 210	52 599	102	x104	A4 c1	0.5	347	300
America, South · Amérique du Sud										
Argentina Argentine	15−V−91	32 615 528	15 937 980	16 677 548	32 547	*34 180	A3 c1	1.2	2 780 400	12
Bolivia Bolivie	3−VI−92	6 420 792	3 171 265	3 249 527	6 573	*7 237	A2 c3	2.4	1 098 581	7
Brazil[23] Brésil[23]	1−IX−91	146 825 475 [3]	72 485 122 [3]	74 340 353 [3]	144 723	*153 725	A3 c1	1.5	8 511 965	18
Chile Chili	22−IV−92	13 348 401	6 553 254	6 795 147	13 173	*13 994	A2 b1	1.5	756 626	18
Colombia Colombie	15−X−85	27 837 932	13 777 700	14 060 232	32 300	*34 520	A9 b3	1.7	1 138 914	30
Ecuador[24] Equateur[24]	25−XI−90	9 648 189	4 796 412	4 851 777	10 264	*11 221	A4 b3	2.2	283 561	40
Falkland Is. (Malvinas)[25 26] Iles Falkland (Malvinas)[25 26]	5−III−91	2 050	1 095	955	x2	x2	A3 d	0.0	12 173	−
French Guyana[3] Guyane française[3]	15−III−90	114 808	59 798	55 010	x117	x141	A4 c1	4.7	90 000	2
Guyana Guyana	12−V−80	758 619	375 841	382 778	x796	x825	A14b1	0.9	214 969	4
Paraguay Paraguay	26−VIII−92	4 152 588	2 085 905	2 066 683	4 219	*4 700	A2 c2	2.7	406 752	12
Peru[23] Pérou[23]	11−VII−93	*22 048 356	*10 956 375	*11 091 981	21 550	*23 088	A13c2	1.7	1 285 216	18
Suriname Suriname	1−VII−80	352 041	173 083	178 958	404	x418	A14c2	0.9	163 265	3
Uruguay[9] Uruguay[9]	23−X−85	2 955 241	1 439 021	1 516 220	3 094	*3 167	A9 b3	0.6	177 414	18
Venezuela[23] Venezuela[23]	20−X−90	18 105 265	9 019 757	9 085 508	19 325	*21 177	A4 c1	2.3	912 050	23
Asia · Asie										
Afghanistan Afghanistan	23−VI−79	13 051 358 [27]	6 712 377 [27]	6 338 981 [27]	27 16121	x18 879	A15c3	([11])	652 090	29

8

Population by sex, rate of population increase, surface area and density [*cont.*]
Population selon le sexe, taux d'accroissement de la population,
superficie et densité [*suite*]

Country or area Pays ou zone	Latest Census Dernier recensement Date	Both sexes Les deux sexes	Male Masculin	Female Féminin	Midyear estimates (thousands) Estimations au milieu de l'année (milliers) 1990	1994	Type[1] 1994	Annual rate of increase Taux d'accrois- sement annuel % 1990–94	Surface area (km²) Superficie (km²) 1994	Density Densité 1994[2]
Armenia Arménie	12–I–89	3 304 776 [3]	1 619 308 [3]	1 685 468 [3]	3 545	x3 548	A5 b1	0.0	29 800	119
Azerbaijan Azerbaïdjan	12–I–89	7 021 178 [3]	3 423 793 [3]	3 597 385 [3]	7 153	x7 472	A5 b1	1.1	86 600	86
Bahrain Bahreïn	16–XI–91	508 037	294 346	213 691	486	x549	A3 c1	3.1	694	791
Bangladesh Bangladesh	12–III–91	*104 766 143	*53 918 319	*50 847 824	x108 118	x117 787	A3 c1	2.1	143 998	818
Bhutan Bhoutan	XI–69	1 034 774	...	...	x1 544	x1 614	A25c3	1.1	47 000	34
Brunei Darussalam[9][28] Brunéi Darussalam[9][28]	7–VIII–91	260 482	137 616	122 866	253	x280	A3 c2	2.5	5 765	49
Cambodia[29] Cambodge[29]	17–IV–62	5 728 771	2 862 939	2 865 832	8 568	*9 568	A32c3	2.8	181 035	53
China[30] Chine[30]	1–VII–90	1 160 044 618	...	...	x1 155 305	x1 208 842	A4 c3	1.1	9 596 961	126
Cyprus Chypre	1–X–92	1 602 025 [31]	299 614 [31]	302 411 [31]	681	x734	A18b2	1.9	9 251	79
East Timor Timor oriental	31–X–90	747 750	386 939	360 811	x740	x800	A4 c1	1.9	14 874	54
Georgia Géorgie	12–I–89	5 400 841 [3]	2 562 040 [3]	2 838 801 [3]	5 464	x5 450	A5 b1	–0.1	69 700	78
Hong Kong[32] Hong–kong[32]	15–III–91	5 522 281	2 811 991	2 710 290	5 705	*6 061	A8 b2	1.5	1 075 [33]	5 639
India[34] Inde[34]	1–III–91	846 302 688	439 230 458	407 072 230	834 697	x918 570	A3 c1	2.4	3 287 590	279
Indonesia[35] Indonésie[35]	31–X–90	179 378 946	...	...	179 830	*192 217	A4 c1	1.7	1 904 569	101
Iran, Islamic Republic of Iran, Rép. islamique d'	1–X–91	55 837 163	28 768 450	27 068 713	54 496	*59 778	A3 c1	2.3	1 633 188	37
Iraq Iraq	17–X–87	16 335 199	8 395 889	7 939 310	17 373	x19 925	A7 c1	3.4	438 317	45
Israel[3][36] Israël[3][36]	4–VI–83	4 037 620	2 011 590	2 026 030	4 660	*5 383	A11b1	3.6	21 056	256
Japan[37] Japon[37]	1–X–90	123 611 167	60 696 724	62 914 443	123 537	*124 961	A4 b1	0.3	377 801	331
Jordan[38] Jordanie[38]	10–XII–94	* 4 095 579 [39]	* 2 135 883 [39]	*1 959 696 [39]	x4 259	x5 198	A15b3	5.0	97 740	53
Kazakstan Kazakstan	12–I–89	16 536 511	8 012 985	8 523 526	16 670	x17 027	A5 b1	0.5	2 717 300	6
Korea, Dem. People's Rep. Corée, Rép. pop. dém. de	1–V–44	...	...	...	x21 774	x23 483	D31c3	1.9	120 538	195
Korea, Republic of[9][40] Corée, Rép. de[9][40]	1–XI–90	43 410 899	21 782 154	21 628 745	42 869	*44 453	A4 c1	0.9	99 274	448
Kuwait Koweït	21–IV–85	1 697 301	965 297	732 004	2 125	*1 620	A9 c1	–6.8	17 818	91
Kyrgyzstan Kirghizistan	12–I–89	4 257 755 [3]	2 077 623 [3]	2 180 132 [3]	4 395	*4 596	A5 b1	1.1	198 500	23
Lao People's Dem. Rep. Rép. dém. populaire lao	1–III–85	3 584 803	1 757 115	1 827 688	x4 202	x4 742	A9 c3	3.0	236 800	20
Lebanon[41] Liban[41]	15–XI–70	2 126 325 [42]	1 080 015 [42]	1 046 310 [42]	x2 555	x2 915	B24c3	3.3	10 400	280
Macau[43] Macao[43]	30–VIII–91	*385 089	...	...	335	x398	A3 c1	4.3	18	22111
Malaysia Malaisie	14–VIII–91	*17 566 982	*8 861 124	*8 705 858	17 764	*19 489	A3 c2	2.3	329 758	59
Maldives Maldives	8–III–90	213 215	109 336	103 879	216	*246	A4 c1	3.2	298	825
Mongolia Mongolie	5–I–89	2 043 400	...	...	x2 177	x2 363	A5 c1	2.0	1 566 500	2

8
Population by sex, rate of population increase, surface area and density [cont.]
Population selon le sexe, taux d'accroissement de la population,
superficie et densité [suite]

Country or area Pays ou zone	Latest Census Dernier recensement				Midyear estimates (thousands) Estimations au milieu de l'année (milliers)			Annual rate of increase Taux d'accrois- sement annuel %	Surface area (km²) Superficie (km²)	Density Densité
	Date	Both sexes Les deux sexes	Male Masculin	Female Féminin	1990	1994	Type[1] 1994	1990–94	1994	1994[2]
Myanmar Myanmar	31–III–83	35 307 913 [3]	17 518 255 [3]	17 789 658 [3]	x41 813	x45 555	A11c2	2.1	676 578	67
Nepal[3] Népal[3]	22–VI–91	18 491 097	9 220 974	9 270 123	18 111	x21 360	A3 c1	4.1	147 181	145
Oman Oman	1–XII–93	*2 017 591	...	...	2 000	x2 077	A1 c1	0.9	212 457	10
Pakistan[44] Pakistan[44]	1–III–81	84 253 644	44 232 677	40 020 967	112 049	*126 610	A13c1	3.1	796 095	159
Palestine[45] Palestine[45]	18–XI–31	1 035 821	524 268 [46]	509 028 [46]	...	...	..	...	...	...
Gaza Strip[47] Zone de Gaza[47]	14–IX–67	356 261	172 511	183 750					378	...
Philippines[3] Philippines[3]	1–V–90	60 559 116	30 443 187	30 115 929	61 480	*67 038	A4 c2	2.2	300 000	223
Qatar Qatar	16–III–86	369 079	247 852	121 227	486	x540	A8 c3	2.6	11 000	49
Saudi Arabia Arabie saoudite	27–IX–92	*16 929 294	*9 466 541	*7 462 753	14 870	x17 451	A2 c3	4.0	2 149 690	8
Singapore[48] Singapour[48]	30–VI–90	2 705 115	1 370 059	1 335 056	2 705	*2 930	A4 b2	2.0	618	4 741
Sri Lanka Sri Lanka	17–III–81	14 846 750	7 568 253	7 278 497	16 993	*17 865	A13c1	1.3	65 610	272
Syrian Arab Republic[49] Rép. arabe syrienne[49]	7–IX–81	9 046 144	4 621 852	4 424 292	12 116	*13 844	A13c1	3.3	185 180	75
Tajikistan Tadjikistan	12–I–89	5 092 603 [3]	2 530 245 [3]	2 562 358 [3]	5 303	x5 933	A5 b1	2.8	143 100	41
Thailand[3] Thaïlande[3]	1–IV–90	*54 532 300	*27 031 200	*27 501 100	56 082	*59 396	A14c1	1.4	513 115	116
Turkey Turquie	21–X–90	56 473 035	28 607 047	27 865 988	56 098	*61 183	A4 c1	2.2	774 815	79
Turkmenistan Turkménistan	12–I–89	3 522 717 [3]	1 735 179 [3]	1 787 538 [3]	3 670	x4 010	A5 b1	2.2	488 100	8
United Arab Emirates[50] Emirats arabes unis[50]	15–XII–80	1 043 225	720 360	322 865	x1 671	x1 861	A14c3	2.7	83 600	22
Uzbekistan Ouzbékistan	12–I–89	19 810 077 [3]	9 784 156 [3]	10 025 921 [3]	20 531	x22 349	A5 b1	2.1	447 400	50
Viet Nam Viet Nam	1–IV–89	*64 411 713	*31 336 568	*33 075 145	66 233	*72 510	A5 c3	2.3	331 689	219
Yemen Yémen	16–XII–94	*14 561 330	...	...	11 279	*12 672	..	2.9	527 968	24
Europe · Europe										
Albania Albanie	12–IV–89	3 182 417	*1 638 900	*1 543 500	3 256	x3 414	A5 b1	1.2	28 748	119
Andorra Andorre	XI–54	5 664	...	...	53	*65	A40c3	5.3	453	143
Austria[3] Autriche[3]	15–V–91	7 795 786	3 753 989	4 041 797	7 718	*8 031	A3 b1	1.0	83 859	96
Belarus Bélarus	12–I–89	10 151 806 [3]	4 749 324 [3]	5 402 482 [3]	10 260	*10 355	A5 b1	0.2	207 600	50
Belgium[3] Belgique[3]	1–III–91	9 978 681	...	...	9 967	x10 080	A3 b1	0.3	30 519	330
Bosnia–Herzegovina[3] Bosnie–Herzégovine[3]	31–III–91	4 365 639	...	...	x4 308	x3 527	A3 b1	–5.0	51 129	69
Bulgaria Bulgarie	4–XII–92	*8 472 724	...	...	8 991	*8 443	A2 b1	–1.6	110 912 [51]	76
Channel Islands Iles Anglo–Normandes	21–IV–91	142 949	69 159	73 790	x142	x147	A8 b1	0.9	195	754
Guernsey[52] Guernesey[52]	21–IV–91	58 867	28 297	30 570	60	...		...	78	...

8
Population by sex, rate of population increase, surface area and density [*cont.*]
Population selon le sexe, taux d'accroissement de la population,
superficie et densité [*suite*]

Country or area Pays ou zone	Latest Census Dernier recensement Date	Both sexes Les deux sexes	Male Masculin	Female Féminin	Midyear estimates (thousands) Estimations au milieu de l'année (milliers) 1990	1994	Type[1] 1994	Annual rate of increase Taux d'accrois- sement annuel % 1990–94	Surface area (km²) Superficie (km²) 1994	Density Densité 1994[2]
Jersey Jersey	10–III–91	84 082	40 862	43 220	...	...		...	116	...
Croatia Croatie	31–III–91	4 784 265	2 318 623	2 465 642	4 778	x4 504	A3 b1	−1.5	88 117	51
Czech Republic Rép. tchéque	3–III–91	10 302 215	4 999 935	5 302 280	10 363	*10 333	A3 b1	−0.1	78 864	131
Denmark[3][53] Danemark[3][53]	1–I–91	5 146 469	2 536 391	2 610 078	5 140	*5 205	A3 a1	0.3	43 094	121
Estonia Estonie	12–I–89	1 565 662[3]	731 392[3]	834 270[3]	1 571	*1 499	A5 b1	−1.2	45 100	33
Faeroe Islands[3] Iles Féroe[3]	22–IX–77	41 969	21 997	19 972	47	x47	A17b1	−0.2	1 399	34
Finland[3] Finlande[3]	31–XII–90	4 998 478	2 426 204	2 572 274	4 986	*5 095	A4 b1	0.5	338 145	15
France[34][55] France[54][55]	5–III–90	56 634 299[56]	27 553 788[56]	29 080 511[56]	56 735	x57 747	A4 b1	0.4	551 500	105
Germany † Allemagne †	...	...	...	...	79 365	*81 410	..	0.6	356 733	228
Federal Rep. of Germany[3] Rép. féd. d'Allemagne[3]	25–V–87	61 077 042	29 322 923	31 754 119	63 253	*61 175	A6 b1	−0.8	248 647	246
former German Dem Rep.[3] ancienne R. d. allemande[3]	31–XII–81	16 705 635	7 849 112	8 856 523	16 247	x16 213	A13b1	−0.1	108 333	150
Gibraltar[57] Gibraltar[57]	9–XI–81	29 616	14 992	14 624	31	x28	A3 b1	−2.4	6	4 667
Greece Grèce	17–III–91	10 259 900[58]	5 055 408[58]	5 204 492[58]	10 161[59]	10 426[59]	A3 b2	0.6	131 990	79
Holy See Saint–Siège	30–IV–48	890	548	342	x1	x1	D6 d	0.0	0[60]	2 273
Hungary Hongrie	1–I–90	10 374 823	4 984 904	5 389 919	10 365	*10 261	A4 b1	−0.3	93 032	110
Iceland[3] Islande[3]	1–XII–70	204 930	103 621	101 309	255	*266	A24a1	1.1	103 000	3
Ireland Irlande	21–IV–91	3 525 719	1 753 418	1 772 301	3 503	*3 571	A3 b2	0.5	70 284	51
Isle of Man Ile de Man	14–IV–91	69 788	33 693	36 095	x69	x73	A3 b1	1.4	572	128
Italy Italie	20–X–91	59 103 833	...	...	57 661[3]	*57 193[3]	A3 b1	−0.2	301 268	190
Latvia Lettonie	12–I–89	2 666 567[3]	1 238 806[3]	1 427 761[3]	2 671	*2 548	A5 b1	−1.2	64 600	39
Liechtenstein Liechtenstein	2–XII–80	25 215	...	...	x29	*31	A14b1	1.4	160	192
Lithuania Lithuanie	12–I–89	3 674 802[3]	1 738 953[3]	1 935 849[3]	3 722	*3 721	A5 b1	−0.0	65 200	57
Luxembourg[3] Luxembourg[3]	31–III–91	384 634	188 570	196 064	382	x401	A3 b2	1.2	2 586	155
Malta[61] Malte[61]	16–XI–85	345 418	169 832	175 586	354	x364	A9 b2	0.7	316	1 152
Monaco[3] Monaco[3]	4–III–82	27 063	12 598	14 465	x30	x31	A12c1	0.8	1[62]	20805
Netherlands[3] Pays–Bas[3]	28–II–71	13 060 115	...	...	14 952	*15 380	A23a1	0.7	40 844	377
Norway[3] Norvège[3]	3–XI–90	4 247 546	2 099 881	2 147 665	4 241	*4 325	A4 a1	0.5	323 877	13
Poland[63] Pologne[63]	6–XII–88	37 878 641	18 464 373	19 414 268	38 119	*38 544	A6 b1	0.3	323 250	119
Portugal[64] Portugal[64]	15–IV–91	9 862 540	4 754 632	5 107 908	9 896	x9 830	A3 b1	−0.2	91 982	107
Republic of Moldova Moldova, Rép. de	12–I–89	4 337 592	2 058 160	2 279 432	4 364	*4 350	A5 b1	−0.1	33 700	129

8

Population by sex, rate of population increase, surface area and density [*cont.*]
Population selon le sexe, taux d'accroissement de la population,
superficie et densité [*suite*]

Country or area Pays ou zone	Latest Census Dernier recensement				Midyear estimates (thousands) Estimations au milieu de l'année (milliers)			Annual rate of increase Taux d'accrois- sement annuel %	Surface area (km^2) Superficie (km^2)	Density Densité
	Date	Both sexes Les deux sexes	Male Masculin	Female Féminin	1990	1994	Type[1] 1994	1990–94	1994	1994[2]
Romania Roumanie	7–I–92	22 810 035	11 213 763	11 596 272	23 207	*22 736	A2 b2	−0.5	238 391	95
Russian Federation Fédération de Russie	12–I–89	147 021 869[3]	68 713 869[3]	78 308 000[3]	148 292	*147 997	A5 b1	−0.0	17075400	9
San Marino Saint–Marin	30–XI–76	19 149	9 654	9 495	23	*25	A18a2	1.5	61	402
Slovakia Slovaquie	3–III–91	5 274 335	2 574 061	2 700 274	5 298	*5 347	A3 b1	0.2	49 012	109
Slovenia Slovénie	31–III–91	1 965 986	952 611	1 013 375	1 998	x1 942	A3 b1	−0.7	20 256	96
Spain[65] Espagne[65]	1–III–91	39 433 942	19 338 083	20 095 859	38 959	*39 143	A3 c1	0.1	505 992	77
Svalbard and Jan Mayen Isl.[66] Svalbard et Ile Jan–Mayen[66]	1–XI–60	3 431	2 545	886	...	...	..	...	62 422	...
Sweden Suède	1–IX–90	8 587 353	4 242 351	4 345 002	8 559	*8 780	A4 a1	0.6	449 964	20
Switzerland Suisse	4–XII–90	6 873 687	3 390 446	3 483 241	6 712	*6 995	A4 b1	1.0	41 284	169
TFYR of Macedonia[3] L'ex–R.y. Macédoine[3]	31–III–91	2 033 964	1 027 352	1 006 612	2 028	x2 142	A3 b1	1.4	25 713	83
Ukraine Ukraine	12–I–89	51 452 034[3]	23 745 108[3]	27 706 926[3]	51 839	*51 910	A5 b1	0.0	603 700	86
United Kingdom[67] Royaume–Uni[67]	21–IV–91	*56 352 200	...	...	57 561	x58 091	A13b1	0.2	244 100	238
Yugoslavia[3] Yougoslavie[3]	31–III–91	*10 337 504	...	...	10 529	*10 515	A3 b1	−0.0	102 173	103
Oceania · Océanie										
American Samoa[3] [20] Samoa américaines[3] [20]	1–IV–90	46 773	24 023	22 750	47	x53	A4 b1	2.9	199	266
Australia Australie	30–VI–91	16 850 540	8 362 815	8 487 725	17 065	*17 843	A3 b1	1.1	7 741 220	2
Christmas Island Iles Christmas	30–VI–81	2 871	1 918	953	...	...	..	...	135	...
Cocos (Keeling) Islands Iles des Cocos (Keeling)	30–VI–81	555	298	257	...	...	..	...	14	...
Cook Islands[68] Iles Cook[68]	1–XII–91	18 617	...	...	18	x19	A3 b1	1.1	236	81
Fiji Fidji	31–VIII–86	715 375	362 568	352 807	731	*784	A8 b1	1.7	18 274	43
French Polynesia[69] Polynésie française[69]	6–IX–88	188 814	98 345	90 469	197	x215	A6 c1	2.2	4 000	54
Guam[3] [20] Guam[3] [20]	1–IV–90	133 152	70 945	62 207	134	*146	A4 b1	2.1	549	266
Kiribati[70] Kiribati[70]	7–XI–90	72 298	...	...	x72	x77	A4 c1	1.7	726	106
Marshall Islands Iles Marshall	13–XI–88	43 380	...	...	46	*54	A6 c1	3.9	181	299
Micronesia, Federated States of Micronésie, Etats fédérés de	18–IX–94	104 724	53 500	51 224	101	*104	A0 c1	1.0	702	149
Nauru Nauru	1992	9 919	...	...	x10	x11	A2 d	2.4	21	524
New Caledonia[71] Nouvelle–Calédonie[71]	4–IV–89	164 173	83 862	80 311	170	*183	A5 c1	1.8	18 575	10
New Zealand[72] Nouvelle–Zélande[72]	5–III–91	*3 434 952	...	...	3 363	*3 493	A3 b1	1.0	270 534	13
Niue Nioué	IX–91	2 239	...	...	x2	x2	A3 d	0.0	260	8
Norfolk Island Ile Norfolk	30–VI–86	2 367	1 170	1 197	...	...	..	...	36	...

8

Population by sex, rate of population increase, surface area and density [cont.]

Population selon le sexe, taux d'accroissement de la population,
superficie et densité [suite]

Country or area Pays ou zone	Latest Census Dernier recensement		Male Masculin	Female Féminin	Midyear estimates (thousands) Estimations au milieu de l'année (milliers)		Type[1] 1994	Annual rate of increase Taux d'accrois- sement annuel % 1990–94	Surface area (km²) Superficie (km²) 1994	Density Densité 1994[2]
	Date	Both sexes Les deux sexes			1990	1994				
Northern Mariana Islands Iles Mariannes du Nord	1–IV–90	43 345	...	...	26 [10]	x47	A4 c1	([11])	464	101
Palau Palaos	1990	15 122	...	...	x15	x17	A4 c1	3.1	459	37
Papua New Guinea[73] Papouasie–Nouv.–Guinée[73]	11–VII–90	3 761 954	...	...	3 699	*3 997	A14c3	1.9	462 840	9
Pitcairn Pitcairn	31–XII–91	66	...	...	–	x0	A3 b1	...	5	...
Samoa Samoa	XI–91	161 298	...	...	164	*164	A3 c1	–0.0	2 831	58
Solomon Islands [74] Iles Salomon [74]	23–XI–86	285 176	147 972	137 204	x320	x366	A8 c1	3.4	28 896	13
Tokelau Tokélau	1–X–82	1 552	751	801	x2	x2	A3 b1	0.0	12	167
Tonga Tonga	28–XI–86	94 649	47 611	47 038	x97	x98	A8 c1	0.4	747	131
Tuvalu Tuvalu	27–V–79	7 300	...	...	x9	x9	A3 c1	0.0	26	346
Vanuatu Vanuatu	16–V–89	142 419	73 384	69 035	147	x165	A5 c1	2.9	12 189	14
Wallis and Futuna Islands Iles Wallis et Futuna	1990	13 705	...	...	x14	x14	A4 c1	0.0	200	70

Source:
Demographic statistics database of the Statistics Division of
the United Nations Secretariat.

Source:
Base de données pour les statistiques démographique de la
Division de statistique du Secrétariat de l'ONU.

† For detailed descriptions of data pertaining to former
  Czechoslovakia, Germany, SFR Yugoslavia and former USSR,
  see Annex I – Country or area nomenclature, regional and
  other groupings.

* Provisional.
x Estimate prepared by the Population Division of the United
  Nations.
1 For explanation of code, see technical notes to this chapter.
2 Population per squre kilometre of surface area in 1994.
  Figures are merely the quotients of population divided by
  surface area and are not to be considered either as
  reflecting density in the urban sense or as indicating the
  supporting power of a territory's land and resources.
3 De jure population.
4 Including the enclave of Cabinda.
5 Comprising Chagos Archipelago (formerly dependency of
  Mauritius).
6 Census of Chagos Archipelago taken 30 June 1962 gave
  total population of 747 persons.
7 Excluding Mayotte.
8 Comprising Bioko (which includes Pagalu)
  and Rio Muni (which includes Corisco and Elobeys).
9 Mid–year estimates have been adjusted for
  under–enumeration, estimated as follows:

† Pour les descriptions en détails des données relatives à l'ancienne
  Tchécoslovaquie, l'Allemagne, la Rfs Yougoslavie et l'ancienne
  URSS, voir l'Annexe I – Nomenclautre des pays ou zones,
  groupements régionaux et autres groupements.

* Données provisoires.
x Estimation établie par la Division de la population de
  l'Organisation des Nations Unies.
1 Pour l'explication du code, voir la remarque générale concerment
  ce chapître.
2 Nombre d'habîtants au kilomètre carré en 1994. Il s'agit
  simplement du quotient du chiffre de la population divisé
  par celui de la superficie: il ne faut pas y voir d'indication de la densité au
  sens urbain du terme ni de l'effectif de population que les terres
  et les ressources du territoire sont capables de nourrir.
3 Population de droit.
4 Y compris l'enclave de Cabinda.
5 Comprend l'archipel de Chagos (ancienne dépendance de
  Maurice).
6 Le recensement de la population de l'archipel de Chagos au 30 juin 1962
  a donnée comme population total 747 personnes.
7 Non compris Mayotte.
8 Comprend Bioko (qui comprend Pagalu) et Rio Muni (qui
  comprend Corisco et Elobeys).
9 Les estimations au milieu de l'année tiennent compte d'un ajustement
  destiné à compenser les lacunes du dénombrement. Les données de
  recensement ne tiennent pas compte de cet ajustement. En voici le détail:

8
Population by sex, rate of population increase, surface area and density [*cont.*]
Population selon le sexe, taux d'accroissement de la population,
superficie et densité [*suite*]

	Percentage adjustment	Adjusted census total		Adjustement (en pourcentage)	Chiffre de recensement ajusté
Brunei Darussalam	1.06	...	Brunéi Darussalam	1,06	...
Guatemala	13.7	...	Guatemala	13,7	...
Korea, Republic of	1.9	...	Corée, Rép. de	1,9	...
Mozambique	3.8	...	Mozambique	3,8	...
Netherlands Antilles	2.0	...	Antilles néerlandaises	2,0	...
Sierra Leone	10.0	*3 002 426	Sierra Leone	10,0	*3 002 426
Uruguay	2.6	...	Uruguay	2,6	...

10 Estimate not in accord with the latest census and/or the latest estimate.

11 Rate not computed because of apparent lack of comparability between estimates shown for 1990 and 1994.

12 Including an estimate of 224,095 for nomad population.

13 Comprising the islands of Agalega and St. Brandon.

14 Excluding Bophuthatswana, Ciskei, Transkei and Venda.

15 Comprising the Northern Region (former Saguia el Hamra) and Southern Region (former Rio de Oro).

16 De jure population, but excluding persons residing in institutions.

17 Including Carriacou and other dependencies in the Grenadines.

18 Including dependencies: Marie−Galante, la Désirade, les Saintes, Petite−Terre, St. Barthélemy and French part of St. Martin.

19 Comprising Bonaire, Curaçao, Saba, St. Eustatius and Dutch part of St. Martin.

20 Including armed forces in the area.

21 Including Bequia and other islands in the Grenadines.

22 De jure population, but excluding civilian citizens absent from country for extended period of time. Census figures also exclude armed forces overseas.

23 Excluding Indian jungle population.

24 Excluding nomadic Indian tribes.

25 Excluding dependencies, of which South Georgia (area 3,755 km^2) had an estimated population of 499 in 1964 (494 males, 5 females). The other dependencies namely, the South Sandwich group (surface area 337 km^2) and a number of smaller islands, are presumed to be uninhabited.

26 A dispute exists between the governments of Argentina and the United Kingdom of Great Britain and Northern Ireland concerning sovereignty over the Falkland Islands (Malvinas).

27 Excluding nomad population.

28 Excluding transients afloat.

29 Excluding foreign diplomatic personnel and their dependants.

30 This total population of China, as given in the communiqué of the State Statistical Bureau releasing the major figures of the census, includes a population of 6,130,000 for Hong Kong and Macau.

31 For government controlled areas.

32 Comprising Hong Kong island, Kowloon and the New (leased) Territories.

33 Land area only. Total including ocean area within administrative boundaries is 2,916 km^2.

34 Including data for the Indian−held part of Jammu and Kashmir, the final status of which has not yet been determined.

35 Figures provided by Indonesia including East Timor, shown separately.

36 Including data for East Jerusalem and Israeli residents in certain other territories under

10 L'estimation ne s'accorde avec le dernier recensement, et/ou avec la dernière estimation.

11 On n'a pas calculé le taux parce que les estimations pour 1990 et 1994 ne paraissent pas comparables.

12 Y compris une estimation de 224 095 personnes pour la population nomade

13 Y compris les îles Agalega et Saint−Brandon.

14 Non compris Bophuthatswana, Ciskei, Transkei et Venda.

15 Comprend la région septentrionale (ancien Saguia−el−Hamura) et la région méridionale (ancien Rio de Oro).

16 Population de droit, mais non compris les personnes dans les institutions.

17 Y compris Carriacou et les autres dépendances du groupe des îles Grenadines.

18 Y compris les dépendances: Marie−Galante, la Désirade, les Désirade, les Saintes, Petite−Terre, Saint−Barthélemy et la partie française de Saint−Martin.

19 Comprend Bonaire, Curaçao, Saba, Saint−Eustache et la partie néederlandaise de Saint−Martin.

20 Y compris les militaires en garnison sur le territoire.

21 Y compris Bequia et des autres îles dans les Grenadines.

22 Population de droit, mais non compris les civils hors du pays pendant une période prolongée. Les chiffres de recensement ne comprennent pas également les militaires à l'étranger.

23 Non compris les Indiens de la jungle.

24 Non compris les tribus d'Indiens nomades.

25 Non compris les dépendances, parmi lesquelles figure la Georgie du Sud (3 755 km^2) avec une population estimée à 499 personnes en 1964 (494 du sexe masculin et 5 du sexe féminin). Les autres dépendances, c'est−à−dire le groupe des Sandwich de Sud (superficie: 337 km^2) et certaines petite−îles, sont présumées inhabitées.

26 La souveraineté sur les îles Falkland (Malvinas) fait l'objet d'un différend entre le Gouvernement argentin et le Gouvernement du Royaume−Uni de Grande−Bretagne et d'Irlande du Nord.

27 Non compris la population nomade.

28 Non compris les personnes de passage à bord des navires.

29 Non compris le personnel diplomatique étranger et les membres de leur famille les accompagnant.

30 Le chiffre indiqué pour la population totale de la Chine, qui figure dans le communiqué du Bureau du statistique de l'Etat publiant les principaux chiffres du recensement, comprennent la population de Hong−kong et Macao qui s'élève à 6 130 000 personnes.

31 Pour les zones controlées par le Gouvernement.

32 Comprend les îles de Hong−kong, Kowloon et les Nouveaux Territoires (à bail).

33 Superficie terrestre seulement. La superficie totale, qui comprend la zone maritime se trouvant à l'intérieur des limites administratives, est de 2 916 km^2.

34 Y compris les données pour la partie du Jammu et du Cacehmire occupée par l'Inde dont le statut définitif n'a pas encore été déterminé.

8
Population by sex, rate of population increase, surface area and density [*cont.*]
Population selon le sexe, taux d'accroissement de la population,
superficie et densité [*suite*]

occupation by Israeli military forces since June 1967.
37 Comprising Hokkaido, Honshu, Shikoku, Kyushu. Excluding
    diplomatic personnel outside the country and foreign
    military and civilian personnel and their dependants
    stationed in the area.
38 Including military and diplomatic personnel and their families
    abroad, numbering 933 at 1961 census, but excluding foreign
    military and diplomatic personnel and their families in the
    country, numbering 389 at 1961 census. Also including
    registered Palestinian refugees number 654,092 and 722,687 at
    30 June 1963 and 31 May 1967, respectively.
39 Excluding data for Jordanian territory under
    occupation since June 1967 by Israeli military forces.
40 Excluding alien armed forces, civilian aliens employed
    by armed forces, foreign diplomatic personnel and their
    dependants and Korean diplomatic personnel and their
    dependants outside the country.
41 Excluding Palestinian refugees in camps.
42 Based on results of sample survey.
43 Comprising Macau City and islands of Taipa and Coloane.
44 Excluding data for Jammu and Kashmir, the final
    status of which has not yet been determined,
    Junagardh, Manavadar, Gilgit and Baltistan.
45 Former mandated territory administered by the United
    Kingdom until 1948.
46 Excluding United Kingdom armed forces, numbering 2,507.
47 Comprising that part of Palestine under Egyptian
    administration following the Armistice of 1949 until
    June 1967, when it was occupied by Israeli military forces.
48 Excluding transients afloat and non—locally domiciled military
    and civilian services personnel and their dependants and visitors,
    numbering 5,553, 5,187 and 8,895 respectively at 1980 census.
49 Including Palestinian refugees numbering 193,000 on 1 July 1977.
50 Comprising 7 sheikdoms of Abu Dhabi, Dubai, Sharjah,
    Ajaman, Umm al Qaiwain, Ras al Khaimah and Fujairah,
    and the area lying within the modified Riyadh line as
    announced in October 1955.
51 Excluding surface area of frontier rivers.
52 Including dependencies: Alderey, Brechou, Herm,
    Jethou, Lithou and Sark Island.
53 Excluding Faeroe Islands and Greenland, shown separately.
54 Excluding Overseas Departments, namely French Guiana,
    Guadeloupe, Martinique and Réunion, shown separately.
55 De jure population, but excluding diplomatic personnel
    outside the country and including foreign diplomatic
    personnel not living in embassies or consulates.
56 Excluding military personnel stationed outside the
    country who do not have a personal residence in France.
57 Excluding armed forces.
58 Including armed forces stationed outside the country,
    but excluding alien armed forces stationed in the area.
59 Including armed forces stationed outside the country
    and alien armed forces stationed in the area.
60 Surface area is 0.44 km².
61 Including Gozo and Comino Islands and civilian
    nationals temporarily outside the country.
62 Surface area is 1.49 km².
63 Excluding civilian aliens within the country, but
    including civilian nationals temporarily outside the country.
64 Including the Azores and Madeira Islands.
65 Including the Balearic and Canary Islands, and Alhucemas,
    Ceuta, Chafarinas, Melilla and Penon de Vélez de la Gomera.
66 Inhabited only during the winter season. Census data are for
    total population while estimates refer to Norwegian population
    only. Included also in the de jure population of Norway.
67 Excluding Channel Islands and Isle of Man, shown separately.
68 Excluding Niue, shown separately, which is part of

35 Les chiffres fournis par l'Indonesie comprennent le Timor
    oriental, qui fait l'objet d'une rubrique distincte.
36 Y compris les données pour Jérusalem−Est et les résidents israéliens dans
    certains autres territoires occupés depuis juin 1967 par les forces
    armées israéliennes.
37 Comprend Hokkaido, Honshu, Shikoku, Kyushu. Non compris le
    personnel diplomatique hors du pays, les militaires et agents civils étrangers
    en poste sur le territoire et les membres de leur famille les accompagnant.
38 Y compris les militaires et le personnel diplomatique à l'étranger et
    les membres de leur famille les accompagnant, au nombre de 933
    personnes au recensement de 1961, mais non compris les militaires et
    le personnel diplomatique étrangers sur le territoire et les membres
    de leur famille les accompagnant, au nombre de 389 personnes au
    recensement de 1961. Y compris également les réfugiés de Palestine
    immatriculés: 654 092 au 30 juin 1963 et 722 687 au 31 mai 1967.
39 Non compris les données pour le territoire jordanien
    occupé depuis juin 1967 par les forces armées israéliennes.
40 Non compris les militaires étrangers, les civils étrangers employés par les
    armées, le personnel diplomatique étranger et les membres de leur famille
    les accompagnant et le personnel diplomatique coréen hors du pays et les
    membres de leur familles les accompagnant.
41 Non compris les réfugiés de Palestine dans les camps.
42 D'après les résultats d'une enquête par sondage.
43 Comprend la ville de Macao et les îles de Taipa et de Colowane.
44 Non compris les données pour le Jammu et le Cachemire, dont le status
    définitif n'a pas encore été déterminé, le Junagardh, le Manavadar,
    le Gilgit et le Baltistan.
45 Ancien territoire sous mandat administré par le
    Royaume−Uni jusqu'à 1948.
46 Non compris les forces armées du Royaume−Uni au nombre de 2 507
    personnes.
47 Comprend la partie de la Palestine administrée par l'Egypt depuis
    l'armistice de 1949 jusqu'en juin 1967, date laquelle elle a été occupée par
    les forces armées israéliennes.
48 Non compris les personnes de passage à bord de navires,
    les militaires et agents civils non résidents et les membres de leur
    famille les accompagnant, et les visiteurs, soit: 5 553, 5 187 et 8 895
    personnes respectivement au recensement de 1980.
49 Y compris les réfugiés de Palestine au nombre de
    193 000 au 1er juillet 1977.
50 Comprend les sept cheikhats de Abou Dhabi, Dabai, Ghârdja, Adjmân,
    Oumm−al−Quiwaïn, Ras al Khaîma et Foudjaïra, ainsi que la zone
    délimitée par la ligne de Riad modifiée comme il a été announcé
    en octobre 1955.
51 Non compris la surface des cours d'eau frontières.
52 Y compris les dépendances: Aurigny, Brecqhou, Herm,
    Jethou, Lihou et l'île de Sercq.
53 Non compris les îles Féroé et le Groenland, qui
    font l'objet de rubriques distinctes.
54 Non compris les départements d'outre−mer, c'est−à−dire la Guyane
    française, la Guadeloupe, la Martinique et la Réunion, qui font l'objet de
    rubriques distinctes.
55 Population de droit, non compris le personnel diplomatique hors du
    pays et y compris le personnel diplomatique étranger qui ne vit
    pas dans les ambassades ou les consulats.
56 Non compris les militaires en garnison hors du pays et
    sans résidence personnelle en France.
57 Non compris les militaires.
58 Y compris les militaires en garnison hors du pays, mais non compris les
    militaires étrangers en garnison sur le territoire.
    territoire.
59 Y compris les militaires en garnison hors du pays, et les
    militaires étrangers en garnison sur le territoire.
    territoire.
60 Superficie: 0,44 km².
61 Y compris les îles de Gozo et de Comino et les civils
    nationaux temporairement hors du pays.

8
Population by sex, rate of population increase, surface area and density [cont.]
Population selon le sexe, taux d'accroissement de la population,
superficie et densité [suite]

Cook Islands, but because of remoteness is
administered separately.
69 Comprising Austral, Gambier, Marquesas, Rapa, Society
and Tuamotu Islands.
70 Including Christmas, Fanning, Ocean and Washington Islands.
71 Including the islands of Huon, Chesterfield, Loyalty,
Walpole and Belep Archipelago.
72 Including Campbell and Kermadec Islands (population 20
in 1961, surface area 148 km^2) as well as Antipodes,
Auckland, Bounty, Snares, Solander and Three Kings
island, all of which are uninhabited. Excluding
diplomatic personnel and armed forces outside the
country, the latter numbering 1,936 at 1966 census;
also excluding alien armed forces within the country.
73 Comprising eastern part of New Guinea, the Bismarck
Archipelago, Bougainville and Buka of Solomon Islands
group and about 600 smaller islands.
74 Comprising the Solomon islands group (except
Bougainville and Buka which are included with Papua
New Guinea shown separately), Ontong, Java, Rennel
and Santa Cruz Islands.

62 Superficie: 1,49 km^2.
63 Non compris les civils étrangers dans le pays, mais y
compris les civils nationaux temporairement hors du pays.
64 Y compris les Açores et Madère.
65 Y compris les Baléares et les Canaries, Al Hoceima, Ceuta, les
îles Zaffarines, Melilla et Penon de Vélez de la Gomera.
66 N'est habitée pendant la saison d'hiver. Les données de recensement se
rapportent à la populatio totale, mais les estimations ne concernent que la
population norvégienne, comprise également dans la
population de droit de la Norvège.
67 Non compris les îles Anglo−Normandes et l'île de
Man, qui font l'objet de rubriques distinctes.
68 Non compris Nioué, qui fait l'objet d'une rubrique distincte et qui fait
partie des îles Cook, mais qui, en raison de son éloignement, est
administrée séparément.
69 Comprend les îles Australes, Gambier, Marquises, Rapa,
de la Societé et Tuamotou.
70 Y compris les îles Christmas, Fanning, Océan et Washington.
71 Y compris les îles Huon, Chesterfield, Loyauté et
Walpole, et l'archipel Belep.
72 Y compris les îles Campbell et Kermadec (20 habitants en 1961, superficie:
148 km^2) ainsi que les îles Antipodes, Auckland, Bounty, Snares, Solander
et Three Kings, qui sont toutes inhabitées. Non compris le personnel
diplomatique et les militaires hors du pays, ces derniers au nombre de
1 936 au recensement de 1966; non compris également les militaires
étrangers dans le pays.
73 Comprend l'est de la Nouvelle−Guinée, l'archipel Bismarck, Bougainville
et Buka (ces deux dernières du groupe des Salomon) et environ 600 îlots.
74 Comprend les îles Salomon (à l'exception de Bougainville et de Buka dont
la population est comprise dans celle de Papouasie−Nouvelle Guinée
qui font l'objet d'une rubrique distincte), ainsi que les îles Ontong, Java,
Rennel et Santa Cruz.

Technical notes, table 8

Table 8 is based on detailed data on population and its growth and distribution published in the United Nations *Demographic Yearbook* [21], which also provides a comprehensive description of methods of evaluation and limitations of data. A brief explanation of the quality code used for total population estimates in table 8 is given below.

For "Type of estimate", the code indicates the method by which official estimates of population for the year 1994 were prepared, so far as could be ascertained. The letters A–D indicate the nature of the base figure; numerals to capital letters indicate the lapse of time since the establishment of the base figure; letters a–d indicate the method of time adjustment by which the base figure is brought up to date; numerals to small letters indicate the quality of time adjustment.

The details of the code classification for this column are given below:

Nature of base data (capital letter)
A. Complete census of individuals.
B. Sample survey.
C. Partial census or partial registration of individuals.
D. Conjecture.
... Nature of base data not determined.

Recency of base data (subscript numeral following capital letter)
Numeral indicates time elapsed (in years) since establishment of base figure.

Method of time adjustment (lower-case letter)
a. Adjustment by continuous population register.
b. Adjustment based on calculated balance of births, deaths and migration.
c. Adjustment of assumed rate of population increase.
d. No adjustment: base figure held constant at least two consecutive years.
... Method of time adjustment not determined.

Quality of adjustment for types a and b (numeral following letter a or b)
1. Population balance adequately accounted for.
2. Adequacy of accounting for population balance not determined but assumed to be adequate.
3. Population balance not adequately accounted for.

Quality of adjustment for type c (numeral following letter c)
1. Two or more censuses taken at decennial intervals or less.
2. Two or more censuses taken, but latest interval exceeds a decennium.
3. One or no census taken.

Unless otherwise indicated, figures refer to de facto (present-in-area) population for present territory; surface area estimates include inland waters.

Notes techniques, tableau 8

Le *Tableau 8* : est fondé sur des données détaillées sur la population, sa croissance et sa distribution, publiées dans l'*Annuaire démographique des Nations Unies* [21], qui offre également une description complète des méthodes d'évaluation et une indication des limites des données. On trouvera ci-après une brève explication du code de qualité utilisé pour les estimations de la population totale présentées au Tableau 8.

Pour le "Type d'estimation", le code indique, dans la mesure où elle a pu être déterminée, la méthode selon laquelle les estimations officielles de la population ont été établies pour l'année 1994. Les lettres A-D indiquent la nature du chiffre de base; les nombres placés à la droite de ces lettres indiquent le temps écoulé depuis l'établissement du chiffre de base; les lettres a-d indiquent la méthode d'actualisation du chiffre de base; les numéros qui suivent ces lettres en petits caractères indiquent la qualité de l'actualisation.

Le détail de la classification codée est donné ci-dessous :

Nature des données de base (majuscules)
A. Recensement complet de la population.
B. Enquête par échantillonnage.
C. Recensement partiel ou enregistrement partiel de la population.
D. Conjecture.
... La nature des données de base n'est pas déterminée.

Actualité relative des données (nombre en indice suivant la lettre majuscule)
Le nombre indique le temps écoulé (en années) depuis l'établissement du chiffre de base.

Méthode d'actualisation (lettre minuscule)
a. Actualisation par enregistrement continu de la population.
b. Actualisation basée sur le calcul de la balance des naissances, des décès et des migrations.
c. Actualisatin du taux présumé d'accroissement de la population.
d. Absence d'actualisation : le chiffre de base est maintenu constant pendant au moins deux années consécutives.
... Méthode d'actualisation non déterminée.

Qualité de l'actualisation pour les types a et b (chiffre suivant la lettre a ou b)
1. Balance démographique convenablement établie.
2. La qualité de l'établissement de la balance démographique n'est pas déterminée, mais on suppose qu'elle est convenable.
3. Balance démographique non convenablement établie.

Qualité de l'actualisation pour le type c (définie par le chiffre suivant la lettre c)

1. Deux recensements ou plus ont été effectués en dix ans ou moins.
2. Deux recensements ou plus ont été effectués, mais à plus de dix ans d'intervalle.
3. Un recensement effectué ou aucun.

Sauf indication contraire, les chiffres se rapportent à la population effectivement présente sur le territoire tel qu'il est actuellement défini; les estimations de superficie comprennent les étendues d'eau intérieures.

9
Education at the first, second and third levels
Enseignement des premier, second et troisième degrés

Number of students and percentage female
Nombre d'étudiants et étudiantes feminines en pourcentage

Country or area Pays ou zone	Years Années	First level Premier degré Total	%F	Years Années	Second level Second degré Total	%F	Years Années	Third level Troisième degré Total	%F
Africa · Afrique									
Algeria	1985	3481288	44	1985	1823392	42	1989	258995	...
Algérie	1990	4189152	45	1990	2175580	43	1990	285930	...
	1991	4357352	45	1991	2232780	44	1991	298117	...
	1992	4436363	45	1992	2305198	45	1992	303111	...
Angola	1985	974498	45	1985[1]	178910	...	1985	5034	...
Angola	1990	990155	48[2]	1990	186499	...	1990	6534	...
	1991	989443	...	1991	218987	...	1991	6331	...
Benin	1985	444163	34	1985	107172	29	1985	9063	16
Bénin	1990	490129	33	...	...	...	1989	8883	14
	1991	534810	34	...	...	...	1990	10873	13
Botswana	1985	223608	52	1985	36144	53	1985	1938	45[3]
Botswana	1990	283516	52	1990	61767	53	...	...	...
	1991	298812	51	1991	78804	54	...	...	...
	1992	301482	51	1992	81316	53	...	...	...
Burkina Faso	1985	351807	37	1985	53565	34	1985	4085	23
Burkina Faso	1990	504414	38	1990	98929	34[2]	1988	5491	24
	1991	530013	39	1991	105542	34[2]	1989	5675	28
	1992	562644	39	1992	115753	35[2]	1990	5425	23
Burundi	1985	385936	42	1985	25939	34	1985	2783	24
Burundi	1990	633203	46	1990	44207	37	1990	3592	27
	1991	631039	45	1991	48398	38	1991	3830	26
	1992	651086	45	1992	55713	39	1992	4256	26
Cameroon	1985	1705319	46	1985	343720	38	1986	21438	...
Cameroun	1990	1964146	46	1990	500272	41	1988	24539	...
	1993	1823556	...	1993	648082	...	1990	33177	...
Cape Verde	1985	57909	49	1987	6413	48	...	...	...
Cap–Vert	1990	69832	...	1989	7866	50	...	...	...
Central African Rep.	1985	309656	39	1985	59273	27	1985	2651	11
Rép. centrafricaine	1989	323661	39	1989	49147	29	1989	3482	16
Chad	1985	337616	28	1986	44379	16	1984	1643	9
Tchad	1990	525165	31	1988	49439	16	1988[4]	2983	...
	1991	591417	32	...	...	...	...	...	...
	1992	553105	32	...	...	...	...	...	...
Comoros	1985	66084	43	1985	21056	39	...	...	...
Comores	1990	72824	42	...	...	...	1989	248	15
	1992	73827	46	1991	15878	...	1991	223	28
	1993	77837	45	1993	17637	...			
Congo	1985	475805	49	1985	222633	44	1985	10684	16
Congo	1990	503918	47	1990	182967	...	1990	10671	18
	1991	492286	48	1991	191459	43	1991	12045	19
	1993	505925	48	1993	212850	...	1992	13806	...
Côte d'Ivoire	1985	1214511	41	...	...	...	1986	23642	18
Côte d'Ivoire	1990	1414865	41	...	...	...	...	...	...
	1991	1447785	42	...	...	...	...	...	...
	1993	1553540	42	...	...	...	...	...	...
Djibouti	1985	25212	41	1985	7041	39	...	...	...
Djibouti	1990	31706	41	1990	9513	...	...	...	...
	1992	30589	43	1992	9740	43	1991	53	30
	1993	33005	43	1993	10384	42	...	...	...
Egypt	1985	6214250	43	1985	3826601	40	1985	854584	30
Egypte	1990[1]	6964306	44	1990	5507257	43	1990[5]	708417	35
	1992[6]	6791128	45	1992[6]	5515092	45	...	...	...
	1993	7732308	45	1993	6133308	44	...	...	...
Equatorial Guinea									
Guinée équatoriale	1983	61532	...	...	...	...	1990	578	13
Eritrea	1988	128504	47	...	...	...	...	...	...
Erythrée	1990	109087	49	...	...	...	...	...	...
	1992	184492	45	1992	60955	46	...	...	...
	1993	207099	44	1993	66524	42	...	...	...

9

Education at the first, second and third levels
Number of students and percentage female [*cont.*]
Enseignement des premier, second et troisième degrés
Nombre d'étudiants et étudiantes feminines en pourcentage [*suite*]

Country or area Pays ou zone	Years Années	First level Premier degré Total	%F	Years Années	Second level Second degré Total	%F	Years Années	Third level Troisième degré Total	%F
Ethiopia	1985	2448778	39	1985	666169	...	1985	27338	18
Ethiopie	1990	2466464	40	1990	866016	43	1989	33486	18
	1991	2063636	42	1991	782412	45	1990	34076	18
	1992	1855894	41	1992	720779	46	1991[7]	26218	19
Gabon	1985	183607	49	1985	44124	42	1986	4089	29
Gabon	1988	207023	50	1988	47828	47	1987	4050	30
	1991	210000	50	1991	51348	54	1988	4007	31
Gambia	1985[8]	69017	39	1985	15918	30	...	...	...
Gambie	1990	86307	41[2]	1990	20400	33	...	...	...
	1991	90645	41	1991	21786	35	...	...	...
	1992	97262	41	1992	25929	35	...	...	...
Ghana	1985[9]	1505819	...	1985[9]	749980	...	1985[10]	8324	17
Ghana	1990	1945422	45	1989[9]	829518	39	1989[10]	9274	18
	1991	2011602	46	...	...	...	1990[10]	9609	22
Guinea	1985	276438	32	1985[1]	92754	26	1985	8801	14
Guinée	1990	346807	32	1989	78659	25	1987	5923	12
	1992	421869	32	1990	85942	24	...	...	...
	1993	471792	33	1992	106811	25	...	...	...
Guinea-Bissau	1986	77004	35	1986	6450	25	...	...	...
Guinée-Bissau	1988	79035	36	1988	6330	32	1988	404	6
Kenya	1985[1]	4702414	48	1985[1]	457767	38	1985	21756	26
Kenya	1990	5392319	49	...	...	...	1987	26839	28
	1992	5554977	49	...	...	...	1989	31287	...
	1993[2]	5643000	49	...	...	...	...	...	...
Lesotho	1985	314003	56	1985	37343	60	1985	2428	62
Lesotho	1990	351632	55	1991	48615	59	1990	2758	49
	1992	362657	54	1992	53485	59	1992	3704	54
	1993	354275	54	...	...	...	1993	4001	56
Liberia									
Libérie	1986[9]	80048	...	...	...	...	1987	5095	23
Libyan Arab Jamahiriya	1985[1]	1011952	47	1985[1]	143113	47	1985	30000	...
Jamah. arabe libyenne	1990	1175229	48	1990	257120	...	1989	50471	...
	1992	1254242	48	1991	294283	...	1991	72899	46
	1993	1357040	49	1992	310556	...	...	...	...
Madagascar	1984	1625216	48	...	...	...	1985	38310	38
Madagascar	1990	1570721	49	...	...	...	1990	35824	45
	1992	1490317	49	...	...	...	1992	42681	...
	1993	1504668	49	...	...	...	...	...	...
Malawi	1985	942539	43	1985	25737	32	1985	3928	29
Malawi	1990	1400682	45	1990	32275	34	1989	5594	28
	1992	1795451	47	1992	37413	34	1990	6356	...
Mali	1985	292395	37	1986	63768	30	1985	6768	13
Mali	1990	340573	37	1990	78523	32	1986	5536	13
	1992	438302	38	...	...	...	1990	6703	14
	1993	496909	39	1993	111255	34	...	...	...
Mauritania	1985	140871	40	1985	35955	...	1986	5378	...
Mauritanie	1990	167229	42	1990	37653	32	1991	5850	15
	1992	219258	44	1992	43034	33	1992	7501	15
	1993	248048	45	1993	45810	35	1993	8495	17
Mauritius	1985	140714	49	1985	72551	47	1985	1161	36
Maurice	1990	137491	49	1990	79229	50	1989	2179	34
	1992	129738	49	1992	86024	...	1990	3485	37
	1993	125543	49	...	...	...	1991	4032	41
Morocco	1985	2279887	38	1985	1201858	39	1985	181087	32
Maroc	1990[1]	2483691	40	1990[1]	1123531	41	...	...	...
	1991	2578566	40	1991	1168918	41	...	...	...
	1992	2727833	41	1992	1207734	41	...	...	...
Mozambique	1985	1248074	44	1985[1]	151888	31	1985	1442	23
Mozambique	1990[1]	1260218	43	1990	160177	36	1987	2335	22
	1992	1199476	43	1992	159202	38	1992	4600	26
	1993	1227341	42	1993	163747	39	1993	5250	26
Namibia	1986	294985	...	1986	49571	...	...	...	...
Namibie	1990	313970	52	1990	62354	56	...	...	...
	1991	339804	51	1991	73031	...	1991	4157	64
	1992	349167	50	1992	84581	55	...	...	...

9
Education at the first, second and third levels
Number of students and percentage female [*cont.*]
Enseignement des premier, second et troisième degrés
Nombre d'étudiants et étudiantes feminines en pourcentage [*suite*]

Country or area Pays ou zone	Years Années	First level Premier degré Total	%F	Years Années	Second level Second degré Total	%F	Years Années	Third level Troisième degré Total	%F
Niger	1985	275902	36	...	...	...	1984	2863	18
Niger	1990	368732	36	1990	76758	29	1986	3317	18
	1992	379712	38	1991	78070	31	1988	3773	16
	1993	414296	...	1992	80009	33	1989	4506	15
Nigeria	1985[11]	12914870	44	1985	3088711	43	1985	266679	27
Nigéria	1990[11]	13776854	44	1990	3123277	42	1987	276352	24
	1991[11]	14805937	44	1991	3600620	45	1988	304536	25
	1992[11]	15870280	44	1992	4032083	46	1989	335824	24
Réunion	1985	73985	48	1985	69863	54	...	...	...
Réunion	1988	73747	...	1986	69585	53	...	...	...
	1993	70735	49	1993	88605	51	...	...	...
Rwanda	1985	836877	49	1985	46998	42	1985	1987	14
Rwanda	1990	1100437	50	1990	70400	43	1988	2642	20
	1991[1]	1104902	50	1991	94586	44	1989	3389	19
St. Helena Sainte-Hélène	1985	582	55	1985	513	49	...	...	...
Sao Tome and Principe	1986	17010	48	1986	5255	...	...	...	...
Sao Tomé-et-Principe	1989	19822	47	1987	6452	47	...	...	...
Senegal	1985	583890	40	1985[9]	130338	33	1985	13354	...
Sénégal	1990	708448	42	1989[9]	173044	34	...	...	...
	1991	725496	42	1991[9]	191431	35	...	...	...
	1992	738556	43	...	...	...	...	...	...
Seychelles	1985	14368	49	1985[1]	3975	50	...	...	...
Seychelles	1991[1]	10134	49	1990	4396	...	...	...	...
	1993	9873	49	1993	9111	50	...	...	...
	1994	9911	49	1994	9280	50	...	...	...
Sierra Leone	1985	421689	...	1985	94717	...	1985	5690	...
Sierra Leone	1990[12]	367426	41	1990	102474	37	1990	4742	...
Somalia Somalie	1985	196496	34	1985	45686	35	1986	15672	20
South Africa	1986[13]	4737367	49	...	...	...	1989[13]	421152	46
Afrique du Sud	1990	6951777	50	1990	2743184	54	1990[13]	439007	44
	1992[13]	5643707	49	1991	2939270	54	1991[13]	467129	46
	1993[13]	5758389	50	...	...	...	1992[13]	490112	46
Sudan	1985	1738341	40	1985	556587	42	1985	37367	37
Soudan	1990	2042743	43	1990	731624	43	1987	34647	38
	1991	2168180	43	1991	718298	44	1989	60134	40
Swaziland	1985	139345	50	1985	31109	...	1985	2732	...
Swaziland	1990	166454	50	...	...	...	1990	3198	43
	1992	180285	49	...	...	...	1991	3224	47
	1993	186271	49	...	...	...	1992	3023	42
Togo	1985	462858	38	1985	97120	24	1986	6223	13
Togo	1990	646962	40	1989	127704	25	1989	7826	13
	1991	652548	40	1990	125545	25	1992	8438	12
	1993	663126	40	...	...	...	1993	9120	12
Tunisia	1985	1291490	45	1985	457630	40	1985	41594	36
Tunisie	1990	1405665	46	1990	564540	43	1990	68535	39
	1992	1440960	46	1992	639403	45	1992	87780	41
	1993	1476329	47	1993	688004	46	1993	96101	42
Uganda	1985[14]	2117000	...	1985[14]	179185	...	1985	10103	23
Ouganda	1990[2 14]	2470000	44	1990[14]	267520	36	1990	17578	28
	1991[14]	2576537	46	1992[14]	256669	37	1992	21489	29
	1993[2 14]	2456352	44	1993[14]	261415	...	1993	24122	30
United Republic of Tanzania	1985[15]	3169759	50	...	...	...	1985[3 16]	4863	15
Rép.-Unie de Tanzanie	1990[15]	3379000	50	1990[15]	167150	42	1986[3 16]	4987	14
	1992[15]	3603488	49	1992[15]	189827	44	1987	6071	13
	1993[15]	3736734	49	1993[15]	196723	44	1989	5254	...
Zaire	1985	4650756	39	1985	959934	30	1985	40878	...
Zaïre	1990	4562430	43	1991	1097095	32	1986	45731	...
	1992	4870933	44	1992	1218760	32	1987	52800	...
	1993	4939297	43	1993	1341446	31	1988	61422	...
Zambia	1985	1348318	47	1985	140743	...	1986	14492	...
Zambie	1990	1461206	...	1988	170299	37	1990	15343	...

9
Education at the first, second and third levels
Number of students and percentage female [*cont.*]
Enseignement des premier, second et troisième degrés
Nombre d'étudiants et étudiantes feminines en pourcentage [*suite*]

Country or area Pays ou zone	Years Années	First level Premier degré Total	%F	Years Années	Second level Second degré Total	%F	Years Années	Third level Troisième degré Total	%F
Zimbabwe	1985	2214963	48	1985	482000	...	1985	30843	...
Zimbabwe	1990	2116414	50	1990	661066	47	1990	49361	...
	1992	2301642	50	1992	657344	44	1991	43950	27
	1993	2376048	48	1993	639559	44	1992	61553	27
America, North · Amerique du Nord									
Antigua and Barbuda									
Antigua−et−Barbuda	1991	9298	49	1991	5845	50	...	...	...
Bahamas	1985	32848	49	1985	27604	52	1985	4531	...
Bahamas	1990	32873	...	1991	29559	50	1986	4932	...
	1992	33917	50	1992	29863	50	1987	5305	68
	1993	33340	...	1993	28363	...			
Barbados	1984	30161	48	...	...	...	...	...	...
Barbade	1988	29584	49	1988	25422	51	1988	4244	59
	1989	28516	49	...	...	...	1989	4242	60
	1991	26662	49	1989	24004	47	1991	6888	55
Belize	1985[14]	39212	48	1985	7048	54	...	...	...
Belize	1990[14]	46023	48	1990	7904	53	...	...	...
	1991[14]	46874	48	1991	8901	55	...	...	...
	1992	48397	48	1992	9457	51	...	...	...
Bermuda									
Bermudes	1984	5398	50	...					
British Virgin Islands	1984	2069	48	...	...	...	...	...	...
Iles Vierges brit.	1990	2340	47	1990	1124	53	...	...	...
	1993	2502	48	1991	1134	55	...	...	...
	1994	2625	48	1993	1309	51	...	...	...
Canada	1985	2254887	48	1985	2250941	49	1985	1639410	45[17]
Canada	1990	2339723	48	1990	2292497	49	1990	1916801	54
	1991	2398225	48	1991	2331483	49	1992	2021550	53
	1992	2438436	48	1992	2392064	49	1993	2011485	53
Costa Rica	1985	362877	48	1985	112531	52	1985[18]	63771	...
Costa Rica	1990	435205	49	1990	130553	50	1990[18]	74681	...
	1992	471049	49	1992	151513	50	1991[18]	80442	...
	1993	484958	49	1993	160291	51	1992[18]	88324	...
Cuba	1985	1077213	47	1985	1156555	51	1985	235224	54
Cuba	1990	887737	48	1990	1002338	52	1990	242434	57
	1992	942431	49	1992	819712	52	1991	224568	58
	1993	983459	49	1993	725800	52	1992	198474	58
Dominica	1985	12340	48	1985	7370	54	1984	60	67
Dominique	1990	12836	49	...	...	...	1990	430	41
	1992	12795	49	...	...	...	1991	658	55
	1993	12822	50	...	...	...	1992	484	43
Dominican Republic	1985	1219681	50	1985	463511	...	1985	123748	...
République dominicaine	1989[9 19]	1032055	49	...	...	...	...	...	...
	1993	1336211	50	1993[1]	232999	58	...	...	...
El Salvador	1984	883329	50	1989	95078	50	1985	70499	44
El Salvador	1989	1016181	50	1991	94268	55	1988	77120	...
	1992	1028877	50	1992	105093	53	1989	80818	31[20]
	1993	1042256	49	1993	118115	52	1990	78211	33
Grenada	1985	16538	44	1985	9571	53	...	...	...
Grenade	1990	19811	45	1990	9776	53	...	...	...
	1991	21365	44	1991	9896	54	...	...	...
	1992	22345	49[2]	1992	10213	54	...	...	...
Guadeloupe	1985	42734	...	1985	51634	53	...	...	...
Guadeloupe	1990	38531	49	1990	49846	53	...	...	...
	1991	38255	49	1991	50556	52	...	...	...
	1992	37765	49	1992	50850	50	...	...	...
Guatemala	1985	1016474	45	1985	204049	...	1985[21]	48283	...
Guatemala	1991	1249413	46	1987	241053	...	1986[21]	51860	...
	1993	1393921	46	1991	294907	...	...	...	...
	1994	1449981	...	1993	334383	47	...	...	...
Haiti	1985	872500	47	1985	143758	...	1985	6288	26
Haïti	1990	555433	48	...	...	...	...	...	...

9
Education at the first, second and third levels
Number of students and percentage female [cont.]
Enseignement des premier, second et troisième degrés
Nombre d'étudiants et étudiantes feminines en pourcentage [suite]

Country or area Pays ou zone	Years Années	First level Premier degré Total	%F	Years Années	Second level Second degré Total	%F	Years Années	Third level Troisième degré Total	%F
Honduras	1985	765809	50	1985	184112	...	1985	36620	...
Honduras	1988	863313	50	1986	179444	...	1989	44849	39
	1991	908446	50	1991	194083	55	1990	44233	...
	1993	990352	50	1993	203192	...	...	...	...
Jamaica	1985	340059	...	1985	237713	52	1985	10969	...
Jamaïque	1990[8]	323378	50	1990[9]	225240	52	1990	16018	...
	1992	333104	49[2]	1992	235071	51	1991	15646	...
Martinique	1986	33492	48	1985	47500	...	...	...	...
Martinique	1990	32744	...	1989	43480	53	...	...	...
	1991	32747	48	1991	46373	52	...	...	...
	1992	32585	49	1992	43928	54	...	...	...
Mexico	1985	15124160	49	1985	6549105	48	1985	1207779	...
Mexique	1990	14401588	49	1990	6704297	50	1990	1310835	...
	1992	14425669	48	1992	6782886	49	1992	1302590	45
	1993	14469450	48	1993	6977086	50	1993	1358271	46
Montserrat	1985	1351	49	1985	1069	51	...	...	...
Monteserrat	1990	1593	...	1989	866	55	...	...	...
	1991	1570	47	1991	837	49	...	...	...
	1993	1525	46	1992	888	...	...	...	...
Netherlands Antilles Antilles néerlandaises	1991	22410	...	1991	14987	...	...	...	...
Nicaragua	1985	561551	52	1985	128499	67	1985	29001	56
Nicaragua	1990	632882	51	1990	168888	58	1990	30733	52
	1992	703854	50	...	...	...	1991	31499	49
	1993	737476	50	1993	203962	53	1992	35730	50
Panama	1985	340135	48	1985	184536	52	1985	55303	58
Panama	1990	351021	48	1990	195903	51	1989	50762	...
	1991	349858	...	1991	198138	...	1990	53235	...
	1992	352994	...	1992	201047	...	1991	58625	...
St. Kitts and Nevis	1985	7810	...	1985	4197	49[2]	1985	212	42
St. Kitts−Nevis	1989	7665	48	1988	4204	52	1987	194	40
	1991	7236	48	1991	4396	51	1991	325	37
	1992	7068	49	1992	4402	51	1992	394	55
Saint Lucia	1985	32817	49	1985	6833	61	1986	367	55
Sainte−Lucie	1990	33006	49	1990	8230	59	1987	389	54
	1991	32622	48	1991	9419	61	...	...	...
	1992	32545	48	1992	10356	63	1992	870	61
St. Pierre and Miquelon	1985	558	47	1985	821	53	...	...	...
St. Pierre et Miquelon	1989	556	...	1986	800	53	...	...	...
St. Vincent and the Grenadines	1985[22]	24561	49	1985[23]	6782	59	1985	736	69
Saint−Vincent−et−Grenadines	1989[22]	25742	47	1987[23]	7237	60	1986	795	64
	1990	22030	49	1990	10719	55	1989	677	68
	1993	21386	49	...	...	...	...	...	...
Trinidad and Tobago	1985[14]	168308	50	1985[24]	95302	...	1985	6582	39
Trinité−et−Tobago	1990[14]	193992	49	1990[24]	97493	50	1990	7249	44
	1992[14]	197030	49	1991[24]	97804	50	1991	7513	40[25]
	1993[14]	195013	49	1992[24]	100278	50	1992	8170	41
Turks and Caicos Is.	1984[9]	1429	49	1984	707	...	...	...	...
Iles Turques et Caïques	1993[9]	1211	50	1993	1032	50	...	...	...
United States	1985[26]	20214000	49	1985[27]	20633000	49	1985	12247055	52
Etats−Unis	1989[26]	22279000	49	1989[27]	19276000	49	1990	13710150	54
	1990[26]	22429000	48	1990[27]	19270000	49	1992	14422975	...
	1993[26]	23694000	49	1993[27]	20578000	49	1993	14473106	...
US Virgin Islands	1985	20548	...	1985	7948	...	1985	2602	72
Iles Vierges américaines	1990[9]	15256	51	1990[9]	5848	59	1990	2466	75
	...	...	...	...	...	...	1992	2924	74
America, South · Amerique du Sud									
Argentina	1985	4589291	49	1985	1800049	52	1985	846145	53
Argentine	1988	4998963	51	1987	1897711	52	1986	902882	53
	1991	5041090	49	1988	1974119	52	1987	958542	53
	1993	4990486	...	1991	2262378	51	1991	1077212	...
Bolivia	1986	1204534	47	1986	209293	46	...	...	...
Bolivie	1989	1225843	47	1989	207824	46	...	...	...
	1990	1278775	47	1990	219232	46	1989	128800	...

9
Education at the first, second and third levels
Number of students and percentage female [*cont.*]
Enseignement des premier, second et troisième degrés
Nombre d'étudiants et étudiantes feminines en pourcentage [*suite*]

Country or area	Years	First level Premier degré		Years	Second level Second degré		Years	Third level Troisième degré	
Pays ou zone	Années	Total	%F	Années	Total	%F	Années	Total	%F
Brazil	1985	24769736	...	1985	3016175	...	1986	1451191	...
Brésil	1990	28943619	...	1990	3498777	...	1990	1540080[16]	52
	1991	29203724	...	1991	3770230	...	1992	1535788[16]	54
	1992	30106084	...	1992	4085631	...	1993	1594668[16]	54
Chile	1985	2062344	49	1985	667797	52	1985	197437	43
Chili	1990	1991178	49	1990	719819	51	1990	255358	...
	1992	2034839	49	1992	675073	51	1992	317728	...
	1993	2066046	49	1993	652815	51	1993	327435	...
Colombia	1985	4039533	50	1985	1934032	50	1985	391490	49
Colombie	1990	4246658	...	1989	2282816	50	1987	434628	49
	1992	4525959	49	1992	2686515	54	1989	474787	52
	1993	4599132	50	1993	2796007	54	1991	510649	51
Ecuador	1985	1738549	49	1985[1]	730226	50	1984	280594	...
Equateur	1990	1846338	...	...	...	...	1990	206541	...
	1991	2019850	...	...	...	...	...	...	...
	1992	1986753	49	1992	814359	50	...	...	...
Falkland Islands (Malvinas)									
Iles Falkland (Malvinas)	1980	223	58	1980	90	56	...	...	...
French Guiana	1989	13272	...	1989	10125	...	...	...	...
Guyane française	1990	14256	...	1990	10722	...	...	...	...
	1993	15839	48	1993	13869	...	...	...	...
Guyana	1985	113857	49	1985	76546	51	1985	2328	48
Guyana	1987	114700	49[2]	1986	76012	51	1989	4665	43
	1988	118015	49[2]	...	...	...	1993	8257	47
Paraguay	1985	570775	48	1985	150736	...	1985	32090	...
Paraguay	1990	687331	48	1990	163734	50	1989	31117	...
	1992	749336	48	1992	192775	50	1990	32884	...
	1993	798981	48	1993	214272	51	1993	42654	45
Peru	1985	3711592	48	1985	1427261	47	1985	452462	...
Pérou	1990	3855282	...	1990	1697943	...	1989	656258	...
	1993	3914291	...	1993	1719854	...	1990	681801	...
	1994	4030018	...	1994	1775703	...	1992	777918	...
Suriname	1985	69963	48	1985	37630	53	1985	2751	54
Suriname	1990	60085	49	1990	33561	53	1988	3665	51
	1992	79162	48	1992	30016	53	1989	4009	53
	1993	87882	49	...	...	...	1990	4319	53
Uruguay	1985	356002	49	1985	213774	...	1989	69428	...
Uruguay	1990	346416	49	1990	265947	...	1990	71612	...
	1992	338020	49	1992	272622	...	1991	73660	...
	1993	338204	49	1993	266840	...	1992	68227	...
Venezuela	1985[28]	3539890	50	1985	268580	56	1985	443064	41
Venezuela	1990[28]	4052947	50	1990	281419	57	1989	528857	...
	1991[28]	4190047	50	1991	289430	57	1990	550030	...
	1992[28]	4222035	50	1992	298534	57	1991	550783	...
Asia · Asie									
Afghanistan	1985	580499	31	...	...	...	1986	22306	14
Afghanistan	1989	726287	33	...	...	...	1987	17509	...
	1993[1]	786532	25	...	...	...	1990	24333	31
Armenia	...	...	...	...	...	...	1985	54800	...
Arménie	...	...	...	...	...	...	1990	69485	...
	1993	193915	50	1993	380113	52	1991	67019	...
Azerbaijan	...	...	...	...	...	...	1985	105900	...
Azerbaïdjan	...	...	...	...	...	...	1990	105100	...
	1992	553862	48	1992	891839	...	1991	107900	...
	1993	580266	47	1993	869045	...	1992	100985	38
Bahrain	1985	57330	49	1985	38577	48	1985	4180	60
Bahreïn	1990	66597	49	1990	47005	50	1990	6868	56
	1992	68898	49	1992	51513	50	1991	7147	58
	1993	70513	49	1993	54193	50	1992	7763	57
Bangladesh	1985	8920293	40	1985	3125219	28	1985	461073	19
Bangladesh	1990	11939949	45	1990	3592995	33[2]	1990	434309	16
Bhutan	1985	45395	34	1985	6094	...	...	...	...
Bhoutan	1988	55340	37	...	...	...	...	...	...
	1993	56773	43	...	...	...	...	...	...
	1994	60089	43	...	...	...	...	...	...

9

Education at the first, second and third levels
Number of students and percentage female [cont.]
Enseignement des premier, second et troisième degrés
Nombre d'étudiants et étudiantes feminines en pourcentage [suite]

Country or area Pays ou zone	Years Années	First level Premier degré Total	%F	Years Années	Second level Second degré Total	%F	Years Années	Third level Troisième degré Total	%F
Brunei Darussalam	1985	34815	...	1985	20462	...	1984	607	62
Brunéi Darussalam	1989	39862	48	1991	25699	50	1986	601	50
	1992	39782	47	1992	26836	51	1987	945	51
	1993	41134	47	1993	28210	51	1992	1388	57
Cambodia	...	...	...	...	...	...	1985	2213	...
Cambodge	...	...	...	...	...	...	1990	6659	...
China	1985	133701800	45	1985	50926400	40	1985[3]	1778608	30
Chine	1990	122413800	46	1990	51054100	42	1990[3]	2146853	33
	1992	122012800	47	1992	53544000	43	1992[3]	2270772	33
	1993	124212400	47	1993	53837300	44	1993	4505215	29
Cyprus	1985[29]	50990	48	1985[29]	46159	49	1985	3134	48
Chypre	1990[29]	62962	48	1990[29]	44614	49	1990	6554	52
	1992[29]	64313	48	1992[29]	51641	49	1992	6263	49
	1993[29]	64907	48	1993[29]	54687	49	1993	6732	54
Georgia	...	...	...	...	...	...	1985	88500	...
Géorgie	...	...	...	...	...	...	1990	103900	...
Hong Kong	1985	534903	48	1985	450367	50	1984	76844	35
Hong-kong	1990	526700	...	1986	455738	49	1991	85214	40
	1991	517100	...	1987	458444	49	1992	88950	42
India	1985	87440514	40	1985	44484544	33	1986	4806179	30
Inde	1990	99118320	41	...	...	...	1987	4275859	31
	1992	105370216	43	1992	62245635	37	1988	4528956	32
	1993	108200539	43	1993	64115978	37	1990	4950974	33
Indonesia	1985	29897115	48	1985	9479086	...	1984	980162	32
Indonésie	1990	29753576	49	1990	10965430	45	1989	1515689	...
	1991	29577704	49	1991	10920580	45	1991	1885038	...
	1992	29598790	48	1992	10969305	44	1992	1973094	14
Iran, Islamic Rep. of	1985	6788323	44	1990	5084832	41	1985[9]	184442	29
Iran, Rép. islamique d'	1990	9369646	46	1991	5619057	42	1990[9]	312076	27
	1992	9937369	47	1992	6322988	43	1992[9]	374734	28
	1993	9862817	47	1993	7059037	43	1993[9]	436564	28
Iraq	1985	2816326	45	1985	1190833	35	1985	169665	36
Iraq	1990	3328212	44	1988	1166859	38	1987	183608	40
	1992	2857467	45	1992	1144938	38	1988	209818	38
Israel	1985	699476	49	1985	251466	51	1985	116062	47
Israël	1990	724502	49	1990	309098	51	1988	117454	47
	1991	748069	49	1991	326319	51	...	...	...
	1992	763511	49	1992	334290	51	...	...	...
Japan	1985	11095372	49	1985	11058133	49	1985	2347463	35
Japon	1990	9373295	49	1989	11143930	49	1988	2588470	38
	1992	8947226	49	1990	11025720	49	1989	2683035	39
	1993	8768881	49	1991	10676866	49	1991	2899143	40
Jordan	1985	530906	48	1985	335835	48	1985	53753	45
Jordanie	1990[1]	926445	48	1990[1]	100953	47	1990	80442	48
	1992[30]	1014295	49	1992	113910	50	1992	88506	49
	1993	1036079	49	1993	123825	50	1993	85936	48
Kazakstan	...	...	...	...	...	...	1985	273400	...
Kazakstan	...	...	...	...	...	...	1990	289791	...
	...	...	...	...	...	...	1991	290840	...
	1993	1227130	49	...	...	...	1993	272091	52
Korea, Dem. People's Rep. Corée, Rép. pop. dém. de	1987	1543000	49				1987	390000	34
Korea, Republic of	1985	4856752	49	1985	4934975	47	1985[31]	1455759	30
Corée, République de	1990	4868520	49	1990	4559557	48	1990	1691429	32
	1993	4336252	48	1993	4479463	48	1992	1858568	34
	1994	4099395	48	1994	4568829	48	1993	2099021	36
Kuwait	1985	172975	49	1985	239581	47	1985	23678	54
Koweït	1990	124996	48	1991	167331	49	1987	25521	55
	1992	122930	49	1992	177675	49	1988	26080	57
	1993	129956	49	1993	187941	49	1991	28399	61
Kyrgyzstan	...	...	...	...	...	...	1985	58200	...
Kirghizistan	...	...	...	...	...	...	1990	59466	...
	...	...	...	...	...	...	1991	58649	...
	...	...	...	...	...	...	1993	55229	...

9
Education at the first, second and third levels
Number of students and percentage female [*cont.*]
Enseignement des premier, second et troisième degrés
Nombre d'étudiants et étudiantes feminines en pourcentage [*suite*]

Country or area Pays ou zone	Years Années	First level Premier degré Total	%F	Years Années	Second level Second degré Total	%F	Years Années	Third level Troisième degré Total	%F
Lao People's Dem. Rep.	1985	523347	45	1985	113630	41	1985	5382	36
République dém. pop. lao	1989	563734	43	1989	137898	40	1989	4730	32
	1992	637359	44	1992	140777	38	1992	5016	27
	1993	681044	43	1993	155366	39	1993	8881	30
Lebanon	1988[30]	346534	48	...	...	...	1985	79500	...
Liban	1991	345662	48	...	...	...	1986	83891	...
	1993	360858	49	...	...	...	1991	85495	48
Macau	1990	34972	48	1989	16687	52	1989	8824	36
Macao	1991	37872	48	1991	18978	52	1990	7425	41
	1992	40665	48	1992	20383	53	1991	7420	43
Malaysia	1985	2199096	49	1985	1294990	49	1985	93249	44
Malaisie	1990	2455522	49	1990	1420173	50	1988	120714	41
	1992	2652397	49	1992	1566790	51	1989	109345	42
	1993	2718906	49	1993	1572837	51[2]	1990	124259	...
Maldives	1986	39775	...	...	...	...	...	...	...
Maldives	1992	45333	49	...	...	...	...	...	...
	1993	48321	49	...	...	...	...	...	...
Mongolia	1985	153100	...	...	...	...	1985	40099	...
Mongolie	1989	165400	...	...	...	...	1990	31006	...
	1990	166200	50	...	...	...	1991	28209	...
Myanmar	1985	4710616	48	1985	1283586	...	...	...	...
Myanmar	1988	5202508	48	1987	1358788	..	1987	202381	...
	1989	4848158	48	...	...	...	1991	195333	...
	1990	5384539	49	...	...	...	1992	244208	...
Nepal	1985[1]	1812098	30	1985	496921[1]	23	1985[32]	54452	...
Népal	1990	2788644	36	1990	708663	29	1989	102130	20
	1991	2884275	37	1991	773808	30	1990	93753	23
	1992	3034710	38	1992	855137	32	1991	110239	24
Oman	1985	177541	44	1985	48096	32	1985	990	38
Oman	1990	262989	47	1990	102021	44	1989	5377	44
	1992	289911	47	1992	140761	46	1990	5962	44
	1993	297209	48	1993	163004	47	1991	7322	49
Pakistan	1985[33]	7094059	33	1985	2923188	27	1985	267742	26
Pakistan	1989[33]	8614857	34	1989	3665079	28	1989	304922	28
	1990[33]	8855997	34	1990	3983462	29	1991	221313	20
Palestine · Palestine									
Gaza Strip	1986	109521	...	1986	59241	...	1986	5313	...
Zone de Gaza	1989	117821	48	1989	68033	46	1989	6548	31
	1991	127257	...	1991	73124	...	1991	4711	44
	1993	141902	48	1993	75494	...	...	...	...
Philippines	1985	8925959	49	1985	3214159	50	1985	1402000	...
Philippines	1990	10427077	...	1990	4033597	...	1990	1709486	...
	1993	10731453	...	1993	4590037	...	1991	1656815	59
	1994	10898857	...	1994	4803643	...	...	...	...
Qatar	1985	40636	48	1985	22574	50	1985	5344	62
Qatar	1990	48650	48	1990	30031	50	1990	6485	69
	1992	49059	48	1992	35013	50	1992	7283	71
	1993	52016	48	1993	36292	49	1993	7351	71
Saudi Arabia	1985	1344076	43	1985	603127	38	1985	113529	39
Arabie saoudite	1990	1876916	46	1990	892585	44	1990	153967	43
	1991	1922254	46	1991	965305	44	1991	163688	40
	1992	2025948	47	1992	1073361	44	1992	192625	46
Singapore	1985	278060	47	...	...	...	...	...	...
Singapour	1990	257932	...	...	...	...	...	...	...
	1991	260286	...	...	...	...	...	...	...
Sri Lanka	1985	2242645	48	1985	1462794	52	1985	59377	40
Sri Lanka	1990[1]	2112023	48	1990[1]	2081842	51	1986	61628	41
	1992	2059203	48	1992	2185277	51	...	...	...
	1993	2012702	48	1993	2246642	51	...	...	...
Syrian Arab Republic	1985	2029752	46	1985	870383	40	1985	179473	35
Rép. arabe syrienne	1990	2452086	46	1990	914250	41	1989	214173	38
	1992[30]	2573181	47	1992[30]	916950	44	1990	221628	39
	1993	2624594	47	1993	923030	44	...	...	...

9
Education at the first, second and third levels
Number of students and percentage female [*cont.*]
Enseignement des premier, second et troisième degrés
Nombre d'étudiants et étudiantes feminines en pourcentage [*suite*]

Country or area Pays ou zone	Years Années	First level Premier degré Total	%F	Years Années	Second level Second degré Total	%F	Years Années	Third level Troisième degré Total	%F
Tajikistan	...	...	...	...	...	...	1985	55100	...
Tadjikistan	1992	519100	48	1992	736700	48	1990	69301	...
	1993	570300	49	1993	652700	47	1991	69844	...
Thailand	1985	7150489	...	1989	2117903	50	1985	1026952	...
Thaïlande	1990	6956717	49	1990	2230403	48	1987	884237	...
	1991	6906935	49	1991	2444092	48	1989	952012	...
	1992	6758091	49	1992	2717672	49	1992	1156174	53
Turkey	1985	6635858	47	1985	2927692	35	1985	469992	32
Turquie	1990	6861711	47	1990	3808142	37	1990	749921	34
	1991	6878923	47	1991	3987423	38	1992	915765	35
	1992	6707725	47	1992	4299810	38	1993	1143083	37
Turkmenistan	...	...	...	...	...	...	1985	38800	...
Turkménistan	...	...	...	...	...	...	1990	41800	...
United Arab Emirates	1985	152125	48	1985	62082	48	1985	7772	58
Emirats arabes unis	1990	228980	48	1990	107881	50	1989	8491	69
	1992	238469	48	1992	129683	51	1990	10196	70
	1993	251182	48	1993	145143	51	1991	10405	75
Uzbekistan	...	...	...	...	...	...	1985	285500	...
Ouzbékistan	...	...	...	...	...	...	1990	343887	...
	1993	1852841	49	1993	3135851	49	1991	340402	...
Viet Nam	1985	8125836	48	...	...	...	1988	175856	...
Viet Nam	1990	8862292	...	1989	3651719	...	1989	185788	...
	1992	9476441	...	...	...	...	...	...	...
	1993	9725095	...	...	...	...	...	...	...
Yemen									
Yémen							1991	53082	17
former Dem. Yemen	1985	334309	30	1985	36282	30	1985	5239	42
ancienne Yémen dém.	1990[34]	379908	38	1987	38926	30	1987	3999	42
former Yemen Arab Rep.	1985	981127	20	1985	146133	11	1985	12589	...
anc. Yémen rép. arabe	1990	1291372	24	1990	420697	15	1988	23457	...
Europe · Europe									
Albania	1985	543775	48	1985	177679	45	1985	21995	45
Albanie	1989	550656	48	1988	194124	45	1990	22059	52
	1990	551294	48	1989	202864	44	1992	22835	52
	1993	535713	49	1990	205774	45	1993	30185	53
Austria	1985	343823	48	1985	847188	47	1985	173215	45
Autriche	1990	370210	49	1990	746272	47	1990	205767	46
	1992	382663	49	1992	768176	47	1992	221389	47
	1993	381628	49	1993	778006	47	1993	227444	47
Belarus	1985	796600	...	1985	716700	...	1985	181900	...
Bélarus	1990[1]	614800	...	1990[1]	968200	...	1990	191584	52
	1992	635100	49	1992	970300	...	1992	187639	51
	1993	634600	49	1993	993900	...	1993	178016	52
Belgium	1985	730288	49	1985	824997	49	1985	247499	46
Belgique	1990	719372	49	1990	769438	49	1989	271007	48
	1991	711521	49	1991	765672	49	1990	276248	48
Bulgaria	1985	1080979	48	1985	374565	49	1985	113795	55
Bulgarie	1990	960681	48	1990[1]	391550	50	1990	188479	51
	1992	877189	48	1992	374514	50	1992	195447	57
	1993	839419	48	1993	363138	50	1993	206179	59
Croatia	1985[35]	520576	49	1990[35]	186090	51	1985	55886[16]	...
Croatie	1990[35]	431586	49	1991[35]	173727	...	1990	72342[16]	...
	1992[35]	436755	49	1992[35]	190926	51	1992	77689[16]	48
	1993[35]	441837	49	1993[35]	207013	51	1993	82361[16]	48
former Czechoslovakia †	1985[1]	2074403	49	1985	744059	51	1985	169344	43
ancienne Tchécoslovaquie †	1990	1924001	49	1990	864215	51	1990	190409	44
	1991	1898470	49	1991	848721	50	1991	177110	46
Czech Republic	1985	694659	...	...	...	...	1985	109273	...
République tchèque	1990	546036	...	...	...	...	1990	118194	...
	1992	528750	49	1992	1181026	50	1992	116560	44
	1993	521285	49	1993	1119738	50	1993	129391	44

9
Education at the first, second and third levels
Number of students and percentage female [*cont.*]
Enseignement des premier, second et troisième degrés
Nombre d'étudiants et étudiantes feminines en pourcentage [*suite*]

Country or area Pays ou zone	Years Années	First level Premier degré Total	%F	Years Années	Second level Second degré Total	%F	Years Années	Third level Troisième degré Total	%F
Denmark	1985	402707	49	1985	487526	49	1985	116319	49
Danemark	1990	340267	49	1990	464555	49	1990	142968	52
	1991	327024	49	1991	455639	49	1991	150159	53
	1992	325157	49	1992	455677	50	1992	157006	52
Estonia	...	...	...	...	...	...	1985	23500	...
Estonie	...	...	...	...	...	...	1990	25900	...
	1992	119409	49	1992	121798	51	1992	24464	50
	1993	118136	49	1993	120983	52	1993	24768	51
Finland	1985	379339	49	1985	424076	53	1985	127976	49
Finlande	1990	390587	49	1990	426864	53	1990	165714	52
	1992	392754	49	1992	463121	54	1992	188162	53
	1993	390892	49	1993	459108	53	1993	197367	53
France	1985	4115846	48	1985	5371593	51	1985	1278581	50
France	1990	4149143	48	1990	5521862	50	1990	1698938	53
	1992	4060408	48	1992	5573582	50	1992	1951994	54
	1993	4060607	48	1993	5737358	50	1993	2074591	55
Germany †	1990	3431385	...	1990	7398011	...	1990	2048627	...
Germany †	1992	3469959	49	1992	7662797	48	1992	1823100	40
	1993	3524219	49	1993	7796256	48	1993	1875099	40
former German Dem. Rep.	1985	859830	48	1985	1519152	48	1985	432672	54
ancienne R. dém. allemande	1990	870118	...	1990	1425404	...	1987	437919	52
	1991	847970	49	1991	1507080	48	1988	438930	52
Federal Republic of Germany	1985	2271546	49	1985	7101250	48	1985	1550211	42
Rép. féd. d'Allemagne	1990	2561267	49	1990	5972607	48	1990	1799394	40
	1991	2590082	49	1991	5992998	48	1991	1867491	41
Gibraltar									
Gibraltar	1984	2830	48	1984	1806	49	...	...	...
Greece	1985	887735	48	1985	813534	48	1985	181901	49
Grèce	1989	834688	48	1989	843732	48	1990	195213	50
	1990	813353	48	1990	851353	48	1991	196112	50
Holy See	...	...	...	...	...	...	1985[36]	9775	33
Saint–Siège	...	...	...	...	...	...	1990[36]	10938	32
	...	...	...	...	...	...	1991[36]	11681	31
	...	...	...	...	...	...	1992[36]	12253	32
Hungary	1985	1297818	49	1985	422323	49	1985	99344	54
Hongrie	1990	1130656	49	1990	514076	49	1990	102387	50
	1992	1044164	...	1991	531051	49	1992	117460	51
	1993	1009416	49	1993	529445	50	1993	133956	53
Iceland	1985	24603	49	1985	27559	47	1985	4724	55
Islande	1990	25878	49	1990	29465	48	1989	5005	56
	1991	25809	49	1991	29985	48	1990	5225	...
	1992	25234	49	1992	30233	49	1991	6161	59
Ireland	1985	420236	49	1985	338256	51	1985	70301	43
Irlande	1990	416747	49	1990	345941	51	1990	90296	46
	1991	408567	49	1991	352408	51	1991	101108	47
	1992	398736	49	1992	362230	51	1992	108394	48
Italy	1985	3703108	49	1985	5361579	49	1985	1185304	46
Italie	1990	3055883	49	1990	5117897	49	1990	1452286	48
	1992	2959564	49	1992	4892194	49	1992	1615150	51
	1993	2863003	49	1993	4715635	49	1993	1681949	51
Latvia	...	...	...	...	...	...	1985	43900	...
Lettonie	...	...	...	...	...	...	1990	46000	...
	1992	133846	49	1992	242644	51	1992	41138	53
	1993	132059	49	1993	245130	51	1993	37907	56
Lithuania	...	...	...	...	...	...	1985	65300	...
Lituanie	1992	207522	48	1992	337890	50	1990	65600	...
	1993	212246	48	1993	329764	50	1993	70460	58
Luxembourg	1985	22003	49	1985	25656	48	1985[37]	759	34
Luxembourg	1990	23465	51	1987	22496	49	1986[37]	709	30
Malta	1985	36240	47	1985	27779	48	1985	1474	33
Malte	1990	36899	48	1990	32544	47	1989	2511	42
	1991	35626	48	1991	34358	46	1990	3123	44
	1992	35488	48	1992	34619	46	1992	4662	48

9

Education at the first, second and third levels
Number of students and percentage female [*cont.*]
Enseignement des premier, second et troisième degrés
Nombre d'étudiants et étudiantes feminines en pourcentage [*suite*]

Country or area Pays ou zone	Years Années	First level Premier degré Total	%F	Years Années	Second level Second degré Total	%F	Years Années	Third level Troisième degré Total	%F
Monaco	1990	1773	51	1990	2785	49	...	...	...
Monaco	1991	1761	49	1991	2858	49	...	...	...
	1993	1815	49	1993	2835	49	...	...	...
Netherlands	1985	1109590	49	1985	1620011	48	1985	404866	41
Pays-Bas	1990	1082022	50	1990	1401739	47	1990	478869	44
	1991	1040158	49	1991	1377768	47	1991	493563	45
	1992	1046192	50	1992	1369507	48	1992	506580	46
Norway	1985	335373	49	1985	387990	50	1985	94658	52
Norvège	1990	309432	49	1990	370779	50	1990	142521	53
	1992	307461	49	1992	380916	48	1992	166499	54
	1993	309889	49	1993	380315	48	1993	176722	54
Poland	1985	4801307	48	1985	1567641	51	1985	454190	56
Pologne	1990	5189118	49	1990	1887667	50	1990	544893	56
	1992	5231769	49	1992	2030842	50	1992	584177	56
	1993	5194245	49	1993	2109161	50	1993	693993	57
Portugal	1985	1235312	48	1985	580248	...	1985[38]	103585	54
Portugal	1990	1019794	48	1990	670035	53	1990	185762	56
	1991	1004848	48	1991	778432	...	1991	190856	60
Republic of Moldova	1991	306933	49	1991	448404	...	1985	53200	...
République de Moldova	1992	265704	49	1992	375554	...	1990	54700	...
	1993	266047	49	1993	377047	...	1993	72986	...
Romania	1985	3030666	49	1985[39]	1537548	46	1985	159798	45
Roumanie	1990	1253480	49	1990	2837948	49	1988	159465	48
	1991	1211239	49	1991	2606305	49	1989	164507	...
	1992	1201229	49	1992	2451624	49	1992	235669	47
Russian Federation	1985	6579000	49	1985	13341000	...	1985	5400000	57
Fédération de Russie	1990	7596000	49	1990	13956000	...	1990	5100000	55
	1993	7738000	49	1992	13724000	...	1992	4692000	55
	1994	7849000	49	1993	13732000	...	1993	4587045	55
San Marino	1985	1411	49	1985	1248	48	...	...	...
Saint-Marin	1990	1212	47	1990	1182	52	...	...	...
	1992	1190	48	1992	1159	48	...	...	...
	1993	1166	49	1993	1157	48	...	...	...
Slovakia	1992	350604	49	1992	657010	50	1992	66002	48
Slovakia	1993	345594	49	1993	658228	50	1993	72726	49
Slovenia	...	...	...	...	...	...	1991	38388	53
Slevenia	1992	104441	49	1992	211426	49	1992	39264	54
	1993	102120	49	1993	211739	49	1993	40239	55
Spain	1985	3483948	48	1985	4555541	51	1985	935126	49
Espagne	1990	2820497	48	1990	4755322	50	1990	1222089	51
	1992	2554083	48	1992	4744204	51	1991	1301748	51
	1993	2447859	48	1993	4734401	51	1992	1370689	52
Sweden	1985	612704	...	1985	624835	...	1985	176589	52
Suède	1990	578359	49	1990	588474	50	1990	192611	54
	1992	594891	49	1992	602703	49	1991	207265	54
	1993	600392	49	1993	607219	49	1992	226830	54
Switzerland	1985	376512	49	1985	634750	46	1985	110111	32
Suisse	1990	404154	49	1990	567396	47	1990	137486	35
	1992	420089	49	1992	561470	47	1992	146266	36
	1993	423399	49	1993	558920	48	1993	148664	37
TFYR Macedonia	1985	273219	...	1985	77023	...	1985	38065	...
L'ex-R.y. Macédonie	1990	266813	...	1990	70696	...	1990	26515	52
	1992	261540	48	1992	73381	49	1992	26405	52
	1993	260659	48	1993	74583	49	1993	27340	53
Ukraine	1985	3739900	...	1985	3401100	...	1985	853100	...
Ukraine	1990[1]	3990500	...	1990	3407500	...	1989	902100	...
	1992	4102100	49	1992	3281500	...	1990	894700	50[16]
	1993[1]	2658800	49	1993[1]	4124900	...	1991	890192	50[16]
United Kingdom	1985	4296000	49	1985	4877000	50	1985	1032491	46
Royaume-Uni	1990	4532500	49	1990	4335600	50	1990	1258188	48
	1991	4559500	49	1991	4433500	50	1991	1385072	49
	1992	5023200	49	1992	4537000	50	1992	1528389	50
Yugoslavia, SFR †	1985	1448562	48	1985	2352985	47	1985	350334	46
Yougoslavie, Rfs †	1990	1392789	48	1990	2344331	48	1990	327092	51

9
Education at the first, second and third levels
Number of students and percentage female [*cont.*]
Enseignement des premier, second et troisième degrés
Nombre d'étudiants et étudiantes feminines en pourcentage [*suite*]

Country or area Pays ou zone	Years Années	First level Premier degré Total	%F	Years Années	Second level Second degré Total	%F	Years Années	Third level Troisième degré Total	%F
Yugoslavia	1990	466692	49	1990	788170	49	...	...	...
Yougoslavie	1991	470669	49	1991	816143	49	1991	133331	52
	1992	473902	49	1992	831506	49	1992	143268	53
Oceania · Océanie									
American Samoa	1985	7704	47	1985	3342	47	1985	758	52
Samoa américaine	1989	8574	47	1989	3437	48	1987	897	55
	1991	7884	48	1991	3643	46	1988	909	54
Australia	1985	1542101	49	1985	1278272	49	1985	370048	48
Australie	1990	1583024	49	1990	1278163	50	1990	485075	53
	1992	1623012	49	1992	1294596	49	1992	559365	53
	1993	1633797	49	1993	1282309	49	1993	964159[40]	48
Cook Islands	1985	2713	...	...	...	...	...	...	...
Iles Cook	1988	2376	...	...	...	...	...	...	...
Fiji	1985	127286	49	1985	45093	50	1985	2313	38
Fidji	1990	143552	...	...	...	...	1989	3509	...
	1991	144924	49	1991	61614	48	1991	7908	...
	1992	145630	49	1992	66890	49	...	...	...
French Polynesia	1987	27259	47	1986	17878	55	...	...	...
Polynésie française	1990	28270	48	1990	20311	53	...	...	...
	1992	29132	48	1992	22366	55	1991	301	50
Guam	1985	16783	...	1985	14557	...	1986	7052	53
Guam	1988	15516	...	1988	16017	...	...	...	...
Kiribati	1985	13440	49	1985	2196	50	...	...	...
Kiribati	1990	14709	50	1990	3003	49	...	...	...
	1992	16020	49	1992	3357	52	...	...	...
	1993	16316	49	...	...	...	...	...	...
Nauru									
Nauru	1985	1451	47	1985	482	50	...	...	...
New Caledonia	1985	22517	48	1985	18351	52	1985	761	44
Nouvelle—Calédonie	1990	22958	48	1990	20673	52	...	...	...
	1991	22325	48	1991	21908	52	...	...	...
New Zealand	1985	329337	49	1985	354080	50	1985	95793	46
Nouvelle—zélande	1990	318568	48	1990	340915	49	1990	111504	52
	1992	317286	48	1992	350112	49	1992	146215	54
	1993	322984	49	1993[41]	376947	49	1993	162932	54
Niue	1985	503	...	1985	321	...	...	...	...
Nioué	1988[1]	453	49	1988[1]	194	45	...	...	...
	1991[1]	371	...	1991[1]	302	53	...	...	...
Papua New Guinea	1989	417818	44	1987	63391	35	1985	5068	23
Papouasie—Nouv.—Guinée	1990	415195	44	1990	65643	38	1986	6397	24
	1991	422348	45	1991	68506	39	...	...	...
	1992	443552	45	1992	69596	39	...	...	...
Samoa	1986	31412	48	1986	20604	...	...	...	...
Samoa	1989	37833	48	...	...	...	...	...	...
Solomon Islands	1985	38716	...	1990	5636	37	...	...	...
Iles Salomon	1990	47598	44	1991	6363	36	...	...	...
	1992	53320	44	1992	6666	37	...	...	...
	1993	57264	44	1993	7351	36	...	...	...
Tokelau									
Tokélaou	1991	361	50	1983	488	60	...	...	...
Tonga	1985	17019	48	1985	15232	51	1985	705	56
Tonga	1990	16522	48	1990	14749	48	...	...	...
	1992	16658	48	1991	14825	49	...	...	...
	1993	16792	48	1993	16570	48	...	...	...
Tuvalu	1986	1280	49	...	...	...	...	...	...
Tuvalu	1990[9]	1485	48	1990	345	52	...	...	...
Vanuatu	1985	22897	...	...	...	...	...	...	...
Vanuatu	1990[42]	24471	47	...	...	...	...	...	...
	1991[42]	24952	47	1991	4184	43	...	...	...
	1992[42]	26267	47	...	...	...	...	...	...

Source:
United Nations Educational, Scientific and Cultural Organization
(Paris).

Source:
Organisation des Nations Unies pour l'éducation, la science et la culture
(Paris).

9
Education at the first, second and third levels
Number of students and percentage female [*cont.*]
Enseignement des premier, second et troisième degrés
Nombre d'étudiants et étudiantes feminines en pourcentage [*suite*]

† For detailed descriptions of data pertaining to former Czechoslovakia, Germany, SFR Yugoslavia and former USSR, see Annex I – Country or area nomenclature, regional and other groupings.

1 Due to a change in classification, data are not comparable with those of previous years.
2 Estimated data.
3 Data refer to full–time education only.
4 Data do not include the University of Law.
5 Data exclude private institutions.
6 Data do not include Al Azhar.
7 Data do not include Asmara University and Kotebe college.
8 Data do not include Action aid schools.
9 Data refer to public education only (for second level: Ghana, Senegal: General + vocational education; Madagascar: General education).
10 Data refer to universities and equivalent institutions.
11 For 1990, data refer to the period January – October of the following year. For the other years, data refer to the period from October of the year indicated to August of the following year.
12 Data on enrollment refer to approximately 95% of the total number of schools.
13 Excluding Transkei, Bophuthatswana, Venda and Ciskei.
14 Data refer to government–maintained and aided schools only (for second level: in general education only).
15 Data refer to Tanzania mainland only.
16 Data exclude post–graduate students.
17 Data do not include trade and vocational programmes.
18 Data refer only to institutions recognized by the National Council for Higher Education.
19 Data include intermediate education (grades 7 and 8 of "traditional" education).
20 Data exclude la Universidad Nacional de El Salvador.
21 Data refer to the University of San Carlos only.
22 Data include secondary classes attached to primary schools.
23 Data do not include secondary classes attached to primary schools.
24 Data include courses in vocational and technical education.
25 Data on female students in universities refer to nationals only.
26 Revised data series corresponding to grades 1 to 6.
27 Revised data series.
28 Data refer to grades 1 to 9 (basic education).
29 Not including Turkish schools.
30 Including UNRWA schools.
31 Data do not include Air and Correspondence Courses.
32 Data refer to public universities only.
33 Including education preceding the first level.
34 Not including schools for nomads.
35 Data do not include schools in the war areas.
36 Data refer to students enrolled in higher institutions under the authority of the Holy See.
37 Data refer to students enrolled in institutions located in Luxembourg. At university level, the majority of students pursue their studies in the following countries: Austria, Belgium, France, Germany and Switzerland.
38 Excluding the University of Porto.
39 Data include correspondence courses.
40 Data include Vocational Education and Training Institutes (VETS).
41 Data include part–time students in vocational education.
42 Data do not include independent private schools.

† Pour les descriptions en détails des données relatives à l'ancienne Tchécoslovaquie, l'Allemagne, la Rfs Yougoslavie et l'ancienne URSS, voir l'Annexe I – Nomenclature des pays ou zones, groupements régionaux et autres groupements.

1 Suite à un changement de classification, les données ne sont pas comparables à celles des années antérieures.
2 Données estimées.
3 Les données se réfèrent à l'enseignement à plein temps seulement.
4 Les données ne comprennent pas l'Université des Sciences juridiques.
5 Les données excluent les institutions privées.
6 Les données ne comprennent pas Al Azhar.
7 Les données ne comprennent pas l'Université Asmara et le collège Kotebe.
8 Les données n'incluent pas les écoles de Action aid.
9 Les données se réfèrent à l'enseignement public seulement. (pour le second degré: Ghana et Sénégal, l'enseignement général et technique; Madagascar, l'enseignement général).
10 Les données se réfèrent aux universités et établissements équivalents.
11 Pour l'année 1990, les données se réfèrent à la période janvier–octobre de l'année suivant l'année indiquée. Pour les autres années, les données se réfèrent à la période allant du mois d'octobre de l'année indiquée au mois d'août de l'année suivante.
12 Les données relatives aux élèves se réfèrent à environ 95% du nombre total des écoles.
13 Non compris Transkei, Bophuthatswana, Venda and Ciskei.
14 Les données se réfèrent aux écoles publiques et subventionnées seulement (pour le second degré: l'enseignement général).
15 Les données se réfèrent à la Tanzanie continentale seulement.
16 Les données excluent le niveau universitaire supérieur.
17 Les données incluent les programmes d'enseignement techniques et commerciaux.
18 Les données se réfèrent seulement aux institutions reconnues par le Conseil National pour l'Education supérieure.
19 Les données incluent l'enseignement intermédiaire (septième et huitième années d'études de l'enseignement 'tradicional').
20 Les données excluent la Universidad Nacional de El Salvador.
21 Les données se réfèrent à l'Université de San Carlos seulement.
22 Les données incluent les classes secondaires rattachées aux écoles primaires.
23 Les données n'incluent pas les classes secondaires rattachées aux écoles primaires.
24 Les données incluent des cours d'enseignement professionnel et technique.
25 Les données relatives aux étudiantes des universités se réfèrent aux étudiantes nationales seulement.
26 Les données ont été revisées et se réfèrent aux classes allant de la première à la sixième année d'études.
27 Les données ont été revisées.
28 Les données se réfèrent aux années d'études 1 à 9 (enseignement de base).
29 Non compris les écoles turques.
30 Y compris les écoles de l'UNRWA.
31 Les données n'incluent pas 'Air and Correspondence Courses'.
32 Les données se réfèrent aux universités publiques seulement.
33 Y compris l'enseignement précédant le premier degré.
34 les données n'incluent pas les écoles de nomades.
35 les données n'incluent pas les écoles dans les zones de guerre.
36 Les données se réfèrent aux étudiants dans les institutions du troisième degré sous l'autorité du Saint–Siège.
37 Les données se réfèrent seulement aux étudiants inscrits dans les institutions du Luxembourg. La plus grande partie des étudiants luxembourgeois poursuivent leurs études universitaires dans les pays suivants : Allemagne, Autriche, Belgique, France, et Suisse.
38 Non compris l'Université de Porto.
39 Les données incluent les cours par correspondance.
40 Les données incluent l'Education Technique et les instituts de Formation Professionnelle *VETS*.
41 Pour l'enseignement technique, les données incluent les étudiants à temps partiel.
42 Les données n'incluent pas les écoles privées indépendantes.

10
Public expenditure on education at current market prices
Dépenses publiques afférentes à l'enseignement aux prix courants du marché

Country or area Pays ou zone (Currency unit · Unité monétaire)	Years Années	Total educational expenditure Dépenses totales d'éducation			Current educational expenditure Dépenses ordinaires d'éducation		
		Amount Montant (000 000)	% of GNP % du PNB	% total gov't exp. % dép. totales gouv.	Amount Montant (000 000)	% of GNP % du PNB	% current gov't exp. % dép. ordinaires gouv.
Africa · Afrique							
Algeria	1985	24 248	8.5	20.7	16 814	5.9	26.2
Algérie	1990 [1]	29 504	5.7	21.1	24 953	4.8	29.7
(dinar)	1992 [1]	53 516	5.4	16.3	...	...	...
	1993 [1]	80 841	7.2	19.6	70 134	6.3	23.1
Angola							
Angola	1985	9 643	...	10.8	9 419	...	14.0
(new kwanza · nouveau kwanza)	1990 [2]	12 076	...	10.7	10 856	...	...
Botswana	1985	111	6.8	15.4	88	5.4	18.6
Botswana	1990 [2]	437	7.6	17.0	311	5.4	21.1
(pula)	1991	553	8.2	18.7	426	6.3	22.9
	1992 [2]	597	7.5	14.8	485	6.1	21.2
Burkina Faso	1985	12 901	2.3	21.0	12 292	2.2	22.4
Burkina Faso	1989	18 780	2.7	17.5	18 727	2.7	21.9
(CFA franc · franc CFA)	1992 [3]	11 934	1.5	...	11 002	1.4	...
Burundi	1985 [2]	3 467	2.5	15.5	3 212	2.4	17.1
Burundi	1990 [2]	6 570	3.4	16.7	6 370	3.3	19.4
(franc)	1991 [2]	7 403	3.5	17.7	7 208	3.4	20.2
	1992 [2]	8 361	3.7	11.9	8 023	3.6	24.2
Cameroon	1985 [2]	109 344	3.0	14.8	90 045	2.5	20.9
Cameroun	1990 [2]	107 968	3.4	19.6	97 948	3.1	26.9
(CFA franc · franc CFA)	1991 [2]	91 889	3.0	16.9	81 719	2.7	21.6
Cape Verde							
Cap–Vert	1985	341	3.6	...	325	3.5	15.2
(escudo)	1991	903	4.4	19.9	890	4.3	20.0
Central African Rep.	1986	9 553	2.8	...	9 313	2.8	25.6
Rép. centrafricaine	1989	8 305	2.3	...	8 097	2.2	12.8
(CFA franc · franc CFA)	1990	9 862	2.8	...	9 622	2.8	...
Chad							
Tchad	1991	8 284	2.3	...	8 212	2.3	...
(CFA franc · franc CFA)	1993	8 768	2.6	6.8	...	...	...
Comoros [2]	1985	...	...	...	2 105	4.1	23.1
Comores [2]	1990	...	...	...	2 666	4.0	24.3
(CFA franc · franc CFA)	1992	...	...	...	2 829	4.1	22.0
	1993	...	...	...	2 938	4.2	20.5
Congo	1984	44 442	5.1	9.8	41 033	4.7	14.7
Congo	1990	37 899	5.6	14.4	36 906	5.4	18.0
(CFA franc · franc CFA)	1991	57 092	8.6	...	56 537	8.5	19.3
Côte d'Ivoire							
Côte d'Ivoire	1985	...	...	...	179 447	6.3	...
(CFA franc · franc CFA)	1992 [2]	...	...	...	153 004	6.7	...
Djibouti	1985 [2]	1 690	2.7	7.5	1 690	2.7	...
Djibouti	1990	2 614	3.4	10.5	2 614	3.4	10.5
(franc)	1991	2 872	3.8	11.1	2 872	3.8	11.1
Egypt [4]	1985	1 878	6.3	...	1 775	5.9	10.8
Egypte [4]	1990	3 737	4.9	...	3 229	4.2	...
(pound · livre)	1991	4 557	4.7	9.7	3 941	4.1	11.0
	1992	5 839	5.0	11.0	4 683	4.0	11.0
Equatorial Guinea							
Guinée équatoriale							
(CFA franc · franc CFA)	1993	734	1.8	5.6	721	1.7	5.8
Ethiopia	1985	420	4.3	9.5	354	3.6	14.3
Ethiopie	1990	600	4.9	9.4	494	4.0	11.1
(birr)	1992	704	5.1	11.9	564	4.1	17.8
	1993	1 107	6.4	...	790	4.5	...
Gabon							
Gabon	1985	69 500	4.5	9.4	47 500	3.1	21.7
(CFA franc · franc CFA)	1992 [3]	41 529	3.2	...	34 407	2.6	...

10
Public expenditure on education at current market prices [cont.]
Dépenses publiques afférentes à l'enseignement aux prix courants du marché [suite]

Country or area Pays ou zone (Currency unit · Unité monétaire)	Years Années	Total educational expenditure Dépenses totales d'éducation			Current educational expenditure Dépenses ordinaires d'éducation		
		Amount Montant (000 000)	% of GNP % du PNB	% total gov't exp. % dép. totales gouv.	Amount Montant (000 000)	% of GNP % du PNB	% current gov't exp. % dép. ordinaires gouv.
Gambia	1985	31	3.2	...	25	2.6	16.4
Gambie	1990	95	3.8	11.0	73	2.9	11.6
(dalasi)	1991	78	2.7	12.9	75	2.6	13.2
Ghana	1985 [2]	8 675	2.6	19.0	...	...	...
Ghana	1989	47 791	3.5	24.3	43 857	3.2	29.5
(cedi)	1990	61 900	3.1	24.3	53 664	2.7	27.1
Guinea	1984	1 491	...	15.3	1 486	...	17.2
Guinée	1990	23 483	1.4	...	...	...	...
(franc)	1992	61 123	2.4	...	...	...	...
	1993	65 434	2.2	...	...	...	...
Guinea—Bissau Guinée—Bissau							
(peso)	1984	...	...	...	539	3.3	11.2
Kenya	1985	6 171	6.4	...	5 789	6.0	...
Kenya	1990 [2]	12 473	6.7	16.1	11 238	6.1	19.4
(shilling)	1992 [2]	13 203	5.4	...	12 307	5.1	...
	1993 [2]	20 029	6.7	...	18 999	6.3	...
Lesotho	1984	35	3.7	...	29	3.1	15.1
Lesotho	1990	99	3.7	12.2	81	3.0	17.4
(loti)	1992	204	6.0	...	160	4.7	...
	1993	194	4.9	...	192	4.8	...
Libyan Arab Jamahiriya Jamah. arabe libyenne	1985	575	7.1	19.8	457	5.7	38.1
(dinar)	1986	636	9.6	20.8	506	7.7	37.1
Madagascar Madagascar	1985	52 182	2.9	...	49 806	2.8	...
(franc)	1990 [3]	67 038	1.5	...	64 964	1.5	...
Malawi	1985	64	3.5	9.6	46	2.5	...
Malawi	1990	165	3.4	10.3	117	2.4	9.8
(kwacha)	1992	...	...	...	227	3.5	...
Mali Mali	1985	17 184	3.7	...	17 048	3.7	...
(CFA franc · franc CFA)	1993 [2]	15 369	2.1	13.2	14 994	2.0	...
Mauritania	1985	...	...	...	3 973	8.2	33.2
Mauritanie	1988	...	...	...	3 188	4.8	22.0
(ouguiya)	1993 [2]	...	...	...	4 192	3.9	...
Mauritius Maurice	1985	598	3.8	9.8	555	3.5	12.4
(rupee · roupie)	1990	1 384	3.7	11.8	1 287	3.4	14.0
Morocco [2]	1985	7 697	6.3	22.9	6 079	5.0	28.6
Maroc [2]	1990	11 220	5.5	26.1	10 187	5.0	33.6
(dirham)	1991	12 096	5.2	26.3	10 755	4.6	32.5
	1992	13 564	5.8	26.7	11 944	5.1	32.0
Mozambique [5] Mozambique [5]	1985	4 400	4.2	10.6	4 100	3.9	12.3
(metical)	1990	72 264	6.2	12.0	46 064	4.0	17.5
Namibia Namibie							
(rand)	1990	480	8.6	...	...	...	...
Niger Niger	1989 [1] [2]	19 873	2.9	9.0	15 545	2.3	13.6
(CFA franc · franc CFA)	1991 [1] [2]	20 143	3.1	10.8	19 493	3.0	18.4
Nigeria	1985 [6]	814	1.2	8.7	699	1.0	19.7
Nigéria	1990 [6]	2 121	0.8	...	...	...	...
(naira)	1991 [6]	1 558	0.5	...	...	...	...
	1992 [6]	2 405	0.5	...	...	...	...
Réunion	1985	2 416	...	...	2 292	...	...
Réunion	1990	3 375	...	...	3 343	...	...
(F. franc)	1992 [1]	4 854	...	...	4 814	...	...
	1993	5 208	...	...	5 180	...	...
Rwanda Rwanda	1984	4 997	3.1	25.1	4 887	3.1	28.1
(franc)	1989	7 222	3.7	25.4	6 793	3.5	29.1

10
Public expenditure on education at current market prices [*cont.*]
Dépenses publiques afférentes à l'enseignement aux prix courants du marché [*suite*]

Country or area Pays ou zone (Currency unit · Unité monétaire)	Years Années	Total educational expenditure Dépenses totales d'éducation			Current educational expenditure Dépenses ordinaires d'éducation		
		Amount Montant (000 000)	% of GNP % du PNB	% total gov't exp. % dép. totales gouv.	Amount Montant (000 000)	% of GNP % du PNB	% current gov't exp. % dép. ordinaires gouv.
Sao Tome and Principe							
Sao Tomé et Principe							
(dobra)	1986	100	3.8	18.8	...	...	...
Senegal	1985	...	...	...	46 118	4.2	23.1
Sénégal	1990	...	...	...	60 467	4.1	26.8
(CFA franc · franc CFA)	1992	...	...	...	67 100	4.2	32.8
	1993	...	...	...	67 008	4.2	32.6
Seychelles	1985	125	10.7	21.3	120	10.3	21.9
Seychelles	1990	153	8.1	14.8	153	8.1	18.5
(rupee · roupie)	1991	129	6.8	11.6	...	...	...
	1992	183	8.5	12.9	156	7.3	12.5
Sierra Leone							
Sierra Leone	1985	112	2.4	12.4	106	2.3	15.5
(leone)	1989	604	1.4		577	1.3	...
Somalia [1]							
Somalie [1]							
(shilling)	1985	371	0.5	4.1	274	0.3	...
South Africa	1986	8 108	6.0	...	6 844	5.0	...
Afrique du Sud	1990 [7]	17 153	6.5	...	15 265	5.8	...
(rand)	1992	23 221	7.0	22.1	21 397	6.4	...
Sudan							
Soudan							
(pound · livre)	1985 [1]	...	...	...	580	4.0	15.0
Swaziland	1985	52	5.9	20.3	44	5.0	25.9
Swaziland	1989	101	6.0	22.5	88	5.2	25.1
(lilangeni)	1993 [2]	228	6.8	17.5	187	5.6	21.0
Togo	1985	15 880	5.0	19.4	15 028	4.7	19.2
Togo	1990	24 420	5.6	...	22 720	5.2	...
(CFA franc · franc CFA)	1992	27 004	6.7	21.6	26 307	6.5	29.0
Tunisia	1985	389	5.9	14.1	351	5.3	20.8
Tunisie	1990	648	6.3	13.5	569	5.5	16.3
(dinar)	1992 [2]	789	6.0	14.2	701	5.3	17.6
	1993	895	6.4	...	776	5.5	...
Uganda [2]	1984	288	3.5	...	205	2.5	...
Ouganda [2]	1990	20 188	1.5	11.5	18 527	1.4	15.1
(shilling)	1991	35 026	2.0	15.0	33 012	1.8	16.5
United Rep. of Tanzania							
Rep. Unie de Tanzania	1985	4 234	3.6	14.0	3 643	3.1	15.6
(shilling)	1990	23 426	5.0	11.4	20 599	4.4	...
Zaire							
Zaïre							
(new zaire · nouveau zaïre)	1985	3 291	1.0	7.3	3 239	1.0	7.3
Zambia							
Zambie	1985	293	4.6	13.4	272	4.3	14.3
(kwacha)	1990	2 737	2.6	* 8.7	2 382	2.3	* 8.7
Zimbabwe	1986	726	9.1	15.0	721	9.0	...
Zimbabwe	1990	1 661	10.5	...	1 648 [8]	10.4	...
(dollar)	1992	2 444	10.1	...	...	...	...
	1993	2 914	8.3	...	2 893 [8]	8.3	...
America, North · Amérique du Nord							
Antigua and Barbuda							
Antigua—et—Barbuda							
(E.C. dollar)	1984	12	2.7	...	11	2.6	...
Aruba	1986	47	...	14.1	46	...	15.4
Aruba	1990	77	...	18.0	62	...	19.4
(florin)	1991	76	...	15.9	60	...	16.8
Bahamas	1985	86	4.0	18.0	81	3.8	...
Bahamas	1990	125	4.2	17.8	112	3.7	...
(dollar)	1991	114	3.9	16.3	103	3.5	...
Barbados	1984	139	6.1	...	123	5.4	...
Barbade	1990	269	7.9	22.2	218	6.4	22.1
(dollar)	1992	215	7.0	16.9	192	6.3	17.5
	1993	238	7.5	18.6	230	7.3	20.0

10

Public expenditure on education at current market prices [*cont.*]

Dépenses publiques afférentes à l'enseignement aux prix courants du marché [*suite*]

Country or area Pays ou zone (Currency unit · Unité monétaire)	Years Années	Total educational expenditure Dépenses totales d'éducation			Current educational expenditure Dépenses ordinaires d'éducation		
		Amount Montant (000 000)	% of GNP % du PNB	% total gov't exp. % dép. totales gouv.	Amount Montant (000 000)	% of GNP % du PNB	% current gov't exp. % dép. ordinaires gouv.
Belize							
Belize	1986	...	...	...	18	4.0	...
(dollar)	1991	48	5.7	15.5	38	4.5	21.8
Bermuda	1984	33	3.2	18.4	31	3.0	19.9
Bermudes	1990	53	...	14.5	49	...	15.7
(dollar)	1991	60	...		54	...	...
British Virgin Islands	1985	5	...	16.7	4	...	...
Iles Vierges brit.	1990	8	...	12.2	7	...	...
(US dollar · dollar des E−U)	1991	11	...	15.4	9	...	...
	1992	...	...	...	10	...	...
Canada	1985	30 287	6.6	11.9	30 176 [9]	6.6 [9]	...
Canada	1990	43 487	6.8	14.2	44 319 [9]	6.9 [9]	...
(dollar)	1991	47 764	7.4	...	48 746 [9]	7.6 [9]	...
	1992	49 955	7.6	14.3	51 291 [9]	7.8 [9]	...
Costa Rica	1985	8 181	4.5	22.7	7 787	4.2	26.2
Costa Rica	1990	22 907	4.6	20.8	22 188	4.4	26.3
(colón)	1992	38 552	4.4	21.4	36 636 [2]	4.2 [2]	...
	1993	47 656	4.6	20.2	45 717 [2]	4.4 [2]	...
Cuba [10]							
Cuba [10]	1985	1 690	6.3	...	1 588	5.9	...
(peso)	1990	1 748	6.6	12.3	1 627	6.1	14.4
Dominica	1986	17	5.9	16.7	16	5.7	18.5
Dominique	1989	22	5.8	10.6	20	5.2	19.9
(E.C. dollar)							
Dominican Republic	1985	234	1.8	14.0	204 [2]	1.6 [2]	...
Rép. dominicaine	1992	1 502	1.4	8.9	970 [2]	0.9 [2]	...
(peso)	1993	2 007	1.7	9.9	1 289 [2]	1.1 [2]	...
El Salvador	1984	336	3.0	12.5	293	2.6	16.3
El Salvador	1990	722	1.8	...	715	1.8	...
(colón · colon)	1991	785	1.7	...	780	1.7	...
	1992	884	1.6	...	883	1.6	...
Grenada	1985	...	...	...	19	6.3	...
Grenade	1990	...	...	...	30	5.9	...
(E.C. dollar)	1992	...	...	...	31	5.4	...
	1993	...	...	...	31	5.3	...
Guadeloupe	1990	1 973	...	...	1 952	...	...
Guadeloupe	1991	2 077	...	...	2 022	...	...
(F. franc)	1992 [1]	2 663	...	...	2 627	...	...
	1993	2 776	...	...	2 745	...	...
Guatemala	1984	163	1.8	12.4	160	1.7	23.1
Guatemala	1990 [2]	468	1.4	11.8	...	1.3	...
(quetzal)	1992 [2]	774	1.5	...	...	1.4	...
	1993 [2]	995	1.6	12.8	...	1.7	...
Haiti							
Haïti	1985	118	1.2	16.5	117	1.2	16.7
(gourde)	1990	216	1.4	20.0	216	1.4	20.1
Honduras	1985	290	4.2	13.8	286	4.1	...
Honduras	1989	416	4.2	15.9	404	4.1	...
(lempira)	1991	621	4.1	...	606	4.0	...
Jamaica	1985	550	5.8	12.1	515	5.4	15.8
Jamaïque	1990 [2]	1 472	5.4	12.8	1 276	4.7	17.3
(dollar)	1992	3 086	4.7	11.8	2 714	4.1	17.9
	1993 [2]	5 516	6.2	12.9	5 081	5.7	15.6
Martinique	1990	2 013	...	...	1 994	...	...
Martinique	1992 [1]	2 741	...	...	2 716	...	...
(F.franc)	1993	2 842	...	...	2 814	...	...
Mexico	1985	1 767 324	3.9	...	1 229 314 [2]	2.7 [2]	...
Mexique	1990	26 640 958	4.0	...	16 617 522 [2]	2.5 [2]	...
(new peso · nouveau peso)	1992	48 143 389	4.9	...	32 780 581 [2]	3.3 [2]	...
	1993	62 408 008	6.0	...	43 107 371 [2]	4.2 [2]	...
Montserrat	1990	...	...	...	7	...	18.9
Montserrat	1992	...	...	...	8	...	19.3
(E.C. dollar)	1993	...	...	...	7	...	18.8

10
Public expenditure on education at current market prices [*cont.*]
Dépenses publiques afférentes à l'enseignement aux prix courants du marché [*suite*]

Country or area Pays ou zone (Currency unit · Unité monétaire)	Years Années	Total educational expenditure Dépenses totales d'éducation				Current educational expenditure Dépenses ordinaires d'éducation		
		Amount Montant (000 000)	% of GNP % du PNB	% total gov't exp. % dép. totales gouv.		Amount Montant (000 000)	% of GNP % du PNB	% current gov't exp. % dép. ordinaires gouv.
Netherlands Antilles	1991	151	...	...		...	...	...
Antilles néerlandaises	1992	171	...	...		...	...	...
(guilder · florin)	1993	196	...	...		...	...	...
Nicaragua	1985 [2]	6.409	6.8	10.2		6.196	6.6	12.2
Nicaragua	1991 [3]	242	4.4	12.7		...	...	...
(córdoba · cordoba)	1992 [3]	275	4.1	...		...	...	...
	1993 [3]	324	3.9	12.8		...	...	...
Panama	1985	237	4.8	18.7		231	4.7	19.9
Panama	1990	248	5.2	20.9		241	5.1	22.2
(balboa)	1991	268	5.1	18.8		262	5.0	21.1
	1992	329	5.6	18.9		307	5.2	21.9
St. Kitts and Nevis	1985	12	5.8	18.5		12	5.7	19.1
Saint−Kitts−et−Nevis	1990 [1]	11	2.7	...		11	2.7	...
(E.C. dollar)	1991 [1]	12	2.8	11.6		12	2.7	11.7
	1992	15	3.3	13.5		14	3.1	...
Saint Lucia	1986	38	5.5	...		36	5.2	...
Sainte lucie	1990	...	...	...		54	5.3	...
(E.C. dollar)	1991	...	...	...		55	5.1	...
	1992	...	...	...		63	5.2	...
St. Pierre−Miquelon	1985	41	...	...		37	...	...
St. Pierre−Miquelon	1990 [2]	54	...	...		41	...	...
(F. franc)	1992 [2]	57	...	...		54	...	...
	1993 [2]	64	...	...		57	...	...
St. Vincent and the Grenadines								
Saint−Vincent−et−Grenadines	1986	19	5.8	11.6		18	5.4	16.8
(E.C. dollar)	1990 [1]	34	6.7	13.8		26	5.0	17.2
Trinidad and Tobago	1985	1 042	6.1	...		912	5.3	...
Trinité−et−Tobago	1990	788	4.0	11.6		727	3.7	13.5
(dollar)	1992	811	3.8	10.3		772	3.6	10.7
	1993	836	3.6	...		805	3.5	...
United States								
Etats−Unis	1985	199 372	4.9	15.5		182 875	4.5	16.3
(dollar)	1990	292 944	5.3	12.3		265 074	4.8	12.3
US Virgin Islands								
Iles Vierges américaine								
(US dollar · dollar des E−U)	1984	74	7.5	...		...	...	...
America, South · Amérique du Sud								
Argentina	1985 [2]	740	1.5	8.6		667	1.3	8.9
Argentine	1990 [2]	7 356 595	1.1	10.9		7 062 974	1.1	12.4
(peso)	1992 [11]	6 962	3.1	15.7		...	...	...
	1993 [11]	8 310	3.3	12.4		1 506	0.6	...
Bolivia	1985	43	2.1	...		...	...	...
Bolivie	1990 [1][12]	363	2.7	...		...	...	...
(boliviano)	1991 [1][12]	467	2.7	...		...	...	...
Brazil								
Brésil	1985	50	3.8	...		...	...	...
(cruzeiro)	1989	56 101	4.6	...		...	...	...
Chile	1985	101 493	4.4	15.3		...	...	...
Chili	1990 [13]	232 516	2.7	10.4		225 620	2.6	...
(peso)	1992	407 645	2.8	12.9		392 411	2.7	15.0
	1993	477 307	2.7	...		468 452	2.6	...
Colombia [2]	1985	136 570	2.9	...		127 908	2.7	...
Colombie [2]	1990	526 686	2.8	12.4		...	...	...
(peso)	1992	996 567	3.1	...		...	...	...
	1993	1 396 031	3.5	12.3		1 231 516	3.0	19.2
Ecuador	1985	38 009	3.7	20.6		35 611	3.5	25.8
Equateur	1989	134 554	2.8	19.1		127 394	2.7	24.7
(sucre)	1992	492 252	2.7	19.2		416 411	2.3	24.0
	1993	790 964	3.0	...		720 441	2.7	...
French Guiana	1990	501	...	...		490	...	...
Guyane français	1992 [1]	774	...	...		755	...	...
(F. franc)	1993	851	...	...		833	...	...

10
Public expenditure on education at current market prices [cont.]
Dépenses publiques afférentes à l'enseignement aux prix courants du marché [suite]

Country or area Pays ou zone (Currency unit · Unité monétaire)	Years Années	Total educational expenditure Dépenses totales d'éducation			Current educational expenditure Dépenses ordinaires d'éducation		
		Amount Montant (000 000)	% of GNP % du PNB	% total gov't exp. % dép. totales gouv.	Amount Montant (000 000)	% of GNP % du PNB	% current gov't exp. % dép. ordinaires gouv.
Guyana							
Guyana	1985	162	9.8	10.4	135	8.1	13.0
(dollar)	1990	542	7.8	...	435	6.3	5.2
Paraguay	1985	20 662	1.5	16.7	16 822	1.2	18.8
Paraguay	1990 [2]	74 387	1.2	9.1	72 472	1.1	...
(guaraní)	1992 [2]	249 750	2.6	11.9	223 139	2.3	...
	1993 [2]	338 107	2.8	16.9	312 757	2.6	17.1
Peru							
Pérou							
(inti)	1985	5 042	2.9	15.7	4 855	2.8	17.9
Suriname	1985	158	9.4	...	...	...	...
Suriname	1990	250	8.3	...	249	8.3	...
(guilder · florin)	1992	362	7.3	...	360	7.2	...
	1993	384	...	...	380	...	...
Uruguay	1985	12 565	2.8	9.3	12 068	2.7	9.3
Uruguay	1990	289 354	3.1	15.9	265 660	2.8	16.7
(peso)	1991	572 456	2.9	16.6	530 330	2.7	17.0
	1992	959 087	2.8	15.4	873 317	2.5	15.5
Venezuela	1985	23 068	5.1	20.3	...	...	...
Venezuela	1990	69 352	3.1	12.0	...	...	...
(bolívar)	1991 [2]	136 571	4.6	17.0	...	...	...
	1992	211 659	5.3	23.5	...	...	...
Asia · Asie							
Afghanistan							
Afghanistan							
(afghani)	1990	5 667	...	...	5 282	...	...
Armenia							
Arménie	1990	4	7.3	20.5	...	...	...
(dram)	1993	...	...	...	136	3.5	...
Azerbaijan	1990	1 132	7.7	24.2	...	...	...
Azerbaïdjan	1991	2 066	7.7	24.7	...	...	...
(manat)	1992	16 205	6.5	...	15 704	6.3	...
Bahrain	1985	52	4.0	10.4	49	3.8	14.6
Bahreïn	1990 [1]	65	5.0	...	61	4.7	...
(dinar)	1992 [1]	72	5.0	12.3	68	4.7	14.4
	1993 [1]	71	4.7	12.0	69	4.6	...
Bangladesh [2]	1985	7 782	1.9	9.7	6 005	1.5	15.3
Bangladesh [2]	1990	14 942	2.0	10.3	11 820	1.6	14.4
(taka)	1991	18 184	2.2	11.3	13 816	1.7	15.9
	1992	20 996	2.3	8.7	16 744	1.9	10.4
Bhutan							
Bhoutan	1992	...	...	...	187	2.9	...
(ngultrum)	1993	...	...	...	192	2.7	...
Brunei Darussalam	1984	168	2.1	...	151	1.9	...
Brunéi Darussalam	1990	253	3.9	...	229	3.5	...
(dollar)	1991 [2 12]	235	3.6	...	217	3.3	...
	1992 [2 12]	258	...	...	239	...	...
China	1985	22 489	2.6	12.2	19 770	2.3	...
Chine	1990	43 386	2.3	12.8	40 423	2.2	...
(yuan)	1992	53 874	2.0	12.2	48 976	1.8	13.5
	1993	64 439	1.9	12.2	59 104	1.7	...
Cyprus [14]	1985	55	3.7	12.2	53	3.6	13.4
Chypre [14]	1990	89	3.5	11.3	84	3.3	12.3
(pound · livre)	1992	120	3.9	12.5	112	3.6	13.1
	1993	139	4.3	12.6	127	3.9	12.9
Hong Kong	1984	6 991	...	18.7	6 190	...	23.0
Hong-kong	1990	16 566	...	17.4	...	...	...
(dollar)	1991	19 552	...	18.1	16 915	...	...
	1992	22 022	...	17.3	...	...	...

10
Public expenditure on education at current market prices [cont.]
Dépenses publiques afférentes à l'enseignement aux prix courants du marché [suite]

Country or area Pays ou zone (Currency unit · Unité monétaire)	Years Années	Total educational expenditure Dépenses totales d'éducation			Current educational expenditure Dépenses ordinaires d'éducation		
		Amount Montant (000 000)	% of GNP % du PNB	% total gov't exp. % dép. totales gouv.	Amount Montant (000 000)	% of GNP % du PNB	% current gov't exp. % dép. ordinaires gouv.
India	1985	87 257	3.4	9.4	85 198	3.3	13.0
Inde	1990	207 897	4.0	10.9	205 330	3.9	13.7
(rupee · roupie)	1991	232 425	3.8	11.9	228 878	3.8	13.4
	1992	260 169	3.7	11.5	257 377	3.7	13.4
Indonesia	1990 [2]	2 089 319	1.1	...	1 441 498	0.8	...
Indonésie	1992	5 479 346	2.2	...	3 585 711	1.4	...
(rupiah)	1993 [2]	3 639 295	1.3	...	2 294 724	0.8	...
Iran, Islamic Rep. of	1985	575 519	3.6	17.2	510 081	3.2	20.6
Iran, Rép. islamique d'	1990	1 493 896	4.1	22.4	1 232 097	3.4	28.8
(rial)	1992	3 142 954	4.7	28.2	2 582 561	3.9	31.4
	1993	4 978 516	5.4	22.8	4 068 840	4.4	26.4
Iraq	1985	551	4.0	...	...	...	...
Iraq	1991	804	...	...	711	...	...
(dinar)	1992	902	...	...	896	...	...
Israel	1985	1 876	6.4	8.6	1 720	5.9	8.3
Israël	1990	6 239	5.8	10.5	5 713	5.3	10.4
(new sheqel · nouveau sheqel)	1991	8 157	5.8	10.6	7 420	5.3	10.9
Japan	1985	16 142 654	5.0	17.9	15 280 808 [9]	4.8 [9]	...
Japon	1990	20 258 000	4.7	16.5	...	...	...
(yen)	1991	21 300 000	4.7	16.6	...	...	...
Jordan	1985	105	5.5	13.0	92	4.8	18.9
Jordanie	1990 [1]	101	4.3	8.5	92	3.9	...
(dinar)	1992 [1]	116	3.9	9.1	102	3.4	10.9
	1993 [12]	155	4.6	11.6	139	4.1	13.2
Kazakstan	1985	2 174	6.5	18.9	...	...	...
Kazakstan	1990	3 001	6.5	17.6	...	...	...
(tenge)	1991	6 252	7.7	19.1	...	...	...
	1992	65 247	5.4	25.2	60 549	5.0	...
Korea, Republic of	1985	3 530 101	4.5	...	2 811 861	3.5	...
Corée, République de	1990	6 159 073	3.5	...	5 495 204	3.1	...
(won)	1991	8 543 089	4.0	...	6 728 333	3.1	...
	1992	10 019 080	4.2	14.8	7 996 446	3.4	15.3
Kuwait	1986	360	4.9	12.6	344	4.7	...
Koweït	1989	432	4.6	14.0	...	...	...
(dinar)	1992	450	6.4	11.4	...	...	...
	1993	486	6.1	12.6	...	...	...
Kyrgyzstan	1990	4	8.6	22.4	...	...	...
Kirghizistan	1991	6	6.8	24.1	...	...	...
(som)	1993	227	3.6	20.7	215	3.4	21.0
Lao People's Dem. Rep.							
Rep. dém. pop. lao	1985	463	...	4.5	...	...	...
(kip)	1992	19 922	2.3	...	15 094	1.8	...
Lebanon [2]	1985	1 639	...	16.8	...	...	...
Liban [2]	1989	43 711	2.7	...	...	...	...
(pound · livre)	1992	206 603	2.1	12.5	204 123	2.1	...
	1993	251 874	1.9	...	227 049	1.7	...
Malaysia	1985	4 754	6.6	16.3	4 062	5.6	...
Malaysie	1990 [2]	6 033	5.4	18.3	4 664	4.2	19.3
(ringgit)	1992 [2]	7 702	5.5	16.9	6 656	4.7	19.6
	1993 [2]	8 074	5.1	...	7 085	4.5	...
Maldives	1986	24	4.4	* 7.2	20	3.7	...
Maldives	1990	79	6.3	* 10.0	...	...	...
(rufiyaa)	1992	220	12.0	* 16.0	...	...	...
	1993	183	8.1	13.6	132	5.8	18.0
Mongolia	1985	716	7.8	...	...	...	...
Mongolie	1990	882	8.6	...	...	...	...
(tugrik)	1991	1 598	8.5	...	...	...	...
Myanmar [2]							
Myanmar [2]	1985	1 084	2.0	...	841	1.5	...
(kyat)	1989	2 948	2.4	...	2 699	2.2	...

10
Public expenditure on education at current market prices [*cont.*]
Dépenses publiques afférentes à l'enseignement aux prix courants du marché [*suite*]

Country or area Pays ou zone (Currency unit · Unité monétaire)	Years Années	Total educational expenditure Dépenses totales d'éducation			Current educational expenditure Dépenses ordinaires d'éducation		
		Amount Montant (000 000)	% of GNP % du PNB	% total gov't exp. % dép. totales gouv.	Amount Montant (000 000)	% of GNP % du PNB	% current gov't exp. % dép. ordinaires gouv.
Nepal [15] Népal [15] (rupee · roupie)	1985 1990 1991 1992	1 241 2 079 3 268 4 428	2.6 2.0 2.7 2.9	12.7 8.5 12.3 13.2	... ...	... ...	... ...
Oman Oman (rial)	1985 1990 1992 1993	123 128 151 170	4.0 3.5 3.9 5.8	... 11.1 16.2 15.2	77 117 135 151	2.5 3.2 3.5 5.2	... 18.8 19.3 19.1
Pakistan Pakistan (rupee · roupie)	1985 1990 [16] 1991 [16]	12 645 23 570 27 790	2.5 2.6 2.7	... ...	9 390 19 500 24 090	1.8 2.2 2.3	... ...
Philippines Philippines (peso)	1985 1990 1992 [2] 1993 [2]	7 524 31 067 31 687 36 320	1.4 2.9 2.3 2.4	7.4 10.1	7 026 28 713	1.3 2.7	10.0 11.1 ... ...
Qatar Qatar (riyal)	1985 1990 1992 1993	1 012 929 957 976	4.1 3.4 3.4 3.5	... ...	767 904 896 891	3.1 3.3 3.2 3.2	... ...
Saudi Arabia Arabie saoudite (riyal)	1985 1990 1992 1993	23 540 25 460 30 800 31 590	6.7 6.0 6.4 ...	12.0 17.8 17.0 ...	19 283 24 033 29 428 29 671	5.5 5.7 6.1 ...	... ...
Singapore Singapour (dollar)	1985 1988	1 776 1 718	4.4 3.4	... ...	1 388 1 523	3.4 3.0	... ...
Sri Lanka Sri Lanka (rupee · roupie)	1985 [2] 1990 1992 1993	4 183 8 621 13 883 15 515	2.6 2.7 3.3 3.1	6.9 8.1 8.8 7.8	3 530 7 024 10 598 12 604	2.2 2.2 2.5 2.5	11.4 10.7 10.6 12.5
Syrian Arab Republic Rép. arabe syrienne (pound · livre)	1985 1990 1991 1992 [1]	5 060 10 720 12 025 10 903	6.1 4.2 4.2 ...	11.8 17.3 14.2 11.7	2 799 [1] 9 627	3.4 [1]	... ...
Tajikistan Tajikistan (rouble)	1985 1990 1991 1992	509 786 1 227 7 207	8.6 10.7 9.2 11.2	29.5 24.7 24.4 19.2	479 723 1 190 6 976	8.1 9.8 8.9 10.8	... ...
Thailand Thaïlande (baht)	1985 1990 1991 1992	39 367 77 420 87 976 109 890	3.8 3.6 3.5 4.0	18.5 20.0 19.1 19.6	33 830 64 702 72 182 ...	3.3 3.0 2.9 ...	19.2 21.0 19.9 ...
Turkey Turquie (lira · livre)	1985 1990 [1] 1991 [1] 1992 [1]	627 104 8 506 541 14 943 536 30 357 203	2.3 2.2 2.4 2.8	... ...	523 102 7 580 817 13 604 256 27 895 167	1.9 2.0 2.2 ...	... ...
Turkmenistan Turkménistan (manat)	1985 1989 1990 1991	431 602 655 1 159	7.6 8.5 8.6 7.9	28.0 27.1 21.0 19.7	... ...	... ...	... ...
United Arab Emirates Emirats arabes unis (dirham)	1985 1990 1992 1993	1 738 2 280 2 637 2 657	1.7 1.7 2.0 2.0	10.4 14.6 15.2 15.1	1 637 2 174 2 460 2 457	1.6 1.7 1.8 1.8	10.6 14.3 15.1 14.9
Uzbekistan Ouzbékistan (sum)	1993	486 502	11.0	...	475 863	10.7	...
Yemen Yémen former Yemen Arab Republic ancienne Yémen rép. arabe (rial)	1985	2 039	...	21.8	1 789	...	27.4

10
Public expenditure on education at current market prices [*cont.*]
Dépenses publiques afférentes à l'enseignement aux prix courants du marché [*suite*]

Country or area Pays ou zone (Currency unit · Unité monétaire)	Years Années	Total educational expenditure Dépenses totales d'éducation			Current educational expenditure Dépenses ordinaires d'éducation		
		Amount Montant (000 000)	% of GNP % du PNB	% total gov't exp. % dép. totales gouv.	Amount Montant (000 000)	% of GNP % du PNB	% current gov't exp. % dép. ordinaires gouv.
Europe · Europe							
Albania							
Albanie	1987	946	...	11.2	...	...	...
(lek)	1990	984	...		...	...	...
Andorra							
Andorre							
(peseta)	1986	951	...	15.8	800	...	24.4
Austria	1985	78 639	5.9	7.9	70 847	5.3	8.6
Autriche	1990	97 301	5.4	7.6	89 858	5.0	8.8
(schilling)	1991	107 329	5.6	7.6	98 054	5.1	8.6
	1992	117 519	5.8	7.7	103 693	5.1	8.6
Belarus	1985	1 499	4.8	...	1 264	4.0	...
Bélarus	1990	2 093	5.0	...	1 758	4.2	...
(rouble)	1992	60 520	6.6	19.3	49 528	5.4	20.0
	1993[17]	662 987	5.3	15.9	530 554	4.2	...
Belgium [2]	1985	287 388	6.2	15.2	272 843	5.8	16.0
Belgique [2]	1990	325 282	5.1	...	321 427	5.1	...
(franc)	1991	342 383	5.1	...	338 707	5.0	...
	1992	361 584	5.1	...	358 648	5.1	...
Bulgaria	1985	1 784	5.5	...	1 598	4.9	...
Bulgarie	1990	2 357	5.6	...	2 183	5.2	...
(lev)	1992	11 729	5.9	...	11 211	5.6	...
	1993	16 307	5.8	...	15 210	5.4	...
former Czechoslovakia †	1985	28 201	4.2	7.9	26 959	4.0	8.6
anc. Tchécoslovaquie †	1990	37 323	4.6	8.2	35 482	4.4	8.7
(koruna · couronne)	1991 [2]	33 546	3.5	6.6	30 816	3.2	6.8
Czech Republic							
Rép. tchèque	1992	36 915	4.6	...	33 631	4.2	...
(koruna · couronne)	1993	53 393	5.8	...	49 198	5.4	...
Denmark	1985	42 672	7.2	...			...
Danemark	1989	55 448	7.5	13.0	52 270	7.1	12.9
(krone · couronne)	1991	58 960	7.4	11.8	54 896	6.9	11.5
Estonia							
Estonie	1992	795	5.9	...	729	5.4	...
(kroon · couronne)	1993	1 540	5.9	20.1	1 344	5.1	20.9
Finland	1985	17 682	5.4	11.8	17 604 [9]	5.4 [9]	...
Finlande	1990	28 770	5.7	11.9	29 300 [9]	5.8 [9]	...
(markka)	1991	32 412	6.8	11.9	33 495 [9]	7.1 [9]	...
	1992	33 086	7.2	11.6	34 170 [9]	7.5 [9]	...
France [18]	1985	269 191	5.8	...	254 433	5.4	...
France [18]	1990	351 867	5.4	...	327 427	5.1	...
(franc)	1992	393 004	5.7	...	362 695	5.2	...
	1993	406 772	5.8	...	369 289	5.2	...
Germany † · Allemagne †							
Federal Republic of Germany	1985	83 691	4.6	9.2	75 566	4.1	9.4
Rép. féd. d'Allemagne	1990	98 412	4.0	8.6	88 499	3.6	8.7
(deutsche mark)	1991 [19]	107 497	3.7	11.6	97 255	3.4	12.5
former German Dem. Republic							
ancienne Rép. dém. allemande							
(DDR mark)	1985	...	...	...	12 404	...	...
Gibraltar							
Gibraltar							
(pound · livre)	1984	5	6.0	...	5	6.0	...
Greece							
Grèce	1985	133 091	2.9	7.5	126 749	2.8	8.5
(drachma · drachme)	1990	325 385	3.1	...	306 303	2.9	...
Hungary	1985	54 061	5.5	6.4	48 125	4.9	7.4
Hongrie	1990	122 120	6.1	7.8	110 382	5.5	8.6
(forint)	1992	193 772	7.0	7.7	178 954	6.4	8.6
	1993	229 000	6.7	7.4	215 195	6.3	8.3
Iceland							
Islande	1985	5 684	4.9	13.8	...	...	...
(króna · couronne)	1990	19 747	5.6	...	14 584	4.2	...

10
Public expenditure on education at current market prices [*cont.*]
Dépenses publiques afférentes à l'enseignement aux prix courants du marché [*suite*]

Country or area Pays ou zone (Currency unit · Unité monétaire)	Years Années	Total educational expenditure Dépenses totales d'éducation				Current educational expenditure Dépenses ordinaires d'éducation		
		Amount Montant (000 000)	% of GNP % du PNB	% total gov't exp. % dép. totales gouv.		Amount Montant (000 000)	% of GNP % du PNB	% current gov't exp. % dép. ordinaires gouv.
Ireland	1985	1 058	6.3	8.9		963	5.8	10.5
Irlande	1990	1 372	5.7	10.2		1 303	5.4	12.1
(pound · livre)	1991	1 479	5.8	9.7		1 416	5.6	12.2
	1992	1 645	6.2	...		1 568	5.9	...
Italy	1985	40 533 126	5.0	8.3		36 859 217	4.6	10.0
Italie	1990 [1] [13]	40 846 282	3.2	...		40 400 136	3.1	...
(lira · lire)	1991 [1] [13]	43 141 268	3.1	...		42 664 531	3.0	...
	1992	80 268 000	5.4	...		77 347 968 [8]	5.2	...
Latvia Lettonie								
(lats)	1993	89	6.7	16.8		87	6.6	16.8
Lithuania								
Lituanie	1992	179	5.5	22.1		171	5.2	23.5
(litas)	1993	531	4.4	20.1		499	4.1	32.2
Luxembourg								
Luxembourg	1986	12 269	3.8	15.7		10 712	3.3	15.4
(franc)	1989	16 363	4.1	...		13 440	3.4	...
Malta	1985	17	3.4	7.7		17	3.3	9.1
Malte	1990	32	4.0	8.3		30	3.8	10.9
(lira · lire)	1991	35	4.1	8.5		33	3.9	11.1
	1992	42	4.6	10.9		41	4.5	12.5
Monaco								
Monaco	1989	124	...	5.3		113	...	7.8
(F. franc)	1992	153	...	5.6		140	...	7.7
Netherlands	1985	27 403	6.4	...		24 796 [9]	5.8 [9]	...
Pays−Bas	1990	30 697	6.0	...		29 005 [9]	5.6 [9]	...
(guilder · florin)	1991	31 709	5.9	...		30 231 [9]	5.6 [9]	...
Norway	1985	30 956	6.3	14.3		27 979 [9]	5.7 [9]	...
Norvège	1990	49 655	7.7	14.2		44 109 [9]	6.9 [9]	...
(krone · couronne)	1991	53 100	7.9	14.1		47 807 [9]	0.0 [9]	...
	1992	57 201	8.4	13.6		51 132 [9]	7.5 [9]	...
Poland	1985	497 497	4.9	12.2		405 597	4.0	11.6
Pologne	1990	28 249 871	5.0	14.6		...	...	...
(zloty)	1992	62 442 000	5.5	14.0		58 467 000	5.2	14.2
	1993	83 697 000	5.5	14.0		77 947 000	5.1	15.5
Portugal	1985	152 886	4.0	...		135 612	3.6	...
Portugal	1990 [2]	412 481	4.3	...		378 252	4.0	...
(escudo)	1991 [2]	540 503	4.8	...		508 664	4.5	...
	1992	651 768	5.0	...		610 807	4.7	...
Republic of Modova	1990	794	6.3	19.3		...	...	...
République de Moldova	1991	1 370	5.6	21.4		...	...	...
(leu)	1992	14 073	6.5	26.4		12 923	6.0	28.6
Romania	1985	17 941	2.2	...		17 345	2.1	...
Roumanie	1990	24 270	2.8	7.3		23 881	2.8	9.0
(leu)	1992	216 465	3.6	14.2		208 881	3.5	15.5
	1993 [13]	605 562	3.1	...		...	...	...
Russian federation	1985	14 945	3.1	...		...	...	...
Fédération de Russie	1990	22 237	3.5	...		...	...	...
(rouble)	1992	679 434	4.0	...		...	...	...
	1993	6 917 781	4.4	...		...	...	...
San Marino	1984	11 470	...	10.7		10 474	...	10.3
Saint−Marin	1990	22 048	...	...		21 723	...	...
(lira · lire)	1992	30 915	...	...		29 221	...	...
	1993	34 112	...	...		32 981	...	...
Slovakia								
Slovaquie	1992	19 829	6.6	...		17 575	5.8	...
(koruna · couronne)	1993	19 400	5.7	...		16 966	5.0	...
Slovenia	1991	16 603	4.8	16.1		15 266	4.4	...
Slovénie	1992	55 828	5.6	23.2		52 595	5.3	24.6
(tolar)	1993	83 183	6.2	21.7		76 591	5.7	...

10
Public expenditure on education at current market prices [*cont.*]
Dépenses publiques afférentes à l'enseignement aux prix courants du marché [*suite*]

Country or area Pays ou zone (Currency unit · Unité monétaire)	Years Années	Total educational expenditure Dépenses totales d'éducation			Current educational expenditure Dépenses ordinaires d'éducation		
		Amount Montant (000 000)	% of GNP % du PNB	% total gov't exp. % dép. totales gouv.	Amount Montant (000 000)	% of GNP % du PNB	% current gov't exp. % dép. ordinaires gouv.
Spain	1985	917 076	3.3	...	821 118	2.9	...
Espagne	1990	2 181 935	4.4	9.4	1 936 203	3.9	...
(peseta)	1991	2 445 957	4.5	...	2 165 629	4.0	...
	1992	2 680 764	4.6	9.3	2 423 169	4.2	...
Sweden	1985	65 001	7.7	12.6	57 703	6.8	...
Suède	1990	101 363	7.7	13.8	93 083	7.1	...
(krona · couronne)	1991	113 123	8.0	14.0	103 927	7.4	...
	1992	115 610	8.3	12.6	105 115	7.6	...
Switzerland	1985	11 696	4.8	18.6	10 638	4.4	19.9
Suisse	1989	14 560	4.8	18.7	12 941	4.2	19.6
(franc)	1990	16 215	5.0	...	14 395	4.4	...
	1991	18 106	5.2	18.8	16 061	4.7	19.5
TFYR Macedonia							
L'ex−R.y. Macédoine	1992	605	5.3	...	591	5.2	...
(denar)	1993	2 939	5.0	21.5	2 863	4.9	21.3
Ukraine	1985	6 721	5.2	...	5 708	4.4	...
Ukraine	1990	8 606	5.2	...	6 903	4.2	...
(karbovanets)	1992	327 968	7.8	...	280 690	6.7	...
	1993 [20]	9 006 147	6.1	...	7 430 284	5.1	...
United Kingdom	1985	17 501	4.9	...	16 764	4.7	...
Royaume−Uni	1990	26 677	4.9	...	25 318	4.7	...
(pound · livre)	1991	29 534	5.2	...	28 045	5.0	...
Yugoslavia							
Yugoslavie							
(dinar)	1992	0.292	...	...	0.274	...	...
Yugoslavia, SFR †							
Yugoslavie, Rfs †	1985	42	3.4	...	39	3.1	...
(dinar)	1990	60 318	6.1	...	55 911	5.7	...
Oceania · Océanie							
American Samoa							
Samoa américaines							
(US dollar · dollar des E−U)	1986	23	...	...	23	...	...
Australia	1985	12 925	5.6	12.8	11 848	5.1	14.2
Australie	1990	19 364	5.4	14.8	17 889	4.9	14.8
(dollar)	1991	20 417	5.5	14.1	18 983	5.1	14.6
Cook Islands							
Iles Cook	1986	5	...	9.5	4	...	9.5
(NZ dollar)	1991	8	...	12.4	8	...	12.7
Fiji	1986	85	6.0	...	83	5.9	...
Fidji	1990 [2]	94	4.7	...	93	4.7	...
(dollar)	1991 [2]	105	4.9	...	98	4.6	...
	1992 [2]	128	5.6	18.6	124	5.4	...
French Polynesia	1984 [2]	1 030	9.8	...	935	8.9	...
Polynésia française	1990 [2]	1 205	...	...	1 148	...	...
(F. franc)	1992 [1,2]	1 785	...	...	1 708	...	...
	1993 [2]	1 894	...	...	1 807	...	...
Guam							
Guam							
(US dollar · dollar des E−U)	1985 [1]	60	8.5	...	59	8.3	...
Kiribati	1985	3	6.7	18.5	3	6.7	...
Kiribati	1990	4	6.0	18.3	4	6.0	...
(Australian dollar)	1991	4	6.5	14.8	4	6.5	...
	1992	5	7.4	...	5	7.4	...
New Caledonia	1985	1 007	13.5	...	919	12.3	...
Nouvelle−Calédonie	1990 [2]	1 137	...	...	1 040	...	...
(F. franc)	1992 [1,2]	1 501	...	...	1 458	...	...
	1993 [2]	1 652	...	...	1 606	...	...
New Zealand	1985	2 028	4.7	18.4	1 849	4.3	25.5
Nouvelle−Zélande	1990	4 451	6.5	...	4 252	6.2	...
(dollar)	1991	5 013	7.3	...	4 825	7.0	...
	1992	5 308	7.3	...	5 107	7.0	...

10
Public expenditure on education at current market prices [*cont.*]
Dépenses publiques afférentes à l'enseignement aux prix courants du marché [*suite*]

Country or area Pays ou zone (Currency unit · Unité monétaire)	Years Années	Total educational expenditure Dépenses totales d'éducation				Current educational expenditure Dépenses ordinaires d'éducation		
		Amount Montant (000 000)	% of GNP % du PNB	% total gov't exp. % dép. totales gouv.	Amount Montant (000 000)	% of GNP % du PNB	% current gov't exp. % dép. ordinaires gouv.
Niue	1986	1.394	...	...	1.283	...	...
Nioué	1988	1.366	...	10.8	1.166	...	10.1
(NZ dollar)	1991	1.454	...	10.2	1.164	...	10.8
Samoa							
Samoa							
(tala)	1990	15	4.2	10.7	14	3.9	15.8
Solomon Islands							
Iles Salomon	1984	10	4.7	12.4	4	1.9	8.0
(S.I. dollar)	1991	24	4.2	7.9	24	4.2	13.5
Tonga							
Tonga	1985	4	4.4	16.1	4	4.4	...
(pa'anga)	1992	9	4.8	17.3	...	...	...
Tuvalu							
Tuvalu	1989	0.741	...	18.5	0.741	...	...
(australian dollar)	1990	0.854	...	16.2	...	...	...
Vanuatu	1987	924	7.4	24.6	924	7.4	25.4
Vanuatu	1990	831	4.3	...	831	4.3	19.2
(vatu)	1991	929	4.5	...	929	4.5	18.8
former USSR · ancienne URSS							
former USSR † [21]							
ancienne URSS † [21]	1985	39 866	7.0	...	33 319	5.9	...
(rouble)	1990	57 608	8.2	...	46 030	6.5	...

Source:
United Nations Educational, Scientific and Cultural Organization
(Paris).

† For detailed descriptions of data pertaining to former
Czechoslovakia, Germany, SFR Yugoslavia and former
USSR, see Annex I − Country or area nomenclature,
regional and other groupings.

1 Expenditure on third level education is not included.
2 Data refer to expenditure of the Ministry of Education only.
3 Data refer to expenditure of the Ministry of Primary and
Secondary Education only (Nicaragua: expressed in gold
cordobas).
4 Expenditure relating to Al−Azhar is not included.
5 Data include foreign aid received for education.
6 Data refer to expenditure of the Federal government only.
7 Data do not include expenditure for Transkei, Bophuthatswana,
Venda and Ciskei.
8 Data include capital expenditure on universities.
9 Data refer to public and private expenditure on education.
10 Expenditure on education is calculated as percentage of
global social product.
11 Figures are in pesos (1 austral = 1000 pesos).
12 Expenditure on universities is not included.
13 Data refer to expenditure of education of the central
government only.
14 Expenditure of the Office of Greek Education only.
15 Data refer to regular and development expenditure.
16 Data do not include expenditure on education by other ministries
which are not directly related to education.
17 Data are expressed in B. rouble.
18 Metropolitan France.
19 Data include expenditure for East Berlin.
20 Data are expressed in Karbovanets.
21 Expenditure on education is calculated as percentage of net
material product.

Source:
Organisation des Nations Unies pour l'éducation, la science et
la culture (Paris).

† Pour les descriptions en détails des données relatives à l'ancienne
Tchécoslovaquie, l'Allemagne, la Rfs Yougoslavie et l'ancienne
URSS, voir l'Annexe I − Nomenclature des pays ou zones,
groupements régionaux et autres groupements.

1 Les dépenses relatives à l'enseignement du troisième degré ne sont pas
incluses.
2 Les données se réfèrent aux dépenses du Ministère de l'Education
seulement.
3 Les données de réfèrent aux dépenses du Ministère des enseignements
primaire et secondaire seulement (Nicaragua: exprimées en cordobas or).
4 Les dépenses relatives à Al−Azhar ne sont pas incluses.
5 Les données comprennent l'aide étrangère reçue pour la éducation.
6 Les dépenses se réfèrent aux dépenses du gouvernement fédéral
seulement.
7 Les données ne comprennent pas Transkei, Bophuthatswana, Venda et
Ciskei.
8 Les données comprennent les dépenses en capital des universités.
9 Les données se réfèrent aux dépenses publiques et privées afférentes à
l'enseignement.
10 Les dépenses de l'enseignement sont calculés en pourcentage du produit
social global.
11 Les chiffres sont exprimés en pesos (1 austral = 1 000 pesos).
12 Les dépenses des universités ne sont pas incluses.
13 Les données se réfèrent aux dépenses de l'éducation du gouvernement
central seulement.
14 Dépenses du bureau grec de l'éducation seulement.
15 Les données se réfèrent aux dépenses ordinaires et de developpement.
16 Les données ne comprennent pas les dépenses d'éducation effectuées
par d'autres ministères qui ne sont pas en rapport direct avec
l'enseignement.
17 Les données sont exprimées en B. rouble.
18 France métropolitaine.
19 Les données comprennent les dépenses relatives à Berlin Est.
20 Les données sont exprimées en Karbovanets.
21 Les dépenses de l'enseignement sont calculés en pourcentage du produit
matériel net.

11
Illiterate population by sex
Population analphabète selon le sexe

Country or area Pays ou zone	Year Année	Age group Groupe d'âge	Illiterate population Population analphabète			Percentage of illiterates Percentage d'analphabètes		
			Total	M	F	Total	M	F
Africa · Afrique								
Algeria	1987	15+	6373688	2320756	4052932	50.4	36.6	64.2
Algérie	1995[1]	15+	6582000	2249000	4333000	38.4	26.1	51.0
Angola								
Angola	1985[2]	15+	...	...	...	59.0	51.0	...
Benin	1992	15+	1784235	667174	1116971	70.7	57.6	81.7
Bénin	1995[1]	15+	1792000	713000	1079000	63.0	51.3	74.2
Botswana	1991[3]	15+	340523	164045	176478	45.2	46.8	43.8
Botswana	1995[1]	15+	255000	79000	177000	30.2	19.5	40.1
Burkina Faso								
Burkina Faso	1995[1]	15+	4597000	1972000	2625000	80.8	70.5	90.8
Burundi	1982[2]	10+	...	...	...	66.2	57.2	74.3
Burundi	1995[1]	15+	2221000	835000	1386000	64.7	50.7	77.5
Cameroon								
Cameroun	1995[1]	15+	2712000	908000	1805000	36.6	25.0	47.9
Cape Verde	1990	15+	69930	21363	48567	37.1	25.2	46.7
Cap–Vert	1995[1]	15+	64000	19000	46000	28.4	18.6	36.2
Central African Rep.								
Rép.centrafricaine	1995[1]	15+	760000	285000	475000	40.0	31.5	47.6
Chad								
Tchad	1995[1]	15+	1868000	666000	1202000	51.9	37.9	65.3
Comoros	1980	15+	88780	36429	52351	52.1	44.0	60.0
Comores	1995[1]	15+	143000	60000	83000	42.7	35.8	49.6
Congo	1984	15+	422770	142744	280026	40.4	28.7	51.0
Congo	1995[1]	15+	354000	114000	239000	25.1	16.9	32.8
Côte d'Ivoire	1988	15+	3787385	1636497	2150888	65.9	55.6	76.6
Côte d'Ivoire	1995[1]	15+	4339000	1859000	2480000	59.9	50.1	70.0
Djibouti								
Djibouti	1995[1]	15+	181000	66000	115000	53.8	39.7	67.3
Egypt	1986	15+	14644904	5706276	8938628	54.2	41.6	67.2
Egypte	1995[1]	15+	18954000	7205000	11749000	48.6	36.4	61.2
Equatorial Guinea	1983	15+	58847	16288	42559	38.0	22.6	51.5
Guinée équatoriale	1995[1]	15+	49000	11000	37000	21.5	10.4	31.9
Ethiopia	1984	15+	13533624	5840560	7693064	75.7	67.3	83.6
Ethiopie	1995[1]	15+	19052000	8099000	10953000	64.5	54.5	74.7
Gabon								
Gabon	1995[1]	15+	295000	103000	192000	36.8	26.3	46.7
Gambia								
Gambie	1995[1]	15+	403000	152000	251000	61.4	47.2	75.1
Ghana	1990[2]	15+	4839557	1843221	2996236	59.0	45.7	71.9
Ghana	1995[1]	15+	3387000	1134000	2253000	35.5	24.1	46.5
Guinea								
Guinée	1995[1]	15+	2272000	886000	1386000	64.1	50.1	78.1
Guinea–Bissau								
Guinée–Bissau	1995[1]	15+	282000	98000	185000	45.1	32.0	57.5
Kenya	1989	15+	3179856	1025621	2154235	29.1	19.2	38.5
Kenya	1995[1]	15+	3237000	1005000	2232000	21.9	13.7	30.0
Lesotho								
Lesotho	1995[1]	15+	340000	108000	231000	28.7	18.9	37.7
Liberia								
Libéria	1995[1]	15+	1014000	381000	632000	61.7	46.1	77.6
Libyan Arab Jamah.	1984	15+	646181	192106	454075	39.9	23.1	57.7
Jamah. arabe libyenne	1995[1]	15+	702000	189000	513000	23.8	12.1	37.0
Malawi	1987	15+	2214440	706326	1508114	51.5	34.7	66.5
Malawi	1995[1]	15+	2587000	804000	1784000	43.6	28.1	58.2
Mali	1988	6+	...	...	...	81.2	73.6	88.6
Mali	1995[1]	15+	3917000	1668000	2249000	69.0	60.6	76.9
Mauritania	1988	15+	667342	268955	398387	64.9	53.9	75.4
Mauritanie	1995[1]	15+	806000	319000	487000	62.3	50.4	73.7
Mauritius	1990	15+	149383	54748	94635	20.1	14.8	25.3
Maurice	1995[1]	15+	138000	52000	86000	17.1	12.9	21.2
Morocco	1982	15+	8119233	3187079	4932154	69.7	56.3	82.5
Maroc	1995[1]	15+	9730000	3714000	6016000	56.3	43.4	69.0
Mozambique	1980	15+	4557751	1650952	2906799	72.8	56.0	87.8
Mozambique	1995[1]	15+	5298000	1828000	3470000	59.9	42.3	76.7

11
Illiterate population by sex [*cont.*]
Population analphabète selon le sexe [*suite*]

Country or area Pays ou zone	Year Année	Age group Groupe d'âge	Illiterate population Population analphabète			Percentage of illiterates Percentage d'analphabètes		
			Total	M	F	Total	M	F
Niger	1988	15+	3268685	1467030	1801655	89.1	83.1	94.6
Niger	1995[1]	15+	4081000	1825000	2256000	86.4	79.1	93.4
Nigeria								
Nigéria	1995[1]	15+	26075000	9731000	16344000	42.9	32.7	52.7
Réunion								
Réunion	1982	15+	73220	38861	34359	21.4	23.5	19.5
Rwanda								
Rwanda	1995[1]	15+	1695000	635000	1060000	39.5	30.2	48.4
Saint Helena								
Sainte–Hélène	1987	20+	104	65	39	2.7	3.3	2.1
Sao Tome and Principe								
Sao Tomé–et–Principe	1981	15+	22080	6755	15325	42.6	26.8	57.6
Senegal	1988	15+	2652915	1090771	1562144	73.1	63.1	82.1
Sénégal	1995[1]	15+	3084000	1305000	1779000	66.9	57.0	76.8
Sierra Leone								
Sierra Leone	1995[1]	15+	1727000	668000	1059000	68.6	54.6	81.8
South Africa	1980[4]	15+	3711776	1796523	1915253	23.8	22.5	25.2
Afrique du Sud	1995[1]	15+	4731000	2319000	2412000	18.2	18.1	18.3
Sudan	1983	15+	6551501	2605046	3946455	67.6	55.5	79.0
Soudan	1995[1]	15+	8507000	3327000	5180000	53.9	42.3	65.4
Swaziland	1986	15+	116464	48722	67742	32.7	30.1	34.8
Swaziland	1995[1]	15+	114000	50000	64000	23.3	22.0	24.4
Togo	1981	15+	927712	328497	599215	68.6	53.3	81.5
Togo	1995[1]	15+	1085000	363000	722000	48.3	33.0	63.0
Tunisia	1989	15+	2095943	762085	1333858	42.7	30.8	54.8
Tunisie	1995[1]	15+	1930000	621000	1309000	33.3	21.4	45.4
Uganda	1991	15+	3855388	1348282	2507106	43.9	31.8	55.2
Ouganda	1995[1]	15+	4172000	1409000	2762000	38.2	26.3	49.8
United Rep.Tanzania								
Rép. Unie de Tanzanie	1995[1]	15+	5171000	1618000	3553000	32.2	20.6	43.2
Zaire								
Zaïre	1995[1]	15+	5184000	1491000	3783000	22.7	13.4	32.3
Zambia	1980	15+	1308098	476250	831848	46.5	35.3	56.8
Zambie	1995[1]	15+	1082000	346000	736000	21.8	14.4	28.7
Zimbabwe	1982[5]	15+	852120	292790	559330	22.2	15.8	28.1
Zimbabwe	1995[1]	15+	940000	298000	642000	14.9	9.6	20.1
America, North · Amérique du Nord								
Bahamas								
Bahamas	1995[1]	15+	3000	1000	2000	1.8	1.5	2.0
Barbados								
Barbade	1995[1]	15+	5000	2000	3000	2.6	2.0	3.2
Belize								
Belize	1991	14+	31879	16040	15839	29.7	29.7	29.7
British Virgin Islands								
Iles Vierges britanniques	1991[3]	15+	207	135	72	2.2	1.8	1.3
Canada								
Canada	1986	15+	659745	...	...	3.4	...	...
Costa Rica	1984	15+	112946	55431	57515	7.4	7.3	7.4
Costa Rica	1995[1]	15+	115000	59000	56000	5.2	5.3	5.0
Cuba	1981[6]	10+	...	...	...	3.8	3.8	3.8
Cuba	1995[1]	15+	364000	163000	201000	4.3	3.8	4.7
Dominican Republic	1981	15+	1031629	518236	513809	26.0	26.0	26.0
Rép. dominicaine	1995[1]	15+	908000	465000	443000	17.9	18.0	17.8
El Salvador	1980	15+	818100	...	...	32.7	...	...
El Salvador	1995[1]	15+	975000	432000	543000	28.5	26.5	30.2
Guadeloupe								
Guadeloupe	1982	15+	22359	11231	11128	10.0	10.4	9.6
Guatemala								
Guatemala	1995[1]	15+	2627000	1111000	1516000	44.4	37.5	51.4
Haiti	1982	15+	2004791	926751	1078040	65.2	62.7	67.5
Haïti	1995[1]	15+	2360000	1075000	1285000	55.0	52.0	57.8
Honduras	1985	15+	...	...	...	40.5	39.3	41.6
Honduras	1995[1]	15+	869000	435000	434000	27.3	27.4	27.3
Jamaica	1987	15+	278578	173683	104895	18.2	23.1	13.5
Jamaïque	1995[1]	15+	254000	161000	93000	15.0	19.2	10.9

11
Illiterate population by sex [*cont.*]
Population analphabète selon le sexe [*suite*]

Country or area Pays ou zone	Year Année	Age group Groupe d'âge	Illiterate population Population analphabète			Percentage of illiterates Percentage d'analphabètes		
			Total	M	F	Total	M	F
Martinique								
Martinique	1982	15+	16814	8824	7990	7.2	8.0	6.6
Mexico	1990	15+	6161662	2305113	3856549	12.4	9.6	15.0
Mexique	1995[1]	15+	6246000	2416000	3829000	10.4	8.2	12.6
Netherlands Antilles								
Antilles néerlandaises	1981	15+	10236	4497	5739	6.2	5.8	6.6
Nicaragua								
Nicaragua	1995[1]	15+	822000	398000	424000	34.3	35.4	33.4
Panama	1990	15+	168644	80700	87944	11.2	10.6	11.7
Panama	1995[1]	15+	161000	76000	85000	9.2	8.6	9.8
Puerto Rico [7]								
Porto Rico [7]	1980	15+	239095	107372	131723	10.9	10.3	11.5
Saint Kitts and Nevis								
Saint−Kitts−et−Nevis	1980	15+	674	337	337	2.7	2.9	2.5
Trinidad and Tobago	1990	15+	25910	9159	16751	3.1	2.0	4.4
Trinité−et−Tobago	1995[1]	15+	19000	5000	13000	2.1	1.2	3.0
America, South · Amérique du Sud								
Argentina	1991	15+	895483	416466	479017	4.0	3.8	4.1
Argentine	1995[1]	15+	935000	450000	485000	3.8	3.8	3.8
Bolivia	1992	15+	744846	213713	531133	19.9	11.8	27.5
Bolivie	1995[1]	15+	745000	204000	541000	16.9	9.5	24.0
Brazil	1991	15+	19294646	9300503	9994143	20.1	19.9	20.3
Brésil	1995[1]	15+	18331000	9067000	9263000	16.7	16.7	16.8
Chile	1992	15+	537744	247531	290213	5.7	5.4	6.0
Chili	1995[1]	15+	485000	225000	260000	4.8	4.6	5.0
Colombia	1985[8]	12+	2271338	1076907	1194431	11.9	11.6	12.2
Colombie	1995[1]	15+	2046000	1010000	1037000	8.7	8.8	8.6
Ecuador	1990	15+	691422	274731	416691	11.7	9.5	13.8
Equateur	1995[1]	15+	720000	289000	430000	9.9	8.0	11.8
French Guiana								
Guyane française	1982	15+	8372	4321	4051	17.0	16.4	17.7
Guyana								
Guyana	1995[1]	15+	11000	4000	7000	1.9	1.4	2.5
Paraguay	1982	15+	219120	84340	134780	12.5	9.7	15.2
Paraguay	1995[1]	15+	235000	97000	138000	7.9	6.5	9.4
Peru	1993	15+	1784281	487113	1297168	12.8	7.1	18.3
Pérou	1995[1]	15+	1736000	421000	1315000	11.3	5.5	17.0
Suriname	1985[2]	15+	...	...	...	10.0	10.0	10.0
Suriname	1995[1]	15+	19000	7000	13000	7.0	4.9	9.0
Uruguay	1985	15+	108400	57300	51100	5.0	5.6	4.5
Uruguay	1995[1]	15+	65000	36000	29000	2.7	3.1	2.3
Venezuela	1990	15+	1130567	509864	620703	10.0	9.1	10.8
Venezuela	1995[1]	15+	1244000	571000	673000	8.9	8.2	9.7
Asia · Asie								
Afghanistan								
Afghanistan	1995[1]	15+	8169000	3229000	4940000	68.5	52.8	85.0
Armenia								
Arménie	1989	15+	...	...	...	1.2	0.6	1.9
Azerbaijan								
Azerbaïdjan	1989	15+	...	...	...	2.7	1.1	4.1
Bahrain	1991	15+	55300	24196	31104	15.9	11.4	23.0
Bahreïn	1995[1]	15+	57000	25000	31000	14.8	10.9	20.6
Bangladesh	1981	15+	32923083	14501583	18421500	70.8	60.3	82.0
Bangladesh	1995[1]	15+	45082000	19057000	26025000	61.9	50.6	73.9
Bhutan								
Bhoutan	1995[1]	15+	558000	211000	347000	57.8	43.8	71.9
Brunei Darussalam	1991	15+	20809	6887	13922	12.2	7.5	17.5
Brunéi Darussalam	1995[1]	15+	22000	7000	15000	11.8	7.4	16.6
China	1990	15+	181609097	54359731	127249366	22.2	13.0	31.9
Chine	1995[1]	15+	166173000	46651000	119522000	18.5	10.1	27.3
Cyprus [2]	1980	15+	...	...	...	7.0	3.0	13.0
Chypre [2]	1987	15+	...	...	...	6.0	2.0	9.0
Georgia								
Géorgie	1989	15+	...	...	...	1.0	0.5	1.5

11
Illiterate population by sex [*cont.*]
Population analphabète selon le sexe [*suite*]

Country or area Pays ou zone	Year Année	Age group Groupe d'âge	Illiterate population Population analphabète			Percentage of illiterates Percentage d'analphabètes		
			Total	M	F	Total	M	F
Hong Kong								
Hong-Kong	1995[1]	15+	370000	96000	275000	7.8	4.0	11.8
India [9]	1991	7+	328879000	128362000	200517000	47.8	35.9	60.7
Inde [9]	1995[1]	15+	290705000	108017000	182688000	48.0	34.5	62.3
Indonesia	1990	15+	20899440	6553716	14345714	18.4	11.7	24.7
Indonésie	1995[1]	15+	21507000	6783000	14724000	16.2	10.4	22.0
Iran, Islamic Rep. of	1991	15+	10652344	4113811	6538533	34.3	25.6	43.6
Iran, Rép. islamique d'	1994[2]	15+	9788927	3950690	5838237	27.9	21.6	34.2
Iraq	1985[2]	15-45	...	...	...	10.7	9.8	12.5
Iraq	1995[1]	15+	4848000	1715000	3133000	42.0	29.3	55.0
Israel	1983	15+	224080	67020	157140	8.2	5.0	11.3
Israël	1992	15+	183200	50500	132700	5.1	2.9	7.3
Jordan	1991	15+	373610	105950	267660	16.8	9.2	24.9
Jordanie	1995[1]	15+	414000	105000	309000	13.4	6.6	20.6
Kazakstan								
Kazakstan	1989	15+	276835	49301	227534	2.5	0.9	3.9
Korea, Republic of	1985[2]	15+	...	...	...	3.0	...	...
Corée, République de	1995[1]	15+	697000	124000	573000	2.0	0.7	3.3
Kuwait	1985	15+	273513	141082	132431	25.5	21.8	31.2
Kuwëit	1995[1]	15+	200000	83000	117000	21.4	17.8	25.1
Kyrgyzstan								
Kirghizistan	1989	15+	...	...	...	3.0	1.4	4.5
Lao People's Dem. Rep.	1985[2]	15-45	...	...	...	16.1	8.0	24.2
Rép. dém. pop.lao	1995[1]	15+	1170000	402000	768000	43.4	30.6	55.6
Lebanon								
Liban	1995[1]	15+	151000	50000	101000	7.6	5.3	9.7
Malaysia	1980	15+	2399790	791000	1608790	30.4	20.4	40.3
Malaisie	1995[1]	15+	2057000	682000	1374000	16.5	10.9	21.9
Maldives	1985	15+	8568	4565	4003	8.7	8.8	8.5
Maldives	1995[1]	15+	9000	5000	5000	6.8	6.7	7.0
Mongolia								
Mongolie	1988	15+	256000	85000	170000	17.1	11.4	22.8
Myanmar	1983	15+	4492769	1460457	3032312	21.4	14.2	28.3
Myanmar	1995[1]	15+	4913000	1617000	3296000	16.9	11.3	22.3
Nepal	1991	6+	9073370	3402273	5671097	59.9	45.2	74.4
Népal	1995[1]	15+	9149000	3762000	5387000	72.5	59.1	86.0
Pakistan [10]	1981	15+	34713824	16051771	18662053	74.3	64.6	85.2
Pakistan [10]	1995[1]	15+	48693000	20433000	28260000	62.2	50.0	75.6
Philippines	1990	15+	2349731	1095697	1254034	6.4	6.0	6.8
Philippines	1995[1]	15+	2234000	1047000	1187000	5.4	5.0	5.7
Qatar	1986	15+	64891	45253	19638	24.3	23.2	27.5
Qatar	1995[1]	15+	82000	60000	22000	20.6	20.8	20.1
Saudi Arabia	1982	15+	...	...	...	48.9	28.9	69.2
Arabie Saoudite	1995[1]	15+	3871000	1740000	2131000	37.2	28.5	49.8
Singapore	1990	15+	226677	51307	175370	10.9	4.9	17.0
Singapour	1995[1]	15+	196000	46000	150000	8.9	4.1	13.7
Sri Lanka	1981	15+	1271984	424424	847560	13.2	8.7	18.0
Sri Lanka	1995[1]	15+	1241000	413000	829000	9.8	6.6	12.8
Syrian Arab Republic	1981[11]	15+	1982265	601390	1380875	44.4	26.4	63.0
Rép. arabe syrienne	1995[1]	15+	2259000	556000	1703000	29.2	14.3	44.2
Tajikistan								
Tadjikistan	1989	15+	66973	17189	49784	2.3	1.2	3.4
Thailand	1990	15+	2572127	833682	1738445	6.7	4.4	8.8
Thaïlande	1995[1]	15+	2613000	829000	1784000	6.2	4.0	8.4
Turkey	1990	15+	7615973	1870245	5745728	20.8	10.1	31.5
Turquie	1995[1]	15+	7231000	1737000	5495000	17.7	8.3	27.6
Turkmenistan								
Turkménistan	1989	15+	...	...	...	2.3	1.2	3.4
United Arab Emirates	1985	15+	269983	185397	84586	28.8	27.7	31.3
Emirats arabes unis	1995[1]	15+	272000	192000	80000	20.8	21.1	20.2
Uzbekistan								
Ouzbékistan	1989	15+	...	...	...	2.8	1.5	4.0
Viet Nam								
Viet Nam	1995[1]	15+	2916000	785000	2131000	6.3	3.5	8.8

11
Illiterate population by sex [cont.]
Population analphabète selon le sexe [suite]

Country or area Pays ou zone	Year Année	Age group Groupe d'âge	Illiterate population Population analphabète			Percentage of illiterates Percentage d'analphabètes		
			Total	M	F	Total	M	F
Europe · Europe								
Belarus								
Bélarus	1989	15+	165406	21917	143489	2.1	0.6	3.4
Bulgaria								
Bulgarie	1992	15+	147389	44123	103266	2.1	1.3	2.9
Croatia								
Croatie	1991	15+	124882	22507	102375	3.3	1.2	5.2
Estonia								
Estonie	1989	15+	3329	687	2642	0.3	0.1	0.4
Greece	1981	15+	701056	140544	560512	9.5	3.9	14.7
Grèce	1991	15+	389067	90049	299018	4.8	2.3	7.0
Hungary								
Hongrie	1980	15+	95542	27756	67786	1.1	0.7	1.5
Italy								
Italie	1981	15+	1572556	539781	1032775	3.5	2.5	4.5
Latvia								
Lettonie	1989	15+	11476	2327	9149	0.5	0.2	0.8
Liechtenstein								
Liechtenstein	1981	10+	68	33	35	*0.3	*0.3	*0.3
Lithuania								
Lituanie	1989	15+	44308	10436	33872	1.6	0.8	2.2
Malta								
Malte	1985	20+	33740	16802	16938	14.3	14.8	13.9
Portugal								
Portugal	1981	15+	1506206	524461	981745	20.6	15.2	25.4
Republic of Moldova								
République de Moldova	1989	15+	113193	20078	93115	3.6	1.4	5.6
Romania								
Roumanie	1992	15+	577376	125372	452004	3.3	1.5	5.0
Russian Federation								
Fédération de Russie	1989	15+	2274572	279490	1995082	2.0	0.5	3.2
Spain	1981	15+	1971695	541480	1430215	7.1	4.0	9.9
Espagne	1986	15+	1260789	360483	900306	4.2	2.5	5.8
Ukraine								
Ukraine	1989	15+	...	...	...	1.6	0.5	2.6
Yugoslavia								
Yougoslavie	1991	15+	463291	79258	384033	6.7	2.4	10.8
Yugoslavia, SFR †								
Yougoslavie, Rfs †	1981	15+	1764042	370558	1393484	10.4	4.5	16.1
Oceania · Océanie								
American Samoa [12]								
Samoa américaines [12]	1980	15+	507	240	267	2.7	2.5	2.8
Fiji	1986	15+	56203	21633	34570	12.8	9.8	15.8
Fidji	1995[1]	15+	43000	16000	27000	8.4	6.2	10.7
Guam								
Guam	1990	15+	1004	511	493	1.0	1.0	1.0
Palau [12] [13]								
Palaos [12] [13]	1980	15+	5798	2454	3344	8.1	6.7	9.5
Papua New Guinea								
Papouasie–Nvl–Guinée	1995[1]	15+	724000	257000	467000	27.8	19.0	37.3
former USSR · ancienne URSS								
former USSR †								
ancienne URSS †	1989	15+	4282023	644964	3637059	2.0	0.7	3.2

Source:
United Nations Educational, Scientific and Cultural Organization
(Paris).

Source:
Organisation des Nations Unies pour l'éducation, la science
et la culture (Paris).

† For detailed description of data pertaining to former
Czechoslovakia, Germany, SFR Yugoslavia and former USSR,
see Annex I — Country or area nomenclature, regional and other
groupings.

† Pour les descriptions en détails des données relatives à l'ancienne
Tchécoslovaquie, l'Allemagne, la Rfs Yougoslavie et l'ancienne USSR,
voir l'Annexe I — Nomenclature des pays ou zones, groupements
régionaux et autres groupements.

11
Illiterate population by sex [*cont.*]
Population analphabète selon le sexe [*suite*]

1 The latest estimates of adult illiteracy as assessed by the UNESCO Division of Statistics in 1994.	1 Les estimations sur l'analphabétisme des adultes élaborées en 1994 par la Division des Statistiques de l'UNESCO.
2 National estimates.	2 Estimations nationales.
3 Illiterates are defined as persons with less than five years of schooling.	3 Les analphabètes sont définis comme toute personnes ayant suivi moins de cinq années d'études.
4 Not including Bothuthatswana, Transkei and Veda.	4 Non compris le Bothuthatswana, le Transkei and Veda.
5 Based on a 10% sample of census returns.	5 D'après un échantillon portant sur 10% des bulletins de recensement.
6 Data do not include functionally and physically handicapped.	6 Les données ne comprennent pas les handicapés physiques et fonctionnels.
7 De jure population but not including armed forces stationed in the area.	7 Population de droit mais non compris les militaires en garnison sur le territoire.
8 Including persons of unknown literacy situation.	8 Y compris les personnes dont le niveau d'alphabétisation est inconnu.
9 Including data for Jammu and Kashmir, the final status of which has not yet been determined.	9 Y compris les données pour Jammu et Cachemire dont le statut final n'a pas encore été déterminé.
10 Not including Jammu, Kashmir, the final status of which has not yet been determined, and Junagardh, Manavadar, Gilgit and Baltistan and federally adminstered tribal areas.	10 Non compris le Jammu, le Cachemire dont le statut final n'a pas encore été déterminé, ainsi que le Junagardh, le Manavadar, le Gilgit, le Baltistan et les zones tribales administrées fédérativement.
11 National population only.	11 Population nationale seulement.
12 De jure population but including armed forces stationed in the area.	12 Population de droit mais y compris les militaires en garnison sur le territoire.
13 Including data for Federated States of Micronesia, Marshall Is. and Northern Mariana Is.	13 Y compris les données pour les Etats fédérés de Micronésie, les îles Marshall, et les îles Mariannes du Nord.

Technical notes, tables 9-11

Detailed data on education accompanied by explanatory notes can be found in the UNESCO *Statistical Yearbook*. [29] Brief notes pertaining to major items of statistical information on education shown in the present edition of the United Nations *Statistical Yearbook* are given below.

The tables included in this chapter cover basic data on education at the first, second and third levels. Definitions for the different levels and types of education given below are based on the "Revised recommendations concerning the international standardization of educational statistics" adopted by the General Conference of UNESCO at its twentieth session (1978). [50]

Table 9: Data on education at the first level refer to education whose main function is to provide basic instruction in the tools of learning (for example at elementary and primary schools). Its length may vary from 4 to 9 years, depending on the organization of the school system in each country. Unless otherwise stated, data cover both public and private schools. Figures on teachers refer to both full-time and part-time but exclude classes organized for adults or for handicapped children.

Data on education at the second level refer to education which is based upon at least four years of previous instruction at first level and provides general or specialized instruction, or both (for example at middle and secondary schools, high schools, teachers' training schools at this level, schools of a vocational or technical nature). Unless otherwise stated data cover both public and private schools. In most cases data include part-time teachers.

Data on education at the third level refer to education which requires as a minimum condition of admission the successful completion of education at the second level or proof of equivalent knowledge or experience. It can be given in different types of institutions such as universities, teacher-training institutes and technical institutes. The figures include, as a rule, both full-time and part-time teachers and students. Correspondence courses are not normally included. Figures on teachers include auxiliary teachers (assistants, demonstrators and the like) but exclude staff with no teaching duties (such as administrators and laboratory technicians).

Table 10: Data on total expenditure refer to public expenditure on public education plus subsidies for private education. Total expenditures cover both current and capital expenditure.

Current expenditures include expenditures on administration, emoluments of teachers and supporting teaching staff, school books and other teaching materials, scholarships, welfare services and maintenance of school buildings.

Capital expenditures include outlays on purchases of land, building construction expenditures and so forth. This item also includes loan transactions.

Notes techniques, tableaux 9-11

On trouvera des données détaillées sur l'éducation accompagnées de notes explicatives dans l'*Annuaire statistique* de l'UNESCO [29]. Des notes sommaires concernant les principaux éléments d'information statistique sur l'éducation figurant dans la présente édition de l'*Annuaire statistique* des Nations Unies sont présentées ci-dessous.

Les tableaux de ce chapitre contiennent des données de base sur l'enseignement aux premier, second et troisième degrés. Les définitions des différents niveaux et types d'enseignement données ci-dessous sont fondées sur les "recommandations révisées concernant la normalisation internationale des statistiques de l'éducation" adoptées par la Conférence générale de l'UNESCO à sa vingtième session (1978) [50].

Tableau 9 : Les données relatives à l'enseignement du premier degré portent sur l'enseignement dont la fonction principale est d'offrir les premiers éléments de l'instruction (par exemple, dans les écoles élémentaires ou primaires). Sa durée peut varier de quatre à neuf ans, selon l'organisation du système scolaire de chaque pays. Sauf indication contraire, les données portent à la fois sur les établissements d'enseignement publics et privés. Les chiffres relatifs aux enseignants désignent à la fois ceux qui enseignent à plein temps et à temps partiel mais ne comprennent pas les classes organisées à l'intention des adultes ou des enfants handicapés.

Les données relatives à l'enseignement secondaire se rapportent à un enseignement fondé sur au moins quatre années d'enseignement préalable au niveau primaire et donnant une formation générale ou spécialisée, ou les deux (par exemple, dans les écoles moyennes et secondaires, les lycées, les écoles normales de ce niveau, les écoles professionnelles ou techniques).

Les données relatives à l'enseignement du troisième degré se rapportent à un enseignement qui exige comme condition minimum d'admission l'achèvement avec succès d'un enseignement secondaire complet ou la preuve de connaissances ou d'une expérience équivalentes. Il peut être dispensé dans différents types d'établissement tels que les universités, les instituts de formation pédagogique et les instituts techniques. En règle générale, les chiffres portent à la fois sur les enseignants et les étudiants à plein temps et à temps partiel. Normalement, les cours par correspondance ne sont pas compris. Les données relatives aux enseignants englobent les professeurs auxiliaires (assistants, maîtres de travaux pratiques, etc.), mais pas le personnel n'exerçant pas de fonctions d'enseignement (tel que les administrateurs et les techniciens de laboratoire).

Tableau 10 : Les données relatives aux dépenses totales se rapportent aux dépenses publiques consacrées à l'enseignement public et aux subventions à l'enseignement privé. Les totaux englobent à la fois les dépenses ordinaires et les dépenses d'équipement.

Data include, unless otherwise indicated, educational expenditure at every level of administration. In general, the data do not include development assistance expenditures on education. Data on gross national product (GNP) used to derive the ratio of total public expenditure on education to GNP are World Bank estimates. For certain countries with centrally planned economies, the concept of material product rather than GNP was employed.

Table 11: Except where otherwise stated, data refer to population 15 years of age and over.

Ability to both read and write a simple sentence on everyday life is used as the criterion of literacy; hence semi-literates (persons who can read but not write) are included with illiterates. Persons for whom literacy is not known are excluded from calculations; consequently the percentage of illiteracy for a given country is based on the number of reported illiterates, divided by the total number of reported literates and illiterates. The data are based on population censuses or surveys.

Les dépenses ordinaires comprennent les dépenses d'administration, les émoluments du personnel enseignant et auxiliaire, les manuels scolaires et autres matériels didactiques, les bourses d'études, les services sociaux et l'entretien des bâtiments scolaires.

Les dépenses d'équipement comprennent les dépenses consacrées à l'achat de terrains, à la construction de bâtiments, etc. Les transactions de prêt sont également incluses dans cette rubrique.

Sauf indication contraire, les données comprennent les dépenses effectuées à tous les niveaux administratifs. En règle générale, elles ne comprennent pas les dépenses d'enseignement financées au titre de l'aide au développement. Les données relatives au produit national brut (PNB), utilisées pour déterminer le ratio du volume total de dépenses publiques consacrées à l'éducation au PNB, sont des estimations de la Banque mondiale. Pour certains pays à économie planifiée, on a utilisé la notion de produit matériel à la place du PNB.

Tableau 11 : Sauf indication contraire, les données se réfèrent à la population âgée de 15 ans et plus.

On utilise l'aptitude à lire et à écrire une phrase simple sur la vie quotidienne comme critère d'alphabétisme; par conséquent, les semi-alphabètes (c'est-à-dire les personnes qui savent lire, mais non écrire) sont assimiliés aux analphabètes. Les personnes dont on ne sait pas si elles savent lire ou écrire sont exclues de ces calculs; par conséquent, le pourcentage d'analphabétisme d'un pays donné est fondé sur le nombre d'analphabètes connus divisé par le total des alphabètes et analphabètes connus. Ces données sont fondées sur les recensements ou enquêtes de population.

12
Selected indicators of life expectancy, child-bearing and mortality
Choix d'indicateurs de l'espérance de vie, de la maternité et de la mortalité

Country or area Pays or zone	Year Année	Life expectancy at birth (years) Espérance de vie à la naissance (en années) M	F	Infant mortality per 100,000 live births Mortalité infantile pour 100 000 naissances vivantes	Total fertility rate Taux de fécondité	Child mortality rate Taux de mortalité juvénile Year Année	M	F	Maternal mortality per 100,000 live births Mort. lié à la maternité pour 100 000 naissances vivantes Ratio (1990) Taux (1990)
Africa · Afrique									
Algeria	1980–85	60.0	62.0	88	6.4				
Algérie	1990–95	66.0	68.3	55	3.9				160
Angola	1980–85	40.4	43.6	149	7.0				
Angola	1990–95	44.9	48.1	124	7.2	...	...	...	1500
Benin	1980–85	42.3	45.7	100	7.1				
Bénin	1990–95	45.9	49.3	86	7.1	...	...	...	990
Botswana	1980–85	57.5	61.2	64	5.8				
Botswana	1990–95	63.0	66.7	43	4.9	...	...	...	250
Burkina Faso	1980–85	43.5	46.8	149	6.5				
Burkina Faso	1990–95	45.8	49	130	6.5	...	...	...	930
Burundi	1980–85	46.2	49.6	117	6.8				
Burundi	1990–95	48.4	51.9	102	6.8	...	...	...	1300
Cameroon	1980–85	49.5	52.5	88	6.4				
Cameroun	1990–95	54.5	57.5	63	5.7	...	...	...	550
Cape Verde	1980–85	59.5	61.5	66	6.3				
Cap–Vert	1990–95	63.5	65.5	50	4.3	1990	3.4	3.4	...
Central African Rep.	1980–85	44.1	49.3	114	5.7				
Rép. centrafricaine	1990–95	46.9	51.9	102	5.7	1988	14.9	12.8	700
Chad	1980–85	41.4	44.6	143	5.9				
Tchad	1990–95	45.9	49.1	122	5.9	...	...	...	1500
Comoros	1980–85	51.5	52.5	109	7.1				
Comores	1990–95	55.5	56.5	89	7.1	...	...	...	950
Congo	1980–85	48.0	53.6	87	6.3				
Congo	1990–95	48.9	53.8	84	6.3	...	...	...	890
Côte d'Ivoire	1980–85	48.8	52.3	105	7.4				
Côte d'Ivoire	1990–95	49.7	52.4	92	7.4	...	...	...	810
Djibouti	1980–85	43.4	46.6	132	6.6				
Djibouti	1990–95	46.7	50	115	5.8	...	...	...	570
Egypt	1980–85	55.3	57.8	115	5.1				
Egypte	1990–95	62.4	64.8	67	3.9	1991	10.4[1]	11.1[1]	170
Equatorial Guinea	1980–85	42.4	45.6	137	5.8				
Guinée équatoriale	1990–95	46.4	49.6	117	5.9	...	...	...	820
Eritrea	1980–85	42.0	45.1	140	6.1				
Erythrée	1990–95	48.9	52.1	105	5.8	...	...	...	1400
Ethiopia	1980–85	38.4	41.6	161	6.9				
Ethiopie	1990–95	45.9	49.1	119	7.0	...	...	...	1400
Gabon	1980–85	47.4	50.7	112	4.5				
Gabon	1990–95	51.9	55.2	94	5.3	...	...	...	500
Gambia	1980–85	39.4	42.6	154	6.5				
Gambie	1990–95	43.4	46.6	132	5.6	...	...	...	1100
Ghana	1980–85	50.3	53.8	98	6.5				
Ghana	1990–95	54.2	57.8	81	6.0	...	...	...	740
Guinea	1980–85	40.0	41	157	7.0				
Guinée	1990–95	44.0	45	134	7.0				1600
Guinea–Bissau	1980–85	38.0	41.1	163	5.8				
Guinée–Bissau	1990–95	41.9	45.1	140	5.8	...	...	...	910
Kenya	1980–85	53.9	58.2	81	7.5				
Kenya	1990–95	54.2	57.3	69	6.3	...	...	...	650
Lesotho	1980–85	53.0	58	100	5.7				
Lesotho	1990–95	58.0	63	79	5.2	...	...	...	610
Liberia	1980–85	50.0	53	153	6.8				
Libéria	1990–95	54.0	57	126	6.8	...	...	...	560
Libyan Arab Jamah.	1980–85	56.6	60	97	7.2				
Jamah. arabe libyenne	1990–95	61.6	65	68	6.4	...	...	...	220
Madagascar	1980–85	50.0	53	130	6.6				
Madagascar	1990–95	55.0	58	93	6.1	...	...	...	490
Malawi	1980–85	44.3	45.7	163	7.6				
Malawi	1990–95	45.0	46.2	143	7.2	...	...	...	560

12
Selected indicators of life expectancy, child–bearing and mortality [*cont.*]
Choix d'indicateurs de l'espérance de vie, de la maternité et de la mortalité [*suite*]

Country or area Pays or zone	Year Année	Life expectancy at birth (years) Espérance de vie à la naissance (en années) M	F	Infant mortality per 100,000 live births Mortalité infantile pour 100 000 naissances vivantes	Total fertility rate Taux de fécondité	Child mortality rate Taux de mortalité juvénile Year Année	M	F	Maternal mortality per 100,000 live births Mort. lié à la maternité pour 100 000 naissances vivantes Ratio (1990) Taux (1990)
Mali	1980–85	40.4	43.6	180	7.1				
Mali	1990–95	44.4	47.6	159	7.1	1987[2]	41.5[1]	35.7[1]	1200
Mauritania	1980–85	45.9	49.1	117	6.1				
Mauritanie	1990–95	49.9	53.1	101	5.4	...	...	...	930
Mauritius	1980–85	64.0	69.5	28	2.5				
Maurice	1990–95	66.9	73.8	18	2.4	1993[3]	0.6[4]	0.7[4]	120
Morocco	1980–85	56.6	60.0	97	5.1				
Maroc	1990–95	61.6	65.0	68	3.8	...	...	...	610
Mozambique	1980–85	42.9	46.2	155	6.5				
Mozambique	1990–95	44.9	48.0	148	6.5	...	...	...	1500
Namibia	1980–85	52.5	55.0	84	5.8				
Namibie	1990–95	57.5	60.0	60	5.3	...	...	...	370
Niger	1980–85	40.9	44.1	146	8.1				
Niger	1990–95	44.9	48.1	124	7.4	...	...	...	1200
Nigeria	1980–85	44.9	48.1	99	6.5				
Nigéria	1990–95	48.8	52.0	84	6.5	...	...	...	1000
Réunion	1980–85	65.4	74.5	14	2.9				
Réunion	1990–95	69.4	77.7	8	2.3	1987[5]	0.6[4]	0.6[4]	...
Rwanda	1980–85	44.8	48.2	124	8.1				
Rwanda	1990–95	45.8	48.9	110	6.6	...	...	...	1300
Senegal	1980–85	44.3	46.3	87	6.7				
Sénégal	1990–95	48.3	50.3	68	6.1	...	...	...	1200
Sierra Leone	1980–85	34.0	37.0	189	6.5				
Sierra Leone	1990–95	37.5	40.6	166	6.5	...	...	...	1800
Somalia	1980–85	41.4	44.6	143	7.0				
Somalie	1990–95	45.4	48.6	122	7.0	...	...	...	1600
South Africa	1980–85	55.0	61.0	63	4.8				
Afrique du Sud	1990–95	60.0	66.0	53	4.1	...	...	...	230
Sudan	1980–85	47.8	50.6	92	6.4				
Soudan	1990–95	51.6	54.4	78	5.7	...	...	...	660
Swaziland	1980–85	50.2	54.8	94	6.0				
Swaziland	1990–95	55.2	59.8	75	4.9	...	...	...	560
Togo	1980–85	48.8	52.2	105	6.6				
Togo	1990–95	53.2	56.8	85	6.6	...	...	...	640
Tunisia	1980–85	62.6	63.6	71	4.9				
Tunisie	1990–95	66.9	68.7	43	3.2	1989	7.0[1]	5.9[1]	170
Uganda	1980–85	45.9	49.2	116	7.0				
Ouganda	1990–95	43.6	46.2	115	7.3	...	...	...	1200
United Rep.Tanzania	1980–85	49.3	52.8	98	6.7				
Rép. Unie de Tanzanie	1990–95	50.5	53.6	85	5.9	...	...	...	770
Zaire	1980–85	48.2	51.7	107	6.7				
Zaïre	1990–95	50.4	53.7	93	6.7	...	...	...	870
Zambia	1980–85	50.3	52.6	88	6.9				
Zambie	1990–95	48.0	49.7	104	6.0	...	...	...	940
Zimbabwe	1980–85	54.0	57.8	76	6.2				
Zimbabwe	1990–95	52.4	55.1	67	5.0	...	...	...	570
America, North · Amérique du Nord									
Bahamas	1980–85	65.7	73.6	28	2.8				
Bahamas	1990–95	68.7	77.9	23	2.0	1992	0.5[4]	0.9[4]	100
Barbados	1980–85	70.5	75.5	17	1.9				
Barbade	1990–95	72.9	77.9	9	1.8	1988[3]	0.5[4]	0.5[4]	43
Belize	1980–85	70.4	72.6	39	5.4				
Belize	1990–95	72.4	75.0	33	4.2	...	...	...	...
Canada	1980–85	72.4	79.6	9	1.7				
Canada	1990–95	74.2	80.7	7	1.9	1990	0.4	0.3	6
Costa Rica	1980–85	71.6	76.1	19	3.5				
Costa Rica	1990–95	74.0	78.6	14	3.1	...	...	...	55
Cuba	1980–85	72.3	75.7	17	1.8				
Cuba	1990–95	73.5	77.3	12	1.8	1992	0.7	0.5	95
Dominican Republic	1980–85	63.7	67.6	71	3.9				
Rép. dominicaine	1990–95	67.6	71.7	42	3.1				110

12
Selected indicators of life expectancy, child-bearing and mortality [*cont.*]
Choix d'indicateurs de l'espérance de vie, de la maternité et de la mortalité [*suite*]

Country or area Pays or zone	Year Année	Life expectancy at birth (years) Espérance de vie à la naissance (en années)		Infant mortality per 100,000 live births Mortalité infantile pour 100 000 naissances vivantes	Total fertility rate Taux de fécondité	Child mortality rate Taux de mortalité juvénile Year Année			Maternal mortality per 100,000 live births Mort. lié à la maternité pour 100 000 naissances vivantes Ratio (1990) Taux (1990)
		M	F				M	F	
El Salvador	1980–85	50.7	63.9	77	5.0				
El Salvador	1990–95	63.9	68.8	46	4.0	1986	7.1[1]	6.2[1]	300
Guadeloupe	1980–85	68.9	76.2	15	2.6				
Guadeloupe	1990–95	71.1	78.0	12	2.3	1985[5]	4.8[1]	4.2[1]	...
Guatemala	1980–85	56.8	61.3	70	6.1				
Guatemala	1990–95	62.4	67.3	48	5.4	1985	22.2[1]	20.1[1]	200
Haiti	1980–85	51.2	54.4	108	5.2				
Haïti	1990–95	54.9	58.3	86	4.8	...	...	...	1000
Honduras	1980–85	59.4	63.8	65	6.0				
Honduras	1990–95	65.4	70.1	43	4.9	...	...	...	220
Jamaica	1980–85	69.2	73.6	18	3.6				
Jamaïque	1990–95	71.4	75.8	14	2.4	...	...	...	120
Martinique	1980–85	71.0	78.0	14	2.1				
Martinique	1990–95	72.9	79.4	8	2.0	1990[5]	2.1[14]	2.5[1]	...
Mexico	1980–85	64.6	70.7	49	4.3				
Mexique	1990–95	67.8	73.9	36	3.2	1990	2.5	2.3	110
Netherlands Antilles	1980–85	68.6	73.6	25	2.3				
Antilles néerlandaises	1990–95	70.6	75.6	19	2.1	...	...	...	...
Nicaragua	1980–85	55.8	63.0	86	6.0				
Nicaragua	1990–95	64.8	68.5	52	5.0	...	...	...	160
Panama	1980–85	68.6	73.1	30	3.5				
Panama	1990–95	70.9	75.0	25	2.9	1991	4.9[1]	4.4[1]	55
Puerto Rico	1980–85	70.5	77.5	17	2.5				
Porto Rico	1990–95	71.4	79.3	11	2.2	1992	0.5	0.4	...
Trinidad and Tobago	1980–85	66.2	71.2	31	3.2				
Trinité–et–Tobago	1990–95	69.3	74.0	18	2.4	1990	0.9	0.7	90
United States	1980–85	70.9	78.3	11	1.8				
Etats–Unis	1990–95	72.5	79.3	9	2.1	1991	0.5	0.4	12
United States Virgin Islands	...	...	...	...	...				
Iles Vierges américaines	...	...	...	...	...	1990	1.1[4]	–	...
America, South · Amérique du Sud									
Argentina	1980–85	66.8	73.7	32	3.2				
Argentine	1990–95	68.6	75.7	24	2.8	1993	5.6[1]	4.5[1]	100
Bolivia	1980–85	51.9	55.6	109	5.3				
Bolivie	1990–95	57.7	61.0	75	4.8	...	...	...	650
Brazil	1980–85	61.1	65.7	71	3.7				
Brésil	1990–95	64.0	68.7	58	2.9	1990[6]	6.7[1]	5.3[1]	220
Chile	1980–85	67.4	74.2	24	2.7				
Chili	1990–95	70.4	77.4	16	2.5	1992	0.8	0.6	65
Colombia	1980–85	64.6	69.9	41	3.5				
Colombie	1990–95	66.4	72.3	37	2.7	1991[37]	4.9[1]	3.9[1]	100
Ecuador	1980–85	62.5	66.6	68	4.7				
Equateur	1990–95	66.4	71.4	50	3.5	1993[8]	2.7	2.3	150
Guyana	1980–85	58.4	64.2	63	3.3				
Guyana	1990–95	62.4	68.0	48	2.6	...	...	...	...
Paraguay	1980–85	65.5	69.4	46	4.8				
Paraguay	1990–95	68.1	71.9	38	4.3	1985	5.4[1]	4.8[1]	160
Peru	1980–85	58.4	62.1	82	4.7				
Pérou	1990–95	64.1	67.9	64	3.4	1985[36]	10.8[1]	9.9[1]	280
Suriname	1980–85	64.8	69.7	39	3.4				
Suriname	1990–95	67.8	72.8	28	2.7	...	...	...	...
Uruguay	1980–85	67.8	74.3	33	2.6				
Uruguay	1990–95	69.3	75.7	20	2.3	1990	5.6[1]	4.5[1]	85
Venezuela	1980–85	65.9	71.8	34	4.0				
Venezuela	1990–95	68.9	74.7	23	3.3	1990[6]	7.0[1]	5.7[1]	120
Asia · Asie									
Afghanistan	1980–85	40.0	41.0	183	6.9				
Afghanistan	1990–95	43.0	44.0	163	6.9	...	...	...	1700
Armenia	1980–85	69.3	75.4	22	2.4				
Arménie	1990–95	69.5	75.5	21	2.6	1992[9]	1.3	1.2	50

12
Selected indicators of life expectancy, child–bearing and mortality [*cont.*]
Choix d'indicateurs de l'espérance de vie, de la maternité et de la mortalité [*suite*]

Country or area / Pays or zone	Year / Année	Life expectancy at birth (years) Espérance de vie à la naissance (en années)		Infant mortality per 100,000 live births Mortalité infantile pour 100 000 naissances vivantes	Total fertility rate Taux de fécondité	Child mortality rate Taux de mortalité juvénile Year / Année			Maternal mortality per 100,000 live births Mort. lié à la maternité pour 100 000 naissances vivantes Ratio (1990) Taux (1990)
		M	F				M	F	
Azerbaijan	1980–85	64.3	72.1	33	3.0				
Azerbaïdjan	1990–95	66.5	74.5	28	2.5	...	...	...	22
Bahrain	1980–85	67.1	71.4	22	4.6				
Bahreïn	1990–95	69.8	74.1	18	3.8	1991	3.8[1]	4.3[1]	60
Bangladesh	1980–85	50.1	49.3	128	6.2				
Bangladesh	1990–95	55.6	55.6	108	4.4	1986	43.1[1]	41.1[1]	850
Bhutan	1980–85	43.6	46.6	154	5.9				
Bhoutan	1990–95	49.1	52.4	124	5.9	...	...	...	1600
Brunei Darussalam	1980–85	70.1	73.6	14	3.8				
Brunéi Darussalam	1990–95	72.5	76.3	8	3.1	...	...	...	60
Cambodia	1980–85	45.1	47.9	160	5.1				
Cambodge	1990–95	50.1	52.9	116	5.3	...	...	...	900
China	1980–85	65.5	67.7	52	2.5				
Chine	1990–95	66.7	70.4	44	2.0	...	...	...	95
Cyprus	1980–85	73.0	77.5	16	2.4				
Chypre	1990–95	74.8	79.2	9	2.5	1993[10]	2.2[1]	1.8[1]	5
Korea, Dem. P. R.	1980–85	64.6	71.0	30	2.8				
Corée, R. p. dém. de	1990–95	67.7	73.9	24	2.4	...	...	...	70
East Timor	1980–85	39.2	40.7	183	5.4				
Timor oriental	1990–95	44.1	45.9	149	4.8	...	...	...	...
Georgia	1980–85	66.6	74.4	23	2.3				
Géorgie	1990–95	68.5	76.7	19	2.1	...	...	...	33
Hong Kong	1980–85	72.6	78.3	10	1.8				
Hong–kong	1990–95	75.6	81.8	7	1.2	1993[11]	0.3	0.3	7
India	1980–85	55.5	55.2	106	4.5				
Inde	1990–95	60.3	60.4	82	3.8	...	...	...	570
Indonesia	1980–85	54.5	58.0	90	4.1				
Indonésie	1990–95	61.0	64.5	58	2.9	...	...	...	650
Iran, Islamic Rep. of	1980–85	59.4	63.0	78	6.8				
Iran, Rép. islamique d'	1990–95	67.0	68.0	36	5.0	1986	3.9	1.4	120
Iraq	1980–85	61.5	63.3	78	6.4				
Iraq	1990–95	64.5	67.5	58	5.7	1988	5.7[1]	4.4[1]	310
Israel	1980–85	72.8	76.2	14	3.1				
Israël	1990–95	74.6	78.4	9	2.9	1992[12]	0.4	0.4	7
Japan	1980–85	74.2	79.7	7	1.8				
Japon	1990–95	76.4	82.5	4	1.5	1993[13]	0.5	0.4	18
Jordan	1980–85	61.9	65.5	54	6.8				
Jordanie	1990–95	66.2	69.8	36	5.6	...	...	...	150
Kazakstan	1980–85	61.7	71.9	36	3.0				
Kazakstan	1990–95	65.0	73.9	30	2.5	1991[9]	2.1	1.7	80
Korea, Republic of	1980–85	63.5	71.1	23	2.4				
Corée, République de	1990–95	67.3	74.9	11	1.7	1993[14][15]	0.8	0.7	130
Kuwait	1980–85	69.6	73.7	25	4.9				
Koweït	1990–95	73.3	77.2	18	3.1	1989	0.7	0.6	29
Kyrgyzstan	1980–85	61.3	69.8	44	4.1				
Kirghizistan	1990–95	65.0	72.8	35	3.7	1992[9]	2.9	2.6	110
Lao People's Dem. Rep.	1980–85	44.5	47.5	122	6.7				
Rép. dém. pop. lao	1990–95	49.5	52.5	97	6.7	...	...	...	650
Lebanon	1980–85	63.1	67.0	48	3.8				
Liban	1990–95	66.6	70.5	34	3.1	...	...	...	300
Macau	...	...	...	...	...				
Macao	...	...	...	...	...	1993[16]	0.3[4]	0.2[4]	...
Malaysia	1980–85	66.0	70.0	28	4.2				
Malaisie	1990–95	68.7	73.0	13	3.6	1992	0.8	0.8	80
Maldives	1980–85	58.4	55.8	94	6.8				
Maldives	1990–95	63.4	60.8	60	6.8	1990	3.8	4.3	...
Mongolia	1980–85	57.5	60.0	78	5.3				
Mongolie	1990–95	62.3	65.0	60	3.6	...	...	...	65
Myanmar	1980–85	51.1	54.3	106	4.9				
Myanmar	1990–95	56.0	59.3	84	4.2	...	...	...	580

12
Selected indicators of life expectancy, child-bearing and mortality [*cont.*]
Choix d'indicateurs de l'espérance de vie, de la maternité et de la mortalité [*suite*]

Country or area Pays or zone	Year Année	Life expectancy at birth (years) Espérance de vie à la naissance (en années) M	F	Infant mortality per 100,000 live births Mortalité infantile pour 100 000 naissances vivantes	Total fertility rate Taux de fécondité	Child mortality rate Taux de mortalité juvénile Year Année	M	F	Maternal mortality per 100,000 live births Mort. lié à la maternité pour 100 000 naissances vivantes Ratio (1990) Taux (1990)
Nepal	1980−85	49.0	47.5	122	6.4				
Népal	1990−95	54.0	53.0	99	5.4	...	...	...	1500
Oman	1980−85	61.6	64.6	56	7.2				
Oman	1990−95	67.7	71.8	30	7.2	...	...	...	190
Pakistan	1980−85	55.6	56.9	120	7.0				
Pakistan	1990−95	60.6	62.6	91	6.2	...	...	...	340
Philippines	1980−85	60.2	63.7	60	4.7				
Philippines	1990−95	64.5	68.2	44	3.9	1991[3]	2.8	2.5	280
Qatar	1980−85	65.4	69.8	34	5.5				
Qatar	1990−95	68.8	74.2	20	4.3	...	...	...	...
Saudi Arabia	1980−85	61.4	64.1	58	7.3				
Arabie saoudite	1990−95	68.4	71.4	29	6.4	...	...	...	130
Singapore	1980−85	69.2	74.6	10	1.7				
Singapour	1990−95	72.4	77.4	6	1.7	* 1994[3][17]	1.2[1]	1.1[1]	10
Sri Lanka	1980−85	67.0	71.5	35	3.3				
Sri Lanka	1990−95	69.7	74.2	18	2.5	1989[3]	4.4[1]	3.8[1]	140
Syrian Arab Republic	1980−85	60.8	64.4	59	7.4				
Rép. arabe syrienne	1990−95	65.2	69.2	39	5.9	...	...	...	180
Tajikistan	1980−85	63.3	68.4	62	5.5				
Tadjikistan	1990−95	67.3	73.0	48	4.9	...	...	...	130
Thailand	1980−85	62.6	67.4	44	3.0				
Thaïlande	1990−95	66.3	71.8	37	2.1	1992[3]	2.2[1]	1.7[1]	200
Turkey	1980−85	60.0	64.6	102	4.1				
Turquie	1990−95	64.5	68.6	65	3.4	...	...	...	180
Turkmenistan	1980−85	59.6	66.6	64	4.8				
Turkménistan	1990−95	61.5	68.5	57	4.0	...	...	...	55
Uzbekistan	1980−85	63.1	69.9	50	4.7				
Ouzbékistan	1990−95	66.0	72.2	41	3.9	...	...	...	55
United Arab Emirates	1980−85	67.1	71.4	32	5.2				
Emirats arabes unis	1990−95	72.9	75.3	19	4.2	...	...	...	26
Viet Nam	1980−85	56.7	61.1	63	4.7				
Viet Nam	1990−95	62.9	67.3	42	3.9				160
Yemen	1980−85	45.9	46.4	143	7.6				
Yémen	1990−95	49.9	50.4	119	7.6	...	...	...	1400
Europe · Europe									
Albania	1980−85	68.0	73.0	45	3.4				
Albanie	1990−95	69.2	75.0	30	2.9	...	...	...	65
Andorra	...	...	...	...	...				
Andorre	...	...	...	...	...	1992	3.6[14]	1.3[14]	...
Austria	1980−85	69.6	76.8	12	1.6				
Autriche	1990−95	73.0	79.2	7	1.5	1992	0.4	0.4	10
Belarus	1980−85	65.6	75.2	20	2.1				
Bélarus	1990−95	64.5	75.1	16	1.7	1992[9]	0.9	0.6	37
Belgium	1980−85	70.4	77.2	11	1.6				
Belgique	1990−95	73.0	79.7	6	1.6	...	...	...	10
Bosnia & Herzegovina	1980−85	67.9	73.4	27	2.0				
Bosnie−Herzégovine	1990−95	69.5	75.1	15	1.6	...	...	...	...
Bulgaria	1980−85	68.5	74.3	18	2.0				
Bulgarie	1990−95	67.8	74.9	14	1.5	1992	1.2	0.9	27
Croatia	1980−85	66.4	74.6	18	2.0				
Croatie	1990−95	67.1	75.7	9	1.7	1991	0.4	0.3	...
Czech Republic	1980−85	67.2	74.3	15	2.0				
République tchèque	1990−95	67.8	74.9	9	1.8	1991	0.5	0.4	15
Denmark	1980−85	71.6	77.6	8	1.4				
Danemark	1990−95	72.5	78.2	7	1.7	1992[18]	0.3	0.3	9
Estonia	1980−85	64.8	74.5	20	2.1				
Estonie	1990−95	63.8	74.8	16	1.6	1993[9]	0.8	0.8	41
Finland	1980−85	70.0	77.9	6	1.7				
Finlande	1990−95	71.7	79.6	5	1.9	1990	0.3	0.2[4]	11
France	1980−85	70.8	78.9	9	1.9				
France	1990−95	73.0	80.8	7	1.7	1991[19]	0.4	0.4	15

12
Selected indicators of life expectancy, child-bearing and mortality [cont.]
Choix d'indicateurs de l'espérance de vie, de la maternité et de la mortalité [suite]

Country or area Pays or zone	Year Année	Life expectancy at birth (years) Espérance de vie à la naissance (en années)		Infant mortality per 100,000 live births Mortalité infantile pour 100 000 naissances vivantes	Total fertility rate Taux de fécondité	Child mortality rate Taux de mortalité juvénile			Maternal mortality per 100,000 live births Mort. lié à la maternité pour 100 000 naissances vivantes
		M	F			Year Année	M	F	Ratio (1990) Taux (1990)
Germany	1980–85	70.3	76.8	11	1.5				
Allemagne	1990–95	72.7	79.0	6	1.3	...	...	...	22
Germany, Fed. Rep. of	...	...	...	...	...				
Allemagne, Rep. féd. d'	...	...	...	...	...	1989	0.4	0.3	...
Former German Dem. Rep.	...	...	...	...	...				
Ancienne Rep. dém. allemagne	...	...	...	...	...	1989	0.4	0.4	...
Greece	1980–85	72.8	77.5	15	2.0				
Grèce	1990–95	75.0	80.1	10	1.4	1993	0.3	0.3	10
Hungary	1980–85	65.3	73.0	20	1.8				
Hongrie	1990–95	64.5	73.8	15	1.7	1993	0.6	0.5	30
Iceland	1980–85	73.9	79.8	6	2.3				
Islande	1990–95	75.8	80.8	5	2.2	1993	1.9[14]	0.9[14]	0
Ireland	1980–85	70.4	75.9	9	2.9				
Irlande	1990–95	72.6	78.1	7	2.1	1991[3 20]	0.4	0.3	10
Italy	1980–85	71.4	78.0	13	1.6				
Italie	1990–95	74.2	80.6	8	1.3	1991	0.3	0.3	12
Latvia	1980–85	64.5	74.2	18	2.0				
Lettonie	1990–95	63.3	74.9	14	1.6	1993[9]	1.3	1.0	40
Lithuania	1980–85	66.1	75.7	18	2.0				
Lituanie	1990–95	64.9	76.0	13	1.8	1993[9]	0.8	0.6	36
Luxembourg	1980–85	70.2	77.1	12	1.5				
Luxembourg	1990–95	71.9	79.3	7	1.7	1987	0.6[4]	0.5[4]	0
Malta	1980–85	71.3	75.8	13	2.0				
Malte	1990–95	73.8	78.3	9	2.1	1992	3.0[1]	2.0[14]	0
Netherlands	1980–85	72.8	79.4	8	1.5				
Pays–Bas	1990–95	74.4	80.4	7	1.6	1993	0.4	0.3	12
Norway	1980–85	72.9	79.5	8	1.7				
Norvège	1990–95	73.6	80.3	8	1.9	1992	0.4	0.3	6
Poland	1980–85	67.0	75.0	20	2.3				
Pologne	1990–95	66.7	75.7	15	1.9	1992	0.6	0.5	19
Portugal	1980–85	68.8	75.8	20	2.0				
Portugal	1990–95	71.1	78.0	10	1.6	1993	0.8	0.6	15
Republic of Moldova	1980–85	61.7	68.3	28	2.5				
République de Moldova	1990–95	63.5	71.6	25	2.1	1992[9]	1.6	0.9	60
Romania	1980–85	66.9	72.6	26	2.2				
Roumanie	1990–95	66.6	73.3	23	1.5	1993	1.7	1.3	130
Russian Federation	1980–85	62.1	73.4	26	2.0				
Fédération de Russie	1990–95	61.7	73.6	21	1.5	1993[9]	1.2	1.0	75
Slovakia	1980–85	66.8	74.7	18	2.3				
Slovaquie	1990–95	66.5	75.4	12	1.9	1991	0.6	0.5	...
Slovenia	1980–85	66.9	75.5	14	2.0				
Slovénie	1990–95	67.7	77.6	8	1.5	1991	0.4[4]	0.4[4]	13
Spain	1980–85	72.8	78.9	11	1.9				
Espagne	1990–95	74.6	80.5	7	1.2	1991	0.4	0.4	7
Sweden	1980–85	73.4	79.3	7	1.6				
Suède	1990–95	75.4	81.1	5	2.1	1993	0.3	0.2	7
Switzerland	1980–85	72.9	79.6	8	1.5				
Suisse	1990–95	74.7	81.2	6	1.6	1993	0.3	0.4	6
TFYR Macedonia	1980–85	68.2	72.6	48	2.5				
L'ex–R.y. Macédoine	1990–95	68.8	75.0	27	2.0	1992	0.9	0.9	...
Ukraine	1980–85	64.5	73.8	20	2.0				
Ukraine	1990–95	64.3	74.2	16	1.6	1992[9]	1.1	0.8	50
United Kingdom	1980–85	71.0	77.2	11	1.8				
Royaume–Uni	1990–95	73.6	78.7	7	1.8	1992	0.3	0.3	9
Yugoslavia	1980–85	67.7	72.6	34	2.3				
Yougoslavie	1990–95	69.5	74.5	20	2.0	...	...	...	...
Oceania · Océanie									
Australia	1980–85	71.9	78.7	10	1.9				
Australie	1990–95	74.7	80.6	7	1.9	1993[3]	0.5	0.3	9
Fiji	1980–85	67.0	71.0	31	3.8				
Fidji	1990–95	69.5	73.7	23	3.0	1987[3]	1.1	0.8	90

12
Selected indicators of life expectancy, child-bearing and mortality [cont.]
Choix d'indicateurs de l'espérance de vie, de la maternité et de la mortalité [suite]

Country or area Pays or zone	Year Année	Life expectancy at birth (years) Espérance de vie à la naissance (en années)		Infant mortality per 100,000 live births Mortalité infantile pour 100 000 naissances vivantes	Total fertility rate Taux de fécondité	Child mortality rate Taux de mortalité juvénile			Maternal mortality per 100,000 live births Mort. lié à la maternité pour 100 000 naissances vivantes
		M	F			Year Année	M	F	Ratio (1990) Taux (1990)
French Polynesia	1980–85	64.0	69.0	30	3.8				
Polynésie française	1990–95	67.2	72.8	17	3.2	...	...	...	...
Guam	1980–85	70.8	76.4	11	3.1				
Guam	1990–95	72.8	78.3	8	3.2	...	...	...	...
Marshall Islands	...	...	...						
Iles Marshall	...	...	...	...	...	1989	4.7[14]	3.8[14]	...
New Caledonia	1980–85	67.0	72.0	31	3.1				
Nouvelle–Calédonie	1990–95	69.7	74.7	22	2.7	1989	1.3[4]	1.2[4]	...
New Zealand	1980–85	70.7	76.9	12	2.0				
Nouvelle–Zélande	1990–95	72.5	78.6	9	2.2	1992[3]	0.5	0.4	25
Northern Mariana Islands	...	...	...						
Iles Mariannes du Nord	...	...	...	...	...	1989	0.5[4]	–	...
Papua New Guinea	1980–85	51.2	52.7	72	5.6				
Papouasie–Nvl–Guinée	1990–95	55.2	56.7	68	5.1	...	...	...	930
Samoa	1980–85	62.0	65.0	80	5.7				
Samoa	1990–95	65.9	69.2	64	4.5	...	...	...	35
Solomon Islands	1980–85	65.7	69.6	38	6.4				
Iles Salomon	1990–95	68.4	72.7	27	5.4	...	...	...	...
Vanuatu	1980–85	58.2	61.9	70	5.3				
Vanuatu	1990–95	63.5	67.3	47	4.7	...	...	...	280

Sources:
World Population Prospects, 1994 and Demographic Yearbook, 1994 (United Nations publications); World Health Organization and United Nations Children's Fund.

1   0–4 years old.
2   Based on the results of the population census.
3   Data tabulated by date of registration rather than occurrence.
4   Rates based on 30 or fewer deaths.
5   Excluding live–born infants dying before registration of birth.
6   Excluding Indian jungle population.
7   Based on burial permits.
8   Excluding nomadic Indian tribes.
9   Excluding infants born alive after less than 28 weeks' gestation, of less than 1000 grammes in weight and 35 centimeters in length, who die within seven days of birth.
10   For government controlled areas.
11   Excluding Veitnamese refugees.
12   Including data for East Jerusalem and Israrli residents in certain other territories under occupation by Israeli military forces since June 1967.
13   For Japanese nationals in Japan only; however, rates computed on population including foreigners except foreign military and civilian personnel and their dependants stationed in the area.
14   Excluding alien armed forces, civilian aliens employed by armed forces, and foreign diplomatic personnel and their dependants.
15   Estimates based on the results of the continuous Demographic Sample Survey.
16   Events registered by Health Service only.
17   Excluding transients afloatand non–locally domiciled military and civilian services personnel and their dependants.
18   Excluding Faeroe Islands and Greenland.
19   Including armed forces stationed outside the country.
20   Deaths registered within one year of occurrence.

Sources:
"World Population Prospects, 1994", et l'annuaire démographique, 1994 (publications des Nations Unies); Organisation mondiale de la santé et Fonds des Nations Unies pour l'enfance.

1   De 0 à 4 ans.
2   D'après les résultats du recensement de la population.
3   Données exploitées selon la date de l'enregistrement et non la date de l'événement.
4   Taux basés sur 30 décès ou moins.
5   Non compris les enfants nés vivants, décédés avant l'enregistrement de leur naissance.
6   Non compris les Indiens de la jungle.
7   D'après les permis d'inhumer.
8   Non compris les tribus d'Indiens nomades.
9   Non compris les enfants nés vivants après moins de 28 semaines de gestation, pesant moins de 1000 grammes, mesurant moins de 35 centimètres et décédé dans les sept jours qui ont suivi leur naissance.
10   Pour les zones contrôlées pour le Gouvernement.
11   Non compris les réfugiés du Viet Nam.
12   Y compris les données pour Jérusalem–Est et les résidents israéliens dans certains autres territoires occupés depuis juin 1967 par les forces armées israéliennes.
13   Pour les nationaux japonais seulement; toutefois, les taux sont calculés sur la base d'une population comprenant les étrangers, mais ne comprenant ni les militaires et agents civils étrangers en poste sur le territoire ni les membres de leur famille les accompagnant.
14   Non compris les militaires étrangers, les civils étrangers employés par les forces armées, le personnel diplomatique étranger et les membres de leur famille les accompagnant.
15   Les estimations sont basés sur les résultats d'une enquête démographique pour sondage continue.
16   Evénements enregistrés par le service de santé seulement.
17   Non compris les personnes de passage à bord de navires, les militaires et agents civils domiciliés hors du territoire et les membres de leur famille les accompagnant.
18   Non compris les fles Féroé et le Groenland.
19   Y compris les militaires en garnison hors du pays.
20   Décès enregistrés dans l'année qui suit l'événement.

13

Estimates of cumulative HIV infections, AIDS cases and HIV/AIDS deaths and number of reported AIDS cases

Chiffres estimatifs du nombre cumulé de personnes infectées par le VIH, de cas de SIDA et de décès causés par le VIH ou le SIDA, et nombre de cas déclarés de SIDA

A. Estimated cumulative HIV infections, AIDS cases and HIV/AIDS deaths to mid 1996

Chiffres estimatifs cumulés du nombre de personnes infectées par le VIH, de cas de SIDA et de décès causés par le VIH ou le SIDA jusqu'au milieu de 1996

	Number of cases (million) Nombre de cas (millions)		
	Total	M	F
Cumulative HIV infections **Cumulé de personnes infectées par le VIH**	27.9	...	...
Adults Adultes	25.5	14.9	10.5
Children Enfants	2.4	...	...
Cumulative AIDS cases **Cumulé de cas de SIDA**	7.7	...	...
Adults Adultes	6.1	3.5	2.6
Children Enfants	1.6	...	...
Cumulative HIV/AIDS deaths **Cumulé de décès liés au VIH/SIDA**	5.8	...	...
Adults Adultes	4.5	2.6	1.9
Children Enfants	1.3	...	...

B. Reported and estimated AIDS cases to mid 1996

Cas de SIDA : nombre de cas déclarés, et chiffres estimatifs jusqu'au milieu de 1996

Regions Régions	Cases reported to World Health Organization (cumulative) Cas déclarés à l'Organisation mondiale de la santé (chiffres cumulés)	Estimated cases Chiffres estimatifs
World **Monde**	1 393 649	7 700 000 +
Africa Afrique	499 037	5 929 000
Americas Amériques	690 042	1 001 000
Asia Asie	29 707	539 000
Europe Europe	167 578	231 000
Oceania Océanie	7 285	< 77 000

13 C. Reported AIDS cases • Cas de SIDA déclarés

Country or area Pays ou zone	Total reported to Dec. 1993 Nombre total de cas déclarés jusqu' en déc. 1993	New cases reported for 1994 Nombre de cas nouveaux déclarés pour 1994	New cases reported for 1995 Nombre de cas nouveaux déclarés pour 1995	Cumulative total to Dec. 1995 Nombre total cumulé jusqu'en déc. 1995
Africa · Afrique				
Algeria Algérie	138	79	0	217
Angola Angola	703	157	321	1181
Benin Bénin	742	324	214	1280
Botswana Botswana	1948	968	535	3451
Burkina Faso Burkina Faso	3722	244	0	3966
Burundi Burundi	6880	144	0	7024
Cameroon Cameroun	3958	1417	0	5375
Cape Verde Cap-Vert	82	14	21	117
Central African Rep. Rép. centrafricaine	4240	50	649	4939
Chad Tchad	1597	1268	592	3457
Comoros Comores	10	3	2	15
Congo Congo	6473	1300	0	7773
Côte d'Ivoire Côte d'Ivoire	18670	6566	0	25236
Djibouti Djibouti	453	196	231	880
Egypt Egypte	91	22	16	129
Equatorial Guinea Guinée équatoriale	43	16	98	157
Eritrea Erythrée	669	625	727	2021
Ethiopia Ethiopie	10008	5558	3867	19433
Gabon Gabon	521	204	265	890
Gambia Gambie	295	53	62	410
Ghana Ghana	12656	2330	2578	17564
Guinea Guinée	1005	543	610	2158
Guinea-Bissau Guinée-Bissau	453	254	79	786
Kenya Kenya	49251	6359	6203	63813
Lesotho Lesotho	357	238	341	936
Liberia Libéria	191	0	0	191
Libyan Arab Jamahiriya Jamah. arabe libyenne	12	3	2	17
Madagascar Madagascar	11	7	6	24
Malawi Malawi	31871	4732	5261	41864
Mali Mali	1985	609	454	3048
Mauritania Mauritanie	90	24	16	130
Mauritius Maurice	18	9	0	27

13 C. Reported AIDS cases [cont.] • Cas de SIDA déclarés [suite]

Country or area Pays ou zone	Total reported to Dec. 1993 Nombre total de cas déclarés jusqu' en déc. 1993	New cases reported for 1994 Nombre de cas nouveaux déclarés pour 1994	New cases reported for 1995 Nombre de cas nouveaux déclarés pour 1995	Cumulative total to Dec. 1995 Nombre total cumulé jusqu'en déc. 1995
Morocco Maroc	172	77	57	306
Mozambique Mozambique	826	534	1180	2540
Namibia Namibie	5101	0	0	5101
Niger Niger	1262	467	0	1729
Nigeria Nigéria	961	630	0	1591
Réunion Réunion	65	0	0	65
Rwanda Rwanda	10706	0	0	10706
Sao Tome and Principe Sao Tomé-et-Principe	13	1	4	18
Senegal Sénégal	911	534	128	1573
Seychelles Seychelles	1	9	6	16
Sierra Leone Sierra Leone	111	22	35	168
Somalia Somalie	13	0	0	13
South Africa Afrique du Sud	3862	3870	2805	10337
Sudan Soudan	883	201	257	1341
Swaziland Swaziland	412	120	58	590
Togo Togo	3472	1284	1710	6466
Tunisia Tunisie	166	43	61	270
Uganda Ouganda	41193	4927	2192	48312
United Rep. Tanzania Rép. Unie de Tanzanie	50964	2869	28341	82174
Zaire Zaïre	26161	1398	1875	29434
Zambia Zambie	32308	1692	0	34000
Zimbabwe Zimbabwe	27905	10647	2746	41298
America, North • Amérique du Nord				
Anguilla Anguilla	5	0	0	5
Antigua and Barbuda Antigua-et-Barbuda	34	6	5	45
Aruba Aruba	15	0	6	21
Bahamas Bahamas	1389	322	390	2101
Barbados Barbade	418	119	95	632
Belize Belize	92	18	28	138
Bermuda Bermudes	222	44	49	315
British Virgin Islands Iles Vierges britanniques	7	1	3	11
Canada Canada	10781	1467	987	13235
Cayman Islands Iles Caïmanes	15	3	0	18

13 C. Reported AIDS cases [*cont.*] • Cas de SIDA déclarés [*suite*]

Country or area Pays ou zone	Total reported to Dec. 1993 Nombre total de cas déclarés jusqu' en déc. 1993	New cases reported for 1994 Nombre de cas nouveaux déclarés pour 1994	New cases reported for 1995 Nombre de cas nouveaux déclarés pour 1995	Cumulative total to Dec. 1995 Nombre total cumulé jusqu'en déc. 1995
Costa Rica Costa Rica	586	155	181	922
Cuba Cuba	261	101	78	440
Dominica Dominique	26	5	0	31
Dominican Republic Rép. dominicaine	2446	348	366	3160
El Salvador El Salvador	605	387	380	1372
Grenada Grenade	56	7	13	76
Guadeloupe Guadeloupe	430	110	83	623
Guatemala Guatemala	497	110	104	711
Haiti Haïti	4967	0	0	4967
Honduras Honduras	3416	862	806	5084
Jamaica Jamaïque	669	359	505	1533
Martinique Martinique	260	48	36	344
Mexico Mexique	19281	4048	4310	27639
Montserrat Montserrat	7	0	0	7
Netherlands Antilles Antilles néerlandaises	157	0	76	233
Nicaragua Nicaragua	71	37	9	117
Panama Panama	655	187	203	1045
Saint Kitts and Nevis Saint–Kitts–et–Nevis	40	5	5	50
Saint Lucia Sainte–Lucie	53	13	10	76
St. Vincent and the Grenadines St. Vincent–et–Grenadines	54	8	6	68
Trinidad and Tobago Trinité–et–Tobago	1474	269	340	2083
Turks and Caicos Islands Iles Turques et Caiques	39	0	0	39
United States Etats–Unis	409409	64026	40051	513486
America, South • Amérique du Sud				
Argentina Argentine	4313	2029	1624	7966
Bolivia Bolivie	88	13	8	109
Brazil Brésil	58321	13595	7992	79908
Chile Chili	970	236	223	1429
Colombia Colombie	4453	1324	764	6541
Ecuador Equateur	357	117	69	543
French Guiana Guyane française	373	55	61	489
Guyana Guyana	497	105	96	698
Paraguay Paraguay	143	24	23	190

13 C. Reported AIDS cases [*cont.*] · Cas de SIDA déclarés [*suite*]

Country or area Pays ou zone	Total reported to Dec. 1993 Nombre total de cas déclarés jusqu' en déc. 1993	New cases reported for 1994 Nombre de cas nouveaux déclarés pour 1994	New cases reported for 1995 Nombre de cas nouveaux déclarés pour 1995	Cumulative total to Dec. 1995 Nombre total cumulé jusqu'en déc. 1995
Peru Pérou	2523	718	843	4084
Suriname Suriname	169	20	20	209
Uruguay Uruguay	438	119	127	684
Venezuela Venezuela	3989	518	453	4960
Asia · Asie				
Afghanistan Afghanistan	0	0	0	0
Armenia Arménie				
Azerbaijan Azerbaïdjan	0	1	1	2
Bahrain Bahreïn	15	5	8	28
Bangladesh Bangladesh	1	0	6	7
Bhutan Bhoutan	0	0	0	0
Brunei Darussalam Brunéi Darussalam	2	4	0	6
Cambodia Cambodge	1	9	76	86
China Chine	36	29	52	117
Cyprus Chypre	38	9	3	50
Georgia Géorgie	2	0	0	2
Hong Kong Hong–kong	92	38	45	175
India Inde	494	391	1210	2095
Indonesia Indonésie	51	16	20	87
Iran, Islamic Rep. of Iran, Rép. islamique d'	92	19	7	118
Iraq Iraq	24	12	6	42
Israel Israël	293	31	48	372
Japan Japon	685	204	265	1154
Jordan Jordanie	31	7	2	40
Kazakstan Kazakstan	2	3	0	5
Korea, Dem.People's Rep. Corée, Rép. pop. dém. de	0	0	0	0
Korea, Republic of Corée, République de	16	11	14	41
Kuwait Koweït	10	5	4	19
Kyrgyzstan Kirghizistan	0	0	0	0
Lao People's Dem. Rep. Rép. dém. populaire lao	6	4	4	14
Lebanon Liban	69	14	8	91
Macau Macao	6	2	0	8
Malaysia Malaisie	117	72	142	331

13 C. Reported AIDS cases [*cont.*] • Cas de SIDA déclarés [*suite*]

Country or area Pays ou zone	Total reported to Dec. 1993 Nombre total de cas déclarés jusqu' en déc. 1993	New cases reported for 1994 Nombre de cas nouveaux déclarés pour 1994	New cases reported for 1995 Nombre de cas nouveaux déclarés pour 1995	Cumulative total to Dec. 1995 Nombre total cumulé jusqu'en déc. 1995
Maldives Maldives	0	1	4	5
Mongolia Mongolie	0	0	0	0
Myanmar Myanmar	189	286	618	1093
Nepal Népal	24	8	16	48
Oman Oman	34	14	7	55
Pakistan Pakistan	38	8	9	55
Philippines Philippines	129	56	50	235
Qatar Qatar	69	6	5	80
Saudi Arabia Arabie saoudite	62	38	37	137
Singapore Singapour	75	48	56	179
Sri Lanka Sri Lanka	33	8	17	58
Syrian Arab Republic Rép. arabe syrienne	26	4	6	36
Tajikistan Tadjikistan	0	0	0	0
Thailand Thaïlande	8453	10303	3379	22135
Turkey Turquie	131	33	24	188
Turkmenistan Turkménistan	1	0	0	1
United Arab Emirates Emirats arabes unis	8	0	0	8
Uzbekistan Ouzbékistan	2	0	1	3
Viet Nam Viet Nam	108	109	98	315
Yemen Yémen	8	3	11	22
Europe • Europe				
Albania Albanie				
Austria Autriche	1176	162	177	1515
Belarus Bélarus	10	2	3	15
Belgium Belgique	1631	244	197	2072
Bosnia & Herzegovina Bosnie et Herzégovine	...	...	...	6
Bulgaria Bulgarie	24	10	1	35
Croatia Croatie	60	17	15	92
Czech Republic République tchèque	47	12	13	72
Denmark Danemark	1399	235	209	1843
Estonia Estonie	3	1	3	7
Finland Finlande	147	44	39	230
France France	30768	5505	4422	40695

13 C. Reported AIDS cases [*cont.*] • Cas de SIDA déclarés [*suite*]

Country or area Pays ou zone	Total reported to Dec. 1993 Nombre total de cas déclarés jusqu' en déc. 1993	New cases reported for 1994 Nombre de cas nouveaux déclarés pour 1994	New cases reported for 1995 Nombre de cas nouveaux déclarés pour 1995	Cumulative total to Dec. 1995 Nombre total cumulé jusqu'en déc. 1995
Germany Allemagne	11552	1682	1189	14423
Greece Grèce	953	196	165	1314
Hungary Hongrie	148	23	31	202
Iceland Islande	32	3	3	38
Ireland Irlande	418	64	29	511
Italy Italie	21928	5433	5263	32624
Latvia Lettonie	7	2	3	12
Lithuania Lituanie	5	0	3	8
Luxembourg Luxembourg	77	13	15	105
Malta Malte	29	5	3	37
Monaco Monaco	30	4	3	37
Netherlands Pays–Bas	3045	451	458	3954
Norway Norvège	374	73	64	511
Poland Pologne	222	96	104	422
Portugal Portugal	1972	585	549	3106
Republic of Moldova République de Moldova	4	0	2	6
Romania Roumanie	2756	479	617	3852
Russian Federation Fédération de Russie	143	27	28	198
San Marino Saint–Marin	1	0	0	1
Slovakia Slovaquie	8	3	2	13
Slovenia Slovénie	31	6	15	52
Spain Espagne	25559	6696	5592	37847
Sweden Suède	982	183	181	1346
Switzerland Suisse	4150	577	367	5094
TFYR Macedonia L'ex–R.y. Macédonie	...	...	...	18
Ukraine Ukraine	26	15	34	75
United Kingdom Royaume–Uni	9397	1659	1360	12416
Yugoslavia, SFR Yougoslavie, Rfs	350	83	97	530
Oceania • Océanie				
Australia Australie	5006	909	527	6442
Cook Islands Iles Cook	0	0	0	0
Fiji Fidji	5	2	0	7
French Polynesia Polynésie française	42	3	5	50

13 C. Reported AIDS cases [*cont.*] · Cas de SIDA déclarés [*suite*]

Country or area Pays ou zone	Total reported to Dec. 1993 Nombre total de cas déclarés jusqu' en déc. 1993	New cases reported for 1994 Nombre de cas nouveaux déclarés pour 1994	New cases reported for 1995 Nombre de cas nouveaux déclarés pour 1995	Cumulative total to Dec. 1995 Nombre total cumulé jusqu'en déc. 1995
Guam Guam	19	11	3	33
Kiribati Kiribati	0	0	0	0
Marshall Islands Iles Marshall	2	0	0	2
Micronesia, Federated States of Micronésie, Etats fédérés de	2	0	0	2
Nauru Nauru	0	0	0	0
New Caledonia Nouvelle–Calédonie	36	7	4	47
New Zealand Nouvelle–Zélande	441	42	40	523
Niue Nioué	0	0	0	0
Northern Mariana Islands Iles Mariannes du Nord	4	2	0	6
Palau Palaos	1	0	0	1
Papua New Guinea Papouasie–Nvl–Guinée	83	26	43	152
Samoa Samoa	1	2	1	4
Solomon Islands Iles Salomon	0	0	0	0
Tokelau Tokélaou	0	0	0	0
Tonga Tonga	4	1	0	5
Tuvalu Tuvalu	0	0	0	0
Vanuatu Vanuatu	0	0	0	0
Wallis and Futana Islands Iles Wallis et Futana	0	1	0	1

Source:
World Health Organization (Geneva), UNAIDS (United Nations Children's Fund, United Nations Development Programme, United Nations Population Fund, United Nations Educational, Scientific and Cultural Organization, World Health Organization and World Bank).

Source:
Organisation mondiale de la santé (Gèneve), UNAIDS (Fonds des Nations Unies pour l'enfance, Programme des Nations Unies pour le développement, Fonds des Nations Unies pour la population, Organisation des Nations Unies pour l'éducation, la science et la culture, Organisation mondiale de la santé, la Banque mondiale).

Technical notes, tables 12 and 13

Table 12: "Life expectancy at birth", "Infant mortality rate" and "Total fertility rate" are taken from the estimates and projections prepared by the Population Division of the United Nations Secretariat, published in *World Population Prospects: The 1994 Revision* [27].

"Life expectancy at birth" is an overall estimate of the expected average number of years to be lived by a female or male newborn. Many developing countries lack complete and reliable statistics of births and deaths based on civil registration, so various estimation techniques are used to calculate life expectancy using other sources of data, mainly population censuses and demographic surveys. Life expectancy at birth by sex gives a statistical summary of current differences in male and female mortality across all ages. However, trends and differentials in infant and child mortality rates are predominant influence on trends and differentials in life expectancy at birth in most developing countries. Thus, life expectancy at birth is of limited usefulness in these countries in assessing levels and differentials in male and female mortality at other ages.

"Infant mortality rate" is the total number of deaths in a given year of children less than one year old divided by the total number of live births in the same year, multiplied by 1,000. It is an approximation of the number of deaths per 1,000 children born alive who die within one year of birth. In most developing countries where civil registration data are deficient, the most reliable sources are demographic surveys of households. Where these are not available, other sources and general estimates are made which are necessarily of limited reliability. Where countries lack comprehensive and accurate systems of civil registration, infant mortality statistics by sex are difficult to collect or to estimate with any degree of reliability because of reporting biases, and thus are not shown here.

"Total fertility rate" is the average number of children that would be born alive to a hypothetical cohort of women if, throughout their reproductive years, the age-specific fertility rates for the specified year remained unchanged.

"Child mortality rate" is defined as the annual number of deaths among children aged 1-4 years per 1,000 population of the same age. These series have been compiled by the Statistics Division of the United Nations Secretariat for the *Demographic Yearbook* [21] and are subject to the limitations of national reporting in this field.

Data on maternal mortality are estimated by World Health Organization and United Nations Educational, Scientific and Cultural Organization published in *Revised 1990 Estimates of Maternal Mortality* [33]. The new 1990 estimates were developed using a dual strategy: existing national maternal mortality estimates were adjusted to account for underreporting and misclassification; and a simple model was developed to predict values for countries

Notes techniques, tableaux 12 et 13

Tableau 12: L'"espérance de vie à la naissance", le "taux de mortalité infantile" et le "taux de fécondité" sont proviennent des estimations et projections de la Division de la population du Secrétariat de l'ONU, qui ont publiées dans *World Population Prospects: The 1994 Revision* [27].

L'"espérance de vie à la naissance" est une estimation globale du nombre d'années qu'un nouveau-né de sexe masculin ou féminin vivant, peut s'attendre à vivre. Comme dans beaucoup de pays en développement, les registres d'état civil ne permettent pas d'établir des statistiques fiables et complètes des naissances et des décès, diverses techniques d'estimation ont été utilisées pour calculer l'espérance de vie à partir d'autres sources et notamment des recensements et enquêtes démographiques. Sur la base des statistiques de l'espérance de vie par sexe, on peut calculer la différence entre la longévité des hommes et celle des femmes à tous les âges. Cependant, ce sont les tendances et les écarts des taux de mortalité infantile et juvénile qui influent de façon prépondérante sur les tendances et les écarts de l'espérance de vie à la naissance dans la plupart des pays en développement. Ainsi, l'espérance de vie à la naissance ne revêt qu'une utilité limitée dans ce pays pour évaluer les niveaux et les écarts de la mortalité des femmes et des hommes à des âges plus avancés.

Le "taux de mortalité infantile" correspond au nombre total de décès au cours d'une année donnée des enfants de moins de 5 ans divisé par le nombre total de naissances vivantes au cours de la même année, multiplié par 1 000. Il s'agit d'une approximation du nombre de décès pour 1 000 enfants nés vivants qui meurent la première année. Dans la plupart des pays en développement, où les données d'état civil sont déficientes, les sources les plus fiables sont les enquêtes démographiques auprès des ménages. Lorsque de telles enquêtes ne sont pas réalisées, d'autres sources sont utilisées et des estimations générales sont réalisées qui sont nécessairement d'une fiabilité limitée. Lorsqu'il n'y a pas dans les pays de systèmes complets et exacts d'enregistrement des faits d'état civil, les statistiques de la mortalité infantile par sexe sont difficiles à rassembler ou à estimer avec quelque fiabilité que ce soit en raison des distorsions de la notification; elles ne sont donc pas indiquées ici.

Le "taux de fécondité" est le nombre moyen d'enfants que mettrait au monde une cohorte hypothétique de femmes si, pendant toutes leurs années d'âge reproductif, les taux de fécondité par âge de l'année en question restaient inchangés.

Le "taux de mortalité juvénile" est par définition le nombre de décès d'enfants âgés de 1 à 4 ans pour 1 000 enfants de cet âge. Cette série a été compilée par la Division de statistique du Secrétariat de l'ONU pour l'*Annuaire démographique* [21] et les données qui sont incluses sont présentées sous réserve de mises en garde formulées à leur sujet.

with no data. The model uses two widely available independent variables - general fertility rates and proportion of births that are assisted by a trained person - to predict maternal mortality. A detailed description of the methodology used is found in *Modelling maternal mortality in the developing world* (forthcoming) [39].

Table 13: Data on acquired immunodeficiency syndrome (AIDS) have been compiled and estimated by WHO and UNAIDS (United Nations Children's Fund, United Nations Development Programme, United Nations Population Fund, United Nations Educational, Scientific and Cultural Organization, World Health Organization and World Bank) from official national reports and special studies (unpublished).

Les données concernant la mortalité maternelle sont tirées des chiffres estimatifs de l'OMS et de l'UNICEF, publiés dans "*Revised 1990 Estimates of Maternal Mortality*" [33]. Les nouveaux chiffres de 1990 ont été calculés en combinant deux méthodes : d'une part on a ajusté les chiffres nationaux existants de mortalité maternelle pour tenir compte des déclarations lacunaires et des erreurs de classement; de l'autre, on a mis au point un modèle simple permettant de prédire les taux pour les pays où les données font défaut, à partir de deux variables indépendantes qui sont largement disponibles : les taux globaux de fécondité, et la proportion d'accouchements bénéficiant de l'aide d'une personne qualifiée. On trouvera cette méthode exposée en détail dans Stanton, C. et al (1996) "*Modelling Maternal Mortality in the Developing World*" (à paraître) [39].

Tableau 13 : Les données sur le syndrome d'immuno-déficience acquise (SIDA) ont été compilées et estimées par l'OMS et UNAIDS (Fonds des Nations Unies pour l'enfance, Programme des Nations Unies pour le développement, Fonds des Nations Unies pour la population, Organisation des Nations pour l'éducation, la science et la culture, Organisation mondiale de la santé, la Banque mondiale) sur la base des rapports officiels soumis par les pays et d'études spéciales (non publiées).

14
Daily newspapers
Journaux quotidiens

Country or area	Number Nombre				Circulation Diffusion (estimation) Total (000)				Per 1000 inhabitants Pour 1000 habitants			
Pays ou zone	1980	1985	1990	1992	1980	1985	1990	1992	1980	1985	1990	1992
Africa · Afrique												
Algeria Algérie	4	5	10	5	448	570	1274	1000	24	26	51	38
Angola Angola	4	4	4	4	143	103	*115	*116	20	13	*13	*12
Benin Bénin	1	1	1	1	1	1	12	12	0.3	0.3	3	2
Botswana Botswana	1	1	1	1	19	18	18	40	21	17	14	29
Burkina Faso Burkina Faso	1	2	1	1	2	4	3	*3	0.2	0.4	0.3	*0.3
Burundi Burundi	1	1	1	1	1	2	20	20	0.2	0.4	4	3
Cameroon Cameroun	2	1	2	1	65	35	*80	*50	8	4	*7	*4
Central African Rep. Rép. centrafricaine	–	–	1	1	–	–	*2	*2	–	–	*1	*1
Chad Tchad	1	1	1	1	1	1	2	2	0.2	0.2	0.4	0.4
Congo Congo	1	1	5	6	3	8	*17	*19	2	4	*8	*8
Côte d'Ivoire Côte d'Ivoire	2	1	1	1	81	90	90	90	10	9	8	7
Egypt Egypte	12	12	14	16	1701	2383	*2400	*2426	39	48	*42	*41
Equatorial Guinea Guinée équatoriale	2	2	2	1	*2	*2	*2	*1	*7	*5	*6	*3
Ethiopia Ethiopie	3	3	6	4	40	41	*100	*70	1	1	*2	*1
Gabon Gabon	1	1	1	1	15	20	*20	*20	19	20	*17	*16
Gambia Gambie	–	6	2	2	–	4	*2	*2	–	6	*2	*2
Ghana Ghana	5	5	2	4	*500	*510	200	280	*47	*40	13	18
Guinea–Bissau Guinée–Bissau	1	1	1	1	6	6	6	6	8	7	6	6
Kenya Kenya	3	4	5	5	216	283	*330	*354	13	14	*14	*14
Lesotho Lesotho	3	4	4	2	44	47	20	14	33	30	11	7
Liberia Libéria	3	5	8	8	11	*28	*35	*35	6	*13	*14	*13
Libyan Arab Jamahiriya Jamah. arabe libyenne	3	3	3	4	*55	*65	*70	*71	*18	*17	*15	*15
Madagascar Madagascar	6	7	5	7	55	67	50	48	6	6	4	4
Malawi Malawi	*2	1	1	1	*20	15	25	25	*3	2	3	2
Mali Mali	2	2	2	2	*4	*10	*10	*41	*1	*1	*1	*4
Mauritania Mauritanie	–	–	1	1	–	–	*1	*1	–	–	*0.5	*0.5
Mauritius Maurice	10	7	7	6	80	*70	80	80	83	*69	76	74
Morocco Maroc	11	14	13	14	*270	*320	*320	*335	*14	*15	*13	*13
Mozambique Mozambique	2	2	2	2	54	81	81	81	4	6	6	5
Namibia Namibie	4	3	6	4	27	21	220	209	26	17	163	147

14
Daily newspapers [*cont.*]
Journaux quotidiens [*suite*]

Country or area	Number				Circulation Diffusion (estimation)							
Pays ou zone	Nombre				Total (000)				Per 1000 inhabitants Pour 1000 habitants			
	1980	1985	1990	1992	1980	1985	1990	1992	1980	1985	1990	1992
Niger												
Niger	1	1	1	1	3	4	5	5	1	1	1	1
Nigeria												
Nigéria	16	19	31	26	*1100	*1400	*1700	*1850	*15	*17	*18	*18
Réunion												
Réunion	3	2	3	3	56	49	*55	55	111	89	*91	88
Rwanda												
Rwanda	1	1	1	1	0.3	0.3	0.5	0.5	0.1	0.1	0.1	0.1
Senegal												
Sénégal	1	3	1	1	35	53	50	50	6	8	7	6
Seychelles												
Seychelles	1	1	1	1	3	3	3	3	48	49	46	45
Sierra Leone												
Sierra Leone	1	1	1	1	10	10	10	10	3	3	3	2
Somalia												
Somalie	2	2	1	1	*5	*7	*9	*9	*1	*1	*1	*1
South Africa												
Afrique du Sud	*24	24	22	20	*1400	1440	1340	1248	*48	44	36	32
Sudan												
Soudan	6	5	5	5	105	*250	*610	*620	6	*12	*25	*24
Swaziland												
Swaziland	1	2	3	3	9	10	*11	*12	15	15	*15	*15
Togo												
Togo	3	2	1	2	*16	*11	10	*12	*6	*4	3	*3
Tunisia												
Tunisie	5	6	6	9	272	*280	*345	*410	43	*39	*43	*49
Uganda												
Ouganda	1	1	2	6	25	25	30	*80	2	2	2	*4
United Rep. of Tanzania												
Rép.—Unie de Tanzanie	3	2	3	3	208	101	*200	*220	11	5	*8	*8
Zaire												
Zaïre	5	4	5	9	*60	*50	75	*112	*2	*2	2	*3
Zambia												
Zambie	2	2	2	2	110	95	99	70	19	14	12	8
Zimbabwe												
Zimbabwe	2	3	2	2	133	203	206	195	19	24	21	19
America, North · Amérique du Nord												
Antigua and Barbuda												
Antigua—et—Barbuda	1	1	1	—	6	6	6	—	98	97	94	—
Bahamas												
Bahamas	3	3	3	3	33	39	35	35	157	167	137	133
Barbados												
Barbade	2	2	2	2	39	40	30	41	156	158	117	160
Belize												
Belize	1	1	—	—	3	3	—	—	21	18	—	—
Bermuda												
Bermudes	1	1	1	1	14	18	*18	16	257	321	*295	258
Canada												
Canada	123	117	107	106	5425	5566	*5900	*5800	221	215	*212	*204
Cayman Islands												
Iles Caïmanes	—	—	1	1	—	—	6	8	—	—	212	268
Costa Rica												
Costa Rica	4	6	5	4	251	*280	*306	322	110	*106	*101	101
Cuba												
Cuba	17	17	19	17	1050	1207	1824	1315	108	119	172	122
Dominican Republic												
République dominicaine	7	7	12	11	220	216	*230	*265	39	34	*32	*36
El Salvador												
El Salvador	7	4	5	8	291	243	457	*485	64	51	88	*90
Grenada												
Grenade	1	—	—	—	*4	—	—	—	*45	—	—	—
Guadeloupe												
Guadeloupe	1	2	1	1	*32	*33	*34	35	*98	*94	*87	86
Guatemala												
Guatemala	9	9	5	5	*200	*250	190	180	*29	*31	21	18

14
Daily newspapers [*cont.*]
Journaux quotidiens [*suite*]

Country or area	Number Nombre				Circulation Diffusion (estimation) Total (000)				Per 1000 inhabitants Pour 1000 habitants			
Pays ou zone	1980	1985	1990	1992	1980	1985	1990	1992	1980	1985	1990	1992
Haiti Haïti	4	5	4	4	*36	*50	45	45	*7	*9	7	7
Honduras Honduras	6	7	5	4	212	293	199	*159	59	70	41	*31
Jamaica Jamaïque	3	4	3	3	109	*138	*155	*160	51	*60	*66	*67
Martinique Martinique	1	1	1	1	28	32	32	32	86	94	88	86
Mexico Mexique	317	332	*285	292	8322	9964	*11237	10231	124	132	*133	116
Netherlands Antilles Antilles néerlandaises	8	6	6	6	*52	*54	*54	53	*299	*297	*284	275
Nicaragua Nicaragua	3	3	6	3	136	*160	*180	90	49	*50	*49	23
Panama Panama	5	7	8	8	*110	245	*234	223	*56	113	*98	90
Puerto Rico Porto Rico	4	5	3	3	512	599	456	507	160	178	129	141
Trinidad and Tobago Trinité−et−Tobago	4	4	2	4	*155	173	95	175	*143	149	77	138
United States Etats−Unis	1745	1676	1611	1570	62200	62800	62328	60164	273	263	249	236
US Virgin Islands Iles Vierges américaines	3	3	2	2	17	21	19	22	168	198	166	206
America, South · Amérique du Sud												
Argentina Argentine	220	218	159	190	*4000	*3940	*4000	*4780	*142	*130	*123	*143
Bolivia Bolivie	14	14	17	16	226	*290	*400	*390	42	*49	*61	*57
Brazil Brésil	343	322	356	373	5482	6534	*8100	*8500	45	48	*55	*55
Chile Chili	34	*38	*45	45	...	...	*1997	*2000	...	...	*152	*147
Colombia Colombie	36	*46	45	46	*1400	*1800	*2000	*2100	*53	*61	*62	*63
Ecuador Equateur	18	26	25	36	558	*800	*820	688	70	*88	*80	64
French Guiana Guyane française	1	1	1	1	1	1	1	2	15	11	9	13
Guyana Guyana	1	2	2	2	58	78	*80	80	76	99	*101	99
Paraguay Paraguay	5	6	5	5	*160	*170	*165	168	*51	*46	*38	37
Peru Pérou	66	70	66	59	*1400	*1600	*1700	*1590	*81	*82	*79	*71
Suriname Suriname	4	5	2	3	*45	*55	40	*43	*127	*146	100	*105
Uruguay Uruguay	24	25	30	32	*700	*680	*720	*750	*240	*226	*233	*240
Venezuela Venezuela	66	55	54	82	2937	*2700	*2800	*4200	195	*158	*144	*205
Asia · Asie												
Afghanistan Afghanistan	13	13	14	16	*90	*110	*180	*206	*6	*8	*12	*12
Armenia Arménie	..	..	..	7	..	..	..	*84	..	..	..	*24
Azerbaijan Azerbadjan	..	..	..	6	..	..	..	427	..	..	..	59
Bahrain Bahreïn	3	2	2	3	*14	19	29	*43	*40	45	59	*83
Bangladesh Bangladesh	44	60	52	51	274	591	*700	*710	3	6	*6	*6
Brunei Darussalam Brunéi Darussalam	−	−	1	1	−	−	10	20	−	−	39	74

14
Daily newspapers [*cont.*]
Journaux quotidiens [*suite*]

Country or area	Number Nombre				Circulation Diffusion (estimation) Total (000)				Per 1000 inhabitants Pour 1000 habitants			
Pays ou zone	1980	1985	1990	1992	1980	1985	1990	1992	1980	1985	1990	1992
China Chine	50	70	44	74	34375	*39000	*48000	*50520	34	*36	*42	*43
Cyprus Chypre	12	10	11	9	*80	83	78	77	*127	125	110	107
Hong Kong Hong-kong	41	46	38	49	*3600	*4100	*4250	*4750	*715	*751	*745	*822
India [1] Inde [1]	1173	1802	2281	*2300	14531	19804	*26000	*27500	21	26	*31	*31
Indonesia Indonésie	84	97	64	68	2281	3010	5144	4591	15	18	28	24
Iran, Islamic Rep. of Iran, Rép. islamique d'	*45	15	21	13	*970	*1250	*1500	*1250	*25	*26	*25	*20
Iraq Iraq	5	6	6	6	*340	*600	*650	*660	*26	*39	*36	*35
Israel Israël	36	21	30	31	*1000	*1100	*120	*1240	*258	*260	*258	*246
Japan Japon	151	124	125	121	66258	68296	72524	71690	567	565	587	577
Jordan Jordanie	4	4	4	4	66	155	225	250	23	40	53	53
Korea, Dem.People's Rep. Corée, Rép. pop. dém. de	11	11	11	11	*4000	*4500	*5000	*5000	*219	*226	*230	*221
Korea, Republic of Corée, République de	30	35	39	63	8000	*10000	*12000	*18000	210	*245	*280	*412
Kuwait Koweït	8	8	9	9	305	380	*450	*480	222	221	*210	*248
Lao People's Dem. Rep. République dém. pop. lao	3	3	3	3	*14	*13	*14	*14	*4	*4	*3	*3
Lebanon Liban	14	13	*14	16	*290	*300	*320	*500	*109	*112	*125	*185
Macau Macao	6	9	8	9	*70	*250	*240	*250	*217	*638	*518	*510
Malaysia Malaisie	40	32	45	39	*810	*1500	*2500	*2200	*59	*96	*140	*117
Maldives Maldives	2	2	*2	2	1	2	*3	3	6	8	*12	13
Mongolia Mongolie	2	2	1	3	177	177	162	*208	106	93	74	*92
Myanmar Myanmar	7	7	2	2	*350	511	*300	324	*10	14	*7	7
Nepal Népal	28	28	28	25	*120	*130	*150	*140	*8	*8	*8	*7
Oman Oman	–	3	4	4	–	51	62	79	–	37	35	41
Pakistan Pakistan	106	118	398	274	*1032	1149	1826	809	*12	11	15	6
Philippines Philippines	22	15	47	43	2000	2170	*3400	*3200	41	40	*56	*50
Qatar Qatar	3	4	5	4	*30	60	*80	*70	*131	168	*165	*135
Saudi Arabia Arabie saoudite	11	13	12	13	*350	*450	*600	729	*36	*36	*37	43
Singapore Singapour	12	10	8	10	690	*706	763	*930	286	*285	282	*336
Sri Lanka Sri Lanka	21	17	18	10	450	390	*550	*480	30	24	*32	*27
Syrian Arab Republic Rép. arabe syrienne	7	7	10	11	*114	*163	*260	*290	*13	*16	*21	*22
Tajikistan Tadjikistan	..	..	..	9	..	..	..	116	..	..	..	21
Thailand Thaïlande	27	32	34	41	2680	4350	*4500	*4820	57	85	*81	*85
Turkey Turquie	*400	366	399	...	*2500	3020	4000	...	*56	60	71	...

14
Daily newspapers [*cont.*]
Journaux quotidiens [*suite*]

Country or area	Number Nombre				Circulation Diffusion (estimation) Total (000)				Per 1000 inhabitants Pour 1000 habitants			
Pays ou zone	1980	1985	1990	1992	1980	1985	1990	1992	1980	1985	1990	1992
United Arab Emirates												
Emirats arabes unis	9	13	8	11	152	290	250	*335	149	210	150	*189
Uzbekistan												
Ouzbékistan	..	..	..	12	..	..	..	452	..	..	..	21
Viet Nam												
Viet Nam	4	4	5	4	*520	*540	*560	*570	*10	*9	*8	*8
Yemen												
Yémen	..	..	..	4	..	..	..	236	..	..	..	19
former Democratic Yemen												
ancienne Yémen dém.	3	3	3	..	*14	*15	*15	..	*8	*7	*6	..
former Yemen Arab Rep.												
ancienne Yémen rép. arabe	*3	1	2	..	*84	110	120	..	*13	*14	13	..
Europe · Europe												
Albania												
Albanie	2	2	2	4	145	135	135	*165	54	46	41	*49
Andorra												
Andorre	–	–	–	3	–	–	–	*4	–	–	–	*67
Austria												
Autriche	30	33	25	27	2651	2729	2706	3108	351	361	351	398
Belarus												
Bélarus	27	28	28	10	2343	2446	2937	1899	243	246	288	186
Belgium												
Belgique	26	24	33	33	2289	2171	*3000	*3100	232	220	*301	*310
Bosnia & Herzegovina [2]												
Bosnie–Herzégovine [2]	..	..	..	2	..	..	..	518	..	..	..	131
Bulgaria												
Bulgarie	14	17	24	46	2244	2626	4065	1464	253	293	452	164
Croatia												
Croatie	..	8	9	9	..	....	*2383	*2404	..	....	*528	*532
former Czechoslovakia †												
ancienne Tchécoslovaquie †	30	30	48	..	4798	5124	7943	..	313	331	507	..
Czech Republic												
République tchéque	..	..	..	55	..	..	..	*6000	..	..	..	*583
Denmark												
Danemark	48	47	47	42	1874	1855	1810	1710	366	363	352	332
Estonia												
Estonie	..	..	..	15	..	..	..	....	..	..	..	....
Finland [3]												
Finlande [3]	58	65	66	58	2414	2661	2780	2578	505	543	558	512
France [4]												
France [4]	90	92	79	77	10332	10670	11792	11695	192	193	208	205
Germany † [5]												
Allemagne † [5]	..	..	355	357	..	..	26425	25952	..	..	331	323
Federal Republic of Germany												
Rép. féd. d'Allemagne	329	319	..	..	20611	21108	..	..	335	346	..	..
former German Dem. Rep.												
ancienne Rép. dém. allemande	39	39	..	..	8777	9320	..	..	524	560	..	..
Gibraltar												
Gibraltar	1	1	2	2	2	3	*4	*4	83	107	*150	*150
Greece												
Grèce	128	140	*130	145	*1160	*1205	*1250	*1400	*120	*121	*122	*135
Holy See												
Saint–Siège	1	1	1	1	70	70	70	70	..	..	..	..
Hungary												
Hongrie	27	28	34	28	2648	2717	2460	2896	247	257	237	282
Iceland												
Islande	6	6	6	5	125	113	*13	*135	548	467	*510	*519
Ireland												
Irlande	7	7	7	8	779	685	591	652	229	193	169	186
Italy												
Italie	82	72	76	78	4775	5511	*6000	6068	85	97	*105	106
Latvia												
Lettonie	..	..	..	17	..	..	..	258	..	..	..	98

14
Daily newspapers [cont.]
Journaux quotidiens [suite]

Country or area	Number Nombre				Circulation Diffusion (estimation) Total (000)				Per 1000 inhabitants Pour 1000 habitants			
Pays ou zone	1980	1985	1990	1992	1980	1985	1990	1992	1980	1985	1990	1992
Liechtenstein Liechtenstein	2	2	*2	2	14	14	*18	20	540	504	*621	653
Lithuania Lituanie	..	..	..	18	..	..	..	836	..	..	..	225
Luxembourg Luxembourg	5	4	5	5	135	140	143	145	371	381	375	372
Malta Malte	5	4	3	3	*60	*56	*54	54	*185	*163	*153	150
Monaco Monaco	2	2	1	1	10	*10	8	8	381	*357	267	258
Netherlands Pays—Bas	84	88	45	44	4612	4496	*4500	*4600	326	310	*301	*303
Norway Norvège	85	82	85	82	1892	2120	2588	2600	463	510	610	607
Poland Pologne	43	45	67	72	8407	7714	4889	6085	236	207	128	159
Portugal Portugal	28	25	24	25	*480	413	446	465	*49	42	45	47
Republic of Moldova République de Moldova	..	..	..	5	..	..	...	*205	..	..	..	*47
Romania Roumanie	35	36	65	76	*4024	*3601	*6300	*7500	*181	*158	*272	*324
Russian Federation [5] Fédération Russe [5]	..	..	378	339	..	..	74550	57367	..	..	503	387
San Marino Saint—Marin	3	–	–	–	1	–	–	–	48	–	–	–
Slovakia [5] Slovaquie [5]	..	..	18	21	..	..	1410	1680	..	..	267	317
Slovenia Slovénie	3	3	4	6	198	216	303	308	108	115	158	160
Spain Espagne	111	102	*125	148	3487	3078	*3450	*4100	93	80	*88	*104
Sweden Suède	114	115	107	104	4386	4389	4499	4419	528	526	526	511
Switzerland [6] Suisse [6]	89	97	94	83	2483	3213	3063	2635	393	492	448	377
TFYR Macedonia L'ex—R.y.Macédoine	..	..	2	*2	..	..	*55	*56	..	..	*27	*27
Ukraine Ukraine	..	..	127	90	..	..	13026	6083	..	..	252	118
United Kingdom Royaume—Uni	113	104	*103	101	23472	22495	*22350	*22100	417	397	*389	*383
Yugoslavia, SFR † Yougoslavie, Rfs †	27	27	..	..	2649	2451	..	..	119	106	..	..
Yugoslavia Yougoslavie	12	12	15	10	537	425	366	544	56	43	36	52
Oceania · Océanie												
American Samoa Samoa américaines	2	3	–	–	10	*9	–	–	319	*226	–	–
Australia Australie	62	62	62	69	*4700	*4300	*4200	*4600	*323	*275	*249	*265
Cook Islands Iles Cook	1	1	1	1	2	2	2	2	111	118	111	111
Fiji Fidji	3	3	1	1	64	68	27	27	102	97	37	36
French Polynesia Polynésie française	2	3	2	4	*13	23	21	*24	*86	132	107	*117
Guam Guam	1	1	1	1	18	18	22	25	169	151	161	178
New Caledonia Nouvelle—Calédonie	1	1	1	3	15	19	19	*23	105	123	113	*133
New Zealand Nouvelle—Zélande	32	33	35	31	1059	1075	*1100	*1050	340	331	*327	*305

14
Daily newspapers [*cont.*]
Journaux quotidiens [*suite*]

Country or area	Number Nombre				Circulation Diffusion (estimation)							
					Total (000)				Per 1000 inhabitants Pour 1000 habitants			
Pays ou zone	1980	1985	1990	1992	1980	1985	1990	1992	1980	1985	1990	1992
Papua New Guinea Papouasie−Nouv.−Guinée	1	2	2	2	27	45	49	64	9	13	13	16
Tonga Tonga	−	−	1	1	−	−	7	7	−	−	73	72
former USSR · ancienne URSS												
former USSR † ancienneURSS †	713	727	..	..	*109089	120027	..	..	*423	445	..	..

Source:
United Nations Educational, Scientific and Cultural Organization
(Paris).

† For detaied descriptions of data pertaining to former Czechoslovakia,
  Germany, SFR Yugoslavia and former USSR, see Annex I − Country
  or area nomenclature, regional and other groupings.

1 Data shown for 1990 refer to 1988.
2 Data shown for 1992 refer only to territory that is under the control
   of the Government of the Republic of Bosnia and Herzegovina.
3 Data shown for 1992 do not include newspapers that are distributed
   free of charge.
4 Data shown for 1992 refer to 1991.
5 Data shown for 1990 refer to 1991.
6 Data shown for 1992 refer only to newspapers purchased and do not
   include satellites publications.

Source:
Organisation des Nations Unies pour l'éducation, la science et
la culture (Paris).

† Pour les descriptions en détails des données relatives
  à l'ancienne Tchécoslovaquie, l'Allemagne, la Rfs Yougoslavie
  et l'ancienne URSS, voir l'Annexe I − Nomenclature des pays
  ou zones, groupements régionaux et autres groupements.

1 Les données présentées pour 1990 se réfèrent à 1988.
2 Les données présentées pour 1992 se réfèrent seulement au
   territoire qui est sous le contrôle du governement de la
   République de Bosnie−Herzégovine.
3 Les données présentées pour 1992 n'incluent pas les journaux
   qui sont distribués gratuitement.
4 Les données présentées pour 1992 se réfèrent à 1991.
5 Les données présentées pour 1990 se réfèrent à 1991.
6 Les données préséntées pour 1992 se réfèrent seulement aux
   journaux payants et n'incluent pas les éditions satellites.

15
Non-daily newspapers and periodicals
Journaux non quotidiens et périodiques

Country or area Pays ou zone	Year Année	Non-daily newspapers Journaux non quotidiens			Periodicals Périodiques		
			Circulation Diffusion			Circulation Diffusion	
		Number Nombre	Total (000)	Per 1000 inhabitants Pour 1000 habitants	Number Nombre	Total (000)	Per 1000 inhabitants Pour 1000 habitants
Africa · Afrique							
Algeria Algérie	1990	37	1409	57	48	803	32
Angola Angola	1988	*2	*7	*1	...	...	...
Benin Bénin	1988	*3	*20	*5	...	...	...
Botswana Botswana	1992	4	61	45	14	177	130
Burkina Faso Burkina Faso	1990	10	14	2	37	24	3
Burundi Burundi	1988	*3	*22	*4	...	...	...
Cameroon Cameroun	1988	25	315	29	58	127	*11
Cape Verde Cap–Vert	1988	3	7	21	...	...	...
Central African Republic République centrafricaine	1988	*2	*3	*1	...	...	...
Chad Tchad	1988	1	1	0.2	10	...	...
Congo Congo	1990	3	139	62	3	34	15
Côte d'Ivoire Côte d'Ivoire	1988	*5	*172	*15	...	...	...
Djibouti Djibouti	1988	2	*7	*15	7	6	14
Egypt Egypte	1991	35	1502	26	266	1815	31
Ethiopia Ethiopie	1988	4	40	1	3	14	0.3
Gabon Gabon	1988	1	20	18	...	...	...
Gambia Gambie	1990	6	*7	*8	10	885	958
Ghana Ghana	1990	87	1111	74	121	774	52
Guinea Guinée	1990	*1	*1	*0.2	*3	*5	*1
Guinea–Bissau Guinée–Bissau	1988	*1	*2	*2	...	...	...
Kenya Kenya	1988	*8	*300	*14	...	...	...
Lesotho Lesotho	1988	*3	*45	*26	...	...	...
Liberia Libéria	1988	*8	*25	*10	...	...	...
Libyan Arab Jamahiriya Jamahiriya arabe libyenne	1988	*1	*15	*4	...	...	...
Madagascar Madagascar	1992	37	*168	*13	63	*191	*14
Malawi Malawi	1992	4	133	13	...	...	...
Mauritius Maurice	1992	25	...	...	62	...	...
Morocco Maroc	1988	*5	*35	*2	...	...	...
Mozambique Mozambique	1988	2	*85	*6	5	2263	172
Namibia Namibie	1990	18	71	53	...	...	...

15
Non–daily newspapers and periodicals [*cont.*]
Journaux non quotidiens et périodiques [*suite*]

Country or area Pays ou zone	Year Année	Non–daily newspapers Journaux non quotidiens			Periodicals Périodiques		
			Circulation Diffusion			Circulation Diffusion	
		Number Nombre	Total (000)	Per 1000 inhabitants Pour 1000 habitants	Number Nombre	Total (000)	Per 1000 inhabitants Pour 1000 habitants
Niger Niger	1988	1	5	1	...	...	...
Nigeria Nigéria	1988	11	45	0.4	92	495	5
Reunion Réunion	1988	*4	*20	*34	...	...	...
Rwanda Rwanda	1990	15	*155	*22	15	101	14
St. Helena Saint–Hélène	1988	1	2	250	...	...	...
Sao Tome and Principe Sao Tomé–et–Principe	1988	*2	*2	*18	...	...	...
Senegal Sénégal	1988	10	63	9	...	...	...
Seychelles Seychelles	1988	*4	*9	*138	...	...	...
Sierra Leone Sierra Leone	1988	*6	*65	*17	...	...	...
Somalia Somalie	1988	*4	*13	*2	...	...	...
South Africa Afrique du Sud	1991	10	1527	40	11	2149	57
Sudan Soudan	1988	*10	*135	*6	10	136	6
Swaziland Swaziland	1988	*1	*7	*10	...	...	...
Togo Togo	1988	*1	*5	*2	...	...	...
Tunisia Tunisie	1988	*9	*244	*31	...	...	...
Uganda [1] Uganda [1]	1990	*5	*70	*4	26	158	10
United Republic of Tanzania Rép. Unie de Tanzanie	1988	*9	*450	*19	...	...	...
Zaire Zaïre	1990	77	...	...	...	...	...
Zambia Zambie	1988	*1	*72	*9	...	...	...
Zimbabwe [1] Zimbabwe [1]	1990	16	428	44	28	680	69
America, North · Amérique du Nord							
Antigua and Barbuda Antigua–et–Barbuda	1988	*5	*10	*154	...	...	...
Bahamas Bahamas	1988	*2	*13	*52	...	...	...
Barbados [2] Barbade [2]	1990	4	*95	*370	52	...	...
Belize Belize	1990	7	37	196	...	...	...
Bermuda Bermudes	1990	3	35	566	...	...	...
British Virgin Islands Iles Vierges brit.	1990	2	4	250	...	...	...
Canada [3] Canada [3]	1992	1627	22043	804	1400	37108	1303
Cayman Islands Iles Caïmanes	1988	*1	*4	*167	...	...	...
Costa Rica Costa Rica	1991	12	106	34	...	...	...
Cuba [3] Cuba [3]	1990	4	36	3	160	2797	264

15
Non–daily newspapers and periodicals [*cont.*]
Journaux non quotidiens et périodiques [*suite*]

| Country or area
Pays ou zone | Year
Année | Non-daily newspapers
Journaux non quotidiens | | | Periodicals
Périodiques | | |
| | | Number
Nombre | Circulation
Diffusion | | Number
Nombre | Circulation
Diffusion | |
			Total (000)	Per 1000 inhabitants Pour 1000 habitants		Total (000)	Per 1000 inhabitants Pour 1000 habitants
Dominica Dominique	1992	1	5	63	...	...	...
El Salvador El Salvador	1988	*3	*12	*2	...	...	...
Greenland Groenland	1988	*3	*15	*264	...	...	...
Grenada Grenade	1992	2	*5	*55	...	...	...
Guadeloupe Guadeloupe	1988	*9	*28	*74	...	...	...
Guatemala Guatemala	1988	*1	*7	*1	–	–	–
Haiti Haïti	1988	*4	*16	*3	...	...	...
Honduras Honduras	1988	*1	*5	*1	...	...	...
Martinique Martinique	1988	*7	*28	*80	...	...	...
Mexico Mexique	1992	56	1258	14	182	28016	318
Montserrat Montserrat	1990	2	2	200	...	...	...
Netherlands Antilles Antilles néerlandaises	1988	*1	*3	*16	...	...	...
Nicaragua Nicaragua	1988	*8	*140	*40	...	...	...
Panama Panama	1988	3	*50	*22	8	...	...
Puerto Rico Porto Rico	1988	*4	*106	*31	...	...	...
Saint Kitts and Nevis Saint Kitts–et–Nevis	1993	2	6	*143	10	44	*1048
Saint Lucia Sainte Lucie	1992	3	18	131	...	...	...
Saint Pierre and Miquelon Saint–Pierre et Miquelon	1992	1	2	317	...	...	...
Saint Vincent and the Grenadines Saint Vincent–et–Grenadines	1988	2	11	105	...	...	...
Trinidad and Tobago Trinité–et–Tobago	1990	5	125	101	...	...	...
Turks and Caicos Islands Iles Turques et Caïques	1992	1	10	769	...	...	...
United States Etats–Unis	1993	9816	*71500	*277	...	...	...
United States Virgin Islands Iles Vierges américaines	1988	*2	*4	*33	...	...	...
America, South · Amérique du Sud							
Argentina Argentine	1992	*7	*350	*11	...	...	...
Bolivia Bolivie	1988	*8	*16	*2	...	...	...
Brazil Brésil	1988	*1450	*5000	*35	...	...	...
Chile Chili	1992	48	102	7	417	*3450	*254
Colombia Colombie	1988	*6	*260	*8	...	...	...
Ecuador Equateur	1992	...	...	...	199	...	...
Falkland Islands (Malvinas) Iles Falkland (Malvinas)	1988	*2	*1	*500	...	...	...

15
Non–daily newspapers and periodicals [cont.]
Journaux non quotidiens et périodiques [suite]

Country or area Pays ou zone	Year Année	Non–daily newspapers Journaux non quotidiens			Periodicals Périodiques		
		Number Nombre	Circulation Diffusion Total (000)	Per 1000 inhabitants Pour 1000 habitants	Number Nombre	Circulation Diffusion Total (000)	Per 1000 inhabitants Pour 1000 habitants
French Guiana Guyane française	1988	*2	*7	*66	...	...	...
Guyana Guyana	1988	*6	*84	*106	...	...	...
Paraguay Paraguay	1988	*2	*16	*4	...	...	...
Peru Pérou	1988	*12	*374	*18	45	90	4
Suriname Suriname	1992	1	*5	*12	...	...	...
Uruguay Uruguay	1988	*95	...	...	...	...	...
Venezuela Venezuela	1988	*45	*450	*24	...	...	...
Asia · Asie							
Afghanistan [2] Afghanistan [2]	1988	37	223	15	105	...	...
Armenia Arménie	1992	57	*200	*58	40	5064	1472
Azerbaijan Azerbaïdjan	1992	273	3476	476	49	801	110
Bahrain Bahreïn	1993	5	17	31	26	73	137
Bangladesh Bangladesh	1988	490	916	9	...	...	...
Bhutan Bhoutan	1992	1	11	7	...	...	...
Brunei Darussalam Brunéi Darussalam	1992	2	57	212	15	132	489
China [4] Chine [4]	1992	875	134409	114	6486	205060	173
Cyprus Chypre	1992	30	133	185	37	167	232
Hong Kong [5] Hong–kong [5]	1992	17	...	...	598	...	...
India Inde	1988	*8000	*13000	*16	...	...	...
Indonesia Indonésie	1992	92	3501	19	117	3985	21
Iran, Islamic Rep. of Iran, Rép. islamique d'	1990	50	*470	*8	318	6166	105
Iraq Iraq	1988	*12	*465	*27	...	...	...
Israel Israël	1988	*80	...	...	...	...	...
Japan Japon	1992	*16	*9100	*73	2926	...	...
Jordan Jordanie	1990	6	122	29	31	43	10
Korea, Dem. People's Rep. of Corée, Rép. pop. dém. de	1988	*2	...	...	...	...	...
Kuwait Koweït	1988	59	420	204	...	...	...
Lao People's Dem. Rep. Rép. dém. populaire Lao	1988	*4	*20	*5	...	...	...
Lebanon Liban	1988	*15	*240	*94	...	...	...
Macau Macao	1992	*3	...	...	16	...	...
Malaysia Malaisie	1992	8	1530	81	25	996	53

15
Non–daily newspapers and periodicals [*cont.*]
Journaux non quotidiens et périodiques [*suite*]

Country or area Pays ou zone	Year Année	Non-daily newspapers Journaux non quotidiens			Periodicals Périodiques		
		Number Nombre	Circulation Diffusion Total (000)	Per 1000 inhabitants Pour 1000 habitants	Number Nombre	Circulation Diffusion Total (000)	Per 1000 inhabitants Pour 1000 habitants
Maldives Maldives	1988	*4	*5	*25	...	...	...
Mongolia Mongolie	1990	55	1133	520	45	6361	2920
Myanmar Myanmar	1988	*4	*246	*6	...	...	...
Nepal Népal	1988	*9	*43	*2	...	...	...
Oman Oman	1992	5	...	...	15	...	...
Pakistan [6] Pakistan [6]	1991	719	1957	16	...	...	...
Philippines Philippines	1990	306	*610	*10	1570	*9468	*156
Qatar Qatar	1990	*1	*6	*12	190	120	247
Saudi Arabia Arabie saoudite	1990	6	...	...	...	...	...
Singapore Singapour	1988	*7	*470	*178	...	...	...
Sri Lanka Sri Lanka	1992	80	...	...	...	...	...
Tajikistan Tadjikistan	1992	110	56853	10145	26	481	86
Thailand Thaïlande	1992	395	...	...	1522	...	...
Turkey Turquie	1990	872	1500	27	1325	1325	24
United Arab Emirates [1] Emirats arabes unis [1]	1990	1	30	19	80	922	614
Uzbekistan Ouzbékistan	1992	43	1279	60	61	1598	75
Yemen Yémen Former Democratic Yemen Ancienne Yémem dém.	1988	*5	*43	...	...	...	...
Former Yemen Arab Republic Ancienne Yémem rép. arabe	1988	*7	*40	...	...	...	...
Europe · Europe							
Albania Albanie	1989	42	65	20	143	3477	1074
Andorra Andorre	1992	4	*8	*138	...	...	...
Austria Autriche	1993	141	...	...	2481	...	...
Belarus Bélarus	1992	338	4749	465	155	3765	369
Belgium Belgique	1992	3	*40	*4	13706	...	...
Bosnia & Herzegovina Bosnie–Herzégovine	1992	2	2508	636	...	...	...
Bulgaria [7] Bulgarie [7]	1992	871	8992	1008	745	3097	347
Croatia Croatie	1990	563	*2781	*616	352	6357	1407
former Czechoslovakia † ancienne Tchécoslovaquie †	1990	64	849	54	2513	...	...
Czech Republic Rép. tchèque	1993	168	64	6	1168	...	...
Denmark Danemark	1992	11	1490	289	205	7838	1520

15
Non-daily newspapers and periodicals [*cont.*]
Journaux non quotidiens et périodiques [*suite*]

| Country or area
Pays ou zone | Year
Année | Non-daily newspapers
Journaux non quotidiens | | | Periodicals
Périodiques | | |
| | | Number
Nombre | Circulation
Diffusion | | Number
Nombre | Circulation
Diffusion | |
			Total (000)	Per 1000 inhabitants Pour 1000 habitants		Total (000)	Per 1000 inhabitants Pour 1000 habitants
Estonia [8] Estonie [8]	1993	169	...	...	312	...	...
Faeroe Islands Iles Féroé	1992	7	6	128	...	...	...
Finland Finlande	1993	*171	*1143	*226	5711[9]	...	...
France France	1991	227	3068	54	2672	120018	2106
Germany † Allemagne †	1992	35	5322	66	9010	395036	4916
Federal Republic of Germany [10] Rép. féd. d'Allemagne [10]	1990	34	4562	...	7831	309041	...
former German Dem. Rep. l'ancienne Rép. dém. allemande	1988	30	9431	...	1209	23872	...
Gibraltar Gibraltar	1992	*5	*6	*221	...	...	...
Greece Grèce	1988	1051	...	...	309	...	...
Holy See [1] Saint-Siège [1]	1992	*2	*130	..	48	102	...
Hungary Hongrie	1991	279	4603	446	1203	14927	1447
Iceland Islande	1993	78	...	...	629	...	...
Ireland Irlande	1988	54	1935	549	...	...	...
Italy Italie	1992	230	1277	22	10064	85071	1490
Latvia Lettonie	1992	186	2717	1030	170	1912	725
Liechtenstein Liechtenstein	1991	3	3	97	...	...	...
Lithuania Lituanie	1992	395	2851	767	237	2602	700
Luxembourg [1] Luxembourg [1]	1990	1	3	8	508	...	...
Malta Malte	1992	8	...	...	359	...	...
Monaco [1] Monaco [1]	1992	*1	*8	*267	3	38	1226
Netherlands Pays-Bas	1990	...	...	...	367	19283	1290
Norway Norvège	1992	66	358	84	7010	...	...
Poland Pologne	1993	53	1710	45	2997	57605	1504
Portugal Portugal	1993	173	4068	414	866	7050	717
Republic of Moldova République de Moldova	1992	212	*1269	*289	68	351	80
Romania [3] Roumanie [3]	1990	24	* 812	*35	1379	...	...
Russian Federation Fédération de Russie	1992	4498	86677	585	2592	918218	6201
San Marino Saint-Marin	1992	6	13	542	18	10	417
Slovakia Slovaquie	1992	262	2091	395	424	8725	1648
Slovenia Slovénie	1992	153	...	...	482	...	...
Spain Espagne	1988	85	*3100	*80	...	...	...

15
Non-daily newspapers and periodicals [cont.]
Journaux non quotidiens et périodiques [suite]

Country or area Pays ou zone	Year Année	Non-daily newspapers Journaux non quotidiens			Periodicals Périodiques		
		Number Nombre	Circulation Diffusion Total (000)	Per 1000 inhabitants Pour 1000 habitants	Number Nombre	Circulation Diffusion Total (000)	Per 1000 inhabitants Pour 1000 habitants
Sweden [2] [5] Suède [2] [5]	1992	70	414	48	46	4947	572
Switzerland [2] [11] Suisse [2] [11]	1992	139	1286	184	*3079	...	...
TFYR Macedonia L'ex−R.y. Macédoine	1990	110	10373	5069	74	347	170
Ukraine Ukraine	1992	1605	18194	352	321	3491	68
United Kingdom Royaume−Uni	1988	818	29047	509	...	...	...
Yugoslavia Yougoslavie	1992	599	5088	487	397	747	71
Yugoslavia, SFR † Yougoslavie, Rfs †	1990	2229	21756	914	1361	4197	176
Oceania · Océanie							
American Samoa Samoa américaines	1992	2	4	86	...	...	...
Australia Australie	1988	*460	*17204	*1050	...	...	...
Cook Islands Iles Cook	1988	*1	*2	*83	...	...	...
Fiji Fidji	1988	*7	*99	*138	...	...	...
French Polynesia Polynésie française	1988	*1	*4	*19	...	...	...
Guam Guam	1988	*4	*26	*203	...	...	...
Kiribati Kiribati	1988	*2	*4	*57	...	...	...
New Caledonia Nouvelle−Calédonie	1988	*1	*5	*31	...	...	...
New Zealand Nouvelle−Zélande	1988	139	*1100	*332	...	...	...
Niue [9] Nioué [9]	1992	1	2	950	9	10	4900
Norfolk Island Ile Norfolk	1992	1	1	...	...	...	...
Papua New Guinea Papouasie−Nouv.−Guinée	1988	*4	*78	*21	...	...	...
Samoa Samoa	1988	*5	*23	*143	...	...	...
Solomon Islands Iles Salomon	1988	4	12	40	...	...	...
Tokelau Tokélaou	1988	*1	*2	*750	...	...	...
Tonga Tonga	1988	*2	*9	*96	...	...	...
Tuvalu Tuvalu	1992	1	0.3	*33	...	...	...
Vanuatu Vanuatu	1992	1	2	11	...	...	...
former USSR · ancienne URSS							
former USSR † ancienne URSS †	1989	8092	92710	332	5228	5085133	18203

15
Non–daily newspapers and periodicals [*cont.*]
Journaux non quotidiens et périodiques [*suite*]

Source:
United Nations Educational, Scientific and Cultural Organization
(Paris).

† For detailed descriptions of data pertaining to former
Czechoslovakia, Germany, SFR Yugoslavia and former USSR,
see Annex I – Country or area nomenclature, regional and
other groupings.

1 Data on non–dailies refer to 1988.
2 Data on periodicals refer to 1988.
3 Data on non–dailies refer to 1989.
4 Data on non–dailies include daily newspapers.

5 Data on periodicals refer only to periodicals for the general
public.
6 Data on non–dailies include periodicals.
7 Data on non–daily newspapers include regional editions.
8 Data on non–dailies refer to 1992.
9 Data on periodicals refer to 1990.
10 Data on periodicals refer to 1989.
11 Data on non–dailies include to newspapers purchased and do not
include satellites publications.

Source:
Organisation des Nations Unies pour l'éducation, la science et
la culture (Paris).

† Pour les descriptions en détails des données relatives à
l'ancienne Tchécoslovaquie, l'Allemagne, la Rfs Yugoslavie et
l'ancienne URSS, voir l'Annexe I – Nomenclature des pays ou
zones, groupements régionaux et autres groupements.

1 Les données pour les non–quotidiens se réfèrent à 1988.
2 Les données relatives aux périodiques se réfèrent à 1988.
3 Les données pour les non–quotidiens se réfèrent à 1989.
4 Les données relatives aux non–quotidiens comprennent les
quotidiens.
5 Les données relatives aux périodiques se réfèrent seulement aux
périodiques destinés au grand public.
6 Les données relatives aux non–quotidiens comprennent les
periodiques.
7 Les données relatives aux journaux non–quotidiens comprennent
les éditions régionales.
8 Les données relatives aux non–quotidiens se réfèrent à 1992.
9 Les données relatives aux périodiques se réfèrent à 1990.
10 Les données relatives aux périodiques se réfèrent à 1989.
11 Les données relatives aux non–quotidiens se réfèrent seulement
aux journaux payants et n'incluent pas les éditions satellites.

16
Television and radio receivers
Postes récepteurs de télévision et de radio

Country or area		Number (000) Nombre (000)				Per 1000 inhabitants Pour 1000 habitants			
Pays ou zone	Code §	1980	1985	1990	1993	1980	1985	1990	1993
Africa · Afrique									
Algeria	T	975	1500	1840	2100	52	69	74	79
Algérie	R	3700	4800	5810	6310	197	219	233	236
Angola	T	30	37	57	68	4	5	6	7
Angola	R	145	217	260	295	21	27	28	29
Benin	T	5	15	23	28	1	4	5	6
Bénin	R	230	300	415	461	66	75	90	91
Botswana	T	–	–	20	23	–	–	16	17
Botswana	R	75	115	150	167	83	107	118	119
Burkina Faso	T	20	37	48	54	3	5	5	6
Burkina Faso	R	125	150	235	265	18	19	26	27
Burundi	T	–	0.3	5	9	–	0	1	2
Burundi	R	160	250	320	375	39	53	58	62
Cameroon	T	–	–	270	307	–	–	23	25
Cameroun	R	760	1200	1650	1830	88	120	143	146
Cape Verde	T	–	–	1	1	–	–	3	3
Cap–Vert	R	41	50	59	65	142	161	173	176
Central African Rep.	T	1	5	13	15	0	2	4	5
Rép. centrafricaine	R	120	150	200	227	52	58	68	72
Chad	T	–	–	7	8	–	–	1	1
Tchad	R	750	1150	1350	1470	168	229	243	245
Comoros	T	–	–	0.2	0.2	–	–	0	0
Comores	R	46	56	69	78	120	123	127	129
Congo	T	4	5	13	17	2	3	6	7
Congo	R	100	138	250	280	60	72	112	115
Côte d'Ivoire	T	310	500	703	805	38	50	59	60
Côte d'Ivoire	R	1000	1300	1700	1905	122	131	142	143
Djibouti	T	5	12	22	25	18	31	43	45
Djibouti	R	21	30	41	45	75	77	79	81
Egypt	T	1400	3860	5700	6800	32	78	101	113
Egypte	R	6000	12000	17000	18500	137	241	302	307
Equatorial Guinea	T	1	2	3	4	5	7	9	10
Guinée équatoriale	R	87	128	147	160	401	410	418	422
Ethiopia	T	30	70	115	165	1	2	2	3
Ethiopie	R	3000	8000	9300	10200	82	194	196	197
Gabon	T	9	22	43	48	12	22	38	38
Gabon	R	105	132	165	183	130	134	144	147
Gambia									
Gambie	R	73	105	148	169	114	141	160	162
Ghana	T	57	150	225	265	5	12	15	16
Ghana	R	1700	2500	4000	4420	158	195	266	269
Guinea	T	6	8	40	48	1	2	7	8
Guinée	R	135	180	240	270	30	36	42	43
Guinea–Bissau									
Guinée–Bissau	R	25	30	38	41	31	34	39	40
Kenya	T	62	100	225	280	4	5	10	11
Kenya	R	650	1600	2000	2300	39	80	85	87
Lesotho	T	–	1	10	13	–	0	6	7
Lesotho	R	33	44	56	63	25	28	31	32
Liberia	T	21	35	47	54	11	16	18	19
Libéria	R	335	475	580	645	179	216	225	227
Libyan Arab Jamahiriya	T	186	235	435	504	61	62	96	100
Jamah. arabe libyenne	R	200	800	1020	1140	66	211	224	226
Madagascar	T	45	100	240	272	5	9	19	20
Madagascar	R	1600	1950	2400	2655	177	183	191	192
Malawi									
Malawi	R	260	1500	2000	2375	42	207	214	226
Mali	T	–	1	10	13	–	0	1	1
Mali	R	105	250	400	450	15	32	43	44
Mauritania	T	–	1	45	50	–	0	22	23
Mauritanie	R	150	250	291	318	97	142	145	147
Mauritius	T	92	140	233	242	95	138	220	222
Maurice	R	260	335	385	399	269	330	364	366

16
Television and radio receivers [*cont.*]
Postes récepteurs de télévision et de radio [*suite*]

Country or area Pays ou zone	Code §	Number (000) Nombre (000)				Per 1000 inhabitants Pour 1000 habitants			
		1980	1985	1990	1993	1980	1985	1990	1993
Morocco	T	890	1370	1850	2050	46	63	76	79
Maroc	R	3000	3850	5250	5670	155	176	216	219
Mozambique	T	2	7	40	54	0	1	3	4
Mozambique	R	254	450	650	720	21	33	46	48
Namibia	T	5	16	30	33	5	14	22	23
Namibie	R	..	150	180	205	..	127	133	140
Niger	T	5	12	35	42	1	2	5	5
Niger	R	250	300	460	520	45	45	60	61
Nigeria	T	550	1000	3500	4000	8	12	36	38
Nigéria	R	7000	14500	18700	20650	97	175	194	196
Réunion	T	81	89	98	104	160	161	162	164
Réunion	R	100	122	145	155	198	222	240	244
Rwanda									
Rwanda	R	175	335	450	500	34	55	64	66
Saint Helena									
Sainte-Hélène	R	1	2	2	2	280	263	383	386
Sao Tome and Principe									
Sao Tomé-et-Principe	R	23	27	32	34	245	255	269	270
Senegal	T	8	200	265	290	1	31	36	37
Sénégal	R	360	700	830	920	65	110	113	116
Seychelles	T	–	2	6	6	–	31	86	88
Seychelles	R	21	25	32	35	333	385	457	486
Sierra Leone	T	20	30	42	47	6	8	11	11
Sierra Leone	R	450	775	925	1000	139	216	231	233
Somalia	T	–	1	105	118	–	0	12	13
Somalie	R	112	200	320	370	17	25	37	41
South Africa	T	2010	3000	3700	4000	69	91	100	101
Afrique du Sud	R	8000	10000	11450	12450	274	303	309	314
Sudan	T	800	1100	1800	2121	43	51	73	80
Soudan	R	3500	5375	6280	6860	187	250	255	257
Swaziland	T	1	8	14	16	2	12	19	20
Swaziland	R	81	101	120	132	145	156	161	163
Togo	T	10	15	22	26	4	5	6	7
Togo	R	530	630	740	820	203	208	210	211
Tunisia	T	300	400	625	690	47	55	77	81
Tunisie	R	1000	1185	1550	1700	157	163	192	198
Uganda	T	72	90	180	220	6	6	10	11
Ouganda	R	400	1250	1900	2130	30	83	106	107
United Rep. of Tanzania	T	7	8	40	55	0	0	2	2
Rép.-Unie de Tanzanie	R	290	365	600	720	16	17	23	26
Western Sahara	T	2	4	5	5	18	20	20	21
Sahara occidental	R	22	33	42	48	169	179	182	183
Zaire	T	10	13	40	62	0	0	1	2
Zaïre	R	1500	2800	3600	4000	56	88	96	97
Zambia	T	60	90	210	237	10	13	26	27
Zambie	R	135	500	650	730	24	73	80	82
Zimbabwe	T	73	178	260	290	10	21	26	27
Zimbabwe	R	240	500	832	920	34	60	84	86
America, North · Amérique du Nord									
Anguilla									
Anguilla	R	..	..	2	3	..	..	307	314
Antigua and Barbuda	T	16	19	23	24	262	306	359	369
Antigua-et-Barbuda	R	17	21	26	28	279	339	406	425
Aruba	T	..	..	..	19	..	..	..	275
Aruba	R	..	..	..	40	..	..	..	580
Bahamas	T	31	51	57	61	148	218	223	226
Bahamas	R	102	120	137	146	486	513	535	545
Barbados	T	52	60	70	73	209	237	272	279
Barbade	R	135	200	225	228	542	791	875	877
Belize	T	–	–	31	34	–	–	164	167
Belize	R	71	88	109	118	486	530	577	578
Bermuda	T	30	45	56	57	556	804	918	924
Bermudes	R	60	68	77	79	1111	1214	1254	1268

16
Television and radio receivers [*cont.*]
Postes récepteurs de télévision et de radio [*suite*]

Country or area		Number (000) Nombre (000)				Per 1000 inhabitants Pour 1000 habitants			
Pays ou zone	Code §	1980	1985	1990	1993	1980	1985	1990	1993
British Virgin Islands	T	2	3	3	4	167	204	206	212
Iles Vierges brit.	R	6	7	8	9	458	486	470	472
Canada	T	10617	14028	17000	17800	432	541	612	618
Canada	R	17734	23237	27305	28600	721	896	983	992
Cayman Islands	T	2	4	5	6	106	190	200	201
Iles Caïmanes	R	12	19	25	28	706	910	962	966
Costa Rica	T	155	200	420	465	68	76	138	142
Costa Rica	R	190	650	781	844	83	246	257	258
Cuba	T	1273	1940	1770	1850	131	192	167	170
Cuba	R	2914	3282	3650	3768	300	325	344	346
Dominica	T	–	–	5	5	–	–	70	75
Dominica	R	31	38	42	43	419	528	592	599
Dominican Republic	T	400	500	600	680	70	78	84	90
République dominicaine	R	900	1020	1210	1300	158	160	170	172
El Salvador	T	300	350	475	520	66	74	92	94
El Salvador	R	1550	1900	2125	2280	343	401	411	413
Greenland	T	4	7	11	12	70	132	196	202
Groënland	R	15	19	23	23	300	358	402	406
Grenada	T	–	–	30	31	–	–	330	332
Grenade	R	35	45	54	55	393	500	588	594
Guadeloupe	T	37	77	102	108	113	217	261	262
Guadeloupe	R	50	80	89	94	153	225	227	228
Guatemala	T	175	207	475	530	25	26	52	53
Guatemala	R	350	450	600	680	51	57	65	68
Haiti	T	16	21	30	33	3	4	5	5
Haïti	R	105	140	290	330	20	24	45	48
Honduras	T	65	280	370	415	18	67	76	78
Honduras	R	500	1600	1980	2175	140	382	406	408
Jamaica	T	170	215	310	340	80	93	131	141
Jamaïque	R	800	920	1010	1045	375	398	427	433
Martinique	T	38	44	48	51	117	129	133	137
Martinique	R	62	67	72	75	190	196	200	202
Mexico	T	3820	8500	12350	13500	57	113	146	150
Mexique	R	9000	15000	21500	23000	134	199	254	255
Montserrat	T	–	–	2	2	–	–	148	149
Montserrat	R	6	6	6	6	458	545	573	579
Netherlands Antilles	T	43	58	63	65	247	319	332	333
Antilles néerlandaises	R	175	190	202	208	1006	1044	1065	1066
Nicaragua	T	160	190	240	275	57	59	65	67
Nicaragua	R	670	802	955	1075	239	248	260	261
Panama	T	225	350	400	430	115	162	167	169
Panama	R	300	400	540	575	154	185	225	227
Puerto Rico	T	725	850	930	965	226	253	263	267
Porto Rico	R	2000	2300	2505	2576	624	683	709	712
Saint Kitts and Nevis	T	4	5	9	9	91	116	202	208
Saint–Kitts–et–Nevis	R	...	21	27	27	...	488	643	650
Saint Lucia	T	9	17	25	26	80	135	188	189
Sainte–Lucie	R	81	92	100	105	704	738	752	761
Saint Pierre and Miquelon	T	3	4	4	4	533	600	650	654
Saint–Pierre–et–Miquelon	R	4	4	4	4	583	633	696	700
Saint Vincent and Grenadines	T	5	6	15	16	53	59	140	145
Saint–Vincent–et–Grenadines	R	42	55	70	73	429	539	654	664
Trinidad and Tobago	T	210	320	387	405	194	276	313	317
Trinité–et–Tobago	R	300	500	600	625	277	431	485	489
Turks and Caicos Is.									
Iles Turques et Caïques	R	4	5	6	7	506	510	512	513
United States	T	155800	190000	203000	210500	684	797	812	816
Etats–Unis	R	454500	500000	529440	546800	1996	2097	2118	2120
US Virgin Islands	T	50	59	64	66	515	596	630	635
Iles Vierges américaines	R	82	93	101	104	845	939	990	1000
America, South · Amérique du Sud									
Argentina	T	5140	6500	7100	7420	183	214	218	220
Argentine	R	12000	18000	21800	22700	427	594	670	672

16
Television and radio receivers [*cont.*]
Postes récepteurs de télévision et de radio [*suite*]

Country or area Pays ou zone	Code §	Number (000) Nombre (000)				Per 1000 inhabitants Pour 1000 habitants			
		1980	1985	1990	1993	1980	1985	1990	1993
Bolivia	T	300	420	730	800	56	71	111	113
Bolivie	R	2800	3675	4380	4725	523	623	666	669
Brazil	T	15000	25000	30800	32650	124	185	207	209
Brésil	R	38000	49000	57000	61000	313	363	384	390
Chile	T	1225	1750	2700	2910	110	145	205	211
Chili	R	3250	4000	4500	4765	292	331	342	345
Colombia	T	2250	2750	3600	4000	85	93	111	118
Colombie	R	3300	4000	5600	6020	124	136	173	177
Ecuador	T	500	600	880	970	63	66	86	88
Equateur	R	2425	2850	3330	3580	305	313	324	326
Falkland Islands (Malvinas)									
Iles Falkland (Malvinas)	R	1	1	1	1	400	500	500	503
French Guiana	T	13	17	21	24	191	184	175	179
Guyane française	R	30	59	75	86	441	643	644	645
Guyana	T	—	—	28	32	—	—	35	39
Guyana	R	310	355	387	400	408	449	486	490
Paraguay	T	68	85	300	390	22	23	69	83
Paraguay	R	350	600	730	800	112	162	169	170
Peru	T	895	1500	2080	2260	52	77	96	99
Pérou	R	2750	4000	5420	5800	159	205	251	253
Suriname	T	40	45	55	58	113	119	138	140
Suriname	R	189	230	265	280	532	610	663	676
Uruguay	T	368	500	710	730	126	166	229	232
Uruguay	R	1630	1760	1865	1903	559	585	603	604
Venezuela	T	1710	2250	3100	3400	113	131	159	163
Venezuela	R	5900	7000	8600	9260	391	408	441	443
Asia · Asie									
Afghanistan	T	45	100	137	175	3	7	9	10
Afghanistan	R	1200	1450	1720	2080	75	100	114	118
Bahrain	T	90	170	208	230	259	411	424	430
Bahreïn	R	125	210	269	296	360	507	549	553
Bangladesh	T	80	261	525	670	1	3	5	6
Bangladesh	R	1500	4000	4855	5360	17	41	45	47
Bhutan									
Bhoutan	R	7	18	24	27	6	13	16	17
Brunei Darussalam	T	26	45	60	66	135	199	233	241
Brunéi Darussalam	R	41	55	68	74	212	243	265	270
Cambodia	T	35	52	68	77	5	7	8	8
Cambodge	R	600	800	942	1045	92	106	107	108
China	T	4000	10000	35000	45000	4	9	30	38
Chine	R	55000	120000	209500	219550	55	112	181	184
Cyprus	T	85	92	101	110	135	138	144	152
Chypre	R	162	190	205	215	258	286	292	296
East Timor									
Timor oriental	R	4	5	6	6	7	7	7	8
Hong Kong	T	1114	1275	1550	1660	221	234	272	286
Hong−kong	R	2550	3250	3800	3900	506	596	666	671
India	T	3000	10000	27000	36500	4	13	32	40
Inde	R	26000	50000	67000	72000	38	65	79	80
Indonesia	T	3000	6438	10500	11800	20	38	57	62
Indonésie	R	15000	21500	26500	28300	99	128	145	148
Iran, Islamic Rep. of	T	2000	2600	3620	4050	51	53	61	63
Iran, Rép. islamique d'	R	6400	10000	13428	14730	163	204	228	230
Iraq	T	650	900	1300	1450	50	59	72	75
Iraq	R	2100	3000	3880	4225	161	196	215	217
Israel	T	900	1100	1245	1430	232	260	267	272
Israël	R	950	1800	2180	2510	245	425	468	478
Japan	T	62976	70000	75500	77000	539	579	611	618
Japon	R	79200	95000	111000	113500	678	786	899	911
Jordan	T	171	240	315	375	59	63	74	76
Jordanie	R	550	791	1015	1200	188	206	238	243
Korea, Dem.People's Rep.	T	130	200	330	430	7	10	15	19
Corée, Rép. pop. dém. de	R	1500	2000	2600	2850	82	101	119	124

16
Television and radio receivers [*cont.*]
Postes récepteurs de télévision et de radio [*suite*]

Country or area Pays ou zone	Code §	Number (000) Nombre (000)				Per 1000 inhabitants Pour 1000 habitants			
		1980	1985	1990	1993	1980	1985	1990	1993
Korea, Republic of	T	6300	7721	9000	9500	165	189	210	215
Corée, République de	R	20000	38605	43350	44700	525	946	1011	1013
Kuwait	T	353	450	575	615	257	262	268	346
Koweït	R	390	535	700	725	284	311	327	408
Lao People's Dem. Rep.	T	–	–	22	32	–	–	5	7
République dém. pop. lao	R	350	430	520	580	109	120	124	126
Lebanon	T	750	800	880	970	281	300	344	346
Liban	R	2000	2050	2255	2490	749	768	883	887
Macau	T	–	–	30	36	–	–	88	94
Macao	R	80	99	120	135	331	349	351	352
Malaysia	T	1200	1800	2640	2915	87	115	148	151
Malaisie	R	5650	6600	7680	8280	411	421	429	430
Maldives	T	1	3	5	6	7	17	24	25
Maldives	R	7	19	25	28	44	103	116	118
Mongolia	T	6	45	85	96	3	24	39	41
Mongolie	R	160	200	289	315	96	105	133	136
Myanmar	T	1	20	75	120	0	1	2	3
Myanmar	R	774	2500	3400	3665	23	67	81	82
Nepal	T	–	20	35	55	–	1	2	3
Népal	R	300	450	650	720	20	27	34	35
Oman	T	35	900	1130	1300	32	644	645	653
Oman	R	300	800	1010	1155	272	573	577	580
Pakistan	T	938	1304	1989	2450	11	13	16	18
Pakistan	R	5500	8500	10650	11660	64	83	87	88
Philippines	T	1050	1500	2700	3050	22	27	44	47
Philippines	R	2100	5000	8600	9260	43	91	141	143
Qatar	T	76	120	190	210	331	335	392	397
Qatar	R	90	150	188	206	393	419	388	389
Saudi Arabia	T	2100	3050	3950	4370	219	241	246	255
Arabie saoudite	R	2500	3545	4655	5015	260	280	290	293
Singapore	T	750	850	1020	1065	311	332	377	381
Singapour	R	900	1550	1720	1800	373	606	636	644
Sri Lanka	T	35	450	600	885	2	28	35	49
Sri Lanka	R	1454	2551	3400	3600	98	158	197	201
Syrian Arab Republic	T	385	600	740	850	44	58	60	62
Rép. arabe syrienne	R	1700	2200	3150	3515	195	213	255	257
Thailand	T	1000	4122	5900	6500	21	81	106	113
Thaïlande	R	6550	8000	10300	10900	140	156	185	189
Turkey	T	3500	8000	9750	10500	79	159	174	176
Turquie	R	5000	7000	9000	9650	113	139	160	162
United Arab Emirates	T	89	130	172	192	88	94	103	106
Emirats arabes unis	R	240	380	515	565	236	276	308	311
Viet Nam	T	...	2000	2600	3000	...	33	39	42
Viet Nam	R	5000	6000	6900	7420	93	100	103	104
Yemen	T	..	..	300	365	..	..	27	28
Yémen	R	..	..	310	400	..	..	27	30
former Dem. Yemen	T	35	41	..	..	19	19	..	..
ancienne Yémen dém.	R	118	150	..	..	63	70	..	..
former Yemen Arab Rep.	T	5	28	..	..	1	4	..	..
ancienne Yémen rép. arabe	R	110	150	..	..	17	20	..	..
Europe · Europe									
Albania	T	96	232	280	300	36	78	85	89
Albanie	R	400	493	570	600	150	166	173	177
Andorra	T	4	6	7	22	118	136	138	367
Andorre	R	7	9	11	13	194	200	205	206
Austria	T	2950	3260	3650	3770	391	431	474	479
Autriche	R	3830	4180	4755	4860	507	553	617	618
Belarus	T	2100	2500	2750	2775	218	251	269	272
Bélarus	R	2145	2900	3150	3185	223	291	308	313
Belgium	T	3815	3950	4450	4550	387	401	447	453
Belgique	R	7200	7450	7660	7745	731	756	770	771

16
Television and radio receivers [*cont.*]
Postes récepteurs de télévision et de radio [*suite*]

Country or area Pays ou zone	Code §	Number (000) Nombre (000)				Per 1000 inhabitants Pour 1000 habitants			
		1980	1985	1990	1993	1980	1985	1990	1993
Bulgaria	T	2150	2220	2250	2310	243	248	250	260
Bulgarie	R	3500	3750	3950	3990	395	419	439	450
Croatia	T	940	976	1027	1525	215	218	227	338
Croatie	R	1050	1120	1150	1360	240	251	255	301
former Czechoslovakia †	T	5900	6080	7302	..	385	392	466	..
ancienne Tchècoslovaquie †	R	7800	8050	12418	..	509	519	793	..
Czech Republic	T	..	..	..	4905	..	..	..	476
Républic Tchèque	R	..	..	..	6500	..	..	..	631
Denmark	T	2550	2675	2750	2780	498	523	535	538
Danemark	R	4750	4875	5250	5345	927	953	1021	1035
Estonia	T	..	..	..	560	..	..	..	361
Estonie	R								
Faeroe Islands	T	4	9	11	12	93	196	243	249
Iles Féroé	R	18	22	24	24	407	478	504	511
Finland	T	1980	2300	2470	2550	414	469	495	504
Finlande	R	4000	4830	4960	5040	837	985	995	996
France	T	19000	21500	22800	23700	353	390	402	412
France	R	39900	48000	50370	51200	741	870	888	890
Germany †	T	..	..	44000	45200	..	..	554	559
Allemagne †	R	..	..	69650	72000	..	..	878	890
Federal Republic of Germany	T	27000	29500	..	..	439	483	..	..
Rép. féd. d'Allemagne	R	55000	57500	..	..	893	942	..	..
former German Dem. Rep.	T	8600	12300	..	..	514	739	..	..
ancienne Rép. dém. allemande	R	8970	10250	..	..	536	616	..	..
Gibraltar	T	7	8	10	10	240	282	349	351
Gibraltar	R	33	34	36	36	1124	1199	1289	1294
Greece	T	1650	1896	1970	2100	171	191	192	202
Grèce	R	3310	4000	4250	4320	343	403	415	416
Hungary	T	3320	4250	4330	4360	310	402	418	427
Hongrie	R	5340	6144	6275	6300	499	581	605	617
Iceland	T	65	75	82	88	285	311	322	335
Islande	R	162	185	200	208	711	768	784	791
Ireland	T	785	910	1025	1060	231	256	293	301
Irlande	R	1275	2050	2170	2240	375	577	619	636
Italy	T	22000	23600	24200	24500	390	416	424	429
Italie	R	34000	37000	45500	45800	602	652	798	802
Latvia	T	..	..	..	1200	..	..	..	460
Lettonie	R	..	..	..	1700	..	..	..	651
Liechtenstein	T	7	9	10	10	280	322	332	337
Liechtenstein	R	13	18	19	20	520	656	655	661
Lithuania	T	..	..	..	1420	..	..	..	383
Lituanie	R	..	..	..	1430	..	..	..	385
Luxembourg	T	90	92	97	103	247	251	255	261
Luxembourg	R	200	228	237	250	549	621	622	633
Malta	T	202	235	262	269	623	683	740	745
Malte	R	165	178	186	190	509	517	525	526
Monaco	T	17	19	22	23	630	679	735	739
Monaco	R	26	28	30	31	967	1008	1012	1013
Netherlands	T	5650	6700	7200	7500	399	462	482	491
Pays—Bas	R	9200	12000	13550	13865	650	828	906	907
Norway	T	1430	1640	1790	1835	350	395	422	427
Norvège	R	2700	3230	3370	3430	661	778	794	798
Poland	T	8750	10400	11250	11400	246	280	295	298
Pologne	R	10615	12250	16500	16800	298	329	433	439
Portugal	T	1540	1765	1820	1870	158	178	184	190
Portugal	R	1660	2000	2240	2280	170	202	227	232
Romania	T	4085	4375	4520	4595	184	193	195	200
Roumanie	R	3930	4100	4600	4660	177	180	198	202
Russian Federation	T	..	..	53978	55000	..	..	365	372
Fédération de Russie	R	...	...	49700	49900	...	...	336	338
San Marino	T	6	7	8	8	300	314	350	352
Saint—Marin	R	10	12	14	14	476	527	587	590

16
Television and radio receivers [*cont.*]
Postes récepteurs de télévision et de radio [*suite*]

Country or area Pays ou zone	Code §	Number (000) Nombre (000)				Per 1000 inhabitants Pour 1000 habitants			
		1980	1985	1990	1993	1980	1985	1990	1993
Slovakia	T	..	..	...	2520	..	..	...	474
Slovaquie	R	..	..	..	3015	..	..	..	567
Slovenia	T	460	500	550	575	251	266	287	297
Slovénie	R	500	650	700	730	273	346	365	377
Spain	T	9505	10400	15500	15800	253	270	395	400
Espagne	R	9700	11300	12000	12300	258	294	306	311
Sweden	T	3830	3875	4000	4085	461	464	467	470
Suède	R	7000	7250	7500	7640	842	868	876	879
Switzerland	T	2300	2550	2725	2825	364	390	399	400
Suisse	R	5140	5426	5682	5870	813	830	831	832
The Former Yugoslav Rep. of Macedonia	T	262	310	335	350	146	161	164	165
L'ex–Rép. Yougoslave de Macédoine	R	..	..	365	382	..	..	178	180
Ukraine	T	12722	15190	16950	17500	255	298	328	339
Ukraine	R	28941	36434	41000	41700	579	716	794	809
United Kingdom	T	22600	24500	24900	25200	401	433	434	435
Royaume–Uni	R	53500	57000	65600	66400	950	1007	1143	1146
Yugoslavia	T	1620	1710	1800	1900	170	174	177	179
Yougoslavie	R	1930	2020	2100	2210	203	205	207	207
Yugoslavia, SFR †	T	4245	4500	4720	..	190	195	198	..
Yougoslavie, Rfs †	R	5000	5580	5850	..	224	241	246	..
Oceania · Océanie									
American Samoa	T	6	7	10	11	173	179	211	220
Samoa américaines	R	32	38	47	51	991	974	1003	1006
Australia	T	5600	7000	8200	8610	384	448	486	489
Australie	R	16000	19500	21600	22730	1098	1247	1279	1290
Cook Islands	T	–	–	3	3	–	–	167	176
Iles Cook	R	8	10	12	13	417	612	678	695
Fiji	T	–	–	11	13	–	–	15	17
Fidji	R	300	370	430	460	473	529	592	607
French Polynesia	T	18	27	33	36	121	155	170	172
Polynésie française	R	78	93	108	117	517	532	546	553
Guam	T	63	76	88	95	589	633	657	660
Guam	R	100	150	185	201	935	1250	1381	1396
Kiribati									
Kiribati	R	12	13	15	16	193	195	203	208
Nauru									
Nauru	R	4	5	6	6	557	569	572	575
New Caledonia	T	25	40	45	47	175	258	268	269
Nouvelle–Calédonie	R	69	80	94	98	479	516	560	561
New Zealand	T	1035	1397	1500	1570	332	430	446	451
Nouvelle–zélande	R	2755	2950	3130	3260	885	909	931	935
Niue									
Nioué	R	1	1	1	1	317	358	558	563
Norfolk Island	T	–	–	1	1	–	–	*0	*1
Ile Norfolk	R	2	2	2	2	...	...	...	...
Palau [1]	T	6	8	9	10	500	557	604	606
Palaos [1]	R	85	98	125	135	7083	7000	8333	8438
Papua New Guinea	T	–	–	9	12	–	–	2	3
Papouasie–Nouv.–Guinée	R	180	230	280	310	58	67	73	75
Samoa	T	3	5	6	7	16	31	38	39
Samoa	R	32	68	74	77	201	425	454	461
Solomon Islands	T	–	–	–	2	–	–	–	6
Iles Salomon	R	20	27	38	43	88	100	119	121
Tokelau									
Tokélaou	R	...	1	1	1	...	425	525	600
Tonga	T	–	–	–	2	–	–	–	15
Tonga	R	20	30	53	54	217	330	552	560
Tuvalu									
Tuvalu	R	2	2	3	3	206	237	304	307
Vanuatu	T	–	–	1	2	–	–	9	12
Vanuatu	R	23	36	43	47	197	269	285	292
former USSR · ancienne URSS									
former USSR †	T	76500	82400	..	..	296	305	..	..
ancienne URSS †	R	130000	182800	..	..	504	678	..	..

16
Television and radio receivers [*cont.*]
Postes récepteurs de télévision et de radio [*suite*]

Source:
United Nations Educational, Scientific and Cultural Organization
(Paris).

† For detailed descriptions of data pertaining to former
Czechoslavakia, Germany, SFR Yugoslavia and former USSR,
see Annex I – – Country or nomenclature, regional and other
groupings.

§ T: Estimated number of television receivers in use.
R: Estimated number of radio receivers in use.

1 Including data for Federated States of Micronesia,
Marshall Islands and Northern Mariana Islands.

Source:
Organisation des Nations Unies pour l'éducation, la science et la culture
(Paris).

† Pour les descriptions en détails des données relatives à l'ancienne
Tchécoslovaquie, l'Allemagne, la Rfs Yougoslavie et l'ancienne USSR,
voir l'Annexe I – – Nomenclature des pays ou zones, groupements
régionaux et autres groupements.

§ T: Estimation du nombre de récepteurs de télévision en service.
R: Estimation du nombre de récepteurs de radio en service.

1 Y compris les données pour les Etats fédérés de Micronésie,
les îles Marshall et les îles Mariannes du Nord.

17
Cinemas: number, seating capacity, annual attendance and box office receipts
Cinémas: nombre d'établissements, nombre de sièges, fréquentation annuelle et recettes guichet

Country or area Pays ou zone	Year Année	Cinemas [1] – Cinémas [1]						
		Number Nombre	Seating capacity Sièges		Annual attendance [2] Fréquentation annuelle [2]		Gross receipts Recettes brutes	
			No. (000)	P. 1000	No. (000000)	P. capita P. habitant	Currency Monnaie	Total (000000)
Africa · Afrique								
Algeria Algérie	1988	249	...	...	21.0	0.9	dinar	181
Benin Bénin	1993	23	9.4	1.8	0.7	0.1	CFA Franc	116
Cameroon Cameroun	1991	232	39.9	3.4	...	...	CFA Franc	...
Côte d'Ivoire Côte d'Ivoire	1993	60	70.0	5.3	7.3	0.5	CFA Franc	...
Egypt Egypte	1991	149	126.0	2.2	16.5	0.3	pound	23
Gabon Gabon	1992	5	3.0	2.5	2.0	1.6	CFA Franc	104
Guinea Guinée	1991	80	41.0	6.9	3.9	0.7	franc	793
Kenya Kenya	1993	42	7.0	0.3	5.8	0.2	shilling	...
Madagascar Madagascar	1991	11	...	...	0.4	0.0	franc	209
Mauritius Maurice	1993	16	14.0	12.8	0.7	0.7	rupee	* 22
Morocco Maroc	1993	203	138.0	5.3	20.4	0.8	dirham	...
United Rep. Tanzania Rép.−Unie de Tanzanie	1991	28	12.4	0.5	* 1.9	* 0.1	shilling	148
Zimbabwe Zimbabwe	1991	24	12.2	1.2	1.8	0.2	dollar	7.6
America, North · Amérique du Nord								
Barbados Barbade	1991	4	1.5	...	0.0	0.0	dollar	...
Canada [3] Canada [3]	1990	742	722.0	26.0	79.0	2.8	dollar	439
Cuba [4] Cuba [4]	1993	903	187.9	17.3	23.8	2.2	peso	6.4
Guatemala Guatemala	1988	110	59.0	6.8	7.7	0.9	quetzal	13
Mexico Mexique	1989	1 913	...	...	246.0	3.0	new peso	...
United States Etats−Unis	1991	24 570	...	...	981.9	3.9	dollar	4 803
America, South · Amérique du Sud								
Argentina Argentine	1991	348	69.0	2.1	* 18.0	* 0.5	peso	...
Bolivia Bolivie	1993	130	...	...	* 2.2	* 0.3	boliviano	...
Chile Chili	1993	* 133	* 75.9	* 5.5	* 8.0	* 0.6	peso	...
Colombia Colombie	1988	515	235.0	7.5	41.0	1.3	peso	12 078
Ecuador Equateur	1991	134	75.3	7.2	6.8	0.6	sucre	4 949
Venezuela Venezuela	1993	218	132.0	6.3	19.0	0.9	bolívar	1 896
Asia · Asie								
Armenia Arménie	1993	577	118.5	33.9	...	...	dram	44
Azerbaijan Azerbaïdjan	1993	100	348.0	47.1	1.9	0.3	manat	...
China Chine	1991	139 639	...	...	14 428.4	12.3	yuan	2 365

17
Cinemas: number, seating capacity, annual attendance and box office receipts [*cont.*]
Cinémas: nombre d'établissements, nombre de sièges, fréquentation annuelle et recettes guichet [*suite*]

Country or area Pays ou zone	Year Année	Cinemas [1] – Cinémas [1]			Annual attendance [2] Fréquentation annuelle [2]		Gross receipts Recettes brutes	
		Number Nombre	Seating capacity Sièges					
			No. (000)	P. 1000	No. (000000)	P. capita P. habitant	Currency Monnaie	Total (000000)
Cyprus Chypre	1993	17	8.7	12.0	...	...	pound	...
Georgia Géorgie	1993	290	106.8	19.6	30.4	5.6	lari	91 093
Hong Kong Hong−kong	1989	153	...	...	58.5	10.3	dollar	1 367
India * Inde *	1991	13 448	16 751.4	7.8	4 300.0	5.0	rupee	...
Iran, Islamic Rep. of Iran, Rép. islamique de	1993	277	171.4	2.7	29.0	0.5	rial	12 616
Israel Israël	1994	266	62.5	11.5	10.0	1.8	new sheqel	...
Japan Japon	1993	1 734	...	...	130.7	1.1	yen	163 700
Jordan Jordanie	1993	35	...	...	0.2	0.0	dinar	...
Kazakstan Kazakstan	1993	5 947	...	...	39.3	2.3	tenge	2.3
Korea, Republic of Corée, République de	1993	640	212.0	4.8	...	...	won	...
Kuwait Koweït	1990	14	17.3	8.1	0.3	0.1	dinar	...
Lao People's Dem. Rep. Rép. dém. pop. lao	1991	31	6.6	1.5	1.0	0.2	kip	245
Lebanon Liban	1993	79	26.8	9.5	99.3	35.3	pound	691 733
Malaysia Malaisie	1993	261	157.0	8.2	39.4	2.0	ringgit	...
Mongolia Mongolie	1989	581	...	...	20.1	9.5	tugrik	...
Pakistan Pakistan	1991	702	3.2	...	...	...	rupee	...
Qatar Qatar	1989	4	4.0	8.6	0.3	0.6	riyal	...
Sri Lanka Sri Lanka	1993	259	143.0	8.0	27.2	1.5	rupee	223
Syrian Arab Republic Rép. arabe syrienne	1993	55	28.8	1.7	4.0	0.3	pound	12
Tajikistan Tadjikistan	1993	918	200.2	34.7	12.7	2.2	rouble	235
Thailand Thaïlande	1989	668	8.0	0.1	...	...	baht	...
Turkey Turquie	1991	341	178.0	3.1	16.5	0.3	lira	...
United Arab Emirates Emirats arabes unis	1989	33	30.0	18.6	...	...	dirham	...
Uzbekistan Ouzbékistan	1993	2 777	609.3	27.9	29.0	1.3	sum	1 219
Viet Nam Viet Nam	1988	1 451	...	...	239.9	3.8	dong	...
Europe · Europe								
Albania [4] Albanie [4]	1989	551	28.6	8.9	6.9	2.2	lek	5.5
Austria Autriche	1993	386	70.6	9.0	12.0	1.5	schilling	809
Belarus Bélarus	1993	4 168	744.3	73.1	29.5	2.9	rouble	2 581
Belgium Belgique	1993	409	...	...	18.6	1.9	franc	3 247
Bulgaria Bulgarie	1993	270	122.0	13.8	11.1	1.2	lev	103
Croatia Croatie	1993	132	52.0	11.5	3.7	0.8	kuna	16 196
former Czechoslovakia † anc. Tchècoslovaquie †	1990	2 679	801.2	51.2	50.2	3.2	koruna	386

17

Cinemas: number, seating capacity, annual attendance and box office receipts [*cont.*]

Cinémas: nombre d'établissements, nombre de sièges, fréquentation annuelle et recettes guichet [*suite*]

Country or area Pays ou zone	Year Année	Cinemas [1] – Cinémas [1]			Annual attendance [2] Fréquentation annuelle [2]		Gross receipts Recettes brutes	
		Number Nombre	Seating capacity Sièges				Currency Monnaie	Total (000000)
			No. (000)	P. 1000	No. (000000)	P. capita P. habitant		
Czech Republic République tchèque	1993	1 380	360.0	35.0	21.9	2.1	koruna	433
Denmark Danemark	1993	312	52.0	10.1	10.2	2.0	krone	312
Estonia Estonie	1992	453	69.1	44.2	3.4	2.2	kroon	3.2
Finland Finlande	1993	335	60.8	12.0	5.8	1.1	markka	196
France [5] France [5]	1993	4 713	961.7	16.7	132.7	2.3	franc	4 519
Germany † Allemagne †	1993	3 748	745.7	9.2	130.5	1.6	deutsche mark	1 170
Greece Grèce	1991	584	392.0	38.1	...	...	drachma	...
Hungary Hongrie	1993	633	* 134.0	* 13.1	14.8	1.4	forint	1 504
Iceland Islande	1993	24	6.1	23.2	1.2	4.7	króna	...
Italy Italie	1993	3 567	...	...	92.2	1.6	lira	758 829
Latvia Lettonie	1993	420	...	...	1.8	0.7	lats	...
Lithuania Lituanie	1993	245	53.5	14.4	2.3	0.6	litas	1.15
Luxembourg [6] Luxembourg [6]	1993	17	3.1	7.8	0.7	1.8	franc	134
Malta Malte	1992	10	7.0	19.5	0.3	0.8	lira	...
Monaco Monaco	1990	4	1.6	53.3	0.1	3.7	french franc	3.9
Netherlands Pays–Bas	1991	430	98.8	6.6	14.7	1.0	guilder	182
Norway Norvège	1993	400	96.0	22.3	10.9	2.5	krone	410
Poland Pologne	1993	705	212.0	5.5	14.9	0.4	zloty	346 466
Portugal Portugal	1993	187	66.1	6.7	7.8	0.8	escudo	3 122
Republic of Moldova République de Moldova	1993	76	29.9	6.8	4.7	1.1	leu	0.438
Romania [5] Roumanie [5]	1993	1 470	168.3	7.3	33.7	1.5	leu	...
Russian Federation Fédération de Russie	1993	1 643	285.6	1.9	380.7	2.6	rouble	* 190 000
San Marino Saint–Marin	1993	3	2.0	83.3	0.0	1.7	lira	191
Slovakia Slovaquie	1993	456	150.0	28.2	8.9	1.7	koruna	...
Slovenia Slovénie	1993	94	28.6	14.8	2.3	1.2	tolar	732
Spain Espagne	1993	1 791	...	...	87.7	2.2	peseta	40 579
Sweden Suède	1993	1 169	...	...	15.7	1.8	krona	860
Switzerland Suisse	1993	415	98.6	14.0	15.9	2.3	franc	180
TFYR Macedonia L'ex–R.Y. Macédoine	1992	38	14.0	6.7	0.3	0.2	denar	0.7
Ukraine Ukraine	1993	865	378.3	7.3	126.7	2.5	karbovanets	27 529
United Kingdom Royaume–Uni	1993	1 890	...	...	113.4	2.0	pound	343
Yugoslavia Yugoslavie	1992	170	76.0	7.2	2.3	0.2	dinar	...

17
Cinemas: number, seating capacity, annual attendance and box office receipts [*cont.*]
Cinémas: nombre d'établissements, nombre de sièges, fréquentation annuelle et recettes guichet [*suite*]

Country or area Pays ou zone	Year Année	Cinemas [1] – Cinémas [1]			Annual attendance [2] Fréquentation annuelle [2]		Gross receipts Recettes brutes	
		Number Nombre	Seating capacity Sièges					
			No. (000)	P. 1000	No. (000000)	P. capita P. habitant	Currency Monnaie	Total (000000)
Yugoslavia, SFR † Yugoslavie, Rfs †	1989	1 167	401.0	16.9	44.6	1.9	dinar	643 490
Oceania · Océanie								
Australia Australie	1993	940	298.0	16.9	52.8	3.0	dollar	369
former USSR · ancienne URSS								
former USSR † ancienne URSS †	1990	140 700	...	...	2 900.0	10.3	rouble	...

Source: United Nations Educational, Scientific and Cultural Organization (Paris).

† For detailed descriptions of data pertaining to former Czechoslovakia, Germany, SFR Yugoslavia and former USSR, see Annex I — Country or area nomenclature, regional and other groupings.

1 Includes totals of fixed cinemas, drive−in cinemas and mobile units to the extent information available on each.
2 Annual attendance per inhabitant does not include attendance at mobile units and/or drive−in cinemas.
3 Receipts do not include taxes.
4 Mobile units are non−commercial.
5 Data on seating capacity refer to 35 mm cinemas only.
6 Data do not include receipts of one cinema center of five screens.

Source: Organisation des Nations Unies pour l'éducation, la science et la culture (Paris).

† Pour les descriptions en détails des données relatives à l'ancienne Tchécoslovaquie, l'Allemagne, la Rfs Yougoslavie et l'ancienne URSS, voir l'Annexe I — Nomenclature des pays ou zones, groupements régionaux et autres groupements.

1 Comprend le total des salles fixes, des cinémas pour automobilistes et des cinémas itinérants, dans la mesure où l'on dispose des données correspondant à chacune de ces catégories.
2 La fréquentation annuelle par habitant ne comprend pas la fréquentation des cinémas pour automobilistes et/ou itinérants.
3 Les recettes ne tiennent pas compte des taxes.
4 Les cinémas itinérants ne sont pas commerciaux.
5 Les données sur le nombre de sièges se réfèrent aux cinémas de 35 mm seulement.
6 Les données ne comprennent pas les recettes d'un complexe cinématographique de cinq écrans.

18
Telefax stations and mobile cellular telephone subscribers
Postes de télécopie et abonnés au téléphone mobile cellulaire

Country or area Pays ou zone	Telefax stations Postes de télécopie					Mobile cellular telephone subscribers Abonnés au téléphone mobile cellulaire				
	1990	1991	1992	1993	1994	1990	1991	1992	1993	1994
Africa · Afrique										
Algeria Algérie	...	...	5000	5500	4140	470	4781	4781	4781	1350
Angola Angola	...	...	...	...	...	...	...	...	1100	...
Benin Bénin	144	184	300	500	600	...	...	...	...	...
Botswana [1] Botswana [1]	820	...	235	250	220	...	...	...	...	...
Burundi Burundi	600	...	...	80	...	...	...	...	320	340
Cape Verde Cap–Vert	...	300	...	...	...	...	...	...	...	...
Central African Rep. Rép. centrafricaine	...	...	50	30	30	...	...	...	...	...
Chad Tchad	72	93	128	170	190	...	...	...	...	...
Comoros Comores	27	57	76	100		...	...	...	...	...
Congo Congo	...	...	110	...	...	...	...	...	...	...
Djibouti Djibouti	101	128	124	120	90	...	...	...	...	...
Egypt [2] Egypte [2]	7620	11695	13640	17610	21590	4000	...	4910	6880	7370
Equatorial Guinea Guinée équatoriale	...	...	...	50	100	...	...	...	...	...
Eritrea Erythrée	...	...	130	310	510	...	...	...	...	...
Ethiopia Ethiopie	250[2][3]	260[2][3]	521	760	1060	...	...	...	...	...
Gabon Gabon	191	...	...	...	...	...	...	280	1200	2580
Gambia [1] Gambie [1]	190	361	365	650	700	...	...	204	400	810
Ghana Ghana	1921	2677	3817	4000	4500	...	...	400	1742	3340
Guinea Guinée	...	...	...	...	30	...	...	...	42	310
Guinea–Bissau Guinée–Bissau	...	...	300	380	...	...	...	...	...	...
Kenya [2] Kenya [2]	2000	2500	3000	...	...	...	...	1100	1162	1990
Lesotho Lesotho	283	338	447	...	...	...	...	...	...	...
Malawi Malawi	342	411	680	920	920	...	...	...	...	...
Mauritania Mauritanie	300	...	...	...	...	...	...	...	...	...
Mauritius Maurice	...	1280	1560	1860	1750	2200	2500	2912	4037	5710
Mayotte Mayotte	100	...	...	...	...	...	...	...	...	...
Morocco Maroc	...	...	5000	7500	...	904	1500	3228	6725	13790
Mozambique Mozambique	...	...	1237	2000	7180	...	...	...	...	...
Niger Niger	150	207	268	310	...	...	...	...	...	...
Nigeria Nigéria	...	...	...	...	...	...	...	...	9049	12800
Reunion Réunion	1476	1906	...	...	...	...	2735	...	...	...

18
Telefax stations and mobile cellular telephone subscribers [*cont.*]
Postes de télecopie et abonnés au téléphone mobile cellulaire [*suite*]

Country or area Pays ou zone	Telefax stations Postes de télécopie					Mobile cellular telephone subscribers Abonnés au téléphone mobile cellulaire				
	1990	1991	1992	1993	1994	1990	1991	1992	1993	1994
Rwanda Rwanda	300	321	481	...	...	...	...	...	...	...
Sao Tome and Principe Sao Tomé−et−Principe	...	31	91	130	150	...	...	...	...	...
Senegal Sénégal	...	...	...	...	...	28	...	...	...	100
Seychelles [1] Seychelles [1]	275	347	439	502	510	...	...	...	...	...
Sierra Leone [1] Sierra Leone [1]	23	48	152	500	800	...	...	...	...	...
South Africa Afrique du Sud	...	...	50000	60000	...	5680	7100	12510	40000	340000
Saint Helena Sainte−Hélène	...	20	30	40	...	...	...	...	...	...
Sudan Soudan	...	258	...	...	5000	...	...	...	...	...
Swaziland [1] Swaziland [1]	341	688	793	800	920	...	...	...	...	...
United Rep.Tanzania Rép. Unie de Tanzanie	600	900	2000	...	...	...	...	...	...	370
Togo Togo	335	430	590	1400	4000	...	...	...	...	...
Tunisia Tunisie	25000	5000	10000	15000	20000	953	1239	1889	2269	2710
Uganda [2] Ouganda [2]	698	...	1600	...	...	...	...	...	...	...
Zambia [1] Zambie [1]	460	460	460	460	460	...	...	...	...	...
Zimbabwe [2] Zimbabwe [2]	1487	2000	2000	...	10000	...	...	...	...	...
America, North · Amérique du Nord										
Anguilla Anguilla	...	140	160	190	...	...	...	...	...	...
Antigua and Barbuda [1] Antigua−et−Barbuda [1]	350	...	...	...	...	...	...	...	...	...
Aruba Aruba	...	...	500	...	...	...	...	...	20	...
Bahamas Bahamas	522	569	524	550	...	1922	2020	2600	2400	...
Barbados [1] Barbade [1]	1300	1500	1503	1390	...	...	486	796	1560	...
Belize [1] Belize [1]	...	253	381	540	...	...	...	...	200	830
Bermuda [1] Bermudes [1]	...	...	...	...	...	1112	1440	1936	3400	5130
Canada Canada	300000	450000	500000	525000	...	583000	786000	1022754	1326390	1890000
Cayman Islands [1] Iles Caïmanes [1]	...	150	120	120	...	...	560	990	1260	1810
Costa Rica Costa Rica	1707	2138	2177	2190	2190	...	...	3008	4533	6990
Cuba Cuba	207	300	392	...	...	...	...	234	500	1150
Dominica Dominique	220	238	290	...	...	...	...	...	...	...
Dominican Republic Rép. dominicaine	...	2187	2061	2500	...	3166	5605	7190	11020	20040
El Salvador El Salvador	3500	...	...	...	...	...	...	...	1632	6480
Greenland Groënland	...	...	1150	...	...	...	...	170	440	1110
Grenada Grenade	150	217	272	...	...	150	147	181	282	350
Guadeloupe Guadeloupe	291	...	...	...	...	814	...	...	...	...

18
Telefax stations and mobile cellular telephone subscribers [*cont.*]
Postes de télecopie et abonnés au téléphone mobile cellulaire [*suite*]

Country or area	Telefax stations Postes de télécopie					Mobile cellular telephone subscribers Abonnés au téléphone mobile cellulaire				
Pays ou zone	1990	1991	1992	1993	1994	1990	1991	1992	1993	1994
Guatemala Guatemala	1000	3000	4000	6000	10000	293	1221	2141	2990	10460
Jamaica [1] Jamaïque [1]	...	...	1567	...	...	...	2512	7910	18640	26110
Martinique Martinique	690	...	...	...	...	802	...	...	...	...
Mexico Mexique	...	...	150000	180000	...	34944	170080	311510	385341	569250
Montserrat Montserrat	...	...	...	...	...	...	...	60	60	70
Nicaragua Nicaragua	...	...	...	...	...	...	...	...	320	2180
Puerto Rico Porto Rico	...	...	495590	543250	...	20369	33410	51115	68410	109220
Saint Lucia [1] Sainte−Lucie [1]	...	...	...	...	...	...	...	...	...	520
St. Vincent and Grenadines [1] St. Vincent−et−Grenadine [1]	...	244	336	...	670	...	...	70	83	...
Trinidad and Tobago Trinité−et−Tobago	1806[4]	...	1480[4]	1780[4]	1960[4]	...	426	1277	1679	2600
Turks and Caicos Islands Iles Turques et Caiques	...	...	200	...	...	...	...	...	...	...
United States Etats−Unis	5084000	7210000	9056000	11304000	14052000	5283055[5]	7557148[5]	11032753[5]	16009461[5]	24134420[5]
U.S. Virgin Islands Iles Vierges américaines	...	...	...	...	...	2000	...	2000	...	...
America, South · Amérique du Sud										
Argentina [6] Argentine [6]	...	...	25000	30000	...	12000	25000	46590	115820	202220
Bolivia Bolivie	...	...	...	...	...	...	500	1556	2651	4060
Brazil Brésil	90000	125000	160000	200000	...	667	6700	30729	180220	574000
Chile Chili	5700	...	12457	15000	...	13921	36140	64438	85186	100000
Colombia Colombie	35000	44000	53000	65000	79700	...	...	...	...	101460
Ecuador Equateur	...	...	25000	30000	...	...	...	...	...	17860
Falkland Islands Iles Falkland	...	...	140	...	...	...	...	...	...	...
French Guiana Guyane française	185	...	...	...	...	...	...	...	...	...
Guyana Guyana	195	...	...	...	...	...	...	841	1029	1250
Paraguay Paraguay	1189	1493	1691	...	...	...	...	1500	1500	7660
Peru Pérou	1814	1948	2082	5000	...	1650	5700	21550	36300	52200
Suriname Suriname	200	244	250	500	...	...	...	...	1080	1380
Uruguay Uruguay	...	...	7000	8000	...	...	...	1712	4070	7000
Venezuela Venezuela	...	...	15000	16000	...	7422	16600	78560	182600	319000
Asia · Asie										
Armenia Arménie	...	...	180	220	300	...	...	...	...	...
Azerbaijan Azerbaïdjan	...	...	...	...	2500	...	...	...	...	500
Bahrain Bahreïn	2800[7]	3500[7]	3798[7]	5060[7]	5390[7]	6900	7354	9683	11360	17620
Bangladesh [2] Bangladesh [2]	...	...	1440	2000	2000	...	...	250	500	1100
Bhutan Bhoutan	...	...	130	...	300	...	...	...	...	...

18
Telefax stations and mobile cellular telephone subscribers [*cont.*]
Postes de télecopie et abonnés au téléphone mobile cellulaire [*suite*]

Country or area Pays ou zone	Telefax stations Postes de télécopie					Mobile cellular telephone subscribers Abonnés au téléphone mobile cellulaire				
	1990	1991	1992	1993	1994	1990	1991	1992	1993	1994
Brunei Darussalam Brunéi Darussalam	1145	1221	1233	1230	1500	1770	3025	4103	8304	15620
Cambodia Cambodge	...	...	...	1170	...	...	...	...	2510	6500
China Chine	39268	57899	89271	125000	200000	18319	47544	176943	638000	1566000
Cyprus Chypre	3000	...	6000	7000	...	3156	5131	9739	15288	22940
Georgia Géorgie	...	...	...	420	460	...	...	...	...	...
Hong Kong [1] Hong–kong [1]	111239	138616	196872	233546	256960	133910	189660	233324	290840	484820[8]
India Inde	5000	10000	35000	45000	50000	...	...	...	...	...
Indonesia Indonésie	15000	20000	35000	45000	55000	18096	24528	35546	53438	78020
Iran, Islamic Rep. of [1] Iran, Rép. islamique d' [1]	13000	...	22015	25000	30000	...	...	...	...	9200
Israel Israël	35000	55000	70000	80000	...	15240	23000	36104	64484	140000
Japan [1] Japon [1]	4000000	5000000	5500000	5750000	6000000	868078	1378108	1712545	2131370	4331000[9]
Jordan Jordanie	...	...	27000	29000	31000	1439	1462	1462	1460	1450
Kazakstan Kazakstan	...	...	1070	1500	1990	...	...	...	...	3570
Korea, Dem. People's Rep. Corée, Rép. pop. dém. de	...	...	...	2960	3000	...	...	...	...	...
Korea, Republic of Corée, République de	230000	250000	300000	350000	375000	80000	166108	271868	417780	960260
Kuwait Koweït	...	527	...	25000	...	20735	...	51000	60100	85630
Kyrgyzstan Kirghizistan	...	...	...	...	...	...	...	...	...	100
Lao People's Dem. Rep. Rép. dém. populaire lao	...	150	200	300	500	...	...	290	340	630
Lebanon Liban	...	2000	3000	...	...	...	...	...	...	...
Macau Macao	3548	4336	5608	6660	7170	3197	6596	12414	18048	24720
Malaysia Malaisie	40000	45000	46000	52600	58090	86620	130000	210000	290000	571720
Maldives Maldives	235	...	...	...	480	...	...	...	...	...
Mongolia Mongolie	...	...	...	330	350	...	...	...	...	...
Myanmar Myanmar	...	...	...	...	1410	...	...	...	640	1820
Nepal Népal	500	610	610	590	600	...	...	...	...	...
Oman Oman	...	...	1560	...	...	2730	3672	4721	5616	6750
Pakistan Pakistan	2300	4100	5300	6500	8000	2000	8500	13500	16000	30000
Philippines Philippines	10000	15000	20000	30000	35000	9708	11083	52000	101740	200410
Qatar Qatar	950	2800	4000	4500	8000	3811	4057	4233	4289	9790
Saudi Arabia Arabie saoudite	...	...	50000	75000	...	14851	15331	15828	15910	15960
Singapore [1] Singapour [1]	33269	39354	48343	55580	...	51000	81900	120000	179000	235630
Sri Lanka Sri Lanka	4000	5890	8100	10000	11000	1010	1973	4000	13000	30000
Syrian Arab Republic Rép. arabe syrienne	...	...	...	...	4200	...	...	...	...	...

18
Telefax stations and mobile cellular telephone subscribers [*cont.*]
Postes de télecopie et abonnés au téléphone mobile cellulaire [*suite*]

Country or area	Telefax stations Postes de télécopie					Mobile cellular telephone subscribers Abonnés au téléphone mobile cellulaire				
Pays ou zone	1990	1991	1992	1993	1994	1990	1991	1992	1993	1994
Tajikistan Tadjikistan	...	...	...	...	1200	...	...	...	...	...
Thailand [5] Thaïlande [5]	6324[10]	7540[10]	25000	50000	60000	63220	123550	248716	436000	643000
Turkey Turquie	32882	48311	62876	77190	87610	31809	47828	61395	84187	174780
Turkmenistan Turkménistan	...	...	...	...	...	...	...	...	500	1000
United Arab Emirates Emirats arabes unis	15562	19700	24090	26100	29740	33580	43010	48920	70590	91240
Uzbekistan Ouzbékistan	...	...	570	1920	...	...	...	...	500	...
Viet Nam Viet Nam	500	...	2100	4894	7000	...	...	800	4060	13200
Yemen Yémen	778[10]	805[10]	782[10]	1300[10]	1980[10]	...	...	1550	5170	8190
Europe · Europe										
Albania Albanie	300	500	600	...	...	...	...	...	...	...
Andorra Andorre	...	...	1280	...	...	...	...	770	780	780
Austria Autriche	85000	160000	190000	210000	...	73698	115402	172453	220860	278200
Belarus Bélarus	...	...	1514	3160	...	...	...	...	324	...
Belgium Belgique	67000[4]	93320[4]	150000[4]	165000[4]	...	42880	51420	61460	66929	126940
Bulgaria Bulgarie	...	...	7500	10000	...	...	...	...	1000	...
Croatia Croatie	3320	7067	9079	14322	28350	240	2019	6320	11239	21660
Czech Republic République tchèque	4552	16059	29418	45520	58460	...	1242	4651	11151	20000
Denmark Danemark	100000	150000	170000	185000	...	148220	175943	211060	357590	503500
Estonia Estonie	...	...	1459	2180	10000	...	570	2500	7220	13770
Faeroe Islands Iles Féroé	...	...	1300	1400	...	...	1429	1718	1605	1960
Finland Finlande	75000	92000	105000	115000	124000	225980	283050	354220	459070	649160
France France	580000	650000	750000	1000000	...	283200	375000	436700	572000	603900
Germany Allemagne	696229[4]	946216[4]	1172700[4]	1296000[4]	1446600[4]	272609	532251	974890	1767980	2501400
Gibraltar Gibraltar	122	135	160	180	...	...	...	...	...	...
Greece Grèce	9200	12082	13273	15260	...	...	...	...	48000	167000
Hungary Hongrie	9693	14580	24721	25460	...	2645	8477	23292	45712	143000
Iceland Islande	1343	...	4000	4100	...	10010	12889	15251	17409	21850
Ireland [1] Irlande [1]	53000	60000	75000	80000	...	25000	32000	44000	61100	88000
Italy Italie	170450	190987	201000	202000	...	266000	568000	783000	1207000	2239740
Latvia Lettonie	...	...	596	930	800	...	...	1027	3800	8360
Liechtenstein Liechtenstein	...	...	...	960	...	...	...	...	...	...
Lithuania Lituanie	...	444	3000	1880	2990	...	...	267	1239	4510
Luxembourg Luxembourg	3500	4000	5000	5500	...	824	1130	1139	5082	12900

18
Telefax stations and mobile cellular telephone subscribers [*cont.*]
Postes de télécopie et abonnés au téléphone mobile cellulaire [*suite*]

Country or area Pays ou zone	Telefax stations Postes de télécopie					Mobile cellular telephone subscribers Abonnés au téléphone mobile cellulaire				
	1990	1991	1992	1993	1994	1990	1991	1992	1993	1994
Malta Malte	1456	1900	2224	3200	...	...	2280	3500	5300	7500
Monaco Monaco	...	...	1880	...	...	...	...	...	1150	2560
Netherlands Pays−Bas	180000	325000	372750	400000	...	79000	115000	166000	216000	321000
Norway Norvège	85000	107000	120000	130000	...	196828	227733	280000	397500	588800
Poland Pologne	5824	13156	25068	30000	...	...	...	2800	13570	38940
Portugal Portugal	10500	17700	26761	35340	...	6500	12600	37262	101231	173510
Republic of Moldova République de Moldova	35	122	245	520	510	100	100	160	170	...
Romania Roumanie	4000	5000	10231	1506	...	...	...	...	800	2780
Russian Federation Fédération de Russie	...	6540	13410	26320	...	...	300	6000	10000	27740
San Marino Saint−Marin	...	...	1800	2500	...	...	...	900	1300	1900
Slovakia Slovaquie	2514	7330	16202	27200	37900	...	119	1537	3125	5950
Slovenia Slovénie	73	135	7578	10480	...	...	523	3500	6500	16800
Spain Espagne	144310	176061	195029	215000	...	54700	108451	180296	257250	411930
Sweden Suède	170000	230000	300000	325000	...	461200	568200	656000	811600	1380000
Switzerland Suisse	83000[4]	118000[4]	135000[4]	169000[4]	175000[4]	125047	174557	215061	257703	332170
TFYR Macedonia L'ex−R.y. Macédonie	...	...	1408	1720	1780	...	...	...	...	...
Ukraine Ukraine	682	944	1465	...	...	...	...	...	65	5000
United Kingdom [1] Royaume−Uni [1]	750000	900000	1005000	1300000	...	1114000	1260000	1507000	2266000	3757000
Yugoslavia Yougoslavie	...	7860	8180	12930	13720	...	...	...	...	...
Oceania · Océanie										
American Samoa Samoa américaines	...	...	...	...	...	...	...	700	900	1200
Australia [2] Australie [2]	280000	350000	400000	425000	450000	184943	291459	497000	760000	1250000
Cook Islands Iles Cook	230	...	...	...	...	...	...	...	...	...
Fiji Fidji	1513	2079	2197	2300	2500	...	...	...	...	1100
French Polynesia Polynésie française	800	330	570[11]	800[11]	850	...	...	...	...	...
Guam Guam	...	...	...	...	...	...	867	1301	1907	4100
Kiribati Kiribati	38	76	96	110	130	...	...	...	...	...
Marshall Islands Iles Marshall	50	80	120	140	...	...	...	...	...	280
Micronesia, Fed. States of Micronésie, Etats féd. de	251	299	...	...	...	...	...	...	...	...
Nauru Nauru	...	...	...	...	...	...	...	...	150	450
New Caledonia Nouvelle−Calédonie	1000	1200	1350	1940	2200	...	...	...	...	...
New Zealand [1] Nouvelle−Zélande [1]	28000	35000	40000	45000	50000	54100	72300	100200	143800	229200
Northern Mariana Islands Iles Mariannes du Nord	...	...	1000	1000	1200	...	...	...	730	770

18
Telefax stations and mobile cellular telephone subscribers [*cont.*]
Postes de télécopie et abonnés au téléphone mobile cellulaire [*suite*]

Country or area / Pays ou zone	Telefax stations / Postes de télécopie					Mobile cellular telephone subscribers / Abonnés au téléphone mobile cellulaire				
	1990	1991	1992	1993	1994	1990	1991	1992	1993	1994
Papua New Guinea / Papouasie–Nvl–Guinée	629	1018	1085	840	800	...	...	...	...	...
Samoa / Samoa	...	...	100	300	410	...	...	...	...	...
Solomon Islands [1] / Iles Salomon [1]	126	410	440	650	700	...	...	...	...	140
Tonga / Tonga	83	127	134	170	180	...	...	...	...	...
Tuvalu / Tuvalu	...	...	...	10	...	...	...	...	...	...
Vanuatu / Vanuatu	...	...	...	...	500	...	...	...	...	60
Wallis and Futuna / Iles Wallis et Futuna	50	...	60	90	...	...	...	...	...	...

Source:
International Telecommunications Union (Geneva).

1   Year beginning 1 April.
2   Year ending 30 June.
3   Including Eritrea.
4   According to telefax directory.
5   Source: Cellular Telecommunications Industry Association.
6   Year ending 30 September.
7   Fax lines.
8   Year ending 31 March.
9   Data at September 1994.
10 Fax subscribers.
11 Facsimile machines provided by operator.

Source:
Union internationale des télécommunications (Genève).

1   L'année commençant le 1er avril.
2   L'année finissant le 30 juin.
3   Y compris l'Erythrée.
4   Selon les annuaires de télécopie.
5   Source : "Cellular Telecommunications Industry Association".
6   L'année finissant le 30 septembre.
7   Nombre de télécopie.
8   L'année finissant le 31 mars.
9   Données recueillies au septembre 1994.
10 Abonnés à télécopie.
11 Télécopiérs fournis par l'agent.

19
Telephones
Téléphones
Main telephone lines in operation and per 100 inhabitants
Nombre de lignes téléphoniques en service et pour 100 habitants

Country or area Pays ou zone	Number (000) Nombre (000)					Per 100 inhabitants Pour 100 habitants				
	1990	1991	1992	1993	1994	1990	1991	1992	1993	1994
Africa · Afrique										
Algeria Algérie	794	883	962	1 068	1 122	3.2	3.4	3.7	4.0	4.1
Angola Angola	70	72	49	53	...	0.8	0.8	0.5	0.5	...
Benin Bénin	15	15	16	20	24	0.3	0.3	0.3	0.4	0.5
Botswana[1] Botswana[1]	26	33	36	43	50	2.1	2.5	2.7	3.1	3.5
Burkina Faso Burkina Faso	16	18	20	22	26	0.2	0.2	0.2	0.2	0.3
Burundi Burundi	8	10	13	16	16	0.1	0.2	0.2	0.3	0.3
Cameroon Cameroun	40	42	55	57	...	0.4	0.4	0.5	0.5	...
Cape Verde Cap-Vert	8	9	11	15	19	2.2	2.4	2.9	3.8	4.7
Central African Rep. Rép. centrafricaine	5	5	6	7	7	0.2	0.2	0.2	0.2	0.2
Chad Tchad	4	4	4	5	5	0.1	0.1	0.1	0.1	0.1
Comoros Comores	3	4	4	4	4	0.7	0.7	0.8	0.8	0.9
Congo Congo	16	17	18	19	21	0.7	0.7	0.7	0.8	0.8
Côte d'Ivoire Côte d'Ivoire	73	79	86	94	108	0.6	0.6	0.7	0.7	0.8
Djibouti Djibouti	6	6	7	7	8	1.2	1.2	1.2	1.3	1.3
Egypt[2] Egypte[2]	1 602	1 817	2 028	2 235	2 456	3.1	3.4	3.7	4.0	4.3
Equatorial Guinea Guinée équatoriale	1	1	1	1	3	0.3	0.3	0.3	0.3	0.7
Eritrea Erythrée	...	...	...	13	15	...	...	...	0.4	0.4
Ethiopia incl.Eritrea[2] Ethiopie comp. Erythrée[2]	125	133	127	...	...	0.3	0.3	0.2	...	...
Ethiopia Ethiopie	...	...	...	132	138	...	...	...	0.3	0.3
Gabon Gabon	21	26	28	30	31	1.8	2.3	2.3	2.4	3.0
Gambia[13] Gambie[13]	6	10	14	16	18	0.7	1.1	1.4	1.6	1.7
Ghana Ghana	44	47	48	49	50	0.3	0.3	0.3	0.3	0.3
Guinea Guinée	11	12	11	12	9	0.2	0.2	0.2	0.2	0.1
Guinea-Bissau Guinée-Bissau	6	6	8	9	...	0.6	0.7	0.8	0.8	...

19
Telephones
Main telephone lines in operation and per 100 inhabitants [*cont.*]
Téléphones
Nombre de lignes téléphoniques en service et pour 100 habitants [*suite*]

Country or area Pays ou zone	Number (000) Nombre (000)					Per 100 inhabitants Pour 100 habitants				
	1990	1991	1992	1993	1994	1990	1991	1992	1993	1994
Kenya[2] Kenya[2]	183	200	207	215	229	0.8	0.8	0.8	0.9	0.9
Lesotho Lesotho	12	12	11	12	...	0.7	0.7	0.6	0.6	...
Liberia Libéria	...	3	5	5	...	...	0.1	0.2	0.2	...
Libyan Arab Jamah. Jamah. arabe libyenne	220	233	236	240	...	4.8	5.0	4.8	4.8	...
Madagascar Madagascar	32	36	37	35	34	0.3	0.3	0.3	0.3	0.2
Malawi Malawi	27	29	31	33	33	0.3	0.3	0.3	0.4	0.3
Mali Mali	11	12	13	14	...	0.1	0.1	0.1	0.2	...
Mauritania Mauritanie	6	6	7	8	8	0.3	0.3	0.3	0.4	0.4
Mauritius Maurice	56	64	79	107	129	5.2	5.9	7.2	9.6	11.7
Mayotte Mayotte	3	3	4	4	...	3.1	3.4	3.8	4.0	...
Morocco Maroc	402	497	654	821	993	1.6	1.9	2.5	3.1	3.8
Mozambique Mozambique	47	53	56	62	57	0.3	0.3	0.3	0.4	0.4
Namibia[1] Namibie[1]	53	57	61	70	...	3.7	3.8	4.0	4.5	...
Niger Niger	9	10	10	11	...	0.1	0.1	0.1	0.1	...
Nigeria Nigéria	289	294	321	342	369	0.3	0.3	0.3	0.3	0.3
Réunion Réunion	162	175	188	199	...	27.4	29.1	30.7	32.0	...
Rwanda Rwanda	10	11	12	12	15	0.2	0.2	0.2	0.2	0.2
Saint Helena Sainte-Hélène	1	1	1	2	2	...	15.3	18.7	21.9	26.1
Sao Tome and Principe Sao Tomé-et-Principe	2	2	2	2	2	1.9	1.9	1.9	1.9	2.0
Senegal Sénégal	44	48	58	64	72	0.6	0.6	0.7	0.8	0.9
Seychelles[1] Seychelles[1]	9	9	10	11	12	12.8	13.6	14.6	16.2	17.1
Sierra Leone Sierra Leone	13	14	14	14	16	0.3	0.3	0.3	0.3	0.3
Somalia Somalie	15	15	15	15	15	0.2	0.2	0.2	0.2	0.2
South Africa[1] Afrique du Sud[1]	3 315	3 435	3 524	3 660	3 845	8.7	8.8	8.9	9.0	9.5
Sudan Soudan	62	64	64	64	64	0.3	0.3	0.2	0.2	0.2

19
Telephones
Main telephone lines in operation and per 100 inhabitants [cont.]
Téléphones
Nombre de lignes téléphoniques en service et pour 100 habitants [suite]

Country or area Pays ou zone	Number (000) Nombre (000)					Per 100 inhabitants Pour 100 habitants				
	1990	1991	1992	1993	1994	1990	1991	1992	1993	1994
Swaziland[1] Swaziland[1]	14	15	15	16	19	1.7	1.8	1.8	1.9	2.1
Togo Togo	11	11	15	17	21	0.3	0.3	0.4	0.4	0.5
Tunisia Tunisie	303	337	375	421	474	3.8	4.1	4.5	4.9	5.4
Uganda[2] Ouganda[2]	28	28	30	21	35	0.2	0.2	0.2	0.1	0.2
United Rep.Tanzania Rép. Unie de Tanzanie	73	76	81	85	88	0.3	0.3	0.3	0.3	0.3
Zaire Zaïre	34	35	36	36	36	0.1	0.1	0.1	0.1	0.1
Zambia[1] Zambie[1]	65	69	76	78	80	0.8	0.9	0.9	0.9	0.9
Zimbabwe[2] Zimbabwe[2]	124	126	127	128	135	1.3	1.3	1.2	1.2	1.2
America, North · Amérique du Nord										
Anguilla Anguilla	...	3	3	3	4	...	35.6	38.7	38.0	46.5
Antigua and Barbuda[1] Antigua-et-Barbuda[1]	16	14	17	19	...	24.6	20.9	25.5	28.9	...
Aruba Aruba	19	20	20	21	...	28.4	30.3	30.5	31.3	...
Bahamas Bahamas	70	62	80	76	...	27.4	23.9	30.4	28.6	...
Barbados[1] Barbade[1]	83	78	80	83	87	32.4	30.1	30.9	31.8	33.4
Belize[1] Belize[1]	17	21	25	29	28	9.2	11.0	12.5	14.0	13.4
Bermuda[1] Bermudes[1]	37	39	40	42	47	61.7	63.9	64.7	67.8	75.0
British Virgin Islands Iles Vierges britanniques	...	...	8	8	9	...	...	45.3	46.5	47.1
Canada[4] Canada[4]	15 296	15 815	16 247	16 471	16 756	57.5	58.6	59.2	59.2	57.6
Cayman Islands[1] Iles Caïmanes[1]	12	12	13	14	18	...	43.4	44.0	44.9	58.8
Costa Rica Costa Rica	281	305	327	364	430	9.3	9.8	10.2	11.2	13.0
Cuba Cuba	337	339	337	349	350	3.2	3.2	3.1	3.2	3.2
Dominica Dominique	12	12	14	16	17	16.2	17.2	19.1	22.0	23.5
Dominican Republic Rép. dominicaine	341	411	479	552	605	4.8	5.7	6.6	7.4	7.9
El Salvador El Salvador	125	130	165	174	236	2.4	2.5	3.1	3.2	4.2
Greenland Groënland	17	17	17	18	18	29.9	30.3	30.6	31.7	32.1

19
Telephones
Main telephone lines in operation and per 100 inhabitants [cont.]
Téléphones
Nombre de lignes téléphoniques en service et pour 100 habitants [suite]

Country or area Pays ou zone	Number (000) Nombre (000)					Per 100 inhabitants Pour 100 habitants				
	1990	1991	1992	1993	1994	1990	1991	1992	1993	1994
Grenada Grenade	15	16	19	20	21	16.7	17.8	20.3	22.1	22.8
Guadeloupe Guadeloupe	118	127	139	149	159	30.3	32.1	34.6	36.7	37.8
Guatemala Guatemala	190	202	214	231	245	2.1	2.1	2.2	2.3	2.4
Haiti Haïti	45	45	45	45	...	0.7	0.7	0.7	0.7	...
Honduras Honduras	88	94	105	117	131	1.7	1.8	1.9	2.1	2.4
Jamaica[1] Jamaïque[1]	105	132	167	208	251	4.5	5.5	7.0	8.6	10.3
Martinique Martinique	122	132	141	150	155	33.9	36.5	38.5	40.5	41.4
Mexico Mexique	5 355	6 025	6 754	7 621	8 493	6.6	7.2	8.0	8.8	9.3
Montserrat Montserrat	4	4	4	5	5	...	36.4	39.4	37.8	44.0
Netherlands Antilles Antilles néerlandaises	47	49	49	50	...	24.8	25.3	25.3	25.5	...
Nicaragua Nicaragua	46	50	54	67	85	1.3	1.4	1.4	1.7	2.0
Panama Panama	216	229	243	261	287	8.9	9.3	9.7	10.2	11.1
Puerto Rico[5] Porto Rico[5]	1 002	1 060	1 134	1 207	1 315	26.4	29.9	31.7	33.5	36.1
Saint Kitts and Nevis[1] Saint-Kitts-et-Nevis[1]	10	10	12	12	14	23.1	24.3	27.7	29.6	33.2
Saint Lucia[1] Sainte-Lucie[1]	17	17	20	24	25	11.3	11.2	13.1	15.4	17.2
Saint Pierre and Miquelon Saint-Pierre-et-Miquelon	3	3	3	...	4	...	54.5	57.0	...	60.9
St. Vincent-Grenadines[1] St. Vincent-Grenadines[1]	13	15	16	16	17	12.3	13.6	14.3	15.0	15.5
Trinidad and Tobago Trinité-et-Tobago	165	174	180	192	204	13.3	13.9	14.2	15.0	15.8
Turks and Caicos Islands Iles Turques et Caiques	...	...	3	3	3	...	...	24.6	24.9	24.3
United States[4] Etats-Unis[4]	136 337	139 658	144 057	149 084	156 769	54.6	55.3	56.5	57.8	60.2
United States Virgin Is. Iles Vierges américaines	47	51	54	57	59	46.3	51.6	54.7	57.3	56.5
America, South · Amérique du Sud										
Argentina[6] Argentine[6]	3 087	3 199	3 682	4 092	4 834	9.6	9.8	11.1	12.2	14.1
Bolivia Bolivie	184	185	193	234	...	2.6	2.5	2.6	3.0	...
Brazil Brésil	9 409	10 076	10 670	11 557	12 927	6.3	6.7	6.9	7.4	8.1

19
Telephones
Main telephone lines in operation and per 100 inhabitants [*cont.*]
Téléphones
Nombre de lignes téléphoniques en service et pour 100 habitants [*suite*]

Country or area Pays ou zone	Number (000) Nombre (000)					Per 100 inhabitants Pour 100 habitants				
	1990	1991	1992	1993	1994	1990	1991	1992	1993	1994
Chile Chili	860	1 056	1 283	1 520	1 545	6.5	7.9	9.4	11.0	11.0
Colombia Colombie	2 415	2 633	2 822	3 221	3 518	7.5	8.0	8.4	9.5	9.7
Ecuador Equateur	491	491	531	598	658	4.7	4.6	4.8	5.3	5.9
French Guiana Guyane française	30	34	36	38	40	30.4	33.6	30.4	29.8	28.8
Guyana Guyana	13	16	28	41	44	1.6	2.0	3.5	5.1	5.3
Paraguay Paraguay	112	120	128	142	...	2.6	2.7	2.8	3.1	...
Peru Pérou	565	577	614	673	772	2.6	2.6	2.7	3.0	3.3
Suriname Suriname	37	41	44	47	50	9.1	10.0	10.8	11.6	12.0
Uruguay Uruguay	415	451	492	530	582	13.4	14.5	15.7	16.9	18.4
Venezuela Venezuela	1 488	1 599	1 832	2 083	2 334	7.7	8.1	9.1	10.0	10.9
Asia · Asie										
Afghanistan Afghanistan	36	37	29	29	29	0.2	0.2	0.1	0.1	0.2
Armenia Arménie	560	572	578	583	587	15.8	15.7	15.7	15.6	15.6
Azerbaijan Azerbaïdjan	620	627	657	647	635	8.7	8.7	8.9	8.7	8.5
Bahrain Bahreïn	94	101	113	124	136	18.7	19.5	21.2	22.9	24.8
Bangladesh[2] Bangladesh[2]	242	250	256	268	269	0.2	0.2	0.2	0.2	0.2
Bhutan Bhoutan	2	3	3	4	5	0.3	0.4	0.5	0.6	0.7
Brunei Darussalam Brunéi Darussalam	35	39	48	55	62	13.6	14.8	17.6	19.7	22.1
Cambodia Cambodge	5	4	4	4	5	0.1	0.0	0.0	0.0	0.1
China Chine	6 850	8 451	11 469	17 332	27 230	0.6	0.7	1.0	1.5	2.3
Cyprus Chypre	246	269	291	311	330	35.0	44.6	47.0	49.4	45.0
Georgia Géorgie	540	557	573	571	526	9.9	10.2	10.5	10.5	9.6
Hong Kong[1] Hong-kong[1]	2 475	2 642	2 820	2 992	3 149	43.4	45.9	48.5	51.0	54.0
India Inde	5 075	5 810	6 797	8 026	9 795	0.6	0.7	0.8	0.9	1.1
Indonesia Indonésie	1 066	1 295	1 652	1 909	2 521	0.6	0.7	0.9	1.0	1.3

19

Telephones
Main telephone lines in operation and per 100 inhabitants [cont.]
Téléphones
Nombre de lignes téléphoniques en service et pour 100 habitants [suite]

Country or area Pays ou zone	Number (000) Nombre (000)					Per 100 inhabitants Pour 100 habitants				
	1990	1991	1992	1993	1994	1990	1991	1992	1993	1994
Iran, Islamic Rep. of[1] Iran, Rép. islamique d'[1]	2 199	2 456	2 998	3 598	4 320	3.9	4.3	5.0	5.9	6.6
Iraq Iraq	675	675	675	675	...	3.7	3.6	3.5	3.4	...
Israel Israël	1 626	1 703	1 804	1 958	2 138	35.0	34.3	35.3	37.1	39.4
Japan[17] Japon[17]	54 528	56 260	57 652	58 830	59 870	44.1	45.4	46.4	47.1	48.0
Jordan Jordanie	246	265	278	290	305	7.5	7.2	7.1	7.1	7.2
Kazakstan Kazakstan	1 333	1 425	1 490	1 973	1 987	8.0	8.4	8.8	11.5	11.6
Korea, Dem. P. R. Corée, R. p. dém. de	780	800	840	1 089	...	3.6	3.6	3.7	4.7	...
Korea, Republic of Corée, République de	13 276	14 573	15 593	16 686	17 647	31.0	33.7	35.7	37.9	39.7
Kuwait Koweït	331	322	346	358	373	15.5	22.1	24.5	24.5	22.6
Kyrgyzstan Kirghizistan	314	332	339	367	339	7.2	7.5	7.5	8.1	7.3
Lao People's Dem. Rep. Rép. dém. pop. lao	7	7	9	9	16	0.2	0.2	0.2	0.2	0.4
Lebanon Liban	300	310	350	...	...	8.3	8.4	9.3	...	...
Macau Macao	93	107	121	134	145	27.1	30.1	32.3	34.4	36.8
Malaysia Malaisie	1 586	1 817	2 092	2 411	2 864	8.9	10.0	11.2	12.6	14.7
Maldives Maldives	6	8	9	10	12	2.9	3.4	3.7	4.2	4.8
Mongolia Mongolie	66	68	69	66	69	3.0	3.0	3.0	2.8	2.9
Myanmar Myanmar	70	86	99	119	131	0.2	0.2	0.2	0.3	0.3
Nepal Népal	57	65	69	73	77	0.3	0.3	0.4	0.4	0.4
Oman Oman	105	117	130	148	158	6.9	7.4	7.9	8.6	7.6
Pakistan Pakistan	843	1 116	1 244	1 528	2 048	0.8	1.0	1.0	1.2	1.6
Philippines Philippines	610	648	661	860	1 110	1.0	1.0	1.0	1.3	1.7
Qatar Qatar	92	96	105	111	117	18.9	19.4	20.6	21.4	21.7
Saudi Arabia Arabie saoudite	1 234	1 466	1 568	1 615	1 676	7.8	9.0	9.3	9.3	9.6
Singapore[1] Singapour[1]	1 054	1 101	1 169	1 246	1 332	39.0	39.9	41.5	43.5	47.3
Sri Lanka Sri Lanka	121	126	136	158	181	0.7	0.7	0.8	0.9	1.0

19
Telephones
Main telephone lines in operation and per 100 inhabitants [cont.]
Téléphones
Nombre de lignes téléphoniques en service et pour 100 habitants [suite]

Country or area Pays ou zone	Number (000) Nombre (000)					Per 100 inhabitants Pour 100 habitants				
	1990	1991	1992	1993	1994	1990	1991	1992	1993	1994
Syrian Arab Republic Rép. arabe syrienne	496	502	531	550	588	4.1	4.0	4.1	4.1	4.9
Tajikistan Tadjikistan	240	258	267	265	268	4.5	4.7	4.8	4.7	4.5
Thailand[68] Thaïlande[68]	1 325	1 553	1 790	2 215	2 752	2.4	2.7	3.1	3.8	4.7
Turkey Turquie	6 861	8 152	9 410	10 936	12 212	12.2	14.1	16.0	18.4	20.1
Turkmenistan Turkménistan	220	237	249	265	305	6.0	6.3	6.5	6.7	7.6
United Arab Emirates Emirats arabes unis	396	438	492	553	615	25.0	26.7	29.2	32.1	33.2
Uzbekistan Ouzbékistan	1 403	1 458	1 440	1 452	...	6.8	7.0	6.7	6.6	...
Viet Nam Viet Nam	99	137	153	260	442	0.2	0.2	0.2	0.4	0.6
Yemen Yémen	125	131	143	161	173	1.1	1.0	1.1	1.2	1.3
Europe · Europe										
Albania Albanie	40	42	45	43	48	1.2	1.3	1.3	1.3	1.4
Andorra Andorre	22	23	25	27	28	41.8	40.4	41.8	42.2	44.0
Austria Autriche	3 223	3 344	3 466	3 579	3 681	41.8	42.8	44.0	45.1	46.6
Belarus Bélarus	1 574	1 673	1 744	1 814	...	15.3	16.3	16.9	17.6	...
Belgium Belgique	3 913	4 096	4 264	4 396	4 526	39.3	40.9	42.5	43.7	44.9
Bosnia & Herzegovina Bosnie-Herzégovine	...	...	600	600	250	...	...	13.7	13.7	6.9
Bulgaria Bulgarie	2 175	2 205	2 340	2 410	2 955	25.2	25.7	27.5	27.6	33.5
Croatia Croatie	823	891	955	1 027	1 205	17.3	18.6	19.9	21.5	26.8
Czech Republic République tchèque	1 624	1 707	1 819	1 961	2 151	15.8	16.6	17.6	19.0	20.9
Denmark[9] Danemark[9]	2 911	2 951	3 005	3 060	3 123	56.6	57.3	58.1	58.9	60.4
Estonia Estonie	320	332	335	358	378	20.4	21.2	21.5	23.2	24.5
Faeroe Islands Iles Féroé	23	24	24	23	23	48.1	50.9	50.7	49.5	48.2
Finland Finlande	2 670	2 718	2 742	2 761	2 801	53.6	54.0	54.4	54.4	55.1
France[10] France[10]	28 085	29 100	30 100	30 900	31 600	49.5	51.0	52.5	53.6	54.7
Germany † Allemagne†	31 887	33 560	35 421	36 900	39 200	40.1	42.0	44.0	45.7	48.3

19
Telephones
Main telephone lines in operation and per 100 inhabitants [cont.]
Téléphones
Nombre de lignes téléphoniques en service et pour 100 habitants [suite]

Country or area Pays ou zone	Number (000) Nombre (000)					Per 100 inhabitants Pour 100 habitants				
	1990	1991	1992	1993	1994	1990	1991	1992	1993	1994
Gibraltar Gibraltar	11	12	13	14	15	35.8	41.1	45.3	48.7	54.1
Greece Grèce	3 949	4 190	4 497	4 744	4 976	38.9	40.9	43.7	45.7	47.8
Hungary Hongrie	996	1 128	1 291	1 498	1 732	9.4	10.9	12.5	14.6	17.0
Iceland[11] Islande[11]	131	136	140	144	148	51.2	52.5	53.7	54.4	55.7
Ireland[1] Irlande[1]	983	1 048	1 113	1 170	1 240	28.1	29.7	31.4	32.8	35.0
Italy Italie	22 350	23 071	23 709	24 167	24 542	38.8	39.9	41.0	41.7	42.9
Latvia Lettonie	620	643	652	694	681	23.2	24.2	24.7	26.8	26.4
Liechtenstein Liechtenstein	17	17	18	19	19	56.1	62.5	61.5	62.4	60.6
Lithuania[3] Lituanie[3]	781	814	832	858	898	20.9	21.7	22.2	22.9	24.2
Luxembourg Luxembourg	184	192	206	215	222	48.3	49.7	52.9	54.1	56.4
Malta Malte	128	139	150	158	163	36.0	38.6	41.5	43.0	44.8
Monaco Monaco	24	26	29	30	30	81.3	92.9	104.0	106.5	96.3
Netherlands Pays-Bas	6 940	7 175	7 395	7 630	7 830	46.4	47.6	48.7	49.9	50.9
Norway Norvège	2 132	2 198	2 268	2 335	2 392	50.3	51.7	52.9	54.2	55.4
Poland Pologne	3 293	3 565	3 938	4 419	5 006	8.6	9.3	10.3	11.5	13.1
Portugal Portugal	2 379	2 694	3 014	3 260	3 444	24.3	27.5	30.6	31.1	35.0
Republic of Moldova République de Moldova	462	496	511	524	546	10.7	11.4	11.7	12.0	12.4
Romania Roumanie	2 366	2 445	2 574	2 604	2 806	10.2	10.6	11.3	11.4	12.3
Russian Federation Fédération de Russie	20 700	22 296	22 849	23 475	24 097	14.0	15.0	15.4	15.8	16.2
San Marino Saint-Marin	10	11	14	14	14	51.2	54.0	67.5	61.3	58.7
Slovakia Slovaquie	711	759	821	893	1 004	13.4	14.4	15.5	16.7	18.8
Slovenia Slovénie	422	459	494	516	573	21.1	22.9	24.7	25.9	29.5
Spain Espagne	12 603	13 264	13 792	14 253	14 685	32.4	34.0	35.3	36.4	37.1
Sweden Suède	5 849	5 957	5 929	5 910	5 967	68.3	69.1	68.3	67.8	68.3
Switzerland Suisse	3 943	4 081	4 185	4 266	4 258	58.7	60.1	60.6	61.1	59.7

19
Telephones
Main telephone lines in operation and per 100 inhabitants [cont.]
Téléphones
Nombre de lignes téléphoniques en service et pour 100 habitants [suite]

Country or area Pays ou zone	Number (000) Nombre (000)					Per 100 inhabitants Pour 100 habitants				
	1990	1991	1992	1993	1994	1990	1991	1992	1993	1994
TFYR Macedonia L'ex-R.y. Macédoine	286	290	312	324	337	13.4	13.5	14.4	14.8	16.1
Ukraine Ukraine	7 028	7 344	7 578	7 820	...	13.6	14.1	14.5	15.0	...
United Kingdom[1] Royaume-Uni[1]	25 368	25 920	26 560	27 380	28 389	44.2	45.0	45.9	47.2	48.9
Yugoslavia Yougoslavie	1 682	1 782	1 873	1 923	1 970	16.1	17.0	17.7	18.0	18.4
Oceania · Océanie										
American Samoa Samoa américaines	6	6	6	8	10	14.1	14.1	15.4	20.5	24.4
Australia[2][12] Australie[2][12]	7 787	8 046	8 257	8 540	8 850	45.7	46.5	47.1	48.2	49.6
Cook Islands Iles Cook	3	3	4	4	5	15.0	17.0	21.5	25.1	25.6
Micronesia,Federated States of Micron, Etats fédérés de	2	3	3	6	7	2.4	2.6	2.8	5.6	6.7
Fiji Fidji	42	46	50	54	59	5.8	6.2	6.6	7.1	7.7
French Polynesia Polynésie française	38	41	43	45	47	19.3	20.4	20.9	21.1	21.9
Guam Guam	39	43	46	66	64	29.4	31.8	33.3	46.4	43.4
Kiribati Kiribati	1	1	1	2	2	1.7	1.7	1.8	2.3	2.5
Marshall Islands Iles Marshall	1	1	1	2	3	1.1	1.5	1.7	4.4	5.7
Nauru Nauru	1	1	1	1	2	...	13.3	12.0	14.0	15.7
New Caledonia Nouvelle-Calédonie	28	31	35	39	42	16.9	18.4	20.1	21.9	23.3
New Zealand[1] Nouvelle-Zélande[1]	1 469	1 493	1 534	1 593	1 658	43.7	43.8	44.9	46.0	47.0
Niue Nioué	...	...	0	0	1	...	...	20.0	22.0	25.0
Northern Mariana Islands Iles Marianas du Nord	...	...	13	14	14	...	...	28.8	30.0	31.1
Papua New Guinea Papouasie-Nvl-Guinée	30	34	36	39	40	0.8	0.9	0.9	1.0	1.0
Samoa Samoa	4	4	7	7	8	2.6	2.6	4.0	4.4	4.6
Solomon Islands[1][13] Iles Salomon[1][13]	4	5	5	5	6	1.4	1.4	1.5	1.5	1.6
Tonga Tonga	4	5	5	6	6	4.8	5.6	6.0	6.4	6.6
Tuvalu Tuvalu	0	0	0	0	0	1.3	1.3	1.4	1.6	5.0
Vanuatu Vanuatu	3	3	4	4	4	1.8	2.0	2.3	2.5	2.7

19
Telephones
Main telephone lines in operation and per 100 inhabitants [*cont.*]
Téléphones
Nombre de lignes téléphoniques en service et pour 100 habitants [*suite*]

Country or area Pays ou zone	Number (000) Nombre (000)					Per 100 inhabitants Pour 100 habitants				
	1990	1991	1992	1993	1994	1990	1991	1992	1993	1994
Wallis and Futuna Islands Iles Wallis et Futuna	...	...	0	1	1	...	...	3.5	6.3	7.5

Source:
International Telecommunications Union (Geneva).

† For detailed descriptions of data pertaining to
former Czechoslovakia, Germany, SFR Yugoslavia and former
USSR, see Annex I - Country or area nomenclature, regional
and other groupings.

1 Year beginning 1 April.
2 Year ending 30 June.
3 Excluding public call offices.
4 Access lines.
5 Switched access lines.
6 Year ending 30 September.
7 Telephone subscriptions.
8 Main telephone stations.
9 Number of subscribers.
10 Including ISDN from 1993.
11 Including PABX.
12 Telephone services in operation.
13 Billable lines.

Source:
Union internationale des télécommunications (Genève).

† Pour les descriptions en détails des données
relatives à l'ancienne Tchécoslovaquie, l'Allemagne, la Rfs
Yougoslavie et l'ancienne URSS, voir l'Annexe I -
Nomenclature des pays ou zones, groupements régionaux et
autres groupements.

1 L'année commençant le 1er avril.
2 L'année finissant le 30 juin.
3 Cabines publiques exclues.
4 Lignes d'accès.
5 Lignes d'accès par communication.
6 L'année finissant le 30 septembre.
7 Abonnements téléphoniques.
8 Postes téléphoniques principaux.
9 Nombre d'abonnés.
10 RNIS inclu à partir de 1993.
11 PABX inclu.
12 Les services téléphoniques en exploitation.
13 Lignes payables.

Technical notes, tables 14-19

Tables 14-17 are compiled from the UNESCO *Statistical Yearbook*. [29] The technical notes in the UNESCO *Yearbook* concerning these tables are summarized below.

Table 14: For the purposes of this table, a daily general interest newspaper is defined as a publication devoted primarily to recording general news. It is considered to be "daily" if it appears at least four times a week.

For 1992, it is known or believed that no daily general-interest newspapers are published in the following 37 countries and territories: *Africa*: Cape Verde, Comoros, Djibouti, Eritrea, Guinea, St. Helena, Sao Tome and Principe, Western Sahara; *America, North*: Anguilla, Antigua and Barbuda, Aruba, Belize, British Virgin Islands, Dominica, Greenland, Grenada, Montserrat, St. Kitts and Nevis, St. Lucia, St. Pierre and Miquelon, St. Vincent and the Grenadines, Turks and Caicos Islands. *America, South*: Falkland Islands (Malvinas); *Asia*: Bhutan, Cambodia, East Timor; *Europe*: Faeroe Islands, San Marino; *Oceania*: American Samoa, Kiribati, Nauru, Niue, Norfolk Island, Pacific Islands, Samoa, Solomon Islands, Tokelau, Tuvalu, Vanuatu.

Table 15: For the purposes of this table a non-daily general interest newspaper is defined as a publication which is devoted primarily to recording general news and which is published three times a week or less. Under the category of periodicals are included publications of periodical issue, other than newspapers, containing information of a general or of a specialized nature.

Table 16: Data show the estimated number of television receivers in use (indicated by T) and the estimated number of radio receivers (indicated by R) as well as receivers per 1,000 inhabitants. The figures refer to 31 December of the year stated. In these tables the term "receivers" relates to all types of receivers for broadcasts to the general public, including receivers connected to a redistribution system (wired receivers).

Table 17: The statistics shown in this table refer to fixed cinemas and mobile units regularly used for commercial exhibition of long films of 16 mm and over.

The term fixed cinema used in this table refers to establishments possessing their own equipment and includes indoor cinemas (those with a permanent fixed roof over most of the seating accommodation), outdoor cinemas and drive-ins (establishments designed to enable the audience to watch a film while seated in their automobile). Mobile Units are defined as projection units equipped and used to serve more than one site.

The capacity for fixed cinemas refers to the number of seats in the case of cinema halls and to the number of places for automobiles multiplied by a factor of 4 in the case of drive-ins.

Notes techniques, tableaux 14-19

Tableaux 14-17 ont été établis à partir de l'*Annuaire statistique* de l'UNESCO [29]. Les notes techniques de l'*Annuaire* de l'UNESCO concernant ces tableaux sont résumées ci-dessous.

Tableau 14 : Dans ce tableau, par "journal quotidien d'information générale", on entend une publication qui a essentiellement pour objet de rendre compte des événements courants. Il est considéré comme "quotidien" s'il paraît au moins quatre fois par semaine.

Pour 1992, on sait ou l'on croit savoir qu'il ne paraît aucun journal quotidien d'information générale dans les 37 pays ou territoires suivants : *Afrique* : Cap-Vert, Comores, Djibouti, Erythrée, Guinée, Sahara occidental, Sainte-Hélène, Sao Tomé-et-Principe; *Amérique du Nord* : Anguilla, Antigua-et-Barbuda, Aruba, Bélize, Dominique, Grenade, Groenland, Iles turques et caïques, Iles vierges britanniques, Montserrat, Panama-ancienne zone du Canal, Saint Kitts-et-Nevis, Sainte-Lucie, Saint-Pierre-et-Miquelon, Saint-Vincent-et-Grenadines; *Amérique du Sud* : Iles Falkland (Malvinas), *Asie* : Bhoutan, Cambodge, Timor oriental; *Europe* : Iles Faeroe, Saint-Marin; *Océanie* : Ile Norfolk, Iles du Pacifique, Iles Salomon, Kirabiti, Nauru, Niue, Samoa, Samoa américaines, Tokelau, Tuvalu, Vanuatu.

Tableau 15 : Aux fins de ce tableau, par "journal non quotidien d'information générale", on entend une publication qui a essentiellement pour objet de rendre compte des événements courants et qui est publié trois fois par semaine ou moins. La catégorie périodique comprend les publications périodiques autres que les journaux, contenant des informations de caractère général ou spécialisé.

Tableau 16 : Les données de ces tableaux indiquent le nombre estimatif de récepteurs de télévision en usage (indiqués par un T), et le nombre estimatif de récepteurs de radio (indiqués par R) ainsi que les récepteurs pour 1000 habitants. Les chiffres se rapportent au 31 décembre de l'année indiquée. Dans ces tableaux, le terme "récepteurs" désigne tous les types de récepteur permettant de capter les émissions destinées au grand public, y compris les récepteurs reliés (par fil) à un réseau de redistribution.

Tableau 17 : Les statistiques présentées dans ce tableau concernent les établissements fixes et les cinémas itinérants d'exploitation commerciale de films de long métrage de 16mm et plus.

Dans ce tableau, le terme établissement fixe désigne tout établissement doté de son propre équipement; il englobe les salles fermées (c'est-à-dire celles où un toit fixe recouvre la plupart des places assises), les cinémas de plein air et les cinémas pour automobilistes ou drive-ins (conçus pour permettre aux spectateurs d'assister à la projection sans quitter leur voiture). Les cinémas itinérants sont définis comme groupes mobiles de projection équipés de manière à pouvoir être utilisés dans des lieux différents.

Cinema attendance is calculated from the number of tickets sold during a given year.

As a rule, figures refer only to commercial establishments but in the case of mobile units, it is possible that the figures for some countries may also include non-commercial units. Gross receipts are given in the national currency.

Table 18: The number of telefax stations refers to all types of private equipment (e.g. Group 2, Group 3) connected to the PSTN. Some operators report only the equipment sold, leased or registered by them and therefore the actual number may be higher.

The number of mobile cellular subscribers refers to users of portable telephones subscribing to an automatic public mobile telephone service using cellular technology which provides access to the PSTN.

Table 19: This table shows the number of main lines in operation and the main lines in operation per 100 inhabitants for the years indicated. Main telephone lines refer to the telephone lines connecting a customer's equipment to the PSTN and which have a dedicated port on a telephone exchange. Main telephone lines per 100 inhabitants is calculated by dividing the number of main lines by the population and multipying by 100.

La capacité des cinémas fixes se réfère au nombre de sièges dans les salles de cinéma at au nombre de places d'automobiles multiplié par le facteur 4 dans le cas de drive-ins.

La fréquentation des cinémas est calculée sur la base du nombre de billets vendus au cours d'une année donnée.

En général, des statistiques présentées ne concernent que les établissements commerciaux: toutefois, dans le cas des cinémas itinérants, il se peut que les données relatives à certains pays tiennent compte aussi des établissements non-commerciaux. Les recettes brutes sont indiquées en monnaie nationale.

Tableau 18 : Le nombre de postes de télécopie désigne tous les types d'équipements privés (par exemple, Groupes 2 et 3) reliés au RTPC. Certains exploitants signalent uniquement les équipements qu'ils ont vendus, loués ou enregistrés; par conséquent, leur nombre réel peut être plus élevé.

Les abonnés mobiles désignent les utilisateurs de téléphones portatifs abonnés à un service automatique public de téléphones mobiles cellulaires ayant accès au RTPC.

Tableau 19 : Ce tableau indique le nombre de lignes principales en service et les lignes principales en service pour 100 habitants pour les années indiquées. Les lignes principales sont des lignes téléphoniques qui relient l'equipement terminal de l'abonné au RTPC et qui possèdent un accès individualisé aux équipements d'un central téléphonique. Les lignes principales pour 100 habitants se calculent en divisant le nombre de lignes principales par la population et en multipliant pour 100.

Part Three
Economic Activity

VI
National accounts and industrial production (tables 20-26)
VII
Financial statistics (tables 27 and 28)
VIII
Labour force (tables 29 and 30)
IX
Wages and prices (tables 31-33)
X
Agriculture, hunting, forestry and fishing (tables 34-40)
XI
Manufacturing (tables 41-60)
XII
Transport (tables 61-65)
XIII
Energy (tables 66 and 67)
XIV
Environment (tables 68-70)
XV
Intellectual property; Science and technology (table 71)

Part Three of the *Yearbook* presents statistical series on economic production and consumption for a wide range of economic activities, and other basic series on major economic topics, for all countries or areas of the world for which data are available. Included are basic tables on national accounts, finance, labour force, wages and prices, a wide range of agricultural, mined and manufactured commodities, transport, energy, environment and intellectual property. In most cases, tables present statistics on production; in a few cases, data are presented on stocks and consumption.

International economic topics such as external trade are covered in Part Four.

Troisième partie
Activité économique

VI
Comptabilités nationales et production industrielle (tableaux 20 à 26)
VII
Statistiques financières (tableaux 27 et 28)
VIII
Main-d'oeuvre (tableaux 29 et 30)
IX
Salaires et prix (tableaux 31 à 33)
X
Agriculture, chasse, forêts et pêche (tableaux 34 à 40)
XI
Industries manufacturières (tableaux 41 à 60)
XII
Transports (tableaux 61 à 65)
XIII
Energie (tableaux 66 et 67)
XIV
Environnement (tableaux 68 à 70)
XV
Propriété intellectuelle; Science et technologie (tableau 71)

La troisième partie de l'*Annuaire* présente, pour une large gamme d'activités économiques, des séries statistiques sur la production économique et la consommation, et, pour tous les pays ou zones du monde pour lesquels des données sont disponibles, d'autres séries fondamentales ayant trait à des questions économiques importantes. Y figurent des tableaux de base consacrés à la comptabilité nationale, aux finances, à la main-d'oeuvre, aux salaires et aux prix, à un large éventail de produits agricoles, miniers et manufacturés, aux transports, à l'énergie, l'environnement et à la propriété intellectuelle. On y trouve, dans la plupart des cas, des statistiques sur la production et parfois des données relatives aux stocks et à la consommation.

Les questions économiques internationales comme le commerce extérieur sont traitées dans la quatrième partie.

20
Gross domestic product: total and per capita
Produit intérieur brut : total et par habitant
In US dollars (millions) [1] at current and constant 1990 prices; per capita US$;
real rates of growth

En monnaie dollars de E−u (millions) [1] aux prix courants et constants de 1990; par habitant en dollars de E−u ;
taux de l'accroissement réels

Country or area Pays ou zone	1986	1987	1988	1989	1990	1991	1992	1993	1994
Afghanistan Afghanistan									
At current prices	7 272	7 710	8 479	13 799	18 969	29 390	40 795	63 855	74 328
Per capita	507	540	592	946	1 261	1 868	2 454	3 609	3 937
At constant prices	25 595	22 968	21 067	19 580	18 969	18 763	17 503	17 957	17 418
Growth rates	3.0	−10.3	−8.3	−7.1	−3.1	−1.1	−6.7	2.6	−3.0
Albania Albanie									
At current prices	2 483	2 464	2 549	3 046	2 170	1 526	1 116	1 685	2 391
Per capita	820	794	804	941	660	458	332	497	700
At constant prices	2 244	2 226	2 195	2 411	2 170	1 569	1 417	1 573	1 689
Growth rates	5.6	−0.8	−1.4	9.8	−10.0	−27.7	−9.7	11.0	7.4
Algeria Algérie									
At current prices	63 065	64 479	56 571	53 027	46 333	24 187	22 076	21 546	15 374
Per capita	2 802	2 788	2 384	2 179	1 858	947	845	806	563
At constant prices	45 792	45 287	43 800	44 898	46 333	47 369	48 578	49 402	50 464
Growth rates	1.5	−1.1	−3.3	2.5	3.2	2.2	2.6	1.7	2.2
Andorra Andorre									
At current prices	269	354	424	486	651	724	845	739	745
Per capita	5 973	7 541	8 842	9 721	12 520	13 399	14 571	12 107	11 462
At constant prices	475	522	558	606	651	689	745	774	781
Growth rates	5.1	9.8	6.9	8.7	7.4	5.9	8.1	3.9	0.9
Angola Angola									
At current prices	6 443	7 419	8 009	9 320	10 296	8 252	11 210	7 874	4 097
Per capita	787	882	927	1 047	1 120	866	1 134	766	384
At constant prices	9 120	9 758	10 302	10 342	10 296	10 131	10 466	7 849	8 524
Growth rates	3.2	7.0	5.6	0.4	−0.4	−1.6	3.3	−25.0	8.6
Anguilla Anguilla									
At current prices	25	32	41	51	58	59	65	72	79
Per capita	3 608	4 501	5 793	7 235	8 272	8 391	8 091	9 011	9 933
At constant prices	38	42	48	52	58	55	58	63	67
Growth rates	14.2	11.6	13.6	9.7	10.9	−5.9	7.1	7.5	6.5
Antigua and Barbuda Antigua−et−Barbuda									
At current prices	238	240	286	324	334	360	374	391	368
Per capita	3 835	3 807	4 533	5 139	5 219	5 631	5 754	6 020	5 666
At constant prices	253	275	296	323	334	348	354	366	377
Growth rates	8.4	8.7	7.6	9.0	3.5	4.3	1.7	3.4	3.0
Argentina Argentine									
At current prices	105 876	108 826	126 885	76 637	141 353	189 710	228 990	257 841	281 924
Per capita	3 440	3 485	4 006	2 386	4 343	5 755	6 861	7 633	8 248
At constant prices	149 657	153 525	150 632	141 263	141 353	153 944	167 270	177 361	190 523
Growth rates	7.3	2.6	−1.9	−6.2	0.1	8.9	8.7	6.0	7.4
Armenia Arménie									
At current prices	12 003	13 511	13 772	15 710	15 107	9 107	321	611	414
Per capita	3 689	4 127	4 181	4 733	4 507	2 684	93	175	117
At constant prices	13 616	13 647	13 427	15 821	15 107	13 777	6 572	5 599	5 487
Growth rates	−1.1	0.2	−1.6	17.8	−4.5	−8.8	−52.3	−14.8	−2.0
Australia Australie									
At current prices	176 810	209 353	265 491	292 809	296 046	301 711	296 590	289 390	331 365
Per capita	11 131	12 977	16 203	17 599	17 530	17 608	17 068	16 427	18 561
At constant prices	263 688	277 312	289 681	298 194	296 046	296 956	306 567	319 593	335 527
Growth rates	2.7	5.2	4.5	2.9	−0.7	0.3	3.2	4.3	5.0
Austria Autriche									
At current prices	93 174	117 175	126 861	126 441	158 429	165 153	186 188	182 067	196 549
Per capita	12 300	15 422	16 631	16 500	20 562	21 302	23 849	23 155	24 823
At constant prices	138 367	140 660	146 366	151 973	158 429	163 094	166 110	166 011	170 558
Growth rates	1.2	1.7	4.1	3.8	4.3	2.9	1.9	−0.1	2.7
Azerbaijan Azerbaïdjan									
At current prices	19 432	22 953	23 653	24 949	22 012	15 243	1 247	1 602	1 312
Per capita	2 877	3 352	3 409	3 550	3 093	2 115	171	217	176
At constant prices	21 385	22 649	22 441	24 401	22 012	21 858	16 918	13 010	10 148
Growth rates	−5.9	5.9	−0.9	8.7	−9.8	−0.7	−22.6	−23.1	−22.0

20

Gross domestic product: total and per capita
In US dollars (millions) [1] at current and constant 1990 prices; per capita US$;
real rates of growth [*cont.*]
Produit intérieur brut : total et par habitant
En monnaie dollars de E−u (millions) [1] aux prix courants et constants de 1990; par habitant;
taux de l'accroissement réels [*suite*]

Country or area Pays ou zone	1986	1987	1988	1989	1990	1991	1992	1993	1994
Bahamas Bahamas									
At current prices	2 370	2 625	2 913	3 006	3 134	3 090	3 059	3 215	3 357
Per capita	9 915	10 803	11 746	11 929	12 242	11 885	11 587	11 998	12 342
At constant prices	2 740	2 866	2 932	2 990	3 134	3 034	3 064	3 138	3 229
Growth rates	3.6	4.6	2.3	2.0	4.8	−3.2	1.0	2.4	2.9
Bahrain Bahrēin									
At current prices	3 187	3 170	3 359	3 584	3 903	4 077	4 214	4 382	4 514
Per capita	7 446	7 155	7 318	7 545	7 965	8 073	8 104	8 192	8 223
At constant prices	3 548	3 504	3 762	3 856	3 903	4 081	4 278	4 477	4 455
Growth rates	1.6	−1.2	7.4	2.5	1.2	4.6	4.8	4.7	−0.5
Bangladesh Bangladesh									
At current prices	17 733	19 294	20 786	22 856	24 137	24 770	24 336	26 041	27 520
Per capita	177	189	200	216	223	224	216	226	234
At constant prices	20 755	21 355	21 893	23 344	24 137	25 157	26 285	27 497	28 734
Growth rates	4.2	2.9	2.5	6.6	3.4	4.2	4.5	4.6	4.5
Barbados Barbados									
At current prices	1 316	1 449	1 541	1 697	1 710	1 687	1 577	1 631	1 698
Per capita	5 179	5 703	6 043	6 631	6 655	6 539	6 088	6 273	6 505
At constant prices	1 565	1 672	1 730	1 790	1 710	1 662	1 559	1 578	1 641
Growth rates	10.3	6.8	3.5	3.5	−4.4	−2.8	−6.2	1.2	4.0
Belarus Bélarus									
At current prices	44 955	54 775	55 227	62 973	64 164	49 089	4 731	7 076	5 250
Per capita	4 485	5 431	5 445	6 182	6 283	4 804	463	695	517
At constant prices	58 623	59 045	60 310	65 075	64 164	63 393	56 393	50 427	40 342
Growth rates	6.1	0.7	2.1	7.9	−1.4	−1.2	−11.0	−10.6	−20.0
Belgium Belgique									
At current prices	111 789	139 601	151 327	153 089	192 175	197 475	220 895	210 576	219 391
Per capita	11 330	14 127	15 284	15 426	19 312	19 787	22 063	20 961	21 765
At constant prices	168 125	171 473	179 869	186 130	192 175	196 511	200 166	196 753	201 125
Growth rates	1.4	2.0	4.9	3.5	3.3	2.3	1.9	−1.7	2.2
Belize Belize									
At current prices	228	277	315	363	396	430	468	525	552
Per capita	1 341	1 580	1 759	1 973	2 098	2 219	2 352	2 572	2 630
At constant prices	266	297	323	363	396	413	443	415	422
Growth rates	4.6	11.6	9.0	12.2	9.3	4.2	7.2	−6.3	1.6
Benin Bénin									
At current prices	1 336	1 562	1 620	1 502	1 845	1 898	2 057	1 994	1 457
Per capita	325	369	372	334	398	397	417	392	278
At constant prices	1 773	1 747	1 800	1 787	1 845	1 888	1 918	1 965	2 032
Growth rates	2.2	−1.5	3.0	−0.7	3.3	2.4	1.6	2.5	3.4
Bermuda Bermudes									
At current prices	1 297	1 415	1 502	1 592	1 635	1 680	1 698	1 792	1 881
Per capita	22 746	24 398	25 449	26 540	26 802	27 095	27 381	28 448	29 859
At constant prices	1 621	1 687	1 694	1 695	1 635	1 632	1 596	1 643	1 684
Growth rates	3.7	4.1	0.4	0.0	−3.5	−0.2	−2.2	3.0	2.5
Bhutan Bhoutan									
At current prices	222	278	283	270	283	245	245	238	263
Per capita	158	192	191	178	184	156	155	149	163
At constant prices	216	254	257	269	283	299	312	328	345
Growth rates	10.2	17.8	1.0	4.7	5.3	5.4	4.6	5.2	5.0
Bolivia Bolivie									
At current prices	4 643	4 953	4 834	5 479	5 339	5 841	6 030	6 109	6 272
Per capita	772	806	770	853	812	868	875	865	867
At constant prices	4 789	4 914	5 059	5 202	5 339	5 586	5 741	5 977	6 229
Growth rates	−2.5	2.6	3.0	2.8	2.6	4.6	2.8	4.1	4.2
Bosnia & Herzegovina Bosnie−Herzégovine									
At current prices	8 461	9 384	7 772	10 253	13 012	14 377	1 377	1 222	4 608
Per capita	2 018	2 195	1 789	2 350	3 020	3 453	349	330	1 307
At constant prices	17 344	17 059	16 682	16 943	13 012	11 438	10 054	8 837	7 768
Growth rates	3.8	−1.6	−2.2	1.6	−23.2	−12.1	−12.1	−12.1	−12.1
Botswana Botswana									
At current prices	1 288	1 674	2 076	2 716	3 295	3 460	3 702	3 504	3 847
Per capita	1 155	1 450	1 738	2 199	2 582	2 627	2 724	2 501	2 666

20
Gross domestic product: total and per capita
In US dollars (millions) [1] at current and constant 1990 prices; per capita US$;
real rates of growth [cont.]
Produit intérieur brut : total et par habitant
En monnaie dollars de E−u (millions) [1] aux prix courants et constants de 1990; par habitant;
taux de l'accroissement réels [suite]

Country or area Pays ou zone	1986	1987	1988	1989	1990	1991	1992	1993	1994
At constant prices	2 195	2 390	2 755	3 117	3 295	3 586	3 817	3 804	3 959
Growth rates	7.5	8.9	15.3	13.1	5.7	8.8	6.5	−0.3	4.1
Brazil Brésil									
At current prices	268 082	294 311	328 495	447 473	477 980	404 530	409 221	475 056	602 531
Per capita	1 946	2 095	2 295	3 069	3 219	2 676	2 660	3 036	3 786
At constant prices	469 876	503 439	503 439	503 439	477 980	479 207	475 524	495 167	523 392
Growth rates	7.7	7.1	0.0	0.0	−5.1	0.3	−0.8	4.1	5.7
British Virgin Islands Iles Vierges britanniques									
At current prices	98	117	131	156	163	166	178	181	193
Per capita	6 987	7 777	8 756	9 763	10 164	9 778	10 492	10 048	10 730
At constant prices	113	117	135	150	163	156	160	164	171
Growth rates	1.4	3.8	14.7	11.3	8.6	−4.0	2.3	2.7	4.2
Brunei Darussalam Brunéi Darussalam									
At current prices	2 314	2 753	2 689	2 996	3 590	3 816	3 919	3 948	4 556
Per capita	9 929	11 518	10 976	11 936	13 969	14 511	14 570	14 409	16 270
At constant prices	3 425	3 494	3 532	3 494	3 590	3 721	3 683	3 533	3 731
Growth rates	−2.7	2.0	1.1	−1.1	2.7	3.6	−1.0	−4.1	5.6
Bulgaria Bulgarie									
At current prices	36 621	41 990	46 199	47 118	20 726	7 367	8 355	10 520	9 749
Per capita	4 079	4 669	5 131	5 233	2 305	822	937	1 186	1 106
At constant prices	23 412	24 597	25 190	25 116	20 726	18 301	17 258	16 999	16 985
Growth rates	5.3	5.1	2.4	−0.3	−17.5	−11.7	−5.7	−1.5	−0.1
Burkina Faso Burkina Fasо									
At current prices	1 454	1 788	1 900	1 854	2 581	2 752	2 939	2 815	1 871
Per capita	180	216	223	212	287	298	309	288	186
At constant prices	2 473	2 509	2 560	2 573	2 581	2 743	2 760	2 771	2 798
Growth rates	4.0	1.5	2.1	0.5	0.3	6.3	0.6	0.4	1.0
Burundi Burundi									
At current prices	1 234	1 162	1 089	1 132	1 148	1 129	1 192	1 033	1 067
Per capita	252	231	210	212	209	199	204	171	172
At constant prices	1 047	1 090	1 150	1 160	1 148	1 194	1 217	1 241	1 264
Growth rates	3.8	4.1	5.5	0.9	−1.0	4.0	1.9	2.0	1.8
Cambodia Cambodge									
At current prices	620	625	765	852	861	825	1 549	3 343	4 211
Per capita	79	77	92	99	97	90	165	345	422
At constant prices	796	786	878	861	861	870	930	983	1 036
Growth rates	−5.3	−1.3	11.7	−2.0	0.0	1.0	7.0	5.7	5.3
Cameroon Cameroun									
At current prices	11 857	13 050	12 236	11 012	12 191	11 648	11 844	10 386	6 769
Per capita	1 155	1 235	1 124	983	1 058	983	972	829	526
At constant prices	14 407	13 690	12 702	11 940	12 191	12 046	11 781	10 662	10 481
Growth rates	7.2	−5.0	−7.2	−6.0	2.1	−1.2	−2.2	−9.5	−1.7
Canada Canada									
At current prices	360 868	412 355	488 206	544 892	568 072	582 528	563 691	546 349	543 042
Per capita	13 731	15 474	18 059	19 873	20 441	20 697	19 788	18 959	18 635
At constant prices	508 674	529 734	556 031	569 196	568 072	558 275	562 472	573 287	599 578
Growth rates	3.3	4.1	5.0	2.4	−0.2	−1.7	0.8	1.9	4.6
Cape Verde Cap−Vert									
At current prices	194	248	286	282	328	341	385	338	343
Per capita	616	776	879	848	963	973	1 069	912	900
At constant prices	261	280	302	317	328	346	363	372	382
Growth rates	2.7	7.6	7.6	4.9	3.7	5.3	5.1	2.5	2.6
Cayman Islands Iles Caïmanes									
At current prices	242	283	345	395	492	513	536	559	581
Per capita	10 985	12 283	14 375	15 800	18 910	19 012	19 142	19 260	19 351
At constant prices	320	349	399	434	492	498	507	521	536
Growth rates	7.8	9.3	14.2	8.8	13.2	1.4	1.8	2.7	3.0
Central African Rep. Rép. centrafricaine									
At current prices	1 122	1 201	1 265	1 228	1 492	1 477	1 541	1 506	1 012
Per capita	422	441	454	430	510	492	501	477	313
At constant prices	1 421	1 379	1 416	1 461	1 492	1 490	1 520	1 549	1 642
Growth rates	4.2	−3.0	2.7	3.2	2.1	−0.1	2.0	1.9	6.0
Chad Tchad									
At current prices	817	819	1 044	1 019	1 219	1 290	1 383	1 337	1 003

20

Gross domestic product: total and per capita
In US dollars (millions) [1] at current and constant 1990 prices; per capita US$;
real rates of growth [*cont.*]

Produit intérieur brut : total et par habitant
En monnaie dollars de E−u (millions) [1] aux prix courants et constants de 1990; par habitant;
taux de l'accroissement réels [*suite*]

Country or area Pays ou zone	1986	1987	1988	1989	1990	1991	1992	1993	1994
Per capita	160	157	196	188	220	227	237	222	162
At constant prices	1 034	1 009	1 163	1 214	1 219	1 323	1 424	1 475	1 535
Growth rates	−4.1	−2.4	15.3	4.4	0.4	8.5	7.6	3.6	4.1
Chile Chili									
At current prices	17 715	20 682	24 150	28 182	30 384	34 396	42 748	45 636	51 752
Per capita	1 442	1 655	1 900	2 179	2 310	2 571	3 143	3 302	3 685
At constant prices	23 419	24 964	26 789	29 434	30 384	32 227	35 539	37 778	39 365
Growth rates	5.6	6.6	7.3	9.9	3.2	6.1	10.3	6.3	4.2
China Chine									
At current prices	295 476	321 391	401 072	449 104	387 412	406 090	482 998	599 013	522 188
Per capita	277	296	364	401	341	353	415	510	440
At constant prices	290 215	315 738	345 516	363 099	387 412	423 442	483 570	548 852	613 617
Growth rates	9.6	8.8	9.4	5.1	6.7	9.3	14.2	13.5	11.8
Colombia Colombie									
At current prices	34 943	36 372	39 211	39 541	40 274	41 240	43 650	48 420	63 810
Per capita	1 163	1 188	1 257	1 246	1 247	1 255	1 306	1 425	1 847
At constant prices	34 058	35 887	37 345	38 620	40 274	41 080	42 654	44 018	46 145
Growth rates	5.8	5.4	4.1	3.4	4.3	2.0	3.8	3.2	4.8
Comoros Comores									
At current prices	162	196	207	199	244	245	273	268	190
Per capita	345	403	411	379	449	435	466	441	301
At constant prices	235	239	246	242	244	248	252	254	259
Growth rates	2.1	1.6	2.7	−1.6	0.9	1.8	1.4	1.1	1.8
Congo Congo									
At current prices	1 849	2 298	2 212	2 425	2 840	2 909	2 827	3 071	2 165
Per capita	933	1 126	1 053	1 120	1 272	1 265	1 193	1 257	860
At constant prices	2 701	2 706	2 753	2 802	2 840	2 785	2 814	2 876	2 832
Growth rates	−6.9	0.2	1.8	1.8	1.3	−1.9	1.1	2.2	−1.5
Cook Islands Iles Cook									
At current prices	33	46	52	49	52	55	56	61	71
Per capita	1 945	2 687	2 881	2 740	2 880	2 900	2 935	3 189	3 717
At constant prices	41	42	50	54	52	54	55	56	58
Growth rates	8.2	1.8	19.0	7.1	−3.3	3.9	2.0	1.7	3.5
Costa Rica Costa Rica									
At current prices	4 404	4 533	4 614	5 226	5 710	5 637	6 722	7 557	8 244
Per capita	1 620	1 620	1 604	1 768	1 881	1 811	2 106	2 311	2 463
At constant prices	4 815	5 045	5 218	5 514	5 710	5 839	6 290	6 694	6 996
Growth rates	5.5	4.8	3.4	5.7	3.6	2.3	7.7	6.4	4.5
Côte d'Ivoire Côte d'Ivoir(									
At current prices	9 159	10 088	10 253	9 758	10 795	10 492	11 721	11 487	7 495
Per capita	888	941	922	845	902	845	911	863	544
At constant prices	11 754	11 567	11 358	11 245	10 795	10 978	11 209	11 450	11 645
Growth rates	3.4	−1.6	−1.8	−1.0	−4.0	1.7	2.1	2.2	1.7
Croatia Croatie									
At current prices	14 888	17 314	15 423	19 692	24 395	18 602	12 738	14 659	17 419
Per capita	3 319	3 850	3 422	4 363	5 401	4 117	2 821	3 250	3 867
At constant prices	32 595	32 563	32 260	31 765	24 395	19 293	17 422	16 775	16 915
Growth rates	2.8	−0.1	−0.9	−1.5	−23.2	−20.9	−9.7	−3.7	0.8
Cuba Cuba									
At current prices	19 090	19 262	20 752	20 218	20 874	18 738	15 965	15 233	17 827
Per capita	1 873	1 871	1 996	1 926	1 970	1 752	1 480	1 401	1 627
At constant prices	22 213	21 147	21 610	21 508	20 874	18 642	16 483	14 031	14 131
Growth rates	1.7	−4.8	2.2	−0.5	−3.0	−10.7	−11.6	−14.9	0.7
Cyprus Chypre									
At current prices	3 089	3 701	4 278	4 564	5 560	5 740	6 854	6 505	7 159
Per capita	4 590	5 442	6 228	6 577	7 921	8 085	9 546	8 959	9 754
At constant prices	4 116	4 418	4 800	5 183	5 560	5 609	6 198	6 296	6 620
Growth rates	3.4	7.3	8.7	8.0	7.3	0.9	10.5	1.6	5.1
Czech Republic République tchèque									
At current prices	32 221	36 163	35 755	34 855	31 606	24 308	27 990	31 204	36 007
Per capita	3 127	3 509	3 469	3 382	3 067	2 359	2 718	3 031	3 498
At constant prices	29 824	29 993	30 608	31 995	31 606	27 113	25 381	25 243	25 777
Growth rates	2.1	0.6	2.1	4.5	−1.2	−14.2	−6.4	−0.5	2.1

20

Gross domestic product: total and per capita

In US dollars (millions) [1] at current and constant 1990 prices; per capita US$;

real rates of growth [*cont.*]

Produit intérieur brut : total et par habitant

En monnaie dollars de E−u (millions) [1] aux prix courants et constants de 1990; par habitant;

taux de l'accroissement réels [*suite*]

Country or area Pays ou zone	1986	1987	1988	1989	1990	1991	1992	1993	1994
Denmark Danemark									
At current prices	82 375	102 321	108 751	104 956	129 126	129 425	141 027	134 678	146 109
Per capita	16 105	19 989	21 220	20 451	25 122	25 141	27 352	26 075	28 245
At constant prices	124 771	125 137	126 595	127 308	129 126	130 861	131 940	133 911	139 826
Growth rates	3.6	0.3	1.2	0.6	1.4	1.3	0.8	1.5	4.4
Djibouti Djibouti									
At current prices	363	387	418	428	465	466	486	507	524
Per capita	870	870	886	863	899	873	891	910	926
At constant prices	390	415	440	447	465	459	473	485	493
Growth rates	1.2	6.5	6.1	1.5	4.0	−1.1	3.0	2.4	1.7
Dominica Dominica									
At current prices	112	126	146	157	167	177	189	198	206
Per capita	1 557	1 745	2 023	2 174	2 355	2 498	2 668	2 792	2 902
At constant prices	136	147	160	159	167	170	192	198	204
Growth rates	7.1	7.6	8.7	−0.4	5.3	1.8	12.6	3.3	3.0
Dominican Republic Rép. dominicaine									
At current prices	5 433	5 081	4 638	6 687	7 609	7 884	8 797	9 512	10 347
Per capita	833	762	681	960	1 070	1 087	1 189	1 261	1 347
At constant prices	6 820	7 510	7 672	8 009	7 609	7 667	8 262	8 510	8 892
Growth rates	3.5	10.1	2.2	4.4	−5.0	0.8	7.8	3.0	4.5
Ecuador Equateur									
At current prices	11 264	10 530	10 013	9 822	10 686	11 752	12 656	14 304	17 921
Per capita	1 207	1 101	1 022	979	1 041	1 119	1 178	1 303	1 597
At constant prices	9 956	9 360	10 345	10 372	10 686	11 222	11 622	11 858	12 322
Growth rates	3.1	−6.0	10.5	0.3	3.0	5.0	3.6	2.0	3.9
Egypt Egypte									
At current prices	58 314	74 209	87 299	65 260	43 871	33 054	40 793	41 088	46 828
Per capita	1 143	1 418	1 627	1 187	779	573	692	681	760
At constant prices	33 017	35 612	36 738	40 407	43 871	45 445	47 263	48 114	48 691
Growth rates	2.0	7.9	3.2	10.0	8.6	3.6	4.0	1.8	1.2
El Salvador ElSalvador									
At current prices	3 953	4 628	5 473	6 446	5 113	5 915	5 982	7 683	8 933
Per capita	823	948	1 101	1 272	989	1 120	1 109	1 393	1 584
At constant prices	4 690	4 816	4 893	4 945	5 113	5 294	5 566	5 977	6 335
Growth rates	0.6	2.7	1.6	1.1	3.4	3.5	5.2	7.4	6.0
Equatorial Guinea Guinée équatoriale									
At current prices	107	131	144	132	163	165	185	181	133
Per capita	332	393	423	384	463	457	500	477	342
At constant prices	142	152	160	156	163	169	174	179	174
Growth rates	−3.8	7.5	5.3	−2.8	4.5	3.5	3.2	2.7	−2.9
Eritrea Erythrée									
At current prices	...	...	...	...	...	...	469	335	329
Per capita	...	...	...	...	...	...	144	100	96
At constant prices	...	...	...	...	...	...	510	540	581
Growth rates	...	...	...	...	...	...	1.7	5.9	7.5
Estonia Estonie									
At current prices	7 276	8 537	9 488	10 242	11 977	10 466	1 114	1 658	2 327
Per capita	4 704	5 479	6 051	6 507	7 605	6 662	713	1 068	1 510
At constant prices	107 473	112 802	118 484	128 062	119 775	103 459	88 719	81 091	85 956
Growth rates	0.7	5.0	5.0	8.1	−6.5	−13.6	−14.3	−8.6	6.0
Ethiopia including Eritrea Ethiopie y compris Erythrée									
At current prices	7 001	7 488	7 728	8 151	8 634	9 573	...	...	...
Per capita	158	165	165	169	173	186	...	...	...
At constant prices	7 646	8 377	8 534	8 671	8 634	8 113	...	...	...
Growth rates	6.9	9.6	1.9	1.6	−0.4	−6.0	...	...	...
Ethiopia Ethiopie									
At current prices	...	...	...	...	...	...	7 247	5 192	5 109
Per capita	...	...	...	...	...	...	144	100	96
At constant prices	...	...	...	...	...	...	7 851	8 316	8 941
Growth rates	...	...	...	...	...	...	1.7	5.9	7.5
Fiji Fidji									
At current prices	1 291	1 178	1 110	1 255	1 381	1 475	1 582	1 647	1 826
Per capita	1 825	1 654	1 552	1 743	1 902	2 006	2 120	2 173	2 369

20

Gross domestic product: total and per capita

In US dollars (millions) [1] at current and constant 1990 prices; per capita US$;

real rates of growth [*cont.*]

Produit intérieur brut : total et par habitant

En monnaie dollars de E−u (millions) [1] aux prix courants et constants de 1990; par habitant;

taux de l'accroissement réels [*suite*]

Country or area Pays ou zone	1986	1987	1988	1989	1990	1991	1992	1993	1994
At constant prices	1 182	1 106	1 125	1 274	1 381	1 344	1 397	1 421	1 466
Growth rates	6.8	−6.5	1.8	13.2	8.4	−2.7	3.9	1.7	3.2
Finland Finlande									
At current prices	70 025	88 010	103 840	113 488	134 806	121 382	106 438	84 111	96 822
Per capita	14 230	17 827	20 969	22 844	27 037	24 238	21 148	16 629	19 048
At constant prices	116 806	121 595	127 558	134 789	134 806	125 281	120 832	118 905	123 720
Growth rates	2.4	4.1	4.9	5.7	0.0	−7.1	−3.6	−1.6	4.1
France France									
At current prices	731 912	887 859	962 765	965 452	1 195 432	1 198 835	1 322 096	1 251 696	1 421 066
Per capita	13 195	15 916	17 160	17 112	21 077	21 033	23 089	21 766	24 608
At constant prices	1 046 905	1 070 467	1 118 621	1 166 187	1 195 432	1 204 960	1 219 247	1 206 990	1 241 147
Growth rates	2.5	2.3	4.5	4.3	2.5	0.8	1.2	−1.0	2.8
French Guiana Guyane française									
At current prices	421	612	827	891	1 199	1 312	1 888	2 536	3 175
Per capita	4 389	6 063	7 806	8 026	10 244	10 669	14 638	18 782	22 516
At constant prices	615	745	976	1 082	1 199	1 329	1 752	2 460	2 975
Growth rates	−10.0	21.2	30.9	10.9	10.7	10.9	31.8	40.4	21.0
French Polynesia Polynesie française									
At current prices	2 120	2 342	2 475	2 428	3 007	3 036	3 528	3 857	4 216
Per capita	11 842	12 799	13 166	12 581	15 266	15 029	17 126	18 281	19 608
At constant prices	2 560	2 743	2 808	2 893	3 007	3 125	3 173	3 238	3 351
Growth rates	8.4	7.1	2.4	3.0	4.0	3.9	1.5	2.0	3.5
Gabon Gabon									
At current prices	3 992	3 909	3 917	4 214	5 489	5 434	5 913	5 725	3 959
Per capita	3 921	3 722	3 620	3 783	4 790	4 609	4 875	4 587	3 086
At constant prices	6 400	5 384	5 203	5 334	5 489	5 598	5 708	5 830	5 851
Growth rates	−15.0	−15.9	−3.4	2.5	2.9	2.0	2.0	2.1	0.4
Gambia Gambie									
At current prices	156	210	244	256	300	299	332	348	358
Per capita	202	260	288	290	325	310	331	334	332
At constant prices	262	266	278	294	300	305	321	326	330
Growth rates	2.8	1.7	4.3	5.7	2.2	1.5	5.4	1.4	1.4
Georgia Géorgie									
At current prices	19 537	21 724	23 346	23 114	22 470	10 941	772	1 336	1 396
Per capita	3 692	4 076	4 352	4 284	4 147	2 014	142	245	256
At constant prices	21 700	21 463	22 090	22 546	22 470	17 954	10 718	6 495	4 547
Growth rates	−5.4	−1.1	2.9	2.1	−0.3	−20.1	−40.3	−39.4	−30.0
Germany † Allemagne †									
At current prices	...	...	...	...	...	1 719 513	1 969 455	1 910 761	2 046 537
Per capita	...	...	...	...	...	21 533	24 506	23 631	25 179
At constant prices	...	...	...	...	...	1 700 074	1 737 488	1 717 947	1 767 217
Growth rates	...	...	...	...	...	3.3	2.2	−1.1	2.9
F. R. Germany R.F. Allemagne									
At current prices	886 618	1 107 422	1 193 475	1 183 213	1 501 516	...	...	...	...
Per capita	14 526	18 125	19 504	19 310	24 485	...	...	...	...
At constant prices	1 302 359	1 321 601	1 370 810	1 420 495	1 501 516	...	...	...	...
Growth rates	2.4	1.5	3.7	3.6	5.7	...	...	...	...
former German D. R. anc. R.d. allemande									
At current prices	124 326	154 676	163 779	151 011	144 519	...	...	...	...
Per capita	7 500	9 380	9 989	9 258	8 894	...	...	...	...
At constant prices	156 155	161 354	166 367	170 266	144 519	...	...	...	...
Growth rates	3.9	3.3	3.1	2.3	−15.1	...	...	...	...
Ghana Ghana									
At current prices	5 733	4 853	5 195	5 249	6 226	7 000	6 884	6 059	5 635
Per capita	432	354	367	360	415	452	431	368	333
At constant prices	5 180	5 429	5 732	6 025	6 226	6 556	6 812	7 138	7 710
Growth rates	5.2	4.8	5.6	5.1	3.3	5.3	3.9	4.8	8.0
Greece Grèce									
At current prices	39 397	46 312	53 379	54 211	66 560	70 713	77 809	73 110	77 758
Per capita	3 942	4 606	5 275	5 325	6 501	6 873	7 529	7 045	7 465
At constant prices	62 421	62 132	64 898	67 195	66 560	68 709	69 275	69 661	70 897
Growth rates	1.6	−0.5	4.5	3.5	−1.0	3.2	0.8	0.6	1.8

20

Gross domestic product: total and per capita
In US dollars (millions) [1] at current and constant 1990 prices; per capita US$;
real rates of growth [*cont.*]
Produit intérieur brut : total et par habitant
En monnaie dollars de E−u (millions) [1] aux prix courants et constants de 1990; par habitant;
taux de l'accroissement réels [*suite*]

Country or area Pays ou zone	1986	1987	1988	1989	1990	1991	1992	1993	1994
Grenada Grenade									
At current prices	130	150	166	182	200	210	214	217	224
Per capita	1 442	1 671	1 847	2 000	2 202	2 309	2 352	2 357	2 437
At constant prices	162	171	180	190	200	206	207	204	208
Growth rates	3.9	6.0	5.3	5.7	5.2	2.9	0.6	−1.5	1.6
Guadeloupe Guadeloupe									
At current prices	1 582	2 045	2 187	2 204	2 791	2 909	3 250	3 181	3 362
Per capita	4 370	5 543	5 815	5 755	7 139	7 310	8 005	7 703	7 985
At constant prices	2 242	2 500	2 590	2 707	2 791	2 681	2 728	2 801	2 855
Growth rates	3.6	11.5	3.6	4.5	3.1	−4.0	1.8	2.7	1.9
Guatemala Guatemala									
At current prices	8 447	7 084	7 843	8 410	7 650	9 406	10 434	11 279	12 922
Per capita	1 031	840	903	941	832	994	1 071	1 125	1 252
At constant prices	6 636	6 871	7 138	7 420	7 650	7 930	8 309	8 641	8 969
Growth rates	0.1	3.5	3.9	3.9	3.1	3.7	4.8	4.0	3.8
Guinea Guinée									
At current prices	2 376	2 041	2 384	2 432	2 764	3 016	3 000	2 944	2 997
Per capita	464	388	440	435	480	508	490	467	461
At constant prices	2 216	2 353	2 498	2 630	2 764	2 895	3 048	3 141	3 223
Growth rates	4.1	6.2	6.2	5.3	5.1	4.8	5.3	3.1	2.6
Guinea−Bissau Guinée−Bissau									
At current prices	231	165	155	198	233	234	221	235	192
Per capita	259	182	168	210	242	237	219	228	182
At constant prices	191	202	216	226	233	240	248	255	262
Growth rates	4.6	5.6	6.9	4.5	3.3	3.0	3.0	2.8	3.0
Guyana Guyana									
At current prices	519	344	414	380	396	349	375	467	540
Per capita	656	434	522	479	498	435	464	572	655
At constant prices	471	472	457	441	396	420	453	490	531
Growth rates	0.4	0.4	−3.3	−3.5	−10.1	6.0	7.8	8.2	8.5
Haiti Haïti									
At current prices	2 238	1 968	1 968	1 862	2 488	1 791	1 403	1 415	1 872
Per capita	374	323	316	293	384	271	208	205	266
At constant prices	2 464	2 445	2 464	2 491	2 488	2 505	2 288	2 256	1 959
Growth rates	−0.5	−0.8	0.8	1.1	−0.1	0.7	−8.6	−1.4	−13.2
Holy See Saint−Siège									
At current prices	11	13	15	15	19	20	21	17	18
Per capita	10 623	13 346	14 735	15 266	19 205	20 192	21 379	17 354	17 930
At constant prices	17	18	18	19	19	19	20	19	20
Growth rates	2.8	3.0	4.0	2.9	2.1	1.1	0.7	−0.7	2.3
Honduras Honduras									
At current prices	3 809	4 153	4 626	5 167	6 269	3 021	3 225	3 091	2 922
Per capita	882	932	1 007	1 091	1 285	601	623	579	532
At constant prices	5 412	5 738	6 003	6 262	6 269	6 472	6 836	7 256	7 136
Growth rates	0.7	6.0	4.6	4.3	0.1	3.3	5.6	6.1	−1.7
Hong Kong Hong−kong									
At current prices	40 055	49 305	58 291	67 163	74 785	86 024	100 681	116 034	131 881
Per capita	7 260	8 850	10 372	11 858	13 109	14 982	17 428	19 975	22 590
At constant prices	57 821	65 312	70 516	72 322	74 785	78 567	83 488	88 366	93 223
Growth rates	10.8	13.0	8.0	2.6	3.4	5.1	6.3	5.8	5.5
Hungary Hongrie									
At current prices	26 204	28 799	30 840	31 484	35 680	33 340	37 158	38 483	41 375
Per capita	2 486	2 743	2 949	3 024	3 442	3 233	3 621	3 769	4 072
At constant prices	35 297	36 726	36 702	36 973	35 680	31 393	30 442	30 189	31 155
Growth rates	1.5	4.1	−0.1	0.7	−3.5	−12.0	−3.0	−0.8	3.2
Iceland Islande									
At current prices	3 919	5 405	5 967	5 403	6 242	6 723	6 915	6 076	6 193
Per capita	16 061	21 884	23 962	21 442	24 480	26 058	26 595	23 103	23 280
At constant prices	5 687	6 185	6 164	6 175	6 242	6 324	6 116	6 175	6 345
Growth rates	6.5	8.8	−0.4	0.2	1.1	1.3	−3.3	1.0	2.8
India Inde									
At current prices	232 300	257 070	284 385	281 545	305 949	270 887	271 173	257 878	284 220
Per capita	296	321	348	338	360	312	307	286	309

20

Gross domestic product: total and per capita
In US dollars (millions) [1] at current and constant 1990 prices; per capita US$;
real rates of growth [*cont.*]

Produit intérieur brut : total et par habitant
En monnaie dollars de E−u (millions) [1] aux prix courants et constants de 1990; par habitant;
taux de l'accroissement réels [*suite*]

Country or area Pays ou zone	1986	1987	1988	1989	1990	1991	1992	1993	1994
At constant prices	235 897	247 148	271 674	289 529	305 949	307 435	321 596	332 765	349 071
Growth rates	4.9	4.8	9.9	6.6	5.7	0.5	4.6	3.5	4.9
Indonesia Indonésie									
At current prices	80 061	75 930	84 300	94 452	106 141	116 649	128 471	142 794	154 090
Per capita	470	437	477	525	581	628	681	745	792
At constant prices	82 985	87 072	92 105	98 974	106 141	113 477	120 774	128 576	136 934
Growth rates	5.9	4.9	5.8	7.5	7.2	6.9	6.4	6.5	6.5
Iran, Islamic Rep. of Iran, Rép. islamique d'									
At current prices	206 032	279 162	324 737	385 851	538 138	742 267	1 034 461	75 336	75 716
Per capita	4 041	5 263	5 897	6 764	9 129	12 215	16 550	1 174	1 151
At constant prices	504 609	510 468	466 157	481 616	538 138	599 728	634 076	644 165	656 589
Growth rates	−15.1	1.2	−8.7	3.3	11.7	11.4	5.7	1.6	1.9
Iraq Iraq									
At current prices	48 457	57 586	64 444	67 640	74 945	64 146	68 667	60 672	56 876
Per capita	3 056	3 507	3 792	3 853	4 146	3 456	3 612	3 119	2 855
At constant prices	66 839	79 791	82 227	74 933	74 945	25 392	26 154	26 546	25 219
Growth rates	8.1	19.4	3.1	−8.9	0.0	−66.1	3.0	1.5	−5.0
Ireland Irlande									
At current prices	26 513	31 318	34 513	35 991	44 812	45 371	51 023	47 678	52 146
Per capita	7 462	8 842	9 788	10 251	12 793	12 948	14 532	13 530	14 735
At constant prices	35 213	36 793	38 428	41 274	44 812	46 102	48 411	50 336	53 727
Growth rates	4.7	4.5	4.4	7.4	8.6	2.9	5.0	4.0	6.7
Israel Israël									
At current prices	32 203	38 623	47 112	46 809	54 698	62 512	69 136	69 184	78 229
Per capita	7 494	8 858	10 630	10 335	11 738	12 940	13 728	13 168	14 333
At constant prices	46 576	49 893	51 126	51 359	54 698	58 862	63 177	65 571	69 831
Growth rates	4.4	7.1	2.5	0.5	6.5	7.6	7.3	3.8	6.5
Italy Italie									
At current prices	603 634	759 066	838 823	869 813	1 095 122	1 152 218	1 220 635	991 386	1 024 283
Per capita	10 623	13 346	14 735	15 266	19 205	20 192	21 379	17 354	17 921
At constant prices	970 503	1 000 935	1 041 622	1 072 237	1 095 122	1 108 266	1 116 559	1 109 151	1 134 661
Growth rates	2.9	3.1	4.1	2.9	2.1	1.2	0.8	−0.7	2.3
Jamaica Jamaïque									
At current prices	2 536	3 030	3 540	4 063	4 242	3 645	3 159	3 839	4 007
Per capita	1 089	1 294	1 506	1 725	1 793	1 533	1 320	1 592	1 650
At constant prices	3 397	3 660	3 765	4 023	4 242	4 264	4 323	4 375	4 484
Growth rates	1.7	7.7	2.9	6.8	5.5	0.5	1.4	1.2	2.5
Japan Japon									
At current prices	1 985 574	2 408 912	2 898 385	2 871 825	2 932 088	3 350 137	3 656 889	4 190 396	4 590 940
Per capita	16 344	19 733	23 638	23 328	23 734	27 036	29 434	33 648	36 782
At constant prices	2 416 074	2 515 269	2 671 417	2 797 373	2 932 088	3 056 964	3 090 646	3 084 349	3 152 205
Growth rates	2.6	4.1	6.2	4.7	4.8	4.3	1.1	−0.2	2.2
Jordan Jordanie									
At current prices	6 042	6 390	5 927	4 055	3 936	4 081	4 791	5 225	5 693
Per capita	1 534	1 596	1 461	981	924	918	1 025	1 059	1 095
At constant prices	4 383	4 496	4 474	3 869	3 936	4 006	4 459	4 715	4 938
Growth rates	7.7	2.6	−0.5	−13.5	1.7	1.8	11.3	5.7	4.7
Kazakstan Kazakstan									
At current prices	47 803	53 082	59 950	63 762	71 772	47 714	6 413	11 120	2 048
Per capita	2 993	3 284	3 666	3 859	4 305	2 843	380	656	120
At constant prices	52 403	51 666	56 433	62 121	71 772	65 610	57 081	49 718	37 288
Growth rates	1.6	−1.4	9.2	10.1	15.5	−8.6	−13.0	−12.9	−25.0
Kenya Kenya									
At current prices	7 240	7 971	8 520	8 340	8 533	8 043	7 938	5 539	6 956
Per capita	352	375	387	366	361	328	312	210	254
At constant prices	6 953	7 366	7 823	8 190	8 533	8 655	8 587	8 676	9 016
Growth rates	7.1	6.0	6.2	4.7	4.2	1.4	−0.8	1.0	3.9
Kiribati Kiribati									
At current prices	20	22	30	33	37	39	40	40	46
Per capita	301	319	427	465	507	529	537	527	602
At constant prices	27	27	33	34	37	38	39	39	41
Growth rates	−0.6	−1.2	21.0	4.1	7.0	3.9	1.5	2.0	3.5

20

Gross domestic product: total and per capita
In US dollars (millions) [1] at current and constant 1990 prices; per capita US$;
real rates of growth [*cont.*]
Produit intérieur brut : total et par habitant
En monnaie dollars de E−u (millions) [1] aux prix courants et constants de 1990; par habitant;
taux de l'accroissement réels [*suite*]

Country or area Pays ou zone	1986	1987	1988	1989	1990	1991	1992	1993	1994
Korea, Dem. P. R. Corée, R.p. dém.									
At current prices	17 400	19 400	20 506	21 736	21 712	21 310	23 746	26 231	27 126
Per capita	860	942	977	1 017	997	960	1 050	1 138	1 155
At constant prices	18 902	20 155	21 293	22 546	21 712	21 712	20 626	19 904	19 566
Growth rates	3.8	6.6	5.7	5.9	−3.7	0.0	−5.0	−3.5	−1.7
Korea, Republic of Corée, République de									
At current prices	105 991	131 816	174 940	212 970	244 043	283 904	296 839	330 831	379 623
Per capita	2 569	3 163	4 158	5 015	5 693	6 559	6 792	7 497	8 519
At constant prices	168 633	188 928	210 618	223 581	244 043	264 698	277 373	293 325	317 891
Growth rates	12.4	12.0	11.5	6.2	9.2	8.5	4.8	5.8	8.4
Kuwait Koweït									
At current prices	17 692	22 084	20 690	24 315	18 190	11 201	21 714	25 866	26 593
Per capita	9 678	11 319	10 020	11 378	8 488	5 406	11 204	14 572	16 285
At constant prices	20 934	25 232	19 720	25 986	18 190	10 550	20 044	21 648	22 946
Growth rates	−18.1	20.5	−21.9	31.8	−30.0	−42.0	90.0	8.0	6.0
Kyrgyzstan Kirghizistan									
At current prices	4 316	4 961	5 750	6 093	6 291	4 943	3 996	1 070	1 035
Per capita	1 062	1 199	1 365	1 421	1 442	1 114	885	233	222
At constant prices	4 778	5 010	5 340	6 217	6 291	6 027	5 039	4 212	3 117
Growth rates	−3.0	4.9	6.6	16.4	1.2	−4.2	−16.4	−16.4	−26.0
Lao People's Dem. Rep. Rép. dé. pop. lao									
At current prices	1 653	941	546	675	767	923	1 058	1 191	1 374
Per capita	447	246	139	166	182	213	237	259	290
At constant prices	652	645	633	712	767	805	861	913	990
Growth rates	4.9	−1.1	−1.8	12.5	7.6	5.0	7.0	6.0	8.4
Latvia Lettonie									
At current prices	12 306	13 898	15 354	16 415	18 751	16 380	1 364	2 172	3 030
Per capita	4 677	5 246	5 764	6 143	7 020	6 160	517	832	1 173
At constant prices	16 439	16 685	17 719	19 035	18 751	16 798	10 943	9 316	9 370
Growth rates	4.6	1.5	6.2	7.4	−1.5	−10.4	−34.9	−14.9	0.6
Lebanon Liban									
At current prices	2 987	3 680	2 840	2 317	3 325	4 043	4 246	4 385	4 931
Per capita	1 132	1 416	1 110	912	1 302	1 549	1 574	1 563	1 692
At constant prices	3 016	3 717	2 872	3 064	3 325	4 088	4 287	4 587	4 977
Growth rates	23.3	23.2	−22.7	6.7	8.5	22.9	4.9	7.0	8.5
Lesotho Lesotho									
At current prices	276	370	447	510	638	659	766	792	847
Per capita	172	224	263	293	356	358	405	407	424
At constant prices	453	476	537	605	638	651	661	693	684
Growth rates	2.0	5.1	13.0	12.7	5.3	2.1	1.4	5.0	−1.4
Liberia Libéria									
At current prices	1 037	1 090	1 158	1 194	1 317	1 491	1 671	1 878	2 112
Per capita	457	465	480	479	511	560	607	660	718
At constant prices	1 220	1 242	1 277	1 313	1 317	1 355	1 381	1 411	1 442
Growth rates	−1.2	1.8	2.8	2.8	0.3	2.9	1.9	2.2	2.2
Libyan Arab Jamah. Jamah. arabe libyenne									
At current prices	21 544	25 768	22 774	22 869	26 953	29 423	25 566	22 600	22 050
Per capita	5 473	6 308	5 378	5 213	5 930	6 249	5 244	4 477	4 220
At constant prices	25 594	24 776	24 530	25 212	26 953	28 301	28 725	28 899	29 274
Growth rates	−8.7	−3.2	−1.0	2.8	6.9	5.0	1.5	0.6	1.3
Liechtenstein Liechtenstein									
At current prices	771	974	1 046	1 012	1 289	1 317	1 377	1 336	1 481
Per capita	28 574	34 787	37 360	36 151	44 448	45 403	47 474	44 527	49 368
At constant prices	1 156	1 179	1 213	1 260	1 289	1 289	1 288	1 281	1 296
Growth rates	2.9	2.0	2.9	3.9	2.3	0.0	−0.1	−0.6	1.2
Lithuania Lituanie									
At current prices	13 864	16 288	18 584	19 561	19 365	21 821	1 877	2 513	4 195
Per capita	3 833	4 466	5 058	5 292	5 218	5 871	505	677	1 132
At constant prices	16 459	17 414	19 379	20 021	19 365	16 828	10 215	7 447	7 596
Growth rates	7.8	5.8	11.3	3.3	−3.3	−13.1	−39.3	−27.1	2.0
Luxembourg Luxembourg									
At current prices	4 999	6 095	6 805	7 178	8 989	9 336	10 558	10 092	11 072
Per capita	13 584	16 428	18 195	19 039	23 594	24 249	27 073	25 551	27 611

20

Gross domestic product: total and per capita

In US dollars (millions) [1] at current and constant 1990 prices; per capita US$;

real rates of growth [*cont.*]

Produit intérieur brut : total et par habitant

En monnaie dollars de E−u (millions) [1] aux prix courants et constants de 1990; par habitant;

taux de l'accroissement réels [*suite*]

Country or area Pays ou zone	1986	1987	1988	1989	1990	1991	1992	1993	1994
At constant prices	7 506	7 727	8 168	8 712	8 989	9 265	9 438	9 702	9 973
Growth rates	4.8	2.9	5.7	6.7	3.2	3.1	1.9	2.8	2.8
Madagascar Madagascar									
At current prices	3 258	2 566	2 442	2 498	3 080	2 673	2 996	3 371	2 977
Per capita	296	226	208	205	245	206	223	243	208
At constant prices	2 743	2 775	2 869	2 986	3 080	2 886	2 920	2 981	2 979
Growth rates	2.0	1.2	3.4	4.1	3.1	−6.3	1.2	2.1	−0.1
Malawi Malawi									
At current prices	1 176	1 228	1 369	1 644	2 145	2 192	1 907	2 119	1 410
Per capita	155	153	161	184	229	224	188	201	130
At constant prices	1 860	1 905	1 954	2 052	2 145	2 299	2 099	2 305	2 079
Growth rates	0.4	2.4	2.6	5.0	4.6	7.2	−8.7	9.8	−9.8
Malaysia Malaisie									
At current prices	27 734	31 602	34 696	37 852	42 822	47 111	58 014	64 472	70 543
Per capita	1 722	1 911	2 043	2 171	2 394	2 568	3 087	3 350	3 582
At constant prices	31 124	32 802	35 734	39 022	42 822	46 528	50 160	54 424	58 941
Growth rates	1.1	5.4	8.9	9.2	9.7	8.7	7.8	8.5	8.3
Maldives Maldives									
At current prices	95	91	113	117	139	152	182	215	254
Per capita	502	466	559	559	646	679	790	905	1 032
At constant prices	93	101	110	120	139	150	160	170	180
Growth rates	8.6	8.9	8.7	9.3	16.2	7.6	6.3	6.5	5.7
Mali Mali									
At current prices	1 690	1 999	2 067	2 073	2 510	2 451	2 786	2 781	1 917
Per capita	207	238	239	232	272	258	284	274	183
At constant prices	2 329	2 274	2 280	2 451	2 510	2 505	2 747	2 827	2 895
Growth rates	16.1	−2.4	0.3	7.5	2.4	−0.2	9.7	2.9	2.4
Malta Malte									
At current prices	1 303	1 590	1 833	1 923	2 312	2 496	2 743	2 454	2 692
Per capita	3 754	4 555	5 222	5 463	6 531	7 012	7 640	6 798	7 394
At constant prices	1 781	1 855	2 011	2 175	2 312	2 457	2 572	2 688	2 804
Growth rates	3.9	4.1	8.4	8.2	6.3	6.3	4.7	4.5	4.3
Marshall Islands Iles Marshall									
At current prices	55	62	69	71	77	72	79	85	89
Per capita	1 334	1 465	1 568	1 579	1 664	1 496	1 618	1 705	1 719
At constant prices	57	65	71	72	77	69	69	71	72
Growth rates	22.4	13.2	9.3	0.8	7.0	−9.8	0.1	2.0	2.0
Martinique Martinique									
At current prices	1 996	2 622	2 836	2 835	3 548	3 684	4 143	4 114	4 377
Per capita	5 802	7 534	8 058	7 963	9 856	10 121	11 257	11 089	11 671
At constant prices	2 858	3 068	3 254	3 447	3 548	3 408	3 467	3 561	3 628
Growth rates	4.5	7.3	6.1	5.9	2.9	−4.0	1.8	2.7	1.9
Mauritania Mauritanie									
At current prices	803	910	965	1 006	1 050	1 136	1 146	903	912
Per capita	443	490	507	515	524	553	544	418	411
At constant prices	923	944	964	1 013	1 050	1 085	1 127	1 162	1 193
Growth rates	5.8	2.3	2.1	5.1	3.6	3.4	3.8	3.1	2.7
Mauritius Maurice									
At current prices	1 463	1 831	2 069	2 116	2 559	2 738	3 079	3 112	3 460
Per capita	1 429	1 776	1 991	2 021	2 421	2 566	2 854	2 853	3 134
At constant prices	1 942	2 139	2 284	2 388	2 559	2 665	2 830	4 589	4 810
Growth rates	9.7	10.2	6.8	4.6	7.2	4.1	6.2	62.2	4.8
Mexico Mexique									
At current prices	129 440	140 264	171 770	206 223	244 047	286 631	329 302	361 916	371 223
Per capita	1 675	1 774	2 124	2 494	2 888	3 320	3 734	4 020	4 041
At constant prices	219 235	223 308	226 086	233 631	244 047	252 888	259 971	261 545	270 699
Growth rates	−3.7	1.9	1.2	3.3	4.5	3.6	2.8	0.6	3.5
Micronesia, Fed. States of Micron, Etats fédèrés de									
At current prices	119	144	184	214	242	269	277	275	310
Per capita	1 214	1 435	1 783	2 022	2 241	2 425	2 428	2 335	2 560
At constant prices	167	182	198	222	242	251	255	260	259
Growth rates	6.7	9.0	9.1	12.1	8.8	3.7	1.5	2.0	−0.4

20

Gross domestic product: total and per capita
In US dollars (millions) [1] at current and constant 1990 prices; per capita US$;
real rates of growth [cont.]

Produit intérieur brut : total et par habitant
En monnaie dollars de E−u (millions) [1]   aux prix courants et constants de 1990; par habitant;
taux de l'accroissement réels [suite]

Country or area Pays ou zone	1986	1987	1988	1989	1990	1991	1992	1993	1994
Monaco Monaco									
At current prices	369	462	498	513	632	629	715	674	765
Per capita	13 195	15 916	17 160	17 112	21 064	20 980	23 051	21 736	24 693
At constant prices	528	556	577	619	632	633	659	650	668
Growth rates	2.0	5.3	3.9	7.3	2.0	0.2	4.1	−1.4	2.8
Mongolia Mongolie									
At current prices	2 928	3 378	3 596	3 622	748	1 986	1 111	1 582	686
Per capita	1 492	1 675	1 736	1 704	343	892	489	682	290
At constant prices	699	734	777	763	748	678	614	595	609
Growth rates	10.2	4.9	6.0	−1.8	−2.1	−9.3	−9.5	−3.0	2.3
Montserrat Montserrat									
At current prices	42	56	63	70	67	65	68	71	75
Per capita	3 842	5 051	5 741	6 364	6 061	5 941	6 224	6 474	6 795
At constant prices	53	59	69	75	67	64	65	67	68
Growth rates	5.2	11.6	16.0	9.1	−10.8	−4.0	1.8	2.7	1.9
Morocco Maroc									
At current prices	16 947	18 703	22 079	22 847	25 939	27 755	28 253	26 636	29 093
Per capita	759	820	947	959	1 066	1 116	1 112	1 027	1 098
At constant prices	22 693	22 129	24 462	25 069	25 939	27 544	26 578	26 294	26 925
Growth rates	8.1	−2.5	10.5	2.5	3.5	6.2	−3.5	−1.1	2.4
Mozambique Mozambique									
At current prices	4 134	1 465	1 249	1 349	1 443	1 433	1 242	1 410	1 433
Per capita	302	106	90	96	102	99	84	93	92
At constant prices	1 232	1 291	1 350	1 430	1 443	1 524	1 510	1 644	1 676
Growth rates	1.6	4.8	4.6	6.0	0.9	5.6	−0.9	8.8	2.0
Myanmar Myanmar									
At current prices	8 053	10 325	11 923	18 593	23 971	28 415	37 830	52 839	67 637
Per capita	210	263	298	454	573	665	867	1 185	1 485
At constant prices	26 421	25 363	22 483	23 314	23 971	23 725	26 313	27 871	29 769
Growth rates	−1.1	−4.0	−11.4	3.7	2.8	−1.0	10.9	5.9	6.8
Namibia Namibie									
At current prices	1 459	1 769	1 989	1 979	2 302	2 406	2 768	2 562	2 886
Per capita	1 206	1 423	1 556	1 507	1 706	1 737	1 945	1 754	1 924
At constant prices	2 065	2 112	2 243	2 235	2 302	2 419	2 503	2 585	2 773
Growth rates	3.7	2.3	6.2	−0.4	3.0	5.1	3.5	3.3	7.3
Nauru Nauru									
At current prices	109	119	147	163	176	208	234	242	276
Per capita	12 103	13 231	16 340	18 161	17 632	20 754	23 397	24 197	25 094
At constant prices	138	125	149	166	176	197	200	204	213
Growth rates	0.0	−9.3	19.4	11.1	6.2	11.6	1.5	2.0	4.5
Nepal Népal									
At current prices	2 375	2 715	2 962	2 859	3 099	2 790	2 954	2 982	3 375
Per capita	136	152	162	152	161	141	146	143	158
At constant prices	2 461	2 558	2 747	2 871	3 099	3 240	3 307	3 403	3 637
Growth rates	4.3	3.9	7.4	4.5	8.0	4.6	2.1	2.9	6.9
Netherlands Pays−Bas									
At current prices	178 631	217 495	231 415	228 538	283 518	290 008	320 210	309 227	331 589
Per capita	12 259	14 838	15 689	15 391	18 962	19 258	21 105	20 231	21 536
At constant prices	250 563	253 523	260 151	272 326	283 518	289 933	293 585	294 612	302 313
Growth rates	2.8	1.2	2.6	4.7	4.1	2.3	1.3	0.4	2.6
Netherlands Antilles Antilles néerlandaises									
At current prices	1 076	1 190	1 317	1 397	1 559	1 522	1 589	1 656	1 710
Per capita	5 845	6 435	7 041	7 429	8 203	7 928	8 235	8 494	8 679
At constant prices	1 246	1 329	1 427	1 449	1 559	1 497	1 523	1 564	1 588
Growth rates	−2.8	6.7	7.4	1.5	7.6	−4.0	1.8	2.7	1.5
New Caledonia Nouvelle−Calédonie									
At current prices	1 201	1 488	2 073	2 185	2 529	2 628	2 926	3 116	3 316
Per capita	7 651	9 301	12 795	13 243	15 056	15 460	16 916	17 805	18 631
At constant prices	1 674	1 769	2 382	2 642	2 529	2 629	2 669	2 723	2 818
Growth rates	−1.0	5.7	34.6	11.0	−4.3	3.9	1.5	2.0	3.5
New Zealand Nouvelle−Zélande									
At current prices	28 761	36 903	44 043	42 706	43 625	42 059	40 881	43 699	51 727
Per capita	8 795	11 220	13 314	12 821	12 984	12 381	11 887	12 539	14 649

20

Gross domestic product: total and per capita
In US dollars (millions) [1] at current and constant 1990 prices; per capita US$;
real rates of growth [cont.]

Produit intérieur brut : total et par habitant
En monnaie dollars de E−u (millions) [1] aux prix courants et constants de 1990; par habitant;
taux de l'accroissement réels [suite]

Country or area Pays ou zone	1986	1987	1988	1989	1990	1991	1992	1993	1994
At constant prices	42 890	43 471	43 161	42 986	43 625	43 045	44 321	46 680	48 132
Growth rates	2.1	1.4	−0.7	−0.4	1.5	−1.3	3.0	5.3	3.1
Nicaragua Nicaragua									
At current prices	6 917	3 947	1 248	1 018	2 214	1 740	1 845	1 969	1 851
Per capita	2 090	1 165	360	286	602	457	467	479	433
At constant prices	2 591	2 572	2 252	2 213	2 214	2 210	2 219	2 211	2 285
Growth rates	−1.0	−0.7	−12.5	−1.7	0.0	−0.2	0.4	−0.4	3.3
Niger Niger									
At current prices	1 905	2 233	2 277	2 171	2 506	2 464	2 712	2 594	1 866
Per capita	279	317	314	290	324	308	328	303	211
At constant prices	2 561	2 333	2 376	2 437	2 506	2 556	2 605	2 662	2 769
Growth rates	12.6	−8.9	1.8	2.6	2.8	2.0	1.9	2.2	4.0
Nigeria Nigéria									
At current prices	41 643	27 113	32 013	30 524	32 424	32 697	31 784	31 592	40 803
Per capita	487	308	353	327	337	330	311	300	376
At constant prices	25 617	25 437	27 955	29 968	32 424	33 982	34 994	35 790	36 269
Growth rates	2.5	−0.7	9.9	7.2	8.2	4.8	3.0	2.3	1.3
Norway Norvège									
At current prices	69 471	83 337	89 501	89 997	105 524	105 922	113 115	103 419	109 580
Per capita	16 664	19 909	21 290	21 311	24 882	24 859	26 429	24 056	25 378
At constant prices	101 684	103 709	103 184	103 796	105 524	107 191	110 804	114 475	120 358
Growth rates	4.2	2.0	−0.5	0.6	1.7	1.6	3.4	3.3	5.1
Oman Oman									
At current prices	7 283	7 809	7 610	8 402	10 535	10 188	11 489	11 686	11 835
Per capita	4 978	5 101	4 750	5 016	6 017	5 570	6 018	5 866	5 698
At constant prices	9 312	8 970	9 484	9 798	10 535	11 504	12 284	12 774	12 646
Growth rates	3.3	−3.7	5.7	3.3	7.5	9.2	6.8	4.0	−1.0
Pakistan Pakistan									
At current prices	34 388	38 818	42 756	41 669	47 016	50 897	53 501	55 679	59 288
Per capita	323	352	374	353	386	405	414	419	434
At constant prices	37 784	40 665	42 682	44 585	47 016	50 700	51 673	53 761	55 535
Growth rates	6.5	7.6	5.0	4.5	5.5	7.8	1.9	4.0	3.3
Palau Palaos									
At current prices	37	45	58	68	76	85	86	86	99
Per capita	2 677	3 230	3 856	4 501	5 082	5 307	5 379	5 355	5 833
At constant prices	57	57	68	71	76	79	80	82	85
Growth rates	−0.6	−1.2	21.0	4.1	7.0	3.9	1.5	2.0	3.5
Panama Panama									
At current prices	5 191	5 363	4 605	4 639	5 009	5 496	6 015	6 565	6 591
Per capita	2 347	2 375	1 998	1 973	2 089	2 249	2 415	2 587	2 550
At constant prices	5 562	5 697	4 808	4 788	5 009	5 488	5 955	6 276	6 571
Growth rates	3.3	2.4	−15.6	−0.4	4.6	9.6	8.5	5.4	4.7
Papua New Guinea Papouasie−Nvl−Guinée									
At current prices	2 648	3 144	3 656	3 546	3 221	3 788	4 292	5 090	5 330
Per capita	753	875	995	944	839	965	1 068	1 238	1 267
At constant prices	3 185	3 273	3 369	3 321	3 221	3 528	3 965	4 655	4 804
Growth rates	5.6	2.8	2.9	−1.4	−3.0	9.5	12.4	17.4	3.2
Paraguay Paraguay									
At current prices	5 407	4 534	6 035	4 363	5 265	6 249	6 446	6 723	7 692
Per capita	1 418	1 152	1 485	1 042	1 220	1 406	1 410	1 430	1 593
At constant prices	4 350	4 538	4 827	5 107	5 265	5 395	5 492	5 851	6 098
Growth rates	0.0	4.3	6.4	5.8	3.1	2.5	1.8	6.5	4.2
Peru Pérou									
At current prices	26 713	44 014	38 372	43 136	36 142	42 636	41 790	40 501	49 644
Per capita	1 340	2 163	1 848	2 038	1 674	1 937	1 862	1 770	2 128
At constant prices	43 495	47 182	43 238	38 203	36 142	37 155	36 231	38 593	42 436
Growth rates	9.2	8.5	−8.4	−11.7	−5.4	2.8	−2.5	6.5	10.0
Philippines Philippines									
At current prices	29 868	33 196	37 885	42 575	44 312	45 418	52 976	54 390	63 883
Per capita	534	581	650	715	729	732	835	839	965
At constant prices	36 364	37 931	40 493	43 006	44 312	44 055	44 204	45 149	47 082
Growth rates	3.4	4.3	6.8	6.2	3.0	−0.6	0.3	2.1	4.3

20

Gross domestic product: total and per capita

In US dollars (millions) [1] at current and constant 1990 prices; per capita US$;

real rates of growth [*cont.*]

Produit intérieur brut : total et par habitant

En monnaie dollars de E−u (millions) [1] aux prix courants et constants de 1990; par habitant;

taux de l'accroissement réels [*suite*]

Country or area Pays ou zone	1986	1987	1988	1989	1990	1991	1992	1993	1994
Poland Pologne									
At current prices	68 233	59 008	63 555	75 917	58 976	76 478	84 357	85 995	95 955
Per capita	1 822	1 566	1 679	1 998	1 547	2 002	2 205	2 245	2 503
At constant prices	62 699	63 926	66 568	66 675	58 976	54 864	56 304	58 438	61 360
Growth rates	4.2	2.0	4.1	0.2	−11.6	−7.0	2.6	3.8	5.0
Portugal Portugal									
At current prices	33 598	41 820	47 999	51 699	67 238	77 409	95 029	84 736	86 720
Per capita	3 393	4 225	4 853	5 233	6 814	7 853	9 651	8 613	8 822
At constant prices	56 009	58 951	61 263	64 421	67 238	68 680	69 424	68 590	69 276
Growth rates	4.1	5.3	3.9	5.2	4.4	2.2	1.1	−1.2	1.0
Puerto Rico Porto Rico									
At current prices	23 878	26 178	28 267	30 604	32 287	34 630	36 847	39 265	41 817
Per capita	7 025	7 628	8 156	8 747	9 144	9 725	10 267	10 853	11 469
At constant prices	27 208	28 982	30 413	31 562	32 287	33 761	35 082	36 322	37 271
Growth rates	4.9	6.5	4.9	3.8	2.3	4.6	3.9	3.5	2.6
Qatar Qatar									
At current prices	5 053	5 446	6 038	6 488	7 360	6 884	7 473	7 193	7 031
Per capita	13 091	13 187	13 723	13 983	15 176	13 685	14 455	13 598	13 020
At constant prices	6 448	6 507	6 811	7 169	7 360	7 302	8 011	8 115	8 074
Growth rates	3.7	0.9	4.7	5.3	2.7	−0.8	9.7	1.3	−0.5
Republic of Moldova République de Moldova									
At current prices	12 896	14 808	16 194	17 892	19 041	14 797	994	1 524	1 424
Per capita	3 034	3 458	3 755	4 123	4 365	3 378	226	346	322
At constant prices	14 879	15 522	16 256	18 404	19 041	15 480	11 099	10 566	7 396
Growth rates	5.2	4.3	4.7	13.2	3.5	−18.7	−28.3	−4.8	−30.0
Réunion Réunion									
At current prices	2 723	3 643	3 962	4 015	5 211	5 554	6 120	6 037	6 377
Per capita	4 862	6 381	6 808	6 770	8 627	9 046	9 800	9 522	9 903
At constant prices	4 445	4 645	4 831	5 013	5 211	5 389	5 551	5 705	5 834
Growth rates	4.7	4.5	4.0	3.8	4.0	3.4	3.0	2.8	2.3
Romania Roumanie									
At current prices	52 046	58 207	60 177	53 612	38 244	28 852	19 578	25 963	29 206
Per capita	2 279	2 534	2 607	2 314	1 648	1 244	847	1 128	1 274
At constant prices	42 763	43 120	42 900	40 417	38 244	33 305	28 720	29 007	30 023
Growth rates	2.3	0.8	−0.5	−5.8	−5.4	−12.9	−13.8	1.0	3.5
Russian Federation Fédération de Russie									
At current prices	733 652	829 575	919 989	953 708	967 267	799 143	108 324	172 893	287 591
Per capita	5 090	5 709	6 283	6 474	6 539	5 394	732	1 170	1 951
At constant prices	994 133	998 411	1 042 961	1 047 286	967 267	918 904	785 663	717 310	626 929
Growth rates	−2.1	0.4	4.5	0.4	−7.6	−5.0	−14.5	−8.7	−12.6
Rwanda Rwanda									
At current prices	1 928	2 152	2 327	2 378	2 335	1 701	1 630	1 082	504
Per capita	309	335	352	350	334	237	221	143	65
At constant prices	2 297	2 300	2 301	2 376	2 335	2 265	2 236	1 990	995
Growth rates	4.5	0.1	0.0	3.3	−1.7	−3.0	−1.3	−11.0	−50.0
Saint Kitts and Nevis Saint−Kitts−et−Nevis									
At current prices	83	93	108	117	126	137	145	163	173
Per capita	1 938	2 167	2 578	2 797	3 002	3 250	3 445	3 888	4 217
At constant prices	101	109	116	122	126	131	135	141	146
Growth rates	6.2	7.4	7.0	5.1	3.0	3.9	3.0	4.5	3.2
Saint Lucia Sainte−Lucie									
At current prices	223	240	270	304	333	358	393	405	425
Per capita	1 769	1 872	2 092	2 320	2 503	2 655	2 866	2 913	3 014
At constant prices	256	261	293	320	333	341	365	373	381
Growth rates	5.8	2.2	12.2	9.1	4.1	2.3	7.1	2.3	2.2
St. Vincent−Grenadines St. Vincent−Grenadines									
At current prices	127	142	161	174	194	212	231	244	250
Per capita	1 235	1 366	1 530	1 640	1 817	1 967	2 120	2 222	2 248
At constant prices	147	156	170	182	194	200	210	213	217
Growth rates	7.4	6.3	8.7	7.0	7.0	3.1	4.9	1.4	1.6
Samoa Samoa									
At current prices	71	79	94	87	89	95	101	104	118
Per capita	443	490	583	535	549	579	610	622	700

20

Gross domestic product: total and per capita
In US dollars (millions) [1] at current and constant 1990 prices; per capita US$;
real rates of growth [cont.]

Produit intérieur brut : total et par habitant
En monnaie dollars de E−u (millions) [1] aux prix courants et constants de 1990; par habitant;
taux de l'accroissement réels [suite]

Country or area Pays ou zone	1986	1987	1988	1989	1990	1991	1992	1993	1994
At constant prices	91	92	92	93	89	99	104	107	101
Growth rates	0.6	1.0	−0.2	1.3	−4.5	10.8	5.0	3.5	−5.5
San Marino San Marino									
At current prices	234	307	339	351	442	464	513	417	430
Per capita	10 623	13 346	14 735	15 266	19 205	20 192	21 379	17 354	17 213
At constant prices	391	404	420	432	442	447	450	460	471
Growth rates	2.9	3.1	4.1	2.9	2.1	1.2	0.8	2.2	2.3
Sao Tome and Principe Sao Tomé−et−Principe									
At current prices	64	55	49	46	54	42	27	21	16
Per capita	595	499	433	397	454	349	218	166	120
At constant prices	51	50	51	52	54	56	57	59	60
Growth rates	1.0	−1.5	2.0	1.5	3.8	3.5	2.0	2.8	1.5
Saudi Arabia Arabie saoudite									
At current prices	84 773	72 387	73 552	76 142	82 996	104 670	115 332	121 530	121 762
Per capita	6 347	5 135	4 962	4 917	5 172	6 349	6 855	7 099	6 977
At constant prices	76 132	75 526	72 591	80 086	82 996	97 063	102 860	107 177	108 923
Growth rates	−11.9	−0.8	−3.9	10.3	3.6	17.0	6.0	4.2	1.6
Senegal Sénégal									
At current prices	3 762	4 599	4 980	4 628	5 703	5 492	6 246	5 818	3 995
Per capita	574	682	718	649	778	731	810	736	493
At constant prices	5 064	5 266	5 533	5 456	5 703	5 664	5 904	5 851	5 955
Growth rates	4.6	4.0	5.1	−1.4	4.5	−0.7	4.2	−0.9	1.8
Seychelles Seychelles									
At current prices	209	249	284	305	369	374	434	452	496
Per capita	3 164	3 720	4 174	4 418	5 266	5 348	6 108	6 281	6 798
At constant prices	283	295	311	343	369	377	403	425	425
Growth rates	1.2	4.4	5.3	10.3	7.5	2.2	6.9	5.6	0.0
Sierra Leone Sierra Leone									
At current prices	465	579	894	735	594	615	546	698	809
Per capita	127	155	234	188	149	150	130	162	184
At constant prices	567	582	595	610	594	608	597	582	598
Growth rates	5.5	2.7	2.3	2.5	−2.6	2.3	−1.9	−2.4	2.6
Singapore Singapour									
At current prices	17 757	20 245	24 845	29 463	36 509	42 278	48 548	55 086	66 453
Per capita	6 864	7 739	9 390	11 010	13 497	15 458	17 564	19 723	23 556
At constant prices	25 270	27 648	30 729	33 568	36 509	38 938	41 290	45 396	49 979
Growth rates	1.8	9.4	11.1	9.2	8.8	6.7	6.0	9.9	10.1
Slovakia Slovaquie									
At current prices	14 123	15 847	15 669	15 560	13 568	9 500	10 892	11 056	12 431
Per capita	2 733	3 053	3 005	2 972	2 581	1 801	2 057	2 081	2 331
At constant prices	13 182	13 518	13 771	13 918	13 568	11 304	11 129	10 674	11 190
Growth rates	4.1	2.6	1.9	1.1	−2.5	−16.7	−1.6	−4.1	4.8
Slovenia Slovénie									
At current prices	10 258	12 280	10 775	12 102	17 304	12 719	12 348	12 644	13 994
Per capita	5 433	6 477	5 659	6 333	9 022	6 607	6 395	6 528	7 206
At constant prices	18 994	18 792	18 474	18 150	17 304	15 692	14 844	15 037	15 789
Growth rates	3.1	−1.1	−1.7	−1.8	−4.7	−9.3	−5.4	1.3	5.0
Solomon Islands Iles Salomon									
At current prices	145	146	176	179	177	195	216	222	245
Per capita	520	506	589	576	554	589	630	626	669
At constant prices	144	148	155	166	177	184	199	207	216
Growth rates	−0.7	2.4	5.4	6.9	6.7	3.8	8.2	4.0	4.5
Somalia Somalie									
At current prices	1 650	1 613	1 622	1 140	1 062	614	551	1 006	1 126
Per capita	204	196	193	133	122	70	62	112	124
At constant prices	979	1 078	1 079	1 079	1 062	1 051	925	925	731
Growth rates	−2.2	10.1	0.1	0.0	−1.6	−1.0	−12.0	0.0	−21.0
South Africa Afrique du Sud									
At current prices	62 203	80 806	87 119	89 004	102 115	107 882	114 680	112 447	114 963
Per capita	1 839	2 334	2 459	2 456	2 755	2 846	2 957	2 835	2 835
At constant prices	94 261	96 241	100 283	102 586	102 115	101 717	99 602	100 697	102 812
Growth rates	0.0	2.1	4.2	2.3	−0.5	−0.4	−2.1	1.1	2.1

20

Gross domestic product: total and per capita
In US dollars (millions) [1]   at current and constant 1990 prices; per capita US$;
real rates of growth [cont.]

Produit intérieur brut : total et par habitant
En monnaie dollars de E−u (millions) [1]   aux prix courants et constants de 1990; par habitant;
taux de l'accroissement réels [suite]

Country or area Pays ou zone	1986	1987	1988	1989	1990	1991	1992	1993	1994
Spain Espagne									
At current prices	230 806	292 716	344 748	380 511	491 938	528 339	576 311	478 582	482 788
Per capita	5 973	7 541	8 842	9 721	12 526	13 418	14 608	12 112	12 201
At constant prices	407 536	430 529	452 748	474 200	491 938	502 965	506 451	500 854	510 763
Growth rates	3.2	5.6	5.2	4.7	3.7	2.2	0.7	−1.1	2.0
Sri Lanka Sri Lanka									
At current prices	6 155	6 413	6 878	6 886	7 935	8 937	9 623	10 341	11 758
Per capita	376	387	410	405	461	512	545	578	649
At constant prices	7 013	7 126	7 324	7 469	7 935	8 318	8 682	9 282	9 811
Growth rates	4.3	1.6	2.8	2.0	6.2	4.8	4.4	6.9	5.7
Sudan Soudan									
At current prices	8 056	12 157	10 398	18 347	24 469	27 697	4 167	2 795	1 683
Per capita	365	536	446	767	995	1 097	161	105	62
At constant prices	23 407	23 922	23 132	24 844	24 469	24 640	27 425	26 328	26 328
Growth rates	3.9	2.2	−3.3	7.4	−1.5	0.7	11.3	−4.0	0.0
Suriname Suriname									
At current prices	998	1 098	1 301	1 520	1 728	2 083	2 859	5 923	359
Per capita	2 614	2 837	3 327	3 838	4 321	5 142	6 990	14 306	858
At constant prices	1 639	1 537	1 658	1 728	1 728	1 782	1 863	1 867	1 811
Growth rates	0.8	−6.2	7.8	4.2	0.0	3.1	4.5	0.2	−3.0
Swaziland Swaziland									
At current prices	449	592	692	696	904	874	954	936	1 090
Per capita	673	864	982	961	1 215	1 142	1 212	1 157	1 311
At constant prices	776	757	806	859	904	949	968	946	949
Growth rates	8.9	−2.5	6.6	6.5	5.3	5.0	1.9	−2.2	0.3
Sweden Suède									
At current prices	132 975	161 441	181 897	191 193	229 756	239 327	247 557	185 289	196 598
Per capita	15 870	19 178	21 493	22 464	26 844	27 812	28 619	21 312	22 499
At constant prices	209 928	216 531	221 405	226 667	229 756	227 191	223 961	218 214	222 951
Growth rates	2.3	3.2	2.3	2.4	1.4	−1.1	−1.4	−2.6	2.2
Switzerland Suisse									
At current prices	135 277	170 792	183 428	177 493	226 022	230 875	240 908	232 164	257 402
Per capita	20 525	25 695	27 357	26 229	33 073	33 431	34 514	32 903	36 096
At constant prices	202 621	206 733	212 729	220 944	226 022	225 957	225 272	223 345	226 007
Growth rates	2.9	2.0	2.9	3.9	2.3	0.0	−0.3	−0.9	1.2
Syrian Arab Republic Rép. arabe syrienne									
At current prices	25 461	32 538	16 574	18 610	23 905	27 756	33 018	35 502	40 056
Per capita	2 375	2 929	1 440	1 561	1 936	2 171	2 495	2 592	2 827
At constant prices	21 133	21 536	24 393	22 208	23 904	25 614	28 315	29 425	30 408
Growth rates	−5.0	1.9	13.3	−9.0	7.6	7.2	10.6	3.9	3.3
Tajikistan Tadjikistan									
At current prices	8 421	9 612	11 042	10 772	11 032	7 661	313	677	779
Per capita	1 794	1 988	2 216	2 099	2 087	1 407	56	117	131
At constant prices	9 462	9 616	10 590	10 566	11 032	10 105	6 972	5 766	5 074
Growth rates	−6.1	1.6	10.1	−0.2	4.4	−8.4	−31.0	−17.3	−12.0
Thailand Thaïlande									
At current prices	43 097	50 536	61 668	72 251	85 639	98 744	111 546	124 859	142 794
Per capita	828	954	1 144	1 319	1 541	1 754	1 958	2 168	2 454
At constant prices	55 116	60 363	68 384	76 720	85 639	92 838	100 192	108 389	117 649
Growth rates	5.5	9.5	13.3	12.2	11.6	8.4	7.9	8.2	8.5
TFYR Macedonia L'ex−R.y. Macédoine									
At current prices	3 318	3 812	3 317	4 383	5 431	6 458	3 511	1 579	3 324
Per capita	1 703	1 932	1 660	2 168	2 655	3 118	1 676	745	1 552
At constant prices	6 163	6 084	5 887	6 000	5 431	4 774	4 182	3 680	3 470
Growth rates	7.1	−1.3	−3.2	1.9	−9.5	−12.1	−12.4	−12.0	−5.7
Togo Togo									
At current prices	1 050	1 237	1 389	1 354	1 680	1 749	2 112	2 108	1 679
Per capita	336	385	419	396	476	480	561	543	419
At constant prices	1 433	1 520	1 617	1 678	1 680	1 747	1 798	1 827	2 023
Growth rates	2.7	6.1	6.4	3.8	0.1	4.0	3.0	1.6	10.7
Tonga Tonga									
At current prices	67	80	111	116	124	149	147	163	145
Per capita	727	864	1 179	1 219	1 289	1 537	1 517	1 660	1 482

20

Gross domestic product: total and per capita
In US dollars (millions) [1] at current and constant 1990 prices; per capita US$;
real rates of growth [cont.]

Produit intérieur brut : total et par habitant
En monnaie dollars de E−u (millions) [1]   aux prix courants et constants de 1990; par habitant;
taux de l'accroissement réels [suite]

Country or area Pays ou zone	1986	1987	1988	1989	1990	1991	1992	1993	1994
At constant prices	118	123	126	129	124	128	131	142	134
Growth rates	−2.3	4.4	2.5	2.4	−4.0	3.7	1.9	8.4	−5.4
Trinidad and Tobago Trinité−et−Tobago									
At current prices	4 794	4 798	4 497	4 323	5 068	5 308	5 440	4 670	4 792
Per capita	4 077	4 025	3 726	3 538	4 100	4 243	4 300	3 654	3 709
At constant prices	5 490	5 240	5 034	4 993	5 068	5 195	5 116	5 031	5 356
Growth rates	−3.3	−4.6	−3.9	−0.8	1.5	2.5	−1.5	−1.7	6.5
Tunisia Tunisie									
At current prices	8 821	9 604	10 031	10 004	12 425	12 759	13 805	12 976	13 461
Per capita	1 187	1 265	1 293	1 263	1 538	1 548	1 642	1 514	1 541
At constant prices	10 466	11 072	11 233	12 057	12 425	12 808	13 275	13 614	14 069
Growth rates	−1.6	5.8	1.5	7.3	3.1	3.1	3.7	2.6	3.3
Turkey Turquie									
At current prices	75 729	87 171	90 857	107 142	150 679	151 042	159 096	174 167	135 366
Per capita	1 470	1 655	1 688	1 950	2 686	2 638	2 723	2 922	2 227
At constant prices	122 866	134 048	136 831	138 085	150 679	152 204	160 567	170 074	163 441
Growth rates	7.8	9.1	2.1	0.9	9.1	1.0	5.5	5.9	−3.9
Turkmenistan Turkménistan									
At current prices	8 291	9 916	10 847	11 051	11 411	8 400	1 471	5 036	8 112
Per capita	2 508	2 924	3 118	3 097	3 120	2 243	384	1 284	2 023
At constant prices	9 295	9 919	10 422	10 828	11 411	10 875	10 299	9 269	7 415
Growth rates	1.7	6.7	5.1	3.9	5.4	−4.7	−5.3	−10.0	−20.0
Tuvalu Tuvalu									
At current prices	4	5	6	6	6	7	7	7	8
Per capita	454	566	754	667	701	780	802	798	924
At constant prices	5	6	6	6	6	7	7	7	7
Growth rates	−0.6	10.0	10.4	−4.3	2.5	4.8	1.5	2.0	3.5
Uganda Ouganda									
At current prices	4 665	5 216	5 960	5 267	3 723	3 018	3 244	3 370	5 261
Per capita	299	323	356	304	207	162	168	169	255
At constant prices	3 170	3 387	3 660	3 931	3 734	4 051	4 234	4 504	4 930
Growth rates	0.9	6.9	8.1	7.4	−5.0	8.5	4.5	6.4	9.4
Ukraine Ukraine									
At current prices	184 203	213 972	234 267	244 657	247 447	131 886	25 679	19 435	17 428
Per capita	3 605	4 173	4 554	4 745	4 792	2 553	497	377	339
At constant prices	226 681	231 287	230 075	244 055	247 447	218 744	188 776	161 970	131 195
Growth rates	2.0	2.0	−0.5	6.1	1.4	−11.6	−13.7	−14.2	−19.0
United Arab Emirates Emirats arabes unis									
At current prices	21 674	23 799	23 728	27 506	33 780	33 914	34 977	35 405	38 437
Per capita	15 031	15 834	15 201	17 011	20 216	19 706	19 761	19 496	20 654
At constant prices	24 365	25 890	25 269	28 688	33 780	33 818	34 464	34 809	34 461
Growth rates	−19.0	6.3	−2.4	13.5	17.8	0.1	1.9	1.0	−1.0
United Kingdom Royaume−Uni									
At current prices	562 354	689 455	835 619	841 404	975 524	1 011 545	1 044 665	941 434	1 018 761
Per capita	9 876	12 075	14 592	14 647	16 930	17 501	18 020	16 192	17 471
At constant prices	864 682	905 849	950 978	971 701	975 524	956 237	951 343	970 627	1 007 945
Growth rates	4.4	4.8	5.0	2.2	0.4	−2.0	−0.5	2.0	3.8
United Rep.Tanzania Rép. Unie de Tanzanie									
At current prices	4 782	3 360	3 149	2 633	2 330	2 960	3 561	3 317	3 440
Per capita	212	144	131	106	91	112	131	118	119
At constant prices	1 958	2 058	2 145	2 231	2 330	2 463	2 550	2 656	2 737
Growth rates	3.3	5.1	4.2	4.0	4.5	5.7	3.5	4.2	3.0
United States Etats−Unis									
At current prices	4 230 784	4 496 574	4 853 962	5 204 500	5 489 600	5 656 400	5 937 300	6 259 900	6 649 805
Per capita	17 581	18 516	19 803	21 031	21 965	22 401	23 266	24 270	25 514
At constant prices	4 926 602	5 078 574	5 278 652	5 422 533	5 489 600	5 457 379	5 599 509	5 790 925	6 027 216
Growth rates	2.8	3.1	3.9	2.7	1.2	−0.6	2.6	3.4	4.1
Uruguay Uruguay									
At current prices	5 858	7 329	7 583	7 992	8 355	10 041	11 677	13 404	13 297
Per capita	1 936	2 408	2 478	2 597	2 700	3 227	3 731	4 256	4 199
At constant prices	7 574	8 175	8 174	8 279	8 355	8 511	9 191	9 435	8 496
Growth rates	8.9	7.9	0.0	1.3	0.9	1.9	8.0	2.7	−10.0

20

Gross domestic product: total and per capita
In US dollars (millions) [1] at current and constant 1990 prices; per capita US$;
real rates of growth [cont.]
Produit intérieur brut : total et par habitant
En monnaie dollars de E−u (millions) [1] aux prix courants et constants de 1990; par habitant;
taux de l'accroissement réels [suite]

Country or area Pays ou zone	1986	1987	1988	1989	1990	1991	1992	1993	1994
Uzbekistan Ouzbékistan									
At current prices	40 565	42 809	48 389	48 960	48 694	35 171	2 298	4 617	4 169
Per capita	2 185	2 251	2 484	2 454	2 385	1 683	107	211	187
At constant prices	34 057	32 003	43 293	46 490	48 694	46 259	41 124	40 137	38 532
Growth rates	−19.8	−6.0	35.3	7.4	4.7	−5.0	−11.1	−2.4	−4.0
Vanuatu Vanuatu									
At current prices	115	122	144	141	153	172	181	181	184
Per capita	844	878	1 012	966	1 026	1 124	1 153	1 122	1 117
At constant prices	138	138	139	145	153	159	160	167	159
Growth rates	−2.0	0.4	0.6	4.5	5.2	4.1	0.8	3.8	−4.5
Venezuela Venezuela									
At current prices	60 516	48 029	60 226	43 549	48 598	53 462	60 423	59 995	55 963
Per capita	3 441	2 660	3 249	2 290	2 492	2 676	2 955	2 869	2 618
At constant prices	45 546	47 178	49 924	45 645	48 598	53 326	56 558	56 330	54 488
Growth rates	6.5	3.6	5.8	−8.6	6.5	9.7	6.1	−0.4	−3.3
Viet Nam Viet Nam									
At current prices	26 341	36 659	25 424	6 293	6 472	8 095	9 841	12 863	15 531
Per capita	430	586	398	96	97	119	141	180	213
At constant prices	5 193	5 384	5 702	6 158	6 472	6 858	7 450	8 052	8 764
Growth rates	2.9	3.7	5.9	8.0	5.1	6.0	8.7	8.1	8.8
Yemen Yémen									
At current prices	...	...	...	6 266	7 873	7 465	8 980	11 319	14 552
Per capita	...	...	...	577	696	629	718	858	1 049
At constant prices	...	...	...	8 176	7 873	7 873	8 204	8 688	9 183
Growth rates	...	...	...	...	−3.7	0.0	4.2	5.9	5.7
former Dem. Yemen ancienne Yémen dém.									
At current prices	3 903	4 229	5 491	...	...	...	...	...	...
Per capita	493	515	644	...	...	...	...	...	...
former Yemen Arab Rep. anc. Yémen rép. arabe									
At current prices	899	1 026	1 077	...	...	...	...	...	...
Per capita	409	452	460	...	...	...	...	...	...
Yugoslavia Yougoslavie									
At current prices	19 183	21 965	19 492	25 753	31 901	40 709	27 452	5 813	12 599
Per capita	1 938	2 209	1 951	2 560	3 141	3 956	2 626	547	1 171
At constant prices	35 086	34 508	33 738	34 111	31 901	29 349	21 718	15 637	16 654
Growth rates	3.7	−1.7	−2.2	1.1	−6.5	−8.0	−26.0	−28.0	6.5
Zaire Zaïre									
At current prices	8 146	7 662	8 854	9 023	11 195	9 078	8 208	14 644	9 642
Per capita	249	226	253	249	299	235	206	355	227
At constant prices	0	0	0	0	0	0	0	0	0
Growth rates	4.7	2.6	0.6	−1.4	−2.4	−12.3	−10.4	−16.2	−7.6
Zambia Zambie									
At current prices	2 262	2 265	3 729	4 250	4 077	3 628	3 531	3 402	3 377
Per capita	318	308	489	539	500	431	407	381	367
At constant prices	3 827	3 932	4 008	4 047	4 077	3 997	3 817	4 073	4 114
Growth rates	2.7	2.8	2.0	1.0	0.8	−2.0	−4.5	6.7	1.0
Zimbabwe Zimbabwe									
At current prices	4 974	5 380	6 336	6 510	6 801	6 025	5 565	6 042	6 247
Per capita	573	598	681	678	687	591	532	563	568
At constant prices	5 085	5 083	5 965	6 655	6 801	7 134	6 586	6 724	7 033
Growth rates	0.4	−0.1	17.4	11.6	2.2	4.9	−7.7	2.1	4.6

Source:
National accounts database of the Statistics Division of
the United Nations Secretariat.

† For detailed descriptions of data pertaining to
former Czechoslovakia, Germany, SFR Yugoslavia and former
USSR, see Annex I − Country or area nomenclature, regional
and other groupings.

Source:
Base de données sur les comptes nationaux de la Division de
statistique du Secrétariat de l'ONU.

† Pour les descriptions en détails des données relatives
à l'ancienne Tchécoslovaquie, l'Allemagne, la Rfs
Yougoslavie et l'ancienne URSS, voir l'Annexe I −
Nomenclature des pays ou zones, groupements régionaux
et autres groupements.

20

Gross domestic product: total and per capita
In US dollars (millions) [1] at current and constant 1990 prices; per capita US$;
real rates of growth [*cont.*]

Produit intérieur brut : total et par habitant
En monnaie dollars de E−u (millions) [1] aux prix courants et constants de 1990; par habitant;
taux de l'accroissement réels [*suite*]

1   The exchange rates used for the conversion of national currency data into US dollars are the average market rates as published by the International Monetary Fund in the International Financial Statistics. Official exchange rates were used only when a free market rate was not available. For non−members of the fund, the conversion rates used are the average of United Nations operational rates of exchange. It should be noted that the use of market rates may distort the US dollar income level figures in a number of countries. Therefore, comparability of data both across countries and over time should be dealt with caution.

1 Les taux de change utilisés pour la conversion en dollars des États−Unis des données libellées en monnaie nationale sont les taux moyens du marché publiés par le Fonds monétaire international dans les "Statistiques financières internationales". Le taux de change officiel n'a été utilisé qu'en l'absence d'un taux du marché libre. Pour les pays qui ne sont pas membres du Fonds, les taux de change utilisés sont la moyenne des taux appliqués pour les opérations des Nations Unies. Il est à noter que l'utilisation des taux du marché risque de fausser, dans plusieurs pays, les chiffres du revenu exprimés en dollars des États−Unis. Toute comparaison des données entre pays et à des dates différentes doit être faite avec prudence.

21
Expenditure on gross domestic product at current prices
Dépenses imputées au produit intérieur brut aux prix courants
Percentage distribution
Répartition en pourcentage

Country or area Pays ou zone	Year Année	GDP at current prices (Million nat. cur.) PIB aux prix courants (Mil. monnaie nat.)	% of GDP – en % du PIB					
			Govt. final cons. exp. Consom. finale des admin. publiques	Private final cons. exp. Consom. finale privée	Increase in stocks Variation des stocks	Gross fixed capital form. Formation brute de capital fixe	Exports of goods/ services Exportations de biens et services	Imports of goods/ services Importations de biens et services
Albania	1985	16856	9.3	58.6	0.5	33.2	−1.6[1]	...
Albanie	1989	18674	8.8	61.0	0.4	31.3	−1.5[1]	...
	1990	16812	10.2	72.7	−10.1	34.6	−7.4[1]	...
Algeria	1985	291597	15.8	47.9	1.4	31.8	23.5	20.4
Algérie	1988	334607	19.5	52.4	1.8	26.5	14.9	15.1
	1989	403460	17.5	52.1	3.1	26.9	19.3	18.9
Angola	1985	205400	31.0	47.0	0.7	17.1	32.9	28.7
Angola	1989	278866	28.9	48.2	0.9	11.2	33.8	23.1
	1990	308062	28.5	44.7	0.6	11.1	38.9	23.8
Anguilla	1986	68	13.5	36.3	0.0	54.7	68.3	72.8
Anguilla	1990	156	12.8	29.0	0.0	63.7	70.6	76.1
	1991	159	14.8	...	...	...	...	...
Antigua and Barbuda	1984	468	18.5	69.8	0.0	23.6	73.7	85.6
Antigua−et−Barbuda	1985	541	18.3	71.5	0.0	28.0	75.7	93.5
	1986	642	18.9	69.7	0.0	36.1	75.2	99.9
Argentina	1985	5	76.9[2]	...	...	17.6[3]	11.7	6.3
Argentine	1991	180898	83.8[2]	...	...	14.6[3]	7.7	6.1
	1992	226638	84.8[2]	...	...	16.7[3]	6.6	8.1
Australia [4]	1985	239970[5]	18.7	59.9	0.6	24.7	16.2	19.3
Australie [4]	1992	403852[5]	18.5	62.6	−0.1	19.7	18.9	19.4
	1993	425566[5]	18.1	62.1	0.2	19.5	19.3	19.8
Austria	1985	1348425	18.9	57.5	0.8[5]	22.6	40.7	40.6
Autriche	1992	2046080	18.4	55.1	0.2[5]	25.0	39.3	38.0
	1993	2117841	19.2	55.2	0.4[5]	24.1	37.9	36.8
Bahamas	1989	3006	13.6	76.6	0.4	23.7	47.4	59.5
Bahamas	1991	3090	14.3	77.1	−0.4	20.8	45.8	57.0
	1992	3059	14.6	74.2	0.2	20.8	45.9	55.2
Bahrain	1985	1393	22.5	31.5	−0.7	35.0	100.3	88.6
Bahrëin	1989	1348	26.5	37.5	2.2	28.6	99.6	94.3
	1990	1468	25.8	35.9	4.0	27.3	118.7	102.3
Bangladesh [4]	1985	466227	12.5	84.3	...	12.5	7.3	16.6
Bangladesh [4]	1993	1030361	14.2	78.3	...	14.6	12.3	19.4
	1994	1106608	14.1	77.2	...	15.0	13.1	19.4
Barbados	1985	2410	18.9	58.0	0.3	15.1	67.7	60.1
Barbade	1992	3171	20.2	62.7	−1.5	11.0	50.0	42.4
	1993	3281	22.3	61.6	0.4	13.4	48.1	45.7
Belarus	1990	42733	23.8	47.0	4.6	22.3	46.5	44.3
Bélarus	1992	913962	16.0	50.2	6.6	25.7	60.0	58.5
	1993	10376418	18.5	55.5	6.8	29.4	55.7	65.9
Belgium	1985	4745838	17.2	65.4	−0.7	15.6	76.8	74.3
Belgique	1992	7101672	14.7	62.6	−0.0	19.1	70.1	66.5
	1993	7285204	15.3	62.0	−0.2	17.8	68.8	63.7
Belize	1985	418	22.8	51.4	4.2	17.4	93.7	89.5
Belize	1991	861	19.4	66.3	1.7	28.5	70.7	86.6
	1992	936	18.7	64.4	1.2	29.7	68.7	82.8
Benin	1985	469778	12.5	79.6	2.4	13.4	33.3	41.3
Bénin	1990	502300	13.2	80.4	0.8	13.4	20.4	28.2
	1991	535500	12.0	82.6	0.9	13.6	22.0	31.1
Bermuda [6]	1985	1174	11.7	66.6	...	17.7	59.8	55.8
Bermudes [6]	1991	1680	12.9	69.4	...	13.4	56.9	52.6
	1992	1698	12.8	70.5	...	13.9	58.9	56.1
Bhutan	1985	2392	23.5	63.0	3.4	41.9	15.4	47.2
Bhoutan	1990	4961	19.6	59.8	−0.7	33.7	29.9	42.3
	1991	5569	18.7	59.9	−1.3	35.0	31.3	43.7
Bolivia	1985	2867	8.3	62.5	5.2	11.7	29.0	16.7
Bolivie	1992	23520	11.8	83.1	3.3	15.0	16.8	30.0
	1993	26057	12.7	84.0	3.5	16.4	17.2	33.8

21

Expenditure on gross domestic product at current prices
Percentage distribution *[cont.]*
Dépenses imputées au produit intérieur brut aux prix courants
Répartition en pourcentage *[suite]*

Country or area Pays ou zone	Year Année	GDP at current prices (Million nat. cur.) PIB aux prix courants (Mil. monnaie nat.)	% of GDP − en % du PIB					
			Govt. final cons. exp. Consom. finale des admin. publiques	Private final cons. exp. Consom. finale privée	Increase in stocks Variations des stocks	Gross fixed capital form. Formation de brute capital fixe	Exports of goods/ services Exportations de biens et services	Imports of goods/ services Importations de biens et services
Botswana [4] Botswana [4]	1985	2421	22.0	37.3	−2.7	18.9	71.8	47.3
	1987	3796	27.7	29.4	−21.2	28.5	82.2	46.6
	1988	5472	22.1	22.6	1.0	40.8	67.7	54.2
Brazil Brésil	1985	1	9.9	65.7	2.2	16.9	12.2	7.1
	1991	164486	14.5	64.6	...	19.0	8.5	6.6
	1992	1846813	15.2	62.4	...	19.1	9.7	6.3
British Virgin Islands Iles Vierges brit.	1985	90	18.8	74.5	2.5	37.5	97.1	130.5
	1988	131	20.1	68.9	2.7	34.3	107.6	133.5
	1989	156	20.7	64.9	2.6	31.6	104.8	124.6
Brunei Darussalam Brunéi Darussalam	1982	9126	10.0	5.5	−0.0	12.4	89.3	17.2
	1983	8124	11.4	9.5	−0.0	9.9	88.3	19.0
	1984	8069	31.1	−5.6	0.0	6.5	84.5	16.5
Bulgaria Bulgarie	1985	32595	8.5	61.5	5.8	26.4	−2.1 [1]	...
	1992	200832	8.8	77.1	3.7	16.2	47.1	52.9
	1993	298934	8.6	84.6	2.3	11.9 [3]	37.4	44.7
Burkina Faso Burkina Faso	1983	381013	20.7	86.0	0.7	23.7	14.7	45.7
	1984	390565	19.7	78.9	0.8	23.3	22.6	45.3
	1985	469313	15.5	87.8	3.3	24.2	16.9	47.6
Burundi Burundi	1985	141347	16.1	77.5	0.1	14.2	9.9	17.7
	1991	211898	17.0	83.9	−0.5	18.1	10.0	28.5
	1992	226384	15.6	82.9	0.4	21.1	9.0	29.0
Cameroon [4] Cameroun [4]	1985	4106200	11.3	62.6	0.7	24.8	21.5	20.9
	1989	3420900	10.8	69.2	0.0	17.0	21.4	18.4
	1990	3423600	10.2	68.8	0.0	16.4	21.1	16.5
Canada Canada	1985	474339 [5]	20.1	57.2	0.5	19.9	28.4	26.0
	1992	681344 [5]	21.9	61.1	−0.5	18.8	26.5	27.4
	1993	704829 [5]	21.7	61.1	0.2	18.0	29.5	30.2
Cape Verde Cap−Vert	1985	13081	21.0	87.7	−1.9	45.5	22.1	74.4
	1987	17984	20.4	84.2	1.8	39.2	16.6	62.2
	1988	20640	19.2	86.5	−2.1	37.4	15.5	56.5
Cayman Islands Iles Caïmanes	1985	264 [5]	16.3	62.9	...	20.1	69.7	70.1
	1990	590 [5]	14.2	62.5	...	21.4	64.1	58.5
	1991	616 [5]	15.1	62.5	...	21.8	58.9	52.8
Central African Rep. Rép. centrafricaine	1985	388545	15.1	79.1	3.0	12.4	22.0	31.6
	1987	360942	17.5	80.6	−0.2	12.9	17.8	28.6
	1988	376748	16.1	80.7	0.7	9.8	17.7	25.1
Chile Chili	1985	2651937	12.6	69.9	0.3	16.8	28.2	25.7
	1992	15499840	9.4	62.4	4.1	22.7	29.8	28.3
	1993	18453550	9.7	63.8	3.2	25.6	26.6	28.9
China Chine	1985	896440 [5]	13.2	51.2	8.3	29.5	−4.6 [1]	...
	1993	3451510 [5]	13.0	45.4	5.8	37.6	−1.7 [1]	...
	1994	4500580 [5]	13.2	46.0	3.5	38.6	−2.0 [1]	...
Colombia Colombie	1985	4966000	10.7	69.4	1.5	17.5	14.4	13.6
	1991	26107000	10.3	66.4	1.4	14.6	22.6	15.3
	1992	33143000	11.0	69.9	1.5	15.7	18.9	17.1
Congo Congo	1985	970850	16.4	41.6	1.8	28.5	56.8	45.1
	1988	658964	21.1	60.1	−1.0	19.6	40.6	40.4
	1989	773524	18.7	52.8	−0.5	16.4	47.6	35.0
Costa Rica Costa Rica	1985	197920	15.8	60.1	6.6	19.3	30.7	32.5
	1992	904102	16.0	60.2	8.1	20.8	37.8	43.0
	1993	1074411	16.3	60.3	6.1	23.1	39.3	45.2
Côte d'Ivoire Côte d'Ivoire	1985	3134800	14.1	58.6	1.2	11.8	46.8	32.4
	1990	2939000	17.0	71.8	−1.8	8.5	31.7	27.1
	1991	2960000	16.5	73.0	−1.1	8.6	30.0	27.0
Cyprus Chypre	1985	1482 [5]	14.1	63.8	3.2	27.2	48.7	58.8
	1991	2666 [5]	18.5	65.8	1.5	24.4	47.2	57.3
	1992	3081 [5]	19.2	63.6	2.8	25.7	49.9	61.0
Czech Republic République tchèque	1985	473700	...	...	2.0	25.6	...	...
	1992	791000	20.7	51.4	−1.9	28.5	56.6	55.3
	1993	909700	23.3	54.6	−8.8	26.6	57.4	53.1

21
Expenditure on gross domestic product at current prices
Percentage distribution *[cont.]*
Dépenses imputées au produit intérieur brut aux prix courants
Répartition en pourcentage *[suite]*

Country or area Pays ou zone	Year Année	GDP at current prices (Million nat. cur.) PIB aux prix courants (Mil. monnaie nat.)	Govt. final cons. exp. Consom. finale des admin. publiques	Private final cons. exp. Consom. finale privée	Increase in stocks Variations des stocks	Gross fixed capital form. Formation de brute capital fixe	Exports of goods/ services Exportations de biens et services	Imports of goods/ services Importations de biens et services
Denmark	1985	615072	25.3	54.8	0.8	18.7	36.7	36.3
Danemark	1992	851253	25.7	52.0	−0.1	15.3	36.5	29.5
	1993	873238	26.3	52.4	−0.8	15.1	34.3	27.3
Djibouti	1980	60313	33.6	64.2	1.5	12.9	39.0	51.2
Djibouti	1981	67193	30.8	66.6	−0.3	13.0	44.7	54.8
Dominica	1985	266	22.5	72.4	0.0	28.5	36.5	60.0
Dominique	1990	452	20.3	64.1	1.1	39.7	50.1	75.3
	1991	479	20.0	71.4	1.1	40.2	46.4	79.1
Dominican Republic	1985	13972	8.0	77.5	0.4	19.7	29.3	34.8
Rép. dominicaine	1992	112369	5.1	81.2	0.1	21.0	23.6	31.0
	1993	120572	5.7	76.9	0.2	22.2	23.4	28.4
Ecuador	1985	1109940	11.5	64.5	2.1	16.1	26.8	20.9
Equateur	1992	19414000	7.2	67.7	1.7	19.5	31.5	27.7
	1993	27451000	7.7	70.6	1.2	19.9	26.2	25.5
Egypt [4]	1986	51946	12.8	67.0	2.9	27.4	12.5	22.6
Egypte [4]	1990	110143	10.0	76.3	−0.6	22.4	28.1	36.2
	1991	136190	8.9	80.8	0.1	17.9	29.5	37.2
El Salvador	1985	14331	15.5	81.2	−1.2	12.0	22.3	29.9
El Salvador	1991	47792	11.0	87.5	0.4	13.5	14.8	27.1
	1992	54853	10.6	89.0	0.5	15.7	13.6	29.3
Equatorial Guinea	1985	38067	15.5	80.3	−4.5	12.0	27.3	30.5
Guinée équatoriale	1990	44349	15.3	53.2	−3.1	34.6	59.7	59.7
	1991	46429	14.4	75.9	−2.3	18.4	28.4	34.7
Estonia	1985	495	16.2	64.1	2.6	30.4	55.0	67.9
Estonie	# 1992	14255 [5]	14.6	50.9	6.9	19.3	55.4	53.5
	# 1993	21918	18.5	58.0	2.5	24.3	69.3	72.6
Ethiopia incl. Eritrea [6]	1985	9924	19.7	75.9	...	15.5	11.5	22.6
Ethiopie y comp. Erythrée [6]	1991	13332	28.2	69.9	...	10.7	10.9	19.6
	1992	13508	16.0	86.7	...	9.0	7.7	19.4
Fiji	1985	1316 [5]	19.1	63.7	0.9	18.2	44.4	44.8
Fidji	1992	2377 [5]	18.9	66.5	1.3	11.8	55.4	53.0
	1993	2540 [5]	20.2	66.5	1.6	13.5	56.1	58.5
Finland	1985	331628 [5]	20.2	54.5	−0.1	23.9	29.6	28.5
Finlande	1992	476778 [5]	24.8	57.1	−1.2	18.4	26.9	25.6
	1993	480470 [5]	23.4	56.6	−0.6	14.9	33.2	27.8
France	1985	4700143	19.4	61.1	−0.4	19.3	23.9	23.2
France	1993	7082790	19.8	60.9	−1.5	18.6	22.0	19.8
	1994	7376050	19.6	60.4	−0.3	18.1	22.8	20.6
French Guyana	1985	3173	41.7	68.5	0.1	37.9	53.6	101.8
Guyane française	1990	6526	35.0	64.4	−0.2	47.8	67.3	114.3
	1991	7404	34.4	60.1	1.5	40.5	81.1	117.6
French Polynesia	1985	226772	41.9	52.8	0.4	35.3	8.8	39.2
Polynésie française	1989	281667	40.9	59.4	0.2	23.2	8.8	32.5
	1990	297754	40.4	60.0	0.2	21.2	9.2	30.9
Gabon	1985	1645800	18.6	30.5	...	37.3 [3]	56.9	43.2
Gabon	1988	1013600	21.8	48.1	...	36.2 [3]	37.3	43.4
	1989	1168066	18.4	48.4	...	23.3 [3]	50.3	40.3
Gambia [4]	1985	1085	14.9	...	...	7.1	43.4	46.8
Gambie [4]	1990	2630	14.5	...	...	5.0	...	...
	1991	2948	12.5	...	...	5.3	...	...
Germany † · Allemagne †								
F. R. Germany	1985	1823180	20.1	56.9	0.1	19.5	32.5	29.0
R.f. Allemagne	1992	2813000	17.9	54.6	−0.1	20.9	33.2	26.4
	1993	2853700	17.8	55.7	−0.4	19.3	31.9	24.4
Ghana	1985	343048	9.4	83.0	0.0	9.5	9.7	11.6
Ghana	1991	2574800	11.4	83.9	0.1	12.7	15.7	23.7
	1992	3008800	13.3	84.6	0.1	12.8	16.0	26.8
Greece	1985	4617816 [5]	20.4	65.5	2.2	19.1	21.2	32.8
Grèce	1992	14832170 [5]	19.7	71.9	1.4	18.2	23.2	33.0
	1993	16760352 [5]	19.1	72.5	1.1	17.4	22.1	32.3

21
Expenditure on gross domestic product at current prices
Percentage distribution *[cont.]*
Dépenses imputées au produit intérieur brut aux prix courants
Répartition en pourcentage *[suite]*

Country or area Pays ou zone	Year Année	GDP at current prices (Million nat. cur.) PIB aux prix courants (Mil. monnaie nat.)	% of GDP — en % du PIB					
			Govt. final cons. exp. Consom. finale des admin. publiques	Private final cons. exp. Consom. finale privée	Increase in stocks Variations des stocks	Gross fixed capital form. Formation de brute capital fixe	Exports of goods/ services Exportations de biens et services	Imports of goods/ services Importations de biens et services
Grenada	1985	311	21.9	77.2	−1.7	31.2	47.9	76.4
Grenade	1991	567	18.8	69.2	3.7	40.0	45.4	77.1
	1992	578	19.9	66.5	2.1	32.4	38.6	59.4
Guadeloupe	1985	9802	34.6	95.2	0.3	21.8	7.4	59.3
Guadeloupe	1990	15201	30.8	92.8	1.1	33.9	4.9	63.5
	1991	16415	31.0	87.3	1.0	33.0	6.1	58.4
Guatemala	1985	11180	7.0	83.1	0.5	11.0	18.5	20.1
Guatemala	1992	53949	6.5	85.1	2.8	15.5	17.6	27.4
	1993	63563	6.4	84.8	2.2	16.4	16.7	26.6
Guinea−Bissau	1986	46973	13.7	89.1	1.2	20.0	4.7	28.7
Guinée−Bissau	1991	854985	12.6	100.6	0.9	10.4	13.4	38.0
	1992	1530010	10.7	111.1	...	26.5 [3]	8.2	56.5
Guyana	1985	1964	35.6	53.7	0.0	20.9	53.1	63.3
Guyana	1992	46734	13.7	5.0	0.0	53.7	...	...
	1993	56647	13.0	5.1	0.0	53.2	...	...
Haiti [7]	1985	10047	94.3 [2]	...	...	16.7	27.0	38.0
Haïti [7]	1992	15368	97.0 [2]	...	...	7.9	7.1	12.0
	1993	18124	98.2 [2]	...	...	6.9	6.5	11.7
Honduras	1985	7279	13.1	74.4	0.4	17.0	25.1	29.9
Honduras	1992	18800	11.5	66.6	3.6	22.4	32.2	36.3
	1993	22444	11.2	65.7	3.7	25.3	32.7	38.6
Hong Kong	1985	271655	7.3	61.7	0.5	21.1	109.0	99.6
Hong−kong	1992	779335	8.2	58.0	1.1	27.4	143.0	137.6
	1993	897595	8.1	57.4	0.2	27.5	140.8	133.9
Hungary	1985	1033658	19.5	53.4	2.5	22.5	42.2	40.1
Hongrie	# 1992	2935056	27.1 [2]	57.9	−4.5	19.7	31.5	31.8
	1993	3537835	29.1 [2]	59.7	0.8	18.7	26.5	34.7
Iceland	1985	120898	17.5	63.9	−2.6	21.1	40.3	40.3
Islande	1992	397917	20.2	62.6	−0.1	17.5	30.5	30.6
	1993	410756	20.5	60.6	0.1	15.8	32.9	29.9
India [8]	1985	2622430 [5]	11.1	67.4	3.5	20.7	5.7	8.3
Inde [8]	1992	7028290 [5]	11.2	59.7	1.8	21.5	9.6	10.4
	1993	7863550	11.6	60.3	0.4	20.9	...	...
Indonesia	1985	96997000	11.2	59.0	5.0	23.1	22.2	20.4
Indonésie	1992	260786000	9.5	52.7	7.2	28.4	29.1	26.9
	1993	298026000	10.0	53.0	3.5	29.1	29.7	25.4
Iran, Islamic Republic of [9]	1985	15775000 [5]	15.5	61.0	3.6	17.5	7.9	8.0
Iran, Rép. islamique d' [9]	1991	50107000 [5]	10.7	63.2	11.6	21.6	14.8	19.5
	1992	67811000 [5]	11.8	60.9	9.5	23.1	14.2	16.9
Iraq	1985	15494	28.6	52.3	−4.1	27.8	24.4	28.9
Iraq	1990	23297	26.4	50.5	−4.2	26.7	18.5	17.8
	1991	19940	35.3	48.2	2.6	16.5	2.7	5.3
Ireland	1985	17790	18.6	59.6	0.9	19.0	60.4	58.4
Irlande	# 1992	29987	16.1	58.6	−0.6	15.9	62.4	52.4
	1993	32290	16.0	55.9	−0.6	14.9	67.7	54.0
Israel	1985	30355	34.3	54.3	0.3	17.7	39.7	46.3
Israël	1992	170012	26.4	57.6	0.9	22.2	28.9	35.9
	1993	195797	27.1	59.4	1.3	21.3	31.3	40.4
Italy	1985	810580000	16.4	61.4	1.8	20.7	22.8	23.2
Italie	1992	1504323000	17.6	62.9	0.3	19.1	20.0	19.9
	1993	1560114000	17.7	61.9	−0.2	17.1	23.4	19.9
Jamaica	1985	11203	15.5	69.4	2.3	23.0	58.2	68.5
Jamaïque	1992	72540	9.5	59.7	0.3	28.3	70.4	68.2
	1993	95785	13.1	60.5	0.5	34.3	59.6	68.0
Japan	1985	320419000	9.6	58.9	0.7	27.5	14.5	11.1
Japon	1992	463145000	9.3	57.2	0.4	30.7	10.2	7.8
	1993	465972000	9.6	58.1	0.1	29.8	9.5	7.2
Jordan	1985	1970	26.8	90.6	2.1	19.6	37.2	76.3
Jordanie	1991	2778	26.5	91.4	2.1	21.9	43.1	85.0
	1992	3257	23.7	92.8	1.8	30.1	43.0	91.3

21
Expenditure on gross domestic product at current prices
Percentage distribution [cont.]
Dépenses imputées au produit intérieur brut aux prix courants
Répartition en pourcentage [suite]

			% of GDP — en % du PIB					
Country or area Pays ou zone	Year Année	GDP at current prices (Million nat. cur.) PIB aux prix courants (Mil. monnaie nat.)	Govt. final cons. exp. Consom. finale des admin. publiques	Private final cons. exp. Consom. finale privée	Increase in stocks Variations des stocks	Gross fixed capital form. Formation de brute capital fixe	Exports of goods/ services Exportations de biens et services	Imports of goods/ services Importations de biens et services
Kenya	1985	5042	17.5	58.0	8.1	17.6	25.3	26.3
Kenya	1992	12787	16.2	66.2	0.4	17.1	27.1	27.0
	1993	16063	13.1	65.7	0.7	15.4	42.0	37.0
Kiribati								
Kiribati	1980	21	36.4	92.8	...	...	22.5	95.7
Korea, Republic of	1985	82062000[5]	10.1	58.5	1.0	28.6	34.1	32.8
Corée, Rép. de	1992	240392000[5]	10.9	54.0	0.0	36.6	28.9	29.9
	1993	265548000[5]	10.8	54.1	−1.2	35.5	29.4	29.0
Kuwait	1985	6450	22.4	47.8	−0.9	19.8	53.7	42.7
Koweït	1992	5518	40.7	54.7	...	19.1	42.7	57.2
	1993	6766	32.1	37.5	...	22.9	53.2	45.7
Kyrgyzstan	1985	31[5]	21.6	58.0	6.2	30.5	−16.4[1]	...
Kirghizistan	1991	87[5]	16.9	55.0	14.7	17.0	37.8	39.2
	1992	772[5]	10.2	51.1	41.6	12.3	34.2	45.7
Latvia	1990	62	8.6	52.7	17.1	23.0	47.7	49.0
Lettonie	1992	1005	12.5	39.4	30.1	11.2	79.9	73.1
	1993	1467	22.1	52.5	−4.6	13.8	73.2	57.0
Lebanon	1980	14000	25.1	92.2	...	15.7[3]	39.0	72.0
Liban	1981	16800	25.1	92.2	...	20.6[3]	34.1	72.0
	1982	12599	38.5	125.7	...	9.4[3]	41.7	115.3
Lesotho	1985	551	24.7	152.0	−0.2	49.6	12.7	138.8
Lesotho	1992	2184	18.0	117.9	−0.4	81.8	17.3	134.7
	1993	2587	17.7	108.2	0.0	78.0	17.0	120.9
Liberia	1985	1055[5]	13.0	67.0	0.7	12.0	44.6	30.6
Libéria	1988	1158[5]	11.8	63.3	0.3	10.0	39.0	27.8
	1989	1194[5]	11.9	55.0	0.3	8.1	43.7	23.1
Libyan Arab Jamah.	1983	8805	32.7	39.2	−1.1	25.1	42.1	38.0
Jamah. arabe libyenne	1984	8013	33.6	38.6	0.5	25.3	41.4	39.4
	1985	8277	31.7	37.6	0.4	19.7	37.4	26.7
Lithuania	1985	9190	22.4	56.9	2.0	32.3	61.6	75.3
Lithuanie	1991	38187	12.1	50.8	3.4	24.4	32.2	22.9
	1992	332830	13.0	67.8	−5.1	15.2	32.4	23.2
Luxembourg	1985	205255	15.7	58.7	2.6	17.7	108.6	103.3
Luxembourg	1991	318804	17.1	57.3	2.4	29.0	94.3	100.0
	1992	339450	17.1	56.3	2.5	27.7	89.1	92.7
Madagascar	1985	1553400	13.5	77.8	...	14.0[3]	14.5	19.8
Madagascar	1991	4906400	8.6	92.2	0.0	8.2	17.3	26.2
	1992	5584500	8.2	90.0	0.0	11.6	15.6	25.3
Malawi	1985	1929	17.9	74.1[10]	...	13.5	24.4	29.9
Malawi	1992	6873	18.1	84.1[10]	...	15.7	22.0	39.9
	1993	9330	16.1	83.0[10]	...	10.2	15.6	24.9
Malaysia	1985	77470	15.3	52.0	−2.3	29.8	54.9	49.8
Malaisie	1991	129559	14.2	54.7	1.3	35.6	81.4	87.3
	1992	147784	13.1	51.5	−0.6	34.3	78.0	76.2
Mali	1985	520200	20.2	83.9	−2.4	19.2	18.5	39.4
Mali	1991	691400	15.3	85.1	−2.4	20.0	17.5	35.5
	1992	737400	14.2	82.2	2.7	17.6	17.8	34.6
Malta	1985	476	17.7	70.0	1.7[5]	26.4	72.5	88.3
Malte	1992	875	18.8	60.7	0.0[5]	27.5	91.9	99.0
	1993	938	20.1	60.7	0.9[5]	29.1	95.6	106.4
Martinique	1985	12484	33.7	87.4	−0.5	16.7	11.7	48.9
Martinique	1990	19320	29.7	83.6	1.9	26.7	8.4	50.3
	1991	20787	28.8	84.0	1.4	25.6	7.4	47.1
Mauritania	1985	52665	22.3	67.3	3.9	28.5	58.8	80.8
Mauritanie	1987	67216	13.6	82.6	1.7	20.8	48.3	67.0
	1988	72635	14.2	79.6	1.4	17.0	49.1	61.3
Mauritius	1985	16618	11.5	66.9	4.8	18.7	53.5	55.4
Maurice	1993	54928	12.1	63.8	1.7	28.8	61.1	67.4
	1994	62150	12.7	64.0	0.8	30.9	60.9	69.3

21

Expenditure on gross domestic product at current prices
Percentage distribution *[cont.]*
Dépenses imputées au produit intérieur brut aux prix courants
Répartition en pourcentage *[suite]*

Country or area Pays ou zone	Year Année	GDP at current prices (Million nat. cur.) PIB aux prix courants (Mil. monnaie nat.)	% of GDP — en % du PIB					
			Govt. final cons. exp. Consom. finale des admin. publiques	Private final cons. exp. Consom. finale privée	Increase in stocks Variations des stocks	Gross fixed capital form. Formation de brute capital fixe	Exports of goods/ services Exportations de biens et services	Imports of goods/ services Importations de biens et services
Mexico	1985	47392	9.2	64.5	2.1	19.1	15.4	10.3
Méxique	1992	1019156	10.1	72.2	2.5	20.8	12.6	18.1
	1993	1127584	10.8	71.5	1.6	20.4	12.4	16.7
Montserrat	1984	94	20.6	96.4	2.7	23.7	13.6	56.9
Montserrat	1985	100	20.3	96.3	1.5	24.7	11.7	54.4
	1986	114	18.7	89.5	2.8	33.0	10.1	53.9
Morocco	1985	129510	15.8	65.2	4.0	23.1	24.9	33.1
Maroc	1992	241220	16.9	65.9	0.5	22.8	22.7	28.7
	1993	247680	18.2	66.0	−1.2	22.4	22.5	28.0
Mozambique	1985	147000	15.6	87.1	...	6.8 [3]	−10.2 [1]	...
Mozambique	1991	1967000	19.2	90.4	...	40.8 [3]	22.6	73.0
	1992	2764000	21.6	93.5	...	43.5 [3]	26.7	85.3
Myanmar [8]	1985	55989	88.5 [2]	...	0.1	15.4	4.6	8.6
Myanmar [8]	1991	178553	85.6 [2]	...	0.6	15.1	1.6	3.0
	1992	230935	86.9 [2]	...	0.7	13.4	1.6	2.7
Namibia	1985	2973	29.1	49.1 [11]	−3.5	14.3	62.7	51.7
Namibie	1992	7838	35.4	53.5 [11]	1.9	17.6	53.9	62.2
	1993	8390	34.4	54.7 [11]	−4.5	18.3	58.4	61.4
Nepal [12]	1985	44417	9.8	76.1	1.8	21.1	12.1	21.0
Népal [12]	1991	103948	11.6	81.0	2.2	18.9	13.9	27.7
	1992	126186	10.0	80.6	3.2	18.7	19.5	32.0
Netherlands	1985	425350	15.7	59.5	0.3	19.7	60.8	56.0
Pays−Bas	1992	563080	14.5	60.5	0.2	20.3	52.2	47.8
	1993	574330	14.6	61.0	−0.2	19.7	50.6	45.6
Netherlands Antilles	1983	1910	30.1	72.9	−0.5	15.4	73.6	91.3
Antilles néerlandaises	1984	1929	31.8	71.9	−0.3	13.7	68.4	85.5
	1985	1966	31.9	70.0	0.8	15.0	66.6	84.2
New Caledonia	1985	139650 [5]	37.8	54.8	−1.4	15.4	33.4	39.7
Nouvelle−Calédonie	1991	272235 [5]	32.8	53.8	1.3	23.9	20.1	32.2
	1992	281427 [5]	33.7	56.7	0.1	23.7	16.8	31.4
New Zealand [8]	1985	45777 [5]	16.0	60.9	0.7	26.2	30.5	33.4
Nouvelle−Zélande [8]	1992	76111 [5]	16.5	61.4	2.3	16.5	31.2	28.6
	1993	80865 [5]	15.5	59.9	2.7	18.4	31.0	28.0
Nicaragua	1985	115404	35.7	48.2	2.4	20.7	14.8	21.8
Nicaragua	1986	435742	35.4	55.8	3.1	13.8	12.8	20.8
	1987	2389500	24.7	58.1	3.0	7.9	22.1	15.7
Niger	1985	647100	15.0	78.8	1.0	14.3	21.0	30.1
Niger	1989	692600	18.0	73.0	−0.1	12.3	18.6	21.8
	1990	682300	17.2	74.1	1.1	11.7	16.8	20.9
Nigeria	1985	72355	10.1	74.7	−0.6	7.7	16.7	8.7
Nigéria	1992	549809	3.7	73.5	0.1	10.7	35.8	23.8
	1993	697095	4.0	81.7 [11]	0.1	11.6	27.5	24.9
Norway	1985	500199	18.5	49.1	2.2	22.0	47.1	38.9
Norvège	1992	702955	22.4	51.9	−0.8	19.2	43.1	35.9
	1993	733665	22.1	51.6	−2.3	22.0	43.3	36.5
Oman	1985	3454	27.2	32.6 [10]	...	27.6	49.9	37.2
Oman	1991	3917	35.6	37.9 [10]	...	16.9	47.8	38.2
	1992	4417	39.3	33.4 [10]	...	17.0	48.4	38.1
Pakistan [4]	1985	514532	12.8	76.3	1.7	17.0	12.3	20.1
Pakistan [4]	1992	1341955	13.0	72.1	1.6	19.1	16.2	22.1
	1993	1564974	12.3	72.1	1.6	18.4	15.7	20.0
Panama	1985	4948	21.1	61.0	−0.4	15.6	36.8	34.2
Panama	1992	6015	17.0	59.7	1.7	21.1	38.9	38.5
	1993	6565	16.7	59.4	0.5	24.4	37.0	38.0
Papua New Guinea	1985	2403	23.8	66.6	1.4	18.6	42.5	52.9
Papouasie−Nouv.−Guinée	1991	3606	22.4	60.1	−0.6	28.0	42.3	52.2
	1992	4140	22.5	57.9	0.0	23.8	45.2	49.3
Paraguay	1985	1393890	6.5	76.7	1.3	20.7	21.4	26.6
Paraguay	1991	8280772	6.6	78.3	1.1	23.7	24.7	34.4
	1992	9670838	6.5	78.7	1.0	21.9	21.6	29.8

21
Expenditure on gross domestic product at current prices
Percentage distribution *[cont.]*
Dépenses imputées au produit intérieur brut aux prix courants
Répartition en pourcentage *[suite]*

Country or area Pays ou zone	Year Année	GDP at current prices (Million nat. cur.) PIB aux prix courants (Mil. monnaie nat.)	% of GDP − en % du PIB					
			Govt. final cons. exp. Consom. finale des admin. publiques	Private final cons. exp. Consom. finale privée	Increase in stocks Variations des stocks	Gross fixed capital form. Formation de brute capital fixe	Exports of goods/ services Exportations de biens et services	Imports of goods/ services Importations de biens et services
Peru	1985	197 [13]	11.3	62.4	0.2	21.4	20.0	15.3
Pérou	# 1992	52062	6.7	75.7	1.5	19.2	10.3	13.4
	1993	80529	6.7	73.2	2.8	20.5	10.7	13.9
Philippines	1985	571883 [5]	7.6	73.6	−2.1	16.5	24.0	21.9
Philippines	1993	1475042 [5]	10.1	75.4	0.2	24.3	31.3	40.2
	1994	1687607 [5]	10.0	74.3	0.5	24.8	34.6	42.4
Poland	1985	10445000	18.1	52.7	6.5	21.2	18.2	16.9
Pologne	# 1992	1149442000	20.7	62.6	−1.6	16.8	23.7	22.2
	1993	1557800000	19.5	64.0	−0.3	15.9	22.9	22.0
Portugal	1985	3523945	15.5	67.9	−1.2	21.8	37.3	41.4
Portugal	# 1992	12828682	16.7	65.1	0.9	26.7	25.5	34.8
	1993	13625623	17.2	65.8	0.7	25.1	25.8	34.6
Puerto Rico [4]	1985	21969	14.7	71.7	−0.3	10.6	66.6	63.3
Porto Rico [4]	1992	36847	13.8	61.7	1.2	15.0	67.8	59.5
	1993	39265	13.6	60.9	0.9	14.9	68.4	58.7
Qatar	1985	22398	35.2	25.1	0.1	17.7	51.4	29.5
Qatar	1991	25056	35.7	31.4	1.7	17.4	47.4	33.5
	1992	27202	33.0	30.8	1.0	18.0	51.2	34.0
Réunion	1985	17054	32.8	86.1	−2.5	21.9	6.4	44.7
Réunion	1990	28374	27.1	81.0	−0.3	29.1	3.7	40.7
	1991	31339	27.6	75.9	1.2	29.7	2.8	37.2
Romania	1985	817400 [5]	10.2	50.0	2.9	30.1	4.1 [1]	...
Roumanie	# 1992	6029000 [5]	15.5	61.7	12.4	18.8	−8.4 [1]	...
	1993	19733300 [5]	13.3	62.5	12.1	17.1	−5.1 [1]	...
Rwanda	1985	173700	11.3	80.5	1.7	15.6	10.8	19.9
Rwanda	1991	212900	21.6	82.2	−1.5	11.9	9.8	23.9
	1992	217300	25.1	76.8	−0.0	14.9	7.4	24.2
Saint Kitts−Nevis	1982	158	22.5	74.1	0.0	34.9	51.0	82.5
Saint−Kitts−et−Nevis	1983	154	23.1	91.0	0.0	32.4	51.2	97.6
	1984	167	22.4	77.5	0.0	31.9	55.5	87.3
Saint Lucia	1982	364	24.2	75.5	6.7	33.3	55.0	94.7
Sainte−Lucie	1983	380	25.7	64.1	5.0	24.9	63.5	83.3
	1984	408	25.2	65.3	5.1	25.7	64.0	85.4
Saint Vincent−Grenadines	1985	305	19.8	57.7	3.3	25.0	73.0	78.8
St.−Vincent−et−Grenad.	1989	469	19.6	74.4	2.7	26.7	63.8	87.2
	1990	525	17.8	67.2	1.4	30.3	70.6	87.3
Sao Tome and Principe	1986	2478	30.3	76.1	0.9	13.6	...	50.8
Sao Tomé−et−Principe	1987	3003	24.8	63.1	1.1	15.4	...	43.1
	1988	4221	21.2	71.8	0.0	15.7	...	66.8
Saudi Arabia [4]	1985	313941	36.4	50.5	−3.4 [5]	24.3	36.0	43.9
Arabie saoudite [4]	1991	431920	38.2	39.1	1.2 [5]	18.2	45.7	42.3
	1992	455130	32.7	40.4	2.0 [5]	21.7	43.1	39.9
Senegal	1985	1158200	16.8	84.6	−1.7	11.5	29.7	40.9
Sénégal	1992	1653300	12.5	80.3	0.0	13.4	22.4	28.6
	1993	1647400	12.4	80.5	0.0	13.8	21.7	28.4
Seychelles	1985	1205	34.6	58.2	0.0	22.7	48.2	63.7
Seychelles	1991	1980	28.2	50.7	1.0	21.3	48.1	49.3
	1992	2221	30.4	50.6	0.3	20.9	45.8	48.0
Sierra Leone [4]	1985	7481	6.7	83.4	1.5	9.8	11.4	12.7
Sierra Leone [4]	1989	82837	6.6	84.7	0.5	13.5	19.7	25.1
	1990	150175	10.4	77.9	1.8	10.1	25.4	25.7
Singapore	1985	38924 [5]	14.3	45.1	0.3	42.2	−2.4 [1]	...
Singapour	1992	79083 [5]	9.4	43.0	1.4	39.1	7.2 [1]	...
	1993	89007 [5]	9.4	42.7	3.3	40.5	3.6 [1]	...
Slovakia	1985	203258 [5]	19.6	49.9	2.3	29.4	−1.1 [1]	...
Slovaquie	1992	307800 [5]	23.9	52.8	−5.2	31.7	75.9	80.4
	1993	340200 [5]	25.1	58.5	−5.6	27.5	67.0	73.0
Slovenia	1990	196242	17.1	51.8	0.5	17.3	81.6	68.4
Slovénie	1992	1003605	20.6	53.0	−0.1	19.1	56.1	48.7

21
Expenditure on gross domestic product at current prices
Percentage distribution [cont.]
Dépenses imputées au produit intérieur brut aux prix courants
Répartition en pourcentage [suite]

Country or area Pays ou zone	Year Année	GDP at current prices (Million nat. cur.) PIB aux prix courants (Mil. monnaie nat.)	% of GDP — en % du PIB					
			Govt. final cons. exp. Consom. finale des admin. publiques	Private final cons. exp. Consom. finale privée	Increase in stocks Variations des stocks	Gross fixed capital form. Formation de brute capital fixe	Exports of goods/ services Exportations de biens et services	Imports of goods/ services Importations de biens et services
Solomon Islands Iles Salomon	1985	237	28.1	64.2	5.1	21.1	51.1	69.6
	1987	293	36.3	63.1	2.7	20.4	55.9	78.4
	1988	367	31.4	68.6	2.7	30.0	52.4	85.0
Somalia Somalie	1985	87290	10.6	90.5 [11]	2.9	8.9	4.2	17.0
	1986	118781	9.7	89.1 [11]	1.0	16.8	5.8	22.4
	1987	169608	11.1	88.8 [11]	4.8	16.8	5.9	27.2
South Africa Afrique du Sud	1985	123126 [5]	17.3	53.7	−3.0	23.3	32.2	23.2
	1991	297895 [5]	20.8	60.2	−1.9	18.0	24.9	19.7
	1992	327068 [5]	21.3	62.2	−0.9	15.9	23.9	20.0
Spain Espagne	1985	28200900	14.7	64.1	0.0	19.2	22.7	20.8
	1992	59002100	17.0	63.1	0.9	21.8	17.6	20.4
	1993	60904300	17.5	63.2	0.1	19.8	19.3	20.0
Sri Lanka Sri Lanka	1985	157763 [5]	12.2	74.9	0.1	23.9	26.9	39.6
	1992	421755 [5]	12.8	74.3	0.8	22.9	32.0	41.4
	1993	499708 [5]	13.2	72.8	0.4	24.2	33.8	43.3
Sudan [4] Soudan [4]	1981	6721	10.7	80.8	5.5	19.0	9.4	25.4
	1982	9186	9.3	86.6	0.4	17.4	11.9	25.6
	1983	11329	9.8	83.5	−2.1	16.5	11.5	19.3
Suriname Suriname	1985	1747	33.7	55.0	−3.4	17.9	36.7	39.9
	1991	3708	29.3	52.1	4.3	18.0	17.7	21.4
	1992	5010	24.7	52.4	4.6	18.6	13.0	13.3
Swaziland [12] Swaziland [12]	1985	803	22.8	72.5	1.6	24.6	56.4	78.0
	1990	2340	17.6	51.9	0.7	20.0	75.5	65.8
	1991	2413	19.7	60.0	0.9	18.3	79.4	78.3
Sweden Suède	1985	866601	27.9	51.2	−0.1	19.3	35.3	33.6
	1992	1441723	27.9	53.9	−0.5	17.0	27.9	26.2
	1993	1442181	28.0	54.9	−0.8	14.3	32.8	29.2
Switzerland Suisse	1985	227950	13.3	61.9	0.6	23.8	39.1	38.6
	1992	338765	14.3	58.7	−0.3	23.7	36.1	32.5
	1993	343045	14.3	59.2	−0.9	22.5	36.4	31.4
Syrian Arab Rep. Rép. arabe syrienne	1985	83225	23.8	65.7	...	24.1	12.0	25.4
	1992	370631	14.5	73.7	...	23.2	26.3	37.7
	1993	398515	14.4	73.9	...	25.8	28.6	42.7
Thailand Thaïlande	1985	1056496 [5]	13.5	62.2	1.1	27.2	23.2	25.9
	1992	2833277 [5]	10.0	54.4	0.4	39.3	36.3	40.5
	1993	3161374 [5]	10.3	54.2	0.1	39.9	37.0	41.1
Togo Togo	1984	304800	14.0	66.0	−1.5	21.2	51.9	51.6
	1985	332500	14.2	66.0	5.2	22.9	48.3	56.7
	1986	363600	14.4	69.0	5.3	23.8	35.6	48.2
Tonga [14] Tonga [14]	1981	54	14.2	122.8	2.2	23.9	26.3	67.3 [5]
	1982	64	16.8	121.0	1.4	23.1	25.7	63.9 [5]
	1983	73	14.2	125.9	1.0	28.1	19.7	70.0 [5]
Trinidad and Tobago Trinité−et−Tobago	1985	18071	22.7	54.4	−1.5	20.2	32.6	28.4
	1993	24883	16.2	60.9	0.4	12.7	39.9	30.1
	1994	28390	15.7	61.1	0.4	12.7	41.7	31.7
Tunisia Tunisie	1985	6910	16.5	63.0	−0.2	26.8	32.6	38.7
	1988	8605	16.1	64.6	−0.8	19.5	42.5	42.0
	1989	9497	16.9	64.9	1.6	21.1	42.8	47.4
Turkey Turquie	1985	35095000	8.9	71.0	0.4	21.8	16.4	18.6
	1992	1093368000 [5]	12.9	67.2	0.4	23.0	14.4	17.3
	1993	1913150000 [5]	13.3	67.4	1.1	25.3	14.2	20.0
Uganda Ouganda	1985	27578 [5]	11.6	84.2	0.0	7.7	10.9	12.6
	1993	4026764 [5]	10.2	87.5	0.1	16.0	7.8	20.0
	1994	5152630 [5]	9.6	84.5	0.0	13.3	10.9	18.2
Ukraine Ukraine	1989	153400	17.3	54.5	2.9	25.4	32.1	32.1
	1991	230800 [5]	22.6	70.1	−23.3	26.0	33.9	31.1
United Arab Emirates Emirats arabes unis	1985	99416	19.7	28.5	0.5	24.6	58.0	31.2
	1991	124500	16.9	41.4	1.1	20.7	67.6	47.7
	1992	128400	17.8	45.5	1.2	23.2	69.1	56.8

21
Expenditure on gross domestic product at current prices
Percentage distribution *[cont.]*
Dépenses imputées au produit intérieur brut aux prix courants
Répartition en pourcentage *[suite]*

Country or area Pays ou zone	Year Année	GDP at current prices (Million nat. cur.) PIB aux prix courants (Mil. monnaie nat.)	% of GDP − en % du PIB					
			Govt. final cons. exp. Consom. finale des admin. publiques	Private final cons. exp. Consom. finale privée	Increase in stocks Variations des stocks	Gross fixed capital form. Formation de brute capital fixe	Exports of goods/ services Exportations de biens et services	Imports of goods/ services Importations de biens et services
United Kingdom	1985	356172	21.1	60.6	0.2	17.0	28.8	27.8
Royaume−Uni	1992	595219	22.2	63.9	−0.3	15.8	23.7	25.2
	1993	627701	22.0	64.2	−0.0	15.1	25.3	26.6
United Rep. of Tanzania	1985	120621	15.4	77.2	1.7	14.0	6.2	14.5
Rép.−Unie de Tanzanie	1990	494999	14.3	74.0	3.6	43.9	20.8	56.7
	1991	690421	13.5	76.3	2.9	38.0	17.7	48.3
United States	1985	4016649	18.1	64.7	0.7	19.5	7.4	10.4
Etats−Unis	1992	5937300	17.7	67.3	0.1	15.6	10.6	11.3
	1993	6259900	17.1	67.7	0.3	16.2	10.3	11.6
Uruguay	1985	479	14.4	68.5	1.7	9.6	26.8	21.1
Uruguay	1991	20271	13.5	69.9	1.6	11.9	23.1	19.9
	1992	35346	12.8	72.6	0.7	13.1	22.4	21.5
former USSR †	1986	798500 [15]	20.8	47.2	...	...	...	...
ancienne URSS †	1987	825000 [15]	20.8	47.1	...	...	...	...
	1988	875400 [15]	21.5	47.0	...	...	...	...
Uzbekistan	1987	27269	21.5	58.2	−1.3	29.8	−8.3 [1]	...
Ouzbékistan	1992	443887	20.1	45.3	17.4	26.5	33.9	43.2
	1993	5095202	24.6	57.5	−10.5	25.2	33.8	30.6
Vanuatu	1985	12534 [5]	35.9	56.6	5.5	22.7	51.0	72.3
Vanuatu	1989	16367 [5]	29.8	64.4	3.7	33.4	36.7	64.7
	1990	17899 [5]	28.2	62.9	2.7	40.8	46.4	76.6
Venezuela	1985	464741	10.4	61.8	1.2	17.3	25.0	15.8
Venezuela	# 1993	5449109	8.7	73.2	−0.8	19.5	26.2	26.8
	1994	8310682	7.3	72.7	−5.7	15.8	30.8	20.9
Viet Nam	1989	24308000	17.3	1.7	9.9	27.6	39.4	100.0
Viet Nam	1990	38166000 [5]	17.0	80.9	...	11.5 [3]	−7.7 [1]	...
	1991	69959000 [5]	14.9	80.4	...	11.6 [3]	−5.6 [1]	...
Yemen	1989	61406	26.8	78.7	0.2	18.5	16.6	40.8
Yémen	1990	77159	27.4	75.2	0.9	15.5	13.6	32.6
former Yemen Arab Rep.	1985	30939	17.9	95.0	−0.2	14.7	3.8	31.2
anc. Yémen rép. arabe	1986	37472	18.4	90.7	0.1	13.2	3.1	25.5
former Dem. Yemen	1985	369	53.0	94.5	...	43.1 [3]	10.9	101.4
ancienne Yémen dém	1986	311	58.0	105.3	...	34.9 [3]	7.3	105.4
Yugoslavia, SFR †	1985	1195 [5]	13.9	49.8	17.5	21.8	22.1	23.2
Yougoslavie, SFR †	1989	235395 [5]	14.4	47.4	28.0	14.5	25.3	29.2
	1990	1147787	17.6	66.1	7.3	14.7	23.7	29.4
Zaire	1985	147263	11.6	47.8	7.7	21.7	72.2	61.1
Zaïre	1986	203416	19.0	48.1	8.3	23.0	61.4	59.6
	1987	326946	22.4	77.1	5.3	20.3	63.2	88.2
Zambia	1985	9351	66.0	18.0	...	15.5	29.3	28.9
Zambie	1990	123487	54.7	14.1	...	30.7	34.3	33.8
	1991	234504	60.4	14.3	...	24.6	26.4	25.7
Zimbabwe	1985	7295	21.5	57.5	4.3	15.5	28.8	27.6
Zimbabwe	1988	11441	23.7	49.3	4.0	17.8	30.0	24.8
	1989	13794	23.6	54.5	1.6	17.4	30.0	27.0

Source:
National accounts database of the Statistics Division of the
United Nations Secretariat.

Source:
Base de données sur les comptes nationaux de la division
de statistique du Secrétariat de l'ONU.

† For detailed descriptions of data pertaining to
former Czechoslovakia, Germany, SFR Yugoslavia and former
USSR, see annex I − Country or area nomenclature, regional
and other groupings.

† Pour les descriptions en détails des données relatives
à l'ancienne Tchécoslovaquie, l'Allemagne, la Rfs
Yougoslavie et l'ancienne URSS, voir l'Annexe I −
Nomenclature des pays ou zones, groupements
régionaux et autres groupements.

21
Expenditure on gross domestic product at current prices
Percentage distribution *[cont.]*
Dépenses imputées au produit intérieur brut aux prix courants
Répartition en pourcentage *[suite]*

1 Net exports.	1 Exportations nettes.
2 Including private final consumption expenditure.	2 Y compris dépenses consommation final privée.
3 Gross capital formation.	3 Formation brute de capital.
4 Fiscal year beginning 1 July.	4 L'année fiscale commençant le 1er juillet.
5 Including a statistical discrepancy.	5 Y compris divergence statistique.
6 Fiscal year beginning 7 July.	6 L'année fiscale commençant le 7 juillet.
7 Fiscal year ending 30 September.	7 L'année fiscale finissant le 30 septembre.
8 Fiscal year beginning 1 April.	8 L'année fiscale commençant le 1er avril.
9 Fiscal year beginning 21 March.	9 L'année fiscale commençant le 21 mars.
10 Including increase in stocks.	10 Y compris les variations des stocks.
11 Obtained as a residual.	11 Données résiduelles.
12 Fiscal year ending 15 July.	12 L'année fiscale finissant 15 juillet.
13 Thousand.	13 Milliers.
14 Fiscal year ending 30 June.	14 L'année fiscale finissant le 30 juin.
15 Gross national product.	15 Produit nationale brut.

22
Gross domestic product by kind of economic activity at current prices
Produit intérieur brut par genre d'activité economique aux prix courants
Percentage distribution
Répartition en pourcentage

Country or area Pays ou zone	Year Année	GDP at current prices (Mil. nat.cur.) PIB aux prix courants (Mil. mon.nat.)	Agriculture, hunting, forestry & fishing Agriculture, chasse, sylviculture et pêche	Mining & quarrying Industries extractives	Manufac- turing Manufac- turières	Electricity, gas and water Electricité, gaz et eau	Construc- tion Construc- tion	Wholesale/ retail trade, restaurants and hotels Commerce, restaurants, hôtels	Transport, storage & commu- nication Transports, entrepôts, communi- cations	Other activities Autres activités
						% of GDP – en % du PIB				
Angola	1985	205400	13.4	28.3	9.6	0.2	4.8	12.9[1]	4.8	25.9[1]
Angola	1989	278866	19.1	29.4	6.1	0.2	3.2	11.2[1]	3.0	27.8[1]
	1990	308062	17.9	32.7	5.0	0.1	2.9	10.7[1]	3.2	27.6[1]
Anguilla	1985	53	5.3	1.0	0.9	1.3	13.4	32.1	12.9	33.0
Anguilla	1990	156	3.9	0.4	0.6	1.0	19.8	33.6	10.5	30.3
	1991	159	2.5	0.7	0.7	1.6	17.1	34.2	11.4	31.8
Antigua and Barbuda	1985	541	4.3	0.9	3.8	3.2	6.6	22.5	15.0	43.8
Antigua−et−Barbuda	1987	649[2]	4.5	2.2	3.5	3.5	11.3	24.1	15.6	35.3
	1988	776[2]	4.1	2.2	3.1	4.0	12.7	23.7	14.3	35.9
Argentina	1985	5	7.6	2.0	29.6	2.0	5.7	16.5	0.5	35.7
Argentine	# 1991	180898	6.9	2.1	24.4	1.6	4.7	15.9	5.2	39.5
	1992	226638	6.0	1.8	21.9	1.7	5.3	15.4	5.2	42.7
Australia[3]	1985	239970	4.0	6.5	17.2	3.5	7.6	17.0[1]	7.0	37.2[1]
Australie[3]	1991	389247	3.1	4.2	14.4	3.5	7.1	17.5[1]	7.5	42.7[1]
	1992	405860	3.2	4.3	14.7	3.5	6.9	17.4[1]	7.5	42.5[1]
Austria	1985	1348425	3.3	0.4	26.9	3.0	6.6	15.9	5.8	38.0
Autriche	1992	2046080	2.4	0.3	24.5	2.8	7.5	16.7	6.4	39.4
	1993	2117841	2.3	0.2	23.4	2.8	7.6	16.3	6.3	40.9
Bahamas	1989	3006	2.3	3.3[4]	...	2.1	3.8	28.1	6.6	53.9
Bahamas	1991	3090	3.4	3.3[4]	...	2.5	3.4	25.9	6.6	54.9
	1992	3059	2.9	3.4[4]	...	2.9	3.0	23.0	7.4	57.3
Bahrain	1985	1393	1.2	28.6	10.0	1.8	9.6	8.6	11.9	28.3
Bahrëin	1989	1348	1.2	17.5	17.8	2.1	6.5	10.2	11.3	33.4
	1990	1468	1.0	22.1	17.2	2.0	6.4	10.1	9.6	31.7
Bangladesh[3]	1985	466227	40.4	0.0	9.3	0.6	5.6	9.3	11.7	23.1
Bangladesh[3]	1992	947896	30.5	0.0	9.7	1.8	6.0	8.3	12.9	30.8
	1993	1030361	30.6	0.0	10.0	2.0	5.8	8.0	12.5	31.1
Barbados	1985	2410	5.7	1.2	9.6	3.0	4.9	28.1	7.7	39.9
Barbade	1992	3171	4.6	0.5	6.4	3.3	3.6	25.7	7.8	48.0
	1993	3281	4.5	0.5	6.4	3.1	3.5	26.5	7.8	47.8
Belarus	1990	42733	23.1	0.2	38.0[5]	...	7.8	3.5	6.8	20.5
Bélarus	1992	913962	22.7	0.1	36.6[5]	...	7.0	4.9	8.6	20.2
	1993	10376418	17.7	0.1	32.2[5]	...	7.9	8.3	10.8	23.1
Belgium	1985	4745838[6]	2.2	0.2	23.5	2.5	5.2	16.0	7.9	42.1
Belgique	1992	7101672[6]	1.7	...	...	...	5.4	18.4	8.0	43.4
	1993	7285204[6]	1.6	...	...	...	5.1	18.5	7.9	44.4
Belize	1985	418	17.8	0.3	14.6	2.2	4.7	13.5	8.4	38.5
Belize	1992	936	17.1	0.6	11.7	2.5	6.8	15.0	10.1	36.2
	1993	995	15.3	0.7	11.2	2.9	7.1	14.8	10.7	37.3
Benin	1985	469778	32.0	4.5	7.5	0.7	3.2	15.9[1]	8.0	28.2[1]
Bénin	1988	482434	34.8	0.9	8.3	0.9	3.1	17.5[1]	7.6	27.0[1]
	1989	487525	36.3	0.9	8.8	0.8	3.1	16.8[1]	7.5	25.7[1]
Bhutan	1985	2392	51.7	0.8	5.4	0.3	12.1	8.5	4.4	16.8
Bhoutan	1991	5569	41.9	1.7	9.0	7.5	6.6	6.9	6.9	19.5
	1992	6337	41.4	3.1	9.1	7.3	6.8	7.0	7.1	18.2
Bolivia	1985	2867	29.0	11.8	12.0	0.9	4.2	10.8	10.6	20.6
Bolivie	1992	23520	15.9	6.2	15.1	2.4	4.2	11.7	13.0	31.5
	1993	26057	16.2	5.8	14.5	2.5	4.4	11.9	13.5	31.1
Botswana[3]	1985	2421	5.5	46.8	5.1	2.4	4.0	6.8	2.7	26.7
Botswana[3]	1990	6995	5.2	42.3	4.3	2.3	5.6	13.9	2.5	23.9
	1991	7810	5.1	39.3	4.4	2.3	5.9	15.2	2.8	25.1
Brazil	1985	1	10.5	3.0	30.7	2.1	5.5	8.2	4.8	35.1
Brésil	1988	86	9.2	1.7	28.1	2.5	7.3	7.3	4.9	39.0
	1989	1266	7.8	1.4	27.0	2.2	8.4	7.1	5.1	40.9
British Virgin Islands	1985	90	4.1	0.2	2.6	3.2	6.6	27.4	9.7	46.4
Iles Vierges brit.	1988	131	3.4	0.2	2.8	3.6	5.6	26.1	11.0	47.3
	1989	156	3.0	0.2	2.8	3.3	6.0	25.3	13.6	45.7

22

Gross domestic product by kind of economic activity at current prices
Percentage distribution [cont.]
Produit intérieur brut par genre d'activité économique aux prix courants
Répartition en pourcentage [suite]

Country or area Pays ou zone	Year Année	GDP at current prices (Mil. nat.cur.) PIB aux prix courants (Mil. mon.nat.)	Agriculture, hunting, forestry & fishing Agriculture, chasse, sylviculture et pêche	Mining & quarrying Industries extractives	Manufac- turing Manufac- turières	Electricity, gas and water Electricité, gaz et eau	Construc- tion Construc- tion	Wholesale/ retail trade, restaurants and hotels Commerce, restaurants, hôtels	Transport, storage & commu- nication Transports, entrepôts, communi- cations	Other activities Autres activités
Brunei Darussalam	1985	7752	1.2	59.2	10.1	0.4	2.1	10.6	1.8	14.6
Brunéi Darussalam	1992	6372	3.0	41.7 [4]	...	1.0	4.9	12.3	4.9	32.3
	1993	6475	3.2	37.3 [4]	...	1.0	5.3	12.2	5.1	35.9
Bulgaria	1985	32595	11.9	54.4 [7]	...	...	8.1	5.7	6.1	13.8
Bulgarie	1992	200832	11.7	39.2 [7]	...	...	5.9	10.4	6.5	26.3
	1993	298934	10.0	33.7 [7]	...	...	5.5	10.5	6.6	33.6
Burkina Faso	1983	381013	39.9	0.0	12.6	1.1	2.0	12.2	6.4	25.8
Burkina Faso	1984	390565	42.0	0.1	12.2	1.1	1.3	10.8	7.4	25.1
	1985	455882	46.9	0.1	11.2	0.7	1.2	10.0	6.8	23.2
Burundi	1985	141347	54.8	0.5 [5]	12.1	...	4.0	11.4	2.2	15.0
Burundi	1989	179549	46.0	1.1 [5]	18.1	...	3.2	10.6	3.2	17.8
	1990	196656	51.2	0.8 [5]	16.4	...	3.4	4.8	3.0	20.4
Cameroon [3]	1985	4106200	21.6	12.6	12.0	1.1	6.8	16.0	6.1	23.8
Cameroun [3]	1989	3420900	24.2	9.4	14.2	1.7	4.2	15.2	7.0	24.2
	1990	3423600	25.0	9.1	13.6	1.7	3.8	15.4	7.3	24.1
Canada	1985	474340	2.8	5.7	17.2	3.1	5.5	12.2	6.3	47.2
Canada	1990	662809	2.2	3.2	15.9	2.7	6.3	12.7	5.7	51.3
	1991	667413	2.1	2.7	14.8	3.1	5.8	12.3	5.8	53.6
Cape Verde	1985	13081	15.6	0.9	5.5	0.1	10.7	27.6	14.0	25.5
Cap-Vert	1987	17984	20.1	0.6	5.7	1.0	10.5	24.3	12.8	25.0
	1988	20640	20.2	0.6	5.4	1.0	10.8	24.8	12.6	24.5
Cayman Islands	1985	264	0.4	0.4	2.3	2.3	9.5	20.5	12.5	52.3 [8]
Iles Caïmanes	1990	590	0.3	0.3	1.5	3.1	9.5	24.1	10.7	50.7 [8]
	1991	616	0.3	0.3	1.5	3.1	8.9	22.4	10.6	52.9 [8]
Central African Rep.	1983	251055	39.6	2.5	7.6	0.5	2.0	20.5	4.1	23.2
Rép. centrafricaine	1984	275730	39.6	2.8	7.9	0.9	2.6	21.1	4.2	22.0
	1985	311430	42.0	2.5	7.4	0.8	2.6	21.8	4.2	21.0
Chile	1985	2651937	7.4	13.2	15.7	2.6	4.9	13.4	6.0	36.7
Chili	1987	4540556	8.8	11.4	17.5	2.5	4.8	15.4	6.1	33.5
	1988	5917879	8.5	15.5	18.1	2.5	5.1	13.4	6.0	30.9
Colombia	1985	4966000	17.0	4.2	21.4	2.2	6.9	14.1	8.2	26.2
Colombie	1991	26107000	17.0	8.2	20.4	2.6	5.0	14.4	9.6	22.6
	1992	33143000	15.7	7.1	19.4	2.7	5.7	15.5	10.4	23.5
Congo	1985	970850	7.5	41.0	5.6	1.2	6.1	11.4	7.3	20.0
Congo	1988	658964	13.9	16.8	8.6	1.9	2.6	16.3	11.0	28.9
	1989	773524	13.0	27.9	7.0	1.8	1.8	14.4	9.1	24.9
Cook Islands	1984	43	15.2	0.2	4.9	1.0	2.1	25.9	10.5	40.1
Iles Cook	1985	52	14.3	0.1	4.6	0.1	2.6	26.1	10.9	41.1
	1986	63	12.7	0.1	5.1	1.1	3.7	23.0	12.2	42.1
Costa Rica	1985	197920	18.9	22.1 [4]	...	3.2	3.6	20.5	4.9	26.9
Costa Rica	1992	904102	16.4	20.5 [4]	...	3.5	2.6	21.4	5.3	30.4
	1993	1074411	15.8	19.7 [4]	...	3.7	2.8	20.7	5.6	31.8
Côte d'Ivoire	1981	2291401	28.7	1.2	10.0	1.8	5.6	16.8	7.9	28.0
Côte d'Ivoire	1982	2486544	26.2	2.1	12.1	2.1	5.1	18.4	7.1	26.9
	1984	2855779	27.7	2.9	12.0	1.3	2.2	...	7.5	
Cyprus	1985	1481	7.5	0.5	15.7	2.2	10.0	18.7	9.3	36.0
Chypre	1991	2666	6.2	0.3	14.3	2.1	10.2	20.0	8.7	38.1
	1992	3081	5.8	0.2	13.4	2.0	10.0	21.2	8.6	39.0
Czech Republic	1987	495073	6.7	41.9 [7]	...	...	7.9	12.2	5.4	25.9
République tchèque	1990	567322	7.3	39.3 [7]	...	...	8.1	13.2	4.3	27.8
	1991	716593	5.6	43.9 [7]	...	...	6.3	10.5	4.1	29.7
Denmark	1985	615072	4.9	1.0	17.1	1.1	5.0	13.2	7.0	50.7
Danemark	1992	851253	3.2	0.9	16.7	1.5	4.7	12.3	7.9	52.9
	1993	873236	3.0	0.9	16.3	1.7	4.5	11.9	8.1	53.5
Djibouti	1981	56818	3.7	...	8.3	2.0	7.0	18.6	9.9	50.4
Djibouti	1982	59383	4.3	...	8.1	2.6	7.5	16.3	9.7	51.6
	1983	59997	4.3	...	8.2	3.2	7.6	15.7	9.8	51.2

22
Gross domestic product by kind of economic activity at current prices
Percentage distribution *[cont.]*
Produit intérieur brut par genre d'activité économique aux prix courants
Répartition en pourcentage *[suite]*

Country or area Pays ou zone	Year Année	GDP at current prices (Mil. nat.cur.) PIB aux prix courants (Mil. mon. nat.)	Agriculture, hunting, forestry & fishing Agriculture, chasse, sylviculture et pêche	Mining & quarrying Industries extractives	Manufacturing Manufacturières	Electricity, gas and water Electricité, gaz et eau	Construction Construction	Wholesale/retail trade, restaurants and hotels Commerce, restaurants, hôtels	Transport, storage & communication Transports, entrepôts, communications	Other activities Autres activités
Dominica	1985	266	23.4	0.5	5.4	2.3	5.6	8.9	11.0	42.7
Dominique	1990	452	21.5	0.7	5.9	2.5	6.2	10.8	13.3	39.3
	1991	479	21.2	0.8	5.7	2.7	6.1	11.0	13.5	39.0
Dominican Republic	1985	13972	17.4	4.5	17.4[9][10]	0.8	6.4	16.2[1]	8.3	29.1[1]
Rép. dominicaine	1992	112369	17.5	3.0	14.1[9][10]	0.5	8.2	14.1[1]	6.9	35.8[1]
	1993	120572	17.5	3.0	14.1[9][10]	0.5	8.2	14.1[1]	6.9	35.8[1]
Ecuador	1985	1109940	13.3	17.1	18.9	0.3	4.4	15.6	8.6	21.8
Equateur	1992	19414000	12.7	12.6	22.0	0.1	4.5	21.5	7.8	18.8
	1993	27451000	12.1	10.7	21.7	0.3	4.9	20.2	8.9	21.1
Egypt [3]	1985	40403	12.0	7.9	15.7	1.2[11]	5.7	22.0	8.7	20.8[11]
Egypte [3]	1990	110143	16.2	10.0	15.8	1.3[11]	4.7	19.7	9.8	22.4[11]
	1991	136190	15.2	9.8	15.7	1.5[11]	4.5	19.6	10.4	23.4[11]
El Salvador	1985	14331	18.2	0.1	16.4	2.3	3.0	27.2[1]	4.3	28.4[1]
El Salvador	1991	47792	10.2	0.2	18.7	2.3	2.7	35.0[1]	4.8	26.1[1]
	1992	54853	9.4	0.2	18.9	2.3	2.8	35.8[1]	4.8	25.7[1]
Equatorial Guinea	1985	38067	59.8	...	1.5	1.2	5.4	7.0	1.7	23.6
Guinée équatoriale	1990	44350	51.7	...	1.3	3.3	3.7	7.4	2.1	30.6
	1991	46429	50.2	...	1.3	2.9	2.8	7.1	1.8	33.8
Estonia	1985	495	20.7	...	39.0	...	8.0	7.5	5.6	19.3
Estonie	# 1992	13054	13.6	2.4	21.2	4.1	4.6	15.8	13.1	26.1
	# 1993	21918	10.1	1.7	17.1	3.2	5.9	17.0	11.2	33.9
Ethiopia incl. Eritrea [12]	1985	9924	38.9	0.2	10.1	0.7	4.0	9.7[1]	6.2	30.1[1]
Ethiopie y comp. Eryth. [12]	1991	13332	37.8	0.3	9.5	1.4	3.0	8.6[1]	6.6	32.9[1]
	1992	13508	46.7	0.3	8.4	1.2	2.6	9.5[1]	5.0	26.3[1]
Fiji	1985	1316	16.4	1.1	8.4	3.0	4.9	16.0	9.3	41.0
Fidji	1988	1588	17.6	3.9	8.6	3.3	3.8	17.8	10.3	34.8
	1989	1861	17.5	3.0	9.4	3.0	3.5	20.4	9.1	34.1
Finland	1985	331628	7.3	0.4	22.8	2.5	7.0	11.8	7.1	41.0
Finlande	1992	476778	4.5	0.4	19.4	2.3	5.5	10.2	7.7	50.2
	1993	480470	4.6	0.4	21.2	2.3	4.1	9.9	7.8	49.7
France	1985	4700143	3.9	0.9	22.0	2.5	5.2	14.6	6.1	44.9
France	1992	7010540	2.8	0.5	20.4	2.4	5.2	15.0	5.9	47.7
	1993	7082790	2.3	0.5	19.8	2.5	5.1	15.0	5.9	49.0
French Guiana	1985	3173	6.4	4.9	...	−0.5	10.6	12.8	12.2	53.7
Guyane française	1990	6526	10.0	7.5	...	0.7	12.7	13.4	7.6	48.1
	1991	7404	7.4	7.6	...	0.5	12.0	13.1	12.3	47.1
French Polynesia	1985	226772	3.8	...	8.5	0.8	12.0	...	5.8	27.7
Polynésie française	1989	281667	4.4	...	7.2	1.5	6.6	22.8	...[13]	57.5[13]
	1990	297754	4.7	...	7.3	1.7	6.1	22.7	...[13]	57.6[13]
Gabon	1985	1645800	6.2	46.2	5.3[10]	1.8	6.3	6.6	4.8	22.8
Gabon	1988	1013600	10.7	21.5	6.9[10]	2.8	5.0	13.8	8.6	30.8
	1989	1168066	10.0	31.2	5.5[10]	2.4	5.3	12.0	7.9	25.7
Gambia [3]	1985	1085	25.5	0.0	6.4	0.6	3.7	34.1	9.4	20.2
Gambie [3]	1990	2630	23.1	0.0	6.1	0.8	4.5	39.0	10.0	16.5
	1991	2948	22.9	0.0	5.9	0.9	5.0	38.3	10.6	16.4
Germany † · Allemagne † F.R. Germany	1985	1823180	1.8	0.9	31.7[14]	2.8	5.2	9.8	5.8	42.1
R.f. Allemagne	1992	2813000	1.2	0.4	28.4[14]	2.3	5.4	10.3	5.5	46.6
	1993	2853700	1.0	...	26.2[14]	...	5.6	...	5.5	30.1
Ghana	1984	270561	49.2	1.2	6.4	0.8	2.2	28.3	6.4	5.4
Ghana	1985	343048	44.9	1.1	11.5	1.2	2.9	24.8	5.3	8.3
	1986	550515	44.4	1.6	11.2	1.6	2.4	22.8	4.6	11.4
Greece	1985	4617816	15.5	1.9	16.3	2.3	5.7	11.7[1]	6.7	39.9[1]
Grèce	1992	14832170	12.5	1.1	13.1	2.3	5.7	11.1[1]	6.0	48.2[1]
	1993	16760352	11.8	1.0	13.2	2.2	5.6	11.8[1]	6.1	48.2[1]
Grenada	1985	311	14.2	0.3	4.0	2.1	6.2	15.7	10.1	47.4
Grenade	1990	541	13.2	0.3	4.2	2.4	8.2	15.2	11.1	45.4
	1991	567	12.1	0.3	4.3	2.5	8.5	15.9	11.7	44.6

22

Gross domestic product by kind of economic activity at current prices
Percentage distribution [cont.]
Produit intérieur brut par genre d'activité économique aux prix courants
Répartition en pourcentage [suite]

Country or area Pays ou zone	Year Année	GDP at current prices (Mil. nat.cur.) PIB aux prix courants (Mil. mon.nat.)	Agriculture, hunting, forestry & fishing Agriculture, chasse, sylviculture et pêche	Mining & quarrying Industries extractives	Manufac-turing Manufac-turières	Electricity, gas and water Electricité, gaz et eau	Construc-tion Construc-tion	Wholesale/ retail trade, restaurants and hotels Commerce, restaurants, hôtels	Transport, storage & commu-nication Transports, entrepôts, communi-cations	Other activities Autres activités
Guadeloupe	1985	9802	9.8	4.7 [4]	...	-0.5	4.7	16.7	5.6	58.9
Guadeloupe	1990	15201	6.7	5.3 [4]	...	1.0	7.4	18.1	5.8	55.7
	1991	16415	7.3	6.1 [4]	...	1.4	7.0	16.4	6.0	55.9
Guinea−Bissau	1986	46973	46.8	0.1	14.8	0.0	5.6	19.7	2.8	10.1
Guinée−Bissau	1990	510094	44.6	8.2 [7]	...	...	10.0	25.7	3.7	7.8
	1991	854985	44.7	8.5 [7]	...	...	8.4	25.8	3.9	8.7
Guyana	1985	1964	25.8	2.5	8.1 [5]	...	6.1	6.8 [1]	6.5	44.1 [1]
Guyana	1992	46734	43.8	9.7	3.8 [5]	...	3.0	4.3 [1]	4.9	30.4 [1]
	1993	56647	38.3	14.4	3.5 [5]	...	3.0	4.1 [1]	4.7	32.1 [1]
Honduras	1985	7279	19.3	1.9	12.8	1.6	4.9	11.7	5.6	42.1
Honduras	1992	18800	17.3	1.6	15.3	2.8	5.6	9.4	5.6	42.3
	1993	22444	17.8	1.6	15.4	2.6	6.5	9.2	4.9	42.0
Hong Kong	1985	271655	0.4	0.1	20.7	2.5	4.7	21.3	7.6	42.7
Hong−kong	1992	779335	0.2	0.0	12.8	2.0	4.8	24.5	9.1	46.4
	1993	897595	0.2	0.0	10.5	2.0	4.6	24.4	9.1	49.2
Hungary	1985	1033658	16.1	5.7	26.4 [15]	3.3 [15]	7.2	9.4	7.5	24.4
Hongrie	# 1992	2935056	6.5	1.1	19.9 [15]	3.5 [15]	5.2	11.6	8.4	43.9
	1993	3537835	5.9	0.6	19.6 [15]	3.5 [15]	4.7	11.8	8.0	46.0
Iceland	1985	120899	9.5	...	14.2	4.6	6.1	8.4	6.0	51.1
Islande	1990	363829	9.8	...	13.1	3.2	6.3	10.1	5.9	51.7
	1991	396628	9.6	...	13.0	3.0	6.1	10.3	5.7	52.4
India [16]	1985	2622430	29.4	2.4	15.9	1.9	4.9	11.8	5.4	28.2
Inde [16]	1992	7028290	27.5	2.1	15.8	2.2	5.1	11.6	7.0	28.8
	1993	7863550	27.3	2.2	15.5	2.5	5.1	11.7	7.3	28.4
Indonesia	1985	96997000	23.2	14.0	16.0	0.4	5.5	15.9 [1]	6.3	18.8 [1]
Indonésie	1992	260787000	19.2	11.9	21.7	0.8	6.2	16.4 [1]	6.5	17.4 [1]
	1993	298026000	18.4	8.9	22.4	0.9	6.9	16.6 [1]	7.0	18.9 [1]
Iran, Islamic Rep. of [17]	1985	15775000	19.7	10.1	8.2	0.9	7.4	14.5	7.5	31.7
Iran, Rép. islamique d' [17]	1989	27787000	24.0	6.6	10.5	1.1	4.6	19.9	6.4	26.8
	1990	36645000	23.0	10.8	12.0	1.1	3.9	17.9	7.2	24.1
Iraq	1985	15494	13.9	22.5	9.6	1.3	9.1	12.5	5.0	26.2
Iraq	1990	23297	19.8	14.3	8.8	1.1	7.3	14.8	9.0	24.9
	1991	19940	30.3	0.7	6.4	0.8	4.1	18.1	13.3	26.3
Ireland	1985	17790	8.8	30.2 [7]	...	...	5.4	10.8	4.8	40.0
Irlande	# 1991	28189	6.8	30.9 [7]	...	...	4.8	10.9	5.2	41.3
	1992	29987	7.2	30.8 [7]	...	...	4.7	10.1	5.1	42.2
Israel	1985	21358	4.9	22.5 [4]	...	1.7	4.2	14.2	8.0	44.6 [18]
Israël	1992	117303	2.8	21.1 [4]	...	1.7	8.1	11.1	7.8	47.5 [18]
	1993	134667	2.4	21.5 [4]	...	1.7	7.2	11.6	7.6	48.0 [18]
Italy	1985	810580000 [6]	4.5	24.2 [4]	...	4.6	6.3	19.1 [10]	5.4	35.9
Italie	1992	1504323000 [6]	3.1	20.5 [4]	...	5.7	5.8	18.4 [10]	6.0	40.3
	1993	1560114000 [6]	2.9	20.2 [4]	...	5.7	5.6	18.2 [10]	6.3	41.1
Jamaica	1985	11203	6.0	5.1	20.0	3.2	9.1	23.9	8.3	24.4
Jamaïque	1992	72540	8.0	9.4	19.6	2.5	12.9	23.6	7.7	16.2
	1993	95785	8.4	7.3	18.4	2.3	12.9	23.7	8.0	19.0
Japan	1985	320419000	3.2	0.3	29.5	3.2	7.9	13.4 [1]	6.6	35.9 [1]
Japon	1992	463145000	2.2	0.3	28.0	2.8	10.1	12.8 [1]	6.2	37.6 [1]
	1993	465972000	2.1	0.3	26.8	2.9	10.3	12.5 [1]	6.3	38.8 [1]
Jordan	1985	1970	4.3	3.3	10.4	2.0	7.9	14.7	13.5	43.9
Jordanie	1991	2778	6.3	4.5	12.4	2.2	4.5	9.2	13.2	47.8
	1992	3257	6.3	3.6	13.1	2.2	4.7	8.3	13.1	48.8
Kazakstan	1990	48	29.1	25.9	...	...	11.5	6.3	7.5	19.7
Kazakstan	1992	1239	20.4	27.4	...	...	5.6	3.6	5.6	37.4
	1993	27	12.7	31.0	...	...	9.7	13.1	6.0	27.6
Kenya	1985	5043	28.6	0.2	10.3	1.5	4.7	10.3	5.9	38.4
Kenya	1992	12787	23.2	0.2	9.6	1.2	5.0	11.9	7.1	41.7
	1993	16063	24.5	0.2	8.8	1.1	4.7	12.0	7.0	41.7

22
Gross domestic product by kind of economic activity at current prices
Percentage distribution *[cont.]*
Produit intérieur brut par genre d'activité économique aux prix courants
Répartition en pourcentage *[suite]*

Country or area Pays ou zone	Year Année	GDP at current prices (Mil. nat.cur.) PIB aux prix courants (Mil. mon.nat.)	Agriculture, hunting, forestry & fishing Agriculture, chasse, sylviculture et pêche	Mining & quarrying Industries extractives	Manufac- turing Manufac- turières	Electricity, gas and water Electricité, gaz et eau	Construc- tion Construc- tion	Wholesale/ retail trade, restaurants and hotels Commerce, restaurants, hôtels	Transport, storage & commu- nication Transports, entrepôts, communi- cations	Other activities Autres activités
Korea, Republic of	1985	82062000	12.5	1.1	29.3	3.0	7.6	13.6	7.3	25.7
Corée, Rép. de	1992	240392000	7.4	0.4	27.8	2.2	13.7	12.0	6.8	29.8
	1993	265548000	7.1	0.3	27.1	2.3	13.6	11.9	7.0	30.7
Kuwait	1985	6450	0.6	49.4	5.9	-2.4	4.0	8.8	4.2	29.4
Kowëit	1992	5518	0.4	32.6	9.2	-1.4	3.8	8.9	4.3	42.2
	1993	6766	0.5	43.9	8.7	-0.9	3.2	5.6	3.5	35.6
Kyrgyzstan	1990	42	32.5	26.7 [7]	...	...	7.4	5.3	5.7	22.4
Kirghizistan	1991	87	39.2	21.0 [7]	...	...	6.6	5.5	4.9	22.8
	1992	772	37.1	34.3 [7]	...	...	3.2	4.8	3.4	17.1
Latvia	1990	62	21.1	0.2	33.2	1.7	9.4	6.6	10.5	17.4
Lettonie	1992	1005	16.5	0.1	26.4	1.4	4.7	13.6	16.6	20.8
	1993	1467	10.7	0.2	20.9	6.8	3.9	8.7	21.0	27.8
Lebanon	1980	14000	9.2	...	12.2	5.1	3.2	28.6	3.8	38.0
Liban	1981	16800	8.5	...	13.0	5.4	3.4	28.3	3.7	37.5
	1982	12600	8.5	...	13.0	5.4	3.4	28.3	3.7	37.5
Lesotho	1985	551	17.6	0.3	9.1 [9]	0.7	14.2	9.4	2.6	46.1
Lesotho	1992	2184	8.2	0.1	12.1 [9]	1.6	22.1	8.2	2.8	44.8
	1993	2587	11.0	0.1	12.6 [9]	2.0	21.5	8.4	2.6	41.8
Liberia	1985	1055	33.3	12.2	6.1	1.6	3.1	5.7	6.8	31.3
Libéria	1988	1158	35.6	9.9	6.9	1.6	2.5	5.5	6.8	31.1
	1989	1194	34.4	10.2	6.8	1.6	2.2	5.3	6.6	32.8
Libyan Arab Jamah.	1983	8805	2.9	47.0 [19]	3.1	0.9	10.0	5.8	4.4	25.8
Jaman. arabe libyenne	1984	8013	3.2	39.2 [19]	3.7	1.1	10.6	7.6	5.0	29.4
	1985	8277	3.4	40.4 [19]	4.4	1.2	11.1	6.8	4.8	27.8
Lithuania	1985	9190	27.8	36.9 [7]	...	...	11.5	4.5	8.1	11.3
Lithuanie	1990	12897	27.7	36.9 [7]	...	...	10.5	4.9	8.0	12.0
	1992	332830	15.9	42.3 [7]	...	...	5.5	8.7	6.1	16.8
Luxembourg	1985	205255 [6]	2.6	0.1	30.0	2.4	5.4	16.6	5.4	37.6
Luxembourg	1990	300409 [6]	1.9	0.3	25.8	1.7	7.2	16.5	6.8	39.8
	1991	318804 [6]	1.4	0.3	24.2	1.7	7.5	16.4	6.9	41.5
Madagascar	1983	1221100	43.0	15.2 [7 20]	...	...	...	...	...	...
Madagascar	1984	1369100	42.4	15.6 [7 20]	...	...	...	...	...	...
	1985	1553400	42.0	16.4 [7 20]	...	...	...	...	...	...
Malawi	1984	1398	35.4 [21]	...	17.6	1.7	1.9	6.4	4.6	32.5
Malawi	1985	1655	32.3 [21]	...	16.3	1.4	2.0	11.9	4.4	31.5
	1986	1793	32.6 [21]	...	19.1	1.1	1.9	10.9	3.3	31.1
Malaysia Malaisie	1983	69941	18.7	13.9	19.1	1.5	5.5	11.6	5.2	24.4
Maldives	1984	543	30.9	2.1	5.6 [5]	...	7.5	16.2	18.7	19.1
Maldives	1985	613	28.8	1.9	5.5 [5]	...	8.0	15.9	22.1	17.9
	1986	697	30.5	1.7	5.5 [5]	...	7.6	14.8	22.8	17.0
Mali	1985	520200	38.2	2.7	7.0 [9]	4.2 [20]	...	17.5	5.2	25.2
Mali	1991	691400	44.1	1.6	6.6 [9]	4.1 [20]	...	19.3	4.7	19.4
	1992	737400	45.2	1.5	6.7 [9]	4.2 [20]	...	18.5	4.8	19.1
Malta	1985	476	4.1	4.4 [20]	26.7	4.7	...	14.0 [1]	5.0	41.2 [1]
Malte	1992	875	2.7	2.9 [20]	21.9	7.1	...	12.6 [1]	6.0	46.9 [1]
	1993	938	2.7	2.7 [20]	21.3	6.7	...	12.2 [1]	6.3	48.1 [1]
Martinique	1985	12484	7.8	6.0 [4]	...	2.0	3.7	16.8	4.8	58.8
Martinique	1990	19320	5.6	7.7 [4]	...	2.4	4.8	18.5	6.0	55.0
	1991	20787	5.5	7.7 [4]	...	2.4	5.2	18.5	6.2	54.5
Mauritania	1985	52665	20.0	10.8	11.5 [5]	...	7.0	13.1	6.1	31.6
Mauritanie	1988	72635	29.0	6.9	11.7 [5]	...	5.6	11.8	4.6	30.4
	1989	83520	30.9	9.4	9.3 [5]	...	5.8	...	4.5	...
Mauritius	1985	16618	12.7	0.1	21.7	2.4	4.6	11.5	9.1	37.8
Maurice	1993	54928	8.2	0.1	19.4	2.2	6.3	14.8	9.9	39.0
	1994	62150	7.8	0.1	19.6	2.0	6.5	14.9	9.9	39.1

22
Gross domestic product by kind of economic activity at current prices
Percentage distribution [cont.]
Produit intérieur brut par genre d'activité économique aux prix courants
Répartition en pourcentage [suite]

% of GDP – en % du PIB

Country or area Pays ou zone	Year Année	GDP at current prices (Mil. nat.cur.) PIB aux prix courants (Mil. mon.nat.)	Agriculture, hunting, forestry & fishing Agriculture, chasse, sylviculture et pêche	Mining & quarrying Industries extractives	Manufac- turing Manufac- turières	Electricity, gas and water Electricité, gaz et eau	Construc- tion Construc- tion	Wholesale/ retail trade, restaurants and hotels Commerce, restaurants, hôtels	Transport, storage & commu- nication Transports, entrepôts, communi- cations	Other activities Autres activités
Mexico	1985	47392	9.1	4.6 [22]	23.4	0.9	4.4	28.1	6.7	22.8
Mexique	1992	1019156	7.0	2.1 [22]	21.2	1.5	4.8	24.0	9.3	30.2
	1993	1127584	6.8	1.7 [22]	20.1	1.5	5.3	22.6	9.7	32.3
Montserrat	1985	90 [2]	4.8	1.3	5.7	3.7	7.9	18.0	11.5	47.2
Montserrat	1986	103 [2]	4.3	1.4	5.6	3.7	11.3	18.7	11.6	43.4
	1987	118 [2]	4.1	1.3	5.7	3.2	11.5	22.1	11.1	41.0
Morocco	1985	129510	16.6	4.3	18.6	4.8 [15]	5.7	14.1	6.4	29.5
Maroc	1992	241220	14.9	2.3	18.1	7.2 [15]	5.0	13.4	6.3	32.7
	1993	247680	14.3	2.1	18.0	7.5 [15]	4.7	13.5	6.7	33.1
Myanmar [16]	1985	55989	48.2	1.0	9.9	0.5 [11]	1.7	23.9 [1]	4.0	10.9 [1]
Myanmar [16]	1991	178553	57.8	0.6	7.3	0.2 [11]	2.2	22.6 [1]	2.7	6.7 [1]
	1992	230935	59.8	0.6	7.4	0.2 [11]	1.8	22.5 [1]	2.1	5.6 [1]
Namibia	1985	2973	8.8	28.5	4.8	1.9	2.6	7.8	4.5	41.1
Namibie	1992	7838	9.1	14.3	6.2	2.1	2.2	9.0	4.5	52.6
	1993	8390	10.0	10.5	7.8	1.2	2.4	9.2	4.7	54.3
Nepal [23]	1985	44417	53.9	0.3	4.5	0.4	8.1	4.1	6.2	22.5
Népal [23]	1992	126186	48.7	0.1	7.4	0.8	8.1	6.0	6.1	22.8
	1993	144959	45.9	0.2	7.8	1.0	8.2	6.0	6.8	24.1
Netherlands	1985	425350	3.9	8.3	17.7	1.8	4.6	12.6 [24]	6.0	45.0
Pays–Bas	1992	563078	3.6	3.0	18.1	1.6	5.1	14.6 [24]	6.5	48.1
	1993	574333	3.2	2.7	17.5	1.7	5.2	14.6	6.6	48.8
Netherlands Antilles	1983	1910	0.8 [14]	...	7.6	3.3	8.9	21.8	12.8	44.9
Antilles néerlandaises	1984	1929	1.0 [14]	...	7.1	3.7	9.1	21.6	11.1	46.4
	1985	1966	0.9 [14]	...	7.1	3.4	8.0	23.1	10.8	46.8
New Caledonia	1985	139650	1.8	15.6	4.7	2.3	3.4	23.8 [1]	3.4	45.0 [1]
Nouvelle–Calédonie	1991	272235	1.9	11.4	6.5	2.2	5.7	22.2 [1]	5.3	44.7 [1]
	1992	281427	1.8	8.0	6.6	2.3	5.5	23.7 [1]	5.6	46.4 [1]
New Zealand [16]	1985	45777	9.0	1.3	21.7	3.2	5.6	18.6	7.7	33.0
Nouvelle–Zélande [16]	1989	71411	8.7	1.2	18.4	3.0	4.5	14.1	8.3	41.9
	1990	73127	7.7	1.4	17.6	2.9	3.8	15.6	8.3	42.9
Niger	1985	647141	36.7	8.1	7.1	2.2	3.5	15.8	4.2	22.4
Niger	1986	643362	36.0	7.4	7.7	2.5	4.5	14.1	4.1	23.7
	1987	649846	33.7	7.6	8.7	2.8	5.1	13.7	4.1	24.3
Nigeria	1985	72355	36.8	17.3	8.6	0.7	2.1	13.4	5.4	15.7
Nigéria	1992	549809	26.5	46.6	5.7	0.3	1.1	11.5	1.7	6.7
	1993	697095	33.3	35.5	6.2	0.2	1.2	14.6	2.2	6.8
Norway	1985	500201	3.0	18.2	14.0	3.7	5.4	10.8	7.6	37.3
Norvège	1990	660552	3.1	13.4	13.7	4.1	4.4	11.1	9.8	40.4
	1991	686686	2.9	13.3	13.5	4.0	3.9	11.0	10.4	41.0
Oman	1985	3454	2.7	48.8	2.4	1.1	7.0	12.4	2.9	22.8
Oman	1991	3917	3.7	42.6	4.3	1.6	3.9	13.8	3.7	26.3
	1992	4417	3.3	42.7	4.3	1.5	4.0	13.9	3.6	26.6
Pakistan [3]	1985	514532	25.0	0.6	14.7	2.1	3.7	14.1 [1]	8.0	31.7 [1]
Pakistan [3]	1992	1341955	22.2	0.6	15.5	2.9	3.7	14.6 [1]	9.5	31.2 [1]
	1993	1564974	22.3	0.6	15.5	2.9	3.5	14.3 [1]	9.3	31.6 [1]
Panama	1985	4948	10.1	0.1	8.5	4.3	4.6	14.0	12.9	45.4
Panama	1992	6015	10.9	0.1	8.3	3.5	5.0	12.9	13.8	45.4
	1993	6565	10.2	0.2	8.1	3.9	6.1	12.7	13.3	45.7
Papua New Guinea	1985	2403	33.3	10.0	10.9	1.9	3.9	9.9 [1]	5.0	25.2 [1]
Papua New Guinea	1990	3076	29.0	14.7	9.0	1.7	5.0	9.6 [1]	6.2	24.8 [1]
	1991	3606	26.0	17.0	9.6	1.6	6.2	9.9 [1]	6.7	22.9 [1]
Paraguay	1985	1393890	28.9	0.4	16.2	2.2	5.9	25.9 [1]	4.2	16.3 [1]
Paraguay	1988	3319124	29.6	0.5	16.8	2.5	4.9	27.5 [1]	4.0	14.2 [1]
	1989	4608400	29.6	0.5	17.0	2.4	5.6	27.4 [1]	3.8	13.7 [1]
Peru	1985	197 [25]	9.4	9.9	24.3	1.2	7.1	18.0	6.2	24.0
Pérou	# 1992	52062	7.4	1.9	23.7	0.7	8.6	17.5	4.9	35.4
	1993	80529	7.7	1.8	23.8	0.8	9.3	17.5	4.3	34.8

22

Gross domestic product by kind of economic activity at current prices
Percentage distribution [cont.]
Produit intérieur brut par genre d'activité économique aux prix courants
Répartition en pourcentage [suite]

Country or area Pays ou zone	Year Année	GDP at current prices (Mil. nat.cur.) PIB aux prix courants (Mil. mon.nat.)	% of GDP – en % du PIB							
			Agriculture, hunting, forestry & fishing Agriculture, chasse, sylviculture et pêche	Mining & quarrying Industries extractives	Manufac- turing Manufac- turières	Electricity, gas and water Electricité, gaz et eau	Construc- tion Construc- tion	Wholesale/ retail trade, restaurants and hotels Commerce, restaurants, hôtels	Transport, storage & commu- nication Transports, entrepôts, communi- cations	Other activities Autres activités
Philippines	1985	571883	24.6	2.1	25.2	2.8	5.1	15.7	5.5	19.1
Philippines	1993	1475042	21.6	1.1	23.7	2.5	5.4	15.7	5.4	24.6
	1994	1687607	22.0	1.0	23.3	2.7	5.7	15.3	5.0	24.9
Poland	1990	591518000	8.4	44.9 [7]	...	...	9.2	12.7	4.9	19.8
Pologne	1991	824330000	6.9	40.2 [7]	...	...	10.2	13.1	5.6	24.0
Portugal	1985	3523945	8.0	30.4 [4]	...	3.5	5.7	22.4	7.7	22.4
Portugal	# 1988	6909628	5.6	27.9 [4]	...	4.2	5.6	18.5	6.5	31.8
	1989	8140498	6.0	27.7 [4]	...	3.6	5.2	18.1	6.4	24.7
Puerto Rico [3]	1985	21969	1.7	0.1	38.9	3.1	1.4 [26]	16.2	5.6	33.1
Porto Rico [3]	1992	36847	1.1	0.1	41.4	2.9	2.2 [26]	15.5	5.2	31.6
	1993	39265	1.0	0.1	41.5	2.8	2.1 [26]	15.5	5.0	31.9
Qatar	1985	22398	1.0	42.8	7.9	0.9	5.9	5.3	2.0	34.3
Qatar	1991	25056	0.9	32.5	13.3	1.2	4.1	6.7	3.1	38.1
	1992	27202	0.9	35.8	12.7	1.1	4.1	6.7	2.9	35.7
Réunion	1985	17054	4.1	7.6 [4]	...	4.1	5.5	16.0	4.7	58.0
Réunion	1990	28374	3.9	8.8 [4]	...	4.6	5.7	19.9	3.9	53.3
	1991	31339	3.6	8.8 [4]	...	3.9	6.9	19.3	4.5	53.0
Romania	1985	817400	14.9	46.0 [7]	...	...	6.7	5.9	6.6	19.9
Roumanie	# 1992	6029000	19.0	38.3 [7]	...	...	4.8	14.3	8.5	15.0
	1993	19733300	21.1	34.4 [7]	...	...	4.7	12.5	6.7	20.6
Rwanda	1985	173700	41.8	0.3	13.7	0.5	8.7	12.2	4.9	17.8
Rwanda	1988	177940	37.9	0.2	14.0	0.7	6.9	12.7	7.1	20.5
	1989	190220	39.8	0.4	13.1	0.5	6.8	12.8	6.8	19.8
Saint Kitts–Nevis	1985	172 [2]	9.6	0.3	12.8	1.0	8.8	20.8	12.3	34.5
Saint–Kitts–et–Nevis	1988	279 [2]	10.0	0.3	15.9	1.0	10.3	20.6	14.5	27.4
	1989	302 [2]	9.2	0.4	15.7	0.9	11.8	20.6	14.4	27.0
Saint Lucia	1985	389 [2]	15.0	0.6	8.5	3.9	6.9	22.7	10.4	32.0
Sainte–Lucie	1986	427 [2]	16.6	0.6	8.0	3.9	7.5	22.1	9.9	31.6
	1987	446 [2]	14.4	0.6	7.9	4.2	8.1	23.4	9.6	31.9
Saint Vincent–Grenadines	1985	305	16.3	0.2	9.6	3.3	6.4	11.1	15.3	38.0
St.–Vincent–et–Gren.	1989	469	14.5	0.2	9.2	4.0	7.6	11.1	16.9	36.5
	1990	525	16.0	0.2	7.3	4.1	8.1	11.8	17.8	34.7
Sao Tome and Principe	1986	2478	26.6	...	2.1	0.3	3.1	17.7	4.8	45.4
Sao Tomé–et–Principe	1987	3003	29.4	...	1.2	1.3	3.5	15.9	5.2	43.4
	1988	4221	28.9	...	1.6	0.9	3.8	16.9	3.7	44.2
Saudi Arabia [3]	1985	313941	4.4	28.7	7.8	0.1	12.3	9.6	7.6	29.5
Arabie saoudite [3]	1987	275453	6.6	23.6	8.7	0.2	12.1	10.1	8.0	30.6
	1988	281971	7.3	22.5	8.8	0.3	11.2	9.5	8.1	32.4
Senegal	1985	1158500	18.7	0.3	12.8	1.8	2.8	25.0	10.0	28.6
Sénégal	1992	1653300	19.5	0.4	13.0	2.1	3.3	23.8	10.2	27.7
	1993	1647400	18.5	0.3	13.1	2.1	3.3	24.3	10.5	27.9
Seychelles	1985	1205	5.8	0.0	9.7	2.6	6.1	24.7	14.1	37.1
Seychelles	1990	1967	4.8	0.0	10.1	1.4	4.8	27.0	12.0	39.9
	1991	1980	4.8	0.0	10.8	2.1	5.1	25.0	14.9	37.2
Sierra Leone [3]	1985	7481	39.1	17.5	4.3	0.2	2.3	14.0	8.1	14.5
Sierra Leone [3]	1989	82837	36.9	7.0	7.0	0.2	1.9	24.7	10.7	11.6
	1990	150175	35.0	9.4	8.7	0.1	1.2	20.1	8.9	16.7
Singapore	1985	38924	0.7	0.3	23.6	2.0	10.6	17.0	13.4	32.3
Singapour	1992	79083	0.2	0.1	27.9	1.7	7.6	18.4	12.6	31.5
	1993	89007	0.2	0.0	27.5	1.7	7.4	17.8	12.1	33.3
Slovenia	1985	178	5.1	1.1	36.5	2.8	5.6	9.6	7.3	32.0
Slovénie	1992	1005261	4.9	1.7	29.7	2.4	3.8	12.9	6.5	38.1
	1993	1434974	4.5	1.0	27.6	2.6	4.2	12.9	7.3	39.8
Solomon Islands	1984	221	48.1	−0.2	3.3	0.8	3.4	9.5	4.7	30.4
Iles Salomon	1985	236	45.6	−0.6	3.4	0.9	3.8	9.4	4.6	32.9
	1986	250	43.3	−1.0	4.0	1.0	4.6	7.5	5.2	35.4

184 National accounts and industrial production   Comptabilités nationales et production industrielle

22

Gross domestic product by kind of economic activity at current prices
Percentage distribution [cont.]
Produit intérieur brut par genre d'activité économique aux prix courants
Répartition en pourcentage [suite]

% of GDP – en % du PIB

Country or area Pays ou zone	Year Année	GDP at current prices (Mil. nat.cur.) PIB aux prix courants (Mil. mon.nat.)	Agriculture, hunting, forestry & fishing Agriculture, chasse, sylviculture et pêche	Mining & quarrying Industries extractives	Manufacturing Manufacturières	Electricity, gas and water Electricité, gaz et eau	Construction Construction	Wholesale/retail trade, restaurants and hotels Commerce, restaurants, hôtels	Transport, storage & communication Transports, entrepôts, communications	Other activities Autres activités
Somalia Somalie	1985	87290	63.6	0.3	4.7	0.1	2.2	9.7	6.5	12.9
	1986	118781	59.3	0.3	5.3	0.2	2.5	9.8	6.9	15.7
	1987	169608	62.5	0.3	4.9	−0.5	2.8	10.3	6.5	13.2
South Africa Afrique du Sud	1985	123126	5.3	13.5	21.1	3.9	3.4	10.8	8.1	34.0
	1991	297895	4.4	9.1	22.3	3.9	2.8	12.1	7.6	37.8
	1992	327068	3.5	8.7	22.5	3.9	2.7	12.4	7.5	38.8
Spain Espagne	1985	28200900	5.9	1.0	26.7	2.9	6.7	20.2	5.6	31.0
	1992	59002100	3.4	...	17.9	...	8.6	...	...	...
	1993	60904300	3.5	...	17.0	...	8.2	...	...	...
Sri Lanka Sri Lanka	1985	157763	24.4	0.8	16.6	1.9	7.6	18.4	11.0	19.3
	1992	421755	21.1	1.0	17.1	1.8	6.5	21.0	10.2	21.3
	1993	499708	20.8	1.1	17.0	2.1	6.8	20.5	9.9	21.8
Sudan [3] Soudan [3]	1981	6721	35.7	0.1	6.9	1.1	5.7	14.1	10.3	26.0
	1982	9186	30.4	0.1	7.3	1.0	6.6	15.4	10.1	29.2
	1983	11329	29.5	0.0	7.7	1.5	5.9	17.5	9.5	28.4
Suriname Suriname	1985	1747	8.2	5.4	11.8	4.2	5.6	15.3	6.5	43.0
	1991	3708	10.9	2.4	10.7	3.9	6.6	19.2	5.3	41.1
	1992	5010	13.7	2.1	10.2	3.0	7.0	21.7	5.2	37.2
Swaziland [27] Swaziland [27]	1985	803	16.9	2.2	13.3	2.7	3.1	10.4	5.4	45.9
	1987	1118	13.7	1.7	21.1	2.7	2.8	10.1	6.6	41.3
	1988	1325	13.8	1.2	20.0	2.6	2.8	10.7	6.2	42.7
Sweden Suède	1985	866601	3.3	0.4	21.5	2.6	5.9	10.7	5.4	50.1
	1992	1441723	2.0	0.2	17.1	3.0	6.4	9.7	6.2	55.4
	1993	1442181	2.0	0.3	18.1	3.0	5.7	9.4	6.1	55.6
Switzerland Suisse	1985	227950	3.6	...	25.8	2.2	7.6	18.3	6.4	35.1
	1990	313990	3.1	...	24.4	1.9	8.4	19.4	5.9	37.5
	1991	331075	3.0	...	23.5	1.9	8.1	17.2	6.1	40.2
Syrian Arab Rep. Rép. arabe syrienne	1985	83225	21.0	7.1	7.7	0.2	6.8	22.2	9.8	25.0
	1992	370631	31.3	9.1	4.4	0.9	3.7	25.7	9.3	15.6
	1993	398515	30.8	8.3	5.2	0.6	4.2	25.4	9.7	15.8
Thailand Thaïlande	1985	1056496	15.8	2.5	21.9	2.4	5.1	23.9	7.4	21.0
	1992	2833277	12.0	1.5	28.0	2.3	6.7	22.1	7.2	20.2
	1993	3161374	10.0	1.5	28.5	2.4	6.9	22.0	7.5	21.3
Togo Togo	1980	238872	26.6	9.2	7.0	1.7	5.8	19.2	6.4	...
	1981	258000	26.9	8.8	6.3	1.6	4.3	20.5	6.7	...
Tonga [27] Tonga [27]	1981	64	27.6	0.6	7.0	0.5	3.1	11.5	7.0	...
	1982	64	32.9	0.6	8.1	13.1	3.0	16.5	7.3	...
	1983	73	33.4	0.6	6.9	0.6	3.4	17.1	6.7	...
Trinidad and Tobago Trinité−et−Tobago	1985	18071	3.0	22.1	8.7	1.0	12.1	14.2	8.8	30.1
	1992	23118	2.4	15.4	13.2	1.5	9.6	17.0	9.4	31.4
	1993	24883	2.3	14.4	14.0	1.7	8.8	18.9	8.7	31.3
Tunisia Tunisie	1985	6910	15.2	10.1	11.8	1.7	6.1	18.5 [1]	5.2	31.3 [1]
	1988	8605	11.8	7.9	14.1	1.7	4.4	20.5 [1]	6.6	33.0 [1]
	1989	9497	12.1	8.0	14.5	1.6	4.7	20.4 [1]	6.6	32.1 [1]
Turkey Turquie	1985	35095481	19.7	1.6	18.3	1.8	5.8	19.1	12.7	20.1
	1992	1093368044	15.0	1.4	21.6	2.6	6.8	18.5	12.2	21.8
	1993	1913150236	14.4	1.1	21.6	2.7	7.1	18.8	11.9	22.5
Uganda Ouganda	1985	27579 [2]	53.5	0.1	4.3	0.4	2.8	13.2	2.5	23.2
	1993	4026764 [2]	45.4	0.3	5.9	0.9	6.0	11.5	3.9	26.2
	1994	5152629 [2]	48.6	0.2	5.6	1.1	5.0	11.3	3.4	24.8
United Arab Emirates Emirats arabes unis	1985	99416	1.4	45.3	9.3	2.2	8.9	8.8	4.2	19.9
	1989	100976	1.9	38.7	8.6	2.2	9.5	10.6	5.6	23.0
	1990	124008	1.6	46.7	7.5	1.9	8.1	9.1	4.8	20.4
United Kingdom Royaume−Uni	1985	356172	1.7	6.4	21.6	2.3	5.2	11.4	6.8	44.7
	1992	595219	1.6	1.8	18.8	2.2	5.0	12.5	7.4	50.8
	1993	627701	1.7	1.9	18.8	2.2	4.7	12.5	7.4	50.8

22
Gross domestic product by kind of economic activity at current prices
Percentage distribution [cont.]
Produit intérieur brut par genre d'activité économique aux prix courants
Répartition en pourcentage [suite]

Country or area Pays ou zone	Year Année	GDP at current prices (Mil. nat.cur.) PIB aux prix courants (Mil. mon.nat.)	Agriculture, hunting, forestry & fishing Agriculture, chasse, sylviculture et pêche	Mining & quarrying Industries extractives	Manufacturing Manufacturières	Electricity, gas and water Electricité, gaz et eau	Construction Construction	Wholesale/ retail trade, restaurants and hotels Commerce, restaurants, hôtels	Transport, storage & communication Transports, entrepôts, communications	Other activities Autres activités
United Rep. of Tanzania	1985	120621	50.8	0.2	5.5 [9]	0.9	1.7	11.8	5.8	23.3
Rép.−Unie de Tanzanie	1990	494999	47.2	1.0	3.7 [9]	1.5	2.6	11.4	7.3	25.3
	1991	690421	52.0	1.0	3.0 [9]	1.2	2.1	12.1	6.8	21.9
United States	1985	4016600	2.1	3.3	20.0	3.2	4.5	16.5	6.2	44.1
Etats Unis	# 1992	5937400	2.0	1.5	18.0	2.9	3.8	15.9	6.0	49.9
	1993	6260000	1.7	1.4	18.0	2.9	3.8	15.9	6.1	50.2
Uruguay	1985	479	13.6	0.2	29.4	3.4	3.0	12.5	6.0	31.9
Uruguay	1990	9698	11.5	0.2	26.2	2.8	3.1	12.2	6.5	37.5
	1991	19135	9.8	0.2	25.1	2.8	3.8	12.5	6.4	39.4
Uzbekistan	1990	32430	33.4	22.7 [7]	...	...	10.6	3.8	5.9	23.5
Ouzbékistan	1992	443887	35.4	26.6 [7]	...	...	9.5	5.5	5.2	17.7
	1993	5095202	27.9	22.4 [7]	...	...	9.0	6.2	5.5	29.0
Vanuatu	1985	12534	29.5	...	3.8	1.6	2.7	32.3	7.0	23.2
Vanuatu	1988	15006	19.5	...	4.7	1.4	5.7	33.1	8.1	27.5
	1989	16367	19.2	...	5.4	1.6	5.8	32.1	8.4	27.6
Venezuela	1985	464741	5.8	13.5 [28]	21.9 [29]	1.5 [15]	6.1	15.9	5.3	30.0
Venezuela	1993	5449109	5.0	15.3 [28]	17.7 [29]	2.7 [15]	6.3	19.1	7.4	26.6
	1994	8310682	4.8	16.3 [28]	17.0 [29]	2.8 [15]	5.0	18.7	7.2	28.3
Viet Nam	1986	512000	36.1	27.5 [7]	...	...	2.7	12.9	1.4	19.5
Viet Nam	# 1990	38166000	38.6	19.9 [7]	...	...	3.8	12.1	3.2	22.4
	1991	69959000	40.8	20.3 [7]	...	...	3.3	11.7	3.8	20.1
Yemen	1989	61406	23.9	6.4	9.5	1.9	4.6	12.7	8.5	32.5
Yémen	1990	77159	20.9	9.1	8.5	1.8	4.4	12.4	7.8	35.0
Yemen, former Arab Rep.	1985	30939	26.0	0.8	10.9	0.8	5.0	13.5	11.3	31.8
anc. Yémen rép. arabe	1986	37472	28.5	1.4	12.3	0.9	3.4	13.1	11.0	29.5
former Dem. Yemen	1987	391	11.9	7.3 [7]	...	...	8.2	12.9	8.2	51.4
ancienne Yémen dém.	1988	411	12.8	7.3 [7]	...	...	9.5	11.4	8.5	50.5
Yugoslavia, SFR †	1985	1195	11.5	2.8	34.5	2.2	6.9	10.9	7.4	23.7
Yougoslavie, SFR †	1989	235395	10.8	2.3	39.5	1.6	6.1	6.3	10.0	23.3
	1990	1147787	10.8	2.1	26.2	1.5	6.6	7.2	10.3	35.2
Zambia	1985	9351	8.7	24.9	18.9	1.2	4.0	9.1	5.8	27.5
Zambie	1990	123487	11.5	20.5	20.7	0.5	5.1	10.6	5.6	25.6
	1991	234504	12.0	14.4	26.3	0.8	4.7	10.2	6.7	24.8
Zimbabwe	1985	7295	18.0	4.6	20.4	2.0 [15]	2.1	10.7	5.9	36.4
Zimbabwe	1990	16674	14.3	4.1	24.8	2.4 [15]	2.2	9.4	6.4	36.5
	1991	21818	17.0	4.3	25.6	2.4 [15]	2.3	8.7	5.7	34.0

Source:
National accounts database of the Statistics Division of the
United Nations Secretariat.

† For detailed descriptions of data pertaining to
former Czechoslovakia, Germany, SFR Yugoslavia and former
USSR, see annex I − Country or area nomenclature, regional
and other groupings.

1 Restaurants and hotels are included in "other activities".
2 Gross domestic product in factor values.
3 Fiscal year beginning 1 July.
4 Including manufacturing.
5 Including electricity, gas and water.
6 The breakdown by kind of economic activity used in this table is
according to the classification NACE/CLIO.
7 Including manufacturing and electricity, gas and water.
8 Excluding banks and insurance companies registered in Cayman

Source:
Base de données sur les comptes nationaux de la division
de statistique du Secrétariat de l'ONU.

† Pour les descriptions en détails des données relatives
a l'ancienne Tchécoslovaquie, l'Allemagne, la Rfs
Yougoslavie et l'ancienne URSS, voir l'Annexe I −
Nomenclature des pays ou zones, groupements
regionaux et autres groupements.

1 Restaurants et hôtels sont incluses dans "autres activités".
2 Produit intérieur brut au coût de facteurs.
3 L'année fiscale commençant le 1er juillet.
4 Y compris les industries manufacturières.
5 Y compris l'électricité, le gaz et l'eau.
6 La ventilation par branche utilisée est conforme à la
nomenclature NACE/CLIO.
7 Y compris les industries manufacturières, l'électricité,
le gaz et l'eau.

22
Gross domestic product by kind of economic activity at current prices
Percentage distribution *[cont.]*
Produit intérieur brut par genre d'activité économique aux prix courants
Répartition en pourcentage *[suite]*

Islands but with no physical presence in the Islands.
9   Including handicrafts.
10   Including repair services.
11   Electricity only. Gas and water are included in "other activities".
12   Fiscal year ending 7 July.
13   Trasnport, storage and communication are included in "other activities".
14   Including quarrying (Netherlands Antilles: and mining).
15   Excluding gas (Hungary: included in manufacturing).
16   Fiscal year beginning 1 April.
17   Fiscal year beginning 21 March.
18   Including a statistical discrepancy.
19   Including gas and oil production.
20   Including construction.
21   Including non−monetary output.
22   Including basic petroleum manufacturing.
23   Fiscal year ending 15 July.
24   Including real estate brokers.
25   Thousand.
26   Contract construction only.
27   Fiscal year ending 30 June.
28   Including crude petroleum and natural gas production.
29   Including petroleum refining.

8   Non compris les banques et les compagnies d'assurances enregistrées aux îles Caïmanes, mais sans présence matérielle dans ce territoire.
9   Y compris l'artisanat.
10   Y compris les services de répartion.
11   Seulement électricité. Le gaz et l'eau sont incluses dans autres activités".
12   L'année fiscale finissant le 7 juillet.
13   Transports, entrepôts et communications sont incluses dans "autres activités".
14   Y compris les carrières (Antilles néerlandaises : industries extractives).
15   Non compris le gaz (Hongrie : est incluse dans manufacturières).
16   L'année fiscale commençant le 1er avril.
17   L'année fiscale commençant le 21 mars.
18   Y compris erreurs et omissions.
19   Y compris la production de gaz et de pétrole.
20   Y compris construction.
21   Y compris la production non commercialisée.
22   Y compris la production de pétrole.
23   L'année fiscale finissant le 15 juillet.
24   Y compris les agences immobilières.
25   Milliers.
26   Construction sous contrat seulement.
27   L'année fiscale finissant le 30 juin.
28   Y compris la production de pétrole brut et de gas naturel.
29   Y compris le raffinage du pétrole.

23
Relationships between the principal national accounting aggregates
Relations entre les principaux agrégats de comptabilité nationale
As percentage of GDP
En pourcentage du PIB

As percentage of GDP − En pourcentage du PIB

Country or area Pays ou zone	Year Année	GDP at current prices (Mil. nat.cur.) PIB aux prix courants (Mil. mon.nat.)	Plus: NFI from the rest of world Plus : Rev. net des facteurs reçu du reste du monde	Equals: Gross national product Égal : Produit national brut	Less: Consump. of Fixed Capital Moins : Consomm. de capital fixe	Equals: National Income Égal : Revenu national	Plus: Net Curr. transfer from the rest of the world Plus : Transferts courants nets reçus du reste du monde	Equals: National Disposable Income Égal : Revenu national disponible	Less: Final Consump-tion Moins : Consom-mation finale	Equals: Net savings Égal : Épargne nette
Algeria	1985	291597	−2.3	97.7	9.7	88.1	0.6	88.7	63.7	25.0
Algiers	1988	334607	−3.5	96.5	9.7	86.7	0.6	87.4	71.9	15.5
	1989	403460	−3.3	96.7	8.2	88.5	1.0	89.5	69.6	19.9
Angola	1985	205400	−4.4	95.6	...	...	−0.4	...	78.0	...
Angola	1989	278866	−10.5	89.5	...	...	−1.6	...	77.1	...
	1990	308062	−12.4	87.6	...	...	−4.2	...	73.2	...
Armenia	1985	8101	...	...	...	75.8	...	...	...	...
Arménie	1990	9693	...	...	...	72.0	...	...	...	...
	1991	11567	...	...	...	97.1	...	...	...	...
Australia [1]	1985	239970	−3.2	96.8	15.6	81.2	0.3	81.5	78.5	3.0
Australie [1]	1992	403852	−3.4	96.6	15.5	81.1	0.2	81.3	81.1	0.1
	1993	425566	−3.4	96.6	15.2	81.4	0.1	81.5	80.2	1.3
Austria	1985	1348425	−0.5	99.5	12.4	87.1	0.2	87.2	76.4	10.8
Autriche	1992	2046080	−0.5	99.5	12.3	87.2	−0.9	86.3	73.5	12.8
	1993	2117841	−0.4	99.6	12.8	86.8	−1.2	85.6	74.3	11.3
Bahamas	1990	3134	−4.3	95.7	...	...	0.4	...	87.8	...
Bahamas	1991	3090	−5.4	94.6	...	...	0.6	...	91.4	...
	1992	3059	−4.9	95.1	...	...	0.4	...	88.8	...
Bahrain	1985	1393	−7.9	92.1	14.6	77.5	−6.3	71.1	53.9	17.2
Bahrëin	1989	1348	−7.3	92.7	16.7	76.0	−5.6	70.5	63.9	6.5
	1990	1468	−8.8	91.2	15.6	75.6	−7.0	68.6	61.7	7.0
Bangladesh [1]	1985	466227	2.6	102.6	6.9	95.7	3.9	99.6	96.8	2.8
Bangladesh [1]	1992	947896	4.1	104.1	7.2	96.9	3.4	100.3	93.3	6.9
	1993	1030361	4.4	104.4	7.3	97.1	3.2	100.3	92.5	7.8
Belgium	1985	4745838	−1.6	98.4	9.6	88.8	−0.6	88.2	82.6	5.6
Belgique	1992	7101672	−0.6	99.4	9.7	89.7	−0.8	88.9	77.3	11.6
	1993	7285204	0.5	100.5	9.6	90.9	−1.0	89.9	77.2	12.7
Belize	1985	418	−4.7	95.3	7.0	88.3	...	...	...	...
Belize	1992	936	−2.4	97.6	6.3	91.3	...	...	...	...
	1993	995	−2.3	97.7	6.5	91.3	...	...	...	...
Benin	1987	469554	−1.8	98.2	...	...	8.7	...	96.5	...
Bénin	1988	482434	−2.1	97.9	...	...	9.3	...	95.3	...
	1989	487525	−2.5	97.5	...	...	10.9	...	95.9	...
Bermuda [2]	1985	1174	3.2	103.2	...	...	...	...	...	...
Bermudes [2]	1991	1680	0.1	100.1	...	...	...	...	...	...
	1992	1698	0.9	100.9	...	...	...	...	...	...
Bhutan	1985	2392	−18.8	81.2	5.8	75.4	5.0	80.5	86.4	−6.0
Bhoutan	1991	5569	−7.9	92.1	9.3	82.8	4.0	86.8	78.6	8.2
	1992	6337	−6.9	93.1	9.4	83.7	...	...	...	...
Bolivia	1985	2867	−5.8	94.2	0.0	94.2	1.3	95.5	70.9	24.7
Bolivie	1986	8924	−3.4	96.6	0.0	96.6	1.7	98.4	77.5	20.8
Botswana [1]	1985	2421	−13.3	86.7	14.5	72.2	3.0	75.2	59.2	16.0
Botswana [1]	1986	2810	−9.0	91.0	15.4	75.6	1.6	77.2	60.9	16.4
	1987	3796	−12.3	87.7	15.2	72.6	−3.1	69.5	57.1	12.3
Brazil	1985	1	−5.4	94.6	...	...	0.1	...	75.6	...
Brésil	1991	164486	−2.7	97.3	...	...	...	...	...	...
	1992	1846813	−2.3	97.7	...	...	...	...	...	...
Burkina Faso	1984	390565	−0.4	99.6	...	...	11.5	...	98.6	...
Burkina Faso	1985	455882	−0.4	99.6	...	...	9.9	...	103.3	...
Burundi	1985	141347	−1.0	99.0	2.5	96.5	1.4	97.9	93.6	4.4
Burundi	1991	211898	−1.0	99.0	...	...	...	...	...	...
	1992	226384	−3.9	98.7	...	...	...	...	...	...

23
Relationships between the principal national accounting aggregates
As percentage of GDP *[cont.]*
Relations entre les princiterpaux agrégates de comptabilité nationale
En pourcentage du PIB *[suite]*

As percentage of GDP – En pourcentage du PIB

Country or area Pays ou zone	Year Année	GDP at current prices (Mil. nat.cur.) PIB aux prix courants (Mil. mon.nat.)	Plus: NFI from the rest of world Plus : Rev. net des facteurs reçu du reste du monde	Equals: Gross national product Égal : Produit national brut	Less: Consump. of Fixed Capital Moins : Consomm. de capital fixe	Equals: National Income Égal : Revenu national	Plus: Net Curr. transfer from the rest of the world Plus : Transferts courants nets reçus du reste du monde	Equals: National Disposable Income Égal : Revenu national disponible	Less: Final Consump-tion Moins : Consom-mation finale	Equals: Net savings Égal : Épargne nette
Cameroon [1]	1985	4106200	−3.3	96.7	4.2	92.5	−0.3	92.2	73.9	18.2
Cameroun [1]	1987	3644500	−2.7	97.3	6.4	90.9	−2.0	88.8	79.0	9.8
	1988	3513000	−3.4	96.6	6.6	90.0	−1.7	88.3	80.0	8.3
Canada	1985	474339	−3.0	97.0	11.8	85.2 [3]	−0.1	85.1	77.2	7.8
Canada	1992	681344	−3.6	96.4	12.4	83.6 [3]	−0.2	83.5	83.0	0.4
	1993	704829	−3.4	96.6	12.3	83.9 [3]	−0.1	83.7	82.8	0.9
Cape Verde	1985	13081	−2.2	97.8	...	...	52.3	...	...	...
Cap−Vert	1987	17984	−0.8	99.2	...	...	40.5	...	...	...
	1988	20640	1.6	101.6	...	...	37.5	...	...	...
Cayman Islands	1985	264	−7.6	92.4	7.6	84.8	2.3	87.1	79.2	8.0
Iles Caïmanes	1990	590	−10.3	89.7	7.1	82.5	2.5	85.1	76.8	8.3
	1991	616	−9.4	90.6	7.6	83.0	2.4	85.4	77.6	7.8
Chile	1985	2651937	−12.2	84.5	...	...	0.8	...	77.7	...
Chili	1992	15499840	−4.5	95.5	...	...	1.0	...	71.8	...
	1993	18453550	−3.4	96.6	...	...	0.8	...	73.5	...
China	1985	896440	0.3	100.3	9.3	91.0	0.1	91.1	64.4	26.7
Chine	1992	2663540	0.1	100.1	9.4	90.7	0.2	90.9	59.9	31.0
	1993	3451510	−0.1	99.9	10.5	89.4	0.2	89.6	58.5	31.1
Colombia	1985	4966000	−4.1	95.9	...	...	1.3	...	80.1	...
Colombie	1991	26107000	−4.7	95.3	...	...	4.1	...	76.7	...
	1992	33143000	−3.9	96.1	...	...	3.6	...	81.0	...
Congo	1985	970850	−10.6	89.4	17.2	72.2	−1.3	70.9	58.0	12.9
Congo	1987	690523	−11.1	88.9	23.8	65.1	−1.6	63.5	77.2	−13.6
	1988	658964	−13.7	86.3	22.0	64.4	−1.8	62.5	81.2	−18.7
Costa Rica	1985	197920	−7.1	92.9	2.8	90.1	1.4	91.5	75.9	15.6
Costa Rica	1992	904102	−2.8	97.2	2.5	94.7	2.1	96.9	76.2	20.7
	1993	1074411	−2.6	97.4	2.4	95.0	1.9	96.9	76.6	20.3
Côte d'Ivoire	1981	2291401	−7.5	92.5	9.2	83.3	−3.5	79.8	82.6	−2.9
Côte d'Ivoire	1982	2486544	−8.7	91.3	8.4	83.0	−4.2	78.7	81.2	−2.4
Cyprus	1985	1481	1.7	101.7	10.8	90.9	1.7	92.6	78.0	12.9 [3]
Chypre	1991	2666	1.7	101.7	10.7	91.0	0.7	91.7	84.3	7.6 [3]
	1992	3081	1.5	101.5	10.7	90.8	0.5	91.4	82.8	8.7 [3]
Denmark	1985	615072	−4.3	95.7	8.9	86.8	−0.7	86.1	80.1	6.0
Danemark	1992	851253	−3.7	96.3	9.4	86.9	−0.7	86.2	77.8	8.4
	1993	873237	−3.3	96.7	9.6	87.1	−0.8	86.3	78.8	7.6
Djibouti	1983	59997	−9.8	90.2	...	...	...	...	...	...
Djibouti	1984	60234	−11.0	89.0	...	...	...	...	...	...
Dominica	1985	266	−1.3	98.7	...	...	...	...	...	...
Dominique	1990	452	1.1	101.1	...	...	...	...	...	...
	1991	479	1.0	101.0	...	...	...	...	...	...
Dominican Republic	1985	13972	−5.1	94.9	6.0	89.0	7.9	96.9	85.5	11.4
Rép. dominicaine	1992	112369	−2.7	97.3	6.0	91.3	4.8	96.2	86.3	10.4
	1993	120572	−4.1	95.9	5.9	89.9	4.6	94.5	82.6	12.6
Ecuador	1985	1110000	−7.4	92.6	12.3	80.4	0.2	80.5	75.9	4.6
Equateur	1992	19414000	−4.8	95.2	15.5	79.7	1.0	80.7	75.0	5.7
	1993	27451000	−4.0	96.0	15.9	80.1	0.9	80.9	78.3	2.7
Egypt [1]	1980	17149	4.3	104.3	...	...	1.5	...	81.6	...
Egypte [1]	1981	20222	1.3	101.3	...	...	1.3	...	81.7	...
El Salvador	1985	14331	−2.5	97.5	4.1	93.4	6.0	99.4	96.7	2.7
El Salvador	1991	47792	−1.7	98.3	4.1	94.2	12.1	106.3	98.5	7.7
	1992	54853	−0.9	99.1	4.1	95.0	14.3	109.3	99.5	9.7
Estonia	1985	495	0.0	100.0	20.2	79.8	0.0	79.8	80.4	−0.6
Estonie	# 1992	14255	2.6	102.6	4.5	98.1	4.9	103.0	71.9	31.1
	# 1993	21918	0.4	100.4	12.2	88.2	6.4	94.6	76.5	17.5 [3]
Ethiopia incl. Eritrea [4]	1985	9924	−0.7	99.3	...	...	...	...	...	...
Ethiopie y comp.Erythrée [4]	1991	13332	−0.7	99.3	...	...	...	...	...	...
	1992	13508	−0.6	99.4	...	...	...	...	...	...

23
Relationships between the principal national accounting aggregates
As percentage of GDP *[cont.]*
Relations entre les printicpaux agrégates de comptabilité nationale
En pourcentage du PIB *[suite]*

As percentage of GDP – En pourcentage du PIB

Country or area Pays ou zone	Year Année	GDP at current prices (Mil. nat.cur.) PIB aux prix courants (Mil. mon.nat.)	Plus: NFI from the rest of world Plus : Rev. net des facteurs reçu du reste du monde	Equals: Gross national product Égal : Produit national brut	Less: Consump. of Fixed Capital Moins : Consomm. de capital fixe	Equals: National Income Égal : Revenu national	Plus: Net Curr. transfer from the rest of the world Plus : Transferts courants nets reçus du reste du monde	Equals: National Disposable Income Égal : Revenu national disponible	Less: Final Consump- tion Moins : Consom- mation finale	Equals: Net savings Égal : Épargne nette
Fiji	1985	1316	-2.7	97.3	7.2	90.0	-0.5	89.6	82.9	6.7
Fidji	1992	2377	-1.7	98.3	7.7	90.6	-0.8	89.8	85.4	4.4
	1993	2540	-0.6	99.4	7.2	92.2	-0.5	91.8	86.7	5.0
Finland	1985	331628	-2.0	98.0	14.6	83.3	-0.4	82.9	74.7	8.2
Finlande	1992	476778	-4.2	95.8	17.2	78.7	-1.8	76.9	81.9	-5.1
	1993	480470	-4.8	95.2	17.4	77.8	-1.6	76.2	80.0	-3.8
France	1985	4700143	-0.5	99.5	12.5	86.9	-0.1	86.8	80.5	6.4
France	1993	7082790	-0.8	99.2	13.1	86.2	-0.4	85.8	80.7	5.1
	1994	7376050	-0.7	99.3	12.9	86.4	-0.4	86.0	79.9	6.1
French Guiana	1985	3173	-4.8	95.2	...	...	45.3	...	110.2	...
Guyane française	1990	6526	-1.9	98.1	...	...	36.3	...	99.4	...
	1991	7404	-5.8	94.2	...	...	35.9	...	94.5	...
Gabon	1985	1645800	-5.6	94.4	9.9	84.5	-3.2	81.3	49.1	32.3
Gabon	1988	1013600	-7.4	92.6	12.0	80.6	-7.6	73.0	69.9	3.1
	1989	1168066	-8.6	91.4	14.5	76.9	-6.1	70.8	66.8	4.0
Gambia [1]	1985	1085	-6.1	93.9	11.5	82.4	17.3	99.7	...	...
Gambie [1]	1990	2630	-2.4	97.6	10.4	87.2	17.0	104.2	...	...
	1991	2948	-2.6	97.4	10.2	87.2	18.4	105.6	...	...
Germany † · Allemagne † F.R. Germany	1985	1823180	0.6	100.6	12.9	87.7	-1.7	86.0	76.9	9.1
R.f. Allemagne	1992	2813000	0.2	100.2	12.8	87.5	-5.6	81.8	72.5	9.4
	1993	2853700	-0.4	99.6	13.3	86.3	-5.8	80.6	73.5	7.1
Ghana	1985	343048	-1.7	98.3	4.8	93.6	2.2	95.7	92.4	3.4
Ghana	1991	2574800	-1.7	98.3	5.1	93.2	...	...	...	...
	1992	3008800	-1.5	98.5	5.2	93.3	...	...	...	...
Greece	1985	4617816	-0.7	99.3	8.7	90.5	4.2	94.7	85.9	4.4 [3]
Grèce	1992	14832170	-0.3	99.7	8.6	91.1	5.9	96.9	91.7	6.7 [3]
	1993	16760352	0.6	100.6	8.6	91.9	6.6	98.6	91.6	6.9 [3]
Grenada	1985	311	-1.1	98.9	...	...	...	...	...	...
Grenade	1986	350	-0.8	99.2	...	...	...	...	...	...
Guadeloupe	1985	9802	-3.7	96.3	...	...	37.1	...	129.8	...
Guadeloupe	1990	15201	-2.5	97.5	...	...	37.3	...	123.6	...
	1991	16415	-3.4	96.6	...	...	35.4	...	118.3	...
Guatemala	1985	11180	-3.0	97.0	...	...	0.3	...	90.1	...
Guatemala	1992	53949	-0.6	99.4	...	...	3.8	...	91.5	...
	1993	63563	-0.2	99.8	...	...	3.2	...	91.2	...
Guinea–Bissau	1986	46973	-1.7	98.3	...	...	2.9	...	102.8	...
Guinée–Bissau	1987	92375	-0.5	99.5	...	...	4.1	...	100.8	...
Guyana	1985	1964	-12.5	87.5	6.4	81.1	1.0	82.1	89.4	-7.2
Guyana	1992	46734	-17.7	82.3	...	...	...	...	...	...
	1993	56647	-17.6	82.4	...	...	...	...	...	...
Haiti [5]	1985	10047	-1.0	99.0	2.7	96.3	7.2	103.6	94.3	9.3
Haïti [5]	1992	15368	-0.7	99.3	1.3	98.1	4.4	102.5	97.0	5.5
	1993	18124	-0.4	99.6	1.1	98.5	5.6	104.2	98.2	5.9
Honduras	1985	7279	-5.3	94.7	6.7	88.0	4.0	92.0	87.4	4.6
Honduras	1992	18800	-9.9	90.1	6.5	83.7	6.4	90.0	78.1	11.9
	1993	22444	-9.3	90.7	6.1	84.6	5.0	89.5	76.9	12.6
Iceland	1985	120899	-4.0	96.0	12.8	83.2	-0.0	83.2	81.4	1.8
Islande	1992	397917	-2.8	97.2	12.9	84.2	-0.1	84.1	82.8	1.3
	1993	410755	-2.9	97.1	13.3	83.8	-0.1	83.6	81.1	2.6
India [2]	1985	2622430	-0.5	99.5	10.0	89.5	1.1	90.5	78.6	9.8 [3]
Inde [2]	1992	7028290	-1.7	98.3	10.3	88.0	1.2	89.2	70.9	9.7 [3]
	1993	7863550	-1.5	98.5	10.2	88.3	1.0	89.3	71.9	10.0 [3]
Indonesia	1985	96997000	-4.1	95.9	5.0	90.9	...	...	...	...
Indonésie	1991	227502000	-4.8	95.2	5.0	90.2	...	...	...	...
	1992	260786000	-4.7	95.3	5.0	90.3	...	...	...	...

23
Relationships between the principal national accounting aggregates
As percentage of GDP *[cont.]*
Relations entre les printicpaux agrégates de comptabilité nationale
En pourcentage du PIB *[suite]*

As percentage of GDP – En pourcentage du PIB

Country or area Pays ou zone	Year Année	GDP at current prices (Mil. nat.cur.) PIB aux prix courants (Mil. mon.nat.)	Plus: NFI from the rest of world Plus : Rev. net des facteurs reçu du reste du monde	Equals: Gross national product Égal : Produit national brut	Less: Consump. of Fixed Capital Moins : Consomm. de capital fixe	Equals: National Income Égal : Revenu national	Plus: Net Curr. transfer from the rest of the world Plus : Transferts courants nets reçus du reste du monde	Equals: National Disposable Income Égal : Revenu national disponible	Less: Final Consump-tion Moins : Consom-mation finale	Equals: Net savings Égal : Épargne nette
Iran, Islamic Rep. of [6]	1985	15775000	−0.2	99.8	11.8	88.0	0.0	88.0	76.5	8.9 [3]
Iran, Rép. islamique d' [6]	1991	50107000	0.9	100.9	...	...	...	...	...	...
	1992	67811000	0.3	100.3	...	...	...	...	...	...
Iraq	1985	15494	−3.6	96.4	8.3	88.1	−1.0	87.1	80.9	6.2
Iraq	1990	23297	−3.3	96.7	8.8	87.9	−0.2	87.6	76.8	10.8
	1991	19940	−3.3	96.7	9.6	87.1	0.6	87.7	83.5	4.3
Ireland	1985	17790	−11.0	89.0	9.7	79.3	5.2	84.5	78.1	6.3
Irlande #	1992	29987	−11.0	89.0	9.6	79.4	4.3	83.7	74.8	8.9
	1993	32290	−11.5	88.5	9.4	79.0	4.3	83.3	71.9	11.4
Israel	1985	30355	−8.0	92.0	15.6	76.4	20.8	97.2	88.6	8.6
Israël	1992	170012	−2.9	97.1	13.2	83.9	9.7	93.7	84.0	9.7
	1993	195797	−2.7	97.3	13.7	83.6	9.5	93.1	86.5	6.6
Italy	1985	810580000	−0.7	99.3	12.4	87.0	0.2	87.1	77.9	9.2
Italie	1992	1504323000	−1.7	98.3	12.0	86.3	−0.6	85.7	80.5	5.2
	1993	1560114000	−1.6	98.4	12.3	86.1	−0.8	85.3	79.6	5.7
Jamaica	1985	11203	−13.1	86.9	9.7	77.3	7.4	84.6	84.9	−0.3
Jamaïque	1988	18748	−10.5	89.5	7.3	82.2	12.6	94.8	77.2	17.6
	1989	22224	−11.1	88.9	7.9	81.1	7.9	89.0	76.5	12.5
Japan	1985	320419000	0.4	100.4	13.6	86.7 [3]	−0.1	86.6	68.5	18.1
Japon	1992	463145000	0.9	100.9	15.7	84.9 [3]	−0.1	84.8	66.5	18.3
	1993	465972000	0.9	100.9	15.7	84.6 [3]	−0.1	84.5	67.7	16.8
Jordan	1985	1970	−0.2	99.8	10.0	89.7	28.7	118.4	117.4	1.0
Jordanie	1991	2778	−8.0	92.0	10.5	81.5	20.6	102.1	117.9	−15.8
	1992	3257	−5.7	94.3	10.6	83.7	22.8	106.5	116.4	−9.9
Kenya	1985	5043	−3.6	96.4	...	...	1.0	...	75.5	...
Kenya	1992	12787	−4.9	95.1	...	...	5.2	...	82.4	...
	1993	16063	−7.0	93.0	...	...	4.4	...	78.9	...
Korea, Republic of	1985	82062000	−3.4	96.6	10.0	86.6	1.2	87.8	68.6	19.2
Corée, Rép. de	1992	240392000	−0.7	99.3	10.0	89.3	0.2	89.6	64.8	24.8
	1993	265548000	−0.6	99.4	10.1	89.3	0.4	89.7	64.9	24.8
Kuwait	1985	6450	21.5	121.5	7.4	114.1	−7.3	106.8	70.2	36.6
Koweït	1992	5518	27.0	127.0	9.1	118.0	...	...	95.4	...
	1993	6766	18.5	118.5	7.7	110.8	...	...	69.6	...
Latvia	1985	42	−5.1	94.9	10.4	84.5	...	...	...	...
Lettonie	1992	1005	0.1	100.1	1.5	98.6	7.0	105.7	51.9	53.8
	1993	1467	−0.1	99.9	9.8	90.1	3.5	93.7	74.6	19.1
Lesotho	1985	551	93.3	193.3	...	...	29.8	...	176.7	...
Lesotho	1992	2184	59.2	159.2	...	...	59.8	...	135.9	...
	1993	2587	53.8	153.8	...	...	50.1	...	125.9	...
Liberia	1985	1055	−11.7	88.3	8.1	80.2	...	...	...	...
Libéria	1988	1158	−15.8	84.2	8.3	75.9	...	...	...	...
	1989	1194	−15.1	84.9	8.5	76.4	...	...	...	...
Libyan Arab Jamah.	1984	8013	−7.3	92.7	5.7	87.0	−0.3	86.7	72.2	14.5
Jaman. arabe libyenne	1985	8277	−3.3	96.7	5.8	90.9	−0.2	90.7	69.2	21.4
Luxembourg	1985	205255	40.7	140.7	11.7	129.0	−2.2	126.9	74.5	52.4
Luxembourg	1991	318804	35.8	135.8	10.7	125.2	−2.2	123.0	74.3	48.7
	1992	339450	36.1	136.1	10.6	125.5	−2.5	123.0	73.4	49.6
Malawi	1985	1929	−4.7	95.3	5.7	89.6	...	...	...	...
Malawi	1992	6873	−2.0	98.0	...	...	...	...	...	...
	1993	9330	−1.8	98.2	...	...	...	...	...	...
Malaysia	1985	77470	−7.1	92.9	...	92.9	−0.0	92.9	67.3	25.6
Malaisie	1991	129559	−4.6	95.4	...	95.4	0.1	95.4	68.9	26.5
	1992	147784	−5.1	94.9	...	94.9	0.1	95.0	64.5	30.5
Mali	1985	520200	0.1	100.1	...	...	10.7	...	104.1	...
Mali	1991	691400	−1.3	98.7	4.0	94.8	13.2	108.0	100.4	7.6
	1992	737400	−1.2	98.8	3.5	95.3	11.4	106.7	96.4	10.2

23
Relationships between the principal national accounting aggregates
As percentage of GDP *[cont.]*
Relations entre les printicpaux agrégates de comptabilité nationale
En pourcentage du PIB *[suite]*

As percentage of GDP – En pourcentage du PIB

Country or area Pays ou zone	Year Année	GDP at current prices (Mil. nat.cur.) PIB aux prix courants (Mil. mon.nat.)	Plus: NFI from the rest of world Plus: Rev. net des facteurs reçu du reste du monde	Equals: Gross national product Égal: Produit national brut	Less: Consump. of Fixed Capital Moins: Consomm. de capital fixe	Equals: National Income Égal: Revenu national	Plus: Net Curr. transfer from the rest of the world Plus: Transferts courants nets reçus du reste du monde	Equals: National Disposable Income Égal: Revenu national disponible	Less: Final Consump-tion Moins: Consom-mation finale	Equals: Net savings Égal: Épargne nette
Malta	1985	476	8.1	108.1	4.5	103.6	2.6	106.3	87.7	18.6
Malte	1991	807	6.2	106.2	4.7	101.5	2.0	103.5	79.5	24.0
	1992	875	4.8	104.8	4.8	99.9	1.3	101.3	79.5	21.7
Martinique	1985	12484	−3.6	96.4	...	...	32.6	...	121.1	...
Martinique	1990	19320	−4.2	95.8	...	...	33.7	...	113.3	...
	1991	20787	−4.4	95.6	...	...	30.7	...	112.8	...
Mauritania	1985	52665	−10.1	89.9	...	...	16.0	...	89.6	...
Mauritanie	1988	72635	−5.6	94.4	...	...	7.9	...	93.7	...
	1989	83500	−3.6	96.4	...	...	9.0	...	...	...
Mauritius	1985	16618	−4.2	95.8	...	95.8	3.3	99.1	78.4	20.7
Maurice	1992	47926	0.4	100.4	...	100.4	3.0	103.3	74.8	28.6
	1993	54928	0.1	100.1	...	100.1	3.2	103.3	75.8	27.5
Mexico	1985	47392	−4.5	95.5	11.2	84.3	0.7	85.0	73.7	11.2
Mexique	1992	1019156	−2.6	97.4	9.6	87.8	0.9	88.7	82.3	6.4
	1993	1127584	−2.7	97.3	10.0	87.3	0.8	88.0	82.3	5.8
Morocco	1985	129510	−5.9	94.1	...	...	7.9	...	81.1	...
Maroc	1992	241220	−3.6	96.4	...	...	8.6	...	82.8	...
	1993	247680	−4.4	95.6	...	...	8.1	...	84.2	...
Mozambique	1985	147000	0.0	100.0	2.7	97.3	...	...	...	...
Mozambique	1986	167000	0.6	100.6	...	...	...	...	...	...
Myanmar [2]	1985	55989	−1.0	99.0	9.0	89.9	...	...	...	...
Myanmar [2]	1991	178553	−0.2	99.8	5.2	94.7	...	...	...	...
	1992	230935	−0.1	99.9	4.5	95.5	...	...	...	...
Namibia	1985	2973	−21.1	78.9	...	...	21.1	...	78.1	...
Namibie	1992	7838	1.4	101.4	...	...	12.8	...	88.9	...
	1993	8390	1.9	101.9	...	...	9.9	...	89.1	...
Nepal [7]	1985	44417	1.5	101.5	4.6	96.9	0.2	97.1	86.0	11.1
Népal [7]	1989	77740	2.0	102.0	4.8	97.1	0.2	97.3	89.9	7.4
	1990	91008	2.1	102.1	5.0	97.2	0.2	97.3	92.7	4.7
Netherlands	1985	425350	−0.0	100.0	10.9	89.1	−0.5	88.6	75.2	13.4
Pays–Bas	1992	563080	−0.4	99.6	11.5	88.1	−1.0	87.1	75.0	12.1
	1993	574330	−0.1	99.9	11.6	88.3	−1.2	87.1	75.5	11.5
Netherlands Antilles	1981	2404	10.4	110.4	7.8	102.6	9.2	111.8	97.8	14.0
Antilles néerlandaises	1982	2558	11.9	111.9	8.1	103.9	12.8	116.7	102.3	14.3
New Zealand [2]	1985	45777	−5.5	94.5	8.4	86.1	0.5	86.6	76.9	9.7
Nouvelle–Zélande [2]	1992	76111	−4.0	96.0	9.5	86.5	0.5	87.0	77.9	9.1
	1993	80865	−4.0	96.0	9.3	86.8	0.4	87.2	75.4	11.8
Nicaragua	1982	28350	−4.9	95.1	4.2	91.0	...	...	...	...
Nicaragua	1983	32920	−2.0	98.0	4.5	93.5	...	...	...	...
Niger	1983	687142	−3.1	96.9	9.3	87.6	1.1	88.7	88.8	−0.2
Niger	1984	638406	−3.8	96.2	10.4	85.7	1.6	87.4	88.2	−0.8
Nigeria	1985	72355	−2.4	97.6	6.1	91.5	−1.1	90.3	84.9	5.5
Nigéria	1992	549809	−11.7	88.3	3.0	85.3	2.3	87.6	77.2	10.4
	1993	697095	−10.5	89.5	2.5	87.0	2.6	89.6	85.7	3.9
Norway	1985	500200	−1.9	98.1	13.3	84.8	−1.0	83.8	67.6	16.3
Norvège	1992	702954	−3.1	96.9	14.8	82.0	−1.6	80.5	74.3	6.1
	1993	733664	−3.1	96.9	14.9	82.0	−1.4	80.7	73.6	7.1
Oman	1985	3454	−11.6	88.4	...	...	...	...	...	...
Oman	1991	3917	−10.8	89.2	...	...	...	...	...	...
	1992	4417	−13.0	87.0	...	...	...	...	...	...
Pakistan [1]	1985	514532	8.0	108.0	6.1	101.9	...	...	89.1	...
Pakistan [1]	1992	1341955	1.1	101.1	6.3	94.8	...	...	85.2	...
	1993	1564974	0.9	100.9	6.4	94.6	...	...	84.4	...
Panama	1985	4948	−0.9	99.1	8.1	91.0	2.2	93.2	82.1	11.1
Panama	1992	6015	−2.9	97.1	8.1	89.1	5.0	94.1	76.7	17.4
	1993	6565	−0.8	99.2	7.7	91.5	2.7	94.2	76.1	18.2

23
Relationships between the principal national accounting aggregates
As percentage of GDP [cont.]
Relations entre les printicpaux agrégates de comptabilité nationale
En pourcentage du PIB [suite]

As percentage of GDP − En pourcentage du PIB

Country or area Pays ou zone	Year Année	GDP at current prices (Mil. nat.cur.) PIB aux prix courants (Mil. mon.nat.)	Plus: NFI from the rest of world Plus : Rev. net des facteurs reçu du reste du monde	Equals: Gross national product Égal : Produit national brut	Less: Consump. of Fixed Capital Moins : Consomm. de capital fixe	Equals: National Income Égal : Revenu national	Plus: Net Curr. transfer from the rest of the world Plus : Transferts courants nets reçus du reste du monde	Equals: National Disposable Income Égal : Revenu national disponible	Less: Final Consumption Moins : Consommation finale	Equals: Net savings Égal : Épargne nette
Papua New Guinea	1985	2403	−3.7	96.3	9.3	87.0	5.4	92.5	90.4	2.0
Papua New Guinea	1991	3606	−3.3	96.7	11.6	85.2	3.4	88.6	82.5	6.1
	1992	4140	−2.7	97.3	...	...	...	...	...	...
Paraguay	1985	1393890	−0.9	99.1	10.4	88.6	0.0	88.6	83.2	5.4
Paraguay	1991	8280772	1.4	101.4	8.3	93.1	0.0	93.1	84.9	8.2
	1992	9670838	0.2	100.2	8.0	92.3	0.0	92.3	85.2	7.1
Peru	1985	197 [8]	−5.1	94.9	5.6	89.4	0.5	89.9	73.7	16.2
Pérou #	1992	52062	−2.1	97.9	...	...	...	...	82.4	...
	1993	80529	...	...	...	...	...	...	79.9	...
Philippines	1985	571883	−2.8	97.2	9.9	87.3	1.2	88.5	81.2	6.5 [3]
Philippines	1993	1475042	3.0	103.0	9.0	94.1	1.2	95.2	85.5	7.8 [3]
	1994	1687607	3.8	103.8	10.6	93.2	1.6	94.8	84.3	9.1 [3]
Portugal	1985	3523945	−5.6	94.4	...	94.4	10.0	104.4	83.4	21.0
Portugal #	1992	12828682	0.6	100.6	...	100.6	6.8	107.5	81.8	25.7
	1993	13625623	−0.1	99.9	...	99.9	6.8	106.7	83.0	23.7
Puerto Rico [1]	1985	21969	−27.8	72.2	6.0	66.2	17.0	83.2	86.4	−3.2
Porto Rico [1]	1992	36847	−32.0	68.0	6.7	61.2	13.7	75.0	75.5	−0.5
	1993	39265	−32.6	67.4	6.7	60.7	13.9	74.5	74.5	0.1
Republic of Moldova	1985	9	...	...	17.8	82.2	...	...	...	...
Rép. de Moldova	1990	13	...	...	14.3	85.7	...	...	...	...
	1991	23	...	...	...	81.5	...	...	...	...
Réunion	1985	17054	−1.3	98.7	...	98.7	42.5	141.2	118.9	22.3
Réunion	1990	28374	−2.5	97.5	...	97.5	44.3	141.7	108.1	33.6
	1991	31339	0.7	100.7	...	100.7	42.7	143.4	103.5	39.9
Russian Federation	1985	476000	...	81.5	...	...	...	...	...	...
Féderation de Russie	1991	1300000	...	90.5	...	...	...	...	...	...
	1992	18063000	...	91.9	...	...	...	...	...	...
Rwanda	1985	173700	−1.0	99.0	5.4	93.6	3.8	97.4	91.8	5.6
Rwanda	1988	177940	−2.0	98.0	6.9	91.0	2.9	93.9	93.6	0.4
	1989	190220	−1.2	98.8	7.6	91.2	2.4	93.6	95.4	−1.7
Saint Kitts−Nevis	1983	154	−1.4	98.6	...	...	19.8	...	...	...
Saint−Kitts−et−Nevis	1984	167	−0.5	99.5	...	...	18.9	...	...	...
Saint Vincent−Grenadines	1985	305	−1.7	98.3	...	...	...	...	...	...
St.−Vincent−et−Gren.	1989	469	−4.5	95.5	...	...	...	...	...	...
	1990	525	−5.8	94.2	...	...	...	...	...	...
Saudi Arabia [1]	1983	371200	4.3	104.3	...	...	...	...	71.5	...
Arabie saoudite [1]	1984	330900	4.4	104.4	...	...	...	...	79.1	...
Senegal	1985	1152000	−3.2	96.8	13.7	83.1	5.9	89.0	...	...
Sénégal	1986	1307000	−4.2	95.8	13.7	82.0	5.4	87.4	...	...
	1987	1374600	−4.9	95.1	6.5	88.6	5.3	93.9	...	...
Seychelles	1985	1205	−3.5	96.5	6.2	90.3	8.0	98.3	92.8	5.5
Seychelles	1991	1980	−4.1	95.9	11.1	84.9	6.7	91.6	78.9	12.7
	1992	2221	−3.1	96.9	...	...	...	...	...	...
Sierra Leone [1]	1985	7481	0.8	100.8	6.8	94.0	1.4	95.4	90.0	5.3
Sierra Leone [1]	1989	82837	0.8	100.8	5.9	94.9	0.5	95.5	91.3	4.2
	1990	150175	−5.0	95.0	5.6	89.4	0.7	90.1	88.4	1.7
Singapore	1985	38924	3.6	103.6	14.9	88.7	−1.2	87.5	59.4	27.6 [3]
Singapour	1992	79083	1.7	101.7	13.9	87.8	−1.2	86.6	52.4	34.2 [3]
	1993	89007	1.4	101.4	13.7	87.7	−1.3	86.4	52.1	33.8 [3]
Solomon Islands	1985	235	−4.3	95.7	6.7	89.0	5.9	94.9	92.2	2.7
Iles Salomon	1988	131	8.8	108.8	10.8	98.0	1.6	99.6	88.9	10.6
	1989	156	8.5	108.5	14.9	93.6	1.5	95.0	85.6	9.4
Somalia	1985	87290	−2.2	97.8	...	...	10.1	...	101.1	...
Somalie	1986	118781	−3.7	96.3	...	...	14.2	...	98.8	...
	1987	169608	−3.2	96.8	...	...	21.3	...	99.9	...

23
Relationships between the principal national accounting aggregates
As percentage of GDP *[cont.]*
  Relations entre les printicpaux agrégates de comptabilité nationale
  En pourcentage du PIB *[suite]*

As percentage of GDP – En pourcentage du PIB

Country or area Pays ou zone	Year Année	GDP at current prices (Mil. nat.cur.) PIB aux prix courants (Mil. mon.nat.)	Plus: NFI from the rest of world Plus : Rev. net des facteurs reçu du reste du monde	Equals: Gross national product Égal : Produit national brut	Less: Consump. of Fixed Capital Moins : Consomm. de capital fixe	Equals: National Income Égal : Revenu national	Plus: Net Curr. transfer from the rest of the world Plus : Transferts courants nets reçus du reste du monde	Equals: National Disposable Income Égal : Revenu national disponible	Less: Final Consumption Moins : Consommation finale	Equals: Net savings Égal : Épargne nette
South Africa	1985	123126	−4.9	95.1	16.0	79.2	0.0	79.2	71.0	8.6
Afrique du Sud	1991	297895	−3.2	96.8	15.8	81.0	0.1	81.1	81.0	2.4
	1992	327068	−2.8	97.2	15.3	81.9	0.1	82.0	83.5	0.9
Spain	1985	28200900	−1.2	98.8	12.7	86.1	0.6	86.7	78.8	7.9
Espagne	1992	59002100	−1.2	98.8	10.9	87.9	0.4	88.3	80.1	8.2
	1993	60904300	−1.1	98.9	11.4	87.5	0.5	88.0	80.7	7.2
Sri Lanka	1985	157763	−2.2	97.8	4.8	93.0	4.6	97.6	87.0	8.9 [3]
Sri Lanka	1992	421755	−1.9	98.1	4.6	93.6	4.8	98.4	87.1	12.7 [3]
	1993	499708	−1.2	98.8	4.8	94.0	5.4	99.4	85.9	14.4 [3]
Sudan [1]	1983	11329	−2.7	97.3	11.0	86.3	4.5	90.8	93.4	−2.6
Soudan [1]	1984	6721	−1.7	98.3	9.5	88.8	5.9	94.7	91.5	3.2
Suriname	1985	1747	−0.1	99.9	11.1	88.8	−0.5	88.3	88.7	−0.4
Suriname	1991	3708	−0.5	99.5	11.2	88.2	−0.4	87.9	81.3	6.5
	1992	5010	−0.3	99.7	11.3	88.4	−0.3	88.2	77.2	11.0
Swaziland [9]	1985	803	9.5	109.5	...	...	2.5	...	95.3	...
Swaziland [9]	1987	1118	0.1	100.1	...	...	3.3	...	71.4	...
	1988	1325	3.8	103.8	...	...	2.7	...	63.0	...
Sweden	1985	866601	−2.4	97.6	12.7	85.0	−1.0	83.9	79.1	4.8
Suède	1992	1441723	−3.7	96.3	13.4	82.9	−1.1	81.9	81.8	0.0
	1993	1442181	−4.0	96.0	14.1	82.0	−0.8	81.2	82.9	−1.7
Switzerland	1985	227950	5.9	105.9	10.3	95.6	−0.9	94.7	75.2	19.5
Suisse	1992	338765	4.0	104.0	10.5	93.5	−1.2	92.2	73.0	19.2
	1993	343045	4.1	104.1	10.6	93.6	−1.2	92.3	73.5	18.8
Tajikistan	1989	6639	4.0	104.0	17.1	86.9	...	...	...	...
Tadjikistan	1990	7347	5.5	105.5	14.7	90.8	...	...	...	...
	1991	13407	0.9	100.9	8.5	92.4	...	...	...	...
Thailand	1985	1056496	−1.7	98.3	8.8	89.5	0.6	90.1	75.7	14.3
Thaïlande	1992	2833277	−1.8	98.2	10.1	88.1	0.4	88.5	64.3	24.2
	1993	3161374	−1.9	98.1	10.8	87.4	0.3	87.7	64.5	23.1
Togo	1985	332500	...	...	...	84.8	...	...	...	...
Togo	1986	363600	...	...	...	85.7	...	...	...	...
Tonga [9]	1982	64	6.9	106.9	4.5	102.3	35.8	138.2	137.9	24.5 [3]
Tonga [9]	1983	73	4.4	104.4	4.0	100.4	27.1	126.5	140.0	6.2 [3]
Trinidad and Tobago	1985	18071	−4.8	95.3	8.7	86.6	−0.8	85.7	77.1	8.6
Trinité−et−Tobago	1992	23118	−8.4	91.6	11.3	80.3	−0.3	80.0	75.3	4.7
	1993	24883	−7.4	92.6	11.3	81.3	−0.1	81.1	77.1	4.1
Tunisia	1985	6910	−1.0	99.0	11.3	87.7	0.0	87.7	79.6	8.1
Tunisie	1988	8605	0.6	100.6	11.2	89.4	0.0	89.4	80.8	8.6
	1989	9497	0.7	100.7	10.8	89.9	0.0	89.9	81.9	8.1
Turkey	1985	35095000	0.7	100.7	5.5	95.2	0.0	95.2	80.0	15.3
Turquie	1992	1093368000	1.0	101.0	5.5	95.5	0.0	95.5	80.1	15.4
	1993	1913150000	0.8	100.8	5.5	95.4	0.0	95.4	80.7	14.7
Ukraine	1989	153400	1.6	101.6	17.3	84.3	5.9	90.2	71.8	18.3
Ukraine	1991	230800	2.7	102.7	15.3	87.4	3.3	90.7	92.7	−2.0
United Arab Emirates	1985	99416	0.4	100.4	17.1	83.3	−1.0	82.3	48.2	34.1
Emirats arabes unis	1989	100976	0.4	100.4	15.0	85.4	−0.7	84.7	61.7	23.0
	1990	124008	−1.0	99.0	13.0	86.0	−8.9	77.1	54.9	22.2
United Kingdom	1985	356172	0.3	100.3	11.8	88.5	−0.9	87.6	81.8	5.8
Royaume−Uni	1992	595219	−0.3	99.7	10.8	89.0	−0.9	88.1	86.0	2.1
	1993	627701	−0.1	99.9	10.4	89.5	−0.8	88.7	86.3	2.4
United Rep. of Tanzania	1985	120621	−0.6	99.4	2.1	97.4	2.5	99.9	92.6	7.3
Rép.−Unie de Tanzanie	1990	494999	−8.2	91.8	2.9	88.9	27.3	116.2	88.4	27.9
	1991	690421	−6.0	94.0	2.1	91.8	27.6	119.4	89.8	29.7
United States	1985	4016649	0.5	100.5	13.0	87.5	−0.4	87.1	82.8	4.6 [3]
Etats Unis	1992	5937300	0.3	100.3	12.6	87.6	−0.5	87.1	85.0	1.9 [3]
	1993	6259900	0.3	100.3	12.2	88.0	−0.5	87.5	84.8	2.7 [3]

23
Relationships between the principal national accounting aggregates
As percentage of GDP [cont.]
Relations entre les printicpaux agrégates de comptabilité nationale
En pourcentage du PIB [suite]

As percentage of GDP — En pourcentage du PIB

Country or area Pays ou zone	Year Année	GDP at current prices (Mil. nat.cur.) PIB aux prix courants (Mil. mon.nat.)	Plus: NFI from the rest of world Plus : Rev. net des facteurs reçu du reste du monde	Equals: Gross national product Égal : Produit national brut	Less: Consump. of Fixed Capital Moins : Consomm. de capital fixe	Equals: National Income Égal : Revenu national	Plus: Net Curr. transfer from the rest of the world Plus : Transferts courants nets reçus du reste du monde	Equals: National Disposable Income Égal : Revenu national disponible	Less: Final Consumption Moins : Consommation finale	Equals: Net savings Égal : Épargne nette
Uruguay	1985	479	−7.4	92.6	...	...	0.2	...	83.0	...
Uruguay	1990	9698	−3.9	96.1	...	...	0.1	...	81.1	...
	1991	19135	−2.5	97.5	...	...	0.3	...	83.3	...
Vanuatu	1985	12534	3.2	103.2	...	...	27.2	...	92.5	...
Vanuatu	1989	16367	3.4	103.4	...	...	17.3	...	94.3	...
	1990	17899	7.2	107.2						
Venezuela	1985	464741	−3.5	96.5	7.9	88.7	−0.3	88.4	72.3	16.1
Venezuela	1993	5449109	−2.9	97.1	8.0	89.1	−0.5	88.6	81.9	6.7
	1994	8310682	−2.9	97.1	7.9	89.2	−0.0	89.2	80.0	9.2
Viet Nam										
Viet Nam	1989	24308000	−2.0	98.0	6.8	91.1	9.4	100.6	100.2	0.4
Yemen	1989	61406	2.4	102.4	4.1	98.3	6.0	104.3	105.5	−1.2
Yémen	1990	77159	2.1	102.1	5.4	96.7	14.1	110.8	102.6	8.2
Yemen, former Arab Rep.	1985	30939	20.3	...	2.7	...	...	117.6	113.0	4.6
anc. Yémen rép. arabe	1986	37472	19.4	...	2.8	...	...	116.6	109.1	7.5
former Dem. Yemen	1984	374	1.6	101.6	5.6	96.0	46.0	142.0	139.3	2.6
ancienne Yémen dém.	1985	369	1.9	101.9	5.9	96.0	40.8	136.8	147.4	−10.7
Yugoslavia, SFR †	1985	1195	2.4	102.4	11.1	91.3	...	...	63.7	...
Yougoslavie, SFR †	1989	235395	6.9	106.9	12.1	94.8	...	...	61.9	...
	1990	1147787	8.7	108.7	11.2	97.5	...	...	83.7	...
Zaire	1984	99723	−11.5	88.5	2.5	86.0	...	...	...	...
Zaïre	1985	147263	−2.8	97.2	2.9	94.3	...	...	...	...
Zambia	1985	7072	−10.0	90.0	13.2	76.8	−1.2	75.6	84.6	−9.0
Zambie	1987	19778	−11.4	88.6	17.3	71.3	0.5	71.8	82.0	−10.3
	1988	27725	−14.2	85.8	14.5	71.4	1.0	72.4	79.8	−7.4
Zimbabwe	1985	7295	−3.9	96.1	...	...	0.5	...	79.0	...
Zimbabwe	1988	11441	−4.2	95.8	...	...	0.8	...	73.0	...
	1989	13794	−3.9	96.1	...	...	0.9	...	78.0	...

Source:
National accounts database of the Statistics Division of the United Nations Secretariat.

† For detailed descriptions of data pertaining to former Czechoslovakia, Germany, SFR Yugoslavia and former USSR, see annex I — Country or area nomenclature, regional and other groupings.

1   Fiscal year beginning 1 July.
2   Fiscal year beginning 1 April.
3   Including statistical discrepancy.
4   Fiscal year ending 7 July.
5   Fiscal year ending 30 September.
6   Fiscal year beginning 21 March.
7   Fiscal year ending 15 July.
8   Thousand.
9   Fiscal year ending 30 June.

Source:
Base de données sur les comptes nationaux de la division de statistique du Secrétariat de l'ONU.

† Pour les descriptions en détails des données relatives a l'ancienne Tchécoslovaquie, l'Allemagne, la Rfs Yougoslavie et l'ancienne URSS, voir l'Annexe I — Nomenclature des pays ou zones, groupements regionaux et autres groupements.

1   L'années fiscales commençant le 1 juillet.
2   L'années fiscales commençant le 1 avril.
3   Y compris le divergence statistique.
4   L'années fiscales finissant le 7 juillet.
5   L'années fiscales finissant la 30 septembre.
6   L'années fiscales commençant la 21 mars.
7   L'années fiscales finissant le 15 juillet.
8   Milliers.
9   L'années fiscales finissant la 30 juin.

24
Government final consumption expenditure by function at current prices
Consommation finale des administrations publiques par fonction aux prix courants

Percentage distribution
Répartition en pourcentage

Country or area	Year	Govt. final consumption expenditures Consommation finale des administrations (M. nat'l. curr.)	General public services Adminis— tration publique générale	Defence Defence	Public order & safety Sûreté publique	Education Enseigne— ment	Health Santé	Social services Services sociaux	Economic services Services écono— miques	Other functions Autres fonctions
Anguilla	1985	8	22.8	...	12.4	23.9	14.8	1.8	8.9	15.5
Anguilla	1990	20	19.3	...	12.3	23.6	15.7	2.4	13.9	12.8
	1991	23	25.9	...	11.6	22.2	15.3	2.5	10.7	11.9
Antigua and Barbuda [1]	1984	67	22.8	2.2	11.4	15.8	9.7	8.4	22.5	7.1
Antigua—et—Barbuda [1]	1985	81	25.1	2.2	11.4	14.0	11.5	6.6	20.9	8.2
	1986	108	26.1	2.3	11.6	14.7	10.0	7.2	21.2	6.9
Australia [2]	1985	44755	13.0	13.9	6.6	23.2	17.3	3.5	16.6	5.9
Australie [2]	1991	71324	14.5	12.1	7.2	21.3	17.5	5.5	16.2	5.7
	1992	74344	14.7	12.2	7.1	21.3	16.9	5.7	15.9	6.1
Austria	1985	254999	16.5	6.6	4.8	22.0	23.5	18.4	6.2	2.1
Autriche	1992	377059	16.8	4.9	4.5	22.2	26.5	18.5	4.5	2.0
	1993	405598	...	4.8	...	...	...	...	...	...
Bahamas	1985	295	12.2	3.4	12.5	27.5	20.0	2.4	20.7	1.0
Bahamas #	1991	443	16.5	4.1	13.5	22.3	18.7	4.7	19.0	1.4
	1992	448	17.9	4.0	13.4	23.4	17.9	5.1	17.0	1.6
Belarus	1990	10160	...	55.7	2.2	12.9	7.1[3]	...	4.3	15.7
Bélarus	1991	18174	...	45.9	9.4	15.3	13.3[3]	...	3.5	10.7
	1992	146200	...	15.2	17.9	24.9	19.7[3]	...	4.2	12.5
Belgium	1984	760210	14.4	15.2	8.6	38.1	2.9	5.9	7.7	6.5
Belgique	1985	815164	14.9	15.2	8.6	37.5	2.9	5.9	7.7	6.6
	1986	846686	14.8	15.2	9.3	36.6	2.8	5.9	7.9	6.5
Belize [4]	1989	229	12.7	4.3	5.3	16.5	7.9	0.7	40.3	12.4
Belize [4]	1990	279	12.7	3.4	7.9	15.3	6.8	3.3	37.5	13.2
	1991	321	16.6	3.4	7.0	16.8	6.6	4.0	32.6	13.1
Bermuda [4]	1985	138	36.9	2.0	...	21.3	3.7	3.6	27.1	5.3
Bermudes [4]	1991	217	34.6	1.8	...	22.7	4.1	3.8	27.2	5.8
	1992	218	34.9	1.5	...	22.6	4.2	3.8	27.4	5.5
Bolivia										
Bolivie	1980	19[5]	12.3	15.5	5.9	25.2	3.7	9.9	26.4	1.1
British Virgin Islands [1]	1985	17	23.3	...	10.8	23.6	14.9	1.8	20.7	4.9
Iles Vierges brit. [1]	1986	19	21.8	...	11.4	22.7	14.5	2.4	22.1	5.1
	1987	21	23.3	...	11.0	21.1	15.8	2.6	20.2	6.0
Brunei Darussalam	1982	914	22.9	41.4	5.5	14.2	5.0	0.2	5.0	5.8
Brunéi Darussalam	1983	922	24.6	35.3	6.0	15.2	5.7	0.2	5.5	7.5
	1984	2512	69.3	12.8	2.7	6.5	2.6	0.1	2.5	3.4
Burkina Faso	1982	38198	8.2	28.3	8.7	16.6	10.0[3]	...	9.9	18.3
Burkina Faso	1983	38864	8.1	28.7	9.1	18.3	10.5[3]	...	10.5	14.7
	1984	38760	7.3	30.4	8.7	19.0	10.3[3]	...	10.8	13.4
Cameroon [2]	1985	465500	29.9	11.6[6]	...	17.6	5.6	0.6	11.3	23.3
Cameroun [2]	1987	391000	28.3	14.7[6]	...	21.6	6.1	0.8	7.3	21.0
	1988	378400	35.5	12.4[6]	...	21.5	6.0	0.9	6.2	17.6
Cayman Islands [7]	1985	45	31.1	...	15.6	15.6	15.6	2.2	17.8	2.2
Iles Caïmanes [7]	1990	94	26.6	...	14.9	14.9	16.0	4.3	19.1	4.3
	1991	103	27.2	...	14.6	14.6	14.6	5.8	20.4	2.9
Colombia	1985	531264	31.3	11.6	...	28.6	9.8	6.3	10.9	1.7
Colombie	1990	2076459	30.8	12.1	...	26.3	9.8	7.2	12.1	1.6
	1991	2684541	29.7	11.5	...	26.9	9.4	7.4	12.8	2.2
Cyprus	1985	209	14.0	6.0	14.3	23.3	11.8	14.1	11.6	4.9
Chypre	1991	494	11.4	26.5[8]	9.9	17.7	9.2	12.8	8.4	4.2
	1992	591	10.4	32.3[8]	8.8	16.3	9.5	11.6	7.0	4.2
Denmark	1985	155481	11.7	8.4[6]	...	23.6	19.7	22.4	8.8	5.3
Danemark	1989	196546	11.8	7.9[6]	...	23.8	19.8	24.1	7.8	4.8
	1990	202504	11.3	8.0[6]	...	23.7	19.8	24.3	8.0	4.9
Ecuador	1985	137000	10.8	18.3	5.5	31.4	6.3	5.1	11.7	10.9
Equateur	1991	1009000	13.0	15.0	7.1	27.8	4.6	6.2	14.9	11.5
	1992	1498000	12.8	15.9	7.3	26.8	3.9	7.8	16.1	9.3

24
Government final consumption expenditure by function at current prices
Percentage distribution [cont.]
Consommation finale des administrations publiques par fonction aux prix courants
Répartition en pourcentage [suite]

Country or area	Year	Govt. final consumption expenditures Consommation finale des administrations (M. nat'l. curr.)	Per cent — Pourcentage							
			General public services Administration publique générale	Defence Défence	Public order & safety Sûreté publique	Education Enseignement	Health Santé	Social services Services sociaux	Economic services Services économiques	Other functions Autres fonctions
Estonia	1992	2084	10.4	2.1	8.4	34.1	16.9	3.1	19.4	5.5
Estonie	1993	4054	11.7	3.3	11.4	37.5	10.8	4.8	7.9	12.5
Fiji	1985	252	28.6	6.0	...	27.8	12.3	0.4	22.6	2.4
Fidji	1988	264	33.0	10.6	...	23.9	10.6	0.4	18.9	2.7
	1989	304	28.9	12.2	...	25.7	10.9	0.3	18.8	3.3
Finland	1985	66967	9.5	7.7	5.8	25.2	22.8	14.6	7.0	7.4
Finlande	1992	118453	9.2	8.0	5.5	25.0	22.1	15.9	7.8	6.6
	1993	112542	8.8	7.7	5.4	24.8	21.9	16.0	8.5	6.9
France	1985	910315	13.0	16.5	4.5	25.7	16.5	8.1	6.6	9.1
France	1989	1106075	13.0	16.3	4.6	25.3	17.1	7.6	6.2	9.9
	1990	1170435	11.9	16.6	4.6	25.7	17.0	7.8	6.3	9.8
Gambia [1][2]	1985	265	22.6	...	...	10.3[9]	5.6	0.1	45.8	15.7
Gambie [1][2]	1990	819	22.0	...	...	12.9[9]	6.4	0.1	18.6	40.1
	1991	804	22.2	...	...	12.6[9]	5.7	0.1	24.1	35.3
Germany † · Allemagne †										
F.R. Germany	1985	365720	10.2	13.6	7.7	19.8	30.1	10.2	4.5	3.9
R.f. Allemagne	1989	418820	10.4	12.8	7.9	19.1	30.1	11.3	4.3	4.0
	1990	444070	10.4	11.9	7.9	18.9	30.7	12.0	4.2	3.9
Greece	1985	942050	39.2	30.8	...	14.6	9.9	1.6	3.9[10]	...
Grèce	1990	2250732	40.9	24.9	...	15.5	11.7	1.4	4.2[10]	...
	1991	2554988	42.5	24.6	...	15.5	11.6	1.3	4.1[10]	...
Guinea–Bissau	1986	6423	44.0	...	...	18.4	11.8	0.9	22.7	2.2
Guinée–Bissau	1987	10776	44.0	...	...	18.4	11.8	1.2	22.7	1.9
Honduras	1985	1046	37.4	18.0	...	25.7	9.1	...	...	13.6
Honduras	1988	1468	29.7	18.0	...	27.5	11.9	...	...	12.9
	1989	1607	25.6	17.2	...	27.9	11.9	...	...	17.4
Hungary	1992	796694	15.7	6.5	7.8	21.8	16.0	9.2	9.5	13.5
Hongrie	1993	1030317	15.6	12.8	7.5	20.1	14.2	8.5	7.9	13.3
Iceland	1985	21129	6.8	0.0	7.0	20.0	34.2	5.6	11.9	14.5
Islande	1992	80375	8.0	0.0	6.4	19.8	33.0	7.7	9.5	15.6
	1993	84818	8.0	0.0	6.3	19.3	32.0	7.7	9.9	16.7
India [1][4]	1985	241870	22.2[6]	35.8	...	14.7	7.2	2.7	13.6	3.8
Inde [1][4]	1991	575300	24.7[6]	32.7	...	15.6	6.6	3.5	13.6	3.3
	1992	648370	25.4[6]	32.4	...	15.5	6.8	3.4	13.3	3.2
Iran, Islamic Rep. of [11]	1985	2443000	2.3	38.0	6.8	20.1	6.6	7.5	8.4	10.2
Iran, Rép. islamique d' [11]	1989	3294000	3.9	33.9	4.7	24.5	8.4	8.3	6.1	10.1
	1990	4054000	3.3	27.7	5.6	25.9	7.4	9.6	7.2	13.3
Israel [4]	1985	11662	5.9	54.4	3.5	15.9	8.0	1.4	2.1	8.8
Israël [4]	1986	15220	6.6	50.6	4.0	17.1	8.6	1.5	2.3	9.4
	1987	20599	6.2	53.3	3.9	16.1	7.9	1.5	2.1	9.0
Italy	1985	133265000	15.2	12.6	9.4	28.1	18.7	4.3	6.7	4.9
Italie	1992	264149000	16.3	10.5	10.0	27.3	21.1	4.2	6.0	4.5
	1993	275966000	17.2	10.6	10.5	26.3	20.8	4.2	6.0	4.5
Japan	1985	31038000	26.2[6]	9.5	...	36.3	3.9	5.6	10.0	8.5
Japon	1992	43686000	27.1[6]	9.7	...	33.6	4.6	6.1	9.0	9.8
	1993	44987000	27.3[6]	9.4	...	33.1	4.7	6.3	8.8	10.4
Jordan	1985	411	63.6[6][12]	...	...	15.9	5.2	0.6	4.6	5.4
Jordanie	1986	461	65.5[6][12]	...	...	15.7	5.4	0.5	4.7	3.8
	1987	460	63.5[6][12]	...	...	16.9	5.7	0.5	5.1	4.2
Kenya	1985	880	17.4	14.3	...	37.3	10.8	20.2[10]	...	...
Kenya	1992	2074	25.4	10.8	...	42.6	9.8	11.3[10]	...	...
	1993	2109	27.1	5.5	...	43.8	9.9	13.7[10]	...	...
Korea, Republic of	1985	8305000	14.8	43.1	9.7	22.4	1.3	2.2	3.5	3.0
Corée, Rép. de	1992	26110000	16.0	33.6	11.5	24.1	1.3	5.0	4.5	4.0
	1993	28563000	16.0	32.6	11.4	24.8	1.4	5.0	4.5	4.3
Kuwait	1985	1445	51.3[6][12]	...	...	23.3	12.6	2.1	3.7	7.1
Koweït	1986	1404	48.0[6][12]	...	...	24.9	13.3	2.3	4.1	7.4
	1987	1371	45.5[6][12]	...	...	25.4	13.8	2.5	4.1	8.8

24
Government final consumption expenditure by function at current prices
Percentage distribution [cont.]
Consommation finale des administrations publiques par fonction aux prix courants
Répartition en pourcentage [suite]

Country or area	Year	Govt. final consumption expenditures Consommation finale des administrations (M. nat'l. curr.)	Per cent — Pourcentage General public services Administration publique générale	Defence Défense	Public order & safety Sûreté publique	Education Enseignement	Health Santé	Social services Services sociaux	Economic services Services économiques	Other functions Autres fonctions
Lesotho	1985	136	22.7	...	31.6	4.1	11.4[3]	...	23.3	6.8
Lesotho	1992	394	19.5	...	30.2	5.2	12.6[3]	...	24.4	8.1
	1993	458	20.5	...	29.1	6.1	13.1[3]	...	23.5	7.6
Libyan Arab Jamah. Jamah. arabe libyenne	1980	2351	68.8[6][12]	...	...	11.5	7.4	2.3	7.7	2.2
Malaysia	1985	11844	16.3	20.3	9.4	27.6	9.3	4.5[10]	12.5	...
Malaisie	1991	18391	12.8	23.6	9.3	28.8	9.1	4.6[10]	11.7	...
	1992	19304	12.7	22.4	9.6	29.5	9.4	4.6[10]	11.8	...
Maldives	1984	103	30.4	15.6[6]	...	14.6	7.9	6.8	13.9	10.8
Maldives	1985	121	29.9	15.0[6]	...	14.5	7.9	5.6	11.8	15.3
	1986	139	32.3	16.3[6]	...	16.2	8.3	5.3	5.6	15.9
Malta	1985	84	12.8	17.4[6]	...	23.1	25.0	2.5	3.3	15.8
Malte	1991	147	14.6	12.6[6]	...	29.2	23.9	5.5	3.1	11.2
	1992	164	14.7	11.9[6]	...	29.6	24.7	4.6	3.0	11.5
Mauritius	1985	1915	15.6	2.0	12.9	23.0	17.5	2.9	20.5	5.6
Maurice	1992	5499	19.9	2.6	15.2	20.6	17.2	2.7	13.1	8.5
	1993	6620	20.9	3.1	14.8	20.3	17.3	2.4	13.6	7.5
Montserrat	1983	18	15.1	0.4	10.9	17.7	17.4	9.2	27.0	2.1
Montserrat	1984	19	19.6	0.3	10.5	19.3	15.9	6.6	27.2	0.5
	1985	20	18.7	0.3	11.3	22.4	15.3	4.8	24.5	2.7
Nepal [13]	1985	4445	13.0	12.4	10.3	28.1	5.3	0.0	24.1	3.3
Népal [13]	1987	6571	14.9	11.5	7.2	24.3	7.7	0.4	30.5	3.5
	1988	7303	14.4	7.0	10.4	22.7	3.6	1.6	34.9	5.2
Netherlands	1985	67670	...	17.6	...	31.8	...	4.6	...	45.9[14]
Pays—Bas	1988	71160	...	18.2	...	30.7	...	4.9	...	46.2[14]
	1989	72490	...	18.0	...	30.3	...	4.9	...	46.8[14]
Netherlands Antilles	1980	568	14.4	3.6	8.7	26.6	7.4[15]	17.8	11.6	9.8
Antilles néerlandaises	1981	649	16.4	1.7	10.6	27.7	7.4[15]	17.7	10.2	8.3
	1982	727	17.9	0.2	11.2	27.3	7.1[15]	17.9	9.6	8.7
New Zealand [4]	1985	7345	...	11.2	...	2.3	20.3	...	...	...
Nouvelle—Zélande [4]	1992	12572	...	8.2	...	26.0	18.3	...	...	...
	1993	12530	...	8.0	...	26.4	18.7	...	...	...
Norway	1985	92653	7.5	15.6	4.0	26.0	23.2	8.8	11.5	3.3
Norvège	1990	139115	7.9	15.9	4.2	25.7	22.4	10.0	10.5	3.4
	1991	147478	8.1	15.1	4.3	25.7	22.6	10.5	10.2	3.5
Oman	1985	938	...	82.5[6]	...	9.1	4.9	...	3.6	...
Oman	1991	1395	...	79.8[6]	...	12.5	5.2	...	2.4	...
	1992	1735	...	82.5[6]	...	10.8	4.7	...	2.1	...
Pakistan [2]	1985	65662	59.1[12]	...	7.5	9.8	4.5	3.0	12.9	3.1
Pakistan [2]	1992	174680	52.9[12]	...	6.9	10.9	4.6	4.7	15.6	4.4
	1993	192095	52.0[12]	...	6.8	11.2	4.4	5.3	15.7	4.6
Panama	1985	1044	31.0[12]	...	...	24.8	7.6	20.8	10.9	5.0
Panama	1992	1022	29.0[12]	...	...	28.5	12.3	19.4	5.5	5.3
	1993	1096	31.5[12]	...	...	27.7	12.1	18.2	5.6	4.8
Peru	1985	22[5]	57.4[12]	...	...	24.7	8.3	1.9	6.0	1.6
Pérou	1990	557	55.8[12]	...	...	18.0	6.6	2.0	5.0	5.0
	1991	1821	53.5[12]	...	...	37.8	9.9	2.4	6.3	4.6
Portugal	1985	546899	12.4	16.2	9.7	24.7	22.5	4.8	6.5	3.2
Portugal	# 1988	1020829	12.5	9.9	14.9	29.4	17.2	4.5	8.0	3.6
	1989	1226693	11.9	10.1	13.1	29.3	15.8	4.7	10.4	4.9
Saint Vincent—Grenadines	1985	63	9.3	0.0	13.0	26.6	18.7	6.9	24.3	1.3
St.—Vincent—et—Grenad.	1988	91	14.9	0.0	11.0	25.7	19.1	5.4	22.8	1.1
	1989	94	10.7	0.0	11.3	26.1	22.4	6.5	21.5	1.5
Seychelles	1989	475	9.4	11.5	4.9	29.7	11.8	2.6	17.1	13.0
Seychelles	1990	544	9.5	10.2	5.1	29.2	12.8	3.5	18.3	11.5
	1991	558	10.3	11.0	5.7	26.4	13.7	5.2	17.0	10.7
Sierra Leone [1][2]	1985	900	15.1	3.9	...	10.1	4.3	0.3	38.7	27.4
Sierra Leone [1][2]	1989	7620	14.4	7.3	...	10.2	5.0	1.4	45.9	15.9
	1990	32337	11.9	5.6	...	6.2	2.1	0.6	27.9	45.6

24
Government final consumption expenditure by function at current prices
Percentage distribution *[cont.]*
Consommation finale des administrations publiques par fonction aux prix courants
Répartition en pourcentage *[suite]*

Country or area	Year	Govt. final consumption expenditures Consommation finale des administrations (M. nat'l. curr.)	General public services Administration publique générale	Defence Défence	Public order & safety Sûreté publique	Education Enseignement	Health Santé	Social services Services sociaux	Economic services Services économiques	Other functions Autres fonctions
Slovenia	1990	34226	39.6	0.7	...	21.3	27.6	7.6	...	3.2
Slovénie	1992	213669	34.1	7.6	...	19.8	28.6	7.0	...	2.9
	1993	297449	40.5[12]	...	...	24.3	28.8	2.0	...	4.4
Spain	1985	4151700	3.9	13.3	7.5	17.9	23.6	10.9	5.9	17.0
Espagne	1989	6831300	5.8	11.5	7.4	18.6	24.5	10.3	6.6	15.4
	1990	7814600	7.8	9.8	7.4	19.1	23.8	10.7	6.7	14.6
Sri Lanka	1985	19170	32.0	24.3	...	16.5	8.7	11.6	6.2	0.9
Sri Lanka	1992	53965	20.2	25.9	...	13.7	8.4	19.5	11.6	0.6
	1993	65745	23.7	22.5	...	15.0	8.1	19.3	9.0	2.3
Sudan [2]	1981	720	25.2[6]	18.6	...	30.9	9.7	...	12.4	3.3
Soudan [2]	1982	854	27.7[6]	19.0	...	27.7	8.6	...	14.4	2.7
	1983	1113	32.4[6]	22.5	...	23.7	5.1	...	14.4	2.0
Sweden	1985	241754	9.0	9.6	4.6	20.5	24.0	17.0	8.0	7.3
Suède	1991	394394	9.2	10.1	5.3	18.9	23.1	19.2	7.5	6.8
	1992	402508	9.9	8.6	5.5	19.1	18.7	22.9	8.0	7.3
Thailand	1985	142923	19.8	42.3[6]	...	27.1	7.1	0.5	2.1	1.1
Thaïlande	1992	282739	19.8	36.0[6]	...	30.4	8.7	0.6	2.2	2.3
	1993	325525	20.5	34.0[6]	...	31.2	9.3	0.6	1.9	2.3
Tonga [16]	1985	21	20.7	4.2	7.0	13.6	12.2	1.9	31.9	8.5
Tonga [16]	1986	27	22.7	3.7	7.1	13.8	11.9	1.9	29.0	9.7
	1987	32	26.9	3.4	6.9	13.1	10.3	1.9	26.3	11.3
Trinidad and Tobago	1985	4109	14.7	...	13.8	19.5	17.0	0.5	28.3	6.3
Trinité−et−Tobago	1992	4117	19.2	...	14.5	18.8	16.2	0.5	24.4	6.3
	1993	4019	19.6	...	14.8	18.9	15.8	0.6	23.9	6.3
Ukraine	1989	26600	...	52.3	...	20.3	15.0[3]	...	4.1	8.3
Ukraine	1991	52100	...	41.3	...	25.9	20.3[3]	...	3.6	8.8
United Kingdom	1985	75296	5.0	23.7	7.7	19.9	22.3	6.8	6.3	8.4
Royaume−Uni	1992	131926	6.2	17.9	9.5	20.4	25.2	7.8	5.4	7.7
	1993	138266	5.8	17.1	9.8	20.1	25.8	8.2	5.9	7.3
United Rep. of Tanzania [1][2]	1985	27440	21.4	13.3	7.8	6.5	4.8	0.5	23.6	22.1
Rép.−Unie de Tanzanie [1][2]	1990	134691	23.4	8.6	7.8	6.6	4.9	0.4	15.9	32.3
	1991	207000	17.2	6.2	6.2	6.9	4.9	0.4	22.1	35.9
Vanuatu	1985	4501	15.3	5.5[6]	...	17.4	9.2[3]	...	14.8	37.8
Vanuatu	1988	4969	17.1	6.8[6]	...	21.1	8.4[3]	...	18.3	28.4
	1989	4881	15.9	7.7[6]	...	17.5	8.1[3]	...	24.6	26.3
Venezuela	1985	48547	...	...	...	29.1	11.2	...	...	...
Venezuela	1992	379426	...	...	...	21.1	11.2	...	...	...
	1993	472636	...	...	...	21.0	10.4	...	...	...
Zimbabwe [1]	1985	1559	47.8[6][12]	...	...	28.7	10.5	...	9.5	3.5
Zimbabwe [1]	1990	7425	28.1	13.1	...	19.9	6.5	3.1	20.8	3.5
	1991	7788	16.7	14.3	...	26.7	7.4	4.1	23.0	4.5

Source:
National accounts database of the Statistics Division of the
United Nations Secretariat.

† For detailed descriptions of data pertaining to
former Czechoslovakia, Germany, SFR Yugoslavia and former
USSR, see annex I − Country or area nomenclature, regional
and other groupings.

1 Central government estimates only (India: incl. state government;
 Zimbabwe: incl. local government).
2 Fiscal year beginning 1 July.
3 Including social services.
4 Fiscal year beginning 1 April.
5 Thousand.
6 Including public order and safety.

Source:
Base de données sur les comptes nationaux de la division
de statistique du Secrétariat de l'ONU.

† Pour les descriptions en détails des données relatives
à l'ancienne Tchécoslovaquie, l'Allemagne, la Rfs
Yougoslavie et l'ancienne URSS, voir l'Annexe I −
Nomenclature des pays ou zones, groupements régionaux
et autres groupements.

1 Administration centrale seulement (Inde : y compris
 administration des États ; Zimbabwe : y compris
 administration locales).
2 L'année fiscale commençant le 1er juillet.
3 Services sociaux compris.
4 L'année fiscale commençant le 1er avril.
5 Milliers.

24
Government final consumption expenditure by function at current prices
Percentage distribution *[cont.]*
Consommation finale des administrations publiques par fonction aux prix courants
Répartition en pourcentage *[suite]*

7 Total government current expenditure only.	6 Y compris l'ordre public et la sécurité.
8 Including military expenditure of government.	7 Dépenses publiques courants seulement.
9 Including recreational, cultural and religious affairs.	8 Y compris les dépenses militaires de l'État.
10 Including "other functions" (Kenya: including economic services).	9 Loisirs, affaires culturelles et religieuses.
11 Fiscal year beginning 21 March.	10 Y compris les "autres fonctions" (Kenya : services économique compris).
12 Including defence.	11 L'année fiscale commençant le 21 mars.
13 Fiscal year ending 15 July.	12 Défense comprise.
14 Including general public services, health services and economic services.	13 L'année fiscale finissant le 15 juillet.
15 Including housing and community amenities.	14 Y compris l'administration publique générale, les soins de santé et les services économiques.
16 Fiscal year ending 30 June.	15 Y compris logement et aménagements cóllectif.
	16 L'année fiscale finissant le 30 juin.

25
Private final consumption expenditure by type and purpose at current prices
Consommation finale privée par catégorie de dépenses et par fonction aux prix courants

Percentage distribution
Répartition en pourcentage

Per cent – Pourcentage

Country or area Pays ou zone	Year Année	Private final consump. expend. Consomma- tion finale privée (M. nat.curr.)	Food, beverages, & tobacco Alimentation boissons et tabac	Clothing/ footwear Articles d'habille- ment et chaussures	Gross rent fuel and power Loyers bruts, chauffuge et éclairage	Furniture household equip. and operation Muebles articles de ménager et dépenses d'entretien courant de la maison	Medical and health expenses Soins med. et dépenses de santé	Transport and communi- cation Transports et communi- cations	Recreation entertain- ment and education services Loisirs, spectacles et ensei- gnement	Other functions Autres fonctions
Australia [1] Australie [1]	1985	143738	22.4	6.7[2]	19.5	7.5	6.4	14.8	9.0	13.8
	1991	242750	20.6	5.7[2]	20.6	6.6	7.2	15.0	9.7	14.7
	1992	253952	20.7	5.5[2]	20.4	6.6	7.3	14.9	9.8	14.7
Austria Autriche	1985	775529	23.5	11.0	19.6	7.1	5.0	17.2	6.1	10.6
	1992	1127091	20.7	9.4	19.1	8.1	6.0	17.9	8.0	10.8
	1993	1168262	20.4	9.0	19.7	8.3	6.1	17.4	8.0	11.1
Belgium Belgique	1985	3105122	21.5	7.5	18.9	9.8	10.4	12.5	6.0	13.3
	1992	4445416	17.7	7.7	16.8	10.6	11.8	13.2	6.3	15.9
	1993	4514296	17.2	7.5	17.8	10.3	12.2	12.8	6.3	16.0
Bolivia Bolivie	1985	1793	52.1	3.6	7.8	5.2	2.1	14.8	3.4	11.0
	1986	6214	47.7	3.3	8.0	6.7	2.5	16.5	4.2	11.1
	1988	8591	40.1	5.1	12.5	9.7	2.1	17.7	3.0	10.0
Canada Canada	1985	271099	17.4	6.1	22.2	9.1	4.2	15.9	10.5	14.5
	1992	416353	15.8	5.1	24.2	8.6	4.5	14.1	11.0	16.6
	1993	430806	15.5	5.1	24.4	8.6	4.5	14.1	11.1	16.6
Cape Verde Cap-Vert	1985	11470	60.7	3.2	13.8	7.7	0.8	8.3	5.9	−0.4
	1987	15134	60.4	2.9	13.6	7.2	0.6	10.1	5.8	−0.5
	1988	17848	62.6	2.5	13.5	6.9	0.5	8.8	5.6	−0.5
Colombia Colombie	1985	3446000	37.1	6.4	12.3	5.5	5.9	14.0	5.5	13.2
	1991	17348000	34.6	4.5	10.5	5.8	6.2	18.0	5.7	14.7
	1992	23183000	34.2	4.5	10.0	5.7	6.4	18.5	5.4	15.3
Cyprus Chypre	1985	946	36.6	13.2	11.3	14.4	3.6	19.8	9.7	−7.1
	1991	1754	33.3	13.6	9.5	13.2	4.0	21.5	10.1	−4.3
	1992	1961	34.0	13.6	9.3	14.3	4.2	21.3	10.6	−6.5
Denmark Danemark	1985	337215	23.2	5.9	25.1	6.8	1.8	17.5	9.6	9.9
	1992	442968	21.2	5.2	28.1	6.2	2.2	15.4	10.0	11.9
	1993	457904	20.4	5.1	28.7	6.0	2.2	15.3	10.1	12.1
Ecuador Equateur	1985	715659	38.4	10.9	7.2	6.0	3.8	12.5[3]	...	21.2
	1992	13147000	38.7	9.5	5.1	7.2	4.5	12.7[3]	...	22.4
	1993	19374000	37.8	9.2	5.2	6.6	4.6	13.9[3]	...	22.6
Fiji Fidji	1985	838	32.6	4.8	13.6	8.4	1.8	13.1	4.3	21.5
	1990	1366	29.5	7.7	12.2	7.2	1.9	11.3	3.7	26.4
	1991	1484	29.6	7.5	12.5	7.5	1.9	11.1	3.4	26.5
Finland Finlande	1985	180887	24.9	5.3	18.0	6.7	3.7	16.2	8.7	16.4
	1992	272114	22.5	4.6	21.3	5.7	4.9	13.7	8.9	18.3
	1993	271753	22.1	4.5	23.6	5.5	5.0	13.8	8.8	16.7
France France	1985	2871097	20.6	7.0[4]	19.0	8.3	8.6	16.8	7.0	12.6
	1992	4208390	18.6	6.2[4]	20.3	7.6	10.0	16.3	7.5	13.5
	1993	4310136	18.5	6.0[4]	21.1	7.5	10.3	15.9	7.5	13.4
Germany † · Allemagne † F.R. Germany R.f. Allemagne	1985	1036530	22.5[5]	8.2	21.8	8.4	3.2	14.9[3]	9.6	11.3
	1992	1536320	20.0[5]	7.8	20.2	9.3	3.5	17.3[3]	10.2	11.8
	1993	1588900	19.4[5]	7.7	21.2	9.1	3.5	16.2[3]	9.9	12.9
Greece Grèce	1985	3025492	41.1	9.0	11.4	8.8	3.8	14.6	6.1	5.0
	1992	10669224	37.7	8.3	13.2	7.9	4.0	16.1	5.6	7.3
	1993	12147952	37.9	8.0	14.1	7.7	4.4	15.3	5.5	7.1
Honduras Honduras	1984	4742	45.2	9.1	22.5	8.3	7.0	3.0	2.4	2.5
	1985	5033	45.2	9.1	22.5	8.3	7.0	3.0	2.4	2.5
	1986	5421	45.1	9.1	22.5	8.3	7.0	3.0	2.4	2.6

25
Private final consumption expenditure by type and purpose at current prices
Percentage distribution *[cont.]*
Consommation finale privée par catégorie de dépenses et par fonction aux prix courants
Répartition en pourcentage *[suite]*

Per cent — Pourcentage

Country or area Pays ou zone	Year Année	Private final consump. exp. Consomma- tion finale privée (M. nat.curr.)	Food, beverages, & tobacco Alimentation boissons et tabac	Clothing/ footwear Articles d'habille- ment et chaussures	Gross rent fuel and power Loyers bruts, chauffuge et éclairage	Furniture household equip. and operation Muebles articles de ménager et dépenses d'entretien courant de la maison	Medical and health expenses Soins med. et dépenses de santé	Transport and communi- cation Transports et communi- cation	Recreation entertain- ment and education services Loisirs, spectacles et ensei- gnement	Other functions Autres fonctions
Hong Kong	1985	167483	21.5	17.2[4]	15.3	10.8	6.0	7.2	9.1	13.0
Hong kong	1992	451670	15.1	21.2[4]	14.6	12.8	5.5	9.8	7.9	13.0
	1993	515312	14.2	22.1[4]	14.5	12.0	5.5	10.4	8.6	12.7
Hungary	1985	552294	47.5[5]	9.9	9.5	9.1	0.7	10.0	6.7	6.6
Hungary	# 1992	1700597	37.7[5]	6.9	17.1	8.1	1.6	14.8	6.7	9.6
	1993	2110620	36.5[5]	6.6	16.6	7.9	1.7	15.1	7.0	10.5
Iceland	1985	77240	24.8	9.2	18.9	9.7	1.5	15.0	8.2	12.7
Islande	1992	249044	24.5	7.8	17.6	7.7	1.9	14.1	10.2	16.2
	1993	248952	24.8	7.3	18.2	7.3	2.2	13.9	10.5	15.8
India [6]	1985	1768520	55.3	11.6	12.1	4.4	2.9	7.5	3.0	3.2
Inde [6]	1992	4194180	54.2	9.3	10.2	4.3	2.4	12.7	3.6	3.3
	1993	4744490	53.5	9.9	10.0	4.2	2.3	13.1	3.5	3.4
Iran, Islamic Rep. of	1985	9627000	43.2[5]	9.3	24.4	6.1	4.3	6.3	1.6	5.0
Iran, Rép. islamique d'	1989	18448000	46.5[5]	12.0	23.4	5.5	3.4	4.6	1.4	3.1
	1990	24071000	42.4[5]	11.7	24.8	6.4	3.8	5.0	1.7	4.2
Ireland	1985	10598	40.6	7.3	11.8	6.9	3.6	13.1	9.6	7.1
Irlande	# 1992	17575	36.2	6.7	12.1	7.2	4.0	13.0	11.8	9.0
	1993	18065	35.6	7.2	12.4	7.0	4.2	13.2	12.1	8.3
Israel	1985	16487	28.7	6.1	22.9	9.6	5.4	11.7	7.1	8.5
Israël	1992	97889	23.8	5.0	22.5	10.1	6.8	13.3	7.5	11.0
	1993	116317	22.8	5.4	22.9	10.0	6.7	13.1	7.8	11.3
Italy	1985	498048000	25.3	10.3	15.0	9.1	5.6	12.6	8.4	13.7
Italie	1992	946937000	20.0	9.8	15.9	9.4	6.8	12.2	8.9	17.0
	1993	965390000	20.2	9.4	16.7	9.2	7.1	11.8	8.9	16.6
Jamaica	1985	7772	50.5	4.5	15.3	7.0	2.9	17.3	3.1	−0.5
Jamaïque	1987	9849	52.1	6.0	14.5	6.9	3.4	15.8	2.9	−1.4
	1988	11388	49.6	5.8	13.1	6.8	3.5	15.3	2.8	3.2
Japan	1985	188760000	22.0	6.6	18.6	6.1	10.4	9.6	9.7	17.1
Japon	1992	264824000	19.8	5.9	19.7	5.9	10.7	9.5	10.1	18.4
	1993	270919000	19.4	5.6	20.3	5.8	11.0	9.4	10.4	18.0
Jordan	1984	1375	41.6	6.1	6.7	5.1	4.2	6.0	6.4	24.0
Jordanie	1985	1415	40.3	5.7	6.5	4.8	4.1	5.9	6.4	26.3
	1986	1238	40.7	5.6	6.5	4.9	4.1	5.9	6.4	25.9
Kenya										
Kenya	1980	1606	49.3	7.7	12.6	9.4	2.2	8.4	4.1	6.2
Korea, Republic of	1985	47875000	39.4	5.1	11.1	5.1	6.2	10.1	10.8	12.3
Corée, République de	1991	109655000	34.7	4.4	11.1	6.0	7.3	10.9	11.2	14.4
	1992	123746000	33.6	4.2	11.3	5.8	7.3	11.3	11.3	15.2
Luxembourg	1985	120523	24.3	6.9	21.9	9.6	7.0	17.7	3.6	9.1
Luxembourg	1990	166543	19.9	6.3	20.3	11.1	7.7	18.0	4.5	12.3
	1991	182597	19.1	6.0	20.4	11.1	7.6	19.7	4.3	11.8
Malaysia										
Malaisie	1983	36458	31.7	4.2	10.0	7.5	2.5	20.3	11.3	12.5
Malta	1985	333	42.5	9.9	6.9	10.1	3.8	17.4	6.4	3.1
Malte	1991	495	39.6	9.6	7.0	12.5	4.4	20.8	9.5	−3.4
	1992	531	38.3	8.4	7.3	11.9	4.2	21.4	8.7	−0.1
Mexico	1985	30575	38.5	9.7	8.4	13.3	4.0	9.2	5.5	11.3
Mexique	1992	735865	33.7	7.1	12.8	10.4	4.2	12.2	5.2	14.4
	1993	805684	33.2	6.6	13.2	10.0	4.3	12.2	5.6	14.8
Netherlands	1985	252910	16.6	7.2	18.7	6.4	12.5	12.4	9.5	14.5
Pays−Bas	1992	340720	14.7	6.8	18.2	6.9	12.8	12.8	10.1	17.6
	1993	350280	14.4	6.6	18.9	6.9	12.9	12.6	10.1	17.6
New Zealand [6]	1985	27868	18.3	5.9	18.5	9.5	4.8	18.7	8.4	15.9
Nouvelle−Zélande [6]	1989	43454	18.4	5.0	21.6	8.5	5.7	16.7	8.2	15.9
	1990	45642	19.0	4.8	22.2	8.0	5.9	15.6	8.1	16.3

25

Private final consumption expenditure by type and purpose at current prices
Percentage distribution *[cont.]*
Consommation finale privée par catégorie de dépenses et par fonction aux prix courants
Répartition en pourcentage *[suite]*

Per cent — Pourcentage

Country or area Pays ou zone	Year Année	Private final consump. exp. Consomma-tion finale privée (M. nat.curr.)	Food, beverages, & tobacco Alimentation boissons et tabac	Clothing/ footwear Articles d'habille-ment et chaussures	Gross rent fuel and power Loyers bruts, chauffuge et éclairage	Furniture household equip. and operation Muebles articles de ménager et dépenses d'entretien courant de la maison	Medical and health expenses Soins med. et dépenses de santé	Transport and communi-cation Transports et communi-cation	Recreation entertain-ment and education services Loisirs, spectacles et ensei-gnement	Other functions Autres fonctions
Norway Norvège	1985	245439	25.1	7.8	16.6	7.8	3.8	16.8	8.2	13.9
	1990	336065	25.3	6.8	19.1	6.9	4.7	13.1	8.9	15.2
	1991	349705	25.4	6.8	19.4	6.7	5.2	12.4	9.1	14.9
Peru Pérou	1985	123 [7]	38.2	8.4	2.2	11.8	4.0	9.3	9.2	16.8
	1989	79	32.9	10.1	1.3	10.1	5.1	5.1	12.7	21.5
	1990	4768	31.0	9.0	1.1	10.6	7.4	7.9	13.9	24.4
Philippines Philippines	1985	421093	59.2	3.8	3.7	13.3	...	4.9	...	15.2
	1993	1112374	57.8	3.7	4.2	14.0	...	4.7	...	15.7
	1994	1254011	57.7	3.5	4.1	13.9	...	4.4	...	16.5
Portugal Portugal	1985	2393244	39.5	9.8	5.2	9.1	4.8	15.5	6.1	9.9
	# 1988	4437451	33.3	10.0	7.1	8.9	5.2	17.5	6.1	11.7
	1989	5140404	34.1	10.0	7.3	9.0	5.1	16.5	6.5	11.5
Puerto Rico [1] Porto Rico [1]	1985	15746	26.4	8.6	15.4	7.3	6.4	15.7	6.6	13.6
	1992	22721	22.1	7.8	15.3	7.5	9.6	14.2	7.5	16.0
	1993	23913	21.9	7.6	15.1	7.2	9.8	14.6	7.5	16.2
Sierra Leone [1] Sierra Leone [1]	1984	4002	63.7	3.9	14.9	3.3	0.9	8.0	2.2	3.0
	1985	6238	64.5	3.0	14.9	2.7	0.9	6.9	1.8	5.2
	1986	16267	66.7	2.7	13.9	2.2	1.1	8.1	1.4	4.0
Singapore Singapour	1985	17553	29.2	8.9	12.4	11.5	4.0	15.3	14.0	4.7
	1992	33974	20.9	7.9	15.5	10.1	5.3	16.5	17.2	6.6
	1993	38042	19.6	7.5	15.7	9.7	5.2	17.1	16.1	9.1
South Africa Afrique du Sud	1985	66167	34.0	7.0	12.1	10.4	4.2	16.7[8]	6.0	9.5
	1991	179283	37.6	7.5	9.4	10.1	4.9	14.9[8]	6.3	9.3
	1992	203407	38.3	7.2	9.5	9.9	4.8	14.5[8]	6.2	9.4
Spain Espagne	1985	18080000	26.6	9.2	15.5	7.2	3.8	14.4	7.0	16.4
	1992	37219900	21.3	9.0	13.1	6.9	4.6	16.3	6.8	22.0
	1993	38510800	21.0	8.5	13.7	6.8	4.9	15.9	7.0	22.2
Sri Lanka Sri Lanka	1985	118101	54.4	6.8	5.7	4.5	1.5	15.8	4.7	6.6
	1991	276384	55.6	5.8	4.3	4.7	1.5	13.9	3.7	8.6
	1992	313525	54.6	7.8	4.3	3.3	1.5	14.9	3.0	8.9
Sudan Soudan	1981	5431	62.3	5.5	15.7	4.6	5.2	2.3	1.1	3.3
	1982	7957	59.9	7.5	15.2	5.6	5.3	2.5	1.1	2.9
	1983	9465	64.2	5.3	15.1	5.4	4.1	1.5	0.7	3.7
Sweden Suède	1985	443671	23.4	7.2	25.6	6.0	2.5	15.3	9.5	10.6
	1992	777324	18.9	6.2	29.9	5.5	3.0	15.3	9.4	11.8
	1993	792077	19.2	5.6	31.7	5.2	3.4	15.1	9.1	10.6
Switzerland Suisse	1985	141015	27.4	4.5	19.7	5.1	8.6	10.9	9.4[5]	14.4
	1992	198835	25.2	4.0	19.5	4.4	10.6	11.1	9.6[5]	15.7
	1993	203115	24.6	3.7	20.0	4.3	11.0	11.1	9.5[5]	15.6
Thailand Thaïlande	1985	657365	38.7	11.3	11.5	8.0	6.5	11.2	4.6	8.2
	1992	1540283	32.4	12.6	8.3	10.4	7.5	14.7	4.9	9.2
	1993	1714681	30.5	12.7	8.1	10.6	7.3	16.2	5.1	9.5
United Kingdom Royaume-Umi	1985	215972	24.7	6.9	20.0	6.5	1.2	16.9	9.3	14.5
	1992	380237	20.8	5.8	18.9	6.4	1.6	16.5	9.9	20.0
	1993	403297	20.2	5.8	19.1	6.5	1.6	16.7	10.1	20.1
United States Etats-Unis	1985	2598435	13.5	6.2	19.3	6.1	14.0	16.3	9.1	15.4
	1992	3996900	11.9	6.1	18.4	5.8	17.6	13.9	10.3	16.0
	1993	4235900	11.5	6.0	18.2	5.9	18.0	14.1	10.4	16.0
Vanuatu Vanuatu	1985	7091	45.6	7.0	8.3	2.9	...	18.3	...	11.2
	1988	9562	46.6	5.5	7.4	2.7	...	22.5	...	9.1
	1989	10545	46.0	4.9	7.9	2.8	...	22.9	...	8.9
Venezuela Venezuela	1985	287321	32.1	10.3	14.1	3.5	2.4	7.2	3.1	27.4
	1993	3989102	38.3	5.8	8.7	4.0	2.4	8.4	2.2	30.1
	1994	6039119	38.9	5.6	8.8	4.0	2.7	8.2	2.4	29.4

25
Private final consumption expenditure by type and purpose at current prices
Percentage distribution *[cont.]*
Consommation finale privée par catégorie de dépenses et par fonction aux prix courants
Répartition en pourcentage *[suite]*

Per cent — Pourcentage

Country or area Pays ou zone	Year Année	Private final consump. exp. Consomma- tion finale privée (M. nat.curr.)	Food, beverages, & tobacco Alimentation boissons et tabac	Clothing/ footwear Articles d'habille- ment et chaussures	Gross rent fuel and power Loyers bruts, chauffage et éclairage	Furniture household equip. and operation Muebles articles de ménager et dépenses d'entretien courant de la maison	Medical and health expenses Soins med. et dépenses de santé	Transport and communi- cation Transports et communi- cation	Recreation entertain- ment and education services Loisirs, spectacles et ensei- gnement	Other functions Autres fonctions
Zimbabwe	1985	3894	34.6	11.4	16.9	7.7	4.2	1.9[9]	6.5	17.0
Zimbabwe	1986	4521	31.8	10.6	15.5	11.6	5.2	1.3[9]	5.8	18.2
	1987	4387	29.7	10.2	15.1	12.7	7.0	1.0[9]	6.5	17.8

Source:
National accounts database of the Statistics Division of the
United Nations Secretariat.

†   For detailed descriptions of data pertaining to
former Czechoslovakia, Germany, SFR Yugoslavia and former
USSR, see annex I — Country or area nomenclature, regional
and other groupings.

1   Fiscal year beginning 1 July.
2   Including drapery.
3   Including fuel.
4   Including personal effects.
5   Including expenditures in restaurants, cafes and hotels
   (Germany: excluding hotels).
6   Fiscal year beginning 1 April.
7   Thousand.
8   Incluidng packaged tours.
9   Including personal transport equipment only.
   Communication is included in "Other functions".

Source:
Base de données sur les comptes nationaux de la Division de
statistique du Secrétariat de l'ONU.

†   Pour les descriptions en détails des données relatives
à l'ancienne Tchécoslovaquie, l'Allemagne, la Rfs
Yougoslavie et l'ancienne URSS, voir l'Annexe I —
Nomenclature des pays ou zones, groupements régionaux et
autres groupements.

1   L'année fiscale commençant le 1er juillet.
2   Y compris les tissus d'ameublement.
3   Y compris le carburant.
4   Y compris les effets personnels.
5   Y compris les dépenses faites dans les restaurants, les cafés
   et hôtels (Allemagne : hôtels exclus).
6   L'année fiscale commençant le 1er avril.
7   Milliers.
8   Voyages organisés compris.
9   Y compris seulement le matériel de transport individuel.
   Les communications sont incluses dans "les autres fonctions".

26
Index numbers of industrial production
Indices de la production industrielle
1980=100

Country or area and industry [SITC] Pays ou zone et industrie [CITI]	1985	1986	1987	1988	1989	1990	1991	1992	1993	1994
Africa · Afrique										
Algeria Algérie										
Total industry [2−4]										
Total, industrie [2−4]	**156**	**164**	**166**	**167**	**165**	**168**	**163**	**157**	**156**	**146**
Total mining [2]										
Total, industries extractives [2]	**124**	**132**	**128**	**122**	**124**	**126**	**115**	**118**	**105**	**103**
Total manufacturing [3]										
Total, industries manufacturières [3]	**179**	**189**	**186**	**188**	**181**	**183**	**174**	**163**	**160**	**146**
Food, beverages, tobacco										
Aliments, boissons, tabac	145	160	165	168	171	173	171	162	172	165
Textiles										
Textiles	166	162	154	138	140	147	143	149	140	117
Petroleum products										
Produits pétroliers	186	206	200	207	206	213	213	216	210	194
Non−metallic mineral products										
Produits minéraux non métalliques	141	147	155	158	153	151	150	157	148	132
Electricity [4]										
Électricité [4]	**174**	**186**	**199**	**216**	**226**	**239**	**259**	**273**	**293**	**300**
Côte d'Ivoire Côte d'Ivoire										
Total industry [2−4]										
Total, industrie [2−4]	**112**	**120**	**120**	**116**	**114**	**108**	**105**	**104**	**106**	**110**
Total mining [2]										
Total, industries extractives [2]	**111**	**103**	**88**	**56**	**14**	**12**	**10**	**8**	**3**	**3**
Total manufacturing [3]										
Total, industries manufacturières [3]	**113**	**123**	**121**	**118**	**115**	**124**	**121**	**121**	**121**	**123**
Food, beverages, tobacco										
Aliments, boissons, tabac	114	129	129	122	132	123	130	161	189	165
Textiles and clothing										
Textiles, habillement	122	120	126	140	145	118	112	109	114	116
Chemicals and petroleum										
Produits chimiques et pétrole	109	112	117	129	117	119	116	114	114	132
Metal products										
Produits métalliques	92	124	94	87	89	71	61	65	60	63
Electricity and water [4]										
Électricité et eau [4]	110	120	124	136	133	122	114	118	134	142
Egypt Egypte										
Total industry [2−4]										
Total, industrie [2−4]	**152**	**139**	**144**	**146**	**142**	**136**	**144**	**137**	**141**	**140**
Total mining [2]										
Total, industries extractives [2]	**146**	**142**	**142**	**145**	**141**	**143**	**146**	**150**	**154**	**155**
Total manufacturing [3]										
Total, industries manufacturières [3]	**152**	**136**	**142**	**143**	**139**	**130**	**138**	**126**	**129**	**132**
Food, beverages, tobacco										
Aliments, boissons, tabac	210	237	203	197	233	185	187	190	227	235
Textiles										
Textiles	145	149	130	108	112	114	122	112	105	105
Chemicals, coal, petroleum products										
Produits chimiques, houillers, pétroliers	168	143	184	185	169	171	180	165	165	170
Basic metals										
Métaux de base	134	148	169	169	182	179	201	162	160	174
Metal products										
Produits métalliques	206	179	185	190	182	162	158	142	142	150
Electricity [4]										
Électricité [4]	**185**	**167**	**178**	**198**	**189**	**190**	**222**	**227**	**238**	**241**
Ethiopia[1] **Ethiopie**[1]										
Total manufacturing [3]										
Total, industries manufacturières [3]	**143**	**152**	**157**	**151**	**142**	**103**	...	...	...	...
Food, beverages, tobacco										
Aliments, boissons, tabac	165	167	170	166	151	122	...	...	...	...

26
Index numbers of industrial production [*cont.*]
Indices de la production industrielle [*suite*]
1980=100

Country or area and industry [SITC] Pays ou zone et industrie [CITI]	1985	1986	1987	1988	1989	1990	1991	1992	1993	1994
Textiles										
Textiles	116	127	135	115	124	78	...	...	...	...
Chemicals										
Produits chimiques	156	238	188	152	122	62	...	...	...	...
Metal products										
Produits métalliques	130	139	144	108	92	57	...	...	...	...
Ghana Ghana										
Total industry [2−4]										
Total, industrie [2−4]	**74**	**83**	**87**	**94**	**103**	**111**	...	...	...	...
Total mining [2]										
Total, industries extractives [2]	**88**	**82**	**88**	**94**	**114**	**134**	...	...	...	...
Total manufacturing [3]										
Total, industries manufacturières [3]	**71**	**79**	**82**	**90**	**101**	**106**	...	...	...	...
Food, beverages, tobacco										
Aliments, boissons, tabac	74	82	94	101	94	101	...	...	...	...
Chemical and rubber products										
Produits chimiques ou en caoutchouc	92	110	150	194	177	166	...	...	...	...
Non−metallic mineral products										
Produits minéraux non métalliques	122	91	95	141	192	225	...	...	...	...
Electricity [4]										
Electricité [4]	**103**	**153**	**160**	**161**	**99**	**109**	...	...	...	...
Kenya Kenya										
Total mining [2]										
Total, industries extractives [2]	**187**	**169**	**210**	**234**	**297**	**283**	**271**	**248**	**293**	...
Total manufacturing [3] [2]										
Total, industries manufacturières [3] [2]	**120**	**128**	**135**	**143**	**141**	**149**	**154**	**156**	**169**	**172**
Food, beverages, tobacco										
Aliments, boissons, tabac	119	130	143	151	151	155	157	159	159	149
Textiles										
Textiles	108	116	119	122	122	126	136	136	156	116
Chemicals, coal, petroleum products										
Produits chimiques, houillers, pétroliers	121	130	140	156	156	178	227	216	213	202
Metal products										
Produits métalliques	92	92	94	106	106	113	139	130	119	128
Malawi Malawi										
Total industry [2−4] [3]										
Total, industrie [2−4] [3]	**103**	**105**	**101**	**107**	**116**	**132**	**139**	**137**	**128**	**123**
Total manufacturing [3]										
Total, industries manufacturières [3]	**101**	**102**	**95**	**102**	**110**	**126**	**132**	**129**	**119**	**111**
Food, beverages, tobacco										
Aliments, boissons, tabac	139	149	151	148	176	189	172	188	188	191
Textiles [4]										
Textiles [4]	122	115	104	108	112	129	193	167	134	121
Electricity and water [4]										
Electricité et eau [4]	**123**	**132**	**144**	**146**	**157**	**175**	**185**	**198**	**200**	**212**
Morocco Maroc										
Total industry [2−4] [5]										
Total, industrie [2−4] [5]	**118**	**120**	**122**	**135**	**125**	**139**	**135**	**140**	**139**	**150**
Total mining [2] [6]										
Total, industries extractives [2] [6]	**120**	**118**	**117**	**134**	**101**	**118**	**103**	**108**	**106**	**115**
Total manufacturing [3] [7]										
Total, industries manufacturières [3] [7]	**116**	**121**	**124**	**135**	**137**	**149**	**152**	**155**	**154**	**167**
Food, beverages, tobacco										
Aliments, boissons, tabac	105	110	95	101	100	102	107	107	115	119
Textiles										
Textiles	117	128	143	152	151	157	162	167	161	152
Chemicals and petroleum products										
Produits chimiques et pétroliers	122	122	109	119	119	125	121	132	133	145
Basic metals										
Métaux de base	81	67	124	146	169	167	178	172	167	175

26
Index numbers of industrial production [cont.]
Indices de la production industrielle [suite]
1980=100

Country or area and industry [SITC] Pays ou zone et industrie [CITI]	1985	1986	1987	1988	1989	1990	1991	1992	1993	1994
Metal products										
Produits métalliques	80	77	97	101	110	117	122	121	115	117
Electricity and water [4] [8]										
Electricité et eau [4] [8]	**120**	**121**	**125**	**135**	**144**	**153**	**148**	**162**	**165**	**178**
Nigeria Nigéria										
Total industry [2−4]										
Total, industrie [2−4]	**122**	**107**	**127**	**133**	**152**	**159**	**169**	**166**	**158**	**150**
Total mining [2]										
Total, industries extractives [2]	**125**	**116**	**112**	**119**	**136**	**144**	**150**	**150**	**151**	**146**
Total manufacturing [3]										
Total, industries manufacturières [3]	**139**	**109**	**182**	**188**	**215**	**227**	**248**	**236**	**202**	**184**
Electricity [4]										
Electricité [4]	**135**	**158**	**160**	**169**	**223**	**168**	**169**	**188**	**192**	**196**
Senegal Sénégal										
Total industry [2−4]										
Total, industrie [2−4]	**118**	**106**	**118**	**124**	**112**	**118**	**102**	**110**	**104**	**105**
Total mining [2]										
Total, industries extractives [2]	**125**	**130**	**115**	**149**	**147**	**130**	**100**	**133**	**103**	**97**
Total manufacturing [3] [5]										
Total, manufactures [3] [5]	**117**	**101**	**117**	**119**	**105**	**115**	**101**	**104**	**102**	**104**
Food, beverages, tobacco										
Aliments, boissons, tabac	88	73	114	145	130	135	82	112	110	128
Textiles										
Textiles	150	91	124	140	73	89	80	81	72	67
Chemicals, coal, petroleum products [9]										
Produits chimiques, houillers, pétroliers [9]	85	83	98	95	80	94	106	98	99	133
Electricity and water [4]										
Electricité et eau [4]	**120**	**128**	**148**	**144**	**140**	**139**	**140**	**157**	**151**	**154**
South Africa Afrique du Sud										
Total industry [2−4]										
Total, industrie [2−4]	107	106	105	108	108	108	106	104	106	107
Total mining [2]										
Total, industries extractives [2]	**105**	**102**	**97**	**100**	**98**	**96**	**95**	**96**	**98**	**96**
Total manufacturing [3]										
Total, industries manufacturières [3]	**105**	**104**	**108**	**110**	**112**	**112**	**108**	**105**	**104**	**107**
Food, beverages, tobacco										
Aliments, boissons, tabac	117	118	115	117	121	131	129	130	124	121
Textiles										
Textiles	91	94	88	87	86	78	75	72	74	77
Chemicals										
Produits chimiques	104	106	105	113	117	118	116	113	113	116
Basic metals										
Métaux de base	92	89	88	100	106	99	89	82	81	86
Metal products										
Produits métalliques	96	91	92	100	102	102	96	93	91	93
Electricity [4]										
Electricité [4]	**132**	**136**	**141**	**146**	**152**	**155**	**157**	**157**	**163**	**170**
Tunisia Tunisie										
Total industry [2−4] [5]										
Total, industrie [2−4] [5]	**112**	**114**	**114**	**118**	**120**	**120**	**124**	**125**	**122**	**122**
Total mining [2] [10]										
Total, industries extractives [2] [10]	**80**	**98**	**106**	**107**	**117**	**108**	**108**	**103**	**88**	**96**
Total manufacturing [3] [11]										
Total, industries manufacturières [3] [11]	**121**	**123**	**125**	**134**	**136**	**142**	**139**	**142**	**144**	**147**
Food, beverages, tobacco										
Aliments, boissons, tabac	125	132	133	143	144	147	150	157	157	164
Textiles										
Textiles	118	112	127	134	134	128	112	115	121	125
Chemicals and petroleum products										
Produits chimiques et pétroliers	114	127	134	150	157	163	166	165	168	183
Basic metals										
Métaux de base	96	112	107	107	105	108	111	107	105	105

26
Index numbers of industrial production [*cont.*]
Indices de la production industrielle [*suite*]
1980=100

Country or area and industry [SITC] Pays ou zone et industrie [CITI]	1985	1986	1987	1988	1989	1990	1991	1992	1993	1994
Metal products										
Produits métalliques	135	103	94	101	109	125	125	120	118	109
Electricity and water [4] [12]										
Electricité et eau [4] [12]	**124**	**122**	**118**	**117**	**118**	**112**	**124**	**126**	**117**	**113**
Zambia Zambie										
Total industry [2−4]										
Total, industrie [2−4]	**99**	**97**	**96**	**97**	**96**	**96 ·**	**93**	**98**	**88**	**78**
Total mining [2] [13]										
Total, industries extractives [2] [13]	**87**	**86**	**84**	**81**	**82**	**79**	**72**	**80**	**71**	**61**
Total manufacturing [3] [14]										
Total, manufactures [3] [14]	**115**	**113**	**117**	**123**	**122**	**125**	**125**	**127**	**115**	**103**
Food, beverages, tobacco										
Aliments, boissons, tabac	102	100	104	113	108	125	128	159	...	...
Textiles and clothing										
Textiles, habillement	152	133	114	147	156	161	145	134	...	...
Basic metals										
Métaux de base	96	90	92	92	67	50	50	57	...	...
Electricity and water [4]										
Electricité et eau [4]	109	106	91	91	73	84	94	82	85	88
Zimbabwe Zimbabwe										
Total industry [2−4] [5]										
Total, industrie [2−4] [5]	**108**	**113**	**118**	**122**	**129**	**134**	**137**	**127**	**118**	**129**
Total mining [2]										
Total, industries extractives [2]	**97**	**99**	**103**	**102**	**107**	**108**	**109**	**107**	**104**	**113**
Total manufacturing [3]										
Total, manufactures [3]	**112**	**115**	**118**	**124**	**131**	**139**	**143**	**130**	**119**	**131**
Food, beverages, tobacco										
Aliments, boissons, tabac	106	112	121	124	124	138	142	144	124	128
Textiles										
Textiles	175	190	196	203	208	217	226	176	192	206
Chemicals and petroleum products										
Produits chimiques et pétroliers	122	122	119	131	146	159	159	138	129	149
Basic metals and metal products										
Métaux de base et produits métalliques	100	98	92	101	113	117	118	107	82	99
Electricity [4]										
Electricité [4]	**111**	**132**	**171**	**177**	**208**	**202**	**186**	**180**	**159**	**175**
America, North · Amérique du Nord										
Barbados Barbade										
Total industry [2−4]										
Total, industrie [2−4]	**96**	**102**	**97**	**102**	**106**	**110**	**108**	**101**	**99**	**104**
Total mining [2]										
Total, industries extractives [2]	**166**	**156**	**144**	**135**	**127**	**134**	**128**	**128**	**137**	**140**
Total manufacturing [3]										
Total, industries manufacturières [3]	**87**	**93**	**87**	**93**	**97**	**101**	**98**	**90**	**87**	**93**
Food, beverages, tobacco										
Aliments, boissons, tabac	85	89	95	93	94	104	110	105	110	116
Wearing apparel										
Habillement	96	77	90	93	72	60	48	31	26	16
Chemicals and petroleum products										
Produits chimiques et pétroliers	88	99	92	104	116	120	114	95	99	100
Electricity and gas [4]										
Electricité et gaz [4]	**132**	**139**	**145**	**157**	**162**	**164**	**168**	**170**	**171**	**177**
Canada [15] **Canada** [15]										
Total industry [2−4]										
Total, industrie [2−4]	**115**	**115**	**120**	**125**	**128**	**128**	**126**	**127**	**130**	**135**
Total mining [2]										
Total, industries extractives [2]	**117**	**113**	**123**	**134**	**131**	**130**	**132**	**136**	**140**	**146**
Total manufacturing [3]										
Total, industries manufacturières [3]	**112**	**113**	**118**	**124**	**126**	**121**	**112**	**114**	**119**	**128**
Food, beverages, tobacco										
Aliments, boissons, tabac	106	104	105	106	103	103	103	106	107	110
Textiles										
Textiles	104	115	116	117	116	109	104	104	108	118

26
Index numbers of industrial production [*cont.*]
Indices de la production industrielle [*suite*]
1980=100

Country or area and industry [SITC] Pays ou zone et industrie [CITI]	1985	1986	1987	1988	1989	1990	1991	1992	1993	1994
Paper and paper products										
Papier, produits en papier	97	102	108	109	104	101	97	97	100	105
Chemicals, coal, petroleum products										
Produits chimiques, houillers, pétroliers	114	116	125	133	139	141	128	134	140	143
Basic metals										
Métaux de base	111	107	119	125	121	114	115	118	130	133
Metal products										
Produits métalliques	119	120	125	138	144	138	125	126	134	153
Electricity, gas and water [4]										
Electricité, gaz, eau [4]	**120**	**123**	**127**	**129**	**128**	**122**	**128**	**127**	**130**	**136**
Costa Rica [16] Costa Rica [16]										
Total industry [2−4]										
Total, industrie [2−4]	**104**	**111**	**118**	**120**	**125**	**150**	**151**	**165**	**177**	**...**
Total mining [2]										
Total, industries extractives [2]	**90**	**88**	**84**	**87**	**98**	**97**	**106**	**129**	**135**	**...**
Total manufacturing [3]										
Total, industries manufacturières [3]	**101**	**108**	**114**	**117**	**121**	**124**	**127**	**140**	**149**	**...**
Electricity, gas and water [4]										
Electricité, gaz et eau [4]	**129**	**137**	**147**	**151**	**159**	**169**	**177**	**187**	**198**	**...**
El Salvador [17] El Salvador [17]										
Total industry [2−4]										
Total, industrie [2−4]	**91**	**93**	**96**	**98**	**101**	**104**	**107**	**118**	**116**	**126**
Total mining [2]										
Total, industries extractives [2]	**103**	**103**	**103**	**128**	**128**	**128**	**140**	**148**	**163**	**183**
Total manufacturing [3]										
Total, industries manufacturières [3]	**88**	**90**	**93**	**96**	**98**	**101**	**107**	**118**	**116**	**125**
Food, beverages, tobacco										
Aliments, boissons, tabac	102	103	105	109	111	114	118	171	175	181
Textiles										
Textiles	47	56	59	53	57	59	61	66	60	65
Chemical products and petroleum										
Produits chimiques et pétroliers	91	94	96	96	104	106	119	136	124	135
Basic metals										
Métaux de base	103	120	122	124	122	134	137	145	141	164
Metal products										
Produits métalliques	67	68	71	72	70	74	76	83	82	99
Electricity, gas and water [4]										
Electricité, gaz et eau [4]	**107**	**109**	**111**	**113**	**114**	**121**	**60**	**63**	**69**	**73**
Honduras [18] Honduras [18]										
Total industry [2−4]										
Total, industrie [2−4]	**116**	**119**	**123**	**132**	**138**	**140**	**143**	**151**	**160**	**157**
Total mining [2]										
Total, industries extractives [2]	**135**	**126**	**77**	**105**	**118**	**109**	**114**	**126**	**130**	**136**
Total manufacturing [3]										
Total, industries manufacturières [3]	**110**	**115**	**122**	**128**	**133**	**134**	**136**	**145**	**154**	**151**
Food, beverages, tobacco										
Aliments, boissons, tabac	128	130	130	148	151	193	246	284	316	...
Textiles										
Textiles	152	149	153	158	181	236	332	396	460	...
Chemicals										
Produits chimiques	120	120	120	126	145	144	208	360	405	...
Electricity [4]										
Electricité [4]	**148**	**158**	**185**	**208**	**217**	**246**	**248**	**250**	**269**	**250**
Mexico Méxique										
Total industry [2−4] [19]										
Total, industrie [2−4] [19]	**112**	**108**	**113**	**115**	**122**	**128**	**132**	**135**	**135**	**135**
Total mining [2]										
Total, industries extractives [2]	**129**	**126**	**131**	**131**	**131**	**136**	**137**	**139**	**139**	**139**
Total manufacturing [3]										
Total, manufactures [3]	**108**	**104**	**108**	**111**	**118**	**124**	**129**	**132**	**131**	**135**
Food, beverages, tobacco										
Aliments, boissons, tabac	115	117	118	117	124	128	133	135	135	134

26
Index numbers of industrial production [*cont.*]
Indices de la production industrielle [*suite*]
1980=100

Country or area and industry [SITC] Pays ou zone et industrie [CITI]	1985	1986	1987	1988	1989	1990	1991	1992	1993	1994
Textiles [4]										
Textiles [4]	98	92	92	96	97	95	91	91	88	86
Chemicals, coal, petroleum products [9]										
Produits chimiques, houillers, pétroliers [9]	119	116	121	123	132	140	148	153	148	157
Basic metals										
Métaux de base	97	89	102	108	113	120	117	116	124	129
Metal products										
Produits métalliques	101	94	103	113	125	132	146	146	145	155
Electricity, gas and water										
Electricité, gaz et eau	**135**	**140**	**148**	**156**	**169**	**178**	**185**	**195**	**202**	**213**
Panama Panama										
Total mining [2]										
Total, industries extractives [2]	**79**	**81**	**87**	**51**	**48**	**62**	**104**	**144**	**177**	...
Total manufacturing [3]										
Total, industries manufacturières [3]	**110**	**113**	**121**	**92**	**97**	**109**	**117**	**128**	**137**	**141**
Food, beverages, tobacco										
Aliments, boissons, tabac	105	105	112	97	104	111	116	122	130	140
Textiles										
Textiles	93	97	96	68	95	110	112	99	111	111
Non-metallic mineral products										
Produits minéraux non-métalliques	89	108	116	46	45	62	96	120	159	174
Basic metals										
Métaux de base	62	70	107	36	34	58	85	98	114	98
Metal products										
Produits métalliques	120	128	145	76	75	104	99	105	117	130
Trinidad and Tobago Trinité-et-Tobago										
Total industry [2-4] [3]										
Total, industrie [2-4] [3]	**99**	**121**	**125**	**120**	**121**	**124**	**138**	**151**	**141**	**162**
Total manufacturing [3] [5]										
Total, industries manufacturières [3][5]	**94**	**116**	**119**	**114**	**115**	**118**	**132**	**144**	**135**	**155**
Food, beverages, tobacco										
Aliments, boissons, tabac	85	88	89	87	89	90	91	91	86	90
Textiles										
Textiles	43	53	38	29	33	42	38	39	25	22
Chemicals and petroleum products										
Produits chimiques et pétroliers	64	67	70	72	70	71	69	72	70	71
Metal products										
Produits métalliques	56	64	54	50	46	45	61	66	56	68
Electricity [4]										
Electricité [4]	**154**	**171**	**181**	**183**	**181**	**188**	**198**	**210**	**208**	**220**
United States Etats-Unis										
Total industry [2-4]										
Total, industrie [2-4]	**112**	**113**	**119**	**124**	**126**	**126**	**124**	**128**	**132**	**140**
Total mining [2]										
Total, industries extractives [2]	**99**	**92**	**91**	**92**	**91**	**93**	**91**	**90**	**89**	**91**
Total manufacturing [3]										
Total, industries manufacturières [3]	**116**	**120**	**127**	**133**	**135**	**135**	**132**	**137**	**142**	**152**
Food, beverages, tobacco										
Aliments, boissons, tabac	111	113	116	118	119	121	122	124	125	130
Textiles										
Textiles	99	105	112	110	112	108	108	116	123	127
Paper and paper products										
Papier, produits en papier	116	124	131	135	138	138	139	144	150	156
Chemicals, coal, petroleum products										
Produits chimiques, houillers, pétroliers	109	115	121	127	130	133	131	135	136	142
Basic metals										
Métaux de base	89	83	90	98	97	96	89	92	97	105
Metal products										
Produits métalliques	117	118	122	132	135	134	131	139	149	165
Electricity and gas [4]										
Electricité et gaz [4]	**104**	**100**	**104**	**109**	**113**	**115**	**117**	**117**	**121**	**123**

26
Index numbers of industrial production [*cont.*]
Indices de la production industrielle [*suite*]
1980=100

Country or area and industry [SITC] Pays ou zone et industrie [CITI]	1985	1986	1987	1988	1989	1990	1991	1992	1993	1994
America, South · Amérique du Sud										
Argentina Argentine										
Total industry [2−4] [5]										
Total, industrie [2−4] [5]	**86**	**96**	**98**	**93**	**87**	**89**	**99**	...	...	...
Total mining [2]										
Total, industries extractives [2]	**94**	**87**	**93**	**100**	**103**	**109**	**103**	...	...	...
Total manufacturing [3]										
Total, industries manufacturières [3]	**85**	**95**	**96**	**92**	**85**	**87**	**97**	...	...	...
Food, beverages, tobacco										
Aliments, boissons, tabac	105	113	114	112	110	113	125	...	...	...
Textiles										
Textiles	91	110	104	106	100	103	120	...	...	...
Chemicals, coal, petroleum products										
Produits chimiques, houillers, pétroliers	89	101	104	103	94	102	109	...	...	...
Basic metals										
Métaux de base	77	99	110	114	103	109	112	...	...	...
Metal products										
Produits métalliques	74	77	82	75	63	59	70	...	...	...
Electricity and gas [4]										
Electricité et gaz [4]	**125**	**129**	**136**	**126**	**120**	**131**	**134**	...	...	...
Bolivia Bolivie										
Total industry [2−4] [5]										
Total, industrie [2−4] [5]	**67**	**65**	**66**	**73**	**79**	**87**	**92**	**94**	**101**	**108**
Total mining [2]										
Total, industries extractives [2]	**59**	**42**	**43**	**62**	**73**	**85**	**86**	**88**	**96**	**100**
Total manufacturing [3]										
Total, industries manufacturières [3]	**64**	**67**	**69**	**72**	**76**	**82**	**88**	**89**	**95**	**100**
Electricity [4]										
Electricité [4]	**133**	**134**	**126**	**132**	**135**	**144**	**154**	**165**	**182**	**211**
Brazil Brésil										
Total industry [2−4]										
Total, industrie [2−4]	**99**	**110**	**111**	**107**	**110**	**100**	**98**	**94**	**101**	**109**
Total mining [2]										
Total, industries extractives [2]	**176**	**182**	**181**	**182**	**189**	**194**	**196**	**197**	**198**	**208**
Total manufacturing [3] [21]										
Total, manufactures [3] [21]	**97**	**108**	**109**	**105**	**108**	**98**	**96**	**92**	**99**	**107**
Food, beverages, tobacco										
Aliments, boissons, tabac	106	108	114	112	115	117	124	122	124	127
Textiles										
Textiles	89	101	100	94	94	85	87	83	83	86
Chemicals and petroleum products										
Produits chimiques et pétroliers	121	123	130	126	· 125	115	106	106	110	118
Basic metals [22]										
Métaux de base [22]	95	106	107	104	109	95	90	89	96	106
Chile Chili										
Total industry [2−4] [5]										
Total, industrie [2−4] [5]	**109**	**115**	**118**	**126**	**136**	**136**	**148**	**162**	**166**	**173**
Total mining [2] [23]										
Total, industries extractives [2] [23]	**129**	**130**	**131**	**137**	**148**	**150**	**167**	**177**	**184**	**196**
Total manufacturing [3]										
Total, manufactures [3]	**98**	**106**	**110**	**119**	**129**	**128**	**136**	**152**	**155**	**158**
Food, beverages, tobacco										
Aliments, boissons, tabac	116	125	121	128	140	134	136	157	163	176
Textiles										
Textiles	105	124	130	124	126	118	130	125	120	110
Chemicals and petroleum products										
Produits chimiques et pétroliers	93	103	108	120	134	133	140	154	162	173
Basic metals										
Métaux de base	107	111	114	122	129	131	128	139	136	130
Metal products										
Produits métalliques	68	75	86	92	104	105	106	134	149	152
Electricity [4]										
Electricité [4]	**118**	**126**	**133**	**144**	**151**	**156**	**168**	**188**	**198**	**215**

26
Index numbers of industrial production [*cont.*]
Indices de la production industrielle [*suite*]
1980=100

Country or area and industry [SITC] Pays ou zone et industrie [CITI]	1985	1986	1987	1988	1989	1990	1991	1992	1993	1994
Colombia Colombie										
Total manufacturing [3]										
Total, industries manufacturières [3]	**104**	**112**	**120**	**122**	**125**	**133**	**133**	**142**	**146**	**151**
Food, beverages, tobacco										
Aliments, boissons, tabac	114	116	119	118	118	130	123	130	136	135
Textiles										
Textiles	104	115	125	118	112	115	115	123	121	123
Chemicals, coal, petroleum products										
Produits chimiques, houillers, pétroliers	134	152	164	163	165	168	174	157	163	167
Basic metals										
Métaux de base	106	116	134	143	141	145	140	156	163	185
Metal products										
Produits métalliques	87	96	104	117	109	115	105	119	140	152
Ecuador Equateur										
Total manufacturing [3]										
Total, industries manufacturières [3]	**113**	**117**	**120**	**126**	**131**	**140**	**158**	**166**	**169**	**172**
Food, beverages, tobacco										
Aliments, boissons, tabac	96	99	102	102	105	110	121	121	119	126
Textiles										
Textiles	98	95	91	94	96	100	100	89	77	82
Chemicals, coal, petroleum products										
Produits chimiques, houillers, pétroliers	123	128	128	132	128	145	185	189	206	228
Basic metals										
Métaux de base	150	142	129	146	129	132	167	167	184	204
Metal products										
Produits métalliques	122	136	136	149	163	174	205	235	251	298
Paraguay Paraguay										
Total manufacturing [3]										
Total, industries manufacturières [3]	**102**	**101**	**106**	**114**	**148**	**102**	**78**	**81**	**75**	**80**
Food, beverages, tobacco										
Aliments, boissons, tabac	111	116	123	111	148	152	112	124	110	124
Textiles										
Textiles	169	115	95	196	215	224	106	77	104	94
Chemicals, coal, petroleum products										
Produits chimiques, houillers, pétroliers	74	67	76	87	78	81	65	62	84	68
Basic metals										
Métaux de base	271	254	560	622	615	509	220	217	244	152
Metal products										
Produits métalliques	212	192	190	181	168	145	144	140	113	88
Peru Pérou										
Total manufacturing [3]										
Total, industries manufacturières [3]	**89**	**105**	**120**	**104**	**84**	**82**	**88**	**86**	**90**	**104**
Food, beverages, tobacco										
Aliments, boissons, tabac	94	114	132	118	94	95	101	101	101	117
Textiles										
Textiles	113	121	134	126	116	104	101	94	89	107
Chemicals, coal, petroleum products										
Produits chimiques, houillers, pétroliers	83	103	124	111	78	78	82	80	87	93
Basic metals										
Métaux de base	99	96	100	78	86	77	90	91	96	105
Metal products										
Produits métalliques	55	81	102	70	42	46	50	41	38	49
Uruguay Uruguay										
Total manufacturing [3]										
Total, manufactures [3]	**75**	**84**	**93**	**91**	**89**	**98**	**90**	**90**	**84**	**86**
Food, beverages, tobacco										
Aliments, boissons, tabac	95	96	97	101	103	103	104	110	105	111
Textiles										
Textiles	85	99	106	101	96	100	108	109	98	99
Chemicals, coal, petroleum products										
Produits chimiques, houillers, pétroliers	75	83	97	100	99	102	100	96	76	78
Metal products										
Produits métalliques	48	62	85	75	69	69	68	64	60	76

26
Index numbers of industrial production [*cont.*]
Indices de la production industrielle [*suite*]
1980=100

Country or area and industry [SITC] Pays ou zone et industrie [CITI]	1985	1986	1987	1988	1989	1990	1991	1992	1993	1994
Asia · Asie										
Bangladesh [24] **Bangladesh** [24]										
Total industry [2–4]										
Total, industrie [2–4]	127	146	148	153	172	176	194	219	240	267
Total mining [2]										
Total, industries extractives [2]	199	236	277	295	315	325	359	394	386	458
Total manufacturing [3]										
Total, industries manufacturières [3]	126	144	145	148	167	171	189	214	235	262
Food, beverages, tobacco										
Aliments, boissons, tabac	108	124	127	129	156	158	151	145	163	179
Textiles										
Textiles	77	89	88	87	91	80	80	82	78	73
Basic metals [14]										
Métaux de base [14]	55	50	45	51	57	44	34	36	64	104
Electricity [4]										
Électricité [4]	180	210	246	285	304	326	350	363	379	402
Cyprus Chypre										
Total industry [2–4]										
Total, industrie [2–4]	116	119	131	142	147	154	156	162	151	156
Total mining [2]										
Total, industries extractives [2]	71	64	68	66	55	55	54	58	67	73
Total manufacturing [3] [25]										
Total, manufactures [3] [25]	115	118	130	138	144	151	152	156	140	145
Food, beverages, tobacco										
Aliments, boissons, tabac	126	125	137	146	157	168	168	178	164	174
Textiles										
Textiles	95	94	102	124	113	125	118	136	124	120
Chemicals										
Produits chimiques	140	156	166	221	234	212	201	223	217	238
Metal products										
Produits métalliques	134	123	141	157	143	141	147	157	164	165
Electricity, gas and water [4]										
Électricité, gaz et eau [4]	123	134	150	167	181	198	196	228	248	264
India Inde										
Total industry [2–4]										
Total, industrie [2–4]	140	149	165	178	188	209	213	221	223	240
Total mining [2]										
Total, industries extractives [2]	164	176	184	194	210	216	221	223	227	241
Total manufacturing [3]										
Total, industries manufacturières [3]	135	143	160	173	181	205	206	214	214	231
Food, beverages, tobacco										
Aliments, boissons, tabac	125	129	129	136	137	153	160	162	156	...
Textiles										
Textiles	109	107	114	107	108	122	132	138	149	...
Chemicals and petroleum products										
Produits chimiques et du pétroliers	149	172	197	227	238	254	254	268	283	...
Basic metals										
Métaux de base	133	140	156	169	167	180	195	194	203	...
Metal products										
Produits métalliques	146	157	194	209	227	279	264	275	255	...
Electricity [4]										
Électricité [4]	149	164	178	192	216	233	253	266	284	308
Indonesia Indonésie										
Total mining [2]										
Total, industries extractives [2]	83	87	87	84	93	91	100	81	97	98
Total manufacturing [3]										
Total, industries manufacturières [3]	130	145	162	185	208	236	262	291	324	381
Food, beverages, tobacco										
Aliments, boissons, tabac	116	132	147	168	177	204	182	186	221	276
Textiles										
Textiles	97	127	134	163	184	221	233	253	252	268
Chemicals										
Produits chimiques	169	175	163	144	174	187	184	222	282	291

26
Index numbers of industrial production [cont.]
Indices de la production industrielle [suite]
1980=100

Country or area and industry [SITC] Pays ou zone et industrie [CITI]	1985	1986	1987	1988	1989	1990	1991	1992	1993	1994
Iran, Islamic Rep. of [26] **Iran, Rép. islamique d'** [26]										
Total manufacturing [3] [7] [27]										
Total, manufactures [3] [7] [27]	152	121	113	104	109	130	160	170	...	...
Food and beverages										
Aliments et boissons	125	110	104	98	97	111	121	136	...	...
Textiles										
Textiles	148	135	118	105	96	103	117	123	...	...
Chemicals										
Produits chimiques	141	140	131	123	137	186	189	195	...	...
Non−metallic mineral products										
Produits minéraux non−métalliques	145	138	144	136	142	162	180	192	...	...
Israel Israël										
Total industry [2−4] [28]										
Total, industrie [2−4] [28]	120	124	130	126	124	132	141	153	162	175
Total mining [2] [29]										
Total, industries extractives [2] [29]	108	118	126	115	118	125	136	142	146	162
Total manufacturing [3]										
Total, industries manufacturières [3]	120	124	130	126	124	132	141	153	163	175
Food and beverages										
Aliments et boissons	125	144	161	161	157	159	161	166	179	190
Textiles										
Textiles	99	98	99	92	92	97	104	107	107	116
Chemicals and petroleum products										
Produits chimiques et du pétroliers	128	131	146	148	156	163	170	188	206	228
Basic metals										
Métaux de base	85	83	86	90	85	106	118	124	129	148
Metal products										
Produits métalliques	123	111	122	118	114	120	128	138	145	154
Japan Japon										
Total industry [2−4]										
Total, industrie [2−4]	118	118	122	134	142	148	150	141	134	136
Total mining [2]										
Total, industries extractives [2]	94	94	86	82	79	75	77	76	75	74
Total manufacturing [3]										
Total, manufactures [3]	119	118	122	134	142	148	150	141	135	136
Food and beverages										
Aliments et boissons	101	102	103	106	108	108	109	109	108	108
Textiles										
Textiles	98	94	92	93	92	90	88	85	76	73
Chemicals and petroleum products										
Produits chimiques et du pétroliers	107	107	111	120	127	134	136	136	134	140
Basic metals										
Métaux de base	101	96	100	108	111	115	116	107	104	104
Metal products										
Produits métalliques	142	143	149	169	182	193	200	181	172	177
Electricity and gas [4]										
Electricité et gaz [4]	120	120	126	132	139	149	155	158	159	169
Jordan Jordanie										
Total industry [2−4] [28]										
Total, industrie [2−4] [28]	155	157	172	158	166	169	158	179	193	204
Total mining [2] [30]										
Total, industries extractives [2] [30]	155	160	175	144	170	149	132	128	129	139
Total manufacturing [3]										
Total, industries manufacturières [3]	145	150	168	152	160	164	156	181	197	208
Food and beverages										
Aliments et boissons	108	80	84	95	93	98	94	133	137	135
Textiles										
Textiles	149	132	149	156	133	142	123	106	117	114
Chemicals and petroleum products										
Produits chimiques et du pétroliers	135	139	145	135	154	165	149	162	156	156

26
Index numbers of industrial production [*cont.*]
Indices de la production industrielle [*suite*]
1980=100

Country or area and industry [SITC] Pays ou zone et industrie [CITI]	1985	1986	1987	1988	1989	1990	1991	1992	1993	1994
Basic metals										
Métaux de base	155	162	172	152	138	137	153	183	144	122
Korea, Rep. of Corée, Rép. de										
Total industry [2−4]										
Total, industrie [2−4]	**165**	**199**	**238**	**269**	**278**	**302**	**331**	**350**	**366**	**406**
Total mining [2]										
Total, industries extractives [2]	**116**	**124**	**126**	**126**	**112**	**102**	**102**	**88**	**82**	**80**
Total manufacturing [3]										
Total, industries manufacturières [3]	**168**	**205**	**246**	**279**	**288**	**314**	**344**	**364**	**380**	**421**
Food, beverages, tobacco										
Aliments, boissons, tabac	150	164	183	205	219	232	251	257	261	282
Textiles										
Textiles	124	149	166	171	166	165	162	156	142	142
Chemicals and petroleum products										
Produits chimiques et du pétroliers	146	164	192	237	259	295	350	421	464	497
Basic metals										
Métaux de base	189	210	239	259	282	316	350	366	407	441
Metal products										
Produits métalliques	268	342	429	504	497	571	628	665	685	776
Electricity and gas [4]										
Electricité et gaz [4]	**156**	**174**	**198**	**230**	**254**	**289**	**322**	**360**	**401**	**464**
Malaysia Malaisie										
Total industry [2−4]										
Total, industrie [2−4]	**138**	**152**	**164**	**188**	**210**	**236**	**262**	**284**	**312**	**349**
Total mining [2]										
Total, industries extractives [2]	**163**	**189**	**194**	**218**	**235**	**247**	**259**	**266**	**270**	**281**
Total manufacturing [3] [31]										
Total, manufactures [3] [31]	**122**	**130**	**147**	**169**	**193**	**223**	**254**	**281**	**317**	**363**
Food, beverages, tobacco										
Aliments, boissons, tabac	123	129	136	145	164	175	170	178	190	202
Textiles										
Textiles	92	103	118	122	147	164	173	201	263	328
Chemicals										
Produits chimiques	111	126	143	148	154	157	202	187	197	213
Basic metals										
Métaux de base	131	102	125	166	198	226	256	305	344	398
Metal products										
Prcduits métalliques	149	183	218	269	317	418	528	592	704	856
Electricity [4]										
Electricité [4]	**143**	**157**	**169**	**188**	**210**	**239**	**270**	**308**	**346**	**394**
Mongolia Mongolie										
Total manufacturing [3]										
Total, industries manufacturières [3]	**156**	**168**	**176**	**182**	**187**	**183**	**156**	**...**	**...**	**...**
Food, beverages, tobacco										
Aliments, boissons, tabac	137	142	144	148	152	139	152	...	...	...
Textiles										
Textiles	227	240	246	244	276	248	197	...	...	...
Chemicals										
Produits chimiques	130	150	162	192	198	187	162	...	...	...
Metal products										
Produits métalliques	159	165	184	186	186	158	146	...	...	...
Electricity [4]										
Electricité [4]	**181**	**202**	**214**	**217**	**224**	**236**	**211**	**...**	**...**	**...**
Pakistan [24] Pakistan [24]										
Total industry [2−4]										
Total, industrie [2−4]	**160**	**170**	**186**	**191**	**204**	**218**	**232**	**238**	**245**	**245**
Total mining [2]										
Total, industries extractives [2]	**183**	**187**	**212**	**218**	**250**	**275**	**278**	**278**	**275**	**269**
Total manufacturing [3]										
Total, industries manufacturières [3]	**154**	**165**	**179**	**183**	**192**	**206**	**218**	**228**	**237**	**238**
Electricity and gas [4]										
Electricité et gaz [4]	**163**	**182**	**209**	**211**	**218**	**255**	**282**	**302**	**308**	**329**

26
Index numbers of industrial production [*cont.*]
Indices de la production industrielle [*suite*]
1980=100

Country or area and industry [SITC] Pays ou zone et industrie [CITI]	1985	1986	1987	1988	1989	1990	1991	1992	1993	1994
Philippines Philippines										
Total industry [2−4] [5]										
Total, industrie [2−4] [5]	**231**	**258**	**296**	**358**	**408**	**451**	**515**	**540**	**571**	**617**
Total mining [2]										
Total, industries extractives [2]	**85**	**71**	**87**	**92**	**125**	**157**	**195**	**262**	**197**	**152**
Total manufacturing [3] [2]										
Total, industries manufacturières [3] [2]	**241**	**291**	**333**	**406**	**459**	**506**	**577**	**597**	**643**	**703**
Food, beverages, tobacco										
Aliments, boissons, tabac	272	264	288	343	379	411	468	504	521	570
Textiles										
Textiles	166	221	256	274	288	289	322	317	338	340
Non−metallic mineral products										
Produits minéraux non−métalliques	173	182	213	256	310	355	468	474	544	550
Metal products										
Produits métalliques	357	598	669	826	953	1072	1198	1326	1461	1520
Electricity and water [4]										
Electricité et gaz [4]	**126**	**130**	**141**	**148**	**152**	**154**	**158**	**159**	**165**	**190**
Singapore Singapour										
Total manufacturing [3]										
Total, industries manufacturières [3]	**107**	**116**	**136**	**162**	**178**	**196**	**206**	**211**	**232**	**262**
Food, beverages, tobacco										
Aliments, boissons, tabac	90	93	96	112	132	132	140	150	154	171
Textiles										
Textiles	30	30	35	37	39	36	39	34	30	29
Chemicals, coal, petroleum products										
Produits chimiques, houillers, pétroliers	136	145	143	149	169	198	216	211	232	244
Basic metals										
Métaux de base	123	124	129	136	139	151	144	150	163	162
Metal products										
Produits métalliques	103	108	132	158	182	181	196	196	198	221
Sri Lanka Sri Lanka										
Total manufacturing [3] [34]										
Total, manufactures [3] [34]	**144**	**155**	**141**	**138**	**147**	**175**	**172**	**172**	**177**	**200**
Food, beverages, tobacco										
Aliments, boissons, tabac	96	115	102	92	109	114	116	111	134	142
Textiles and clothing										
Textiles, habillement	177	188	218	282	364	487	531	564	600	636
Chemicals and rubber products										
Produits chimiques et en caoutchouc	131	116	104	108	84	115	101	113	135	144
Basic metals										
Métaux de base	61	84	73	102	94	142	134	90	102	133
Metal products										
Produits métalliques	60	55	80	78	102	132	98	133	164	191
Syrian Arab Rep. Rép. arabe syrienne										
Total industry [2−4]										
Total, industrie [2−4]	**136**	**141**	**151**	**151**	**170**	**186**	**199**	**212**	**216**	**225**
Total mining [2]										
Total, industries extractives [2]	**101**	**125**	**143**	**181**	**229**	**270**	**310**	**338**	**343**	**343**
Total manufacturing [3]										
Total, industries manufacturières [3]	**163**	**161**	**165**	**147**	**153**	**163**	**165**	**174**	**179**	**189**
Food, beverages, tobacco										
Aliments, boissons, tabac	147	150	131	121	123	136	148	150	142	150
Textiles										
Textiles	118	133	118	92	102	100	93	107	108	116
Non−metallic mineral products										
Produits minéraux non−métalliques	191	191	174	145	171	134	141	155	171	177
Electricity and water [4]										
Electricité et eau [4]	**183**	**172**	**191**	**224**	**237**	**258**	**276**	**255**	**289**	**348**
Turkey Turquie										
Total industry [2−4]										
Total, industrie [2−4]	**148**	**166**	**183**	**186**	**193**	**211**	**217**	**227**	**246**	**231**
Total mining [2]										
Total, industries extractives [2]	**136**	**151**	**158**	**150**	**169**	**179**	**197**	**190**	**173**	**187**

26
Index numbers of industrial production [*cont.*]
Indices de la production industrielle [*suite*]
1980=100

Country or area and industry [SITC] Pays ou zone et industrie [CITI]	1985	1986	1987	1988	1989	1990	1991	1992	1993	1994
Total manufacturing [3]										
Total, industries manufacturières [3]	**152**	**168**	**187**	**188**	**192**	**211**	**214**	**223**	**243**	**223**
Food, beverages, tobacco										
Aliments, boissons, tabac	156	154	164	167	176	187	202	194	206	211
Textiles										
Textiles	170	191	209	216	226	231	210	221	226	230
Chemicals, coal, petroleum products										
Produits chimiques, houillers, pétroliers	178	210	248	244	251	261	256	261	270	254
Basic metals										
Métaux de base	187	220	244	241	247	288	264	279	317	302
Metal products										
Produits métalliques	208	224	244	232	228	298	330	364	428	305
Electricity, gas and water [4]										
Electricité, gaz et eau [4]	**146**	**152**	**170**	**184**	**199**	**221**	**229**	**257**	**282**	**299**
Europe · Europe										
Austria Autriche										
Total industry [2−4]										
Total, industrie [2−4]	**109**	**110**	**112**	**116**	**123**	**132**	**134**	**132**	**130**	**136**
Total mining [2]										
Total, industries extractives [2]	**110**	**108**	**112**	**101**	**100**	**104**	**94**	**84**	**76**	**71**
Total manufacturing [3]										
Total, industries manufacturières [3]	**109**	**110**	**110**	**116**	**124**	**133**	**136**	**135**	**132**	**138**
Food, beverages, tobacco										
Aliments, boissons, tabac	112	115	116	118	124	135	143	145	146	151
Textiles										
Textiles	91	91	86	90	94	98	99	96	85	84
Chemicals and petroleum products										
Produits chimiques et pétroliers	116	113	118	131	136	138	139	140	136	146
Basic metals										
Métaux de base	107	102	102	112	118	115	108	105	101	110
Metal products										
Produits métalliques	118	123	119	127	140	157	162	160	156	165
Electricity, gas and water [4]										
Electricité, gaz et eau [4]	**110**	**110**	**123**	**119**	**123**	**125**	**128**	**126**	**131**	**131**
Belgium Belgique										
Total industry [2−4] [32]										
Total, industrie [2−4] [32]	**104**	**105**	**107**	**114**	**118**	**122**	**119**	**119**	**113**	**115**
Total mining [2] [32] [33]										
Total, industries extractives [2] [32] [33]	**84**	**75**	**65**	**56**	**45**	**32**	**33**	**36**	**32**	**33**
Total manufacturing [3] [32] [34]										
Total, manufactures [3] [32] [34]	**104**	**105**	**108**	**115**	**120**	**125**	**127**	**123**	**122**	**125**
Food, beverages, tobacco										
Aliments, boissons, tabac	118	120	124	127	118	139	143	144	145	143
Textiles										
Textiles	104	105	105	106	107	105	95	100	90	91
Chemicals and petroleum products										
Produits chimiques et pétroliers	112	117	119	126	118	132	132	144	139	137
Basic metals										
Métaux de base	92	86	88	99	105	101	99	84	81	80
Metal products										
Produits métalliques	105	106	106	113	114	122	121	115	110	112
Electricity, gas and water [4] [32]										
Electricité, gaz et eau [4] [32]	**107**	**110**	**118**	**122**	**126**	**133**	**134**	**136**	**134**	**136**
Bulgaria Bulgarie										
Total industry [2−4]										
Total, industrie [2−4]	**124**	**129**	**134**	**141**	**139**	**116**	**90**	**76**	**74**	**78**
Total mining [2] [9] [38]										
Total, industries extractives [2] [9] [38]	**105**	**109**	**109**	**108**	**108**	**96**	**74**	**74**	**77**	...
Total manufacturing [3] [35]										
Total, manufactures [3] [35]	**124**	**130**	**135**	**142**	**140**	**116**	**89**	**74**	**64**	...
Food, beverages, tobacco										
Aliments, boissons, tabac	111	107	106	115	114	107	84	73	56	51

26
Index numbers of industrial production [*cont.*]
Indices de la production industrielle [*suite*]
1980=100

Country or area and industry [SITC] Pays ou zone et industrie [CITI]	1985	1986	1987	1988	1989	1990	1991	1992	1993	1994
Textiles										
Textiles	117	114	121	131	136	138	96	84	70	67
Chemicals										
Produits chimiques	125	140	133	163	138	104	85	70	62	86
Basic metals										
Métaux de base	115	119	120	122	118	99	59	55	68	77
Metal products										
Produits métalliques	149	138	151	184	177	140	105	78	63	58
Electricity and steam [4]										
Electricité et vapeur [4]	**124**	**127**	**133**	**140**	**137**	**124**	**116**	**102**	**103**	**99**
former Czechoslovakia † ancienne Tchécoslovaquie †										
Total industry [2−4]										
Total, industrie [2−4]	**115**	**119**	**121**	**124**	**125**	**120**	**90**	**79**	**...**	**...**
Total mining [2]										
Total, industries extractives [2]	**101**	**101**	**102**	**103**	**100**	**91**	**77**	**69**	**...**	**...**
Total manufacturing [3] [34]										
Total, manufactures [3] [34]	**116**	**119**	**122**	**125**	**126**	**121**	**89**	**74**	**...**	**...**
Food, beverages, tobacco										
Aliments, boissons, tabac	107	109	110	110	113	111	96	87	...	...
Textiles										
Textiles	111	114	115	118	120	120	78	67	...	...
Chemicals, coal, petroleum products										
Produits chimiques, houillers, pétroliers	117	115	120	123	123	128	94	88	...	...
Basic metals										
Métaux de base	104	105	107	108	108	107	81	69	...	...
Metal products										
Produits métalliques	139	146	152	156	156	150	102	75	...	...
Electricity, gas and water [4]										
Electricité, gaz et eau [4]	112	118	120	122	124	123	118	119	...	...
Denmark Danemark										
Total industry [2−4] [32]										
Total, industrie [2−4] [28] [32]	**122**	**131**	**127**	**129**	**133**	**133**	**133**	**137**	**134**	**148**
Total mining [2] [32]										
Total, industries extractives [2] [32]	**110**	**138**	**122**	**124**	**132**	**116**	**114**	**116**	**106**	**112**
Total manufacturing [3] [36] [1] [32]										
Total, manufactures [3] [36] [1] [32]	**122**	**131**	**127**	**129**	**133**	**133**	**133**	**137**	**134**	**148**
Food, beverages, tobacco										
Aliments, boissons, tabac	117	122	120	123	122	126	135	134	134	...
Textiles										
Textiles	116	120	116	111	113	106	106	105	91	...
Chemicals, coal, petroleum products										
Produits chimiques, houillers, pétroliers	127	134	134	137	137	138	139	148	148	...
Basic metals										
Métaux de base	97	93	87	91	103	96	93	92	79	...
Metal products										
Produits métalliques	125	136	129	131	138	139	141	143	137	...
Finland Finlande										
Total industry [2−4]										
Total, industrie [2−4]	**116**	**118**	**124**	**129**	**133**	**132**	**120**	**122**	**129**	**143**
Total mining [2]										
Total, industries extractives [2]	**123**	**127**	**124**	**134**	**146**	**143**	**132**	**127**	**124**	**138**
Total manufacturing [3]										
Total, industries manufacturières [3]	**116**	**118**	**124**	**128**	**133**	**132**	**118**	**120**	**127**	**142**
Food, beverages, tobacco										
Aliments, boissons, tabac	110	114	116	120	122	122	121	121	125	129
Textiles										
Textiles	79	75	78	73	70	64	52	53	55	59
Paper and paper products										
Papier, produits en papier	113	116	121	129	130	132	128	133	144	157
Chemicals, coal, petroleum products										
Produits chimiques, houillers, pétroliers	110	109	118	125	129	132	128	130	129	147
Basic metals										
Métaux de base	120	121	125	132	136	139	138	154	168	181

26
Index numbers of industrial production [*cont.*]
Indices de la production industrielle [*suite*]
1980=100

Country or area and industry [SITC] Pays ou zone et industrie [CITI]	1985	1986	1987	1988	1989	1990	1991	1992	1993	1994
Metal products Produits métalliques	132	135	146	152	163	161	134	142	155	188
Electricity, gas and water [4] **Electricité, gaz et eau** [4]	**121**	**121**	**130**	**133**	**134**	**136**	**141**	**141**	**147**	**156**
France France										
Total industry [2−4] **Total, industrie** [2−4]	**101**	**101**	**103**	**108**	**112**	**114**	**114**	**114**	**111**	**115**
Total mining [2] **Total, industries extractives** [2]	**86**	**81**	**81**	**77**	**75**	**72**	**72**	**67**	**64**	**62**
Total manufacturing [3] **Total, manufactures** [3]	**97**	**98**	**99**	**104**	**108**	**110**	**108**	**108**	**104**	**109**
Food, beverages, tobacco Aliments, boissons, tabac	106	105	108	111	113	118	120	121	123	123
Textiles Textiles	86	84	81	80	80	77	72	71	66	69
Chemicals, coal, petroleum products Produits chimiques, houillers, pétroliers	109	109	112	119	125	126	128	134	135	143
Basic metals Métaux de base	82	80	80	86	88	88	85	84	76	84
Metal products Produits métalliques	92	92	94	101	107	110	107	103	95	100
Electricity and gas [4] **Electricité et gaz** [4]	**130**	**136**	**142**	**145**	**150**	**154**	**168**	**171**	**175**	**175**
Germany † Allemagne †										
Germany, Fed. Rep. of Allemagne, Rép. féd. d'										
Total industry [2−4] [37] **Total, industrie** [2−4] [37]	**104**	**107**	**107**	**111**	**117**	**123**	**100**	**98**	**90**	**94**
Total mining [2] [37] **Total, industries extractives** [2] [37]	**93**	**91**	**87**	**85**	**84**	**84**	**100**	**93**	**86**	**83**
Total manufacturing [3] **Total, manufactures** [3]	**104**	**107**	**107**	**112**	**118**	**124**	**100**	**98**	**90**	**94**
Food, beverages, tobacco Aliments, boissons, tabac	105	108	109	113	116	129	138	137	136	...
Textiles Textiles	94	95	94	92	93	95	94	87	77	...
Chemicals, coal, petroleum products Produits chimiques, houillers, pétroliers	104	103	104	111	112	115	117	120	118	...
Basic metals Métaux de base	97	92	90	99	102	98	97	91	83	...
Metal products Produits métalliques	111	116	117	120	130	137	141	136	121	...
Electricity, gas and water [4] [37] **Electricité, gaz et eau** [4] [37]	**112**	**111**	**115**	**118**	**121**	**125**	**100**	**100**	**98**	**99**
former German Dem. Rep. ancienne Rép. dém. allemande										
Total industry [2−4] **Total, industrie** [2−4]	**119**	**123**	**126**	**130**	**133**	**94**	**...**	**...**	**...**	**...**
Total mining [2] [38] **Total, industries extractives** [2] [38]	**118**	**120**	**119**	**120**	**116**	**82**	**...**	**...**	**...**	**...**
Total manufacturing [3] [34] [35] [38] **Total, manufactures** [3] [34] [35] [38]	**119**	**123**	**127**	**131**	**135**	**95**	**...**	**...**	**...**	**...**
Food, beverages, tobacco Aliments, boissons, tabac	110	113	113	114	115	66	...	...	...	...
Textiles Textiles	109	111	114	117	119	74	...	...	...	...
Chemicals, coal, petroleum products Produits chimiques, houillers, pétroliers	112	113	114	119	122	65	...	...	...	...
Basic metals Métaux de base	112	113	117	117	116	69	...	...	...	...
Metal products Produits métalliques	134	141	149	158	165	75	...	...	...	...
Electricity and gas [4] **Electricité et gaz** [4]	**118**	**121**	**122**	**123**	**123**	**93**	**...**	**...**	**...**	**...**

26
Index numbers of industrial production [*cont.*]
Indices de la production industrielle [*suite*]
1980=100

Country or area and industry [SITC] Pays ou zone et industrie [CITI]	1985	1986	1987	1988	1989	1990	1991	1992	1993	1994
Greece Grèce										
Total industry [2−4]										
Total, industrie [2−4]	**107**	**107**	**106**	**111**	**113**	**110**	**109**	**108**	**105**	**106**
Total mining [2] [39]										
Total, industries extractives [2] [39]	**183**	**185**	**182**	**189**	**180**	**174**	**172**	**161**	**150**	**149**
Total manufacturing [3] [40]										
Total, manufactures [3] [40]	**101**	**100**	**98**	**103**	**106**	**103**	**102**	**100**	**97**	**98**
Food, beverages, tobacco										
Aliments, boissons, tabac	116	111	102	112	120	114	121	128	128	132
Textiles										
Textiles	95	102	104	101	99	95	86	79	74	74
Chemicals, coal, petroleum products										
Produits chimiques, houillers, pétroliers	115	115	117	125	132	133	124	126	126	132
Basic metals										
Métaux de base	88	86	85	95	96	93	96	92	86	89
Metal products										
Produits métalliques	84	87	79	83	82	83	85	88	80	76
Electricity and gas [4]										
Electricité et gaz [4]	**123**	**126**	**136**	**144**	**151**	**155**	**152**	**163**	**167**	**176**
Hungary Hongrie										
Total industry [2−4]										
Total, industrie [2−4]	**110**	**112**	**116**	**116**	**111**	**102**	**82**	**74**	**77**	**84**
Total mining [2] [38]										
Total, industries extractives [2] [38]	**99**	**99**	**99**	**95**	**88**	**78**	**69**	**56**	**55**	**46**
Total manufacturing [3] [38] [41]										
Total, manufactures [3] [38] [41]	**110**	**112**	**117**	**117**	**111**	**101**	**76**	**63**	**65**	**71**
Food, beverages, tobacco										
Aliments, boissons, tabac	109	111	114	111	112	109	106	92	89	92
Textiles										
Textiles	101	102	104	107	103	85	58	43	38	38
Chemicals, coal, petroleum products										
Produits chimiques, houillers, pétroliers	125	128	134	142	135	120	96	81	81	82
Basic metals										
Métaux de base	107	110	111	116	124	107	71	53	49	54
Metal products										
Produits métalliques	119	123	129	130	132	110	89	64	74	92
Electricity and gas [4]										
Electricité et gaz [4]	**120**	**123**	**130**	**129**	**130**	**132**	**125**	**104**	**102**	**103**
Ireland Irlande										
Total industry [2−4]										
Total, industrie [2−4]	**128**	**131**	**143**	**158**	**176**	**184**	**190**	**208**	**220**	**246**
Total mining [2]										
Total, industries extractives [2]	**72**	**79**	**85**	**69**	**89**	**84**	**77**	**71**	**83**	**84**
Total manufacturing [3] [7]										
Total, manufactures [3] [7]	**131**	**135**	**149**	**167**	**187**	**196**	**202**	**222**	**234**	**264**
Food, beverages, tobacco										
Aliments, boissons, tabac	117	121	132	139	145	149	156	167	173	186
Textiles										
Textiles	93	92	95	99	103	111	111	117	119	123
Chemicals										
Produits chimiques	166	165	172	200	240	247	301	353	388	464
Basic metals										
Métaux de base	130	120	120	136	150	158	141	128	134	128
Metal products										
Produits métalliques	158	166	201	244	282	300	291	326	345	398
Electricity, gas and water [4]										
Electricité, gaz et eau [4]	**133**	**127**	**124**	**128**	**135**	**144**	**155**	**160**	**169**	**178**
Italy Italie										
Total industry [2−4] [32]										
Total, industrie [2−4] [32]	**97**	**100**	**104**	**110**	**114**	**114**	**113**	**112**	**110**	**116**
Total mining [2] [32]										
Total, industries extractives [2] [32]	**100**	**105**	**118**	**130**	**128**	**130**	**128**	**124**	**129**	**133**

26
Index numbers of industrial production [cont.]
Indices de la production industrielle [suite]
1980=100

Country or area and industry [SITC] Pays ou zone et industrie [CITI]	1985	1986	1987	1988	1989	1990	1991	1992	1993	1994
Total manufacturing [3] [32] **Total, manufactures [3] [32]**	**96**	**100**	**103**	**109**	**113**	**112**	**111**	**110**	**108**	**113**
Food, beverages, tobacco Aliments, boissons, tabac	105	109	115	119	120	121	122	126	126	...
Textiles Textiles	97	101	105	106	112	110	111	110	105	...
Chemicals, coal, petroleum products Produits chimiques, houillers, pétroliers	90	93	96	98	98	99	94	96	93	...
Basic metals Métaux de base	93	93	96	104	108	104	104	104	100	...
Metal products Produits métalliques	101	110	113	122	128	127	119	113	106	...
Electricity, gas and water [4] [32] **Electricité, gaz et eau [4] [32]**	103	107	113	116	121	125	128	130	129	134
Luxembourg Luxembourg										
Total industry [2−4] [32] **Total, industrie [2−4] [32]**	**121**	**124**	**122**	**133**	**144**	**143**	**143**	**142**	**138**	**146**
Total mining [2] [32] **Total, industries extractives [2] [32]**	**29**	**29**	**33**	**36**	**40**	**44**	**49**	**56**	**50**	**46**
Total manufacturing [3] [32] [42] **Total, manufactures [3] [32] [42]**	**122**	**124**	**123**	**134**	**144**	**143**	**143**	**142**	**135**	**143**
Food, beverages, tobacco Aliments, boissons, tabac	129	134	130	128	133	138	140	142	140	143
Chemicals Produits chimiques	143	204	269	268	308	280	294	338	360	436
Basic metals [14] Métaux de base [14]	102	97	90	102	104	100	97	92	90	87
Metal products Produits métalliques	151	155	147	161	176	183	183	172	166	176
Electricity and gas [4] [32] **Electricité et gaz [4] [32]**	**126**	**132**	**138**	**148**	**154**	**158**	**164**	**163**	**167**	**175**
Malta Malte										
Total industry [2−4] **Total, industrie [2−4]**	**120**	**127**	**131**	**142**	**167**	**189**	**213**	**243**	**254**	...
Total mining [2] **Total, industries extractives [2]**	**64**	**84**	**95**	**91**	**170**	**195**	**294**	**298**	**311**	...
Total manufacturing [3] **Total, industries manufacturières [3]**	**118**	**128**	**132**	**144**	**169**	**191**	**214**	**244**	**260**	...
Food, beverages, tobacco Aliments, boissons, tabac	146	152	167	178	186	182	177	185	...	...
Metal products [43] Produits métalliques [43]	135	153	165	214	277	352	391	464	...	...
Electricity and water [4] **Electricité et eau [4]**	**132**	**143**	**160**	**176**	**188**	**202**	**226**	**240**	**252**	...
Netherlands Pays−Bas										
Total industry [2−4] **Total, industrie [2−4]**	**106**	**106**	**107**	**109**	**113**	**117**	**119**	**118**	**117**	**119**
Total mining [2] **Total, industries extractives [2]**	**93**	**86**	**89**	**79**	**81**	**82**	**89**	**90**	**91**	**89**
Total manufacturing [3] **Total, industries manufacturières [3]**	**109**	**111**	**113**	**118**	**123**	**126**	**126**	**126**	**123**	**128**
Food, beverages, tobacco Aliments, boissons, tabac	105	112	112	113	119	125	130	129	126	129
Textiles Textiles	100	95	96	98	100	104	99	93	92	97
Chemicals, coal, petroleum products [44] Produits chimiques, houillers, pétroliers [44]	130	134	135	147	150	155	151	149	150	156
Basic metals Métaux de base	110	108	99	108	114	107	109	110	109	117
Metal products Produits métalliques	110	110	112	112	119	126	126	125	120	124
Electricity, gas and water [4] **Electricité, gaz et eau [4]**	**108**	**112**	**114**	**118**	**118**	**121**	**124**	**126**	**128**	**129**

26
Index numbers of industrial production [*cont.*]
Indices de la production industrielle [*suite*]
1980=100

Country or area and industry [SITC] Pays ou zone et industrie [CITI]	1985	1986	1987	1988	1989	1990	1991	1992	1993	1994
Norway Norvège										
Total industry [2-4]										
Total, industrie [2-4]	**125**	**128**	**137**	**141**	**155**	**157**	**161**	**171**	**177**	**190**
Total mining [2]										
Total, industries extractives [2]	**139**	**148**	**165**	**181**	**230**	**242**	**267**	**297**	**317**	**356**
Total manufacturing [3]										
Total, industries manufacturières [3]	**110**	**111**	**112**	**110**	**111**	**111**	**109**	**111**	**113**	**121**
Food, beverages, tobacco										
Aliments, boissons, tabac	92	92	93	92	93	91	94	94	95	104
Textiles										
Textiles	76	77	72	63	58	59	59	57	55	61
Paper and paper products										
Papier, produits en papier	137	136	135	136	145	143	142	139	148	162
Chemicals, coal, petroleum products										
Produits chimiques, houillers, pétroliers	182	178	189	192	203	230	219	224	234	241
Basic metals										
Métaux de base	123	121	127	136	138	138	136	137	138	152
Metal products										
Produits métalliques	102	104	105	101	102	102	100	106	109	115
Electricity and gas [4]										
Electricité et gaz [4]	**118**	**111**	**119**	**125**	**136**	**139**	**127**	**134**	**137**	**130**
Poland Pologne										
Total industry [2-4] [32]										
Total, industrie [2-4] [32]	**99**	**103**	**106**	**111**	**110**	**81**	**74**	**77**	**82**	**92**
Total mining [2] [32]										
Total, industries extractives [2] [32]	**104**	**104**	**106**	**105**	**106**	**78**	**76**	**72**	**69**	**72**
Total manufacturing [3] [32]										
Total, manufactures [3] [32]	**97**	**102**	**105**	**111**	**108**	**80**	**72**	**75**	**83**	**94**
Food, beverages, tobacco										
Aliments, boissons, tabac	94	98	100	101	94	70	69	75	85	...
Textiles										
Textiles	88	89	90	98	102	61	49	48	53	...
Chemicals, coal, petroleum products										
Produits chimiques, houillers, pétroliers	98	102	106	112	107	79	73	73	79	...
Basic metals										
Métaux de base	89	91	90	93	89	69	54	51	51	...
Metal products										
Produits métalliques	106	114	122	132	131	100	75	75	85	...
Electricity, gas and water [4] [32]										
Electricité, gaz et eau [4] [32]	**128**	**136**	**135**	**135**	**134**	**122**	**126**	**120**	**107**	**112**
Portugal Portugal										
Total industry [2-4]										
Total, industrie [2-4]	**119**	**127**	**133**	**138**	**147**	**161**	**163**	**160**	**154**	**153**
Total mining [2]										
Total, industries extractives [2]	**109**	**98**	**86**	**95**	**236**	**422**	**428**	**426**	**408**	**378**
Total manufacturing [3] [34]										
Total, manufactures [3] [34]	**117**	**128**	**135**	**138**	**141**	**150**	**150**	**146**	**140**	**139**
Food, beverages, tobacco										
Aliments, boissons, tabac	98	101	107	116	122	131	132	123	126	123
Chemicals, coal, petroleum products										
Produits chimiques, houillers, pétroliers	119	130	136	145	151	162	136	127	117	120
Basic metals										
Métaux de base	104	105	113	121	119	120	107	116	108	114
Metal products										
Produits métalliques	85	85	87	92	92	100	99	96	87	87
Electricity and gas [4]										
Electricité et gaz [4]	127	130	132	146	168	184	194	197	199	196
Romania Roumanie										
Total industry [2-4]										
Total, industrie [2-4]	**96**	**98**	**96**	**95**	**90**	**69**	**53**	**40**	**40**	**41**
Total mining [2]										
Total, industries extractives [2]	**106**	**106**	**102**	**109**	**107**	**78**	**64**	**64**	**64**	**65**

26
Index numbers of industrial production [*cont.*]
Indices de la production industrielle [*suite*]
1980=100

Country or area and industry [SITC] Pays ou zone et industrie [CITI]	1985	1986	1987	1988	1989	1990	1991	1992	1993	1994
Total manufacturing [3]										
Total, manufactures [3]	**95**	**97**	**94**	**94**	**88**	**68**	**52**	**37**	**37**	**38**
Food, beverages, tobacco										
Aliments, boissons, tabac	108	112	121	121	121	106	88	73	63	71
Textiles										
Textiles	114	121	123	125	124	106	92	65	63	62
Chemicals, coal, petroleum products										
Produits chimiques, houillers, pétroliers	119	129	124	130	125	99	64	56	58	54
Basic metals										
Métaux de base	117	127	121	124	121	95	70	49	52	54
Metal products										
Produits métalliques	129	137	141	145	134	127	95	68	69	72
Electricity, gas and water [4]										
Electricité, gaz et eau [4]	**106**	**114**	**112**	**117**	**113**	**86**	**78**	**62**	**66**	**66**
Spain Espagne										
Total industry [2−4] [32]										
Total, industrie [2−4] [32]	**103**	**107**	**112**	**115**	**120**	**120**	**119**	**115**	**110**	**118**
Total mining [2] [32]										
Total, industries extractives [2] [32]	**130**	**124**	**107**	**102**	**110**	**104**	**99**	**96**	**90**	**97**
Total manufacturing [3] [32]										
Total, industries manufacturières [3] [32]	**101**	**105**	**111**	**114**	**119**	**119**	**117**	**113**	**107**	**116**
Food, beverages, tobacco										
Aliments, boissons, tabac	117	116	125	129	127	133	136	131	133	138
Textiles										
Textiles	96	104	108	100	105	102	97	91	83	93
Chemicals, coal, petroleum products										
Produits chimiques, houillers, pétroliers	104	107	108	109	115	116	112	112	110	123
Basic metals										
Métaux de base	107	99	98	101	108	104	104	99	97	107
Metal products										
Produits métalliques	91	99	110	120	130	130	127	122	109	119
Electricity and water [4] [32]										
Electricité et eau [4] [32]	**115**	**117**	**122**	**127**	**133**	**136**	**139**	**140**	**136**	**137**
Sweden Suède										
Total industry [2−4] [28] [32]										
Total, industrie [2−4] [28] [32]	**110**	**110**	**114**	**117**	**120**	**121**	**115**	**113**	**114**	**127**
Total mining [2] [32]										
Total, industries extractives [2] [32]	**103**	**102**	**103**	**100**	**94**	**95**	**99**	**94**	**90**	**95**
Total manufacturing [3] [32]										
Total, industries manufacturières [3] [32]	**110**	**111**	**114**	**117**	**121**	**121**	**114**	**113**	**114**	**127**
Food, beverages, tobacco										
Aliments, boissons, tabac	104	104	104	106	108	108	105	102	106	110
Textiles										
Textiles	96	94	94	92	88	96	90	77	69	72
Paper and paper products										
Papier, produits en papier	108	111	118	120	120	118	117	118	122	130
Chemicals, coal, petroleum products										
Produits chimiques, houillers, pétroliers	113	111	123	130	130	128	130	134	144	156
Basic metals										
Métaux de base	109	103	105	113	114	103	99	101	106	113
Metal products										
Produits métalliques	119	118	120	124	131	135	125	121	126	150
Switzerland Suisse										
Total industry [2−4] [3]										
Total, industrie [2−4] [3]	**103**	**107**	**108**	**117**	**119**	**122**	**123**	**122**	**122**	**131**
Total manufacturing [3]										
Total, industries manufacturières [3]	**103**	**106**	**107**	**117**	**120**	**123**	**124**	**123**	**122**	**132**
Food, beverages, tobacco										
Aliments, boissons, tabac	101	102	104	106	109	111	113	113	114	117
Textiles										
Textiles	105	107	105	106	104	99	96	94	90	101
Chemicals, coal, petroleum products										
Produits chimiques, houillers, pétroliers	123	125	129	146	169	171	173	179	193	221

26
Index numbers of industrial production [*cont.*]
Indices de la production industrielle [*suite*]
1980=100

Country or area and industry [SITC] Pays ou zone et industrie [CITI]	1985	1986	1987	1988	1989	1990	1991	1992	1993	1994
Basic metals										
Métaux de base	101	103	105	115	116	117	110	110	104	114
Metal products										
Produits métalliques	94	99	99	106	106	114	121	116	109	115
Electricity and gas [4]										
Electricité et gaz [4]	114	116	121	123	110	112	116	119	123	132
United Kingdom Royaume Uni										
Total industry [2−4]										
Total, industrie [2−4]	**108**	**111**	**115**	**120**	**123**	**123**	**118**	**118**	**121**	**127**
Total mining [2]										
Total, industries extractives [2]	**117**	**117**	**117**	**109**	**94**	**90**	**94**	**97**	**104**	**119**
Total manufacturing [3]										
Total, manufactures [3]	**102**	**103**	**108**	**116**	**121**	**121**	**114**	**114**	**115**	**120**
Food, beverages, tobacco										
Aliments, boissons, tabac	101	102	104	107	107	109	107	108	108	110
Textiles										
Textiles	97	79	83	83	80	78	70	70	69	69
Chemicals, coal, petroleum products										
Produits chimiques, houillers, pétroliers	115	119	123	129	135	134	139	143	146	150
Basic metals										
Métaux de base	100	98	106	119	118	112	102	98	98	100
Metal products										
Produits métalliques	102	86	88	97	104	104	97	95	95	102
Electricity, gas and water [4]										
Electricité, gaz et eau [4]	**108**	**119**	**122**	**122**	**122**	**125**	**132**	**134**	**140**	**141**
Yugoslavia, SFR † Yougoslavie, Rfs †										
Total industry [2−4]										
Total, industrie [2−4]	**114**	**119**	**120**	**119**	**120**	**107**	**98**	...	...	...
Total mining [2]										
Total, industries extractives [2]	**115**	**116**	**117**	**116**	**113**	**108**	**102**	...	...	...
Total manufacturing [3]										
Total, industries manufacturières [3]	**114**	**117**	**119**	**117**	**120**	**106**	**94**	...	...	...
Food, beverages, tobacco										
Aliments, boissons, tabac	108	110	113	109	83	108	90	...	...	...
Textiles										
Textiles	109	116	117	115	112	92	65	...	...	...
Chemicals, coal, petroleum products										
Produits chimiques, houillers, pétroliers	118	126	128	134	131	118	84	...	...	...
Basic metals										
Métaux de base	127	129	124	128	131	113	78	...	...	...
Metal products										
Produits métalliques	122	131	131	129	132	110	65	...	...	...
Electricity and gas [4]										
Electricité et gaz [4]	**119**	**124**	**128**	**132**	**131**	**131**	**131**	...	...	...
Oceania · Océanie										
Australia [24] Australie [24]										
Total industry [2−4] [45]										
Total, industrie [2−4] [45]	**109**	**110**	**119**	**125**	**126**	**126**	**125**	**129**	**136**	**146**
Total mining [2] [45] [46]										
Total, industries extractives [2] [45] [46]	**140**	**133**	**150**	**155**	**169**	**177**	**181**	**182**	**185**	**193**
Total manufacturing [3] [45]										
Total, industries manufacturières [3] [45]	**101**	**104**	**110**	**117**	**115**	**113**	**110**	**114**	**123**	**134**
Food, beverages, tobacco										
Aliments, boissons, tabac	101	104	109	111	112	114	117	126	136	...
Textiles										
Textiles	107	112	111	113	108	109	113	101	85	...
Chemicals, coal, petroleum products										
Produits chimiques, houillers, pétroliers	104	109	118	120	119	124	124	125	136	...
Basic metals										
Métaux de base	105	106	110	116	128	132	133	133	141	...
Metal products										
Produits métalliques	95	96	103	111	108	103	98	105	117	...

26
Index numbers of industrial production [*cont.*]
Indices de la production industrielle [*suite*]
1980=100

Country or area and industry [SITC] Pays ou zone et industrie [CITI]	1985	1986	1987	1988	1989	1990	1991	1992	1993	1994
Electricity and water [4] [45]										
Electricité et eau [4] [45]	**124**	**127**	**133**	**140**	**147**	**150**	**152**	**154**	**157**	**162**
Fiji Fidji										
Total industry [2−4]										
Total, industrie [2−4]	**103**	**123**	**110**	**117**	**128**	**138**	**141**	**144**	**152**	**160**
Total mining [2]										
Total, industries extractives [2]	**241**	**369**	**370**	**552**	**545**	**532**	**355**	**478**	**489**	**445**
Total manufacturing [3]										
Total, industries manufacturières [3]	**98**	**118**	**102**	**103**	**114**	**126**	**133**	**129**	**139**	**146**
Food, beverages, tobacco										
Aliments, boissons, tabac	95	126	117	112	128	124	128	132	132	144
Electricity [4]										
Electricité [4]	**129**	**138**	**136**	**147**	**157**	**166**	**172**	**186**	**192**	**206**
New Zealand [47] **Nouvelle−Zélande** [47]										
Total industry [2−4] [3] [19]										
Total, industrie [2−4] [3] [19]	115	116	118	120	119	121	120	119	122	128
Total manufacturing [3]										
Total, industries manufacturières [3]	122	116	118	114	112	112	106	105	110	116
Electricity, gas and water [4]										
Electricité, gaz et eau [4]	118	122	124	125	128	133	134	139	135	145
former USSR · ancienne URSS										
former USSR † ancienne URSS †										
Total industry [2−4] [48]										
Total, industrie [2−4] [48]	**119**	**125**	**129**	**134**	**136**	**135**	**124**	...	...	...
Total mining [2] [49]										
Total, industries extractives [2] [49]	**107**	**111**	**113**	**116**	**115**	**111**	**99**	...	...	...
Total manufacturing [3] [34] [50]										
Total, manufactures [3] [34] [50]	**120**	**126**	**131**	**136**	**139**	**138**	**126**	...	...	...
Food, beverages, tobacco										
Aliments, boissons, tabac	112	111	115	119	123	124	127	...	...	...
Textiles										
Textiles	106	108	110	114	117	115	110	...	...	...
Chemicals, coal, petroleum products										
Produits chimiques, houillers, pétroliers	115	120	124	129	131	130	127	...	...	...
Basic metals										
Métaux de base	113	118	121	125	125	122	113	...	...	...
Metal products										
Produits métalliques	135	144	152	160	164	165	170	...	...	...
Electricity and steam [4]										
Electricité et vapeur [4]	**120**	**123**	**129**	**132**	**133**	**135**	**134**	...	...	...

Source:
Industrial statistics database of the Statistics Division of the United Nations Secretariat.

† For detailed descriptions of data pertaining to former Czechoslovakia, Germany, SFR Yugoslavia and former USSR, see Annex I − Country or area nomenclature, regional and other groupings.

1 Index numbers of gross domestic product (at constant prices of 1978/79).
2 Excluding basic metals.
3 Excluding mining.
4 Including clothing and footwear.
5 Calculated by the Statistics Division of the United Nations.
6 Excluding coal, crude petroleum, stone quarrying, clay and sand pits.
7 Excluding petroleum refineries.
8 Including coal mining, crude petroleum and petroleum refineries.
9 Including rubber and plastic products.
10 Covers phosphate rock, sea salt, ferrous and non−ferrous minerals only.
11 Excluding petroleum refineries, wearing apparels, leather, wood

Source:
Base de données de statistiques industrielles de la Division de statistique du Secrétariat de l'ONU.

† Pour les descriptions en détails des données relatives à l'ancienne Tchécoslovaquie, l'Allemagne, la Rfs Yougoslavie et et l'ancienne URSS, voir l'Annexe I − Nomenclature des pays ou zones, groupements régionaux et autres groupements.

1 Indices du produit intérieur brut (aux prix constants de 1978/79).
2 Non compris les métaux de base.
3 Non compris les mines.
4 Y compris l'industrie d'habillement et des chaussures.
5 Calculé par la Division de Statistique de l'Organisation des Nations Unies.
6 Non compris l'extraction du charbon, de pétrole brut, de la pierre às batir.
7 Non compris les raffineries de pétrole.
8 Y compris l'extraction du charbon, de pétrole brut et les raffineries de pétrole.
9 Y compris l'industrie du caoutchouc et articles en matière plastique.
10 Le phosphate de chaux, le sel−marin et les minarais ferreux et

26
Index numbers of industrial production [*cont.*]
Indices de la production industrielle [*suite*]
1980=100

and plastic industries.
12 Including petroleum, natural gas and petroleum refineries.
13 Including non—ferrous metal basic industries.
14 Excluding non—ferrous metal basic industries.
15 Gross Domestic Product by industry at factor cost at 1986 prices.
16 Index numbers of gross domestic product (at constant prices of 1966).
17 Index numbers of gross domestic product (at constant prices of 1962).
18 Index numbers of gross domestic product (at constant prices of 1978).
19 Including construction.
20 Beginning 1992, based on ISIC, Rev. 3.
21 Excluding wood, furniture, printing and publishing.
22 Manufacture of fabricated metal products, except machinery and equipment, is included in basic metals.
23 Excluding the extraction of natural gas.
24 Figures relate to 12 months beginning 1 July of year stated.
25 Excluding coal, petroleum products and basic metals.
26 Figures relate to 12 months beginning 21 March of year stated.
27 Excluding tobacco industry.
28 Excluding electricity, gas and water.
29 Extraction of non—metallic minerals only.
30 Phosphate, potash and stone quarrying only.
31 Excluding fur and leather products, footwear, furniture and fixture.
32 Beginning 1990, based on ISIC, Rev. 3.
33 Excluding metal mining.
34 Excluding publishing.
35 Including logging and fishing.
36 Excluding shipbuilding and repairing.
37 Beginning 1991, base: 1991=100 and data based on ISIC, Rev. 3.
38 Stone quarrying, clay and sand pits are included in manufacturing. Coal briquetting is included in mining.
39 Including magnesite roasting.
40 Including car repairs.
41 Including waterworks and gasworks, excluding publishing.
42 Excluding paper and paper products.
43 Including basic metals.
44 Including plastic products.
45 Based on ISIC, Rev. 3.
46 Excluding services to mining.
47 Gross domestic product at constant 1982—1983 prices. Annual figures: average of four quarters ending 31 March of the year stated.
48 Including logging, motion picture production, cleaning and dyeing.
49 Excluding oil and natural gas drilling, prospecting and preparing sites for the extraction of minerals.
50 Including commercial fishing and the processing and cold storage of fish and fish products by factory—type vessels.

non—ferreux seulement.
11 Non compris les raffineries de pétrole et les industries d'habillement du cuir, du bois et du matière plastique.
12 Y compris l'extraction de pétrole brut, les raffineries de pétrole et les produits de gaz naturel.
13 Y compris la métallurgie de base de métaux non—ferreux.
14 Non compris la métallurgie de base de métaux non—ferreux.
15 Produit intérieur brut par industrie au coût des facteurs aux prix de 1986.
16 Indices du produit intérieur brut (aux prix constants de 1966).
17 Indices du produit intérieur brut (aux prix constants de 1962).
18 Indices du produit intérieur brut (aux prix constants de 1978).
19 Y compris la construction.
20 Tirées de la CITI, Rev. 3 à partir de 1992.
21 Non compris l'industrie du bois et du meuble, l'imprimerie et l'édition.
22 Fabrication d'ouvrages en métaux, à l'exclusion des machines et du matériel est comprise dans les industries des métaux de base.
23 Non compris l'extraction du gaz naturel.
24 Les chiffres se rapportent à 12 mois commençant le 1er juillet de l'année indiquée.
25 Non compris les produits dérivés du charbon, des produits pétroliers et des métaux de base.
26 Les chiffres se rapportent à 12 mois commençant le 21 mars de l'année indiquée.
27 Non compris l'industrie du tabac.
28 Non compris l'electricité, gaz et eau.
29 Extraction des minéraux non—métalliques seulement.
30 Le phosphate, la potasse et l'extraction de la pierre á bâtir seulement.
31 Non compris l'industrie de la fourrure et du cuir, la fabrication des chaussures.
32 Tirées de la CITI, Rev. 3 à partir de 1990.
33 Non compris l'extraction des minerais métalliques.
34 Non compris l'édition.
35 Y compris l'exploitation forestière et la pêche.
36 Non compris la construction navale et la réparation des navires.
37 A partir de 1991, on a adoptée 1991=100 comme base de référence et les données sont tirées de la CITI, Rev. 3.
38 L'extraction de la pierre à bâtir, de l'argile et du sable est comprise dans les industries manufacturières. La fabrication des briquettes de charbon est comprise dans les industries extractives.
39 Y compris le rôtissage du magnésite.
40 Y compris la réparation des véhicules automobiles.
41 Y compris les usines des eaux et les usines à gaz, non compris l'édition.
42 Non compris le papier et les ouvrages en papier.
43 Y compris les métaux de base.
44 Y compris articles en matière plastique.
45 Tirées de la CITI, Rev. 3.
46 Non compris les services relatifs aux mines.
47 Produit intérieur brut aux prix constants de 1982—1983. Chiffres annuels : moyennes de quatre trimestres finissant le 31 mars de l'année.
48 Y compris l'exploitation forestière, la production cinématographique, le nettoyage et la teinture.
49 L'exploitation des puits de pétrole et des puits de gaz naturel, la prospection et la préparation du terrain avant l'extraction des minéraux ne sont pas comprises.
50 Y compris la pêche commerciale, le traitement des poissons et des produits poissonniers et les entrepôts frigorifiques dans les usines flottantes.

Technical Notes, tables 20-26

Detailed internationally comparable data on national accounts are compiled and published annually by the Statistics Division, Department for Economic and Social Information and Policy Analysis, of the United Nations Secretariat. Data of the national accounts aggregates for countries or areas are based on the concepts and definitions contained in *A System of National Accounts* [53], Studies in Methods, Series F, No. 2, Rev. 3. A summary of the conceptual framework, classifications and definitions of trasactions is found in the annual United Nations publication, *National Accounts Statistics: Main Aggregates and Detailed Tables* [26].

The national accounts data shown in this publication offer in the form of analytical tables a summary of some selected principal national accounts aggregates based on official detailed national accounts data of some 180 countries and areas. Every effort has been made to present the estimates of the various countries or areas in a form designed to facilitate international comparability. Differences in concept, scope, coverage and classification are footnoted. Detailed footnotes identifying these differences are also available in the national accounts yearbook mentioned above. Such differences should be taken into account if misleading comparisons among countries or areas are to be avoided.

Table 20 shows total and per capita gross domestic product (GDP) expressed in United States dollars at current prices and total GDP at constant 1990 prices and its corresponding rates of growth. The table is designed to facilitate international comparisons of levels of income generated in production. In order to have a comparable coverage for as many countries as possible, the official GDP national currency data are supplemented by estimates prepared by the Statistical Division, based on a variety of data derived from national and international sources. National currency data are converted to United States dollars using the average market rates as published by the International Monetary Fund in the *International Financial Statistics* [13]. Official exchange rates are used only when market rate is not available. For non-members of the Fund, the conversion rates are the average of United Nations operational rates of exchange. It should be noted that the conversion from local currency into US dollars introduces deficiencies of comparability over time and between countries which should be taken into account when using the data. The comparability over time is distorted when there are large and discrepant fluctuations in the exchange rates vis-a-vis domestic inflation. Per capita GDP data are likewise affected by the same distortions resulting from exchange rate conversion. Per capita takes the growth of the population into account as well.

Notes techniques, tableaux 20 à 26

La Division de statistique du Département de l'information économique et sociale et de l'analyse des politiques du Secrétariat de l'Organisation des Nations Unies établit et publie chaque année des données détaillées sur les comptes nationaux se prêtant à des comparaisons internationales. Les données relatives aux agrégats des différents pays et territoires sont établies à l'aide des concepts et des définitions figurant dans le *Système de comptabilité nationale* [53], études méthodologiques, série F, No 2, Rev. 3. On trouvera un résumé de l'appareil conceptuel des classifications et des définitions des transactions dans *National Accounts Statistics: Main Aggregates and Detailed Tables* [26], publication annuelle des Nations Unies.

Les comptes nationaux figurant dans cette publication présentent, sous forme de tableaux analytiques, un résumé de certains agrégats importants calculés à partir des comptes nationaux détaillés d'environ 180 pays et territoires. Tout a été fait pour présenter des estimations relatives aux divers pays ou territoires sous une forme facilitant les comparaisons internationales. Les différences de définition, de portée, de couverture et de classification sont indiquées dans les notes en bas de page. Des notes détaillées précisant ces différences figurent également dans l'annuaire des comptes nationaux mentionné plus haut.

En raison de ces différences, l'interprétation des comparaisons entre pays et territoires doit être prudente.

Le *tableau 20* donne le produit intérieur brut (PIB) total et par habitant, exprimé en dollars des États-Unis à prix courants et le PIB total aux prix constants de 1990, ainsi que les taux de croissance correspondants. Le tableau est conçu pour faciliter les comparaisons internationales du revenu engendré par la production. À l'aide des données les plus diverses provenant de sources nationales et internationales, la Division de statistique établit des estimations destinées à compléter les chiffres officiels du PIB exprimé dans la monnaie nationale de façon à rendre possible une comparaison d'autant de pays que possible. Les données libellées en monnaie nationale sont converties en dollars des États-Unis à l'aide des taux moyens du marché publiés par le Fonds monétaire international dans les *Statistiques financières internationales* [13]. Le taux de change officiel n'est utilisé que si l'on ne dispose pas d'un taux du marché. Pour les pays qui ne sont pas membres du Fonds, les taux de change utilisés sont la moyenne des taux de change retenus pour les opérations des Nations Unies. Il est à noter que cette opération de conversion des monnaies nationales en dollars des Etats-Unis fausse la comparaison des données dans le temps et entre pays et toute interprétation des données doit donc en tenir compte. Les comparaisons dans le temps sont faussées quand l'évolution des taux de change s'écarte nettement de celle de l'inflation intérieure. De même, le PIB

The GDP constant price series based primarily on data officially provided by countries and partly based on estimates made by the Statistical Division are transformed into index numbers and rebased to 1990=100. The resulting data are then converted into US dollars at the rate prevailing in the base year 1990. The growth rates are based on the estimates of GDP at constant 1990 prices. The rate of the year in question is obtained by dividing the GDP of that year by the GDP of the preceeding year.

Table 21 features the distribution of GDP by expenditure breakdown at current prices. It shows what portion of income is spent by the government and by the private sector on consumption, what is spent on investment and what revenues are obtained from exports after deducting the expenditure on imports. The percentages are derived from official data of countries as reported to the United Nations and published in the annual national accounts yearbook.

Table 22 shows the distribution of GDP originating from each industry component based on the *International Standard Industrial Classification of All Economic Activities* [46]. This table reflects the economic structure of production in the country. The percentages are based on official GDP estimates broken down by kind of economic activity at current prices: agriculture, hunting, forestry and fishing; mining and quarrying; manufacturing; electricity, gas and water; construction; wholesale, retail trade, restaurants and hotel; transport, storage and communication; and other activities comprised of financial and community services, producers of government services, other producers and import duties and taxes.

Table 23 presents the relationships between the principal national accounting aggregates, namely: gross domestic product (GDP), gross national product (GNP), national income (NI), national disposable income (NDI) and net saving. The ratio of each aggregate to GDP is derived cumulatively by adding net factor income from the rest of the world (GNP); deducting consumption of fixed capital (NI); adding net current transfers from the rest of the world (NDI); and, deducting final consumption to arrive at net saving.

Table 24 presents the distribution of total government final consumption expenditure by function at current prices. The breakdown by function includes: general public services; defence; public order and safety; education; health; social serives; economic services; and other function which include housing, community amenities, recreational, cultural and religious affairs. The government expenditure is equal to the service produced by general government for its own use. These services are not sold, they are valued in the GDP at their cost to the government.

Table 25 shows the distribution of total private final consumption expenditure by type and purpose at current prices. Private consumption expenditure measures the expenditure of all resident non-government units which includes all housholds and private non-profit institutions

par habitant est susceptible d'être affecté par les mêmes distorsions liées au taux de change. Les données exprimées par habitant tiennent compte aussi de l'accroissement de la population.

La série de statistiques du PIB à prix constants est fondée principalement sur des données officiellement communiquées par les pays et en partie sur des estimations effectuées par la Division de statistique; les données permettent de calculer des indices, la base 100 étant retenue pour 1990. Les données ainsi obtenues sont alors converties en dollars des États-Unis au taux de change de l'année de base (1990). Les taux de croissance sont calculés à partir des estimations du PIB aux prix constants de 1990. Le taux de croissance de l'année en question est obtenu en divisant le PIB de l'année par celui de l'année précédente.

Le *tableau 21* donne la répartition du PIB par catégorie de dépenses aux prix courants. Il indique quelle est la fraction du revenu national qui est consacrée à la consommation par les administrations et par le secteur privé, quelle est celle qui est affectée à l'investissement, et quelles recettes proviennent des exportations une fois les importations déduites. Les pourcentages sont calculés à partir des données officiellement communiquées par les pays à l'Organisation des Nations Unies et sont publiés dans l'annuaire des comptes nationaux.

Le *tableau 22* donne la répartition du PIB par secteur industriel, selon le classement proposé par la *Classification internationale type, par industrie, de toutes les branches d'activité économique (CITI) [46]*. Ce tableau donne donc la structure économique de la production dans chaque pays. Les pourcentages sont établis à partir des estimations officielles du PIB, ventilées entre les diverses branches d'activité économique aux prix courants : agriculture, chasse, forêts et pêche; industries minières et extractives; industrie manufacturière; électricité, gaz et eau; construction; commerce de gros et de détail, restaurants et hôtels; transports, entrepôts et communications; autres activités, y compris les services financiers, les services communautaires, les services fournis par les administrations, divers autres services et les droits et taxes d'importation.

Le *tableau 23* présente les liens existant entre les principaux agrégats de comptabilité ationale, à savoir: le produit intérieur brut (PIB), le produit national brut (PNB), le revenu national, le revenu national disponible et l'épargne nette. On détermine successivement chaque agrégat par rapport au PIB en ajoutant le revenu net des facteurs reçus de l'étranger, ce qui donne le PNB; en déduisant la consommation de capital fixe, on obtient le revenu national; en ajoutant le solde des transferts courants reçus de l'étranger, on obtient le revenu national disponible; en éeduisant la consommation finale, on obtient l'épargne nette.

Le *tableau 24* donne la répartition des dépenses de consommation finale des administrations, par fonction, aux prix courants. La répartition par fonction est la suivante : administration publique générale; défense; ordre public et sécurité; éducation; santé; services sociaux; services

serving households. The percentage shares include: food, beverages and tobacco; clothing and footwear; gross rent, fuel and power; furniture, furnishings and household equipment; medical care and health expenses; transport and communication; recreational, entertainment, education and cultural services; and other fuctions which include miscellaneous goods and services, purchases abroad by resident households deducting the expenditure of non-resident in the domestic market and the expenditure of private non-profit insitutions serving households.

Table 26: Detailed descriptions of national practices in the compilation of production index numbers are given in the United Nations *1977 Supplement to the Statistical Yearbook and Monthly Bulletin of Statistics.* [49] Some differences in national practice in compilation, as well as major deviations from ISIC in the scope of the indexes, are indicated in the footnotes to this table.

économiques; et autres fonctions incluant le logement, les aménagements collectifs, les équipements de loisir et les activités culturelles et religieuses. Les dépenses des administrations sont considérées comme égales aux services produits par l'administration pour son propre usage. Ces services ne sont pas vendus et ils sont évalués, dans le PIB, à leur coût pour l'administration.

Le *tableau 25* donne la répartition des dépenses totales de consommation finale privée par type et par objet aux prix courants. Les dépenses privées de consommation mesurent donc les dépenses de toutes les entités résidentes autres que les administrations, y compris tous les ménages et les entités privées à but non lucratif fournissant des services aux ménages. La répartition en pourcentage distingue les rubriques suivantes : aliments, boissons et tabac, articles d'habillement et chaussures, loyer brut, combustible et électricité, mobilier et équipement des ménages, soins médicaux et dépenses de santé, services de loisir, éducatifs et culturels, autres fonctions, y compris les biens et services divers, achats à l'étranger effectués par les ménages résidents, moins les dépenses des non-résidents sur le marché intérieur, et dépenses des institutions privées à but non lucratif fournissant des services aux ménages.

Tableau 26 : Des descriptions détaillées des pratiques nationales employées pour la compilation des indices de production sont données dans le *Supplément 1977 à l'Annuaire statistique et au Bulletin mensuel de statistique des Nations Unies* [49]. Certaines différences dans la méthode nationale de compilation, ainsi que les écarts importants par rapport à la CITI dans la portée des indices, sont indiqués dans les notes figurant au bas de ce tableau.

27
Rates of discount of central banks
Taux d'escompte des banques centrales
Per cent per annum, end of period
Pour cent par année, fin de la période

Country or area Pays ou zone	1986	1987	1988	1989	1990	1991	1992	1993	1994	1995
Aruba Aruba	9.50	9.50	9.50	9.50	9.50	9.50	9.50	9.50	9.50	9.50
Australia Australie	16.92	14.95	13.20	17.23	15.24	10.99	6.96	5.83	5.75	5.75
Austria Autriche	4.00	3.00	4.00	6.50	6.50	8.00	8.00	5.25	4.50	3.00
Bahamas Bahamas	7.50	7.50	9.00	9.00	9.00	9.00	7.50	7.00	6.50	6.50
Bangladesh Bangladesh	10.75	10.75	10.75	10.75	9.75	9.25	8.50	6.00	5.50	6.00
Barbados Barbade	8.00	8.00	8.00	13.50	13.50	18.00	12.00	8.00	9.50	12.50
Belgium Belgique	8.00	7.00	7.75	10.25	10.50	8.50	7.75	5.25	4.50	3.00
Belize Belize	12.00	12.00	10.00	12.00	12.00	12.00	12.00	12.00	12.00	12.00
Benin Bénin	8.50	8.50	9.50	11.00	11.00	11.00	12.50	10.50	10.00	7.50
Botswana Botswana	9.00	8.50	6.50	6.50	8.50	12.00	14.25	14.25	13.50	13.00
Brazil Brésil	89.00	401.00	2 282.00	38 341.00	1 082.80	2 494.30	1 489.00	5 756.80	56.40	39.00
Burkina Faso Burkina Faso	8.50	8.50	9.50	11.00	11.00	11.00	12.50	10.50	10.00	7.50
Burundi Burundi	5.00	7.00	7.00	7.00	8.00	10.70	9.80	9.80	9.40	9.90
Cameroon Cameroun	8.00	8.00	9.50	10.00	11.00	10.75	12.00	11.50	# 7.75	8.60
Canada Canada	8.49	8.66	11.17	12.47	11.78	7.67	7.36	4.11	7.43	5.79
Central African Rep. Rép. centrafricaine	8.00	8.00	9.50	10.00	11.00	10.75	12.00	11.50	# 7.75	8.60
Chad Tchad	8.00	8.00	9.50	10.00	11.00	10.75	12.00	11.50	# 7.75	8.60
Colombia Colombie	33.80	34.80	34.30	36.90	# 46.50	45.00	34.40	33.50	44.90	40.40
Comoros Comores	10.00	8.50	8.50	...	...	...	...	...	...	...
Congo Congo	8.00	8.00	9.50	10.00	11.00	10.75	12.00	11.50	# 7.75	8.60
Costa Rica Costa Rica	27.50	31.38	31.50	31.61	37.80	42.50	29.00	35.00	37.75	38.50
Côte d'Ivoire Côte d'Ivoire	8.50	8.50	9.50	11.00	11.00	11.00	12.50	10.50	10.00	7.50
Croatia Croatie	...	...	...	...	...	...	1 889.39	34.49	8.50	8.50
Cyprus Chypre	6.00	6.00	6.00	6.50	6.50	6.50	6.50	6.50	6.50	6.50
Czech Republic République tchèque	...	...	...	...	...	...	...	8.00	8.50	9.50

27
Rates of discount of central banks
Per cent per annum, end of period [cont.]
Taux d'escompte des banques centrales
Pour cent par année, fin de la période [suite]

Country or area Pays ou zone	1986	1987	1988	1989	1990	1991	1992	1993	1994	1995
Denmark Danemark	7.00	7.00	7.00	7.00	8.50	9.50	9.50	6.25	5.00	4.25
Ecuador Equateur	23.00	23.00	23.00	32.00	35.00	49.00	49.00	33.57	44.88	59.41
Egypt Egypte	13.00	13.00	13.00	14.00	14.00	20.00	18.40	16.50	14.00	13.50
Equatorial Guinea Guinée équatoriale	8.00	8.00	9.50	10.00	11.00	10.75	12.00	11.50	# 7.75	8.60
Ethiopia Ethiopie	6.00	3.00	3.00	3.00	3.00	3.00	5.25	12.00	12.00	12.00
Fiji Fidji	8.00	11.00	11.00	8.00	8.00	8.00	6.00	6.00	6.00	6.00
Finland Finlande	7.00	7.00	8.00	8.50	8.50	8.50	9.50	5.50	5.25	4.88
France France	9.50	9.50	9.50	...	...	...	...	...	...	...
Gabon Gabon	8.00	8.00	9.50	10.00	11.00	10.75	12.00	11.50	# 7.75	8.60
Gambia Gambie	20.00	21.00	19.00	15.00	16.50	15.50	17.50	13.50	13.50	14.00
Germany † Allemagne† F. R. Germany[1] R. f. Allemagne[1]	... 3.50	... 2.50	... 3.50	... 6.00	... 6.00	8.00 ...	8.25 ...	5.75 ...	4.50 ...	3.00 ...
Ghana Ghana	20.50	23.50	26.00	26.00	33.00	20.00	30.00	35.00	33.00	45.00
Greece Grèce	20.50	20.50	19.00	19.00	19.00	19.00	19.00	21.50	20.50	18.00
Guatemala Guatemala	9.00	9.00	9.00	13.00	18.50	16.50	...	...	...	...
Guinea Guinée	9.00	10.00	10.00	13.00	15.00	19.00	19.00	17.00	17.00	18.00
Guinea-Bissau Guinée-Bissau	...	...	...	...	42.00	42.00	45.50	41.00	26.00	39.00
Guyana Guyana	14.00	14.00	14.00	35.00	30.00	32.50	24.30	17.00	20.30	17.30
Honduras Honduras	24.00	24.00	24.00	24.00	28.20	30.10	26.10	...	...	...
Hungary Hongrie	10.50	10.50	14.00	17.00	22.00	22.00	21.00	22.00	25.00	28.00
Iceland Islande	21.00	49.20	24.10	38.40	21.00	21.00	# 16.60	...	4.70	5.90
India Inde	10.00	10.00	10.00	10.00	10.00	12.00	12.00	12.00	12.00	12.00
Ireland Irlande	13.25	9.25	8.00	12.00	11.25	10.75	...	7.00	6.25	6.50
Israel Israël	31.40	26.80	30.90	15.00	13.00	14.20	10.40	9.80	17.00	14.20
Italy Italie	12.00	12.00	12.50	13.50	12.50	12.00	12.00	8.00	7.50	9.00

27
Rates of discount of central banks
Per cent per annum, end of period [cont.]
Taux d'escompte des banques centrales
Pour cent par année, fin de la période [suite]

Country or area Pays ou zone	1986	1987	1988	1989	1990	1991	1992	1993	1994	1995
Jamaica Jamaïque	21.00	21.00	21.00	21.00	21.00	...	...	...	...	...
Japan Japon	3.00	2.50	2.50	4.25	6.00	4.50	3.25	1.75	1.75	0.50
Jordan Jordanie	6.25	6.25	* 6.25	8.00	* 8.50	8.50	8.50	8.50	8.50	8.50
Kenya Kenya	12.50	12.50	16.02	16.50	19.43	20.27	20.46	45.50	21.50	24.50
Korea, Republic of Corée, République de	7.00	7.00	8.00	7.00	7.00	7.00	7.00	5.00	5.00	5.00
Kuwait Koweït	6.00	6.00	7.50	7.50	...	7.50	7.50	5.80	7.00	7.30
Lao People's Dem. Rep. Rép. dém. pop. lao	...	...	...	...	...	...	23.67	25.00	30.00	32.08
Latvia Lettonie	...	...	...	...	...	...	...	27.00	25.00	24.00
Lebanon Liban	21.85	21.85	21.84	21.84	21.84	18.04	16.00	20.22	16.49	19.01
Lesotho Lesotho	9.50	9.00	15.50	17.00	15.75	18.00	15.00	13.50	13.50	15.50
Libyan Arab Jamah. Jamah. arabe libyenne	5.00	5.00	5.00	5.00	5.00	5.00	5.00	5.00	...	...
Madagascar Madagascar	11.50	11.50	11.50	...	...	...	...	...	...	...
Malawi Malawi	11.00	14.00	11.00	11.00	14.00	13.00	20.00	25.00	40.00	50.00
Malaysia Malaisie	3.89	3.20	4.12	4.89	7.23	7.70	7.10	5.24	4.51	6.47
Mali Mali	8.50	8.50	9.50	11.00	11.00	11.00	12.50	10.50	10.00	7.50
Malta Malte	6.00	5.50	5.50	5.50	5.50	5.50	5.50	5.50	5.50	5.50
Mauritania Mauritanie	6.50	6.50	6.50	7.00	7.00	7.00	7.00	...	...	...
Mauritius Maurice	11.00	10.00	10.00	12.00	12.00	11.30	8.30	8.30	13.80	11.40
Mongolia Mongolie	...	...	...	...	...	...	...	628.80	180.00	150.00
Morocco Maroc	8.50	8.50	8.50	...	...	...	...	...	7.00	...
Namibia Namibie	...	...	...	...	...	20.50	16.50	14.50	15.50	17.50
Nepal Népal	11.00	11.00	11.00	11.00	11.00	13.00	13.00	11.00	11.00	...
Netherlands Pays-Bas	4.50	3.75	4.50	7.00	7.25	8.50	7.75	5.00	...	...
Netherlands Antilles Antilles néerlandaises	8.00	6.00	6.00	6.00	6.00	6.00	6.00	6.00	5.00	...
New Zealand Nouvelle-Zélande	24.60	18.55	15.10	15.00	13.25	8.30	9.15	5.70	9.75	9.80

27
Rates of discount of central banks
Per cent per annum, end of period [*cont.*]
Taux d'escompte des banques centrales
Pour cent par année, fin de la période [*suite*]

Country or area Pays ou zone	1986	1987	1988	1989	1990	1991	1992	1993	1994	1995
Nicaragua Nicaragua	...	...	12 874.60	311.00	10.00	15.00	15.00	11.80	10.50	10.20
Niger Niger	8.50	8.50	8.50	11.00	11.00	11.00	12.50	10.50	10.00	7.50
Nigeria Nigéria	10.00	12.75	12.75	18.50	18.50	15.50	17.50	26.00	13.50	13.50
Norway Norvège	14.80	13.80	12.00	11.00	10.50	10.00	11.00	7.00	6.75	6.75
Pakistan Pakistan	10.00	10.00	10.00	10.00	10.00	10.00	10.00	...	...	
Papua New Guinea Papouasie-Nvl-Guinée	11.40	8.80	10.80	...	...	...	...	# 6.39	...	...
Paraguay Paraguay	...	...	10.00	21.00	30.00	18.00	18.00	18.00	18.00	18.00
Peru Pérou	36.10	29.80	748.00	865.60	289.60	67.70	48.50	28.60	16.10	18.40
Philippines Philippines	10.00	10.00	10.00	12.00	14.00	14.00	14.30	9.40	8.30	10.83
Poland Pologne	4.00	4.00	6.00	104.00	48.00	36.00	32.00	29.00	28.00	25.00
Portugal Portugal	17.00	14.96	13.71	14.33	14.50	14.50	19.77	14.27	10.05	8.93
Rwanda Rwanda	9.00	9.00	9.00	9.00	14.00	14.00	11.00	11.00	11.00	16.00
Senegal Sénégal	8.50	8.50	9.50	11.00	11.00	11.00	12.50	10.50	10.00	7.50
Slovakia Slovaquie	...	...	...	...	...	...	...	12.00	12.00	9.75
Slovenia Slovénie	...	...	...	...	...	...	25.00	18.00	16.00	10.00
Somalia Somalie	12.00	12.00	45.00	45.00	...	...	...	...	...	...
South Africa Afrique du Sud	9.50	9.50	14.50	18.00	18.00	17.00	14.00	12.00	13.00	15.00
Spain Espagne	11.84	13.50	12.40	14.52	14.71	12.50	13.25	9.00	7.38	9.00
Sri Lanka Sri Lanka	11.00	10.00	10.00	14.00	15.00	17.00	17.00	17.00	17.00	...
Swaziland Swaziland	9.50	9.00	11.00	12.00	12.00	13.00	12.00	11.00	12.00	15.00
Sweden Suède	7.50	7.50	8.50	10.50	11.50	8.00	# 10.00	5.00	7.00	7.00
Switzerland Suisse	4.00	2.50	3.50	6.00	6.00	7.00	6.00	4.00	3.50	1.50
Syrian Arab Republic Rép. arabe syrienne	5.00	5.00	5.00	5.00	5.00	5.00	5.00	5.00	5.00	...
Thailand Thaïlande	8.00	8.00	8.00	8.00	12.00	11.00	11.00	9.00	9.50	10.50
Togo Togo	8.50	8.50	9.50	11.00	11.00	11.00	12.50	10.50	10.00	7.50

27

Rates of discount of central banks
Per cent per annum, end of period [cont.]
Taux d'escompte des banques centrales
Pour cent par année, fin de la période [suite]

Country or area Pays ou zone	1986	1987	1988	1989	1990	1991	1992	1993	1994	1995
Trinidad and Tobago Trinité-et-Tobago	5.97	7.50	9.50	9.50	9.50	11.50	13.00	13.00	13.00	13.00
Tunisia Tunisie	9.25	9.25	9.25	11.37	11.88	11.88	11.38	8.88	8.88	8.88
Turkey Turquie	48.00	45.00	54.00	54.00	45.00	45.00	...	...	...	...
Uganda Ouganda	36.00	31.00	45.00	55.00	50.00	46.00	41.00	24.00	15.00	15.00
Ukraine Ukraine	...	...	...	...	...	...	80.00	240.00	252.00	110.00
United Rep.Tanzania Rép. Unie de Tanzanie	6.50	11.31	12.67	15.17	...	...	...	14.50	34.63	48.42
United States Etats-Unis	5.50	6.00	6.50	7.00	6.50	3.50	3.00	3.00	4.75	5.25
Uruguay Uruguay	138.40	143.40	154.50	219.60	251.60	219.00	162.40	164.30	182.30	178.70
Venezuela Venezuela	8.00	8.00	8.00	45.00	43.00	43.00	52.20	71.25	48.00	49.00
Zaire Zaïre	26.00	29.00	37.00	50.00	45.00	55.00	55.00	95.00	145.00	125.00
Zambia Zambie	30.00	15.00	15.00	...	...	...	47.00	72.50	20.48	...
Zimbabwe Zimbabwe	9.00	9.00	9.00	9.00	10.25	20.00	...	28.50	29.50	29.50

Source:
International Monetary Fund (Washington, DC).

† For detailed descriptions of data pertaining to
former Czechoslovakia, Germany, SFR Yugoslavia and former
USSR, see Annex I - Country or area nomenclature, regional
and other groupings.

1 Data cover the former Federal Republic of Germany and the
former German Democratic Republic beginning July 1990.

Source:
Fonds monétaire international (Washington, DC).

† Pour les descriptions en détails des données
relatives à l'ancienne Tchécoslovaquie, l'Allemagne, la Rfs
Yougoslavie et l'ancienne URSS, voir l'Annexe I -
Nomenclature des pays ou zones, groupements régionaux et
autres groupements.

1 Les données se rapportent à l'ancienne République Fédéral
Allemagne et à l'ancienne République Démocratique Allemande
à partir de juillet 1990.

28
Short-term rates
Taux à court terme
Treasury bill and money market rates: per cent per annum
Taux des bons du Trésor et du marché monétaire : pour cent par année

Country or area Pays ou zone	1986	1987	1988	1989	1990	1991	1992	1993	1994	1995
Antigua and Barbuda Antigua-et-Barbuda										
Treasury bill										
Bons du Trésor	7.00	7.00	7.00	7.00	7.00	7.00	7.00	7.00	7.00	7.00
Argentina Argentine										
Money market										
Marché monétaire	135.00	253.00	524.00	..[1]	..[2]	71.00	15.00	6.00	8.00	...
Australia Australie										
Treasury bill										
Bons du Trésor	15.39	12.80	12.14	16.80	14.15	9.96	6.27	5.00	5.69	7.63
Money market										
Marché monétaire	15.75	13.06	11.90	16.75	14.81	10.47	6.44	5.11	5.18	7.44
Austria Autriche										
Money market										
Marché monétaire	5.19	4.35	4.59	7.46	8.53	9.10	9.35	7.22	5.03	4.36
Bahamas Bahamas										
Treasury bill										
Bons du Trésor	3.47	2.40	4.46	5.21	5.85	6.49	5.32	3.96	1.88	3.01
Bahrain Bahreïn										
Treasury bill										
Bons du Trésor	...	6.40	7.40	9.10	...	5.90	3.80	3.30	4.80	6.10
Money market										
Marché monétaire	7.20	7.10	7.90	9.20	8.50	6.30	4.00	3.50	5.20	6.20
Barbados Barbade										
Treasury bill										
Bons du Trésor	4.42	4.84	4.75	4.90	7.07	9.34	10.88	5.44	7.26	8.01
Belgium Belgique										
Treasury bill										
Bons du Trésor	8.09	7.00	6.61	8.45	9.62	9.23	9.36	8.52	5.56	4.67
Money market										
Marché monétaire	6.64	5.67	5.04	7.00	8.29	# 9.38	9.38	8.21	5.72	4.80
Belize Belize										
Treasury bill										
Bons du Trésor	10.81	8.80	8.32	7.36	7.37	6.71	5.37	4.59	4.27	4.10
Benin Bénin										
Money market										
Marché monétaire	8.58	8.37	8.72	10.07	10.98	10.94	11.44	...	...	...
Brazil Brésil										
Treasury bill										
Bons du Trésor	151.00	195.00	483.00	381.80	...	...	...	...	...	...
Burkina Faso Burkina Faso										
Money market										
Marché monétaire	8.58	8.37	8.72	10.07	10.98	10.94	11.44	...	...	...
Canada Canada										
Treasury bill										
Bons du Trésor	8.97	8.15	9.48	12.05	12.81	8.73	6.59	4.84	5.54	6.89
Money market										
Marché monétaire	8.16	8.50	10.35	12.06	11.62	7.40	6.79	3.79	5.54	5.71
Côte d'Ivoire Côte d'Ivoire										
Money market										
Marché monétaire	8.58	8.37	8.72	10.07	10.98	10.94	11.44	...	...	...
Croatia Croatie										
Money market										
Marché monétaire	...	...	...	...	...	...	951.20	1 370.50	26.93	21.13

28
Short-term rates
Treasury bill and money market rates: per cent per annum [cont.]
Taux à court terme
Taux des bons du Trésor et du marché monétaire : pour cent par année [suite]

Country or area Pays ou zone	1986	1987	1988	1989	1990	1991	1992	1993	1994	1995
Denmark Danemark										
Treasury bill										
Bons du Trésor	9.59	10.99	9.19	...	...	...	...	...	...	...
Money market										
Marché monétaire	9.22	10.20	8.52	9.66	10.97	9.78	11.35	# 11.49	6.30	6.19
Dominica Dominique										
Treasury bill										
Bons du Trésor	6.50	6.50	6.50	6.50	6.50	6.50	6.50	6.40	6.40	6.40
Ethiopia Ethiopie										
Treasury bill										
Bons du Trésor	3.00	3.00	3.00	3.00	3.00	3.00	5.25	12.00	12.00	12.00
Fiji Fidji										
Treasury bill										
Bons du Trésor	6.36	9.76	1.78	2.75	4.40	5.61	3.65	2.91	2.69	3.15
Money market										
Marché monétaire	6.55	9.02	1.49	2.34	2.92	4.28	3.06	2.91	4.10	3.95
Finland Finlande										
Money market										
Marché monétaire	11.90	10.03	9.97	12.56	14.00	13.08	13.25	7.77	5.35	5.75
France France										
Treasury bill										
Bons du Trésor	...	8.22	7.82	9.34	# 10.18	9.69	10.49	8.41	5.79	6.58
Money market										
Marché monétaire	7.74	7.98	7.52	9.07	9.85	9.49	10.35	8.75	5.69	6.35
Germany † Allemagne†										
Treasury bill										
Bons du Trésor	...	...	...	...	...	8.27	8.32	6.22	5.05	4.40
Money market										
Marché monétaire	...	...	...	...	...	8.84	9.42	7.49	5.35	4.50
F. R. Germany R. f. Allemagne										
Treasury bill[3]										
Bons du Trésor[3]	3.86	3.28	3.62	6.28	8.13	...	...	...	...	...
Money market[3]										
Marché monétaire[3]	4.57	3.72	4.01	6.59	7.92	...	...	...	...	...
Ghana Ghana										
Treasury bill										
Bons du Trésor	18.47	21.71	19.76	19.84	21.78	29.23	19.38	30.95	27.72	35.38
Greece Grèce										
Treasury bill										
Bons du Trésor	17.00	17.30	16.30	16.50	18.50	18.80	17.70	18.20	...	...
Grenada Grenade										
Treasury bill										
Bons du Trésor	6.50	6.50	6.50	6.50	6.50	6.50	6.50	6.50	6.50	6.50
Guyana Guyana										
Treasury bill										
Bons du Trésor	12.80	11.30	11.00	15.20	30.00	30.90	25.70	16.80	17.70	17.50
Hungary Hongrie										
Treasury bill										
Bons du Trésor	...	...	18.00	20.50	30.10	34.50	22.70	17.20	26.90	32.00
Iceland Islande										
Treasury bill										
Bons du Trésor	...	...	26.39	23.00	12.92	14.25	# 11.30	8.35	4.95	7.22
Money market										
Marché monétaire	...	31.52	34.49	21.58	12.73	14.85	12.37	8.61	4.96	6.58

28
Short-term rates
Treasury bill and money market rates: per cent per annum [*cont.*]
Taux à court terme
Taux des bons du Trésor et du marché monétaire : pour cent par année [*suite*]

Country or area Pays ou zone	1986	1987	1988	1989	1990	1991	1992	1993	1994	1995
India Inde										
Money market										
Marché monétaire	9.97	9.83	...	...	15.57	19.35	15.23	8.64	7.14	15.57
Indonesia Indonésie										
Money market										
Marché monétaire	13.00	14.52	15.00	12.57	14.37	15.12	12.14	...	...	...
Ireland Irlande										
Treasury bill										
Bons du Trésor	11.85	10.70	7.81	9.70	10.90	10.12	...	# 9.06	5.87	6.19
Money market										
Marché monétaire	12.28	10.84	7.84	9.55	11.10	10.45	15.12	10.49	# 5.75	5.45
Israel Israël										
Treasury bill										
Bons du Trésor	19.90	20.00	16.00	12.90	15.10	14.50	11.80	10.50	11.80	14.40
Italy Italie										
Treasury bill										
Bons du Trésor	11.40	10.73	11.13	12.58	12.38	12.54	14.32	10.58	9.17	10.85
Money market										
Marché monétaire	13.41	11.51	11.29	12.69	12.38	# 12.21	14.02	10.20	8.51	10.46
Jamaica Jamaïque										
Treasury bill										
Bons du Trésor	20.88	18.16	18.50	19.10	26.21	25.56	34.36	28.85	42.98	27.65
Japan Japon										
Money market										
Marché monétaire	4.79	3.51	3.62	4.87	7.24	7.46	4.58	# 3.06	2.20	1.21
Kenya Kenya										
Treasury bill										
Bons du Trésor	13.22	12.86	13.48	13.86	14.78	16.59	16.53	49.80	23.32	18.29
Korea, Republic of Corée, République de										
Money market										
Marché monétaire	9.70	8.90	9.60	13.30	14.00	17.00	14.30	12.10	12.50	12.60
Kuwait Koweït										
Treasury bill										
Bons du Trésor	5.69	5.48	6.01	8.28	...	...	...	...	...	...
Money market										
Marché monétaire	7.53	6.08	6.12	8.70	...	...	...	7.43	6.27	7.43
Lao People's Dem. Rep. Rép. dém. pop. lao										
Treasury bill										
Bons du Trésor	...	...	...	...	...	...	...	...	...	20.46
Latvia Lettonie										
Treasury bill										
Bons du Trésor	...	...	...	...	...	...	...	...	...	28.24
Lebanon Liban										
Treasury bill										
Bons du Trésor	18.67	26.91	25.17	18.84	18.84	17.47	22.40	18.27	15.09	19.40
Lesotho Lesotho										
Treasury bill										
Bons du Trésor	11.21	10.75	11.42	15.75	16.33	15.75	14.20	...	# 9.44	12.40
Lithuania Lituanie										
Treasury bill										
Bons du Trésor	...	...	...	...	...	...	...	...	...	26.90
Libyan Arab Jamah. Jamah. arabe libyenne										
Money market										
Marché monétaire	4.00	4.00	4.00	4.00	4.00	4.00	4.00	4.00	...	...

28

Short-term rates

Treasury bill and money market rates: per cent per annum [*cont.*]

Taux à court terme

Taux des bons du Trésor et du marché monétaire : pour cent par année [*suite*]

Country or area Pays ou zone	1986	1987	1988	1989	1990	1991	1992	1993	1994	1995
Luxembourg Luxembourg										
Money market										
Marché monétaire	7.30	6.71	7.16	10.02	9.67	9.10	8.93	8.09	5.16	4.25
Malawi Malawi										
Treasury bill										
Bons du Trésor	12.75	14.25	15.75	15.75	12.92	11.50	15.62	23.54	27.68	46.30
Malaysia Malaisie										
Money market										
Marché monétaire	4.19	3.12	4.11	4.72	6.81	7.83	8.01	6.53	5.07	...
Maldives Maldives										
Money market										
Marché monétaire	9.00	8.67	8.50	7.33	7.00	...	...	...	...	...
Mali Mali										
Money market										
Marché monétaire	8.58	8.37	8.72	10.07	10.98	10.94	11.44	...	...	...
Malta Malte										
Treasury bill										
Bons du Trésor	...	4.50	4.24	4.24	4.25	4.46	4.58	4.60	4.29	4.65
Mauritius Maurice										
Money market										
Marché monétaire	11.10	10.30	...	...	13.30	12.20	9.10	7.70	10.20	10.40
Mexico Mexique										
Treasury bill										
Bons du Trésor	...	103.07	69.14	44.99	34.76	19.28	15.62	15.03	14.10	48.44
Money market										
Marché monétaire	88.01	95.59	69.01	# 47.43	37.36	23.58	18.87	17.39	16.47	50.52
Morocco Maroc										
Treasury bill										
Bons du Trésor	10.50	10.50	10.50	10.50	9.50	9.50	...	...	...	...
Money market										
Marché monétaire	9.44	...	...	...	...	...	...	...	12.29	10.06
Namibia Namibie										
Treasury bill										
Bons du Trésor	...	...	...	...	...	...	13.88	12.16	11.35	13.91
Nepal Népal										
Treasury bill										
Bons du Trésor	5.00	5.00	5.00	5.62	7.93	8.80	9.00	4.50	6.50	...
Netherlands Pays-Bas										
Treasury bill										
Bons du Trésor	5.49	5.18	4.34	6.80	...	...	...	...	...	...
Money market										
Marché monétaire	5.83	5.16	4.48	6.99	8.29	9.01	9.27	7.10	5.14	4.22
Netherlands Antilles Antilles néerlandaises										
Treasury bill										
Bons du Trésor	7.34	6.36	5.79	5.96	6.10	...	...	4.83	4.48	5.46
New Zealand Nouvelle-Zélande										
Treasury bill										
Bons du Trésor	19.97	20.49	...	13.51	13.78	9.74	6.72	6.21	6.69	8.82
Money market										
Marché monétaire	24.10	17.40	14.18	14.10	12.61	7.59	7.59	4.96	9.44	8.77
Niger Niger										
Money market										
Marché monétaire	8.58	8.37	8.72	10.07	10.98	10.94	11.44	...	...	...

28
Short-term rates
Treasury bill and money market rates: per cent per annum [cont.]
Taux à court terme
Taux des bons du Trésor et du marché monétaire : pour cent par année [suite]

Country or area Pays ou zone	1986	1987	1988	1989	1990	1991	1992	1993	1994	1995
Norway Norvège Money market Marché monétaire	14.15	14.66	13.29	11.31	11.45	10.58	13.70	7.63	5.70	5.54
Pakistan Pakistan Money market Marché monétaire	6.59	6.25	6.31	6.30	7.29	7.64	7.51	11.00	8.36	11.52
Papua New Guinea Papouasie-Nvl-Guinée Treasury bill Bons du Trésor	12.32	10.44	10.12	10.50	11.40	10.33	8.88	6.25	6.85	...
Philippines Philippines Treasury bill Bons du Trésor	16.08	11.51	14.67	18.65	23.67	21.48	16.02	12.45	12.71	11.76
Poland Pologne Treasury bill Bons du Trésor	...	...	...	...	...	...	44.00	33.20	28.80	25.60
Money market Marché monétaire	...	...	...	...	...	49.90	# 29.50	24.50	23.30	25.80
Portugal Portugal Treasury bill Bons du Trésor	15.56	13.89	12.96	...	13.51	14.20	12.88	...	...	...
Money market Marché monétaire	14.52	13.69	12.34	12.68	13.12	15.50	# 17.48	13.25	10.62	8.91
Russian Federation Fédération de Russie Treasury bill Bons du Trésor	...	...	...	...	...	...	...	...	...	168.00
Saint Kitts and Nevis Saint-Kitts-et-Nevis Treasury bill Bons du Trésor	6.50	6.50	6.50	6.50	6.50	6.50	6.50	6.50	6.50	6.50
Saint Lucia Sainte-Lucie Treasury bill Bons du Trésor	7.00	7.00	7.00	7.00	7.00	7.00	7.00	7.00	7.00	7.00
St. Vincent-Grenadines St. Vincent-Grenadines Treasury bill Bons du Trésor	6.50	6.50	6.50	6.50	6.50	6.50	6.50	6.50	6.50	6.50
Senegal Sénégal Money market Marché monétaire	8.58	8.37	8.72	10.07	10.98	10.94	11.44	...	...	...
Seychelles Seychelles Treasury bill Bons du Trésor	12.91	15.15	13.90	13.41	* 13.17	13.30	13.28	13.18	12.51	12.39
Sierra Leone Sierra Leone Treasury bill Bons du Trésor	14.50	16.50	18.00	22.00	47.50	50.67	78.63	28.64	12.19	14.73
Singapore Singapour Money market Marché monétaire	4.27	3.89	4.30	5.34	6.61	4.76	2.74	2.50	3.68	2.56
Solomon Islands Iles Salomon Treasury bill Bons du Trésor	12.00	11.33	11.00	11.00	11.00	13.71	13.50	12.15	11.25	12.50
South Africa Afrique du Sud Treasury bill Bons du Trésor	10.43	8.71	12.03	16.84	17.80	16.68	13.77	11.31	10.93	13.53
Money market Marché monétaire	10.92	9.50	13.90	18.77	19.46	17.02	14.11	10.83	10.24	13.07

28
Short-term rates
Treasury bill and money market rates: per cent per annum [cont.]
Taux à court terme
Taux des bons du Trésor et du marché monétaire : pour cent par année [suite]

Country or area Pays ou zone	1986	1987	1988	1989	1990	1991	1992	1993	1994	1995
Spain Espagne										
Treasury bill										
Bons du Trésor	8.63	8.03	# 10.79	13.57	14.17	12.45	12.44	10.53	8.11	9.79
Money market										
Marché monétaire	11.50	16.07	11.30	14.39	14.76	13.20	13.01	...	...	...
Sri Lanka Sri Lanka										
Treasury bill										
Bons du Trésor	10.47	7.30	13.59	14.81	14.08	13.75	16.19	16.52	12.68	...
Money market										
Marché monétaire	12.95	13.14	18.65	22.19	21.56	25.42	21.63	25.65	18.54	...
Swaziland Swaziland										
Treasury bill										
Bons du Trésor	9.76	5.96	7.28	10.16	11.14	12.67	12.34	8.25	8.35	10.87
Money market										
Marché monétaire	...	...	...	8.39	10.50	10.61	10.25	9.73	7.01	8.52
Sweden Suède										
Treasury bill										
Bons du Trésor	9.83	9.39	10.08	11.50	13.66	11.59	12.85	8.35	7.40	8.75
Money market										
Marché monétaire	10.15	9.16	10.08	11.52	13.45	11.81	18.42	9.08	7.36	8.54
Switzerland Suisse										
Treasury bill										
Bons du Trésor	3.54	3.18	3.01	6.60	8.32	7.74	7.76	4.75	3.97	2.78
Money market										
Marché monétaire	3.17	2.51	2.22	6.50	8.33	7.73	7.47	4.94	3.85	2.89
Thailand Thaïlande										
Treasury bill										
Bons du Trésor	6.76	3.63	5.08	...	...	...	...	...	...	...
Money market										
Marché monétaire	8.07	5.91	8.66	9.82	12.73	10.58	7.06	6.49	7.16	10.28
Togo Togo										
Money market										
Marché monétaire	8.58	8.37	8.72	10.07	10.98	10.94	11.44	...	...	...
Trinidad and Tobago Trinité-et-Tobago										
Treasury bill										
Bons du Trésor	3.99	4.63	...	7.13	7.50	7.67	9.26	9.45	...	8.41
Tunisia Tunisie										
Money market										
Marché monétaire	9.95	10.00	9.15	9.40	11.53	11.79	11.73	10.48	8.81	8.81
Turkey Turquie										
Treasury bill										
Bons du Trésor	...	41.92	54.56	48.01	43.46	67.01	72.17	...	...	...
Money market										
Marché monétaire	...	39.82	60.62	40.66	51.91	72.75	65.35	62.83	136.47	72.30
Uganda Ouganda										
Treasury bill										
Bons du Trésor	30.67	30.50	33.00	42.17	41.00	34.17	...	# 21.30	12.52	8.75
United Kingdom Royaume-Uni										
Treasury bill										
Bons du Trésor	10.36	9.25	9.78	10.99	14.04	10.80	8.00	5.18	5.21	6.38
Money market										
Marché monétaire	10.68	9.66	10.31	13.62	14.64	11.77	9.39	5.46	4.76	5.98
United States Etats-Unis										
Treasury bill										
Bons du Trésor	5.97	5.83	6.67	8.11	7.51	5.41	3.46	3.02	4.27	5.51

28
Short-term rates
Treasury bill and money market rates: per cent per annum [cont.]
Taux à court terme
Taux des bons du Trésor et du marché monétaire : pour cent par année [suite]

Country or area Pays ou zone	1986	1987	1988	1989	1990	1991	1992	1993	1994	1995
Money market Marché monétaire	6.80[4]	6.66[4]	7.61[4]	9.22[4]	8.10[4]	5.70[4]	3.52[4]	3.02[4]	4.20	5.84
Vanuatu Vanuatu										
Money market Marché monétaire	6.96	6.50	7.50	7.08	7.00	7.00	5.92	6.00	6.00	...
Zambia Zambie										
Treasury bill Bons du Trésor	24.25	16.50	15.17	18.50	25.92	...	...	124.03	...	...
Zimbabwe Zimbabwe										
Treasury bill Bons du Trésor	8.71	8.73	8.38	8.17	8.39	13.34	...	33.04	29.22	27.98
Money market Marché monétaire	9.10	9.30	9.07	8.73	8.68	17.36	...	34.18	30.90	29.64

Source:
International Monetary Fund (Washington, DC).

† For detailed descriptions of data pertaining to former Czechoslovakia, Germany, SFR Yugoslavia and former USSR, see Annex I - Country or area nomenclature, regional and other groupings.

1 Rate = 1,387,179.00.
2 Rate = 9,695,422.00.
3 Data cover the former Federal Republic of Germany and the former German Democratic Republic beginning July 1990.

4 Federal funds rate.

Source:
Fonds monétaire international (Washington, DC).

† Pour les descriptions en détails des données relatives à l'ancienne Tchécoslovaquie, l'Allemagne, la Rfs Yougoslavie et l'ancienne URSS, voir l'Annexe I - Nomenclature des pays ou zones, groupements régionaux et autres groupements.

1 Taux = 1 387 179.00.
2 Taux = 9 695 422.00.
3 Les données se rapportent à l'ancienne République Fédéral Allemagne et à l'ancienne République Démocratique Allemande à partir de juillet 1990.

4 Taux des fonds du système fédérale.

Technical notes, tables 27 and 28

Detailed information and current figures relating to tables 27 and 28 are contained in *International Financial Statistics*, published monthly by the International Monetary Fund [13] and in the United Nations *Monthly Bulletin of Statistics*. [25]

Table 27: Rates shown represent those rates at which the central bank either discounts or makes advances against eligible commercial paper and/or government securities for commercial banks or brokers. For countries with more than one rate applicable to such discounts or advances, the rate shown is the one at which the largest proportion of central bank credit operations is understood to be transacted.

Table 28: Rates shown represent short-term money market rates - the rate at which short-term borrowings are effected between financial institutions or the rate at which short-term government paper is issued or traded in the market. Typical standardized names for these rates are *Money Market Rate* and *Treasury Bill Rate*, respectively.

Notes techniques, tableaux 27 et 28

Les informations détaillées et les chiffres courants concernant les tableaux 27 et 28 figurent dans les *Statistiques financières internationales* publiées chaque mois par le Fonds monétaire international [13] et dans le *Bulletin mensuel de statistique* des Nations Unies [25].

Tableau 27 : Les taux indiqués représentent les taux pratiqués par la banque centrale à l'escompte, ou pour avance de fonds, dans toute transaction portant sur des effets de commerce ou des obligations de l'Etat détenus par les banques commerciales ou des courtiers. Pour les pays où il existe plus d'un taux applicable à de telles transactions, le tableau indique le taux que la Banque centrale semble pratiquer pour la plupart de ses opérations de crédit.

Tableau 28 : Les taux indiqués représentent le marché monétaire à court terme - le taux auquel les emprunts à court terme sont effectués entre les institutions financières, ou le taux auquel les effets publics à court terme sont émis ou négociés sur le marché. Ces taux sont normalement dénommés *taux du marché monétaire* et *taux des bons du Trésor*, respectivement.

29
Employment by industry
Emploi par industrie

Persons employed, by branch of economic activity (000s)
Personnes employées, par branches d'activité économique (000s)

Country or area Pays ou zone	Year Année	Total employment (000s) Emploi total (000s)		Agriculture, hunting, forestry and fishing Agriculture, chasse sylviculture, pêche		Mining and quarrying Industries extractives		Manufacturing Industries manufacturières		Electricity, gas, water Electricité, gaz, eau	
		M	F	M	F	M	F	M	F	M	F
Albania [1] [2]	1985	462.3	313.4	93.6	76.8	...	...	145.5[34]	120.4[34]	...	...
Albanie [1] [2]	1991	494.1	356.4	107.2	88.0	...	...	151.2[34]	141.1[34]	...	...
Australia [6] [7] [8]	1985[9]	4126.4	2571.1	302.4	112.1	90.8	8.9	825.4	290.5	125.8	11.5
Australie [6] [7] [8]	1994	4545.4	3375.2	281.0	122.6	76.6	9.7	811.5	294.5	77.3	13.0
Austria [7] [10]	1985	1957.4	1277.1	157.3	133.6	12.7	1.5	663.8	249.3	37.6	4.3
Autriche [7] [10]	1993	2078.8	1496.6	129.3	117.2	9.3	0.9	658.0	244.8	31.8	4.1
Bahrain [11] [12]	1988	80.5	5.9	2.2	0.1	0.9	0.0	17.0	0.6	2.7	0.0
Bahreïn [11] [12]	1994	104.0	11.8	0.9	0.3	0.5	...	22.4	3.7	3.3	0.7
Barbados [6] [7]	1985	52.0	40.1	4.9	2.9	...	...	5.5	6.5	2.1	0.2
Barbade [6] [7]	1994	54.1	46.6	3.5	2.4	...	...	5.2	4.8	0.9	0.1
Belarus [14]	1985	5112.4	...	1287.2	...	33.7	...	1431.7	...	24.8	...
Bélarus [14]	1994	4696.0	...	995.7	...	27.2	...	1245.6	...	38.7	...
Belgium [7] [15] [16]	1985	2234.3	1326.5	83.7	25.3	23.3	0.4	615.3	187.5	28.5	3.0
Belgique [7] [15] [16]	1992	2236.0	1517.1	68.5	26.4	6.3	0.3	576.1	175.6	25.7	3.4
Belize [17]	1993	43.4	18.7	14.7	0.9	0.3	0.0	5.0	2.2	1.0	0.2
Belize [17]	1994	43.0	19.0	13.3	0.8	0.3	0.0	5.0	1.7	1.0	0.2
Bermuda [9] [16]	1985	17.4	14.8	0.2	0.0	0.1	0.0	0.8	0.4	0.4	0.1
Bermudes [9] [16]	1994	17.1	17.0	0.4	0.0	0.1	0.0	0.7	0.4	0.4	0.1
Bolivia [6] [18]	1989	477.3	370.5	13.4	3.0	14.5	1.7	76.1	32.4	3.9	0.1
Bolivie [6] [18]	1992	616.3	432.1	16.7	5.4	18.8	0.9	136.5	67.0	8.2	1.1
Botswana [6] [16]	1985	82.9	33.9	3.4	0.6	6.9	0.4	7.4	2.7	1.8	0.1
Botswana [6] [16]	1992	145.6	81.9	4.2	1.8	7.3	0.4	16.1	9.5	2.3	0.3
Brazil [6] [16] [20] [21]	1985	35820.0	17940.0	12070.0	3319.0	761.0[4] [22]	87.0[4] [22]	5824.0	2083.0	...	...
Brésil [6] [16] [20] [21]	1990	40018.0	22083.0	11235.0	2945.0	764.0[4] [22]	96.0[4] [22]	6774.0	2637.0	...	...
British Virgin Islands [9] [14] [28]	1985	5.1	...	0.1	...	0.0	...	0.2	...	0.2	...
Iles Vierges brit. [9] [14] [28]	1987	6.6	...	0.1	...	0.0	...	0.4	...	0.2	...
Bulgaria [14] [29]	1985	4459.5	...	934.8[30]	...	109.6	...	1522.5	...	30.1	...
Bulgarie [14] [29]	1994	3157.9	...	698.1[30]	...	...	...	934.9	...	...	...
Burundi [14] [16] [33]	1985	44.7	...	6.5	...	0.5	...	5.6	...	1.0	...
Burundi [14] [16] [33]	1991	44.7	...	6.6	...	0.3	...	6.2	...	0.9	...
Canada [6] [7]	1985	6428.0	4794.0	427.0	147.0	163.0	26.0	1416.0[34]	544.0[34]	100.0[22]	22.0[22]
Canada [6] [7]	1993	6753.0	5630.0	395.0	155.0	129.0	20.0	1297.0[34]	503.0[34]	108.0[22]	34.0[22]
Central African Rep. [11] [14]	1985	19.8	...	4.3	...	...	...	7.8	...	0.9	...
Rép. centrafricaine [11] [14]	1990	13.0	...	2.3	...	...	...	4.0	...	0.8	...
Chad [9]	1986	8.4	0.5	1.6	0.1	...	...	0.5	0.0	0.5	0.0
Tchad [9]	1991	11.8	0.7	1.3	0.1	0.2	0.0	5.2	0.1	0.0	0.0
Chile [6] [7] [36]	1985	2620.9	1099.7	707.5	43.6	84.3	1.8	373.9	120.8	23.7	2.3
Chili [6] [7] [36]	1994	3373.5	1614.8	720.1	88.8	82.9	3.5	594.9	223.9	30.6	3.0
China [16] [37]	1985	60795.0	29100.0	5055.0	2776.0	...	...	25221.0[3] [4]	12924.0[3] [4]	...	...
Chine [16] [37]	1989	66867.0	34220.0	5076.0	2867.0	6218.0	1589.0	20292.0	13144.0	1089.0	395.0
Colombia [16] [38] [39]	1985	1916.5	1183.4	33.5	8.6	9.3	1.4	443.5	247.4	19.9	3.2
Colombie [16] [38] [39]	1992	2819.5	2021.7	53.0	15.4	15.0	4.3	660.8	477.9	27.1	5.4
Costa Rica [6] [16] [39]	1985	613.3	213.4	216.3	9.5	...	...	89.5[3]	41.7[3]	...	...
Costa Rica [6] [16] [39]	1994	801.2	336.4	226.4	17.2	2.1	...	131.6	71.9	14.7	2.2
Côte d'Ivoire [14] [41]	1985	406.0	...	60.0	...	...	...	67.8[3] [4]	...	...	...
Côte d'Ivoire [14] [41]	1990	385.0	...	53.3	...	...	...	60.0[3] [4]	...	...	...
Croatia	1985	888.1	620.5	58.8	18.1	10.3	1.6	317.4	219.2	23.9	5.0
Croatie	1993	601.6	506.8	42.9	14.6	5.8	1.1	214.2	156.4	21.9	4.9
Cuba [2]	1985	1988.3	1175.3	432.9[42]	110.7[42]	...	...	481.8[3] [43]	213.3[3] [43]	14.3[44]	4.8[44]
Cuba [2]	1988	2135.6	1309.8	519.4	142.7	29.9	5.3	452.2	230.9	29.2	9.7
Cyprus [6]	1985	139.5	82.3	19.4	16.9	1.0	...	24.3	20.5	1.4	0.1
Chypre [6]	1993	163.8	106.6	19.3	15.7	0.7	...	25.0	20.5	1.4	0.1
Denmark [46] [47]	1985	1410.3	1143.2	129.8	39.0	4.1	0.2	352.3	163.0	16.3	2.4
Danemark [46] [47]	1993[48]	1383.1	1200.9	100.5	31.3	1.8	0.7	346.6	155.1	13.9	2.3
Ecuador [16] [18] [20]	1990	1499.9	830.6	153.9[3]	21.1[3]	...	...	285.4	132.2	...	...
Equateur [16] [18] [20]	1994	1665.2	1032.3	164.0	24.7	14.95	1.2	268.6	146.2	10.9	1.4
Egypt [6] [16] [49]	1989	10808.0	4117.7	3734.6	2600.6	41.9	1.4	1614.1	344.6	88.7	11.2
Egypte [6] [16] [49]	1992[50]	11232.1	3166.8	3876.2	1658.8	42.6	2.3	1718.4	296.2	136.5	10.8

Construction Construction		Trade, restaurants and hotels Commerce, restaurants, hôtels		Transport, storage, communications Transports, entrepôts, communications		Finance, insurance, real est.,bus. services Services financières, immob.,et apparentées		Community, social and personal services Services à collectivité services soc. et pers.	
M	F	M	F	M	F	M	F	M	F
67.8	6.3	26.9	28.9	31.3	5.8	15.5	9.6	81.7[5]	65.6[5]
69.7	6.4	27.7	29.6	32.1	6.4	12.8	13.9	93.4[5]	71.0[5]
421.1	58.9	849.2	709.2	417.2	95.0	413.1	326.6	682.7	962.5
490.0	79.6	1066.1	948.5	384.2	126.5	537.5	488.7	800.1	1278.1
241.1	22.6	244.1	333.9	170.3	38.0	92.5	86.4	331.9	403.7
280.7	25.1	273.2	401.1	188.1	44.4	133.7	131.6	366.4	516.0
29.3	0.2	13.1	0.8	4.1	0.4	4.4	1.5	7.4	2.2
33.0	0.3	19.3	1.6	8.3	2.3	5.0	1.6	10.0	2.1
6.9[13]	0.2[13]	9.3	10.8	4.0	1.1	1.4	1.8	17.9	16.6
7.4[13]	0.3[13]	6.9	8.4	3.1	1.1	2.2	4.1	10.8	19.8
355.1	...	321.4	...	424.9	...	27.7	...	1038.8	...
328.9	...	422.3	...	318.0	...	40.9	...	1099.7	...
192.3	11.0	301.4	285.2	223.1	36.5	157.5	98.5	609.2	679.1
229.6	15.7	318.0	316.2	211.3	45.8	196.8	144.8	603.7	788.8
3.8	0.1	1.1	2.0	2.9	0.5	0.3	0.6	1.6	1.1
3.5	0.1	1.3	1.9	3.2	0.5	0.5	0.7	1.4	1.4
2.2	0.2	5.6	5.4	1.5	0.7	1.7	2.7	4.8	5.2
1.5	0.1	5.2	5.5	1.6	0.7	1.8	3.3	5.3	6.9
52.7	1.2	76.6	168.3	59.2	5.4	16.4	6.8	164.4	151.6
95.9	1.3	121.8	183.4	70.7	4.8	26.5	13.9	120.4	154.3
11.0	0.5	10.5	7.8	5.0	0.7	4.8	2.1	32.2[19]	19.1[19]
28.9	4.8	18.4	22.5	7.5	2.7	11.4	6.2	49.4[19]	33.8[19]
3069.0	56.0	3997.0[23]	1871.0[23]	1782.0[24]	151.0[24]	1210.0[5][25]	548.0[5][25]	7107.0[26][27]	9825.0[26][27]
3726.0	97.0	5060.0[23]	2916.0[23]	2246.0[24]	194.0[24]	1151.0[5][25]	565.0[5][25]	9062.0[26][27]	12633.0[26][27]
0.5	...	0.6	...	0.4	...	0.2	...	2.9	...
0.5	...	0.6	...	0.4	...	0.3	...	4.1	...
346.2	...	393.8	...	296.5[24]	...	59.1	...	766.9[31][32]	...
177.8	...	389.2	...	230.8[24]	...	68.0	...	659.1[31][32]	...
7.1	...	4.2	...	2.8	...	1.6	...	13.3	...
2.4	...	3.8	...	2.9	...	1.9	...	17.7	...
514.0	66.0	1373.0	1241.0	576.0	178.0	530.0	599.0	1329.0[32][35]	1971.0[32][35]
585.0	75.0	1514.0	1398.0	559.0	208.0	699.0	767.0	1468.0[32][35]	2469.0[32][35]
1.6	...	3.6	...	0.9	...	...	...	0.0	...
1.3	...	4.3	...	1.5	...	0.3	...	...	...
1.1	0.0	1.2	0.0	1.2	0.1	0.1	0.1	1.9	0.1
1.0	0.0	0.6	0.1	0.9	0.1	0.3	0.0	2.1	0.3
141.7	3.8	396.0	248.5	200.2	14.1	105.1	45.6	588.1	619.1
350.7	10.2	530.0	410.7	328.2	43.1	192.5	106.0	542.8	725.6
4602.0	1192.0	5028.0	3407.0	4623.0	1225.0	599.0	331.0	14837.0	7021.0
4550.0	1233.0	5639.0	4167.0	4947.0	1453.0	864.0	492.0	17396.0	8637.0
184.0	10.9	481.2	299.9	179.6	18.1	135.6	74.9	438.8	518.2
288.3	16.3	680.0	552.7	266.2	32.1	216.0	130.0	604.4	781.3
41.9	0.2	105.4[40]	51.0[40]	47.0[4]	4.2[4]	...	...	108.5	105.7
73.1	1.4	126.1	83.6	51.3	7.1	37.7	12.9	130.8	137.2
18.8	...	28.5	...	57.3	...	...	...	173.2[40]	...
17.4	...	25.9	...	53.5	...	...	...	174.9[40]	...
124.4	14.6	102.4	132.7	110.1	26.9	21.3	26.5	119.5	175.9
58.3	8.7	73.6	101.2	74.8	23.7	16.2	24.7	93.9	171.5
258.0	37.4	211.2	195.6	176.4	48.4	28.9[45]	27.0[45]	384.8	538.1
280.1	42.5	223.3	213.2	187.4	54.8	33.5[45]	29.6[45]	380.6	581.1
19.8	1.6	28.0	19.3	10.1	2.5	6.7	4.5	25.5	16.2
21.9	1.4	37.3	30.5	12.1	4.1	10.3	9.1	33.1	24.5
156.2	14.7	207.0	184.9	132.8	46.9	99.6	92.9	308.3	597.6
131.9	15.9	216.5	185.6	132.5	51.5	134.6	122.9	300.2	632.0
164.1	4.7	327.7	303.2	143.1[4]	13.1[4]	77.7	29.8	347.4	326.5
165.6	6.1	411.9	402.7	146.9	9.6	75.6	36.4	406.8	404.0
973.0	17.2	1102.6	237.4	734.3	45.9	209.0	46.3	2302.4	813.1
863.4	20.8	1148.5	183.6	734.8	42.9	191.3	45.8	2515.1	905.1

29
Employment by industry [*cont.*]
Emploi par industrie [*suite*]

Country or area Pays ou zone	Year Année	Total employment (000s) Emploi total (000s)		Persons employed, by branch of economic activity (000s) Personnes employées, par branches d'activité économique (000s)							
				Agriculture, hunting, forestry and fishing Agriculture, chasse sylviculture, pêche		Mining and quarrying Industries extractives		Manufacturing Industries manufacturières		Electricity, gas, water Electricité, gaz, eau	
		M	F	M	F	M	F	M	F	M	F
El Salvador [20]	1985 [18]	900.7	472.5	411.5	57.1	0.8	...	135.3	98.6	6.8	0.5
El Salvador [20]	1992	1134.4	647.2	542.2	96.1	2.3	0.3	167.4	141.3	9.7	1.9
Estonia [14]	1985	810.9	...	107.7	...	...	...	273.3[3 4]	...	...	...
Estonie [14]	1994	461.7	...	40.2	...	11.6	...	109.4	...	14.3	...
Ethiopia [12 51]	1987 [52]	414.6	124.8	93.2	23.3	2.1	0.2	67.2	29.5	11.1	1.4
Ethiopie [12 51]	1993	504.6	178.3	82.7	17.2	0.4	0.1	96.3	39.0	18.2	3.6
Fiji [16]	1985	61.1	20.0	2.2	0.3	1.2	0.1	11.6	2.8	2.2	0.1
Fidji [16]	1990	65.0	27.1	2.0	0.3	1.6	0.1	12.4	8.6	2.0	0.1
Finland [1 46]	1985	1294.0	1173.0	173.0	106.0	8.0	2.0	353.0	204.0	25.0	7.0
Finlande [1 46]	1994	1065.0	981.0	110.0	57.0	5.0	...	271.0	127.0	19.0	4.0
France [15]	1985	12545.1	8905.4	1004.4	525.7	...	...	5080.8[3 4 53]	1687.8[3 4 53]	...	...
France [15]	1993	12446.3	9629.9	748.7	352.1	...	...	4551.8[3 4 53]	1479.8[3 4 53]	...	...
French Polynesia [14]	1985	40.1	...	0.6	...	0.1	...	1.8	...	0.3	...
Polynésie française [14]	1989	41.7	...	0.9	...	0.1	...	2.2	...	0.4	...
Gambia [12 16]	1985	20.6	3.5	0.8	0.1	...	...	1.3	0.0	1.1	0.1
Gambie [12 16]	1987	21.1	5.0	1.4	0.6	...	...	1.9	0.5	0.8	0.1
Germany † · Allemagne †											
F. R. Germany [7 16]	1985	16402.0	10225.0	671.0	591.0	265.0	18.0	6027.0	2441.0	230.0	35.0
R. f. Allemagne [7 16]	1994	17270.0	12127.0	555.0	375.0	177.0	16.0	6032.0	2392.0	223.0	51.0
former German D. R. [7 16]	1991	4156.0	3605.0	331.0	199.0	129.0	44.0	1393.0	856.0	100.0	41.0
anc. R. d. allemande [7 16]	1994	3717.0	2961.0	159.0	102.0	57.0	16.0	845.0	373.0	72.0	28.0
Ghana [14 16]	1985	464.3	...	56.4	...	25.2	...	51.7	...	8.0	...
Ghana [14 16]	1991	186.3	...	14.7	...	17.1	...	20.6	...	1.7	...
Gibraltar [16 56 57]	1985	8.2	3.5	...	...	...	...	2.2	0.5	0.2	...
Gibraltar [16 56 57]	1992	9.9	4.8	...	...	...	...	0.4	0.1	0.3	0.0
Greece [15 36 58]	1985	2371.4	1217.3	576.1	460.8	26.8	2.0	485.0[59]	193.7[59]	27.9	3.7
Grèce [15 36 58]	1992	2403.2	1281.3	468.7	338.0	17.6	0.7	487.3[59]	211.4[59]	30.9	5.8
Guam [105]	1985	22.6	15.9	0.1	...	...	...	0.7	0.4	...	...
Guam [105]	1987 [16]	25.8	18.3	0.2	...	...	...	1.0	0.7	...	...
Guatemala [14 29]	1985	631.7	...	233.6	...	2.1	...	78.2	...	13.0[22]	...
Guatemala [14 29]	1993	823.2	...	214.6	...	2.4	...	136.7	...	11.1[22]	...
Honduras [20]	1985	162.1	118.6	2.5	0.3	0.6	0.5	32.2	22.4	2.6	0.4
Honduras [20]	1992 [18]	1152.0	522.7	607.6	32.3	5.4	358.0	125.4	125.0	6.8	1.1
Hong Kong [6 7 63]	1985	1613.0	930.4	27.1	14.4	0.5	0.2	491.7	427.1	15.5	1.5
Hong–kong [6 7 63]	1994	1822.7	1092.7	14.0	4.1	0.3	...	368.3	201.9	17.0	2.3
Hungary	1985	2653.3	2467.7	662.5	426.5	...	...	853.2[3 4]	684.8[3 4]	...	...
Hongrie	1992	2185.2	2131.3	364.8	204.7	...	...	718.2[3 4]	599.6[3 4]	...	...
Iceland [14 65]	1985	120.7	...	13.4	...	...	...	27.3[3]	...	1.1	...
Islande [14 65]	1990	124.6	...	13.1	...	...	...	23.3[3]	...	1.1	...
India [16 52 66 67]	1985	21416.0	3162.0	872.0	433.0	999.0	87.0	5597.0	586.0	778.0	21.0
Inde [16 52 66 67]	1989	22417.0	3545.0	903.0	467.0	975.0	78.0	5670.0	575.0	880.0	28.0
Indonesia [1 20]	1985 [68]	39950.6	22506.5	22074.2	12067.6	346.2	69.4	3170.1	2625.8	65.0	4.7
Indonésie [1 20]	1992	47644.6	30459.5	25629.5	17224.0	489.9	104.9	4187.1	3660.5	157.5	15.8
Ireland [7 16]	1985	744.3	332.0	149.9	17.9	9.7	0.4	145.9	56.7	13.6	1.6
Irlande [7 16]	1991	748.1	377.0	141.9	12.3	6.1	0.5	157.8	63.4	12.5	1.5
Israel [6 7 69]	1985	836.0	513.4	56.6	15.5	...	...	231.7[3]	74.7[3]	9.9	1.9
Israël [6 7 69]	1994	1090.3	781.1	48.3	14.0	...	...	285.4[3]	110.7[3]	17.1	3.2
Italy [15 58 70]	1985	14064.0	6830.0	1485.0	812.0	193.0[4]	16.0[4]	3234.0[71]	1532.0[71]	...	...
Italie [15 58 70]	1994	12972.0	7030.0	998.0	574.0	267.0[4]	27.0[4]	3120.0[71]	1421.0[71]	...	...
Jamaica [6 58]	1985	475.0	306.7	212.4	67.4	5.6	1.0	73.3	25.3	...	...
Jamaïque [6 58]	1992	517.5	389.9	185.0	60.5	4.2	0.4	57.6	41.6	...	...
Japan [17]	1985	35030.0	23040.0	2650.0	2440.0	70.0	10.0	8790.0	5740.0	290.0	40.0
Japon [17]	1993	38400.0	26100.0	2070.0	1760.0	50.0	10.0	9450.0	5850.0	300.0	50.0
Jordan [12 16 56]	1985	128.2	35.8	...	...	6.1	0.1	23.4	2.8	4.3	0.2
Jordanie [12 16 56]	1993	240.4	70.7	...	...	7.4	0.2	48.4	5.7	11.9	0.4
Kazakstan [14 106]	1985	7136.0	...	1617.0	...	225.0	...	1232.0	...	66.0	...
Kazakstan [14 106]	1992	7356.0	...	1762.0	...	257.0	...	1160.0	...	83.0	...
Kenya [16 75]	1985	943.5	230.9	197.7	43.2	4.7	0.1	143.0	15.8	16.3	1.4
Kenya [16 75]	1991	1117.1	324.6	207.6	64.4	3.5	0.9	167.0	21.9	19.2	3.2

Construction Construction		Trade, restaurants and hotels Commerce, restaurants, hôtels		Transport, storage, communications Transports, entrepôts, communications		Finance, insurance, real est.,bus. services Services financières, immob.,et apparentées		Community, social and personal services Services à collectivité services soc. et pers.	
M	F	M	F	M	F	M	F	M	F
50.4	1.9	74.4	161.4	47.5	1.9	20.1	11.1	148.9	140.0
79.2	1.8	123.6	184.0	56.5	4.5	12.2	7.8	139.3	209.4
70.7	...	74.8	...	77.4	...	4.2	...	190.8	...
29.4	...	56.7	...	43.2	...	27.1	...	129.7	...
38.3	4.4	8.5	6.0	25.3	5.1	19.2	6.9	149.7	48.1
23.3	4.3	18.9	11.4	21.2	6.9	15.2	6.4	228.6	89.5
6.9	0.1	10.4	4.4	6.9	1.0	3.0	1.8	16.9	9.4
5.6	0.1	10.1	4.8	8.2	1.3	3.6	2.1	19.6	9.7
161.0	18.0	148.0	207.0	133.0	53.0	65.0	91.0	226.0	485.0
103.0	10.0	133.0	161.0	120.0	41.0	84.0	91.0	216.0	487.0
...	...	6459.9[40 54 55]	6691.9[40 54 55]	...	...	...	...	...	...
...	...	7145.8[40 54 55]	7798.0[40 54 55]	...	...	...	...	...	...
5.3	...	8.3	...	2.6	...	2.4	...	18.7	...
5.3	...	9.5	...	9.7	...	2.8	...	15.3	...
2.9	0.1	4.0	0.7	2.4	0.2	0.9	0.2	7.2	2.1
2.9	0.0	3.7	0.8	2.7	0.4	0.8	0.3	7.0	2.3
1694.0	192.0	1737.0	2208.0	1166.0	346.0	1024.0	885.0	3588.0	3509.0
1846.0	255.0	1905.0	2541.0	1230.0	459.0	1422.0	1282.0	3881.0	4756.0
562.0	88.0	322.0	619.0	387.0	218.0	147.0	191.0	785.0	1350.0
907.0	100.0	368.0	570.0	325.0	155.0	214.0	241.0	770.0	1377.0
23.2	...	23.1	...	20.2	...	25.0	...	231.5	...
7.8	...	7.5	...	10.4	...	8.4	...	98.1	...
2.0	0.1	1.4	1.0	0.5	0.1	0.3	0.3	1.3	1.2
3.0	0.2	1.8	1.4	0.5	0.1	0.6	0.9	2.5	1.7
240.4	2.2	364.7	206.2	225.4	24.1	83.5	49.1	340.9	275.1
242.5	3.7	423.9	263.4	220.7	29.5	120.1	80.5	391.5	348.1
2.6	0.1	3.7[60]	3.3[60]	1.3[4]	0.5[4]	0.6	1.2	3.6[61]	2.9[61]
4.2	0.2	4.0[60]	4.0[60]	1.5[4]	0.7[4]	0.8	1.2	4.0[61]	3.7[61]
14.1	...	58.4[62]	...	20.3	...	...	...	212.0[35]	...
26.4	...	102.6[62]	...	25.2	...	...	...	304.2[35]	...
13.9	0.5	38.1	30.6	11.3	1.8	7.8	4.6	52.8	57.9
70.0	2.6	130.8	151.1	45.7	6.3	19.6	10.4	140.1	193.5
182.9	8.9	378.2	195.6	181.3	25.3	86.0	61.5	249.9	195.9
214.7	11.0	475.4	363.9	289.1	58.0	197.6	133.5	246.1	318.1
284.9	66.9	177.4	331.4	290.1	108.1	...	...	384.7[40 64]	631.8[40 64]
211.2	60.1	205.4	412.3	250.4	123.6	...	...	435.2[40 64]	791.0[40 64]
11.5	...	18.1	...	8.2	...	8.3	...	32.8	...
12.4	...	18.1	...	8.4	...	10.0	...	38.2	...
1154.0	62.0	383.0	25.0	2837.0	111.0	1080.0	121.0	7716.0	1716.0
1157.0	58.0	404.0	31.0	2895.0	130.0	1204.0	152.0	8280.0	2025.0
2043.4	52.2	4577.4	4767.8	1933.7	24.6	201.5	49.0	5506.9	2810.4
2259.4	104.0	5604.6	5495.7	2439.7	72.5	376.9[3 4 53 54]	184.9[3 4 53 54]	6447.5	3525.5
75.0	2.8	115.5	75.8	56.3	11.9	46.1	30.8	129.3	132.2
76.3	3.5	113.9	85.7	52.3	12.9	51.0	43.5	133.7	151.3
67.3	4.9	108.6	59.1	69.1	17.2	69.7	61.4	214.9	277.0
111.5	6.5	162.2	118.6	83.8	25.2	111.2	95.2	262.3	405.0
1843.0	77.0	2822.0	1544.0	968.0	123.0	467.0	249.0	3052.0	2477.0
1554.0	88.0	2663.0	1557.0	914.0	168.0	959.0	557.0	2496.0	2638.0
33.1[34]	0.6[34]	...	...	29.0[4 22]	6.4[4 22]	38.3[72]	75.4[72]	81.8	130.1
62.4[34]	0.6[34]	...	...	28.5[4 22]	8.7[4 22]	84.6[72]	134.1[72]	91.8	139.3
4540.0	760.0	6930.0[60]	6250.0[60]	2990.0	440.0	2270.0	1640.0	6340.0[61]	5630.0[61]
5370.0	1030.0	7300.0[60]	7180.0[60]	3300.0	640.0	3020.0	2450.0	7360.0[61]	7020.0[61]
5.5	0.2	9.2[23 73]	0.7[23 73]	9.4	1.0	6.8	2.8	63.5	28.1
7.5	0.2	22.2[73]	1.7[73]	22.7	2.2	10.5	3.5	109.9	56.8
622.0	...	451.0	...	828.0	...	41.0[74]	...	1630.0	...
681.0	...	437.0	...	665.0	...	46.0[74]	...	1906.0	...
48.6	1.3	75.6	14.1	48.8	6.9	42.5	10.9	366.3	137.2
68.3	4.2	97.1	19.6	65.6	10.6	51.4	14.9	437.4	185.0

29
Employment by industry [cont.]
Emploi par industrie [suite]

| | | Persons employed, by branch of economic activity (000s) Personnes employées, par branches d'activité économique (000s) | | | | | | | | | |
| | | Total employment (000s) Emploi total (000s) | | Agriculture, hunting, forestry and fishing Agriculture, chasse sylviculture, pêche | | Mining and quarrying Industries extractives | | Manufacturing Industries manufacturières | | Electricity, gas, water Electricité, gaz, eau | |
Country or area Pays ou zone	Year Année	M	F	M	F	M	F	M	F	M	F
Korea, Republic of [6][7]	1985	9137.0	5833.0	2114.0	1619.0	150.0	5.0	2153.0	1351.0	38.0	3.0
Corée, République de [6][7]	1994	11832.0	8005.0	1427.0	1272.0	37.0	3.0	2930.0	1765.0	59.0	12.0
Latvia											
Lettonie	1992	703.0	642.0	177.0	92.0	2.0	1.0	169.0	152.0	11.0	5.0
Lithuania	1985	888.9	970.8	231.5	135.3	...	...	281.2[3][4]	289.2[3][4]	...	...
Lituanie	1993	846.4	931.8	263.3	164.5	2.6	1.4	198.5[3][4]	221.1[3][4]	24.2	9.2
Luxembourg [1]	1985	106.7	54.2	4.4	2.3	0.2	...	33.2	5.1	1.2	0.1
Luxembourg [1]	1990	125.0	64.6	4.3	1.9	0.2	...	33.1	4.1	1.2	0.2
Macau [6][58]	1989 [16]	95.4	66.6	0.9	0.1	...	...	23.9	35.5	1.6	0.4
Macao [6][58]	1993	99.6	71.8	0.3	0.1	0.0	...	17.6	25.2	0.6	0.1
Madagascar [11][14]	1986	259.0	...	68.0	...	4.5[77]	...	45.0[13]	...	9.0	...
Madagascar [11][14]	1991	285.9	...	76.3	...	4.5[77]	...	93.1[13]	...	11.5	...
Malawi	1985	348.1	67.1	162.2	31.1	0.3	0.0	41.1	19.1	4.1	0.4
Malawi	1991	487.9	106.5	243.4	77.6	0.8	0.0	70.3	6.5	6.3	0.6
Malaysia [6][80]	1985	3700.5	1952.8	1057.3	660.1	39.7	4.7	479.4	371.0	30.4	1.1
Malaisie [6][80]	1993	4853.8	2529.6	1077.0	481.6	34.0	3.6	960.7	766.3	54.6	5.7
Malta [1][16]	1985	85.1	27.7	4.8	0.6	1.4	0.1	22.2[34]	11.7[34]	1.3[22]	0.1[22]
Malte [1][16]	1991	96.0	34.3	2.9	0.4	0.6	...	25.0[34]	10.9[34]	1.8[22]	0.1[22]
Mauritius [12][16]	1985	139.3	64.4	36.0[83]	12.3[83]	0.1	0.1	21.0[84]	35.1[84]	3.8	0.1
Maurice [12][16]	1994	188.6	103.8	30.0[83]	11.7[83]	0.1	0.1	41.9[84]	62.8[84]	3.4	0.2
Mexico	1991	21266.0	9277.0	7186.0	1004.0	188.0	30.0	3132.0	1674.0	130.0	21.0
Mexique	1993	22748.0	10085.0	7721.0	1122.0	165.0	6.0	3372.0	1706.0	87.0	12.0
Montserrat [6][14]	1985	5.1	...	0.5	...	0.0	...	0.5	...	0.1	...
Montserrat [6][14]	1987	5.2	...	0.5	...	0.0	...	0.6	...	0.1	...
Morocco [7][18]	1991	2590.9	809.1	109.2	23.2	39.1	1.9	634.8	378.0	28.6	2.7
Maroc [7][18]	1992	2733.5	760.8	104.0	21.1	43.9	1.5	548.4	340.9	30.5	2.5
Mozambique [14]	1987	192.7	...	15.1	...	5.0	...	111.6	...	3.8	...
Mozambique [14]	1988	201.6	...	16.9	...	4.9	...	117.0	...	2.9	...
Myanmar [6][14]	1985	14792.0	...	9772.0	...	85.0	...	1234.0	...	16.0	...
Myanmar [6][14]	1994	16817.0	...	11551.0	...	87.0	...	1250.0	...	17.0	...
Netherlands [1]	1985 [7]	3414.0	1730.0	214.0	54.0	10.0	1.0	822.0	171.0	39.0	5.0
Pays–Bas [1]	1994 [80]	3979.0	2713.0	193.0	71.0	9.0	...	855.0	220.0	40.0	7.0
Netherlands Antilles [6][14][85]	1985	60.3	...	0.5	...	0.2	...	5.6	...	1.4	...
Antilles néerlandaises [6][14][85]	1989 [86]	43.8	...	...	...	0.4[87]	...	4.2	...	0.9	...
New Caledonia [14]	1985	33.4	...	1.6	...	1.0	...	4.6[4]	...	...	...
Nouvelle–Calédonie [14]	1989	44.4	...	2.1	...	1.1	...	4.6	...	0.6	...
New Zealand [6][7]	1986	904.0	641.0	116.0	49.0	6.0	1.0	217.0	101.0	14.0	2.0
Nouvelle–Zélande [6][7]	1993	838.0	657.0	108.0	49.0	4.0	...	175.0	80.0	9.0	2.0
Nicaragua [14]	1985	289.8	...	32.4	...	2.4	...	57.0	...	5.4	...
Nicaragua [14]	1992	214.7	...	28.0	...	1.3	...	33.4	...	6.1	...
Niger	1985	20.9	1.6	1.0	0.0	4.1	0.0	2.3	0.2	1.6	0.0
Niger	1991	22.1	2.0	1.8	0.1	3.0	0.1	1.7	0.1	4.2	0.3
Norway [1][88]	1985 [9]	1149.0	865.0	106.0	41.0	18.0	4.0	261.0	88.0	16.0	3.0
Norvège [1][88]	1994	1102.0	932.0	80.0	27.0	19.0	6.0	224.0	79.0	18.0	4.0
Pakistan [6][20][89]	1985	24360.0	2601.0	11677.0	1954.0	46.0	...	3390.0	296.0	183.0	3.0
Pakistan [6][20][89]	1994	28465.0	4638.0	12516.0	3225.0	33.0	...	3105.0	504.0	275.0	4.0
Panama [6][7][16]	1985	441.8	185.2	176.0	8.7	0.3	0.1	47.7	18.9	7.7	1.4
Panama [6][7][16]	1992	560.5	234.6	202.0	7.2	1.7	0.4	53.7	21.8	7.8	2.0
Paraguay [6]	1985 [39][90]	230.7	176.3	10.2	0.9	0.8	...	49.0	30.1	2.8	0.8
Paraguay [6]	1994 [18][20]	616.0	433.6	36.9	3.5	1.8	...	126.7	53.1	10.1	1.7
Peru [15][58][91]	1987	1233.3	827.8	10.5	5.9	13.0	0.6	314.9	138.5	5.5	0.6
Pérou [15][58][91]	1994 [47]	1643.6	1038.6	8.0	3.4	6.4	0.9	376.6	138.5	12.8	4.2
Philippines [7]	1985 [36]	12758.0	7569.0	7434.0	2651.0	120.0	9.0	989.0	937.0	67.0	12.0
Philippines [7]	1994 [16]	15985.0	9181.0	8446.0	2803.0	95.0	6.0	1391.0	1191.0	83.0	18.0
Poland [6][14]	1985	18531.4	...	5169.2	...	587.3	...	4895.6	...	181.0	...
Pologne [6][14]	1992	15462.3	...	3860.8	...	477.9	...	3589.7	...	149.6	...
Portugal [15][93]	1985 [39]	2554.4	1724.8	528.7	489.5	22.4	1.6	629.1	407.4	26.6	3.2
Portugal [15][93]	1993 [58]	2486.0	1971.6	262.7	252.9	19.0	0.7	598.2	444.4	25.8	6.3
Puerto Rico [6][65]	1985	486.0	290.0	39.0	1.0	...	...	75.0	65.0	10.0	1.0
Porto Rico [6][65]	1994	612.0	414.0	34.0	1.0	1.0	...	95.0	70.0	15.0	3.0

Construction Construction		Trade, restaurants and hotels Commerce, restaurants, hôtels		Transport, storage, communications Transports, entrepôts, communications		Finance, insurance, real est.,bus. services Services financières, immob.,et apparentées		Community, social and personal services Services à collectivité services soc. et pers.	
M	F	M	F	M	F	M	F	M	F
846.0	65.0	1628.0	1750.0	640.0	62.0	370.0	194.0	1199.0	785.0
1616.0	161.0	2554.0	2645.0	901.0	106.0	850.0	645.0	1458.0	1398.0
78.0	11.0	62.0	125.0	70.0	35.0	34.0	41.0	41.0	31.0
151.0	29.4	32.4	121.2	103.6	45.2	1.2	8.2	85.9	336.9
107.7	19.1	35.1	155.8	66.3	33.6	19.0	31.1	152.3	289.7
13.1	0.8	17.2	17.3	9.0	1.8	9.3[74]	7.5[74]	19.1[5][76]	19.3[5][76]
17.7	1.1	20.9	19.3	10.6	2.3	9.1[74]	7.7[74]	27.9[5][76]	28.0[5][76]
13.3	0.9	20.0	11.6	6.2	0.9	3.7	2.9	24.8	13.4
15.3	1.8	25.0	19.5	8.7	1.8	4.4	4.8	27.4	18.1
27.8	...	...	...	24.2	...	33.4[78]	...	151.8	...
28.4	...	...	...	26.1	...	37.6[78]	...	169.2	...
22.9	0.3	35.9	3.5	22.9	1.3	11.3	1.5	47.5[79]	10.0[79]
44.1	0.5	26.3	3.1	20.9	1.4	15.2	1.8	60.6[79]	15.1[79]
396.0	23.4	620.7	373.6	219.0	25.3	142.0	76.9	715.2	416.5
508.1	30.7	770.5	495.7	309.5	34.4	208.1	121.9	931.2	589.7
5.1	0.1	8.5[23]	3.0[23]	7.2	0.8	2.2[81]	1.4[81]	32.6[32][35][82]	9.6[32][35][82]
5.8	0.1	9.9[23]	3.7[23]	8.4	1.1	2.9[81]	2.1[81]	38.9[32][35][82]	15.9[32][35][82]
4.7	0.1	7.3	1.9	7.8	0.6	3.6	1.4	50.3	12.8
13.2	0.2	17.7	5.7	12.5	1.7	8.1	3.4	58.7	18.1
1822.0	50.0	3264.0	2886.0	1041.0	100.0	602.0	343.0	3741.0	3135.0
1816.0	63.0	3646.0	3246.0	1243.0	119.0	657.0	423.0	3837.0	3368.0
0.8	...	0.7	...	0.3	...	0.2	...	2.0	...
0.9	...	0.7	...	0.3	...	0.2	...	2.0	...
261.1	3.0	649.2	63.3	171.8	9.1	52.7	22.9	639.3[59]	304.0[59]
278.1	3.8	698.6	62.8	189.8	10.3	52.8	23.3	779.8[59]	293.0[59]
19.6	...	5.5	...	29.8	...	...	...	2.2	...
21.5	...	6.4	...	29.3	...	...	...	2.7	...
240.0	...	1444.0	...	488.0	...	885.0	...	628.0[5]	...
292.0	...	1450.0	...	420.0	...	1264.0	...	486.0[5]	...
362.0	24.0	547.0	359.0	272.0	51.0	292.0	166.0	831.0	885.0
364.0	29.0	654.0	573.0	323.0	96.0	425.0	279.0	1032.0	1339.0
5.3	...	14.2	...	4.1	...	4.8	...	23.8	...
3.9	...	10.7	...	3.8	...	4.3	...	15.5	...
3.1	...	5.6	...	1.6	...	2.8	...	9.2	...
5.5	...	7.4	...	1.9	...	3.3	...	11.6	...
92.0	11.0	140.0	155.0	78.0	31.0	64.0	70.0	172.0	218.0
72.0	9.0	162.0	155.0	66.0	25.0	77.0	72.0	164.0	265.0
15.7	...	24.6	...	17.2	...	14.7	...	119.6	...
6.6	...	21.5	...	8.8	...	11.2	...	96.3	...
4.2	0.2	1.7	0.3	2.3	0.1	1.7	0.4	2.0	0.3
2.3	0.0	2.1	0.3	2.9	0.5	0.6	0.2	3.5	0.5
140.0	10.0	159.0	188.0	129.0	46.0	72.0	57.0	246.0	427.0
111.0	8.0	163.0	185.0	116.0	48.0	92.0	68.0	276.0	508.0
1502.0	8.0	3074.0	37.0	1394.0	8.0	226.0	11.0	2701.0	284.0
2251.0	44.0	4273.0	136.0	1808.0	19.0	265.0	5.0	3882.0	696.0
31.8	1.5	51.4	35.7	31.6	5.8	14.1	10.3	69.2	99.8
42.1	0.9	104.4	52.9	40.8	6.5	21.7	13.9	85.4	128.9
33.0	0.2	44.4	48.3	19.8	2.5	15.6	8.2	55.0	85.3
89.2	...	151.1	159.0	48.7	6.2	30.5	16.8	121.0	193.4
112.8	7.1	309.4	318.7	118.4	14.2	73.4	24.1	275.4	318.3
158.6	5.5	419.4	462.5	183.2	16.3	140.4	66.4	338.2	340.8
668.0	10.0	861.0[23]	1789.0[23]	871.0	41.0	221.0	130.0	1526.0[92]	1988.0[92]
1166.0	21.0	1201.0[23]	2362.0[23]	1343.0	58.0	296.0	198.0	1959.0[92]	2521.0[92]
1394.6	...	1640.2	...	1394.6	...	390.8	...	2698.1	...
1131.8	...	1827.3	...	1023.5	...	405.0	...	2895.8	...
344.0	10.2	351.0	240.6	155.1	31.9	83.6	36.6	413.1	503.5
349.5	15.8	498.1	369.1	160.9	47.0	182.1	117.9	389.7	717.6
36.0	1.0	107.0[60]	43.0[60]	30.0	6.0	14.0	12.0	176.0[61]	161.0[61]
52.0	1.0	130.0[60]	77.0[60]	34.0	7.0	17.0	18.0	237.0[61]	235.0[61]

29
Employment by industry [*cont.*]
Emploi par industrie [*suite*]

		Total employment (000s) Emploi total (000s)		Persons employed, by branch of economic activity (000s) Personnes employées, par branches d'activité économique (000s)							
				Agriculture, hunting, forestry and fishing Agriculture, chasse sylviculture, pêche		Mining and quarrying Industries extractives		Manufacturing Industries manufacturières		Electricity, gas, water Electricité, gaz, eau	
Country or area Pays ou zone	Year Année	M	F	M	F	M	F	M	F	M	F
Rep. of Moldova [6] [14] Rép. de Moldova [6] [14]	1985	2080.0	...	777.0	...	...	...	414.0	...	12.0	...
	1992	2050.0	...	820.0	...	...	...	394.0	...	14.0	...
Romania [6] Roumanie [6]	1985 [2]	5828.3	4757.8	1318.2	1741.3	225.9	45.3	2020.0	1582.8	44.2	9.6
	1993	5415.3	4646.7	1742.3	1878.8	216.8	42.4	1430.8	1175.5	128.8	36.3
Russian Federation [14] Fédération de Russie [14]	1990	75324.7	...	10499.1	...	1235.9	...	20181.9	...	595.1	...
	1992	72071.1	...	11078.9	...	1252.8	...	18682.8	...	669.3	...
San Marino [58] Saint-Marin [58]	1985	6.5	4.0	0.2	0.1	...	...	2.5	1.5	...	...
	1993	8.6	5.6	0.2	0.1	...	...	3.2	1.5	...	...
Seychelles [14] [94] Seychelles [14] [94]	1985	18.2	...	2.3	...	...	...	1.1	...	0.6	...
	1989	22.3	...	2.2	...	...	...	2.5[95]	...	...	...
Sierra Leone [12] [14] [66] Sierra Leone [12] [14] [66]	1985	69.4	...	6.0	...	6.3	...	8.1	...	2.2	...
	1988	70.2	...	7.3	...	5.8	...	8.6	...	2.7	...
Singapore [7] [16] Singapour [7] [16]	1985	785.3	449.2	6.6	2.0	2.1	0.5	174.9	139.3	7.1	1.1
	1993	952.3	639.7	3.6	0.3	0.3	...	247.8	181.7	5.9	1.6
Slovakia [96] Slovaquie	1985	1325.0	1100.0	225.0	145.0	22.0	6.0	452.0	329.0	25	8.0
	1992	1264.0	911.0[97]	169.0	87.0[97]	24.0	4.0[97]	353.0	236.0[97]	32	9.0[97]
Slovenia [29] Slovénie	1985	511.6	426.8	40.3	43.4	11.8	1.1	227.8	173.6	9.3	2.6
	1993 [1]	402.7	363.5	32.7	38.5	8.7	0.7	173.9	127.3	9.3	2.4
Solomon Islands [14] [16] Iles Salomon [14] [16]	1985	24.0	...	8.0	...	...	...	1.8[3]	...	0.3[44]	...
	1992	26.8	...	6.4	...	...	...	2.0[3]	...	0.4[44]	...
South Africa [14] [16] [98] Afrique du Sud [14] [16] [98]	1985	5036.4	...	...	...	724.6	...	1429.0	...	66.2	...
	1993	4950.5	...	...	...	561.7	...	1400.5	...	42.5	...
Spain [15] [65] Espagne [15] [65]	1985	7553.1	3087.9	1439.2	509.8	87.8	2.4	1922.6	495.9	78.3	6.0
	1993 [48]	7850.3	3987.3	869.7	328.1	55.6	2.6	1859.4	542.3	73.5	6.5
Sri Lanka [20] [36] Sri Lanka [20] [36]	1985	3581.3	1550.4	1690.4	840.5	58.1	8.6	359.5	288.9	20.8	0.7
	1994 [99]	3542.2	1606.2	1445.2	746.4	30.3	0.5	371.0	411.1	19.7	...
Suriname [36] Suriname [36]	1990	50.2	31.4	2.3	0.7	2.4	0.2	6.5	2.0	0.3	0.1
	1993	53.3	34.2	2.5	0.6	2.3	...	6.8	1.0	1.4	0.2
Swaziland [16] Swaziland [16]	1985	52.7	20.2	18.2	4.9	2.3	0.1	7.8	2.8	1.2	0.1
	1986	55.0	21.4	18.1	5.0	2.3	0.1	7.5	3.4	1.3	0.1
Sweden [15] Suède [15]	1985 [88]	2276.0	2022.0	154.0	54.0	13.0	2.0	713.0	256.0	34.0	6.0
	1994 [100]	2016.0	1911.0	101.0	35.0	8.0	1.0	527.0	193.0	26.0	6.0
Switzerland [6] Suisse [6]	1986	2157.0	1273.0	137.0	57.0	22.0	2.0	630.0[4]	237.0[4]	...	...
	1994	2248.0	1525.0	93.0	50.0	24.0	3.0	573.0[4]	210.0[4]	...	...
Syrian Arab Republic [6] [16] [20] Rép. arabe syrienne [6] [16] [20]	1984	1945.9	300.5	429.3	142.7	17.4	0.3	301.7	34.9	18.2	1.1
	1991	2710.3	539.6	625.0	292.0	6.7	...	421.5	34.6	7.9	0.6
TFYR Macedonia [47] L'ex-R.y. Macédoine [47]	1985 [2]	323.0	168.0	31.0	10.0	11.0	1.0	107.0	71.0	9.0	1.0
	1994	248.0	148.0	25.0	9.0	9.0	1.0	83.0	56.0	10.0	1.0
Thailand [6] [16] Thaïlande [6] [16]	1985 [101]	13971.5	10749.1	9385.7	6890.0	47.2	22.2	1143.9[34]	1013.7[34]	90.3[22]	13.3[22]
	1991 [102]	16850.9	14287.5	10089.6	8687.7	41.5	12.8	1717.5[34]	1747.5[34]	92.3[22]	17.9[22]
Togo [14] Togo [14]	1985	61.2	...	5.3	...	2.5	...	5.2	...	2.3	...
	1992	60.7	...	4.4	...	3.1	...	7.3	...	2.4	...
Trinidad and Tobago [7] Trinité-et-Tobago [7]	1985	263.6	128.6	32.6	9.7	...	...	42.2[3]	15.8[3]	...	...
	1993	261.8	142.8	37.7	8.0	13.1	1.9	28.1	12.2	6.2	0.9
Turkey [6] [16] [39] Turquie [6] [16] [39]	1985	2378.6	229.3	45.8	4.1	123.2	1.2	1009.0	151.8	100.7	1.7
	1993	3570.6	405.6	65.7	4.5	141.4	0.9	1424.1	217.7	171.5	3.8
United Kingdom [9] [16] [65] [103] Royaume-Uni [9] [16] [65] [103]	1985	14289.0	10250.0	497.0	119.0	304.0	26.0	3919.0	1621.0	243.0	60.0
	1993	13741.0	11576.0	427.0	120.0	...	...	4936.0[3] [4] [53]	1629.0[3] [4] [53]	...	...
United States [6] [65] Etats-Unis [6] [65]	1985	59891.0	47259.0	2667.0	671.0	795.0	144.0	14127.0	6752.0	1212.0[22]	274.0[22]
	#1994	66450.0	56610.0	2689.0	897.0	564.0	105.0	13686.0	6471.0	1236.0[22]	309.0[22]
US Virgin Islands [14] [108] Iles Vierges amé [14] [108]	1985	37.1	...	0.2	...	...	...	2.1	...	...	...
	1993	48.9	...	0.1	...	...	...	2.9	...	...	...
Uruguay [15] [18] [58] Uruguay [15] [18] [58]	1986 [36]	626.2	395.0	...	...	50.5	5.4	131.5	82.6	...	...
	1993	679.2	476.8	40.7	4.5	1.9	0.1	149.2	89.9	13.1	2.9
Venezuela [6] [7] Venezuela [6] [7]	1985	3692.2	1413.9	795.5	30.7	62.5	6.4	584.4	206.0	52.9	10.6
	1993 [36]	4815.6	2219.3	719.8	36.3	60.4	8.8	794.9	295.5	47.2	9.7
Zambia [14] [36] Zambie [14] [36]	1985	361.5	...	35.1	...	57.5	...	48.5	...	8.2	...
	1989	359.6	...	37.2	...	54.2	...	50.9	...	8.7	...
Zimbabwe [75] Zimbabwe [75]	1985	865.6	189.4	209.1	67.3	53.1	1.2	158.0	11.6	7.4	0.3
	1994 [16]	1018.0	252.2	228.7	94.8	49.9	1.6	184.9	18.0	8.1	0.3

Construction Construction		Trade, restaurants and hotels Commerce, restaurants, hôtels		Transport, storage, communications Transports, entrepôts, communications		Finance, insurance, real est.,bus. services Services financières, immob.,et apparentées		Community, social and personal services Services à collectivité services soc. et pers.	
M	F	M	F	M	F	M	F	M	F
132.0	...	115.0	...	145.0	...	8.0	...	403.0	...
120.0	...	111.0	...	102.0	...	9.0	...	422.0	...
693.1	94.5	236.0	381.4	606.2	114.4	12.2	16.5	672.5[5]	772.0[5]
500.7	73.3	332.5	383.2	451.5	140.4	235.3	246.9	376.6[5]	669.9[5]
8168.1	...	5085.8	...	5818.2	...	401.6	...	19607.1	...
7246.6	...	4914.2	...	5631.8	...	493.6	...	18641.8	...
0.9	0.0	0.8	0.8	0.1	0.0	0.1	0.1	2.0	1.4
1.2	0.0	1.2	1.3	0.2	0.1	0.2	0.2	2.4	2.4
1.7[3]	...	3.1	...	2.3	...	0.8	...	3.6	...
1.7[3]	...	4.4	...	3.1	...	0.7	...	4.6	...
9.1	...	4.0	...	7.5	...	2.3	...	23.9	...
7.3	...	3.3	...	7.7	...	1.8	...	25.7	...
100.7	9.2	176.9	113.0	101.3	23.8	54.3	53.5	158.9	106.8
91.1	11.0	216.2	147.4	131.0	35.8	88.1	85.3	167.6	176.5
210.0	32.0	73.0	192.0	111.0	45.0	42.0	39.0	165.0	303.0
161.0	37.0[97]	143.0	113.0[97]	109.0	52.0[97]	105.0	65.0[97]	168.0	308.0[97]
62.0	8.1	36.4	66.4	45.0	12.6	14.0	16.4	65.2	102.5
29.8	4.5	29.7	55.2	32.5	10.4	14.3	19.3	71.8	105.2
1.5	...	2.6	...	2.1	...	0.5	...	7.1	...
1.1	...	3.2	...	1.4	...	1.2	...	11.1	...
410.1[107]	...	755.7	...	425.5	...	160.9	...	1064.5[79]	...
374.5[107]	...	764.4	...	303.1	...	191.5	...	1312.4[79]	...
762.0	14.0	1185.0	767.2	554.8	57.5	342.5	101.6	1167.8	1126.8
1046.1	42.3	1596.5	1095.5	606.5	88.4	554.5	372.2	1188.6	1509.3
216.4	10.6	411.1	102.8	213.0	7.0	50.0	15.1	378.5	252.9
171.6	...	560.4	105.9	197.4	8.0	59.1	38.5	546.4	279.0
4.2	0.0	7.0	5.8	4.6	0.4	1.6	1.3	19.3	19.9
4.3	0.4	7.2	0.6	4.1	0.2	1.2	2.1	20.7	22.6
3.5	0.1	4.0	3.0	4.8	0.6	2.1	1.2	8.8	7.3
5.1	0.2	4.3	3.1	4.9	0.7	2.2	1.2	9.2	7.6
236.0	24.0	287.0	304.0	213.0	87.0	174.0	147.0	453.0	1141.0
202.0	18.0	292.0	276.0	187.0	84.0	213.0	166.0	457.0	1131.0
297.0	22.0	329.0	378.0	160.0	44.0	211.0	135.0	370.0	398.0
243.0	35.0	341.0	405.0	175.0	60.0	302.0	179.0	496.0	582.0
361.8	4.8	243.4	9.4	122.6	5.1	13.1	4.2	438.5	98.0
334.3	6.4	369.0	9.3	158.4	8.6	20.2	4.5	767.4	183.7
50.0	3.0	35.0	26.0	21.0	4.0	7.0	6.0	39.0	44.0
30.0	3.0	20.0	18.0	18.0	3.0	6.0	6.0	36.0	49.0
478.4	96.6	1127.7[23 73]	1409.0[23 73]	485.4	49.4	...	...	1205.3[32 35 92]	1251.5[32 35 92]
998.1	180.1	1648.3[23 73]	1828.8[23 73]	739.0	94.9	...	...	1515.0[32 35 92]	1710.6[32 35 92]
5.6	...	8.2[40]	...	4.5	...	...	...	27.6	...
2.3	...	7.9[40]	...	4.8	...	...	...	28.5	...
66.1[4]	5.6[4]	43.4	50.2	24.8	3.4	...	...	54.5[40]	43.8[40]
39.7	4.6	35.5	35.6	25.2	4.8	15.4	12.5	60.5	62.2
559.2	4.7	153.6	19.9	117.4	4.8	17.9	3.3	251.8	37.7
566.3	10.2	385.3	61.4	216.4	14.0	39.3	9.1	560.7	84.0
1358.0	134.0	2336.0	2558.0	1154.0	277.0	1257.0	1071.0	2911.0	4369.0
...	...	8125.0[40 54 55]	9809.0[40 54 55]	...	...	...	...	...	...
6370.0	617.0	11742.0[60]	10554.0[60]	4301.0	1761.0	4942.0	6062.0	13734.0[35 61]	20425.0[35 61]
6775.0	718.0	13564.0[60]	12136.0[60]	4987.0	2160.0	6352.0	7213.0	16598.0[35 61]	26601.0[35 61]
1.9	...	11.2	...	2.4[4]	...	2.7	...	3.2	...
5.4	...	14.9	...	2.7[4]	...	3.3	...	5.7	...
48.7	0.4	110.1	63.9	68.3	8.4	33.4	15.1	183.7	219.2
80.4	1.7	126.5	90.7	55.2	9.1	38.7	25.5	173.5	252.3
340.7	9.5	688.1	313.8	310.7	27.8	166.9	90.9	689.4	718.2
611.5	25.0	989.1	576.6	415.6	46.4	273.5	186.2	900.1	1033.1
29.3	...	28.2	...	24.2	...	22.6	...	108.0	...
20.8	...	26.6	...	26.1	...	24.7	...	110.2	...
44.1	0.7	66.2	12.1	46.9	3.1	10.1[81]	5.2[81]	270.7[104]	87.9[104]
82.8	6.1	89.0	16.9	48.6	4.7	15.7[81]	7.0[81]	310.3[104]	102.8[104]

29
Employment by industry [*cont.*]
Emploi par industrie [*suite*]

Source:
International Labour Office (Geneva).

† For detailed descriptions of data pertaining to former
Czechoslovakia, Germany, SFR Yugoslavia and former USSR,
see Annex I — Country or area nomenclature, regional and
other groupings.

1   Including armed forces.
2   State sector (Estonia, Romania, TFYR Macedonia: and
cooperative sector).
3   Including mining and quarrying.
4   Including electricity, gas and water.
5   Including activities not adequately defined.
6   Civilian labour force employed.
7   Persons aged 15 years and over.
8   Data classified according to ANZSIC; previously
classified by ASIC.
9   Excluding unpaid family workers.
10 Including armed forces, except conscripts not employed
before their military service.
11 Private sector.
12 Establishments with 10 or more persons employed (Gambia,
Jordan: 5 or more persons; Sierra Leone: 6 or more persons).
13 Including quarrying.
14 Both sexes.
15 Including professional army; Excluding compulsory
military service.
16 One month of each year.
17 Persons aged 15 to 69 years.
18 Urban areas.
19 Including local and central government.
20 Persons aged 10 years and over.
21 Excluding rural population of Rondônia, Acre, Amazonas,
Roraima, Pará and Amapá.
22 Including sanitary services.
23 Excluding restaurants and hotels.
24 Excluding storage.
25 Including international and other extra−territorial bodies.
26 Including restaurants, hotels and storage.
27 Excluding sanitary services and international bodies.
28 Excluding own−account workers.
29 Excluding armed forces.
30 Including veterinary services.
31 Excluding veterinary services, radio and TV broadcasting.
32 Excluding repair and installation services.
33 Bujumbura.
34 Including repair and installation services.
35 Excluding sanitary services.
36 One quarter of each year.
37 State owned enterprises.
38 7 main cities of the country.
39 Persons aged 12 years and over.
40 Including financing, insurance, real estate and business services.
41 Modern sector.
42 Excluding hunting and fishing.
43 Including fishing, water and gas.
44 Excluding gas and water (Solomon Islands: excl. gas only).
45 Including petroleum and gas extraction.
46 Persons aged 15 to 74 years.
47 Average of less than 12 months.
48 Data classified according to ISIC, Rev. 3.
49 Persons aged 6 years and over.
50 Average of four surveys.
51 Year ending in September of the year indicated.

Source:
Bureau international du travail (Genève).

† Pour les descriptions en détails des données relatives à l'ancienne
Tchécoslovaquie, l'Allemagne, la Rfs Yougoslavie et l'ancienne URSS,
voir l'Annexe I — Nomenclature des pays ou zones, groupements
régionaux et autres groupements.

1   Y compris les forces armées.
2   Secteur d'Etat (Estonie, Roumanie, L'ex−R.y.Macédoine:
et secteur de coopératif).
3   Y compris les industries extractives.
4   Y compris l'électricité, le gaz et l'eau.
5   Y compris les activités mal désignées.
6   Main−d'œuvre civile occupée.
7   Personnes âgées de 15 ans et plus.
8   Données classifiées selon l'ANZSIC; précédemment
classifiées par l'ASIC.
9   Non compris les travailleurs familiaux non rémunérés.
10 Y compris les forces armées, sauf les conscrits n'ayant pas travaillé avant
leur service militaire.
11 Secteur privé.
12 Etablissements occupant 10 personnes et plus (Gambie, Jordanie: 5 et plus
personnes; Sierra leone: 6 et plus personnes).
13 Y compris les carrières.
14 Les deux sexes.
15 Y compris les militaires de carrière; non compris les militaires du
contingent.
16 Un mois de chaque année.
17 Personnes âgées de 15 à 69 ans.
18 Régions urbaines.
19 Y compris le gouvernement local et central.
20 Personnes âgées de 10 ans et plus.
21 Non compris la population rurale de Rondônia, Acre, Amazonas, Roraima,
Pará et Amapá.
22 Y compris les services sanitaires.
23 Non compris les restaurants et hôtels.
24 Non compris les entrepôts.
25 Y compris les organisations internationales et autres organismes
extra−territoriaux.
26 Y compris les restaurants, hôtels et entrepôts..
27 Non compris les services sanitaires et les organismes internationaux.
28 Non compris les travailleurs à leur propre compte.
29 Non compris les forces armées.
30 Y compris les services vétérinaires.
31 Non compris les services vétérinaires, la radiodiffusion et télévision.
32 Non compris les services de réparation et d'installation.
33 Bujumbura.
34 Y compris les services de réparation et d'installation.
35 Non compris les services sanitaires.
36 Un trimestre de chaque année.
37 Entreprises d'Etat.
38 7 villes principales du pays.
39 Personnes âgées de 12 ans et plus.
40 Y compris les banques, les assurances, les affaires immobilières et les
services aux entreprises.
41 Secteur moderne.
42 Non compris la chasse et la pêche.
43 Y compris la pêche, l'eau et le gaz.
44 Non compris le gaz et l'eau (Iles Salomon: non compris le gaz seulement).
45 Y compris l'extraction du pétrole et du gaz.
46 Personnes âgées de 15 à 74 ans.
47 Moyenne de moins de douze mois.
48 Données classifiées selon la CITI, Rév. 3.
49 Personnes âgées de 6 ans et plus.

52 Public sector.
53 Including construction.
54 Including transport, storage and communication.
55 Including community, social and personal services.
56 Non–agricultural activities.
57 Excluding mining and quarrying.
58 Persons aged 14 years and over.
59 Including repairs.
60 Excluding hotels.
61 Including hotels.
62 Including finance and insurance.
63 Including unpaid family workers.
64 Non–material activities.
65 Persons aged 16 years and over.
66 Including working proprietors.
67 Establishments of non–agricultural private sector with 10 or more persons employed.
68 Intercensal Population Survey results.
69 Including the residents of East Jerusalem.
70 Including permanent members of institutional households.
71 Industrial transformations.
72 Including trade, restaurants and hotels.
73 Including financing, insurance and real estate.
74 Excluding real estate and business services.
75 Excluding small establishments in rural areas.
76 Including real estate and business services.
77 Excluding quarrying.
78 Including trade.
79 Excluding domestic services.
80 Persons aged 15 to 64 years.
81 Excluding business services.
82 Including restaurants and hotels and business services.
83 Including sugar and tea factories.
84 Excluding sugar and tea factories.
85 Excluding Aruba.
86 Curaçao.
87 Including agriculture, hunting, forestry and fishing.
88 Persons aged 16 to 74 years.
89 July of preceding year to June of current year.
90 Asunción metropolitan area.
91 Lima.
92 Including restaurants and hotels.
93 Including the Azores and Madeira.
94 Excluding domestic workers, self–employed and family workers.
95 Including electricity and water.
96 Socialised sector.
97 Excluding women on maternity leave, apprentices and armed forces.
98 Excluding Transkei, Bophuthatswana, Venda and Ciskei.
99 Excluding Northern and Eastern provinces.
100 Persons aged 16 to 64 years.
101 Persons aged 11 years and over.
102 Persons aged 13 years and over.
103 Excluding employees in private domestic services.
104 Including business services.
105 Multiple job–holders are counted at each establishment.
106 Including members of producers' cooperatives.
107 Private construction.
108 Based on an establishment survey plus an estimation for agriculture.

50 Moyenne de quatre enquêtes.
51 Année se terminant en septembre de l'année indiquée.
52 Secteur public.
53 Y compris la construction.
54 Y compris les transports, les entrepôts at les communications.
55 Y compris les services à collectivité, les services social et personnel.
56 Activités non agricoles.
57 Non compris les industries extractives.
58 Personnes âgées de 14 ans et plus.
59 Y compris les réparations.
60 Non compris les hôtels.
61 Y compris les hôtels.
62 Y compris les banques et les assurances.
63 Y compris les travailleurs familiaux non rémunérés.
64 Activités non matérielles.
65 Personnes âgées de 16 ans et plus.
66 Y compris les propriétaires exploitants.
67 Etablissements du secteur privé non agricole occupant 10 personnes et plus.
68 Résultats de l'enquête intercensitaire de population.
69 Y compris les résidents de Jérusalem–Est.
70 Y compris les membres permanents des ménages collectifs.
71 Transformations industrielles.
72 Y compris le commerce, les restaurants et les hôtels.
73 Y compris les banques, les assurances, les affaires immobilières.
74 Non compris les affaires immobilières et les services aux entreprises.
75 Non compris les petites entreprises des zones rurales.
76 Y compris les affaires immobilières et les services aux entreprises.
77 Non compris les carrières.
78 Y compris le commerce.
79 Non compris les services domestiques.
80 Personnes âgées de 15 à 64 ans.
81 Non compris les services aux entreprises.
82 Y compris les restaurants, hôtels et les services aux entreprises.
83 Y compris les fabriques de sucre et de thé.
84 Non compris les fabriques de sucre et de thé.
85 Non compris Aruba.
86 Curaçao.
87 Y compris l'agriculture, la chasse, la sylviculture et la pêche.
88 Personnes âgées de 16 à 74 ans.
89 Juillte de l'année précédente à juin de l'année en cours.
90 Région métropolitaine d'Asunción.
91 Lima.
92 Y compris les restaurants et les hôtels.
93 Y compris les Açores and Madère.
94 Non compris le personnel domestique, les travailleurs indépandants et les travailleurs familiaux.
95 Y compris l'électricité et l'eau.
96 Secteur socialisé.
97 Non compris les femmes en congé de maternité, les apprentis et les forces armées.
98 Non compris Transkei, Bophuthatswana, Venda et Ciskei.
99 Non compris les provinces du Nord et de l'Est.
100 Personnes âgées de 16 à 64 ans.
101 Personnes âgées de 11 ans et plus.
102 Personnes âgées de 13 ans et plus.
103 Non compris les personnes occupées à des services domestiques privés.
104 Y compris les services aux entreprises.
105 Les personnes qui occupent plus d'un emploi sont comptées dans chaque établissement.
106 Y compris les membres des coopératives de production.
107 Construction privée.
108 Basée sur une enquête auprès des établissements plus une estimation pour l'agriculture.

30
Unemployment
Chômage

Number (thousands) and percentage of unemployed
Nombre (milliers) et pourcentage des chômeurs

Country or area § Pays ou zone §	1985	1986	1987	1988	1989	1990	1991	1992	1993	1994
Albania Albanie										
MF [IV]	94.0	92.0	89.4	105.8	113.4	150.7	139.8	...	...	...
% MF [IV]	6.7	6.4	6.1	7.0	7.3	9.5	9.1	...	...	...
Algeria Algérie										
MF [I] [12]	...	...	...	...	946.0	1156.0	1261.0	1482.0	...	...
M [I] [12]	...	...	...	...	876.0	1069.0	1155.0	1348.0	...	...
F [I] [12]	...	...	...	...	70.0	87.0	106.0	134.0	...	...
% MF [I] [12]	...	...	...	...	17.0	19.7	21.1	23.8	...	...
% M [I] [12]	...	...	...	...	17.2	...	21.7	24.2	...	...
% F [I] [12]	...	...	...	...	15.9	...	17.0	20.3	...	...
Argentina Argentine										
MF [I] [23]	216.2	177.8[1]	230.5	251.2	322.6	...	...	...	519.7	...
M [I] [23]	143.0	107.7[1]	126.8	137.2	195.2	...	...	...	267.4	...
F [I] [23]	73.3	70.1[1]	103.7	114.0	127.4	...	...	...	252.2	...
% MF [I] [23]	5.3	4.4[1]	5.3	5.9	7.3	...	...	...	10.1	...
% M [I] [23]	...	...	4.5	5.2	7.0	...	...	...	8.5	...
% F [I] [23]	...	...	6.6	7.2	7.7	...	...	...	12.7	...
Australia Australie										
MF [I] [2]	602.9[4]	# 613.1	628.9	576.2	...	584.8[5]	814.5[5]	925.1[5]	939.2[5]	855.5[5]
M [I] [2]	355.9[4]	# 351.8	361.0	321.1	# 276.5[5]	332.3[5]	489.5[5]	566.2[5]	574.0[5]	505.6[5]
F [I] [2]	246.9[4]	# 261.3	267.9	255.1	# 231.6[5]	252.5[5]	325.0[5]	358.9[5]	365.1[5]	349.9[5]
% MF [I] [2]	8.3[4]	# 8.1	8.1	7.2	# 6.2[5]	6.9[5]	9.6[5]	10.8[5]	10.9[5]	9.8[5]
% M [I] [2]	7.9[4]	# 7.7	7.8	6.8	# 5.7[5]	6.7[5]	9.9[5]	11.4[5]	11.5[5]	10.0[5]
% F [I] [2]	8.4[4]	# 8.7	8.6	7.9	# 6.8[5]	7.2[5]	9.2[5]	10.0[5]	10.1[5]	9.4[5]
Austria Autriche										
MF [I] [2]	120.7[6]	105.8[6]	# 130.2	122.0	108.6	114.8	125.4	132.4	158.8	...
M [I] [2]	73.8[6]	64.7[6]	# 74.3	66.5	58.2	63.0	70.9	74.4	88.1	...
F [I] [2]	46.9[6]	41.1[6]	# 55.9	55.5	50.4	51.8	54.5	58.0	70.7	...
MF [III] [27]	139.5[6]	152.0[6]	164.5	158.6	149.2	165.8	185.0	193.1	222.3	214.9
M [III] [27]	84.2[6]	88.9[6]	95.0	89.8	81.0	89.0	99.0	107.2	126.7	120.6
F [III] [27]	55.3[6]	63.1[6]	69.5	68.8	68.2	76.8	86.0	85.9	95.6	84.4
% MF [I] [2]	...	...	3.8	3.7	3.1	3.2	3.5	3.7	4.3	...
% M [I] [2]	...	...	3.6	3.3	2.8	3.0	3.3	3.5	4.1	...
% F [I] [2]	...	...	4.1	4.0	3.6	3.6	3.7	3.8	4.5	...
% MF [III] [27]	4.8[6]	5.2[6]	5.6	5.3	5.0	5.4	5.8	5.9	6.8	6.5
% M [III] [27]	4.9[6]	5.1[6]	5.5	5.1	4.6	4.9	5.3	5.7	6.7	6.4
% F [III] [27]	4.7[6]	5.2[6]	5.7	5.6	5.5	6.0	6.5	6.2	6.9	6.7
Azerbaijan Azerbaïdjan										
MF [III] [78]	...	...	...	...	...	...	4.0	6.4	19.5	23.6
M [III] [78]	...	...	...	...	...	...	1.5	2.8	7.7	9.2
F [III] [78]	...	...	...	...	...	...	2.5	3.6	11.8	14.4
Bahamas Bahamas										
MF [I] [12]	...	# 13.5	...	13.7	14.9	...	16.0	20.0	18.0	18.4
M [I] [12]	...	# 5.7	...	5.4	7.4	...	8.4	9.8	9.2	9.2
F [I] [12]	...	# 7.8	...	8.3	7.5	...	7.7	10.2	8.7	9.3
% MF [I] [12]	...	# 12.2	...	11.0	11.7	...	12.3	14.8	13.1	13.3
% M [I] [12]	...	# 9.7	...	8.2	11.0	...	12.2	13.8	12.8	12.6
% F [I] [12]	...	# 15.0	...	14.2	12.5	...	12.4	16.0	13.4	14.0
Bahrain Bahreïn										
MF [III] [9 10]	6.3	6.7	4.0	4.5	3.4	3.0	3.3	3.0	3.6	4.2
M [III] [9 10]	...	...	3.1	3.6	2.5	2.1	2.4	2.2	2.9	2.7
F [III] [9 10]	...	...	0.9	0.9	0.9	0.8	0.9	0.9	0.7	1.4
Barbados Barbade										
MF [I] [2]	21.2	20.7	21.4	21.2[11]	17.1[11]	18.6[11]	20.9	28.7	30.9	28.2
M [I] [2]	8.6	8.0	8.4	7.7[11]	5.9[11]	6.6[11]	8.6	13.2	14.0	12.1
F [I] [2]	12.6	12.7	13.0	13.5[11]	11.2[11]	12.0[11]	12.3	15.5	16.9	16.1
% MF [I] [2]	18.7	17.7	17.9	17.4[11]	13.7[11]	15.0[11]	17.1	23.0	24.5	21.9
% M [I] [2]	14.1	13.0	13.3	12.3[11]	9.1[11]	10.3[11]	13.3	20.4	21.5	18.3
% F [I] [2]	24.0	23.0	23.1	22.9[11]	18.7[11]	20.2[11]	21.4	25.7	27.7	25.6

30
Unemployment
Number (thousands) and percentage of unemployed [*cont.*]
Chômage
Nombre (milliers) et pourcentage des chômeurs [*suite*]

Country or area [§] Pays ou zone [§]	1985	1986	1987	1988	1989	1990	1991	1992	1993	1994
Belarus Bélarus										
MF [III] [17]	...	...	...	...	...	...	2.3	24.0	66.3	101.2
M [III] [17]	...	...	...	...	...	...	0.5	4.4	22.3	36.7
F [III] [17]	...	...	...	...	...	...	1.8	19.6	44.0	64.5
% MF [III] [17]	...	...	...	...	...	...	...	0.5	1.4	1.8
% M [III] [17]	...	...	...	...	...	...	...	0.1	0.5	...
% F [III] [17]	...	...	...	...	...	...	...	0.4	0.9	...
Belgium Belgique										
MF [I] [1 12]	455.3	450.2	444.8	396.0	326.1	285.2	282.4	315.9	335.1	405.3
M [I] [1 12]	185.8	176.3	177.8	167.2	128.0	109.2	110.8	137.1	149.1	188.5
F [I] [1 12]	269.5	273.9	267.0	228.8	198.1	176.0	171.6	178.8	186.0	216.8
MF [III] [7]	558.3	516.8	500.8	459.4	419.3	402.8	429.5	472.9	549.7	588.7
M [III] [7]	246.0	217.6	208.9	187.8	167.5	161.3	178.0	199.1	237.5	257.0
F [III] [7]	312.3	299.1	292.0	271.6	251.8	241.5	251.5	273.8	312.2	331.6
% MF [I] [1 12]	11.4	11.3	11.3	10.1	8.3	7.2	7.0	7.7	8.2	9.7
% M [I] [1 12]	7.5	7.1	7.3	7.0	5.3	· 4.5	4.5	5.6	6.1	7.7
% F [I] [1 12]	17.9	17.9	17.6	15.1	13.0	11.4	10.7	10.7	11.1	12.7
% MF [III] [7]	13.6	12.6	12.2	11.1	10.1	9.6	10.2	11.2	13.0	* 13.9
% M [III] [7]	9.9	8.9	8.6	7.7	6.9	6.6	7.3	8.1	9.7	* 10.5
% F [III] [7]	19.1	18.1	17.4	16.0	14.7	13.9	14.3	15.3	17.4	* 18.5
Belize Belize										
MF [I] [13]	...	...	...	...	...	...	...	...	6.7	7.7
M [I] [13]	...	...	...	...	...	...	...	...	3.5	4.3
F [I] [13]	...	...	...	...	...	...	...	...	3.2	3.5
% MF [I] [13]	...	...	...	...	...	...	...	...	9.8	11.1
% M [I] [13]	...	...	...	...	...	...	...	...	7.5	9.0
% F [I] [13]	...	...	...	...	...	...	...	...	14.5	15.1
Bermuda Bermudes										
MF [III] [7]	0.0	0.0	0.1	0.1	· 0.0	0.1	0.2	...	...	...
Bolivia Bolivie										
MF [I] [14]	58.2	46.2	78.0	...	96.1	67.3	33.7	42.8	...	...
M [I] [14]	...	...	...	...	51.1	37.2	20.4	27.9	...	...
F [I] [14]	...	...	...	...	45.0	30.0	13.3	14.9	...	...
MF [IV] [15]	370.9	415.4	430.7	388.4	443.2	433.4	...	...	...	...
M [IV] [15]	323.2	362.0	365.1	329.3	375.7	366.6	...	...	...	...
F [IV] [15]	47.6	53.4	65.6	59.1	67.5	66.9	...	...	...	...
% MF [I] [14]	...	...	...	...	...	7.3	5.8	5.4	...	...
% M [I] [14]	...	...	...	...	...	6.9	5.6	5.4	...	...
% F [I] [14]	...	...	...	...	...	7.8	6.0	5.5	...	...
% MF [IV] [15]	18.0	20.0	20.5	18.0	20.0	19.0	...	...	...	...
Brazil Brésil										
MF [I] [1 15 16]	1875.3	1380.2	2133.0	2319.4	1891.0	2367.5	...	...	...	...
M [I] [1 15 16]	1171.5	854.1	1315.3	1410.3	1244.0	1582.4	...	...	...	...
F [I] [1 15 16]	703.8	526.1	817.7	909.1	647.0	785.1	...	...	...	...
% MF [I] [1 15 16]	3.4	2.4	3.6	3.8	3.0	3.7	...	...	...	...
% M [I] [1 15 16]	3.2	2.3	3.4	3.6	3.1	3.8	...	...	...	...
% F [I] [1 15 16]	3.8	2.7	4.0	4.2	2.9	3.4	...	...	...	...
Bulgaria Bulgarie										
MF [III] [17 17]	...	...	...	...	...	65.1	419.1	576.9	626.1	488.4
M [III] [17 17]	...	...	...	...	...	22.7	190.7	274.5	298.4	223.0
F [III] [17 17]	...	...	...	...	...	42.4	228.4	302.4	327.7	265.4
% MF [III] [17 17]	...	...	...	...	...	1.7	11.1	15.3	16.4	12.4
Burkina Faso Burkina Faso										
MF [III] [10 18]	32.5	32.0[19]	35.3	# 34.6	38.1	42.0	34.8	29.8	29.6	26.6
M [III] [10 18]	28.8	26.8[19]	30.4	# 29.3	32.4	37.4	30.4	25.9	24.9	24.0
F [III] [10 18]	3.8	4.7[19]	4.9	# 5.3	5.7	4.6	4.4	3.9	4.6	2.7
Burundi Burundi										
MF [III] [10 20]	1.9	6.8	8.2	9.3	11.1	14.5	13.8	7.3	...	...
M [III] [10 20]	1.7	6.0	7.4	8.4	9.8	...	9.6	...	...	...
F [III] [10 20]	0.3	0.8	0.8	0.9	1.3	...	4.2	...	...	...
Canada Canada										
MF [I] [2 21]	1381.0	1283.0	1208.0	1082.0	1065.0	1164.0	1492.0	1640.0	1649.0	1541.0
M [I] [2 21]	787.0	723.0	662.0	578.0	578.0	649.0	866.0	966.0	952.0	885.0
F [I] [2 21]	594.0	560.0	546.0	503.0	487.0	515.0	626.0	674.0	697.0	656.0

30
Unemployment
Number (thousands) and percentage of unemployed [*cont.*]
Chômage
Nombre (milliers) et pourcentage des chômeurs [*suite*]

Country or area § Pays ou zone §	1985	1986	1987	1988	1989	1990	1991	1992	1993	1994
% MF [I] [2 21]	10.5	9.6	8.9	7.8	7.5	8.1	10.4	11.3	11.2	10.4
% M [I] [2 21]	10.4	9.4	8.6	7.4	7.3	8.1	10.9	12.1	11.8	10.8
% F [I] [2 21]	10.7	9.8	9.3	8.3	7.8	8.1	9.7	10.4	10.6	9.9
Central African Rep. Rép. centrafricaine										
MF [III] [10 22]	8.2	9.7	8.9[1]	9.1	7.8	7.8	7.7	5.8	5.6	...
M [III] [10 22]	7.5	7.8	8.1[1]	8.3	7.2	7.1	7.2	5.2	5.2	...
F [III] [10 22]	0.7	0.9	0.8[1]	0.8	0.6	0.7	0.5	0.5	0.4	...
Chile Chili										
MF [I] [2 11]	# 516.5	374.2	343.5	286.1	249.8	268.9	253.6	217.1	233.6	311.3
M [I] [2 11]	# 346.7	250.0	222.5	177.4	162.4	184.8	168.6	132.1	147.6	193.9
F [I] [2 11]	# 169.8	124.0	120.9	108.6	87.4	84.0	85.0	85.1	86.0	117.4
% MF [I] [2 11]	# 12.1	8.8	7.9	6.3	5.3	5.6	5.3	4.4	4.5	5.9
% M [I] [2 11]	# 11.7	8.4	7.3	5.6	5.0	5.7	5.1	4.1	4.2	5.4
% F [I] [2 11]	# 13.4	9.7	9.3	7.8	6.1	5.7	5.8	5.6	5.1	6.8
China Chine										
MF [IV] [1 14 23]	2385.0	2644.0	2766.0	2960.0	3779.0	3832.0	3522.0	3603.0	4201.0	4764.0
M [IV] [1 14 23]	783.0	805.0	953.0	1001.0	1942.0	1313.0	1207.0	1298.0	1394.0	1258.0
F [IV] [1 14 23]	1186.0	1288.0	1398.0	1452.0	1837.0	1814.0	1677.0	1700.0	1925.0	1752.0
% MF [IV] [1 14 23]	1.8	2.0	2.0	2.0	2.6	2.5	2.3	2.3	2.6	2.8
% M [IV] [1 14 23]	0.6	0.6	0.7	0.7	1.3	0.9	0.8	...	0.9	0.8
% F [IV] [1 14 23]	0.9	1.0	1.0	1.0	1.3	1.2	1.1	...	1.2	1.1
Colombia Colombie										
MF [I] [1 24 25]	499.9	482.8	429.0	403.0	356.5	491.6	501.6	486.6	407.8	418.0
M [I] [1 24 25]	228.7	221.1	190.7	175.5	159.5	232.8	216.8	196.6	158.8	156.6
F [I] [1 24 25]	271.2	261.8	238.3	227.5	197.1	258.8	254.8	290.0	249.0	261.4
Costa Rica Costa Rica										
MF [I] [1 25]	60.8	56.7	# 54.5	54.9	38.7	49.5	59.1	44.0	46.9	49.4
M [I] [1 25]	42.5	40.3	# 33.1	31.9	23.4	31.7	35.5	26.4	28.9	28.7
F [I] [1 25]	18.3	16.5	# 21.4	23.1	15.3	17.8	23.5	17.6	18.0	20.7
% MF [I] [1 25]	6.8	6.2	# 5.6	5.5	3.8	4.6	5.5	4.1	4.1	4.2
% M [I] [1 25]	6.5	6.0	# 4.7	4.4	3.2	4.2	4.8	3.5	3.6	3.5
% F [I] [1 25]	7.9	6.9	# 7.9	8.0	5.3	5.9	7.4	5.4	5.3	5.8
Côte d'Ivoire Côte d'Ivoire										
MF [III] [7 8 26]	86.4	92.0	107.8	120.6	128.5	140.3	136.9	114.9	...	...
M [III] [7 8 26]	62.5	...	73.2	81.9	89.4	99.0	...	88.2	...	...
F [III] [7 8 26]	23.9	...	34.6	38.7	39.1	41.3	...	26.7	...	...
Croatia Croatie										
MF [III] [7]	120.0	123.0	123.0	135.0	140.0	161.0	254.0	267.0	251.0	...
M [III] [7]	46.0	48.0	48.0	55.0	57.0	70.0	121.0	126.0	113.0	...
F [III] [7]	74.0	75.0	75.0	80.0	83.0	91.0	133.0	141.0	138.0	...
% MF [III] [7]	7.0	7.0	6.0	7.0	7.0	8.0	15.0	17.0	17.0	...
% M [III] [7]	4.0	4.0	4.0	5.0	5.0	6.0	13.0	15.0	14.0	...
% F [III] [7]	10.0	10.0	9.0	10.0	10.0	11.0	18.0	20.0	20.0	...
Cyprus Chypre										
MF [III] [7 12]	8.3	9.2	8.7	7.4	6.2	5.1	8.3	5.2	7.6	8.0
M [III] [7 12]	4.6	4.8	4.4	3.7	2.9	2.5	3.8	2.4	3.2	3.7
F [III] [7 12]	3.7	4.4	4.3	3.7	3.3	2.6	4.5	2.8	4.4	4.3
% MF [III] [7 12]	3.3	3.7	3.4	2.8	2.3	1.8	3.0	1.8	2.6	2.7
% M [III] [7 12]	2.9	2.9	2.7	2.2	1.7	1.4	2.2	1.3	1.8	2.0
% F [III] [7 12]	4.2	5.0	4.7	3.8	3.3	2.5	4.3	2.5	4.0	3.8
Czech Republic République tchèque										
MF [I] [2 7 27]	...	...	...	...	...	...	...	...	199.6	201.5
M [I] [2 7 27]	...	...	...	...	...	...	...	...	87.1	95.2
F [I] [2 7 27]	...	...	...	...	...	...	...	...	112.5	106.3
MF [III] [7 8]	...	...	...	...	...	39.0	222.0	135.0	185.0	166.0
M [III] [7 8]	...	...	...	...	...	19.0	95.0	57.0	81.0	70.0
F [III] [7 8]	...	...	...	...	...	20.0	127.0	78.0	104.0	96.0
% MF [I] [2 7 27]	...	...	...	...	...	...	...	...	3.8	3.8
% M [I] [2 7 27]	...	...	...	...	...	...	...	...	3.1	3.4
% F [I] [2 7 27]	...	...	...	...	...	...	...	...	4.6	4.4
% MF [III] [7 8]	...	...	...	...	...	0.7	4.1	2.6	3.5	3.2
% M [III] [7 8]	...	...	...	...	...	0.7	3.5	2.2	3.0	2.5
% F [III] [7 8]	...	...	...	...	...	0.8	4.8	3.0	4.1	4.0

30
Unemployment
Number (thousands) and percentage of unemployed [*cont.*]
       Chômage
       Nombre (milliers) et pourcentage des chômeurs [*suite*]

Country or area § Pays ou zone §	1985	1986	1987	1988	1989	1990	1991	1992	1993	1994
Denmark Danemark										
MF [I] [11][28]	199.5	153.6	200.0	207.9	253.9	242.4	264.8	261.8	308.8	221.9[29]
M [I] [11][28]	88.6	62.0	92.0	99.0	124.3	122.8	129.3	127.9	159.2	107.0[29]
F [I] [11][28]	110.9	91.6	108.0	108.9	129.6	119.7	135.5	134.0	149.6	115.0[29]
MF [III] [7][30]	251.8	220.4	221.9	243.9	264.9	271.7	296.1	318.3	348.8	343.4
M [III] [7][30]	110.9	90.8	96.1	108.8	120.0	124.0	137.2	148.8	168.6	163.9
F [III] [7][30]	140.9	129.6	125.7	135.1	145.0	147.7	158.9	169.5	180.2	179.6
% MF [III] [7][30]	9.1	7.9	7.9	8.7	9.5	9.7	10.6	11.3	12.4	12.2
% M [III] [7][30]	7.5	6.1	6.4	7.3	8.1	8.4	9.2	10.0	11.3	11.0
% F [III] [7][30]	11.0	10.0	9.6	10.3	11.1	11.3	12.1	12.9	13.7	13.6
Ecuador Equateur										
MF [I] [1][14][15]	...	...	89.5[25][31]	155.4[25]	187.0[25]	# 150.5	237.0	263.2	240.8	207.2
M [I] [1][14][15]	...	...	39.8[25][31]	73.0[25]	88.1[25]	# 67.3	91.9	105.3	108.6	101.8
F [I] [1][14][15]	...	...	49.7[25][31]	82.3[25]	98.9[25]	# 83.2	145.2	157.9	132.3	105.4
% MF [I] [1][14][15]	...	...	7.2[25][31]	7.0[25]	7.9[25]	# 6.1	8.5	8.9	8.3	7.1
% M [I] [1][14][15]	...	...	5.2[25][31]	5.1[25]	5.9[25]	# 4.3	5.4	6.0	6.2	5.8
% F [I] [1][14][15]	...	...	10.4[25][31]	10.3[25]	11.1[25]	# 9.1	13.2	13.2	11.5	9.3
Egypt Egypte										
MF [I] [1][32]	...	...	...	...	1107.9	1346.5	1463.4	1415.7[33]	...	...
M [I] [1][32]	...	...	...	...	615.9	602.3	692.2	768.1[33]	...	...
F [I] [1][32]	...	...	...	...	492.0	744.2	771.2	647.6[33]	...	...
% MF [I] [1][32]	...	...	...	...	6.9	8.6	9.6	9.0[33]	...	...
% M [I] [1][32]	...	...	...	...	5.4	5.2	5.9	6.4[33]	...	...
% F [I] [1][32]	...	...	...	...	10.7	17.9	21.3	17.0[33]	...	...
El Salvador El Salvador										
MF [I] [15]	280.2	# 28.3[34]	...	# 74.1[14]	72.0	97.9	72.5[1]	81.0	...	...
M [I] [15]	128.0	# 14.5[34]	...	# 50.9[14]	46.2	54.8	43.9[1]	47.5	...	...
F [I] [15]	152.3	# 13.8[34]	...	# 23.2[14]	25.8	43.1	28.6[1]	33.5	...	...
% MF [I] [15]	16.9	# 7.9[34]	...	# 9.4[14]	8.4	10.0	7.5[1]	7.9	...	...
% M [I] [15]	12.4	# 7.5[34]	...	# 11.0[14]	10.0	10.1	8.3[1]	8.4	...	...
% F [I] [15]	24.3	# 8.5[34]	...	# 7.1[14]	6.8	9.8	6.6[1]	7.2	...	...
Estonia Estonie										
MF [III] [7][17]	...	...	...	...	...	...	0.9	14.9	16.3	15.3
M [III] [7][17]	...	...	...	...	...	...	0.3	7.5	7.5	6.4
F [III] [7][17]	...	...	...	...	...	...	0.6	7.4	8.8	8.9
% MF [III] [7][17]	...	...	...	...	...	...	0.1	1.7	1.9	2.2
% M [III] [7][17]	...	...	...	...	...	...	0.1	1.6	1.7	...
% F [III] [7][17]	...	...	...	...	...	...	0.2	1.8	2.1	...
Ethiopia Ethiopie										
MF [III] [7][35][36]	56.4	52.6	58.2	55.3	51.3	44.2	44.3	70.9	62.9	...
M [III] [7][35][36]	33.3	30.7	37.9	34.1	28.6	25.8	24.9	52.1	40.4	...
F [III] [7][35][36]	23.1	21.9	20.3	21.2	22.7	18.4	19.4	18.8	22.6	...
Fiji Fidji										
MF [IV] [2]	18.6	18.2	23.0	23.0	15.0	16.0	15.0	14.2	15.8	16.5
% MF [IV] [2]	8.1	7.5	9.3	9.4	6.1	6.4	5.9	5.4	5.9	6.0
Finland Finlande										
MF [I] [37][38]	129.0	138.0	130.0	116.0	89.0	88.0	193.0	328.0	444.0	456.0
M [I] [37][38]	73.0	82.0	78.0	67.0	48.0	54.0	124.0	203.0	259.0	259.0
F [I] [37][38]	56.0	56.0	53.0	48.0	41.0	34.0	69.0	125.0	184.0	196.0
MF [III] [2][7][38][39]	129.0	136.0	130.0	119.0	97.0	94.0	181.0	319.0	436.0	...
M [III] [2][7][38][39]	71.0	76.0	74.0	65.0	50.0	52.0	108.0	186.0	245.0	...
F [III] [2][7][38][39]	58.0	60.0	56.0	54.0	47.0	42.0	73.0	133.0	191.0	...
% MF [I] [37][38]	5.0	5.4	5.1	4.5	3.5	3.4	7.6	13.0	17.7	18.2
% M [I] [37][38]	5.5	6.1	5.8	5.1	3.6	4.0	9.2	15.2	19.5	19.6
% F [I] [37][38]	4.6	4.6	4.3	4.0	3.3	2.8	5.7	10.5	15.7	16.7
France France										
MF [III] [7][17]	2458.4	2516.6	2621.7	2562.9	2531.9	2504.7	2709.1	2911.2	3172.0	3329.2
M [III] [7][17]	1272.5	1275.1	1297.7	1224.8	1177.4	1148.7	1266.4	1404.6	1603.9	1664.5
F [III] [7][17]	1185.9	1241.5	1324.0	1338.1	1354.5	1355.9	1442.7	1506.6	1568.1	1664.7
MF [IV]	2473.6	2520.3	2567.2	2456.0	2323.0	2204.9	2348.9	2590.7	2929.0	3164.0
M [IV]	1179.1	1190.5	1169.3	1092.5	998.9	947.8	1031.8	1168.3	1401.0	1522.0
F [IV]	1294.5	1329.9	1398.0	1363.5	1324.1	1257.0	1317.1	1422.5	1528.0	1642.0
% MF [IV]	10.2	10.4	10.5	10.0	9.4	8.9	9.4	10.3	11.6	12.5
% M [IV]	8.4	8.5	8.4	7.8	7.1	6.7	7.3	8.3	10.0	10.8
% F [IV]	12.7	12.9	13.3	12.9	12.4	11.7	12.0	12.9	13.7	14.5

30
Unemployment
Number (thousands) and percentage of unemployed [cont.]
Chômage
Nombre (milliers) et pourcentage des chômeurs [suite]

Country or area [§] Pays ou zone [§]	1985	1986	1987	1988	1989	1990	1991	1992	1993	1994
French Guiana Guyane française										
MF [III] [10 17 40]	4.2[1]	3.7	3.4	3.3	3.8	4.4	4.7	6.9	8.1	...
M [III] [10 17 40]	2.1[1]	1.8	1.6	1.6	1.9	2.3	2.5	4.0	4.7	...
F [III] [10 17 40]	2.1[1]	1.8	1.9	1.7	2.0	2.1	2.2	3.0	3.4	...
% MF [III] [10 17 40]	13.5[1]	12.0	11.0	10.6	12.2	13.9	9.7	...	...	...
% M [III] [10 17 40]	10.5[1]	9.2	8.4	...	9.4	11.7	8.2	...	...	...
% F [III] [10 17 40]	18.5[1]	16.7	15.4	...	16.8	17.6	11.6	...	...	...
French Polynesia Polynésie française										
MF [III] [10 12]	0.9	1.0	0.5	0.7	0.6	0.6	...	...	...	...
Germany † Allemagne †										
F. R. Germany R. f. Allemagne										
MF [I] [12]	2385.0	2290.0	2359.0	2314.0	2147.0	1971.0	1676.0	1788.0	2322.0	2691.0
M [I] [12]	1177.0	1127.0	1236.0	1145.0	1046.0	943.0	852.0	930.0	1267.0	1511.0
F [I] [12]	1209.0	1163.0	1123.0	1169.0	1101.0	1028.0	824.0	858.0	1055.0	1181.0
MF [III] [7 37]	2304.0	2288.0	2228.8	2241.6	2037.8	1883.1	1689.4	1808.3	2270.3	2556.0
M [III] [7 37]	1289.1	1200.0	1207.4	1198.8	1069.8	967.7	897.7	982.8	1277.1	1461.6
F [III] [7 37]	1015.0	1028.0	1021.4	1042.8	968.0	915.4	791.7	825.5	993.3	1094.3
% MF [I] [12]	9.2	8.8	9.0	8.7	8.0	7.0	6.0	6.2	7.2	8.4
% M [I] [12]	7.5	7.2	7.8	7.2	6.5	5.7	5.2	5.6	6.7	8.0
% F [I] [12]	11.8	11.2	10.7	11.0	10.2	8.8	7.1	7.2	8.0	8.9
% MF [III] [7 37]	9.3	9.0	8.9	8.7	7.9	7.2	6.3	6.6	8.2	9.2
% M [III] [7 37]	8.6	8.0	8.0	7.8	6.9	6.3	5.8	6.2	8.0	9.2
% F [III] [7 37]	10.4	10.5	10.2	10.0	9.4	8.4	7.0	7.2	8.4	9.2
former German D. R. anc. R. d. allemande										
MF [I] [12]	...	...	...	...	...	...	966.0	1397.0	1477.0	1469.0
M [I] [12]	...	...	...	...	...	...	399.0	492.0	525.0	540.0
F [I] [12]	...	...	...	...	...	...	568.0	905.0	952.0	929.0
MF [III] [7 37]	...	...	...	...	...	...	912.8	1170.3	1148.8	1142.1
M [III] [7 37]	...	...	...	...	...	...	382.9	429.1	414.5	401.5
F [III] [7 37]	...	...	...	...	...	...	530.0	741.2	734.3	740.6
% MF [I] [12]	...	...	...	...	...	...	11.5	17.8	19.4	19.2
% M [I] [12]	...	...	...	...	...	...	9.3	12.3	13.5	13.8
% F [I] [12]	...	...	...	...	...	...	13.9	23.5	25.5	24.9
% MF [III] [7 37]	...	...	...	...	...	...	10.3	14.8	15.8	16.0
% M [III] [7 37]	...	...	...	...	...	...	8.5	10.5	11.0	10.9
% F [III] [7 37]	...	...	...	...	...	...	12.3	19.6	21.0	21.5
Ghana Ghana										
MF [III] [7 41]	24.2	25.8	...	28.7	27.4	30.2	30.7	30.6	...	...
M [III] [7 41]	19.2	22.5	...	26.1	24.7	26.6	27.5	27.5	...	...
F [III] [7 41]	5.1	3.3	...	2.6	2.7	3.2	3.3	3.1	...	...
Gibraltar Gibraltar										
MF [III] [7 42]	0.5	0.5	0.3	0.5	0.6	...	...	...	...	...
M [III] [7 42]	0.3	0.4	0.2	0.5	0.5	...	...	...	...	...
F [III] [7 42]	0.1	0.1	0.1	0.1	0.1	...	...	...	...	...
Greece Grèce										
MF [I] [11 12]	303.9	286.9	286.2	303.4	296.0	280.8	301.1	349.8	398.2	...
M [I] [11 12]	141.9	127.1	127.9	121.5	114.6	107.1	120.8	137.9	164.5	...
F [I] [11 12]	162.0	159.9	158.3	181.9	181.4	173.7	180.3	211.9	233.7	...
MF [III] [27]	89.0	110.5	117.9	115.3	133.9	140.2	173.2	184.7	175.9	179.8
M [III] [27]	51.2	61.0	64.1	58.7	64.6	68.1	83.9	89.7	87.9	87.3
F [III] [27]	37.8	49.4	53.9	56.6	69.3	72.1	89.3	95.0	87.9	92.4
% MF [I] [11 12]	7.8	7.4	7.4	7.7	7.5	7.0	7.7	8.7	9.7	...
% M [I] [11 12]	5.7	5.1	5.1	4.9	4.6	4.3	4.8	5.4	6.4	...
% F [I] [11 12]	11.7	11.6	11.4	12.5	12.4	11.7	12.9	14.2	15.2	...
% MF [III] [27]	5.1	6.1	6.4	6.0	6.5	6.4	7.3	7.6	7.1	7.2
Greenland Groënland										
MF [III] [7]	2.4	...	...	...	...	...	...	1.9	1.8	2.6
Guadeloupe Guadeloupe										
MF [III] [7 17]	24.2	27.2	27.8	29.5	30.8	29.4[1]	34.3[1]	...	...	...
M [III] [7 17]	11.4	12.2	11.7	11.5	13.5	11.7[1]	13.9[1]	...	...	...
F [III] [7 17]	12.8	15.0	16.1	18.0	21.3	17.6[1]	20.4[1]	...	...	...
% MF [III] [7 17]	22.0	27.0	23.0	24.0	24.0	17.0	19.9	...	...	...
% M [III] [7 17]	19.0	22.0	16.0	16.0	16.0	...	...	...	...	...
% F [III] [7 17]	27.0	33.0	31.0	33.0	34.0	...	...	...	...	...

30
Unemployment
Number (thousands) and percentage of unemployed [*cont.*]
Chômage
Nombre (milliers) et pourcentage des chômeurs [*suite*]

Country or area [§] Pays ou zone [§]	1985	1986	1987	1988	1989	1990	1991	1992	1993	1994
Guam Guam										
MF [I] [17]	2.7	2.2	1.6	1.6	1.1	1.3	1.7	1.8	2.6	...
% MF [I] [17]	7.8	6.1	4.4	4.2	2.8	2.8	3.5	3.9	5.5	...
Guatemala Guatemala										
MF [III] [7 15 43]	2.7	2.7	2.2	1.9	1.7	1.8	1.7	1.6	1.0	...
M [III] [7 15 43]	1.7	1.8	1.4	1.3	1.2	1.3	1.0	1.1	0.7	...
F [III] [7 15 43]	1.0	0.9	0.8	0.6	0.5	0.5	0.7	0.5	0.3	...
Haiti Haïti										
MF [IV] [15]	...	...	...	561.8	...	339.7	...	...	...	...
M [IV] [15]	...	...	...	265.0	...	191.3	...	...	...	...
F [IV] [15]	...	...	...	296.7	...	148.3	...	...	...	...
Hong Kong Hong-kong										
MF [I] [2 44]	83.6	76.1	47.5	38.0	30.0	37.0	50.3	54.7	56.9	57.2
M [I] [2 44]	58.6	51.1	29.8	24.1	19.3	23.5	33.7	35.3	36.2	38.5
F [I] [2 44]	25.1	24.9	17.7	13.8	10.7	13.5	16.6	19.4	20.7	18.7
% MF [I] [2 44]	3.2	2.8	1.7	1.4	1.1	1.3	1.8	2.0	2.0	1.9
% M [I] [2 44]	3.5	3.0	1.7	1.4	1.1	1.3	1.9	2.0	2.0	2.1
% F [I] [2 44]	2.6	2.5	1.8	1.4	1.1	1.3	1.6	1.9	2.0	1.7
Hungary Hongrie										
MF [I] [28]	...	...	...	...	...	...	...	444.2	518.9	451.2
M [I] [28]	...	...	...	...	...	...	...	265.9	316.0	274.8
F [I] [28]	...	...	...	...	...	...	...	178.3	202.9	176.4
MF [III] [17]	...	...	...	...	...	79.5	406.1	663.0	632.1	519.6
M [III] [17]	...	...	...	...	...	49.1	239.0	390.0	376.1	302.6
F [III] [17]	...	...	...	...	...	30.4	167.1	273.0	256.0	217.0
% MF [I] [28]	...	...	...	...	...	...	...	9.9	12.1	10.9
% M [I] [28]	...	...	...	...	...	...	...	11.0	13.5	12.1
% F [I] [28]	...	...	...	...	...	...	...	8.7	10.4	9.4
% MF [III] [17]	...	...	...	...	...	1.7	8.5	12.3	12.1	10.4
% M [III] [17]	...	...	...	...	...	1.8	9.2	14.0	14.2	11.7
% F [III] [17]	...	...	...	...	...	1.4	7.6	10.5	10.1	8.9
Iceland Islande										
MF [I] [11 45]	...	...	...	...	...	...	3.6	6.2	7.6	7.7
M [I] [11 45]	...	...	...	...	...	...	1.7	2.9	3.8	4.0
F [I] [11 45]	...	...	...	...	...	...	1.9	3.2	3.8	3.8
MF [III] [7 17]	1.1	0.8	0.6	0.8	2.1	2.3	1.9	3.9	5.6	...
M [III] [7 17]	0.5	0.4	0.3	0.3	0.9	1.1	1.0	1.9	2.7	...
F [III] [7 17]	0.7	0.4	0.3	0.5	1.2	1.2	0.9	1.9	2.9	...
% MF [I] [11 45]	...	...	...	...	...	...	2.5	4.3	5.3	5.3
% M [I] [11 45]	...	...	...	...	...	...	2.3	3.8	5.0	5.1
% F [I] [11 45]	...	...	...	...	...	...	2.9	4.9	5.6	5.5
% MF [III] [7 17]	0.9	0.7	0.4	0.6	1.7	1.8	1.5	3.0	4.3	...
% M [III] [7 17]	0.6	0.5	0.3	0.4	1.2	1.4	1.3	2.6	3.6	...
% F [III] [7 17]	1.3	0.8	0.6	0.9	2.2	2.2	1.7	3.6	5.4	...
India Inde										
MF [III] [10 12]	24861.0[46]	28261.0[46]	30542.0[46]	# 30050.0[1]	32776.0[1]	34632.0[1]	36300.0[1]	36758.0[1]	...	...
M [III] [10 12]	20628.0[46]	23476.0[46]	25251.0[46]	# 24590.0[1]	26668.0[1]	27932.0[1]	28992.0[1]	29105.0[1]	...	...
F [III] [10 12]	4233.0[46]	4785.0[46]	5291.0[46]	# 5461.0[1]	6109.0[1]	6700.0[1]	7308.0[1]	7653.0[1]	...	...
Indonesia Indonésie										
MF [I] [15]	1368.0[47]	1855.0	1843.0	2106.0	2083.0	1952.0	2032.0	2199.0	...	...
M [I] [15]	898.0[47]	1127.0	1148.0	1269.0	1251.0	1155.0	1147.0	1292.0	...	...
F [I] [15]	470.0[47]	728.0	695.0	837.0	832.0	796.0	885.0	907.0	...	...
MF [III] [10 48]	785.2	855.0	1017.2	1352.4	1518.5	1238.7	1042.3	...	...	...
M [III] [10 48]	552.3	586.3	672.8	900.8	991.7	735.9	...	...	...	...
F [III] [10 48]	233.0	268.7	344.4	451.6	526.8	502.9	...	...	...	...
Ireland Irlande										
MF [I] [12]	226.0	227.4	231.6	218.5	202.2	178.9	208.4	221.0	* 230.0	* 221.0
M [I] [12]	172.8	173.7	176.3	169.6	157.3	138.1	156.3	...	...	...
F [I] [12]	53.2	53.8	55.2	49.0	44.9	40.8	52.1	...	...	...
MF [III] [7 17]	230.6	236.4	247.3	241.4	231.6	224.7	254.0	283.1	294.0	...
M [III] [7 17]	170.2	172.0	176.2	169.7	160.0	152.1	170.5	187.2	194.0	...
F [III] [7 17]	60.4	64.4	71.1	71.7	71.6	72.6	83.5	96.0	101.0	...
% MF [I] [12]	17.4	17.4	17.6	16.7	15.6	13.7	15.6	16.3	* 16.7	* 15.8
% M [I] [12]	18.8	19.0	19.4	18.6	17.6	15.5	17.3	...	...	...
% F [I] [12]	13.8	13.7	13.6	12.3	11.3	9.9	12.1	...	...	...

30
Unemployment
Number (thousands) and percentage of unemployed [*cont.*]
Chômage
Nombre (milliers) et pourcentage des chômeurs [*suite*]

Country or area [§] Pays ou zone [§]	1985	1986	1987	1988	1989	1990	1991	1992	1993	1994
% MF [III] [7 17]	17.7	18.1	18.8	18.4	17.9	17.2	19.0	...	...	...
% M [III] [7 17]	18.5	18.8	19.3	18.4	17.9	17.0	18.8	...	...	...
% F [III] [7 17]	15.7	16.4	17.7	17.9	17.9	17.6	19.5	...	...	...
Isle of Man Ile de Man										
MF [III] [7]	2.2	2.1	1.6	0.9	0.6	0.6	1.0	1.4	1.7	...
M [III] [7]	1.5	1.4	1.1	0.6	0.4	0.4	0.7	1.0	1.2	...
F [III] [7]	0.7	0.7	0.6	0.3	0.2	0.1	0.3	0.4	0.4	...
% MF [III] [7]	8.0	7.7	5.9	3.4	2.0	2.1	# 3.0[49]	4.3[49]	5.0[49]	...
% M [III] [7]	8.8	8.4	6.3	3.7	2.3	2.6	# 3.9[49]	5.4[49]	6.3[49]	...
% F [III] [7]	6.7	6.6	5.3	2.9	1.6	1.3	# 1.9[49]	2.7[49]	3.1[49]	...
Israel Israël										
MF [I] [2 50 51]	97.0	104.2	90.1	100.0	142.5	158.0	187.4	207.5	194.9	158.3
M [I] [2 50 51]	56.5	59.1	47.6	53.0	75.7	82.2	89.9	99.7	96.2	71.7
F [I] [2 50 51]	40.1	45.2	42.5	47.0	66.8	75.8	97.5	107.8	98.7	86.6
% MF [I] [2 50 51]	6.7	7.1	6.1	6.4	8.9	9.6	10.6	11.2	10.0	7.8
% M [I] [2 50 51]	6.3	6.5	5.2	5.7	7.9	8.4	8.6	9.2	8.5	6.2
% F [I] [2 50 51]	7.2	7.9	7.3	7.6	10.3	11.3	13.4	13.9	12.1	10.0
Italy Italie										
MF [I] [12]	2382.0	2611.0	2832.0	2885.0	2865.0	2621.0	2653.0	2799.0	...	2678.0
M [I] [12]	1024.0	1115.0	1228.0	1240.0	1220.0	1102.0	1142.0	1226.0	...	1335.0
F [I] [12]	1358.0	1496.0	1604.0	1645.0	1646.0	1519.0	1511.0	1573.0	...	1343.0
% MF [I] [12]	10.3	11.1	11.9	12.0	12.0	11.0	10.9	11.5	...	11.3
% M [I] [12]	6.8	7.4	8.1	8.1	8.1	7.3	7.5	8.1	...	8.7
% F [I] [12]	16.7	17.8	18.5	15.4	18.7	17.1	16.8	17.3	...	15.7
Jamaica Jamaïque										
MF [I] [12]	260.8	250.5	224.3	203.3	177.4	166.6	168.7	171.5	...	...
M [I] [12]	88.4	85.3	77.0	68.0	54.1	52.8	54.2	55.7	...	...
F [I] [12]	172.4	165.2	147.3	135.3	123.3	113.8	114.5	115.8	...	...
% MF [I] [12]	25.0	23.6	21.0	18.9	16.8	15.7	15.7	15.9	...	...
% M [I] [12]	15.7	15.0	13.2	11.9	9.5	9.3	9.4	9.7	...	...
% F [I] [12]	36.0	33.8	30.4	27.0	25.2	23.1	22.8	22.9	...	...
Japan Japon										
MF [I] [2]	1560.0	1670.0	1730.0	1550.0	1420.0	1340.0	1360.0	1420.0	1660.0	...
M [I] [2]	930.0	990.0	1040.0	910.0	830.0	770.0	780.0	820.0	950.0	...
F [I] [2]	630.0	670.0	690.0	640.0	590.0	570.0	590.0	600.0	710.0	...
% MF [I] [2]	2.6	2.8	2.8	2.5	2.3	2.1	2.1	2.2	2.5	...
% M [I] [2]	2.6	2.7	2.8	2.5	2.2	2.0	2.0	2.1	2.4	...
% F [I] [2]	2.7	2.8	2.8	2.6	2.3	2.2	2.2	2.2	2.6	...
Kazakstan Kazakstan										
MF [III] [7]	...	...	...	...	...	...	6.0	70.0	78.1	...
M [III] [7]	...	...	...	...	...	...	2.0	21.0	27.7	...
F [III] [7]	...	...	...	...	...	...	4.0	49.0	50.4	...
% MF [III] [7]	...	...	...	...	...	...	0.1	0.9	1.0	...
Korea, Republic of Corée, République de										
MF [I] [2]	622.0	611.0	519.0	435.0	463.0	454.0	436.0	465.0	550.0	489.0
M [I] [2]	480.0	480.0	397.0	315.0	329.0	321.0	288.0	305.0	375.0	334.0
F [I] [2]	141.0	131.0	122.0	120.0	134.0	133.0	149.0	160.0	175.0	155.0
% MF [I] [2]	4.0	3.8	3.1	2.5	2.6	2.4	2.3	2.4	2.8	2.4
% M [I] [2]	5.0	4.9	3.9	3.0	3.1	2.9	2.5	2.6	3.2	2.7
% F [I] [2]	2.4	2.1	1.8	1.7	1.8	1.8	1.9	2.1	2.2	1.9
Kyrgyzstan Kirghizistan										
MF [III] [7]	...	...	...	...	...	...	...	1.8	2.9	12.6
M [III] [7]	...	...	...	...	...	...	...	0.5	0.9	4.9
F [III] [7]	...	...	...	...	...	...	...	1.3	2.0	7.7
Latvia Lettonie										
MF [III] [17]	...	...	...	...	...	...	...	31.3	76.7	84.0
M [III] [17]	...	...	...	...	...	...	...	12.9	35.9	40.4
F [III] [17]	...	...	...	...	...	...	...	18.4	40.8	43.6
% MF [III] [17]	...	...	...	...	...	...	...	2.3	5.8	6.5
% M [III] [17]	...	...	...	...	...	...	...	1.8	5.2	6.2
% F [III] [17]	...	...	...	...	...	...	...	2.8	6.4	6.9

30
Unemployment
Number (thousands) and percentage of unemployed [*cont.*]
Chômage
Nombre (milliers) et pourcentage des chômeurs [*suite*]

Country or area [§] Pays ou zone [§]	1985	1986	1987	1988	1989	1990	1991	1992	1993	1994
Lithuania Lituanie										
MF [III] [78]	...	...	...	...	...	...	4.8	66.5	65.5	78.0
M [III] [78]	...	...	...	...	...	...	...	...	33.5	36.7
F [III] [78]	...	...	...	...	...	...	...	...	32.0	41.3
% MF [III] [78]	...	...	...	...	...	...	0.3	3.5	3.5	4.4
% M [III] [78]	...	...	...	...	...	...	...	...	3.8	3.8
% F [III] [78]	...	...	...	...	...	...	...	...	3.3	3.8
Luxembourg Luxembourg										
MF [III] [752]	2.6	2.3	2.7	2.5	2.3	2.1	2.3	2.7	3.5	...
M [III] [752]	1.3	1.2	1.5	1.5	1.4	1.2	1.4	1.5	2.0	...
F [III] [752]	1.3	1.1	1.2	1.0	0.9	0.9	0.9	1.2	1.5	...
% MF [III] [752]	1.7	1.5	1.7	1.6	1.4	1.3	1.4	1.6	...	...
% M [III] [752]	1.3	1.2	1.5	1.5	1.4	1.1	1.3	1.5	...	...
% F [III] [752]	2.3	1.8	2.0	1.7	1.5	1.5	1.5	1.9	...	...
Macau Macao										
MF [I] [12]	...	...	...	...	6.2[1]	5.3[1]	5.3[1]	3.8	3.7	...
M [I] [12]	...	...	...	...	2.6[1]	2.5[1]	2.6[1]	2.1	2.2	...
F [I] [12]	...	...	...	...	3.6[1]	2.8[1]	2.7[1]	1.8	1.5	...
% MF [I] [12]	...	...	...	...	3.7[1]	3.2[1]	3.0[1]	2.2	2.1	...
% M [I] [12]	...	...	...	...	2.7[1]	2.5[1]	2.5[1]	2.1	2.2	...
% F [I] [12]	...	...	...	...	5.1[1]	4.1[1]	3.7[1]	2.4	2.0	...
Madagascar Madagascar										
MF [III] [1 10 53]	28.8	24.2	18.4	16.1	15.7	...	...	...	...	...
Malaysia Malaisie										
MF [III] [2 10]	80.7[1]	86.9[1]	# 82.5	82.8	75.6	61.2	48.6	45.2	35.6	...
Malta Malte										
MF [III] [1 754]	9.9	8.5	5.6	5.2	4.8	5.1	4.9	5.6	6.1	...
M [III] [1 754]	7.8	6.6	4.6	4.2	4.1	4.3	4.0	4.5	5.3	...
F [III] [1 754]	2.2	1.9	1.0	1.0	0.8	0.8	0.9	1.1	0.9	...
% MF [III] [1 754]	8.1	6.8	4.4	4.0	3.7	3.8	3.6	4.0	4.5	...
% M [III] [1 754]	8.4	6.9	4.8	4.3	4.1	4.4	4.0	4.4	5.2	...
% F [III] [1 754]	7.2	6.2	3.1	3.1	2.3	2.3	2.6	3.0	2.5	...
Mauritius Maurice										
MF [III] [2 755]	64.8	54.6	46.8	27.7	18.1	12.8	10.6	7.9	6.7	7.1
M [III] [2 755]	48.8	42.2	36.3	19.9	11.8	7.3	5.2	3.4	2.6	2.7
F [III] [2 755]	16.0	12.4	10.5	7.8	6.3	5.5	5.4	4.6	4.1	4.4
Mexico Mexique										
MF [I] [25]	...	...	...	723.9	...	...	694.9	...	819.1	...
M [I] [25]	...	...	...	393.6	...	...	373.1	...	495.4	...
F [I] [25]	...	...	...	330.3	...	...	321.8	...	323.7	...
% MF [I] [25 34]	4.4[14]	4.3	3.9	2.5	3.0	2.8	2.2	2.8[14]	2.4[14]	3.8[14]
% M [I] [25 34]	3.5[14]	3.7	3.4	2.0	2.6	2.6	1.7	2.7[14]	2.1[14]	3.7[14]
% F [I] [25 34]	5.7[14]	5.3	4.8	3.6	3.8	3.1	3.4	3.2[14]	3.1[14]	4.0[14]
Morocco Maroc										
MF [I] [2 14]	...	...	...	...	...	601.2	695.5	649.9	...	...
M [I] [2 14]	...	...	...	...	...	401.4	459.3	400.7	...	...
F [I] [2 14]	...	...	...	...	...	199.8	236.2	249.2	...	...
% MF [I] [2 14]	...	...	14.7	13.9	16.3	15.4	17.0	16.0	...	...
% M [I] [2 14]	...	...	13.4	12.8	15.0	13.9	15.1	13.0	...	...
% F [I] [2 14]	...	...	18.5	17.3	19.8	19.6	22.6	25.3	...	...
Myanmar Myanmar										
MF [III] [756]	338.0[1]	354.4[1]	331.4	312.7	485.8	555.3	559.0	502.6	518.2	541.5
Netherlands Pays–Bas										
MF [I] [37]	620.5[2]	...	# 622.0	609.0	558.0	516.0	490.0	386.0	# 437.0[57]	492.0
M [I] [37]	362.9[2]	...	# 290.0	291.0	261.0	227.0	226.0	181.0	# 217.0[57]	254.0
F [I] [37]	257.6[2]	...	# 332.0	318.0	297.0	288.0	264.0	205.0	# 220.0[57]	239.0
MF [III] [737]	761.0	710.7	685.5	# 433.0	390.0	346.0	319.0	336.0	415.0	486.0
M [III] [737]	498.0	453.5	428.7	# 278.0	241.0	209.0	187.0	195.0	240.0	283.0
F [III] [737]	263.0	257.2	256.8	# 155.0	149.0	137.0	132.0	141.0	175.0	203.0
% MF [I] [37]	10.8[2]	...	# 10.0	9.0	8.0	7.5	7.0	5.5	# 6.2[57]	6.8
% M [I] [37]	9.6[2]	...	# 7.0	7.0	6.0	5.4	5.3	4.3	# 5.2[57]	6.0
% F [I] [37]	13.0[2]	...	# 14.0	13.0	12.0	10.7	9.5	7.3	# 7.6[57]	8.1

30
Unemployment
Number (thousands) and percentage of unemployed [*cont.*]
Chômage
Nombre (milliers) et pourcentage des chômeurs [*suite*]

Country or area [§] Pays ou zone [§]	1985	1986	1987	1988	1989	1990	1991	1992	1993	1994
% MF [III] [7 37]	12.9	12.0	11.5	# 6.5	5.8	5.0	4.5	5.3	6.5	7.6
% M [III] [7 37]	13.0	11.8	11.1	# 6.8	5.8	5.0	4.4	4.9	6.0	7.0
% F [III] [7 37]	12.8	12.3	12.1	# 6.1	5.8	5.1	4.7	6.1	7.3	8.3
Netherlands Antilles Antilles néerlandaises										
MF [IV] [59]	17.2[58]	17.9[58]	17.6[58]	13.3	11.7	11.2	9.4	...	...	...
M [IV] [59]	7.3[58]	7.8[58]	...	...	...	5.7	4.3	...	...	...
F [IV] [59]	9.9[58]	10.1[58]	...	...	...	5.5	5.1	...	...	...
% MF [IV] [59]	22.2[58]	...	24.6[58]	24.4	21.0	19.8	16.4	...	...	...
% M [IV] [59]	15.9[58]	...	...	...	...	17.2	13.1	...	...	...
% F [IV] [59]	31.3[58]	...	...	...	...	23.6	20.9	...	...	...
New Caledonia Nouvelle–Calédonie										
MF [III] [7 17]	1.5[60]	1.6[60]	# 4.5	5.0	5.2	5.7	6.3	6.6	6.8	...
New Zealand Nouvelle–Zélande										
MF [I] [2]	...	64.2	66.0	89.0	112.6	124.6	167.4	168.9	157.2	138.4
M [I] [2]	...	33.0	36.6	51.3	66.0	74.0	99.8	100.7	93.3	80.9
F [I] [2]	...	31.1	29.4	37.7	46.5	50.5	67.6	68.2	63.9	57.5
MF [III] [7 41 61]	53.2	67.2	88.1	120.9	153.6	163.8	196.0	216.9	212.7	...
M [III] [7 41 61]	33.5	45.0	60.8	84.6	106.6	112.1	135.9	149.8	143.2	...
F [III] [7 41 61]	19.7	22.2	27.3	36.4	47.0	51.7	60.1	67.1	69.4	...
% MF [I] [2]	...	4.0	4.0	5.6	7.1	7.8	10.3	10.3	9.5	8.2
% M [I] [2]	...	3.6	3.9	5.6	7.3	8.2	10.9	10.9	10.0	8.5
% F [I] [2]	...	4.6	4.3	5.6	6.9	7.2	9.6	9.5	8.9	7.7
Nicaragua Nicaragua										
MF [IV] [15]	34.6	51.8	66.6	71.8	107.2	145.6	194.2	...	...	...
M [IV] [15]	18.6	27.9	35.9	38.9	57.8	78.5	104.8	...	...	...
F [IV] [15]	16.0	23.9	30.7	32.9	49.4	67.1	89.4	...	...	...
% MF [IV] [15]	3.2	4.7	5.8	6.0	8.4	11.1	14.0	...	...	...
% M [IV] [15]	2.6	3.8	4.7	4.9	6.9	9.0	11.3	...	...	...
% F [IV] [15]	4.6	6.5	8.0	8.3	12.0	15.4	19.4	...	...	...
Niger Niger										
MF [III] [7]	29.0	27.7	27.2	26.1	24.6	20.9	20.9	...	...	...
M [III] [7]	28.2	26.7	25.7	24.8	23.4	19.9	19.9	...	...	...
F [III] [7]	0.8	1.0	1.5	1.3	1.3	1.1	1.0	...	...	...
Nigeria Nigéria										
MF [III] [2 7]	28.3	32.5	57.3	60.5	57.6	57.1	60.2	64.0	68.6	...
Norway Norvège										
MF [I] [45]	53.0	42.0	45.0	69.0	106.0	112.0	116.0	126.0	127.0	116.0
M [I] [45]	25.0	18.0	21.0	36.0	61.0	66.0	68.0	76.0	77.0	70.0
F [I] [45]	28.0	24.0	25.0	33.0	45.0	46.0	48.0	50.0	50.0	46.0
MF [III] [7 17]	51.4	36.2	32.4	49.3	82.9	92.7[62]	100.7	114.4	118.2	110.3
M [III] [7 17]	29.8	20.2	18.4	30.0	51.6	57.1[62]	62.8	71.0	73.3	65.7
F [III] [7 17]	21.7	16.0	14.0	19.3	31.4	35.6[62]	37.9	43.3	44.8	44.5
% MF [I] [45]	2.6	2.0	2.1	3.2	4.9	5.2	5.5	5.9	6.0	5.4
% M [I] [45]	2.2	1.5	1.7	3.0	5.1	5.6	5.9	6.5	6.6	6.0
% F [I] [45]	3.1	2.5	2.6	3.4	4.7	4.8	5.0	5.1	5.2	4.7
% MF [III] [7 17]	2.5	1.8	1.5	2.3	3.8	4.3[62]	4.7	5.4	5.5	5.2
Pakistan Pakistan										
MF [I] [15 35]	1042.0	1018.0	903.0	937.0	966.0	996.0[63]	1999.0	1928.0	1595.0	* 1645.0
M [I] [15 35]	1005.0	970.0	862.0	907.0	935.0	964.0[63]	1238.0	1185.0	1077.0	* 1111.0
F [I] [15 35]	37.0	48.0	41.0	30.0	31.0	32.0[63]	761.0	743.0	518.0	* 534.0
MF [III] [10 64]	212.3	224.6	247.6	265.5	251.8	238.8	221.7	204.3	...	...
% MF [I] [15 35]	3.7	3.6	3.1	3.1	3.1	3.1[63]	6.3	5.9	4.7	* 4.7
% M [I] [15 35]	4.0	3.9	3.3	3.4	3.4	3.4[63]	4.5	4.3	3.8	* 3.8
% F [I] [15 35]	1.5	1.7	1.1	0.9	0.9	0.9[63]	16.8	14.2	10.3	* 10.3
Panama Panama										
MF [I] [12]	88.3	75.7	91.1	127.8	133.7	...	136.0	134.4	124.7	133.3
M [I] [12]	46.3	42.9	48.5	74.9	75.0	...	71.4	65.6	60.2	66.7
F [I] [12]	41.9	32.9	42.7	52.9	58.7	...	64.6	68.7	64.5	66.6
% MF [I] [12]	12.3	10.5	11.8	16.3	16.3	...	16.0	14.7	13.3	13.8
% M [I] [12]	9.5	8.7	9.4	14.0	13.7	...	12.6	10.8	9.7	10.5
% F [I] [12]	18.5	14.5	16.7	21.4	21.6	...	22.6	22.3	20.2	20.1

30

Unemployment
Number (thousands) and percentage of unemployed [*cont.*]
Chômage
Nombre (milliers) et pourcentage des chômeurs [*suite*]

Country or area [§] Pays ou zone [§]	1985	1986	1987	1988	1989	1990	1991	1992	1993	1994
Paraguay Paraguay										
MF [I] [14 25 34]	22.0	26.7	24.8	22.2	32.0	34.1	26.6	29.1	30.5[15]	# 48.1
M [I] [14 25 34]	12.4	15.1	16.1	12.8	19.3	20.3	16.6	20.2	19.1[15]	# 31.7
F [I] [14 25 34]	9.6	11.6	8.7	9.4	12.7	13.8	10.0	8.9	11.4[15]	# 16.5
% MF [I] [14 25 34]	5.1	6.1	5.5	4.7	6.1	6.6	5.1	5.3	5.1[15]	# 4.4
% M [I] [14 25 34]	5.1	6.3	6.5	4.8	6.6	6.6	5.4	6.4	5.5[15]	# 4.9
% F [I] [14 25 34]	5.1	5.8	4.3	4.6	5.6	6.5	4.7	3.8	4.5[15]	# 3.7
Peru Pérou										
MF [I] [12 65]	...	111.7	103.5	...	186.7	...	146.3	251.0	285.9	263.0[11]
M [I] [12 65]	...	40.9	48.6	...	84.8	...	73.7	120.9	147.6	124.3[11]
F [I] [12 65]	...	70.8	54.9	...	101.9	...	72.6	130.2	138.3	138.6[11]
% MF [I] [12 65]	...	5.3	4.8	...	7.9	...	5.8	9.4	9.9	8.9[11]
% M [I] [12 65]	...	3.4	3.8	...	6.0	...	4.8	7.5	8.3	7.0[11]
% F [I] [12 65]	...	8.0	6.2	...	10.7	...	7.3	12.5	12.2	11.8[11]
Philippines Philippines										
MF [I] [12]	1316.0[11]	1438.0[11]	# 2085.0	1954.0	2009.0	1993.0	2267.0	2263.0	2379.0	2317.0
M [I] [12]	644.0[11]	686.0[11]	# 1163.0	1131.0	1101.0	1099.0	1290.0	1303.0	1384.0	1362.0
F [I] [12]	672.0[11]	752.0[11]	# 922.0	823.0	908.0	893.0	977.0	959.0	995.0	955.0
% MF [I] [12]	6.1[11]	6.4[11]	# 9.1	8.3	8.4	8.1	9.0	8.6	8.9	8.4
% M [I] [12]	4.8[11]	4.9[11]	# 8.1	7.6	7.3	7.1	8.1	7.9	8.2	7.9
% F [I] [12]	8.2[11]	8.9[11]	# 10.9	9.5	10.3	9.8	10.5	9.8	10.0	9.4
Poland Pologne										
MF [III] [17]	...	...	...	...	...	1126.1	2155.6	2509.3	2889.6	2838.0
M [III] [17]	...	...	...	...	...	552.4	1021.5	1170.5	1382.3	1343.0
F [III] [17]	...	...	...	...	...	573.7	1134.1	1338.8	1507.3	1495.0
% MF [III] [17]	...	...	...	...	...	6.3	11.8	13.6	16.4	16.0
% M [III] [17]	...	...	...	...	...	5.8	10.6	11.9	15.0	14.7
% F [III] [17]	...	...	...	...	...	7.1	13.5	15.5	17.9	17.3
Portugal Portugal										
MF [I]	397.0[15]	393.4[15]	329.0[15]	...	243.3[15]	231.1[15]	207.5[15]	# 194.1[12]	257.5[12]	...
M [I]	171.0[15]	176.2[15]	143.4[15]	...	95.1[15]	90.0[15]	77.6[15]	# 90.7[12]	120.0[12]	...
F [I]	225.9[15]	217.2[15]	185.6[15]	...	148.3[15]	141.1[15]	129.9[15]	# 103.4[12]	137.5[12]	...
% MF [I]	8.5[15]	8.3[15]	7.0[15]	...	5.0[15]	4.7[15]	4.1[15]	# 4.1[12]	5.5[12]	...
% M [I]	6.3[15]	6.4[15]	5.2[15]	...	3.4[15]	3.2[15]	2.8[15]	# 3.4[12]	4.6[12]	...
% F [I]	11.6[15]	10.9[15]	9.3[15]	...	7.2[15]	6.6[15]	5.8[15]	# 5.0[12]	6.5[12]	...
Puerto Rico Porto Rico										
MF [I] [17 39]	216.0	194.0	178.0	165.0	163.0	160.0	186.0	197.0	206.0	175.0
M [I] [17 39]	160.0	145.0	130.0	120.0	118.0	115.0	131.0	139.0	144.0	121.0
F [I] [17 39]	56.0	50.0	48.0	45.0	45.0	45.0	55.0	58.0	62.0	54.0
% MF [I] [17 39]	21.8	18.9	16.8	15.0	14.6	14.1	16.0	16.6	17.0	14.6
% M [I] [17 39]	24.8	22.0	19.4	17.4	16.9	16.2	17.9	19.0	19.5	16.5
% F [I] [17 39]	16.2	13.5	12.4	10.8	10.8	10.7	12.6	12.8	13.2	11.5
Republic of Moldova République de Moldova										
MF [III] [17]	...	...	...	...	...	...	0.1	15.0	14.1	20.6
M [III] [17]	...	...	...	...	...	...	...	5.9	5.5	7.7
F [III] [17]	...	...	...	...	...	...	0.1	9.1	8.9	12.9
% MF [III] [17]	...	...	...	...	...	...	...	0.7	0.7	1.1
Réunion Réunion										
MF [III] [17 17]	45.0	51.6	52.8	56.7	59.5	53.8	59.3	80.1	80.2	...
M [III] [17 17]	28.2	26.8	25.8	29.2	30.2	28.4	30.4	41.9	43.1	...
F [III] [17 17]	19.6	24.5	26.3	29.2	27.3	25.4	28.8	38.2	37.1	...
% MF [III] [7 17]	...	...	...	...	...	23.0	25.4	34.3	34.4	...
Romania Roumanie										
MF [III] [17]	...	...	...	...	...	...	337.4	929.0	1164.7	...
M [III] [17]	...	...	...	...	...	...	129.0	366.0	479.2	...
F [III] [17]	...	...	...	...	...	...	208.4	563.0	685.5	...
% MF [III] [17]	...	...	...	...	...	...	3.0	8.4	10.2	...
% M [III] [17]	...	...	...	...	...	...	2.2	6.2	8.1	...
% F [III] [17]	...	...	...	...	...	...	4.0	10.7	12.6	...
Russian Federation Fédération de Russie										
MF [III] [17]	...	...	...	...	...	...	61.9	577.7	...	...
M [III] [17]	...	...	...	...	...	...	18.8	160.7	...	...
F [III] [17]	...	...	...	...	...	...	43.1	417.0	...	...

30

Unemployment

Number (thousands) and percentage of unemployed [*cont.*]

Chômage

Nombre (milliers) et pourcentage des chômeurs [*suite*]

Country or area [§] Pays ou zone [§]	1985	1986	1987	1988	1989	1990	1991	1992	1993	1994
% MF [III] [17]	...	...	...	...	...	...	0.1	0.8	...	...
% M [III] [17]	...	...	...	...	...	...	0.1	0.5	...	...
% F [III] [17]	...	...	...	...	...	...	0.1	1.1	...	...
Saint Helena Sainte–Hélène										
MF [III] [7]	...	...	...	...	0.2	0.2	0.2	0.2	0.2	...
M [III] [7]	...	...	...	...	0.0	0.1	0.1	0.1	0.1	...
F [III] [7]	...	...	...	...	0.1	0.1	0.1	0.1	0.1	...
Saint Pierre and Miquelon Saint–Pierre–et–Miquelon										
MF [III] [7 66]	0.3	0.3	0.3	0.4	0.3		...	· ...	0.4	...
San Marino Saint–Marin										
MF [IV] [8 12]	0.7	0.7	0.7	0.7	0.6	0.6	0.5	0.5	0.6	...
M [IV] [8 12]	0.2	0.2	0.2	0.2	0.1	0.2	0.1	0.1	0.2	...
F [IV] [8 12]	0.5	0.5	0.5	0.5	0.5	0.5	0.3	0.4	0.4	...
% MF [IV] [8 12]	6.9	6.9	6.2	6.0	5.3	5.5	4.3	4.2	5.1	...
% M [IV] [8 12]	3.0	3.2	2.8	2.7	2.1	2.4	2.3	2.0	2.6	...
% F [IV] [8 12]	12.5	12.0	10.9	10.5	9.5	9.7	6.9	7.1	8.1	...
Senegal Sénégal										
MF [III] [10 26 67]	10.8	10.2	8.1	17.3	8.3	10.4	14.4	12.0	10.2	...
M [III] [10 26 67]	9.0	8.4	6.4	15.0	7.1	8.3	13.1	10.0	9.0	...
F [III] [10 26 67]	1.8	1.9	1.8	2.4	1.2	2.1	1.3	2.0	1.2	...
Singapore Singapour										
MF [I] [12]	53.2	84.1	62.4	46.2	30.7	25.8[68]	30.0	43.4	43.7	43.8
M [I] [12]	34.1	57.5	42.1	32.3	20.2	17.6[68]	18.7	26.4	25.2	24.9
F [I] [12]	19.1	26.6	20.3	13.8	10.4	8.2[68]	11.3	17.0	18.5	18.9
MF [III] [7 12]	9.2	9.5	8.1	4.5	2.7	1.7	1.2	1.0	1.0	...
M [III] [7 12]	5.6	6.5	5.6	3.2	1.9	1.2	0.8	0.7	0.7	...
F [III] [7 12]	3.6	2.9	2.5	1.4	0.8	0.5	0.4	0.3	0.3	...
% MF [I] [12]	4.1	6.5	4.7	3.3	2.2	1.7[68]	1.9	2.7	2.7	2.6
% M [I] [12]	4.2	7.0	5.1	3.8	2.3	1.9[68]	2.0	2.7	2.6	2.5
% F [I] [12]	4.1	5.5	4.0	2.6	1.9	1.3[68]	1.8	2.6	2.8	2.8
Slovakia Slovaquie										
MF [I] [2]	...	...	...	...	...	...	...	...	305.7[11]	336.6
M [I] [2]	...	...	...	...	...	...	...	...	171.5[11]	180.0
F [I] [2]	...	...	...	...	...	...	...	...	134.2[11]	153.7
MF [III] [7]	...	...	...	...	...	...	...	...	323.2	...
M [III] [7]	...	...	...	...	...	...	169.0	285.5	167.2	...
F [III] [7]	...	...	...	...	...	...	83.4	141.1	156.0	...
% MF [I] [2]	...	...	...	...	...	...	85.6	144.4	12.2[11]	13.3
% M [I] [2]	...	...	...	...	...	...	...	...	12.7[11]	13.3
% F [I] [2]	...	...	...	...	...	...	...	...	11.7[11]	13.3
% MF [III] [7]	...	...	...	...	...	...	6.6	11.4	12.7	...
% M [III] [7]	...	...	...	...	...	...	6.3	11.1	12.5	...
% F [III] [7]	...	...	...	...	...	...	6.9	11.7	12.9	...
Slovenia Slovénie										
MF [III] [2 7]	14.7	14.2	15.2	21.3	28.2	44.6	75.1	102.6	129.1	127.1
M [III] [2 7]	6.8	6.9	7.8	11.3	14.4	23.2	41.5	57.5	72.5	70.0
F [III] [2 7]	7.9	7.3	7.4	10.1	13.8	21.4	33.6	45.1	56.6	57.0
% MF [III] [2 7]	...	1.4	1.5	2.2	2.9	4.7	8.2	11.5	14.4	14.4
% M [III] [2 7]	...	1.3	1.5	2.1	2.8	4.5	8.5	12.1	15.3	15.1
% F [III] [2 7]	...	1.7	1.7	2.3	3.1	4.8	7.9	10.8	13.5	13.7
South Africa Afrique du Sud										
MF [III] [7 69]	...	...	...	122.1	116.5	110.7	247.8	287.8	313.3	...
M [III] [7 69]	...	...	...	82.7	80.0	77.3	176.6	201.1	...	...
F [III] [7 69]	...	...	...	39.4	36.5	33.3	71.2	86.7	...	...
Spain Espagne										
MF [I] [17]	2938.5	2933.0	2937.7	2847.9	2560.8	2441.2	2463.7	2788.5	3481.3	3738.1
M [I] [17]	1907.1	1852.1	1641.3	1464.5	1263.0	1166.1	1191.9	1384.5	1836.7	1911.9
F [I] [17]	1031.5	1080.8	1296.4	1383.4	1297.8	1275.1	1271.8	1404.1	1644.6	1826.2
MF [III] [7 52]	2642.0	2758.7	2924.1	2858.3	2550.3	2350.0	2289.0	2259.9	2537.9	...
M [III] [7 52]	1599.3	1572.2	1525.4	1359.7	1087.5	942.5	910.7	954.2	1193.0	...
F [III] [7 52]	1042.7	1186.4	1398.8	1498.6	1462.8	1407.5	1378.3	1305.7	1344.9	...
% MF [I] [17]	21.6	21.2	20.5	19.5	17.3	16.3	16.4	18.4	22.7	24.2
% M [I] [17]	20.2	19.4	17.1	15.2	13.0	12.0	12.3	14.3	19.0	18.8
% F [I] [17]	25.0	25.3	27.5	27.7	25.4	24.2	23.8	25.6	29.2	31.4

30
Unemployment
Number (thousands) and percentage of unemployed [*cont.*]
Chômage
Nombre (milliers) et pourcentage des chômeurs [*suite*]

Country or area [§] Pays ou zone [§]	1985	1986	1987	1988	1989	1990	1991	1992	1993	1994
% MF [III] [7 52]	19.5	20.0	20.4	19.5	17.2	15.7	15.2	14.9	16.6	...
% M [III] [7 52]	16.9	16.5	15.9	14.1	11.2	9.7	9.4	9.9	12.3	...
% F [III] [7 52]	25.5	28.0	29.7	30.0	28.6	26.7	25.8	23.8	23.9	...
Sri Lanka Sri Lanka										
MF [I] [11 15]	840.3	...	...	...	...	1005.1	843.3[70]	817.6[70]	874.1[70]	813.3[70]
M [I] [11 15]	433.2	...	...	...	...	395.8	380.0[70]	408.7[70]	349.3[70]	390.5[70]
F [I] [11 15]	407.0	...	...	...	...	609.2	463.3[70]	409.0[70]	524.8[70]	422.8[70]
% MF [I] [11 15]	...	...	...	...	...	14.4	14.1[70]	14.1[70]	14.7[70]	13.6[70]
% M [I] [11 15]	...	...	...	...	...	9.1	10.0[70]	10.6[70]	9.1[70]	9.9[70]
% F [I] [11 15]	...	...	...	...	...	23.5	21.2[70]	21.0[70]	25.2[70]	20.8[70]
Sudan Soudan										
MF [III] [10]	48.8	63.1	...	...	25.5	70.1	# 19.9[71]	5.3[71]	...	...
M [III] [10]	36.6	48.6	...	...	15.5	44.4	# 10.2[71]	3.7[71]	...	...
F [III] [10]	12.3	14.5	...	...	9.9	25.7	# 9.7[71]	1.6[71]	...	...
Suriname Suriname										
MF [I]	...	14.7	19.3	20.4	15.4	15.4[11]	...	18.5	17.0[11]	...
M [I]	...	7.9	11.0	11.5	7.6	7.2[11]	...	9.1	8.6[11]	...
F [I]	...	6.9	8.3	8.9	7.9	8.2[11]	...	9.4	8.4[11]	...
MF [III] [7]	17.0	13.4	# 2.8[72]	3.0	2.4	3.9	3.7	1.4	1.0	...
M [III] [7]	8.6	7.3	# 1.3[72]	1.4	1.2	1.2	1.1	0.5	0.4	...
F [III] [7]	8.3	6.1	# 1.5[72]	1.6	1.2	2.8	2.6	0.9	0.6	...
% MF [I]	...	...	...	...	...	15.8[11]	...	17.2	16.3[11]	...
% M [I]	...	...	...	...	...	12.5[11]	...	13.7	13.9[11]	...
% F [I]	...	...	...	...	...	20.6[11]	...	24.6	19.7[11]	...
Sweden Suède										
MF [I] [52]	125.0[45]	98.0	92.0	78.0	67.0	75.0	133.0	233.0	# 356.0	340.0
M [I] [52]	65.0[45]	51.0	48.0	40.0	34.0	40.0	77.0	145.0	# 219.0	202.0
F [I] [52]	60.0[45]	47.0	44.0	38.0	33.0	36.0	55.0	88.0	# 137.0	138.0
MF [III] [7 52]	84.9	84.2	78.1	61.1	56.3	66.4	114.6	214.5	326.1	331.7
M [III] [7 52]	42.3	42.4	38.9	31.2	29.2	35.6	66.5	131.4	193.7	191.1
F [III] [7 52]	42.6	41.9	39.2	29.9	27.1	30.9	48.1	83.2	131.4	140.6
% MF [I] [52]	2.8[45]	2.2	2.1	1.8	1.5	1.6	3.0	5.3	# 8.2	8.0
% M [I] [52]	2.8[45]	2.2	2.1	1.8	1.5	1.7	3.3	6.3	# 9.7	9.1
% F [I] [52]	2.9[45]	2.2	2.1	1.8	1.5	1.6	2.6	4.2	# 6.6	6.7
% MF [III] [7 52]	2.5	2.5	2.3	1.7	1.6	1.9	3.2	5.9	8.7	8.8
% M [III] [7 52]	2.6	2.4	2.2	1.8	1.6	2.0	3.9	...	...	10.4
% F [III] [7 52]	2.6	2.5	2.2	1.7	1.6	1.7	2.7	...	...	7.3
Switzerland Suisse										
MF [I] [2 11]	...	...	...	...	...	...	68.0	110.0	144.0	147.0
M [I] [2 11]	...	...	...	...	...	...	27.0	50.0	67.0	75.0
F [I] [2 11]	...	...	...	...	...	...	41.0	60.0	79.0	72.0
MF [III] [27]	30.4	25.7	24.7	22.3	17.5	18.1	39.2	92.3	163.1	171.0
M [III] [27]	16.4	13.4	12.5	11.4	9.1	9.8	22.7	54.7	96.6	98.0
F [III] [27]	13.9	12.4	12.1	10.9	8.4	8.3	16.5	37.6	66.6	73.1
% MF [I] [2 11]	...	...	...	...	...	...	1.8	2.9	3.7	3.8
% M [I] [2 11]	...	...	...	...	...	...	1.2	2.3	3.0	3.4
% F [I] [2 11]	...	...	...	...	...	...	2.5	3.6	4.7	4.3
% MF [III] [27]	1.0	0.8	0.8	0.7	0.6	0.5	1.1	2.5	4.5	4.7
% M [III] [27]	0.8	0.7	0.6	0.6	0.5	0.4	1.1	2.5	4.4	4.4
% F [III] [27]	1.2	1.1	1.1	1.0	0.8	0.6	1.2	2.7	4.7	5.2
Syrian Arab Republic Rép. arabe syrienne										
MF [I] [1 15]	...	...	...	...	177.3	...	235.4	...	...	...
M [I] [1 15]	...	...	...	...	130.8	...	147.3	...	...	...
F [I] [1 15]	...	...	...	...	46.5	...	88.2	...	...	...
% MF [I] [1 15]	...	...	...	...	5.8	...	6.8	...	...	...
% M [I] [1 15]	...	...	...	...	5.1	...	5.2	...	...	...
% F [I] [1 15]	...	...	...	...	9.5	...	14.0	...	...	...
Thailand Thaïlande										
MF [I] [1 74]	994.6[73]	968.7[73]	1721.6[73]	929.2[73]	# 433.1	710.0	869.3	...	...	...
M [I] [1 74]	456.2[73]	463.9[73]	672.7[73]	419.3[73]	# 204.5	347.4	350.1	...	...	...
F [I] [1 74]	538.4[73]	504.8[73]	1048.9[73]	509.8[73]	# 228.6	362.5	519.1	...	...	...
% MF [I] [1 74]	3.7[73]	3.5[73]	5.9[73]	3.1[73]	# 1.4	2.2	2.7	...	...	...
% M [I] [1 74]	6.9[73]	3.1[73]	4.3[73]	2.6[73]	# 1.2	2.1	2.0	...	...	...
% F [I] [1 74]	4.4[73]	3.9[73]	7.6[73]	3.6[73]	# 1.6	2.4	3.5	...	...	...

30
Unemployment
Number (thousands) and percentage of unemployed [*cont.*]
Chômage
Nombre (milliers) et pourcentage des chômeurs [*suite*]

Country or area [§] Pays ou zone [§]	1985	1986	1987	1988	1989	1990	1991	1992	1993	1994
TFYR Macedonia L'ex—R.y. Macédoine										
MF [III] [10]	136.0	141.0	141.0	140.0	150.0	156.0	165.0	172.0	175.0	186.0
M [III] [10]	61.0	64.0	66.0	66.0	72.0	76.0	82.0	87.0	89.0	96.0
F [III] [10]	75.0	77.0	75.0	74.0	78.0	80.0	83.0	85.0	86.0	90.0
% MF [III] [10]	21.6	21.7	21.5	21.4	22.6	23.6	26.0	27.8	29.3	32.0
% M [III] [10]	15.8	16.3	16.5	16.9	18.3	19.4	21.7	23.8	25.3	27.9
% F [III] [10]	30.9	30.2	29.1	28.2	28.8	29.7	32.3	33.7	35.2	37.8
Trinidad and Tobago Trinité—et—Tobago										
MF [I] [2]	72.8	81.2	# 106.6[6]	104.7[6]	103.4[6]	93.6[6]	91.2[6]	99.2[6]	99.9[6]	...
M [I] [2]	46.4	51.5	# 65.7[6]	66.5[6]	64.8[6]	55.1[6]	49.6[6]	54.3[6]	56.3[6]	...
F [I] [2]	26.4	29.7	# 40.9[6]	38.2[6]	38.6[6]	38.5[6]	41.5[6]	44.9[6]	43.7[6]	...
% MF [I] [2]	15.5	17.2	# 22.3[6]	22.0[6]	22.0[6]	20.0[6]	18.5[6]	19.6[6]	19.8[6]	...
% M [I] [2]	15.0	16.4	# 20.7[6]	21.6[6]	20.8[6]	17.8[6]	15.7[6]	17.0[6]	17.6[6]	...
% F [I] [2]	17.0	18.9	# 25.3[6]	23.6[6]	24.5[6]	24.2[6]	23.4[6]	23.9[6]	23.4[6]	...
Tunisia Tunisie										
MF [III] [10 56]	84.0	80.2	83.7	91.5	105.9	...	...	...	...	...
M [III] [10 56]	69.1	65.8	67.3	72.8	80.5	...	...	...	...	...
F [III] [10 56]	14.9	14.3	16.4	18.7	25.5	...	...	...	...	...
Turkey Turquie										
MF [I] [1 25]	2040.0	...	...	1709.0	1802.0	1572.0	1714.0	1656.0	1659.0	...
M [I] [1 25]	1431.0	...	...	1081.0	1196.0	1085.0	1253.0	1184.0	1191.0	...
F [I] [1 25]	609.0	...	...	627.0	607.0	487.0	461.0	472.0	467.0	...
MF [III] [7 12 46]	935.0	1053.0	1124.0	1155.0	1076.0	980.0	859.0	840.0	683.0	* 469.0
M [III] [7 12 46]	782.0	877.0	929.0	952.0	888.0	809.0	707.0	695.0	572.0	* 382.0
F [III] [7 12 46]	153.0	177.0	195.0	204.0	189.0	171.0	152.0	145.0	111.0	* 87.0
% MF [I] [1 25]	11.2	...	...	8.3	8.5	7.4	8.3	7.8	7.9	...
% M [I] [1 25]	11.3	...	...	7.7	8.4	7.5	8.8	8.1	8.2	...
% F [I] [1 25]	11.1	...	...	9.6	8.8	7.2	7.1	7.2	7.2	...
United Kingdom Royaume—Uni										
MF [I] [17]	3076.0	3073.0	2979.0	2489.0	2063.0	1949.0	2385.0	2732.0	2891.0	...
M [I] [17]	1862.0	1857.0	1789.0	1465.0	1207.0	1149.0	1494.0	1846.0	1967.0	...
F [I] [17]	1214.0	1217.0	1190.0	1005.0	857.0	800.0	891.0	886.0	924.0	...
MF [II] [39 75 76 77 78]	3271.2	# 3292.9	2953.4	# 2370.4	# 1798.7	1664.5	2291.9	2778.6	2919.2	...
M [II] [39 75 76 77 78]	2251.7	# 2254.7	2045.8	# 1650.5	# 1290.8	1232.3	1737.1	2126.0	2236.0	...
F [II] [39 75 78]	1019.5	# 1036.6	907.6	# 719.9	507.9	432.2	554.9	652.6	683.1	...
% MF [I] [17]	11.2	11.2	10.7	8.8	7.2	6.8	8.3	9.6	10.2	...
% M [I] [17]	11.6	11.6	11.1	9.0	7.4	7.0	9.2	11.5	12.4	...
% F [I] [17]	10.7	10.6	10.2	8.4	7.0	6.5	7.2	7.2	7.5	...
% MF [II] [39 75 76 77 78]	11.8	# 11.8	10.6	# 8.4	# 6.3	5.9	8.1	9.9	10.4	...
% M [II] [39 75 76 77 78]	13.7	# 13.8	12.5	# 10.1	# 7.9	7.6	10.7	13.3	...	...
% F [II] [39 75 78]	9.1	# 9.0	7.8	# 6.1	4.2	3.5	4.6	5.4	...	...
United States Etats—Unis										
MF [I] [17]	8312.0	8237.0	7425.0	6701.0	6528.0	6874.0	8426.0	9384.0	8734.0	# 7996.0
M [I] [17]	4521.0	4530.0	4101.0	3655.0	3525.0	3799.0	4817.0	5380.0	4932.0	# 4367.0
F [I] [17]	3791.0	3707.0	3324.0	3046.0	3003.0	3075.0	3609.0	4005.0	3801.0	# 3629.0
% MF [I] [17]	7.2	7.0	6.2	5.5	5.3	5.5	6.7	7.4	6.8	# 6.1
% M [I] [17]	7.0	6.9	6.2	5.5	5.2	5.6	7.0	7.8	7.1	# 6.2
% F [I] [17]	7.4	7.1	6.2	5.6	5.4	5.4	6.3	6.9	6.5	# 6.0
United States Virgin Is. Iles Vierges américaines										
MF [III] [7 79]	2.6	2.1	1.4	1.5	1.7	1.3	1.4	1.1	1.9	...
% MF [III] [7 79]	6.0	4.7	3.0	3.3	3.7	2.8	2.8	3.5	3.5	...
Uruguay Uruguay										
MF [I] [12 14]	...	122.0[11]	108.7	104.1	98.4	105.7	111.0	112.8	105.0	...
M [I] [12 14]	...	58.1[11]	48.6	46.3	44.9	50.6	52.6	49.6	46.9	...
F [I] [12 14]	...	63.9[11]	60.1	57.8	53.5	55.1	58.4	63.2	58.1	...
% MF [I] [12 14]	...	10.7[11]	9.1	8.6	8.0	8.5	9.0	9.0	8.3	...
% M [I] [12 14]	...	8.5[11]	6.7	6.3	6.1	6.9	7.2	6.9	6.5	...
% F [I] [12 14]	...	13.9[11]	12.6	11.9	10.8	10.9	11.6	11.9	10.9	...

30
Unemployment
Number (thousands) and percentage of unemployed [cont.]
Chômage
Nombre (milliers) et pourcentage des chômeurs [suite]

Country or area [§] Pays ou zone [§]	1985	1986	1987	1988	1989	1990	1991	1992	1993	1994
Venezuela **Venezuela**										
MF [I] [2]	766.8	667.4	575.3	478.2	621.1	741.7	701.0	579.8	497.9	...
M [I] [2]	577.3	502.2	448.9	367.3	469.5	535.8	478.6	415.1	366.3	...
F [I] [2]	189.6	165.8	124.6	110.6	151.9	205.8	222.5	164.7	131.6	...
% MF [I] [2]	13.1	11.0	9.2	7.3	9.2	10.4	9.5	7.5	6.4	...
% M [I] [2]	13.5	11.4	9.9	7.8	9.8	10.9	9.6	8.1	7.1	...
% F [I] [2]	11.6	9.9	7.2	6.1	7.6	9.3	9.4	6.9	5.6	...

Source:
International Labour Office (Geneva).

Source:
Bureau international du Travail (Genève).

[§]   I = Labour force sample surveys and general
    household sample surveys.
    II = Social insurance statistics.
    III = Employment office statistics.
    IV = Official estimates.

[§]   I = Enquêtes par sondage sur la main-d'oeuvre et enquêtes
    générales par sondage auprès des ménages
    II = Statistiques d'assurances sociales.
    III = Statistiques des bureaux de placement.
    IV = Evaluations officielles.

[†]   For detailed descriptions of data pertaining to former
    Czechoslovakia, Germany, SFR Yugoslavia and former
    USSR, see Annex I — Country or area nomenclature,
    regional and other groupings.

[†]   Pour les descriptions en détails des données relatives à l'ancienne
    Tchécoslovaquie, l'Allemagne, la Rfs Yougoslavie et l'ancienne URSS,
    voir l'Annexe I — Nomenclature des pays ou zones, groupements
    régionaux et autres groupements.

1   One month of each year.
2   Persons aged 15 years and over.
3   Gran Buenos Aires.
4   Including unpaid family workers who worked for less than 15
    hours.
5   Beginning 1989, based on the 1991 Census of Population and
    Housing.
6   Excluding the unemployed not previously employed.
7   Registered unemployed.
8   31 st. Dec. of each year.
9   Private sector.
10 Applications for work (incl. persons in employment).
11 Average of less than twelve months.
12 Persons aged 14 years and over.
13 Persons aged 15 to 69 years.
14 Urban areas.
15 Persons aged 10 years and over.
16 Excluding the rural population of Rondônia, Acre, Amazonas,
    Roraima, Pará and Amapá.
17 Persons aged 16 years and over.
18 Prior to 1989, three employment offices. Beginning 1989,
    four employment offices.
19 Including unemployed not registered by sex.
20 Bujumbura.
21 Revised survey.
22 Bangui.
23 Young people aged 16 to 25 years.
24 7 main cities of the country.
25 Persons aged 12 years and over.
26 Persons aged 14 to 55 years.
27 Year ending in February of the following year.
28 Persons aged 15 to 74 years.
29 Persons aged 15 to 66 years.
30 Persons aged 16 to 66 years.
31 Quito, Guayaquil and Cuenca.
32 Persons aged 12 to 64 years.
33 Average of four surveys.
34 Metropolitan area (Paraguay: Ascunción metropolitan area;
    Mexico: Mexico city, Monterrey and Guadalajara).
35 Year ending in June of the year indicated.
36 Persons aged 18 to 55 years.

1   Un mois de chaque année.
2   Personnes âgées de 15 ans et plus.
3   Gran Buenos Aires.
4   Y compris les travailleurs familiaux non rémunérés qui ont travaillé
    moins de 15 heures.
5   A partir de 1989, basées sur le recensement de la population et de
    l'habitat de 1991.
6   Non compris les chômeurs n'ayant jamais travaillé précédemment.
7   Les chômeurs n'ayant jamais travaillé précédemment.
8   31 déc. de chaque année.
9   Secteur privé.
10 Demandeurs d'emploi (y compris les pesonnes d'un emploi).
11 Moyenne de moins de douze mois.
12 Personnes âgées de 14 ans et plus.
13 Personnes âgées de 15 à 69 ans.
14 Les régions urbaines.
15 Personnes âgées de 10 ans et plus.
16 Non compris la population rurale de Rondônia, Acre, Amazonas,
    Roraima, Pará and Amapá.
17 Personnes âgées de 16 ans et plus.
18 Avant 1989, trois bureau de placement. A partir de 1989, quatre
    bureau de placement.
19 Y compris chômeure non répartis par sexe.
20 Bujumbura.
21 Enquête révisée.
22 Bangui.
23 Jeunes gens de 16 à 25 ans.
24 7 villes principales du pays.
25 Personnes âgées de 12 ans et plus.
26 Personnes âgées de 14 à 55 ans.
27 Année se terminant en février de l'année suivante.
28 Personnes âgées de 15 à 74 ans.
29 Personnes âgées de 15 à 66 ans.
30 Personnes âgées de 16 à 66 ans.
31 Quito, Guayaquil et Cuenca.
32 Personnes âgées de 12 à 64 ans.
33 Moyenne de quatre enquêtes.
34 Région métropolitaine (Paraguay: Région métropolitaine d'Asuncion;
    Mexique: la ville de Mexique, de Monterrey et de Guadalajara).
35 Année se terminant en juin de l'année indiquée.
36 Personnes âgées de 18 à 55 ans.

30
Unemployment
Number (thousands) and percentage of unemployed [*cont.*]
Chômage
Nombre (milliers) et pourcentage des chômeurs [*suite*]

37 Persons aged 15 to 64 years.
38 Excluding elderly unemployment pensioners no longer seeking work.
39 Excluding persons temporarily laid off.
40 Cayenne and Kourou.
41 Persons aged 15 to 60 years.
42 Persons aged 15 to 65 years.
43 Guatemala city only.
44 Excluding unpaid family workers who worked for one hour or more.
45 Persons aged 16 to 74 years.
46 Annual averages.
47 Intercensal Population Survey results.
48 Persons aged 10 to 56 years.
49 Rates calculated on basis of 1991 census.
50 Including the residents of East Jerusalem.
51 Including persons who did not work in the country during the previous 12 months.
52 Persons aged 16 to 64 years.
53 6 provincial capitals.
54 Persons aged 16 to 61 years.
55 Excluding Rodrigues.
56 Persons aged 18 years and over.
57 Persons working or seeking work for less than 12 hours per week are no longer included.
58 Excluding Aruba.
59 Curaçao.
60 Noumea.
61 Including students seeking vacation work.
62 Annual average calculated using December data as at 12 Dec.
63 Computed from 1987−88 survey results.
64 Persons aged 18 to 60 years.
65 Lima.
66 Persons aged 16 to 60 years.
67 Dakar.
68 Population census.
69 Excluding Transkei, Bophuthatswana, Venda, Ciskei; elsewhere persons enumerated at de facto dwelling place.
70 Excluding Northern and Eastern provinces.
71 Khartoum province.
72 Change in registration system; unemployed must re−register every 3 months.
73 Persons aged 11 years and over.
74 Persons aged 13 years and over.
75 Beginning Sept. 1988, excluding most under 18−year−olds.
76 Beginning Sept. 1989, excluding some men formerly employed in the coalmining industry.
77 Excluding some categories of men aged 60 and over.
78 Claimants at unemployment benefits offices.
79 Persons aged 16 to 65 years.

37 Personnes âgées de 15 à 64 ans.
38 Non compris les chômeurs indemnisés âgés ne recherchant plus de travail.
39 Non compris les personnes temporairement mises à pied.
40 Cayenne et Kourou.
41 Personnes âgées de 15 à 60 ans.
42 Personnes âgées de 15 à 65 ans.
43 Ville de Guatemala seulement.
44 Non compris les travailleurs familiaux non rémunérés ayant travaillé une heure ou plus.
45 Personnes âgées de 16 à 74 ans.
46 Moyennes annuelles.
47 Résultats de l'enquête intercensitaire de population.
48 Personnes âgées de 10 à 56 ans.
49 Taux calculés sur la base du Recensement de 1991.
50 Y compris les résidents de Jérusalem−Est.
51 Y compris les personnes qui n'ont pas travaillé dans le pays pendant les 12 mois précédents.
52 Personnes âgées de 16 à 64 ans.
53 6 chefslieux de province.
54 Personnes âgées de 16 à 61 ans.
55 Non compris Rodrigues.
56 Personnes âgées de 18 ans et plus.
57 Ne sont plus comprises les personnes qui travaillent, ou qui cherchent moins de 12 heures de travail par semaine.
58 Non compris Aruba.
59 Curaçao.
60 Nouméa.
61 Y compris les étudiants qui cherchent un emploi pendant les vacances.
62 Moyenne annuelle calculée en utilisant pour le mois de décembre les données du 12 déc.
63 Calculé sur la base de résultats de l'enquête de 1987−88.
64 Personnes âgées de 18 à 60 ans.
65 Lima.
66 Personnes âgées de 16 à 60 ans.
67 Dakar.
68 Recensement de population.
69 Non compris Transkei, Bophuthatswana, Venda, Ciskei; ailleurs personnes énumérées aux logis de facto.
70 Non compris les provinces du Nord et de l'Est.
71 Province de Khartoum.
72 Modification du système d'enregistrement les chômeurs doivent se réinscrire tous les 3 mois.
73 Personnes âgées de 11 ans et plus.
74 Personnes âgées de 13 ans et plus.
75 A partir de sept. 1988, non compris la plupart des moins de 18 ans.
76 Dès sept. 1989, non compris certains hommes ayant précédemment travaillé dans l'industrie charbonnière.
77 Non compris certaines catégories d'hommes âgés de 60 ans et plus.
78 Demandeurs auprès des bureaux de prestations de chômage.
79 Personnes âgées de 16 à 65 ans.

Technical notes, tables 29 and 30

Detailed data on labour force and related topics are published in the ILO *Year Book of Labour Statistics*.[11] The series shown in the *Statistical Yearbook* give an overall picture of the availability and disposition of labour resources and, in conjunction with other macro-economic indicators, can be useful for an overall assessment of economic performance. The ILO *Year Book of Labour Statistics* provides a comprehensive description of the methodology underlying the labour series. Brief definitions of the major categories of labour statistics are given below.

"Employment" is defined to include persons above a specified age who, during a specified period of time, were in one of the following categories:

(a) "Paid employment", comprising persons who perform some work for pay or profit during the reference period or persons with a job but not at work due to temporary absence, such as vacation, strike, education leave;

(b) "Self-employment", comprising employers, own-account workers, members of producers' cooperatives, persons engaged in production of goods and services for own consumption and unpaid family workers;

(c) Members of the armed forces. Students, homemakers and others mainly engaged in non-economic activities during the reference period who, at the same time, were in paid employment or self-employment are considered as employed on the same basis as other categories.

"Unemployment" is defined to include persons above a certain age and who during a specified period of time were:

(a) "Without work", i.e. were not in paid employment or self-employment;

(b) "Currently available for work", i.e. were available for paid employment or self-employment during the reference period; and

(c) "Seeking work", i.e. had taken specific steps in a specified period to find paid employment or self-employment.

The following categories of persons are not considered to be unemployed:

(a) Persons intending to establish their own business or farm, but who had not yet arranged to do so and who were not seeking work for pay or profit;

(b) Former unpaid family workers not at work and not seeking work for pay or profit.

For various reasons, national definitions of employment and unemployment often differ from the recommended international standard definitions and thereby limit international comparability. Intercountry comparisons are also complicated by a variety of types of data collection systems used to obtain information on employed and unemployed persons.

Notes techniques, tableaux 29 et 30

Des données détaillées sur la main-d'oeuvre et des sujets connexes sont publiées dans l'*Annuaire des Statistiques du Travail* du BIT [11]. Les séries indiqués dans l'*Annuaire des Statistiques* donnent un tableau d'ensemble des disponibilités de main-d'oeuvre et de l'emploi de ces ressources et, combinées à d'autres indicateurs économiques, elles peuvent être utiles pour une évaluatation générale de la performance économique. L'*Annuaire des statistiques du Travail* du BIT donne une description complète de la méthodologie employée pour établir les séries sur la main-d'oeuvre. On trouvera ci-dessous quelques brèves définitions des grandes catégories de statistiques du travail.

Le terme "Emploi" désigne les personnes dépassant un âge déterminé qui, au cours d'une période donnée, se trouvaient dans l'une des catégories suivantes :

(a) La catégorie "emploi rémunéré", composée des personnes faisant un certain travail en échange d'une rémunération ou d'un profit pendant la période de référence, ou les personnes ayant un emploi, mais qui ne travaillaient pas en raison d'une absence temporaire (vacances, grève, congé d'études);

(b) La catégorie "emploi indépendant" regroupe les employeurs, les travailleurs indépendants, les membres de coopératives de producteurs et les personnes s'adonnant à la production de biens et de services pour leur propre consommation et la main-d'oeuvre familiale non rémunérée;

(c) Les membres des forces armées, les étudiants, les aides familiales et autres personnes qui s'adonnaient essentiellement à des activités non économiques pendant la période de référence et qui, en même temps, avaient un emploi rémunéré ou indépendant, sont considérés comme employés au même titre que les personnes des autres catégories.

Par "chômeurs", on entend les personnes dépassant un âge déterminé et qui, pendant une période donnée, éaient :

(a) "sans emploi", c'est-à-dire sans emploi rémunéré ou indépendant;

(b) "disponibles", c'est-à-dire qui pouvaient être engagées pour un emploi rémunéré ou pouvaient s'adonner à un emploi indépendant au cours de la période de référence; et

(c) "à la recherche d'un emploi", c'est-à-dire qui avaient pris des mesures précises à un certain moment pour trouver un emploi rémunéré ou un emploi indépendant.

Ne sont pas considérés comme chômeurs :

(a) Les personnes qui, pendant la période de référence, avaient l'intention de créer leur propre entreprise ou exploitation agricole, mais n'avaient pas encore pris les dispositions nécessaires à cet effet et qui n'étaient pas à la recherche d'un emploi en vue d'une rémunération ou d'un profit;

Table 29 presents absolute figures on the distribution of employed persons by major divisions of economic activity. Data are arranged as far as possible according to the major divisions of economic activity of the *International Standard Industrial Classification of All Economic Activities*. [46] The column for total employment includes economic activities not adequately defined. The four main sources of these statistics are: labour force sample surveys and general household sample surveys, social insurance statistics, establishment surveys and official estimates.

Table 30: Figures are presented in absolute numbers and in percentages. Data are normally annual averages of monthly, quarterly or semi-annual data.

The series generally represent the total number of persons wholly unemployed or temporarily laid off. Percentage figures, where given, are calculated by comparing the number of unemployed to the total members of that group of the labour force on which the unemployment data are based.

(b)   Les anciens travailleurs familiaux non rémunérés qui n'avaient pas d'emploi et n'étaient pas à la recherche d'un emploi en vue d'une rémunération ou d'un profit.

Pour diverses raisons, les définitions nationales de l'emploi et du chômage diffèrent souvent des définitions internationales types recommandées, limitant ainsi les possibilités de comparaison entre pays. Ces comparaisons se trouvent en outre compliquées par la diversité des systèmes de collecte de données utilisés pour recueillir des informations sur les personnes employées et les chômeurs.

Le *Tableau 29* présente des chiffres en valeur absolue sur la répartition des personnes employées par branche d'activité économique. Les données sont présentées autant que possible selon les principales divisions de l'activité économique de la *Classification internationale type, par Industrie, de toutes les branches d'activité économique* [46]. La colonne indiquant l'emploi total englobe les activités économiques non convenablement définies. Les quatre sources principales de ces statistiques sont : les enquêtes par sondage sur la main-d'oeuvre et les enquêtes générales par sondage auprès des ménages, les statistiques d'assurances sociales, les enquêtes auprès des établissements et les évaluations officielles.

Tableau 30 : Les chiffres sont présentés en valeur absolue et en pourcentage. Les données sont normalement des moyennes annuelles des données mensuelles, trimestrielles ou semestrielles.

Les séries représentent généralement le nombre total des chômeurs complets ou des personnes temporairement mises à pied. Les données en pourcentage, lorsqu'elles figurent au tableau, sont calculées par comparaison du nombre de chômeurs au nombre total des personnes du groupe de main-d'oeuvre sur lequel sont basées les données relatives au chômage.

31
Earnings in manufacturing
Gains dans les industries manufacturières
By hour, day, week or month
Par heure, jour, semaine ou mois

Country or area and unit Pays ou zone et unité	1985	1986	1987	1988	1989	1990	1991	1992	1993	1994
Albania: lek Albanie : lek										
MF - month mois[1,2,3]	521.0	528.0	533.0	533.0	542.0	554.0	* 665.0	...	...	...
Antigua and Barbuda: EC dollar Antigua-et-Barbuda : dollar des Caraïbes orientales										
MF - week semaine	...	...	456.3	502.0	416.0	...	505.0	505.0	...	...
Argentina: Argentine peso Argentine : peso argentin										
MF - hour heure[4,5]	0.4[6]	0.8[6]	1.7[6]	7.7[6]	186.6[6]	5 383.7[6]	13.0[6,7]	# 1.5	1.6	1.7
Australia: Australian dollar Australie : dollar australien										
MF - hour heure[8,9]	...	...	...	...	...	12.9	13.3	13.7	14.0	* 15.9
M - hour heure[8,9]	...	...	...	...	...	13.5	13.8	14.2	14.6	* 16.6
F - hour heure[8,9]	...	...	...	...	...	11.1	11.7	12.0	12.4	* 13.5
Austria: Austrian schilling Autriche : schilling autrichien										
MF - month mois[2,10]	16 395.0	17 116.0	17 646.0	18 318.0	19 130.0	20 496.0	21 547.0	22 784.0	23 758.0	24 743.0
Azerbaijan: Azeri manat Azerbaïdjan : manat azeri										
MF - month mois[1]	181.9	184.4	188.1	196.8	209.4	218.7	400.2	3 282.6	3 109.2	20 585.0
Bahrain: Bahrain dinar Bahreïn : dinar de Bahreïn										
MF - month mois[1,3,12]	256.0[11]	...	304.0	248.0	241.0	225.0	220.0	204.0	190.0	188.0
Barbados: Barbados dollar Barbade : dollar de la Barbade										
MF - week semaine	...	...	...	238.5[8]	235.3[8]	251.5[8]	255.7	...	...	...
Belarus: Belarussian rouble Bélarus : rouble bélarussien										
MF - month mois[1]	191.0[13]	197.0[13]	204.0[13]	226.0[13]	249.0[13]	283.0[13]	596.0	5 852.0	68 866.0	115 536.0
Belgium: Belgian franc Belgique : franc belge										
MF - hour heure[8,10]	293.8	295.3	302.2	309.8	327.1	342.4	363.1	379.6	395.9	...
M - hour heure[8,10]	312.5	314.2	321.2	329.3	348.2	364.0	385.7	403.8	420.7	...
F - hour heure[8,10]	232.3	232.7	239.9	245.3	257.6	271.2	287.7	300.2	313.4	...
Bolivia: boliviano Bolivie : boliviano										
MF - month mois[1,8]	67.0	172.0	279.0	371.0	437.0	493.0	621.0	690.0	761.0	* 906.0
Botswana: pula Botswana : pula										
MF - month mois[1,8,14]	249.2	282.4	278.3	330.9	345.0	383.0	403.0	511.0	606.0	551.0
Brazil: real Brésil : real										
MF - month mois[1]	1.6	3.5	10.9	75.6	1 110.7	26 076.0	136 699.0	1 562.0[7]	...	...
Bulgaria: lev Bulgarie : lev										
MF - month mois[1,3]	227.0	239.9	243.8	262.8	281.8	335.8	916.9	2 244.2[2]	3 481.2[2]	5 239.0[2]
Burundi: Burundi franc Burundi : franc burundais										
MF - month mois[1,15,16]	17 421.0	17 532.0	17 600.0	...	...	...	...	...	...	...
Canada: Canadian dollar Canada : dollar canadien										
MF - hour heure[17]	11.6	12.0	12.4	12.9	13.6	14.3	14.9	15.5	15.8	...
Chile: Chilean peso Chili : peso chilien										
MF - month mois[8,10,18]	24 409.0	29 157.0	34 137.0	41 497.0	50 432.0	64 447.0	83 908.0	102 514.0	118 612.0	...
China: yuan renminbi Chine : yuan renminbi										
MF - month mois[1]	92.6	106.4	118.1	148.5	166.8	174.2	191.3	231.2	279.0	356.9

31
Earnings in manufacturing
By hour, day, week or month [cont.]
Gains dans les industries manufacturières
Par heure, jour, semaine ou mois [suite]

Country or area and unit / Pays ou zone et unité	1985	1986	1987	1988	1989	1990	1991	1992	1993	1994
Colombia: Colombian peso Colombie : peso colombien										
MF - month mois[1][19]	317.9	393.6	483.1	614.1	788.3	...	...	...	...	...
Cook Islands: Cook Islands dollar Iles Cook : dollar des îles de Cook										
MF - week semaine[1][8]	...	...	...	...	134.0	137.0	...	...	* 187.0	
M - week semaine[1][8]	...	...	...	...	134.0	160.0	...	...	* 194.0	...
F - week semaine[1][8]	...	...	...	...	87.0	111.0	...	...	* 177.0	...
Costa Rica: Costa Rican colón Costa Rica : colón costa-ricien										
MF - month mois[1][8][20]	8 673.0	9 588.0	# 13 211.0	14 658.0	16 784.0	20 037.0	27 229.0	32 949.0	38 631.0	44 720.0
M - month mois[1][8][20]	9 422.0	10 370.0	# 14 207.0	16 573.0	18 534.0	21 887.0	30 152.0	36 427.0	42 225.0	49 059.0
F - month mois[1][8][20]	6 932.0	7 815.0	# 11 021.0	11 102.0	13 505.0	16 262.0	21 733.0	26 282.0	30 556.0	35 335.0
Croatia: kuna Croatie : kuna										
MF - month mois[1]	4.2[21]	8.7[21]	18.0[21]	48.0[21]	764.0[21]	4 218.0[21]	7 447.0[21]	34 024.0[21]	518.0	1 186.0
Cuba: Cuban peso Cuba : peso cubain										
MF - month mois[13]	193.0[2][22]	# 189.0[2]	183.0[2]	# 183.0	...	...	...	...	...	...
Cyprus: Cyprus pound Chypre : livre chypriote										
MF - week semaine[8][15][18][23]	52.4	54.0	58.1	61.9	68.0	74.2	80.3	89.0	101.0	104.1
M - week semaine[8][15][18][23]	70.1	72.5	76.7	80.6	89.4	98.8	105.6	116.4	134.2	132.3
F - week semaine[8][15][18][23]	39.1	40.7	44.3	47.7	52.1	56.8	63.0	69.9	75.8	81.2
Czech Republic: Czech koruna République tchèque : couronne tchèque										
MF - month mois[1][24]	3 015.0	3 055.0	3 112.0	3 172.0	3 239.0	3 325.0	3 882.0	4 565.0	5 717.0	6 649.0
M - month mois[1][24]	...	...	3 560.0	3 628.0	3 705.0	3 803.0	4 440.0	5 221.0	6 539.0	7 605.0
F - month mois[1][24]	...	...	2 416.0	2 463.0	2 515.0	2 582.0	3 014.0	3 544.0	4 439.0	5 163.0
Denmark: Danish krone Danemark : couronne danoise										
MF - hour heure[11][23][25]	75.8	78.7	86.8	92.1	96.0	99.9	104.6	108.3	...	...
M - hour heure[11][23][25]	78.3	81.5	90.2	95.6	99.6	103.8	108.5	112.2	...	...
F - hour heure[11][23][25]	67.1	69.2	75.9	80.7	84.3	87.8	92.1	95.4	...	...
Ecuador: sucre Equateur : sucre										
MF - hour heure	90.0	117.3	145.8	223.3	337.0	467.9	669.4	1 088.6	1 676.1	...
Egypt: Egyptian pound Egypte : livre égyptienne										
MF - week semaine[8][12]	29.0	33.0	38.0	41.0	46.0	54.0	55.0	62.0	...	...
M - week semaine[8][12]	30.0	34.0	39.0	43.0	48.0	56.0	57.0	64.0	...	...
F - week semaine[8][12]	22.0	25.0	28.0	31.0	34.0	38.0	41.0	48.0	...	...
El Salvador: El Salvador colón El Salvador : colón salvadorien										
MF - hour heure	3.3[26]	3.2	3.2	3.2	3.3	3.3	4.1	4.6	...	...
M - hour heure	3.6[26]	3.5	3.3	3.3	3.4	3.4	4.5	4.8	...	...
F - hour heure	2.9[26]	3.0	3.0	3.0	3.1	3.2	3.7	4.5	...	...
Estonia: Estonian kroon Estonie : couronne estonienne										
MF - month mois[1]	230.0[27]	237.2[27]	246.2[27]	268.0[27]	292.6[27]	359.8[27]	850.7[27]	527.0	* 1 036.0	...
Fiji: Fiji dollar Fidji : dollar des Fidji										
MF - day jour[8]	12.2	11.8	12.3	12.6	11.4	11.4	12.0	12.9	13.5	13.9

31
Earnings in manufacturing
By hour, day, week or month [cont.]
Gains dans les industries manufacturières
Par heure, jour, semaine ou mois [suite]

Country or area and unit Pays ou zone et unité	1985	1986	1987	1988	1989	1990	1991	1992	1993	1994
Finland: Finnish markka **Finlande : markka finlandais**										
MF - hour heure[2]	32.1	34.0	36.5	39.7	43.5	47.7	50.7	52.3	53.5	...
M - hour heure[2]	34.6	36.6	39.2	42.6	46.7	51.1	53.9	55.4	56.8	...
F - hour heure[2]	26.6	28.3	30.3	32.9	35.8	39.5	42.1	43.4	44.4	...
France: French franc **France : franc français**										
MF - hour heure[8]	# 37.8	39.3	41.0	# 41.8	43.4	45.5	47.5	49.4	50.6	43.7
M - hour heure[8]	# 40.2	41.6	43.4	# 44.4	46.2	48.4	50.5	52.4	53.7	...
F - hour heure[8]	# 31.8	33.0	34.4	# 35.1	36.3	38.2	39.7	41.2	42.5	...
French Polynesia: CFP franc **Polynésie française : franc CFP**										
MF - month mois	70 000.0	77 700.0	82 000.0	84 000.0	86 500.0	...	...	...	...	...
Gambia: dalasi **Gambie : dalasi**										
MF - day jour[1 8 12]	# 12.3	11.5	11.1	...	...	...	...	...	...	...
Germany † Allemagne† **F. R. Germany: deutsche mark** **R. f. Allemagne : deutsche mark**										
MF - hour heure[15]	16.2	16.8	17.5	18.3	19.1	20.1	21.3	22.5	23.8	24.6
M - hour heure[15]	17.2	17.9	18.6	19.5	20.3	21.3	22.6	23.8	25.0	25.8
F - hour heure[15]	12.5	13.0	13.6	14.2	14.7	15.5	16.5	17.5	18.5	19.0
former German D. R.: mark **anc. R. d. allemande : mark**										
MF - hour heure	...	...	...	...	...	...	9.4	11.9	13.9	15.5
M - hour heure	...	...	...	...	...	...	9.7	12.3	14.4	16.2
F - hour heure	...	...	...	...	...	...	8.4	10.5	11.9	13.0
Ghana: cedi **Ghana : cedi**										
MF - month mois[1 8]	5 059.0	8 787.0	15 216.0	21 411.0	36 793.0	45 045.0	34 226.0	...	...	...
Gibraltar: Gibraltar pound **Gibraltar : livre de Gibraltar**										
MF - week semaine[8]	140.9	150.2	152.7	190.6	190.1	238.5	214.1	239.4	...	...
M - week semaine[8]	149.0	157.9	158.7	203.3	194.3	247.7	254.4	254.5	...	...
F - week semaine[8]	97.5	108.5	118.6	122.0	137.7	151.7	148.8	161.7	...	...
Greece: drachma **Grèce : drachme**										
MF - hour heure[10 12]	# 314.2	354.1	388.2	459.7	554.0	661.3	772.1	878.2	970.8	1 097.9
M - hour heure[10 12]	# 347.2	393.2	430.2	509.2	614.5	733.8	854.7	967.5	1 063.6	1 200.1
F - hour heure[10 12]	# 269.5	302.3	333.7	397.4	481.0	575.3	673.2	765.3	851.4	963.4
Guam: US dollar **Guam : dollar des Etats-Unis**										
MF - hour heure[3 8]	6.2	6.3	6.0	6.3	7.3	8.1	9.1	9.3	10.1	...
Guatemala: quetzal **Guatemala : quetzal**										
MF - month mois[1]	266.9	296.9	331.2	365.2	435.1	473.6	577.9	686.2	775.2	...
Hong Kong: Hong Kong dollar **Hong-kong : dollar de Hong Kong**										
MF - day jour	98.3	106.4	119.4	136.9	157.0	179.5	200.7	218.6	242.0	266.6
M - day jour	115.1	125.9	143.3	166.1	191.7	224.5	249.9	274.8	314.5	333.5
F - day jour	91.2	98.1	108.2	123.7	140.3	155.8	173.6	189.6	207.0	226.3

31
Earnings in manufacturing
By hour, day, week or month [*cont.*]
Gains dans les industries manufacturières
Par heure, jour, semaine ou mois [*suite*]

Country or area and unit Pays ou zone et unité	1985	1986	1987	1988	1989	1990	1991	1992	1993	1994
Hungary: forint Hongrie : forint										
MF - month mois[24]	5 366.0[28]	5 716.0[28]	6 214.0[28]	7 761.0	9 121.0	11 167.0	13 992.0	17 636.0	21 751.0	...
India: Indian rupee Inde : roupie indienne										
MF - month mois[22]	740.2	890.7	862.9	913.2	841.2	* 1 045.5	* 1 094.9	...	...	...
Ireland: Irish pound Irlande : livre irlandaise										
MF - hour heure[8][29]	# 4.2	4.5	4.7	4.9	5.1	5.4	5.6	5.9	6.2	...
M - hour heure[8][23]	# 4.8	5.1	5.3	5.5	5.7	6.0	6.3	6.6	7.0	...
F - hour heure[8][23]	# 3.2	3.5	3.6	3.8	4.0	4.2	4.4	4.7	5.0	...
Isle of Man: pound sterling Ile de Man : livre sterling										
MF - week semaine[18]	...	...	...	...	...	...	...	207.0	225.0	238.0
M - week semaine[18]	...	...	...	...	...	...	...	...	276.0	252.0
F - week semaine[18]	...	...	...	...	...	...	...	...	148.0	199.0
Israel: new sheqel Israël : nouveau sheqel										
MF - month mois[1][30][31]	...	...	...	...	...	2 669.0	3 080.0	3 514.0	3 917.0	4 388.0
Italy: Italian lira Italie : lire italienne										
MF - hour heure[32]	...	...	...	...	...	100.0	109.5	115.7	120.5	124.3
Jamaica: Jamaican dollar Jamaïque : dollar jamaïquain										
MF - week semaine[1]	...	271.9	309.4	345.9	391.8	450.6[11]	701.0	895.0	...	...
Japan: yen Japon : yen										
MF - month mois[1][15][33]	299 531.0	305 414.0	313 170.0	318 663.0	336 648.0	352 020.0	368 011.0	372 594.0	371 356.0	...
M - month mois[1][15][33]	367 182.0	373 324.0	381 138.0	393 804.0	414 981.0	436 135.0	450 336.0	454 482.0	...	...
F - month mois[1][15][33]	154 571.0	158 550.0	163 944.0	164 673.0	173 097.0	180 253.0	193 112.0	198 058.0	...	...
Jordan: Jordanian dinar Jordanie : dinar jordanien										
MF - day jour[18]	4.0	4.2	4.5	4.2	4.4	4.6	4.6	4.8	4.9	...
M - day jour[18]	4.0	4.4	4.7	4.3	4.6	4.8	4.9	5.0	5.1	...
F - day jour[18]	2.5	2.7	2.7	2.7	2.8	2.7	3.0	2.9	3.1	...
Kazakstan: tenge Kazakstan : tenge										
MF - month mois[1]	199.0[27]	204.0[27]	209.0[27]	229.0[27]	250.0[27]	277.0[27]	489.0[27]	5 675.0[27]	144.0	...
Kenya: Kenya shilling Kenya : shilling kényen										
MF - month mois[18][18]	1 928.7	2 078.1	2 293.8	2 469.7	2 797.5	3 064.6	3 324.2	...	...	...
M - month mois[18][18]	2 025.2	2 137.8	2 376.7	2 576.0	2 890.9	3 159.8	3 430.1	...	...	...
F - month mois[18][18]	1 531.0	1 554.3	1 551.1	1 751.7	2 001.7	2 317.7	2 515.8	...	...	...
Korea, Republic of: won of the Rep. of Korea Corée, République de : won de la Rép. de Corée										
MF - month mois[17][15][18]	270.0	294.0	329.0	393.0	492.0	591.0	690.0	799.0	# 885.0[34]	# 1 022.0[34]
M - month mois[17][15][18]	347.0	375.0	413.0	491.0	609.0	724.0	843.0	964.0	# 1 056.0[34]	...
F - month mois[17][15][18]	163.0	182.0	208.0	250.0	307.0	364.0	428.0	497.0	# 551.0[34]	...
Latvia: lats Lettonie : lats										
MF - month mois[13]	...	...	...	...	...	1.6[27]	3.2[27]	2.2[27]	46.8	...
M - month mois[13][27]	...	...	...	...	...	...	...	23.5	...	...
F - month mois[13][27]	...	...	...	...	...	...	...	20.2	...	...

31
Earnings in manufacturing
By hour, day, week or month [*cont.*]
Gains dans les industries manufacturières
Par heure, jour, semaine ou mois [*suite*]

Country or area and unit Pays ou zone et unité	1985	1986	1987	1988	1989	1990	1991	1992	1993	1994
Lithuania: litas Lituanie : litas										
MF - month mois[1,3]	...	...	...	...	...	...	...	5 884.0	...	...
Luxembourg: Luxembourg franc Luxembourg : franc luxembourgeois										
MF - hour heure[8,10]	320.0	332.2	339.2	357.0	374.0	379.0	400.0	425.0	446.0	...
M - hour heure[8,10]	331.1	344.3	352.4	375.0	393.0	399.0	420.0	446.0	466.0	...
F - hour heure[8,10]	207.3	209.1	217.2	218.0	234.0	248.0	265.0	278.0	300.0	...
Macau: Macao pataca Macao : pataca de Macao										
MF - month mois[20]	...	...	...	...	1 859.0[8]	2 058.0[8]	2 232.0[8]	2 509.0	2 926.0	...
M - month mois[20]	...	...	...	...	...	...	...	3 321.0	3 865.0	...
F - month mois[20]	...	...	...	...	...	...	...	2 222.0	2 447.0	...
Malawi: Malawi kwacha Malawi : kwacha malawien										
MF - month mois[1]	90.2	101.3	125.8	135.7	147.0	176.8	* 137.6	...	...	...
Malaysia: ringgit Malaisie : ringgit										
MF - month mois[1]	638.0	636.0	627.0	620.0	640.0	660.0	719.0	794.0	...	...
M - month mois[1]	825.0	844.0	838.0	848.0	864.0	885.0	952.0	1 037.0	...	...
F - month mois[1]	407.0	400.0	401.0	393.0	420.0	443.0	495.0	558.0	...	...
Mauritius: Mauritian rupee Maurice : roupie mauricienne										
MF - day jour[8,36,37]	33.8[35]	34.4[35]	37.6[35]	45.5	52.6	60.5	83.3	92.5	108.0	121.8
Mexico: Mexican new peso Mexique : peso nouveau mexicain										
MF - hour heure	# 314.0[38]	527.0[38]	1 337.0[38]	2 666.0[38]	3 257.0[38]	4 152.0[38]	5 217.0[38]	6 391.0[38]	7.0	8.0
Myanmar: kyat Myanmar : kyat										
M - month mois[1,11]	260.1	282.2	325.7	533.1	729.5	...	631.9	880.5	985.3	...
F - month mois[1,11]	256.8	243.6	261.1	496.9	705.6	...	670.9	866.8	940.2	...
Netherlands: Netherlands guilder Pays-Bas : florin néerlandais										
MF - hour heure[1,8,29]	19.0	19.4	19.9	20.3	20.8	21.5	22.3	22.7	23.4	...
M - hour heure[1,8,23]	20.1	20.5	21.0	21.5	21.9	22.8	23.5	23.9	24.5	...
F - hour heure[1,8,23]	15.0	15.4	15.6	16.1	16.5	17.1	17.8	18.3	19.0	...
New Zealand: New Zealand dollar Nouvelle-Zélande : dollar néo-zélandais										
MF - hour heure[1,39]	8.4	10.1	11.0	12.0	12.6	13.4	13.9	14.1	14.2	14.5
M - hour heure[1,39]	9.1	10.9	11.9	12.9	13.5	14.4	14.8	15.0	15.1	15.4
F - hour heure[1,39]	6.4	7.8	8.6	9.6	10.2	10.8	11.2	11.6	11.6	11.9
Nicaragua: córdoba Nicaragua : córdoba										
MF - hour heure[1]	...	...	...	...	5.8[7,40]	590.1[7,40]	4.7	8.0	...	...
Norway: Norwegian krone Norvège : couronne norvégienne										
MF - hour heure[18,23]	61.5	67.7	78.6	83.0	87.3	92.5	97.3	100.4	103.2	106.1
M - hour heure[18,23]	63.3	69.7	81.0	85.4	89.5	94.6	99.5	102.7	105.4	108.5
F - hour heure[18,23]	52.9	58.4	67.8	72.0	76.5	81.8	86.7	89.2	91.8	94.6
Pakistan: Pakistan rupee Pakistan : roupie pakistanaise										
MF - month mois[1]	881.6	1 026.4	1 115.4	1 130.9	1 289.7	...	...	...	...	...
Panama: balboa Panama : balboa										
MF - month mois[1]	...	...	464.0	462.0	459.0	455.0	...	...	...	...

31
Earnings in manufacturing
By hour, day, week or month [cont.]
Gains dans les industries manufacturières
Par heure, jour, semaine ou mois [suite]

Country or area and unit Pays ou zone et unité	1985	1986	1987	1988	1989	1990	1991	1992	1993	1994
Paraguay: guaraní Paraguay : guaraní										
MF - month mois[1]	53 100.0	67 466.0	...	115 897.0	177 464.0	220 548.0	273 537.0	298 682.0	380 096.0	480 081.0
M - month mois[1]	54 216.0	68 493.0	...	118 473.0	170 222.0	234 234.0	292 787.0	342 552.0	407 117.0	507 072.0
F - month mois[1]	47 127.0	62 324.0	...	105 252.0	212 743.0	155 744.0	196 738.0	177 754.0	298 952.0	389 558.0
Peru: nuevo sol Pérou : nouveau sol										
MF - day jour[10 42]	26.7[8 41]	# 80.6[41]	161.0[41]	758.2[41]	18 636.6[41]	0.3	6.0	10.1	14.8	21.9
Philippines: Philippine peso Philippines : peso philippin										
MF - month mois[1 12 43]	1 951.0	2 183.0	2 537.0	2 995.0	3 441.0	4 263.0	4 831.0	...	...	...
Poland: zloty Pologne : zloty										
MF - month mois[1 18]	19 901.0[13]	24 076.0[13]	29 382.0[13]	54 708.0[13]	212 170.0[3]	996.0[7 13]	1 620.0[7]	2 679.0[7]	...	...
Portugal: Portugese escudo Portugal : escudo portugais										
MF - hour heure	...	...	...	...	281.0	324.0	370.0	419.0	436.0	...
M - hour heure	...	...	...	...	320.0	368.0	419.0	480.0	486.0	...
F - hour heure	...	...	...	...	222.0	254.0	295.0	326.0	390.0	...
Puerto Rico: US dollar Porto Rico : dollar des Etats-Unis										
MF - hour heure	5.2	5.3	5.4	5.6	5.8	6.0	6.3	6.6	7.0	7.2
Republic of Moldova: Moldovan leu République de Moldova : leu moldove										
MF - month mois[1]	185.6[27]	182.4[27]	188.2[27]	212.2[27]	244.4[27]	287.6[27]	475.2[27]	3 676.2[27]	37.8	143.2
Romania: Romanian leu Roumanie : leu roumain										
MF - month mois[28]	2 718.0[3]	2 728.0[3]	2 719.0[3]	2 835.0[3]	2 920.0[3]	3 146.0[3]	6 842.0[3]	17 959.0	54 245.0	...
San Marino: Italian lira Saint-Marin : lire italienne										
MF - day jour[1]	65 742.0	72 911.0	76 133.0	...	84 782.0	84 835.0	102 579.0	111 611.0	113 772.0	...
Seychelles: Seychelles rupee Seychelles : roupie des Seychelles										
MF - month mois[1]	1 956.0[22]	2 003.0[22]	2 075.0[22]	1 863.0[22 44]	1 975.0[22 44]	2 187.0[22 44]	2 259.0[22 44]	2 349.0[44]	2 454.0[44]	...
Sierra Leone: leone Sierra Leone : leone										
MF - week semaine[11 23]	45.7	79.7	80.5	...	...	...	...	...	...	...
Singapore: Singapore dollar Singapour : dollar de Singapour										
MF - month mois[1 45]	...	975.8	1 008.8	1 115.9	1 242.9	1 395.0	1 551.8	1 686.2	1 817.8	1 995.3
M - month mois[1 45]	...	...	...	...	1 623.0	1 797.5	1 970.1	2 127.4	2 266.2	2 473.8
F - month mois[1 45]	...	...	...	...	876.2	983.3	1 096.8	1 190.7	1 294.5	1 415.4
Slovakia: Slovak koruna Slovaquie : couronne slovaque										
MF - month mois[1]	2 912.0	2 973.0	3 017.0	3 088.0	3 156.0	3 262.0	...	...	...	...
Slovenia: tolar Slovénie : tolar										
MF - month mois[1]	7.0	16.0	35.0	110.0	1 895.0	8 696.0	14 742.0	43 321.0	62 473.0	...
South Africa: rand Afrique du Sud : rand										
MF - month mois[1 46]	805.0	911.0	1 045.0	1 215.0	1 438.0	1 660.0	1 890.0	2 195.0	2 446.0	...
Spain: peseta Espagne : peseta										
MF - hour heure[1]	564.0	620.0	678.0	735.0	780.0	902.0	994.0	1 080.0	1 159.0	1 221.0
Sri Lanka: Sri Lanka rupee Sri Lanka : roupie sri-lankaise										
MF - hour heure[11]	5.1	5.5	6.0	6.6	7.5	9.5	11.2	11.8	13.7	15.1

31
Earnings in manufacturing
By hour, day, week or month [cont.]
Gains dans les industries manufacturières
Par heure, jour, semaine ou mois [suite]

Country or area and unit Pays ou zone et unité	1985	1986	1987	1988	1989	1990	1991	1992	1993	1994
M - hour heure[11]	5.9	5.8	6.4	6.9	8.2	9.8	11.7	12.3	14.1	15.6
F - hour heure[11]	4.3	4.5	4.6	4.8	5.4	8.9	9.4	10.4	12.7	13.8
Sudan: Sudanese pound Soudan : livre soudanaise										
MF - month mois[10]	...	...	...	248.2	...	375.4	...	1 210.3	...	...
Swaziland: lilangeni Swaziland : lilangeni										
M - month mois[4 8]	881.0	946.0	1 032.0	941.0	1 040.0	1 380.0	1 415.0	1 486.0	...	...
F - month mois[4 8]	265.0	572.0	577.0	404.0	561.0	1 001.0	845.0	835.0	...	...
Sweden: Swedish krona Suède : couronne suédoise										
MF - hour heure[11 18 23]	58.6	62.7	67.0	72.2	79.3	87.3	91.7	98.3	98.5	...
M - hour heure[11 18 23]	59.8	63.9	68.5	73.8	81.1	89.5	93.8	100.7	100.7	...
F - hour heure[11 18 23]	53.7	57.8	61.7	66.4	72.6	79.5	83.7	90.1	90.1	...
Switzerland: Swiss franc Suisse : franc suisse										
M - hour heure[8 15 23]	19.0	19.9	20.5	21.3	22.1	23.4	25.0	26.2	26.8	...
F - hour heure[8 15 23]	12.8	13.4	13.8	14.3	15.0	15.9	17.0	17.8	18.4	...
Thailand: baht Thaïlande : baht										
MF - month mois[1 8 47]	2 826.0	2 631.0	...	...	2 996.0	3 357.0	3 688.0	4 016.0	4 258.0	4 230.0
Tonga: pa'anga Tonga : pa'anga										
MF - week semaine[1 8]	26.4	28.6	30.8	33.8	43.0	42.6	51.4	51.3	...	...
Turkey: Turkish lira Turquie : livre turque										
MF - day jour[1 8 31]	...	...	...	8 461.0	17 820.5	30 582.2	61 620.4	88 144.3	135 236.0	...
M - day jour[1 8 31]	...	...	...	8 642.9	18 679.1	31 231.1	62 140.3	91 204.1	138 746.1	...
F - day jour[1 8 31]	...	...	...	6 877.3	13 830.0	25 299.5	56 660.2	84 558.2	122 720.8	...
Ukraine: karbovanets Ukraine : karbovanets										
MF - month mois[1 13]	201.5[2]	193.5	198.2	215.8	...	...	...	...	...	...
former USSR†: rouble ancienne URSS† : rouble										
MF - month mois[12 13]	203.3	208.1	213.6	232.2	253.9	...	...	...	...	...
United Kingdom: pound sterling Royaume-Uni : livre sterling										
MF - hour heure[2 8 48 49]	3.6	3.9	4.1	4.4	4.8	5.2	5.6	6.0	6.2	6.3
M - hour heure[2 8 48 49]	3.9	4.1	4.4	4.7	5.1	5.5	6.0	6.4	6.6	6.7
F - hour heure[2 8 48 49]	2.6	2.8	3.0	3.2	3.4	3.8	4.1	4.3	4.5	4.6
United States: US dollar Etats-Unis : dollar des Etats-Unis										
MF - hour heure[50]	9.5	9.7	9.9	# 10.2[34]	10.5	10.8	11.2	11.5	11.7	12.1
United States Virgin Is.: US dollar Iles Vierges américaines : dollar des Etats-Unis										
MF - hour heure	9.4	9.6	9.4	9.9	10.9	11.9	12.5	13.7	15.0	...
Uruguay: Uruguayan peso Uruguay : peso uruguayen										
MF - month mois[1 51]	169.8	322.2	572.5	949.3	1 751.6	3 453.2	7 371.5	12 564.4	20 197.5	...
Yugoslavia, SFR†: Yugoslavian dinar Yougoslavie, Rfs† : dinar yougoslave										
MF - month mois[1 13]	3.9	8.0	16.6	44.6	773.0	...	...	...	...	...
Zimbabwe: Zimbabwe dollar Zimbabwe : dollar zimbabwéen										
MF - month mois[1 52]	435.4	471.2	527.9	590.3	665.5	796.1	928.1	1 123.3	1 242.1	1 456.7[11]

31
Earnings in manufacturing
By hour, day, week or month [*cont.*]

Gains dans les industries manufacturières
Par heure, jour, semaine ou mois [*suite*]

Source:
International Labour Office (Geneva).

† For detailed descriptions of data pertaining to
former Czechoslovakia, Germany, SFR Yugoslavia and former
USSR, see Annex I – Country or area nomenclature, regional
and other groupings.

1 Employees.
2 Including mining and quarrying (Bulgaria: and electricity,
gas and water; Cuba: and fishing and gas; Finland: and
electricity; United Kingdom: quarrying only).

3 State sector (Cuba: civilian; Bahrain and Guam: private
sector only; Bulgaria and Romania: and cooperative sector).

4 Skilled workers only.
5 Basic wages from collective agreements.
6 Australes: 1 peso = 10,000 australes.
7 Figures in thousands.
8 One month of each year.
9 Full-time adult non-managerial employees.

10 Wage earners.
11 Average of less than twelve months.
12 Establishments with 10 or more persons employed (Gambia: 5
or more persons; Hungary: 20 persons or more).
13 Socialized sector.
14 Citizens only.
15 Including family allowances (Germany: paid directly by the
employers; Japan: and mid and end of year bonuses).

16 Bujumbura only.
17 Paid by the hour.
18 Including the value of payments in kind (Sweden: including
holidays and sick-leave payments).

19 Index of monthly earnings; base: 1980 = 100.
20 Labour force sample survey.
21 Dinars; 1 kuna = 1,000 dinars.
22 Including electricity and water (Cuba: water only; India:
and gas and services).
23 Adults only.
24 Enterprises with 25 or more employees (Hungary: 20 or more
employees; Czech Republic: in 1991, enterprises with 100 or
more employees).
25 Excluding vacation pay.
26 Department of San Salvador only.
27 Roubles (Estonia: 1 kroon = 10 roubles; Kazakstan: 1 tenge =
500 roubles; Latvia: 1 lat = 200 roubles; Republic of
Moldova: 1 leu = 417 roubles).
28 Net earnings after deduction of income taxes.
29 Including juveniles.
30 Including payments subject to income tax.
31 Insurance statistics.
32 Index of hourly wage rates (1990=100).
33 1985: sample design revised.
34 New industrial classification.
35 Including workers on piece rates of pay.
36 Excluding sugar and tea factories.
37 Daily rates of pay.
38 Pesos: 1 new peso = 1,000 pesos.

Source:
Bureau international du Travail (Genève).

† Pour les descriptions en détails des données
relatives à l'ancienne Tchécoslovaquie, l'Allemagne, la Rfs
Yougoslavie et l'ancienne URSS, voir l'Annexe I –
Nomenclature des pays ou zones, groupements régionaux et
autres groupements.

1 Salariés.
2 Y compris les industries extractives (Bulgarie: et
l'électricité, le gaz et l'eau; Cuba: et la pêche et le gaz;
Finlande: et l'électricité; Royaume-Uni: y compris les
carrières seulement).
3 Secteur d'etat (Cuba: civils; Bahreïn et Guam: secteur privé
seulement; Bulgarie et Roumanie: et compris secteur de
coopératif).
4 Ouvriers qualifiés seulement.
5 Salaires de base fixés par conventions collectives.
6 Australes: 1 peso = 10,000 australes.
7 Données in milliers.
8 Un mois de chaque année.
9 Salariés adultes à plein temps, non compris les cadres
dirigeants.
10 Ouvriers.
11 Moyenne de moins de douze mois.
12 Etablissements occupant 10 personnes et plus (Gambie: 5
personnes et plus; Hongrie: 20 personnes et plus).
13 Secteur socialisé.
14 Nationaux seulement.
15 Y compris les allocations familiales (Allemagne: payées
directement par les employeurs; Japon: et les primes de
milieu et de fin d'année).
16 Bujumbura seulement.
17 Rémunérés à l'heure.
18 Y compris la valeur des paiements en nature (Suède: y
compris les versements pour les vacances et congés de
maladie).
19 Indices; base: 1980 = 100.
20 Enquête par sondage sur la main-d'oeuvre.
21 Dinars; 1 kuna = 1,000 dinars.
22 Y compris l'électricité et l'eau (Cuba: l'eau seulement;
Inde: et le gaz et les services).
23 Adultes seulement.
24 Les entreprises occupant 25 salariés et plus (Hongrie: 20
salariés et plus; République tchèque: en 1991, les
entreprises occupant 100 salariés et plus).
25 Non compris les versements pour congés payés.
26 Département de San Salvador seulement.
27 Roubles (Estonie: 1 couronne = 10 roubles; Kazakstan: 1
tenge = 500 roubles; Lettonie: 1 lat = 200 roubles;
République de Moldova: 1 leu = 417 roubles).
28 Gains nets après déduction de l'impôt sur le revenu.
29 Y compris les jeunes gens.
30 Y compris les versements soumis à l'impôt sur le revenu.
31 Statistiques d'assurances.
32 Indice des taux de salaire horaire (1990=100).
33 1985: plan d'échantillonnage révisé.
34 Nouvelle classification industrielle.
35 Y compris les travailleurs aux pièces.
36 Non compris les fabriques de sucre et de thé.
37 Rémunérés sur la base de taux de salaire journaliers.
38 Pesos: 1 nouveau peso = 1,000 pesos.

31
Earnings in manufacturing
By hour, day, week or month [*cont.*]

Gains dans les industries manufacturières
Par heure, jour, semaine ou mois [*suite*]

39 Establishments with the equivalent of more than 2 full-time paid employees.
40 Old córdobas: 1 new córdoba = 1,000 old córdobas.

41 Intís: 1 new sol = 1 million intís.
42 Lima only.
43 Computed on the basis of annual wages.
44 Earnings are exempted from income tax.
45 Social security statistics.
46 Including employers' non-statutory contributions to certain funds.
47 Average wage rates for normal/usual hours of work.

48 Full-time workers on adult rates of pay.

49 Excluding Northern Ireland.
50 Private sector: production and construction workers and non-supervisory employees.
51 Index of average monthly earnings (Oct.-Dec. 1984=100).
52 Including employers' contributions to pension, provident and other funds.

39 Etablissements occupant plus de l'équivaut de 2 salariés plein temps.
40 Anciens córdobas: 1 nouveau córdoba = 1,000 anciens córdobas.
41 Intís: 1 nouveau sol = 1 million d'Intís.
42 Lima seulement.
43 Calculés sur la base de salaires annuels.
44 Les gains sont exempts de l'impôts sur le revenu.
45 Statistiques de la sécurité sociale.
46 Y compris les cotisations des employeurs certains fonds privés.
47 Taux de salaire moyens pour la durée normale/usuelle du travail.
48 Travailleurs à plein temps rémunérés sur la base de taux de salaire pour adultes.
49 Non compris l'Irlande du Nord.
50 Secteur privée: ouvriers à la production, travailleurs à la construction et salariés sans activité de surveillance.
51 Indices des gains mensuels moyens (oct.-déc. 1984=100).
52 Y compris les cotisations des employeurs aux fonds de pension, de prévoyance et autres fonds.

32
Producers prices and wholesale prices
Prix à la production et des prix de gros
Index numbers: 1990 = 100
Indices : 1990 = 100

Country or area and groups	1988	1989	1990	1991	1992	1993	1994	Pays ou zone et groupes
Argentina								**Argentine**
Domestic supply[1][2]	0	6	100	210	223	227	228	Offre intérieure[1][2]
Domestic production	0	6	100	212	226	230	231	Production intérieure
Agricultural products[3]	0	6	100	195	230	243	223	Produits agricoles[3]
Industrial products[3][4]	0	6	100	215	225	228	232	Produits industriels[3][4]
Import products[4]	0	8	100	188	188	189	198	Produits importés[4]
Australia								**Australie**
Industrial products[3][4][5]	85	91	100	101	102	104	106	Produits industriels[3][4][5]
Exported goods	105	105	100	94	92	93	91	Produits exportés
Raw materials	87	96	100	97	102	102	100	Matières premières
Austria								**Autriche**
Domestic supply[2][6][7]	96	97	100	101	101	100	101	Offre intérieure[2][6][7]
Agricultural products	93	93	100	102	91	89	91	Produits agricoles
Producers' material[2][6][7]	95	99	100	99	98	97	98	Matériaux de production[2][6][7]
Consumers' goods[2][6]	94	95	100	102	103	103	105	Biens de consommation[2][6]
Capital goods[2][6]	100	98	100	101	102	99	100	Biens d'équipement[2][6]
Bangladesh								**Bangladesh**
Domestic supply[2][6][7]	86	92	100	104	108	110	117	Offre intérieure[2][6][7]
Agricultural products[2][6][8]	85	92	100	102	104	106	115	Produits agricoles[2][6][8]
Industrial products[2][6][8]	86	93	100	110	117	119	122	Produits industriels[2][6][8]
Raw materials[6]	79	90	100	103	108	110	...	Matières premières[6]
Finished goods[6]	86	90	100	104	114	117	118	Produits finis[6]
Belgium								**Belgique**
Domestic supply	94	99	100	99	99	98	99	Offre intérieure
Agricultural products[3]	97	102	100	101	104	102	104	Produits agricoles[3]
Industrial products	94	100	100	99	99	97	99	Produits industriels
Intermediate products	93	99	100	97	95	93	94	Produits intermédiaires
Consumers' goods	96	100	100	101	104	103	101	Biens de consommation
Capital goods	94	97	100	103	105	106	107	Biens d'équipement
Bolivia								**Bolivie**
Domestic supply	70	83	100	119	137	...	...	Offre intérieure
Agricultural products	68	81	100	117	136	...	...	Produits agricoles
Industrial products	72	85	100	119	135	...	...	Produits industriels
Import products	69	83	100	122	140	...	...	Produits importés
Brazil								**Brésil**
Domestic supply[9][10]	0	0	0	9	100	2 165	51 441	Offre intérieure[9][10]
Agricultural products[9][10]	0	0	0	12	100	2 238	68 799	Produits agricoles[9][10]
Industrial products[9][10]	0	0	0	10	100	2 181	47 619	Produits industriels[9][10]
Raw materials[9][10]	0	0	0	10	100	2 163	50 194	Matières premières[9][10]
Producers' material[9][10]	0	0	0	9	100	2 151	49 041	Matériaux de production[9][10]
Consumers' goods[9][10]	0	0	0	11	100	2 139	55 556	Biens de consommation[9][10]
Capital goods[10]	0	0	0	8	100	2 078	46 373	Biens d'équipement[10]
Canada								**Canada**
Agricultural products[3]	98	103	100	94	93	...	...	Produits agricoles[3]
Industrial products[3][4]	98	100	100	99	99	103	105	Produits industriels[3][4]
Raw materials[11]	93	96	100	94	95	100	108	Matières premières[11]

32
Producers prices and wholesale prices
Index numbers: 1990 = 100 [cont.]
Prix à la production et des prix de gros
Indices : 1990 = 100 [suite]

Country or area and groups	1988	1989	1990	1991	1992	1993	1994	Pays ou zone et groupes
Intermediate products	99	101	100	97	97	100	102	Produits intermédiaires
Finished goods	95	97	100	102	104	107	108	Produits finis
Chile								**Chili**
Domestic supply	71	82	100	122	136	147	159	Offre intérieure
Domestic production	70	81	100	123	140	151	163	Production intérieure
Agricultural products	66	81	100	122	140	150	163	Produits agricoles
Industrial products[7]	71	80	100	123	140	153	166	Produits industriels [7]
Import products	79	87	100	112	116	128	136	Produits importés
Colombia								**Colombie**
Domestic supply[26]	61	77	100	123	145	164	198	Offre intérieure [26]
Domestic production[6]	61	76	100	125	149	170	208	Production intérieure [6]
Agricultural products[6]	64	82	100	130	154	172	236	Produits agricoles [6]
Industrial products[6]	61	76	100	123	145	165	191	Produits industriels [6]
Import products[6]	62	79	100	113	123	136	150	Produits importés [6]
Exported goods[6]	65	62	100	97	102	112	156	Produits exportés [6]
Raw materials[6]	64	79	100	118	144	176	201	Matières premières [6]
Intermediate products[6]	61	79	100	121	139	155	188	Produits intermédiaires [6]
Finished goods[6]	72	93	100	128	158	183	223	Produits finis [6]
Costa Rica								**Costa Rica**
Domestic supply	76	87	100	89	...	...	...	Offre intérieure
Croatia								**Croatie**
Industrial products[10]	...	0	4	11	100	1 613	2 865	Produits industriels [10]
Producers' material[10]	...	0	4	10	100	1 649	2 865	Matériaux de production [10]
Consumers' goods[10]	...	0	6	12	100	1 559	2 915	Biens de consommation [10]
Capital goods[10]	...	0	4	9	100	1 595	2 653	Biens d'équipement [10]
Cyprus								**Chypre**
Industrial products	90	95	100	104	107	110	112	Produits industriels
Czech Republic								**République tchèque**
Agricultural products	...	...	100	98	105	113	120	Produits agricoles
Denmark								**Danemark**
Domestic supply[39]	94	99	100	101	100	99	100	Offre intérieure [39]
Domestic production[312]	93	98	100	101	101	100	100	Production intérieure [312]
Import products[9]	93	99	100	100	98	97	100	Produits importés [9]
Producers' material	93	99	100	101	99	99	100	Matériaux de production
Consumers' goods	95	99	100	102	101	99	101	Biens de consommation
Dominican Republic								**Rép. dominicaine**
Domestic supply[6713]	33	53	100	125	134	...	...	Offre intérieure [6713]
Industrial products	44	67	100	100	115	...	...	Produits industriels
Ecuador								**Equateur**
Agricultural products	43	73	100	138	215	...	...	Produits agricoles
Industrial products	37	66	100	151	230	...	...	Produits industriels
Egypt								**Egypte**
Domestic supply[67]	67	86	100	118	133	131	162	Offre intérieure [67]
Raw materials[6]	57	77	100	120	147	170	106	Matières premières [6]
Intermediate products[6]	57	74	100	123	143	143	146	Produits intermédiaires [6]
Finished goods[6]	67	81	100	121	139	150	162	Produits finis [6]

32
Producers prices and wholesale prices
Index numbers: 1990 = 100 [cont.]
Prix à la production et des prix de gros
Indices : 1990 = 100 [suite]

Country or area and groups	1988	1989	1990	1991	1992	1993	1994	Pays ou zone et groupes
Capital goods[6]	69	85	100	137	192	212	153	Biens d'équipement[6]
El Salvador								**El Salvador**
Domestic supply[14]	77	84	100	107	109	118	127	Offre intérieure[14]
Finland								**Finlande**
Domestic supply	92	97	100	100	101	105	106	Offre intérieure
Domestic production	91	96	100	100	100	101	103	Production intérieure
Import products	95	99	100	101	108	119	119	Produits importés
Raw materials	92	98	100	97	98	104	105	Matières premières
Finished goods	93	98	100	101	104	108	109	Produits finis
Consumers' goods	94	97	100	103	106	109	110	Biens de consommation
Capital goods	88	94	100	103	103	104	105	Biens d'équipement
France								**France**
Agricultural products	93	100	100	101	93	89	88	Produits agricoles
Germany †								**Allemagne†**
Domestic supply[15]	...	...	...	100	101	102	102	Offre intérieure[15]
Import products[15]	...	...	...	100	98	96	97	Produits importés[15]
Exported goods[15]	...	...	...	100	101	101	102	Produits exportés[15]
Finished goods[15]	...	...	...	100	103	104	105	Produits finis[15]
Producers' material[15]	...	...	...	100	101	101	101	Matériaux de production[15]
Consumers' goods[15]	...	...	...	100	103	104	105	Biens de consommation[15]
Capital goods[15]	...	...	...	100	103	104	105	Biens d'équipement[15]
F. R. Germany								**R. f. Allemagne**
Domestic production	97	101	100	100	100	99	100	Production intérieure
Agricultural products[16]	96	105	100	99	97	89	91	Produits agricoles[16]
Industrial products	95	98	100	102	104	104	104	Produits industriels
Import products	98	102	100	100	97	95	96	Produits importés
Exported goods	100	103	100	101	106	106	107	Produits exportés
Raw materials	97	105	100	96	93	90	93	Matières premières
Intermediate products	97	101	100	100	99	98	99	Produits intermédiaires
Greece								**Grèce**
Domestic supply[17 18 19]	76	86	100	117	130	145	158	Offre intérieure[17 18 19]
Domestic production[20 21]	74	84	100	119	133	149	162	Production intérieure[20 21]
Agricultural products[20 22]	70	81	100	123	125	132	150	Produits agricoles[20 22]
Industrial products[20 21]	75	84	100	118	135	153	165	Produits industriels[20 21]
Import products[17 18 19]	79	89	100	115	129	145	158	Produits importés[17 18 19]
Exported goods[20 21 23]	80	94	100	111	118	131	186	Produits exportés[20 21 23]
Honduras								**Honduras**
Domestic supply	61	62	100	134	148	166	...	Offre intérieure
Domestic production	...	...	100	142	160	185	...	Production intérieure
Agricultural products	...	...	100	146	157	199	...	Produits agricoles
Import products	...	...	100	122	128	138	...	Produits importés
India								**Inde**
Domestic supply	87	92	100	112	125	137	151	Offre intérieure
Agricultural products	91	94	100	116	138	147	160	Produits agricoles
Industrial products[4]	85	92	100	111	122	133	141	Produits industriels[4]

32
Producers prices and wholesale prices
Index numbers: 1990 = 100 [cont.]
Prix à la production et des prix de gros
Indices : 1990 = 100 [suite]

Country or area and groups	1988	1989	1990	1991	1992	1993	1994	Pays ou zone et groupes
Raw materials[24]	87	91	100	118	131	138	153	Matières premières[24]
Indonesia								**Indonésie**
Domestic supply[6][19]	84	91	100	105	111	115	121	Offre intérieure [6][19]
Domestic production	88	94	100	109	117	126	138	Production intérieure
Agricultural products[6]	85	93	100	108	118	131	156	Produits agricoles [6]
Industrial products[4][6]	89	94	100	110	117	124	131	Produits industriels [4][6]
Import products[6]	86	93	100	105	109	110	113	Produits importés [6]
Exported goods[6]	74	82	100	96	100	99	99	Produits exportés [6]
Raw materials[6]	...	86	100	98	101	103	108	Matières premières [6]
Intermediate products[6]	...	70	100	108	113	118	123	Produits intermédiaires [6]
Finished goods[6]	...	94	100	107	112	118	125	Produits finis [6]
Producers' material[6]	...	90	100	103	107	111	116	Matériaux de production[6]
Consumers' goods[6]	...	93	100	107	112	118	127	Biens de consommation [6]
Capital goods[6]	...	96	100	109	113	117	121	Biens d'équipement[6]
Iran, Islamic Rep. of								**Iran, Rép. islamique d'**
Domestic production[2][8]	68	82	100	126	170	192	302	Production intérieure[2][8]
Agricultural products[2][8]	...	95	100	128	162	171	268	Produits agricoles [2][8]
Industrial products[2][8]	55	66	100	124	166	188	291	Produits industriels [2][8]
Import products[2][8]	66	74	100	121	168	193	314	Produits importés [2][8]
Exported goods[2][8]	85	88	100	153	163	167	248	Produits exportés [2][8]
Raw materials[2][8]	72	78	100	126	149	155	287	Matières premières[2][8]
Ireland								**Irlande**
Domestic supply[3][17][25]	97	103	100	101	102	107	108	Offre intérieure[3][17][25]
Agricultural products[3][25]	107	113	100	96	98	104	106	Produits agricoles [3][25]
Industrial products[3][4][25]	97	102	100	101	103	107	108	Produits industriels [3][4][25]
Capital goods[8]	92	97	100	103	104	107	110	Biens d'équipement[8]
Israel								**Israël**
Industrial products[21]	74	92	100	117	129	139	150	Produits industriels[21]
Italy								**Italie**
Domestic supply[2][19]	87	93	100	105	107	113	117	Offre intérieure [2][19]
Agricultural products[3][8]	86	95	100	109	107	105	109	Produits agricoles [3][8]
Industrial products[3][21]	88	93	100	105	107	114	119	Produits industriels [3][21]
Producers' material	87	92	100	104	108	111	116	Matériaux de production
Consumers' goods	89	95	100	107	112	115	120	Biens de consommation
Capital goods	89	95	100	105	106	112	116	Biens d'équipement
Japan								**Japon**
Domestic supply[2][6]	96	98	100	101	102	102	95	Offre intérieure [2][6]
Domestic production[6]	97	99	100	102	101	99	97	Production intérieure [6]
Agricultural products[6][8]	98	99	100	101	102	101	98	Produits agricoles [6][8]
Industrial products[6][8]	97	99	100	102	101	101	97	Produits industriels [6][8]
Import products[6][17]	94	98	100	99	96	96	98	Produits importés [6][17]
Exported goods[23]	102	104	100	102	101	95	105	Produits exportés [23]
Raw materials[6]	87	94	100	96	103	106	80	Matières premières [6]
Intermediate products[6]	96	98	100	101	100	100	93	Produits intermédiaires [6]
Finished goods[6]	98	99	100	101	102	102	98	Produits finis [6]
Producers' material[6]	94	97	100	100	97	101	92	Matériaux de production[6]

32
Producers prices and wholesale prices
Index numbers: 1990 = 100 [*cont.*]

Prix à la production et des prix de gros
Indices : 1990 = 100 [*suite*]

Country or area and groups	1988	1989	1990	1991	1992	1993	1994	Pays ou zone et groupes
Consumers' goods[6]	99	99	100	102	103	103	99	Biens de consommation[6]
Capital goods[6]	96	99	100	101	101	99	97	Biens d'équipement[6]
Jordan								**Jordanie**
Domestic supply[2 6]	65	87	100	105	110	111	112	Offre intérieure[2 6]
Korea, Republic of								**Corée, République de**
Domestic supply	95	96	100	105	107	109	112	Offre intérieure
Agricultural products[8 26]	87	88	100	111	115	114	128	Produits agricoles[8 26]
Industrial products	96	98	100	104	106	108	109	Produits industriels
Raw materials	91	93	100	109	106	108	110	Matières premières
Intermediate products	99	99	100	103	105	106	108	Produits intermédiaires
Finished goods	91	94	100	107	109	111	116	Produits finis
Producers' material	99	99	100	104	106	107	103	Matériaux de production
Consumers' goods	91	93	100	108	110	113	119	Biens de consommation
Capital goods	93	99	100	103	106	108	110	Biens d'équipement
Luxembourg								**Luxembourg**
Industrial products	95	102	100	97	95	94	94	Produits industriels
Import products	93	96	100	100	103	106	107	Produits importés
Exported goods	95	103	100	97	93	91	89	Produits exportés
Intermediate products	95	104	100	95	90	88	88	Produits intermédiaires
Consumers' goods[27]	97	100	100	106	111	113	101	Biens de consommation[27]
Capital goods	92	97	100	104	105	105	106	Biens d'équipement
Mexico								**Mexique**
Domestic supply[7 28]	72	81	100	119	133	142	151	Offre intérieure[7 28]
Agricultural products	51	70	100	123	151	159	167	Produits agricoles
Exported goods	64	78	100	99	106	104	117	Produits exportés
Raw materials	74	85	100	117	124	129	138	Matières premières
Consumers' goods[8 28]	71	81	100	123	139	150	158	Biens de consommation[8 28]
Capital goods[8 28 29]	80	86	100	120	132	143	150	Biens d'équipement[8 28 29]
Netherlands								**Pays-Bas**
Agricultural products[16 30]	97	105	100	101	98	94	94	Produits agricoles[16 30]
Industrial products	97	101	100	102	103	102	102	Produits industriels
Import products	94	101	100	98	94	91	92	Produits importés
Exported goods[23]	95	101	100	100	97	94	95	Produits exportés[23]
Raw materials	98	104	100	99	96	93	95	Matières premières
Intermediate products	98	102	100	101	101	99	100	Produits intermédiaires
Producers' material	96	102	100	98	95	92	94	Matériaux de production
Consumers' goods	96	99	100	103	106	107	105	Biens de consommation
Capital goods	96	98	100	101	102	102	104	Biens d'équipement
New Zealand								**Nouvelle-Zélande**
Domestic supply[3 31]	90	97	100	100	102	106	107	Offre intérieure[3 31]
Agricultural products	82	99	100	89	98	102	105	Produits agricoles
Industrial products	90	96	100	101	103	107	108	Produits industriels
Intermediate products	...	...	100	101	103	105	...	Produits intermédiaires
Finished goods[6]	...	...	100	100	102	105	...	Produits finis[6]
Norway								**Norvège**
Domestic supply	92	97	100	103	103	103	105	Offre intérieure

32
Producers prices and wholesale prices
Index numbers: 1990 = 100 [cont.]
Prix à la production et des prix de gros
Indices : 1990 = 100 [suite]

Country or area and groups	1988	1989	1990	1991	1992	1993	1994	Pays ou zone et groupes
Import products	93	99	100	98	97	97	98	Produits importés
Exported goods	86	96	100	97	89	89	87	Produits exportés
Raw materials	91	101	100	99	96	92	96	Matières premières
Finished goods	94	97	100	100	98	99	101	Produits finis
Consumers' goods	92	96	100	105	106	106	108	Biens de consommation
Pakistan								**Pakistan**
Domestic supply[2 6 7]	86	93	100	113	121	133	144	Offre intérieure [2 6 7]
Agricultural products[6]	87	94	100	111	122	136	159	Produits agricoles [6]
Industrial products[6]	81	89	100	116	122	127	151	Produits industriels [6]
Raw materials[6]	88	95	100	112	121	134	177	Matières premières [6]
Panama								**Panama**
Domestic supply	89	91	100	100	103	100	108	Offre intérieure
Peru								**Pérou**
Domestic supply	0	2	100	363	639	942	1 111	Offre intérieure
Domestic production	0	2	100	407	640	...	1 117	Production intérieure
Agricultural products[32]	0	2	100	450	720	1 089	1 378	Produits agricoles [32]
Industrial products[48]	0	1	100	395	618	936	1 051	Produits industriels [48]
Import products	0	1	100	393	626	962	1 050	Produits importés
Capital goods	0	11	100	427	689	1 036	1 276	Biens d'équipement
Philippines								**Philippines**
Domestic supply[33]	82	91	100	113	119	...	...	Offre intérieure [33]
Romania								**Roumanie**
Industrial products	81	81	100	308	862	2 103	4 016	Produits industriels
Singapore								**Singapour**
Domestic supply[7]	96	98	100	94	92	89	87	Offre intérieure [7]
Domestic production[3 4 34]	94	96	100	95	91	83	80	Production intérieure [3 4 34]
Agricultural products[3 34]	96	96	100	...	...	...	...	Produits agricoles [3 34]
Import products[17 34]	101	101	100	95	94	92	91	Produits importés [17 34]
Exported goods	100	100	100	95	88	86	83	Produits exportés
Slovakia								**Slovaquie**
Agricultural products	77	100	100	104	111	127	139	Produits agricoles
South Africa								**Afrique du Sud**
Domestic supply[35]	77	89	100	111	121	129	139	Offre intérieure [35]
Domestic production[36]	77	89	100	112	123	131	143	Production intérieure [36]
Agricultural products	92	96	100	110	129	137	155	Produits agricoles
Industrial products[4]	77	89	100	111	120	128	139	Produits industriels [4]
Import products	78	91	100	108	113	118	125	Produits importés
Spain								**Espagne**
Domestic supply[19]	95	99	100	101	103	105	110	Offre intérieure [19]
Producers' material	97	101	100	99	99	101	107	Matériaux de production
Consumers' goods	93	97	100	104	107	110	115	Biens de consommation
Capital goods	92	96	100	103	105	107	109	Biens d'équipement
Sri Lanka								**Sri Lanka**
Domestic supply	75	82	100	109	119	128	134	Offre intérieure
Domestic production	65	79	100	112	118	125	141	Production intérieure
Import products	70	79	100	106	110	116	121	Produits importés
Exported goods	95	88	100	108	127	141	132	Produits exportés

32
Producers prices and wholesale prices
Index numbers: 1990 = 100 [cont.]
Prix à la production et des prix de gros
Indices : 1990 = 100 [suite]

Country or area and groups	1988	1989	1990	1991	1992	1993	1994	Pays ou zone et groupes
Producers' material	69	82	100	109	...	...	...	Matériaux de production
Consumers' goods	78	92	100	109	120	129	130	Biens de consommation
Capital goods	62	72	100	113	118	134	156	Biens d'équipement
Sweden								**Suède**
Domestic supply[2 19 37]	89	96	100	101	100	106	111	Offre intérieure [2 19 37]
Domestic production[3 21 22]	89	96	100	102	101	103	107	Production intérieure [3 21 22]
Import products[19 37]	91	97	100	101	99	112	117	Produits importés [19 37]
Exported goods[19 37]	90	97	100	101	99	108	113	Produits exportés [19 37]
Producers' material	89	96	100	102	101	106	111	Matériaux de production
Switzerland								**Suisse**
Domestic supply[2 7]	94	99	100	100	100	101	100	Offre intérieure [2 7]
Domestic production[2 7]	95	98	100	101	102	103	102	Production intérieure [2 7]
Agricultural products[3]	99	99	100	101	97	95	97	Produits agricoles [3]
Import products[7]	94	101	100	98	96	96	96	Produits importés [7]
Raw materials	95	100	100	99	99	98	103	Matières premières
Consumers' goods	95	97	100	102	103	104	104	Biens de consommation
Syrian Arab Republic								**Rép. arabe syrienne**
Domestic supply	72	82	100	114	117	126	145	Offre intérieure
Raw materials	60	84	100	114	119	150	143	Matières premières
Intermediate products	85	93	100	140	118	119	150	Produits intermédiaires
Finished goods	41	66	100	111	114	96	106	Produits finis
Consumers' goods	47	79	100	102	104	113	102	Biens de consommation
Thailand								**Thaïlande**
Domestic supply[2 9]	92	96	100	106	106	106	109	Offre intérieure [2 9]
Agricultural products	93	98	100	112	114	108	113	Produits agricoles
Industrial products[4]	91	95	100	107	107	105	108	Produits industriels [4]
Exported goods[9]	99	101	100	101	103	101	115	Produits exportés [9]
Raw materials	98	103	100	109	109	100	110	Matières premières
Intermediate products	91	95	100	108	108	108	109	Produits intermédiaires
Finished goods	91	95	100	106	108	110	115	Produits finis
Consumers' goods	91	95	100	107	110	111	119	Biens de consommation
Trinidad and Tobago								**Trinité-et-Tobago**
Domestic supply	91	99	100	100	101	106	...	Offre intérieure
Tunisia								**Tunisie**
Agricultural products	85	91	100	106	111	122	122	Produits agricoles
Industrial products	88	96	100	102	103	105	108	Produits industriels
Turkey								**Turquie**
Domestic supply[2 19 38]	40	67	100	155	252	399	880	Offre intérieure [2 19 38]
Agricultural products	36	65	100	151	245	398	788	Produits agricoles
Industrial products	42	69	100	155	248	388	891	Produits industriels
United Kingdom								**Royaume-Uni**
Agricultural products[5]	92	98	100	105	108	119	125	Produits agricoles [5]
Industrial products[4 5]	89	95	100	105	107	110	113	Produits industriels [4 5]
Raw materials	95	100	100	99	97	102	104	Matières premières

32
Producers prices and wholesale prices
Index numbers: 1990 = 100 [cont.]
Prix à la production et des prix de gros
Indices : 1990 = 100 [suite]

Country or area and groups	1988	1989	1990	1991	1992	1993	1994	Pays ou zone et groupes
Finished goods	90	94	100	105	109	113	116	Produits finis
United States								**Etats-Unis**
Domestic supply[2]	92	97	100	100	101	102	104	Offre intérieure[2]
Agricultural products[3]	94	99	100	94	92	96	95	Produits agricoles[3]
Industrial products[3][39]	92	96	100	101	101	103	104	Produits industriels[3][39]
Raw materials	88	95	100	93	92	94	93	Matières premières
Intermediate products	94	98	100	100	100	102	103	Produits intermédiaires
Finished goods	91	95	100	102	103	105	105	Produits finis
Consumers' goods	90	95	100	102	103	104	104	Biens de consommation
Capital goods	93	97	100	103	105	107	109	Biens d'équipement
Uruguay								**Uruguay**
Domestic supply[3][29][40]	28	48	100	209	291	384	515	Offre intérieure[3][29][40]
Agricultural products[40]	35	60	100	150	363	381	523	Produits agricoles[40]
Industrial products[29][40]	28	48	100	195	305	416	554	Produits industriels[29][40]
Venezuela								**Venezuela**
Domestic supply[6][7]	40	79	100	122	151	205	363	Offre intérieure[6][7]
Domestic production[6][29]	38	77	100	123	155	211	372	Production intérieure[6][29]
Agricultural products[6][7]	45	64	100	135	168	211	316	Produits agricoles[6][7]
Industrial products[6][7]	39	80	100	121	150	204	367	Produits industriels[6][7]
Import products[6][7]	44	83	100	119	140	189	341	Produits importés[6][7]
Zambia								**Zambie**
Agricultural products	24	52	100	...	...	...	...	Produits agricoles
Industrial products	25	46	100	204	...	...	...	Produits industriels
Exported goods	28	45	100	227	...	...	...	Produits exportés
Producers' material	25	53	100	...	...	...	...	Matériaux de production
Consumers' goods	22	50	100	103	...	...	...	Biens de consommation
Capital goods	25	42	100	50	...	...	...	Biens d'équipement
Zimbabwe								**Zimbabwe**
Domestic supply	74	85	100	141	214	258	314	Offre intérieure
Domestic production	74	85	100	141	214	257	...	Production intérieure

Source:
Price statistics database of the Statistics Division of the United Nations Secretariat.

† For detailed descriptions of data pertaining to former Czechoslovakia, Germany, SFR Yugoslavia and former USSR, see Annex I - Country or area nomenclature, regional and other groupings.

1 Domestic agricultural products only.
2 Including exported products.
3 Including production of exported products.
4 Manufacturing industry only.
5 Prices relate only to products for sale or transfer to other sectors or for use as capital equipment.
6 Prices are collected from wholesalers.
7 Exclusive of products of mining and quarrying.
8 Including imported products.
9 Agricultural products and products of manufacturing industry.

Source:
Base de données pour les statistiques des prix de la Division de statistique du Secrétariat de l'ONU.

† Pour les descriptions en détails des données relatives à l'ancienne Tchécoslovaquie, l'Allemagne, la Rfs Yougoslavie et l'ancienne URSS, voir l'Annexe I - Nomenclature des pays ou zones, groupements régionaux et autres groupements.

1 Produits agricoles intérieurs seulement.
2 Y compris les produits exportés.
3 Y compris les produits exportés.
4 Industries manufacturiéres seulement.
5 Uniquement les prix des produits destinés à être vendus ou transférés à d'autres secteurs ou à être utilisés comme biens d'équipement.
6 Prix recueillis auprès des grossistes.
7 Non compris les produits des industries extractives.
8 Y compris les produits importés.
9 Produits agricoles et produits des industries manufacturières.

32
Producers prices and wholesale prices
Index numbers: 1990 = 100 [cont.]

Prix à la production et des prix de gros
Indices : 1990 = 100 [suite]

10 Base: 1992 = 100.
11 Valued at purchasers' values.
12 Agricultural production and manufacturing industry.
13 Sto. Domingo.
14 San Salvador.
15 Base: 1991 = 100.
16 Excluding forestry, fishing and hunting.
17 Imports are valued c.i.f.
18 Finished products only.
19 Exclusive of products of electricity, gas and water.

20 Production of finished goods only.
21 Excluding electricity, gas and water.
22 Including mining and quarrying.
23 Exports are valued f.o.b.
24 Primary articles include food articles, non-food articles and minerals.
25 Excluding Value Added Tax.
26 Including marine foods.
27 Beginning 1994, durable goods only.
28 Mexico City.
29 Excluding mining and quarrying.
30 Crop growing production only, excluding live stock production.
31 Output price index.
32 Excluding fishing.
33 Manila.
34 Not a sub-division of the domestic supply index.
35 Exclusive of products of gold mining.
36 Excluding gold mining.
37 Excluding agricultural products.
38 Exclusive of industrial finished goods.
39 Excluding foods and feeds production.
40 Montevideo.

10 Base : 1992 = 100.
11 A la valeur d'acquisition.
12 Production agricole et industries manufacturières.
13 Saint-Domingue.
14 San Salvador.
15 Base : 1991 = 100.
16 Non compris sylviculture, pêche et chasse.
17 Les importations sont évaluées à leur valeur c.a.f.
18 Produits finis uniquement.
19 Non compris les produits de l'électricité, du gaz et de l'eau.
20 Production de produits finis uniquements.
21 Non compris l'électricité, le gaz et l'eau.
22 Y compris les industries extractives.
23 Les exportations sont évaluées f.o.b.
24 Les articles premiéres comprennent des articles des produits alimentaires, non alimentaires et des mineraux.
25 Non compris taxe sur la valeur ajoutée.
26 Y compris l'alimentation marine.
27 A compter de 1994, biens durables seulement.
28 Mexico.
29 Non compris les industries extractives.
30 Cultures uniquement, non compris les produits de l'élevage.

31 Indice des prix de production.
32 Non compris la pêche.
33 Manila.
34 Pas un élément de l'indice de l'offre intérieure.
35 Non compris les produits de l'extraction de l'or.
36 Non compris l'extraction de l'or.
37 Non compris les produits agricoles.
38 Non compris les produits finis industriels.
39 Non compris les produits alimentaires et d'affouragement.
40 Montevideo.

33
Consumer price index numbers
Indices des prix à la consommation
All items and food; 1990 = 100
Ensemble et aliments; 1990 = 100

Country or area Pays ou zone	1985	1986	1987	1988	1989	1990	1991	1992	1993	1994
Afghanistan[12] **Afghanistan**[12]	27	26	31	40	68	100	144	...	...	...
Food[1] Aliments[1]	22	22	27	33	56	100	...	...	...	...
Albania[4] **Albanie**[4]	...	...	...	...	22[3]	23[3]	46[3]	100	185	227
Food[4] Aliments[4]	...	...	...	...	21[3]	21[3]	45[3]	100	187	214
Algeria[5] **Algérie**[5]	61	69	74	78	86	100	126	166	200	258
Food[5] Aliments[5]	59	69	75	77	84	100	120	151	188	265
American Samoa[2] **Samoa américaines**[2]	80	81	85	89	93	100	104	109	109	...
Food Aliments	81	83	85	89	94	100	104	108	107	...
Angola[67] **Angola**[67]	...	...	...	...	...	...	100	399	5 905	61 982
Food[67] Aliments[67]	...	...	...	...	...	...	100	409	6 856	70 425
Anguilla **Anguilla**	83	84	87	91	95	100	105	108	...	...
Food Aliments	78	81	82	87	95	100	104	107	...	...
Antigua and Barbuda **Antigua-et-Barbuda**	81	82	85	90	94	100	106	...	...	...
Food Aliments	79	78	83	87	94	100	106	...	...	...
Argentina[8 9 10] **Argentine**[8 9 10]	5	10	23	100	3 295	79 531	216 062	269 861	298 498	310 967
Food[8 9 10] Aliments[8 9 10]	5	10	23	100	3 187	71 040	185 492	241 460	266 327	270 038
Aruba **Aruba**	84	85	88	91	95	100	106	110	115	123
Food Aliments	72	74	80	85	92	100	105	109	113	120
Australia **Australie**	68	75	81	87	93	100	103	104	106	108
Food Aliments	71	77	82	88	96	100	104	105	107	109
Austria **Autriche**	90	91	93	94	97	100	103	108	111	115
Food Aliments	92	95	95	96	97	100	104	108	111	113
Azerbaijan **Azerbaïdjan**	...	...	...	...	...	100	207	2 092	25 711	453 423
Food Aliments	...	...	...	...	...	100	198	2 133	29 547	529 872
Bahamas **Bahamas**	78	82	87	91	96	100	107	113	117	118
Food Aliments	70	79	83	88	93	100	109	111	112	111
Bahrain **Bahrein**	101[11]	99	97	97	99	100	101	101	104	104
Food Aliments	105[11]	105	100	99	100	100	102	102	102	101

33
Consumer price index numbers
All items and food; 1990 = 100 [*cont.*]
Indices des prix à la consommation
Ensemble et aliments; 1990 = 100 [*suite*]

Country or area Pays ou zone	1985	1986	1987	1988	1989	1990	1991	1992	1993	1994
Bangladesh[12][13][14]										
Bangladesh[12][13][14]	**63**	**70**	**77**	**84**	**93**	**100**	**107**	**112**	**112**	**116**
Food[12][13][14]										
Aliments[12][13][14]	65	74	82	87	94	100	106	110	108	112
Barbados										
Barbade	**83**	**84**	**87**	**91**	**97**	**100**	**106**	**113**	**114**	**114**
Food										
Aliments	77	79	83	88	96	100	105	105	105	105
Belarus										
Bélarus	**90**	**93**	**94**	**94**	**96**	**100**	**# 194**[15]	**2 078**	**26 818**	**622 203**
Food										
Aliments	87	93	97	97	97	100	# 188[15]	2 173	32 920	814 304
Belgium										
Belgique	**90**	**91**	**93**	**94**	**97**	**100**	**103**	**106**	**109**	**111**
Food										
Aliments	92	94	94	94	96	100	102	102	101	103
Belize										
Belize	**90**	**90**	**92**	**95**	**97**	**100**	**106**	**# 102**[7]	**104**[7]	**106**[7]
Food										
Aliments	89	89	91	94	98	100	106	# 103[7]	105[7]	106[7]
Benin										
Bénin	**78**	**82**	**85**	**90**	**94**	**100**	**104**	**107**	**110**	**113**
Food										
Aliments	113	106	105	104	101	100	100	# 106[7]	...	...
Bermuda										
Bermudes	**78**	**82**	**85**	**90**	**94**	**100**	**104**	**107**	**110**	**113**
Food										
Aliments	78	80	84	88	95	100	103	104	106	107
Bolivia[7][16]										
Bolivie[7][16]	...	...	...	...	...	...	**100**	**113**	**123**	**132**
Food[7][16]										
Aliments[7][16]	...	...	...	...	...	...	100	115	122	133
Botswana										
Botswana	**62**	**68**	**74**	**80**	**90**	**100**	**112**	**130**	**149**	**164**
Food										
Aliments	62	68	75	82	90	100	112	133	151	165
Brazil[18]										
Brésil[18]	**0**[17]	**0**[17]	**1**[17]	**8**[17]	**100**[17]	**# 2**[4]	**9**[4]	**100**[4]	**2 020**[4]	**52 581**[4]
Food[18]										
Aliments[18]	0[17]	0[17]	1[17]	7[17]	100[17]	# 2[4]	9[4]	100[4]	1 995[4]	54 511[4]
British Virgin Islands										
Iles Vierges britanniques	**84**	**86**	**87**	**91**	**95**	**100**	**106**	**110**	...	...
Food										
Aliments	87	89	88	92	97	100	107	109	...	...
Brunei Darussalam										
Brunéi Darussalam	**93**[12]	**94**[12]	**96**[12]	**97**[12]	**98**[12]	**100**[12]	**102**	**103**	**107**	**110**
Food										
Aliments	96[12]	97[12]	98[12]	99[12]	100[12]	100[12]	103	103	106	107
Bulgaria										
Bulgarie	**90**[17]	**93**[17]	**93**[17]	**94**[17]	**100**[17]	**# 100**	**439**	**787**	**1 450**	**2 842**
Food										
Aliments	93[17]	97[17]	97[17]	98[17]	100[17]	# 100	475	830	1 614	3 287
Burkina Faso[19]										
Burkina Faso[19]	**103**	**100**	**97**	**101**	**101**	**100**	**103**	**101**	**101**	**126**
Food[19]										
Aliments[19]	116	107	95	106	101	100	110	101	96	113

33
Consumer price index numbers
All items and food; 1990 = 100 [*cont.*]
Indices des prix à la consommation
Ensemble et aliments; 1990 = 100 [*suite*]

Country or area Pays ou zone	1985	1986	1987	1988	1989	1990	1991	1992	1993	1994
Burundi[20]										
Burundi[20]	73	75	80	84	93	100	109	# 102[7]	112[7]	128[7]
Food[20]										
Aliments[20]	79	74	73	79	93	100	107	# 98[7]	114[7]	134[7]
Cameroon[10 21]										
Cameroun[10 21]	81	87	98	100	98[11]	100[11]	102	103	...	...
Food[10 21]										
Aliments[10 21]	93	94	100	100	93[11]	83[11]	83	81	...	...
Canada										
Canada	80	84	87	91	95	100	106	107	109	109
Food										
Aliments	82	86	90	93	96	100	105	104	106	107
Cape Verde[2 22]										
Cap-Vert[2 22]	72	79	83	86	90	100	110	# 125[17 23]	138[17 23]	141[17 23]
Food[22]										
Aliments[22]	67	76	79	81	89	100	112	# 134[17]	146[17]	145[17]
Cayman Islands										
Iles Caïmanes	78	80	83	88	93	100	108	111	...	...
Food										
Aliments	83	85	86	88	92	100	103	103	...	...
Central African Rep.[2 24]										
Rép. centrafricaine[2 24]	109	111	104	100	100	100	97	96	94	117
Food[24]										
Aliments[24]	114	114	103	98	99	100	96	95	91	113
Chad[25]										
Tchad[25]	128[26]	106[26]	100[11 26]	# 105	100	100	...	...	...	...
Food[25]										
Aliments[25]	158[26]	117[26]	100[11 26]	# 110	100	100	...	...	...	...
Chile[27]										
Chili[27]	41	49	59	68	79	100	122	141	159	177
Food[27]										
Aliments[27]	38	47	58	66	79	100	126	148	165	181
China										
Chine	60	65	70	85	99	100	105	113	133	166
Food										
Aliments	60	64	70	85	99	100	103	114	132	174
Colombia[28]										
Colombie[28]	33	39	48	61	77	100	130	167	203	250
Food[28]										
Aliments[28]	32	38	48	63	79	100	130	168	194	234
Congo[29]										
Congo[29]	98	98	99	97	97	100	98	94	99	141
Food[29]										
Aliments[29]	107	104	105	99	99	100	96	88	94	139
Cook Islands[30]										
Iles Cook[30]	76[10]	83[10]	92[10]	100[10]	# 95	100	106	110	118	121
Food[30]										
Aliments[30]	76[10]	84[10]	92[10]	100[10]	# 96	100	102	106	113	115
Costa Rica[8 31]										
Costa Rica[8 31]	45	51	60	72	84	100	129	157	172	195
Food[8 31]										
Aliments[8 31]	47	52	60	72	85	100	126	156	173	197
Côte d'Ivoire[7 28 32]										
Côte d'Ivoire[7 28 32]	80	86	92	98	99[11]	98[11]	100	...	...	...
Food[7 28 32]										
Aliments[7 28 32]	82	90	101	113	114[11]	98[11]	100	...	...	...

33
Consumer price index numbers
All items and food; 1990 = 100 [cont.]
Indices des prix à la consommation
Ensemble et aliments; 1990 = 100 [suite]

Country or area Pays ou zone	1985	1986	1987	1988	1989	1990	1991	1992	1993	1994
Croatia **Croatie**	**0**	**0**	**0**	**1**	**14**	**100**	**# 224**[15]	**1 646**	**26 105**	**53 818**
Food Aliments	0	0	0	1	16	100	# 223[15]	1 832	26 709	53 627
Cyprus **Chypre**[33]	**86**	**87**	**89**	**92**	**96**	**100**	**105**	**112**	**117**	**123**
Food[33] Aliments[33]	83	85	88	91	96	100	107	115	117	126
former Czechoslovakia† **anc. Tchécoslovaquie†**	**89**	**89**	**90**	**90**	**91**	**100**	**158**	**175**	**...**	**...**
Food Aliments	90	90	90	90	90	100	145	157	...	...
Czech Republic[7] **République tchèque**[7]	**..**	**...**	**...**	**...**	**...**	**...**	**100**	**111**	**134**	**148**
Food[7] Aliments[7]	...	...	...	...	...	...	100	109	127	139
Denmark **Danemark**	**83**	**86**	**89**	**93**	**98**	**100**	**102**	**105**	**106**	**108**
Food Aliments	90	91	92	96	100	100	100	102	102	105
Dominica **Dominique**	**82**	**84**	**89**	**90**	**97**	**100**	**106**	**111**	**113**	**115**
Food Aliments	83	84	91	94	102	100	105	114	117	115
Dominican Republic[17 34] **Rép. dominicaine**[17 34]	**37**	**41**	**48**	**69**	**100**	**...**	**...**	**...**	**...**	**...**
Food[17] Aliments[17]	33	37	44	68	100	...	...	...	...	...
Ecuador **Equateur**	**15**	**19**	**24**	**38**	**67**	**100**	**149**	**230**	**333**	**424**
Food Aliments	14	17	22	36	68	100	149	229	325	405
Egypt **Egypte**[33]	**41**	**50**	**60**	**71**	**86**	**100**	**120**	**136**	**153**	**165**
Food[33] Aliments[33]	37	47	57	69	86	100	117	126	136	149
El Salvador[16] **El Salvador**[16 33]	**35**	**46**	**57**	**69**	**81**	**100**	**114**	**127**	**151**	**167**
Food[16 33] Aliments[16 33]	29	39	48	63	79	100	118	133	167	193
Estonia **Estonie**	**...**	**...**	**...**	**...**	**...**	**100**	**302**	**3 553**	**6 744**	**9 960**
Food Aliments	...	...	...	...	...	100	333	3 453	6 004	8 011
Ethiopia[2 35] **Ethiopie**[2 35]	**94**	**84**	**82**	**88**	**95**	**100**	**136**	**150**	**155**	**167**
Food[35] Aliments[35]	104	88	83	89	95	100	141	158	160	177
Faeroe Islands **Iles Féroé**	**87**	**87**	**87**	**90**	**95**	**100**	**104**	**106**	**111**	**...**
Food Aliments	79	82	86	88	95	100	105	...	...	...
Falkland Is. (Malvinas)[36] **Iles Falkland (Malvinas)**[36]	**85**[2 10]	**91**[2 10]	**93**[2 10]	**100**[2 10]	**...**	**# 100**[23]	**105**[23]	**112**[23]	**113**[23]	**...**
Food[36] Aliments[36]	79[10]	81[10]	82[10]	92[10]	94	# 100	104	...	...	...

33
Consumer price index numbers
All items and food; 1990 = 100 [cont.]
Indices des prix à la consommation
Ensemble et aliments; 1990 = 100 [suite]

Country or area Pays ou zone	1985	1986	1987	1988	1989	1990	1991	1992	1993	1994
Fiji										
Fidji	**72**	**74**	**78**	**87**	**93**	**100**	**107**	**112**	**118**	**119**
Food										
Aliments	68	67	71	84	92	100	102	101	108	108
Finland										
Finlande	**79**	**81**	**84**	**88**	**94**	**100**	**104**	**107**	**110**	**111**
Food										
Aliments	86	89	91	93	96	100	103	103	102	102
France										
France	**86**	**88**	**91**	**93**	**97**	**100**	**103**	**106**	**108**	**110**
Food										
Aliments	86	89	91	92	96	100	103	104	104	105
French Guiana [37]										
Guyane française [37]	**85**	**87**	**91**	**93**	**97**	**100**	**102**	**105**	...	...
Food [37]										
Aliments [37]	86	87	91	92	96	100	101	102	...	...
French Polynesia										
Polynésie française	**92**	**93**	**94**	**96**	**99**	**100**	**101**	**102**	**104**	**106**
Food										
Aliments	98	95	92	94	98	100	99	100	102	105
Gabon [7 38]										
Gabon [7 38]	**90**	**96**	**95**	**87**	**93**	**100** [11]	**100**	**91**	**91**	**124**
Food [7 38]										
Aliments [7 38]	91	96	96	83	91	101 [11]	100	84	85	111
Gambia [39]										
Gambie [39]	**38**	**60**	**74**	**82**	**89**	**100**	**119**	**119**	**127**	**129**
Food [39]										
Aliments [39]	37	59	73	82	88	100	108	118	128	126
Germany † [7 40]										
Allemagne† [7 33 40]	...	...	...	...	...	**87** [11]	**100**	**111**	**121**	**125**
Food [7 33 40]										
Aliments [7 33 40]	...	...	...	...	...	93 [11]	100	103	104	106
F. R. Germany										
R. f. Allemagne [33]	**94**	**93**	**94**	**95**	**97**	**100**	**104**	**108**	**112**	**115**
Food [33]										
Aliments [33]	95	95	95	95	97	100	103	106	108	110
former German D. R. [17]										
anc. R. d. allemande [17]	**100**	**100**	**100**	**100**	**100**	...	...	...	...	...
Food [17]										
Aliments [17]	100	100	100	100	100	...	...	...	...	...
Ghana										
Ghana	**25**	**32**	**44**	**58**	**73**	**100**	**118**	**130**	**163**	**203**
Food										
Aliments	26	31	43	57	71	100	109	120	150	189
Gibraltar										
Gibraltar	**80**	**83**	**87**	**90**	**94**	**100**	**108**	**115**	**121**	**121**
Food										
Aliments	80	83	87	90	94	100	107	112	114	113
Greece										
Grèce	**45**	**55**	**64**	**73**	**83**	**100**	**120**	**138**	**158**	**176**
Food										
Aliments	46	55	62	69	83	100	119	136	153	173
Greenland										
Groënland	**78**	**82**	**84**	**91**	**95**	**100**	**104**	**106**	**107**	**108**
Food										
Aliments	83	83	86	88	94	100	105	106	107	108

33
Consumer price index numbers
All items and food; 1990 = 100 [cont.]
Indices des prix à la consommation
Ensemble et aliments; 1990 = 100 [suite]

Country or area Pays ou zone	1985	1986	1987	1988	1989	1990	1991	1992	1993	1994
Grenada										
Grenade	**89**	**90**	**89**	**92**	**97**	**100**	**103**	**107**	**110**	**112**
Food[33]										
Aliments[33]	83	85	85	89	96	100	102	102	107	112
Guadeloupe[16]										
Guadeloupe[16]	**88**	**91**	**93**	**95**	**97**	**100**	**103**	**106**	**108**[41]	**110**
Food[16]										
Aliments[16]	89	92	95	96	97	100	102	103	106[41]	108
Guam										
Guam	**70**	**72**	**75**	**79**	**88**	**100**	**110**	**121**	**132**	**...**
Food										
Aliments	58	63	69	77	85	100	118	136	160	...
Guatemala[16]										
Guatemala[16]	**37**	**51**	**57**	**64**	**71**	**100**	**133**	**142**	**162**	**182**
Food[16]										
Aliments[16]	33	46	53	60	67	100	131	138	157	182
Guinea[42]										
Guinée[42]	**...**	**...**	**51**	**65**	**84**	**100**	**119**	**140**	**149**	**156**
Food[42]										
Aliments[42]	...	...	50	67	78	100	116	135	148	155
Guinea-Bissau Guinée-Bissau										
Food[43]										
Aliments[43]	...	14[11]	26	42	75	100	158	...	...	...
Guyana[10][16]										
Guyana[10][16]	**52**	**56**	**71**	**100**	**167**[11]	**...**	**...**	**...**	**...**	**...**
Food[10][16]										
Aliments[10][16]	48	52	68	100	170[11]	...	...	...	...	...
Haiti[8]										
Haïti[8]	**81**	**84**	**74**	**77**	**83**	**100**	**115**	**131**	**166**	**249**
Food[8]										
Aliments[8]	85	88	71	76	81	100	115	126	160	208
Honduras										
Honduras	**66**	**68**	**70**	**74**	**81**	**100**	**134**	**146**	**161**	**196**
Food										
Aliments	63	65	65	70	79	100	144	153	172	219
Hong Kong										
Hong-kong	**71**	**73**	**77**	**83**	**91**	**100**	**112**	**122**	**133**	**143**
Food										
Aliments	70	71	74	81	91	100	111	121	130	138
Hungary										
Hongrie	**50**	**53**	**57**	**66**	**78**	**100**	**135**	**166**	**203**	**242**
Food										
Aliments	49	50	54	63	74	100	122	146	188	232
Iceland[44]										
Islande[44]	**40**	**48**	**57**	**72**	**87**	**100**	**107**	**111**	**115**	**117**
Food[44]										
Aliments[44]	39	48	56	74	89	100	103	104	106	104
India[45]										
Inde[45]	**66**	**72**	**78**	**85**[11]	**92**	**100**	**114**	**127**	**136**	**150**
Food[45]										
Aliments[45]	66	72	79	85[11]	92	100	116	131	139	155
Indonesia										
Indonésie	**75**[17]	**80**[17]	**87**[17]	**94**[17]	**100**[17]	**# 100**	**109**	**118**	**129**	**140**
Food										
Aliments	68[17]	74[17]	82[17]	93[17]	100[17]	# 100	108	116	125	138

33
Consumer price index numbers
All items and food; 1990 = 100 [cont.]
Indices des prix à la consommation
Ensemble et aliments; 1990 = 100 [suite]

Country or area Pays ou zone	1985	1986	1987	1988	1989	1990	1991	1992	1993	1994
Iran, Islamic Rep. of Iran, Rép. islamique d'	**39**	**46**	**59**	**76**	**93**	**100**	**118**	**148**	**180**	**236**
Food[33] Aliments[33]	46	58	71	81	97	100	119	159	193	255
Iraq Iraq	**55**	**56**	**63**	**77**	**82**	**# 100**[15]	**287**[11]	...	...	...
Food Aliments	47	47	58	72	77	# 100[15]	364[11]	...	...	...
Ireland Irlande	**85**	**88**	**91**	**93**	**97**	**100**	**103**	**106**	**108**	**111**
Food Aliments	85	89	91	94	98	100	101	103	104	107
Isle of Man Ile de Man	**77**	**79**	**82**	**86**	**92**	**100**	**107**	**112**	**115**	...
Food Aliments	72	75	79	85	91	100	108	113	118	...
Israel Israël	**34**	**51**	**61**	**71**	**85**	**100**	**119**	**133**	**148**	**166**
Food Aliments	36	56	65	76	92	100	114	129	135	150
Italy Italie	**76**	**80**	**84**	**88**	**94**	**100**	**106**	**112**[46]	**117**[46]	**121**[46]
Food Aliments	78	82	85	89	94	100	107	112	114	118
Jamaica Jamaïque	**54**	**62**	**66**	**72**	**82**	**100**	**151**	**268**	...	...
Food Aliments	49	58	62	68	82	100	155	275	...	...
Japan Japon	**94**	**94**	**94**	**95**	**97**	**100**	**103**	**105**	**106**	**107**
Food Aliments	94	94	93	94	96	100	105	105	107	107
Jordan Jordanie	**64**	**64**	**64**	**69**	**86**	**100**	**108**	**113**	**118**	**120**
Food Aliments	65	66	65	69	83	100	111	114	115	124
Kazakstan[4] Kazakstan[4]	...	...	...	...	...	...	3	100	2 265	...
Food[4] Aliments[4]	...	...	...	...	...	...	5	100	2 297	...
Kenya[28 47] Kenya[28 47]	**69**	**72**	**75**	**82**	**90**	**# 100**	**119**	**155**	**225**	**291**
Food[28 47] Aliments[28 47]	73	76	78	84	92	# 100	124	167	242	317
Kiribati[48] Kiribati[48]	**79**	**84**	**90**	**92**	**96**	**100**	**106**	**109**	**116**	...
Food[48] Aliments[48]	80	86	91	94	97	100	104	107	113	...
Korea, Republic of Corée, République de	**77**	**79**	**81**	**87**	**92**	**100**	**109**	**116**	**122**	**129**
Food Aliments	73	75	77	85	91	100	112	119	124	135
Kuwait[17] Koweït[17]	**94**	**95**	**95**	**97**	**100**	**110**[11]	**120**[11]	**119**	...	...
Food[17] Aliments[17]	98	98	96	96	100	112[11]	124[11]	121	...	...

33
Consumer price index numbers
All items and food; 1990 = 100 [cont.]
Indices des prix à la consommation
Ensemble et aliments; 1990 = 100 [suite]

Country or area Pays ou zone	1985	1986	1987	1988	1989	1990	1991	1992	1993	1994
Kyrgyzstan[4] **Kirghizistan**[4] Food[4]	...	...	...	...	...	...	...	**100**	**1 309**	**4 948**
Aliments[4]	...	...	...	...	...	...	...	100	1 079	3 394
Latvia[49] **Lettonie**[49] Food[49]	...	...	...	...	...	...	**100**	**1 052**	**2 199**	**2 989**
Aliments[49]	...	...	...	...	...	...	100	848	1 104	1 471
Lesotho **Lesotho** Food[33]	**53**	**63**	**70**	**78**	**90**	**100**	**118**	**138**	**157**	**169**
Aliments[33]	55	65	74	81	90	100	118	146	161	171
Liberia[17 50] **Libéria**[17 50] Food[10 50]	**79**	**82**	**86**	**94**	**100**	**108**[11]	...	...	...	...
Aliments[10 50]	85	84	84	100	110[11]	125[11]		...	...	...
Lithuania **Lituanie** Food	**94**[17]	**96**[17]	**99**[17]	**98**[17]	**100**[17]	**# 100**	**316**	**3 546**	**18 093**	**31 156**
Aliments	88[17]	95[17]	101[17]	100[17]	100[17]	# 100	318	3 295	16 528	26 610
Luxembourg **Luxembourg** Food	**92**[2]	**92**[2]	**92**[23]	**93**[23]	**96**[23]	**100**[23]	**# 103**[23 46]	**106**[23]	**110**[23]	**113**[23]
Aliments	91	94	92	93	96	100	# 103	104	104	105
Macau[2] **Macao**[2] Food	**74**	**76**	**79**	**85**	**93**	**100**	**110**	**118**	**126**	**134**
Aliments	73	73	76	83	92	100	109	118	126	135
Madagascar[2 51] **Madagascar**[2 51] Food[51]	**49**	**56**	**65**	**82**	**90**	**100**	**109**	**124**	**137**	**190**
Aliments[51]	53	62	67	80	88	100	109	127	138	193
Malawi[2 28 52] **Malawi**[2 28 52] Food[28 52]	**42**	**47**	**59**	**80**	**89**	**100**	**111**	**139**	...	...
Aliments[28 52]	40	46	58	77	89	100	113	145	...	...
Malaysia **Malaisie** Food	**91**	**91**	**92**	**94**	**97**	**# 100**[15]	**104**	**109**	**113**	**117**
Aliments	89	90	89	93	96	# 100[15]	105	112	114	120
Mali[53] **Mali**[53] Food[10 53]	...	...	...	**100**	**99**	**100**	**101**	**96**	**95**	...
Aliments[10 53]	...	...	...	102	99	100	103	94	93	...
Malta **Malte** Food	**93**	**95**	**95**	**96**	**97**	**100**	**103**	**# 102**[7]	**106**[7]	**110**[7]
Aliments	94	96	97	97	96	100	102	# 100[7]	...	...
Marshall Islands[4 54] **Iles Marshall**[4 54] Food[4 54]	...	...	...	...	...	...	...	**100**	**105**	...
Aliments[4 54]	...	...	...	...	...	...	...	100	103	...
Martinique **Martinique** Food[33]	**85**	**88**	**91**	**94**	**96**	**100**	**103**	**107**	**111**	**113**
Aliments[33]	87	90	94	95	96	100	103	107	109	111

33
Consumer price index numbers
All items and food; 1990 = 100 [cont.]
Indices des prix à la consommation
Ensemble et aliments; 1990 = 100 [suite]

Country or area Pays ou zone	1985	1986	1987	1988	1989	1990	1991	1992	1993	1994
Mauritius **Maurice**	**98**[26]	**99**[26]	**# 72**	**78**	**88**	**100**	**107**	**112**	**124**	**133**
Food Aliments	95[26]	98[26]	# 71	79	90	100	104	# 100[4]	114[4]	124[4]
Mexico **Mexique**	**7**	**13**	**31**	**66**	**79**	**100**	**123**	**142**	**156**	**166**
Food[33] Aliments[33]	7	14	32	66	80	100	120	134	142	150
Morocco **Maroc**	**80**	**86**	**89**	**91**	**# 94**[15]	**100**	**108**	**114**	**120**	**126**
Food[33] Aliments[33]	83	90	91	91	# 93[15]	100	109	116	123	132
Myanmar[55] **Myanmar**[55]	**42**	**46**	**57**	**67**	**85**	**100**	**132**	**161**	**213**	**264**
Food[55] Aliments[55]	40	43	54	65	84	100	138	168	234	281
Namibia[56] **Namibie**[56]	**55**	**62**	**70**	**78**	**90**	**100**	**112**	**133**	**144**	**159**
Food[56] Aliments[56]	47	54	63	72	86	100	105	126	134	152
Nepal **Népal**	**59**	**70**	**77**	**83**	**91**	**100**	**116**	**135**	**146**	**158**
Food Aliments	57	70	78	...	93	100	118	140	147	159
Netherlands **Pays-Bas**	**96**	**97**	**96**	**97**	**98**	**# 100**[15]	**103**	**106**	**109**	**112**
Food Aliments	99	98	97	97	98	# 100[15]	103	106	107	109
Netherlands Antilles[57] **Antilles néerlandaises**[57]	**86**	**87**	**91**	**93**	**96**	**100**	**104**	**105**	**108**	**110**
Food[57] Aliments[57]	76	77	81	87	93	100	107	110	114	117
New Caledonia[58] **Nouvelle-Calédonie**[58]	**89**	**91**	**91**	**94**	**98**	**100**	**104**	**107**	**109**	**113**
Food[58] Aliments[58]	94	93	92	96	100	100	103	106	110	114
New Zealand **Nouvelle-Zélande**	**64**	**72**	**84**	**89**	**94**	**100**	**103**	**104**	**105**	**107**
Food Aliments	64	71	81	86	93	100	101	101	102	102
Nicaragua **Nicaragua**	**1**[26]	**10**[26]	**100**[26]	**...**	**1**	**100**	**2 842**	**3 767**	**...**	**...**
Food Aliments	1[26]	9[26]	100[26]	...	1	100	2 851	3 503	...	...
Niger[2][59] **Niger**[2][59]	**116**	**113**	**105**	**104**	**101**	**100**	**92**	**# 98**[7]	**...**	**...**
Food[59] Aliments[59]	131	124	110	105	99	100	88	# 97[7]	...	...
Nigeria[60] **Nigéria**[60]	**...**	**38**	**44**	**62**	**93**	**100**	**113**	**163**	**257**	**403**
Food[60] Aliments[60]	...	35	41	63	96	100	112	164	259	380
Niue **Nioué**	**71**	**76**	**81**	**86**	**94**	**100**	**105**	**110**	**112**	**...**
Food Aliments	75	81	86	89	94	100	104	107	110	...

33
Consumer price index numbers
All items and food; 1990 = 100 [cont.]
Indices des prix à la consommation
Ensemble et aliments; 1990 = 100 [suite]

Country or area Pays ou zone	1985	1986	1987	1988	1989	1990	1991	1992	1993	1994
Northern Mariana Islands[61] **Iles Marianas du Nord**[61] Food[61]	**102**	**107**	...	**120**	**116**	**100**	**107**	**117**	**122**	...
Aliments[61]	94	96	...	104	99	100	107	112	116	...
Norway **Norvège** Food	**74**	**79**	**86**	**92**	**96**	**100**	**103**	**106**	**108**	**110**
Aliments	75	82	89	94	97	100	102	103	102	103
Oman[62] **Oman**[62] Food[62]	...	...	...	...	...	**100**	**105**	**106**	**107**	...
Aliments[62]	89	97	97	99	100	# 100[15]	103	102	101	...
Pakistan **Pakistan** Food	**72**	**75**	**78**	**85**	**92**	**100**	**112**	**122**	**134**	**151**
Aliments	70	72	76	85	92	100	111	123	135	154
Panama[63] **Panama**[63] Food[63]	**98**	**98**	**99**	**99**[11]	**99**	**100**	**101**	**103**	**104**	**105**
Aliments[63]	95	96	98	99[11]	99	100	102	106	106	108
Papua New Guinea **Papouasie-Nvl-Guinée** Food	**78**	**82**	**85**	**90**	**94**	**100**	**107**	**112**	**117**	**120**
Aliments	81	83	85	88	91	100	108	111	114	116
Paraguay[64] **Paraguay**[64] Food[64]	**29**	**38**	**47**	**57**	**72**	**100**	**124**	**143**	**169**	**204**
Aliments[64]	26	37	46	57	68	100	120	138	162	195
Peru[8][65] **Pérou**[8][65] Food[8][65]	**0**[17]	**0**[17]	**0**[17]	**3**[17]	**# 1**	**100**	**510**	**884**	**1 314**	**1 626**
Aliments[8][65]	0[17]	0[17]	1[17]	4[17]	# 1	100	448	770	1 150	1 357
Philippines **Philippines** Food[33]	**70**	**70**	**72**	**78**	**88**	**100**	**119**	**129**	**139**	**152**
Aliments[33]	70	69	71	78	89	100	115	123	131	142
Poland **Pologne** Food	**2**	**2**	**3**	**4**	**15**	**100**	**170**	**244**	**330**	**436**
Aliments	2	2	3	4	16	100	151	207	274	363
Portugal[2] **Portugal**[2] Food	**59**	**65**	**72**	**78**	**88**	**100**	**111**	**# 109**[7]	**116**[7]	**122**[7]
Aliments	59	65	71	77	88	100	110	# 107[7]	110[7]	115[7]
Puerto Rico **Porto Rico** Food	**87**	**86**	**89**	**91**	**95**	**100**	**103**	**106**	**109**	**113**
Aliments	82	83	85	88	92	100	105	111	118	127
Qatar **Qatar** Food	...	**88**	**90**	**94**	**97**	**100**	**104**	...	...	...
Aliments	...	91	93	95	99	100	106	...	...	...
Republic of Moldova[49] **République de Moldova**[49] Food[49]	...	...	...	...	...	...	**100**	**1 209**	**23 014**	**135 087**
Aliments[49]	...	...	...	...	...	...	100	1 188	20 382	...

33
Consumer price index numbers
All items and food; 1990 = 100 [*cont.*]
Indices des prix à la consommation
Ensemble et aliments; 1990 = 100 [*suite*]

Country or area Pays ou zone	1985	1986	1987	1988	1989	1990	1991	1992	1993	1994
Réunion[16] Réunion[16]	87	89	91	93	96	100[41]	104	107	111	114
Food[16] Aliments[16]	94	96	97	95	98	100[41]	105	107	111	112
Romania Roumanie	90	91	92	94	95	100	275	# 310[7]	1 105[7]	2 617[7]
Food Aliments	90	91	92	94	96	100	299	# 337[7]	1 174[7]	2 774[7]
Russian Federation[7] Fédération de Russie[7]	...	...	...	...	...	...	100	1 629	15 869	64 688
Food[7] Aliments[7]	...	...	...	...	...	...	100	1 690	16 750	67 338
Rwanda Rwanda	90	89	92	95	96	100	120	131	147	...
Food Aliments	87	79	85	93	95	100	114	122	...	...
Saint Helena Sainte-Hélène	98[10]	94[10]	97[10]	# 93	97	100	104	109	118	123
Food Aliments	94[10]	93[10]	97[10]	# 92	96	100	102	106	112	116
Saint Kitts and Nevis[66] Saint-Kitts-et-Nevis[66]	90	90	91	91	96	100	104	107	...	...
Food[66] Aliments[66]	92	92	93	93	98	100	106	111	...	...
Saint Lucia Sainte-Lucie	83	85	91	92	96	100	106	112	112	115
Food Aliments	81	83	93	92	96	100	108	113	113	118
Saint Pierre and Miquelon[11] Saint-Pierre-et-Miquelon[11]	88	86	87	90	96	100	...	...	...	...
Food[11] Aliments[11]	89	86	87	90	99	100	...	...	...	...
St. Vincent-Grenadines[67] St. Vincent-Grenadines[67]	87	88	91	91	93	100	106	110	115	115
Food[67] Aliments[67]	88	89	92	93	93	100	109	113	116	116
Samoa[2] Samoa[2]	68	72	75	82	87	100	99	107	109	129
Food Aliments	68	72	74	81	83	100	92	102	102	127
San Marino Saint-Marin	75	80	84	88	94	100	107	115	121	# 110[4]
Food Aliments	77	83	85	89	95	100	105	111	118	# 111[4]
Saudi Arabia[68] Arabie saoudite[68]	101	98	96	97	98	100	105	104	105	106
Food[33][68] Aliments[33][68]	99	98	96	96	98	100	108	112	113	111
Senegal[69] Sénégal[69]	99	105	101	99	100	100	98	98	98	129
Food[69] Aliments[69]	101	108	99	99	100	100	97	96	94	131
Seychelles Seychelles	91	91	93	95	96	100	102	105	107	109
Food Aliments	89	89	92	94	95	100	103	104	107	100

33
Consumer price index numbers
All items and food; 1990 = 100 [cont.]
Indices des prix à la consommation
Ensemble et aliments; 1990 = 100 [suite]

Country or area Pays ou zone	1985	1986	1987	1988	1989	1990	1991	1992	1993	1994
Sierra Leone[70]										
Sierra Leone[70]	4	8	22	29	47	100	183	259	...	...
Food[70]										
Aliments[70]	4	8	21	28	47	100	186	264	...	...
Singapore										
Singapour	94	93	93	95	97	100	103	106	108	112
Food										
Aliments	98	97	97	98	99	100	102	103	104	107
Slovakia										
Slovaquie	89	89	89	90	91	100	161	177	219	248
Food										
Aliments	90	90	90	90	90	100	147	158	191	222
Slovenia[7 16]										
Slovénie[7 16]	...	0	0	1	7	47	100	307	408	494
Food[7 16]										
Aliments[7 16]	...	0	0	1	8	47	100	306	384	473
Solomon Islands[71]										
Iles Salomon[71]	54	61	68	79	91	100	114	126	137	156
Food[71]										
Aliments[71]	54	60	65	78	92	100	117	130	142	158
South Africa										
Afrique du Sud	49	58	68	76	87	100	115	131	144	157
Food										
Aliments	45	55	67	78	86	100	120	150	160	182
Spain										
Espagne	73	80	84	88	94	100	106	112	117	123
Food[33]										
Aliments[33]	72	80	84	87	94	100	104	107	109	115
Sri Lanka[72]										
Sri Lanka[72]	56	60	65	74	82	100	112	125	140	151
Food[72]										
Aliments[72]	55	59	64	74	81	100	112	125	139	152
Sudan[28]										
Soudan[28]	14	18	23	35	60	100	224	478	...	...
Food[28 33]										
Aliments[28 33]	13	18	23	34	59	100	236	457	...	...
Suriname[73]										
Suriname[73]	42	50	76	82	82	100	126	181	441	2 065
Food[73]										
Aliments[73]	32	40	73	76	77	100	119	184	485	2 365
Swaziland[28]										
Swaziland[28]	...	...	...	...	89	100	102	122	137	157
Food[28]										
Aliments[28]	...	...	...	...	85	100	114	128	145	172
Sweden										
Suède	74	77	80	85	91	100	109	112	117	120
Food[33]										
Aliments[33]	76	81	84	88	93	100	105	99	100	102
Switzerland										
Suisse	88	89	90	92	95	100	106	110	114	115
Food										
Aliments	89	90	91	93	95	100	105	106	106	106
Syrian Arab Republic[74]										
Rép. arabe syrienne[74]	...	...	60	78	90	100	109	121	137	158
Food[74]										
Aliments[74]	...	...	57	75	84	100	106	113	126	154

33
Consumer price index numbers
All items and food; 1990 = 100 [cont.]
Indices des prix à la consommation
Ensemble et aliments; 1990 = 100 [suite]

Country or area Pays ou zone	1985	1986	1987	1988	1989	1990	1991	1992	1993	1994
Thailand[75] **Thaïlande**[75]	**83**	**84**	**86**	**90**	**94**	**100**	**106**	**110**	**114**	**120**
Food[75] Aliments[75]	79	80	81	86	93	100	107	112	114	122
TFYR Macedonia **L'ex-R.y. Macédoine**	**0**	**0**	**0**	**1**	**14**	**100**	**211**	**3 397**	**15 692**	**35 826**
Food Aliments	0	0	0	1	16	100	205	3 462	15 434	34 419
Togo[76] **Togo**[76]	**96**	**100**	**100**	**100**	**99**	**100**	**101**	...	...	...
Food[76] Aliments[76]	101	105	104	119	98	100	96	...	...	...
Tonga[2] **Tonga**[2]	**62**	**75**	**79**	**87**	**90**	**100**	**109**	**118**	**119**	...
Food Aliments	67	84	87	95	94	100	108	121	·116	...
Trinidad and Tobago **Trinité-et-Tobago**	**63**	**68**	**75**	**81**	**90**	**100**	**104**	**111**	**123**	...
Food Aliments	47	52	62	70	85	100	106	115	137	...
Tunisia **Tunisie**	**72**	**77**	**82**	**87**	**94**	**100**	**108**	**114**	**119**	**# 125**[15]
Food Aliments	71	75	80	86	94	100	109	113	116	# 122[15]
Turkey **Turquie**	**11**	**15**	**# 22**[15]	**38**	**62**	**100**	**166**	**282**	**469**	**967**
Food[33] Aliments[33]	12	15	# 20[15]	36	61	100	167	286	468	983
Tuvalu[77] **Tuvalu**[77]	**74**	**80**	...	**94**	**96**	**100**	**106**	**100**	**102**	...
Food[77] Aliments[77]	77	83	...	99	98	100	106	97	...	...
Uganda[16] **Ouganda**[16]	...	...	...	...	...	**100**	**128**	**197**	**207**	**228**
Food[16] Aliments[16]	...	...	...	...	...	100	124	205	197	228
Ukraine[17] **Ukraine**[17]	**95**	**97**	**98**	**98**	**100**	...	...	...	...	...
Food[17] Aliments[17]	91	95	100	99	100	...	...	...	...	...
former USSR†[78] **ancienne URSS†**[78]	**89**	**91**	**92**	**93**	**95**	**100**	...	...	...	...
Food[78] Aliments[78]	87	91	95	97	98	100	...	...	...	...
United Kingdom **Royaume-Uni**	**75**	**78**	**81**	**85**	**91**	**100**	**106**	**110**	**112**	**114**
Food Aliments	80	82	85	88	93	100	105	108	109	111
United Rep.Tanzania[79] **Rép. Unie de Tanzanie**[79]	**25**	**33**	**43**	**56**	**74**	**100**	**129**	**157**	**197**	**254**
Food[79] Aliments[79]	24	32	42	57	74	100	132	160	197	260
United States **Etats-Unis**	**82**	**84**	**87**	**91**	**95**	**100**	**104**	**107**	**111**	**113**
Food Aliments	80	83	86	90	95	100	104	105	107	110

33

Consumer price index numbers
All items and food; 1990 = 100 [*cont.*]

Indices des prix à la consommation
Ensemble et aliments; 1990 = 100 [*suite*]

Country or area Pays ou zone	1985	1986	1987	1988	1989	1990	1991	1992	1993	1994
Uruguay[80]										
Uruguay[80]	6	10	16	26	47	100	202	340	524	759
Food[80]										
Aliments[80]	5	10	16	25	45	100	185	297	449	632
Vanuatu[16]										
Vanuatu[16]	66	70	81	89	95	100	106	111	115	117
Food[16]										
Aliments[16]	71	75	85	95	98	100	103	104	108	109
Venezuela[8 81]										
Venezuela[8 81]	21	23	30	39	71	100	134	176	244	392
Food[8 81]										
Aliments[8 81]	13	15	22	30	68	100	138	180	240	379
Yugoslavia[82]										
Yougoslavie[82]	...	...	...	...	...	# 100[15]	222	20 021	...	...
Food[82]										
Aliments[82]	...	...	...	...	...	# 100[15]	200	19 217	...	...
Yugoslavia, SFR†										
Yougoslavie, Rfs†	0	0	0	1	15	100	218	...	...	...
Food										
Aliments	0	0	0	1	16	100	204	...	...	...
Zambia[28]										
Zambie[28]	6	9	13	21	47	100	193	573	1 655	...
Food[28]										
Aliments[28]	6	9	13	21	48	100	191	608	1 781	...
Zimbabwe[28]										
Zimbabwe[28]	...	...	...	...	...	100	123	175	224	273
Food[28]										
Aliments[28]	...	...	...	...	...	100	113	193	267	337

Source:
International Labour Office (Geneva).

Source:
Bureau international du Travail (Genève).

† For detailed descriptions of data pertaining to
former Czechoslovakia, Germany, SFR Yugoslavia and former
USSR, see Annex I - Country or area nomenclature, regional
and other groupings.

† Pour les descriptions en détails des données
relatives à l'ancienne Tchécoslovaquie, l'Allemagne, la Rfs
Yougoslavie et l'ancienne URSS, voir l'Annexe I -
Nomenclature des pays ou zones, groupements régionaux et
autres groupements.

1 Kabul.
2 Excluding "Rent".
3 One month of each year.
4 Index base: 1992 = 100.
5 Algiers.
6 Luanda.
7 Index base: 1991 = 100.
8 Metropolitan area.
9 Buenos Aires.
10 Index base: 1988 = 100.
11 Average of less than twelve months.
12 Government officials.
13 Middle income group.
14 Dhaka.
15 Series replacing former series.
16 Urban areas.
17 Index base: 1989 = 100.
18 Sao Paulo.
19 Ouagadougou.
20 Bujumbura.
21 Yaounde, Africans.

1 Kaboul.
2 Non compris le groupe "Loyer".
3 Un mois de chaque année.
4 Indices base : 1992 = 100.
5 Algers.
6 Luanda.
7 Indices base : 1991 = 100.
8 Région métropolitaine.
9 Buenos Aires.
10 Indices base : 1988 = 100.
11 Moyenne de moins de douze mois.
12 Fonctionnaires.
13 Familles à revenu moyen.
14 Dhaka.
15 Série remplaçant la précédente.
16 Régions urbaines.
17 Indices base : 1989 = 100.
18 Sao Paulo.
19 Ouagadougou.
20 Bujumbura.
21 Yaoundé, Africains.

33

Consumer price index numbers
All items and food; 1990 = 100 [*cont.*]

Indices des prix à la consommation
Ensemble et aliments; 1990 = 100 [*suite*]

22 Praia.	22 Praya.
23 Including rent.	23 Y compris loyer.
24 Bangui.	24 Bangui.
25 N'Djamena.	25 N'Djamena.
26 Index base: 1987 = 100.	26 Indices base : 1987 = 100.
27 Santiago.	27 Santiago.
28 Low income group.	28 Familles à revenu modique.
29 Brazzaville, Africains.	29 Brazzaville, Africains.
30 Rarotonga.	30 Rarotonga.
31 San José.	31 San José.
32 Abidjan, Africans.	32 Abidjan, Africains.
33 Including tobacco.	33 Y compris le tabac.
34 Including direct taxes.	34 Y compris les impôts directs.
35 Addis Ababa.	35 Addis Abéba.
36 Stanley.	36 Stanley.
37 Cayenne.	37 Cayenne.
38 Libreville, Africans.	38 Libreville, Africains.
39 Banjul, Kombo St. Mary.	39 Banjul, Kombo St. Mary.
40 5 new Länder and Berlin (East).	40 5 nouveau Länder et Berlin (Est).
41 All households.	41 Ensemble des ménages.
42 Conakry.	42 Conakry.
43 Bissau.	43 Bissau.
44 Reykjavik.	44 Reykjavik.
45 Industrial workers.	45 Travailleurs de l'industrie.
46 Excluding tobacco.	46 Non compris tabac.
47 Nairobi.	47 Nairobi.
48 Tarawa.	48 Tarawa.
49 Index base: 1991 = 100.	49 Indices base : 1991 = 100.
50 Monrovia.	50 Monrovia.
51 Antananarivo, Madagascans.	51 Antananarivo, Malgaches.
52 Blantyre.	52 Blantyre.
53 Bamako.	53 Bamako.
54 Majuro.	54 Majuro.
55 Yangon.	55 Yangon.
56 Windhoek.	56 Windhoek.
57 Curaçao.	57 Curaçao.
58 Nouméa.	58 Nouméa.
59 Niamey, Africans.	59 Niamey, Africains.
60 Rural and urban areas.	60 Régions rurales et urbaines.
61 Saipan.	61 Saipan.
62 Muscat.	62 Muscat.
63 Panama City.	63 Panamá.
64 Asuncion.	64 Asunción.
65 Lima.	65 Lima.
66 Saint Kitts.	66 Saint Kitts.
67 St. Vincent.	67 St. Vincent.
68 All cities.	68 Ensemble des villes.
69 Dakar.	69 Dakar.
70 Freetown.	70 Freetown.
71 Honiara.	71 Honiara.
72 Colombo.	72 Colombo.
73 Paramaribo.	73 Paramaribo.
74 Damascus.	74 Damas.
75 Bangkok Metrolopis.	75 Bangkok.
76 Lomé.	76 Lomé.
77 Funafuti.	77 Funafuti.
78 Including Belarus and Ukraine shown separately in this table.	78 Y compris le Bélarus et l'Ukraine, figurant séparément dans ce tableau.
79 Tanganyika only.	79 Tanganyika seulement.
80 Montevideo.	80 Montevideo.
81 Caracas.	81 Caracas.
82 Serbia and Montenegro.	82 Serbie et Monténegro.

Technical notes, tables 31-33

In *Table 31*, the series generally relate to the average earnings of wage earners in manufacturing industries. Earnings generally include bonuses, cost of living allowances, taxes, social insurance contributions payable by the employed person and, in some cases, payments in kind, and normally exclude social insurance contributions payable by the employers, family allowances and other social security benefits. The time of year to which the figures refer is not the same for all countries. Unless otherwise stated, the series relate to wage earners of both sexes, irrespective of age.

Some of the series do not conform to the above for one or more of the following reasons: inclusion of salaried employees, inclusion of non-manufacturing industries and use of wage rates instead of earnings.

In the case of countries with widely fluctuating exchange rates or with multiple exchange systems it is advisable to consult table 80 on exchange rates.

For international definitions, further details and current figures, see the International Labour Office *Year Book of Labour Statistics*, *Bulletin of Labour Statistics* and the United Nations *Monthly Bulletin of Statistics*. [11, 25]

In *table 32*, producer prices are prices at which producers sell their output on the domestic market or for export. Wholesale prices, in the strict sense, are prices at which wholesalers sell on the domestic market or for export. In practice, many national wholesale price indexes are a mixture of producer and wholesale prices for domestic goods representing prices for purchases in large quantities from either source. In addition, these indexes may cover the prices of goods imported in quantity for the domestic market either by producers or by retail or wholesale distribution.

Producer or wholesale price indexes normally cover the prices of the characteristic products of agriculture, forestry and fishing, mining and quarrying, manufacturing, and electricity, gas and water supply. Prices are normally measured in terms of transaction prices, including non-deductible indirect taxes less subsidies, in the case of domestically-produced goods and import duties and other non-deductible indirect taxes less subsidies in the case of imported goods.

The Laspeyres index number formula is generally used and, for the purpose of the presentation, the national index numbers have been recalculated, where necessary, on the reference base 1990=100.

The price index numbers for each country are arranged according to the following scheme:

(a) Components of supply
   Domestic supply
   Domestic production for domestic market

Notes techniques, tableaux 31-33

Au *Tableau 31*, les séries se rapportent généralement aux gains moyens des salariés des industries manufacturières. Ces gains, en général, comprennent normalement les primes, les indemnités de vie chère, les impôts, les cotisations des travailleurs à une caisse d'assurance sociale et, dans certains cas, des paiements en nature; ils excluent normalement les contributions de l'employeur à la caisse d'assurance sociale, les allocations familiales et autres prestations de la sécurité sociale. La période de l'année à laquelle se rapportent les chiffres n'est pas la même pour tous les pays. Sauf indication contraire, les séries se rapportent aux salariés des deux sexes et ne tiennent pas compte de l'âge.

Certaines des séries s'écartent des normes indiquées ci-dessus pour une ou plusieurs des raisons suivantes : l'inclusion des employés salariés, l'inclusion des industries non manufacturières et l'utilisation des taux de rémunération au lieu des gains.

Dans le cas des pays à larges fluctuations des cours des changes ou à système de changes multiples, il est recommandé de consulter le tableau 80 sur les cours de changes.

Pour les définitions internationales, plus de détails et pour les chiffres courants, voir l'*Annuaire des Statistiques du Travail*, le *Bulletin des statistiques du travail* du Bureau international du travail et le *Bulletin mensuel de statistique* des Nations Unies [11, 25].

Au *tableau 32*, les prix à la production sont les prix auxquels les producteurs vendent leur production sur le marché intérieur ou à l'exportation. Les prix de gros, au sens strict du terme, sont les prix auxquels les grossistes vendent sur le marché intérieur ou à l'exportation. En pratique, les indices nationaux des prix de gros combinent souvent les prix à la production et les prix de gros de biens nationaux représentant les prix d'achat par grandes quantités au producteur ou au grossiste. En outre, ces indices peuvent s'appliquer aux prix de biens importés en quantités pour être vendus sur le marché intérieur par les producteurs, les détaillants ou les grossistes.

Les indices de prix de gros ou de prix à la production comprennent aussi en général les prix des produits provenant de l'agriculture, de la sylviculture et de la pêche, des industries extractives (mines et carrières), de l'industrie manufacturière ainsi que les prix de l'électricité, de gaz et de l'eau. Les prix sont normalement ceux auxquels s'effectue la transaction, y compris les impôts indirects non déductibles, mais non compris les subventions dans le cas des biens produits dans le pays et y compris les taxes à l'importation et autres impôts indirects non déductibles, mais non compris les subventions dans le cas des biens importés.

On utilise généralement la formule de Laspeyres et, pour la présentation, on a recalculé les indices nationaux, le cas échéant, en prenant comme base de référce 1990=100.

Agricultural products
Industrial products
Import products
Exported goods
(b)   Stage of processing
Raw materials
Intermediate products
Finished goods
(c)   End-use
Producers' material
Consumers' goods
Capital goods
Description of the general methods used in compiling
the related national indexes is given in the United Nations
*1977 Supplement to the Statistical Yearbook and the
Monthly Bulletin of Statistics.*[49]

In *table 33*, unless otherwise stated, the index covers all
the main classes of expenditure on all items and on food.
Monthly data for many of these series and descriptions of
them may be found in the United Nations *Monthly Bulletin
of Statistics* and the United Nations *1977 Supplement to the
Statistical Yearbook and the Monthly Bulletin of
Statistics.*[49]

Les indices des prix pour chaque pays sont présentés
suivant la classification ci-après :
(a)   Eléments de l'offre
Offre intérieure
Production nationale pour le marché intérieur
Produits agricoles
Produits industriels
Produits importés
Produits exportés
(b)   Stade de la transformation
Matières premières
Produits intermédiaires
Produits finis
(c)   Utilisation finale
Biens de production
Biens de consommation
Biens d'équipement
Les méthodes générales utilisées pour calculer les indices
nationaux correspondants sont exposées dans : *1977
Supplément à l'Annuaire statistique et au Bulletin mensuel
de statistique* des Nations Unies [49].

Au *tableau 33*, sauf indication contraire, les indices
donnés englobent tous les groupes principaux de dépenses
pour l'ensemble et les aliments. Les données mensuelles pour
plusieurs de ces séries et définitions figurent dans le *Bulletin
mensuel de statistique* (ONU) et dans le *1977 Supplément à
l'Annuaire statistique et au Bulletin mensuel de statistique*
des Nations Unies [49].

34
Agricultural production
Production agricole
Index numbers: 1979-81 = 100
Indices : 1979-81 = 100

Country or area Pays ou zone	Agriculture Agriculture					Food Produit alimentaires				
	1990	1991	1992	1993	1994	1990	1991	1992	1993	1994
Africa · Afrique										
Algeria Algérie	150	178	182	174	180	150	177	182	173	179
Angola Angola	103	108	112	108	95	107	112	117	113	99
Benin Bénin	166	179	179	185	194	159	170	171	174	180
Botswana Botswana	115	117	112	105	108	115	117	112	105	108
Burkina Faso Burkina Faso	149	180	181	185	188	145	178	179	183	187
Burundi Burundi	127	130	134	127	105	129	132	136	133	106
Cameroon Cameroun	116	115	110	110	113	117	114	111	114	115
Cape Verde Cap-Vert	194	152	114	121	122	194	152	114	121	122
Central African Rep. Rép. centrafricaine	123	126	129	132	135	123	128	132	136	137
Chad Tchad	128	140	136	130	136	118	129	134	131	135
Comoros Comores	126	150	129	139	137	126	150	129	139	137
Congo Congo	118	109	111	115	115	118	109	112	115	116
Côte d'Ivoire Côte d'Ivoire	139	135	134	143	143	143	142	147	156	155
Egypt Egypte	138	144	152	158	154	150	157	165	170	168
Ethiopia Ethiopie	111	110	115	...	...	111	111	116	...	...
Gabon Gabon	121	121	122	122	123	121	121	122	122	123
Gambia Gambie	108	120	104	110	126	108	120	103	109	119
Ghana Ghana	127	158	161	176	179	128	160	162	178	180
Guinea Guinée	128	133	141	150	158	125	131	139	148	157
Guinea-Bissau Guinée-Bissau	136	137	137	142	151	137	137	138	143	152
Kenya Kenya	146	144	139	131	141	147	145	142	129	145
Lesotho Lesotho	123	96	82	99	121	124	94	79	98	122
Liberia Libéria	79	72	76	68	67	93	91	91	87	86
Libyan Arab Jamah. Jamah. arabe libyenne	122	128	120	84	43	122	128	120	84	43
Madagascar Madagascar	122	123	124	128	124	123	125	126	130	126

34
Agricultural production
Index numbers: 1979-81 = 100 [cont.]
Production agricole
Indices : 1979-81 = 100 [suite]

Country or area Pays ou zone	Agriculture Agriculture					Food Produit alimentaires				
	1990	1991	1992	1993	1994	1990	1991	1992	1993	1994
Malawi Malawi	110	120	96	126	107	101	111	86	117	97
Mali Mali	126	138	132	138	147	122	134	126	135	144
Mauritania Mauritanie	118	122	113	115	120	118	122	113	115	120
Mauritius Maurice	115	116	122	120	115	116	117	122	121	116
Morocco Maroc	171	198	149	152	204	171	198	149	152	205
Mozambique Mozambique	107	101	84	95	95	111	105	86	98	98
Namibia Namibie	95	100	101	105	110	97	102	104	107	112
Niger Niger	105	125	124	123	127	105	125	124	123	127
Nigeria Nigéria	167	174	189	197	204	167	174	189	197	203
Réunion Réunion	106	117	118	106	106	106	118	119	106	106
Rwanda Rwanda	113	117	118	110	100	110	117	114	109	101
Sao Tome and Principe Sao Tomé-et-Principe	69	77	97	99	97	69	77	98	99	98
Senegal Sénégal	135	144	139	160	162	135	143	139	160	162
Sierra Leone Sierra Leone	126	126	118	115	114	121	121	112	110	109
Somalia Somalie	115	90	76	85	102	115	90	76	85	101
South Africa Afrique du Sud	103	106	86	99	99	104	107	86	102	101
Sudan Soudan	92	118	129	113	138	91	120	132	116	141
Swaziland Swaziland	126	130	114	124	123	126	131	115	121	120
Togo Togo	139	138	140	164	151	136	131	131	156	143
Tunisia Tunisie	144	173	160	169	149	144	174	161	169	149
Uganda Ouganda	143	146	147	155	161	143	146	148	155	161
United Rep.Tanzania Rép. Unie de Tanzanie	125	122	117	116	116	127	123	118	117	118
Zaire Zaïre	138	143	147	152	147	138	143	148	152	147
Zambia Zambie	129	136	118	157	140	128	133	117	153	139
Zimbabwe Zimbabwe	129	130	84	120	135	127	119	66	105	128

34
Agricultural production
Index numbers: 1979-81 = 100 [cont.]
Production agricole
Indices : 1979-81 = 100 [suite]

Country or area Pays ou zone	Agriculture Agriculture					Food Produit alimentaires				
	1990	1991	1992	1993	1994	1990	1991	1992	1993	1994
America, North · Amérique du Nord										
Antigua and Barbuda Antigua-et-Barbuda	110	114	117	117	118	109	114	117	117	118
Bahamas Bahamas	98	104	96	96	97	98	104	96	96	97
Barbados Barbade	78	69	66	64	70	78	69	66	64	70
Belize Belize	119	124	125	134	138	119	124	125	134	138
Canada Canada	128	128	124	123	128	129	129	126	124	129
Costa Rica Costa Rica	137	138	145	145	147	138	136	143	149	154
Cuba Cuba	109	112	94	77	75	108	111	94	75	74
Dominica Dominique	151	151	153	153	154	151	151	153	153	154
Dominican Republic Rép. dominicaine	121	125	126	128	135	125	131	136	139	148
El Salvador El Salvador	87	87	94	95	90	107	106	115	116	117
Grenada Grenade	84	82	82	84	84	84	82	82	84	84
Guadeloupe Guadeloupe	98	109	114	120	120	98	109	114	120	120
Guatemala Guatemala	116	117	115	114	115	143	144	144	144	147
Haiti Haïti	96	93	87	85	86	97	94	89	86	87
Honduras Honduras	133	129	135	138	143	126	128	132	138	133
Jamaica Jamaïque	118	119	123	117	120	117	118	123	117	120
Martinique Martinique	137	125	131	126	130	137	125	131	126	130
Mexico Mexique	115	119	117	125	126	115	120	119	128	131
Netherlands Antilles Antilles néerlandaises	39	77	21	54	54	39	77	21	54	54
Nicaragua Nicaragua	72	78	79	76	82	93	86	90	96	99
Panama Panama	114	122	123	120	122	112	120	121	118	120
Puerto Rico Porto Rico	98	102	97	93	91	97	101	96	92	89
Saint Lucia Sainte-Lucie	178	152	179	173	174	178	152	179	173	174
St. Vincent-Grenadines St. Vincent-Grenadines	164	152	168	169	177	164	152	168	169	178

34
Agricultural production
Index numbers: 1979-81 = 100 [*cont.*]
Production agricole
Indices : 1979-81 = 100 [*suite*]

Country or area Pays ou zone	Agriculture Agriculture					Food Produit alimentaires				
	1990	1991	1992	1993	1994	1990	1991	1992	1993	1994
Trinidad and Tobago Trinité-et-Tobago	101	100	93	104	112	102	102	95	107	115
United States Etats-Unis	106	105	114	104	121	106	104	115	104	120
America, South · Amérique du Sud										
Argentina Argentine	111	115	118	112	121	110	114	119	112	122
Bolivia Bolivie	131	144	139	145	159	134	147	141	147	162
Brazil Brésil	130	133	140	141	150	134	137	146	147	158
Chile Chili	135	138	143	149	156	136	139	144	150	157
Colombia Colombie	136	140	141	142	137	143	143	140	145	151
Ecuador Equateur	143	150	153	159	164	142	149	153	159	165
Guyana Guyana	80	91	97	99	103	81	92	99	100	104
Paraguay Paraguay	177	164	155	170	167	171	155	157	175	175
Peru Pérou	116	119	110	117	132	119	123	115	122	139
Suriname Suriname	92	105	105	108	112	92	105	105	108	112
Uruguay Uruguay	115	116	123	119	124	113	114	124	119	126
Venezuela Venezuela	132	136	141	139	147	132	136	143	141	148
Asia · Asie										
Afghanistan Afghanistan	77	79	75	76	78	78	79	75	76	78
Bangladesh Bangladesh	125	129	130	130	132	127	130	132	131	134
Bhutan Bhoutan	105	107	109	110	111	105	106	108	110	111
Brunei Darussalam Brunéi Darussalam	157	145	140	148	151	157	145	140	149	151
Cambodia Cambodge	194	194	202	209	195	191	189	196	203	189
China Chine	159	167	173	182	189	157	163	171	181	190
Cyprus Chypre	101	77	113	137	128	101	77	113	137	128
Hong Kong Hong-kong	114	113	113	113	112	114	113	113	113	112
India Inde	148	152	159	162	166	149	154	161	164	168

34
Agricultural production
Index numbers: 1979-81 = 100 [cont.]
Production agricole
Indices : 1979-81 = 100 [suite]

Country or area Pays ou zone	Agriculture Agriculture					Food Produit alimentaires				
	1990	1991	1992	1993	1994	1990	1991	1992	1993	1994
Indonesia Indonésie	158	161	171	174	174	161	165	176	179	179
Iran, Islamic Rep. of Iran, Rép. islamique d'	169	182	202	207	212	170	184	205	211	216
Iraq Iraq	146	101	119	132	129	147	101	119	133	130
Israel Israël	124	108	113	111	122	137	125	129	128	139
Japan Japon	98	91	96	81	100	101	94	99	84	104
Jordan Jordanie	176	185	219	240	244	178	189	222	244	248
Korea, Dem. P. R. Corée, R. p. dém. de	128	125	116	108	111	127	124	115	106	109
Korea, Republic of Corée, République de	113	105	114	108	114	115	107	116	109	116
Lao People's Dem. Rep. Rép. dém. pop. lao	156	138	154	146	174	156	137	153	145	174
Lebanon Liban	167	184	193	192	203	172	189	199	197	209
Macau Macao	105	87	80	92	104	105	87	80	92	104
Malaysia Malaisie	184	198	204	223	227	224	244	256	285	291
Maldives Maldives	128	122	126	125	126	128	122	126	125	126
Mongolia Mongolie	115	118	102	96	94	117	120	102	97	95
Myanmar Myanmar	118	119	125	137	144	121	122	127	140	147
Nepal Népal	159	159	152	163	169	161	161	155	166	172
Pakistan Pakistan	155	167	166	171	173	150	156	163	170	172
Philippines Philippines	119	116	117	119	123	119	116	117	119	124
Saudi Arabia Arabie saoudite	583	530	584	574	507	595	540	596	585	516
Singapore Singapour	93	73	56	42	39	94	73	56	42	39
Sri Lanka Sri Lanka	101	96	93	98	102	103	97	98	100	105
Syrian Arab Republic Rép. arabe syrienne	125	126	145	135	140	125	123	140	134	138
Thailand Thaïlande	124	132	135	135	133	119	128	126	126	124
Turkey Turquie	133	134	134	135	133	134	136	135	136	134
Viet Nam Viet Nam	152	156	165	175	178	151	155	163	173	175

34
Agricultural production
Index numbers: 1979-81 = 100 [*cont.*]
Production agricole
Indices : 1979-81 = 100 [*suite*]

Country or area Pays ou zone	Agriculture Agriculture					Food Produit alimentaires				
	1990	1991	1992	1993	1994	1990	1991	1992	1993	1994
Yemen Yémen	117	105	130	137	134	117	105	129	137	135
Europe · Europe										
Albania Albanie	116	89	105	107	107	119	92	109	111	110
Austria Autriche	112	113	110	111	113	112	113	110	111	113
Belgium-Luxembourg Belgique-Luxembourg	110	130	139	145	145	110	130	139	145	145
Bulgaria Bulgarie	92	86	79	63	59	98	91	86	69	65
former Czechoslovakia† anc. Tchécoslovaquie†	126	118	112	...	...	126	119	113	...	...
Denmark Danemark	135	136	121	133	130	135	136	120	133	130
Finland Finlande	122	110	100	107	108	122	110	100	107	108
France France	106	105	112	103	101	106	106	112	103	101
Germany † Allemagne†	117	115	107	109	105	117	115	107	109	105
Greece Grèce	97	115	113	112	112	93	111	106	104	105
Hungary Hongrie	108	115	87	79	83	109	116	87	80	84
Iceland Islande	83	88	90	80	82	84	88	90	81	83
Ireland Irlande	123	127	130	130	124	123	126	130	130	124
Italy Italie	98	107	107	103	101	97	106	107	103	101
Malta Malte	120	128	127	134	134	120	128	127	134	134
Netherlands Pays-Bas	113	118	121	129	125	113	117	121	129	125
Norway Norvège	119	114	106	119	116	119	114	106	119	116
Poland Pologne	119	114	102	108	92	121	116	104	111	94
Portugal Portugal	136	139	119	103	109	136	139	119	103	109
Romania Roumanie	89	89	73	85	90	89	90	73	86	91
Spain Espagne	125	120	122	115	109	125	119	122	115	110
Sweden Suède	108	93	86	97	89	108	93	86	97	89
Switzerland Suisse	111	112	113	109	107	111	112	113	109	107

34
Agricultural production
Index numbers: 1979-81 = 100 [cont.]
Production agricole
Indices : 1979-81 = 100 [suite]

Country or area Pays ou zone	Agriculture Agriculture					Food Produit alimentaires				
	1990	1991	1992	1993	1994	1990	1991	1992	1993	1994
United Kingdom Royaume-Uni	111	114	112	103	103	110	114	112	103	103
Yugoslavia, SFR† Yougoslavie, Rfs†	95	99	...	...	...	96	99	...	...	...
Oceania · Océanie										
Australia Australie	116	114	124	130	112	112	107	119	129	110
Fiji Fidji	120	107	112	114	117	120	108	113	114	118
French Polynesia Polynésie française	96	95	92	96	93	98	97	94	97	95
New Caledonia Nouvelle-Calédonie	99	100	104	106	106	101	104	108	111	111
New Zealand Nouvelle-Zélande	102	106	109	106	108	108	114	118	117	120
Papua New Guinea Papouasie-Nvl-Guinée	129	128	132	136	138	130	130	137	139	140
Samoa Samoa	100	89	87	94	95	100	88	87	94	95
Solomon Islands Iles Salomon	129	135	139	134	146	129	135	140	134	146
Tonga Tonga	87	85	86	85	86	87	85	86	85	86
Vanuatu Vanuatu	123	107	102	106	108	124	107	103	107	109
former USSR† · ancienne URSS†										
former USSR† ancienne URSS†	120	106	...	...	...	122	108	...	...	...

Source:
Food and Agriculture Organization of the United Nations (Rome).

† For detailed descriptions of data pertaining to former Czechoslovakia, Germany, SFR Yugoslavia and former USSR, see Annex I - Country or area nomenclature, regional and other groupings.

Source:
Organisation des Nations Unies pour l'alimentation et l'agriculture (Rome).

† Pour les descriptions en détails des données relatives à l'ancienne Tchécoslovaquie, l'Allemagne, la Rfs Yougoslavie et l'ancienne URSS, voir l'Annexe I - Nomenclature des pays ou zones, groupements régionaux et autres groupements.

35
Cereals
Céréales
Production: thousand metric tons
Production : milliers de tonnes métriques

Country or area Pays ou zone	1985	1986	1987	1988	1989	1990	1991	1992	1993	1994
World *Monde*	1 822 721	1 835 803	1 768 183	1 725 543	1 868 766	1 946 554	1 876 297	1 960 172	1 891 578	1 950 599
Africa **Afrique**	83 465	87 918	80 281	92 888	96 362	88 194	99 291	83 988	95 399	104 737
Algeria Algérie	2 919	2 404	2 066	1 038	2 006	1 629	3 812	3 333	2 012	2 195
Angola Angola	325 [1]	356	382	352	289	264	386	465	335	274
Benin Bénin	535	497	401	557	565	546	587	609	628	646
Botswana Botswana	19	22	23	106	76	54	45	15	34	50
Burkina Faso Burkina Faso	1 583	1 890	1 637	2 101	1 952	1 518	2 455	2 477	2 495	2 509
Burundi Burundi	256	266	285	288	255	293	299	309	* 299	213
Cameroon Cameroun	815	1 094	715	900	858	816	1 003	905 [1]	970 [1]	985 [1]
Cape Verde Cap-Vert	1	12	21	17	10	11	3	5	12	6 [1]
Central African Rep. Rép. centrafricaine	111	178	126	143	124	105	100	100	101	92 [1]
Chad Tchad	704	687	563	782	582	602	812	976	747	963
Comoros Comores	17	17	16	17	19	19	20	20	21	19 [1]
Congo Congo	16	22	20	21	26	26	26 [1]	27	27 [1]	27 [1]
Côte d'Ivoire Côte d'Ivoire	1 089	1 049	1 086	1 144	1 193	1 239	1 286	1 340	1 539	1 359
Egypt Egypte	8 561	8 754	9 445	9 764	11 102	13 028	13 854	14 440	14 961	14 766
Eritrea Erythrée	...	...	...	...	...	...	...	...	* 73	72 [1]
Ethiopia Ethiopie	...	...	...	...	...	...	...	...	6 956	6 734
Ethiopia incl.Eritrea Ethiopie comp. Erythrée	4 820	6 504	6 195	6 384	6 355	6 457 [1]	6 305 [1]	7 070 [1]	...	...
Gabon Gabon	14	21	25	25	21	23 [1]	24 [1]	25	25 [1]	27 [1]
Gambia Gambie	116	102	92	100	96	90	111	96	97	109
Ghana Ghana	921	867	1 057	1 146	1 184	844	1 436	1 254	1 645	1 450
Guinea Guinée	739	814	801	760	802	859	913	949	1 065	1 172
Guinea-Bissau Guinée-Bissau	158 [1]	162	153 [1]	150	148	167	179	169	181	201 [1]
Kenya Kenya	2 901	3 371	2 866	3 285	3 178	2 729	2 770	2 833	2 006	3 481

35
Cereals
Production: thousand metric tons [cont.]
Céréales
Production : milliers de tonnes métriques [suite]

Country or area Pays ou zone	1985	1986	1987	1988	1989	1990	1991	1992	1993	1994
Lesotho Lesotho	167	132	146	234	200	238	133	80	154	258
Liberia Libéria	289	288	298	298	294	100[1]	109[1]	102[1]	* 65	* 50
Libyan Arab Jamah. Jamah. arabe libyenne	235	285	276	283	322	273	298[1]	283[1]	273[1]	263[1]
Madagascar Madagascar	2 320	2 385	2 338	2 307	2 542	2 577	2 489	2 617	2 727	2 517
Malawi Malawi	1 423	1 364	1 255	1 489	1 588	1 413	1 680	670	2 137	1 110
Mali Mali	1 719	1 728	1 639	2 197	2 157	1 771	2 415	1 819	2 138	2 705
Mauritania Mauritanie	108	127	152	174	184	103	105	107	169	188
Mauritius Maurice	5	8	4	4	2	2	2	2	2	2[1]
Morocco Maroc	5 312	7 825	4 337	7 959	7 429	6 276	8 668	2 952	2 930	9 789
Mozambique Mozambique	746[1]	829	569	562	607	734	546	239	766	819
Namibia Namibie	63	81	69	83	97	99	114	33	76	120
Niger Niger	1 849	1 834	1 439	2 389	1 842	1 480	2 384	2 253	2 155	2 221[1]
Nigeria Nigéria	11 911	12 744	12 626	14 560	15 122	13 733	13 059	12 734	13 919	13 517
Réunion Réunion	12	13	11	13	13	11	13	16	14	15[1]
Rwanda Rwanda	337	297	292	292	262	306	329	292	181	158[1]
Sao Tome and Principe Sao Tomé-et-Principe	1	1	1	2	2	3	4	4	* 4	4[1]
Senegal Sénégal	1 249	887	1 054	867	1 067	977	946	856	1 086	952
Sierra Leone Sierra Leone	488	577	517	547	574	562	560	535	540	515
Somalia Somalie	514	586	543	601	654	581[1]	256	209	165	405
South Africa Afrique du Sud	10 870	11 352	11 483	11 347	14 884	11 016	10 810	4 616	12 405	14 422
Sudan Soudan	4 036	3 799	1 699	5 132	1 975	1 716	4 590	5 438	3 093	4 805
Swaziland Swaziland	178	164	101	118	138	99	142	58	77	67
Togo Togo	371	366	368	504	566	484	465	495	634	526
Tunisia Tunisie	2 098	624	1 917	295	641	1 638	2 556	2 199	1 917	660
Uganda Ouganda	1 171	1 058	1 220	1 398	1 636	1 580	1 576	1 743	1 881	2 036

35
Cereals
Production: thousand metric tons [cont.]
Céréales
Production : milliers de tonnes métriques [suite]

Country or area Pays ou zone	1985	1986	1987	1988	1989	1990	1991	1992	1993	1994
United Rep.Tanzania Rép. Unie de Tanzanie	3 622	3 864	4 029	3 685	4 791	3 842	3 792	3 538	3 876	3 534
Zaire Zaïre	1 141	1 193	1 256	1 332	1 415	1 487	1 538	1 585	1 752	1 798[1]
Zambia Zambie	1 193	1 319	1 158	2 055	1 967	1 210	1 225	613	1 757	1 168
Zimbabwe Zimbabwe	3 416	3 096	1 505	3 080	2 553	2 560	2 060	481	2 278	2 764
America, North Amerique du Nord	428 103	401 245	361 080	268 807	359 438	400 337	362 520	434 970	343 052	437 420
Bahamas[1] Bahamas[1]	1	1	1	1	1	1	1	1	1	1
Barbados[1] Barbade[1]	2	2	2	2	2	2	2	2	2	2
Belize Belize	25	23	28	29	24	22[1]	22[1]	25[1]	26[1]	26[1]
Canada Canada	48 239	56 965	51 682	35 788	48 402	56 797	53 850	49 513	51 416	47 054
Costa Rica Costa Rica	381	342	299	315	246	281	260	272	204	215[1]
Cuba Cuba	620	667	562	585	632	533	462	371	277	277[1]
Dominican Republic Rép. dominicaine	608	560	613	547	554	488	526	628	504	610
El Salvador El Salvador	697	631	647	807	802	825	729	992	910	943
Guatemala Guatemala	1 283	1 402	1 390	1 389	1 422	1 426	1 382	1 515	1 454	1 507
Haiti Haïti	445	476	462	469	453	361	400	442	370	380
Honduras Honduras	502	550	534	527	619	685	693	688	693	639
Jamaica Jamaïque	8	7	6	4	3	2	3	4	6	6[1]
Mexico Mexique	27 403	23 553	23 636	21 067	21 424	25 562	23 673	26 897	27 311	27 412
Nicaragua Nicaragua	506	478	455	506	484	488	388	498	566	623
Panama Panama	301	293	304	298	328	345	337	337	337	327
Puerto Rico Porto Rico	5	6	2	2	0	0	0	0	0	0
St. Vincent-Grenadines St. Vincent-Grenadines	1[1]	1[1]	1[1]	1	1	1	1[1]	1[1]	1[1]	1[1]
Trinidad and Tobago Trinité-et-Tobago	7	7	10	10	15	17	18[1]	25	22	21[1]
United States Etats-Unis	347 069	315 281	280 447	206 461	284 026	312 502	279 773	352 757	258 952	357 377
America, South Amérique du Sud	77 838	78 255	82 946	82 189	79 357	68 362	74 007	85 070	83 969	87 330

35

Cereals
Production: thousand metric tons [*cont.*]
Céréales
Production : milliers de tonnes métriques [*suite*]

Country or area Pays ou zone	1985	1986	1987	1988	1989	1990	1991	1992	1993	1994
Argentina Argentine	28 098	26 465	22 893	22 342	18 040	19 726	21 663	25 504	25 197	24 668
Bolivia Bolivie	973	839	865	834	845	788	1 011	893	1 078	1 047
Brazil Brésil	36 011	37 319	44 112	42 921	43 943	32 490	36 682	44 058	42 981	45 930
Chile Chili	2 360	2 675	2 819	2 800	3 148	2 981	2 864	2 901	2 643	2 619
Colombia Colombie	3 144	3 067	3 206	3 555	4 007	4 314	3 948	3 674	3 522	3 703
Ecuador Equateur	832	1 127	1 297	1 489	1 439	1 383	1 444	1 624	1 801	1 937
French Guiana Guyane française	8	9	13	14	16	22	29	24	27	25[1]
Guyana Guyana	281	243	229	229	240	146	253	250	249	343[1]
Paraguay Paraguay	1 152	1 143	1 447	1 595	1 550	1 612	717	857	962	941
Peru Pérou	1 829	1 891	2 354	2 369	2 443	1 792	1 773	1 507	1 998	2 396
Suriname Suriname	299	300	272	265	261	196	229	261	217	225
Uruguay Uruguay	1 028	925	1 021	1 291	1 488	1 130	1 144	1 538	1 435	1 428
Venezuela Venezuela	1 822	2 250	2 418	2 485	1 937	1 780	2 250	1 978	1 860	2 069
Asia **Asie**	**753 890**	**773 905**	**762 856**	**800 976**	**830 027**	**871 982**	**861 493**	**886 746**	**899 209**	**898 644**
Afghanistan Afghanistan	* 3 242	3 084	3 394	2 997	2 834	2 705	2 724	2 420[1]	2 540	2 662[1]
Armenia Arménie	...	...	...	...	...	...	...	272	344	240
Azerbaijan Azerbaïdjan	...	...	...	...	...	...	...	1 257	1 136	1 012
Bangladesh Bangladesh	24 135	24 266	24 304	24 450	27 886	27 747	28 462	28 654	28 175	28 741
Bhutan Bhoutan	167	164	140	95	95	106	106	106	106[1]	106[1]
Brunei Darussalam Brunéi Darussalam	1	1	1	1	1[1]	1[1]	1[1]	1[1]	1[1]	1[1]
Cambodia Cambodge	1 854	2 144	1 853	2 541	2 726	2 588	2 460	2 281	2 443	1 864[1]
China Chine	339 794	352 006	359 159	351 747	367 560	404 332	395 015	400 164	405 888	397 212
Cyprus Chypre	112	68	126	158	148	109	65	182	205	148
Gaza Strip Zone de Gaza	1	1[1]	1[1]	1[1]	1[1]	1[1]	1[1]	1[1]	1[1]	1[1]
Georgia Géorgie	...	...	...	...	...	...	...	498	393	353

35

Cereals
Production: thousand metric tons [cont.]
Céréales
Production : milliers de tonnes métriques [suite]

Country or area Pays ou zone	1985	1986	1987	1988	1989	1990	1991	1992	1993	1994
India Inde	165 682	164 955	156 114	183 867	199 413	193 919	193 101	201 923	205 420	212 482
Indonesia Indonésie	43 362	45 647	45 234	48 328	50 918	51 913	50 944	56 235	54 641	52 862
Iran, Islamic Rep. of Iran, Rép. islamique d'	10 728	11 899	12 197	12 103	10 787	13 686	14 447	15 820	16 293	17 522
Iraq Iraq	2 932	2 281	1 728	2 591	1 497	3 455	2 673	3 092	2 310	2 520
Israel Israël	163	203	326	223	209	303	190	267	229	157
Japan Japon	15 856	15 805	14 527	13 867	14 318	14 449	13 070	14 286	10 737	15 787
Jordan Jordanie	85	43	117	129	82	130	108	148	93	119
Kazakstan Kazakstan	...	...	...	...	...	...	...	29 649	21 533	16 395
Korea, Dem. P. R. Corée, R. p. dém. de	6 333	7 114	6 629	6 371	6 509	5 866	5 406	4 912	4 374	4 525
Korea, Republic of Corée, République de	8 808	8 638	8 467	9 164	8 950	8 434	7 852	7 845	7 135	7 588
Kuwait Koweït	3	3	4[1]	4	4[1]	3[1]	0[1]	2[1]	2[1]	2[1]
Kyrgyzstan Kirghizistan	...	...	...	...	...	...	...	1 516	1 606	1 047
Lao People's Dem. Rep. Rép. dém. pop. lao	1 431	1 491	1 243	1 054	1 448	1 558	1 292	1 561	1 298	1 730
Lebanon Liban	34	47[1]	70	73	79	82	83	88	76	67
Malaysia Malaisie	1 873	1 773	1 730	1 815	1 873	1 995	2 175	2 106	* 2 069	* 2 080
Mongolia Mongolie	884	869	689	814	841	720	597	496	492	443
Myanmar Myanmar	15 067	14 861	14 239	13 645	14 256	14 421	13 649	15 340	17 260	19 607
Nepal Népal	4 374	3 999	4 759	5 307	5 672	5 847	5 520	4 919	5 723	5 929
Oman Oman	1	4	4	4	5	5	5[1]	5[1]	5[1]	3[1]
Pakistan Pakistan	17 699	20 866	18 454	19 240	21 018	20 957	21 138	22 117	23 872	22 256
Philippines Philippines	12 728	13 338	12 818	13 399	13 981	14 739	14 329	13 688	14 332	15 550
Qatar Qatar	2	2	3	3	3	3	4	4	5	5[1]
Saudi Arabia Arabie saoudite	2 188	2 461	2 929	3 692	3 932	4 137	4 573	4 659	5 042	4 509
Sri Lanka Sri Lanka	2 702	2 639	2 177	2 524	2 101	2 579	2 430	2 374	2 607	2 620
Syrian Arab Republic Rép. arabe syrienne	2 543	3 167	2 300	5 001	1 404	3 100	3 288	4 361	5 387	5 660

35
Cereals
Production: thousand metric tons [*cont.*]
Céréales
Production : milliers de tonnes métriques [*suite*]

Country or area Pays ou zone	1985	1986	1987	1988	1989	1990	1991	1992	1993	1994
Tajikistan Tadjikistan	...	...	...	...	...	...	...	277	275	254
Thailand Thaïlande	25 615	23 401	21 414	26 167	25 240	21 170	23 873	24 347	23 483	22 576
Turkey Turquie	26 493	29 358	29 282	30 894	23 499	30 201	31 148	29 157	31 749	27 001
Turkmenistan Turkménistan	...	...	...	...	...	...	...	708	989	1 573
United Arab Emirates Emirats arabes unis	5	6	6	5	6	8	8	7[1]	7[1]	7
Uzbekistan Ouzbékistan	...	...	...	...	...	...	...	2 252	2 135	2 306
Viet Nam Viet Nam	16 466	16 578	15 669	17 820	19 840	19 901	20 299	22 343	24 337	23 455
Yemen Yémen	484	700	718	843	864	767	448	811	825	802
Europe **Europe**	**283 557**	**282 227**	**275 011**	**285 805**	**292 553**	**284 701**	**303 482**	**254 823**	**259 309**	**261 214**
Albania Albanie	995	1 046	1 026	998	1 033	897	441	429	682	692[1]
Austria Autriche	5 551	5 108	4 965	5 359	5 009	5 290	5 045	4 323	4 206	* 4 681
Belarus Bélarus	...	...	...	...	...	...	...	* 7 061	* 7 315	5 930
Belgium-Luxembourg Belgique-Luxembourg	2 225	2 401	2 060	2 352	2 375	2 122	2 217	2 170	2 336	2 273
Bosnia & Herzegovina Bosnie-Herzégovine	...	...	...	...	...	...	...	1 361[1]	1 205[1]	1 110
Bulgaria Bulgarie	5 384	8 492	7 278	7 820	9 527	8 115	8 974	6 560	5 832	6 424
Croatia Croatie	...	...	...	...	...	...	...	2 355	2 733	2 595
former Czechoslovakia† anc. Tchécoslovaquie†	11 775	10 805	11 777	11 907	12 047	12 626	11 939	10 196	...	...
Czech Republic République tchèque	...	...	...	...	...	...	...	...	6 477	6 777
Denmark Danemark	7 956	7 969	7 184	8 068	8 795	9 607	9 231	6 954	8 203	7 885
Estonia Estonie	...	...	...	...	...	...	...	592	801	661
Finland Finlande	3 642	3 520	2 183	2 826	3 809	4 296	3 429	2 603	3 340	3 400
France France	55 989	50 387	52 961	56 059	57 615	55 111	60 330	60 638	55 632	53 641
Germany † Allemagne†	37 555	37 257	35 061	36 932	36 881	37 580	39 268	34 758	35 588	36 353
Greece Grèce	4 492	5 286	5 183	5 624	5 827	4 463	6 223	5 047	4 922	4 896
Hungary Hongrie	14 809	14 301	14 168	14 966	15 417	12 561	15 797	9 981	8 520	11 911

35
Cereals
Production: thousand metric tons [*cont.*]
Céréales
Production : milliers de tonnes métriques [*suite*]

Country or area Pays ou zone	1985	1986	1987	1988	1989	1990	1991	1992	1993	1994
Ireland Irlande	2 096	1 955	2 108	2 078	1 919	1 966	1 964	2 015	1 686	1 700
Italy Italie	18 029	18 698	18 400	17 400	17 133	17 411	19 219	19 891	19 690	18 918
Latvia Lettonie	...	...	...	...	...	...	...	1 127	1 199	799
Lithuania Lituanie	...	...	...	...	...	...	...	2 184	2 598	2 412
Malta Malte	9	9[1]	9[1]	9	9	9[1]	9[1]	9[1]	9[1]	9[1]
Netherlands Pays-Bas	1 132	1 266	1 107	1 222	1 368	1 361	1 252	1 350	1 466	1 355
Norway Norvège	1 302	1 109	1 285	1 066	1 180	1 568	1 482	1 010	1 402	1 268
Poland Pologne	23 741	25 036	26 060	24 504	26 958	28 014	27 812	19 962	23 417	21 763
Portugal Portugal	1 380	1 641	1 727	1 450	1 833	1 388	1 796	1 338	1 433	1 546
Republic of Moldova République de Moldova	...	...	...	...	...	...	...	1 976	3 219	1 423
Romania Roumanie	19 503	19 725	16 889	19 286	18 379	17 174	19 307	12 288	15 493	17 512
Russian Federation Fédération de Russie	...	...	...	...	...	...	...	103 795	96 171	78 709
Slovakia Slovaquie	...	...	...	...	...	...	...	...	3 223	3 730
Slovenia Slovénie	...	...	...	...	...	...	...	426	452	409[1]
Spain Espagne	20 972	16 520	20 697	23 834	19 698	18 762	19 457	14 479	17 476	15 341
Sweden Suède	5 629	5 811	5 170	4 743	5 493	6 380	5 160	3 760	5 242	4 571
Switzerland Suisse	1 054	960	939	1 244	1 411	1 268	1 313	1 213	1 291	1 218
TFYR Macedonia L'ex-R.y. Macédoine	...	...	...	...	...	...	...	624	479	656
Ukraine Ukraine	...	...	...	...	...	...	...	35 548	42 725	32 862
United Kingdom Royaume-Uni	22 486	24 509	21 698	21 063	22 729	22 569	22 635	22 063	19 464	19 670
Yugoslavia Yougoslavie	...	...	...	...	...	...	...	7 019	7 411	8 910
Yugoslavia, SFR† Yougoslavie, Rfs†	15 850	18 416	15 077	14 996	16 110	14 166	19 183	...	...	...
Oceania **Océanie**	**26 169**	**25 253**	**20 987**	**22 678**	**23 027**	**23 870**	**19 545**	**25 863**	**28 203**	**15 278**
Australia Australie	24 944	24 031	19 959	21 870	22 319	22 967	18 701	25 097	27 398	14 462
Fiji Fidji	29	26	24	34	33	28	31	24	22	32[1]

35
Cereals
Production: thousand metric tons [*cont.*]
Céréales
Production : milliers de tonnes métriques [*suite*]

Country or area Pays ou zone	1985	1986	1987	1988	1989	1990	1991	1992	1993	1994
New Caledonia Nouvelle-Calédonie	2	2	1	1	1	1	1	1	1[1]	1[1]
New Zealand Nouvelle-Zélande	1 184	1 188	1 000	769	671	869	809	737	778	779[1]
Papua New Guinea Papouasie-Nvl-Guinée	2	2	2	3[1]	3[1]	3[1]	3[1]	3[1]	3[1]	3[1]
Solomon Islands Iles Salomon	6	2	...	...	...	...	...	...	...	...
Vanuatu[1] Vanuatu[1]	1	1	1	1	1	1	1	1	1	1
former USSR† **ancienne URSS†**	**169 700**	**187 001**	**185 021**	**172 201**	**188 002**	**209 109**	**155 960**	...	...	...

Source:
Food and Agriculture Organization of the United Nations
(Rome).

† For detailed descriptions of data pertaining to
former Czechoslovakia, Germany, SFR Yugoslavia and former
USSR, see Annex I - Country or area nomenclature, regional
and other groupings.

1 FAO estimate.

Source:
Organisation des Nations Unies pour l'alimentation et
l'agriculture (Rome).

† Pour les descriptions en détails des données
relatives à l'ancienne Tchécoslovaquie, l'Allemagne, la Rfs
Yougoslavie et l'ancienne URSS, voir l'Annexe I -
Nomenclature des pays ou zones, groupements régionaux et
autres groupements.

1 Estimation de la FAO.

36
Oil crops, in oil equivalent
Cultures d'huile, en équivalent d'huile
Production: thousand metric tons
Production : milliers de tonnes métriques

Country or area Pays ou zone	1985	1986	1987	1988	1989	1990	1991	1992	1993	1994
World **Monde**	**64 776**	**64 920**	**67 854**	**68 424**	**72 280**	**75 679**	**77 395**	**78 657**	**79 711**	**87 691**
Africa **Afrique**	**4 696**	**5 160**	**5 246**	**5 455**	**5 472**	**5 640**	**5 768**	**5 636**	**5 956**	**5 995**
Algeria Algérie	58	70	67	58	53	70[1]	52[1]	75[1]	75[1]	63[1]
Angola Angola	53	56	58	59	59	62	65	69	70	70
Benin Bénin	86	71	63	73	63	67	67	65	81	69
Botswana Botswana	1	0	0	1	1	1	1[1]	1[1]	1[1]	1[1]
Burkina Faso Burkina Faso	95	94	81	93	88	88	73	77[1]	78[1]	79[1]
Burundi Burundi	7	8	8	8	7	8	8	8	8	7
Cameroon Cameroun	189	192	187	196	232	245	222	212	213	214
Cape Verde Cap-Vert	2	2	2	2	2	2	2	1[1]	1[1]	1[1]
Central African Rep. Rép. centrafricaine	47	65	57	62	64	59	51	55	56	57
Chad Tchad	45	51	54	55	75	62	61	72	85	88
Comoros Comores	7	7	6	6	6	6	7	7	7	7[1]
Congo Congo	25	25	26	26	27	26	26	25	25[1]	25[1]
Côte d'Ivoire Côte d'Ivoire	297	339	351	320	322	348	353	382	379	376
Egypt Egypte	173	172	157	158	141	153	163	178	201	169
Equatorial Guinea[1] Guinée équatoriale[1]	7	7	7	7	7	7	7	7	7	7
Eritrea[1] Erythrée[1]	...	...	...	...	...	...	...	...	4	4
Ethiopia incl.Eritrea Ethiopie comp. Erythrée	120	116	121	127	133	138	144	145	...	...
Gabon Gabon	6	8	9	10	10	10	10[1]	9[1]	8[1]	8[1]
Gambia Gambie	28	39	42	35	45	27	31	21	29	32
Ghana Ghana	143	170	167	185	199	178	171	193	202	214
Guinea Guinée	85	84	81	87	87	87	87	95	97	98[1]
Guinea-Bissau Guinée-Bissau	19	24	20[1]	18	18	18	18	17	18	18[1]

36
Oil crops, in oil equivalent
Production: thousand metric tons [cont.]
Cultures d'huile, en équivalent d'huile
Production : milliers de tonnes métriques [suite]

Country or area Pays ou zone	1985	1986	1987	1988	1989	1990	1991	1992	1993	1994
Kenya Kenya	20	20	22	23	25	25	28	25	25	25
Liberia Libéria	40[1]	41[1]	41[1]	41[1]	41[1]	36[1]	31	31	31[1]	31[1]
Libyan Arab Jamah. Jamah. arabe libyenne	33	* 31	17	18	19	20	20[1]	19[1]	16[1]	15[1]
Madagascar Madagascar	31	32	30	31	33	32	31	29	33	30
Malawi Malawi	45	59	56	50	26	17	25	13	25	17
Mali Mali	75	90	89	107	109	114	102	94	99	104
Mauritania Mauritanie	1	1	1	2[1]	2[1]	2[1]	2[1]	2[1]	1[1]	1[1]
Mauritius Maurice	1	1	1	1	1	1	1	1	0	0[1]
Morocco Maroc	103	117	158	163	136	162	134	182	153	160
Mozambique Mozambique	107	110	112	113	114	115	115	105	105	102
Niger Niger	18	20	14	16	9	6	15	19	20	21
Nigeria Nigéria	1 212	1 385	1 340	1 448	1 524	1 658	1 700	1 759	1 799	1 798
Rwanda Rwanda	7	7	7	6	5	4	5	8	7[1]	5[1]
Sao Tome and Principe Sao Tomé-et-Principe	5	6	5	5	5	4	4	6	6[1]	6[1]
Senegal Sénégal	205	281	321	246	283	238	247	200	216	232
Seychelles [1] Seychelles [1]	2	2	2	1	1	1	1	0	0	0
Sierra Leone Sierra Leone	74	76	75	73	71	71	73	76	78	79[1]
Somalia Somalie	30	24	25	25	26	24	19	10[1]	12	13
South Africa Afrique du Sud	189	173	221	291	270	305	317	131	204	185
Sudan Soudan	230	286	330	370	217	151	162	308	266	446
Swaziland Swaziland	2	3	2[1]	4	5	5[1]	4[1]	3[1]	7[1]	7[1]
Togo Togo	37	37	39	39	36	44	39	41	41	41[1]
Tunisia Tunisie	118	128	112	62	146	184	294	151	234	150[1]
Uganda Ouganda	60	67	66	72	82	97	97	101	108	111

36
Oil crops, in oil equivalent
Production: thousand metric tons [*cont.*]
Cultures d'huile, en équivalent d'huile
Production : milliers de tonnes métriques [*suite*]

Country or area Pays ou zone	1985	1986	1987	1988	1989	1990	1991	1992	1993	1994
United Rep.Tanzania Rép. Unie de Tanzanie	111	128	129	125	120	123	136	129	128	128
Zaire Zaïre	341	343	359	382	395	411	419	428	438	422[1]
Zambia Zambie	28	24	27	28	25	24	23	11	33	20
Zimbabwe Zimbabwe	76	67	80	124	106	104	103	39	79	96
America, North **Amerique du Nord**	**14 982**	**13 966**	**14 214**	**12 156**	**13 437**	**13 965**	**15 108**	**15 359**	**14 498**	**19 464**
Canada Canada	1 774	1 924	1 881	1 885	1 478	1 783	2 045	1 749	2 551	3 366
Costa Rica Costa Rica	44	53	56	69	81	84	87	86	95	102[1]
Cuba Cuba	7	8	8	8	8	8[1]	8[1]	7[1]	8[1]	8[1]
Dominica[1] Dominique[1]	2	2	2	2	2	1	2	2	2	2
Dominican Republic Rép. dominicaine	20	25	24	29	32	31	31	28	34[1]	34[1]
El Salvador El Salvador	26	20	17	18	18	19	18	18	18	18
Grenada Grenade	1	1[1]	1[1]	1[1]	1[1]	1[1]	1[1]	1[1]	1[1]	1[1]
Guatemala Guatemala	35	35	34	40	34	40	45	48	48	50
Haiti Haïti	22	23	22	21	20	19	17	14	14[1]	14[1]
Honduras Honduras	72	83	84	81	86	90	88	91	86	88
Jamaica Jamaïque	18	24	26	27	12	11	13	16	16[1]	16[1]
Mexico Mexique	505	432	499	421	488	428	404	331	303	326
Nicaragua Nicaragua	24	20	20	17	17	22	23	20	18	21
Panama Panama	3	3	3	3	3	3	3	3	3[1]	3[1]
Puerto Rico Porto Rico	1	1	1	1	1	1	1	1	1	1
Saint Lucia[1] Sainte-Lucie[1]	4	4	4	3	3	4	3	5	5	5
St. Vincent-Grenadines St. Vincent-Grenadines	3	3	3	3	3[1]	3	3[1]	3[1]	3[1]	3[1]
Trinidad and Tobago[1] Trinité-et-Tobago[1]	5	6	6	5	4	5	5	7	7	7

36
Oil crops, in oil equivalent
Production: thousand metric tons [*cont.*]
Cultures d'huile, en équivalent d'huile
Production : milliers de tonnes métriques [*suite*]

Country or area Pays ou zone	1985	1986	1987	1988	1989	1990	1991	1992	1993	1994
United States Etats-Unis	12 413	11 297	11 522	9 521	11 147	11 413	12 311	12 929	11 284	15 399
America, South Amérique du Sud	7 855	7 295	7 078	8 400	9 025	9 336	8 605	8 987	9 308	10 293
Argentina Argentine	2 878	3 319	2 491	3 341	2 814	3 808	3 952	3 707	3 409	3 860
Bolivia Bolivie	21	33	28	34	54	55	86	82	108	149
Brazil Brésil	4 141	3 074	3 589	3 906	4 914	4 196	3 344	4 091	4 580	5 039
Chile Chili	26	58	52	64	55	32	36	34	16	15
Colombia Colombie	208	235	235	291	325	369	413	377	399	412
Ecuador Equateur	112	157	174	168	218	207	218	204	218	218
Guyana Guyana	5	6	* 6	6	6[1]	7[1]	7[1]	7[1]	7[1]	7[1]
Paraguay Paraguay	327	244	336	381	428	460	384	337	427	434
Peru Pérou	50	53	49	62	67	58	53	46	45	52
Suriname Suriname	10	8	6	4	5	3	3	4	3[1]	3[1]
Uruguay Uruguay	20	39	33	29	30	27	29	31	26	27[1]
Venezuela Venezuela	56	69	80	114	108	114	80	69	70	75
Asia Asie	27 044	27 926	28 647	30 581	31 687	34 661	35 062	36 947	38 798	40 746
Afghanistan Afghanistan	32	33	29	29	28	26	30	30	30	30
Azerbaijan Azerbaïdjan	...	...	...	...	...	...	...	37	38[1]	38[1]
Bangladesh Bangladesh	161	151	142	145	142	145	146	155	156	154
Bhutan Bhoutan	1[1]	1[1]	1[1]	1	1	1[1]	1[1]	1[1]	1[1]	1[1]
Cambodia Cambodge	13	13	14	13	15	15	19	20	20[1]	20[1]
China Chine	9 319	8 966	9 659	8 727	8 300	9 716	10 091	9 826	10 886	11 840
Cyprus Chypre	3	3	2	4	3	3	2	5	3	3
Gaza Strip Zone de Gaza	1	* 1	* 1	* 1	* 0	* 1	* 1	* 1	0[1]	0[1]
Georgia Géorgie	...	...	...	...	...	...	...	5	2	6[1]

36
Oil crops, in oil equivalent
Production: thousand metric tons [*cont.*]
Cultures d'huile, en équivalent d'huile
Production : milliers de tonnes métriques [*suite*]

Country or area Pays ou zone	1985	1986	1987	1988	1989	1990	1991	1992	1993	1994
India Inde	4 919	4 769	4 922	6 923	7 195	7 238	7 440	8 598	8 124	8 569
Indonesia Indonésie	3 447	3 682	3 808	4 151	4 413	5 210	5 450	6 011	6 330	6 879
Iran, Islamic Rep. of Iran, Rép. islamique d'	74	76	68	81	79	98	88	86	82	89
Iraq Iraq	11	12	12	14	19	36	17	27	43	41[l]
Israel Israël	48	41	32	36	31	35	28	40	30	29
Japan Japon	64	69	76	67	68	59	52	50	32	36
Jordan Jordanie	4	7	5	16	6	14	9	18	7	15[l]
Kazakstan Kazakstan	...	...	...	...	...	...	...	94	69	77
Korea, Dem. P. R. Corée, R. p. dém. de	78[l]	80[l]	83[l]	83[l]	78[l]	85[l]	82	76	72	76
Korea, Republic of Corée, République de	75	75	79	88	85	76	64	64	60	60
Kyrgyzstan Kirghizistan	...	...	...	...	...	...	...	* 6	6[l]	7[l]
Lao People's Dem. Rep. Rép. dém. pop. lao	6	3	4	4	5	5	6	7	7	8
Lebanon Liban	8	12	17	11	12	16	13	26	14[l]	15[l]
Malaysia Malaisie	4 893	5 356	5 310	5 893	7 069	7 142	7 134	7 421	8 628	8 415
Maldives Maldives	1	1	1	1	2	* 2	* 2	2	* 2	2[l]
Myanmar Myanmar	439	432	426	378	297	317	329	278	328	311
Nepal Népal	34	34	35	39	41	41	40	39	41	42
Pakistan Pakistan	550	589	619	616	643	700	889	676	601	595
Philippines Philippines	1 182	1 532	1 434	1 103	1 091	1 504	1 201	1 299	1 259	1 265
Saudi Arabia Arabie saoudite	1	1	2	2	2	2	2	2	2	2
Singapore Singapour	1	1	1	0[l]	0[l]	0[l]	0[l]	0[l]	0[l]	0[l]
Sri Lanka Sri Lanka	279	307	232	197	250	255	220	230	211	225
Syrian Arab Republic Rép. arabe syrienne	107	156	109	180	90	172	131	216	168	182
Tajikistan Tadjikistan	...	...	...	...	...	...	...	70	65[l]	68[l]

36
Oil crops, in oil equivalent
Production: thousand metric tons [*cont.*]
Cultures d'huile, en équivalent d'huile
Production : milliers de tonnes métriques [*suite*]

Country or area Pays ou zone	1985	1986	1987	1988	1989	1990	1991	1992	1993	1994
Thailand Thaïlande	457	485	507	584	658	663	651	690	738	743
Turkey Turquie	659	816	813	953	844	836	677	757	648	777
Turkmenistan Turkménistan	...	...	...	...	...	...	...	140	123	141
Uzbekistan Ouzbékistan	...	...	...	...	...	...	...	419	433	406
Viet Nam Viet Nam	167	184	200	202	214	211	242	252	265	286
Yemen Yémen	* 5	5	4	4	5	5	5	6	7	7
Europe **Europe**	**6 190**	**6 591**	**8 375**	**7 374**	**7 803**	**7 566**	**8 762**	**7 691**	**7 332**	**7 688**
Albania Albanie	26	21	21	15	20	12	10	6	6	5[1]
Austria Autriche	8	10	35	54	60	62	84	94	108	109[1]
Belarus Bélarus	...	...	...	...	...	...	...	44	45	46
Belgium-Luxembourg Belgique-Luxembourg	5	6	8	7	8	11	12	11	10	12
Bosnia & Herzegovina[1] Bosnie-Herzégovine[1]	...	...	...	...	...	...	...	2	3	3
Bulgaria Bulgarie	156	210	175	157	195	166	189	250	187	246
Croatia Croatie	...	...	...	...	...	...	...	37	38	39
former Czechoslovakia† anc. Tchécoslovaquie†	127	139	152	169	180	178	230	211	...	...
Czech Republic République tchèque	...	...	...	...	...	...	...	...	149	179
Denmark Danemark	191	217	195	177	229	278	254	142	146	130
Estonia[1] Estonie[1]	...	...	...	...	...	...	...	1	1	1
Finland Finlande	31	43	31	42	44	41	33	46	45	38
France France	1 147	1 163	2 064	1 837	1 595	1 743	1 909	1 520	1 263	1 528
Germany † Allemagne†	419	499	585	597	677	764	1 094	984	1 086	1 132
Greece Grèce	508	430	430	463	474	306	497	454	450	461
Hungary Hongrie	325	411	382	344	353	331	385	338	293	293
Ireland Irlande	5	2	6	4	4	7	8	* 6	* 2	2[1]

36

Oil crops, in oil equivalent
Production: thousand metric tons [*cont.*]
Cultures d'huile, en équivalent d'huile
Production : milliers de tonnes métriques [*suite*]

Country or area Pays ou zone	1985	1986	1987	1988	1989	1990	1991	1992	1993	1994
Italy Italie	934	733	1 233	941	1 147	722	1 285	856	930	933
Latvia Lettonie	...	...	...	...	...	...	...	1	0[1]	0[1]
Lithuania Lituanie	...	...	...	...	...	...	...	4	4[1]	4[1]
Malta Malte	0[1]	0[1]	0[1]	0[1]	0	0[1]	0[1]	0[1]	0[1]	0[1]
Netherlands Pays-Bas	13	9	13	11	11	12	11	6	5	4[1]
Norway Norvège	4	4	4	3	3	3	2	3	5	5[1]
Poland Pologne	385	462	421	426	563	434	371	269	212	269
Portugal Portugal	72	98	80	55	94	71	118	59	77	70
Republic of Moldova République de Moldova	...	...	...	...	...	...	...	80	79	61
Romania Roumanie	363	438	388	362	346	264	291	341	308	402
Russian Federation Fédération de Russie	...	...	...	...	...	...	...	1 432	1 289	1 206
Slovakia Slovaquie	...	...	...	...	...	...	...	...	49	57
Slovenia Slovénie	...	...	...	...	...	...	...	2	2	2[1]
Spain Espagne	835	944	1 289	988	1 051	1 308	1 099	1 267	1 157	988
Sweden Suède	130	131	88	100	148	148	101	99	126	74
Switzerland Suisse	14	14	17	18	19	16	18	16	18	13
TFYR Macedonia L'ex-R.y. Macédoine	...	...	...	...	...	...	...	16	8	8
Ukraine Ukraine	...	...	...	...	...	...	...	928	869	647
United Kingdom Royaume-Uni	313	336	478	374	344	465	514	493	477	533
Yugoslavia Yougoslavie	...	...	...	...	...	...	...	161	170	153
Yugoslavia, SFR† Yougoslavie, Rfs†	177	273	280	229	237	227	245	...	...	...
Oceania **Océanie**	**773**	**738**	**665**	**662**	**678**	**646**	**739**	**776**	**795**	**798**
American Samoa [1] Samoa américaines [1]	1	1	1	1	1	1	1	1	1	1
Australia Australie	269	228	188	228	227	176	276	252	263	246

36
Oil crops, in oil equivalent
Production: thousand metric tons [*cont.*]
Cultures d'huile, en équivalent d'huile
Production : milliers de tonnes métriques [*suite*]

Country or area Pays ou zone	1985	1986	1987	1988	1989	1990	1991	1992	1993	1994
Cocos (Keeling) Islands[1] Iles des Cocos (Keeling)[1]	1	1	1	1	1	1	1	1	1	1
Cook Islands Iles Cook	1[1]	1[1]	1[1]	1[1]	1[1]	1[1]	1[1]	0	1	0
Fiji Fidji	28	34	25	23	25	33	26	32	26[1]	26[1]
French Polynesia[1] Polynésie française[1]	14	14	15	12	12	13	11	11	11	11
Guam[1] Guam[1]	4	4	5	5	5	5	5	5	5	6
Kiribati[1] Kiribati[1]	9	7	7	14	10	6	9	9	8	8
New Caledonia[1] Nouvelle-Calédonie[1]	2	2	2	2	2	2	2	2	2	1
New Zealand Nouvelle-Zélande	0[1]	3	3	2	1	1	1	1	1	1[1]
Palau[1] Palaos[1]	23	23	23	18	18	18	18	18	18	18
Papua New Guinea Papouasie-Nvl-Guinée	283	282	281	246	270	272	284	332	346	359
Samoa Samoa	23[1]	25	22[1]	21[1]	21[1]	18[1]	12[1]	13[1]	17[1]	17[1]
Solomon Islands Iles Salomon	64	58	40	44	48	49	52	59	56	63
Tonga Tonga	7	10	6	5	4	4	4	4[1]	4[1]	4[1]
Vanuatu Vanuatu	42	45	45	40	32	47	35	34	34[1]	34[1]
former USSR† ancienne URSS†	3 236	3 244	3 628	3 796	4 177	3 865	3 351	...	...	...

Source:
Food and Agriculture Organization of the United Nations (Rome).

† For detailed descriptions of data pertaining to former Czechoslovakia, Germany, SFR Yugoslavia and former USSR, see Annex I - Country or area nomenclature, regional and other groupings.

1 FAO estimate.

Source:
Organisation des Nations Unies pour l'alimentation et l'agriculture (Rome).

† Pour les descriptions en détails des données relatives à l'ancienne Tchécoslovaquie, l'Allemagne, la Rfs Yougoslavie et l'ancienne URSS, voir l'Annexe I - Nomenclature des pays ou zones, groupements régionaux et autres groupements.

1 Estimation de la FAO.

37
Livestock
Cheptel

Thousand head
Milliers de têtes

Country or area	1987	1988	1989	1990	1991	1992	1993	1994	Pays ou zone
World									***Monde***
Cattle	1266654	1259574	1272870	1283298	1285143	1281377	1281606	1288124	**Bovine**
Sheep	1136599	1146249	1173970	1183392	1159298	1133372	1096050	1086661	**Ovine**
Pigs	837 507	830 401	845 941	852 434	863 575	864 673	869 537	875 407	**Porcine**
Horses	60 281	60 337	60 732	60 773	61 168	60 738	59 592	58 158	**Chevaline**
Asses	41 718	42 297	42 676	43 202	43 398	43 676	43 688	43 772	**Asine**
Mules	14 358	14 500	14 671	14 744	14 855	15 004	15 066	14 952	**Mulassière**
Africa									**Afrique**
Cattle	176 269	178 965	183 111	188 497	190 098	189 658	189 244	192 180	**Bovine**
Sheep	193 931	194 237	200 011	202 067	201 874	206 843	205 785	208 845	**Ovine**
Pigs	13 842	14 354	15 495	16 487	17 602	18 923	20 484	21 080	**Porcine**
Horses	4 296	4 372	4 419	4 565	4 642	4 688	4 763	4 758	**Chevaline**
Asses	12 071	12 322	12 253	12 685	13 029	13 271	13 340	13 408	**Asine**
Mules	1 306	1 300	1 314	1 342	1 369	1 403	1 421	1 394	**Mulassière**
Algeria									**Algérie**
Cattle	1 416	1 435	1 405	1 393	1 300	1 334	1 350[1]	1 370[1]	Bovine
Sheep	16 148	16 429	17 316	17 698	16 891	17 723	17 800[1]	17 850[1]	Ovine
Pigs [1]	5	5	5	5	5	6	6	6	Porcine [1]
Horses	84	85	86	81	82	77	78[1]	78[1]	Chevaline
Asses	354	327	322	299	* 298	310[1]	315[1]	315[1]	Asine
Mules	127	113	101	100	* 101	110[1]	115[1]	115[1]	Mulassière
Angola									**Angola**
Cattle	3 300	3 200	3 100	3 100[1]	3 150	3 200	3 250[1]	3 280[1]	Bovine
Sheep	250[1]	250[1]	240	240	240	250	255[1]	255[1]	Ovine
Pigs	770[1]	770[1]	800	800	805	810	815[1]	820[1]	Porcine
Horses [1]	1	1	1	1	1	1	1	1	Chevaline [1]
Asses [1]	5	5	5	5	5	5	5	5	Asine [1]
Benin									**Bénin**
Cattle	896	925	943	1 080	1 088	1 095[1]	1 100[1]	1 223	Bovine
Sheep	831	821	846	869	893	920[1]	940[1]	940[1]	Ovine
Pigs	420	437	459	462	515	530[1]	550[1]	555	Porcine
Horses [1]	6	6	6	6	6	6	6	6	Chevaline [1]
Asses [1]	1	1	1	1	1	1	1	1	Asine [1]
Botswana									**Botswana**
Cattle	2 263	2 408	2 543	2 696	2 844	2 800[1]	2 700[1]	2 800[1]	Bovine
Sheep	240	259	286	317	320[1]	325[1]	325[1]	344[1]	Ovine
Pigs	11	13	15	16	16[1]	16[1]	16[1]	17[1]	Porcine
Horses	24	29	32	34	34[1]	34[1]	34[1]	35[1]	Chevaline
Asses	144[1]	148	151	152[1]	153[1]	153[1]	153[1]	155[1]	Asine
Mules	3[1]	2	2	3[1]	3[1]	3[1]	3[1]	3[1]	Mulassière
Burkina Faso									**Burkina Faso**
Cattle	3 711	3 785	3 860	3 937	4 015	4 096	4 178	4 261	Bovine
Sheep	4 619	4 757	4 900	5 050	5 198	5 352	5 520	5 686	Ovine
Pigs	459	477	496	516	518	530	540	551	Porcine
Horses	21	22	22	22	22	22	23	23[1]	Chevaline
Asses	387	395	403	411	419	427	436[1]	445[1]	Asine
Burundi									**Burundi**
Cattle	422	429	423	432	409	420[1]	420[1]	380[1]	Bovine
Sheep	313	350	327	361	381	390[1]	390[1]	350[1]	Ovine
Pigs	80	115	91	103	92	100[1]	100[1]	80[1]	Porcine
Cameroon									**Cameroun**
Cattle	4 362	4 471	4 582	4 697	4 700[1]	4 730[1]	4 867[1]	4 867[1]	Bovine
Sheep	2 597	2 897	3 170	* 3 500	3 550[1]	3 560[1]	3 770[1]	3 770[1]	Ovine
Pigs	1 178	1 237	1 299	1 364	1 370[1]	1 380[1]	1 380[1]	1 380[1]	Porcine
Horses	15	13	14[1]	14[1]	15[1]	15[1]	15[1]	15[1]	Chevaline
Asses	25	33	35[1]	35[1]	36[1]	36[1]	36[1]	36[1]	Asine
Cape Verde									**Cap−Vert**
Cattle	13	18	19	19	16	18	18	18	Bovine
Sheep	4	5	6	8	4	6[1]	6[1]	7[1]	Ovine
Pigs	80	85	91	99	100[1]	102[1]	105[1]	111[1]	Porcine
Horses	0[1]	1	1	1[1]	0	1[1]	1[1]	1[1]	Chevaline
Asses	6	7	11	11[1]	13	11[1]	11[1]	12[1]	Asine
Mules	1[1]	1	2	2[1]	2	2[1]	2[1]	2[1]	Mulassière

37
Livestock
Thousand head [*cont.*]
Cheptel
Milliers de têtes [*suite*]

Country or area	1987	1988	1989	1990	1991	1992	1993	1994	Pays ou zone
Central African Rep.									**Rép. centrafricaine**
Cattle	2 306	2 398	2 495	2 595	2 677	2 680	2 776	2 800[1]	Bovine
Sheep	117	122	128	134	139	145	151	152[1]	Ovine
Pigs	371	382	393	442	454	467	481	480[1]	Porcine
Chad									**Tchad**
Cattle	4 002	4 098	4 197	4 297	4 400	4 506	4 517	4 621	Bovine
Sheep	1 800	1 815	1 870	1 926	1 983	2 028	2 089	2 152	Ovine
Pigs	12	13	13	14	15	15	16	17	Porcine
Horses	186	188	192	179	182	206	210	214	Chevaline
Asses	222	234	259	264	269	243	248	253	Asine
Comoros									**Comores**
Cattle	44	45	47	48[1]	48[1]	49[1]	50[1]	50[1]	Bovine
Sheep	12	12	13	13[1]	14[1]	14[1]	15[1]	15[1]	Ovine
Asses [1]	4	4	4	4	5	5	5	5	Asine [1]
Congo									**Congo**
Cattle	70	69	62	70	64	65[1]	67[1]	68[1]	Bovine
Sheep	97	101	101	104	107	110[1]	111[1]	111[1]	Ovine
Pigs	47	50	44	50[1]	52[1]	55[1]	56[1]	56[1]	Porcine
Côte d'Ivoire									**Côte d'Ivoire**
Cattle	917	992	1 049	1 108	1 145	1 180	1 205	1 232	Bovine
Sheep	1 051	1 090	1 115	1 134	1 161	1 190	1 219	1 251	Ovine
Pigs	335	342	351	360	372	382	392	404	Porcine
Djibouti									**Djibouti**
Cattle [1]	140	160	180	195	190	190	190	190	Bovine [1]
Sheep [1]	412	414	400	430	470	470	470	470	Ovine [1]
Asses [1]	8	8	8	8	8	8	8	8	Asine [1]
Egypt									**Egypte**
Cattle	2 300[1]	2 780	2 721	2 618	2 973	2 970[1]	2 977	3 070[1]	Bovine
Sheep	3 793	3 908	3 481	3 364	3 084	3 385	3 707	* 3 382	Ovine
Pigs	22[1]	21[1]	23	24	24	28[1]	27[1]	27	Porcine
Horses	9[1]	10[1]	10[1]	10[1]	10[1]	10[1]	10[1]	10[1]	Chevaline
Asses	1 600[1]	1 500[1]	1 158	1 380[1]	1 530	1 550[1]	1 600[1]	1 650[1]	Asine
Mules	1[1]	1[1]	1[1]	1[1]	1[1]	1[1]	1[1]	1[1]	Mulassière
Equatorial Guinea									**Guinée équatoriale**
Cattle [1]	5	5	5	5	5	5	5	5	Bovine [1]
Sheep [1]	35	35	35	35	36	36	36	36	Ovine [1]
Pigs [1]	5	5	5	5	5	5	5	5	Porcine [1]
Eritrea									**Erythrée**
Cattle [1]	...	...	...	...	...	...	1 550	1 550	Bovine [1]
Sheep [1]	...	...	...	...	...	...	1 510	1 510	Ovine [1]
Ethiopia									**Ethiopie**
Cattle [1]	...	...	...	...	...	...	29 450	29 450	Bovine [1]
Sheep [1]	...	...	...	...	...	...	21 700	21 700	Ovine [1]
Pigs [1]	...	...	...	...	...	...	20	20	Porcine [1]
Horses [1]	...	...	...	...	...	...	2 750	2 750	Chevaline [1]
Asses [1]	...	...	...	...	...	...	5 200	5 200	Asine [1]
Mules [1]	...	...	...	...	...	...	630	630	Mulassière [1]
Ethiopia incl.Eritrea									Ethiopie comp. Erythrée
Cattle	* 27 000	* 27 000	* 28 900	30 000[1]	30 000[1]	31 000[1]	...	...	Bovine
Sheep	* 24 000	* 24 000	* 24 000	* 22 960	23 000[1]	23 200[1]	...	...	Ovine
Pigs [1]	18	18	19	19	20	20	...	...	Porcine [1]
Horses [1]	2 500	2 550	2 600	2 650	2 700	2 750	...	...	Chevaline [1]
Asses [1]	4 700	4 800	4 900	5 000	5 100	5 200	...	...	Asine [1]
Mules [1]	530	550	570	590	610	630	...	...	Mulassière [1]
Gabon									**Gabon**
Cattle	21	24	27	31	33	35	37	38[1]	Bovine
Sheep	149	153	157	160[1]	165[1]	170[1]	170[1]	170[1]	Ovine
Pigs	141	147	159	160[1]	162[1]	164[1]	165[1]	165[1]	Porcine
Gambia									**Gambie**
Cattle	350[1]	387	390[1]	400[1]	390[1]	400[1]	400[1]	414[1]	Bovine
Sheep	157[1]	163	140[1]	121	121	121[1]	121[1]	121[1]	Ovine
Pigs	11[1]	11	11[1]	11[1]	11[1]	11[1]	11[1]	11[1]	Porcine
Horses	17[1]	17	18	16	16	16[1]	16[1]	16[1]	Chevaline
Asses	40[1]	40	41	37	31	30[1]	30[1]	30[1]	Asine
Ghana									**Ghana**
Cattle	1 170	1 145	1 136	1 145	1 195	1 159	* 1 392	* 1 680	Bovine

37
Livestock
Thousand head [*cont.*]
Cheptel
Milliers de têtes [*suite*]

Country or area	1987	1988	1989	1990	1991	1992	1993	1994	Pays ou zone
Sheep	1 989	2 046	2 212	2 224	2 162	2 126	* 2 920	* 3 288	Ovine
Pigs	399	478	559	474	454	413	* 496	* 595	Porcine
Horses	2	2	2	1	1	2	2[1]	2[1]	Chevaline
Asses	14	10	11	10	12	13	13[1]	13[1]	Asine
Guinea									**Guinée**
Cattle	1 500[1]	1 500[1]	1 436	1 472	1 530[1]	1 612	1 650[1]	1 658[1]	Bovine
Sheep	440[1]	435[1]	432	420	425[1]	431	435[1]	435[1]	Ovine
Pigs	28[1]	25[1]	24	22	27[1]	32	33[1]	33[1]	Porcine
Horses	2[1]	2[1]	2	2[1]	2[1]	2[1]	2[1]	2[1]	Chevaline
Asses	2[1]	1[1]	1	1[1]	1[1]	1[1]	1[1]	1[1]	Asine
Guinea—Bissau									**Guinée—Bissau**
Cattle	350[1]	370[1]	400	410	425[1]	450	475[1]	494[1]	Bovine
Sheep	210[1]	220[1]	230[1]	242	245[1]	250	255[1]	263[1]	Ovine
Pigs	290[1]	290[1]	290[1]	290[1]	290	300	310[1]	312[1]	Porcine
Horses	1[1]	1[1]	2	2	2	2	2[1]	2[1]	Chevaline
Asses	4[1]	5[1]	5	5	5	5	5[1]	5[1]	Asine
Kenya									**Kenya**
Cattle	12 645	13 050	13 457	13 793	13 000[1]	12 000[1]	11 000[1]	11 000[1]	Bovine
Sheep	* 6 040	* 6 167	* 6 325	* 6 516	6 500[1]	6 000[1]	5 500[1]	5 500[1]	Ovine
Pigs	94	97	100	105	105[1]	105[1]	105[1]	107[1]	Porcine
Horses [1]	2	2	2	2	2	2	2	2	Chevaline [1]
Lesotho									**Lesotho**
Cattle	625	627	583	650	660[1]	600[1]	650[1]	663[1]	Bovine
Sheep	1 704	1 650	1 505	1 641	1 676	1 600[1]	1 665[1]	1 691[1]	Ovine
Pigs	70[1]	72[1]	73[1]	74[1]	75[1]	75[1]	76[1]	78[1]	Porcine
Horses	129	116	104	121[1]	122[1]	122[1]	123[1]	123[1]	Chevaline
Asses	148	131	151	155[1]	158[1]	160[1]	162[1]	168[1]	Asine
Mules [1]	1	1	1	1	1	1	1	1	Mulassière [1]
Liberia									**Libéria**
Cattle [1]	42	42	40	38	37	36	36	36	Bovine [1]
Sheep [1]	240	240	230	220	215	210	210	210	Ovine [1]
Pigs [1]	140	140	130	120	120	120	120	120	Porcine [1]
Libyan Arab Jamah.									**Jamah. arabe libyenne**
Cattle	90	95	102	120	125[1]	130[1]	70[1]	50[1]	Bovine
Sheep	4 500	4 500	5 000	5 200	5 500[1]	5 000[1]	4 000[1]	3 500[1]	Ovine
Horses	20	25	20	20	25[1]	24[1]	22[1]	20[1]	Chevaline
Asses [1]	61	61	62	62	62	60	55	50	Asine [1]
Madagascar									**Madagascar**
Cattle	10 220	10 232	10 243	10 254	* 10 265	* 10 276	10 287	* 10 288	Bovine
Sheep	670[1]	683	700[1]	* 737	* 721	730[1]	735[1]	740[1]	Ovine
Pigs	1 532	1 412	1 400	1 431	* 1 461	* 1 493	* 1 525	* 1 558	Porcine
Malawi									**Malawi**
Cattle	1 055	860	850[1]	* 836	* 899	* 967	970[1]	980[1]	Bovine
Sheep	170[1]	170[1]	175[1]	* 177	* 186	* 195	195[1]	196[1]	Ovine
Pigs	313	250	240[1]	* 233	* 235	* 238	240[1]	245[1]	Porcine
Asses	1	1	2[1]	2[1]	2[1]	2[1]	2[1]	2[1]	Asine
Mali									**Mali**
Cattle	4 589	4 738	4 826	4 996	5 198	5 373	5 380	5 542	Bovine
Sheep	* 5 329	5 527	5 771	6 086	6 359	6 658	4 926	5 173	Ovine
Pigs	56	58	55	56	67	75	62	63	Porcine
Horses	54	56	55	77	83	85	92	101	Chevaline
Asses	348	510	517	575	590	600	600	611	Asine
Mauritania									**Mauritanie**
Cattle	1 220	1 260	1 300	1 350	1 400	1 200	1 000[1]	1 011[1]	Bovine
Sheep	* 4 200	* 4 500	* 4 800	* 5 100	5 300[1]	* 5 100	4 800[1]	4 800[1]	Ovine
Horses [1]	16	17	17	18	18	18	18	18	Chevaline [1]
Asses	149[1]	149[1]	150[1]	151[1]	153[1]	154[1]	155[1]	155[1]	Asine
Mauritius									**Maurice**
Cattle	32	33	34	33	34[1]	33	34[1]	34[1]	Bovine
Sheep	7	7	7	7	6[1]	7	7[1]	7[1]	Ovine
Pigs	13	10	10	13	14	14	15	17[1]	Porcine
Morocco									**Maroc**
Cattle	3 178	3 137	3 324	3 346	3 183	3 269	2 924	2 431	Bovine
Sheep	16 136	12 733	13 761	13 514	13 308	17 201	16 302	15 594	Ovine
Pigs [1]	9	9	9	9	9	9	10	10	Porcine [1]
Horses	198	198	184	194	188	186	180	156	Chevaline

37
Livestock
Thousand head [cont.]
Cheptel
Milliers de têtes [suite]

Country or area	1987	1988	1989	1990	1991	1992	1993	1994	Pays ou zone
Asses	854	904	918	912	896	940	946	880	Asine
Mules	524	511	515	523	528	536	547	519	Mulassière
Mozambique									**Mozambique**
Cattle [1]	1 350	1 360	1 370	1 380	1 370	1 250	1 250	1 250	Bovine [1]
Sheep [1]	117	119	120	121	118	118	118	119	Ovine [1]
Pigs [1]	155	160	165	170	165	170	170	174	Porcine [1]
Asses [1]	20	20	20	20	20	20	20	20	Asine [1]
Namibia									**Namibie**
Cattle	1 835	1 970	2 014	2 087	2 212	2 206	2 037	2 036	Bovine
Sheep	2 811	3 046	3 242	3 328	3 295	2 863	2 768	2 620	Ovine
Pigs	19[1]	18[1]	20	18	17	15	20	18	Porcine
Horses	49[1]	50[1]	47	52	53[1]	55	58	59	Chevaline
Asses	68[1]	68[1]	68[1]	68[1]	68[1]	* 70	71[1]	71[1]	Asine
Mules	6[1]	6[1]	6[1]	6[1]	6[1]	* 7	7[1]	7[1]	Mulassière
Niger									**Niger**
Cattle	1 495	1 563	1 636	1 711	1 790	* 1 909	* 1 947	* 1 986	Bovine
Sheep	2 676	2 900	2 950	3 098	3 253	* 3 500	* 3 570	* 3 700	Ovine
Pigs [1]	37	37	37	37	38	38	39	39	Porcine [1]
Horses	76	78	80	82[1]	82[1]	82[1]	82[1]	82[1]	Chevaline
Asses	382	397	412	431	449	450[1]	450[1]	450[1]	Asine
Nigeria									**Nigéria**
Cattle	13 415	13 759	14 170	14 640	15 140	15 700	16 316	16 717[1]	Bovine
Sheep	11 107	11 575	11 971	12 460	13 000	13 500	14 000[1]	14 455[1]	Ovine
Pigs	2 400[1]	2 600[1]	3 000[1]	3 410	4 263	5 328	6 660	6 926	Porcine
Horses	214[1]	212[1]	210[1]	208	206[1]	205[1]	204[1]	204[1]	Chevaline
Asses	830[1]	860[1]	900[1]	936	960[1]	1 000[1]	1 000[1]	1 033[1]	Asine
Réunion									**Réunion**
Cattle	19	19	18	20	22	23	25	25	Bovine
Sheep	3	2	2	2	2	2	2[1]	2[1]	Ovine
Pigs	99	97	84	86	94	92	86	86[1]	Porcine
Rwanda									**Rwanda**
Cattle	583	579	594	582	600[1]	610[1]	610[1]	610[1]	Bovine
Sheep	363	364	393	389	390[1]	395[1]	400[1]	400[1]	Ovine
Pigs	105	126	120	116	120[1]	130[1]	130[1]	130[1]	Porcine
Saint Helena									**Sainte−Hélène**
Cattle	1	1	1	1	1	1	1	1	Bovine
Sheep	1	2	2	2	1	1	1	1	Ovine
Pigs	1	1	1	1	1	1	1	1	Porcine
Sao Tome and Principe									**Sao Tomé−et−Principe**
Cattle [1]	3	3	4	4	4	· 4	4	4	Bovine [1]
Sheep [1]	2	2	2	2	2	2	2	2	Ovine [1]
Pigs [1]	3	3	3	3	3	3	2	2	Porcine [1]
Senegal									**Sénégal**
Cattle	2 543	2 465	2 540	2 622	2 687	2 700[1]	2 750[1]	2 800[1]	Bovine
Sheep	3 326	3 120	3 300[1]	3 400[1]	* 3 800	* 4 200	* 4 400	* 4 600	Ovine
Pigs	285	288	291	295	300[1]	310[1]	320[1]	329[1]	Porcine
Horses	338	360	380[1]	440	453	431	498	500[1]	Chevaline
Asses	278	290	300[1]	303	328	362	364	379[1]	Asine
Seychelles									**Seychelles**
Cattle	2[1]	2[1]	2[1]	2[1]	2[1]	2[1]	2[1]	2[1]	Bovine
Pigs [1]	16	17	17	18	18	18	18	18	Porcine [1]
Sierra Leone									**Sierra Leone**
Cattle	333[1]	333	333	333	333	349	360	362[1]	Bovine
Sheep	280[1]	264	267	271	274	288	302	302[1]	Ovine
Pigs	50[1]	50[1]	50[1]	50[1]	50[1]	50[1]	50[1]	51[1]	Porcine
Somalia									**Somalie**
Cattle	4 770	4 983	4 800[1]	3 800[1]	3 300[1]	3 000[1]	4 000[1]	5 000	Bovine
Sheep	13 195	14 304	14 350[1]	12 000[1]	10 000[1]	9 000[1]	11 000[1]	13 000	Ovine
Pigs [1]	10	10	10	10	7	2	6	9	Porcine [1]
Horses [1]	1	1	1	1	1	1	1	1	Chevaline [1]
Asses [1]	25	25	25	25	25	20	23	24	Asine [1]
Mules [1]	23	23	24	24	23	18	20	21	Mulassière [1]
South Africa									**Afrique du Sud**
Cattle	* 11 799	11 820[1]	11 850[1]	* 13 398	* 13 512	13 074	12 503	12 584	Bovine
Sheep	* 29 753	* 29 640	* 30 935	* 32 665	* 32 580	30 955	28 930	29 134	Ovine
Pigs	* 1 455	1 460[1]	1 470[1]	1 480[1]	1 490[1]	1 529	1 493	1 511	Porcine

37
Livestock
Thousand head [*cont.*]
Cheptel
Milliers de têtes [*suite*]

Country or area	1987	1988	1989	1990	1991	1992	1993	1994	Pays ou zone
Horses [1]	230	230	230	230	230	230	230	230	Chevaline [1]
Asses [1]	210	210	210	210	210	210	210	210	Asine [1]
Mules [1]	14	14	14	14	14	14	14	14	Mulassière [1]
Sudan									**Soudan**
Cattle	19 738	19 858	20 167	20 583	21 028	* 21 600	21 600[1]	21 751[1]	Bovine
Sheep	18 807	19 207	19 668	20 168	20 700	* 22 600	22 500[1]	22 870[1]	Ovine
Horses [1]	21	20	21	22	22	23	23	23	Chevaline [1]
Asses [1]	660	650	670	675	680	681	670	675	Asine [1]
Mules [1]	1	1	1	1	1	1	1	1	Mulassière [1]
Swaziland									**Swaziland**
Cattle	641	640	679	716	740	753	608	620[1]	Bovine
Sheep	28	26	25	24	24	28	27	27[1]	Ovine
Pigs	21	18	19	24	28	31	30	32[1]	Porcine
Horses	1	1	1	1	1	1	1	1[1]	Chevaline
Asses	13	12	12	12	12	12	12	12[1]	Asine
Togo									**Togo**
Cattle	235	255	250[1]	243	247	251	248	250[1]	Bovine
Sheep	1 094	1 175	1 147	1 144	1 200	1 200	1 200	1 250[1]	Ovine
Pigs	245	385	433	709	709	800[1]	850[1]	934[1]	Porcine
Horses	2	2[1]	2[1]	2[1]	2[1]	2[1]	2[1]	2[1]	Chevaline
Asses	2	3	4	3	3[1]	3[1]	3[1]	4[1]	Asine
Tunisia									**Tunisie**
Cattle	666	634	626	622	631	* 636	659	660[1]	Bovine
Sheep	5 707	5 581	5 548	5 966	6 290	6 400[1]	7 110	7 100[1]	Ovine
Pigs	4[1]	3[1]	5[1]	7	6[1]	6[1]	6[1]	6[1]	Porcine
Horses [1]	55	55	55	55	56	56	56	56	Chevaline [1]
Asses [1]	218	220	224	226	229	229	230	230	Asine [1]
Mules [1]	75	76	77	78	79	80	81	81	Mulassière [1]
Uganda									**Ouganda**
Cattle	3 905	4 260	4 417	4 913	5 000[1]	5 100[1]	5 200[1]	5 100[1]	Bovine
Sheep	1 400[1]	1 300[1]	1 320[1]	1 350[1]	* 1 380	* 1 560	* 1 760	1 980[1]	Ovine
Pigs	470	452	716	824	850[1]	880[1]	900[1]	880[1]	Porcine
Asses [1]	17	17	17	17	17	17	17	17	Asine [1]
United Rep.Tanzania									**Rép. Unie de Tanzanie**
Cattle	12 777	12 866	12 956	13 047	13 138	* 13 217	* 13 296	* 13 376	Bovine
Sheep	3 512	3 526	3 541	3 557	3 556	* 3 706	* 3 828	* 3 955	Ovine
Pigs	290[1]	300[1]	310[1]	320[1]	* 330	* 330	* 335	* 335	Porcine
Asses [1]	171	172	173	174	175	176	177	178	Asine [1]
Zaire									**Zaïre**
Cattle	1 386	1 434	1 484	1 535	1 586	1 600[1]	1 650[1]	1 696[1]	Bovine
Sheep	849	874	900	927	974	980[1]	985[1]	1 012[1]	Ovine
Pigs	858	918	982	1 050	1 118	1 120[1]	1 130[1]	1 185[1]	Porcine
Horses	...	...	...	...	...	...	...	...	Chevaline
Zambia									**Zambie**
Cattle	2 601	2 638	2 672	* 2 878	* 2 984	* 3 095	* 3 204	3 300[1]	Bovine
Sheep	* 47	* 51	55	* 60	* 62	* 63	* 67	69[1]	Ovine
Pigs	196	207	297	295[1]	296[1]	290[1]	293[1]	295[1]	Porcine
Asses	1[1]	1[1]	1	2[1]	2[1]	2[1]	2[1]	2[1]	Asine
Zimbabwe									**Zimbabwe**
Cattle	5 918	5 805	5 850	6 218	6 374	4 700	4 000[1]	4 500[1]	Bovine
Sheep	569	673	569	600	584	550[1]	530[1]	550[1]	Ovine
Pigs	216	238	304	290	305	285[1]	270[1]	280[1]	Porcine
Horses [1]	22	23	23	24	24	24	23	24	Chevaline [1]
Asses [1]	100	101	102	103	104	104	103	104	Asine [1]
Mules [1]	1	1	1	1	1	1	1	1	Mulassière [1]
America, North									**Amerique du Nord**
Cattle	164 582	162 077	161 297	159 426	159 446	159 248	161 066	163 354	**Bovine**
Sheep	18 376	18 570	18 633	18 818	18 225	16 270	16 168	17 529	**Ovine**
Pigs	85 959	87 425	89 004	85 411	86 519	90 575	91 845	93 056	**Porcine**
Horses	14 112	14 434	14 493	14 326	14 596	14 383	13 456	12 740	**Chevaline**
Asses	3 652	3 658	3 689	3 688	3 687	3 684	3 692	3 703	**Asine**
Mules	3 631	3 645	3 654	3 664	3 675	3 684	3 695	3 707	**Mulassière**
Antigua and Barbuda									**Antigua—et—Barbuda**
Cattle	18[1]	18[1]	16[1]	16[1]	16[1]	16[1]	16[1]	16[1]	Bovine
Sheep	13[1]	13[1]	13[1]	12[1]	13[1]	13[1]	13[1]	13[1]	Ovine
Pigs [1]	4	4	4	4	4	4	4	4	Porcine [1]

37
Livestock
Thousand head [cont.]
Cheptel
Milliers de têtes [suite]

Country or area	1987	1988	1989	1990	1991	1992	1993	1994	Pays ou zone
Horses [1]	1	1	1	1	1	1	1	1	Chevaline [1]
Asses [1]	2	2	2	1	2	2	2	2	Asine [1]
Bahamas									**Bahamas**
Cattle [1]	5	5	5	5	6	6	6	6	Bovine [1]
Sheep [1]	40	40	40	40	40	40	40	40	Ovine [1]
Pigs [1]	15	15	15	15	15	15	15	15	Porcine [1]
Barbados									**Barbade**
Cattle	18[1]	18[1]	20	23[1]	23[1]	25[1]	25[1]	25[1]	Bovine
Sheep	40[1]	40[1]	39	40[1]	40[1]	41[1]	41[1]	41[1]	Ovine
Pigs	32[1]	30[1]	29	29[1]	30[1]	30[1]	30[1]	30[1]	Porcine
Horses	1[1]	1[1]	1	1[1]	1[1]	1[1]	1[1]	1[1]	Chevaline
Asses [1]	2	2	2	2	2	2	2	2	Asine [1]
Mules [1]	2	2	2	2	2	2	2	2	Mulassière [1]
Belize									**Belize**
Cattle	* 49	* 50	* 50	* 51	* 51	* 54	* 58	59[1]	Bovine
Sheep	4[1]	4[1]	4[1]	4[1]	4[1]	4[1]	4[1]	4[1]	Ovine
Pigs	25[1]	26[1]	26[1]	26[1]	26[1]	26[1]	26[1]	26[1]	Porcine
Horses [1]	5	5	5	5	5	5	5	5	Chevaline [1]
Mules [1]	4	4	4	4	4	4	4	4	Mulassière [1]
Bermuda									**Bermudes**
Cattle	1[1]	1[1]	1[1]	1[1]	1[1]	1[1]	1[1]	1	Bovine
Pigs [1]	2	1	1	1	1	1	1	1	Porcine [1]
Horses	0	0[1]	1	1[1]	1[1]	1[1]	1[1]	1	Chevaline
British Virgin Islands									**Iles Vierges britanniques**
Cattle [1]	2	2	2	2	2	2	2	2	Bovine [1]
Sheep	6	6[1]	6[1]	6[1]	6[1]	6[1]	6[1]	6[1]	Ovine
Pigs	2	2[1]	2[1]	2[1]	2[1]	2[1]	2[1]	2[1]	Porcine
Canada									**Canada**
Cattle	10 667	10 756	10 984	11 220	11 289	11 713	11 786	12 306	Bovine
Sheep	485	521	560	595	628	654	662	691	Ovine
Pigs	9 998	10 801	10 951	10 392	10 172	10 498	10 841	11 200	Porcine
Horses [1]	400	405	415	415	415	420	420	425	Chevaline [1]
Mules [1]	4	4	4	4	4	4	4	4	Mulassière [1]
Cayman Islands									**Iles Caïmanes**
Cattle	2	2	2	2	1	1	1[1]	1[1]	Bovine
Costa Rica									**Costa Rica**
Cattle	* 2 294	2 190	* 2 168	* 2 201	* 2 175	* 2 132	* 2 122	* 1 694	Bovine
Sheep	3	3	3[1]	3[1]	3[1]	3[1]	3[1]	3[1]	Ovine
Pigs	* 160	* 237	237[1]	241[1]	244[1]	245[1]	244[1]	252[1]	Porcine
Horses	114[1]	114[1]	114[1]	114[1]	114[1]	114[1]	114[1]	114[1]	Chevaline
Asses [1]	7	7	7	7	7	7	7	7	Asine [1]
Mules	5[1]	5[1]	5[1]	5[1]	5[1]	5[1]	5[1]	5[1]	Mulassière
Cuba									**Cuba**
Cattle	5 007	4 984	4 927	4 920	4 920[1]	4 700[1]	4 500[1]	4 500[1]	Bovine
Sheep [1]	382	382	385	385	385	350	310	310	Ovine [1]
Pigs [1]	1 996	2 125	2 401	2 002	1 903	1 703	1 603	1 503	Porcine [1]
Horses	718	703	630	629	629[1]	625[1]	580[1]	580[1]	Chevaline
Asses	4	4	5	5	5[1]	5[1]	5[1]	5[1]	Asine
Mules	31	32	31	31	32[1]	32[1]	32[1]	32[1]	Mulassière
Dominica									**Dominique**
Cattle [1]	9	9	9	9	9	9	9	9	Bovine [1]
Sheep [1]	7	8	7	8	8	8	8	8	Ovine [1]
Pigs [1]	5	5	5	5	5	5	5	5	Porcine [1]
Dominican Republic									**Rép. dominicaine**
Cattle	2 092	2 129	2 245	* 2 240	* 2 365	* 2 356	* 2 371	2 450[1]	Bovine
Sheep	* 95	* 100	* 110	115[1]	120[1]	122[1]	128[1]	134[1]	Ovine
Pigs	389	409	429	431[1]	* 769	750[1]	850[1]	900[1]	Porcine
Horses	300[1]	310[1]	310[1]	315[1]	320[1]	320[1]	329[1]	334[1]	Chevaline
Asses [1]	140	142	142	143	143	143	145	146	Asine [1]
Mules [1]	130	132	132	133	133	133	135	136	Mulassière [1]
El Salvador									**El Salvador**
Cattle	1 088	1 144	1 176	1 220	1 243	1 257	1 197	1 256	Bovine
Sheep	5[1]	5[1]	5[1]	5[1]	5[1]	5[1]	5[1]	5[1]	Ovine
Pigs	418	377	289	317	308	* 315	* 325	* 325	Porcine
Horses	93[1]	93[1]	94[1]	94[1]	95[1]	95[1]	96[1]	96[1]	Chevaline

37
Livestock
Thousand head [*cont.*]
Cheptel
Milliers de têtes [*suite*]

Country or area	1987	1988	1989	1990	1991	1992	1993	1994	Pays ou zone
Asses [1]	2	2	2	3	3	3	3	3	Asine [1]
Mules [1]	23	23	23	23	23	23	24	24	Mulassière [1]
Greenland									**Groënland**
Sheep	21[1]	21[1]	21[1]	22[1]	22[1]	22[1]	22[1]	22[1]	Ovine
Grenada									**Grenade**
Cattle [1]	4	4	4	4	4	4	4	4	Bovine [1]
Sheep [1]	12	12	11	11	12	12	12	12	Ovine [1]
Pigs [1]	3	3	3	3	3	3	3	3	Porcine [1]
Asses [1]	1	1	1	1	1	1	1	1	Asine [1]
Guadeloupe									**Guadeloupe**
Cattle	76	74	74	68	67	64	56	56[1]	Bovine
Sheep	5[1]	6[1]	4	3	4	3	4	4[1]	Ovine
Pigs	41	43	38	32	27[1]	30[1]	30[1]	30[1]	Porcine
Horses [1]	1	1	1	1	1	1	1	1	Chevaline [1]
Guatemala									**Guatemala**
Cattle	2 004	2 071	2 047	2 032	2 077	2 097	* 2 236	* 2 210	Bovine
Sheep	490[1]	431	425	434	438	430	440	440[1]	Ovine
Pigs	611	631	611	609	587	650	715	720[1]	Porcine
Horses [1]	110	112	112	113	114	114	116	118	Chevaline [1]
Asses [1]	9	9	9	9	9	9	9	9	Asine [1]
Mules	38[1]	38[1]	38[1]	38[1]	38[1]	38[1]	38[1]	38[1]	Mulassière
Haiti									**Haïti**
Cattle	1 200[1]	1 150[1]	1 100[1]	1 000[1]	900[1]	800	800[1]	800[1]	Bovine
Sheep [1]	87	87	86	86	86	86	85	85	Ovine [1]
Pigs	450[1]	400[1]	350[1]	300[1]	250[1]	200[1]	200[1]	200[1]	Porcine
Horses [1]	420	430	432	435	430	400	400	400	Chevaline [1]
Asses	216[1]	216[1]	217[1]	215[1]	214[1]	210[1]	210[1]	210	Asine
Mules	84[1]	85[1]	85[1]	83[1]	82[1]	81[1]	80[1]	80	Mulassière
Honduras									**Honduras**
Cattle	* 2 532	* 2 489	2 424	* 2 424	* 2 388	* 2 351	2 077	* 2 286	Bovine
Sheep	* 7	8[1]	9[1]	10[1]	11[1]	12[1]	13	14[1]	Ovine
Pigs	* 567	* 600	* 590	* 590	587	591	596	603[1]	Porcine
Horses [1]	171	175	180	200	210	220	172	177	Chevaline [1]
Asses [1]	22	22	22	22	22	22	22	23	Asine [1]
Mules [1]	69	69	69	69	69	69	69	69	Mulassière [1]
Jamaica									**Jamaïque**
Cattle [1]	290	290	290	310	320	320	330	335	Bovine [1]
Sheep [1]	3	2	2	2	3	2	2	2	Ovine [1]
Pigs [1]	190	195	215	220	150	180	180	180	Porcine [1]
Horses [1]	4	4	4	4	4	4	4	4	Chevaline [1]
Asses [1]	23	23	23	23	23	23	23	23	Asine [1]
Mules [1]	10	10	10	10	10	10	10	10	Mulassière [1]
Martinique									**Martinique**
Cattle	37	35	37	37	37	35	36[1]	36[1]	Bovine
Sheep [1]	95	98	102	110	118	113	110	110	Ovine [1]
Pigs	49[1]	51[1]	51[1]	53[1]	55[1]	53[1]	49[1]	49[1]	Porcine
Horses	2[1]	2[1]	2[1]	2[1]	2[1]	2[1]	2[1]	2[1]	Chevaline
Mexico									**Mexique**
Cattle	* 31 156	* 31 240	33 068	32 054	31 460	* 30 157	* 30 649	* 30 702	Bovine
Sheep	5 926	5 761	5 863	5 480[1]	5 000[1]	5 300[1]	5 876	* 5 905	Ovine
Pigs	18 722	15 884	16 157	15 203	15 786	16 502	16 832	* 18 000	Porcine
Horses	6 150[1]	6 160[1]	6 170[1]	6 170[1]	6 175[1]	6 180[1]	6 185[1]	6 191[1]	Chevaline
Asses	3 184[1]	3 185[1]	3 186[1]	3 187[1]	3 188[1]	3 189[1]	3 190[1]	3 200[1]	Asine
Mules	3 150[1]	3 160[1]	3 170[1]	3 180[1]	3 190[1]	3 200[1]	3 210[1]	3 220[1]	Mulassière
Montserrat									**Montserrat**
Cattle [1]	9	9	9	10	10	10	10	10	Bovine [1]
Sheep	4[1]	4[1]	4[1]	5[1]	5[1]	5[1]	5[1]	5[1]	Ovine
Pigs	1[1]	1[1]	1[1]	1[1]	1[1]	1[1]	1[1]	1[1]	Porcine
Netherlands Antilles									**Antilles néerlandaises**
Cattle [1]	1	1	1	1	1	1	1	1	Bovine [1]
Sheep [1]	6	5	6	6	7	7	7	7	Ovine [1]
Pigs [1]	3	3	3	3	2	3	3	3	Porcine [1]
Asses [1]	3	3	3	3	3	3	3	3	Asine [1]
Nicaragua									**Nicaragua**
Cattle	* 1 885	* 1 700	1 800[1]	1 680[1]	* 1 600	* 1 640	* 1 645	1 650[1]	Bovine
Sheep	3[1]	4[1]	4[1]	4[1]	4[1]	4[1]	4[1]	4[1]	Ovine

37

Livestock
Thousand head [*cont.*]
Cheptel
Milliers de têtes [*suite*]

Country or area	1987	1988	1989	1990	1991	1992	1993	1994	Pays ou zone
Horses	255[1]	250[1]	250[1]	250[1]	250[1]	250[1]	248[1]	247[1]	Chevaline
Asses [1]	8	8	8	8	8	8	8	8	Asine [1]
Mules [1]	45	45	45	45	45	45	45	46	Mulassière [1]
Panama									**Panama**
Cattle	1 410	1 423	1 417	1 388	1 399	1 427	1 437	1 437[1]	Bovine
Pigs	229	211	202	226	256	292	290[1]	295[1]	Porcine
Horses	141[1]	144[1]	147[1]	151[1]	156	155[1]	156[1]	157[1]	Chevaline
Mules	3[1]	3[1]	4[1]	4[1]	4	4[1]	4[1]	4[1]	Mulassière
Puerto Rico									**Porto Rico**
Cattle	520	559	586	601	599	429	429	429	Bovine
Sheep [1]	7	7	7	7	7	8	8	8	Ovine [1]
Pigs	199	195	199	203	209	197	194	196	Porcine
Horses [1]	22	22	22	22	23	23	23	24	Chevaline [1]
Asses [1]	2	2	2	2	2	2	2	2	Asine [1]
Mules [1]	2	2	3	3	3	3	3	3	Mulassière [1]
Saint Kitts and Nevis									**Saint−Kitts−et−Nevis**
Cattle [1]	5	5	5	5	5	5	5	5	Bovine [1]
Sheep [1]	15	15	15	15	15	15	14	14	Ovine [1]
Pigs [1]	2	2	2	2	2	2	2	2	Porcine [1]
Saint Lucia									**Sainte−Lucie**
Cattle	12[1]	12[1]	12[1]	12[1]	12[1]	12[1]	12[1]	12[1]	Bovine
Sheep	15[1]	15[1]	16[1]	16[1]	16[1]	16[1]	16[1]	16[1]	Ovine
Pigs	12[1]	12[1]	12[1]	12[1]	12[1]	12[1]	13[1]	13[1]	Porcine
Horses [1]	1	1	1	1	1	1	1	1	Chevaline [1]
Asses [1]	1	1	1	1	1	1	1	1	Asine [1]
Mules [1]	1	1	1	1	1	1	1	1	Mulassière [1]
Saint Pierre and Miquelon									**Saint−Pierre−et−Miquelon**
Pigs	1	1	0	0	0[1]	0[1]	...	...	Porcine
St. Vincent−Grenadines									**St. Vincent−Grenadines**
Cattle	6	7	7	6	6	6[1]	6[1]	6[1]	Bovine
Sheep	15	14	13	13	12	12[1]	12[1]	12[1]	Ovine
Pigs	10[1]	12	11	10	9	9[1]	9[1]	9[1]	Porcine
Asses [1]	1	1	1	1	1	1	1	1	Asine [1]
Trinidad and Tobago									**Trinité−et−Tobago**
Cattle [1]	60	70	65	60	60	55	55	55	Bovine [1]
Sheep [1]	12	13	13	14	14	14	14	14	Ovine [1]
Pigs [1]	72	65	50	54	54	54	48	48	Porcine [1]
Horses [1]	1	1	1	1	1	1	1	1	Chevaline [1]
Asses [1]	2	2	2	2	2	2	2	2	Asine [1]
Mules [1]	2	2	2	2	2	2	2	2	Mulassière [1]
United States									**Etats−Unis**
Cattle	102 118	99 622	96 740	95 816	96 393	97 556	99 176	100 988	Bovine
Sheep	10 572	10 945	10 858	11 364	11 200	8 965	8 305	9 600	Ovine
Pigs	51 001	54 384	55 469	53 821	54 477	57 649	58 202	57 904	Porcine
Horses [1]	5 203	5 500	5 600	5 400	5 650	5 450	4 600	3 860	Chevaline [1]
Asses [1]	24	26	55	53	52	51	56	56	Asine [1]
Mules [1]	28	28	28	28	28	28	28	28	Mulassière [1]
United States Virgin Is.									**Iles Vierges américaines**
Cattle	5	8[1]	8[1]	8[1]	8[1]	8[1]	8[1]	8[1]	Bovine
Sheep	3	3[1]	3[1]	3[1]	3[1]	3[1]	3[1]	3[1]	Ovine
Pigs	3	3[1]	3[1]	3[1]	3[1]	3[1]	3[1]	3[1]	Porcine
America, South									**Amérique du Sud**
Cattle	258 219	262 877	266 268	269 901	274 269	278 803	279 629	279 656	**Bovine**
Sheep	104 030	105 220	105 384	104 457	102 788	101 540	92 876	94 054	**Ovine**
Pigs	51 045	51 540	51 781	52 329	53 019	52 943	49 867	49 846	**Porcine**
Horses	13 876	13 988	14 508	14 787	14 932	14 960	14 912	14 493	**Chevaline**
Asses	3 884	3 919	3 978	4 020	4 050	4 059	4 076	4 105	**Asine**
Mules	3 237	3 279	3 321	3 356	3 370	3 395	3 433	3 451	**Mulassière**
Argentina									**Argentine**
Cattle	51 683	* 50 782	* 49 500	* 50 582	* 50 080	* 50 020	* 50 856	* 50 000	Bovine
Sheep	28 750	29 167	* 29 345	* 28 571	* 26 500	* 25 706	18 468	20 000	Ovine
Pigs	3 700[1]	3 400[1]	2 800[1]	2 500[1]	2 600[1]	2 100[1]	2 200[1]	2 200[1]	Porcine
Horses	* 3 000	* 2 900	* 3 200	* 3 400	* 3 400	* 3 300	* 3 300	3 369[1]	Chevaline
Asses [1]	90	90	90	90	90	90	90	90	Asine [1]
Mules [1]	167	168	170	172	172	173	174	175	Mulassière [1]

37
Livestock
Thousand head [*cont.*]
Cheptel
Milliers de têtes [*suite*]

Country or area	1987	1988	1989	1990	1991	1992	1993	1994	Pays ou zone
Bolivia									**Bolivie**
Cattle	5 239	5 402	5 476	5 543	5 607	5 779	5 794	6 012	Bovine
Sheep	7 246	7 505	7 701	7 676	7 342	7 472	7 512	7 789	Ovine
Pigs	1 902	2 019	2 127	2 176	2 177	2 226	2 273	2 331	Porcine
Horses [1]	315	315	320	320	320	322	322	324	Chevaline [1]
Asses [1]	610	620	630	630	630	631	631	636	Asine [1]
Mules [1]	80	80	80	80	80	81	81	81	Mulassière [1]
Brazil									**Brésil**
Cattle	135 720	139 599	144 154	147 102	152 136	154 229	* 152 300	* 151 600	Bovine
Sheep	19 860	20 085	20 041	20 015	20 128	19 956	20 000[1]	20 500[1]	Ovine
Pigs	32 480	32 121	33 015	33 623	34 290	34 522	* 31 050	* 30 450	Porcine
Horses	5 855	5 971	6 098	6 122	6 237	6 329	6 300[1]	5 800[1]	Chevaline
Asses	1 295	1 304	1 322	1 343	1 364	1 350[1]	1 360[1]	1 370[1]	Asine
Mules	1 952	1 984	2 009	2 033	2 035	2 046	2 080[1]	2 090[1]	Mulassière
Chile									**Chili**
Cattle	3 371	3 466	3 466	3 336	3 404	3 461	3 557	3 692	Bovine
Sheep	5 500	5 300	4 721	4 887	4 801	4 689	4 629	4 649	Ovine
Pigs	1 300	1 360	1 057	1 125	1 251	1 226	1 288	1 407	Porcine
Horses [1]	490[1]	490[1]	500[1]	520[1]	530[1]	530[1]	500[1]	450[1]	Chevaline
Asses [1]	28	28	28	28	28	28	28	28	Asine [1]
Mules [1]	10	10	10	10	10	10	10	10	Mulassière [1]
Colombia									**Colombie**
Cattle	23 971	24 245	24 415	24 384	24 350	24 772	25 324	* 25 700	Bovine
Sheep	2 576	2 542	2 545	2 547	2 550	2 553	2 540	2 540[1]	Ovine
Pigs	2 511	2 580	2 600	2 640	2 642	2 644	2 635	2 635[1]	Porcine
Horses	1 898	1 936	1 974	1 975[1]	1 980[1]	2 000[1]	2 000[1]	2 000[1]	Chevaline
Asses	682	693	703	703[1]	705[1]	705[1]	710[1]	710[1]	Asine
Mules	606	612	618	618[1]	620[1]	620[1]	622[1]	622[1]	Mulassière
Ecuador									**Equateur**
Cattle	3 884	3 997	4 177	4 359	4 516	4 682	* 4 819	4 963[1]	Bovine
Sheep	1 293	1 226	1 329	1 420	1 501	1 565	1 631	1 728	Ovine
Pigs	1 620	1 922	2 092	2 220	2 327	2 425	* 2 540	2 540[1]	Porcine
Horses	404	427	460	492	516	512	510[1]	535[1]	Chevaline
Asses	215	221	242	253	259	262	263[1]	274[1]	Asine
Mules	113	116	124	131	141	151	152[1]	158[1]	Mulassière
Falkland Is. (Malvinas)									**Iles Falkland (Malvinas)**
Cattle	6	6	6	5	5	5	5	5	Bovine
Sheep	692	705	745	740	729	713	721	727	Ovine
Horses	2	2	2	2	2	2	1	1	Chevaline
French Guiana									**Guyane française**
Cattle	17	15	16	16	15	10	10	10[1]	Bovine
Sheep	3[1]	4[1]	4	* 4	* 4	4	* 4	4[1]	Ovine
Pigs	10	9	8	9	9	11	10	10[1]	Porcine
Guyana									**Guyana**
Cattle [1]	130	140	140	130	140	190	190	190	Bovine [1]
Sheep [1]	126	127	128	129	130	130	130	131	Ovine [1]
Pigs [1]	65	60	50	40	35	36	50	50	Porcine [1]
Horses [1]	2	2	2	2	2	2	2	2	Chevaline [1]
Asses [1]	1	1	1	1	1	1	1	1	Asine [1]
Paraguay									**Paraguay**
Cattle	7 374	7 780	8 074	8 254	7 627	7 886	8 000[1]	8 000[1]	Bovine
Sheep	411	432	451	457	357	365	378	386	Ovine
Pigs	1 809	2 108	2 305	2 444	2 580	2 700[1]	2 950[1]	3 300[1]	Porcine
Horses	323	328	334	335	320	327	339	370	Chevaline
Asses [1]	31	31	31	31	31	31	31	31	Asine [1]
Mules [1]	14	14	14	14	14	14	14	14	Mulassière [1]
Peru									**Pérou**
Cattle	4 161	4 174	4 234	4 102	4 042	3 972	3 924	4 000	Bovine
Sheep	13 075	12 922	12 970	12 257	12 226	11 912	11 915	* 11 600	Ovine
Pigs	2 222	2 376	2 434	2 400	2 417	2 396	2 312	2 405	Porcine
Horses	655[1]	655[1]	660[1]	660[1]	660[1]	665[1]	665[1]	666[1]	Chevaline
Asses	490[1]	490[1]	490[1]	500[1]	500[1]	520[1]	520[1]	523[1]	Asine
Mules	220[1]	220[1]	220[1]	222[1]	222[1]	224[1]	224[1]	225[1]	Mulassière
Suriname									**Suriname**
Cattle	76	84	89	92	92	96	97[1]	98[1]	Bovine

37
Livestock
Thousand head [cont.]
Cheptel
Milliers de têtes [suite]

Country or area	1987	1988	1989	1990	1991	1992	1993	1994	Pays ou zone
Sheep	6	8	8	10	9	9	9[1]	9[1]	Ovine
Pigs	19	21	25	32	31	38	36[1]	37[1]	Porcine
Uruguay									**Uruguay**
Cattle	9 945	10 331	9 446	8 723	8 889	9 508	10 093	* 10 316	Bovine
Sheep	24 006	24 689	24 872	25 220	25 986	25 941	24 414	* 23 441	Ovine
Pigs	220	215	215	215	215[1]	220[1]	223[1]	230[1]	Porcine
Horses	437	466	462	465[1]	470[1]	475[1]	477[1]	479[1]	Chevaline
Asses [1]	1	1	1	1	1	1	1	1	Asine [1]
Mules [1]	4	4	4	4	4	4	4	4	Mulassière [1]
Venezuela									**Venezuela**
Cattle	12 641	12 856	13 076	13 272	* 13 368	* 14 192	* 14 660	* 15 071	Bovine
Sheep	488	508	523	525[1]	525[1]	525[1]	525[1]	550[1]	Ovine
Pigs	3 187	3 349	3 053	2 904	2 445[1]	2 400[1]	2 300[1]	2 250[1]	Porcine
Horses	495[1]	495[1]	495[1]	495[1]	495[1]	495[1]	495[1]	495[1]	Chevaline
Asses [1]	440	440	440	440	440	440	440	440	Asine [1]
Mules [1]	72	72	72	72	72	72	72	72	Mulassière [1]
Asia									**Asie**
Cattle	387 347	382 066	386 675	390 809	392 931	396 159	402 136	410 118	**Bovine**
Sheep	321 664	326 039	342 120	345 373	342 604	341 381	336 104	340 102	**Ovine**
Pigs	413 031	406 263	421 155	433 214	444 638	454 462	472 926	482 889	**Porcine**
Horses	17 109	16 767	16 617	16 447	16 307	16 188	16 050	16 007	**Chevaline**
Asses	20 732	21 077	21 460	21 487	21 320	21 382	21 316	21 325	**Asine**
Mules	5 783	5 912	6 036	6 062	6 141	6 247	6 242	6 124	**Mulassière**
Afghanistan									**Afghanistan**
Cattle	1 500[1]	1 500[1]	1 500[1]	1 500[1]	1 500[1]	1 500[1]	1 500[1]	1 500[1]	Bovine
Sheep	12 000[1]	14 150	14 150	14 170	14 200	14 200[1]	14 200[1]	14 200[1]	Ovine
Horses	400[1]	387[1]	374[1]	362[1]	350	340[1]	320[1]	300[1]	Chevaline
Asses	1 300	1 280[1]	1 260[1]	1 240[1]	1 220[1]	1 200[1]	1 180[1]	1 160[1]	Asine
Mules	30[1]	29[1]	28[1]	27[1]	26[1]	25[1]	24[1]	23[1]	Mulassière
Armenia									**Arménie**
Cattle	...	...	...	...	...	499	499	502	Bovine
Sheep	...	...	...	...	...	854	724	* 720	Ovine
Pigs	...	...	...	...	...	84	81	80[1]	Porcine
Horses	...	...	...	...	...	9	9	9[1]	Chevaline
Asses	...	...	...	...	...	3	4[1]	3[1]	Asine
Azerbaijan									**Azerbaïdjan**
Cattle	...	...	...	...	...	1 716	1 791	1 621	Bovine
Sheep	...	...	...	...	...	5 088	* 4 701	* 4 339	Ovine
Pigs	...	...	...	...	...	* 140	* 123	115[1]	Porcine
Horses [1]	...	...	...	...	...	35	33	30	Chevaline [1]
Asses [1]	...	...	...	...	...	5	6	5	Asine [1]
Bahrain									**Bahreïn**
Cattle	9[1]	* 12	* 13	* 14	15[1]	15[1]	16[1]	16[1]	Bovine
Sheep	15[1]	* 18	* 19	* 21	24[1]	26[1]	29[1]	29[1]	Ovine
Bangladesh									**Bangladesh**
Cattle	22 567	22 789	23 015	23 244	23 259	23 480	23 923	* 24 130	Bovine
Sheep	770	803	837	873	902	940	989	* 1 070	Ovine
Bhutan									**Bhoutan**
Cattle	387	393	387	406[1]	413[1]	422[1]	429[1]	435[1]	Bovine
Sheep	36	47	48	49[1]	50[1]	52[1]	54[1]	59[1]	Ovine
Pigs	70	66	63	72[1]	73[1]	74[1]	74[1]	75[1]	Porcine
Horses	26	26	26	25[1]	27[1]	28[1]	29[1]	30[1]	Chevaline
Asses [1]	18	18	18	18	18	18	18	18	Asine [1]
Mules [1]	9	9	9	9	9	10	10	10	Mulassière [1]
Brunei Darussalam									**Brunéi Darussalam**
Cattle	* 1	* 1	* 1	* 1	* 1	1[1]	1[1]	1[1]	Bovine
Pigs	* 15	* 17	* 15	* 14	* 14	14[1]	14[1]	14[1]	Porcine
Cambodia									**Cambodge**
Cattle	1 852	1 891	2 095	2 181	2 257	2 468	2 468[1]	2 589[1]	Bovine
Pigs	1 251	1 500	1 737	1 515	1 550	2 043	2 043[1]	2 154[1]	Porcine
Horses [1]	14	15	16	17	18	19	20	21	Chevaline [1]
China									**Chine**
Cattle	70 964	73 963	77 025	79 495	81 326	82 721	85 781	90 906	Bovine
Sheep	99 009	102 656	110 571	113 508	112 816	110 855	109 720	111 649	Ovine
Pigs	344 248	334 862	349 172	360 594	370 975	379 735	393 965	402 846	Porcine
Horses	10 988	10 691	10 541	10 295	10 175	10 095	10 018	9 960	Chevaline

37
Livestock
Thousand head [*cont.*]
Cheptel
Milliers de têtes [*suite*]

Country or area	1987	1988	1989	1990	1991	1992	1993	1994	Pays ou zone
Asses	10 689	10 846	11 052	11 136	11 198	11 158	10 983	10 886	Asine
Mules	5 113	5 248	5 366	5 391	5 494	5 606	5 610	5 498	Mulassière
Cyprus									**Chypre**
Cattle	44	45	46	49	55	55	56	61	Bovine
Sheep	325	310	300	310	290	295	285	285[1]	Ovine
Pigs	225	266	284	281	278	296	342	370[1]	Porcine
Horses	1	1	1	1[1]	1[1]	1[1]	1[1]	1[1]	Chevaline
Asses	6	6	5	5[1]	5[1]	5[1]	5[1]	5[1]	Asine
Mules	2	2	2	2[1]	2[1]	2[1]	2[1]	2[1]	Mulassière
Gaza Strip									**Zone de Gaza**
Cattle	3	3	3[1]	3[1]	3[1]	3[1]	3[1]	3[1]	Bovine
Sheep	20	24	24[1]	24[1]	24[1]	24[1]	24[1]	24[1]	Ovine
Georgia									**Géorgie**
Cattle	...	...	...	...	...	* 1 216	* 1 130	1 050[1]	Bovine
Sheep	...	...	...	...	...	* 1 400	1 350[1]	* 1 300	Ovine
Pigs	...	...	...	...	...	* 782	* 688	650[1]	Porcine
Horses [1]	...	...	...	...	...	20	20	18	Chevaline [1]
Asses [1]	...	...	...	...	...	2	2	2	Asine [1]
Hong Kong									**Hong-kong**
Cattle	2	1	1	2	2	2	2	2	Bovine
Pigs	353	358	350	304	234	175	104	97	Porcine
Horses	1	1	1	1	1	1	1	1	Chevaline
India									**Inde**
Cattle	199 528	* 190 791	* 190 614	* 191 750	* 193 328	* 192 650	* 192 700	* 192 980	Bovine
Sheep *	45 750	42 702	43 204	43 706	44 207	44 407	44 608	44 809	Ovine *
Pigs	10 760	10 900[1]	11 050[1]	11 200[1]	11 330[1]	11 480[1]	11 630[1]	11 780[1]	Porcine
Horses [1]	950	953	955	960	965	970	980	990	Chevaline [1]
Asses [1]	1 300	1 328	1 400	1 450	1 500	1 500	1 550	1 600	Asine [1]
Mules [1]	134	135	138	139	140	141	142	144	Mulassière [1]
Indonesia									**Indonésie**
Cattle	9 742	9 776	10 095	10 410	10 665	11 000[1]	11 300[1]	* 11 595	Bovine
Sheep	5 363	5 825	5 910	6 006	6 108	6 200[1]	6 300[1]	* 6 411	Ovine
Pigs	6 340	6 484	6 946	7 136	7 612	8 000[1]	8 350[1]	* 8 720	Porcine
Horses	658	675	683	683	695	700[1]	705[1]	* 714	Chevaline
Iran, Islamic Rep. of									**Iran, Rép. islamique d'**
Cattle	6 500[1]	6 368	7 918	7 532	6 697	* 6 900	7 000[1]	7 100[1]	Bovine
Sheep	41 000	40 665	45 000	44 581	44 681	* 45 000	45 200[1]	45 400[1]	Ovine
Horses	276[1]	274[1]	271	255	255	255[1]	255[1]	255[1]	Chevaline
Asses	2 000[1]	1 970[1]	2 014	1 860	1 860	1 900[1]	1 900[1]	1 900[1]	Asine
Mules	138[1]	137[1]	* 136	135[1]	134[1]	134[1]	133[1]	133[1]	Mulassière
Iraq									**Iraq**
Cattle	1 580[1]	1 600[1]	* 1 578	1 520[1]	1 150[1]	1 130[1]	1 120[1]	1 100[1]	Bovine
Sheep	9 000	* 9 000	* 8 981	8 631[1]	6 500[1]	6 400[1]	6 300[1]	6 320[1]	Ovine
Horses	55[1]	55[1]	58[1]	60[1]	18[1]	20[1]	20[1]	21[1]	Chevaline
Asses	400[1]	410[1]	415[1]	416[1]	150[1]	155[1]	160[1]	162[1]	Asine
Mules	25[1]	26[1]	26[1]	27[1]	10[1]	12[1]	13[1]	13[1]	Mulassière
Israel									**Israël**
Cattle	325	345	348	342	331	349	357	362[1]	Bovine
Sheep	306	372	394	380	375	360	330	330[1]	Ovine
Pigs [1]	130	130	130	115	100	100	100	100	Porcine [1]
Horses [1]	4	4	4	4	4	4	4	4	Chevaline [1]
Asses [1]	5	5	5	5	5	5	5	5	Asine [1]
Mules [1]	2	2	2	2	2	2	2	2	Mulassière [1]
Japan									**Japon**
Cattle	4 694	4 667	4 682	4 760	4 873	4 980	5 024	4 989	Bovine
Sheep	27	29	30	31	30	29	27	25	Ovine
Pigs	11 354	11 725	11 866	11 817	11 335	10 966	10 783	10 621	Porcine
Horses	22	22	22	23	24	26	27	28	Chevaline
Jordan									**Jordanie**
Cattle	29	30	29	35[1]	40[1]	40[1]	40[1]	42[1]	Bovine
Sheep	1 219	1 279	1 523	1 556	1 900[1]	1 900[1]	2 000[1]	2 100[1]	Ovine
Horses	3	3	4	4[1]	4[1]	4[1]	4[1]	4[1]	Chevaline
Asses	19	19	19	19[1]	19[1]	19[1]	19[1]	19[1]	Asine
Mules	3	3	3	3[1]	3[1]	3[1]	3[1]	3[1]	Mulassière
Kazakstan									**Kazakstan**
Cattle	...	...	...	...	...	9 084	9 576	9 347	Bovine

37
Livestock
Thousand head [*cont.*]
Cheptel
Milliers de têtes [*suite*]

Country or area	1987	1988	1989	1990	1991	1992	1993	1994	Pays ou zone
Sheep	...	...	...	...	...	33 908	* 33 732	* 33 524	Ovine
Pigs	...	...	...	...	...	2 794	2 591	2 445	Porcine
Horses [1]	...	...	...	...	...	1 510	1 500	1 400	Chevaline [1]
Asses [1]	...	...	...	...	...	45	45	40	Asine [1]
Korea, Dem. P. R.									**Corée, R. p. dém. de**
Cattle [1]	1 200	1 250	1 280	1 300	1 300	1 300	1 300	1 330	Bovine [1]
Sheep [1]	368	372	380	385	390	390	390	396	Ovine [1]
Pigs [1]	3 050	3 100	3 145	3 200	3 300	3 300	3 300	3 368	Porcine [1]
Horses [1]	42	43	44	44	45	46	46	47	Chevaline [1]
Asses [1]	3	3	3	3	3	3	3	3	Asine [1]
Mules [1]	2	2	2	2	2	2	2	2	Mulassière [1]
Korea, Republic of									**Corée, République de**
Cattle	2 386	2 039	2 051	2 126	2 269	2 527	2 813	3 200	Bovine
Sheep	3	3	3	3	3	4	4[1]	4[1]	Ovine
Pigs	4 281	4 852	4 801	4 528	5 046	5 463	5 928	6 300	Porcine
Horses	3	4	5	5	5	5	6[1]	6[1]	Chevaline
Kuwait									**Koweït**
Cattle	28	24	20	18[1]	1[1]	5[1]	12[1]	12[1]	Bovine
Sheep	282	280	305	200[1]	50[1]	100[1]	150[1]	150[1]	Ovine
Horses [1]	3	3	4	3	0	0	0	0	Chevaline [1]
Kyrgyzstan									**Kirghizistan**
Cattle	...	...	...	...	...	1 095	1 122	1 061	Bovine
Sheep	...	...	...	...	...	9 200	* 8 480	* 7 077	Ovine
Pigs	...	...	...	...	...	299	247	165	Porcine
Horses [1]	...	...	...	...	...	315	310	300	Chevaline [1]
Asses [1]	...	...	...	...	...	10	10	10	Asine [1]
Lao People's Dem. Rep.									**Rép. dém. pop. lao**
Cattle	703	764	817	842	899	993	1 010	* 1 137	Bovine
Pigs	1 420	1 268	1 350	1 372	1 469	1 561	1 559	1 605	Porcine
Horses	42[1]	42[1]	43[1]	44[1]	36	29	29[1]	29[1]	Chevaline
Lebanon									**Liban**
Cattle	61	59	59	65[1]	70	73[1]	77[1]	80[1]	Bovine
Sheep	208	204	210	220[1]	238	240[1]	250[1]	258[1]	Ovine
Pigs	49	47	49	45[1]	44	42[1]	40[1]	41[1]	Porcine
Horses	5[1]	5[1]	6[1]	8[1]	10	11[1]	12[1]	13[1]	Chevaline
Asses	14[1]	16[1]	18[1]	19[1]	21	22[1]	23[1]	24[1]	Asine
Mules	6[1]	6[1]	7[1]	7[1]	8	8[1]	8[1]	9[1]	Mulassière
Macau									**Macao**
Pigs [1]	1	1	1	1	1	1	1	1	Porcine [1]
Malaysia									**Malaisie**
Cattle	663	637	661	668	701	718	* 735	686	Bovine
Sheep	130	150	183	205	247	276	308	336[1]	Ovine
Pigs	2 261	2 113	2 345	2 678	2 708	2 843	2 983	3 098[1]	Porcine
Horses [1]	5	5	5	5	5	5	5	5	Chevaline [1]
Mongolia									**Mongolie**
Cattle	2 480	2 526	2 541	2 693	2 849	2 822	2 731	2 779	Bovine
Sheep	13 194	13 234	13 451	14 265	15 083	14 721	13 779	14 392	Ovine
Pigs	80	120	171	192	135	83	49	49	Porcine
Horses	2 018	2 047	2 103	2 200	2 262	2 259	2 200	2 100[1]	Chevaline
Myanmar									**Myanmar**
Cattle	9 919	10 091	9 126	9 298	9 382	9 470	9 584	9 691	Bovine
Sheep	304	313	269	276	279	284	305	304	Ovine
Pigs	3 059	3 199	2 449	2 243	2 372	2 514	2 529	2 589	Porcine
Horses	136	138	119	121	118	116	120	121[1]	Chevaline
Mules [1]	9	9	9	9	9	9	9	9	Mulassière [1]
Nepal									**Népal**
Cattle	6 363	6 343	6 285	6 281	6 255	6 246	6 237	6 546	Bovine
Sheep	837	873	910	892	906	912	911	914	Ovine
Pigs	476	516	548	574	592	599	630	612	Porcine
Oman									**Oman**
Cattle	135[1]	136[1]	136[1]	137	138[1]	140[1]	142[1]	144[1]	Bovine
Sheep	137[1]	138[1]	139[1]	140[1]	143[1]	145[1]	148[1]	149[1]	Ovine
Asses [1]	24	25	25	25	26	26	26	26	Asine [1]
Pakistan									**Pakistan**
Cattle	17 575	17 609	17 643	17 677	17 711	17 745	17 779	* 18 146	Bovine
Sheep	23 868	24 463	25 072	25 698	26 338	26 995	27 668	* 28 975	Ovine

37
Livestock
Thousand head [*cont.*]
Cheptel
Milliers de têtes [*suite*]

Country or area	1987	1988	1989	1990	1991	1992	1993	1994	Pays ou zone
Horses	454	378	373	368	363	358	354	354[1]	Chevaline
Asses	2 938	3 202	3 309	3 420	3 534	3 653	3 775	3 904[1]	Asine
Mules	65	71	72	72	73	74	75	77[1]	Mulassière
Philippines									**Philippines**
Cattle	1 747	1 700	1 682	1 629	1 680	1 729	1 781	* 1 825	Bovine
Sheep [1]	30	30	30	30	30	30	30	30	Ovine [1]
Pigs	7 038	7 581	7 909	7 990	8 006	8 022	7 954	* 8 227	Porcine
Horses	195[1]	200[1]	200[1]	200[1]	200[1]	200[1]	210[1]	210[1]	Chevaline
Qatar									**Qatar**
Cattle	9	10	10	10	9	11	12	12[1]	Bovine
Sheep	121	123	126	130	122	142	166	170[1]	Ovine
Horses	1	1	1	1	1	1	1	1[1]	Chevaline
Saudi Arabia									**Arabie saoudite**
Cattle	195	195	194	193	198	202	202	203[1]	Bovine
Sheep	6 812	6 194	6 173	6 383	6 553	6 890	6 973	* 7 257	Ovine
Horses [1]	3	3	3	3	3	3	3	3	Chevaline [1]
Asses [1]	107	106	105	104	103	102	100	98	Asine [1]
Singapore									**Singapour**
Pigs	459	321	350[1]	300[1]	250[1]	200[1]	150[1]	150[1]	Porcine
Sri Lanka									**Sri Lanka**
Cattle	1 808	1 788	1 820	1 773	1 477	1 568	1 600[1]	1 600[1]	Bovine
Sheep	28	28	30	26	20	17	19[1]	19[1]	Ovine
Pigs	97	95	94	85	84	91	90[1]	90[1]	Porcine
Horses [1]	2	2	2	2	2	2	2	2	Chevaline [1]
Syrian Arab Republic									**Rép. arabe syrienne**
Cattle	710	763	800	787	771	765	707	770[1]	Bovine
Sheep	12 669	13 691	14 011	14 509	15 194	14 665	11 000	12 000[1]	Ovine
Pigs [1]	1	1	1	1	1	1	1	1	Porcine [1]
Horses	41	40	43	41	39	37	38[1]	38[1]	Chevaline
Asses	184	177	178	168	161	158	160[1]	160[1]	Asine
Mules	28	27	27	26	25	27	27[1]	27[1]	Mulassière
Tajikistan									**Tadjikistan**
Cattle	...	...	...	...	...	1 222	1 244	1 250	Bovine
Sheep	...	...	...	...	...	2 172	2 081	2 000[1]	Ovine
Pigs	...	...	...	...	...	56	46	40[1]	Porcine
Horses	...	...	...	...	...	48	53[1]	50[1]	Chevaline
Asses [1]	...	...	...	...	...	36	36	35	Asine [1]
Thailand									**Thaïlande**
Cattle	4 969	5 072	5 285	5 459	5 631	5 815	7 190	7 593	Bovine
Sheep	95	131	156	162	166	176	136	98	Ovine
Pigs	4 209	4 685	4 679	4 728	4 859	4 655	* 5 435	* 4 931	Porcine
Horses	19	19	18	20	20	19	20	162	Chevaline
Asses	0[1]	0[1]	0[1]	0[1]	0[1]	0[1]	0[1]	0[1]	Asine
Mules	0[1]	0[1]	0[1]	0[1]	0[1]	0[1]	0[1]	0[1]	Mulassière
Turkey									**Turquie**
Cattle	12 713	12 713	12 562	12 173	11 377	11 973	11 951	11 910	Bovine
Sheep	43 758	43 796	45 384	43 647	40 553	40 433	39 416	37 541	Ovine
Pigs	8	7	9	8	12	10	12	9	Porcine
Horses	600	590	557	545	513	496	483	450	Chevaline
Asses	1 188	1 153	1 119	1 084	985	944	895	841	Asine
Mules	216	205	208	210	202	192	181	172	Mulassière
Turkmenistan									**Turkménistan**
Cattle	...	...	...	...	...	777	1 004	1 104	Bovine
Sheep	...	...	...	...	...	5 380	* 6 000	* 6 000	Ovine
Pigs	...	...	...	...	...	237	212	159	Porcine
Horses [1]	...	...	...	...	...	20	22	20	Chevaline [1]
Asses [1]	...	...	...	...	...	26	26	25	Asine [1]
United Arab Emirates									**Emirats arabes unis**
Cattle	44	46	46	49	53	55[1]	60[1]	65	Bovine
Sheep	207	222	238	254	272	295[1]	320[1]	333	Ovine
Uzbekistan									**Ouzbékistan**
Cattle	...	...	...	...	...	5 113	5 275	5 291	Bovine
Sheep	...	...	...	...	...	8 275	8 407	8 600[1]	Ovine
Pigs	...	...	...	...	...	654	529	391	Porcine
Horses	...	...	...	...	...	113	123	120[1]	Chevaline
Asses	...	...	...	...	...	143	158	150[1]	Asine

37

Livestock
Thousand head [*cont.*]
Cheptel
Milliers de têtes [*suite*]

Country or area	1987	1988	1989	1990	1991	1992	1993	1994	Pays ou zone
Viet Nam									**Viet Nam**
Cattle	2 784	2 979	3 127	3 202	3 117	3 136	3 320	3 438[1]	Bovine
Pigs	11 796	12 051	11 643	12 221	12 261	12 194	14 861	15 043[1]	Porcine
Horses	137	136	133	143	141	134	133	134[1]	Chevaline
Yemen									**Yémen**
Cattle	1 120	1 137	1 170	1 175	1 117	1 139	1 163	1 128	Bovine
Sheep	3 488	3 602	3 720	3 756	3 568	3 640	3 715	3 715	Ovine
Horses	3[1]	3[1]	3[1]	3[1]	3[1]	3[1]	3[1]	3[1]	Chevaline
Asses	524[1]	500	500	500	500	500	500	* 500	Asine
Europe									**Europe**
Cattle	127 546	124 698	124 980	124 394	120 283	113 783	109 076	107 158	Bovine
Sheep	142 981	144 350	144 943	145 957	142 452	138 834	133 776	130 692	Ovine
Pigs	189 440	188 627	185 671	181 328	181 766	173 937	168 847	167 983	Porcine
Horses	4 509	4 387	4 303	4 253	4 302	4 313	4 270	4 185	Chevaline
Asses	1 069	1 012	987	1 013	993	949	918	906	Asine
Mules	399	363	344	319	300	274	273	276	Mulassière
Albania									**Albanie**
Cattle	671	695	699	633	640	596	655	630[1]	Bovine
Sheep	1 432	1 525	1 592	1 646	1 696	1 795	1 912	1 900[1]	Ovine
Pigs	214	196	181	220	148	90	93	86[1]	Porcine
Horses	* 94	* 99	* 101	57	56	44	58	58[1]	Chevaline
Asses	53[1]	53[1]	53[1]	104	106	104	114	113[1]	Asine
Mules	23[1]	23[1]	23[1]	20	20	20	26	25[1]	Mulassière
Austria									**Autriche**
Cattle	2 637	2 590	2 541	2 562	2 534	2 532	2 334	* 2 430	Bovine
Sheep	256	261	256	287	309	323	334	324[1]	Ovine
Pigs	3 801	3 947	3 874	3 773	3 638	3 629	3 820	* 3 800	Porcine
Horses	44	45	44	48	49	57	65	65[1]	Chevaline
Belarus									**Bélarus**
Cattle	...	...	...	...	...	6 577	6 221	5 851	Bovine
Sheep	...	...	...	...	...	* 373	336	* 289	Ovine
Pigs	...	...	...	...	...	4 703	4 308	4 175	Porcine
Horses	...	...	...	...	...	212	215	215[1]	Chevaline
Asses [1]	...	...	...	...	...	8	8	8	Asine [1]
Belgium–Luxembourg									**Belgique–Luxembourg**
Cattle	3 190	3 159	3 174	3 257	3 360	3 311	3 303	3 289	Bovine
Sheep	168	174	170	174	177	170	163	160	Ovine
Pigs	5 838	5 958	6 310	6 511	6 496	6 597	6 963	6 948	Porcine
Horses	24	23	22	21	21	21	21	21	Chevaline
Bosnia & Herzegovina									**Bosnie–Herzégovine**
Cattle [1]	...	...	...	...	...	500	425	390	Bovine [1]
Sheep [1]	...	...	...	...	...	854	718	600	Ovine [1]
Pigs [1]	...	...	...	...	...	590	550	223	Porcine [1]
Horses [1]	...	...	...	...	...	70	56	50	Chevaline [1]
Bulgaria									**Bulgarie**
Cattle	1 678	1 649	1 613	1 575	1 457	1 310	974	750	Bovine
Sheep	9 563	8 886	8 609	8 130	7 938	6 703	4 814	3 763	Ovine
Pigs	4 050	4 034	4 119	4 352	4 187	3 141	2 680	2 071	Porcine
Horses	121	123	122	119	115	114	114	113	Chevaline
Asses	341	333	329	329	329	329	303	297	Asine
Mules	26	25	24	22	19	17	21	23	Mulassière
Croatia									**Croatie**
Cattle	...	...	...	...	...	590	590	519	Bovine
Sheep	...	...	...	...	...	539	524	444	Ovine
Pigs	...	...	...	...	...	1 183	1 262	1 347	Porcine
Horses	...	...	...	...	...	27	22	22	Chevaline
Asses	...	...	...	...	...	13	12	7	Asine
Mules [1]	...	...	...	...	...	4	3	3	Mulassière [1]
former Czechoslovakia†									**anc. Tchécoslovaquie †**
Cattle	5 073	5 044	5 075	5 129	4 923	4 347	...	...	Bovine
Sheep	1 104	1 075	1 047	1 051	1 030	886	...	...	Ovine
Pigs	6 833	7 235	7 384	7 498	7 090	7 139	...	...	Porcine
Horses	46	45	44	42	39	34	...	...	Chevaline
Czech Republic									**République tchèque**
Cattle	...	...	...	...	...	...	2 512	* 2 113	Bovine
Sheep	...	...	...	...	...	...	254	196	Ovine

37
Livestock
Thousand head [*cont.*]
Cheptel
Milliers de têtes [*suite*]

Country or area	1987	1988	1989	1990	1991	1992	1993	1994	Pays ou zone
Pigs	...	...	...	...	...	...	4 599	4 071	Porcine
Horses	...	...	...	...	...	...	19	18	Chevaline
Denmark									**Danemark**
Cattle	2 490	2 323	2 232	2 241	2 222	2 180	2 115	2 082	Bovine
Sheep	70	73	86	100	122	102	87	82	Ovine
Pigs	9 422	9 048	9 120	9 282	9 767	10 345	10 870	10 864	Porcine
Horses	29	34	35	38	34	29	24	17	Chevaline
Estonia									**Estonie**
Cattle	...	...	...	...	...	708	615	463	Bovine
Sheep	...	...	...	...	...	142	124	83	Ovine
Pigs	...	...	...	...	...	799	541	424	Porcine
Horses	...	...	...	...	...	8	7	5	Chevaline
Faeroe Islands									**Iles Féroé**
Cattle	2[1]	2[1]	2[1]	2[1]	2[1]	2[1]	2[1]	2[1]	Bovine
Sheep	66	67[1]	67[1]	67[1]	67[1]	68[1]	68[1]	69[1]	Ovine
Finland									**Finlande**
Cattle	1 485	1 434	1 379	1 363	1 315	1 263	1 232	1 230	Bovine
Sheep	66	63	59	61	57	61	62	79	Ovine
Pigs	1 309	1 291	1 327	1 348	1 290	1 357	1 309	1 300	Porcine
Horses	39	36	40	44	45	49	49	49	Chevaline
France									**France**
Cattle	21 967	21 340	21 377	21 394	21 450	20 970	20 328	20 112	Bovine
Sheep	12 044	11 495	11 208	11 209	11 170	10 640	10 380	10 452	Ovine
Pigs	12 419	12 643	12 410	12 276	12 013	12 068	12 564	13 383	Porcine
Horses	268	266	269	319	322	328	329	332	Chevaline
Asses	24[1]	25[1]	25[1]	25[1]	25[1]	25[1]	25[1]	25[1]	Asine
Mules	12[1]	12[1]	12[1]	13	13	12	12	13	Mulassière
Germany †									**Allemagne †**
Cattle	21 109	20 607	20 369	20 288	19 488	17 134	15 897	15 891	Bovine
Sheep	4 030	4 070	4 099	4 135	3 239	2 488	2 369	* 2 360	Ovine
Pigs	37 342	36 172	35 053	34 178	30 819	26 063	26 075	26 044	Porcine
Horses	472	469	477	484[1]	491	492[1]	531	530[1]	Chevaline
Greece									**Grèce**
Cattle	725	683	677	654	624	616	629	608	Bovine
Sheep	8 258	8 612	8 670	8 723	8 660	9 694	9 659	* 9 604	Ovine
Pigs	1 061	998	1 011	1 001	996	1 125	1 040	1 143	Porcine
Horses	74	57	53	49	45	40[1]	40[1]	40[1]	Chevaline
Asses	188	157	147	137	127	115[1]	110[1]	110[1]	Asine
Mules	89	75	70	65	60	55[1]	50[1]	50[1]	Mulassière
Hungary									**Hongrie**
Cattle	1 725	1 664	1 690	1 598	1 571	1 420	1 159	1 002	Bovine
Sheep	2 337	2 336	2 215	2 069	1 865	1 808	1 752	1 280	Ovine
Pigs	8 687	8 216	8 327	7 660	8 000	5 993	5 364	5 002	Porcine
Horses	95	88	76	75	76	75	73	72	Chevaline
Asses	5	5[1]	4[1]	4[1]	4	4[1]	4[1]	4[1]	Asine
Iceland									**Islande**
Cattle	69	71	73	75	78	75	76[1]	77[1]	Bovine
Sheep	624	587	561	549	511	500	500[1]	500[1]	Ovine
Pigs	18[1]	18[1]	17[1]	19[1]	19[1]	20[1]	21[1]	22[1]	Porcine
Horses	59	64	69	72	74	75	78[1]	82[1]	Chevaline
Ireland									**Irlande**
Cattle	5 670	5 633	5 699	5 969	6 101	6 158	6 265	6 308	Bovine
Sheep	3 672	4 301	4 991	5 714	5 864	5 988	6 125	5 991	Ovine
Pigs	980	960	1 015	1 110	1 249	1 346	1 423	1 487	Porcine
Horses	55	53	52	54	53[1]	53[1]	53[1]	53[1]	Chevaline
Asses	17[1]	16[1]	16[1]	15[1]	15[1]	14[1]	14[1]	14[1]	Asine
Mules	1[1]	1[1]	1[1]	1[1]	1[1]	1[1]	1[1]	1[1]	Mulassière
Italy									**Italie**
Cattle	8 819	8 794	8 737	8 746	8 140	8 004	7 783	7 683[1]	Bovine
Sheep	11 451	11 457	11 569	10 848	10 848	10 435	10 403	* 10 370	Ovine
Pigs	9 278	9 383	9 359	9 254	8 837	8 549	8 307	* 8 200	Porcine
Horses	253	250	256	271	288	316	330[1]	338[1]	Chevaline
Asses	91	86	81	74	51	* 37	30[1]	30[1]	Asine
Mules	52	50	47	43	33	* 23	20[1]	20[1]	Mulassière
Latvia									**Lettonie**
Cattle	...	...	...	...	...	1 383	1 144	995[1]	Bovine

37

Livestock
Thousand head [*cont.*]
Cheptel
Milliers de têtes [*suite*]

Country or area	1987	1988	1989	1990	1991	1992	1993	1994	Pays ou zone
Sheep	...	...	...	...	...	184	165	133[1]	Ovine
Pigs	...	...	...	...	...	1 246	867	737[1]	Porcine
Horses	...	...	...	...	...	30	28	28[1]	Chevaline
Liechtenstein									**Liechtenstein**
Cattle	6	6	6	6	6	6	6[1]	6[1]	Bovine
Sheep	2	2	2	3	3	3	3[1]	3[1]	Ovine
Pigs	3	3	3	3	4	3	3[1]	3[1]	Porcine
Lithuania									**Lituanie**
Cattle	...	...	...	...	...	2 197	1 701	1 650	Bovine
Sheep	...	...	...	...	...	58	52	* 48	Ovine
Pigs	...	...	...	...	...	2 180	1 360	1 200[1]	Porcine
Horses	...	...	...	...	...	80	78[1]	78[1]	Chevaline
Malta									**Malte**
Cattle	18[1]	19[1]	21	21[1]	22[1]	22[1]	22	20	Bovine
Sheep	6[1]	6[1]	6	6[1]	6[1]	6[1]	* 6	* 6	Ovine
Pigs	95[1]	98[1]	101	101[1]	102[1]	107[1]	109[1]	111[1]	Porcine
Horses	1[1]	1[1]	1	1[1]	1[1]	1[1]	1[1]	1[1]	Chevaline
Asses	1[1]	1[1]	1	1[1]	1[1]	1[1]	1[1]	1[1]	Asine
Netherlands									**Pays-Bas**
Cattle	4 895	4 546	4 772	4 926	5 057	* 4 876	* 4 794	* 4 629	Bovine
Sheep	985	* 1 169	* 1 405	* 1 702	* 1 882	* 1 954	* 2 000	2 174[1]	Ovine
Pigs	14 349	* 14 226	* 13 820	* 13 634	* 13 788	* 13 727	* 13 709	* 13 991	Porcine
Horses	64	64[1]	64[1]	65[1]	65[1]	65[1]	65[1]	66[1]	Chevaline
Norway									**Norvège**
Cattle	945	932	949	953	974	984	1 008	1 003	Bovine
Sheep	2 248	2 210	2 183	2 211	2 211	2 363	2 316	2 316[1]	Ovine
Pigs	779	745	657	710	721	766	745	745[1]	Porcine
Horses	16	17	17	19	21	21	21	22[1]	Chevaline
Poland									**Pologne**
Cattle	10 523	10 322	10 733	10 049	8 844	8 221	7 643	7 696	Bovine
Sheep	4 739	4 377	4 409	4 158	3 234	1 870	1 268	870	Ovine
Pigs	18 546	19 605	18 835	19 464	21 868	22 086	18 860	19 466	Porcine
Horses	1 141	1 051	973	941	939	900	841	* 721	Chevaline
Portugal									**Portugal**
Cattle *	1 332	1 332	1 356	1 335	1 341	1 416	1 345	1 322	Bovine *
Sheep	* 5 100	* 5 298	* 5 354	* 5 567	* 5 673	* 5 640	6 125	5 991	Ovine
Pigs	* 2 454	2 455	2 331	2 598	2 664	2 564	1 423	1 487	Porcine
Horses	26[1]	26[1]	26[1]	26[1]	26[1]	25[1]	25[1]	25[1]	Chevaline
Asses	170[1]	170[1]	170[1]	170[1]	170[1]	170[1]	170[1]	170[1]	Asine
Mules	80[1]	80[1]	80[1]	80[1]	80[1]	80[1]	80[1]	80[1]	Mulassière
Republic of Moldova									**République de Moldova**
Cattle	...	...	...	...	...	1 000	971	916	Bovine
Sheep	...	...	...	...	...	1 239	1 294	1 373	Ovine
Pigs	...	...	...	...	...	1 753	1 487	1 165	Porcine
Horses	...	...	...	...	...	48	51	55	Chevaline
Asses	...	...	...	...	...	2	2	2	Asine
Romania									**Roumanie**
Cattle	6 703	6 559	6 416	6 291	5 381	4 355	3 683	3 597	Bovine
Sheep	17 219	16 839	16 210	15 435	14 062	13 879	12 079	11 499	Ovine
Pigs	14 095	14 328	14 351	11 671	12 003	10 954	9 852	9 262	Porcine
Horses	686	693	702	663	670	749	721	751	Chevaline
Asses [1]	36	36	36	35	35	35	34	34	Asine [1]
Russian Federation									**Fédération de Russie**
Cattle	...	...	...	...	...	54 677	52 226	48 900	Bovine
Sheep	...	...	...	...	...	52 195	48 183	41 078	Ovine
Pigs	...	...	...	...	...	35 384	31 520	28 600	Porcine
Horses	...	...	...	...	...	2 590	2 556	2 500[1]	Chevaline
Asses	...	...	...	...	...	22	22	20[1]	Asine
Mules [1]	...	...	...	...	...	1	1	...	Mulassière [1]
Slovakia									**Slovaquie**
Cattle	...	...	...	...	...	...	1 182	916	Bovine
Sheep	...	...	...	...	...	...	* 561	397	Ovine
Pigs	...	...	...	...	...	...	2 269	2 179	Porcine
Horses	...	...	...	...	...	...	13[1]	12	Chevaline
Slovenia									**Slovénie**
Cattle	...	...	...	...	...	484	504	504[1]	Bovine

37
Livestock
Thousand head [*cont.*]
Cheptel
Milliers de têtes [*suite*]

Country or area	1987	1988	1989	1990	1991	1992	1993	1994	Pays ou zone
Sheep	...	...	...	...	...	28	21	21[1]	Ovine
Pigs	...	...	...	...	...	529	602	620[1]	Porcine
Horses	...	...	...	...	...	11	8	8[1]	Chevaline
Spain									**Espagne**
Cattle	4 795	5 061	5 185	5 126	5 063	4 976	5 018	5 000	Bovine
Sheep	22 994	23 064	22 739	24 037	24 625	24 615	23 872	23 838	Ovine
Pigs	17 303	16 614	16 911	16 002	17 247	18 260	18 234	18 188	Porcine
Horses	248	247[1]	245[1]	260[1]	273[1]	263[1]	263[1]	262[1]	Chevaline
Asses	120[1]	105[1]	100[1]	90[1]	90[1]	90[1]	90[1]	90[1]	Asine
Mules	110[1]	90[1]	80[1]	70[1]	70[1]	60[1]	60[1]	60[1]	Mulassière
Sweden									**Suède**
Cattle	1 656	1 662	1 688	1 718	1 707	1 773	1 871	1 830	Bovine
Sheep	397	395	401	406	419	447	471	483	Ovine
Pigs	2 234	2 274	2 264	2 264	2 201	2 279	2 268	2 168	Porcine
Horses	57[1]	58[1]	58[1]	58[1]	77	78[1]	79[1]	86	Chevaline
Switzerland									**Suisse**
Cattle	1 858	1 837	1 850	1 855	1 829	1 783	1 745	1 700[1]	Bovine
Sheep	355	367	371	395	409	415	424	425[1]	Ovine
Pigs	1 917	1 941	1 869	1 787	1 723	1 706	1 692	1 680[1]	Porcine
Horses	48	49	48	45	49	52	54	55[1]	Chevaline
Asses	2	2	2[1]	2[1]	2[1]	2[1]	2[1]	2[1]	Asine
TFYR Macedonia									**L'ex−R.y. Macédoine**
Cattle	...	...	...	...	...	285	280	276	Bovine
Sheep	...	...	...	...	...	2 351	2 420	2 444	Ovine
Pigs	...	...	...	...	...	173	182	181	Porcine
Horses	...	...	...	...	...	65	62	62[1]	Chevaline
Ukraine									**Ukraine**
Cattle	...	...	...	...	...	23 728	22 457	21 607	Bovine
Sheep	...	...	...	...	...	7 259	6 597	6 118	Ovine
Pigs	...	...	...	...	...	17 839	16 175	15 298	Porcine
Horses	...	...	...	...	...	717	707	716	Chevaline
Asses [1]	...	...	...	...	...	19	19	15	Asine [1]
United Kingdom									**Royaume−Uni**
Cattle	12 476	11 855	11 909	11 922	11 641	11 620	11 708	* 11 735	Bovine
Sheep	25 976	27 820	29 103	29 678	28 944	29 493	29 333	* 29 300	Ovine
Pigs	7 955	7 915	7 627	7 383	7 520	7 705	7 869	* 7 910	Porcine
Horses [1]	165	168	168	169	170	172	173	174	Chevaline [1]
Asses [1]	10	10	10	10	10	10	10	10	Asine [1]
Yugoslavia									**Yougoslavie**
Cattle	...	...	...	...	...	1 975	1 991	1 809	Bovine
Sheep	...	...	...	...	...	2 715	2 752	2 752	Ovine
Pigs	...	...	...	...	...	3 844	* 4 092	4 000[1]	Porcine
Horses	...	...	...	...	...	89	82	82	Chevaline
Yugoslavia, SFR †									**Yougoslavie, Rfs †**
Cattle	5 030	4 881	4 759	4 705	4 514	...	...	...	Bovine
Sheep	7 819	7 824	7 564	7 596	7 431	...	...	...	Ovine
Pigs	8 459	8 323	7 396	7 231	7 378	...	...	...	Porcine
Horses	384	362	340	314	303	...	...	...	Chevaline
Asses	* 13	* 14	* 13	18	29	...	...	...	Asine
Mules	5[1]	5[1]	5[1]	4[1]	4[1]	...	...	...	Mulassière
Oceania									**Océanie**
Cattle	30 588	30 591	30 939	31 883	32 472	32 735	33 480	34 049	Bovine
Sheep	213 407	217 049	222 179	228 156	218 407	200 779	189 116	182 758	Ovine
Pigs	4 688	4 788	4 736	4 702	4 603	4 883	4 794	4 910	Porcine
Horses	479	504	489	474	470	454	429	430	Chevaline
Asses	9	8	9	9	10	10	9	9	Asine
American Samoa									**Samoa américaines**
Pigs	13[1]	13[1]	13	11[1]	11[1]	11[1]	11[1]	11[1]	Porcine
Australia									**Australie**
Cattle	21 915	21 851	22 434	23 162	23 662	23 880	24 062	24 732	Bovine
Sheep	149 157	152 443	161 603	170 297	163 238	148 203	138 102	132 609	Ovine
Pigs	2 611	2 706	2 671	2 648	2 531	2 792	2 646	2 740	Porcine
Horses	313	335	317	310	308	289	272	272[1]	Chevaline
Asses	2	1	2	2	3	3	2	2[1]	Asine
Cook Islands									**Iles Cook**
Pigs	17[1]	16	16	17	17	18	25	28	Porcine

37
Livestock
Thousand head [*cont.*]
Cheptel
Milliers de têtes [*suite*]

Country or area	1987	1988	1989	1990	1991	1992	1993	1994	Pays ou zone
Fiji									**Fidji**
Cattle	261[1]	265[1]	268[1]	273[1]	280	288[1]	315	334	Bovine
Sheep	...	...	...	...	...	...	5	6	Ovine
Pigs	80[1]	83[1]	86[1]	88[1]	91	97[1]	110	115	Porcine
Horses [1]	41	42	42	43	43	43	43	44	Chevaline [1]
French Polynesia									**Polynésie française**
Cattle	8	8	9	7	7[1]	7[1]	8[1]	8[1]	Bovine
Pigs	32	32	32	32	34[1]	36[1]	38	38[1]	Porcine
Horses	2	2[1]	2[1]	2	2[1]	2[1]	2[1]	2[1]	Chevaline
Guam									**Guam**
Pigs [1]	14	14	5	4	4	4	4	4	Porcine [1]
Kiribati									**Kiribati**
Pigs [1]	10	10	9	9	9	9	9	9	Porcine [1]
Nauru									**Nauru**
Pigs [1]	2	2	2	3	3	3	3	3	Porcine [1]
New Caledonia									**Nouvelle—Calédonie**
Cattle	130[1]	136	121	120	125	125	125[1]	125[1]	Bovine
Sheep	2	3[1]	3	4[1]	4	4[1]	4[1]	4[1]	Ovine
Pigs	35	36[1]	36[1]	37[1]	38	39[1]	39[1]	39[1]	Porcine
Horses	10[1]	10[1]	11[1]	11[1]	11	12[1]	12[1]	13[1]	Chevaline
New Zealand									**Nouvelle—Zélande**
Cattle	7 999	8 058	7 828	8 034	8 100	8 144	8 675	* 8 550	Bovine
Sheep	64 244	64 600	60 569	57 852	55 162	52 568	51 000	* 50 135	Ovine
Pigs	426	414	411	395	407	411	430	430[1]	Porcine
Horses	94	97	98	94	91	88	80	80[1]	Chevaline
Niue									**Nioué**
Pigs	1[1]	2[1]	2	2	2[1]	2[1]	2[1]	2[1]	Porcine
Palau									**Palaos**
Cattle [1 2]	12	12	12	13	13	14	14	14	Bovine [1 2]
Pigs [1 2]	29	30	30	30	31	31	32	33	Porcine [1 2]
Papua New Guinea									**Papouasie—Nvl—Guinée**
Cattle	105[1]	* 101	101[1]	103[1]	105[1]	105[1]	105[1]	105[1]	Bovine
Sheep	3[1]	3[1]	3[1]	4[1]	4[1]	4[1]	4[1]	4[1]	Ovine
Pigs 1	960	975	990	1 000	1 000	1 010	1 022	1 033	Porcine [1]
Horses	1[1]	1[1]	1[1]	1[1]	2[1]	2[1]	2[1]	2[1]	Chevaline
Samoa									**Samoa**
Cattle	24	24	24	24[1]	25[1]	24[1]	25[1]	26[1]	Bovine
Pigs	193	193	193	185[1]	180[1]	175[1]	178[1]	179[1]	Porcine
Horses	3[1]	3[1]	3	3[1]	3[1]	3[1]	3[1]	3[1]	Chevaline
Asses	7[1]	7[1]	7[1]	7[1]	7[1]	7[1]	7[1]	7[1]	Asine
Solomon Islands									**Iles Salomon**
Cattle	14	* 13	* 13	* 13	* 13	13[1]	13[1]	13[1]	Bovine
Pigs	* 51	* 52	* 52	* 53	* 53	54[1]	55[1]	55[1]	Porcine
Tokelau									**Tokélaou**
Pigs [1]	1	1	1	1	1	1	1	1	Porcine [1]
Tonga									**Tonga**
Cattle	* 10	10	12	* 10	* 10	10[1]	10[1]	10[1]	Bovine
Pigs	105[1]	120	94	94[1]	94[1]	94[1]	94[1]	94[1]	Porcine
Horses	* 11	11	11	* 6	* 6	12[1]	11[1]	11[1]	Chevaline
Tuvalu									**Tuvalu**
Pigs	8	8	11	11	13	13[1]	13[1]	13[1]	Porcine
Vanuatu									**Vanuatu**
Cattle	110	113	116	123[1]	130	125[1]	128[1]	132[1]	Bovine
Pigs	77	58	58	60	60	59[1]	59[1]	59[1]	Porcine
Horses	3	3[1]	3[1]	3[1]	3[1]	3[1]	3[1]	3[1]	Chevaline
Wallis and Futuna Islands									**Iles Wallis et Futuna**
Pigs	24[1]	24[1]	24[1]	24[1]	25[1]	25[1]	25[1]	25[1]	Porcine
former USSR †									**ancienne URSS †**
Cattle	122 103	118 300	119 600	118 388	115 643	...	...	...	Bovine
Sheep	142 210	140 783	140 700	138 564	132 949	...	...	...	Ovine
Pigs	79 501	77 403	78 100	78 963	75 428	...	...	...	Porcine
Horses	5 900	5 885	5 904	5 921	5 919	...	...	...	Chevaline
Asses	300	300	300[1]	300[1]	310[1]	...	...	...	Asine
Mules	1	1	1	1	1	...	...	...	Mulassière

37
Livestock
Thousand head [*cont.*]
Cheptel
Milliers de têtes [*suite*]

Source:
Food and Agriculture Organization of the United Nations (Rome).

† For detailed descriptions of data pertaining to former Czechoslovakia, Germany, SFR Yugoslavia and former USSR, see Annex I − Country or area nomenclature, regional and other groupings.

1 FAO estimate.
2 Including data for Federated States of Micronesia, Marshall Islands, and Northern Mariana Islands.

Source:
Organisation des Nations Unies pour l'alimentation et l'agriculture (Rome).

† Pour les descriptions en détails des données relatives à l'ancienne Tchécoslovaquie, l'Allemagne, la Rfs Yougoslavie et l'ancienne URSS, voir l'Annexe I − Nomenclature des pays ou zones, groupements régionaux et autres groupements.

1 Estimation de la FAO.
2 Y compris les données pour les Etats fédérés de Micronésie, les îles Marshall et les îles Mariannes du Nord.

38
Roundwood
Bois rond

Production (solid volume of roundwood without bark): million cubic metres
Production (volume solide de bois rond sans écorce) : millions de mètres cubes

Country or area Pays ou zone	1984	1985	1986	1987	1988	1989	1990	1991	1992	1993
World *Monde*	3 154.0	3 189.1	3 276.9	3 353.5	3 413.3	3 472.1	3 521.0	3 413.9	3 416.3	3 404.4
Africa Afrique	433.6	448.2	460.2	473.3	486.3	499.6	514.7	526.2	539.7	553.1
Algeria Algérie	1.8[1]	1.9[1]	1.9[1]	2.0[1]	2.1[1]	2.1[1]	2.2[1]	2.2	2.3	2.4[1]
Angola Angola	5.2	5.3	5.4	5.5	5.7	5.8	6.0	6.2[1]	6.4[1]	6.6[1]
Benin Bénin	4.2	4.3	4.5	4.6	4.7	4.9[1]	5.0	5.2[1]	5.4[1]	5.5[1]
Botswana[1] Botswana[1]	1.1	1.1	1.2	1.2	1.2	1.3	1.3	1.4	1.4	1.4
Burkina Faso Burkina Faso	7.5	7.7	7.9[1]	8.1[1]	8.3[1]	8.5[1]	8.7[1]	9.0[1]	9.3[1]	9.5[1]
Burundi Burundi	3.6[1]	3.7[1]	3.8[1]	3.9[1]	4.0[1]	4.1	4.2	4.4	4.5[1]	4.6[1]
Cameroon Cameroun	11.7	12.2	12.5	12.8	13.0	13.5	14.1	14.3	14.4	14.7[1]
Central African Rep. Rép. centrafricaine	3.3	3.4	3.4	3.5	3.5	3.5	3.5	3.4	3.7	3.7
Chad Tchad	3.5[1]	3.6[1]	3.6[1]	3.7[1]	3.8[1]	3.9[1]	3.9	4.0	4.2	4.3
Congo Congo	2.5	2.6	2.8	3.0	3.4	3.5	3.6	3.3	3.5	3.6[1]
Côte d'Ivoire Côte d'Ivoire	12.3	12.0	12.1	12.0	11.8	12.2	13.3	13.1	13.3	13.7
Egypt[1] Egypte[1]	1.9	2.0	2.0	2.1	2.1	2.2	2.2	2.3	2.4	2.4
Equatorial Guinea Guinée équatoriale	0.5	0.6	0.6[1]	0.7	0.6	0.6	0.6	0.6	0.6	0.6
Ethiopia Ethiopie	36.7	37.5	38.4	39.5	40.6	41.8	43.0	44.3	45.6	47.0
Gabon Gabon	3.6	3.5	3.5	3.5[1]	3.8	3.9	4.2	4.3[1]	4.3[1]	4.4[1]
Gambia Gambie	0.9	0.9	0.9[1]	0.9[1]	0.9[1]	0.9[1]	0.9[1]	0.9[1]	0.9[1]	1.0[1]
Ghana Ghana	16.4	16.5	16.6	16.7	16.9	17.0	17.5	16.9	16.8	17.2
Guinea Guinée	3.4[1]	3.5[1]	3.6	3.7	3.8	3.9	4.0	4.1	4.4	4.5
Guinea-Bissau[1] Guinée-Bissau[1]	0.6	0.6	0.6	0.6	0.6	0.6	0.6	0.6	0.6	0.6
Kenya Kenya	28.5	29.5[1]	30.5[1]	31.6[1]	32.7	33.8	34.9	36.1[1]	37.3[1]	38.6[1]
Lesotho[1] Lesotho[1]	0.5	0.5	0.5	0.6	0.6	0.6	0.6	0.6	0.6	0.7
Liberia Libéria	4.2	4.5	5.3	5.6	5.9	6.0[1]	6.1[1]	5.7	6.1	6.2[1]
Libyan Arab Jamah.[1] Jamah. arabe libyenne[1]	0.6	0.6	0.6	0.6	0.6	0.6	0.6	0.6	0.6	0.6

38
Roundwood
Production (solid volume of roundwood without bark): million cubic metres [cont.]
Bois rond
Production (volume solide de bois rond sans écorce) : millions de mètres cubes [suite]

Country or area Pays ou zone	1984	1985	1986	1987	1988	1989	1990	1991	1992	1993
Madagascar Madagascar	6.8[1]	7.0[1]	7.2[1]	7.4[1]	7.6[1]	7.9	8.1	8.3[1]	8.6[1]	8.9[1]
Malawi Malawi	6.6	6.9	7.2[1]	7.6[1]	8.1[1]	8.5	9.0	9.4[1]	9.8	10.1
Mali Mali	4.7	4.8	5.0	5.1	5.3	5.4[1]	5.6[1]	5.8[1]	6.0[1]	6.1[1]
Morocco Maroc	2.0[1]	2.2	2.0	2.0[1]	1.9	2.1	2.0	2.5	2.4	2.0
Mozambique Mozambique	15.0	15.2	15.6	15.9	15.9	15.9	15.9	16.0	16.0	16.0
Niger[1] Niger[1]	4.1	4.2	4.4	4.5	4.7	4.8	5.0	5.1	5.3	5.5
Nigeria Nigéria	89.5[1]	92.5	95.4	98.3[1]	101.4[1]	104.5[1]	108.1	111.4[1]	114.7[1]	118.1[1]
Rwanda Rwanda	5.6	5.8	5.8[1]	5.8[1]	5.8[1]	6.6	5.6	5.6	5.7	5.7[1]
Senegal Sénégal	4.0	4.4	4.6	4.6	4.5	4.4	4.9	4.9	4.9	5.0[1]
Sierra Leone Sierra Leone	2.7[1]	2.7	2.8	2.9[1]	2.9[1]	3.0[1]	3.1	3.1	3.2[1]	3.3[1]
Somalia[1] Somalie[1]	7.3	7.5	7.6	7.8	7.9	8.1	8.3	8.5	8.8	9.0
South Africa Afrique du Sud	19.0	19.0[1]	18.6	19.0	19.4	19.4[1]	20.1	19.7	19.8[1]	19.8[1]
Sudan Soudan	19.2[1]	19.7[1]	20.3[1]	20.9[1]	21.5[1]	22.2	22.8	23.4[1]	24.1[1]	24.8[1]
Swaziland Swaziland	2.2[1]	2.2[1]	2.2[1]	2.2[1]	2.2[1]	2.2[1]	2.2[1]	2.3	2.3[1]	2.3[1]
Togo Togo	0.7	0.8	0.8	0.8	0.8	0.9	0.9	1.2	1.3	1.3[1]
Tunisia Tunisie	2.8	2.9	2.9	3.0	3.0	3.1	3.2	3.3	3.3	3.4
Uganda Ouganda	11.8[1]	12.1[1]	12.5[1]	12.9[1]	13.3	13.7	14.2	14.6[1]	15.1[1]	15.6[1]
United Rep.Tanzania Rép. Unie de Tanzanie	26.3	27.2	28.3	29.5	30.5[1]	31.6[1]	32.6[1]	33.8[1]	34.9[1]	36.1[1]
Zaire Zaïre	31.2	35.0	36.1	37.2	38.8	39.5	40.8	42.0	43.2[1]	44.5[1]
Zambia Zambie	10.3[1]	10.8[1]	11.2[1]	11.7[1]	12.2[1]	12.6	13.2	13.7	13.8	13.8[1]
Zimbabwe Zimbabwe	7.1	7.2	7.3	7.6	7.9	7.9[1]	7.9[1]	8.0	8.0[1]	8.1[1]
America, North Amérique du Nord	691.2	686.3	720.7	741.0	749.7	754.5	759.1	713.0	734.8	743.5
Bahamas[1] Bahamas[1]	0.1	0.1	0.1	0.1	0.1	0.1	0.1	0.1	0.1	0.1
Belize Belize	0.2	0.2	0.2	0.2	0.2[1]	0.2[1]	0.2[1]	0.2[1]	0.2[1]	0.2[1]
Canada Canada	167.5	168.7	177.1	176.4	176.7	173.6	180.7	165.9	172.3	180.0

38
Roundwood
Production (solid volume of roundwood without bark): million cubic metres [cont.]
Bois rond
Production (volume solide de bois rond sans écorce) : millions de mètres cubes [suite]

Country or area Pays ou zone	1984	1985	1986	1987	1988	1989	1990	1991	1992	1993
Costa Rica Costa Rica	3.4	3.5[1]	3.6[1]	3.9	4.0	3.9	4.0	4.0	4.2	4.3
Cuba Cuba	3.3	3.3	3.4	3.2	3.3	3.1	3.1	3.1[1]	3.1[1]	3.1[1]
Dominican Republic Rép. dominicaine	1.0[1]	1.0[1]	1.0[1]	1.0[1]	1.0[1]	1.0	1.0	1.0[1]	1.0[1]	1.0[1]
El Salvador[1] El Salvador[1]	5.5	5.6	5.6	5.7	5.9	6.0	6.1	6.2	6.4	6.5
Guatemala Guatemala	9.8	10.0	10.2	10.4	10.7	11.0	11.3	11.3[1]	11.3[1]	11.3[1]
Haïti[1] Haïti[1]	5.2	5.3	5.4	5.5	5.6	5.7	5.8	5.9	6.1	6.2
Honduras Honduras	5.1[1]	5.4	5.5	5.8	6.0	6.0	6.1	6.2	6.2	6.5
Jamaica Jamaïque	0.1	0.3[1]	0.6	0.7	0.7	0.7	0.7	0.6	0.5	0.5
Mexico Mexique	20.1	20.7	20.6[1]	21.3[1]	21.4[1]	22.8[1]	22.7	22.6[1]	23.0[1]	23.3[1]
Nicaragua Nicaragua	2.9	3.0	3.0	3.1	3.2	3.2	3.3	3.4	3.6	3.7[1]
Panama Panama	0.9[1]	1.0[1]	0.9[1]	0.9[1]	0.9[1]	1.0[1]	1.0[1]	1.0	1.0	1.0[1]
Trinidad and Tobago Trinité-et-Tobago	0.1	0.1	0.1	0.1[1]	0.1	0.1	0.1	0.1	0.1	0.0
United States Etats-Unis	466.1	458.3	483.5	502.6	509.9	516.0	512.8	481.4	495.8	495.8[1]
America, South Amérique du Sud	302.2	309.6	318.4	325.6	332.8	342.4	344.4	352.9	364.4	369.9
Argentina Argentine	11.3	11.1	10.8	10.9	11.5	11.3	11.3	11.3[1]	11.9	11.9[1]
Bolivia Bolivie	1.3[1]	1.4[1]	1.4[1]	1.4[1]	1.5	1.5	1.5	1.5[1]	1.5	1.6
Brazil Brésil	230.6	236.0	241.0	245.8	250.8	260.6	259.2	265.7[1]	268.9[1]	272.1[1]
Chile Chili	15.5	16.2	17.2	18.0	19.1	19.3	22.4	24.3	30.6	32.2
Colombia Colombie	17.6	18.1	18.9	19.2	19.5	19.8	20.1	20.3	20.6[1]	20.9[1]
Ecuador Equateur	5.8	6.3	6.6	6.9	7.0	7.2	7.7	7.3	7.5	7.5[1]
French Guiana[1] Guyane française[1]	0.3	0.3	0.3	0.3	0.3	0.3	0.3	0.3	0.3	0.3
Guyana Guyana	0.2	0.2	0.2	0.2	0.2[1]	0.2[1]	0.2	0.2	0.2	0.2[1]
Paraguay Paraguay	7.5	7.7	8.2	8.5	8.4	8.4[1]	8.4[1]	8.5[1]	8.5[1]	8.5[1]
Peru Pérou	7.7	7.7	8.5	8.7	8.8	8.6	7.7	7.8	7.9	8.3
Suriname Suriname	0.2	0.2	0.2	0.2	0.2	0.2	0.1	0.1	0.2	0.2[1]

38
Roundwood
Production (solid volume of roundwood without bark): million cubic metres [*cont.*]
Bois rond
Production (volume solide de bois rond sans écorce) : millions de mètres cubes [*suite*]

Country or area Pays ou zone	1984	1985	1986	1987	1988	1989	1990	1991	1992	1993
Uruguay Uruguay	3.1	3.3	3.7	3.9	3.7	3.6	3.8	3.9	4.1	4.1[1]
Venezuela Venezuela	1.1	1.3	1.4	1.6	1.8	1.6	1.9	1.8	2.2	2.2
Asia **Asie**	**978.1**	**993.5**	**1 017.2**	**1 043.0**	**1 065.0**	**1 080.6**	**1 084.0**	**1 100.8**	**1 123.6**	**1 144.5**
Afghanistan[1] Afghanistan[1]	5.8	5.8	5.8	5.8	6.0	6.2	6.5	6.8	7.3	7.8
Bangladesh Bangladesh	26.7	27.2	28.0	28.4	29.1	29.7	30.2	31.0	31.7[1]	32.5[1]
Bhutan[1] Bhoutan[1]	1.4	1.3	1.3	1.4	1.3	1.4	1.4	1.4	1.5	1.5
Brunei Darussalam Brunéi Darussalam	0.3[1]	0.3[1]	0.3[1]	0.3[1]	0.3[1]	0.3	0.3	0.3[1]	0.3[1]	0.3[1]
Cambodia[1] Cambodge[1]	5.2	5.3	5.5	5.6	5.7	5.9	6.0	6.4	6.9	7.0
China Chine	258.4[1]	265.3[1]	271.4[1]	276.5[1]	279.6[1]	281.8[1]	280.0[1]	282.3[1]	290.1	300.7
Cyprus Chypre	0.1	0.1	0.1	0.1	0.1	0.1	0.1	0.1	0.1	0.0
Hong Kong[1] Hong-kong[1]	0.2	0.2	0.2	0.2	0.2	0.2	0.2	0.2	0.2	0.2
India[1] Inde[1]	243.1	248.6	253.3	258.0	262.8	267.5	272.4	277.3	282.4	287.4
Indonesia Indonésie	155.6	154.7	161.2	167.7[1]	173.9[1]	178.4[1]	176.4[1]	182.5[1]	185.7[1]	188.1[1]
Iran, Islamic Rep. of Iran, Rép. islamique d'	6.7[1]	6.7[1]	6.7[1]	6.7[1]	7.1	7.2	7.2	7.4	7.4	7.5
Iraq[1] Iraq[1]	0.1	0.1	0.1	0.1	0.1	0.1	0.1	0.1	0.2	0.2
Israel Israël	0.1[1]	0.1[1]	0.1[1]	0.1[1]	0.1[1]	0.1	0.1	0.1[1]	0.1[1]	0.1[1]
Japan Japon	33.1	40.1	38.4	38.2	38.0	38.2	37.0	35.5	34.2	32.6
Korea, Dem. P. R.[1] Corée, R. p. dém. de[1]	4.5	4.5	4.5	4.6	4.6	4.6	4.7	4.7	4.8	4.8
Korea, Republic of Corée, République de	7.7	6.7	6.7[1]	6.9[1]	6.8[1]	6.8	6.5[1]	6.5[1]	6.5[1]	6.5[1]
Lao People's Dem. Rep. Rép. dém. pop. lao	3.5	3.7	3.7	3.8[1]	4.0[1]	4.1[1]	4.3	4.6	4.5	4.9
Lebanon Liban	0.5[1]	0.5[1]	0.5[1]	0.5	0.5	0.5	0.5	0.5	0.5	0.5[1]
Malaysia Malaisie	39.7	37.5	39.1	44.5	48.7	51.0	50.0	50.3	54.1	54.3[1]
Mongolia Mongolie	2.4[1]	2.4[1]	2.4[1]	2.4[1]	2.4[1]	2.0	1.6	1.3	1.0	0.9
Myanmar Myanmar	18.6	19.2	19.5	19.8	20.1	20.5	21.5	22.3	22.9	22.5
Nepal Népal	15.9[1]	16.4[1]	16.8[1]	17.3[1]	17.7[1]	18.2[1]	18.6	19.1	19.6[1]	20.1[1]

38
Roundwood
Production (solid volume of roundwood without bark): million cubic metres [cont.]
Bois rond
Production (volume solide de bois rond sans écorce) : millions de mètres cubes [suite]

Country or area Pays ou zone	1984	1985	1986	1987	1988	1989	1990	1991	1992	1993
Pakistan Pakistan	20.1[1]	21.0	21.6[1]	22.2	22.9	24.0	25.7	26.2	27.1	27.8
Philippines Philippines	36.1	35.5	36.2	37.6	38.1	38.3	38.4	38.7	39.2	39.6
Singapore[1] Singapour[1]	...	...	...	...	0.2	0.2	0.2	0.2	0.1	0.1
Sri Lanka Sri Lanka	8.6	8.5	8.6	8.8[1]	8.9[1]	9.0	9.0	9.1	9.3	9.4[1]
Syrian Arab Republic Rép. arabe syrienne	0.0[1]	0.0[1]	0.0[1]	0.1	0.1[1]	0.1	0.1	0.1	0.1	0.1
Thailand Thaïlande	35.7	36.1	36.7	37.3	37.6	37.0	37.0	37.2	37.6	38.0
Turkey Turquie	19.7	16.3	17.9	16.8	16.8	15.5	15.8	15.3	15.4	15.4[1]
Viet Nam Viet Nam	28.2[1]	29.2[1]	30.1[1]	31.0[1]	31.2[1]	31.6[1]	31.9	32.7	32.9	33.5[1]
Yemen[1] Yémen[1]	0.3	0.3	0.3	0.3	0.3	0.3	0.3	0.3	0.3	0.3
Europe **Europe**	**345.7**	**345.4**	**347.3**	**346.6**	**354.3**	**369.0**	**391.1**	**321.6**	**312.6**	**323.2**
Albania Albanie	2.3[1]	2.3[1]	2.3[1]	2.3[1]	2.3[1]	2.3[1]	2.1	2.6[1]	2.6[1]	2.6[1]
Austria Autriche	14.2	14.2	13.7	13.6	15.0	16.3	16.8	15.6	12.8	12.9
Belarus Bélarus	...	...	...	...	...	...	...	...	11.4	10.0
Belgium-Luxembourg Belgique-Luxembourg	3.1	3.3	3.3	3.7	4.0	4.8	5.6	4.8	4.2	4.2
Bulgaria Bulgarie	4.8	4.8	4.5	3.6	3.5	4.2	4.1	3.7	3.6	3.6
Croatia Croatie	...	...	...	...	...	...	...	...	2.1	2.1[1]
former Czechoslovakia† anc. Tchécoslovaquie†	18.9	19.0	18.9	18.7	18.1	18.2	18.2	15.3	...	...
Czech Republic République tchèque	...	...	...	...	...	...	...	...	10.3	10.3
Denmark Danemark	2.6	2.3	2.3	2.1	2.2	2.1	2.3	2.3	2.2	2.2
Estonia Estonie	...	...	...	...	...	...	...	...	2.1	2.4
Finland Finlande	40.5	41.7	40.7	41.9	44.9	47.1	43.2	34.9	38.5	39.6
France France	38.8	38.9	39.9	41.1	43.0	44.7	45.4	44.2	42.6	44.1
Germany † Allemagne†	...	...	...	...	...	...	...	36.6	36.0	36.2
F. R. Germany R. f. Allemagne	30.7	30.7[1]	30.3	31.0	32.6	36.9	73.5	...	...	...
former German D. R. anc. R. d. allemande	10.6	10.9	10.8	10.6	10.9	11.3	11.3[1]	...	...	...

38

Roundwood
Production (solid volume of roundwood without bark): million cubic metres [cont.]
Bois rond
Production (volume solide de bois rond sans écorce) : millions de mètres cubes [suite]

Country or area Pays ou zone	1984	1985	1986	1987	1988	1989	1990	1991	1992	1993
Greece Grèce	2.7	3.0	3.2	2.9	3.1	2.5	2.5	2.5	2.9	2.8
Hungary Hongrie	6.3	6.8	7.0	6.8	6.6	6.6	6.1	5.6	5.0	4.7
Ireland Irlande	1.3	1.3	1.2	1.3	1.4	1.5	1.6	1.7	2.0	1.8
Italy Italie	9.2	9.4	9.6	9.1	9.1	8.8	8.0	8.4	9.5	9.9
Latvia Lettonie	...	...	...	...	...	...	...	...	2.5	4.6
Netherlands Pays-Bas	0.9	1.1	1.1	1.2	1.3	1.3	1.4	1.1	1.7	1.4
Norway Norvège	10.0	9.5	9.9	10.4	11.0	11.5	11.8	11.3	10.1	10.1[1]
Poland Pologne	24.0	23.3	24.3	23.3	22.8	21.4	17.8	17.2	18.9	18.8
Portugal Portugal	8.5	9.4	9.9	9.4	9.5	10.3	11.3	10.9	11.7	11.6
Romania Roumanie	24.1	23.0	20.7	19.9	18.2	16.3	13.3	13.7	13.1	9.5
Russian Federation Fédération de Russie	...	...	...	...	...	...	...	...	281.5	207.5
Slovakia Slovaquie	...	...	...	...	...	...	...	...	4.8	5.3
Slovenia Slovénie	...	...	...	...	...	...	...	...	1.8	1.2
Spain Espagne	14.6	14.0	15.0	15.5	15.2	18.3	16.0	14.9	15.9	14.8
Sweden Suède	53.0	51.5	52.4	53.1	53.9	55.9	53.5	51.9	64.8	63.0
Switzerland Suisse	5.0	4.2	4.7	4.6	4.6	4.6	6.3	4.6	4.6	4.6[1]
United Kingdom Royaume-Uni	3.9	4.8	5.2	5.5	6.1	6.5	6.4	6.4	6.0	6.2
Yugoslavia, SFR† Yougoslavie, Rfs†	15.9	15.9	16.1	15.2	15.2	15.6	12.8	11.5	...	...
Oceania **Océanie**	**35.3**	**38.1**	**39.2**	**38.5**	**38.8**	**39.4**	**41.3**	**43.0**	**43.8**	**45.7**
Australia Australie	18.0	19.7	20.0	19.6[1]	19.8	19.5	20.1	19.5	19.6	20.5
Fiji Fidji	0.2	0.2	0.2	0.3	0.3	0.3	0.3[1]	0.3[1]	0.3[1]	0.3[1]
New Zealand Nouvelle-Zélande	8.8	9.8	10.3	9.7	9.8	10.7	12.0	14.3	15.1	15.9
Papua New Guinea Papouasie-Nvl-Guinée	7.6	7.6	7.9[1]	8.2[1]	8.2[1]	8.2[1]	8.2	8.2[1]	8.2[1]	8.2[1]
Samoa[1] Samoa[1]	0.1	0.1	0.1	0.1	0.1	0.1	0.1	0.1	0.1	0.1
Solomon Islands Iles Salomon	0.5	0.5	0.6	0.4	0.4	0.4	0.5	0.5[1]	0.5[1]	0.5[1]

38
Roundwood
Production (solid volume of roundwood without bark): million cubic metres [*cont.*]
Bois rond
Production (volume solide de bois rond sans écorce) : millions de mètres cubes [*suite*]

Country or area Pays ou zone	1984	1985	1986	1987	1988	1989	1990	1991	1992	1993
Vanuatu[1] Vanuatu[1]	0.0	0.0	0.0	0.1	0.1	0.1	0.1	0.1	0.1	0.1
former USSR† ancienne URSS†	367.9	368.0	373.9	385.5	386.4	386.4	386.4	356.4	297.5[2]	224.5[2]

Source:
Food and Agriculture Organization of the United Nations (Rome).

† For detailed descriptions of data pertaining to former Czechoslovakia, Germany, SFR Yugoslavia and former USSR, see Annex I - Country or area nomenclature, regional and other groupings.

1 FAO estimate.
2 Excluding Belarus, Estonia, Latvia and Russian Federation (shown separately).

Source:
Organisation des Nations Unies pour l'alimentation et l'agriculture (Rome).

† Pour les descriptions en détails des données relatives à l'ancienne Tchécoslovaquie, l'Allemagne, la Rfs Yougoslavie et l'ancienne URSS, voir l'Annexe I - Nomenclature des pays ou zones, groupements régionaux et autres groupements.

1 Estimation de la FAO.
2 Non compris Bélarus, Estonie, Lettonie, et Fédération de Russie(dont les chiffres de production sont données séparément).

39
Fish catches
Quantités pêchées
All fishing areas: thousand metric tons
Toutes les zones de pêche : milliers de tonnes métriques

Country or area Pays ou zone	1984	1985	1986	1987	1988	1989	1990	1991	1992	1993
World *Monde*	83 850.7	86 335.1	92 754.1	94 297.5	98 889.9	100 115.4	97 431.8	97 401.8	98 785.2	101 417.5
Afghanistan[1] Afghanistan[1]	1.3	1.2	1.1	1.0	1.0	1.0	1.1	1.1	1.2	1.2
Albania Albanie	8.0	11.4	11.9	13.1	14.6	12.0	15.0	3.9	3.1	3.5[1]
Algeria Algérie	65.6	66.1	65.5	94.4	106.7	99.7	91.1	80.1	95.9	90.5[1]
American Samoa Samoa américaines	0.2	0.1	0.1	0.1	0.1	0.1	0.0	0.0	0.1	0.1[1]
Angola Angola	72.2	74.0	57.4	82.9	101.8	111.3	107.0	75.2	74.5	80.7
Anguilla Anguilla	0.3[1]	0.3[1]	0.4	0.4	0.4	0.4	0.4	0.4	0.4	0.3
Antigua and Barbuda Antigua-et-Barbuda	1.5	2.4	2.4[1]	2.4[1]	2.4[1]	2.4[1]	2.2[1]	2.4[1]	2.3[1]	2.4[1]
Argentina Argentine	315.2	406.8	420.7	559.8	493.4	486.6	555.6	640.6	705.2	930.6
Armenia Arménie	...	...	...	...	...	...	...	4.5	4.5[1]	4.3[1]
Aruba Aruba	0.8[1]	0.8	0.7[1]	0.6[1]	0.6[1]	0.5[1]	0.4[1]	0.4[1]	0.3	0.3[1]
Australia[2] Australie[2]	169.4[1]	161.4	180.3	204.8	213.3	181.8	220.4	237.3	233.9	218.3
Austria Autriche	4.4	4.5	4.6	4.6	5.1	5.0	4.8	4.5	4.1	4.6
Azerbaijan Azerbaïdjan	...	...	...	...	...	...	...	39.7	39.0[1]	36.0[1]
Bahamas Bahamas	5.3	7.6	5.9	7.1	7.2	8.1	7.5	9.2	9.9	10.0
Bahrain Bahreïn	5.6	7.8	8.1	7.8	6.7	9.2	8.1	7.6	8.0	9.0
Bangladesh Bangladesh	756.0	775.6	796.9	817.0	829.9	843.6	847.8	892.7	966.7	1 047.2
Barbados Barbade	5.8	3.9	4.2	3.7	9.1	2.5	3.0	2.1	3.3	2.9
Belarus Bélarus	...	...	...	...	...	...	...	15.5	15.0[1]	14.0[1]
Belgium-Luxembourg Belgique-Luxembourg	48.2	45.1	39.5	40.4	41.8	39.9	41.6	40.2	37.4	36.4
Belize Belize	1.3	1.4	1.5	1.5	1.5	1.8	1.5	1.6	2.2	2.1
Benin Bénin	35.3[1]	36.4[1]	38.8[1]	41.9	37.3	41.9	41.7[1]	41.0[1]	40.0[1]	39.0[1]
Bermuda Bermudes	0.5	0.7	0.8	0.8	0.8	0.8	0.5	0.4	0.4	0.4
Bhutan[1] Bhoutan[1]	0.3	0.3	0.3	0.3	0.3	0.3	0.3	0.3	0.4	0.4
Bolivia Bolivie	4.1	4.2	3.9	4.3	4.4	6.0	7.4	5.4	5.2	6.2

39
Fish catches
All fishing areas: thousand metric tons [*cont.*]
Quantités pêchées
Toutes les zones de pêche : milliers de tonnes métriques [*suite*]

Country or area Pays ou zone	1984	1985	1986	1987	1988	1989	1990	1991	1992	1993
Bosnia & Herzegovina[1] Bosnie-Herzégovine[1]	...	...	...	...	...	...	...	...	3.0	2.5
Botswana Botswana	1.5	1.5	1.7	1.9	1.9	1.9	1.9[1]	1.9[1]	1.9[1]	2.0[1]
Brazil Brésil	960.6	967.6	957.6	948.0	830.1	850.0	802.9[1]	800.0[1]	790.0[1]	780.0[1]
British Virgin Islands Iles Vierges britanniques	1.0	1.1	1.2	1.2	1.3	1.4	1.4	1.4	1.4[1]	1.3[1]
Brunei Darussalam Brunéi Darussalam	3.4	4.0	4.1	3.9	2.0	2.3	2.4	1.7	1.7	1.7
Bulgaria Bulgarie	115.5	100.2	109.7	111.7	118.0	103.0	57.1	57.9	32.1	21.6
Burkina Faso Burkina Faso	7.4	7.4	7.6	7.8	7.9	8.0	7.0	7.0	7.5	7.5
Burundi Burundi	11.4	11.4	11.8	12.0	11.7	10.8	17.4	21.0	23.0	22.0
Cambodia Cambodge	64.4	70.6	73.7	82.1	86.0	82.1	111.4	117.8	111.2	108.9
Cameroon Cameroun	87.3	86.0	84.0	82.5	82.5[1]	77.6	77.6[1]	78.0[1]	82.0	80.0[1]
Canada Canada	1 284.1	1 453.3	1 512.8	1 567.9	1 611.7	1 574.6	1 625.7	1 544.0	1 275.4	1 171.0
Cape Verde Cap-Vert	10.7	10.2	6.4	6.9	6.2	8.5	7.1	7.4	7.5[1]	7.1[1]
Cayman Islands Iles Caïmanes	0.4	0.4	0.5	1.1	0.4	0.6[1]	0.8[1]	0.8	0.8	0.7
Central African Rep. Rép. centrafricaine	13.3	13.3	13.2	13.1	13.1	13.1	13.1	13.6	13.3	13.5[1]
Chad Tchad	50.0[1]	55.0[1]	60.0[1]	70.0[1]	60.0[1]	65.0[1]	60.0[1]	65.0[1]	70.0[1]	80.0
Chile Chili	4 499.3	4 804.4	5 571.6	4 814.6	5 209.9	6 454.2	5 195.4	6 002.8	6 501.8	6 038.0
China Chine	5 926.8	6 778.8	8 000.1	9 346.2	10 358.7	11 220.0	12 095.4	13 135.0	15 007.5	17 567.9
Colombia Colombie	79.1	71.5	83.4	85.5	89.1	98.3	128.0	109.2	158.5	146.4
Comoros Comores	5.0[1]	5.2[1]	5.3[1]	5.3[1]	5.5[1]	6.8	8.0	8.8[1]	8.0	7.0[1]
Congo Congo	32.8	29.9	31.6	37.9	42.0	45.8	48.2	45.6	40.0	41.5
Cook Islands Iles Cook	1.0[1]	1.0[1]	1.0[1]	1.1[1]	1.1[1]	1.1[1]	1.2[1]	1.1	1.0	1.0[1]
Costa Rica Costa Rica	16.4	20.3	20.8	17.1[1]	17.0[1]	17.3[1]	17.5[1]	17.9	18.1	17.7
Côte d'Ivoire Côte d'Ivoire	88.1	110.7	104.4	101.7	89.5	99.2	104.4	85.1	87.3	70.2
Croatia Croatie	...	...	...	...	...	...	...	...	32.8	30.3
Cuba Cuba	199.6	219.8	244.4	214.6	231.3	192.1	188.2	171.1	109.4	93.4

39
Fish catches
All fishing areas: thousand metric tons [*cont.*]
Quantités pêchées
Toutes les zones de pêche : milliers de tonnes métriques [*suite*]

Country or area Pays ou zone	1984	1985	1986	1987	1988	1989	1990	1991	1992	1993
Cyprus Chypre	2.3	2.4	2.6	2.6	2.6	2.6	2.7	2.7	2.8	2.9
Czech Republic République tchèque	...	...	...	...	...	...	...	...	...	24.4
former Czechoslovakia† anc. Tchécoslovaquie†	19.7	20.0	21.3	20.7	21.2	21.6	22.6	21.9	24.1	...
Denmark Danemark	1 851.5	1 797.0	1 849.8	1 707.8	1 974.4	1 929.3	1 518.2	1 793.3	1 995.5	1 534.1
Djibouti Djibouti	0.4	0.4	0.4	0.4	0.5	0.4	0.4	0.3[1]	0.3[1]	0.3[1]
Dominica Dominique	0.7[1]	0.6	0.6	0.7[1]	0.7[1]	0.7[1]	0.7[1]	0.6	0.8	0.8
Dominican Republic Rép. dominicaine	14.6	18.3	17.2	20.4	12.9	21.8	20.1	17.3	13.6	14.1
Ecuador Equateur	882.8	1 086.9	1 003.4	680.1	876.0	739.9	391.2	384.1	347.1	330.7
Egypt Egypte	163.8	215.9	229.1	231.0	284.2	293.5	313.0	299.9	287.1	302.8
El Salvador El Salvador	12.2	16.1	20.5	21.5	11.7	11.6	9.2	11.3	12.6	13.0
Equatorial Guinea Guinée équatoriale	4.0	3.6	4.4	4.0[1]	4.0[1]	4.0[1]	3.7[1]	3.5[1]	3.6[1]	3.8[1]
Eritrea[1] Erythrée[1]	...	...	...	...	...	...	...	...	...	2.5
Estonia Estonie	...	...	...	...	...	...	...	358.1	132.0	146.9
Ethiopia Ethiopie	4.3[1]	4.0[1]	4.1[1]	4.0[1]	4.1	4.3	5.0	4.3	4.6	4.2
Faeroe Islands Iles Féroé	347.4	374.0	352.2	391.0	359.9[1]	308.6	289.3	246.0	270.8	261.6
Falkland Is. (Malvinas) Iles Falkland (Malvinas)	...	0.0	0.0	0.0	2.6	4.6	6.0	1.5	1.9	1.6
Fiji Fidji	27.7	27.3	26.4	34.2	30.7	31.8	33.8	30.5	30.9	31.4
Finland Finlande	171.3	171.9	156.8	155.6	165.2	154.7	139.8	126.9	148.1	152.5
France France	786.3	832.2	874.2	849.1	889.0	850.9	863.7	816.8	816.8	823.0[1]
French Guiana Guyane française	2.2	2.5	3.3	5.3	5.5	6.5	6.5	7.1	7.0	7.0
French Polynesia Polynésie française	2.8	2.3	2.3	2.3	2.9	3.1	3.0	2.4	2.5[1]	8.1
Gabon Gabon	21.0	21.0	20.2	22.2[1]	22.1[1]	20.5[1]	22.0[1]	22.0[1]	24.0[1]	28.3
Gambia Gambie	11.9	10.7	13.3	14.6	13.9	19.8	17.9	23.7	22.7	20.5
Gaza Strip Zone de Gaza	1.6	0.4	0.5	0.5	0.5	0.5	0.5	0.5	0.5	0.5
Georgia Géorgie	...	...	...	...	...	...	...	60.8	40.0[1]	37.0[1]

39
Fish catches
All fishing areas: thousand metric tons [*cont.*]
Quantités pêchées
Toutes les zones de pêche : milliers de tonnes métriques [*suite*]

Country or area Pays ou zone	1984	1985	1986	1987	1988	1989	1990	1991	1992	1993
Germany † Allemagne†	553.2	425.9	415.4	399.3	393.5	412.3	390.7	303.4	307.2	316.4
Ghana Ghana	269.1	276.0	319.5	382.0	361.9	361.7	392.8	366.3	426.4	371.2
Greece Grèce	108.2	114.8	124.7	134.6	126.9	140.1	146.4	156.8	179.2	199.6
Greenland Groënland	86.3	94.9	102.9	100.4	120.3	168.8	143.3	113.4	113.3	113.6
Grenada Grenade	1.6	1.7	2.7	2.2	2.0	1.7	1.8	2.0	2.0	2.1
Guadeloupe Guadeloupe	9.0	8.4	8.5	8.6	8.2	8.5	8.6	7.9	7.9	8.0
Guam Guam	0.4	0.5	0.6	0.5	0.6	0.6	0.7	0.8	0.7	0.6
Guatemala Guatemala	3.0	2.8	2.2	2.5	2.9	3.8	7.1	6.8	7.2	7.7
Guinea[1] Guinée[1]	28.0	30.0	33.0	35.0	35.0	35.2	36.2	38.8	38.3	40.0
Guinea-Bissau Guinée-Bissau	2.8	3.7[1]	3.7[1]	4.1[1]	4.7[1]	5.4[1]	5.4[1]	5.0[1]	5.2[1]	5.4[1]
Guyana Guyana	37.2	37.6	37.4	36.8	36.5	35.3	36.9	40.8	41.4	40.0[1]
Haiti[1] Haïti[1]	7.0	6.4	6.0	5.8	5.5	5.5	5.2	5.2	5.0	5.6
Honduras Honduras	8.4	9.7	20.6	23.1	20.0	17.4	15.9	21.4	19.1	24.4
Hong Kong Hong-kong	199.7	198.2	213.6	228.1	238.2	242.5	234.5	230.9	229.5	226.8
Hungary Hongrie	39.2	36.9	36.1	36.8	38.3	35.5	33.9	29.4	29.4	23.4
Iceland Islande	1 535.0	1 680.4	1 658.6	1 632.7	1 757.7	1 502.4	1 508.1	1 050.3	1 577.2	1 718.5
India Inde	2 864.5	2 826.1	2 923.2	2 906.6	3 125.4	3 640.3	3 794.2	4 044.2	4 232.1	4 324.2
Indonesia Indonésie	2 251.9	2 338.0	2 457.0	2 583.9	2 795.2	2 948.4	3 044.2	3 251.8	3 441.5	3 637.7
Iran, Islamic Rep. of Iran, Rép. islamique d'	115.8	118.5	151.7	212.0	235.0	260.2	269.5	275.7	334.2	343.9
Iraq[1] Iraq[1]	21.0	21.5	20.6	20.5	18.0	18.6	16.0	14.4	23.5	23.5
Ireland Irlande	209.9	230.7	231.6	251.0	257.8	201.8	236.4	262.0	272.5	305.0
Israel Israël	24.4	27.3	25.2	28.4	28.2	26.5	23.6	20.7	19.2	18.7
Italy Italie	580.5	591.4	570.7	565.0	580.4	551.5	525.2	560.5	556.7	552.0
Jamaica Jamaïque	9.7	10.5	10.8	10.7	9.7	10.7	10.6[1]	10.6[1]	10.7[1]	11.0[1]
Japan Japon	12 021.5	11 409.3	11 976.5	11 857.6	11 966.1	11 173.4	10 354.2	9 301.1	8 502.2	8 128.1

39
Fish catches
All fishing areas: thousand metric tons [*cont.*]
Quantités pêchées
Toutes les zones de pêche : milliers de tonnes métriques [*suite*]

Country or area Pays ou zone	1984	1985	1986	1987	1988	1989	1990	1991	1992	1993
Jordan Jordanie	0.0[1]	0.0[1]	0.1	0.1	0.1	0.1	0.1	0.0	0.0	0.1
Kazakstan Kazakstan	...	...	...	...	...	...	...	82.7	80.0[1]	75.0[1]
Kenya Kenya	91.0	106.0	119.8	131.2	138.3	146.5	201.8	198.7	163.0	185.4
Kiribati Kiribati	16.4	21.0	27.5	36.1	23.9	34.1	29.4[1]	29.6[1]	30.5[1]	29.3[1]
Korea, Dem. P. R.[1] Corée, R. p. dém. de[1]	1 649.9	1 700.0	1 700.2	1 712.3	1 717.0	1 737.6	1 752.8	1 743.1	1 778.1	1 780.0
Korea, Republic of Corée, République de	2 476.8	2 649.9	3 103.4	2 876.6	2 731.5	2 840.6	2 843.1	2 521.2	2 695.6	2 749.0
Kuwait Koweït	9.6	10.1	7.6	7.7	10.8	7.7	4.5	2.0	7.9	8.6
Kyrgyzstan Kirghizistan	...	...	...	...	...	...	...	1.2	1.2[1]	1.1[1]
Lao People's Dem. Rep. Rép. dém. pop. lao	26.0[1]	26.0[1]	26.0[1]	28.0[1]	28.0[1]	28.0[1]	28.0[1]	29.0[1]	30.0	30.4
Latvia Lettonie	...	...	...	...	...	...	...	416.2	158.0	142.2
Lebanon Liban	1.5[1]	1.7[1]	1.9	1.9	1.8	1.8	1.5	1.8	1.8[1]	2.2[1]
Liberia Libéria	14.7	11.5	16.1	18.7	16.1	14.8	6.5	9.6	8.9	7.8
Libyan Arab Jamah.[1] Jamah. arabe libyenne[1]	7.8	9.7	9.7	8.6	9.7	7.8	8.8	8.1	8.9	8.8
Lithuania Lituanie	...	...	...	...	...	...	...	475.0	192.5	119.9
Macau Macao	11.8[1]	12.4[1]	8.0	3.5	2.5	3.5	2.6	2.3	2.7	1.9
Madagascar Madagascar	67.5	69.2	84.3	92.4	101.1	97.7	104.6	101.2	106.4	115.0
Malawi Malawi	65.1	62.1	72.9	88.6	78.8	70.8	74.1	63.7	64.0[1]	65.0[1]
Malaysia Malaisie	669.6	639.7	621.9	619.3[1]	612.4[1]	609.6[1]	604.0[1]	620.0[1]	650.0[1]	680.0[1]
Maldives Maldives	55.1	61.9	59.3	57.0	71.5	71.2	78.7	80.7	82.2	90.0
Mali Mali	54.7	54.2	61.0	55.7	55.9	71.8	70.5	68.8	68.5	64.4
Malta Malte	1.2	2.5	1.1	1.0	0.8	0.9	6.4	5.2	5.3	5.6
Marshall Islands Iles Marshall	0.2[1]	0.2[1]	0.2[1]	0.2[1]	0.2[1]	0.2[1]	0.2[1]	0.2	0.2	0.3
Martinique Martinique	5.2	4.6	4.1	3.2	3.1	3.3	3.4	6.6	4.7	4.6[1]
Mauritania Mauritanie	93.8	103.3	98.2	99.4	97.6	92.6[1]	80.5[1]	86.7[1]	93.9[1]	92.8[1]
Mauritius Maurice	10.6	12.4	12.9	18.2	17.2	17.2	14.7	18.9	19.2	21.1

39
Fish catches
All fishing areas: thousand metric tons [cont.]
Quantités pêchées
Toutes les zones de pêche : milliers de tonnes métriques [suite]

Country or area Pays ou zone	1984	1985	1986	1987	1988	1989	1990	1991	1992	1993
Mayotte Mayotte	0.6[1]	0.7[1]	0.8	1.2	1.4[1]	1.7	1.4	1.3	1.1	0.4
Mexico Mexique	1 108.2	1 226.5	1 315.7	1 419.3	1 372.6	1 469.9	1 400.9	1 453.3	1 247.6	1 200.7
Micronesia,Federated States of Micron, Etats fédérés de	1.8	3.4	3.5	3.6	2.6	2.1[1]	2.1[1]	1.4	1.5[1]	1.6[1]
Mongolia Mongolie	0.4	0.4	0.4	0.4	0.3	0.3	0.1	0.1	0.1[1]	0.1[1]
Montserrat Montserrat	0.1[1]	0.1[1]	0.1[1]	0.1	0.1	0.0	0.2	0.1	0.1	0.1[1]
Morocco Maroc	467.5	473.2	595.4	494.2	551.7	520.4	565.6	593.1	548.1	622.4
Mozambique Mozambique	35.8	36.3	42.4	39.6	35.4	31.1[1]	36.4[1]	29.3	31.6	30.2
Myanmar[2] Myanmar[2]	613.7	648.8	686.5	685.9	704.5	733.8	743.8	769.2	800.0[1]	836.9
Namibia Namibie	12.9[1]	13.7[1]	14.9[1]	32.4	33.4	21.2	262.4	206.2	294.5	329.8
Nauru Nauru	0.2[1]	0.2[1]	0.2[1]	0.2[1]	0.2[1]	0.2[1]	0.2[1]	0.2	0.4	0.5
Nepal[2] Népal[2]	4.9	9.1	9.4	10.7	12.1	12.5	14.5	15.6	16.5	16.9
Netherlands Pays-Bas	432.4	504.2	454.8	446.1	399.6	452.5	459.9	444.3	439.3	486.9
Netherlands Antilles[1] Antilles néerlandaises[1]	1.0	1.0	1.1	1.1	1.2	1.2	1.2	1.1	1.2	1.2
New Caledonia Nouvelle-Calédonie	3.3	2.7	4.0	4.8	3.7	3.3	5.3	4.9	4.0	3.5
New Zealand Nouvelle-Zélande	218.3	213.5	217.7	246.3	291.9	333.6	371.9	417.1	503.2	470.4
Nicaragua Nicaragua	4.3	4.2	2.5	5.0	4.7	4.6	3.1	5.7	6.7	8.8
Niger Niger	3.0	2.0	2.4	2.3	2.5	4.8	3.4	3.2	2.1	2.2
Nigeria Nigéria	263.2[1]	244.5	271.5	260.9	279.4[1]	299.7[1]	316.3	267.2	318.4	355.5
Niue Nioué	0.1	0.1	0.1	0.1	0.1	0.1	0.1	0.1	0.1	0.1
Northern Mariana Islands Iles Marianas du Nord	0.3	0.2	0.3	0.2	0.2	0.2	0.2	0.1	0.1	0.1[1]
Norway Norvège	2 465.8	2 119.0	1 915.0	1 949.5	1 839.9	1 908.4	1 744.9	2 168.5	2 547.0	2 561.8
Oman Oman	105.2	101.2	96.4	136.1	165.6	117.7	120.2	117.8	112.3	116.5
Pakistan Pakistan	372.3	408.4	415.7	427.7	445.4	446.2	479.0	515.5	553.1	621.7
Palau Palaos	1.3	1.4[1]	1.4[1]	1.5[1]	1.5[1]	1.4[1]	1.4[1]	1.4	1.4[1]	1.5[1]
Panama Panama	131.1	289.2	131.5	155.5	125.1	190.4	143.7	149.8	148.8	158.2

39
Fish catches
All fishing areas: thousand metric tons [*cont.*]
Quantités pêchées
Toutes les zones de pêche : milliers de tonnes métriques [*suite*]

Country or area Pays ou zone	1984	1985	1986	1987	1988	1989	1990	1991	1992	1993
Papua New Guinea[1] Papouasie-Nvl-Guinée[1]	17.8	25.5	25.0	25.1	25.0	25.2	25.0	24.3	24.8	24.8
Paraguay Paraguay	5.0	7.5	13.0	10.0	10.0	11.0	12.5	13.0	18.0	16.0[1]
Peru Pérou	3 319.9	4 138.1	5 616.2	4 587.4	6 641.7	6 853.8	6 875.0	6 949.4	6 871.2	8 450.6
Philippines Philippines	1 933.2	1 865.0	1 916.3	1 988.7	2 010.4	2 098.8	2 209.6	2 316.5	2 272.0	2 263.8
Poland Pologne	719.2	683.5	645.2	670.9	654.9	564.8	473.0	457.4	505.9	423.0
Portugal Portugal	302.0	317.5	408.7	389.6	346.4	332.1	322.0	325.6	300.1	274.2
Puerto Rico Porto Rico	2.4	1.5	1.3	1.3	1.7	2.1	2.2	2.6	2.2	1.9
Qatar Qatar	3.2	2.5	2.0	2.7	3.1	4.4	5.7	8.1	7.8	7.0
Republic of Moldova République de Moldova	...	...	...	...	...	...	...	5.2	5.0[1]	4.7[1]
Réunion Réunion	2.6	2.1	1.7	1.8	2.1	2.0	1.9	2.2	2.4	2.7
Romania Roumanie	232.1	237.6	271.1	264.3	267.6	224.8	127.7	125.0	95.4	34.9
Russian Federation Fédération de Russie	...	...	...	...	...	...	...	7 046.8	5 611.2	4 461.4
Rwanda Rwanda	0.8	0.9	1.5	1.7	1.3	1.5	2.5	3.6	3.7	3.6[1]
Saint Helena Sainte-Hélène	0.7	0.6	0.6	0.7	0.8	1.0	0.8	0.6	0.7	0.7
Saint Kitts and Nevis[1] Saint-Kitts-et-Nevis[1]	1.4	1.6	1.6	1.7	1.7	1.7	1.7	1.8	1.7	1.7
Saint Lucia Sainte-Lucie	0.9	1.1	0.8	0.7	0.8	0.8	0.9	0.9	1.0	1.1
Saint Pierre and Miquelon Saint-Pierre-et-Miquelon	12.0	12.3	23.8	23.7	14.0	18.5	19.1	19.2	13.8	0.2
St. Vincent-Grenadines St. Vincent-Grenadines	0.5[1]	0.5	0.6	0.7	4.7	5.9	9.0	8.1	2.3	1.8
Samoa Samoa	3.7[1]	3.6	3.2	3.1	2.5	1.9	0.6	0.6	1.3	1.6
Sao Tome and Principe Sao Tomé-et-Principe	4.4	4.0	2.8	2.8	2.9	3.1	3.6	2.2	2.0	2.2[1]
Saudi Arabia Arabie saoudite	40.0[1]	43.7	45.5	47.9	47.1	53.4[1]	42.3[1]	41.9	47.9	49.4
Senegal Sénégal	247.3	246.0	255.6	255.0	260.7	287.1	297.9	319.7	370.3	377.7[1]
Seychelles Seychelles	3.8	4.1	4.5	3.9	4.3	4.4	5.4	8.2	6.9[1]	7.0[1]
Sierra Leone Sierra Leone	52.7[1]	53.5[1]	53.3[1]	53.2[1]	53.3[1]	53.9[1]	51.7[1]	61.4	61.6	62.0
Singapore Singapour	26.2	23.9	21.4	16.9	15.2	12.6	13.3	13.1	11.6	11.7

39
Fish catches
All fishing areas: thousand metric tons [*cont.*]
Quantités pêchées
Toutes les zones de pêche : milliers de tonnes métriques [*suite*]

Country or area Pays ou zone	1984	1985	1986	1987	1988	1989	1990	1991	1992	1993
Slovakia Slovaquie	...	...	...	...	...	...	...	...	...	2.8
Slovenia Slovénie	...	...	...	...	...	...	...	...	3.7	3.0
Solomon Islands Iles Salomon	48.9	44.0	55.5	44.6	55.1	57.0	54.8	69.3	47.0[1]	45.4[1]
Somalia Somalie	19.9	16.8	16.9[1]	17.5[1]	18.2[1]	18.2[1]	17.5[1]	16.1[1]	15.3[1]	14.9[1]
South Africa Afrique du Sud	735.5	777.1	821.2	1 427.2	1 302.3	878.5	537.6	501.0	696.4	563.2
Spain Espagne	1 440.6	1 482.8	1 489.0	1 525.5	1 593.4	1 560.0[1]	1 400.0[1]	1 320.0[1]	1 330.0[1]	1 290.0
Sri Lanka Sri Lanka	169.2	179.2	181.5	185.7	197.5	205.3	165.4	198.0	206.1	220.9
Sudan Soudan	29.8	26.3	23.9	27.2	29.2	30.3	31.7	33.3	31.7[1]	31.7[1]
Suriname Suriname	4.1	4.1	3.7	5.2	3.7	6.2	6.5	7.4	10.9	9.5
Swaziland[1] Swaziland[1]	0.1	0.1	0.1	0.1	0.1	0.1	0.1	0.1	0.1	0.1
Sweden Suède	274.6	239.7	215.3	214.5	251.0	257.7	260.1	245.0	314.7	347.8
Switzerland Suisse	4.1	4.6	4.7	4.5	4.2	4.5	4.2	4.8	3.9	3.2
Syrian Arab Republic Rép. arabe syrienne	5.3	5.9	5.3	5.4	5.5	5.1	5.8[1]	5.5[1]	5.4[1]	5.6[1]
Tajikistan Tadjikistan	...	...	...	...	...	...	...	3.9	3.9[1]	3.7[1]
Thailand Thaïlande	2 127.2	2 226.5	2 537.2	2 779.6	2 642.4	2 700.2	2 786.4	2 967.8	3 240.2	3 348.1
TFYR Macedonia L'ex-R.y. Macédoine	...	...	...	...	...	...	...	1.8	1.5[1]	1.4
Togo Togo	14.5	15.5	14.8	15.2	15.5	16.5	15.8	12.5	10.8	17.0
Tokelau Tokélaou	0.2[1]	0.2[1]	0.2[1]	0.2[1]	0.2[1]	0.2[1]	0.2[1]	0.2	0.2	0.2[1]
Tonga Tonga	2.6	2.7	3.0	2.8	2.7	2.7	1.7	2.0	2.3	2.5
Trinidad and Tobago Trinité-et-Tobago	3.6	5.5	4.1	6.6[1]	7.4[1]	8.0[1]	8.4[1]	12.2	15.0	10.6
Tunisia Tunisie	76.9	91.1	92.8	99.3	103.6	95.1	88.6	87.6	88.5	83.8
Turkey Turquie	566.9	578.1	582.9	628.0	674.2	455.9	384.9	364.6	454.3	550.6
Turkmenistan Turkménistan	...	...	...	...	...	...	...	43.0	40.0[1]	37.0[1]
Turks and Caicos Islands Iles Turques et Caiques	1.2	1.3	1.4	1.2	1.2	1.2	1.0	1.1	1.2	1.5
Tuvalu Tuvalu	0.8	0.3	0.7	0.9	1.4	0.5	0.5	0.5	0.5	1.5

39
Fish catches
All fishing areas: thousand metric tons [*cont.*]
Quantités pêchées
Toutes les zones de pêche : milliers de tonnes métriques [*suite*]

Country or area Pays ou zone	1984	1985	1986	1987	1988	1989	1990	1991	1992	1993
Uganda Ouganda	212.3	160.8	197.6	200.0	214.3	212.2	245.2	254.9	250.0[1]	219.8
Ukraine Ukraine	...	...	...	...	...	...	...	926.0	525.8	371.3
former USSR† ancienne URSS†	10 592.9	10 522.8	11 260.0	11 159.6	11 332.1	11 310.1	10 389.0	...	...	...
United Arab Emirates Emirats arabes unis	72.7	72.3	79.3	85.2	89.5	91.2	95.1	92.3	95.0	92.5[1]
United Kingdom Royaume-Uni	847.8	901.3	859.2	953.3	945.7	832.3	778.0	827.1	834.8	905.7
United Rep.Tanzania Rép. Unie de Tanzanie	277.2	300.6	309.9	342.3	393.0	377.1	414.0	326.8	331.6	345.0
United States Etats-Unis	4 987.6	4 947.6	5 183.1	5 988.7	5 952.9	5 774.8	5 867.7	5 485.8	5 588.5	5 923.3
United States Virgin Is. Iles Vierges américaines	0.7	0.6	0.9	0.9	0.7	0.8	0.7	0.9	0.9[1]	0.9[1]
Uruguay Uruguay	133.0	138.4	140.7	137.8	107.3	121.7	90.8	143.7	125.8	118.8
Vanuatu Vanuatu	2.9	3.5	3.2	3.2	3.3[1]	3.3[1]	3.3[1]	3.5	2.7	2.9
Venezuela Venezuela	259.7	264.0	284.6	297.8	285.7	328.9	331.9	358.3	329.9	390.3
Viet Nam Viet Nam	776.3	808.0	824.7	871.4	900.0[1]	930.0[1]	960.0[1]	1 020.0[1]	1 080.3	1 100.0[1]
Wallis and Futuna Islands Iles Wallis et Futuna	0.1[1]	0.1[1]	0.1[1]	0.1	0.1	0.1	0.1	0.1	0.1	0.2
Yemen Yémen	65.7	71.3	72.7	72.4	73.2[1]	72.9[1]	77.9	83.4	80.7	86.7
Yugoslavia Yougoslavie	...	...	...	...	...	...	...	...	7.6	6.5
Yugoslavia, SFR† Yougoslavie, Rfs†	73.4	75.0	77.5	81.3	71.8	71.7	65.5	35.6[1]	...	...
Zaire Zaïre	148.3	148.5	156.5[1]	162.0[1]	162.0[1]	166.0[1]	162.0[1]	160.0[1]	150.0[1]	147.3[1]
Zambia Zambie	64.6	67.7	68.2	63.6	60.6	66.8	64.8	65.4	67.3	65.3
Zimbabwe Zimbabwe	16.4	17.4	18.9	19.2	22.2	24.0	25.8	22.2	21.7	21.8

Source:
Food and Agriculture Organization of the United Nations (Rome).

† For detailed descriptions of data pertaining to former Czechoslovakia, Germany, SFR Yugoslavia and former USSR, see Annex I - Country or area nomenclature, regional and other groupings.

1 FAO estimate.
2 Data refer to a split year period.

Source:
Organisation des Nations Unies pour l'alimentation et l'agriculture (Rome).

† Pour les descriptions en détails des données relatives à l'ancienne Tchécoslovaquie, l'Allemagne, la Rfs Yougoslavie et l'ancienne URSS, voir l'Annexe I - Nomenclature des pays ou zones, groupements régionaux et autres groupements.

1 Estimation de la FAO.
2 Les données se réfèrent à une année fractionnée.

40
Fertilizers
Engrais
Nitrogenous, phosphate and potash: thousand metric tons
Azotés, phosphatés et potassiques : milliers de tonnes métriques

Country or area	Production Production					Consumption Consommation				
Pays ou zone	1989/90	1990/91	1991/92	1992/93	1993/94	1989/90	1990/91	1991/92	1992/93	1993/94
World Monde										
Nitrogenous fertilizers										
Engrais azotés	84 862.1	81 899.9	80 606.4	80 539.7	79 470.7	79 142.2	77 245.0	75 491.2	74 519.6	72 760.6
Phosphate fertilizers										
Engrais phosphatés	39 732.6	38 978.7	38 574.9	34 485.7	31 689.3	37 392.6	36 278.6	35 292.6	30 909.3	28 812.8
Potash fertilizers										
Engrais potassiques	28 327.8	26 710.8	24 980.2	23 557.4	20 378.5	26 885.5	24 523.1	23 568.5	20 685.6	19 098.4
Africa Afrique										
Nitrogenous fertilizers										
Engrais azotés	2 143.0	2 241.3	2 410.3	2 402.9	2 624.2	2 043.9	2 098.5	2 111.5	2 120.9	2 339.7
Phosphate fertilizers										
Engrais phosphatés	2 442.6	2 611.3	2 392.7	2 342.2	2 499.9	1 077.0	1 104.9	1 021.4	986.6	1 155.0
Potash fertilizers										
Engrais potassiques	...	...	...	...	...	488.7	481.6	466.3	471.1	498.1
Algeria Algérie										
Nitrogenous fertilizers										
Engrais azotés	* 88.0	90.4	73.2	88.3	* 79.1	* 46.3	* 63.2	* 41.0	* 46.6	* 74.0
Phosphate fertilizers										
Engrais phosphatés	* 45.3	53.7	34.6	* 33.5	* 40.9	* 47.7	46.3	34.6	* 31.9	* 34.8
Potash fertilizers *										
Engrais potassiques *	...	...	...	...	...	23.0	29.0	20.0	18.2	22.3
Angola Angola										
Nitrogenous fertilizers										
Engrais azotés	...	...	...	...	...	9.2	* 2.5	* 2.3	* 3.1	* 2.0
Phosphate fertilizers *										
Engrais phosphatés *	...	...	...	...	...	8.0	5.0	2.3	3.0	3.0
Potash fertilizers										
Engrais potassiques	...	...	...	...	...	6.4	* 2.0	* 2.3	* 3.0	* 2.5
Benin Bénin										
Nitrogenous fertilizers										
Engrais azotés	...	...	...	...	...	* 1.1	5.1	5.0	6.2	* 6.0
Phosphate fertilizers										
Engrais phosphatés	...	...	...	...	...	* 1.1	3.4	4.3	5.8	* 6.0
Potash fertilizers										
Engrais potassiques	...	...	...	...	...	* 1.1	2.5	2.5	3.3	* 4.0
Botswana Botswana										
Nitrogenous fertilizers *										
Engrais azotés *	...	...	...	...	...	0.3	0.3	0.3	0.3	0.4
Phosphate fertilizers *										
Engrais phosphatés *	...	...	...	...	...	0.4	0.4	0.4	0.4	0.4
Potash fertilizers *										
Engrais potassiques *	...	...	...	...	...	0.2	0.2	0.2	0.2	0.2
Burkina Faso Burkina Faso										
Nitrogenous fertilizers										
Engrais azotés	...	...	...	...	...	8.2	9.2	* 9.0	* 9.3	* 9.0
Phosphate fertilizers										
Engrais phosphatés	...	0.1	0.2	0.3	* 0.3	7.9	7.5	* 6.8	* 8.0	* 8.0
Potash fertilizers										
Engrais potassiques	...	...	...	...	...	4.5	4.4	4.0	4.0	* 4.0
Burundi Burundi										
Nitrogenous fertilizers										
Engrais azotés	...	...	...	...	...	* 2.0	* 1.0	* 0.1	1.8	1.4
Phosphate fertilizers *										
Engrais phosphatés *	...	...	...	...	...	2.4	1.0	0.3	3.0	2.4
Potash fertilizers										
Engrais potassiques	...	...	...	...	...	* 0.3	* 0.1	* 0.1	0.4	0.1

40
Fertilizers
Nitrogenous, phosphate and potash: thousand metric tons [cont.]
Engrais
Azotés, phosphatés et potassiques : milliers de tonnes métriques [suite]

Country or area Pays ou zone	Production Production					Consumption Consommation				
	1989/90	1990/91	1991/92	1992/93	1993/94	1989/90	1990/91	1991/92	1992/93	1993/94
Cameroon Cameroun										
Nitrogenous fertilizers										
Engrais azotés	...	...	...	...	...	* 18.2	* 8.1	* 10.0	12.6	10.2
Phosphate fertilizers										
Engrais phosphatés	...	...	...	...	...	* 4.4	* 2.7	* 2.8	2.9	5.2
Potash fertilizers										
Engrais potassiques	...	...	...	...	...	* 6.0	* 6.0	* 5.0	3.9	6.7
Central African Rep. Rép. centrafricaine										
Nitrogenous fertilizers										
Engrais azotés	...	...	...	...	...	0.7	* 0.8	* 0.8	* 0.9	* 1.0
Phosphate fertilizers										
Engrais phosphatés	...	...	...	...	...	0.0	...	...	* 0.1	* 0.2
Potash fertilizers										
Engrais potassiques	...	...	...	...	...	0.0	* 0.1	* 0.1	* 0.1	* 0.1
Chad Tchad										
Nitrogenous fertilizers										
Engrais azotés	...	...	...	...	...	2.0	* 2.0	* 3.4	4.2	2.1
Phosphate fertilizers										
Engrais phosphatés	...	...	...	...	...	1.1	* 1.9	* 2.6	2.6	1.6
Potash fertilizers										
Engrais potassiques	...	...	...	...	...	1.8	* 1.9	* 2.6	3.3	1.6
Comoros Comores										
Nitrogenous fertilizers *										
Engrais azotés *	...	...	...	...	...	...	...	0.1	0.1	0.1
Congo Congo										
Nitrogenous fertilizers										
Engrais azotés	...	...	...	...	...	0.2	0.6	* 1.3	* 1.1	* 1.0
Phosphate fertilizers										
Engrais phosphatés	...	...	...	...	...	0.2	0.4	...	...	...
Potash fertilizers										
Engrais potassiques	...	...	...	...	...	0.2	0.5	* 0.1	* 0.9	* 1.0
Côte d'Ivoire Côte d'Ivoire										
Nitrogenous fertilizers *										
Engrais azotés *	...	...	...	...	...	10.0	13.5	21.0	30.0	30.0
Phosphate fertilizers *										
Engrais phosphatés *	2.5	2.5	2.5	2.5	2.5	11.0	8.2	8.5	15.5	14.0
Potash fertilizers *										
Engrais potassiques *	...	...	...	...	...	18.0	14.0	14.0	10.0	10.0
Egypt Egypte										
Nitrogenous fertilizers										
Engrais azotés	* 678.0	676.1	823.6	749.5	809.8	754.1	745.1	* 775.0	721.7	858.5
Phosphate fertilizers										
Engrais phosphatés	* 217.4	* 194.9	163.1	* 126.5	114.1	164.9	184.1	* 150.0	* 104.0	113.3
Potash fertilizers										
Engrais potassiques	...	...	...	...	...	* 46.1	35.5	* 38.4	27.4	27.8
Ethiopia Ethiopie										
Nitrogenous fertilizers										
Engrais azotés	...	...	...	...	...	...	...	...	...	61.0
Phosphate fertilizers										
Engrais phosphatés	...	...	...	...	...	...	...	...	...	90.0
Potash fertilizers										
Engrais potassiques	...	...	...	...	...	...	...	...	...	0.5
Ethiopia incl.Eritrea Ethiopie comp. Erythrée										
Nitrogenous fertilizers *										
Engrais azotés *	...	...	...	...	...	38.0	42.1	43.0	56.0	...
Phosphate fertilizers *										
Engrais phosphatés *	...	...	...	...	...	59.0	69.7	56.0	79.0	...

40
Fertilizers
Nitrogenous, phosphate and potash: thousand metric tons [cont.]
Engrais
Azotés, phosphatés et potassiques : milliers de tonnes métriques [suite]

Country or area Pays ou zone	Production Production					Consumption Consommation				
	1989/90	1990/91	1991/92	1992/93	1993/94	1989/90	1990/91	1991/92	1992/93	1993/94
Potash fertilizers * Engrais potassiques *	...	...	...	...	...	...	...	...	0.4	...
Gabon Gabon										
Nitrogenous fertilizers Engrais azotés	...	...	...	...	...	* 0.4	0.1	* 0.2	* 0.1	* 0.1
Phosphate fertilizers Engrais phosphatés	...	...	...	...	...	* 0.1	0.5	* 0.1	* 0.1	* 0.1
Potash fertilizers * Engrais potassiques *	...	...	...	...	...	0.7	0.5	0.3	0.3	0.2
Gambia Gambie										
Nitrogenous fertilizers Engrais azotés	...	...	...	...	...	0.7	* 0.2	* 0.3	* 0.2	* 0.2
Phosphate fertilizers Engrais phosphatés	...	...	...	...	...	0.7	* 0.2	* 0.3	* 0.4	* 0.4
Potash fertilizers Engrais potassiques	...	...	...	...	...	0.7	* 0.2	* 0.3	* 0.2	* 0.2
Ghana Ghana										
Nitrogenous fertilizers Engrais azotés	...	...	...	...	...	5.8	* 8.0	* 7.0	* 7.0	* 3.0
Phosphate fertilizers Engrais phosphatés	...	...	...	...	...	1.2	* 3.0	* 0.2	* 2.0	* 2.0
Potash fertilizers Engrais potassiques	...	...	...	...	...	1.5	* 2.0	* 0.8	* 1.1	* 1.0
Guinea Guinée										
Nitrogenous fertilizers Engrais azotés	...	...	...	...	...	0.4	0.7	1.4	0.3	1.1
Phosphate fertilizers Engrais phosphatés	...	...	...	...	...	0.1	0.1	0.1	0.1	0.3
Potash fertilizers Engrais potassiques	...	...	...	...	...	0.3	0.3	0.4	0.1	0.2
Guinea-Bissau Guinée-Bissau										
Nitrogenous fertilizers Engrais azotés	...	...	...	...	...	0.4	0.2	* 0.2	* 0.1	* 0.1
Phosphate fertilizers Engrais phosphatés	...	...	...	...	...	0.3	0.2	0.2	0.1	* 0.1
Potash fertilizers Engrais potassiques	...	...	...	...	...	0.2	0.1	0.1	* 0.1	* 0.2
Kenya Kenya										
Nitrogenous fertilizers * Engrais azotés *	...	...	...	...	...	45.0	57.0	51.1	46.0	62.0
Phosphate fertilizers * Engrais phosphatés *	...	...	...	...	...	62.0	51.0	35.6	46.0	52.0
Potash fertilizers * Engrais potassiques *	...	...	...	...	...	9.8	8.0	8.7	8.0	6.0
Lesotho Lesotho										
Nitrogenous fertilizers * Engrais azotés *	...	...	...	...	...	0.5	0.5	0.8	0.7	1.0
Phosphate fertilizers * Engrais phosphatés *	...	...	...	...	...	4.0	4.0	4.0	4.0	4.0
Potash fertilizers * Engrais potassiques *	...	...	...	...	...	0.1	0.1	1.1	1.0	1.2
Liberia Libéria										
Nitrogenous fertilizers * Engrais azotés *	...	...	...	...	...	0.1	0.1	...	...	...
Phosphate fertilizers * Engrais phosphatés *	...	...	...	...	...	0.2	0.1	...	...	...
Potash fertilizers * Engrais potassiques *	...	...	...	...	...	2.4	0.1	...	...	...

40

Fertilizers

Nitrogenous, phosphate and potash: thousand metric tons [*cont.*]

Engrais

Azotés, phosphatés et potassiques : milliers de tonnes métriques [*suite*]

Country or area Pays ou zone	Production Production					Consumption Consommation				
	1989/90	1990/91	1991/92	1992/93	1993/94	1989/90	1990/91	1991/92	1992/93	1993/94
Libyan Arab Jamah. Jamah. arabe libyenne										
Nitrogenous fertilizers Engrais azotés	* 124.0	* 89.0	* 172.5	285.7	* 268.7	* 30.0	* 35.0	* 35.0	* 30.0	* 30.0
Phosphate fertilizers * Engrais phosphatés *	...	...	...	...	...	47.0	41.0	47.5	59.0	71.0
Potash fertilizers * Engrais potassiques *	...	...	...	...	...	1.8	1.6	2.3	0.4	5.0
Madagascar Madagascar										
Nitrogenous fertilizers Engrais azotés	...	...	...	...	...	2.5	4.4	3.7	3.9	4.3
Phosphate fertilizers Engrais phosphatés	...	...	...	...	...	1.0	2.5	2.3	1.6	1.2
Potash fertilizers Engrais potassiques	...	...	...	...	...	2.7	4.0	3.4	2.1	2.8
Malawi Malawi										
Nitrogenous fertilizers * Engrais azotés *	...	...	...	...	...	30.3	30.0	46.0	51.8	60.0
Phosphate fertilizers * Engrais phosphatés *	...	...	...	...	...	18.0	13.0	16.0	14.0	21.0
Potash fertilizers * Engrais potassiques *	...	...	...	...	...	6.5	5.0	8.0	8.0	5.0
Mali Mali										
Nitrogenous fertilizers * Engrais azotés *	...	...	...	...	...	8.7	9.2	9.5	10.7	12.0
Phosphate fertilizers * Engrais phosphatés *	...	...	...	...	...	9.1	6.0	5.5	9.0	10.0
Potash fertilizers * Engrais potassiques *	...	...	...	...	...	...	...	...	3.0	3.0
Mauritania Mauritanie										
Nitrogenous fertilizers Engrais azotés	...	...	...	...	...	* 1.7	* 3.5	* 4.5	6.2	4.0
Phosphate fertilizers Engrais phosphatés	...	...	...	...	...	* 0.6	* 0.4	0.7	1.1	0.6
Mauritius Maurice										
Nitrogenous fertilizers Engrais azotés	* 9.0	12.0	12.4	14.6	12.6	* 11.5	11.2	11.2	11.3	9.9
Phosphate fertilizers Engrais phosphatés	...	...	...	...	...	* 4.7	3.8	3.9	3.6	4.0
Potash fertilizers Engrais potassiques	...	...	...	...	...	* 16.0	12.8	12.5	11.8	12.1
Morocco Maroc										
Nitrogenous fertilizers Engrais azotés	* 273.1	* 344.1	* 346.0	* 296.5	* 388.0	148.3	144.2	147.5	130.4	* 130.0
Phosphate fertilizers Engrais phosphatés	* 935.8	* 1 179.9	* 1 070.0	* 997.2	1 235.0	116.6	* 125.0	119.2	* 104.9	* 105.0
Potash fertilizers Engrais potassiques	...	...	...	...	...	55.9	56.3	* 45.4	* 55.0	* 55.0
Mozambique Mozambique										
Nitrogenous fertilizers * Engrais azotés *	...	...	...	...	...	1.7	2.2	2.1	3.0	2.0
Phosphate fertilizers * Engrais phosphatés *	...	...	...	...	...	0.3	0.2	1.7	1.2	0.2
Potash fertilizers * Engrais potassiques *	...	...	...	...	...	0.4	0.2	1.3	0.7	0.5
Niger Niger										
Nitrogenous fertilizers Engrais azotés	...	...	...	...	...	1.8	1.4	0.2	* 0.9	* 1.0

40
Fertilizers
Nitrogenous, phosphate and potash: thousand metric tons [cont.]
Engrais
Azotés, phosphatés et potassiques : milliers de tonnes métriques [suite]

Country or area Pays ou zone	Production Production					Consumption Consommation				
	1989/90	1990/91	1991/92	1992/93	1993/94	1989/90	1990/91	1991/92	1992/93	1993/94
Phosphate fertilizers Engrais phosphatés	...	...	...	...	...	0.7	0.7	0.2	* 0.4	* 0.4
Potash fertilizers Engrais potassiques	...	...	...	...	...	0.3	0.2	0.1	* 0.1	* 0.1
Nigeria Nigéria										
Nitrogenous fertilizers Engrais azotés	* 272.4	* 284.0	231.0	271.0	* 267.0	197.4	210.0	212.0	270.1	* 220.0
Phosphate fertilizers Engrais phosphatés	44.1	50.2	57.9	76.2	44.2	93.5	96.1	110.6	95.8	155.9
Potash fertilizers Engrais potassiques	...	...	...	...	...	87.1	94.2	106.6	129.8	* 130.0
Réunion Réunion										
Nitrogenous fertilizers Engrais azotés	...	...	...	...	...	5.7	* 3.6	* 5.0	5.2	* 5.5
Phosphate fertilizers Engrais phosphatés	...	...	...	...	...	3.7	* 2.7	* 3.0	5.0	* 5.0
Potash fertilizers Engrais potassiques	...	...	...	...	...	5.3	* 5.8	* 6.0	4.8	* 5.0
Rwanda Rwanda										
Nitrogenous fertilizers Engrais azotés	...	...	...	...	...	0.3	1.2	0.7	0.4	* 2.0
Phosphate fertilizers Engrais phosphatés	...	...	...	...	...	0.1	1.0	0.5	0.1	* 0.1
Potash fertilizers Engrais potassiques	...	...	...	...	...	0.1	0.7	0.4	0.1	...
Senegal Sénégal										
Nitrogenous fertilizers Engrais azotés	14.4	15.7	26.8	* 25.0	* 24.0	6.2	6.0	8.6	* 9.0	* 14.0
Phosphate fertilizers Engrais phosphatés	27.5	* 50.0	46.4	* 33.0	* 38.0	3.2	2.7	5.1	* 6.0	* 6.0
Potash fertilizers Engrais potassiques	...	...	...	...	...	3.2	3.4	1.7	* 2.0	5.0
Sierra Leone Sierra Leone										
Nitrogenous fertilizers Engrais azotés	...	...	...	...	...	0.9	* 0.6	* 0.2	* 0.6	* 1.0
Phosphate fertilizers Engrais phosphatés	...	...	...	...	...	0.4	* 0.4	* 0.2	* 0.4	* 1.0
Potash fertilizers Engrais potassiques	...	...	...	...	...	0.3	* 0.3	* 0.2	* 0.4	* 1.0
Somalia Somalie										
Nitrogenous fertilizers * Engrais azotés *	...	...	...	...	...	1.4	1.7	...	...	...
Phosphate fertilizers * Engrais phosphatés *	...	...	...	...	...	0.8	0.5	...	...	...
Potash fertilizers * Engrais potassiques *	...	...	...	...	...	0.5	0.5	...	...	...
South Africa Afrique du Sud										
Nitrogenous fertilizers Engrais azotés	* 400.0	* 430.0	* 425.0	* 410.0	* 490.0	375.2	* 377.6	* 357.8	* 363.0	* 411.6
Phosphate fertilizers Engrais phosphatés	* 375.0	* 380.0	* 339.0	* 340.0	* 340.0	273.0	277.0	* 259.0	* 243.0	301.2
Potash fertilizers Engrais potassiques	...	...	...	...	...	127.8	137.0	* 123.0	* 127.0	* 130.9
Sudan Soudan										
Nitrogenous fertilizers Engrais azotés	...	...	...	...	...	46.9	73.7	76.8	* 59.4	* 59.0
Phosphate fertilizers Engrais phosphatés	...	...	...	...	...	2.4	15.6	16.4	* 15.0	* 8.0

40

Fertilizers
Nitrogenous, phosphate and potash: thousand metric tons [*cont.*]
Engrais
Azotés, phosphatés et potassiques : milliers de tonnes métriques [*suite*]

| Country or area | Production | | | | | Consumption | | | | |
Pays ou zone	1989/90	1990/91	1991/92	1992/93	1993/94	1989/90	1990/91	1991/92	1992/93	1993/94
Swaziland Swaziland										
Nitrogenous fertilizers										
Engrais azotés	...	...	...	...	...	* 7.0	7.1	* 6.0	* 6.7	* 6.3
Phosphate fertilizers										
Engrais phosphatés	...	...	...	...	...	* 2.0	2.4	* 2.5	* 2.5	* 2.3
Potash fertilizers										
Engrais potassiques	...	...	...	...	...	* 3.0	3.2	* 3.0	* 3.2	* 3.0
Togo Togo										
Nitrogenous fertilizers										
Engrais azotés	...	...	...	...	...	* 6.5	* 5.0	5.5	5.9	* 4.0
Phosphate fertilizers										
Engrais phosphatés	...	...	...	...	...	* 4.5	* 5.0	3.7	3.7	* 3.0
Potash fertilizers										
Engrais potassiques	...	...	...	...	...	* 1.0	* 1.5	2.6	2.6	* 2.0
Tunisia Tunisie										
Nitrogenous fertilizers										
Engrais azotés	206.3	202.0	209.4	202.0	196.9	* 49.5	* 36.7	* 52.0	54.7	* 55.0
Phosphate fertilizers										
Engrais phosphatés	753.5	657.1	631.1	687.1	646.4	* 45.9	* 44.2	* 45.0	48.1	* 49.0
Potash fertilizers *										
Engrais potassiques *	...	...	...	...	...	8.3	2.0	2.0	3.0	3.0
Uganda Ouganda										
Nitrogenous fertilizers										
Engrais azotés	...	...	...	...	...	0.3	0.1	* 0.5	* 0.4	* 1.3
Phosphate fertilizers										
Engrais phosphatés	...	...	...	...	...	0.1	* 0.1	* 0.3	* 0.1	* 0.3
Potash fertilizers										
Engrais potassiques	...	...	...	...	...	0.1	...	* 0.4	* 0.3	* 0.5
United Rep.Tanzania Rép. Unie de Tanzanie										
Nitrogenous fertilizers										
Engrais azotés	* 4.1	3.4	2.9	...	...	* 28.7	36.7	33.6	33.1	* 37.0
Phosphate fertilizers										
Engrais phosphatés	* 3.0	1.5	2.9	...	...	* 16.3	11.7	11.3	10.0	* 8.0
Potash fertilizers										
Engrais potassiques	...	...	...	...	...	* 4.0	2.9	4.7	4.8	* 5.0
Zaire Zaïre										
Nitrogenous fertilizers *										
Engrais azotés *	...	...	...	...	...	4.0	4.0	4.0	1.0	3.0
Phosphate fertilizers *										
Engrais phosphatés *	...	...	...	...	...	1.4	0.5	1.8	0.2	0.1
Potash fertilizers *										
Engrais potassiques *	...	...	...	...	...	2.5	1.7	2.4	1.1	1.0
Zambia Zambie										
Nitrogenous fertilizers										
Engrais azotés	* 1.9	* 6.0	4.7	* 3.7	* 6.3	* 51.8	* 38.0	40.1	* 57.3	* 58.0
Phosphate fertilizers										
Engrais phosphatés	...	...	...	...	...	* 19.4	* 15.9	15.4	* 18.2	* 19.2
Potash fertilizers										
Engrais potassiques	...	...	...	...	...	* 8.0	* 5.7	7.0	* 9.0	* 8.3
Zimbabwe Zimbabwe										
Nitrogenous fertilizers										
Engrais azotés	71.7	88.6	82.7	* 56.6	* 81.8	82.2	95.0	75.7	* 57.6	* 84.7
Phosphate fertilizers										
Engrais phosphatés	38.4	41.4	45.0	* 45.9	* 38.5	35.7	46.6	40.5	* 34.6	* 44.8
Potash fertilizers										
Engrais potassiques	...	...	...	...	...	30.6	35.1	32.3	* 16.0	* 30.0

40
Fertilizers
Nitrogenous, phosphate and potash: thousand metric tons [*cont.*]
Engrais
Azotés, phosphatés et potassiques : milliers de tonnes métriques [*suite*]

Country or area	Production Production					Consumption Consommation				
Pays ou zone	1989/90	1990/91	1991/92	1992/93	1993/94	1989/90	1990/91	1991/92	1992/93	1993/94
America, North Amerique du Nord										
Nitrogenous fertilizers										
Engrais azotés	17 185.7	17 745.9	18 343.5	18 683.9	19 503.1	13 252.9	13 369.7	13 376.1	13 415.0	15 022.8
Phosphate fertilizers										
Engrais phosphatés	10 499.5	10 888.5	12 079.6	11 479.3	10 851.9	5 093.5	4 953.7	4 987.6	5 077.8	5 256.0
Potash fertilizers										
Engrais potassiques	7 780.5	8 528.2	7 951.9	8 227.0	7 983.0	5 509.7	5 294.8	5 145.9	5 268.2	5 381.4
Bahamas Bahamas										
Nitrogenous fertilizers *										
Engrais azotés *	...	...	...	...	...	0.2	...	0.2	0.2	0.2
Phosphate fertilizers *										
Engrais phosphatés *	...	...	...	...	...	0.2	...	...	...	...
Potash fertilizers *										
Engrais potassiques *	...	...	...	...	...	0.1	0.1	0.1	0.1	0.1
Barbados Barbade										
Nitrogenous fertilizers *										
Engrais azotés *	...	...	...	...	...	1.5	1.5	1.5	2.0	1.5
Phosphate fertilizers *										
Engrais phosphatés *	...	...	...	...	...	0.1	0.2	0.2	0.2	0.2
Potash fertilizers *										
Engrais potassiques *	...	...	...	...	...	1.4	1.0	1.0	1.0	1.0
Belize Belize										
Nitrogenous fertilizers *										
Engrais azotés *	...	...	...	...	...	1.9	1.5	1.5	2.0	2.0
Phosphate fertilizers *										
Engrais phosphatés *	...	...	...	...	...	1.2	1.7	2.0	2.4	2.5
Potash fertilizers *										
Engrais potassiques *	...	...	...	...	...	1.8	1.9	1.7	1.9	2.0
Bermuda Bermudes										
Nitrogenous fertilizers										
Engrais azotés	...	...	...	...	...	* 0.1	...	...	* 0.1	0.1 [1]
Canada Canada										
Nitrogenous fertilizers										
Engrais azotés	2 706.0	2 842.8	2 904.2	2 971.7	3 488.7	1 197.2	1 157.8	1 253.3	1 317.5	1 783.8
Phosphate fertilizers										
Engrais phosphatés	440.0	354.0	437.0	395.5	400.5	609.2	578.2	592.2	615.9	636.8
Potash fertilizers										
Engrais potassiques	* 6 773.5	7 520.2	7 013.9	7 289.0	* 7 141.0	359.8	337.9	310.3	327.6	316.2
Costa Rica Costa Rica										
Nitrogenous fertilizers *										
Engrais azotés *	24.0	30.2	39.4	41.9	38.0	63.0	55.6	62.4	65.0	60.0
Phosphate fertilizers *										
Engrais phosphatés *	...	...	...	...	...	14.0	15.0	20.0	18.0	20.0
Potash fertilizers										
Engrais potassiques	...	...	...	...	...	* 30.0	* 38.0	* 38.0	41.8	* 30.0
Cuba Cuba										
Nitrogenous fertilizers										
Engrais azotés	145.9	* 140.0	* 120.0	* 100.0 [1]	* 70.0	* 366.7	* 283.0	* 240.0	* 192.0	* 120.0
Phosphate fertilizers										
Engrais phosphatés	14.9	* 7.0	* 7.0	* 6.0	* 6.0	83.0	* 82.0	* 65.0	* 20.7	* 22.3
Potash fertilizers										
Engrais potassiques	...	...	...	...	...	211.7	* 215.0	* 60.0	* 36.5	* 30.0
Dominica Dominique										
Nitrogenous fertilizers *										
Engrais azotés *	...	...	...	...	...	2.0	2.2	2.4	2.0	2.0
Phosphate fertilizers *										
Engrais phosphatés *	...	...	...	...	...	1.2	0.6	1.3	1.3	1.3

40

Fertilizers
Nitrogenous, phosphate and potash: thousand metric tons [*cont.*]
Engrais
Azotés, phosphatés et potassiques : milliers de tonnes métriques [*suite*]

Country or area Pays ou zone	Production Production					Consumption Consommation				
	1989/90	1990/91	1991/92	1992/93	1993/94	1989/90	1990/91	1991/92	1992/93	1993/94
Potash fertilizers * Engrais potassiques *	...	...	...	...	...	1.2	0.6	1.3	1.3	1.3
Dominican Republic Rép. dominicaine										
Nitrogenous fertilizers Engrais azotés	...	...	...	...	...	32.8	47.0	* 51.0	* 45.0	* 42.0
Phosphate fertilizers Engrais phosphatés	...	...	...	...	...	* 20.0	18.8	* 22.0	* 25.6	* 26.0
Potash fertilizers * Engrais potassiques *	...	...	...	...	...	20.0	23.0	24.0	20.0	20.0
El Salvador El Salvador										
Nitrogenous fertilizers Engrais azotés	5.5	11.2	9.2	...	...	56.2	53.2	55.4	53.7	* 61.0
Phosphate fertilizers Engrais phosphatés	0.1	0.1	0.1	8.9	10.4	17.9	18.9	19.1	* 10.0	14.3
Potash fertilizers Engrais potassiques	...	...	...	...	...	4.0	3.2	3.0	* 2.4	2.1
Guadeloupe Guadeloupe										
Nitrogenous fertilizers * Engrais azotés *	...	...	...	...	...	3.9	3.1	3.4	4.0	1.0
Phosphate fertilizers * Engrais phosphatés *	...	...	...	...	...	2.5	1.4	3.6	1.2	1.0
Potash fertilizers * Engrais potassiques *	...	...	...	...	...	2.5	1.4	1.8	3.4	4.0
Guatemala Guatemala										
Nitrogenous fertilizers * Engrais azotés *	7.0	7.0	8.0	8.5	...	90.5	88.0	98.0	100.0	99.0
Phosphate fertilizers * Engrais phosphatés *	7.0	7.0	7.0	1.9	...	18.0	27.0	27.0	35.0	35.0
Potash fertilizers * Engrais potassiques *	...	...	...	...	...	16.0	17.0	18.0	30.0	30.0
Haiti Haïti										
Nitrogenous fertilizers * Engrais azotés *	...	...	...	...	...	2.3	0.9	2.7	4.2	4.0
Phosphate fertilizers * Engrais phosphatés *	...	...	...	...	...	0.7	...	...	...	...
Potash fertilizers * Engrais potassiques *	...	...	...	...	...	0.7	0.1	0.1	0.1	0.1
Honduras Honduras										
Nitrogenous fertilizers Engrais azotés	...	...	...	...	...	20.3	11.1	* 20.0	* 20.9	* 33.0
Phosphate fertilizers Engrais phosphatés	...	...	...	...	...	6.0	2.1	8.0	* 12.0	* 23.0
Potash fertilizers Engrais potassiques	...	...	...	...	...	7.2	1.8	7.6	* 8.0	* 9.0
Jamaica Jamaïque										
Nitrogenous fertilizers * Engrais azotés *	...	...	...	...	...	16.0	7.4	9.2	4.2	6.0
Phosphate fertilizers * Engrais phosphatés *	...	...	...	...	...	4.1	3.6	3.8	3.8	5.4
Potash fertilizers * Engrais potassiques *	...	...	...	...	...	11.0	8.1	12.7	13.0	12.0
Martinique Martinique										
Nitrogenous fertilizers Engrais azotés	...	...	...	...	...	* 6.4	* 8.1	* 6.6	7.0	* 6.0
Phosphate fertilizers Engrais phosphatés	...	...	...	...	...	* 4.5	* 5.2	* 2.7	2.2	* 2.0
Potash fertilizers Engrais potassiques	...	...	...	...	...	* 8.0	* 11.8	* 8.0	11.7	* 12.0

40

Fertilizers

Nitrogenous, phosphate and potash: thousand metric tons [*cont.*]

Engrais

Azotés, phosphatés et potassiques : milliers de tonnes métriques [*suite*]

Country or area Pays ou zone	Production Production					Consumption Consommation				
	1989/90	1990/91	1991/92	1992/93	1993/94	1989/90	1990/91	1991/92	1992/93	1993/94
Mexico Mexique										
Nitrogenous fertilizers * Engrais azotés *	1 497.9	1 358.9	1 465.0	1 346.0	1 249.0	1 292.8	1 346.3	1 130.0	1 230.0	1 276.0
Phosphate fertilizers * Engrais phosphatés *	447.5	383.3	488.4	383.0	212.0	354.3	373.8	380.0	298.0	352.0
Potash fertilizers * Engrais potassiques *	...	...	...	...	...	92.8	78.5	73.0	88.0	125.0
Nicaragua Nicaragua										
Nitrogenous fertilizers Engrais azotés	...	...	...	...	...	21.9	31.8	26.6	* 26.0	* 21.0
Phosphate fertilizers Engrais phosphatés	...	...	...	...	...	7.6	6.1	6.2	* 0.4	* 6.0
Potash fertilizers Engrais potassiques	...	...	...	...	...	5.8	2.1	* 2.0	* 4.9	...
Panama Panama										
Nitrogenous fertilizers Engrais azotés	...	...	...	...	...	18.4	21.7	* 16.0	* 23.7	* 26.2
Phosphate fertilizers Engrais phosphatés	...	...	...	...	...	4.0	5.1	4.2	* 3.0	* 3.5
Potash fertilizers Engrais potassiques	...	...	...	...	...	10.9	11.9	5.1	* 8.8	* 2.0
Saint Kitts and Nevis Saint-Kitts-et-Nevis										
Nitrogenous fertilizers Engrais azotés	...	...	...	...	...	0.4	0.4	* 0.5	* 0.5	* 1.0
Phosphate fertilizers Engrais phosphatés	...	...	...	...	...	0.2	0.2	* 0.3	* 0.3	* 0.3
Potash fertilizers Engrais potassiques	...	...	...	...	...	0.3	0.3	* 0.3	* 0.3	...
Saint Lucia Sainte-Lucie										
Nitrogenous fertilizers Engrais azotés	...	...	...	...	...	2.9	2.4	* 3.0	* 3.0	* 3.0
Phosphate fertilizers Engrais phosphatés	...	...	...	...	...	2.1	1.7	* 1.8	* 1.8	* 2.0
Potash fertilizers Engrais potassiques	...	...	...	...	...	2.2	1.7	* 1.7	* 1.7	* 2.0
St. Vincent-Grenadines St. Vincent-Grenadines										
Nitrogenous fertilizers * Engrais azotés *	...	...	...	...	...	1.5	0.5	0.5	0.5	1.0
Phosphate fertilizers * Engrais phosphatés *	...	...	...	...	...	0.9	0.9	0.9	1.0	...
Potash fertilizers * Engrais potassiques *	...	...	...	...	...	0.9	0.9	0.9	0.9	0.9
Trinidad and Tobago Trinité-et-Tobago										
Nitrogenous fertilizers Engrais azotés	* 223.4	* 231.8	* 240.7	209.8	* 242.4	* 5.0	* 6.0	* 7.0	* 7.0	* 3.0
Phosphate fertilizers Engrais phosphatés	...	...	...	...	...	* 0.2	* 0.2	0.6	* 0.8	* 0.6
Potash fertilizers * Engrais potassiques *	...	...	...	...	...	1.6	1.6	1.6	1.3	2.6
United States Etats-Unis										
Nitrogenous fertilizers Engrais azotés	12 576.0	13 124.0	13 557.0	14 006.0	14 415.0	10 047.9	10 239.3	10 383.9	10 303.6	11 469.0
Phosphate fertilizers Engrais phosphatés	9 590.0	10 137.0	* 11 140.0	10 684.0	10 223.0	3 941.4	3 810.7	3 826.4	4 023.9	4 101.5
Potash fertilizers Engrais potassiques	1 007.0	1 008.0	938.0	938.0	842.0	4 719.9	4 537.0	4 573.7	4 663.5	4 779.1

40
Fertilizers
Nitrogenous, phosphate and potash: thousand metric tons [*cont.*]
Engrais
Azotés, phosphatés et potassiques : milliers de tonnes métriques [*suite*]

Country or area Pays ou zone	Production Production					Consumption Consommation				
	1989/90	1990/91	1991/92	1992/93	1993/94	1989/90	1990/91	1991/92	1992/93	1993/94
United States Virgin Is. **Iles Vierges américaines**										
Nitrogenous fertilizers * Engrais azotés *	...	...	...	...	...	1.0	1.0	1.0	1.0	1.0
Phosphate fertilizers * Engrais phosphatés *	...	...	...	...	...	0.3	0.3	0.3	0.3	0.3
America, South **Amérique du Sud**										
Nitrogenous fertilizers Engrais azotés	**1 430.3**	**1 372.8**	**1 351.1**	**1 214.9**	**1 323.2**	**1 791.7**	**1 734.4**	**1 669.9**	**1 879.7**	**2 039.5**
Phosphate fertilizers Engrais phosphatés	**1 215.0**	**1 209.6**	**1 260.9**	**1 175.2**	**1 330.8**	**1 861.3**	**1 693.4**	**1 757.1**	**1 848.0**	**2 089.8**
Potash fertilizers Engrais potassiques	**109.4**	**68.1**	**138.1**	**112.6**	**211.9**	**1 623.8**	**1 528.2**	**1 528.3**	**1 694.6**	**1 886.5**
Argentina **Argentine**										
Nitrogenous fertilizers Engrais azotés	* 50.0	* 40.5	42.1	32.7	47.8	* 99.4	* 101.4	* 96.0	* 146.1	* 186.2
Phosphate fertilizers Engrais phosphatés	...	...	...	...	...	* 42.7	* 51.5	69.0	* 83.6	* 107.4
Potash fertilizers Engrais potassiques	...	...	...	...	...	* 11.0	* 12.6	20.1	13.1	* 14.0
Bolivia **Bolivie**										
Nitrogenous fertilizers Engrais azotés	...	...	...	...	...	4.6	2.3	3.6	5.5	* 6.0
Phosphate fertilizers Engrais phosphatés	...	...	...	...	...	5.3	2.5	3.5	7.6	* 6.8
Potash fertilizers Engrais potassiques	...	...	...	...	...	0.3	0.3	0.7	0.7	* 0.8
Brazil **Brésil**										
Nitrogenous fertilizers Engrais azotés	748.5	737.2	704.3	664.6	709.2	823.3	779.3	781.5	865.5	1 014.8
Phosphate fertilizers Engrais phosphatés	1 109.4	* 1 090.7	* 1 139.4	1 075.7	1 253.7	1 296.2	* 1 201.6	* 1 247.4	1 346.1	1 546.1
Potash fertilizers Engrais potassiques	109.4	68.1	101.1	77.3	173.9	1 263.7	1 183.2	1 206.0	1 372.8	1 589.4
Chile **Chili**										
Nitrogenous fertilizers Engrais azotés	* 130.0	* 126.0	* 119.7	* 126.0	* 130.0	158.3	152.9	* 161.0	* 190.0	* 195.0
Phosphate fertilizers Engrais phosphatés	* 4.0	* 5.0	* 4.0	* 4.0	* 5.0	125.9	113.8	* 111.6	* 130.0	* 140.0
Potash fertilizers Engrais potassiques	...	...	* 37.0	* 35.3	* 38.0	27.7	28.8	* 37.0	* 40.0	* 50.0
Colombia **Colombie**										
Nitrogenous fertilizers Engrais azotés	95.7	* 99.7	* 100.0	* 60.0	* 60.0	* 269.0	* 312.0	* 271.0	280.7	* 267.0
Phosphate fertilizers Engrais phosphatés	* 39.0	* 40.0	* 28.0	* 29.0	* 24.0	* 121.8	* 126.7	* 120.0	98.0	* 105.0
Potash fertilizers Engrais potassiques	...	...	...	...	...	153.5	* 163.8	* 150.0	160.0	* 142.7
Ecuador **Equateur**										
Nitrogenous fertilizers Engrais azotés	...	...	...	...	...	41.1	36.7	* 45.0	* 57.4	* 49.0
Phosphate fertilizers Engrais phosphatés	...	...	...	...	...	21.9	* 10.6	* 16.8	* 27.0	* 29.0
Potash fertilizers Engrais potassiques	...	...	...	...	...	14.4	19.9	* 24.1	* 30.3	* 18.0
French Guiana **Guyane française**										
Nitrogenous fertilizers * Engrais azotés *	...	...	...	...	...	0.3	0.7	0.9	0.6	0.6

40

Fertilizers
Nitrogenous, phosphate and potash: thousand metric tons [cont.]
Engrais
Azotés, phosphatés et potassiques : milliers de tonnes métriques [suite]

Country or area Pays ou zone	Production Production					Consumption Consommation				
	1989/90	1990/91	1991/92	1992/93	1993/94	1989/90	1990/91	1991/92	1992/93	1993/94
Phosphate fertilizers										
Engrais phosphatés	...	...	...	...	...	* 0.2	* 0.2	* 0.2	0.3	* 0.3
Potash fertilizers										
Engrais potassiques	...	...	...	...	...	* 0.2	* 0.2	* 0.2	0.1	* 0.1
Guyana Guyana										
Nitrogenous fertilizers *										
Engrais azotés *	...	...	...	...	...	12.0	8.0	13.0	10.5	10.0
Phosphate fertilizers *										
Engrais phosphatés *	...	...	...	...	...	1.8	2.2	1.6	0.9	1.0
Potash fertilizers *										
Engrais potassiques *	...	...	...	...	...	2.5	1.8	1.0	0.8	1.0
Paraguay Paraguay										
Nitrogenous fertilizers										
Engrais azotés	...	...	...	...	...	3.5	3.7	4.3	4.8	* 9.9
Phosphate fertilizers										
Engrais phosphatés	...	...	...	...	...	12.8	11.2	* 13.4	* 14.6	* 16.1
Potash fertilizers										
Engrais potassiques	...	...	...	...	...	3.4	3.1	2.7	2.5	* 6.0
Peru Pérou										
Nitrogenous fertilizers										
Engrais azotés	36.2	32.4	20.0	14.6	14.1	113.2	* 104.1	58.6	* 113.0	* 124.0
Phosphate fertilizers										
Engrais phosphatés	4.0	4.7	3.0	3.5	1.1	18.8	12.8	11.2	10.8	* 23.0
Potash fertilizers										
Engrais potassiques	...	...	...	...	...	19.8	8.3	5.7	4.8	5.3
Suriname Suriname										
Nitrogenous fertilizers										
Engrais azotés	...	...	...	...	...	1.3	* 0.6	* 0.6	* 2.6	* 3.0
Phosphate fertilizers										
Engrais phosphatés	...	...	...	...	...	0.2	* 0.2	* 0.2	* 0.1	* 0.1
Potash fertilizers										
Engrais potassiques	...	...	...	...	...	0.2	* 0.2	* 0.2	* 0.2	* 0.2
Uruguay Uruguay										
Nitrogenous fertilizers										
Engrais azotés	...	...	...	...	...	24.5	27.7	28.3	30.0[1]	* 37.0
Phosphate fertilizers										
Engrais phosphatés	8.6	* 12.0	* 17.0	* 17.0	* 17.0	42.3	41.2	46.5	* 45.0	* 52.0
Potash fertilizers										
Engrais potassiques	...	...	...	...	...	3.8	3.0	4.0	* 4.3	* 5.0
Venezuela Venezuela										
Nitrogenous fertilizers *										
Engrais azotés *	370.0	337.0	365.0	317.0	362.0	241.1	205.0	206.0	173.0	137.0
Phosphate fertilizers										
Engrais phosphatés	* 50.0	* 57.2	* 69.5	* 46.0	* 30.0	171.3	* 119.0	* 115.6	* 84.0	* 63.0
Potash fertilizers										
Engrais potassiques	...	...	...	...	...	123.4	* 103.0	* 76.7	* 65.0	* 54.0
Asia Asie										
Nitrogenous fertilizers										
Engrais azotés	31 400.8	31 969.8	32 280.1	34 012.6	33 910.4	35 909.7	37 186.8	37 908.3	39 802.5	37 527.2
Phosphate fertilizers										
Engrais phosphatés	9 041.4	9 656.7	10 462.2	10 247.5	9 246.3	12 763.6	13 832.7	15 161.4	14 462.5	12 936.6
Potash fertilizers										
Engrais potassiques	2 167.4	2 183.6	2 165.4	2 256.5	2 281.2	4 471.4	5 176.8	5 756.4	5 064.9	4 761.5
Afghanistan Afghanistan										
Nitrogenous fertilizers										
Engrais azotés	55.2	* 53.0	* 48.8	* 42.0	* 40.0	50.0	* 44.1	* 45.0	36.2	* 40.0
Phosphate fertilizers *										
Engrais phosphatés *	...	...	...	...	...	5.6	0.4	5.8	6.9	...

40

Fertilizers
Nitrogenous, phosphate and potash: thousand metric tons [*cont.*]
Engrais
Azotés, phosphatés et potassiques : milliers de tonnes métriques [*suite*]

Country or area Pays ou zone	Production Production					Consumption Consommation				
	1989/90	1990/91	1991/92	1992/93	1993/94	1989/90	1990/91	1991/92	1992/93	1993/94
Armenia Arménie										
Nitrogenous fertilizers *										
Engrais azotés *	...	...	...	...	...	...	...	...	15.0	15.0
Phosphate fertilizers *										
Engrais phosphatés *	...	...	...	...	...	...	...	...	5.0	...
Potash fertilizers *										
Engrais potassiques *	...	...	...	...	...	...	...	...	5.0	...
Azerbaijan Azerbaïdjan										
Nitrogenous fertilizers *										
Engrais azotés *	...	...	...	...	...	...	...	...	50.0	34.0
Phosphate fertilizers *										
Engrais phosphatés *	...	...	...	61.0	40.0	...	...	...	20.0	15.0
Potash fertilizers *										
Engrais potassiques *	...	...	...	62.0	50.0	...	...	...	5.0	5.0
Bahrain Bahreïn										
Nitrogenous fertilizers										
Engrais azotés	...	...	...	...	...	0.2	0.3	* 0.3	* 0.3	* 0.3
Phosphate fertilizers										
Engrais phosphatés	...	...	...	...	...	0.1	0.2	* 0.2	* 0.2	* 0.2
Potash fertilizers										
Engrais potassiques	...	...	...	...	...	0.1	0.2	* 0.2	* 0.2	* 0.2
Bangladesh Bangladesh										
Nitrogenous fertilizers										
Engrais azotés	677.8	653.6	756.8	918.6	1 003.8	629.8	608.6	704.6	683.9	735.8
Phosphate fertilizers										
Engrais phosphatés	67.3	50.9	50.0	40.1	49.2	221.1	236.3	216.3	212.0	149.7
Potash fertilizers										
Engrais potassiques	...	...	...	...	...	56.1	88.2	82.2	73.4	62.4
Bhutan Bhoutan										
Nitrogenous fertilizers *										
Engrais azotés *	...	...	...	...	...	0.1	0.1	0.1	0.1	0.1
Brunei Darussalam Brunéi Darussalam										
Nitrogenous fertilizers *										
Engrais azotés *	...	...	...	...	...	0.1	1.4	1.4	1.5	1.5
Phosphate fertilizers *										
Engrais phosphatés *	...	...	...	...	...	0.1	1.4	1.5	1.5	1.5
Potash fertilizers *										
Engrais potassiques *	...	...	...	...	...	0.2	1.4	1.5	1.5	1.5
Cambodia Cambodge										
Nitrogenous fertilizers										
Engrais azotés	...	...	...	...	...	...	* 1.6	4.2	* 5.0	* 10.0
Phosphate fertilizers *										
Engrais phosphatés *	3.5	3.7	...	...	...	3.5	6.2	1.5	1.5	4.5
Potash fertilizers *										
Engrais potassiques *	...	...	...	...	...	0.3	...	...	0.1	0.1
China Chine										
Nitrogenous fertilizers										
Engrais azotés	14 515.0	14 914.5	15 372.5	15 958.0	15 532.9	* 18 855.3	* 19 449.8	20 020.1	* 20 716.0	* 18 003.3
Phosphate fertilizers										
Engrais phosphatés	3 807.7	4 196.0	4 677.5	4 700.0	4 170.0	* 5 272.1	* 5 878.5	7 326.3	6 758.0	* 5 545.0
Potash fertilizers										
Engrais potassiques	56.0	47.0	97.0	152.9	117.2	* 1 300.8	* 1 699.1	2 402.4	1 993.8	* 1 531.0
Cyprus Chypre										
Nitrogenous fertilizers										
Engrais azotés	11.2	...	...	...	...	12.5	12.4	12.2	15.4	14.5
Phosphate fertilizers										
Engrais phosphatés	24.1	...	...	...	...	8.3	8.3	8.1	9.8	9.7

40
Fertilizers
Nitrogenous, phosphate and potash: thousand metric tons [*cont.*]
Engrais
Azotés, phosphatés et potassiques : milliers de tonnes métriques [*suite*]

Country or area Pays ou zone	Production Production					Consumption Consommation				
	1989/90	1990/91	1991/92	1992/93	1993/94	1989/90	1990/91	1991/92	1992/93	1993/94
Potash fertilizers Engrais potassiques	...	...	...	...	...	1.7	2.0	1.8	2.6	2.0
Georgia Géorgie										
Nitrogenous fertilizers * Engrais azotés *	...	...	...	76.0	58.6	...	...	...	62.0	48.9
Phosphate fertilizers * Engrais phosphatés *	...	...	...	...	...	...	...	...	10.0	5.0
India Inde										
Nitrogenous fertilizers Engrais azotés	6 747.4	6 993.1	7 301.5	7 430.6	7 231.2	7 385.9	7 997.2	8 046.3	8 426.1	8 764.9
Phosphate fertilizers Engrais phosphatés	1 834.0	2 088.9	2 596.4	2 355.8	1 874.2	3 052.9	3 258.8	3 355.6	2 907.8	2 669.7
Potash fertilizers Engrais potassiques	...	...	...	...	...	1 168.0	1 328.0	1 360.6	883.9	910.2
Indonesia Indonésie										
Nitrogenous fertilizers Engrais azotés	2 369.0	* 2 348.3	* 2 302.4	* 2 513.1	* 2 357.4	* 1 474.0	* 1 496.0	* 1 552.0	* 1 696.3	* 1 700.0
Phosphate fertilizers Engrais phosphatés	551.3	588.8	* 500.9	* 437.0	* 542.5	* 598.0	* 585.0	* 584.0	* 593.4	* 540.0
Potash fertilizers Engrais potassiques	...	...	...	...	...	* 274.0	* 306.0	* 271.7	* 290.0	387.0
Iran, Islamic Rep. of Iran, Rép. islamique d'										
Nitrogenous fertilizers * Engrais azotés *	308.1	376.2	451.0	571.7	427.2	668.3	558.1	658.6	834.0	600.0
Phosphate fertilizers * Engrais phosphatés *	49.7	80.5	162.0	186.8	91.5	512.4	587.0	482.6	487.6	321.1
Potash fertilizers * Engrais potassiques *	...	...	...	...	...	0.2	15.9	15.0	28.0	25.0
Iraq Iraq										
Nitrogenous fertilizers Engrais azotés	* 450.0	* 409.0	* 95.0	* 130.0	* 150.0	138.4	* 130.0	* 95.0	* 130.0	* 150.0
Phosphate fertilizers Engrais phosphatés	* 415.0	* 207.0	* 30.0	* 80.0	* 100.0	75.1	* 75.0	* 39.7	* 80.0	* 120.9
Potash fertilizers Engrais potassiques	...	...	...	...	...	1.9	* 4.2	...	...	* 11.0
Israel Israël										
Nitrogenous fertilizers Engrais azotés	* 75.0	* 75.0	* 75.0	* 75.0	* 75.0	53.8	49.6	41.3	43.4	* 44.0
Phosphate fertilizers Engrais phosphatés	* 180.0	* 200.0	* 185.0	* 210.0	* 190.0	21.4	20.7	20.0	21.5	* 22.0
Potash fertilizers Engrais potassiques	* 1 301.0	* 1 295.0	* 1 250.0	* 1 296.0	* 1 342.0	33.9	32.1	32.3	32.9	* 32.0
Japan Japon										
Nitrogenous fertilizers Engrais azotés	946.0	957.0	931.0	906.0	868.0	641.0	612.0	574.0	572.0	600.0
Phosphate fertilizers Engrais phosphatés	445.0	429.0	425.0	393.0	384.0	728.0	690.0	695.0	699.0	728.0
Potash fertilizers Engrais potassiques	...	...	...	...	...	569.0	537.0	494.0	513.0	489.0
Jordan Jordanie										
Nitrogenous fertilizers Engrais azotés	108.5	107.3	107.8	99.6	84.6	* 15.0	* 10.0	14.8	0.5	3.3
Phosphate fertilizers Engrais phosphatés	277.2	274.2	275.5	254.6	216.2	* 5.0	4.6	4.6	1.4	8.5
Potash fertilizers Engrais potassiques	810.4	841.6	818.4	807.6	822.1	* 4.0	* 1.4	1.1	* 1.4	* 2.0

40

Fertilizers
Nitrogenous, phosphate and potash: thousand metric tons [*cont.*]
Engrais
Azotés, phosphatés et potassiques : milliers de tonnes métriques [*suite*]

Country or area Pays ou zone	Production Production					Consumption Consommation				
	1989/90	1990/91	1991/92	1992/93	1993/94	1989/90	1990/91	1991/92	1992/93	1993/94
Kazakstan Kazakstan										
Nitrogenous fertilizers *										
Engrais azotés *	...	...	...	64.0	29.0	...	...	...	150.0	70.0
Phosphate fertilizers *										
Engrais phosphatés *	...	...	...	400.0	282.0	...	...	...	315.0	231.0
Potash fertilizers *										
Engrais potassiques *	...	...	...	12.6	13.0	...	...	...	10.0	10.0
Korea, Dem. P. R. Corée, R. p. dém. de										
Nitrogenous fertilizers *										
Engrais azotés *	660.0	660.0	660.0	660.0	660.0	644.0	655.4	659.0	652.5	500.0
Phosphate fertilizers *										
Engrais phosphatés *	137.0	137.0	137.0	130.0	130.0	163.2	158.9	148.5	130.0	130.0
Potash fertilizers										
Engrais potassiques	...	...	...	...	...	7.5	* 18.1	* 3.6	...	...
Korea, Republic of Corée, République de										
Nitrogenous fertilizers										
Engrais azotés	583.4	554.4	* 570.5	* 623.3	* 621.4	455.0	465.2	* 473.5	* 486.6	* 477.3
Phosphate fertilizers										
Engrais phosphatés	* 393.8	414.4	398.0	* 421.8	* 447.0	235.1	228.0	242.8	219.1	* 226.5
Potash fertilizers *										
Engrais potassiques *	...	...	...	...	...	231.1	222.7	233.7	258.0	269.9
Kuwait Koweït										
Nitrogenous fertilizers										
Engrais azotés	* 386.4	* 204.0	...	118.4	* 292.8	* 0.8	* 1.0	...	* 0.8	* 1.0
Kyrgyzstan Kirghizistan										
Nitrogenous fertilizers *										
Engrais azotés *	...	...	...	...	...	...	...	...	25.3	22.0
Phosphate fertilizers *										
Engrais phosphatés *	...	...	...	...	...	...	...	...	1.7	1.0
Potash fertilizers *										
Engrais potassiques *	...	...	...	...	...	...	...	...	5.0	5.0
Lao People's Dem. Rep. Rép. dém. pop. lao										
Nitrogenous fertilizers										
Engrais azotés	...	...	...	...	...	* 0.1	* 1.1	1.7	3.1	* 3.1
Phosphate fertilizers										
Engrais phosphatés	...	...	...	...	...	* 0.1	* 0.3	0.8	0.2	...
Potash fertilizers										
Engrais potassiques	...	...	...	...	...	* 0.1	* 0.1	0.0	0.0	* 0.1
Lebanon Liban										
Nitrogenous fertilizers *										
Engrais azotés *	...	...	...	...	...	14.0	11.0	12.4	14.2	18.0
Phosphate fertilizers *										
Engrais phosphatés *	15.0	34.0	40.0	55.0	50.0	10.0	12.0	15.0	17.0	14.0
Potash fertilizers *										
Engrais potassiques *	...	...	...	...	...	3.6	2.4	2.3	3.9	4.2
Malaysia Malaisie										
Nitrogenous fertilizers										
Engrais azotés	* 249.0	* 211.0	* 325.0	* 303.0	* 292.0	288.0	* 313.0	* 320.0	* 295.0	* 303.0
Phosphate fertilizers										
Engrais phosphatés	...	...	...	...	...	150.1	* 163.5	* 166.2	* 160.0	* 170.0
Potash fertilizers										
Engrais potassiques	...	...	...	...	...	* 391.0	475.0	* 480.0	* 510.0	* 560.0
Mongolia Mongolie										
Nitrogenous fertilizers										
Engrais azotés	...	...	...	...	...	10.0	9.1	* 10.0	* 2.0	* 0.5
Phosphate fertilizers										
Engrais phosphatés	...	...	...	...	...	3.5	3.7	* 4.0	* 3.5	...

40
Fertilizers
Nitrogenous, phosphate and potash: thousand metric tons [*cont.*]
Engrais
Azotés, phosphatés et potassiques : milliers de tonnes métriques [*suite*]

Country or area Pays ou zone	Production Production					Consumption Consommation				
	1989/90	1990/91	1991/92	1992/93	1993/94	1989/90	1990/91	1991/92	1992/93	1993/94
Potash fertilizers										
Engrais potassiques	...	...	...	...	...	3.6	1.8	* 2.0	* 0.6	...
Myanmar Myanmar										
Nitrogenous fertilizers										
Engrais azotés	* 88.3	* 60.0	46.7	54.3	99.4	63.7	* 53.0	62.7	71.5	160.5
Phosphate fertilizers										
Engrais phosphatés	...	...	...	...	...	17.3	14.8	14.5	12.9	23.7
Potash fertilizers										
Engrais potassiques	...	...	...	...	...	1.8	2.9	1.3	2.6	7.0
Nepal Népal										
Nitrogenous fertilizers										
Engrais azotés	...	...	...	...	...	49.2	52.0	* 55.0	60.3	55.3
Phosphate fertilizers										
Engrais phosphatés	...	...	...	...	...	16.7	19.1	* 22.7	19.5	16.2
Potash fertilizers										
Engrais potassiques	...	...	...	...	...	1.3	1.6	1.2	1.2	1.3
Oman Oman										
Nitrogenous fertilizers										
Engrais azotés	...	...	...	...	...	2.4	4.8	4.9	* 5.0	* 5.0
Phosphate fertilizers										
Engrais phosphatés	...	...	...	...	...	1.1	1.5	1.5	* 1.5	* 2.0
Potash fertilizers										
Engrais potassiques	...	...	...	...	...	1.8	3.1	1.8	* 1.5	* 2.0
Pakistan Pakistan										
Nitrogenous fertilizers										
Engrais azotés	1 156.3	1 120.3	1 045.0	1 227.3	1 565.9	1 467.6	1 471.6	1 462.9	1 635.4	1 659.4
Phosphate fertilizers										
Engrais phosphatés	105.1	104.7	106.0	104.8	92.9	382.5	388.5	393.3	488.2	464.3
Potash fertilizers										
Engrais potassiques	...	...	...	...	...	40.1	32.8	23.3	24.1	23.2
Philippines Philippines										
Nitrogenous fertilizers										
Engrais azotés	127.0	* 120.8	143.2	* 142.3	* 157.6	376.0	400.6	298.6	* 360.3	* 400.0
Phosphate fertilizers										
Engrais phosphatés	191.0	199.4	191.9	* 153.0	* 185.0	84.1	105.0	71.3	* 72.5	* 96.5
Potash fertilizers										
Engrais potassiques	...	...	...	...	...	77.1	82.5	67.5	* 69.7	* 61.7
Qatar Qatar										
Nitrogenous fertilizers										
Engrais azotés	359.0	350.1	* 367.5	379.9	380.1	1.2	1.4	* 1.5	* 1.5	* 2.0
Saudi Arabia Arabie saoudite										
Nitrogenous fertilizers										
Engrais azotés	* 428.4	* 584.0	* 658.0	713.9	* 831.7	* 265.0	* 273.0	* 284.0	291.9	* 250.0
Phosphate fertilizers										
Engrais phosphatés	...	* 27.0	* 200.0	* 146.0	* 132.0	175.0	* 193.0	* 200.0	218.2	* 190.0
Potash fertilizers										
Engrais potassiques	...	...	...	...	...	* 35.0	* 23.0	* 24.0	28.6	* 15.0
Singapore Singapour										
Nitrogenous fertilizers *										
Engrais azotés *	...	...	...	...	...	2.6	2.6	2.6	2.6	2.6
Phosphate fertilizers *										
Engrais phosphatés *	...	...	...	...	...	0.5	0.5	0.5	0.5	0.5
Potash fertilizers *										
Engrais potassiques *	...	...	...	...	...	2.5	2.5	2.5	2.5	2.5
Sri Lanka Sri Lanka										
Nitrogenous fertilizers										
Engrais azotés	...	...	...	...	...	108.5	92.4	95.8	102.2	114.6

40
Fertilizers
Nitrogenous, phosphate and potash: thousand metric tons [cont.]
Engrais
Azotés, phosphatés et potassiques : milliers de tonnes métriques [suite]

Country or area Pays ou zone	Production Production					Consumption Consommation				
	1989/90	1990/91	1991/92	1992/93	1993/94	1989/90	1990/91	1991/92	1992/93	1993/94
Phosphate fertilizers Engrais phosphatés	6.8	9.1	5.5	7.2	* 8.5	40.7	29.2	30.9	30.4	38.4
Potash fertilizers Engrais potassiques	...	...	...	...	...	61.6	49.6	50.5	51.1	57.1
Syrian Arab Republic Rép. arabe syrienne										
Nitrogenous fertilizers Engrais azotés	* 108.1	31.8	* 15.0	45.2	77.4	153.6	184.8	* 180.0	204.1	230.0
Phosphate fertilizers Engrais phosphatés	14.9	21.3	* 25.0	...	...	91.6	111.9	* 120.0	139.0	138.9
Potash fertilizers Engrais potassiques	...	...	...	...	...	4.6	6.5	* 8.9	5.9	5.9
Tajikistan Tadjikistan										
Nitrogenous fertilizers * Engrais azotés *	...	...	...	48.0	19.0	...	...	...	64.0	39.0
Phosphate fertilizers * Engrais phosphatés *	...	...	...	...	...	...	...	...	56.0	25.0
Potash fertilizers * Engrais potassiques *	...	...	...	...	...	...	...	...	8.0	5.0
Thailand Thaïlande										
Nitrogenous fertilizers Engrais azotés	...	...	...	...	...	494.9	576.5	485.5	* 586.9	* 646.0
Phosphate fertilizers Engrais phosphatés	...	...	...	...	...	188.8	318.3	235.5	* 295.6	* 305.7
Potash fertilizers Engrais potassiques	...	...	...	...	...	117.8	148.9	* 125.0	* 157.5	* 174.3
Turkey Turquie										
Nitrogenous fertilizers Engrais azotés	700.0	947.1	748.9	831.4	* 856.3	1 140.4	1 199.7	1 099.5	1 206.1	* 1 335.2
Phosphate fertilizers Engrais phosphatés	468.0	524.8	387.9	474.4	* 489.2	599.7	624.8	619.6	658.1	* 787.0
Potash fertilizers Engrais potassiques	...	...	...	...	...	58.0	63.0	47.5	63.3	* 85.0
Turkmenistan Turkménistan										
Nitrogenous fertilizers * Engrais azotés *	...	...	...	79.0	82.0	...	...	...	100.0	83.0
Phosphate fertilizers * Engrais phosphatés *	...	...	...	130.0	100.0	...	...	...	65.0	50.0
Potash fertilizers * Engrais potassiques *	...	...	...	...	...	...	...	...	10.0	10.0
United Arab Emirates Emirats arabes unis										
Nitrogenous fertilizers Engrais azotés	266.4	228.3	237.8	232.3	* 259.7	7.8	9.2	14.2	* 19.0	* 20.0
Phosphate fertilizers * Engrais phosphatés *	...	...	...	...	...	1.6	1.2	1.3	1.3	4.7
Potash fertilizers * Engrais potassiques *	...	...	...	...	...	2.7	2.1	2.0	2.0	3.0
Uzbekistan Ouzbékistan										
Nitrogenous fertilizers * Engrais azotés *	...	...	...	1 018.0	922.0	...	...	...	410.0	357.0
Phosphate fertilizers * Engrais phosphatés *	...	...	...	310.0	276.0	...	...	...	260.0	256.0
Potash fertilizers * Engrais potassiques *	...	...	...	...	...	...	...	...	60.0	60.0
Viet Nam Viet Nam										
Nitrogenous fertilizers Engrais azotés	25.3	* 11.0	20.7	* 36.8	* 46.0	424.0	* 419.0	598.6	* 628.8	* 668.0
Phosphate fertilizers Engrais phosphatés	55.0	66.0	68.5	* 98.0	* 94.0	* 97.7	103.3	128.8	* 213.2	* 205.6

40

Fertilizers
Nitrogenous, phosphate and potash: thousand metric tons [*cont.*]
Engrais
Azotés, phosphatés et potassiques : milliers de tonnes métriques [*suite*]

Country or area Pays ou zone	Production Production					Consumption Consommation				
	1989/90	1990/91	1991/92	1992/93	1993/94	1989/90	1990/91	1991/92	1992/93	1993/94
Potash fertilizers										
Engrais potassiques	...	...	...	...	...	* 20.0	22.2	* 15.9	* 60.0	* 35.0
Yemen Yémen										
Nitrogenous fertilizers										
Engrais azotés	...	...	...	...	...	16.5	19.1	* 16.0	* 12.0	* 8.0
Phosphate fertilizers										
Engrais phosphatés	...	...	...	...	...	0.8	2.8	* 3.0	* 1.1	* 2.0
Potash fertilizers										
Engrais potassiques	...	...	...	...	...	* 0.1	0.5	* 0.6	* 1.5	* 1.0
Europe Europe										
Nitrogenous fertilizers										
Engrais azotés	18 140.6	15 207.7	13 927.1	13 498.6	12 930.0	15 728.4	13 683.1	12 103.6	11 365.3	11 244.9
Phosphate fertilizers										
Engrais phosphatés	6 802.4	5 308.5	4 254.3	3 889.8	3 522.6	7 372.0	6 058.0	4 856.7	4 434.1	4 168.0
Potash fertilizers										
Engrais potassiques	8 037.9	6 895.7	6 193.7	5 999.7	5 195.4	8 148.8	6 642.3	5 335.6	4 602.0	4 498.4
Albania Albanie										
Nitrogenous fertilizers										
Engrais azotés	79.9	* 73.4	* 22.3	* 5.7	* 9.3	79.9	* 73.4	* 22.3	* 14.8	* 8.8
Phosphate fertilizers										
Engrais phosphatés	24.3	* 25.5	* 7.7	* 4.0	* 2.0	24.3	* 25.5	* 7.7	* 8.7	* 2.1
Potash fertilizers *										
Engrais potassiques *	...	...	...	...	...	2.3	3.1	1.3	...	1.1
Austria Autriche										
Nitrogenous fertilizers										
Engrais azotés	* 230.0	* 227.0	* 233.0	* 210.0	* 220.0	135.6	* 135.0	* 132.0	* 124.0	* 125.0
Phosphate fertilizers										
Engrais phosphatés	* 85.0	* 70.0	* 71.0	* 76.0	* 80.0	74.4	* 74.0	* 72.0	* 65.0	* 61.0
Potash fertilizers										
Engrais potassiques	...	...	...	...	...	97.8	* 94.0	* 93.1	* 78.0	* 76.0
Belarus Bélarus										
Nitrogenous fertilizers *										
Engrais azotés *	...	...	...	580.0	464.0	...	...	...	250.0	227.0
Phosphate fertilizers *										
Engrais phosphatés *	...	...	...	101.0	68.0	...	...	...	295.0	225.0
Potash fertilizers *										
Engrais potassiques *	...	...	...	3 311.0	1 947.0	...	...	...	850.0	400.0
Belgium-Luxembourg Belgique-Luxembourg										
Nitrogenous fertilizers *										
Engrais azotés *	678.0	725.0	760.0	709.0	688.0	190.5	186.0	182.0	173.0	169.0
Phosphate fertilizers										
Engrais phosphatés	* 332.5	* 362.0	* 340.0	* 340.0	318.0	* 86.5	* 78.0	* 65.0	* 55.0	* 51.0
Potash fertilizers *										
Engrais potassiques *	...	...	...	...	...	131.0	120.0	115.0	103.5	100.0
Bosnia & Herzegovina Bosnie-Herzégovine										
Nitrogenous fertilizers *										
Engrais azotés *	...	...	...	10.0	...	...	...	...	10.0	...
Bulgaria Bulgarie										
Nitrogenous fertilizers										
Engrais azotés	926.0	911.1	760.4	681.5	649.0	* 495.0	* 450.0	377.3	189.2	180.4
Phosphate fertilizers										
Engrais phosphatés	168.8	46.6	36.9	37.1	44.6	220.3	132.6	61.1	26.4	41.1
Potash fertilizers										
Engrais potassiques	...	...	...	...	...	91.6	97.0	33.2	21.4	* 10.0
Croatia Croatie										
Nitrogenous fertilizers										
Engrais azotés	...	...	...	* 280.0	* 270.0	...	...	...	133.5	147.6

40

Fertilizers
Nitrogenous, phosphate and potash: thousand metric tons [cont.]
Engrais
Azotés, phosphatés et potassiques : milliers de tonnes métriques [suite]

Country or area Pays ou zone	Production Production					Consumption Consommation				
	1989/90	1990/91	1991/92	1992/93	1993/94	1989/90	1990/91	1991/92	1992/93	1993/94
Phosphate fertilizers * Engrais phosphatés *	...	...	...	118.8	79.9	...	...	...	50.0	37.0
Potash fertilizers * Engrais potassiques *	...	...	...	...	...	...	...	...	56.0	41.0
former Czechoslovakia† anc. Tchécoslovaquie†										
Nitrogenous fertilizers Engrais azotés	* 675.0	* 604.0	* 450.6	* 423.0	...	704.8	* 588.3	* 289.0	* 300.0	...
Phosphate fertilizers Engrais phosphatés	* 320.0	311.3	* 47.1	* 44.5	...	* 437.0	* 359.0	* 75.0	* 76.6	...
Potash fertilizers Engrais potassiques	...	...	...	...	...	460.6	* 355.9	* 65.0	* 63.6	...
Czech Republic République tchèque										
Nitrogenous fertilizers Engrais azotés	...	...	...	...	186.0	...	...	...	...	220.1
Phosphate fertilizers Engrais phosphatés	...	...	...	...	27.7	...	...	...	...	* 46.5
Denmark Danemark										
Nitrogenous fertilizers * Engrais azotés *	200.4	184.9	138.0	120.0	120.0	400.4	394.9	369.5	332.9	326.0
Phosphate fertilizers * Engrais phosphatés *	136.2	81.1	75.0	65.0	60.0	94.8	88.6	76.0	64.0	54.0
Potash fertilizers * Engrais potassiques *	...	...	...	...	...	155.4	149.7	134.7	109.5	105.0
Estonia Estonie										
Nitrogenous fertilizers * Engrais azotés *	...	...	...	42.0	16.0	...	...	...	39.0	30.0
Phosphate fertilizers Engrais phosphatés	...	...	...	* 22.4	* 0.9	...	...	...	25.7	12.0
Potash fertilizers * Engrais potassiques *	...	...	...	...	...	...	...	...	48.0	23.0
Finland Finlande										
Nitrogenous fertilizers Engrais azotés	* 277.6	* 268.0	* 254.0	* 228.0	* 231.0	231.5	206.8	166.5	174.0	171.0
Phosphate fertilizers Engrais phosphatés	* 183.3	* 171.9	* 162.3	* 139.0	* 130.0	143.1	117.2	* 76.0	82.0	* 82.0
Potash fertilizers Engrais potassiques	...	...	...	...	...	140.9	119.1	88.9	90.0	* 88.0
France France										
Nitrogenous fertilizers Engrais azotés	1 572.0	1 524.0	1 636.0	1 344.0	1 524.0	2 660.0	2 492.0	2 569.0	2 154.0	2 222.0
Phosphate fertilizers Engrais phosphatés	1 025.0	916.0	926.0	726.0	697.0	1 494.0	1 349.0	1 253.0	1 029.0	1 014.0
Potash fertilizers Engrais potassiques	* 1 199.4	* 1 292.4	* 1 129.0	* 1 141.0	* 890.0	1 949.0	1 842.0	1 741.0	1 348.0	1 375.0
Germany† Allemagne†										
Nitrogenous fertilizers Engrais azotés	2 133.8	* 1 165.0	* 1 095.0	* 1 327.0	* 1 267.0	2 253.5	* 1 788.0	* 1 720.0	* 1 680.0	* 1 612.0
Phosphate fertilizers Engrais phosphatés	* 594.7	* 294.0	* 212.0	* 187.0	165.0	* 950.7	* 609.0	* 519.0	* 490.0	415.0
Potash fertilizers Engrais potassiques	* 5 491.2	* 4 462.0	* 3 902.0	* 3 525.0	* 2 860.0	* 1 387.1	* 875.0	* 729.0	673.0	* 645.0
Greece Grèce										
Nitrogenous fertilizers Engrais azotés	* 407.0	396.2	379.9	* 342.0	* 312.0	425.7	426.6	408.3	* 393.0	* 337.0
Phosphate fertilizers Engrais phosphatés	* 198.0	* 198.6	* 191.8	* 168.0	* 122.0	188.8	187.3	* 176.0	* 178.0	* 133.0
Potash fertilizers Engrais potassiques	...	...	...	...	...	73.2	71.3	67.2	53.0	* 48.0

40

Fertilizers
Nitrogenous, phosphate and potash: thousand metric tons [*cont.*]
Engrais
Azotés, phosphatés et potassiques : milliers de tonnes métriques [*suite*]

Country or area Pays ou zone	Production Production 1989/90	1990/91	1991/92	1992/93	1993/94	Consumption Consommation 1989/90	1990/91	1991/92	1992/93	1993/94
Hungary Hongrie										
Nitrogenous fertilizers										
Engrais azotés	591.2	421.5	224.5	188.0	167.3	583.0	358.0	159.5	144.4	152.1
Phosphate fertilizers										
Engrais phosphatés	220.0	* 109.0	51.0	5.4	5.9	266.0	127.0	24.2	14.3	11.8
Potash fertilizers										
Engrais potassiques	...	...	...	...	...	372.0	186.0	37.4	* 20.0	* 33.0
Iceland Islande										
Nitrogenous fertilizers										
Engrais azotés	10.3	10.1	13.0	10.7	* 9.6	10.4	11.8	12.1	14.0	* 12.8
Phosphate fertilizers										
Engrais phosphatés	...	...	...	...	...	5.2	5.8	6.1	5.3	* 4.0
Potash fertilizers										
Engrais potassiques	...	...	...	...	...	4.6	4.8	4.5	3.9	* 4.0
Ireland Irlande										
Nitrogenous fertilizers										
Engrais azotés	* 296.7	* 279.0	* 250.0	* 307.0	* 335.0	* 378.5	* 370.0	358.0	* 353.0	* 401.0
Phosphate fertilizers										
Engrais phosphatés	...	...	...	...	...	* 145.5	* 138.5	136.2	* 137.0	* 136.0
Potash fertilizers										
Engrais potassiques	...	...	...	...	...	* 182.3	* 183.8	178.1	175.0	* 173.0
Italy Italie										
Nitrogenous fertilizers										
Engrais azotés	1 168.6	862.0	916.9	986.0	654.0	827.3	879.0	906.7	906.0	* 873.0
Phosphate fertilizers										
Engrais phosphatés	266.0	426.7	389.0	331.0	251.9	607.9	644.6	662.8	613.0	535.6
Potash fertilizers										
Engrais potassiques	130.5	6.0	126.1	13.1	...	377.7	424.3	416.4	397.0	341.6
Latvia Lettonie										
Nitrogenous fertilizers *										
Engrais azotés *	...	...	...	18.0	...	...	...	...	63.0	40.0
Phosphate fertilizers *										
Engrais phosphatés *	...	...	...	60.0	...	...	...	...	45.0	2.3
Potash fertilizers *										
Engrais potassiques *	...	...	...	...	...	...	...	...	60.0	53.0
Lithuania Lituanie										
Nitrogenous fertilizers *										
Engrais azotés *	...	...	...	207.0	177.0	...	...	...	88.0	30.0
Phosphate fertilizers *										
Engrais phosphatés *	...	...	...	50.0	39.0	...	...	...	18.0	10.0
Potash fertilizers *										
Engrais potassiques *	...	...	...	...	...	...	...	...	50.0	40.0
Malta Malte										
Nitrogenous fertilizers										
Engrais azotés	...	...	...	...	...	0.4	* 0.7	* 0.7	* 1.2	* 1.0
Phosphate fertilizers										
Engrais phosphatés	...	...	...	...	...	0.0	0.0	...	...	...
Potash fertilizers										
Engrais potassiques	...	...	...	...	...	0.0	0.0	...	...	...
Netherlands Pays-Bas										
Nitrogenous fertilizers										
Engrais azotés	1 847.9	* 1 875.0	1 820.9	1 817.1	* 1 574.0	412.4	* 390.0	* 391.8	389.9	* 374.0
Phosphate fertilizers										
Engrais phosphatés	* 378.4	* 365.0	* 345.0	* 287.0	* 256.0	76.1	* 74.0	* 75.0	* 70.0	* 67.0
Potash fertilizers										
Engrais potassiques	...	...	...	...	...	98.3	* 94.6	* 94.0	* 81.8	* 82.0

40

Fertilizers

Nitrogenous, phosphate and potash: thousand metric tons [cont.]

Engrais

Azotés, phosphatés et potassiques : milliers de tonnes métriques [suite]

Country or area Pays ou zone	Production Production					Consumption Consommation				
	1989/90	1990/91	1991/92	1992/93	1993/94	1989/90	1990/91	1991/92	1992/93	1993/94
Norway Norvège										
Nitrogenous fertilizers										
Engrais azotés	* 494.0	517.4	* 512.0	431.0	* 432.0	* 110.4	* 110.8	110.9	109.3	* 108.0
Phosphate fertilizers										
Engrais phosphatés	229.9	228.7	211.9	211.0	* 225.0	* 36.6	* 34.8	33.9	31.4	* 32.0
Potash fertilizers										
Engrais potassiques	...	...	...	...	...	* 65.5	55.0	62.9	60.2	* 64.0
Poland Pologne										
Nitrogenous fertilizers										
Engrais azotés	1 642.6	1 303.0	1 104.7	1 081.4	1 143.1	* 1 478.6	735.2	619.0	683.3	* 757.7
Phosphate fertilizers										
Engrais phosphatés	946.0	467.0	252.4	329.0	* 281.0	751.8	410.6	222.5	* 232.3	* 243.0
Potash fertilizers										
Engrais potassiques	...	...	...	...	...	1 003.1	606.7	293.4	276.9	* 281.0
Portugal Portugal										
Nitrogenous fertilizers *										
Engrais azotés *	133.0	126.0	116.0	122.0	108.0	145.4	150.1	135.0	127.0	130.0
Phosphate fertilizers *										
Engrais phosphatés *	76.7	63.3	39.0	37.0	30.0	81.1	80.3	75.4	77.0	72.0
Potash fertilizers *										
Engrais potassiques *	...	...	...	...	...	47.5	48.0	40.7	36.0	35.0
Republic of Moldova République de Moldova										
Nitrogenous fertilizers *										
Engrais azotés *	...	...	...	...	...	...	...	...	64.7	60.0
Phosphate fertilizers *										
Engrais phosphatés *	...	...	...	...	...	...	...	...	46.1	40.0
Potash fertilizers *										
Engrais potassiques *	...	...	...	...	...	...	...	...	24.0	15.0
Romania Roumanie										
Nitrogenous fertilizers										
Engrais azotés	2 035.4	* 1 249.1	* 823.0	1 084.4	* 1 008.8	778.2	* 656.1	* 274.0	481.5	238.3
Phosphate fertilizers										
Engrais phosphatés	647.7	* 387.3	* 228.0	* 260.1	* 246.4	360.0	* 313.1	* 145.0	193.4	131.4
Potash fertilizers										
Engrais potassiques	...	...	...	...	...	240.0	* 133.9	* 43.0	27.3	15.8
Russian Federation Fédération de Russie										
Nitrogenous fertilizers *										
Engrais azotés *	...	...	...	5 708.0	5 000.0	...	...	...	2 622.0	2 051.0
Phosphate fertilizers *										
Engrais phosphatés *	...	...	...	3 000.0	2 500.0	...	...	...	1 300.0	900.0
Potash fertilizers *										
Engrais potassiques *	...	...	...	3 454.0	2 597.0	...	...	...	1 348.0	900.0
Slovakia Slovaquie										
Nitrogenous fertilizers										
Engrais azotés	...	...	...	...	175.0	...	...	...	...	64.9
Phosphate fertilizers										
Engrais phosphatés	...	...	...	...	...	...	...	...	...	16.5
Slovenia Slovénie										
Phosphate fertilizers *										
Engrais phosphatés *	...	...	...	...	...	...	...	...	15.0	16.0
Potash fertilizers *										
Engrais potassiques *	...	...	...	...	...	...	...	...	14.0	20.3
Spain Espagne										
Nitrogenous fertilizers										
Engrais azotés	966.7	869.6	862.2	655.5	737.3	1 109.4	1 063.1	998.7	817.6	937.4
Phosphate fertilizers										
Engrais phosphatés	368.2	293.0	270.6	296.3	365.3	559.4	534.2	501.7	423.2	496.5

40
Fertilizers
Nitrogenous, phosphate and potash: thousand metric tons [*cont.*]
Engrais
Azotés, phosphatés et potassiques : milliers de tonnes métriques [*suite*]

Country or area Pays ou zone	Production Production					Consumption Consommation				
	1989/90	1990/91	1991/92	1992/93	1993/94	1989/90	1990/91	1991/92	1992/93	1993/94
Potash fertilizers Engrais potassiques	728.7	642.3	542.6	790.6	890.4	383.3	378.6	381.4	330.4	392.1
Sweden Suède										
Nitrogenous fertilizers Engrais azotés	154.4	176.0	147.5	106.9	110.6	221.5	211.7	* 185.0	210.8	226.1
Phosphate fertilizers Engrais phosphatés	108.0	108.0	79.6	12.9	14.2	69.7	57.8	* 46.0	46.5	53.5
Potash fertilizers Engrais potassiques	...	...	...	...	...	71.4	58.7	* 61.0	50.4	53.6
Switzerland Suisse										
Nitrogenous fertilizers Engrais azotés	30.2	26.7	29.0	24.4	22.0	70.3	63.4	* 63.0	* 64.0	* 63.0
Phosphate fertilizers Engrais phosphatés	2.4	2.5	3.1	2.1	2.8	39.4	38.3	37.0	36.0	* 31.0
Potash fertilizers Engrais potassiques	...	...	...	...	...	67.4	66.2	* 59.0	* 58.0	* 56.0
TFYR Macedonia L'ex-R.y. Macédoine										
Nitrogenous fertilizers * Engrais azotés *	...	...	...	...	...	...	...	...	3.0	3.0
Phosphate fertilizers * Engrais phosphatés *	...	...	...	...	...	...	...	...	3.0	3.0
Potash fertilizers * Engrais potassiques *	...	...	...	...	...	...	...	...	9.0	· 6.0
Ukraine Ukraine										
Nitrogenous fertilizers * Engrais azotés *	...	...	...	2 543.0	2 072.0	...	...	...	1 338.0	841.0
Phosphate fertilizers * Engrais phosphatés *	...	...	...	591.0	324.0	...	...	...	532.0	262.0
Potash fertilizers * Engrais potassiques *	...	...	...	122.0	100.0	...	...	...	822.0	253.0
United Kingdom Royaume-Uni										
Nitrogenous fertilizers * Engrais azotés *	1 070.0	980.0	930.0	751.0	803.0	1 582.0	1 525.0	1 365.0	1 219.0	1 268.0
Phosphate fertilizers Engrais phosphatés	* 172.0	* 128.0	* 90.0	* 102.0	* 81.0	* 428.0	* 380.0	* 371.0	* 360.0	366.0
Potash fertilizers Engrais potassiques	* 488.0	* 493.0	* 494.0	* 530.0	* 555.0	* 525.0	* 465.0	* 441.0	* 420.0	437.0
Yugoslavia Yougoslavie										
Nitrogenous fertilizers Engrais azotés	...	...	...	252.9	174.0	...	...	...	115.0	77.0
Phosphate fertilizers Engrais phosphatés	...	...	...	110.6	36.9	...	...	...	52.0	16.0
Potash fertilizers Engrais potassiques	...	...	...	...	...	...	...	...	46.0	15.0
Yugoslavia, SFR† Yougoslavie, Rfs†										
Nitrogenous fertilizers Engrais azotés	519.8	* 433.6	* 448.2	...	...	443.7	417.3	* 288.3	...	...
Phosphate fertilizers Engrais phosphatés	319.3	253.0	225.0	...	...	231.2	* 199.0	* 139.0	...	...
Potash fertilizers Engrais potassiques	...	...	...	...	...	221.8	* 209.6	* 154.3	...	...
Oceania Océanie										
Nitrogenous fertilizers Engrais azotés	289.8	278.0	290.0	343.7	340.2	497.6	503.9	543.9	595.2	638.7
Phosphate fertilizers Engrais phosphatés	716.6	437.2	439.7	626.4	608.0	1 050.2	806.0	913.9	1 105.9	1 173.1

40
Fertilizers
Nitrogenous, phosphate and potash: thousand metric tons [*cont.*]
Engrais
Azotés, phosphatés et potassiques : milliers de tonnes métriques [*suite*]

Country or area Pays ou zone	Production Production					Consumption Consommation				
	1989/90	1990/91	1991/92	1992/93	1993/94	1989/90	1990/91	1991/92	1992/93	1993/94
Potash fertilizers Engrais potassiques	...	...	...	...	...	262.1	254.2	245.1	279.9	293.4
Australia Australie Nitrogenous fertilizers										
Engrais azotés	* 230.0	215.0	233.0	280.0	261.0	* 440.3	* 439.4	* 462.3	* 488.0	* 518.0
Phosphate fertilizers Engrais phosphatés	* 511.0	* 269.6	229.0	322.0	* 300.0	* 790.5	* 578.9	* 640.0	* 782.0	* 810.0
Potash fertilizers * Engrais potassiques *	...	...	...	...	...	162.6	145.4	142.1	150.0	160.0
Fiji Fidji Nitrogenous fertilizers *										
Engrais azotés *	...	...	...	...	...	13.2	12.0	10.0	8.5	9.0
Phosphate fertilizers Engrais phosphatés	...	...	...	...	...	2.7	* 3.0	* 2.0	* 2.5	* 2.7
Potash fertilizers Engrais potassiques	...	...	...	...	...	7.2	* 8.0	* 2.0	* 2.1	* 2.9
French Polynesia Polynésie française Nitrogenous fertilizers *										
Engrais azotés *	...	...	...	...	...	0.3	0.3	0.3	0.4	0.4
Phosphate fertilizers * Engrais phosphatés *	...	...	...	...	...	0.3	0.3	0.3	0.4	0.4
Potash fertilizers * Engrais potassiques *	...	...	...	...	...	0.3	0.3	0.2	0.2	0.2
New Caledonia Nouvelle-Calédonie Nitrogenous fertilizers *										
Engrais azotés *	...	...	...	...	...	0.5	1.0	0.4	0.3	0.3
Phosphate fertilizers * Engrais phosphatés *	...	...	...	...	...	0.5	0.5	0.5	0.5	1.0
Potash fertilizers * Engrais potassiques *	...	...	...	...	...	0.2	0.3	0.3	0.3	0.3
New Zealand Nouvelle-Zélande Nitrogenous fertilizers										
Engrais azotés	* 59.8	* 63.0	* 57.0	63.7	79.2	* 37.0	* 45.8	* 64.4	* 90.0	* 103.0
Phosphate fertilizers Engrais phosphatés	* 205.6	* 167.6	* 210.7	304.4	308.0	253.2	220.3	* 268.9	* 318.0	* 356.0
Potash fertilizers Engrais potassiques	...	...	...	...	...	85.7	96.3	* 98.5	* 125.0	* 128.0
Papua New Guinea Papouasie-Nvl-Guinée Nitrogenous fertilizers *										
Engrais azotés *	...	...	...	...	...	6.3	5.4	6.5	8.0	8.0
Phosphate fertilizers * Engrais phosphatés *	...	...	...	...	...	3.0	3.0	2.2	2.5	3.0
Potash fertilizers * Engrais potassiques *	...	...	...	...	...	6.2	3.9	2.0	2.3	2.0
former USSR† ancienne URSS† Nitrogenous fertilizers										
Engrais azotés	14 272.0	13 084.4	* 12 004.2	...	...	9 918.0	8 668.7	* 7 778.0	...	...
Phosphate fertilizers Engrais phosphatés	9 015.0	8 866.9	* 7 685.6	...	...	8 175.0	7 830.0	* 6 594.6	...	...
Potash fertilizers Engrais potassiques	10 232.6	9 035.2	* 8 531.0	...	...	6 381.0	5 145.2	* 5 090.8	...	...

Source:
Food and Agriculture Organization of the United Nations (Rome).

Source:
Organisation des Nations Unies pour l'alimentation et l'agriculture (Rome).

40
Fertilizers
Nitrogenous, phosphate and potash: thousand metric tons [*cont.*]
Engrais
Azotés, phosphatés et potassiques : milliers de tonnes métriques [*suite*]

† For detailed descriptions of data pertaining to former Czechoslovakia, Germany, SFR Yugoslavia and former USSR, see Annex I - Country or area nomenclature, regional and other groupings.

1 FAO estimate.

† Pour les descriptions en détails des données relatives à l'ancienne Tchécoslovaquie, l'Allemagne, la Rfs Yougoslavie et l'ancienne URSS, voir l'Annexe I - Nomenclature des pays ou zones, groupements régionaux et autres groupements.

1 Estimation de la FAO.

Technical notes, tables 34-40

The series shown on agriculture and fishing have been furnished by the Food and Agriculture Organization of the United Nations (FAO). They refer to the following three topics:

(a)   Long-term trends in growth of agricultural output and food supply;

(b)   Output of principal agricultural commodities and in a few cases consumption;

(c)   Basic means of production.

Agricultural output is defined to include all crop and livestock products except those used for seed and fodder and other intermediate uses in agriculture; for example deductions are made for eggs used for hatching. Intermediate input of seeds and fodder and similar items refer to both domestically produced and imported commodities.

Detailed data and technical notes are published by FAO in its yearbooks.[5, 8]

The index-numbers of agricultural output and food production are calculated by the Laspeyres formula with the base year period 1979-1981. The latter is provided in order to diminish the impact of annual fluctuations in agricultural output during base years on the indices for the period. Production quantities of each commodity are weighted by 1979-1981 average national producer prices and summed for each year. The index numbers are based on production data for a calendar year. These may differ in some instances from those actually produced and published by the individual countries themselves due to variations in concepts, coverage, weights and methods of calculation. Efforts have been made to estimate these methodological differences to achieve a better international comparability of data. The series include a large amount of estimates made by FAO in cases where no official or semi-official figures are available from the countries.

In *table 34*, The "Agriculture" relates to the production of all crops and livestock products. The "Food Index" includes those commodities which are considered edible and contain nutrients.

In *table 35*, Cereals, production data relate to crops harvested for grain only. Cereals harvested for hay, green feed or used for grazing are excluded.

Table 36: Oil crops, or oil-bearing crops, are those crops yielding seeds, nuts or fruits which are used mainly for the extraction of culinary or industrial oils, excluding essential oils. In this table, data for oil crops represent the total production of oil seeds, oil nuts and oil fruits harvested in the year indicated and expressed in terms of oil equivalent and cake/meal equivalent. That is to say, these figures do not relate to the actual production of vegetable oils and cake/meal, but to the potential

Notes techniques, tableaux 34-40

Les séries présentées sur l'agriculture et la pêche ont été fournies par l'Organisation des Nations Unies pour l'alimentation et l'agriculture (FAO). Elles portent sur les trois aspects suivants :

(a)   Les tendances à long terme de la croissance de la production agricole et des approvisionnements alimentaires;

(b)   La production des principales denrées agricoles et, dans certains cas, la consommation;

(c)   Les moyens essentiels de production.

La production agricole se définit comme comprenant l'ensemble des produits agricoles et des produits de l'élevage à l'exception de ceux utilisés comme semences et comme aliments pour les animaux, et pour les autres utilisations intermédiaires en agriculture; par exemple, on déduit les oeufs utilisés pour la reproduction. L'apport intermédiaire de semences et d'aliments pour les animaux et d'autres éléments similaires se rapportent à la fois à des produits locaux et importés.

Des données détaillées et des notes techniques sont publiées par la FAO dans ses annuaires [5, 8].

Les indices de la production agricole et de la production alimentaire sont calculés selon la formule de Laspeyres avec les années 1979-1981 pour période de base. Le choix d'une période de plusieurs années permet de diminuer l'incidence des fluctuations annuelles de la production agricole pendant les années de base sur les indices pour cette période. Les quantités produites de chaque denrée sont pondérées par les prix nationaux moyens à la production de 1979-1981, et additionnées pour chaque année. Les indices sont fondés sur les données de production d'une année civile. Ils peuvent différer dans certains cas des indices effectivement établis et publiés par les pays eux-mêmes par suite de différences dans les concepts, la couverture, les pondérations et les méthodes de calcul. On s'est efforcé d'estimer ces différences méthodologiques afin de rendre les données plus facilement comparables à l'échelle internationale. Les séries comprennent une grande quantité d'estimations faites par la FAO dans les cas où les pays n'avaient pas fourni de chiffres officiels ou semi-officiels.

Au *Tableau 34*, l'"Agriculture" se rapporte à la production de tous les produits de l'agriculture et de l'élevage. L'"Indice des produits alimentaires" comprend les produits considérés comme comestibles et qui contiennent des éléments nutritifs.

Au *Tableau 35*, Céréales : les données sur la production se rapportent uniquement aux céréales récoltées pour le grain; celles cultivées pour le foin, le fourrage vert ou le pâturage en sont exclues.

Tableau 36 : On désigne sous le nom de cultures oléagineuses l'ensemble des cultures produisant des graines, des noix ou des fruits, essentiellement destinées à l'extraction

production if the total amounts produced from all oil crops were processed into oil and cake/meal in producing countries in the same year in which they were harvested. Naturally, the total production of oil crops is never processed into oil in its entirety, since depending on the crop, important quantities are also used for seed, feed and food. However, although oil and cake/meal extraction rates vary from country to country, in this table the same extraction rate for each crop has been applied for all countries. Moreover. it should be borne in mind that the crops harvested during the latter months of the year are generally processed into oil during the following year. In spite of these deficiencies in coverage, extraction rates and time reference the data reported here are useful as they provide a valid indication of year-to-year changes in the size of total oil-crop production. The actual production of vegetable oils in the world is about 80 percent of the production reported here. In addition, about two million tonnes of vegetable oils are produced every year from crops which are not included among those defined above. The most important of these oils are maize-germ oil and rice-bran oil. The actual world production of cake/meal derived from oil crops is also about 80 percent of the production reported in the table.

In *table 37*, Livestock, data refer to livestock numbers grouped into twelve-month periods ending 30 September of the year stated and cover all animals irrespective of their age and place or purpose of their breeding.

In *table 39*, the data cover as far as possible both sea and inland fisheries and are expressed in terms of live weight. They generally include crustaceans and molluscs but exclude seaweed and aquatic mammals such as whales and dolphins. Data include landings by domestic craft in foreign ports and exclude the landings by foreign craft in domestic ports. The flag of the vessel is considered as the paramount indication of the nationality of the catch.

In *table 40*, data generally refer to the fertilizer year 1 July-30 June.

Nitrogenous fertilizers: data refer to the nitrogen content of commercial inorganic fertilizers.

Phosphate fertilizers: data refer to commercial phosphoric acid (P_2O_5) and cover the P_2O_5 of superphosphates, ammonium phosphate and basic slag.

Potash fertilizers: data refer to K_2O content of commercial potash, muriate, nitrate and sulphate of potash, manure salts, kainit and nitrate of soda potash.

d'huiles alimentaires ou industrielles, à l'exclusion des huiles essentielles. Dans ce tableau, les chiffres se rapportent à la production totale de graines, noix et fruits oléagineux récoltés au cours de l'année de référence et sont exprimés en équivalent d'huile et en équivalent de tourteau/farine. En d'autres termes, ces chiffres ne se rapportent pas à la production effective mais à la production potentielle d'huiles végétales et de tourteau/farine dans l'hypothèse où les volumes totaux de produits provenant de toutes les cultures d'oléagineux seraient transformés en huile et en tourteau/farine dans les pays producteurs l'année même où ils ont été récoltés. Bien entendu, la production totale d'oléagineux n'est jamais transformée intégralement en huile, car des quantités importantes qui varient suivant les cultures sont également utilisées pour les semailles, l'alimentation animale et l'alimentation humaine. Toutefois, bien que les taux d'extraction d'huile et de tourteau/farine varient selon les pays, on a appliqué dans ce tableau le même taux à tous les pays pour chaque oléagineux. En outre, il ne faut pas oublier que les produits récoltés au cours des derniers mois de l'année sont généralement transformés en huile dans le courant de l'année suivante.

En dépit de ces imperfections qui concernent le champ d'application, les taux d'extraction et les périodes de référence, les chiffres présentés ici sont utiles, car ils donnent une indication valable des variations de volume que la production totale d'oléagineux enregistre d'une année à l'autre. La production mondiale effective d'huiles végétales atteint 80 pour cent environ de la production indiquée ici. En outre, environ 2 millions de tonnes d'huiles végétales sont produites chaque année à partir de cultures non comprises dans les catégories définies ci-dessus. Les principales sont l'huile de germs de maïs et l'huile de son de riz. La production mondiale effective tourteau/farine d'oléagineux représente environ 80 pour cent de production indiquée dans le tableau.

Au *Tableau 37*, Elevage : les statistiques sur les effectifs du cheptel sont groupées en périodes de 12 mois se terminant le 30 septembre de l'année indiquée et s'entendent de tous les animaux, quels que soient leur âge et l'emplacement ou le but de leur élevage.

Au *Tableau 39*, les données englobent autant que possible la pêche maritime et intérieure, et sont exprimées en poids vif. Elles comprennent, en général, crustacés et mollusques, mais excluent les plantes marines et les mammifères aquatiques (baleines, dauphins, etc.). Les données comprennent les quantités débarquées par des bateaux nationaux dans des ports étrangers et excluent les quantités débarquées par des bateaux étrangers dans des ports nationaux. Le pavillon du navire est considéré comme la principale indication de la nationalité de la prise.

Au *Tableau 40,* Engrais : les données se rapportent en général à une période d'un an comptée du 1er juillet au 30 juin.

Engrais azotés : les données se rapportent à la teneur en azote des engrais commerciaux inorganiques.

Engrais phosphatés : les données se rapportent à l'acide phosphorique (P_2O_5) et englobent la teneur en (P_2O_5) des superphosphates, du phosphate d'ammonium et des scories de déphosphoration.

Engrais potassiques: les données se rapportent à la teneur en K_2O des produits potassiques commerciaux, muriate, nitrate et sulfate de potasse, sels d'engrais, kainite et nitrate de soude potassique.

41
Sugar
Sucre

Production and consumption: thousand metric tons; consumption per capita: kilograms
Production et consommationa : milliers de tonnes métriques ; consommation par habitant : kilogrammes

Country or area Pays ou zone	1985	1986	1987	1988	1989	1990	1991	1992	1993	1994
World Monde										
Production	98 365	100 018	103 528	104 591	107 184	110 894	112 100	117 565	112 378	110 289
Consumption	97 859	101 251	105 657	105 863	107 296	108 417	108 865	112 804	111 755	113 798
Consumption per cap.(kg)	20	21	21	21	21	21	20	21	20	20
Africa · Afrique										
Algeria Algérie										
Production *	0	0	0	0	0	0	0	0	0	0
Consumption *	600	585	630	675	710	810	850	880	850	825
Consumption per cap.(kg)	28	26	27	29	29	32	33	33	31	30
Angola Angola										
Production *	50	50	30	30	25	25	30	25	20	20
Consumption *	100	100	77	75	90	95	100	110	110	95
Consumption per cap.(kg)	11	11	8	8	9	10	11	10	11	9
Benin Bénin										
Production *	5	5	5	5	7	5	5	4	5	4
Consumption *	30	30	20	20	15	15	20	25	30	35
Consumption per cap.(kg)	8	7	5	5	3	3	4	5	6	7
Botswana Botswana										
Consumption	37	37	40	45	45	50	55	50	45	45
Consumption per cap.(kg)	34	33	34	37	36	38	41	37	31	30
Burkina Faso Burkina Faso										
Production *	10	10	25	25	20	30	26	27	25	28
Consumption *	35	35	30	30	40	35	30	30	30	31
Consumption per cap.(kg)	5	5	4	4	5	4	3	3	3	3
Burundi Burundi										
Production	0	0	0	3	9	8	14	10	10	12
Consumption	7	12	15	14	15	17	11	15	17	20
Consumption per cap.(kg)	2	2	3	3	3	3	2	3	3	3
Cameroon Cameroun										
Production	* 50	* 40	* 28	67	* 35	* 75	* 70	* 70	* 65	* 65
Consumption	* 60	* 45	* 40	63	* 40	* 75	* 80	* 80	* 80	* 83
Consumption per cap.(kg)	6	4	4	6	4	7	7	7	6	6
Cape Verde Cap−Vert										
Consumption *	9	10	15	13	12	11	13	14	16	15
Consumption per cap.(kg)	27	30	43	39	36	32	37	39	43	39
Central African Rep. Rép. centrafricaine										
Consumption *	7	10	5	4	3	3	3	3	4	4
Consumption per cap.(kg)	3	4	2	1	1	1	1	1	1	1
Chad Tchad										
Production	* 8	* 10	* 20	* 20	* 25	* 25	* 30	* 30	32	* 32
Consumption *	30	18	20	20	30	50	40	40	40	43
Consumption per cap.(kg)	6	4	4	4	5	9	7	7	6	7
Comoros Comores										
Consumption	3	3	3	3	3	3	4	4	4	3
Consumption per cap.(kg)	7	6	6	6	6	6	7	7	7	5
Congo Congo										
Production	* 25	* 32	* 35	* 40	* 35	* 35	21	30	26	* 29
Consumption	* 20	* 20	* 20	* 20	* 25	* 20	* 17	18	16	* 17
Consumption per cap.(kg)	12	10	10	10	12	9	7	8	7	7
Côte d'Ivoire Côte d'Ivoire										
Production	* 125	* 120	* 165	* 165	* 160	* 160	* 155	* 160	* 155	141
Consumption	* 125	* 125	* 130	* 155	* 155	* 160	* 160	* 165	* 165	126
Consumption per cap.(kg)	13	12	12	14	13	13	13	13	12	9
Djibouti Djibouti										
Consumption	8	9	9	10	10	10	9	12	10	11
Consumption per cap.(kg)	19	20	23	21	20	19	17	22	18	19
Egypt Egypte										
Production *	900	950	1 000	1 035	947	955	1 060	1 060	1 090	1 190
Consumption *	1 600	1 650	1 650	1 775	1 650	1 725	1 745	1 750	1 675	1 700
Consumption per cap.(kg)	33	35	34	35	32	33	32	32	30	29
Ethiopia Ethiopie										
Production	191	193	* 195	169	183	* 184	* 161	165	* 185	95
Consumption	144	159	* 160	139	162	* 160	* 160	* 160	* 160	* 145
Consumption per cap.(kg)	3	4	4	3	3	3	3	3	3	3

41

Sugar
Production and consumption: thousand metric tons; consumption per capita: kilograms [cont.]
Sucre
Production et consommation : milliers de tonnes métriques ; consommation par habitant : kilogrammes [suite]

Country or area Pays ou zone	1985	1986	1987	1988	1989	1990	1991	1992	1993	1994
Gabon Gabon										
Production	* 12	18	* 19	* 20	* 15	* 20	* 22	* 25	* 20	* 19
Consumption *	18	16	16	17	17	18	18	18	19	19
Consumption per cap.(kg)	16	15	15	15	15	15	14	15	15	15
Gambia Gambie										
Consumption *	30	30	30	33	33	33	35	35	35	35
Consumption per cap.(kg)	47	46	38	40	37	35	37	40	34	32
Ghana Ghana										
Consumption *	30	55	65	80	80	90	95	105	120	123
Consumption per cap.(kg)	2	4	5	6	6	6	6	7	7	7
Guinea Guinée										
Production *	5	5	10	10	20	20	18	18	10	10
Consumption *	35	50	55	40	50	50	55	60	65	65
Consumption per cap.(kg)	6	10	11	8	9	9	9	10	10	10
Guinea−Bissau Guinée−Bissau										
Consumption	3	3	3	4	4	3	3	3	2	3
Consumption per cap.(kg)	3	3	3	4	4	3	3	3	2	3
Kenya Kenya										
Production	* 260	* 200	449	447	480	496	471	404	414	329
Consumption	* 420	* 420	436	502	532	585	537	600	609	620
Consumption per cap.(kg)	21	20	20	21	21	22	21	22	22	21
Liberia Libéria										
Production	3	3	3	3	3	1	1	1	1	1
Consumption	10	15	15	17	15	11	6	6	6	8
Consumption per cap.(kg)	5	7	7	7	6	5	2	2	2	3
Libyan Arab Jamah. Jamah. arabe libyenne										
Consumption *	150	190	175	160	150	155	160	160	160	160
Consumption per cap.(kg)	42	48	43	38	34	37	37	36	34	33
Madagascar Madagascar										
Production	99	98	107	122	120	118	96	97	104	83
Consumption	84	81	82	79	76	87	87	88	85	90
Consumption per cap.(kg)	8	8	8	7	7	8	8	7	7	7
Malawi Malawi										
Production	154	168	181	187	173	204	210	209	137	213
Consumption	62	73	89	108	107	124	130	152	162	149
Consumption per cap.(kg)	8	10	12	13	13	15	14	17	18	15
Mali Mali										
Production	21	21	17	21	22	* 25	* 30	* 25	* 25	* 25
Consumption	* 44	47	* 55	* 50	* 70	* 75	* 80	* 80	* 80	* 85
Consumption per cap.(kg)	5	6	7	6	8	9	8	8	8	8
Mauritania Mauritanie										
Consumption *	25	40	70	65	70	55	60	60	55	65
Consumption per cap.(kg)	13	22	38	34	36	27	29	28	26	29
Mauritius Maurice										
Production	684	748	733	672	602	661	648	681	604	530
Consumption	39	40	40	41	40	41	42	41	39	39
Consumption per cap.(kg)	38	41	38	37	37	38	40	38	36	36
Morocco Maroc										
Production	433	352	* 450	590	469	* 520	518	509	520	454
Consumption	707	725	* 700	756	740	* 775	778	810	830	854
Consumption per cap.(kg)	32	33	30	32	31	32	31	32	33	32
Mozambique Mozambique										
Production	* 60	* 40	* 25	* 40	* 25	* 32	* 25	* 30	* 20	* 20
Consumption *	90	90	60	45	50	45	45	50	70	73
Consumption per cap.(kg)	6	6	4	3	3	3	3	3	5	4
Niger Niger										
Consumption *	30	30	30	25	20	25	25	23	25	25
Consumption per cap.(kg)	5	4	4	3	3	3	3	3	3	3
Nigeria Nigéria										
Production *	50	45	40	31	55	55	60	50	50	55
Consumption *	600	625	625	425	370	415	480	600	625	600
Consumption per cap.(kg)	6	6	6	4	4	4	5	6	6	6
Réunion Réunion										
Production	228	244	226	252	171	192	215	227	183	...

41

Sugar
Production and consumption: thousand metric tons; consumption per capita: kilograms [*cont.*]
Sucre
Production et consommation : milliers de tonnes métriques ; consommation par habitant : kilogrammes [*suite*]

Country or area Pays ou zone	1985	1986	1987	1988	1989	1990	1991	1992	1993	1994
Rwanda Rwanda										
Production	2	2	4	5	3	3	4	4	4	3
Consumption	17	19	12	12	10	10	11	12	12	7
Consumption per cap.(kg)	3	3	2	2	2	1	2	2	2	1
Senegal Sénégal										
Production	* 65	73	* 71	* 72	* 70	* 80	* 85	* 90	* 90	* 95
Consumption	* 75	71	* 80	* 85	* 90	* 98	* 115	* 128	* 135	* 145
Consumption per cap.(kg)	12	11	12	12	12	13	15	16	17	17
Sierra Leone Sierra Leone										
Production	* 5	* 5	* 6	* 5	* 5	* 5	* 5	* 3	* 4	* 4
Consumption *	18	16	17	17	16	18	18	19	19	20
Consumption per cap.(kg)	5	4	5	5	4	5	4	5	4	4
Somalia Somalie										
Production *	54	30	35	40	47	35	30	20	20	25
Consumption *	90	90	80	60	50	40	37	43	47	70
Consumption per cap.(kg)	19	11	10	7	6	5	4	5	5	8
South Africa Afrique du Sud										
Production	2 540[2]	2 248	2 235	2 470	2 293	2 226	2 462	1 715	1 282	1 777
Consumption	1 368	1 381	1 433	1 417	1 390	1 433	1 382	1 327	1 303	1 480
Consumption per cap.(kg)	43	40	41	39	38	38	38	34	33	37
Sudan Soudan										
Production *	450	550	485	415	405	445	490	515	485	510
Consumption *	470	550	500	470	450	455	475	480	500	515
Consumption per cap.(kg)	22	25	26	19	18	18	19	18	18	18
Swaziland Swaziland										
Production	396	537	461	464	504	527	517	495	458	474
Consumption	22	* 24	* 35	* 41	* 49	* 47	* 52	* 73	* 103	* 141
Consumption per cap.(kg)	35	36	50	58	67	61	68	69	77	172
Togo Togo										
Production	–	0	* 4	* 5	* 5	* 5	* 5	* 5	* 5	* 5
Consumption *	50	50	40	40	35	35	30	30	19	* 28
Consumption per cap.(kg)	17	16	12	12	10	10	8	8	5	7
Tunisia Tunisie										
Production	17	21	27	26	22	25	22	28	25	25
Consumption	212	189	212	202	192	212	215	246	250	258
Consumption per cap.(kg)	30	25	28	26	24	26	26	28	28	30
Uganda Ouganda										
Production *	20	10	20	40	40	25	45	40	50	50
Consumption *	22	30	70	70	70	35	45	46	55	60
Consumption per cap.(kg)	1	2	4	4	4	2	2	2	3	3
United Rep. Tanzania Rép. Unie de Tanzanie										
Production *	105	100	95	80	100	115	115	105	120	130
Consumption *	126	115	100	85	90	100	115	120	120	115
Consumption per cap.(kg)	6	5	4	4	4	4	4	4	4	4
Zaire Zaïre										
Production	* 65	* 55	* 75	* 75	* 90	* 85	* 88	* 90	* 85	* 85
Consumption *	90	95	120	120	110	95	95	100	105	105
Consumption per cap.(kg)	3	3	4	4	3	3	3	3	3	3
Zambia Zambie										
Production	143	127	139	146	143	135	134	155	147	* 150
Consumption	122	105	114	123	114	116	105	111	86	105
Consumption per cap.(kg)	17	16	16	16	15	14	13	13	10	11
Zimbabwe Zimbabwe										
Production	456	507	459	453	502	493	346[3]	9	51	524
Consumption	225	238	253	270	283	297	294	234	229	253
Consumption per cap.(kg)	27	28	29	30	31	32	29	29	22	20
America, North · Amerique du Nord										
Bahamas Bahamas										
Consumption	10	10	12	9	10	11	10	10	10	9
Consumption per cap.(kg)	41	40	48	38	40	42	39	39	37	35
Barbados Barbade										
Production	101	113	84	81	67	70	67	* 55	* 48	* 51
Consumption	14	14	13	14	13	12	11	* 12	* 11	* 13
Consumption per cap.(kg)	54	54	53	57	52	49	42	46	42	48

41

Sugar
Production and consumption: thousand metric tons; consumption per capita: kilograms [*cont.*]
Sucre
Production et consommation : milliers de tonnes métriques ; consommation par habitant : kilogrammes [*suite*]

Country or area Pays ou zone	1985	1986	1987	1988	1989	1990	1991	1992	1993	1994
Belize Belize										
Production	110	105	88	89	94	108	103	108	108	108
Consumption	6	6	7	7	7	9	9	9	11	13
Consumption per cap.(kg)	39	39	39	40	42	46	47	47	54	63
Bermuda Bermudes										
Consumption	2	2	2	4	2	2	2	2	2	2
Consumption per cap.(kg)	37	37	33	67	30	33	33	27	33	24
Canada Canada										
Production *	* 60	* 106	* 147	* 110	* 117	* 140	* 150	* 125	* 124	175
Consumption	* 1 050	* 1 100	1 120	* 1 100	* 1 050	* 1 050	* 1 100	* 1 120	* 1 150	1 175
Consumption per cap.(kg)	41	43	44	42	40	41	41	41	40	40
Costa Rica Costa Rica										
Production	* 230	220	* 230	237	* 220	246	279	301	* 305	* 325
Consumption	* 150	164	* 166	* 170	* 168	178	183	186	* 190	* 193
Consumption per cap.(kg)	60	61	60	59	59	60	60	60	61	61
Cuba Cuba										
Production	7 889	7 467	7 232	8 119	7 579	8 445	7 233	7 219	4 246	4 017
Consumption [4]	887[5]	762	772	746	882	937	956	942	796	664
Consumption per cap.(kg)	65	75	75	72	84	88	89	87	73	61
Dominican Republic Rép. dominicaine										
Production	921	895	816	777	693	590	628	593	621	579
Consumption	304	294	351	223	244	201	251	277	290	295
Consumption per cap.(kg)	49	46	52	32	35	29	35	28	38	38
El Salvador El Salvador										
Production	279	292	262	178	196	* 220	186	233	* 250	* 275
Consumption	159	176	161	173	163	* 165	* 150	116	* 165	* 170
Consumption per cap.(kg)	33	34	32	34	31	32	28	21	30	31
Guadeloupe Guadeloupe										
Production	53[1]	65[1]	63[1]	76[6]	78[6]	26[6]	53[6]	38[6]	63[6]	* 67[6]
Guatemala Guatemala										
Production	583	651	639	720	735	939	1 038	1 165	1 226	1 131
Consumption	279	300	320	332	353	360	348	368	391	416
Consumption per cap.(kg)	35	37	38	38	39	39	37	38	39	40
Haiti Haïti										
Production	* 50	* 40	35	* 30	* 30	* 35	* 25	* 20	* 20	* 15
Consumption *	62	60	55	55	70	85	90	95	85	85
Consumption per cap.(kg)	12	11	10	10	13	15	14	14	12	12
Honduras Honduras										
Production	235	227	* 190	* 180	* 180	* 205	175	* 185	* 190	* 185
Consumption	120	114	* 120	* 150	* 160	* 175	161	* 170	* 175	* 180
Consumption per cap.(kg)	27	29	26	31	32	34	31	31	31	31
Jamaica Jamaïque										
Production	209	199	189	222	205	209	234	228	219	223
Consumption	97	102	108	113	125	114	116	117	123	120
Consumption per cap.(kg)	46	44	47	48	53	48	48	48	50	48
Martinique Martinique										
Production	9[1]	8[6]	8[6]	8[6]	7[6]	6[6]	7[6]	6[6]	7[6]	* 7[6]
Mexico Mexique										
Production	3 492	4 068	4 061	3 909	3 570	3 384	3 744	3 745	* 4 360	* 4 025
Consumption	3 548	3 451	3 657	4 070	4 023	4 424	4 200	4 520	* 4 300	* 4 350
Consumption per cap.(kg)	45	43	45	49	48	55	52	54	47	47
Netherlands Antilles Antilles néerlandaises										
Consumption *	8	9	8	8	9	10	10	10	9	9
Consumption per cap.(kg)	30	32	32	32	36	40	44	44	39	39
Nicaragua Nicaragua										
Production	240	256	199	209	160	212	* 225	* 190	* 185	* 210
Consumption	146	157	151	136	* 150	* 150	* 140	* 135	* 150	* 155
Consumption per cap.(kg)	45	47	43	38	40	39	35	33	35	35
Panama Panama										
Production	160	139	* 100	* 90	* 110	* 90	* 130	* 130	* 120	* 130
Consumption	79	80	* 70	* 80	* 85	* 90	* 90	* 95	* 95	* 98
Consumption per cap.(kg)	36	36	31	35	36	37	36	38	37	38
Saint Kitts and Nevis Saint-Kitts-et-Nevis										
Production	27	28	25	26	25	* 25	20	* 20	* 25	* 30
Consumption	2	2	2	2	2	* 2	2	* 2	* 2	* 2
Consumption per cap.(kg)	43	44	51	50	41	40	40	41	41	43

41

Sugar

Production and consumption: thousand metric tons; consumption per capita: kilograms [*cont.*]

Sucre

Production et consommation : milliers de tonnes métriques ; consommation par habitant : kilogrammes [*suite*]

Country or area Pays ou zone	1985	1986	1987	1988	1989	1990	1991	1992	1993	1994
Trinidad and Tobago Trinité—et—Tobago										
Production	80	95	88	94	100	122	104	114	108	127
Consumption	65	63	71	67	60	63	61	55	59	63
Consumption per cap.(kg)	55	52	58	53	48	49	49	48	47	48
United States Etats—Uni										
Production	5 415	5 685	6 631	6 429	6 206	5 740	6 477	6 805	7 045	6 921
Consumption	7 290	7 036	7 385	7 420	7 561	7 848	7 887	8 098	8 192	8 454
Consumption per cap.(kg)	32	29	30	30	31	32	32	33	33	33
America, South · Amerique du Sud										
Argentina Argentine										
Production	1 188	1 120	1 063	1 283	1 017	1 351	* 1 560	1 379	1 093	1 202
Consumption	974 [7]	1 093	1 104	895	914	1 070	* 1 140	1 174	* 1 200	1 296
Consumption per cap.(kg)	31	35	34	27	28	33	35	36	36	38
Bolivia Bolivie										
Production	* 175	* 180	161	162	* 170	* 225	* 230	* 220	* 220	* 235
Consumption	* 189	* 170	134	* 175	* 170	* 185	* 185	* 190	* 200	* 205
Consumption per cap.(kg)	29	26	20	28	26	28	28	28	28	28
Brazil Brésil										
Production	8 455	7 999	9 266	7 874	* 7 326	* 8 007	9 453	9 925	10 097	12 270
Consumption	6 080	6 589	6 573	6 241	* 7 401	* 6 615	7 276	* 7 349	* 7 575	* 7 874
Consumption per cap.(kg)	45	48	47	45	52	46	50	49	50	51
Chile Chili										
Production	351	481	437	443	445	371	360	525	490	505
Consumption	402	440 [8]	467	466	498	508	518	588	598	615
Consumption per cap.(kg)	34	35	37	36	38	39	39	44	44	46
Colombia Colombie										
Production	1 367	1 272	1 293	1 364	1 523	1 593	1 633	1 813	1 833	1 964
Consumption [9]	1 044	1 101	1 208	1 143	1 163	1 195	1 318	1 262	1 158	1 140
Consumption per cap.(kg)	35	39	42	35	36	36	39	37	33	32
Ecuador Equateur										
Production	* 300	286	341	292	300	334	* 335	387	366	312
Consumption	* 324	353	383	313	327	360	* 375	439	361	* 400
Consumption per cap.(kg)	35	38	40	32	33	35	36	41	33	36
Guyana Guyana										
Production	258	261	234	178	170	134	168	255	255	265
Consumption	31	35	45	38	34	29	26	24	22	23
Consumption per cap.(kg)	40	43	56	47	41	35	32	29	31	31
Paraguay Paraguay										
Production	* 80	* 80	* 112	* 112	* 118	89	* 105	* 95	* 105	* 100
Consumption	* 85	* 90	* 100	* 100	* 110	79	* 90	* 91	* 100	* 103
Consumption per cap.(kg)	22	24	26	25	26	19	21	20	22	22
Peru Pérou										
Production	* 710	585	* 560	571	* 625	* 590	* 580	* 480	* 440	* 510
Consumption	* 650	733	* 850	* 750	* 725	* 650	* 675	* 700	* 720	* 745
Consumption per cap.(kg)	33	36	41	35	33	29	31	31	32	32
Suriname Suriname										
Production *	7	10	10	10	10	10	5	5	5	7
Consumption *	16	16	14	15	15	18	18	18	16	17
Consumption per cap.(kg)	43	42	35	37	38	45	45	43	39	40
Uruguay Uruguay										
Production	* 90	98	103	63	88	* 84	79	73	* 35	22
Consumption	* 95	82	83	78	68	* 75	88	92	* 95	100
Consumption per cap.(kg)	32	27	30	26	22	24	28	30	30	32
Venezuela Venezuela										
Production	495	588	634	521	569	542	567	570	* 510	* 525
Consumption	705	758	777	853	706	732	731	642	* 725	* 750
Consumption per cap.(kg)	41	43	43	46	39	37	37	34	35	35
Asia · Asie										
Afghanistan Afghanistan										
Production	* 3	0	0	0	0	0	0	0	0	0
Consumption	80	80	80	80	55	39	40	50	50	46
Consumption per cap.(kg)	4	4	4	5	4	2	2	3	2	2
Armenia Arménie										
Consumption	..	..	..	..	..	..	..	* 70	* 60	* 50
Azerbaijan Azerbaïdjan										
Consumption	..	..	..	..	..	..	..	* 220	* 205	*190

41
Sugar
Production and consumption: thousand metric tons; consumption per capita: kilograms [*cont.*]
Sucre
Production et consommation : milliers de tonnes métriques ; consommation par habitant : kilogrammes [*suite*]

Country or area Pays ou zone	1985	1986	1987	1988	1989	1990	1991	1992	1993	1994
Bangladesh Bangladesh										
Production	94	* 180	* 200	* 200	* 130	* 190	* 250	* 220	220	* 235
Consumption *	330	340	340	300	275	250	275	285	300	315
Consumption per cap.(kg)	3	3	3	3	3	2	2	2	3	3
Brunei Darussalam Brunéi Darussalam										
Consumption	6	6	7	8	8	10	9	8	8	8
Consumption per cap.(kg)	27	30	30	33	32	39	35	28	28	28
Cambodia Cambodge										
Consumption *	5	5	5	5	5	5	5	10	15	20
Consumption per cap.(kg)	1	1	1	1	1	1	1	1	2	3
China Chine										
Production	* 4 800	* 5 700	* 5 450	* 4 875	* 5 350	* 6 250	6 944	8 864	8 093	6 325
Consumption *	6 350	6 700	7 000	7 200	7 150	7 125	7 350	7 615	7 720	7 900
Consumption per cap.(kg)	6	6	7	6	6	6	6	6	7	7
Cyprus Chypre										
Consumption	* 20	21	21	17	* 20	* 25	* 27	* 28	* 28	* 29
Consumption per cap.(kg)	30	30	30	24	29	36	38	39	39	40
Georgia Géorgie										
Production	..	..	..	..	..	..	..	*15	* 10	0
Consumption	..	..	..	..	..	..	..	* 153	* 140	* 125
Hong Kong Hong−kong										
Consumption *	130	135	140	145	148	150	153	155	158	160
Consumption per cap.(kg)	24	24	25	26	26	26	27	27	27	26
India Inde										
Production	7 016	7 594	9 215	10 207	* 9 912	12 068	13 113	13 873	* 11 750	* 11 900
Consumption	8 974	8 694	9 732	10 175	* 10 575	11 075	11 721	12 387	* 12 989	* 13 700
Consumption per cap.(kg)	12	12	13	13	13	13	14	14	15	15
Indonesia Indonésie										
Production	1 705	2 150	* 2 200	* 2 205	2 171	2 346	2 438	* 2 350	* 2 490	* 2 450
Consumption	1 794	2 123	* 2 350	* 2 545	* 2 600	* 2 650	2 629	* 2 750	* 2 850	* 2 900
Consumption per cap.(kg)	11	13	14	15	15	15	14	15	15	15
Iran, Islamic Rep. of Iran, Rép. islamique d'										
Production *	700	600	600	725	600	620	710	975	935	950
Consumption *	1 300	1 300	1 300	1 150	1 000	1 200	1 400	1 500	1 550	1 600
Consumption per cap.(kg)	29	27	26	22	19	22	25	26	27	27
Iraq Iraq										
Consumption *	600	600	600	575	600	450	300	325	350	375
Consumption per cap.(kg)	38	37	37	33	34	25	16	17	18	19
Israel Israël										
Consumption *	250	250	250	250	260	265	280	295	305	315
Consumption per cap.(kg)	59	58	57	56	58	57	57	58	58	58
Japan Japon										
Production	928	953	960	944	998	982	1 005	1 023	861	826
Consumption	2 891	2 738	2 690	2 905	2 801	2 833	2 846	2 773	2 678	2 657
Consumption per cap.(kg)	24	23	22	24	23	23	23	22	22	22
Jordan Jordanie										
Consumption	* 135	* 140	* 150	* 160	* 160	* 170	* 175	* 185	171	183
Consumption per cap.(kg)	39	39	40	41	39	40	41	43	39	45
Kazakstan Kazakstan										
Production	..	..	..	..	..	..	..	*105	*100	* 87
Consumption	..	..	..	..	..	..	..	* 495	* 460	* 400
Korea, Dem. P. R. Corée, R.p. dém. de										
Consumption	120	120	120	120	120	120	120	125	125	81
Consumption per cap.(kg)	6	6	6	6	6	6	5	6	5	3
Korea, Republic of Corée, République de										
Consumption [10]	548	643	668	765	839	817	857	860	852	* 864
Consumption per cap.(kg)	13	15	16	18	20	19	20	18	19	19
Kuwait Koweït										
Consumption *	65	68	65	60	60	60	40	48	50	55
Consumption per cap.(kg)	38	38	35	31	29	28	19	34	34	34
Kyrgyzstan Kirghizistan										
Production	..	..	..	..	..	..	..	* 15	* 10	* 23
Consumption	..	..	..	..	..	..	..	* 135	* 145	* 130
Lao People's Dem. Rep. Rép. dém. pop. lao										
Consumption *	6	6	6	6	6	7	8	9	11	13
Consumption per cap.(kg)	2	2	2	2	2	2	2	2	2	3

41

Sugar
Production and consumption: thousand metric tons; consumption per capita: kilograms [*cont.*]

Sucre
Production et consommation : milliers de tonnes métriques ; consommation par habitant : kilogrammes [*suite*]

Country or area Pays ou zone	1985	1986	1987	1988	1989	1990	1991	1992	1993	1994
Lebanon Liban										
Consumption *	70	70	95	110	110	110	115	115	113	118
Consumption per cap.(kg)	26	26	35	43	43	43	44	43	40	40
Macau Macao										
Consumption	3	3	3	3	3	3	3	4	5	6
Consumption per cap.(kg)	8	7	10	9	9	9	9	11	13	15
Malaysia Malaisie										
Production *	70	70	90	90	100	110	105	105	105	110
Consumption	* 600	* 615	* 625	* 635	* 640	* 670	* 700	* 730	* 755	* 776
Consumption per cap.(kg)	38	38	35	38	37	38	39	39	40	40
Maldives Maldives										
Consumption	6	9	9	9	7	9	8	8	8	10
Consumption per cap.(kg)	31	47	45	45	33	41	34	34	33	38
Mongolia Mongolie										
Consumption	42	45	45	50	50	50	55	50	45	43
Consumption per cap.(kg)	22	23	23	25	24	23	24	22	19	18
Myanmar Myanmar										
Production	* 59	54	50	27	31	38	35	50	47	48
Consumption *	55	55	42	30	27	34	36	42	47	50
Consumption per cap.(kg)	3	1	1	1	1	1	1	1	1	1
Nepal Népal										
Production	25	15	20	20	15	15	25	20	25	25
Consumption	35	40	35	40	35	40	40	40	41	40
Consumption per cap.(kg)	2	2	2	2	2	2	2	2	2	2
Pakistan Pakistan										
Production	* 1 450	1 151	* 1 425	1 943	2 052	1 989	2 198	* 2 630	* 2 770	3 044
Consumption	* 1 400	* 1 750	* 2 005	1 978	2 089	2 290	2 662	* 2 720	* 2 775	* 2 900
Consumption per cap.(kg)	* 15	* 18	19	19	19	20	23	23	23	23
Philippines Philippines										
Production	1 665	1 514	1 304	1 495	1 878	1 686	1 911	1 919	2 091	2 098
Consumption	1 340	1 180	1 438	1 225	1 471	1 582	1 565	1 643	1 739	1 922
Consumption per cap.(kg)	25	21	25	21	25	26	25	26	27	29
Saudi Arabia Arabie saoudite										
Consumption *	400	350	380	400	450	475	475	500	520	535
Consumption per cap.(kg)	41	29	28	29	31	32	31	31	32	31
Singapore Singapour										
Consumption *	130	145	175	200	193	195	200	210	210	220
Consumption per cap.(kg)	51	56	67	76	72	72	73	75	73	75
Sri Lanka Sri Lanka										
Production	* 17	35	* 30	24	* 29	* 30	67	60	69	* 40
Consumption *	350	315	320	330	345	350	360	360	405	430
Consumption per cap.(kg)	22	20	20	21	21	21	21	23	23	24
Syrian Arab Republic Rép. arabe syrienne										
Production *	50	50	40	40	30	50	75	100	100	110
Consumption *	385	385	385	375	370	395	430	450	460	495
Consumption per cap.(kg)	32	36	35	33	32	33	34	35	35	36
Tajikistan Tadjikistan										
Consumption	..	..	..	..	..	..	..	* 110	* 115	* 100
Thailand Thaïlande										
Production	2 393	2 718	2 532	2 638	4 338	3 542	4 248	5 078	3 825	4 168
Consumption	721	744	883	886	981	1 105	1 189	1 264	1 368	1 480
Consumption per cap.(kg)	14	14	16	16	18	20	21	22	23	25
Turkey Turquie										
Production	1 398	1 414	1 857	1 414	1 565	1 565	2 052	* 2 081	* 2 179	* 1 810
Consumption	1 348	1 483	1 658	1 534	1 641	1 715	1 737	* 1 752	* 1 810	* 1 795
Consumption per cap.(kg)	27	29	32	29	30	31	30	30	30	29
Turkmenistan Turkménistan										
Consumption	..	..	..	..	..	..	..	* 100	* 105	* 95
Uzbekistan Ouzbékistan										
Consumption	..	..	..	..	..	..	..	* 475	* 450	* 375
Viet Nam Viet Nam										
Production *	470	440	440	460	465	465	475	495	510	475
Consumption *	450	475	500	500	500	520	510	520	570	590
Consumption per cap.(kg)	4	8	8	8	8	8	8	8	8	8

41

Sugar
Production and consumption: thousand metric tons; consumption per capita: kilograms [*cont.*]
Sucre
Production et consommation : milliers de tonnes métriques ; consommation par habitant : kilogrammes [*suite*]

Country or area Pays ou zone	1985	1986	1987	1988	1989	1990	1991	1992	1993	1994
Yemen Yémen										
Consumption *	..	..	..	..	..	..	250	265	275	285
Consumption per cap.(kg)	..	..	..	..	..	..	22	22	22	23
former Yemen Arab Rep. anc. arabe rép. de Yémen										
Consumption *	..	..	220	240	195	195	..	..	..	..
Consumption per cap.(kg)	..	..	..	32	25	24	..	..	..	..
former Dem. Rep. of Yemen anc. dém. rép. de Yémen										
Consumption *	..	..	65	65	45	55	..	..	..	..
Consumption per cap.(k	..	..	..	26	19	23	..	..	..	..
Europe · Europe										
Albania Albanie										
Production	33	* 35	* 40	* 45	25	17	* 15	* 17	* 10	* 10
Consumption	55	* 58	* 60	* 65	68	70	* 68	* 65	* 85	* 80
Consumption per cap.(kg)	19	19	20	21	21	22	21	19	25	24
Austria Autriche										
Production	468	307	390	357	390	432	507	436	497	501
Consumption [11]	348	357	370	375	373	396	425	426	412	406
Consumption per cap.(kg)	46	47	49	49	49	51	54	54	52	50
Belarus Bélarus										
Production	..	..	..	..	..	..	..	117	129	* 90
Consumption	..	..	..	..	..	..	..	347	425	* 385
Belgium [1] Belgique [1]										
Production	961	915	915	910	1 312	1 023	1 121	959	...	...
Bosnia−Herzegovina Bosnie−Herzégovine										
Production	..	..	..	..	..	..	..	..	25	15
Consumption	..	..	..	..	..	..	..	..	* 30	* 30
Bulgaria Bulgarie										
Production *	58	40	35	40	76	35	65	35	15	10
Consumption	471	432	482	420	401	289	160	* 180	* 195	* 245
Consumption per cap.(kg)	53	48	47	45	32	18	20	20	23	29
Croatia Croatie										
Production	..	..	..	..	..	..	..	..	90	80
Consumption	..	..	..	..	..	..	..	..	* 150	* 155
former Czechoslovakia † anc. Tchécoslovaquie †										
Production	* 840	* 850	* 775	* 660	* 756	717	* 790	743	..	..
Consumption	* 800	* 800	* 750	* 750	* 800	741	* 800	* 795	..	..
Consumption per cap.(kg)	52	52	48	48	51	48	51	51	..	..
Czech Republic République tchèque										
Production	..	..	..	..	..	..	..	..	624	470
Consumption	..	..	..	..	..	..	..	..	* 485	435
Consumption per cap.(kg)	..	..	..	..	..	..	..	..	5	39
Denmark [6] Danemark [6]										
Production	574	547	422	549	530	572	527	446	542	510
Estonia Estonie										
Production	..	..	..	..	..	..	..	0	* 5	0
Consumption	..	..	..	..	..	..	..	* 72	* 68	* 63
Finland Finlande										
Production	103	133	70	147	173	169	163	153	154 [12]	113 [12]
Consumption	202 [13]	209 [13]	207 [13]	223 [13]	217	189	213	227	242	219
Consumption per cap.(kg)	41	43	42	45	44	38	42	45	48	43
France [6] France [6]										
Production	3 953	3 734	3 973	4 372	4 198	4 595	4 422	4 687	5 037	4 988
Germany † Allemagne †										
Production [6]	..	..	..	..	..	..	4 224	4 401	4 352	* 3 940
F. R. Germany [6] R.f. Allemagne [6]										
Production	3 454	3 479	2 963	3 004	3 337	3 396	..	..	..	..
former German D. R. anc. R.d. allemande										
Production	798	805	750	658	610	..	..	..	..	..
Consumption	757	746	740	787	782	..	..	..	..	..
Consumption per cap.(kg	46	45	45	47	47	..	..	..	..	..
Gibraltar Gibraltar										
Consumption	1	1	1	1	2	3	3	3	3	3
Consumption per cap.(kg)	33	33	33	33	67	75	79	76	74	74
Greece [6] Grèce [6]										
Production	345	312	197	235	421	312	* 297	* 385	* 333	* 272

41

Sugar
Production and consumption: thousand metric tons; consumption per capita: kilograms [*cont.*]
Sucre
Production et consommation : milliers de tonnes métriques ; consommation par habitant : kilogrammes [*suite*]

Country or area Pays ou zone	1985	1986	1987	1988	1989	1990	1991	1992	1993	1994
Hungary Hongrie										
Production	579	510	538	513	630	580	* 700	391	248[14]	434
Consumption	518	513	555	488	572	657	* 575	608	382	398
Consumption per cap.(kg)	50	49	52	46	54	61	56	59	37	39
Iceland Islande										
Consumption	11	12	* 13	* 14	* 15	* 14	* 14	* 15	* 15	16
Consumption per cap.(kg)	48	52	52	56	60	54	54	58	58	58
Ireland [6] Irlande [6]										
Production	189	202	242	212	233	245	* 232	* 223	* 192	* 230
Italy [6] Italie [6]										
Production	1 352	1 868	1 867	1 607	1 879	1 586	1 641	2 032	* 1 544	* 1 620
Latvia Lettonie										
Production	..	..	..	..	..	..	..	* 30	* 35	* 25
Consumption	..	..	..	..	..	..	..	* 151	* 145	* 140
Lithuania Lituanie										
Production	..	..	..	..	..	..	..	85	* 70	59
Consumption	..	..	..	..	..	..	..	116	* 110	* 105
Malta Malte										
Consumption	17	15	15	15	17	18	13	17	17	18
Consumption per cap.(kg)	52	44	44	43	50	51	37	46	47	47
Netherlands [6] Pays–Bas [6]										
Production	1 000	1 325	1 064	1 075	1 240	1 304	* 1 137	* 1 295	* 1 232	* 1 023
Norway Norvège										
Consumption	175	170	173	158	168	171	177	178	177	184
Consumption per cap.(kg)	42	41	41	38	40	40	42	41	41	42
Poland Pologne										
Production	1 841	* 1 881	* 1 820	1 823	1 864	2 212	1 618	1 566	2 201	* 1 495
Consumption	1 690	* 1 646	* 1 800	1 903	1 634	1 624	1 660	1 618	1 691	* 1 705
Consumption per cap.(kg)	45	44	48	50	43	43	43	42	44	44
Portugal Portugal										
Production [6]	9	4	2	1	1	1	* 2	* 2	4[15]	4[15]
Consumption *	330	...	...	...	...	...	...	...	...	...
Consumption per cap.(kg)	32	...	...	...	...	...	...	...	...	...
Republic of Moldova République de Moldova										
Production	..	..	..	..	..	..	..	* 180	* 220	* 167
Consumption	..	..	..	..	..	..	..	* 203	* 205	* 175
Russian Federation Fédération de Russie										
Production	..	..	..	..	..	..	..	2 437	* 2 717	1 650
Consumption	..	..	..	..	..	..	..	* 6 145	* 5 850	* 5 250
Romania Roumanie										
Production	* 540	451	438	363	473	408	344	280	141	206
Consumption *	650	525	495	475	540	555	565	615	475	480
Consumption per cap.(kg)	29	23	22	21	23	24	24	24	21	21
Slovakia Slovaquie										
Production	..	..	..	..	..	..	..	..	*150	*130
Consumption	..	..	..	..	..	..	..	..	*190	*175
Consumption per cap.(kg)	..	..	..	..	..	..	..	..	4	...
Slovenia Slovénie										
Production	..	..	..	..	..	..	..	..	50	35
Consumption	..	..	..	..	..	..	..	..	* 85	* 90
Spain Espagne										
Production	1 090	# 1 111[6]	1 093[6]	1 306[6]	953[6]	994[6]	949[6]	935[6]	1 338[6]	* 1 087[6]
Consumption	* 960	...	...	...	...	...	...	...	...	...
Consumption per cap.(kg)	25	...	...	...	...	...	...	...	...	...
Sweden Suède										
Production [16]	350	391	274	385	424	445	266	333	413	370
Consumption	390	387	372	383	377	379	380	382	388	457
Consumption per cap.(kg)	46	47	44	45	44	44	44	44	44	52
Switzerland Suisse										
Production	139	129	123	150	152	160	136	137	* 150	* 130
Consumption	287[17]	289[17]	287[17]	282	291	305	307	311	* 310	* 310
Consumption per cap.(kg)	43	46	43	42	43	46	46	46	45	44
TFYR Macedonia L'ex–r.p. Macédonie										
Production	..	..	..	..	..	..	..	..	10	8
Consumption	..	..	..	..	..	..	..	..	* 20	* 20

41

Sugar

Production and consumption: thousand metric tons; consumption per capita: kilograms [*cont.*]

Sucre

Production et consommation : milliers de tonnes métriques ; consommation par habitant : kilogrammes [*suite*]

Country or area Pays ou zone	1985	1986	1987	1988	1989	1990	1991	1992	1993	1994
Ukraine Ukraine										
Production	..	..	..	..	..	..	...	3 824	* 4 160	3 632
Consumption	..	..	..	..	..	..	...	* 2 881	* 2 575	2 492
United Kingdom [6] Royaume−Uni [6]										
Production [18]	1 315	1 433	1 333	1 417	1 377	1 349	1 326	1 604	* 1 558	* 1 35*9
Yugoslavia Yougoslavie										
Production	..	..	..	..	..	..	..	..	* 300	* 250
Consumption *	..	..	..	..	..	..	..	..	300	305
Consumption per cap.(kg)	..	..	..	..	..	..	..	..	29	29
Yugoslavia, SFR † Yougoslavie, Rfs †										
Production	933	801	* 920	691	930	* 945	* 900	* 500	..	..
Consumption *	950	950	950	900	907	950	810	725	..	..
Consumption per cap.(kg)	41	41	41	38	38	40	34	30	..	..
Oceania · Océanie										
Australia Australie										
Production	3 439	3 439	3 511	3 759	3 887	3 612	3 195	4 363	4 488	5 217
Consumption	764	818	817	844	882	864	835	829	909	927
Consumption per cap.(kg)	49	51	50	51	53	51	48	47	51	52
Fiji Fidji										
Production	367	508	426	377	466	378	456	451	451	543
Consumption	36	35	36	38	37	40	44	45	46	43[19]
Consumption per cap.(kg)	51	48	49	53	51	54	59	60	60	56
New Zealand Nouvelle−Zélande										
Consumption *	170	165	170	170	173	175	175	178	180	183
Consumption per cap.(kg)	52	51	52	52	52	52	52	52	52	52
Papua New Guinea Papouasie−Nvl−Guinée										
Production	30	10	24	51	30	28	* 35	* 30	* 30	* 35
Consumption	27	30	30	29	29	27	* 27	* 27	* 28	* 30
Consumption per cap.(kg)	8	9	7	8	8	7	7	7	7	8
Samoa Samoa										
Production	3	2	2	2	2	2	2	2	2	2
Consumption	3	3	3	3	3	3	3	3	3	4
Consumption per cap.(kg)	20	19	19	14	14	13	13	12	12	14
former USSR · ancienne URSS										
former USSR † ancienne URSS †										
Production	8 261	8 696	9 565	8 913	9 533	9 159	6 898	..	..	..
Consumption *	12 610	14 050	14 950	14 350	13 150	13 400	11 908	..	..	..
Consumption per cap.(kg)	45	50	53	50	46	46	41	..	..	..

Source:
International Sugar Organization (London).

Source:
L'organisation internationale du sucre (Londres).

† For detailed descriptions of data pertaining to
former Czechoslovakia, Germany, SFR Yugoslavia and former
USSR, see Annex I − Country or area nomenclature, regional
and other groupings.

1   Official figures communicated directly to the Statistics
Division of the United Nations.
2   Excluding high−test molasses to a reported equivalent of raw sugar:
1984 − 6,278 t; 1985 − 74,219 t.
3   3,268 t lost in fire.
4   Including non−human consumption: 1984 − 31,119 t; 1985 − 77,946 t;
1986 − 8,831 t; 1987 − 64,646 t; 1988 − 46,834 t; 1989 − 167,173 t;
1990 − 129,608 t; 1991 − 92,446 t; 1994 − 92,313 t.
5   Including 149,293 t destroyed in hurricane kate.
6   Source: Food and Agriculture Organization of the United
Nations.
7   Excluding 100,348 t adjustment for loss.

† Pour les descriptions en détails des données relatives
à l'ancienne Tchécoslovaquie, l'Allemagne, la Rfs
Yougoslavie et l'ancienne URSS, voir l'Annexe I −
Nomenclature des pays ou zones, groupements régionaux et
autres groupments.

1   Données officielles fournies directement de la Division de
statistique des Nations Unies.
2   Á l'exclusion des mélasses interverties, en équivalent de
sucre brut : 1984 : 6 278 t; 1985 : 74 219 t.
3   Dont 3 268 tonnes détruites par le feu.
4   Dont consommation non humaine : 1984 − 31 119 t;
1985 − 77 946 t; 1986 − 8 831 t; 1987 − 64 646 t;
1988 − 46 834 t; 1989 − 167 173 t; 1990 − 129 608 t;
1991 − 92 446 t; 1994 − 92 313 t.
5   Dont 149 293 tonnes détruites par l'ouragan Kate.
6   Source: Organisation des Nations Unies pour l'alimentation
et l'agriculture.

41

Sugar
Production and consumption: thousand metric tons; consumption per capita: kilograms [*cont.*]

Sucre
Production et consommation : milliers de tonnes métriques ; consommation par habitant : kilogrammes [*suite*]

8 Excluding consumption in Free Zone.
9 Including non−human consumption: 1986 − 98,608 t; 1987 − 147,262 t; 1988 − 122,058 t; 1989 − 52,230 t; 1991 − 13,541 t; 1992 − 8,938 t; 1993 − 8,344 t; 1994 − 12,178 t.
10 Including sugar used for mono−sodium glutamate and L−hysinproduction: 1987 − 44,600 t; 1988 − 92,200 t; 1989 − 94,500 t; 1990 − 89,400 t; 1991 − 77,300 t; 1992 − 75,800 t; 1993 − 89,800 t; 1994 − estimated 89,000 t.
11 Including non−human consumption: 1984 − 9,002 t; 1986 − 7,862 t; 1987 − 9,989 t; 1988 − 12,384 t; 1989 − 8,288 t; 1990 − 5,387 t; 1991 − 11,799 t; 1993 − 9,348 t.
12 Of which 1,041 t of sugar produced from imported Estonian beet in 1993 and 1,145 t in 1994.
13 Including sugar for non−human consumption: 1984 − 16,775 t; 185 − 12,812 t; 1986 − 26,552 t; 1987 − 31,312 t; 1988 − 20,912 t.
14 In addition, 140,412 t of sugar manufactured from Thick (beet) juice were imported from Poland.
15 FAO estimate.
16 Including sales from government stocks: 1984 − 3,602 t; 1985 − 3,181 t; 1986 − 3,775 t; 1988 − 4,324 t; 1989 − 2,771 t.
17 Calculated by Switzerland.
18 Sugar produced from home−grown beet.
19 Includes 11 572t sold to Other Pacific Nations.

7 Non compris un ajustement de 100 348 t pour pertes.
8 Non compris la consommation dans la Zone libre.
9 Dont consommation non humaine : 1986 − 98 608 t; 1987 − 147 262 t; 1988 − 122 058 t; 1989 − 52 230 t; 1991 − 13 541 t; 1992 − 8 938 t; 1993 − 8 344 t; 1994 − 12 1778 t.
10 Y compris le sucre utilisé pour fabriquer du glutamate de monosodium et de la L−lysine : 1987 − 44 600 t; 1988 − 92 200 t; 1989 − 94 500 t; 1990 − 89 400 t; 1991 − 77 300 t; 1992 − 75 800 t; 1993 − 89 800 t; 1994 − 89 000 t (chiffre estimatif).
11 Y compris la consommation non humaine : 1984 − 9 002 t; 1986 − 7 862 t; 1987 − 9 989 t; 1988 − 12 384 t; 1989 − 8 288 t; 1990 − 5 387 t; 1991 − 11 799 t; 1993 − 9 478 t.
12 Dont 1 041 tonnes de sucre à l'aide de betteraves importées d'Estonie en 1993 et 1 145 t en 1994.
13 Y compris le sucre pour la consommation non humaine : 1984 − 16 775 t; 1985 − 12 812 t; 1986 − 26 552 t; 1987 − 31 312 t; 1988 − 20 912 t.
14 En outre, 140 412 t de sucre fabriqué à partir du jus de betteraves épais importé de Pologne.
15 Estimation de la FAO.
16 Dont ventes par prélèvement dans les réserves publiques : 1984 − 3 602 t; 1985 − 3 181 t; 1986 − 3 775 t; 1988 − 4 324 t; 1989 − 2 771 t.
17 Données calculées par la Suisse.
18 Sucre provenant de bettraves récoltées localement.
19 Y compris 11 572 tonnes vendues à d'autres pays du Pacifique.

42
Meat
Viande
Production: thousand metric tons
Production : milliers de tonnes métriques

Country or area Pays ou zone	1985	1986	1987	1988	1989	1990	1991	1992	1993	1994
World **Monde**	**117 990**	**120 881**	**123 781**	**128 035**	**129 782**	**133 347**	**135 238**	**136 117**	**137 644**	**141 938**
Beaf and veal **Boeuf et veau**	**49 803**	**51 103**	**51 798**	**52 032**	**52 381**	**53 815**	**54 428**	**53 579**	**52 654**	**53 041**
Pork **Porc**	**59 931**	**61 449**	**63 369**	**67 092**	**68 127**	**69 934**	**71 019**	**72 778**	**75 193**	**78 954**
Mutton and lamb **Mouton et agneau**	**8 257**	**8 330**	**8 615**	**8 911**	**9 275**	**9 598**	**9 791**	**9 761**	**9 798**	**9 943**
Africa **Afrique**	**5 112**	**5 076**	**5 181**	**5 257**	**5 448**	**5 625**	**5 802**	**5 934**	**5 935**	**5 708**
Beaf and veal **Boeuf et veau**	**3 395**	**3 334**	**3 304**	**3 330**	**3 381**	**3 499**	**3 635**	**3 714**	**3 664**	**3 437**
Pork **Porc**	**428**	**464**	**502**	**518**	**557**	**598**	**629**	**683**	**738**	**719**
Mutton and lamb **Mouton et agneau**	**1 289**	**1 278**	**1 375**	**1 410**	**1 509**	**1 529**	**1 538**	**1 537**	**1 532**	**1 552**
Algeria[1] **Algérie**[1]	**153**	**155**	**189**	* **200**	* **222**	* **232**	* **242**	* **244**	**240**	**243**
Beaf and veal Boeuf et veau	67	66	74	* 81	* 85	* 89	* 89	* 90	91[1]	92[1]
Mutton and lamb[1] Mouton et agneau[1]	86	88	115	119	* 137	* 142	* 152	154	149	151
Angola[1] **Angola**[1]	**78**	**82**	**82**	**83**	**81**	**81**	**81**	**82**	**83**	**83**
Beaf and veal Boeuf et veau[1]	54	57	57	57	54	54	54	55	56	56
Pork[1] Porc[1]	20	21	21	21	22	22	22	22	22	23
Mutton and lamb[1] Mouton et agneau[1]	4	4	4	5	5	5	5	5	5	5
Benin[1] **Bénin**[1]	**24**	**23**	**23**	**24**	**24**	**26**	**27**	**28**	**28**	**29**
Beaf and veal[1] Boeuf et veau[1]	13	13	13	13	14	15	16	16	16	16
Pork[1] Porc[1]	4	4	5	5	5	5	6	6	6	6
Mutton and lamb[1] Mouton et agneau[1]	7	5	5	5	6	6	6	6	6	6
Botswana[1] **Botswana**[1]	**50**	**49**	**41**	**40**	**43**	**49**	**51**	**56**	**46**	**47**
Beaf and veal[1] Boeuf et veau[1]	46	44	36	34	37	42	44	49	39	39
Pork[1] Porc[1]	0	0	0	0	1	1	1	1	1	1
Mutton and lamb[1] Mouton et agneau[1]	4	4	5	5	6	7	7	7	7	7
Burkina Faso[1] **Burkina Faso**[1]	**58**	**61**	**64**	**66**	**69**	**72**	**74**	**75**	**77**	**78**
Beaf and veal[1] Boeuf et veau[1]	33	34	36	37	37	36	37	39	40	40
Pork[1] Porc[1]	5	5	5	6	6	6	6	6	6	7
Mutton and lamb[1] Mouton et agneau[1]	21	22	23	24	26	29	30	31	31	32
Burundi[1] **Burundi**[1]	**16**	**19**	**19**	**22**	**20**	**22**	**21**	**22**	**22**	**19**
Beaf and veal[1] Boeuf et veau[1]	9	11	11	11	11	11	11	11	11	10

42
Meat
Production: thousand metric tons [cont.]
Viande
Production : milliers de tonnes métriques [suite]

Country or area Pays ou zone	1985	1986	1987	1988	1989	1990	1991	1992	1993	1994
Pork[1] Porc[1]	3	4	5	7	5	6	5	6	6	5
Mutton and lamb[1] Mouton et agneau[1]	4	4	4	4	4	4	4	4	4	4
Cameroon[1] **Cameroun[1]**	**84**	**90**	**96**	**106**	**111**	**116**	**117**	**118**	**121**	**122**
Beaf and veal Boeuf et veau	56	53	62	68	71[1]	72[1]	73[1]	73[1]	74[1]	75[1]
Pork[1] Porc[1]	14	17	14	15	16	16	17	17	17	17
Mutton and lamb[1] Mouton et agneau[1]	15	19	20	22	25	27	28	28	30	30
Cape Verde[1] **Cap-Vert[1]**	**2**	**3**	**3**	**3**	**4**	**4**	**4**	**4**	**4**	**4**
Pork[1] Porc[1]	2	2	2	3	3	3	3	3	3	3
Mutton and lamb[1] Mouton et agneau[1]	0	0	0	0	0	0	0	0	1	1
Central African Rep.[1] **Rép. centrafricaine[1]**	**40**	**41**	*** 46**	*** 49**	*** 51**	*** 53**	*** 55**	**56**	**60**	**61**
Beaf and veal Boeuf et veau	30[1]	31[1]	* 35	* 37	* 39	* 40	42[1]	43[1]	45[1]	45[1]
Pork Porc	6[1]	7[1]	* 7	* 7	* 7	* 8	* 8	8[1]	10[1]	10[1]
Mutton and lamb[1] Mouton et agneau[1]	4	4	* 5	* 5	* 5	* 5	5	5	6	6
Chad[1] **Tchad[1]**	**44**	**70**	**69**	**74**	**75**	**79**	**82**	**85**	**88**	**92**
Beaf and veal[1] Boeuf et veau[1]	29	52	51	56	57	62	63	65	67	70
Mutton and lamb[1] Mouton et agneau[1]	16	18	18	18	18	17	19	20	21	21
Comoros[1] **Comores[1]**	**1**	**1**	**1**	**1**	**1**	**1**	**1**	**1**	**1**	**1**
Beaf and veal[1] Boeuf et veau[1]	1	1	1	1	1	1	1	1	1	1
Congo[1] **Congo[1]**	**4**	**5**	**5**	**5**	**4**	**5**	**5**	**5**	**5**	**5**
Beaf and veal[1] Boeuf et veau[1]	2	2	2	2	1	2	2	2	2	2
Pork[1] Porc[1]	2	2	2	2	2	2	2	2	3	3
Mutton and lamb[1] Mouton et agneau[1]	1	1	1	1	1	1	1	1	1	1
Côte d'Ivoire[1] **Côte d'Ivoire[1]**	**66**	**63**	**59**	**59**	**57**	**54**	**56**	**58**	**59**	**65**
Beaf and veal[1] Boeuf et veau[1]	44	41	37	37	34	31	33	34	34	40
Pork[1] Porc[1]	13	13	13	14	14	14	15	15	16	16
Mutton and lamb[1] Mouton et agneau[1]	9	9	8	8	9	9	8	9	9	9
Djibouti[1] **Djibouti[1]**	**5**	**6**	**6**	**6**	**6**	**6**	**7**	**7**	**7**	**7**
Beaf and veal[1] Boeuf et veau[1]	1	2	2	2	2	2	3	3	3	3
Mutton and lamb[1] Mouton et agneau[1]	4	4	4	4	4	4	4	4	5	5

42

Meat
Production: thousand metric tons [*cont.*]
Viande
Production : milliers de tonnes métriques [*suite*]

Country or area Pays ou zone	1985	1986	1987	1988	1989	1990	1991	1992	1993	1994
Egypt[1] **Egypte**[1]	**317**	**335**	**359**	**386**	**382**	**394**	**417**	**433**	**454**	**441**
Beaf and veal[1] Boeuf et veau[1]	237	251	272	294	297	304	331	342	359	348
Pork Porc	3	3	2[1]	2[1]	2[1]	2[1]	3[1]	3[1]	3[1]	3[1]
Mutton and lamb Mouton et agneau	77	81	85	89	83[1]	88[1]	83[1]	88[1]	93[1]	91[1]
Eritrea[1] **Erythrée**[1]	...	...	...	...	...	...	...	...	**25**	**25**
Beaf and veal[1] Boeuf et veau[1]	...	...	...	...	...	...	...	...	15	15
Mutton and lamb[1] Mouton et agneau[1]	...	...	...	...	...	...	...	...	10	10
Ethiopia[1] **Ethiopie**[1]	...	...	...	...	...	...	...	...	**370**	**370**
Beaf and veal[1] Boeuf et veau[1]	...	...	...	...	...	...	...	...	230	230
Pork Porc	...	...	...	...	...	...	...	...	1	1
Mutton and lamb[1] Mouton et agneau[1]	...	...	...	...	...	...	...	...	139	139
Ethiopia incl.Eritrea[1] **Ethiopie comp. Erythrée**[1]	**366**	**458**	*** 353**	*** 353**	*** 387**	*** 394**	*** 395**	**394**	...	...
Beaf and veal Boeuf et veau	216[1]	310[1]	* 206	* 206	* 237	* 245	* 245	244[1]	...	...
Pork[1] Porc[1]	1	1	1	1	1	1	1	1	...	...
Mutton and lamb[1] Mouton et agneau[1]	149	147	* 146	* 146	* 149	* 148	149	149	...	...
Gabon[1] **Gabon**[1]	**3**	**3**	**3**	**4**	**4**	**4**	**4**	**4**	**4**	**4**
Beaf and veal[1] Boeuf et veau[1]	0	1	1	1	1	1	1	1	1	1
Pork[1] Porc[1]	2	2	2	2	2	2	2	2	2	2
Mutton and lamb[1] Mouton et agneau[1]	1	1	1	1	1	1	1	1	1	1
Gambia[1] **Gambie**[1]	**6**	**6**	**7**	**7**	**7**	**7**	**7**	**7**	**7**	**7**
Beaf and veal[1] Boeuf et veau[1]	4	5	5	6	6	6	6	6	6	6
Mutton and lamb[1] Mouton et agneau[1]	1	1	1	1	1	1	1	1	1	1
Ghana[1] **Ghana**[1]	**38**	**39**	**39**	**41**	**44**	**41**	**42**	**40**	**50**	**59**
Beaf and veal[1] Boeuf et veau[1]	20	20	20	20	20	20	21	20	24	29
Pork[1] Porc[1]	9	11	9	11	12	11	10	9	11	13
Mutton and lamb[1] Mouton et agneau[1]	9	9	10	10	12	11	11	11	15	17
Guinea[1] **Guinée**[1]	**16**	**16**	**16**	**16**	**15**	**16**	**16**	**17**	**18**	**18**
Beaf and veal[1] Boeuf et veau[1]	13	13	13	13	13	13	13	14	15	15
Pork[1] Porc[1]	1	1	1	1	1	0	1	1	1	1

42

Meat
Production: thousand metric tons [*cont.*]
Viande
Production : milliers de tonnes métriques [*suite*]

Country or area Pays ou zone	1985	1986	1987	1988	1989	1990	1991	1992	1993	1994
Mutton and lamb[1] Mouton et agneau[1]	2	2	2	2	2	2	3	3	3	3
Guinea-Bissau[1] **Guinée-Bissau**[1]	**12**	**12**	**13**	**13**	**13**	**13**	**14**	**14**	**15**	**15**
Beaf and veal[1] Boeuf et veau[1]	3	3	3	3	3	3	3	4	4	4
Pork[1] Porc[1]	9	9	9	9	9	9	9	9	10	10
Mutton and lamb[1] Mouton et agneau[1]	1	1	1	1	1	1	1	1	1	1
Kenya[1] **Kenya**[1]	**246**	**250**	**270**	**294**	**286**	**312**	**307**	**289**	**266**	**272**
Beaf and veal Boeuf et veau	192[1]	199	219	238	228	250[1]	245[1]	230[1]	210[1]	215[1]
Pork[1] Porc[1]	5	5	5	5	5	5	5	5	5	5
Mutton and lamb[1] Mouton et agneau[1]	49	46	46	50	54	56	56	53	51	52
Lesotho[1] **Lesotho**[1]	**21**	**22**	**22**	**22**	**23**	**23**	**24**	**23**	**24**	**24**
Beaf and veal[1] Boeuf et veau[1]	12	12	12	13	13	13	14	13	13	13
Pork[1] Porc[1]	3	3	3	3	3	3	3	3	3	3
Mutton and lamb[1] Mouton et agneau[1]	6	7	7	7	7	7	8	7	7	7
Liberia[1] **Libéria**[1]	**7**	**7**	**7**	**7**	**7**	**6**	**6**	**6**	**6**	**6**
Beaf and veal[1] Boeuf et veau[1]	2	1	1	1	1	1	1	1	1	1
Pork[1] Porc[1]	4	4	4	4	4	4	4	4	4	4
Mutton and lamb[1] Mouton et agneau[1]	1	1	1	1	1	1	1	1	1	1
Libyan Arab Jamah.[1] **Jamah. arabe libyenne**[1]	**78**	**74**	**66**	**73**	**64**	**59**	**66**	**58**	**45**	**35**
Beaf and veal[1] Boeuf et veau[1]	31	32	25	28	22	19	25	20	13	9
Mutton and lamb[1] Mouton et agneau[1]	47	42	42	45	42	40	41	38	32	26
Madagascar[1] **Madagascar**[1]	**179**	**181**	**188**	**192**	**194**	**196**	**199**	**200**	**202**	**203**
Beaf and veal[1] Boeuf et veau[1]	134	134	138	141	142	143	143	143	143	143
Pork[1] Porc[1]	36	38	41	42	44	45	47	48	49	50
Mutton and lamb[1] Mouton et agneau[1]	9	9	9	9	9	9	9	9	9	9
Malawi[1] **Malawi**[1]	**21**	**31**	**32**	**30**	**29**	**30**	**30**	**31**	**31**	**31**
Beaf and veal[1] Boeuf et veau[1]	10	16	16	16	16	17	17	17	18	18
Pork[1] Porc[1]	7	11	13	10	10	9	9	10	10	10
Mutton and lamb[1] Mouton et agneau[1]	4	3	3	3	3	4	4	4	4	4
Mali[1] **Mali**[1]	**87**	**96**	**96**	**104**	**112**	**117**	**122**	**128**	**134**	**139**

42

Meat
Production: thousand metric tons [cont.]
Viande
Production : milliers de tonnes métriques [suite]

Country or area Pays ou zone	1985	1986	1987	1988	1989	1990	1991	1992	1993	1994
Beaf and veal[1] Boeuf et veau[1]	54	62	61	65	69	72	74	78	81	83
Pork[1] Porc[1]	2	2	2	2	2	2	2	2	3	3
Mutton and lamb[1] Mouton et agneau[1]	31	33	33	37	41	44	46	48	50	53
Mauritania[1] **Mauritanie[1]**	* 34	* 33	* 33	* 34	* 36	* 38	* 41	38	38	38
Beaf and veal Boeuf et veau	* 17	* 15	* 15	* 16	* 16	* 17	* 20	18	18[1]	18[1]
Mutton and lamb[1] Mouton et agneau[1]	17	18	18	18	20	21	21	20	20	20
Mauritius[1] **Maurice[1]**	2	2	2	3	3	3	3	4	4	4
Beaf and veal Boeuf et veau	1	1	1	2	2	2	2	2	3	3[1]
Pork Porc	1	1	1	1	1	1	1	1	1	1
Morocco[1] **Maroc[1]**	152	161	225	198	266	258	270	267	241	211
Beaf and veal Boeuf et veau	85[1]	94[1]	140[1]	122[1]	150	145	165	160	154	134
Pork Porc	0	0	1	1	1	1	1	1[1]	1[1]	1[1]
Mutton and lamb Mouton et agneau	67	67[1]	84	76[1]	115[1]	112[1]	104[1]	107[1]	86	76
Mozambique[1] **Mozambique[1]**	50	51	53	54	55	56	62	52	52	52
Beaf and veal[1] Boeuf et veau[1]	37	38	38	39	40	41	47	36	36	36
Pork[1] Porc[1]	10	11	11	12	12	12	12	12	12	12
Mutton and lamb[1] Mouton et agneau[1]	3	3	3	3	3	3	3	3	3	3
Namibia[1] **Namibie[1]**	49	51	53	55	60	57	65	69	69	71
Beaf and veal[1] Boeuf et veau[1]	35	35	36	38	41	39	45	48	48	50
Pork[1] Porc[1]	2	2	3	3	3	3	2	2	2	2
Mutton and lamb[1] Mouton et agneau[1]	12	14	14	15	16	16	18	19	19	19
Niger[1] **Niger[1]**	37	53	60	64	67	65	67	70	71	74
Beaf and veal Boeuf et veau	17[1]	24[1]	30[1]	29[1]	30	32[1]	34[1]	35[1]	36[1]	38[1]
Pork[1] Porc[1]	1	1	1	1	1	1	1	1	1	1
Mutton and lamb[1] Mouton et agneau[1]	19	28	29	34	36	31	32	33	34	35
Nigeria[1] **Nigéria[1]**	621	495	500	483	492	497	535	583	646	660
Beaf and veal Boeuf et veau	438	283	267	236	218	204	205	210	219[1]	219[1]
Pork[1] Porc[1]	59	75	90	97	112	128	159	199	249	259
Mutton and lamb[1] Mouton et agneau[1]	124	136	143	150	162	165	170	174	178	182

42
Meat
Production: thousand metric tons [cont.]
Viande
Production : milliers de tonnes métriques [suite]

Country or area Pays ou zone	1985	1986	1987	1988	1989	1990	1991	1992	1993	1994
Réunion[1] Réunion[1]	7	7	8	8	9	9	9	9	9	9
Beaf and veal Boeuf et veau	1	1	1	1	1	1	1[1]	1[1]	1[1]	1[1]
Pork Porc	5	6	6	7	7	8	8[1]	8[1]	8[1]	8[1]
Rwanda[1] Rwanda[1]	21	20	19	21	21	21	22	22	22	22
Beaf and veal[1] Boeuf et veau[1]	15	14	12	14	14	14	14	14	14	14
Pork[1] Porc[1]	2	2	2	3	3	3	3	3	3	3
Mutton and lamb[1] Mouton et agneau[1]	4	4	4	4	5	5	5	5	5	5
Senegal[1] Sénégal[1]	58	66	66	65	68	72	76	78	80	82
Beaf and veal[1] Boeuf et veau[1]	38	40	39	40	41	43	44	44	45	46
Pork[1] Porc[1]	5	7	6	6	7	7	7	7	7	7
Mutton and lamb[1] Mouton et agneau[1]	15	19	20	19	20	23	25	27	28	29
Seychelles[1] Seychelles[1]	1	1	1	1	1	1	1	1	1	1
Pork[1] Porc[1]	1	1	1	1	1	1	1	1	1	1
Sierra Leone[1] Sierra Leone[1]	9	8	8	8	9	9	9	9	9	9
Beaf and veal[1] Boeuf et veau[1]	5	5	5	5	5	5	5	5	5	5
Pork[1] Porc[1]	2	2	2	2	2	2	2	2	2	2
Mutton and lamb[1] Mouton et agneau[1]	1	1	1	1	1	1	1	1	1	1
Somalia[1] Somalie[1]	117	105	130	137	141	130	105	84	95	111
Beaf and veal[1] Boeuf et veau[1]	42	35	44	50	51	44	36	33	37	44
Mutton and lamb[1] Mouton et agneau[1]	75	69	86	87	90	86	69	51	57	66
South Africa[1] Afrique du Sud[1]	* 924	* 877	* 910	901	* 890	* 959	* 991	* 1 041	* 987	744
Beaf and veal Boeuf et veau	* 638	* 616	* 628	615[1]	* 603	* 661	* 700	* 745	* 691	472
Pork Porc	120[1]	120[1]	122[1]	123[1]	* 121	* 130	* 123	* 129	* 130	100
Mutton and lamb[1] Mouton et agneau[1]	166	141	160	163	167	168	168	167	166	172
Sudan Soudan	371	337[1]	301[1]	304	312	322	338	359[1]	369[1]	370[1]
Beaf and veal Boeuf et veau	267	248[1]	210[1]	205	211	218	231	250[1]	258[1]	258[1]
Mutton and lamb Mouton et agneau	104	89	92	99	101	104	107	109[1]	111[1]	112[1]
Swaziland[1] Swaziland[1]	18	19	19	15	16	15	17	18	19	19
Beaf and veal Boeuf et veau	14[1]	15[1]	15[1]	12[1]	12[1]	11	13	14	15	15[1]

42
Meat
Production: thousand metric tons [cont.]
Viande
Production : milliers de tonnes métriques [suite]

Country or area Pays ou zone	1985	1986	1987	1988	1989	1990	1991	1992	1993	1994
Pork[1]										
Porc[1]	1	1	1	1	1	1	1	1	1	1
Mutton and lamb[1]										
Mouton et agneau[1]	3	3	3	3	3	3	3	3	3	3
Togo[1]										
Togo[1]	**13**	**13**	**14**	**16**	**17**	**22**	**22**	**24**	**24**	**26**
Beaf and veal[1]										
Boeuf et veau[1]	5	5	5	5	5	5	5	5	5	5
Pork[1]										
Porc[1]	4	3	3	5	6	10	10	11	12	13
Mutton and lamb[1]										
Mouton et agneau[1]	4	5	5	6	6	7	7	7	7	7
Tunisia[1]										
Tunisie[1]	**80**	**81**	**83**	**73**	**73**	**74**	**77**	**78**	**80**	**81**
Beaf and veal										
Boeuf et veau	36	39	38	34	34	34	36	38	38	39
Mutton and lamb										
Mouton et agneau	44	42	45	39	39	40	41	41	41	42[1]
Uganda[1]										
Ouganda[1]	*** 123**	**95**	**100**	**101**	**130**	**146**	**149**	**153**	**157**	**145**
Beaf and veal										
Boeuf et veau	90	60	59	64[1]	73[1]	81[1]	83[1]	84[1]	86[1]	80[1]
Pork										
Porc	* 11	13[1]	25	23[1]	39[1]	45[1]	46[1]	48[1]	49[1]	40[1]
Mutton and lamb[1]										
Mouton et agneau[1]	* 22	22	16	14	18	20	21	22	23	25
United Rep.Tanzania[1]										
Rép. Unie de Tanzanie[1]	**200**	**208**	**209**	**224**	**233**	**235**	**238**	**241**	**244**	**246**
Beaf and veal[1]										
Boeuf et veau[1]	163	170	171	186	194	195	197	199	200	202
Pork[1]										
Porc[1]	8	8	8	9	9	9	9	9	9	9
Mutton and lamb[1]										
Mouton et agneau[1]	29	29	30	30	31	31	32	33	34	35
Zaïre[1]										
Zaïre[1]	**62**	**65**	**68**	**70**	**74**	**77**	**81**	**81**	**82**	**85**
Beaf and veal										
Boeuf et veau	23	24	25	26	26	27[1]	28[1]	29[1]	30[1]	30[1]
Pork[1]										
Porc[1]	29	31	33	34	36	38	40	40	40	42
Mutton and lamb[1]										
Mouton et agneau[1]	10	10	10	11	11	12	12	12	12	13
Zambia[1]										
Zambie[1]	**39**	**40**	**42**	**43**	**46**	**48**	**49**	**52**	**53**	**54**
Beaf and veal[1]										
Boeuf et veau[1]	32	32	33	34	34	36	37	41	41	42
Pork[1]										
Porc[1]	6	6	6	7	9	9	10	9	9	9
Mutton and lamb[1]										
Mouton et agneau[1]	2	2	2	2	2	2	2	2	2	2
Zimbabwe[1]										
Zimbabwe[1]	**99**	**90**	**103**	**99**	**93**	**100**	**101**	**111**	**93**	**86**
Beaf and veal[1]										
Boeuf et veau[1]	84	73	84	79	72	78	80	90	75	67
Pork[1]										
Porc[1]	8	8	10	11	11	11	11	11	8	9

42

Meat
Production: thousand metric tons [*cont.*]
Viande
Production : milliers de tonnes métriques [*suite*]

Country or area Pays ou zone	1985	1986	1987	1988	1989	1990	1991	1992	1993	1994
Mutton and lamb[1] Mouton et agneau[1]	6	8	9	9	9	10	10	10	9	10
America, North **Amerique du Nord**	**23 111**	**23 046**	**22 715**	**23 310**	**22 931**	**22 459**	**22 906**	**23 680**	**23 554**	**24 689**
Beaf and veal Boeuf et veau	13 544	14 136	13 695	13 683	13 368	13 118	13 201	13 339	13 292	14 086
Pork Porc	9 321	8 670	8 794	9 394	9 318	9 089	9 447	10 086	10 011	10 356
Mutton and lamb Mouton et agneau	246	241	226	233	245	252	257	256	251	247
Antigua and Barbuda[1] **Antigua-et-Barbuda[1]**	**1**	**1**	**1**	**1**	**1**	**1**	**1**	**1**	**1**	**1**
Beaf and veal[1] Boeuf et veau[1]	1	1	1	1	0	1	1	1	1	1
Barbados[1] **Barbade[1]**	**5**	**4**	**5**	**4**	**5**	**5**	**5**	**5**	**5**	**5**
Beaf and veal Boeuf et veau	0	0	0	0	1	1	1	1	1	1[1]
Pork[1] Porc[1]	4	4	4	4	4	4	4	4	4	4
Mutton and lamb[1] Mouton et agneau[1]	0	0	0	0	0	0	0	0	0	0
Belize[1] **Belize[1]**	**2**	**2**	**3**	**2**	**2**	**2**	**2**	**2**	**2**	**2**
Beaf and veal Boeuf et veau	1	1	1	1	1	1[1]	1[1]	1[1]	1[1]	1[1]
Pork[1] Porc[1]	1	1	1	1	1	1	1	1	1	1
Canada **Canada**	**2 125**	**2 130**	**2 083**	**2 137**	**2 138**	**2 033**	**1 995**	**2 129**	***2 086**	**2 146**
Beaf and veal Boeuf et veau	1 029	1 028	953	947	952	900	867	910	883	930
Pork Porc	1 088	1 094	1 122	1 182	1 177	1 124	1 119	1 209	1 192	1 205
Mutton and lamb Mouton et agneau	8	8	8	8	9	9	10	10	* 11	11
Costa Rica[1] **Costa Rica[1]**	**106**	***102**	**107**	***102**	**100**	**102**	**111**	**100**	**102**	***114**
Beaf and veal Boeuf et veau	94	* 92	97	* 86	86	87	94	81	82	* 92
Pork Porc	12	10	10	16	14	14	17	19	20	22[1]
Cuba[1] **Cuba[1]**	**220**	**230**	**227**	**227**	**229**	**232**	**232**	**186**	**166**	**167**
Beaf and veal Boeuf et veau	142	148	140	141	138	141[1]	140[1]	112[1]	100[1]	100[1]
Pork Porc	76	80	85	84	89[1]	89[1]	90[1]	72[1]	65[1]	66[1]
Mutton and lamb[1] Mouton et agneau[1]	2	2	2	2	2	2	2	2	1	1
Dominican Republic[1] **Rép. dominicaine[1]**	**78**	**81**	**85**	**99**	**104**	**106**	**125**	**129**	**141**	**150**
Beaf and veal Boeuf et veau	63	64	67	79	81	82	84	83	86	90[1]
Pork[1] Porc[1]	13	14	17	18	20	21	38	43	53	57
Mutton and lamb[1] Mouton et agneau[1]	2	2	2	2	2	2	2	3	3	3

42
Meat
Production: thousand metric tons [*cont.*]
Viande
Production : milliers de tonnes métriques [*suite*]

Country or area Pays ou zone	1985	1986	1987	1988	1989	1990	1991	1992	1993	1994
El Salvador[1]										
El Salvador[1]	**35**	**36**	**33**	**36**	**36**	**35**	**31**	**30**	**33**	*** 34**
Beaf and veal										
Boeuf et veau	21	22	19	22	28	27	24	22	25	* 26
Pork[1]										
Porc[1]	14	14	14	13	8	7	8	8	8	8
Guadeloupe										
Guadeloupe	**7**	**7**	**7**	**6**	*** 6**	**6**	*** 5**	**5**[1]	**5**[1]	**5**[1]
Beaf and veal										
Boeuf et veau	4	4	3	3	3	3	3	3	3[1]	3[1]
Pork										
Porc	3	3	3	3	* 2	2	* 2	2[1]	2[1]	2[1]
Guatemala[1]										
Guatemala[1]	**69**	**53**	**64**	**66**	**80**	**78**	**65**	**76**	**78**	*** 74**
Beaf and veal										
Boeuf et veau	49	34	46	48	61	61	49	55	57	* 53
Pork										
Porc	16	16	14	14	15	14	13	16	17	17[1]
Mutton and lamb[1]										
Mouton et agneau[1]	4	4	4	4	4	4	4	4	4	4
Haiti[1]										
Haïti[1]	**52**	**52**	**49**	**47**	**45**	**41**	**36**	**32**	**32**	**32**
Beaf and veal[1]										
Boeuf et veau[1]	32	30	29	28	27	24	22	20	20	20
Pork[1]										
Porc[1]	16	18	16	15	14	13	10	9	9	9
Mutton and lamb[1]										
Mouton et agneau[1]	4	4	4	4	4	4	4	4	4	4
Honduras[1]										
Honduras[1]	**46**	**38**	*** 56**	*** 58**	*** 59**	*** 59**	**58**	**58**	**58**	**60**
Beaf and veal										
Boeuf et veau	35	27	* 45	* 46	* 46	* 46	45[1]	44[1]	45[1]	46[1]
Pork										
Porc	10	11	* 11	* 12	* 13	13	13	13	13	14[1]
Jamaica[1]										
Jamaïque[1]	**22**	**22**	**22**	**23**	**23**	**24**	**23**	*** 22**	**23**	**23**
Beaf and veal										
Boeuf et veau	14	15	14	14	13	15	16	* 15	16[1]	16[1]
Pork										
Porc	7	6	6	7	8	7	5	* 5	6[1]	6[1]
Mutton and lamb[1]										
Mouton et agneau[1]	2	2	2	2	2	2	2	2	2	2
Martinique[1]										
Martinique[1]	**5**	**5**	**5**	**5**	**5**	**5**	**5**	**5**	**5**	**5**
Beaf and veal										
Boeuf et veau	3	3	3	3	2	3	3	3	2	2[1]
Pork[1]										
Porc[1]	2	2	2	2	2	2	2	2	2	2
Mutton and lamb[1]										
Mouton et agneau[1]	1	1	0	0	0	0	0	0	0	0
Mexico										
Mexique	**2 279**	**2 269**	**2 245**	*** 2 188**	**1 951**	**1 932**	**2 066**	**2 138**	**2 148**	**2 307**
Beaf and veal										
Boeuf et veau	927	1 248	1 273	1 271	1 163	1 114	1 189	1 247	1 256	1 365
Pork										
Porc	1 293	959	915	861	727	757	812	820	822	873
Mutton and lamb										
Mouton et agneau	59	62	58	* 56	62	61	66	71	70	69

42
Meat
Production: thousand metric tons [cont.]
Viande
Production : milliers de tonnes métriques [suite]

Country or area Pays ou zone	1985	1986	1987	1988	1989	1990	1991	1992	1993	1994
Montserrat[1]										
Montserrat[1]	1	1	1	1	1	1	1	1	1	1
Beaf and veal[1]										
Boeuf et veau[1]	1	1	1	1	1	1	1	1	1	1
Nicaragua[1]										
Nicaragua[1]	58	52	44	44	* 63	68	55	57	58	* 68
Beaf and veal										
Boeuf et veau	45	37	30	33	50	57	45	48	48	* 59
Pork										
Porc	13[1]	14[1]	14	11	* 13	10	9[1]	9[1]	10[1]	10[1]
Panama										
Panama	71	73	68	64	67	76	72	68	75	76[1]
Beaf and veal										
Boeuf et veau	59	59	58	54	57	64	61	56	59	60[1]
Pork										
Porc	12	13	10	10	10	12	11	13	16	16[1]
Puerto Rico[1]										
Porto Rico[1]	43	51	52	45	45	50	49	39	36	34
Beaf and veal										
Boeuf et veau	24	25	28	22	20	21	19	21	19	18
Pork										
Porc	18	25	24	22	25	28	30	18	17	15
Saint Lucia[1]										
Sainte-Lucie[1]	1	1	1	1	1	1	1	1	1	1
Beaf and veal[1]										
Boeuf et veau[1]	1	1	1	1	1	1	1	1	1	1
Pork[1]										
Porc[1]	1	1	1	1	1	1	1	1	1	1
St. Vincent-Grenadines[1]										
St. Vincent-Grenadines[1]	1	1	1	1	1	1	1	1	1	1
Pork[1]										
Porc[1]	1	1	1	1	1	1	1	1	1	1
Trinidad and Tobago[1]										
Trinité-et-Tobago[1]	5	5	5	5	4	4	4	4	3	3
Beaf and veal										
Boeuf et veau	1	1	1	2	1	1	1	1	1	1[1]
Pork										
Porc	3	3	3	3	2	2	2	2	2	2[1]
Mutton and lamb[1]										
Mouton et agneau[1]	1	1	0	0	0	0	0	0	0	0
United States										
Etats-Unis	17 873	17 824	17 547	18 145	17 963	17 595	17 956	18 587	18 488	19 377
Beaf and veal										
Boeuf et veau	10 996	11 292	10 884	10 879	10 633	10 465	10 534	10 612	10 584	11 199
Pork										
Porc	6 715	6 379	6 520	7 114	7 173	6 965	7 258	7 817	7 751	8 027
Mutton and lamb										
Mouton et agneau	162	153	143	152	157	165	164	158	153	151
United States Virgin Is.[1]										
Iles Vierges américaines[1]	1	1	0	1	1	1	1	1	1	1
Beaf and veal[1]										
Boeuf et veau[1]	1	1	0	0	0	0	1	1	1	1
America, South										
Amérique du Sud	8 823	8 629	8 941	9 560	9 946	10 207	10 354	10 354	10 173	10 633
Beaf and veal										
Boeuf et veau	6 914	6 641	6 738	7 149	7 645	7 804	7 888	7 762	7 605	7 946
Pork										
Porc	1 593	1 656	1 867	2 066	1 949	2 038	2 106	2 245	2 219	2 321

42
Meat
Production: thousand metric tons [*cont.*]
Viande
Production : milliers de tonnes métriques [*suite*]

Country or area Pays ou zone	1985	1986	1987	1988	1989	1990	1991	1992	1993	1994
Mutton and lamb **Mouton et agneau**	**316**	**333**	**336**	**346**	**352**	**366**	**360**	**347**	**349**	**366**
Argentina[1] **Argentine**[1]	**3 145**	**3 087**	**2 996**	**2 917**	**2 898**	**2 898**	**2 971**	*** 2 699**	*** 2 734**	*** 2 822**
Beaf and veal Boeuf et veau	2 848	2 813	2 700	2 590	2 626	2 635	2 700	2 487	2 508	* 2 590
Pork Porc	193	170	200	237	181	171	180	* 140	* 155	155[1]
Mutton and lamb[1] Mouton et agneau[1]	104	104	96	90	91	92	91	72	71	* 77
Bolivia[1] **Bolivie**[1]	**195**	**185**	**196**	**211**	**207**	**214**	**214**	**211**	**208**	**217**
Beaf and veal Boeuf et veau	125	115	121	131	135	130	132	127	133	139
Pork[1] Porc[1]	55	54	57	61	54	65	65	67	58	60
Mutton and lamb[1] Mouton et agneau[1]	15	16	18	19	19	18	16	17	17	19
Brazil[1] **Brésil**[1]	**3 081**	**2 872**	**3 342**	*** 3 785**	*** 3 906**	*** 4 098**	*** 4 159**	*** 4 468**	*** 4 337**	*** 4 569**
Beaf and veal Boeuf et veau	2 223	1 958	2 262	2 581	2 748	2 836	2 885	3 062	3 005	* 3 160
Pork Porc	780[1]	825[1]	986[1]	* 1 100	* 1 050	* 1 150	* 1 160	* 1 291	* 1 215	* 1 290
Mutton and lamb[1] Mouton et agneau[1]	79	89	94	104	108	112	* 114	* 115	* 117	* 119
Chile[1] **Chili**[1]	**259**	**270**	**282**	**315**	**352**	**385**	**376**	**355**	**389**	**417**
Beaf and veal Boeuf et veau	175	177	175	197	221	242	230	200	224	240
Pork Porc	66	75	88	100	113	123	129	138	147	161
Mutton and lamb[1] Mouton et agneau[1]	18	17	19	18	17	19	18	17	18	17
Colombia **Colombie**	**740**	*** 788**	*** 755**	*** 814**	**943**[1]	*** 941**[1]	*** 913**[1]	**818**[1]	**721**[1]	**756**[1]
Beaf and veal Boeuf et veau	609	652	621	669	805	* 795	* 768	670	573	609
Pork Porc	118	123	* 122	* 131	126	133	133	135	134	133
Mutton and lamb Mouton et agneau	13	* 12	* 13	* 13	12[1]	13[1]	12[1]	13[1]	13[1]	13[1]
Ecuador[1] **Equateur**[1]	**159**	**162**	**164**	**165**	**167**	**215**	**218**	**227**	**229**	**239**
Beaf and veal Boeuf et veau	89	90	92	95	98	140	137	140	137	145[1]
Pork[1] Porc[1]	65	68	68	65	64	71	76	82	87	90
Mutton and lamb[1] Mouton et agneau[1]	6	5	4	4	5	5	5	5	5	5
Falkland Is. (Malvinas)[1] **Iles Falkland (Malvinas)**[1]	**1**	**1**	**1**	**1**	**1**	**1**	**1**	**1**	**1**	**1**
Mutton and lamb[1] Mouton et agneau[1]	1	1	1	1	1	1	1	1	1	1
French Guiana[1] **Guyane française**[1]	**2**	**2**	**1**	**1**	**1**	**1**	**2**	**1**	**1**	**1**
Beaf and veal[1] Boeuf et veau[1]	0	1	1	1	1	1	1	1	0	0

42

Meat
Production: thousand metric tons [*cont.*]
Viande
Production : milliers de tonnes métriques [*suite*]

Country or area Pays ou zone	1985	1986	1987	1988	1989	1990	1991	1992	1993	1994
Pork Porc	1	1	1	1	1	1	1	1	1	1[1]
Guyana[1] Guyana[1]	3	3	4	4	4	3	4	6	6	6
Beaf and veal Boeuf et veau	2	2	2	2	2	2	3	4[1]	4	4[1]
Pork Porc	1	1	1	1	1	1	0	1	1	1[1]
Mutton and lamb[1] Mouton et agneau[1]	1	1	1	1	1	1	1	1	1	1
Paraguay[1] Paraguay[1]	225	228	213	244	* 290	* 311	* 372	* 398	* 423	* 432
Beaf and veal Boeuf et veau	115	118	101	131	* 172	* 189	* 219	* 233	* 225	* 225
Pork[1] Porc[1]	107	107	108	109	114	118	150	162	195	203
Mutton and lamb[1] Mouton et agneau[1]	3	3	3	3	3	3	3	3	3	4
Peru * Pérou *	197	192	217	235	231	232	221	227	225	222[1]
Beaf and veal Boeuf et veau	101	90	107	117	112	117	109	111	107	103
Pork * Porc *	70	77	83	91	91	82	84	88	91	93
Mutton and lamb Mouton et agneau	26	25	27	28	29	33	28	28	27	27[1]
Suriname[1] Suriname[1]	3	3	3	3	4	4	5	4	4	4
Beaf and veal Boeuf et veau	1	1	1	1	2	2	3	3	3[1]	3[1]
Pork Porc	2	1	1	1	2	2	2	1	2[1]	2[1]
Uruguay Uruguay	395	392	350	402	464	416	* 434	* 447	399	* 457
Beaf and veal Boeuf et veau	332	324	279	326	386	333	350	360	310	* 359
Pork Porc	18	17	19	20	20	22	22	22	23	* 23
Mutton and lamb Mouton et agneau	45	52	53	56	58	61	* 63	* 64	66	* 75
Venezuela Venezuela	418	444	417	464	478	* 490[1]	* 463[1]	* 492[1]	* 496[1]	* 490[1]
Beaf and veal Boeuf et veau	294	300	276	307	338	* 382	* 351	* 365	* 377	* 370
Pork Porc	117	136	133	148	132	* 99	* 103	* 118	* 110	* 110
Mutton and lamb Mouton et agneau	7	7	8	8	8	9[1]	9[1]	9[1]	9[1]	10[1]
Asia Asie	30 736	32 723	33 948	36 084	37 907	40 384	42 758	45 374	48 681	53 493
Beaf and veal Boeuf et veau	5 636	6 073	6 416	6 466	6 752	7 146	7 580	8 011	8 698	8 975
Pork Porc	22 162	23 620	24 350	26 313	27 625	29 504	31 233	33 313	35 753	40 041
Mutton and lamb Mouton et agneau	2 938	3 029	3 182	3 305	3 530	3 734	3 945	4 049	4 230	4 477
Afghanistan Afghanistan	195[1]	* 183	185[1]	191[1]	197[1]	203[1]	203[1]	203[1]	203[1]	203[1]

42
Meat
Production: thousand metric tons [cont.]
Viande
Production : milliers de tonnes métriques [suite]

Country or area Pays ou zone	1985	1986	1987	1988	1989	1990	1991	1992	1993	1994
Beaf and veal Boeuf et veau	68[1]	68	65[1]	65[1]	65[1]	65[1]	65[1]	65[1]	65[1]	65[1]
Mutton and lamb Mouton et agneau	127[1]	* 115	120[1]	126[1]	132[1]	138[1]	138[1]	138[1]	138[1]	138[1]
Armenia **Arménie**	...	...	...	...	...	...	...	57	37	32[1]
Beaf and veal Boeuf et veau	...	...	...	...	...	...	...	33	21	18[1]
Pork Porc	...	...	...	...	...	...	...	16	10	8[1]
Mutton and lamb Mouton et agneau	...	...	...	...	...	...	...	9	6	6[1]
Azerbaijan[1] **Azerbaïdjan**[1]	...	...	...	...	...	...	...	87	* 80	77
Beaf and veal Boeuf et veau	...	...	...	...	...	...	...	50	* 42	40[1]
Pork Porc	...	...	...	...	...	...	...	5	* 8	7[1]
Mutton and lamb[1] Mouton et agneau[1]	...	...	...	...	...	...	...	32	30	30
Bahrain[1] **Bahreïn**[1]	6	6	7	7	8	8	8	8	8	8
Beaf and veal[1] Boeuf et veau[1]	1	1	1	1	1	1	1	1	1	1
Mutton and lamb[1] Mouton et agneau[1]	5	5	6	6	7	7	7	7	7	8
Bangladesh **Bangladesh**	188	194	199	205	* 211	218	223	230	240	248[1]
Beaf and veal Boeuf et veau	135	137	138	140	* 141	143	143	145	147	148[1]
Mutton and lamb Mouton et agneau	53	57	61	65	* 70	75	80	86	93	100[1]
Bhutan[1] **Bhoutan**[1]	6	6	7	7	7	7	7	7	7	7
Beaf and veal[1] Boeuf et veau[1]	5	5	5	5	5	5	6	6	6	6
Pork[1] Porc[1]	1	1	1	1	1	1	1	1	1	1
Brunei Darussalam[1] **Brunéi Darussalam**[1]	2	2	2	2	2	2	2	2	2	2
Beaf and veal[1] Boeuf et veau[1]	2	1	1	1	1	1	1	1	2	2
Pork[1] Porc[1]	1	1	0	1	0	0	0	0	0	0
Cambodia[1] **Cambodge**[1]	67	66	70	79	89	82	85	103	104	109
Beaf and veal[1] Boeuf et veau[1]	25	25	26	26	28	29	30	31	33	34
Pork[1] Porc[1]	42	41	44	53	61	53	54	72	72	75
China * **Chine ***	18 442	20 043	20 802	22 852	24 185	26 149	28 369	30 547	33 429	37 891
Beaf and veal * Boeuf et veau *	471	593	796	963	1 078	1 261	1 540	1 808	2 341	2 505
Pork Porc	17 378	18 828	19 287	21 087	22 145	23 820	25 649	27 488	29 714	* 33 835
Mutton and lamb * Mouton et agneau *	593	622	719	802	962	1 068	1 180	1 251	1 374	1 551

42

Meat
Production: thousand metric tons [cont.]
Viande
Production : milliers de tonnes métriques [suite]

Country or area Pays ou zone	1985	1986	1987	1988	1989	1990	1991	1992	1993	1994
Cyprus Chypre	**34**	**35**	**38**	**40**	**42**	**44**	**43**	**45**	**51**	**55**[1]
Beaf and veal Boeuf et veau	3	4	4	4	4	4	5	5	5	5[1]
Pork Porc	24	23	25	27	29	31	32	34	39	43
Mutton and lamb Mouton et agneau	7	8	9	9	8	8	7	7	7	7[1]
Gaza Strip Zone de Gaza	* 2	* 2	* 2	* 2	* 2	* 3	* 2	* 2	3[1]	3[1]
Beaf and veal Boeuf et veau	* 1	* 1	* 1	* 1	* 1	* 1	* 1	* 1	1[1]	1[1]
Mutton and lamb Mouton et agneau	* 1	* 1	* 1	* 1	* 1	* 2	* 1	* 1	1[1]	1[1]
Georgia Géorgie	...	...	...	...	...	...	...	* 91	* 86[1]	78[1]
Beaf and veal Boeuf et veau	...	...	...	...	...	...	...	* 38	* 36	32[1]
Pork Porc	...	...	...	...	...	...	...	* 47	* 44	40[1]
Mutton and lamb Mouton et agneau	...	...	...	...	...	...	...	* 6	6[1]	6[1]
Hong Kong Hong-kong	**221**[1]	**237**[1]	**238**[1]	**240**[1]	**231**[1]	**227**[1]	**206**[1]	**195**[1]	**181**	**195**
Beaf and veal Boeuf et veau	38	40	40	40	37	39	38	35	32	29
Pork Porc	182	197	197	200[1]	194[1]	188	168	160	149	166
India[1] Inde[1]	**2 854**	**2 894**	**3 141**	**3 001**	**3 098**	**3 290**	**3 376**	**3 418**	**3 496**	**3 545**
Beaf and veal[1] Boeuf et veau[1]	1 954	1 981	2 206	2 086	2 168	2 319	2 361	2 398	2 458	2 496
Pork[1] Porc[1]	364	368	373	378	383	389	392	397	403	408
Mutton and lamb[1] Mouton et agneau[1]	536	546	563	538	547	583	623	623	635	641
Indonesia[1] Indonésie[1]	**672**	**729**	*** 713**	*** 731**	*** 804**	*** 850**	**896**	**955**	*** 1 025**	*** 1 063**
Beaf and veal Boeuf et veau	227	239	* 216[1]	* 192	* 227	* 223	240[1]	280[1]	* 313[1]	* 322[1]
Pork[1] Porc[1]	369	413	418	462	495	545	572	589	622	649
Mutton and lamb Mouton et agneau	76[1]	78[1]	* 79[1]	* 77[1]	* 82[1]	* 83[1]	84[1]	86[1]	* 91	* 92
Iran, Islamic Rep. of[1] Iran, Rép. islamique d'[1]	**461**	**483**	**483**	**493**	*** 526**	*** 550**	*** 585**	*** 630**	**639**	**640**
Beaf and veal[1] Boeuf et veau[1]	177	180	183	190	* 211	* 220	* 245	* 280	285	286
Mutton and lamb Mouton et agneau	284[1]	303[1]	300[1]	304[1]	* 315	* 330	* 340	* 350	354[1]	355[1]
Iraq[1] Iraq[1]	**81**	**77**	**78**	**78**	**76**	**74**	**57**	**56**	**55**	**52**
Beaf and veal[1] Boeuf et veau[1]	49	46	47	47	46	44	33	32	31	29
Mutton and lamb[1] Mouton et agneau[1]	32	31	31	31	31	29	24	24	24	24
Israel Israël	*** 45**	*** 45**	*** 47**	*** 51**	*** 50**	*** 51**	*** 53**[1]	*** 52**[1]	**52**[1]	**53**[1]

42

Meat
Production: thousand metric tons [cont.]
Viande
Production : milliers de tonnes métriques [suite]

Country or area Pays ou zone	1985	1986	1987	1988	1989	1990	1991	1992	1993	1994
Beaf and veal										
Boeuf et veau	32	32	33	35	36	36	* 38	* 37	37[l]	38[l]
Pork										
Porc	9	8	9	9	9	9	9[l]	9[l]	9[l]	9[l]
Mutton and lamb										
Mouton et agneau	* 4	* 5	* 5	* 6	* 6	* 6	* 6	* 6	6[l]	6[l]
Japan										
Japon	**2 087**	**2 111**	**2 147**	**2 149**	**2 142**	**2 105**	**2 058**	**2 026**	**2 027**	*** 2 006**[l]
Beaf and veal										
Boeuf et veau	555	559	565	570	548	549	575	592	593	* 605
Pork										
Porc	1 532	1 552	1 582	1 579	1 594	1 555	1 483	1 434	1 433	* 1 400
Mutton and lamb										
Mouton et agneau	0	0	0	0	0	0	0	0	0	1[l]
Jordan										
Jordanie	**10**	**6**	**8**	**8**	**9**	*** 10**	*** 16**	*** 16**	*** 18**[l]	**19**[l]
Beaf and veal										
Boeuf et veau	1	1	1	1	1	* 1	* 1	* 1	2[l]	2[l]
Mutton and lamb										
Mouton et agneau	9	5	7	7	8	* 9	* 15	* 15	* 17	18[l]
Kazakstan *[l]										
Kazakstan *[l]	...	...	...	...	...	...	...	1 059	1 064	1 067
Beaf and veal *										
Boeuf et veau *	...	...	...	...	...	...	...	596	630	615
Pork *										
Porc *	...	...	...	...	...	...	...	217	197	225
Mutton and lamb[l]										
Mouton et agneau[l]	...	...	...	...	...	...	...	246	237	227
Korea, Dem. P. R.[l]										
Corée, R. p. dém. de[l]	**189**	**195**	**206**	**209**	**211**	**213**	**210**	**206**	**183**	**185**
Beaf and veal[l]										
Boeuf et veau[l]	38	39	41	42	44	45	45	45	30	31
Pork[l]										
Porc[l]	148	153	161	164	164	164	161	158	150	151
Mutton and lamb[l]										
Mouton et agneau[l]	3	3	3	3	4	4	4	4	3	3
Korea, Republic of[l]										
Corée, République de[l]	**601**	**531**	**586**	**603**	**606**	**679**	**664**	*** 928**	*** 1 002**	*** 1 059**
Beaf and veal										
Boeuf et veau	166	208	208	177	125	128	132	174	204	* 203
Pork										
Porc	434	322	377	425	480	550	530	* 752	* 796	* 854
Mutton and lamb[l]										
Mouton et agneau[l]	1	1	1	1	1	1	2	2	2	2
Kuwait[l]										
Koweït[l]	*** 35**	*** 36**	*** 35**	*** 35**	**35**	**18**	**9**	**18**	**26**	**26**
Beaf and veal										
Boeuf et veau	2	2[l]	2	2	1	1[l]	0[l]	0[l]	1[l]	1[l]
Mutton and lamb[l]										
Mouton et agneau[l]	* 33	* 33	* 33	* 33	34	17	9	17	25	25
Kyrgyzstan[l]										
Kirghizistan[l]	...	...	...	...	...	...	...	189	* 168	154
Beaf and veal										
Boeuf et veau	...	...	...	...	...	...	...	88	* 76	70[l]
Pork										
Porc	...	...	...	...	...	...	...	36	* 33	30[l]
Mutton and lamb[l]										
Mouton et agneau[l]	...	...	...	...	...	...	...	65	59	54

42

Meat
Production: thousand metric tons [*cont.*]
Viande
Production : milliers de tonnes métriques [*suite*]

Country or area Pays ou zone	1985	1986	1987	1988	1989	1990	1991	1992	1993	1994
Lao People's Dem. Rep.[1] **Rép. dém. pop. lao[1]**	**32**	**34**	**36**	**35**	**33**	**33**	**34**	**36**	**38**	**40**
Beaf and veal[1] Boeuf et veau[1]	14	15	15	15	12	12	12	13	14	14
Pork[1] Porc[1]	18	19	21	19	21	21	22	23	25	26
Lebanon[1] **Liban[1]**	**26**	**23**	**21**	**20**	**15**	**13**	**25**	**25**	**25**	**26**
Beaf and veal[1] Boeuf et veau[1]	18	15	13	8	7	7	15	15	16	16
Pork[1] Porc[1]	0	0	1	1	1	1	1	1	1	i
Mutton and lamb[1] Mouton et agneau[1]	8	8	8	11	7	5	9	9	9	9
Macau[1] **Macao[1]**	**8**	**8**	**8**	**9**	**9**	**9**	**8**	**8**	**8**	**9**
Beaf and veal[1] Boeuf et veau[1]	1	1	1	2	2	2	1	1	1	1
Pork Porc	7	7	6	7	7	8[1]	8[1]	8[1]	8[1]	8[1]
Malaysia[1] **Malaisie[1]**	**170**	**175**	**191**	**180**	**202**	**235**	**243**	**240**	**238**	**249**
Beaf and veal[1] Boeuf et veau[1]	16	15	15	17	15	15	18	18	18	18
Pork[1] Porc[1]	153	159	175	163	186	219	225	222	219	231
Mutton and lamb[1] Mouton et agneau[1]	1	1	1	1	1	1	1	1	1	1
Mongolia **Mongolie**	**187**	**201**	**196**	**190**	**200**	**206**	**224**	**194**	**163**[1]	**162**[1]
Beaf and veal Boeuf et veau	68	75	73	73	73	66	84	76	48[1]	48[1]
Pork Porc	2	2	3	4	6	8	4	2	5[1]	5[1]
Mutton and lamb Mouton et agneau	116	123	121	112	122	132	136	116	110[1]	109[1]
Myanmar[1] **Myanmar[1]**	**190**	*** 193**	*** 196**	*** 199**	**189**	**193**	**198**	**205**	**209**	**213**
Beaf and veal[1] Boeuf et veau[1]	99	101	103	105	105	106	109	110	111	112
Pork[1] Porc[1]	83	85	86	87	77	80	83	88	91	94
Mutton and lamb Mouton et agneau	8[1]	* 7	* 7	* 7	7	7	7	7	7	7
Nepal[1] **Népal[1]**	**125**	**128**	**130**	**135**	**139**	**140**	**142**	**143**	**144**	**149**
Beaf and veal[1] Boeuf et veau[1]	90	92	93	96	98	98	99	100	100	104
Pork Porc	7	7	8	9	9	10	10	10	10	11
Mutton and lamb Mouton et agneau	28	29	29	31	31	32	32	33	33	34
Oman[1] **Oman[1]**	**13**	**13**	**13**	**15**	**18**	**18**	**19**	**18**	**19**	**20**
Beaf and veal[1] Boeuf et veau[1]	3	3	3	3	3	3	3	3	3	3
Mutton and lamb[1] Mouton et agneau[1]	10	10	10	12	15	15	16	16	16	17

42

Meat
Production: thousand metric tons [cont.]
Viande
Production : milliers de tonnes métriques [suite]

Country or area Pays ou zone	1985	1986	1987	1988	1989	1990	1991	1992	1993	1994
Pakistan										
Pakistan	**831**	**915**	**969**	**1 025**	**1 085**	**1 151**	**1 215**	**1 287**	*** 1 363**	*** 1 443**
Beaf and veal										
Boeuf et veau	466	546	574	602	632	667	696	731	* 768	* 806
Mutton and lamb										
Mouton et agneau	365	369	395	423	453	484	519	556	595	* 637
Philippines[1]										
Philippines[1]	**503**	**576**	**628**	**705**	*** 798**	*** 860**	*** 848**	*** 877**	*** 852**	*** 889**
Beaf and veal										
Boeuf et veau	87	96	108	113	* 132	* 125	* 129	* 138	* 129	* 133
Pork										
Porc	397	460	500	566	639	709	691	* 710	* 690	* 720
Mutton and lamb[1]										
Mouton et agneau[1]	19	19	20	25	27	27	28	29	33	36
Qatar[1]										
Qatar[1]	**7**	**18**	**11**	**13**	**7**	**11**	**14**	**11**	**13**	**13**
Mutton and lamb[1]										
Mouton et agneau[1]	7	18	10	13	7	11	14	10	13	13
Saudi Arabia										
Arabie saoudite	**94**	**102**	*** 97**	*** 107**	*** 110**	*** 111**	*** 106**	*** 112**[1]	*** 114**[1]	*** 118**[1]
Beaf and veal										
Boeuf et veau	25	25	* 18	* 24	* 25	* 28	* 27	* 28	* 29	* 30
Mutton and lamb										
Mouton et agneau	69	77	* 79	* 83	* 85	* 83	* 79	84[1]	85[1]	88[1]
Singapore										
Singapour	**74**	**74**[1]	**79**	**75**	**76**	**77**	**82**	**85**	**86**	*** 91**[1]
Pork										
Porc	72	72	77	74	75	76	81	84	85	* 90
Mutton and lamb										
Mouton et agneau	1	1	1	1	1	1	1	1	1	1[1]
Sri Lanka[1]										
Sri Lanka[1]	*** 42**	**36**	**45**	**36**	**36**	**50**	**28**	**41**	**41**	**42**
Beaf and veal[1]										
Boeuf et veau[1]	* 38	32	41	32	32	46	24	37	38	38
Pork										
Porc	1	1	1	1	1	2	2	2[1]	2[1]	2[1]
Mutton and lamb[1]										
Mouton et agneau[1]	* 3	3	2	2	2	2	2	2	2	2
Syrian Arab Republic[1]										
Rép. arabe syrienne[1]	**118**	**126**	**132**	**144**	**143**	**152**	**162**	**146**	**127**	**130**
Beaf and veal[1]										
Boeuf et veau[1]	30	30	30	31	32	32	33	29	30	30
Mutton and lamb										
Mouton et agneau	88[1]	95	101[1]	113[1]	112[1]	120	129	118	97[1]	100[1]
Tajikistan[1]										
Tadjikistan[1]	...	...	...	...	...	...	...	64	* 61	58
Beaf and veal										
Boeuf et veau	...	...	...	...	...	...	...	41	* 37	35[1]
Pork										
Porc	...	...	...	...	...	...	...	4	* 6	5[1]
Mutton and lamb[1]										
Mouton et agneau[1]	...	...	...	...	...	...	...	19	18	18
Thailand[1]										
Thaïlande[1]	**602**	**502**	**554**	**562**	**563**	**576**	**612**	**596**	**650**	**663**
Beaf and veal[1]										
Boeuf et veau[1]	224	226	227	228	227	237	271	252	298	306
Pork[1]										
Porc[1]	378	276	326	334	335	338	340	343	351	356

42

Meat
Production: thousand metric tons [*cont.*]
Viande
Production : milliers de tonnes métriques [*suite*]

Country or area Pays ou zone	1985	1986	1987	1988	1989	1990	1991	1992	1993	1994
Mutton and lamb[1] Mouton et agneau[1]	1	1	1	1	1	1	1	1	1	1
Turkey * [1] **Turquie *** [1]	**713**	**851**	**723**	**710**	**756**	**742**	**715**	**674**	**666**	**656**
Beaf and veal Boeuf et veau	333	466	341	329	381	372	348	309	303	* 294[1]
Pork[1] Porc[1]	1	0	0	0	0	0	0	0	0	0
Mutton and lamb Mouton et agneau	* 380	* 385	* 382	* 380	* 375	* 370	* 367	* 365	* 363[1]	362[1]
Turkmenistan[1] **Turkménistan**[1]	...	...	...	...	...	...	...	86	52	54
Beaf and veal Boeuf et veau	...	...	...	...	...	...	...	46	18	18
Pork Porc	...	...	...	...	...	...	...	6	8	7[1]
Mutton and lamb[1] Mouton et agneau[1]	...	...	...	...	...	...	...	34	26	29
United Arab Emirates[1] **Emirats arabes unis**[1]	**26**	**26**	**31**	**32**	**28**	**31**	**34**	**35**	**35**	**35**
Beaf and veal[1] Boeuf et veau[1]	5	6	6	5	5	5	6	6	6	6
Mutton and lamb[1] Mouton et agneau[1]	21	21	25	27	23	26	28	29	29	29
Uzbekistan **Ouzbékistan**	...	...	...	...	...	...	...	427	* 366[1]	338[1]
Beaf and veal Boeuf et veau	...	...	...	...	...	...	...	323	* 265	250[1]
Pork Porc	...	...	...	...	...	...	...	36	* 46	38[1]
Mutton and lamb Mouton et agneau	...	...	...	...	...	...	...	68	55[1]	50[1]
Viet Nam[1] **Viet Nam**[1]	**698**	**762**	**816**	**827**	**885**	**904**	**892**	**908**	**1 048**	**1 084**
Beaf and veal[1] Boeuf et veau[1]	135	134	142	162	168	172	173	174	167	173
Pork Porc	561	625	671	662	714	729	716	730[1]	878	907[1]
Mutton and lamb[1] Mouton et agneau[1]	2	3	3	3	3	3	3	3	3	3
Yemen **Yémen**	*** 65**	**65**[1]	**65**[1]	*** 67**	*** 68**	*** 70**[1]	*** 67**[1]	*** 68**[1]	*** 70**[1]	*** 71**[1]
Beaf and veal Boeuf et veau	* 29	30[1]	30[1]	* 30	* 31	* 32	* 31	* 31	* 32	* 33
Mutton and lamb Mouton et agneau	36	35[1]	35[1]	37	37	38[1]	36[1]	37[1]	38[1]	38[1]
Europe **Europe**	**32 735**	**33 192**	**33 845**	**33 832**	**33 441**	**34 443**	**34 276**	**33 359**	**33 359**	**31 646**
Beaf and veal Boeuf et veau	11 127	11 207	11 269	10 609	10 381	11 257	11 541	10 981	10 329	9 567
Pork Porc	20 224	20 631	21 187	21 821	21 579	21 646	21 205	20 941	21 600	20 747
Mutton and lamb Mouton et agneau	1 384	1 354	1 390	1 403	1 480	1 540	1 530	1 438	1 431	1 332
Albania[1] **Albanie**[1]	*** 37**	*** 36**	*** 37**	*** 42**	*** 45**	*** 52**	*** 51**	*** 53**	*** 57**	**57**
Beaf and veal Boeuf et veau	17	15	17	19	20	22	25	* 24	* 25	26[1]

42

Meat
Production: thousand metric tons [*cont.*]
Viande
Production : milliers de tonnes métriques [*suite*]

Country or area Pays ou zone	1985	1986	1987	1988	1989	1990	1991	1992	1993	1994
Pork										
Porc	10	11	11	12	12	18	13	16	18	17[1]
Mutton and lamb[1]										
Mouton et agneau[1]	* 10	* 9	* 9	* 11	* 13	* 12	* 13	* 13	* 14	14
Austria										
Autriche	* 701[1]	* 698[1]	* 705[1]	* 745	* 735	* 747	* 759[1]	* 773	* 760	762[1]
Beaf and veal										
Boeuf et veau	221	231	230	219	212	224	236	239	216	222[1]
Pork										
Porc	* 476	* 462	* 470	* 522	* 518	* 517	* 517	* 527	* 538	534[1]
Mutton and lamb										
Mouton et agneau	* 3[1]	* 4[1]	* 5[1]	5	5	6	6[1]	6	6	6[1]
Belarus										
Bélarus	...	...	...	...	...	...	...	824	* 751[1]	* 744[1]
Beaf and veal										
Boeuf et veau	...	...	...	...	...	...	...	495	* 442	430[1]
Pork										
Porc	...	...	...	...	...	...	...	323	* 305	* 310
Mutton and lamb										
Mouton et agneau	...	...	...	...	...	...	...	5	4[1]	4[1]
Belgium-Luxembourg										
Belgique-Luxembourg	1 059	1 081	1 121	1 137	1 143	1 114	1 305	1 316	1 378	* 1 359
Beaf and veal										
Boeuf et veau	326	326	326	317	305	323	381	359	373	* 358
Pork										
Porc	725	747	788	813	830	784	915	951	1 001	* 996
Mutton and lamb										
Mouton et agneau	8	8	7	7	7	7	8	6	4	* 5
Bosnia & Herzegovina[1]										
Bosnie-Herzégovine[1]	...	...	...	...	...	...	...	104	91	58
Beaf and veal[1]										
Boeuf et veau[1]	...	...	...	...	...	...	...	43	37	30
Pork[1]										
Porc[1]	...	...	...	...	...	...	...	50	44	20
Mutton and lamb[1]										
Mouton et agneau[1]	...	...	...	...	...	...	...	10	10	8
Bulgaria										
Bulgarie	563	* 591	581	586	608	590	543	506	* 455[1]	369
Beaf and veal										
Boeuf et veau	134	130	129	122	125	121	108	135	* 126[1]	99
Pork										
Porc	334	372	372	394	412	406	362	311	* 265	214
Mutton and lamb										
Mouton et agneau	94	* 89	80	71	72	63	73	60	* 64[1]	55
Croatia										
Croatie	...	...	...	...	...	...	...	123	143	88
Beaf and veal										
Boeuf et veau	...	...	...	...	...	...	...	40	36	31
Pork										
Porc	...	...	...	...	...	...	...	81	105	57
Mutton and lamb										
Mouton et agneau	...	...	...	...	...	...	...	2	2	0
former Czechoslovakia†										
anc. Tchécoslovaquie†	1 247	1 254	1 281	1 331	1 352	1 326	1 190	1 162	...	...
Beaf and veal										
Boeuf et veau	413	412	412	405	407	403	354	319	...	...
Pork										
Porc	823	832	858	915	934	913	827	834	...	...

42
Meat
Production: thousand metric tons [*cont.*]
Viande
Production : milliers de tonnes métriques [*suite*]

Country or area Pays ou zone	1985	1986	1987	1988	1989	1990	1991	1992	1993	1994
Mutton and lamb Mouton et agneau	11	10	11	11	11	10	9	8	...	...
Czech Republic **République tchèque**	...	...	...	...	...	...	...	...	834	706
Beaf and veal Boeuf et veau	...	...	...	...	...	...	...	...	216	174
Pork Porc	...	...	...	...	...	...	...	...	615	530
Mutton and lamb Mouton et agneau	...	...	...	...	...	...	...	...	3	2
Denmark **Danemark**	**1 320**	**1 388**	**1 384**	**1 385**	**1 369**	**1 412**	**1 486**	**1 589**	**1 709**	**1 712**
Beaf and veal Boeuf et veau	236	243	235	217	205	202	213	217	203	189
Pork Porc	1 083	1 144	1 149	1 167	1 163	1 208	1 272	1 370	1 504	1 521
Mutton and lamb Mouton et agneau	1	1	1	1	1	1	2	2	2	2
Estonia **Estonie**	...	...	...	...	...	...	...	97	79	141[1]
Beaf and veal Boeuf et veau	...	...	...	...	...	...	...	45	43	60[1]
Pork Porc	...	...	...	...	...	...	...	50	35	78[1]
Mutton and lamb Mouton et agneau	...	...	...	...	...	...	...	2	1	3[1]
Faeroe Islands[1] **Iles Féroé**[1]	**1**	**1**	**1**	**1**	**1**	**1**	**1**	**1**	**1**	**1**
Mutton and lamb[1] Mouton et agneau[1]	0	0	1	1	1	1	1	1	1	1
Finland **Finlande**	**300**	**300**	**310**	**290**	**291**	**306**	**300**	**295**	**277**	**280**
Beaf and veal Boeuf et veau	126	125	127	115	110	118	122	117	106	108
Pork Porc	172	174	181	174	180	187	177	176	169	171
Mutton and lamb Mouton et agneau	2	1	1	1	1	1	1	1	1	1
France **France**	**3 743**	**3 770**	**3 874**	**3 857**	**3 693**	**3 833**	**3 968**	**4 094**	**4 081**	**3 930**
Beaf and veal Boeuf et veau	1 893	1 911	1 963	1 828	1 673	1 912	2 026	2 079	1 909	1 667
Pork Porc	1 662	1 677	1 729	1 852	1 844	1 727	1 773	1 859	2 017	2 116
Mutton and lamb Mouton et agneau	188	182	182	177	176	194	170	156	155	147
Germany † **Allemagne†**	* 6 656	* 6 855	* 6 881	6 692	6 474	6 619	6 149	5 557	5 468	5 090[1]
Beaf and veal Boeuf et veau	* 1 993	* 2 110	* 2 099	1 988	1 953	2 112	2 181	1 829	1 681	1 500[1]
Pork Porc	* 4 620	* 4 703	* 4 734	4 663	4 478	4 457	3 918	3 684	3 747	3 550[1]
Mutton and lamb Mouton et agneau	* 43	* 42	* 48	41	43	50	50	44	40	40[1]
Greece **Grèce**	349	352[1]	358[1]	358[1]	363[1]	364[1]	* 362[1]	* 357[1]	* 363[1]	* 358[1]
Beaf and veal Boeuf et veau	84	85[1]	85[1]	84[1]	84[1]	83[1]	81[1]	80[1]	80[1]	* 85[1]

42

Meat
Production: thousand metric tons [cont.]
Viande
Production : milliers de tonnes métriques [suite]

Country or area Pays ou zone	1985	1986	1987	1988	1989	1990	1991	1992	1993	1994
Pork										
Porc	138	142	141	140	139	140	153	153	154	* 145
Mutton and lamb										
Mouton et agneau	126	125	132	134	139	141	* 128	* 124	* 129	* 128
Hungary										
Hongrie	**1 165**	**1 118**	**1 171**	**1 137**	**1 135**	**1 137**	**1 059**	*** 890**	**771**[1]	**664**[1]
Beaf and veal										
Boeuf et veau	146	124	129	110	114	114	123	123	59	62[1]
Pork										
Porc	1 011	986	1 037	1 022	1 014	1 018	931	764	710[1]	600[1]
Mutton and lamb										
Mouton et agneau	9	8	5	5	7	5	6	* 3	2	2[1]
Iceland										
Islande	**18**	**19**	**18**	**16**	**16**	**15**	**15**	**15**	**15**[1]	**15**[1]
Beaf and veal										
Boeuf et veau	3	3	3	3	3	3	3	3	3[1]	3[1]
Pork										
Porc	2	2	2	2	3	3	3	2	2[1]	3[1]
Mutton and lamb										
Mouton et agneau	13	13	13	11	10	10	9	9	9	9
Ireland										
Irlande	**632**	**693**	**672**	**656**	**639**	**758**	**825**	**864**	**838**	*** 756**
Beaf and veal										
Boeuf et veau	448	509	484	459	432	515	554	564	526	* 441
Pork										
Porc	135	137	141	148	144	157	179	204	213	* 220
Mutton and lamb										
Mouton et agneau	48	46	48	50	63	86	92	96	99	* 95
Italy										
Italie	**2 462**	**2 420**	**2 476**	**2 507**	**2 520**	**2 583**	**2 599**	**2 645**[1]	*** 2 640**[1]	*** 2 583**[1]
Beaf and veal										
Boeuf et veau	1 205	1 180	1 175	1 165	1 146	1 165	1 182	1 218[1]	1 188[1]	* 1 180[1]
Pork										
Porc	1 187	1 172	1 231	1 269	1 295	1 333	1 333	1 342	1 371	* 1 320
Mutton and lamb										
Mouton et agneau	70	67	70	73	79	85	85	86	* 81[1]	* 82[1]
Latvia										
Lettonie	...	...	...	...	...	...	...	**224**	**125**[1]	**121**[1]
Beaf and veal										
Boeuf et veau	...	...	...	...	...	...	...	120	67	62
Pork										
Porc	...	...	...	...	...	...	...	101	54	56
Mutton and lamb										
Mouton et agneau	...	...	...	...	...	...	...	4	4[1]	4[1]
Lithuania										
Lituanie	...	...	...	...	...	...	...	**340**[1]	*** 363**	**336**[1]
Beaf and veal										
Boeuf et veau	...	...	...	...	...	...	...	176	* 183	175[1]
Pork										
Porc	...	...	...	...	...	...	...	163	* 179	160[1]
Mutton and lamb										
Mouton et agneau	...	...	...	...	...	...	...	1[1]	1	1[1]
Malta										
Malte	**8**	**9**[1]	**9**[1]	**10**[1]	**10**	**10**	**10**[1]	**10**[1]	**10**[1]	**10**[1]
Beaf and veal										
Boeuf et veau	1	1[1]	2[1]	2	2	2	2[1]	2[1]	2	2
Pork										
Porc	7	7[1]	8[1]	8	8	8	8[1]	8[1]	9	9[1]

42
Meat
Production: thousand metric tons [*cont.*]
Viande
Production : milliers de tonnes métriques [*suite*]

Country or area Pays ou zone	1985	1986	1987	1988	1989	1990	1991	1992	1993	1994
Netherlands **Pays-Bas**	**1 933**	**1 994**	*** 2 062**[1]	**2 151**[1]	*** 2 106**[1]	*** 2 197**[1]	*** 2 232**[1]	**2 238**[1]	**2 377**[1]	*** 2 297**[1]
Beaf and veal Boeuf et veau	511	539	540	507	486	521	* 623	635	611	* 600
Pork Porc	1 412	1 443	1 511	1 631	1 606	1 661	* 1 591	1 585	1 747	* 1 677
Mutton and lamb Mouton et agneau	11	11	* 11[1]	13[1]	* 14[1]	* 15[1]	* 18[1]	18[1]	19[1]	20[1]
Norway **Norvège**	**183**	**186**	**196**	**191**	**183**	**189**	**189**	**200**	**198**	**201**[1]
Beaf and veal Boeuf et veau	74	75	78	77	75	81	80	85	83	84
Pork Porc	84	85	92	90	84	83	85	91	90	92
Mutton and lamb Mouton et agneau	25	26	26	25	24	24	24	25	25	25[1]
Poland **Pologne**	**2 236**	**2 511**	**2 495**	**2 544**	**2 513**	**2 609**	**2 643**	**2 602**	**2 401**	*** 2 067**[1]
Beaf and veal Boeuf et veau	724	752	735	689	637	725	663	544	480	450[1]
Pork Porc	1 486	1 728	1 729	1 828	1 854	1 855	1 947	2 036	1 903	* 1 609
Mutton and lamb Mouton et agneau	26	31	30	26	22	29	33	23	18	8[1]
Portugal **Portugal**	**299**	**302**	**330**	**326**	**369**	**424**	**420**	**414**	**450**	*** 444**[1]
Beaf and veal Boeuf et veau	100	105	105	115	131	116	127	122	115	* 114
Pork Porc	174	171	199	183	211	279	263	265	307	* 302
Mutton and lamb Mouton et agneau	24	26	26	28	27	28	30	27	27	28[1]
Republic of Moldova **République de Moldova**	...	...	...	...	...	...	...	193	152	* 101[1]
Beaf and veal Boeuf et veau	...	...	...	...	...	...	...	75	68	* 42
Pork Porc	...	...	...	...	...	...	...	114	79	* 57
Mutton and lamb Mouton et agneau	...	...	...	...	...	...	...	4	4	2[1]
Romania *[1] **Roumanie ***[1]	**1 169**	**1 122**	**1 168**	**1 091**	**1 114**	**1 195**	**1 228**	**1 121**	**1 175**	**1 149**
Beaf and veal * Boeuf et veau *	232	191	206	191	220	317	317	250	351	333
Pork Porc	* 853	* 851	* 872	* 818	* 798	788	834	789	* 750	* 738
Mutton and lamb[1] Mouton et agneau[1]	* 84	* 81	* 90	* 82	* 97	* 91	* 77	* 82	75	78
Russian Federation * **Fédération de Russie ***	...	...	...	...	...	...	...	**6 746**	**6 150**[1]	**6 095**[1]
Beaf and veal Boeuf et veau	...	...	...	...	...	...	...	3 631	3 359	3 350[1]
Pork Porc	...	...	...	...	...	...	...	2 783	2 432[1]	* 2 400
Mutton and lamb * Mouton et agneau *	...	...	...	...	...	...	...	332	359	345[1]
Slovakia * **Slovaquie ***	...	...	...	...	...	...	...	...	**326**	**276**

42
Meat
Production: thousand metric tons [cont.]
Viande
Production : milliers de tonnes métriques [suite]

Country or area Pays ou zone	1985	1986	1987	1988	1989	1990	1991	1992	1993	1994
Beaf and veal										
Boeuf et veau	...	...	...	...	...	...	...	...	67	32
Pork *										
Porc *	...	...	...	...	...	...	...	...	255	243
Mutton and lamb										
Mouton et agneau	...	...	...	...	...	...	...	...	* 4	0
Slovenia[1]										
Slovénie[1]	...	...	...	...	...	...	...	80	86	87
Beaf and veal										
Boeuf et veau	...	...	...	...	...	...	...	38	38	39[1]
Pork										
Porc	...	...	...	...	...	...	...	41	47	48[1]
Spain										
Espagne	**1 998**	**2 050**	**2 164**	**2 404**	**2 384**	**2 537**	**2 630**	**2 686**	**2 817**	**2 841**
Beaf and veal										
Boeuf et veau	401	440	450	450	459	514	509	538	488	472
Pork										
Porc	1 388	1 399	1 489	1 722	1 703	1 789	1 877	1 916	2 089	2 125
Mutton and lamb										
Mouton et agneau	210	211	225	231	222	234	244	232	241	244
Sweden										
Suède	**495**	**462**	**427**	**432**	**451**	**441**	**409**	**412**	**436**	**439**
Beaf and veal										
Boeuf et veau	158	147	135	127	139	145	137	130	142	139
Pork										
Porc	332	309	288	299	307	291	268	278	289	296
Mutton and lamb										
Mouton et agneau	5	5	5	5	5	5	4	4	4	4
Switzerland										
Suisse	**459**	**461**	**454**	**438**	**441**	**439**	**444**	**435**	**422**	**406**[1]
Beaf and veal										
Boeuf et veau	170	171	172	154	157	164	173	165	155	147
Pork										
Porc	285	286	278	279	280	270	265	264	260	253
Mutton and lamb										
Mouton et agneau	5	5	5	5	5	5	6	6	6	6[1]
TFYR Macedonia										
L'ex-R.y. Macédoine	...	...	...	...	...	...	...	35[1]	43	41
Beaf and veal										
Boeuf et veau	...	...	...	...	...	...	...	8	8	9
Pork										
Porc	...	...	...	...	...	...	...	15[1]	21	19
Mutton and lamb										
Mouton et agneau	...	...	...	...	...	...	...	12	13	13
Ukraine										
Ukraine	...	...	...	...	...	...	...	2 870	2 422	2 376
Beaf and veal										
Boeuf et veau	...	...	...	...	...	...	...	1 656	1 379	1 421
Pork										
Porc	...	...	...	...	...	...	...	1 180	1 013	910
Mutton and lamb										
Mouton et agneau	...	...	...	...	...	...	...	35	30	45
United Kingdom										
Royaume-Uni	**2 454**	**2 335**	**2 421**	**2 285**	**2 283**	**2 318**	**2 384**	**2 284**	**2 215**	**2 186**
Beaf and veal										
Boeuf et veau	1 179	1 062	1 118	946	978	1 002	1 020	959	859	877

42
Meat
Production: thousand metric tons [*cont.*]
Viande
Production : milliers de tonnes métriques [*suite*]

Country or area Pays ou zone	1985	1986	1987	1988	1989	1990	1991	1992	1993	1994
Pork										
Porc	971	983	1 007	1 017	939	946	979	970	1 008	1 032
Mutton and lamb										
Mouton et agneau	304	290	296	322	366	370	385	355	348	278
Yugoslavia										
Yougoslavie	...	...	...	...	...	...	...	**500**	**525**	*** 415**[1]
Beaf and veal										
Boeuf et veau	...	...	...	...	...	...	...	117	145	95[1]
Pork										
Porc	...	...	...	...	...	...	...	357	350	290[1]
Mutton and lamb										
Mouton et agneau	...	...	...	...	...	...	...	26	29	* 30
Yugoslavia, SFR†*										
Yougoslavie, Rfs†*	**1 248**	**1 187**	**1 252**	**1 224**	**1 202**	**1 230**	**1 075**	...	...	...
Beaf and veal										
Boeuf et veau	333	317	317	301	309	352	* 301	...	...	...
Pork *										
Porc *	853	807	870	853	824	810	716	...	...	...
Mutton and lamb										
Mouton et agneau	62	63	65	70	69	67	* 57	...	...	...
Oceania										
Océanie	**3 423**	**3 434**	**3 672**	**3 780**	**3 615**	**3 752**	**3 969**	**4 061**	**3 987**	**4 000**
Beaf and veal										
Boeuf et veau	**1 816**	**1 872**	**2 095**	**2 180**	**2 053**	**2 177**	**2 322**	**2 359**	**2 400**	**2 414**
Pork										
Porc	**349**	**361**	**370**	**386**	**397**	**406**	**402**	**430**	**423**	**440**
Mutton and lamb										
Mouton et agneau	**1 257**	**1 201**	**1 207**	**1 214**	**1 165**	**1 170**	**1 245**	**1 273**	**1 164**	**1 146**
Australia[1]										
Australie[1]	**2 097**	**2 239**	**2 398**	**2 482**	**2 353**	**2 634**	**2 757**	**2 811**	**2 815**	**2 830**
Beaf and veal										
Boeuf et veau	1 310	1 385	1 521	1 588	1 491	1 677	1 760	1 791	1 826	1 825
Pork										
Porc	260	271	283	297	308	317	312	336	328	344
Mutton and lamb[1]										
Mouton et agneau[1]	527	583	594	597	553	640	685	684	661	661
Fiji[1]										
Fidji[1]	**13**	**14**	**14**	**15**	**15**	**15**	**15**	**16**	**17**	**17**
Beaf and veal[1]										
Boeuf et veau[1]	10	11	11	11	11	11	12	12	12	13
Pork[1]										
Porc[1]	3	3	3	3	3	3	3	3	3	4
Mutton and lamb										
Mouton et agneau	1	1	1	1	1	1	1	1	1	1
French Polynesia[1]										
Polynésie française[1]	**1**	**1**	**1**	**1**	**1**	**1**	**1**	**1**	**1**	**1**
Pork										
Porc	1	1	1	1	1	1	1	1	1	1[1]
Kiribati[1]										
Kiribati[1]	**1**	**1**	**1**	**1**	**1**	**1**	**1**	**1**	**1**	**1**
Pork[1]										
Porc[1]	1	1	1	1	1	1	1	1	1	1
New Caledonia[1]										
Nouvelle-Calédonie[1]	**4**	**4**	**3**	**3**	**3**	**4**	**4**	**5**	**5**	**5**
Beaf and veal										
Boeuf et veau	3	3	2	2	2	3	3	3	4	3[1]

42

Meat
Production: thousand metric tons [*cont.*]
Viande
Production : milliers de tonnes métriques [*suite*]

Country or area Pays ou zone	1985	1986	1987	1988	1989	1990	1991	1992	1993	1994
Pork Porc	1	1	1	1	1	1	1	1	1	1[1]
New Zealand **Nouvelle-Zélande**	1 263[1]	1 133[1]	1 210	1 233	1 197	1 050	1 143	1 180	1 100	* 1 097[1]
Beaf and veal Boeuf et veau	487	468	555	572	541	479	540	545	550	* 565
Pork Porc	48	48	44	46	45	43	44	48	48	48[1]
Mutton and lamb Mouton et agneau	729[1]	617[1]	611	616	611	528	559	587	502	* 484[1]
Palau[12] **Palaos**[12]	1	1	1	1	1	1	1	1	1	1
Pork[12] Porc[12]	1	1	1	1	1	1	1	1	1	1
Papua New Guinea[1] **Papouasie-Nvl-Guinée**[1]	27	28	28	28	29	29	29	30	30	31
Beaf and veal[1] Boeuf et veau[1]	2	2	2	2	2	2	2	2	2	2
Pork[1] Porc[1]	25	26	26	26	27	27	27	28	28	28
Samoa[1] **Samoa**[1]	* 4	4	4	4	5	5	5	4	5	5
Beaf and veal Boeuf et veau	* 1	1	1	1	1	1	1[1]	1[1]	1[1]	1[1]
Pork[1] Porc[1]	3	3	4	4	4	4	4	4	4	4
Solomon Islands[1] **Iles Salomon**[1]	2	2	2	3	3	3	3	3	3	3
Beaf and veal[1] Boeuf et veau[1]	1	1	1	1	1	1	1	1	1	1
Pork[1] Porc[1]	2	2	2	2	2	2	2	2	2	2
Tonga[1] **Tonga**[1]	2	2	2	2	2	2	2	2	2	2
Pork[1] Porc[1]	1	1	1	1	2	2	2	2	1	2
Vanuatu[1] **Vanuatu**[1]	5	5	5	5	5	5	6	6	6	6
Beaf and veal Boeuf et veau	2	2	3	3	3	3	3	3[1]	4[1]	4[1]
Pork[1] Porc[1]	3	3	3	2	2	2	2	2	3	3
former USSR†* **ancienne URSS†***	14 050	14 781	15 480	16 211	16 494	16 476	15 174	...	...	...
Beaf and veal Boeuf et veau	7 370	7 840	8 281	8 616	8 800	8 814	8 261	...	...	...
Pork Porc	5 853	6 047	6 299	6 595	6 700	6 654	5 997	...	...	...
Mutton and lamb * Mouton et agneau *	827	894	900	1 000	994	1 008	916	...	...	...

42

Meat
Production: thousand metric tons [*cont.*]
Viande
Production : milliers de tonnes métriques [*suite*]

Source:
Food and Agriculture Organization of the United Nations
(Rome).

† For detailed descriptions of data pertaining to
former Czechoslovakia, Germany, SFR Yugoslavia and former
USSR, see Annex I - Country or area nomenclature, regional
and other groupings.

1 FAO estimate.
2 Including data for Federated States of Micronesia, Marshall
  Is. and Northern Mariana Is.

Source:
Organisation des Nations Unies pour l'alimentation et
l'agriculture (Rome).

† Pour les descriptions en détails des données
relatives à l'ancienne Tchécoslovaquie, l'Allemagne, la Rfs
Yougoslavie et l'ancienne URSS, voir l'Annexe I -
Nomenclature des pays ou zones, groupements régionaux et
autres groupements.

1 Estimation de la FAO.
2 Y compris les données pour les Etats fédérés de Micronésie,
  les îles Marshall et les îles Mariannes du Nord.

43

Beer

Bière

Production: thousand hectolitres

Production : milliers d'hectolitres

Country or area Pays ou zone	1984	1985	1986	1987	1988	1989	1990	1991	1992	1993
Total	946 983	954 969	974 134	991 638	1 035 968	1 059 320	1 099 783	1 147 223	1 153 282	1 182 110
Algeria Algérie	520	526	503	491	475	365	325	301	337	420
Angola Angola	* 650	653	583	466	...	...	...	...	...	...
Argentina Argentine	4 079	3 827	5 452	5 847	5 229	6 102	6 170	7 979	9 518	10 305
Armenia Arménie	..	..	..	..	..			419	149	20
Australia[12] Australie[12]	18 729	18 553	18 627	18 589	18 912	19 508	19 390	19 155	18 623	18 050
Austria Autriche	8 440	8 836	9 017	8 638	8 938	9 174	9 799	9 971	10 176	11 465
Azerbaijan Azerbaïdjan	..	..	..	..	..	..	..	5 159	1 855	1 478
Barbados Barbade	58	55	63	73	76	80	77	66	63	67
Belarus Bélarus	..	..	..	..	..	..	..	3 389	2 736	2 146
Belgium Belgique	14 311	13 931	13 715	13 988	13 792	13 164	14 141	13 799	14 259	...
Belize Belize	24	23	21	22	24	27	34	36	38	57
Bolivia Bolivie	701	606	803	...	1 179	965	1 031	1 278	1 333	...
Botswana Botswana	667	...	...	830	1 002	1 076	1 214	1 283	1 290	1 374
Brazil Brésil	25 980	27 092	34 005	33 893	36 445	42 343	43 849	54 545	43 509	45 336
Bulgaria Bulgarie	5 764	5 838	6 023	6 212	6 332	6 720	6 507	4 880	4 695	4 247
Burkina Faso Burkina Faso	701	525	422	389	401	398	350	394	71	258
Burundi Burundi	798	817	897	937	953	919	1 107	981	1 007	1 044
Cameroon Cameroun	3 976	4 904	5 308	5 857	5 105	...	...	...	...	...
Canada Canada	23 558	23 237	23 547	...	...	...	...	...	...	...
Central African Rep. Rép. centrafricaine	218	276	280	299	...	...	...	...	...	...
Chad Tchad	135	152	118	107	109	115	116	144	129	117
Chile Chili	1 781	1 892	2 050	2 548	2 650	2 765	2 653	2 788	3 349	3 631
China[3] Chine[3]	22 400	31 000	41 301	54 043	65 600	64 339	69 221	83 800	102 064	119 207
Colombia Colombie	...	15 509	16 915	15 355	11 973	14 027	15 098	...	...	...

43

Beer
Production: thousand hectolitres [*cont.*]
Bière
Production : milliers d'hectolitres [*suite*]

Country or area Pays ou zone	1984	1985	1986	1987	1988	1989	1990	1991	1992	1993
Congo Congo	906	882	897	762	744	618	566	686	708	759
Côte d'Ivoire Côte d'Ivoire	1 245	...	...	...	...	...	...	...	...	...
Croatia Croatie	..	..	..	..		..	..	2 248	2 720	...
Cuba Cuba	2 607	2 736	2 931	3 288	3 324	3 333	...	...	...	...
Cyprus Chypre	232	247	257	271	296	318	342	331	370	341
former Czechoslovakia† anc. Tchécoslovaquie†	23 768	22 354	22 789	22 228	22 670	23 333	21 966	20 579	..	
Czech Republic République tchèque	..	..	..	..		..	..	..	18 982	17 414
Denmark[4] Danemark[4]	8 671	8 286	9 064	8 754	9 160	9 217	9 362	...	9 775	...
Dominican Republic Rép. dominicaine	945	1 038	1 099	1 269	...	...	...	...	...	...
Ecuador Equateur	...	...	...	...	...	...	...	...	1 826	...
Egypt Egypte	360	423	460	470	510	490	500	440	420	350
Estonia Estonie	..	..	..	..	..	..	..	68	43	42
Ethiopia[5] Ethiopie[5]	613	818	797	797	877	777	500	435	428	522
Fiji Fidji	185	178	160	148	157	175	194	183	173	167
Finland Finlande	2 968	3 110	3 238	3 509	3 752	3 947	4 151	4 418	4 685	4 579
France France	20 280	19 300	19 000	...	...	...	...	...	...	...
French Polynesia Polynésie française	94	95	118	120	125	121	121	124	129	...
Gabon Gabon	769	850	888	879	851	786	819	814	785	...
Germany † Allemagne†	..	..	..	..	..	..	..	112 071	114 089	111 075
F. R. Germany R. f. Allemagne	87 309	87 895	88 476	86 962	87 044	87 761	99 150	..	..	..
former German D. R. anc. R. d. allemande	24 500	24 288	24 316	24 128	24 521	24 843	15 885	..	..	..
Ghana Ghana	452	429	546	589	614	...	...	...	...	...
Greece Grèce	2 969	3 262	3 103	3 461	4 524	3 869	3 961	3 772	4 025	...
Grenada Grenade	12	14	16	17	20	21	25	...	...	...
Guatemala Guatemala	672	715	613	795	869	...	...	...	...	...

43
Beer
Production: thousand hectolitres [cont.]
Bière
Production : milliers d'hectolitres [suite]

Country or area Pays ou zone	1984	1985	1986	1987	1988	1989	1990	1991	1992	1993
Guyana Guyana	77	80	80	95	134	106	104	124	143	145
Honduras Honduras	511	* 500	* 548	...	...	...	...	...	...	...
Hungary Hongrie	7 962	8 740	8 963	9 045	9 425	9 722	9 918	9 570	9 162	7 877
Iceland Islande	2	4	3	4	5	44	35	30	32	41
India[6] Inde[6]	1 923	2 030	2 036	1 492	1 635	1 972	1 915	2 136	2 233	3 024
Indonesia Indonésie	847	797	718	833	957	953	1 042	1 044	1 145	...
Ireland[7] Irlande[7]	4 214	4 352	4 479	4 360	4 624	5 094	5 236	...	...	...
Israel Israël	415	511	523	536	556	511	567	...	...	...
Italy Italie	9 201	10 381	11 372	11 503	11 589	10 615	11 248	11 049	10 489	...
Jamaica Jamaïque	517	568	632	700	809	852	887	715	828	786
Japan[8] Japon[8]	45 978	48 522	50 754	54 922	58 572	62 869	65 636	69 157	70 106	69 642
Jordan Jordanie	50	46	45	46	45	46	...	...	...	...
Kazakstan Kazakstan	..	..	..	..	..	..	..	31 330	23 011	...
Kenya Kenya	2 280	2 630	3 010	3 070	3 140	3 154	3 311	3 140	3 686	1 742
Korea, Republic of Corée, République de	7 626	7 919	8 040	8 789	10 312	12 108	13 045	15 928	15 673	15 252
Kyrgyzstan Kirghizistan	..	..	..	..	..	..	..	445	310	213
Latvia Lettonie	..	..	..	..	..	..	..	1 295	859	546
Lebanon * Liban *	...	...	...	...	...	...	130	...	...	...
Liberia Libéria	111	97	106	136	158	...	...	...	...	...
Lithuania Lituanie	..	..	..	..	..	..	..	1 412	1 426	1 164
Luxembourg Luxembourg	634	738	732	662	635	618	600	572	569	558
Madagascar Madagascar	229	241	255	240	201	232	298	236	226	228
Malawi Malawi	622	658	627	675	659	757	752	763	...	...
Malaysia Malaisie	998	1 026	* 1 013	988	1 115	1 263	1 401	1 413	...	...
Mali Mali	...	...	...	...	...	34	34	38	41	40

43

Beer
Production: thousand hectolitres [cont.]
Bière
Production : milliers d'hectolitres [suite]

Country or area Pays ou zone	1984	1985	1986	1987	1988	1989	1990	1991	1992	1993
Mauritius Maurice	166	172	188	238	261	254	281	291	295	292
Mexico Mexique	25 616	27 215	27 353	31 482	33 261	37 355	38 734	41 092	42 262	43 780
Mongolia Mongolie	97	89	65	50	49	67	...	...	...	...
Morocco [9] Maroc [9]	393	411	...	...	...	...	...	...	...	...
Mozambique Mozambique	375	228	230	214	297	413	353	227	211	204
Myanmar [10] Myanmar [10]	40	57	50	17	10	21	24	30	19	24
Nepal [11] Népal [11]	23	60	37	52	63	73	...	...	...	...
Netherlands [4] Pays-Bas [4]	17 050	17 530	17 990	17 550	17 437	18 908	20 055	19 863	20 419	20 591
New Zealand [4] Nouvelle-Zélande [4]	3 839	3 863	4 062	4 087	3 925	3 916	3 890	3 627	3 637	3 519
Nicaragua Nicaragua	522	...	...	...	...	...	...	...	...	...
Nigeria Nigéria	7 355	8 052	10 160	6 695	9 167	8 179	7 877	8 108	11 438	16 860
Norway Norvège	1 944	1 991	...	2 198	2 238	2 229	2 281	...	2 273	...
Panama Panama	734	796	925	1 014	871	1 042	1 162	1 219	1 163	1 204
Papua New Guinea * Papouasie-Nvl-Guinée *	474	550	555	...	...	...	...	...	...	...
Paraguay Paraguay	753	768	887	918	903	1 060	1 070	1 150	1 140	1 710
Peru Pérou	5 388	5 724	7 477	8 559	7 018	5 548	5 732	...	...	...
Philippines Philippines	19 030	11 395	8 780	1 175	...	...	...	...	...	...
Poland Pologne	9 867	11 078	11 307	11 897	12 238	12 082	11 294	13 633	14 139	12 585
Portugal Portugal	3 682	3 795	4 128	4 977	5 619	6 874	6 919	6 309	6 860	...
Puerto Rico [1] Porto Rico [1]	347	266	261	266	349	525	625	644	545	397
Republic of Moldova République de Moldova	..	..	..	..	..	..	..	660	410	297
Romania Roumanie	9 845	9 847	10 603	10 364	10 655	11 513	10 527	9 803	10 014	9 929
Russian Federation Fédération de Russie	..	..	..	..	..	..	..	32 700	27 900	24 700
Rwanda Rwanda	576	631	578	596	711	...	...	...	...	...
Saint Kitts and Nevis Saint-Kitts-et-Nevis	9	10	11	14	15	17	17	17	...	...

43
Beer
Production: thousand hectolitres [cont.]
Bière
Production : milliers d'hectolitres [suite]

Country or area Pays ou zone	1984	1985	1986	1987	1988	1989	1990	1991	1992	1993
Sao Tome and Principe * Sao Tomé-et-Principe *	17	31	30	29	...	...	...	...	...	...
Senegal Sénégal	164	168	197	157	170	...	...	...	...	...
Seychelles Seychelles	38	41	42	47	50	52	53	59	70	65
Sierra Leone Sierra Leone	102	60	31	50	40	...	...	...	...	...
Slovakia Slovaquie	..	..	..	..	..	..	..	4 082	3 686	3 967
Slovenia Slovénie	..	..	..	...	..	..	..	2 203	1 783	...
South Africa Afrique du Sud	12 400	12 284	13 751	16 710	18 330	18 610	17 750	17 710	18 290	...
Spain Espagne	21 464	22 475	23 510	24 788	26 141	27 546	27 940	26 482	24 279	...
Sri Lanka Sri Lanka	61	74	85	92	* 92	60		...	...	...
Suriname Suriname	150	142	112	124	99	117	122	122	70	106
Sweden Suède	3 616	3 784	3 979	4 106	4 391	4 722	4 711	4 663	4 969	...
Switzerland[4] Suisse[4]	4 078	4 076	4 087	4 045	4 049	4 121	4 143	4 137	4 020	3 804
Syrian Arab Republic Rép. arabe syrienne	89	94	101	91	83	95	99	99	102	104
Tajikistan Tadjikistan	..	..	..	..	..	..	..	364	135	82
Thailand Thaïlande	1 639	1 052	863	973	1 303	1 801	2 635	2 840	3 252	4 153
TFYR Macedonia L'ex-R.y. Macédoine	..	..	..	..	..	..	..	928	861	...
Togo Togo	359	423	464	452	...	...	...	...	...	...
Trinidad and Tobago Trinité-et-Tobago	347	274	246	371	349	527	412	487	402	...
Tunisia Tunisie	396	373	355	347	405	394	426	407	494	601
Turkey Turquie	2 622	1 965	1 890	2 470	2 671	2 994	3 544	4 188	4 843	5 524
Turkmenistan Turkménistan	..	..	..	..	..	..	..	5	4	3
Uganda Ouganda	148	81	66	169	215	195	194	195	187	239
Ukraine Ukraine	..	..	..	..	..	..	..	13 093	10 997	9 086
former USSR† ancienne URSS†	65 385	65 721	48 907	50 711	55 811	60 182	62 507	..	..	..
United Kingdom Royaume-Uni	60 105	59 655	59 439	59 895	60 156	54 950	70 800	...	...	...

43
Beer
Production: thousand hectolitres [cont.]
Bière
Production : milliers d'hectolitres [suite]

Country or area Pays ou zone	1984	1985	1986	1987	1988	1989	1990	1991	1992	1993
United Rep.Tanzania Rép. Unie de Tanzanie	670	758	652	588	530	537	450	498	493	570
United States[7] Etats-Unis[7]	228 955	228 960	230 588	229 321	231 985	232 510	236 670	...	237 029	237 345
Uruguay Uruguay	...	468	678	709	603	...	...	...	...	817
Uzbekistan Ouzbékistan	..	..	..	..	..	..	..	1 759	1 434	1 363
Viet Nam Viet Nam	845	866	872	840	976	892	1 000	1 312	1 685	...
Yemen Yémen	..	..	..	..	..	..	50	100	40	...
former Dem. Yemen anciennce Yémen dém.	66	70	59	50	...	...	...	..	..	..
Yugoslavia Yougoslavie	..	..	..	..	..	..	..	...	4 413	...
Yugoslavia, SFR† Yougoslavie, Rfs†	10 925	10 656	11 643	12 054	11 970	11 286	...	..	..	..
Zaire Zaïre	3 699	4 222	4 284	...	...	...	...	...	...	...
Zambia Zambie	* 4 169	* 717[12]	* 782[12]	714[12]	825[12]	...	...	...	...	...
Zimbabwe Zimbabwe	920	1 100	...	...	...	...	...	...	...	...

Source:
Industrial statistics database of the Statistics Division of
the United Nations Secretariat.

† For detailed descriptions of data pertaining to
former Czechoslovakia, Germany, SFR Yugoslavia and former
USSR, see Annex I - Country or area nomenclature, regional
and other groupings.

1 Twelve months ending 30 June of year stated.

2 Excluding light beer containing less than 1.15% by volume of
alcohol.
3 Original data in metric tons.
4 Sales.
5 Twelve months ending 7 July of the year stated.

6 Production by large and medium scale establishments only.
7 Twelve months ending 30 September of year stated.

8 Twelve months beginning 1 April of year stated.

9 Including some carbonated drinks.
10 Government production only.
11 Twelve months beginning 16 July of year stated.

12 Incomplete coverage.

Source:
Base de données pour les statistiques industrielles de la
Division de statistique du Secrétariat de l'ONU.

† Pour les descriptions en détails des données
relatives à l'ancienne Tchécoslovaquie, l'Allemagne, la Rfs
Yougoslavie et l'ancienne URSS, voir l'Annexe I -
Nomenclature des pays ou zones, groupements régionaux et
autres groupements.

1 Période de douze mois finissant le 30 juin de l'année
indiquée.
2 Non compris la biére légère contenant moins de 1.15 p. 100
en poids d'alcohol.
3 Données d'origine exprimées en tonnes.
4 Ventes.
5 Période de douze mois finissant le 7 juillet de l'année
indiquée.
6 Production des grandes et moyennes entreprises seulement.
7 Période de douze mois finissant le 30 septembre de l'année
indiquée.
8 Période de douze mois commençant le 1er avril de l'année
indiquée.
9 Y compris certaines boissons gazeuses.
10 Production de l'Etat seulement.
11 Période de douze mois commençant le 16 juillet de i'année
indiquée.
12 Couverture incomplète.

44
Cigarettes
Cigarettes
Production: millions
Production : millions

Country or area Pays ou zone	1984	1985	1986	1987	1988	1989	1990	1991	1992	1993
Total	4 597 295	4 743 118	4 839 700	4 978 118	5 077 419	5 093 145	5 240 085	5 173 439	5 143 924	5 194 538
Albania Albanie	6 200[1]	5 348	5 624	5 467	5 310	6 184	4 947	1 703	...	...
Algeria[2] Algérie[2]	18 000	18 500	20 223	17 699	17 016	15 850	18 775	17 848	16 426	16 260
Angola[1] Angola[1]	2 400	2 400	2 400	2 400	2 400	2 400	2 400	2 400	2 400	...
Argentina Argentine	30 843[2]	31 092[2]	# 2 004	1 883	1 693	1 677	1 657	1 727	1 845	1 929
Armenia Arménie	..	..	..	..	..	..	..	6 614	3 927	1 878
Australia[3] Australie[3]	32 667	32 453	...	...	34 106	34 736	36 263	34 977	* 34 000	...
Austria Autriche	14 907	16 051	15 354	15 067	14 324	14 402	14 961	16 406	15 836	16 247
Azerbaijan Azerbaïdjan	..	..	..	..	..	..	..	7 256	4 855	5 277
Bangladesh[4] Bangladesh[4]	14 843	14 393	14 365	14 762	14 031	14 088	12 289	13 604	12 535	11 516
Barbados[2] Barbade[2]	238	200	199	162	149	143	135	124	115	133
Belarus Bélarus	..	..	..	..	..	..	..	15 009	8 847	8 670
Belgium[5] Belgique[5]	29 422	30 184	28 619	28 953	28 683	27 489	27 758	27 303	29 576	27 173
Belize Belize	65	74	78	81	94	95	101	104	104	105
Bolivia Bolivie	368[1]	533[1]	899[1]	900[1]	95	101	97	102	116	...
Brazil[1] Brésil[1]	127 800	146 300	168 000	161 400	157 900	162 700	173 987	175 396	169 000	...
Bulgaria Bulgarie	92 055[3]	93 975[3]	89 918[3]	90 300	86 800	82 600	73 000	73 300	71 000	...
Burkina Faso Burkina Faso	660	671	510	430	533	609	822	983	979	943
Burundi Burundi	334	293	257	284	333	286	384	450	453	517
Cambodia[1] Cambodge[1]	4 100	4 150	4 175	4 175	4 200	4 200	4 200	4 200	4 200	...
Cameroon Cameroun	2 319	2 128	3 800[1]	4 770[1]	4 800[1]	4 800[1]	4 900[1]	5 000[1]	5 000[1]	...
Canada Canada	61 600	63 486	55 632	54 030	53 858[1]	48 792[1]	46 111[1]	46 815[1]	45 500[1]	...
Central African Rep. Rép. centrafricaine	413	539	407	460	...	...	...	...	...	...
Chad Tchad	298	308	225	187	204	187	248	476	415	499

44
Cigarettes
Production: millions [*cont.*]
Cigarettes
Production : millions [*suite*]

Country or area Pays ou zone	1984	1985	1986	1987	1988	1989	1990	1991	1992	1993
Chile Chili	8 107	8 053	8 296	8 183	9 061	9 686	10 011	10 000	10 790	10 516
China Chine	1 066 000[1]	1 180 000[1]	1 296 500[1]	1 440 500[1]	1 545 000[1]	1 597 530	1 648 765	1 613 245	1 642 340	1 655 630
Colombia[1] Colombie[1]	23 400	24 050	24 181	21 987	18 253	16 570	14 490	13 585	13 250	...
Congo[2] Congo[2]	903	1 027	888	787	770	709	* 645	581	431	...
Costa Rica[1] Costa Rica[1]	2 200	2 200	2 000	2 135	2 135	2 050	2 030	2 000	2 000	...
Côte d'Ivoire Côte d'Ivoire	3 210	4 000[1]	4 200[1]	4 400[1]	4 500[1]	4 500[1]	4 500[1]	4 500[1]	4 500[1]	...
Croatia Croatie	..	..	..	..	..	..	..	11 655	12 833	...
Cuba Cuba	18 697	17 961	16 841	15 398	16 885	16 520	...	...	...	...
Cyprus Chypre	2 586	2 366	1 914	3 717	4 412	3 935	4 601	5 497	6 177	3 530
former Czechoslovakia† anc. Tchécoslovaquie†	24 603	23 840	24 998	25 365	25 502	25 428	26 708	28 190	..	
Denmark[6] Danemark[6]	10 583	10 966	11 246	11 162	11 144	11 209	11 387	11 407	11 439	...
Dominica Dominique	27	29	29	...	...	...	...	...	...	...
Dominican Republic Rép. dominicaine	3 696	3 826	4 164	4 473	4 802[1]	4 473[1]	4 805[1]	4 376[1]	4 582[1]	...
Ecuador Equateur	5 000	4 800	3 967	* 4 600	* 4 600	* 4 600	* 4 600	* 4 600	3 000	...
Egypt Egypte	44 599	47 520	44 394	47 500	43 846	43 208	39 837	40 154	42 516	38 844
El Salvador[1] El Salvador[1]	2 500	2 300	2 100	2 100	1 967	1 970	1 655	1 620	1 620	...
Estonia Estonie	..	..	..	..	..	..	..	3 577	1 780	2 630
Ethiopia[7] Ethiopie[7]	2 036	2 229	2 619	3 040	2 972	2 711	2 258	2 416	1 879	1 932
Fiji Fidji	513	513	478	466	466	505	532	515	484	505
Finland Finlande	8 345	8 185	8 540	9 061	9 619	8 931	8 974	8 180	8 106	7 237
France France	60 729	67 376	59 122	54 120	* 53 307	* 54 225	53 000	* 50 311	* 49 000	...
Gabon Gabon	341	355	368	280	422	319	253	359	399	...
Germany † Allemagne†	..	..	..	..	..	..	..	...	...	204 730†
F. R. Germany R. f. Allemagne	160 680	163 267	166 665	157 586	159 499	159 477	177 905	..	..	
former German D. R. anc. R. d. allemande	28 018	26 909	27 364	27 625	28 576	28 625	22 469	..	..	..

44
Cigarettes
Production: millions [cont.]
Cigarettes
Production : millions [suite]

Country or area Pays ou zone	1984	1985	1986	1987	1988	1989	1990	1991	1992	1993
Ghana Ghana	2 008	1 942	1 826	1 734	1 831	1 616	1 805	* 2 100	* 2 100	...
Greece Grèce	25 699	27 635	27 118	28 859	26 244	26 123	26 175	27 700	* 29 250	...
Grenada Grenade	25	24	23	22	23	24	22	...	...	...
Guatemala Guatemala	1 968	1 988	1 926	2 270	1 858[1]	1 997[1]	1 955[1]	1 907[1]	2 001[1]	...
Guyana Guyana	373	467	481	477	470	266	247	307	318	302
Haiti Haïti	886	806	829	903	870[1]	870[1]	870[1]	870[1]	870[1]	...
Honduras Honduras	2 145	2 311	2 300[1]	2 278[1]	2 319[1]	2 582[1]	2 862[1]	2 300[1]	2 200[1]	...
Hong Kong[5] Hong-kong[5]	8 681	12 496	11 841	15 309	24 000	20 901	21 700	32 721	36 513	...
Hungary Hongrie	26 679	26 430	26 351	26 541	26 171	26 540	28 212	26 124	26 835	28 728
India[8] Inde[8]	86 217	80 600	74 991	64 782	54 013	58 066	61 162	65 130	61 413	71 686
Indonesia Indonésie	95 634	102 300	114 312	124 432	136 271	148 000	155 000	153 000	156 422	...
Iran, Islamic Rep. of[9] Iran, Rép. islamique d'[9]	16 154	16 168	15 239	15 068	13 790	9 923	12 319	* 11 565	* 10 543	...
Iraq[1] Iraq[1]	7 000	7 000	10 000	13 000	20 250	27 000	26 000	13 000	5 794	...
Ireland Irlande	7 391	8 037	6 825	6 659	6 420	6 161	6 218	6 377	* 7 850	...
Israel Israël	6 714	6 709	6 723	6 888	5 882	5 245	5 440	* 5 650	* 5 650	...
Italy[2] Italie[2]	80 452	78 774	75 541	70 447	67 394	67 942	61 736	57 634	53 799	54 943
Jamaica Jamaïque	1 270	1 314	* 1 140	1 273	1 303	1 383	1 380	1 219	1 299	1 224
Japan[10] Japon[10]	306 867	303 000	309 200	273 700	267 000	268 400	268 100	275 000	279 000	...
Jordan Jordanie	5 027	3 905	3 732	4 378	3 678	2 926	3 185	3 719	3 091	3 465
Kazakstan Kazakstan	..	..	..	..	..	..	..	9 536	8 997	10 664
Kenya Kenya	5 391	5 409	5 821	6 372	6 641	6 661	6 647	6 473	7 193	7 267
Korea, Republic of Corée, République de	77 984	75 532	78 694	81 816	86 014	86 759	91 923	94 336	96 648	96 887
Kyrgyzstan Kirghizistan	..	..	..	..	..	..	..	4 015	3 120	3 428
Lao People's Dem. Rep.[1] Rép. dém. pop. lao[1]	1 100	1 125	1 200	1 200	1 200	1 200	1 200	1 200	1 200	...
Latvia Lettonie	..	..	..	..	..	..	..	4 765	3 435	2 589

44
Cigarettes
Production: millions [*cont.*]
Cigarettes
Production : millions [*suite*]

Country or area Pays ou zone	1984	1985	1986	1987	1988	1989	1990	1991	1992	1993
Lebanon[1] Liban[1]	200	1 800	* 1 800	2 500	3 500	4 000	4 000	4 000	4 000	...
Liberia Libéria	123	82	92	22[1]	22[1]	22[1]	22[1]	22[1]	22[1]	...
Libyan Arab Jamah.[1] Jamah. arabe libyenne[1]	3 500	3 500	3 500	3 500	3 500	3 500	3 500	3 500	3 500	...
Lithuania Lituanie	..	..	..	..	..	..	..	6 438	5 269	3 435
Madagascar Madagascar	2 137[2]	2 368[2]	2 188[2]	2 669[2]	1 817[2]	2 341[2]	1 476	1 950[2]	2 223[2]	2 304
Malawi Malawi	824	857	874	908	956	* 1 080	1 061	951	* 1 000	...
Malaysia[2] Malaisie[2]	14 671	13 839	13 706	13 729	15 904	16 169	17 331	17 498	16 574	15 568
Malta[1] Malte[1]	1 129	1 300	1 300	1 400	1 425	1 450	1 475	1 475	1 475	...
Mauritius Maurice	1 253[2]	1 418[2]	1 266[2]	1 392[2]	1 304[2]	1 050	1 000	1 110	1 060	1 190
Mexico Mexique	51 666	54 332	49 898	54 644	50 507	53 920	55 380	54 680	55 988	52 977
Morocco Maroc	548	593	663	671	684	615	640	602	515	...
Mozambique Mozambique	792	710	1 053	899	670	1 044	1 030	217	124	377
Myanmar[11] Myanmar[11]	2 515	3 506	1 574	553	952	505	979	682	396	426
Nepal Népal	4 252	4 741	5 600	6 046	5 664	6 706	...	...	...	...
Netherlands Pays-Bas	47 761	51 321	53 339	59 801	61 693	63 148	71 992	74 767	78 479	71 254
New Zealand Nouvelle-Zélande	6 236	5 654	5 223	5 361	5 355	4 270	4 489	4 014	3 466	3 381
Nicaragua Nicaragua	2 318	2 400[1]	2 400[1]	2 400[1]	2 400[1]	2 400[1]	2 400[1]	2 400[1]	2 400[1]	...
Nigeria Nigéria	9 000[1]	9 100[1]	9 600[1]	6 106	8 676	9 284	10 380	9 405	8 608	9 384
Norway[1] Norvège[1]	790	1 082	1 400	1 400	1 655	1 750	1 480	1 730	1 825	...
Pakistan[4] Pakistan[4]	40 096	38 921	39 593	39 929	40 697	31 567	32 279	29 887	29 673	29 947
Panama Panama	911	873	873	825	671	637	814	771	806	907
Paraguay Paraguay	878	834	750	1 134	* 2 730	2 730	992	827	777	...
Peru Pérou	3 489	3 102	3 741	3 420	2 671	2 439	2 672	...	...	...
Philippines[4] Philippines[4]	58 600	62 300	60 700	61 072	66 850[1]	69 700[1]	71 500[1]	70 710[1]	75 400[1]	...
Poland Pologne	86 363	90 021	94 212	98 666	89 681	81 342	91 497	90 407	86 571	99 704

44

Cigarettes
Production: millions [*cont.*]
Cigarettes
Production : millions [*suite*]

Country or area Pays ou zone	1984	1985	1986	1987	1988	1989	1990	1991	1992	1993
Portugal Portugal	14 798[2]	14 900[2]	15 166[2]	15 481[2]	15 129[2]	15 424[2]	17 547	17 361	15 619	...
Republic of Moldova République de Moldova	..	..	..	..	..	..	..	9 164	8 582	8 790
Romania[3] Roumanie[3]	32 888[1]	32 471[1]	31 013	32 918	33 349	22 121	18 090	17 722	17 781	23 272
Russian Federation Fédération de Russie	..	..	..	..	..	..	..	144 000	148 000	146 000
Rwanda Rwanda	696	698	649	698	458	...	...	...	...	...
Senegal Sénégal	2 501[2]	2 979[2]	3 300[2]	1 872[2]	1 348[2]	3 350[1]	3 350[1]	3 350[1]	3 350[1]	...
Seychelles Seychelles	65	56	60	68	61	58	67	69	62	65
Sierra Leone Sierra Leone	1 341	1 189	940	1 100	933	1 200[1]	1 200[1]	1 200[1]	1 200[1]	...
Singapore[1] Singapour[1]	3 000	2 400	2 000	2 340	4 700	5 982	9 620	10 500	11 760	...
Slovenia Slovénie	..	..	..	..	..	..	..	4 798	5 278	...
South Africa Afrique du Sud	32 501	31 704	30 680	17 773	28 002	36 665	40 792	40 163	35 563	34 499
Spain Espagne	83 884	80 495	81 705	87 362	85 612	75 817	75 995	81 843	76 696	...
Sri Lanka Sri Lanka	5 200	6 168	6 111	5 894	5 028	5 136	5 621	5 789	5 359	...
Sudan Soudan	1 884[2]	2 700	2 200	2 200	1 800	750[1]	750[1]	750[1]	750[1]	...
Suriname Suriname	521	514	557	492	501	526	487	337	419	454
Sweden Suède	10 420	10 090	10 197	10 103	10 208	10 107	9 648	9 594	9 841	...
Switzerland Suisse	25 449	23 150	23 555	24 863	27 075	28 059	31 771	32 943	33 740	34 713
Syrian Arab Republic[2] Rép. arabe syrienne[2]	11 274	12 127	12 112	9 143	7 056	6 345	6 855	7 974	8 093	7 185
Tajikistan Tadjikistan	..	..	..	..	..	..	..	4 467	2 607	1 901
Thailand Thaïlande	29 170	29 192	29 530	31 407	33 992	37 365	38 180	39 697	40 691	42 043
Trinidad and Tobago Trinité-et-Tobago	1 064[2]	987[2]	920[2]	583[2]	766[2]	726[2]	701[2]	881[2]	656[2]	880
Tunisia Tunisie	5 527	6 334	8 097	6 937	7 125	6 571	6 852	7 790	7 797	6 965
Turkey Turquie	62 085	62 000	59 740	58 617	60 153	46 570	63 055	71 106	67 549	74 845
Uganda Ouganda	966	1 416	1 420	1 435	1 638	1 586	1 290	1 688	1 575	1 412
Ukraine Ukraine	..	..	..	..	..	..	..	66 645	60 990	40 571

44

Cigarettes
Production: millions [cont.]
Cigarettes
Production : millions [suite]

Country or area Pays ou zone	1984	1985	1986	1987	1988	1989	1990	1991	1992	1993
former USSR[†] ancienne URSS[†]	373 793	381 274	383 878	378 475	358 218	343 288	313 082	..	..	..
United Kingdom[2][12] Royaume-Uni[2][12]	93 400	88 600	83 300	89 900	87 900	104 155	112 000	127 000	* 126 538	...
United Rep.Tanzania Rép. Unie de Tanzanie	4 000	2 666	2 748	2 635	2 785	2 845	3 742	3 870	3 789	3 893
United States[4] Etats-Unis[4]	668 800	655 300	652 000	689 400	694 500	677 200	709 700	694 500	703 134	687 317
Uruguay Uruguay	3 800[1]	3 098	3 583	3 383	3 446	3 900[1]	3 900[1]	3 900[1]	3 900[1]	3 736
Uzbekistan Ouzbékistan	..	..	..	..	..	..	..	4 897	4 150	4 151
Venezuela[1] Venezuela[1]	20 643	19 760	18 400	18 100	18 824	20 599	23 560	24 236	24 400	...
Viet Nam Viet Nam	21 236	21 012	22 364	19 630	17 754	23 288	24 990	25 960	* 24 600	...
former Dem. Yemen anciennce Yémen dém.	1 202	1 467	1 147	1 193	...	...	...	..	..	..
Yugoslavia Yougoslavie	..	..	..	..	..	..	..	...	15 654	...
Yugoslavia, SFR[†] Yougoslavie, Rfs[†]	55 965	57 652	55 787	56 128	60 169	51 287	58 200	..	..	..
Zaire Zaïre	3 500	3 525	3 600	4 500[1]	5 200	5 200[1]	5 200[1]	5 200[1]	5 200[1]	...
Zambia[1] Zambie[1]	1 400	1 400	1 450	1 500	1 500	1 500	1 500	1 500	1 500	...
Zimbabwe[1] Zimbabwe[1]	2 300	2 318	2 300	2 420	2 560	2 518	2 600	3 240	3 025	...

Source:
Industrial statistics database of the Statistics Division of
the United Nations Secretariat.

† For detailed descriptions of data pertaining to
former Czechoslovakia, Germany, SFR Yugoslavia and former
USSR, see Annex I - Country or area nomenclature, regional
and other groupings.

1 Source: US Department of Agriculture, (Washington, DC).
2 Original data in units of weight. Computed on the basis of
   one million cigarettes per ton.
3 Including cigars.
4 Twelve months ending 30 June of year stated.

5 Including cigarillos.
6 Sales.
7 Twelve months ending 7 July of the year stated.

8 Production by large and medium scale establishments only.
9 Production by establishments employing 50 or more persons.
10 Twelve months beginning 1 April of year stated.

11 Government production only.
12 Sales by manufacturers employing 25 or more persons.

Source:
Base de données pour les statistiques industrielles de la
Division de statistique du Secrétariat de l'ONU.

† Pour les descriptions en détails des données
relatives à l'ancienne Tchécoslovaquie, l'Allemagne, la Rfs
Yougoslavie et l'ancienne URSS, voir l'Annexe I -
Nomenclature des pays ou zones, groupements régionaux et
autres groupements.

1 Source: "US Department of Agriculture," (Washington, DC).
2 Données d'origine exprimées en poids. Calcul sur la base
   d'un million cigarettes par tonne.
3 Y compris les cigares.
4 Période de douze mois finissant le 30 juin de l'année
   indiquée.
5 Y compris les cigarillos.
6 Ventes.
7 Période de douze mois finissant le 7 juillet de l'année
   indiquée.
8 Production des grandes et moyennes entreprises seulement.
9 Production des établissements occupant 50 personnes ou plus.
10 Période de douze mois commençant le 1er avril de l'année
   indiquée.
11 Production de l'Etat seulement.
12 Ventes des fabricants employant 25 personnes ou plus.

45
Fabrics
Tissus

Woven cotton and wool, cellulosic and non-cellulosic fibres: million square metres

Tissus de coton, laines, fibres cellulosiques et non cellulosiques : millions de mètres carrés

Country or area Pays ou zone	1984	1985	1986	1987	1988	1989	1990	1991	1992	1993
A. Cotton • Coton										
Total	**70 416**	**73 304**	**89 415**	**81 173**	**91 310**	**99 887**	**85 013**	**94 897**	**94 860**	**97 835**
Afghanistan[1] Afghanistan[1]	45	45	58	53	32	...	...	...	...	...
Algeria Algérie	* 105	* 103	* 87	* 88	80[2]	75[2]	75[2]	64[2]	83[2]	...
Armenia Arménie	..	..	..	..	..	..	..	10	5	2
Australia[34] Australie[34]	33	37	39	38	39	36	40	36	39	41
Austria Autriche	64	85	85	93	89	88	108	100	86	83
Azerbaijan Azerbaïdjan	..	..	..	..	..	..	..	120	114	115
Bangladesh[3] Bangladesh[3]	* 70	* 75	* 70	* 70	63	63	63	63	63	...
Belarus Bélarus	..	..	..	..	..	..	..	144	119	92
Belgium Belgique	361[5]	373[5]	388[5]	379[5]	340[5]	386	399	379	337	331
Bolivia * Bolivie *	1	1	2	...	...	...	...	...	...	...
Brazil[2] Brésil [2]	1 780	2 170	2 352	2 359	2 157	2 179	1 901	1 631		
Bulgaria[6] Bulgarie[6]	374	356	352	358	370	367	254	138	102	83
Cameroon[2] Cameroun[2]	61	29	29	19	...	...	...	...	...	...
Central African Rep. * Rép. centrafricaine *	4	...	...	...	...	...	...	...	...	...
Chad Tchad	60	37	39	34	48	57	58	60	81	...
Chile[2] Chili[2]	49	54	62	61	39	38	31	31	25	...
China[2] Chine[2]	16 372	15 202	19 685	20 679	22 454	22 613	22 556	21 719	21 726	23 295
Côte d'Ivoire[7] Côte d'Ivoire[7]	118	...	...	...	...	...	...	...	...	...
Croatia Croatie	..	..	..	..	..	..	..	30	29	...
Cuba[8] Cuba[8]	156	177	183	202	203	184	...	...	...	...
former Czechoslovakia†[6] anc. Tchécoslovaquie†[6]	624	631	634	634	629	624	629	464		
Czech Republic République tchèque	..	..	..	..	..	..	..	..	293	225
Dominican Republic[9] Rép. dominicaine[9]	13	13	11	13	...	...	...	...	...	...

45
Fabrics
Woven cotton and wool, cellulosic and non-cellulosic fibres: million square metres [cont.]
Tissus
Tissus de coton, laines, fibres cellulosiques et non cellulosiques : millions de mètres carrés [suite]

Country or area Pays ou zone	1984	1985	1986	1987	1988	1989	1990	1991	1992	1993
Egypt Egypte	* 899[2]	* 740[2]	* 726[2]	* 694[2]	589	601	603	609	613	329
Estonia Estonie	..	..	..	..	..	..	..	168	111	55
Ethiopia[10] Ethiopie[10]	85	79	84	87	96	68	65	32	30	36
Finland[6] Finlande[6]	73	80	53	70	* 58	46	41	24	20	21
France[11] France[11]	907	861	841	843	820	841	808	751	736	665
Germany † Allemagne† F. R. Germany[6] R. f. Allemagne[6] former German D. R. anc. R. d. allemande	.. 943 294	.. 990 298	.. 946 308	.. 1 014 287	.. 962 304	.. 943 304	.. 896 213	929	763	687 .. ..
Ghana[6] Ghana[6]	12	15	...	...	...	...	...	...	...	...
Greece Grèce	281[11]	288[11]	305[11]	* 381	* 382	* 394	...	...	...	...
Haiti Haïti	1	1	1	1	...	...	...	.	...	...
Honduras[12] Honduras[12]	11	10	...	...	...	...	...	...	...	...
Hong Kong Hong-kong	659	639	760	* 850	867	734	* 818	753	807	755
Hungary[6] Hongrie[6]	278	287	292	292	295	247	206	133	86	78
India Inde	10 547	12 610	12 367	12 912	12 269	13 750	15 177	16 478	17 582	19 648
Indonesia[2][13] Indonésie[2][13]	* 1 135	* 1 274	* 3 038	* 2 253	15 293	18 527	4 284	...	...	...
Ireland[6][14] Irlande[6][14]	34	...	...	...	...	...	...	...	...	...
Italy[11] Italie[11]	1 665	1 626	1 633	1 611	1 554	1 618	1 618	1 525	1 353	1 293
Jamaica[2] Jamaïque[2]	* 2	1	2	1	0	0	3	4	3	...
Japan[15] Japon[15]	2 090	2 061	1 974	1 837	1 885	1 915	1 765	1 603	1 465	1 205
Jordan[9] Jordanie[9]	2	* 2	1	2	...	...	...	...	...	...
Kazakstan Kazakstan	..	..	..	..	..	..	..	134	135	136
Kenya Kenya	51	54	51	51	46	38	45	27	31	40
Korea, Republic of[6] Corée, République de[6]	395	482	559	567	623	648	620	608	483	480
Kyrgyzstan Kirghizistan	..	..	..	..	..	..	..	119	119	65

45

Fabrics
Woven cotton and wool, cellulosic and non-cellulosic fibres: million square metres [*cont.*]
Tissus
Tissus de coton, laines, fibres cellulosiques et non cellulosiques : millions de mètres carrés [*suite*]

Country or area Pays ou zone	1984	1985	1986	1987	1988	1989	1990	1991	1992	1993
Latvia Lettonie	..	..	..	..	..	..	..	45	22	0
Lithuania Lituanie	..	..	..	..	..	..	..	106	89	48
Macau Macao	...	...	...	...	...	...	...	...	15
Madagascar Madagascar	82	78	81	75	68	72	59[2]	57[2]	50	42
Mexico[11 12] Mexique[11 12]	460	511	504	626	424	...	...	...	...	...
Myanmar[16] Myanmar[16]	109	68	* 53	* 36	* 31	21	47[2]	28[2]	27[2]	...
Nepal Népal	10 533	12 000	21 386	11 897	8 467	...	...	...	...	...
Netherlands[6 11] Pays-Bas[6 11]	114	105	101	93	79	86	79	72	...	...
Nicaragua[2] Nicaragua[2]	31	...	...	...	...	...	...	...	...	...
Niger * Niger *	7	6	31	39	20	...	...	...	...	...
Nigeria Nigéria	267[12]	285[12]	102[12]	323[12]	331	279	316	395	420	393
Norway Norvège	19[6]	16[6]	16[6]	16[6]	14[6]	14[11]	* 14[11]	7[11]	...	...
Pakistan[12 17] Pakistan[12 17]	297	272	253	238	282	270	295	293	308	325
Paraguay Paraguay	7	* 11	* 14	* 7	14	16	18[2]	23[2]	23[2]	...
Philippines[2 6] Philippines[2 6]	184	191	* 217	* 304	* 478	* 535	...	...	...	...
Poland[6 18] Pologne[6 18]	868	887	878	801	839	811	474	332	290	284
Portugal[11] Portugal[11]	523	542	619	561	503	562	547	511	355	...
Republic of Moldova République de Moldova	..	..	..	..	..	..	..	165	150	1
Romania[6] Roumanie[6]	697	695	727	705	689	709	536	437	289	271
Russian Federation Fédération de Russie	..	..	..	..	..	..	..	5 949	3 799	2 822
Senegal * Sénégal *	8	3	...	3	...	...	...	...	...	...
Slovakia Slovaquie	..	..	..	..	..	..	..	..	...	78
Slovenia[18] Slovénie[18]	..	..	..	..	..	..	..	102	78	...
South Africa Afrique du Sud	147	139	158	172	163	188	175	170	138	166
Spain[11] Espagne[11]	576	604	583	640	662	705	698	705	...	...

45

Fabrics
Woven cotton and wool, cellulosic and non-cellulosic fibres: million square metres [cont.]
Tissus
Tissus de coton, laines, fibres cellulosiques et non cellulosiques : millions de mètres carrés [suite]

Country or area Pays ou zone	1984	1985	1986	1987	1988	1989	1990	1991	1992	1993
Sri Lanka[2][12] Sri Lanka[2][12]	30	44	49	46	* 49	36	19	14	...	...
Sweden * Suède *	56[11]	57[11]	54[11]	53[11]	67	65	...	...	...	...
Switzerland[2] Suisse[2]	127	130	131	130	110	101	103	81	77	74
Syrian Arab Republic *[11] Rép. arabe syrienne *[11]	273	158	289	180	173	215	194	201	187	...
Tajikistan Tadjikistan	..	..	..	..	..	..	..	102	58	57
Thailand[6] Thaïlande[6]	784	825	881	...	...	...	...	...	...	...
TFYR Macedonia L'ex-R.y. Macédoine	..	..	..	..	..	..	..	25	21	...
Turkey[2][19] Turquie[2][19]	685	589	390	399	422	660	714	626	710	...
Turkmenistan Turkménistan	..	..	..	..	..	..	..	28	29	29
Uganda[6][9] Ouganda[6][9]	...	10	10	10	11	12	8	9	10	7
Ukraine Ukraine	..	..	..	..	..	..	..	561	509	262
former USSR†[6] ancienne URSS†[6]	8 313	8 580	8 770	8 721	8 670	8 906	8 647	..	..	..
United Kingdom Royaume-Uni	305	315	308	280	240	* 246	* 198	* 185	...	...
United Rep.Tanzania Rép. Unie de Tanzanie	...	54	48	60	44	46	46	38	49	40
United States Etats-Unis	3 346	3 278	3 648	3 990	3 873	3 837	3 732	3 682	3 846	...
Uzbekistan Ouzbékistan	..	..	..	..	..	..	..	392	474	482
Viet Nam Viet Nam	435	439	427	432	458	403	380	335[2]	...	...
former Yemen Arab Rep.[2] anc. Yémen rép. arabe[2]	7	7	...	...	...	...	...	...	...	...
former Dem. Yemen anciennce Yémen dém.	4	3	3	3	...	...	...	..	..	...
Yugoslavia Yougoslavie	..	..	..	..	..	..	..	...	39	...
Yugoslavia, SFR†[20] Yougoslavie, Rfs†[20]	318	344	358	366	351	339	...	..	..	...
Zaire *[12] Zaïre *[12]	58	50	...	...	...	...	...	...	...	...
Zambia Zambie	16	21	18	...	...	11	...	...	...	...

B. Wool · Laines

Total	3 395	3 391	3 418	3 379	3 520	3 453	3 215	2 956	2 723	2 294

45

Fabrics
Woven cotton and wool, cellulosic and non-cellulosic fibres: million square metres [*cont.*]
Tissus
Tissus de coton, laines, fibres cellulosiques et non cellulosiques : millions de mètres carrés [*suite*]

Country or area Pays ou zone	1984	1985	1986	1987	1988	1989	1990	1991	1992	1993
Afghanistan * [1] Afghanistan * [1]	1	0	0	0	0	...	...	...	...	...
Algeria Algérie	15	18	18	12	7[2]	10[2]	13[2]	16[2]	13[2]	...
Armenia Arménie	..	..	..	..	..	..	..	4	3	1
Australia[3] Australie[3]	10	11	11	11	11	10	8	8	8	8
Austria Autriche	16	16	15	13	11	9	9	8	8	5
Azerbaijan Azerbaïdjan	..	..	..	..	..	..	..	10	7	6
Belarus Bélarus	..	..	..	..	..	..	..	49	39	40
Belgium [21] Belgique[21]	11	10	9	6	5	5	5	6	4	4
Bulgaria[6] Bulgarie[6]	61	61	64	66	52	51	47	26	22	23
China Chine	298	360[2]	416[2]	438[2]	472[2]	461[2]	487[2]	514[2]	558[2]	354[2]
Croatia Croatie	..	..	..	..	..	..	..	5	1	...
Cuba[22] Cuba[22]	0	0	0	0	0	0	...	...	...	...
former Czechoslovakia†[6] anc. Tchécoslovaquie†[6]	85	87	85	85	86	87	77	56	..	
Czech Republic République tchèque	..	..	..	..	..	..	..	..	46	40
Denmark [12 23] Danemark[12 23]	...	...	1	1	* 1	1	1	1	1	
Ecuador * [2] Equateur * [2]	...	...	...	2	3	...	...	...	...	
Egypt Egypte	20[2]	22[2]	26[2]	24[2]	39[2]	* 28	23	23	23	9
Estonia Estonie	..	..	..	..	..	..	..	7	4	1
Finland [6] Finlande[6]	3	2	2	1	* 1	1	* 0	* 0	* 0	* 0
France France	41	45	39	29	19	21	16	14	13	9
Germany † Allemagne†	..	..	..	..	..	..	..	121	119	97
F. R. Germany[6] R. f. Allemagne[6]	87	104	102	100	104	109	108	..	..	
former German D. R. anc. R. d. allemande	41	41	42	44	47	50	38	..	..	
Greece[6 11] Grèce[6 11]	4	5	5	4	3	4	2	3	...	...
Hungary[6] Hongrie[6]	24	23	22	18	17	21	11	7	4	3

45

Fabrics
Woven cotton and wool, cellulosic and non-cellulosic fibres: million square metres [cont.]
Tissus
Tissus de coton, laines, fibres cellulosiques et non cellulosiques : millions de mètres carrés [suite]

Country or area Pays ou zone	1984	1985	1986	1987	1988	1989	1990	1991	1992	1993
India *[2 24] Inde *[2 24]	221	140	117	107	139	149	...	...	...	...
Ireland[6] Irlande[6]	3	3	3	2	2	2	2	...	...	...
Italy[11] Italie[11]	480	497	448	436	457	457	418	428	445	426
Japan[12 15] Japon[12 15]	327	326	313	331	353	351	335	345	326	287
Kazakstan Kazakstan	..	..	..	..	..	..	..	31	23	20
Kenya Kenya	3	4	3	4	3	1	0	...	...	0
Korea, Republic of[6] Corée, République de[6]	12	14	16	16	19	21	20	20	20	19
Kyrgyzstan Kirghizistan	..	..	..	..	..	..	..	13	11	9
Latvia Lettonie	..	..	..	..	..	..	..	11	8	2
Lithuania Lituanie	..	..	..	..	..	..	..	22	17	12
Mexico Mexique	13	13	11	9[11]	7[11]	8[11]	9[11]	8[11]	11[11]	...
Mongolia Mongolie	2	2	2	2	* 2	3[2]	...	...	...	...
Netherlands[6] Pays-Bas[6]	3	4	5	4	4	5	4	4	4	...
New Zealand Nouvelle-Zélande	3	3	2	2	2	...	...	...	...	...
Norway[6 25] Norvège[6 25]	3	3	3	2	2	1	...	...	...	...
Pakistan[3] Pakistan[3]	1	2	2	2	2	...	...	...	...	...
Poland[6 26] Pologne[6 26]	155	158	155	150	152	146	98	67	50	48
Portugal[11] Portugal[11]	27	34	34	35	31	32	34	29	14	...
Romania[6] Roumanie[6]	123	128	137	135	133	141	107	100	69	68
Russian Federation Fédération de Russie	..	..	..	..	..	..	..	492	351	270
Slovakia[6] Slovaquie[6]	..	..	..	..	..	..	..	..	11	10
Slovenia Slovénie	..	..	..	..	..	..	..	15	15	...
South Africa[25] Afrique du Sud[25]	17	16	17	20	19	19	19	15	11	10
Spain[11] Espagne[11]	27	30	32	35	34	40	31	32	...	...
Sweden *[11] Suède *[11]	1	1	1	1	1	1	1	...	...	...

45

Fabrics

Woven cotton and wool, cellulosic and non-cellulosic fibres: million square metres [*cont.*]

Tissus

Tissus de coton, laines, fibres cellulosiques et non cellulosiques : millions de mètres carrés [*suite*]

Country or area Pays ou zone	1984	1985	1986	1987	1988	1989	1990	1991	1992	1993
Switzerland[25] Suisse[25]	14	14	14	12	11	9	9	10	8	7
Syrian Arab Republic[11] Rép. arabe syrienne[11]	4	5	4	1	2	1	2	0	1	2
TFYR Macedonia L'ex-R.y. Macédoine	..	..	..	..	..	..	..	10	9	...
Turkey[2][19] Turquie[2][19]	39	37	27	27	41	29	42	40	35	...
Turkmenistan Turkménistan	..	..	..	..	..	..	..	3	3	3
Ukraine Ukraine	..	..	..	..	..	..	..	79	76	60
former USSR† ancienne URSS†	872	841	842	854	876	890	865	..	..	..
United Kingdom[27] Royaume-Uni[27]	91	91	93	90	89	25	20	...	...	...
United States Etats-Unis	133	116	167	141	159	147	118	142	147	154
Uzbekistan Ouzbékistan	..	..	..	..	..	..	..	1	1	1
Yugoslavia Yougoslavie	..	..	..	..	..	..	..	..	21	...
Yugoslavia, SFR†[20] Yougoslavie, Rfs†[20]	99	101	110	105	104	100	...	..	..	..

C. Cellulosic and non-cellulosic fibres • Fibres cellulosiques et non cellulosiques

Total	19 844	20 510	20 860	20 330	21 337	22 292	23 290	21 097	21 563	20 156
Afghanistan[1][2][28] Afghanistan[1][2][28]	5	6	6	5	3	...	...	...	...	...
Algeria * Algérie *	20	20	...	...	...	...	...	...	...	...
Australia[3] Australie[3]	141	155	161	170	167	192	179	185	186	185
Austria Autriche	84	102	117	95	90	96	101	66	73	47
Belarus[28] Bélarus[28]	..	..	..	..	..	..	..	175	147	135
Belgium[29] Belgique[29]	2 641	2 630	2 762	2 828	3 154	3 639	3 955	3 883	4 259	4 776
Bulgaria[6][30] Bulgarie[6][30]	45	45	46	47	...	...	...	...	...	...
Côte d'Ivoire[2][31] Côte d'Ivoire[2][31]	2	2	...	...	...	...	...	...	...	...
Croatia Croatie	..	..	..	..	..	..	..	12	12	...
Cuba[28] Cuba[28]	16	28	...	...	...	...	...	...	...	...
former Czechoslovakia† anc. Tchécoslovaquie†	110	112	115	117	118	115	113	83	..	..

45

Fabrics
Woven cotton and wool, cellulosic and non-cellulosic fibres: million square metres [*cont.*]
Tissus
Tissus de coton, laines, fibres cellulosiques et non cellulosiques : millions de mètres carrés [*suite*]

Country or area Pays ou zone	1984	1985	1986	1987	1988	1989	1990	1991	1992	1993
Czech Republic[31] République tchèque[31]	..	..	..	..	..	..	..	..	35	29
Ecuador[2 28] Equateur[2 28]	* 1	...	...	...	19	...	...	...	...	...
El Salvador *[28] El Salvador *[28]	29	...	...	...	...	...	...	...	...	...
Ethiopia[10 31] Ethiopie[10 31]	6	6	6	6	6	5	5	3	2	4
Finland[6] Finlande[6]	35	# 42	36	34	* 35	* 34	27	* 17	* 14	* 15
France France	# 1 890	1 919	2 032	1 841	1 962	2 446	2 668	2 763	3 517	2 891
Germany † Allemagne†	..	..	..	..	..	..	..	1 477	1 359	1 153
F. R. Germany[6] R. f. Allemagne[6]	901	1 005	1 039	984	1 343	1 473	1 471	..	..	..
former German D. R. anc. R. d. allemande	253	251	247	256	258	249	...	..	..	..
Greece *[12] Grèce *[12]	87[11]	9[28]	...	...	...	...	...	...	...	...
Hong Kong[32] Hong-kong[32]	...	...	1[31]	1[31]	1[31]	1	0	1	2	2
Hungary[6] Hongrie[6]	90	91	86	82	75	67	45	35	22	20
India Inde	2 451	2 759	...	...	...	...	...	...	...	...
Ireland[6] Irlande[6]	56	27	36	48	...	...	...	...	...	...
Japan[12 15] Japon[12 15]	3 994	3 787	3 560	3 307	3 340	3 365	3 376	3 263	3 175	2 758
Korea, Republic of[31] Corée, République de[31]	1 936	2 145	2 619	2 988	3 157	2 908	3 428	3 479	3 094	2 459
Mexico Mexique	530[28]	584[28]	499[28]	# 368[11]	367[11]	4[11]	4[11]	5[11]	5[11]	...
Nepal[2 31 33] Népal[2 31 33]	8	8	14	18	16	...	...	...	...	...
Netherlands[6] Pays-Bas[6]	130	137[11]	* 179	* 172	* 170	18[11 28]	22[11 28]	26[11 28]	...	...
Norway[31] Norvège[31]	25	...	...	...	...	...	...	...	...	...
Poland[6] Pologne[6]	154	154	146	138	154	148	113	88	98	85
Portugal Portugal	* 26[11 28]	* 21[11 28]	* 20[11 28]	* 14[11 28]	* 13[11 28]	* 19[11 28]	* 15[11 28]	* 15[11 28]	154	...
Republic of Moldova[30] République de Moldova[30]	..	..	..	..	..	..	..	44	22	...
Slovakia Slovaquie	..	..	..	..	..	..	..	26	...	...
Slovenia[28] Slovénie[28]	..	..	..	..	..	..	..	7	6	...

45

Fabrics
Woven cotton and wool, cellulosic and non-cellulosic fibres: million square metres [cont.]
Tissus
Tissus de coton, laines, fibres cellulosiques et non cellulosiques : millions de mètres carrés [suite]

Country or area Pays ou zone	1984	1985	1986	1987	1988	1989	1990	1991	1992	1993
Spain[11] Espagne[11]	589	625	549	...	...	...	...	...	...	...
Sri Lanka[2 19] Sri Lanka[2 19]	1	1	...	...	...	...	...	...	...	...
Sweden[34] Suède[34]	66	70	50	54	10[11]	9[11]	10[11]	6[11]	...	...
Thailand Thaïlande	757	812	875	...	...	...	...	...	...	...
TFYR Macedonia[28] L'ex-R.y. Macédoine[28]	..	..	..	...	...	...	...	5	3	...
Tunisia *[31] Tunisie *[31]	2	2	...	...	...	...	...	...	...	...
former USSR† ancienne URSS†	1 857	1 878	1 895	1 990	2 016	2 049		..	..	..
United Kingdom Royaume-Uni	388	415	436	407	423	...		..	...	...
Yugoslavia[28] Yougoslavie[28]	..	..	..	..		..	..	...	4	...
Yugoslavia, SFR† Yougoslavie, Rfs†	26	31	33	26	30	37	...	..	..	..

Source:
Industrial statistics database of the Statistics Division of
the United Nations Secretariat.

† For detailed descriptions of data pertaining to
former Czechoslovakia, Germany, SFR Yugoslavia and former
USSR, see Annex I - Country or area nomenclature, regional
and other groupings.

1 Twelve months beginning 21 March of year stated.

2 Original data in metres.
3 Twelve months ending 30 June of year stated.

4 Including pile and chenille fabrics of non-cellulosic
fibres.
5 Including cotton blankets and carpets.
6 After undergoing finishing processes.
7 Finished fabrics.
8 Including mixed cotton fabrics.
9 Including cellulosic fabrics.
10 Twelve months ending 7 July of the year stated.

11 Original data in metric tons (Greece: non-cellulosic fibres,
Netherlands: cellulosic fibres).
12 Including finished fabrics and blanketing made of synthetic
fibers.
13 Including synthetic fabrics.
14 Beginning 1985, data are confidential.
15 Shipments.
16 Production by government-owned enterprises only.
17 Factory production only.
18 Including fabrics of cotton substitutes.
19 Government production only.
20 Including woven cellulosic fabrics.

Source:
Base de données pour les statistiques industrielles de la
Division de statistique du Secrétariat de l'ONU.

† Pour les descriptions en détails des données
relatives à l'ancienne Tchécoslovaquie, l'Allemagne, la Rfs
Yougoslavie et l'ancienne URSS, voir l'Annexe I -
Nomenclature des pays ou zones, groupements régionaux et
autres groupements.

1 Période de douze mois commençant le 21 mars de l'année
indiquée.
2 Données d'origine exprimées en mètres.
3 Période de douze mois finissant le 30 juin de l'année
indiquée.
4 Y compris les tissus bouclés et tissus chenille de fibres
non cellulosiques.
5 Y compris les couvertures et les tapis en coton.
6 Après opérations de finition.
7 Tissus finis.
8 Y compris les tissus de cotton mélangé.
9 Y compris les tissus en fibres cellulosiques.
10 Période de douze mois finissant le 7 juillet de l'année
indiquée.
11 Données d'origine exprimées en tonnes (Grèce : fibres non
cellulosiques; Pays-Bas : fibres cellulosiques).
12 Y compris les tissus finis et les couvertures en fibres
synthétiques.
13 Y compris les tissus synthétiques.
14 A partir de 1985, les données sont confidentielles.
15 Expéditions.
16 Production des établissements d'Etat seulement.
17 Production des fabriques seulement.
18 Y compris les tissus de succédanés de coton.
19 Production de l'Etat seulement.
20 Y compris les tissus en fibres cellulosiques.

45

Fabrics
Woven cotton and wool, cellulosic and non-cellulosic fibres: million square metres [*cont.*]

Tissus
Tissus de coton, laines, fibres cellulosiques et non cellulosiques : millions de mètres carrés [*suite*]

21 Including woollen blankets and carpets.	21 Y compris les couvertures et tapis en laine.
22 Including mixed wool fabrics.	22 Y compris les tissues de laine mélangée.
23 Sales.	23 Ventes.
24 Mill production relating to wearable woollen fabrics only.	24 Production des usines correspondant aux tissus d'habillement en laine seulement.
25 Pure woollen fabrics only.	25 Tissus de laine pure seulement.
26 Including fabrics of wool substitutes.	26 Y compris les tissus de succédanés de laine.
27 Deliveries of woollen & worsted fabrics (weight: more than 15% of wool or animal fibres).	27 Quantités livrées de tissus de laine cardée et peignée (poids : plus de 15% de laine ou fibres animales).
28 Cellulosic fibres only.	28 Fibres cellulosiques seulement.
29 Including blankets and carpets of cellulosic and non-cellulosic fibres.	29 Y compris les couvertures et les tapis en fibres cellulosiques et non-cellulosiques.
30 Including silk fabrics.	30 Y compris les tissus de soie.
31 Non-cellulosic fibres only.	31 Fibres non-cellulosiques seulement.
32 1982-1988 data are confidential (cellulosic fibres).	32 1982-1988 les données sont confidentielles (fibres cellulosiques).
33 Twelve months beginning 16 July of year stated.	33 Période de douze mois commençant le 16 juillet de l'année indiquée.
34 Including woven non-cellulosic fabrics.	34 Y compris les tissus en fibres non cellulosiques.

46
Leather footwear
Chaussures de cuir

Production: thousand pairs
Production : milliers de paires

Country or area Pays or zone	1984	1985	1986	1987	1988	1989	1990	1991	1992	1993
Total	4 152 214	4 340 499	4 455 129	4 194 026	4 555 859	4 493 182	4 487 474	4 132 375	4 037 431	4 134 092
Afghanistan Afghanistan	344	380	613	701	607	...	...	...	...	...
Algeria Algérie	18 135	17 909	18 421	18 100	14 689	14 943	16 376	11 824	9 040	7 171
Armenia Arménie	..	..	..	..	..	..	..	11 340	5 661	3 517
Australia[1] Australie[1]	33 675	36 404	35 164	33 743	29 334	29 032	17 901	14 844	13 115	12 399
Austria Autriche	25 453	26 107	23 667	20 729	16 859	16 769	16 553	16 760	14 842	13 229
Azerbaijan Azerbaïdjan	..	..	..	..	..	..	..	10 262	5 221	4 068
Belarus Bélarus	..	..	..	..	..	..	..	45 343	37 207	33 411
Belgium Belgique	5 837	5 343	5 000	4 343	3 916	3 810	3 562	3 454	3 190	2 267
Bolivia Bolivie	1 142	1 302	1 312	...	1 001	938	833	857	1 089	...
Brazil Brésil	145 838	139 251	152 094	135 791	140 795	157 749	141 000	152 925	156 529	190 026
Bulgaria Bulgarie	27 997	29 623	29 932	30 668	32 284	33 206	27 214	17 048	13 421	10 785
Burkina Faso Burkina Faso	# 911	1 318	890	667	470	500	500	1 271	...	...
Cameroon[2] Cameroun[2]	3 572	3 964	2 415	1 725	1 733	1 800	1 800	...	...	...
Canada Canada	45 416	44 394	43 087	38 774	33 901	...	...	...	...	...
Central African Rep. Rép. centrafricaine	582	611	544	159	200	200	200	...	...	...
Chile Chili	6 847	6 357	6 318	6 277	6 614	7 601	6 314	8 481	8 783	8 655
China Chine	638 920	730 610	798 450	618 680	1 055 390	1 103 933	1 202 565	1 328 950	1 613 647	...
Colombia[3] Colombie[3]	...	9 555	12 377	10 731	17 200	12 496	11 284	...	...	...
Congo[4] Congo[4]	995	1 127	535	180	296	147	* 300	...	...	...
Côte d'Ivoire Côte d'Ivoire	5 900	1 600	1 700	1 700	1 800	1 800	1 800	...	...	...
Croatia Croatie	..	..	..	..	..	..	..	11 717	11 240	...
Cuba Cuba	12 473	12 396	13 492	14 183	13 300	11 004	13 400	...	...	...
Cyprus Chypre	12 524	12 277	12 273	13 097	13 377	11 643	10 447	10 591	6 199	3 835

46
Leather footwear
Production: thousand pairs [cont.]
Chaussures de cuir
Production : milliers de paires [suite]

Country or area Pays or zone	1984	1985	1986	1987	1988	1989	1990	1991	1992	1993
former Czechoslovakia† anc. Tchécoslovaquie†	130 584	131 410	124 469	119 427	119 088	120 226	113 596	72 134	..	..
Czech Republic République tchèque	..	..	..	..	..	..	..	..	36 948	32 293
Denmark[3] Danemark[3]	5 100	5 000	5 500	6 000	4 800	4 400	4 400		...	...
Dominican Republic Rép. dominicaine	9 636	9 458	9 611	* 2 500	...		...		...	...
Ecuador Equateur	* 1 400	* 1 400	1 567	1 400	1 500	1 500	1 500	...	1 936	...
Egypt Egypte	65 325	66 328	65 347	66 287	50 438	50 375	48 325	48 311	48 390	48 385
El Salvador El Salvador	# * 3 400	* 3 500	* 3 200	* 3 300	3 600	3 600	3 600		...	...
Estonia Estonie	..	..	..	..	..		..	6 301	3 208	1 035
Ethiopia[6] Ethiopie[6]	8 794[5]	6 030[5]	8 868[5]	11 130[5]	11 409[5]	12 957[5]	5 367	3 374	2 419	3 083
Finland Finlande	7 867	7 407	9 414	8 635	6 860	5 243	4 752	3 683	3 606	3 291
France[2] France[2]	201 809	196 992	194 753	183 209	168 564	169 788	194 700	168 084	160 320	151 124
Germany † Allemagne†	..	..	..	..	..	..	..	84 435	63 672	55 485
F. R. Germany R. f. Allemagne	92 472	86 678	86 629	78 291	71 674	68 697	64 358	..	..	
former German D. R. anc. R. d. allemande	82 425	83 551	85 518	87 980	91 382	91 518	61 822	..	..	..
Greece Grèce	11 180	11 305	11 430	13 900[4]	13 220	12 359	12 260	10 712	9 264	...
Haiti[3] Haïti[3]	528	500	600	500	500	500	500	...	...	...
Hong Kong Hong-kong	# 77 821	80 642	98 178	61 008	134 951	48 710	73 496	...	8 433	...
Hungary Hongrie	49 035	49 756	46 934	44 340	40 063	33 107	27 426	20 757	14 752	12 783
Iceland Islande	77	83	74	60	20	29	39	46	18	...
India[7] Inde[7]	59 212	167 938	193 385	194 455	200 320	198 761	198 404	188 309	187 493	187 148
Indonesia[8] Indonésie[8]	56 765	61 948	73 219	109 345	5 338	5 565	9 749	1 890	...	...
Iran, Islamic Rep. of[9] Iran, Rép. islamique d'[9]	25 602	24 717	21 129	21 946	21 005	21 849	23 374	18 849	17 785	...
Iraq Iraq	4 500[3]	4 200[3]	3 305	4 900[3]	4 669	4 600	4 400	...	4 087	...
Ireland Irlande	2 716	1 914	2 492	2 202	2 097	1 913	1 403	...	...	...
Italy[3] Italie[3]	352 800	371 600	362 000	343 500	327 300	311 900	320 200	...	...	...

46
Leather footwear
Production: thousand pairs [*cont.*]
Chaussures de cuir
Production : milliers de paires [*suite*]

Country or area Pays or zone	1984	1985	1986	1987	1988	1989	1990	1991	1992	1993
Jamaica[3] Jamaïque[3]	600	700	700	700	700	700	700	...	...	...
Japan[10 11] Japon[10 11]	55 707	53 387	51 975	51 984	56 023	53 819	54 054	53 351	52 455	47 703
Kenya Kenya	1 182	1 361	1 465	1 306	1 381	1 696	1 605	1 190	1 480	...
Korea, Republic of Corée, République de	17 368	19 209	22 603	25 807	25 339	24 023	24 440	26 384	25 409	19 085
Kyrgyzstan Kirghizistan	..	..	..	..	..	..	..	9 507	5 751	3 528
Latvia Lettonie	..	..	..	..	..	..	..	7 778	5 738	2 669
Lithuania Lituanie	..	..	..	..	..	..	..	11 154	7 702	3 621
Madagascar[8] Madagascar[8]	2 133	2 172	2 889	1 686	1 036	1 356	807	837	702	306
Malta Malte	1 691	...	...	...	...	...	...	...	...	...
Mexico Mexique	...	...	...	9 943	15 528	15 986	16 249	14 685	14 570	12 926
Mongolia Mongolie	2 677	2 883	3 149	3 517	3 921	4 140	3 000	...	...	...
Mozambique Mozambique	639	599	829	59	374	346	347	242	148	...
Nepal[12] Népal[12]	83	112	121	214	332	124	...	...	...	...
Netherlands[2] Pays-Bas[2]	9 585	9 452	9 349	8 556	6 249	6 197	5 598	5 255	5 289	5 988
New Zealand Nouvelle-Zélande	8 464	7 701	7 396	7 327	5 385	5 073	4 977	4 022	3 765	3 525
Nicaragua Nicaragua	2 549	* 1 000	* 1 000	* 1 100	...	...	...	...	...	...
Nigeria Nigéria	10 118	8 256	6 455	4 574	6 097	3 423	3 779	7 093	4 538	4 554
Norway[4] Norvège[4]	1 600	1 400	1 200	1 000	800	800	900	...	...	...
Panama Panama	1 696	1 852	* 1 400	1 791	1 047	999	1 507	...	...	...
Paraguay Paraguay	5 034	4 790	4 936	5 308	5 053	5 094	5 300	...	...	...
Peru[3] Pérou[3]	2 107	2 179	2 423	1 623	943	904	636	...	...	...
Philippines[3] Philippines[3]	3 880	3 084	5 302	16 128	10 400	10 100	10 000	...	...	...
Poland Pologne	147 076	147 603	146 996	151 619	155 639	150 833	98 200	66 857	55 181	47 905
Portugal Portugal	28 790	31 333	34 167	35 173	37 762	43 667	75 378	39 658	53 990	...
Republic of Moldova République de Moldova	..	..	..	..	..	..	..	20 751	14 504	4 897

46
Leather footwear
Production: thousand pairs [*cont.*]
Chaussures de cuir
Production : milliers de paires [*suite*]

Country or area Pays or zone	1984	1985	1986	1987	1988	1989	1990	1991	1992	1993
Romania Roumanie	96 210	99 732	105 093	102 871	99 751	110 733	80 670	63 196	41 237	42 328
Russian Federation Fédération de Russie	..	..	..	..	..	..	..	336 411	220 415	145 889
Rwanda Rwanda	5	16	21	24	25	...	...	...	...	...
Saint Kitts and Nevis Saint-Kitts-et-Nevis	59	23	24	...	...	...	...	...	...	...
Senegal Sénégal	3 234	2 851	* 1 800	* 2 000	561	186	302	153	644	508
Singapore [4] Singapour [4]	4 755	3 789	* 2 600	* 2 700	2 700	2 800	2 800	...	...	...
Slovakia Slovaquie	..	..	..	..	..	..	..	..	22 875	17 257
Slovenia Slovénie	..	..	..	..	..	..	..	9 124	9 492	
South Africa [2] Afrique du Sud [2]	46 316	47 488	45 789	46 062	44 370	50 658	51 633	49 318	42 251	44 492
Spain Espagne	125 250	113 888	114 621	109 714	117 707	114 089	117 199	115 190	106 959	...
Sri Lanka Sri Lanka	249	263	359	358	328	270	339	276	272	274
Sudan [3] Soudan [3]	8 000	8 500	6 000	5 000	4 000	4 000	4 000	...	...	...
Sweden Suède	4 490	3 826	3 977	4 263	2 518	2 088	1 904	...	...	...
Switzerland Suisse	5 781	5 813	5 462	4 832	4 544	4 285	4 039	3 353	3 035	3 261
Tajikistan Tadjikistan	..	..	..	..	..	..	..	9 000	5 000	4 000
TFYR Macedonia L'ex-R.y. Macédoine	..	..	..	..	..	..	..	4 238	3 786	...
Togo Togo	486	* 521	286	29	100	100	100	...	...	...
Tunisia Tunisie	3 600 [3]	4 000 [3]	5 000 [3]	5 300 [3]	7 000 [3]	9 800	10 380	11 590	13 220	15 800
Turkmenistan Turkménistan	..	..	..	..	..	..	..	2 802	1 999	1 414
Ukraine Ukraine	..	..	..	..	..	..	..	177 336	143 970	...
former USSR† ancienne URSS†	763 514	787 610	800 745	808 993	819 050	826 988	843 245	..	..	..
United Kingdom [13] Royaume-Uni [13]	123 807	128 698	129 017	124 298	120 589	101 318	92 673	...	...	...
United Rep.Tanzania Rép. Unie de Tanzanie	* 1 949	1 324	1 260	609	569	445	459	328	168	55
United States Etats-Unis	303 174	265 098	240 932	230 046	231 595	218 025	184 568	168 992	164 904	171 733
Uzbekistan Ouzbékistan	..	..	..	..	..	..	..	45 443	40 491	40 499

46
Leather footwear
Production: thousand pairs [cont.]
Chaussures de cuir
Production : milliers de paires [suite]

Country or area Pays or zone	1984	1985	1986	1987	1988	1989	1990	1991	1992	1993
Viet Nam Viet Nam	...	...	...	...	5 290	...	5 827	6 188	5 672	...
former Yemen Arab Rep. anc. Yémen rép. arabe	...	240	217	...	...	...	..	...	..	..
former Dem. Yemen anciennce Yémen dém.	219	112	171	239	...	...	...	..	...	..
Yugoslavia Yougoslavie	...	...	...	...	...	...	...	...	16 169	...
Yugoslavia, SFR† Yougoslavie, Rfs†	90 798	93 063	99 503	93 051	86 336	91 616	...	...	...	...
Zaïre[3] Zaïre[3]	900	800	900	900	900	900	900	...	...	...

Source:
Industrial statistics database of the Statistics Division of
the United Nations Secretariat.

† For detailed descriptions of data pertaining to
former Czechoslovakia, Germany, SFR Yugoslavia and former
USSR, see Annex I - Country or area nomenclature, regional
and other groupings.

1 Twelve months ending 30 June of year stated.

2 Including rubber footwear.
3 Source: Food and Agriculture Organization (FAO), (Rome).

4 Including rubber and plastic footwear.

5 Including canvas, plastic and rubber footwear.

6 Twelve months ending 7 July of the year stated.

7 Production by large and medium scale establishments only.
8 Including plastic footwear.
9 Production by establishments employing 50 or more persons.
10 Shipments.
11 Production by establishments employing 10 or more persons.
12 Twelve months beginning 16 July of year stated.

13 Manufacturers' sales.

Source:
Base de données pour les statistiques industrielles de la
Division de statistique du Secrétariat de l'ONU.

† Pour les descriptions en détails des données
relatives à l'ancienne Tchécoslovaquie, l'Allemagne, la Rfs
Yougoslavie et l'ancienne URSS, voir l'Annexe I -
Nomenclature des pays ou zones, groupements régionaux et
autres groupements.

1 Période de douze mois finissant le 30 juin de l'année
indiquée.
2 Y compris les chaussures en caoutchouc.
3 Source: Organisation des Nations Unies pour l'alimentation
et l'agriculture (FAO), (Rome).
4 Y compris les chaussures en caoutchouc et en matière
plastique.
5 Y compris les chaussures en toile, en matière plastique et
en caoutchouc.
6 Période de douze mois finissant le 7 juillet de l'année
indiquée.
7 Production des grandes et moyennes entreprises seulement.
8 Y compris les chaussures en matière plastique.
9 Production des établissements occupant 50 personnes ou plus.
10 Expéditions.
11 Production des établissements occupant 10 personnes ou plus.
12 Période de douze mois commençant le 16 juillet de l'année
indiquée.
13 Ventes des fabricants.

47
Sawnwood
Sciages
Production (sawn): thousand cubic metres
Production (sciés) : milliers de mètres cubes

Country or area Pays ou zone	1984	1985	1986	1987	1988	1989	1990	1991	1992	1993
World *Monde*	**460 969**	**467 785**	**484 294**	**505 292**	**508 014**	**507 108**	**505 468**	**455 823**	**436 535**	**432 410**
Africa **Afrique**	**7 356**	**7 623**	**8 002**	**8 361**	**8 413**	**8 517**	**8 479**	**8 160**	**8 271**	**8 225**
Algeria[1] Algérie[1]	13	13	13	13	13	13	13	13	13	13
Angola Angola	2	5	5	5	5	5	5	5[1]	5[1]	5[1]
Benin Bénin	5	8	11	11[1]	11[1]	14	14[1]	27	24	24[1]
Burkina Faso Burkina Faso	2	2	2	2	2	2	2	2	2[1]	2[1]
Burundi Burundi	4	3	3[1]	3[1]	3[1]	3[1]	2	3	3[1]	3[1]
Cameroon Cameroun	423	454	552	580	492	489	489[1]	489[1]	489[1]	465[1]
Central African Rep. Rép. centrafricaine	58	56	54	52	52[1]	57	63	60	68	60[1]
Chad Tchad	1[1]	1[1]	1[1]	1[1]	1[1]	1[1]	1	2	2	2
Congo Congo	60	50	77	60	57	46	50	54	52	52[1]
Côte d'Ivoire Côte d'Ivoire	679	753	765	775	784	777	753	608	623	587
Equatorial Guinea Guinée équatoriale	24[1]	39	30[1]	10	10	12	12	13	8	10[1]
Ethiopia Ethiopie	45	45	45	45	39	34	22	12	12	12
Gabon Gabon	97	106	100[1]	* 46	* 37	* 30	* 37	* 32	32[1]	32[1]
Gambia[1] Gambie[1]	1	1	1	1	1	1	1	1	1	1
Ghana Ghana	285	345	355	455	455[1]	537	472	400	410	410[1]
Guinea Guinée	90[1]	90[1]	70	70	70	70	70	70	63	65
Guinea-Bissau[1] Guinée-Bissau[1]	16	16	16	16	16	16	16	16	16	16
Kenya Kenya	183	192	173	195	188	185	185[1]	185[1]	185[1]	185[1]
Liberia Libéria	153	169	191	411	411[1]	411[1]	411[1]	411[1]	411[1]	411[1]
Libyan Arab Jamah. Jamah. arabe libyenne[1]	31	31	31	31	31	31	31	31	31	31
Madagascar Madagascar	234	234	234	234[1]	234	234	234	233[1]	238[1]	235[1]
Malawi Malawi	16	19	23	30	31	* 39	* 43	* 43	43[1]	45
Mali Mali	6	4	6	11	13	13[1]	13[1]	13[1]	13[1]	13[1]

47
Sawnwood
Production (sawn): thousand cubic metres [*cont.*]
Sciages
Production (sciés) : milliers de mètres cubes [*suite*]

Country or area Pays ou zone	1984	1985	1986	1987	1988	1989	1990	1991	1992	1993
Mauritius Maurice	0	1	1	4	4	5	4	5	4	5
Morocco Maroc	120[1]	100[1]	90[1]	80[1]	53	83	83[1]	83[1]	83[1]	83[1]
Mozambique Mozambique	37	35	39	42	36	30	26	18	16[1]	30[1]
Niger[1] Niger[1]	...	...	...	...	...	...	...	...	1	4
Nigeria Nigéria	2 512	2 712	2 712	2 712[1]	2 712	2 712	2 729	2 723[1]	2 723[1]	2 723[1]
Réunion Réunion	1[1]	2[1]	2	2	1	1	3	2	2[1]	2[1]
Rwanda Rwanda	12	13	13[1]	13[1]	13[1]	11	8	8	36	36[1]
Sao Tome and Principe Sao Tomé-et-Principe	3[1]	3[1]	3[1]	4[1]	5	5[1]	5[1]	5[1]	5[1]	5[1]
Senegal Sénégal	11[1]	23	20	27	19	15	22	23	23[1]	23[1]
Sierra Leone Sierra Leone	19[1]	14	12	12[1]	12[1]	12[1]	11	9	9[1]	9[1]
Somalia[1] Somalie[1]	14	14	14	14	14	14	14	14	14	14
South Africa Afrique du Sud	1 635	1 510	* 1 734	* 1 734	* 1 873	1 873[1]	* 1 936	* 1 792	1 792[1]	1 792[1]
Sudan Soudan	13	13	13	13[1]	13	5	4	2[1]	3	3[1]
Swaziland[1] Swaziland[1]	103	103	103	103	103	103	103	103	103	103
Togo Togo	1	3	2	4	4	3	6	2	3	3[1]
Tunisia Tunisie	4	6	9	11[1]	12	20	16	17	6	6[1]
Uganda Ouganda	23[1]	23[1]	23[1]	23[1]	28	28[1]	28[1]	28[1]	82	83
United Rep.Tanzania Rép. Unie de Tanzanie	102	109	154	156	156[1]	156[1]	156[1]	156[1]	156[1]	156[1]
Zaire Zaïre	120	118	120	127	135	131	117	105	105[1]	105[1]
Zambia Zambie	50[1]	50[1]	67	51	76	101	81	94	112	112[1]
Zimbabwe Zimbabwe	149	138	114	175	190	190[1]	190[1]	250	250[1]	250[1]
America, North **Amérique du Nord**	**141 747**	**146 633**	**158 018**	**173 170**	**171 995**	**167 166**	**168 302**	**158 270**	**168 642**	**170 286**
Bahamas[1] Bahamas[1]	1	1	1	1	1	1	1	1	1	1
Belize Belize	19[1]	22	14	14[1]	14[1]	14[1]	14[1]	14[1]	14[1]	14[1]
Canada Canada	49 869	54 586	54 853	61 775	60 737	59 245	54 906	52 040	56 318	59 774

47
Sawnwood
Production (sawn): thousand cubic metres [*cont.*]
Sciages
Production (sciés) : milliers de mètres cubes [*suite*]

Country or area Pays ou zone	1984	1985	1986	1987	1988	1989	1990	1991	1992	1993
Costa Rica Costa Rica	412	412	412[1]	503	515	439	412	412	772	798
Cuba Cuba	108	104	108	114	118	130	130[1]	130[1]	130[1]	130[1]
El Salvador[1] El Salvador[1]	46	43	44	47	54	70	70	70	70	70
Guadeloupe[1] Guadeloupe[1]	1	1	1	1	1	1	1	1	1	1
Guatemala Guatemala	103	131	90	90[1]	23[1]	36[1]	37[1]	55[1]	90[1]	90[1]
Haiti[1] Haïti[1]	14	14	14	14	14	14	14	14	14	14
Honduras Honduras	427	436	405	464	447	412	328	303	413	369
Jamaica Jamaïque	31	31[1]	26	30	44	40	40	32	27	22
Martinique Martinique	...	...	...	1	2	1	1[1]	1[1]	1	1[1]
Mexico Mexique	1 975	2 205	2 143	2 410	2 528[1]	2 447[1]	2 366	* 2 696	2 696[1]	2 696[1]
Nicaragua Nicaragua	222[1]	222[1]	222[1]	180[1]	140[1]	110[1]	80	80[1]	61	65
Panama Panama	46	45	30[1]	25[1]	18	50[1]	48[1]	16	37	37[1]
Trinidad and Tobago Trinité-et-Tobago	21	18	22	19	21	80	53	42	59	36
United States Etats-Unis	88 451	88 361	99 632	107 481	107 317	104 075	109 800	102 363	107 937	106 167
America, South **Amérique du Sud**	**24 298**	**24 598**	**25 169**	**26 132**	**26 065**	**25 732**	**25 282**	**25 890**	**26 676**	**26 668**
Argentina Argentine	934[1]	901[1]	978[1]	1 139[1]	950[1]	950[1]	950[1]	950[1]	1 472	1 472[1]
Bolivia Bolivie	46	40	57	62[1]	51	102	102	125[1]	230	268
Brazil[1] Brésil[1]	17 781	17 781	18 063	18 063	18 179	18 179	17 179	18 628	18 628	18 628
Chile Chili	2 001	2 194	2 026	2 677	2 710	2 684	3 327	3 218	3 020	3 113
Colombia Colombie	603[1]	655[1]	813	813[1]	813[1]	813[1]	813[1]	813[1]	813[1]	813[1]
Ecuador Equateur	1 212	1 215	1 258	1 265	1 280	1 492	1 641	865	908	902[1]
French Guiana[1] Guyane française[1]	19	19	19	19	19	19	19	19	19	19
Guyana Guyana	60	65	60	57	57[1]	57[1]	50[1]	10[1]	10[1]	15[1]
Paraguay Paraguay	834	758	766	862	906	510[1]	228	313	313[1]	313[1]
Peru Pérou	482	535	615	628	546	392	499	477	500	555

47
Sawnwood
Production (sawn): thousand cubic metres [cont.]
Sciages
Production (sciés) : milliers de mètres cubes [suite]

Country or area Pays ou zone	1984	1985	1986	1987	1988	1989	1990	1991	1992	1993
Suriname Suriname	57	73	61[1]	42[1]	73[1]	44	44	40	43	43[1]
Uruguay Uruguay	59	54	117	169	185	201	229	205	269	269[1]
Venezuela Venezuela	210[1]	308	336	336[1]	296	* 290	201	227	451	258
Asia Asie	**97 156**	**99 740**	**100 851**	**105 657**	**105 992**	**107 947**	**104 713**	**100 069**	**97 203**	**102 083**
Afghanistan[1] Afghanistan[1]	400	400	400	400	400	400	400	400	400	400
Bangladesh Bangladesh	154[1]	99	79	79[1]	79[1]	79[1]	79[1]	79[1]	79[1]	79[1]
Bhutan[1] Bhoutan[1]	6	6	5	5	3	5	35	35	35	35
Brunei Darussalam[1] Brunéi Darussalam[1]	90	90	90	90	90	90	90	90	90	90
Cambodia Cambodge	43[1]	43[1]	43[1]	43[1]	43[1]	43[1]	71	122	132[1]	127[1]
China[1] Chine[1]	25 791	27 234	26 702	26 577	26 522	25 177	23 160	20 521	19 317	25 268
Cyprus Chypre	59	63	59	57	55	60	22	16	14	17
Hong Kong Hong-kong	248[1]	248[1]	248[1]	248[1]	248[1]	587	421	421[1]	421[1]	439
India Inde	15 907[1]	17 460[1]	17 460[1]	17 460[1]	17 460[1]	17 460[1]	17 460[1]	17 460	17 460[1]	17 460[1]
Indonesia Indonésie	6 620	7 118	7 549	9 887	10 290	10 357	9 145	8 638	8 438	8 338
Iran, Islamic Rep. of Iran, Rép. islamique d'	172[1]	186[1]	202[1]	219[1]	239	262	169	173	187	170
Iraq[1] Iraq[1]	8	8	8	8	8	8	8	8	8	8
Japan Japon	28 667	28 472	29 105	30 159	* 30 138	* 30 542	29 781[1]	28 264[1]	27 277[1]	26 260[1]
Korea, Dem. P. R.[1] Corée, R. p. dém. de[1]	280	280	280	280	280	280	280	280	280	280
Korea, Republic of Corée, République de	2 974	3 018	3 563	4 145	4 014	4 194	3 897	4 041	3 513	3 199
Lao People's Dem. Rep. Rép. dém. pop. lao	26	16[1]	16	30[1]	40[1]	100[1]	100[1]	300[1]	150[1]	242
Lebanon Liban	22[1]	22[1]	22[1]	18	16	18	13	11	9	9[1]
Malaysia Malaisie	5 933	5 494	5 525	6 285	6 662	8 275	8 849	8 993	9 369	9 385[1]
Mongolia Mongolie	470[1]	470[1]	470[1]	470[1]	470[1]	553	509	270	125	125[1]
Myanmar Myanmar	664	615	568	392	283	375	296	282[1]	302	339
Nepal Népal	220[1]	220[1]	220[1]	220[1]	220[1]	220[1]	570	620	620[1]	620[1]

47
Sawnwood
Production (sawn): thousand cubic metres [*cont.*]
Sciages
Production (sciés) : milliers de mètres cubes [*suite*]

Country or area Pays ou zone	1984	1985	1986	1987	1988	1989	1990	1991	1992	1993
Pakistan Pakistan	578	589	647	659	755	1 022	1 450	1 520	1 450	1 520
Philippines Philippines	1 234	1 062	977	1 233	1 033	975	846	729	673	490
Singapore [1] Singapour [1]	211	191	175	152	120	90	55	30	25	25
Sri Lanka Sri Lanka	23 [1]	23 [1]	20 [1]	20 [1]	20 [1]	20 [1]	10	5	5	5 [1]
Syrian Arab Republic [1] Rép. arabe syrienne [1]	9	9	9	9	9	9	9	9	9	9
Thailand Thaïlande	1 036	958	1 027	1 095	1 044	1 259	1 170	939	1 076	715
Turkey Turquie	4 923	4 923	4 923 [1]	4 923 [1]	4 923 [1]	4 923 [1]	4 923 [1]	4 928	4 891	5 580 [1]
Viet Nam Viet Nam	389 [1]	424 [1]	459 [1]	494 [1]	529 [1]	564 [1]	896	885	849	849 [1]
Europe **Europe**	**87 749**	**85 199**	**84 381**	**84 213**	**85 259**	**87 385**	**88 082**	**78 707**	**73 799**	**76 643**
Albania Albanie	200 [1]	200 [1]	200 [1]	200 [1]	200 [1]	200 [1]	382	382 [1]	382 [1]	382 [1]
Austria Autriche	6 315	6 001	5 818	5 944	6 478	6 920	7 509	7 239	7 020	6 786
Belarus Bélarus	...	...	...	...	...	...	...	...	1 693	1 545
Belgium-Luxembourg Belgique-Luxembourg	746	795	824	909	1 009	1 164	1 194	1 244	1 184	1 184
Bulgaria Bulgarie	1 483	1 515	1 338	1 490	1 459	1 402	1 108	1 114	324	253
Croatia Croatie	...	...	...	...	...	...	...	...	651	691 [1]
former Czechoslovakia† anc. Tchécoslovaquie†	5 227	5 219	5 251	5 186	5 128	4 860	4 764	3 621	...	...
Czech Republic République tchèque	...	...	...	...	...	...	...	...	2 650	2 650
Denmark Danemark	829 [1]	879	879 [1]	861 [1]	861 [1]	861 [1]	861 [1]	861	620	583
Estonia Estonie	...	...	...	...	...	...	...	...	300	300 [1]
Finland Finlande	8 265	7 333	7 143	7 563	7 823	7 763	7 503	5 983	6 983	8 367
France France	9 038	9 087	9 318	9 612	10 248	10 655	10 960	10 974	10 488	9 080
Germany † Allemagne†	...	...	...	...	...	...	...	13 322	13 496	13 066
F. R. Germany R. f. Allemagne	9 825	9 541	9 805	9 754	10 395	11 388	12 203	...	...	...
former German D. R. anc. R. d. allemande	2 491	2 491	2 431	2 465	2 489	2 521	2 521 [1]	...	...	...
Greece Grèce	321	305	454	428	410	417	355	387	337	337 [1]

47
Sawnwood
Production (sawn): thousand cubic metres [*cont.*]
Sciages
Production (sciés) : milliers de mètres cubes [*suite*]

Country or area Pays ou zone	1984	1985	1986	1987	1988	1989	1990	1991	1992	1993
Hungary Hongrie	1 322	1 284	1 277	1 225	1 237	1 253	1 068	936	667	548
Ireland Irlande	290	300	300[1]	300[1]	300[1]	356	386	386[1]	345	665
Italy Italie	2 234	2 599	1 919	1 905	2 095	1 998	1 950	1 850	1 823	1 717
Latvia Lettonie	...	...	...	...	...	...	...	...	740	446
Netherlands Pays-Bas	335	412	425	387	435	465	455	425	405	371
Norway Norvège	2 364	2 230	2 260	2 362	2 387	2 492	2 413	2 263	2 362	2 362[1]
Poland Pologne	6 765	6 639	6 645	6 442	5 577	4 878	4 129	3 205	4 082	4 180
Portugal Portugal	2 606	1 860	2 070	2 095	2 088	2 090	2 090	485	1 550	1 494
Romania Roumanie	4 868	4 425	3 538	2 858	2 758	2 850	2 911	2 233	2 460	2 460[1]
Russian Federation Fédération de Russie	...	...	...	...	...	...	...	...	53 370	40 000
Slovakia[1] Slovaquie[1]	...	...	...	...	...	...	...	...	...	80
Slovenia Slovénie	...	...	...	...	...	...	...	...	403	441
Spain Espagne	2 150	2 383	2 613	2 643	2 427	2 993	3 267	3 162	2 468	2 721
Sweden Suède	12 382	11 531	11 641	11 524	11 267	11 487	12 018	11 463	12 128	12 738
Switzerland Suisse	1 515	1 689	1 719	1 650	1 693	1 700	1 985	1 727	1 525	1 410
United Kingdom Royaume-Uni	1 520	1 717	1 807	1 823	1 919	2 191	2 271	2 241	2 097	2 078
Yugoslavia, SFR† Yougoslavie, Rfs†	4 658	4 764	4 706	4 587	4 577	4 481	3 779	3 204	...	...
Oceania **Océanie**	**5 362**	**5 791**	**5 874**	**5 259**	**5 489**	**5 561**	**5 610**	**5 427**	**5 841**	**6 214**
Australia Australie	3 003	3 216	3 220	3 131	3 342	3 165	3 151	2 858	3 041	3 185
Fiji Fidji	80[1]	91[1]	78	88	103	94	94[1]	141[1]	91[1]	91[1]
New Caledonia Nouvelle-Calédonie	4[1]	4[1]	4[1]	4[1]	5	5	5[1]	3	2	2[1]
New Zealand Nouvelle-Zélande	2 109	2 320	2 412	1 876	1 881	2 135	2 198	2 263	2 544	2 773
Papua New Guinea Papouasie-Nvl-Guinée	124[1]	* 117	117[1]	117[1]	117[1]	117[1]	117[1]	117[1]	117[1]	117[1]
Samoa[1] Samoa[1]	21	21	21	21	21	21	21	21	21	21
Solomon Islands Iles Salomon	17	17	15	13	12	16	16[1]	16[1]	16[1]	16[1]

47
Sawnwood
Production (sawn): thousand cubic metres [*cont.*]
    Sciages
    Production (sciés) : milliers de mètres cubes [*suite*]

Country or area Pays ou zone	1984	1985	1986	1987	1988	1989	1990	1991	1992	1993
Tonga Tonga	1[1]	1	2	2[1]	2[1]	1[1]	1[1]	1[1]	1[1]	1[1]
Vanuatu Vanuatu	3[1]	4[1]	6	7	7[1]	7[1]	7[1]	7[1]	7[1]	7[1]
former USSR† **ancienne URSS†**	97 300	98 200	102 000	102 500	104 800	104 800	105 000	79 300	56 103[2]	42 291[2]

Source:
Food and Agriculture Organization of the United Nations
(Rome).

† For detailed descriptions of data pertaining to
former Czechoslovakia, Germany, SFR Yugoslavia and former
USSR, see Annex I - Country or area nomenclature, regional
and other groupings.

1 FAO estimate.
2 Excluding Belarus, Estonia, Latvia and Russian Federation
(shown separately).

Source:
Organisation des Nations Unies pour l'alimentation et
l'agriculture (Rome).

† Pour les descriptions en détails des données
relatives à l'ancienne Tchécoslovaquie, l'Allemagne, la Rfs
Yougoslavie et l'ancienne URSS, voir l'Annexe I -
Nomenclature des pays ou zones, groupements régionaux et
autres groupements.

1 Estimation de la FAO.
2 Non compris Bélarus, Estonie, Lettonie, et Fédération de
Russie(dont les chiffres de production sont données
séparément).

48
Paper and paperboard
Papiers et cartons
Production: thousand metric tons
Production : milliers de tonnes métriques

Country or area Pays ou zone	1984	1985	1986	1987	1988	1989	1990	1991	1992	1993
World *Monde*	189 998	192 941	203 297	214 664	227 576	233 167	240 122	243 448	244 925	253 586
Africa **Afrique**	2 030	2 139	2 331	2 373	2 603	2 756	2 734	2 694	2 641	2 338
Algeria Algérie	135	110	120	120[1]	120[1]	120[1]	* 91	* 91	91[1]	91[1]
Cameroon[1] Cameroun[1]	5	5	5	5	5	5	5	5	5	5
Egypt Egypte	* 145	* 145	145[1]	* 160	160[1]	* 216	* 223	208	201	201[1]
Ethiopia Ethiopie	10	10	10	12	10	10	8	6	3	3
Kenya Kenya	75	75	85	89	100	108	* 93	* 92	176	176[1]
Libyan Arab Jamah. Jamah. arabe libyenne	5[1]	* 6	* 6	6[1]	6[1]	6[1]	6[1]	6[1]	6[1]	6[1]
Madagascar Madagascar	10	10	15	8	6[1]	6[1]	6	5	5	6
Morocco Maroc	101	* 107	* 109	105[1]	103[1]	102[1]	* 119	* 117	102	99
Mozambique Mozambique	1[1]	* 2	* 2	2[1]	2[1]	2[1]	* 1	2[1]	2[1]	1[1]
Nigeria Nigéria	15	41	76	76[1]	95	73	79	65	62	62
South Africa Afrique du Sud	1 422	1 489	* 1 611	1 600	1 800	1 899	* 1 904	* 1 905	* 1 800	* 1 500
Sudan Soudan	9[1]	9[1]	9[1]	* 10	10[1]	10[1]	* 4	* 3	3[1]	3[1]
Tunisia Tunisie	28	48	53	62	70	82	78	72	64	64[1]
Uganda Ouganda	0[1]	* 2	* 2	2[1]	2[1]	2[1]	* 3	* 3	3[1]	3[1]
United Rep.Tanzania Rép. Unie de Tanzanie	...	...	...	29	28	28[1]	25	25[1]	25[1]	25[1]
Zaire Zaïre	2	2[1]	3	3	2[1]	1	1[1]	1[1]	3	3[1]
Zambia Zambie	3[1]	2	5	3	2	4	2	2	4	4[1]
Zimbabwe Zimbabwe	64	76	* 75	81	82	82[1]	86	86[1]	86[1]	86[1]
America, North **Amérique du Nord**	79 067	78 007	82 415	86 379	89 823	89 614	91 519	92 389	94 724	97 715
Canada Canada	14 222	14 448	15 259	16 044	16 639	16 555	16 466	16 559	16 585	17 557
Costa Rica Costa Rica	13	13	13[1]	13[1]	17	18	19	19[1]	19[1]	19[1]
Cuba Cuba	122	132	150	148	141	168	* 123	* 118	* 60	* 57
Dominican Republic Rép. dominicaine	10	10[1]	10[1]	10[1]	10[1]	10[1]	10[1]	10[1]	10[1]	7

48
Paper and paperboard
Production: thousand metric tons [*cont.*]
Papiers et cartons
Production : milliers de tonnes métriques [*suite*]

Country or area Pays ou zone	1984	1985	1986	1987	1988	1989	1990	1991	1992	1993
El Salvador[1] El Salvador[1]	16	16	16	17	17	17	17	17	17	17
Guatemala Guatemala	18	14	17	14	14	14	14	14[1]	14[1]	14[1]
Jamaica Jamaïque	18	15[1]	11[1]	2	3	4	4	4	5	3
Mexico Mexique	2 239	2 376	2 469	2 573	3 375	3 294[1]	2 873	2 896[1]	* 2 825	* 2 763
Panama Panama	43[1]	24	26	26[1]	20	20	28	* 28	28[1]	28[1]
United States Etats-Unis	62 366	60 959	64 444	67 532	69 587	69 514	71 965	72 724	75 161	77 250
America, South **Amérique du Sud**	**6 292**	**6 505**	**7 235**	**7 644**	**7 685**	**7 609**	**7 686**	**8 034**	**8 312**	**8 685**
Argentina Argentine	942	864	998	1 027	974[1]	917	891	* 963	976	976[1]
Bolivia Bolivie	1[1]	1[1]	1[1]	2	2[1]	2[1]	5	...	...	...
Brazil Brésil	3 768	4 022	4 525	4 712	4 685	4 806	4 844	4 888	4 913	5 352
Chile Chili	381	385	388	442	449	438	462	486	552	572
Colombia Colombie	413	* 446	457	488	501	501[1]	494	521	629	595
Ecuador Equateur	34[1]	34	34	34	35	35	44	129	160	160[1]
Paraguay Paraguay	13[1]	8	8	10	11	11[1]	12	13	13	13[1]
Peru Pérou	138	* 150	149	209	260	311	263	327	327	327[1]
Uruguay Uruguay	45	45	64	66	59	63	61	75	83	83[1]
Venezuela Venezuela	* 557	551	612	654	708	524	610	632	659	607
Asia **Asie**	**35 038**	**38 182**	**41 044**	**45 125**	**49 395**	**53 162**	**57 045**	**60 254**	**63 168**	**67 395**
Bangladesh Bangladesh	149	* 104	* 113	* 114	96	97	92	97	97[1]	97[1]
China Chine	9 514	11 197	12 601	14 231	15 700	16 487	17 328	18 525	19 929	23 816[1]
Hong Kong Hong-kong	36	* 40	* 40	40[1]	40[1]	40[1]	* 80	* 115	* 120	* 193
India Inde	1 557	1 559	1 806	1 871	1 977	2 050	2 185	2 362	2 528	2 626
Indonesia Indonésie	* 403	500	* 611	813	974	1 158	* 1 438	* 1 755	* 2 263	2 600[1]
Iran, Islamic Rep. of Iran, Rép. islamique d'	78[1]	78[1]	80[1]	90[1]	100	142[1]	* 211	* 235	190	175
Iraq Iraq	28[1]	28[1]	28[1]	28[1]	28[1]	28[1]	55	13	13[1]	13[1]

48
Paper and paperboard
Production: thousand metric tons [*cont.*]
Papiers et cartons
Production : milliers de tonnes métriques [*suite*]

Country or area Pays ou zone	1984	1985	1986	1987	1988	1989	1990	1991	1992	1993
Israel Israël	148	131	151	160	170	179	194	200	215	* 213
Japan Japon	19 345	20 469	21 062	22 537	24 625	26 809	28 088	29 053	28 324	27 764
Jordan Jordanie	7	13	* 14	12	10	12	* 15	* 15	15[1]	29
Korea, Dem. P. R.[1] Corée, R. p. dém. de[1]	80	80	80	80	80	80	80	80	80	80
Korea, Republic of Corée, République de	2 207	2 312	2 773	3 163	3 659	4 018	4 524	4 922	5 504	5 804
Lebanon Liban	45[1]	* 45	42	42[1]	37	37[1]	37[1]	42	42[1]	42[1]
Malaysia Malaisie	50	* 53	* 73	97	120	251	* 275	* 293	* 636	* 663
Myanmar Myanmar	10[1]	15[1]	23	9	8	10	11	11[1]	11[1]	15
Nepal Népal	2[1]	* 0	* 2	2[1]	2[1]	2[1]	13	13	13	13[1]
Pakistan Pakistan	73	82	80	96	147	151	229	206	229	206
Philippines Philippines	290	268	218	358	314	239	245	395	570	* 487
Singapore Singapour	* 10	* 10	10[1]	10[1]	10[1]	10[1]	* 80	* 85	85[1]	85[1]
Sri Lanka Sri Lanka	23[1]	23	25	25[1]	28[1]	17	16	23	26	29
Syrian Arab Republic Rép. arabe syrienne	3[1]	* 5	* 5	10[1]	19	19[1]	19[1]	1	1[1]	1[1]
Thailand Thaïlande	437	466	432[1]	465	514	520	877	958	1 150	1 306
Turkey Turquie	488	644	710	813	681	751	891	747	1 013	1 013[1]
Viet Nam Viet Nam	55[1]	60[1]	65[1]	59	56	56[1]	62	108	115	125
Europe **Europe**	**55 523**	**55 762**	**57 610**	**60 407**	**64 697**	**66 686**	**67 652**	**67 653**	**67 182**	**69 864**
Albania Albanie	8[1]	8[1]	8[1]	8[1]	26	26	44	44[1]	44[1]	44[1]
Austria Autriche	1 922	2 127	2 183	2 396	2 650	2 754	2 932	3 090	3 252	3 301
Belarus[1] Bélarus[1]	...	...	...	...	...	...	...	...	267	175
Belgium-Luxembourg Belgique-Luxembourg	847	843	850	1 031	1 133	1 170	1 196	1 233	1 147	1 147[1]
Bulgaria Bulgarie	445	454	458	456	477	438	322	258	153	153[1]
former Czechoslovakia† anc. Tchécoslovaquie†	1 237	1 259	1 255	1 273	1 266	1 305	1 300	1 087	...	...
Czech Republic République tchèque	...	...	...	...	...	...	...	...	688	624

48
Paper and paperboard
Production: thousand metric tons [*cont.*]
Papiers et cartons
Production : milliers de tonnes métriques [*suite*]

Country or area Pays ou zone	1984	1985	1986	1987	1988	1989	1990	1991	1992	1993
Denmark Danemark	332	302	293	326	343[l]	326	335	356	317	317[l]
Estonia Estonie	...	...	...	...	...	...	...	...	42	42[l]
Finland Finlande	7 318	7 447	7 549	8 011	8 652	8 754	8 967	8 776	9 147	9 990
France France	5 566	5 150	5 583	5 581	6 313	6 754	7 049	7 442	7 691	7 824
Germany † Allemagne†	...	...	...	...	...	...	...	13 018	12 941	13 034
F. R. Germany R. f. Allemagne	9 145	9 178	9 409	9 938	10 576	11 259	11 873	...	...	...
former German D. R. anc. R. d. allemande	1 293	1 297	1 320	1 340	1 362	1 351	1 351[l]	...	...	...
Greece Grèce	294	282	283	280	280	280	361	387	387[l]	750
Hungary Hongrie	506	494	517	522	535	504	443	364	348	292
Ireland Irlande	20	* 22	37	29	33	34	35	36	36[l]	36
Italy Italie	4 722	4 587	4 631	4 882	5 512	5 640	5 587	5 795	6 040	6 019
Latvia Lettonie	...	...	...	...	...	...	...	...	45	10
Lithuania Lituanie	...	...	...	...	...	...	...	...	50	50[l]
Netherlands Pays-Bas	1 885	1 956	2 088	2 168	2 460	2 572	2 770	2 862	2 835	2 855
Norway Norvège	1 562	1 604	1 573	1 590	1 670	1 789	1 819	1 784	1 683	1 968
Poland Pologne	1 257	1 292	1 327	1 380	1 448	1 406	1 064	1 066	1 147	1 171
Portugal Portugal	671	706	590	628	681	740	780	877	959	876
Romania Roumanie	806	801	811	816	819	739	547	359	359[l]	359[l]
Russian Federation Fédération de Russie	...	...	...	...	...	...	...	...	5 765	4 464
Slovenia Slovénie	...	...	...	...	...	...	...	...	413	401
Spain Espagne	2 952	2 913	3 152	3 251	3 408	3 446	3 446	3 576	3 449	3 348
Sweden Suède	6 870	7 001	7 364	7 812	8 161	8 363	8 419	8 349	8 378	8 781
Switzerland Suisse	986	1 014	1 087	1 147	1 216	1 259	1 295	1 259[l]	1 305	1 332
United Kingdom Royaume-Uni	3 591	3 712	3 941	4 184	4 295	4 475	4 824	4 951	5 152	5 243

48
Paper and paperboard
Production: thousand metric tons [*cont.*]
Papiers et cartons
Production : milliers de tonnes métriques [*suite*]

Country or area Pays ou zone	1984	1985	1986	1987	1988	1989	1990	1991	1992	1993
Yugoslavia, SFR† Yougoslavie, Rfs†	1 288	1 313	1 301	1 358	1 381	1 302	894	685	...	...
Oceania **Océanie**	**2 214**	**2 316**	**2 267**	**2 170**	**2 492**	**2 605**	**2 768**	**2 833**	**2 728**	**2 848**
Australia Australie	1 520	1 546	1 596	1 526	1 792	1 870	2 011	2 018	1 990	2 012
New Zealand Nouvelle-Zélande	694	* 770	671	644	700	735	757	815	738	836
former USSR† **ancienne URSS†**	**9 835**	**10 031**	**10 395**	**10 566**	**10 881**	**10 735**	**10 718**	**9 590**	**6 169**[2]	**4 741**[2]

Source:
Food and Agriculture Organization of the United Nations
(Rome).

† For detailed descriptions of data pertaining to
former Czechoslovakia, Germany, SFR Yugoslavia and former
USSR, see Annex I - Country or area nomenclature, regional
and other groupings.

1 FAO estimate.
2 Excluding Belarus, Estonia, Latvia, Lithuania and Russian
Federation (shown separately).

Source:
Organisation des Nations Unies pour l'alimentation et
l'agriculture (Rome).

† Pour les descriptions en détails des données
relatives à l'ancienne Tchécoslovaquie, l'Allemagne, la Rfs
Yougoslavie et l'ancienne URSS, voir l'Annexe I -
Nomenclature des pays ou zones, groupements régionaux et
autres groupements.

1 Estimation de la FAO.
2 Non compris Bélarus, Estonie, Lettonie, Lituanie et
Fédération de Russie(dont les chiffres de production sont
données séparément).

49

Tires

Pneumatiques : enveloppes

Production: thousands
Production : milliers

Country or area Pays ou zone	1984	1985	1986	1987	1988	1989	1990	1991	1992	1993
Total	**749 184**	**748 434**	**767 277**	**807 906**	**866 115**	**878 807**	**862 284**	**833 041**	**893 071**	**831 904**
Argentina Argentine	5 357	3 904	4 579	4 974	5 297	4 594	4 677	4 568	5 365	6 038
Armenia Arménie	..	..	..	..	..	..	..	485	...	...
Australia[12] Australie[12]	6 165	5 846	6 600	5 576	7 450	7 450	7 600	...	...	...
Azerbaijan Azerbaïdjan	..	..	..	..	..	..	..	271	222	134
Belarus Bélarus	..	..	..	..	..	..	..	3 367	2 862	1 916
Brazil[3] Brésil[3]	21 020	22 827	24 376	28 224	29 255	29 215	29 162	28 926	30 306	...
Bulgaria Bulgarie	1 666	1 659	1 668	1 857	1 693	1 762	1 795	1 125	1 034	783
Canada[4] Canada[4]	25 519	26 655	28 765	27 200	25 032	20 664	21 692	...	...	...
Chile Chili	913	858	862	1 221	1 347	1 562	1 632	1 825	2 002	2 198
China[5] Chine[5]	15 690	19 260	19 243	23 332	29 910	32 262	32 091	38 723	51 834	6 391
Colombia Colombie	1 950	1 856	1 851	1 955	1 915	1 875	1 408	* 1 705	...	...
Croatia Croatie	..	..	..	..	..	..	..	34	...	...
Cuba Cuba	328	345	319	232	320	230	...	...	...	...
Cyprus Chypre	119	105	91	* 91	* 92	89	* 99	* 72	38	* 38
former Czechoslovakia† anc. Tchécoslovaquie†	4 621	4 547	4 737	4 858	5 058	5 263	5 315	4 733	..	..
Czech Republic République tchèque	..	..	..	..	..	..	..	..	3 123	3 655
Ecuador Equateur	...	...	...	97	32	...	42	...	812	...
Egypt Egypte	775	845	1 011	1 038	1 006	1 126	1 171	1 243	1 186	1 162
Finland[6] Finlande[6]	1 427	1 339	...	...	...	...	...	...	...	...
France France	47 817	47 316	51 138	49 344	54 043	61 678	54 536	57 876	59 928	53 390
Germany † Allemagne†	..	..	..	..	..	..	..	...	50 993	45 595
F. R. Germany R. f. Allemagne	39 254	40 475	42 826	47 083	48 644	49 467	48 247	..	..	..
former German D. R. anc. R. d. allemande	5 576	6 003	6 183	6 275	6 328	6 259	4 052	..	..	..
Hungary Hongrie	552	578	635	674	686	736	605	425	355	146

49

Tires
Production: thousands [*cont.*]
Pneumatiques : enveloppes
Production : milliers [*suite*]

Country or area Pays ou zone	1984	1985	1986	1987	1988	1989	1990	1991	1992	1993
India Inde	5 952	5 042	6 383	5 616	7 537	8 066	8 460	8 312	8 756	...
Indonesia Indonésie	3 406	3 420	4 740	4 791	* 6 564	* 8 028	10 080	...	10 661	...
Iran, Islamic Rep. of Iran, Rép. islamique d'[7]	4 782	3 577	3 573	4 587	4 638	4 814	6 012	4 998	3 387	...
Israel Israël	1 009	930	744	920	573	751	778	...	...	...
Italy Italie	27 460	27 955	30 860	32 005	32 053	33 625	30 767	32 447	29 978	29 138
Jamaica Jamaïque	207	208	215	263	242	286	347	326	308	359
Japan Japon	131 199	135 745	135 323	139 086	150 562	155 038	153 226	153 677	154 900	142 595
Kenya[8] Kenya[8]	...	...	725	617	631	797	813	462	474	456
Korea, Republic of Corée, République de	15 126	15 207	18 214	20 060	24 250	24 535	28 129	33 710	38 120	42 285
Malaysia[5] Malaisie[5]	3 700	3 622	3 846	5 173	6 222	6 156	6 764	7 970	8 540	9 486
Mexico Mexique	9 779	10 472	9 330	10 164	10 474	11 038	11 855	12 148	12 568	11 295
Morocco Maroc	834	779	821	943	...	...	...	...	...	...
Mozambique Mozambique	51	80	60	22	17	29	23	5	...	...
New Zealand[9] Nouvelle-Zélande[9]	1 282	1 222	1 389	1 565	1 650	1 460	1 550	...	...	...
Nigeria Nigéria	1 604	2 154	* 2 941	...	...	...	...	...	...	...
Pakistan[1] Pakistan[1]	238	307	412	382	679	907	915	952	784	712
Panama Panama	49	37	...	22	23	23	246	...	...	...
Peru Pérou	782	784	914	946	868	710	637	561	...	...
Philippines Philippines	1 450	1 300	934	1 159	* 1 968	* 2 016	2 208	...	...	...
Poland Pologne	5 902	6 254	6 217	6 020	6 276	6 025	4 704	4 516	5 607	6 479
Portugal Portugal	2 154	2 286	2 385	2 754	3 261	3 292	2 976	2 184	...	...
Romania[9] Roumanie[9]	5 882	5 642	5 789	5 247	5 552	4 804	3 702	2 822	2 877	3 401
Russian Federation Fédération de Russie	..	..	..	..	..	..	..	33 522	33 682	31 208
Slovenia Slovénie	..	..	..	..	..	..	..	3 289	4 133	...
South Africa Afrique du Sud	5 825	5 041	5 432	6 066	6 813	6 817	7 478	7 236	7 136	7 413

49

Tires
Production: thousands [cont.]
      Pneumatiques: enveloppes
      Production : milliers [suite]

Country or area Pays ou zone	1984	1985	1986	1987	1988	1989	1990	1991	1992	1993
Spain Espagne	20 610	19 386	20 034	23 204	24 323	24 696	23 361	23 812	25 670	...
Sri Lanka Sri Lanka	164	180	200	330	228	339	382	392	276	184
Sweden Suède	2 741	2 996	3 001	2 852	* 2 980	* 2 915	* 2 162	2 158	2 517	...
Thailand Thaïlande	2 177	2 126	2 264	3 063	3 980	4 320	4 183	4 518	...	...
TFYR Macedonia L'ex-R.y. Macédoine	..	..	..	..	..	..	..	1	...	
Tunisia Tunisie	205	261	358	374	471	505	579	596	526	602
Turkey Turquie	4 690	4 922	4 871	6 260	12 088	6 633	4 754	7 541	8 463	9 137
Ukraine Ukraine	..	..	..	..	..	..	..	7 859	7 886	7 699
former USSR†[10] ancienne URSS†[10]	63 737	65 171	66 023	67 802	69 125	69 705	...	..	..	..
United Kingdom Royaume-Uni	24 120	24 216	25 644	27 624	30 204	31 080	29 376	28 500	30 408	...
United Rep.Tanzania Rép. Unie de Tanzanie	...	113	139	197	188	213	208	185	158	190
United States Etats-Unis	209 375	195 972	190 296	202 980	211 356	212 868	210 660	202 391	230 250	...
Venezuela Venezuela	2 985	4 492	4 989	5 447	5 203	4 177	3 951	4 787	4 713	...
Yugoslavia Yougoslavie	..	..	..	..	..	..	..	...	2 782	...
Yugoslavia, SFR†[2] Yougoslavie, Rfs†[2]	9 858	11 194	11 632	11 718	12 548	13 201	12 744	..	..	..

Source:
Industrial statistics database of the Statistics Division of
the United Nations Secretariat.

† For detailed descriptions of data pertaining to
former Czechoslovakia, Germany, SFR Yugoslavia and former
USSR, see Annex I - Country or area nomenclature, regional
and other groupings.

1 Twelve months ending 30 June of year stated.

2 Including motorcycle tires.
3 Including tires for motorcycles and bicycles.

4 Source: International Rubber Study Group, (London).
5 Tires of all types.
6 Beginning 1986, data are confidential.
7 Production by establishments employing 50 or more persons.
8 Including retreaded tires.
9 Including tires for vehicles operating off-the-road.
10 Including tires for agricultural vehicles, motorcycles and
   scooter.

Source:
Base de données pour les statistiques industrielles de la
Division de statistique du Secrétariat de l'ONU.

† Pour les descriptions en détails des données
relatives à l'ancienne Tchécoslovaquie, l'Allemagne, la Rfs
Yougoslavie et l'ancienne URSS, voir l'Annexe I -
Nomenclature des pays ou zones, groupements régionaux et
autres groupements.

1 Période de douze mois finissant le 30 juin de l'année
   indiquée.
2 Y compris les pneumatiques pour motocyclettes.
3 Y compris les pneumatiques pour motocyclettes et
   bicyclettes.
4 Source: "International Rubber Study Group", (Londres).
5 Pneumatiques de tous genres.
6 A partir de 1986, les données sont confidentielles.
7 Production des établissements occupant 50 personnes ou plus.
8 Y compris les pneumatiques rechapés.
9 Y compris les pneumatiques pour véhicules tous terrains.
10 Y compris les pneumatiques pour véhicules agricoles,
   motocyclettes et scooters.

50
Cement
Ciment
Production: thousand metric tons
Production : milliers de tonnes métriques

Country or area Pays ou zone	1984	1985	1986	1987	1988	1989	1990	1991	1992	1993
Total	925 142	939 621	985 570	1 034 014	1 100 461	1 136 331	1 142 676	1 161 021	1 214 188	1 273 639
Afghanistan[1] Afghanistan[1]	112	128	103	104	70	* 100	100	109	...	...
Albania Albanie	* 860[2]	642	709	708	746	753	644	311	...	...
Algeria Algérie	5 538	6 096	6 448	7 541	7 195	6 778	6 337	6 323	7 093	6 951
Angola Angola	126	205	354[2]	354[2]	1 000[2]	1 000[2]	1 000[2]	998[2]	370[2]	...
Argentina Argentine	5 220	4 795	5 553	6 302	6 028	4 449	3 612	4 399	5 051	5 647
Armenia Arménie	..	..	..	..	..	..	..	1 507	368	198
Australia Australie	4 655	5 680	6 106	5 920	6 158	6 901	7 075	6 110	5 731	6 225
Austria Autriche	4 899	4 560	4 569	4 518	4 763	4 749	4 903	5 017	5 029	4 941
Azerbaijan Azerbaïdjan	..	..	..	..	..	..	..	923	827	643
Bangladesh[3] Bangladesh[3]	273	240	292	310	310	344	337	275	272	207
Barbados Barbade	64	148	199	147	185	225	213	144	71	64
Belarus Bélarus	..	..	..	..	..	..	..	2 402	2 263	1 908
Belgium Belgique	5 708	5 537	5 760	5 689	6 451	6 720	6 924	7 184	8 073	7 569
Benin[2] Bénin[2]	300	300	300	300	200	250	272	272	...	...
Bolivia Bolivie	220	241	343	386	466	501	523	621	630	...
Brazil Brésil	19 497	20 635	25 252	25 468	25 329	25 921	25 850	27 491	23 902	24 845
Bulgaria Bulgarie	5 717	5 296	5 702	5 494	5 535	5 036	4 710	2 374	2 132	2 007
Cameroon Cameroun	694	785	779	707	586	...	...	...	...	...
Canada Canada	9 387	10 192	10 611	12 603	12 350	12 591	11 745	9 372	8 592	9 394
Chile Chili	1 390	1 430	1 441	1 500	1 885	2 010	2 115	2 251	2 660	3 024
China Chine	123 020	145 950	166 060	186 249	210 140	210 295	209 711	244 656	308 217	367 878
Colombia Colombie	5 280	5 412	5 916	5 892	6 312	6 648	6 360	6 389	6 792	...
Congo Congo	* 45	62	2	38	86	121	90	102	124	95
Costa Rica[4] Costa Rica[4]	350	350	306	285	309	315	...	...	...	...

50

Cement
Production: thousand metric tons [*cont.*]
   Ciment
   Production : milliers de tonnes métriques [*suite*]

Country or area Pays ou zone	1984	1985	1986	1987	1988	1989	1990	1991	1992	1993
Côte d'Ivoire Côte d'Ivoire	552	535	775[2]	652[2]	700[2]	700[2]	500[2]	499[2]	...	...
Croatia Croatie	..	..	..	..	..	..	..	1 742	1 771	...
Cuba Cuba	3 347	3 182	3 305	3 535	3 566	3 759	3 696	2 599	...	...
Cyprus Chypre	853	659	857	854	868	1 042	1 133	1 134	1 132	1 089
former Czechoslovakia† anc. Tchécoslovaquie†	10 530	10 265	10 298	10 369	10 974	10 888	10 215	8 299	..	..
Czech Republic République tchèque	..	..	..	..	..	..	..	..	6 145	5 402
Denmark[5] Danemark[5]	1 668	1 983	2 029	1 886	1 681	2 000	1 656	2 019	2 072	...
Dominican Republic Rép. dominicaine	1 109	1 001	952	1 209	1 235	* 1 269	* 1 189	* 998	...	...
Ecuador Equateur	1 755	2 008	2 118	2 875	2 126	* 1 548	1 792	1 774	2 072	...
Egypt Egypte	4 600	5 275	7 612	8 762	9 794	12 480	14 111	16 427	15 454	12 576
El Salvador[4] El Salvador[4]	399	450	460	480	455	447	444	448	...	...
Estonia Estonie	..	..	..	..	..	..	..	905	483	354
Ethiopia[6] Ethiopie[6]	165	228	270	350	406	412	324	270	237	377
Fiji Fidji	98	93	92	59	44	58	78	79	84	80
Finland Finlande	1 656	1 695	1 495	1 579	1 619	1 693	1 649	1 343	1 133	835
France France	22 724	22 224	21 584	23 544	* 25 374	25 994	26 497	25 089	21 584	19 320
Gabon Gabon	207	244	210	141	132[2]	115[2]	115[2]	113[2]	120	...
Germany † Allemagne†	..	..	..	..	..	..	..	...	37 331	36 649
F. R. Germany R. f. Allemagne	28 909	25 758	26 580	25 268	26 215	28 499	30 456	..	..	..
former German D. R. anc. R. d. allemande	11 555	11 608	11 988	12 430	12 510	12 229	7 316	..	..	..
Ghana Ghana	235	356	219	294	412	* 565	* 675	* 675	...	...
Greece Grèce	13 521	12 855	12 542	11 869	12 777	12 319	13 142	13 151	12 761	...
Guadeloupe Guadeloupe	188	194	197	222	200[2]	200[2]	200[2]	200[2]	...	...
Guatemala Guatemala	455	574	1 392	1 260	* 880	* 591	* 611	* 623	...	...
Haiti Haïti	248	263	248	254	245	234	226	* 226	...	...

50

Cement
Production: thousand metric tons [*cont.*]
Ciment
Production : milliers de tonnes métriques [*suite*]

Country or area Pays ou zone	1984	1985	1986	1987	1988	1989	1990	1991	1992	1993
Honduras Honduras	368	348	360	375	268	321	326	402	...	...
Hong Kong Hong-kong	1 847	1 835	2 236	2 226	2 189	2 141	1 808	1 677	1 644	1 712
Hungary Hongrie	4 145	3 678	3 846	4 153	3 873	3 857	3 933	2 529	2 236	2 533
Iceland Islande	114	117	115	127	* 134	* 116	114	106	100	86
India Inde	29 541	31 971	34 983	37 135	41 136	44 197	46 170	52 013	53 936	57 033
Indonesia Indonésie	8 893	9 940	11 323	11 814	12 096	15 660	15 972	16 153	14 048	...
Iran, Islamic Rep. of[7] Iran, Rép. islamique d'[7]	12 064	11 954	12 148	12 852	11 926	12 587	14 429	14 775	14 889	...
Iraq Iraq	8 000[2]	8 000[2]	7 992	9 780	9 162	12 500	13 000	* 5 000	2 453	...
Ireland Irlande	1 377	1 457	1 250	1 446	* 1 685	* 1 624	* 1 624	* 1 601	...	...
Israel Israël	1 889	1 596	1 624	2 226	2 326	2 289	2 868	* 2 902	...	...
Italy Italie	38 307	37 155	36 393	37 788	38 220	39 692	40 544	40 301	41 034	33 771
Jamaica Jamaïque	259	241	247	261	339	361	421	390	480	441
Japan Japon	78 860	72 847	71 264	71 551	77 554	79 717	84 445	89 564	88 252	88 046
Jordan Jordanie	2 026	2 022	1 837	2 472	1 780	1 930	1 733	1 675	2 651	3 437
Kazakstan Kazakstan	..	..	..	..	..	..	..	7 575	6 436	3 963
Kenya Kenya	1 134	1 115	1 174	1 243	1 201	1 316	1 515	1 423	1 507	1 417
Korea, Dem. P. R.[2] Corée, R. p. dém. de[2]	* 8 000	* 8 000	* 8 000	* 9 000	11 800	16 300	16 300	16 329	...	...
Korea, Republic of Corée, République de	20 413	20 509	23 530	25 946	29 611	30 821	33 914	39 167	44 444	47 313
Kuwait Koweït	1 184	1 067	1 014	882	984	1 108	800	* 299	...	...
Kyrgyzstan Kirghizistan	..	..	..	..	..	..	..	1 320	1 096	672
Latvia Lettonie	..	..	..	..	..	..	..	720	340	114
Lebanon[2] Liban[2]	1 250	* 1 000	* 900	* 900	* 900	* 900	907	907	...	...
Liberia Libéria	86	104	97	95	130	* 85	50	...	...	...
Libyan Arab Jamah.[2] Jamah. arabe libyenne[2]	6 000	6 500	2 077	2 700	2 700	2 700	2 700	2 722	...	...
Lithuania Lituanie	..	..	..	..	..	..	..	3 126	1 485	727

50

Cement
Production: thousand metric tons [cont.]
Ciment
Production : milliers de tonnes métriques [suite]

Country or area Pays ou zone	1984	1985	1986	1987	1988	1989	1990	1991	1992	1993
Luxembourg Luxembourg	340	295	389	509	563	590	636	688	695	719
Madagascar Madagascar	37	28	32	44	33	24	29	32	30	36
Malawi Malawi	70	62	69	75	62	79	101	112	108	...
Malaysia Malaisie	3 469	3 128	3 569	3 316	3 861	4 794	5 881	7 451	8 366	8 797
Mali Mali	25[2]	19[2]	20[2]	22[2]	25[2]	0	4	11	16	14
Martinique Martinique	189	191	209	221	247	244	277	291	...	...
Mexico Mexique	18 702	20 255	19 825	23 482	23 606	24 210	24 683	25 208	27 114	28 626
Mongolia Mongolie	141	151	425	541	502	513	510	* 399	...	...
Morocco Maroc	3 573	3 704	3 709	3 879	4 260	4 641	5 381	5 777	6 223	6 175
Mozambique Mozambique	105	77	73	73	64	79	80	63	73	60
Myanmar[8] Myanmar[8]	310	429	444	389	349	441	420	443	472	400
Nepal Népal	32	96	152	215	217	114	107	* 99	...	...
Netherlands Pays-Bas	3 176	2 911	3 099	2 929	3 418	3 546	3 682	3 571	3 296	3 142
New Caledonia Nouvelle-Calédonie	* 41	31	40	* 58	63	67	64	* 68	90	100
New Zealand Nouvelle-Zélande	823	863	895	880	793	729	681	581	599	...
Nicaragua[4] Nicaragua[4]	280	245	284	265	256	225	* 140	* 140	...	...
Niger[2] Niger[2]	38	38	26	29	40	27	27	28	...	...
Nigeria Nigéria	2 184	3 348	3 624	3 085	4 017	4 229	2 974	3 418	3 367	3 247
Norway Norvège	1 547	1 343	1 752	1 703	1 667	1 380	1 260	1 293	1 242	...
Pakistan[3] Pakistan[3]	4 503	4 732	5 773	6 508	7 072	7 125	7 488	7 762	8 321	8 558
Panama Panama	304[2]	305[2]	336[2]	383	179	169[2]	* 300[2]	* 300[2]	...	...
Paraguay Paraguay	109	46	179	269	256	256	344	343	476	480
Peru Pérou	1 947	1 757	2 207	2 584	2 514	2 105	2 184	2 124	2 052	...
Philippines Philippines	3 660	3 072	3 288	3 984	4 092	3 624	6 360	6 804	6 540	...
Poland Pologne	16 649	14 990	15 831	16 090	16 984	17 125	12 518	12 012	11 908	12 200

50
Cement
Production: thousand metric tons [cont.]
Ciment
Production : milliers de tonnes métriques [suite]

Country or area Pays ou zone	1984	1985	1986	1987	1988	1989	1990	1991	1992	1993
Portugal Portugal	5 514	5 279	5 425	5 853	6 471	6 673	7 188	7 342	# 13 149	...
Puerto Rico[3] Porto Rico[3]	881	865	896	1 094	1 163	1 257	1 305	1 296	1 266	1 303
Qatar Qatar	313	385	324	293	291	295	267	367	354	400
Republic of Moldova République de Moldova	..	..	..	..	..	..	..	1 809	705	110
Réunion Réunion	...	...	...	...	...	322	336	...	...	...
Romania Roumanie	12 991	11 189	13 054	12 435	13 124	12 225	9 468	6 692	6 271	6 240
Russian Federation Fédération de Russie	..	..	..	..	..	..	..	77 463	61 699	49 903
Rwanda Rwanda	8	32	47	57	51	* 68	* 60	* 60	...	...
Saudi Arabia Arabie saoudite	7 504	9 232	9 232	* 8 595	* 9 525	* 9 500	* 10 000	* 12 002	...	...
Senegal Sénégal	414	408	372	362	393	391	471	503	602	591
Sierra Leone Sierra Leone	0	17	34	24	...	9	...	...	...	...
Singapore Singapour	2 511	1 897	1 875	1 550	1 684	1 704	1 848	2 199	...	...
Slovakia Slovaquie	..	..	..	..	..	..	..	..	3 374	2 656
Slovenia Slovénie	..	..	..	..	..	..	..	1 801	1 568	...
South Africa Afrique du Sud	8 084	6 880	6 246	5 999	6 760	7 261	6 563	6 147	5 850	5 818
Spain Espagne	25 435	21 876	22 007	23 012	24 372	27 375	28 092	27 576	24 612	...
Sri Lanka Sri Lanka	401	380	558	619	633	596	579	620	553	466
Sudan Soudan	200	148	175	178	110	* 150	150	168	...	...
Suriname Suriname	50	79	61	40	34	52	55	24	14	14
Sweden Suède	2 393	2 101	2 044	2 238	4 427	4 541	5 000	4 493	2 289	...
Switzerland Suisse	4 181	4 254	4 393	4 617	4 965	5 461	5 206	4 716	4 260	...
Syrian Arab Republic Rép. arabe syrienne	4 279	4 357	4 316	3 870	3 330	3 976	3 049	2 843	3 246	3 667
Tajikistan Tadjikistan	..	...	..	..	..	..	..	1	1	0
Thailand Thaïlande	8 271	7 951	8 005	9 870	11 519	15 024	18 054	19 164	21 711	26 300
TFYR Macedonia L'ex-R.y. Macédoine	..	..	..	..	..	..	..	606	516	...

50
Cement
Production: thousand metric tons [cont.]
Ciment
Production : milliers de tonnes métriques [suite]

Country or area Pays ou zone	1984	1985	1986	1987	1988	1989	1990	1991	1992	1993
Togo Togo	243	284	338[2]	370[2]	378[2]	389[2]	400[2]	399[2]	...	...
Trinidad and Tobago Trinité-et-Tobago	406	329	338	326	360	384	438	486	482	...
Tunisia Tunisie	2 777	3 033	2 962	3 215	3 600	3 984	4 311	4 195	4 184	4 508
Turkey Turquie	15 738	17 581	20 004	21 980	22 568	23 704	24 404	25 842	28 336	31 241
Turkmenistan Turkménistan	..	..	..	..	..	..	..	904	1 050	1 118
Uganda Ouganda	25	12	16	16	15	17	27	27	38	52
Ukraine Ukraine	..	..	..	..	..	..	..	21 745	20 121	15 012
former USSR† ancienne URSS†	129 866	130 772	135 119	137 404	139 499	140 436	137 321	..	..	..
United Arab Emirates[2] Emirats arabes unis[2]	4 005	4 205	2 748	3 106	2 980	3 112	3 110	3 012	...	...
United Kingdom Royaume-Uni	13 481	13 339	13 413	14 311	16 506	16 849	14 736	12 002	...	...
United Rep.Tanzania Rép. Unie de Tanzanie	369	376	435	498	592	595	664	1 022	677	749
United States Etats-Unis	70 452	70 284	71 112	67 380	71 544	71 308	70 944	* 65 052	70 848	...
Uruguay Uruguay	374	317	329	420	435	* 465	469	458	552	610
Uzbekistan Ouzbékistan	..	..	..	..	..	..	..	6 191	5 934	5 278
Venezuela Venezuela	4 783	5 121	5 875	5 975	6 199	5 259	5 996	6 336	6 585	...
Viet Nam Viet Nam	1 296	1 503	1 526	1 665	1 954	2 088	2 534	3 127	3 926	...
Yemen Yémen	..	..	..	..	..	..	..	718	820	...
former Yemen Arab Rep. anc. Yémen rép. arabe	709	698	708	* 760	* 646	* 700	* 700	..	..	..
Yugoslavia Yougoslavie	..	..	..	..	..	..	..	...	2 036	...
Yugoslavia, SFR† Yougoslavie, Rfs†	9 315	9 028	9 128	8 963	8 840	8 560	7 956	..	..	..
Zaire Zaïre	534	444[2]	445[2]	492[2]	495[2]	460[2]	460[2]	449[2]	...	...
Zambia Zambie	220	316	334	375	405	385	432	376	...	...
Zimbabwe Zimbabwe	650	614	659	811	776	827	924	949	829	816

50

Cement
Production: thousand metric tons [*cont.*]

Ciment
Production : milliers de tonnes métriques [*suite*]

Source:
Industrial statistics database of the Statistics Division of
the United Nations Secretariat.

†   For detailed descriptions of data pertaining to
former Czechoslovakia, Germany, SFR Yugoslavia and former
USSR, see Annex I - Country or area nomenclature, regional
and other groupings.

1   Twelve months beginning 21 March of year stated.

2   Source: US Bureau of Mines, (Washington, DC).
3   Twelve months ending 30 June of year stated.

4   Source: United Nations Economic Commission for Latin America
(ECLA), (Santiago).
5   Sales.
6   Twelve months ending 7 July of the year stated.

7   Production by establishments employing 50 or more persons.
8   Government production only.

Source:
Base de données pour les statistiques industrielles de la
Division de statistique du Secrétariat de l'ONU.

†   Pour les descriptions en détails des données
relatives à l'ancienne Tchécoslovaquie, l'Allemagne, la Rfs
Yougoslavie et l'ancienne URSS, voir l'Annexe I -
Nomenclature des pays ou zones, groupements régionaux et
autres groupements.

1   Période de douze mois commençant le 21 mars de l'année
indiquée.
2   Source: "US Bureau of Mines," (Washington, DC).
3   Période de douze mois finissant le 30 juin de l'année
indiquée.
4   Source: Commission économique des Nations Unies pour
l'Amérique Latine (CEPAL), (Santiago).
5   Ventes.
6   Période de douze mois finissant le 7 juillet de l'année
indiquée.
7   Production des établissements occupant 50 personnes ou plus.
8   Production de l'Etat seulement.

51
Sulphuric acid
Acide sulfurique
Production: thousand metric tons
Production : milliers de tonnes métriques

Country or area Pays ou zone	1984	1985	1986	1987	1988	1989	1990	1991	1992	1993
Total	**137 135**	**132 394**	**131 381**	**134 410**	**142 264**	**140 161**	**134 755**	**126 693**	**121 341**	**110 945**
Albania Albanie	...	73	85	80	81	82	68	21	...	...
Algeria Algérie	249	...	...	30	61	49	39	46	52	55
Argentina Argentine	254	235	251	253	258	214	209	243	219	206
Australia[1] Australie[1]	1 706	1 783	1 788	1 680	1 818	1 904	1 464	986	816	868
Azerbaijan Azerbaïdjan	..	..	..	..	..	..	..	552	269	141
Bangladesh[1] Bangladesh[1]	4	4	6	8	5	6	5	6	4	7
Belarus Bélarus	..	..	..	..	..	..	..	998	616	399
Belgium[2] Belgique[2]	2 247	2 107	1 957	2 069	2 136	1 956	1 906	1 936	1 906	1 593
Bolivia Bolivie	1	0	0	...	1	1	1	1	0	...
Brazil Brésil	3 484	3 660	3 820	4 004	4 049	3 809	3 451	3 634	3 257	3 724
Bulgaria Bulgarie	908	810	807	689	840	846	522	356	404	409
Canada Canada	4 043	3 890	3 536	3 437	3 805	3 560	...	...	...	...
China Chine	8 172	6 764	7 631	9 833	11 113	11 533	11 969	13 329	14 087	13 365
Colombia Colombie	...	62	68	68	75	95	76	...	...	...
Côte d'Ivoire Côte d'Ivoire	1	...	...	...	...	...	...	...	...	...
Croatia Croatie	..	..	..	..	..	..	..	187	278	178
Cuba Cuba	336	373	395	370	391	377	...	...	...	...
Cyprus Chypre	0	0	0	17	2	1	0	0	...	...
former Czechoslovakia† anc. Tchécoslovaquie†	1 246	1 298	1 292	1 264	1 249	1 142	1 089	682	..	..
Czech Republic République tchèque	..	..	..	..	..	..	..	..	522	383
Denmark[3][4] Danemark[3][4]	27	36	23	33	91	122	90	37	38	...
Egypt Egypte	55	46	55	60	54	60	92	101	111	122
Estonia Estonie	..	..	..	..	..	..	..	460	46	...
Finland Finlande	1 165	1 207	1 100	870	1 179	1 129	1 010	1 015	1 087	1 179

51
Sulphuric acid
Production: thousand metric tons [cont.]
Acide sulfurique
Production : milliers de tonnes métriques [suite]

Country or area Pays ou zone	1984	1985	1986	1987	1988	1989	1990	1991	1992	1993
France France	4 531	4 321	3 954	3 558	4 081	4 187	3 771	3 627	2 871	2 357
Germany † Allemagne†	..	..	..	..	..	..	..	3 064	...	...
F. R. Germany R. f. Allemagne	4 309	4 199	4 105	4 070	4 053	4 028	3 221		..	..
former German D. R. anc. R. d. allemande	885	883	883	867	799	835	431		..	..
Greece Grèce	1 155	1 086	952	912	987	1 023	950	841	617	...
Hungary[5] Hongrie[5]	587	556	564	592	529	502	263	141	99	77
India Inde	2 683	* 2 626	2 877	3 159	3 416	3 293	3 272	3 904	4 183	3 742
Indonesia Indonésie	44	58	46	71	...	...	40	52	52	...
Iran, Islamic Rep. of * [6] Iran, Rép. islamique d' * [6]	200	200	200	200	200	...	...	...	...	...
Israel Israël	189	178	182	143	164	161	154	...	...	...
Italy Italie	2 636	2 724	2 605	2 724	2 499	2 212	2 038	1 853	1 733	1 430
Japan Japon	6 458	6 580	6 562	6 541	6 767	6 885	6 887	7 057	7 100	6 937
Kazakstan Kazakstan	..	..	..	..	..	..	..	2 815	2 349	...
Korea, Republic of Corée, République de	1 975	2 028	...	...	...	...	...	...	...	...
Kuwait Koweït	4	5	* 5	5	5	...	...	...	...	...
Lithuania Lituanie	..	..	..	..	..	..	..	368	141	129
Mexico Mexique	3 196	2 222	2 149	# 582	534	414	455	362	195	150
Morocco[7] Maroc[7]	758	660	...	...	...	...	...	...	...	...
Netherlands Pays-Bas	1 609	1 508	1 209	1 043	1 144	...	...	...	...	...
Norway Norvège	460	448	484	516	796	...	...	...	615	...
Pakistan[1] Pakistan[1]	81	78	80	78	79	79	90	93	98	100
Peru Pérou	205	213	209	175	174	193	183	...	...	...
Philippines Philippines	40	62	25	...	37	...	...	...	...	...
Poland Pologne	2 769	2 863	2 965	3 149	3 154	3 115	1 721	1 088	1 244	1 145
Portugal Portugal	553	497	448	331	293	289	260	51	...	...

51
Sulphuric acid
Production: thousand metric tons [*cont.*]
Acide sulfurique
Production : milliers de tonnes métriques [*suite*]

Country or area Pays ou zone	1984	1985	1986	1987	1988	1989	1990	1991	1992	1993
Romania Roumanie	1 915	1 835	1 971	1 693	1 825	1 687	1 111	745	572	527
Russian Federation Fédération de Russie	..	..	..	..	..	..	..	11 597	9 704	8 243
Saudi Arabia Arabie saoudite	71	* 73	* 84	...	...	...	...	...	...	...
Slovenia Slovénie	..	..	..	..	..	..	..	86	121	...
Spain Espagne	3 683	3 391	3 577	3 318	3 440	3 325	2 848	1 628	1 724	...
Sweden Suède	927	958	1 014	992	962	902	855	928	...	...
Syrian Arab Republic Rép. arabe syrienne	5	4	5	5	4	7	8	8	10	10
Thailand[7] Thaïlande[7]	63	66	78	81	60	64	72	82	...	...
TFYR Macedonia L'ex-R.y. Macédoine	...	...	...	...	...	...	..	102	95	...
Tunisia Tunisie	2 716	2 559	3 016	3 172	3 316	...	...	...	...	...
Turkey[8] Turquie[8]	353	514	583	102	313	313	295	205	248	273
Ukraine Ukraine	..	..	..	..	..	..	..	4 186	3 000	1 843
former USSR† ancienne URSS†	25 338	26 037	27 847	28 531	29 372	28 276	27 267	..	..	..
United Kingdom Royaume-Uni	2 654	2 525	2 330	2 335	2 257	1 977	...	...	...	...
United States[9] Etats-Unis[9]	37 914	35 964	32 650	35 612	38 628	39 282	40 222	39 432	40 387	35 693
Uzbekistan Ouzbékistan	..	..	..	..	..	..	..	2 393	1 476	1 361
Venezuela Venezuela	158	156	164	197	172	163	210	277	253	...
Viet Nam Viet Nam	...	...	14	14	17	10	8	9	7	...
Yugoslavia Yougoslavie	..	..	..	..	..	..	..	...	302	...
Yugoslavia, SFR† Yougoslavie, Rfs†	1 471	1 489	1 595	1 592	1 713	1 617	...	..	..	..
Zaire * Zaïre *	153	150	...	...	...	...	...	...	...	...
Zambia Zambie	314	240	199	304	276	...	...	...	...	...

Source:
Industrial statistics database of the Statistics Division of

Source:
Base de données pour les statistiques industrielles de la

51
Sulphuric acid
Production: thousand metric tons [*cont.*]

Acide sulfurique
Production : milliers de tonnes métriques [*suite*]

the United Nations Secretariat.

† For detailed descriptions of data pertaining to
former Czechoslovakia, Germany, SFR Yugoslavia and former
USSR, see Annex I - Country or area nomenclature, regional
and other groupings.

1 Twelve months ending 30 June of year stated.

2 Production by establishments employing 5 or more persons.
3 Sales.
4 Excluding quantities consumed by superphosphate industry.

5 Including regenerated sulphuric acid.
6 Source: US Bureau of Mines, (Washington, DC).
7 Strength of acid not known.
8 Output of steel industry only.
9 Including data for government-owned, but privately-operated
plants.

Division de statistique du Secrétariat de l'ONU.

† Pour les descriptions en détails des données
relatives à l'ancienne Tchécoslovaquie, l'Allemagne, la Rfs
Yougoslavie et l'ancienne URSS, voir l'Annexe I -
Nomenclature des pays ou zones, groupements régionaux et
autres groupements.

1 Période de douze mois finissant le 30 juin de l'année
indiquée.
2 Production des établissements occupant 5 personnes ou plus.
3 Ventes.
4 Non compris les quantités utilisées par l'industrie des
superphosphates.
5 Y compris l'acide sulfurique régénéré.
6 Source: "US Bureau of Mines," (Washington, DC).
7 Titre de l'acide inconnu.
8 Production de l'industrie sidérurgique seulement.
9 Y compris les données relatives à des usines appartenant à
l'Etat mais exploitées par des entreprises privées.

52
Soap, washing powders and detergents
Savons, poudres pour lessives et détersifs
Production: thousand metric tons
Production : milliers de tonnes métriques

Country or area Pays ou zone	1984	1985	1986	1987	1988	1989	1990	1991	1992	1993
Total	**18 864**	**20 159**	**20 842**	**21 672**	**22 159**	**23 431**	**23 953**	**20 245**	**18 543**	**20 256**
Albania [1] Albanie [1]	...	3	4	7	5	7	5	1	...	...
Algeria Algérie	111	111	151	193	225	231	263	235	185	92 [2]
Argentina [3] Argentine [3]	144	141	132	124	132	84	153	162	178	189
Armenia Arménie	..	..	..	..	..	..	..	12	1	0
Australia [4] Australie [4]	346	346	304	322	342	...	...	...	...	...
Austria Autriche	114	115	129	145	142	146	153	162	188	155
Azerbaijan Azerbaïdjan	..	..	..	..	..	..	..	101	69	50
Belarus Bélarus	..	..	..	..	..	..	..	71 [5]	58	45
Belgium Belgique	337	337	345	393	401	406	417	440	423	420
Bolivia Bolivie	3 [2]	7 [2]	1 [2]	...	5	5	6	4	4	...
Bulgaria Bulgarie	28	27	27	30	26 [2]	28 [2]	24 [2]	17 [2]	15 [2]	4 [2]
Burkina Faso [2] Burkina Faso [2]	12	13	10	13	11	10	14	26	14	14
Burundi [2] Burundi [2]	3	3	3	3	2	3	3	3	3	5
Cameroon Cameroun	31 [2]	26 [2]	31	39 [2]	23 [2]	...	...	...	...	...
Central African Rep. [2] Rép. centrafricaine [2]	1	...	...	0	...	...	...	...	...	...
Chad [2] Tchad [2]	...	1	1	4	3	4	4	3	3	3
Chile Chili	49	45	52	59	65	69	69	73	73	77
China Chine	1 752	2 000	2 271	2 310	2 514	2 576	2 581	2 367	1 006	2 728
Colombia [2] Colombie [2]	...	145	141	137	165	148	179	...	...	...
Congo [2] Congo [2]	6	2	2	2	1	1	3	5	3	1
Côte d'Ivoire Côte d'Ivoire	65	...	...	...	...	...	...	...	...	...
Croatia Croatie	..	..	..	..	..	..	..	67	52	...
Cuba [6] Cuba [6]	97	87	95	77	67	67	...	...	...	...
Cyprus Chypre	9	9	9	* 9	* 9	11	* 13	* 15	14	* 14

52
Soap, washing powders and detergents
Production: thousand metric tons [cont.]

Savons, poudres pour lessives et détersifs
Production : milliers de tonnes métriques [suite]

Country or area Pays ou zone	1984	1985	1986	1987	1988	1989	1990	1991	1992	1993
former Czechoslovakia† anc. Tchécoslovaquie†	112	118	122	128	131	134	138	105	..	
Czech Republic² République tchèque²	..	..	..	..	..	..	..	..	24	29
Denmark⁷ Danemark⁷	212	216	209²	...	...	...	...	...	...	...
Dominica² Dominique²	4	6	6	7	...	...	...	...	...	...
Dominican Republic Rép. dominicaine	39	39	47	32²	...	...	...	...	...	...
Ecuador Equateur	...	...	...	47	47	...	95	...	57	...
Egypt Egypte	462	485	347	379	339	399	417	370	358	382
Estonia¹ Estonie¹	..		..	..		..		28	4	3
Ethiopia²⁸ Ethiopie²⁸	14	13	15	21	16	12	9	0	5	17
Fiji² Fidji²	7	6	7	7	8	6	7	7	...	...
Finland Finlande	# 65	66	82	82	90	98	93	81	72	77
France France	752	760	818	784	749	808	811	781	822	778
Gabon Gabon	57	138	137	129	130	132	136	153	170	...
Germany † Allemagne†	..	..	..	..	..	..	..	122²	113²	140
F. R. Germany R. f. Allemagne	1 724⁹¹⁰	1 733⁹¹⁰	106²	106²	101²	113²	126²	..	..	..
former German D. R. anc. R. d. allemande	486	498	499	518	476	527	291			
Ghana² Ghana²	6	12	19	31	36	...	...	...	...	...
Greece Grèce	125	137	139	150	156	163	159	150	154	...
Guyana Guyana	1	0	0	1	1	1²	0²	1	1	1
Haiti² Haïti²	14	13	13	...	...	...	...	...	...	...
Hong Kong¹ Hong-kong¹	29	26	43	36	35	62	84	56	46	...
Hungary Hongrie	116	114	125	127	126	130	144	103	92	92
Iceland¹ Islande¹	3	3	3	3	2	3	3	1	2	0
India¹¹ Inde¹¹	941	# 1 545	1 652	1 753	1 639	1 740	1 794	1 794	1 752	1 771
Indonesia Indonésie	131	193	260	248	250	0¹	502	455	568	...

52
Soap, washing powders and detergents
Production: thousand metric tons [cont.]
Savons, poudres pour lessives et détersifs
Production : milliers de tonnes métriques [suite]

Country or area Pays ou zone	1984	1985	1986	1987	1988	1989	1990	1991	1992	1993
Iran, Islamic Rep. of[12] Iran, Rép. islamique d'[12]	254	262	155	169[1]	149[1]	169[1]	212[1]	196[1]	171[1]	...
Israel[2] Israël[2]	6	6	6	6	5	4	4	...	...	...
Jamaica Jamaïque	12	12	13	12	18	16	16	13	11	10
Japan[13] Japon[13]	1 067	1 078	1 101	1 157	1 174	1 245	1 311	1 370	1 394	1 310
Jordan Jordanie	38	23	56	53	18[2]	26[2]	...	...	...	...
Kazakstan[2] Kazakstan[2]	..	..	..	..	..	..	..	38	24	...
Kenya Kenya	22[2]	23[2]	55	55	71	79	73	63	60	62
Korea, Republic of Corée, République de	263	# 359	401	427	473	473	523	508	503	461
Kuwait[1] Koweït[1]	2	1	1	2	2	3	...	...	1	7
Latvia[5] Lettonie[5]	..	..	..	..	..	..	..	18	8	3
Liberia[2] Libéria[2]	5	4	3	...	...	...	...	...	...	...
Lithuania Lituanie	..	..	..	..	..	..	..	39	20	8
Madagascar[2] Madagascar[2]	13	12	13	15	13	15	14	16	16	19
Malaysia[14] Malaisie[14]	34	42	48	51	63	67	80	88	102	105
Mali[2] Mali[2]	...	...	...	...	...	9	10	11	10	9
Mexico Mexique	869	827	901	999	955	1 099	1 166	1 231	1 257	1 176
Mongolia[2] Mongolie[2]	5	4	4	4	3	3	...	...	...	...
Morocco[2] Maroc[2]	28	20	...	...	...	...	...	...	...	...
Mozambique Mozambique	13	9	9	14	12[2]	12[2]	9[2]	9[2]	7[2]	11[2]
Myanmar[2][15] Myanmar[2][15]	28	50	38	18	18	12	15	23	18	...
Nepal[2][16] Népal[2][16]	8	9	11	12	17	...	...	...	...	...
Netherlands[1] Pays-Bas[1]	266	274	...	...	...	...	...	...	...	...
New Zealand[17] Nouvelle-Zélande[17]	33	32	36	...	...	...	...	...	...	...
Nicaragua[2] Nicaragua[2]	40	...	...	...	...	...	...	...	...	...
Nigeria Nigéria	143	158	78	214	207	249	241	243	262	303

52
Soap, washing powders and detergents
Production: thousand metric tons [cont.]
Savons, poudres pour lessives et détersifs
Production : milliers de tonnes métriques [suite]

Country or area Pays ou zone	1984	1985	1986	1987	1988	1989	1990	1991	1992	1993
Norway Norvège	57	51[1]	8[2]	62	56	55	7[2]	...	6[2]	...
Pakistan[14] Pakistan[14]	39	49	48	57	59	103	59	75	86	89
Panama Panama	14	15	...	17	14	17	13	...	...	...
Paraguay[2] Paraguay[2]	12	12	12	12	10	8	8	7	6	...
Peru Pérou	53	49	85	91	88	74	80	...	...	...
Philippines Philippines	186	198	220	221	...	...	...	...	...	...
Poland[18] Pologne[18]	241	273	309	315	339	331	215	199	174	195
Portugal Portugal	190	173	173	180	191	209	213	178	# 148	...
Republic of Moldova République de Moldova	..	..	..	..	..	..	..	23	12	7
Romania[19] Roumanie[19]	53	50	54	51	46	46	49	37	20	25
Russian Federation Fédération de Russie	..	..	..	..	..	..	..	1 106	882	699
Rwanda[2] Rwanda[2]	12	16	12	* 6	* 6	...	...	...	...	...
Sao Tome and Principe[2] Sao Tomé-et-Principe[2]	0	0	0	1	...	...	...	...	...	...
Senegal[2] Sénégal[2]	35	30	...	33	33	26	37	37	42	36
Sierra Leone[2] Sierra Leone[2]	4	1	2	3	...	...	...	1	2	3
Singapore Singapour	25	24	24	26	28	28	...	...	...	...
Slovakia[1] Slovaquie[1]	..	..	..	..	..	..	..	..	...	28
Slovenia Slovénie	..	..	..	..	..	..	..	64	47	...
South Africa[20] Afrique du Sud[20]	200	216	225	236	250	241	263	280	285	276
Spain[20] Espagne[20]	1 145	1 137	1 078	1 170	1 262	1 282	1 376	1 414	1 489	...
Sri Lanka[2 15] Sri Lanka[2 15]	3	5	4	4	4	...	...	...	...	...
Sweden Suède	174	178	180	186	184[1]	185[1]	158[1]	127[1]	121[1]	...
Switzerland[2 7 21] Suisse[2 7 21]	145	145	149	159	161	163	168	165	156	152
Syrian Arab Republic Rép. arabe syrienne	60	71	71	66	34	31	40	38	44	57
Tajikistan[2] Tadjikistan[2]	..	..	..	..	..	..	..	13	11	3

52
Soap, washing powders and detergents
Production: thousand metric tons [cont.]
Savons, poudres pour lessives et détersifs
Production : milliers de tonnes métriques [suite]

Country or area Pays ou zone	1984	1985	1986	1987	1988	1989	1990	1991	1992	1993
Thailand Thaïlande	93[1]	109[1]	107[1]	111[1]	178	197	190	196	...	...
TFYR Macedonia[2] L'ex-R.y. Macédoine[2]	..	..	..	..	..	..	..	19	16	...
Trinidad and Tobago Trinité-et-Tobago	2	3	3	4	4	3	2	2	2	...
Turkey Turquie	241	230	269	282	297	449	442	379	380	434
Turkmenistan Turkménistan							..	25	21	9
Ukraine[2][5] Ukraine[2][5]	..	..	..	..	..	..	..	272	265	188
former USSR†[5] ancienne URSS†[5]	2 632	2 615	2 659	2 728	2 866	3 128	3 209	..	..	..
United Kingdom[1][22] Royaume-Uni[1][22]	1 030	1 128	1 192	1 166	1 284	1 415	...	...	...	...
United Rep.Tanzania Rép. Unie de Tanzanie	...	14	15	19	21	20	23	24	20	22
Uzbekistan Ouzbékistan	..	..	..	..	..	..	..	134	102	89
Viet Nam[2] Viet Nam[2]	38	51	72	47	52	40	55	68	72	...
Yemen[2] Yémen[2]	..	..	..	..	..	..	..	..	39	...
former Yemen Arab Rep.[2] anc. Yémen rép. arabe[2]	6	8	19	...	...	...	...	..	..	...
Yugoslavia Yougoslavie	..	..	..	..	..	..	..	...	92	...
Yugoslavia, SFR† Yougoslavie, Rfs†	286	288	312	340	369	412	...	..	..	..
Zambia Zambie	10	10	11	...	...	...	...	...	...	...

Source:
Industrial statistics database of the Statistics Division of
the United Nations Secretariat.

† For detailed descriptions of data pertaining to
former Czechoslovakia, Germany, SFR Yugoslavia and former
USSR, see Annex I - Country or area nomenclature, regional
and other groupings.

Source:
Base de données pour les statistiques industrielles de la
Division de statistique du Secrétariat de l'ONU.

† Pour les descriptions en détails des données
relatives à l'ancienne Tchécoslovaquie, l'Allemagne, la Rfs
Yougoslavie et l'ancienne URSS, voir l'Annexe I -
Nomenclature des pays ou zones, groupements régionaux et

52
Soap, washing powders and detergents
Production: thousand metric tons [*cont.*]

Savons, poudres pour lessives et détersifs
Production : milliers de tonnes métriques [*suite*]

autres groupements.

1 Washing powders and detergents only.	1 Poudres pour lessives et détersifs seulement.
2 Soap only.	2 Savons seulement.
3 Excluding liquid toilet soap.	3 Non compris le savon liquide de toilette.
4 Twelve months ending 30 June of year stated.	4 Période de douze mois finissant le 30 juin de l'année indiquée.
5 Soap data are in terms of 40 per cent fat content.	5 Les données des savons sont sur la base de 40 p. 100 de matières grasses.
6 Excluding washing powder.	6 Non compris poudres pour lessives.
7 Sales.	7 Ventes.
8 Twelve months ending 7 July of the year stated.	8 Période de douze mois finissant le 7 juillet de l'année indiquée.
9 Excluding surface-active organic agents.	9 Non compris les produits organiques tensio-actifs.
10 Beginning 1986, washing powders and detergents data are confidential.	10 A partir de 1986, les données des poudres pour lessives et détersifs sont confidentielles.
11 Production by large and medium scale establishments only.	11 Production des grandes et moyennes entreprises seulement.
12 Soap production by establishments employing 10 or more persons; washing powders/detergents prod. by estab. employing 50 or more.	12 Savons prod. des établissements occupant 10 personnes ou plus; poudres pour lessives et détersifs prod. des étab. occu.50 ou plus.
13 For washing powder and detergent, surface-active agents only.	13 Pour les poudres pour lessives et détersifs, produits tensio-actifs seulement.
14 Soap: toilet soap only.	14 Les Savons: Savons de toilette seulement.
15 Government production only.	15 Production de l'Etat seulement.
16 Twelve months beginning 16 July of year stated.	16 Période de douze mois commençant le 16 juillet de l'année indiquée.
17 Soap: data refer to soap flakes and powder only.	17 Les savons: données se rapportant aux savons en paillettes et en poudre seulement.
18 Excluding detergents.	18 Non compris les détersifs.
19 On the basis of 100 per cent active substances.	19 Sur la base de 100 p. 100 de substances actives.
20 Synthetic detergents in powder form.	20 Détersifs synthétiques en poudre.
21 Including other cleaning products.	21 Y compris les autres produits de nettoyage.
22 Estimates of manufacturers' sales of finished detergents for washing purposes, in terms of actual weight sold.	22 Estimations des ventes de détersifs pour lessives par les fabricants, sur la base du poids de produits effectivement ecoulé.

53
Pig iron and crude steel
Fonte et acier brut
Production: thousand metric tons
Production : milliers de tonnes métriques

Country or area Pays ou zone	1984	1985	1986	1987	1988	1989	1990	1991	1992	1993
A. Pig-iron • Fonte										
Total	**484 853**	**494 268**	**490 491**	**497 715**	**525 101**	**522 712**	**507 815**	**478 171**	**476 849**	**475 671**
Algeria Algérie	1 191	1 477	1 262	1 493	1 515	1 315	1 054	893	944	925[1]
Argentina Argentine	844	1 310	1 623	1 752	1 596	2 100	1 908	1 366	971	980
Australia[2] Australie[2]	5 258	5 341	5 925	5 783	5 455	5 875	6 188	5 600	6 394	6 445
Austria[1] Autriche[1]	3 745	3 704	3 349	3 451	3 665	3 823	3 452	3 439	3 067[3]	3 000[3]
Belgium[1] Belgique[1]	8 968	8 720	8 048	8 242	9 147	8 863	9 416	9 353	8 524	8 179
Brazil Brésil	17 230	18 961	20 163	20 944	23 454	24 363	21 141	22 695	23 152	23 982
Bulgaria Bulgarie	1 583	1 712	1 605	1 657	1 442	1 487	1 143	961	849	1 014
Canada Canada	9 643	9 660	9 246	9 720	9 490	10 200	7 344	8 268	8 621	6 588
Chile[1] Chili[1]	594	580	591	617	778	679	722	700	750[3]	700[3]
China Chine	40 010	43 840	50 638	55 032	57 040	58 200	62 380	67 000	75 890	87 389
Colombia Colombie	252	234	317	326	309	297	347	300	308[3]	238[3]
Croatia[1] Croatie[1]	..	..	..	..	..	..	..	69	...	...
former Czechoslovakia† anc. Tchécoslovaquie†	9 562	9 562	9 573	9 788	9 706	9 911	9 667	8 480	..	..
Czech Republic[1] République tchèque[1]	..	..	..	..	..	..	..	..	4 889	4 511
Egypt Egypte	159	87	121	147	132	112	108	113	60	92
Finland[1] Finlande[1]	2 034	# 1 890	1 871	2 063	2 173	2 284	2 283	2 332	2 452	2 595
France France	14 710	15 072	13 776	13 157	14 463	14 724	14 100	13 416	12 264	12 396
Germany † Allemagne†	..	..	..	..	..	..	..	...	27 577[1]	26 322[1]
F. R. Germany R. f. Allemagne	29 737	31 143	28 593	28 116	31 890	32 112	29 585	..	..	..
former German D. R. anc. R. d. allemande	2 343	2 565	2 726	2 743	2 774	2 722	2 128	..	..	..
Greece[13] Grèce[13]	138	140	160	160	160	160	160	160	...	...
Hungary Hongrie	2 096	2 095	2 054	2 108	2 093	1 954	1 697	1 314	1 179	1 407[1]
India Inde	9 382	9 701	10 460	10 808	11 602	1 336	1 496	1 587	1 845	2 250

53

Pig iron and crude steel
Production: thousand metric tons [*cont.*]
Fonte et acier brut
Production : milliers de tonnes métriques [*suite*]

Country or area Pays ou zone	1984	1985	1986	1987	1988	1989	1990	1991	1992	1993
Iran, Islamic Rep. of[1] Iran, Rép. islamique d'[1]	1 208	1 122	850	976	1 012	* 1 000	* 1 000	1 952[3]	2 053[3]	1 961[3]
Italy Italie	11 631	12 062	11 916	11 334	11 348	11 762	11 852	10 561	10 432	11 188
Japan Japon	80 403	80 569	74 651	73 418	79 295	80 196	80 229	79 985	73 144	73 738
Kazakstan[4] Kazakstan[4]	..	..	..	..	..	..	..	4 953	4 666	3 552
Korea, Dem. P. R.[3] Corée, R. p. dém. de[3]	5 700	5 800	5 800	5 800	6 500	6 500	6 500	6 500	6 600	6 600
Korea, Republic of Corée, République de	8 763	8 822	9 004	10 858	12 567	14 937	15 477	18 883	19 581	22 193
Luxembourg[1] Luxembourg[1]	2 768	2 754	2 650	2 305	2 520	2 684	2 645	2 463	2 255	2 412
Mexico Mexique	5 339	5 089	5 048	# 1 412	1 489	2 076	2 378	2 313[1]	2 220[1]	2 515[1]
Morocco[13] Maroc[13]	15	15	15	15	15	15	15	15	15	15
Netherlands[1] Pays-Bas[1]	4 926	4 819	4 628	4 575	4 994	5 163	4 960	4 697	4 842	5 405
Norway[1] Norvège[1]	572	610	564	364	367	240	54[3]	61[3]	80[3]	80[3]
Peru[3] Pérou[3]	66	163	216	185	202	199	93	207	147	147
Poland Pologne	9 533	9 335	10 096	10 024	9 837	9 075	8 352	6 297	6 315	6 105
Portugal Portugal	382	424	429	431	445	377	339[13]	251[13]	402[13]	385[13]
Romania Roumanie	9 557	9 212	9 330	8 673	8 941	9 052	6 355	4 525	3 110	3 190
Russian Federation Fédération de Russie	..	..	..	..	..	..	..	48 628	45 990	40 744
Slovakia[1] Slovaquie[1]	..	..	..	..	..	..	..	..	...	3 205
South Africa Afrique du Sud	5 455	7 179	7 406	7 398	6 171[3]	6 543[3]	6 257[3]	6 968[3]	6 498[3]	6 500[3]
Spain Espagne	5 319	5 455	4 862	4 854	4 650	5 479	5 748	5 600[1]	5 076[13]	5 000[13]
Sweden Suède	2 203	2 415	2 428	2 365	2 527	2 648	2 696	2 851	2 883	2 600[3]
Switzerland Suisse	54[5]	66[5]	147	140	134	141	129	105	102	82
TFYR Macedonia[1] L'ex-R.y. Macédoine[1]	..	..	..	..	..	..	..	..	13	...
Tunisia[4] Tunisie[4]	147	141	149	168	133	155	148	162	147	154
Turkey Turquie	226	280	351	342	366	300	354	332	286	291
Ukraine Ukraine	..	..	..	..	..	..	..	36 435	35 163	27 022

53
Pig iron and crude steel
Production: thousand metric tons [cont.]
Fonte et acier brut
Production : milliers de tonnes métriques [suite]

Country or area Pays ou zone	1984	1985	1986	1987	1988	1989	1990	1991	1992	1993
former USSR†[6] ancienne URSS†[6]	110 893	109 977	113 840	113 877	114 558	113 928	110 166	..	..	..
United Kingdom Royaume-Uni	9 420	10 167	9 632	11 916	12 943	12 551	12 320	12 100[1]	11 351[13]	11 000[13]
United States Etats-Unis	47 090	45 763	40 176	43 851	50 571	50 687	49 668	44 123	47 377	48 155
Venezuela Venezuela	326	441	493	473	503	455	314	...	...	...
Yugoslavia[1] Yougoslavie[1]	..	..	..	..	..	..	..	...	512	
Yugoslavia, SFR† Yougoslavie, Rfs†	2 855	3 120	3 063	2 867	2 916	2 899	2 313[5]	..	..	
Zimbabwe[1] Zimbabwe[1]	400	674	644	575	600	520	521	535[3]	507[3]	500[3]

B. Crude steel • Acier brut

	1984	1985	1986	1987	1988	1989	1990	1991	1992	1993
Total	**717 758**	**726 091**	**721 134**	**742 565**	**783 859**	**788 288**	**774 232**	**728 188**	**714 106**	**713 401**
Albania Albanie	...	233	209	137	210	205	143	28	...	...
Algeria Algérie	1 130	1 215	1 123	1 380	1 303	945	769	797[7]	768[7]	798[7]
Angola[38] Angola[38]	10	10	10	10	10	10	10	10	10	9
Argentina Argentine	2 508	2 775	3 116	3 463	3 527	* 3 874	* 3 624[8]	2 972[8]	2 664[8]	2 832[8]
Australia[2] Australie[2]	4 639	6 301	6 826	6 188	6 093	6 651	7 576	7 141	# 5 205	6 218
Austria Autriche	4 870	4 661	4 292	4 301[5]	4 376[5]	4 901[5]	4 449[5]	4 186[5]	3 953[5]	4 149[5]
Azerbaijan Azerbaïdjan	..	..	..	..	..	..	..	1 127	809	461
Bangladesh[28] Bangladesh[28]	73	101	96	82	70	86	90	...	...	...
Belarus Bélarus	..	..	..	..	..	..	..	1 123	1 105[5]	946[5]
Belgium Belgique	11 413	10 781	9 803	9 844	11 306	11 053	11 546	11 419	10 386	10 237
Brazil Brésil	18 476	20 563	21 343	22 228	24 747	25 084	20 631	22 668	23 951	25 201
Bulgaria Bulgarie	2 878	2 944	2 965	3 045	2 875	2 899	2 184	1 615	1 551	1 941
Canada Canada	14 699	13 459	14 081	14 737	14 778	* 15 005	* 12 281	13 079	14 027	* 10 902
Chile[89] Chili[89]	692	689	706	726	899	800	772	805	1 013	1 063
China Chine	45 618	49 454	54 795	58 928	62 147	64 209	68 858	73 881	84 252	89 556
Colombia Colombie	507	525	632	691	777	711	733	700	657	715

53
Pig iron and crude steel
Production: thousand metric tons [*cont.*]
Fonte et acier brut
Production : milliers de tonnes métriques [*suite*]

Country or area Pays ou zone	1984	1985	1986	1987	1988	1989	1990	1991	1992	1993
Croatia[8] Croatie[8]	..	..	..	..	..	..	..	214	102	74[5]
Cuba[8] Cuba[8]	325	401	412	402	321	314	270	270	200[3]	100[3]
former Czechoslovakia† anc. Tchécoslovaquie†	14 831	15 036	15 112	15 416	15 379	15 465	14 775	12 071	..	..
Czech Republic République tchèque	..	..	..	..	..	..	..	..	7 349	6 762
Denmark[5] Danemark[5]	548	528	632	606	650	624	610	633	591	603
Ecuador[8] Equateur[8]	17	18	17	25	24	23	20	20	...	...
Egypt[3] Egypte[3]	1 153	954	1 003	1 436	2 028	2 117	2 328	2 541[8]	2 500[8]	2 500[8]
Finland Finlande	2 632	2 518	2 586	2 669	2 798	2 921	2 860	2 890	3 077	3 257
France France	19 000	18 808	17 857	17 689	19 108	19 535	19 304	18 708	18 190	17 313
Germany † Allemagne†	..	..	..	..	..	..	..	41 997	39 962	37 705
F. R. Germany R. f. Allemagne	39 389	40 488	37 134	36 248	41 023	41 078	38 433	..	..	..
former German D.R.[8] anc. R. d. allemande[8]	7 573	7 853	7 967	8 243	8 131	7 829	5 339	..	..	..
Greece Grèce	895	985	1 009	908	959	960	999	980	924	980
Hungary Hongrie	3 643	3 545	3 601	3 495	3 480	3 263	2 924	2 043	1 687[5]	1 752[58]
India Inde	10 348	11 187	11 427	12 262	13 019	15 522	16 479	17 577	18 723	18 616
Indonesia[7] Indonésie[7]	1 000	1 200	1 500	* 1 453	* 2 050	* 2 000	* 2 100	...	...	...
Iran, Islamic Rep. of[7] Iran, Rép. islamique d'[7]	784	764	741	783	883	* 1 000	* 1 000	...	...	...
Iraq[8] Iraq[8]	...	...	...	...	...	...	...	...	1 940	...
Ireland Irlande	166	203	208	220	200	324	325	293	257	326
Israel[3] Israël[3]	92	100	110	116	120	118	144	160	160	160
Italy Italie	24 110	23 898	22 882	22 858	23 943	25 507	25 647	25 270	24 924	25 967
Japan Japon	105 586	105 278	98 275	98 513	105 680	107 907	110 339	109 648	98 132	99 632
Kazakstan Kazakstan	..	..	..	..	..	..	..	6 377	6 063	...
Korea, Dem. P. R.[3] Corée, R. p. dém. de[3]	6 500	6 500	6 500	6 700	6 800	7 300	8 000	8 000	8 100	8 100
Korea, Republic of Corée, République de	13 118	13 614	14 634	16 894	19 233	21 992	23 247	26 126	28 177	33 141

53
Pig iron and crude steel
Production: thousand metric tons [cont.]
Fonte et acier brut
Production : milliers de tonnes métriques [suite]

Country or area Pays ou zone	1984	1985	1986	1987	1988	1989	1990	1991	1992	1993
Latvia Lettonie	..	..	..	..	..	..	..	374	246	300
Lithuania Lituanie	..	..	..	..	..	..	..	4	3	2
Luxembourg[8] Luxembourg[8]	3 987	3 945	3 705	3 302	3 661	3 721	3 560	3 379	3 068	3 293
Mexico Mexique	7 293	7 174	6 960	7 211	7 312[8]	7 329[8]	8 221[8]	7 462[8]	7 848[8]	8 188[8]
Morocco[3] Maroc[3]	6	6	6	6	7	7	7	7	7	7
Netherlands Pays-Bas	5 739	5 517	5 283	5 083	5 518	5 681	5 412	5 171	5 439	6 000
New Zealand[8] Nouvelle-Zélande[8]	274	228	291	409[3]	460[3]	608[3]	765[3]	700[3]	759[3]	850[3]
Nigeria[8] Nigéria[8]	187	254	200	200	192	213	220	200	140[3]	140[3]
Norway Norvège	927	579	837	853	903	677	376[5]	438[5]	446[5]	505[5]
Peru Pérou	337	414	486	503	496	364	284	404	343	417
Philippines[3] Philippines[3]	250	260	260	250	300	300	300	250	250	250
Poland Pologne	15 180	15 361	16 283	16 263	* 15 943	12 466[8]	11 501[8]	9 512[5]	9 336[5]	9 005[5]
Portugal Portugal	690	665	717	1 099	1 239	* 1 061	717[5]	547[5]	749[5]	775[5]
Republic of Moldova République de Moldova	..	..	..	..	..	..	..	623	653	497
Romania Roumanie	15 229	14 587	15 026	14 631	15 057	15 165	10 624	7 509	5 614	5 598
Russian Federation Fédération de Russie	..	..	..	..	..	..	..	77 100	67 028	58 346
Saudi Arabia[3 8] Arabie saoudite[3 8]	842	1 106	1 100	1 365	1 614	1 810	1 833	1 850	1 900	2 000
Slovakia Slovaquie	..	..	..	..	..	..	..	..	4 498	3 922
Slovenia Slovénie	..	..	..	..	..	..	..	289	401	...
South Africa Afrique du Sud	7 827	8 582	8 127	9 123	8 837	9 337	8 691	9 358	9 061[3]	8 610[3]
Spain Espagne	13 379	14 679	* 12 137	* 11 629	* 11 679	* 12 564	* 12 818	12 846[5]	12 270[5]	12 967[5]
Sweden Suède	4 674	4 851	4 719	4 683	4 779	4 692	4 455[5]	4 252[5]	4 358[5]	4 591[5]
Switzerland[5 8] Suisse[5 8]	978	987	1 075	866	989	1 064	1 105	955	1 050	...
Thailand[3] Thaïlande[3]	381	447	463	534	552	689	685	711	779	800
TFYR Macedonia L'ex-R.y. Macédoine	..	..	..	..	..	..	..	209	162	...

53
Pig iron and crude steel
Production: thousand metric tons [*cont.*]
Fonte et acier brut
Production : milliers de tonnes métriques [*suite*]

Country or area Pays ou zone	1984	1985	1986	1987	1988	1989	1990	1991	1992	1993
Tunisia[7] Tunisie[7]	166	160	181	188	159	188	176	193	182	182
Turkey Turquie	4 113	4 737	5 989	10 188	11 481	10 809	12 225	12 323	13 241	12 575
Uganda Ouganda	6	8	8	0	0	0	0	...	...	...
Ukraine Ukraine	..	..	..	..	..	..	..	46 767	43 285	33 709
former USSR† ancienne URSS†	163 097	163 808	170 098	171 417	172 217	168 421	162 326	..	..	..
United Kingdom Royaume-Uni	15 122	15 722	14 725	17 414	18 950	18 740	17 841	16 511[5]	16 212[5]	16 625[5]
United States[10] Etats-Unis[10]	83 940	80 067	74 032	80 876	91 765	* 88 852	89 726	79 738	84 322	88 793
Uruguay[9] Uruguay[9]	41	39	31	30	29	37	34	44[3]	53[3]	53[3]
Venezuela Venezuela	2 770	3 060	3 402	3 721	3 650	3 404	3 140	2 933	2 446	2 568
Viet Nam[8] Viet Nam[8]	...	...	64	70	74	85	101	149	196	190[3]
Yugoslavia Yougoslavie	..	..	..	..	..	..	...		96	...
Yugoslavia, SFR† Yougoslavie, Rfs†	4 236	4 476	4 524	4 368	4 488	4 542	3 608	..	..	..
Zimbabwe[3,8] Zimbabwe[3,8]	391	463	490	515	500	650	580	581	547	400

Source:
Industrial statistics database of the Statistics Division of the United Nations Secretariat.

† For detailed descriptions of data pertaining to former Czechoslovakia, Germany, SFR Yugoslavia and former USSR, see Annex I - Country or area nomenclature, regional and other groupings.

1 Pig-iron for steel making only.
2 Twelve months ending 30 June of year stated.

3 Source: US Bureau of Mines, (Washington, DC).
4 Foundry pig iron only.
5 Source: Annual Bulletin of Steel Statistics for Europe, United Nations Economic Commission of Europe (Geneva).

6 Including other ferro-alloys.
7 Crude steel for casting only.
8 Ingots only.
9 Source: "Instituto Latino Americano del Fierro y el Acero", (Santiago).
10 Excluding steel for castings made in foundries operated by companies not producing ingots.

Source:
Base de données pour les statistiques industrielles de la Division de statistique du Secrétariat de l'ONU.

† Pour les descriptions en détails des données relatives à l'ancienne Tchécoslovaquie, l'Allemagne, la Rfs Yougoslavie et l'ancienne URSS, voir l'Annexe I - Nomenclature des pays ou zones, groupements régionaux et autres groupements.

1 La fonte d'affinage seulement.
2 Période de douze mois finissant le 30 juin de l'année indiquée.
3 Source: "US Bureau of Mines," (Washington, DC).
4 La fonte de moulage seulement.
5 Source: Bulletin annuel de statistiques de l'acier pour l'Europe, Commission économique des Nations Unies pour l'Europe (Genève).
6 Y compris les autres ferro-alliages.
7 L'acier brut pour moulages seulement.
8 Les lingots seulement.
9 Source: "Instituto Latino Americano del Fierro y el Acero", (Santiago).
10 Non compris l'acier pour les moulages fabriqués dans des fonderies exploitées par des entreprises ne produisant pas de lingots.

54
Aluminium
Aluminium

Production: thousand metric tons
Production : milliers de tonnes métriques

Country or area Pays ou zone	1984	1985	1986	1987	1988	1989	1990	1991	1992	1993
Total	18 233.0	17 937.0	18 949.0	19 261.0	20 338.0	20 736.0	21 125.0	18 082.0	18 499.0	18 753.0
Argentina **Argentine**	**145.3**	**143.5**	**151.2**	**160.5**	**161.2**	**167.3**	**169.0**	**175.5**	**172.1**	**189.7**
Primary 1re fusion	137.8	139.9	147.6	152.5	154.1	162.0	163.0	166.3	153.0	170.6
Secondary[1] 2ème fusion[1]	7.5	3.6	3.6	8.0	7.1	5.3	6.0	9.2	19.1	19.1
Australia[2] **Australie[2]**	**681.8**	**926.4**	*** 925.0**	*** 960.0**	*** 1 120.5**	*** 1 289.2**	*** 1 268.0**	**1 264.6**	**1 234.0**	**1 268.0**
Primary[2] 1re fusion[2]	617.9	822.3	870.0	921.0	1 074.0	1 240.8	1 235.1	1 235.0	1 194.0	1 228.0
Secondary[2] 2ème fusion[2]	63.9	104.1	55.0	39.0[1]	46.5[1]	48.4[1]	32.9	29.6	40.0[1]	40.0[1]
Austria **Autriche**	**380.7**	**285.0**	**283.7**	**322.3**	**391.1**	**334.1**	**246.3**	**205.9**	**...**	**...**
Primary 1re fusion	151.9	152.7	148.8	156.1	165.9	169.0	159.1	...	...	...
Secondary[3] 2ème fusion[3]	228.8	132.4	134.9	166.1	225.2	165.2	87.2	...	...	...
Azerbaijan **Azerbaïdjan**	**..**	**..**	**..**	**..**	**..**	**..**	**..**	**31.7**	**21.3**	**14.3**
Primary 1re fusion	..	..	..	..	..	..	..	25.9	19.6	13.6
Secondary 2ème fusion	..	..	..	..	..	..	..	5.8	1.7	0.7
Bahrain[14] **Bahreïn[14]**	**177.3**	**174.8**	**178.2**	**180.3**	**182.8**	**186.4**	**212.0**	**213.7**	**292.5**	**448.0**
Belgium[15] **Belgique[15]**	**2.0**	**2.0**	**2.0**	**3.2**	**3.2**	**3.2**	**3.0**	**3.0**	**0.0**	**0.0**
Brazil **Brésil**	**503.9**	**594.2**	**805.3**	**893.8[1]**	**938.4[1]**	**954.5[1]**	**995.6[1]**	**1 206.0[1]**	**1 260.4[1]**	**1 248.8[1]**
Primary 1re fusion	455.0	549.4	757.4	843.5[1]	873.5[1]	887.9[1]	930.6[1]	1 139.0[1]	1 193.3[1]	1 172.0[1]
Secondary 2ème fusion	48.9	44.8	48.0	50.3[1]	64.9[1]	66.6[1]	65.0[1]	66.4[1]	67.1[1]	76.8[1]
Cameroon[4] **Cameroun[4]**	**125.4**	**81.8**	**51.0**	**79.0**	**80.0**	**87.3**	**87.5**	**85.6**	**82.5**	**86.5**
Canada[1] **Canada[1]**	**1 286.0**	**1 347.3**	**1 420.2**	**1 582.2**	**1 590.6**	**1 615.2**	**1 635.1**	**1 889.3**	**2 057.8**	**2 394.9**
Primary[1] 1re fusion[1]	1 222.0	1 282.3	1 355.2	1 540.4	1 534.5	1 554.8	1 567.4	1 821.6	1 971.8	2 308.9
Secondary[1] 2ème fusion[1]	64.0	65.0	65.0	41.7	56.1	60.4	67.7	67.7	86.0	86.0
China[4] **Chine[4]**	**400.0**	**410.0**	**410.0**	**615.0**	**718.4**	**758.4**	**854.3**	**900.0**	**1 096.4**	**1 255.4**
Croatia **Croatie**	**..**	**..**	**..**	**..**	**..**	**..**	**..**	**54.5**	**29.0**	**...**
former Czechoslovakia† **anc. Tchécoslovaquie†**	**66.0**	**66.0**	**66.1**	**66.4**	**67.4**	**69.3**	**69.8**	**66.3**	**..**	**..**
Primary 1re fusion	31.6	31.7	33.1	32.4	31.4	32.6	30.1	49.4	..	..
Secondary 2ème fusion	34.4	34.3	33.0	34.0	36.0	36.7	39.7	16.9	..	..

54
Aluminium
Production: thousand metric tons [cont.]
Aluminium
Production : milliers de tonnes métriques [suite]

Country or area Pays ou zone	1984	1985	1986	1987	1988	1989	1990	1991	1992	1993
Denmark [5] **Danemark** [5]	14.2	16.4	16.4	16.4	16.4	16.4	10.6	12.0	14.1	14.0
Egypt [4][6] **Egypte** [4][6]	128.4	135.5	114.0	148.7	142.6	146.2	141.1	141.0	139.4	138.8
Finland **Finlande**	# 1.6	1.0	0.2	0.2	* 2.0	* 4.1	* 4.9	* 4.2	* 4.5	* 3.7
France [7] **France** [7]	504.0	457.3	* 495.2	568.2	541.0	554.8	533.4	471.8	636.7	627.3
Primary 1re fusion	341.0	293.1	321.8	381.8	328.0	329.3	325.2	254.6	414.3	424.5
Secondary [7] 2ème fusion [7]	163.0	164.3	173.4	186.3	213.0	225.5	208.3	217.2	222.4	202.8
Germany † **Allemagne†**	..	..	..	..	..	..	..	739.9	654.4	610.4
Primary 1re fusion	..	..	..	..	..	..	..	690.3	602.8	551.9
Secondary 2ème fusion	..	..	..	..	..	..	..	49.5	51.9	58.5
F. R. Germany R. f. Allemagne	815.1	789.7	805.3	773.7	787.0	784.7	759.6	..	..	..
Primary 1re fusion	777.2	745.5	765.1	737.7	744.1	742.2	720.3 [8]	..	..	..
former German D. R. [7] anc. R. d. allemande [7]	125.9	127.1	125.0	122.3	115.8	107.7	82.8	..	..	..
Primary [7] 1re fusion [7]	67.8	65.7	66.0	67.9	61.2	53.9	41.2	..	..	..
Secondary [7] 2ème fusion [7]	58.1	61.4	59.0	54.5	54.6	53.8	41.6	..	..	..
Ghana [4] **Ghana** [4]	0.0	48.6	124.6	150.0	161.0	169.0	174.0	175.0	179.9	175.4
Greece **Grèce**	189.0	175.5	175.9	223.6	207.9	209.1	225.9	175.1	174.5	...
Hungary **Hongrie**	89.0	86.9	86.4	85.2	83.8	85.1	81.1	...	...	...
Primary 1re fusion	74.2	73.9	73.9	73.5	74.7	75.2	75.2	63.3	26.9	28.9
Secondary 2ème fusion	14.8	13.0	12.5	11.7	9.1	9.9	5.9	...	...	...
Iceland [4] **Islande** [4]	80.4	73.4	75.9	83.5	82.0	88.7	86.8	88.8	89.5	94.5
India [4] **Inde** [4]	268.3	259.9	234.9	245.3	289.7	425.3	427.6	504.3	499.0	...
Indonesia [4] **Indonésie** [4]	206.9	216.8	220.0	219.9	180.0	196.9	192.1	173.0	213.5	202.1
Iran, Islamic Rep. of **Iran, Rép. islamique d'**	54.0	58.0	52.4	48.6	53.2	28.5	73.0	109.5	118.7	106.6
Primary 1re fusion	42.0	43.0	37.4	33.6	38.2	19.9 [1]	59.4 [1]	70.1 [1]	79.3 [1]	91.5 [1]
Secondary [1] 2ème fusion [1]	12.0	15.0	15.0	15.0	15.0	8.6	13.6	39.4	39.4	15.1
Italy **Italie**	513.2	506.1	543.6	567.6	604.1	609.5	581.4	566.0	513.8	501.7
Primary 1re fusion	230.2	224.1	242.6	232.6	226.3	219.5	231.8	218.0	160.7	155.6

54
Aluminium
Production: thousand metric tons [*cont.*]
Aluminium
Production : milliers de tonnes métriques [*suite*]

Country or area Pays ou zone	1984	1985	1986	1987	1988	1989	1990	1991	1992	1993
Secondary 2ème fusion	283.0	282.0	301.0	335.0	377.8	390.0	349.6	348.0	353.1	346.1
Japan[7] **Japon**[7]	**1 131.4**	**1 098.5**	**1 013.6**	**1 085.1**	**1 053.3**	**1 081.5**	**1 140.6**	**1 148.5**	**1 112.2**	**1 044.2**
Primary 1re fusion	291.1	231.3	148.3	52.8	49.0	50.7	50.5	52.1	38.5	38.5
Secondary[7] 2ème fusion[7]	840.3	867.2	865.3	1 032.3	1 004.3	1 030.8	1 090.1	1 096.4	1 073.7	1 005.6
Korea, Republic of[4] **Corée, République de**[4]	**18.3**	**17.1**	**18.3**	**16.8**	**16.1**	**15.7**	**13.3**	**13.6**	...	...
Mexico **Mexique**	**63.2**	**65.1**	**62.6**	**88.1**	**79.9**	**80.8**	**113.6**	**106.6**	**101.0**	**109.1**
Primary 1re fusion	43.6	42.8	46.2	79.3	75.4	67.6	56.8	42.8	17.4	25.5
Secondary[1] 2ème fusion[1]	19.6	22.3	16.4	8.8	4.5	13.2	56.8	63.8	83.6	83.6
Netherlands **Pays-Bas**	**309.1**	**312.9**	**362.6**	**377.3**	**394.1**	**409.4**	**392.1**	**367.8**	**377.6**	**383.3**
Primary 1re fusion	249.2	250.6	265.8	275.9	278.2	279.2	257.9	253.6	227.3	228.3
Secondary 2ème fusion	59.9	62.3	96.8	101.4	115.9	130.2	134.2	114.3	150.2	155.1
New Zealand **Nouvelle-Zélande**	**246.6**	**242.3**	**240.3**	**256.0**[1]	**258.7**[1]	**262.0**[1]	**264.5**[1]	**263.2**[1]	**249.6**[1]	**284.1**[1]
Primary 1re fusion	242.9	240.8	236.3	252.0[1]	255.6[1]	257.5[1]	259.7[1]	258.5[1]	242.9[1]	277.4[1]
Secondary[1] 2ème fusion[1]	3.7	1.5	4.0	4.0	3.1	4.5	4.8	4.7	6.7	6.7
Norway **Norvège**	**770.7**	**748.7**	**733.0**	**805.0**	**845.4**	**874.5**	**874.1**	**865.2**	**878.1**	**927.5**[1]
Primary 1re fusion	765.1	742.7	725.8	797.8	838.2	867.3	867.1	858.2	838.1	887.5
Secondary 2ème fusion	5.6	6.0	7.2	7.2	7.2	7.2	7.0[1]	7.0[1]	40.0[1]	40.0[1]
Poland[4] **Pologne**[4]	**46.0**	**47.0**	**47.5**	**47.5**	**47.7**	**47.8**	**46.0**	**45.8**	**43.6**	**46.9**
Portugal[5] **Portugal**[5]	**2.4**	**2.5**	**2.1**	**2.3**	**2.5**	**4.0**	**9.3**	**8.1**	**8.4**	...
Romania[79] **Roumanie**[79]	**264.0**	**265.0**	**269.0**	**275.2**	**279.0**	**280.2**	**178.3**	**167.5**	**119.5**	**117.2**
Primary[9] 1re fusion[9]	244.0	247.0	253.0	260.5	265.6	269.1	168.0	158.2	112.0	112.4
Secondary 2ème fusion	20.0	18.0	16.0	14.7	13.4	11.2	10.3	9.2	7.5	4.9
Slovakia **Slovaquie**	..	..	..	..	..	..	..	..	...	**19.2**
Primary 1re fusion	..	..	..	..	..	..	..	..	...	17.8
Secondary 2ème fusion	..	..	..	..	..	..	..	..	...	1.4
Slovenia **Slovénie**	..	..	..	..	..	..	..	**90.2**	**84.8**	...
South Africa[14] **Afrique du Sud**[14]	**167.4**	**165.0**	**169.6**	**170.6**	**170.4**	**165.9**	**170.0**	**170.0**	**174.0**	**176.0**

54

Aluminium
Production: thousand metric tons [*cont.*]
Aluminium
Production : milliers de tonnes métriques [*suite*]

Country or area Pays ou zone	1984	1985	1986	1987	1988	1989	1990	1991	1992	1993
Spain[1] **Espagne**[1]	**421.4**	**412.6**	**402.9**	**411.0**	**378.9**	**430.0**	**442.0**	**451.2**	**455.5**	**455.6**
Primary[1] 1re fusion[1]	380.8	370.1	354.7	341.0	293.9	352.4	355.3	355.2	359.0	355.9
Secondary[1] 2ème fusion[1]	40.6	42.5	48.2	70.0	85.0	77.6	86.7	96.0	96.5	99.7
Suriname[4] **Suriname**[4]	**23.0**	**28.8**	**28.7**	**1.9**	**9.8**	**28.4**	**31.3**	**30.7**	**32.4**	**30.1**
Sweden[1] **Suède**[1]	**113.6**	**114.1**	**109.9**	**111.5**	**130.6**	**130.0**	**126.3**	**115.4**	**93.7**	**101.4**
Primary[1] 1re fusion[1]	82.8	83.7	77.1	81.5	98.6	97.0	96.3	96.9	77.2	82.4
Secondary[1] 2ème fusion[1]	30.8	30.4	32.8	30.0	32.0	33.0	30.0	18.5	16.5	19.0
Switzerland[4] **Suisse**[4]	**79.2**	**72.7**	**80.3**	**73.2**	**71.8**	**71.3**	**71.6**	**65.9**	**52.1**	**36.4**
TFYR Macedonia **L'ex-R.y. Macédoine**	...	..	..	..	..	..	..	6.0	5.8	...
Turkey[4] **Turquie**[4]	**37.9**	**54.1**	**60.0**	**41.7**	**56.7**	**57.2**	**60.0**	**56.0**	...	...
former USSR†[10] **ancienne URSS†**[10]	*** 2 550.0**	*** 2 700.0**	*** 2 850.0**	*** 3 000.0**	*** 3 000.0**	*** 3 000.0**	...	..	..	..
Primary[10] 1re fusion[10]	* 2 100.0	* 2 200.0	* 2 300.0	* 2 400.0	* 2 400.0	* 2 400.0	...	..	..	..
Secondary[10] 2ème fusion[10]	* 450.0	* 500.0	* 550.0	* 600.0	* 600.0	* 600.0	...	..	..	..
United Kingdom[9] **Royaume-Uni**[9]	**431.8**	**403.0**	**392.3**	**411.1**	**405.9**	**366.9**	**362.8**	**349.8**[1]	...	...
Primary[9] 1re fusion[9]	287.9	275.4	275.9	294.4	300.2	297.3	289.8	293.5[1]	244.2[1]	239.1[1]
Secondary 2ème fusion	143.9	127.6	116.4	116.7	105.8	69.5	73.0	56.3	...	...
United States[7] **Etats-Unis**[7]	**5 859.0**	**5 262.0**	**4 810.0**	**5 329.0**	**6 066.0**	**6 084.0**	**6 441.0**	**6 407.0**	**6 798.0**	**6 638.8**
Primary 1re fusion	4 099.0	3 500.0	3 037.0	3 343.0	3 944.0	4 030.0	4 048.0	4 121.0	4 042.0	3 694.8
Secondary[7] 2ème fusion[7]	1 760.0	1 762.0	1 773.0	1 986.0	2 122.0	2 054.0	2 393.0	2 286.0	2 756.0	2 944.0
Venezuela **Venezuela**	**399.2**	**416.8**	**431.4**	**440.2**	**453.3**	**575.6**	**608.8**	**620.0**	**542.2**	**602.3**
Primary 1re fusion	385.2	402.8	421.4	430.2	443.3	565.6	598.8	610.0	507.5	567.6
Secondary[1] 2ème fusion[1]	14.0	14.0	10.0	10.0	10.0	10.0	10.0	10.0	34.7	34.7
Yugoslavia **Yougoslavie**	..	..	..	..	..	..	..	...	**66.9**	...
Primary 1re fusion	..	..	..	..	..	..	..	...	66.9	...
Secondary 2ème fusion	..	..	..	..	..	..	..	...	0.1	...
Yugoslavia, SFR† **Yougoslavie, Rfs†**	**301.6**	**316.1**	**319.7**	**281.1**	**313.3**	**331.7**	**291.0**	..	..	..
Primary 1re fusion	292.3	306.3	309.2	280.6	312.7	331.0	* 290.0	..	..	..

54

Aluminium
Production: thousand metric tons [*cont.*]
Aluminium
Production : milliers de tonnes métriques [*suite*]

Country or area Pays ou zone	1984	1985	1986	1987	1988	1989	1990	1991	1992	1993
Secondary 2ème fusion	9.3	9.7	10.5	0.5	0.7	0.6	* 1.0	..	..	..

Source:
Industrial statistics database of the Statistics Division of
the United Nations Secretariat.

† For detailed descriptions of data pertaining to
former Czechoslovakia, Germany, SFR Yugoslavia and former
USSR, see Annex I - Country or area nomenclature, regional
and other groupings.

1 Source: World Metal Statistics (London).
2 Twelve months ending 30 June of year stated.

3 Secondary aluminium produced from old scrap only.

4 Primary metal production only.
5 Secondary metal production only.
6 Including aluminum plates, shapes and bars.
7 Including alloys.
8 Source: "Metallgesellschaft Aktiengesellschaft",
(Frankfurt).
9 Including pure content of virgin alloys.
10 Source: US Bureau of Mines, (Washington, DC).

Source:
Base de données pour les statistiques industrielles de la
Division de statistique du Secrétariat de l'ONU.

† Pour les descriptions en détails des données
relatives à l'ancienne Tchécoslovaquie, l'Allemagne, la Rfs
Yougoslavie et l'ancienne URSS, voir l'Annexe I -
Nomenclature des pays ou zones, groupements régionaux et
autres groupements.

1 Source: "World Metal Statistics," (Londres).
2 Période de douze mois finissant le 30 juin de l'année
indiquée.
3 Aluminium de deuxième fusion obtenu à partir de vieux
déchets seulement.
4 Production du métal de première fusion seulement.
5 Production du métal de deuxième fusion seulement.
6 Y compris les tôles, les profilés et les barres d'aluminium.
7 Y compris les alliages.
8 Source: "Metallgesellschaft Aktiengesellschaft",
(Francfort).
9 Y compris la teneur pure des alliages de première fusion.
10 Source: "US Bureau of Mines," (Washington, DC).

55
Radio and television receivers
Radiodiffusion et télévision : postes récepteurs
Production: thousands
Production : milliers

Country or area Pays ou zone	Radio receivers Radiodiffusion : postes récepteurs					Television receivers Télévision : postes récepteurs				
	1989	1990	1991	1992	1993	1989	1990	1991	1992	1993
Total	**148 455**	**144 284**	**133 273**	**123 010**	**115 168**	**121 524**	**128 330**	**137 943**	**130 669**	**132 217**
Albania Albanie	30	...	...	...	...	23	18	5	...	...
Algeria Algérie	120	213	215	192	12	212	283	176	218	258
Argentina Argentine	...	...	...	...	...	674	310	607	1 386	1 612
Armenia Arménie	..	..	167	50	8	..	..	...	...	...
Australia[12] Australie[12]	...	...	...	...	...	162	158	...	...	...
Azerbaijan Azerbaïdjan	..	..	7	0	...	...	...	...	5 913	...
Bangladesh Bangladesh	102	68	21	16	7	79	83	57	44	61
Belarus Bélarus	..	..	932	721	768	..	..	1 103	798	610
Belgium[34] Belgique[34]	859	986	556	416	408	979	1 084	886	620	559
Brazil Brésil	7 210	5 151	5 333	5 486	4 097	2 920	3 196	3 265	...	...
Bulgaria Bulgarie	52	43	16	5	1	185	219	108	64	26
Chad Tchad	9	13	7	7	...	...	...	...	...	...
Chile Chili	...	...	...	...	...	24	0	0	...	...
China Chine	18 347[5]	21 030[5]	19 691[5]	16 489[5]	17 542[5]	27 665	26 847	26 914	28 678	30 330
Colombia Colombie	...	...	...	...	...	130	135	...	...	...
Croatia Croatie	...	..	3	1	...	..	..	3	...	...
Cuba Cuba	173	...	...	...	...	71	...	...	...	...
former Czechoslovakia† anc. Tchécoslovaquie†	173[6]	187[6]	73[6]	..	..	524	504	208	..	..
Denmark[7] Danemark[7]	...	...	...	...	...	125	122	117	...	...
Ecuador Equateur	...	...	...	...	...	...	...	...	11	...
Egypt Egypte	43	59	39	36	13	194	333	264	260	269
Finland Finlande	...	...	...	* 4	* 5	413	412	327	269	321
France France	2 039	2 059	1 865	1 679	2 083	2 447	2 838	2 549	2 799	2 523

55
Radio and television receivers
Production: thousands [*cont.*]
Radiodiffusion et télévision : postes récepteurs
Production : milliers [*suite*]

Country or area Pays ou zone	Radio receivers Radiodiffusion : postes récepteurs					Television receivers Télévision : postes récepteurs				
	1989	1990	1991	1992	1993	1989	1990	1991	1992	1993
Germany † Allemagne†	..	..	...	4 703	4 623	..	..	...	...	2 800
F. R. Germany R. f. Allemagne	4 975	5 955	..	..	..	3 236	3 595	..	..	..
former German D. R. anc. R. d. allemande	1 151	522	..	..	..	775	632	..	..	..
Greece Grèce	...	...	...	...	...	37	10	2	...	...
Hong Kong Hong-kong	...	8 182	6 145	6 508	...	683	1 177	749	...	...
Hungary Hongrie	145	83	14	1	...	502	492	217	274	204
India Inde	672[8]	647[8]	286[8]	245[8]	152[8]	1 237	1 322	1 217	1 254	1 540
Indonesia Indonésie	1 905[9]	4 436[9]	4 659[9]	2 863[9]	...	525	700	725	700	...
Iran, Islamic Rep. of[10] Iran, Rép. islamique d'[10]	217[11 12]	232[11 12]	183[11 12]	99[11 12]	...	407	598	744	723	...
Iraq Iraq	...	...	...	...	...	...	...	...	16	...
Italy Italie	...	...	...	...	...	2 391	2 312	2 435	2 151	2 432
Japan Japon	17 052	15 647	16 247	13 711	11 382	13 983	15 132	15 640	14 253	12 840
Kazakstan Kazakstan	..	..	86	97	72	...	...	5	36	20
Kenya Kenya	...	...	...	...	...	2 077	4 186	...	...	...
Korea, Republic of Corée, République de	1 112	1 468	836	619	550	15 469	16 201	16 129	16 311	15 956
Kyrgyzstan Kirghizistan	..	..	...	...	...	..	..	8 000	2 000	1 694
Latvia Lettonie	..	..	1 230	630	124	...	...	...	...	...
Lithuania Lituanie	..	..	...	...	...	..	..	516	445	423
Malaysia Malaisie	28 450	37 019	31 920	31 360	34 537	2 375	3 238	4 838	5 553	6 629
Mexico Mexique	...	...	...	...	...	536	633	490	435	299
Mozambique Mozambique	97	12	19	...	...	...	...	...	...	...
Myanmar[13] Myanmar[13]	7	4	1	1	...	0	...	...	...	...
Pakistan Pakistan	...	...	...	...	...	211	200	182	145	162
Peru Pérou	...	...	...	...	...	55	...	...	...	...

55
Radio and television receivers
Production: thousands [*cont.*]
Radiodiffusion et télévision : postes récepteurs
Production : milliers [*suite*]

Country or area Pays ou zone	Radio receivers Radiodiffusion : postes récepteurs					Television receivers Télévision : postes récepteurs				
	1989	1990	1991	1992	1993	1989	1990	1991	1992	1993
Poland Pologne	2 523	1 433	589	334	329	772	748	438	652	855
Portugal Portugal	1 071	1 435	1 522	...	...	304	329	318	238	...
Republic of Moldova République de Moldova	..	..	5	3	5	..	..	173	176	167
Romania Roumanie	526	384	384	79	70	511	401	389	318	431
Russian Federation Fédération de Russie	..	..	5 537	4 015	2 806	..	..	4 439	3 672	3 987
Singapore Singapour	...	...	...	...	...	3 040	...	...	...	...
Slovakia Slovaquie	..	..	..	...	2[6]	..	..	..	...	165
Slovenia Slovénie	..	..	0	0	...	..	..	101	55	...
South Africa Afrique du Sud	941	775	...	...	...	344	373	486	376	321
Spain Espagne	15	10	28	...	...	2 100	2 466	2 807	2 544	...
Sweden Suède	...	...	...	...	...	333	284	224	13	...
Syrian Arab Republic Rép. arabe syrienne	...	...	...	...	...	90	18	17	20	20
Thailand Thaïlande	933	1 105	1 062	...	...	1 476	2 351	2 426	...	...
Trinidad and Tobago Trinité-et-Tobago	6	2	3	3	...	2	7	13	16	...
Tunisia Tunisie	17	22	21	27	2	112	115	124	153	...
Turkey Turquie	108	100	43	22	74	999	1 994	2 567	2 111	1 922
Ukraine Ukraine	..	..	892	860	797	..	..	3 616	2 570	1 919
former USSR† ancienne URSS†	8 561	9 168	..	..	..	9 938	10 540	..	..	..
United Kingdom[14] Royaume-Uni[14]	34	...	...	...	...	...	...	...	...	...
United Rep.Tanzania Rép. Unie de Tanzanie	56	71	102	108	95	...	...	...	...	...
United States Etats-Unis	3 408[4]	3 014[4]	3 504[4]	4 006[4]	...	15 478[4]	13 982[4]	12 865	13 972	14 297
Yugoslavia Yougoslavie	..	..	...	1	...	..	..	...	64	...
Yugoslavia, SFR† Yougoslavie, Rfs†	86	...	..	..	..	503	...	..	..	..

55
Radio and television receivers
Production: thousands[*cont.*]

Radiodiffusion et télévision : postes récepteurs
Production : milliers [*suite*]

Source:
Industrial statistics database of the Statistics Division of
the United Nations Secretariat.

† For detailed descriptions of data pertaining to
former Czechoslovakia, Germany, SFR Yugoslavia and former
USSR, see Annex I - Country or area nomenclature, regional
and other groupings.

1 Twelve months ending 30 June of year stated.

2 Colour television receivers only.
3 Production by establishments employing 5 or more persons.
4 Shipments.
5 Portable battery sets only.
6 Including record players.
7 Sales.
8 Production by large and medium scale establishments only.
9 Including radio with tape recording unit.

10 Production by establishments employing 50 or more persons.
11 Including sound reproducers.
12 Including tape recorders.
13 Government production only.
14 Including car tape-players.

Source:
Base de données pour les statistiques industrielles de la
Division de statistique du Secrétariat de l'ONU.

† Pour les descriptions en détails des données
relatives à l'ancienne Tchécoslovaquie, l'Allemagne, la Rfs
Yougoslavie et l'ancienne URSS, voir l'Annexe I -
Nomenclature des pays ou zones, groupements régionaux et
autres groupements.

1 Période de douze mois finissant le 30 juin de l'année
indiquée.
2 Récepteurs de télévision en couleur seulement.
3 Production des établissements occupant 5 personnes ou plus.
4 Expéditions.
5 Appareils portatifs à piles seulement.
6 Y compris les tourne-disques.
7 Ventes.
8 Production des grandes et moyennes entreprises seulement.
9 Y compris les récepteurs de radio avec appareil enregistreur
à bande magnétique incorporés.
10 Production des établissements occupant 50 personnes ou plus.
11 Y compris les lecteurs de son.
12 Y compris les magnétophones.
13 Production de l'Etat seulement.
14 Y compris les lecteurs de cassettes pour automobiles.

56
Passenger cars
Voitures de tourisme
Production: thousands
Production : milliers

Country or area Pays ou zone	1984	1985	1986	1987	1988	1989	1990	1991	1992	1993
Total	**30 385**	**31 971**	**32 413**	**32 804**	**33 842**	**34 691**	**34 900**	**33 515**	**33 699**	**30 896**
Argentina[1] Argentine[1]	142	118	138	159	136	108	81	114	221	287
Australia[1,2] Australie[1,2]	341	376	365	302	315	333	386	311	269	275
Austria Autriche	7	7	7	7	7	7	15	14	...	...
Brazil Brésil	679	759	815	683	782	# 313[3]	267[3]	293[3]	338[3]	392[3]
Canada Canada	1 022	1 075	1 061	810	1 008	984	940	890	901	838
China Chine	6	9	* 10	* 12	* 11	...	...	* 40	...	...
former Czechoslovakia† anc. Tchécoslovaquie†	180	184	185	172	164	189	191	177	..	..
Egypt Egypte	20	21	19	18	19	13	10	9	7	4
Finland[1] Finlande[1]	32	39	43	46	45	37	30	39	13	7
France France	2 909	2 631	2 773	3 052	3 228	3 415	3 293	3 190	3 326	2 837
Germany † Allemagne†	..	..	..	..	..	..	..	4 647	4 895	3 875
F. R. Germany R. f. Allemagne	3 783	4 165	4 269	4 348	4 312	4 536	4 634	..	..	..
former German D. R. anc. R. d. allemande	202	210	218	217	218	217	145	..	..	..
India[4] Inde[4]	64	89	101	123	157	178	177	164	162	211
Indonesia Indonésie	...	...	...	...	15	16	18	25	28	...
Italy[4] Italie[4]	1 439	1 384	1 653	1 712	1 883	1 971	1 873	1 632	1 475	1 116
Japan Japon	7 073	7 647	7 810	7 891	8 198	9 052	9 948	9 753	9 379	8 494
Korea, Republic of Corée, République de[1]	167	262	457	778	868	846	935	1 119	1 259	1 528
Mexico[1] Mexique[1]	247	285	198	278	345	448	611	730	799	851
Netherlands[1] Pays-Bas[1]	109	108	119	125	120	133	122	84	95	80
Poland Pologne	278	283	290	293	293	285	266	167	219	334
Romania Roumanie	125	134	124	129	141	144	100	84	74	93
Russian Federation Fédération de Russie	..	..	..	..	..	..	..	1 030	963	956

56
Passenger cars
Production: thousands [*cont.*]
Voitures de tourisme
Production : milliers [*suite*]

Country or area Pays ou zone	1984	1985	1986	1987	1988	1989	1990	1991	1992	1993
Slovakia Slovaquie	..	..	..	..	..	..	..	..	...	5
Slovenia Slovénie	..	..	..	..	..	..	..	79	84	...
Spain Espagne	1 137	1 220	1 290	1 444	* 1 498	1 651	1 696	1 787	1 817	...
Sweden Suède	378	402	415	416	259	240	216	178	205	...
Ukraine Ukraine	..	..	..	..	..	..	..	156	135	140
United Kingdom Royaume-Uni	909	1 048	1 019	1 143	1 227	1 308	1 302	1 340	1 291	...
United States[5] Etats-Unis[5]	7 622	8 002	7 516	7 085	7 105	6 808	6 081	5 441	5 684	...
Yugoslavia Yougoslavie	..	..	..	..	..	..	..	...	22	...
Yugoslavia, SFR† Yougoslavie, Rfs†	187	177	185	219	226	227	289	..	..	..

Source:
Industrial statistics database of the Statistics Division of
the United Nations Secretariat.

† For detailed descriptions of data pertaining to
former Czechoslovakia, Germany, SFR Yugoslavia and former
USSR, see Annex I - Country or area nomenclature, regional
and other groupings.

1 Including assembly.
2 Twelve months ending 30 June of year stated.

3 Excluding station wagons.
4 Excluding ordinance production.
5 Factory sales.

Source:
Base de données pour les statistiques industrielles de la
Division de statistique du Secrétariat de l'ONU.

† Pour les descriptions en détails des données
relatives à l'ancienne Tchécoslovaquie, l'Allemagne, la Rfs
Yougoslavie et l'ancienne URSS, voir l'Annexe I -
Nomenclature des pays ou zones, groupements régionaux et
autres groupements.

1 Y compris le montage.
2 Période de douze mois finissant le 30 juin de l'année
indiquée.
3 Non compris les stations-wagons.
4 Non compris la production d'artillerie.
5 Ventes des fabriques.

57
Refrigerators for household use
Réfrigérateurs ménagers

Production: thousands
Production : milliers

Country or area Pays or zone	1984	1985	1986	1987	1988	1989	1990	1991	1992	1993
Total	40 873	42 802	45 363	49 255	55 656	54 470	52 735	53 353	52 523	55 275
Algeria Algérie	100	102	104	225	382	369	387	388	317	183
Antigua and Barbuda Antigua-et-Barbuda	1	1	1	1	1	...	...	...	...	...
Argentina Argentine	253	162	209	207	162	...	...	...	...	...
Australia[1] Australie[1]	265	252	328	289	386	380	346	363	372	393
Azerbaijan Azerbaïdjan	..	..	..	..	..	..	..	313	223	...
Belarus Bélarus	..	..	..	..	..	..	..	743	740	738
Brazil Brésil	1 491	1 706	2 220	2 366	1 875	2 381	2 441	2 445	1 704	2 098
Bulgaria Bulgarie	135	122	118	111	111	101	82	65	106	81
Canada Canada	439	510	569	...	...	...	...	...	...	...
Chile Chili	42	32	46	60	59	79	89	86	136	192
China Chine	587	1 448	2 250	4 013	7 576	6 708	4 631	4 699	4 858	5 967
Cuba Cuba	22	26	17	5	7	9	...	...	...	...
former Czechoslovakia† anc. Tchécoslovaquie†	446	480	524	526	551	502	449	515	..	..
Denmark[2] Danemark[2]	814	915	902	817	* 217	257	278	269	294	...
Dominican Republic Rép. dominicaine	16	11	16	...	...	...	...	...	...	...
Ecuador Equateur	30	45	54	57	125	...	...	...	66	...
Egypt Egypte	457	514	536	601	693	477	246	260	232	204
Finland Finlande	...	# 149	141	165	194	198	166	150	144	128
France France	469	436	490	612	650	614	596	556	566	487
Germany † Allemagne†	..	..	..	..	..	..	..	4 226	4 298	3 838
F. R. Germany R. f. Allemagne	2 667	2 788	3 009	3 024	3 411	3 614	4 037	..	..	..
former German D. R. anc. R. d. allemande	895	973	1 018	1 075	1 124	1 140	1 005	..	..	..
Greece Grèce	118	139	148	130	114	130	119	85	80	...
Guyana Guyana	...	6	6	4	6	7	6	10	6	5

57
Refrigerators for household use
Production: thousands [cont.]
Réfrigérateurs ménagers
Production : milliers [suite]

Country or area Pays or zone	1984	1985	1986	1987	1988	1989	1990	1991	1992	1993
Hungary Hongrie	473	457	438	462	469	390	438	443	483	520
India Inde	553	661	582	595	961	991	1 220	1 133	997	1 257
Indonesia Indonésie	97	108	137	100	98	115	196	194	...	...
Iran, Islamic Rep. of[3] Iran, Rép. islamique d'[3]	726	721	435	354	326	351	651	818	879	...
Iraq Iraq	...	...	220	...	90	...	...	...	35	...
Italy Italie	3 576	3 357	3 590	3 794	3 942	4 082	4 199	4 484	4 285	4 753
Japan Japon	4 936	5 354	4 497	5 008	5 177	5 018	5 048	5 212	4 425	4 351
Kazakstan Kazakstan	..	..	..	..	..	..	..	...	...	13
Kenya Kenya	...	...	1	2	2	21	21	...	...	...
Korea, Republic of Corée, République de	1 819	1 864	2 336	3 123	3 931	2 803	2 827	3 228	3 296	3 585
Kyrgyzstan Kirghizistan	..	..	..	..	..	..	..	...	1	...
Lithuania Lituanie	..	..	..	..	..	..	..	265	166	276
Malaysia Malaisie	157	149	* 154	145	197	185	212	266	288	250
Mexico Mexique	357	336	329	282	264	372	396	487	541	525
Mozambique Mozambique	...	2	2	2	3	3	1	...	...	...
Nigeria Nigéria	...	...	79	59	...	...	...	...	...	...
Peru Pérou	52	54	60	78	54	32	45	...	...	...
Philippines Philippines	146	146	140	236	...	...	...	...	...	...
Poland Pologne	543	578	569	506	484	516	604	553	500	588
Portugal Portugal	227	209	192	311	382	376	464	529	# 125	...
Republic of Moldova République de Moldova	..	..	..	..	..	..	..	118	55	58
Romania[4] Roumanie[4]	402	400	404	420	442	470	393	389	402	435
Russian Federation Fédération de Russie	..	..	..	..	..	..	..	3 566	2 972	3 049
Singapore Singapour	45	37	...	...	...	...	...	...	...	...
Slovakia Slovaquie	..	..	..	..	..	..	..	..	552	175

57
Refrigerators for household use
Production: thousands [cont.]
Réfrigérateurs ménagers
Production : milliers [suite]

Country or area Pays or zone	1984	1985	1986	1987	1988	1989	1990	1991	1992	1993
Slovenia Slovénie	..	..	..	..	..	..	..	720	661	...
South Africa[5] Afrique du Sud[5]	172	146	205	211	306	338	352	356	318	333
Spain Espagne	1 105	1 082	1 169	1 136	1 210	1 268	1 285	1 410	1 322	...
Sweden Suède	513	510	559	580	626	631	584	562	562	...
Syrian Arab Republic Rép. arabe syrienne	111	76	43	32	22	89	40	85	129	150
Thailand Thaïlande	...	...	...	...	548	730	855	789	...	
TFYR Macedonia L'ex-R.y. Macédoine	..	..	..	..	..	..	..	136	139	...
Trinidad and Tobago Trinité-et-Tobago	22	10	14	17	14	12	14	13	10	...
Tunisia Tunisie	46	48	44	39	37	...	...	82	123	141
Turkey Turquie	501	488	659	834	862	815	986	1 019	1 040	1 254
Ukraine Ukraine	..	..	..	..	..	..	..	883	838	757
former USSR†[4] ancienne URSS†[4]	5 667	5 860	5 948	5 984	6 231	6 465	6 499	..	..	
United Kingdom Royaume-Uni	1 228	1 266	1 254	1 281	1 405	1 244	1 312	...	...	...
United States Etats-Unis	6 317[6,7]	6 419[6,7]	6 940[6,7]	7 231[6,7]	7 968[6,7]	8 013[6,7]	7 015[6,7]	7 599	9 676	10 306
Uzbekistan Ouzbékistan	..	..	..	..	..	..	..	212	...	...
Yugoslavia Yougoslavie	..	..	..	..	..	..	..	...	85	...
Yugoslavia, SFR†[8] Yougoslavie, Rfs†[8]	746	732	885	738	1 164	971	...	..	..	..

Source:
Industrial statistics database of the Statistics Division of the United Nations Secretariat.

Source:
Base de données pour les statistiques industrielles de la Division de statistique du Secrétariat de l'ONU.

† For detailed descriptions of data pertaining to former Czechoslovakia, Germany, SFR Yugoslavia and former USSR, see Annex I - Country or area nomenclature, regional and other groupings.

1 Twelve months ending 30 June of year stated.

2 Sales.
3 Production by establishments employing 50 or more persons.
4 Including freezers.
5 Including deep freezers and deep freeze-refrigerator combinations.
6 Electric domestic refrigerators only.
7 Shipments.
8 Including refrigerators other than domestic.

† Pour les descriptions en détails des données relatives à l'ancienne Tchécoslovaquie, l'Allemagne, la Rfs Yougoslavie et l'ancienne URSS, voir l'Annexe I - Nomenclature des pays ou zones, groupements régionaux et autres groupements.

1 Période de douze mois finissant le 30 juin de l'année indiquée.
2 Ventes.
3 Production des établissements occupant 50 personnes ou plus.
4 Y compris les congélateurs.
5 Y compris congélateurs-conservateurs et congélateurs combinés avec un réfrigérateur.
6 Réfrigérateurs électriques de ménage seulement.
7 Expéditions.
8 Y compris les réfrigérateurs autres que ménagers.

58
Washing machines for household use
Machines et appareils à laver, à usage domestique
Production: thousands
Production : en milliers

Country or area Pays or zone	1984	1985	1986	1987	1988	1989	1990	1991	1992	1993
Total	**35 750**	**40 081**	**41 899**	**44 468**	**47 705**	**45 976**	**45 971**	**44 067**	**41 575**	**44 639**
Argentina Argentine	171	103	188	156	137	...	...	...	...	...
Armenia Arménie	..	..	..	..	..	..	..	74	9	0
Australia[1] Australie[1]	...	276	282	400	394	397	330	326	296	308
Austria Autriche	71	72	83	80	80	72	77	...	...	...
Belarus Bélarus	..	..	..	..	..	..	..	57	62	71
Belgium[2 3] Belgique[2 3]	158	124	113	109	109	81	60	99	138	49
Brazil Brésil	344	419	576	630	559	578	552	948	849	1 167
Bulgaria Bulgarie	141	156	159	172	169	177	90	74	69	42
Canada Canada	368	407	417	...	...	...	...	...	...	...
Chile Chili	50	43	62	71	81	108	124	134	189	213
China Chine	5 781	8 872	8 934	9 902	10 468	8 254	6 627	6 872	7 079	8 959
Croatia Croatie	..	..	..	..	..	..	..	1	1	...
former Czechoslovakia† anc. Tchécoslovaquie†	423	445	452	460	463	454	451	376	..	..
Ecuador Equateur	4	1	...	2	2	...	...	...	...	...
Egypt Egypte	313	268	194	178	248	212	179	202	198	200
France[3] France[3]	1 370	1 262	1 444	1 288	1 561	1 670	1 636	1 645	1 713	1 943
Germany † · Allemagne† F. R. Germany[4] R. f. Allemagne[4]	1 692	1 827	1 986	2 113	2 194	2 430	...	..	..	..
former German D. R. anc. R. d. allemande	525	502	495	497	503	521	556	..	..	..
Greece Grèce	46	59	81	61	46	48	...	...	...	...
Hungary Hongrie	392	385	404	404	436	383	315	220	219	...
Indonesia Indonésie	10	12	13	13	16	10	17	19	27	...
Iran, Islamic Rep. of[5] Iran, Rép. islamique d'[5]	...	...	49	62	8	41	36	80	102	...
Israel[6] Israël[6]	11	11	13	11	9	8	13	...	...	...

58
Washing machines for household use
Production: thousands [*cont.*]

Machines et appareils à laver, à usage domestique
Production : en milliers [*suite*]

Country or area Pays or zone	1984	1985	1986	1987	1988	1989	1990	1991	1992	1993
Italy Italie	3 393	3 692	3 991	4 140	4 368	4 338	4 372	5 044	5 140	5 693
Japan Japon	5 277	5 092	4 661	4 772	5 118	5 141	5 576	5 587	5 225	5 163
Kazakstan Kazakstan	..	..	..	..	..	..	..	391	370	255
Korea, Republic of Corée, République de	646	635	902	1 303	1 903	1 864	2 163	2 157	1 896	2 199
Kyrgyzstan Kirghizistan	..	..	..	..	..	..	..	209	94	77
Latvia Lettonie	..	..	..	..	..	..	..	427	18	18
Mexico Mexique	314	322	268	# 345	463	442	558	611	646	568
Myanmar[7][8] Myanmar[7][8]	2	0	...	...	...	...	...	...	...	...
Peru Pérou	11	10	18	28	17	10	11	...	...	...
Philippines Philippines	0	48	9	17	...	...	...	...	...	...
Poland Pologne	730	739	773	779	761	811	482	336	363	402
Portugal Portugal	...	...	...	...	...	16	34	7	...	...
Republic of Moldova République de Moldova	..	..	..	..	..	..	..	194	102	123
Romania Roumanie	208	210	263	242	236	204	205	188	159	166
Russian Federation Fédération de Russie	..	..	..	..	..	..	..	5 541	4 289	3 901
Slovakia Slovaquie	..	..	..	..	..	..	..	..	122	100
Slovenia Slovénie	..	..	..	..	..	..	..	318	188	...
South Africa Afrique du Sud	66	54	60	45	52	68	109	87	44	52
Spain Espagne	1 100	1 083	1 217	1 407	1 552	1 378	1 425	1 522	1 540	...
Sweden Suède	69	68	77	76	109	104	107	103	91	...
Syrian Arab Republic Rép. arabe syrienne	52	49	33	65	42	34	44	29	41	47
Turkey Turquie	213	345	643	408	665	621	743	837	802	980
Ukraine Ukraine	..	..	..	..	..	..	..	830	805	643
former USSR† ancienne URSS†	4 534	5 068	5 383	5 779	6 104	6 698	7 818	..	..	..
United Kingdom Royaume-Uni	1 349	1 430	1 317	1 343	1 351	...	...	...	...	...

58
Washing machines for household use
Production: thousands [*cont.*]
Machines et appareils à laver, à usage domestique
Production : en milliers [*suite*]

Country or area Pays or zone	1984	1985	1986	1987	1988	1989	1990	1991	1992	1993
United States[3] Etats-Unis[3]	5 006	5 456	5 783	6 100	6 441	6 375	6 428	6 404	6 566	6 739
Uzbekistan Ouzbékistan	..	..	..	..	..	..	..	13	9	10
Yugoslavia Yougoslavie	..	..	..	..	..	..	..	...	68	...
Yugoslavia, SFR†[9] Yougoslavie, Rfs†[9]	533	487	534	593	604	529	...	..	..	..

Source:
Industrial statistics database of the Statistics Division of
the United Nations Secretariat.

† For detailed descriptions of data pertaining to
former Czechoslovakia, Germany, SFR Yugoslavia and former
USSR, see Annex I - Country or area nomenclature, regional
and other groupings.

1 Twelve months ending 30 June of year stated.

2 Production by establishments employing 5 or more persons.
3 Shipments.
4 Automatic washing machines only.
5 Production by establishments employing 50 or more persons.
6 Marketed local production.
7 Data refer to assembly.
8 Government production only.
9 Including drying machines.

Source:
Base de données pour les statistiques industrielles de la
Division de statistique du Secrétariat de l'ONU.

† Pour les descriptions en détails des données
relatives à l'ancienne Tchécoslovaquie, l'Allemagne, la Rfs
Yougoslavie et l'ancienne URSS, voir l'Annexe I -
Nomenclature des pays ou zones, groupements régionaux et
autres groupements.

1 Période de douze mois finissant le 30 juin de l'année
indiquée.
2 Production des établissements occupant 5 personnes ou plus.
3 Expéditions.
4 Machines à laver automatiques seulement.
5 Production des établissements occupant 50 personnes ou plus.
6 Production locale commercialisée.
7 Données se rapportant à l'assemblage.
8 Production de l'Etat seulement.
9 Y compris les machines à sécher.

59
Machine tools
Machines-outils
Production: number
Production : nombre

Country or area Pays ou zone	1984	1985	1986	1987	1988	1989	1990	1991	1992	1993
A. Drilling and boring machines • Perceuses										
Total	**165 491**	**158 811**	**152 917**	**146 815**	**156 113**	**150 939**	**140 778**	**157 624**	**135 103**	**129 312**
Algeria Algérie	211	209	352	347	261	32	412	210	122	30
Austria Autriche	1 881	1 593	1 780	1 114	1 201	1 443	...	...	...	...
Azerbaijan Azerbaïdjan	..	..	..	..	..	..	..	326	237	72
Bangladesh Bangladesh	...	...	...	...	117	125	131	...	...	...
Belgium Belgique	37 528	...	36 893	...	...	...	...	...	...	...
Bulgaria Bulgarie	4 731	6 563	7 565	7 092	7 095	6 496	4 729	1 959	996	759
Croatia Croatie	..	..	..	..	..	..	..	458	346	...
former Czechoslovakia† anc. Tchécoslovaquie†	1 492	1 514	1 280	987	974	871	901	1 133	..	..
Denmark[1] Danemark[1]	...	185	165	125	* 305	338	348	394	223	...
Finland Finlande	...	...	51	...	103	74	59	42	54	78
France[2] France[2]	3 081	3 769	3 406	2 441	2 459	...	2 500	1 460	1 212	...
Germany † Allemagne†	..	..	..	..	..	..	..	...	15 085	21 222
F. R. Germany[3] R. f. Allemagne[3]	...	12 997	14 790	16 196	14 504	14 336	14 158	..	..	..
Hungary Hongrie	4 147	5 744	8 188	5 557	4 108	2 027	1 929	1 257	75	78
Indonesia Indonésie	...	...	...	...	112	139	89	527	1 000	...
Iran, Islamic Rep. of Iran, Rép. islamique d'	3 184	2 200	...	...	...	...	...	...	...	...
Japan Japon	41 224	36 807	27 968	24 077	32 954	39 152	40 171	33 929	22 973	14 496
Korea, Republic of Corée, République de	...	3 971	5 514	7 909	8 974	8 347	7 662	8 150	7 336	7 416
Mexico Mexique	...	...	...	5 760	6 312	4 518	2 138	2 187	855	487
Poland Pologne	11 130	10 439	12 636	12 394	12 193	5 339	2 238	2 995	1 858	1 348
Russian Federation Fédération de Russie	..	..	..	..	..	..	..	16 020	12 835	10 607
Slovenia Slovénie	..	..	..	..	..	..	..	114	60	...
Spain Espagne	5 012	7 423	4 193	6 004	4 702	5 043	3 688	2 567	2 060	...

59
Machine tools
Production: number [*cont.*]
Machines-outils
Production : nombre [*suite*]

Country or area Pays ou zone	1984	1985	1986	1987	1988	1989	1990	1991	1992	1993
Sweden Suède	7 371	7 717	7 278	6 796	...	...	...	...	...	...
Turkey Turquie	...	...	...	140	172	22	8	57	0	52
Ukraine Ukraine	..	..	..	..	..	..	..	8 904	11 113	12 996
United States[4] Etats-Unis[4]	12 526	10 259	8 515	7 708	10 236	10 508	8 828	7 603	7 542	7 182
Viet Nam Viet Nam	...	...	50	30	...	...	...	...	...	...
Yugoslavia Yougoslavie	..	..	..	..	..	..	..	...	607	...
Yugoslavia, SFR† Yougoslavie, Rfs†	2 279	2 507	3 057	2 045	2 098	2 355	...	..	..	..

B. Lathes • Tours

Total	145 524	145 194	136 068	131 673	139 127	148 218	146 356	145 534	118 965	106 963
Algeria Algérie	138	149	161	120	110	150	270	273	310	194
Armenia Arménie	..	..	..	..	..	..	..	2 633	1 079	486
Austria Autriche	1 613	1 939	1 719	1 709	2 143	4 556	1 726	1 647	1 421	915
Bangladesh Bangladesh	...	...	...	...	202	214	223	...	...	...
Belarus Bélarus	...	...	...	...	...	...	...	...	162	332
Bulgaria Bulgarie	5 564	5 477	5 912	4 886	4 953	5 438	5 014	4 744	3 587	2 197
China Chine	55 675	...	...	...	...	...	...	...	...	...
Croatia Croatie	..	..	..	..	..	..	..	584	463	...
former Czechoslovakia† anc. Tchécoslovaquie†	7 254	7 157	6 011	6 185	6 055	6 393	6 020	5 853	..	..
Czech Republic République tchèque	..	..	..	..	..	..	..	..	1 017	641
Denmark[1] Danemark[1]	...	...	...	18	* 5	...	545	384	279	...
Finland Finlande	...	...	...	...	2	2	4	1	1	1
France[4] France[4]	1 077	1 284	1 356	1 273	1 012	...	1 400	988	942	11
Germany † Allemagne†	..	..	..	..	..	..	..	...	7 689	4 733
F. R. Germany R. f. Allemagne	6 772	6 864	7 011	7 046	6 637	7 155	7 612	..	..	..
former German D. R.[5] anc. R. d. allemande[5]	3 225	2 598	2 522	2 466	2 482	2 481	...	..	..	..

59
Machine tools
Production: number [*cont.*]
        Machines-outils
        Production : nombre [*suite*]

Country or area Pays ou zone	1984	1985	1986	1987	1988	1989	1990	1991	1992	1993
Hungary Hongrie	1 113	952	971	894	894	943	663	304	63	135
Indonesia Indonésie	...	...	...	...	36	19	2	45	42	...
Japan Japon	31 455	33 527	25 424	21 066	28 257	32 748	32 659	26 216	16 155	12 343
Korea, Republic of Corée, République de	6 020	5 206	6 209	7 898	8 605	9 156	10 597	11 324	6 643	6 931
Lithuania Lituanie	...	...	...	...	...	..	..	95	110	164
Poland Pologne	4 701	4 474	4 676	4 104	3 970	3 824	5 178	2 184	1 105	910
Portugal Portugal	141	157	167	169	147	124	101	87	...	...
Romania Roumanie	...	5 148	5 083	5 038	4 958	4 747	3 702	2 883	1 583	489
Russian Federation Fédération de Russie	..	..	..	..	..	..	..	9 850	7 079	6 506
Slovakia Slovaquie	..	..	..	..	..	..	..	..	...	1 637
Spain Espagne	1 674	1 264	1 336	1 599	1 484	2 074	1 353	1 265	925	...
Sweden[6] Suède[6]	500	431	349	296	113	...	...	...	...	...
Turkey Turquie	180	71	144	114	91	47	34	23	2	10
Ukraine Ukraine	..	..	..	..	..	..	..	3 300	2 420	1 619
United Kingdom Royaume-Uni	...	...	...	...	...	5 275	5 742	...	...	...
United States[4] Etats-Unis[4]	4 300	3 836	3 057	3 045	3 317	3 789	3 247	2 658	2 409	2 739
Yugoslavia Yougoslavie	..	..	..	..	..	..	..	...	338	...
Yugoslavia, SFR† Yougoslavie, Rfs†	2 887	3 176	2 429	2 331	2 470	2 059	...	..	..	...

C. Milling machines • Fraiseuses

Total	**68 060**	**70 803**	**66 136**	**63 044**	**64 582**	**67 053**	**62 491**	**47 583**	**47 143**	**43 940**
Algeria Algérie	92	97	162	119	92	44	267	150	103	81
Armenia Arménie	..	..	..	..	..	..	..	759	410	...
Austria Autriche	682	713	554	564	828	1 142	458	526	844	223
Bangladesh Bangladesh	...	...	...	...	134	139	144	...	...	...
Belarus Bélarus	..	..	..	..	..	..	..	150	56	13

59
Machine tools
Production: number [*cont.*]
Machines-outils
Production : nombre [*suite*]

Country or area Pays ou zone	1984	1985	1986	1987	1988	1989	1990	1991	1992	1993
Bulgaria Bulgarie	1 209	1 981	1 320	1 307	1 453	1 450	1 240	961	432	324
China Chine	11 134	...	...	...	...	...	...	...	...	...
Croatia Croatie	..	..	..	..	..	..	..	212	168	...
former Czechoslovakia† anc. Tchécoslovaquie†	2 548	2 260	2 278	2 299	2 208	1 596	1 470	1 176	..	..
Czech Republic République tchèque	..	..	..	..	..	..	..	..	1 358	...
Denmark [1] Danemark[1]	...	...	320	252	* 103	292	...	201	200	...
Finland Finlande	...	...	...	...	100	100	...	...	...	...
France [4] France[4]	1 665	1 434	1 451	966	570	...	700	496	401	7
Germany † · Allemagne† F. R. Germany[7] R. f. Allemagne[7]	...	...	...	...	...	...	12 150	..	..	..
former German D. R. anc. R. d. allemande	3 429	3 335	3 081	3 007	3 298	3 135	3 051	..	..	..
Greece Grèce	853	594	618	1 404	1 674	1 890	1 805	1 452	...	...
Hungary Hongrie	53	39	39	42	22	66	136	297	256	50
Indonesia Indonésie	...	...	...	...	...	...	21	...	...	...
Japan Japon	10 723	11 399	7 258	4 859	6 959	8 612	8 492	7 584	3 913	2 007
Korea, Republic of Corée, République de	2 261	2 428	2 994	3 740	2 802	3 062	3 775	3 994	2 509	2 824
Lithuania Lituanie	..	..	..	..	..	..	..	1 303	1 035	450
Poland Pologne	1 442	1 500	1 546	1 462	1 387	1 448	1 196	834	500	248
Portugal Portugal	107	95	79	98	148	134	...	...	...	...
Romania Roumanie	...	2 618	2 924	2 733	2 209	2 073	1 196	1 355	764	425
Russian Federation Fédération de Russie	..	..	..	..	..	..	..	4 233	4 144	3 424
Slovakia Slovaquie	..	..	..	..	..	..	..	..	...	6 852
Slovenia Slovénie	..	..	..	..	..	..	..	13	12	...
Spain Espagne	5 041	6 823	6 519	6 984	6 533	8 057	7 062	4 169	4 553	...
Sweden Suède	412	293	...	...	...	...	98	...	48	...

59
Machine tools
Production: number [cont.]
Machines-outils
Production : nombre [suite]

Country or area Pays ou zone	1984	1985	1986	1987	1988	1989	1990	1991	1992	1993
Turkey Turquie	...	...	...	211	157	52	169	403	39	85
Ukraine Ukraine	..	..	..	..	..	..	..	1 208	1 040	752
United Kingdom Royaume-Uni	1 596	...	...	...	...	...	...	...	...	...
United States[4] Etats-Unis[4]	7 981	8 308	8 133	6 277	7 717	6 872	4 787	2 772	2 581	3 386
Yugoslavia, SFR† Yougoslavie, Rfs†	1 145	1 260	1 320	1 367	1 074	921	...	..	..	..

D. Metal-working presses • Presses pour le travail des métaux

Total	**63 670**	**55 079**	**56 112**	**51 784**	**58 173**	**59 990**	**58 394**	**53 284**	**83 142**	**43 161**
Armenia Arménie	..	..	..	..	..	..	..	206	45	100
Austria Autriche	69	79	31	31	27	52	...	...	...	...
Brazil Brésil	1 384	1 824	2 136	2 312	1 499	1 415	1 182	1 853	1 194	1 763
Bulgaria Bulgarie	...	824	863	871	...	...	...	...	...	...
former Czechoslovakia† anc. Tchécoslovaquie†	1 540	1 581	1 614	1 689	1 410	1 486	1 424	920	..	..
Czech Republic République tchèque	..	..	..	..	..	..	..	106	47	
Finland Finlande	2 803	...	...	...	* 118	121	126	98	17	6
France[4] France[4]	1 166	1 082	1 015	787	1 883	781	1 300	1 235	1 385	970
Germany † Allemagne†	..	..	..	..	..	..	..	17 726	55 997	18 939
F. R. Germany R. f. Allemagne	14 153	13 289	15 804	13 620	14 372	16 460	16 643	..	..	..
former German D. R. anc. R. d. allemande	...	...	2 513	2 671	2 136	2 366	1 781	..	..	..
Greece Grèce	475	324	947	484	296	405	328	320	355	...
Japan Japon	21 351	19 023	16 185	15 395	20 449	21 574	22 571	19 173	12 458	9 516
Latvia Lettonie	..	..	..	..	..	..	..	3	...	...
Mexico Mexique	...	...	...	11	5	...	...	...	...	...
Netherlands[89] Pays-Bas[89]	187	280	328	...	...	...	...	...	...	...
Poland Pologne	67	64	49	170	66	63	50	44	13	11
Portugal Portugal	132	110	146	240	295	315	255	102	# 688	...

59
Machine tools
Production: number [*cont.*]
    Machines-outils
    Production : nombre [*suite*]

Country or area Pays ou zone	1984	1985	1986	1987	1988	1989	1990	1991	1992	1993
Slovakia Slovaquie	..	..	..	..	..	..	..	..	261	184
Slovenia Slovénie	..	..	..	..	..	..	..	119	92	...
Spain Espagne	3 332	1 647	2 239	1 846	2 483	2 035	1 600	2 152	1 687	...
Ukraine Ukraine	..	..	..	..	..	..	..	666	268	277
United Kingdom Royaume-Uni	552	...	...	...	...	...	...	...	...	...
United States[4] Etats-Unis[4]	10 814	9 137	9 439	8 134	9 593	8 959	7 285	5 912	5 822	6 326
Yugoslavia Yougoslavie	..	..	..	..	..	..	..	...	1 046	...
Yugoslavia, SFR† Yougoslavie, Rfs†	1 783	1 961	1 773	2 236	1 871	2 280	...	..	..	..

Source:
Industrial statistics database of the Statistics Division of
the United Nations Secretariat.

† For detailed descriptions of data pertaining to
former Czechoslovakia, Germany, SFR Yugoslavia and former
USSR, see Annex I - Country or area nomenclature, regional
and other groupings.

1 Sales.
2 Limited coverage.
3 1982-1984, data are confidential (drilling and boring
   machines).
4 Shipments.
5 Excluding turning lathes for clock-makers.
6 Excluding automatic lathes not numerically controlled.
7 1982-1989 data are confidential (milling machines).
8 Excluding mechanical presses.
9 Industrial sales.

Source:
Base de données pour les statistiques industrielles de la
Division de statistique du Secrétariat de l'ONU.

† Pour les descriptions en détails des données
relatives à l'ancienne Tchécoslovaquie, l'Allemagne, la Rfs
Yougoslavie et l'ancienne URSS, voir l'Annexe I -
Nomenclature des pays ou zones, groupements régionaux et
autres groupements.

1 Ventes.
2 Couverture limitée.
3 1982-1984, les données sont confidentielles (perceuses).

4 Expéditions.
5 Non compris les tours d'horloger.
6 Non compris les tours automatiques sans contrôle numérique.
7 1982-1989 les données sont confidentielles.
8 Non compris les presses à commande mécanique.
9 Ventes industrielles.

60
Lorries (trucks)
Camions
Production: number
Production : nombre

Country or area Pays ou zone	1984	1985	1986	1987	1988	1989	1990	1991	1992	1993
A. Assembled • Assemblés										
Total	**524 489**	**452 006**	**403 178**	**412 118**	**511 664**	**575 324**	**672 459**	**703 298**	**680 258**	**697 877**
Algeria[1] Algérie[1]	6 619	5 722	6 671	5 785	3 326	3 656	3 564	3 164	2 434	2 304
Bangladesh Bangladesh	...	...	551	457	809	806	504	528	...	...
Belgium[23] Belgique[23]	38 951	37 455	54 245	54 374	69 396	75 357	65 667	88 937	70 532	56 244
Chile Chili	2 556	3 528	3 016	* 4 548	6 012[4]	8 377[4]	8 028[4]	9 400[4]	14 352[4]	...
Colombia[4] Colombie[4]	11 220	5 878	8 056	8 869	13 718	13 572	12 660	8 900	10 116	...
Cuba Cuba	562	870	688	475	469	542	...	...	...	...
Denmark[5] Danemark[5]	109	237	...	...	...	...	...	...	...	...
Greece Grèce	4 685	3 081	3 152	3 459	3 322	2 897	1 715	1 534	1 920	...
Indonesia Indonésie	770	1 000	920	925	...	...	...	...	...	...
Iran, Islamic Rep. of[6] Iran, Rép. islamique d'[6]	83 576	57 025	29 481	16 744	5 477	8 086	22 198	32 672	34 547	...
Iraq Iraq	...	297	557	...	...	...	...	...	...	...
Israel Israël	2 146	1 130	1 152	971	615	1 174	1 074	...	...	...
Kenya Kenya	...	...	2 120	1 947	2 086	1 679	1 701	1 296	...	...
Malaysia[7] Malaisie[7]	26 740	35 772	* 17 318	12 594	18 999	38 607	60 798	78 926	26 867	28 129
Morocco[4] Maroc[4]	2 847	3 373	3 768	2 256	8 256	9 621	10 784	12 775	11 976	9 734
Myanmar Myanmar	567[8]	798[8]	560	480	204	229	166	117	85	172
Netherlands Pays-Bas	2 709	2 605	3 135	3 959	4 036	4 092	...	...	...	...
New Zealand[7] Nouvelle-Zélande[7]	24 997	24 185	15 964	12 873	...	...	* 13 500	* 13 500	* 10 210	...
Nigeria Nigéria	1 958	2 091	6 150	3 747	...	...	...	...	...	...
Pakistan[9] Pakistan[9]	14 601	15 255	13 851	12 666	12 326	13 756	13 324	13 911	13 270	12 687
Peru[4] Pérou[4]	2 671	3 246	5 637	8 378	4 736	3 019	2 921	2 000	2 000	...
Philippines Philippines	# 271	44	111	780	1 008	...	...	...	...	...
Portugal Portugal	7 076	9 174	14 068	23 481	55 291	61 996	...	...	...	...

60
Lorries (trucks)
Production: number [*cont.*]
Camions
Production : nombre [*suite*]

Country or area Pays ou zone	1984	1985	1986	1987	1988	1989	1990	1991	1992	1993
Slovenia Slovénie	..	..	..	..	..	..	..	611	...	...
South Africa Afrique du Sud	123 070	94 461	77 929	93 534	108 663	119 591	107 922	97 178	93 599	96 772
Thailand[4] Thaïlande[4]	81 850	58 244	53 116	68 815	97 722	155 094	236 221	206 172	* 235 000	...
Trinidad and Tobago[4] Trinité-et-Tobago[4]	3 631	3 173	...	911	1 356	381	1 124	1 711	1 698	...
Tunisia Tunisie	9 798	7 328	2 890	2 607	1 115	478	1 024	1 065	768	922
Turkey Turquie	23 217	25 025	19 935	20 966	20 048	19 045	27 014	29 967	37 195	49 827
United Kingdom Royaume-Uni	1 315	1 168	1 142	1 170	1 628	...	...	...	...	...
United Rep.Tanzania[1] Rép. Unie de Tanzanie[1]	...	481	353	333	341	470	637	479	171	40
Venezuela Venezuela	40 000	44 000	52 000	41 000	46 000	6 000	12 000	24 000	30 000	...
Yugoslavia, SFR† Yougoslavie, Rfs†	48	...	...	79	918	434	451	..	..	..
Zaire Zaïre	2 335	...	...	...	...	...	...	...	...	...

B. Produced · Fabriqués

Total	11 353 622	11 954 262	11 855 205	12 451 709	13 515 735	12 793 757	11 812 401	10 842 593	11 482 501	11 102 802
Argentina[10] Argentine[10]	15 842[11]	12 767[11]	30 267	30 963	25 494	18 368	16 869	22 388	36 999	50 805
Armenia Arménie	..	..	..	..	..	..	..	6 823	3 171	1 247
Australia[9][12] Australie[9][12]	10 747	28 947	25 912	20 462	22 303	29 557	25 958	17 666	14 550	15 459
Austria Autriche	776	487	147	416	798	557	736	5 168	4 089	3 565
Azerbaijan Azerbaïdjan	..	..	..	..	..	..	..	3 246	402	...
Belarus Bélarus	..	..	..	..	..	..	..	38 178	32 951	30 771
Brazil Brésil	161 323[13]	181 469[13]	212 860[13]	206 523[13]	244 076[13]	# 62 699[14]	51 597[14]	49 295[14]	32 025[14]	47 876[14]
Bulgaria[10] Bulgarie[10]	6 456	6 860	6 748	7 346	6 811	7 888	7 285	2 778	945	406
Canada[15] Canada[15]	807 848	855 609	784 892	825 187	1 018 317	949 200	789 932	789 600	901 000	838 000
China Chine	181 800	269 000	229 100	298 400	403 300	363 400	289 700	382 500	476 700	597 897
former Czechoslovakia† anc. Tchécoslovaquie†	42 739	44 680	47 002	47 669	45 468	46 177	49 006	26 507	..	..
Czech Republic République tchèque	..	..	..	..	..	..	..	..	14 030	8 727

60
Lorries (trucks)
Production: number [*cont.*]
Camions
Production : nombre [*suite*]

Country or area Pays ou zone	1984	1985	1986	1987	1988	1989	1990	1991	1992	1993
Egypt Egypte	3 278	3 082	3 345	2 580	1 745	1 475	1 371	1 127	1 529	1 208
Finland[10] Finlande[10]	20	# 315	360	390	771	852	910	545	578	435
France France	412 757	* 448 692	495 372	* 502 901	535 571	577 495	539 796	461 640	494 124	373 200
Germany † Allemagne† F. R. Germany	..	..	..	..	..	..	..	356 059	325 901	240 014
R. f. Allemagne former German D. R. anc. R. d. allemande	236 876 43 105	262 199 45 305	267 147 44 887	243 760 41 897	258 314 39 572	274 496 38 786	315 010 31 360	..	..	..
Hungary Hongrie	201	736	1 025	1 406	748	162	154	11	30	...
India[15] Inde[15]	75 739	85 352	76 992	105 996[11]	119 868[11]	115 200[11]	145 200[11]	146 400[11]	141 600[11]	...
Indonesia Indonésie	...	...	...	...	20	1 145	1 280	26	174	...
Italy Italie	150 550	171 245	169 985	191 096	219 805	240 807	234 393	229 860	194 616	155 476
Japan Japon	4 308 257	4 535 947	4 399 699	4 297 737	4 431 099	3 918 400	3 486 618	3 433 790	3 053 477	2 674 941
Korea, Republic of[10] Corée, République de[10]	63 117	71 217	86 385	109 427	129 956	169 703	238 520	246 522	294 550	312 110
Kyrgyzstan Kirghizistan	..	..	..	..	..	..	..	23 621	14 818	5 026
Mexico[10] Mexique[10]	94 591	132 389	115 611	112 002	145 895	184 725	199 123	238 804	269 591	216 817
Netherlands Pays-Bas	7 360	7 799	8 086	9 407	9 753	9 994	11 305	10 316	10 034	9 538
Poland[16] Pologne[16]	46 903	49 114	46 088	45 550	46 834	43 853	38 956	20 100	17 657	18 811
Romania Roumanie	16 485	20 788	14 485	12 715	16 556	13 515	8 457	7 592	4 456	4 433
Russian Federation Fédération de Russie	..	..	..	..	..	..	..	378 089	410 234	389 858
Slovakia Slovaquie	...	...	...	...	...	...	...	...	...	744
Slovenia Slovénie	..	..	..	..	..	..	..	1 513	377	...
Spain Espagne	107 828	155 744	204 999	254 250	313 200[15]	343 899[15]	302 400[15]	244 164	256 070	...
Sweden Suède	* 53 775	* 54 648	* 59 618	62 335	76 507[15]	81 670[15]	74 400[15]	75 000[15]	...	...
Ukraine Ukraine	..	..	..	..	..	..	..	25 096	33 386	23 052
former USSR†*[17] ancienne URSS†*[17]	849 600	926 000	942 000	958 000	974 000	900 000	...	..	..	
United Kingdom[16][18] Royaume-Uni[16][18]	202 965	243 792	210 994	227 389	294 633	326 590[11]	273 600[11]	222 000[11]	240 000[11]	...

60
Lorries (trucks)
Production: number [*cont.*]
Camions
Production : nombre [*suite*]

Country or area Pays ou zone	1984	1985	1986	1987	1988	1989	1990	1991	1992	1993
United States[19] Etats-Unis[19]	3 435 890	3 323 372	3 355 863	3 821 410	4 120 574	4 061 950	3 720 000	3 372 000	4 118 578	...
Yugoslavia Yougoslavie	..	..	..	..	..	..	..	...	4 169	...
Yugoslavia, SFR† Yougoslavie, Rfs†	15 778	15 772	14 483	13 723	13 747	11 194	9 989	..	..	..

Source:
Industrial statistics database of the Statistics Division of
the United Nations Secretariat.

† For detailed descriptions of data pertaining to
former Czechoslovakia, Germany, SFR Yugoslavia and former
USSR, see Annex I - Country or area nomenclature, regional
and other groupings.

1 Including buses.
2 Production by establishments employing 5 or more persons.
3 Shipments.
4 Including motor coaches and buses.
5 Sales.
6 Production by establishments employing 50 or more persons.
7 Including vans and buses.
8 Government production only.
9 Twelve months ending 30 June of year stated.

10 Including assembly.
11 Including buses and motor coaches.
12 Finished and partly finished.
13 Incomplete coverage.
14 Trucks only.
15 Excluding ordinance production.
16 Including special-purpose vehicles.
17 Excluding production for armed forces.
18 Including electrically-powered vehicles.
19 Factory sales.

Source:
Base de données pour les statistiques industrielles de la
Division de statistique du Secrétariat de l'ONU.

† Pour les descriptions en détails des données
relatives à l'ancienne Tchécoslovaquie, l'Allemagne, la Rfs
Yougoslavie et l'ancienne URSS, voir l'Annexe I -
Nomenclature des pays ou zones, groupements régionaux et
autres groupements.

1 Y compris les autobus.
2 Production des établissements occupant 5 personnes ou plus.
3 Expéditions.
4 Y compris les autocars et autobus.
5 Ventes.
6 Production des établissements occupant 50 personnes ou plus.
7 Y compris les autobus et les camionnettes.
8 Production de l'Etat seulement.
9 Période de douze mois finissant le 30 juin de l'année
   indiquée.
10 Y compris le montage.
11 Y compris les autocars et autobus.
12 Finis et semi-finis.
13 Couverture incomplète.
14 Les camions seulement.
15 Non compris la production d'artillerie.
16 Y compris véhicules à usages spéciaux.
17 Non compris production destinée aux forces armées.
18 Y compris les véhicules à propulsion électrique.
19 Ventes des fabriques.

Technical notes, tables 41-60

Industrial activity comprises mining and quarrying, manufacturing and the production of electricity, gas and water. These activities correspond to the major divisions 2, 3 and 4 respectively of the *International Standard Industrial Classification of All Economic Activities*.[46]

Many of the tables are based on data compiled for the United Nations *Industrial Commodity Statistics Yearbook*. [23] Exceptions are indicated in notes at the end of the tables.

The methods used by countries for the computation of industrial output are, as a rule, consistent with the recommendations on this subject by the United Nations and provide a satisfactory basis for comparative analysis.[45] In some cases, however, the definitions and procedures underlying computations of output differ from approved guidelines. The differences, where known, are indicated in the footnotes to each table.

A. *Food, beverages and tobacco*

Table 41 covers the production of centrifugal sugar from both beet and cane and the figures are expressed as far as possible in terms of raw sugar. However, where exact information about polarisation is lacking, data are expressed in terms of sugar "tel quel" and are footnoted accordingly. Unless otherwise stated, the data refer to calendar years.

The consumption data relate to the apparent consumption of centrifugal sugar in the country concerned, including sugar used for the manufacture of sugar-containing products whether exported or not and sugar used for purposes other than human consumption as food. Unless otherwise specified the statistics are expressed in terms of raw value (i.e. sugar polarizing at 96 degrees). However, where exact information is lacking, data are expressed in terms of sugar "tel quel" and are footnoted accordingly. The world and regional totals also include data for countries whose sugar consumption was less than 10 thousand metric tons.

Table 42 refers to meat from animals slaughtered within the national boundaries irrespective of the origin of the animals. Production figures of beef and veal (including buffalo meat), pork (including bacon and ham) and mutton and lamb (including goat meat), are in terms of carcass weight, excluding edible offals, tallow and lard. All data refer to total meat production, i.e from both commercial and farm slaughter.

Table 43 refers to beer made from malt, including ale, stout, porter.

Table 44 refers to cigarettes only.

Notes techniques, tableaux 41-60

L'activité industrielle comprend les industries extractives (mines et carrières), les industries manufacturières et la production d'électricité, de gaz et d'eau. Ces activités correspondent aux grandes divisions 2, 3 et 4, respectivement, de la *Classification internationale type par industrie de toutes les branches d'activité économique* [46].

Un grand nombre de ces tableaux sont établis sur la base de données compilées pour l'*Annuaire de statistiques industrielles par produit* des Nations Unies [23]. Les exceptions sont indiquées dans des notes au bas des tableaux.

En règle générale, les méthodes employées par les pays pour le calcul de leur production industrielle sont conformes aux recommandations des Nations Unies à ce sujet et offrent une base satisfaisante pour une analyse comparative [45]. Toutefois, dans certains cas, les définitions des méthodes sur lesquelles reposent les calculs de la production diffèrent des directives approuvées. Lorsqu'elles sont connues, les différences sont indiquées dans les notes au bas des tableaux.

A. *Alimentation, boisson et tabacs*

Le *Tableau 41* porte sur la production de sucre centrifugé à partir de la betterave et de la canne à sucre, et les chiffres sont exprimés autant que possible en sucre brut. Toutefois, en l'absence d'informations exactes sur la polarisation, les données sont exprimées en sucre tel quel, accompagnées d'une note au bas du tableau. Sauf indication contraire, les chiffres se rapportent à des années civiles.

Les données de la consommation se rapportent à la consommation apparente de sucre centrifugé dans le pays en question, y compris le sucre utilisé pour la fabrication de produits à base de sucre, exportés ou non, et le sucre utilisé à d'autres fins que pour la consommation alimentaire humaine. Sauf indication contraire, les statistiques sont exprimés en valeur brute (sucre polarisant à 96°). Toutefois, en l'absence d'informations exactes, les données sont exprimées en sucre tel quel, accompagnées d'une note au bas du tableau. Les totaux mondiaux et régionaux comprennent également les données relatives aux pays où la consommation de sucre est inférieure à 10.000 tonnes métriques.

Le *Tableau 42* indique la production de viande provenant des animaux abattus à l'intérieur des frontières nationales, quelle que soit leur origine. Les chiffres de production de viande de boeuf et de veau (y compris la viande de buffle), de porc (y compris le bacon et le jambon) et de mouton et d'agneau (y compris la viande de chèvre) se rapportent à la production en poids de carcasses et ne comprennent pas le saindoux, le suif et les abats comestibles. Toutes les données se rapportent à la production totale de viande, c'est-à-dire à la fois aux animaux abattus à des fins commerciales et des animaux sacrifiés à la ferme.

B. *Textile, wearing apparel and leather industries*
   In *table 45, Fabrics of cotton and of wool*: data refer to woollen and worsted fabrics, woven fabrics of cotton at loom stage before undergoing finishing processes such as bleaching, dyeing, printing, mercerizing, lazing, etc. Fabrics of fine hair are excluded.
   Woven fabrics of cellulosic and non-cellulosic fibres: fabrics of continuous and discontinuous rayon and acetate fibres and non-cellulosic fibres other than textile glass fibres, including pile and chenille fabrics at loom stage.
   In table 46, data refer to total production of leather footwear for children, men and women and all other footwear such as footwear with outer soles of wood or cork, sports footwear and orthopedic leather footwear. House slippers and sandals of various types are included. Rubber footwear, however, are excluded.

C. *Wood and wood products; paper and paper products*
   Table 47 refers to aggregate of sawnwood-coniferous, non-coniferous and sleepers. Data cover wood planed, unplaned, grooved, tongued and the like, sawn lengthwise or produced by a profile-chipping process, and planed wood which may also be finger-jointed, tongued or grooved, chamfered, rabbeted, V-jointed, beaded and so on. Wood flooring is excluded. Sleepers may be sawn or hewn.
   Table 48 refers to the production of all paper and paper board. Data cover newsprint, printing and writing paper, construction paper and paperboard, household and sanitary paper, special thin paper, wrapping and packaging paper and paperboard.

D. *Chemicals and related products*
   Table 49 refers to the production of rubber tires for passenger cars and commercial vehicles. Unless otherwise stated, data do not cover tires for vehicles operating off the road, motorcycles, bicycles and animal-drawn road vehicles, or the production of inner tubes.
   Table 50 refers to all hydraulic cements used for construction (portland, metallurgic, aluminous, natural, and so on).
   In *table 51*, data refer to H_2SO_4 in terms of pure monohydrate sulphuric acid, including the sulphuric acid equivalent of oleum or fuming sulphuric acid.
   In *table 52*, data on soaps refer to normal soaps of commerce, including both hard and soft soaps. Included are, in particular, household soaps, toilet soaps, transparent soaps, shaving soaps, medicated soaps, disinfectant soaps, abrasive soaps, resin and naphthenate soaps, and industrial soaps.
   Washing powders and detergents refer to organic surface—active agents, surface—active preparations and washing preparations whether or not containing soap.

   Tableau 43 : Bière produite à partir du malte, y compris ale, stout et porter (bière anglaise, blonde et brune).
   Le *Tableau 44* se rapporte seulement aux cigarettes.

B. *Textile, habillement et cuir*
   Au *tableau 45, Tissus de coton et de laine* : données se rapportent aux tissus de laine cardée ou peignée, tissus de coton, avant les operations de finition, c'est-à-dire avant d'être blanchis teints, imprimés, mercerisés, glacés, etc. A l'exclusion des tissus de poils fins.
   Tissus de fibres cellulosiques et non-cellulosiques : tissus sortant du metier à tisser de fibres de rayonne et d'acetate et tissus composés de fibres non cellulosiques, autres que les fibres de verre, continues ou discontinues; cette rubrique comprend les velours, peluches, tissus boucles et tissus chenille.
   Au *tableau 46*, les données se rapportent à la production totale de chaussures de cuir pour enfants, hommes et dames et toutes les autres chaussures telles que chaussures à semelles en bois ou en liège, chaussures pour sports et orthopediques en cuir. Chaussures en caoutchouc ne sont pas compris.

C. *Bois et produits dérivés; papier et produits dérivés*
   Les données du *Tableau 47* sont un agrégat des sciages de bois de cônifères et de non-cônifères et des traverses de chemins de fer. Elles comprennent les bois rabotés, non rabotés, rainés, languetés, etc. sciés en long ou obtenus à l'aide d'un procédé de profilage par enlèvement de copeaux et les bois rabotés qui peuvent être également à joints digitiformes languetés ou rainés, chanfreinés, à feuillures, à joints en V, à rebords, etc. Cette rubrique ne comprend pas les éléments de parquet en bois. Les traverses de chemin de fer comprennent les traverses sciées ou équaries à la hache.
   Le *Tableau 48* se rapporte à la production de tout papier et carton. Les données comprennent le papier journal, les papiers d'impression et d'écriture, les papiers et cartons de construction, les papiers de ménage et les papiers hygiéniques, les papiers minces spéciaux, les papiers d'empaquetage et d'emballage et carton.

D. *Produits chimiques et apparentés*
   Le *Tableau 49* se rapporte à la production de pneus en caoutchouc pour voitures particulières et véhicules utilitaires. Sauf indication contraire, elles ne couvrent pas les pneus pour véhicules non routiers, motocyclettes, bicyclettes et véhicules routiers à traction animale, ni la production de chambres à air.
   Le *Tableau 50* se rapporte à tous les ciments hydrauliques utilisés dans la construction (portland, métallurgique, alumineux, naturel, etc.).
   Au *tableau 51*, les données se rapportent au H_2SO_4 sur la base de l'acide sulfurique monohydraté, y compris l'équivalent en acide sulfurique de l'oléum ou acide sulfurique fumant.

E. *Basic metal industries*

Table 53 includes foundry and steel making pig-iron. Figures on crude steel include both ingots and steel for castings. In selected cases data are obtained from the United States of America Bureau of Mines (Washington, DC), Instituto Latino-Americano del Ferro y el Acero (Santiago) and the United Nations Economic Commission for Europe. Detailed references to sources of data are given in the United Nations *Industrial Commodity Statistics Yearbook*.[23]

Table 54 refers to aluminium obtained by electrolytic reduction of alumina (primary) and remelting metal waste or scrap (secondary).

F. *Non-metallic mineral products and fabricated metal products, machinery and equipment*

Table 55 refers to total production of radio and television receivers of all kinds.

In *table 56*, passenger cars include three-and four-wheeled road motor vehicles other than motor-cycle combinations intended for the transport of passengers and seating not more than nine persons (including the driver), which are manufactured wholly or mainly from domestically-produced parts and passenger cars shipped in "knocked-down" form for assembly abroad.

In *table 57*, data refer to refrigerators of the compression type or of the absorption type, of the sizes commonly used in private households. Insulated cabinets to contain an active refrigerating element (block ice) but no machine are excluded.

In *table 58*, these washing machines usually include electrically-driven paddles or rotating cylinders (for keeping the cleaning solution circulating through the fabrics) or alternative devices. Washing machines with attached wringers or cetrifugal spin driers, and centrifugal spin driers designed as independent units, are included.

Table 59, *machine-tools* presented in this table include drilling and boring machines, lathes, milling machines, and metal-working presses. Drilling and boring machines refer to metal-working machines fitted with a baseplate, stand or other device for mounting on the floor, or on a bench, wall or another machine. Lathes refer to metal-working lathes of all kinds, whether or not automatic, including slide lathes, vertical lathes, capstan and turret lathes, production (or copying) lathes. Milling machines refer to metal-working machines designed to work a plane or profile surface by means of rotating tools, known as milling cutters. Metal-working presses are mechanical, hydraulic and pneumatic presses used for forging, stamping, cutting out etc. Forge hammers are excluded. Detailed product definitions are given in the United Nations *Industrial Commodity Statistics Yearbook* [23].

Au *tableau 52*, les savons se rapportent aux produits commercialemenmt désignés sous le nom de savon, y compris les savons durs et les savons mous. Cette rubrique comprend notamment: les savons de ménage, les savons de toilette, les savons translucides, les savons à barbe, les savons médicinaux, les savons désinfectants, les savons abrasifs, les savons de résines ou de naphténates et les savons industriels.

Les poudres pour lessives et les détersifs se rapportent aux produits organiques tensio—actifs, préparations tensio—actives et préparations pour lessives contenant ou non du savon.

E. *Industries métallurgiques de base*

Les données du *tableau 53* se rapportent à la production de fonte et d'acier. Les données sur l'acier brut comprennent les lingots et l'acier pour moulage. Dans certains cas, les données proviennent du United States of America Bureau of Mines (Washington, DC), de l'Instituto Latino-Americano del Ferro y el Acero (Santiago) et de la United States Economic Commission for Europe. Pour plus de détails sur les sources de données, se reporter à *l'Annuaire des statistiques industrielles par produit* des Nations Unies [23].

Le *Tableau 54* se rapporte à la production d'aluminium obtenue par réduction électrolytique de l'alumine (production primaire) et par refusion de déchets métalliques (production secondaire).

F. *Produits minéraux non métalliques et fabrications métallurgiques, machines et équipements*

Tableau 55 : Production totale de postes récepteurs de radiodiffusion et de télévision de toutes sortes.

Tableau 56 : Les voitures de tourime comprennent les véhicules automobiles routiers à trois ou quatre roues, autres que les motocycles, destinés au transport de passagers, dont le nombre de places assises (y compris celle du conducteur) n'est pas supérieur à neuf et qui sont construits entièrement ou principalement avec des pièces fabriqués dans le pays, et les voitures destinées au transport de passagers exportées en pièces détachées pour être montées à l'étranger.

Au *tableau 57*, les données se rapportent aux appareils frigorifiques du type à compression ou à absorption de la taille des appareils communément utilisés dans les ménages. Cette rubrique ne comprend pas les glacières conçues pour contenir un élément frigorifique actif (glace en bloc) mais non un équipement frigorifique.

Au *tableau 58*, ces machines à laver comprennent généralement des pales ou des cylindres rotatifs (destinés à assurer le brassage continu du liquide et du linge) ou des dispositifs à mouvements alternés, mus électriquement. Cette rubrique comprend les machines à laver avec essoreuses à rouleau ou essoreuses centrifuges et les essoreuses centrifuges conçues comme des appareils indépendants.

In *table 60, lorries assembled from imported parts* include road motor vehicles designed for the conveyance of goods, including vehicles specially equipped for the transport of certain goods, which are assembled wholly or mainly from imported parts. Articulated vehicles (that is, units made up of a road motor vehicle and a semi-trailer) are included. Ambulances, prison vans and special purpose lorries and vans, such as fire-engines are excluded.

Lorries produced include road motor vehicles designed for the conveyance of goods, including vehicles specially equipped for the transport of certain goods, which are manufactured wholly or mainly from domestically-produced parts. Articulated vehicles (that is, units made up of a road motor vehicle and a semi-trailer) are included. Ambulances, prison vans, and special purpose lorries and vans, such as fire-engines, are excluded.

Tableau 59, machines-outils présentés dans ce tableau comprennent les perceuses, tours, fraiseuses, et presses pour le travail des métaux. Perceuses se rapportent aux machines-outils pour le travail des métaux, munies d'un socle, d'un pied ou d'un autre dispositif permettant de les fixer au sol, à un établi, à une paroi ou à une autre machine. Tours se rapportent aux tours à métaux, de tous types, automatiques ou non, y compris les tours parallèles, les tours verticaux, les tours à revolver, les tours à reproduire. Fraiseuses se rapportent aux machines-outils pour le travail des métaux conçues pour usiner une surface plane ou un profil au moyen d'outils tournants appelés fraises. Presses pour le travail des métaux se rapportent aux presses à commande mécanique, hydraulique et penumatique servant à forger, à estamper, à matricer etc. Cette rubrique ne comprend pas les outils agissant par chocs. Pour plus de détails sur les description des produits se reporter à l'*Annuaire des statistiques industrielles par produit* [23] des Nations Unies.

Au *tableau 60, camions assemblés à partir de pièces importées* comprennent les véhicules automobiles routiers conçus pour le transport des marchandises, y compris les véhicules spécialement équipés pour le transport de certaines marchandises, et qui sont montés entièrement ou principalement avec des pièces importées. Les véhicules articulés (c'est-à-dire les ensembles composés d'un véhicule automobile routier et d'une semi-remorque) sont compris dans cette rubrique. Cette rubrique ne comprend pas les ambulances, les voitures cellulaires et les camions à usages spéciaux, tels que les voitures-pompes à incendie.

Camions fabriqués comprennent les véhicules automobiles routiers conçus pour le transport des marchandises, y compris les véhicules spécialement équipés pour le transport de certaines marchandises, et qui sont montés entièrement ou principalement avec des pièces importées. Les véhicules articulés (c'est-à-dire les ensembles composés d'un véhicule automobile routier et d'une semi-remorque) sont compris dans cette rubrique. Cette rubrique ne comprend pas les ambulances, les voitures cellulaires et les camions à usages spéciaux, tels que les voitures-pompes à incendie.

61
Railways: traffic
Chemins de fer : trafic
Passenger and net ton-kilometres: millions
Voyageurs et tonnes-kilomètres : millions

Country or area Pays ou zone	1985	1986	1987	1988	1989	1990	1991	1992	1993	1994
Albania Albanie										
Passenger-kilometres										
Voyageurs-kilomètres	564	619	662	703	753	779	...	...	...	...
Net ton-kilometres										
Tonnes-kilomètres	605	622	629	626	674	584	...	...	...	...
Algeria Algérie										
Passenger-kilometres										
Voyageurs-kilomètres	2 011	2 035	1 972	2 439	2 724	2 991	3 192	...	...	...
Net ton-kilometres										
Tonnes-kilomètres	3 048	2 934	2 937	2 814	2 698	2 690	2 710	...	...	...
Angola Angola										
Passenger-kilometres										
Voyageurs-kilomètres	331	326	...	...	...	...	...	...	...	...
Net ton-kilometres										
Tonnes-kilomètres	1 615	1 720	...	...	...	...	...	...	...	...
Argentina Argentine										
Passenger-kilometres[1]										
Voyageurs-kilomètres[1]	10 743	12 459	12 475	10 271	10 533	10 512	8 045	6 749	5 836	* 6 460
Net ton-kilometres										
Tonnes-kilomètres	9 501	8 761	7 952	8 983	8 237	7 578	5 460	4 388	4 477	6 613
Armenia Arménie										
Passenger-kilometres										
Voyageurs-kilomètres	490	486	493	417	381	316	320	446	435	...
Net ton-kilometres										
Tonnes-kilomètres	5 140	4 958	5 139	4 803	5 120	4 884	4 177	1 280	451	...
Austria Autriche										
Passenger-kilometres										
Voyageurs-kilomètres	7 499	7 542	7 568	7 994	8 663	9 017	9 428	9 799	9 599	9 384
Net ton-kilometres										
Tonnes-kilomètres	12 066	11 436	11 263	11 331	11 962	12 796	12 981	12 321	11 922	13 164
Bangladesh Bangladesh										
Passenger-kilometres[2]										
Voyageurs-kilomètres[2]	6 031	6 005	6 027	5 052	4 338	5 070	4 587	5 348	...	...
Net ton-kilometres[2]										
Tonnes-kilomètres [2]	813	612	503	678	666	643	651	718	...	...
Belarus Bélarus										
Passenger-kilometres[3]										
Voyageurs-kilomètres[3]	13 731	14 199	14 965	15 989	16 525	16 852	15 795	18 017	19 500	16 063
Net ton-kilometres										
Tonnes-kilomètres	73 243	77 943	79 862	82 231	81 734	75 430	65 551	56 441	42 919	27 963
Belgium Belgique										
Passenger-kilometres										
Voyageurs-kilomètres	6 572	6 069	6 270	6 348	6 400	6 539	6 771	6 798	6 694	6 638
Net ton-kilometres										
Tonnes-kilomètres	8 254	7 423	7 266	7 694	8 049	8 354	8 153	8 074	7 568	8 084
Benin Bénin										
Passenger-kilometres										
Voyageurs-kilomètres	150	167	120	...	...	...	...	...	...	...
Net ton-kilometres										
Tonnes-kilomètres	179	186	191	...	...	...	...	...	...	...
Bolivia Bolivie										
Passenger-kilometres										
Voyageurs-kilomètres	748	657	500	369	386	388	350	334	288	276
Net ton-kilometres										
Tonnes-kilomètres	494	464	505	424	512	541	683	710	692	782
Botswana Botswana										
Net ton-kilometres										
Tonnes-kilomètres	1 297[4]	1 328[4]	1 401[4]	755[4]	964[4]	888	...	...	585	569

61

Railways: traffic
Passenger and net ton-kilometres: millions [cont.]
Chemins de fer : trafic
Voyageurs et tonnes-kilomètres : millions [suite]

Country or area Pays ou zone	1985	1986	1987	1988	1989	1990	1991	1992	1993	1994
Brazil Brésil										
Passenger-kilometres										
Voyageurs-kilomètres	16 362	15 782	15 273	13 891[5]	18 813[5]	18 202	18 859	15 667	14 038	...
Net ton-kilometres[6]										
Tonnes-kilomètres[6]	99 881	103 877	109 433	119 754	125 046	120 439	121 414	116 569	124 740	...
Bulgaria Bulgarie										
Passenger-kilometres										
Voyageurs-kilomètres	7 785	8 004	8 075	8 143	7 601	7 793	4 866	5 393	5 837	5 059
Net ton-kilometres[6]										
Tonnes-kilomètres[6]	18 172	18 327	17 842	17 585	17 034	14 132	8 685	7 758	7 702	7 774
Cameroon Cameroun										
Passenger-kilometres										
Voyageurs-kilomètres	440	433	466	495	458	442	530	445	352	...
Net ton-kilometres										
Tonnes-kilomètres	999	758	622	685	743	684	679	613	653	...
Canada Canada										
Passenger-kilometres										
Voyageurs-kilomètres	3 040	2 831	2 709	2 989	3 178	2 004	1 426	1 439	1 413	1 440
Net ton-kilometres[6]										
Tonnes-kilomètres[6]	245 284	246 722	272 122	274 571	252 075	250 117	262 425	252 454	257 805	288 864
Chile Chili										
Passenger-kilometres										
Voyageurs-kilomètres	1 522	1 274	1 176	1 013	1 058	1 077	1 125	1 010	938	816
Net ton-kilometres										
Tonnes-kilomètres	2 577	2 555	2 657	2 809	2 946	2 787	2 717	2 715	2 464	2 371
China Chine										
Passenger-kilometres[7]										
Voyageurs-kilomètres[7]	241 600	258 696	284 304	326 000	303 700	261 263	282 810	315 224	348 330	363 605
Net ton-kilometres[7]										
Tonnes-kilomètres[7]	812 600	876 504	947 196	987 740	1 039 423	1 062 238	1 097 200	1 157 555	1 195 464	1 245 750
Colombia Colombie										
Passenger-kilometres										
Voyageurs-kilomètres	228	178	171	148	152	141	79	16	...	...
Net ton-kilometres[6]										
Tonnes-kilomètres[6]	777	691	563	464	361	391	298	243	459	666
Congo Congo										
Passenger-kilometres										
Voyageurs-kilomètres	437	456	400	419	434	410	435	...	...	...
Net ton-kilometres										
Tonnes-kilomètres	518	536	449	477	467	421	397	...	...	...
Côte d'Ivoire Côte d'Ivoire										
Passenger-kilometres[8]										
Voyageurs-kilomètres[8]	1 008	1 015	* 1 021	...	...	...	...	...	...	...
Net ton-kilometres[6,8]										
Tonnes-kilomètres[6,8]	544	562	578	...	...	...	...	...	...	...
Croatia Croatie										
Passenger-kilometres										
Voyageurs-kilomètres	4 063	4 077	3 962	3 833	3 664	3 429	1 503	981	951	962
Net ton-kilometres										
Tonnes-kilomètres	8 674	8 098	7 698	7 211	7 419	6 535	3 617	1 776	1 592	1 563
Cuba Cuba										
Passenger-kilometres										
Voyageurs-kilomètres	2 257	2 200	2 189	2 627	2 891	...	...	...	...	...
Net ton-kilometres										
Tonnes-kilomètres	2 409	2 155	2 105	2 087	2 048	...	...	...	...	...
former Czechoslovakia† anc. Tchécoslovaquie†										
Passenger-kilometres										
Voyageurs-kilomètres	19 839	19 935	20 029	19 408	19 669	19 335	19 263	...	...	...

61
Railways: traffic
Passenger and net ton-kilometres: millions [*cont.*]
Chemins de fer : trafic
Voyageurs et tonnes-kilomètres : millions [*suite*]

Country or area Pays ou zone	1985	1986	1987	1988	1989	1990	1991	1992	1993	1994
Net ton-kilometres Tonnes-kilomètres	73 598	75 152	73 525	75 294	71 985	64 326	49 933	...	...	...
Czech Republic République tchèque										
Passenger-kilometres Voyageurs-kilomètres	...	...	...	...	...	...	...	11 753	8 548	8 481
Net ton-kilometres Tonnes-kilomètres	...	...	...	...	...	...	...	31 116	25 579	24 401
Denmark Danemark										
Passenger-kilometres Voyageurs-kilomètres	4 564	4 643	4 720	4 728	4 611	4 729	4 659	4 648	4 596	...
Net ton-kilometres[9] Tonnes-kilomètres[9]	1 768	1 800	1 644	1 671	1 723	1 787	1 858	1 870	1 751	...
Ecuador Equateur										
Passenger-kilometres Voyageurs-kilomètres	53	55	63	77	83	82	53	53	39	27
Net ton-kilometres Tonnes-kilomètres	9	7	8	8	6	5	2	3	3	9
Egypt Egypte										
Passenger-kilometres[10] Voyageurs-kilomètres[10]	16 853	18 485	23 796	26 064	27 083	28 684	20 950	36 644	...	...
Net ton-kilometres[10] Tonnes-kilomètres[10]	2 756	2 908	3 021	3 029	2 853	3 045	3 162	3 229	...	...
El Salvador El Salvador										
Passenger-kilometres Voyageurs-kilomètres	5	5	6	6	5	6	8	6	6	6
Net ton-kilometres Tonnes-kilomètres	25	24	39	36	22	38	35	38	35	30
Estonia Estonie										
Passenger-kilometres Voyageurs-kilomètres	1 649	1 721	1 764	1 722	1 562	1 510	1 273	950	722	537
Net ton-kilometres Tonnes-kilomètres	6 446	6 736	7 134	7 989	9 609	6 977	6 545	3 646	4 152	3 612
Ethiopia Ethiopie										
Passenger-kilometres[11 12] Voyageurs-kilomètres[11 12]	275	276	315	342	298	277	291	204	230	...
Net ton-kilometres[11 12] Tonnes-kilomètres[11 12]	144	166	150	141	129	126	122	84	...	...
Finland Finlande										
Passenger-kilometres Voyageurs-kilomètres	3 224	2 676	3 106	3 147	3 208	3 331	3 230	3 057	3 007	3 037
Net ton-kilometres[13] Tonnes-kilomètres[13]	8 066	6 951	7 402	7 815	7 958	8 357	7 634	7 848	9 259	9 949
France France										
Passenger-kilometres Voyageurs-kilomètres	62 070	59 860	59 970	63 290	64 490	63 740	62 300	62 980	58 430	58 930
Net ton-kilometres[14] Tonnes-kilomètres[14]	55 780	51 690	51 330	52 290	53 270	51 530	51 480	50 400	45 900	49 740
Georgia Géorgie										
Passenger-kilometres Voyageurs-kilomètres	3 724	3 684	3 614	3 442	2 858	2 497	2 135	1 210	1 003	...
Net ton-kilometres Tonnes-kilomètres	13 487	13 132	12 500	13 020	12 671	12 355	9 916	3 677	1 750	...
Germany † Allemagne†										
Passenger-kilometres Voyageurs-kilomètres	...	...	...	...	...	61 985	57 034	57 240	58 003	61 327
Net ton-kilometres Tonnes-kilomètres	...	...	...	...	...	103 093	82 220	72 848	66 646	71 814

61
Railways: traffic
Passenger and net ton-kilometres: millions [*cont.*]
Chemins de fer : trafic
Voyageurs et tonnes-kilomètres : millions [*suite*]

Country or area Pays ou zone	1985	1986	1987	1988	1989	1990	1991	1992	1993	1994
F. R. Germany R. f. Allemagne										
Passenger-kilometres										
Voyageurs-kilomètres	43 451	42 129	39 965	41 760	42 023	...	...	...	...	...
Net ton-kilometres										
Tonnes-kilomètres	63 873	57 916	58 947	59 922	61 981	...	...	...	...	...
former German D. R. anc. R. d. allemande										
Passenger-kilometres										
Voyageurs-kilomètres	22 451	22 402	22 563	22 775	23 588	...	...	...	...	...
Net ton-kilometres										
Tonnes-kilomètres	57 582	57 916	58 096	59 374	58 027	...	...	...	...	...
Ghana Ghana										
Passenger-kilometres										
Voyageurs-kilomètres	244	294	318	...	...	...	...	...	...	...
Net ton-kilometres										
Tonnes-kilomètres	80	101	114	...	...	...	...	...	...	...
Greece Grèce										
Passenger-kilometres										
Voyageurs-kilomètres	1 732	1 950	1 973	1 963	2 011	1 978	1 995	2 004	1 726	1 399
Net ton-kilometres[15]										
Tonnes-kilomètres[15]	733	702	599	604	657	647	606	563	523	325
Guatemala Guatemala										
Passenger-kilometres										
Voyageurs-kilomètres	27 967	19 874	15 596	9 094	10 213	15 960	12 531	...	...	...
Net ton-kilometres										
Tonnes-kilomètres	72 725	78 218	74 859	48 185	51 546	44 134	47 233	...	...	...
Hong Kong Hong-kong										
Passenger-kilometres[16]										
Voyageurs-kilomètres[16]	1 781	1 934	2 105	2 360	2 469	2 533	2 912	3 121	3 269	3 497
Net ton-kilometres										
Tonnes-kilomètres	52	69	72	70	69	70	65	61	51	47
Hungary Hongrie										
Passenger-kilometres										
Voyageurs-kilomètres	10 463	10 452	10 486	10 758	10 414	11 403[17]	9 861	9 184	8 432	8 508
Net ton-kilometres										
Tonnes-kilomètres	21 814	22 095	21 253	20 573	19 364	16 781[18]	11 938	10 015	7 708	7 707
India Inde										
Passenger-kilometres[4]										
Voyageurs-kilomètres[4]	240 614	256 535	269 389	263 731	280 848	295 644	314 564	...	...	...
Net ton-kilometres[4]										
Tonnes-kilomètres[4]	196 600	214 096	222 528	222 374	229 602	235 785	250 238	...	...	...
Indonesia Indonésie										
Passenger-kilometres										
Voyageurs-kilomètres	6 774	7 327	7 516	7 863	8 426	9 290	9 514	10 458	12 337	13 610
Net ton-kilometres										
Tonnes-kilomètres	1 333	1 465	1 759	2 359	2 921	3 190	3 470	3 779	3 955	3 843
Iran, Islamic Rep. of Iran, Rép. islamique d'										
Passenger-kilometres										
Voyageurs-kilomètres	5 585	4 638	3 674	4 661	4 752	4 573	4 585	5 298	6 422	...
Net ton-kilometres										
Tonnes-kilomètres	6 888	7 316	8 625	8 047	7 963	9 409	7 701	8 002	9 124	...
Iraq Iraq										
Passenger-kilometres										
Voyageurs-kilomètres	1 118	1 005	1 150	1 570	...	...	...	...	...	...
Net ton-kilometres[19]										
Tonnes-kilomètres[19]	1 245	1 294	1 534	2 023	...	...	...	...	...	...
Ireland Irlande										
Passenger-kilometres										
Voyageurs-kilomètres	1 023	1 075	1 191	1 181	1 226	1 223	1 243	1 222	1 111	1 102

61
Railways: traffic
Passenger and net ton-kilometres: millions [*cont.*]
Chemins de fer : trafic
Voyageurs et tonnes-kilomètres : millions [*suite*]

Country or area Pays ou zone	1985	1986	1987	1988	1989	1990	1991	1992	1993	1994
Net ton-kilometres Tonnes-kilomètres	601	574	563	545	556	582	600	633	575	569
Israel Israël										
Passenger-kilometres Voyageurs-kilomètres	209	179	173	166	151	168	178	198	214	238
Net ton-kilometres Tonnes-kilomètres	942	952	1 062	1 032	1 016	1 041	1 091	1 098	1 072	1 089
Italy Italie										
Passenger-kilometres Voyageurs-kilomètres	39 194	40 500	41 395	43 343	44 443	45 513	46 427	48 361	47 101	...
Net ton-kilometres[19] Tonnes-kilomètres[19]	18 024	17 410	18 625	19 567	20 587	21 217	21 680	21 830	20 226	...
Jamaica Jamaïque										
Passenger-kilometres Voyageurs-kilomètres[20]	25	42	29	22	24	-	-	-	-	...
Net ton-kilometres[20] Tonnes-kilomètres[20]	62	117	123	72	18	-	-	-	-	...
Japan Japon										
Passenger-kilometres Voyageurs-kilomètres	328 450	333 425	341 439	356 468	369 642	383 735	396 472	403 245	401 864	402 513
Net ton-kilometres Tonnes-kilomètres	22 099	20 917	20 307	22 911	24 767	26 656	27 292	26 899	25 619	25 946
Jordan Jordanie										
Passenger-kilometres Voyageurs-kilomètres	1	1	1	1	1	2	2	2	2	2
Net ton-kilometres Tonnes-kilomètres	692	771	720	625	610	711	791	797	711	676
Kazakstan Kazakstan										
Passenger-kilometres Voyageurs-kilomètres	15 749	16 922	17 888	18 637	18 921	19 734	19 365	19 671	20 507	17 362
Net ton-kilometres Tonnes-kilomètres	382 507	397 907	404 583	416 875	409 573	406 963	374 230	286 109	192 258	146 778
Kenya Kenya										
Passenger-kilometres Voyageurs-kilomètres	4 842	1 478	1 558	828	732	699	658	563	464	...
Net ton-kilometres Tonnes-kilomètres	1 858	1 831	1 702	1 755	1 910	1 808	1 865	1 627	1 312	...
Korea, Republic of Corée, République de										
Passenger-kilometres Voyageurs-kilomètres	22 595	23 563	24 457	25 978	27 390	29 864	33 470	34 787	33 693	31 912
Net ton-kilometres Tonnes-kilomètres	12 296	12 813	13 061	13 784	13 605	13 663	14 494	14 256	14 658	14 070
Latvia Lettonie										
Passenger-kilometres[17] Voyageurs-kilomètres[17]	5 214	5 573	5 679	5 761	5 449	5 366	3 930	3 656	2 359	1 794
Net ton-kilometres[9] Tonnes-kilomètres[9]	19 933	20 691	21 380	21 689	21 132	18 538	16 739	10 115	9 852	9 520
Lithuania Lituanie										
Passenger-kilometres Voyageurs-kilomètres	3 417	3 494	3 565	3 665	3 470	3 640	3 225	2 740	2 700	1 574
Net ton-kilometres Tonnes-kilomètres	20 927	21 076	21 205	22 595	21 749	19 258	17 748	11 337	11 030	8 849
Luxembourg Luxembourg										
Passenger-kilometres Voyageurs-kilomètres	283	278	269	277	280	261	...	...	...	...
Net ton-kilometres Tonnes-kilomètres	645	604	593	639	704	709	713	672	647	686

61
Railways: traffic
Passenger and net ton-kilometres: millions [*cont.*]
Chemins de fer : trafic
Voyageurs et tonnes-kilomètres : millions [*suite*]

Country or area Pays ou zone	1985	1986	1987	1988	1989	1990	1991	1992	1993	1994
Madagascar Madagascar										
Passenger-kilometres Voyageurs-kilometres	178	208	209	242	204	198	...	...	...	...
Net ton-kilometres[6] Tonnes-kilomètres[6]	208	188	174	174	207	209	...	...	...	...
Malawi Malawi[4]										
Passenger-kilometres[4] Voyageurs-kilomètres[4]	123	112	113	113	112	107	92	* 72	...	...
Net ton-kilometres[4] Tonnes-kilomètres[4]	99	132	95	71	70	76	56	52	49	...
Malaysia Malaisie[21]										
Passenger-kilometres[21] Voyageurs-kilomètres[21]	1 409	1 369	1 425	1 518	1 701	1 830	1 763	1 618	1 543	1 367
Net ton-kilometres[21] Tonnes-kilomètres[21]	1 018	1 042	1 119	1 326	1 361	1 405	1 262	1 081	1 157	1 464
Mali Mali										
Passenger-kilometres Voyageurs-kilomètres	173	177	196	177	184	184	...	...	...	...
Net ton-kilometres Tonnes-kilomètres	241	225	199	227	279	273	...	...	...	...
Mauritania Mauritanie										
Net ton-kilometres Tonnes-kilomètres	13 929	13 396	13 434	14 931	16 623	...	...	...	...	...
Mexico Mexique										
Passenger-kilometres Voyageurs-kilomètres	6 015	5 874	5 828	5 619	5 383	5 336	4 725	4 794	3 219	1 855
Net ton-kilometres Tonnes-kilomètres	45 306	40 608	40 475	41 177	38 570	36 408	32 986	34 229	35 901	37 468
Mongolia Mongolie										
Passenger-kilometres Voyageurs-kilomètres	436	467	486	531	579	...	...	...	...	...
Net ton-kilometres Tonnes-kilomètres	5 960	6 333	6 180	6 241	5 956	...	...	...	...	...
Morocco Maroc										
Passenger-kilometres[22] Voyageurs-kilomètres[22]	1 933	1 958	2 069	2 092	2 168	2 237	2 345	2 233	1 904	1 881
Net ton-kilometres[22] Tonnes-kilomètres[22]	4 562	4 953	4 880	5 706	4 519	5 107	4 523	5 001	4 415	4 679
Mozambique Mozambique										
Passenger-kilometres Voyageurs-kilomètres	161	183	105	75	74	...	...	...	...	...
Net ton-kilometres Tonnes-kilomètres	290	301	353	306	403	...	...	...	...	...
Myanmar Myanmar										
Passenger-kilometres Voyageurs-kilomètres	3 834	3 554	4 486	3 830	3 920	4 374	4 482	4 606	4 706	4 390
Net ton-kilometres[6] Tonnes-kilomètres[6]	600	507	545	356	458	524	579	601	663	726
Netherlands Pays-Bas										
Passenger-kilometres Voyageurs-kilomètres	9 007	8 919	9 396	9 664	10 235	11 060	15 195	14 980	14 788	14 439
Net ton-kilometres Tonnes-kilomètres	3 274	3 050	3 010	3 194	3 108	3 070	3 038	2 764	2 681	2 830
New Zealand Nouvelle-Zélande										
Net ton-kilometres Tonnes-kilomètres	3 192[23]	3 051[23]	2 912[23]	2 924[23]	2 682[23]	2 744[10]	2 364[10]	2 475[10]	2 629[10]	2 992[10]

61
Railways: traffic
Passenger and net ton-kilometres: millions [*cont.*]
Chemins de fer : trafic
Voyageurs et tonnes-kilomètres : millions [*suite*]

Country or area Pays ou zone	1985	1986	1987	1988	1989	1990	1991	1992	1993	1994
Nicaragua Nicaragua										
Passenger-kilometres										
Voyageurs-kilomètres	26	22	15	14	12	3	3	6	...	...
Net ton-kilometres *										
Tonnes-kilomètres *	4	...	...	...	...	...	...	...	...	...
Nigeria Nigéria										
Passenger-kilometres										
Voyageurs-kilomètres	2 978	2 587	2 344	1 500	973	953	517	434	555	...
Net ton-kilometres										
Tonnes-kilomètres	577	525	469	403	303	237	209	120	161	141
Norway Norvège										
Passenger-kilometres										
Voyageurs-kilomètres	2 241	2 225	2 187	2 110	2 136	2 136	2 153	2 201	2 201	2 341
Net ton-kilometres										
Tonnes-kilomètres	2 932	3 015	2 822	2 617	2 780	2 354	2 675	2 294	2 873	2 678
Pakistan Pakistan										
Passenger-kilometres[2]										
Voyageurs-kilomètres[2]	16 848	16 919	18 544	19 732	20 373	19 963	18 159	16 759	16 274	18 044
Net ton-kilometres[2]										
Tonnes-kilomètres[2]	8 272	7 819	8 033	8 364	7 226	5 704	5 964	5 860	5 940	5 666
Panama Panama										
Passenger-kilometres										
Voyageurs-kilomètres	282 978[24]	260 906[24]	232 386[24]	149 243[24]	205 585[24]	44 260[25]	62 951[25]	54 234[25]	46 440[25]	51 250[25]
Net ton-kilometres[26]										
Tonnes-kilomètres[26]	...	33 718	34 776	10 282	35 299	30 020	37 856	48 380	42 482	38 173
Paraguay Paraguay										
Passenger-kilometres										
Voyageurs-kilomètres	2	2	2	2	2	2	1	1	1	...
Net ton-kilometres										
Tonnes-kilomètres	13	17	17	18	14	4	3	3	3	...
Peru Pérou										
Passenger-kilometres[6]										
Voyageurs-kilomètres[6]	476	490	594	596	659	469	320	226	165	241
Net ton-kilometres[6]										
Tonnes-kilomètres[6]	1 049	1 022	1 148	971	929	848	825	817	844	898
Philippines Philippines										
Passenger-kilometres										
Voyageurs-kilomètres	146	173	219	230	230	264	228	121	102	...
Net ton-kilometres										
Tonnes-kilomètres	13	15	16	15	13	36	12	9	5	...
Poland Pologne										
Passenger-kilometres										
Voyageurs-kilomètres	51 978	48 526	48 285	52 134	55 888	50 373	40 115	32 571	30 865	27 610
Net ton-kilometres										
Tonnes-kilomètres	120 642	121 775	121 381	122 204	111 140	83 530	65 146	73 333	78 437	81 736
Portugal Portugal										
Passenger-kilometres										
Voyageurs-kilomètres	5 725	5 803	5 907	6 036	5 908	5 664	5 692	5 494	5 397	5 149
Net ton-kilometres										
Tonnes-kilomètres	1 306	1 448	1 615	1 708	1 719	1 588	1 784	1 767	1 786	1 826
Republic of Moldova République de Moldova										
Passenger-kilometres										
Voyageurs-kilomètres	1 648	1 685	1 766[3]	1 616	1 514	1 464	1 280	1 718[3]	1 661[3]	...
Net ton-kilometres										
Tonnes-kilomètres	16 614	16 890	15 820	15 989	15 632	15 007	11 883	7 861	4 965	...
Romania Roumanie										
Passenger-kilometres[17]										
Voyageurs-kilomètres[17]	31 082	32 304	33 520	34 643	35 456	30 582	25 429	24 269	19 402	18 313

61
Railways: traffic
Passenger and net ton-kilometres: millions [*cont.*]
Chemins de fer : trafic
Voyageurs et tonnes-kilomètres : millions [*suite*]

Country or area Pays ou zone	1985	1986	1987	1988	1989	1990	1991	1992	1993	1994
Net ton-kilometres Tonnes-kilomètres	74 215	79 092	78 070	80 607	81 131	57 253	37 853	28 170	25 170	24 704
Russian Federation Fédération de Russie										
Passenger-kilometres Voyageurs-kilomètres	246 300	257 900	264 300	272 500	270 100	274 400	255 000	253 200	272 200	227 100
Net ton-kilometres Tonnes-kilomètres	2 506 000	2 585 000	2 581 000	2 606 000	2 557 000	2 523 000	2 326 000	1 967 000	1 608 000	1 195 000
Saudi Arabia Arabie saoudite										
Passenger-kilometres Voyageurs-kilomètres	72	71	81	92	156	141	145	126	139	...
Net ton-kilometres Tonnes-kilomètres	415	321	491	470	797	351	480	453	451	...
Senegal Sénégal										
Passenger-kilometres Voyageurs-kilomètres	139	143	155	139	143	183	173	...	...	...
Net ton-kilometres Tonnes-kilomètres	468	492	524	478	535	612	485	...	...	...
South Africa Afrique du Sud										
Passenger-kilometres[23 27] Voyageurs-kilomètres[23 27]	24 009	23 032	21 413	...	138 555	120 542	103 781	89 466	71 573	...
Net ton-kilometres[23 27] Tonnes-kilomètres[23 27]	90 162	93 331	92 178	...	95 736	90 716	85 524	88 586	89 716	...
Spain Espagne										
Passenger-kilometres Voyageurs-kilomètres	17 231	17 034	16 600	16 959	15 999	16 733	16 353	17 422	16 486	16 139
Net ton-kilometres[6] Tonnes-kilomètres[6]	12 074	11 729	11 892	12 145	12 048	11 613	10 808	9 582	8 132	9 047
Sri Lanka Sri Lanka[28]										
Passenger-kilometres[28] Voyageurs-kilomètres[28]	2 111	1 972	1 881	1 859	1 734	2 781	2 698	2 613	2 822	3 265
Net ton-kilometres[28] Tonnes-kilomètres[28]	247	203	195	197	162	164	170	177	159	155
Sudan Soudan										
Passenger-kilometres Voyageurs-kilomètres	849	924	982	* 900	* 920	* 985	* 1 020	* 1 130	* 1 183	...
Net ton-kilometres Tonnes-kilomètres	1 860	1 813	1 904	* 1 900	* 1 920	* 1 970	* 2 030	* 2 120	* 2 240	...
Sweden Suède										
Passenger-kilometres Voyageurs-kilomètres	6 803	6 363	6 215	6 289	6 361	6 353	5 745	5 583	5 975	...
Net ton-kilometres Tonnes-kilomètres	18 420	18 553	18 406	18 687	19 156	19 599	18 815	18 609	17 337	...
Switzerland Suisse										
Passenger-kilometres Voyageurs-kilomètres	10 163	10 095	11 695	11 998	12 283	12 678	13 834	13 209	13 384	13 836
Net ton-kilometres Tonnes-kilomètres	7 379	7 279	7 124	7 875	8 560	8 794	8 659	8 212	7 821	8 586
Syrian Arab Republic Rép. arabe syrienne										
Passenger-kilometres Voyageurs-kilomètres	944	904	1 029	1 133	1 113	1 140	1 314	1 254	855	769
Net ton-kilometres Tonnes-kilomètres	1 251	1 418	1 508	1 569	1 350	1 265	1 238	1 699	1 097	1 190
Tajikistan Tadjikistan										
Passenger-kilometres Voyageurs-kilomètres	...	...	...	...	...	...	...	103	...	...
Net ton-kilometres Tonnes-kilomètres	...	...	...	...	...	...	...	604	...	...
Thailand Thaïlande										
Passenger-kilometres[28] Voyageurs-kilomètres[28]	9 140	9 274	9 583	10 301	10 935	11 612	12 820	14 136	14 718	14 496

61
Railways: traffic
Passenger and net ton-kilometres: millions [*cont.*]
Chemins de fer : trafic
Voyageurs et tonnes-kilomètres : millions [*suite*]

Country or area Pays ou zone	1985	1986	1987	1988	1989	1990	1991	1992	1993	1994
Net ton-kilometres[28] Tonnes-kilomètres[28]	2 718	2 583	2 729	2 867	3 065	3 291	3 365	3 075	3 059	3 072
Togo Togo										
Passenger-kilometres Voyageurs-kilomètres	102	109	117	...	...	...	...	...	...	...
Net ton-kilometres[9] Tonnes-kilomètres[9]	10	11	12	...	...	...	...	...	...	...
Tunisia Tunisie										
Passenger-kilometres[15] Voyageurs-kilomètres[15]	744	750	798	1 014	1 039	1 019	1 020	1 078	1 057	1 038
Net ton-kilometres[6 29] Tonnes-kilomètres[6 29]	1 710	1 877	1 986	2 156	2 064	1 834	1 813	2 015	2 012	2 225
Turkey Turquie										
Passenger-kilometres Voyageurs-kilomètres	6 489	6 052	6 174	6 708	6 845	6 410	6 048	6 259	7 147	6 335
Net ton-kilometres Tonnes-kilomètres	7 959	7 396	7 403	8 149	7 707	8 031	8 093	8 383	8 517	8 339
Uganda Ouganda										
Passenger-kilometres Voyageurs-kilomètres	234	195	212	118	69	108	60	...	...	...
Net ton-kilometres Tonnes-kilomètres	60	71	77	83	90	103	139	...	...	...
Ukraine Ukraine										
Passenger-kilometres Voyageurs-kilomètres	66 954	68 580	71 425	72 859	73 218	76 038	70 968	76 196	75 896	70 882
Net ton-kilometres Tonnes-kilomètres	497 916	506 123	496 001	504 689	497 333	473 953	402 290	337 761	246 356	200 422
former USSR† ancienne URSS†										
Passenger-kilometres Voyageurs-kilomètres	91	100	108	113	113	114	...	...	...	...
Net ton-kilometres Tonnes-kilomètres	1 288	1 281	1 251	1 316	1 336	1 276	...	...	...	...
United Kingdom Royaume-Uni										
Passenger-kilometres[4 30] Voyageurs-kilomètres[4 30]	30 381	31 099	33 140	34 322	33 648	33 191	32 466	31 718	30 363	28 656
Net ton-kilometres[4 30] Tonnes-kilomètres[4 30]	16 000	16 600	17 451	18 100	16 400	16 000	15 300	15 550	13 765	12 979
United Rep.Tanzania Rép. Unie de Tanzanie										
Passenger-kilometres Voyageurs-kilomètres	1 194	1 024	647	855	832	809	990	...	...	...
Net ton-kilometres Tonnes-kilomètres	660	814	789	936	990	956	983	...	...	...
United States Etats-Unis										
Passenger-kilometres[31] Voyageurs-kilomètres[31]	17 649	8 069	8 639	9 154	9 402	9 726	10 101	9 800	9 974	9 529
Net ton-kilometres[32] Tonnes-kilomètres[32]	1 280 394	1 283 736	1 388 388	1 603 853	1 632 284	1 664 690	1 672 589	1 557 180	1 619 258	1 752 903
Uruguay Uruguay										
Passenger-kilometres[33] Voyageurs-kilomètres[33]	241	196	140	-	-	-	-	-	-	...
Net ton-kilometres Tonnes-kilomètres	185	210	210	213	243	204	203	215	178	...
Venezuela Venezuela										
Passenger-kilometres Voyageurs-kilomètres	8	17	22	29	38	64	55	47	44	...
Net ton-kilometres Tonnes-kilomètres	14	12	18	40	39	35	40	36	26	...

61
Railways: traffic
Passenger and net ton-kilometres: millions [*cont.*]
Chemins de fer : trafic
Voyageurs et tonnes-kilomètres : millions [*suite*]

Country or area Pays ou zone	1985	1986	1987	1988	1989	1990	1991	1992	1993	1994
Yugoslavia Yougoslavie										
Passenger-kilometres[34]										
Voyageurs-kilomètres[34]	...	...	...	...	...	...	...	2 800	3 379	2 525
Net ton-kilometres[6][34]										
Tonnes-kilomètres[6][34]	...	...	...	...	...	...	...	4 409	1 699	1 387
Yugoslavia, SFR† Yougoslavie, Rfs†										
Passenger-kilometres										
Voyageurs-kilomètres	4 198	4 542	4 356	4 213	4 654	4 794	2 935	...	...	...
Net ton-kilometres[6]										
Tonnes-kilomètres[6]	9 638	9 259	8 738	8 395	8 707	7 744	5 760	...	...	...
Zaire Zaïre										
Passenger-kilometres										
Voyageurs-kilomètres	504	511	522	465	467	469	...	...	...	...
Net ton-kilometres										
Tonnes-kilomètres	1 599	1 624	1 681	1 670	1 687	1 655	...	...	...	...
Zambia Zambie										
Passenger-kilometres										
Voyageurs-kilomètres	488	496	510	512	596	...	...	...	...	...
Net ton-kilometres										
Tonnes-kilomètres	1 401	1 407	1 420	1 431	...	...	...	...	...	...
Zimbabwe Zimbabwe										
Net ton-kilometres[10][35]										
Tonnes-kilomètres[10][35]	6 200	6 574	5 451	5 551	5 287	5 590	5 413	5 887	4 581	4 489

Source:
Transport statistics database of the Statistics Division of
the United Nations Secretariat.

† For detailed descriptions of data pertaining to
former Czechoslovakia, Germany, SFR Yugoslavia and former
USSR, see Annex I - Country or area nomenclature, regional
and other groupings.

1 Including urban, suburban and interurban railways.

2 Twelve months beginning 1 July of year stated.

3 Including passengers carried without revenues.
4 Twelve months beginning 1 April of year stated.
5 Including urban railways traffic.

6 Including service traffic.
7 May include service traffic.
8 Abidjan-Ouagadougou line, which lies in Burkina Faso.

9 Including passengers' baggage and parcel post (Latvia: also
mail).
10 Twelve months ending 30 June of year stated.
11 Including traffic of Djibouti portion of Djibouti-Addis
Ababa line.
12 Twelve months beginning 7 July of year stated.
13 Beginning 1984, excluding local transport.
14 Including passengers' baggage.
15 Including military traffic (Greece: also government
traffic).
16 Kowloon - Canton Railway only.
17 Including military, government and railway personnel

Source:
Base de données pour les statistiques des transports de la
Division de statistique du Secrétariat de l'ONU.

† Pour les descriptions en détails des données
relatives à l'ancienne Tchécoslovaquie, l'Allemagne, la Rfs
Yougoslavie et l'ancienne URSS, voir l'Annexe I -
Nomenclature des pays ou zones, groupements régionaux et
autres groupements.

1 Y compris les chemins de fer urbains, suburbans, et
interurbans.
2 Douze mois commençant le premier juillet de l'année
indiquée.
3 Y compris passagers transportés gratuitement.
4 Douze mois commençant le premier avril de l'année indiquée.
5 Y compris les lignes situées a l'intérieur d'une
agglomération urbaine.
6 Y compris le trafic de service.
7 Le trafic de service peut être compris.
8 Ligne Abidjan-Ouagadougou dont un tronçon passe en Burkina
Faso.
9 Y compris les bagages des voyageurs et les colis postaux
(Lettonie : courrier aussi).
10 Douze mois finissant le 30 juin de l'année indiquée.
11 Y compris le trafic de la ligne Djibouti-Addis Abéba en
Djibouti.
12 Douze mois commençant le 7 juillet de l'année indiquée.
13 A compter de 1984 non compris le transport local.
14 Y compris les bagages des voyageurs.
15 Y compris le trafic militaire (Grèce: et de l'Etat aussi).

16 Chemin de fer de Kowloon - Canton seulement.
17 Y compris le militaires, les fonctionnaires et le personnel

61
Railways: traffic
Passenger and net ton-kilometres: millions [*cont.*]
Chemins de fer : trafic
Voyageurs et tonnes-kilomètres : millions [*suite*]

(Latvia: railway personnel only; Romania: military and government only).

18 Excluding suburban railways.
19 Excluding livestock.
20 Beginning 1990, railway closed.
21 Peninsular Malaysia only.
22 Principal railways.
23 Twelve months ending 31 March of year stated.
24 Panama Railway and National Railway of Chiriqui.

25 National Railway of Chiriqui only.
26 Panama Railway only.
27 Including Namibia.
28 Twelve months ending 30 September of year stated.
29 Ordinary goods only.
30 Excluding Northern Ireland.
31 Excluding commuter railroads beginning 1986.

32 Class I railways only.
33 Beginning 1988, passenger transport suspended.
34 Source: Monthly Review of Economic Statistics, 1996.
   Federal Statistics Office, Yugoslavia.
35 Including traffic in Botswana.

de chemin de fer (Lettonie : le personnel de chemins de fer seulement ; Roumanie : les militaires et les fonctionnaires seulement).

18 Non compris les lignes de banlieues.
19 Non compris le bétail.
20 A compter de 1990, les chemins de fer fermés.
21 Malasie péninsulaire seulement.
22 Chemins de fer principaux.
23 Douze mois finissant le 31 mars de l'année indiquée.
24 Chemin de fer de Panama et chemin de fer national de Chiriqui.
25 Chemin de fer national de Chiriqui seulement.
26 Chemin de fer de Panama seulement.
27 Y compris Namibie.
28 Douze mois finissant le 30 septembre de l'année indiquée.
29 Petite vitesse seulement.
30 Non compris l'Irlande du Nord.
31 A compter de 1986 non compris les chemins de fer de banlieue.
32 Réseaux de catégorie 1 seulement.
33 Transport passager interrompu à partir de 1988.
34 Source: Monthly Review of Economic Statistics, 1996.
   Federal Statistics Office, Yugoslavia.
35 Y compris le trafic en Botswana.

62
Motor vehicles in use
Véhicules automobiles en circulation
Passenger cars and commercial vehicles: thousand units
Voitures de tourisme et véhicules utilitaires : milliers de véhicules

Country or area Pays or zone	1985	1986	1987	1988	1989	1990	1991	1992	1993	1994
World Monde										
Passenger cars[1]										
Voitures de tourisme[1]	373 667.2	393 351.7	395 129.4	409 513.3	422 240.4	441 957.6	451 927.6	445 741.8	458 488.7	...
Commercial vehicles[1]										
Véhicules utilitaires[1]	115 164.7	120 859.7	124 036.9	129 537.2	133 831.3	137 869.4	141 929.8	139 575.4	146 501.2	...
Afghanistan Afghanistan										
Passenger cars[1]										
Voitures de tourisme[1]	32.0	31.1	31.0	31.0	31.0	31.0	31.0	31.0	31.0	...
Commercial vehicles[1]										
Véhicules utilitaires[1]	25.5	24.8	24.8	25.0	25.0	25.0	25.0	25.0	25.0	
Albania Albanie										
Commercial vehicles										
Véhicules utilitaires	2.5	2.5	2.5	2.8	2.8	* 2.8	...	...	...	
Algeria Algérie										
Passenger cars										
Voitures de tourisme	611.0	639.0	667.0	725.0[1]	725.0[1]	725.0[1]	725.0[1]	725.0[1]	725.0[1]	
Commercial vehicles										
Véhicules utilitaires	300.0	317.0	324.0	480.0[1]	480.0[1]	480.0[1]	480.0[1]	480.0[1]	480.0[1]	...
American Samoa Samoa américaines										
Passenger cars										
Voitures de tourisme	3.6	3.7	3.8	3.9	4.2	4.3	4.2	5.0	4.6	4.6
Commercial vehicles										
Véhicules utilitaires	0.4	0.4	0.3	0.5	0.3	0.4	0.3	0.3	0.5	0.4
Angola Angola										
Passenger cars[1]										
Voitures de tourisme[1]	125.9	122.4	122.0	122.0	122.0	122.0	122.0	122.0	122.0	...
Commercial vehicles[1]										
Véhicules utilitaires[1]	42.3	41.5	41.0	41.0	41.0	41.0	41.0	42.2	42.9	...
Antigua and Barbuda Antigua-et-Barbuda										
Passenger cars										
Voitures de tourisme	11.0	12.4	14.2	15.4	17.1	18.1	19.2	13.5	14.8	15.1
Commercial vehicles										
Véhicules utilitaires	2.0	2.4	2.7	3.3	3.9	4.3	3.8	3.5	4.6	4.8
Argentina Argentine										
Passenger cars										
Voitures de tourisme	3 878.2	4 037.9	4 137.2	4 079.8	4 235.1	4 283.7	4 405.0	4 809.0	4 856.0	4 427.0
Commercial vehicles										
Véhicules utilitaires	1 432.0	1 459.2	1 483.5	1 470.6	1 483.8	1 500.8	1 554.0	1 648.0	1 664.0	1 239.0
Australia Australie										
Passenger cars[2]										
Voitures de tourisme[2]	6 842.5	6 985.4	7 072.8	7 243.6	7 442.2	7 672.2	7 734.1	7 913.2	8 050.0	8 209.0
Commercial vehicles[2]										
Véhicules utilitaires[2]	1 838.2	1 881.1	1 949.9	1 977.6	2 047.3	2 104.3	1 915.4	2 041.3	2 043.0	2 151.0
Austria Autriche										
Passenger cars[3]										
Voitures de tourisme[3]	2 530.8	2 609.4	2 684.8	2 784.8	2 902.9	2 991.3	3 100.0	3 244.9	3 367.6	3 479.6
Commercial vehicles[3 4]										
Véhicules utilitaires[3 4]	580.2	591.6	605.8	624.9	643.1	648.3	657.6	674.6	685.7	698.2
Bahamas Bahamas										
Passenger cars										
Voitures de tourisme	54.1	54.5	59.3	69.0[1]	69.0[1]	69.0[1]	69.0[1]	44.7[1]	46.1[1]	...
Commercial vehicles										
Véhicules utilitaires	8.5	9.5	12.6	14.0[1]	14.0[1]	14.0[1]	14.0[1]	11.5[1]	11.9[1]	...
Bahrain Bahreïn										
Passenger cars										
Voitures de tourisme	79.4	82.8	84.9	90.3	94.9	98.6	102.5	108.0	117.8	125.5
Commercial vehicles										
Véhicules utilitaires	21.8	22.3	23.0	21.3	22.7	24.2	28.3	25.0	28.2	29.4

62
Motor vehicles in use
Passenger cars and commercial vehicles: thousand units [cont.]
Véhicules automobiles en circulation
Voitures de tourisme et véhicules utilitaires : milliers de véhicules [suite]

Country or area Pays or zone	1985	1986	1987	1988	1989	1990	1991	1992	1993	1994
Bangladesh Bangladesh										
Passenger cars										
Voitures de tourisme	29.4	30.9	32.4	34.2	37.8	42.1	44.2	45.6	46.6	...
Commercial vehicles										
Véhicules utilitaires	42.4	44.2	45.9	47.7	49.5	51.9	54.9	57.4	59.5	...
Barbados Barbade										
Passenger cars[3]										
Voitures de tourisme[3]	32.8	34.8	37.0	38.7	43.1	41.9	42.5	41.0	45.5	42.6
Commercial vehicles[3,5]										
Véhicules utilitaires[3,5]	4.8	4.7	5.1	4.3	4.8	6.8	8.6	6.6	6.6	6.8
Belgium Belgique										
Passenger cars										
Voitures de tourisme	3 300.5	3 336.2	3 453.1	3 567.4	3 688.1	3 814.6	3 934.0	3 991.6	4 079.5	4 208.1
Commercial vehicles										
Véhicules utilitaires	318.9	326.9	344.1	358.7	377.7	396.0	414.3	420.0	427.7	444.4
Belize Belize										
Passenger cars[6]										
Voitures de tourisme[6]	...	...	...	...	...	2.6	2.8	2.5	2.2	1.3
Commercial vehicles[6]										
Véhicules utilitaires[6]	...	...	...	...	...	1.0	1.2	1.0	0.8	0.7
Benin Bénin										
Passenger cars										
Voitures de tourisme	25.0	25.0	26.0	22.0[1]	22.0[1]	22.0[1]	22.0[1]	22.0[1]	22.0[1]	...
Commercial vehicles										
Véhicules utilitaires	12.0	12.0	13.0	12.0[1]	12.0[1]	12.0[1]	12.0[1]	12.2[1]	12.3[1]	...
Bermuda Bermudes										
Passenger cars										
Voitures de tourisme	17.8	17.7	18.2	18.9	19.5	19.7	20.1	19.7	20.1	20.7
Commercial vehicles										
Véhicules utilitaires	3.2	3.2	3.3	3.4	3.6	3.8	3.6	3.9	4.0	4.0
Bolivia Bolivie										
Passenger cars[1]										
Voitures de tourisme[1]	33.2	33.0	74.7	75.0	250.0	261.1	261.0	261.0	261.0	...
Commercial vehicles[1]										
Véhicules utilitaires[1]	46.9	46.6	135.8	136.0	54.0	55.9	58.0	63.0	66.3	...
Botswana Botswana										
Passenger cars										
Voitures de tourisme	14.7	17.0	17.5	18.2	19.5	22.7	21.5	23.8	26.8	27.6
Commercial vehicles										
Véhicules utilitaires	37.0	38.6	40.2	46.1	50.5	58.5	63.0	66.7	74.2	81.9
Brazil Brésil										
Passenger cars										
Voitures de tourisme	9 527.3	* 9 885.2	* 10 035.5	* 10 274.4	10 475.3	10 597.5	12 128.0[1]	7 855.5[1]	8 098.4[1]	...
Commercial vehicles										
Véhicules utilitaires	2 410.0	* 2 350.0	* 2 373.6	* 2 417.8	2 451.6	2 472.5	1 075.0[1]	1 170.8[1]	1 839.0[1]	...
British Virgin Islands Iles Vierges britanniques										
Passenger cars[7]										
Voitures de tourisme[7]	3.6	4.0	4.3	4.8	5.5	6.2	6.5	6.9	6.7	7.0
Brunei Darussalam Brunéi Darussalam										
Passenger cars										
Voitures de tourisme	78.6	83.4	87.8	92.1	98.8	106.6	114.1	122.0	134.0	...
Commercial vehicles										
Véhicules utilitaires	9.7	10.0	10.2	10.4	10.8	11.4	11.9	13.7	14.5	...
Bulgaria Bulgarie										
Passenger cars										
Voitures de tourisme	1 064.0	1 117.7	1 173.6	1 220.8	1 270.0	1 317.4	1 359.0	1 411.3	1 505.5	1 587.9
Commercial vehicles										
Véhicules utilitaires	...	...	...	...	187.3	195.4	209.8	224.5	243.2	255.4

62
Motor vehicles in use
Passenger cars and commercial vehicles: thousand units [cont.]
Véhicules automobiles en circulation
Voitures de tourisme et véhicules utilitaires : milliers de véhicules [suite]

Country or area Pays or zone	1985	1986	1987	1988	1989	1990	1991	1992	1993	1994
Burkina Faso Burkina Faso										
Passenger cars										
Voitures de tourisme	22.3	...	...	...	19.9	22.4	25.0	27.4	29.9	32.0
Commercial vehicles										
Véhicules utilitaires	22.4	24.0	25.0	25.5	17.8	19.3	21.0	22.2	23.4	24.0
Burundi Burundi										
Passenger cars										
Voitures de tourisme	9.2	11.1	12.2	13.0	13.9	15.0	16.4	17.5	18.5	17.5
Commercial vehicles										
Véhicules utilitaires	5.6	7.5	8.4	9.0	9.7	10.4	11.3	11.8	12.3	10.2
Cameroon Cameroun										
Passenger cars										
Voitures de tourisme	77.1	80.8	78.3	73.7	68.7	63.4	57.2	90.0[1]	90.0[1]	...
Commercial vehicles										
Véhicules utilitaires	43.5	44.9	43.9	41.0	37.7	34.3	30.9	79.0[1]	79.0[1]	...
Canada Canada										
Passenger cars[3]										
Voitures de tourisme[3]	11 118.1	11 477.0	11 772.5	12 086.0	12 811.3	12 622.0	13 061.1	13 322.5	13 477.9	13 639.4
Commercial vehicles[3]										
Véhicules utilitaires[3]	3 148.5	3 212.0	3 567.8	3 765.9	3 458.4	3 931.3	3 679.8	3 688.0	3 712.4	3 764.9
Cape Verde Cap-Vert										
Passenger cars										
Voitures de tourisme	2.0	2.0	2.0	...	...	10.0[8]	10.0[8]	10.0[8]	...	...
Commercial vehicles										
Véhicules utilitaires	1.0	1.0	1.0	...	...	4.5[8]	5.0[8]	5.0[8]	...	...
Cayman Islands Iles Caïmanes										
Passenger cars										
Voitures de tourisme	7.9	8.0	9.8	9.1	9.7	10.7	10.8	11.3	11.6	12.3
Commercial vehicles										
Véhicules utilitaires	1.6	1.7	2.1	1.9	2.1	2.4	2.6	2.6	2.7	2.8
Central African Rep. Rép. centrafricaine										
Passenger cars										
Voitures de tourisme	19.1	15.1	12.1	12.4	11.1	12.2	9.2	8.0	10.4	11.9
Commercial vehicles										
Véhicules utilitaires	5.6	4.7	4.2	4.1	3.2	3.0	2.3	1.7	2.4	2.8
Chad Tchad										
Passenger cars										
Voitures de tourisme	11.0	11.0	11.0	...	...	8.5[8]	8.5[8]	9.0[8]	...	...
Commercial vehicles										
Véhicules utilitaires	3.0	3.0	3.0	...	...	6.5[8]	6.5[8]	7.0[8]	...	...
Chile Chili										
Passenger cars										
Voitures de tourisme	624.9	590.7	618.5	669.1	661.3	710.4	765.5	826.8	896.5	914.0
Commercial vehicles[9]										
Véhicules utilitaires[9]	257.9	242.1	267.9	297.0	169.6[10]	178.2[10]	192.0[10]	198.8[10]	211.0[10]	208.3[10]
Colombia Colombie										
Passenger cars[11]										
Voitures de tourisme[11]	805.5	842.0	...	645.0[1]	715.3[1]	715.0[1]	715.0[1]	715.0[1]	761.7[1]	...
Commercial vehicles[11]										
Véhicules utilitaires[11]	390.9	400.6	...	617.0[1]	665.3[1]	665.0[1]	665.0[1]	665.0[1]	672.6[1]	...
Comoros Comores										
Passenger cars										
Voitures de tourisme	1.0	1.0	1.0	...	...	...	...	...	...	...
Commercial vehicles										
Véhicules utilitaires	4.0	4.0	4.0	...	...	...	...	...	...	...
Congo Congo										
Passenger cars[1]										
Voitures de tourisme[1]	25.8	26.1	26.0	26.0	26.0	26.0	26.0	26.0	26.0	...

62
Motor vehicles in use
Passenger cars and commercial vehicles: thousand units [*cont.*]
Véhicules automobiles en circulation
Voitures de tourisme et véhicules utilitaires : milliers de véhicules [*suite*]

Country or area Pays or zone	1985	1986	1987	1988	1989	1990	1991	1992	1993	1994
Commercial vehicles[1] Véhicules utilitaires[1]	19.6	20.0	20.0	20.0	20.0	20.0	20.0	20.1	20.1	...
Costa Rica Costa Rica										
Passenger cars[3] Voitures de tourisme[3]	111.5	119.1	127.2	135.0	143.9	168.8	180.8	204.2	220.1	238.5
Commercial vehicles[3] Véhicules utilitaires[3]	69.5	76.3	84.2	89.6	94.6	95.1	96.3	110.3	114.9	127.1
Côte d'Ivoire Côte d'Ivoire										
Passenger cars Voitures de tourisme	176.0	178.0	178.0	168.0[1]	155.0[1]	155.0[1]	155.0[1]	155.3[1]	155.3[1]	...
Commercial vehicles Véhicules utilitaires	99.0	90.0	90.0	91.0[1]	90.0[1]	90.0[1]	90.0[1]	90.3[1]	90.3[1]	...
Croatia Croatie										
Passenger cars Voitures de tourisme	652.7	693.2	716.3	756.1	796.2	795.4	735.7	669.8	646.2	698.4
Commercial vehicles Véhicules utilitaires	77.3	82.6	82.9	68.1	69.4	68.0	58.4	53.6	55.0	68.5
Cuba Cuba										
Passenger cars Voitures de tourisme	206.3	217.2	229.5	241.3	...	...	...	...	...	...
Commercial vehicles Véhicules utilitaires	172.8	184.2	194.9	208.4	...	...	...	...	...	...
Cyprus Chypre										
Passenger cars[3] Voitures de tourisme[3]	125.7	131.6	142.6	152.7	165.4	178.2	189.7	197.8	203.2	210.0[12]
Commercial vehicles[3] Véhicules utilitaires[3]	47.3	50.7	56.5	61.8	68.8	76.6	84.3	89.2	92.6	97.1
former Czechoslovakia† anc. Tchécoslovaquie†										
Passenger cars Voitures de tourisme	2 726.3	2 812.4	2 904.0	3 000.0	3 122.3	3 242.3	3 341.8	...	...	...
Commercial vehicles Véhicules utilitaires	388.2	400.8	413.0	423.0	446.7	461.6	474.7	...	...	...
Czech Republic République tchèque										
Passenger cars Voitures de tourisme	...	...	...	...	...	...	...	2 522.8	2 693.9	2 917.3
Commercial vehicles Véhicules utilitaires	...	...	...	...	...	...	...	336.2	330.0	336.2
Denmark Danemark										
Passenger cars[3][13] Voitures de tourisme[3][13]	1 513.3	1 571.1	1 601.6	1 610.3	1 611.7	1 603.8	1 607.0	1 617.5	1 630.3	1 622.3
Commercial vehicles[3][13] Véhicules utilitaires[3][13]	270.3	286.2	298.0	305.0	306.5	305.9	312.7	319.9	329.4	339.7
Djibouti Djibouti										
Passenger cars Voitures de tourisme	6.0	7.0	7.0	...	...	13.0[8]	13.0[8]	13.0[8]	...	...
Commercial vehicles Véhicules utilitaires	1.0	1.0	1.0	...	...	2.0[8]	2.5[8]	3.0[8]	...	...
Dominica Dominique										
Passenger cars Voitures de tourisme	1.0	1.3	1.8	2.0	2.2	3.0	3.0	2.6	2.5	2.8
Commercial vehicles Véhicules utilitaires	1.0	1.2	1.8	2.0	2.5	3.1	3.4	2.8	2.7	2.8
Dominican Republic Rép. dominicaine										
Passenger cars Voitures de tourisme	100.0[14]	132.9[14]	151.7[14]	...	129.7[14]	148.0	144.7	138.2	174.4	...
Commercial vehicles Véhicules utilitaires	57.2	76.6	84.2	...	87.5	89.9	94.3	93.5	111.4	...

62
Motor vehicles in use
Passenger cars and commercial vehicles: thousand units [cont.]
Véhicules automobiles en circulation
Voitures de tourisme et véhicules utilitaires : milliers de véhicules [suite]

Country or area Pays or zone	1985	1986	1987	1988	1989	1990	1991	1992	1993	1994
Ecuador Equateur										
Passenger cars										
Voitures de tourisme	121.3	136.5	140.7	146.5	176.2	165.6	181.2	194.5	202.4	219.8
Commercial vehicles										
Véhicules utilitaires	176.0	185.1	188.5	190.2	221.6	207.3	206.0	232.7	231.4	243.4
Egypt Egypte										
Passenger cars										
Voitures de tourisme	900.0	933.0	965.0	980.0	1 019.0	1 054.0	1 081.0	1 117.0	1 143.0	1 225.0
Commercial vehicles										
Véhicules utilitaires	293.0	315.0	332.0	350.0	353.0	380.0	389.0	408.0	422.0	445.0
El Salvador El Salvador										
Passenger cars[1]										
Voitures de tourisme[1]	52.9	52.1	52.0	52.0	52.0	52.0	53.0	20.9	21.6	...
Commercial vehicles[1]										
Véhicules utilitaires[1]	64.8	64.0	65.0	65.0	65.0	65.0	65.0	32.1	33.1	...
Estonia Estonie										
Passenger cars										
Voitures de tourisme	173.0	182.0	194.0	206.0	222.0	242.0	261.1	283.5	317.4	337.8
Ethiopia Ethiopie										
Passenger cars[15]										
Voitures de tourisme[15]	41.1	41.2	48.3	43.5	42.8	38.5	40.2	40.0[1]	40.0[1]	...
Commercial vehicles[15]										
Véhicules utilitaires[15]	18.2	18.7	10.9	21.8	21.6	20.3	20.2	18.8[1]	20.3[1]	...
Fiji Fidji										
Passenger cars[16]										
Voitures de tourisme[16]	32.4	33.6	34.4	34.9	37.5	40.2	42.0	44.0	45.3	47.7
Commercial vehicles[17]										
Véhicules utilitaires[17]	25.6	26.7	27.3	27.9	29.1	30.9	32.7	34.5	35.3	36.8
Finland Finlande										
Passenger cars										
Voitures de tourisme	1 546.1	1 619.8	1 698.7	1 795.9	1 908.9	1 939.9	1 922.5	1 936.3	1 872.9	1 872.6
Commercial vehicles										
Véhicules utilitaires	188.7	196.6	207.4	222.9	254.0	273.5	273.4	271.2	261.4	257.5
France France										
Passenger cars										
Voitures de tourisme	21 090.0	21 500.0	21 970.0	22 520.0	23 010.0	23 550.0	23 810.0	24 020.0	24 385.0	24 900.0
Commercial vehicles										
Véhicules utilitaires	3 209.0	3 298.0	3 419.0	3 547.0	3 674.0	3 810.0	3 922.0	4 099.0	4 036.0	4 027.0
French Guiana Guyane française										
Passenger cars[1]										
Voitures de tourisme[1]	22.4	23.4	24.0	24.0	24.0	25.0	27.0	27.7	29.1	...
Commercial vehicles[1]										
Véhicules utilitaires[1]	6.7	6.9	7.0	7.0	8.0	9.0	10.0	10.4	10.6	...
Gabon Gabon										
Passenger cars										
Voitures de tourisme	16.0	16.0	17.0	...	...	22.0[8]	23.0[8]	23.0[8]	...	...
Commercial vehicles										
Véhicules utilitaires	11.0	11.0	11.0	...	...	16.0[8]	17.0[8]	17.0[8]	...	...
Gambia Gambie										
Passenger cars										
Voitures de tourisme	4.2	3.8	3.9	4.5	5.3	6.5[8]	6.0[8]	7.0[8]	...	...
Commercial vehicles										
Véhicules utilitaires	1.6	1.4	1.4	1.5	2.0	1.5[8]	2.5[8]	3.0[8]	...	...
Georgia Géorgie										
Passenger cars										
Voitures de tourisme	...	...	425.7	440.8	448.7	481.9	479.0	479.0	468.8	...
Commercial vehicles										
Véhicules utilitaires	...	...	74.8	75.7	75.9	86.3	94.0	66.7	56.0	...

62
Motor vehicles in use
Passenger cars and commercial vehicles: thousand units [cont.]
Véhicules automobiles en circulation
Voitures de tourisme et véhicules utilitaires : milliers de véhicules [suite]

Country or area Pays or zone	1985	1986	1987	1988	1989	1990	1991	1992	1993	1994
Germany † Allemagne†										
Passenger cars										
Voitures de tourisme	...	...	...	...	...	...	...	...	...	39 765.4
Commercial vehicles										
Véhicules utilitaires	...	...	...	...	...	...	...	...	...	3 150.7
F. R. Germany R. f. Allemagne										
Passenger cars										
Voitures de tourisme	25 844.5	26 917.4	27 908.2	28 878.2	29 755.4	30 684.8	31 321.7	32 007.0	32 652.0	...
Commercial vehicles										
Véhicules utilitaires	1 629.0	1 664.3	1 704.4	1 753.0	1 811.9	1 895.4	1 985.8	2 134.6	2 826.0	...
former German D. R. anc. R. d. allemande										
Passenger cars										
Voitures de tourisme	3 306.2	3 462.2	3 600.4	* 3 743.6	* 3 898.9	4 817.0	* 6 300.0	* 7 000.0	* 6 500.0	...
Commercial vehicles[4]										
Véhicules utilitaires[4]	656.8	668.5	685.3	* 706.0	* 732.3	774.8	* 1 000.0	* 700.0	* 500.0	...
Ghana Ghana										
Passenger cars[1]										
Voitures de tourisme[1]	59.1	58.3	58.0	58.0	66.0	82.2	90.0	90.0	90.0	...
Commercial vehicles[1]										
Véhicules utilitaires[1]	45.5	45.7	46.0	46.0	40.0	42.1	43.0	44.2	44.7	...
Gibraltar Gibraltar										
Passenger cars										
Voitures de tourisme	10.6	13.0	13.1	15.5	17.7	19.8	18.1	24.0	18.0	18.5
Commercial vehicles										
Véhicules utilitaires	1.0	1.0	1.6	2.0	2.3	2.5	2.6	2.9	1.1	1.2
Greece Grèce										
Passenger cars										
Voitures de tourisme	1 263.4	1 359.2	1 428.5	1 503.9	1 605.1	1 735.5	1 777.5	1 829.1	1 958.5	2 074.1
Commercial vehicles										
Véhicules utilitaires	619.2	645.7	663.8	697.1	732.2	784.2	811.2	8 205.0	848.9	849.1
Greenland Groënland										
Passenger cars[3]										
Voitures de tourisme[3]	1.7	2.1	2.0	2.1	2.0	2.0	1.9	2.0	2.1	1.9
Commercial vehicles[3]										
Véhicules utilitaires[3]	1.4	1.3	1.6	1.5	1.6	1.2	1.5	1.5	1.4	1.6
Guadeloupe Guadeloupe										
Passenger cars										
Voitures de tourisme	89.4	71.3[1]	79.0[1]	79.0[1]	83.0[1]	86.0[1]	89.0[1]	94.7[1]	101.6[1]	...
Commercial vehicles										
Véhicules utilitaires	28.3	28.1[1]	31.0[1]	31.0[1]	33.0[1]	34.0[1]	35.0[1]	36.0[1]	37.5[1]	...
Guam Guam										
Passenger cars										
Voitures de tourisme	60.6	54.9	55.9	56.2	62.0	...	72.8	76.7	74.7	...
Commercial vehicles										
Véhicules utilitaires	16.4	15.1	19.5	16.7	22.8	...	29.7	30.2	30.6	...
Guatemala Guatemala										
Passenger cars[1]										
Voitures de tourisme[1]	96.7	95.1	95.0	95.0	95.0	95.0	95.0	98.7	102.0	...
Commercial vehicles[1]										
Véhicules utilitaires[1]	93.7	92.7	93.0	93.0	93.0	93.0	93.0	95.0	96.8	...
Guinea Guinée										
Passenger cars										
Voitures de tourisme	11.0	11.0	11.0	50.1	57.7	60.9	65.6	23.1[8]	...	...
Commercial vehicles										
Véhicules utilitaires	11.0	12.0	12.0	24.6	25.9	27.8	29.0	13.0[8]	...	...
Guinea-Bissau Guinée-Bissau										
Passenger cars										
Voitures de tourisme	4.0	4.0	4.0	...	...	3.3[8]	3.3[8]	3.5[8]	...	...

62
Motor vehicles in use
Passenger cars and commercial vehicles: thousand units [*cont.*]
Véhicules automobiles en circulation
Voitures de tourisme et véhicules utilitaires : milliers de véhicules [*suite*]

Country or area Pays or zone	1985	1986	1987	1988	1989	1990	1991	1992	1993	1994
Commercial vehicles Véhicules utilitaires	3.0	3.0	3.0	...	...	2.4[8]	2.4[8]	2.5[8]	...	...
Guyana Guyana										
Passenger cars[1] Voitures de tourisme[1]	29.4	28.9	20.3	22.0	24.0	24.0	24.0	24.0	24.0	...
Commercial vehicles[1] Véhicules utilitaires[1]	11.7	11.7	8.5	9.0	9.0	9.0	9.0	9.0	9.0	...
Haiti Haïti										
Passenger cars Voitures de tourisme	26.1	19.5	19.7	20.6	27.7	* 25.8	32.0[1]	32.0[1]	32.0[1]	...
Commercial vehicles Véhicules utilitaires	10.7	13.0	22.6	22.8	22.8	* 9.6	21.0[1]	21.0[1]	21.0[1]	...
Honduras Honduras										
Passenger cars Voitures de tourisme	34.2[3]	26.8[1]	27.0[1]	27.0[1]	27.0[1]	38.6	43.7	68.5	...	...
Commercial vehicles Véhicules utilitaires	...	50.2[1]	51.0[1]	52.0[1]	52.0[1]	80.4	92.9	102.0	...	...
Hong Kong Hong-kong										
Passenger cars Voitures de tourisme	160.9	155.6	162.3	177.4	197.2	214.9	229.3	254.6	277.5	297.3
Commercial vehicles Véhicules utilitaires	81.4	91.7	107.3	118.4	126.1	131.8	132.4	134.4	135.6	137.0
Hungary Hongrie										
Passenger cars Voitures de tourisme	1 435.9	1 538.9	1 660.3	1 789.6	1 732.4	1 944.6	2 015.5	2 058.3	2 091.6	2 176.9
Commercial vehicles Véhicules utilitaires	223.4	238.3	254.2	259.6	267.8	288.5	289.6	259.3	266.8	297.1
Iceland Islande										
Passenger cars Voitures de tourisme	103.0	112.3	120.1	125.2	124.3	119.7	120.9	120.1	116.2	116.2
Commercial vehicles Véhicules utilitaires	14.2	13.1	12.9	13.2	13.5	14.5	16.0	6.0	15.6	15.6
India Inde										
Passenger cars Voitures de tourisme	1 606.5	1 780.0	2 006.9	2 295.3	2 486.3	2 694.0[18]	2 954.0[18]	3 205.0[18]	3 330.0[18]	...
Commercial vehicles[19] Véhicules utilitaires[19]	2 113.3	2 101.8	2 543.5	2 855.2	3 073.0	3 425.2	3 740.6	2 396.7[1]	...	...
Indonesia Indonésie										
Passenger cars Voitures de tourisme	990.7[9]	1 064.0[9]	1 170.1[9]	1 073.1[9]	1 182.2[9]	1 313.2	1 494.6	1 590.8	1 700.5	1 890.3
Commercial vehicles Véhicules utilitaires	1 072.6	1 138.9	1 257.1	1 278.3	1 387.3	1 492.8	1 592.7	1 666.0	1 729.0	1 903.6
Iran, Islamic Rep. of Iran, Rép. islamique d'										
Passenger cars[11][20] Voitures de tourisme[11][20]	1 851.0	1 919.0	1 958.0	1 981.0	2 000.0	1 557.0[1]	1 557.0[1]	1 557.0[1]	1 557.0[1]	...
Commercial vehicles[11][20] Véhicules utilitaires[11][20]	760.0	819.0	853.0	862.0	870.0	533.0[1]	561.0[1]	584.1[1]	588.9[1]	...
Iraq Iraq										
Passenger cars[21] Voitures de tourisme[21]	447.5	491.8	551.4	630.3	671.7	732.7	660.1	670.2	672.4	...
Commercial vehicles[21] Véhicules utilitaires[21]	236.6	246.7	256.1	260.1	272.6	288.2	295.0	299.5	309.3	...
Ireland Irlande										
Passenger cars[22][23] Voitures de tourisme[22][23]	715.3[24]	717.2[24]	742.8[24]	755.7[24]	779.8[24]	802.7[24]	843.2	865.4	898.3	947.2
Commercial vehicles[25] Véhicules utilitaires[25]	98.7	106.9	116.6	124.4	135.9	149.5	155.2	152.0	142.9	143.9

62
Motor vehicles in use
Passenger cars and commercial vehicles: thousand units [*cont.*]
Véhicules automobiles en circulation
Voitures de tourisme et véhicules utilitaires : milliers de véhicules [*suite*]

Country or area Pays or zone	1985	1986	1987	1988	1989	1990	1991	1992	1993	1994
Israel Israël										
Passenger cars										
Voitures de tourisme	621.0	655.8	704.4	761.4	786.3	811.7	857.4	932.4	988.6	1 057.5
Commercial vehicles										
Véhicules utilitaires	123.2	129.0	140.4	152.5	157.9	161.9	174.1	195.0	217.1	251.7
Italy Italie										
Passenger cars										
Voitures de tourisme	22 494.6	23 495.5	24 320.2	25 290.3	26 267.4	27 415.8	28 519.0	29 497.0[1]	29 497.0[1]	29 600.0[1]
Commercial vehicles										
Véhicules utilitaires	2 308.8	2 428.2	2 002.7	2 120.5	2 350.0	2 416.7	2 529.6	2 763.0[1]	2 663.0[1]	2 745.5[1]
Jamaica Jamaïque										
Passenger cars										
Voitures de tourisme	42.9	44.5	52.9	63.1	64.8	68.5	77.8	73.0	81.1	86.8
Commercial vehicles										
Véhicules utilitaires	26.1	20.7	23.0	26.9	24.5	28.2	29.8	30.5	36.2	41.3
Japan Japon[26][27]										
Passenger cars[26][27]										
Voitures de tourisme[26][27]	27 844.0	28 654.0	29 478.0	30 776.0	32 621.0	34 924.0	37 076.0	38 964.0	40 772.0	42 679.0
Commercial vehicles[26]										
Véhicules utilitaires[26]	17 377.0	18 346.0	19 401.0	20 592.0	21 330.0	21 571.0	21 575.0	21 383.0	21 132.0	20 916.0
Jordan Jordanie[3]										
Passenger cars[3]										
Voitures de tourisme[3]	143.4	149.8	153.6	158.9	159.9	172.0	166.8	181.5	175.3	164.0
Commercial vehicles[3]										
Véhicules utilitaires[3]	55.8	57.8	60.9	63.2	63.4	68.3	61.4	51.5	63.8	75.3
Kenya Kenya										
Passenger cars										
Voitures de tourisme	126.2[3][11]	127.4[3][11]	133.3[3][11]	141.8	150.0	157.7	163.5	·165.4	171.5	...
Commercial vehicles										
Véhicules utilitaires	103.8[3][11]	102.9[3][11]	110.8[3][11]	118.9	149.0	138.6	150.1	168.4	172.8	...
Korea, Republic of Corée, République de										
Passenger cars										
Voitures de tourisme	556.7	664.2	844.4	1 118.0	1 558.7	2 074.9	2 727.9	3 461.1	4 271.3	5 148.7
Commercial vehicles										
Véhicules utilitaires	541.0	627.2	746.9	895.0	1 092.3	1 308.4	1 505.1	1 745.1	1 976.6	2 226.7
Kuwait Koweït										
Passenger cars										
Voitures de tourisme	417.4	410.0	429.2	458.1	488.0	...	554.7	579.8	600.0	629.7
Commercial vehicles										
Véhicules utilitaires	140.4	133.6	135.2	132.9	134.3	...	149.8	151.1	147.0	148.7
Latvia Lettonie										
Passenger cars										
Voitures de tourisme	214.5	226.1	236.3	251.3	264.1	282.7	328.5	350.0	367.5	251.6
Commercial vehicles										
Véhicules utilitaires	71.5	73.1	74.1	74.9	76.9	79.0	83.3	93.0	72.1	73.5
Lebanon Liban[21]										
Passenger cars[21]										
Voitures de tourisme[21]	...	...	...	...	...	...	...	...	943.1	1 035.1
Commercial vehicles[21]										
Véhicules utilitaires[21]	...	...	...	...	...	...	...	...	77.3	80.8
Lesotho Lesotho										
Passenger cars										
Voitures de tourisme	6.1[3]	6.7[3]	5.0	...	...	...	...	...	...	...
Commercial vehicles										
Véhicules utilitaires	14.6[3]	16.3[3]	* 13.0	...	...	...	...	...	...	...
Liberia Libéria										
Passenger cars										
Voitures de tourisme	16.0	17.0	18.0	...	...	...	...	...	...	...

62
Motor vehicles in use
Passenger cars and commercial vehicles: thousand units [*cont.*]
Véhicules automobiles en circulation
Voitures de tourisme et véhicules utilitaires : milliers de véhicules [*suite*]

Country or area Pays or zone	1985	1986	1987	1988	1989	1990	1991	1992	1993	1994
Commercial vehicles										
Véhicules utilitaires	14.0	15.0	15.0	...	...	...	...	...	...	...
Libyan Arab Jamah. Jamah. arabe libyenne										
Passenger cars										
Voitures de tourisme	420.0	428.0	433.0	448.0[8]	448.0[8]	448.0[8]	450.0[8]	448.0[8]	...	...
Commercial vehicles										
Véhicules utilitaires	210.0	216.0	223.0	322.0[8]	322.0[8]	322.0[8]	330.0[8]	322.0[8]	...	...
Lithuania Lituanie										
Passenger cars										
Voitures de tourisme	341.2	370.5	390.8	417.7	452.0	493.0	530.8	565.3	597.7	652.8
Commercial vehicles										
Véhicules utilitaires	94.2	95.7	97.1	38.3	99.7	105.9	107.7	112.5	115.1	118.2
Luxembourg Luxembourg										
Passenger cars										
Voitures de tourisme	151.6	156.0	162.5	168.5	177.0	183.4	191.6	200.7	208.8	217.8
Commercial vehicles[4]										
Véhicules utilitaires[4]	30.5	31.3	32.0	32.7	34.2	35.9	38.0	40.2	42.2	45.6
Macau Macao										
Passenger cars[9]										
Voitures de tourisme[9]	17.9	19.5	19.6	21.0	22.4	24.7	26.2	29.9	32.6	34.0
Commercial vehicles[9]										
Véhicules utilitaires[9]	4.4	4.8	4.9	5.3	6.3	6.4	6.5	6.5	6.6	6.3
Madagascar Madagascar										
Passenger cars										
Voitures de tourisme	46.0	46.0	46.0	...	45.0	46.6[1]	47.0[1]	47.0[1]	...	...
Commercial vehicles										
Véhicules utilitaires	45.0	48.0	47.0	...	32.0	33.1[1]	33.0[1]	33.3[1]	...	...
Malawi Malawi										
Passenger cars[3]										
Voitures de tourisme[3]	24.7	15.5[1]	26.3	26.9	30.0	35.3	# 6.6[28]	5.3[28]	...	...
Commercial vehicles[3]										
Véhicules utilitaires[3]	2.4	15.6[1]	2.6	2.8	3.1	3.3	2.7	2.7	...	...
Malaysia Malaisie										
Passenger cars										
Voitures de tourisme[29]	1 384.0	1 453.6	1 504.2	1 578.9	1 689.4	1 845.6	2 024.8	2 158.2	2 298.8	2 333.0
Commercial vehicles[29]										
Véhicules utilitaires[29]	311.1	330.1	339.0	351.9	374.6	407.1	446.8	447.7	502.7	422.0
Mali Mali										
Passenger cars										
Voitures de tourisme	19.0	19.0	19.0	20.0	21.0[1]	21.0[1]	21.0[1]	21.0[1]	21.0[1]	...
Commercial vehicles										
Véhicules utilitaires	13.0	13.0	13.0	13.0	8.0[1]	8.0[1]	8.0[1]	8.4[1]	8.6[1]	...
Malta Malte										
Passenger cars										
Voitures de tourisme	82.3	85.6	89.5	97.6	110.6	109.2	121.6	125.0	152.6	170.6
Commercial vehicles										
Véhicules utilitaires	18.2	17.8	17.2	19.3	19.6	20.5	21.7	35.4	50.9	55.7
Martinique Martinique										
Passenger cars[1]										
Voitures de tourisme[1]	74.6	77.0	80.0	84.0	80.0	92.0	96.0	102.6	108.3	...
Commercial vehicles[1]										
Véhicules utilitaires[1]	25.3	26.0	27.0	28.0	29.0	30.0	31.0	31.9	32.2	...
Mauritania Mauritanie										
Passenger cars										
Voitures de tourisme	11.0	11.0	12.0	8.0[1]	8.0[1]	8.0[1]	8.0[1]	8.0[1]	8.0[1]	...
Commercial vehicles										
Véhicules utilitaires	5.0	6.0	6.0	5.0[1]	5.0[1]	5.0[1]	5.0[1]	5.5[1]	5.7[1]	...

62
Motor vehicles in use
Passenger cars and commercial vehicles: thousand units [*cont.*]
Véhicules automobiles en circulation
Voitures de tourisme et véhicules utilitaires : milliers de véhicules [*suite*]

Country or area Pays or zone	1985	1986	1987	1988	1989	1990	1991	1992	1993	1994
Mauritius Maurice										
Passenger cars										
Voitures de tourisme	33.1	34.2	36.5	39.4	42.1	45.5	50.0	53.9	57.4	53.2[1]
Commercial vehicles										
Véhicules utilitaires	10.8	11.2	12.2	13.7	15.1	16.9	19.1	20.9	22.5	11.1[1]
Mexico Mexique										
Passenger cars										
Voitures de tourisme	5 102.4	5 202.9	5 336.2	5 806.9	6 219.1	6 893.3	7 497.1	7 749.6	8 172.4	8 451.1
Commercial vehicles										
Véhicules utilitaires	2 033.4	2 213.0	2 292.0	2 435.9	2 704.1	2 982.0	3 501.0	3 505.7	3 580.0	3 839.4
Morocco Maroc										
Passenger cars[9]										
Voitures de tourisme[9]	508.3	527.4	554.0	588.9	634.4	669.6	707.1	778.9	849.3	864.6
Commercial vehicles[9]										
Véhicules utilitaires[9]	239.9	247.7	255.1	263.1	272.4	282.9	295.5	302.3	316.7	317.0
Mozambique Mozambique										
Passenger cars										
Voitures de tourisme	46.0	45.0	45.0	# 84.0[1]	84.0[1]	84.0[1]	84.0[1]	84.0[1]	84.0[1]	...
Commercial vehicles										
Véhicules utilitaires	18.0	18.0	18.0	# 24.0[1]	24.0[1]	25.0[1]	26.0[1]	26.2[1]	26.8[1]	...
Myanmar Myanmar										
Passenger cars[3]										
Voitures de tourisme[3]	59.8	60.9	60.4	64.9	71.3	78.1	88.6	100.2	115.9	125.4
Commercial vehicles[3]										
Véhicules utilitaires[3]	51.9	53.5	50.7	51.6	53.7	54.9	56.6	59.7	66.6	58.2
Netherlands Pays-Bas										
Passenger cars[3,30]										
Voitures de tourisme[3,30]	4 901.i	4 949.9	5 117.7	5 250.6	5 371.4	5 509.2	5 569.1	5 658.3	5 755.4	5 883.9
Commercial vehicles[30]										
Véhicules utilitaires[30]	428.2[3,31]	463.8	506.5[3]	538.2[3]	556.8[3]	582.1[3]	604.6[3]	644.9[3]	679.2[3]	687.3[3]
New Caledonia Nouvelle-Calédonie										
Passenger cars[1]										
Voitures de tourisme[1]	43.8	46.4	48.0	50.0	53.0	54.0	55.0	56.7	58.5	...
Commercial vehicles[1]										
Véhicules utilitaires[1]	16.3	16.7	17.0	18.0	19.0	19.0	20.0	21.2	22.6	...
New Zealand Nouvelle-Zélande										
Passenger cars[32]										
Voitures de tourisme[32]	1 495.1	1 531.4	...	1 382.3	1 438.7	1 497.7	1 548.1	1 551.4	1 571.8	1 611.8
Commercial vehicles[32]										
Véhicules utilitaires[32]	302.1	373.8	...	289.2	289.2	306.6	309.6	317.8	332.3	353.0
Nicaragua Nicaragua										
Passenger cars[1]										
Voitures de tourisme[1]	31.9	31.1	31.0	30.0	31.1	31.1	31.0	31.3	31.3	...
Commercial vehicles[1]										
Véhicules utilitaires[1]	28.3	27.9	28.0	42.0	43.0	43.0	43.0	43.6	43.6	...
Niger Niger										
Passenger cars										
Voitures de tourisme	35.0	35.0	35.0	...	...	17.0[8]	18.0[8]	16.0[1]	16.0[1]	...
Commercial vehicles										
Véhicules utilitaires	9.0	9.0	9.0	...	...	18.0[8]	18.0[8]	18.0[1]	18.0[1]	...
Nigeria Nigéria										
Passenger cars										
Voitures de tourisme	350.0	391.0	337.0	308.0	259.0	273.0	144.6	185.5	189.2	227.0
Commercial vehicles										
Véhicules utilitaires	34.0	132.0	126.0	103.0	81.0	84.0	17.7	20.6	23.1	22.3
Norway Norvège										
Passenger cars[3,33]										
Voitures de tourisme[3,33]	1 514.0	1 592.2	1 623.1	1 622.0	1 612.7	1 612.0	1 614.6	1 619.4	1 633.0	1 653.7

62
Motor vehicles in use
Passenger cars and commercial vehicles: thousand units [*cont.*]
Véhicules automobiles en circulation
Voitures de tourisme et véhicules utilitaires : milliers de véhicules [*suite*]

Country or area Pays or zone	1985	1986	1987	1988	1989	1990	1991	1992	1993	1994
Commercial vehicles[3][33] Véhicules utilitaires[3][33]	249.7	282.8	303.2	313.9	320.4	330.6	334.3	341.6	352.5	366.3
Oman Oman										
Passenger cars[21] Voitures de tourisme[21]	128.3	145.0	104.3	110.1	119.9	134.9	158.0	173.0	180.0	...
Commercial vehicles[21][34] Véhicules utilitaires[21][34]	98.9	107.0	65.9	66.9	70.2	75.0	78.3	81.9	85.5	...
Pakistan Pakistan										
Passenger cars[3] Voitures de tourisme[3]	452.1	500.2	540.4	590.5	660.0	715.0	746.1	855.4	916.1	955.1
Commercial vehicles[3] Véhicules utilitaires[3]	153.2	172.8	175.0	194.4	259.6	269.1	279.8	310.8	332.4	359.5
Panama Panama										
Passenger cars Voitures de tourisme	129.0	134.3	129.4	129.5	120.8	132.9	144.2	149.9	161.2	...
Commercial vehicles Véhicules utilitaires	40.3	41.9	44.6	41.2	40.0	42.2	47.3	50.4	55.0	...
Papua New Guinea Papouasie-Nvl-Guinée										
Passenger cars[3] Voitures de tourisme[3]	16.0	16.6	17.1	...	...	...	...	11.5[8]	...	...
Commercial vehicles[3][35] Véhicules utilitaires[3][35]	26.6	27.0	26.1	...	...	...	...	29.8[8]	...	...
Paraguay Paraguay										
Passenger cars Voitures de tourisme	104.9	111.9	122.5	80.2	149.2	165.2	190.9	221.1	250.7	...
Commercial vehicles Véhicules utilitaires	22.0	23.2	27.2	18.9	25.2	25.7	30.7	34.9	37.7	...
Peru Pérou										
Passenger cars Voitures de tourisme	376.0	377.2	377.4	376.8	372.8	368.2	379.1	402.4	418.6	444.2
Commercial vehicles Véhicules utilitaires	220.3	226.5	233.4	239.8	239.5	237.4	244.9	270.6	288.8	316.6
Philippines Philippines										
Passenger cars Voitures de tourisme	347.9	356.7	358.8	376.6	413.0	454.6[1]	456.6	483.6	531.2	...
Commercial vehicles Véhicules utilitaires	514.5	526.7	554.7	598.2	671.7	764.9[1]	829.7	916.7	1 024.0	...
Poland Pologne										
Passenger cars Voitures de tourisme	3 671.4	3 964.0	4 231.7	4 519.1	4 846.4	5 260.6	6 112.2	6 504.7	6 770.6	7 153.1
Commercial vehicles[36] Véhicules utilitaires[36]	864.3	914.4	955.0	1 010.5	1 069.6	1 138.1	1 240.2	1 299.5	1 321.9	1 395.1
Portugal Portugal										
Passenger cars[24][37][38] Voitures de tourisme[24][37][38]	1 701.7	1 813.0	1 947.3	2 152.5	2 343.4	2 552.3	2 774.7	3 049.8	3 295.1	3 532.0
Commercial vehicles[24][38] Véhicules utilitaires[24][38]	669.1[29]	705.9[29]	607.9	669.6	739.2	812.8	881.2[9]	964.0	1 050.1	1 158.6
Puerto Rico Porto Rico										
Passenger cars[2] Voitures de tourisme[2]	1 195.0	1 114.3	1 227.0	1 304.2	1 289.6	1 305.1	1 321.9	1 347.0	1 393.3	...
Commercial vehicles[2] Véhicules utilitaires[2]	147.5	146.3	158.3	171.8	172.8	188.4	192.1	201.5	239.6	...
Qatar Qatar										
Passenger cars Voitures de tourisme	80.0	85.4	91.0	97.3	100.2	105.8	114.5	123.6	132.1	137.6
Commercial vehicles Véhicules utilitaires	33.4	36.8	39.3	41.7	43.7	46.8	53.9	57.5	61.5	65.8

62
Motor vehicles in use
Passenger cars and commercial vehicles: thousand units [*cont.*]
Véhicules automobiles en circulation
Voitures de tourisme et véhicules utilitaires : milliers de véhicules [*suite*]

Country or area Pays or zone	1985	1986	1987	1988	1989	1990	1991	1992	1993	1994
Republic of Moldova République de Moldova										
Passenger cars										
Voitures de tourisme	148.1	163.1	171.3	184.9	195.7	209.0	218.1	166.3[39]	166.4[39]	169.4[39]
Commercial vehicles[40]										
Véhicules utilitaires[40]	16.1	16.3	16.1	15.6	15.2	15.0	14.3	10.1[39]	8.9[39]	7.8[39]
Réunion Réunion										
Passenger cars										
Voitures de tourisme	101.6	106.6	114.6	125.9	139.0	146.4	155.9	173.2[1]	181.8[1]	...
Commercial vehicles										
Véhicules utilitaires	45.0	48.5	53.3	50.0[1]	53.0[1]	55.0[1]	58.0[1]	61.6[1]	61.7[1]	
Rwanda Rwanda										
Passenger cars										
Voitures de tourisme	6.1	6.7	7.1	7.2	7.9	7.2	15.0[8]	7.9[8]	...	...
Commercial vehicles										
Véhicules utilitaires	6.3	7.0	7.3	7.9	7.0	7.0	10.0[8]	2.0[8]	...	...
Saint Kitts and Nevis Saint-Kitts-et-Nevis										
Passenger cars										
Voitures de tourisme	3.1	3.3	3.3	3.4	3.9	4.1	3.7	...	...	...
Commercial vehicles										
Véhicules utilitaires	0.9	1.0	1.0	1.2	1.5	1.6	2.2	...	...	...
Saint Lucia Sainte-Lucie										
Passenger cars										
Voitures de tourisme	5.4	5.5	6.0	6.5	7.2	8.1	8.6	9.9[8]	...	...
Commercial vehicles										
Véhicules utilitaires	3.7	4.2	5.1	5.5	5.9	6.3	...	9.1[8]	...	...
St. Vincent-Grenadines St. Vincent-Grenadines										
Passenger cars										
Voitures de tourisme	4.9	5.1	4.9	5.2	5.3	5.3	5.3	5.0	5.4	5.7
Commercial vehicles										
Véhicules utilitaires	2.0	2.3	2.4	2.6	2.7	2.8	2.8	2.0	3.1	3.2
Samoa Samoa										
Passenger cars										
Voitures de tourisme	2.0	2.1	1.8	1.9	2.0	...	5.0[1]	5.0[1]	5.0[1]	...
Commercial vehicles										
Véhicules utilitaires	2.8	2.0	2.5	2.5	3.9	...	1.0[1]	1.8[1]	1.8[1]	...
Sao Tome and Principe Sao Tomé-et-Principe										
Passenger cars										
Voitures de tourisme	2.2	2.4	2.6	...	...	...	...	...	...	...
Commercial vehicles										
Véhicules utilitaires	0.3	0.3	0.3	...	...	...	...	...	...	...
Saudi Arabia Arabie saoudite										
Passenger cars[21]										
Voitures de tourisme[21]	2 165.7	2 245.0	2 332.3	2 419.4	2 550.5	2 664.1	...	...	...	...
Commercial vehicles[21]										
Véhicules utilitaires[21]	1 966.2	2 023.4	2 082.9	2 141.9	2 204.2	2 272.8	1 592.0	1 681.9	...	...
Senegal Sénégal										
Passenger cars										
Voitures de tourisme	63.0	63.0	63.0	...	...	...	...	...	* 65.4	
Commercial vehicles										
Véhicules utilitaires	36.0	36.0	36.0	...	...	...	...	...	* 24.0	...
Seychelles Seychelles										
Passenger cars										
Voitures de tourisme	3.5	3.5	3.4	3.6	4.0	4.3	4.7	4.9	6.1	6.6
Commercial vehicles										
Véhicules utilitaires	1.3	1.0	1.0	1.0	1.0	1.2	1.3	1.5	1.8	2.0
Sierra Leone Sierra Leone										
Passenger cars										
Voitures de tourisme	31.0	33.0	33.0	23.0[1]	23.0[1]	35.9[1]	36.0[1]	36.0[1]	36.0[1]	...

62
Motor vehicles in use
Passenger cars and commercial vehicles: thousand units [*cont.*]
Véhicules automobiles en circulation
Voitures de tourisme et véhicules utilitaires : milliers de véhicules [*suite*]

Country or area Pays or zone	1985	1986	1987	1988	1989	1990	1991	1992	1993	1994
Commercial vehicles Véhicules utilitaires	14.0	15.0	15.0	7.0[1]	7.0[1]	11.8[1]	12.0[1]	12.0[1]	12.0[1]	...
Singapore Singapour										
Passenger cars Voitures de tourisme	236.2	234.6	236.1	251.4	271.2	286.8	300.1	302.8	321.9	340.6
Commercial vehicles Véhicules utilitaires	118.3	114.3	113.7	117.4	122.8	126.9	130.1	131.5	135.2	136.8
Somalia Somalie										
Passenger cars Voitures de tourisme	6.0	5.0	5.0	...	...	20.0[8]	10.5[8]	10.5[8]	...	...
Commercial vehicles Véhicules utilitaires	7.0	8.0	8.0	...	...	12.0[8]	12.0[8]	11.5[8]	...	...
South Africa Afrique du Sud										
Passenger cars Voitures de tourisme	3 096.6[23]	3 237.2[23]	3 286.8[23]	3 222.4[23]	3 498.2[23]	3 599.8[23]	3 698.2[23]	3 739.2[23]	3 488.6[1]	...
Commercial vehicles Véhicules utilitaires	1 461.6[41]	1 433.9[41]	1 454.9[41]	1 456.7[41]	1 462.5[41]	1 486.9[41]	1 519.9[41]	1 551.4[41]	1 784.9[1]	...
Spain Espagne										
Passenger cars Voitures de tourisme	9 273.7	9 643.3	10 218.5	10 787.5	11 467.7	11 995.6	12 537.1	13 102.3	13 440.7	13 733.8
Commercial vehicles Véhicules utilitaires	1 610.3	1 762.5	1 911.9	2 073.4	2 269.3	2 446.9	2 615.0	2 773.4	2 859.6	2 952.8
Sri Lanka Sri Lanka[3]										
Passenger cars[3] Voitures de tourisme[3]	148.6	155.2	147.8	155.2	163.8	173.5	180.1	189.5	197.3	210.1
Commercial vehicles[3] Véhicules utilitaires[3]	132.4	141.3	135.4	139.2	142.1	146.0	152.7	159.9	166.3	175.3
Sudan Soudan										
Passenger cars Voitures de tourisme	171.0	177.0	185.0	...	...	116.0[8]	116.0[8]	116.0[8]	...	...
Commercial vehicles Véhicules utilitaires	23.0	23.0	24.0	...	...	56.9[8]	57.0[8]	57.0[8]	...	...
Suriname Suriname										
Passenger cars[3] Voitures de tourisme[3]	31.6	32.1	32.1	35.1	36.6	36.2	38.7	42.6	46.6	42.1
Commercial vehicles Véhicules utilitaires	12.8	13.2	13.0	13.4	14.0	14.4	15.5	16.0	18.2	17.2
Swaziland Swaziland										
Passenger cars Voitures de tourisme	19.6	20.9	22.6	23.5	25.3	26.9	21.3[8]	22.0[8]	...	...
Commercial vehicles Véhicules utilitaires	20.1	20.6	21.9	23.6	24.4	26.3	15.9[8]	16.0[8]	...	...
Sweden Suède										
Passenger cars[3] Voitures de tourisme[3]	3 151.2	3 253.6	3 366.6	3 482.7	3 578.0	3 600.5	3 619.4	3 586.7	3 566.0	...
Commercial vehicles Véhicules utilitaires	552.1	567.1	584.9	611.6	643.8	658.0	656.9	649.1	643.0	...
Switzerland Suisse										
Passenger cars[3][24] Voitures de tourisme[3][24]	2 617.2	2 678.9	2 732.7	2 745.5	2 895.8	2 985.4	3 057.8	3 091.2	3 109.5	3 165.0
Commercial vehicles[3][24] Véhicules utilitaires[3][24]	211.3	217.8	228.7	252.2	270.8	283.4	291.3	291.3	288.8	292.4
Syrian Arab Republic Rép. arabe syrienne										
Passenger cars Voitures de tourisme	120.1	123.9	125.3	124.3	124.7	126.0	126.9	128.0	149.8	159.1
Commercial vehicles Véhicules utilitaires	109.2	116.8	117.3	126.4	118.0	118.5	121.9	136.7	162.3	188.4

62
Motor vehicles in use
Passenger cars and commercial vehicles: thousand units [*cont.*]
Véhicules automobiles en circulation
Voitures de tourisme et véhicules utilitaires : milliers de véhicules [*suite*]

Country or area Pays or zone	1985	1986	1987	1988	1989	1990	1991	1992	1993	1994
Thailand Thaïlande										
Passenger cars[24][42]										
Voitures de tourisme[24][42]	739.4	789.1	930.7	949.1	1 000.4	1 222.4	1 279.2	1 396.6	1 598.2	1 798.8
Commercial vehicles[24][43]										
Véhicules utilitaires[24][43]	821.8	895.5	1 045.3	1 085.8	1 253.8	1 457.4	1 541.2	1 763.5	2 091.1	2 384.1
Togo Togo										
Passenger cars										
Voitures de tourisme	2.1	2.2	2.6	# 25.0[1]	25.0[1]	25.0[1]	25.0[1]	25.0[1]	25.0[1]	...
Commercial vehicles										
Véhicules utilitaires	0.8	0.8	0.9	# 15.0[1]	15.0[1]	15.0[1]	16.0[1]	16.1[1]	16.1[1]	...
Tonga Tonga										
Passenger cars										
Voitures de tourisme	0.9	1.1	1.4	1.6	1.4	2.0	2.8	3.3[8]	...	...
Commercial vehicles										
Véhicules utilitaires	1.7	2.1	2.4	3.5	2.2	2.6	3.1	3.7[8]	...	...
Trinidad and Tobago Trinité-et-Tobago										
Passenger cars										
Voitures de tourisme	...	...	...	...	...	...	...	...	118.1	128.5
Commercial vehicles										
Véhicules utilitaires	...	...	...	...	...	...	...	...	32.6	33.6
Tunisia Tunisie										
Passenger cars										
Voitures de tourisme	241.0	252.6	261.1	269.5	279.8	292.5	302.6	313.5	325.0	...
Commercial vehicles										
Véhicules utilitaires	153.4	160.1	165.8	170.5	176.9	186.2	197.3	209.4	222.0	...
Turkey Turquie										
Passenger cars										
Voitures de tourisme	983.4	1 087.2	1 193.0	1 310.3	1 434.8	1 649.9	1 864.3	2 181.4	2 619.9	2 861.6
Commercial vehicles[44]										
Véhicules utilitaires[44]	381.1	401.8	414.9	427.3	438.0	452.9	469.0	490.9	518.4	530.4
Uganda Ouganda										
Passenger cars										
Voitures de tourisme	10.0	12.0	12.0	13.0	13.0	13.0	17.0	17.8[1]	17.8[1]	...
Commercial vehicles										
Véhicules utilitaires	10.0	11.0	12.0	13.0	14.0	15.0	20.0	25.2[1]	25.3[1]	...
Ukraine Ukraine										
Passenger cars										
Voitures de tourisme	2 447.0	2 619.0	2 816.0	3 012.0	3 195.0	3 362.0	3 657.0	3 884.8	4 206.5	4 384.1
former USSR† ancienne URSS†										
Passenger cars										
Voitures de tourisme	6 670.6	7 082.9	7 539.2	7 955.5	8 438.1	8 963.9	9 712.6	10 531.3	11 518.2	...
United Arab Emirates Emirats arabes unis										
Passenger cars[21]										
Voitures de tourisme[21]	196.2	182.8	189.3	201.7	239.2	224.9	241.3	257.8	297.1	...
Commercial vehicles[21]										
Véhicules utilitaires[21]	36.2	43.8	45.5	48.6	47.4	53.0	43.4	60.4	72.8	...
United Kingdom Royaume-Uni										
Passenger cars[45]										
Voitures de tourisme[45]	17 737.1	18 355.1	18 859.1	19 940.0	20 925.0	21 485.0	21 515.0	# 20 973.0	21 291.0	21 740.0
Commercial vehicles[45]										
Véhicules utilitaires[45]	1 983.8	2 011.1	2 053.4	2 193.7	2 563.0	2 520.0	2 438.0	# 3 008.0	2 990.0	2 994.0
United Rep.Tanzania Rép. Unie de Tanzanie										
Passenger cars										
Voitures de tourisme	49.0	49.0	49.0	49.0	49.0	44.0	44.0[1]	44.0[1]	44.0[1]	...
Commercial vehicles										
Véhicules utilitaires	33.0	33.0	33.0	33.0	33.0	54.0	55.0[1]	57.2[1]	59.9[1]	...

62
Motor vehicles in use
Passenger cars and commercial vehicles: thousand units [*cont.*]
Véhicules automobiles en circulation
Voitures de tourisme et véhicules utilitaires : milliers de véhicules [*suite*]

Country or area Pays or zone	1985	1986	1987	1988	1989	1990	1991	1992	1993	1994
United States Etats-Unis										
Passenger cars										
Voitures de tourisme	131 864.0	135 431.0	137 323.0	141 251.7	143 081.4	143 549.6	142 955.6	144 213.4	146 314.2	147 171.0
Commercial vehicles										
Véhicules utilitaires	39 196.0	40 166.0	41 119.0	43 145.0	44 179.1	45 105.8	45 416.3	46 148.8	47 749.1	48 298.0
Uruguay Uruguay										
Passenger cars										
Voitures de tourisme	306.3	318.4	332.7	350.2	360.3	379.6	389.6	418.0	425.6	...
Commercial vehicles										
Véhicules utilitaires	46.5	47.0	46.6	49.8	50.2	49.9	48.6	45.0	44.4	...
Vanuatu Vanuatu										
Passenger cars										
Voitures de tourisme	2.3 [3 28]	3.8 [1]	4.0 [1]	4.0 [1]	4.0 [1]	4.0 [1]	4.5 [3 28]	4.0 [1]	4.0 [1]	...
Commercial vehicles										
Véhicules utilitaires	1.2	2.4 [1]	2.0 [1]	2.0 [1]	2.0 [1]	2.0 [1]	2.1 [3 28]	2.2 [1]	2.3 [1]	...
Venezuela Venezuela										
Passenger cars										
Voitures de tourisme	1 598.0	1 656.0	1 718.0	1 740.0	1 615.0	1 582.0	1 540.0	1 566.0	1 579.0	...
Commercial vehicles										
Véhicules utilitaires	418.0	430.0	448.0	421.0	459.0	464.0	449.0	456.0	460.0	...
Yemen Yémen										
Passenger cars[21]										
Voitures de tourisme[21]	...	...	...	...	90.5	94.9	118.3	140.6	176.1	...
Commercial vehicles[21]										
Véhicules utilitaires[21]	...	...	...	...	185.9	190.3	208.3	227.1	256.7	...
former Dem. Yemen anciennce Yémen dém.										
Passenger cars										
Voitures de tourisme	25.6	26.5	27.6	28.6	...	...	...	...	...	...
Commercial vehicles										
Véhicules utilitaires	29.2	31.2	32.4	33.9	...	...	...	...	...	...
Yugoslavia, SFR† Yougoslavie, Rfs†										
Passenger cars										
Voitures de tourisme	1 080.1	1 133.1	1 177.3	1 225.0	1 309.7	1 405.5	...	...	...	...
Commercial vehicles										
Véhicules utilitaires	102.0	111.2	117.4	121.4	127.2	132.5	...	...	...	...
Zaire Zaïre										
Passenger cars										
Voitures de tourisme	92.0	92.0	92.0	130.7	137.9	145.1	...	...	...	...
Commercial vehicles										
Véhicules utilitaires	80.0	80.0	80.0	76.8	84.8	92.8	...	...	...	...
Zambia Zambie										
Passenger cars[11]										
Voitures de tourisme[11]	71.8	74.0	75.2	96.0 [1]	96.0 [1]	96.0 [1]	96.0 [1]	96.0 [1]	96.0 [1]	...
Commercial vehicles[11]										
Véhicules utilitaires[11]	35.2	37.7	39.1	67.0 [1]	68.0 [1]	68.0 [1]	68.0 [1]	68.0 [1]	68.0 [1]	...
Zimbabwe Zimbabwe										
Passenger cars										
Voitures de tourisme	241.0	266.0	274.0	276.0	285.0	290.0	300.0	* 310.0	...	...
Commercial vehicles										
Véhicules utilitaires	78.0	80.0	81.0	81.0	82.0	83.0	85.0	* 88.0	...	...

Source:
Transport statistics database of the Statistics Division of
the United Nations Secretariat.

† For detailed descriptions of data pertaining to
former Czechoslovakia, Germany, SFR Yugoslavia and former
USSR, see Annex I - Country or area nomenclature, regional
and other groupings.

Source:
Base de données pour les statistiques des transports de la
Division de statistique du Secrétariat de l'ONU.

† Pour les descriptions en détails des données
relatives à l'ancienne Tchécoslovaquie, l'Allemagne, la Rfs
Yougoslavie et l'ancienne URSS, voir l'Annexe I -
Nomenclature des pays ou zones, groupements régionaux et
autres groupements.

62

Motor vehicles in use
Passenger cars and commercial vehicles: thousand units [*cont.*]
Véhicules automobiles en circulation
Voitures de tourisme et véhicules utilitaires : milliers de véhicules [*suite*]

1 Source: World Automotive Market Report, Auto and Truck International (Illinois).	1 Source: "World Automotive Market Report, Auto and Truck International" (Illinois).
2 Twelve months beginning 1 July of year indicated.	2 Douze mois à compte de 1 juillet de l'année indiquée.
3 Including vehicles operated by police or other governmental security organizations.	3 Y compris véhicules de la police ou d'autres services gouvernementaux d'ordre public.
4 Including farm tractors.	4 Y compris tracteurs agricoles.
5 Including jeeps.	5 Y compris jeeps.
6 Excluding government vehicles.	6 Non compris les véhicules des administrations publiques.
7 Including commercial vehicles.	7 Y compris véhicules utilitaires.
8 Source: AAMA Motor Vehicle Facts and figures, American Automobile Manufacturers Association (Michigan).	8 Source: "AAMA Motor Vehicle Facts and Figures", "American Automobile Manufacturers Association" (Michigan).
9 Including special-purpose vehicles.	9 Y compris véhicules à usages spéciaux.
10 Excluding pick-ups.	10 Non compris fourgonnettes.
11 Including vehicles no longer in circulation.	11 Y compris véhicules retirés de la circulation.
12 Including licensed driver-training cars.	12 Y compris les voitures-écoles homologuées.
13 Including Faeroe Islands.	13 Y compris les Iles Féroé.
14 Excluding jeeps.	14 Non compris jeeps.
15 Twelve months ending 7 July of year indicated.	15 Douze mois finissant le 7 juillet de l'année indiquée.
16 Including private and government cars, rental and hired cars.	16 Y compris les voitures particulières et celles des administrations publiques, les voitures de location et de louage.
17 Including pick-ups, ambulances, light and heavy fire engines and all other vehicles such as trailers, cranes, loaders, forklifts, etc.	17 Y compris les fourgonnettes, les ambulances, les voitures de pompiers légères et lourdes, et tous autres véhicules tels que remoques, grues, chargeuses, chariots élévateurs à fourches, etc.
18 Source: India Pocketbook of Transport Statistics, 1994.	18 Source: "India Pocketbook of Transport Statistics, 1994".
19 Including 3-wheeled passengers and goods vehicles.	19 Y compris véhicules à trois roues (passagers et marchandises).
20 Twelve months ending 20 March of year indicated.	20 Douze mois finissant le 20 mars de l'année indiquée.
21 Source: United Nations Economic and Social Commission for Western Asia (ESCWA).	21 Source: Commission économiques et sociale pour l'Asie occidentale (CESAO).
22 Including school buses.	22 Y compris l'autobus de l'école.
23 Passenger cars include mini-buses equipped for transport of nine to fifteen passengers.	23 Voitures de tourisme comprennent mini-buses ayant une capacité de neuf à quinze passagers.
24 Twelve months ending 30 September of year indicated.	24 Douze mois finissant le 30 septembre de l'année indiquée.
25 Including large public service excavators and trench diggers.	25 Y compris les grosses excavatrices et machines d'excavation de tranchées de travaux publics.
26 Excluding small vehicles.	26 Non compris véhicules petites.
27 Including cars with a seating capacity of up to 10 persons.	27 Y compris véhicules comptant jusqu'à 10 places.
28 Limited coverage.	28 Portée limitée.
29 Excluding tractors.	29 Non compris tracteurs.
30 Excluding diplomatic corps vehicles.	30 Non compris véhicules des diplomates.
31 Twelve months ending 31 July of year indicated.	31 Douze mois finissant le 31 juillet de l'année indiquée.
32 Twelve months ending 31 March of year indicated.	32 Douze mois finissant le 31 mars de l'année indiquée.
33 Including hearses (Norway: registered before 1981).	33 Y compris corbillards (Norvège: enregistrés avant de 1981).
34 Trucks only.	34 Camión seulement.
35 Including ambulances.	35 Y compris ambulances.
36 Excluding buses and tractors, but including special lorries.	36 Non compris autobus et tracteurs, mais y compris camions spéciaux.
37 Including light miscellaneous vehicles.	37 Y compris les véhicules légers divers.
38 Excluding Madeira and Azores.	38 Non compris Madère et Azores.
39 Excluding Transnistria region.	39 Non compris région de Transnistria.
40 Refers to motor vehicles for general use owned by Ministry of Transport.	40 Désigne les véhicules à moteur d'usage général appartenant au Ministère des transports.
41 Commercial vehicles include hearses, ambulances, fire-engines and jeeps specifically registered as commercial vehicles.	41 Véhicules utilitaires comprennent corbillards, ambulances, voitures de pompiers et jeeps spécifiquement immatriculés comme véhicules utilitaires.
42 Including micro-buses and passenger pick-ups.	42 Y compris les microbus et les camionnettes de transport de passagers.
43 Including pick-ups, taxis, cars for hire, small rural buses.	43 Y compris les camionnettes, les taxis, les voitures de louage, les petits autobus ruraux.
44 Excluding tractors and semi-trailer combinations.	44 Non compris ensembles tracteur-remorque et semi-remorque.
45 Figures prior to 1992 were derived from vehicle taxation class; beginning 1992, figures derived from vehicle body type.	45 Les chiffres antérieurs à 1992 ont été calculés selon les catégories fiscales de véhicules; à partir de 1992, ils ont été calculés selon les types de carrosserie.

63
Merchant shipping: fleets
Transports maritimes : flotte marchande
Total, Oil tankers and Ore and bulk carrier fleets: thousand gross registered tons
Total, Pétroliers et Minéraliers et transporteurs de vracs : milliers de tonneaux de jauge brute

Flag Pavillon	1985	1986	1987	1988	1989	1990	1991	1992	1993	1994
A. Total · Totale										
World Monde	**416 269**	**404 910**	**403 498**	**403 406**	**410 481**	**423 627**	**436 027**	**445 169**	**457 915**	**475 859**
Steam Vapeur	89 857	76 896	72 228	67 989	65 070	63 974	62 662	56 800	...	...
Motor Moteur	326 412	328 014	331 270	335 417	345 410	359 653	373 364	388 200	...	...
Africa · Afrique										
Algeria Algérie	1 347	882	893	897	848	906	921	921	921	936
Angola Angola	91	92	92	91	93	93	93	94	88	90
Benin Bénin	5	5	5	5	5	5	2	2	1	1
Cameroon Cameroun	76	77	58	57	33	33	34	35	36	36
Cape Verde Cap-Vert	14	14	15	17	18	21	22	22	23	22
Comoros Comores	1	1	2	1	2	2	3	2	2	2
Congo Congo	8	8	8	8	8	9	9	9	10	9
Côte d'Ivoire Côte d'Ivoire	142	121	119	119	83	82	82	75	103	62
Djibouti Djibouti	3	3	3	3	3	3	3	3	4	4
Egypt Egypte	953	1 063	1 074	1 227	1 230	1 257	1 257	1 122	1 149	1 262
Equatorial Guinea Guinée équatoriale	6	6	6	6	6	6	6	7	2	3
Ethiopia incl.Eritrea Ethiopie comp. Erythrée	57	67	73	74	77	75	84	70	...	...
Ethiopia Ethiopie	...	...	...	...	...	...	...	...	69	83
Gabon Gabon	98	98	24	25	25	24	25	25	36	28
Gambia Gambie	3	3	4	4	2	2	3	2	2	3
Ghana Ghana	163	166	142	125	126	126	135	135	118	106
Guinea Guinée	7	7	7	7	8	9	9	5	6	8
Guinea-Bissau Guinée-Bissau	4	4	4	4	4	4	4	4	4	5
Kenya Kenya	8	9	8	8	8	7	13	14	16	16
Liberia Libéria	58 180	52 649	51 412	49 734	47 893	54 700	52 427	55 918	53 919	57 648

63
Merchant shipping: fleets
Total, Oil tankers and Ore and bulk carrier fleets: thousand gross registered tons [*cont.*]
Transports maritimes : flotte marchande
Total, Pétroliers et Minéraliers et transporteurs de vracs : milliers de tonneaux de jauge brute [*suite*]

Flag Pavillon	1985	1986	1987	1988	1989	1990	1991	1992	1993	1994
Libyan Arab Jamah. Jamah. arabe libyenne	854	825	817	830	831	835	840	720	721	739
Madagascar Madagascar	74	74	64	92	70	74	73	45	34	36
Mauritania Mauritanie	17	23	30	37	40	41	42	43	44	42
Mauritius Maurice	38	152	163	157	130	99	82	122	194	206
Morocco Maroc	461	416	418	437	454	488	483	479	393	362
Mozambique Mozambique	41	43	36	36	38	40	37	39	36	36
Namibia Namibie	...	...	...	...	...	...	0	17	36	44
Nigeria Nigéria	443	564	594	587	500	496	493	516	515	473
Réunion Réunion	...	...	21	21	21	21	21	21	...	...
Saint Helena Sainte-Hélène	4	4	4	4	3	3	...	...	...	...
Sao Tome and Principe Sao Tomé-et-Principe	1	1	1	1	1	1	1	3	3	3
Senegal Sénégal	51	50	46	49	51	52	55	58	66	50
Seychelles Seychelles	2	4	3	3	3	3	4	4	4	4
Sierra Leone Sierra Leone	6	7	9	14	18	21	21	26	26	24
Somalia Somalie	29	16	18	13	11	17	17	17	18	17
South Africa Afrique du Sud	632	600	533	486	397	352	340	336	346	331
Sudan Soudan	96	96	97	97	97	58	45	45	64	57
Togo Togo	54	55	60	515	43	52	22	12	12	1
Tunisia Tunisie	284	286	285	281	282	278	276	280	269	141
United Rep.Tanzania Rép. Unie de Tanzanie	51	51	32	32	32	32	39	41	43	43
Zaire Zaïre	85	66	56	56	56	56	56	29	15	15
America, North · Amérique du Nord										
Anguilla Anguilla	4	4	4	3	3	3	5	5	4	3
Antigua and Barbuda Antigua-et-Barbuda	1	1	52	323	392	359	811	802	1 063	1 507
Bahamas Bahamas	3 907	5 985	9 105	8 963	11 579	13 626	17 541	20 616	21 224	22 915

63
Merchant shipping: fleets
Total, Oil tankers and Ore and bulk carrier fleets: thousand gross registered tons [cont.]
Transports maritimes : flotte marchande
Total, Pétroliers et Minéraliers et transporteurs de vracs : milliers de tonneaux de jauge brute [suite]

Flag Pavillon	1985	1986	1987	1988	1989	1990	1991	1992	1993	1994
Barbados Barbade	8	8	8	8	8	8	8	51	49	76
Belize Belize	1	1	1	1	1	1	...	37	148	280
Bermuda Bermudes	981	1 208	1 925	3 774	4 076	4 258	3 037	3 338	3 140	2 904
British Virgin Islands Iles Vierges britanniques	9	8	8	7	7	7	7	7	6	5
Canada Canada	3 344	3 160	2 971	2 902	2 825	2 744	2 685	2 610	2 541	2 490
Cayman Islands Iles Caïmanes	414	1 390	706	477	411	415	395	363	383	383
Costa Rica Costa Rica	20	13	15	15	13	14	14	8	8	8
Cuba Cuba	965	959	966	912	900	836	770	671	626	444
Dominica Dominique	3	2	2	2	3	2	2	2	4	2
Dominican Republic Rép. dominicaine	47	42	44	48	44	36	12	12	13	12
El Salvador El Salvador	4	4	4	4	4	2	2	2	2	1
Greenland Groënland	...	...	40	50	56	57	57	55	...	...
Grenada Grenade	0	0	1	1	1	1	1	1	1	1
Guadeloupe Guadeloupe	...	...	2	3	4	4	5	6	...	...
Guatemala Guatemala	16	9	5	5	5	5	1	2	1	1
Haiti Haïti	3	3	1	1	1	1	1	1	1	1
Honduras Honduras	357	555	506	582	691	712	816	1 045	1 116	1 206
Jamaica Jamaïque	9	9	13	14	14	14	14	11	11	7
Martinique Martinique	...	...	7	7	8	8	1	1	...	...
Mexico Mexique	1 467	1 520	1 532	1 448	1 388	1 320	1 196	1 114	1 125	1 179
Montserrat Montserrat	1	1	1	1	1	1	1	1	...	...
Netherlands Antilles[1] Antilles néerlandaises[1]	...	...	395	432	421	455	568	841	1 039	1 047
Nicaragua Nicaragua	18	23	13	14	5	5	5	4	4	4
Panama Panama	40 674	41 305	43 255	44 604	47 365	39 298	44 949	52 486	57 619	64 710
Puerto Rico Porto Rico	...	...	76	58	57	21	16	9	...	...

63
Merchant shipping: fleets
Total, Oil tankers and Ore and bulk carrier fleets: thousand gross registered tons [cont.]
Transports maritimes : flotte marchande
Total, Pétroliers et Minéraliers et transporteurs de vracs : milliers de tonneaux de jauge brute [suite]

Flag Pavillon	1985	1986	1987	1988	1989	1990	1991	1992	1993	1994
Saint Kitts and Nevis Saint-Kitts-et-Nevis	1	0	1	0	0	0	0	0	0	0
Saint Lucia Sainte-Lucie	2	3	2	2	2	2	2	2	2	2
Saint Pierre and Miquelon Saint-Pierre-et-Miquelon	...	...	3	4	4	4	3	6	...	...
St. Vincent-Grenadines St. Vincent-Grenadines	235	510	700	900	1 486	1 937	4 221	4 698	5 287	5 420
Trinidad and Tobago Trinité-et-Tobago	19	19	19	24	22	22	22	24	23	27
Turks and Caicos Islands Iles Turques et Caiques	3	4	3	4	3	3	5	4	4	3
United States Etats-Unis	19 518	19 900	20 086	20 758	20 263	19 744	18 565	14 435	14 087	13 655
America, South · Amérique du Sud										
Argentina Argentine	2 457	2 117	1 901	1 877	1 833	1 890	1 709	873	773	716
Brazil Brésil	6 057	6 212	6 324	6 123	6 078	6 016	5 883	5 348	5 216	5 283
Chile Chili	454	567	547	604	590	616	619	580	624	721
Colombia Colombie	366	380	424	412	379	372	313	250	238	142
Ecuador Equateur	444	438	421	428	402	385	384	348	286	270
Falkland Is. (Malvinas) Iles Falkland (Malvinas)	7	7	7	7	8	10	10	14	15	16
French Guiana Guyane française	...	...	0	1	1	1	1	1	...	...
Guyana Guyana	23	23	22	15	15	15	16	17	17	15
Paraguay Paraguay	43	43	42	39	39	37	35	33	31	33
Peru Pérou	818	754	788	675	638	617	605	433	411	321
Suriname Suriname	15	13	11	11	11	13	13	13	13	8
Uruguay Uruguay	173	150	144	170	100	104	105	127	149	125
Venezuela Venezuela	985	998	999	982	1 087	935	970	871	971	920
Asia · Asie										
Azerbaijan Azerbaïdjan	...	...	...	...	...	...	...	637	667	621
Bahrain Bahreïn	48	52	44	54	55	47	262	138	103	167
Bangladesh Bangladesh	358	379	411	432	439	464	456	392	388	380
Brunei Darussalam Brunéi Darussalam	1	2	352	354	355	358	348	364	365	366

63
Merchant shipping: fleets
Total, Oil tankers and Ore and bulk carrier fleets: thousand gross registered tons [*cont.*]
Transports maritimes : flotte marchande
Total, Pétroliers et Minéraliers et transporteurs de vracs : milliers de tonneaux de jauge brute [*suite*]

Flag Pavillon	1985	1986	1987	1988	1989	1990	1991	1992	1993	1994
Cambodia Cambodge	...	...	...	...	...	...	...	4	6	6
China Chine	10 568	11 557	12 341	12 920	13 514	13 899	14 299	13 899	14 945	15 827
Cyprus Chypre	8 196	10 617	15 650	18 390	18 134	18 336	20 298	20 487	22 842	23 293
Georgia Géorgie	...	...	...	...	...	...	...	...	0	439
Hong Kong Hong-kong	6 858	8 180	8 035	7 329	6 151	6 565	5 876	7 267	7 664	7 703
India Inde	6 605	6 540	6 726	6 161	6 315	6 476	6 517	6 546	6 575	6 485
Indonesia Indonésie	1 936	2 086	2 121	2 126	2 035	2 179	2 337	2 367	2 440	2 678
Iran, Islamic Rep. of Iran, Rép. islamique d'	2 380	2 911	3 977	4 337	4 733	4 738	4 583	4 571	4 444	3 803
Iraq Iraq	1 012	1 016	1 002	953	1 056	1 044	931	902	902	885
Israel Israël	550	557	515	546	505	530	604	664	652	646
Japan Japon	39 940	38 488	35 932	32 074	28 030	27 078	26 407	25 102	24 248	22 102
Jordan Jordanie	48	42	33	32	32	42	135	61	71	61
Kazakstan Kazakstan	...	...	...	...	...	...	...	...	...	9
Korea, Dem. P. R. Corée, R. p. dém. de	513	407	407	406	396	442	511	602	671	696
Korea, Republic of Corée, République de	7 169	7 184	7 214	7 334	7 832	7 783	7 821	7 407	7 047	7 004
Kuwait Koweït	2 350	2 581	2 088	735	1 865	1 855	1 373	2 258	2 218	2 017
Lao People's Dem. Rep. Rép. dém. pop. lao	0	0	0	0	0	0	0	0	3	3
Lebanon Liban	505	485	461	405	384	307	274	293	249	258
Macau Macao	...	...	3	4	3	3	3	3	2	2
Malaysia Malaisie	1 773	1 744	1 689	1 608	1 668	1 717	1 755	2 048	2 166	2 728
Maldives Maldives	133	85	100	104	94	78	42	52	55	68
Myanmar Myanmar	116	126	239	273	582	827	1 046	947	711	683
Oman Oman	17	15	25	25	24	23	23	15	16	15
Pakistan Pakistan	451	434	394	366	366	354	358	380	360	375
Philippines Philippines	4 594	6 922	8 681	9 312	9 385	8 515	8 626	8 470	8 466	9 413

63
Merchant shipping: fleets
Total, Oil tankers and Ore and bulk carrier fleets: thousand gross registered tons [*cont.*]
Transports maritimes : flotte marchande
Total, Pétroliers et Minéraliers et transporteurs de vracs : milliers de tonneaux de jauge brute [*suite*]

Flag Pavillon	1985	1986	1987	1988	1989	1990	1991	1992	1993	1994
Qatar Qatar	353	307	306	309	306	359	485	392	431	557
Saudi Arabia Arabie saoudite	3 137	2 978	2 692	2 269	2 119	1 683	1 321	1 016	998	1 064
Singapore Singapour	6 505	6 268	7 098	7 209	7 273	7 928	8 488	9 905	11 035	11 895
Sri Lanka Sri Lanka	635	622	594	410	287	350	333	285	294	294
Syrian Arab Republic Rép. arabe syrienne	58	63	63	64	74	80	109	144	209	279
Thailand Thaïlande	586	533	511	515	539	615	725	917	1 116	1 374
Turkey Turquie	3 684	3 424	3 336	3 281	3 240	3 719	4 107	4 136	5 044	5 453
Turkmenistan Turkménistan	...	...	...	...	...	...	...	...	...	23
United Arab Emirates Emirats arabes unis	869	654	732	825	839	750	889	884	804	1 016
Viet Nam Viet Nam	299	339	360	338	358	470	574	616	728	773
Yemen Yémen	...	...	...	...	...	17	17	16	24	25
former Yemen Arab Rep. anc. Yémen rép. arabe	3	7	200	196	196	...	...	...	...	...
former Dem. Yemen anciennce Yémen dém.	12	13	12	11	11	...	...	...	...	...
Europe · Europe										
Albania Albanie	56	56	56	56	56	56	59	59	59	59
Austria Autriche	134	125	194	201	204	139	139	140	160	134
Belgium Belgique	2 400	2 420	2 268	2 118	2 044	1 954	314	241	218	233
Bulgaria Bulgarie	1 322	1 385	1 551	1 392	1 375	1 360	1 367	1 348	1 314	1 295
Channel Islands Iles Anglo-Normandes	...	...	23	15	10	8	4	3	3	3
Croatia Croatie	...	...	...	...	...	...	...	210	193	247
former Czechoslovakia† anc. Tchécoslovaquie†	184	198	157	158	191	326	361	238	...	...
Czech Republic République tchèque	...	...	...	...	...	...	...	...	228	173
Denmark Danemark	4 942	4 651	4 714	4 322	4 785	5 008	5 698	5 269	5 293	5 698
Estonia Estonie	...	...	...	...	...	...	...	680	686	695
Faeroe Islands Iles Féroé	103	115	119	130	121	124	115	111	100	100
Finland Finlande	1 974	1 470	1 122	838	944	1 069	1 053	1 197	1 354	1 404

63
Merchant shipping: fleets
Total, Oil tankers and Ore and bulk carrier fleets: thousand gross registered tons [cont.]
Transports maritimes : flotte marchande
Total, Pétroliers et Minéraliers et transporteurs de vracs : milliers de tonneaux de jauge brute [suite]

Flag Pavillon	1985	1986	1987	1988	1989	1990	1991	1992	1993	1994
France[2] France[2]	8 237	5 936	5 264	4 395	4 286	3 721	3 879	3 869	4 252	4 242
Germany † Allemagne† F. R. Germany	...	...	...	...	...	...	5 971	5 360	4 979	5 696
R. f. Allemagne	6 177	5 565	4 318	3 917	3 967	4 301	...	...	...	...
former German D. R. anc. R. d. allemande	1 434	1 519	1 494	1 443	1 500	1 437	...	...	...	...
Gibraltar Gibraltar	583	1 613	2 827	3 042	2 611	2 008	1 410	492	384	331
Greece Grèce	31 032	28 391	23 560	21 979	21 324	20 522	22 753	25 739	29 134	30 162
Hungary Hongrie	77	86	77	76	76	98	104	92	45	45
Iceland Islande	180	176	174	175	183	177	168	177	174	175
Ireland Irlande	194	149	154	173	167	181	195	199	184	190
Isle of Man Ile de Man	...	...	1 914	2 137	2 111	1 824	1 937	1 628	1 563	2 093
Italy Italie	8 343	7 897	7 817	7 794	7 602	7 991	8 122	7 513	7 030	6 818
Latvia Lettonie	...	...	...	...	...	...	...	1 207	1 155	1 034
Lithuania Lituanie	...	...	...	...	...	...	...	668	639	661
Luxembourg Luxembourg	...	...	...	2	4	3	1 703	1 656	1 327	1 143
Malta Malte	1 856	2 015	1 726	2 686	3 329	4 519	6 916	11 005	14 163	15 455
Netherlands Pays-Bas	4 301	4 324	3 514	3 294	3 234	3 330	3 305	3 346	3 086	3 349
Norway Norvège	15 339	9 295	6 359	9 350	15 597	23 429	23 586	22 231	21 536	22 388
Poland Pologne	3 315	3 457	3 470	3 489	3 416	3 369	3 348	3 109	2 646	2 610
Portugal Portugal	1 437	1 114	1 045	985	723	851	887	972	1 002	882
Romania Roumanie	3 024	3 234	3 264	3 561	3 783	4 005	3 828	2 981	2 867	2 689
Russian Federation Fédération de Russie	...	...	...	...	...	...	...	16 302	16 814	16 504
Slovakia Slovaquie	...	...	...	...	...	...	...	...	...	6
Slovenia Slovénie	...	...	...	...	...	...	...	2	2	9
Spain[3] Espagne[3]	6 256	5 422	4 949	4 415	3 962	3 807	3 617	2 643	1 752	1 560
Sweden Suède	3 162	2 517	2 270	2 116	2 167	2 775	3 174	2 884	2 439	2 797
Switzerland Suisse	342	346	355	259	220	287	286	346	300	336

63
Merchant shipping: fleets
Total, Oil tankers and Ore and bulk carrier fleets: thousand gross registered tons [*cont.*]
Transports maritimes : flotte marchande
Total, Pétroliers et Minéraliers et transporteurs de vracs : milliers de tonneaux de jauge brute [*suite*]

Flag Pavillon	1985	1986	1987	1988	1989	1990	1991	1992	1993	1994
Ukraine Ukraine	...	...	...	...	...	...	...	5 222	5 265	5 279
United Kingdom Royaume-Uni	14 344	11 567	6 568	6 108	5 525	4 887	4 670	4 081	4 117	4 430
Yugoslavia Yougoslavie	...	...	...	...	...	...	...	2	2	2
Yugoslavia, SFR† Yougoslavie, Rfs†	2 699	2 873	3 165	3 476	3 681	3 816	3 293	...	...	...
Oceania · Océanie										
Australia Australie	2 088	2 368	2 405	2 366	2 494	2 512	1 709	2 689	2 862	3 012
Cook Islands Iles Cook	...	...	...	4	5	6	7	5	5	5
Micronesia,Federated States of Micron, Etats fédérés de	...	...	...	...	...	6	8	9	9	9
Fiji Fidji	31	30	35	37	62	55	50	64	39	31
French Polynesia Polynésie française	...	...	21	18	17	20	20	23	...	...
Guam Guam	...	...	3	3	3	4	1	1	...	...
Kiribati Kiribati	2	3	3	4	4	4	4	5	5	5
Marshall Islands Iles Marshall	...	...	...	...	...	1 551	1 698	1 676	2 198	2 149
Nauru Nauru	67	67	66	60	41	32	15	5	1	...
New Caledonia Nouvelle-Calédonie	...	...	12	12	13	14	14	14	...	...
New Zealand Nouvelle-Zélande	296	314	334	332	252	254	269	238	218	246
Papua New Guinea Papouasie-Nvl-Guinée	29	31	36	38	37	37	36	46	47	47
Samoa Samoa	26	26	26	26	27	27	6	6	6	6
Solomon Islands Iles Salomon	6	6	6	9	8	8	8	8	7	8
Tonga Tonga	17	16	18	14	35	52	40	11	12	10
Tuvalu Tuvalu	1	1	1	1	2	1	1	12	70	51
Vanuatu Vanuatu	138	165	540	790	920	2 164	2 173	2 064	1 946	1 998
Wallis and Futuna Islands Iles Wallis et Futuna	...	...	39	44	59	39	42	80	80	105
former USSR† · ancienne URSS†										
former USSR† ancienne URSS†	24 745	24 961	25 232	25 784	25 854	26 737	26 405	...	...	...

63
Merchant shipping: fleets
Total, Oil tankers and Ore and bulk carrier fleets: thousand gross registered tons [*cont.*]
Transports maritimes : flotte marchande
Total, Pétroliers et Minéraliers et transporteurs de vracs : milliers de tonneaux de jauge brute [*suite*]

Flag Pavillon	1985	1986	1987	1988	1989	1990	1991	1992	1993	1994
B. Oil tankers • Pétroliers										
World *Monde*	**138 448**	**128 426**	**127 600**	**127 843**	**129 578**	**134 836**	**138 897**	**138 149**	**143 077**	**144 595**
Africa • Afrique										
Algeria Algérie	594	119	134	119	40	39	39	32	32	35
Angola Angola	2	2	2	2	2	2	2	2	2	2
Cape Verde Cap-Vert	...	...	...	0	0	1	1	0	0	0
Côte d'Ivoire Côte d'Ivoire	1	1	1	1	0	0	0	0	0	1
Egypt Egypte	97	99	95	255	244	263	262	170	195	245
Ethiopia incl.Eritrea Ethiopie comp. Erythrée	3	1	1	1	1	4	4	4	4	4
Gabon Gabon	74	74	0	0	0	0	1	1	1	1
Ghana Ghana	...	...	1	1	1	1	1	1	1	1
Kenya Kenya	...	...	...	...	...	...	4	4	4	4
Liberia Libéria	31 585	28 675	28 249	27 961	26 667	28 763	26 700	27 440	26 273	28 275
Libyan Arab Jamah. Jamah. arabe libyenne	745	708	708	708	581	707	581	581	581	579
Madagascar Madagascar	10	8	9	9	5	5	5	9	9	9
Morocco Maroc	62	10	10	10	10	10	10	14	14	14
Mozambique Mozambique	0	1	1	1	1	1	1	1	1	0
Nigeria Nigéria	154	223	227	227	225	225	225	235	236	245
Senegal Sénégal	4	1	1	0	...	...	...	...	...	...
Sierra Leone Sierra Leone	...	...	0	0	0	0	1	1	1	1
South Africa Afrique du Sud	38	39	21	21	20	1	1	1	1	1
Sudan Soudan	...	...	1	1	1	1	1	1	1	1
Tunisia Tunisie	132	132	132	132	27	27	27	27	6	6
United Rep.Tanzania Rép. Unie de Tanzanie	4	4	4	4	3	3	3	4	5	4
America, North • Amérique du Nord										
Antigua and Barbuda Antigua-et-Barbuda	...	...	...	2	47	11	14	5	7	2

63
Merchant shipping: fleets
Total, Oil tankers and Ore and bulk carrier fleets: thousand gross registered tons [*cont.*]
Transports maritimes : flotte marchande
Total, Pétroliers et Minéraliers et transporteurs de vracs : milliers de tonneaux de jauge brute [*suite*]

Flag Pavillon	1985	1986	1987	1988	1989	1990	1991	1992	1993	1994
Bahamas Bahamas	3 010	4 201	5 357	4 556	6 110	6 780	8 738	9 812	9 680	10 393
Barbados Barbade	...	...	...	...	...	...	...	44	44	44
Belize Belize	...	...	...	...	...	...	...	4	9	59
Bermuda Bermudes	220	301	895	2 836	3 273	3 285	1 987	2 058	1 838	1 569
Canada Canada	281	279	272	259	260	242	233	162	153	153
Cayman Islands Iles Caïmanes	46	737	218	75	43	79	72	31	31	6
Cuba Cuba	68	68	68	68	80	80	78	71	67	71
Dominican Republic Rép. dominicaine	1	1	1	1	1	1	1	1	1	1
Honduras Honduras	51	67	58	51	87	112	149	144	119	85
Jamaica Jamaïque	...	...	...	2	2	2	2	2	2	2
Mexico Mexique	540	606	587	522	533	507	507	479	478	425
Netherlands Antilles Antilles néerlandaises	...	...	...	...	...	...	...	32	32	32
Nicaragua Nicaragua	3	1	...	...	...	...	...	...	...	...
Panama Panama	8 414	9 192	9 966	10 659	11 418	10 080	13 976	16 454	18 273	18 649
St. Vincent-Grenadines St. Vincent-Grenadines	...	83	96	141	203	295	378	834	1 112	941
Turks and Caicos Islands Iles Turques et Caiques	1	1	1	1	0	0	1	1	1	1
United States Etats-Unis	7 472	7 296	7 428	7 949	7 956	8 532	8 069	5 493	5 013	4 500
America, South · Amérique du Sud										
Argentina Argentine	842	654	585	586	543	568	542	221	107	124
Brazil Brésil	1 834	1 938	1 943	1 849	1 838	1 897	1 947	1 930	2 068	2 112
Chile Chili	15	15	15	19	28	26	26	4	4	41
Colombia Colombie	32	36	12	14	14	14	11	6	6	6
Ecuador Equateur	160	157	159	159	120	120	116	112	75	77
Paraguay Paraguay	3	3	3	3	1	1	1	2	2	2
Peru Pérou	183	147	197	197	197	190	177	131	131	68

63
Merchant shipping: fleets
Total, Oil tankers and Ore and bulk carrier fleets: thousand gross registered tons [*cont.*]
Transports maritimes : flotte marchande
Total, Pétroliers et Minéraliers et transporteurs de vracs : milliers de tonneaux de jauge brute [*suite*]

Flag Pavillon	1985	1986	1987	1988	1989	1990	1991	1992	1993	1994
Suriname Suriname	0	0	...	...	1	2	2	2	2	2
Uruguay Uruguay	96	76	77	118	47	47	47	46	46	46
Venezuela Venezuela	498	470	470	463	463	463	478	455	437	420
Asia · Asie										
Azerbaijan Azerbaïdjan	...	...	...	...	...	...	...	197	222	180
Bahrain Bahreïn	3	3	3	2	2	2	2	2	2	55
Bangladesh Bangladesh	38	40	50	60	49	50	51	51	51	51
China Chine	1 476	1 701	1 751	1 826	1 790	1 810	1 840	1 721	2 117	2 278
Cyprus Chypre	3 327	4 481	4 984	5 618	5 639	5 390	5 996	4 677	4 960	4 634
Georgia Géorgie	...	...	...	...	...	...	...	...	...	220
Hong Kong Hong-kong	440	884	1 095	945	827	1 000	756	880	818	697
India Inde	1 717	1 814	1 828	1 772	1 718	1 734	1 805	2 009	2 112	2 337
Indonesia Indonésie	491	617	644	660	580	582	595	594	608	646
Iran, Islamic Rep. of Iran, Rép. islamique d'	918	1 242	2 347	2 717	3 102	3 101	2 945	2 944	2 765	2 135
Iraq Iraq	747	777	770	729	831	829	725	720	719	719
Israel Israël	1	1	1	1	1	0	0	1	1	1
Japan Japon	14 089	12 365	10 798	9 628	7 879	7 584	7 204	7 167	7 249	6 421
Jordan Jordanie	...	...	...	...	...	...	50	50	50	50
Korea, Dem. P. R. Corée, R. p. dém. de	171	59	59	13	13	13	13	112	115	115
Korea, Republic of Corée, République de	1 002	977	963	951	808	593	543	612	620	524
Kuwait Koweït	1 290	1 629	1 261	133	1 092	1 101	1 044	1 706	1 548	1 343
Lebanon Liban	14	14	25	25	14	14	2	2	2	2
Malaysia Malaisie	224	238	241	180	163	179	249	256	257	382
Maldives Maldives	1	2	3	3	5	5	5	6	6	6
Myanmar Myanmar	3	3	3	3	2	6	9	3	3	3

63
Merchant shipping: fleets
Total, Oil tankers and Ore and bulk carrier fleets: thousand gross registered tons [cont.]
Transports maritimes : flotte marchande
Total, Pétroliers et Minéraliers et transporteurs de vracs : milliers de tonneaux de jauge brute [suite]

Flag Pavillon	1985	1986	1987	1988	1989	1990	1991	1992	1993	1994
Oman Oman	0	0	0	0	...	0	0	...	1	0
Pakistan Pakistan	44	43	43	43	43	43	43	50	50	50
Philippines Philippines	562	656	755	480	403	372	376	388	414	419
Qatar Qatar	112	112	112	112	108	160	160	125	125	177
Saudi Arabia Arabie saoudite	1 578	1 604	1 636	1 300	1 214	928	561	265	277	210
Singapore Singapour	2 049	1 653	2 305	2 443	2 553	3 165	3 543	4 182	4 684	4 959
Sri Lanka Sri Lanka	137	140	98	5	8	78	78	74	74	74
Thailand Thaïlande	147	62	69	77	73	85	100	172	184	190
Turkey Turquie	1 582	1 037	846	828	793	777	772	828	903	954
Turkmenistan Turkménistan	...	...	...	...	...	...	...	...	...	1
United Arab Emirates Emirats arabes unis	629	372	396	450	441	332	334	458	326	502
Viet Nam Viet Nam	38	40	41	15	18	18	91	15	91	94
Yemen Yémen	...	...	...	...	...	2	2	2	2	2
former Yemen Arab Rep. anc. Yémen rép. arabe	...	...	193	193	193	...	...	...	...	...
former Dem. Yemen anciennce Yémen dém.	2	2	2	2	2	...	...	...	...	...
Europe · Europe										
Belgium Belgique	232	266	224	252	273	272	12	2	2	3
Bulgaria Bulgarie	312	317	441	292	285	288	293	283	284	256
Croatia Croatie	...	...	...	...	...	...	...	7	7	19
Denmark Danemark	2 199	2 044	2 166	2 053	2 041	2 024	2 061	834	787	788
Estonia Estonie	...	...	...	...	...	...	...	6	6	10
Faeroe Islands Iles Féroé	...	...	...	...	...	...	...	1	1	1
Finland Finlande	926	597	457	211	155	245	209	256	307	303
France France	4 346	2 603	2 465	1 953	1 944	1 717	1 674	1 696	1 869	1 957

63
Merchant shipping: fleets
Total, Oil tankers and Ore and bulk carrier fleets: thousand gross registered tons [*cont.*]
Transports maritimes : flotte marchande
Total, Pétroliers et Minéraliers et transporteurs de vracs : milliers de tonneaux de jauge brute [*suite*]

Flag Pavillon	1985	1986	1987	1988	1989	1990	1991	1992	1993	1994
Germany † Allemagne† F. R. Germany R. f. Allemagne	...	...	...	...	...	...	249	89	89	83
	1 394	750	317	265	283	228	...	...	...	...
former German D. R. anc. R. d. allemande	36	36	36	36	36	6	...	...	...	...
Gibraltar Gibraltar	167	856	1 834	2 318	2 060	1 552	1 123	319	276	271
Greece Grèce	9 366	10 259	9 247	8 492	8 229	7 856	9 095	10 876	13 273	13 386
Iceland Islande	3	3	2	2	2	1	1	0	2	2
Ireland Irlande	9	8	15	15	19	19	19	8	8	9
Isle of Man Ile de Man	...	...	...	...	...	...	...	801	744	1 059
Italy Italie	3 601	2 561	2 631	2 670	2 461	2 560	2 685	2 115	1 949	2 181
Latvia Lettonie	...	...	...	...	...	...	...	533	536	483
Lithuania Lituanie	...	...	...	...	...	...	...	17	12	13
Luxembourg Luxembourg	...	...	...	2	2	2	264	107	55	3
Malta Malte	329	515	312	977	1 405	1 646	2 412	3 086	5 176	5 699
Monaco Monaco	3	...	...	...	...	...	...	...	...	...
Netherlands Pays-Bas	745	931	774	615	575	590	618	364	407	403
Norway Norvège	7 263	3 304	2 785	4 397	7 074	10 794	10 904	9 220	9 265	8 962
Poland Pologne	318	318	317	235	154	154	136	89	89	88
Portugal Portugal	860	533	533	486	323	393	460	657	723	552
Romania Roumanie	384	384	384	523	596	645	679	520	446	438
Russian Federation Fédération de Russie	...	...	...	...	...	...	...	2 436	2 507	2 378
Spain Espagne	2 906	2 372	2 104	1 616	1 486	1 472	1 488	917	452	430
Sweden Suède	894	504	370	191	211	534	862	692	368	370
Ukraine Ukraine	...	...	...	...	...	...	...	80	80	84
United Kingdom Royaume-Uni	5 937	4 394	2 822	2 835	2 604	2 367	2 316	1 179	1 176	1 185

63
Merchant shipping: fleets
Total, Oil tankers and Ore and bulk carrier fleets: thousand gross registered tons [*cont.*]
Transports maritimes : flotte marchande
Total, Pétroliers et Minéraliers et transporteurs de vracs : milliers de tonneaux de jauge brute [*suite*]

Flag Pavillon	1985	1986	1987	1988	1989	1990	1991	1992	1993	1994
Yugoslavia, SFR† Yougoslavie, Rfs†	217	308	317	312	312	306	264	...	...	...
Oceania · Océanie										
Australia Australie	588	662	702	702	678	677	708	780	780	779
Fiji Fidji	5	5	5	5	5	4	4	4	3	3
Marshall Islands Iles Marshall	...	...	...	...	...	...	...	1 146	1 601	1 560
New Caledonia Nouvelle-Calédonie	...	...	...	...	...	...	...	1	...	...
New Zealand Nouvelle-Zélande	73	73	73	80	80	80	80	73	54	54
Papua New Guinea Papouasie-Nvl-Guinée	2	2	2	2	1	2	2	3	3	3
Vanuatu Vanuatu	...	26	248	252	175	233	233	184	24	15
Wallis and Futuna Islands Iles Wallis et Futuna	...	...	...	...	...	...	...	50	50	75
former USSR† · ancienne URSS†										
former USSR† ancienne URSS†	4 591	4 087	4 207	4 368	4 128	4 167	4 068	...	...	...

C. Ore and bulk carrier fleets · Minéraliers et transporteurs de vracs

World *Monde*	133 983	132 908	131 028	129 635	129 482	133 190	135 884	139 042	140 915	144 914
Africa · Afrique										
Algeria Algérie	57	57	57	77	95	153	172	172	172	172
Egypt Egypte	273	343	369	356	343	343	343	343	343	420
Gabon Gabon	...	...	...	...	...	...	...	...	11	11
Liberia Libéria	20 773	18 028	16 788	15 647	14 374	16 099	15 629	17 035	15 640	15 970
Mauritius Maurice	16	125	97	81	39	47	47	80	116	120
Morocco Maroc	125	125	92	92	92	92	92	92	...	...
Nigeria Nigéria	...	...	...	...	...	...	...	1	1	1
South Africa Afrique du Sud	129	125	88	88	...	...	...	...	...	...
Tunisia Tunisie	37	37	37	37	37	37	37	37	37	37

63
Merchant shipping: fleets
Total, Oil tankers and Ore and bulk carrier fleets: thousand gross registered tons [*cont.*]
Transports maritimes : flotte marchande
Total, Pétroliers et Minéraliers et transporteurs de vracs : milliers de tonneaux de jauge brute [*suite*]

Flag Pavillon	1985	1986	1987	1988	1989	1990	1991	1992	1993	1994
America, North · Amérique du Nord										
Antigua and Barbuda Antigua-et-Barbuda	...	...	...	...	3	3	3	43	90	93
Bahamas Bahamas	405	902	2 105	2 368	2 822	3 698	4 872	4 312	4 515	4 269
Bermuda Bermudes	258	319	432	294	157	161	199	213	147	165
Canada Canada	2 000	1 851	1 654	1 590	1 550	1 462	1 414	1 425	1 377	1 371
Cayman Islands Iles Caïmanes	117	283	184	103	111	89	54	69	100	136
Cuba Cuba	62	62	62	62	62	62	62	31	30	1
Dominican Republic Rép. dominicaine	9	11	11	11	11	11	...	...	...	...
Honduras Honduras	...	...	25	60	103	56	57	92	90	118
Mexico Mexique	310	311	328	271	226	178	48	...	...	...
Netherlands Antilles[1] Antilles néerlandaises[1]	...	...	...	...	...	...	...	113	131	146
Panama Panama	17 431	17 400	17 733	17 924	17 513	13 293	13 669	17 327	19 280	22 169
St. Vincent-Grenadines St. Vincent-Grenadines	171	298	406	391	540	651	1 004	1 816	1 798	1 939
United States Etats-Unis	2 075	2 020	1 989	1 935	1 884	2 140	2 168	1 550	1 539	1 546
America, South · Amérique du Sud										
Argentina Argentine	505	515	457	465	459	502	365	62	62	62
Brazil Brésil	2 748	2 802	2 894	2 859	2 943	2 971	2 855	2 378	2 199	2 214
Chile Chili	240	314	278	320	295	296	296	279	297	306
Colombia Colombie	47	29	92	92	81	81	81	63	63	...
Ecuador Equateur	11	11	...	22	22	27	27	22	22	22
Peru Pérou	192	190	160	134	129	129	129	64	49	31
Venezuela Venezuela	75	86	86	109	157	147	147	96	147	147
Asia · Asie										
Bahrain Bahreïn	17	17	12	12	12	...	...	...	8	8
China Chine	3 531	3 871	4 143	4 391	4 726	4 907	5 206	5 405	5 714	5 960

63
Merchant shipping: fleets
Total, Oil tankers and Ore and bulk carrier fleets: thousand gross registered tons [*cont.*]
Transports maritimes : flotte marchande
Total, Pétroliers et Minéraliers et transporteurs de vracs : milliers de tonneaux de jauge brute [*suite*]

Flag Pavillon	1985	1986	1987	1988	1989	1990	1991	1992	1993	1994
Cyprus Chypre	2 741	3 739	6 788	8 789	8 821	9 226	10 234	10 816	12 277	12 317
Georgia Géorgie	...	...	...	...	...	...	...	...	...	170
Hong Kong Hong-kong	5 428	6 090	5 748	5 355	4 363	4 396	3 925	4 864	5 466	5 570
India Inde	2 954	2 943	3 152	2 729	3 025	3 182	3 134	2 912	2 939	2 740
Indonesia Indonésie	128	129	129	129	145	138	149	170	170	170
Iran, Islamic Rep. of Iran, Rép. islamique d'	777	1 109	1 080	1 068	1 059	1 059	1 059	1 047	1 049	1 048
Israel Israël	64	74	42	42	32	32	22	22	22	23
Japan Japon	13 900	13 895	12 611	10 847	9 234	8 788	8 652	8 509	7 336	6 615
Jordan Jordanie	26	26	26	25	25	25	13	...	10	10
Korea, Dem. P. R. Corée, R. p. dém. de	64	64	54	89	68	79	79	84	130	128
Korea, Republic of Corée, République de	4 258	4 269	4 140	4 227	4 492	4 708	4 463	3 931	3 575	3 659
Lebanon Liban	131	131	116	84	91	44	44	55	46	46
Malaysia Malaisie	468	456	378	378	347	347	319	449	556	798
Maldives Maldives	54	45	43	43	43	32	21	19	11	11
Myanmar Myanmar	...	...	80	112	355	518	569	553	415	358
Pakistan Pakistan	12	12	...	...	...	...	...	17	17	88
Philippines Philippines	2 756	4 805	6 388	6 906	6 987	6 344	6 262	6 040	5 999	6 496
Saudi Arabia Arabie saoudite	387	373	193	170	170	26	...	12	12	12
Singapore Singapour	2 258	2 478	2 465	2 287	2 083	2 190	2 132	2 626	2 889	3 209
Sri Lanka Sri Lanka	229	242	256	135	37	103	93	93	93	93
Syrian Arab Republic Rép. arabe syrienne	...	...	...	...	...	...	14	24	32	48
Thailand Thaïlande	13	28	16	...	10	10	32	69	158	224
Turkey Turquie	1 129	1 353	1 419	1 360	1 413	1 932	2 331	2 263	3 036	3 253
United Arab Emirates Emirats arabes unis	9	9	9	22	24	34	32	60	27	47

63
Merchant shipping: fleets
Total, Oil tankers and Ore and bulk carrier fleets: thousand gross registered tons [*cont.*]
Transports maritimes : flotte marchande
Total, Pétroliers et Minéraliers et transporteurs de vracs : milliers de tonneaux de jauge brute [*suite*]

Flag Pavillon	1985	1986	1987	1988	1989	1990	1991	1992	1993	1994
Viet Nam Viet Nam	14	14	14	14	14	14	21	21	21	21
Europe · Europe										
Austria Autriche	63	63	128	128	136	71	71	63	85	49
Belgium Belgique	1 365	1 416	1 350	1 164	1 091	979	...	...	...	...
Bulgaria Bulgarie	525	572	620	612	612	611	601	613	589	578
Croatia Croatie	...	...	...	...	...	...	...	32	3	19
former Czechoslovakia† anc. Tchécoslovaquie†	103	116	75	75	96	241	276	153	...	...
Czech Republic République tchèque	...	...	...	...	...	...	...	...	153	112
Denmark Danemark	423	290	251	163	326	353	525	563	498	569
Estonia Estonie	...	...	...	...	...	...	...	160	160	160
Finland Finlande	280	121	70	70	78	120	89	72	71	71
France France	1 400	957	858	698	641	357	406	343	463	462
Germany † Allemagne†	...	...	...	...	...	...	695	377	308	285
F. R. Germany R. f. Allemagne	768	559	402	344	318	397	...	...	...	...
former German D. R. anc. R. d. allemande	323	353	362	338	324	324	...	...	...	...
Gibraltar Gibraltar	...	...	716	560	398	344	192	73	58	28
Greece Grèce	15 324	13 202	10 557	10 060	9 987	9 783	10 802	11 638	12 482	12 988
Iceland Islande	...	...	...	...	...	4	...	0	0	0
Ireland Irlande	57	...	...	...	...	9	9	3	3	3
Isle of Man Ile de Man	...	...	...	...	...	...	...	304	171	223
Italy Italie	3 041	3 059	2 792	2 561	2 351	2 346	2 228	2 200	1 829	1 549
Lithuania Lituanie	...	...	...	...	...	...	...	112	116	111
Luxembourg Luxembourg	...	...	...	...	...	...	993	879	669	555
Malta Malte	806	952	882	1 019	1 172	1 774	2 772	5 103	5 854	6 196
Netherlands Pays-Bas	699	524	318	295	328	328	359	244	98	99

63
Merchant shipping: fleets
Total, Oil tankers and Ore and bulk carrier fleets: thousand gross registered tons [cont.]
Transports maritimes : flotte marchande
Total, Pétroliers et Minéraliers et transporteurs de vracs : milliers de tonneaux de jauge brute [suite]

Flag Pavillon	1985	1986	1987	1988	1989	1990	1991	1992	1993	1994
Norway Norvège	3 930	2 479	1 085	1 684	4 170	7 283	7 091	5 912	4 924	4 865
Poland Pologne	1 337	1 499	1 551	1 604	1 610	1 603	1 636	1 667	1 524	1 511
Portugal Portugal	158	231	286	267	178	223	197	75	27	85
Romania Roumanie	1 439	1 590	1 590	1 667	1 758	1 891	1 698	1 082	1 089	980
Russian Federation Fédération de Russie	...	...	...	...	...	...	...	1 903	1 821	1 757
Spain Espagne	1 321	1 175	1 060	1 105	955	850	732	504	223	59
Sweden Suède	394	271	134	127	176	383	415	209	119	45
Switzerland Suisse	247	264	284	210	183	252	252	312	268	307
Ukraine Ukraine	...	...	...	...	...	...	...	1 199	1 195	1 196
United Kingdom Royaume-Uni	3 014	2 150	1 492	1 286	1 249	749	743	122	104	74
Yugoslavia, SFR† Yougoslavie, Rfs†	1 115	1 182	1 369	2 212	1 915	2 018	1 707	...	...	...
Oceania · Océanie										
Australia Australie	932	1 185	1 173	1 178	1 106	1 112	1 004	987	1 030	1 049
Marshall Islands Iles Marshall	...	...	...	...	...	...	...	440	506	539
Nauru Nauru	37	37	37	37	17	17	...	...	...	...
New Zealand Nouvelle-Zélande	...	...	26	26	26	26	13	22	25	25
Vanuatu Vanuatu	106	77	208	361	482	1 133	1 132	1 052	1 117	1 008
former USSR† · ancienne URSS†										
former USSR† ancienne URSS†	2 974	3 433	3 535	3 805	4 115	4 183	3 902	...	...	...

Source:
Lloyd's Register of Shipping (London).

Source:
"Lloyd's Register of Shipping" (Londres).

† For detailed descriptions of data pertaining to
former Czechoslovakia, Germany, SFR Yugoslavia and former
USSR, see Annex I - Country or area nomenclature, regional
and other groupings.

† Pour les descriptions en détails des données
relatives à l'ancienne Tchécoslovaquie, l'Allemagne, la Rfs
Yougoslavie et l'ancienne URSS, voir l'Annexe I -
Nomenclature des pays ou zones, groupements régionaux et
autres groupements.

1 Including Aruba.
2 Including French Antarctic Territory.
3 Including Canary Islands.

1 Y compris Aruba.
2 Y compris Territoire antarctiques française.
3 Y compris Iles Canaries.

64
International maritime transport
Transports maritimes internationaux
Vessels entered and cleared: thousand net registered tons
Navires entrés et sortis : milliers de tonneaux de jauge nette

Country or area Pays ou zone	1985	1986	1987	1988	1989	1990	1991	1992	1993	1994
Algeria Algérie										
Vessels entered Navires entrés	51 012	49 408	48 657	49 213	50 721	44 659	...	...	...	...
Vessels cleared Navires sortis	50 962	49 161	48 516	48 992	50 646	44 611	...	...	...	...
American Samoa Samoa américaines										
Vessels entered[1] Navires entrés[1]	851	...	...	...	...	...	848	618	440	581
Argentina Argentine										
Vessels entered[2] Navires entrés[2]	37 850	34 044	29 294	32 535	31 253	38 283	36 664[3]	11 379[4]	20 092[5]	12 345[4]
Vessels cleared[2] Navires sortis[2]	50 962	49 161	48 516	48 992	50 646	44 611	...	...	...	...
Bangladesh Bangladesh										
Vessels entered[6] Navires entrés[6]	5 456	5 372	5 646	5 184	5 655	991	1 169	859	875	...
Vessels cleared[6] Navires sortis[6]	4 795	3 833	3 254	3 323	3 796	664	695	629	571	...
Belgium Belgique										
Vessels entered Navires entrés	88 098	87 458	90 822	96 548	190 157	204 857	211 767	236 323	229 915	239 678
Vessels cleared Navires sortis	77 086	72 235	75 037	76 919	155 017	162 236	165 185	189 286	190 795	201 448
Brazil Brésil										
Vessels entered Navires entrés	52 206	63 499	65 519	61 992	59 643	61 852	65 461	65 794	74 314	...
Vessels cleared Navires sortis	143 333	134 303	145 425	159 468	169 512	170 917	166 047	164 152	173 624	...
Brunei Darussalam Brunéi Darussalam										
Vessels entered Navires entrés	24 542	1 215 694	938 919	1 056 590	1 266 208	1 310 080	1 376 212	1 583 776	1 695 497	...
Vessels cleared Navires sortis	10 524	1 211 898	930 574	1 056 590	1 265 100	1 306 281	1 371 748	1 582 087	1 685 075	...
Cameroon Cameroun										
Vessels entered[2 7] Navires entrés[2 7]	6 362	6 427	6 059	5 562	5 333	5 521	5 426	5 344	5 279	...
Canada Canada										
Vessels entered[8] Navires entrés[8]	67 643	62 523	61 975	67 688	68 940	64 163	58 690	58 724	56 769	60 417
Vessels cleared[8] Navires sortis[8]	116 796	109 616	114 546	120 442	116 769	114 272	116 974	109 263	108 587	116 279
Cape Verde Cap-Vert										
Vessels entered Navires entrés	3 539	4 054	4 493	...	...	...	...	...	...	...
Colombia Colombie										
Vessels entered[2] Navires entrés[2]	16 092	17 497	19 691	18 781	20 410	22 713	23 732	21 927	24 874	28 138
Vessels cleared Navires sortis	15 799	17 218	19 331	18 826	20 437	22 448	23 809	22 056	24 967	27 919
Congo Congo										
Vessels entered Navires entrés	7 564	7 504	7 181	7 793	7 386	7 148	6 480	...	...	...
Costa Rica Costa Rica										
Vessels entered Navires entrés	...	...	...	...	...	...	...	3 178	3 556	...
Vessels cleared Navires sortis	...	...	...	...	...	...	...	2 486	2 713	...

64
International maritime transport
Vessels entered and cleared: thousand net registered tons [*cont.*]
Transports maritimes internationaux
Navires entrés et sortis : milliers de tonneaux de jauge nette [*suite*]

Country or area Pays ou zone	1985	1986	1987	1988	1989	1990	1991	1992	1993	1994
Croatia Croatie										
Vessels entered										
Navires entrés	35 214	35 591	35 047	41 072	39 948	43 736	30 801	27 591	29 753	34 438
Vessels cleared										
Navires sortis	28 555	30 109	30 132	36 309	34 715	35 624	29 133	24 542	27 701	33 305
Cuba Cuba										
Vessels entered										
Navires entrés	12 400	12 900	15 400	12 100	...	...	...	...	...	...
Vessels cleared										
Navires sortis	12 100	12 700	15 300	12 000	...	...	...	...	...	...
Cyprus Chypre										
Vessels entered										
Navires entrés	11 436	12 429	12 839	13 231	14 793	14 964	12 860	14 791	14 918	15 350
Djibouti Djibouti										
Vessels entered[2]										
Navires entrés[2]	4 197	...	...	...	...	...	...	...	...	...
Dominican Republic Rép. dominicaine										
Vessels entered[2]										
Navires entrés[2]	8 969	9 094	9 219	9 344	9 469	9 594	9 719	9 844	9 969	...
Vessels cleared										
Navires sortis	8 996	9 111	9 226	9 340	9 455	9 569	9 684	9 798	9 913	...
Ecuador Equateur										
Vessels entered										
Navires entrés	12 653	12 694	12 524	16 303	17 008	17 484	21 152	20 806	22 610	28 976
Egypt Egypte										
Vessels entered										
Navires entrés	37 805	37 865	30 976	20 966	23 252	23 629	21 457	18 488	23 125	23 806
Vessels cleared										
Navires sortis	34 537	34 751	27 729	11 132	11 157	10 184	12 259	13 716	13 706	16 029
El Salvador El Salvador										
Vessels entered										
Navires entrés	2 341	...	...	...	2 357	2 208	2 270	3 008	3 012	3 393
Vessels cleared										
Navires sortis	909	...	...	...	604	551	589	834	938	861
Estonia Estonie										
Vessels entered										
Navires entrés	...	...	...	...	...	...	...	...	3 419	2 376[9]
Vessels cleared										
Navires sortis	...	...	...	...	...	...	...	...	3 087	3 813[9]
Fiji Fidji										
Vessels entered										
Navires entrés	699	1 590	2 025	1 739	2 603	3 012	...	...	...	...
Finland Finlande										
Vessels entered										
Navires entrés	55 740	65 098	68 203	70 420	85 265	102 500	112 418	119 238	117 003	111 934
Vessels cleared										
Navires sortis	55 713	65 509	68 807	70 877	84 438	102 995	111 948	119 040	121 946	117 143
France France										
Vessels entered										
Navires entrés	1 475 319	1 597 747	1 619 267	1 554 890	1 564 075	1 681 491	1 751 943	1 825 276	1 861 742	1 941 433
Gambia Gambie										
Vessels entered[1]										
Navires entrés[1]	659	954	892	982	969	...	...	...	...	...
Germany † Allemagne†										
Vessels entered										
Navires entrés	...	...	...	...	...	...	...	225 984	221 741	223 363
Vessels cleared										
Navires sortis	...	...	...	...	...	...	...	199 441	196 456	201 316

64
International maritime transport
Vessels entered and cleared: thousand net registered tons [*cont.*]
Transports maritimes internationaux
Navires entrés et sortis : milliers de tonneaux de jauge nette [*suite*]

Country or area Pays ou zone	1985	1986	1987	1988	1989	1990	1991	1992	1993	1994
F. R. Germany R. f. Allemagne										
Vessels entered										
Navires entrés	138 149	147 513	155 938	162 784	169 542	171 906	181 086	...	...	...
Vessels cleared										
Navires sortis	119 678	123 942	135 987	141 305	150 792	150 514	156 178	...	...	...
former German D. R. anc. R. d. allemande										
Vessels entered										
Navires entrés	10 343	11 023	10 324	10 469	10 820	8 713	...	...	...	...
Vessels cleared										
Navires sortis	14 778	14 486	14 480	15 076	14 303	8 327	...	...	...	...
Gibraltar Gibraltar										
Vessels entered										
Navires entrés	176	251	403	304	231	209	291	321	307	276
Greece Grèce										
Vessels entered										
Navires entrés	27 800	28 700	31 365	31 638	31 608	35 152	36 679	37 789	32 429	33 049
Vessels cleared										
Navires sortis	26 276	24 777	23 917	24 448	25 365	22 262	20 118	20 401	18 467	21 087
Guadeloupe Guadeloupe										
Vessels entered[2]										
Navires entrés[2]	1 235	1 099	1 255	1 458	1 618	2 557	2 579	...	...	...
Guatemala Guatemala										
Vessels entered										
Navires entrés	1 345	1 544	1 826	1 877	2 018	2 111	2 349	...	...	...
Vessels cleared										
Navires sortis	1 424	1 562	1 557	1 579	1 705	1 772	1 740	...	...	...
Haïti Haïti										
Vessels entered										
Navires entrés	728	725	707	734	709	1 975	...	...	...	347
Hong Kong Hong-kong										
Vessels entered[10]										
Navires entrés[10]	91 608	98 137	106 396	115 736	126 308	131 802	140 121	161 109	184 901	201 626
Vessels cleared[10]										
Navires sortis[10]	91 631	98 078	106 451	115 641	126 562	131 636	140 198	161 292	184 658	201 124
India Inde										
Vessels entered[11 12]										
Navires entrés[11 12]	35 566	33 563	30 171	27 894	28 593	34 260	18 892	...	...	...
Vessels cleared[11 12]										
Navires sortis[11 12]	26 924	28 386	26 253	31 031	34 529	35 666	23 423	...	...	...
Indonesia Indonésie										
Vessels entered										
Navires entrés	54 814	63 589	65 245	82 125	82 846	109 490	113 380	128 571	140 861	155 880
Vessels cleared										
Navires sortis	15 886	20 302	21 449	21 601	22 798	26 105	34 903	38 178	41 993	48 874
Ireland Irlande										
Vessels entered[2]										
Navires entrés[2]	20 455	20 915	22 557	25 630	25 940	31 769	32 892	33 857	36 408	37 896
Israel Israël										
Vessels entered[2 13]										
Navires entrés[2 13]	13 232	14 408	15 857	15 962	15 853	17 771	20 033	22 358	26 401[14]	28 981[14]
Italy Italie										
Vessels entered										
Navires entrés	152 426	155 299	161 403	160 251	161 145	173 360	184 693	175 940	168 545	180 175
Vessels cleared										
Navires sortis	63 165	65 509	65 863	67 927	67 170	74 000	80 303	79 600	84 044	91 288
Jamaica Jamaïque										
Vessels entered										
Navires entrés	...	...	...	...	...	...	...	...	9 892	...

64
International maritime transport
Vessels entered and cleared: thousand net registered tons [*cont.*]
Transports maritimes internationaux
Navires entrés et sortis : milliers de tonneaux de jauge nette [*suite*]

Country or area Pays ou zone	1985	1986	1987	1988	1989	1990	1991	1992	1993	1994
Japan Japon Vessels entered[2] Navires entrés[2]	352 589	345 284	347 605	361 530	378 291	385 110	402 190	398 240	397 582	410 164
Jordan Jordanie Vessels entered Navires entrés	2 122	2 012	1 908	1 981	1 834	1 678	1 690	2 041	2 143	1 910
Vessels cleared Navires sortis	549	665	647	602	612	544	385	392	347	576
Kenya Kenya Vessels entered[2 7] Navires entrés[2 7]	5 743	6 134	6 172	6 133	6 091	6 134	5 897	7 112	7 102	...
Korea, Republic of Corée, République de Vessels entered Navires entrés	179 760	201 857	238 186	252 390	262 791	279 004	317 046	348 767	383 311	430 872
Vessels cleared Navires sortis	179 286	204 090	240 505	254 627	264 114	278 423	316 670	350 906	381 545	429 538
Macau Macao Vessels entered Navires entrés	11 482	...	...	...	...	...	...	...	...	...
Madagascar Madagascar Vessels entered[2] Navires entrés[2]	1 302	1 383	1 400	1 494	1 654	2 161	...	...	...	...
Vessels cleared[2] Navires sortis[2]	1 301	1 355	1 430	1 500	1 639	2 160	...	...	...	...
Malaysia Malaisie Vessels entered[15] Navires entrés[15]	69 032	55 197[16]	59 900[16]	79 521	86 033	95 724	101 170	108 170	109 300	110 330
Vessels cleared[15] Navires sortis[15]	69 012	54 925[16]	59 709[16]	79 735	85 301	94 713	101 230	109 070	109 000	110 650
Malta Malte Vessels entered Navires entrés	2 016	2 370	2 327	2 726	2 681	4 068	5 087	7 049	6 802	7 657
Vessels cleared Navires sortis	763	888	880	942	897	1 670	2 377	3 160	3 534	2 467
Mauritius Maurice Vessels entered[2] Navires entrés[2]	2 715	2 988	3 733	4 064	4 195	4 364	6 157	5 277	5 271	5 500
Vessels cleared Navires sortis	2 696	3 051	3 464	3 677	3 978	4 357	6 188	5 447	5 219	5 550
Mexico Mexique Vessels entered Navires entrés	10 619	9 009	10 880	14 262	17 318	19 274	18 209	20 887	19 731	17 233
Vessels cleared Navires sortis	84 139	82 796	88 950	90 432	84 575	89 111	93 680	97 356	93 357	94 210
Myanmar Myanmar Vessels entered Navires entrés	821	866	636	597	212	610	698	879	1 278	1 587
Vessels cleared Navires sortis	960	1 243	1 311	750	683	577	667	1 205	1 408	1 612
Netherlands Pays-Bas Vessels entered Navires entrés	213 668	215 340	210 547	220 323	232 153	365 350[9]	374 428[9]	383 164[9]	375 906[9]	403 355[9]
Vessels cleared Navires sortis	209 119	212 823	180 611	190 524	200 373	224 415[9]	232 349[9]	239 572[9]	237 817[9]	258 152[9]
New Caledonia Nouvelle-Calédonie Vessels entered Navires entrés	2 526	...	...	...	...	...	...	...	...	...
Vessels cleared Navires sortis	2 524	...	...	...	...	...	...	...	...	...

64
International maritime transport
Vessels entered and cleared: thousand net registered tons [*cont.*]
Transports maritimes internationaux
Navires entrés et sortis : milliers de tonneaux de jauge nette [*suite*]

Country or area Pays ou zone	1985	1986	1987	1988	1989	1990	1991	1992	1993	1994
New Zealand Nouvelle-Zélande										
Vessels entered Navires entrés	14 607	13 388	14 113	27 844[9]	30 890[9]	32 592[9]	38 069[9]	27 983[9]	37 603[9]	39 700[9]
Vessels cleared Navires sortis	14 613	13 365	14 107	27 247[9]	29 753[9]	31 967[9]	36 158[9]	27 508[9]	35 128[9]	37 421[9]
Nicaragua Nicaragua										
Vessels entered Navires entrés	1 326	...	...	...	...	...	...	...	...	...
Vessels cleared Navires sortis	442	...	...	...	...	...	...	...	...	...
Nigeria Nigéria										
Vessels entered Navires entrés	50 879	47 038	50 879	42 852	40 354	41 600	42 970	26 780	...	...
Vessels cleared Navires sortis	...	...	...	...	...	41 490	35 750	25 020	...	...
Norway Norvège										
Vessels entered Navires entrés	48 734	...	...	...	...	...	...	...	...	...
Pakistan Pakistan										
Vessels entered[6] Navires entrés[6]	14 493	14 736	15 168	15 190	15 331	15 057	16 289	19 401	18 785	20 195
Vessels cleared[6] Navires sortis[6]	7 155	6 899	7 141	6 728	7 265	6 743	7 692	7 382	7 284	8 287
Panama Panama										
Vessels entered Navires entrés	1 204	1 322	1 362	1 019	1 141	1 337	1 583	1 916	2 134	2 443
Vessels cleared Navires sortis	1 247	1 134	1 228	1 159	1 210	1 377	1 412	1 470	1 514	1 610
Peru Pérou										
Vessels entered Navires entrés	3 038	4 241	5 547	5 989	4 075	4 363	6 115	7 012	6 066	7 145
Vessels cleared Navires sortis	10 386	11 501	10 478	8 854	9 873	9 076	9 815	8 852	9 187	...
Philippines Philippines										
Vessels entered Navires entrés	18 395	19 380	21 787	24 130	25 729	30 441	28 969	29 876	32 388	...
Vessels cleared Navires sortis	18 927	20 282	20 593	20 830	20 441	22 810	22 442	19 411	22 431	...
Poland Pologne										
Vessels entered Navires entrés	11 279	11 467	12 989	14 394	15 129	12 959	13 116	15 573	15 544	14 816
Vessels cleared Navires sortis	18 320	17 939	18 298	19 844	19 477	21 131	18 277	20 031	23 222	25 552
Portugal Portugal										
Vessels entered[2][17] Navires entrés[2][17]	25 860	30 333	29 202	32 404	32 836	35 757	34 909	36 415	32 654	34 544
Réunion Réunion										
Vessels entered[2] Navires entrés[2]	1 892	1 995	2 189	2 391	2 547	2 728	2 792	...	...	...
Saint Helena Sainte-Hélène										
Vessels entered Navires entrés	91	276	174	79	49	78	216	244	319	254
Saint Lucia Sainte-Lucie										
Vessels entered Navires entrés	2 257	2 255	2 408	2 329	2 276	2 063	...	...	...	...
Vessels cleared Navires sortis	2 252	2 256	3 126	...	...	...	...	...	...	...

64
International maritime transport
Vessels entered and cleared: thousand net registered tons [*cont.*]
Transports maritimes internationaux
Navires entrés et sortis : milliers de tonneaux de jauge nette [*suite*]

Country or area Pays ou zone	1985	1986	1987	1988	1989	1990	1991	1992	1993	1994
St. Vincent-Grenadines St. Vincent-Grenadines										
Vessels entered										
Navires entrés	1 179	1 224	1 309	1 374	1 499	1 185	1 143	1 233	1 336	1 037
Vessels cleared										
Navires sortis	1 150	1 182	1 184	1 278	1 428	1 120	1 083	...	...	...
Samoa Samoa										
Vessels entered										
Navires entrés	453	434	659	523	499	501	527	425	530	...
Senegal Sénégal										
Vessels entered										
Navires entrés	9 750	5 258	9 872	...	...	...	8 985	9 447	9 625	...
Vessels cleared										
Navires sortis	9 824	5 237	9 858	...	...	...	8 987	9 477	9 769	...
Seychelles Seychelles										
Vessels entered										
Navires entrés	578	796	909	916	959	953	769	778	871	764
Singapore Singapour										
Vessels entered[9]										
Navires entrés[9]	36 531	40 722	42 560	44 855	49 107	60 347	70 345	81 334	92 655	101 107
Vessels cleared[9]										
Navires sortis[9]	...	...	...	...	...	...	70 119	81 245	92 477	101 017
South Africa Afrique du Sud										
Vessels entered[9]										
Navires entrés[9]	13 803	14 864	13 172	13 992	14 510	15 138	13 396	13 309	13 437	13 037
Vessels cleared[9]										
Navires sortis[9]	343 381	348 288	333 902	351 390	371 946	389 880	402 011	439 645	441 053	472 025
Spain Espagne										
Vessels entered										
Navires entrés	93 553	100 658	104 011	108 637	119 595	125 881	132 398	134 847	130 171	137 951
Vessels cleared										
Navires sortis	48 992	47 549	43 967	45 349	43 301	43 208	43 226	43 255	46 942	47 813
Sri Lanka Sri Lanka										
Vessels entered										
Navires entrés	13 608	15 422	13 870	14 161	17 084	20 148	20 545	22 087	24 955	25 120
Syrian Arab Republic Rép. arabe syrienne										
Vessels entered[2 7]										
Navires entrés[2 7]	2 576	2 257	2 093	2 184	2 150	2 087	2 446	2 836	3 525	3 433
Vessels cleared[2]										
Navires sortis[2]	2 531	2 053	2 084	2 100	2 100	2 143	2 351	2 992	3 459	3 537
Thailand Thaïlande										
Vessels entered										
Navires entrés	17 933	16 809	21 622	25 215	33 514	38 587	40 880	47 641	39 652	...
Vessels cleared										
Navires sortis	18 460	21 211	19 547	23 029	26 574	23 224	22 740	23 584	23 011	...
Tonga Tonga										
Vessels entered										
Navires entrés	1 765	1 765	1 778	1 611	1 874	1 816	1 950	...	...	...
Turkey Turquie										
Vessels entered										
Navires entrés	50 004	52 736	63 456	64 447	83 749	62 689	47 818	46 990	56 687	52 925
Vessels cleared										
Navires sortis	44 814	51 152	60 477	63 695	81 515	60 651	45 719	45 961	55 329	51 303
Ukraine Ukraine										
Vessels entered										
Navires entrés	...	...	...	...	...	...	19 236	16 640	5 072	3 381
Vessels cleared										
Navires sortis	...	...	...	...	...	...	40 142	45 374	29 120	25 189

64
International maritime transport
Vessels entered and cleared: thousand net registered tons [cont.]
Transports maritimes internationaux
Navires entrés et sortis : milliers de tonneaux de jauge nette [suite]

Country or area Pays ou zone	1985	1986	1987	1988	1989	1990	1991	1992	1993	1994
United States Etats-Unis										
Vessels entered[8][18]										
Navires entrés[8][18]	294 110	321 761	344 710	364 140	379 130	379 612	320 439	321 169	340 507	363 896
Vessels cleared[8][18]										
Navires sortis[8][18]	273 444	265 475	289 767	318 264	325 520	323 183	298 837	293 452	277 520	281 709
Venezuela Venezuela										
Vessels entered										
Navires entrés	21 337	20 579	22 663	26 101	17 529	15 774	19 882	19 758	22 087	...
Vessels cleared										
Navires sortis	7 044	13 320	8 826	8 223	6 641	18 294	11 500	15 194	17 211	...
former Dem. Yemen anciennce Yémen dém.										
Vessels entered[2]										
Navires entrés[2]	9 315	8 344	8 788	...	...	...	...	...	...	...
Vessels cleared[2]										
Navires sortis[2]	1 921	1 737	1 892	...	...	...	...	...	...	...
Yugoslavia, SFR† Yougoslavie, Rfs†										
Vessels entered										
Navires entrés	1 754	1 445	1 215	2 289	3 318	3 190	1 180	...	...	...
Vessels cleared										
Navires sortis	1 265	1 170	1 410	2 137	2 893	3 244	1 128	...	...	...

Source:
Transport statistics database of the Statistics Division of
the United Nations Secretariat.

† For detailed descriptions of data pertaining to
former Czechoslovakia, Germany, SFR Yugoslavia and former
USSR, see Annex I - Country or area nomenclature, regional
and other groupings.

1 Twelve months ending 30 June of year stated.
2 Including vessels in ballast.
3 Comprises Buenos Aires, Bahía Blanca, La Plata, Quequén, Mar
 del Plata, Paraná Inferior, Paraná Medio and Rosario.
4 Buenos Aires only.
5 Comprising Buenos Aires, Rosario, Lib. Gral. San Martín,
 Quequén and La Plata.
6 Twelve months beginning 1 July of year stated.

7 All entrances counted.
8 Including Great Lakes international traffic (Canada: also
 St. Lawrence).
9 Gross registered tons (Singapore: vessels exceeding 75 GRT).

10 Including ocean-going vessels and river vessels as well as
 vessels in ballast.
11 Twelve months beginning 1 April of year stated.
12 Excluding minor and intermediate ports.
13 Excluding tankers.
14 Including fuel.
15 Data for Sarawak include vessels in ballast and all
 entrances counted.
16 Peninsular Malaysia and Sarawak only.
17 Including traffic with Portuguese overseas provinces.

18 Excluding traffic with United States Virgin Islands.

Source:
Base de données pour les statistiques des transports de la
Division de statistique du Secrétariat de l'ONU.

† Pour les descriptions en détails des données
relatives à l'ancienne Tchécoslovaquie, l'Allemagne, la Rfs
Yougoslavie et l'ancienne URSS, voir l'Annexe I -
Nomenclature des pays ou zones, groupements régionaux et
autres groupements.

1 Douze mois finissant le 30 juin de l'année indiquée.
2 Y compris navires sur lest.
3 Buenos aires, Bahía Blanca, La Plata, Quequén, Mar del
 Plata, Paraná Inferior, Paraná Medio et Rosario.
4 Buenos Aires seulement.
5 Buenos Aires, Rosario, Lib. Gral. San Martín, Quequén et La
 Plata.
6 Douze mois commençant le premier juillet de l'année
 indiquée.
7 Toutes entrées comprises.
8 Y compris trafic international des Grands Lacs (Canada: et
 du St. Laurent).
9 Tonneaux de jauge bruts (Singapour: navires dépassant 75
 TJB).
10 Y compris les grandes navigations et les navigations
 fluviales et aussi les navires sur lest.
11 Douze mois commençant le premier avril de l'année indiquée.
12 Non compris les ports petits et moyens.
13 Non compris les bateaux citernes.
14 Y compris carburant.
15 Les données pour Sarawak comprennent navires sur lest et
 toutes entrées comprises.
16 Malaisie péninsulaire et Sarawak seulement.
17 Y compris le trafic avec les provinces portugaises
 d'outre-mer.
18 Non compris le trafic avec les Iles Vierges américaines.

65
Civil Aviation
Aviation civile

Passengers on scheduled services (000); Kilometres (million)
Passagers sur les services réguliers (000); Kilomètres (millions)

Country or area and traffic	Total Totale 1980	1992	1993	1994	International Internationaux 1980	1992	1993	1994	Pays ou zone et trafic
World									**Monde**
Kilometres flown	**9362**	**15639**	**17047**	**18063**	**3613**	**6844**	**7283**	**7768**	**Kilomètres parcourus**
Passengers carried	**748978**	**1144674**	**1138471**	**1225067**	**163222**	**299612**	**318424**	**343712**	**Passagers transportés**
Passengers km	**1089343**	**1926442**	**1946231**	**2091659**	**466532**	**982662**	**1046796**	**1140155**	**Passagers−km**
Total ton−km	**130999**	**241811**	**249442**	**272656**	**64279**	**143607**	**155432**	**172755**	**Total tonnes−km**
Africa [1]									**Afrique** [1]
Kilometres flown	**351**	**410**	**437**	**461**	**236**	**295**	**312**	**332**	**Kilomètres parcourus**
Passengers carried	**21235**	**25555**	**24445**	**26088**	**9003**	**12753**	**12307**	**13134**	**Passagers transportés**
Passengers km	**29724**	**42841**	**43290**	**47235**	**22434**	**34921**	**35293**	**38747**	**Passagers−km**
Total ton−km	**3544**	**5078**	**5202**	**5643**	**2811**	**4294**	**4404**	**4789**	**Total tonnes−km**
Algeria									**Algérie**
Kilometres flown	28	27	36	36	19	14	20	19	Kilomètres parcourus
Passengers carried	2950	3551	3254	3241	1500	1711	1676	1257	Passagers transportés
Passengers km	2300	3234	2901	2706	1600	2161	1991	1546	Passagers−km
Total ton−km	220	310	296	268	156	210	207	159	Total tonnes−km
Angola									**Angola**
Kilometres flown	8	10	9	13	4	8	7	10	Kilomètres parcourus
Passengers carried	635	440	334	519	51	105	84	140	Passagers transportés
Passengers km	553	1196	948	1594	295	1020	816	1396	Passagers−km
Total ton−km	69	147	113	197	46	132	102	180	Total tonnes−km
Benin [2]									**Bénin** [2]
Kilometres flown	2	2	2	2	2	2	2	2	Kilomètres parcourus
Passengers carried	61	66	68	69	61	66	68	69	Passagers transportés
Passengers km	178	201	207	215	178	201	207	215	Passagers−km
Total ton−km	35	34	33	34	35	34	33	34	Total tonnes−km
Botswana									**Botswana**
Kilometres flown	1	3	3	2	0	2	2	2	Kilomètres parcourus
Passengers carried	39	111	123	101	20	77	87	73	Passagers transportés
Passengers km	15	76	75	58	7	58	61	46	Passagers−km
Total ton−km	1	8	8	6	1	6	6	4	Total tonnes−km
Burkina Faso [2]									**Burkina Faso** [2]
Kilometres flown	2	3	3	3	2	2	3	3	Kilomètres parcourus
Passengers carried	73	127	128	130	65	102	104	105	Passagers transportés
Passengers km	183	233	239	247	181	225	231	239	Passagers−km
Total ton−km	36	37	36	37	35	36	35	37	Total tonnes−km
Burundi									**Burundi**
Kilometres flown	0	0	0	0	0	0	0	0	Kilomètres parcourus
Passengers carried	11	9	9	9	11	7	7	7	Passagers transportés
Passengers km	5	2	2	2	5	2	2	2	Passagers−km
Total ton−km	1	0	0	0	1	0	0	0	Total tonnes−km
Cameroon									**Cameroun**
Kilometres flown	7	5	5	6	5	4	4	4	Kilomètres parcourus
Passengers carried	480	363	275	295	126	182	150	162	Passagers transportés
Passengers km	477	477	402	436	358	405	335	365	Passagers−km
Total ton−km	72	53	58	64	60	45	52	57	Total tonnes−km
Cape Verde									**Cap−Vert**
Kilometres flown	1	3	3	3	0	1	1	1	Kilomètres parcourus
Passengers carried	75	100	100	118	0	24	24	28	Passagers transportés
Passengers km	12	169	169	173	0	145	145	145	Passagers−km
Total ton−km	1	16	16	17	0	13	13	13	Total tonnes−km
Central African Rep. [2]									**Rép. centrafricaine** [2]
Kilometres flown	3	3	3	3	2	2	2	2	Kilomètres parcourus
Passengers carried	136	120	122	123	61	66	68	69	Passagers transportés
Passengers km	190	213	219	227	178	201	207	215	Passagers−km
Total ton−km	36	35	35	36	35	34	33	34	Total tonnes−km
Chad [2]									**Tchad** [2]
Kilometres flown	3	2	2	2	2	2	2	2	Kilomètres parcourus
Passengers carried	106	83	85	86	61	69	71	72	Passagers transportés
Passengers km	210	208	214	222	178	202	208	216	Passagers−km
Total ton−km	39	35	34	35	35	34	33	34	Total tonnes−km

65

Civil Aviation
Passengers on scheduled services (000); Kilometres (million) [cont.]
Aviation civile
Passagers sur les services réguliers (000); Kilomètres (millions) [suite]

Country or area and traffic	Total Totale				International Internationaux				Pays ou zone et trafic
	1980	1992	1993	1994	1980	1992	1993	1994	
Comoros									**Comores**
Kilometres flown	...	0	0	0	...	0	0	0	Kilomètres parcourus
Passengers carried	...	26	26	26	...	5	5	5	Passagers transportés
Passengers km	...	3	3	3	...	1	1	1	Passagers−km
Total ton−km	...	0	0	0	...	0	0	0	Total tonnes−km
Congo [2]									**Congo** [2]
Kilometres flown	3	3	3	3	2	2	2	2	Kilomètres parcourus
Passengers carried	117	229	231	232	67	71	73	74	Passagers transportés
Passengers km	197	250	256	264	182	203	209	217	Passagers−km
Total ton−km	37	39	38	40	36	34	33	35	Total tonnes−km
Côte d'Ivoire [2]									**Côte d'Ivoire** [2]
Kilometres flown	3	4	4	3	2	3	3	3	Kilomètres parcourus
Passengers carried	151	195	186	157	61	152	149	140	Passagers transportés
Passengers km	215	297	295	282	178	277	277	274	Passagers−km
Total ton−km	39	43	41	40	35	41	40	40	Total tonnes−km
Egypt									**Egypte**
Kilometres flown	31	44	44	54	27	38	40	48	Kilomètres parcourus
Passengers carried	2028	3609	2881	3538	1270	2075	1836	2401	Passagers transportés
Passengers km	2870	6323	5277	6324	2536	5629	4786	5765	Passagers−km
Total ton−km	299	687	606	763	268	625	562	712	Total tonnes−km
Equatorial Guinea									**Guinée équatoriale**
Kilometres flown	0	0	0	0	0	0	0	0	Kilomètres parcourus
Passengers carried	13	14	14	14	13	14	14	14	Passagers transportés
Passengers km	7	7	7	7	7	7	7	7	Passagers−km
Total ton−km	1	1	1	1	1	1	1	1	Total tonnes−km
Ethiopia									**Ethiopie**
Kilometres flown	11	26	23	24	10	22	19	20	Kilomètres parcourus
Passengers carried	243	756	752	716	186	447	435	429	Passagers transportés
Passengers km	647	1725	1717	1607	597	1577	1571	1480	Passagers−km
Total ton−km	85	264	259	267	78	248	244	254	Total tonnes−km
Gabon									**Gabon**
Kilometres flown	6	6	6	6	5	4	4	4	Kilomètres parcourus
Passengers carried	331	471	302	481	95	145	152	154	Passagers transportés
Passengers km	374	536	570	719	313	450	480	660	Passagers−km
Total ton−km	61	77	82	96	54	68	73	90	Total tonnes−km
Gambia									**Gambie**
Kilometres flown	...	1	1	1	...	1	1	1	Kilomètres parcourus
Passengers carried	...	19	19	19	...	19	19	19	Passagers transportés
Passengers km	...	50	50	50	...	50	50	50	Passagers−km
Total ton−km	...	5	5	5	...	5	5	5	Total tonnes−km
Ghana									**Ghana**
Kilometres flown	4	5	4	5	3	5	4	5	Kilomètres parcourus
Passengers carried	279	206	152	182	179	200	152	182	Passagers transportés
Passengers km	330	352	387	478	304	350	387	478	Passagers−km
Total ton−km	34	62	61	72	32	61	61	72	Total tonnes−km
Guinea									**Guinée**
Kilometres flown	1	1	1	2	1	1	1	1	Kilomètres parcourus
Passengers carried	80	23	24	45	24	20	21	30	Passagers transportés
Passengers km	34	33	35	33	12	31	32	27	Passagers−km
Total ton−km	3	4	4	4	1	3	4	4	Total tonnes−km
Guinea−Bissau									**Guinée−Bissau**
Kilometres flown	1	1	1	1	0	0	0	0	Kilomètres parcourus
Passengers carried	22	21	21	21	8	8	8	8	Passagers transportés
Passengers km	8	10	10	10	4	6	6	6	Passagers−km
Total ton−km	1	1	1	1	0	1	1	1	Total tonnes−km
Kenya									**Kenya**
Kilometres flown	12	14	15	16	10	12	13	13	Kilomètres parcourus
Passengers carried	393	721	770	754	204	380	413	417	Passagers transportés
Passengers km	863	1333	1459	1737	782	1205	1325	1591	Passagers−km
Total ton−km	98	174	191	215	90	162	178	202	Total tonnes−km
Lesotho									**Lesotho**
Kilometres flown	1	1	1	1	0	1	1	1	Kilomètres parcourus
Passengers carried	52	26	23	27	10	20	19	22	Passagers transportés
Passengers km	11	9	9	9	4	8	8	8	Passagers−km
Total ton−km	1	1	1	1	0	1	1	1	Total tonnes−km

65
Civil Aviation
Passengers on scheduled services (000); Kilometres (million) [*cont.*]
Aviation civile
Passagers sur les services réguliers (000); Kilomètres (millions) [*suite*]

Country or area and traffic	Total Totale				International Internationaux				Pays ou zone et trafic
	1980	1992	1993	1994	1980	1992	1993	1994	
Liberia									**Libéria**
Kilometres flown	2	0	...	...	...	...	...	...	Kilomètres parcourus
Passengers carried	50	32	...	...	...	...	...	...	Passagers transportés
Passengers km	17	7	...	...	...	...	...	...	Passagers−km
Total ton−km	2	1	...	...	...	...	...	...	Total tonnes−km
Libyan Arab Jamah.									**Jamah. arabe libyenne**
Kilometres flown	12	11	6	4	7	3	...	...	Kilomètres parcourus
Passengers carried	1169	1350	853	641	468	178	...	...	Passagers transportés
Passengers km	1101	1116	565	425	632	344	...	...	Passagers−km
Total ton−km	116	96	44	34	70	35	...	...	Total tonnes−km
Madagascar									**Madagascar**
Kilometres flown	7	6	7	7	2	3	3	3	Kilomètres parcourus
Passengers carried	448	344	419	451	54	79	94	106	Passagers transportés
Passengers km	379	432	499	567	226	325	368	424	Passagers−km
Total ton−km	54	66	72	74	38	56	60	61	Total tonnes−km
Malawi									**Malawi**
Kilometres flown	2	2	2	3	1	1	2	2	Kilomètres parcourus
Passengers carried	94	121	132	142	52	52	63	69	Passagers transportés
Passengers km	68	79	266	289	56	53	234	255	Passagers−km
Total ton−km	7	9	15	28	6	6	13	26	Total tonnes−km
Mali [2]									**Mali** [2]
Kilometres flown	2	2	2	2	1	2	2	2	Kilomètres parcourus
Passengers carried	71	66	68	69	42	66	68	69	Passagers transportés
Passengers km	97	201	207	215	82	201	207	215	Passagers−km
Total ton−km	9	34	33	34	8	34	33	34	Total tonnes−km
Mauritania [2]									**Mauritanie** [2]
Kilometres flown	3	3	4	3	2	2	3	3	Kilomètres parcourus
Passengers carried	141	213	215	216	76	89	91	92	Passagers transportés
Passengers km	218	275	281	289	188	224	230	238	Passagers−km
Total ton−km	39	41	40	41	36	36	35	36	Total tonnes−km
Mauritius									**Maurice**
Kilometres flown	3	18	17	18	3	17	17	17	Kilomètres parcourus
Passengers carried	84	578	582	636	77	551	550	601	Passagers transportés
Passengers km	185	2799	2677	2972	181	2782	2658	2951	Passagers−km
Total ton−km	20	342	334	372	20	341	333	370	Total tonnes−km
Morocco									**Maroc**
Kilometres flown	21	42	45	45	20	40	42	42	Kilomètres parcourus
Passengers carried	947	2169	2140	2184	906	1884	1775	1788	Passagers transportés
Passengers km	1868	4297	4395	4573	1855	4197	4264	4433	Passagers−km
Total ton−km	209	399	449	369	208	390	437	356	Total tonnes−km
Mozambique									**Mozambique**
Kilometres flown	6	4	4	5	3	3	3	3	Kilomètres parcourus
Passengers carried	282	225	206	221	52	88	84	91	Passagers transportés
Passengers km	467	382	411	443	260	248	282	307	Passagers−km
Total ton−km	51	44	47	52	29	29	34	38	Total tonnes−km
Namibia									**Namibie**
Kilometres flown	...	6	7	7	...	4	4	5	Kilomètres parcourus
Passengers carried	...	163	179	199	...	134	149	170	Passagers transportés
Passengers km	...	535	687	751	...	508	659	725	Passagers−km
Total ton−km	...	59	84	93	...	57	81	90	Total tonnes−km
Niger [2]									**Niger** [2]
Kilometres flown	3	2	2	2	2	2	2	2	Kilomètres parcourus
Passengers carried	111	66	68	69	61	66	68	69	Passagers transportés
Passengers km	199	201	207	215	178	201	207	215	Passagers−km
Total ton−km	37	34	33	34	35	34	33	34	Total tonnes−km
Nigeria									**Nigéria**
Kilometres flown	24	12	11	12	11	7	6	6	Kilomètres parcourus
Passengers carried	1939	647	608	650	301	230	208	225	Passagers transportés
Passengers km	1877	990	913	985	996	672	608	662	Passagers−km
Total ton−km	179	103	96	100	99	72	67	70	Total tonnes−km
Rwanda									**Rwanda**
Kilometres flown	...	0	0	0	...	0	0	0	Kilomètres parcourus
Passengers carried	...	9	9	9	...	4	4	4	Passagers transportés
Passengers km	...	2	2	2	...	1	1	1	Passagers−km
Total ton−km	...	0	0	0	...	0	0	0	Total tonnes−km

65
Civil Aviation
Passengers on scheduled services (000); Kilometres (million) [*cont.*]
Aviation civile
Passagers sur les services réguliers (000); Kilomètres (millions) [*suite*]

Country or area and traffic	Total Totale				International Internationaux				Pays ou zone et trafic
	1980	1992	1993	1994	1980	1992	1993	1994	
Sao Tome and Principe									**Sao Tomé−et−Principe**
Kilometres flown	...	0	0	0	...	0	0	0	Kilomètres parcourus
Passengers carried	...	22	22	22	...	13	13	13	Passagers transportés
Passengers km	...	8	8	8	...	4	4	4	Passagers−km
Total ton−km	...	1	1	1	...	0	0	0	Total tonnes−km
Senegal [2]									**Sénégal** [2]
Kilometres flown	3	3	3	3	2	2	3	2	Kilomètres parcourus
Passengers carried	113	138	140	141	71	110	112	113	Passagers transportés
Passengers km	196	222	216	224	182	214	208	216	Passagers−km
Total ton−km	37	36	35	36	36	35	34	36	Total tonnes−km
Seychelles									**Seychelles**
Kilometres flown	0	4	7	6	0	4	6	6	Kilomètres parcourus
Passengers carried	15	239	289	297	0	68	97	112	Passagers transportés
Passengers km	2	438	626	685	0	430	618	677	Passagers−km
Total ton−km	0	57	70	77	0	56	69	76	Total tonnes−km
Sierra Leone									**Sierra Leone**
Kilometres flown	1	0	0	1	0	0	0	1	Kilomètres parcourus
Passengers carried	56	17	18	14	26	17	18	14	Passagers transportés
Passengers km	86	51	55	66	77	51	55	66	Passagers−km
Total ton−km	9	5	5	6	8	5	5	6	Total tonnes−km
Somalia									**Somalie**
Kilometres flown	4	...	...	...	2	...	...	...	Kilomètres parcourus
Passengers carried	90	...	...	...	70	...	...	...	Passagers transportés
Passengers km	140	...	...	...	120	...	...	...	Passagers−km
Total ton−km	13	...	...	...	11	...	...	...	Total tonnes−km
South Africa									**Afrique du Sud**
Kilometres flown	67	73	92	97	37	36	43	47	Kilomètres parcourus
Passengers carried	4116	4685	5582	5802	801	969	1130	1225	Passagers transportés
Passengers km	8920	9511	11529	12352	6088	6229	7554	8184	Passagers−km
Total ton−km	1074	1116	1357	1374	778	785	955	949	Total tonnes−km
Sudan									**Soudan**
Kilometres flown	11	12	12	13	7	5	6	7	Kilomètres parcourus
Passengers carried	519	480	408	432	311	303	225	239	Passagers transportés
Passengers km	710	511	580	615	530	396	454	481	Passagers−km
Total ton−km	76	85	91	96	58	55	59	62	Total tonnes−km
Swaziland									**Swaziland**
Kilometres flown	1	1	1	1	1	1	1	1	Kilomètres parcourus
Passengers carried	31	57	58	65	31	57	58	65	Passagers transportés
Passengers km	30	42	44	48	30	42	44	48	Passagers−km
Total ton−km	3	4	4	4	3	4	4	4	Total tonnes−km
Togo [2]									**Togo** [2]
Kilometres flown	2	2	2	2	2	2	2	2	Kilomètres parcourus
Passengers carried	65	66	68	69	65	66	68	69	Passagers transportés
Passengers km	179	201	207	215	179	201	207	215	Passagers−km
Total ton−km	35	34	33	34	35	34	33	34	Total tonnes−km
Tunisia									**Tunisie**
Kilometres flown	14	15	17	20	13	15	17	19	Kilomètres parcourus
Passengers carried	978	1250	1351	1391	898	1219	1345	1385	Passagers transportés
Passengers km	1241	1673	1877	1977	1213	1663	1875	1975	Passagers−km
Total ton−km	123	168	173	197	120	167	172	197	Total tonnes−km
Uganda									**Ouganda**
Kilometres flown	3	1	1	2	2	1	1	2	Kilomètres parcourus
Passengers carried	83	32	40	63	43	32	40	63	Passagers transportés
Passengers km	68	17	24	52	58	17	24	52	Passagers−km
Total ton−km	15	2	2	5	14	2	2	5	Total tonnes−km
United Rep.Tanzania									**Rép. Unie de Tanzanie**
Kilometres flown	8	4	3	3	3	2	2	2	Kilomètres parcourus
Passengers carried	388	216	188	199	94	56	57	64	Passagers transportés
Passengers km	284	174	157	165	180	99	83	87	Passagers−km
Total ton−km	28	18	16	17	18	10	8	8	Total tonnes−km
Zaire									**Zaïre**
Kilometres flown	10	4	4	6	4	3	3	4	Kilomètres parcourus
Passengers carried	439	116	84	178	92	53	39	93	Passagers transportés
Passengers km	834	295	218	480	464	200	150	355	Passagers−km
Total ton−km	110	56	42	87	64	40	31	67	Total tonnes−km

65
Civil Aviation
Passengers on scheduled services (000); Kilometres (million) [cont.]
Aviation civile
Passagers sur les services réguliers (000); Kilomètres (millions) [suite]

Country or area and traffic	Total Totale				International Internationaux				Pays ou zone et trafic
	1980	1992	1993	1994	1980	1992	1993	1994	
Zambia									**Zambie**
Kilometres flown	11	5	4	4	9	4	3	3	Kilomètres parcourus
Passengers carried	257	246	219	235	114	127	102	110	Passagers transportés
Passengers km	467	509	393	428	425	470	359	391	Passagers−km
Total ton−km	89	63	47	54	85	59	44	51	Total tonnes−km
Zimbabwe									**Zimbabwe**
Kilometres flown	6	14	13	10	4	11	10	8	Kilomètres parcourus
Passengers carried	412	678	558	605	180	278	215	253	Passagers transportés
Passengers km	362	880	735	666	286	736	600	543	Passagers−km
Total ton−km	33	171	154	209	27	159	143	198	Total tonnes−km
America, North [1]									**Amérique du Nord** [1]
Kilometres flown	**5074**	**8025**	**8143**	**8671**	**812**	**1762**	**1806**	**1862**	**Kilomètres parcourus**
Passengers carried	**336928**	**507124**	**511691**	**560005**	**38722**	**66013**	**68079**	**70687**	**Passagers transportés**
Passengers km	**467284**	**836380**	**845301**	**902312**	**112763**	**258832**	**264690**	**277117**	**Passagers−km**
Total ton−km	**53930**	**96172**	**97986**	**106250**	**14695**	**33683**	**34867**	**38069**	**Total tonnes−km**
Antigua and Barbuda									**Antigua−et−Barbuda**
Kilometres flown	...	10	11	11	...	10	11	11	Kilomètres parcourus
Passengers carried	...	914	955	1000	...	914	955	1000	Passagers transportés
Passengers km	...	213	225	240	...	213	225	240	Passagers−km
Total ton−km	...	19	20	22	...	19	20	22	Total tonnes−km
Bahamas									**Bahamas**
Kilometres flown	10	4	4	4	4	2	2	2	Kilomètres parcourus
Passengers carried	345	835	862	862	160	380	397	397	Passagers transportés
Passengers km	539	188	191	191	459	132	132	132	Passagers−km
Total ton−km	52	17	18	18	44	12	12	12	Total tonnes−km
Barbados									**Barbade**
Kilometres flown	1	...	...	...	1	...	...	...	Kilomètres parcourus
Passengers carried	46	...	...	...	46	...	...	...	Passagers transportés
Passengers km	330	...	...	...	330	...	...	...	Passagers−km
Total ton−km	30	...	...	...	30	...	...	...	Total tonnes−km
Canada									**Canada**
Kilometres flown	338	383	369	397	114	159	166	189	Kilomètres parcourus
Passengers carried	22453	16818	17516	18105	5530	6171	6601	7044	Passagers transportés
Passengers km	36234	41253	40426	43490	16293	24160	24936	27360	Passagers−km
Total ton−km	4095	5109	5151	5532	1944	3173	3355	3700	Total tonnes−km
Costa Rica									**Costa Rica**
Kilometres flown	8	14	17	19	8	13	17	19	Kilomètres parcourus
Passengers carried	431	623	690	773	332	535	645	732	Passagers transportés
Passengers km	495	1202	1429	1611	485	1197	1425	1607	Passagers−km
Total ton−km	68	165	188	213	67	165	188	213	Total tonnes−km
Cuba									**Cuba**
Kilometres flown	15	12	11	13	7	7	7	8	Kilomètres parcourus
Passengers carried	676	733	624	731	120	177	183	221	Passagers transportés
Passengers km	932	1370	1321	1556	666	1042	1069	1259	Passagers−km
Total ton−km	95	149	138	174	72	123	118	150	Total tonnes−km
Dominican Republic									**Rép. dominicaine**
Kilometres flown	6	4	3	2	6	4	3	2	Kilomètres parcourus
Passengers carried	466	323	328	300	466	323	328	300	Passagers transportés
Passengers km	550	283	280	234	550	283	280	234	Passagers−km
Total ton−km	60	26	28	24	60	26	28	24	Total tonnes−km
El Salvador									**El Salvador**
Kilometres flown	6	29	17	17	6	29	17	17	Kilomètres parcourus
Passengers carried	265	683	723	734	265	683	723	734	Passagers transportés
Passengers km	289	1563	1738	1573	289	1563	1738	1573	Passagers−km
Total ton−km	41	175	203	217	41	175	203	217	Total tonnes−km
Guatemala									**Guatemala**
Kilometres flown	4	6	6	6	4	6	6	6	Kilomètres parcourus
Passengers carried	119	230	240	252	119	230	240	252	Passagers transportés
Passengers km	159	366	384	411	159	366	384	411	Passagers−km
Total ton−km	21	52	56	58	21	52	56	58	Total tonnes−km
Honduras									**Honduras**
Kilometres flown	7	5	4	5	7	5	4	5	Kilomètres parcourus
Passengers carried	508	438	409	449	369	245	409	255	Passagers transportés
Passengers km	387	309	362	323	369	275	362	289	Passagers−km
Total ton−km	43	40	50	42	41	36	50	38	Total tonnes−km

65
Civil Aviation
Passengers on scheduled services (000); Kilometres (million) [*cont.*]
Aviation civile
Passagers sur les services réguliers (000); Kilomètres (millions) [*suite*]

Country or area and traffic	Total Totale				International Internationaux				Pays ou zone et trafic
	1980	1992	1993	1994	1980	1992	1993	1994	
Jamaica									**Jamaïque**
Kilometres flown	15	12	13	13	13	11	11	12	Kilomètres parcourus
Passengers carried	723	983	1038	1011	660	900	942	929	Passagers transportés
Passengers km	1207	1460	1488	1430	1200	1448	1474	1419	Passagers—km
Total ton—km	115	151	155	150	115	150	154	149	Total tonnes—km
Mexico									**Mexique**
Kilometres flown	157	219	237	264	63	92	90	92	Kilomètres parcourus
Passengers carried	12890	15532	16485	18791	2777	3976	3703	3540	Passagers transportés
Passengers km	13870	19553	20790	23521	6594	9119	8436	8235	Passagers—km
Total ton—km	1383	1851	1978	2299	665	909	848	862	Total tonnes—km
Nicaragua									**Nicaragua**
Kilometres flown	2	3	2	1	1	2	2	1	Kilomètres parcourus
Passengers carried	115	159	34	44	50	110	34	44	Passagers transportés
Passengers km	76	186	58	72	60	170	58	72	Passagers—km
Total ton—km	8	24	9	17	7	22	9	17	Total tonnes—km
Panama									**Panama**
Kilometres flown	7	5	8	6	6	5	8	6	Kilomètres parcourus
Passengers carried	355	283	320	368	307	283	320	368	Passagers transportés
Passengers km	409	340	380	405	395	340	380	405	Passagers—km
Total ton—km	40	43	50	43	38	43	50	43	Total tonnes—km
Trinidad and Tobago									**Trinité—et—Tobago**
Kilometres flown	16	25	26	32	16	24	25	32	Kilomètres parcourus
Passengers carried	877	1354	1389	1642	633	950	985	1216	Passagers transportés
Passengers km	1505	3077	3232	4112	1485	3050	3205	4084	Passagers—km
Total ton—km	160	346	364	406	158	344	362	404	Total tonnes—km
United States									**Etats—Unis**
Kilometres flown	4469	7284	7405	7869	543	1384	1427	1451	Kilomètres parcourus
Passengers carried	295281	466157	468974	513756	25744	49180	50611	52656	Passagers transportés
Passengers km	409520	764118	772048	822152	82678	214628	219691	228880	Passagers—km
Total ton—km	47644	87917	89486	96941	11319	28353	29327	32074	Total tonnes—km
America, South [1]									**Amérique du Sud** [1]
Kilometres flown	**498**	**702**	**734**	**769**	**199**	**311**	**332**	**359**	**Kilomètres parcourus**
Passengers carried	**34008**	**42195**	**42581**	**45368**	**6049**	**9342**	**10136**	**11352**	**Passagers transportés**
Passengers km	**38628**	**61450**	**62546**	**68685**	**19547**	**36709**	**38422**	**43455**	**Passagers—km**
Total ton—km	**4790**	**8490**	**8843**	**9725**	**2907**	**5881**	**6142**	**6929**	**Total tonnes—km**
Argentina									**Argentine**
Kilometres flown	94	93	78	88	39	37	35	38	Kilomètres parcourus
Passengers carried	5589	6711	5104	6253	1300	1787	1661	1999	Passagers transportés
Passengers km	8031	11696	9231	11250	4413	7178	6072	7410	Passagers—km
Total ton—km	939	1319	1117	1289	599	899	780	942	Total tonnes—km
Bolivia									**Bolivie**
Kilometres flown	14	11	11	14	9	7	8	10	Kilomètres parcourus
Passengers carried	1342	1214	1117	1175	268	412	423	424	Passagers transportés
Passengers km	944	1069	1092	1139	570	780	843	866	Passagers—km
Total ton—km	121	107	120	151	89	81	96	123	Total tonnes—km
Brazil									**Brésil**
Kilometres flown	203	326	333	345	58	106	112	124	Kilomètres parcourus
Passengers carried	13008	16388	16599	17885	1330	2707	3062	3372	Passagers transportés
Passengers km	15572	27897	29555	32139	6008	15144	16866	18760	Passagers—km
Total ton—km	1956	3796	4084	4496	945	2320	2514	2835	Total tonnes—km
Chile									**Chili**
Kilometres flown	25	65	72	81	19	45	48	53	Kilomètres parcourus
Passengers carried	669	1906	2360	2962	299	589	717	1014	Passagers transportés
Passengers km	1875	3854	4425	5398	1362	2495	2772	3531	Passagers—km
Total ton—km	324	879	1018	1142	267	739	844	947	Total tonnes—km
Colombia									**Colombie**
Kilometres flown	45	69	91	98	22	37	41	46	Kilomètres parcourus
Passengers carried	4808	5414	6930	7686	752	758	853	1004	Passagers transportés
Passengers km	4198	4590	5437	5675	2203	2268	2426	2666	Passagers—km
Total ton—km	532	952	1029	1156	339	733	750	866	Total tonnes—km
Ecuador									**Equateur**
Kilometres flown	21	24	24	20	11	13	12	9	Kilomètres parcourus
Passengers carried	701	1120	1243	1126	255	356	491	338	Passagers transportés
Passengers km	975	1604	1800	1410	851	1298	1401	1055	Passagers—km
Total ton—km	131	214	245	162	115	178	199	119	Total tonnes—km

65
Civil Aviation
Passengers on scheduled services (000); Kilometres (million) [*cont.*]
   Aviation civile
   Passagers sur les services réguliers (000); Kilomètres (millions) [*suite*]

Country or area and traffic	Total Totale				International Internationaux				Pays ou zone et trafic
	1980	1992	1993	1994	1980	1992	1993	1994	
Guyana									**Guyana**
Kilometres flown	1	2	2	2	...	2	2	2	Kilomètres parcourus
Passengers carried	28	115	115	115	...	54	54	54	Passagers transportés
Passengers km	6	224	224	224	...	208	208	208	Passagers−km
Total ton−km	1	23	23	23	...	21	21	21	Total tonnes−km
Paraguay									**Paraguay**
Kilometres flown	4	9	8	8	3	8	7	6	Kilomètres parcourus
Passengers carried	129	314	337	324	109	279	303	290	Passagers transportés
Passengers km	262	1141	1273	1235	246	1121	1253	1215	Passagers−km
Total ton−km	26	125	139	123	24	122	136	120	Total tonnes−km
Peru									**Pérou**
Kilometres flown	25	19	22	27	9	8	11	14	Kilomètres parcourus
Passengers carried	1980	1218	1362	1895	221	231	336	431	Passagers transportés
Passengers km	1974	1528	1926	2601	822	848	1205	1639	Passagers−km
Total ton−km	217	179	214	257	98	111	143	164	Total tonnes−km
Suriname									**Suriname**
Kilometres flown	3	4	5	3	2	3	4	3	Kilomètres parcourus
Passengers carried	144	216	96	149	120	200	80	138	Passagers transportés
Passengers km	245	604	304	541	240	600	300	539	Passagers−km
Total ton−km	26	71	31	76	25	71	30	76	Total tonnes−km
Uruguay									**Uruguay**
Kilometres flown	4	5	5	5	3	5	5	5	Kilomètres parcourus
Passengers carried	478	430	503	529	433	430	503	529	Passagers transportés
Passengers km	178	490	400	645	160	490	400	645	Passagers−km
Total ton−km	17	46	40	62	15	46	40	62	Total tonnes−km
Venezuela									**Venezuela**
Kilometres flown	61	76	82	78	26	41	47	50	Kilomètres parcourus
Passengers carried	5133	7149	6814	5267	960	1540	1653	1760	Passagers transportés
Passengers km	4367	6753	6880	6426	2671	4278	4676	4921	Passagers−km
Total ton−km	501	779	784	788	392	560	589	653	Total tonnes−km
Asia [1]									**Asie** [1]
Kilometres flown	**1270**	**2562**	**2803**	**3094**	**777**	**1611**	**1750**	**1928**	**Kilomètres parcourus**
Passengers carried	**106119**	**240753**	**251664**	**275758**	**34301**	**80867**	**86321**	**95088**	**Passagers transportés**
Passengers km	**158192**	**407368**	**433238**	**480701**	**108019**	**285073**	**305536**	**341214**	**Passagers−km**
Total ton−km	**20458**	**56739**	**61986**	**69619**	**15977**	**45540**	**50270**	**56725**	**Total tonnes−km**
Afghanistan									**Afghanistan**
Kilometres flown	3	4	4	6	3	2	1	3	Kilomètres parcourus
Passengers carried	76	212	197	238	51	92	83	102	Passagers transportés
Passengers km	163	205	197	263	155	151	145	192	Passagers−km
Total ton−km	36	27	25	36	35	22	20	29	Total tonnes−km
Azerbaijan									**Azerbaïdjan**
Kilometres flown	...	0	23	23	...	0	2	2	Kilomètres parcourus
Passengers carried	...	1455	1383	1380	...	16	60	57	Passagers transportés
Passengers km	...	3511	1738	1731	...	33	122	115	Passagers−km
Total ton−km	...	339	184	183	...	3	15	14	Total tonnes−km
Bahrain									**Bahreïn**
Kilometres flown	7	16	18	21	7	16	18	21	Kilomètres parcourus
Passengers carried	522	981	1080	1151	522	981	1080	1151	Passagers transportés
Passengers km	714	1922	2210	2439	714	1922	2210	2439	Passagers−km
Total ton−km	91	252	297	354	91	252	297	354	Total tonnes−km
Bangladesh									**Bangladesh**
Kilometres flown	12	15	17	19	10	13	15	17	Kilomètres parcourus
Passengers carried	614	1051	1083	1216	270	624	667	770	Passagers transportés
Passengers km	1179	2303	2556	2936	1113	2215	2470	2844	Passagers−km
Total ton−km	126	290	278	425	119	282	270	416	Total tonnes−km
Bhutan									**Bhoutan**
Kilometres flown	...	0	0	0	...	0	0	0	Kilomètres parcourus
Passengers carried	...	9	9	9	...	9	9	9	Passagers transportés
Passengers km	...	5	5	5	...	5	5	5	Passagers−km
Total ton−km	...	0	0	0	...	0	0	0	Total tonnes−km
Brunei Darussalam									**Brunéi Darussalam**
Kilometres flown	...	10	16	20	...	10	16	20	Kilomètres parcourus
Passengers carried	...	410	604	769	...	410	604	769	Passagers transportés
Passengers km	...	900	1623	2029	...	900	1623	2029	Passagers−km
Total ton−km	...	111	211	277	...	111	211	277	Total tonnes−km

65
Civil Aviation
Passengers on scheduled services (000); Kilometres (million) [cont.]
Aviation civile
Passagers sur les services réguliers (000); Kilomètres (millions) [suite]

Country or area and traffic	Total Totale				International Internationaux				Pays ou zone et trafic
	1980	1992	1993	1994	1980	1992	1993	1994	
China									**Chine**
Kilometres flown	47	290	367	431	10	72	81	86	Kilomètres parcourus
Passengers carried	2568	27345	31312	37498	360	4500	4667	4909	Passagers transportés
Passengers km	3578	40605	45000	51395	913	11162	11171	11748	Passagers−km
Total ton−km	443	4284	4848	5535	134	1677	1842	1892	Total tonnes−km
Cyprus									**Chypre**
Kilometres flown	10	19	19	21	10	19	19	21	Kilomètres parcourus
Passengers carried	441	947	1011	1234	441	947	1011	1234	Passagers transportés
Passengers km	798	2095	2179	2810	798	2095	2179	2810	Passagers−km
Total ton−km	92	223	230	291	92	223	230	291	Total tonnes−km
Georgia									**Géorgie**
Kilometres flown	...	...	...	4	...	...	...	3	Kilomètres parcourus
Passengers carried	...	...	...	223	...	...	...	150	Passagers transportés
Passengers km	...	...	...	283	...	...	...	217	Passagers−km
Total ton−km	...	...	...	26	...	...	...	20	Total tonnes−km
India									**Inde**
Kilometres flown	85	114	104	134	43	48	46	55	Kilomètres parcourus
Passengers carried	6603	11127	9442	11518	1668	2457	2194	2505	Passagers transportés
Passengers km	10765	16718	14396	17581	6765	8932	7858	9567	Passagers−km
Total ton−km	1353	1919	1661	2145	966	1169	1032	1355	Total tonnes−km
Indonesia									**Indonésie**
Kilometres flown	88	192	218	215	24	70	80	83	Kilomètres parcourus
Passengers carried	5059	11177	12009	12290	922	2773	2932	3285	Passagers transportés
Passengers km	5907	18758	19846	21166	2774	12076	12850	14431	Passagers−km
Total ton−km	625	2213	2416	2666	337	1538	1700	1999	Total tonnes−km
Iran, Islamic Rep. of									**Iran, Rép. islamique d'**
Kilometres flown	16	32	34	38	8	11	12	13	Kilomètres parcourus
Passengers carried	1998	4896	5352	5803	396	730	750	704	Passagers transportés
Passengers km	2071	4867	5045	5238	995	1914	1868	1726	Passagers−km
Total ton−km	210	510	519	554	109	235	223	228	Total tonnes−km
Iraq									**Iraq**
Kilometres flown	13	0	...	0	12	0	...	...	Kilomètres parcourus
Passengers carried	620	53	...	31	434	12	...	...	Passagers transportés
Passengers km	1161	35	...	20	1083	15	...	...	Passagers−km
Total ton−km	157	3	...	2	150	1	...	...	Total tonnes−km
Israel									**Israël**
Kilometres flown	30	55	59	64	28	50	54	59	Kilomètres parcourus
Passengers carried	1483	2391	2569	2980	1043	1857	2014	2345	Passagers transportés
Passengers km	4727	8361	8747	9662	4590	8203	8581	9544	Passagers−km
Total ton−km	724	1603	1654	1832	712	1588	1638	1820	Total tonnes−km
Japan									**Japon**
Kilometres flown	365	569	583	628	150	286	284	306	Kilomètres parcourus
Passengers carried	45145	81378	80064	83913	4499	11589	11260	12700	Passagers transportés
Passengers km	51217	108082	106983	118011	22254	55324	53979	62822	Passagers−km
Total ton−km	6184	14542	14721	16247	3778	9882	10031	11363	Total tonnes−km
Jordan									**Jordanie**
Kilometres flown	21	31	35	36	21	31	35	36	Kilomètres parcourus
Passengers carried	1113	1109	1186	1220	1070	1076	1145	1170	Passagers transportés
Passengers km	2607	3572	4000	4155	2595	3564	3990	4143	Passagers−km
Total ton−km	316	503	580	625	315	502	579	624	Total tonnes−km
Kazakstan									**Kazakstan**
Kilometres flown	...	0	16	16	...	0	1	1	Kilomètres parcourus
Passengers carried	...	5273	706	702	...	10	85	81	Passagers transportés
Passengers km	...	9713	1810	1787	...	10	400	377	Passagers−km
Total ton−km	...	913	172	170	...	1	39	37	Total tonnes−km
Korea, Dem. P. R.									**Corée, R. p. dém. de**
Kilometres flown	3	3	3	3	0	1	1	1	Kilomètres parcourus
Passengers carried	192	235	242	242	20	35	36	36	Passagers transportés
Passengers km	90	189	197	197	17	103	108	108	Passagers−km
Total ton−km	10	20	21	21	2	10	11	11	Total tonnes−km
Korea, Republic of									**Corée, République de**
Kilometres flown	61	188	218	241	55	150	173	195	Kilomètres parcourus
Passengers carried	3567	19767	21426	24932	2105	5633	6372	7368	Passagers transportés
Passengers km	10833	28004	34083	39579	10240	22935	28762	33422	Passagers−km
Total ton−km	1850	5825	7246	8191	1797	5327	6717	7586	Total tonnes−km

65
Civil Aviation
Passengers on scheduled services (000); Kilometres (million) [cont.]
Aviation civile
Passagers sur les services réguliers (000); Kilomètres (millions) [suite]

Country or area and traffic	Total Totale 1980	1992	1993	1994	International Internationaux 1980	1992	1993	1994	Pays ou zone et trafic
Kuwait									**Koweït**
Kilometres flown	20	29	33	35	20	29	33	35	Kilomètres parcourus
Passengers carried	1076	1409	1554	1756	1076	1409	1554	1756	Passagers transportés
Passengers km	2114	3529	4054	4509	2114	3529	4054	4509	Passagers–km
Total ton–km	265	538	632	696	265	538	632	696	Total tonnes–km
Kyrgyzstan									**Kirghizistan**
Kilometres flown	...	...	8	8	...	...	1	1	Kilomètres parcourus
Passengers carried	...	...	464	464	...	...	10	10	Passagers transportés
Passengers km	...	...	568	568	...	...	41	41	Passagers–km
Total ton–km	...	...	52	52	...	...	3	3	Total tonnes–km
Lao People's Dem. Rep.									**Rép. dém. pop. lao**
Kilometres flown	0	1	1	1	0	1	1	1	Kilomètres parcourus
Passengers carried	13	119	119	119	13	30	30	30	Passagers transportés
Passengers km	7	46	46	46	7	19	19	19	Passagers–km
Total ton–km	1	4	4	4	1	2	2	2	Total tonnes–km
Lebanon									**Liban**
Kilometres flown	43	19	18	19	43	19	18	19	Kilomètres parcourus
Passengers carried	930	600	677	706	930	600	677	706	Passagers transportés
Passengers km	1571	1285	1459	1588	1571	1285	1459	1588	Passagers–km
Total ton–km	680	272	260	284	680	272	260	284	Total tonnes–km
Malaysia									**Malaisie**
Kilometres flown	41	111	115	126	22	69	74	84	Kilomètres parcourus
Passengers carried	4516	12757	13077	14250	1822	5081	5597	6402	Passagers transportés
Passengers km	4076	15714	17445	20335	2916	12625	14431	17024	Passagers–km
Total ton–km	501	2113	2178	2507	384	1824	1898	2205	Total tonnes–km
Maldives									**Maldives**
Kilometres flown	1	0	0	0	1	...	...	0	Kilomètres parcourus
Passengers carried	27	9	9	38	27	...	...	6	Passagers transportés
Passengers km	20	3	3	7	20	...	...	3	Passagers–km
Total ton–km	2	0	0	1	2	...	...	0	Total tonnes–km
Mongolia									**Mongolie**
Kilometres flown	0	11	12	12	0	2	2	2	Kilomètres parcourus
Passengers carried	0	591	630	630	0	40	43	43	Passagers transportés
Passengers km	0	438	491	491	0	107	115	115	Passagers–km
Total ton–km	0	42	45	45	0	10	12	12	Total tonnes–km
Myanmar									**Myanmar**
Kilometres flown	6	4	4	4	1	0	0	0	Kilomètres parcourus
Passengers carried	481	319	319	319	64	19	19	19	Passagers transportés
Passengers km	218	140	140	140	56	14	14	14	Passagers–km
Total ton–km	21	14	14	14	6	2	2	2	Total tonnes–km
Nepal									**Népal**
Kilometres flown	6	9	7	10	3	5	7	7	Kilomètres parcourus
Passengers carried	380	680	633	683	164	365	356	347	Passagers transportés
Passengers km	234	721	772	812	196	670	729	764	Passagers–km
Total ton–km	22	71	87	88	19	67	83	84	Total tonnes–km
Oman									**Oman**
Kilometres flown	7	17	19	26	7	16	18	23	Kilomètres parcourus
Passengers carried	522	1081	1180	1512	522	981	1080	1282	Passagers transportés
Passengers km	714	1987	2275	2802	714	1922	2210	2631	Passagers–km
Total ton–km	91	258	303	386	91	252	297	371	Total tonnes–km
Pakistan									**Pakistan**
Kilometres flown	50	68	68	71	37	44	44	48	Kilomètres parcourus
Passengers carried	3029	5681	5647	5664	1501	2251	2269	2360	Passagers transportés
Passengers km	5696	10095	9898	10409	4522	7574	7533	8059	Passagers–km
Total ton–km	763	1332	1322	1400	643	1067	1069	1150	Total tonnes–km
Philippines									**Philippines**
Kilometres flown	42	68	70	72	26	46	49	50	Kilomètres parcourus
Passengers carried	3246	6137	6526	6851	997	2113	2229	2356	Passagers transportés
Passengers km	5959	12882	13496	13977	4880	10918	11343	11686	Passagers–km
Total ton–km	709	1602	1687	1769	612	1409	1478	1546	Total tonnes–km
Qatar									**Qatar**
Kilometres flown	7	16	18	21	7	16	18	21	Kilomètres parcourus
Passengers carried	522	981	1080	1151	522	981	1080	1151	Passagers transportés
Passengers km	714	1922	2210	2439	714	1922	2210	2439	Passagers–km
Total ton–km	91	252	297	354	91	252	297	354	Total tonnes–km

65

Civil Aviation

Passengers on scheduled services (000); Kilometres (million) [*cont.*]

Aviation civile

Passagers sur les services réguliers (000); Kilomètres (millions) [*suite*]

Country or area and traffic	Total Totale				International Internationaux				Pays ou zone et trafic
	1980	1992	1993	1994	1980	1992	1993	1994	
Saudi Arabia									**Arabie saoudite**
Kilometres flown	91	106	114	117	47	59	64	66	Kilomètres parcourus
Passengers carried	9241	11155	11864	11922	2348	3602	3800	3684	Passagers transportés
Passengers km	9938	17563	18572	18250	4958	12003	12646	12215	Passagers–km
Total ton–km	1069	2283	2415	2477	591	1718	1816	1862	Total tonnes–km
Singapore									**Singapour**
Kilometres flown	69	158	181	201	69	158	181	201	Kilomètres parcourus
Passengers carried	3827	8477	9271	9929	3827	8477	9271	9929	Passagers transportés
Passengers km	14719	37045	41262	44947	14719	37045	41262	44947	Passagers–km
Total ton–km	1959	5783	6826	7586	1959	5783	6826	7586	Total tonnes–km
Sri Lanka									**Sri Lanka**
Kilometres flown	8	24	22	21	8	24	22	21	Kilomètres parcourus
Passengers carried	235	1046	994	1067	235	1046	994	1067	Passagers transportés
Passengers km	691	4104	3624	3683	691	4104	3624	3683	Passagers–km
Total ton–km	72	485	436	448	72	485	436	448	Total tonnes–km
Syrian Arab Republic									**Rép. arabe syrienne**
Kilometres flown	11	9	10	10	10	8	9	9	Kilomètres parcourus
Passengers carried	465	552	485	464	383	492	443	428	Passagers transportés
Passengers km	948	966	817	820	908	928	801	806	Passagers–km
Total ton–km	101	101	86	88	98	97	85	86	Total tonnes–km
Tajikistan									**Tadjikistan**
Kilometres flown	...	...	0	0	...	...	0	0	Kilomètres parcourus
Passengers carried	...	...	783	783	...	...	1	1	Passagers transportés
Passengers km	...	...	2231	2231	...	...	5	5	Passagers–km
Total ton–km	...	...	205	205	...	...	0	0	Total tonnes–km
Thailand									**Thaïlande**
Kilometres flown	42	115	116	124	37	98	98	106	Kilomètres parcourus
Passengers carried	2459	8547	10197	11405	1924	5343	6203	6775	Passagers transportés
Passengers km	6276	20427	22874	25242	5988	18616	20609	22619	Passagers–km
Total ton–km	812	2815	3167	3552	789	2637	2941	3288	Total tonnes–km
Turkey									**Turquie**
Kilometres flown	15	64	80	91	8	47	58	68	Kilomètres parcourus
Passengers carried	1254	4959	6077	6872	377	2158	2512	2675	Passagers transportés
Passengers km	1103	6060	7519	8576	689	4653	5669	6307	Passagers–km
Total ton–km	113	670	842	989	72	541	676	791	Total tonnes–km
Turkmenistan									**Turkménistan**
Kilometres flown	...	...	—	—	...	...	—	—	Kilomètres parcourus
Passengers carried	...	...	748	748	...	...	—	—	Passagers transportés
Passengers km	...	...	1562	1562	...	...	—	—	Passagers–km
Total ton–km	...	...	143	143	...	...	—	—	Total tonnes–km
United Arab Emirates									**Emirats arabes unis**
Kilometres flown	7	50	64	68	7	50	64	68	Kilomètres parcourus
Passengers carried	522	2509	2936	3162	522	2509	2936	3162	Passagers transportés
Passengers km	714	6298	7794	8267	714	6298	7794	8267	Passagers–km
Total ton–km	91	899	1126	1225	91	899	1126	1225	Total tonnes–km
Uzbekistan									**Ouzbékistan**
Kilometres flown	...	2	2	2	...	2	2	2	Kilomètres parcourus
Passengers carried	...	4032	2217	2217	...	24	32	32	Passagers transportés
Passengers km	...	8125	4855	4855	...	102	127	127	Passagers–km
Total ton–km	...	774	447	447	...	16	18	18	Total tonnes–km
Viet Nam									**Viet Nam**
Kilometres flown	0	3	3	3	0	2	2	2	Kilomètres parcourus
Passengers carried	6	204	211	211	6	130	137	137	Passagers transportés
Passengers km	3	201	209	209	3	125	133	133	Passagers–km
Total ton–km	0	18	19	19	0	11	12	12	Total tonnes–km
Yemen									**Yémen**
Kilometres flown	6	13	13	13	6	11	11	11	Kilomètres parcourus
Passengers carried	310	800	848	791	255	519	551	531	Passagers transportés
Passengers km	291	1124	1217	1183	280	1016	1099	1084	Passagers–km
Total ton–km	27	114	124	119	26	104	113	110	Total tonnes–km
Europe [1]									**Europe** [1]
Kilometres flown	**1892**	**3137**	**3321**	**3506**	**1488**	**2487**	**2652**	**2815**	**Kilomètres parcourus**
Passengers carried	**128802**	**218962**	**228396**	**243642**	**69391**	**120218**	**128621**	**139290**	**Passagers transportés**
Passengers km	**203021**	**366713**	**393604**	**429439**	**173908**	**311259**	**336096**	**369067**	**Passagers–km**
Total ton–km	**27042**	**52391**	**56946**	**63094**	**24200**	**46957**	**51208**	**57034**	**Total tonnes–km**

65
Civil Aviation
Passengers on scheduled services (000); Kilometres (million) [*cont.*]
Aviation civile
Passagers sur les services réguliers (000); Kilomètres (millions) [*suite*]

Country or area and traffic	Total Totale				International Internationaux				Pays ou zone et trafic
	1980	1992	1993	1994	1980	1992	1993	1994	
Albania									**Albanie**
Kilometres flown	...	...	...	0	...	...	...	0	Kilomètres parcourus
Passengers carried	...	...	...	9	...	...	...	9	Passagers transportés
Passengers km	...	...	...	2	...	...	...	2	Passagers—km
Total ton—km	...	...	...	0	...	...	...	0	Total tonnes—km
Austria									**Autriche**
Kilometres flown	22	62	72	79	22	61	70	76	Kilomètres parcourus
Passengers carried	1284	3024	3297	3748	1267	2935	3212	3491	Passagers transportés
Passengers km	1120	4867	5629	5933	1115	4832	5595	5868	Passagers—km
Total ton—km	118	568	669	703	118	564	665	697	Total tonnes—km
Belarus									**Bélarus**
Kilometres flown	...	...	1	1	...	...	1	1	Kilomètres parcourus
Passengers carried	...	...	805	805	...	...	42	42	Passagers transportés
Passengers km	...	...	2604	2604	...	...	98	98	Passagers—km
Total ton—km	...	...	237	237	...	...	9	9	Total tonnes—km
Belgium									**Belgique**
Kilometres flown	55	76	99	107	55	76	99	107	Kilomètres parcourus
Passengers carried	1974	3146	3651	4193	1974	3146	3651	4193	Passagers transportés
Passengers km	4852	6203	6484	7496	4852	6203	6484	7496	Passagers—km
Total ton—km	842	965	1081	1209	842	965	1081	1209	Total tonnes—km
Bulgaria									**Bulgarie**
Kilometres flown	13	22	26	26	7	20	24	24	Kilomètres parcourus
Passengers carried	1788	814	916	789	486	673	776	702	Passagers transportés
Passengers km	775	1636	2241	2085	515	1575	2180	2025	Passagers—km
Total ton—km	80	163	231	220	55	157	225	214	Total tonnes—km
Croatia									**Croatie**
Kilometres flown	...	2	5	7	...	2	3	6	Kilomètres parcourus
Passengers carried	...	215	432	624	...	84	191	306	Passagers transportés
Passengers km	...	123	255	405	...	78	171	279	Passagers—km
Total ton—km	...	12	26	41	...	8	17	28	Total tonnes—km
former Czechoslovakia †									**anc. Tchécoslovaquie †**
Kilometres flown	25	26	...	...	16	24	...	...	Kilomètres parcourus
Passengers carried	1461	974	...	...	585	810	...	...	Passagers transportés
Passengers km	1539	2135	...	...	1190	2059	...	...	Passagers—km
Total ton—km	154	219	...	...	124	212	...	...	Total tonnes—km
Czech Republic									**République tchèque**
Kilometres flown	...	...	25	24	...	...	25	24	Kilomètres parcourus
Passengers carried	...	...	1025	1072	...	...	1016	1067	Passagers transportés
Passengers km	...	...	1900	1976	...	...	1897	1975	Passagers—km
Total ton—km	...	...	196	201	...	...	196	200	Total tonnes—km
Denmark [3]									**Danemark [3]**
Kilometres flown	33	60	65	65	27	47	52	52	Kilomètres parcourus
Passengers carried	3330	4720	5077	5456	1354	2551	2835	3038	Passagers transportés
Passengers km	3296	4506	4913	5112	2637	3763	4130	4293	Passagers—km
Total ton—km	423	538	579	603	359	462	502	523	Total tonnes—km
Estonia									**Estonie**
Kilometres flown	...	4	4	4	...	3	4	4	Kilomètres parcourus
Passengers carried	...	146	128	157	...	112	109	157	Passagers transportés
Passengers km	...	102	86	92	...	96	82	92	Passagers—km
Total ton—km	...	10	8	9	...	9	8	9	Total tonnes—km
Finland									**Finlande**
Kilometres flown	36	62	63	67	24	42	44	49	Kilomètres parcourus
Passengers carried	2512	3898	3947	4492	969	1841	2074	2572	Passagers transportés
Passengers km	2139	4639	5529	6720	1603	3755	4712	5871	Passagers—km
Total ton—km	243	535	662	804	194	458	590	730	Total tonnes—km
France [4]									**France [4]**
Kilometres flown	276	441	471	511	213	311	322	353	Kilomètres parcourus
Passengers carried	19521	33607	35221	38060	9952	13580	13877	15445	Passagers transportés
Passengers km	34130	56701	60056	68019	25938	37308	38196	44581	Passagers—km
Total ton—km	5131	9293	9808	11360	4317	7315	7533	8858	Total tonnes—km
Germany †									**Allemagne †**
Kilometres flown	...	468	474	501	...	392	399	421	Kilomètres parcourus
Passengers carried	...	27578	29363	30964	...	15435	16555	17247	Passagers transportés
Passengers km	...	48965	52941	56903	...	44063	47808	51689	Passagers—km
Total ton—km	...	9166	10109	11243	...	8653	9542	10670	Total tonnes—km

65
Civil Aviation
Passengers on scheduled services (000); Kilometres (million) [*cont.*]
Aviation civile
Passagers sur les services réguliers (000); Kilomètres (millions) [*suite*]

Country or area and traffic	Total Totale				International Internationaux				Pays ou zone et trafic
	1980	1992	1993	1994	1980	1992	1993	1994	
F. R. Germany									**R. f. Allemagne**
Kilometres flown	196	...	...	...	168	...	...	...	Kilomètres parcourus
Passengers carried	13046	...	...	...	7458	...	...	...	Passagers transportés
Passengers km	21056	...	...	...	18932	...	...	...	Passagers – km
Total ton – km	3524	...	...	...	3299	...	...	...	Total tonnes – km
Greece									**Grèce**
Kilometres flown	40	58	62	64	30	43	47	49	Kilomètres parcourus
Passengers carried	4891	5466	5478	5813	1656	2137	2290	2545	Passagers transportés
Passengers km	5062	7262	7899	8429	4030	6263	6964	7453	Passagers – km
Total ton – km	521	772	848	904	427	673	755	807	Total tonnes – km
Hungary									**Hongrie**
Kilometres flown	16	22	24	26	16	22	24	26	Kilomètres parcourus
Passengers carried	874	1029	1217	1325	874	1029	1217	1325	Passagers transportés
Passengers km	1020	1125	1484	1653	1020	1125	1484	1653	Passagers – km
Total ton – km	111	110	147	169	111	110	147	169	Total tonnes – km
Iceland									**Islande**
Kilometres flown	11	18	19	21	9	16	17	18	Kilomètres parcourus
Passengers carried	542	767	801	1031	300	510	552	774	Passagers transportés
Passengers km	1295	1840	1968	2297	1235	1775	1905	2232	Passagers – km
Total ton – km	142	203	219	254	136	196	212	247	Total tonnes – km
Ireland									**Irlande**
Kilometres flown	22	43	39	42	21	41	37	40	Kilomètres parcourus
Passengers carried	1830	5006	4650	4826	1636	4662	4354	4516	Passagers transportés
Passengers km	2049	4461	4209	4920	2009	4400	4157	4863	Passagers – km
Total ton – km	271	501	467	537	266	496	463	532	Total tonnes – km
Italy									**Italie**
Kilometres flown	139	236	246	248	96	161	172	174	Kilomètres parcourus
Passengers carried	9956	21767	21880	22933	4191	8480	8559	9460	Passagers transportés
Passengers km	14076	28667	29702	31738	11209	21719	22751	24730	Passagers – km
Total ton – km	1813	3878	4044	4257	1535	3235	3393	3600	Total tonnes – km
Latvia									**Lettonie**
Kilometres flown	...	2	4	6	...	1	4	6	Kilomètres parcourus
Passengers carried	...	66	111	133	...	32	111	133	Passagers transportés
Passengers km	...	133	106	145	...	41	106	145	Passagers – km
Total ton – km	...	13	11	15	...	4	11	15	Total tonnes – km
Lithuania									**Lituanie**
Kilometres flown	...	12	5	7	...	12	5	7	Kilomètres parcourus
Passengers carried	...	557	150	195	...	554	150	195	Passagers transportés
Passengers km	...	756	154	241	...	755	154	241	Passagers – km
Total ton – km	...	72	15	23	...	72	15	23	Total tonnes – km
Luxembourg									**Luxembourg**
Kilometres flown	3	7	8	9	3	7	8	9	Kilomètres parcourus
Passengers carried	162	461	471	533	162	461	471	533	Passagers transportés
Passengers km	55	286	290	361	55	286	290	361	Passagers – km
Total ton – km	5	27	27	33	5	27	27	33	Total tonnes – km
Malta									**Malte**
Kilometres flown	6	11	13	21	6	11	13	21	Kilomètres parcourus
Passengers carried	401	693	797	1010	401	693	797	1010	Passagers transportés
Passengers km	602	1111	1250	1821	602	1111	1250	1821	Passagers – km
Total ton – km	59	104	117	180	59	104	117	180	Total tonnes – km
Monaco									**Monaco**
Kilometres flown	0	0	0	0	0	0	0	0	Kilomètres parcourus
Passengers carried	44	44	44	44	44	44	44	44	Passagers transportés
Passengers km	1	1	1	1	1	1	1	1	Passagers – km
Total ton – km	0	0	0	0	0	0	0	0	Total tonnes – km
Netherlands [5]									**Pays – Bas** [5]
Kilometres flown	109	221	247	263	107	219	246	262	Kilomètres parcourus
Passengers carried	4984	10088	11775	12895	4633	10011	11704	12817	Passagers transportés
Passengers km	14643	33351	38544	42435	14596	33302	38495	42382	Passagers – km
Total ton – km	2347	5556	6512	7320	2342	5552	6507	7315	Total tonnes – km
Norway [3]									**Norvège** [3]
Kilometres flown	58	96	102	106	27	46	50	48	Kilomètres parcourus
Passengers carried	4804	9469	10383	11133	1354	2591	2842	3004	Passagers transportés
Passengers km	4068	6584	7266	7663	2637	3736	4092	4259	Passagers – km
Total ton – km	493	718	791	836	359	459	498	522	Total tonnes – km

65

Civil Aviation
Passengers on scheduled services (000); Kilometres (million) [*cont.*]
Aviation civile
Passagers sur les services réguliers (000); Kilomètres (millions) [*suite*]

Country or area and traffic	Total Totale				International Internationaux				Pays ou zone et trafic
	1980	1992	1993	1994	1980	1992	1993	1994	
Poland									**Pologne**
Kilometres flown	35	31	37	38	26	29	34	36	Kilomètres parcourus
Passengers carried	1711	1102	1270	1452	931	985	1106	1246	Passagers transportés
Passengers km	2232	2873	3335	3690	1934	2827	3272	3611	Passagers–km
Total ton–km	207	293	357	396	182	289	351	389	Total tonnes–km
Portugal									**Portugal**
Kilometres flown	39	69	72	74	30	56	58	59	Kilomètres parcourus
Passengers carried	1978	4109	4379	4360	971	2512	2632	2543	Passagers transportés
Passengers km	3459	7790	8089	7880	2793	6665	6928	6648	Passagers–km
Total ton–km	424	882	913	904	349	760	787	771	Total tonnes–km
Republic of Moldova									**République de Moldova**
Kilometres flown	...	0	0	0	...	0	0	0	Kilomètres parcourus
Passengers carried	...	571	312	312	...	1	2	2	Passagers transportés
Passengers km	...	1826	1078	1078	...	3	4	4	Passagers–km
Total ton–km	...	176	100	100	...	0	0	0	Total tonnes–km
Romania									**Roumanie**
Kilometres flown	20	25	24	30	13	20	19	26	Kilomètres parcourus
Passengers carried	1112	919	979	1243	383	615	615	900	Passagers transportés
Passengers km	1209	2042	1810	2584	916	1898	1657	2442	Passagers–km
Total ton–km	109	174	161	252	83	162	148	239	Total tonnes–km
Russian Federation									**Fédération de Russie**
Kilometres flown	...	134	974	870	...	134	162	179	Kilomètres parcourus
Passengers carried	...	62174	36229	29333	...	2872	3856	4068	Passagers transportés
Passengers km	...	116139	76683	65144	...	12269	15362	14914	Passagers–km
Total ton–km	...	12085	7825	6744	...	1423	1777	1835	Total tonnes–km
Slovakia									**Slovaquie**
Kilometres flown	...	...	1	1	...	...	1	1	Kilomètres parcourus
Passengers carried	...	...	18	23	...	...	10	10	Passagers transportés
Passengers km	...	...	10	12	...	...	7	7	Passagers–km
Total ton–km	...	...	1	1	...	...	1	1	Total tonnes–km
Slovenia									**Slovénie**
Kilometres flown	...	3	5	6	...	3	5	6	Kilomètres parcourus
Passengers carried	...	188	291	340	...	180	276	338	Passagers transportés
Passengers km	...	196	278	329	...	195	275	329	Passagers–km
Total ton–km	...	19	28	33	...	19	28	33	Total tonnes–km
Spain									**Espagne**
Kilometres flown	164	246	248	234	96	148	148	135	Kilomètres parcourus
Passengers carried	15089	23386	22279	21992	5137	6657	6956	6754	Passagers transportés
Passengers km	15517	27480	27105	26654	10290	18198	18551	18181	Passagers–km
Total ton–km	1808	3081	3025	3003	1267	2144	2168	2154	Total tonnes–km
Sweden [3]									**Suède** [3]
Kilometres flown	66	114	120	125	41	69	76	74	Kilomètres parcourus
Passengers carried	5209	9924	9730	10808	2031	3703	4042	4386	Passagers transportés
Passengers km	5342	8247	8428	9417	3955	5518	5945	6405	Passagers–km
Total ton–km	666	932	993	1064	538	689	757	790	Total tonnes–km
Switzerland									**Suisse**
Kilometres flown	98	158	165	174	97	152	160	169	Kilomètres parcourus
Passengers carried	5930	8256	9152	9338	5221	7281	8134	8281	Passagers transportés
Passengers km	10831	16472	17509	18858	10773	16236	17299	18651	Passagers–km
Total ton–km	1419	2704	2990	3288	1413	2674	2965	3262	Total tonnes–km
TFYR Macedonia									**L'ex–R.y. Macédoine**
Kilometres flown	...	...	5	5	...	...	5	5	Kilomètres parcourus
Passengers carried	...	...	187	203	...	...	187	203	Passagers transportés
Passengers km	...	...	292	319	...	...	292	319	Passagers–km
Total ton–km	...	...	28	29	...	...	28	29	Total tonnes–km
Ukraine									**Ukraine**
Kilometres flown	...	134	35	19	...	4	8	15	Kilomètres parcourus
Passengers carried	...	4906	1278	769	...	117	178	549	Passagers transportés
Passengers km	...	7906	1790	1294	...	334	511	1101	Passagers–km
Total ton–km	...	760	171	133	...	32	49	115	Total tonnes–km
United Kingdom [6]									**Royaume–Uni** [6]
Kilometres flown	426	684	729	804	370	592	636	709	Kilomètres parcourus
Passengers carried	25551	47563	50188	55475	18489	35831	38061	42450	Passagers transportés
Passengers km	56750	115199	124882	139088	54026	110462	119950	133752	Passagers–km
Total ton–km	6742	15710	17387	19699	6503	15308	16970	19250	Total tonnes–km

65
Civil Aviation
Passengers on scheduled services (000); Kilometres (million) [*cont.*]
Aviation civile
Passagers sur les services réguliers (000); Kilomètres (millions) [*suite*]

Country or area and traffic	Total Totale 1980	1992	1993	1994	International Internationaux 1980	1992	1993	1994	Pays ou zone et trafic
Oceania [1]									**Océanie** [1]
Kilometres flown	**277**	**532**	**558**	**628**	**100**	**238**	**255**	**269**	Kilomètres parcourus
Passengers carried	**18133**	**31672**	**35231**	**36933**	**3254**	**7379**	**8705**	**9182**	Passagers transportés
Passengers km	**32195**	**64468**	**73902**	**80719**	**20881**	**43118**	**50131**	**53597**	Passagers−km
Total ton−km	**3727**	**7894**	**8995**	**9938**	**2554**	**5776**	**6633**	**7161**	Total tonnes−km
Australia									**Australie**
Kilometres flown	200	377	402	445	59	144	157	156	Kilomètres parcourus
Passengers carried	13649	23887	26929	26816	1961	4786	5705	5455	Passagers transportés
Passengers km	25555	49612	57343	61124	15769	30568	36015	36747	Passagers−km
Total ton−km	2900	6024	6896	7442	1897	4140	4781	4945	Total tonnes−km
Fiji									**Fidji**
Kilometres flown	7	12	10	12	3	8	5	8	Kilomètres parcourus
Passengers carried	322	426	424	465	90	274	281	298	Passagers transportés
Passengers km	250	1009	983	1101	141	989	964	1080	Passagers−km
Total ton−km	26	125	126	155	14	123	125	153	Total tonnes−km
Kiribati									**Kiribati**
Kilometres flown	...	1	1	1	...	0	0	0	Kilomètres parcourus
Passengers carried	...	25	26	26	...	2	3	3	Passagers transportés
Passengers km	...	9	10	10	...	5	6	6	Passagers−km
Total ton−km	...	2	2	2	...	1	1	1	Total tonnes−km
Marshall Islands									**Iles Marshall**
Kilometres flown	...	2	2	9	...	1	1	6	Kilomètres parcourus
Passengers carried	...	96	44	42	...	40	16	14	Passagers transportés
Passengers km	...	53	49	41	...	43	39	31	Passagers−km
Total ton−km	...	9	10	12	...	8	9	10	Total tonnes−km
Nauru									**Nauru**
Kilometres flown	5	3	3	3	5	3	3	3	Kilomètres parcourus
Passengers carried	64	117	117	117	64	117	117	117	Passagers transportés
Passengers km	107	206	206	206	107	206	206	206	Passagers−km
Total ton−km	10	20	20	20	10	20	20	20	Total tonnes−km
New Zealand									**Nouvelle−Zélande**
Kilometres flown	52	116	121	136	29	77	81	92	Kilomètres parcourus
Passengers carried	3497	5784	6291	7716	1041	1968	2244	2934	Passagers transportés
Passengers km	5725	12679	14163	16946	4563	10828	12194	14770	Passagers−km
Total ton−km	731	1618	1823	2170	599	1430	1622	1951	Total tonnes−km
Papua New Guinea									**Papouasie−Nvl−Guinée**
Kilometres flown	11	17	13	19	4	4	5	5	Kilomètres parcourus
Passengers carried	559	954	866	1113	99	165	181	196	Passagers transportés
Passengers km	520	699	733	837	301	390	409	445	Passagers−km
Total ton−km	57	82	82	94	33	49	50	55	Total tonnes−km
Solomon Islands									**Iles Salomon**
Kilometres flown	1	2	2	2	0	1	1	1	Kilomètres parcourus
Passengers carried	42	69	75	79	0	8	27	28	Passagers transportés
Passengers km	39	13	62	65	0	4	50	53	Passagers−km
Total ton−km	3	1	7	5	0	0	6	4	Total tonnes−km
Tonga									**Tonga**
Kilometres flown	...	1	1	1	...	...	...	...	Kilomètres parcourus
Passengers carried	...	35	35	53	...	...	...	...	Passagers transportés
Passengers km	...	7	7	11	...	...	...	...	Passagers−km
Total ton−km	...	1	1	1	...	...	...	...	Total tonnes−km
Vanuatu									**Vanuatu**
Kilometres flown	...	1	2	2	...	1	2	2	Kilomètres parcourus
Passengers carried	...	59	67	70	...	59	67	70	Passagers transportés
Passengers km	...	129	142	143	...	129	142	143	Passagers−km
Total ton−km	...	13	14	15	...	13	14	15	Total tonnes−km

65
Civil Aviation
Passengers on scheduled services (000); Kilometres (million) [*cont.*]
Aviation civile
Passagers sur les services réguliers (000); Kilomètres (millions) [*suite*]

Source:
International Civil Aviation Organization (ICAO) (Montreal).

† For detailed descriptions of data pertaining to former
Czechoslovakia, Germany, SFR Yugoslavia and former USSR
USSR, see Annex I — Country or area nomenclature, regional
and other groupings.

1 Regional totals add to world totals. However, individual
country statistics do not add to regional totals because (i)
not all countries are shown, and (ii) the stastistics of
France, the Netherlands and the United Kingdom have been
distributed between two or more regions; France (Europe,
Asia and Pacific, Africa, America: North and South),
Netherlands (Europe and America: North and South), United
Kingdom (Europe, Asia and Pacific, America: North and
South).
2 Includes apportionment (1/10) of the traffic of Air Afrique,
a multinational airline with headquarters in Côte d'Ivoire
and operated by 10 African States until 1991. From 1992
includes apportionment (1/11) of the traffic of Air Afrique
and operated by 11 African States.
3 Includes an apportionment of international operations
performed by Scandinavian Airlines System (SAS), Denmark
(2/7), Norway (2/7), Sweden (3/7).
4 Including data for airlines based in the territories and
dependencies of France.
5 Including data for airlines based in the territories and
dependencies of Netherlands.
6 Including data for airlines based in the territories and
dependencies of United Kingdom.

Source:
Organisation de l'aviation civile internationale (OACI) (Montréal).

† Pour les descriptions en détails des données relatives à
l'ancienne Tchécoslovaquie, l'Allemagne, la Rfs Yougoslavie et
l'ancienne URSS, voir l'Annexe I — Nomenclature des pays ou
zones, groupements régionaux et autres groupements.

1 Les totaux régionaux s'ajoutent pour donner les totaux mondiaux. En
revanche, les statistiques de chaque pays ne s'additionnent pas pour
donner des totaux régionaux car (i) tous les pays ne sont pas indiqués
et (ii) les statistiques de la France, des Pays—Bas et du
Royaume—Uni concernent deux régions ou plus; France (Europe,
Asie et Pacifique, Afrique, Amérique : Nord et Sud), Pays—Bas
(Europe et Amérique : Nord et Sud), Royaume—Uni (Europe, Asie
et Pacifique, Amérique : Nord et Sud).
2 Ces chiffres comprennent une partie du trafic (1/10) assurée
par Air Afrique, compagnie aérienne multinationale dont le
siège est situé en Côte d'Ivoire et est exploitée conjointement
par 10 Etats Africains jusqu'à 1991. A partir de 1992 ces
chiffres comprennent une partie du trafic (1/11) assurée par
Air Afrique et est exploitée conjointement par 11 Etats
Africains.
3 Y compris une partie des vols internationaux effectués par
le SAS, Danemark (2/7), Norvège (2/7) et Suède (3/7).
4 Y compris les données relatives aux compagnies aériennes
ayant des bases d'opérations dans les territoires et
dépendances de France.
5 Y compris les données relatives aux compagnies aériennes
ayant des bases d'opérations dans les territoires et
dépendances des Pays—Bas.
6 Y compris les données relatives aux compagnies aériennes
ayant des bases d'opération dans les territoires et
dépendances du Royaume—Uni.

Technical notes, tables 61-65

Table 61: Data refer to domestic and international traffic on all railway lines within each country shown, except railways entirely within an urban unit, and plantation, industrial mining, funicular and cable railways. The figures relating to passenger-kilometres include all passengers except military, government and railway personnel when carried without revenue. Those relating to ton-kilometres are freight net ton-kilometres and include both fast and ordinary goods services but exclude service traffic, mail, baggage and non-revenue governmental stores.

Table 62: For years in which a census or registration took place the census or registration figure is shown; for other years, unless otherwise indicated, the officially estimated number of vehicles in use is shown. The time of year to which the figures refer is variable. Special purpose vehicles such as two- or three-wheeled cycles and motorcycles, trams, trolley-buses, ambulances, hearses, military vehicles operated by police or other governmental security organizations are excluded. Passenger cars includes vehicles seating not more than nine persons (including the driver), such as taxis, jeeps and station wagons. Commercial vehicles includes: vans, lorries (trucks), buses, tractor and semi-trailer combinations but excluding trailers and farm tractors.

Table 63: Data refer to merchant fleets registered in each country on 30 June of the year stated (1983-1991). Beginning 1992, data refer to end of the year merchant fleets. They are given in gross registered tons (100 cubic feet or 2.83 cubic metres) and represent the total volume of all the permanently enclosed spaces of the vessels to which the figures refer. Vessels without mechanical means of propulsion are excluded, but sailing vessels with auxiliary power are included.

Part A of the table refers to the total of merchant fleets registered. Part B shows data for oil tanker fleets and part C data for ore-oil and bulk carrier fleets.

Table 64: The figures for vessels entered and cleared, unless otherwise stated, represent the sum of the net registered tonnage of sea-going foreign and domestic merchant vessels (power and sailing) entered with cargo from or cleared with cargo to a foreign port and refer to only one entrance or clearance for each foreign voyage. The data where possible exclude vessels "in ballast", i.e. entering without unloading or clearing without loading goods.

Notes techniques, tableaux 61-65

Tableau 61 : Les données se rapportent au trafic intérieur et international de toutes les lignes de chemins de fer du pays indiqué, à l'exception des lignes situées entièrement à l'intérieur d'une agglomération urbaine ou desservant une plantation ou un complexe industriel minier, des funiculaires et des téléfériques. Les chiffres relatifs aux voyageurs-kilomètres se rapportent à tous les voyageurs sauf les militaires, les fonctionnaires et le personnel des chemins de fer, qui sont transportés gratuitement. Les chiffres relatifs aux tonnes-kilomètres se rapportent aux tonnes-kilomètres nettes de fret et comprennent les services rapides et ordinaires de transport de marchandises, à l'exception des transports pour les besoins du service, du courrier, des bagages et des marchandises transportées gratuitement pour les besoins de l'Etat.

Tableau 62 : Pour les années où a eu lieu un recensement ou un enregistrement des véhicules, le chiffre indiqué est le résultat de cette opération; pour les autres années, sauf indication contraire, le chiffre indiqué correspond à l'estimation officielle du nombre de véhicules en circulation. L'époque de l'année à laquelle se rapportent les chiffres varie. Les véhicules à usage spécial, tels que les cycles à deux ou trois roues et motocyclettes, les tramways, les trolley-bus, les ambulances, les corbillards, les véhicules militaires utilisés par la police ou par d'autres services publics de sécurité ne sont pas compris dans ces chiffres. Les voitures de tourisme comprennent les véhicules automobiles dont le nombre de places assises (y compris celle du conducteur) n'est pas supérieur à neuf, tels que les taxis, jeeps et breaks. Les véhicules utilitaires comprennent les fourgons, camions, autobus et autocars, les ensembles tracteurs-remorques et semi-remorques, mais ne comprennent pas les remorques et les tracteurs agricoles.

Tableau 63 : Les données se rapportent à la flotte marchande enregistrée dans chaque pays au 30 juin de l'année indiquée (1983-1991). A partir de 1992, les données se rapportent à la flotte marchande à la fin de l'année. Elles sont exprimées en tonneaux de jauge brute (100 pieds cubes ou 2,83 mètres cubes) et représentent le volume total de tous les espaces clos en permanence dans les navires auxquels elle s'appliquent. Elles excluent les navires sans moteur, mais pas les voiliers avec moteurs auxiliaires.

Les données de la Partie A du tableau se rapportent au total de la flotte marchande enregistrée. Celles de la Partie B se rapportent à la flotte des pétroliers, et celles de la Partie C à la flotte des minéraliers et des transporteurs de vrac et d'huile.

Table 65: Data for total services cover both domestic and international scheduled services operated by airlines registered in each country. Scheduled services include supplementary services occasioned by overflow traffic on regularly scheduled trips and preparatory flights for newly scheduled services. Freight means all goods, except mail and excess baggage, carried for remuneration.

Tableau 64 : sauf indication contraire, les données relatives aux navires entrés et sortis représentent la jauge nette totale des navires marchands de haute mer (à moteur ou à voile) nationaux ou étrangers, qui entrent ou sortent chargés, en provenance ou à destination d'un port étranger. On ne compte qu'une seule entrée et une seule sortie pour chaque voyage international. Dans la mesure du possible, le tableau exclut les navires sur lest (c'est-à-dire les navires entrant sans décharger ou sortant sans avoir chargé).

Tableau 65 : Les données relatives au total des services se rapportent aux services réguliers, intérieurs ou internationaux, des compagnies de transport aérien enregistrées dans chaque pays. Les services réguliers comprennent aussi les vols supplémentaires nécessités par un surcroît d'activité des services réguliers et les vols préparatoires en vue de nouveaux services réguliers. Par fret, on entend toutes les marchandises transportées contre paiement, mais non le courrier et les excédents de bagage.

66
Production, trade and consumption of commercial energy
Production, commerce et consommation d'énergie commerciale
Thousand metric tons of coal equivalent and kilograms per capita
Milliers de tonnes métriques d'équivalent houille et kilogrammes par habitant

Country or area	Year	Primary energy production – Production d'énergie primaire					Changes in stocks Variations des stocks	Imports Importations	Exports Exportations
		Total Totale	Solids Solides	Liquids Liquides	Gas Gaz	Electricity Electricité			
Africa	**1991**	**739 200**	**142 767**	**485 853**	**99 936**	**10 644**	**1 599**	**70 076**	**491 896**
	1992	**733 690**	**139 919**	**484 157**	**98 976**	**10 639**	**−3 105**	**73 204**	**488 387**
	1993	**732 121**	**145 381**	**474 028**	**103 073**	**9 639**	**−3 893**	**75 773**	**476 466**
	1994	**732 327**	**146 096**	**468 581**	**107 056**	**10 594**	**−2 760**	**80 118**	**470 362**
Algeria	1991	160 182	15	88 355	71 776	36	157	1 576	113 827
	1992	153 602	15	84 015	69 547	24	−670	1 768	112 222
	1993	156 534	20	84 763	71 708	43	−761	1 744	111 847
	1994	153 015	20	84 865	68 110	20	−514	1 270	106 639
Angola	1991	35 713	..	35 324	222	167	..	21	33 403
	1992	37 527	..	37 137	222	169	..	21	35 332
	1993	36 386	..	35 994	223	169	..	21	34 046
	1994	36 457	..	36 065	222	170	..	21	33 896
Benin	1991	421	..	421	..	..	..	259	432
	1992	426	..	426	..	..	..	266	436
	1993	431	..	431	..	..	..	268	442
	1994	443	..	443	..	..	..	278	444
Burkina Faso	1991	2	..	..	..	2	..	433	0
	1992	2	..	..	..	2	..	439	0
	1993	6	..	..	..	6	..	446	0
	1994	9	..	..	..	9	..	457	0
Burundi	1991	21	5	..	..	16	..	110	..
	1992	19	6	..	..	13	..	97	..
	1993	23	6	..	..	17	..	106	..
	1994	24	6	..	..	18	..	112	..
Cameroon	1991	11 341	1	11 012	..	328	−164	23	9 646
	1992	10 025	1	9 698	..	326	−14	23	8 166
	1993	9 197	1	8 870	..	326	7	24	7 321
	1994	8 150	1	7 823	..	326	0	24	6 275
Cape Verde	1991	..	..	..	..	..	..	49	0
	1992	..	..	..	..	..	..	51	0
	1993	..	..	..	..	..	..	51	0
	1994	..	..	..	..	..	..	56	0
Central African Rep.	1991	9	..	..	..	9	3	120	..
	1992	10	..	..	..	10	1	123	..
	1993	10	..	..	..	10	1	126	..
	1994	10	..	..	..	10	...	134	..
Chad	1991	..	..	..	..	..	1	55	...
	1992	..	..	..	..	..	3	63	...
	1993	..	..	..	..	..	4	75	...
	1994	..	..	..	..	..	4	78	...
Comoros	1991	0	..	..	..	0	..	31	..
	1992	0	..	..	..	0	..	31	..
	1993	0	..	..	..	0	..	31	..
	1994	0	..	..	..	0	..	32	..
Congo	1991	11 524	0	11 462	3	59	121	17	10 491
	1992	12 417	0	12 361	4	52	130	22	11 371
	1993	12 497	0	12 441	4	53	126	22	11 340
	1994	13 141	0	13 081	7	53	131	22	11 453
Côte d'Ivoire	1991	611	..	457	..	154	..	4 717	381
	1992	593	..	464	..	129	..	4 770	383
	1993	598	..	463	..	135	..	4 826	383
	1994	614	..	478	..	135	..	4 846	391
Djibouti	1991	..	..	..	..	..	..	753	..
	1992	..	..	..	..	..	..	762	..
	1993	..	..	..	..	..	..	770	..
	1994	..	..	..	..	..	..	780	..
Egypt	1991	78 995	..	67 597	10 339	1 060	714	1 122	39 339
	1992	80 737	..	68 510	11 179	1 049	857	1 076	39 243
	1993	83 087	..	69 201	12 839	1 047	714	1 340	39 404
	1994	82 121	..	67 033	14 039	1 049	714	1 632	37 358

Bunkers – Soutes			Consumption – Consommation							
Air Avion	Sea Maritime	Unallocated Nondistribué	Per capita Par habitant	Total Totale	Solids Solides	Liquids Liquides	Gas Gaz	Electricity Electricité	Année	Pays ou zone
3 157	**5 254**	**19 855**	**442**	**287 513**	**103 872**	**119 457**	**53 594**	**10 590**	**1991**	**Afrique**
3 230	**5 078**	**29 915**	**423**	**283 390**	**101 192**	**121 773**	**50 027**	**10 398**	**1992**	
3 390	**5 070**	**29 709**	**431**	**297 152**	**107 184**	**125 565**	**55 080**	**9 322**	**1993**	
3 508	**5 278**	**26 948**	**436**	**309 110**	**107 959**	**127 159**	**63 692**	**10 300**	**1994**	
236	287	7 141	1 571	40 109	1 145	12 355	26 655	−45	1991	Algérie
236	230	6 250	1 420	37 103	1 235	13 808	22 149	−90	1992	
236	259	6 568	1 502	40 129	1 340	13 862	25 037	−109	1993	
295	288	4 316	1 583	43 262	1 280	16 169	25 931	−118	1994	
228	985	228	93	889	0	500	222	167	1991	Angola
236	985	100	91	896	0	505	222	169	1992	
239	971	250	88	902	0	509	223	169	1993	
236	964	491	83	890	0	499	222	170	1994	
25	..	0	47	224	..	199	..	25	1991	Bénin
25	..	0	47	231	..	202	..	29	1992	
27	..	0	45	231	..	202	..	29	1993	
27	..	9	46	242	..	212	..	30	1994	
..	..	..	47	435	0	433	..	2	1991	Burkina Faso
..	..	..	46	441	0	439	..	2	1992	
..	..	..	46	452	0	446	..	6	1993	
..	..	..	46	466	0	457	..	9	1994	
3	..	..	23	128	5	104	..	19	1991	Burundi
3	..	..	19	113	6	91	..	16	1992	
3	..	..	21	126	6	98	..	21	1993	
3	..	..	22	134	6	104	..	23	1994	
19	..	73	151	1 790	1	1 461	..	328	1991	Cameroun
19	..	78	148	1 798	1	1 471	..	326	1992	
22	..	71	144	1 800	1	1 473	..	326	1993	
22	..	62	141	1 815	1	1 488	..	326	1994	
0	7	..	117	41	0	41	..	..	1991	Cap–Vert
0	0	..	142	51	0	51	..	..	1992	
0	0	..	138	51	0	51	..	..	1993	
0	0	..	147	56	0	56	..	..	1994	
18	..	..	37	109	..	100	..	9	1991	Rép. centrafricaine
18	..	..	37	114	..	104	..	10	1992	
18	..	..	37	117	..	107	..	10	1993	
18	..	..	39	126	..	116	..	10	1994	
24	..	..	5	29	0	29	..	..	1991	Tchad
24	..	..	6	37	0	37	..	..	1992	
27	..	..	7	44	0	44	..	..	1993	
28	..	..	7	45	0	45	..	..	1994	
0	..	..	55	31	..	31	..	0	1991	Comores
0	..	..	53	31	..	31	..	0	1992	
0	..	..	51	31	..	31	..	0	1993	
0	..	..	52	33	..	32	..	0	1994	
0	8	33	386	887	0	818	3	66	1991	Congo
0	11	123	339	803	0	734	4	65	1992	
0	11	194	347	848	0	778	4	66	1993	
0	11	705	343	862	0	788	7	67	1994	
104	14	1 306	284	3 523	..	3 369	..	154	1991	Côte d'Ivoire
109	7	1 071	295	3 793	..	3 665	..	129	1992	
107	10	1 815	233	3 109	..	2 974	..	135	1993	
107	10	1 439	255	3 512	..	3 377	..	135	1994	
96	491	..	311	166	..	166	..	..	1991	Djibouti
93	496	..	317	173	..	173	..	..	1992	
94	497	..	321	179	..	179	..	..	1993	
94	501	..	327	185	..	185	..	..	1994	
221	1 713	2 301	622	35 829	978	23 452	10 339	1 060	1991	Egypte
221	1 699	3 015	623	36 777	942	23 608	11 179	1 049	1992	
348	1 699	2 790	654	39 472	1 251	24 335	12 839	1 047	1993	
368	1 956	2 795	658	40 561	1 311	24 161	14 039	1 049	1994	

66
Production, trade and consumption of commercial energy
Thousand metric tons of coal equivalent and kilograms per capita [cont.]
Production, commerce et consommation d'énergie commerciale
Milliers de tonnes métriques d'équivalent houille et kilogrammes par habitant [suite]

Country or area	Year	Primary energy production – Production d'energie primaire					Changes in stocks Variations des stocks	Imports Importations	Exports Exportations
		Total Totale	Solids Solides	Liquids Liquides	Gas Gaz	Electricity Electricité			
Equatorial Guinea	1991	0	..	..	..	0	..	58	..
	1992	0	..	..	..	0	..	58	..
	1993	0	..	..	..	0	..	58	..
	1994	0	..	..	..	0	..	60	..
Ethiopia	1991	217	..	..	..	217	30	1 655	209
	1992	221	..	..	..	221	40	1 660	213
	1993	237	..	..	..	237	12	1 634	219
	1994	223	..	..	..	223	2	1 650	228
Gabon	1991	21 510	..	21 316	107	87	..	58	20 102
	1992	22 174	..	21 951	136	87	..	61	20 774
	1993	21 740	..	21 522	131	87	..	56	20 354
	1994	22 805	..	22 601	117	88	..	64	20 519
Gambia	1991	..	..	..	..	..	..	97	3
	1992	..	..	..	..	..	..	97	3
	1993	..	..	..	..	..	..	103	3
	1994	..	..	..	..	..	..	113	3
Ghana	1991	750	..	...	..	750	..	1 775	123
	1992	751	..	...	..	751	..	1 817	127
	1993	751	..	...	..	751	..	1 832	120
	1994	752	..	...	..	752	..	1 849	120
Guinea	1991	22	..	..	..	22	..	507	..
	1992	23	..	..	..	23	..	507	..
	1993	23	..	..	..	23	..	520	..
	1994	22	..	..	..	22	..	533	..
Guinea–Bissau	1991	..	..	..	..	..	..	109	0
	1992	..	..	..	..	..	..	110	0
	1993	..	..	..	..	..	..	116	0
	1994	..	..	..	..	..	..	119	0
Kenya	1991	706	..	..	..	706	0	3 144	922
	1992	677	..	..	..	677	0	3 519	933
	1993	701	..	..	..	701	0	3 852	872
	1994	697	..	..	..	697	0	3 707	647
Liberia	1991	20	..	..	..	20	..	156	1
	1992	20	..	..	..	20	..	156	1
	1993	21	..	..	..	21	..	172	1
	1994	22	..	..	..	22	..	172	1
Libyan Arab Jamah.	1991	113 963	..	105 256	8 707	..	−2 685	9	96 124
	1992	109 756	..	100 742	9 014	..	−4 155	9	93 872
	1993	104 213	..	95 745	8 468	..	−4 178	8	87 645
	1994	106 419	..	97 911	8 508	..	−3 231	9	87 219
Madagascar	1991	41	..	..	..	41	0	562	70
	1992	42	..	..	..	42	0	567	79
	1993	43	..	..	..	43	−10	580	85
	1994	43	..	..	..	43	1	593	34
Malawi	1991	92	..	..	..	92	..	298	0
	1992	95	..	..	..	95	..	299	0
	1993	96	..	..	..	96	..	311	0
	1994	97	..	..	..	97	..	312	0
Mali	1991	23	..	..	..	23	..	224	..
	1992	26	..	..	..	26	..	230	..
	1993	27	..	..	..	27	..	237	..
	1994	28	..	..	..	28	..	241	..
Mauritania	1991	3	..	..	..	3	..	1 398	..
	1992	3	..	..	..	3	..	1 485	..
	1993	3	..	..	..	3	..	1 499	..
	1994	3	..	..	..	3	..	1 511	..
Mauritius	1991	9	..	..	..	9	−32	898	0
	1992	14	..	..	..	14	−27	986	0
	1993	13	..	..	..	13	−21	1 034	0
	1994	13	..	..	..	13	−24	1 045	0

Bunkers – Soutes			Consumption – Consommation							
Air Avion	Sea Maritime	Unallocated Nondistribué	Per capita Par habitant	Total Totale	Solids Solides	Liquids Liquides	Gas Gaz	Electricity Electricité	Année	Pays ou zone
..	..	..	164	59	..	58	..	0	1991	Guinée équatoriale
..	..	..	160	59	..	58	..	0	1992	
..	..	..	156	59	..	58	..	0	1993	
..	..	..	154	60	..	60	..	0	1994	
81	4	13	31	1 534	0	1 317	..	217	1991	Ethiopie
84	6	6	30	1 531	0	1 310		221	1992	
84	6	−11	30	1 562	0	1 325	..	237	1993	
85	7	18	29	1 533	0	1 310	..	223	1994	
40	111	283	875	1 032	..	838	107	87	1991	Gabon
42	36	253	931	1 129	..	906	136	87	1992	
43	39	252	889	1 109	..	891	131	87	1993	
46	41	1 144	873	1 120	..	915	117	88	1994	
..	..	..	98	94	..	94	..	..	1991	Gambie
..	..	..	94	94	..	94	..	..	1992	
..	..	..	96	100	..	100	..	..	1993	
..	..	..	102	110	..	110	..	..	1994	
37	28	108	144	2 230	3	1 502	..	724	1991	Ghana
38	0	135	142	2 267	3	1 548	..	716	1992	
37	0	123	140	2 303	3	1 583	..	716	1993	
37	0	119	137	2 325	3	1 608	..	714	1994	
18	...	..	86	511	..	489	..	22	1991	Guinée
18	...	..	84	512	..	489	..	23	1992	
19	...	..	83	524	..	501	..	23	1993	
19	...	..	82	536	..	514	..	22	1994	
9	..	..	102	100	..	100	..	..	1991	Guinée–Bissau
9	..	..	101	102	..	102	..	..	1992	
9	..	..	104	107	..	107	..	..	1993	
10	..	..	104	109	..	109	..	..	1994	
0	182	85	109	2 661	133	1 806	..	722	1991	Kenya
0	199	165	114	2 899	159	2 033	..	706	1992	
0	236	377	116	3 068	132	2 202	..	735	1993	
0	194	269	120	3 293	110	2 453	..	729	1994	
6	17	0	57	151	..	131	..	20	1991	Libéria
6	17	0	55	151	..	131	..	20	1992	
6	17	0	59	169	..	147	..	21	1993	
6	17	0	57	169	..	147	..	22	1994	
310	142	5 285	3 143	14 798	5	8 189	6 604	..	1991	Jamah.arabe libyenne
295	113	4 714	3 062	14 927	5	8 358	6 564	..	1992	
295	127	4 758	3 085	15 573	4	9 232	6 338	..	1993	
295	113	4 586	3 339	17 447	5	10 904	6 538	..	1994	
1	19	18	38	496	15	440	..	41	1991	Madagascar
1	19	9	37	502	15	444	..	42	1992	
1	17	23	37	506	16	447	..	43	1993	
1	17	14	40	567	16	508	..	43	1994	
16	..	..	38	374	11	271	..	92	1991	Malawi
16	..	..	37	378	12	271	..	95	1992	
18	..	..	37	389	15	278	..	96	1993	
18	..	..	36	391	15	280	..	97	1994	
21	..	..	24	226	..	203	..	23	1991	Mali
22	..	..	24	233	..	208	..	26	1992	
22	..	..	24	242	..	215	..	27	1993	
22	..	..	24	247	..	219	..	28	1994	
18	13	155	592	1 215	6	1 206	..	3	1991	Mauritanie
18	14	125	632	1 331	6	1 322	..	3	1992	
18	14	136	617	1 334	6	1 325	..	3	1993	
19	17	130	608	1 348	6	1 339	..	3	1994	
200	107	..	562	632	66	557	..	9	1991	Maurice
215	102	..	633	709	72	623	..	14	1992	
218	89	..	678	760	63	685	..	13	1993	
221	89	..	678	772	65	694	..	13	1994	

66
Production, trade and consumption of commercial energy
Thousand metric tons of coal equivalent and kilograms per capita [*cont.*]
Production, commerce et consommation d'énergie commerciale
Milliers de tonnes métriques d'équivalent houille et kilogrammes par habitant [*suite*]

Country or area	Year	Primary energy production – Production d'energie primaire					Changes in stocks	Imports	Exports
		Total Totale	Solids Solides	Liquids Liquides	Gas Gaz	Electricity Electricité	Variations des stocks	Imports Importations	Exports Exportations
Morocco	1991	773	551	17	52	153	−320	9 989	0
	1992	742	576	16	32	118	355	11 073	0
	1993	705	604	14	32	54	18	11 699	0
	1994	798	650	11	33	103	144	13 039	0
Mozambique	1991	48	42	..	..	6	..	540	0
	1992	46	40	..	..	6	..	538	0
	1993	46	40	..	..	6	..	534	0
	1994	46	40	..	..	6	..	510	0
Niger	1991	172	172	..	..	..	..	329	..
	1992	170	170	..	..	..	..	339	..
	1993	172	172	..	..	..	..	345	..
	1994	174	174	..	..	..	..	355	..
Nigeria	1991	141 923	138	135 199	5 858	728	2 999	1 034	116 290
	1992	146 480	87	139 762	5 886	744	471	1 047	114 462
	1993	143 565	41	136 063	6 724	737	...	1 040	112 337
	1994	143 875	50	130 043	13 045	737	...	3 295	114 608
Réunion	1991	57	..	..	..	57	..	730	1
	1992	61	..	..	..	61	..	719	1
	1993	61	..	..	..	61	..	756	0
	1994	62	..	..	..	62	..	771	0
Rwanda	1991	20	..	..	0	20	..	226	0
	1992	21	..	..	0	21	..	229	0
	1993	19	..	..	0	19	..	239	0
	1994	20	..	..	0	20	..	241	0
Sao Tome − Principe	1991	1	..	..	..	1	..	34	..
	1992	1	..	..	..	1	..	35	..
	1993	1	..	..	..	1	..	35	..
	1994	1	..	..	..	1	..	37	..
Senegal	1991	..	..	..	..	..	..	1 716	49
	1992	..	..	..	..	..	..	1 701	49
	1993	..	..	..	..	..	..	1 711	54
	1994	..	..	..	..	..	..	1 721	55
Seychelles	1991	..	..	..	..	..	..	220	..
	1992	..	..	..	..	..	..	230	..
	1993	..	..	..	..	..	..	236	..
	1994	..	..	..	..	..	..	239	..
Sierra Leone	1991	..	..	..	..	..	..	376	4
	1992	..	..	..	..	..	..	381	4
	1993	..	..	..	..	..	..	489	4
	1994	..	..	..	..	..	..	498	4
St.Helena and Depend.	1991	0	0	..	..	..	..	3	..
	1992	0	0	..	..	..	..	3	..
	1993	0	0	..	..	..	..	3	..
	1994	0	0	..	..	..	..	3	..
South Africa Customs Un.	1991	141 787	135 843	..	2 388	3 556	−3	22 603	42 870
	1992	139 056	133 043	..	2 457	3 556	0	23 613	42 880
	1993	144 030	138 763	..	2 491	2 776	0	24 298	42 970
	1994	145 452	139 260	..	2 525	3 668	0	24 298	43 319
Sudan	1991	115	..	..	..	115	..	1 843	53
	1992	115	..	..	..	115	..	1 866	50
	1993	115	..	..	..	115	..	1 817	12
	1994	116	..	..	..	116	..	1 830	12
Togo	1991	1	0	..	..	1	..	300	9
	1992	1	0	..	..	1	..	295	9
	1993	1	0	..	..	1	..	303	9
	1994	1	0	..	..	1	..	316	9
Tunisia	1991	7 973	...	7 476	484	13	556	4 291	5 346
	1992	7 742	11	7 223	500	8	−72	4 491	5 721
	1993	7 169	15	6 693	453	8	70	4 613	4 995
	1994	6 773	9	6 306	450	8	136	5 396	5 090

Bunkers – Soutes			Consumption – Consommation							
Air Avion	Sea Maritime	Unallocated Nondistribué	Per capita Par habitant	Total Totale	Solids Solides	Liquids Liquides	Gas Gaz	Electricity Electricité	Année	Pays ou zone
102	4	859	407	10 116	2 041	7 791	52	232	1991	Maroc
103	64	1 538	384	9 755	1 748	7 742	32	233	1992	
111	0	1 338	422	10 937	2 004	8 723	32	177	1993	
118	0	1 229	466	12 345	2 218	9 878	33	216	1994	
53	36	...	35	498	62	390	..	46	1991	Mozambique
52	36	...	34	496	60	390	..	46	1992	
52	36	...	33	492	60	386	..	46	1993	
49	36	...	30	472	60	366	..	46	1994	
22	..	..	60	479	172	284	..	23	1991	Niger
22	..	..	59	487	170	294	..	23	1992	
22	..	..	58	495	172	300	..	24	1993	
22	..	..	57	507	174	308	..	24	1994	
523	570	635	221	21 940	105	15 248	5 858	728	1991	Nigéria
531	548	11 041	200	20 473	74	13 768	5 886	744	1992	
523	556	9 821	203	21 368	48	13 859	6 724	737	1993	
523	527	8 834	209	22 678	56	8 839	13 045	737	1994	
16	1	..	1 249	767	..	710	..	57	1991	Réunion
18	1	..	1 216	759	..	698	..	61	1992	
18	1	..	1 259	798	..	737	..	61	1993	
21	1	..	1 259	811	..	749	..	62	1994	
13		..	32	233	..	211	0	21	1991	Rwanda
12		..	32	238	..	216	0	22	1992	
12		..	33	246	..	226	0	20	1993	
13		..	32	248	..	226	0	21	1994	
0	..	..	289	35	..	34		1	1991	Sao Tomé–et–Principe
0	..	..	290	36	..	35	..	1	1992	
0	..	..	283	36	..	35	..	1	1993	
0	..	..	292	38	..	37	..	1	1994	
152	189	38	171	1 287	..	1 287		..	1991	Sénégal
152	186	22	168	1 292	..	1 292		..	1992	
155	186	10	165	1 307	..	1 307		..	1993	
156	191	−2	163	1 321	..	1 321		..	1994	
27	126	..	957	67	..	67	..	..	1991	Seychelles
44	112	..	1 042	74	..	74	..	..	1992	
47	112	..	1 069	77	..	77	..	..	1993	
47	112	..	1 096	80	..	80	..	..	1994	
25	107	69	42	171	0	171	..	..	1991	Sierra Leone
25	107	68	42	177	0	177	..	..	1992	
25	97	170	45	193	0	193	..	..	1993	
25	94	175	45	200	0	200	..	..	1994	
0	..	..	500	3	0	3	..	..	1991	Ste–Hélène et dépend
0	..	..	500	3	0	3	..	..	1992	
0	..	..	500	3	0	3	..	..	1993	
0	..	..	500	3	0	3	..	..	1994	
...	...	886	2 791	120 637	93 196	21 686	2 388	3 367	1991	Un.douan.d'Afr.mérid
...	...	847	2 689	118 941	90 393	22 725	2 457	3 367	1992	
...	...	686	2 754	124 674	96 113	23 601	2 491	2 469	1993	
...	...	151	2 726	126 281	96 260	24 135	2 525	3 361	1994	
47	10	234	64	1 613	0	1 498	..	115	1991	Soudan
47	10	240	63	1 634	0	1 519	..	115	1992	
49	10	232	61	1 629	0	1 514	..	115	1993	
49	10	231	60	1 644	0	1 529	..	116	1994	
..	..	0	80	292	0	258	..	33	1991	Togo
..	..	0	76	287	0	249	..	39	1992	
..	..	0	76	295	0	256	..	39	1993	
..	..	0	77	308	0	269	..	39	1994	
115	1	2	757	6 243	99	4 761	1 367	15	1991	Tunisie
227	1	25	753	6 331	122	4 802	1 399	7	1992	
236	1	11	755	6 468	142	5 058	1 261	7	1993	
251	1	138	750	6 553	132	5 176	1 235	10	1994	

66
Production, trade and consumption of commercial energy
Thousand metric tons of coal equivalent and kilograms per capita [cont.]
Production, commerce et consommation d'énergie commerciale
Milliers de tonnes métriques d'équivalent houille et kilogrammes par habitant [suite]

| Country or area | Year | Primary energy production – Production d'énergie primaire | | | | | Changes in stocks | Imports | Exports |
		Total Totale	Solids Solides	Liquids Liquides	Gas Gaz	Electricity Electricité	Variations des stocks	Imports Importations	Exports Exportations
Uganda	1991	95	..	..	..	95	..	440	18
	1992	96	..	..	..	96	..	451	18
	1993	96	..	..	..	96		462	18
	1994	97	..	..	..	97		474	18
United Rep. Tanzania	1991	80	4	..	..	76	..	1 069	35
	1992	81	4	..	..	77	..	1 035	35
	1993	81	4	..	..	77		1 048	37
	1994	81	4	..	..	77		1 061	37
Western Sahara	1991	..	..	..	..	..	..	98	..
	1992	..	..	..	..	..	..	100	..
	1993	..	..	..	..	..		97	..
	1994	..	..	..	..	..		97	..
Zaire	1991	2 727	80	1 960	..	687	..	1 584	1 647
	1992	2 723	85	1 853	..	786	..	1 569	1 643
	1993	2 641	92	1 828	..	721		1 596	1 655
	1994	2 693	93	1 921	..	679	..	1 616	1 706
Zambia	1991	1 270	320	..	..	950	..	793	247
	1992	1 284	333	..	..	951	..	800	247
	1993	1 289	337	..	..	951		807	247
	1994	1 272	320	..	..	951		807	247
Zimbabwe	1991	5 979	5 596	..	..	383	221	1 627	252
	1992	5 913	5 548	..	..	365	−25	1 615	109
	1993	5 493	5 285	..	..	208	124	1 778	46
	1994	5 760	5 469	..	..	291	−125	1 792	27
America, North	**1991**	**2 998 549**	**806 924**	**982 558**	**844 630**	**364 437**	**10 530**	**761 757**	**473 007**
	1992	**3 009 953**	**800 638**	**974 208**	**871 064**	**364 043**	**−14 304**	**800 901**	**482 373**
	1993	**2 972 565**	**748 099**	**958 265**	**894 657**	**371 544**	**4 877**	**874 913**	**464 803**
	1994	**3 236 232**	**945 519**	**961 865**	**939 485**	**389 363**	**45 965**	**916 678**	**484 886**
Antigua and Barbuda	1991	..	..	..	..	..	..	200	10
	1992	..	..	..	..	..	..	200	10
	1993	..	..	..	..	..		210	10
	1994	..	..	..	..	..		220	10
Aruba	1991	..	..	..	..	..	..	853	0
	1992	..	..	..	..	..	..	750	0
	1993	..	..	..	..	..		788	0
	1994	..	..	..	..	..		791	0
Bahamas	1991	..	..	..	..	..	129	4 862	3 569
	1992	..	..	..	..	..	−101	4 361	3 286
	1993	..	..	..	..	..	−79	4 197	3 144
	1994	..	..	..	..	..	−69	4 049	3 003
Barbados	1991	119	..	89	30	..	13	855	268
	1992	122	..	93	29	..	10	512	64
	1993	125	..	90	35	..	−24	510	23
	1994	118	..	89	29	..	−3	504	29
Belize	1991	..	..	..	..	..	39	182	0
	1992	..	..	..	..	..	...	141	0
	1993	..	..	..	..	..	...	140	0
	1994	..	..	..	..	..	...	133	0
Bermuda	1991	..	..	..	..	..	...	259	0
	1992	..	..	..	..	..	..	213	0
	1993	..	..	..	..	..	..	243	0
	1994	..	..	..	..	..	..	240	0
British Virgin Islds	1991	..	..	..	..	..	..	23	..
	1992	..	..	..	..	..	..	25	..
	1993	..	..	..	..	..	..	25	..
	1994	..	..	..	..	..	..	25	..
Canada	1991	403 277	55 294	130 302	148 233	69 447	−2 844	56 108	172 577
	1992	416 238	49 183	135 595	162 645	68 815	−8 722	54 599	184 453
	1993	451 136	53 598	143 947	178 600	74 991	122	57 427	198 438
	1994	482 338	54 509	150 688	196 772	80 369	170	61 121	218 494

Bunkers – Soutes			Consumption – Consommation							
Air Avion	Sea Maritime	Unallocated Nondistribué	Per capita Par habitant	Total Totale	Solids Solides	Liquids Liquides	Gas Gaz	Electricity Electricité	Année	Pays ou zone
0	..	..	28	517	..	436	..	82	1991	Ouganda
0	..	..	27	528	..	446	..	82	1992	
0	..	..	27	540	..	458	..	82	1993	
0	..	..	27	552	..	470	..	83	1994	
40	31	16	39	1 028	4	948	..	76	1991	Rép.Unie de Tanzanie
40	31	9	37	1 001	4	920	..	77	1992	
40	31	−2	36	1 022	4	941	..	77	1993	
41	31	−3	36	1 035	4	954	..	77	1994	
6	0	..	388	93	..	93	..	..	1991	Sahara occidental
6	0	..	376	94	..	94	..	..	1992	
6	0	..	349	91	..	91	..	..	1993	
6	0	..	335	91	..	91	..	..	1994	
155	50	45	62	2 415	299	1 434	..	681	1991	Zaïre
152	45	36	60	2 414	303	1 472	..	639	1992	
155	45	45	57	2 337	310	1 473	..	553	1993	
158	48	37	55	2 359	315	1 491	..	553	1994	
52	..	42	205	1 722	316	638	..	768	1991	Zambie
52	..	45	201	1 740	329	642	..	769	1992	
50	..	52	195	1 746	333	644	..	770	1993	
50	..	61	187	1 721	316	635	..	770	1994	
78	..	...	692	7 055	5 210	1 246	..	598	1991	Zimbabwe
0	..	...	711	7 444	5 532	1 399	..	512	1992	
0	..	...	662	7 101	5 159	1 499	..	444	1993	
...	..	...	695	7 650	5 605	1 543	..	502	1994	
1 942	32 911	26 527	7 469	3 215 389	701 802	1 304 552	844 295	364 741	1991	**Amérique du Nord**
2 009	33 298	30 377	7 505	3 277 100	707 744	1 323 131	881 885	364 339	1992	
1 880	31 386	28 268	7 488	3 316 264	684 748	1 364 357	895 572	371 587	1993	
2 067	32 289	37 844	7 906	3 549 859	841 670	1 390 106	928 717	389 365	1994	
52	0	0	2 156	138	..	138	..	..	1991	Antigua−et−Barbuda
52	0	0	2 123	138	..	138	..	..	1992	
55	0	0	2 231	145	..	145	..	..	1993	
62	0	0	2 277	148	..	148	..	..	1994	
..	..	536	4 731	317	..	317	..	..	1991	Aruba
..	..	428	4 721	321	..	321	..	..	1992	
..	..	446	4 957	342	..	342	..	..	1993	
..	..	446	5 000	345	..	345	..	..	1994	
46	277	0	3 292	841	1	840	..	..	1991	Bahamas
46	270	0	3 258	860	1	859	..	..	1992	
46	270	0	3 049	817	1	816	..	..	1993	
46	263	0	2 967	807	1	806	..	..	1994	
159	...	16	2 008	518	0	488	30	..	1991	Barbade
131	...	−44	1 834	472	0	443	29	..	1992	
119	...	13	1 862	503	0	468	35	..	1993	
164	...	21	1 586	411	0	382	29	..	1994	
16	0	..	655	127	..	127	..	0	1991	Belize
15	0	..	638	127	..	127	..	0	1992	
13	0	..	623	127	..	127	..	0	1993	
13	0	..	567	119	..	119	..	0	1994	
25	0	..	3 774	234	0	234	..	..	1991	Bermudes
22	0	..	3 081	191	0	191	..	..	1992	
22	0	..	3 508	221	0	221	..	..	1993	
22	0	..	3 460	218	0	218	..	..	1994	
..	..	..	1 353	23	..	23	..	..	1991	Iles Vierges brit.
..	..	..	1 471	25	..	25	..	..	1992	
..	..	..	1 389	25	..	25	..	..	1993	
..	..	..	1 389	25	..	25	..	..	1994	
1 151	948	−5 727	10 416	293 279	35 257	103 168	87 670	67 184	1991	Canada
1 257	839	−7 028	10 530	300 038	36 056	106 037	92 208	65 738	1992	
1 147	816	−4 747	10 853	312 789	34 357	109 674	97 135	71 623	1993	
1 229	915	−4 004	11 211	326 655	34 268	113 502	105 514	74 974	1994	

66
Production, trade and consumption of commercial energy
Thousand metric tons of coal equivalent and kilograms per capita [*cont.*]
Production, commerce et consommation d'énergie commerciale
Milliers de tonnes métriques d'équivalent houille et kilogrammes par habitant [*suite*]

Country or area	Year	Primary energy production – Production d'energie primaire					Changes in stocks Variations des stocks	Imports Importations	Exports Exportations
		Total Totale	Solids Solides	Liquids Liquides	Gas Gaz	Electricity Electricité			
Cayman Islands	1991	..	..	..	..	..	..	138	..
	1992	..	..	..	..	..	..	141	..
	1993	..	..	..	..	..	..	142	..
	1994	..	..	..	..	..	..	145	..
Costa Rica	1991	446		..		446	−43	1 511	120
	1992	437		..		437	14	1 789	141
	1993	487		..		487	30	1 888	178
	1994	858	..	..		858	63	2 343	93
Cuba	1991	1 131	..	1 068	49	13	0	12 683	171
	1992	1 399		1 337	49	13	0	12 127	170
	1993	1 456		1 393	51	13	0	12 107	146
	1994	1 516	..	1 451	52	13	0	12 357	126
Dominica	1991	2		..		2	..	28	..
	1992	2		..		2	..	28	..
	1993	2		..		2	..	30	..
	1994	2		..		2	..	34	..
Dominican Republic	1991	78		..		78	−41	4 414	..
	1992	270		..		270	−33	4 888	..
	1993	217		..		217	−12	4 846	..
	1994	230		..		230	−13	5 020	..
El Salvador	1991	680		..		680	11	1 404	19
	1992	657		..		657	−1	1 559	23
	1993	712		..		712	48	1 851	27
	1994	867	..	..		867	49	2 072	30
Greenland	1991	0	0	..		..	..	267	9
	1992	0	0	..		..	..	239	10
	1993	...	...	..		..	..	247	10
	1994	...	...	..		..	..	249	10
Grenada	1991	..		..		..	1	65	..
	1992	..		..		..	1	68	..
	1993	..		..		..	1	71	..
	1994	..		..		..	−1	78	..
Guadeloupe	1991	..		..		..	..	710	0
	1992	..		..		..	..	732	0
	1993	..		..		..	..	739	0
	1994	..	..	..		..	..	762	0
Guatemala	1991	564	..	289	11	264	7	1 990	227
	1992	709	..	437	12	260	4	2 421	354
	1993	751	..	503	12	236	63	2 421	421
	1994	785	..	521	13	251	75	2 817	331
Haiti	1991	23	..	..		23	−24	432	..
	1992	23	..	..		23	14	407	..
	1993	20	..	..		20	0	300	..
	1994	20	..	..		20	...	252	..
Honduras	1991	260		..		260	33	1 164	46
	1992	260	..	..		260	0	1 299	0
	1993	278	..	..		278	0	1 180	0
	1994	301		..		301	−10	1 380	...
Jamaica	1991	15		..		15	−133	3 659	96
	1992	13		..		13	22	3 765	77
	1993	11		..		11	−20	3 825	87
	1994	10		..		10	−69	4 013	66
Martinique	1991	..		..		..	..	1 089	254
	1992	..		..		..	..	1 189	257
	1993	..		..		..	..	1 198	268
	1994	..		..		..	..	1 216	270
Mexico	1991	271 598	4 983	223 328	32 350	10 937	519	11 962	108 277
	1992	279 542	4 724	223 834	39 180	11 805	−782	15 350	110 414
	1993	278 231	4 648	223 409	38 343	11 831	−1 682	13 972	111 788
	1994	283 065	6 215	224 864	39 833	12 153	499	14 335	104 629

Bunkers – Soutes			Consumption – Consommation							
Air Avion	Sea Maritime	Unallocated Nondistribué	Per capita Par habitant	Total Totale	Solids Solides	Liquids Liquides	Gas Gaz	Electricity Electricité	Année	Pays ou zone
9	..	..	4 778	129	..	129	..	..	1991	Iles Caïmanes
9	..	..	4 714	132	..	132	..	..	1992	
9	..	..	4 586	133	..	133	..	..	1993	
10	..	..	4 500	135	..	135	..	..	1994	
..	...	72	583	1 808	..	1 360	..	448	1991	Costa Rica
..	...	45	633	2 026	..	1 597	..	429	1992	
..	...	31	653	2 136	..	1 649	..	486	1993	
..	...	148	868	2 898	..	2 041	..	857	1994	
90	0	608	1 210	12 945	148	12 734	49	13	1991	Cuba
90	0	739	1 162	12 528	182	12 283	49	13	1992	
90	0	860	1 146	12 467	182	12 222	51	13	1993	
83	...	1 136	1 143	12 529	182	12 282	52	13	1994	
0	..	..	423	30	..	28	..	2	1991	Dominique
0	..	..	423	30	..	28	..	2	1992	
0	..	..	451	32	..	30	..	2	1993	
0	..	..	507	36	..	34	..	2	1994	
...	..	194	598	4 339	57	4 204	..	78	1991	Rép. dominicaine
...	..	−67	710	5 257	139	4 848	..	270	1992	
...	..	25	669	5 049	120	4 712	..	217	1993	
...	..	259	651	5 004	104	4 669	..	230	1994	
...	...	37	382	2 017	..	1 337	..	681	1991	El Salvador
...	...	36	400	2 159	..	1 495	..	664	1992	
...	...	23	447	2 466	..	1 744	..	721	1993	
...	...	20	503	2 840	..	1 962	..	878	1994	
..	..	..	4 625	259	0	259	..	..	1991	Groënland
..	..	..	4 000	228	0	228	..	..	1992	
..	..	..	4 158	237	...	237	..	..	1993	
..	..	..	4 103	238	...	238	..	..	1994	
1	...	..	681	62	..	62	..	..	1991	Grenade
3	...	..	692	63	..	63	..	..	1992	
3	...	..	717	66	..	66	..	..	1993	
3	...	..	837	77	..	77	..	..	1994	
127	...	..	1 467	584	..	584	..	..	1991	Guadeloupe
117	...	..	1 515	615	..	615	..	..	1992	
109	...	..	1 525	630	..	630	..	..	1993	
112	...	..	1 544	650	..	650	..	..	1994	
...	...	78	237	2 240	..	1 965	11	264	1991	Guatemala
...	...	140	270	2 631	..	2 359	12	260	1992	
...	...	71	261	2 617	..	2 369	12	236	1993	
...	...	225	288	2 971	..	2 708	13	251	1994	
49	...	..	65	431	25	382	..	23	1991	Haïti
29	...	..	57	387	26	338	..	23	1992	
15	...	..	44	306	10	276	..	20	1993	
9	...	..	38	264	...	243	..	20	1994	
...	...	21	264	1 325	0	1 089	..	236	1991	Honduras
...	...	87	284	1 471	0	1 212	..	260	1992	
...	...	...	273	1 458	..	1 178	..	280	1993	
...	...	...	308	1 691	...	1 388	..	303	1994	
44	...	157	1 476	3 510	51	3 444	..	15	1991	Jamaïque
66	...	−38	1 525	3 650	66	3 571	..	13	1992	
59	...	−13	1 544	3 723	55	3 657	..	11	1993	
44	...	−44	1 657	4 025	64	3 951	..	10	1994	
..	39	18	2 137	778	..	778	..	..	1991	Martinique
..	40	80	2 207	812	..	812	..	..	1992	
..	46	80	2 167	804	..	804	..	..	1993	
..	53	87	2 149	806	..	806	..	..	1994	
106	61	10 607	1 900	163 991	5 336	113 357	34 533	10 765	1991	Mexique
106	566	9 012	1 992	175 575	5 411	115 747	42 741	11 676	1992	
106	566	8 412	1 922	173 013	5 969	115 293	40 056	11 695	1993	
106	566	5 026	2 031	186 573	7 166	126 272	41 084	12 051	1994	

66

Production, trade and consumption of commercial energy
Thousand metric tons of coal equivalent and kilograms per capita [*cont.*]
Production, commerce et consommation d'énergie commerciale
Milliers de tonnes métriques d'équivalent houille et kilogrammes par habitant [*suite*]

Country or area	Year	Primary energy production – Production d'énergie primaire					Changes in stocks Variations des stocks	Imports Importations	Exports Exportations
		Total Totale	Solids Solides	Liquids Liquides	Gas Gaz	Electricity Electricité			
Montserrat	1991	..	..	..	..	..	..	18	..
	1992							19	
	1993	..	..	..	..	..	..	19	..
	1994				..	..		19	..
Netherland Antilles	1991	..		..	..	..	−294	19 272	12 745
	1992						172	20 408	12 289
	1993	..	..	..	..	..	22	22 220	13 164
	1994	..	..	..	..	..	15	22 303	13 327
Nicaragua	1991	604	..	..	..	604	28	964	26
	1992	606	..	..	..	606	−4	1 138	1
	1993	669	..	..	..	669	28	1 078	7
	1994	679	..	..	..	679	−44	835	6
Panama	1991	250	..	..	..	250	73	2 269	626
	1992	232	..	..	..	232	166	3 172	1 147
	1993	282	..	..	..	282	26	3 226	1 409
	1994	294	..	..	..	294	928	3 741	470
Puerto Rico	1991	36	..	..	..	36	520	10 076	1 450
	1992	37	..	..	..	37	683	10 729	1 063
	1993	38	..	..	..	38	679	11 407	1 058
	1994	40	..	..	..	40	−387	11 444	1 036
Saint Lucia	1991	..	..	..	..	..	..	78	..
	1992				..	..	..	81	..
	1993						..	82	..
	1994	..	..	..	..	..	..	90	..
St.Kitts−Nevis	1991	..	..	..	..	..	0	35	..
	1992	..	..	..	..	..	0	35	..
	1993	..	..	..	..	..	0	40	..
	1994	..	..	..	..	..	0	47	..
St.Pierre−Miquelon	1991	..	..	..	..	..	..	113	..
	1992	..	..	..	..	..	..	106	..
	1993	..	..	..	..	..	..	58	..
	1994	..	..	..	..	..	..	60	..
S.Vincent−Grenadines	1991	2	..	..	..	2	..	37	..
	1992	2	..	..	..	2	..	40	..
	1993	3	..	..	..	3	..	49	..
	1994	3	..	..	..	3	..	58	..
Trinidad and Tobago	1991	18 624	..	10 645	7 979	..	171	2 959	10 231
	1992	17 933	..	10 027	7 906	..	79	4 056	10 984
	1993	16 052	..	9 151	6 901	..	−300	2 928	10 017
	1994	17 605	..	9 684	7 921	..	89	2 482	9 817
United States	1991	2 300 841	746 646	616 837	655 977	281 380	11 656	597 178	143 416
	1992	2 291 470	746 731	602 886	661 243	280 609	−6 101	631 937	138 984
	1993	2 222 094	689 852	579 773	670 715	281 754	5 690	701 089	106 048
	1994	2 447 502	884 795	574 568	694 864	293 274	44 381	736 973	114 652
U.S. Virgin Islands	1991	..	..	..	..	..	710	23 899	18 871
	1992						272	22 377	18 644
	1993	..	..	..	..	..	284	24 360	18 557
	1994	..	..	..	..	..	292	24 472	18 487
America, South	1991	**493 041**	**30 680**	**331 722**	**81 270**	**49 369**	**3 107**	**84 321**	**221 643**
	1992	**500 850**	**28 029**	**341 430**	**81 219**	**50 172**	**1 979**	**87 058**	**221 807**
	1993	**527 276**	**28 811**	**360 134**	**84 373**	**53 957**	**125**	**96 591**	**244 492**
	1994	**561 383**	**30 764**	**383 158**	**90 923**	**56 537**	**−1 309**	**101 198**	**263 040**
Antarctic Fisheries	1991	..	..	..	..	..	..	101	..
	1992	..	..	..	..	..	..	101	..
	1993	..	..	..	..	..	..	101	..
	1994	..	..	..	..	..	..	101	..
Argentina	1991	73 187	246	37 816	30 220	4 905	105	5 058	7 367
	1992	78 415	181	42 520	30 680	5 035	751	5 268	9 866
	1993	82 493	141	44 951	31 556	5 845	218	5 459	11 862
	1994	90 748	293	50 010	34 000	6 444	140	7 353	19 713

	Bunkers – Soutes		Consumption – Consommation							
Air Avion	Sea Maritime	Unallocated Nondistribué	Per capita Par habitant	Total Totale	Solids Solides	Liquids Liquides	Gas Gaz	Electricity Electricité	Année	Pays ou zone
..	1	..	1 455	16	..	16	..	..	1991	Montserrat
..	1	..	1 636	18	..	18	..	..	1992	
..	1	..	1 636	18	..	18	..	..	1993	
..	1	..	1 636	18	..	18	..	..	1994	
66	2 451	2 810	7 781	1 494	..	1 494	..	..	1991	Antilles néerland.
66	2 451	4 221	6 254	1 207	..	1 207	..	..	1992	
87	2 410	5 426	5 703	1 112	..	1 112	..	..	1993	
86	2 434	5 208	6 259	1 233	..	1 233	..	..	1994	
...	..	26	391	1 488	..	877	..	611	1991	Nicaragua
...	..	95	418	1 653	..	1 042	..	611	1992	
...	..	43	406	1 669	..	1 006	..	664	1993	
...	..	30	356	1 522	..	845	..	677	1994	
0	...	0	745	1 820	49	1 424	80	267	1991	Panama
0	...	55	817	2 036	54	1 653	79	250	1992	
0	...	−17	823	2 090	58	1 659	80	293	1993	
0	...	−465	1 212	3 103	52	2 673	80	298	1994	
...	214	−200	2 294	8 128	192	7 900	..	36	1991	Porto Rico
...	214	172	2 430	8 634	154	8 443	..	37	1992	
...	200	−300	2 719	9 808	160	9 610	..	38	1993	
...	214	−583	3 081	11 203	172	10 991	..	40	1994	
0	..	..	578	78	..	78	..	..	1991	Sainte−Lucie
0	..	..	591	81	..	81	..	..	1992	
0	..	..	590	82	..	82	..	..	1993	
0	..	..	638	90	..	90	..	..	1994	
..	..	..	833	35	..	35	..	..	1991	St−Kitts−Nevis
..	..	..	833	35	..	35	..	..	1992	
..	..	..	952	40	..	40	..	..	1993	
..	..	..	1 146	47	..	47	..	..	1994	
..	65	..	8 000	48	0	48	..	..	1991	St.Pierre−Miquelon
..	61	..	7 500	45	0	45	..	..	1992	
..	23	..	5 833	35	0	35	..	..	1993	
..	26	..	5 500	33	0	33	..	..	1994	
0	..	..	361	39	..	37	..	2	1991	S.Vincent−Grenadines
0	..	..	385	42	..	40	..	2	1992	
0	..	..	473	52	..	49	..	3	1993	
0	..	..	541	60	..	58	..	3	1994	
0	...	338	8 667	10 843	0	2 864	7 979	..	1991	Trinité−et−Tobago
0	...	244	8 443	10 681	0	2 775	7 906	..	1992	
0	...	150	7 130	9 112	0	2 211	6 901	..	1993	
78	319	53	7 530	9 729	0	1 808	7 921	..	1994	
0	28 661	16 994	10 680	2 697 292	660 563	1 038 671	719 887	284 116	1991	Etats−Unis
0	28 661	22 226	10 731	2 739 636	665 450	1 051 234	738 861	284 092	1992	
0	26 824	16 502	10 730	2 768 119	643 606	1 087 924	751 045	285 285	1993	
0	27 252	29 445	11 395	2 968 744	799 416	1 094 942	786 846	298 758	1994	
...	194	−58	42 757	4 183	123	4 060	..	..	1991	Iles Vierges amér.
...	194	−27	31 981	3 294	205	3 089	..	..	1992	
...	230	1 263	38 702	4 025	230	3 795	..	..	1993	
...	244	838	44 337	4 611	245	4 366	..	..	1994	
1 383	**3 961**	**18 436**	**1 102**	**328 833**	**25 665**	**172 884**	**81 017**	**49 268**	**1991**	**Amérique du Sud**
1 341	**3 762**	**24 392**	**1 102**	**334 626**	**26 126**	**177 323**	**81 176**	**50 001**	**1992**	
1 452	**3 955**	**22 399**	**1 137**	**351 444**	**26 327**	**187 432**	**83 895**	**53 791**	**1993**	
1 720	**4 164**	**22 606**	**1 184**	**372 359**	**27 844**	**197 275**	**90 944**	**56 296**	**1994**	
..	94	..	7 000	7	..	7	..	..	1991	Pêcheries antarctiq.
..	94	..	7 000	7	..	7	..	..	1992	
..	94	..	7 000	7	..	7	..	..	1993	
..	94	..	7 000	7	..	7	..	..	1994	
0	687	5 069	1 973	65 018	1 013	26 194	32 798	5 013	1991	Argentine
0	696	5 330	2 009	67 041	1 108	27 076	33 503	5 353	1992	
0	555	5 978	2 053	69 340	889	28 516	33 913	6 021	1993	
0	558	4 184	2 150	73 506	1 274	28 565	37 104	6 563	1994	

66
Production, trade and consumption of commercial energy
Thousand metric tons of coal equivalent and kilograms per capita [*cont.*]
Production, commerce et consommation d'énergie commerciale
Milliers de tonnes métriques d'équivalent houille et kilogrammes par habitant [*suite*]

Country or area	Year	Primary energy production – Production d'energie primaire					Changes in stocks Variations des stocks	Imports Importations	Exports Exportations
		Total Totale	Solids Solides	Liquids Liquides	Gas Gaz	Electricity Electricité			
Bolivia	1991	5 440	..	1 861	3 408	170	58	1	2 845
	1992	5 719	..	1 872	3 681	166	−33	15	2 852
	1993	5 599	..	1 779	3 651	169	−264	180	2 864
	1994	6 563	..	2 038	4 354	171	−67	110	2 889
Brazil	1991	81 235	3 293	45 629	5 026	27 287	−737	57 817	4 164
	1992	82 816	3 003	46 312	5 413	28 088	−1 907	58 238	4 838
	1993	85 563	2 917	47 288	5 907	29 452	2 174	67 307	7 583
	1994	88 407	3 297	49 128	6 123	29 859	−2 211	67 285	7 430
Chile	1991	7 988	2 607	1 677	2 092	1 613	958	10 426	129
	1992	7 884	1 938	1 509	2 381	2 057	121	10 802	87
	1993	7 562	1 610	1 496	2 291	2 165	168	11 356	4
	1994	7 510	1 407	1 538	2 485	2 081	628	14 110	146
Colombia	1991	61 546	21 914	30 844	5 414	3 373	2 172	1 677	32 933
	1992	60 145	20 336	31 973	5 085	2 751	277	2 632	31 313
	1993	61 837	20 162	33 145	5 093	3 436	−3 157	3 723	36 656
	1994	63 914	20 918	32 995	6 034	3 967	−1 372	2 755	33 886
Ecuador	1991	22 656	..	21 638	395	624	0	371	15 272
	1992	26 936	..	25 946	382	608	0	514	16 721
	1993	29 825	..	28 724	380	721	0	300	18 179
	1994	26 196	..	25 076	337	783	0	674	19 956
Falkland Is. (Malvinas)	1991	5	5	..	..	..	..	12	..
	1992	5	5	..	..	..	..	12	..
	1993	5	5	..	..	..	..	12	..
	1994	5	5	..	..	..	..	12	..
French Guiana	1991	..	..	..	..	..	..	413	..
	1992	..	..	..	..	..	..	433	..
	1993	..	..	..	..	..	..	432	..
	1994	..	..	..	..	..	..	432	..
Guyana	1991	1	..	..	..	1	..	543	..
	1992	1	..	..	..	1	..	510	..
	1993	1	..	..	..	1	..	511	..
	1994	1	..	..	..	1	..	515	..
Paraguay	1991	3 608	..	..	..	3 608	−44	940	3 292
	1992	3 331	..	..	..	3 331	−49	1 172	3 076
	1993	3 858	..	..	..	3 858	−111	1 206	3 484
	1994	4 399	..	..	..	4 399	181	1 603	4 026
Peru	1991	10 423	59	8 262	691	1 412	−162	3 424	3 480
	1992	10 539	88	8 318	931	1 203	−94	3 426	3 459
	1993	10 814	88	9 004	320	1 402	−84	2 908	3 487
	1994	10 899	107	9 136	226	1 430	98	3 101	3 179
Suriname	1991	553	...	380	..	173	0	655	71
	1992	563	...	384	..	178	0	661	76
	1993	567	...	387	..	180	0	664	74
	1994	563	0	389	..	174	−1	666	74
Uruguay	1991	751	..	..	..	751	91	2 486	220
	1992	973	..	..	..	973	−10	2 851	417
	1993	896	..	..	..	896	−374	2 178	283
	1994	917	..	..	..	917	175	2 298	206
Venezuela	1991	225 648	2 556	183 615	34 024	5 454	666	498	151 869
	1992	223 524	2 479	182 596	32 668	5 782	2 922	526	149 102
	1993	238 256	3 889	193 361	35 174	5 831	1 554	354	160 015
	1994	261 262	4 738	212 848	37 365	6 311	1 120	285	171 535
Asia	1991	3 270 390	1 117 517	1 657 646	314 831	180 396	35 596	1 092 226	1 335 731
	1992	3 740 223	1 262 102	1 825 123	463 384	189 614	30 894	1 289 110	1 587 405
	1993	3 859 803	1 292 608	1 871 548	487 891	207 756	32 896	1 324 260	1 646 831
	1994	4 016 714	1 357 630	1 926 956	513 966	218 162	17 051	1 359 273	1 663 946
Afghanistan	1991	454	94	5	270	85	18	846	0
	1992	318	8	0	252	59	19	488	0
	1993	309	7	0	243	58	19	472	0
	1994	297	6	0	233	58	18	453	0

Bunkers – Soutes			Consumption – Consommation							
Air Avion	Sea Maritime	Unallocated Nondistribué	Per capita Par habitant	Total Totale	Solids Solides	Liquids Liquides	Gas Gaz	Electricity Electricité	Année	Pays ou zone
0	..	−18	380	2 556	0	1 748	637	171	1991	Bolivie
0	..	165	399	2 750	0	1 727	856	167	1992	
0	..	257	414	2 921	0	1 867	884	170	1993	
0	..	330	487	3 522	0	1 875	1 473	173	1994	
700	1 113	11 857	807	121 955	15 672	70 643	5 034	30 613	1991	Brésil
647	1 201	11 176	813	125 099	15 086	73 561	5 409	31 038	1992	
690	1 501	10 616	834	130 307	15 371	76 193	5 907	32 836	1993	
822	1 773	12 667	850	135 209	15 828	79 511	6 123	33 748	1994	
0	106	464	1 256	16 757	3 660	9 453	2 032	1 613	1991	Chili
0	42	427	1 325	18 009	3 120	10 495	2 338	2 057	1992	
0	0	397	1 323	18 349	3 129	10 833	2 222	2 165	1993	
0	0	547	1 450	20 299	3 755	12 181	2 282	2 081	1994	
...	187	1 549	804	26 382	4 528	13 066	5 414	3 373	1991	Colombie
...	181	1 878	872	29 127	6 094	15 156	5 085	2 793	1992	
...	28	−1 495	987	33 527	6 154	18 807	5 093	3 473	1993	
...	28	−262	995	34 388	6 013	18 357	6 034	3 985	1994	
57	256	−670	772	8 111	..	7 093	395	624	1991	Equateur
68	265	1 858	795	8 537	..	7 548	382	608	1992	
63	269	3 317	756	8 296	..	7 195	380	721	1993	
60	295	−2 099	772	8 658	..	7 538	337	783	1994	
..	0	..	8 500	17	5	12	..	..	1991	Il. Falkland (Malvinas)
..	0	..	8 500	17	5	12	..	..	1992	
..	0	..	8 500	17	5	12	..	..	1993	
..	0	..	8 500	17	5	12	..	..	1994	
22	..	..	3 179	391	..	391	..	..	1991	Guyane française
22	..	..	3 186	411	..	411	..	..	1992	
24	..	..	3 022	408	..	408	..	..	1993	
24	..	..	2 894	408	..	408	..	..	1994	
15	4	..	654	524	0	523	..	1	1991	Guyana
13	4	..	610	493	0	490	..	3	1992	
13	4	..	605	494	0	492	..	2	1993	
15	4	..	602	497	0	494	..	2	1994	
3	..	−1	289	1 298	..	982	..	316	1991	Paraguay
3	..	−5	321	1 477	..	1 170	..	307	1992	
3	..	−56	371	1 744	..	1 340	..	404	1993	
3	..	−40	380	1 833	..	1 459	..	374	1994	
0	...	−223	488	10 752	358	8 292	691	1 412	1991	Pérou
0	...	−344	488	10 944	405	8 406	931	1 203	1992	
0	...	−607	477	10 926	400	8 803	320	1 402	1993	
0	...	75	456	10 648	520	8 472	226	1 430	1994	
0	...	296	2 077	841	0	668	..	173	1991	Suriname
0	...	294	2 088	854	0	676	..	178	1992	
0	...	313	2 039	844	0	664	..	180	1993	
0	...	316	2 010	840	0	666	..	174	1994	
53	251	265	757	2 356	0	1 825	..	531	1991	Uruguay
57	342	445	821	2 571	1	2 013	..	557	1992	
55	489	108	799	2 515	0	1 894	..	621	1993	
59	311	0	780	2 465	0	1 751	..	713	1994	
532	1 355	−152	3 594	71 876	429	31 994	34 024	5 429	1991	Venezuela
531	1 031	3 168	3 295	67 296	307	28 584	32 668	5 737	1992	
604	1 109	3 571	3 436	71 756	379	30 408	35 174	5 794	1993	
737	1 194	6 890	3 746	80 072	449	35 986	37 365	6 272	1994	
17 197	43 498	162 618	867	2 767 976	1 269 657	995 073	322 872	180 373	1991	Asie
19 115	46 996	186 219	953	3 158 705	1 385 005	1 133 674	449 417	190 609	1992	
19 818	50 322	176 038	967	3 258 159	1 425 881	1 163 187	460 378	208 713	1993	
20 501	52 750	167 899	1 009	3 453 839	1 506 431	1 211 140	516 835	219 433	1994	
9	..	0	82	1 273	94	824	270	85	1991	Afghanistan
9	..	0	48	779	8	444	252	75	1992	
9	..	0	44	753	7	428	243	74	1993	
7	..	0	39	725	6	412	233	74	1994	

66
Production, trade and consumption of commercial energy
Thousand metric tons of coal equivalent and kilograms per capita [*cont.*]
Production, commerce et consommation d'énergie commerciale
Milliers de tonnes métriques d'équivalent houille et kilogrammes par habitant [*suite*]

Country or area	Year	Primary energy production – Production d'energie primaire					Changes in stocks Variations des stocks	Imports Importations	Exports Exportations
		Total Totale	Solids Solides	Liquids Liquides	Gas Gaz	Electricity Electricité			
Bahrain	1991	10 558	..	3 665	6 893	..	79	15 212	15 175
	1992	10 543	..	3 650	6 893	..	91	15 623	15 989
	1993	12 289	..	3 612	8 677	..	45	14 716	14 338
	1994	12 072	..	3 574	8 498	..	75	14 595	14 523
Bangladesh	1991	6 562	..	177	6 282	103	−123	2 953	0
	1992	6 943	..	182	6 664	98	−30	2 935	3
	1993	7 467	..	185	7 208	75	−23	3 140	4
	1994	8 222	..	161	7 956	104	−90	3 101	0
Bhutan	1991	195	2	..	..	193	..	57	174
	1992	201	2	..	..	199	..	59	180
	1993	201	2	..	..	199	..	60	180
	1994	208	2	..	..	206	..	67	182
Brunei Darussalam	1991	24 418	..	10 996	13 422	..	−1 194	105	21 678
	1992	25 399	..	12 057	13 343	..	−1 194	0	22 514
	1993	25 112	..	11 924	13 188	..	−1 223	0	22 439
	1994	25 758	..	12 190	13 567	..	−1 161	0	22 867
Cambodia	1991	8	..	..	..	8	..	220	..
	1992	8	..	..	..	8	..	226	..
	1993	9	..	..	..	9	..	226	..
	1994	9	..	..	..	9	..	232	..
China	1991	1 014 037	775 942	201 383	21 347	15 365	8 626	19 490	55 453
	1992	1 037 003	796 609	202 962	20 975	16 458	422	32 390	58 456
	1993	1 069 992	820 425	207 447	22 545	19 575	4 806	35 657	54 240
	1994	1 142 633	884 759	208 654	23 353	25 867	−6 664	41 212	53 372
Cyprus	1991	..	..	..	..	..	95	2 316	0
	1992	..	..	..	..	..	63	2 600	0
	1993	..	..	..	..	..	186	2 767	0
	1994	..	..	..	..	..	236	2 920	0
Hong Kong	1991	..	..	..	..	..	166	18 683	4 041
	1992	..	..	..	..	..	212	22 857	5 273
	1993	..	..	..	..	..	−219	26 461	7 522
	1994	..	..	..	..	..	473	28 027	7 816
India	1991	264 694	193 004	45 738	14 956	10 996	7 091	50 593	564
	1992	267 355	199 137	41 578	15 551	11 090	3 827	64 995	619
	1993	275 411	209 524	39 521	15 696	10 670	2 113	66 924	604
	1994	296 523	217 339	45 703	22 665	10 817	−1 128	68 129	99
Indonesia	1991	228 095	13 715	147 004	64 781	2 595	9 591	13 668	123 447
	1992	234 734	21 147	142 890	67 871	2 826	4 264	18 020	132 563
	1993	244 348	27 584	143 592	70 355	2 818	6 532	17 937	131 554
	1994	255 309	28 549	144 619	79 263	2 878	611	18 350	150 640
Iran, Islamic Rep. of	1991	284 646	986	248 507	34 286	867	8 606	10 041	179 278
	1992	285 518	971	250 092	33 285	1 171	−1 428	10 744	185 266
	1993	276 400	970	249 407	24 816	1 207	−7 902	7 549	191 083
	1994	317 541	980	261 857	53 790	915	296	7 763	194 470
Iraq	1991	22 163	..	19 677	2 449	38	−3 159	1	3 904
	1992	40 020	..	36 911	3 022	86	3 407	0	5 480
	1993	50 350	..	46 882	3 395	74	6 283	0	5 491
	1994	57 432	..	53 142	4 221	69	8 324	0	5 578
Israel	1991	48	..	16	31	1	−551	17 281	1 832
	1992	45	..	13	28	4	1 274	21 830	1 909
	1993	44	..	11	28	4	201	24 187	3 932
	1994	39	..	6	29	4	−1 158	23 632	4 173
Japan	1991	105 591	7 084	1 073	2 988	94 446	1 540	520 639	7 351
	1992	107 042	6 685	1 192	3 022	96 143	−500	529 865	9 550
	1993	117 893	5 989	1 082	3 085	107 736	2 337	527 893	10 711
	1994	121 775	5 753	1 033	3 182	111 807	5 339	558 838	11 895
Jordan	1991	11	..	10	..	1	−211	4 450	67
	1992	6	..	4	..	2	103	5 452	0
	1993	3	..	0	..	3	223	5 448	0
	1994	5	..	3	..	2	−144	5 565	0

Bunkers – Soutes			Consumption – Consommation							
Air Avion	Sea Maritime	Unallocated Nondistribué	Per capita Par habitant	Total Totale	Solids Solides	Liquids Liquides	Gas Gaz	Electricity Electricité	Année	Pays ou zone
0	...	2 945	15 020	7 570	0	677	6 893	..	1991	Bahreïn
0	...	2 399	14 812	7 687	0	794	6 893	..	1992	
0	...	3 170	17 667	9 452	...	775	8 677	..	1993	
0	...	2 705	17 058	9 365	...	866	8 498	..	1994	
0	7	653	81	8 978	129	2 464	6 282	103	1991	Bangladesh
0	0	404	84	9 501	121	2 619	6 664	98	1992	
0	0	324	89	10 301	139	2 879	7 208	75	1993	
0	0	1 020	88	10 394	0	2 333	7 956	104	1994	
..	..	..	50	78	18	38	..	22	1991	Bhoutan
..	..	..	51	80	18	40	..	22	1992	
..	..	..	51	81	19	40	..	22	1993	
..	..	..	58	93	20	46	..	27	1994	
..	..	−496	17 243	4 535	0	1 244	3 291	..	1991	Brunéi Darussalam
..	..	−533	17 149	4 613	0	1 207	3 406	..	1992	
..	..	−227	15 047	4 123	0	1 243	2 881	..	1993	
..	..	−211	15 225	4 263	0	1 273	2 990	..	1994	
..	..	0	25	228	0	220	..	8	1991	Cambodge
..	..	0	25	234	0	226	..	8	1992	
..	..	0	24	234	0	226	..	9	1993	
..	..	0	24	241	0	232	..	9	1994	
..	...	36 429	812	933 020	754 087	141 870	21 347	15 716	1991	Chine
..	...	37 669	836	972 846	777 908	156 894	20 975	17 069	1992	
..	...	35 135	860	1 011 467	801 994	166 715	22 545	20 214	1993	
..	1 218	43 378	920	1 092 541	875 124	168 448	23 353	25 616	1994	
283	80	25	2 765	1 833	15	1 818	..	..	1991	Chypre
364	84	24	2 929	2 066	26	2 040	..	..	1992	
340	71	33	3 062	2 136	31	2 105	..	..	1993	
349	88	26	3 424	2 221	27	2 194	..	..	1994	
2 373	1 696	..	1 837	10 406	7 363	3 419	..	−376	1991	Hong−kong
3 100	2 265	..	2 098	12 007	7 807	4 810	..	−610	1992	
3 389	2 469	..	2 260	13 301	9 043	4 756	..	−498	1993	
3 560	2 415	..	2 451	13 764	6 460	6 506	..	798	1994	
892	344	16 809	334	289 589	193 530	69 928	14 956	11 175	1991	Inde
899	356	22 498	344	304 151	203 013	74 349	15 551	11 238	1992	
921	248	20 347	353	318 102	214 321	77 238	15 696	10 847	1993	
943	0	21 035	374	343 703	227 315	82 724	22 665	10 998	1994	
385	293	33 064	406	74 983	5 750	47 637	19 001	2 595	1991	Indonésie
485	300	32 898	435	82 244	5 331	49 512	24 574	2 826	1992	
590	315	32 617	473	90 679	9 051	50 782	28 028	2 818	1993	
663	329	30 970	466	90 447	3 514	53 176	30 878	2 878	1994	
9	597	10 106	1 581	96 090	1 558	62 707	30 959	867	1991	Iran, Rép.islamique d'
7	682	9 812	1 631	101 923	1 318	66 150	33 285	1 171	1992	
7	839	6 307	1 459	93 615	1 229	67 029	24 150	1 207	1993	
7	739	6 243	1 879	123 550	1 280	67 566	53 790	915	1994	
0	0	1 569	1 069	19 850	1	17 363	2 449	38	1991	Iraq
0	0	−282	1 652	31 415	0	28 307	3 022	86	1992	
0	0	4 933	1 729	33 642	0	30 174	3 395	74	1993	
0	0	8 450	1 761	35 079	...	30 790	4 221	69	1994	
481	309	860	2986	14 398	4 050	10 360	31	−43	1991	Israël
599	268	1 375	3 270	16 451	4 946	11 516	28	−39	1992	
674	273	1 775	3 299	17 376	5 654	11 729	28	−36	1993	
546	268	2 043	3 266	17 799	6 027	11 780	29	−37	1994	
6 391	8 276	17 961	4 719	584 710	119 760	296 658	73 847	94 446	1991	Japon
6 655	8 250	23 605	4 744	589 348	118 275	299 887	75 043	96 143	1992	
6 701	9 588	24 026	4 757	592 423	116 087	292 738	75 862	107 736	1993	
7 030	9 824	25 202	4 980	621 323	119 098	309 178	81 240	111 807	1994	
159	..	174	957	4 272	..	4 271	..	1	1991	Jordanie
290	..	216	1 036	4 848	..	4 846	..	2	1992	
333	..	−106	1 011	5 000	..	4 998	..	3	1993	
304	..	140	1 012	5 270	..	5 269	..	2	1994	

66

Production, trade and consumption of commercial energy
Thousand metric tons of coal equivalent and kilograms per capita [*cont.*]
Production, commerce et consommation d'énergie commerciale
Milliers de tonnes métriques d'équivalent houille et kilogrammes par habitant [*suite*]

Country or area	Year	Primary energy production – Production d'energie primaire					Changes in stocks Variations des stocks	Imports Importations	Exports Exportations
		Total Totale	Solids Solides	Liquids Liquides	Gas Gaz	Electricity Electricité			
Korea,Dem.Ppl's.Rep.	1991	87 700	83 800	..	..	3 900	..	8 907	489
	1992	88 348	85 400	..	..	2 948	..	8 621	464
	1993	91 148	88 200	..	..	2 948	..	8 221	464
	1994	90 287	87 400	..	..	2 887	..	8 048	438
Korea, Republic of	1991	31 218	9 678	..		21 540	−1 225	126 179	13 205
	1992	29 292	7 693	..		21 598	1 364	149 619	17 828
	1993	28 405	6 069	..		22 336	6 181	169 939	19 122
	1994	27 073	4 781	..		22 292	5 116	181 556	16 950
Kuwait [1]	1991	15 779	..	13 220	2 559		0	1 251	9 653
	1992	81 546	..	78 058	3 488		14	76	84 237
	1993	147 420	..	139 139	8 281		74	1	151 575
	1994	156 609	..	148 661	7 948		58	0	176 313
Lao People's Dem. Rep.	1991	110	1	..		109	..	123	81
	1992	107	1			106	..	133	78
	1993	106	1			105	..	133	78
	1994	107	1			106	..	144	78
Lebanon	1991	61		..		61	..	4 428	0
	1992	68		..		68	..	5 191	0
	1993	113		..		113	..	4 981	0
	1994	118		..		118	..	5 405	0
Macau	1991	..	..	..	..	..	−21	500	0
	1992	..				..	−1	518	0
	1993	..		..		..	4	572	0
	1994	..		..		..	14	610	0
Malaysia	1991	66 214	180	44 450	21 039	546	−412	14 057	48 226
	1992	69 246	80	45 735	22 896	535	−1 718	12 941	47 970
	1993	76 354	397	45 923	29 429	605	194	16 924	49 166
	1994	78 780	174	45 428	32 502	676	950	17 493	47 115
Maldives	1991	..		..		..	..	97	46
	1992	..		..		..	..	93	50
	1993	..		..		..	..	107	50
	1994	..		..		..	..	113	60
Mongolia	1991	3 018	3 018	...	..	..	..	994	198
	1992	2 912	2 912	...		..	..	903	165
	1993	2 869	2 869	...		..	..	886	165
	1994	2 928	2 928	...		..	..	905	168
Myanmar	1991	2 419	51	1 024	1 192	152	14	57	2
	1992	2 456	49	1 048	1 173	186	−144	275	0
	1993	2 688	47	983	1 449	209	−105	426	0
	1994	3 048	51	993	1 809	194	−96	582	0
Nepal	1991	106	..	..	..	106	−41	413	49
	1992	110	..	..		110	−50	526	49
	1993	102	..	..		102	−38	564	44
	1994	107	..	..		107	−28	643	50
Oman	1991	54 010	..	50 380	3 630	..	−229	30	47 957
	1992	57 296		52 810	4 486	..	−647	150	51 194
	1993	60 838	..	55 407	5 431	..	−251	402	53 568
	1994	66 645	..	57 770	8 875	..	−531	58	55 592
Pakistan	1991	25 759	2 063	4 669	16 635	2 391	..	12 861	487
	1992	27 042	2 450	4 448	17 697	2 446	..	14 472	527
	1993	28 032	2 207	4 323	18 693	2 810	..	16 241	636
	1994	28 787	2 387	4 033	19 794	2 572	..	18 396	416
Philippines	1991	8 888	853	236		7 799	−503	19 480	355
	1992	9 461	1 122	597		7 741	344	21 914	574
	1993	9 679	1 132	714		7 833	562	20 991	690
	1994	9 517	1 169	428		7 919	597	22 243	740
Qatar	1991	38 300	..	28 328	9 972		87	0	26 679
	1992	48 338		33 041	15 297		240	0	31 050
	1993	48 522		30 548	17 974		−22	0	29 329
	1994	47 741	..	29 767	17 974		−210	0	28 681

Bunkers – Soutes			Consumption – Consommation							
Air Avion	Sea Maritime	Unallocated Nondistribué	Per capita Par habitant	Total Totale	Solids Solides	Liquids Liquides	Gas Gaz	Electricity Electricité	Année	Pays ou zone
...	...	−360	4 348	96 478	86 095	6 483	..	3 900	1991	Corée,Rép.pop.dém.de
...	...	−646	4 296	97 151	87 720	6 483	..	2 948	1992	
...	...	−895	4 330	99 800	90 420	6 432	..	2 948	1993	
...	...	−930	4 208	98 826	89 572	6 367	..	2 887	1994	
733	3 494	10 679	3 004	130 513	35 691	68 279	5 003	21 540	1991	Corée, République de
892	4 533	13 478	3 210	140 816	34 136	78 538	6 544	21 598	1992	
836	5 543	12 966	3 471	153 696	37 343	85 842	8 175	22 336	1993	
904	6 046	11 524	3 776	168 089	40 138	94 990	10 669	22 292	1994	
181	14	−917	3 908	8 097	..	5 538	2 559	..	1991	Koweït [1]
404	99	−13 768	5 489	10 637	..	7 148	3 488	..	1992	
298	185	−19 703	8 447	14 994	..	6 713	8 281	..	1993	
472	242	−36 553	9 846	16 078	..	8 129	7 948	..	1994	
..	..	..	35	151	1	120	..	31	1991	Rép. dém. pop. lao
..	..	..	36	163	1	130	..	31	1992	
..	..	..	35	162	1	130	..	31	1993	
..	..	..	36	172	1	141	..	31	1994	
118	14	−8	1 672	4 365	0	4 299	..	66	1991	Liban
133	14	42	1 879	5 070	0	4 997	..	72	1992	
162	0	...	1 758	4 932	111	4 702	..	119	1993	
200	0	...	1 826	5 323	112	5 093	..	118	1994	
..	..	..	1 466	522	0	510	..	12	1991	Macao
..	..	..	1 405	520	0	506	..	14	1992	
..	..	..	1 477	567	0	553	..	14	1993	
..	..	..	1 497	596	0	579	..	17	1994	
0	156	25	1 759	32 276	2 288	20 223	9 221	543	1991	Malaisie
0	104	1 263	1 840	34 568	2 383	20 551	11 100	533	1992	
0	86	2 773	2 133	41 059	2 030	23 144	15 278	608	1993	
0	86	3 010	2 292	45 113	1 968	24 932	17 530	682	1994	
..	..	..	229	51	..	51		..	1991	Maldives
..	..	..	186	43	..	43		..	1992	
..	..	..	239	57	..	57		..	1993	
..	..	..	211	52	..	52		..	1994	
...	..	...	1 713	3 814	2 824	979	..	10	1991	Mongolie
...	..	...	1 606	3 650	2 751	889	..	9	1992	
...	..	...	1 549	3 590	2 708	857	..	24	1993	
...	..	...	1 551	3 665	2 765	875	..	25	1994	
10	36	14	56	2 400	63	991	1 193	152	1991	Myanmar
3	22	359	57	2 492	62	1 071	1 173	186	1992	
3	1	276	66	2 939	59	1 221	1 449	209	1993	
3	7	305	75	3 411	62	1 345	1 809	194	1994	
..	..	..	26	511	67	343	..	102	1991	Népal
..	..	..	31	637	92	436	..	109	1992	
..	..	..	32	661	100	454	..	107	1993	
..	..	..	34	728	115	502	..	111	1994	
419	354	26	3 014	5 513	..	1 882	3 630	..	1991	Oman
251	156	44	3 378	6 448	..	1 962	4486	..	1992	
282	170	16	3 742	7 455	..	2 024	5 431	..	1993	
239	187	−8	5 405	11 226	..	2 350	8 875	..	1994	
217	26	1 216	292	36 675	3 024	14 624	16 635	2 391	1991	Pakistan
214	18	1 162	306	39 592	3 508	15 941	17 697	2 446	1992	
231	21	1 136	318	42 248	3 191	17 556	18 693	2 810	1993	
190	24	1 207	332	45 346	3 470	19 509	19 794	2 572	1994	
554	77	1 960	417	25 925	2 346	15 780	..	7 799	1991	Philippines
654	96	3 132	418	26 575	1 921	16 913	..	7 741	1992	
700	114	1 478	418	27 125	1 977	17 315	..	7 833	1993	
722	143	1 340	426	28 217	2 106	18 192	..	7 919	1994	
127	..	113	22 453	11 294	..	1 322	9 972	..	1991	Qatar
103	..	119	32 545	16 826	..	1 529	15 297	..	1992	
103	..	59	36 015	19 052	..	1 078	17 974	..	1993	
147	..	113	35 204	19 010	..	1 036	17 974	..	1994	

66

Production, trade and consumption of commercial energy
Thousand metric tons of coal equivalent and kilograms per capita [*cont.*]
Production, commerce et consommation d'énergie commerciale
Milliers de tonnes métriques d'équivalent houille et kilogrammes par habitant [*suite*]

Country or area	Year	Primary energy production – Production d'energie primaire					Changes in stocks Variations des stocks	Imports Importations	Exports Exportations
		Total Totale	Solids Solides	Liquids Liquides	Gas Gaz	Electricity Electricité			
Saudi Arabia [1]	1991	653 169	..	609 051	44 118	..	9 148	0	527 222
	1992	673 054	..	627 244	45 810	..	10 776	0	534 345
	1993	653 007	..	605 210	47 797	..	11 126	0	514 130
	1994	656 067	..	605 872	50 195	..	14 042	0	507 726
Singapore	1991	..	..	..	..	..	599	89 218	47 080
	1992	..	..	..	..	..	1 742	95 165	47 489
	1993	..	..	..	..	..	2 091	104 776	53 419
	1994	..	..	..	..	..	−8 476	104 705	59 836
Sri Lanka	1991	383	..	..	..	383	−43	2 670	149
	1992	356	..	..	..	356	−8	2 897	8
	1993	466	..	..	..	466	−49	3 094	95
	1994	502	..	..	..	502	−55	3 296	129
Syrian Arab Republic	1991	38 564	..	35 260	2 536	768	503	340	19 678
	1992	40 757	..	37 227	2 623	907	1 644	835	20 632
	1993	42 100	..	38 679	2 597	824	158	645	22 815
	1994	45 495	..	41 931	2 730	835	−716	649	26 615
Thailand	1991	20 292	5 477	4 670	9 580	565	161	28 893	1 289
	1992	21 792	5 740	5 262	10 269	522	474	31 700	1 364
	1993	23 243	5 806	5 403	11 578	456	635	36 878	1 338
	1994	24 439	6 382	5 409	12 093	556	−624	40 380	1 619
Turkey	1991	26 278	16 882	6 233	265	2 897	−1 959	39 279	3 913
	1992	25 316	15 626	6 108	233	3 349	247	41 908	2 609
	1993	26 591	16 531	5 559	235	4 266	−246	48 062	2 700
	1994	26 655	17 287	5 279	234	3 854	1 150	48 592	311
United Arab Emirates	1991	196 870	..	162 506	34 364	..	857	608	156 268
	1992	184 208	..	154 691	29 517	..	571	734	147 086
	1993	178 817	..	148 288	30 529	..	−594	1 047	141 534
	1994	190 621	..	156 791	33 830	..	369	561	150 245
Viet Nam	1991	10 677	4 329	5 650	3	694	−243	3 734	6 757
	1992	13 362	4 792	7 842	3	725	−185	4 167	9 352
	1993	16 676	5 899	9 016	3	1 758	695	5 014	10 221
	1994	17 672	5 600	10 141	3	1 927	−271	5 597	11 984
Yemen	1991	13 548	..	13 548	..	..	32	3 514	12 474
	1992	11 714	..	11 714	..	..	33	5 890	10 950
	1993	16 735	..	16 735	..	..	...	4 585	14 716
	1994	23 277	..	23 277	..	..	14	534	18 631
Europe	**1991**	**1 485 727**	**487 561**	**319 480**	**308 734**	**369 953**	**8 541**	**1 528 460**	**582 838**
	1992	**3 261 907**	**814 057**	**922 991**	**1 036 177**	**488 682**	**31 915**	**1 865 892**	**1 165 872**
	1993	**3 153 371**	**744 997**	**874 077**	**1 041 301**	**492 996**	**5 594**	**1 794 297**	**1 148 937**
	1994	**3 085 530**	**677 309**	**883 089**	**1 029 018**	**496 113**	**17 880**	**1 725 590**	**1 200 668**
Albania	1991	2 360	544	1 207	172	438	214	200	317
	1992	1 538	183	836	124	395	143	60	119
	1993	1 445	108	811	119	407	114	0	95
	1994	1 414	85	764	102	463	179	0	...
Austria	1991	8 421	774	1 896	1 730	4 020	−82	26 965	2 176
	1992	8 719	659	1 747	1 881	4 432	973	26 980	1 584
	1993	8 960	629	1 711	1 949	4 670	305	26 678	1 846
	1994	8 462	517	1 644	1 769	4 532	−877	26 778	2 341
Belgium	1991	17 170	1 113	..	13	16 044	485	90 270	28 198
	1992	16 859	564	..	8	16 287	533	91 419	28 421
	1993	16 040	332	..	6	15 702	−856	87 825	26 814
	1994	15 530	290	..	1	15 238	74	90 898	26 737
Bulgaria	1991	12 299	7 006	83	12	5 198	63	20 141	143
	1992	12 219	7 555	76	43	4 545	75	16 534	359
	1993	12 819	7 250	61	78	5 430	249	23 996	1 196
	1994	13 108	7 115	51	65	5 877	−430	19 663	2 909
former Czechoslovakia †	1991	60 724	50 645	200	642	9 237	..	37 666	5 598
Denmark	1991	15 381	0	10 130	5 156	94	−1 100	25 338	12 934
	1992	16 551	0	11 078	5 359	114	464	24 556	14 465
	1993	17 918	0	11 805	5 983	130	−1 732	23 801	15 760
	1994	19 695	0	13 024	6 527	144	−1 190	25 743	17 330

Bunkers – Soutes			Consumption – Consommation							
Air Avion	Sea Maritime	Unallocated Nondistribué	Per capita Par habitant	Total Totale	Solids Solides	Liquids Liquides	Gas Gaz	Electricity Electricité	Année	Pays ou zone
1 483	12 457	14 204	5 377	88 655	..	44 537	44 118	..	1991	Arabie saoudite [1]
1 621	13 045	19 420	5 578	93 847	..	48 036	45 810	..	1992	
1 769	13 004	15 967	5 667	97 012	..	49 214	47 797	..	1993	
1 769	12 692	19 163	5 769	100 676	..	50 481	50 195	..	1994	
1 105	11 708	8 530	7 454	20 195	17	20 179		0	1991	Singapour
1 179	12 488	8 721	8 953	23 545	25	23 521	..	0	1992	
1 238	13 269	9 336	9 314	25 422	27	25 401	..	−6	1993	
1 268	14 049	10 739	9 823	27 290	36	27 265	..	−11	1994	
57	443	122	133	2 325	3	1 939	..	383	1991	Sri Lanka
74	404	125	150	2 651	2	2 293		356	1992	
97	486	266	149	2 665	2	2 197		466	1993	
100	487	232	160	2 904	3	2 399	..	502	1994	
463	...	1 396	1 319	16 864	2	13 558	2 536	768	1991	Rép. arabe syrienne
389	...	1 746	1 298	17 180	2	13 648	2 623	907	1992	
279	...	1 940	1 282	17 554	2	14 132	2 597	824	1993	
295	...	1 834	1 278	18 117	2	14 551	2 730	835	1994	
0	0	1 467	819	46 268	5 876	30 179	9 580	633	1991	Thaïlande
0	0	1 612	880	50 043	6 277	32 921	10 269	576	1992	
0	0	1 765	981	56 383	6 795	37 481	11 578	529	1993	
0	0	1 392	1 075	62 431	7 688	41 993	12 093	657	1994	
335	192	3 139	1 047	59 937	24 226	27 246	5 537	2 928	1991	Turquie
376	158	3 297	1 036	60 537	22 120	29 628	5 455	3 334	1992	
457	142	4 077	1 133	67 523	23 185	34 056	6 062	4 220	1993	
368	159	3 003	1 157	70 254	23 132	36 924	6 412	3 788	1994	
324	668	−487	23 153	39 846	..	10 231	29 616	..	1991	Emirats arabes unis
324	654	788	20 067	35 518	..	10 602	24 916	..	1992	
310	683	964	20 356	36 967	..	10 976	25 991	..	1993	
354	682	406	21 025	39 127	..	11 144	27 983	..	1994	
..	..	2	116	7 894	3 428	3 769	3	694	1991	Viet Nam
..	..	2	120	8 360	3 437	4 194	3	725	1992	
..	..	2	151	10 771	3 979	5 031	3	1 758	1993	
..	..	2	159	11 553	4 015	5 607	3	1 927	1994	
90	229	875	283	3 362	..	3 362	..	..	1991	Yémen
90	214	2 024	343	4 293	..	4 293	..	..	1992	
90	157	1 730	351	4 627	..	4 627	..	..	1993	
60	143	407	328	4 555	..	4 555	..	..	1994	
31 094	51 101	17 301	4 626	2 323 312	613 169	863 219	474 124	372 800	1991	Europe
32 962	74 390	98 389	5 138	3 724 270	942 961	1 183 312	1 110 309	487 688	1992	
35 957	53 808	78 661	4 997	3 624 711	870 720	1 149 222	1 112 147	492 622	1993	
37 857	52 074	88 936	4 700	3 413 705	807 594	1 068 334	1 042 525	495 252	1994	
..	..	277	526	1 753	694	716	172	171	1991	Albanie
..	..	217	333	1 120	193	476	124	327	1992	
..	..	222	299	1 014	83	475	119	337	1993	
..	..	207	301	1 028	85	378	102	463	1994	
271	..	615	4 180	32 405	5 351	15 249	7 692	4 114	1991	Autriche
290	..	420	4 154	32 431	4 700	14 747	8 483	4 500	1992	
283	..	241	4 192	32 963	4 122	15 311	8 950	4 580	1993	
298	..	526	4 162	32 953	4 232	15 076	8 504	4 431	1994	
1 322	6 108	1 956	6 945	69 370	14 153	25 536	13 864	15 817	1991	Belgique
1 304	6 070	2 939	6 897	69 011	13 306	25 038	14 365	16 303	1992	
1 172	6 245	2 852	6 732	67 637	12 244	24 486	14 931	15 976	1993	
1 167	5 981	3 308	6 861	69 161	13 244	24 835	15 520	15 728	1994	
..	299	1 018	3 449	30 916	10 983	7 878	6 596	5 459	1991	Bulgarie
..	387	628	3 060	27 303	10 647	5 969	5 810	4 877	1992	
..	283	4 265	3 475	30 821	11 207	8 739	5 432	5 443	1993	
..	377	1 195	3 257	28 721	10 331	7 064	5 406	5 868	1994	
..	..	3 489	5 690	89 303	51 409	12 171	16 249	9 459	1991	Tchec.anc †
884	1 248	317	5 149	26 435	11 796	11 886	2 901	−148	1991	Danemark
864	1 309	−124	4 669	24 130	9 642	10 872	3 041	574	1992	
884	1 947	−243	4 855	25 103	10 300	10 988	3 540	275	1993	
899	2 149	−395	5 150	26 644	11 334	11 778	4 151	−451	1994	

66

Production, trade and consumption of commercial energy
Thousand metric tons of coal equivalent and kilograms per capita [*cont.*]

Production, commerce et consommation d'énergie commerciale
Milliers de tonnes métriques d'équivalent houille et kilogrammes par habitant [*suite*]

Country or area	Year	Primary energy production – Production d'energie primaire					Changes in stocks Variations des stocks	Imports Importations	Exports Exportations
		Total Totale	Solids Solides	Liquids Liquides	Gas Gaz	Electricity Electricité			
Faeroe Islands	1991	9	...	..	..	9	..	272	..
	1992	9	...	..	..	9	..	305	..
	1993	10	0	..	..	10	..	273	..
	1994	10	0	..	..	10	..	276	..
Finland	1991	10 819	1 950	..	..	8 869	−756	26 892	4 013
	1992	10 868	1 857	..	..	9 011	−1 802	25 743	5 348
	1993	10 179	1 119	..	..	9 060	−1 464	26 720	4 860
	1994	11 708	3 043	..	..	8 665	3 232	32 207	5 080
France incl. Monaco	1991	149 408	10 687	4 907	3 169	130 645	3 930	206 062	26 343
	1992	163 293	9 767	4 783	3 052	145 690	4 659	203 292	26 975
	1993	161 946	8 982	4 629	3 212	145 122	−718	194 735	30 549
	1994	159 387	7 817	4 664	3 221	143 685	700	188 714	32 073
Germany †	1991	235 124	151 742	4 863	21 480	57 039	2 442	277 783	24 000
	1992	227 538	140 006	4 684	21 255	61 594	11 297	290 394	26 092
	1993	210 871	125 474	4 376	21 352	59 668	1 299	294 170	26 935
	1994	200 675	115 708	4 196	21 664	59 105	9 829	303 886	30 081
Gibraltar	1991	..	..	..	..	..	47	740	0
	1992	..	..	..	..	..	78	1 322	0
	1993	..	..	..	..	..	82	1 373	1
	1994	..	..	..	..	..	72	1 380	0
Greece	1991	11 657	9 854	1 199	214	390	2 462	29 076	6 618
	1992	11 259	9 783	985	197	294	1 286	32 396	7 006
	1993	12 013	10 744	806	146	318	475	29 766	4 947
	1994	11 783	10 594	762	73	354	−2 295	28 504	4 880
Hungary	1991	20 158	6 013	3 522	5 499	5 123	−683	19 395	1 017
	1992	19 053	5 567	3 116	5 163	5 207	−865	17 419	1 384
	1993	18 195	4 533	2 959	5 558	5 146	692	19 787	1 752
	1994	17 836	4 396	2 836	5 365	5 239	111	19 450	2 537
Iceland	1991	863	..	..	..	863	−15	883	..
	1992	811	..	..	..	811	55	1 014	..
	1993	865	..	..	..	865	−29	1 006	..
	1994	873	..	..	..	873	−2	1 047	..
Ireland	1991	4 733	1 572	..	3 042	118	−3	10 759	132
	1992	4 778	1 635	..	3 014	130	−209	10 679	1 137
	1993	5 170	1 621	..	3 423	126	−34	10 901	1 107
	1994	5 335	1 704	..	3 482	149	−473	11 527	1 431
Italy and San Marino	1991	39 814	356	6 190	23 763	9 504	−2 823	215 649	29 167
	1992	40 046	362	6 431	23 387	9 866	3 469	224 443	29 290
	1993	41 845	362	6 630	24 891	9 961	−1 991	216 093	31 634
	1994	43 399	88	6 994	26 263	10 054	357	211 307	28 986
Luxembourg	1991	98	..	..	..	98	−32	5 324	99
	1992	75	..	..	..	75	−41	5 439	67
	1993	57	..	..	..	57	−26	5 431	51
	1994	85	..	..	..	85	−0	5 374	78
Malta	1991	..	..	..	..	..	..	831	0
	1992	..	..	..	..	..	..	834	0
	1993	..	..	..	..	..	..	849	0
	1994	..	..	..	..	..	..	835	0
Netherlands	1991	104 621	0	5 364	98 001	1 255	1 017	133 049	114 512
	1992	104 532	0	4 802	98 286	1 445	1 219	130 634	113 867
	1993	106 194	0	4 705	99 990	1 500	1 075	132 110	117 195
	1994	102 621	0	6 275	94 827	1 519	1 327	133 273	111 558
Norway, Svalbard, and Jan Mayen Is.	1991	185 726	316	134 123	37 704	13 583	−371	6 482	159 903
	1992	206 192	375	152 894	38 543	14 380	775	5 484	179 013
	1993	218 585	257	163 800	39 848	14 681	1 562	6 355	187 711
	1994	241 339	289	184 098	43 094	13 859	568	6 870	210 273
Poland	1991	132 132	127 746	227	3 739	419	1 144	28 494	21 717
	1992	128 861	124 501	286	3 636	439	1 003	28 962	20 713
	1993	132 325	126 891	336	4 659	439	−1 964	29 727	23 391
	1994	134 558	129 321	406	4 366	465	870	29 984	28 286

| Bunkers – Soutes | | | Consumption – Consommation | | | | | | | |
Air Avion	Sea Maritime	Unallocated Nondistribué	Per capita Par habitant	Total Totale	Solids Solides	Liquids Liquides	Gas Gaz	Electricity Electricité	Année	Pays ou zone
..	..	..	5 979	281	0	272	..	9	1991	Iles Feroe
..	..	..	6 681	314	0	305	..	9	1992	
..	..	..	6 043	284	0	273	..	10	1993	
..	..	..	6 106	287	0	276	..	10	1994	
442	786	−397	6 720	33 624	7 728	12 338	3 793	9 765	1991	Finlande
391	990	−1 346	6 554	33 030	7 029	12 028	3 931	10 042	1992	
375	777	−1 781	6 757	34 133	7 709	12 350	4 082	9 992	1993	
388	605	−3 007	7 389	37 617	9 490	14 145	4 513	9 468	1994	
4 251	3 792	5 811	5 460	311 342	30 092	113 657	43 446	124 148	1991	France y comp.Monaco
4 886	3 664	4 590	5 617	321 811	26 466	113 078	43 184	139 082	1992	
4 984	3 492	6 196	5 427	312 180	20 803	109 335	44 602	137 576	1993	
5 253	3 095	9 365	5 152	297 614	20 750	98 139	44 858	135 926	1994	
6 636	2 970	4 155	5 920	472 704	158 848	165 268	91 620	56 968	1991	Allemagne †
7 370	2 509	6 800	5 774	463 865	149 276	164 014	89 634	60 941	1992	
7 422	3 155	3 893	5 719	462 339	139 714	168 590	94 259	59 775	1993	
7 716	2 911	9 045	5 474	444 978	123 198	166 243	100 435	59 393	1994	
10	649	..	1 214	34	0	34	..	−0	1991	Gibraltar
6	1 214	..	857	24	0	24	..	0	1992	
6	1 219	..	2 357	66	0	66	..	−1	1993	
6	1 207	..	3 393	95	...	95	..	0	1994	
1 017	3 359	−2 117	2 858	29 393	11 090	17 620	214	469	1991	Grèce
1 030	3 858	−2 522	3 180	32 997	11 476	20 956	197	369	1992	
1 358	4 502	−3 243	3 268	33 742	12 176	21 002	146	417	1993	
1 219	4 782	−1 883	3 204	33 583	12 205	20 905	73	401	1994	
..	..	1 644	3 643	37 574	8 765	10 155	12 626	6 027	1991	Hongrie
..	..	1 680	3 340	34 273	7 430	10 110	11 099	5 633	1992	
..	..	1 439	3 340	34 099	6 605	10 100	11 944	5 450	1993	
..	..	1 377	3 273	33 260	6 201	9 997	11 818	5 489	1994	
91	...	..	6 465	1 670	87	719	..	863	1991	Islande
108	28	..	6 269	1 634	62	762	..	811	1992	
85	45	..	6 722	1 769	64	840	..	865	1993	
99	42	..	6 703	1 782	96	812	..	873	1994	
481	49	51	4 221	14 783	4 721	6 902	3 042	118	1991	Irlande
435	23	138	3 972	13 934	4 714	6 077	3 014	130	1992	
343	78	−27	4 145	14 604	4 726	6 329	3 423	126	1993	
545	56	63	4 311	15 239	4 509	7 099	3 485	149	1994	
3 079	3 562	−8 466	4 044	230 945	18 826	130 585	67 720	13 814	1991	Italie y compris
3 088	3 491	−7 175	4 067	232 326	17 405	135 462	68 282	14 202	1992	Saint−Marin
3 554	3 480	−6 568	3 986	227 829	15 407	131 030	66 587	14 805	1993	
3 712	3 365	−7 512	3 949	225 798	16 253	130 528	64 680	14 672	1994	
196	..	..	13 400	5 159	1 424	2 471	709	555	1991	Luxembourg
189	..	..	13 585	5 300	1 357	2 639	739	563	1992	
189	..	..	13 352	5 274	1 387	2 564	768	554	1993	
239	..	..	12 810	5 142	1 218	2 517	775	632	1994	
74	43	..	2 006	714	253	461	..	..	1991	Malte
74	43	..	1 997	717	256	461	..	..	1992	
74	43	..	2 028	732	256	476	..	..	1993	
74	43	..	1 973	718	256	462	..	..	1994	
2 311	16 179	−6 272	7 294	109 923	11 509	41 347	54 687	2 380	1991	Pays−Bas
2 746	16 343	−6 959	7 117	107 951	11 363	41 233	52 844	2 510	1992	
3 000	16 927	−12 711	7 378	112 819	12 114	43 739	54 201	2 765	1993	
3 132	16 152	−7 391	7 203	111 117	12 343	43 213	52 751	2 817	1994	
115	563	2 608	6 883	29 391	1 125	12 206	2 818	13 242	1991	Norvège,Savalbard,
118	704	2 351	6 701	28 716	1 149	11 541	2 718	13 307	1992	et Ile Jan−Mayen
124	753	2 650	7 488	32 140	1 219	11 810	5 386	13 725	1993	
130	823	4 258	7 443	32 158	1 417	11 329	5 569	13 843	1994	
..	262	2 402	3 536	135 103	107 409	16 304	11 293	97	1991	Pologne
..	415	2 367	3 485	133 324	105 516	16 715	11 150	−57	1992	
..	146	1 291	3 634	139 187	108 635	18 698	11 711	143	1993	
..	128	810	3 507	134 448	102 622	20 011	11 482	136	1994	

66

Production, trade and consumption of commercial energy
Thousand metric tons of coal equivalent and kilograms per capita [*cont.*]
Production, commerce et consommation d'énergie commerciale
Milliers de tonnes métriques d'équivalent houille et kilogrammes par habitant [*suite*]

Country or area	Year	Primary energy production – Production d'energie primaire					Changes in stocks Variations des stocks	Imports Importations	Exports Exportations
		Total Totale	Solids Solides	Liquids Liquides	Gas Gaz	Electricity Electricité			
Portugal	1991	1 292	158	..	..	1 133	97	23 801	3 085
	1992	759	129	..	..	630	166	27 074	4 448
	1993	1 195	115	..	..	1 079	152	26 215	4 394
	1994	1 443	86	..	..	1 357	−352	27 736	5 950
Romania	1991	49 406	9 713	9 700	28 243	1 750	−1 533	25 654	3 669
	1992	46 151	10 106	9 448	25 159	1 437	1 568	23 203	3 267
	1993	46 530	10 894	10 125	23 943	1 568	−397	21 877	4 034
	1994	43 997	11 118	9 700	21 577	1 603	−421	23 554	7 173
Spain	1991	44 800	16 716	2 071	1 890	24 123	−1 586	103 919	16 735
	1992	42 620	15 644	2 040	1 642	23 294	956	108 229	14 157
	1993	41 089	14 569	1 600	927	23 993	354	103 914	14 023
	1994	39 923	14 134	1 370	285	24 133	401	108 669	12 624
Sweden	1991	36 369	26	4	* ..	36 338	−996	39 030	13 525
	1992	33 171	364	1		32 806	−993	38 798	11 307
	1993	32 411	337	0	..	32 074	−218	40 649	14 572
	1994	34 806	319	7	..	34 479	784	41 544	13 057
Switzerland,Liechtenstein	1991	12 645	..	..	14	12 631	476	25 604	4 131
	1992	12 899	..	..	4	12 895	−549	24 841	3 855
	1993	13 176	..	..	3	13 173	−1 148	23 192	4 156
	1994	13 959	..	..	1	13 958	−627	23 569	4 307
United Kingdom	1991	308 337	78 228	130 854	72 204	27 050	6 142	124 878	104 418
	1992	308 315	70 045	135 191	73 549	29 530	2 228	123 371	107 684
	1993	319 711	55 802	143 654	86 333	33 924	−358	124 735	121 456
	1994	347 703	39 905	181 851	92 305	33 642	−17 169	107 821	145 114
Yugoslavia, SFR †	1991	21 363	12 400	2 937	2 047	3 979		23 304	389
Oceania	**1991**	**239 911**	**150 721**	**49 260**	**32 245**	**7 685**	**219**	**28 543**	**122 294**
	1992	**247 032**	**159 558**	**45 124**	**34 929**	**7 421**	**−593**	**31 396**	**132 608**
	1993	**249 606**	**160 970**	**44 950**	**36 850**	**6 837**	**−3 149**	**37 818**	**140 200**
	1994	**261 258**	**173 518**	**42 668**	**38 573**	**6 500**	**−5 202**	**38 875**	**149 956**
American Samoa	1991	..	..	..	..	..	..	267	..
	1992	..	..	..	..	..	..	274	..
	1993	..	..	..	..	..	..	273	..
	1994	..	..	..	..	..	..	266	..
Australia	1991	215 244	148 544	39 257	25 465	1 978	342	18 279	112 463
	1992	221 656	157 174	34 828	27 718	1 936	−345	21 216	122 539
	1993	224 705	158 458	34 322	29 828	2 096	−3 259	27 128	129 501
	1994	236 996	170 914	31 996	32 020	2 066	−5 162	27 626	139 340
Cook Islands	1991	..	..	..	..	..	..	22	..
	1992	..	..	..	..	..	..	22	..
	1993	..	..	..	..	..	..	22	..
	1994	..	..	..	..	..	..	22	..
Fiji	1991	47	..	..	..	47	−27	565	194
	1992	48	..	..	..	48	...	573	178
	1993	48	..	..	..	48	...	567	171
	1994	50	..	..	..	50	...	563	171
French Polynesia	1991	9	..	..	..	9	..	400	..
	1992	11	..	..	..	11	..	403	..
	1993	12	..	..	..	12	..	404	..
	1994	12	..	..	..	12	..	318	..
Guam	1991	..	..	..	..	..	..	861	0
	1992	..	..	..	..	..	..	861	0
	1993	..	..	..	..	..	..	854	0
	1994	..	..	..	..	..	..	847	0
Kiribati	1991	..	..	..	..	..	..	10	..
	1992	..	..	..	..	..	..	10	..
	1993	..	..	..	..	..	..	10	..
	1994	..	..	..	..	..	..	10	..
Nauru	1991	..	..	..	..	..	..	69	..
	1992	..	..	..	..	..	..	70	..
	1993	..	..	..	..	..	..	70	..
	1994	..	..	..	..	..	..	70	..

Bunkers – Soutes			Consumption – Consommation							
Air Avion	Sea Maritime	Unallocated Nondistribué	Per capita Par habitant	Total Totale	Solids Solides	Liquids Liquides	Gas Gaz	Electricity Electricité	Année	Pays ou zone
721	895	959	1 960	19 334	3 874	14 316	..	1 145	1991	Portugal
778	878	736	2 118	20 827	4 089	15 943	..	795	1992	
764	744	763	2 092	20 594	4 476	15 017	..	1 101	1993	
422	708	1 477	2 132	20 975	4 671	14 838	..	1 466	1994	
..	..	2 511	3 037	70 413	14 156	19 351	34 290	2 616	1991	Roumanie
..	..	1 348	2 732	63 171	14 876	16 064	30 278	1 953	1992	
..	..	4 203	2 631	60 566	14 448	15 211	29 108	1 798	1993	
..	..	2 486	2 544	58 313	14 875	14 834	26 913	1 692	1994	
2 133	5 622	6 114	3 033	119 700	29 634	57 138	8 888	24 039	1991	Espagne
1 666	5 697	5 638	3 111	122 736	28 348	61 809	9 206	23 373	1992	
3 036	4 974	8 003	2 900	114 612	26 067	55 299	9 097	24 149	1993	
2 750	4 499	9 094	3 018	119 223	25 967	58 189	10 586	24 361	1994	
422	1 143	1 810	6 915	59 495	3 382	19 052	881	36 179	1991	Suède
483	1 307	−760	7 013	60 623	3 456	23 629	996	32 541	1992	
607	1 316	−1	6 537	56 785	3 816	19 854	1 113	32 001	1993	
615	1 551	974	6 779	59 369	3 831	20 010	1 016	34 511	1994	
1 384	12	13	4 653	32 233	453	16 253	3 240	12 288	1991	Suisse, Liechtenstein
1 492	25	−137	4 728	33 054	297	17 333	3 056	12 368	1992	
1 576	25	−284	4 521	32 044	253	16 297	3 206	12 288	1993	
1 677	26	−75	4 500	32 219	256	16 300	3 161	12 503	1994	
5 253	3 561	−4 217	5 503	318 058	90 951	117 360	80 682	29 065	1991	Royaume–Uni
5 632	3 633	−645	5 400	313 153	84 869	115 850	80 853	31 580	1992	
6 122	3 548	−928	5 411	314 606	74 206	112 781	91 642	35 977	1993	
7 516	3 317	5 751	5 335	310 996	69 303	110 408	95 191	35 716	1994	
0	0	3 021	1 727	41 257	14 456	15 974	6 687	4 139	1991	Yougoslavie, Rfs †
3 406	**1 637**	**−7 446**	**5 525**	**148 346**	**57 790**	**56 307**	**26 564**	**7 685**	**1991**	**Oceanie**
3 594	**1 668**	**−11 167**	**5 585**	**152 318**	**60 233**	**56 964**	**27 700**	**7 421**	**1992**	
3 788	**1 772**	**−10 787**	**5 618**	**155 602**	**58 634**	**61 776**	**28 356**	**6 837**	**1993**	
3 851	**2 066**	**−9 662**	**5 658**	**159 124**	**63 938**	**59 963**	**28 724**	**6 500**	**1994**	
..	130	..	2 854	137	..	137	..	..	1991	Samoa americaines
..	130	..	2 880	144	..	144	..	..	1992	
..	130	..	2 784	142	..	142	..	..	1993	
..	130	..	2 547	135	..	135	..	..	1994	
2 081	847	−6 602	7 261	124 391	55 749	46 880	19 784	1 978	1991	Australie
2 208	901	−10 145	7 349	127 714	58 071	47 218	20 489	1 936	1992	
2 386	984	−10 080	7 515	132 300	56 620	52 250	21 334	2 096	1993	
2 459	1 087	−9 030	7 609	135 928	61 811	49 881	22 170	2 066	1994	
12	..	..	526	10	..	10	..	..	1991	Iles Cook
12	..	..	526	10	..	10	..	..	1992	
12	..	..	526	10	..	10	..	..	1993	
12	..	..	526	10	..	10	..	..	1994	
59	40	..	434	345	18	280	..	47	1991	Fidji
41	40	..	484	361	20	293	..	48	1992	
41	40	..	479	363	20	295	..	48	1993	
37	40	..	473	365	20	295	..	50	1994	
59	46	..	1 505	304	..	294	..	9	1991	Polynésie française
59	46	..	1 495	308	..	297	..	11	1992	
59	46	..	1 469	310	..	299	..	12	1993	
7	51	..	1 265	272	..	260	..	12	1994	
12	144	...	5 146	705	..	705	..	..	1991	Guam
12	144	...	5 036	705	..	705	..	..	1992	
12	144	...	4 847	698	..	698	..	..	1993	
12	144	...	4 701	691	..	691	..	..	1994	
..	..	..	135	10	..	10	..	..	1991	Kiribati
..	..	..	133	10	..	10	..	..	1992	
..	..	..	132	10	..	10	..	..	1993	
..	..	..	130	10	..	10	..	..	1994	
7	..	..	6 100	61	..	61	..	..	1991	Nauru
7	..	..	6 300	63	..	63	..	..	1992	
7	..	..	6 300	63	..	63	..	..	1993	
7	..	..	5 727	63	..	63	..	..	1994	

66

Production, trade and consumption of commercial energy

Thousand metric tons of coal equivalent and kilograms per capita [*cont.*]

Production, commerce et consommation d'énergie commerciale

Milliers de tonnes métriques d'équivalent houille et kilogrammes par habitant [*suite*]

Country or area	Year	Primary energy production – Production d'energie primaire					Changes in stocks Variations des stocks	Imports Importations	Exports Exportations
		Total Totale	Solids Solides	Liquids Liquides	Gas Gaz	Electricity Electricité			
New Caledonia	1991	42	..	..	..	42	..	825	22
	1992	42	..	..	..	42	..	814	17
	1993	42	..	..	..	42	..	814	17
	1994	42	..	..	..	42	..	792	17
New Zealand	1991	17 262	2 177	2 861	6 678	5 546	−97	5 188	2 451
	1992	17 538	2 384	2 726	7 108	5 320	−248	5 086	2 282
	1993	16 918	2 512	2 915	6 916	4 575	110	5 612	2 776
	1994	16 133	2 603	2 816	6 448	4 266	−40	6 321	2 551
Niue	1991	..	..	..	..	..	..	1	..
	1992	..	..	..	..	..	..	1	..
	1993	..	..	..	..	..	..	1	..
	1994	..	..	..	..	..	..	1	..
Palau [2]	1991	4	..	..	..	4	..	133	..
	1992	4	..	..	..	4	..	135	..
	1993	4	..	..	..	4	..	132	..
	1994	4	..	..	..	4	..	132	..
Papua New Guinea	1991	7 301	..	7 142	102	57	..	1 128	7 163
	1992	7 729	..	7 570	102	57	..	1 127	7 592
	1993	7 875	..	7 713	106	57	..	1 122	7 735
	1994	8 018	..	7 856	106	57	..	1 098	7 878
Samoa	1991	2	..	..	..	2	..	60	..
	1992	3	..	..	..	3	..	62	..
	1993	3	..	..	..	3	..	62	..
	1994	3	..	..	..	3	..	59	..
Solomon Islands	1991	..	..	..	..	..	..	80	..
	1992	..	..	..	..	..	..	79	..
	1993	..	..	..	..	..	..	77	..
	1994	..	..	..	..	..	..	76	..
Tonga	1991	..	..	..	..	..	..	49	..
	1992	..	..	..	..	..	..	47	..
	1993	..	..	..	..	..	..	53	..
	1994	..	..	..	..	..	..	55	..
Vanuatu	1991	..	..	..	..	..	..	31	..
	1992	..	..	..	..	..	..	29	..
	1993	..	..	..	..	..	..	29	..
	1994	..	..	..	..	..	..	29	..
Wake Island	1991	..	..	..	..	..	..	575	..
	1992	..	..	..	..	..	..	586	..
	1993	..	..	..	..	..	..	586	..
	1994	..	..	..	..	..	..	590	..
former USSR †	1991	2 217 666	433 974	740 707	935 323	107 661	..	4 484	285 499

Source:
Energy statistics database of the Statistics Division of the United Nations Secretariat.

Source:
Base de données pour les statistiques énergétiques de la Division de statistique du Secrétariat de l'ONU.

† For detailed descriptions of data pertaining to former Czechoslovakia, Germany, SFR Yugoslavia and former USSR, see annex I − Country or area nomenclature, regional and other groupings.

† Pour les descriptions en détails des données relatives à l'ancienne Tchécoslovaquie, l'Allemagne, la Rfs Yougoslavie et l'ancienne URSS, voir l'Annexe I − Nomenclature des pays ou zones, groupements régionaux et autres groupements.

1 Part Neutral Zone.
2 Including data for Federated States of Micronesia, Marshall Is. and Northern Mariana Is.

1 Part Zone neutrel.
2 Y compris les données pour les Etats fédérés de Micronésie, les iles Marshall et les iles Mariannes du Nord.

Bunkers – Soutes			Consumption – Consommation							
Air Avion	Sea Maritime	Unallocated Nondistribué	Per capita Par habitant	Total Totale	Solids Solides	Liquids Liquides	Gas Gaz	Electricity Electricité	Année	Pays ou zone
22	13	..	4 765	810	176	592	..	42	1991	Nouvelle−Calédonie
22	13	..	4 647	804	170	592	..	42	1992	
22	13	..	4 594	804	170	592	..	42	1993	
22	13	..	4 393	782	165	575	..	42	1994	
544	411	−844	5 869	19 984	1 845	5 915	6 678	5 546	1991	Nouvelle−Zélande
618	389	−1 022	5 989	20 607	1 971	6 207	7 108	5 320	1992	
628	410	−707	5 524	19 314	1 822	6 000	6 916	4 575	1993	
675	597	−632	5 487	19 304	1 940	6 649	6 448	4 266	1994	
0	..	..	500	1	..	1	..	..	1991	Nioué
0	..	..	500	1	..	1	..	..	1992	
0	..	..	500	1	..	1	..	..	1993	
0	..	..	500	1	..	1	..	..	1994	
22	..	..	520	115	..	111	..	4	1991	Palaos [2]
22	..	..	518	117	..	113	..	4	1992	
22	..	..	494	114	..	110	..	4	1993	
22	..	..	481	114	..	110	..	4	1994	
38	4	0	312	1 223	1	1 063	102	57	1991	Papouasie−Nvl−Guinée
37	4	0	304	1 223	1	1 063	102	57	1992	
37	4	0	297	1 222	1	1 058	106	57	1993	
29	4	0	286	1 204	1	1 041	106	57	1994	
..	..	..	384	63	0	60	..	2	1991	Samoa
..	..	..	394	65	0	62	..	3	1992	
..	..	..	389	65	0	62	..	3	1993	
..	..	..	367	62	0	59	..	3	1994	
3	...	...	233	77	..	77	..	..	1991	Iles Salomon
3	...	...	222	76	..	76	..	..	1992	
3	...	...	212	75	..	75	..	..	1993	
3	...	...	199	73	..	73	..	..	1994	
4	..	..	454	44	0	44	..	..	1991	Tonga
4	..	..	443	43	0	43	..	..	1992	
4	..	..	500	49	0	49	..	..	1993	
4	..	..	510	50	0	50	..	..	1994	
..	0	..	203	31	0	31	..	..	1991	Vanuatu
..	0	..	185	29	0	29	..	..	1992	
..	0	..	180	29	0	29	..	..	1993	
..	0	..	176	29	0	29	..	..	1994	
542	..	..	34 000	34	..	34	..	..	1991	Ile de Wake
549	..	..	37 000	37	..	37	..	..	1992	
554	..	..	32 000	32	..	32	..	..	1993	
561	..	..	29 000	29	..	29	..	..	1994	
..	...	69 353	6 415	1 867 297	411 963	536 625	813 424	105 286	1991	ancienne URSS †

67
Production of selected energy commodities
Production des principaux biens de l'énergie

Thousand metric tons of coal equivalent
Milliers de tonnes métriques d'équivalent houille

Country or area Pays ou zone	Year Anneé	Hard coal, lignite & peat Houille, lignite et tourbe	Briquettes & cokes Agglo- mérés et cokes	Crude petroleum & NGL Pétrole brut et GNL	Light petroleum products Produits pétroliers légers	Heavy petroleum products Produits pétroliers lourds	Other petroleum products Autres produits pétroliers	LPG & refinery gas GLP et gaz de raffinerie	Natural gas Gaz naturel	Electricity Electricité
World Monde	1991	3 170 143	361 567	4 567 227	1 667 052	2 232 985	316 761	249 763	2 616 970	2 030 750
	1992	3 204 302	336 210	4 593 034	1 692 458	2 222 440	329 840	254 394	2 585 749	2 056 175
	1993	3 120 866	327 571	4 583 003	1 733 142	2 231 219	330 884	250 773	2 648 146	2 092 719
	1994	3 330 835	321 096	4 666 316	1 747 398	2 205 918	335 595	258 248	2 719 022	2 161 968
Africa Afrique	1991	142 767	3 602	485 853	57 044	91 723	4 466	2 770	99 936	43 141
	1992	139 919	3 552	484 157	56 881	92 224	4 588	2 809	98 976	43 531
	1993	145 381	3 749	474 028	57 589	93 645	4 550	2 779	103 073	44 211
	1994	146 096	3 853	468 581	56 919	90 739	4 665	3 047	107 056	46 035
Algeria Algérie	1991	15	0	88 355	10 338	19 303	494	855	71 776	2 131
	1992	15	0	84 015	10 561	19 613	515	824	69 547	2 246
	1993	20	0	84 763	11 035	19 188	544	668	71 708	2 385
	1994	20	0	84 865	12 758	18 226	558	808	68 110	2 443
Angola Angola	1991	..	..	35 324	473	1 399	20	26	222	226
	1992	..	..	37 137	485	1 399	21	26	222	228
	1993	..	..	35 994	491	1 385	21	28	223	228
	1994	..	..	36 065	478	1 370	21	28	222	229
Benin Bénin	1991	..	..	421	..	..	..	..	..	1
	1992	..	..	426	..	..	..	..	..	1
	1993	..	..	431	..	..	..	..	..	1
	1994	..	..	443	..	..	..	..	..	1
Burkina Faso Burkina Faso	1991	..	0		..	..	..	..	..	24
	1992	..	0		..	..	..	..	..	25
	1993	..	...		..	..	..	..	..	26
	1994	..	...		..	..	..	..	..	27
Burundi Burundi	1991	5	0		..	..	..	..	..	17
	1992	6	0		..	..	..	..	..	13
	1993	6	0		..	..	..	..	..	17
	1994	6	0		..	..	..	..	..	18
Cameroon Cameroun	1991	1	..	11 012	833	621	75	30	..	337
	1992	1	..	9 698	841	627	75	30	..	335
	1993	1	..	8 870	845	623	81	33	..	335
	1994	1	..	7 823	851	631	86	31	..	337
Cape Verde Cap−Vert	1991	..	..	..	..	..	..	..	..	4
	1992	..	..	..	..	..	..	..	..	5
	1993	..	..	..	..	..	..	..	..	5
	1994	..	..	..	..	..	..	..	..	5
Central African Republic Rép. centrafricaine	1991	..	..	..	..	..	..	..	..	12
	1992	..	..	..	..	..	..	..	..	12
	1993	..	..	..	..	..	..	..	..	12
	1994	..	..	..	..	..	..	..	..	12
Chad Tchad	1991	..	..	..	..	..	..	..	..	11
	1992	..	..	..	..	..	..	..	..	10
	1993	..	..	..	..	..	..	..	..	11
	1994	..	..	..	..	..	..	..	..	10
Comoros Comores	1991	..	..	..	..	..	..	..	..	2
	1992	..	..	..	..	..	..	..	..	2
	1993	..	..	..	..	..	..	..	..	2
	1994	..	..	..	..	..	..	..	..	2
Congo Congo	1991	0	..	11 462	256	597	16	6	3	59
	1992	0	..	12 361	255	509	16	6	4	53
	1993	0	..	12 441	265	537	17	6	4	53
	1994	0	..	13 081	273	546	19	6	7	53
Côte d'Ivoire Côte d'Ivoire	1991	..	..	457	1 572	1 799	123	26	..	223
	1992	..	..	464	1 781	1 891	129	23	..	227
	1993	..	..	463	1 421	1 545	139	26	..	235
	1994	..	..	478	1 712	1 651	142	26	..	235

67
Production of selected energy commodities
Thousand metric tons of coal equivalent [*cont.*]
Production des principaux biens de l'énergie
Milliers de tonnes métriques d'équivalent houille [*suite*]

Country or area Pays ou zone	Year Anneé	Hard coal, lignite & peat Houille, lignite et tourbe	Briquettes & cokes Agglo− mérés et cokes	Crude petroleum & NGL Pétrole brut et GNL	Light petroleum products Produits pétroliers légers	Heavy petroleum products Produits pétroliers lourds	Other petroleum products Autres produits pétroliers	LPG & refinery gas GLP et gaz de raffinerie	Natural gas Gaz naturel	Electricity Electricité
Djibouti	1991	..	..	..	..	..	..	..	..	22
Djibouti	1992	..	..	..	..	..	..	..	..	22
	1993	..	..	..	..	..	..	..	..	22
	1994	..	..	..	..	..	..	..	..	23
Egypt	1991	..	1 201	67 597	9 590	22 544	1 537	513	10 339	5 470
Egypte	1992	..	1 152	68 510	8 998	22 223	1 559	510	11 179	5 541
	1993	..	1 401	69 201	9 708	23 500	1 614	598	12 839	5 831
	1994	..	1 476	67 033	9 762	24 699	1 673	636	14 039	5 886
Equatorial Guinea	1991	..	..	..	..	..	..	..	..	2
Guinée équatoriale	1992	..	..	..	..	..	..	..	..	2
	1993	..	..	..	..	..	..	..	..	2
	1994	..	..	..	..	..	..	..	..	2
Ethiopia	1991	..	..	..	309	742	14	10	..	227
Ethiopie	1992	..	..	..	310	744	14	11	..	230
	1993	..	..	..	313	743	14	12	..	247
	1994	..	..	..	316	753	16	11	..	233
Gabon	1991	..	..	21 316	487	753	22	11	107	112
Gabon	1992	..	..	21 951	478	743	23	11	136	113
	1993	..	..	21 522	496	732	28	12	131	113
	1994	..	..	22 601	514	741	30	12	117	115
Gambia	1991	..	..	..	..	..	..	..	..	9
Gambie	1992	..	..	..	..	..	..	..	..	9
	1993	..	..	..	..	..	..	..	..	9
	1994	..	..	..	..	..	..	..	..	9
Ghana	1991	..	..	...	561	702	110	25	..	756
Ghana	1992	..	..	...	570	711	103	26	..	756
	1993	..	..	...	582	718	77	26	..	756
	1994	..	..	...	591	724	81	28	..	758
Guinea	1991	..	..	..	..	..	..	..	..	64
Guinee	1992	..	..	..	..	..	..	..	..	65
	1993	..	..	..	..	..	..	..	..	66
	1994	..	..	..	..	..	..	..	..	65
Guinea−Bissau	1991	..	..	..	..	..	..	..	..	5
Guinée−Bissau	1992	..	..	..	..	..	..	..	..	5
	1993	..	..	..	..	..	..	..	..	5
	1994	..	..	..	..	..	..	..	..	6
Kenya	1991	..	..	..	1 113	1 703	162	40	..	725
Kenya	1992	..	..	..	1 193	1 791	215	44	..	695
	1993	..	..	..	1 121	1 707	169	42	..	717
	1994	..	..	..	1 114	1 674	158	47	..	723
Liberia	1991	..	..	..	0	0	0	0	..	55
Libéria	1992	..	..	..	0	0	0	0	..	57
	1993	..	..	..	0	0	0	0	..	59
	1994	..	..	..	0	0	0	0	..	60
Libyan Arab Jamahiriya	1991	..	..	105 256	7 006	12 770	128	264	8 707	2 076
Jamah. arabe libyenne	1992	..	..	100 742	7 058	12 756	143	280	9 014	2 082
	1993	..	..	95 745	6 815	12 738	128	311	8 468	2 088
	1994	..	..	97 911	7 100	12 883	143	357	8 508	2 186
Madagascar	1991	..	0	..	85	160	12	2	..	72
Madagascar	1992	..	0	..	89	164	12	2	..	73
	1993	..	0	..	94	170	12	2	..	74
	1994	..	0	..	95	172	12	2	..	74
Malawi	1991	..	..	..	..	..	..	..	..	94
Malawi	1992	..	..	..	..	..	..	..	..	97
	1993	..	..	..	..	..	..	..	..	98
	1994	..	..	..	..	..	..	..	..	99
Mali	1991	..	..	..	..	..	..	..	..	31
Mali	1992	..	..	..	..	..	..	..	..	33
	1993	..	..	..	..	..	..	..	..	35
	1994	..	..	..	..	..	..	..	..	35

67
Production of selected energy commodities
Thousand metric tons of coal equivalent [*cont.*]
Production des principaux biens de l'énergie
Milliers de tonnes métriques d'équivalent houille [*suite*]

Country or area Pays ou zone	Year Anneé	Hard coal, lignite & peat Houille, lignite et tourbe	Briquettes & cokes Agglo– mérés et cokes	Crude petroleum & NGL Pétrole brut et GNL	Light petroleum products Produits pétroliers légers	Heavy petroleum products Produits pétroliers lourds	Other petroleum products Autres produits pétroliers	LPG & refinery gas GLP et gaz de raffinerie	Natural gas Gaz naturel	Electricity Electricité
Mauritania	1991	..	..	..	396	649	129	50	..	18
Mauritanie	1992	..	..	..	423	719	140	59	..	18
	1993	..	..	..	432	716	139	56	..	18
	1994	..	..	..	436	720	140	59	..	18
Mauritius	1991	..	..	..	..	..	..	..	..	102
Maurice	1992	..	..	..	..	..	..	..	..	114
	1993	..	..	..	..	..	..	..	..	121
	1994	..	..	..	..	..	..	..	..	123
Morocco	1991	551	0	17	1 567	5 476	331	350	52	1 129
Maroc	1992	576	0	16	1 791	6 050	321	364	32	1 193
	1993	604	0	14	1 664	6 264	272	384	32	1 215
	1994	650	0	11	1 568	6 739	403	407	33	1 323
Mozambique	1991	42	..	..	...	...	...	...	..	60
Mozambique	1992	40	..	..	...	...	...	...	..	60
	1993	40	..	..	...	...	...	...	..	60
	1994	40	..	..	...	...	...	...	..	60
Niger	1991	172	..	..	..	..	...	..	..	21
Niger	1992	170	..	..	..	..	..	..	..	21
	1993	172	..	..	..	..	..	..	..	21
	1994	174	..	..	..	..	..	..	..	22
Nigeria	1991	138	..	135 199	8 249	8 249	...	85	5 858	1 757
Nigéria	1992	87	..	139 762	7 320	7 641	...	93	5 886	1 822
	1993	41	..	136 063	7 189	7 765	...	93	6 724	1 817
	1994	50	..	130 043	3 734	3 829	...	93	13 045	1 817
Réunion	1991	..	..	..	..	..	..	..	..	121
Réunion	1992	..	..	..	..	..	..	..	..	134
	1993	..	..	..	..	..	..	..	..	139
	1994	..	..	..	..	..	..	..	..	140
Rwanda	1991	..	..	..	..	..	..	..	0	21
Rwanda	1992	..	..	..	..	..	..	..	0	22
	1993	..	..	..	..	..	..	..	0	20
	1994	..	..	..	..	..	..	..	0	20
St.Helena and dep.	1991	0	..	..	..	..	..	..	..	1
Ste–Hélène et dép.	1992	0	..	..	..	..	..	..	..	1
	1993	0	..	..	..	..	..	..	..	1
	1994	0	..	..	..	..	..	..	..	1
Sao Tome and Principe	1991	..	..	..	..	..	..	..	..	2
Sao Tomé–et–Principe	1992	..	..	..	..	..	..	..	..	2
	1993	..	..	..	..	..	..	..	..	2
	1994	..	..	..	..	..	..	..	..	2
Senegal	1991	..	..	..	464	729	16	5	..	93
Sénégal	1992	..	..	..	473	741	16	5	..	94
	1993	..	..	..	483	745	16	5	..	94
	1994	..	..	..	494	749	17	5	..	94
Seychelles	1991	..	..	..	..	..	..	..	..	13
Seychelles	1992	..	..	..	..	..	..	..	..	14
	1993	..	..	..	..	..	..	..	..	14
	1994	..	..	..	..	..	..	..	..	15
Sierra Leone	1991	..	..	..	79	164	33	..	..	28
Sierra Leone	1992	..	..	..	81	166	33	..	..	28
	1993	..	..	..	88	168	36	..	..	29
	1994	..	..	..	88	168	36	..	..	29
Somalia	1991	..	..	..	...	...	...	...	..	32
Somalie	1992	..	..	..	...	...	...	...	..	32
	1993	..	..	..	...	...	...	...	..	32
	1994	..	..	..	...	...	...	...	..	32
S.Africa Customs Un.	1991	135 843	1 843	..	11 858	9 608	1 049	216	2 388	23 151
Un.douan.d'Afr.merid	1992	133 043	1 848	..	12 338	10 170	1 052	213	2 457	23 090
	1993	138 763	1 848	..	12 575	10 794	1 043	227	2 491	23 398
	1994	139 260	1 862	..	13 060	10 833	928	238	2 525	24 963

67
Production of selected energy commodities
Thousand metric tons of coal equivalent [*cont.*]
Production des principaux biens de l'énergie
Milliers de tonnes métriques d'équivalent houille [*suite*]

Country or area Pays ou zone	Year Anneé	Hard coal, lignite & peat Houille, lignite et tourbe	Briquettes & cokes Agglomérés et cokes	Crude petroleum & NGL Pétrole brut et GNL	Light petroleum products Produits pétroliers légers	Heavy petroleum products Produits pétroliers lourds	Other petroleum products Autres produits pétroliers	LPG & refinery gas GLP et gaz de raffinerie	Natural gas Gaz naturel	Electricity Electricité
Sudan	1991	..	..	..	339	922	140	9	..	163
Soudan	1992	..	..	..	341	917	145	9	..	163
	1993	..	..	..	351	919	148	9	..	163
	1994	..	..	..	356	922	149	9	..	164
Togo	1991	0	..	..	...	...	..	..	..	11
Togo	1992	0	..	..	...	...	..	..	..	11
	1993	0	..	..	...	...	..	..	..	11
	1994	0	..	..	...	...	..	..	..	11
Tunisia	1991	...	..	7 476	801	1 503	..	222	484	705
Tunisie	1992	11	..	7 223	818	1 306	..	247	500	759
	1993	15	..	6 693	922	1 353	..	214	453	788
	1994	9	..	6 306	924	1 362	..	218	450	795
Uganda	1991	..	..	..	..	..	..	..	..	96
Ouganda	1992	..	..	..	..	..	..	..	..	97
	1993	..	..	..	..	..	..	..	..	97
	1994	..	..	..	..	..	..	..	..	98
United Rep. Tanzania	1991	4	..	..	249	547	3	8	..	111
Rép.−Unie de Tanzanie	1992	4	..	..	255	552	3	9	..	111
	1993	4	..	..	265	556	3	9	..	111
	1994	4	..	..	269	560	3	9	..	112
Western Sahara	1991	..	..	..	..	..	..	..	..	10
Sahara occidental	1992	..	..	..	..	..	..	..	..	10
	1993	..	..	..	..	..	..	..	..	10
	1994	..	..	..	..	..	..	..	..	11
Zaire	1991	80	..	1 960	141	348	17	2	..	690
Zaïre	1992	85	..	1 853	144	354	20	2	..	788
	1993	92	..	1 828	152	342	20	2	..	723
	1994	93	..	1 921	156	348	22	2	..	681
Zambia	1991	320	32	..	279	435	35	16	..	955
Zambie	1992	333	32	..	280	438	33	16	..	956
	1993	337	31	..	282	436	29	16	..	956
	1994	320	30	..	270	439	29	16	..	956
Zimbabwe	1991	5 596	526	..	..	..	..	..	..	1 085
Zimbabwe	1992	5 548	520	..	..	..	..	..	..	1 058
	1993	5 285	469	..	..	..	..	..	..	939
	1994	5 469	486	..	..	..	..	..	..	901
America, North	1991	806 924	25 988	982 558	690 329	426 823	130 009	91 580	844 630	659 424
Amérique du Nord	1992	800 638	25 401	974 208	695 221	429 768	129 087	95 872	871 064	665 336
	1993	748 099	24 992	958 265	715 567	437 126	137 792	94 906	894 657	678 073
	1994	945 519	25 601	961 865	714 424	441 394	136 022	96 589	939 485	709 254
Antigua and Barbuda	1991	..	..	..	0	...	...	...	..	12
Antigua−et−Barbuda	1992	..	..	..	0	...	...	...	..	12
	1993	..	..	..	0	...	...	...	..	12
	1994	..	..	..	0	...	...	...	..	12
Aruba	1991	..	..	..	..	..	..	..	..	42
Aruba	1992	..	..	..	..	..	..	..	..	43
	1993	..	..	..	..	..	..	..	..	43
	1994	..	..	..	..	..	..	..	..	44
Bahamas	1991	..	..	..	0	0	..	0	..	119
Bahamas	1992	..	..	..	0	0	..	0	..	120
	1993	..	..	..	0	0	..	0	..	120
	1994	..	..	..	0	0	..	0	..	121
Barbados	1991	..	..	89	94	289	9	3	30	65
Barbade	1992	..	..	93	94	236	3	3	29	66
	1993	..	..	90	96	269	7	3	35	67
	1994	..	..	89	91	259	9	3	29	70
Belize	1991	..	..	..	..	..	..	..	..	13
Belize	1992	..	..	..	..	..	..	..	..	14
	1993	..	..	..	..	..	..	..	..	14
	1994	..	..	..	..	..	..	..	..	14

67
Production of selected energy commodities
Thousand metric tons of coal equivalent [*cont.*]
Production des principaux biens de l'énergie
Milliers de tonnes métriques d'équivalent houille [*suite*]

Country or area Pays ou zone	Year Anneé	Hard coal, lignite & peat Houille, lignite et tourbe	Briquettes & cokes Agglo–mérés et cokes	Crude petroleum & NGL Pétrole brut et GNL	Light petroleum products Produits pétroliers légers	Heavy petroleum products Produits pétroliers lourds	Other petroleum products Autres produits pétroliers	LPG & refinery gas GLP et gaz de raffinerie	Natural gas Gaz naturel	Electricity Electricité
Bermuda	1991	..	..	..	..	..	..	..	..	63
Bermudes	1992	..	..	..	..	..	..	..	..	64
	1993	..	..	..	..	..	..	..	..	64
	1994	..	..	..	..	..	..	..	..	64
British Virgin Islands	1991	..	..	..	..	..	..	..	..	6
Iles Vierges brittaniques	1992	..	..	..	..	..	..	..	..	6
	1993	..	..	..	..	..	..	..	..	6
	1994	..	..	..	..	..	..	..	..	6
Canada	1991	55 294	3 385	130 302	53 773	43 069	12 342	8 463	148 233	83 508
Canada	1992	49 183	3 468	135 595	52 929	41 024	12 303	8 932	162 645	84 017
	1993	53 598	3 418	143 947	53 661	42 661	13 356	8 518	178 600	88 352
	1994	54 509	3 442	150 688	55 034	42 984	12 461	8 469	196 772	94 888
Cayman Islands	1991	..	..	..	..	..	..	..	..	29
Iles Caïmanes	1992	..	..	..	..	..	..	..	..	29
	1993	..	..	..	..	..	..	..	..	29
	1994	..	..	..	..	..	..	..	..	29
Costa Rica	1991	..	..	..	140	365	9	3	..	468
Costa Rica	1992	..	..	..	184	553	1	5	..	509
	1993	..	..	..	155	577	14	5	..	539
	1994	..	..	..	234	548	23	6	..	964
Cuba	1991	..	17	1 068	2 296	4 695	596	248	49	1 565
Cuba	1992	..	13	1 337	2 251	4 291	583	244	49	1 367
	1993	..	13	1 393	2 176	4 294	533	239	51	1 358
	1994	..	13	1 451	2 206	4 297	526	239	52	1 349
Dominica	1991	..	..	..	..	..	..	..	..	4
Dominique	1992	..	..	..	..	..	..	..	..	4
	1993	..	..	..	..	..	..	..	..	4
	1994	..	..	..	..	..	..	..	..	4
Dominican Republic	1991	..	..	..	924	1 731	..	42	..	478
Rép. dominicaine	1992	..	..	..	909	1 883	..	39	..	686
	1993	..	..	..	812	1 900	..	47	..	722
	1994	..	..	..	857	1 674	..	54	..	759
El Salvador	1991	..	..	..	243	753	20	53	..	759
El Salvador	1992	..	..	..	294	772	26	54	..	733
	1993	..	..	..	369	847	21	59	..	792
	1994	..	..	..	453	920	21	62	..	960
Greenland	1991	0	..	..	..	..	..	..	..	26
Groenland	1992	0	..	..	..	..	..	..	..	27
	1993	...	..	..	..	..	..	..	..	31
	1994	...	..	..	..	..	..	..	..	31
Grenada	1991	..	..	..	..	..	..	..	..	7
Grenade	1992	..	..	..	..	..	..	..	..	8
	1993	..	..	..	..	..	..	..	..	8
	1994	..	..	..	..	..	..	..	..	9
Guadeloupe	1991	..	..	..	..	..	..	..	..	101
Guadeloupe	1992	..	..	..	..	..	..	..	..	111
	1993	..	..	..	..	..	..	..	..	118
	1994	..	..	..	..	..	..	..	..	123
Guatemala	1991	..	..	289	206	696	..	8	11	306
Guatemala	1992	..	..	437	236	804	..	12	12	344
	1993	..	..	503	236	747	..	16	12	380
	1994	..	..	521	248	819	..	20	13	388
Haiti	1991	..	..	..	..	..	..	..	..	58
Haïti	1992	..	..	..	..	..	..	..	..	53
	1993	..	..	..	..	..	..	..	..	48
	1994	..	..	..	..	..	..	..	..	44
Honduras	1991	..	..	..	148	405	..	8	..	285
Honduras	1992	..	..	..	145	359	..	6	..	284
	1993	..	..	..	...	...	..	...	..	303
	1994	..	..	..	...	...	..	...	..	326

67
Production of selected energy commodities
Thousand metric tons of coal equivalent [*cont.*]
Production des principaux biens de l'énergie
Milliers de tonnes métriques d'équivalent houille [*suite*]

Country or area Pays ou zone	Year Anneé	Hard coal, lignite & peat Houille, lignite et tourbe	Briquettes & cokes Agglo-mérés et cokes	Crude petroleum & NGL Pétrole brut et GNL	Light petroleum products Produits pétroliers légers	Heavy petroleum products Produits pétroliers lourds	Other petroleum products Autres produits pétroliers	LPG & refinery gas GLP et gaz de raffinerie	Natural gas Gaz naturel	Electricity Electricité
Jamaica	1991	..	..	..	344	882	33	32	..	261
Jamaïque	1992	..	..	..	451	1 245	29	44	..	270
	1993	..	..	..	319	712	26	28	..	466
	1994	..	..	..	351	805	26	37	..	482
Martinique	1991	..	..	..	370	607	..	26		91
Martinique	1992	..	..	..	391	620	..	26		97
	1993	..	..	..	385	628	..	28		105
	1994	..	..	..	402	611	..	31		111
Mexico	1991	4 983	2 139	223 328	33 210	52 714	3 114	4 222	32 350	22 629
Mexique	1992	4 724	2 014	223 834	31 902	58 118	3 065	3 805	39 180	23 361
	1993	4 648	1 850	223 409	32 836	58 354	3 087	4 680	38 343	23 834
	1994	6 215	1 891	224 864	38 679	58 313	3 097	5 055	39 833	25 352
Montserrat	1991	..	..	..	..	..	..	..	..	2
Montserrat	1992	..	..	..	..	..	..	..	..	2
	1993	..	..	..	..	..	..	..	..	2
	1994	..	..	..	..	..	..	..	..	2
Netherlands Antilles	1991	..	..	..	3703	9 272	2 815	70		98
Antilles néerlandaises	1992			..	3 784	9 700	3 182	78		105
	1993			..	3 920	10 154	3 447	90		108
	1994			..	3 969	10 286	3 415	95		108
Nicaragua	1991	..		..	206	638	17	38	..	686
Nicaragua	1992	..		..	208	661	33	52	..	711
	1993			..	212	614	36	45	..	775
	1994			..	206	537	36	41	..	789
Panama	1991	..		..	309	1 234	6	46	..	357
Panama	1992	..		..	415	2 065	19	70	..	370
	1993	..		..	402	1 985	23	69	..	404
	1994	..		..	431	1 637	14	64	..	430
Puerto Rico	1991	..		..	4 823	4 060	2 526	140	..	1 932
Porto Rico	1992	..		..	4 408	3 920	2 279	109	..	2 019
	1993	..		..	4 830	3 999	2 315	171	..	2 032
	1994	..		..	5 481	4 285	2 242	140	..	2 196
Saint Kitts and Nevis	1991	..	..	..	..	..	..	..	..	10
Saint−Kitts−et−Nevis	1992	..	..	..	..	..	..	..	..	10
	1993	..	..	..	..	..	..	..	..	11
	1994	..	..	..	..	..	..	..	..	11
Saint Lucia	1991	..	..	..	..	..	..	..	..	13
Sainte−Lucie	1992	..	..	..	..	..	..	..	..	13
	1993	..	..	..	..	..	..	..	..	13
	1994	..	..	..	..	..	..	..	..	14
St.Pierre and Miquelon	1991	..	..	..	..	..	..	..	..	6
St.−Pierre−et−Miquelon	1992	..	..	..	..	..	..	..	..	6
	1993	..	..	..	..	..	..	..	..	5
	1994	..	..	..	..	..	..	..	..	5
St. Vincent and Grenadines	1991	..	..	..	..	..	..	..	..	7
St.−Vincent−et−Grenad.	1992	..	..	..	..	..	..	..	..	7
	1993	..	..	..	..	..	..	..	..	8
	1994	..	..	..	..	..	..	..	..	8
Trinidad and Tobago	1991	..	..	10 645	1 880	5 782	99	368	7 979	457
Trinité−et−Tobago	1992		..	10 027	1 704	6 083	50	370	7 906	488
	1993		..	9 151	1 881	5 482	47	283	6 901	469
	1994		..	9 684	2 209	4 744	242	289	7 921	489
Turks and Caicos Islands	1991	..	..	..	..	..	..	..	..	1
Iles Turques et Caïques	1992	..	..	..	..	..	..	..	..	1
	1993	..	..	..	..	..	..	..	..	1
	1994	..	..	..	..	..	..	..	..	1
United States	1991	746 646	20 446	616 837	581 722	289 758	101 678	77 453	655 977	544 839
Etats−Unis	1992	746 731	19 905	602 886	589 583	288 109	101 517	81 729	661 243	549 258
	1993	689 852	19 711	579 773	607 840	294 462	106 221	80 314	670 715	556 706
	1994	884 795	20 255	574 568	597 856	299 063	107 613	81 595	694 864	578 921

67

Production of selected energy commodities
Thousand metric tons of coal equivalent [*cont.*]
Production des principaux biens de l'énergie
Milliers de tonnes métriques d'équivalent houille [*suite*]

Country or area Pays ou zone	Year Anneé	Hard coal, lignite & peat Houille, lignite et tourbe	Briquettes & cokes Agglo— mérés et cokes	Crude petroleum & NGL Pétrole brut et GNL	Light petroleum products Produits pétroliers légers	Heavy petroleum products Produits pétroliers lourds	Other petroleum products Autres produits pétroliers	LPG & refinery gas GLP et gaz de raffinerie	Natural gas Gaz naturel	Electricity Electricité
U.S. Virgin Islands	1991	..	..	..	5 937	9 870	6 747	357	..	123
Iles Vierges américaines	1992	..	..	..	5 334	9 325	5 997	295	..	125
	1993	..	..	..	5 435	9 441	6 147	311	..	128
	1994	..	..	..	5 717	9 613	6 297	388	..	130
America, South	**1991**	**30 680**	**8 719**	**331 722**	**78 908**	**137 511**	**10 671**	**14 201**	**81 270**	**59 750**
Amérique du Sud	**1992**	**28 029**	**8 785**	**341 430**	**81 336**	**131 779**	**11 618**	**15 489**	**81 219**	**61 600**
	1993	**28 811**	**9 048**	**360 134**	**87 371**	**130 866**	**11 356**	**16 240**	**84 373**	**65 866**
	1994	**30 764**	**8 980**	**383 158**	**89 754**	**133 901**	**11 867**	**17 436**	**90 923**	**68 502**
Argentina	1991	246	706	37816	11 094	17 676	2 264	1 967	30 220	8 571
Argentine	1992	181	630	42 520	11 475	18 403	2 817	2 155	30 680	8 673
	1993	141	494	44 951	11 598	18 152	2 878	2 234	31 556	9 608
	1994	293	638	50 010	12 059	16 641	2 722	2 437	34 000	10 193
Bolivia	1991	..	..	1 861	749	549	26	79	3 408	279
Bolivie	1992	..	..	1 872	699	521	32	71	3 681	296
	1993	..	..	1 779	721	503	25	72	3 651	300
	1994	..	..	2 038	742	532	27	75	4 354	353
Brazil	1991	3 293	7 277	45 629	24 796	46 068	4 579	7 953	5 026	29 147
Brésil	1992	3 003	7 344	46 312	25 266	47 532	5 114	8 546	5 413	30 131
	1993	2 917	7 653	47 288	27 829	45 989	4 265	9 137	5 907	31 475
	1994	3 297	7 491	49 128	28 168	49 871	5 002	9 923	6 123	32 035
Chile	1991	2 607	433	1 677	3 068	5 014	137	534	2 092	2 452
Chili	1992	1 938	445	1 509	3 175	5 172	172	622	2 381	2 747
	1993	1 610	467	1 496	3 569	5 430	202	663	2 291	2 949
	1994	1 407	465	1 538	3 715	5 820	181	651	2 485	3 102
Colombia	1991	21 914	302	30 844	6 796	9 102	280	1 210	5 414	4 503
Colombie	1992	20 336	366	31 973	6 939	8 610	338	1 569	5 085	4 421
	1993	20 162	433	33 145	8 904	9 801	414	1 571	5 093	4 950
	1994	20 918	385	32 995	8 254	8 315	395	1 791	6 034	5 340
Ecuador	1991	..	..	21 638	2 521	5 972	182	294	395	856
Equateur	1992	..	..	25 946	2 466	5 890	172	340	382	880
	1993	..	..	28 724	2 427	6 042	206	396	380	915
	1994	..	..	25 076	2 342	6 469	236	393	337	1 003
Falkland Is. (Malvinas)	1991	5	..	..	..	..	..	..	..	1
Iles Falkland (Malvinas)	1992	5	..	..	..	..	..	..	..	1
	1993	5	..	..	..	..	..	..	..	1
	1994	5	..	..	..	..	..	..	..	1
French Guiana	1991	..	..	..	..	..	..	..	..	50
Guyane francaise	1992	..	..	..	..	..	..	..	..	55
	1993	..	..	..	..	..	..	..	..	55
	1994	..	..	..	..	..	..	..	..	55
Guyana	1991	..	..	..	..	..	..	..	..	31
Guyana	1992	..	..	..	..	..	..	..	..	29
	1993	..	..	..	..	..	..	..	..	29
	1994	..	..	..	..	..	..	..	..	30
Paraguay	1991	..	..	..	143	265	...	14	..	3 611
Paraguay	1992	..	..	..	124	328	...	3	..	3 334
	1993	..	..	..	154	257	...	3	..	3 864
	1994	..	..	..	145	276	...	6	..	4 405
Peru	1991	59	...	8 262	3 330	7 308	102	303	691	1 780
Pérou	1992	88	...	8 318	3 432	7 117	70	310	931	1 615
	1993	88	...	9 004	3 517	7 579	82	312	320	1 760
	1994	107	...	9 136	3 385	6 749	80	301	226	1 863
Suriname	1991	...	..	380	..	..	..	..	..	208
Suriname	1992	...	..	384	..	..	..	..	..	210
	1993	...	..	387	..	..	..	..	..	212
	1994	0	..	389	..	..	..	..	..	207
Uruguay	1991	..	0	..	521	1 055	103	87	..	862
Uruguay	1992	..	0	..	430	1 046	106	85	..	1 093
	1993	..	1	..	114	374	39	31	..	980
	1994	..	1	..	0	0	0	0	..	936

67
Production of selected energy commodities
Thousand metric tons of coal equivalent [*cont.*]
Production des principaux biens de l'énergie
Milliers de tonnes métriques d'équivalent houille [*suite*]

Country or area Pays ou zone	Year Anneé	Hard coal, lignite & peat Houille, lignite et tourbe	Briquettes & cokes Agglo— mérés et cokes	Crude petroleum & NGL Pétrole brut et GNL	Light petroleum products Produits pétroliers légers	Heavy petroleum products Produits pétroliers lourds	Other petroleum products Autres produits pétroliers	LPG & refinery gas GLP et gaz de raffinerie	Natural gas Gaz naturel	Electricity Electricité
Venezuela	1991	2 556	0	183 615	25 889	44 502	2 999	1 761	34 024	7 399
Venezuela	1992	2 479	0	182 596	27 328	37 159	2 797	1 786	32 668	8 116
	1993	3 889	0	193 361	28 536	36 739	3 246	1 821	35 174	8 769
	1994	4 738	0	212 848	30 944	39 227	3 223	1 857	37 365	8 981
Asia	**1991**	**1 117 517**	**152 517**	**1 657 646**	**343 747**	**644 856**	**54 829**	**51 224**	**314 831**	**423 834**
Asie	**1992**	**1 262 102**	**155 802**	**1 825 123**	**390 804**	**738 012**	**59 229**	**57 900**	**463 384**	**473 265**
	1993	**1 292 608**	**164 853**	**1 871 548**	**414 454**	**765 893**	**61 945**	**60 816**	**487 891**	**503 960**
	1994	**1 357 630**	**167 731**	**1 926 956**	**429 632**	**789 450**	**64 688**	**65 001**	**513 966**	**539 884**
Afghanistan	1991	94	35	5	..	..	..	..	270	125
Afghanistan	1992	8	0	0	..	..	..	..	252	86
	1993	7	0	0	..	..	..	..	243	85
	1994	6	0	0	..	..	..	..	233	84
Armenia	1992	..	..	..	..	..	..	..	6	1 106
Arménie	1993	..	..	..	..	..	..	..	...	773
	1994	..	..	..	..	..	..	..	...	695
Azerbaijan	1992	..	..	15 877	3 200	6 089	681	107	9 118	2 428
Azerbaidjan	1993	..	..	15 204	3 101	7 227	493	98	7 883	2 346
	1994	..	..	14 052	3 039	5 875	475	96	7 389	2 162
Bahrain	1991	..	..	3 665	7 310	10 656	678	47	6 893	429
Bahreïn	1992	..	..	3 650	7 616	11 279	660	39	6 893	431
	1993	..	..	3 612	6 713	9 935	481	36	8 677	532
	1994	..	..	3 574	6 595	10 363	549	37	8 498	559
Bangladesh	1991	..	..	177	667	673	24	12	6 282	1 097
Bangladesh	1992	..	..	182	633	593	33	12	6 664	1 174
	1993	..	..	185	831	719	32	14	7 208	1 212
	1994	..	..	161	617	371	49	20	7 956	1 302
Bhutan	1991	2	..	..	..	..	..	..	..	194
Bhoutan	1992	2	..	..	..	..	..	..	..	200
	1993	2	..	..	..	..	..	..	..	200
	1994	2	..	..	..	..	..	..	..	207
Brunei Darussalam	1991	..	..	10 996	346	226	..	3	13 422	153
Brunéi Darussalam	1992	..	..	12 057	356	256	..	3	13 343	154
	1993	..	..	11 924	377	264	..	5	13 188	158
	1994	..	..	12 190	410	255	..	5	13 567	162
Cambodia	1991	..	..	..	0	0	..	..	..	20
Cambodge	1992	..	..	..	0	0	..	..	..	21
	1993	..	..	..	0	0	..	..	..	22
	1994	..	..	..	0	0	..	..	..	23
China	1991	775 942	71 311	201 383	42 163	87 308	8 268	9 184	21 347	83 227
Chine	1992	796 609	77 444	202 962	46 838	91 746	8 930	10 104	20 975	92 796
	1993	820 425	90 382	207 447	53 035	97 107	9 504	10 629	22 545	103 736
	1994	884 759	94 873	208 654	48 956	93 627	9 774	12 895	23 353	117 493
Cyprus	1991	..	..	..	239	756	40	70	..	255
Chypre	1992	..	..	..	208	739	34	68	..	295
	1993	..	..	..	206	810	48	66	..	317
	1994	..	..	..	255	917	50	83	..	329
Georgia	1992	167	..	143	..	..	..	..	14	1 415
Géorgie	1993	100	..	143	..	..	..	..	14	1 247
	1994	28	..	106	..	..	..	..	12	836
Hong Kong	1991	..	..	..	..	..	..	..	..	3 917
Hong—kong	1992	..	..	..	..	..	..	..	..	4 309
	1993	..	..	..	..	..	..	..	..	4 416
	1994	..	..	..	..	..	..	..	..	3 285
India	1991	193 004	9 582	45 738	22 048	38 344	7 479	3 736	14 956	40 144
Inde	1992	199 137	9 610	41 578	22 330	40 501	7 727	3 885	15 551	42 541
	1993	209 524	9 700	39 521	22 958	41 252	7 052	4 166	15 696	45 113
	1994	217 339	9 886	45 703	24 986	42 492	7 410	4 264	22 665	48 613
Indonesia	1991	13 715	0	147004	19 354	31 974	1 945	8 339	64 781	7 536
Indonésie	1992	21 147	0	142 890	19 605	33 243	2 050	11 811	67 871	7 880
	1993	27 584	0	143 592	19 555	33 994	2 086	12 019	70 355	8 433
	1994	28 549	0	144 619	20 683	34 716	2 129	12 096	79 263	8 774

67
Production of selected energy commodities
Thousand metric tons of coal equivalent [cont.]
Production des principaux biens de l'énergie
Milliers de tonnes métriques d'équivalent houille [suite]

Country or area Pays ou zone	Year Anneé	Hard coal, lignite & peat Houille, lignite et tourbe	Briquettes & cokes Agglo-mérés et cokes	Crude petroleum & NGL Pétrole brut et GNL	Light petroleum products Produits pétroliers légers	Heavy petroleum products Produits pétroliers lourds	Other petroleum products Autres produits pétroliers	LPG & refinery gas GLP et gaz de raffinerie	Natural gas Gaz naturel	Electricity Electricité
Iran, Islamic Republic of	1991	986	192	248 507	16 503	36 124	4 446	1 554	34 286	7 877
Iran, Rép. islamique d'	1992	971	21	250 092	17 205	38 677	4 433	1 709	33 285	8 429
	1993	970	33	249 407	18 587	40 839	4 719	2 020	24 816	9 337
	1994	980	36	261 857	18 596	40 846	4 577	2 331	53 790	9 720
Iraq	1991	..	..	19 677	5 047	13 605	766	264	2 449	2 556
Iraq	1992	..	..	36 911	7 717	22 102	962	622	3 022	3 108
	1993	..	..	46 882	8 156	22 434	991	932	3 395	3 231
	1994	..	..	53 142	8 495	22 720	1 034	932	4 221	3 324
Israel	1991	..	..	16	3 596	7 491	272	336	31	2 643
Israël	1992	..	..	13	4 558	8 682	379	451	28	3 032
	1993	..	..	11	5 954	9 348	405	595	28	3 194
	1994	..	..	6	6 229	9 260	379	645	29	3 478
Japan	1991	7 084	42 272	1 073	100 142	137 033	14 677	17 651	2 988	164 125
Japon	1992	6 685	40 281	1 192	107 039	143 917	14 989	18 433	3 022	167 459
	1993	5 989	38 731	1 082	112 111	146 176	15 505	18 607	3 085	175 318
	1994	5 753	37 960	1 033	115 416	155 277	16 126	19 089	3 182	187 653
Jordan	1991	..	..	10	1 139	1 875	211	227	..	457
Jordanie	1992			4	1 379	2 368	207	263	..	543
	1993	..	..	0	1 350	2 638	230	271	..	585
	1994	..	..	3	1 356	2 521	228	281	..	623
Kazakstan	1992	107 866	2 849	38 240	7 985	14 870	..	..	9 398	10 274
Kazakstan	1993	95 861	2 245	32 799	5 889	13 454	..	..	7 744	9 678
	1994	89 692	1 800	31 869	3 995	11 319	..	..	4 691	8 297
Korea, Dem. People's Rep.	1991	83 800	3 240	..	1 809	2 408	..	..	..	6 572
Corée, Rép. pop. dém. de	1992	85 400	3 240	..	1 809	2 408	..	..	..	4 668
	1993	88 200	3 240	..	1 787	2 393	..	..	..	4 668
	1994	87 400	3 195	..	1 765	2 379	..	..	..	4 545
Korea, Republic of	1991	9 678	18 806	..	20 163	57 220	2 494	1 700	..	30 245
Corée, Rép. de	1992	7 693	15 540	..	26 563	68 967	3 214	1 956	..	32 217
	1993	6 069	13 809	..	28 536	74 139	3 244	1 865	..	34 534
	1994	4 781	13 186	..	31 889	75 907	3 579	1 963	..	37 431
Kuwait, part Neutral Zone	1991	..	..	13 220	1 670	2 990	30	36	2 559	1 336
Koweït et prt. Zone Neut.	1992	..	..	78 058	5 749	17 348	43	43	3 488	2 099
	1993	..	..	139 139	9 437	19 331	360	357	8 281	2 236
	1994	..	..	148 661	14 844	32 715	529	512	7 948	2 844
Kyrgyzstan	1992	1 297	..	163	..	..	..	..	83	1 472
Kirghizistan	1993	995	..	126	..	..	..	..	49	1 385
	1994	461	..	126	..	..	..	..	45	1 589
Lao People's Dem. Rep.	1991	1	..	..	..	..	..	..	..	114
Rép. dém. populaire Lao	1992	1	..	..	..	..	..	..	..	112
	1993	1	..	..	..	..	..	..	..	111
	1994	1	..	..	..	..	..	..	..	111
Lebanon	1991	..	...	..	148	594	..	6	..	295
Liban	1992	..	...	..	100	354	..	3	..	479
	1993	..	0	..	...	...	..	...	..	597
	1994	..	...	..	...	...	..	...	..	633
Macau	1991	..	..	..	..	..	..	..	..	109
Macao	1992	..	..	..	..	..	..	..	..	122
	1993	..	..	..	..	..	..	..	..	146
	1994	..	..	..	..	..	..	..	..	157
Malaysia	1991	180	..	44 450	4 151	9 168	384	553	21 039	3 481
Malaisie	1992	80	..	45 735	4 263	8 743	404	489	22 896	3 917
	1993	397	..	45 923	4 671	9 404	424	499	29 429	4 370
	1994	174	..	45 428	5 253	10 504	454	513	32 502	4 910
Maldives	1991	..	..	..	..	..	..	..	..	3
Maldives	1992	..	..	..	..	..	..	..	..	4
	1993	..	..	..	..	..	..	..	..	5
	1994	..	..	..	..	..	..	..	..	6
Mongolia	1991	3 018	..	..	...	..	..	..	..	418
Mongolie	1992	2 912	..	..	...	...	..	..	..	405
	1993	2 869	..	..	...	...	..	..	..	393
	1994	2 928	..	..	...	...	..	..	..	401

67
Production of selected energy commodities
Thousand metric tons of coal equivalent [*cont.*]
Production des principaux biens de l'énergie
Milliers de tonnes métriques d'équivalent houille [*suite*]

Country or area Pays ou zone	Year Anneé	Hard coal, lignite & peat Houille, lignite et tourbe	Briquettes & cokes Agglo- mérés et cokes	Crude petroleum & NGL Pétrole brut et GNL	Light petroleum products Produits pétroliers légers	Heavy petroleum products Produits pétroliers lourds	Other petroleum products Autres produits pétroliers	LPG & refinery gas GLP et gaz de raffinerie	Natural gas Gaz naturel	Electricity Electricité
Myanmar	1991	51	..	1 024	261	700	68	5	1 192	329
Myanmar	1992	49	..	1 048	284	672	58	6	1 173	368
	1993	47	..	983	309	678	63	5	1 449	416
	1994	51		993	359	723	75	3	1 809	430
Nepal	1991	..		..	..	..	..	..	..	110
Nepal	1992	..	..	..	..	..	..	..	..	114
	1993	..	..	..	..	..	..	..	..	108
	1994			..	..	..	..	..	..	112
Oman	1991	..	..	50 380	1 186	3 501	22	67	3 630	681
Oman	1992	..		52 810	954	3 135	23	61	4 486	766
	1993	..		55 407	795	2 580	40	48	5 431	896
	1994	..		57 770	1 089	4 058	36	53	8 875	965
Pakistan	1991	2 063	652	4 669	3 230	5 466	577	70	16 635	5 910
Pakistan	1992	2 450	663	4 448	3 248	5 344	571	70	17 697	6 463
	1993	2 207	644	4 323	3 292	4 934	696	56	18 693	6 927
	1994	2 387	688	4 033	3 215	5 213	627	62	19 794	7 143
Philippines	1991	853	..	236	4 107	10 006	289	371	..	9 504
Philippines	1992	1 122	..	597	4 644	10 597	153	388	..	9 468
	1993	1 132	..	714	4 956	11 177	163	404	..	9 557
	1994	1 169	..	428	5 172	11 621	170	427	..	9 668
Qatar	1991	..	..	28 328	1 152	2 353	..	93	9 972	574
Qatar	1992	..	..	33 041	1 193	2 639	..	78	15 297	637
	1993	..	..	30 548	1 138	2 185	..	115	17 974	683
	1994	..	..	29 767	1 449	2 417	..	135	17 974	719
Saudi Arabia, pt. Neutral Zone	1991	..	..	609 051	31 998	64 149	2 045	1 414	44 118	6 298
Arabie saoudie,p.Zone nuet.	1992	..	..	627 244	33 854	68 659	2 289	1 507	45 810	6 832
	1993	..	..	605 210	34 355	70 181	2 460	1 476	47 797	7 779
	1994	..	..	605 872	36 028	67 566	2 961	1 399	50 195	8 200
Singapore	1991	..	..	..	26 090	39 680	1 828	738	..	2 039
Singapour	1992	..	..	..	26 562	41 608	2 092	761	..	2 155
	1993	..	..	..	27 794	44 619	2 171	808	..	2 329
	1994		..	..	29 516	47 630	2 442	870	..	2 540
Sri Lanka	1991	..	..	..	689	1 561	80	83	..	415
Sri Lanka	1992	..	..	..	577	1 242	67	69	..	436
	1993	..	..	..	850	1 655	93	88	..	489
	1994	..	..	..	816	1 883	100	90	..	539
Syrian Arab Republic	1991	..	..	35 260	3 141	13 382	485	236	2 536	1 496
Rép. arabe syrienne	1992	..	..	37 227	3 021	12 782	510	255	2 623	1 543
	1993	..	..	38 679	3 029	12 801	395	253	2 597	1 552
	1994	..	..	41 931	3 065	13 049	436	264	2 730	1 818
Tajikistan	1992	167	10	89	84	..	..	..	83	2 066
Tadjikistan	1993	167	4	60	59	..	..	..	57	2 179
	1994	117	2	46	...	..	..	..	39	2 088
Thailand	1991	5 477	..	4 670	5 783	10 939	300	322	9 580	6 448
Thaïlande	1992	5 740	..	5 262	6 365	13 327	398	502	10 269	7 334
	1993	5 806	..	5 403	7 259	15 412	432	640	11 578	8 146
	1994	6 382	..	5 409	8 612	18 449	448	720	12 093	9 146
Turkey	1991	16 882	3 388	6 233	7 283	21 885	1 754	1 653	265	7 501
Turquie	1992	15 626	3 265	6 108	7 894	22 161	1 697	1 751	233	8 349
	1993	16 531	3 103	5 559	8 597	23 689	2 833	1 935	235	9 152
	1994	17 287	2 984	5 279	9 092	22 966	2 007	1 993	234	9 708
Turkmenistan	1992	..	..	8 271	1 396	5 176	..	..	69 620	1 619
Turkmenistan	1993	..	..	7 722	1 090	3 776	..	..	75 698	1 552
	1994	..	..	5 856	900	3 105	..	..	41 130	1 289
United Arab Emirates	1991	..	..	162 506	5 034	8 094	29	398	34 364	2 115
Emirats arabes unis	1992	..	..	154 691	5 165	8 101	58	404	29 517	2 145
	1993	..	..	148 288	5 461	8 236	86	466	30 529	2 159
	1994	..	..	156 791	5 763	9 023	86	622	33 830	2 318
Uzbekistan	1992	1 883	..	4 879	2 232	4 884	636	..	49 582	6 254
Ouzbekistan	1993	1 534	..	5 808	2 418	6 003	672	..	52 167	6 037
	1994	1 531	..	8 083	2 445	6 096	685	..	54 757	5 872

67
Production of selected energy commodities
Thousand metric tons of coal equivalent [*cont.*]
Production des principaux biens de l'énergie
Milliers de tonnes métriques d'équivalent houille [*suite*]

Country or area Pays ou zone	Year Anneé	Hard coal, lignite & peat Houille, lignite et tourbe	Briquettes & cokes Agglomérés et cokes	Crude petroleum & NGL Pétrole brut et GNL	Light petroleum products Produits pétroliers légers	Heavy petroleum products Produits pétroliers lourds	Other petroleum products Autres produits pétroliers	LPG & refinery gas GLP et gaz de raffinerie	Natural gas Gaz naturel	Electricity Electricité
Viet Nam	1991	4 329	..	5 650	16	39	1	..	3	1 142
Viet Nam	1992	4 792	..	7 842	16	39	1	..	3	1 204
	1993	5 899	..	9 016	16	39	1	..	3	1 996
	1994	5 600	..	10 141	16	39	1	..	3	2 161
Yemen	1991	..	..	13 548	1 735	3 625	61	78	..	215
Yémen	1992	..	..	11 714	2 148	4 305	68	78	..	222
	1993	..	..	16 735	2 327	4 717	88	93	..	240
	1994	..	..	23 277	1 345	3 008	76	93	..	241
Europe	1991	487 561	105 375	319 480	330 231	524 437	75 683	54 687	308 734	555 112
Europe	1992	814 057	138 435	922 991	440 203	811 535	121 370	79 073	1 036 177	785 849
	1993	744 997	120 970	874 077	428 905	783 851	111 120	72 622	1 041 301	774 268
	1994	677 309	111 019	883 089	427 481	730 057	113 888	72 405	1 029 018	771 882
Albania	1991	544	220	1 207	189	527	41	..	172	461
Albanie	1992	183	45	836	128	348	20	..	124	412
	1993	108	25	811	112	363	31	..	119	428
	1994	85	1	764	101	277	50	..	102	479
Austria	1991	774	1 482	1 896	4 175	6 469	1 255	611	1 730	6 324
Autriche	1992	659	1 414	1 747	4 288	7 284	1 546	512	1 881	6 287
	1993	629	1 363	1 711	4 076	7 603	1 541	457	1 949	6 470
	1994	517	1 393	1 644	4 379	7 368	1 605	545	1 769	6 554
Belarus	1992	1 359	..	2 857	5 285	19 276	1 619	407	346	4 618
Bélarus	1993	950	..	2 864	3 913	13 708	1 071	340	345	4 099
	1994	1 132		2 857	3 792	11 453	849	276	349	3 857
Belgium	1991	1 113	4 893	..	13 393	26 234	6 096	1 481	13	19 495
Belgique	1992	564	4 584	..	13 504	25 187	6 926	1 236	8	19 682
	1993	332	4 000	..	12 440	24 869	6 864	1 270	6	19 005
	1994	290	3 755	..	12 978	24 202	7 370	1 732	1	18 975
Bosnia Herzegovina	1992	416	..	..	..	..	..	..	..	614
Bosnie–Herzégovine	1993	312	..	..	..	..	..	..	..	430
	1994	539	..	..	..	..	..	..	..	236
Bulgaria	1991	7 006	1 470	83	910	3 992	264	397	12	8 059
Bulgarie	1992	7 555	1 603	76	727	1 867	198	241	43	7 247
	1993	7 250	1 805	61	2 621	5 331	221	353	78	8 142
	1994	7 115	1 655	51	2 882	6 226	188	373	65	8 497
Croatia	1992	120	366	2 985	1 430	3 610	320	368	2 092	1 092
Croatie	1993	109	380	3 083	1 965	4 228	496	533	2 370	1 150
	1994	99	249	2 632	2 124	3 941	602	488	2 079	1 016
former Czechoslovakia † anciene Tchécoslovaquie †	1991	50 645	8 700	200	2 705	9 557	3 265	482	642	16 152
Czech Republic	1992	41 673	5 741	117	1 962	4 696	2 381	126	200	10 329
République tchéque	1993	40 757	5 365	159	1 784	4 351	2 449	119	269	10 373
	1994	37 177	5 187	183	1 697	4 556	2 168	117	273	10 438
Denmark	1991	0	0	10 130	2 871	8 340	29	565	5 156	4 463
Danemark	1992	0	0	11 078	2 752	8 900	29	609	5 359	3 789
	1993	0	0	11 805	2 751	9 039	0	631	5 983	4 144
	1994	0	0	13 024	2 969	9 194	0	663	6 527	5 048
Estonia	1992	5 226	27	..	..	387	..	..	..	1 453
Estonie	1993	4 119	29	..	..	252	..	..	..	1 120
	1994	4 075	33	..	..	212	..	..	..	1 124
Faeroe Islands	1991	...	...	..	..	..	..	..	..	25
Iles Féroe	1992	...	...	..	..	..	..	..	..	25
	1993	0	0	..	..	..	..	..	..	24
	1994	0	0	..	..	..	..	..	..	24
Finland	1991	1 950	424	..	6 044	7 916	564	1 125	..	11 974
Finlande	1992	1 857	448	..	6 308	7 476	560	1 201	..	11 880
	1993	1 119	639	..	6 080	7 164	406	1 170	..	12 460
	1994	3 043	684	..	7 583	7 801	879	1 293	..	12 882
France incl. Monaco	1991	10 687	7 799	4 907	39 679	61 523	11 296	7 327	3 169	138 179
France y compris Monaco	1992	9 767	7 559	4 783	38 818	60 139	10 769	7 233	3 052	151 991
	1993	8 982	6 836	4 629	39 299	63 548	10 326	7 439	3 212	149 466
	1994	7 817	6 106	4 664	39 777	59 218	10 901	7 233	3 221	147 938

67
Production of selected energy commodities
Thousand metric tons of coal equivalent [*cont.*]
Production des principaux biens de l'énergie
Milliers de tonnes métriques d'équivalent houille [*suite*]

Country or area Pays ou zone	Year Anneé	Hard coal, lignite & peat Houille, lignite et tourbe	Briquettes & cokes Agglomérés et cokes	Crude petroleum & NGL Pétrole brut et GNL	Light petroleum products Produits pétroliers légers	Heavy petroleum products Produits pétroliers lourds	Other petroleum products Autres produits pétroliers	LPG & refinery gas GLP et gaz de raffinerie	Natural gas Gaz naturel	Electricity Electricité
Germany † Allemagne †	1991	151 742	41 928	4 863	51 500	77 887	14 417	8 688	21 480	102 917
	1992	140 006	26 955	4 684	52 937	86 068	14 772	9 426	21 255	105 468
	1993	125 474	22 300	4 376	56 910	88 894	13 603	10 142	21 352	102 741
	1994	115 708	19 157	4 196	58 384	90 597	14 539	11 094	21 664	102 483
Gibraltar Gibraltar	1991	..	...	..	..	..	..	..	..	10
	1992	..	...	..	..	..	..	..	..	11
	1993	..	...	..	..	..	..	..	..	11
	1994	..	0	..	..	..	..	..	..	11
Greece Grèce	1991	9 854	64	1 199	7 221	12 379	1 086	1 226	214	4 399
	1992	9 783	32	985	8 179	12 972	865	1 205	197	4 595
	1993	10 744	21	806	7 286	10 983	1 023	1 215	146	4 716
	1994	10 594	20	762	8 514	12 914	879	1 336	73	4 990
Hungary Hongrie	1991	6 013	2 141	3 522	3 771	6 052	955	440	5 499	7 096
	1992	5 567	662	3 116	3 692	6 243	719	409	5 163	7 356
	1993	4 533	443	2 959	3 625	6 895	835	433	5 558	7 458
	1994	4 396	353	2 836	3 842	5 943	1 115	387	5 365	7 607
Iceland Islande	1991	..	..	..	..	..	..	..	..	864
	1992	..	..	..	..	..	..	..	..	812
	1993	..	..	..	..	..	..	..	..	865
	1994	..	..	..	..	..	..	..	..	874
Ireland Irlande	1991	1 572	0	..	569	1 906	9	98	3 042	1 861
	1992	1 635	0	..	603	2 120	6	119	3 014	1 967
	1993	1 621	0	..	599	2 033	0	106	3 423	2 016
	1994	1 704	0	..	794	2 378	14	112	3 482	2 101
Italy and San Marino Italie y comp. Saint−Marin	1991	356	6 057	6 190	38 992	78 953	7 054	7 022	23 763	30 786
	1992	362	5 413	6 431	41 952	80 737	7 677	6 654	23 387	31 608
	1993	362	4 929	6 630	41 708	78 950	7 535	7 761	24 891	31 413
	1994	88	5 291	6 994	42 722	75 798	8 161	8 022	26 263	32 242
Latvia Lettonie	1992	133	..	..	..	..	..	..	..	471
	1993	109	..	..	..	..	..	..	..	482
	1994	207	..	..	..	..	..	..	..	545
Lithuania Lituanie	1992	35	..	91	1 493	3 387	397	191	..	5 938
	1993	17	..	104	2 241	4 754	299	249	..	4 783
	1994	30	..	133	1 889	3 438	412	238	..	3 151
Luxembourg Luxembourg	1991	..	0	..	..	..	..	..	..	174
	1992	..	0	..	..	..	..	..	..	147
	1993	..	0	..	..	..	..	..	..	131
	1994	..	0	..	..	..	..	..	..	146
Malta Malte	1991	..	0	..	..	..	..	..	..	157
	1992	..	0	..	..	..	..	..	..	174
	1993	..	0	..	..	..	..	..	..	184
	1994	..	0	..	..	..	..	..	..	184
Netherlands Pays−Bas	1991	0	2 851	5 364	42 123	44 846	7 986	8 059	98 001	9 949
	1992	0	2 841	4 802	41 962	47 389	6 105	9 281	98 286	10 428
	1993	0	2 800	4 705	43 162	48 214	7 555	9 495	99 990	10 439
	1994	0	2 806	6 275	45 241	45 685	8 752	10 267	94 827	10 774
Norway, Svalbard & Jan Mayen Is. Norvège,Svalbd., île J.Mayen	1991	316	0	134 123	6 468	10 534	323	1 184	37 704	13 636
	1992	375	0	152 894	7 551	11 641	507	1 379	38 543	14 434
	1993	257	0	163 800	7 407	11 417	393	1 333	39 848	14 740
	1994	289	0	184 098	7 489	12 185	253	1 438	43 094	13 928
Poland Pologne	1991	127 746	11 075	227	4 693	10 256	1 292	625	3 739	16 548
	1992	124 501	10 736	286	5 846	10 605	1 537	667	3 636	16 306
	1993	126 891	9 943	336	6 516	11 914	1 302	684	4 659	16 444
	1994	129 321	11 065	406	6 995	11 910	1 194	644	4 366	16 625
Portugal Portugal	1991	158	230	..	4 679	8 268	1 025	851	..	3 675
	1992	129	257	..	5 254	10 307	451	925	..	3 701
	1993	115	256	..	4 764	10 186	576	888	..	3 837
	1994	86	277	..	6 534	11 528	824	1 167	..	3 891
Republic of Moldova République de Moldova	1992	..	..	..	..	..	..	..	..	1 382
	1993	..	..	..	..	..	..	..	..	1 261
	1994	..	..	..	..	..	..	..	..	1 011

67
Production of selected energy commodities
Thousand metric tons of coal equivalent [*cont.*]
Production des principaux biens de l'énergie
Milliers de tonnes métriques d'équivalent houille [*suite*]

Country or area Pays ou zone	Year Anneé	Hard coal, lignite & peat Houille, lignite et tourbe	Briquettes & cokes Agglo— mérés et cokes	Crude petroleum & NGL Pétrole brut et GNL	Light petroleum products Produits pétroliers légers	Heavy petroleum products Produits pétroliers lourds	Other petroleum products Autres produits pétroliers	LPG & refinery gas GLP et gaz de raffinerie	Natural gas Gaz naturel	Electricity Electricité
Romania	1991	9 713	2 504	9 700	5 283	12 740	1 366	1 219	28 243	6 991
Roumanie	1992	10 106	2 770	9 448	4 952	10 827	1 570	1 402	25 159	6 657
	1993	10 894	2 410	10 125	5 195	10 681	1 733	1 541	23 943	6 814
	1994	11 118	2 530	9 700	6 203	11 604	1 798	1 781	21 577	6 773
Russian Federation	1992	241 872	30 275	570 386	84 607	220 835	40 423	21 371	703 674	153 652
Fédération de Russie	1993	220 337	26 053	502 053	70 403	203 695	32 029	13 144	691 909	147 062
	1994	196 364	23 899	451 016	59 722	170 114	30 849	10 158	678 521	131 948
Slovakia	1992	1 497	1 876	100	1 205	3 149	1 595	146	409	5 526
Slovaquie	1993	978	1 743	96	1 175	3 889	1 079	155	282	5 969
	1994	1 004	1 759	86	1 193	4 009	935	149	321	6 057
Slovenia	1992	1 159	..	3	416	445	141	..	20	2 472
Slovénie	1993	1 065	..	3	376	435	18	..	16	2 420
	1994	1 010	..	3	233	306	4	..	15	2 698
Spain	1991	16 716	3 275	2 071	22 848	45 392	6 393	4 981	1 890	32 946
Espagne	1992	15 644	3 047	2 040	23 664	46 868	7 461	5 189	1 642	33 341
	1993	14 569	3 157	1 600	22 449	43 224	7 521	4 462	927	33 167
	1994	14 134	3 093	1 370	23 532	43 833	8 030	4 781	285	33 593
Sweden	1991	26	1 064	4	6 293	16 239	1 371	395	..	37 191
Suède	1992	364	1 097	1	6 820	17 485	1 314	452	..	33 790
	1993	337	1 088	0	6 657	18 429	1 614	463	..	32 993
	1994	319	1 093	7	7 912	17 890	1 492	424	..	35 743
Switzerland, Liechtenstein	1991	..	...	..	2 138	3 968	221	520	14	12 808
Suisse, Liechtenstein	1992	..	...	..	1 852	3 691	203	473	4	13 092
	1993	..	...	..	2 043	4 165	180	538	3	13 309
	1994	..	...	..	2 105	4 181	208	565	1	14 121
TFYR Macedonia	1992	2 695	..	..	255	986	..	23	..	745
L'ex – r.p. Macédonie	1993	2 663	..	..	646	1 104	..	28	..	636
	1994	2 641	..	..	118	139	..	3	..	677
Ukraine	1992	110 354	23 941	6 390	8 221	36 764	2 831	1 270	24 154	49 358
Ukraine	1993	95 725	18 833	6 068	6 775	20 849	1 640	902	22 574	46 951
	1994	78 467	14 036	5 999	3 662	11 285	881	489	21 517	56 379
United Kingdom	1991	78 228	7 512	130 854	59 700	59 622	7 683	6 595	72 204	57 193
Royaume–Uni	1992	70 045	6 745	135 191	61 745	57 940	7 987	6 481	73 549	58 523
	1993	55 802	6 551	143 654	63 419	61 684	8 472	6 756	86 333	61 903
	1994	39 905	6 576	181 851	61 709	58 948	8 629	6 609	92 305	61 921
Yugoslavia	1992	8 414	..	1 664	1 795	1 906	443	78	981	4 474
Yugoslavie	1993	7 838	..	1 640	511	1 001	306	16	1 116	4 208
	1994	8 035	..	1 540	406	923	306	19	956	4 340
Yugoslavia, SFR † Yugoslavie, Rfs †	1991	12 400	1 686	2 937	3 988	10 836	1 692	797	2 047	10 781
Oceania	**1991**	**150 721**	**4 187**	**49 260**	**26 891**	**18 931**	**3 964**	**3 340**	**32 245**	**26 333**
Océanie	**1992**	**159 558**	**4 236**	**45 124**	**28 014**	**19 122**	**3 947**	**3 251**	**34 929**	**26 593**
	1993	**160 970**	**3 959**	**44 950**	**29 255**	**19 837**	**4 119**	**3 410**	**36 850**	**26 341**
	1994	**173 518**	**3 911**	**42 668**	**29 188**	**20 377**	**4 463**	**3 770**	**38 573**	**26 412**
American Samoa	1991	..	..	..	..	..	..	..	..	13
Samoa américaines	1992	..	..	..	..	..	..	..	..	13
	1993	..	..	..	..	..	..	..	..	13
	1994	..	..	..	..	..	..	..	..	14
Australia	1991	148 544	4 180	39257	23 245	16 315	3 682	3 063	25 465	19 267
Australie	1992	157 174	4 236	34 828	24 294	16 497	3 612	2 905	27 718	19 623
	1993	158 458	3 959	34 322	25 439	17 136	3 760	3 056	29 828	20 114
	1994	170 914	3 911	31 996	25 427	17 381	4 138	3 365	32 020	20 532
Cook Islands	1991	..	..	..	..	..	..	..	..	2
Iles Cook	1992	..	..	..	..	..	..	..	..	2
	1993	..	..	..	..	..	..	..	..	2
	1994	..	..	..	..	..	..	..	..	2
Fiji	1991	..	..	..	..	..	..	..	..	58
Fidji	1992	..	..	..	..	..	..	..	..	58
	1993	..	..	..	..	..	..	..	..	59
	1994	..	..	..	..	..	..	..	..	64

67
Production of selected energy commodities
Thousand metric tons of coal equivalent [*cont.*]
Production des principaux biens de l'énergie
Milliers de tonnes métriques d'équivalent houille [*suite*]

Country or area Pays ou zone	Year Anneé	Hard coal, lignite & peat Houille, lignite et tourbe	Briquettes & cokes Agglo— mérés et cokes	Crude petroleum & NGL Pétrole brut et GNL	Light petroleum products Produits pétroliers légers	Heavy petroleum products Produits pétroliers lourds	Other petroleum products Autres produits pétroliers	LPG & refinery gas GLP et gaz de raffinerie	Natural gas Gaz naturel	Electricity Electricité
French Polynesia	1991	..	..	..	...	..	..	..	..	37
Polynésie française	1992	..	..	..	...	..	..	..	..	39
	1993	..	..	..	...	..	..	..	..	40
	1994	..	..	..	...	..	..	..	..	41
Guam	1991	..	..	..	...	..	..	...	..	98
Guam	1992	..	..	..	...	..	..	...	..	98
	1993	..	..	..	...	..	..	...	..	98
	1994	..	..	..	...	..	..	...	..	98
Kiribati	1991	..	..	..	...	..	..	..	..	1
Kiribati	1992	..	..	..	...	..	..	..	..	1
	1993	..	..	..	...	..	..	..	..	1
	1994	..	..	..	...	..	..	..	..	1
Nauru	1991	..	..	..	...	..	..	..	..	4
Nauru	1992	..	..	..	...	..	..	..	..	4
	1993	..	..	..	...	..	..	..	..	4
	1994	..	..	..	...	..	..	..	..	4
New Caledonia	1991	..	..	..	...	..	..	..	..	143
Nouvelle—Caledonie	1992	..	..	..	...	..	..	..	..	144
	1993	..	..	..	...	..	..	..	..	144
	1994	..	..	..	...	..	..	..	..	144
New Zealand	1991	2 177	7	2 861	3 646	2 616	282	277	6 678	6 449
Nouvelle—Zélande	1992	2 384	0	2 726	3 720	2 625	336	345	7 108	6 348
	1993	2 512	0	2 915	3 816	2 701	359	354	6 916	5 604
	1994	2 603	0	2 816	3 760	2 996	325	406	6 448	5 249
Palau [1]	1991	..	..	..	...	..	..	..	..	25
Palaos [1]	1992	..	..	..	...	..	..	..	..	25
	1993	..	..	..	...	..	..	..	..	25
	1994	..	..	..	...	..	..	..	..	25
Papua New Guinea	1991	..	..	7 142	...	..	..	..	102	220
Papouasie—Nouv.—Guinée	1992	..	..	7 570	...	..	..	..	102	220
	1993	..	..	7 713	...	..	..	..	106	220
	1994	..	..	7 856	...	..	..	..	106	220
Samoa	1991	..	..	..	...	..	..	..	..	6
Samoa	1992	..	..	..	...	..	..	..	..	7
	1993	..	..	..	...	..	..	..	..	7
	1994	..	..	..	...	..	..	..	..	8
Solomon Islands	1991	..	..	..	...	..	..	..	..	4
Iles Salomon	1992	..	..	..	...	..	..	..	..	4
	1993	..	..	..	...	..	..	..	..	4
	1994	..	..	..	...	..	..	..	..	4
Tonga	1991	..	..	..	...	..	..	..	..	3
Tonga	1992	..	..	..	...	..	..	..	..	3
	1993	..	..	..	...	..	..	..	..	3
	1994	..	..	..	...	..	..	..	..	4
Vanuatu	1991	..	..	..	...	..	..	..	..	3
Vanuatu	1992	..	..	..	...	..	..	..	..	4
	1993	..	..	..	...	..	..	..	..	4
	1994	..	..	..	...	..	..	..	..	4
former USSR † ancienne URSS †	1991	433 974	61 180	740 707	139 902	388 703	37 140	31 962	935 323	263 154

Source:
Energy statistics database of the Statistics Division of the
United Nations Secretariat.

Source:
Base de données pour les statistiques énergétiques de la Division
de statistique du Secrétariat de l'ONU.

† For detailed descriptions of data pertaining to
former Czechoslovakia, Germany, SFR Yugoslavia and former
USSR, see annex I – Country or area nomenclature, regional
and other groupings.

† Pour les descriptions en détails des données relatives à l'ancienne
Tchécoslovaquie, l'Allemagne, la Rfs Yougoslavie et l'ancienne URSS,
voir l'Annexe I – Nomenclature des pays ou zones, groupements
régionaux et autres groupements.

1 Including data for Federated States of Micronesia, Marshall Is.
and Northern Mariana Is.

1 Y compris les données pour les Etats fédérés de Micronésie, les îles
Marshall et les îles Mariannes du Nord.

Technical notes, tables 66 and 67

Tables 66 and 67: Data are presented in metric tons of coal equivalent (TCE), to which the individual energy commodities are converted in the interests of international uniformity and comparability.

The procedure to convert from original units to TCE is as follows:

Data in original unit (metric tons, TJ, kWh,m³) x special factors = TCE

For special factors used to convert the commodities into coal equivalent and detailed description of methods, see the United Nations *Energy Statistics Yearbook* and related methodological publications. [22, 41, 42]

Table 66: The data on production refer to the first stage of production. Thus, for hard coal the data refer to mine production; for briquettes to the output of briquetting plants; for crude petroleum and natural gas to production at oil and gas wells; for natural gas liquids to production at wells and processing plants; for refined petroleum products to gross refinery output; for cokes and coke-oven gas to the output of ovens; for other manufactured gas to production at gas works, blast furnaces or refineries; and for electricity to the gross production of generating plants.

International trade of energy commodities is based on the "general trade" system, that is, all goods entering and leaving the national boundary of a country are recorded as imports and exports.

Bunkers refers to fuels supplied to ships and aircraft engaged in international transportation, irrespective of the carrier's flag.

In general, data on stocks refer to changes in stocks of producers, importers and/or industrial consumers at the beginning and end of each year.

Data on consumption refer to "apparent consumption" and are derived from the formula "production + imports – exports – bunkers +/- stock changes". Accordingly, the series on apparent consumption may in some cases represent only an indication of the magnitude of actual gross inland availability.

Table 67: Definitions of the energy commodities are as follows:

— Hard coal: Coal with a high degree of coalification, and with a gross calorific value above 24 MJ/kg (5,700 kcal/kg) on an ash-free but moist basis, and with a reflectance index of vitrinite of 0.5 and above;

— Lignite: Coal with a low degree of coalification which has retained the anatomical structure of the vegetable matter from which it was formed. Its gross calorific value is less than 24 MJ/kg (5,700 kcal/kg) on an ash-free but moist basis, and its reflectance index of vitrinite is less than 0.5;

Notes techniques, tableaux 66 et 67

Tableaux 66 et 67 : Les données relatives aux divers produits énergétiques ont été converties en tonnes métriques d'équivalent houille (TEC), dans un souci d'uniformité et pour permettre les comparaisons entre la production de différents pays.

La méthode de conversion utilisée pour passer des unités de mesure d'origine à l'unité commune est la suivante :

Données en unités d'origine (tonnes métriques, TJ, kWh, m³) x facteurs de conversion = TEC

Pour les facteurs spéciaux utilisés pour convertir les produits énergétiques en équivalent houille et pour des descriptions détaillées des méthodes appliquées, se reporter à l'*Annuaire des statistiques de l'énergie* des Nations Unies et aux publications méthodologiques connexes [22, 41, 42].

Tableau 66 : Les données relatives à la production se rapportent au premier stade de production. Ainsi, pour la houille, les données se rapportent à la production minière; pour les briquettes, à la production des briquetteries; pour le pétrole brut et le gaz naturel, à la production des gisements de pétrole et de gaz; pour les condensats de gaz naturel, à la production au puits et aux installations de traitement; pour les produits pétroliers raffinés, à la production brute des raffineries; pour les cokes et le gaz des fours à coke, à la production des fours; pour les autres gaz manufacturés, à la production des usines à gaz, des hauts fourneaux ou des raffineries; et pour l'électricité, à la production brute des centrales.

Le commerce international des produits énergétiques est fondé sur le système du "commerce général", c'est-à-dire que tous les biens entrant sur le territoire national d'un pays ou en sortant sont respectivement enregistrés comme importations et exportations.

Les soutages se rapportent aux carburants fournis aux navires et aux avions assurant des transports internationaux, quel que soit leur pavillon.

En général, les variations des stocks se rapportent aux différences entre les stocks des producteurs, des importateurs ou des consommateurs industriels au début et à la fin de chaque année.

Les données sur la consommation se rapportent à la "consommation apparente" et sont obtenues par la formule "production + importations - exportations - soutage +/- variations des stocks". En conséquence, les séries relatives à la consommation apparente peuvent occasionnellement ne donner qu'une indication de l'ordre de grandeur des disponibilités intérieures brutes réelles.

Tableau 67 : Les définitions des produits énergétiques sont données ci-après :

— Peat: Solid fuel formed from the partial decomposition of dead vegetation under conditions of high humidity and limited air access (initial stage of coalification). Included is only that portion of peat used as fuel;

— Briquettes include the following commodities:

Patent fuel (hard coal briquettes): In the briquetting process, coal fines are moulded into artifacts of even shape under the influence of pressure and temperature with the admixture of binders.

Lignite briquettes: Lignite, after crushing and drying, is moulded under high pressure and without the admixture of binders to form artifacts of even shape;

Peat briquettes: Raw peat, after crushing and drying, is moulded under high pressure and without the admixture of binders to form artifacts of even shape;

— Coke: The solid residue obtained from the distillation of hard coal or lignite in the total absence of air (carbonization);

— Crude petroleum: Mineral oil consisting of a mixture of hydrocarbons of natural origin, yellow to black in colour, of variable specific gravity and viscosity, including crude mineral oils extracted from bituminous minerals (shale, bituminous sand, etc.). Data for crude petroleum include lease (field) condensate (separator liquids) which is recovered from gaseous hydrocarbons in lease separation facilities;

— Natural gas liquids (NGL): Liquid or liquefied hydrocarbons produced in the manufacture, purification and stabilization of natural gas. Their characteristics vary, ranging from those of butane and propane to heavy oils. Specifically included are natural gasolene, liquefied petroleum gas (LPG) from plants and plant condensate;

— Light petroleum products: Light products are defined (from the technological point of view) as liquid products obtained by distillation of crude petroleum at temperatures between 30 and 350°C, and/or having a specific gravity within the range of 0.625 to around 0.830;

— Heavy petroleum products: Heavy products are defined (from the technological point of view) as products obtained by distillation of crude petroleum at temperatures above 350°C and having a specific gravity higher than 0.830. Excluded are products which are not used for energy purposes, such as insulating oils, lubricants, paraffin wax, bitumen and petroleum coke;

— Liquefied petroleum gas (LPG): Hydrocarbons which are gaseous under conditions of normal temperature and pressure but are liquefied by compression or cooling to facilitate storage, handling and transportation;

— Refinery gas: Non-condensable gas collected in petroleum refineries which is generally used wholly as refinery fuel. It is also known as still gas;

– Houille : Charbon à haut degré de houillification et de pouvoir calorifique brut supérieur à 24 MJ/kg (5.700 kcal/kg) mesuré sans cendre, mais sur base humide, pour lequel l'indice de réflectance du vitrain est égal ou supérieur à 0,5;

– Lignite : Charbon d'un faible degré de houillification qui a gardé la structure anatomique des végétaux dont il est issu. Son pouvoir calorifique brut est inférieur à 24 MK/kg (5.700 kcal/kg) mesuré sans cendre, mais sur base humide, et son indice de réflectance du vitrain est égal ou inférieur à 0,5;

— Tourbe : Combustible solide issu de la décomposition partielle de végétaux morts dans des conditions de forte humidité et de faible circulation d'air (phase initiale de la houillification). N'est prise en considération ici que la tourbe utilisée comme combustible;

— Briquettes comprennent les produits suivants :

Agglomérés (briquettes de houille) : Par briquetage, les fines de charbon sont moulées en pains de forme régulière par compression et chauffage avec adjonction de liants.

Briquettes de lignite : Le lignite, après broyage et séchage, est moulé par compression, sans addition de liant, en pains de forme régulière.

Briquettes de tourbe : La tourbe brute, après broyage et séchage, est moulée par compression, sans addition de liant, en pains de forme régulière;

– Coke : Résidu solide obtenu lors de la distillation de houille ou de lignite en l'absence totale d'air (carbonisation);

– Pétrole brut : Huile minérale constituée d'un mélange d'hydrocarbures d'origine naturelle, de couleur variant du jaune au noir, d'une densité et d'une viscosité variables. Figurent également dans cette rubrique les huiles minérales brutes extraites de minéraux bitumeux (schiste, sable, etc.). Les données relatives au pétrole brut comprennent les condensats directement récupérés sur les sites d'exploitation des hydrocarbures gazeux (dans les installations prévues pour la séparation des phases liquide et gazeuse);

— Condensats de gaz naturel (GNL) : Hydrocarbures liquides ou liquéfiés produits lors de la fabrication, de la purification et de la stabilisation de gaz naturel. Leurs caractéristiques varient et se classent entre celles des gaz butane et propane et celles des huiles lourdes. Sont inclus en particulier dans cette rubrique l'essence naturelle, les gaz de pétrole liquéfiés (GPL) obtenus en usine et les condensats d'usine;

— Produits pétroliers légers : Les produits légers sont définis (du point de vue technologique) comme des produits liquides obtenus par distillation du pétrole brut à des températures comprises entre 30 et 350°C et/ou ayant une densité comprise entre 0,625 et 0,830 environ;

— Natural gas: A mixture of hydrocarbon compounds and small quantities of non-hydrocarbons existing in the gaseous phase, or in solution with oil in natural underground reservoirs at reservoir conditions;

— Electricity production: Refers to gross production, which includes the consumption by station auxiliaries and any losses in the transformers that are considered integral parts of the station. Excluded is electricity produced from pumped storage.

— Produits pétroliers lourds : Les produits lourds sont définis (du point de vue technologique) comme des produits obtenus par distilation du pétrole brut à des températures supérieures à 350°C et ayant une densité supérieure à 0,830. En sont exclus les produits qui ne sont pas utilisés à des fins énergétiques, tels que les huiles isolantes, les lubrifiants, les paraffines, le bitume et le coke de pétrole;

– Gaz de pétrole liquéfié (GPL) : Hydrocarbures qui sont à l'état gazeux dans des conditions de température et de pression normales mais sont liquéfiés par compression ou refroidissement pour en faciliter l'entreposage, la manipulation et le transport;

— Gaz de raffinerie : Comprend les gaz non condensables obtenus dans les raffineries de pétrole et qui sont généralement utilisés en totalité comme combustible de raffinerie. Ce produit est également appelé gaz de distillation;

– Gaz naturel : Mélanges de composés d'hydrocarbures et de petites quantités de composants autres que des hydrocarbures existant en phase gazeuse ou en solution huileuse dans des roches réservoirs souterraines naturelles, dans les conditions du réservoir;

– Production d'électricité : Se rapporte à la production brute qui comprend la consommation des équipements auxiliaires des centrales et les pertes au niveau des transformateurs considérés comme faisant partie intégrante de ces centrales. Elle ne comprend pas l'électricité produite à partir d'une accumulation par pompage.

68
Selected indicators of natural resources
Choix d'indicateurs concernant certaines ressources naturelles

Forest and other wooded land; wildlife species; and production in % of energy reserves
Forêt et autres terres boisées; espèces sauvages; et production en pourcentage des réserves énergétiques

Country or area Pays ou zone	Forest and other wooded land (1990) Forêt et autres terres boisées (1990) Total 10^3ha	Annual change Change annuel (1980–1990) 10^3ha	Forest Forêt 10^3ha	% of land % de la terre	Other wooded land Autres terres boisées 10^3ha	Wildlife species (1994) Espèces sauvages (1994) Number of threatened species Nombre d'espèces menacées	Number of extinct species Nombre d'espèces disparues	Production in % of energy reserves (1994) Production en % des réserves énergétiques (1994) Coal Houille	Natural gas Gaz naturel	Crude oil Pétrole brut
Africa • Afrique										
Algeria Algérie	3945	...	2039	1	1906	24	1	...	1.4	4.8
Angola Angola	77198	...	23194	19	54004	37	...	...	0.3	3.4
Benin Bénin	11497	...	4961	45	6536	11	...	...	...	7.8
Botswana Botswana	26561	...	14262	25	12299	13	...	...	...	...
Burkina Faso Burkina Faso	13813	...	4436	16	9377	8	...	...	...	...
Burundi Burundi	1314	...	325	13	989	12	...	...	...	...
Cameroon Cameroun	35905	...	20366	44	15539	62	...	...	...	10.1
Cape Verde Cap–Vert	78	...	16	4	62	6	1	...	...	...
Central African Republic Rép. centrafricaine	46753	...	30568	49	16185	13	...	...	...	...
Chad Tchad	32450	...	11438	9	21012	17	...	...	...	...
Comoros Comores	41	...	11	5	30	16	...	...	...	...
Congo Congo	25285	...	19902	58	5383	20	...	...	...	8.1
Côte d'Ivoire Côte d'Ivoire	18952	...	10967	34	7985	33	...	...	...	4.8
Djibouti Djibouti	1320	...	22	1	1298	8	...	...	...	...
Egypt Egypte	34	...	34	0	0	31	...	...	1.5	9.9
Equatorial Guinea Guinée équatoriale	2719	...	1829	65	890	23	...	...	...	...
Eritrea Erythrée	...	...	...	...	...	6	...	...	...	...
Ethiopia Ethiopie	41991	...	14354	13	27637	41	...	...	...	...
Gabon Gabon	19966	...	18256	71	1710	21	...	...	0.6	8.7
Gambia Gambie	286	...	98	10	188	5	...	...	...	...
Ghana Ghana	18013	...	9608	42	8405	24	...	...	...	...
Guinea Guinée	17484	...	6696	27	10788	29	...	...	...	...
Guinea–Bissau Guinée–Bissau	2162	...	2022	72	140	10	...	...	...	...
Kenya Kenya	16816	...	1305	2	15511	44[1]	1	...	...	...
Lesotho Lesotho	23	...	7	0	16	10[2]	...	...	...	...
Liberia Libéria	6632	...	4639	48	1993	32	...	...	...	...
Libyan Arab Jamahiriya Jamah. arabe libyenne	846	...	400	0	446	12	...	...	0.5	1.1

68

Selected indicators of natural resources
Forest and other wooded land; wildlife species; and production in % of energy reserves [*cont.*]
Choix d'indicateurs concernant certaines ressources naturelles
Forêt et autres terres boisées; espèces sauvages; et production en pourcentage des réserves énergétiques [*suite*]

Country or area Pays ou zone	Forest and other wooded land (1990) Forêt et autres terres boisées (1990)				Wildlife species (1994) Espèces sauvages (1994)		Production in % of energy reserves (1994) Production en % des réserves énergétiques (1994)		
	Total	Annual change Change annuel (1980–1990)	Forest Forêt	% of land % de la terre	Other wooded land Autres terres boisées	Number of threatened species Nombre d'espèces menacées	Number of extinct species Nombre d'espèces disparues	Coal Houille	Natural gas Gaz naturel	Crude oil Pétrole brut
	10³ha	10³ha	10³ha		10³ha					
Madagascar Madagascar	23225	...	15999	28	7226	99	2	...	...	...
Malawi Malawi	3724	...	3612	38	112	17		...	...	...
Mali Mali	28791	...	12158	10	16633	18		...	...	...
Mauritania Mauritanie	4536	...	556	1	3980	16		...	...	...
Mauritius Maurice	44	...	12	6	32	37	46	...	...	...
Morocco Maroc	5744	...	3864	5	1880	26	...	1.0	0.8	...
Mozambique Mozambique	55881	...	17357	22	38524	33	...	...	...	...
Namibia Namibie	26296	...	12569	15	13727	26	...	...	...	...
Niger Niger	10442	...	2562	2	7880	13	...	0.2	...	...
Nigeria Nigéria	65654	...	15785	17	49869	34	...	0.1	0.3	5.4
Réunion Réunion	135	...	100	40	35	26	16	...	...	...
Rwanda Rwanda	946	...	252	10	694	22	...	...	...	...
Saint Helena Sainte–Hélène	9	...	1	3	8	15	23	...	...	...
Sao Tome and Principe Sao Tomé–et–Principe	...	...	...	...	...	16	...	...[3]	...	...
Senegal Sénégal	13400	...	7656	40	5744	20	...	...	...	...
Seychelles Seychelles	4	...	4	13	0	21	2	...	...	...
Sierra Leone Sierra Leone	6969	...	1895	26	5074	29	...	...	...	...
Somalia Somalie	15945	...	758	1	15187	23	...	...	...	...
South Africa Afrique du Sud	41543	...	8208	7	33335	223[2]	6	0.3[3]	1.1[3]	...
Sudan Soudan	68955	...	43179	18	25776	29	...	...	...	...
Swaziland Swaziland	146	...	146	8	0	11	...	...	...	...
Togo Togo	4566	...	1370	25	3196	13	1	...	...	...
Tunisia Tunisie	569	...	569	4	0	15	...	...	0.3	9.7
Uganda Ouganda	16023	...	6366	32	9657	27	...	...	...	...
United Rep. Tanzania Rép. Unie de Tanzanie	68497	...	33709	38	34788	61[1]	1	...	...	...
Western Sahara Sahara occidental	...	...	...	...	...	9	...	...	...	...
Zaire Zaïre	166076	...	113317	50	52759	54	...	0.1	...	5.4
Zambia Zambie	60337	...	32349	44	27988	19	...	...	...	...

68

Selected indicators of natural resources
Forest and other wooded land; wildlife species; and production in % of energy reserves [*cont.*]
Choix d'indicateurs concernant certaines ressources naturelles
Forêt et autres terres boisées; espèces sauvages; et production en pourcentage des réserves énergétiques [*suite*]

Country or area Pays ou zone	Forest and other wooded land (1990) Forêt et autres terres boisées (1990)				Other wooded land Autres terres boisées 10^3ha	Wildlife species (1994) Espèces sauvages (1994)		Production in % of energy reserves (1994) Production en % des réserves énergétiques (1994)		
	Total		Forest Forêt			Number of threatened species Nombre d'espèces menacées	Number of extinct species Nombre d'espèces disparues	Coal Houille	Natural gas Gaz naturel	Crude oil Pétrole brut
	10^3ha	Annual change Change annuel (1980– 1990) 10^3ha	10^3ha	% of land % de la terre						
Zimbabwe Zimbabwe	26144	...	8981	23	17163	18	...	0.7	...	...
America, North • Amérique du Nord										
Anguilla Anguilla	...	...	...	...	...	5	...	...	...	...
Antigua and Barbuda Antigua–et–Barbuda	26	...	10	23	16	6	...	...	...	...
Aruba Aruba	...	...	...	...	...	4	...	...	...	...
Bahamas Bahamas	186	...	186	19	0	14	2	...	...	...
Barbados Barbade	5	...	0	0	5	3	1	...	...	1.5
Belize Belize	2117	...	1998	88	119	12	...	...	...	...
Bermuda Bermudes	1	...	0	0	1	3	...	...	...	...
British Virgin Islands Iles Vierges britanniques	5	...	3	20	2	8	...	...	...	...
Canada Canada	453300	...	247164	27	206136	43	4	0.8	6.8	13.4
Cayman Islands Iles Caïmanes	6	...	0	0	6	3	4	...	...	...
Costa Rica Costa Rica	1569	...	1456	29	113	36	...	...	...	...
Cuba Cuba	3262	...	1960	18	1302	36	6	...	1.4	7.3
Dominica Dominique	50	...	44	59	6	6	...	...	...	...
Dominican Republic Rép. dominicaine	1530	...	1084	22	446	29	7	...	...	...
El Salvador El Salvador	890	...	127	6	763	9	...	...	...	...
Greenland Groënland	...	...	...	...	...	3	1	...	...	...
Grenada Grenade	11	...	6	18	5	5	...	...	...	...
Guadeloupe Guadeloupe	93	...	93	55	0	8	2	...	...	...
Guatemala Guatemala	9465	...	4253	39	5212	23	1	...	3.2	0.6
Haiti Haïti	139	...	31	1	108	26	8	...	...	...
Honduras Honduras	6054	...	4608	41	1446	18	1	...	...	...
Jamaica Jamaïque	653	...	254	23	399	30	2	...	...	...
Martinique Martinique	71	...	43	41	28	7	3	...	...	...
Mexico Mexique	129057	...	48695	26	80362	209	17	0.9	1.4	2.3
Montserrat Montserrat	4	...	3	25	1	5	...	...	...	...
Netherland Antilles Antilles néerlandaises	7	...	0	0	7	7	...	...	...	...

68

Selected indicators of natural resources
Forest and other wooded land; wildlife species; and production in % of energy reserves [*cont.*]
Choix d'indicateurs concernant certaines ressources naturelles
Forêt et autres terres boisées; espèces sauvages; et production en pourcentage des réserves énergétiques [*suite*]

Country or area Pays ou zone	Forest and other wooded land (1990) Forêt et autres terres boisées (1990) Total 10³ha	Annual change Change annuel (1980–1990) 10³ha	Forest Forêt 10³ha	% of land % de la terre	Other wooded land Autres terres boisées 10³ha	Wildlife species (1994) Espèces sauvages (1994) Number of threatened species Nombre d'espèces menacées	Number of extinct species Nombre d'espèces disparues	Production in % of energy reserves (1994) Production en % des réserves énergétiques (1994) Coal Houille	Natural gas Gaz naturel	Crude oil Pétrole brut
Nicaragua Nicaragua	7732	...	6027	51	1705	16		...		...
Panama Panama	3266	...	3123	41	143	29	...	...	...	...
Puerto Rico Porto Rico	336		324	37	12	20	1	...	...	...
Saint Kitts and Nevis Saint–Kitts–et–Nevis	24	...	13	36	11	6		...	...	...
Saint Lucia Sainte–Lucie	34	...	5	8	29	9	1			
Saint Pierre and Miquelon Saint–Pierre–et–Miquelon	1		0	0	1	...	...	...	...	...
Saint Vincent and the Grenadines St. Vincent–Grenadines	12	...	11	28	1	6	1			
Trinidad and Tobago Trinité–et–Tobago	236	...	168	33	68	9		...	...	2.2	9.0
Turks and Caicos Islands Iles Turques et Caiques	...	...	...	...	...	6	...	...	...	...
United States Etats–Unis	295989	−316.5	209573	23	86416	1141[4]	87	0.6	11.5	10.2
United States Virgin Islands Iles Vierges américaines	14	...	14	41	0	6	1	...	...	...
America, South • Amérique du Sud										
Argentina Argentine	50936		34436	13	16500	74	1	...	4.8	11.4
Bolivia Bolivie	57977	...	49345	46	8632	53		...	2.7	6.7
Brazil Brésil	671921		566007	67	105914	181	2	...	3.0	6.4
Chile Chili	16583	...	8033	11	8550	91	...	0.3	1.8	1.4
Colombia Colombie	63231	...	54190	52	9041	101	2	0.5	2.4	5.0
Ecuador Equateur	15576	...	12007	43	3569	112	1	...	...	6.3
Falkland Islands (Malvinas) Iles Falkland (Malvinas)	...	...	...	...	...	2	1			...
French Guiana Guyane française	8318	...	7997	91	321	14		...	...	...
Guyana Guyana	18755	...	18424	94	331	15	...	...	...	...
Paraguay Paraguay	19256	...	12868	32	6388	33		...	...	...
Peru Pérou	84844	...	68090	53	16754	97	...	...	0.2	5.8
Suriname Suriname	15093	...	14776	95	317	12	...	...	...	2.5
Uruguay Uruguay	933	...	813	5	120	14	...	...	...	...
Venezuela Venezuela	69436	...	45943	52	23493	44	...	1.1	0.6	1.5
Asia • Asie										
Afghanistan Afghanistan	2614	...	1199	2	1415	22	...	...	0.2	...

68
Selected indicators of natural resources
Forest and other wooded land; wildlife species; and production in % of energy reserves [*cont.*]
Choix d'indicateurs concernant certaines ressources naturelles
Forêt et autres terres boisées; espèces sauvages; et production en pourcentage des réserves énergétiques [*suite*]

Country or area Pays ou zone	Forest and other wooded land (1990) Forêt et autres terres boisées (1990)					Wildlife species (1994) Espèces sauvages (1994)		Production in % of energy reserves (1994) Production en % des réserves énergétiques (1994)		
	Total		Forest Forêt		Other wooded land Autres terres boisées	Number of threatened species Nombre d'espèces menacées	Number of extinct species Nombre d'espèces disparues	Coal Houille	Natural gas Gaz naturel	Crude oil Pétrole brut
	10^3ha	Annual change Change annuel (1980–1990) 10^3ha	10^3ha	% of land % de la terre	10^3ha					
Armenia Arménie	...	...	...	...	...	21		...	...	...
Azerbaijan Azerbaïdjan	...	...	...	...	...	22	...	...	...	6.1
Bahrain Bahreïn	0	...	0	0	0	4	...	...	3.9	8.6
Bangladesh Bangladesh	1472	...	1004	8	468	61	...	...	1.8	3.6
Bhutan Bhoutan	3168	...	2813	60	355	34	...	...	...	...
Brunei Darussalam Brunéi Darussalam	458	...	458	87	...	28	...	...	2.3	4.6
Cambodia Cambodge	13724	...	12170	69	1554	46	...	...	...	...
China Chine	162029	...	133799	14	28230	166	1	1.5	1.1	4.5
Cyprus Chypre	280	0.2	140	15	140	9	...	...	...	...
Georgia Géorgie	...	...	...	...	...	29	...	...	0.4	...
Hong Kong Hong–kong	...	...	...	...	...	14	...	...	...	...
India Inde	82648	...	64959	22	17689	155	2	0.5	2.5	4.1
Indonesia Indonésie	145108	...	115674	64	29434	301	1	0.2	3	13.1
Iran, Islamic Republic of Iran, Rép. islamique d'	11437	...	1737	1	9700	37	...	0.5	0.2	1.4
Iraq Iraq	192	...	83	0	109	23	...	...	0.1	0.3
Israel Israël	124	...	102	5	22	24	2	...	4.5	0.7
Japan Japon	24718	−4.8	24158	66	560	146	30	0.9	7.6	7.1
Jordan Jordanie	173	...	51	1	122	16	...	...	...	...
Kazakstan Kazakstan	...	...	...	...	...	41	...	...	0.2	3.1
Korea D. People's R. Corée, R. p. dém. de	7370	...	6170	51	1200	23	...	19.7	...	...
Korea, Republic of Corée, République de	6291	...	6291	64	0	25	...	4.0	...	...
Kuwait Koweït	5	...	5	0	0	7	...	...	0.4	0.7
Kyrgyzstan Kirghizistan	...	...	...	...	...	13	...	...	0.8	0.7
Lao People's Dem. Rep. Rép. dém. pop. lao	21436	...	13177	57	8259	54	...	...	...	...
Lebanon Liban	144	...	78	8	66	14	...	...	...	...
Malaysia Malaisie	22248	...	17664	54	4584	81	...	4.4	1.2	5.4
Maldives Maldives	...	...	...	...	...	4	...	...	...	...
Mongolia Mongolie	13741	...	9406	6	4335	25	...	...	...	...

68
Selected indicators of natural resources
Forest and other wooded land; wildlife species; and production in % of energy reserves [cont.]
Choix d'indicateurs concernant certaines ressources naturelles
Forêt et autres terres boisées; espèces sauvages; et production en pourcentage des réserves énergétiques [suite]

Country or area Pays ou zone	Forest and other wooded land (1990) Forêt et autres terres boisées (1990)				Other wooded land Autres terres boisées 10^3ha	Wildlife species (1994) Espèces sauvages (1994)		Production in % of energy reserves (1994) Production en % des réserves énergétiques (1994)		
	Total		Forest Forêt			Number of threatened species Nombre d'espèces menacées	Number of extinct species Nombre d'espèces disparues	Coal Houille	Natural gas Gaz naturel	Crude oil Pétrole brut
	10^3ha	Annual change Change annuel (1980–1990) 10^3ha	10^3ha	% of land % de la terre						
Myanmar Myanmar	49774	...	29091	44	20683	83	1	...	0.5	10.0
Nepal Népal	5751	...	5079	37	672	56	1	...	...	...
Oman Oman	0	...	0	0	0	17	...	...	1.3	6.1
Pakistan Pakistan	3128	...	2023	3	1105	40	...	0.5	2.6	10.3
Philippines Philippines	13640	...	8034	27	5606	166	3	0.7	...	0.9
Qatar Qatar	...	...	...	...	...	3	...	...	0.2	3.4
Saudi Arabia Arabie saoudite	902	...	202	0	700	24	...	...	0.7	1.2
Singapore Singapour	4	...	4	7	0	13	...	...	...	...
Sri Lanka Sri Lanka	3998	...	1885	29	2113	47	...	...	...	...
Syrian Arab Republic Rép. arabe syrienne	484	...	245	1	239	17	...	...	0.8	8.6
Tajikistan Tadjikistan	...	...	...	...	...	18	...	...	0.5	...
Thailand Thaïlande	14968	...	13264	26	1704	93	1	1.7	5.4	13.4
Turkey Turquie	20199	3.1	8856	11	11343	66	...	0.8	1.8	5.6
Turkmenistan Turkménistan	...	...	...	...	...	22	...	...	1.2	6.3
United Arab Emirates Emirats arabes unis	60	...	60	1	0	8	...	...	0.4	0.9
Uzbekistan Ouzbékistan	...	...	...	...	...	21	...	...	...	...
Viet Nam Viet Nam	23499	...	9782	30	13717	84	1	3.7	...	10.4
Yemen Yémen	1921	...	9	0	1912	19	...	...	...	2.9
Europe • Europe										
Albania Albanie	1449	0.1	1046	38	403	19	...	...	4.3	2.4
Andorra Andorre	...	...	...	...	...	3	...	...	...	...
Austria Autriche	3877	14.2	3877	47	0	70	5	7.5	6.0	7.3
Belarus Bélarus	6256	27.3	6016	29	240	28	...	...	...	...
Belgium Belgique	620	1.9	620	20	0	35	...	...	...	...
Bosnia and Herzegovina Bosnie–Herzégovine						2	...	...	...	...
Bulgaria Bulgarie	3683	7.8	3386	31	298	38	...	1.1	2.5	5.1
Croatia Croatie	...	...	...	...	...	4	...	...	5.0	7.1
former Czechoslovakia † anc. Tchécoslovaquie †	4491	2	4491	36	0	7	...	1.2	...	...

68
Selected indicators of natural resources
Forest and other wooded land; wildlife species; and production in % of energy reserves [cont.]
Choix d'indicateurs concernant certaines ressources naturelles
Forêt et autres terres boisées; espèces sauvages; et production en pourcentage des réserves énergétiques [suite]

Country or area Pays ou zone	Forest and other wooded land (1990) Forêt et autres terres boisées (1990)				Other wooded land Autres terres boisées 10³ha	Wildlife species (1994) Espèces sauvages (1994)		Production in % of energy reserves (1994) Production en % des réserves énergétiques (1994)		
	Total		Forest Forêt			Number of threatened species Nombre d'espèces menacées	Number of extinct species Nombre d'espèces disparues	Coal Houille	Natural gas Gaz naturel	Crude oil Pétrole brut
	10³ha	Annual change Change annuel (1980–1990) 10³ha	10³ha	% of land % de la terre						
Czech Republic République tchèque	...	...	...	...	...	42	...	...	4.1	6.4
Denmark Danemark	466	1	466	11	0	23	1	...	3.3	9.0
Estonia Estonie	...	...	...	...	...	24		...	...	...
Finland Finlande	23373	5.5	20112	66	3261	34		...	...	...
France France	14154	8	13110	24	1044	109	3	6.6	6.4	14.8
Germany † Allemagne †	10735	46.9	10490	30	245	68	3	0.6	5.6	5.8
Gibraltar Gibraltar	...	...	...	...	...	3		...	...	...
Greece Grèce	6032	0.9	2512	19	3520	53	...	1.9	0.5	8.9
Hungary Hongrie	1675	8.2	1675	18	0	47	...	0.3	5.0	10.4
Iceland Islande	123	...	...	...	123	3	1			
Ireland Irlande	429	4.8	396	6	33	9	...	...	18.1	...
Italy Italie	8550	...	6750	22	1800	69	2	0.9	7.6	11.1
Latvia Lettonie	...	...	...	...	...	30		...	...	...
Liechtenstein Liechtenstein	...	...	...	...	...	8		...	...	...
Lithuania Lituanie	...	...	...	...	...	30		...	...	1.2
Luxembourg Luxembourg	88	0.1	85	33	3	13	...	...	...	...
Malta Malte	...	...	...	...	...	10		...	...	...
Netherlands Pays–Bas	334	1	334	10	0	27	...	...	4.5	27.1
Norway Norvège	9565	...	8697	28	868	27	...	...	1.5	8.6
Poland Pologne	8672	5	8672	28	0	49	...	0.5	3.7	5.7
Portugal Portugal	3102	13.8	2755	32	347	106	13	4.9	...	...
Republic of Moldova Moldova, Rép. de	...	...	...	...	...	27	...	...	...	...
Romania Roumanie	6265	0.2	6190	27	75	47	...	1.3	4.1	3.1
Russian Federation Fédération de Russie	...	...	...	...	...	94	3	...	1.2	4.7
Slovakia Slovaquie	...	...	...	...	...	42	...	...	3.6	...
Slovenia Slovénie	...	...	...	...	...	8	...	...	...	...
Spain Espagne	25622	0.9	8388	17	17234	119	1	1.9	1.0	...
Sweden Suède	28015	...	24437	60	3578	41	...	...	...	...

68

Selected indicators of natural resources
Forest and other wooded land; wildlife species; and production in % of energy reserves [*cont.*]
Choix d'indicateurs concernant certaines ressources naturelles
Forêt et autres terres boisées; espèces sauvages; et production en pourcentage des réserves énergétiques [*suite*]

Country or area Pays ou zone	Forest and other wooded land (1990) Forêt et autres terres boisées (1990)				Other wooded land Autres terres boisées 10^3ha	Wildlife species (1994) Espèces sauvages (1994)		Production in % of energy reserves (1994) Production en % des réserves énergétiques (1994)		
	Total		Forest Forêt			Number of threatened species Nombre d'espèces menacées	Number of extinct species Nombre d'espèces disparues	Coal Houille	Natural gas Gaz naturel	Crude oil Pétrole brut
	10^3ha	Annual change Change annuel (1980–1990) 10^3ha	10^3ha	% of land % de la terre						
Switzerland Suisse	1186	6.6	1130	28	56	53	...	...	...	...
Ukraine Ukraine	9239	24	9213	16	26	45[1]	...	...	1.6	1.8
United Kingdom Royaume–Uni	2380	24.2	2207	9	173	23	2	2.2	11.4	20.9
Yugoslavia Yougoslavie	...	...	...	...	...	...	1	...	1.8	9.8
Yugoslavia, SFR † Yougoslavie, Rfs †	9454	34.5	8371	33	1083	53	...	0.3		
Oceania • Océanie										
American Samoa Samoa américaines	14	...	0	0	14	12	1	...	...	...
Australia Australie	145613	0.6	39837	5	105776	582	31	0.3	4.3	11.2
Christmas Island Ile Christmas	...	...	...	...	...	...	2			
Cook Islands Iles Cook	...	...	...	...	...	8	14	...	...	...
Fiji Fidji	859	...	853	47	6	22	...	...	...	...
French Polynesia Polynésie française	115	...	0	0	115	35	81	...	...	...
Guam Guam	10	...	0	0	10	62	3	...	...	...
Kiribati Kiribati	2	...	0	0	2	7	...	...	...	...
Marshall Islands Iles Marshall	...	...	...	...	...	8	...	...	...	...
Micronesia, Federated States of Etats fédérés de Micron	...	...	...	...	...	71	3	...	...	...
Nauru Nauru	...	...	...	...	...	1	...	...	...	...
New Caledonia Nouvelle–Calédonie	1289	...	710	39	579	27	7	...	...	...
New Zealand Nouvelle–Zélande	7472	...	7472	28	0	115	19	5.0	5.2	11.0
Niue Nioué	6	...	0	0	6	2	...	...	...	...
Norfolk Island Ile Norfolk	...	...	...	...	...	...	1	...	...	...
Northern Mariana Islands Iles Mariannes du Nord	...	...	...	...	...	25	...	...	...	...
Palau Palaos	40	...	0	0	40	68	1	0.7	...	0.9
Papua New Guinea Papouasie–Nvl–Guinée	42115	...	36030	80	6085	143	2	...	0.0	17.7
Pitcairn Pitcairn	...	...	...	...	...	7	...	...	...	...
Samoa Samoa	164	...	133	47	31	...	...	...	...	...
Solomon Islands Iles Salomon	2455	...	2410	86	45	39	3	...	...	...
Tokelau Tokélaou	...	...	...	...	...	4	...	...	...	...

68
Selected indicators of natural resources
Forest and other wooded land; wildlife species; and production in % of energy reserves [*cont.*]
Choix d'indicateurs concernant certaines ressources naturelles
Forêt et autres terres boisées; espèces sauvages; et production en pourcentage des réserves énergétiques [*suite*]

Country or area Pays ou zone	Forest and other wooded land (1990) Forêt et autres terres boisées (1990)				Other wooded land Autres terres boisées 10^3ha	Wildlife species (1994) Espèces sauvages (1994)		Production in % of energy reserves (1994) Production en % des réserves énergétiques (1994)		
	Total					Number of threatened species Nombre d'espèces menacées	Number of extinct species Nombre d'espèces disparues	Coal Houille	Natural gas Gaz naturel	Crude oil Pétrole brut
	10^3ha	Annual change Change annuel (1980– 1990) 10^3ha	Forest Forêt 10^3ha	% of land % de la terre						
Tonga Tonga	8	...	0	0	8	8	1	...	...	...
Tuvalu Tuvalu	...	...	...	...	...	7	...	...	...	...
Vanuatu Vanuatu	809	...	809	66	0	17	...	...	...	...
former USSR • ancienne URSS										
former USSR † ancienne URSS †	926035	...	739729	36	186306		...	0.3	...	...

Source:
Food and Agriculture Organization of the United Nations (Rome); World Conservation Monitoring Centre (Cambridge, U.K.); Energy statistics database of the Statistics Division of the United Nations Secretariat.

† For detailed descriptions of data pertaining to former Czechoslovakia, Germany, SFR Yugoslavia and former USSR, see Annex I – Country or area nomenclature, regional and other groupings.

1 The estimate for fishes does not include a large number of cichlids in Lake Victoria for which we have insufficient data on the country range of individual species. A total of 250 haplochromine and 2 tilapiine cichlid fishes in Lake Victoria is given in the 1990 Red List, but recent estimates suggest >300 haplochromine species are present of which some 200 may be critically threatened.
2 The figure for invertebrates does not include 62 earthworms of the genra Microscolex and Udeina which occur in Lesotho and South Africa but for which we have insufficient data on the range of individual species.
3 South African Customs Union.
4 The invertebrate total does not include species of the insect genra Intodacnus and Oodemus for which we lack data on the number of registered species.

Source:
Organisation des Nations Unies pour l'alimentation et l'agriculture (Rome); Centre mondial de surveillance pour la conservation (Cambridge, Royaume–Uni); Base de données pour les statistiques énergétiques de la Division de Statistique du Secrétariat de l'ONU.

† Pour les descriptions en détails des données relatives à l'ancienne Tchécoslovaquie, l'Allemagne, la Rfs Yougoslavie et l'ancienne URSS, voir l'Annexe I – Nomenclature des pays ou zones, groupements régionaux et autres groupements.

1 Les estimations relatives aux poissons n'incluent pas un grand nombre des cichlidés du lac Victoria pour lesquels on ne dispose pas de données suffisantes sur la répartition des espèces individuelles. Un total de 250 haplochromis et 2 tilapies dans le lac Victoria est indiqué dans la Liste rouge de 1990, mais des estimations récentes donnent à penser que plus de 300 espèces d'haplochromis sont présentes, parmi lesquelles 200 pourraient être menacées d'extinction.
2 Le chiffre pour les invertébrés ne couvre pas 62 espèces de vers de terre du genre Microscolex et Udeina présents au Lesotho et en Afrique du Sud mais pour lesquels on ne dispose pas de données suffisantes sur la répartition des diverses espèces.
3 Union douanière d'Afrique australe.
4 Le total donné pour les invertébrés ne couvre pas les espèces d'insectes du genre Intodacnus et Oodemus pour lesquels on ne dispose pas de données suffisantes sur le nombre d'espèces identifiées.

69
Selected indicators of environmental protection
Choix d'indicateurs de la protection de l'environnement
Access to safe drinking water and sanitation services; and protected area as % of land area

Accès à l'eau salubre et à des services d'assainissement; et aires protégées en pourcentage de la superficie totale

Country or area Pays ou zone	Access to safe drinking water (% pop.) Accès à l'eau salubre (% pop.)				Access to sanitation services (% pop.) Accès à des services d'assainissement (% pop.)				Protected area as % of land area Aires protégées en pourcentage de la superficie totale
	1990	1992	1993	1994	1990	1992	1993	1994	1994
Africa · Afrique									
Algeria Algérie	...	...	...	...	...	...	...	...	5.00
Angola Angola	39.6	...	...	32.0	...	...	...	16.0	2.12
Benin Bénin	54.8	...	50.0	...	...	...	20.0	...	6.90
Botswana Botswana	90.4	...	...	...	...	...	...	...	18.54
Burkina Faso Burkina Faso	...	...	78.0	...	...	...	18.0	...	9.71
Burundi Burundi	46.5	52.0	...	...	...	51.0	...	...	3.19
Cameroon Cameroun	43.7	...	...	...	...	...	...	...	4.31
Cape Verde Cap–Vert	51.0[1]	...	...	...	24.0[1]	...	...	...	...
Central African Republic Rép. centrafricaine	23.6	...	...	...	46.0[1]	...	...	...	9.77
Chad Tchad	...	...	...	24.0	...	...	...	21.0	8.95
Congo Congo	...	...	...	...	...	...	...	...	3.44
Cote d'Ivoire Côte d'Ivoire	69.3	...	72.0	...	...	...	...	54.0	6.18
Djibouti Djibouti	...	...	90.0	...	...	...	90.0	...	0.43
Egypt Egypte	89.8	...	64.0	...	...	...	11.0	...	0.79
Equatorial Guinea Guinée équatoriale	35.4	...	...	96.0	...	...	...	54.0	...
Ethiopia Ethiopie	...	...	...	...	...	...	...	...	5.45
Gabon Gabon	...	...	...	...	...	...	...	...	3.90
Gambia Gambie	76.7	...	76.0	...	...	...	37.0	...	2.15
Ghana Ghana	...	...	...	56.0	...	...	...	42.0	4.63
Guinea Guinée	52.3	...	...	49.0	...	...	...	...	0.67
Guinea–Bissau Guinée–Bissau	...	...	...	53.0	...	...	...	20.0	...
Kenya Kenya	...	...	53.0	...	...	...	77.0	...	6.01
Lesotho Lesotho	...	...	...	52.0	...	...	...	6.0	0.22
Liberia Libéria	...	...	...	30.0	...	...	...	18.0	1.16
Libyan Arab Jamahiriya Jamah. arabe libyenne	...	...	...	...	...	...	...	...	0.10
Madagascar Madagascar	...	...	...	29.0	...	...	...	15.0	1.88
Malawi Malawi	...	...	...	45.0	...	...	...	53.0	11.25
Mali Mali	11.2	...	37.0	...	...	...	31.0	...	3.24
Mauritania Mauritanie	...	...	...	...	...	...	...	...	1.69

69
Selected indicators of environmental protection
Access to safe drinking water and sanitation services; and protected area as % of land area [*cont.*]
Choix d'indicateurs de la protection de l'environnement
Accès à l'eau salubre et à des services d'assainissement; et aires protégées en pourcentage de la superficie totale [*suite*]

Country or area Pays ou zone	Access to safe drinking water (% pop.) Accès à l'eau salubre (% pop.)				Access to sanitation services (% pop.) Accès à des services d'assainissement (% pop.)				Protected area as % of land area Aires protégées en pourcentage de la superficie totale
	1990	1992	1993	1994	1990	1992	1993	1994	1994
Mauritius Maurice	99.0	...	...	...	100.0	...	...	...	2.16
Morocco Maroc	55.6	...	52.0	...	...	...	40.0	...	0.79
Mozambique Mozambique	...	...	...	32.0	...	...	...	...	0.00
Namibia Namibie	47.2	...	...	...	34.0[1]	...	...	...	12.4
Niger Niger	53.2	...	...	53.0	...	...	...	15.0	7.09
Nigeria Nigéria	41.5	...	39.0	...	...	...	36.0	...	3.22
Rwanda Rwanda	68.5	...	...	...	...	...	...	...	12.42
Senegal Sénégal	43.9	...	50.0	...	...	...	58.0	...	11.09
Seychelles Seychelles	...	...	...	...	...	...	...	...	93.79
Sierra Leone Sierra Leone	40.0	...	...	...	...	...	...	...	1.13
Somalia Somalie	...	...	...	...	...	...	...	...	0.29
South Africa Afrique du Sud	...	...	...	...	...	...	...	46.0	5.85
Sudan Soudan	...	...	51.0	...	...	...	22.0	...	3.74
Swaziland Swaziland	...	...	43.0	...	...	...	36.0	...	2.64
Togo Togo	...	63.0	...	...	...	...	...	...	11.39
Tunisia Tunisie	99.0[1]	...	...	...	...	96.0	...	...	0.27
Uganda Ouganda	33.4	...	...	34.0	...	...	...	57.0	8.07
United Rep. Tanzania Rép. Unie de Tanzanie	...	...	...	...	...	...	...	...	14.78
Zaire Zaïre	39.1	27.0	...	...	...	...	9.0	...	4.23
Zambia Zambie	83.5	...	...	43.0	...	...	...	23.0	8.46
Zimbabwe Zimbabwe	...	...	...	...	...	...	...	...	7.86
America, North · Amérique du Nord									
Antigua and Barbuda Antigua−et−Barbuda	...	...	...	...	...	...	...	...	13.86
Bahamas Bahamas	94.1	...	...	...	...	...	...	...	8.97
Barbados Barbade	100.0	...	...	...	...	...	...	...	...
Belize Belize	72.8	...	...	89.0	...	...	...	57.0	14.07
British Virgin Islands Iles Vierges britanniques	100.0	...	...	...	...	...	...	...	...
Canada Canada	...	...	...	...	...	...	...	...	8.32
Costa Rica Costa Rica	...	92.0	...	...	...	92.0	...	...	12.55
Cuba Cuba	97.7	...	...	93.0	...	...	...	66.0	7.80
Dominica Dominique	...	...	...	...	...	...	...	...	9.15

69

Selected indicators of environmental protection
Access to safe drinking water and sanitation services; and protected area as % of land area [*cont.*]
Choix d'indicateurs de la protection de l'environnement
Accès à l'eau salubre et à des services d'assainissement; et aires protégées en pourcentage de la superficie totale [*suite*]

Country or area Pays ou zone	Access to safe drinking water (% pop.) Accès à l'eau salubre (% pop.)				Access to sanitation services (% pop.) Accès à des services d'assainissement (% pop.)				Protected area as % of land area Aires protégées en pourcentage de la superficie totale
	1990	1992	1993	1994	1990	1992	1993	1994	1994
Dominican Republic Rép. dominicaine	67.4	...	71.0	...	...	...	78.0	...	21.64
El Salvador El Salvador	46.6	...	55.0	...	...	...	68.0	...	0.24
Greenland Groënland	...	...	...	...	...	...	...	...	44.95
Guatemala Guatemala	79.1	...	...	...	...	...	...	...	7.65
Haiti Haïti	61.3	...	...	28.0	...	...	...	24.0	0.35
Honduras Honduras	41.0	...	...	65.0	...	...	...	65.0	7.70
Jamaica Jamaïque	64.3	...	...	...	...	...	...	...	0.13
Mexico Mexique	...	...	83.0	...	...	...	67.0	...	4.93
Nicaragua Nicaragua	54.3	...	...	...	...	...	...	...	6.10
Panama Panama	...	83.0	...	...	...	86.0	...	...	16.89
Saint Kitts and Nevis Saint−Kitts−et−Nevis	...	...	...	...	...	...	...	...	10.00
Saint Lucia Sainte−Lucie	...	...	...	...	...	...	...	...	2.41
St. Vincent & the Grenadines St. Vincent−Grenadines	...	...	...	...	...	...	...	...	21.3
Trinidad and Tobago Trinité−et−Tobago	96.4	...	...	...	...	...	...	...	3.07
United States Etats−Unis	...	...	...	...	...	...	...	...	11.12
America, South · Amérique du Sud									
Argentina Argentine	...	...	...	...	...	...	...	...	1.57
Bolivia Bolivie	53.4	55.0	...	...	...	41.0	...	...	8.40
Brazil Brésil	86.7	...	...	...	82.0[1]	...	...	...	3.78
Chile Chili	...	85.0	...	...	...	68.0	...	...	18.26
Colombia Colombie	85.3	...	76.0	...	...	...	63.0	...	8.22
Ecuador Equateur	54.5	...	70.0	...	...	...	64.0	...	24.08
Guyana Guyana	...	61.0	...	...	...	81.0	...	...	0.27
Paraguay Paraguay	32.4	...	...	...	...	...	...	...	3.65
Peru Pérou	53.0	...	59.0	...	...	...	46.0	...	3.25
Suriname Suriname	...	...	...	...	...	...	...	...	4.49
Uruguay Uruguay	...	...	...	...	...	...	...	...	0.17
Venezuela Venezuela	79.0	...	...	...	58.0	...	...	...	28.86
Asia · Asie									
Afghanistan Afghanistan	22.5	...	...	12.0	...	...	...	8.0	0.33
Armenia Arménie	...	...	...	...	...	...	...	...	7.18

69
Selected indicators of environmental protection
Access to safe drinking water and sanitation services; and protected area as % of land area [*cont.*]
Choix d'indicateurs de la protection de l'environnement
Accès à l'eau salubre et à des services d'assainissement; et aires protégées en pourcentage de la superficie totale [*suite*]

Country or area Pays ou zone	Access to safe drinking water (% pop.) Accès à l'eau salubre (% pop.)				Access to sanitation services (% pop.) Accès à des services d'assainissement (% pop.)				Protected area as % of land area Aires protégées en pourcentage de la superficie totale
	1990	1992	1993	1994	1990	1992	1993	1994	1994
Azerbaijan Azerbaïdjan	...	...	...	...	...	...	...	...	2.20
Bahrain Bahreïn	100.0	...	...	...	...	...	...	...	...
Bangladesh Bangladesh	78.2	...	...	92.0	...	...	...	33.0	0.67
Bhutan Bhoutan	33.9	...	...	21.0	...	...	...	21.0	20.72
Brunei Darussalam Brunéi Darussalam	...	...	...	...	...	...	...	...	19.97
China Chine	71.3	...	69.0	...	...	...	21.0	...	6.05
Cyprus Chypre	100.0	...	...	...	...	...	...	...	8.14
Georgia Géorgie	...	...	...	...	...	...	...	...	2.68
Hong Kong Hong-kong	99.8	...	...	...	...	...	...	...	...
India Inde	73.4	...	...	74.0	...	...	...	26.0	4.53
Indonesia Indonésie	33.6	...	62.0	...	...	...	51.0	...	9.67
Iran, Islamic Republic of Iran, Rép. islamique d'	...	83.0	...	...	...	67.0	...	...	5.04
Iraq Iraq	77.7	...	...	44.0	...	...	...	36.0	...
Israel Israël	...	...	...	...	...	...	...	...	14.82
Japan Japon	...	...	...	...	...	...	...	...	7.46
Jordan Jordanie	99.1	...	...	...	95.0[1]	...	...	...	3.02
Kazakstan Kazakstan	...	...	...	...	...	...	...	...	0.33
Korea D. People's R. Corée, R. p. dém. de	...	...	...	...	...	...	...	...	0.47
Korea, Republic of Corée, République de	93.0	...	...	...	...	...	...	...	7.05
Kuwait Koweït	...	...	...	...	...	...	...	...	1.11
Kyrgyzstan Kirghizistan	...	...	...	...	...	...	...	...	1.43
Lao People's Dem. Rep. Rép. dém. pop. lao	28.3	...	...	...	...	24.0	...	...	...
Lebanon Liban	...	...	...	100.0	...	...	...	100.0	0.34
Macau Macao	100.0	...	...	...	...	...	...	...	...
Malaysia Malaisie	78.4	...	...	...	...	...	...	...	4.46
Maldives Maldives	70.0	...	89.0	...	...	...	44.0	...	...
Mongolia Mongolie	80.0	...	...	...	...	...	...	...	3.94
Myanmar Myanmar	73.7	...	38.0	...	...	...	41.0	...	0.26
Nepal Népal	36.7	...	...	...	20.0[1]	...	...	...	7.84
Oman Oman	...	63.0	...	...	...	...	...	...	13.74

69

Selected indicators of environmental protection
Access to safe drinking water and sanitation services; and protected area as % of land area [*cont.*]
Choix d'indicateurs de la protection de l'environnement
Accès à l'eau salubre et à des services d'assainissement; et aires protégées en pourcentage de la superficie totale [*suite*]

Country or area Pays ou zone	Access to safe drinking water (% pop.) Accès à l'eau salubre (% pop.)				Access to sanitation services (% pop.) Accès à des services d'assainissement (% pop.)				Protected area as % of land area Aires protégées en pourcentage de la superficie totale
	1990	1992	1993	1994	1990	1992	1993	1994	1994
Pakistan									
Pakistan	54.8	...	...	60.0	...	...	...	30.0	4.63
Philippines									
Philippines	81.1	87.0	...	...	...	78.0	...	...	2.02
Qatar									
Qatar	100.0	...	...	...	...	76.0	...	...	0.14
Saudi Arabia									
Arabie saoudite	...	...	...	...	...	...	...	...	2.58
Singapore									
Singapour	100.0	...	...	...	...	...	...	...	4.54
Sri Lanka									
Sri Lanka	60.0	46.0	...	...	52.0[1]	...	...	...	12.13
Syrian Arab Republic									
Rép. arabe syrienne	...	...	85.0	...	...	...	56.0	...	...
Tajikistan									
Tadjikistan	...	...	...	...	...	...	...	...	0.60
Thailand									
Thaïlande	...	...	...	...	...	...	...	...	13.66
Turkey									
Turquie	...	...	...	...	...	...	...	...	1.05
Turkmenistan									
Turkménistan	...	...	...	...	...	...	...	...	2.28
Uzbekistan									
Ouzbékistan	...	...	...	...	...	...	...	...	0.55
Viet Nam									
Viet Nam	35.6	...	...	36.0	...	...	...	21.0	4.03
Europe · Europe									
Albania									
Albanie	...	...	...	...	...	...	...	...	1.18
Austria									
Autriche	...	...	...	...	...	...	...	...	23.92
Belarus									
Bélarus	...	...	...	...	...	...	...	...	1.17
Belgium									
Belgique	...	...	...	...	...	...	...	...	2.53
Bosnia and Herzegovina									
Bosnie–Herzégovine	...	...	...	...	...	...	...	...	0.49
Bulgaria									
Bulgarie	...	...	...	...	...	...	...	...	3.34
Croatia									
Croatie	...	...	...	...	...	...	...	...	6.82
Czech Republic									
République tchèque	...	...	...	...	...	...	...	...	13.53
Denmark									
Danemark	...	...	...	...	...	...	...	...	32.24
Estonia									
Estonie	...	...	...	...	...	...	...	...	9.76
Finland									
Finlande	...	...	...	...	...	...	...	...	8.10
France									
France	...	...	...	...	...	...	...	...	10.30
Germany †									
Allemagne †	...	...	...	...	...	...	...	...	25.77
Greece									
Grèce	...	...	...	...	...	...	...	...	1.69
Hungary									
Hongrie	...	...	...	...	...	...	...	...	6.17
Iceland									
Islande	...	...	...	...	...	...	...	...	8.91

69
Selected indicators of environmental protection
Access to safe drinking water and sanitation services; and protected area as % of land area [*cont.*]
Choix d'indicateurs de la protection de l'environnement
Accès à l'eau salubre et à des services d'assainissement; et aires protégées en pourcentage de la superficie totale [*suite*]

Country or area Pays ou zone	Access to safe drinking water (% pop.) Accès à l'eau salubre (% pop.)				Access to sanitation services (% pop.) Accès à des services d'assainissement (% pop.)				Protected area as % of land area Aires protégées en pourcentage de la superficie totale
	1990	1992	1993	1994	1990	1992	1993	1994	1994
Ireland Irlande	...	...	...	...	...	...	...	...	0.68
Italy Italie		...							7.55
Latvia Lettonie	...	...	...	...	...	...	...	...	12.16
Liechtenstein Liechtenstein	...	...	...	...	...	...	...	...	37.5
Lithuania Lituanie	...	...	...	...	...	...	...	...	9.73
Luxembourg Luxembourg	...	...	...	...	...	...	...	...	13.93
Netherlands Pays-Bas	...	...	...	...	...	...	...	...	9.44
Norway Norvège									17.09
Poland Pologne	...	...	...	...	...	...	...	...	9.80
Portugal Portugal	...	...	...	...	...	...	...	...	6.31
Republic of Moldova Moldova, Rép. de	...	...	...	...	...	...	...	...	0.18
Romania Roumanie	...	...	...	...	...	...	...	...	4.57
Russian Federation Fédération de Russie	...	...	...	...	...	...	...	...	3.84
Slovakia Slovaquie									72.36
Slovenia Slovénie	...	...	...	...	...	...	...	...	5.34
Spain Espagne	...	...	...	...	...	...	...	...	8.41
Sweden Suède									6.78
Switzerland Suisse	...	...	...	...	...	...	...	...	17.7
TFYR Macedonia L'ex-R.y. Macédoine	...	...	...	...					8.42
Ukraine Ukraine	...								0.87
United Kingdom Royaume-Uni	...	...	...	...	...	...	...	...	20.94
Yugoslavia Yougoslavie	...	...	...	...	...	...	...	...	3.40
Oceania · Océanie									
Australia Australie	...	...	...	...	...	...	...	...	12.18
Cook Islands Iles Cook	100.0	...	...	...	...	...	...	...	...
Fiji Fidji	79.3	...	100.0	...	...	...	100.0		1.03
French Polynesia Polynésie française	63.0	...	...	...	...	...	...	...	...
Kiribati Kiribati	72.9	...	96.0	...	...	96.0	...	...	38.93
Marshall Islands Iles Marshall	73.9	...	...	...	...	...	...	...	...
New Zealand Nouvelle-Zélande	...	...	...	...		...	...	...	23.19

69

Selected indicators of environmental protection
Access to safe drinking water and sanitation services; and protected area as % of land area [*cont.*]
Choix d'indicateurs de la protection de l'environnement
Accès à l'eau salubre et à des services d'assainissement; et aires protégées en pourcentage de la superficie totale [*suite*]

Country or area Pays ou zone	Access to safe drinking water (% pop.) Accès à l'eau salubre (% pop.)				Access to sanitation services (% pop.) Accès à des services d'assainissement (% pop.)				Protected area as % of land area Aires protégées en pourcentage de la superficie totale
	1990	1992	1993	1994	1990	1992	1993	1994	1994
Niue Nioué	100.0	100.0	...	...	...	...	100.0	...	...
Northern Mariana Islands Iles Mariannes du Nord	...	...	...	...	...	...	...	...	3.23
Palau Palaos	100.0	...	...	...	...	...	...	...	2.44
Papua New Guinea Papouasie−Nvl−Guinée	32.8	...	28.0	...	...	...	22.0	...	0.18
Samoa Samoa	81.8	...	...	...	...	...	...	...	...
Solomon Islands Iles Salomon	60.7	...	...	...	...	...	...	...	...
Tokelau Tokélaou	90.0	...	...	...	...	...	...	...	...
Tonga Tonga	96.0	...	97.0	...	...	...	97.0	...	...
Tuvalu Tuvalu	...	...	100.0	...	...	...	89.0	...	...

Source:
World Health Organization (Geneva); World Conservation Monitoring Centre (Cambridge, U.K.).

1   Data refer to 1991.

Source:
Organisation mondiale de la santé (Gèneve); Centre mondial de surveillance pour la conservation (Cambridge, Royaume−Uni).

1   Les données se rèfèrent à 1991.

70
CO_2 emission estimates
Estimations des émissions de CO_2

From fossil fuel combustion, cement production and gas flared (thousand metric tons of carbon)
Dues à la combustion de combustibles fossiles, à la production de ciment et au gaz brûlés à la torche
(milliers tonnes métriques de carbone)

Country or area Pays ou zone	1983	1984	1985	1986	1987	1988	1989	1990	1991	1992
Africa · Afrique										
Algeria Algérie	13902	18955	19330	20575	22409	22334	21270	22023	21744	21608
Angola Angola	1386	1356	1276	1263	1242	1388	1355	1369	1307	1235
Benin Bénin	126	140	161	145	145	136	146	153	156	167
Botswana Botswana	284	288	320	366	424	446	464	584	588	593
Burkina Faso Burkina Faso	119	120	122	123	132	141	147	147	152	152
Burundi Burundi	37	39	41	41	47	44	53	55	61	52
Cameroon Cameroun	1780	1632	1725	520	480	576	586	603	609	609
Cape Verde Cap–Vert	10	31	23	16	21	19	21	23	23	29
Central African Rep. Rép. centrafricaine	40	40	44	44	71	63	68	54	57	59
Chad Tchad	56	59	59	57	62	65	65	68	69	69
Comoros Comores	12	11	13	12	13	14	14	18	18	18
Congo Congo	591	497	131	522	529	541	537	550	554	1084
Côte d'Ivoire Côte d'Ivoire	1278	1453	1464	1643	2101	1746	1736	1693	1685	1722
Djibouti Djibouti	82	85	90	91	95	100	97	96	95	355
Egypt Egypte	15533	17377	17322	19391	19753	20286	20457	21887	22507	22925
Equatorial Guinea Guinée équatoriale	13	19	18	22	25	28	30	31	33	32
Ethiopia Ethiopie	493	445	488	599	696	713	744	804	798	793
Gabon Gabon	1402	1686	1724	1393	1418	1429	1472	1497	1269	1520
Gambia Gambie	44	47	47	44	49	50	49	52	54	54
Ghana Ghana	965	669	885	812	852	879	853	955	961	1032
Guinea Guinée	254	260	265	266	263	270	273	275	280	280
Guinea–Bissau Guinée–Bissau	33	36	39	41	41	46	49	55	56	57
Kenya Kenya	1272	1179	1029	1136	1412	1307	1417	1590	1323	1458
Liberia Libéria	192	191	195	198	207	220	177	127	76	76
Libyan Arab Jamahiriya Jamah. arabe libyenne	7653	7222	8028	8817	8466	9578	10268	11145	11335	10786
Madagascar Madagascar	173	234	287	309	349	347	247	266	294	258
Malawi Malawi	156	149	150	144	145	143	148	165	177	178
Maldives Maldives	14	16	18	22	22	23	23	26	26	27
Mali Mali	114	120	111	104	98	106	114	115	118	121
Mauritania Mauritanie	247	231	174	125	885	872	768	717	738	783
Mauritius Maurice	163	171	193	219	255	248	287	315	331	370

70

CO$_2$ emission estimates
From fossil fuel combustion, cement production and gas flared (thousand metric tons of carbon) [*cont.*]

Estimations des émissions de CO$_2$
Dues à la combustion de combustibles fossiles, à la production de ciment et au gaz brûlés à la torche (milliers tonnes métriques de carbone) [*suite*]

Country or area Pays ou zone	1983	1984	1985	1986	1987	1988	1989	1990	1991	1992
Morocco Maroc	4854	4865	4880	5111	5463	5793	6248	6425	6680	7463
Mozambique Mozambique	539	416	314	268	269	277	285	273	274	272
Niger Niger	264	272	273	246	274	270	284	287	291	296
Nigeria Nigéria	16343	18988	19062	20046	16178	19660	21760	24479	26008	26341
Réunion Réunion	193	213	213	231	255	268	281	297	302	307
Rwanda Rwanda	105	98	100	98	109	112	114	117	119	123
Saint Helena Sainte—Hélène	1	1	1	1	1	1	1	1	1	1
Sao Tome and Principe Sao Tomé—et—Principe	15	14	15	16	16	18	18	18	19	20
Senegal Sénégal	697	818	665	653	593	618	779	743	761	767
Seychelles Seychelles	27	27	41	45	55	54	64	33	33	41
Sierra Leone Sierra Leone	185	162	172	174	123	113	90	93	116	118
Somalia Somalie	241	189	228	248	233	237	223	5	1	4
South Africa Afrique du Sud	70545	75379	76446	78402	78189	80265	80449	79292	79597	79228
Sudan Soudan	1054	1038	1003	954	998	1028	909	944	929	945
Swaziland Swaziland	75	92	122	126	121	121	121	117	90	73
Togo Togo	126	141	130	165	179	186	186	188	196	200
Tunisia Tunisie	3073	3146	3255	3290	3204	3373	3560	3775	3736	3701
Uganda Ouganda	167	159	161	188	199	232	222	231	255	260
United Rep. Tanzania Rép. Unie de Tanzanie	605	647	642	626	650	639	687	707	706	574
Western Sahara Sahara occidental	47	49	47	49	50	49	51	54	54	54
Zaire Zaïre	1084	1067	973	903	1025	1050	1086	1132	1129	1141
Zambia Zambie	895	772	755	793	741	861	713	662	662	677
Zimbabwe Zimbabwe	2879	2731	2824	3614	4197	4435	4457	4189	4832	5097
America, North · Amérique du Nord										
Antigua and Barbuda Antigua—et—Barbuda	18	40	68	68	75	78	78	82	79	79
Aruba Aruba	...	...	...	28	120	166	139	466	489	427
Bahamas Bahamas	550	506	412	385	388	420	531	532	486	496
Barbados Barbade	187	204	230	250	257	258	270	290	329	264
Belize Belize	47	47	52	56	62	68	82	69	72	72
Bermuda Bermudes	121	119	121	113	155	174	212	161	134	109
British Virgin Islands Iles Vierges britanniques	10	9	10	11	12	13	13	13	13	14
Canada Canada	105354	108825	107111	104008	107368	114603	118441	111571	108836	111862

70

CO$_2$ emission estimates
From fossil fuel combustion, cement production and gas flared (thousand metric tons of carbon) [cont.]

Estimations des émissions de CO$_2$
Dues à la combustion de combustibles fossiles, à la production de ciment et au gaz brûlés à la torche
(milliers tonnes métriques de carbon) [suite]

Country or area Pays ou zone	1983	1984	1985	1986	1987	1988	1989	1990	1991	1992
Cayman Islands Iles Caïmanes	46	50	52	55	59	61	70	68	74	75
Costa Rica Costa Rica	575	546	618	712	752	802	798	772	903	1039
Cuba Cuba	8284	8724	8684	8971	9082	9535	9853	8848	7657	7812
Dominica Dominique	11	12	13	13	13	15	16	16	16	16
Dominican Republic Rép. dominicaine	2137	2015	1973	2215	2661	2691	2831	2572	2806	2797
El Salvador El Salvador	519	432	545	542	669	673	705	714	880	969
Greenland Groënland	97	153	137	87	63	147	128	151	149	131
Grenada Grenade	17	17	18	21	22	28	28	33	33	33
Guadeloupe Guadeloupe	222	239	243	259	275	306	308	312	315	318
Guatemala Guatemala	859	933	960	916	1002	1047	1094	1234	1274	1544
Haiti Haïti	204	205	213	217	236	249	264	260	249	214
Honduras Honduras	546	542	520	504	594	679	740	701	732	835
Jamaica Jamaïque	1750	1351	1367	1217	1339	1125	1737	2139	2149	2195
Martinique Martinique	278	403	329	371	447	434	370	375	369	391
Mexico Mexique	77917	75354	76601	74824	78283	77867	81606	85551	88705	90844
Montserrat Montserrat	6	6	7	8	8	9	9	9	9	10
Netherlands Antilles Antilles néerlandaises	1567[1]	1573[1]	1525[1]	1349	1104	938	...	...	761	1107
Nicaragua Nicaragua	544	504	542	570	681	636	421	577	551	681
Panama Panama	927	807	768	796	927	696	688	714	881	1154
Puerto Rico Porto Rico	3867	3551	3675	4416	5416	4172	3442	3193	3264	3589
Saint Lucia Sainte−Lucie	28	30	34	35	39	44	44	44	44	272
Saint Kitts and Nevis Saint−Kitts−et−Nevis	14	14	14	16	15	18	18	18	20	20
Saint Pierre and Miquelon Saint−Pierre−et−Miquelon	9	10	9	13	14	18	28	25	28	26
St. Vincent and the Grenadines St. Vincent−Grenadines	11	18	18	18	21	18	21	22	21	23
Trinidad and Tobago Trinité−et−Tobago	4404	4748	5635	4728	4762	4324	4290	4617	5615	5634
Turks and Caicos Islands Iles Turques et Caiques	0	0	0	0	0	0	0	0	0	0
US Virgin Islands Iles Vierges américaines	2060	1400	1490	1371	1576	1480	1861	2221	2431	2309
United States Etats−Unis	1143714	1184227	1202453	1224096	1268062	1340168	1347634	1322212	1317297	1332246
America, South · Amérique du Sud										
Argentina Argentine	28005	28416	26649	27555	30663	32393	31307	29961	31670	31933
Bolivia Bolivie	1169	1101	1125	1030	1098	1184	1360	1501	1564	1810

70

CO$_2$ emission estimates
From fossil fuel combustion, cement production and gas flared (thousand metric tons of carbon) [*cont.*]

Estimations des émissions de CO$_2$
Dues à la combustion de combustibles fossiles, à la production de ciment et au gaz brûlés à la torche (milliers tonnes métriques de carbone) [*suite*]

Country or area Pays ou zone	1983	1984	1985	1986	1987	1988	1989	1990	1991	1992
Brazil Brésil	44473	44520	47675	52621	55186	55570	56908	55419	58508	59245
Chile Chili	6101	6379	6082	6067	6352	7613	9184	9854	9289	9481
Colombia Colombie	13331	13194	13050	13251	13648	14198	14412	15208	15826	16783
Ecuador Equateur	5333	5796	5236	4083	4049	4581	4186	4630	4873	5155
Falkland Islands (Malvinas) Iles Falkland (Malvinas)	6	6	8	9	9	11	11	10	10	10
French Guiana Guyane française	103	95	99	98	111	129	143	180	144	152
Guyana Guyana	332	380	383	282	277	269	205	219	228	228
Paraguay Paraguay	393	414	428	466	528	615	640	617	610	715
Peru Pérou	5522	5570	5107	5856	6824	6824	6195	5799	5713	6080
Suriname Suriname	375	424	435	479	480	507	497	482	554	548
Uruguay Uruguay	1029	933	889	857	945	1287	1309	1066	1217	1375
Venezuela Venezuela	25815	26317	26457	27918	28816	29924	29157	31000	31047	31775
Asia · Asie										
Afghanistan Afghanistan	677	762	948	846	839	768	743	716	668	380
Armenia Arménie	...	...	...	...	...	...	...	...	...	1146
Azerbaijan Azerbaïdjan	...	...	...	...	...	...	...	...	...	17434
Bahrain Bahreïn	2252	2445	2737	3192	3299	3385	3300	3598	3493	3475
Bangladesh Bangladesh	2247	2484	2768	3098	3200	3678	3843	4241	4217	4699
Bhutan Bhoutan	8	14	17	15	28	30	17	35	35	36
Brunei Darussalam Brunéi Darussalam	733	519	704	623	902	1409	1608	1588	1680	1834
Cambodia Cambodge	100	112	114	118	119	123	123	123	126	130
China Chine	455215	494786	536666	564391	602467	646047	657086	660736	694154	728161
Cyprus Chypre	844	867	846	967	1125	1126	1184	1270	1223	1360
Georgia Géorgie	...	...	...	...	...	...	...	...	...	3777
Hong Kong Hong-kong	5569	5921	6092	6793	7494	8225	8617	7245	7997	9434
India Inde	118457	122502	134286	144167	152739	164699	179237	186187	199508	210000
Indonesia Indonésie	30981	31816	33555	35240	34482	34321	39109	42398	46525	50378
Iraq Iraq	9947	10210	10959	12031	13335	17350	18804	13442	11894	17611
Iran, Islamic Rep. of Iran, Rép. islamique d'	36904	37965	40301	37475	40009	44535	48784	57808	61162	64268
Israel Israël	6545	7138	7464	7610	7864	8530	8976	9559	9767	11355
Japan Japon	233413	252146	245751	245530	243312	267409	274791	289064	294749	298436
Jordan Jordanie	2008	2278	2309	2530	2639	2544	2524	2779	2726	3087

70

CO$_2$ emission estimates
From fossil fuel combustion, cement production and gas flared (thousand metric tons of carbon) [*cont.*]

Estimations des émissions de CO$_2$
Dues à la combustion de combustibles fossiles, à la production de ciment et au gaz brûlés à la torche
(milliers tonnes métriques de carbone) [*suite*]

Country or area Pays ou zone	1983	1984	1985	1986	1987	1988	1989	1990	1991	1992
Kazakstan Kazakstan	...	...	...	...	...	...	...	...	...	81327
Korea, Dem.People's Rep. Corée, R. p. dém. de	37637	40515	43429	47197	52854	60535	64233	67117	68109	69255
Korea, Republic of Corée, République de	38517	41901	46371	47059	49488	56897	60409	65995	73015	79103
Kuwait [2] Koweït [2]	5893	7736	7952	9630	8583	8570	9125	7313	3334	4359
Kyrgyzstan Kirghizistan	...	...	...	...	...	...	...	...	...	4196
Lao People's Dem. Rep. Rép. dém. pop. lao	48	49	54	56	56	56	63	63	69	74
Lebanon Liban	1996	1923	2197	2116	2172	2088	2196	2483	2592	3016
Macau Macao	179	156	198	239	263	262	280	280	297	295
Malaysia Malaisie	10359	9465	9820	10798	10997	11491	13180	15104	16695	19239
Mongolia Mongolie	1859	1713	2389	2573	2808	3068	2801	2744	2667	2533
Myanmar Myanmar	1400	1629	1663	1731	1241	1346	1339	1383	1166	1197
Nepal Népal	136	193	186	192	238	272	249	172	264	354
Oman Oman	2024	2096	2269	2546	2456	2757	2731	3059	3193	2739
Pakistan Pakistan	10974	11674	12859	13489	14586	15865	16486	18304	18768	19624
Philippines Philippines	9676	8601	8043	8277	9084	10806	11067	12110	12473	13564
Qatar Qatar	3011	3293	3319	3563	3081	3194	3815	3683	4615	7652
Saudi Arabia [2] Arabie saoudite [2]	37630	36744	41518	49303	42708	43544	46601	48334	58333	60213
Singapore Singapour	10252	8439	8267	8900	8179	9042	10021	11442	12227	13589
Sri Lanka Sri Lanka	1332	1059	1076	1008	1110	949	948	1052	1136	1357
Syrian Arab Republic Rép. arabe syrienne	6798	8155	7179	7777	9105	9340	8925	9784	11103	11574
Tajikistan Tadjikistan	...	...	...	...	...	...	...	...	...	1084
Thailand Thaïlande	11573	12538	13234	13506	15447	18211	21442	25979	28665	30698
Turkey Turquie	25985	26821	30713	34344	36613	32206	36785	39680	39223	39708
Turkmenistan Turkménistan	...	...	...	...	...	...	...	...	...	11533
United Arab Emirates Emirats arabes unis	7912	7759	11243	12088	13683	14048	15355	15465	17301	19273
Uzbekistan Ouzbékistan	...	...	...	...	...	...	...	...	...	33639
Viet Nam Viet Nam	5286	4802	5810	6331	7123	6376	4817	6172	5516	5874
Yemen Yémen	...	...	...	...	...	...	...	1031	2080	2752
former Dem. Yemen anc. Yémen dém.	1047	1152	1500	1395	1453	1690	1772	...	...	...
former Yemen Arab Rep. anc. Yémen rép. arabe	678	804	861	860	812	841	859	...	...	...
Europe · Europe										
Albania Albanie	1975	2000	2036	2105	1933	1870	1807	1702	1373	1083

70

CO$_2$ emission estimates
From fossil fuel combustion, cement production and gas flared (thousand metric tons of carbon) [*cont.*]

Estimations des émissions de CO$_2$
Dues à la combustion de combustibles fossiles, à la production de ciment et au gaz brûlés à la torche
(milliers tonnes métriques de carbone) [*suite*]

Country or area Pays ou zone	1983	1984	1985	1986	1987	1988	1989	1990	1991	1992
Austria Autriche	14078	14676	14715	14524	14724	14130	14478	15445	15921	15440
Belarus Bélarus	...	...	...	...	...	...	...	...	...	27846
Belgium Belgique	26427	27107	27254	26398	26239	24039	25352	26711	28323	27775
Bosnia and Herzegovina Bosnie−Herzégovine	...	...	...	...	...	...	...	...	...	4109
Bulgaria Bulgarie	23929	23106	23708	24197	24216	23043	22940	20432	16445	14836
Croatia Croatie	...	...	...	...	...	...	...	...	...	4424
former Czechoslovakia † anc. Tchécoslovaquie †	64756	66935	65119	65677	65003	63367	62129	57571	52226	...
Czech Republic République tchèque	...	...	...	...	...	...	...	...	...	37011
Denmark Danemark	14351	14562	17338	16964	16834	15049	13038	13918	17211	14710
Estonia Estonie	...	...	...	...	...	...	...	...	...	5700
Faeroe Islands Iles Féroé	133	136	141	134	136	145	158	168	157	158
Finland Finlande	11347	11242	12993	14780	14717	13720	14248	13946	14168	11238
France [3] France [3]	108731	104705	103279	98164	95412	87787	96169	96601	102306	98820
Germany † Allemagne †	...	...	...	...	...	...	...	...	241444	239666
Federal Rep. of Germany R. f. Allemagne	183390	187014	184643	184989	180872	182867	179213	183931	...	...
former German Dem. Rep. anc. R. d. allemande	83521	86014	90216	91123	91040	88945	88012	81641	...	...
Gibraltar Gibraltar	3	3	4	5	7	10	10	16	18	13
Greece Grèce	15106	15514	16322	15925	16936	18026	19665	19487	19944	20158
Hungary Hongrie	22773	23259	21946	21075	21199	19893	19273	17888	17328	16351
Iceland Islande	423	495	446	485	497	521	530	552	491	485
Ireland Irlande	6754	6800	6969	7801	8142	8234	7790	8136	8343	8420
Italy [4] Italie [4]	93598	95770	97686	95118	99343	101499	106717	108223	109970	111272
Latvia Lettonie	...	...	...	...	...	...	...	...	...	4034
Lithuania Lituanie	...	...	...	...	...	...	...	...	...	6006
Luxembourg Luxembourg	2183	2345	2391	2357	2277	2371	2541	2636	2820	2874
Malta Malte	267	366	324	358	366	421	457	455	454	455
Netherlands Pays−Bas	30410	32802	35014	33072	33593	32649	37591	38035	38309	37944
Norway Norvège	11012	11164	11441	13639	12170	12688	11043	14282	15807	16443
Poland Pologne	114445	119298	122428	124377	127773	122212	116090	95184	94207	93311
Portugal Portugal	8172	7821	8372	8115	8735	8852	11164	11411	11612	12877
Republic of Moldova Moldova, Rép. de	...	...	...	...	...	...	...	...	...	3878

70

CO$_2$ emission estimates
From fossil fuel combustion, cement production and gas flared (thousand metric tons of carbon) [*cont.*]

Estimations des émissions de CO$_2$
Dues à la combustion de combustibles fossiles, à la production de ciment et au gaz brûlés à la torche
(milliers tonnes métriques de carbone) [*suite*]

Country or area Pays ou zone	1983	1984	1985	1986	1987	1988	1989	1990	1991	1992
Romania Roumanie	53402	50294	51537	53578	56294	56333	56929	42320	37257	33325
Russian Federation Fédération de Russie	...	...	...	...	...	...	...	...	...	573999
Slovakia Slovaquie	...	...	...	...	...	...	...	...	...	10098
Slovenia Slovénie	...	...	...	...	...	...	...	...	...	1502
Spain Espagne	53200	49781	51783	47295	48628	49993	56944	57842	60011	60916
Sweden Suède	15416	15091	16449	16248	15732	15617	14990	13637	14310	15501
Switzerland Suisse	10901	10668	10845	11477	10959	11069	10723	11654	11470	11927
TFYR Macedonia L'ex−R.y. Macédoine	...	...	...	...	...	...	...	...	...	1119
Ukraine Ukraine	...	...	...	...	...	...	...	...	...	166851
United Kingdom Royaume−Uni	151153	143853	153283	155878	156980	155967	158217	155465	159054	154543
Yugoslavia Yougoslavie	30520	32245	33053	34607	34022	35392	35204	35132	23806	...
Yugoslavia, SFR † Yougoslavie, Rfs †	...	...	...	...	...	...	...	...	...	10425
Oceania · Océanie										
American Samoa Samoa américaines	114	63	59	59	55	69	69	78	78	82
Australia Australie	56730	59407	60861	60925	64650	65786	69870	72608	71177	73127
Christmas Island Ile Christmas	22	...	...	...	...	...	...	...	...	...
Cook Islands Iles Cook	14	6	6	6	6	6	6	6	6	6
Fiji Fidji	196	159	158	164	130	151	172	222	185	194
French Polynesia Polynésie française	110	121	157	162	163	152	160	167	168	170
Guam Guam	535	301	342	359	380	392	396	409	409	409
Kiribati Kiribati	6	6	6	5	6	6	6	6	6	6
Nauru Nauru	34	34	34	34	34	34	34	36	36	37
New Caledonia Nouvelle−Calédonie	314	327	396	382	397	421	461	441	486	478
New Zealand Nouvelle−Zélande	4985	5344	5901	6425	6560	6686	7031	6451	6857	7145
Niue Nioué	1	1	1	1	1	1	1	1	1	1
Palau Palaos	42	42	43	43	43	49	61	64	64	64
Papua New Guinea Papouasie−Nvl−Guinée	548	558	580	563	637	600	614	623	616	616
Samoa Samoa	31	31	31	31	31	31	33	34	34	35
Solomon Islands Iles Salomon	39	39	41	42	44	42	44	44	44	44
Tonga Tonga	13	13	13	13	15	19	19	21	25	24
Vanuatu Vanuatu	15	15	33	16	12	17	16	18	18	17

70

CO$_2$ emission estimates
From fossil fuel combustion, cement production and gas flared (thousand metric tons of carbon) [cont.]

Estimations des émissions de CO$_2$
Dues à la combustion de combustibles fossiles, à la production de ciment et au gaz brûlés à la torche
(milliers tonnes métriques de carbone) [suite]

Country or area Pays ou zone	1983	1984	1985	1986	1987	1988	1989	1990	1991	1992
Wake Island Ile de Wake	22	22	22	22	22	22	22	22	19	21
former USSR ancienne URSS †	944142	954642	1033379	1033768	1077352	1109178	1082160	1012979	977396	...

Source:
Carbon Dioxide Information Analysis Center (Oak Ridge, Tennessee).

†   For detailed descriptions of data pertaining to former
     Czechoslovakia, Germany, SFR Yugoslavia and former
     USSR, see Annex I – Country or area nomenclature,
     regional and other groupings.

1   Including Aruba.
2   Part Neutral Zone.
3   Including Monaco.
4   Including San Marino.

Source:
Carbon Dioxide Information Analysis Center (Oak Ridge, Tennessee).

†   Pour les descriptions en détails des données relatives à l'ancienne
     Tchécoslovaquie, l'Allemagne, la Rfs Yougoslavie et l'ancienne
     URSS, voir l'Annexe I – Nomenclature des pays ou zones,
     groupements régionaux et autres groupements.

1   Y compris l'Aruba.
2   Part Zone Neutrel.
3   Y compris Monaco.
4   Y compris Saint–Marin.

Technical notes, tables 68-70

Table 68: The Food and Agriculture Organization of the United Nations (FAO) undertakes periodic assessments of the world's forest resources. The data in the table are published in *Forest Resources Assessment 1990* [7].

For the developed countries forest land is that with tree crown cover (stand density) of more than 20% of the area. Continuous forest with trees usually growing more than 7 m in height and able to produce wood. This includes both closed and open forest formulations. Other wooded land is land which has some forestry characteristics but is not forest as defined earlier. It includes open woodland and scrub, shrub and brushland. It excludes land occupied by "Trees outside the forest".

For the developing countries forests are ecological systems with a minimum crown coverage of land surface (here assumed as 10%) and generally associated with wild flora, fauna and natural soil conditions and not subject to agronomic practices. Only forest areas more than a minimum area of 100 ha are considered. Forests are further subdivided into natural forests and plantation forests. Other wooded land includes the following two categories: (i) forest fallow which refers to all complexes of woody vegetation deriving from the clearing of natural forest for shifting agriculture; and (ii) shrubs which refer to vegetation types where the dominant woody elements are shrubs with more than 50 cm and less that 5 metres height on maturity.

When available, annual change data from 1980 to 1990 are shown for the total of forest and other wooded land.

Data on the numbers of threatened species are compiled by the World Conservation Monitoring Centre (WCMC) from the 1994 IUCN Red List of Threatened Animals and are published in the *Biodiversity Data Sourcebook* [31]. This list provides a catalogue of those animal species - mammals, birds, reptiles, amphibians, fishes and invertebrates - that are considered to be globally threatened. Each species is assigned an IUCN status category which is determined by a review of the factors affecting it and the extent of the effect that these factors are having throughout its range. The categories comprise endangered, vulnerable, rare, indeterminate and insufficiently known.

Data on the numbers of extinct species are also compiled by the WCMC. The figures include species listed as Ex and Ex?: Ex being those that have not been definitely located in the wild during the past 50 years; and Ex? being those where it is virtually certain that the taxon has become extinct. They also include species that are known or believed to have become extinct since 1600 AD or thereabouts and which have never appeared in previous Red Lists nor been given a status category.

Notes techniques, tableaux 68-70

Tableau 68 : L'Organisation des Nations Unies pour l'alimentation et l'agriculture (FAO) procède à des évaluations périodiques des ressources forestières mondiales. Les données figurant dans le tableau sont publiées dans "Forest Resources Assessment 1990" [7].

Dans les pays développés, on considère qu'un espace forestier est une zone où la couronne d'arbres (densité de peuplement) correspond à plus de 20 % de la superficie avec une forêt continue dont les arbres atteignent généralement des hauteurs supérieures à 7 mètres et peuvent produire du bois. Cela inclut les forêts-parcs et les forêts denses. On appelle terres boisées des terres qui présentent certaines caractéristiques des forêts, mais ne correspondent pas à la définition des forêts donnée plus haut. Cela inclut les forêts claires et les broussailles, les maquis et les taillis. Cela n'inclut pas les terres où poussent des "arbres en dehors de forêt".

Dans les pays en développement, la forêt est un écosystème dont une superficie minimale est couverte par une couronne d'arbres (ici 10 % de la superficie) et généralement associée à une flore et une faune sauvages; le sol y est normalement à l'état naturel et elle ne fait l'objet d'aucune pratique culturale. On ne tient compte que de zones forestières supérieures à une superficie de 100 hectares. Les forêts se divisent en forêts naturelles et plantations. D'autres catégories de terres boisées sont notamment : i) les friches forestières qui correspondent à tous les systèmes de végétation ligneuse découlent du déboisement d'une forêt naturelle effective pour un nouveau mode d'agriculture; et ii) des brousses, c'est-à-dire des types de végétation dont les éléments ligneux dominants sont des bosquets dont la hauteur à maturité est comprise entre 50 centimètres et 5 mètres.

Dans la mesure du possible, les données reflétant des changements annuels entre 1980 et 1990 sont indiquées pour le total des forêts et autres terres boisées.

Les données relatives au nombre d'espèces menacées sont compilées pour le Centre mondial de surveillance pour la conservation de la liste rouge 1994 des animaux menacés tenue par l'Union internationale pour la conservation de la nature et de ses ressources (UICN) et sont publiées dans "Biodiversity Data Sourcebook" [31]. La liste recense les diverses espèces de mammifères, d'oiseaux, de reptiles, d'amphibiens, de poissons et d'invertébrés qui sont considérées comme menacées dans le monde entier. Chaque espèce est affectée à l'une des catégories d'espèces UICN suivantes, choisie sur la base des facteurs qui l'influencent et de tous les effets qu'exercent ces facteurs : espèces éteintes; espèces en voie de disparition; espèces vulnérables; espèces rares; espèces en situation indéterminée; et espèces en situation insuffisamment connue.

The data on production of energy refer to the first stage of production; accordingly, for hard coal and lignite the data refer to mine production; for crude oil and natural gas to production at oil and gas wells. These data are compiled by the United Nations Statistics Division and published in the *Energy Statistics Yearbook* [22]. The data on reserves refer to proved recoverable reserves of coal, crude oil and natural gas and are compiled by the World Energy Council and published in the *Survey of Energy Resources* [32]. Proved recoverable reserves are the tonnage of the proved amount in place that can be recovered (extracted from the earth in raw form) in the future under present and expected economic conditions and existing technological limits. The ratio of production data to reserves means the annual percentage share of energy commodities produced in the total proved recoverable reserves known in 1993.

Table 69: The World Health Organization compiles data on access to safe drinking water and sanitation services. Although there is a wide variation in the definition of service coverage between countries, access to safe drinking water in urban areas is generally taken to mean the existence of piped water to housing units or to public standpipes within 200 m of the dwelling. In rural areas reasonable access implies that fetching water does not take up a disproportionate part of the day. Safe drinking water includes treated surface water and untreated water from protected springs, boreholes and wells.

Access to sanitation services is generally considered to mean access to a sanitary facility in the dwelling (i.e., connection to public sewers or household disposal systems such as pit privies, pour flush latrines and septic tanks) or located within a convenient distance (e.g., communal toilets).

Although no data are available on the access to safe drinking water and sanitation services for the developed countries, the situation observed indicates that a very small proportion of people, in particular in the remote areas, in those countries do not have such access.

Information on protected areas is routinely collated by the World Conservation Monitoring Centre and is published in the *Biodiversity Data Sourcebook.* [31] Countries vary considerably in their mechanisms for creating and maintaining systems of protected areas. In order to facilitate international comparisons for protected areas, the IUCN have developed a classification system for the different types of designated protected areas. Protected areas which fall into IUCN management categories I to V, inclusive can be considered as having been established with conservation aims in mind. These categories are:

    (i)   Strict Nature Reserve/Scientific Reserve
    (ii) National Park
    (iii) Natural Monument/Natural Landmark
    (iv) Managed Nature Reserve/Wildlife Sanctuary
    (v) Protected Landscapes and Seascapes

Les données relatives au nombre d'espèces éteintes sont également compilés par le Centre mondial de surveillance pour la conservation. Les chiffres indiqués couvrent des espèces désignées par le symbole Ex et Ex? : le symbole Ex désigne des espèces qui n'ont pu être observées en liberté au cours des 50 dernières années; le symbole Ex? indique que l'on est presque certain que le groupe taxonomique est effectivement éteint. Les données concernent également des espèces qui sont (ou que l'on soupçonne) éteintes depuis le XVIIe siècle et qui n'ont jamais figuré sur la Liste rouge ni été inscrites dans une autre catégorie.

Les données sur la production d'énergie se réfèrent à la première étape du processus, soit la production à la mine pour la houille et le lignite et la production à la tête de puits pour le pétrole brut et le gaz naturel. Ces données sont compilées par la Division de statistique des Nations Unies et sont publiées dans *l'Annuaire des statistiques de l'énergie* [22]. Les données relatives aux réserves se réfèrent aux réserves récupérables prouvées de charbon, de pétrole et de gaz naturel et sont compilées pour *le Conseil mondial d'énergie* et sont publiées dans "*Survey of Energy Resources*" [32]. Les réserves récupérables prouvées représentent le tonnage en place qu'il sera possible d'extraire du sol sous forme brute dans les conditions économiques actuelles et prévisibles et dans les limites techniques existantes. Le rapport production/réserves correspond au pourcentage annuel des matières énergétiques produites par rapport au total des réserves récupérables prouvées connues en 1991.

Tableau 69 : L'Organisation mondiale de la santé (OMS) compile des données relatives à l'accès à l'eau salubre et aux services d'assainissement. Bien que la définition de la desserte varie beaucoup d'un pays à l'autre, on entend généralement par « accès à l'eau salubre » l'existence en milieu urbain de conduites d'eau alimentant soit les unités d'habitation soit des fontaines publiques situées dans un rayon de 200 mètres du logement. En milieu rural l'accès à l'eau salubre est considéré comme raisonnable dans la mesure où la corvée d'eau n'occupe pas une partie disproportionnée de la journée. L'eau salubre comprend les eaux superficielles traitées et les eaux non traitées provenant de sources, forages et puits protégés.

L'accès à des services d'assainissement est généralement défini comme la présence dans le logement de lieux d'aisance raccordés au tout-à-l'égout ou à un système local pour l'évacuation des déchets humains (cabinet à fosse, cabinet à chasse d'eau et fosse septique) ou l'existence de lieux d'aisance d'accès commode situés à proximité (par exemple, toilettes collectives).

Bien que l'on ne dispose pas de données relatives à l'accès à l'eau potable et à des services d'assainissement dans les pays développés, la situation observée donne à penser que seule une très faible proportion de la population, en particulier dans les zones reculées de ces pays, n'est pas desservie.

Table 70: Emissions of CO_2 data are calculated by the Carbon Dioxide Information Analysis Center located at the Oak Ridge National Laboratory. National emissions of CO_2 from industrial sources are derived from UN consumption data for gas, liquid and solid fuels plus cement manufacturing and gas flaring statistics to which appropriate emission factors have been applied. Emissions are in units of 1000 metric tons of carbon; to convert carbon into carbon dioxide, multiply data by 3.67. Full details of the procedures for calculating emissions are given in *Estimates of Global, Regional, and National Annual C0₂ Emissions from Fossil-Fuel Burning, Hydraulic Cement Production, and Gas Flaring: 1950-1992* [3]. Relative to the other industrial sources for which $C0_2$ emissions are calculated, statistics on gas flaring activities are sparse and sporadic. In countries where gas flaring activities account for a considerable proportion of the total CO_2 emission, the sporadic nature of gas flaring statistics may produce spurious or misleading trends in national CO_2 emissions over the period covered by the table.

Des données concernant les aires protégées sont régulièrement colligées par le Centre mondial mixte PNUE/UICN/WWF de surveillance pour la conservation et sont publiées dans *"Biodiversity Data Sourcebook"* [31]. Les mécanismes nationaux pour la création et l'entretien de systèmes pour les aires protégées varient considérablement d'un pays à l'autre. Dans le but de faciliter les comparaisons à l'échelle internationale, l'UICN a mis au point une classification qui répartit les divers types d'aires protégées. Les données concernent les aires protégées, qui relèvent des catégories de gestion I à V de l'UICN (aires ayant été créées dans un souci de conservation) :

(i) Réserves scientifiques ou strictement naturelles;
(ii) Parcs nationaux;
(iii) Monuments ou éléments topographiques naturels;
(iv) Réserves naturelles aménagées ou refuges animaliers;
(v) Paysages naturels protégés, y compris les paysages marins.

Tableau 70 : Les données des émissions CO_2 sont calculées par "Carbon Dioxide Information Analysis Center" situé à "Oak Ridge National Laboratory". Les valeurs établies à l'échelon national pour les émissions CO_2 sont tirées des données de l'ONU concernant les combustibles gazeux, liquides et solides et des statistiques relatives à la fabrication de ciment et à la combustion de gaz de torche, multipliées par des coefficients appropriés pour le calcul des émissions. Les émissions sont indiquées en millions de tonnes de carbone; pour convertir le carbone en dioxyde de carbone, il convient de multiplier la valeur indiquée par un coefficient de 3,67. Tous les détails concernant le calcul des émissions figurent dans *"Estimates of Global, Regional, and National Annual C0₂ Emissions from Fossil-Fuel Burning, Hydraulic Cement Production, and Gas Flaring: 1950-1992"* [3]. Par rapport aux autres sources industrielles dont on calcule les émissions de CO_2, les statistiques concernant la combustion de gaz de torche sont peu nombreuses et sporadiques. Dans les pays ou la combustion de gaz de torche est responsable d'une part considérable des émissions totales de CO_2, le caractère sporadique des statistiques concernant cette activité risque d'induire des tendances parasites ou inexactes dans les valeurs relatives aux émissions de CO_2 à l'échelon national pendant la période considérée dans le tableau.

71
Patents
Brevets
Applications, grants, patents in force: number
Demandes, délivrances, brevets en vigueur : nombre

Country or area Pays ou zone	Applications for patents Demandes de brevets			Grants of patents Brevets délivrés			Patents in force Brevets en vigueur		
	1991	1992	1993	1991	1992	1993	1991	1992	1993
African Intellectual Prop. Org[1] Org. africaine de la prop. intel.[1]	4 463	6 102	8 458	150	392	159	1 853	1 791	1 423
Algeria Algérie	139	144	121	617	83	...	...	...	...
Argentina Argentine	...	2 453	...	406	663	3 479	...	...	...
Armenia Arménie	...	...	214	...	...	...	...	...	...
Australia Australie	27 672	28 927	30 729	12 636	12 899	12 728	67 845	70 516	72 809
Austria Autriche	43 535	48 352	51 491	13 354	14 956	16 787	23 798	21 818	19 477
Bahamas Bahamas	28	31	...	...	31	...	...	...	...
Bahrain Bahreïn	...	31	...	...	26	...	...	...	...
Bangladesh Bangladesh	113	161	107	78	61	76	597	595	559
Barbados Barbade	4 336	5 875	8 365	...	...	...	...	...	...
Belarus Bélarus	...	...	5 715	...	...	237	...	...	237
Belgium Belgique	42 047	45 260	46 520	14 291	17 026	19 074	86 075	100 081	81 494
Bolivia Bolivie	...	...	88	...	...	1	...	...	...
Botswana Botswana	68	89	107	39	29	42	...	...	...
Brazil Brésil	12 769	14 180	16 944	2 419	1 822	2 649	...	...	...
Brunei Darussalam Brunéi Darussalam	...	...	88	...	...	251	...	...	1 384
Bulgaria Bulgarie	5 584	7 136	9 512	417	394	1	1 591	824	837
Burundi Burundi	...	2	1	...	2	...	129	14	15
Canada Canada	38 380	44 064	47 752	15 473	18 332	14 580	333 370	331 158	320 000
Chile Chili	1 000	1 139	...	506	460	...	7 879	7 756	79
China Chine	11 423	14 409	19 618	4 122	3 966	6 556	...	...	...
Colombia Colombie	612	695	907	425	248	280	...	...	...
Costa Rica Costa Rica	...	...	120	...	...	6	...	...	...
Croatia Croatie	...	1 489	1 249	...	...	...	...	...	...

71
Patents
Applications, grants, patents in force: number [cont.]
Brevets
Demandes, délivrances, brevets en vigueur : nombre [suite]

Country or area Pays ou zone	Applications for patents Demandes de brevets			Grants of patents Brevets délivrés			Patents in force Brevets en vigueur		
	1991	1992	1993	1991	1992	1993	1991	1992	1993
Cuba Cuba	24	20	14	3	11	12	388	170	...
Cyprus Chypre	53	57	...	54	57	...	688	727	...
Czech Republic République tchèque	...	...	11 804	...	...	860	...	...	15 150
former Czechoslovakia† anc. Tchécoslovaquie†	5 934	10 715	...	1 401	1 751	...	...	18 582	...
Denmark Danemark	39 764	44 351	47 088	2 609	3 773	6 629	12 213	14 206	16 466
Ecuador Equateur	88	107	121	102	60	45	342	372	371
Egypt Egypte	787	818	831	403	290	341	...	...	...
El Salvador El Salvador	36	108	85	6	24	61	...	...	258
European Patent Office[2] Office européen de brevets[2]	66 822	70 747	70 278	26 643	30 408	36 667	...	...	...
Finland Finlande	12 099	14 927	15 647	2 683	2 695	2 721	16 629	18 367	18 721
France France	79 075	82 038	82 141	35 581	38 215	44 291	114 249	296 316	296 433
Gambia Gambie	62	81	98	35	26	34	...	...	...
Georgia Géorgie	...	428	1 027	...	...	19	...	...	19
Germany † Allemagne†	109 187	115 209	117 768	43 190	...	52 008	244 488	253 267	261 229
Ghana Ghana	87	101	158	37	24	31	...	...	...
Greece Grèce	32 359	35 958	36 907	3 688	6 361	7 835	...	...	6 174
Guatemala Guatemala	95	73	81	123	65	19	1 390	1 317	...
Haiti Haïti	8	...	...	8	...	...	...	...	...
Honduras Honduras	19	30	...	...	24	...	441	465	...
Hong Kong Hong-kong	1 092	1 259	1 195	1 079	1 069	1 438	...	...	...
Hungary Hongrie	9 950	10 931	12 779	2 305	2 112	1 409	19 433	...	...
Iceland Islande	133	149	146	30	48	6	317	339	314
India Inde	3 595	3 424	3 720	1 572	1 469	1 551	11 126	10 031	9 765
Indonesia Indonésie	1 336	4 027	...	...	...	...	...	...	...
Iran, Islamic Rep. of Iran, Rép. islamique d'	427	400	442	286	205	149	...	...	...

71
Patents
Applications, grants, patents in force: number [*cont.*]
Brevets
Demandes, délivrances, brevets en vigueur : nombre [*suite*]

Country or area Pays ou zone	Applications for patents Demandes de brevets			Grants of patents Brevets délivrés			Patents in force Brevets en vigueur		
	1991	1992	1993	1991	1992	1993	1991	1992	1993
Iraq Iraq	...	174	192	...	66	63	...	1 119	1 122
Ireland Irlande	4 580	14 681	36 792	860	764	1 574	6 279	6 109	6 893
Israel Israël	3 717	3 727	3 953	2 346	2 681	2 198	10 863	11 837	12 182
Italy Italie	53 300	64 664	65 170	19 503	27 228	32 511	...	...	...
Jamaica Jamaïque	41	65	...	11	3	...	422	418	...
Japan Japon	380 453	384 456	380 035	36 100	92 100	88 400	579 695	601 635	631 063
Kazakstan Kazakstan	...	445	9 449	...	...	...	...	...	325
Kenya Kenya	131	110	175	47	58	54	1 777	...	...
Korea, Dem. P. R. Corée, R. p. dém. de	4 549	6 170	8 379	37	27	...	121	141	...
Korea, Republic of Corée, République de	36 154	40 157	47 344	8 691	10 502	11 446	28 271	39 487	47 704
Kuwait Koweït	...	...	...	...	...	107	...	...	...
Latvia Lettonie	...	661	2 666	...	...	355	...	...	354
Lesotho Lesotho	59	82	97	29	25	34	...	...	...
Liberia Libéria	17	...	35	17	...	30	490	...	...
Libyan Arab Jamah. Jamah. arabe libyenne	47	...	36	...	...	...	...	...	...
Lithuania Lituanie	29	251	1 449	...	13	383	...	13	389
Luxembourg Luxembourg	35 978	39 965	43 503	7 337	8 680	10 293	23 133	...	...
Macau Macao	...	3	...	...	...	2	...	33	35
Madagascar Madagascar	4 343	5 880	8 350	...	...	...	...	...	...
Malawi Malawi	4 402	5 947	8 443	74	57	50	350	383	387
Malaysia Malaisie	2 427	2 410	2 882	...	1 134	1 281	...	2 840	4 124
Malta Malte	27	25	24	24	12	20	134	...	146
Mauritius Maurice	10	12	6	11	9	4	142	120	119
Mexico Mexique	5 271	7 695	8 212	1 360	3 160	6 183	18 155	18 732	24 784

71
Patents
Applications, grants, patents in force: number [cont.]
        Brevets
        Demandes, délivrances, brevets en vigueur : nombre [suite]

Country or area Pays ou zone	Applications for patents Demandes de brevets			Grants of patents Brevets délivrés			Patents in force Brevets en vigueur		
	1991	1992	1993	1991	1992	1993	1991	1992	1993
Monaco Monaco	4 728	29 622	32 717	49	89	115	396	441	461
Mongolia Mongolie	1 163	4 940	8 385	38	33	50	61	122	172
Morocco Maroc	356	...	298	303	372	352	...	6 593	6 614
Namibia Namibie	133	...	133	124	...	102	1 151	...	...
Nepal Népal	...	3	9	...	6	2	...	29	31
Netherlands Pays-Bas	51 412	55 885	58 822	17 610	20 346	23 264	81 602	88 750	94 379
New Zealand Nouvelle-Zélande	4 533	4 546	12 588	3 598	2 988	2 886	...	...	...
Nicaragua Nicaragua	...	42	36	...	4	2	...	87	89
Norway Norvège	12 572	14 104	14 675	2 821	2 998	2 609	16 046	16 600	16 537
Pakistan Pakistan	524	622	636	524	436	476	...	...	...
Panama Panama	87	84	100	46	40	26	1 519	1 548	1 578
Paraguay Paraguay	...	64	101	...	24	26	...	811	...
Peru Pérou	247	283	288	193	260	114	892	1 149	...
Philippines Philippines	1 921	...	...	944	...	...	17 044	...	...
Poland Pologne	8 817	11 371	13 756	3 788	3 851	2 941	...	...	18 733
Portugal Portugal	3 555	13 402	42 932	453	1 253	1 694	3 731	6 205	8 629
Republic of Moldova République de Moldova	...	...	103	...	...	...	...	...	...
Romania Roumanie	7 184	8 318	10 952	2 127	2 100	1 713	23 820	22 898	22 626
Russian Federation Fédération de Russie	1 203	59 239	43 717	...	7 897	13 214	...	22 779	44 321
Rwanda Rwanda	1	2	...	1	2	...	82	69	...
Saint Lucia Sainte-Lucie	...	1	...	...	1	...	...	...	...
Saudi Arabia Arabie saoudite	519	626	750	...	...	...	...	...	...
Singapore Singapour	1 104	1 354	1 426	1 091	1 281	1 395	...	...	...
Slovakia Slovaquie	...	...	9 459	...	...	4	...	...	12 894

71
Patents
Applications, grants, patents in force: number [cont.]
Brevets
Demandes, délivrances, brevets en vigueur : nombre [suite]

Country or area Pays ou zone	Applications for patents Demandes de brevets			Grants of patents Brevets délivrés			Patents in force Brevets en vigueur		
	1991	1992	1993	1991	1992	1993	1991	1992	1993
Slovenia Slovénie	...	420	696	...	33	379	...	...	412
South Africa Afrique du Sud	10 202	10 128	9 807	5 885	6 125	5 096	...	...	...
Spain Espagne	48 929	53 605	56 733	9 781	14 021	15 815	...	106 536	17 359
Sri Lanka Sri Lanka	4 494	6 044	8 517	104	58	85	770	828	954
Sudan Soudan	4 411	5 986	8 473	37	56	34	...	...	...
Swaziland Swaziland	60	126	98	28	70	33	...	...	...
Sweden Suède	48 568	52 726	55 641	16 767	18 672	21 115	53 327	88 240	89 757
Switzerland Suisse	48 496	52 941	55 557	16 808	17 967	20 637	101 275	102 360	103 794
TFYR Macedonia L'ex-R.y. Macédoine	...	...	128	...	...	...	...	...	...
Thailand Thaïlande	1 987	1 962	3 345	153	199	451	...	655	...
Trinidad and Tobago Trinité-et-Tobago	...	67	91	...	67	91	...	873	964
Tunisia Tunisie	128	...	142	180	...	138	4 090	...	1 788
Turkey Turquie	1 205	1 252	1 226	694	674	804	6 351	6 369	...
Uganda Ouganda	74	96	104	42	42	38	1 679	...	...
Ukraine Ukraine	...	579	19 365	...	226	1 942	...	226	2 168
former USSR† ancienne URSS†	30 180	...	...	1 215	...	...	6 956	...	...
United Kingdom Royaume-Uni	95 533	99 241	101 242	34 074	37 827	42 586	...	...	...
United States Etats-Unis	177 388	187 291	191 386	96 514	97 443	98 344	...	1 160 613	1 131 239
Uruguay Uruguay	171	179	176	125	...	119	...	...	...
Uzbekistan Ouzbékistan	...	...	3 768	...	...	13	...	...	17
Venezuela Venezuela	1 361	1 540	1 675	593	481	2 103	...	...	...
Viet Nam Viet Nam	62	83	5 008	23	35	16	117	68	83
Yugoslavia Yougoslavie	..	1 125	838	..	375	283	..	5 143	4 418
Yugoslavia, SFR† Yougoslavie, Rfs†	2 010	..	...	1 400	...	...	10 900	...	...
Zambia Zambie	120	161	173	73	48	76	878	892	925

71

Patents

Applications, grants, patents in force: number [*cont.*]

Brevets

Demandes, délivrances, brevets en vigueur : nombre [*suite*]

Country or area Pays ou zone	Applications for patents Demandes de brevets			Grants of patents Brevets délivrés			Patents in force Brevets en vigueur		
	1991	1992	1993	1991	1992	1993	1991	1992	1993
Zimbabwe Zimbabwe	270	302	293	222	194	194	1 549	1 616	1 494

Source:
World Intellectual Property Organization (Geneva).

† For detailed descriptions of data pertaining to
former Czechoslovakia, Germany, SFR Yugoslavia and former
USSR, see Annex I - Country or area nomenclature, regional
and other groupings.

1 Members of the African Intellectual Property Organization
(OAPI), which includes Benin, Burkina Faso, Cameroon,
Central African Republic, Chad, Congo, Côte d'Ivoire, Gabon,
Guinea, Mali, Mauritania, Niger, Senegal, Togo.
2 In 1992, the European Patent Office (EPO) was constituted by
the following member countries: Austria, Belgium, Denmark,
France, Germany, Greece, Ireland, Italy, Liechtenstein,
Luxembourg, Monaco, Netherlands, Portugal, Spain, Sweden,
Switzerland, United Kingdom.

Source:
Organisation mondiale de la propriété intellectuelle
(Genève).

† Pour les descriptions en détails des données
relatives à l'ancienne Tchécoslovaquie, l'Allemagne, la Rfs
Yougoslavie et l'ancienne URSS, voir l'Annexe I -
Nomenclature des pays ou zones, groupements régionaux et
autres groupements.

1 Les membres de l'Organisation africaine de la propriété
intellectuelle (OAPI): Bénin, Burkina Faso, Cameroun, Congo,
Côte d'Ivoire, Gabon, Guinée, Mali, Mauritanie, Niger,
République centrafricaine, Sénégal, Tchad, Togo.
2 En 1992, l'Office européen de brevets (OEB) comprenait les
pays membres suivants: Allemagne, Autriche, Belgique,
Danemark, Espagne, France, Grèce, Irlande, Italie,
Liechtenstein, Luxembourg, Monaco, Pays-Bas, Portugal,
Royaume-Uni, Suède, Suisse.

Technical notes, table 71

Table 71: Data on patents include patent applications filed directly with the office concerned and grants made on the basis of such applications; inventors' certificates; patents of importation, including patents of introduction, revalidation patents and "patentes précautionales"; petty patents; patents applied and granted under the Patent Cooperation Treaty (PCT), the European Patent Convention, the Havana Agreement, the Harare Protocol of the African Regional Industrial Property Organization (ARIPO) and the African Intellectual Property Organization (OAPI). The data are compiled and published by World Intellectual Property Organization [34].

Notes techniques, tableau 71

Tableau 71 : Les données relatives aux brevets comprennent les demandes de brevet déposées directement au bureau intéressé et les délivrances effectuées sur la base de ces demandes; les brevets d'invention; les brevets d'importation; y compris les brevets d'introduction, les brevets de revalidation et les "patentes précautionales"; les petits brevets, les brevets demandés et délivrés en vertu du traité de coopération sur les brevets, de la Convention européenne relative aux brevets, de l'Accord de la Havane, du Protocole d'Hararé de l'Organisation régionale africaine de la propriété industrielle (ARIPO) et de l'Organisation africaine de la propriété intellectuelle (OAPI). Les données sont compilées et publiées par l'Organisation mondiale de la propriété intellectuelle [34].

Part Four
International Economic Relations

XVI
International merchandise trade (tables 72-75)
XVII
International tourism (tables 76-78)
XVIII
Balance of payments (table 79)
XIX
International finance (tables 80 and 81)
XX
Development assistancè (tables 82-84)

Part Four of the *Yearbook* presents statistics on international economic relations in areas of international merchandise trade, international tourism, balance of payments and assistance to developing countries. The series cover all countries or areas of the world for which data are available.

Quatrième partie
Relations économiques internationales

XVI
Commerce international des marchandises (tableaux 72 à 75)
XVII
Tourisme international (tableaux 76 à 78)
XVIII
Balance des paiements (tableau 79)
XIX
Finances internationales (tableaux 80 et 81)
XX
Aide au développement (tableaux 82 à 84)

La quatrième partie de l'*Annuaire* présente des statistiques sur les relations économiques internationales dans les domaines du commerce international des marchandises, du tourisme international, de la balance des paiements et de l'assistance aux pays en développement. Les séries couvrent tous les pays ou les zones du monde pour lesquels des données sont disponibles.

72
Total imports and exports
Importations et exportations totales
Value in million US dollars
Valeur en millions de dollars E-U

Region, country or area Region, pays ou zone	1985	1986	1987	1988	1989	1990	1991	1992	1993	1994
A. Imports c.i.f. • Importations c.i.f.										
World *Monde*	2 005 154	2 198 079	2 558 957	2 913 533	3 134 590	3 547 715	3 538 135	3 791 395	3 720 494	4 220 489
Developed economies[1][2] Econ. développées[1][2]	1 375 428	1 551 022	1 840 364	2 076 864	2 244 189	2 573 741	2 586 312	2 700 031	2 541 198	2 864 527
Developing economies[2] Econ. en dévelop.[2]	458 972	460 918	523 477	628 472	690 955	778 671	858 150	994 604	1 086 022	1 232 880
OPEC+ OPEP+	100 662	88 617	87 374	102 047	102 567	111 483	128 064	158 444	155 618	157 495
LDC+ PMA+	17 983	18 822	18 985	20 953	21 203	23 560	22 150	23 495	24 154	25 970
Other[3] Autres[3]	170 754	186 139	195 116	208 197	199 445	195 303	93 673	96 760	93 274	123 082
America • Amérique										
Developed economies **Economies développées**	**424 448**	**454 036**	**505 296**	**554 997**	**595 229**	**615 676**	**605 871**	**653 774**	**709 563**	**805 392**
Canada[4] Canada[4]	80 642	85 494	92 596	112 718	119 796	123 247	124 782	129 268	139 039	155 076
United States Etats-Unis	352 463	382 295	424 442	459 542	492 922	516 987	508 363	553 923	603 438	689 215
Developing economies **Econ. en dévelop.**	**80 256**	**84 622**	**88 334**	**102 739**	**107 195**	**118 056**	**133 070**	**159 845**	**172 178**	**201 322**
LAIA+[5] ALAI+[5]	**53 423**	**56 400**	**61 383**	**75 403**	**76 651**	**85 984**	**104 255**	**129 637**	**140 530**	**168 241**
Argentina[6] Argentine[6]	3 814	4 724	5 818	5 322	4 203	4 077	8 275	14 872	16 784	21 527
Bolivia[6] Bolivie[6]	691	674	766	591	611	687	970	1 090	1 206	1 209
Brazil[6] Brésil[6]	14 332	15 557	16 581	16 055	19 875	22 524	22 950	23 068	27 740	35 997
Chile[6] Chili[6]	3 072	3 436	4 396	5 292	7 144	7 678	8 094	10 129	11 125	11 825
Colombia[6] Colombie[6]	4 141	3 862	4 322	5 002	5 004	5 590	4 906	6 516	9 832	11 883
Ecuador Equateur	1 767	1 810	2 252	1 714	1 855	1 862	2 397	2 501	2 562	3 690
Mexico Mexique	13 994	11 997	12 731	19 591	24 438	29 969	38 124	48 998	50 147	60 979
Paraguay[6] Paraguay[6]	502	578	595	574	760	1 352	1 460	1 422	1 689	2 370
Peru[4][6] Pérou[4][6]	1 835	2 909	3 562	3 348	2 749	3 470	4 195	4 861	4 859	6 691
Uruguay[6] Uruguay[6]	708	870	1 142	1 157	1 203	1 343	1 637	2 045	2 326	2 786
Venezuela[4] Venezuela[4]	8 240	9 610	8 814	16 304	8 818	7 443	11 256	14 145	12 269	9 291
CACM+ MCAC+	**5 087**	**4 773**	**5 478**	**5 719**	**6 116**	**6 473**	**6 840**	**8 599**	**9 272**	**9 758**
Costa Rica[6] Costa Rica[6]	1 098	1 148	1 383	1 410	1 717	1 990	1 877	2 440	2 885	3 025

Region, country or area Region, pays ou zone	1985	1986	1987	1988	1989	1990	1991	1992	1993	1994
B. Exports f.o.b. • Exportations f.o.b.										
World *Monde*	1 933 836	2 129 766	2 491 653	2 827 862	3 022 411	3 423 462	3 417 944	3 654 786	3 639 197	4 143 832
Developed economies[1][2] Econ. développées [1][2]	1 281 238	1 492 000	1 745 835	1 991 385	2 127 912	2 455 967	2 490 902	2 635 489	2 558 269	2 874 428
Developing economies[2] Econ. en dévelop.[2]	482 738	453 963	544 685	627 374	703 548	795 760	836 311	926 561	983 735	1 138 068
OPEC+ OPEP+	153 249	112 727	122 012	122 877	144 386	179 393	169 049	181 324	177 793	187 225
LDC+ PMA+	10 807	10 525	11 628	12 498	13 501	14 614	13 747	14 409	14 045	15 261
Other[3] Autres[3]	169 860	183 802	201 133	209 103	190 951	171 735	90 731	92 735	97 193	131 337
America • Amérique										
Developed economies **Economies développées**	301 111	303 730	340 551	422 276	468 159	496 668	521 619	553 187	577 042	639 002
Canada[4] Canada[4]	90 953	90 325	98 171	117 112	121 835	127 634	127 163	134 441	145 182	165 380
United States Etats-Unis	218 815	227 158	254 122	322 427	363 812	393 592	421 730	448 163	464 773	512 521
Developing economies **Econ. en dévelop.**	101 530	89 472	94 719	110 343	123 522	131 955	127 648	131 881	137 391	159 298
LAIA+[5] **ALAI+[5]**	83 742	71 444	78 538	93 551	105 643	113 332	111 684	116 551	121 873	142 558
Argentina[6] Argentine [6]	8 396	6 852	6 360	9 135	9 579	12 353	11 978	12 235	13 118	15 659
Bolivia[6] Bolivie[6]	623	638	570	600	822	926	849	710	728	1 032
Brazil[6] Brésil[6]	25 639	22 349	26 224	33 494	34 383	31 414	31 620	35 793	38 597	43 558
Chile[6] Chili[6]	3 804	4 191	5 224	7 052	8 080	8 373	8 942	10 007	9 199	11 539
Colombia[6] Colombie[6]	3 552	5 102	4 642	5 037	5 717	6 766	7 232	6 917	7 116	8 399
Ecuador Equateur	2 905	2 172	1 928	2 192	2 354	2 714	2 852	3 007	2 904	3 820
Mexico Mexique	22 112	16 347	20 887	20 765	23 048	27 131	27 318	27 704	30 241	34 530
Paraguay[6] Paraguay[6]	304	233	353	510	1 009	959	737	657	725	817
Peru[4][6] Pérou[4][6]	2 979	2 531	2 661	2 701	3 488	3 231	3 329	3 484	3 515	4 555
Uruguay[6] Uruguay[6]	909	1 088	1 189	1 405	1 599	1 693	1 605	1 703	1 645	1 913
Venezuela[4] Venezuela [4]	12 533	9 956	8 510	10 669	15 573	17 783	15 233	14 343	14 095	16 744
CACM+ **MCAC+**	3 794	4 021	3 801	3 951	4 189	4 354	4 455	4 741	5 203	5 775
Costa Rica [6] Costa Rica[6]	976	1 121	1 158	1 246	1 415	1 448	1 598	1 829	2 049	2 215

72
Total imports and exports
Value in million US dollars [cont.]
Importations et exportations totales
Valeur en millions de dollars E-U [suite]

Region, country or area Region, pays ou zone	1985	1986	1987	1988	1989	1990	1991	1992	1993	1994
El Salvador[6] El Salvador[6]	961	935	994	1 007	1 161	1 263	1 406	1 699	1 912	2 249
Guatemala[6] Guatemala[6]	1 175	959	1 447	1 557	1 654	1 649	1 851	2 532	2 599	2 604
Honduras[6] Honduras[6]	888	875	827	940	969	935	955	1 037	1 130	1 056
Nicaragua Nicaragua	964	857	827	805	615	638	751	892	746	824
Other America **Autres pays d'Amérique**	**21 746**	**23 448**	**21 473**	**21 617**	**24 428**	**25 598**	**21 975**	**21 609**	**22 376**	**23 324**
Antigua and Barbuda Antigua-et-Barbuda	112	207	222	225	...	...	...	...	...	...
Aruba[6] Aruba[6]	...	192	236	336	387	536	481	...	...	...
Bahamas Bahamas	3 078	3 289	3 041	2 264	3 001	2 920	1 801	...	...	...
Barbados Barbade	602	587	515	579	673	700	695	521	574	611
Belize Belize	128	122	143	181	216	211	256	274	281	260
Bermuda Bermudes	402	492	420	488	535	595	510	562	534	551
Cayman Islands[6] Iles Caïmanes[6]	147	161	195	231	259	288	267	...	...	...
Cuba[6] Cuba[6]	8 758	11 139	7 584	7 579	8 124	6 745	3 690	2 185	...	...
Dominica Dominique	55	56	66	88	107	118	110	111	...	...
Dominican Republic[4] Rép. dominicaine[4]	1 487	1 433	1 830	1 849	2 258	2 062	1 988	2 501	2 436	2 626
French Guiana[6] Guyane française[6]	257	295	394	507	568	785	769	669	524	676
Greenland Groënland	296	360	507	519	399	447	408	457	...	...
Grenada[6] Grenade[6]	69	84	89	92	99	105	121	107	...	...
Guadeloupe[6] Guadeloupe[6]	620	762	1 038	1 243	1 251	1 650	1 644	1 509	1 393	1 539
Guyana[6] Guyana[6]	...	...	...	...	...	...	328	440	485	...
Haiti Haïti	442	360	399	344	291	332	464	286	359	260
Jamaica Jamaïque	1 111	971	1 238	1 455	1 853	1 924	1 811	1 675	2 097	2 161
Martinique[6] Martinique[6]	683	879	1 119	1 290	1 317	1 779	1 695	1 750	1 556	1 642
Montserrat[6] Montserrat[6]	18	...	25	27	37	48	35	34	...	...
Netherlands Antilles[6,7] Antilles néerlandaises[6,7]	2 256	1 112	1 502	1 403	1 610	2 141	2 139	1 868	1 947	...
Panama[6,8] Panama[6,8]	1 392	1 229	1 306	751	986	1 539	1 695	2 024	2 188	2 404

Region, country or area Region, pays ou zone	1985	1986	1987	1988	1989	1990	1991	1992	1993	1994
El Salvador[6] El Salvador[6]	679	755	591	609	498	582	588	598	732	844
Guatemala[6] Guatemala[6]	1 057	1 044	987	1 022	1 108	1 163	1 202	1 295	1 340	1 522
Honduras[6] Honduras[6]	780	854	791	842	859	831	792	802	814	843
Nicaragua Nicaragua	302	247	273	233	311	331	275	218	267	352
Other America Autres pays d'Amérique	13 994	14 007	12 381	12 842	13 690	14 269	11 508	10 590	10 315	10 965
Antigua and Barbuda Antigua-et-Barbuda	13	20	17	22	...	...	...	...	...	...
Aruba[6] Aruba[6]	...	24	26	31	23	28	26	...	...	...
Bahamas Bahamas	2 728	2 701	2 728	2 164	2 786	2 678	1 517	...	...	...
Barbados Barbade	347	275	156	176	187	214	205	189	180	184
Belize Belize	90	93	103	116	125	133	122	141	136	151
Bermuda Bermudes	23	65	29	31	50	60	55	85	...	...
Cayman Islands[6] Iles Caïmanes[6]	2	3	2	2	2	4	3	...	...	...
Cuba[6] Cuba[6]	6 531	7 615	5 402	5 518	5 392	4 910	3 550	2 050	...	...
Dominica Dominique	28	43	48	54	45	55	54	56	...	...
Dominican Republic[4] Rép. dominicaine[4]	735	718	711	890	924	735	658	562	511	633
French Guiana[6] Guyane française[6]	38	32	54	51	57	93	70	96	95	136
Greenland Groënland	174	257	346	391	418	454	341	333	...	...
Grenada[6] Grenade[6]	23	31	32	33	28	27	23	20	...	...
Guadeloupe[6] Guadeloupe[6]	72	104	93	158	112	118	147	130	128	152
Guyana[6] Guyana[6]	166	222	267	230	227	256	247	290	414	456
Haïti Haïti	168	184	214	179	144	160	190	73	80	87
Jamaica Jamaïque	566	589	706	880	998	1 158	1 097	1 048	1 069	1 191
Martinique[6] Martinique[6]	162	216	194	196	200	278	216	247	191	218
Monteserrat[6] Montserrat[6]	3	...	4	2	1	1	1	2	...	...
Netherlands Antilles[6 7] Antilles néerlandaises[6 7]	1 679	924	1 308	1 134	1 454	1 790	1 599	1 559	1 283	...
Panama[6 8] Panama[6 8]	336	349	358	307	318	340	358	502	553	583

72
Total imports and exports
Value in million US dollars [cont.]
Importations et exportations totales
Valeur en millions de dollars E-U [suite]

Region, country or area Region, pays ou zone	1985	1986	1987	1988	1989	1990	1991	1992	1993	1994
Saint Kitts and Nevis[6] Saint-Kitts-et-Nevis[6]	51	63	79	93	102	111	...	...	...	...
Saint Lucia[6] Sainte-Lucie[6]	125	155	179	220	274	271	295	313	...	...
St. Pierre and Miquelon[6] St.-Pierre-et-Miquelon[6]	...	...	...	62	84	86	81	76	70	71
St. Vincent-Grenadines[6] St. Vincent-Grenadines[6]	79	87	...	...	127	136	140	132	134	135
Suriname[6] Suriname[6]	299	327	294	351	443	...	...	...	...	...
Trinidad and Tobago[6] Trinité-et-Tobago[6]	1 538	1 350	1 219	1 128	1 221	1 109	1 410	1 168	1 463	1 130

Europe • Europe

Region, country or area Region, pays ou zone	1985	1986	1987	1988	1989	1990	1991	1992	1993	1994
Developed economies[9] Economies développées[9]	770 084	917 044	1 121 954	1 263 032	1 358 907	1 642 844	1 663 321	1 728 440	1 501 884	1 680 844
EEC+[10] CEE+[10]	656 369	775 170	949 221	1 071 805	1 157 214	1 406 329	1 444 343	1 510 939	1 308 063	1 454 840
Belgium-Luxembourg[6] Belgique-Luxembourg[6]	56 211	68 729	83 550	92 453	98 596	120 325	121 060	125 153	112 255	125 617
Denmark[6][11] Danemark[6][11]	18 072	22 822	25 429	25 944	26 696	32 230	32 411	35 185	30 546	34 882
France[6][12] France[6][12]	108 379	129 435	158 499	177 288	190 963	233 207	230 832	238 875	200 750	230 638
F.R. Germany†[6] R.f. Allemagne†[6]	158 856[10]	191 379[10]	228 281[10]	250 839[10]	269 763[10]	345 342[10]	389 516	403 268	348 908	381 306
Greece[6] Grèce[6]	10 140	11 353	13 164	12 324	16 149	19 780	21 582	23 232	22 007	21 489
Ireland Irlande	10 019	11 559	13 639	15 571	17 423	20 682	20 756	22 483	21 794	25 818
Italy[6] Italie[6]	87 718	99 404	125 692	138 582	153 010	181 983	182 750	188 456	148 308	167 694
Netherlands[6] Pays-Bas[6]	65 382	75 690	91 495	99 522	104 467	126 195	127 256	134 422	121 594	131 118
Portugal[6] Portugal[6]	7 655	9 648	13 966	17 941	19 205	25 358	26 425	30 348	24 320	26 941
Spain[6] Espagne[6]	29 965	35 086	49 119	60 533	70 957	87 722	93 330	99 765	81 888	92 503
United Kingdom[12] Royaume-Uni[12]	109 593	126 367	154 407	189 719	199 220	224 550	209 864	221 638	206 321	226 172
EFTA+ AELE+	109 981	137 360	167 189	185 336	195 837	228 940	216 431	214 699	191 328	223 177
Austria[6] Autriche[6]	20 996	26 852	32 683	36 565	38 935	49 092	50 804	54 122	48 616	55 340
Finland Finlande	13 256	15 335	18 964	21 949	24 631	26 993	21 787	21 163	18 069	23 245
Iceland[6] Islande[6]	904	1 115	1 590	1 598	1 402	1 679	1 761	1 684	1 342	1 472
Norway Norvège	15 560	20 307	22 641	23 223	23 680	27 219	25 576	25 916	23 892	27 303
Sweden Suède	28 553	32 697	40 709	45 631	48 981	54 266	50 001	50 050	42 687	51 732

Region, country or area Region, pays ou zone	1985	1986	1987	1988	1989	1990	1991	1992	1993	1994
Saint Kitts and Nevis[6] Saint-Kitts-et-Nevis[6]	20	25	28	27	29	28	...	...	...	...
Saint Lucia[6] Sainte-Lucie[6]	57	87	80	116	109	127	110	123	...	...
St. Pierre and Miquelon[6] St.-Pierre-et-Miquelon[6]	...	...	...	13	30	26	30	25	1	12
St. Vincent-Grenadines[6] St. Vincent-Grenadines[6]	63	64	...	...	75	83	67	78	58	43
Suriname[6] Suriname[6]	329	335	306	409	542	...	...	...	...	...
Trinidad and Tobago[6] Trinité-et-Tobago[6]	2 147	1 386	1 462	1 413	1 578	1 960	1 775	1 691	1 662	1 866

Europe · Europe

Region, country or area Region, pays ou zone	1985	1986	1987	1988	1989	1990	1991	1992	1993	1994
Developed economies[9] Economies développées[9]	755 087	927 077	1 114 635	1 237 815	1 313 146	1 594 274	1 575 321	1 661 666	1 536 258	1 747 726
EEC+[10] CEE+[10]	642 181	790 034	949 948	1 055 064	1 120 195	1 354 678	1 357 075	1 437 119	1 329 196	1 507 361
Belgium-Luxembourg[6] Belgique-Luxembourg[6]	53 762	68 960	83 308	92 149	100 095	118 328	118 355	123 564	119 530	137 272
Denmark[6][11] Danemark[6][11]	16 941	21 214	25 598	27 657	28 113	35 135	36 011	41 067	37 172	41 422
France[6][12] France[6][12]	101 709	124 863	148 402	167 813	173 073	210 169	213 441	231 913	206 231	236 072
F.R. Germany†[6] R.f. Allemagne†[6]	183 979 [10]	243 473 [10]	293 894 [10]	323 898 [10]	341 440 [10]	410 678 [10]	402 764	422 706	380 313	426 573
Greece[6] Grèce[6]	4 543	5 649	6 531	5 430	7 544	8 106	8 675	9 839	8 777	9 392
Ireland Irlande	10 362	12 586	15 996	18 745	20 694	23 747	24 223	28 532	29 022	34 252
Italy[6] Italie[6]	76 741	97 631	116 413	127 886	140 623	170 385	169 536	178 164	167 746	190 019
Netherlands[6] Pays-Bas[6]	68 418	80 512	93 096	103 586	108 285	131 783	133 689	139 966	131 183	146 495
Portugal[6] Portugal[6]	5 684	7 242	9 321	10 990	12 801	16 419	16 318	18 369	15 418	17 901
Spain[6] Espagne[6]	24 249	27 231	34 199	40 340	43 463	55 646	60 197	64 342	62 872	73 293
United Kingdom[12] Royaume-Uni[12]	101 414	106 975	131 210	145 482	153 299	185 326	185 306	190 542	181 559	204 009
EFTA+ AELE+	109 582	132 808	159 565	177 540	187 377	224 667	216 569	222 594	205 410	238 551
Austria[6] Autriche[6]	17 247	22 529	27 175	31 062	32 485	41 138	41 126	44 377	40 200	45 031
Finland Finlande	13 618	16 334	19 539	22 167	23 306	26 558	23 018	23 939	23 474	29 673
Iceland[6] Islande[6]	816	1 099	1 374	1 424	1 386	1 591	1 549	1 528	1 400	1 623
Norway Norvège	19 989	18 095	21 493	22 425	27 112	34 045	34 116	35 193	31 778	34 685
Sweden Suède	30 467	37 267	44 509	49 751	51 552	57 542	55 229	56 154	49 864	61 301

72
Total imports and exports
Value in million US dollars [*cont.*]
Importations et exportations totales
Valeur en millions de dollars E-U [*suite*]

Region, country or area Region, pays ou zone	1985	1986	1987	1988	1989	1990	1991	1992	1993	1994
Switzerland Suisse[6]	30 711	41 053	50 602	56 372	58 207	69 691	66 502	61 763	56 722	64 085
Other Europe **Autres pays d'Europe**	**1 115**	**1 351**	**1 832**	**2 024**	**2 002**	**2 445**	**2 547**	**2 801**	**2 493**	**2 827**
Faeroe Islands Iles Féroé	248	336	513	478	346	338	303	334	219	...
Gibraltar Gibraltar	147	164	231	...	...	...	...	...	...	...
Malta Malte	759	887	1 140	1 353	1 480	1 961	2 114	2 349	2 166	2 448
Developing economies[13] **Econ. en dévelop.[13]**	**12 164**	**11 750**	**12 603**	**13 154**	**14 802**	**18 890**	**11 804**	**16 456**	**14 194**	**15 073**
Croatia Croatie	...	...	...	...	...	...	...	4 501	4 667	5 231
Slovenia Slovénie	...	...	...	...	...	...	...	6 142	6 529	7 304
TFYR Macedonia L'ex-R.y. Macédoine	...	...	...	...	...	...	...	1 206	1 199	...
Yugoslavia, SFR†[6] **Yougoslavie, Rfs†[6]**	**12 164**	**11 750**	**12 603**	**13 154**	**14 802**	**18 890**	**11 804**	...	...	...
Eastern Europe **Europe de l'est**	**79 875**	**88 861**	**90 232**	**91 499**	**75 795**	**65 764**	**46 298**	**51 139**	**55 215**	**62 495**
Bulgaria Bulgarie	13 656[4]	15 249[4]	16 211[4]	16 582[4]	14 881[4]	12 893[4]	3 017[4]	5 228	4 315	4 316
former Czechoslovakia†[4][14] l'anc. Tchécoslovaquie†[4][14]	11 152	13 358	14 883	14 593	14 277	13 106	10 014	12 530	...	...
Czech Republic[4] République tchèque[4]	...	...	...	...	...	...	...	...	12 694	14 956
former German D. R.†[4][15] anc. R. d. allemande†[4][15]	23 433	27 414	28 786	29 647	17 778	...	...	...	...	...
Hungary Hongrie	8 223	9 599	9 842	9 345	8 710	8 671	11 416	11 106	12 520	14 384
Poland[4] Pologne[4]	11 855	11 535	11 215	12 712	10 659	8 413	15 757	15 701	18 834	21 383
Romania[6] Roumanie[6]	11 267	11 437	8 978	8 254	9 122	9 843	5 793	6 260	6 522	7 109
Slovakia[16] Slovaquie[16]	...	...	...	...	...	...	...	...	6 360	6 503
former USSR†[4][17] **ancienne URSS†[4][17]**	**83 140**	**88 871**	**96 061**	**107 229**	**114 567**	**120 651**	**43 458**	...	...	...
former USSR-Europe[18] anc. URSS-Europe[18]	...	...	...	...	...	...	...	41 542	34 214	55 411
Belarus Bélarus	...	...	...	...	...	...	...	1 061	747	...
Estonia Estonie	...	...	...	...	...	...	...	412	897	1 663
Latvia Lettonie	...	...	...	...	...	...	...	843	872	1 251
Lithuania Lituanie	...	...	...	...	...	...	...	125	2 279	2 353

Region, country or area Region, pays ou zone	1985	1986	1987	1988	1989	1990	1991	1992	1993	1994
Switzerland[6] Suisse[6]	27 446	37 484	45 474	50 712	51 536	63 793	61 532	61 403	58 694	66 238
Other Europe **Autres pays d'Europe**	**603**	**774**	**983**	**1 098**	**1 223**	**1 549**	**1 677**	**1 954**	**1 653**	**1 813**
Faeroe Islands Iles Féroé	179	249	345	348	346	418	435	439	327	...
Gibraltar Gibraltar	62	65	85	...	...	...	...	...	...	...
Malta Malte	400	497	605	714	844	1 130	1 252	1 543	1 348	1 519
Developing economies[13] **Econ. en dévelop.[13]**	**10 642**	**10 298**	**11 425**	**12 597**	**13 363**	**14 312**	**9 548**	**15 150**	**11 800**	**12 370**
Croatia Croatie	...	...	...	...	...	...	...	4 597	3 914	4 259
Slovenia Slovénie	...	...	...	...	...	...	...	6 681	6 083	6 828
TFYR Macedonia L'ex-R.y. Macédoine	...	...	...	...	...	...	...	1 199	1 055	...
Yugoslavia, SFR†[6] **Yougoslavie, Rfs†[6]**	**10 642**	**10 298**	**11 425**	**12 597**	**13 363**	**14 312**	**9 548**	...	...	...
Eastern Europe **Europe de l'est**	**82 579**	**86 556**	**93 168**	**98 544**	**81 778**	**67 558**	**44 456**	**44 668**	**45 097**	**52 708**
Bulgaria Bulgarie	13 348[4]	14 192[4]	15 905[4]	17 223[4]	16 013[4]	13 347[4]	3 835[4]	4 268	3 582	4 157
former Czechoslovakia†[4][14] l'anc. Tchécoslovaquie†[4][14]	11 510	13 227	14 723	14 894	14 440	11 882	10 878	11 656	...	...
Czech Republic[4] République tchèque[4]	...	...	...	...	...	...	...	...	13 209	14 280
former German D. R.†[4][15] anc. R. d. allemande†[4][15]	25 268	27 729	29 871	30 672	17 334	...	...	...	...	...
Hungary Hongrie	8 538	9 166	9 555	9 950	9 582	9 779	10 199	10 676	8 887	10 690
Poland[4] Pologne[4]	11 489	12 074	12 205	13 960	13 466	13 627	14 903	13 324	14 143	17 042
Romania[6] Roumanie[6]	12 167	9 763	10 492	11 392	10 487	5 775	4 266	4 363	4 892	6 151
Slovakia[16] Slovaquie[16]	...	...	...	...	...	...	...	...	5 469	6 592
former USSR†[4][17] **ancienne URSS†[4][17]**	**87 281**	**97 247**	**107 966**	**110 559**	**109 173**	**104 177**	**46 274**	...	...	...
former USSR-Europe[18] anc. URSS-Europe[18]	...	...	...	...	...	...	...	48 068	52 096	78 629
Belarus Bélarus	...	...	...	...	...	...	...	751	715	...
Estonia Estonie	...	...	...	...	...	...	...	445	805	1 302
Latvia Lettonie	...	...	...	...	...	...	...	896	963	962
Lithuania Lituanie	...	...	...	...	...	...	...	308	2 025	2 029

72

Total imports and exports
Value in million US dollars [*cont.*]
Importations et exportations totales
Valeur en millions de dollars E-U [*suite*]

Region, country or area Region, pays ou zone	1985	1986	1987	1988	1989	1990	1991	1992	1993	1994
Republic of Moldova Rép. de Moldova	...	...	...	...	...	...	...	164	181	669
Russian Federation Fédération de Russie	...	...	...	...	...	...	...	36 984	26 807	38 650
Ukraine Ukraine	...	...	...	...	...	...	...	1 953	2 431	9 989

Africa · Afrique

Region, country or area Region, pays ou zone	1985	1986	1987	1988	1989	1990	1991	1992	1993	1994
South Africa[4 19 20] Afrique du Sud[4 19 20]	10 921	12 372	14 623	17 612	17 664	17 665	17 837	18 714	19 090	22 470
Developing economies **Econ. en dévelop.**	**55 033**	**56 287**	**55 065**	**61 111**	**62 567**	**72 329**	**69 029**	**73 915**	**71 002**	**75 167**
Northern Africa **Afrique du Nord**	**26 628**	**29 596**	**27 377**	**31 297**	**32 632**	**37 843**	**33 700**	**36 268**	**36 724**	**39 685**
Algeria[6] Algérie[6]	9 841	9 234	7 028	7 403	9 123	9 574	7 438	8 648	...	...
Egypt[6 21] Egypte[6 21]	5 495	8 680	7 596	8 657	7 434	9 202	8 310	8 325	8 214	10 218
Libyan Arab Jamah. Jamah. arabe libyenne	4 101	4 193	4 722	5 878	5 049	5 599	5 356	...	...	...
Morocco[6] Maroc[6]	3 850	3 803	4 229	4 773	5 493	6 925	6 894	7 356	7 162	7 188
Sudan[22] Soudan[22]	756	961	929	1 059	...	...	...	...	...	...
Tunisia Tunisie	2 757	2 891	3 039	3 689	4 387	5 513	5 189	6 431	6 214	6 581
Other Africa **Autres Pays d'Afrique**	**28 405**	**26 692**	**27 688**	**29 814**	**29 935**	**34 486**	**35 329**	**37 647**	**34 279**	**35 482**
CACEU+[23] **UDEAC+[23]**	**2 718**	**3 334**	**3 188**	**2 768**	**2 696**	**3 094**	**2 575**	**2 698**	**2 731**	**2 075**
Cameroon[6 23] Cameroun[6 23]	1 152	1 704	1 723	1 271	1 261	1 400	1 173	1 163	1 106	732
Central African Rep.[6 23] Rép. centrafricaine[6 23]	113	167	204	141	150	154	93	146	126	142
Congo[6 23] Congo[6 23]	598	597	529	564	517	617	474	690	583	...
Gabon[6 23] Gabon[6 23]	855	866	732	791	767	922	834	700	917	740
ECOWAS+ **CEDEAO+**	**15 183**	**11 561**	**11 481**	**12 269**	**11 971**	**14 049**	**17 119**	**18 537**	**15 339**	**15 378**
Benin[6] Bénin[6]	343	387	348	326	206	...	...	...	...	...
Burkina Faso[6] Burkina Faso[6]	333	405	434	454	391	540	536	...	...	...
Cape Verde[6] Cap-Vert[6]	84	107	100	106	112	136	147	180	154	...
Côte d'Ivoire Côte d'Ivoire	1 750	2 055	2 243	2 081	2 133	2 098	2 125	2 354	...	...
Gambia Gambie	93	105	127	137	161	188	202	217	261	208
Ghana Ghana	866	1 046	1 166	904	1 277	...	...	2 175	...	...

Region, country or area Région, pays ou zone	1985	1986	1987	1988	1989	1990	1991	1992	1993	1994
Republic of Moldova Rép. de Moldova	...	...	...	...	...	...	...	119	174	565
Russian Federation Fédération de Russie	...	...	...	...	...	...	...	42 376	44 297	63 243
Ukraine Ukraine	...	...	...	...	...	...	...	3 173	3 116	9 708

Africa • Afrique

Region, country or area Région, pays ou zone	1985	1986	1987	1988	1989	1990	1991	1992	1993	1994
South Africa[4][19][20] Afrique du Sud[4][19][20]	15 814	17 777	20 553	20 755	21 318	22 834	22 288	22 416	23 339	24 082
Developing economies **Econ. en dévelop.**	**62 024**	**47 645**	**51 235**	**50 329**	**57 488**	**75 413**	**71 272**	**69 355**	**63 694**	**69 704**
Northern Africa **Afrique du Nord**	**31 091**	**22 153**	**24 650**	**22 882**	**27 045**	**37 298**	**35 499**	**32 668**	**30 957**	**33 918**
Algeria[6] Algérie[6]	12 841	7 831	8 565	7 711	9 485	12 675	12 657	11 137	...	...
Egypt[6][21] Egypte[6][21]	1 838	2 214	2 037	2 120	2 565	2 582	3 790	3 063	2 252	3 475
Libyan Arab Jamah. Jamah. arabe libyenne	12 314	7 748	8 765	6 684	8 239	13 877	11 213	...	...	...
Morocco[6] Maroc[6]	2 165	2 433	2 807	3 626	3 337	4 265	4 285	3 977	3 428	4 005
Sudan[22] Soudan[22]	367	333	504	509	671	...	...	...	...	...
Tunisia Tunisie	1 738	1 760	2 139	2 395	2 930	3 527	3 699	4 019	3 802	4 657
Other Africa **Autres Pays d'Afrique**	**30 933**	**25 492**	**26 585**	**27 447**	**30 443**	**38 116**	**35 773**	**36 686**	**32 737**	**35 787**
CACEU+[23] **UDEAC+[23]**	**3 853**	**2 896**	**2 740**	**3 123**	**4 251**	**5 311**	**5 155**	**5 217**	**5 381**	**4 917**
Cameroon[6][23] Cameroun[6][23]	722	782	806	924	1 273	2 002	1 834	1 840	1 901	1 369
Central African Rep.[6][23] Rép. centrafricaine[6][23]	92	66	130	66	134	120	47	108	110	150
Congo[6][23] Congo[6][23]	1 087	777	517	937	1 245	975	1 031	1 187	1 070	...
Gabon[6][23] Gabon[6][23]	1 952	1 271	1 286	1 195	1 599	2 213	2 243	2 082	2 300	2 314
ECOWAS+ **CEDEAO+**	**18 884**	**13 712**	**14 329**	**13 498**	**14 744**	**20 264**	**19 142**	**20 019**	**16 343**	**18 878**
Benin[6] Bénin[6]	152	104	114	71	97	...	...	...	...	...
Burkina Faso[6] Burkina Faso[6]	70	83	155	142	95	151	105	...	...	...
Cape Verde[6] Cap-Vert[6]	6	4	8	3	7	6	6	5	4	...
Côte d'Ivoire Côte d'Ivoire	2 946	3 355	3 112	2 771	2 852	3 072	2 711	2 878	...	...
Gambia Gambie	43	35	40	58	27	31	38	57	66	35
Ghana Ghana	623	876	957	1 008	1 018	...	...	1 252	...	...

72
Total imports and exports
Value in million US dollars [*cont.*]
Importations et exportations totales
Valeur en millions de dollars E-U [*suite*]

Region, country or area Région, pays ou zone	1985	1986	1987	1988	1989	1990	1991	1992	1993	1994
Guinea-Bissau[6] Guinée-Bissau[6]	...	...	...	65	79	86	76	181	61	63
Liberia[6] Libéria[6]	284	259	308	272	...	...	...	...	...	...
Mali[6] Mali[6]	300	444	374	504	340	608	...	...	...	...
Mauritania[6] Mauritanie[6]	233	221	235	240	222	...	...	...	...	...
Niger[6] Niger[6]	369	368	311	387	363	389	355	...	...	...
Nigeria Nigéria	8 890	4 433	3 917	4 784	4 195	5 692	9 072	8 772	7 513	...
Senegal[6] Sénégal[6]	812	962	1 023	1 080	1 221	1 314	1 100	1 173	...	...
Sierra Leone Sierra Leone	154	132	137	156	182	155	163	156	147	150
Togo[6] Togo[6]	288	312	424	487	472	581	444	395	179	222
Rest of Africa **Afrique N.D.A.**	**10 504**	**11 796**	**13 019**	**14 778**	**15 269**	**17 343**	**15 635**	**16 411**	**16 209**	**18 028**
Angola[6] Angola[6]	671	619	443	989	1 140	...	...	...	...	...
Burundi[6] Burundi[6]	189	202	206	206	188	235	255	221	196	224
Chad[6] Tchad[6]	166	212	226	252	235	286	251	244	201	186
Comoros[6] Comores[6]	37	37	52	53	43	52	58	69	...	...
Djibouti Djibouti	201	184	205	201	196	215	214	219	...	...
Equatorial Guinea[6] Guinée équatoriale[6]	20	52	58	61	55	61	117	92	60	...
Ethiopia Ethiopie	993	1 102	1 066	1 129	951	1 081	472	859	787	1 033
Kenya Kenya	1 436	1 613	1 755	1 975	2 148	2 124	1 799	1 828	1 711	2 196
Madagascar[6] Madagascar[6]	402	353	302	383	372	651	435	448	468	441
Malawi Malawi	295	258	295	420	507	575	703	735	545	495
Mauritius Maurice	529	684	1 013	1 289	1 326	1 618	1 559	1 624	1 716	1 930
Mozambique[6] Mozambique[6]	424	543	642	736	808	878	899	855	955	...
Réunion[6] Réunion[6]	841	1 137	1 464	1 662	1 732	2 160	2 129	2 315	2 057	2 365
Rwanda Rwanda	299	350	352	370	333	285	308	288	296	...
Seychelles Seychelles	99	105	114	159	165	187	173	191	238	207
Somalia[6] Somalie[6]	112	284	132	...	...	...	...	...	...	...

Region, country or area Région, pays ou zone	1985	1986	1987	1988	1989	1990	1991	1992	1993	1994
Guinea-Bissau[6] Guinée-Bissau[6]	...	...	...	16	14	19	20	12	16	33
Liberia[6] Libéria[6]	436	408	382	396	...	...	...	...	...	...
Mali[6] Mali[6]	124	212	179	214	247	359	...	...	...	...
Mauritania[6] Mauritanie[6]	374	349	428	354	437	...	...	...	...	...
Niger[6] Niger[6]	259	317	312	289	244	283	312	...	...	...
Nigeria Nigéria	12 567	6 715	7 382	6 958	7 880	12 961	12 321	12 600	9 923	...
Senegal[6] Sénégal[6]	554	625	606	591	693	762	653	683	...	...
Sierra Leone Sierra Leone	130	142	129	106	138	138	145	149	118	116
Togo[6] Togo[6]	190	204	244	242	245	268	253	275	136	162
Rest of Africa **Afrique N.D.A.**	**8 196**	**8 884**	**9 516**	**10 826**	**11 448**	**12 541**	**11 476**	**11 450**	**11 014**	**11 992**
Angola[6] Angola[6]	2 224	1 319	2 147	2 494	2 989	3 910	3 413	3 714	...	...
Burundi[6] Burundi[6]	112	154	90	133	78	75	91	73	62	121
Chad[6] Tchad[6]	62	99	109	159	155	188	194	183	132	157
Comoros[6] Comores[6]	16	20	12	21	18	18	25	22	...	...
Djibouti Djibouti	14	20	28	23	25	25	17	16	...	...
Equatorial Guinea[6] Guinée équatoriale[6]	17	35	42	49	41	62	83	41	62	...
Ethiopia Ethiopie	333	455	355	429	440	298	189	169	199	372
Kenya Kenya	958	1 200	961	1 071	970	1 031	1 107	1 362	1 374	1 593
Madagascar[6] Madagascar[6]	274	315	333	274	321	319	305	278	261	333
Malawi Malawi	248	245	277	288	267	417	469	396	319	325
Mauritius Maurice	440	676	880	997	987	1 194	1 195	1 301	1 299	1 347
Mozambique[6] Mozambique[6]	77	79	97	103	105	126	162	139	132	...
Réunion[6] Réunion[6]	97	135	169	158	161	190	150	213	168	171
Rwanda Rwanda	131	188	112	109	95	114	93	67	55	...
Seychelles Seychelles	28	18	22	32	34	57	49	48	51	52
Somalia[6] Somalie[6]	91	89	104	...	...	...	...	...	...	...

72
Total imports and exports
Value in million US dollars [cont.]
Importations et exportations totales
Valeur en millions de dollars E-U [suite]

Region, country or area Region, pays ou zone	1985	1986	1987	1988	1989	1990	1991	1992	1993	1994
Uganda Ouganda	298	307	848	887	390	293	196	515	...	879
United Rep.Tanzania Rép. Unie de Tanzanie	860	938	929	823	989	1 364	1 546	1 453	1 498	1 504
Zaire[6] Zaïre[6]	792	875	756	763	850	888	711	420	372	382
Zambia[4] Zambie[4]	653	648	735	828	924	1 260	961	988	...	...
Zimbabwe[4] Zimbabwe[4]	1 031	1 133	1 205	1 304	1 627	1 850	2 037	2 202	1 817	2 241

Asia • Asie

Region, country or area Region, pays ou zone	1985	1986	1987	1988	1989	1990	1991	1992	1993	1994
Developed economies Economies développées	138 926	136 419	163 233	199 071	220 304	247 822	251 336	248 321	257 951	293 165
Israel[6 24 25] Israël[6 24 25]	10 136	10 813	14 348	15 018	14 347	16 794	18 849	20 262	22 623	25 237
Japan Japon	130 515	127 588	151 075	187 411	209 755	235 423	237 289	233 265	241 652	275 268
Developing economies[26] Econ. en dévelop.[26]	308 048	304 413	363 130	446 689	501 350	564 185	638 768	738 925	823 412	935 643
Asia Middle East Moyen-Orient d'Asie	86 366	73 803	80 147	81 693	87 461	98 302	106 598	135 662	140 518	136 219
Non petroleum exports Petrole non compris	...	...	...	...	...	...	...	...	...	...
Bahrain Bahreïn	3 107	2 405	2 714	2 593	3 134	3 712	4 115	4 263	3 858	3 737
Cyprus Chypre	1 247	1 274	1 484	1 857	2 285	2 569	2 622	3 301	2 534	3 018
Iran, Islamic Rep. of[6 27] Iran, Rép. islamique d'[6 27]	11 629	9 107	9 228	8 272	...	...	...	30 676	...	...
Iraq[6] Iraq[6]	7 619	6 360	3 854	5 960	6 956	4 834	...	...	...	...
Jordan Jordanie	2 733	2 432	2 703	2 705	2 126	2 603	2 508	3 255	3 539	3 382
Kuwait[6] Koweït[6]	6 188	5 687	5 496	6 146	6 297	3 923	4 761	7 251	7 042	6 680
Oman Oman	3 153	2 384	1 822	2 202	2 257	2 681	3 194	3 769	4 114	3 915
Qatar[6] Qatar[6]	1 139	1 099	1 134	1 267	1 326	1 695	1 720	2 015	1 891	...
Saudi Arabia[6] Arabie saoudite[6]	23 622	19 109	20 110	21 784	21 154	24 069	29 079	33 698	28 198	23 338
Syrian Arab Republic[6] Rép. arabe syrienne[6]	3 967	2 728	7 112	2 231	2 097	2 400	2 768	3 490	4 140	5 467
Turkey[6] Turquie[6]	11 344	11 105	14 158	14 335	15 792	22 302	21 047	22 872	29 174	23 270
United Arab Emirates Emirats arabes unis	6 548	6 422	7 226	8 521	10 010	11 199	13 746	17 410	19 520	...
Yemen[28] Yémen[28]	1 998	1 640	1 378	...	...	...	...	...	...	...

Region, country or area Région, pays ou zone	1985	1986	1987	1988	1989	1990	1991	1992	1993	1994
Uganda Ouganda	387	436	319	274	250	152	200	143	179	410
United Rep.Tanzania Rép. Unie de Tanzanie	246	361	289	275	365	331	342	412	450	519
Zaire[6] Zaïre[6]	950	1 100	975	1 120	1 254	999	830	427	369	419
Zambia[4] Zambie[4]	482	741	873	1 178	1 344	1 312	1 076	1 088	...	...
Zimbabwe[4] Zimbabwe [4]	1 110	1 301	1 425	1 646	1 546	1 729	1 530	1 442	...	1 882

Asia · Asie

Region, country or area Région, pays ou zone	1985	1986	1987	1988	1989	1990	1991	1992	1993	1994
Developed economies Economies développées	181 736	215 985	237 615	269 743	280 922	294 829	322 281	347 824	370 787	406 589
Israel[6 24 25] Israël[6 24 25]	6 260	7 154	8 454	8 198	10 738	11 576	11 921	13 119	14 825	16 881
Japan Japon	177 202	210 813	231 351	264 903	273 983	287 648	315 163	339 911	362 286	397 048
Developing economies[26] Econ. en dévelop. [26]	306 585	304 502	384 878	451 144	506 154	571 342	624 793	706 710	766 672	892 275
Asia Middle East Moyen-Orient d'Asie	97 688	75 428	89 546	88 250	100 863	120 208	111 090	122 434	119 862	124 017
Non petroleum exports[31] Petrole non compris[31]	18 780	26 781	27 840	30 203	28 241	59 657	33 791	37 213	29 251	27 749
Bahrain Bahreïn	2 897	2 199	2 430	2 411	2 831	3 761	3 513	3 465	3 710	3 454
Cyprus Chypre	476	504	621	711	795	948	954	984	867	968
Iran, Islamic Rep. of[6 27] Iran, Rép. islamique d'[6 27]	13 449	6 642	...	...	...	...	...	...	...	...
Iraq Iraq	...	...	...	...	...	...	...	...	...	...
Jordan Jordanie	791	733	932	1 000	1 107	1 063	1 130	1 219	1 246	1 424
Kuwait[6] Koweït[6]	10 600	7 221	8 266	7 759	11 502	6 956	1 088	6 567	10 245	11 228
Oman Oman	3 938	1 834	2 491	2 476	4 068	5 508	4 871	5 428	5 299	5 545
Qatar[6] Qatar[6]	3 542	...	...	...	2 687	3 529	3 107	3 736	3 181	...
Saudi Arabia[6] Arabie saoudite[6]	27 481	20 187	23 199	24 377	28 382	44 417	47 797	50 280	42 395	...
Syrian Arab Republic[6] Rép. arabe syrienne[6]	1 637	1 325	3 870	1 345	3 006	4 212	3 430	3 093	3 146	3 547
Turkey[6] Turquie[6]	7 958	7 457	10 191	11 662	11 625	12 959	13 594	14 716	15 343	18 106
United Arab Emirates Emirats arabes unis	13 124	15 837	...	...	...	...	...	...	...	...
Yemen[28] Yémen[28]	54	37	101	...	...	...	...	...	...	...

72
Total imports and exports
Value in million US dollars [cont.]
Importations et exportations totales
Valeur en millions de dollars E-U [suite]

Region, country or area Region, pays ou zone	1985	1986	1987	1988	1989	1990	1991	1992	1993	1994
Other Asia[29] Autres pays d'Asie[29]	221 682	230 610	282 983	364 996	413 889	465 883	532 170	600 533	680 076	795 756
Afghanistan[30] Afghanistan[30]	1 194	1 404	996	900	822	936	616	...	...	...
Bangladesh Bangladesh	2 505	2 546	2 715	3 042	3 651	3 618	3 412	3 731	3 994	4 701
Brunei Darussalam[6] Brunéi Darussalam[6]	615	656	641	744	859	1 001	1 208	1 176	1 201	1 695
China Chine	42 983	43 639	43 393	55 279	58 512	52 570	62 577	76 376	103 093	114 577
Hong Kong Hong-kong	29 703	35 367	48 465	63 896	72 155	82 474	100 255	123 430	138 658	161 777
India Inde	15 935	15 413	16 678	19 103	20 550	23 583	20 445	23 594	22 789	26 843
Indonesia[6] Indonésie[6]	10 262	10 718	12 891	13 249	16 360	21 837	25 869	27 280	28 328	31 985
Korea, Republic of[6] Corée, République de[6]	31 070	31 599	41 157	51 969	61 477	69 740	81 496	81 794	83 784	102 428
Lao People's Dem. Rep.[6] Rép. dém. pop. lao[6]	131	131	146	162	...	...	...	...	...	...
Macau Macao	779	890	1 121	1 290	1 478	1 534	1 843	1 948	1 999	2 090
Malaysia Malaisie	12 253	10 806	12 681	16 507	22 481	29 259	36 649	39 854	45 657	59 581
Maldives Maldives	53	45	81	90	113	138	161	189	185	222
Mongolia[6] Mongolie[6]	1 096	1 140	1 105	1 114	963	924	361	418	362	223
Myanmar Myanmar	284	304	268	244	191	270	646	651	814	878
Nepal Népal	455	460	571	679	582	686	765	792	880	1 177
Pakistan Pakistan	5 890	5 374	5 822	6 590	7 143	7 376	8 439	9 379	9 501	8 889
Philippines Philippines	5 459	5 394	7 144	8 721	11 171	13 041	12 786	15 449	18 754	22 546
Singapore Singapour	26 288	25 511	32 566	43 862	49 657	60 774	66 093	72 132	85 229	102 670
Sri Lanka Sri Lanka	1 990	1 948	2 057	2 240	2 239	2 689	3 062	3 505	3 993	4 777
Thailand Thaïlande	9 252	9 181	12 987	20 286	25 785	33 031	37 579	40 680	46 076	54 438
Viet Nam Viet Nam	1 857	2 155	2 455	2 757	2 566	2 752	2 338	2 541	3 924	5 000
former USSR-Asia anc. URSS-Asie	...	...	...	...	...	...	...	2 730	2 818	3 668
Armenia Arménie	...	...	...	...	...	...	...	60	85	...
Azerbaizan Azerbadjan	...	...	...	...	...	...	...	333	241	727

Region, country or area Region, pays ou zone	1985	1986	1987	1988	1989	1990	1991	1992	1993	1994
Other Asia[29] **Autres pays d'Asie**[29]	**208 897**	**229 074**	**295 332**	**362 894**	**405 291**	**451 134**	**513 702**	**579 769**	**642 878**	**763 853**
Afghanistan[30] Afghanistan[30]	567	552	512	395	236	235	188	...	...	...
Bangladesh Bangladesh	986	880	1 067	1 291	1 305	1 671	1 689	2 098	2 278	2 661
Brunei Darussalam[6] Brunéi Darussalam[6]	2 972	1 797	1 902	1 708	1 883	2 213	2 682	2 370	2 198	2 296
China Chine	27 612	31 612	39 543	47 541	51 925	61 323	70 463	80 541	90 973	119 830
Hong Kong Hong-kong	30 187	35 439	48 476	63 163	73 140	82 160	98 577	119 512	135 248	151 395
India Inde	9 144	9 391	11 299	13 235	15 872	17 970	17 727	19 641	21 573	25 022
Indonesia[6] Indonésie[6]	18 590	16 075	17 135	19 465	22 160	25 674	29 142	33 967	36 823	40 054
Korea, Republic of[6] Corée, République de[6]	30 164	34 747	47 358	60 993	62 384	64 879	71 736	76 575	82 189	96 111
Lao People's Dem. Rep.[6] Rép. dém. pop. lao[6]	54	60	62	81	...	...	...	...	...	...
Macau Macao	906	1 046	1 397	1 492	1 644	1 694	1 655	1 749	1 763	1 834
Malaysia Malaisie	15 316	13 688	17 958	21 082	25 048	29 453	34 350	40 772	47 131	58 755
Maldives Maldives	23	25	31	40	45	52	54	40	35	46
Mongolia[6] Mongolie[6]	689	716	718	739	722	661	348	389	381	324
Myanmar Myanmar	304	288	219	166	210	325	419	531	586	764
Nepal Népal	161	142	151	191	159	209	263	374	389	363
Pakistan Pakistan	2 740	3 384	4 172	4 522	4 709	5 589	6 528	7 317	6 688	7 365
Philippines Philippines	4 607	4 771	5 649	7 032	7 755	8 068	8 767	9 752	11 089	13 304
Singapore Singapour	22 815	22 495	28 692	39 305	44 661	52 730	58 964	63 435	74 008	96 826
Sri Lanka Sri Lanka	1 333	1 216	1 398	1 477	1 568	1 913	1 988	2 462	2 851	3 209
Thailand Thaïlande	7 122	8 877	11 714	15 956	20 090	23 071	28 439	32 467	36 963	45 236
Viet Nam Viet Nam	699	823	854	1 038	1 946	2 404	2 087	2 581	2 985	3 600
former USSR-Asia **anc. URSS-Asie**	...	...	...	...	...	...	...	4 507	3 932	4 405
Armenia Arménie	...	...	...	...	...	...	...	12	29	...
Azerbaizan Azerbadjan	...	...	...	...	...	...	...	754	351	625

72
Total imports and exports
Value in million US dollars [*cont.*]
Importations et exportations totales
Valeur en millions de dollars E-U [*suite*]

Region, country or area Region, pays ou zone	1985	1986	1987	1988	1989	1990	1991	1992	1993	1994
Georgia Géorgie	...	...	...	...	...	...	...	...	...	330
Kazakstan Kazakstan	...	...	...	...	...	...	...	469	358	514
Kyrgyzstan Kirghizistan	...	...	...	...	...	...	...	70	112	...
Tajikistan Tadjikistan	...	...	...	...	...	...	...	...	374	328
Turkmenistan Turkménistan	...	...	...	...	...	...	...	543	501	...
Uzbekistan Ouzbékistan	...	...	...	...	...	...	...	929	947	1 127

Oceania • Océanie

Region, country or area Region, pays ou zone	1985	1986	1987	1988	1989	1990	1991	1992	1993	1994
Developed economies **Economies développées**	**31 049**	**31 151**	**35 258**	**42 152**	**52 085**	**49 734**	**47 948**	**50 783**	**52 710**	**62 657**
Australia Australie	25 900	26 109	29 321	36 101	44 944	42 024	41 651	43 808	45 478	53 425
New Zealand Nouvelle-Zélande	5 993	6 065	7 276	7 342	8 784	9 501	8 408	9 218	9 636	11 913
Developing economies **Econ. en dévelop.**	**3 472**	**3 846**	**4 345**	**4 779**	**5 041**	**5 210**	**5 480**	**5 462**	**5 236**	**5 675**
American Samoa[6] Samoa américaines[6]	296	313	346	339	378	360	372	418	...	...
Cook Islands[4,6] Iles Cook[4,6]	25	26	34	42	44	51	55	59	...	...
Fiji Fidji	442	435	379	462	579	754	652	631	720	829
French Polynesia[6] Polynésie française[6]	549	736	827	808	791	929	915	894	852	881
Kiribati[4,6] Kiribati[4,6]	15	14	18	22	23	27	26	37	...	...
New Caledonia[6] Nouvelle-Calédonie[6]	348	458	626	604	766	883	863	917	849	842
Papua New Guinea[4] Papouasie-Nvl-Guinée[4]	1 008	1 068	1 262	1 593	1 546	1 271	1 615	1 521	1 306	1 521
Samoa Samoa	51	47	62	76	75	81	94	110	105	81
Solomon Islands[6] Iles Salomon[6]	83	72	81	98	114	95	110	97	101	...
Tonga Tonga	41	41	48	56	54	62	59	63	61	69
Vanuatu Vanuatu	70	57	70	71	71	96	83	82	79	87

Source:
Trade statistics database of the Statistics Division of the
United Nations Secretariat.
+   For Member States of this grouping, see
    Annex I - Other groupings.

Source:
Base de données pour les statistiques du commerce extérieur
de la Division de statistique du Secrétariat de l'ONU.
+   Les Etats membres de ce groupement, voir
    annexe I - Autres groupements.

Region, country or area Région, pays ou zone	1985	1986	1987	1988	1989	1990	1991	1992	1993	1994
Georgia Géorgie	...	...	...	...	...	...	...	...	...	209
Kazakstan Kazakstan	...	...	...	...	...	...	...	1 398	1 271	1 095
Kyrgyzstan Kirghizistan	...	...	...	...	...	...	...	76	112	...
Tajikistan Tadjikistan	...	...	...	...	...	...	...	...	263	356
Turkmenistan Turkménistan	...	...	...	...	...	...	...	1 145	1 049	...
Uzbekistan Ouzbékistan	...	...	...	...	...	...	...	869	707	1 006

Oceania • Océanie

	1985	1986	1987	1988	1989	1990	1991	1992	1993	1994
Developed economies **Economies développées**	**27 491**	**27 432**	**32 481**	**40 796**	**44 367**	**47 362**	**49 393**	**50 396**	**50 842**	**57 028**
Australia Australie	22 613	22 573	26 624	33 238	37 134	39 760	41 855	42 839	42 704	47 525
New Zealand Nouvelle-Zélande	5 722	5 882	7 196	8 849	8 875	9 394	9 649	9 799	10 542	12 185
Developing economies **Econ. en dévelop.**	**1 957**	**2 046**	**2 428**	**2 960**	**3 020**	**2 738**	**3 051**	**3 465**	**4 179**	**4 420**
American Samoa[6] Samoa américaines[6]	202	254	288	368	308	311	327	318	...	...
Cook Islands[4][6] Iles Cook[4][6]	3	5	7	4	3	5	5	3	...	...
Fiji Fidji	307	336	380	372	442	498	451	443	450	550
French Polynesia[6] Polynésie française[6]	41	41	83	75	89	111	127	107	148	226
Kiribati[4][6] Kiribati[4][6]	4	2	2	5	5	3	3	5	...	...
New Caledonia[6] Nouvelle-Calédonie[6]	271	191	225	464	675	449	444	409	356	355
Papua New Guinea[4] Papouasie-Nvl-Guinée[4]	928	1 031	1 241	1 451	1 300	1 177	1 459	1 927	2 584	2 630
Samoa Samoa	16	11	12	15	13	9	6	6	6	4
Solomon Islands[6] Iles Salomon[6]	70	65	64	81	74	70	83	101	96	...
Tonga Tonga	5	6	6	8	9	11	13	12	17	14
Vanuatu Vanuatu	31	17	18	20	22	19	18	24	23	25

† For detailed descriptions of data pertaining to former Czechoslovakia, Germany, SFR Yugoslavia and former USSR, see Annex I – Country or area nomenclature, regional and other groupings.

† Pour les descriptions en détails des données relatives à l'ancienne Tchécoslovaquie, l'Allemagne, la Rfs Yougoslavie et l'ancienne URSS, voir l'Annexe I – Nomenclature des pays ou zones, groupements régionaux et autres groupements.

72
Total imports and exports
Value in million US dollars [cont.]

Importations et exportations totales
Valeur en millions de dollars E-U [suite]

1 United States, Canada, Developed Economies of Europe, Israel, Japan, Australia, New Zealand and South African Customs Union.
2 This classification is intended for statistical convenience and does not necessarily express a judgement about the stage reached by a particular country in the development process.
3 Prior to January 1992, includes Eastern Europe and the former USSR. Beginning January 1992, includes Eastern Europe and the European countries of the former USSR.
4 Imports F.O.B.
5 Latin American Integration Association. Formerly Latin American Free Trade Association.
6 Country or area using special trade system. See technical notes for explanation of trade systems.
7 Prior to 1986, includes Aruba.
8 Excluding trade of the free zone of Colon.
9 Prior to January 1991, includes trade conducted in accordance with the supplementary protocol to the treaty on the basis of relations between the Federal Republic of Germany and the former German Democratic Republic.
10 Excludes trade conducted in accordance with the supplementary protocol to the treaty on the basis of relations between the Federal Republic of Germany and the former German Democratic Republic.
11 Prior to 1983, General trade.
12 Including monetary gold.
13 Beginning January 1992, data refer to Bosnia and Herzegovina, Croatia, Slovenia, TFYR Macedonia and the Federal Republic of Yugoslavia. Prior to 1992, data refer to the Socialist Federal Republic of Yugoslavia.
14 Beginning 1985, data are not comparable to those shown for prior periods due to revisions of the Koruna to US dollar exchange rate.
15 For 1989, data are not comparable to those shown for prior periods due to revisions of the Mark to US dollar exchange rate.
16 Imports and exports are valued at foreign contract prices.
17 For 1991, data for the former USSR are converted to US dollars using commercial exchange rate and are not comparable to those shown for prior periods.
18 Excluding inter-trade among countries of the region, except for Estonia, Latvia and Lithuania.
19 Excluding exports of gold bullion and gold coin.
20 The South African Customs Union comprising Botswana, Lesotho, Namibia, South Africa and Swaziland. Trade between the component countries is excluded.
21 Import figures exclude petroleum imported without stated value.

1 Etats-Unis, Canada, Pays à économie développés d'Europe, Israel, Japon, Australie, Nouvelle-Zéalande et l'union douaniere de l'Afrique du Sud.
2 Cette classification est utilisée pour plus de commodité dans la présentation des statistiques et n'implique pas nécessairement un jugement quant au stage de développement auquel est parvenu un pays donné.
3 Avant janvier 1992, y compris l'Europe de l'est et l'ancienne URSS. A partir de janvier 1992, y compris l'Europe de l'est et les pays européennes de l'ancienne URSS.
4 Importations F.O.B.
5 Association Latino-Américaine d'intégration. Antérieurement Association Latino-Américaine de libre-Echange.
6 Pays ou zone utilisant un système spécial du commerce. Pour l'explication du système de commerce, voir les notes techniques.
7 Avant 1986, comprend Aruba.
8 Non compris le commerce de la zone libre de Colon.
9 Avant janvier 1991, Y compris le commerce effectué en accord avec le protocole additionnel au traite définissant la base des relations entre la République Fédérale d'Allemagne et l'ancienne République Démocratique Allemande.
10 Non compris le commerce effectué en accord avec le protocole additionnel au traite définissant la base des relations entre la République fédérale d'allemagne et l'ancienne République démocratique allemande.
11 Avant 1983, commerce général.
12 Y compris l'or monétaire.
13 A partir de janvier 1992, les données se rapportent aux Bosnie-Herzegovine, Croatie, Slovénie, TARY Macédonie et la république fédérative de Yougoslavie. Avant 1992, les données se rapportent à la république fédérative socialiste de Yougoslavie.
14 A partir de l'année 1985, les données ne sont pas comparables aux données des périodes antérieurs à cause des révisions de taux de change de Koruna au dollar de E-U.
15 Les données de 1989 ne sont pas comparables aux données des périodes antérieurs à cause des révisions de taux de change de mark au dollar de E-U.
16 Importations et exportations sont valuées du prix de contract étranger.
17 Les données de 1991 de l'ancienne URSS sont converties en dollars des E.U. en utilisant le taux de change commercial de rouble et ne sont pas comparables aux données des périodes antérieures.
18 Non compris le commerce avec les autres pays de la région, excepte pour Estonie, Lettonie et Lituanie.
19 Non compris les exportations de Lingots et pièces d'or.
20 L'union douaniere de l'Afrique Meridionale comprend Botswana, Lesotho, Namibie, Afrique du Sud et Swaziland. Non compris le commerce entre ces pays.
21 Non compris le petrole brut dont la valeur à la importation n'est pas stipulée.

22 Excluding exports of camels to Egypt.
23 Inter-trade among the members of Customs and Economic Union of Central Africa is excluded.
24 Imports and exports net of returned goods. The figures also exclude Judea and Samaria and the Gaza area.

25 Excluding military imports.
26 Prior to January 1992, excludes Armenia, Azerbaijan, Georgia, Kazakstan, Kyrgyzstan, Tajikistan, Turkmenistan and Uzbekistan. Total developing Asia re-calculated for all periods shown in the table according to the current composition.
27 Year ending 20 December of the year stated.
28 Comprises trade of the former Democratic Yemen and former Yemen Arab Republic including any intertrade between them.

29 Includes Peoples Democratic Republic of Korea.
30 Year beginning 21 March of the year stated.
31 Data refer to total exports less petroleum exports of Asia Middle East countries where petroleum, in this case, is the sum of SITC groups 333, 334 and 335.

22 Non compris les exportations des chameaux en Egypte.
23 Non compris le commerce entre les pays membres du UDEAC.

24 Importations et exportations nets. Ne comprennent pas les marchandises retournées. Sont également exclués les données de la Judee et de Samaria et ainsi que la zone de Gaza.
25 Non compris les importations des economats militaires.
26 Avant janvier 1992, non compris Arménie, Azerbaidjan, Géorgie, Kazakstan, Kirghizistan, Tadjikistan, Turkménistan et Ouzbékistan. Total Asie en voie de développement avait été recalculé pour toutes les périodes données au tableau suivant la composition présente.
27 Année finissant le 20 décembre de l'année indiquée.
28 Y compris le commerce de l'ancienne République populaire Démocratique de Yémen, le commerce de l'ancienne République Arabe de Yémen et le commerce entre eux.
29 Y compris la République Democratique de Corée.
30 Année commençant le 21 mars de l'année indiquée.
31 Les données se rapportent aux exportations totales moins les exportations pétroliers de moyen-orient d'Asie. Dans ce cas, le pétrole est la somme des groupes CTCI 333, 334 et 335.

International merchandise trade   Commerce international des marchandises

73
World exports by commodity classes and by regions
Exportations mondiales par classes de marchandises et par régions

In million US dollars f.o.b.

Exports from	Year	World Monde /1,2,3	Developed economies Econ. développées /2,3,4	Developing economies Economies en voie de développement /1,3,4 Total	OPEC+ OPEP+	Eastern Europe and former USSR Europe de l'Est et l'ancienne URSS Total /2,3,7	fmr USSR anc URSS /10	Europe Total /2	EEC+ CEE+ /2	EFTA+ AELE+	Developed Economies South Africa Afrique du Sud
									Total trade (SITC, Rev. 2 and Rev. 3, 0-9) /6		
World /1,2,3	1980	2027619	1336782	500519	128126	140018	60473	879151	747478	129893	13310
	1990	3416417	2445616	777981	110332	155056	73460	1581440	1357824	219303	12676
	1991	3433554	2443255	849681	126210	108344	52538	1581396	1369526	207334	13797
	1992	3703953	2589010	971639	145076	99754	43334	1656370	1440440	211224	14973
	1993	3689744	2495003	1043584	137884	105742	43772	1486386	1287100	194470	15033
Developed economies /2,3,4	1980	1270951	891580	314408	99885	42215	21562	650038	542021	106417	12566
	1990	2445179	1894309	478702	80173	49921	26401	1325757	1129507	192620	11525
	1991	2507026	1901616	526521	92264	56780	27611	1343578	1155722	184035	12075
	1992	2670288	1986604	588766	102995	62774	25590	1403174	1212610	186417	12438
	1993	2574782	1844562	629912	93977	66427	26161	1225278	1051584	169573	12204
Developing economies /1,3,4	1980	601281	400761	153859	22857	19838	12065	188284	174508	13612	743
	1990	788617	482424	263991	27189	27576	19021	193652	178583	14734	1149
	1991	835388	498362	306244	32266	22063	15624	198361	182109	15570	1708
	1992	940789	552201	365848	39969	14752	8414	207497	191108	15909	2502
	1993	1013186	593336	395695	41869	16786	9803	210599	194979	14968	2766
OPEC+	1980	326196	234055	69160	3976	1472	182	115783	107649	8081	3
	1990	172056	114320	47453	3002	2775	714	52575	50384	2127	5
	1991	162360	111680	45091	4025	1676	362	50479	47292	3132	3
	1992	169749	115327	49235	6966	2047	455	47961	45887	2037	16
	1993	176248	118978	52329	7313	2195	546	48128	46124	1968	12
Eastern Europe and the former USSR /2,3,7	1980	155386	44442	32252	5384	77966	26846	40829	30950	9865	1
	1990	182621	68883	35288	2971	77559	28037	62032	49733	11949	2
	1991	91140	43278	16916	1680	29501	9304	39458	31695	7729	14
	1992	92875	50205	17025	2112	22227	9330	45699	36722	8898	33
	1993	101777	57105	17977	2038	22529	7808	50509	40537	9929	63
former USSR /3	1980	76449	24431	19740	1740	32278	.	22672	17260	5413	0
	1990	104177	43065	25520	946	35592	.	38589	32252	6300	0
	1991	46274	...	...	...	...	.	...	...	...	...
	1992	.	.	.	.	.	.	.	.	.	.
	1993	.	.	.	.	.	.	.	.	.	.
former USSR-Europe /8	1980	.	.	.	.	.	.	.	.	.	.
	1990	.	.	.	.	.	.	.	.	.	.
	1991	.	.	.	.	.	.	.	.	.	.
	1992	48535	26766	9521	865	10211	1736	23874	19254	4594	1
	1993	51395	27612	10138	1026	10355	2194	23037	17275	5755	12
Developed economies-Europe /2	1980	801840	615414	149323	60121	31447	14681	540358	446088	92771	7888
	1990	1578081	1313175	205357	48745	40481	19298	1124815	952251	169210	7911
	1991	1585895	1308421	211067	52775	47113	20183	1133526	969655	160272	7895
	1992	1683664	1377787	232947	58296	53753	19446	1194665	1026346	164446	7729
	1993	1540211	1218141	244057	51913	57056	20112	1031860	880243	147857	7474
European Economic Community+ /2	1980	689597	527375	132681	54303	23888	10829	462282	384556	76305	7168
	1990	1351043	1122944	179795	43351	30039	13640	962609	820585	138967	7360
	1991	1367722	1125231	185025	46926	38950	17324	975825	839691	132834	7392
	1992	1455380	1186772	205560	52490	44694	16797	1030060	889136	137302	7158
	1993	1328530	1045885	215060	46270	47473	16955	886213	758433	124231	6780
European Free Trade Association+	1980	111610	87481	16588	5777	7541	3852	77552	61041	16434	719
	1990	225512	188908	25431	5330	10402	5625	160973	130477	30199	551
	1991	216495	181726	25876	5757	8147	2845	156338	128648	27391	503
	1992	226335	189343	27200	5720	9020	2612	163073	135747	27073	570
	1993	210008	170851	28807	5569	9558	3135	144387	120579	23598	693
Other developed economies	1980	469112	276166	165086	39764	10768	6881	109681	95933	13646	4678
	1990	867098	581133	273345	31428	9440	7103	200941	177257	23411	3613
	1991	921132	593195	315455	39489	9667	7428	210053	186068	23763	4180
	1992	986624	608818	355819	44699	9021	6144	208509	186264	21971	4709
	1993	1034570	626420	385856	42064	9371	6049	193419	171341	21716	4729

International merchandise trade   Commerce international des marchandises

En millions de dollars E.-U. f.o.b.

| Economies développées /2,3,4 | | | | Developing economies — Economies en voie de développement /1,3,4 | | | | | | ← Exportations vers | |
Canada	USA E-U	Japan Japon	Australia New Zealand Australie Nouvelle-Zélande	Africa Afrique	America Amerique Total	LAIA+ ALADI+	Asia Asie Mid.East Moyen Orient	Other Autres /9	Oceania Océanie	Année	Exportations en provenance de ↓

Commerce total (CTCI, Rev. 2 et Rev. 3, 0-9) /6

Canada	USA E-U	Japon	Aust/NZ	Afrique	Total	ALADI+	Moyen Orient	Autres /9	Océanie	Année	En provenance de
50753	237607	125386	24138	81953	123134	85316	97427	174596	2949	1980	Monde /1,2,3
110804	491100	192567	44130	79732	136414	90206	102789	433927	4992	1990	
113157	474485	202795	42854	81921	150083	106027	113112	484983	5163	1991	
116348	537372	200522	46892	82410	177529	132592	131725	560376	5352	1992	
124663	593237	209193	48588	78184	190511	143186	131688	625397	5110	1993	
43164	122873	40326	17303	63595	76234	60154	67019	97209	2118	1980	Economies dévelopées /2,3,4
100711	308228	102237	34229	58967	95224	70093	69039	238206	3721	1990	
101350	299509	100473	31542	57476	109527	82713	78738	266711	3747	1991	
104623	320278	97352	34050	61107	129801	100388	89294	295928	4056	1992	
111537	347152	98063	34596	57830	135297	103879	86525	337899	3845	1993	
7359	113313	83253	6729	14194	41837	24455	24234	70225	831	1980	Economies en voie de développement /1,3,4
9790	180214	86708	9744	17336	32523	19300	28998	182003	1269	1990	
11600	173471	100476	11206	22699	36784	22866	31735	212109	1415	1991	
11382	215289	101091	12743	19625	46522	31647	38405	255747	1294	1992	
12715	242738	108792	13884	18591	54139	38620	40476	278077	1250	1993	
4549	57398	53656	2665	3629	23840	12721	9631	30482	9	1980	OPEP+
1244	37207	22121	1142	3565	7910	3593	8893	26168	18	1990	
1656	27664	30253	1588	6767	6712	2340	8637	22221	79	1991	
977	34001	30380	1951	3132	8230	5059	9992	27288	47	1992	
1128	36314	31296	2063	3199	9406	6122	10425	28680	43	1993	
230	1421	1807	107	4164	5063	706	6174	7162	0	1980	Europe de l'Est et l'ancienne URSS /2,3,7
303	2658	3622	157	3428	8667	813	4752	13718	2	1990	
207	1505	1846	106	1747	3772	448	2639	6163	1	1991	
343	1805	2079	99	1678	1205	557	4026	8702	3	1992	
411	3348	2338	108	1764	1074	688	4687	9421	15	1993	
46	233	1464	14	1380	3679	130	2210	4574	0	1980	l'ancienne URSS /3
111	1189	3114	62	1515	7406	305	2554	10910	0	1990	
...	...	...	...	...	...	...	...	...	...	1991	
.	.	.	.	.	.	.	.	.	.	1992	
.	.	.	.	.	.	.	.	.	.	1993	
.	.	.	.	.	.	.	.	.	.	1980	l'ancienne URSS-Europe /8
.	.	.	.	.	.	.	.	.	.	1990	
.	.	.	.	.	.	.	.	.	.	1991	
180	910	1746	12	577	613	204	2296	5807	0	1992	
253	2102	2024	12	481	487	224	2878	5990	0	1993	
5777	44042	8181	6129	49626	25478	19374	41359	25147	519	1980	Economies développées-Europe /2
14653	111276	34453	12229	45991	29615	19951	46023	69869	1283	1990	
13981	101419	32719	10454	44179	32364	22440	50607	73134	1111	1991	
13356	109480	31630	11331	45941	37454	26657	56828	83146	1409	1992	
12183	113615	31523	11314	41864	39540	28075	55276	98073	1099	1993	
4953	38619	6672	5309	45716	22214	16875	36698	21653	487	1980	Communauté Economique Européenne+ /2
11832	95908	28486	10149	42727	25706	16942	40479	58953	1241	1990	
11492	87418	27126	8750	40719	28328	19414	44732	61834	1073	1991	
10890	94519	26351	9375	42726	32891	23365	50810	70860	1380	1992	
9951	98332	26381	9412	38798	35120	24921	49446	83721	1070	1993	
821	5393	1509	819	3870	3260	2498	4653	3493	32	1980	Association Européenne de Libre Echange+
2806	15310	5954	2078	3203	3903	3008	5523	10874	42	1990	
2486	13923	5577	1703	3380	4022	3025	5845	11261	38	1991	
2464	14846	5267	1952	3137	4553	3284	5991	12214	29	1992	
2221	15170	5126	1901	2991	4410	3146	5809	14268	29	1993	
37387	78831	32145	11174	13969	50756	40781	25660	72062	1599	1980	Autres economies développées
86059	196953	67784	22000	12976	65609	50142	23016	168337	2438	1990	
87369	198090	67754	21088	13297	77168	60273	28131	193577	2636	1991	
91267	210798	65722	22719	15166	92348	73730	32466	212781	2647	1992	
99353	233536	66540	23282	15965	95757	75804	31250	239827	2746	1993	

International merchandise trade   Commerce international des marchandises

73
World exports by commodity classes and by regions (continued)
Exportations mondiales par classes de marchandises et par régions (suite)

In million US dollars f.o.b.

Exports to → Exports from	Year	World Monde /1,2,3	Developed economies Econ. dévelop- pées /2,3,4	Developing economies Economies en voie de développement /1,3,4		Eastern Europe and former USSR Europe de l'Est et l'ancienne URSS		Europe			Developed Economies South Africa Afrique du Sud
				Total	OPEC⁺ OPEP⁺	Total /2,3,7	fmr USSR anc URSS /10	Total /2	EEC⁺ CEE⁺ /2	EFTA⁺ AELE⁺	

Total trade (SITC, Rev. 2 and Rev. 3, 0-9) /6(continued)

Exports from	Year	World	Developed	Total	OPEC	Eastern Total	fmr USSR	Europe Total	EEC	EFTA	South Africa
Canada	1980	64935	55286	7601	1869	1776	1317	9447	8565	880	175
	1990	126897	115641	10176	1630	1081	964	12209	10269	1927	143
	1991	126762	114385	10981	1848	1396	1290	11737	10250	1475	109
	1992	134617	122615	10774	1762	1227	1059	11469	9576	1891	118
	1993	144731	134065	10103	1835	563	394	9757	8267	1478	128
United States	1980	216592	128821	82805	17465	3850	1510	65064	57849	7185	2487
	1990	374449	242222	127479	13418	4226	3072	103832	93049	10666	1750
	1991	400984	249153	146869	18587	4673	3500	109122	97514	11524	2131
	1992	424871	252611	166710	21324	5252	3584	107457	97340	10032	2470
	1993	439223	256469	176835	20045	5575	3520	103184	91237	11755	2195
Japan	1980	129807	61602	64619	18482	3585	2778	21436	18120	3264	1809
	1990	286947	170164	113476	13575	3308	2563	62412	53846	8437	1518
	1991	314525	177648	134015	16474	2862	2115	68325	59557	8651	1670
	1992	339651	186080	151727	18995	1844	1128	71584	62952	8488	1757
	1993	360911	188795	169913	17263	2203	1581	64117	56910	7084	2032
Australia, New Zealand	1980	26673	15513	8291	1809	1513	1276	4334	4161	165	126
	1990	47784	29518	16846	2654	715	500	7866	6819	1042	105
	1991	49817	29828	18621	2490	591	505	7210	6315	890	173
	1992	50801	28791	19858	2349	196	82	7483	6762	694	239
	1993	50951	28359	21483	2601	308	231	6717	6197	515	252
Developing economies-Africa	1980	113844	80850	10152	1021	2159	713	47564	45073	2434	17
	1990	73188	60652	10257	1691	1882	985	44845	43734	979	313
	1991	71773	59839	10062	1982	1212	559	44610	42981	1309	293
	1992	69412	57027	10749	2196	922	262	41975	39935	1839	346
	1993	68542	56218	10856	1977	789	217	40737	39332	1185	367
Developing economies-America	1980	102399	65023	28619	3392	6964	5192	25696	23602	2025	161
	1990	134319	94243	30748	4200	6358	4300	32296	29951	2301	337
	1991	131279	90034	34416	4531	4838	4113	30997	29097	1861	346
	1992	154253	108793	43207	4954	937	313	31486	29511	1962	472
	1993	165685	114700	48806	5068	945	471	29167	27168	1955	331
Developing economies-Europe /5	1980	8977	3286	1659	851	4033	2489	2807	2385	417	0
	1990	14391	8444	1888	747	4059	2681	7572	6587	978	1
	1991	9548	5601	1247	495	2700	1786	5024	4370	649	0
	1992	13952	8774	4156	296	992	436	8288	7149	1134	2
	1993	12134	8144	2849	189	1010	473	7534	6811	696	3
Developing economies-Middle East	1980	212886	152746	55890	6223	1252	313	84029	77803	6224	0
	1990	113349	59820	43480	6120	4030	2224	30595	28454	2115	51
	1991	104875	59046	39062	6623	3322	1841	28454	25416	3018	59
	1992	111079	64463	40855	9794	2659	790	28220	26320	1860	57
	1993	115375	66487	43040	10251	2947	909	28764	26846	1855	63
Developing economies-Other Asia	1980	161009	96944	57308	11370	5429	3358	27427	24889	2508	565
	1990	450556	257017	177059	14426	11247	8832	77681	69246	8309	445
	1991	514602	281234	220822	18633	9938	7310	88613	79625	8689	1009
	1992	588844	310440	266355	22722	9237	6609	96798	87516	9063	1624
	1993	647363	344599	289258	24370	11096	7733	103712	94174	9241	2002
former USSR-Asia /9	1980	.	.	.	.	.	.	.	.	.	.
	1990	.	.	.	.	.	.	.	.	.	.
	1991	.	.	.	.	.	.	.	.	.	.
	1992	4453	502	2683	843	377	.	425	366	58	0
	1993	3848	498	2397	759	349	.	394	321	73	0
Developing economies-Oceania	1980	2165	1911	232	0	0	0	760	757	3	0
	1990	2814	2249	560	4	0	0	663	611	52	2
	1991	3311	2607	636	2	53	15	664	621	43	0
	1992	3250	2703	528	7	4	4	729	677	52	0
	1993	4087	3188	886	14	0	0	685	649	37	0

En millions de dollars E.-U. f.o.b.

Economies développées /2,3,4				Developing economies Economies en voie de développement /1,3,4						← Exportations vers	
Canada	USA E-U	Japan Japon	Australia New Zealand Australie Nouvelle-Zélande	Africa Afrique	America Amerique		Asia Asie		Oceania Océanie		Exportations en provenance de ↓
					Total	LAIA+ ALADI+	Mid.East Moyen Orient	Other Autres /9		Année	
Commerce total (CTCI, Rev. 2 et Rev. 3, 0-9) /6(suite)											
.	41183	3726	660	932	3288	2396	681	2628	13	1980	Canada
.	95217	7038	909	903	2325	1675	961	5911	27	1990	
.	95501	6243	674	820	2329	1751	1007	6764	21	1991	
.	104056	6198	669	722	2769	2198	840	6408	16	1992	
.	116784	6558	718	682	2856	2296	916	5612	16	1993	
34102	.	20574	4651	6357	38021	31668	10266	27224	184	1980	Etats-Unis
78212	.	46130	9406	6068	52280	41969	10234	58051	289	1990	
79055	.	46111	9181	6562	61326	50671	13719	64523	376	1991	
83217	.	45836	9973	7287	73118	61378	15399	70110	489	1992	
91865	.	46030	9243	6991	75293	62380	15668	78260	404	1993	
2437	31747	.	4065	5958	8537	5923	13114	36480	407	1980	Japon
6726	90893	.	8106	3835	9712	5354	9570	89255	853	1990	
7251	92091	.	7574	3973	12243	6791	11583	105257	784	1991	
7090	96489	.	8158	4648	15053	8936	14201	117071	708	1992	
6328	106353	.	8975	5263	15914	9605	12569	135325	804	1993	
539	2804	6053	1627	611	358	267	1507	4754	991	1980	Australie, Nouvelle-Zélande
765	5503	11880	3365	601	707	610	1891	12319	1263	1990	
738	5218	12994	3449	498	727	583	1475	14440	1448	1991	
799	4685	11883	3657	324	775	659	1500	15833	1422	1992	
1002	4268	12034	4041	589	953	859	1548	16879	1508	1993	
191	30643	2180	51	2349	3546	1575	1841	1518	3	1980	Economies en voie de développement-Afrique
680	13140	1401	58	4991	1037	797	1804	1856	5	1990	
400	12771	1288	47	4941	1085	896	1352	2112	2	1991	
278	12531	1494	61	5187	1218	1100	1630	2206	3	1992	
402	12636	1729	65	5211	1329	1196	1516	2293	8	1993	
2763	30933	4577	167	2295	22152	11524	1593	2128	62	1980	Economies en voie de développement-Amérique
2036	51551	7182	451	1618	20338	13052	2314	6205	30	1990	
2929	47523	7432	437	1696	23317	16037	2201	6978	53	1991	
2358	67158	6527	431	1885	28860	20255	2497	9848	33	1992	
2886	75238	6292	461	1632	34033	24622	2320	10743	42	1993	
28	393	31	12	735	65	36	628	228	2	1980	Economies en voie de développement-Europe /5
62	691	39	66	715	110	47	788	273	2	1990	
41	458	26	44	475	73	31	518	180	1	1991	
43	379	31	22	257	69	35	360	238	1	1992	
39	484	48	23	151	60	28	283	160	1	1993	
2610	20397	43306	2394	3458	12033	9537	11714	27571	111	1980	Economies en voie de développement-Moyen Orient
178	15262	12954	729	2860	3831	1716	12396	23791	3	1990	
806	7266	21377	996	6117	2484	303	11992	18068	58	1991	
538	13054	21305	1187	2260	2690	2586	14126	21499	0	1992	
568	14152	21575	1269	2229	2884	2797	14764	22879	0	1993	
1743	30653	32588	3843	5357	4036	1777	8458	38638	570	1980	Economies en voie de développement-Autres Pays d'Asie
6817	99158	64517	7899	7152	7204	3688	11697	149495	1056	1990	
7409	104981	69707	8872	9468	9822	5597	15669	184323	1119	1991	
8150	121656	71170	10163	10036	13684	7672	19784	221530	1162	1992	
8805	139645	78381	10929	9368	15833	9977	21590	241213	1108	1993	
.	.	.	.	.	.	.	.	.	.	1980	l'ancienne URSS asiatique /9
.	.	.	.	.	.	.	.	.	.	1990	
.	.	.	.	.	.	.	.	.	.	1991	
0	39	38	0	32	119	37	1803	729	0	1992	
0	39	66	0	37	128	40	1525	706	0	1993	
24	296	570	261	0	6	5	0	143	83	1980	Economies en voie de développement-Océanie
16	412	614	542	0	3	1	0	382	174	1990	
15	472	646	811	2	3	2	2	448	181	1991	
16	512	565	881	0	0	0	7	426	94	1992	
15	583	768	1137	0	0	0	2	791	93	1993	

International merchandise trade   Commerce international des marchandises

73
World exports by commodity classes and by regions (continued)
Exportations mondiales par classes de marchandises et par régions (suite)

In million US dollars f.o.b.

Food and raw materials (SITC, Rev. 2 and Rev. 3, 0 - 4)

Exports from / Year	World Monde /1,2,3	Developed economies Econ. développées /2,3,4	Developing economies Economies en voie de développement /1,3,4 Total	OPEC+ OPEP+	Eastern Europe and former USSR Europe de l'Est et l'ancienne URSS Total /2,3,7	fmr USSR anc URSS /10	Europe Total /2	EEC+ CEE+ /2	EFTA+ AELE+	Developed Economies South Africa Afrique du Sud
World /1,2,3 1980	825446	572234	170675	25173	44842	15974	344831	310618	33552	1252
1990	826551	583286	181346	21761	46181	17407	365026	331480	32433	1147
1991	788519	563565	178552	21796	32827	15978	352343	320329	30588	1207
1992	818331	582648	192511	25466	30430	13406	361976	328431	32235	1907
1993	800855	556698	197886	25973	29843	12096	329592	297011	31114	1472
Developed economies /2,3,4 1980	300150	220222	55821	15339	11930	6051	165278	147969	16784	905
1990	423478	334823	72363	12886	10367	6065	241572	217858	22865	754
1991	426651	335354	73118	12390	12127	7265	246220	222307	23004	783
1992	444847	346989	77644	12367	14234	8418	253338	228741	23595	1247
1993	424703	321920	78686	12751	12929	6926	224011	201264	21609	944
Developing economies /1,3,4 1980	470279	326254	105768	9496	13344	8240	155297	144840	10327	347
1990	334890	213419	98352	8202	13967	8874	91466	87494	3791	393
1991	325343	208990	100070	9118	10162	7197	88349	83792	4055	421
1992	332810	210671	110618	12736	6203	2753	85659	81364	4040	646
1993	336472	210057	114937	12878	6619	3180	83529	79261	3961	524
OPEC+ 1980	319143	230756	65596	2225	1436	162	113666	105729	7884	1
1990	149575	102736	37781	826	2474	583	46649	45684	920	4
1991	137965	98674	34064	1355	1366	252	43604	42245	1307	1
1992	140622	100923	34690	3388	1853	336	41110	39530	1546	9
1993	143255	102282	36306	3592	1991	417	40885	39421	1431	10
Eastern Europe and the former USSR /2,3,7 1980	55017	25758	9087	338	19568	1683	24256	17809	6441	0
1990	68184	35043	10631	672	21846	2468	31988	26128	5777	0
1991	36525	19221	5364	288	10539	1517	17775	14231	3529	2
1992	40675	24988	4249	363	9993	2235	22980	18326	4599	14
1993	39679	24721	4263	345	10295	1990	22052	16487	5544	5
former USSR /3 1980	44273	20034	8081	91	16158	.	18839	14185	4654	0
1990	...	...	...	...	...	.	...	...	...	...
1991	...	...	...	...	...	.	...	...	...	...
1992	.	.	.	.	.	.	.	.	.	.
1993	.	.	.	.	.	.	.	.	.	.
former USSR-Europe /8 1980	.	.	.	.	.	.	.	.	.	.
1990	.	.	.	.	.	.	.	.	.	.
1991	.	.	.	.	.	.	.	.	.	.
1992	28516	18311	2500	159	7137	551	16637	13584	3035	0
1993	28035	17723	2820	156	7105	625	15372	11458	3909	1
Developed economies-Europe /2 1980	177685	145882	21732	9321	5769	2489	136298	120813	14996	433
1990	264301	228765	24981	6808	5804	2422	206846	185322	20722	446
1991	269413	232516	24694	6843	7294	2996	213129	191454	20815	467
1992	284169	243866	26067	6933	10165	4940	223237	200811	21485	487
1993	261780	219740	27576	6969	10199	4855	198835	178062	19690	425
European Economic Community+ /2 1980	152142	123281	19929	8479	4634	1974	114643	101852	12324	335
1990	224438	192527	22876	6244	4478	1874	173951	157382	15836	435
1991	230594	197010	22728	6331	6133	2734	180647	163763	16086	454
1992	243738	207012	24099	6435	8765	4564	189612	171960	16778	456
1993	224276	186032	25423	6402	8749	4379	168545	152022	15484	406
European Free Trade Association+ 1980	25338	22406	1798	838	1135	515	21480	18798	2660	97
1990	39427	35847	2093	556	1325	548	32536	27607	4860	12
1991	38346	35084	1949	500	1159	260	32108	27345	4702	13
1992	39937	36438	1942	485	1398	374	33250	28502	4682	30
1993	37091	33370	2129	555	1450	475	29979	25744	4191	19
Other developed economies 1980	122465	74341	34089	6018	6161	3562	28979	27156	1788	473
1990	159177	106059	47382	6079	4564	3643	34726	32536	2143	308
1991	157238	102837	48424	5547	4833	4269	33091	30853	2189	316
1992	160678	103123	51578	5435	4069	3478	30102	27930	2110	760
1993	162923	102180	51111	5782	2730	2071	25176	23202	1919	519

International merchandise trade   Commerce international des marchandises

En millions de dollars E.-U. f.o.b.

← Exportations vers

Economies développées /2,3,4				Developing economies / Economies en voie de développement /1,3,4							Exportations en provenance de ↓
Canada	USA E-U	Japan Japon	Australia New Zealand Australie Nouvelle-Zélande	Africa Afrique	America Amerique — Total	LAIA+ ALADI+	Asia Asie — Mid.East Moyen Orient	Other Autres /9	Oceania Océanie	Année	Exportations en provenance de ↓

Produits alimentaires et matières brutes (CTCI, Rev. 2 et Rev. 3, 0 - 4)

Canada	USA E-U	Japon	Aust. N-Z	Afrique	Amérique Total	LAIA+	Moyen Orient	Autres /9	Océanie	Année	Exportations en provenance de
12144	109363	97051	6014	21985	46142	26801	24364	69311	1295	1980	Monde /1,2,3
14963	107569	87447	5309	21195	33144	18657	25258	94629	1496	1990	
14811	92534	94923	5653	23010	32161	18976	23825	94157	1618	1991	
14468	102112	94228	5844	20251	34962	23750	27058	105119	1479	1992	
14880	108081	94133	6245	19779	37127	25220	27979	108219	1440	1993	
6575	23706	21508	1625	13612	13103	9522	9449	17822	674	1980	Economies dévelopées /2,3,4
12419	39861	36209	2841	11883	13997	9299	11212	32509	951	1990	
11750	37196	35514	2647	11281	15344	10620	10514	33725	1008	1991	
11987	40936	35454	2682	11650	17155	12334	10487	36242	970	1992	
12330	44462	35788	2799	11434	17340	12221	11038	36549	977	1993	
5553	85384	74338	4383	7851	31326	17186	14252	49474	620	1980	Economies en voie de développement /1,3,4
2508	66706	49266	2444	8237	16299	9135	12578	59352	544	1990	
3020	54879	58493	2992	11234	15473	8193	12527	59161	610	1991	
2386	60690	57381	3149	8151	17477	11216	15325	67340	509	1992	
2423	62719	56732	3433	7923	19478	12795	15490	70055	462	1993	
4542	57141	52792	2614	3390	23598	12515	7498	29535	9	1980	OPEP+
1111	34448	19667	835	3151	6941	3015	5570	21246	4	1990	
1490	25019	27216	1310	5879	5685	1701	5362	16427	60	1991	
755	30239	27257	1515	2508	6788	4109	5553	19313	2	1992	
831	31574	27412	1536	2548	7422	4649	5833	19938	5	1993	
16	274	1205	6	521	1713	93	663	2015	0	1980	Europe de l'Est et l'ancienne URSS /2,3,7
36	1002	1972	24	1075	2848	223	1469	2769	0	1990	
41	459	916	14	495	1344	163	784	1270	0	1991	
94	485	1392	13	449	331	201	1246	1537	0	1992	
127	900	1613	13	422	309	204	1451	1616	0	1993	
2	51	1137	4	327	1526	10	427	1885	0	1980	l'ancienne URSS /3
...	...	...	...	...	...	...	...	...	...	1990	
...	...	...	...	...	...	...	...	...	...	1991	
.	.	.	.	.	.	.	.	.	.	1992	
.	.	.	.	.	.	.	.	.	.	1993	
.	.	.	.	.	.	.	.	.	.	1980	l'ancienne URSS-Europe /8
.	.	.	.	.	.	.	.	.	.	1990	
.	.	.	.	.	.	.	.	.	.	1991	
74	308	1286	5	169	134	55	851	1223	0	1992	
104	725	1515	6	167	119	61	1038	1328	0	1993	
804	6436	1266	405	9857	2967	1517	6032	2123	87	1980	Economies développées-Europe /2
2979	13114	3970	802	8204	3421	1767	6414	5283	186	1990	
2718	10690	4139	685	7718	3548	1965	6560	5636	174	1991	
2659	11881	4242	713	7961	3866	2114	6434	6594	176	1992	
2498	12444	4186	664	7714	4142	2236	6722	7567	164	1993	
744	5902	1096	367	9155	2798	1398	5516	1897	86	1980	Communauté Economique Européenne+ /2
2173	11283	3462	735	7619	3189	1596	5941	4880	185	1990	
1863	9364	3538	637	7179	3271	1768	6102	5217	173	1991	
1782	10301	3714	669	7454	3633	1953	5982	6074	175	1992	
1748	10614	3557	624	7189	3888	2054	6255	6912	164	1993	
60	514	170	38	699	170	119	512	226	1	1980	Association Européenne de Libre Echange+
806	1812	495	67	584	231	170	464	401	1	1990	
854	1295	586	48	536	277	196	446	417	0	1991	
876	1551	518	44	504	228	156	437	516	1	1992	
750	1815	620	40	522	249	177	453	653	0	1993	
5771	17270	20241	1220	3756	10136	8005	3418	15699	588	1980	Autres economies développées
9440	26748	32239	2039	3680	10576	7532	4798	27226	765	1990	
9031	26506	31374	1962	3563	11796	8656	3954	28089	835	1991	
9329	29056	31212	1969	3690	13289	10220	4053	29648	795	1992	
9832	32018	31603	2134	3721	13198	9985	4316	28981	813	1993	

International merchandise trade   Commerce international des marchandises

73
World exports by commodity classes and by regions (continued)
Exportations mondiales par classes de marchandises et par régions (suite)

In million US dollars f.o.b.

Food and raw materials (SITC, Rev. 2 and Rev. 3, 0 - 4)(continued)

Exports from / Year	World Monde /1,2,3	Developed economies Econ. développées /2,3,4	Developing economies Economies en voie de développement /1,3,4 Total	OPEC+ OPEP+	Eastern Europe and former USSR Europe de l'Est et l'ancienne URSS Total /2,3,7	fmr USSR anc URSS /10	Europe Total /2	EEC+ CEE+ /2	EFTA+ AELE+	Developed Economies South Africa Afrique du Sud
Canada 1980	28989	23881	3500	664	1441	1146	5277	4892	384	78
1990	40312	34808	4557	905	946	875	5642	4957	672	90
1991	39646	33653	4755	798	1238	1190	5240	4553	676	66
1992	41892	35728	5203	800	961	911	4720	4140	578	64
1993	42551	38100	4273	815	179	117	3608	3122	478	74
United States 1980	64022	37540	22307	3314	3059	1085	19497	18311	1172	288
1990	76749	45462	28151	3246	2915	2337	17537	16580	930	165
1991	75131	43711	28351	3019	2902	2553	17094	16106	957	158
1992	77865	44590	30168	2954	2807	2429	16472	15560	882	567
1993	74988	42549	30015	3312	2147	1678	13924	13073	830	354
Japan 1980	3693	1003	2517	542	172	75	414	372	38	71
1990	4929	1184	3628	201	117	82	450	413	37	36
1991	5179	1195	3893	210	90	58	459	424	34	40
1992	5777	1280	4434	266	63	54	455	418	38	35
1993	6243	1269	4916	296	58	50	415	375	40	32
Australia, New Zealand 1980	19822	11068	5709	1494	1469	1256	2992	2907	78	31
1990	26725	16481	9304	1722	538	349	4722	4571	146	12
1991	27786	16918	9843	1514	539	466	4518	4315	200	48
1992	28513	16693	10165	1312	125	40	4727	4479	231	89
1993	32654	15632	10295	1260	197	143	3882	3672	206	52
Developing economies-Africa 1980	106923	75673	8954	795	1936	553	43464	41066	2342	13
1990	60048	51400	6897	767	1295	505	36947	36004	832	177
1991	59334	51321	6678	873	758	209	37306	35918	1081	177
1992	55811	47342	7094	961	705	111	33776	32460	1125	196
1993	54713	46270	7217	886	672	122	32789	31566	1013	180
Developing economies-America 1980	80823	53865	19140	1866	6641	5104	20633	18892	1675	80
1990	84317	60001	16000	2196	5854	4009	21409	19792	1579	182
1991	78610	55931	16770	2044	4524	3855	20774	19465	1274	162
1992	78276	55627	21303	2177	825	270	20981	19831	1141	317
1993	79300	54583	23198	2342	767	375	19196	17975	1210	145
Developing economies-Europe /5 1980	1940	1068	278	101	594	338	990	852	137	0
1990	2392	1558	269	53	564	333	1438	1198	239	0
1991	1582	1031	177	36	374	221	953	795	157	0
1992	2528	1119	1177	29	220	38	1068	941	124	0
1993	2254	1135	899	20	220	36	1035	926	109	0
Developing economies-Middle East 1980	205616	149855	51779	3599	1122	218	81821	75884	5937	0
1990	92005	49441	35366	2505	2144	624	22007	21413	583	13
1991	83463	47645	30940	2883	1631	571	19137	18169	960	17
1992	88351	52960	30690	5241	1851	397	18921	17886	1028	13
1993	91981	55528	31973	5524	1943	419	20015	18942	1066	15
Developing economies-Other Asia 1980	73215	44247	25421	3135	3052	2027	7878	7638	233	253
1990	94274	49536	39459	2681	4111	3402	9168	8627	521	21
1991	100369	51515	45084	3282	2875	2341	9664	8966	547	66
1992	105932	52106	49971	4328	2603	1937	10433	9808	580	119
1993	105315	50397	50894	4092	3017	2229	10053	9440	535	183
former USSR-Asia /9 1980	.	.	.	.	.	.	.	.	.	.
1990	.	.	.	.	.	.	.	.	.	.
1991	.	.	.	.	.	.	.	.	.	.
1992	2359	353	1689	703	207	.	326	283	43	0
1993	2111	337	1483	629	291	.	300	241	59	0
Developing economies-Oceania 1980	1763	1546	196	0	0	0	511	508	3	0
1990	1855	1483	361	0	0	0	497	460	37	0
1991	1986	1546	421	0	0	0	514	478	36	0
1992	1912	1518	384	1	0	0	481	438	43	0
1993	2910	2144	756	13	0	0	441	412	29	0

International merchandise trade   Commerce international des marchandises

En millions de dollars E.-U. f.o.b.

Economies développées /2,3,4				Developing economies Economies en voie de développement /1,3,4						← Exportations vers	
Canada	USA E-U	Japan Japon	Australia New Zèaland Australie Nouvelle-Zélande	Africa Afrique	America Amerique		Asia Asie		Oceania Océanie		Exportations ↓ en provenance de ↓
					Total	LAIA + ALADI +	Mid.East Moyen Orient	Other Autres /9		Année	

Produits alimentaires et matières brutes (CTCI, Rev. 2 et Rev. 3, 0 - 4)(suite)

.	15036	3230	229	580	1300	805	207	1370	2	1980	Canada
.	23146	5636	251	511	902	659	514	2621	1	1990	
.	23143	4999	162	518	946	722	345	2931	1	1991	
.	25793	4948	174	417	1161	957	336	3287	1	1992	
.	28875	5322	181	363	1099	913	323	2476	6	1993	
5234	.	11791	406	2465	8419	6902	1565	9422	67	1980	Etats-Unis
9026	.	17562	711	2162	9091	6406	2796	13748	94	1990	
8616	.	16669	725	2186	10130	7354	2519	13282	106	1991	
8938	.	17401	699	2422	11338	8604	2605	13619	102	1992	
9389	.	17610	765	2513	11180	8263	2835	13343	85	1993	
86	346	.	81	218	174	131	296	1764	64	1980	Japon
67	526	.	103	38	49	36	94	3354	89	1990	
63	538	.	93	42	126	109	85	3540	96	1991	
42	647	.	98	33	107	89	109	4082	98	1992	
39	681	.	99	44	78	60	128	4568	90	1993	
446	1859	5214	501	482	235	160	1335	3133	455	1980	Australie, Nouvelle-Zélande
266	2684	7815	955	516	479	388	1363	6333	577	1990	
282	2473	8595	965	407	537	426	972	7276	626	1991	
313	2341	8219	973	236	603	497	856	7876	592	1992	
373	2133	8100	1062	277	751	665	875	7762	629	1993	
177	30067	1706	50	1789	3445	1485	1717	1168	3	1980	Economies en voie de développement-Afrique
646	12434	942	46	3218	947	723	1200	1010	4	1990	
315	12158	921	36	3063	977	811	815	1282	2	1991	
223	11908	865	46	3357	1102	1008	805	1353	3	1992	
343	11702	936	49	3276	1196	1085	798	1470	5	1993	
2476	26397	3512	52	1618	14325	5599	1304	1578	55	1980	Economies en voie de développement-Amérique
1247	32383	4299	148	1018	10463	6124	1403	2897	13	1990	
1387	28564	4551	166	1057	10839	6461	1250	3424	41	1991	
1061	28636	4158	163	1290	12556	7020	1493	5888	24	1992	
926	29853	4008	175	1210	14198	8342	1590	6128	36	1993	
3	61	9	2	122	17	5	107	31	1	1980	Economies en voie de développement-Europe /5
9	90	6	8	139	12	7	80	38	0	1990	
6	59	4	5	91	8	5	51	27	0	1991	
5	33	4	5	71	23	2	49	7	0	1992	
5	73	11	6	29	23	1	61	8	0	1993	
2606	20263	42806	2351	3104	12027	9531	8436	27106	111	1980	Economies en voie de développement-Moyen Orient
110	14294	12431	557	2148	3790	1691	7376	21535	1	1990	
736	6413	20415	889	5049	2420	258	7242	15880	58	1991	
446	11958	20577	1006	1551	2633	2552	8199	18084	0	1992	
478	12961	20962	1065	1533	2839	2758	8569	18809	0	1993	
268	8344	25775	1699	1217	1507	560	2688	19463	389	1980	Economies en voie de développement-Autres Pays d'Asie
485	7159	31080	1564	1713	1088	590	2518	33586	452	1990	
562	7300	32077	1787	1974	1230	657	3168	38206	432	1991	
639	7745	31299	1792	1882	1163	634	4773	41689	424	1992	
656	7632	30153	1611	1876	1222	608	4470	42944	363	1993	
.	.	.	.	.	.	.	.	.	.	1980	l'ancienne URSS asiatique /9
.	.	.	.	.	.	.	.	.	.	1990	
.	.	.	.	.	.	.	.	.	.	1991	
0	10	17	0	17	66	25	1467	140	0	1992	
0	10	28	0	26	76	30	1232	149	0	1993	
24	252	530	229	0	5	5	0	129	62	1980	Economies en voie de développement-Océanie
11	346	508	121	0	0	0	0	285	75	1990	
13	385	525	109	0	0	0	1	344	76	1991	
12	409	479	137	0	0	0	6	319	58	1992	
15	499	662	527	0	0	0	2	696	58	1993	

International merchandise trade   Commerce international des marchandises

73
World exports by commodity classes and by regions (continued)
Exportations mondiales par classes de marchandises et par régions (suite)

In million US dollars f.o.b.

Exports to → / Exports from	Year	World Monde /1,2,3	Developed economies Econ. dévelop-pées /2,3,4	Developing economies Economies en voie de développement /1,3,4 Total	OPEC+ OPEP+	Eastern Europe and former USSR Europe de l'Est et l'ancienne URSS Total /2,3,7	fmr USSR anc URSS /10	Europe Total /2	EEC+ CEE+ /2	EFTA+ AELE+	Developed Economies South Africa Afrique du Sud
										Manufactured goods (SITC, Rev. 2 and Rev. 3, 5 - 8)	
World /1,2,3	1980	1118891	720226	311522	98646	76649	36050	504574	413714	89762	11807
	1990	2492516	1806114	574579	86040	99298	54540	1183323	1000754	179470	11254
	1991	2559650	1829974	649864	101732	70117	35114	1201270	1028005	170206	12290
	1992	2793485	1957276	757229	116441	66545	27962	1269394	1093496	172588	12748
	1993	2785620	1872498	822518	108889	73323	29902	1117072	958254	155532	13232
Developed economies /2,3,4	1980	928175	639288	251300	82766	29902	15318	464795	379063	84677	11412
	1990	1958255	1520582	391539	65129	38472	19659	1063436	896340	164363	10509
	1991	2014492	1527369	436238	77494	43515	19704	1076919	918304	155742	10999
	1992	2148029	1598259	493105	87970	47179	16355	1128247	967404	157765	10891
	1993	2064360	1465864	532860	78935	52167	18496	965811	821802	141078	10953
Developing economies /1,3,4	1980	126175	71632	46956	13299	6369	3766	31434	28257	3144	394
	1990	445309	264376	163561	18857	13566	10115	100674	89809	10722	742
	1991	502628	285174	204434	22998	11854	8400	108429	97083	11170	1280
	1992	596827	334882	252220	26966	8400	5635	119384	108209	10962	1839
	1993	664454	376093	276990	28757	10141	6607	124501	113417	10749	2228
OPEC+	1980	6852	3141	3539	1749	36	19	2073	1876	196	2
	1990	22141	11420	9389	2135	300	131	5826	4619	1188	1
	1991	23716	12527	10786	2618	297	107	6556	4938	1616	2
	1992	28670	14146	14194	3549	193	119	6766	6286	477	7
	1993	32276	16282	15721	3716	203	129	6938	6421	515	2
Eastern Europe and the former USSR /2,3,7	1980	64542	9305	13267	2581	40378	16965	8345	6395	1942	1
	1990	88952	21157	19481	2055	47259	24766	19213	14606	4385	2
	1991	42531	17430	9192	1240	14748	7009	15921	12619	3294	11
	1992	48629	24135	11904	1506	10966	7009	15921	12619	3294	11
	1992	48629	24135	11904	1506	10966	5972	15921	12619	3294	11
	1993	56806	30541	12668	1197	11015	4799	26761	23035	3706	50
former USSR /3	1980	18920	1323	6994	971	10604	.	1130	860	270	0
	1990	...	...	...	...	...		...	...	...	...
	1991	...	...	...	...	...		...	...	...	...
	1992	.	.	.	.	.		.	.	.	.
	1993	.	.	.	.	.		.	.	.	.
former USSR-Europe /8	1980	.	.	.	.	.	.	.	.	.	.
	1990	.	.	.	.	.	.	.	.	.	.
	1991	.	.	.	.	.	.	.	.	.	.
	1992	17446	7625	6293	484	2312	480	6517	5309	1200	0
	1993	19261	8220	6321	378	2181	663	6127	4857	1267	5
Developed economies-Europe /2	1980	610138	459221	125168	49840	25446	12131	395250	318804	75456	7317
	1990	1288640	1071492	177022	40873	34024	16538	906782	758204	146054	7348
	1991	1289935	1062580	182212	44814	39022	16744	908693	769222	136761	7320
	1992	1372633	1120568	202854	49901	42793	14066	959701	816394	140419	7151
	1993	1244168	976354	212969	44126	46096	14881	812484	684195	125655	6954
European Economic Community+ /2	1980	524266	394373	110575	44884	19028	8794	339399	276667	61797	6695
	1990	1102518	918394	153700	36101	24930	11435	778249	655023	120929	6814
	1991	1111455	915653	158237	39504	32036	14151	784151	667410	114265	6832
	1992	1185380	966911	177522	44619	35143	11796	829183	708399	118080	6613
	1993	1070773	838478	186216	39069	37981	12208	697766	588798	106497	6281
European Free Trade Association+	1980	85444	64498	14546	4920	6400	3337	55515	41821	13639	622
	1990	185033	152167	23204	4716	9054	5071	127661	102326	25108	534
	1991	177279	145887	23827	5230	6972	2581	123556	100846	22476	487
	1992	185805	152407	25171	5208	7613	2234	129362	106885	22295	537
	1993	172139	136811	26587	4994	8090	2652	113773	94464	19147	672
Other developed economies	1980	318037	180067	126132	32925	4456	3187	69545	60259	9221	4095
	1990	669615	449090	214517	24255	4448	3120	156655	138137	18309	3161
	1991	724557	464790	254026	32680	4493	2960	168227	149082	18981	3679
	1992	775397	477691	290251	38069	4387	2288	168547	151010	17346	3740
	1993	820192	489510	319891	34809	6072	3615	153327	137607	15422	3999

International merchandise trade   Commerce international des marchandises

En millions de dollars E.-U. f.o.b.

Economies développées /2,3,4				Developing economies / Economies en voie de développement /1,3,4						Exportations vers	
Canada	USA E-U	Japan Japon	Australia New Zealand Australie Nouvelle-Zélande	Africa Afrique	America Amerique Total	LAIA⁺ ALADI⁺	Asia Asie Mid.East Moyen Orient	Other Autres /9	Oceania Océanie	Année	Exportations en provenance de ↓

Articles manufacturés (CTCI, Rev. 2 et Rev. 3, 5 - 8)

Canada	USA E-U	Japan	Australia NZ	Africa	America Total	LAIA ALADI	Mid.East	Other /9	Oceania	Année	Exportations en provenance de
35514	121503	25249	17562	57155	74050	56752	68912	100233	1556	1980	Monde /1,2,3
91954	371638	99850	37366	57354	98407	68805	74512	327202	3223	1990	
93307	370352	103189	35300	57899	113502	84082	85898	379031	3225	1991	
98250	421776	101827	39163	61068	138256	105609	101496	442480	3568	1992	
105638	470516	110284	40509	57130	149008	114709	100642	503246	3354	1993	
33575	93828	16539	15248	48923	61158	48996	56265	76642	1359	1980	Economies dévelopées /2,3,4
84559	259163	62458	30336	46316	77603	58142	55565	197959	2530	1990	
86641	252521	61112	27736	45432	90384	69212	65235	223780	2455	1991	
89166	268469	58178	30241	48665	108506	84891	76184	249724	2796	1992	
95231	291216	58240	30596	45259	113799	88514	73242	291010	2567	1993	
1773	27110	8565	2236	6110	10303	7230	9940	20133	196	1980	Economies en voie de développement /1,3,4
7170	111516	36833	6918	9016	16077	10123	16239	121022	692	1990	
8520	117135	41632	7484	11400	21180	14607	19081	151569	770	1991	
8839	152044	43017	8839	11270	28909	20365	22756	186101	770	1992	
10131	176926	51362	9819	10583	34491	25716	24700	204829	773	1993	
6	225	783	51	237	242	206	2131	926	0	1980	OPEP⁺
133	2714	2437	307	373	966	576	3224	4782	15	1990	
165	2595	2990	215	860	1021	635	3220	5641	19	1991	
221	3721	2992	435	581	1442	950	4346	7767	46	1992	
296	4687	3828	527	616	1983	1473	4541	8532	38	1993	
166	565	146	79	2122	2588	526	2707	3458	0	1980	Europe de l'Est et l'ancienne URSS /2,3,7
225	959	559	111	2022	4728	541	2708	8221	2	1990	
146	696	445	81	1067	1938	263	1582	3682	0	1991	
244	1263	632	83	1133	842	353	2556	6656	3	1992	
277	2374	682	93	1288	718	479	2699	7408	14	1993	
34	132	18	8	790	1741	115	1004	2220	0	1980	l'ancienne URSS /3
...	...	...	...	...	...	...	...	...	...	1990	
...	...	...	...	...	...	...	...	...	...	1991	
.	.	.	.	.	.	.	.	.	.	1992	
										1993	
.	.	.	.	.	.	.	.	.	.	1980	l'ancienne URSS-Europe /8
.	.	.	.	.	.	.	.	.	.	1990	
.	.	.	.	.	.	.	.	.	.	1991	
102	555	405	6	331	450	147	1232	4180	0	1992	
143	1308	467	7	266	325	161	1308	4294	0	1993	
4803	36812	6807	5553	39017	21988	17419	34802	22529	421	1980	Economies développées-Europe /2
11443	97254	30218	11275	37264	25815	17903	38274	63606	1086	1990	
11068	89951	28239	9654	35923	28370	20106	42103	66378	928	1991	
10549	96712	27065	10508	37391	33072	24118	48921	75264	1225	1992	
9578	100363	27042	10533	33666	34915	25442	47516	89155	928	1993	
4041	31931	5471	4777	35840	18898	15045	30670	19383	390	1980	Communauté Economique Européenne⁺ /2
9437	83786	24784	9269	34604	22155	15079	33242	53143	1045	1990	
9444	77321	23265	8002	33029	24626	17290	36693	55542	891	1991	
8961	83349	22328	8598	34699	28758	21001	43369	63536	1197	1992	
8096	86923	22545	8674	31141	30765	22485	42163	75505	900	1993	
760	4871	1336	775	3138	3085	2374	4128	3145	32	1980	Association Européenne de Libre Echange⁺
1991	13429	5433	2005	2600	3655	2823	5020	10422	41	1990	
1623	12583	4973	1651	2818	3730	2815	5391	10798	37	1991	
1587	13277	4736	1906	2616	4310	3114	5540	11659	28	1992	
1470	13341	4491	1859	2454	4145	2954	5344	13568	28	1993	
28772	57017	9732	9694	9906	39171	31577	21463	54113	938	1980	Autres economies développées
73116	161909	32240	19061	9052	51787	40239	17292	134353	1444	1990	
75573	162569	32873	18082	9508	62014	49106	23132	157402	1527	1991	
78618	171758	31113	19733	11274	75433	60772	27263	174461	1570	1992	
85653	190854	31198	20063	11593	78884	63073	25727	201855	1639	1993	

International merchandise trade   Commerce international des marchandises

73
World exports by commodity classes and by regions (continued)
Exportations mondiales par classes de marchandises et par régions (suite)

In million US dollars f.o.b.

Exports from	Year	World Monde /1,2,3	Developed economies Econ. développées /2,3,4	Developing economies Economies en voie de développement /1,3,4 Total	OPEC+ OPEP+	Eastern Europe and former USSR Europe de l'Est et l'ancienne URSS Total /2,3,7	fmr USSR anc URSS /10	Europe Total /2	EEC+ CEE+ /2	EFTA+ AELE+	Developed Economies South Africa Afrique du Sud

Manufactured goods (SITC, Rev. 2 and Rev. 3, 5 - 8)(continued)

Exports from	Year	World	Developed economies	Developing Total	OPEC+	Eastern Total	fmr USSR	Europe Total	EEC+	EFTA+	South Africa
Canada	1980	33888	29401	4050	1200	332	169	3728	3354	372	97
	1990	78831	73854	4881	700	97	52	5161	4561	600	53
	1991	79418	73896	5393	1033	129	72	5682	5178	504	42
	1992	84610	79250	5121	946	239	121	5597	5072	525	51
	1993	93869	87888	5608	1002	373	266	5214	4729	480	53
United States	1980	144093	84501	57529	13488	784	424	42242	36909	5319	2115
	1990	282461	186994	93940	9613	1227	719	81125	72480	8574	1496
	1991	309827	195955	112164	14811	1586	896	86720	77403	9273	1868
	1992	329192	197684	129334	17647	2174	1047	85438	77281	8109	1776
	1993	341238	198169	139864	16053	3139	1739	78600	70877	7557	1729
Japan	1980	124501	59710	61493	17874	3298	2595	20600	17397	3154	1734
	1990	277438	166243	108156	13284	3039	2332	60859	52629	8102	1477
	1991	304343	173359	128320	16165	2663	1954	66686	58320	8250	1616
	1992	328521	181490	145293	18638	1737	1036	69896	61561	8196	1708
	1993	348557	183810	162636	16865	2110	1501	62423	55414	6889	1988
Australia, New Zealand	1980	5712	3159	2330	288	18	0	1008	967	40	72
	1990	10817	6860	3929	512	25	13	1388	1302	85	44
	1991	11863	7048	4779	587	32	22	1370	1286	83	59
	1992	12552	7047	5389	671	30	18	1543	1431	111	84
	1993	13829	7104	6136	668	23	14	1346	1263	83	114
Developing economies-Africa	1980	6182	4472	1184	225	223	160	3421	3330	89	3
	1990	12789	8944	3322	922	586	479	7664	7500	143	124
	1991	11981	8099	3346	1087	453	349	6945	6720	213	112
	1992	12816	8879	3605	1231	217	151	7533	7331	193	141
	1993	13480	9650	3593	1089	117	95	7718	7545	164	180
Developing economies-America	1980	20776	11004	9425	1513	323	88	5013	4667	343	81
	1990	48845	33605	14671	1998	503	289	10580	9957	617	155
	1991	51299	33387	17534	2467	308	252	9869	9287	577	185
	1992	74386	52177	21820	2760	112	43	9972	9389	579	155
	1993	84683	58896	25494	2719	177	95	9211	8492	687	186
Developing economies-Europe /5	1980	7001	2185	1379	749	3437	2150	1813	1529	280	0
	1990	11955	6848	1617	694	3490	2345	6100	5359	735	1
	1991	7941	4545	1070	459	2326	1565	4049	3556	489	0
	1992	11378	7633	2957	266	770	396	7201	6190	1008	2
	1993	9731	7002	1939	169	789	437	6493	5880	586	2
Developing economies-Middle East	1980	7110	2739	4103	2622	130	94	2153	1881	270	0
	1990	21163	10236	7970	3572	1885	1599	8498	6964	1519	38
	1991	20936	10980	8025	3689	1679	1269	9052	7188	1852	43
	1992	22465	11344	9982	4520	807	392	9225	7188	817	43
	1993	23127	10811	10949	4718	1003	491	8678	8374	776	49
Developing economies-Other Asia	1980	84754	50911	30835	8190	2257	1274	18804	16619	2161	310
	1990	349946	204302	135814	11667	7102	5402	67678	59881	7700	422
	1991	409772	227696	174282	15294	7036	4951	78367	70192	8031	940
	1992	475133	254341	213725	18184	6489	4648	85206	76686	8355	1498
	1993	532851	289240	234928	20062	8055	5489	92157	83418	8528	1811
former USSR-Asia /9	1980	.	.	.	.	.	.	.	.	.	.
	1990	.	.	.	.	.	.	.	.	.	.
	1991	.	.	.	.	.	.	.	.	.	.
	1992	1203	148	978	138	58	.	99	83	16	0
	1993	1120	159	904	126	58	.	94	80	14	0
Developing economies-Oceania	1980	352	321	30	0	0	0	229	229	0	0
	1990	612	441	168	4	0	0	155	147	8	0
	1991	700	467	178	1	53	15	148	141	8	2
	1992	648	509	131	6	4	4	248	239	7	0
	1993	583	495	87	0	0	0	244	236	8	0

International merchandise trade   Commerce international des marchandises

En millions de dollars E.-U. f.o.b.

← Exportations vers

Economies développées /2,3,4				Developing economies / Economies en voie de développement /1,3,4						Année	Exportations en provenance de ↓
Canada	USA E-U	Japan Japon	Australia New Zealand Australie Nouvelle-Zélande	Africa Afrique	America Amerique Total	LAIA+ ALADI+	Asia Asie Mid.East Moyen Orient	Other Autres /9	Oceania Océanie		

Articles manufacturés (CTCI, Rev. 2 et Rev. 3, 5 - 8)(suite)

.	24592	494	430	348	1966	1581	469	1237	10	1980	Canada
.	66823	1105	633	365	1321	954	432	2707	21	1990	
.	66468	1136	493	287	1315	993	654	3096	16	1991	
.	71895	1154	477	287	1562	1219	490	2754	12	1992	
.	80852	1175	519	302	1703	1355	583	3000	9	1993	
26338	.	8589	4167	3628	28645	24027	8035	16737	104	1980	Etats-Unis
66127	.	27793	8147	3748	40291	33478	6931	42527	155	1990	
68074	.	28536	7804	4227	48089	40999	10542	48862	220	1991	
71363	.	27448	8661	4726	58345	50186	12159	53615	318	1992	
79154	.	27525	7887	4340	60683	51553	12189	62252	268	1993	
2346	30961	.	3972	5721	8324	5766	12771	34222	336	1980	Japon
6634	88862	.	7937	3786	9593	5270	9442	84338	752	1990	
7158	89819	.	7406	3923	12035	6618	11450	100072	669	1991	
7007	93969	.	7970	4604	14853	8769	14045	111155	595	1992	
6236	103473	.	8767	5212	15717	9462	12389	128588	700	1993	
48	523	426	1078	107	61	45	137	1537	488	1980	Australie, Nouvelle-Zélande
98	1309	1867	2151	51	53	46	158	3151	515	1990	
104	1386	1938	2188	51	95	64	171	3841	618	1991	
123	1321	1569	2398	57	120	111	191	4387	635	1992	
134	1349	1527	2622	48	134	125	173	5130	650	1993	
13	551	473	1	548	100	90	123	350	0	1980	Economies en voie de développement-Afrique
33	652	454	9	1734	90	73	602	848	1	1990	
85	560	366	10	1845	107	84	537	827	0	1991	
55	569	552	14	1784	117	92	823	852	1	1992	
59	878	789	14	1893	133	111	716	822	2	1993	
283	4446	1058	114	676	7777	5898	286	548	7	1980	Economies en voie de développement-Amérique
751	18909	2855	303	599	9810	6899	910	3296	18	1990	
1525	18625	2864	280	635	12389	9519	951	3535	12	1991	
1230	38144	2362	266	594	16244	13190	1005	3937	10	1992	
1901	44997	2275	284	420	19754	16221	727	4586	6	1993	
25	304	22	10	613	48	31	520	197	2	1980	Economies en voie de développement-Europe /5
53	598	33	58	575	98	39	707	235	2	1990	
35	396	22	39	384	65	26	467	153	1	1991	
37	344	27	16	183	44	32	312	229	1	1992	
34	410	37	17	122	37	26	222	151	1	1993	
3	118	420	43	351	6	5	3275	464	0	1980	Economies en voie de développement-Moyen Orient
68	926	513	171	701	38	22	4918	2229	2	1990	
69	805	920	43	1065	62	44	4676	2172	0	1991	
91	1062	681	178	701	57	34	5829	3345	0	1992	
90	1165	563	201	693	46	39	6139	4015	0	1993	
1449	21648	6552	2058	3922	2372	1205	5737	18563	168	1980	Economies en voie de développement-Autres Pays d'Asie
6260	90368	32889	6251	5407	6040	3087	9101	114322	595	1990	
6805	96665	37361	6981	7469	8556	4932	12450	144786	678	1991	
7423	111837	39313	8278	8008	12446	7018	14787	177641	725	1992	
8047	129411	47602	9214	7455	14520	9318	16895	195201	731	1993	
.	.	.	.	.	.	.	.	.	.	1980	l'ancienne URSS asiatique /9
.	.	.	.	.	.	.	.	.	.	1990	
.	.	.	.	.	.	.	.	.	.	1991	
0	29	20	0	15	52	12	334	576	0	1992	
0	29	36	0	11	52	10	289	551	0	1993	
0	43	40	8	0	1	1	0	10	19	1980	Economies en voie de développement-Océanie
5	64	89	127	0	1	1	0	92	74	1990	
2	86	100	131	2	2	2	1	96	78	1991	
4	88	82	87	0	0	0	1	97	33	1992	
0	65	97	89	0	0	0	0	54	33	1993	

International merchandise trade   Commerce international des marchandises

73
World exports by commodity classes and by regions (continued)
Exportations mondiales par classes de marchandises et par régions (suite)

Source:
International Trade statistics database of the Statistical Division of the
United Nations Secretariat.

+ For member states of this grouping, see Annex I:- Other groupings.

1/ Excluding the inter-trade between China, the Democratic People's
   Republic of Korea, Mongolia and Viet Nam in 1980. The figures
   shown for other years are based on the import statistics of China.

2/ Excluding the trade conducted in accordance with the
   supplementary protocol to the treaty on the basis of relations
   between the Federal Republic of Germany (FRG) and the former
   German Democratic Republic (GDR). Data reported by FRG are as
   follows:

   Value in million United States dollars

	1980	1990
FRG to GDR	2911	13379
FRG from GDR	3072	5129

3/ Exports of the former USSR for which country of destination is not
   available are included in the totals for the World, the 'Developed

economies', the 'Developing economies' and 'Eastern Europe and
former USSR' but are excluded from the regional components of
these groupings.

4/ This classification is intended for statistical convenience and does
   not, necessarily, express a judgement about the stage reached by a
   particular country in the development process.

5/ Includes the Socialist Federal Republic of Yugoslavia only.

6/ Section 9 of the SITC, which comprises commodities and
   transactions not classified elsewhere, is included in the total trade
   but is not shown separately in this table.

7/ Beginning 1992, includes Eastern Europe and the European
   countries of the former USSR.

8/ Includes Belarus, Estonia, Latvia, Lithuania, Republic of Moldova,
   the Russian Federation, and Ukraine.

9/ Beginning 1992, includes Armenia, Azerbaijan, Georgia,
   Kazakhstan, Kyrgyzstan, Tajikistan, Turkmenistan, and Uzbekistan.

10/ Prior to 1992, data refer to the former USSR. Beginning 1992,
    data refer to the European countries of the former USSR.

Source:
Base de données pour les statistiques du commerce international de la Division de statistique du Secrétariat de l'ONU.

+ Les etats membres de ce groupement, voir annexe I:- Autres groupements.

1/ Non compris le commerce entre la Chine, la République populaire démocratique de Corée, la Mongolie et le Viet Nam en 1980. Les chiffres indiqués pour les autres années sont bases sur les statistiques d'importations de la Chine.

2/ Non compris le commerce effectué en accord avec le protocole additionnel au traité définissant la base des relations entre la République fédérale d'Allemagne (RfA) et l'ancienne République démocratique allemande (Rda). Les données fournies par RfA sont les suivantes:

Valeur en millions de dollars des E.-U.

	1980	1990
de RfA vers Rda	2911	13379
de RfA en prov. de Rda	3072	5129

3/ Les exportations en provenance de l'ancienne URSS dont les pays de destination ne sont pas disponibles sont comprises dans les totaux du Monde, des 'Économies développées', des 'Economies en voie de développement' et de 'Europe de l'Est et l'ancienne URSS', mais ils ne sont pas comprises dans chaque partie composant ces régions.

4/ Cette classification est utilisée pour plus de commodité dans la présentation des statistiques et n'implique pas nécessairement un jugement quant au stade de développement auquel est parvenu un pays donné.

5/ Y compris la République fédérative socialiste de Yougoslavie seuleument.

6/ Section 9 de la CTCI, qui représente les articles et transactions non classes ailleurs est comprise dans le commerce total mais n'est pas présentée séparément dans ce tableau.

7/ A partir de janvier 1992, y compris de l'Europe de l'est et les pays européens de l'ancienne URSS.

8/ Y compris Bélarus, Estonie, Lettonie, Lituanie, République de Moldova, Fédération de Russie, et Ukraine.

9/ A partir de l'année 1992, y compris Azerbaïdjan, Arménie, Géorgie, Kazakhstan, Kirghizistan, Tadjikistan, Turkménistan, et Ouzbékistan.

10/ Avant l'année 1992, les données se rapportent à l'ancienne URSS. A partir de l'année 1992, les données se rapportent aux pays européens de l'ancienne URSS.

74
Total imports and exports: index numbers
Importations et exportations totales: indices

1990 = 100

Country or area Pays ou zone	1985	1986	1987	1988	1989	1990	1991	1992	1993	1994
A. Imports: Quantum index • Importations: Indice du quantum										
Australia Australie	77	74	76	89	108	100	99	107	114	133
Austria Autriche	69	71	75	82	90	100	101	107	106	119
Belgium-Luxembourg Belgique-Luxembourg	73	80	88	88	94	100	104	105	...	...
Bolivia Bolivie	...	...	...	...	...	...	...	...	...	...
Brazil Brésil	68	92	90	80	92	100	110	...	...	...
Bulgaria Bulgarie	127	132	130	137	130	100	83	...	...	...
Canada Canada	72	80	89	95	100	100	102	109	120	138
Denmark Danemark	90	96	95	94	94	100	105	109	101	129
Dominica Dominique	57	63	75	80	93	100	89	...	...	...
Dominican Republic Rép. dominicaine	...	...	...	...	...	...	...	...	...	...
Ecuador Equateur	...	...	...	...	...	...	...	...	...	...
Ethiopia Ethiopie	...	...	...	...	...	...	...	...	...	...
Faeroe Islands Iles Féroé	112	136	146	146	125	100	100	...	...	...
Finland Finlande	75	80	86	94	104	100	83	81	78	...
France France	72	77	82	90	95	100	102	104	97	114
Germany † Allemagne†	70	75	79	84	90	100	113	115	104	113
Greece Grèce	71	72	81	66	89	100	113	130	143	...
Guatemala Guatemala	70	57	88	62	92	100	117	125	133	...
Honduras Honduras	...	...	...	...	...	...	...	...	...	...
Hong Kong Hong-kong	44	49	65	82	90	100	119	145	55	187
Hungary Hongrie	99	102	104	104	105	100	105	98	119	...
Iceland Islande	88	95	118	112	100	100	105	97	84	...
India Inde	65	85	90	96	97	100	91	120	...	...
Indonesia Indonésie	...	...	...	...	...	...	...	...	...	...

Country or area Pays ou zone	1985	1986	1987	1988	1989	1990	1991	1992	1993	1994
A. Exports: Quantum index • Exportations: Indice du quantum										
Australia Australie	81	84	94	89	94	100	115	121	128	139
Austria Autriche	70	71	72	80	90	100	106	111	108	119
Belgium-Luxembourg Belgique-Luxembourg	77	83	89	90	94	100	104	104	...	...
Bolivia Bolivie	84	94	81	82	94	100	101	99	93	95
Brazil Brésil	96	79	92	109	109	100	104	...	...	...
Bulgaria Bulgarie	133	128	130	133	130	100	70	...	...	...
Canada Canada	80	84	93	94	96	100	101	110	121	140
Denmark Danemark	80	82	83	87	92	100	106	111	108	99
Dominica Dominique	62	83	96	107	88	100	94	...	...	...
Dominican Republic Rép. dominicaine	109	91	111	114	117	100	95	90	93	...
Ecuador Equateur	98	105	68	100	98	100	106	108	121	138
Ethiopia Ethiopie	96	111	104	106	115	100	57	50	...	...
Faeroe Islands Iles Féroé	86	86	83	89	102	100	104	...	...	...
Finland Finlande	92	93	94	97	97	100	91	99	117	...
France France	79	78	81	88	95	100	105	108	106	118
Germany † Allemagne†	82	83	86	92	99	100	100	102	98	112
Greece Grèce	86	101	103	77	105	100	114	147	143	...
Guatemala Guatemala	81	113	90	91	101	100	125	145	136	...
Honduras Honduras	115	107	123	109	99	100	88	102	90	79
Hong Kong[4] Hong-kong[4]	43	50	66	84	92	100	117	140	48	176
Hungary Hongrie	96	94	97	104	104	100	95	96	84	...
Iceland Islande	86	95	99	98	101	100	92	91	96	...
India Inde	52	59	71	74	91	100	114	116	...	...
Indonesia Indonésie	91	98	94	93	102	100	128	117	126	213

74
Total imports and exports: index numbers
[*cont.*]

Importations et exportations totales: indices
1990 = 100 [*suite*]

Country or area Pays ou zone	1985	1986	1987	1988	1989	1990	1991	1992	1993	1994
A. Imports: Quantum index [cont.] • Importations: Indice du quantum [suite]										
Ireland Irlande	72	75	80	83	94	100	101	106	112	127
Israel Israël	73	86	96	97	92	100	116	130	146	166
Italy Italie	72	75	83	88	96	100	104	108	96	108
Japan Japon	63	69	75	87	94	100	104	104	107	121
Jordan Jordanie	101	106	110	116	96	100	99	135	148	144
Kenya Kenya	72	85	89	100	105	100	93	76	97	102
Korea, Republic of Corée, République de	51	56	67	77	88	100	117	119	127	154
Malaysia Malaisie	...	...	...	...	...	...	...	...	...	...
Morocco Maroc	66	66	68	74	87	100	112	128	120	...
Netherlands Pays-Bas	77	80	85	90	95	100	104	106	110	115
New Zealand Nouvelle-Zélande	76	75	85	77	93	100	90	100	104	121
Norway[1] Norvège[1]	94	108	106	95	90	100	102	106	107	122
Pakistan Pakistan	77	75	77	100	105	100	105	122	124	119
Panama Panama	...	...	...	...	...	...	...	...	...	...
Peru Pérou	...	...	...	...	...	...	...	...	...	...
Philippines Philippines	41	49	64	78	93	100	102	...	...	...
Poland Pologne	113	118	124	136	138	100	156	...	210	238
Portugal Portugal	43	52	66	81	88	100	106	119	...	...
Rwanda Rwanda	...	...	...	...	...	...	...	...	...	...
Seychelles Seychelles	60	64	63	87	97	100	95	107	147	...
Singapore Singapour	50	54	62	79	87	100	107	114	137	...
Solomon Islands Iles Salomon	...	...	...	...	...	...	...	...	...	...
South Africa Afrique du Sud	88	85	89	109	109	100	100	103	107	122
Spain Espagne	44	52	63	78	91	100	112	121	118	130
Sri Lanka Sri Lanka	105	120	106	101	95	100	114	125	144	162

Country or area Pays ou zone	1985	1986	1987	1988	1989	1990	1991	1992	1993	1994
A. Exports:Quantum index [cont.] • Exportations:Indice du quantum [suite]										
Ireland Irlande	65	69	79	83	92	100	106	120	132	154
Israel Israël	82	91	101	96	100	100	98	107	121	140
Italy Italie	81	82	84	89	97	100	100	104	112	125
Japan Japon	88	87	87	91	95	100	102	104	101	103
Jordan Jordanie	72	74	88	102	104	100	88	96	104	112
Kenya Kenya	81	93	90	95	94	100	103	103	99	112
Korea, Republic of Corée, République de	60	67	83	93	94	100	110	119	127	146
Malaysia Malaisie	76	82	86	92	98	100	97	96	86	84
Morocco Maroc	66	66	72	84	92	100	108	101	105	...
Netherlands Pays-Bas	77	80	83	91	95	100	105	108	115	118
New Zealand Nouvelle-Zélande	93	91	94	97	95	100	110	113	118	130
Norway[1] Norvège [1]	67	69	78	81	93	100	106	115	121	136
Pakistan Pakistan	56	75	82	90	94	100	113	124	112	139
Panama Panama	97	94	94	79	93	100	95	97	116	...
Peru Pérou	118	106	96	85	100	100	103	...	...	...
Philippines Philippines	60	70	75	83	93	100	103	...	...	...
Poland Pologne	77	81	85	92	92	100	103	...	96	114
Portugal Portugal	56	61	68	74	89	100	101	107	...	...
Rwanda Rwanda	67	76	94	72	72	100	87	78	...	...
Seychelles Seychelles	18	17	44	93	102	100	136	126	106	...
Singapore Singapour	46	53	62	83	92	100	113	123	145	...
Solomon Islands Iles Salomon	94	116	85	94	92	100	106	...	...	...
South Africa Afrique du Sud	90	93	91	98	106	100	100	88	107	116
Spain Espagne	76	72	77	85	89	100	111	117	135	160
Sri Lanka Sri Lanka	83	89	87	84	86	100	104	120	137	153

74
Total imports and exports: index numbers
[cont.]

Importations et exportations totales: indices
1990 = 100 [suite]

Country or area Pays ou zone	1985	1986	1987	1988	1989	1990	1991	1992	1993	1994
A. Imports: Quantum index [cont.] · Importations: Indice du quantum [suite]										
Sweden Suède	80	83	89	94	100	100	93	95	97	108
Switzerland Suisse	75	82	88	93	98	100	99	94	93	102
Syrian Arab Republic Rép. arabe syrienne	161	152	114	98	92	100	163	143	225	...
Thailand Thaïlande	41	40	49	68	82	100	109	117	131	147
Trinidad and Tobago Trinité-et-Tobago	128	131	103	87	106	100	...	...	...	...
Tunisia Tunisie	77	93	68	85	101	100	94	104	115	...
Turkey Turquie	68	76	86	87	87	100	96	98	134	105
former USSR† ancienne URSS†	84	79	78	81	102	100	...	...	...	...
United Kingdom Royaume-Uni	70	75	80	92	100	100	95	101	101	108
United States Etats-Unis	79	87	90	93	98	100	98	106	117	131
B. Imports: Unit value index · Importations: Indice du valeur unitaire										
Australia[2] Australie[2]	86	94	99	97	96	100	101	106	114	111
Austria Autriche	113	103	99	100	103	100	100	99	96	94
Bangladesh Bangladesh	77	86	95	89	90	100	121	...	...	...
Belgium-Luxembourg Belgique-Luxembourg	112	94	88	94	102	100	99	95	...	...
Bolivia Bolivie	...	...	...	...	...	...	...	...	...	...
Brazil[3] Brésil[3]	90	70	82	89	96	100	93	...	...	...
Canada Canada	101	101	97	98	98	100	99	103	109	116
Colombia[3] Colombie[3]	30	38	47	60	80	100	121	129	145	157
Denmark Danemark	111	103	96	97	105	100	100	97	94	107
Dominica Dominique	79	77	85	92	94	100	104	...	...	...
Ecuador Equateur	...	...	...	...	...	...	...	...	...	...
Ethiopia Ethiopie	...	...	...	...	...	...	...	...	...	...
Faeroe Islands Iles Féroé	108	101	116	99	103	100	100	...	...	...
Finland Finlande	105	95	93	95	98	100	102	113	129	...

Country or area Pays ou zone	1985	1986	1987	1988	1989	1990	1991	1992	1993	1994
A. Exports:Quantum index [cont.] · Exportations:Indice du quantum [suite]										
Sweden Suède	90	93	96	99	101	100	98	99	107	114
Switzerland Suisse	82	86	86	91	96	100	99	103	104	109
Syrian Arab Republic Rép. arabe syrienne	45	44	46	51	78	100	104	105	158	...
Thailand Thaïlande	59	48	57	72	89	100	119	134	149	176
Trinidad and Tobago Trinité-et-Tobago	95	94	92	95	94	100	...	...	...	...
Tunisia Tunisie	82	92	95	96	110	100	110	111	121	...
Turkey Turquie	65	71	88	101	95	100	107	110	117	134
former USSR† ancienne URSS†	89	98	102	107	113	100	...	...	...	...
United Kingdom Royaume-Uni	80	83	87	88	94	100	101	103	103	115
United States[5] Etats-Unis[5]	63	63	71	84	93	100	106	113	116	126
B. Exports: Unit value index · Exportations: Indice du valeur unitaire										
Australia[2] Australie[2]	79	80	84	94	98	100	91	93	94	92
Austria Autriche	109	105	103	103	100	100	97	95	91	89
Bangladesh Bangladesh	105	89	83	97	96	100	105	...	...	...
Belgium-Luxembourg Belgique-Luxembourg	106	96	90	98	106	100	98	97	...	...
Bolivia Bolivie	156	131	104	99	110	100	96	76	64	64
Brazil[3] Brésil[3]	87	93	93	102	101	100	96	...	...	...
Canada Canada	98	95	94	98	101	100	96	99	104	111
Colombia[3] Colombie[3]	37	57	54	70	73	100	117	118	134	174
Denmark Danemark	102	98	97	96	103	100	101	99	97	89
Dominica Dominique	81	91	91	99	93	100	105	...	...	...
Ecuador Equateur	128	76	86	72	85	100	88	97	75	83
Ethiopia Ethiopie	110	146	107	111	108	100	97	104	...	...
Faeroe Islands Iles Féroé	97	97	103	100	99	100	110	...	...	...
Finland Finlande	90	88	89	94	101	100	100	106	113	...

74
Total imports and exports: index numbers
[*cont.*]

Importations et exportations totales: indices
1990 = 100 [*suite*]

Country or area Pays ou zone	1985	1986	1987	1988	1989	1990	1991	1992	1993	1994
B. Imports: Unit value index [cont.] • Importations: Indice du valeur unitaire [suite]										
France France	111	93	92	95	101	100	99	95	90	94
Germany † Allemagne†	120	101	95	96	103	100	102	99	93	95
Greece Grèce	61	68	68	82	92	100	109	110	111	...
Guatemala Guatemala	101	101	100	128	117	100	96	123	119	...
Honduras Honduras	...	...	...	...	...	...	...	...	...	...
Hong Kong Hong-kong	83	87	90	94	98	100	102	102	66	104
Hungary Hongrie	73	77	78	81	91	100	146	161	176	...
Iceland Islande	44	49	53	63	83	100	103	104	113	...
India Inde	65	54	60	69	86	100	122	125	...	...
Indonesia Indonésie	...	...	...	...	...	...	...	...	...	...
Ireland Irlande	104	93	93	99	105	100	102	100	105	109
Israel[3] Israël[3]	74	74	81	87	93	100	95	95	92	94
Italy Italie	111	91	90	94	101	100	99	99	110	115
Japan Japon	146	92	85	81	90	100	91	84	74	69
Jordan Jordanie	62	47	48	51	74	100	100	95	96	94
Kenya Kenya	65	62	63	69	83	100	111	54	87	187
Korea, Republic of[3] Corée, République de[3]	88	91	88	98	100	100	104	108	107	108
Malaysia Malaisie	...	...	...	...	...	...	...	...	...	...
Mauritius Maurice	86	69	72	79	96	100	82	107	118	126
Mexico Mexique	...	...	...	...	...	100	100	101	102	...
Morocco Maroc	102	91	89	91	91	100	96	92	101	...
Netherlands Pays-Bas	122	101	94	94	101	100	100	97	93	92
New Zealand Nouvelle-Zélande	100	97	93	92	99	100	101	108	107	104
Norway[1] Norvège[1]	88	88	91	93	99	100	98	96	97	...

Country or area Pays ou zone	1985	1986	1987	1988	1989	1990	1991	1992	1993	1994
B. Exports:Unit value index [cont.] • Exportations:Indice du valeur unitaire [suite]										
France France	98	94	93	96	102	100	100	97	94	100
Germany † Allemagne†	102	99	96	96	101	100	99	99	94	93
Greece Grèce	57	62	67	80	92	100	109	106	109	...
Guatemala Guatemala	109	81	94	96	106	100	79	77	85	...
Honduras Honduras	98	127	100	107	105	100	98	77	78	89
Hong Kong [4] Hong-kong [4]	85	87	90	93	98	100	103	104	66	105
Hungary Hongrie	71	72	74	79	91	100	131	143	160	...
Iceland Islande	42	51	58	68	85	100	108	104	107	...
India Inde	60	58	65	78	93	100	111	142	...	...
Indonesia Indonésie	125	87	88	82	82	100	88	84	77	85
Ireland Irlande	104	97	97	104	110	100	99	97	104	104
Israel [3] Israël [3]	72	74	78	89	92	100	100	101	102	100
Italy Italie	91	87	88	92	98	100	103	104	115	120
Japan Japon	116	98	92	90	97	100	100	100	96	95
Jordan Jordanie	58	50	46	53	84	100	111	107	108	113
Kenya Kenya	84	90	75	86	92	100	128	85	259	266
Korea, Republic of [3] Corée, République de [3]	72	76	80	91	100	100	104	109	111	114
Malaysia Malaisie	103	77	90	99	101	100	102	...	...	...
Mauritius Maurice	63	67	75	80	89	100	85	114	123	129
Mexico Mexique	...	...	...	...	...	100	92	92	89	...
Morocco Maroc	90	91	88	97	96	100	100	95	95	...
Netherlands Pays-Bas	122	103	94	94	100	100	98	95	93	93
New Zealand Nouvelle-Zélande	81	79	84	89	101	100	96	104	106	102
Norway [1] Norvège [1]	118	88	85	85	96	100	96	88	88	...

74
Total imports and exports: index numbers
[cont.]

Importations et exportations totales: indices
1990 = 100 [suite]

Country or area Pays ou zone	1985	1986	1987	1988	1989	1990	1991	1992	1993	1994
	B. Imports: Unit value index [cont.] • Importations: Indice du valeur unitaire [suite]									
Pakistan Pakistan	73	65	76	78	92	100	107	110	118	138
Panama Panama	...	...	...	...	...	...	...	...	...	...
Peru Pérou	...	...	...	...	...	...	...	...	...	...
Philippines [3] Philippines [3]	81	73	74	76	83	100	108	...	...	...
Poland [2] Pologne [2]	2	2	3	5	14	100	136	...	182	231
Portugal Portugal	86	79	84	90	97	100	100	95	...	...
Rwanda Rwanda	...	...	...	...	...	...	...	...	...	...
Seychelles Seychelles	118	103	102	100	96	100	97	93	85	...
Singapore Singapour	105	93	101	101	101	100	97	93	92	...
Solomon Islands Iles Salomon	...	...	...	...	...	...	...	...	...	...
South Africa Afrique du Sud	62	72	75	83	93	100	110	117	127	141
Spain [2] Espagne [2]	128	105	101	101	103	100	97	96	101	107
Sri Lanka Sri Lanka	48	44	53	66	79	100	104	113	123	129
Sweden [2] Suède [2]	96	88	91	94	99	100	101	99	112	117
Switzerland Suisse	105	94	90	93	101	100	100	102	100	95
Syrian Arab Republic Rép. arabe syrienne	69	82	83	102	99	100	101	98	93	...
Thailand Thaïlande	102	76	81	89	95	100	104	105	105	107
Trinidad and Tobago Trinité-et-Tobago	50	68	77	86	99	100	...	...	...	...
Tunisia Tunisie	71	70	77	81	89	100	99	94	94	...
Turkey Turquie	102	86	92	92	95	100	97	95	89	90
United Kingdom Royaume-Uni	93	89	91	94	98	100	101	102	111	115
United States Etats-Unis	87	84	89	94	97	100	100	101	100	102
Venezuela [2] Venezuela [2]	19	23	38	44	83	100	119	140	189	341
Yugoslavia, SFR†[3] Yougoslavie, Rfs†[3]	82	74	78	89	90	100	...	...	...	...

Country or area Pays ou zone	1985	1986	1987	1988	1989	1990	1991	1992	1993	1994
	B. Exports: Unit value index [cont.] • Exportations: Indice du valeur unitaire [suite]									
Pakistan Pakistan	62	65	79	84	91	100	104	106	116	136
Panama Panama	106	93	103	93	95	100	101	...	...	...
Peru[3] Pérou[3]	85	69	86	95	104	100	88	87	73	84
Philippines[3] Philippines[3]	75	73	80	91	92	100	115	...	...	...
Poland[2] Pologne[2]	2	2	3	5	16	100	118	...	191	246
Portugal Portugal	74	77	83	92	97	100	100	98	...	...
Rwanda Rwanda	195	209	111	...	115	100	131	105	...	...
Seychelles Seychelles	169	110	112	112	94	100	88	101	102	...
Singapore Singapour	114	98	101	100	100	100	95	88	86	...
Solomon Islands Iles Salomon	66	59	89	107	108	100	95	...	...	...
South Africa Afrique du Sud	58	66	69	79	95	100	106	112	122	131
Spain[2] Espagne[2]	96	95	97	99	103	100	99	100	104	109
Sri Lanka Sri Lanka	55	48	60	70	83	100	102	115	127	128
Sweden[2] Suède[2]	86	86	88	92	98	100	101	98	108	113
Switzerland Suisse	95	92	92	93	99	100	103	103	103	102
Syrian Arab Republic Rép. arabe syrienne	95	70	65	62	77	100	98	68	67	...
Thailand Thaïlande	81	82	88	95	98	100	103	104	105	109
Trinidad and Tobago Trinité-et-Tobago	68	66	70	66	84	100	...	...	...	...
Tunisia Tunisie	76	68	78	83	95	100	97	95	96	...
Turkey Turquie	...	...	...	...	...	...	...	...	...	...
United Kingdom Royaume-Uni	93	86	89	92	97	100	101	103	115	118
United States[5] Etats-Unis[5]	88	88	90	97	99	100	101	101	101	104
Venezuela[2] Venezuela[2]	16	10	19	20	60	100	94	108	127	...
Yugoslavia, SFR†[3] Yougoslavie, Rfs†[3]	74	72	76	88	90	100	...	...	...	...

74
Total imports and exports: index numbers
[*cont.*]

Importations et exportations totales: indices
1990 = 100 [*suite*]

Country or area Pays ou zone	1985	1986	1987	1988	1989	1990	1991	1992	1993	1994

C. Terms of trade • Termes de l'échange

Country or area Pays ou zone	1985	1986	1987	1988	1989	1990	1991	1992	1993	1994
Australia Australie	92	85	85	97	102	100	90	88	82	83
Austria Autriche	96	102	104	103	97	100	97	96	95	95
Bangladesh Bangladesh	136	103	87	109	107	100	87	...	...	...
Belgium-Luxembourg Belgique-Luxembourg	95	102	102	104	104	100	99	102	...	...
Brazil Brésil	97	133	113	115	105	100	103	...	...	...
Canada Canada	97	94	97	100	103	100	97	96	95	96
Colombia Colombie	123	150	115	117	91	100	97	91	92	111
Denmark Danemark	92	95	101	99	98	100	101	102	103	83
Dominica Dominique	103	118	107	108	99	100	101	...	...	...
Faeroe Islands Iles Féroé	90	96	89	101	96	100	110	...	...	...
Finland Finlande	86	93	96	99	103	100	98	94	88	...
France France	88	101	101	101	101	100	101	102	104	106
Germany † Allemagne†	85	98	101	100	98	100	97	100	101	98
Greece Grèce	93	91	99	98	100	100	100	96	98	...
Guatemala Guatemala	108	80	94	75	91	100	82	63	71	...
Hong Kong Hong-kong	102	100	100	99	100	100	101	102	100	101
Hungary Hongrie	97	94	95	98	100	100	90	89	91	...
Iceland Islande	95	104	109	108	102	100	105	100	95	...
India Inde	92	107	108	113	108	100	91	114	...	...
Ireland Irlande	100	104	104	105	105	100	97	97	99	95
Israel Israël	97	100	96	102	99	100	105	106	111	106
Italy Italie	82	96	98	98	97	100	104	105	105	104
Japan Japon	79	107	108	111	108	100	110	119	130	138
Jordan Jordanie	94	106	96	104	114	100	111	113	113	120

Country or area Pays ou zone	1985	1986	1987	1988	1989	1990	1991	1992	1993	1994
D. Purchasing power of exports • Pouvoir d'achat des exportations										
Australia Australie	74	71	80	86	96	100	104	106	106	115
Austria Autriche	68	72	75	82	87	100	103	107	102	113
Bangladesh Bangladesh	...	...	...	...	...	...	...	...	...	...
Belgium-Luxembourg Belgique-Luxembourg	73	85	91	94	98	100	103	106	...	...
Brazil Brésil	93	105	104	125	115	100	107	...	...	...
Canada Canada	78	79	90	94	99	100	98	106	115	134
Colombia Colombie	...	...	...	...	...	...	...	...	...	...
Denmark Danemark	74	78	84	86	90	100	107	113	111	82
Dominica Dominique	64	98	103	115	87	100	95	...	...	...
Faeroe Islands Iles Féroé	77	83	74	90	98	100	114	...	...	...
Finland Finlande	79	86	90	96	100	100	89	93	102	...
France France	70	79	82	89	96	100	106	110	111	126
Germany † Allemagne†	70	81	87	92	97	100	97	102	99	110
Greece Grèce	80	92	101	75	105	100	114	142	140	...
Guatemala Guatemala	87	91	85	68	92	100	103	91	97	...
Hong Kong Hong-kong	44	50	66	83	92	100	118	143	48	178
Hungary Hongrie	93	88	92	101	104	100	85	85	76	...
Iceland Islande	82	99	108	106	103	100	96	91	91	...
India Inde	48	63	77	84	98	100	104	132	...	...
Ireland Irlande	65	72	82	87	96	100	103	116	131	147
Israel Israël	80	91	97	98	99	100	103	114	134	149
Italy Italie	66	78	82	87	94	100	104	109	117	130
Japan Japon	70	93	94	101	102	100	112	124	131	142
Jordan Jordanie	67	79	84	106	118	100	98	108	117	135

74
Total imports and exports: index numbers
[cont.]

Importations et exportations totales: indices
1990 = 100 [suite]

Country or area Pays ou zone	1985	1986	1987	1988	1989	1990	1991	1992	1993	1994
C. Terms of trade [cont.] · Termes de l'échange [suite]										
Kenya Kenya	129	145	119	125	111	100	115	157	298	142
Korea, Republic of Corée, République de	82	84	91	93	100	100	100	101	104	106
Mauritius Maurice	73	97	104	101	93	100	104	107	104	102
Mexico Mexique	...	...	...	...	...	100	92	91	87	...
Morocco Maroc	88	100	99	107	105	100	104	103	94	...
Netherlands Pays-Bas	100	102	100	100	99	100	98	98	100	101
New Zealand Nouvelle-Zélande	81	81	90	97	102	100	95	96	99	98
Norway Norvège	134	100	93	91	97	100	98	92	91	...
Pakistan Pakistan	85	100	104	108	99	100	97	96	98	99
Philippines Philippines	93	100	108	120	111	100	106	...	...	...
Poland Pologne	100	100	100	100	114	100	87	...	105	106
Portugal Portugal	86	97	99	102	100	100	100	103	...	...
Seychelles Seychelles	143	107	110	112	98	100	91	109	120	...
Singapore Singapour	109	105	100	99	99	100	98	95	93	...
South Africa Afrique du Sud	94	92	92	95	102	100	96	96	96	93
Spain Espagne	75	90	96	98	100	100	102	104	103	102
Sri Lanka Sri Lanka	115	109	113	106	105	100	98	102	103	99
Sweden Suède	90	98	97	98	99	100	100	99	96	97
Switzerland Suisse	90	98	102	100	98	100	103	101	103	107
Syrian Arab Republic Rép. arabe syrienne	138	85	78	61	78	100	97	69	72	...
Thailand Thaïlande	79	108	109	107	103	100	99	99	100	102
Trinidad and Tobago Trinité-et-Tobago	136	97	91	77	85	100	...	...	...	...

Country or area Pays ou zone	1985	1986	1987	1988	1989	1990	1991	1992	1993	1994
D. Purchasing power of exp.[cont.] • Pouvoir d'achat des exportations [suite]										
Kenya Kenya	105	135	107	118	104	100	119	162	295	159
Korea, Republic of Corée, République de	49	56	75	86	94	100	110	120	132	154
Mauritius Maurice	...	...	...	...	...	...	...	...	...	...
Mexico Mexique	...	...	...	...	...	...	...	...	...	...
Morocco Maroc	58	66	71	90	97	100	113	104	99	...
Netherlands Pays-Bas	77	82	83	91	94	100	103	106	115	119
New Zealand Nouvelle-Zélande	75	74	85	94	97	100	105	109	117	128
Norway Norvège	90	69	73	74	90	100	104	105	110	...
Pakistan Pakistan	48	75	85	97	93	100	110	119	110	137
Philippines Philippines	56	70	81	99	103	100	110	...	...	...
Poland Pologne	77	81	85	92	105	100	89	...	101	121
Portugal Portugal	48	59	67	76	89	100	101	110	...	...
Seychelles Seychelles	26	18	48	104	100	100	123	137	127	...
Singapore Singapour	50	56	62	82	91	100	111	116	136	...
South Africa Afrique du Sud	84	85	84	93	108	100	96	84	103	108
Spain Espagne	57	65	74	83	89	100	113	122	139	163
Sri Lanka Sri Lanka	95	97	98	89	90	100	102	122	141	152
Sweden Suède	81	91	93	97	100	100	98	98	103	110
Switzerland Suisse	74	84	88	91	94	100	102	104	107	117
Syrian Arab Republic Rép. arabe syrienne	62	38	36	31	61	100	101	73	114	...
Thailand Thaïlande	47	52	62	77	92	100	118	133	149	179
Trinidad and Tobago Trinité-et-Tobago	129	91	84	73	80	100	...	...	...	...

74

Total imports and exports: index numbers
[*cont.*]

Importations et exportations totales: indices
1990 = 100 [*suite*]

Country or area Pays ou zone	1985	1986	1987	1988	1989	1990	1991	1992	1993	1994
C. Terms of trade [cont.] • *Termes de l'échange* [suite]										
Tunisia Tunisie	107	97	101	102	107	100	98	101	102	...
United Kingdom Royaume-Uni	100	97	98	98	99	100	100	101	104	103
United States Etats-Unis	101	105	101	103	102	100	101	100	101	102
Venezuela Venezuela	84	43	50	45	72	100	79	77	67	...
Yugoslavia, SFR† Yougoslavie, Rfs†	90	97	97	99	100	100	...	...	...	...

Source:
Trade statistics database of the Statistics Division of the
United Nations Secretariat.

† For detailed descriptions of data pertaining to
former Czechoslovakia, Germany, SFR Yugoslavia and former
USSR, see Annex I – Country or area nomenclature, regional
and other groupings.

1 Excluding ships.
2 Price index numbers; for the United States, beginning 1989
and for Australia, beginning 1981.
3 Calculated in terms of US dollars.

Source:
Base de données pour les statistiques du commerce extérieur
de la Division de statistique du Secrétariat de l'ONU.

† Pour les descriptions en détails des données
relatives à l'ancienne Tchécoslovaquie, l'Allemagne, la Rfs
Yougoslavie et l'ancienne URSS, voir l'Annexe I –
Nomenclature des pays ou zones, groupements régionaux et
autres groupements.

1 Non compris les navires.
2 Indices des prix; pour les Etats-Unis à partir de 1989 et
pour l'Australie à partir de 1981.
3 Calculés en dollars des Etats-Unis.

Country or area Pays ou zone	1985	1986	1987	1988	1989	1990	1991	1992	1993	1994
D. Purchasing power of exp.[cont.] • Pouvoir d'achat des exportations [suite]										
Tunisia Tunisie	88	89	96	98	117	100	108	112	124	...
United Kingdom Royaume-Uni	80	80	85	86	93	100	101	104	107	118
United States Etats-Unis	64	66	72	87	95	100	107	113	117	128
Venezuela Venezuela	...	...	...	...	...	...	...	...	...	...
Yugoslavia, SFR† Yougoslavie, Rfs†	...	...	...	...	...	...	...	...	...	...

4 Domestic exports only.
5 Excludes military exports.

4 Seulement exportations domestiques.
5 Non compris les exportations militaires.

75
Manufactured goods exports
Exportations des produits manufacturés
1990 = 100

Region, country or area Région, pays ou zone	1985	1986	1987	1988	1989	1990	1991	1992	1993	1994
Unit value indices in US dollars • Indices de valeur unitaire en dollars des E-U										
Total[1]	66	77	86	93	92	100	100	103	99	...
Developed economies **Econ. développées**	63	76	85	92	91	100	100	103	97	99
America, North **Amérique du Nord**	85	86	90	96	99	100	102	100	99	99
Canada Canada	87	87	90	96	101	100	99	90	88	85
United States[2] Etats-Unis[2]	85	88	90	95	98	100	102	103	103	104
Europe **Europe**	57	72	82	88	87	100	98	101	91	93
EC+ **CE+**	58	72	82	88	87	100	98	102	92	94
Belgium-Luxembourg[3] Belgique-Luxembourg[3]	58	74	76	89	89	100	97	99	90	93
Denmark Danemark	56	71	85	88	84	100	96	102	92	96
France France	62	73	84	88	86	100	96	100	94	98
Germany † Allemagne†	55	73	86	89	87	100	98	103	93	94
Greece Grèce	63	70	78	86	87	100	95	94	...	...
Ireland[4] Irlande[4]	63	76	81	88	91	100	95	97	96	89
Italy[3] Italie[3]	54	68	80	85	86	100	99	102	89	86
Netherlands[3] Pays-Bas[3]	57	71	83	88	86	100	96	100	92	92
Portugal[4] Portugal[4]	60	66	82	88	85	100	101	106	98	84
Spain[4] Espagne[4]	55	71	68	83	83	100	95	109	85	86
United Kingdom Royaume-Uni	60	70	81	91	88	100	101	102	98	103
EFTA **AELE**	57	72	84	90	88	100	97	99	85	91
Austria[5] Autriche[5]	60	76	90	95	85	100	95	99	90	96
Finland Finlande	54	65	76	85	89	100	95	88	74	82
Iceland[4] Islande[4]	57	66	75	99	103	100	88	86	76	80
Norway Norvège	58	66	78	96	99	100	95	92	80	82
Sweden Suède	57	71	83	89	90	100	100	101	82	...

75
Manufactured goods exports
[*cont.*]

Exportations des produits manufacturés
1990 = 100 [*suite*]

Region, country or area Région, pays ou zone	1985	1986	1987	1988	1989	1990	1991	1992	1993	1994
Switzerland[3] Suisse[3]	55	73	88	88	84	100	98	103	88	99
Other **Autres**	**70**	**83**	**91**	**101**	**100**	**100**	**107**	**113**	**120**	**129**
Australia Australie	67	67	77	97	102	100	92	86	81	88
Israel Israël	69	72	76	86	92	100	101	101	102	101
Japan Japon	70	85	92	102	100	100	108	115	124	134
New Zealand Nouvelle-Zélande	66	72	84	107	105	100	94	89	89	98
South Africa Afrique du Sud	61	68	84	89	95	100	96	101	100	101
Developing economies[7] **Econ. en dévelop.[7]**	**80**	**79**	**88**	**97**	**98**	**100**	**100**	**103**	**104**	**...**

Unit value indices in 'SDR'[6] · Indices de valeur unitaire en 'DTS'[6]

Total[1]	89	89	90	93	98	100	99	99	96	...
Developed economies **Econ. développées**	85	88	89	93	96	100	99	99	95	94
Developing economies[7] **Econ. en dévelop.[7]**	107	92	92	98	104	100	99	100	101	...

Unit value indices in national currency · Indices de valeur unitaire en monnaie nationale

America, North · Amérique du Nord

Canada Canada	103	104	102	101	102	100	97	94	97	99
United States[2] Etats-Unis[2]	85	88	90	95	98	100	102	103	103	104
Europe · Europe **EC+ · CE+**										
Denmark Danemark	96	94	94	96	100	100	99	100	97	99
France France	102	93	93	96	101	100	99	97	98	100
Germany † Allemagne†	100	98	96	97	101	100	100	100	95	94
Greece Grèce	55	62	67	77	90	100	110	114	...	...
Netherlands[3] Pays-Bas[3]	103	96	92	95	101	100	99	97	94	92
United Kingdom Royaume-Uni	83	85	88	91	96	100	102	104	117	120
EFTA · AELE Austria[5] Autriche[5]	109	103	101	104	99	100	98	96	93	96
Finland Finlande	88	87	88	94	101	100	100	106	112	112

75
Manufactured goods exports
[*cont.*]

Exportations des produits manufacturés
1990 = 100 [*suite*]

Region, country or area Région, pays ou zone	1985	1986	1987	1988	1989	1990	1991	1992	1993	1994
Norway Norvège	79	79	84	101	110	100	98	92	92	93
Sweden Suède	83	85	88	93	98	100	102	100	108	...
Other · Autres Australia Australie	75	79	86	96	101	100	92	92	93	94
Japan Japon	116	98	93	91	96	100	101	101	95	95
New Zealand Nouvelle-Zélande	80	81	85	97	104	100	97	99	98	99
South Africa Afrique du Sud	52	60	66	78	97	100	103	111	127	139

Quantum indices · Indices de volume

Region, country or area Région, pays ou zone	1985	1986	1987	1988	1989	1990	1991	1992	1993	1994
Total[1]	**71**	**74**	**80**	**87**	**94**	**100**	**105**	**110**	**115**	**...**
Developed economies **Econ. développées**	**77**	**78**	**82**	**88**	**95**	**100**	**103**	**107**	**108**	**120**
America, North **Amérique du Nord**	**65**	**66**	**72**	**83**	**90**	**100**	**106**	**114**	**121**	**137**
Canada Canada	78	81	85	95	94	100	102	119	136	163
United States Etats-Unis	61	60	68	80	88	100	107	113	117	130
Europe **Europe**	**78**	**80**	**84**	**89**	**96**	**100**	**103**	**105**	**106**	**119**
EC+ **CE+**	**77**	**79**	**84**	**89**	**96**	**100**	**103**	**106**	**105**	**119**
Belgium-Luxembourg Belgique-Luxembourg	72	75	89	87	95	100	102	104	112	126
Denmark Danemark	81	82	84	90	93	100	106	114	111	119
France France	72	76	80	87	94	100	107	112	104	116
Germany † Allemagne†	81	82	85	91	99	100	102	104	100	111
Greece Grèce	85	101	106	85	106	100	109	127	...	...
Ireland Irlande	65	65	77	85	93	100	108	122	124	151
Italy Italie	82	83	86	91	97	100	101	103	112	132
Netherlands Pays-Bas	78	83	85	90	95	100	105	106	107	122
Portugal Portugal	54	65	68	75	90	100	101	110	99	130
Spain Espagne	75	66	85	84	94	100	114	109	132	157

75
Manufactured goods exports
[*cont.*]

Exportations des produits manufacturés
1990 = 100 [*suite*]

Region, country or area Région, pays ou zone	1985	1986	1987	1988	1989	1990	1991	1992	1993	1994
United Kingdom Royaume-Uni	75	76	82	86	94	100	100	101	95	107
EFTA **AELE**	**80**	**83**	**85**	**90**	**95**	**100**	**99**	**102**	**110**	**117**
Austria Autriche	66	70	71	78	90	100	104	109	107	102
Finland Finlande	88	90	94	93	96	100	90	99	117	133
Iceland Islande	96	102	114	114	108	100	91	94	102	131
Norway Norvège	85	87	91	83	89	100	103	106	105	114
Sweden Suède	88	91	92	98	100	100	97	98	108	...
Switzerland Suisse	77	81	81	91	96	100	98	100	112	111
Other **Autres**	**87**	**86**	**87**	**91**	**95**	**100**	**102**	**104**	**104**	**106**
Australia Australie	67	69	82	82	88	100	121	138	162	170
Israel Israël	72	80	91	94	97	100	98	110	126	146
Japan Japon	88	87	87	91	96	100	102	103	101	103
New Zealand Nouvelle-Zélande	88	86	87	85	92	100	112	120	132	152
South Africa Afrique du Sud	85	91	86	91	96	100	109	107	113	95
Developing economies[7] **Econ. en dévelop.[7]**	**51**	**58**	**71**	**80**	**92**	**100**	**112**	**126**	**144**	**...**

Value (thousand million US $) • Valeur (millards de dollars E-U)

	1985	1986	1987	1988	1989	1990	1991	1992	1993	1994
Total[1]	1 138.30	1 363.80	1 648.70	1 927.00	2 088.80	2 402.30	2 514.30	2 724.30	2 729.00	...
Developed economies **Econ. développées**	955.64	1 159.00	1 370.80	1 579.50	1 688.20	1 957.20	2 014.90	2 146.00	2 064.30	2 333.70
America, North **Amérique du Nord**	199.19	205.06	232.91	286.97	319.63	361.29	389.25	413.80	435.11	489.84
Canada Canada	53.86	56.19	59.81	72.19	74.46	78.83	79.42	84.61	93.87	108.90
United States Etats-Unis	145.34	148.87	173.11	214.78	245.17	282.46	309.83	329.19	341.24	380.94
Europe **Europe**	571.06	734.12	894.89	1 011.50	1 075.30	1 289.10	1 290.50	1 372.70	1 244.10	1 423.30
EC+ **CE+**	486.97	624.17	762.34	861.55	919.91	1 103.00	1 112.10	1 185.50	1 070.80	1 226.20
Belgium-Luxembourg Belgique-Luxembourg	39.75	52.29	64.09	73.83	80.42	95.18	93.84	97.60	95.90	110.83

75
Manufactured goods exports
[*cont.*]

Exportations des produits manufacturés
1990 = 100 [*suite*]

Region, country or area Region, pays ou zone	1985	1986	1987	1988	1989	1990	1991	1992	1993	1994
Denmark Danemark	9.61	12.35	14.92	16.63	16.61	21.14	21.40	24.66	21.65	24.30
France France	73.71	92.19	111.69	126.05	134.56	165.29	169.44	184.58	162.83	187.20
Germany † Allemagne†	161.58	217.32	264.48	293.10	309.59	362.01	361.85	387.53	334.59	377.61
Greece Grèce	2.37	3.15	3.69	3.25	4.12	4.45	4.59	5.31	4.82	4.73
Ireland Irlande	6.66	8.16	10.26	12.31	13.95	16.50	16.96	19.56	19.60	22.07
Italy Italie	67.77	86.09	104.04	115.83	125.92	150.63	150.98	158.35	150.13	170.84
Netherlands Pays-Bas	35.54	46.82	56.91	63.55	65.51	80.23	80.89	85.31	79.18	89.86
Portugal Portugal	4.32	5.62	7.34	8.72	10.09	13.20	13.39	15.38	12.88	14.48
Spain Espagne	17.57	20.11	24.62	29.90	33.18	42.63	46.08	50.61	47.54	57.53
United Kingdom Royaume-Uni	68.08	80.09	100.29	118.37	125.96	151.77	152.62	156.62	141.64	166.70
EFTA **AELE**	**83.75**	**109.51**	**132.01**	**149.37**	**154.64**	**185.03**	**177.28**	**185.80**	**172.14**	**197.15**
Austria Autriche	15.06	20.17	24.28	27.94	29.07	37.89	37.53	40.66	36.70	37.00
Finland Finlande	10.88	13.57	16.56	18.17	19.77	22.98	19.65	20.05	20.05	25.11
Iceland Islande	0.16	0.20	0.25	0.33	0.32	0.29	0.23	0.23	0.23	0.31
Norway Norvège	6.96	8.30	10.08	11.40	12.55	14.22	13.84	13.84	12.05	13.35
Sweden Suède	24.80	31.49	37.54	43.03	43.92	48.90	47.50	48.49	43.13	...
Switzerland Suisse	25.89	35.79	43.30	48.50	49.01	60.76	58.52	62.53	59.98	66.70
Other Europe · Autres pays d'Europe Malta Malte	0.34	0.43	0.54	0.63	0.77	1.00	1.12	1.38	1.21	...
Other **Autres**	**185.39**	**219.85**	**243.03**	**280.94**	**293.25**	**306.87**	**335.15**	**359.52**	**385.08**	**420.51**
Australia Australie	3.69	3.83	5.23	6.60	7.44	8.28	9.19	9.83	10.85	12.36
Israel Israël	5.26	6.10	7.29	8.44	9.42	10.52	10.47	11.74	13.48	15.50
Japan Japon	170.78	203.36	222.81	257.07	266.59	277.44	304.34	328.52	348.56	381.06
New Zealand Nouvelle-Zélande	1.48	1.56	1.85	2.31	2.45	2.54	2.67	2.73	2.98	3.78
South Africa Afrique du Sud	4.19	4.99	5.85	6.52	7.35	8.10	...	6.70	9.21	...
Developing economies[7] **Econ. en dévelop.**[7]	**182.69**	**204.80**	**277.91**	**346.48**	**400.60**	**445.10**	**499.36**	**578.22**	**664.73**	...

75

Manufactured goods exports
[*cont.*]

Exportations des produits manufacturés
1990 = 100 [*suite*]

Source:
Trade statistics database of the Statistics Division of the
United Nations Secretariat.
+   For Member States of this grouping, see
    Annex I - Other groupings.

†   For detailed descriptions of data pertaining to
former Czechoslovakia, Germany, SFR Yugoslavia and former
USSR, see Annex I - Country or area nomenclature, regional
and other groupings.

1 Excludes trade of the countries of Eastern Europe and the
   former USSR.
2 Beginning 1989 derived from price indices; national unit
   value index discontinued.

3 Derived from sub-indices using current weights. Indices for
   Belgium, beginning 1988, and for Switzerland, beginning
   1987, are calculated by the United Nations Statistical
   Division.

4 Indices are calculated by the United Nations Statistics
   Division for the years beginning 1981.
5 Series linked at 1988 by a factor calculated by the United
   Nations Statistics Division.
6 Special drawing right.
7 Includes the Socialist Federal Republic of Yugoslavia.

Source:
Base de données pour les statistiques du commerce extérieur
de la Division de statistique de la secrétariat de l'ONU.
+   Les Etats membres de ce groupement, voir
    annexe I - Autres groupements.

†   Pour les descriptions en détails des données
relatives à l'ancienne Tchécoslovaquie, l'Allemagne, la Rfs
Yougoslavie et l'ancienne URSS, voir l'Annexe I -
Nomenclature des pays ou zones, groupements régionaux et
autres groupements.

1 Non compris le commerce des pays de l'Europe de l'Est et
   l'ancienne URSS.
2 A partir de l'année 1989 calculés à partir des indices des
   prix; l'indice de la valeur unitaire nationale est
   discontinué.

3 Calculé à partir de sous-indices à coéfficients de
   pondération correspondant à la période en cours. Les indices
   pour la Belgique, à partir de 1988, et pour la Suisse, à
   partir de 1987, sont calculés par la Division de statistique
   des Nations Unies.
4 Les indices sont calculés par la Division de statistique des
   Nations Unies pour les années à partir de 1981.
5 Les séries sont enchaînés à 1988 par un facteur calculé par
   la Division de statistique des Nations Unies.
6 Le droit de tirage spécial.
7 Y compris la République socialiste fédérative de
   Yougoslavie.

Technical notes, tables 72-75

Tables 72-75: Current data (annual, monthly and/or quarterly) for most of the series are published regularly by the Statistical Division in the United Nations *Monthly Bulletin of Statistics* [25]. More detailed descriptions of the tables and notes on methodology appear in the United Nations 1977 *Supplement to the Statistical Yearbook and Monthly Bulletin of Statistics, International Trade Statistics: Concepts and Definitions* [47, 49] and the *International Trade Statistics Yearbook*.[24] More detailed data including series for individual countries showing the value in national currencies for imports and exports and notes on these series are to be found in the *International Trade Statistics Yearbook* [24] and in the *Monthly Bulletin of Statistics*.[25]

Data are obtained from national published sources, from data supplied by the Governments for use in the following United Nations publications: *Commodity Trade Statistics* [19], *Monthly Bulletin of Statistics* and *Statistical Yearbook*; and from publications of other United Nations agencies.

Territory

The statistics reported by a country refer to the customs area of the country. In most cases, this coincides with the geographical area of the country.

System of trade

Two systems of recording trade are in common use, differing mainly in the way warehoused and re-exported goods are recorded:

(a) Special trade (S): special imports are the combined total of imports for direct domestic consumption (including transformation and repair) and withdrawals from bonded warehouses or free zones for domestic consumption. Special exports comprise exports of national merchandise, namely, goods wholly or partly produced or manufactured in the country, together with exports of nationalized goods. (Nationalized goods are goods which, having been included in special imports, are then exported without transformation);

(b) General trade (G): general imports are the combined total of imports for direct domestic consumption and imports into bonded warehouses or free zones. General exports are the combined total of national exports and re-exports. Re-exports, in the general trade system, consist of the outward movement of nationalized goods plus goods which, after importation, move outward from bonded warehouses or free zones without having been transformed;

(c) Semi-special trade (Sl): semi-special imports are general imports less all re-exports; semi-special exports are exports of domestic produce.

Notes techniques, tableaux 72-75

Tableaux 72-75 : La Division de statistique des Nations Unies publie régulièrement des données courantes (annuelles, mensuelles et/ou trimestrielles) pour la plupart des séries de ces tableaux dans le *Bulletin mensuel de statistique* [25] des Nations Unies. Des descriptions plus détaillées des tableaux et des notes méthodologiques figurent dans *1977 Supplément à l'Annuaire statistique et au Bulletin mensuel de statistique* des Nations Unies, dans la publication *Statistiques du Commerce international, Concepts et définitions* [47, 49] et dans l'*Annuaire statistique du Commerce international* [24]. Des données plus détaillées, comprenant des séries indiquant la valeur en monnaie nationale des importations et des exportations des divers pays et les notes accompagnant ces séries figurent dans l'*Annuaire statistique du Commerce international* [24] et dans le *Bulletin mensuel de statistique*.[25]

Les données proviennent de publications nationales et des informations fournies par les gouvernements pour les publications suivantes des Nations Unies : *"Commodity Trade Statistics"* [19], Bulletin mensuel de statistique et Annuaire statistique", ainsi que de publications d'autres institutions des Nations Unies.

Territoire

Les statistiques fournies par pays se rapportent au territoire douanier de ce pays. Le plus souvent, ce territoire coïncide avec l'étendue géographique du pays.

Système de commerce

Deux systèmes d'enregistrement du commerce sont couramment utilisés, qui ne diffèrent que par la façon dont sont enregistrées les marchandises entreposées et les marchandises réexportées :

(a) Commerce spécial (S) : les importations spéciales représentent le total combiné des importations destinées directement à la consommation intérieure (transformations et réparations comprises) et les marchandises retirées des entrepôts douaniers ou des zones franches pour la consommation intérieure. Les exportations spéciales comprennent les exportations de marchandises nationales, c'est-à-dire des biens produits ou fabriqués en totalité ou en partie dans le pays, ainsi que les exportations de biens nationalisés. (Les biens nationalisés sont des biens qui, ayant été inclus dans les importations spéciales, sont ensuite réexportés tels quels.)

(b) Commerce général (G) : les importations générales sont le total combiné des importations destinées directement à la consommation intérieure et des importations placées en entrepôt douanier ou destinées aux zones franches. Les exportations générales sont le total combiné des exportations de biens nationaux et des réexportations. Ces dernières, dans le système du commerce général, comprennent les exportations de biens nationalisés et de biens qui, après avoir été importés, sortent des entrepôts de douane ou des zones franches sans avoir été transformés.

Direct transit trade, i.e., goods merely being trans-shipped or moving through the country for the purpose of transport only, is excluded from the statistics of both special and general trade.

Valuation

Goods are, in general, valued according to the transaction value. In the case of imports, the transaction value is the value at which the goods were purchased by the importer plus the cost of transportation and insurance to the frontier of the importing country (a c.i.f. valuation). In the case of exports, the transaction value is the value at which the goods were sold by the exporter, including the cost of transportation and insurance, to bring the goods onto the transporting vehicle at the frontier of the exporting country (a f.o.b. valuation).

Currency conversion

Conversion of values from national currencies into United States dollars is done by means of external trade conversion factors which are generally weighted averages of exchange rates, the weight being the corresponding monthly or quarterly value of imports or exports.

Coverage

The statistics relate to merchandise trade. Merchandise trade is defined to include, as far as possible, all goods which add to or subtract from the material resources of a country as a result of their movement into or out of the country. Thus, ordinary commercial transactions, government trade (including foreign aid, war reparations and trade in military goods), postal trade and all kinds of silver (except silver coin after its issue), are included in the statistics. Since their movement affects monetary rather than material resources, monetary gold, together with currency and titles of ownership after their issue into circulation, are excluded.

Commodity classification

The commodity classification of trade is in accordance with the United Nations *Standard International Trade Classification* (SITC).[52]

World and regional totals

The regional, economic and world totals have been adjusted: (a) to include estimates for countries or areas for which full data are not available; (b) to include insurance and freight for imports valued f.o.b.; (c) to include countries or areas not listed separately; (d) to approximate special trade; (e) to approximate calendar years; and (f) where possible, to eliminate incomparabilities owing to geographical changes, by adjusting the figures for periods before the change to be comparable to those for periods after the change.

(c)   Commerce semi-spécial (SI) : les importations semi-spéciales sont les importations générales moins l'ensemble des réexportations; les exportations semi-spéciales sont les exportations de produits du pays.

Le transit direct, c'est-à-dire les marchandises uniquement transbordées ou transportées à travers le pays, est exclu aussi bien du commerce général que du commerce spécial.

Evaluation

En général, les marchandises sont évaluées à la valeur de la transaction. Dans le cas des importations, cette valeur est celle à laquelle les marchandises ont été achetées par l'importateur plus le coût de leur transport et de leur assurance jusqu'à la frontière du pays importateur (valeur c.a.f.). Dans le cas des exportations, la valeur de la transaction est celle à laquelle les marchandises ont été vendues par l'exportateur, y compris le coût de transport et d'assurance des marchandises jusqu'à leur chargement sur le véhicule de transport à la frontière du pays exportateur (valeur f.o.b.).

Conversion des monnaies

Le conversion en dollars des Etats-Unis de valeurs exprimées en monnaie nationale se fait par application de coefficients de conversion du commerce extérieur, qui sont généralement les moyennes pondérées des taux de change, le poids étant la valeur mensuelle ou trimestrielle correspondante des importations ou des exportations.

Couverture

Les statistiques se rapportent au commerce des marchandises. Le commerce des marchandises se définit comme comprenant, dans toute la mesure du possible, toutes les marchandises qui ajoutent ou retranchent aux ressources matérielles d'un pays par suite de leur importation ou de de leur exportation par ce pays. Ainsi, les transactions commerciales ordinaires, le commerce pour le compte de l'Etat (y compris l'aide extérieure, les réparations pour dommages de guerre et le commerce des fournitures militaires), le commerce par voie postale et les transactions de toutes sortes sur l'argent (à l'exception des transactions sur les pièces d'argent après leur émission) sont inclus dans ces statistiques. La monnaie or ainsi que la monnaie et les titres de propriété après leur mise en circulation sont exclus, car leurs mouvements influent sur les ressources monétaires plutôt que sur les ressources matérielles.

Classification par marchandise

La classification par marchandise du commerce extérieur est celle adoptée dans la *Classification type por le commerce international* des Nations Unies (CTCI) [52].

Totaux mondiaux et régionaux

Les totaux économiques régionaux et mondiaux ont été ajustés de manière : (a) à inclure les estimations pour les pays ou régions pour lesquels on ne disposait pas de données complètes; (b) à inclure l'assurance et le fret dans la valeur f.o.b. des importations; (c) à inclure les pays ou régions

Quantum and unit value index numbers

These index numbers show the changes in the volume of imports or exports (quantum index) and the average price of imports or exports (unit value index).

Description of tables

Table 73: The purpose of this table is to provide data on the network of flows of broad groups of commodities within and between important economic and geographic areas of the world. The regional analysis in this table is in accordance with that of table 72.

Export data in this table are largely comparable to data shown in table 72 except that table 72 contains revised data for total exports which may not be available at the commodity/destination level needed for this table. Also, the regional totals shown in table 72 have been adjusted to exclude the re-exports of countries comprising each region. This adjustment is not made in this table since re-exports are often not available by commodity and by destination.

The commodity classification is in accordance with the United Nations *Standard International Trade Classification* (SITC), Revision 2 for 1980 through 1987 except for countries which report trade data only in terms of the SITC, Revised. Beginning in 1988 the commodity classification is in accordance with SITC, Revision 3 where data are available from countries. [52]

The data approximate total exports of all countries and areas of the world with the exception of the inter-trade of the centrally planned economies of Asia in 1980 and trade conducted in accordance with the supplementary protocol to the treaty on the basis of relations between the Federal Republic of Germany and the former German Democratic Republic. They are based on official export figures converted, where necessary, to US dollars. Where official figures are not available estimates based on the imports reported by partner countries and on other subsidiary data are used. Some official national data have been adjusted (a) to approximate the commodity groupings of SITC; and (b) to approximate calendar years.

The data include special category (confidential) exports, ships' stores and bunders and exports of minor importance, the destination of which cannot be determined. These data are included in the world totals for each commodity group and in total exports, but are excluded from all regions of destination. Approximately 1 ½ percent of total exports are not distributed. All data are generally in accordance with the special trade system.

Table 74: These index numbers show the changes in the volume (quantum index) and the average price (unit value index) of total imports and exports. The terms of trade figures are calculated by dividing export unit value indices by the corresponding import unit value indices. The product of the net terms of trade and the quantum index of exports is called the index of the purchasing power of exports. The footnotes to countries appearing in table 72 also apply to the index numbers in this table.

non indiqués séparément; (d) à donner une approximation du commerce spécial; (e) à les ramener à des années civiles; et (f) à éliminer, dans la mesure du possible, les données non comparables par suite de changements géographiques, en ajustant les chiffres correspondant aux périodes avant le changement de manière à les rendre comparables à ceux des périodes après le changement.

Indices de quantum et de valeur unitaire

Ces indices indiquent les variations du volume des importations ou des exportations (indice de quantum) et du prix moyen des importations ou des exportations (indice de valeur unitaire).

Description des tableaux

Tableau 73 : Ce tableau a pour but de fournir des données sur l'ensemble des flux de grandes catégories de marchandises à l'intérieur des grandes régions économiques et géographiques du monde et entre ces régions. L'analyse régionale de ce tableau est conforme à celle de tableau 72.

Les données de ce tableau sur les exportations sont en grande partie comparables aux données fournies au tableau 72; toutefois, celui-ci présente des données révisées pour les totaux des exportations qui ne sont pas nécessairement disponibles au niveau des marchandises/destinations présentées au tableau 72. En outre, les totaux régionaux indiqués au tableau 72 ont été ajustés de manière à exclure les réexportations effectuées par les pays composant chaque région. Cet ajustement n'apparaît pas sur ce tableau, car il est fréquent que l'on ne dispose pas des chiffres des réexportations par marchandise et par destination.

La classification des marchandises est conforme à la *Classification type pour le commerce international* (CTCI), Révision 2 des Nations Unies pour les années 1980 à 1987, sauf pour les pays qui ne fournissent de statistiques commerciales que sur la base de la CTCI révisée. A partir de 1988, la classification des marchandises est conforme à la CTCI, Révision 3, pour les pays qui ont fourni des données [52].

Les données fournissent une approximation des exportations totales de tous les pays et régions du monde à l'exception du commerce intrarégional des économies à planification centrale d'Asie en 1980 et des échanges commerciaux effectués selon le protocole supplémentaire du traité sur la base des relations entre la République fédérale d'Allemagne et l'ancienne République démocratique allemande. Elles sont fondées sur les chiffres officiels des exportations convertis, le cas échéant, en dollars des Etats-Unis. En l'absence de chiffres officiels, on a utilisé des estimations fondées sur les importations notifiées par les pays partenaires et sur d'autres données subsidiaires. Certaines données nationales officielles ont été ajustées : a) sur la base des groupements de marchandises de la CTCI; et b) sur la base des années civiles.

Ces données englobent les catégories spéciales (confidentielles) d'exportation, les marchandises à bord des navires et les exportations d'importance mineure, dont la

Table 75: Manufactured goods are here defined to comprise sections 5 through 8 of the Standard International Trade Classification. These sections are: chemicals and related products, manufactured goods classified chiefly by material, machinery and transport equipment and miscellaneous manufactured articles. The economic and geographic groupings in this table are in accordance with those of table 72, although table 72 includes more detailed geographical sub-groups which make up the groupings "other developed market economies" and "developing market economies" of this table.

The unit value indices are obtained from national sources, except those of a few countries which the United Nations Statistics Division compiles using their quantity and value figures. For countries that do not compiles indices for manufactured goods exports conforming to the above definition, sub-indices are aggregated to approximate an index of SITC sections 5-8. Unit value indices obtained from national indices are rebased, where necessary, so that 1990=100. Indices in national currency are converted into US dollars using conversion factors obtained by dividing the weighted average exchange rate of a given currency in the current period by the weighted average exchange rate in the base period. All aggregate unit value indices are current period weighted.

The indices in SDRs are calculated by multiplying the equivalent aggregate indices in United States dollars by conversion factors obtained by dividing the SDR/$US exchange rate in the current period by the rate in the base period.

The quantum indices are derived from the value data and the unit value indices. All aggregate quantum indices are base period weighted.

destination ne peut être déterminée. Ces données sont comprises dans les totaux mondiaux pour chaque classe de marchandises et dans les exportations totales, mais sont exclues de ceux des régions de destination. Environ 1,5 % des exportations totales ne sont pas distribuées. Dans l'ensemble, les données sont conformes au système du commerce spécial.

Tableau 74 : Ces indices indiquent les variations du volume (indice de quantum) et du prix moyen (indice de valeur unitaire) des importations et des exportations totales. Les chiffres relatifs aux termes de l'échange se calculent en divisant les indices de valeur unitaire des exportations par les indices correspondants de valeur unitaire des importations. Le produit de la valeur nette des termes de l'échange et de l'indice du quantum des exportations est appelé indice du pouvoir d'achat des exportations. Les notes figurant au bas du tableau 72 concernant certains pays s'appliquent également aux indices du présent tableau.

Tableau 75 : Les produits manufacturés se définissent comme correspondant aux sections 5 à 8 de la Classification type pour le commerce international. Ces sections sont : produits chimiques et produits connexes, biens manufacturés classés principalement par matière première, machines et équipements de transport et articles divers manufacturés. Les groupements économiques et géographiques de ce tableau sont conformes à ceux du tableau 72; toutefois, le tableau 72 comprend des subdivisions géographiques plus détaillées qui composent les groupements "autres pays développés à économie de marché" et "pays en développement à économie de marché" du présent tableau.

Les indices de valeur unitaire sont obtenus de sources nationales, à l'exception de ceux de certains pays que la Division de statistique des Nations Unies compile en utilisant les chiffres de ces pays relatifs aux quantités et aux valeurs. Pour les pays qui n'établissent pas d'indices conformes à la définition ci-dessus pour leurs exportations de produits manufacturés, on fait la synthèse de sous-indices de manière à établir un indice proche de celui des sections 5-8 de la CTCI. Le cas échéant, les indices de valeur unitaire obtenus à partir des indices nationaux sont ajustés sur la base 1990=100. On convertit les indices en monnaie nationale en indices en dollars des Etats-Unis en utilisant des facteurs de conversion obtenus en divisant la moyenne pondérée des taux de change d'une monnaie donnée pendant la période courante par la moyenne pondérée des taux de change de la période de base. Tous les indices globaux de valeur unitaire sont pondérés pour la période courante.

On calcule les indices en DTS en multipliant les indices globaux équivalents en dollars des Etats-Unis par les facteurs de conversion obtenus en divisant le taux de change DTS/dollars EU de la période courante par le taux correspondant de la période de base.

On détermine les indices de quantum à partir des données de valeur et des indices de valeur unitaire. Tous les indices globaux de quantum sont pondérés par rapport à la période de base.

76
Tourist arrivals by region of origin
Arrivées de touristes par région de provenance

Country or area of destination and region of origin	1990	1991	1992	1993	1994	Pays ou zone de destination et région de provenance
Albania[1]	**29 997**	**12 883**	**28 430**	**45 152**	**28 439**	**Albanie**[1]
Africa	...	...	...	39	47	Afrique
Americas	401	501	954	3 736	2 584	Amériques
Europe	29 569	12 382	27 148	39 728	25 262	Europe
Asia, East and South East/Oceania	27	...	138	683	404	Asie, Est et Sud-Est et Océanie
Southern Asia	...	...	...	411	34	Asie du Sud
Western Asia	...	...	190	555	108	Asie occidentale
Algeria[23]	**1 136 918**	**1 193 210**	**1 119 548**	**1 127 545**	**804 713**	**Algérie**[23]
Africa	407 807	519 807	437 076	395 459	252 121	Afrique
Americas	5 764	4 606	5 146	5 116	2 813	Amériques
Europe	227 355	158 957	151 180	144 248	60 383	Europe
Asia, East and South East/Oceania	8 338	13 945	6 390	5 459	3 123	Asie, Est et Sud-Est et Océanie
Western Asia	36 551	25 367	24 304	21 711	17 786	Asie occidentale
Region not specified	451 103	470 528	495 452	555 552	468 487	Région non spécifiés
American Samoa[4]	**47 337**	**39 746**	**31 444**	**...**	**...**	**Samoa américaines**[4]
Americas	10 623	8 418	6 334	...	...	Amériques
Europe	1 331	1 304	732	...	...	Europe
Asia, East and South East/Oceania	35 224	29 928	24 172	...	...	Asie, Est et Sud-Est et Océanie
Region not specified	159	96	206	...	...	Région non spécifiés
Angola[2]	**...**	**...**	**...**	**20 582**	**10 943**	**Angola**[2]
Africa	...	...	...	...	1 308	Afrique
Americas	...	...	...	669	1 209	Amériques
Europe	...	...	...	10 580	8 019	Europe
Asia, East and South East/Oceania	...	...	...	...	301	Asie, Est et Sud-Est et Océanie
Southern Asia	...	...	...	...	66	Asie du Sud
Region not specified	...	...	...	9 333	40	Région non spécifiés
Anguilla	**31 181**	**31 002**	**32 076**	**37 658**	**43 705**	**Anguilla**
Americas	28 617	28 279	29 177	34 355	39 836	Amériques
Europe	2 002	2 077	2 105	2 405	2 742	Europe
Region not specified	562	646	794	898	1 127	Région non spécifiés
Antigua and Barbuda[56]	**197 046**	**196 571**	**209 902**	**240 185**	**254 708**	**Antigua-et-Barbuda**[56]
Americas	136 918	128 771	136 255	149 743	144 877	Amériques
Europe	57 105	64 133	70 008	86 874	105 851	Europe
Region not specified	3 023	3 667	3 639	3 568	3 980	Région non spécifiés
Argentina[6]	**2 727 987**	**2 870 346**	**3 030 913**	**3 532 053**	**3 866 474**	**Argentine**[6]
Americas	2 360 626	2 462 876	2 513 991	2 933 378	3 228 136	Amériques
Europe	260 848	290 447	365 963	443 665	480 218	Europe
Region not specified	106 513	117 023	150 959	155 010	158 120	Région non spécifiés
Aruba	**432 762**	**501 324**	**541 714**	**562 034**	**582 136**	**Aruba**
Americas	387 253	443 338	485 525	506 134	528 294	Amériques
Europe	40 695	54 703	53 118	52 698	51 968	Europe
Asia, East and South East/Oceania	...	78	199	170	188	Asie, Est et Sud-Est et Océanie
Region not specified	4 814	3 205	2 872	3 032	1 686	Région non spécifiés
Australia[267]	**2 215 300**	**2 370 650**	**2 603 260**	**2 996 000**	**3 362 240**	**Australie**[267]
Africa	17 400	17 400	23 300	37 300	42 900	Afrique
Americas	316 900	336 300	323 700	345 300	361 700	Amériques
Europe	556 400	537 400	582 900	644 000	730 000	Europe
Asia, East and South East/Oceania	1 293 800	1 451 400	1 641 000	1 933 700	2 190 600	Asie, Est et Sud-Est et Océanie
Southern Asia	19 200	16 450	15 960	15 900	19 640	Asie du Sud
Western Asia	9 100	8 200	11 100	13 400	15 000	Asie occidentale

76

Tourist arrivals by region of origin [*cont.*]

Arrivées de touristes par région de provenance [*suite*]

Country or area of destination and region of origin	1990	1991	1992	1993	1994	Pays ou zone de destination et région de provenance
Region not specified	2 500	3 500	5 300	6 400	2 400	Région non spécifiés
Austria[8]	**19 011 397**	**19 091 828**	**19 098 478**	**18 256 766**	**17 893 824**	**Autriche**[8]
Africa	24 955	22 609	27 503	26 852	24 891	Afrique
Americas	1 067 420	617 796	785 532	684 482	707 257	Amériques
Europe	16 713 190	17 740 096	17 507 575	16 687 035	16 264 037	Europe
Asia, East and South East/Oceania	350 433	276 872	299 204	280 846	305 863	Asie, Est et Sud-Est et Océanie
Southern Asia	28 000	16 000	15 000	13 000	18 288	Asie du Sud
Western Asia	97 000	74 000	77 000	74 000	79 438	Asie occidentale
Region not specified	730 399	344 455	386 664	490 551	494 050	Région non spécifiés
Bahamas	**1 561 600**	**1 427 035**	**1 398 895**	**1 488 680**	**...**	**Bahamas**
Americas	1 437 765	1 287 005	1 246 165	1 326 995	...	Amériques
Europe	96 625	112 045	122 140	133 085	...	Europe
Asia, East and South East/Oceania	10 635	16 320	17 350	15 580	...	Asie, Est et Sud-Est et Océanie
Region not specified	16 575	11 665	13 240	13 020	...	Région non spécifiés
Bahrain[2]	**1 429 584**	**1 767 948**	**1 701 704**	**2 035 735**	**2 582 895**	**Bahreïn**[2]
Africa	1 499	1 310	2 428	7 414	9 097	Afrique
Americas	26 230	39 502	52 514	64 727	71 851	Amériques
Europe	83 860	83 807	110 875	140 867	156 446	Europe
Asia, East and South East/Oceania	104 654	115 497	136 649	73 440	87 371	Asie, Est et Sud-Est et Océanie
Southern Asia	108 304	135 961	144 206	227 932	256 576	Asie du Sud
Western Asia	1 100 992	1 391 804	1 254 952	1 521 320	2 001 107	Asie occidentale
Region not specified	4 045	67	80	35	447	Région non spécifiés
Bangladesh[6]	**115 369**	**113 242**	**110 475**	**126 785**	**140 122**	**Bangladesh**[6]
Africa	...	565	1 664	1 446	1 540	Afrique
Americas	8 616	7 322	9 663	10 414	12 211	Amériques
Europe	15 041	16 892	22 728	29 079	33 348	Europe
Asia, East and South East/Oceania	13 969	18 206	20 712	23 358	24 050	Asie, Est et Sud-Est et Océanie
Southern Asia	44 890	66 280	53 142	59 428	65 793	Asie du Sud
Western Asia	1 922	2 193	2 566	3 055	3 166	Asie occidentale
Region not specified	30 931	1 784	...	5	14	Région non spécifiés
Barbados	**432 067**	**394 222**	**385 472**	**395 979**	**425 632**	**Barbade**
Americas	274 021	236 898	227 422	227 771	226 762	Amériques
Europe	152 803	153 954	154 277	162 057	190 595	Europe
Asia, East and South East/Oceania	1 126	...	...	1 484	1 239	Asie, Est et Sud-Est et Océanie
Region not specified	4 117	3 370	3 773	4 667	7 036	Région non spécifiés
Belgium * [8]	**3 221 566**	**2 992 170**	**3 219 998**	**3 285 000**	**3 304 000**	**Belgique** * [8]
Africa	71 861	59 786	40 329	34 168	33 341	Afrique
Americas	213 293	162 442	196 041	175 282	187 501	Amériques
Europe	2 832 276	2 679 146	2 839 679	2 909 961	2 930 980	Europe
Asia, East and South East/Oceania	103 353	86 523	109 078	109 875	122 405	Asie, Est et Sud-Est et Océanie
Region not specified	783	4 273	34 871	55 714	29 773	Région non spécifiés
Belize[2]	**256 925**	**255 872**	**271 581**	**315 562**	**357 385**	**Belize**[2]
Americas	229 011	222 963	232 979	274 192	311 247	Amériques
Europe	23 119	27 344	34 718	37 331	41 145	Europe
Asia, East and South East/Oceania	2 270	1 825	2 010	1 942	2 981	Asie, Est et Sud-Est et Océanie
Region not specified	2 525	3 740	1 874	2 097	2 012	Région non spécifiés
Benin[2]	**248 063**	**388 949**	**401 851**	**653 079**	**542 000**	**Bénin**[2]
Africa	203 580	319 205	352 386	603 000	498 000	Afrique
Americas	4 313	6 758	4 794	4 905	4 000	Amériques
Europe	34 990	54 281	38 497	39 389	35 000	Europe

76
Tourist arrivals by region of origin [cont.]
Arrivées de touristes par région de provenance [suite]

Country or area of destination and region of origin	1990	1991	1992	1993	1994	Pays ou zone de destination et région de provenance
Asia, East and South East/Oceania	5 180	8 705	6 174	5 785	5 000	Asie, Est et Sud-Est et Océanie
Bermuda[4]	**433 776**	**384 695**	**374 497**	**412 473**	**415 996**	**Bermudes**[4]
Americas	396 776	350 268	341 671	378 660	376 997	Amériques
Europe	25 027	24 851	24 460	26 602	30 725	Europe
Asia, East and South East/Oceania	902	1 041	880	955	1 267	Asie, Est et Sud-Est et Océanie
Region not specified	11 071	8 535	7 486	6 256	7 007	Région non spécifiés
Bhutan	**1 538**	**2 106**	**2 763**	**2 984**	**3 971**	**Bhoutan**
Africa	...	...	...	...	14	Afrique
Americas	...	544	616	751	806	Amériques
Europe	...	807	1 229	1 323	1 918	Europe
Asia, East and South East/Oceania	...	722	728	725	1 217	Asie, Est et Sud-Est et Océanie
Southern Asia	...	33	...	66	16	Asie du Sud
Region not specified	1 538	...	190	119	...	Région non spécifiés
Bolivia[9]	**217 071**	**220 902**	**244 583**	**268 968**	**319 578**	**Bolivie**[9]
Africa	650	733	621	460	669	Afrique
Americas	118 190	130 635	149 818	163 474	193 821	Amériques
Europe	83 375	77 140	82 602	93 660	111 834	Europe
Asia, East and South East/Oceania	14 856	12 394	11 542	11 374	13 254	Asie, Est et Sud-Est et Océanie
Botswana[2]	**844 295**	**899 005**	**916 126**	**961 844**	**924 395**	**Botswana**[2]
Africa	759 197	813 629	817 437	863 839	831 000	Afrique
Americas	10 854	10 527	12 673	13 139	11 395	Amériques
Europe	65 473	64 921	76 674	73 872	72 000	Europe
Asia, East and South East/Oceania	8 771	9 928	9 342	10 994	10 000	Asie, Est et Sud-Est et Océanie
Brazil	**1 091 067**	**1 192 216**	**1 474 864**	**1 563 936**	**1 612 419**	**Brésil**
Africa	27 956	21 047	23 697	19 475	16 318	Afrique
Americas	682 380	827 699	1 067 324	1 221 173	1 203 681	Amériques
Europe	330 741	307 351	341 532	290 521	342 413	Europe
Asia, East and South East/Oceania	43 553	31 987	36 587	28 499	42 877	Asie, Est et Sud-Est et Océanie
Western Asia	3 381	2 375	3 213	2 008	2 332	Asie occidentale
Region not specified	3 056	1 757	2 511	2 260	4 798	Région non spécifiés
British Virgin Islands	**160 046**	**147 030**	**116 944**	**236 992**	**238 660**	**Iles Vierges britanniques**
Americas	141 164	135 169	96 468	211 742	209 086	Amériques
Europe	11 806	9 356	9 931	19 831	22 536	Europe
Region not specified	7 076	2 505	10 545	5 419	7 038	Région non spécifiés
Brunei Darussalam[2]	**376 636**	**343 944**	**411 876**	**488 909**	**...**	**Brunéi Darussalam**[2]
Americas	5 501	5 310	5 149	5 320	...	Amériques
Europe	10 836	11 724	14 611	16 229	...	Europe
Asia, East and South East/Oceania	354 016	323 332	387 682	463 503	...	Asie, Est et Sud-Est et Océanie
Southern Asia	4 680	2 422	3 059	2 497	...	Asie du Sud
Region not specified	1 603	1 156	1 375	1 360	...	Région non spécifiés
Bulgaria[2]	**10 329 537**	**6 818 449**	**6 123 844**	**8 302 472**	**10 068 181**	**Bulgarie**[2]
Africa	14 001	13 617	16 124	12 274	8 532	Afrique
Americas	17 195	18 153	26 394	26 591	29 641	Amériques
Europe	10 162 128	6 000 815	5 948 922	7 939 655	9 730 612	Europe
Asia, East and South East/Oceania	16 065	11 538	15 819	15 098	16 005	Asie, Est et Sud-Est et Océanie
Southern Asia	55 862	48 383	35 926	12 267	12 144	Asie du Sud
Western Asia	39 951	41 582	52 578	40 779	48 060	Asie occidentale
Region not specified	24 335	684 361	28 081	255 808	223 187	Région non spécifiés
Burkina Faso[1]	**73 814**	**80 100**	**92 118**	**111 115**	**132 551**	**Burkina Faso**[1]
Africa	31 058	32 528	37 150	45 741	56 671	Afrique

76
Tourist arrivals by region of origin [*cont.*]
Arrivées de touristes par région de provenance [*suite*]

Country or area of destination and region of origin	1990	1991	1992	1993	1994	Pays ou zone de destination et région de provenance
Americas	4 158	5 557	5 861	6 650	8 609	Amériques
Europe	33 211	36 242	38 425	46 844	59 436	Europe
Asia, East and South East/Oceania	784	1 223	1 401	1 743	3 636	Asie, Est et Sud-Est et Océanie
Western Asia	210	321	640	595	...	Asie occidentale
Region not specified	4 393	4 229	8 641	9 542	4 199	Région non spécifiés
Burundi[3]	**109 418**	**125 000**	**86 000**	**75 000**	**29 316**	**Burundi**[3]
Africa	51 426	59 000	41 000	36 000	14 072	Afrique
Americas	6 564	8 000	6 000	5 250	2 052	Amériques
Europe	41 579	47 000	32 000	27 750	10 847	Europe
Asia, East and South East/Oceania	9 849	10 000	7 000	6 000	2 345	Asie, Est et Sud-Est et Océanie
Region not specified	...	1 000	...	...	...	Région non spécifiés
Cambodia[4]	**17 000**	**25 000**	**88 000**	**118 183**	**176 617**	**Cambodge**[4]
Americas	...	...	...	9 072	24 000	Amériques
Europe	...	...	...	27 741	36 603	Europe
Asia, East and South East/Oceania	...	...	...	80 917	114 014	Asie, Est et Sud-Est et Océanie
Western Asia	...	...	...	453	2 000	Asie occidentale
Region not specified	17 000	25 000	88 000	...	...	Région non spécifiés
Cameroon[1]	**89 094**	**83 826**	**62 057**	**81 350**	**...**	**Cameroun**[1]
Africa	24 705	24 539	14 851	21 654	...	Afrique
Americas	8 538	6 642	4 595	6 218	...	Amériques
Europe	51 416	48 729	40 702	50 069	...	Europe
Asia, East and South East/Oceania	2 121	2 078	682	1 508	...	Asie, Est et Sud-Est et Océanie
Western Asia	1 519	975	583	1 069	...	Asie occidentale
Region not specified	795	863	644	832	...	Région non spécifiés
Canada	**15 209 200**	**14 912 100**	**14 740 800**	**15 105 100**	**15 971 300**	**Canada**
Africa	49 600	46 100	47 600	48 700	50 200	Afrique
Americas	12 523 000	12 267 700	12 065 900	12 283 400	12 819 700	Amériques
Europe	1 685 600	1 695 200	1 723 900	1 856 400	1 993 900	Europe
Asia, East and South East/Oceania	817 200	781 800	777 000	788 000	962 300	Asie, Est et Sud-Est et Océanie
Southern Asia	63 400	55 500	52 200	49 700	56 400	Asie du Sud
Western Asia	7 800	7 100	8 200	9 200	10 800	Asie occidentale
Region not specified	62 600	58 700	66 000	69 700	78 000	Région non spécifiés
Cayman Islands[4]	**253 158**	**237 351**	**241 843**	**287 277**	**341 491**	**Iles Caïmanes**[4]
Americas	238 103	218 712	217 261	259 553	301 860	Amériques
Europe	13 134	15 249	17 961	20 465	30 549	Europe
Asia, East and South East/Oceania	1 439	1 065	1 242	1 580	1 269	Asie, Est et Sud-Est et Océanie
Region not specified	482	2 325	5 379	5 679	7 813	Région non spécifiés
Chad	**9 156**[2]	**20 501**[2]	**16 991**[2]	**21 227**[2]	**18 933**[1]	**Tchad**
Africa	7 607	10 720	10 145	12 678	6 586	Afrique
Americas	120	1 229	1 143	1 428	2 263	Amériques
Europe	1 294	8 340	5 485	6 852	9 918	Europe
Asia, East and South East/Oceania	135	206	218	269	67	Asie, Est et Sud-Est et Océanie
Western Asia	...	...	...	...	99	Asie occidentale
Region not specified	...	6	...	...	...	Région non spécifiés
Chile	**942 892**	**1 349 149**	**1 283 287**	**1 412 495**	**1 622 766**	**Chili**
Americas	817 808	1 220 250	1 151 810	1 251 008	1 427 762	Amériques
Europe	97 354	103 354	102 219	133 141	162 029	Europe
Asia, East and South East/Oceania	13 706	13 938	5 889	7 952	16 791	Asie, Est et Sud-Est et Océanie
Region not specified	14 024	11 607	23 369	20 394	16 184	Région non spécifiés
China[6 10]		**1 747 315**	**2 710 103**	**4 006 427**	**4 655 857**	**5 182 060**	**Chine**[6 10]

76
Tourist arrivals by region of origin [cont.]
Arrivées de touristes par région de provenance [suite]

Country or area of destination and region of origin	1990	1991	1992	1993	1994	Pays ou zone de destination et région de provenance
Africa	11 138	15 334	23 589	24 000	24 685	Afrique
Americas	304 187	418 498	495 404	564 087	633 111	Amériques
Europe	450 639	795 754	1 529 787	1 612 791	1 479 622	Europe
Asia, East and South East/Oceania	912 856	1 372 517	1 844 945	2 329 836	2 908 999	Asie, Est et Sud-Est et Océanie
Southern Asia	56 105	87 049	89 035	103 059	105 982	Asie du Sud
Western Asia	6 773	6 835	12 812	10 089	12 640	Asie occidentale
Region not specified	5 617	14 116	10 855	11 995	17 021	Région non spécifiés
Colombia[3]	**812 796**	**856 862**	**1 075 891**	**1 047 249**	**...**	**Colombie**[3]
Americas	766 276	799 442	993 512	961 797	...	Amériques
Europe	43 331	53 323	76 320	79 124	...	Europe
Asia, East and South East/Oceania	2 588	3 367	3 950	4 631	...	Asie, Est et Sud-Est et Océanie
Southern Asia	49	44	264	224	...	Asie du Sud
Western Asia	54	107	147	277	...	Asie occidentale
Region not specified	498	579	1 698	1 196	...	Région non spécifiés
Comoros[4]	**7 627**	**16 942**	**18 921**	**23 671**	**27 061**	**Comores**[4]
Africa	1 526	6 641	7 656	9 545	7 958	Afrique
Americas	176	247	222	318	285	Amériques
Europe	5 520	9 684	10 381	13 012	18 405	Europe
Asia, East and South East/Oceania	297	370	662	796	413	Asie, Est et Sud-Est et Océanie
Region not specified	108	...	...	...	...	Région non spécifiés
Congo[11]	**32 547**	**32 945**	**36 072**	**34 027**	**30 338**	**Congo**[11]
Africa	12 670	11 261	14 533	13 709	12 223	Afrique
Americas	1 665	1 910	2 257	2 129	1 898	Amériques
Europe	17 534	18 809	17 939	16 922	15 087	Europe
Region not specified	678	965	1 343	1 267	1 130	Région non spécifiés
Cook Islands[12]	**34 218**	**39 984**	**50 009**	**52 868**	**57 321**	**Iles Cook**[12]
Americas	6 762	8 325	9 716	11 816	11 707	Amériques
Europe	6 015	8 417	13 702	17 524	20 310	Europe
Asia, East and South East/Oceania	21 330	23 126	26 418	23 348	25 005	Asie, Est et Sud-Est et Océanie
Region not specified	111	116	173	180	299	Région non spécifiés
Costa Rica	**435 037**	**504 649**	**610 591**	**684 005**	**761 448**	**Costa Rica**
Africa	244	299	314	468	491	Afrique
Americas	367 964	425 505	509 852	555 616	615 454	Amériques
Europe	58 738	69 087	90 320	115 871	131 737	Europe
Asia, East and South East/Oceania	6 711	7 278	8 144	9 669	10 594	Asie, Est et Sud-Est et Océanie
Region not specified	1 380	2 480	1 961	2 381	3 172	Région non spécifiés
Côte d'Ivoire[4]	**196 528**	**200 000**	**217 000**	**159 262**	**156 632**	**Côte d'Ivoire**[4]
Africa	104 752	100 587	118 982	88 441	85 659	Afrique
Americas	10 622	11 000	17 014	11 418	12 331	Amériques
Europe	73 212	80 990	73 391	53 942	53 397	Europe
Asia, East and South East/Oceania	3 912	3 407	3 954	2 027	2 109	Asie, Est et Sud-Est et Océanie
Southern Asia	444	393	803	597	500	Asie du Sud
Western Asia	3 586	3 623	2 856	1 681	1 509	Asie occidentale
Region not specified	...	...	...	1 156	1 127	Région non spécifiés
Croatia[8]	**7 049 128**	**1 346 320**	**1 270 855**	**1 520 980**	**2 292 758**	**Croatie**[8]
Americas	163 928	22 996	15 472	20 896	27 178	Amériques
Europe	6 805 511	1 281 460	1 239 292	1 479 808	2 241 434	Europe
Asia, East and South East/Oceania	27 418	5 411	1 622	2 286	4 795	Asie, Est et Sud-Est et Océanie
Region not specified	52 271	36 453	14 469	17 990	19 351	Région non spécifiés
Cuba[2]	**340 329**	**424 041**	**460 610**	**546 023**	**617 284**	**Cuba**[2]

76
Tourist arrivals by region of origin [*cont.*]
Arrivées de touristes par région de provenance [*suite*]

Country or area of destination and region of origin	1990	1991	1992	1993	1994	Pays ou zone de destination et région de provenance
Africa	2 395	1 880	2 979	1 674	...	Afrique
Americas	163 795	207 359	226 135	288 051	268 514	Amériques
Europe	168 788	196 767	218 363	246 084	300 807	Europe
Asia, East and South East/Oceania	1 858	1 505	1 661	1 876	...	Asie, Est et Sud-Est et Océanie
Region not specified	3 493	16 530	11 472	8 338	47 963	Région non spécifiés
Cyprus	**1 561 479**	**1 385 129**	**1 991 000**	**1 841 000**	**2 069 000**	**Chypre**
Africa	19 000	17 000	20 810	14 290	10 000	Afrique
Americas	22 197	30 000	38 830	36 210	41 000	Amériques
Europe	1 354 342	1 200 313	1 764 750	1 653 575	1 883 000	Europe
Western Asia	158 994	130 000	114 230	105 000	111 000	Asie occidentale
Region not specified	6 946	7 816	52 380	31 925	24 000	Région non spécifiés
former Czechoslovakia†[2]	**46 586 782**	**64 801 030**	**83 477 428**	**..**	**..**	**anc. Tchécoslovaquie†[2]**
Europe	40 002 463	47 105 508	63 492 132	..	..	Europe
Region not specified	6 584 319	17 695 522	19 985 296	..	..	Région non spécifiés
Denmark * [1]	**1 508 167**	**1 656 417**	**1 716 110**	**1 642 500**	**1 647 860**	**Danemark * [1]**
Americas	110 972	80 944	84 778	81 111	84 861	Amériques
Europe	1 260 806	1 451 640	1 499 582	1 422 055	1 418 805	Europe
Asia, East and South East/Oceania	30 000	25 944	30 806	27 778	28 694	Asie, Est et Sud-Est et Océanie
Region not specified	106 389	97 889	100 944	111 556	115 500	Région non spécifiés
Dominica	**45 087**	**46 312**	**46 959**	**51 937**	**56 522**	**Dominique**
Americas	34 919	35 651	35 864	39 637	43 043	Amériques
Europe	9 329	9 396	9 940	11 550	12 675	Europe
Asia, East and South East/Oceania	...	21	12	28	43	Asie, Est et Sud-Est et Océanie
Region not specified	839	1 244	1 143	722	761	Région non spécifiés
Dominican Republic[2 3]	**1 305 361**	**1 180 819**	**1 415 147**	**1 608 579**	**1 716 789**	**Rép. dominicaine[2 3]**
Region not specified	1 305 361	1 180 819	1 415 147	1 608 579	1 716 789	Région non spécifiés
Ecuador[2 6]	**362 072**	**364 585**	**403 242**	**471 367**	**481 547**	**Equateur[2 6]**
Africa	289	383	446	525	566	Afrique
Americas	292 433	295 819	323 233	378 568	387 923	Amériques
Europe	60 314	58 844	68 337	80 067	80 343	Europe
Asia, East and South East/Oceania	8 992	9 513	11 191	12 194	12 702	Asie, Est et Sud-Est et Océanie
Region not specified	44	26	35	13	13	Région non spécifiés
Egypt[2]	**2 600 117**	**2 214 277**	**3 206 940**	**2 507 762**	**2 581 988**	**Egypte[2]**
Africa	326 584	172 572	204 138	187 148	152 872	Afrique
Americas	179 144	119 863	224 479	187 476	182 378	Amériques
Europe	1 123 161	889 950	1 664 906	1 205 740	1 243 629	Europe
Asia, East and South East/Oceania	125 905	87 522	162 156	131 389	160 220	Asie, Est et Sud-Est et Océanie
Southern Asia	18 275	12 238	25 148	26 465	20 732	Asie du Sud
Western Asia	826 218	931 248	924 897	767 307	819 142	Asie occidentale
Region not specified	830	884	1 216	2 237	3 015	Région non spécifiés
El Salvador[6]	**194 268**	**198 918**	**314 482**	**267 425**	**181 332**	**El Salvador[6]**
Africa	...	7	88	86	86	Afrique
Americas	182 546	184 645	290 646	242 547	157 903	Amériques
Europe	10 002	12 333	20 712	21 421	19 923	Europe
Asia, East and South East/Oceania	1 463	1 931	3 027	3 358	3 418	Asie, Est et Sud-Est et Océanie
Western Asia	...	2	9	13	2	Asie occidentale
Region not specified	257	...	...	...	...	Région non spécifiés
Ethiopia[3 13]	**79 346**	**81 581**	**83 213**	**93 072**	**97 577**	**Ethiopie[3 13]**
Africa	24 073	24 777	25 290	28 386	27 809	Afrique
Americas	8 144	8 352	8 513	9 495	11 807	Amériques

76
Tourist arrivals by region of origin [*cont.*]
Arrivées de touristes par région de provenance [*suite*]

Country or area of destination and region of origin	1990	1991	1992	1993	1994	Pays ou zone de destination et région de provenance
Europe	21 069	21 582	21 993	24 570	31 614	Europe
Asia, East and South East/Oceania	5 306	5 454	5 515	6 143	7 318	Asie, Est et Sud-Est et Océanie
Southern Asia	2 088	2 136	2 181	2 419	2 245	Asie du Sud
Western Asia	7 504	7 746	7 916	8 842	6 831	Asie occidentale
Region not specified	11 162	11 534	11 805	13 217	9 953	Région non spécifiés
Fiji [6]	**278 996**	**259 350**	**278 534**	**287 462**	**318 874**	**Fidji** [6]
Americas	55 366	47 084	47 404	55 004	57 369	Amériques
Europe	43 984	42 820	46 308	50 019	54 919	Europe
Asia, East and South East/Oceania	178 369	168 705	183 873	181 306	205 110	Asie, Est et Sud-Est et Océanie
Region not specified	1 277	741	949	1 133	1 476	Région non spécifiés
Finland * [1]	**649 509**	**579 168**	**590 199**	**680 980**	**751 442**	**Finlande *** [1]
Africa	5 100	3 000	3 010	1 611	1 861	Afrique
Americas	64 562	47 472	48 358	52 355	54 097	Amériques
Europe	528 089	482 972	480 425	561 042	624 693	Europe
Asia, East and South East/Oceania	24 055	21 067	21 145	33 542	42 393	Asie, Est et Sud-Est et Océanie
Southern Asia	...	...	...	1 920	2 408	Asie du Sud
Western Asia	...	...	...	1 129	1 362	Asie occidentale
Region not specified	27 703	24 657	37 261	29 381	24 628	Région non spécifiés
France [14]	**52 785 000**	**55 041 000**	**59 740 000**	**60 565 000**	**61 312 000**	**France** [14]
Africa	1 500 000	1 232 000	...	...	1 068 000	Afrique
Americas	3 300 000	2 748 000	2 604 000	2 669 000	3 914 000	Amériques
Europe	46 835 000	49 616 000	52 537 000	53 176 000	52 921 000	Europe
Asia, East and South East/Oceania	900 000	941 000	449 000	326 000	1 702 000	Asie, Est et Sud-Est et Océanie
Western Asia	250 000	...	...	...	336 000	Asie occidentale
Region not specified	...	504 000	4 150 000	4 394 000	1 371 000	Région non spécifiés
French Polynesia [6]	**132 361**	**120 938**	**123 619**	**147 847**	**166 086**	**Polynésie française** [6]
Africa	150	132	145	195	178	Afrique
Americas	51 592	44 144	46 098	55 878	55 561	Amériques
Europe	46 615	44 508	46 078	58 157	71 078	Europe
Asia, East and South East/Oceania	33 655	31 827	30 865	33 246	38 587	Asie, Est et Sud-Est et Océanie
Southern Asia	37	27	28	18	144	Asie du Sud
Western Asia	103	108	115	193	150	Asie occidentale
Region not specified	209	192	290	160	388	Région non spécifiés
Gabon	**108 000**	**128 000**	**133 000**	**115 000**	**...**	**Gabon**
Africa	14 000	19 900	21 400	22 000	...	Afrique
Americas	6 200	6 400	6 600	...	...	Amériques
Europe	81 400	97 600	99 700	93 000	...	Europe
Asia, East and South East/Oceania	6 400	4 100	5 300	...	...	Asie, Est et Sud-Est et Océanie
Gambia	**101 419**	**65 881**	**63 940**	**89 997**	**78 000**	**Gambie**
Africa	39 000	677	968	1 444	1 887	Afrique
Americas	581	444	918	868	627	Amériques
Europe	61 000	62 810	59 976	85 148	71 793	Europe
Asia, East and South East/Oceania	78	...	...	...	...	Asie, Est et Sud-Est et Océanie
Region not specified	760	1 950	2 078	2 537	3 693	Région non spécifiés
Germany † [8 15 16]	**15 626 858**	**14 294 604**	**15 913 214**	**14 347 710**	**14 493 812**	**Allemagne†** [8 15 16]
Africa	180 461	140 803	149 816	142 338	122 206	Afrique
Americas	2 871 511	1 986 074	2 153 047	1 898 706	1 867 609	Amériques
Europe	10 934 518	10 700 494	11 884 139	10 692 563	10 646 280	Europe
Asia, East and South East/Oceania	1 411 521	1 214 491	1 378 983	1 263 462	1 405 353	Asie, Est et Sud-Est et Océanie
Western Asia	...	...	...	...	57 259	Asie occidentale

76
Tourist arrivals by region of origin [*cont.*]
Arrivées de touristes par région de provenance [*suite*]

Country or area of destination and region of origin	1990	1991	1992	1993	1994	Pays ou zone de destination et région de provenance
Region not specified	228 847	252 742	347 229	350 641	395 105	Région non spécifiés
Ghana	**145 780**	**172 464**	**213 316**	...	...	**Ghana**
Africa	45 797	69 048	72 579	...	...	Afrique
Americas	11 823	15 573	17 915	...	...	Amériques
Europe	40 687	47 152	52 879	...	...	Europe
Asia, East and South East/Oceania	7 770	7 416	10 260	...	...	Asie, Est et Sud-Est et Océanie
Western Asia	773	1 311	1 618	...	...	Asie occidentale
Region not specified	38 930	31 964	58 065	...	...	Région non spécifiés
Greece[17]	**8 873 310**	**8 036 127**	**9 331 360**	**9 412 823**	**10 712 810**	**Grèce**[17]
Africa	44 000	31 475	31 604	28 929	24 594	Afrique
Americas	382 623	255 770	378 191	343 344	360 062	Amériques
Europe	8 109 849	7 525 649	8 628 436	8 782 981	10 058 266	Europe
Asia, East and South East/Oceania	274 932	177 816	242 840	207 407	225 557	Asie, Est et Sud-Est et Océanie
Southern Asia	4 451	4 226	6 794	7 615	6 458	Asie du Sud
Western Asia	57 455	41 191	43 495	42 547	37 873	Asie occidentale
Grenada[3]	**76 447**	**85 000**	**87 554**	**93 919**	**108 957**	**Grenade**[3]
Americas	40 225	44 093	44 974	48 805	50 575	Amériques
Europe	16 778	22 127	23 687	25 296	37 533	Europe
Asia, East and South East/Oceania	769	657	476	839	680	Asie, Est et Sud-Est et Océanie
Western Asia	28	20	32	31	99	Asie occidentale
Region not specified	18 647	18 103	18 385	18 948	20 070	Région non spécifiés
Guadeloupe[1]	**125 663**	**132 253**	**121 278**	**124 321**	**144 568**	**Guadeloupe**[1]
Americas	16 608	11 263	10 576	12 918	12 803	Amériques
Europe	108 564	120 469	110 120	110 901	131 192	Europe
Region not specified	491	521	582	502	573	Région non spécifiés
Guam[5]	**780 404**	**737 260**	**876 742**	**784 018**	**1 086 720**	**Guam**[5]
Americas	52 199	50 897	60 442	61 895	66 847	Amériques
Europe	2 643	1 998	2 643	2 278	...	Europe
Asia, East and South East/Oceania	710 627	671 837	798 831	709 983	993 467	Asie, Est et Sud-Est et Océanie
Region not specified	14 935	12 528	14 826	9 862	26 406	Région non spécifiés
Guatemala	**508 514**	**512 620**	**541 025**	**561 917**	**537 374**	**Guatemala**
Americas	411 871	405 595	419 051	431 673	410 050	Amériques
Europe	84 585	93 630	105 747	115 883	112 442	Europe
Asia, East and South East/Oceania	8 202	9 400	10 741	11 821	12 297	Asie, Est et Sud-Est et Océanie
Southern Asia	246	241	546	536	255	Asie du Sud
Western Asia	281	268	186	206	300	Asie occidentale
Region not specified	3 329	3 486	4 754	1 798	2 030	Région non spécifiés
Guyana[4]	...	...	**74 879**	**107 127**	**112 824**	**Guyana**[4]
Americas	...	...	62 972	97 336	102 834	Amériques
Europe	...	...	6 763	7 892	8 041	Europe
Region not specified	...	...	5 144	1 899	1 949	Région non spécifiés
Haiti	**120 000**	**119 000**	**89 500**	**76 700**	**70 000**	**Haïti**
Americas	107 000	110 900	83 500	70 400	64 500	Amériques
Europe	10 000	7 600	5 700	6 000	5 300	Europe
Region not specified	3 000	500	300	300	200	Région non spécifiés
Honduras[2]	**290 353**	**226 121**	**243 544**	**261 475**	**290 237**	**Honduras**[2]
Africa	101	125	92	145	444	Afrique
Americas	268 329	201 464	217 576	227 437	248 125	Amériques
Europe	18 049	20 277	21 049	27 151	34 791	Europe
Asia, East and South East/Oceania	3 874	4 255	4 827	6 737	6 835	Asie, Est et Sud-Est et Océanie

76
Tourist arrivals by region of origin [*cont.*]
Arrivées de touristes par région de provenance [*suite*]

Country or area of destination and region of origin	1990	1991	1992	1993	1994	Pays ou zone de destination et région de provenance
Region not specified	...	...	...	5	42	Région non spécifiés
Hong Kong[2]	**6 580 850**	**6 795 413**	**8 010 524**	**8 937 500**	**9 331 156**	**Hong-kong[2]**
Africa	46 958	55 355	56 101	65 532	65 861	Afrique
Americas	807 649	822 394	924 223	1 008 289	1 026 395	Amériques
Europe	755 298	809 722	962 322	1 078 786	1 157 542	Europe
Asia, East and South East/Oceania	4 814 284	4 947 045	5 895 152	6 625 324	6 914 323	Asie, Est et Sud-Est et Océanie
Southern Asia	138 515	142 529	152 356	136 948	141 042	Asie du Sud
Western Asia	13 510	14 313	17 895	18 895	19 343	Asie occidentale
Region not specified	4 636	4 055	2 475	3 726	6 650	Région non spécifiés
Hungary[6 18]	**20 510 000**	**21 860 000**	**20 188 000**	**22 804 000**	**21 425 000**	**Hongrie[6 18]**
Africa	23 000	17 000	20 000	20 000	20 000	Afrique
Americas	239 000	236 000	304 000	317 000	310 000	Amériques
Europe	20 158 000	21 431 000	19 688 000	22 333 000	20 889 000	Europe
Asia, East and South East/Oceania	90 000	175 000	176 000	134 000	204 000	Asie, Est et Sud-Est et Océanie
Region not specified	...	1 000	...	...	2 000	Région non spécifiés
Iceland	**141 718**	**143 459**	**142 560**	**157 326**	**179 241**	**Islande**
Africa	329	344	297	251	300	Afrique
Americas	24 138	23 901	23 319	26 973	27 674	Amériques
Europe	114 364	116 332	115 608	125 759	145 467	Europe
Asia, East and South East/Oceania	2 343	2 668	3 029	3 922	5 412	Asie, Est et Sud-Est et Océanie
Southern Asia	116	123	138	176	152	Asie du Sud
Western Asia	35	62	78	105	99	Asie occidentale
Region not specified	393	29	91	140	137	Région non spécifiés
India[6]	**1 707 158**	**1 677 508**	**1 867 651**	**1 764 830**	**1 886 433**	**Inde[6]**
Africa	58 154	59 616	68 154	59 526	61 315	Afrique
Americas	176 995	165 321	208 211	219 527	244 743	Amériques
Europe	630 049	562 731	658 496	683 579	732 289	Europe
Asia, East and South East/Oceania	206 958	176 705	214 242	214 269	250 400	Asie, Est et Sud-Est et Océanie
Southern Asia	520 920	591 210	579 079	466 399	480 986	Asie du Sud
Western Asia	112 470	118 924	135 957	118 430	115 506	Asie occidentale
Region not specified	1 612	3 001	3 512	3 100	1 194	Région non spécifiés
Indonesia	**2 177 566**	**2 569 870**	**3 064 161**	**3 403 138**	**4 006 312**	**Indonésie**
Africa	1 973	3 095	3 263	6 558	9 957	Afrique
Americas	127 278	129 335	157 872	190 310	211 529	Amériques
Europe	484 383	481 684	561 657	659 726	798 870	Europe
Asia, East and South East/Oceania	1 536 557	1 926 663	2 302 369	2 490 260	2 919 596	Asie, Est et Sud-Est et Océanie
Southern Asia	14 415	16 324	23 825	26 688	35 101	Asie du Sud
Western Asia	12 960	12 769	15 175	29 596	31 259	Asie occidentale
Iran, Islamic Rep. of	**153 615**	**212 096**	**278 553**	**304 069**	**362 032**	**Iran, Rép. islamique d'**
Africa	1 442	1 804	4 264	2 955	2 447	Afrique
Americas	1 392	2 121	3 904	3 531	2 652	Amériques
Europe	37 073	61 205	122 699	131 702	166 225	Europe
Asia, East and South East/Oceania	11 767	12 237	16 815	13 367	14 864	Asie, Est et Sud-Est et Océanie
Southern Asia	83 308	97 755	83 429	98 788	122 215	Asie du Sud
Western Asia	18 620	36 965	47 406	53 714	53 624	Asie occidentale
Region not specified	13	9	36	12	5	Région non spécifiés
Iraq[2]	**747 625**	**267 743**	**504 473**	**...**	**...**	**Iraq[2]**
Africa	10 470	3 430	15 124	...	...	Afrique
Americas	6 955	1 123	1 924	...	...	Amériques

76
Tourist arrivals by region of origin [cont.]
Arrivées de touristes par région de provenance [suite]

Country or area of destination and region of origin	1990	1991	1992	1993	1994	Pays ou zone de destination et région de provenance
Europe	55 104	4 737	6 086	...	...	Europe
Asia, East and South East/Oceania	11 159	3 955	2 062	...	...	Asie, Est et Sud-Est et Océanie
Southern Asia	33 107	1 316	2 924	...	...	Asie du Sud
Western Asia	597 013	194 646	474 291	...	...	Asie occidentale
Region not specified	33 817	58 536	2 062	...	...	Région non spécifiés
Ireland[6]	**3 666 000**	**3 571 000**	**3 724 000**	**3 888 000**	**4 309 000**	**Irlande[6]**
Americas	443 000	356 000	417 000	422 000	494 000	Amériques
Europe	3 099 000	3 107 000	3 189 000	3 342 000	3 656 000	Europe
Asia, East and South East/Oceania	69 000	54 000	57 000	56 000	68 000	Asie, Est et Sud-Est et Océanie
Region not specified	55 000	54 000	61 000	68 000	91 000	Région non spécifiés
Israel[6]	**1 063 406**	**943 259**	**1 509 520**	**1 655 642**	**1 838 703**	**Israël[6]**
Africa	26 571	20 712	32 271	36 687	42 642	Afrique
Americas	314 216	285 722	440 580	470 796	490 658	Amériques
Europe	625 178	547 453	906 468	997 521	1 121 122	Europe
Asia, East and South East/Oceania	36 628	31 750	57 221	62 722	77 208	Asie, Est et Sud-Est et Océanie
Southern Asia	4 018	2 289	3 834	5 653	8 027	Asie du Sud
Western Asia	52 287	50 350	60 747	71 342	86 465	Asie occidentale
Region not specified	4 508	4 983	8 399	10 921	12 581	Région non spécifiés
Italy[5]	**20 862 965**	**20 241 217**	**20 424 982**	**21 025 353**	**24 663 870**	**Italie[5]**
Africa	52 300	42 592	39 958	46 538	43 527	Afrique
Americas	3 031 405	2 283 300	2 810 758	2 930 963	3 403 719	Amériques
Europe	15 686 006	16 078 258	15 350 782	15 624 015	18 375 293	Europe
Asia, East and South East/Oceania	1 084 923	924 599	1 201 218	1 344 342	1 615 904	Asie, Est et Sud-Est et Océanie
Western Asia	107 207	98 745	98 020	107 568	112 317	Asie occidentale
Region not specified	901 124	813 723	924 246	971 927	1 113 110	Région non spécifiés
Jamaica	**840 777**	**844 607**	**909 010**	**978 715**	**976 635**	**Jamaïque**
Africa	461	676	908	999	856	Afrique
Americas	709 918	669 036	700 413	752 655	766 923	Amériques
Europe	121 049	159 849	187 874	202 362	183 172	Europe
Asia, East and South East/Oceania	7 091	12 638	17 052	19 778	23 359	Asie, Est et Sud-Est et Océanie
Southern Asia	359	372	304	445	364	Asie du Sud
Region not specified	1 899	2 036	2 459	2 476	1 961	Région non spécifiés
Japan[26]	**3 235 860**	**3 532 651**	**3 581 540**	**3 410 447**	**3 468 055**	**Japon[26]**
Africa	10 392	11 510	10 816	11 096	10 459	Afrique
Americas	711 410	727 072	717 762	680 429	681 482	Amériques
Europe	527 810	532 995	545 403	527 931	536 692	Europe
Asia, East and South East/Oceania	1 903 099	2 159 126	2 241 154	2 142 289	2 191 810	Asie, Est et Sud-Est et Océanie
Southern Asia	78 209	97 936	62 234	44 325	42 833	Asie du Sud
Western Asia	2 178	1 893	2 340	2 503	2 729	Asie occidentale
Region not specified	2 762	2 119	1 831	1 874	2 050	Région non spécifiés
Jordan[2]	**2 633 262**	**2 227 688**	**3 242 985**	**3 098 938**	**3 224 752**	**Jordanie[2]**
Africa	64 613	43 620	69 927	91 707	46 098	Afrique
Americas	38 538	23 978	39 250	51 512	69 878	Amériques
Europe	206 125	194 566	284 032	307 687	312 998	Europe
Asia, East and South East/Oceania	56 112	16 462	25 920	35 822	43 439	Asie, Est et Sud-Est et Océanie
Southern Asia	252 596	24 333	25 772	20 942	30 881	Asie du Sud
Western Asia	2 013 911	1 920 340	2 793 236	2 586 486	2 716 188	Asie occidentale
Region not specified	1 367	4 389	4 848	4 782	5 270	Région non spécifiés
Kenya[6 18]	**814 400**	**817 550**	**782 000**	**826 000**	**863 400**	**Kenya[6 18]**
Africa	142 100	228 020	213 000	227 000	246 700	Afrique

76
Tourist arrivals by region of origin [*cont.*]
Arrivées de touristes par région de provenance [*suite*]

Country or area of destination and region of origin	1990	1991	1992	1993	1994	Pays ou zone de destination et région de provenance
Americas	77 700	67 830	67 000	70 774	72 100	Amériques
Europe	427 400	470 010	443 000	477 479	481 200	Europe
Asia, East and South East/Oceania	31 400	33 290	25 302	30 263	44 900	Asie, Est et Sud-Est et Océanie
Southern Asia	12 500	17 650	16 914	19 586	14 500	Asie du Sud
Region not specified	123 300	750	16 784	898	4 000	Région non spécifiés
Kiribati[2]	**3 332**	**2 935**	**3 747**	**4 225**	**3 888**	**Kiribati**[2]
Americas	642	372	572	971	835	Amériques
Europe	10	64	137	191	190	Europe
Asia, East and South East/Oceania	2 261	2 202	2 613	2 679	2 565	Asie, Est et Sud-Est et Océanie
Region not specified	419	297	425	384	298	Région non spécifiés
Korea, Republic of[2 3]	**2 958 839**	**3 196 340**	**3 231 081**	**3 331 226**	**3 580 024**	**Corée, République de**[2 3]
Africa	5 123	6 856	7 912	6 346	7 626	Afrique
Americas	370 143	358 570	375 706	370 688	382 096	Amériques
Europe	199 445	255 352	286 927	331 762	388 273	Europe
Asia, East and South East/Oceania	1 996 645	2 173 857	2 158 409	2 221 003	2 397 260	Asie, Est et Sud-Est et Océanie
Southern Asia	58 827	82 535	83 040	67 207	74 981	Asie du Sud
Western Asia	5 415	5 716	6 013	7 071	9 623	Asie occidentale
Region not specified	323 241	313 454	313 074	327 149	320 165	Région non spécifiés
Kuwait[2]	...	...	**1 568 221**	**1 128 321**	...	**Koweït**[2]
Africa	...	...	490	140 366	...	Afrique
Americas	...	...	17 506	20 798	...	Amériques
Europe	...	...	22 682	41 980	...	Europe
Asia, East and South East/Oceania	...	...	235 123	439 711	...	Asie, Est et Sud-Est et Océanie
Western Asia	...	...	1 292 361	485 443	...	Asie occidentale
Region not specified	...	...	59	23	...	Région non spécifiés
Lebanon	...	...	**177 503**	**265 710**	**335 181**	**Liban**
Africa	...	...	7 193	9 682	12 133	Afrique
Americas	...	...	26 468	34 301	40 565	Amériques
Europe	...	...	56 721	86 207	117 717	Europe
Asia, East and South East/Oceania	...	...	20 052	23 783	26 513	Asie, Est et Sud-Est et Océanie
Southern Asia	...	...	11 993	15 684	19 601	Asie du Sud
Western Asia	...	...	55 076	96 053	118 652	Asie occidentale
Lesotho[2]	**242 456**	**357 458**	**416 882**	**348 943**	**253 310**	**Lesotho**[2]
Africa	235 845	349 437	408 569	341 480	247 279	Afrique
Americas	1 570	1 608	1 609	1 236	1 021	Amériques
Europe	3 970	5 246	5 499	4 667	4 014	Europe
Asia, East and South East/Oceania	1 026	1 167	1 205	1 560	996	Asie, Est et Sud-Est et Océanie
Southern Asia	45	...	...	...	...	Asie du Sud
Libyan Arab Jamah.[2]	...	...	**251 515**	**658 551**	**1 493 737**	**Jamah. arabe libyenne**[2]
Africa	...	...	134 315	232 758	1 027 628	Afrique
Americas	...	...	...	2 411	1 983	Amériques
Europe	...	...	...	34 302	33 270	Europe
Asia, East and South East/Oceania	...	...	...	9 552	10 312	Asie, Est et Sud-Est et Océanie
Southern Asia	...	...	...	...	4 478	Asie du Sud
Western Asia	...	...	22 126	365 485	416 066	Asie occidentale
Region not specified	...	...	95 074	14 043	...	Région non spécifiés
Liechtenstein[1]	**77 528**	**71 046**	**71 710**	**64 717**	**61 741**	**Liechtenstein**[1]
Africa	249	169	196	241	164	Afrique
Americas	10 984	6 824	7 377	6 047	5 780	Amériques
Europe	63 476	61 638	61 400	56 539	53 998	Europe

76
Tourist arrivals by region of origin [*cont.*]
Arrivées de touristes par région de provenance [*suite*]

Country or area of destination and region of origin	1990	1991	1992	1993	1994	Pays ou zone de destination et région de provenance
Asia, East and South East/Oceania	2 630	2 237	2 650	1 862	1 736	Asie, Est et Sud-Est et Océanie
Region not specified	189	178	87	28	63	Région non spécifiés
Lithuania[1]	..	...	**319 211**	**284 172**	**196 949**	**Lituanie**[1]
Africa	..	...	120	139	169	Afrique
Americas	..	...	4 325	11 070	12 973	Amériques
Europe	..	...	313 601	269 185	179 815	Europe
Asia, East and South East/Oceania	..	...	1 165	3 778	3 992	Asie, Est et Sud-Est et Océanie
Luxembourg[8]	**820 476**	**861 284**	**796 051**	**831 130**	**761 818**	**Luxembourg**[8]
Africa	6 547	5 614	5 627	5 705	...	Afrique
Americas	50 026	37 296	39 132	37 604	36 281	Amériques
Europe	749 260	804 801	737 433	770 402	703 680	Europe
Asia, East and South East/Oceania	14 534	13 525	13 859	10 256	...	Asie, Est et Sud-Est et Océanie
Region not specified	109	48	...	7 163	21 857	Région non spécifiés
Macau[2]	**5 942 210**	**7 488 610**	**7 699 178**	**7 829 311**	**7 833 754**	**Macao**[2]
Africa	2 896	3 404	3 412	5 622	5 551	Afrique
Americas	104 104	123 757	130 893	136 093	139 019	Amériques
Europe	181 147	207 096	230 269	239 162	237 501	Europe
Asia, East and South East/Oceania	5 631 024	7 103 936	7 197 386	7 298 612	7 290 689	Asie, Est et Sud-Est et Océanie
Southern Asia	10 636	8 214	10 532	13 055	13 184	Asie du Sud
Western Asia	...	...	...	707	503	Asie occidentale
Region not specified	12 403	42 203	126 686	136 060	147 307	Région non spécifiés
Madagascar	**52 923**	**34 891**	**53 654**	**55 102**	**66 136**	**Madagascar**
Africa	10 149	7 151	5 923	7 197	7 345	Afrique
Americas	3 867	2 547	2 522	4 210	4 715	Amériques
Europe	36 702	23 931	42 709	40 875	50 875	Europe
Asia, East and South East/Oceania	2 205	1 262	2 500	2 820	3 201	Asie, Est et Sud-Est et Océanie
Malawi[18]	**129 912**	**127 004**	**149 834**	**152 701**	...	**Malawi**[18]
Africa	105 366	102 436	110 350	115 131	...	Afrique
Americas	4 077	3 650	4 811	...	...	Amériques
Europe	15 603	15 563	27 023	25 880	...	Europe
Region not specified	4 866	5 355	7 650	11 690	...	Région non spécifiés
Malaysia[19]	**7 445 908**	**5 847 213**	**6 016 209**	**6 503 860**	**7 197 231**	**Malaisie**[19]
Africa	...	...	13 365	23 106	29 755	Afrique
Americas	174 986	135 344	112 177	120 180	132 479	Amériques
Europe	455 061	420 833	343 897	373 214	401 200	Europe
Asia, East and South East/Oceania	6 481 732	4 967 844	5 313 828	5 782 170	6 421 900	Asie, Est et Sud-Est et Océanie
Southern Asia	108 411	71 411	94 488	42 153	52 278	Asie du Sud
Western Asia	33 876	47 815	24 214	24 413	26 880	Asie occidentale
Region not specified	191 842	203 966	114 240	138 624	132 739	Région non spécifiés
Maldives[4]	**195 156**	**196 112**	**235 852**	**241 020**	**279 436**	**Maldives**[4]
Africa	296	321	480	975	10 405	Afrique
Americas	2 167	2 008	2 060	2 311	3 990	Amériques
Europe	152 041	147 045	165 961	174 403	192 509	Europe
Asia, East and South East/Oceania	24 011	27 632	44 601	36 576	44 789	Asie, Est et Sud-Est et Océanie
Southern Asia	16 632	19 093	22 750	26 618	27 718	Asie du Sud
Region not specified	9	13	...	137	25	Région non spécifiés
Mali[1]	**43 913**	**37 962**	**37 843**	**30 877**	**27 661**	**Mali**[1]
Africa	13 669	16 589	17 907	8 660	10 121	Afrique
Americas	3 895	2 705	2 998	3 961	5 288	Amériques
Europe	22 330	16 452	14 103	13 763	8 914	Europe

76
Tourist arrivals by region of origin [cont.]
Arrivées de touristes par région de provenance [suite]

Country or area of destination and region of origin	1990	1991	1992	1993	1994	Pays ou zone de destination et région de provenance
Asia, East and South East/Oceania	954	517	462	135	123	Asie, Est et Sud-Est et Océanie
Western Asia	179	182	147	33	71	Asie occidentale
Region not specified	2 886	1 517	2 226	4 325	3 144	Région non spécifiés
Malta[18]	**871 675**	**895 036**	**1 002 381**	**1 063 217**	**...**	**Malte**[18]
Africa	1 569	2 083	3 489	8 000	...	Afrique
Americas	15 456	13 934	15 891	16 507	...	Amériques
Europe	793 481	806 184	912 801	973 000	...	Europe
Asia, East and South East/Oceania	8 388	7 822	9 030	8 710	...	Asie, Est et Sud-Est et Océanie
Southern Asia	1 589	1 890	1 855	5 000	...	Asie du Sud
Western Asia	37 566	48 730	40 759	52 000	...	Asie occidentale
Region not specified	13 626	14 393	18 556	...	...	Région non spécifiés
Marshall Islands	**...**	**6 741**	**8 000**	**5 055**	**4 909**	**Iles Marshall**
Americas	...	2 851	3 377	1 981	1 929	Amériques
Europe	...	449	410	238	134	Europe
Asia, East and South East/Oceania	...	3 379	4 124	2 752	1 705	Asie, Est et Sud-Est et Océanie
Region not specified	...	62	89	84	1 141	Région non spécifiés
Martinique[4]	**281 517**	**315 132**	**320 693**	**366 353**	**419 007**	**Martinique**[4]
Americas	62 668	82 723	59 164	59 240	60 165	Amériques
Europe	216 746	231 464	259 117	303 480	349 953	Europe
Region not specified	2 103	945	2 412	3 633	8 889	Région non spécifiés
Mauritius	**291 550**	**300 670**	**335 400**	**374 630**	**400 526**	**Maurice**
Africa	135 320	139 460	141 710	149 750	138 498	Afrique
Americas	3 460	2 920	3 050	3 640	3 369	Amériques
Europe	128 840	134 260	164 660	193 620	230 512	Europe
Asia, East and South East/Oceania	15 740	15 540	17 780	16 880	17 698	Asie, Est et Sud-Est et Océanie
Southern Asia	8 190	8 490	8 200	10 740	10 449	Asie du Sud
Mexico[3]	**17 176 000**	**16 281 000**	**17 273 000**	**16 534 000**	**17 113 500**	**Mexique**[3]
Americas	16 951 000	15 793 000	16 750 000	15 930 000	16 578 900	Amériques
Europe	189 000	328 000	363 000	473 000	409 000	Europe
Asia, East and South East/Oceania	36 000	40 000	33 000	37 000	46 000	Asie, Est et Sud-Est et Océanie
Region not specified	...	120 000	127 000	94 000	79 600	Région non spécifiés
Monaco[1]	**244 640**	**239 043**	**245 592**	**208 206**	**216 889**	**Monaco**[1]
Africa	637	430	375	447	369	Afrique
Americas	38 133	25 075	31 100	29 336	30 558	Amériques
Europe	181 601	190 443	189 870	154 524	157 389	Europe
Asia, East and South East/Oceania	10 048	8 438	9 411	8 903	10 838	Asie, Est et Sud-Est et Océanie
Western Asia	2 674	2 224	2 641	3 250	3 119	Asie occidentale
Region not specified	11 547	12 433	12 195	11 746	14 616	Région non spécifiés
Mongolia	**147 236**	**...**	**...**	**...**	**...**	**Mongolie**
Africa	20	...	...	...	...	Afrique
Americas	1 117	...	...	...	...	Amériques
Europe	137 622	...	...	...	...	Europe
Asia, East and South East/Oceania	8 218	...	...	...	...	Asie, Est et Sud-Est et Océanie
Southern Asia	153	...	...	...	...	Asie du Sud
Western Asia	8	...	...	...	...	Asie occidentale
Region not specified	98	...	...	...	...	Région non spécifiés
Montserrat	**12 780**	**16 700**	**17 260**	**20 994**	**21 285**	**Montserrat**
Americas	9 680	12 700	14 060	17 473	17 176	Amériques
Europe	1 900	2 500	2 800	2 981	3 374	Europe
Region not specified	1 200	1 500	400	540	735	Région non spécifiés

76
Tourist arrivals by region of origin [cont.]
Arrivées de touristes par région de provenance [suite]

Country or area of destination and region of origin	1990	1991	1992	1993	1994	Pays ou zone de destination et région de provenance
Morocco[3]	**4 024 197**	**4 162 239**	**4 389 753**	**4 027 356**	**3 465 437**	**Maroc**[3]
Africa	1 538 478	2 133 777	1 731 985	1 305 879	755 189	Afrique
Americas	115 408	69 085	118 112	120 491	122 700	Amériques
Europe	1 189 981	853 125	1 284 411	1 396 133	1 285 847	Europe
Asia, East and South East/Oceania	18 315	14 768	17 990	19 117	24 903	Asie, Est et Sud-Est et Océanie
Western Asia	83 179	92 041	65 201	63 016	62 388	Asie occidentale
Region not specified	1 078 836	999 443	1 172 054	1 122 720	1 214 410	Région non spécifiés
Myanmar	**21 598**	**22 647**	**26 607**	**48 425**	**80 408**	**Myanmar**
Americas	3 205	2 273	3 157	3 975	7 236	Amériques
Europe	14 918	15 803	16 667	20 230	25 729	Europe
Asia, East and South East/Oceania	3 070	4 024	3 676	9 692	37 191	Asie, Est et Sud-Est et Océanie
Southern Asia	405	547	3 107	14 528	10 252	Asie du Sud
Nepal	**254 885**	**292 995**	**334 353**	**293 567**	**326 531**	**Népal**
Africa	611	956	1 263	985	915	Afrique
Americas	28 215	26 229	30 083	27 895	29 161	Amériques
Europe	117 607	118 065	139 655	128 978	138 787	Europe
Asia, East and South East/Oceania	42 217	45 910	50 307	44 501	47 423	Asie, Est et Sud-Est et Océanie
Southern Asia	65 629	100 077	112 351	90 219	109 859	Asie du Sud
Region not specified	606	1 758	694	989	386	Région non spécifiés
Netherlands[8]	**5 795 100**	**5 841 900**	**6 082 900**	**5 756 700**	**6 177 700**	**Pays-Bas**[8]
Africa	57 700	55 500	52 700	50 500	49 600	Afrique
Americas	690 400	552 000	605 700	564 100	664 700	Amériques
Europe	4 690 900	4 922 000	5 053 100	4 801 800	5 052 300	Europe
Asia, East and South East/Oceania	356 100	312 400	371 400	340 300	411 100	Asie, Est et Sud-Est et Océanie
New Caledonia[34]	**86 870**	**80 930**	**78 264**	**80 753**	**85 103**	**Nouvelle-Calédonie**[34]
Africa	165	169	147	247	245	Afrique
Americas	1 663	1 326	1 329	1 381	1 463	Amériques
Europe	29 855	28 895	27 936	28 771	33 701	Europe
Asia, East and South East/Oceania	55 187	50 540	48 852	50 354	49 694	Asie, Est et Sud-Est et Océanie
New Zealand[23]	**976 010**	**963 470**	**1 055 681**	**1 156 978**	**1 322 565**	**Nouvelle-Zélande**[23]
Africa	3 094	2 872	4 866	7 903	13 258	Afrique
Americas	178 743	168 035	163 670	179 387	198 092	Amériques
Europe	170 739	177 172	201 763	223 407	250 985	Europe
Asia, East and South East/Oceania	564 112	575 043	645 664	708 662	824 981	Asie, Est et Sud-Est et Océanie
Southern Asia	3 626	2 457	2 949	2 506	3 741	Asie du Sud
Western Asia	1 906	1 568	2 155	2 757	3 837	Asie occidentale
Region not specified	53 790	36 323	34 614	32 356	27 671	Région non spécifiés
Nicaragua	**106 462**	**145 872**	**166 914**	**197 565**	**237 652**	**Nicaragua**
Africa	201	105	107	102	96	Afrique
Americas	83 318	118 312	140 390	171 807	208 207	Amériques
Europe	17 755	23 105	22 862	22 354	25 514	Europe
Asia, East and South East/Oceania	1 401	3 730	3 025	2 676	3 472	Asie, Est et Sud-Est et Océanie
Southern Asia	299	472	411	515	270	Asie du Sud
Western Asia	122	148	119	111	93	Asie occidentale
Region not specified	3 366	...	...	...	...	Région non spécifiés
Niger[4]	**20 729**	**16 198**	**13 070**	**11 486**	**10 835**	**Niger**[4]
Africa	6 552	6 900	5 540	5 266	4 877	Afrique
Americas	1 814	1 574	1 189	1 076	1 240	Amériques
Europe	11 557	6 749	5 773	4 785	4 164	Europe
Asia, East and South East/Oceania	524	564	344	284	330	Asie, Est et Sud-Est et Océanie

76
Tourist arrivals by region of origin [cont.]
Arrivées de touristes par région de provenance [suite]

Country or area of destination and region of origin	1990	1991	1992	1993	1994	Pays ou zone de destination et région de provenance
Western Asia	174	...	111	45	130	Asie occidentale
Region not specified	108	411	113	30	94	Région non spécifiés
Nigeria[2]	**226 242**	**308 065**	**271 854**	**294 302**	**327 189**	**Nigéria**[2]
Africa	186 664	272 104	225 847	244 924	272 115	Afrique
Americas	1 656	2 387	2 596	2 995	3 055	Amériques
Europe	28 318	25 913	33 687	36 000	41 685	Europe
Asia, East and South East/Oceania	3 810	3 643	3 834	3 833	4 079	Asie, Est et Sud-Est et Océanie
Southern Asia	4 191	2 661	4 443	4 910	4 512	Asie du Sud
Western Asia	1 574	1 320	1 402	1 000	1 535	Asie occidentale
Region not specified	29	37	45	640	208	Région non spécifiés
Niue[4]	**1 047**	**993**	**1 668**	**3 446**	**3 961**	**Nioué**[4]
Americas	23	21	81	256	316	Amériques
Europe	17	35	42	194	181	Europe
Asia, East and South East/Oceania	1 004	934	1 542	2 972	3 409	Asie, Est et Sud-Est et Océanie
Region not specified	3	3	3	24	55	Région non spécifiés
Northern Mariana Islands[2]	**435 454**	**429 745**	**505 295**	**545 803**	**596 033**	**Iles Marianas du Nord**[2]
Africa	17	28	35	23	26	Afrique
Americas	70 521	75 123	80 161	79 426	81 826	Amériques
Europe	1 611	1 776	1 840	2 190	2 201	Europe
Asia, East and South East/Oceania	362 986	352 265	422 776	463 577	511 673	Asie, Est et Sud-Est et Océanie
Southern Asia	280	490	378	236	235	Asie du Sud
Western Asia	30	63	105	102	34	Asie occidentale
Region not specified	9	...	...	249	38	Région non spécifiés
Norway *[1]	**1 954 821**	**2 113 951**	**2 375 452**	**2 556 162**	**2 830 000**	**Norvège ***[1]
Americas	215 272	175 125	213 813	195 738	242 920	Amériques
Europe	1 408 293	1 659 428	1 785 513	1 903 914	2 053 591	Europe
Asia, East and South East/Oceania	42 248	42 500	49 920	60 434	79 106	Asie, Est et Sud-Est et Océanie
Region not specified	289 008	236 898	326 206	396 076	454 383	Région non spécifiés
Oman[1]	**148 759**	**160 525**	**192 296**	**344 000**	**358 000**	**Oman**[1]
Africa	5 524	6 714	7 006	10 000	14 000	Afrique
Americas	7 956	7 648	9 725	14 000	19 000	Amériques
Europe	58 170	56 970	69 742	96 000	100 000	Europe
Asia, East and South East/Oceania	29 352	40 035	47 136	46 000	48 000	Asie, Est et Sud-Est et Océanie
Western Asia	20 506	27 732	30 641	45 000	37 000	Asie occidentale
Region not specified	27 251	21 426	28 046	133 000	140 000	Région non spécifiés
Pakistan	**423 842**	**438 088**	**352 112**	**379 165**	**454 353**	**Pakistan**
Africa	6 495	8 925	10 013	12 975	13 328	Afrique
Americas	42 290	41 921	39 649	47 650	58 824	Amériques
Europe	145 560	127 932	133 499	176 341	239 390	Europe
Asia, East and South East/Oceania	33 597	35 431	34 901	38 974	36 910	Asie, Est et Sud-Est et Océanie
Southern Asia	177 500	200 629	111 438	79 748	83 954	Asie du Sud
Western Asia	18 400	23 175	22 566	23 418	21 924	Asie occidentale
Region not specified	...	75	46	59	23	Région non spécifiés
Palau	**...**	**32 700**	**36 117**	**40 497**	**40 548**	**Palaos**
Africa	...	...	...	11	10	Afrique
Americas	...	6 411	8 032	8 232	9 795	Amériques
Europe	...	1 202	1 541	1 714	2 190	Europe
Asia, East and South East/Oceania	...	23 922	25 385	30 385	28 431	Asie, Est et Sud-Est et Océanie
Southern Asia	...	...	...	149	61	Asie du Sud
Western Asia	...	...	...	5	36	Asie occidentale

76
Tourist arrivals by region of origin [cont.]
Arrivées de touristes par région de provenance [suite]

Country or area of destination and region of origin	1990	1991	1992	1993	1994	Pays ou zone de destination et région de provenance
Region not specified	...	1 165	1 159	1	25	Région non spécifiés
Panama[2]	**230 960**	**296 756**	**311 937**	**316 813**	**342 790**	**Panama**[2]
Africa	222	175	228	191	273	Afrique
Americas	206 198	267 871	281 216	282 035	305 746	Amériques
Europe	16 999	19 528	19 751	22 558	25 269	Europe
Asia, East and South East/Oceania	7 507	9 155	10 719	12 003	11 451	Asie, Est et Sud-Est et Océanie
Western Asia	34	27	23	26	51	Asie occidentale
Papua New Guinea	**40 742**	**37 346**	**42 816**	**33 552**	**38 739**	**Papouasie-Nvl-Guinée**
Africa	161	94	89	...	...	Afrique
Americas	5 286	6 011	5 866	4 025	4 510	Amériques
Europe	7 497	6 138	5 980	4 656	6 773	Europe
Asia, East and South East/Oceania	26 484	23 285	30 561	24 749	27 239	Asie, Est et Sud-Est et Océanie
Southern Asia	1 314	1 818	318	...	...	Asie du Sud
Region not specified	...	...	2	122	217	Région non spécifiés
Paraguay[6 7 20]	**280 454**	**361 410**	**334 497**	**404 491**	**406 409**	**Paraguay**[6 7 20]
Americas	230 786	290 610	267 798	323 957	327 159	Amériques
Europe	30 317	41 634	38 668	48 053	48 972	Europe
Asia, East and South East/Oceania	12 144	15 830	14 952	18 202	18 369	Asie, Est et Sud-Est et Océanie
Region not specified	7 207	13 336	13 079	14 279	11 909	Région non spécifiés
Peru	**316 873**	**232 012**	**216 534**	**271 901**	**386 120**	**Pérou**
Africa	566	531	392	483	729	Afrique
Americas	159 689	132 763	134 070	172 272	243 155	Amériques
Europe	131 718	82 102	66 147	80 071	112 839	Europe
Asia, East and South East/Oceania	23 701	15 659	14 885	18 115	28 170	Asie, Est et Sud-Est et Océanie
Southern Asia	904	760	845	751	891	Asie du Sud
Western Asia	220	152	178	171	187	Asie occidentale
Region not specified	75	45	17	38	149	Région non spécifiés
Philippines[2 3]	**1 024 520**	**951 365**	**1 152 952**	**1 372 097**	**1 573 821**	**Philippines**[2 3]
Africa	...	387	766	1 219	1 244	Afrique
Americas	245 496	216 482	252 300	307 989	352 483	Amériques
Europe	168 321	131 825	154 620	183 194	205 958	Europe
Asia, East and South East/Oceania	412 389	452 119	588 860	705 128	800 874	Asie, Est et Sud-Est et Océanie
Southern Asia	16 039	15 826	16 829	18 357	20 377	Asie du Sud
Western Asia	12 441	17 249	18 991	17 775	18 115	Asie occidentale
Region not specified	169 834	117 477	120 586	138 435	174 770	Région non spécifiés
Poland[2]	**18 210 747**	**36 845 777**	**49 015 200**	**60 951 100**	**74 252 791**	**Pologne**[2]
Africa	...	...	8 700	8 000	8 966	Afrique
Americas	...	149 200	166 000	173 100	234 324	Amériques
Europe	15 794 055	36 371 400	48 664 100	60 598 200	73 841 082	Europe
Asia, East and South East/Oceania	...	21 000	50 300	66 300	44 643	Asie, Est et Sud-Est et Océanie
Southern Asia	...	...	7 300	11 300	10 083	Asie du Sud
Western Asia	...	...	27 300	29 900	39 565	Asie occidentale
Region not specified	2 416 692	304 177	91 500	64 300	74 128	Région non spécifiés
Portugal[6]	**8 019 919**	**8 656 956**	**8 884 143**	**8 433 900**	**9 132 400**	**Portugal**[6]
Africa	102 030	101 006	94 834	...	...	Afrique
Americas	413 000	347 000	363 428	286 800	306 900	Amériques
Europe	7 423 471	8 137 170	8 352 341	7 899 700	8 550 500	Europe
Asia, East and South East/Oceania	54 146	45 909	45 477	32 500	34 700	Asie, Est et Sud-Est et Océanie
Region not specified	27 272	25 871	28 063	214 900	240 300	Région non spécifiés
Puerto Rico[4]	**2 559 737**	**2 612 991**	**2 656 628**	**2 854 468**	**3 042 375**	**Porto Rico**[4]

76
Tourist arrivals by region of origin [cont.]
Arrivées de touristes par région de provenance [suite]

Country or area of destination and region of origin	1990	1991	1992	1993	1994	Pays ou zone de destination et région de provenance
Americas	1 833 283	1 860 290	1 869 739	2 023 934	2 146 364	Amériques
Region not specified	726 454	752 701	786 889	830 534	896 011	Région non spécifiés
Réunion	**200 276**	**186 026**	**217 350**	**241 691**	...	**Réunion**
Africa	39 277	40 083	43 182	44 575	...	Afrique
Americas	...	...	1 239	884	...	Amériques
Europe	154 246	141 635	163 950	190 290	...	Europe
Asia, East and South East/Oceania	...	...	506	1 187	...	Asie, Est et Sud-Est et Océanie
Southern Asia	...	...	708	150	...	Asie du Sud
Region not specified	6 753	4 308	7 765	4 605	...	Région non spécifiés
Romania[2]	**6 533 315**	**5 360 179**	**6 280 027**	**5 785 575**	**5 898 081**	**Roumanie**[2]
Africa	15 017	9 289	6 375	5 000	4 108	Afrique
Americas	52 911	50 865	50 298	63 343	59 938	Amériques
Europe	6 326 809	5 088 953	6 070 430	5 625 022	5 748 333	Europe
Asia, East and South East/Oceania	29 790	33 918	31 339	30 808	34 670	Asie, Est et Sud-Est et Océanie
Southern Asia	22 770	26 606	20 073	9 991	8 763	Asie du Sud
Western Asia	32 679	34 747	39 428	39 879	35 687	Asie occidentale
Region not specified	53 339	115 801	62 084	11 532	6 582	Région non spécifiés
Russian Federation[2]	..	...	**3 009 488**	**5 895 917**	**4 642 899**	**Fédération de Russie**[2]
Africa	..	...	33 445	28 926	12 676	Afrique
Americas	..	...	245 542	331 572	148 627	Amériques
Europe	..	...	1 683 606	4 192 445	3 658 892	Europe
Asia, East and South East/Oceania	..	...	888 304	1 206 527	773 541	Asie, Est et Sud-Est et Océanie
Southern Asia	..	...	90 106	54 506	19 301	Asie du Sud
Western Asia	..	...	40 711	39 042	26 788	Asie occidentale
Region not specified	..	...	27 774	42 899	3 074	Région non spécifiés
Saint Kitts and Nevis[5]	**75 689**	**83 903**	**89 719**	**86 329**	**96 410**	**Saint-Kitts-et-Nevis**[5]
Americas	67 434	75 513	79 439	75 071	83 387	Amériques
Europe	7 356	7 530	9 865	10 828	12 562	Europe
Asia, East and South East/Oceania	30	51	42	45	31	Asie, Est et Sud-Est et Océanie
Region not specified	869	809	373	385	430	Région non spécifiés
Saint Lucia[4][6]	**140 987**	**152 081**	**176 173**	**194 136**	**218 567**	**Sainte-Lucie**[4][6]
Americas	96 086	92 328	101 910	114 591	139 233	Amériques
Europe	42 624	57 924	72 357	77 112	76 983	Europe
Region not specified	2 277	1 829	1 906	2 433	2 351	Région non spécifiés
St. Vincent-Grenadines	**53 913**	**51 629**	**53 316**	**56 691**	**54 982**	**St. Vincent-Grenadines**
Americas	39 139	37 088	36 596	38 820	37 854	Amériques
Europe	14 277	14 013	16 292	17 323	16 593	Europe
Region not specified	497	528	428	548	535	Région non spécifiés
Samoa	**47 642**	**34 953**	**37 507**	**48 228**	**50 144**	**Samoa**
Americas	4 686	3 940	4 384	6 526	6 419	Amériques
Europe	5 936	3 416	3 754	5 347	4 640	Europe
Asia, East and South East/Oceania	33 879	25 311	27 720	35 068	36 953	Asie, Est et Sud-Est et Océanie
Region not specified	3 141	2 286	1 649	1 287	2 132	Région non spécifiés
San Marino[2]	**2 912 264**	**3 112 995**	**3 208 290**	**3 072 030**	**3 104 231**	**Saint-Marin**[2]
Europe	2 330 290	...	...	...	...	Europe
Region not specified	581 974	3 112 995	3 208 290	3 072 030	3 104 231	Région non spécifiés
Saudi Arabia[2]	**1 982 149**	**2 290 213**	**2 688 643**	**2 738 304**	...	**Arabie saoudite**[2]
Africa	390 889	302 350	559 458	518 316	...	Afrique
Americas	16 706	21 493	25 086	25 679	...	Amériques
Europe	50 684	39 637	60 611	61 434	...	Europe

76
Tourist arrivals by region of origin [cont.]
Arrivées de touristes par région de provenance [suite]

Country or area of destination and region of origin	1990	1991	1992	1993	1994	Pays ou zone de destination et région de provenance
Asia, East and South East/Oceania	1 523 870	1 926 733	2 043 488	2 132 875	...	Asie, Est et Sud-Est et Océanie
Senegal[1]	**245 881**	**233 512**	**245 581**	**167 770**	**239 629**	**Sénégal** [1]
Africa	37 127	38 031	48 110	39 633	47 352	Afrique
Americas	11 005	8 514	11 150	11 125	10 226	Amériques
Europe	193 694	180 963	181 651	112 420	175 984	Europe
Asia, East and South East/Oceania	2 824	3 494	2 866	2 574	2 855	Asie, Est et Sud-Est et Océanie
Western Asia	967	2 064	1 461	1 029	1 029	Asie occidentale
Region not specified	264	446	343	989	2 183	Région non spécifiés
Seychelles[5]	**103 770**	**90 050**	**98 577**	**116 180**	**109 901**	**Seychelles** [5]
Africa	15 789	18 759	12 072	13 510	10 967	Afrique
Americas	2 614	2 406	2 497	3 779	3 367	Amériques
Europe	81 374	64 986	79 516	94 267	90 080	Europe
Asia, East and South East/Oceania	1 837	1 979	1 979	2 690	3 316	Asie, Est et Sud-Est et Océanie
Southern Asia	348	487	684	525	600	Asie du Sud
Western Asia	1 808	1 433	1 829	1 409	1 571	Asie occidentale
Sierra Leone[4]	**28 468**	**25 989**	**19 334**	**21 223**	**23 600**	**Sierra Leone** [4]
Africa	7 403	6 817	5 030	7 068	6 900	Afrique
Americas	3 745	3 407	2 543	2 685	3 200	Amériques
Europe	9 231	8 371	6 268	5 620	7 500	Europe
Region not specified	8 089	7 394	5 493	5 850	6 000	Région non spécifiés
Singapore[21]	**5 322 854**	**5 414 651**	**5 989 940**	**6 425 778**	**6 898 951**	**Singapour** [21]
Africa	52 687	52 070	60 773	87 151	90 480	Afrique
Americas	370 551	354 021	399 293	425 515	469 812	Amériques
Europe	1 204 795	1 168 235	1 246 682	1 316 740	1 322 675	Europe
Asia, East and South East/Oceania	3 168 213	3 313 223	3 763 560	4 101 333	4 521 300	Asie, Est et Sud-Est et Océanie
Southern Asia	454 088	459 272	444 573	412 716	409 112	Asie du Sud
Western Asia	30 506	26 501	30 248	31 975	33 843	Asie occidentale
Region not specified	42 014	41 329	44 811	50 348	51 729	Région non spécifiés
Slovenia[8]	..	..	**616 380**	**624 371**	**748 273**	**Slovénie** [8]
Americas	..	..	8 922	12 026	16 539	Amériques
Europe	..	..	598 056	602 810	719 319	Europe
Asia, East and South East/Oceania	..	..	1 930	2 581	3 107	Asie, Est et Sud-Est et Océanie
Region not specified	..	..	7 472	6 954	9 308	Région non spécifiés
Solomon Islands	**9 195**	**11 105**	**12 446**	**11 570**	**11 919**	**Iles Salomon**
Americas	758	1 115	1 359	1 302	1 057	Amériques
Europe	791	1 327	1 580	1 500	1 521	Europe
Asia, East and South East/Oceania	6 929	8 636	9 467	8 715	9 302	Asie, Est et Sud-Est et Océanie
Region not specified	717	27	40	53	39	Région non spécifiés
South Africa[6][22]	**1 029 094**	**1 709 554**	**2 891 721**	**3 358 193**	**3 896 547**	**Afrique du Sud** [6][22]
Africa	535 274	1 193 446	2 327 456	2 699 147	3 123 319	Afrique
Americas	66 972	67 104	75 013	91 722	115 621	Amériques
Europe	366 412	382 772	408 619	442 624	476 169	Europe
Asia, East and South East/Oceania	54 080	56 002	68 164	88 618	115 411	Asie, Est et Sud-Est et Océanie
Southern Asia	3 609	7 171	9 520	14 773	19 497	Asie du Sud
Western Asia	1 270	1 291	1 848	3 022	5 421	Asie occidentale
Region not specified	1 477	1 768	1 101	18 287	41 109	Région non spécifiés
Spain[23]	**52 044 056**	**53 494 964**	**55 330 716**	**57 263 351**	**61 428 034**	**Espagne** [23]
Africa	2 384 172	2 058 685	2 251 149	2 379 669	...	Afrique
Americas	1 497 189	1 270 138	1 552 234	1 457 888	1 925 449	Amériques
Europe	44 335 013	46 236 764	47 322 066	49 474 766	51 390 029	Europe
Asia, East and South East/Oceania	435 061	377 701	429 123	457 025	...	Asie, Est et Sud-Est et Océanie

76
Tourist arrivals by region of origin [cont.]
Arrivées de touristes par région de provenance [suite]

Country or area of destination and region of origin	1990	1991	1992	1993	1994	Pays ou zone de destination et région de provenance
Southern Asia	44 003	41 268	36 946	42 726	...	Asie du Sud
Western Asia	40 459	30 424	31 930	31 997	...	Asie occidentale
Region not specified	3 308 159	3 479 984	3 707 268	3 419 280	8 112 556	Région non spécifiés
Sri Lanka[6]	**297 888**	**317 703**	**393 669**	**392 250**	**407 511**	**Sri Lanka**[6]
Africa	490	279	573	480	597	Afrique
Americas	8 802	11 617	13 332	14 262	16 362	Amériques
Europe	198 132	198 413	256 485	257 883	260 886	Europe
Asia, East and South East/Oceania	58 488	63 668	73 605	61 890	62 904	Asie, Est et Sud-Est et Océanie
Southern Asia	29 142	41 122	46 257	54 813	62 850	Asie du Sud
Western Asia	2 834	2 604	3 417	2 922	3 912	Asie occidentale
Sudan	**32 789**	**15 649**[4]	**...**	**...**	**...**	**Soudan**
Africa	2 036	1 423	...	...	...	Afrique
Americas	2 585	1 328	...	...	...	Amériques
Europe	10 678	4 513	...	...	...	Europe
Asia, East and South East/Oceania	1 858	1 111	...	...	...	Asie, Est et Sud-Est et Océanie
Southern Asia	1 174	726	...	...	...	Asie du Sud
Western Asia	5 701	2 818	...	...	...	Asie occidentale
Region not specified	8 757	3 730	...	...	...	Région non spécifiés
Suriname[4 6]	**28 478**	**...**	**16 321**	**18 060**	**...**	**Suriname**[4 6]
Americas	3 725	...	1 302	1 005	...	Amériques
Europe	23 836	...	14 014	16 638	...	Europe
Region not specified	917	...	1 005	417	...	Région non spécifiés
Swaziland[1]	**262 826**	**264 376**	**263 477**	**271 680**	**...**	**Swaziland**[1]
Africa	221 350	222 654	223 489	229 624	...	Afrique
Americas	5 500	5 533	4 616	5 224	...	Amériques
Europe	30 474	30 654	28 266	30 327	...	Europe
Asia, East and South East/Oceania	2 917	2 935	3 778	3 454	...	Asie, Est et Sud-Est et Océanie
Region not specified	2 585	2 600	3 328	3 051	...	Région non spécifiés
Sweden *[1]	**730 519**	**622 241**	**646 059**	**674 954**	**753 379**	**Suède** *[1]
Americas	41 264	30 090	33 326	35 256	38 987	Amériques
Europe	629 243	537 447	561 338	580 150	649 989	Europe
Asia, East and South East/Oceania	10 792	9 982	9 546	11 173	11 703	Asie, Est et Sud-Est et Océanie
Region not specified	49 220	44 722	41 849	48 375	52 700	Région non spécifiés
Switzerland[8]	**10 521 446**	**10 111 086**	**10 264 793**	**9 901 324**	**...**	**Suisse**[8]
Africa	135 085	112 510	101 435	99 180	...	Afrique
Americas	1 582 359	1 029 113	1 220 609	1 117 476	...	Amériques
Europe	7 800 483	8 108 576	7 943 683	7 690 118	...	Europe
Asia, East and South East/Oceania	671 244	551 031	634 125	604 843	...	Asie, Est et Sud-Est et Océanie
Southern Asia	52 021	41 916	39 939	40 534	...	Asie du Sud
Western Asia	20 043	18 412	18 645	17 158	...	Asie occidentale
Region not specified	260 211	249 528	306 357	332 015	...	Région non spécifiés
Syrian Arab Republic[2 6]	**1 442 441**	**1 570 161**	**1 739 884**	**1 909 916**	**2 101 082**	**Rép. arabe syrienne**[2 6]
Africa	31 835	20 171	32 075	32 974	33 088	Afrique
Americas	14 034	12 185	15 739	15 688	20 248	Amériques
Europe	231 540	282 736	293 780	306 949	340 389	Europe
Asia, East and South East/Oceania	7 315	4 434	6 246	9 942	12 806	Asie, Est et Sud-Est et Océanie
Southern Asia	200 878	123 863	160 249	125 950	188 017	Asie du Sud
Western Asia	922 848	1 095 355	1 184 427	1 357 097	1 435 222	Asie occidentale
Region not specified	33 991	31 417	47 368	61 316	71 312	Région non spécifiés

76

Tourist arrivals by region of origin [*cont.*]

Arrivées de touristes par région de provenance [*suite*]

Country or area of destination and region of origin	1990	1991	1992	1993	1994	Pays ou zone de destination et région de provenance
Thailand[6]	**5 298 860**	**5 086 899**	**5 136 443**	**5 760 533**	**6 166 496**	**Thaïlande**[6]
Africa	31 943	35 625	38 509	51 355	50 226	Afrique
Americas	381 894	326 812	354 910	359 726	373 610	Amériques
Europe	1 343 618	1 207 670	1 310 148	1 435 993	1 549 119	Europe
Asia, East and South East/Oceania	3 171 445	3 116 983	3 044 763	3 533 134	3 825 797	Asie, Est et Sud-Est et Océanie
Southern Asia	313 902	344 223	331 648	314 646	305 071	Asie du Sud
Western Asia	56 058	55 586	56 465	65 679	62 673	Asie occidentale
TFYR Macedonia	..	...	**219 062**	**208 191**	**185 414**	**L'ex-R.y. Macédoine**
Americas	..	...	1 717	3 615	4 783	Amériques
Europe	..	...	215 143	201 656	177 825	Europe
Asia, East and South East/Oceania	...	...	534	815	1 011	Asie, Est et Sud-Est et Océanie
Region not specified	..	...	1 668	2 105	1 795	Région non spécifiés
Togo[1]	**103 246**	**65 098**	**48 559**	**24 244**	**43 767**	**Togo**[1]
Africa	48 399	37 582	28 533	13 710	22 423	Afrique
Americas	6 953	3 059	2 229	1 307	2 791	Amériques
Europe	44 660	22 198	16 192	7 508	15 689	Europe
Asia, East and South East/Oceania	3 173	2 194	439	350	642	Asie, Est et Sud-Est et Océanie
Western Asia	...	...	1 111	1 294	2 159	Asie occidentale
Region not specified	61	65	55	75	63	Région non spécifiés
Tonga[4]	**20 917**	**22 007**	**23 020**	**25 513**	**28 408**	**Tonga**[4]
Americas	4 892	5 339	5 481	5 498	6 302	Amériques
Europe	3 175	3 617	3 725	5 374	5 643	Europe
Asia, East and South East/Oceania	12 793	12 996	13 740	14 569	16 375	Asie, Est et Sud-Est et Océanie
Southern Asia	39	34	41	64	79	Asie du Sud
Region not specified	18	21	33	8	9	Région non spécifiés
Trinidad and Tobago	**194 521**	**220 206**	**234 759**	**248 815**	**265 915**	**Trinité-et-Tobago**
Americas	144 901	158 451	176 200	187 831	199 726	Amériques
Europe	38 226	49 342	46 459	46 971	58 094	Europe
Region not specified	11 394	12 413	12 100	14 013	8 095	Région non spécifiés
Tunisia[6]	**3 203 787**	**3 224 015**	**3 539 950**	**3 655 698**	**3 855 546**	**Tunisie**[6]
Africa	590 922	911 836	973 650	845 529	793 069	Afrique
Americas	12 608	8 060	13 839	20 182	24 275	Amériques
Europe	1 705 451	1 086 564	1 770 827	2 037 350	2 255 836	Europe
Western Asia	841 523	1 179 395	674 808	582 512	581 091	Asie occidentale
Region not specified	53 283	38 160	106 826	170 125	201 275	Région non spécifiés
Turkey[2]	**5 389 308**	**5 517 897**	**7 076 096**	**6 500 638**	**6 670 618**	**Turquie**[2]
Africa	56 265	31 150	46 575	53 603	76 426	Afrique
Americas	273 436	108 828	236 205	335 850	355 586	Amériques
Europe	4 438 965	4 839 064	6 295 747	5 602 018	5 564 772	Europe
Asia, East and South East/Oceania	106 635	59 980	82 050	99 244	123 045	Asie, Est et Sud-Est et Océanie
Southern Asia	280 425	267 638	182 826	166 427	285 370	Asie du Sud
Western Asia	229 917	208 448	230 308	238 514	257 330	Asie occidentale
Region not specified	3 665	2 789	2 385	4 982	8 089	Région non spécifiés
Turks and Caicos Islands	**48 756**	**55 248**	**52 345**	**67 303**	**71 652**	**Iles Turques et Caiques**
Americas	31 991	43 390	45 140	57 629	61 743	Amériques
Europe	5 017	7 045	6 605	8 171	8 308	Europe
Region not specified	11 748	4 813	600	1 503	1 601	Région non spécifiés
Tuvalu	**671**	**969**	**862**	**929**	**1 185**	**Tuvalu**
Americas	76	84	164	98	131	Amériques
Europe	129	142	176	135	200	Europe
Asia, East and South East/Oceania	433	732	472	637	788	Asie, Est et Sud-Est et Océanie

76
Tourist arrivals by region of origin [cont.]
Arrivées de touristes par région de provenance [suite]

Country or area of destination and region of origin	1990	1991	1992	1993	1994	Pays ou zone de destination et région de provenance
Region not specified	33	11	50	59	66	Région non spécifiés
United Arab Emirates[1][23]	**632 903**	**716 642**	**944 350**	**1 087 733**	**1 239 377**	**Emirats arabes unis**[1][23]
Africa	25 617	21 843	34 619	39 280	47 400	Afrique
Americas	19 616	46 145	35 271	41 510	43 720	Amériques
Europe	151 280	147 250	192 426	295 746	398 781	Europe
Asia, East and South East/Oceania	90 780	100 178	121 981	136 581	132 269	Asie, Est et Sud-Est et Océanie
Southern Asia	144 631	139 544	210 513	182 320	185 377	Asie du Sud
Western Asia	200 979	261 682	349 540	392 296	431 830	Asie occidentale
former USSR†[2]	**7 203 635**	**6 894 713**	..	..	...	**ancienne URSS†**[2]
Africa	37 000	26 883	..	..	..	Afrique
Americas	282 658	233 340	..	..	..	Amériques
Europe	6 006 950	5 636 062	..	..	..	Europe
Asia, East and South East/Oceania	449 650	532 316	..	..	..	Asie, Est et Sud-Est et Océanie
Southern Asia	88 504	150 202	..	..	..	Asie du Sud
Western Asia	107 000	139 354	..	..	..	Asie occidentale
Region not specified	231 873	176 556	..	..	..	Région non spécifiés
United Kingdom[2][18]	**18 013 000**	**17 125 000**	**18 535 000**	**19 398 000**	**21 034 000**	**Royaume-Uni**[2][18]
Africa	553 000	535 000	536 000	553 000	602 000	Afrique
Americas	3 936 000	3 125 000	3 664 000	3 672 000	3 890 000	Amériques
Europe	11 060 000	11 392 000	12 034 000	12 827 000	13 859 000	Europe
Asia, East and South East/Oceania	1 310 000	1 035 000	1 174 000	1 076 000	1 258 000	Asie, Est et Sud-Est et Océanie
Western Asia	466 000	447 000	481 000	539 000	602 000	Asie occidentale
Region not specified	688 000	591 000	646 000	731 000	823 000	Région non spécifiés
United Rep.Tanzania[2]	**153 000**	**186 800**	**201 744**	**230 158**	**261 579**	**Rép. Unie de Tanzanie**[2]
Africa	59 691	72 878	78 708	89 790	102 041	Afrique
Americas	34 005	41 517	44 838	51 151	58 133	Amériques
Europe	55 072	67 238	72 618	82 834	94 138	Europe
Asia, East and South East/Oceania	4 232	5 167	5 580	6 383	7 267	Asie, Est et Sud-Est et Océanie
United States	**39 539 010**	**42 985 520**	**47 261 029**	**45 778 817**	**45 504 325**	**Etats-Unis**
Africa	137 140	138 601	149 835	168 969	176 966	Afrique
Americas	27 356 619	29 910 948	32 725 458	30 786 103	29 968 266	Amériques
Europe	6 857 674	7 568 226	8 463 801	8 864 733	8 744 679	Europe
Asia, East and South East/Oceania	4 872 916	5 076 571	5 614 004	5 642 339	6 286 421	Asie, Est et Sud-Est et Océanie
Southern Asia	165 808	155 591	149 893	144 344	151 575	Asie du Sud
Western Asia	148 853	135 583	158 038	172 329	176 418	Asie occidentale
United States Virgin Is.[1]	**370 008**	**376 371**	**385 575**	**448 950**	**431 969**	**Iles Vierges américaines**[1]
Africa	...	...	225	301	...	Afrique
Americas	354 218	357 881	366 366	421 273	396 909	Amériques
Europe	8 593	8 916	12 472	14 358	14 416	Europe
Asia, East and South East/Oceania	...	...	804	854	...	Asie, Est et Sud-Est et Océanie
Region not specified	7 197	9 574	5 708	12 164	20 644	Région non spécifiés
Uruguay[2][3]	**1 267 040**	**1 509 962**	**1 801 672**	**2 003 000**	**2 175 457**	**Uruguay**[2][3]
Americas	954 038	1 211 452	1 498 913	1 629 132	1 771 017	Amériques
Europe	45 283	44 971	47 779	52 542	59 236	Europe
Asia, East and South East/Oceania	1 918	1 667	1 680	2 647	4 669	Asie, Est et Sud-Est et Océanie
Western Asia	1 449	702	943	...	123	Asie occidentale
Region not specified	264 352	251 170	252 357	318 679	340 412	Région non spécifiés
Vanuatu	**34 728**	**39 548**	**42 673**	**44 478**	**42 140**	**Vanuatu**
Americas	1 082	1 300	1 343	1 351	1 140	Amériques

76
Tourist arrivals by region of origin [*cont.*]
Arrivées de touristes par région de provenance [*suite*]

Country or area of destination and region of origin	1990	1991	1992	1993	1994	Pays ou zone de destination et région de provenance
Europe	1 301	1 236	2 282	2 190	2 295	Europe
Asia, East and South East/Oceania	30 601	35 246	38 445	39 953	38 218	Asie, Est et Sud-Est et Océanie
Region not specified	1 744	1 766	603	984	487	Région non spécifiés
Venezuela	**524 533**	**598 328**	**445 613**	**396 141**	**428 811**	**Venezuela**
Africa	571	446	1 040	610	776	Afrique
Americas	296 412	335 016	245 828	208 340	227 558	Amériques
Europe	219 319	254 796	191 237	179 857	194 981	Europe
Asia, East and South East/Oceania	4 411	4 611	4 206	4 154	4 404	Asie, Est et Sud-Est et Océanie
Southern Asia	610	891	648	568	615	Asie du Sud
Western Asia	1 809	879	1 085	1 064	1 151	Asie occidentale
Region not specified	1 401	1 689	1 569	1 548	1 326	Région non spécifiés
Viet Nam[4]	...	...	**440 000**	**601 527**	**940 707**	**Viet Nam**[4]
Americas	...	...	14 563	23 361	42 438	Amériques
Europe	...	...	25 866	64 959	133 560	Europe
Asia, East and South East/Oceania	...	...	116 542	162 205	310 389	Asie, Est et Sud-Est et Océanie
Region not specified	...	...	283 029	351 002	454 320	Région non spécifiés
Yemen[1]	**51 849**	**43 656**	**72 164**	**69 795**	**39 929**	**Yémen**[1]
Africa	2 052	2 653	3 346	2 101	1 377	Afrique
Americas	3 370	3 806	7 117	6 549	3 594	Amériques
Europe	30 081	21 689	43 777	46 466	26 809	Europe
Asia, East and South East/Oceania	4 366	5 021	6 922	5 038	3 097	Asie, Est et Sud-Est et Océanie
Western Asia	11 980	10 487	11 002	9 641	5 052	Asie occidentale
Yugoslavia[8]	**1 185 663**	**378 600**	**155 564**	**76 555**	**90 619**	**Yougoslavie**[8]
Americas	39 557	12 023	4 694	2 636	2 064	Amériques
Europe	1 090 844	338 173	141 126	68 671	84 107	Europe
Asia, East and South East/Oceania	13 984	4 966	1 559	1 249	826	Asie, Est et Sud-Est et Océanie
Region not specified	41 278	23 438	8 185	3 999	3 622	Région non spécifiés
Zambia[2]	**141 004**	**171 507**	**158 759**	**157 254**	**134 000**	**Zambie**[2]
Africa	105 343	141 327	98 656	116 141	82 000	Afrique
Americas	5 441	3 594	1 332	5 311	7 000	Amériques
Europe	22 588	19 257	24 086	23 949	27 000	Europe
Asia, East and South East/Oceania	3 875	3 481	28 782	8 373	6 000	Asie, Est et Sud-Est et Océanie
Southern Asia	2 679	2 883	3 930	3 145	8 000	Asie du Sud
Western Asia	62	79	253	213	...	Asie occidentale
Region not specified	1 016	886	1 720	122	4 000	Région non spécifiés
Zimbabwe[24]	**606 000**	**664 000**	**737 885**	**942 723**	**1 099 332**	**Zimbabwe**[24]
Africa	436 220	513 580	641 004	787 539	949 283	Afrique
Americas	18 585	14 650	13 658	26 337	30 330	Amériques
Europe	81 827	63 556	67 396	105 017	104 021	Europe
Asia, East and South East/Oceania	16 054	15 775	15 380	23 489	15 232	Asie, Est et Sud-Est et Océanie
Region not specified	53 314	56 439	447	341	466	Région non spécifiés

Source:
World Tourism Organization (Madrid).

† For detailed descriptions of data pertaining to former Czechoslovakia, Germany, SFR Yugoslavia and former USSR, see Annex I - Country or area nomenclature, regional and other groupings.

1 International tourist arrivals in hotels and similar establishments.

Source:
Organisation mondiale du tourisme (Madrid).

† Pour les descriptions en détails des données relatives à l'ancienne Tchécoslovaquie, l'Allemagne, la Rfs Yougoslavie et l'ancienne URSS, voir l'Annexe I - Nomenclature des pays ou zones, groupements régionaux et autres groupements.

1 Arrivées de touristes internationaux dans les hôtels et établissements assimilés.

76

Tourist arrivals by region of origin
[*cont.*]

Arrivées de touristes par région de provenance
[*suite*]

2 International visitor arrivals at frontiers (including tourists and same-day visitors).	2 Arrivées de visiteurs internationaux aux frontières (y compris touristes et visiteurs de la journée).
3 Including nationals of the country residing abroad.	3 Y compris les nationaux du pays résidant à l'étranger.
4 Air arrivals.	4 Arrivées par voie aérienne.
5 Air and sea arrivals.	5 Arrivées par voie aérienne et maritime.
6 Excluding nationals of the country residing abroad.	6 A l'exclusion des nationaux du pays résidant à l'étranger.
7 Excluding crew members.	7 A l'exclusion des membres des équipages.
8 International tourist arrivals at collective tourism establishments.	8 Arrivées de touristes internationaux dans les établissements d'hébergement collectifs.
9 International tourist arrivals in hotels of regional capitals.	9 Arrivées de trousites internationaux dans les hôtel des capitales de département.
10 Excluding ethnic Chinese arriving from Hong Kong, Macau and Taiwan.	10 A l'exclusion des arrivées de personnes d'ethnie chinoise en provenance de Hong-kong, Macao et Taïwan.
11 International visitor arrivals at all means of accommodation in Brazzaville, Pointe Noire, Loubomo, Owando and Sibiti.	11 Arrivées des touristes internationaux dans l'ensemble des moyens d'hébergement de Brazzaville, Pointe Noire, Loubomo, Owando et Sibiti.
12 Air arrivals at Rarotonga.	12 Arrivées par voie aérienne à Rarotonga.
13 International tourist arrivals at Addis Ababa, Asmara and Assab.	13 Arrivées de touristes internationaux à Addis Abeba, Asmara et Assab.
14 Since 1989 "survey at frontiers and car study realized by SOFRES".	14 A partir de 1989 "enquête aux frontières et étude autocar réalisée par la SPFRES".
15 From 1992, including camping sites.	15 A partir de 1992 les chiffres incluent les terrains de camping.
16 The data relate to the territory of the Federal Republic of Germany prior to 3 October 1990. As of 1990, tourists from the former German Democratic Republic will be regarded as domestic tourists.	16 Les données se réfèrent au territoire de la République fédéral d'Allemagne avant le 3 octobre 1990. A partir de 1990, les touristes en provenance de l'ancienne Répulique Démocratique Allemande seront considérés comme des touristes nationaux.
17 Data based on surveys.	17 Données obtenues au moyen d'enquêtes.
18 Departures.	18 Départs.
19 Foreign tourist departures; includes Singapore residents crossing the frontier by road through Johore Causeway.	19 Départs de touristes étrangers; y compris les résidents de Singapour traversant la frontière par voie terrestre a travers le Johore Causeway.
20 Arrivals by air and land.	20 Arrivées par voies aérienne et terrestre.
21 Excluding Malaysian citizens arriving by land and cruise passengers, but including excursionists (same-day visitors).	21 A l'exclusion des arrivées de malaisiens par voie terrestre et de passagers en croisière, mais y compris les excursionnistes (visiteurs de la journée).
22 Beginning Jan. 1992, contract and border traffic concession workers are included.	22 A partir de jan. 1992 les données incluent les travailleurs contractuels et ceux de la zone frontière.
23 Dubai only.	23 Dubai seulement.
24 Excluding transit passengers.	24 A l'exclusion des passagers en transit.

77
Tourist arrivals and international tourism receipts
Arrivées de touristes et recettes touristiques internationales

Country or area Pays ou zone	Number of tourist arrivals (000) Nombre d'arrivées de touristes (000)					Tourist receipts (million US dollars) Recettes touristiques (millions de dollars E-U)				
	1990	1991	1992	1993	1994	1990	1991	1992	1993	1994
World *Monde*	459 233	466 044	503 617	518 254	546 269	264 708	271 827	308 596	314 001	346 703
Africa Afrique	17 597	18 201	20 829	20 699	20 887	7 207	6 916	8 655	7 358	7 921
Algeria Algérie	1 137	1 193	1 120	1 128	805	64	84	75	55	49
Angola Angola	46	46	40	21	11	13	...	...	20	13
Benin Bénin	110	117	130	140	142	28	29	32	38	55
Botswana Botswana	543	592	590	607	637	19	13	24	31	35
Burkina Faso Burkina Faso	74	80	92	111	133	8	8	9	8	22
Burundi Burundi	109	125	86	75	29	4	4	3	3	3
Cameroon Cameroun	89	84	62	81	84	53	73	59	47	49
Cape Verde Cap-Vert	24	20	19	27	31	6	8	7	10	10
Central African Rep. Rép. centrafricaine	6	6	6	6	6	3	3	3	6	6
Chad Tchad	9	21	17	21	19	12	10	21	23	36
Comoros Comores	8	17	19	24	27	2	9	8	8	9
Congo Congo	33	33	36	34	30	8	8	7	6	3
Côte d'Ivoire Côte d'Ivoire	196	200	217	159	157	51	62	66	53	43
Djibouti Djibouti	33	33	28	25	22	6	6	10	13	10
Egypt Egypte	2 411	2 112	2 944	2 291	2 356	1 994	2 029	2 730	1 332	1 384
Equatorial Guinea Guinée équatoriale	...	...	...	...	...	1	2	2	2	2
Ethiopia Ethiopie	79	82	83	93	98	26	20	23	20	23
Gabon Gabon	108	128	133	115	103	3	4	5	4	5
Gambia Gambie	100	66	64	90	78	26	30	27	26	27
Ghana Ghana	146	172	213	257	248	81	118	167	206	218
Guinea Guinée	100	28	33	93	94	30	13	11	6	6
Kenya Kenya	814	805	782	826	863	466	432	442	413	505
Lesotho Lesotho	171	182	155	130	97	17	18	19	17	17

77
Tourist arrivals and international tourism receipts
[*cont.*]

Arrivées de touristes et recettes touristiques internationales
[*suite*]

Country or area Pays ou zone	Number of tourist arrivals (000) Nombre d'arrivées de touristes (000)					Tourist receipts (million US dollars) Recettes touristiques (millions de dollars E-U)				
	1990	1991	1992	1993	1994	1990	1991	1992	1993	1994
Libyan Arab Jamah. Jamah. arabe libyenne	96	90	89	63	54	6	5	6	7	7
Madagascar Madagascar	53	35	54	55	66	40	27	39	41	54
Malawi Malawi	130	127	150	153	154	16	12	8	7	5
Mali Mali	44	38	38	31	28	47	11	11	13	18
Mauritania Mauritanie	...	...	...	...	...	9	12	8	8	8
Mauritius Maurice	292	301	335	375	401	244	252	299	301	356
Morocco Maroc	4 024	4 162	4 390	4 027	3 465	1 259	1 052	1 360	1 243	1 231
Namibia Namibie	...	...	...	...	...	69	87	106	156	184
Niger Niger	21	16	13	11	11	17	16	17	16	16
Nigeria Nigéria	190	214	237	192	193	25	39	29	31	34
Réunion Réunion	200	186	217	242	263	...	...	...	...	...
Rwanda Rwanda	16	3	5	2	1	10	4	4	2	2
Sao Tome and Principe Sao Tomé-et-Principe	4	3	3	3	5	2	2	2	2	2
Senegal Sénégal	246	234	246	168	240	167	171	182	173	115
Seychelles Seychelles	104	90	99	116	110	120	99	117	116	119
Sierra Leone Sierra Leone	98	96	89	91	72	19	18	17	18	10
Somalia Somalie	46	46	20	20	15	...	...	...	...	...
South Africa Afrique du Sud	1 029	1 710	2 892	3 358	3 897	992	1 131	1 226	1 327	1 424
Sudan Soudan	33	16	17	15	12	21	8	5	3	3
Swaziland Swaziland	294	279	280	288	298	25	26	32	30	29
Togo Togo	103	65	49	24	44	58	49	39	18	18
Tunisia Tunisie	3 204	3 224	3 540	3 656	3 856	953	685	1 074	1 114	1 302
Uganda Ouganda	69	69	76	103	119	10	15	38	50	61
United Rep.Tanzania Rép. Unie de Tanzanie	153	187	202	230	262	65	95	120	147	192
Zaire Zaïre	55	33	22	22	18	7	7	7	6	5

77
Tourist arrivals and international tourism receipts
[*cont.*]

Arrivées de touristes et recettes touristiques internationales
[*suite*]

Country or area Pays ou zone	Number of tourist arrivals (000) Nombre d'arrivées de touristes (000)					Tourist receipts (million US dollars) Recettes touristiques (millions de dollars E-U)				
	1990	1991	1992	1993	1994	1990	1991	1992	1993	1994
Zambia Zambie	141	171	159	157	134	41	35	51	44	43
Zimbabwe Zimbabwe	606	664	738	943	1 099	64	75	108	138	153
America, North Amérique du Nord	84 935	87 318	93 159	92 528	94 539	63 710	70 135	77 465	82 320	85 973
Anguilla Anguilla	31	31	32	38	44	35	31	35	43	51
Antigua and Barbuda Antigua-et-Barbuda	197	197	210	240	255	298	314	329	372	394
Aruba Aruba	433	501	542	562	582	348	386	442	464	451
Bahamas Bahamas	1 562	1 427	1 399	1 489	1 516	1 333	1 193	1 244	1 304	1 333
Barbados Barbade	432	394	385	396	426	494	460	463	528	598
Belize Belize	88	87	113	117	129	51	53	60	70	74
Bermuda Bermudes	435	386	375	413	416	490	456	443	505	524
British Virgin Islands Iles Vierges britanniques	160	147	117	237	239	132	109	100	186	188
Canada Canada	15 209	14 912	14 741	15 105	15 971	5 612	5 886	5 712	5 897	6 309
Cayman Islands Iles Caïmanes	253	237	242	287	341	234	220	228	252	328
Costa Rica Costa Rica	435	505	610	684	761	275	331	431	577	626
Cuba Cuba	327	418	455	544	617	243	387	567	729	850
Dominica Dominique	45	46	47	52	57	20	24	25	28	31
Dominican Republic Rép. dominicaine	1 305	1 181	1 415	1 609	1 717	890	877	1 054	1 234	1 148
El Salvador El Salvador	194	199	314	267	181	145	157	128	121	86
Grenada Grenade	76	85	88	94	109	38	42	38	45	60
Guadeloupe Guadeloupe	331	370	341	453	556	197	234	269	370	490
Guatemala Guatemala	509	513	541	562	537	185	211	243	265	258
Haiti Haïti	144	119	90	77	70	82	71	38	78	46
Honduras Honduras	202	198	230	222	198	29	31	32	32	33
Jamaica Jamaïque	841	845	909	979	977	740	764	858	942	919
Martinique Martinique	282	315	321	366	419	240	255	282	332	379

77
Tourist arrivals and international tourism receipts
[cont.]

Arrivées de touristes et recettes touristiques internationales
[suite]

Country or area Pays ou zone	Number of tourist arrivals (000) Nombre d'arrivées de touristes (000)					Tourist receipts (million US dollars) Recettes touristiques (millions de dollars E-U)				
	1990	1991	1992	1993	1994	1990	1991	1992	1993	1994
Mexico Mexique	17 176	16 281	17 273	16 534	17 113	5 467	5 881	6 085	6 167	6 318
Montserrat Montserrat	13	17	17	21	21	11	12	14	17	19
Nicaragua Nicaragua	106	146	167	198	238	12	16	21	30	40
Panama Panama	214	277	291	298	319	172	202	222	228	244
Puerto Rico Porto Rico	2 560	2 613	2 657	2 854	3 042	1 366	1 436	1 520	1 628	1 737
Saint Kitts and Nevis Saint-Kitts-et-Nevis	73	83	88	84	94	63	74	67	69	75
Saint Lucia Sainte-Lucie	141	152	176	194	219	154	173	208	221	224
St. Vincent-Grenadines St. Vincent-Grenadines	54	52	53	57	55	56	53	53	52	51
Trinidad and Tobago Trinité-et-Tobago	195	220	235	250	266	95	101	109	82	80
Turks and Caicos Islands Iles Turques et Caiques	49	55	52	67	72	37	50	48	53	57
United States Etats-Unis	39 539	42 986	47 261	45 779	45 504	43 007	48 384	54 742	57 875	60 406
United States Virgin Is. Iles Vierges américaines	463	470	478	550	540	705	787	822	908	919
America, South **Amérique du Sud**	**8 635**	**9 658**	**10 403**	**11 495**	**12 637**	**5 771**	**6 650**	**7 300**	**8 366**	**9 111**
Argentina Argentine	2 728	2 870	3 031	3 532	3 866	1 976	2 336	3 090	3 614	3 970
Bolivia Bolivie	217	221	245	269	320	84	91	107	115	135
Brazil Brésil	1 091	1 192	1 475	1 564	1 612	1 444	1 559	1 307	1 385	1 352
Chile Chili	943	1 349	1 283	1 412	1 623	540	700	706	744	833
Colombia Colombie	813	857	1 076	1 047	1 207	406	468	705	755	794
Ecuador Equateur	362	365	403	471	482	188	189	192	230	252
Guyana Guyana	64	73	75	107	113	27	30	31	45	47
Paraguay Paraguay	280	361	334	404	406	112	165	154	204	197
Peru Pérou	317	232	217	272	386	259	268	188	265	402
Suriname Suriname	28	30	16	18	18	1	1	2	8	11
Uruguay Uruguay	1 267	1 510	1 802	2 003	2 175	238	333	381	447	632

77
Tourist arrivals and international tourism receipts
[*cont.*]

Arrivées de touristes et recettes touristiques internationales
[*suite*]

Country or area Pays ou zone	Number of tourist arrivals (000) Nombre d'arrivées de touristes (000)					Tourist receipts (million US dollars) Recettes touristiques (millions de dollars E-U)				
	1990	1991	1992	1993	1994	1990	1991	1992	1993	1994
Venezuela Venezuela	525	598	446	396	429	496	510	437	554	486
Asia **Asie**	**63 600**	**65 252**	**76 389**	**83 200**	**91 396**	**42 803**	**42 155**	**51 409**	**57 959**	**67 394**
Afghanistan Afghanistan	8	8	6	6	5	1	1	1	1	1
Azerbaijan Azerbaïdjan	..	...	212	298	321	..	...	42	60	64
Bahrain Bahreïn	1 376	1 674	1 419	1 761	2 270	135	162	177	222	302
Bangladesh Bangladesh	115	113	110	127	140	11	9	8	15	19
Bhutan Bhoutan	2	2	3	3	4	2	2	3	3	3
Brunei Darussalam Brunéi Darussalam	377	344	412	489	527	35	35	35	36	36
Cambodia Cambodge	17	25	88	118	177	...	...	50	48	70
China Chine	10 484	12 464	16 512	18 982	21 070	2 218	2 845	3 948	4 683	7 323
Cyprus Chypre	1 561	1 385	1 991	1 841	2 069	1 258	1 026	1 539	1 396	1 700
Hong Kong Hong-kong	6 581	6 795	8 011	8 938	9 331	5 032	5 078	6 037	7 562	8 317
India Inde	1 707	1 678	1 868	1 765	1 886	1 513	1 757	2 120	2 001	2 265
Indonesia Indonésie	2 178	2 570	3 064	3 403	4 006	2 105	2 522	3 278	3 988	4 785
Iran, Islamic Rep. of Iran, Rép. islamique d'	154	212	279	304	362	61	88	121	131	153
Iraq Iraq	748	268	504	400	330	55	20	20	15	12
Israel Israël	1 063	943	1 509	1 656	1 839	1 382	1 306	1 842	2 110	2 266
Japan Japon	1 879	2 104	2 103	1 925	1 915	3 578	3 435	3 588	3 557	3 477
Jordan Jordanie	572	436	661	765	844	512	317	462	563	582
Korea, Dem. P. R. Corée, R. p. dém. de	115	116	117	120	126	...	...	...	...	...
Korea, Republic of Corée, République de	2 959	3 196	3 231	3 331	3 580	3 559	3 426	3 272	3 475	3 806
Kuwait Koweït	15	4	65	73	73	132	253	273	83	101
Kyrgyzstan Kirghizistan	..	...	9	10	11	..	...	2	2	2
Lao People's Dem. Rep. Rép. dém. pop. lao	14	38	88	103	146	3	8	18	34	43

77
Tourist arrivals and international tourism receipts
[*cont.*]

Arrivées de touristes et recettes touristiques internationales
[*suite*]

Country or area Pays ou zone	Number of tourist arrivals (000) Nombre d'arrivées de touristes (000)					Tourist receipts (million US dollars) Recettes touristiques (millions de dollars E-U)				
	1990	1991	1992	1993	1994	1990	1991	1992	1993	1994
Lebanon Liban	...	...	178	266	335	...	...	...	600	672
Macau Macao	2 513	3 047	3 180	3 915	4 489	1 473	1 761	2 234	2 460	2 688
Malaysia Malaisie	7 446	5 847	6 016	6 504	7 197	1 667	1 530	1 768	1 876	3 189
Maldives Maldives	195	196	236	241	280	89	95	138	146	181
Mongolia Mongolie	147	147	140	150	151	5	5	3	4	4
Myanmar Myanmar	21	22	27	48	83	9	13	16	19	24
Nepal Népal	255	293	334	294	327	109	126	110	157	172
Oman Oman	149	161	192	344	358	69	63	85	86	88
Pakistan Pakistan	424	438	352	379	454	156	163	120	111	117
Philippines Philippines	893	849	1 043	1 246	1 414	1 306	1 281	1 674	2 122	2 282
Qatar Qatar	136	143	141	160	241	...	...	...	...	...
Saudi Arabia Arabie saoudite	827	720	750	993	1 017	1 884	1 000	1 000	1 121	1 140
Singapore Singapour	4 842	4 913	5 446	5 804	6 268	4 596	4 560	5 580	6 289	7 067
Sri Lanka Sri Lanka	298	318	394	392	408	132	157	201	208	224
Syrian Arab Republic Rép. arabe syrienne	562	622	684	703	718	300	410	600	730	800
Thailand Thaïlande	5 299	5 087	5 136	5 761	6 166	4 326	3 923	4 829	5 013	5 762
Turkey Turquie	4 799	5 158	6 549	5 904	6 034	3 225	2 654	3 639	3 959	4 321
United Arab Emirates[1] Emirats arabes unis[1]	633	717	944	1 088	1 239	...	...	...	...	...
Viet Nam Viet Nam	250	300	440	670	1 018	85	85	80	85	85
Yemen Yémen	52	44	72	70	40	40	21	47	45	41
Europe **Europe**	**279 285**	**280 384**	**297 025**	**304 024**	**319 545**	**138 115**	**138 341**	**155 582**	**149 967**	**166 458**
Albania Albanie	30	13	28	45	28	7	5	9	8	5
Austria Autriche	19 011	19 092	19 098	18 257	17 894	13 410	13 800	14 526	13 566	13 160
Belgium Belgique	5 147	4 928	5 204	5 120	5 309	3 721	3 612	4 101	4 054	5 182

77
Tourist arrivals and international tourism receipts
[cont.]

Arrivées de touristes et recettes touristiques internationales
[suite]

Country or area Pays ou zone	Number of tourist arrivals (000) Nombre d'arrivées de touristes (000)					Tourist receipts (million US dollars) Recettes touristiques (millions de dollars E-U)				
	1990	1991	1992	1993	1994	1990	1991	1992	1993	1994
Bulgaria Bulgarie	4 500	4 000	3 750	3 827	4 055	320	44	215	307	358
Croatia Croatie	7 049	1 346	1 271	1 521	2 293	1 704	300	543	832	1 427
Czech Republic République tchèque	7 278	7 565	10 900	11 500	17 000	419	714	1 126	1 558	1 966
Denmark Danemark	1 275	1 429	1 543	1 569	1 585	3 322	3 475	3 784	3 052	3 174
Estonia Estonie	..	...	372	470	550	..	...	27	50	92
Finland Finlande	866	786	790	798	833	1 170	1 247	1 360	1 239	1 436
France France	52 497	55 041	59 740	60 565	61 312	20 185	21 375	25 051	23 565	25 629
Germany †[2] Allemagne†[2]	17 045	15 648	15 913	14 348	14 494	11 471	11 666	10 996	10 429	11 091
Gibraltar Gibraltar	132	97	88	80	82	112	98	82	90	91
Greece Grèce	8 873	8 036	9 331	9 413	10 713	2 587	2 567	3 272	3 335	3 905
Hungary Hongrie	20 510	21 860	20 188	22 804	21 425	824	1 002	1 231	1 181	1 428
Iceland Islande	142	143	143	157	179	139	136	128	128	137
Ireland Irlande	3 666	3 571	3 724	3 888	4 309	1 453	1 514	1 620	1 600	1 765
Italy Italie	26 679	25 878	26 113	26 379	27 480	20 016	18 421	21 450	20 521	23 927
Latvia Lettonie	..	...	35	75	90	..	...	7	15	18
Liechtenstein Liechtenstein	78	71	72	65	62	...	...	...	...	...
Lithuania Lituanie	..	...	325	324	222	..	...	103	102	70
Luxembourg Luxembourg	820	861	796	831	762	290	285	287	290	291
Malta Malte	872	895	1 002	1 063	1 176	495	542	566	607	639
Monaco Monaco	245	239	246	208	217	...	...	...	...	...
Netherlands Pays-Bas	5 795	5 842	6 083	5 757	6 178	3 636	4 246	5 237	4 690	5 612
Norway Norvège	1 955	2 114	2 375	2 556	2 830	1 570	1 646	1 975	1 849	2 157
Poland Pologne	3 400	11 350	16 200	17 000	18 800	358	2 800	4 100	4 500	6 150
Portugal Portugal	8 020	8 657	8 884	8 434	9 132	3 555	3 710	3 721	4 102	4 087

77
Tourist arrivals and international tourism receipts
[*cont.*]

Arrivées de touristes et recettes touristiques internationales
[*suite*]

Country or area Pays ou zone	Number of tourist arrivals (000) Nombre d'arrivées de touristes (000)					Tourist receipts (million US dollars) Recettes touristiques (millions de dollars E-U)				
	1990	1991	1992	1993	1994	1990	1991	1992	1993	1994
Republic of Moldova République de Moldova	..	...	226	56	21	..	...	4	2	2
Romania Roumanie	3 009	3 000	3 798	2 911	2 796	106	145	262	197	414
Russian Federation Fédération de Russie	..	...	3 009	5 896	4 643	..	...	752	1 474	1 161
San Marino Saint-Marin	582	582	583	585	533	...	...	...	...	...
Slovakia Slovaquie	822	635	566	653	902	70	135	213	390	568
Slovenia Slovénie	650	250	616	624	748	721	275	671	734	932
Spain Espagne	37 441	38 539	39 638	40 085	43 232	18 593	19 004	22 181	19 425	21 853
Sweden Suède	731	623	650	659	673	2 916	2 704	3 055	2 650	2 826
Switzerland Suisse	13 200	12 600	12 800	12 400	12 200	6 789	7 026	7 463	7 011	7 570
TFYR Macedonia L'ex-R.y. Macédoine	562	294	219	208	185	45	9	11	13	29
Ukraine Ukraine	..	...	581	685	772	..	...	173	188	230
United Kingdom Royaume-Uni	18 013	17 125	18 535	19 398	21 034	14 940	13 070	13 932	14 031	15 176
Yugoslavia Yougoslavie	1 186	379	156	77	91	419	134	88	23	31
Oceania Océanie	**5 181**	**5 231**	**5 812**	**6 308**	**7 265**	**7 102**	**7 630**	**8 185**	**8 031**	**9 846**
American Samoa Samoa américaines	47	40	31	40	41	10	10	10	10	10
Australia Australie	2 215	2 370	2 603	2 996	3 362	4 088	4 484	4 405	4 655	5 955
Cook Islands Iles Cook	34	40	50	53	57	16	21	27	33	40
Fiji Fidji	279	259	279	287	319	199	194	218	236	298
French Polynesia Polynésie française	132	121	124	148	166	171	150	170	200	235
Guam Guam	780	737	877	784	1 087	936	1 093	1 579	950	1 095
Kiribati Kiribati	3	3	4	4	4	1	1	1	1	1
Marshall Islands Iles Marshall	5	7	8	5	5	...	3	3	3	2
New Caledonia Nouvelle-Calédonie	87	81	78	81	85	94	94	93	95	102
New Zealand Nouvelle-Zélande	976	963	1 056	1 157	1 323	1 019	1 021	1 032	1 165	1 357

77
Tourist arrivals and international tourism receipts
[*cont.*]

Arrivées de touristes et recettes touristiques internationales
[*suite*]

Country or area Pays ou zone	Number of tourist arrivals (000) Nombre d'arrivées de touristes (000)					Tourist receipts (million US dollars) Recettes touristiques (millions de dollars E-U)				
	1990	1991	1992	1993	1994	1990	1991	1992	1993	1994
Niue Nioué	1	1	2	3	4	...	...	...	...	...
Northern Mariana Islands Iles Marianas du Nord	426	422	496	534	588	455	450	528	571	624
Palau Palaos	33	33	36	40	41	...	...	...	...	...
Papua New Guinea Papouasie-Nvl-Guinée	41	37	43	34	39	41	41	49	45	55
Samoa Samoa	48	35	38	48	50	20	18	17	21	23
Solomon Islands Iles Salomon	9	11	12	12	12	4	5	6	6	6
Tonga Tonga	21	22	23	26	28	9	10	9	10	10
Tuvalu Tuvalu	1	1	1	1	1	...	...	...	...	...
Vanuatu Vanuatu	35	40	43	44	42	39	35	38	30	33
former USSR† ancienne URSS†	7 204	6 895	..	..	..	2 752	2 634	..	..	..

Source:
World Tourism Organization (Madrid).

† For detailed descriptions of data pertaining to
former Czechoslovakia, Germany, SFR Yugoslavia and former
USSR, see Annex I - Country or area nomenclature, regional
and other groupings.

1 Dubai only.
2 The data relate to the territory of the Federal Republic of
Germany prior to 3 October 1990. As of 1990, tourists from
the former German Democratic Republic will be regarded as
domestic tourists.

Source:
Organisation mondiale du tourisme (Madrid).

† Pour les descriptions en détails des données
relatives à l'ancienne Tchécoslovaquie, l'Allemagne, la Rfs
Yougoslavie et l'ancienne URSS, voir l'Annexe I -
Nomenclature des pays ou zones, groupements régionaux et
autres groupements.

1 Dubai seulement.
2 Les données se réfèrent au territoire de la République
fédéral d'Allemagne avant le 3 octobre 1990. A partir de
1990, les touristes en provenance de l'ancienne Répulique
Démocratique Allemande seront considérés comme des touristes
nationaux.

78
International tourism expenditures
Dépenses provenant du tourisme international
Million US dollars
Millions de dollars E-U

Country or area Pays ou zone	1985	1986	1987	1988	1989	1990	1991	1992	1993	1994
World *Monde*	101 438	125 400	156 191	185 053	198 637	246 205	246 157	277 206	271 880	302 092
Africa **Afrique**	2 852	2 752	3 225	3 731	4 228	4 586	5 541	5 434	5 679	5 532
Algeria Algérie	606	440	239	294	212	149	140	163	163	135
Angola Angola	...	...	15	15	37	38	65	75	66	50
Benin Bénin	8	10	12	13	10	12	10	12	13	19
Botswana Botswana	17	19	26	32	49	41	49	54	59	52
Burkina Faso Burkina Faso	20	19	28	30	30	32	22	37	35	30
Burundi Burundi	9	14	17	15	14	17	18	21	20	4
Cameroon Cameroun	130	205	244	283	321	279	414	228	225	212
Cape Verde Cap-Vert	...	...	4	3	3	5	3	6	8	9
Central African Rep. Rép. centrafricaine	24	31	41	45	45	51	43	51	50	43
Chad Tchad	20	30	47	32	33	36	32	30	12	11
Comoros Comores	7	13	5	5	5	6	7	6	6	5
Congo Congo	63	67	79	126	86	113	106	93	68	36
Côte d'Ivoire Côte d'Ivoire	106	195	233	235	168	169	163	168	160	118
Djibouti Djibouti	...	...	...	...	...	...	...	7	7	6
Egypt Egypte	106	52	78	43	87	129	225	918	1 048	1 067
Equatorial Guinea Guinée équatoriale	...	...	...	...	8	8	9	9	9	8
Ethiopia Ethiopie	4	5	6	6	10	11	7	10	11	9
Gabon Gabon	83	131	132	134	124	137	112	143	154	143
Gambia Gambie	2	2	3	5	5	8	15	13	14	14
Ghana Ghana	10	11	12	12	13	13	14	17	20	20
Guinea Guinée	...	...	...	29	23	30	27	17	28	29
Kenya Kenya	15	22	24	23	27	38	24	29	48	115

78
International tourism expenditures
Million US dollars [cont.]
Dépenses provenant du tourisme international
Millions de dollars E-U [suite]

Country or area Pays ou zone	1985	1986	1987	1988	1989	1990	1991	1992	1993	1994
Lesotho Lesotho	5	8	9	11	10	12	11	11	7	7
Libyan Arab Jamah. Jamah. arabe libyenne	409	149	322	428	512	424	877	154	206	210
Madagascar Madagascar	24	31	26	30	38	40	32	21	25	23
Malawi Malawi	8	7	6	3	10	16	27	24	11	15
Mali Mali	37	49	57	58	56	62	60	65	60	54
Mauritania Mauritanie	17	18	25	23	31	23	26	31	20	20
Mauritius Maurice	19	26	51	64	79	94	110	142	128	140
Morocco Maroc	88	100	132	164	153	184	190	242	245	302
Namibia Namibie	...	...	...	...	...	65	71	74	73	75
Niger Niger	9	9	34	35	32	44	40	30	29	21
Nigeria Nigéria	200	90	55	41	416	576	839	348	234	144
Rwanda Rwanda	11	14	15	16	17	23	17	17	17	18
Sao Tome and Principe Sao Tomé-et-Principe	1	1	1	1	2	2	2	2	2	1
Senegal Sénégal	38	49	55	76	72	105	105	112	106	70
Seychelles Seychelles	9	10	12	13	17	20	12	16	16	17
Sierra Leone Sierra Leone	1	6	17	3	4	4	4	3	4	4
South Africa Afrique du Sud	413	603	838	958	936	1 117	1 148	1 544	1 721	1 678
Sudan Soudan	43	32	35	99	144	51	12	33	33	30
Swaziland Swaziland	11	12	14	18	10	14	20	17	27	21
Togo Togo	22	27	29	34	34	43	45	48	30	28
Tunisia Tunisie	126	107	95	119	134	179	129	166	203	216
Uganda Ouganda	...	9	13	11	10	8	18	18	40	78
United Rep.Tanzania Rép. Unie de Tanzanie	16	15	23	23	23	22	68	82	102	105
Zaire Zaïre	35	45	22	16	17	16	16	16	16	12

78
International tourism expenditures
Million US dollars [*cont.*]
Dépenses provenant du tourisme international
Millions de dollars E-U [*suite*]

Country or area Pays ou zone	1985	1986	1987	1988	1989	1990	1991	1992	1993	1994
Zambia Zambie	22	31	46	49	98	54	87	56	56	58
Zimbabwe Zimbabwe	58	38	48	58	63	66	70	55	44	50
America, North **Amérique du Nord**	**32 410**	**33 821**	**38 566**	**43 484**	**47 604**	**55 264**	**54 544**	**58 194**	**59 290**	**63 098**
Antigua and Barbuda Antigua-et-Barbuda	13	14	15	16	16	18	20	23	23	24
Aruba Aruba	17	12	22	23	28	40	47	51	57	65
Bahamas Bahamas	123	132	153	172	184	196	200	187	171	192
Barbados Barbade	23	29	36	37	45	47	44	41	52	50
Belize Belize	5	5	5	7	8	7	8	14	21	20
Bermuda Bermudes	76	81	77	109	121	119	126	134	140	143
Canada Canada	4 130	4 294	5 304	6 460	8 044	10 401	11 367	11 289	10 629	11 676
Costa Rica Costa Rica	53	60	71	72	114	148	149	223	267	300
Dominica Dominique	3	2	2	2	4	4	5	6	5	4
Dominican Republic Rép. dominicaine	84	89	95	75	85	101	109	115	118	123
El Salvador El Salvador	89	74	76	75	93	61	57	58	61	70
Grenada Grenade	3	4	4	5	4	5	5	4	4	4
Guatemala Guatemala	61	82	95	109	126	100	67	103	116	129
Haiti Haïti	43	37	42	34	33	32	33	25	20	15
Honduras Honduras	27	30	35	37	38	38	37	38	39	39
Jamaica Jamaïque	32	35	44	57	114	114	71	87	82	81
Mexico Mexique	2 258	2 178	2 366	3 202	4 248	5 519	5 814	6 107	5 562	5 363
Montserrat Montserrat	...	...	...	...	2	2	2	1	3	3
Nicaragua Nicaragua	6	4	6	2	1	15	28	30	34	38
Panama Panama	73	83	90	89	86	99	109	120	129	131
Puerto Rico Porto Rico	411	416	488	533	589	630	689	736	776	797

78
International tourism expenditures
Million US dollars [cont.]
Dépenses provenant du tourisme international
Millions de dollars E-U [suite]

Country or area Pays ou zone	1985	1986	1987	1988	1989	1990	1991	1992	1993	1994
Saint Kitts and Nevis Saint-Kitts-et-Nevis	2	2	3	3	3	4	5	5	5	6
Saint Lucia Sainte-Lucie	44	15	15	21	13	17	18	21	20	23
St. Vincent-Grenadines St. Vincent-Grenadines	7	4	4	4	5	4	4	4	3	3
Trinidad and Tobago Trinité-et-Tobago	219	165	158	168	119	112	113	115	115	90
United States Etats-Unis	24 558	25 913	29 310	32 114	33 418	37 349	35 322	38 552	40 713	43 562
America, South **Amérique du Sud**	**3 461**	**4 421**	**4 070**	**4 202**	**4 060**	**5 361**	**5 901**	**6 860**	**8 555**	**9 306**
Argentina Argentine	671	888	890	975	1 014	1 171	1 739	2 211	2 445	2 500
Bolivia Bolivie	38	27	56	63	106	130	129	141	137	140
Brazil Brésil	1 145	1 464	1 249	1 084	750	1 505	1 214	1 221	1 958	2 947
Chile Chili	269	319	353	423	397	426	409	535	560	639
Colombia Colombie	169	611	454	538	494	454	509	641	644	756
Ecuador Equateur	196	156	170	167	169	175	177	178	190	203
Paraguay Paraguay	47	48	51	54	50	58	118	135	138	176
Peru Pérou	154	179	201	240	263	296	263	255	268	323
Suriname Suriname	13	12	8	10	10	12	16	11	3	3
Uruguay Uruguay	162	174	129	139	167	111	100	104	129	190
Venezuela Venezuela	597	543	509	509	640	1 023	1 227	1 428	2 083	1 429
Asia **Asie**	**14 875**	**17 534**	**22 228**	**32 704**	**39 475**	**44 720**	**46 803**	**55 319**	**57 342**	**65 332**
Afghanistan Afghanistan	2	1	1	1	1	1	1	1	1	1
Bahrain Bahreïn	125	59	80	77	77	94	98	141	130	146
Bangladesh Bangladesh	45	54	53	99	123	78	83	111	153	210
Cambodia Cambodge	...	...	...	...	...	...	...	...	4	7
China Chine	314	308	387	633	429	470	511	2 512	2 797	3 036
Cyprus Chypre	39	54	67	81	78	111	113	132	133	176

78
International tourism expenditures
Million US dollars [cont.]
Dépenses provenant du tourisme international
Millions de dollars E-U [suite]

Country or area Pays ou zone	1985	1986	1987	1988	1989	1990	1991	1992	1993	1994
India Inde	354	302	352	397	416	393	394	394	400	408
Indonesia Indonésie	591	570	511	592	722	836	969	1 166	1 539	1 900
Iran, Islamic Rep. of Iran, Rép. islamique d'	508	247	246	69	129	340	734	1 109	578	570
Israel Israël	549	801	1 043	1 161	1 261	1 442	1 551	1 674	2 313	2 896
Japan Japon	4 814	7 229	10 760	18 682	22 490	24 928	23 983	26 837	26 860	30 715
Jordan Jordanie	424	445	444	475	422	336	282	350	345	394
Korea, Republic of Corée, République de	606	613	704	1 354	2 602	3 166	3 784	3 794	3 259	4 088
Kuwait Koweït	1 988	1 941	2 257	2 358	2 250	1 837	2 012	1 797	1 819	2 146
Kyrgyzstan Kirghizistan	..	..	..	..	..	..	...	...	...	2
Lao People's Dem. Rep. Rép. dém. pop. lao	...	...	...	1	2	1	6	10	11	18
Macau Macao	20	22	24	26	32	39	49	57	71	103
Malaysia Malaisie	1 158	1 669	1 234	1 306	1 365	1 450	1 584	1 770	1 838	1 737
Maldives Maldives	5	6	6	8	10	15	19	22	29	32
Mongolia Mongolie	...	...	...	...	...	1	2	4	3	3
Myanmar Myanmar	19	1	1	1	8	16	24	24	24	24
Nepal Népal	29	29	35	44	48	45	38	52	93	112
Oman Oman	...	47	47	47	47	47	47	47	47	47
Pakistan Pakistan	202	221	248	338	337	440	555	679	633	398
Philippines Philippines	37	56	88	76	77	111	61	102	130	196
Singapore Singapour	613	645	795	930	1 334	1 804	1 944	2 417	3 022	3 665
Sri Lanka Sri Lanka	46	55	63	68	69	74	97	111	121	167
Syrian Arab Republic Rép. arabe syrienne	302	160	131	170	194	223	256	260	300	400
Thailand Thaïlande	280	296	381	602	750	854	1 266	1 590	2 090	2 906
Turkey Turquie	324	314	448	358	565	520	592	776	934	866

78
International tourism expenditures
Million US dollars [cont.]
Dépenses provenant du tourisme international
Millions de dollars E-U [suite]

Country or area Pays ou zone	1985	1986	1987	1988	1989	1990	1991	1992	1993	1994
Yemen Yémen	52	18	37	47	81	64	70	101	80	78
Europe **Europe**	**45 484**	**64 118**	**84 726**	**96 879**	**98 132**	**130 683**	**128 022**	**146 010**	**135 784**	**153 240**
Albania Albanie	...	...	...	...	...	4	3	5	6	4
Austria Autriche	2 723	4 026	5 592	6 307	6 266	7 723	7 392	8 393	8 180	9 330
Belgium Belgique	2 050	2 889	3 881	4 577	4 254	5 477	5 543	6 714	6 338	7 782
Bulgaria Bulgarie	...	...	69	74	113	189	128	313	257	242
Croatia Croatie	..	..	..	..	..	729	231	158	298	552
former Czechoslovakia† anc. Tchécoslovaquie†	300	349	409	399	..	..	..	..	..	
Czech Republic République tchèque	..	..	..	..	300	455	274	467	525	832
Denmark Danemark	1 410	2 119	2 860	3 087	2 932	3 676	3 377	3 779	3 214	3 583
Estonia Estonie	..	..	..	..	..	..	...	19	25	48
Finland Finlande	777	1 060	1 506	1 842	2 040	2 740	2 742	2 449	1 617	1 727
France France	4 557	6 513	8 493	9 715	10 031	12 424	12 321	13 914	12 836	13 875
Germany †[1] Allemagne†[1]	12 809	18 000	23 341	24 564	23 553	32 180	34 250	35 702	36 345	43 398
Greece Grèce	368	494	508	735	816	1 090	1 015	1 186	1 003	1 125
Hungary Hongrie	126	150	158	550	947	477	443	640	741	925
Iceland Islande	94	129	213	200	176	277	292	287	257	249
Ireland Irlande	429	685	839	961	989	1 163	1 128	1 361	1 224	1 575
Italy Italie	2 283	2 910	4 536	5 929	6 774	14 045	11 648	16 530	13 053	12 181
Latvia Lettonie	..	..	..	..	..	..	...	13	29	31
Lithuania Lituanie	..	..	..	..	..	..	...	...	...	50
Malta Malte	50	69	102	120	107	137	132	138	154	176
Netherlands Pays-Bas	3 448	4 901	6 408	6 701	6 461	7 376	8 149	9 649	8 974	10 983
Norway Norvège	1 722	2 511	3 067	3 532	2 986	3 679	3 413	3 870	3 565	3 930

78
International tourism expenditures
Million US dollars [cont.]
Dépenses provenant du tourisme international
Millions de dollars E-U [suite]

Country or area Pays ou zone	1985	1986	1987	1988	1989	1990	1991	1992	1993	1994
Poland Pologne	184	186	203	251	215	423	143	132	181	316
Portugal Portugal	235	329	421	533	583	867	1 024	1 165	2 058	1 705
Romania Roumanie	64	22	30	33	35	103	143	260	195	449
Slovakia Slovaquie	..	..	..	..	131	181	119	155	262	284
Slovenia Slovénie	..	..	..	..	..	..	..	282	304	312
Spain Espagne	1 010	1 513	1 938	2 440	3 080	4 254	4 530	5 542	4 706	4 188
Sweden Suède	1 967	2 821	3 784	4 565	4 961	6 134	6 291	6 969	4 464	4 878
Switzerland Suisse	2 399	3 368	4 339	5 019	4 907	5 817	5 682	6 068	5 915	6 325
United Kingdom Royaume-Uni	6 369	8 942	11 939	14 636	15 344	19 063	17 609	19 850	19 058	22 185
Yugoslavia, SFR† Yougoslavie, Rfs†	110	132	90	109	131	..	..	..	..	..
Oceania **Océanie**	**2 356**	**2 754**	**3 376**	**4 053**	**5 138**	**5 591**	**5 346**	**5 389**	**5 230**	**5 584**
Australia Australie	1 918	2 058	2 427	2 965	4 103	4 535	4 247	4 301	4 100	4 339
Fiji Fidji	18	24	53	35	31	31	36	35	39	55
Kiribati Kiribati	...	...	...	2	2	2	2	2	2	2
New Zealand Nouvelle-Zélande	389	637	852	988	944	958	987	977	1 003	1 101
Papua New Guinea Papouasie-Nvl-Guinée	21	22	32	48	42	50	57	57	69	70
Samoa Samoa	1	2	2	1	2	2	2	2	2	2
Solomon Islands Iles Salomon	4	6	6	9	10	11	12	11	11	11
Tonga Tonga	3	3	3	3	3	1	2	3	3	3
Vanuatu Vanuatu	2	2	1	2	1	1	1	1	1	1

Source:
World Tourism Organization (Madrid).

Source:
Organisation mondiale du tourisme (Madrid).

† For detailed descriptions of data pertaining to

† Pour les descriptions en détails des données

78

International tourism expenditures
Million US dollars [*cont.*]

Dépenses provenant du tourisme international
Millions de dollars E-U [*suite*]

former Czechoslovakia, Germany, SFR Yugoslavia and former USSR, see Annex I - Country or area nomenclature, regional and other groupings.

relatives à l'ancienne Tchécoslovaquie, l'Allemagne, la Rfs Yougoslavie et l'ancienne URSS, voir l'Annexe I - Nomenclature des pays ou zones, groupements régionaux et autres groupements.

1 The data relate to the territory of the Federal Republic of Germany prior to 3 October 1990. As of 1990, tourists from the former German Democratic Republic will be regarded as domestic tourists.

1 Les données se réfèrent au territoire de la République fédéral d'Allemagne avant le 3 octobre 1990. A partir de 1990, les touristes en provenance de l'ancienne Répulique Démocratique Allemande seront considérés comme des touristes nationaux.

Technical notes, tables 76-78

Tables 76 and 77: For statistical purposes, the term "international visitor" describes "any person who travels to a country other than that in which he/she has his/her usual residence but outside his/her usual environment for a period not exceeding 12 months and whose main purpose of visit is other than the exercise of an activity remunerated from within the country visited".

International visitors include:

(a) *Tourists*, (overnight visitor): "a visitor who stays at least one night in a collective or private accommodation in the country visited"; and

(b) *Same-day visitors*: "a visitor who does not spend the night in a collective or private accommodation in the country visited".

Unless otherwise stated, same-day visitors are not included in these tables.

The figures do not therefore include immigrants, residents in a frontier zone, persons domiciled in one country or area and working in an adjoining country or area, members of the armed forces and diplomats and consular representatives when they travel from their country of origin to the country in which they are stationed and vice-versa.

The figures also exclude persons in transit who do not formally enter the country through passport control, such as air transit passengers who remain for a short period in a designated area of the air terminal or ship passengers who are not permitted to disembark. This category would include passengers transferred directly between airports or other terminals. Other passengers in transit through a country are classified as visitors.

These data are based generally on a frontier check. In the absence of frontier check figures, data based on arrivals at accommodation establishments are given but these are not strictly comparable with frontier check data as they exclude certain types of tourists such as campers and tourists staying in private houses, while on the other hand they may contain some duplication when a tourist moves from one establishment to another.

Unless otherwise stated, table 76 shows the number of tourist arrivals at frontiers classified by their region of origin. Totals correspond to the total number of arrivals from the regions indicated in the table. However, these totals may not correspond to the number of tourist arrivals shown in table 77. The later excludes same-day visitors whereas they may be included in table 76. More detailed information will be found in *Yearbook of Tourism Statistics*, published by the World Tourism Organization. [35]

Notes techniques, tableaux 76-78

Tableaux 76 et 77 : A des fins statistiques, l'expression *"visiteur international"* désigne "toute personne qui se rend dans un pays autre que celui où elle a son lieu de résidence habituelle, mais différent de son environnement habituel, pour une période de 12 mois au maximum, dans un but principal autre que celui d'y exercer une profession rémunérée".

Entrent dans cette catégorie :

(a) Les *touristes* (visiteurs passant la nuit), c'est à dire "les visiteurs qui passent une nuit au moins en logement collectif ou privé dans le pays visité";

(b) Les *visiteurs ne restant que la journée*, c'est à dire "les visiteurs qui ne passent pas la nuit en logement collectif ou privé dans le pays visité".

Sauf indication contraire, les visiteurs ne restant que la journée ne sont pas inclus dans ces tableaux.

Par conséquent, ces chiffres ne comprennent pas les immigrants, les résidents frontaliers, les personnes domiciliées dans une zone ou un pays donné et travaillant dans une zone ou pays limitrophe, les membres des forces armées et les membres des corps diplomatique et consulaire lorsqu'ils se rendent de leur pays d'origine au pays où ils sont en poste, et vice versa.

Ne sont pas non plus inclus les voyageurs en transit, qui ne pénètrent pas officiellement dans le pays en faisant contrôler leurs passeports, tels que les passagers d'un vol en escale, qui demeurent pendant un court laps de temps dans une aire distincte de l'aérogare, ou les passagers d'un navire qui ne sont pas autorisés à débarquer. Cette catégorie com-prend également les passagers transportés directement d'une aérogare à l'autre ou à un autre terminal. Les autres passa-gers en transit dans un pays sont classés parmi les visiteurs.

Ces données reposent en général sur un contrôle à la frontière. A défaut, les données sont tirées des établissements d'hébergement, mais elles ne sont alors pas strictement comparables à celles du contrôle à la frontière, en ce qu'elles excluent, d'une part, certaines catégories de touristes telles que les campeurs et les touristes séjournant dans des maisons privées, et que, d'autre part, elles peuvent compter deux fois le même touriste si celui-ci change d'établissement d'hébergement.

Sauf indication contraire, le tableau 76 indique le nombre d'arrivées de touristes par région de provenance. Les totaux correspondent au nombre total d'arrivées de touristes des régions indiquées sur le tableau. Les chiffres totaux peuvent néanmoins, ne pas coïncider avec le nombre des arrivées de touristes indiqué dans le tableau 77, qui ne comprend pas les visiteurs ne restant que la journée, lesquels peuvent au contraire être inclus dans les chiffres du tableau 76. Pour plus de renseignements, consulter l'*Annuaire des statistiques du tourisme* publié par l'Organisation mondiale du tourisme [35].

Unless otherwise stated the data on tourist receipts have been supplied by the World Tourism Organization. Tourist receipts are defined as "expenditure of international inbound visitors including their payments to national carriers for international transport. They should also include any other prepayments made for goods/services received in the destination country. They should in practice also include receipts from same-day visitors, except in cases when these are so important as to justify a separate classification. It is also recommended that, for the sake of consistancy with the Balance of Payments recommendations of the International Monetary Fund, international fare receipts be classified separately.

Table 78: International tourism expenditure are defined as "expenditure of outbound visitors in other countries including their payments to foreign carriers for international transport. They should in practice also include expenditure of residents travelling abroad as same-day visitors, except in cases when these are so important as to justify a separate classification. It is also recommended that, for the sake of consistency with the Balance of Payments recommendations of the International Monetary Fund, international fare expenditure be classified separately".

For more detailed statistics on the number of tourists and expenditures, see *Yearbook of Tourism Statistics* published by the World Tourism Organization.[35] For detailed definitions of tourist receipts, see *Balance of Payments Yearbook* published by the International Monetary Fund.[12]

For detailed information on methods of collection for frontier statistics, accommodation statistics and foreign exchange statistics see *Methodological Supplement to World Travel and Tourism Statistics* published by the World Tourism Organization.[58; see also 51 and 55.]

Sauf indication contraire, les données sur les recettes du tourisme ont été fournies par l'Organisation mondiale du tourisme et sont définies comme "les sommes dépensées par les visiteurs internationaux arrivant dans le pays, y compris les sommes versées aux transporteurs nationaux en paiement de transports internationaux. Il faut également y inclure tout autre versement effectué à l'avance pour des biens ou services à recevoir dans le pays de destination. Dans la pratique, il faut également y inclure les recettes provenant de visiteurs ne restant que la journée, sauf dans les cas où elles sont suffisamment importantes pour justifier une classification distincte. Il est recommandé aussi, dans un souci de cohérence avec les recommandations du Fonds monétaire international visant la balance des paiements, de classer à part les recettes au titre des transports internationaux".

Tableau 78 : Les dépenses du tourisme international sont définies comme étant les dépenses effectuées par les résidents du pays en visite à l'étranger, y compris les sommes versées aux transporteurs étrangers en règlement des transports internationaux. En pratique, ce poste devrait également inclure les dépenses des résidents qui voyagent à l'étranger pour la journée, sauf dans le cas où ces dépenses sont suffisamment importantes pour justifier une classification distincte. Il est recommandé aussi, dans un souci de cohérence avec les recommandations du Fonds monétaire international visant la balance des paiements, de classer à part les dépenses au titre des transports internationaux.

Pour des statistiques plus détaillées sur le nombre de touristes et les dépenses, voir l'*Annuaire des statistiques du tourisme* publié par l'Organisation mondiale du tourisme [35]. Pour des définitions détaillées des recettes touristiques, voir *"Balance of Payments Yearbook"* publié par le Fonds monétaire international [12].

Pour plus de renseignements sur les méthodes de collecte de données statistiques sur les contrôles aux frontières, l'hébergement et les mouvements de devises, voir *"Supplément méthodologique aux statistiques des voyages et du tourisme mondiaux"* publié par l'Organisation mondiale du tourisme [58; voir aussi 51 et 55].

79
Summary of balance of payments
Résumé des balances des paiements
Millions of US dollars
Millions de dollars des E−U

Country or area	1988	1989	1990	1991	1992	1993	1994	Pays ou zone
	Africa· Afrique							
Algeria								**Algérie**
Goods: Exports fob	7 620.0	9 534.0	12 965.0	12 330.0	...	...	...	Biens : exportations,fàb
Goods: Imports fob	−6 685.0	−8 390.0	−8 786.0	−6 862.0	...	...	...	Biens : importations,fàb
Serv. & Income: Credit	541.0	607.0	570.0	463.0	...	...	...	Serv. & revenu : crédit
Serv. & Income: Debit	−3 907.0	−3 371.0	−3 662.0	−3 781.0	...	...	...	Serv. & revenu : débit
Current Trans.,nie: Credit	477.0	603.0	400.0	269.0	...	...	...	Transf. cour.,nia : crédit
Current Transfers: Debit	−86.0	−62.0	−67.0	−53.0	...	...	...	Transf. courants : débit
Capital Acct.,nie: Credit	0.0	0.0	0.0	0.0	...	...	...	Compte de cap.,nia : crédit
Capital Account: Debit	0.0	0.0	0.0	0.0	...	...	...	Compte de capital : débit
Financial Account,nie	744.0	755.0	−1 094.0	−1 020.0	...	...	...	Compte d'op. fin., nia
Net Errors and Omissions	337.0	−448.0	−336.0	−299.0	...	...	...	Erreurs et omissions nettes
Reserves and Related Items	959.0	774.0	10.0	−1 047.0	...	...	...	Rés. et postes appareutés
Angola								**Angola**
Goods: Exports fob	2 492.0	3 014.0	3 883.9	3 449.3	3 832.8	2 900.5	...	Biens : exportations,fàb
Goods: Imports fob	−1 372.0	−1 338.0	−1 578.2	−1 347.2	−1 988.0	−1 462.6	...	Biens : importations,fàb
Serv. & Income: Credit	128.0	150.0	119.1	186.3	158.6	117.1	...	Serv. & revenu : crédit
Serv. & Income: Debit	−1 749.0	−1 954.0	−2 583.2	−2 896.2	−2 840.4	−2 489.3	...	Serv. & revenu : débit
Current Trans.,nie: Credit	42.0	65.0	65.6	111.1	170.9	253.4	...	Transf. cour.,nia : crédit
Current Transfers: Debit	−10.0	−69.0	−142.7	−82.9	−68.7	−87.6	...	Transf. courants : débit
Capital Acct.,nie: Credit	0.0	0.0	0.0	0.0	0.0	0.0	...	Compte de cap.,nia : crédit
Capital Account: Debit	0.0	0.0	0.0	0.0	0.0	0.0	...	Compte de capital : débit
Financial Account,nie	−199.0	−120.0	−954.3	−947.2	−445.9	−274.3	...	Compte d'op. fin., nia
Net Errors and Omissions	−257.0	−678.0	−19.1	26.9	43.0	−277.1	...	Erreurs et omissions nettes
Reserves and Related Items	925.0	930.0	1 208.9	1 499.9	1 137.7	1 319.9	...	Rés. et postes appareutés
Benin								**Bénin**
Goods: Exports fob	376.4	214.7	287.2	336.8	371.4	341.1	301.0	Biens : exportations,fàb
Goods: Imports fob	−507.6	−316.6	−427.9	−482.4	−560.6	−538.9	−365.8	Biens : importations,fàb
Serv. & Income: Credit	99.4	87.8	114.6	122.6	142.8	137.4	103.9	Serv. & revenu : crédit
Serv. & Income: Debit	−174.2	−149.8	−174.1	−169.4	−220.3	−192.5	−151.6	Serv. & revenu : débit
Current Trans.,nie: Credit	160.8	252.7	231.4	199.6	244.1	257.8	159.6	Transf. cour.,nia : crédit
Current Transfers: Debit	−6.7	−7.2	−12.5	−13.8	−16.6	−19.1	−10.6	Transf. courants : débit
Capital Acct.,nie: Credit	0.0	0.0	0.0	0.0	0.0	0.0	0.0	Compte de cap.,nia : crédit
Capital Account: Debit	0.0	0.0	0.0	0.0	0.0	0.0	0.0	Compte de capital : débit
Financial Account,nie	−25.2	2.8	54.3	47.0	−39.9	30.4	−34.4	Compte d'op. fin., nia
Net Errors and Omissions	12.3	−150.2	−63.1	21.6	1.6	−56.4	54.0	Erreurs et omissions nettes
Reserves and Related Items	64.9	65.9	−10.0	−61.9	77.5	40.1	−56.0	Rés. et postes appareutés
Botswana								**Botswana**
Goods: Exports fob	1 468.9	1 819.7	1 795.4	1 871.1	1 743.9	1 722.2	1 878.4	Biens : exportations,fàb
Goods: Imports fob	−986.9	−1 185.1	−1 610.9	−1 604.0	−1 556.6	−1 455.4	−1 350.0	Biens : importations,fàb
Serv. & Income: Credit	330.4	355.3	618.6	685.9	722.5	728.7	399.3	Serv. & revenu : crédit
Serv. & Income: Debit	−785.6	−711.6	−898.0	−802.7	−789.8	−586.5	−754.1	Serv. & revenu : débit
Current Trans.,nie: Credit	301.8	266.8	392.0	455.5	391.1	352.3	370.0	Transf. cour.,nia : crédit
Current Transfers: Debit	−134.7	−53.2	−262.1	−276.0	−275.6	−275.1	−295.1	Transf. courants : débit
Capital Acct.,nie: Credit	...	7.0	4.3	4.6	7.2	9.7	6.5	Compte de cap.,nia : crédit
Capital Account: Debit		−0.7	−0.9	−1.0	−0.5	−1.3	−0.4	Compte de capital : débit
Financial Account,nie	−25.3	113.0	89.7	130.4	284.6	−30.7	16.1	Compte d'op. fin., nia
Net Errors and Omissions	213.7	−34.7	398.8	261.0	−124.8	332.3	264.0	Erreurs et omissions nettes
Reserves and Related Items	−382.3	−576.5	−526.9	−724.7	−401.9	−796.1	−534.7	Rés. et postes appareutés
Burkina Faso								**Burkina Faso**
Goods: Exports fob	240.0	184.6	280.5	269.1	287.5	276.5	225.9	Biens : exportations,fàb
Goods: Imports fob	−477.4	−441.7	−542.5	−490.5	−642.3	−643.4	−365.1	Biens : importations,fàb
Serv. & Income: Credit	72.8	69.2	86.3	84.9	72.9	66.2	0.0	Serv. & revenu : crédit
Serv. & Income: Debit	−269.9	−209.8	−242.6	−282.2	−291.7	−289.5	−106.6	Serv. & revenu : débit
Current Trans.,nie: Credit	452.0	571.6	430.2	413.1	568.6	555.5	273.9	Transf. cour.,nia : crédit
Current Transfers: Debit	−64.1	−74.6	−97.9	−97.7	−92.2	−83.3	−19.5	Transf. courants : débit
Capital Acct.,nie: Credit	0.0	0.0	0.0	0.0	0.0	0.0	0.0	Compte de cap.,nia : crédit
Capital Account: Debit	0.0	0.0	0.0	0.0	0.0	0.0	0.0	Compte de capital : débit
Financial Account,nie	63.5	−228.6	71.7	104.8	118.3	73.3	−3.5	Compte d'op. fin., nia
Net Errors and Omissions	1.1	−5.9	0.1	−5.7	−11.3	56.9	−25.5	Erreurs et omissions nettes
Reserves and Related Items	−18.1	135.2	14.3	4.2	−9.9	−12.1	20.4	Rés. et postes appareutés

79
Summary of balance of payments
Millions of US dollars
Résumé des balances des paiements
Millions de dollars des E−U

Country or area	1988	1989	1990	1991	1992	1993	1994	Pays ou zone
Burundi								**Burundi**
Goods: Exports fob	124.4	93.2	72.9	90.7	79.3	75.0	125.4	Biens : exportations,fàb
Goods: Imports fob	−166.1	−151.4	−189.0	−195.9	−181.8	−172.8	−174.5	Biens : importations,fàb
Serv. & Income: Credit	14.8	24.2	24.9	35.4	31.5	25.4	22.7	Serv. & revenu : crédit
Serv. & Income: Debit	−140.7	−119.1	−152.2	−162.0	−164.9	−137.7	−122.6	Serv. & revenu : débit
Current Trans.,nie: Credit	103.4	142.7	175.5	198.1	180.6	183.8	183.2	Transf. cour.,nia : crédit
Current Transfers: Debit	−5.9	−1.1	−1.3	−1.7	−1.9	−1.8	−1.6	Transf. courants : débit
Capital Acct.,nie: Credit	0.0	0.0	0.0	0.0	0.0	0.0	0.0	Compte de cap.,nia : crédit
Capital Account: Debit	−0.5	−0.6	−0.5	−0.7	−0.8	−1.2	−0.2	Compte de capital : débit
Financial Account,nie	84.3	64.4	78.0	70.4	98.7	52.5	33.4	Compte d'op. fin., nia
Net Errors and Omissions	−6.6	−14.3	−11.5	−1.6	−15.1	−13.0	−40.7	Erreurs et omissions nettes
Reserves and Related Items	−7.1	−38.0	3.2	−32.6	−25.5	−10.2	−25.2	Rés. et postes appareutés
Cameroon								**Cameroun**
Goods: Exports fob	1 841.2	1 853.8	2 125.4	1 957.5	1 934.1	1 507.7	...	Biens : exportations,fàb
Goods: Imports fob	−1 220.8	−1 136.8	−1 347.2	−1 173.1	−983.3	−1 005.3	...	Biens : importations,fàb
Serv. & Income: Credit	473.1	492.5	390.5	424.3	449.3	407.9	...	Serv. & revenu : crédit
Serv. & Income: Debit	−1 412.3	−1 463.2	−1 611.2	−1 565.0	−1 731.2	−1 410.6	...	Serv. & revenu : débit
Current Trans.,nie: Credit	63.8	88.0	82.3	57.0	141.0	65.2	...	Transf. cour.,nia : crédit
Current Transfers: Debit	−176.0	−132.3	−117.5	−105.4	−148.3	−130.2	...	Transf. courants : débit
Capital Acct.,nie: Credit	6.4	5.0	2.9	8.0	17.1	6.4	...	Compte de cap.,nia : crédit
Capital Account: Debit	...	−0.1	−0.1	−0.1	−0.1	−0.1	...	Compte de capital : débit
Financial Account,nie	38.7	319.4	−226.9	−362.2	−346.4	−304.6	...	Compte d'op. fin., nia
Net Errors and Omissions	221.8	−160.7	−168.2	26.9	−640.7	−16.2	...	Erreurs et omissions nettes
Reserves and Related Items	164.1	134.3	870.2	732.2	1 308.6	879.9	...	Rés. et postes appareutés
Cape Verde								**Cap−Vert**
Goods: Exports fob	3.3	6.7	5.6	4.1	4.4	...	...	Biens : exportations,fàb
Goods: Imports fob	−101.8	−106.9	−119.5	−132.2	−173.3	...	...	Biens : importations,fàb
Serv. & Income: Credit	45.0	57.3	61.3	54.3	59.1	...	...	Serv. & revenu : crédit
Serv. & Income: Debit	−24.2	−32.5	−36.9	−23.2	−31.1	...	...	Serv. & revenu : débit
Current Trans.,nie: Credit	80.2	72.9	79.5	94.7	143.0	...	...	Transf. cour.,nia : crédit
Current Transfers: Debit	−2.0	−2.1	−1.9	−5.7	−5.7	...	...	Transf. courants : débit
Capital Acct.,nie: Credit	0.0	0.0	0.0	0.0	0.0	...	...	Compte de cap.,nia : crédit
Capital Account: Debit	0.0	0.0	0.0	0.0	0.0	...	...	Compte de capital : débit
Financial Account,nie	−1.7	−1.1	5.1	2.7	6.1	...	...	Compte d'op. fin., nia
Net Errors and Omissions	−0.7	−1.2	5.2	−7.3	5.5	...	...	Erreurs et omissions nettes
Reserves and Related Items	1.9	6.9	1.7	12.6	−8.0	...	...	Rés. et postes appareutés
Central African Rep.								**Rép. centrafricaine**
Goods: Exports fob	133.7	148.1	150.5	125.6	115.9	132.5	145.9	Biens : exportations,fàb
Goods: Imports fob	−179.1	−186.0	−241.6	−178.7	−189.0	−158.1	−130.6	Biens : importations,fàb
Serv. & Income: Credit	62.3	66.3	69.9	56.0	51.5	53.8	33.1	Serv. & revenu : crédit
Serv. & Income: Debit	−172.2	−165.8	−190.9	−155.7	−174.9	−155.1	−136.5	Serv. & revenu : débit
Current Trans.,nie: Credit	156.7	138.3	164.2	129.7	151.0	152.4	92.6	Transf. cour.,nia : crédit
Current Transfers: Debit	−36.0	−34.2	−41.2	−38.8	−37.6	−38.3	−29.2	Transf. courants : débit
Capital Acct.,nie: Credit	0.0	0.0	0.0	0.0	0.0	0.0	0.0	Compte de cap.,nia : crédit
Capital Account: Debit	0.0	0.0	0.0	0.0	0.0	0.0	0.0	Compte de capital : débit
Financial Account,nie	9.5	20.2	69.3	24.5	18.7	1.3	52.8	Compte d'op. fin., nia
Net Errors and Omissions	11.7	1.4	1.4	−1.9	26.2	6.3	−15.0	Erreurs et omissions nettes
Reserves and Related Items	13.4	11.9	18.5	39.1	38.2	5.3	−13.1	Rés. et postes appareutés
Chad								**Tchad**
Goods: Exports fob	145.9	155.4	230.3	193.5	182.3	151.8	...	Biens : exportations,fàb
Goods: Imports fob	−228.4	−240.3	−259.5	−249.9	−243.0	−215.2	...	Biens : importations,fàb
Serv. & Income: Credit	80.8	43.6	43.9	39.8	44.3	51.4	...	Serv. & revenu : crédit
Serv. & Income: Debit	−233.4	−220.8	−252.0	−219.2	−239.0	−250.8	...	Serv. & revenu : débit
Current Trans.,nie: Credit	301.4	241.4	239.3	215.5	222.3	192.4	...	Transf. cour.,nia : crédit
Current Transfers: Debit	−40.8	−35.2	−47.7	−45.3	−52.5	−46.2	...	Transf. courants : débit
Capital Acct.,nie: Credit	0.0	0.0	0.0	0.0	0.0	0.0	...	Compte de cap.,nia : crédit
Capital Account: Debit	0.0	0.0	0.0	0.0	0.0	0.0	...	Compte de capital : débit
Financial Account,nie	24.2	74.4	56.1	59.9	40.0	74.0	...	Compte d'op. fin., nia
Net Errors and Omissions	−83.7	11.1	−33.3	−13.0	9.2	−0.1	...	Erreurs et omissions nettes
Reserves and Related Items	34.0	−29.6	22.9	18.6	36.5	42.7	...	Rés. et postes appareutés
Comoros								**Comores**
Goods: Exports fob	21.5	18.1	17.9	24.4	...	...	...	Biens : exportations,fàb
Goods: Imports fob	−44.3	−35.7	−45.2	−53.6	...	...	...	Biens : importations,fàb
Serv. & Income: Credit	18.6	21.8	20.2	27.5	...	...	...	Serv. & revenu : crédit
Serv. & Income: Debit	−46.2	−42.6	−46.9	−48.1	...	...	...	Serv. & revenu : débit
Current Trans.,nie: Credit	48.4	49.2	49.4	47.4	...	...	...	Transf. cour.,nia : crédit

79
Summary of balance of payments
Millions of US dollars
Résumé des balances des paiements
Millions de dollars des E-U

Country or area	1988	1989	1990	1991	1992	1993	1994	Pays ou zone
Current Transfers: Debit	−4.5	−5.5	−4.7	−6.5	...	...	...	Transf. courants : débit
Capital Acct.,nie: Credit	0.0	0.0	0.0	0.0	...	...	...	Compte de cap.,nia : crédit
Capital Account: Debit	0.0	0.0	0.0	0.0	...	...	...	Compte de capital : débit
Financial Account,nie	4.2	7.5	13.7	0.6	...	...	...	Compte d'op. fin., nia
Net Errors and Omissions	−1.4	−7.6	−9.2	1.7	...	...	...	Erreurs et omissions nettes
Reserves and Related Items	3.7	−5.4	4.9	6.6	...	...	...	Rés. et postes appareutés
Congo								**Congo**
Goods: Exports fob	843.2	1 160.5	1 388.7	1 107.7	1 178.7	1 119.1	951.5	Biens : exportations,fàb
Goods: Imports fob	−522.7	−532.0	−512.7	−494.5	−438.2	−500.1	−558.5	Biens : importations,fàb
Serv. & Income: Credit	99.8	97.5	113.9	118.1	78.6	67.5	87.9	Serv. & revenu : crédit
Serv. & Income: Debit	−873.4	−857.3	−1 244.0	−1 188.2	−1 117.2	−1 230.4	−1 337.0	Serv. & revenu : débit
Current Trans.,nie: Credit	79.8	119.7	86.3	74.1	54.8	50.5	25.6	Transf. cour.,nia : crédit
Current Transfers: Debit	−72.0	−73.4	−83.4	−78.7	−73.3	−59.3	−37.6	Transf. courants : débit
Capital Acct.,nie: Credit	0.0	0.0	0.0	0.0	0.0	0.0	0.0	Compte de cap.,nia : crédit
Capital Account: Debit	0.0	0.0	0.0	0.0	0.0	0.0	0.0	Compte de capital : débit
Financial Account,nie	−62.0	−325.4	−72.0	9.6	−153.8	−16.6	665.2	Compte d'op. fin., nia
Net Errors and Omissions	40.6	8.5	−40.6	−6.3	40.4	149.3	−58.7	Erreurs et omissions nettes
Reserves and Related Items	466.8	401.8	363.9	458.2	429.9	420.0	261.7	Rés. et postes appareutés
Côte d'Ivoire								**Côte d'Ivoire**
Goods: Exports fob	2 691.3	2 696.8	2 912.6	2 705.0	2 946.8	2 652.3	2 874.6	Biens : exportations,fàb
Goods: Imports fob	−1 769.4	−1 777.1	−1 818.8	−1 781.6	−1 952.1	−1 801.4	−1 566.1	Biens : importations,fàb
Serv. & Income: Credit	627.5	541.7	648.2	674.6	668.1	622.7	446.7	Serv. & revenu : crédit
Serv. & Income: Debit	−2 335.1	−2 226.3	−2 775.2	−2 565.7	−2 577.0	−2 226.2	−1 699.7	Serv. & revenu : débit
Current Trans.,nie: Credit	208.8	316.0	370.2	413.7	404.6	237.0	288.4	Transf. cour.,nia : crédit
Current Transfers: Debit	−664.4	−518.5	−551.3	−520.0	−503.2	−400.5	−330.7	Transf. courants : débit
Capital Acct.,nie: Credit	0.0	0.0	0.0	0.0	0.0	0.0	0.0	Compte de cap.,nia : crédit
Capital Account: Debit	0.0	0.0	0.0	0.0	0.0	0.0	0.0	Compte de capital : débit
Financial Account,nie	−137.7	−304.4	−177.8	−141.1	−417.5	−339.4	278.8	Compte d'op. fin., nia
Net Errors and Omissions	−24.4	−38.8	−109.6	−102.2	46.6	40.3	−250.2	Erreurs et omissions nettes
Reserves and Related Items	1 403.3	1 310.6	1 501.7	1 317.4	1 383.6	1 215.4	−41.8	Rés. et postes appareutés
Djibouti								**Djibouti**
Goods: Exports fob	...	...	...	...	192.0	211.2	...	Biens : exportations,fàb
Goods: Imports fob	...	...	...	...	−383.4	−402.3	...	Biens : importations,fàb
Serv. & Income: Credit	...	...	...	...	174.4	183.9	...	Serv. & revenu : crédit
Serv. & Income: Debit	...	...	...	...	−95.9	−94.8	...	Serv. & revenu : débit
Current Trans.,nie: Credit	...	...	...	...	117.7	106.4	...	Transf. cour.,nia : crédit
Current Transfers: Debit	...	...	...	...	−93.6	−92.8	...	Transf. courants : débit
Capital Acct.,nie: Credit	...	...	...	...	0.0	0.0	...	Compte de cap.,nia : crédit
Capital Account: Debit	...	...	...	...	0.0	0.0	...	Compte de capital : débit
Financial Account,nie	...	...	...	...	60.8	6.5	...	Compte d'op. fin., nia
Net Errors and Omissions	...	...	...	...	11.4	73.3	...	Erreurs et omissions nettes
Reserves and Related Items	...	...	...	...	16.5	8.4	...	Rés. et postes appareutés
Egypt								**Egypte**
Goods: Exports fob	2 770.0	3 119.0	3 924.0	4 164.0	3 670.0	3 545.0	4 044.0	Biens : exportations,fàb
Goods: Imports fob	−9 378.0	−8 841.0	−10 303.0	−9 831.0	−8 901.0	−9 923.0	−9 997.0	Biens : importations,fàb
Serv. & Income: Credit	4 983.0	4 912.0	6 828.0	7 643.0	8 631.0	9 005.0	9 400.0	Serv. & revenu : crédit
Serv. & Income: Debit	−3 858.0	−4 672.0	−5 667.0	−5 507.0	−7 664.0	−7 334.0	−7 759.0	Serv. & revenu : débit
Current Trans.,nie: Credit	4 436.0	4 183.0	5 417.0	5 434.0	7 076.0	7 006.0	4 622.0	Transf. cour.,nia : crédit
Current Transfers: Debit	...	−10.0	−14.0	0.0	0.0	0.0	−279.0	Transf. courants : débit
Capital Acct.,nie: Credit	0.0	0.0	0.0	0.0	0.0	0.0	0.0	Compte de cap.,nia : crédit
Capital Account: Debit	0.0	0.0	0.0	0.0	0.0	0.0	0.0	Compte de capital : débit
Financial Account,nie	1 308.0	361.0	−11 039.0	−4 706.0	−168.0	−762.0	−1 450.0	Compte d'op. fin., nia
Net Errors and Omissions	−362.0	414.0	630.0	730.0	716.0	−1 519.0	255.0	Erreurs et omissions nettes
Reserves and Related Items	102.0	533.0	10 224.0	2 073.0	−3 360.0	−18.0	1 164.0	Rés. et postes appareutés
Equatorial Guinea								**Guinée équatoriale**
Goods: Exports fob	44.7	32.7	37.8	35.8	...	...	...	Biens : exportations,fàb
Goods: Imports fob	−56.5	−43.6	−53.2	−59.6	...	...	...	Biens : importations,fàb
Serv. & Income: Credit	5.9	5.8	4.5	6.2	...	...	...	Serv. & revenu : crédit
Serv. & Income: Debit	−56.6	−39.8	−46.0	−52.4	...	...	...	Serv. & revenu : débit
Current Trans.,nie: Credit	46.9	38.1	56.4	63.4	...	...	...	Transf. cour.,nia : crédit
Current Transfers: Debit	−4.9	−14.3	−18.5	−17.9	...	...	...	Transf. courants : débit
Capital Acct.,nie: Credit	0.0	0.0	0.0	0.0	...	...	...	Compte de cap.,nia : crédit
Capital Account: Debit	0.0	0.0	0.0	0.0	...	...	...	Compte de capital : débit
Financial Account,nie	4.9	10.0	11.7	32.2	...	...	...	Compte d'op. fin., nia
Net Errors and Omissions	−1.7	−4.5	−2.4	−30.7	...	...	...	Erreurs et omissions nettes
Reserves and Related Items	17.4	15.5	9.7	23.2	...	...	...	Rés. et postes appareutés

79
Summary of balance of payments
Millions of US dollars
Résumé des balances des paiements
Millions de dollars des E−U

Country or area	1988	1989	1990	1991	1992	1993	1994	Pays ou zone
Ethiopia								**Ethiopie**
Goods: Exports fob	400.0	443.8	292.0	167.6	169.9	198.8	...	Biens : exportations,fàb
Goods: Imports fob	−956.0	−817.9	−912.1	−470.8	−992.7	−706.0	...	Biens : importations,fàb
Serv. & Income: Credit	288.8	301.9	313.8	282.7	289.9	301.7	...	Serv. & revenu : crédit
Serv. & Income: Debit	−402.9	−408.4	−436.5	−381.0	−472.4	−377.4	...	Serv. & revenu : débit
Current Trans.,nie: Credit	443.2	337.5	451.3	505.9	887.4	532.6	...	Transf. cour.,nia : crédit
Current Transfers: Debit	−0.7	−1.3	−2.2	−1.3	−2.0	−1.2	...	Transf. courants : débit
Capital Acct.,nie: Credit	0.0	0.0	0.0	0.0	0.0	0.0	...	Compte de cap.,nia : crédit
Capital Account: Debit	−0.3	−0.1	0.0	0.0	0.0	0.0	...	Compte de capital : débit
Financial Account,nie	299.6	222.0	230.0	−204.1	−65.4	79.4	...	Compte d'op. fin., nia
Net Errors and Omissions	−94.0	−32.0	−134.6	−254.9	−80.9	−13.7	...	Erreurs et omissions nettes
Reserves and Related Items	22.3	−45.5	198.3	355.9	266.2	−14.2	...	Rés. et postes appareutés
Gabon								**Gabon**
Goods: Exports fob	1 195.6	1 626.0	2 488.8	2 227.9	2 259.2	2 326.2	2 349.4	Biens : exportations,fàb
Goods: Imports fob	−791.2	−751.7	−805.1	−861.0	−886.3	−845.1	−756.5	Biens : importations,fàb
Serv. & Income: Credit	228.1	308.0	261.7	352.0	394.8	343.2	231.5	Serv. & revenu : crédit
Serv. & Income: Debit	−1 103.7	−1 248.6	−1 643.3	−1 524.3	−1 793.7	−1 681.0	−1 381.1	Serv. & revenu : débit
Current Trans.,nie: Credit	53.8	42.3	58.9	44.0	51.4	48.0	59.3	Transf. cour.,nia : crédit
Current Transfers: Debit	−198.1	−168.3	−193.3	−163.8	−193.4	−240.5	−182.8	Transf. courants : débit
Capital Acct.,nie: Credit	0.0	0.0	0.0	0.0	0.0	0.0	0.0	Compte de cap.,nia : crédit
Capital Account: Debit	0.0	0.0	0.0	0.0	0.0	0.0	0.0	Compte de capital : débit
Financial Account,nie	716.6	61.1	−366.5	−303.8	−220.6	−382.8	−480.4	Compte d'op. fin., nia
Net Errors and Omissions	−101.9	35.0	−38.0	8.6	−55.1	−13.6	6.7	Erreurs et omissions nettes
Reserves and Related Items	0.8	96.1	236.8	220.4	443.8	445.5	153.9	Rés. et postes appareutés
Gambia								**Gambie**
Goods: Exports fob	83.1	100.2	110.6	142.9	147.0	157.0	125.0	Biens : exportations,fàb
Goods: Imports fob	−105.9	−125.4	−140.5	−185.0	−177.8	−214.5	−181.6	Biens : importations,fàb
Serv. & Income: Credit	63.7	67.7	59.1	84.3	85.7	85.4	95.3	Serv. & revenu : crédit
Serv. & Income: Debit	−61.4	−66.4	−64.9	−83.5	−74.2	−79.7	−72.2	Serv. & revenu : débit
Current Trans.,nie: Credit	54.5	46.4	60.0	58.6	60.5	50.0	45.9	Transf. cour.,nia : crédit
Current Transfers: Debit	−7.3	−7.5	−2.7	−4.1	−4.0	−3.6	−4.2	Transf. courants : débit
Capital Acct.,nie: Credit	0.0	0.0	0.0	0.0	0.0	0.0	0.0	Compte de cap.,nia : crédit
Capital Account: Debit	0.0	0.0	0.0	0.0	0.0	0.0	0.0	Compte de capital : débit
Financial Account,nie	9.6	9.5	−6.1	20.8	18.7	39.4	33.1	Compte d'op. fin., nia
Net Errors and Omissions	−11.3	−20.8	−11.7	−16.7	−36.7	−22.7	−35.1	Erreurs et omissions nettes
Reserves and Related Items	−24.8	−3.7	−3.8	−17.3	−19.2	−11.4	−6.2	Rés. et postes appareutés
Ghana								**Ghana**
Goods: Exports fob	881.0	807.2	890.6	997.6	986.4	1 063.7	1 226.8	Biens : exportations,fàb
Goods: Imports fob	−993.4	−1 002.2	−1 205.0	−1 318.7	−1 456.7	−1 728.0	−1 579.9	Biens : importations,fàb
Serv. & Income: Credit	77.7	81.9	93.1	110.3	128.9	156.3	159.3	Serv. & revenu : crédit
Serv. & Income: Debit	−399.6	−407.8	−418.5	−462.8	−505.1	−568.3	−542.8	Serv. & revenu : débit
Current Trans.,nie: Credit	377.8	432.2	426.3	434.1	484.8	532.0	487.3	Transf. cour.,nia : crédit
Current Transfers: Debit	−8.6	−9.1	−10.1	−11.3	−13.6	−13.6	−14.5	Transf. courants : débit
Capital Acct.,nie: Credit	0.0	0.0	0.0	0.0	0.0	0.0	0.0	Compte de cap.,nia : crédit
Capital Account: Debit	−0.7	−0.8	−0.5	−0.9	−1.0	−1.0	−1.0	Compte de capital : débit
Financial Account,nie	209.0	178.6	259.2	338.1	321.6	648.1	511.2	Compte d'op. fin., nia
Net Errors and Omissions	71.2	57.7	21.3	165.2	−177.8	53.4	−153.0	Erreurs et omissions nettes
Reserves and Related Items	−214.4	−137.7	−56.4	−251.6	232.5	−142.6	−93.4	Rés. et postes appareutés
Guinea								**Guinée**
Goods: Exports fob	511.9	595.6	671.2	687.1	517.1	561.1	515.7	Biens : exportations,fàb
Goods: Imports fob	−510.6	−531.5	−585.7	−694.9	−608.4	−582.6	−685.3	Biens : importations,fàb
Serv. & Income: Credit	63.8	112.3	170.0	160.1	167.6	196.1	159.4	Serv. & revenu : crédit
Serv. & Income: Debit	−373.2	−438.2	−528.7	−529.2	−471.4	−427.4	−395.4	Serv. & revenu : débit
Current Trans.,nie: Credit	121.3	143.5	118.8	136.2	193.5	260.3	192.1	Transf. cour.,nia : crédit
Current Transfers: Debit	−34.7	−61.3	−48.6	−48.2	−61.2	−64.2	−72.5	Transf. courants : débit
Capital Acct.,nie: Credit	0.0	198.7	0.0	0.0	8.0	5.0	0.0	Compte de cap.,nia : crédit
Capital Account: Debit	...	...	...	...	...	...	...	Compte de capital : débit
Financial Account,nie	34.8	−158.9	53.8	10.4	67.4	62.7	40.3	Compte d'op. fin., nia
Net Errors and Omissions	57.3	−50.5	50.4	117.5	33.4	−124.6	139.4	Erreurs et omissions nettes
Reserves and Related Items	129.4	190.5	98.8	160.9	153.9	113.7	106.3	Rés. et postes appareutés
Guinea−Bissau								**Guinée−Bissau**
Goods: Exports fob	15.9	14.2	19.3	20.4	6.5	16.0	...	Biens : exportations,fàb
Goods: Imports fob	−58.9	−68.9	−68.1	−67.5	−83.5	−53.8	...	Biens : importations,fàb
Serv. & Income: Debit	−37.0	−49.0	−35.5	−47.3	−43.8	−40.4	...	Serv. & revenu : débit
Current Trans.,nie: Credit	11.6	10.9	23.9	19.4	17.3	14.4	...	Transf. cour.,nia : crédit
Current Transfers: Debit	0.0	0.0	0.0	−4.1	−0.6	−1.7	...	Transf. courants : débit

79
Summary of balance of payments
Millions of US dollars
Résumé des balances des paiements
Millions de dollars des E−U

Country or area	1988	1989	1990	1991	1992	1993	1994	Pays ou zone
Capital Acct.,nie: Credit	26.9	41.6	29.0	32.7	28.5	36.6	...	Compte de cap.,nia : crédit
Capital Account: Debit	0.0	0.0	0.0	0.0	0.0	0.0	...	Compte de capital : débit
Financial Account,nie	−3.4	−7.0	1.2	−8.8	2.1	−13.6	...	Compte d'op. fin., nia
Net Errors and Omissions	1.4	−8.5	−4.0	−16.3	22.1	−16.2	...	Erreurs et omissions nettes
Reserves and Related Items	43.6	66.7	34.3	71.3	51.5	58.7	...	Rés. et postes appareutés
Kenya								**Kenya**
Goods: Exports fob	1 072.7	1 001.5	1 090.2	1 185.3	1 099.4	1 253.6	...	Biens : exportations,fàb
Goods: Imports fob	−1 802.2	−1 963.4	−2 005.3	−1 697.3	−1 594.3	−1 492.8	...	Biens : importations,fàb
Serv. & Income: Credit	819.0	933.2	1 143.1	1 020.3	1 052.9	1 075.9	...	Serv. & revenu : crédit
Serv. & Income: Debit	−895.5	−933.2	−1 122.9	−1 067.4	−937.7	−925.3	...	Serv. & revenu : débit
Current Trans.,nie: Credit	372.9	420.6	422.9	396.7	392.9	276.0	...	Transf. cour.,nia : crédit
Current Transfers: Debit	−39.1	−49.1	−55.1	−51.1	−193.4	−63.0	...	Transf. courants : débit
Capital Acct.,nie: Credit	11.8	11.2	7.6	3.6	83.5	28.5	...	Compte de cap.,nia : crédit
Capital Account: Debit	−0.3	−0.2	−0.8	−0.4	−0.4	−0.4	...	Compte de capital : débit
Financial Account,nie	382.3	633.9	360.9	96.6	−270.1	1.9	...	Compte d'op. fin., nia
Net Errors and Omissions	34.7	67.7	66.9	69.6	110.3	257.5	...	Erreurs et omissions nettes
Reserves and Related Items	43.6	−121.9	92.5	43.9	256.9	−411.8	...	Rés. et postes appareutés
Lesotho								**Lesotho**
Goods: Exports fob	63.7	66.4	59.5	67.2	109.2	134.0	143.5	Biens : exportations,fàb
Goods: Imports fob	−559.4	−592.6	−672.6	−803.5	−932.6	−868.1	−810.2	Biens : importations,fàb
Serv. & Income: Credit	417.0	412.9	495.6	517.7	537.6	481.5	407.4	Serv. & revenu : crédit
Serv. & Income: Debit	−84.0	−91.2	−103.2	−104.3	−115.4	−93.3	−103.6	Serv. & revenu : débit
Current Trans.,nie: Credit	197.0	281.7	362.3	492.8	542.1	376.5	472.1	Transf. cour.,nia : crédit
Current Transfers: Debit	−58.8	−66.8	−76.4	−86.6	−103.3	−1.3	−0.9	Transf. courants : débit
Capital Acct.,nie: Credit	0.0	0.0	0.0	0.0	0.0	0.0	0.0	Compte de cap.,nia : crédit
Capital Account: Debit	0.0	0.0	0.0	0.0	0.0	0.0	0.0	Compte de capital : débit
Financial Account,nie	−8.0	−20.2	−45.0	−60.8	−67.0	55.2	33.0	Compte d'op. fin., nia
Net Errors and Omissions	26.5	1.9	−2.8	20.1	79.2	17.8	−20.3	Erreurs et omissions nettes
Reserves and Related Items	6.1	7.9	−17.2	−42.4	−49.9	−102.3	−120.9	Rés. et postes appareutés
Libyan Arab Jamah.								**Jamah. arabe libyenne**
Goods: Exports fob	5 653.0	7 274.0	11 352.0	...	...	...	...	Biens : exportations,fàb
Goods: Imports fob	−5 762.0	−6 509.0	−7 575.0	...	...	...	...	Biens : importations,fàb
Serv. & Income: Credit	890.0	564.0	783.0	...	...	...	...	Serv. & revenu : crédit
Serv. & Income: Debit	−2 074.0	−1 869.0	−1 878.0	...	...	...	...	Serv. & revenu : débit
Current Trans.,nie: Credit	7.0	6.0	7.0	...	...	...	...	Transf. cour.,nia : crédit
Current Transfers: Debit	−541.0	−493.0	−488.0	...	...	...	...	Transf. courants : débit
Capital Acct.,nie: Credit	0.0	0.0	0.0	...	...	...	...	Compte de cap.,nia : crédit
Capital Account: Debit	0.0	0.0	0.0	...	...	...	...	Compte de capital : débit
Financial Account,nie	163.0	1 188.0	−1 006.0	...	...	...	...	Compte d'op. fin., nia
Net Errors and Omissions	271.0	130.0	−37.0	...	...	...	...	Erreurs et omissions nettes
Reserves and Related Items	1 392.0	−292.0	−1 158.0	...	...	...	...	Rés. et postes appareutés
Madagascar								**Madagascar**
Goods: Exports fob	284.0	321.0	318.0	334.0	324.0	332.0	447.0	Biens : exportations,fàb
Goods: Imports fob	−319.0	−320.0	−566.0	−440.0	−465.0	−510.0	−545.0	Biens : importations,fàb
Serv. & Income: Credit	131.0	150.0	168.0	126.0	153.0	165.0	183.0	Serv. & revenu : crédit
Serv. & Income: Debit	−443.0	−437.0	−418.0	−380.0	−401.0	−416.0	−442.0	Serv. & revenu : débit
Current Trans.,nie: Credit	225.0	230.0	270.0	195.0	254.0	288.0	182.0	Transf. cour.,nia : crédit
Current Transfers: Debit	−30.0	−29.0	−36.0	−20.0	−22.0	−19.0	−22.0	Transf. courants : débit
Capital Acct.,nie: Credit	1.0	2.0	3.0	4.0	3.0	2.0	2.0	Compte de cap.,nia : crédit
Capital Account: Debit	0.0	0.0	0.0	0.0	0.0	0.0	0.0	Compte de capital : débit
Financial Account,nie	−22.0	−49.0	−18.0	−42.0	−111.0	−139.0	−158.0	Compte d'op. fin., nia
Net Errors and Omissions	53.0	−42.0	2.0	−12.0	−60.0	−3.0	19.0	Erreurs et omissions nettes
Reserves and Related Items	118.0	174.0	278.0	234.0	326.0	301.0	334.0	Rés. et postes appareutés
Malawi								**Malawi**
Goods: Exports fob	293.5	268.8	406.4	475.5	399.9	317.5	362.6	Biens : exportations,fàb
Goods: Imports fob	−253.0	−204.8	−280.3	−415.8	−415.0	−340.2	−639.0	Biens : importations,fàb
Serv. & Income: Credit	48.1	41.0	45.9	45.9	34.8	32.2	24.1	Serv. & revenu : crédit
Serv. & Income: Debit	−290.8	−316.7	−346.8	−430.9	−405.0	−267.5	−146.0	Serv. & revenu : débit
Current Trans.,nie: Credit	169.2	208.0	134.1	159.0	155.2	167.9	139.7	Transf. cour.,nia : crédit
Current Transfers: Debit	−38.6	−33.9	−35.1	−42.9	−37.7	−11.9	−15.4	Transf. courants : débit
Capital Acct.,nie: Credit	0.0	0.0	0.0	0.0	0.0	0.0	0.0	Compte de cap.,nia : crédit
Capital Account: Debit	0.0	0.0	0.0	0.0	0.0	0.0	0.0	Compte de capital : débit
Financial Account,nie	68.9	92.0	128.6	104.3	93.6	188.9	122.0	Compte d'op. fin., nia
Net Errors and Omissions	62.9	−106.2	−24.3	120.6	127.6	−62.8	117.1	Erreurs et omissions nettes
Reserves and Related Items	−60.2	51.7	−28.7	−15.7	46.5	−24.0	35.1	Rés. et postes appareutés

79
Summary of balance of payments
Millions of US dollars
Résumé des balances des paiements
Millions de dollars des E−U

Country or area	1988	1989	1990	1991	1992	1993	1994	Pays ou zone
Mali								**Mali**
Goods: Exports fob	251.5	269.3	337.9	355.9	335.9	341.1	319.7	Biens : exportations,fàb
Goods: Imports fob	−359.1	−338.8	−432.4	−446.9	−484.5	−446.5	−421.6	Biens : importations,fàb
Serv. & Income: Credit	88.0	75.6	99.6	81.5	87.8	100.5	72.2	Serv. & revenu : crédit
Serv. & Income: Debit	−372.1	−353.7	−456.1	−411.8	−449.6	−426.7	−365.2	Serv. & revenu : débit
Current Trans.,nie: Credit	235.7	232.1	291.9	333.0	344.9	300.2	275.8	Transf. cour.,nia : crédit
Current Transfers: Debit	−77.6	−75.0	−90.6	−87.7	−87.6	−81.9	−45.2	Transf. courants : débit
Capital Acct.,nie: Credit	142.0	107.8	105.8	137.5	143.6	111.9	111.7	Compte de cap.,nia : crédit
Capital Account: Debit	0.0	0.0	0.0	0.0	0.0	0.0	0.0	Compte de capital : débit
Financial Account,nie	138.8	96.9	77.6	52.8	3.0	−25.8	−5.9	Compte d'op. fin., nia
Net Errors and Omissions	−1.5	−1.5	1.1	14.6	−31.0	30.1	−5.1	Erreurs et omissions nettes
Reserves and Related Items	−45.7	−12.6	65.6	−29.0	137.6	97.2	63.7	Rés. et postes appareutés
Mauritania								**Mauritanie**
Goods: Exports fob	437.6	447.9	443.9	435.8	406.8	403.0	399.7	Biens : exportations,fàb
Goods: Imports fob	−348.9	−349.3	−382.9	−399.1	−461.3	−400.4	−352.3	Biens : importations,fàb
Serv. & Income: Credit	39.4	39.2	30.6	33.2	21.3	22.2	27.1	Serv. & revenu : crédit
Serv. & Income: Debit	−306.7	−251.6	−187.0	−185.9	−209.0	−282.5	−228.8	Serv. & revenu : débit
Current Trans.,nie: Credit	123.3	130.0	120.2	118.9	157.4	110.3	113.3	Transf. cour.,nia : crédit
Current Transfers: Debit	−40.8	−34.7	−34.3	−32.8	−33.4	−26.5	−28.9	Transf. courants : débit
Capital Acct.,nie: Credit	0.0	0.0	0.0	0.0	0.0	0.0	0.0	Compte de cap.,nia : crédit
Capital Account: Debit	0.0	0.0	0.0	0.0	0.0	0.0	0.0	Compte de capital : débit
Financial Account,nie	39.4	16.9	−0.5	26.7	77.9	−134.7	−11.2	Compte d'op. fin., nia
Net Errors and Omissions	−16.0	−3.6	−62.3	19.5	57.4	26.7	−23.5	Erreurs et omissions nettes
Reserves and Related Items	72.6	5.3	72.5	−16.3	−17.0	282.0	104.5	Rés. et postes appareutés
Mauritius								**Maurice**
Goods: Exports fob	1 030.2	1 025.3	1 238.1	1 253.4	1 334.7	1 334.4	1 376.9	Biens : exportations,fàb
Goods: Imports fob	−1 177.8	−1 217.7	−1 494.8	−1 438.5	−1 493.9	−1 576.0	−1 769.7	Biens : importations,fàb
Serv. & Income: Credit	375.4	423.8	539.8	610.8	668.5	636.2	646.9	Serv. & revenu : crédit
Serv. & Income: Debit	−377.8	−411.2	−499.7	−526.9	−602.9	−588.2	−583.9	Serv. & revenu : débit
Current Trans.,nie: Credit	103.3	84.9	108.5	98.6	109.9	115.9	126.4	Transf. cour.,nia : crédit
Current Transfers: Debit	−9.7	−8.7	−11.2	−15.7	−16.4	−14.4	−26.3	Transf. courants : débit
Capital Acct.,nie: Credit	0.0	0.0	0.0	0.0	0.0	0.0	0.0	Compte de cap.,nia : crédit
Capital Account: Debit	−1.1	−0.9	−0.6	−1.6	−1.4	−1.5	−1.3	Compte de capital : débit
Financial Account,nie	121.2	50.2	138.6	41.8	−14.8	19.3	55.6	Compte d'op. fin., nia
Net Errors and Omissions	121.2	199.8	213.2	168.8	59.6	81.2	131.9	Erreurs et omissions nettes
Reserves and Related Items	−184.8	−145.6	−231.9	−190.8	−43.3	−7.0	43.5	Rés. et postes appareutés
Morocco								**Maroc**
Goods: Exports fob	3 624.0	3 331.0	4 229.0	5 094.0	5 010.0	4 936.0	5 541.0	Biens : exportations,fàb
Goods: Imports fob	−4 384.0	−5 027.0	−6 338.0	−6 858.0	−7 473.0	−7 001.0	−7 648.0	Biens : importations,fàb
Serv. & Income: Credit	1 782.0	1 682.0	2 092.0	1 817.0	2 417.0	2 274.0	2 238.0	Serv. & revenu : crédit
Serv. & Income: Debit	−2 161.0	−2 395.0	−2 516.0	−2 742.0	−2 920.0	−3 024.0	−3 124.0	Serv. & revenu : débit
Current Trans.,nie: Credit	1 663.0	1 669.0	2 383.0	2 356.0	2 614.0	2 361.0	2 355.0	Transf. cour.,nia : crédit
Current Transfers: Debit	−51.0	−46.0	−47.0	−81.0	−81.0	−66.0	−83.0	Transf. courants : débit
Capital Acct.,nie: Credit	1.0	0.0	0.0	0.0	0.0	0.0	0.0	Compte de cap.,nia : crédit
Capital Account: Debit	−7.0	−3.0	−5.0	−5.0	−6.0	−3.0	−4.0	Compte de capital : débit
Financial Account,nie	−226.0	822.0	1 889.0	1 379.0	1 242.0	973.0	1 211.0	Compte d'op. fin., nia
Net Errors and Omissions	22.0	−11.0	9.0	3.0	−10.0	−5.0	1.0	Erreurs et omissions nettes
Reserves and Related Items	−264.0	−21.0	−1 697.0	−963.0	−794.0	−443.0	−488.0	Rés. et postes appareutés
Mozambique								**Mozambique**
Goods: Exports fob	103.0	104.8	126.4	162.3	139.3	...	...	Biens : exportations,fàb
Goods: Imports fob	−662.0	−726.9	−789.7	−808.8	−798.5	...	...	Biens : importations,fàb
Serv. & Income: Credit	156.6	166.7	173.4	202.8	222.6	...	...	Serv. & revenu : crédit
Serv. & Income: Debit	−332.9	−392.3	−373.8	−402.3	−444.1	...	...	Serv. & revenu : débit
Current Trans.,nie: Credit	376.8	387.5	448.4	501.7	499.4	...	...	Transf. cour.,nia : crédit
Current Transfers: Debit	0.0	0.0	0.0	0.0	0.0	...	...	Transf. courants : débit
Capital Acct.,nie: Credit	0.0	0.0	0.0	0.0	0.0	...	...	Compte de cap.,nia : crédit
Capital Account: Debit	0.0	0.0	0.0	0.0	0.0	...	...	Compte de capital : débit
Financial Account,nie	−126.2	−55.0	−83.5	−187.5	−122.9	...	...	Compte d'op. fin., nia
Net Errors and Omissions	84.7	56.7	66.3	−3.9	32.5	...	...	Erreurs et omissions nettes
Reserves and Related Items	400.0	458.5	432.5	535.7	471.7	...	...	Rés. et postes appareutés
Namibia								**Namibie**
Goods: Exports fob	...	...	1 085.7	1 213.6	1 341.5	1 289.6	1 321.4	Biens : exportations,fàb
Goods: Imports fob	...	...	−1 117.8	−1 119.8	−1 262.6	−1 167.5	−1 156.4	Biens : importations,fàb
Serv. & Income: Credit	...	...	302.6	375.2	350.3	408.0	437.9	Serv. & revenu : crédit
Serv. & Income: Debit	...	...	−515.5	−631.6	−696.7	−621.9	−651.1	Serv. & revenu : débit
Current Trans.,nie: Credit	...	...	372.2	391.8	459.7	363.6	366.4	Transf. cour.,nia : crédit

79
Summary of balance of payments
Millions of US dollars
Résumé des balances des paiements
Millions de dollars des E-U

Country or area	1988	1989	1990	1991	1992	1993	1994	Pays ou zone
Current Transfers: Debit	...	...	−124.5	−122.4	−136.7	−127.0	−128.7	Transf. courants : débit
Capital Acct.,nie: Credit	...	...	49.9	39.5	50.1	35.5	24.2	Compte de cap.,nia : crédit
Capital Account: Debit	...	...	−5.4	−5.4	−1.4	−1.2	−1.7	Compte de capital : débit
Financial Account,nie	...	...	−205.6	−185.8	−97.8	−53.6	−124.5	Compte d'op. fin., nia
Net Errors and Omissions	...	...	195.2	32.6	−13.0	−34.3	−12.7	Erreurs et omissions nettes
Reserves and Related Items	...	...	−36.7	12.3	6.7	−91.2	−74.9	Rés. et postes appareutés
Niger								**Niger**
Goods: Exports fob	369.0	311.0	303.4	283.9	265.6	238.4	226.4	Biens : exportations,fàb
Goods: Imports fob	−392.5	−368.6	−337.5	−273.3	−266.3	−244.0	−245.5	Biens : importations,fàb
Serv. & Income: Credit	50.0	57.7	71.3	58.5	52.1	49.8	34.0	Serv. & revenu : crédit
Serv. & Income: Debit	−218.6	−202.5	−256.4	−195.6	−185.5	−175.5	−183.9	Serv. & revenu : débit
Current Trans.,nie: Credit	153.8	141.7	171.2	151.0	142.1	148.7	143.4	Transf. cour.,nia : crédit
Current Transfers: Debit	−45.0	−50.2	−60.6	−49.6	−52.5	−46.3	−52.6	Transf. courants : débit
Capital Acct.,nie: Credit	0.0	0.0	0.0	0.0	0.0	0.0	0.0	Compte de cap.,nia : crédit
Capital Account: Debit	0.0	0.0	0.0	0.0	0.0	0.0	0.0	Compte de capital : débit
Financial Account,nie	26.1	35.7	22.8	−22.3	12.5	−25.0	2.5	Compte d'op. fin., nia
Net Errors and Omissions	43.4	−4.1	−25.2	−40.4	15.6	−9.4	−1.4	Erreurs et omissions nettes
Reserves and Related Items	13.7	79.3	111.2	87.9	16.5	63.4	77.1	Rés. et postes appareutés
Nigeria								**Nigéria**
Goods: Exports fob	6 875.0	7 871.0	13 585.0	12 254.0	11 791.0	9 910.0	9 459.0	Biens : exportations,fàb
Goods: Imports fob	−4 355.0	−3 693.0	−4 932.0	−7 813.0	−7 181.0	−6 662.0	−6 511.0	Biens : importations,fàb
Serv. & Income: Credit	405.0	704.0	1 176.0	1 097.0	1 209.0	1 221.0	420.0	Serv. & revenu : crédit
Serv. & Income: Debit	−3 209.0	−3 919.0	−4 925.0	−5 079.0	−4 304.0	−6 061.0	−5 993.0	Serv. & revenu : débit
Current Trans.,nie: Credit	28.0	157.0	167.0	877.0	817.0	857.0	550.0	Transf. cour.,nia : crédit
Current Transfers: Debit	−40.0	−31.0	−82.0	−132.0	−64.0	−44.0	−52.0	Transf. courants : débit
Capital Acct.,nie: Credit	0.0	0.0	0.0	0.0	0.0	0.0	0.0	Compte de cap.,nia : crédit
Capital Account: Debit	0.0	0.0	0.0	0.0	0.0	0.0	0.0	Compte de capital : débit
Financial Account,nie	−4 611.0	−3 649.0	−4 182.0	−2 633.0	−7 784.0	−1 043.0	329.0	Compte d'op. fin., nia
Net Errors and Omissions	−221.0	−107.0	235.0	−93.0	−122.0	−88.0	−139.0	Erreurs et omissions nettes
Reserves and Related Items	5 129.0	2 667.0	−1 041.0	1 523.0	5 638.0	1 911.0	1 938.0	Rés. et postes appareutés
Rwanda								**Rwanda**
Goods: Exports fob	117.9	104.7	102.6	95.6	68.5	...	...	Biens : exportations,fàb
Goods: Imports fob	−278.6	−254.1	−227.7	−228.1	−240.4	...	...	Biens : importations,fàb
Serv. & Income: Credit	56.9	52.3	46.6	46.5	36.1	...	...	Serv. & revenu : crédit
Serv. & Income: Debit	−165.0	−142.0	−152.0	−128.8	−132.0	...	...	Serv. & revenu : débit
Current Trans.,nie: Credit	153.0	141.6	147.4	209.3	213.6	...	...	Transf. cour.,nia : crédit
Current Transfers: Debit	−29.0	−25.5	−25.1	−28.3	−30.4	...	...	Transf. courants : débit
Capital Acct.,nie: Credit	2.4	2.7	1.7	2.6	0.0	...	...	Compte de cap.,nia : crédit
Capital Account: Debit	−2.0	−2.2	−2.4	−2.9	0.0	...	...	Compte de capital : débit
Financial Account,nie	93.7	53.9	55.7	99.1	62.4	...	...	Compte d'op. fin., nia
Net Errors and Omissions	0.4	1.9	30.3	0.2	18.2	...	...	Erreurs et omissions nettes
Reserves and Related Items	50.4	66.7	22.9	−65.2	4.0	...	...	Rés. et postes appareutés
Sao Tome and Principe								**Sao Tomé−et−Principe**
Goods: Exports fob	9.5	4.9	4.2	...	...	...	...	Biens : exportations,fàb
Goods: Imports fob	−14.1	−13.3	−13.0	...	...	...	...	Biens : importations,fàb
Serv. & Income: Credit	2.0	4.6	3.9	...	...	...	...	Serv. & revenu : crédit
Serv. & Income: Debit	−9.0	−8.8	−9.3	...	...	...	...	Serv. & revenu : débit
Current Trans.,nie: Credit	1.7	2.4	0.7	...	...	...	...	Transf. cour.,nia : crédit
Current Transfers: Debit	−0.8	−1.1	−0.8	...	...	...	...	Transf. courants : débit
Capital Acct.,nie: Credit	0.0	0.0	0.0	...	...	...	...	Compte de cap.,nia : crédit
Capital Account: Debit	0.0	0.0	0.0	...	...	...	...	Compte de capital : débit
Financial Account,nie	6.3	6.7	7.6	...	...	...	...	Compte d'op. fin., nia
Net Errors and Omissions	...	−1.0	−2.7	...	...	...	...	Erreurs et omissions nettes
Reserves and Related Items	4.4	5.6	9.4	...	...	...	...	Rés. et postes appareutés
Senegal								**Sénégal**
Goods: Exports fob	713.2	758.6	893.6	824.2	828.1	718.7	793.8	Biens : exportations,fàb
Goods: Imports fob	−956.0	−998.4	−1 164.3	−1 114.1	−1 199.9	−1 101.5	−1 026.6	Biens : importations,fàb
Serv. & Income: Credit	456.8	522.6	600.8	564.8	595.9	588.3	610.6	Serv. & revenu : crédit
Serv. & Income: Debit	−751.9	−746.5	−805.8	−794.6	−839.2	−787.2	−540.4	Serv. & revenu : débit
Current Trans.,nie: Credit	386.3	367.9	387.1	382.8	412.9	361.3	469.0	Transf. cour.,nia : crédit
Current Transfers: Debit	−109.6	−101.9	−92.6	−89.3	−96.3	−81.2	−84.7	Transf. courants : débit
Capital Acct.,nie: Credit	0.0	0.0	0.0	0.0	0.0	0.0	0.0	Compte de cap.,nia : crédit
Capital Account: Debit	0.0	0.0	0.0	0.0	0.0	0.0	0.0	Compte de capital : débit
Financial Account,nie	149.9	−45.7	15.8	51.0	79.4	42.2	12.4	Compte d'op. fin., nia
Net Errors and Omissions	−3.3	80.1	−62.8	24.3	112.4	111.6	−211.4	Erreurs et omissions nettes
Reserves and Related Items	114.8	163.3	228.1	151.0	106.7	147.8	−22.8	Rés. et postes appareutés

79
Summary of balance of payments
Millions of US dollars
Résumé des balances des paiements
Millions de dollars des E-U

Country or area	1988	1989	1990	1991	1992	1993	1994	Pays ou zone
Seychelles								**Seychelles**
Goods: Exports fob	17.3	34.4	57.2	49.3	48.1	51.3	52.1	Biens : exportations,fàb
Goods: Imports fob	−135.0	−154.2	−166.4	−162.8	−180.5	−216.3	−188.6	Biens : importations,fàb
Serv. & Income: Credit	167.5	148.1	176.3	172.5	199.3	218.5	210.3	Serv. & revenu : crédit
Serv. & Income: Debit	−102.1	−80.4	−98.3	−83.6	−91.1	−109.0	−96.4	Serv. & revenu : débit
Current Trans.,nie: Credit	34.0	22.2	28.6	26.3	31.1	31.8	21.3	Transf. cour.,nia : crédit
Current Transfers: Debit	−10.1	−9.7	−10.3	−9.9	−13.8	−15.1	−13.4	Transf. courants : débit
Capital Acct.,nie: Credit	...	...	...	...	...	...	...	Compte de cap.,nia : crédit
Capital Account: Debit	...	...	...	...	...	...	...	Compte de capital : débit
Financial Account,nie	21.3	44.3	22.9	30.7	−2.5	25.6	22.4	Compte d'op. fin., nia
Net Errors and Omissions	2.8	−5.5	−5.7	−20.8	5.4	3.2	−19.4	Erreurs et omissions nettes
Reserves and Related Items	4.3	0.9	−4.3	−1.8	4.0	10.1	11.7	Rés. et postes appareutés
Sierra Leone								**Sierra Leone**
Goods: Exports fob	107.9	142.0	148.5	149.5	150.4	118.3	...	Biens : exportations,fàb
Goods: Imports fob	−138.2	−160.4	−140.4	−138.6	−139.0	−187.1	...	Biens : importations,fàb
Serv. & Income: Credit	48.8	36.0	61.8	75.5	53.8	60.8	...	Serv. & revenu : crédit
Serv. & Income: Debit	−30.0	−84.7	−146.2	−80.9	−78.0	−67.1	...	Serv. & revenu : débit
Current Trans.,nie: Credit	9.3	7.9	7.1	10.0	8.2	18.6	...	Transf. cour.,nia : crédit
Current Transfers: Debit	−0.6	−0.7	−0.2	−0.2	−0.8	−1.7	...	Transf. courants : débit
Capital Acct.,nie: Credit	0.1	0.1	...	...	0.1	0.1	...	Compte de cap.,nia : crédit
Capital Account: Debit	0.0	0.0	0.0	0.0	0.0	0.0	...	Compte de capital : débit
Financial Account,nie	−6.7	−17.9	−0.8	−1.4	−18.2	49.1	...	Compte d'op. fin., nia
Net Errors and Omissions	−62.5	29.2	49.2	−28.9	39.8	16.6	...	Erreurs et omissions nettes
Reserves and Related Items	71.9	48.4	20.9	14.9	−16.2	−7.5	...	Rés. et postes appareutés
Somalia								**Somalie**
Goods: Exports fob	58.4	67.7	...	...	...	...	...	Biens : exportations,fàb
Goods: Imports fob	−216.0	−346.3	...	...	...	...	...	Biens : importations,fàb
Serv. & Income: Debit	−164.6	−206.4	...	...	...	...	...	Serv. & revenu : débit
Current Trans.,nie: Credit	223.7	331.2	...	...	...	...	...	Transf. cour.,nia : crédit
Current Transfers: Debit	0.0	−2.9	...	...	...	...	...	Transf. courants : débit
Capital Acct.,nie: Credit	0.0	0.0	...	...	...	...	...	Compte de cap.,nia : crédit
Capital Account: Debit	0.0	0.0	...	...	...	...	...	Compte de capital : débit
Financial Account,nie	−105.5	−32.6	...	...	...	...	...	Compte d'op. fin., nia
Net Errors and Omissions	22.4	−0.8	...	...	...	...	...	Erreurs et omissions nettes
Reserves and Related Items	181.7	190.0	...	...	...	...	...	Rés. et postes appareutés
South Africa								**Afrique du Sud**
Goods: Exports fob	22 432.0	22 399.0	23 560.0	23 289.0	23 645.0	24 068.0	24 654.0	Biens : exportations,fàb
Goods: Imports fob	−17 210.0	−16 810.0	−16 778.0	−17 156.0	−18 216.0	−18 287.0	−21 452.0	Biens : importations,fàb
Serv. & Income: Credit	3 244.0	3 544.0	4 392.0	4 486.0	4 669.0	4 443.0	5 064.0	Serv. & revenu : crédit
Serv. & Income: Debit	−7 424.0	−7 756.0	−9 168.0	−8 433.0	−8 816.0	−8 550.0	−8 927.0	Serv. & revenu : débit
Current Trans.,nie: Credit	309.0	325.0	298.0	242.0	215.0	262.0	246.0	Transf. cour.,nia : crédit
Current Transfers: Debit	−148.0	−139.0	−238.0	−186.0	−121.0	−132.0	−196.0	Transf. courants : débit
Capital Acct.,nie: Credit	29.0	23.0	23.0	27.0	25.0	24.0	18.0	Compte de cap.,nia : crédit
Capital Account: Debit	−15.0	−8.0	−12.0	−12.0	−14.0	−23.0	−23.0	Compte de capital : débit
Financial Account,nie	−1 640.0	−1 117.0	344.0	476.0	187.0	−1 608.0	2 364.0	Compte d'op. fin., nia
Net Errors and Omissions	−965.0	−575.0	−1 016.0	−1 228.0	−1 443.0	−3 025.0	−879.0	Erreurs et omissions nettes
Reserves and Related Items	1 386.0	113.0	−1 405.0	−1 506.0	−131.0	2 828.0	−868.0	Rés. et postes appareutés
Sudan								**Soudan**
Goods: Exports fob	427.0	544.4	326.5	302.5	213.4	306.3	523.9	Biens : exportations,fàb
Goods: Imports fob	−948.5	−1 051.0	−648.8	−1 138.2	−810.2	−532.8	−1 045.4	Biens : importations,fàb
Serv. & Income: Credit	171.6	279.6	184.9	79.7	155.5	70.1	77.8	Serv. & revenu : crédit
Serv. & Income: Debit	−341.3	−495.7	−376.0	−326.4	−297.6	−130.7	−239.6	Serv. & revenu : débit
Current Trans.,nie: Credit	334.4	576.7	143.3	127.9	232.7	84.9	121.5	Transf. cour.,nia : crédit
Current Transfers: Debit	−1.1	−4.4	−2.1	−0.2	0.0	0.0	−38.5	Transf. courants : débit
Capital Acct.,nie: Credit	0.0	0.0	0.0	0.0	0.0	0.0	0.0	Compte de cap.,nia : crédit
Capital Account: Debit	0.0	0.0	0.0	0.0	0.0	0.0	0.0	Compte de capital : débit
Financial Account,nie	67.5	117.8	116.9	584.1	316.4	326.6	276.0	Compte d'op. fin., nia
Net Errors and Omissions	3.1	−160.3	10.9	97.9	31.0	−82.6	343.4	Erreurs et omissions nettes
Reserves and Related Items	287.4	192.8	244.4	272.8	158.8	−41.8	−19.1	Rés. et postes appareutés
Swaziland								**Swaziland**
Goods: Exports fob	466.2	493.8	549.6	610.8	664.0	736.8	741.4	Biens : exportations,fàb
Goods: Imports fob	−441.5	−515.8	−587.6	−632.9	−765.3	−771.5	−827.4	Biens : importations,fàb
Serv. & Income: Credit	184.6	213.7	275.5	267.2	281.7	240.1	252.9	Serv. & revenu : crédit
Serv. & Income: Debit	−216.8	−278.3	−267.0	−296.1	−253.8	−280.7	−261.8	Serv. & revenu : débit
Current Trans.,nie: Credit	129.2	142.0	169.7	178.9	219.1	190.7	187.6	Transf. cour.,nia : crédit
Current Transfers: Debit	−56.5	−54.7	−73.7	−80.3	−95.3	−92.0	−95.6	Transf. courants : débit

79
Summary of balance of payments
Millions of US dollars
Résumé des balances des paiements
Millions de dollars des E−U

Country or area	1988	1989	1990	1991	1992	1993	1994	Pays ou zone
Capital Acct.,nie: Credit	0.3	0.7	2.3	0.3	0.4	0.3	0.1	Compte de cap.,nia : crédit
Capital Account: Debit	−0.2	−0.1	0.0	−0.3	−0.1	0.0	0.0	Compte de capital : débit
Financial Account,nie	−58.3	−12.7	−38.3	19.6	38.1	−45.2	−73.0	Compte d'op. fin., nia
Net Errors and Omissions	7.6	62.7	−19.4	−53.7	3.0	−42.1	63.3	Erreurs et omissions nettes
Reserves and Related Items	−14.6	−51.3	−11.1	−13.7	−91.7	63.8	12.4	Rés. et postes appareutés
Togo								**Togo**
Goods: Exports fob	435.3	411.7	513.8	514.4	275.0	136.0	162.2	Biens : exportations,fàb
Goods: Imports fob	−504.5	−470.1	−602.7	−490.1	−417.8	−251.1	−212.0	Biens : importations,fàb
Serv. & Income: Credit	125.9	152.0	181.9	146.1	160.6	87.7	78.7	Serv. & revenu : crédit
Serv. & Income: Debit	−270.7	−259.6	−309.4	−345.0	−261.9	−190.7	−128.6	Serv. & revenu : débit
Current Trans.,nie: Credit	148.4	134.0	145.6	128.7	111.1	54.0	35.1	Transf. cour.,nia : crédit
Current Transfers: Debit	−21.8	−18.8	−29.1	−24.2	−22.7	−13.4	−4.9	Transf. courants : débit
Capital Acct.,nie: Credit	0.0	0.0	0.0	0.0	0.0	0.0	0.0	Compte de cap.,nia : crédit
Capital Account: Debit	0.0	0.0	0.0	0.0	0.0	0.0	0.0	Compte de capital : débit
Financial Account,nie	29.9	−2.8	75.2	67.8	−23.8	−55.1	−16.0	Compte d'op. fin., nia
Net Errors and Omissions	9.4	26.1	−19.3	−45.9	19.2	45.0	−11.6	Erreurs et omissions nettes
Reserves and Related Items	47.9	27.6	43.9	48.1	160.3	187.5	97.1	Rés. et postes appareutés
Tunisia								**Tunisie**
Goods: Exports fob	2 401.0	2 934.0	3 516.0	3 702.0	4 051.0	3 748.0	4 643.0	Biens : exportations,fàb
Goods: Imports fob	−3 503.0	−4 146.0	−5 201.0	−4 901.0	−6 088.0	−5 817.0	−6 217.0	Biens : importations,fàb
Serv. & Income: Credit	1 903.0	1 615.0	1 781.0	1 466.0	2 074.0	2 113.0	2 340.0	Serv. & revenu : crédit
Serv. & Income: Debit	−1 249.0	−1 223.0	−1 388.0	−1 442.0	−1 634.0	−1 661.0	−1 869.0	Serv. & revenu : débit
Current Trans.,nie: Credit	680.0	718.0	847.0	728.0	681.0	728.0	817.0	Transf. cour.,nia : crédit
Current Transfers: Debit	−13.0	−14.0	−24.0	−17.0	−18.0	−18.0	−19.0	Transf. courants : débit
Capital Acct.,nie: Credit	0.0	0.0	0.0	0.0	0.0	0.0	0.0	Compte de cap.,nia : crédit
Capital Account: Debit	−3.0	−7.0	−7.0	−5.0	−5.0	−7.0	−8.0	Compte de capital : débit
Financial Account,nie	198.0	194.0	381.0	337.0	984.0	905.0	375.0	Compte d'op. fin., nia
Net Errors and Omissions	8.0	−24.0	−35.0	105.0	33.0	35.0	271.0	Erreurs et omissions nettes
Reserves and Related Items	−421.0	−46.0	130.0	27.0	−78.0	−26.0	−334.0	Rés. et postes appareutés
Uganda								**Ouganda**
Goods: Exports fob	266.3	277.7	177.8	173.2	151.2	196.7	437.4	Biens : exportations,fàb
Goods: Imports fob	−523.5	−588.3	−491.0	−377.1	−421.9	−453.4	−695.9	Biens : importations,fàb
Serv. & Income: Credit	0.0	0.0	0.0	23.6	38.6	99.9	78.2	Serv. & revenu : crédit
Serv. & Income: Debit	−260.4	−260.5	−243.1	−318.5	−336.0	−335.8	−470.1	Serv. & revenu : débit
Current Trans.,nie: Credit	322.4	311.6	293.0	329.0	468.5	307.7	563.9	Transf. cour.,nia : crédit
Current Transfers: Debit	0.0	0.0	0.0	0.0	0.0	0.0	0.0	Transf. courants : débit
Capital Acct.,nie: Credit	0.0	0.0	0.0	0.0	0.0	42.4	36.1	Compte de cap.,nia : crédit
Capital Account: Debit	0.0	0.0	0.0	0.0	0.0	0.0	0.0	Compte de capital : débit
Financial Account,nie	3.6	213.0	211.8	137.6	114.8	167.2	147.3	Compte d'op. fin., nia
Net Errors and Omissions	154.9	−38.0	9.5	0.6	9.0	−41.8	5.2	Erreurs et omissions nettes
Reserves and Related Items	36.7	84.5	41.9	31.7	−24.2	17.1	−102.1	Rés. et postes appareutés
United Rep.Tanzania								**Rép. Unie de Tanzanie**
Goods: Exports fob	386.5	415.1	407.8	362.2	400.7	462.0	...	Biens : exportations,fàb
Goods: Imports fob	−1 033.0	−1 070.1	−1 186.4	−1 284.7	−1 313.6	−1 299.9	...	Biens : importations,fàb
Serv. & Income: Credit	120.6	122.7	141.1	150.0	155.6	290.2	...	Serv. & revenu : crédit
Serv. & Income: Debit	−471.1	−487.2	−481.1	−502.2	−569.6	−580.4	...	Serv. & revenu : débit
Current Trans.,nie: Credit	642.9	682.0	723.5	856.0	940.0	749.7	...	Transf. cour.,nia : crédit
Current Transfers: Debit	−21.7	−29.8	−30.0	−32.6	−35.0	−30.0	...	Transf. courants : débit
Capital Acct.,nie: Credit	0.0	0.0	0.0	0.0	0.0	0.0	...	Compte de cap.,nia : crédit
Capital Account: Debit	0.0	0.0	0.0	0.0	0.0	0.0	...	Compte de capital : débit
Financial Account,nie	33.9	21.8	126.5	108.1	88.9	75.0	...	Compte d'op. fin., nia
Net Errors and Omissions	−42.0	18.8	216.9	−20.1	44.6	−18.6	...	Erreurs et omissions nettes
Reserves and Related Items	383.9	326.8	81.6	363.3	288.4	352.1	...	Rés. et postes appareutés
Zaire								**Zaïre**
Goods: Exports fob	2 178.0	2 201.0	2 138.0	...	...	...	...	Biens : exportations,fàb
Goods: Imports fob	−1 645.0	−1 683.0	−1 539.0	...	...	...	...	Biens : importations,fàb
Serv. & Income: Credit	186.0	165.0	171.0	...	...	...	...	Serv. & revenu : crédit
Serv. & Income: Debit	−1 458.0	−1 460.0	−1 549.0	...	...	...	...	Serv. & revenu : débit
Current Trans.,nie: Credit	226.0	276.0	217.0	...	...	...	...	Transf. cour.,nia : crédit
Current Transfers: Debit	−67.0	−109.0	−81.0	...	...	...	...	Transf. courants : débit
Capital Acct.,nie: Credit	...	...	...	...	...	...	...	Compte de cap.,nia : crédit
Capital Account: Debit	...	...	...	...	...	...	...	Compte de capital : débit
Financial Account,nie	−11.0	−60.0	−220.0	...	...	...	...	Compte d'op. fin., nia
Net Errors and Omissions	−133.0	111.0	102.0	...	...	...	...	Erreurs et omissions nettes
Reserves and Related Items	724.0	559.0	761.0	...	...	...	...	Rés. et postes appareutés

79
Summary of balance of payments
Millions of US dollars
Résumé des balances des paiements
Millions de dollars des E−U

Country or area	1988	1989	1990	1991	1992	1993	1994	Pays ou zone
Zambia								**Zambie**
Goods: Exports fob	1 189.0	1 340.0	1 254.0	1 172.0	...	...	...	Biens : exportations,fàb
Goods: Imports fob	−687.0	−774.0	−1 511.0	−752.0	...	...	...	Biens : importations,fàb
Serv. & Income: Credit	61.0	86.0	109.0	93.0	...	...	...	Serv. & revenu : crédit
Serv. & Income: Debit	−893.0	−953.0	−825.0	−1 059.0	...	...	...	Serv. & revenu : débit
Current Trans.,nie: Credit	64.0	114.0	398.0	262.0	...	...	...	Transf. cour.,nia : crédit
Current Transfers: Debit	−27.0	−32.0	−18.0	−22.0	...	...	...	Transf. courants : débit
Capital Acct.,nie: Credit	0.0	0.0	0.0	0.0	...	...	...	Compte de cap.,nia : crédit
Capital Account: Debit	−2.0	−3.0	−3.0	−1.0	...	...	...	Compte de capital : débit
Financial Account,nie	23.0	1 827.0	497.0	18.0	...	...	...	Compte d'op. fin., nia
Net Errors and Omissions	40.0	−1 712.0	322.0	110.0	...	...	...	Erreurs et omissions nettes
Reserves and Related Items	232.0	106.0	−222.0	179.0	...	...	...	Rés. et postes appareutés
Zimbabwe								**Zimbabwe**
Goods: Exports fob	1 664.9	1 693.5	1 747.9	1 693.8	1 527.6	1 609.1	...	Biens : exportations,fàb
Goods: Imports fob	−1 163.6	−1 318.3	−1 505.2	−1 645.7	−1 782.1	−1 487.0	...	Biens : importations,fàb
Serv. & Income: Credit	207.7	267.8	287.1	299.6	331.1	407.1	...	Serv. & revenu : crédit
Serv. & Income: Debit	−644.9	−693.1	−781.8	−905.4	−963.2	−850.9	...	Serv. & revenu : débit
Current Trans.,nie: Credit	211.2	211.4	204.0	191.7	347.3	270.6	...	Transf. cour.,nia : crédit
Current Transfers: Debit	−150.1	−144.3	−91.8	−90.9	−64.4	−64.7	...	Transf. courants : débit
Capital Acct.,nie: Credit	0.3	0.2	0.4	0.1	0.2	0.6	...	Compte de cap.,nia : crédit
Capital Account: Debit	−9.0	−7.9	−7.4	−2.9	−1.6	−1.0	...	Compte de capital : débit
Financial Account,nie	48.0	47.8	242.6	536.5	373.4	327.2	...	Compte d'op. fin., nia
Net Errors and Omissions	−63.0	−103.8	−9.9	−31.4	37.2	14.9	...	Erreurs et omissions nettes
Reserves and Related Items	−101.6	46.8	−85.8	−45.2	194.6	−225.9	...	Rés. et postes appareutés
America, North· Amérique du Nord								
Anguilla								**Anguilla**
Goods: Exports fob	...	...	0.4	0.5	0.6	1.1	1.6	Biens : exportations,fàb
Goods: Imports fob	...	...	−28.7	−28.2	−33.6	−34.4	−38.3	Biens : importations,fàb
Serv. & Income: Credit	...	...	42.7	44.0	46.0	54.5	63.0	Serv. & revenu : crédit
Serv. & Income: Debit	...	...	−22.4	−23.3	−30.3	−34.9	−35.2	Serv. & revenu : débit
Current Trans.,nie: Credit	...	...	3.2	4.0	6.1	7.3	5.1	Transf. cour.,nia : crédit
Current Transfers: Debit	...	...	−3.6	−5.0	−8.1	−6.5	−6.7	Transf. courants : débit
Capital Acct.,nie: Credit	...	...	4.3	3.8	6.4	7.0	7.2	Compte de cap.,nia : crédit
Capital Account: Debit	...	...	−0.9	−0.9	−1.0	−1.3	−1.3	Compte de capital : débit
Financial Account,nie	...	...	22.2	9.0	12.2	4.3	8.4	Compte d'op. fin., nia
Net Errors and Omissions	...	...	−14.2	−4.1	3.1	4.0	−4.2	Erreurs et omissions nettes
Reserves and Related Items	...	...	−3.0	0.2	−1.3	−1.2	0.2	Rés. et postes appareutés
Antigua and Barbuda								**Antigua−et−Barbuda**
Goods: Exports fob	28.2	29.1	33.4	49.5	64.7	62.1	44.5	Biens : exportations,fàb
Goods: Imports fob	−204.5	−246.3	−235.4	−258.8	−274.4	−282.6	−298.1	Biens : importations,fàb
Serv. & Income: Credit	238.8	263.0	314.4	322.9	346.3	380.3	400.6	Serv. & revenu : crédit
Serv. & Income: Debit	−112.4	−139.3	−152.9	−148.3	−156.1	−157.7	−165.7	Serv. & revenu : débit
Current Trans.,nie: Credit	9.8	17.3	14.9	9.2	8.5	9.1	10.4	Transf. cour.,nia : crédit
Current Transfers: Debit	−4.9	−5.5	−5.3	−7.9	−9.7	−11.8	−9.5	Transf. courants : débit
Capital Acct.,nie: Credit	5.5	6.7	5.2	6.4	5.7	6.8	6.5	Compte de cap.,nia : crédit
Capital Account: Debit	0.0	0.0	0.0	0.0	0.0	0.0	−0.6	Compte de capital : débit
Financial Account,nie	45.8	76.8	60.6	46.4	40.0	0.5	9.6	Compte d'op. fin., nia
Net Errors and Omissions	−3.7	−1.9	−35.4	−14.4	−8.7	−18.0	10.5	Erreurs et omissions nettes
Reserves and Related Items	−2.6	0.0	0.6	−5.1	−16.4	11.2	−8.1	Rés. et postes appareutés
Aruba								**Aruba**
Goods: Exports fob	87.4	107.5	155.5	878.8	1 069.2	1 154.4	1 296.8	Biens : exportations,fàb
Goods: Imports fob	−354.6	−397.4	−580.8	−1 402.8	−1 446.7	−1 546.5	−1 607.3	Biens : importations,fàb
Serv. & Income: Credit	337.1	364.7	425.8	490.6	585.7	617.5	633.8	Serv. & revenu : crédit
Serv. & Income: Debit	−113.2	−124.9	−157.5	−173.5	−181.6	−193.7	−251.0	Serv. & revenu : débit
Current Trans.,nie: Credit	14.9	18.0	33.8	38.1	45.9	43.4	47.5	Transf. cour.,nia : crédit
Current Transfers: Debit	−15.8	−14.6	−34.9	−40.6	−28.7	−33.3	−38.7	Transf. courants : débit
Capital Acct.,nie: Credit	0.0	0.0	0.0	0.8	0.9	0.9	0.3	Compte de cap.,nia : crédit
Capital Account: Debit	0.0	0.0	0.0	−3.8	−2.4	−2.8	−4.4	Compte de capital : débit
Financial Account,nie	56.8	47.8	172.2	228.8	−24.1	−8.4	−75.4	Compte d'op. fin., nia
Net Errors and Omissions	−12.8	20.4	−2.4	6.5	4.4	2.0	−4.7	Erreurs et omissions nettes
Reserves and Related Items	0.4	−21.5	−11.7	−22.8	−22.6	−33.4	3.2	Rés. et postes appareutés
Bahamas								**Bahamas**
Goods: Exports fob	310.8	312.1	375.7	360.2	342.5	286.8	258.5	Biens : exportations,fàb
Goods: Imports fob	−982.9	−1 136.7	−1 190.2	−1 045.6	−1 069.2	−1 100.5	−1 145.2	Biens : importations,fàb
Serv. & Income: Credit	1 290.5	1 454.4	1 478.2	1 331.0	1 364.4	1 439.1	1 487.8	Serv. & revenu : crédit
Serv. & Income: Debit	−673.4	−715.1	−773.6	−775.3	−708.8	−717.4	−846.4	Serv. & revenu : débit

79
Summary of balance of payments
Millions of US dollars
Résumé des balances des paiements
Millions de dollars des E−U

Country or area	1988	1989	1990	1991	1992	1993	1994	Pays ou zone
Current Trans.,nie: Credit	17.4	21.6	24.7	30.9	31.1	33.1	33.9	Transf. cour.,nia : crédit
Current Transfers: Debit	−28.9	−17.9	−9.9	−8.4	−13.5	−14.4	−12.9	Transf. courants : débit
Capital Acct.,nie: Credit	0.0	0.0	0.0	0.0	0.0	0.0	0.0	Compte de cap.,nia : crédit
Capital Account: Debit	−3.0	−2.7	−4.2	−2.9	−4.2	−4.3	−3.0	Compte de capital : débit
Financial Account,nie	73.2	94.8	57.1	176.9	12.9	9.4	77.2	Compte d'op. fin., nia
Net Errors and Omissions	−4.4	−37.1	51.5	−53.8	16.1	87.2	159.5	Erreurs et omissions nettes
Reserves and Related Items	0.7	26.6	−9.3	−13.0	28.7	−19.0	−9.4	Rés. et postes appareutés
Barbados								**Barbade**
Goods: Exports fob	175.8	185.7	213.1	203.9	190.5	181.5	...	Biens : exportations,fàb
Goods: Imports fob	−518.7	−600.3	−624.1	−617.4	−464.7	−511.3	...	Biens : importations,fàb
Serv. & Income: Credit	607.1	702.2	623.3	628.1	631.8	700.6	...	Serv. & revenu : crédit
Serv. & Income: Debit	−238.2	−268.6	−271.2	−272.8	−254.2	−327.3	...	Serv. & revenu : débit
Current Trans.,nie: Credit	47.4	51.0	54.4	48.8	54.8	43.1	...	Transf. cour.,nia : crédit
Current Transfers: Debit	−31.0	−46.2	−11.9	−15.8	−14.5	−22.3	...	Transf. courants : débit
Capital Acct.,nie: Credit	0.0	0.0	0.0	0.0	0.0	0.0	...	Compte de cap.,nia : crédit
Capital Account: Debit	0.0	0.0	0.0	0.0	0.0	0.0	...	Compte de capital : débit
Financial Account,nie	47.5	−22.4	48.0	17.8	−94.0	1.2	...	Compte d'op. fin., nia
Net Errors and Omissions	−50.4	−44.1	−70.6	−32.6	−21.5	−44.7	...	Erreurs et omissions nettes
Reserves and Related Items	−39.5	42.8	38.9	39.9	−28.3	−20.9	...	Rés. et postes appareutés
Belize								**Belize**
Goods: Exports fob	119.4	124.4	129.2	126.1	140.6	132.0	...	Biens : exportations,fàb
Goods: Imports fob	−161.2	−188.5	−188.4	−223.6	−244.5	−250.5	...	Biens : importations,fàb
Serv. & Income: Credit	82.4	95.5	125.9	131.0	149.3	156.4	...	Serv. & revenu : crédit
Serv. & Income: Debit	−69.0	−81.6	−80.8	−87.3	−104.4	−115.9	...	Serv. & revenu : débit
Current Trans.,nie: Credit	29.4	34.4	33.6	32.3	35.4	33.8	...	Transf. cour.,nia : crédit
Current Transfers: Debit	−3.5	−3.3	−4.2	−4.3	−5.0	−4.3	...	Transf. courants : débit
Capital Acct.,nie: Credit	0.0	0.0	0.0	0.0	0.0	0.0	...	Compte de cap.,nia : crédit
Capital Account: Debit	0.0	0.0	0.0	0.0	0.0	0.0	...	Compte de capital : débit
Financial Account,nie	27.3	25.5	25.1	22.2	22.4	32.8	...	Compte d'op. fin., nia
Net Errors and Omissions	−2.9	9.1	−25.0	−12.8	6.3	1.5	...	Erreurs et omissions nettes
Reserves and Related Items	−21.8	−15.5	−15.4	16.4	−0.1	14.2	...	Rés. et postes appareutés
Canada								**Canada**
Goods: Exports fob	115 431.0	122 969.0	128 440.0	126 153.0	132 115.0	143 953.0	163 813.0	Biens : exportations,fàb
Goods: Imports fob	−107 273.0	−116 984.0	−120 106.0	−122 282.0	−126 415.0	−136 026.0	−151 505.0	Biens : importations,fàb
Serv. & Income: Credit	22 459.0	24 526.0	24 791.0	26 681.0	26 180.0	26 061.0	29 767.0	Serv. & revenu : crédit
Serv. & Income: Debit	−47 980.0	−53 501.0	−54 634.0	−54 246.0	−53 579.0	−56 678.0	−58 998.0	Serv. & revenu : débit
Current Trans.,nie: Credit	2 066.0	2 035.0	2 290.0	2 292.0	2 233.0	2 281.0	2 258.0	Transf. cour.,nia : crédit
Current Transfers: Debit	−2 727.0	−2 835.0	−3 358.0	−3 169.0	−3 125.0	−2 982.0	−2 613.0	Transf. courants : débit
Capital Acct.,nie: Credit	1 100.0	1 257.0	1 251.0	1 260.0	1 297.0	1 293.0	1 265.0	Compte de cap.,nia : crédit
Capital Account: Debit	−179.0	−202.0	−218.0	−273.0	−264.0	−264.0	−264.0	Compte de capital : débit
Financial Account,nie	25 219.0	22 527.0	23 571.0	23 748.0	14 448.0	29 124.0	9 699.0	Compte d'op. fin., nia
Net Errors and Omissions	−558.0	501.0	−1 402.0	−2 649.0	1 304.0	−7 255.0	1 434.0	Erreurs et omissions nettes
Reserves and Related Items	−7 558.0	−293.0	−625.0	2 486.0	5 807.0	492.0	5 144.0	Rés. et postes appareutés
Costa Rica								**Costa Rica**
Goods: Exports fob	1 180.7	1 333.4	1 354.2	1 498.1	1 739.1	1 866.8	2 102.3	Biens : exportations,fàb
Goods: Imports fob	−1 278.6	−1 572.0	−1 796.7	−1 697.6	−2 210.9	−2 626.6	−2 788.6	Biens : importations,fàb
Serv. & Income: Credit	478.1	617.8	739.3	802.8	954.1	1 150.5	1 296.4	Serv. & revenu : crédit
Serv. & Income: Debit	−814.1	−985.5	−912.7	−820.1	−1 026.0	−1 153.0	−1 215.6	Serv. & revenu : débit
Current Trans.,nie: Credit	141.9	130.5	126.0	121.1	168.9	149.3	150.0	Transf. cour.,nia : crédit
Current Transfers: Debit	−11.5	−4.1	−4.1	−3.5	−5.6	−6.2	−7.7	Transf. courants : débit
Capital Acct.,nie: Credit	0.0	0.0	0.0	0.0	0.0	0.0	0.0	Compte de cap.,nia : crédit
Capital Account: Debit	0.0	0.0	0.0	0.0	0.0	0.0	0.0	Compte de capital : débit
Financial Account,nie	−271.9	−182.5	−83.9	155.0	199.4	138.0	−121.6	Compte d'op. fin., nia
Net Errors and Omissions	224.6	208.9	43.4	99.9	201.9	298.0	498.0	Erreurs et omissions nettes
Reserves and Related Items	350.8	453.5	534.5	−155.7	−20.9	183.2	86.8	Rés. et postes appareutés
Dominica								**Dominique**
Goods: Exports fob	57.0	46.3	56.1	55.6	55.1	47.3	44.0	Biens : exportations,fàb
Goods: Imports fob	−77.2	−94.4	−104.0	−96.5	−92.8	−93.9	−95.8	Biens : importations,fàb
Serv. & Income: Credit	25.2	28.6	37.4	40.0	46.7	49.9	54.7	Serv. & revenu : crédit
Serv. & Income: Debit	−27.5	−33.4	−38.9	−40.1	−42.3	−40.2	−47.0	Serv. & revenu : débit
Current Trans.,nie: Credit	13.2	10.2	10.4	11.2	10.9	12.4	14.8	Transf. cour.,nia : crédit
Current Transfers: Debit	−2.9	−2.8	−4.5	−3.9	−3.3	−3.7	−6.4	Transf. courants : débit
Capital Acct.,nie: Credit	12.9	15.6	15.0	14.7	11.3	11.2	8.2	Compte de cap.,nia : crédit
Capital Account: Debit	−1.5	−2.0	−1.5	−1.6	−1.5	−1.5	−0.2	Compte de capital : débit
Financial Account,nie	5.1	32.0	29.3	24.6	24.3	18.1	25.8	Compte d'op. fin., nia

79
Summary of balance of payments
Millions of US dollars
Résumé des balances des paiements
Millions de dollars des E−U

Country or area	1988	1989	1990	1991	1992	1993	1994	Pays ou zone
Net Errors and Omissions	−5.2	0.1	5.8	0.1	−5.0	1.0	−1.4	Erreurs et omissions nettes
Reserves and Related Items	1.0	−0.2	−5.1	−4.2	−3.4	−0.6	3.2	Rés. et postes apparentés
Dominican Republic								**Rép. dominicaine**
Goods: Exports fob	889.7	924.4	734.5	658.3	562.5	511.0	644.0	Biens : exportations,fàb
Goods: Imports fob	−1 608.0	−1 963.8	−1 792.8	−1 728.8	−2 174.3	−2 118.4	−2 275.8	Biens : importations,fàb
Serv. & Income: Credit	1 021.9	1 148.2	1 183.5	1 285.9	1 403.3	1 751.7	1 957.5	Serv. & revenu : crédit
Serv. & Income: Debit	−676.1	−820.5	−775.4	−759.2	−931.2	−1 011.0	−977.6	Serv. & revenu : débit
Current Trans.,nie: Credit	353.6	384.4	370.6	386.5	431.8	441.6	493.2	Transf. cour.,nia : crédit
Current Transfers: Debit	0.0	0.0	0.0	0.0	0.0	0.0	0.0	Transf. courants : débit
Capital Acct.,nie: Credit	0.0	0.0	0.0	0.0	0.0	0.0	0.0	Compte de cap.,nia : crédit
Capital Account: Debit	0.0	0.0	0.0	0.0	0.0	0.0	0.0	Compte de capital : débit
Financial Account,nie	−15.6	160.0	−17.2	−137.7	75.7	−65.0	269.8	Compte d'op. fin., nia
Net Errors and Omissions	35.6	−73.6	−120.7	548.3	569.0	524.2	−497.5	Erreurs et omissions nettes
Reserves and Related Items	−1.1	240.9	417.5	−253.3	63.1	−34.2	386.4	Rés. et postes apparentés
El Salvador								**El Salvador**
Goods: Exports fob	610.6	557.5	643.9	586.8	598.1	731.5	1 252.2	Biens : exportations,fàb
Goods: Imports fob	−966.5	−1 220.2	−1 309.5	−1 291.4	−1 560.5	−1 766.4	−2 407.4	Biens : importations,fàb
Serv. & Income: Credit	352.2	377.1	358.7	341.2	408.8	437.1	422.7	Serv. & revenu : crédit
Serv. & Income: Debit	−471.0	−519.5	−475.8	−474.0	−493.6	−524.5	−574.0	Serv. & revenu : débit
Current Trans.,nie: Credit	347.6	437.6	524.6	627.5	852.8	1 004.7	1 290.9	Transf. cour.,nia : crédit
Current Transfers: Debit	−2.1	−2.1	−2.7	−2.5	−0.7	−0.7	−2.4	Transf. courants : débit
Capital Acct.,nie: Credit	0.0	0.0	0.0	0.0	0.0	0.0	0.0	Compte de cap.,nia : crédit
Capital Account: Debit	0.0	0.0	0.0	0.0	0.0	0.0	0.0	Compte de capital : débit
Financial Account,nie	52.3	118.2	−11.4	−61.1	−4.3	86.6	83.9	Compte d'op. fin., nia
Net Errors and Omissions	−107.1	140.9	299.4	125.6	65.6	90.3	47.3	Erreurs et omissions nettes
Reserves and Related Items	184.1	110.6	−27.1	147.9	133.8	−58.7	−113.0	Rés. et postes apparentés
Grenada								**Grenade**
Goods: Exports fob	33.2	31.1	29.3	26.7	23.3	22.5	25.8	Biens : exportations,fàb
Goods: Imports fob	−92.2	−99.0	−106.3	−113.6	−103.2	−118.1	−125.1	Biens : importations,fàb
Serv. & Income: Credit	55.7	56.7	66.3	74.3	78.6	90.5	105.5	Serv. & revenu : crédit
Serv. & Income: Debit	−36.7	−41.6	−46.9	−45.3	−43.8	−52.2	−55.3	Serv. & revenu : débit
Current Trans.,nie: Credit	13.0	17.4	12.5	13.3	14.3	16.1	19.8	Transf. cour.,nia : crédit
Current Transfers: Debit	−0.8	−0.9	−1.1	−2.0	−2.3	−2.4	−3.5	Transf. courants : débit
Capital Acct.,nie: Credit	20.9	10.7	23.4	18.5	14.8	18.3	23.0	Compte de cap.,nia : crédit
Capital Account: Debit	−7.9	−0.8	−1.3	−1.0	−1.4	−1.4	−1.4	Compte de capital : débit
Financial Account,nie	11.4	33.2	18.5	23.4	18.3	19.0	6.3	Compte d'op. fin., nia
Net Errors and Omissions	−1.7	−7.6	8.1	8.2	9.5	8.1	9.4	Erreurs et omissions nettes
Reserves and Related Items	5.1	0.8	−2.5	−2.5	−8.1	−0.4	−4.5	Rés. et postes apparentés
Guatemala								**Guatemala**
Goods: Exports fob	1 073.3	1 126.1	1 211.4	1 230.0	1 283.7	1 363.2	1 550.1	Biens : exportations,fàb
Goods: Imports fob	−1 413.2	−1 484.4	−1 428.0	−1 673.0	−2 327.8	−2 384.0	−2 546.6	Biens : importations,fàb
Serv. & Income: Credit	227.4	328.7	377.0	522.7	683.1	721.5	761.1	Serv. & revenu : crédit
Serv. & Income: Debit	−525.8	−587.3	−600.3	−523.1	−735.4	−765.6	−838.5	Serv. & revenu : débit
Current Trans.,nie: Credit	227.7	255.1	217.6	276.7	406.2	371.4	456.4	Transf. cour.,nia : crédit
Current Transfers: Debit	−3.4	−5.3	−10.6	−17.0	−15.7	−8.2	−7.8	Transf. courants : débit
Capital Acct.,nie: Credit	0.0	0.0	0.0	0.0	0.0	0.0	0.0	Compte de cap.,nia : crédit
Capital Account: Debit	0.0	0.0	0.0	0.0	0.0	0.0	0.0	Compte de capital : débit
Financial Account,nie	80.5	225.3	−46.2	732.8	610.5	789.2	655.2	Compte d'op. fin., nia
Net Errors and Omissions	−2.4	54.7	36.2	83.3	81.8	85.2	−23.6	Erreurs et omissions nettes
Reserves and Related Items	336.0	87.1	242.9	−632.4	13.6	−172.7	−6.3	Rés. et postes apparentés
Haiti								**Haïti**
Goods: Exports fob	180.4	148.3	265.8	202.0	75.6	81.6	57.4	Biens : exportations,fàb
Goods: Imports fob	−283.9	−259.3	−442.6	−448.6	−214.1	−266.6	−141.2	Biens : importations,fàb
Serv. & Income: Credit	100.7	93.1	59.1	59.6	39.5	37.8	6.7	Serv. & revenu : crédit
Serv. & Income: Debit	−230.5	−219.0	−97.1	−103.3	−48.1	−42.8	−75.1	Serv. & revenu : débit
Current Trans.,nie: Credit	253.6	237.7	192.9	234.2	155.0	173.4	156.2	Transf. cour.,nia : crédit
Current Transfers: Debit	−60.7	−63.5	0.0	0.0	0.0	0.0	0.0	Transf. courants : débit
Capital Acct.,nie: Credit	0.0	0.0	0.0	0.0	0.0	0.0	0.0	Compte de cap.,nia : crédit
Capital Account: Debit	0.0	0.0	0.0	0.0	0.0	0.0	0.0	Compte de capital : débit
Financial Account,nie	26.3	60.1	33.0	25.9	−20.6	−43.7	−15.8	Compte d'op. fin., nia
Net Errors and Omissions	11.8	−13.7	−44.9	40.6	6.4	37.2	−8.8	Erreurs et omissions nettes
Reserves and Related Items	2.3	16.2	33.8	−10.5	6.3	23.0	20.6	Rés. et postes apparentés
Honduras								**Honduras**
Goods: Exports fob	889.4	911.2	895.2	840.6	839.3	853.0	...	Biens : exportations,fàb
Goods: Imports fob	−923.4	−955.7	−907.0	−912.5	−990.2	−943.9	...	Biens : importations,fàb
Serv. & Income: Credit	158.3	174.0	158.0	214.8	263.4	288.2	...	Serv. & revenu : crédit

79
Summary of balance of payments
Millions of US dollars
Résumé des balances des paiements
Millions de dollars des E−U

Country or area	1988	1989	1990	1991	1992	1993	1994	Pays ou zone
Serv. & Income: Debit	−470.8	−492.4	−477.3	−512.6	−586.6	−587.0	...	Serv. & revenu : débit
Current Trans.,nie: Credit	168.4	159.6	106.2	114.3	126.1	84.1	...	Transf. cour.,nia : crédit
Current Transfers: Debit	−3.0	−3.0	−3.0	−3.0	−3.0	−3.0	...	Transf. courants : débit
Capital Acct.,nie: Credit	30.0	35.0	50.0	52.0	60.0	60.0	...	Compte de cap.,nia : crédit
Capital Account: Debit	−10.0	−9.0	−8.5	−7.0	−7.2	−7.2	...	Compte de capital : débit
Financial Account,nie	55.8	−65.2	−4.8	−97.0	22.5	154.4	...	Compte d'op. fin., nia
Net Errors and Omissions	−93.1	−138.9	−107.4	152.0	29.2	−81.8	...	Erreurs et omissions nettes
Reserves and Related Items	198.3	384.3	298.6	158.4	246.5	183.2	...	Rés. et postes appareutés
Jamaica								**Jamaïque**
Goods: Exports fob	898.4	1 028.9	1 190.6	1 196.7	1 116.5	1 105.4	1 247.7	Biens : exportations,fàb
Goods: Imports fob	−1 255.3	−1 618.7	−1 692.7	−1 588.3	−1 541.1	−1 920.5	−1 892.1	Biens : importations,fàb
Serv. & Income: Credit	873.3	980.1	1 134.1	1 051.8	1 179.0	1 377.7	1 432.5	Serv. & revenu : crédit
Serv. & Income: Debit	−990.8	−1 174.9	−1 235.0	−1 168.8	−1 083.3	−1 136.4	−1 220.2	Serv. & revenu : débit
Current Trans.,nie: Credit	587.8	523.8	314.9	294.8	387.2	415.9	505.2	Transf. cour.,nia : crédit
Current Transfers: Debit	−66.8	−21.8	−24.0	−26.3	−29.8	−26.1	−24.7	Transf. courants : débit
Capital Acct.,nie: Credit	0.0	0.0	0.0	0.0	0.0	0.0	0.0	Compte de cap.,nia : crédit
Capital Account: Debit	−15.4	−15.0	−15.9	−15.7	−17.6	−12.9	−12.9	Compte de capital : débit
Financial Account,nie	88.0	98.2	404.5	271.4	354.5	296.4	394.4	Compte d'op. fin., nia
Net Errors and Omissions	−46.0	10.0	29.3	−20.4	−59.9	49.7	−31.4	Erreurs et omissions nettes
Reserves and Related Items	−73.2	189.4	−105.8	4.8	−305.5	−149.2	−398.5	Rés. et postes appareutés
Mexico								**Mexique**
Goods: Exports fob	30 692.0	35 171.0	40 711.0	42 687.0	46 196.0	51 885.0	60 879.0	Biens : exportations,fàb
Goods: Imports fob	−28 081.0	−34 766.0	−41 592.0	−49 966.0	−62 130.0	−65 366.0	−79 346.0	Biens : importations,fàb
Serv. & Income: Credit	9 133.0	10 368.0	11 367.0	12 392.0	12 064.0	12 211.0	13 671.0	Serv. & revenu : crédit
Serv. & Income: Debit	−16 373.0	−19 141.0	−21 912.0	−22 747.0	−23 957.0	−25 770.0	−28 634.0	Serv. & revenu : débit
Current Trans.,nie: Credit	2 270.0	2 559.0	3 990.0	2 765.0	3 404.0	3 656.0	4 042.0	Transf. cour.,nia : crédit
Current Transfers: Debit	−15.0	−16.0	−15.0	−19.0	−19.0	−16.0	−30.0	Transf. courants : débit
Capital Acct.,nie: Credit	0.0	0.0	0.0	0.0	0.0	0.0	0.0	Compte de cap.,nia : crédit
Capital Account: Debit	0.0	0.0	0.0	0.0	0.0	0.0	0.0	Compte de capital : débit
Financial Account,nie	−4 495.0	1 110.0	8 441.0	25 139.0	27 039.0	33 760.0	15 787.0	Compte d'op. fin., nia
Net Errors and Omissions	−3 193.0	4 504.0	1 228.0	−2 278.0	−852.0	−3 128.0	−4 035.0	Erreurs et omissions nettes
Reserves and Related Items	10 062.0	211.0	−2 218.0	−7 973.0	−1 745.0	−7 232.0	17 667.0	Rés. et postes appareutés
Montserrat								**Montserrat**
Goods: Exports fob	2.3	1.3	1.5	1.0	1.6	2.3	2.9	Biens : exportations,fàb
Goods: Imports fob	−23.4	−32.6	−42.4	−34.1	−29.8	−24.2	−30.0	Biens : importations,fàb
Serv. & Income: Credit	15.5	17.0	19.4	19.4	20.5	23.8	27.6	Serv. & revenu : crédit
Serv. & Income: Debit	−9.7	−12.4	−15.2	−13.8	−13.9	−15.2	−19.7	Serv. & revenu : débit
Current Trans.,nie: Credit	...	35.4	18.4	11.7	12.1	9.7	3.3	Transf. cour.,nia : crédit
Current Transfers: Debit	−0.8	−3.3	−4.6	−5.5	−3.4	−6.4	−3.4	Transf. courants : débit
Capital Acct.,nie: Credit	4.6	7.0	4.5	5.2	2.1	5.4	10.1	Compte de cap.,nia : crédit
Capital Account: Debit	0.0	0.0	0.0	0.0	0.0	0.0	0.0	Compte de capital : débit
Financial Account,nie	4.8	−9.2	23.6	5.1	4.7	5.5	−4.3	Compte d'op. fin., nia
Net Errors and Omissions	6.9	−2.9	−2.7	7.4	6.1	−1.2	15.1	Erreurs et omissions nettes
Reserves and Related Items	−0.3	−0.3	−2.6	3.6	−0.1	0.4	−1.6	Rés. et postes appareutés
Netherlands Antilles								**Antilles néerlandaises**
Goods: Exports fob	225.8	313.4	302.7	301.8	332.3	306.0	351.1	Biens : exportations,fàb
Goods: Imports fob	−879.4	−1 017.8	−1 112.3	−1 118.9	−1 168.4	−1 143.8	−1 271.6	Biens : importations,fàb
Serv. & Income: Credit	973.5	1 069.7	1 287.5	1 354.7	1 497.7	1 468.7	1 547.9	Serv. & revenu : crédit
Serv. & Income: Debit	−419.5	−480.5	−627.8	−653.8	−753.5	−736.3	−769.9	Serv. & revenu : débit
Current Trans.,nie: Credit	268.7	260.9	213.1	228.7	217.4	250.3	217.9	Transf. cour.,nia : crédit
Current Transfers: Debit	−94.1	−107.6	−107.3	−118.6	−115.5	−143.7	−173.3	Transf. courants : débit
Capital Acct.,nie: Credit	0.4	0.1	0.5	0.9	1.7	0.8	1.0	Compte de cap.,nia : crédit
Capital Account: Debit	−3.3	−3.3	−2.2	−1.7	−2.3	−1.7	−1.7	Compte de capital : débit
Financial Account,nie	−58.3	−93.7	9.4	−41.5	41.7	32.2	−2.3	Compte d'op. fin., nia
Net Errors and Omissions	19.5	14.6	6.5	6.2	8.2	11.5	24.9	Erreurs et omissions nettes
Reserves and Related Items	−33.4	44.2	29.8	42.2	−59.2	−44.0	75.9	Rés. et postes appareutés
Nicaragua								**Nicaragua**
Goods: Exports fob	235.7	318.7	332.4	268.1	223.1	267.0	351.2	Biens : exportations,fàb
Goods: Imports fob	−718.3	−547.3	−569.7	−688.0	−770.8	−659.4	−784.7	Biens : importations,fàb
Serv. & Income: Credit	39.5	28.8	71.6	79.9	93.7	105.6	108.1	Serv. & revenu : crédit
Serv. & Income: Debit	−402.3	−330.8	−341.1	−509.2	−650.6	−591.1	−644.4	Serv. & revenu : débit
Current Trans.,nie: Credit	130.0	168.9	201.6	844.4	270.6	233.6	240.9	Transf. cour.,nia : crédit
Current Transfers: Debit	0.0	0.0	0.0	0.0	0.0	0.0	0.0	Transf. courants : débit
Capital Acct.,nie: Credit	0.0	0.0	0.0	0.0	0.0	0.0	0.0	Compte de cap.,nia : crédit
Capital Account: Debit	0.0	0.0	0.0	0.0	0.0	0.0	0.0	Compte de capital : débit
Financial Account,nie	303.5	−89.3	−161.1	−543.6	−538.3	−502.8	−209.1	Compte d'op. fin., nia

79
Summary of balance of payments
Millions of US dollars
Résumé des balances des paiements
Millions de dollars des E−U

Country or area	1988	1989	1990	1991	1992	1993	1994	Pays ou zone
Net Errors and Omissions	51.9	−69.2	−181.2	84.7	60.2	128.1	154.3	Erreurs et omissions nettes
Reserves and Related Items	360.0	520.2	647.5	463.7	1 312.0	1 019.0	783.7	Rés. et postes appareutés
Panama								**Panama**
Goods: Exports fob	2 504.7	2 740.8	3 357.6	4 206.9	5 114.6	5 427.6	6 013.4	Biens : exportations,fàb
Goods: Imports fob	−2 411.8	−2 940.7	−3 593.1	−4 715.4	−5 620.2	−5 889.3	−6 457.8	Biens : importations,fàb
Serv. & Income: Credit	2 232.2	2 726.3	2 554.8	2 469.4	2 731.2	2 862.7	2 775.3	Serv. & revenu : crédit
Serv. & Income: Debit	−2 105.6	−3 523.5	−2 835.2	−2 971.4	−3 345.2	−3 248.0	−3 760.3	Serv. & revenu : débit
Current Trans.,nie: Credit	170.5	141.9	307.2	315.0	424.4	304.7	256.6	Transf. cour.,nia : crédit
Current Transfers: Debit	−45.2	−44.2	−29.4	−27.3	−29.0	−33.4	−36.1	Transf. courants : débit
Capital Acct.,nie: Credit	0.0	0.0	0.0	0.0	0.0	0.0	0.0	Compte de cap.,nia : crédit
Capital Account: Debit	0.0	0.0	0.0	0.0	0.0	0.0	0.0	Compte de capital : débit
Financial Account,nie	−770.8	−577.7	−513.5	−587.8	−481.6	−1 317.1	−242.0	Compte d'op. fin., nia
Net Errors and Omissions	−530.7	673.3	503.7	1 001.8	1 315.7	1 615.8	1 047.8	Erreurs et omissions nettes
Reserves and Related Items	956.7	803.8	247.9	308.8	−109.9	277.0	403.1	Rés. et postes appareutés
Saint Kitts and Nevis								**Saint−Kitts−et−Nevis**
Goods: Exports fob	28.4	29.2	28.3	28.6	33.0	31.9	29.3	Biens : exportations,fàb
Goods: Imports fob	−82.0	−90.2	−97.4	−97.1	−84.2	−94.6	−98.3	Biens : importations,fàb
Serv. & Income: Credit	51.3	53.5	57.4	71.0	81.6	85.9	94.5	Serv. & revenu : crédit
Serv. & Income: Debit	−33.5	−41.9	−42.7	−45.2	−54.3	−61.3	−61.5	Serv. & revenu : débit
Current Trans.,nie: Credit	11.8	17.7	17.2	13.9	13.7	14.2	15.2	Transf. cour.,nia : crédit
Current Transfers: Debit	−3.5	−6.7	−9.7	−6.2	−5.7	−6.2	−5.7	Transf. courants : débit
Capital Acct.,nie: Credit	7.8	5.3	3.1	3.8	3.8	3.5	2.6	Compte de cap.,nia : crédit
Capital Account: Debit	−0.2	−0.2	−0.6	0.0	−0.2	−0.2	−0.9	Compte de capital : débit
Financial Account,nie	18.8	51.2	51.1	25.2	23.6	15.2	26.1	Compte d'op. fin., nia
Net Errors and Omissions	1.1	−11.6	−6.4	6.5	−1.7	14.9	1.0	Erreurs et omissions nettes
Reserves and Related Items	0.1	−6.3	−0.1	−0.7	−9.8	−3.4	−2.3	Rés. et postes appareutés
Saint Lucia								**Sainte−Lucie**
Goods: Exports fob	122.3	116.0	131.0	113.9	127.2	123.5	99.9	Biens : exportations,fàb
Goods: Imports fob	−194.5	−240.9	−238.8	−261.4	−270.8	−264.0	−265.6	Biens : importations,fàb
Serv. & Income: Credit	123.6	142.3	156.5	176.8	200.4	209.0	230.9	Serv. & revenu : crédit
Serv. & Income: Debit	−76.9	−87.8	−101.8	−114.8	−120.6	−119.0	−142.2	Serv. & revenu : débit
Current Trans.,nie: Credit	12.7	12.3	13.9	16.9	16.4	21.9	20.5	Transf. cour.,nia : crédit
Current Transfers: Debit	−5.2	−5.2	−6.3	−3.5	−7.4	−12.6	−8.3	Transf. courants : débit
Capital Acct.,nie: Credit	7.9	8.5	3.9	6.6	9.1	4.2	8.5	Compte de cap.,nia : crédit
Capital Account: Debit	0.0	0.0	0.0	0.0	−0.2	−0.3	−1.1	Compte de capital : débit
Financial Account,nie	7.6	52.2	51.4	59.3	59.8	56.1	46.3	Compte d'op. fin., nia
Net Errors and Omissions	4.4	8.2	−3.5	13.9	−7.1	−14.2	15.4	Erreurs et omissions nettes
Reserves and Related Items	−1.9	−5.6	−6.3	−7.7	−6.8	−4.5	−4.2	Rés. et postes appareutés
St. Vincent−Grenadines								**St. Vincent−Grenadines**
Goods: Exports fob	87.4	77.4	85.4	67.4	79.0	57.1	45.7	Biens : exportations,fàb
Goods: Imports fob	−107.6	−112.6	−120.4	−120.4	−116.9	−118.1	−119.4	Biens : importations,fàb
Serv. & Income: Credit	41.6	42.8	49.4	51.0	54.3	51.6	51.7	Serv. & revenu : crédit
Serv. & Income: Debit	−44.4	−45.5	−50.9	−49.3	−47.7	−44.2	−52.6	Serv. & revenu : débit
Current Trans.,nie: Credit	12.3	13.0	14.5	13.8	14.2	14.8	21.3	Transf. cour.,nia : crédit
Current Transfers: Debit	−6.1	−4.7	−4.9	−6.6	−8.8	−8.6	−8.0	Transf. courants : débit
Capital Acct.,nie: Credit	10.2	12.2	18.9	21.7	14.7	7.0	5.4	Compte de cap.,nia : crédit
Capital Account: Debit	−0.3	−0.2	−0.2	−0.3	−0.3	−0.3	−0.4	Compte de capital : débit
Financial Account,nie	3.5	17.5	2.0	20.6	25.2	32.8	57.0	Compte d'op. fin., nia
Net Errors and Omissions	5.3	1.6	11.7	−1.5	−4.3	6.7	−0.5	Erreurs et omissions nettes
Reserves and Related Items	−1.9	−1.4	−5.4	3.5	−9.6	1.3	−0.3	Rés. et postes appareutés
Trinidad and Tobago								**Trinité−et−Tobago**
Goods: Exports fob	1 469.5	1 550.8	1 960.1	1 774.5	1 691.4	1 500.1	1 777.6	Biens : exportations,fàb
Goods: Imports fob	−1 064.2	−1 045.2	−947.6	−1 210.3	−995.6	−952.9	−1 036.6	Biens : importations,fàb
Serv. & Income: Credit	291.6	313.2	368.1	453.9	482.5	393.6	383.3	Serv. & revenu : crédit
Serv. & Income: Debit	−776.2	−849.9	−915.6	−1 025.1	−1 039.8	−832.4	−906.8	Serv. & revenu : débit
Current Trans.,nie: Credit	3.5	5.2	7.8	15.6	11.1	23.7	28.3	Transf. cour.,nia : crédit
Current Transfers: Debit	−12.7	−12.7	−13.9	−13.3	−10.7	−19.0	−27.9	Transf. courants : débit
Capital Acct.,nie: Credit	...	0.4	0.4	0.4	0.4	1.3	1.1	Compte de cap.,nia : crédit
Capital Account: Debit	−20.4	−17.5	−19.6	−16.5	−16.9	−12.8	−7.5	Compte de capital : débit
Financial Account,nie	−141.5	−166.5	−506.3	−226.8	−154.2	98.8	−32.2	Compte d'op. fin., nia
Net Errors and Omissions	21.1	45.4	−112.0	−29.0	−72.6	−41.8	6.3	Erreurs et omissions nettes
Reserves and Related Items	229.4	176.8	178.5	276.5	104.4	−158.6	−185.5	Rés. et postes appareutés
United States								**Etats−Unis**
Goods: Exports fob	320.2	362.2	389.3	416.9	440.4	458.7	504.5	Biens : exportations,fàb
Goods: Imports fob	−447.2	−477.3	−498.3	−491.0	−536.5	−590.1	−668.9	Biens : importations,fàb
Serv. & Income: Credit	240.2	279.9	308.1	301.3	297.0	305.1	334.3	Serv. & revenu : crédit

79
Summary of balance of payments
Millions of US dollars
Résumé des balances des paiements
Millions de dollars des E−U

Country or area	1988	1989	1990	1991	1992	1993	1994	Pays ou zone
Serv. & Income: Debit	−215.3	−242.4	−258.3	−241.5	−230.3	−239.5	−285.7	Serv. & revenu : débit
Current Trans.,nie: Credit	3.7	4.1	8.8	46.8	6.5	5.3	5.2	Transf. cour.,nia : crédit
Current Transfers: Debit	−28.9	−30.4	−42.5	−40.3	−39.1	−39.2	−40.3	Transf. courants : débit
Capital Acct.,nie: Credit	0.2	0.2	0.3	0.3	0.4	0.5	0.5	Compte de cap.,nia : crédit
Capital Account: Debit	0.0	0.0	0.0	0.0	0.0	−0.7	−1.1	Compte de capital : débit
Financial Account,nie	104.3	65.0	14.4	14.3	39.3	−3.2	120.8	Compte d'op. fin., nia
Net Errors and Omissions	−13.0	54.0	44.5	−28.9	−26.4	36.0	−14.3	Erreurs et omissions nettes
Reserves and Related Items	35.8	−15.3	33.7	22.1	48.7	67.1	45.0	Rés. et postes appareutés

America, South · Amérique du Sud

Argentina / **Argentine**

	1988	1989	1990	1991	1992	1993	1994	
Goods: Exports fob	9 134.0	9 573.0	12 354.0	11 978.0	12 235.0	13 117.0	...	Biens : exportations,fàb
Goods: Imports fob	−4 892.0	−3 864.0	−3 726.0	−7 559.0	−13 685.0	−15 545.0	...	Biens : importations,fàb
Serv. & Income: Credit	2 226.0	2 469.0	4 300.0	4 154.0	3 929.0	4 158.0	...	Serv. & revenu : crédit
Serv. & Income: Debit	−8 040.0	−9 491.0	−9 374.0	−10 013.0	−9 774.0	−9 628.0	...	Serv. & revenu : débit
Current Trans.,nie: Credit	2.0	18.0	1 015.0	821.0	798.0	597.0	...	Transf. cour.,nia : crédit
Current Transfers: Debit	−2.0	−10.0	−17.0	−28.0	−49.0	−151.0	...	Transf. courants : débit
Capital Acct.,nie: Credit	0.0	0.0	0.0	0.0	0.0	0.0	...	Compte de cap.,nia : crédit
Capital Account: Debit	0.0	0.0	0.0	0.0	0.0	0.0	...	Compte de capital : débit
Financial Account,nie	431.0	−8 008.0	−5 850.0	160.0	8 838.0	7 397.0	...	Compte d'op. fin., nia
Net Errors and Omissions	−165.0	−249.0	715.0	−341.0	137.0	87.0	...	Erreurs et omissions nettes
Reserves and Related Items	1 306.0	9 562.0	583.0	828.0	−2 429.0	−32.0	...	Rés. et postes appareutés

Bolivia / **Bolivie**

	1988	1989	1990	1991	1992	1993	1994	
Goods: Exports fob	542.5	723.5	830.8	760.3	608.4	715.5	985.1	Biens : exportations,fàb
Goods: Imports fob	−590.9	−729.5	−775.6	−804.2	−1 040.8	−1 111.7	−1 121.9	Biens : importations,fàb
Serv. & Income: Credit	146.5	167.2	164.7	181.6	182.3	190.6	241.0	Serv. & revenu : crédit
Serv. & Income: Debit	−537.8	−581.2	−578.0	−582.8	−526.4	−536.8	−547.8	Serv. & revenu : débit
Current Trans.,nie: Credit	140.0	152.5	161.2	185.8	246.3	241.0	230.4	Transf. cour.,nia : crédit
Current Transfers: Debit	−4.7	−2.6	−2.0	−3.3	−3.7	−4.1	−5.2	Transf. courants : débit
Capital Acct.,nie: Credit	1.3	5.9	0.8	0.5	0.6	1.0	1.2	Compte de cap.,nia : crédit
Capital Account: Debit	0.0	0.0	0.0	0.0	0.0	0.0	0.0	Compte de capital : débit
Financial Account,nie	−48.9	−124.0	76.8	87.4	316.2	206.1	242.9	Compte d'op. fin., nia
Net Errors and Omissions	70.8	−11.5	4.8	80.5	92.0	341.9	−11.0	Erreurs et omissions nettes
Reserves and Related Items	281.2	399.7	116.5	94.2	125.1	−43.5	−14.7	Rés. et postes appareutés

Brazil / **Brésil**

	1988	1989	1990	1991	1992	1993	1994	
Goods: Exports fob	33 773.0	34 375.0	31 408.0	31 619.0	35 793.0	39 630.0	44 102.0	Biens : exportations,fàb
Goods: Imports fob	−14 605.0	−18 263.0	−20 661.0	−21 041.0	−20 554.0	−25 301.0	−33 241.0	Biens : importations,fàb
Serv. & Income: Credit	3 050.0	4 442.0	4 919.0	4 223.0	5 206.0	5 273.0	7 110.0	Serv. & revenu : crédit
Serv. & Income: Debit	−18 153.0	−19 773.0	−20 288.0	−17 765.0	−16 545.0	−21 185.0	−21 547.0	Serv. & revenu : débit
Current Trans.,nie: Credit	127.0	238.0	840.0	1 556.0	2 260.0	1 704.0	2 577.0	Transf. cour.,nia : crédit
Current Transfers: Debit	−36.0	−17.0	−41.0	−42.0	−71.0	−101.0	−154.0	Transf. courants : débit
Capital Acct.,nie: Credit	4.0	27.0	36.0	43.0	54.0	86.0	175.0	Compte de cap.,nia : crédit
Capital Account: Debit	−1.0	−4.0	−1.0	−1.0	0.0	−5.0	−2.0	Compte de capital : débit
Financial Account,nie	−9 210.0	−12 525.0	−5 567.0	−4 129.0	6 516.0	7 604.0	7 965.0	Compte d'op. fin., nia
Net Errors and Omissions	−827.0	−819.0	−296.0	852.0	−1 393.0	−815.0	−442.0	Erreurs et omissions nettes
Reserves and Related Items	5 878.0	12 319.0	9 651.0	4 685.0	−11 266.0	−6 890.0	−6 543.0	Rés. et postes appareutés

Chile / **Chili**

	1988	1989	1990	1991	1992	1993	1994	
Goods: Exports fob	7 053.0	8 080.0	8 372.0	8 942.0	10 008.0	9 199.0	11 603.0	Biens : exportations,fàb
Goods: Imports fob	−4 844.0	−6 502.0	−7 037.0	−7 354.0	−9 236.0	−10 181.0	−10 879.0	Biens : importations,fàb
Serv. & Income: Credit	1 274.0	1 736.0	2 269.0	2 640.0	2 872.0	3 099.0	3 344.0	Serv. & revenu : crédit
Serv. & Income: Debit	−3 899.0	−4 234.0	−4 340.0	−4 460.0	−4 780.0	−4 599.0	−5 068.0	Serv. & revenu : débit
Current Trans.,nie: Credit	219.0	241.0	228.0	359.0	450.0	405.0	374.0	Transf. cour.,nia : crédit
Current Transfers: Debit	−37.0	−26.0	−28.0	−18.0	−19.0	−19.0	−20.0	Transf. courants : débit
Capital Acct.,nie: Credit	0.0	0.0	0.0	0.0	0.0	0.0	0.0	Compte de cap.,nia : crédit
Capital Account: Debit	0.0	0.0	0.0	0.0	0.0	0.0	0.0	Compte de capital : débit
Financial Account,nie	−773.0	1 211.0	3 051.0	836.0	2 875.0	2 778.0	4 600.0	Compte d'op. fin., nia
Net Errors and Omissions	−117.0	−119.0	−144.0	302.0	328.0	−97.0	−741.0	Erreurs et omissions nettes
Reserves and Related Items	1 124.0	−387.0	−2 371.0	−1 247.0	−2 500.0	−585.0	−3 213.0	Rés. et postes appareutés

Colombia / **Colombie**

	1988	1989	1990	1991	1992	1993	1994	
Goods: Exports fob	5 343.0	6 031.0	7 079.0	7 507.0	7 263.0	7 429.0	8 756.0	Biens : exportations,fàb
Goods: Imports fob	−4 516.0	−4 557.0	−5 108.0	−4 548.0	−6 030.0	−9 087.0	−11 040.0	Biens : importations,fàb
Serv. & Income: Credit	1 665.0	1 578.0	1 947.0	1 984.0	2 432.0	2 293.0	2 773.0	Serv. & revenu : crédit
Serv. & Income: Debit	−3 672.0	−4 151.0	−4 402.0	−4 292.0	−4 487.0	−3 903.0	−4 385.0	Serv. & revenu : débit
Current Trans.,nie: Credit	994.0	928.0	1 043.0	1 743.0	1 871.0	1 350.0	1 056.0	Transf. cour.,nia : crédit
Current Transfers: Debit	−30.0	−30.0	−17.0	−45.0	−137.0	−212.0	−193.0	Transf. courants : débit
Capital Acct.,nie: Credit	0.0	0.0	0.0	0.0	0.0	0.0	0.0	Compte de cap.,nia : crédit

79
Summary of balance of payments
Millions of US dollars
Résumé des balances des paiements
Millions de dollars des E−U

Country or area	1988	1989	1990	1991	1992	1993	1994	Pays ou zone
Capital Account: Debit	0.0	0.0	0.0	0.0	0.0	0.0	0.0	Compte de capital : débit
Financial Account,nie	940.0	407.0	26.0	−785.0	283.0	2 609.0	3 023.0	Compte d'op. fin., nia
Net Errors and Omissions	−530.0	157.0	70.0	269.0	14.0	−477.0	174.0	Erreurs et omissions nettes
Reserves and Related Items	−194.0	−363.0	−638.0	−1 834.0	−1 209.0	−2.0	−164.0	Rés. et postes appareutés
Ecuador								**Equateur**
Goods: Exports fob	2 202.0	2 354.0	2 714.0	2 851.0	3 008.0	3 062.0	3 717.0	Biens : exportations,fàb
Goods: Imports fob	−1 583.0	−1 693.0	−1 711.0	−2 207.0	−2 083.0	−2 474.0	−3 282.0	Biens : importations,fàb
Serv. & Income: Credit	457.0	536.0	563.0	587.0	652.0	680.0	797.0	Serv. & revenu : crédit
Serv. & Income: Debit	−1 856.0	−2 010.0	−2 039.0	−2 048.0	−1 912.0	−2 080.0	−2 184.0	Serv. & revenu : débit
Current Trans.,nie: Credit	104.0	106.0	119.0	123.0	134.0	145.0	164.0	Transf. cour.,nia : crédit
Current Transfers: Deoit	−7.0	−9.0	−12.0	−13.0	−14.0	−15.0	−19.0	Transf. courants : débit
Capital Acct.,nie: Credit	0.0	0.0	0.0	0.0	0.0	0.0	0.0	Compte de cap.,nia : crédit
Capital Account: Debit	0.0	0.0	0.0	0.0	0.0	0.0	0.0	Compte de capital : débit
Financial Account,nie	−588.0	−511.0	−806.0	−481.0	−633.0	156.0	−103.0	Compte d'op. fin., nia
Net Errors and Omissions	28.0	115.0	216.0	163.0	−99.0	−56.0	122.0	Erreurs et omissions nettes
Reserves and Related Items	1 243.0	1 112.0	956.0	1 025.0	947.0	582.0	745.0	Rés. et postes appareutés
Paraguay								**Paraguay**
Goods: Exports fob	871.0	1 180.0	1 382.3	1 120.8	1 081.5	1 500.0	1 871.3	Biens : exportations,fàb
Goods: Imports fob	−1 030.1	−1 015.9	−1 635.8	−1 867.6	−1 950.6	−2 710.7	−3 148.0	Biens : importations,fàb
Serv. & Income: Credit	352.6	483.6	604.3	1 012.2	955.2	1 074.3	1 357.6	Serv. & revenu : crédit
Serv. & Income: Debit	−438.8	−415.6	−578.7	−661.8	−720.1	−739.6	−871.7	Serv. & revenu : débit
Current Trans.,nie: Credit	37.7	24.3	55.9	73.7	34.2	42.4	42.4	Transf. cour.,nia : crédit
Current Transfers: Debit	−2.6	−0.8	−0.3	−1.4	−0.3	−0.4	−0.4	Transf. courants : débit
Capital Acct.,nie: Credit	0.2	0.4	0.0	0.0	0.0	...	...	Compte de cap.,nia : crédit
Capital Account: Debit	−0.1	0.0	0.0	0.0	0.0	...	...	Compte de capital : débit
Financial Account,nie	−199.3	−173.9	−75.8	215.0	192.0	323.0	456.6	Compte d'op. fin., nia
Net Errors and Omissions	198.3	−90.6	362.4	472.0	457.7	700.4	686.5	Erreurs et omissions nettes
Reserves and Related Items	211.1	8.5	−114.3	−362.9	−49.6	−189.4	−394.3	Rés. et postes appareutés
Peru								**Pérou**
Goods: Exports fob	2 732.0	3 555.0	3 324.0	3 392.0	3 535.0	3 513.0	4 554.0	Biens : exportations,fàb
Goods: Imports fob	−2 822.0	−2 313.0	−2 930.0	−3 529.0	−4 090.0	−4 084.0	−5 662.0	Biens : importations,fàb
Serv. & Income: Credit	954.0	1 028.0	1 036.0	1 093.0	1 072.0	1 105.0	1 445.0	Serv. & revenu : crédit
Serv. & Income: Debit	−2 359.0	−2 334.0	−2 427.0	−2 215.0	−2 656.0	−2 694.0	−3 026.0	Serv. & revenu : débit
Current Trans.,nie: Credit	161.0	196.0	319.0	446.0	490.0	465.0	441.0	Transf. cour.,nia : crédit
Current Transfers: Debit	0.0	0.0	0.0	0.0	−8.0	−6.0	−7.0	Transf. courants : débit
Capital Acct.,nie: Credit	50.0	39.0	50.0	56.0	60.0	47.0	32.0	Compte de cap.,nia : crédit
Capital Account: Debit	−46.0	−59.0	−75.0	−108.0	−90.0	−126.0	−48.0	Compte de capital : débit
Financial Account,nie	786.0	−265.0	551.0	−6 145.0	1.0	545.0	1 933.0	Compte d'op. fin., nia
Net Errors and Omissions	−2 042.0	−1 647.0	−1 602.0	6 273.0	896.0	13.0	1 715.0	Erreurs et omissions nettes
Reserves and Related Items	2 586.0	1 800.0	1 754.0	737.0	790.0	1 222.0	−1 377.0	Rés. et postes appareutés
Suriname								**Suriname**
Goods: Exports fob	358.4	549.2	465.9	345.9	341.0	298.3	293.6	Biens : exportations,fàb
Goods: Imports fob	−239.4	−330.9	−374.4	−347.1	−272.5	−213.9	−194.3	Biens : importations,fàb
Serv. & Income: Credit	24.0	24.7	22.9	23.7	23.3	46.7	73.5	Serv. & revenu : crédit
Serv. & Income: Debit	−86.1	−98.0	−106.8	−110.3	−106.9	−108.0	−118.2	Serv. & revenu : débit
Current Trans.,nie: Credit	11.3	24.1	35.5	20.4	37.9	26.7	6.2	Transf. cour.,nia : crédit
Current Transfers: Debit	−4.1	−4.6	−5.8	−7.5	−8.6	−5.8	−2.2	Transf. courants : débit
Capital Acct.,nie: Credit	1.5	1.1	0.3	2.3	2.6	3.5	0.2	Compte de cap.,nia : crédit
Capital Account: Debit	−3.0	−2.7	−3.1	−3.4	−5.8	−3.0	−0.4	Compte de capital : débit
Financial Account,nie	−65.9	−172.9	−15.0	32.4	−48.5	−73.1	−84.1	Compte d'op. fin., nia
Net Errors and Omissions	−1.8	9.9	−9.4	−0.5	25.4	41.3	60.0	Erreurs et omissions nettes
Reserves and Related Items	5.2	0.1	−10.3	43.9	12.0	−12.7	−34.3	Rés. et postes appareutés
Uruguay								**Uruguay**
Goods: Exports fob	1 404.5	1 599.0	1 692.9	1 604.7	1 801.4	1 731.6	1 913.4	Biens : exportations,fàb
Goods: Imports fob	−1 112.2	−1 136.2	−1 266.9	−1 543.7	−1 923.2	−2 118.3	−2 584.9	Biens : importations,fàb
Serv. & Income: Credit	463.0	636.5	723.9	830.9	1 055.3	1 278.5	1 528.9	Serv. & revenu : crédit
Serv. & Income: Debit	−754.4	−973.8	−972.1	−889.6	−970.9	−1 188.9	−1 306.6	Serv. & revenu : débit
Current Trans.,nie: Credit	26.0	15.0	15.8	50.1	36.0	61.2	67.4	Transf. cour.,nia : crédit
Current Transfers: Debit	−4.7	−7.0	−7.7	−10.0	−7.4	−7.8	−8.0	Transf. courants : débit
Capital Acct.,nie: Credit	0.0	0.0	0.0	0.0	0.0	0.0	0.0	Compte de cap.,nia : crédit
Capital Account: Debit	0.0	0.0	0.0	0.0	0.0	0.0	0.0	Compte de capital : débit
Financial Account,nie	186.5	−5.9	−85.9	−429.2	−91.5	223.6	385.8	Compte d'op. fin., nia
Net Errors and Omissions	−247.1	−62.6	35.7	468.8	238.3	208.6	93.8	Erreurs et omissions nettes
Reserves and Related Items	38.4	−65.0	−135.7	−82.0	−138.0	−188.5	−89.8	Rés. et postes appareutés
Venezuela								**Venezuela**
Goods: Exports fob	10 217.0	13 059.0	17 623.0	15 159.0	14 202.0	14 779.0	15 890.0	Biens : exportations,fàb

79
Summary of balance of payments
Millions of US dollars
Résumé des balances des paiements
Millions de dollars des E−U

Country or area	1988	1989	1990	1991	1992	1993	1994	Pays ou zone
Goods: Imports fob	−12 080.0	−7 365.0	−6 917.0	−10 259.0	−12 880.0	−11 504.0	−8 199.0	Biens : importations,fàb
Serv. & Income: Credit	2 488.0	2 511.0	3 841.0	3 397.0	2 919.0	2 939.0	2 934.0	Serv. & revenu : crédit
Serv. & Income: Debit	−6 287.0	−5 861.0	−5 966.0	−6 197.0	−7 616.0	−7 839.0	−7 959.0	Serv. & revenu : débit
Current Trans.,nie: Credit	87.0	237.0	444.0	370.0	533.0	452.0	444.0	Transf. cour.,nia : crédit
Current Transfers: Debit	−234.0	−420.0	−746.0	−734.0	−907.0	−820.0	−660.0	Transf. courants : débit
Capital Acct.,nie: Credit	0.0	0.0	0.0	0.0	0.0	0.0	0.0	Compte de cap.,nia : crédit
Capital Account: Debit	0.0	0.0	0.0	0.0	0.0	0.0	0.0	Compte de capital : débit
Financial Account,nie	−2 043.0	−5 432.0	−5 023.0	1 741.0	2 700.0	2 002.0	−3 636.0	Compte d'op. fin., nia
Net Errors and Omissions	3 117.0	1 603.0	−1 742.0	−1 516.0	−299.0	−539.0	−298.0	Erreurs et omissions nettes
Reserves and Related Items	4 735.0	1 668.0	−1 514.0	−1 961.0	1 348.0	530.0	1 484.0	Rés. et postes appareutés

| | | | | Asia · Asie | | | | |

Afghanistan — **Afghanistan**

Country or area	1988	1989	1990	1991	1992	1993	1994	Pays ou zone
Goods: Exports fob	453.8	252.3	...	...	...	...	...	Biens : exportations,fàb
Goods: Imports fob	−731.8	−623.5	...	...	...	...	...	Biens : importations,fàb
Serv. & Income: Credit	92.9	28.3	...	...	...	...	...	Serv. & revenu : crédit
Serv. & Income: Debit	−131.5	−111.3	...	...	...	...	...	Serv. & revenu : débit
Current Trans.,nie: Credit	342.8	312.1	...	...	...	...	...	Transf. cour.,nia : crédit
Current Transfers: Debit	0.0	−1.2	...	...	...	...	...	Transf. courants : débit
Capital Acct.,nie: Credit	0.0	0.0	...	...	...	...	...	Compte de cap.,nia : crédit
Capital Account: Debit	0.0	0.0	...	...	...	...	...	Compte de capital : débit
Financial Account,nie	−4.1	−59.6	...	...	...	...	...	Compte d'op. fin., nia
Net Errors and Omissions	−47.7	182.8	...	...	...	...	...	Erreurs et omissions nettes
Reserves and Related Items	25.6	20.1	...	...	...	...	...	Rés. et postes appareutés

Armenia — **Arménie**

Country or area	1988	1989	1990	1991	1992	1993	1994	Pays ou zone
Goods: Exports fob	...	...	...	...	...	156.2	237.9	Biens : exportations,fàb
Goods: Imports fob	...	...	...	...	...	−254.2	−418.7	Biens : importations,fàb
Serv. & Income: Credit	...	...	...	...	...	17.3	13.4	Serv. & revenu : crédit
Serv. & Income: Debit	...	...	...	...	...	−41.4	−44.3	Serv. & revenu : débit
Current Trans.,nie: Credit	...	...	...	...	...	56.3	106.2	Transf. cour.,nia : crédit
Current Transfers: Debit	...	...	...	...	...	−1.1	−0.7	Transf. courants : débit
Capital Acct.,nie: Credit	...	...	...	...	...	5.1	5.7	Compte de cap.,nia : crédit
Capital Account: Debit	...	...	...	...	...	0.0	0.0	Compte de capital : débit
Financial Account,nie	...	...	...	...	...	53.0	85.5	Compte d'op. fin., nia
Net Errors and Omissions	...	...	...	...	...	15.9	−12.8	Erreurs et omissions nettes
Reserves and Related Items	...	...	...	...	...	−7.2	27.8	Rés. et postes appareutés

Bahrain — **Bahreïn**

Country or area	1988	1989	1990	1991	1992	1993	1994	Pays ou zone
Goods: Exports fob	2 411.4	2 831.1	3 760.6	3 513.0	3 464.4	3 710.1	3 454.3	Biens : exportations,fàb
Goods: Imports fob	−2 334.0	−2 820.2	−3 339.9	−3 703.5	−3 730.3	−3 858.0	−3 736.7	Biens : importations,fàb
Serv. & Income: Credit	1 164.6	1 187.3	1 197.8	1 218.3	1 505.1	1 476.9	1 590.4	Serv. & revenu : crédit
Serv. & Income: Debit	−1 223.4	−1 294.4	−1 558.2	−1 620.7	−1 821.3	−1 187.7	−1 167.5	Serv. & revenu : débit
Current Trans.,nie: Credit	368.1	102.1	458.8	101.9	100.0	204.0	100.0	Transf. cour.,nia : crédit
Current Transfers: Debit	−194.7	−198.9	−272.3	−303.5	−270.7	−322.6	−329.5	Transf. courants : débit
Capital Acct.,nie: Credit	0.0	0.0	0.0	0.0	0.0	0.0	0.0	Compte de cap.,nia : crédit
Capital Account: Debit	0.0	0.0	0.0	0.0	0.0	0.0	0.0	Compte de capital : débit
Financial Account,nie	−214.4	−264.6	456.4	−348.1	317.6	−76.1	−101.9	Compte d'op. fin., nia
Net Errors and Omissions	114.9	269.3	−521.0	1 424.1	353.5	56.1	193.2	Erreurs et omissions nettes
Reserves and Related Items	−92.5	188.5	−182.2	−281.6	81.9	−2.6	−2.2	Rés. et postes appareutés

Bangladesh — **Bangladesh**

Country or area	1988	1989	1990	1991	1992	1993	1994	Pays ou zone
Goods: Exports fob	1 291.0	1 304.8	1 672.4	1 688.7	2 097.9	2 544.7	2 934.5	Biens : exportations,fàb
Goods: Imports fob	−2 734.4	−3 300.1	−3 259.4	−3 074.5	−3 353.8	−3 657.3	−4 367.9	Biens : importations,fàb
Serv. & Income: Credit	332.4	423.1	455.8	501.0	583.5	629.5	802.5	Serv. & revenu : crédit
Serv. & Income: Debit	−793.8	−923.3	−880.3	−862.2	−954.8	−1 108.0	−1 214.6	Serv. & revenu : débit
Current Trans.,nie: Credit	1 633.0	1 396.6	1 614.2	1 811.9	1 808.8	1 951.8	2 091.9	Transf. cour.,nia : crédit
Current Transfers: Debit	−1.5	−0.7	−0.7	−0.3	−0.7	−1.5	−2.2	Transf. courants : débit
Capital Acct.,nie: Credit	0.0	0.0	0.0	0.0	0.0	0.0	0.0	Compte de cap.,nia : crédit
Capital Account: Debit	0.0	0.0	0.0	0.0	0.0	0.0	0.0	Compte de capital : débit
Financial Account,nie	398.6	833.2	697.8	467.6	538.4	268.9	749.8	Compte d'op. fin., nia
Net Errors and Omissions	6.6	−43.1	−75.7	−98.4	−84.0	69.4	−302.7	Erreurs et omissions nettes
Reserves and Related Items	−132.0	309.5	−224.2	−433.8	−635.2	−697.6	−691.3	Rés. et postes appareutés

Cambodia — **Cambodge**

Country or area	1988	1989	1990	1991	1992	1993	1994	Pays ou zone
Goods: Exports fob	...	...	...	...	264.5	283.7	489.7	Biens : exportations,fàb
Goods: Imports fob	...	...	...	...	−443.4	−471.1	−725.9	Biens : importations,fàb
Serv. & Income: Credit	...	...	...	...	49.7	64.4	56.7	Serv. & revenu : crédit
Serv. & Income: Debit	...	...	...	...	−84.2	−137.1	−182.6	Serv. & revenu : débit
Current Trans.,nie: Credit	...	...	...	...	120.4	156.4	121.8	Transf. cour.,nia : crédit
Current Transfers: Debit	...	...	...	...	0.0	−0.2	−0.2	Transf. courants : débit

79
Summary of balance of payments
Millions of US dollars
Résumé des balances des paiements
Millions de dollars des E-U

Country or area	1988	1989	1990	1991	1992	1993	1994	Pays ou zone
Capital Acct.,nie: Credit	...	...	...	...	126.3	123.4	105.2	Compte de cap.,nia : crédit
Capital Account: Debit	...	...	...	...	...	...	...	Compte de capital : débit
Financial Account,nie	...	...	...	...	13.9	2.4	67.6	Compte d'op. fin., nia
Net Errors and Omissions	...	...	...	...	−34.0	−7.3	60.6	Erreurs et omissions nettes
Reserves and Related Items	...	...	...	...	−13.2	−14.7	7.2	Rés. et postes appareutés
China								**Chine**
Goods: Exports fob	41 054.0	43 220.0	51 519.0	58 919.0	69 568.0	75 659.0	102 561.0	Biens : exportations,fàb
Goods: Imports fob	−46 369.0	−48 840.0	−42 354.0	−50 176.0	−64 385.0	−86 313.0	−95 271.0	Biens : importations,fàb
Serv. & Income: Credit	6 327.0	6 497.0	8 872.0	10 698.0	14 844.0	15 583.0	22 357.0	Serv. & revenu : crédit
Serv. & Income: Debit	−5 233.0	−5 575.0	−6 314.0	−7 000.0	−14 781.0	−17 710.0	−23 074.0	Serv. & revenu : débit
Current Trans.,nie: Credit	439.0	401.0	252.0	683.0	978.0	1 182.0	874.0	Transf. cour.,nia : crédit
Current Transfers: Debit	−145.0	−93.0	−97.0	−41.0	−36.0	−103.0	−915.0	Transf. courants : débit
Capital Acct.,nie: Credit	129.0	76.0	124.0	207.0	228.0	108.0	395.0	Compte de cap.,nia : crédit
Capital Account: Debit	−4.0	−3.0	−5.0	−18.0	−15.0	−15.0	−19.0	Compte de capital : débit
Financial Account,nie	7 133.0	3 723.0	3 255.0	8 032.0	−250.0	23 474.0	32 645.0	Compte d'op. fin., nia
Net Errors and Omissions	−957.0	115.0	−3 205.0	−6 767.0	−8 211.0	−10 096.0	−9 100.0	Erreurs et omissions nettes
Reserves and Related Items	−2 374.0	479.0	−12 047.0	−14 537.0	2 060.0	−1 769.0	−30 453.0	Rés. et postes appareutés
Cyprus								**Chypre**
Goods: Exports fob	709.6	796.9	951.6	965.3	985.9	867.9	967.5	Biens : exportations,fàb
Goods: Imports fob	−1 777.4	−2 185.8	−2 507.9	−2 588.8	−3 311.5	−2 378.1	−2 703.2	Biens : importations,fàb
Serv. & Income: Credit	1 562.2	1 799.7	2 227.8	2 114.5	2 745.4	2 543.8	2 853.6	Serv. & revenu : crédit
Serv. & Income: Debit	−663.0	−717.7	−887.9	−977.7	−1 108.7	−962.4	−1 091.8	Serv. & revenu : débit
Current Trans.,nie: Credit	32.6	28.4	27.9	27.5	19.4	18.9	19.3	Transf. cour.,nia : crédit
Current Transfers: Debit	−1.3	−1.6	−1.7	−1.7	−1.6	−1.6	−1.6	Transf. courants : débit
Capital Acct.,nie: Credit	22.9	21.3	22.3	21.8	22.7	20.1	20.3	Compte de cap.,nia : crédit
Capital Account: Debit	−1.9	−1.8	−2.6	−3.7	−4.0	−3.8	−4.5	Compte de capital : débit
Financial Account,nie	166.9	453.5	437.5	255.6	298.5	−42.2	106.3	Compte d'op. fin., nia
Net Errors and Omissions	20.1	35.6	26.8	120.7	129.1	82.2	81.1	Erreurs et omissions nettes
Reserves and Related Items	−70.7	−228.5	−293.8	66.6	224.9	−144.8	−246.9	Rés. et postes appareutés
India								**Inde**
Goods: Exports fob	13 510.0	16 144.0	18 286.0	18 095.0	20 019.0	...	...	Biens : exportations,fàb
Goods: Imports fob	−20 091.0	−22 254.0	−23 437.0	−21 087.0	−22 150.0	...	...	Biens : importations,fàb
Serv. & Income: Credit	4 218.0	4 586.0	5 061.0	5 157.0	5 303.0	...	...	Serv. & revenu : crédit
Serv. & Income: Debit	−7 255.0	−8 152.0	−9 582.0	−9 916.0	−10 614.0	...	...	Serv. & revenu : débit
Current Trans.,nie: Credit	2 768.0	3 093.0	2 853.0	3 736.0	3 353.0	...	...	Transf. cour.,nia : crédit
Current Transfers: Debit	−16.0	−23.0	−17.0	−13.0	−18.0	...	...	Transf. courants : débit
Capital Acct.,nie: Credit	0.0	0.0	0.0	0.0	0.0	...	...	Compte de cap.,nia : crédit
Capital Account: Debit	0.0	0.0	0.0	0.0	0.0	...	...	Compte de capital : débit
Financial Account,nie	7 175.0	7 212.0	5 528.0	3 485.0	4 131.0	...	...	Compte d'op. fin., nia
Net Errors and Omissions	−326.0	−369.0	−633.0	343.0	1 104.0	...	...	Erreurs et omissions nettes
Reserves and Related Items	16.0	−237.0	1 941.0	200.0	−1 128.0	...	...	Rés. et postes appareutés
Indonesia								**Indonésie**
Goods: Exports fob	19 509.0	22 974.0	26 807.0	29 635.0	33 796.0	36 607.0	40 223.0	Biens : exportations,fàb
Goods: Imports fob	−13 831.0	−16 310.0	−21 455.0	−24 834.0	−26 774.0	−28 376.0	−32 322.0	Biens : importations,fàb
Serv. & Income: Credit	1 861.0	2 437.0	2 897.0	3 739.0	4 209.0	5 149.0	6 072.0	Serv. & revenu : crédit
Serv. & Income: Debit	−9 190.0	−10 548.0	−11 655.0	−13 062.0	−14 582.0	−16 023.0	−17 382.0	Serv. & revenu : débit
Current Trans.,nie: Credit	254.0	339.0	418.0	262.0	571.0	537.0	619.0	Transf. cour.,nia : crédit
Current Transfers: Debit	0.0	0.0	0.0	0.0	0.0	0.0	0.0	Transf. courants : débit
Capital Acct.,nie: Credit	0.0	0.0	0.0	0.0	0.0	0.0	0.0	Compte de cap.,nia : crédit
Capital Account: Debit	0.0	0.0	0.0	0.0	0.0	0.0	0.0	Compte de capital : débit
Financial Account,nie	2 217.0	2 918.0	4 495.0	5 697.0	6 129.0	5 772.0	3 839.0	Compte d'op. fin., nia
Net Errors and Omissions	−933.0	−1 315.0	744.0	91.0	−1 279.0	−3 072.0	−265.0	Erreurs et omissions nettes
Reserves and Related Items	113.0	−495.0	−2 251.0	−1 528.0	−2 070.0	−594.0	−784.0	Rés. et postes appareutés
Iran, Islamic Rep. of								**Iran, Rép. islamique d'**
Goods: Exports fob	10 709.0	13 081.0	19 305.0	18 661.0	19 868.0	18 080.0	19 434.0	Biens : exportations,fàb
Goods: Imports fob	−10 608.0	−13 448.0	−18 330.0	−25 190.0	−23 274.0	−19 287.0	−12 617.0	Biens : importations,fàb
Serv. & Income: Credit	467.0	798.0	892.0	881.0	846.0	1 235.0	580.0	Serv. & revenu : crédit
Serv. & Income: Debit	−2 437.0	−3 122.0	−4 040.0	−5 800.0	−5 940.0	−5 743.0	−3 818.0	Serv. & revenu : débit
Current Trans.,nie: Credit	...	2 500.0	2 500.0	2 000.0	1 996.0	1 500.0	1 200.0	Transf. cour.,nia : crédit
Current Transfers: Debit	0.0	0.0	0.0	0.0	0.0	0.0	−2.0	Transf. courants : débit
Capital Acct.,nie: Credit	0.0	0.0	0.0	0.0	0.0	0.0	0.0	Compte de cap.,nia : crédit
Capital Account: Debit	0.0	0.0	0.0	0.0	0.0	0.0	0.0	Compte de capital : débit
Financial Account,nie	320.0	3 261.0	295.0	6 033.0	4 703.0	5 563.0	−2 227.0	Compte d'op. fin., nia
Net Errors and Omissions	539.0	−770.0	−947.0	1 322.0	1 637.0	−1 119.0	−1 318.0	Erreurs et omissions nettes
Reserves and Related Items	1 010.0	−2 300.0	325.0	2 093.0	164.0	−229.0	−1 232.0	Rés. et postes appareutés

79
Summary of balance of payments
Millions of US dollars
Résumé des balances des paiements
Millions de dollars des E−U

Country or area	1988	1989	1990	1991	1992	1993	1994	Pays ou zone
Israel								**Israël**
Goods: Exports fob	10 334.0	11 123.0	12 214.0	12 092.0	13 382.0	14 888.0	16 741.0	Biens : exportations,fàb
Goods: Imports fob	−13 231.0	−13 045.0	−15 305.0	−17 101.0	−18 389.0	−20 518.0	−22 670.0	Biens : importations,fàb
Serv. & Income: Credit	5 247.0	5 743.0	6 186.0	6 389.0	7 514.0	7 390.0	7 787.0	Serv. & revenu : crédit
Serv. & Income: Debit	−7 148.0	−7 616.0	−8 446.0	−8 585.0	−9 276.0	−9 700.0	−11 227.0	Serv. & revenu : débit
Current Trans.,nie: Credit	4 607.0	4 564.0	5 472.0	6 293.0	6 196.0	6 079.0	5 948.0	Transf. cour.,nia : crédit
Current Transfers: Debit	−185.0	−141.0	−189.0	−236.0	−293.0	−354.0	−300.0	Transf. courants : débit
Capital Acct.,nie: Credit	433.0	677.0	624.0	688.0	924.0	950.0	1 254.0	Compte de cap.,nia : crédit
Capital Account: Debit	0.0	0.0	0.0	0.0	0.0	0.0	0.0	Compte de capital : débit
Financial Account,nie	−596.0	−1 042.0	290.0	69.0	−1 681.0	2 365.0	1 388.0	Compte d'op. fin., nia
Net Errors and Omissions	−632.0	1 136.0	−331.0	220.0	166.0	380.0	1 150.0	Erreurs et omissions nettes
Reserves and Related Items	1 170.0	−1 398.0	−515.0	173.0	1 457.0	−1 481.0	−69.0	Rés. et postes appareutés
Japan								**Japon**
Goods: Exports fob	259.8	269.6	280.4	308.1	332.5	352.9	386.0	Biens : exportations,fàb
Goods: Imports fob	−164.8	−192.7	−216.8	−212.0	−207.8	−213.3	−241.6	Biens : importations,fàb
Serv. & Income: Credit	111.8	143.9	166.0	185.7	191.7	201.5	213.7	Serv. & revenu : crédit
Serv. & Income: Debit	−123.1	−159.5	−188.2	−201.6	−200.3	−204.0	−221.4	Serv. & revenu : débit
Current Trans.,nie: Credit	1.1	1.0	1.0	1.4	1.7	1.6	1.8	Transf. cour.,nia : crédit
Current Transfers: Debit	−5.2	−5.3	−6.5	−13.2	−5.5	−6.7	−8.0	Transf. courants : débit
Capital Acct.,nie: Credit	0.0	0.0	0.0	0.0	0.0	0.0	0.0	Compte de cap.,nia : crédit
Capital Account: Debit	0.0	0.0	0.0	−1.2	−1.3	−1.5	−1.9	Compte de capital : débit
Financial Account,nie	−66.2	−47.9	−21.5	−67.5	−99.9	−102.6	−85.5	Compte d'op. fin., nia
Net Errors and Omissions	3.1	−21.8	−20.9	−7.9	−10.4	−0.3	−17.8	Erreurs et omissions nettes
Reserves and Related Items	−16.5	12.8	6.6	8.3	−0.7	−27.7	−25.4	Rés. et postes appareutés
Jordan								**Jordanie**
Goods: Exports fob	1 007.4	1 109.4	1 063.8	1 129.5	1 218.9	1 246.3	1 424.5	Biens : exportations,fàb
Goods: Imports fob	−2 418.7	−1 882.5	−2 300.7	−2 302.2	−2 998.7	−3 145.2	−3 003.8	Biens : importations,fàb
Serv. & Income: Credit	1 461.2	1 278.2	1 514.5	1 465.5	1 561.6	1 672.7	1 634.7	Serv. & revenu : crédit
Serv. & Income: Debit	−1 695.3	−1 298.9	−1 549.7	−1 570.2	−1 784.7	−1 756.6	−1 780.2	Serv. & revenu : débit
Current Trans.,nie: Credit	1 532.0	1 284.5	1 123.1	949.5	1 263.6	1 441.1	1 447.4	Transf. cour.,nia : crédit
Current Transfers: Debit	−180.5	−105.8	−78.2	−65.7	−96.1	−87.4	−120.5	Transf. courants : débit
Capital Acct.,nie: Credit	0.0	0.0	0.0	0.0	0.0	0.0	0.0	Compte de cap.,nia : crédit
Capital Account: Debit	0.0	0.0	0.0	0.0	0.0	0.0	0.0	Compte de capital : débit
Financial Account,nie	374.2	79.5	572.7	2 097.3	615.1	−530.0	188.9	Compte d'op. fin., nia
Net Errors and Omissions	123.4	0.3	75.4	321.4	83.1	298.0	−55.8	Erreurs et omissions nettes
Reserves and Related Items	−203.9	−464.7	−421.0	−2 025.2	137.1	861.1	264.9	Rés. et postes appareutés
Korea, Republic of								**Corée, République de**
Goods: Exports fob	59 648.0	61 408.0	63 123.0	69 581.0	75 169.0	80 950.0	93 676.0	Biens : exportations,fàb
Goods: Imports fob	−48 203.0	−56 811.0	−65 127.0	−76 561.0	−77 315.0	−79 090.0	−96 822.0	Biens : importations,fàb
Serv. & Income: Credit	10 736.0	12 027.0	13 287.0	14 289.0	14 532.0	17 109.0	21 485.0	Serv. & revenu : crédit
Serv. & Income: Debit	−9 936.0	−12 397.0	−14 224.0	−16 443.0	−17 600.0	−19 524.0	−23 754.0	Serv. & revenu : débit
Current Trans.,nie: Credit	2 538.0	2 103.0	2 439.0	2 794.0	3 358.0	3 644.0	3 937.0	Transf. cour.,nia : crédit
Current Transfers: Debit	−245.0	−943.0	−1 243.0	−1 951.0	−2 083.0	−2 073.0	−2 377.0	Transf. courants : débit
Capital Acct.,nie: Credit	6.0	9.0	7.0	7.0	5.0	2.0	8.0	Compte de cap.,nia : crédit
Capital Account: Debit	−359.0	−327.0	−338.0	−335.0	−412.0	−477.0	−445.0	Compte de capital : débit
Financial Account,nie	−4 279.0	−2 640.0	2 866.0	6 714.0	6 969.0	3 188.0	10 610.0	Compte d'op. fin., nia
Net Errors and Omissions	−590.0	691.0	−1 998.0	757.0	1 101.0	−720.0	−1 704.0	Erreurs et omissions nettes
Reserves and Related Items	−9 316.0	−3 120.0	1 208.0	1 148.0	−3 724.0	−3 009.0	−4 614.0	Rés. et postes appareutés
Kuwait								**Koweït**
Goods: Exports fob	7 709.0	11 396.0	6 989.0	1 080.0	6 548.0	10 141.0	11 129.0	Biens : exportations,fàb
Goods: Imports fob	−5 999.0	−6 410.0	−3 810.0	−5 073.0	−7 237.0	−6 954.0	−6 670.0	Biens : importations,fàb
Serv. & Income: Credit	9 021.0	10 556.0	9 863.0	7 085.0	7 401.0	5 788.0	5 187.0	Serv. & revenu : crédit
Serv. & Income: Debit	−4 810.0	−4 912.0	−4 205.0	−5 772.0	−5 252.0	−5 526.0	−5 453.0	Serv. & revenu : débit
Current Trans.,nie: Credit	...	...	...	...	17.0	109.0	94.0	Transf. cour.,nia : crédit
Current Transfers: Debit	−1 319.0	−1 494.0	−4 951.0	−23 798.0	−1 927.0	−1 620.0	−1 799.0	Transf. courants : débit
Capital Acct.,nie: Credit	0.0	0.0	0.0	0.0	0.0	0.0	0.0	Compte de cap.,nia : crédit
Capital Account: Debit	0.0	0.0	0.0	0.0	0.0	0.0	0.0	Compte de capital : débit
Financial Account,nie	−7 340.0	−8 323.0	413.0	38 766.0	11 067.0	−1 090.0	1 839.0	Compte d'op. fin., nia
Net Errors and Omissions	810.0	462.0	−5 196.0	−11 012.0	−8 765.0	−2 333.0	−4 275.0	Erreurs et omissions nettes
Reserves and Related Items	1 928.0	−1 275.0	897.0	−1 276.0	−1 851.0	1 485.0	−53.0	Rés. et postes appareutés
Lao People's Dem. Rep.								**Rép. dém. pop. lao**
Goods: Exports fob	57.8	63.3	78.7	96.6	132.6	240.5	300.4	Biens : exportations,fàb
Goods: Imports fob	−149.4	−193.8	−185.5	−197.9	−232.8	−397.4	−519.1	Biens : importations,fàb
Serv. & Income: Credit	18.2	23.3	25.9	41.1	67.0	95.3	93.9	Serv. & revenu : crédit
Serv. & Income: Debit	−29.2	−28.9	−29.6	−52.0	−75.9	−102.3	−115.1	Serv. & revenu : débit
Current Trans.,nie: Credit	0.0	0.0	0.0	0.0	0.0	0.0	0.0	Transf. cour.,nia : crédit

79
Summary of balance of payments
Millions of US dollars
Résumé des balances des paiements
Millions de dollars des E−U

Country or area	1988	1989	1990	1991	1992	1993	1994	Pays ou zone
Current Transfers: Debit	−0.6	−0.4	−0.3	−2.9	−2.2	−2.0	−3.2	Transf. courants : débit
Capital Acct.,nie: Credit	6.7	8.3	10.9	10.4	8.6	9.5	9.5	Compte de cap.,nia : crédit
Capital Account: Debit	0.0	0.0	0.0	0.0	0.0	0.0	0.0	Compte de capital : débit
Financial Account,nie	−25.2	−4.4	14.2	39.5	−3.0	28.0	8.7	Compte d'op. fin., nia
Net Errors and Omissions	17.4	−31.2	−40.2	−60.3	−16.3	−29.4	44.2	Erreurs et omissions nettes
Reserves and Related Items	104.3	163.8	125.9	125.5	122.0	157.8	180.7	Rés. et postes appareutés
Malaysia								**Malaisie**
Goods: Exports fob	20 980.0	24 776.0	28 806.0	33 712.0	39 823.0	46 226.0	56 906.0	Biens : exportations,fàb
Goods: Imports fob	−15 553.0	−20 498.0	−26 280.0	−33 321.0	−36 673.0	−43 201.0	−55 325.0	Biens : importations,fàb
Serv. & Income: Credit	3 469.0	4 042.0	5 708.0	5 799.0	6 598.0	7 224.0	8 889.0	Serv. & revenu : crédit
Serv. & Income: Debit	−7 237.0	−8 143.0	−9 206.0	−10 462.0	−12 088.0	−13 268.0	−14 780.0	Serv. & revenu : débit
Current Trans.,nie: Credit	288.0	212.0	249.0	215.0	296.0	345.0	290.0	Transf. cour.,nia : crédit
Current Transfers: Debit	−80.0	−74.0	−147.0	−126.0	−124.0	−135.0	−127.0	Transf. courants : débit
Capital Acct.,nie: Credit	0.0	0.0	0.0	0.0	0.0	0.0	0.0	Compte de cap.,nia : crédit
Capital Account: Debit	−58.0	−57.0	−48.0	−51.0	−40.0	−61.0	−43.0	Compte de capital : débit
Financial Account,nie	−1 973.0	1 330.0	1 786.0	5 623.0	8 743.0	10 798.0	1 511.0	Compte d'op. fin., nia
Net Errors and Omissions	−267.0	−358.0	1 085.0	−151.0	79.0	3 414.0	−476.0	Erreurs et omissions nettes
Reserves and Related Items	430.0	−1 230.0	−1 953.0	−1 238.0	−6 615.0	−11 343.0	3 157.0	Rés. et postes appareutés
Maldives								**Maldives**
Goods: Exports fob	44.6	51.3	58.1	59.2	51.1	38.5	...	Biens : exportations,fàb
Goods: Imports fob	−87.3	−111.3	−121.2	−141.8	−167.9	−177.8	...	Biens : importations,fàb
Serv. & Income: Credit	85.3	102.6	124.4	128.9	171.1	181.2	...	Serv. & revenu : crédit
Serv. & Income: Debit	−40.2	−45.2	−56.5	−60.8	−69.4	−77.8	...	Serv. & revenu : débit
Current Trans.,nie: Credit	11.5	18.3	11.2	22.1	14.3	8.3	...	Transf. cour.,nia : crédit
Current Transfers: Debit	−5.0	−5.1	−7.4	−16.6	−18.9	−20.0	...	Transf. courants : débit
Capital Acct.,nie: Credit	0.0	0.0	0.0	0.0	0.0	0.0	...	Compte de cap.,nia : crédit
Capital Account: Debit	0.0	0.0	0.0	0.0	0.0	0.0	...	Compte de capital : débit
Financial Account,nie	−1.5	11.8	8.1	5.4	25.5	24.9	...	Compte d'op. fin., nia
Net Errors and Omissions	6.2	−20.1	−17.8	2.6	−1.0	22.6	...	Erreurs et omissions nettes
Reserves and Related Items	−13.6	−2.3	1.1	1.0	−4.8	0.1	...	Rés. et postes appareutés
Mongolia								**Mongolie**
Goods: Exports fob	829.1	795.8	444.8	346.5	355.8	365.8	...	Biens : exportations,fàb
Goods: Imports fob	−1 701.9	−1 758.9	−941.7	−447.6	−384.9	−344.5	...	Biens : importations,fàb
Serv. & Income: Credit	94.5	43.9	53.2	26.5	35.0	26.8	...	Serv. & revenu : crédit
Serv. & Income: Debit	−254.7	−313.4	−203.2	−71.2	−96.8	−87.9	...	Serv. & revenu : débit
Current Trans.,nie: Credit	0.0	3.9	7.4	41.6	38.7	66.7	...	Transf. cour.,nia : crédit
Current Transfers: Debit	−0.3	0.0	0.0	0.0	−3.5	4.2	...	Transf. courants : débit
Capital Acct.,nie: Credit	0.0	0.0	0.0	0.0	0.0	0.0	...	Compte de cap.,nia : crédit
Capital Account: Debit	0.0	0.0	0.0	0.0	0.0	0.0	...	Compte de capital : débit
Financial Account,nie	1 019.4	1 313.0	541.0	10.8	−44.0	−11.8	...	Compte d'op. fin., nia
Net Errors and Omissions	14.6	45.4	−3.1	−36.4	17.4	−4.8	...	Erreurs et omissions nettes
Reserves and Related Items	−0.7	−129.7	101.6	129.8	82.3	−14.5	...	Rés. et postes appareutés
Myanmar								**Myanmar**
Goods: Exports fob	165.7	222.8	222.6	248.2	...	...	...	Biens : exportations,fàb
Goods: Imports fob	−370.2	−304.3	−524.3	−301.5	...	...	...	Biens : importations,fàb
Serv. & Income: Credit	49.6	59.3	95.9	57.0	...	...	...	Serv. & revenu : crédit
Serv. & Income: Debit	−113.6	−101.4	−264.4	−326.5	...	...	...	Serv. & revenu : débit
Current Trans.,nie: Credit	93.1	55.6	39.0	55.5	...	...	...	Transf. cour.,nia : crédit
Current Transfers: Debit	−0.5	0.0	0.0	−0.1	...	...	...	Transf. courants : débit
Capital Acct.,nie: Credit	0.0	84.0	232.9	0.0	...	...	...	Compte de cap.,nia : crédit
Capital Account: Debit	0.0	0.0	0.0	0.0	...	...	...	Compte de capital : débit
Financial Account,nie	139.7	82.0	185.8	275.0	...	...	...	Compte d'op. fin., nia
Net Errors and Omissions	116.7	52.6	21.4	−53.9	...	...	...	Erreurs et omissions nettes
Reserves and Related Items	−80.5	−150.6	−8.7	46.3	...	...	...	Rés. et postes appareutés
Nepal								**Népal**
Goods: Exports fob	193.8	161.2	217.9	274.5	376.3	397.0	368.7	Biens : exportations,fàb
Goods: Imports fob	−664.9	−568.1	−666.6	−756.9	−752.1	−858.6	−1 158.9	Biens : importations,fàb
Serv. & Income: Credit	240.0	224.3	229.5	266.8	307.3	362.1	613.8	Serv. & revenu : crédit
Serv. & Income: Debit	−165.2	−158.2	−178.5	−200.1	−241.8	−275.5	−327.4	Serv. & revenu : débit
Current Trans.,nie: Credit	130.5	109.2	115.7	121.3	133.6	155.5	160.7	Transf. cour.,nia : crédit
Current Transfers: Debit	−5.6	−11.6	−7.1	−10.1	−4.6	−3.0	−8.7	Transf. courants : débit
Capital Acct.,nie: Credit	0.0	0.0	0.0	0.0	0.0	0.0	0.0	Compte de cap.,nia : crédit
Capital Account: Debit	0.0	0.0	0.0	0.0	0.0	0.0	0.0	Compte de capital : débit
Financial Account,nie	252.7	196.1	304.5	457.1	335.9	283.5	407.3	Compte d'op. fin., nia
Net Errors and Omissions	12.5	5.2	4.9	10.7	0.8	4.6	7.1	Erreurs et omissions nettes
Reserves and Related Items	6.3	42.1	−20.2	−163.4	−155.4	−65.6	−62.5	Rés. et postes appareutés

79
Summary of balance of payments
Millions of US dollars
Résumé des balances des paiements
Millions de dollars des E−U

Country or area	1988	1989	1990	1991	1992	1993	1994	Pays ou zone
Oman								**Oman**
Goods: Exports fob	3 342.0	4 068.0	5 508.0	4 871.0	5 555.0	5 365.0	...	Biens : exportations,fàb
Goods: Imports fob	−2 107.0	−2 225.0	−2 623.0	−3 112.0	−3 627.0	−4 030.0	...	Biens : importations,fàb
Serv. & Income: Credit	270.0	397.0	443.0	417.0	341.0	434.0	...	Serv. & revenu : crédit
Serv. & Income: Debit	−1 095.0	−1 158.0	−1 348.0	−1 547.0	−1 568.0	−1 528.0	...	Serv. & revenu : débit
Current Trans.,nie: Credit	81.0	55.0	39.0	39.0	39.0	57.0	...	Transf. cour.,nia : crédit
Current Transfers: Debit	−801.0	−830.0	−913.0	−913.0	−1 235.0	−1 368.0	...	Transf. courants : débit
Capital Acct.,nie: Credit	0.0	0.0	0.0	0.0	0.0	0.0	...	Compte de cap.,nia : crédit
Capital Account: Debit	0.0	0.0	0.0	0.0	0.0	0.0	...	Compte de capital : débit
Financial Account,nie	221.0	−15.0	−499.0	521.0	314.0	49.0	...	Compte d'op. fin., nia
Net Errors and Omissions	−379.0	33.0	−472.0	253.0	462.0	−39.0	...	Erreurs et omissions nettes
Reserves and Related Items	467.0	−324.0	−135.0	−530.0	−280.0	1 058.0	...	Rés. et postes appareutés
Pakistan								**Pakistan**
Goods: Exports fob	4 405.0	4 796.0	5 380.0	6 381.0	6 881.0	6 760.0	...	Biens : exportations,fàb
Goods: Imports fob	−7 097.0	−7 366.0	−8 094.0	−8 642.0	−9 671.0	−9 312.0	...	Biens : importations,fàb
Serv. & Income: Credit	947.0	1 323.0	1 519.0	1 597.0	1 625.0	1 577.0	...	Serv. & revenu : crédit
Serv. & Income: Debit	−2 393.0	−2 808.0	−3 238.0	−3 559.0	−4 149.0	−4 237.0	...	Serv. & revenu : débit
Current Trans.,nie: Credit	2 747.0	2 757.0	2 820.0	2 877.0	3 485.0	2 308.0	...	Transf. cour.,nia : crédit
Current Transfers: Debit	−30.0	−36.0	−40.0	−49.0	−40.0	−31.0	...	Transf. courants : débit
Capital Acct.,nie: Credit	0.0	0.0	0.0	0.0	0.0	0.0	...	Compte de cap.,nia : crédit
Capital Account: Debit	−1.0	−1.0	−1.0	−1.0	−1.0	−1.0	...	Compte de capital : débit
Financial Account,nie	1 548.0	1 139.0	1 173.0	891.0	2 556.0	2 949.0	...	Compte d'op. fin., nia
Net Errors and Omissions	23.0	−242.0	−103.0	−78.0	120.0	−91.0	...	Erreurs et omissions nettes
Reserves and Related Items	−147.0	439.0	585.0	584.0	−808.0	78.0	...	Rés. et postes appareutés
Philippines								**Philippines**
Goods: Exports fob	7 074.0	7 821.0	8 186.0	8 840.0	9 824.0	11 375.0	13 483.0	Biens : exportations,fàb
Goods: Imports fob	−8 159.0	−10 419.0	−12 206.0	−12 051.0	−14 519.0	−17 597.0	−21 333.0	Biens : importations,fàb
Serv. & Income: Credit	3 592.0	4 586.0	4 842.0	5 623.0	7 497.0	7 497.0	10 550.0	Serv. & revenu : crédit
Serv. & Income: Debit	−3 672.0	−4 274.0	−4 231.0	−4 273.0	−4 618.0	−4 957.0	−6 476.0	Serv. & revenu : débit
Current Trans.,nie: Credit	778.0	832.0	717.0	828.0	825.0	746.0	1 041.0	Transf. cour.,nia : crédit
Current Transfers: Debit	−3.0	−2.0	−3.0	−1.0	−9.0	−47.0	−105.0	Transf. courants : débit
Capital Acct.,nie: Credit	0.0	0.0	0.0	0.0	1.0	0.0	0.0	Compte de cap.,nia : crédit
Capital Account: Debit	0.0	0.0	0.0	0.0	0.0	0.0	0.0	Compte de capital : débit
Financial Account,nie	571.0	1 354.0	2 057.0	2 927.0	3 208.0	3 054.0	4 964.0	Compte d'op. fin., nia
Net Errors and Omissions	493.0	402.0	593.0	−138.0	−520.0	265.0	203.0	Erreurs et omissions nettes
Reserves and Related Items	−674.0	−300.0	45.0	−1 755.0	−1 689.0	−336.0	−2 327.0	Rés. et postes appareutés
Saudi Arabia								**Arabie saoudite**
Goods: Exports fob	24 377.0	28 385.0	44 414.0	47 789.0	50 287.0	42 395.0	42 614.0	Biens : exportations,fàb
Goods: Imports fob	−19 805.0	−19 231.0	−21 525.0	−25 971.0	−30 248.0	−25 873.0	−21 318.0	Biens : importations,fàb
Serv. & Income: Credit	12 748.0	12 943.0	12 230.0	11 608.0	10 844.0	9 492.0	7 273.0	Serv. & revenu : crédit
Serv. & Income: Debit	−15 651.0	−20 891.0	−23 634.0	−40 737.0	−33 725.0	−26 625.0	−20 417.0	Serv. & revenu : débit
Current Trans.,nie: Credit	0.0	0.0	0.0	0.0	0.0	0.0	0.0	Transf. cour.,nia : crédit
Current Transfers: Debit	−9 009.0	−10 742.0	−15 637.0	−20 235.0	−14 898.0	−16 657.0	−18 676.0	Transf. courants : débit
Capital Acct.,nie: Credit	0.0	0.0	0.0	0.0	0.0	0.0	0.0	Compte de cap.,nia : crédit
Capital Account: Debit	0.0	0.0	0.0	0.0	0.0	0.0	0.0	Compte de capital : débit
Financial Account,nie	5 821.0	6 030.0	−1 224.0	27 595.0	12 075.0	18 763.0	10 380.0	Compte d'op. fin., nia
Reserves and Related Items	1 519.0	3 508.0	5 376.0	−49.0	5 664.0	−1 495.0	146.0	Rés. et postes appareutés
Singapore								**Singapour**
Goods: Exports fob	40 704.0	45 720.0	54 763.0	61 236.0	67 129.0	77 801.0	98 689.0	Biens : exportations,fàb
Goods: Imports fob	−40 675.0	−46 012.0	−56 311.0	−61 443.0	−68 388.0	−80 587.0	−96 583.0	Biens : importations,fàb
Serv. & Income: Credit	11 445.0	14 410.0	19 320.0	21 379.0	24 015.0	26 403.0	31 412.0	Serv. & revenu : crédit
Serv. & Income: Debit	−9 292.0	−10 803.0	−14 144.0	−15 985.0	−16 063.0	−17 808.0	−20 791.0	Serv. & revenu : débit
Current Trans.,nie: Credit	132.0	156.0	187.0	186.0	197.0	176.0	194.0	Transf. cour.,nia : crédit
Current Transfers: Debit	−431.0	−528.0	−633.0	−685.0	−736.0	−813.0	−972.0	Transf. courants : débit
Capital Acct.,nie: Credit	0.0	0.0	0.0	0.0	0.0	0.0	0.0	Compte de cap.,nia : crédit
Capital Account: Debit	0.0	0.0	0.0	0.0	0.0	0.0	0.0	Compte de capital : débit
Financial Account,nie	987.0	455.0	4 687.0	745.0	−1 326.0	5 511.0	1 787.0	Compte d'op. fin., nia
Net Errors and Omissions	−1 211.0	−660.0	−2 437.0	−1 235.0	1 271.0	−3 106.0	−9 001.0	Erreurs et omissions nettes
Reserves and Related Items	−1 659.0	−2 738.0	−5 431.0	−4 198.0	−6 100.0	−7 578.0	−4 736.0	Rés. et postes appareutés
Sri Lanka								**Sri Lanka**
Goods: Exports fob	1 477.1	1 505.1	1 853.0	2 003.3	2 301.4	2 785.7	3 201.8	Biens : exportations,fàb
Goods: Imports fob	−2 017.5	−2 055.1	−2 325.6	−2 808.0	−3 016.5	−3 527.8	−4 072.5	Biens : importations,fàb
Serv. & Income: Credit	407.9	404.2	532.6	601.1	689.5	745.8	897.8	Serv. & revenu : crédit
Serv. & Income: Debit	−787.9	−787.1	−899.0	−995.0	−1 069.4	−1 108.6	−1 363.5	Serv. & revenu : débit
Current Trans.,nie: Credit	563.7	546.6	578.8	644.5	730.4	795.4	878.5	Transf. cour.,nia : crédit
Current Transfers: Debit	−37.7	−27.3	−38.3	−40.8	−86.1	−72.6	−88.1	Transf. courants : débit

79
Summary of balance of payments
Millions of US dollars
Résumé des balances des paiements
Millions de dollars des E−U

Country or area	1988	1989	1990	1991	1992	1993	1994	Pays ou zone
Capital Acct.,nie: Credit	0.0	0.0	0.0	0.0	0.0	0.0	0.0	Compte de cap.,nia : crédit
Capital Account: Debit	0.0	0.0	0.0	0.0	0.0	0.0	0.0	Compte de capital : débit
Financial Account,nie	256.0	577.0	478.1	689.0	501.3	994.2	911.7	Compte d'op. fin., nia
Net Errors and Omissions	37.3	−115.0	−115.1	225.6	173.3	130.1	−67.6	Erreurs et omissions nettes
Reserves and Related Items	101.2	−48.3	−64.8	−319.9	−223.9	−742.0	−298.1	Rés. et postes appareutés
Syrian Arab Republic								**Rép. arabe syrienne**
Goods: Exports fob	1 348.0	3 013.0	4 156.0	3 438.0	3 100.0	3 203.0	3 755.0	Biens : exportations,fàb
Goods: Imports fob	−1 986.0	−1 821.0	−2 062.0	−2 354.0	−2 941.0	−3 476.0	−4 569.0	Biens : importations,fàb
Serv. & Income: Credit	689.0	915.0	919.0	1 130.0	1 350.0	1 611.0	1 914.0	Serv. & revenu : crédit
Serv. & Income: Debit	−1 097.0	−1 537.0	−1 723.0	−2 098.0	−2 316.0	−2 317.0	−2 291.0	Serv. & revenu : débit
Current Trans.,nie: Credit	897.0	657.0	476.0	588.0	871.0	494.0	637.0	Transf. cour.,nia : crédit
Current Transfers: Debit	−1.0	−5.0	−3.0	−4.0	−8.0	−8.0	−6.0	Transf. courants : débit
Capital Acct.,nie: Credit	0.0	0.0	0.0	0.0	0.0	0.0	0.0	Compte de cap.,nia : crédit
Capital Account: Debit	0.0	0.0	0.0	0.0	0.0	0.0	0.0	Compte de capital : débit
Financial Account,nie	85.0	−1 708.0	−1 836.0	−515.0	−50.0	599.0	1 028.0	Compte d'op. fin., nia
Net Errors and Omissions	34.0	420.0	110.0	−112.0	70.0	170.0	188.0	Erreurs et omissions nettes
Reserves and Related Items	32.0	66.0	−36.0	−72.0	−76.0	−276.0	−656.0	Rés. et postes appareutés
Thailand								**Thaïlande**
Goods: Exports fob	15 781.0	19 834.0	22 811.0	28 232.0	32 100.0	36 398.0	44 478.0	Biens : exportations,fàb
Goods: Imports fob	−17 856.0	−22 750.0	−29 561.0	−34 222.0	−36 261.0	−40 648.0	−48 187.0	Biens : importations,fàb
Serv. & Income: Credit	5 945.0	7 046.0	8 478.0	9 526.0	10 769.0	12 744.0	14 064.0	Serv. & revenu : crédit
Serv. & Income: Debit	−5 760.0	−6 874.0	−9 222.0	−11 369.0	−13 339.0	−16 276.0	−19 887.0	Serv. & revenu : débit
Current Trans.,nie: Credit	268.0	281.0	278.0	411.0	578.0	1 204.0	1 883.0	Transf. cour.,nia : crédit
Current Transfers: Debit	−31.0	−34.0	−65.0	−150.0	−202.0	−469.0	−770.0	Transf. courants : débit
Capital Acct.,nie: Credit	0.0	0.0	0.0	0.0	0.0	0.0	0.0	Compte de cap.,nia : crédit
Capital Account: Debit	0.0	0.0	−1.0	0.0	0.0	0.0	0.0	Compte de capital : débit
Financial Account,nie	3 840.0	6 599.0	9 098.0	11 759.0	9 797.0	11 246.0	14 146.0	Compte d'op. fin., nia
Net Errors and Omissions	411.0	928.0	1 419.0	431.0	−517.0	−292.0	−1 558.0	Erreurs et omissions nettes
Reserves and Related Items	−2 596.0	−5 029.0	−3 235.0	−4 618.0	−2 925.0	−3 907.0	−4 169.0	Rés. et postes appareutés
Turkey								**Turquie**
Goods: Exports fob	11 929.0	11 780.0	13 026.0	13 667.0	14 891.0	15 611.0	18 390.0	Biens : exportations,fàb
Goods: Imports fob	−13 706.0	−15 999.0	−22 581.0	−21 007.0	−23 081.0	−29 771.0	−22 606.0	Biens : importations,fàb
Serv. & Income: Credit	6 026.0	7 098.0	8 933.0	9 307.0	10 419.0	11 787.0	11 691.0	Serv. & revenu : crédit
Serv. & Income: Debit	−4 812.0	−5 476.0	−6 496.0	−6 816.0	−7 262.0	−7 828.0	−7 936.0	Serv. & revenu : débit
Current Trans.,nie: Credit	2 220.0	3 574.0	4 525.0	5 131.0	4 075.0	3 800.0	3 113.0	Transf. cour.,nia : crédit
Current Transfers: Debit	−61.0	−39.0	−32.0	−32.0	−16.0	−32.0	−21.0	Transf. courants : débit
Capital Acct.,nie: Credit	0.0	0.0	0.0	0.0	0.0	0.0	0.0	Compte de cap.,nia : crédit
Capital Account: Debit	0.0	0.0	0.0	0.0	0.0	0.0	0.0	Compte de capital : débit
Financial Account,nie	−958.0	780.0	4 037.0	−2 397.0	3 648.0	8 963.0	−4 194.0	Compte d'op. fin., nia
Net Errors and Omissions	515.0	969.0	−469.0	948.0	−1 190.0	−2 222.0	1 766.0	Erreurs et omissions nettes
Reserves and Related Items	−1 153.0	−2 710.0	−943.0	1 199.0	−1 484.0	−308.0	−203.0	Rés. et postes appareutés
Yemen								**Yémen**
Goods: Exports fob	...	...	1 384.4	1 196.6	1 094.9	1 166.9	1 810.9	Biens : exportations,fàb
Goods: Imports fob	...	...	−1 475.6	−1 896.8	−1 891.1	−2 086.9	−1 855.6	Biens : importations,fàb
Serv. & Income: Credit	...	...	143.5	157.3	200.0	199.2	192.5	Serv. & revenu : crédit
Serv. & Income: Debit	...	...	−1 186.0	−1 382.8	−1 585.1	−1 630.9	−1 322.5	Serv. & revenu : débit
Current Trans.,nie: Credit	...	...	1 896.8	1 309.1	1 100.2	1 092.8	1 133.6	Transf. cour.,nia : crédit
Current Transfers: Debit	...	...	−24.4	−44.9	−29.0	−25.5	−16.6	Transf. courants : débit
Capital Acct.,nie: Credit	...	...	...	...	...	...	...	Compte de cap.,nia : crédit
Capital Account: Debit	...	...	...	...	...	...	...	Compte de capital : débit
Financial Account,nie	...	...	−284.2	−150.4	−17.5	39.6	−568.0	Compte d'op. fin., nia
Net Errors and Omissions	...	...	−711.4	41.7	−193.4	136.2	−55.6	Erreurs et omissions nettes
Reserves and Related Items	...	...	256.9	770.2	1 321.0	1 108.6	681.3	Rés. et postes appareutés
Europe· Europe								
Albania								**Albanie**
Goods: Exports fob	344.6	393.7	322.1	73.0	70.0	111.6	141.3	Biens : exportations,fàb
Goods: Imports fob	−382.3	−455.8	−455.9	−281.0	−540.5	−601.5	−601.0	Biens : importations,fàb
Serv. & Income: Credit	30.5	40.6	31.5	10.0	22.9	142.5	134.2	Serv. & revenu : crédit
Serv. & Income: Debit	−26.9	−28.4	−31.0	−59.3	−126.8	−192.9	−173.8	Serv. & revenu : débit
Current Trans.,nie: Credit	7.0	10.6	15.0	89.3	524.0	556.9	347.5	Transf. cour.,nia : crédit
Current Transfers: Debit	...	...	...	...	−0.3	−1.7	−5.5	Transf. courants : débit
Capital Acct.,nie: Credit	...	...	...	...	...	...	...	Compte de cap.,nia : crédit
Capital Account: Debit	0.0	0.0	0.0	0.0	0.0	0.0	0.0	Compte de capital : débit
Financial Account,nie	139.3	359.4	−117.7	−181.2	−32.2	44.1	40.2	Compte d'op. fin., nia
Net Errors and Omissions	22.0	4.8	−2.0	125.2	47.4	−10.3	123.9	Erreurs et omissions nettes
Reserves and Related Items	−134.2	−324.9	238.0	224.0	35.5	−48.7	−6.8	Rés. et postes appareutés

79
Summary of balance of payments
Millions of US dollars
Résumé des balances des paiements
Millions de dollars des E−U

Country or area	1988	1989	1990	1991	1992	1993	1994	Pays ou zone
Austria								**Autriche**
Goods: Exports fob	30 158.0	31 960.0	40 414.0	40 353.0	43 929.0	39 845.0	44 645.0	Biens : exportations,fàb
Goods: Imports fob	−34 922.0	−37 512.0	−47 383.0	−48 913.0	−52 332.0	−47 112.0	−53 373.0	Biens : importations,fàb
Serv. & Income: Credit	22 874.0	25 166.0	32 424.0	35 104.0	37 628.0	37 037.0	37 957.0	Serv. & revenu : crédit
Serv. & Income: Debit	−18 320.0	−19 250.0	−24 284.0	−26 353.0	−28 321.0	−29 398.0	−30 384.0	Serv. & revenu : débit
Current Trans.,nie: Credit	1 258.0	1 227.0	1 657.0	1 699.0	1 386.0	1 334.0	1 443.0	Transf. cour.,nia : crédit
Current Transfers: Debit	−1 289.0	−1 343.0	−1 663.0	−1 830.0	−2 369.0	−2 314.0	−2 498.0	Transf. courants : débit
Capital Acct.,nie: Credit	40.0	50.0	63.0	152.0	168.0	177.0	598.0	Compte de cap.,nia : crédit
Capital Account: Debit	−44.0	−62.0	−55.0	−97.0	−252.0	−288.0	−252.0	Compte de capital : débit
Financial Account,nie	415.0	1 367.0	−19.0	−12.0	1 961.0	3 415.0	3 099.0	Compte d'op. fin., nia
Net Errors and Omissions	322.0	−613.0	−1 170.0	731.0	795.0	−493.0	−417.0	Erreurs et omissions nettes
Reserves and Related Items	−491.0	−990.0	15.0	−835.0	−2 593.0	−2 202.0	−819.0	Rés. et postes appareutés
Belgium−Luxembourg								**Belgique−Luxembourg**
Goods: Exports fob	87 436.0	92 123.0	110 188.0	107 990.0	116 841.0	106 302.0	122 879.0	Biens : exportations,fàb
Goods: Imports fob	−84 733.0	−89 845.0	−108 517.0	−105 991.0	−113 141.0	−100 522.0	−115 949.0	Biens : importations,fàb
Serv. & Income: Credit	54 172.0	70 116.0	93 961.0	106 035.0	121 953.0	116 377.0	144 140.0	Serv. & revenu : crédit
Serv. & Income: Debit	−51 529.0	−66 906.0	−89 809.0	−101 063.0	−116 308.0	−108 133.0	−135 092.0	Serv. & revenu : débit
Current Trans.,nie: Credit	2 602.0	2 329.0	3 825.0	4 160.0	4 368.0	4 198.0	4 476.0	Transf. cour.,nia : crédit
Current Transfers: Debit	−4 357.0	−4 217.0	−6 022.0	−6 385.0	−7 063.0	−6 986.0	−7 434.0	Transf. courants : débit
Capital Acct.,nie: Credit	0.0	0.0	0.0	0.0	0.0	0.0	0.0	Compte de cap.,nia : crédit
Capital Account: Debit	0.0	0.0	0.0	0.0	0.0	0.0	0.0	Compte de capital : débit
Financial Account,nie	−3 758.0	−2 664.0	−1 651.0	−3 155.0	−7 806.0	−13 563.0	−10 453.0	Compte d'op. fin., nia
Net Errors and Omissions	61.0	−624.0	−1 572.0	−1 007.0	1 726.0	204.0	−2 349.0	Erreurs et omissions nettes
Reserves and Related Items	104.0	−312.0	−404.0	−584.0	−569.0	2 122.0	−219.0	Rés. et postes appareutés
Bulgaria								**Bulgarie**
Goods: Exports fob	9 283.0	8 268.0	6 113.0	3 737.0	3 956.0	3 727.0	3 935.0	Biens : exportations,fàb
Goods: Imports fob	−9 889.0	−8 960.0	−7 427.0	−3 769.0	−4 169.0	−4 612.0	−3 952.0	Biens : importations,fàb
Serv. & Income: Credit	1 268.0	1 350.0	957.0	456.0	1 195.0	1 265.0	1 341.0	Serv. & revenu : crédit
Serv. & Income: Debit	−1 167.0	−1 504.0	−1 478.0	−570.0	−1 386.0	−1 514.0	−1 523.0	Serv. & revenu : débit
Current Trans.,nie: Credit	183.0	143.0	232.0	123.0	114.0	286.0	357.0	Transf. cour.,nia : crédit
Current Transfers: Debit	−80.0	−66.0	−107.0	−54.0	−71.0	−249.0	−190.0	Transf. courants : débit
Capital Acct.,nie: Credit	0.0	0.0	0.0	0.0	0.0	0.0	0.0	Compte de cap.,nia : crédit
Capital Account: Debit	0.0	0.0	0.0	0.0	0.0	0.0	0.0	Compte de capital : débit
Financial Account,nie	1 545.0	−40.0	−2 814.0	95.0	716.0	754.0	−911.0	Compte d'op. fin., nia
Net Errors and Omissions	−486.0	375.0	70.0	...	−85.0	22.0	37.0	Erreurs et omissions nettes
Reserves and Related Items	−657.0	434.0	4 454.0	−17.0	−271.0	322.0	144.0	Rés. et postes appareutés
Croatia								**Croatie**
Goods: Exports fob	...	...	...	...	...	3 903.8	4 260.4	Biens : exportations,fàb
Goods: Imports fob	...	...	...	...	...	−4 199.7	−4 706.4	Biens : importations,fàb
Serv. & Income: Credit	...	...	...	...	...	1 918.4	2 393.5	Serv. & revenu : crédit
Serv. & Income: Debit	...	...	...	...	...	−1 894.4	−2 303.4	Serv. & revenu : débit
Current Trans.,nie: Credit	...	...	...	...	...	554.9	602.1	Transf. cour.,nia : crédit
Current Transfers: Debit	...	...	...	...	...	−178.9	−142.8	Transf. courants : débit
Capital Acct.,nie: Credit	...	...	...	...	...	...	...	Compte de cap.,nia : crédit
Capital Account: Debit	...	...	...	...	...	...	...	Compte de capital : débit
Financial Account,nie	...	...	...	...	...	42.5	219.7	Compte d'op. fin., nia
Net Errors and Omissions	...	...	...	...	...	29.4	102.6	Erreurs et omissions nettes
Reserves and Related Items	...	...	...	...	...	−175.9	−425.8	Rés. et postes appareutés
former Czechoslovakia†								**anc. Tchécoslovaquie†**
Goods: Exports fob	15 027.0	14 217.0	11 635.0	10 596.0	11 463.0	...	...	Biens : exportations,fàb
Goods: Imports fob	−14 642.0	−14 074.0	−13 057.0	−10 717.0	−13 297.0	...	...	Biens : importations,fàb
Serv. & Income: Credit	3 302.0	3 363.0	3 171.0	3 583.0	4 811.0	...	...	Serv. & revenu : crédit
Serv. & Income: Debit	−2 659.0	−2 679.0	−3 181.0	−2 614.0	−3 148.0	...	...	Serv. & revenu : débit
Current Trans.,nie: Credit	180.0	213.0	318.0	110.0	313.0	...	...	Transf. cour.,nia : crédit
Current Transfers: Debit	−114.0	−105.0	−112.0	−49.0	−172.0	...	...	Transf. courants : débit
Capital Acct.,nie: Credit	0.0	0.0	0.0	0.0	0.0	...	...	Compte de cap.,nia : crédit
Capital Account: Debit	0.0	0.0	0.0	0.0	0.0	...	...	Compte de capital : débit
Financial Account,nie	−893.0	−292.0	643.0	−980.0	−247.0	...	...	Compte d'op. fin., nia
Net Errors and Omissions	6.0	−81.0	−543.0	861.0	−144.0	...	...	Erreurs et omissions nettes
Reserves and Related Items	−207.0	−563.0	1 127.0	−789.0	422.0	...	...	Rés. et postes appareutés
Czech Republic								**République tchèque**
Goods: Exports fob	...	...	...	...	...	13 002.0	14 037.0	Biens : exportations,fàb
Goods: Imports fob	...	...	...	...	...	−13 304.0	−14 955.0	Biens : importations,fàb
Serv. & Income: Credit	...	...	...	...	...	5 269.0	5 692.0	Serv. & revenu : crédit
Serv. & Income: Debit	...	...	...	...	...	−4 373.0	−4 982.0	Serv. & revenu : débit
Current Trans.,nie: Credit	...	...	...	...	...	242.0	298.0	Transf. cour.,nia : crédit

79
Summary of balance of payments
Millions of US dollars
Résumé des balances des paiements
Millions de dollars des E−U

Country or area	1988	1989	1990	1991	1992	1993	1994	Pays ou zone
Current Transfers: Debit	...	...	...	...	...	−154.0	−171.0	Transf. courants : débit
Capital Acct.,nie: Credit	...	...	...	...	...	0.0	0.0	Compte de cap.,nia : crédit
Capital Account: Debit	...	...	...	...	...	0.0	0.0	Compte de capital : débit
Financial Account,nie	...	...	...	...	...	3 043.0	4 504.0	Compte d'op. fin., nia
Net Errors and Omissions	...	...	...	...	...	−98.0	−940.0	Erreurs et omissions nettes
Reserves and Related Items	...	...	...	...	...	−3 063.0	−3 483.0	Rés. et postes appareutés
Denmark								**Danemark**
Goods: Exports fob	27 537.0	28 728.0	36 072.0	36 783.0	40 650.0	37 070.0	41 777.0	Biens : exportations,fàb
Goods: Imports fob	−25 654.0	−26 304.0	−31 197.0	−32 035.0	−33 446.0	−29 073.0	−34 396.0	Biens : importations,fàb
Serv. & Income: Credit	13 300.0	14 288.0	18 841.0	23 119.0	30 064.0	35 410.0	30 026.0	Serv. & revenu : crédit
Serv. & Income: Debit	−16 303.0	−17 687.0	−21 937.0	−25 019.0	−32 119.0	−38 190.0	−33 988.0	Serv. & revenu : débit
Current Trans.,nie: Credit	1 799.0	1 608.0	2 007.0	2 083.0	2 136.0	2 497.0	2 261.0	Transf. cour.,nia : crédit
Current Transfers: Debit	−2 018.0	−1 750.0	−2 415.0	−2 948.0	−3 016.0	−3 005.0	−3 466.0	Transf. courants : débit
Capital Acct.,nie: Credit	0.0	0.0	0.0	0.0	0.0	0.0	0.0	Compte de cap.,nia : crédit
Capital Account: Debit	0.0	0.0	0.0	0.0	0.0	0.0	0.0	Compte de capital : débit
Financial Account,nie	3 275.0	−2 357.0	4 409.0	−3 103.0	−4 138.0	−2 079.0	−2 564.0	Compte d'op. fin., nia
Net Errors and Omissions	−619.0	−347.0	−2 407.0	−2 183.0	−357.0	1 220.0	−1 744.0	Erreurs et omissions nettes
Reserves and Related Items	−1 316.0	3 821.0	−3 374.0	3 303.0	226.0	−3 851.0	2 094.0	Rés. et postes appareutés
Estonia								**Estonie**
Goods: Exports fob	...	...	...	...	460.7	811.7	1 327.4	Biens : exportations,fàb
Goods: Imports fob	...	...	...	...	−551.1	−956.6	−1 688.3	Biens : importations,fàb
Serv. & Income: Credit	...	...	...	...	203.7	361.5	552.6	Serv. & revenu : crédit
Serv. & Income: Debit	...	...	...	...	−174.2	−298.5	−477.1	Serv. & revenu : débit
Current Trans.,nie: Credit	...	...	...	...	97.4	108.4	120.3	Transf. cour.,nia : crédit
Current Transfers: Debit	...	...	...	...	−0.3	−3.2	−5.7	Transf. courants : débit
Capital Acct.,nie: Credit	...	...	...	...	27.4	...	0.5	Compte de cap.,nia : crédit
Capital Account: Debit	...	...	...	...	...	...	−1.1	Compte de capital : débit
Financial Account,nie	...	...	...	...	−1.3	192.3	175.7	Compte d'op. fin., nia
Net Errors and Omissions	...	...	...	...	−4.3	−50.9	13.2	Erreurs et omissions nettes
Reserves and Related Items	...	...	...	...	−57.9	−164.6	−17.5	Rés. et postes appareutés
Finland								**Finlande**
Goods: Exports fob	21 826.0	22 882.0	26 101.0	22 970.0	23 943.0	23 478.0	29 731.0	Biens : exportations,fàb
Goods: Imports fob	−20 694.0	−23 109.0	−25 383.0	−20 738.0	−20 165.0	−17 217.0	−22 245.0	Biens : importations,fàb
Serv. & Income: Credit	6 363.0	6 611.0	8 193.0	6 762.0	6 125.0	5 508.0	7 538.0	Serv. & revenu : crédit
Serv. & Income: Debit	−9 678.0	−11 416.0	−14 898.0	−14 711.0	−14 052.0	−12 465.0	−13 296.0	Serv. & revenu : débit
Current Trans.,nie: Credit	329.0	192.0	252.0	345.0	427.0	475.0	410.0	Transf. cour.,nia : crédit
Current Transfers: Debit	−827.0	−940.0	−1 204.0	−1 326.0	−1 221.0	−903.0	−863.0	Transf. courants : débit
Capital Acct.,nie: Credit	0.0	0.0	0.0	0.0	0.0	0.0	0.0	Compte de cap.,nia : crédit
Capital Account: Debit	−14.0	−15.0	−22.0	−71.0	...	...	0.0	Compte de capital : débit
Financial Account,nie	2 143.0	3 462.0	13 262.0	4 252.0	3 231.0	521.0	4 385.0	Compte d'op. fin., nia
Net Errors and Omissions	807.0	1 276.0	−2 366.0	629.0	−438.0	894.0	−947.0	Erreurs et omissions nettes
Reserves and Related Items	−255.0	1 058.0	−3 935.0	1 886.0	2 150.0	−291.0	−4 714.0	Rés. et postes appareutés
France								**France**
Goods: Exports fob	161 586.0	172 186.0	208 932.0	209 172.0	227 442.0	199 043.0	224 000.0	Biens : exportations,fàb
Goods: Imports fob	−169 242.0	−182 491.0	−222 186.0	−218 886.0	−225 071.0	−191 532.0	−215 892.0	Biens : importations,fàb
Serv. & Income: Credit	88 537.0	101 227.0	132 191.0	149 869.0	179 359.0	185 382.0	200 685.0	Serv. & revenu : crédit
Serv. & Income: Debit	−78 803.0	−87 908.0	−120 684.0	−139 194.0	−168 857.0	−177 707.0	−192 338.0	Serv. & revenu : débit
Current Trans.,nie: Credit	13 012.0	11 524.0	14 795.0	18 756.0	20 726.0	16 745.0	15 856.0	Transf. cour.,nia : crédit
Current Transfers: Debit	−19 709.0	−19 208.0	−22 994.0	−26 238.0	−29 707.0	−22 947.0	−24 224.0	Transf. courants : débit
Capital Acct.,nie: Credit	217.0	235.0	219.0	252.0	929.0	311.0	270.0	Compte de cap.,nia : crédit
Capital Account: Debit	−403.0	−446.0	−4 352.0	−279.0	−268.0	−279.0	−4 911.0	Compte de capital : débit
Financial Account,nie	−1 307.0	10 361.0	24 764.0	−3 066.0	−8 035.0	−16 670.0	−5 016.0	Compte d'op. fin., nia
Net Errors and Omissions	953.0	−6 336.0	264.0	4 420.0	1 907.0	2 647.0	4 016.0	Erreurs et omissions nettes
Reserves and Related Items	5 159.0	857.0	−10 949.0	5 194.0	1 576.0	5 007.0	−2 448.0	Rés. et postes appareutés
Germany †								**Allemagne†**
Goods: Exports fob	...	...	...	403.7	430.6	382.2	429.5	Biens : exportations,fàb
Goods: Imports fob	...	...	...	−385.2	−403.8	−341.5	−379.8	Biens : importations,fàb
Serv. & Income: Credit	...	...	...	135.8	145.4	138.4	139.6	Serv. & revenu : crédit
Serv. & Income: Debit	...	...	...	−134.7	−158.6	−158.9	−172.7	Serv. & revenu : débit
Current Trans.,nie: Credit	...	...	...	16.6	19.4	18.1	20.5	Transf. cour.,nia : crédit
Current Transfers: Debit	...	...	...	−55.0	−54.5	−53.3	−58.6	Transf. courants : débit
Capital Acct.,nie: Credit	...	...	...	0.8	1.1	1.4	1.6	Compte de cap.,nia : crédit
Capital Account: Debit	...	...	...	−1.4	−0.5	−0.9	−1.4	Compte de capital : débit
Financial Account,nie	...	...	...	5.4	52.2	15.8	25.8	Compte d'op. fin., nia

79
Summary of balance of payments
Millions of US dollars
Résumé des balances des paiements
Millions de dollars des E−U

Country or area	1988	1989	1990	1991	1992	1993	1994	Pays ou zone
Net Errors and Omissions	...	...	...	8.0	5.9	−15.4	−6.6	Erreurs et omissions nettes
Reserves and Related Items	...	...	...	6.0	−37.2	14.2	2.0	Rés. et postes appareutés
F. R. Germany [1]								**R. f. Allemagne** [1]
Goods: Exports fob	322.8	340.9	412.0	...	...	...	...	Biens : exportations,fàb
Goods: Imports fob	−246.5	−265.9	−343.5	...	...	...	...	Biens : importations,fàb
Serv. & Income: Credit	80.9	92.7	126.1	...	...	...	...	Serv. & revenu : crédit
Serv. & Income: Debit	−87.9	−90.8	−122.2	...	...	...	...	Serv. & revenu : débit
Current Trans.,nie: Credit	13.9	12.9	15.9	...	...	...	...	Transf. cour.,nia : crédit
Current Transfers: Debit	−33.5	−32.5	−40.1	...	...	...	...	Transf. courants : débit
Capital Acct.,nie: Credit	0.3	0.4	0.4	...	...	...	...	Compte de cap.,nia : crédit
Capital Account: Debit	−0.3	−0.3	−1.7	...	...	...	...	Compte de capital : débit
Financial Account,nie	−67.7	−59.0	−54.5	...	...	...	...	Compte d'op. fin., nia
Net Errors and Omissions	2.7	4.6	14.8	...	...	...	...	Erreurs et omissions nettes
Reserves and Related Item	15.4	−2.8	−7.3	...	...	...	...	Rés. et postes appareutés
Greece								**Grèce**
Goods: Exports fob	6 015.0	6 074.0	6 458.0	6 911.0	6 076.0	5 112.0	5 338.0	Biens : exportations,fàb
Goods: Imports fob	−12 042.0	−13 401.0	−16 564.0	−16 933.0	−17 637.0	−15 611.0	−16 611.0	Biens : importations,fàb
Serv. & Income: Credit	5 363.0	5 111.0	6 875.0	7 643.0	9 252.0	9 141.0	10 312.0	Serv. & revenu : crédit
Serv. & Income: Debit	−3 943.0	−4 328.0	−5 024.0	−5 378.0	−6 306.0	−5 888.0	−6 121.0	Serv. & revenu : débit
Current Trans.,nie: Credit	3 663.0	3 996.0	4 730.0	6 199.0	6 489.0	6 516.0	6 964.0	Transf. cour.,nia : crédit
Current Transfers: Debit	−14.0	−13.0	−12.0	−16.0	−14.0	−17.0	−28.0	Transf. courants : débit
Capital Acct.,nie: Credit	0.0	0.0	0.0	0.0	0.0	0.0	0.0	Compte de cap.,nia : crédit
Capital Account: Debit	0.0	0.0	0.0	0.0	0.0	0.0	0.0	Compte de capital : débit
Financial Account,nie	1 854.0	2 751.0	4 002.0	3 961.0	2 619.0	4 817.0	6 903.0	Compte d'op. fin., nia
Net Errors and Omissions	41.0	−538.0	−185.0	−183.0	−853.0	−631.0	−448.0	Erreurs et omissions nettes
Reserves and Related Items	−937.0	348.0	−280.0	−2 204.0	374.0	−3 439.0	−6 309.0	Rés. et postes appareutés
Hungary								**Hongrie**
Goods: Exports fob	9 989.0	10 493.0	9 151.0	9 688.0	10 097.0	8 119.0	7 648.0	Biens : exportations,fàb
Goods: Imports fob	−9 406.0	−9 450.0	−8 617.0	−9 330.0	−10 108.0	−12 140.0	−11 364.0	Biens : importations,fàb
Serv. & Income: Credit	1 287.0	1 522.0	3 164.0	2 848.0	3 829.0	3 301.0	3 793.0	Serv. & revenu : crédit
Serv. & Income: Debit	−2 559.0	−3 283.0	−4 107.0	−3 669.0	−4 325.0	−4 275.0	−5 040.0	Serv. & revenu : débit
Current Trans.,nie: Credit	117.0	130.0	1 595.0	2 604.0	2 866.0	2 694.0	2 871.0	Transf. cour.,nia : crédit
Current Transfers: Debit	...	...	−808.0	−1 737.0	−2 008.0	−1 961.0	−1 961.0	Transf. courants : débit
Capital Acct.,nie: Credit	0.0	0.0	0.0	0.0	0.0	0.0	0.0	Compte de cap.,nia : crédit
Capital Account: Debit	0.0	0.0	0.0	0.0	0.0	0.0	0.0	Compte de capital : débit
Financial Account,nie	680.0	901.0	−801.0	1 474.0	416.0	6 083.0	3 370.0	Compte d'op. fin., nia
Net Errors and Omissions	50.0	−141.0	10.0	−82.0	2.0	724.0	209.0	Erreurs et omissions nettes
Reserves and Related Items	−158.0	−172.0	413.0	−1 795.0	−770.0	−2 545.0	475.0	Rés. et postes appareutés
Iceland								**Islande**
Goods: Exports fob	1 425.4	1 401.5	1 588.6	1 551.5	1 523.1	1 398.6	1 572.5	Biens : exportations,fàb
Goods: Imports fob	−1 439.4	−1 267.3	−1 509.1	−1 598.9	−1 521.7	−1 217.9	−1 288.2	Biens : importations,fàb
Serv. & Income: Credit	557.8	549.4	639.3	642.4	684.6	675.4	682.1	Serv. & revenu : crédit
Serv. & Income: Debit	−764.1	−764.5	−852.9	−899.1	−887.8	−853.4	−832.8	Serv. & revenu : débit
Current Trans.,nie: Credit	9.0	10.5	16.5	14.5	17.7	18.0	12.2	Transf. cour.,nia : crédit
Current Transfers: Debit	−19.9	−31.6	−28.9	−21.9	−22.3	−20.9	−21.0	Transf. courants : débit
Capital Acct.,nie: Credit	18.4	25.9	25.1	13.1	11.1	11.0	6.1	Compte de cap.,nia : crédit
Capital Account: Debit	−8.7	−7.8	−12.9	−10.9	−12.7	−10.2	−10.1	Compte de capital : débit
Financial Account,nie	226.8	125.0	210.9	299.9	276.2	−48.7	−278.7	Compte d'op. fin., nia
Net Errors and Omissions	−4.1	13.5	−2.3	19.9	1.9	−12.1	0.5	Erreurs et omissions nettes
Reserves and Related Items	−1.2	−54.6	−74.3	−10.5	−70.1	60.2	157.4	Rés. et postes appareutés
Ireland								**Irlande**
Goods: Exports fob	18 389.0	20 356.0	23 356.0	23 660.0	28 107.0	28 728.0	33 658.0	Biens : exportations,fàb
Goods: Imports fob	−14 567.0	−16 352.0	−19 387.0	−19 493.0	−21 065.0	−20 553.0	−24 093.0	Biens : importations,fàb
Serv. & Income: Credit	3 825.0	4 328.0	5 959.0	6 265.0	6 692.0	5 911.0	6 790.0	Serv. & revenu : crédit
Serv. & Income: Debit	−9 119.0	−10 417.0	−12 499.0	−12 175.0	−14 224.0	−13 722.0	−15 393.0	Serv. & revenu : débit
Current Trans.,nie: Credit	1 908.0	1 976.0	2 916.0	3 303.0	2 966.0	2 868.0	2 678.0	Transf. cour.,nia : crédit
Current Transfers: Debit	−460.0	−471.0	−607.0	−701.0	−767.0	−829.0	−921.0	Transf. courants : débit
Capital Acct.,nie: Credit	247.0	231.0	473.0	692.0	878.0	852.0	493.0	Compte de cap.,nia : crédit
Capital Account: Debit	−152.0	−127.0	−101.0	−97.0	−102.0	−89.0	−90.0	Compte de capital : débit
Financial Account,nie	200.0	−1 574.0	−1 905.0	−3 202.0	−6 496.0	−486.0	−4 095.0	Compte d'op. fin., nia
Net Errors and Omissions	322.0	1 115.0	2 544.0	2 210.0	471.0	1 236.0	796.0	Erreurs et omissions nettes
Reserves and Related Items	−592.0	937.0	−748.0	−464.0	3 542.0	−3 915.0	176.0	Rés. et postes appareutés
Italy								**Italie**
Goods: Exports fob	127 859.0	140 556.0	170 304.0	169 465.0	178 155.0	169 153.0	191 440.0	Biens : exportations,fàb
Goods: Imports fob	−128 782.0	−142 219.0	−168 931.0	−169 911.0	−175 070.0	−136 328.0	−155 819.0	Biens : importations,fàb
Serv. & Income: Credit	41 569.0	47 037.0	68 921.0	71 265.0	90 142.0	87 595.0	88 444.0	Serv. & revenu : crédit

79
Summary of balance of payments
Millions of US dollars
Résumé des balances des paiements
Millions de dollars des E−U

Country or area	1988	1989	1990	1991	1992	1993	1994	Pays ou zone
Serv. & Income: Debit	−45 953.0	−54 688.0	−84 715.0	−88 601.0	−115 187.0	−103 835.0	−102 041.0	Serv. & revenu : débit
Current Trans.,nie: Credit	10 037.0	10 552.0	11 386.0	11 990.0	11 673.0	11 172.0	9 130.0	Transf. cour.,nia : crédit
Current Transfers: Debit	−11 910.0	−14 048.0	−14 551.0	−18 857.0	−19 167.0	−18 354.0	−16 221.0	Transf. courants : débit
Capital Acct.,nie: Credit	1 514.0	1 608.0	1 822.0	1 717.0	2 265.0	2 799.0	2 216.0	Compte de cap.,nia : crédit
Capital Account: Debit	−934.0	−696.0	−1 063.0	−1 129.0	−1 445.0	−1 149.0	−1 187.0	Compte de capital : débit
Financial Account,nie	16 710.0	24 738.0	42 638.0	24 213.0	11 554.0	5 260.0	−14 079.0	Compte d'op. fin., nia
Net Errors and Omissions	−1 695.0	−1 568.0	−14 188.0	−6 871.0	−6 912.0	−19 448.0	−307.0	Erreurs et omissions nettes
Reserves and Related Items	−8 416.0	−11 270.0	−11 623.0	6 718.0	23 992.0	3 135.0	−1 575.0	Rés. et postes appareutés
Latvia								**Lettonie**
Goods: Exports fob	...	...	...	...	800.0	1 054.0	1 022.0	Biens : exportations,fàb
Goods: Imports fob	...	...	...	...	−840.0	−1 051.0	−1 322.0	Biens : importations,fàb
Serv. & Income: Credit	...	...	...	...	294.0	550.0	708.0	Serv. & revenu : crédit
Serv. & Income: Debit	...	...	...	...	−157.0	−215.0	−339.0	Serv. & revenu : débit
Current Trans.,nie: Credit	...	...	...	...	97.0	81.0	136.0	Transf. cour.,nia : crédit
Current Transfers: Debit	...	...	...	...	−1.0	−3.0	−3.0	Transf. courants : débit
Capital Acct.,nie: Credit	...	...	...	...	...	...	...	Compte de cap.,nia : crédit
Capital Account: Debit	...	...	...	...	...	...	...	Compte de capital : débit
Financial Account,nie	...	...	...	...	−110.0	67.0	363.0	Compte d'op. fin., nia
Net Errors and Omissions	...	...	...	...	−44.0	−186.0	−508.0	Erreurs et omissions nettes
Reserves and Related Items	...	...	...	...	−37.0	−298.0	−57.0	Rés. et postes appareutés
Lithuania								**Lithuanie**
Goods: Exports fob	...	...	...	...	...	2 025.8	2 029.2	Biens : exportations,fàb
Goods: Imports fob	...	...	...	...	...	−2 180.5	−2 234.1	Biens : importations,fàb
Serv. & Income: Credit	...	...	...	...	...	210.3	343.5	Serv. & revenu : crédit
Serv. & Income: Debit	...	...	...	...	...	−257.2	−389.3	Serv. & revenu : débit
Current Trans.,nie: Credit	...	...	...	...	...	115.9	161.5	Transf. cour.,nia : crédit
Current Transfers: Debit	...	...	...	...	...	0.0	−4.8	Transf. courants : débit
Capital Acct.,nie: Credit	...	...	...	...	...	0.0	12.9	Compte de cap.,nia : crédit
Capital Account: Debit	...	...	...	...	...	0.0	0.0	Compte de capital : débit
Financial Account,nie	...	...	...	...	...	301.5	308.5	Compte d'op. fin., nia
Net Errors and Omissions	...	...	...	...	...	−7.4	−113.5	Erreurs et omissions nettes
Reserves and Related Items	...	...	...	...	...	−208.5	−114.0	Rés. et postes appareutés
Malta								**Malte**
Goods: Exports fob	780.1	891.3	1 192.0	1 324.4	1 603.5	1 400.8	1 605.1	Biens : exportations,fàb
Goods: Imports fob	−1 222.3	−1 327.7	−1 753.0	−1 897.3	−2 104.0	−1 953.8	−2 165.3	Biens : importations,fàb
Serv. & Income: Credit	809.8	835.0	1 027.4	1 088.3	1 161.1	1 160.9	1 227.5	Serv. & revenu : crédit
Serv. & Income: Debit	−465.8	−506.5	−609.2	−638.5	−724.0	−753.1	−845.7	Serv. & revenu : débit
Current Trans.,nie: Credit	170.5	114.5	105.1	114.5	94.1	62.5	98.2	Transf. cour.,nia : crédit
Current Transfers: Debit	−11.2	−16.1	−23.3	−4.9	−4.7	−4.2	−5.6	Transf. courants : débit
Capital Acct.,nie: Credit	7.0	6.0	5.7	6.2	4.4	2.6	0.3	Compte de cap.,nia : crédit
Capital Account: Debit	0.0	0.0	0.0	0.0	0.0	0.0	0.0	Compte de capital : débit
Financial Account,nie	17.2	−46.8	−43.4	16.7	27.3	176.3	380.2	Compte d'op. fin., nia
Net Errors and Omissions	−50.4	64.4	23.9	−93.9	−12.6	45.5	87.6	Erreurs et omissions nettes
Reserves and Related Items	−34.8	−14.2	74.9	84.6	−45.1	−137.6	−382.4	Rés. et postes appareutés
Netherlands								**Pays−Bas**
Goods: Exports fob	103 389.0	108 155.0	130 002.0	130 759.0	137 330.0	127 050.0	140 165.0	Biens : exportations,fàb
Goods: Imports fob	−93 317.0	−98 330.0	−117 944.0	−118 780.0	−125 024.0	−111 589.0	−124 392.0	Biens : importations,fàb
Serv. & Income: Credit	40 683.0	48 683.0	57 182.0	61 448.0	66 915.0	67 345.0	70 000.0	Serv. & revenu : crédit
Serv. & Income: Debit	−41 752.0	−46 556.0	−57 091.0	−61 567.0	−67 532.0	−66 097.0	−66 939.0	Serv. & revenu : débit
Current Trans.,nie: Credit	5 592.0	5 142.0	4 478.0	4 603.0	4 642.0	4 358.0	4 197.0	Transf. cour.,nia : crédit
Current Transfers: Debit	−7 464.0	−7 081.0	−7 421.0	−8 733.0	−8 997.0	−8 847.0	−9 473.0	Transf. courants : débit
Capital Acct.,nie: Credit	293.0	299.0	314.0	343.0	369.0	577.0	560.0	Compte de cap.,nia : crédit
Capital Account: Debit	−490.0	−613.0	−615.0	−625.0	−1 000.0	−1 281.0	−1 487.0	Compte de capital : débit
Financial Account,nie	−668.0	−7 884.0	−4 635.0	−5 828.0	−7 503.0	−9 822.0	−6 489.0	Compte d'op. fin., nia
Net Errors and Omissions	−4 698.0	−1 308.0	−4 003.0	−1 113.0	6 919.0	4 946.0	−5 641.0	Erreurs et omissions nettes
Reserves and Related Items	−1 568.0	−507.0	−268.0	−506.0	−6 118.0	−6 641.0	−500.0	Rés. et postes appareutés
Norway								**Norvège**
Goods: Exports fob	23 075.0	27 171.0	34 313.0	34 212.0	35 162.0	31 989.0	34 922.0	Biens : exportations,fàb
Goods: Imports fob	−23 284.0	−23 401.0	−26 552.0	−25 516.0	−25 860.0	−23 995.0	−26 601.0	Biens : importations,fàb
Serv. & Income: Credit	12 994.0	14 195.0	16 661.0	16 870.0	16 682.0	15 192.0	15 915.0	Serv. & revenu : crédit
Serv. & Income: Debit	−15 544.0	−16 618.0	−18 954.0	−18 994.0	−21 246.0	−19 633.0	−18 971.0	Serv. & revenu : débit
Current Trans.,nie: Credit	168.0	164.0	217.0	239.0	287.0	319.0	266.0	Transf. cour.,nia : crédit
Current Transfers: Debit	−1 305.0	−1 299.0	−1 693.0	−1 780.0	−2 044.0	−1 720.0	−1 886.0	Transf. courants : débit
Capital Acct.,nie: Credit	107.0	101.0	109.0	118.0	143.0	180.0	76.0	Compte de cap.,nia : crédit
Capital Account: Debit	−99.0	−99.0	−78.0	−101.0	−164.0	−165.0	−94.0	Compte de capital : débit
Financial Account,nie	4 900.0	2 056.0	−761.0	−7 581.0	−375.0	3 280.0	−1 321.0	Compte d'op. fin., nia

79
Summary of balance of payments
Millions of US dollars
Résumé des balances des paiements
Millions de dollars des E−U

Country or area	1988	1989	1990	1991	1992	1993	1994	Pays ou zone
Net Errors and Omissions	−1 149.0	−1 305.0	−2 848.0	−219.0	−3 442.0	−1 309.0	−854.0	Erreurs et omissions nettes
Reserves and Related Items	138.0	−965.0	−414.0	2 751.0	855.0	−4 138.0	−1 451.0	Rés. et postes appareutés
Poland								**Pologne**
Goods: Exports fob	13 846.0	12 869.0	15 837.0	14 393.0	13 929.0	13 582.0	17 121.0	Biens : exportations,fàb
Goods: Imports fob	−12 757.0	−12 822.0	−12 248.0	−15 104.0	−14 060.0	−17 087.0	−18 930.0	Biens : importations,fàb
Serv. & Income: Credit	2 743.0	3 611.0	3 803.0	4 260.0	5 501.0	4 780.0	5 068.0	Serv. & revenu : crédit
Serv. & Income: Debit	−5 630.0	−6 676.0	−6 836.0	−6 463.0	−8 940.0	−7 823.0	−6 968.0	Serv. & revenu : débit
Current Trans.,nie: Credit	2 777.0	4 246.0	6 865.0	6 707.0	6 214.0	5 840.0	6 509.0	Transf. cour.,nia : crédit
Current Transfers: Debit	−1 086.0	−2 637.0	−4 354.0	−5 939.0	−5 748.0	−5 080.0	−5 345.0	Transf. courants : débit
Capital Acct.,nie: Credit	0.0	0.0	0.0	0.0	0.0	0.0	0.0	Compte de cap.,nia : crédit
Capital Account: Debit	0.0	0.0	0.0	0.0	0.0	0.0	0.0	Compte de capital : débit
Financial Account,nie	−10 661.0	−1 796.0	−8 731.0	−4 183.0	−1 045.0	2 341.0	2 173.0	Compte d'op. fin., nia
Net Errors and Omissions	−267.0	−110.0	162.0	−745.0	−181.0	219.0	−142.0	Erreurs et omissions nettes
Reserves and Related Items	11 035.0	3 315.0	5 502.0	7 074.0	4 330.0	3 228.0	514.0	Rés. et postes appareutés
Portugal								**Portugal**
Goods: Exports fob	11 015.0	12 843.0	16 458.0	16 391.0	18 348.0	15 928.0	18 492.0	Biens : exportations,fàb
Goods: Imports fob	−16 392.0	−17 585.0	−23 141.0	−24 079.0	−27 735.0	−22 741.0	−25 222.0	Biens : importations,fàb
Serv. & Income: Credit	3 895.0	4 508.0	6 456.0	6 781.0	7 564.0	9 098.0	8 775.0	Serv. & revenu : crédit
Serv. & Income: Debit	−3 906.0	−4 152.0	−5 462.0	−5 784.0	−6 188.0	−8 239.0	−8 459.0	Serv. & revenu : débit
Current Trans.,nie: Credit	4 946.0	5 227.0	6 433.0	7 237.0	9 344.0	8 377.0	7 363.0	Transf. cour.,nia : crédit
Current Transfers: Debit	−624.0	−687.0	−926.0	−1 263.0	−1 518.0	−1 693.0	−1 986.0	Transf. courants : débit
Capital Acct.,nie: Credit	0.0	0.0	0.0	0.0	0.0	0.0	0.0	Compte de cap.,nia : crédit
Capital Account: Debit	0.0	0.0	0.0	0.0	0.0	0.0	0.0	Compte de capital : débit
Financial Account,nie	293.0	4 005.0	2 563.0	4 537.0	−950.0	−2 913.0	728.0	Compte d'op. fin., nia
Net Errors and Omissions	1 640.0	497.0	1 160.0	1 893.0	978.0	−665.0	−1 122.0	Erreurs et omissions nettes
Reserves and Related Items	−867.0	−4 654.0	−3 542.0	−5 713.0	156.0	2 848.0	1 430.0	Rés. et postes appareutés
Romania								**Roumanie**
Goods: Exports fob	11 392.0	10 487.0	5 770.0	4 266.0	4 364.0	4 892.0	6 151.0	Biens : exportations,fàb
Goods: Imports fob	−7 642.0	−8 437.0	−9 114.0	−5 372.0	−5 558.0	−6 020.0	−6 562.0	Biens : importations,fàb
Serv. & Income: Credit	1 023.0	1 015.0	785.0	784.0	713.0	862.0	1 152.0	Serv. & revenu : crédit
Serv. & Income: Debit	−851.0	−551.0	−801.0	−908.0	−1 090.0	−1 122.0	−1 444.0	Serv. & revenu : débit
Current Trans.,nie: Credit	0.0	0.0	138.0	277.0	136.0	231.0	344.0	Transf. cour.,nia : crédit
Current Transfers: Debit	0.0	0.0	−32.0	−59.0	−71.0	−17.0	−61.0	Transf. courants : débit
Capital Acct.,nie: Credit	0.0	0.0	0.0	0.0	0.0	0.0	0.0	Compte de cap.,nia : crédit
Capital Account: Debit	0.0	0.0	0.0	0.0	0.0	0.0	0.0	Compte de capital : débit
Financial Account,nie	−4 223.0	−1 376.0	1 613.0	320.0	1 380.0	969.0	911.0	Compte d'op. fin., nia
Net Errors and Omissions	16.0	114.0	147.0	15.0	−12.0	151.0	−105.0	Erreurs et omissions nettes
Reserves and Related Items	285.0	−1 252.0	1 494.0	677.0	138.0	54.0	−399.0	Rés. et postes appareutés
Russian Federation								**Fédération de Russie**
Goods: Exports fob	...	...	...	...	...	...	67 716.0	Biens : exportations,fàb
Goods: Imports fob	...	...	...	...	...	...	−48 003.0	Biens : importations,fàb
Serv. & Income: Credit	...	...	...	...	...	...	12 453.0	Serv. & revenu : crédit
Serv. & Income: Debit	...	...	...	...	...	...	−20 725.0	Serv. & revenu : débit
Current Trans.,nie: Credit	...	...	...	...	...	...	423.0	Transf. cour.,nia : crédit
Current Transfers: Debit	...	...	...	...	...	...	−495.0	Transf. courants : débit
Capital Acct.,nie: Credit	...	...	...	...	...	...	4 310.0	Compte de cap.,nia : crédit
Capital Account: Debit	...	...	...	...	...	...	−3 470.0	Compte de capital : débit
Financial Account,nie	...	...	...	...	...	...	−33 060.0	Compte d'op. fin., nia
Net Errors and Omissions	...	...	...	...	...	...	−836.0	Erreurs et omissions nettes
Reserves and Related Items	...	...	...	...	...	...	21 687.0	Rés. et postes appareutés
Slovakia								**Slovaquie**
Goods: Exports fob	...	...	...	...	...	5 452.0	6 743.0	Biens : exportations,fàb
Goods: Imports fob	...	...	...	...	...	−6 365.0	−6 634.0	Biens : importations,fàb
Serv. & Income: Credit	...	...	...	...	...	2 124.0	2 416.0	Serv. & revenu : crédit
Serv. & Income: Debit	...	...	...	...	...	−1 890.0	−1 875.0	Serv. & revenu : débit
Current Trans.,nie: Credit	...	...	...	...	...	216.0	166.0	Transf. cour.,nia : crédit
Current Transfers: Debit	...	...	...	...	...	−118.0	−98.0	Transf. courants : débit
Capital Acct.,nie: Credit	...	...	...	...	...	771.0	84.0	Compte de cap.,nia : crédit
Capital Account: Debit	...	...	...	...	...	0.0	0.0	Compte de capital : débit
Financial Account,nie	...	...	...	...	...	−153.0	4.0	Compte d'op. fin., nia
Net Errors and Omissions	...	...	...	...	...	183.0	398.0	Erreurs et omissions nettes
Reserves and Related Items	...	...	...	...	...	−14.0	−1 205.0	Rés. et postes appareutés
Slovenia								**Slovénie**
Goods: Exports fob	...	...	...	...	6 680.9	6 082.9	6 827.9	Biens : exportations,fàb
Goods: Imports fob	...	...	...	...	−5 891.8	−6 237.1	−7 007.6	Biens : importations,fàb
Serv. & Income: Credit	...	...	...	...	1 331.0	1 507.5	1 831.7	Serv. & revenu : crédit

79
Summary of balance of payments
Millions of US dollars
Résumé des balances des paiements
Millions de dollars des E−U

Country or area	1988	1989	1990	1991	1992	1993	1994	Pays ou zone
Serv. & Income: Debit	...	...	...	...	−1 187.9	−1 185.6	−1 238.3	Serv. & revenu : débit
Current Trans.,nie: Credit	...	...	...	...	93.0	158.5	175.0	Transf. cour.,nia : crédit
Current Transfers: Debit	...	...	...	...	−46.9	−138.7	−131.5	Transf. courants : débit
Capital Acct.,nie: Credit	...	...	...	...	0.0	6.7	3.5	Compte de cap.,nia : crédit
Capital Account: Debit	...	...	...	...	0.0	−2.6	−4.2	Compte de capital : débit
Financial Account,nie	...	...	...	...	−13.3	−63.9	131.0	Compte d'op. fin., nia
Net Errors and Omissions	...	...	...	...	−332.4	−2.8	60.0	Erreurs et omissions nettes
Reserves and Related Items	...	...	...	...	−632.6	−124.9	−647.5	Rés. et postes appareutés
Spain								**Espagne**
Goods: Exports fob	40 692.0	44 945.0	55 658.0	60 167.0	65 826.0	62 019.0	73 924.0	Biens : exportations,fàb
Goods: Imports fob	−59 396.0	−70 351.0	−84 815.0	−90 501.0	−96 247.0	−76 965.0	−88 757.0	Biens : importations,fàb
Serv. & Income: Credit	27 147.0	28 393.0	35 754.0	40 094.0	48 036.0	42 575.0	42 825.0	Serv. & revenu : crédit
Serv. & Income: Debit	−16 731.0	−18 527.0	−27 404.0	−32 456.0	−41 297.0	−35 041.0	−36 306.0	Serv. & revenu : débit
Current Trans.,nie: Credit	7 478.0	8 496.0	7 849.0	9 767.0	11 410.0	9 150.0	9 387.0	Transf. cour.,nia : crédit
Current Transfers: Debit	−2 986.0	−3 880.0	−5 050.0	−6 870.0	−9 015.0	−7 506.0	−7 890.0	Transf. courants : débit
Capital Acct.,nie: Credit	48.0	50.0	1 753.0	3 535.0	3 978.0	3 366.0	3 134.0	Compte de cap.,nia : crédit
Capital Account: Debit	−37.0	−59.0	−302.0	−370.0	−493.0	−449.0	−522.0	Compte de capital : débit
Financial Account,nie	14 615.0	18 342.0	22 970.0	32 015.0	5 959.0	−279.0	5 468.0	Compte d'op. fin., nia
Net Errors and Omissions	−2 414.0	−2 693.0	777.0	−1 075.0	−5 965.0	−1 680.0	−1 214.0	Erreurs et omissions nettes
Reserves and Related Items	−8 416.0	−4 716.0	−7 188.0	−14 307.0	17 809.0	4 808.0	−50.0	Rés. et postes appareutés
Sweden								**Suède**
Goods: Exports fob	49 367.0	51 071.0	56 835.0	54 542.0	55 363.0	49 348.0	60 197.0	Biens : exportations,fàb
Goods: Imports fob	−44 487.0	−47 054.0	−53 433.0	−48 185.0	−48 642.0	−41 801.0	−50 636.0	Biens : importations,fàb
Serv. & Income: Credit	15 697.0	18 323.0	23 415.0	24 160.0	24 336.0	19 714.0	23 278.0	Serv. & revenu : crédit
Serv. & Income: Debit	−19 732.0	−23 691.0	−31 220.0	−33 185.0	−37 271.0	−29 615.0	−30 154.0	Serv. & revenu : débit
Current Trans.,nie: Credit	382.0	298.0	386.0	393.0	405.0	456.0	545.0	Transf. cour.,nia : crédit
Current Transfers: Debit	−1 760.0	−2 049.0	−2 321.0	−2 378.0	−3 019.0	−2 263.0	−2 424.0	Transf. courants : débit
Capital Acct.,nie: Credit	29.0	38.0	38.0	38.0	37.0	37.0	37.0	Compte de cap.,nia : crédit
Capital Account: Debit	−263.0	−334.0	−391.0	−101.0	−31.0	−15.0	−14.0	Compte de capital : débit
Financial Account,nie	2 897.0	9 837.0	19 278.0	−1 336.0	10 214.0	11 518.0	6 438.0	Compte d'op. fin., nia
Net Errors and Omissions	−1 190.0	−5 185.0	−5 035.0	5 988.0	5 561.0	−4 851.0	−4 937.0	Erreurs et omissions nettes
Reserves and Related Items	−938.0	−1 254.0	−7 552.0	63.0	−6 953.0	−2 530.0	−2 331.0	Rés. et postes appareutés
Switzerland								**Suisse**
Goods: Exports fob	63 164.0	65 811.0	78 033.0	74 256.0	79 870.0	75 424.0	82 625.0	Biens : exportations,fàb
Goods: Imports fob	−68 359.0	−70 769.0	−85 207.0	−78 853.0	−80 155.0	−73 852.0	−79 294.0	Biens : importations,fàb
Serv. & Income: Credit	36 171.0	38 508.0	47 579.0	47 303.0	47 303.0	46 495.0	49 765.0	Serv. & revenu : crédit
Serv. & Income: Debit	−20 417.0	−23 823.0	−31 134.0	−29 759.0	−29 830.0	−27 385.0	−31 125.0	Serv. & revenu : débit
Current Trans.,nie: Credit	2 054.0	1 919.0	2 357.0	2 367.0	2 531.0	2 484.0	2 571.0	Transf. cour.,nia : crédit
Current Transfers: Debit	−3 768.0	−3 602.0	−4 686.0	−4 939.0	−5 484.0	−5 317.0	−6 046.0	Transf. courants : débit
Capital Acct.,nie: Credit	0.0	0.0	0.0	0.0	0.0	0.0	0.0	Compte de cap.,nia : crédit
Capital Account: Debit	...	...	...	−48.0	−43.0	−41.0	−45.0	Compte de capital : débit
Financial Account,nie	−14 742.0	−7 618.0	−11 459.0	−11 678.0	−15 370.0	−19 062.0	−16 469.0	Compte d'op. fin., nia
Net Errors and Omissions	3 470.0	995.0	5 686.0	2 325.0	5 596.0	1 654.0	−876.0	Erreurs et omissions nettes
Reserves and Related Items	2 426.0	−1 419.0	−1 168.0	−973.0	−4 418.0	−399.0	−1 105.0	Rés. et postes appareutés
Ukraine								**Ukraine**
Goods: Exports fob	...	...	...	...	...	...	13 894.0	Biens : exportations,fàb
Goods: Imports fob	...	...	...	...	...	...	−16 469.0	Biens : importations,fàb
Serv. & Income: Credit	...	...	...	...	...	...	2 803.0	Serv. & revenu : crédit
Serv. & Income: Debit	...	...	...	...	...	...	−1 938.0	Serv. & revenu : débit
Current Trans.,nie: Credit	...	...	...	...	...	...	583.0	Transf. cour.,nia : crédit
Current Transfers: Debit	...	...	...	...	...	...	−36.0	Transf. courants : débit
Capital Acct.,nie: Credit	...	...	...	...	...	...	106.0	Compte de cap.,nia : crédit
Capital Account: Debit	...	...	...	...	...	...	−9.0	Compte de capital : débit
Financial Account,nie	...	...	...	...	...	...	−557.0	Compte d'op. fin., nia
Net Errors and Omissions	...	...	...	...	...	...	423.5	Erreurs et omissions nettes
Reserves and Related Items	...	...	...	...	...	...	1 199.5	Rés. et postes appareutés
United Kingdom								**Royaume−Uni**
Goods: Exports fob	143 078.0	150 696.0	181 729.0	182 579.0	188 451.0	182 081.0	206 456.0	Biens : exportations,fàb
Goods: Imports fob	−181 237.0	−191 239.0	−214 471.0	−200 853.0	−211 879.0	−202 198.0	−222 943.0	Biens : importations,fàb
Serv. & Income: Credit	148 414.0	168 929.0	197 527.0	190 235.0	182 415.0	166 994.0	180 462.0	Serv. & revenu : crédit
Serv. & Income: Debit	−133 242.0	−157 591.0	−189 513.0	−184 769.0	−167 057.0	−155 660.0	−158 887.0	Serv. & revenu : débit
Current Trans.,nie: Credit	6 817.0	6 423.0	7 215.0	12 056.0	8 557.0	8 068.0	8 350.0	Transf. cour.,nia : crédit
Current Transfers: Debit	−13 154.0	−13 879.0	−15 956.0	−14 518.0	−17 663.0	−15 920.0	−16 458.0	Transf. courants : débit
Capital Acct.,nie: Credit	0.0	0.0	0.0	0.0	0.0	0.0	0.0	Compte de cap.,nia : crédit
Capital Account: Debit	0.0	0.0	0.0	0.0	0.0	0.0	0.0	Compte de capital : débit
Financial Account,nie	17 834.0	17 448.0	29 957.0	29 133.0	1 046.0	13 901.0	−22 557.0	Compte d'op. fin., nia

79
Summary of balance of payments
Millions of US dollars
Résumé des balances des paiements
Millions de dollars des E−U

Country or area	1988	1989	1990	1991	1992	1993	1994	Pays ou zone
Net Errors and Omissions	9 996.0	3 617.0	977.0	−269.0	8 507.0	−3 646.0	6 401.0	Erreurs et omissions nettes
Reserves and Related Items	1 495.0	15 597.0	2 535.0	−13 594.0	7 621.0	6 381.0	19 178.0	Rés. et postes appareutés
			Oceania· Océanie					
Australia								**Australie**
Goods: Exports fob	33 413.0	37 160.0	39 642.0	42 362.0	42 813.0	42 637.0	47 331.0	Biens : exportations,fàb
Goods: Imports fob	−34 090.0	−40 511.0	−39 284.0	−38 833.0	−41 173.0	−42 666.0	−50 611.0	Biens : importations,fàb
Serv. & Income: Credit	11 577.0	12 614.0	13 570.0	14 230.0	14 712.0	15 679.0	18 189.0	Serv. & revenu : crédit
Serv. & Income: Debit	−22 366.0	−28 230.0	−30 459.0	−29 083.0	−27 788.0	−25 950.0	−31 926.0	Serv. & revenu : débit
Current Trans.,nie: Credit	1 204.0	1 366.0	1 749.0	1 401.0	1 221.0	1 103.0	1 180.0	Transf. cour.,nia : crédit
Current Transfers: Debit	−1 125.0	−1 171.0	−1 305.0	−1 496.0	−1 326.0	−1 313.0	−1 529.0	Transf. courants : débit
Capital Acct.,nie: Credit	1 790.0	2 213.0	2 077.0	2 212.0	1 657.0	842.0	976.0	Compte de cap.,nia : crédit
Capital Account: Debit	−429.0	−493.0	−517.0	−530.0	−521.0	−502.0	−592.0	Compte de capital : débit
Financial Account,nie	19 365.0	16 670.0	13 401.0	11 364.0	7 849.0	10 509.0	15 976.0	Compte d'op. fin., nia
Net Errors and Omissions	−4 088.0	1 009.0	2 853.0	−1 942.0	−2 180.0	−394.0	51.0	Erreurs et omissions nettes
Reserves and Related Items	−5 251.0	−628.0	−1 727.0	316.0	4 737.0	55.0	955.0	Rés. et postes appareutés
Fiji								**Fidji**
Goods: Exports fob	373.6	439.5	494.7	446.3	438.2	443.6	...	Biens : exportations,fàb
Goods: Imports fob	−389.9	−487.9	−644.6	−549.5	−539.5	−653.5	...	Biens : importations,fàb
Serv. & Income: Credit	291.2	392.0	442.3	474.1	495.0	557.3	...	Serv. & revenu : crédit
Serv. & Income: Debit	−244.8	−301.5	−320.7	−354.5	−371.5	−376.5	...	Serv. & revenu : débit
Current Trans.,nie: Credit	53.5	55.3	41.5	63.9	63.0	70.7	...	Transf. cour.,nia : crédit
Current Transfers: Debit	−12.9	−22.3	−23.0	−27.9	−25.7	−28.6	...	Transf. courants : débit
Capital Acct.,nie: Credit	0.1	0.1	0.6	0.1	0.1	0.2	...	Compte de cap.,nia : crédit
Capital Account: Debit	−12.2	−21.1	−24.6	−30.7	−27.7	−26.3	...	Compte de capital : débit
Financial Account,nie	46.3	−72.4	48.6	2.4	36.8	5.9	...	Compte d'op. fin., nia
Net Errors and Omissions	7.3	4.8	21.1	−14.6	−15.2	−35.0	...	Erreurs et omissions nettes
Reserves and Related Items	−112.1	13.5	−35.8	−9.6	−53.4	42.1	...	Rés. et postes appareutés
Kiribati								**Kiribati**
Goods: Exports fob	5.3	5.2	4.5	3.3	...	...	...	Biens : exportations,fàb
Goods: Imports fob	−22.0	−22.6	−26.9	−25.9	...	...	...	Biens : importations,fàb
Serv. & Income: Credit	20.7	21.7	22.6	24.2	...	...	...	Serv. & revenu : crédit
Serv. & Income: Debit	−15.4	−15.4	−16.7	−16.3	...	...	...	Serv. & revenu : débit
Current Trans.,nie: Credit	18.4	18.6	24.7	29.1	...	...	...	Transf. cour.,nia : crédit
Current Transfers: Debit	−2.0	−1.9	−2.0	−2.3	...	...	...	Transf. courants : débit
Capital Acct.,nie: Credit	0.0	0.0	0.0	0.0	...	...	...	Compte de cap.,nia : crédit
Capital Account: Debit	0.0	0.0	0.0	0.0	...	...	...	Compte de capital : débit
Financial Account,nie	−2.1	−3.9	−3.7	−1.2	...	...	...	Compte d'op. fin., nia
Net Errors and Omissions	−0.1	5.0	4.9	−0.9	...	...	...	Erreurs et omissions nettes
Reserves and Related Items	−2.7	−6.6	−7.4	−10.0	...	...	...	Rés. et postes appareutés
New Zealand								**Nouvelle−Zélande**
Goods: Exports fob	8 831.0	8 846.0	9 190.0	9 555.0	9 735.0	10 468.0	11 984.0	Biens : exportations,fàb
Goods: Imports fob	−6 658.0	−7 873.0	−8 375.0	−7 485.0	−8 108.0	−8 749.0	−10 648.0	Biens : importations,fàb
Serv. & Income: Credit	3 000.0	2 803.0	2 998.0	2 613.0	2 519.0	3 128.0	4 149.0	Serv. & revenu : crédit
Serv. & Income: Debit	−7 186.0	−6 851.0	−7 087.0	−6 296.0	−5 644.0	−6 049.0	−7 956.0	Serv. & revenu : débit
Current Trans.,nie: Credit	309.0	314.0	317.0	321.0	310.0	310.0	334.0	Transf. cour.,nia : crédit
Current Transfers: Debit	−159.0	−156.0	−179.0	−182.0	−182.0	−178.0	−233.0	Transf. courants : débit
Capital Acct.,nie: Credit	228.0	331.0	507.0	586.0	602.0	833.0	1 155.0	Compte de cap.,nia : crédit
Capital Account: Debit	−277.0	−284.0	−294.0	−334.0	−311.0	−291.0	−349.0	Compte de capital : débit
Financial Account,nie	−2 824.0	−264.0	1 664.0	−695.0	122.0	1 644.0	−1 378.0	Compte d'op. fin., nia
Net Errors and Omissions	1 816.0	1 916.0	1 439.0	405.0	−522.0	−2 889.0	1 723.0	Erreurs et omissions nettes
Reserves and Related Items	2 921.0	1 217.0	−179.0	1 511.0	1 477.0	1 773.0	1 220.0	Rés. et postes appareutés
Papua New Guinea								**Papouasie−Nvl−Guinée**
Goods: Exports fob	1 475.3	1 318.5	1 175.2	1 482.1	1 947.7	2 604.4	2 651.0	Biens : exportations,fàb
Goods: Imports fob	−1 384.5	−1 341.3	−1 105.9	−1 403.9	−1 322.9	−1 134.7	−1 324.9	Biens : importations,fàb
Serv. & Income: Credit	240.9	254.9	312.3	373.9	388.9	340.3	257.8	Serv. & revenu : crédit
Serv. & Income: Debit	−761.3	−674.0	−612.8	−863.4	−1 111.1	−1 206.9	−1 031.1	Serv. & revenu : débit
Current Trans.,nie: Credit	249.4	256.3	273.7	361.0	303.6	220.8	225.7	Transf. cour.,nia : crédit
Current Transfers: Debit	−116.2	−127.2	−118.1	−106.2	−111.1	−178.0	−209.3	Transf. courants : débit
Capital Acct.,nie: Credit	10.0	7.2	5.4	21.0	20.7	20.4	19.9	Compte de cap.,nia : crédit
Capital Account: Debit	−50.1	−49.8	−42.7	−21.0	−20.7	−20.4	−19.9	Compte de capital : débit
Financial Account,nie	245.1	265.0	214.4	64.5	−148.3	−715.4	−600.1	Compte d'op. fin., nia
Net Errors and Omissions	37.9	31.6	−79.7	6.8	−18.0	−12.2	28.3	Erreurs et omissions nettes
Reserves and Related Items	53.5	58.7	−21.7	85.2	71.2	81.6	2.5	Rés. et postes appareutés
Samoa								**Samoa**
Goods: Exports fob	15.09	12.87	8.85	6.48	5.82	6.43	...	Biens : exportations,fàb
Goods: Imports fob	−66.57	−66.99	−70.00	−77.62	−89.90	−87.37	...	Biens : importations,fàb

79
Summary of balance of payments
Millions of US dollars
Résumé des balances des paiements
Millions de dollars des E−U

Country or area	1988	1989	1990	1991	1992	1993	1994	Pays ou zone
Serv. & Income: Credit	29.78	35.38	42.26	37.96	42.80	40.11	...	Serv. & revenu : crédit
Serv. & Income: Debit	−20.37	−21.19	−26.25	−37.03	−45.98	−42.64	...	Serv. & revenu : débit
Current Trans.,nie: Credit	52.95	56.29	56.54	44.66	39.07	49.91	...	Transf. cour.,nia : crédit
Current Transfers: Debit	−2.93	−3.54	−4.15	−3.09	−4.32	−5.11	...	Transf. courants : débit
Capital Acct.,nie: Credit	...	...	...	...	...	...	...	Compte de cap.,nia : crédit
Capital Account: Debit	...	...	...	...	...	...	...	Compte de capital : débit
Financial Account,nie	0.49	0.48	9.40	18.60	19.95	15.55	...	Compte d'op. fin., nia
Net Errors and Omissions	1.67	−2.61	−5.66	7.97	19.82	13.82	...	Erreurs et omissions nettes
Reserves and Related Items	−10.10	−10.68	−11.00	2.08	12.72	9.31	...	Rés. et postes appareutés
Solomon Islands								**Iles Salomon**
Goods: Exports fob	81.9	74.7	70.1	83.4	101.7	...	...	Biens : exportations,fàb
Goods: Imports fob	−104.6	−94.3	−77.3	−92.0	−87.4	...	...	Biens : importations,fàb
Serv. & Income: Credit	25.5	30.4	27.7	33.0	37.0	...	...	Serv. & revenu : crédit
Serv. & Income: Debit	−78.3	−87.0	−86.3	−98.7	−88.9	...	...	Serv. & revenu : débit
Current Trans.,nie: Credit	42.9	47.1	43.7	46.8	43.8	...	...	Transf. cour.,nia : crédit
Current Transfers: Debit	−5.1	−4.1	−5.6	−8.4	−7.6	...	...	Transf. courants : débit
Capital Acct.,nie: Credit	0.0	0.0	0.0	0.0	0.0	...	...	Compte de cap.,nia : crédit
Capital Account: Debit	−0.4	−0.2	−0.2	−0.3	−0.4	...	...	Compte de capital : débit
Financial Account,nie	43.8	25.1	22.9	15.1	22.4		...	Compte d'op. fin., nia
Net Errors and Omissions	−10.9	−5.2	−8.6	8.4	−6.2	...	...	Erreurs et omissions nettes
Reserves and Related Items	5.1	13.5	13.7	12.6	−14.4	...	...	Rés. et postes appareutés
Tonga								**Tonga**
Goods: Exports fob	8.7	9.4	11.9	13.4	12.3	16.1	...	Biens : exportations,fàb
Goods: Imports fob	−48.6	−49.7	−50.8	−49.5	−51.3	−56.6	...	Biens : importations,fàb
Serv. & Income: Credit	22.1	31.0	31.5	23.9	20.9	21.5	...	Serv. & revenu : crédit
Serv. & Income: Debit	−27.0	−22.2	−24.2	−23.5	−23.5	−23.5	...	Serv. & revenu : débit
Current Trans.,nie: Credit	36.9	44.1	43.5	41.8	50.6	49.7	...	Transf. cour.,nia : crédit
Current Transfers: Debit	−4.9	−5.1	−6.2	−6.3	−9.4	−13.1	...	Transf. courants : débit
Capital Acct.,nie: Credit	0.1	0.1	0.2	0.5	0.7	1.3	...	Compte de cap.,nia : crédit
Capital Account: Debit	−0.1	−0.4	−0.4	−0.4	−0.2	−0.7	...	Compte de capital : débit
Financial Account,nie	4.4	−8.2	−1.7	3.0	4.4	3.2	...	Compte d'op. fin., nia
Net Errors and Omissions	10.0	−4.6	2.4	−2.1	−3.4	−0.3	...	Erreurs et omissions nettes
Reserves and Related Items	−1.7	5.6	−6.4	−0.9	−1.1	2.4	...	Rés. et postes appareutés
Vanuatu								**Vanuatu**
Goods: Exports fob	15.4	13.7	13.7	14.9	17.8	17.4	20.7	Biens : exportations,fàb
Goods: Imports fob	−57.9	−57.9	−79.3	−74.0	−66.8	−64.7	−83.5	Biens : importations,fàb
Serv. & Income: Credit	63.4	63.7	92.1	91.0	87.5	87.2	92.4	Serv. & revenu : crédit
Serv. & Income: Debit	−58.8	−48.3	−57.2	−76.1	−74.3	−75.2	−85.4	Serv. & revenu : débit
Current Trans.,nie: Credit	26.3	20.4	25.0	31.1	23.3	23.4	28.2	Transf. cour.,nia : crédit
Current Transfers: Debit	−3.5	−3.9	−0.5	−0.5	−0.6	−0.6	−0.7	Transf. courants : débit
Capital Acct.,nie: Credit	18.0	8.9	16.5	19.3	26.6	25.9	30.2	Compte de cap.,nia : crédit
Capital Account: Debit	−0.1	−0.1	0.0	−0.2	−9.4	−5.7	−4.2	Compte de capital : débit
Financial Account,nie	9.9	24.2	13.8	−27.8	23.7	16.1	−10.2	Compte d'op. fin., nia
Net Errors and Omissions	−17.3	−13.0	−19.4	19.3	−27.1	−20.4	6.3	Erreurs et omissions nettes
Reserves and Related Items	4.7	−7.8	−4.7	3.1	−0.8	−3.5	6.1	Rés. et postes appareutés

Source:
International Monetary Fund (Washington, DC).

† For detailed descriptions of data pertaining to
former Czechoslovakia, Germany, SFR Yugoslavia and former
USSR, see Annex I − Country or area nomenclature, regional
and other groupings.

1 Data cover the former Federal Republic of Germany and the
former German Democratic Republic beginning July 1990.

Sources:
Fonds montaire international (Washington, DC).

† Pour les descriptions en détails des données relatives à l'ancienne
Tchécoslovaquie, l'Allemagne, la Rfs Yougoslavie et l'ancienne
URSS, voir l'Annexe I − Nomenclature des pays ou zones,
groupements régionaux et autres groupements.

1 Les données se rapportent à l'ancienne Rép. Fédéral d'Allemagne
et à l'ancienne Rép. dém. Allemande à partir de juillet 1990.

Technical notes, table 79

A balance of payments can be broadly described as the record of an economy's international economic transactions. It shows (a) transactions in goods, services and income between an economy and the rest of the world, (b) changes of ownership and other changes in that economy's monetary gold, special drawing rights (SDRs) and claims on and liabilities to the rest of the world, and (c) unrequited transfers and counterpart entries needed to balance in the accounting sense any entries for the foregoing transactions and changes which are not mutually offsetting.

The balance of payments are presented on the basis of the methodology and presentation of the fifth edition of the *Balance of Payments Manual* (BPM5)[38], published by the International Monetary Fund in September 1993. The BPM5 incorporates several major changes to take account of developments in international trade and finance over the past decade, and to better harmonize the Fund's balance of payments methodology with the methodology of the 1993 *System of National Accounts* (SNA).[54] The Fund's balance of payments has been converted for all periods from the BPM4 basis to the BPM5 basis; thus the time series conform to the BPM5 methodology with no methodological breaks.

The detailed definitions concerning the content of the basic categories of the balance of payments are given in the *Balance of Payments Manual (fiftieth edition)* [38] Brief explanatory notes are given below to clarify the scope of the major items.

Goods: Exports f.o.b. and Goods: Imports f.o.b. are both measured on the "free-on-board" (f.o.b.) basis—that is, by the value of the goods at the border of the exporting country; in the case of imports, this excludes the cost of freight and insurance incurred beyond the border of the exporting country.

Services and income covers transactions in real resources between residents and non-residents other than those classified as merchandise, including (a) shipment and other transportation services, including freight, insurance and other distributive services in connection with the movement of commodities, (b) travel, i.e. goods and services acquired by non-resident travellers in a given country and similar acquisitions by resident travellers abroad, and (c) investment income which covers income of non-residents from their financial assets invested in the compiling economy (debit) and similar income of residents from their financial assets invested abroad (credit).

Notes techniques, tableau 79

La balance des paiements peut se définir d'une façon générale comme le relevé des transactions économiques internationales d'une économie. Elle indique (a) les transactions sur biens, services et revenus entre une économie et le reste du monde, (b) les transferts de propriété et autres variations intervenues dans les avoirs en or monétaire de cette économie, dans ses avoirs en droits de tirages spéciaux (DTS) ainsi que dans ses créances financièes sur le reste du monde ou dans ses engagements financiers envers lui et (c) les "inscriptions de transferts sans contrepartie" et de "contrepartie" destinées à équilibrer, d'un point de vue comptable, les transactions et changements précités qui ne se compensent pas réciproquement.

Les données de balance des paiements sont présentées conformément à la méthodologie et à la classification recommandées dans la cinquième édition du *Manuel de la balance des paiements* [38], publiée en septembre 1993 par le Fonds monétaire international. La cinquième édition fait état de plusieurs changements importants qui ont été opérés de manière à rendre compte de l'évolution des finances et des changes internationaux pendant la décennie écoulée et à harmoniser davantage la méthodologie de la balance des paiements du FMI avec celle du *Système de comptabilité nationale* (SCN) [54] de 1993. Les statistiques incluses dans la balance des paiements du FMI, ont été converties et sont désormais établies, pour toutes les périodes, sur la base de la cinquième et non plus de la quatrième édition; en conséquence, les séries chronologiques sont conformes aux principes de la cinquième édition, sans rupture due à des différences d'ordre méthodologique.

Les définitions détaillées relatives au contenu des postes fondamentaux de la balance des paiements figurent dans le *Manuel de la balance des paiements (Cinquième édition)* [38]. De brèves notes explicatives sont présentées ci-après pour clarifier la portée de ces principales rubriques.

Les Biens : exportations, f.à.b. et Biens : importations, f.à.b. sont évalués sur la base f.à.b. (franco à bord)—c'est-à-dire à la frontière du pays exportateur; dans le cas des importations, cette valeur exclut le coût du fret et de l'assurance au-delà de la frontière du pays exportateur.

Services et revenus : transactions en ressources effectuées entre résidents et non résidents, autres que celles qui sont considérées comme des marchandises, notamment : (a) expéditions et autres services de transport, y compris le fret, l'assurance et les autres services de distribution liés aux mouvements de marchandises; (b) voyages, à savoir les biens et services acquis par des voyageurs non résidents dans un

Current Transfers, n.i.e.: Credit comprise all current transfers received by the reporting country, except those made to the country to finance its "overall balance", hence, the label "n.i.e." (Note: some of the capital and financial accounts labeled "n.i.e." denote that *Exceptional Financing items* and *Liabilities Constituting Foreign Authorities' Reserves* (LCFARs) have been excluded.)

Capital Account, n.i.e.: Credit refers mainly to capital transfers linked to the acquisition of a fixed aset other than transactions relating to debt forgiveness plus the disposal of nonproduced, nonfinancial assets. *Capital Account: Debit* refers mainly to capital transfers linked to the disposal of fixed asets by the donor or to the financing of capital formation by the recipient, plus the acquisition of nonproduced, nonfinancial assets.

Financial Account, n.i.e. is the net sum of the balance of direct investment, portfolio investment, and other investment transactions.

Net Errors and Omissions is a residual category needed to ensure that all debit and credit entries in the balance of payments statement sum to zero and reflects statistical inconsistencies in the recording of the credit and debit entries.

Reserves and Related Items is the sum of transactions in reserve assets, LCFARs, exceptional financing, and use of Fund credit and loans.

pays donné et achats similaires faits par des résidents voyageant à l'étranger; et (c) revenus des investissements, qui correspondent aux revenus que les non-résidents tirent de leurs avoirs financiers placés dans l'économie déclarante (débit) et les revenus similaires que les résidents tirent de leurs avoirs financiers placés à l'étranger (crédit).

Les transfers courants, n.i.a : Crédit englobent tous les transferts courants reçus par l'économie qui établit sa balance des paiements, à l'exception de ceux qui sont destinés à financer sa "balance globale"—c'est ce qui explique la mention "n.i.a." (non inclus ailleurs). (Note : comptes de capital et d'opérations financières portent la mention "n.i.a.", ce qui signifie que les postes de *Financement exceptionnel* et les *Engagements constituant des réserves pour les autorités étrangères* ont été exclus de ces composantes du compte de capital et d'opérations financières.

Le Compte de capital, n.i.a : crédit retrace principalement les transferts de capital liés à l'acquisition d'un actif fixe autres que les transactions ayant trait à des remises de dettes plus les cessions d'actifs non financiers non produits. Le *Compte de capital : débit* retrace principalement les transferts de capital liés à la cession d'actifs fixes par le donateur ou au financement de la formation de capital par le bénéficiaire, plus les acquisitions d'actifs non financiers non produits.

Le solde du *Compte d'op. Fin., n.i.a.* (compte d'opérations financières, n.i.a.) est la somme des soldes des investissements directs, des investissements de portefeuille et des autres investissements.

Le poste des *Erreurs et omissions* nettes est une catégorie résiduelle qui est nécessaire pour assurer que la somme de toutes les inscriptions effectuées au débit et au crédit est égal à zéro et qui laisse apparaître les écarts entre les montants portés au débit et ceux qui sont inscrits au crédit.

Le montant de *Réserves et postes apparentés* est égal à la somme de transactions afférentes aux avoirs de réserve, aux engagements constituant des réserves pour les autorités étrangères, au financement exceptionnel et à l'utilisation des crédits et des prêts du FMI.

80
Exchange rates
Cours des changes
National currency per US dollar
Valeur du dollar des Etats-Unis en monnaie nationale

Country (monetary unit) Pays (unité monétaire)	1986	1987	1988	1989	1990	1991	1992	1993	1994	1995
Afghanistan: afghani Afghanistan : afghani										
End of period										
Fin de période[1]	50.600	50.600	50.600	50.600	50.600	50.600	50.600	50.600	50.600	50.600
Period average[1]										
Moyenne sur période[1]	50.600	50.600	50.600	50.600	50.600	50.600	50.600	50.600	50.600	50.600
Albania: lek Albanie : lek										
End of period										
Fin de période	7.000	...	6.000	6.400	15.000	25.000	97.000	95.000	...	90.800
Period average										
Moyenne sur période	...	...	...	...	...	...	75.030	102.090	94.710	...
Algeria: Algerian dinar Algérie : dinar algérien										
End of period										
Fin de période	4.823	4.936	6.731	8.032	12.191	21.392	22.781	24.123	42.892	52.175
Period average										
Moyenne sur période	4.702	4.850	5.915	7.609	8.957	18.473	21.836	23.345	35.058	47.663
Angola: new kwanza Angola : nouveau kwanza										
End of period										
Fin de période	30.000	30.000	30.000	30.000	30.000	180.000	550.000	6 500.000	509 262.000	...
Period average										
Moyenne sur période	30.000	30.000	30.000	30.000	30.000	55.000	251.000	2 660.000	59 515.000	...
Antigua and Barbuda: EC dollar Antigua-et-Barbuda : dollar des Caraïbes orientales										
End of period										
Fin de période	2.700	2.700	2.700	2.700	2.700	2.700	2.700	2.700	2.700	2.700
Argentina: Argentine peso Argentine : peso argentin										
End of period										
Fin de période	0.126[2]	0.375[2]	1.337[2]	# 0.179	0.558	0.998	0.990	0.998	0.999	1.000
Period average										
Moyenne sur période	0.943[2]	0.214[2]	0.875[2]	# 0.042	0.488	0.954	0.991	0.999	0.999	1.000
Armenia: dram Arménie : dram										
Period average										
Moyenne sur période	...	...	...	...	...	...	...	8.250	287.480	405.870
Aruba: Aruban florin Aruba : florin de Aruba										
End of period										
Fin de période	1.790	1.790	1.790	1.790	1.790	1.790	1.790	1.790	1.790	1.790
Period average										
Moyenne sur période	1.790	1.790	1.790	1.790	1.790	1.790	1.790	1.790	1.790	1.790
Australia: Australian dollar Australie : dollar australien										
End of period										
Fin de période	1.504	1.384	1.169	1.262	1.293	1.316	1.452	1.477	1.287	1.342
Period average										
Moyenne sur période	1.496	1.428	1.280	1.265	1.281	1.284	1.362	1.471	1.368	1.349
Austria: Austrian schilling Autriche : schilling autrichien										
End of period										
Fin de période	13.710	11.250	12.565	11.815	10.677	10.689	11.354	12.143	11.095	10.088
Period average										
Moyenne sur période	15.267	12.642	12.348	13.231	11.370	11.676	10.989	11.632	11.422	10.081
Bahamas: Bahamian dollar Bahamas : dollar des Bahamas										
End of period[1]										
Fin de période[1]	1.000	1.000	1.000	1.000	1.000	1.000	1.000	1.000	1.000	1.000
Bahrain: Bahrain dinar Bahreïn : dinar de Bahreïn										
End of period										
Fin de période	0.376	0.376	0.376	0.376	0.376	0.376	0.376	0.376	0.376	0.376
Period average										
Moyenne sur période	0.376	0.376	0.376	0.376	0.376	0.376	0.376	0.376	0.376	0.376

80
Exchange rates
National currency per US dollar [*cont.*]
Cours des changes
Valeur du dollar des Etats-Unis en monnaie nationale [*suite*]

Country (monetary unit) Pays (unité monétaire)	1986	1987	1988	1989	1990	1991	1992	1993	1994	1995
Bangladesh: taka Bangladesh : taka										
End of period										
Fin de période	30.800	31.200	32.270	32.270	35.790	38.580	39.000	39.850	40.250	40.750
Period average										
Moyenne sur période	30.407	30.950	31.733	32.270	34.569	36.596	38.951	39.567	40.212	40.278
Barbados: Barbados dollar Barbade : dollar de la Barbade										
End of period										
Fin de période	2.011	2.011	2.011	2.011	2.011	2.011	2.011	2.011	2.011	2.011
Belarus: Belarussian rouble Bélarus : rouble bélarussien										
End of period										
Fin de période	...	...	...	...	...	...	...	5 710.000	...	11 500.000
Belgium: Belgian franc Belgique : franc belge										
End of period										
Fin de période	40.410	33.153	37.345	35.760	30.982	31.270	33.180	36.110	31.837	29.415
Period average										
Moyenne sur période	44.672	37.334	36.768	39.404	33.418	34.148	32.149	34.596	33.456	29.480
Belize: Belize dollar Belize : dollar du Belize										
End of period										
Fin de période	2.000	2.000	2.000	2.000	2.000	2.000	2.000	2.000	2.000	2.000
Benin: CFA franc Bénin : franc CFA										
End of period[3]										
Fin de période[3]	322.750	267.000	302.950	289.400	256.450	259.000	275.320	294.770	# 534.600	490.000
Period average[3]										
Moyenne sur période[3]	346.310	300.540	297.850	319.010	272.260	282.110	264.690	283.160	# 555.200	499.150
Bhutan: ngultrum Bhoutan : ngultrum										
End of period										
Fin de période	13.122	12.877	14.949	17.035	18.073	25.834	26.200	31.380	31.380	35.180
Period average										
Moyenne sur période	12.611	12.961	13.917	16.225	17.505	22.742	25.918	30.493	31.374	32.427
Bolivia: boliviano Bolivie : boliviano										
End of period										
Fin de période	1.923	2.210	2.470	2.980	3.400	3.745	4.095	4.475	4.695	4.935
Period average										
Moyenne sur période	1.922	2.055	2.350	2.692	3.173	3.581	3.900	4.265	4.620	4.800
Botswana: pula Botswana : pula										
End of period										
Fin de période	1.838	1.566	1.936	1.872	1.871	2.072	2.257	2.565	2.717	2.822
Period average										
Moyenne sur période	1.879	1.679	1.829	2.015	1.860	2.022	2.110	2.423	2.685	2.772
Brazil: real Brésil : real[1 4]										
End of period[1 4]										
Fin de période[1 4]	5.420	26.270	278.290	# 4.130	64.385	# 0.190	2.202	# 0.049	# 0.846	0.973
Period average[1 4]										
Moyenne sur période[1 4]	4.960	14.260	95.270	# 1.031	24.836	# 0.148	1.641	# 0.032	# 0.639	# 0.918
Brunei Darussalam: Brunei dollar Brunéi Darussalam : dollar du Brunéi										
End of period										
Fin de période	2.190	2.005	1.925	1.925	1.742	1.630	...	...	...	...
Period average										
Moyenne sur période	2.220	2.107	2.013	1.951	1.813	1.730	...	...	...	...
Bulgaria: lev Bulgarie : lev										
End of period										
Fin de période	1.230	1.310	1.700	2.140	2.800	18.300	23.800	31.000	...	67.600
Period average										
Moyenne sur période	0.940	0.870	0.830	0.840	2.190	17.790	23.340	27.590	54.130	...

80
Exchange rates
National currency per US dollar [*cont.*]
Cours des changes
Valeur du dollar des Etats-Unis en monnaie nationale [*suite*]

Country (monetary unit) Pays (unité monétaire)	1986	1987	1988	1989	1990	1991	1992	1993	1994	1995
Burkina Faso: CFA franc Burkina Faso : franc CFA										
End of period[3]										
Fin de période[3]	322.750	267.000	302.950	289.400	256.450	259.000	275.320	294.770	# 534.600	490.000
Period average[3]										
Moyenne sur période[3]	346.310	300.540	297.850	319.010	272.260	282.110	264.690	283.160	# 555.200	499.150
Burundi: Burundi franc Burundi : franc burundais										
End of period										
Fin de période	124.165	114.470	149.940	175.430	165.350	191.100	236.550	264.380	246.940	277.920
Period average										
Moyenne sur période	114.171	123.564	140.395	158.667	171.255	181.513	208.303	242.780	252.662	249.760
Cambodia: riel Cambodge : riel										
End of period										
Fin de période	...	...	...	216.000	600.000	520.000	2 000.000	2 305.000	2 575.000	2 526.000
Period average										
Moyenne sur période	...	...	...	...	...	...	1 266.600	2 689.000	2 545.200	2 450.800
Cameroon: CFA franc Cameroun : franc CFA										
End of period[3]										
Fin de période[3]	322.750	267.000	302.950	289.400	256.450	259.000	275.320	294.770	# 534.600	490.000
Period average[3]										
Moyenne sur période[3]	346.310	300.540	297.850	319.010	272.260	282.110	264.690	283.160	# 555.200	499.150
Canada: Canadian dollar Canada : dollar canadien										
End of period										
Fin de période	1.380	1.300	1.193	1.158	1.160	1.156	1.271	1.324	1.403	1.365
Period average										
Moyenne sur période	1.389	1.326	1.231	1.184	1.167	1.146	1.209	1.290	1.366	1.372
Cape Verde: Cape Verde escudo Cap-Vert : escudo du Cap-Vert										
End of period										
Fin de période	76.565	65.775	73.665	73.045	66.085	66.470	73.089	85.992	81.140	77.455
Period average										
Moyenne sur période	80.145	72.466	72.067	77.978	70.031	71.408	68.018	80.427	81.891	76.853
Central African Rep.: CFA franc Rép. centrafricaine : franc CFA										
End of period[3]										
Fin de période[3]	322.750	267.000	302.950	289.400	256.450	259.000	275.320	294.770	# 534.600	490.000
Period average[3]										
Moyenne sur période[3]	346.310	300.540	297.850	319.010	272.260	282.110	264.690	283.160	# 555.200	499.150
Chad: CFA franc Tchad : franc CFA										
End of period[3]										
Fin de période[3]	322.750	267.000	302.950	289.400	256.450	259.000	275.320	294.770	# 534.600	490.000
Period average[3]										
Moyenne sur période[3]	346.310	300.540	297.850	319.010	272.260	282.110	264.690	283.160	# 555.200	499.150
Chile: Chilean peso Chili : peso chilien										
End of period[1]										
Fin de période[1]	204.730	238.140	247.200	297.370	337.090	374.510	382.120	428.470	402.920	406.910
Period average[1]										
Moyenne sur période[1]	193.016	219.540	245.047	267.155	305.062	349.372	362.588	404.349	420.077	396.783
China: yuan renminbi Chine : yuan renminbi										
End of period										
Fin de période	3.722	3.722	3.722	4.722	5.222	5.434	5.752	5.800	8.446	8.317
Period average										
Moyenne sur période	3.453	3.722	3.722	3.765	4.783	5.323	5.515	5.762	8.619	8.351
Colombia: Colombian peso Colombie : peso colombien										
End of period[1]										
Fin de période[1]	219.000	263.700	335.860	433.920	568.730	706.860	811.770	917.330	831.270	987.650
Period average[1]										
Moyenne sur période[1]	194.261	242.607	299.174	382.568	502.259	633.045	759.282	863.065	844.836	912.826

80
Exchange rates
National currency per US dollar [*cont.*]
Cours des changes
Valeur du dollar des Etats-Unis en monnaie nationale [*suite*]

Country (monetary unit) Pays (unité monétaire)	1986	1987	1988	1989	1990	1991	1992	1993	1994	1995
Comoros: Comorian franc Comores : franc comorien										
End of period[5]										
Fin de période[5]	322.749	266.999	302.949	289.399	256.449	258.999	275.324	294.774	# 400.950	367.500
Period average[5]										
Moyenne sur période[5]	346.307	300.537	297.849	319.009	272.265	282.108	264.692	283.163	# 416.403	374.361
Congo: CFA franc Congo : franc CFA										
End of period[3]										
Fin de période[3]	322.750	267.000	302.950	289.400	256.450	259.000	275.320	294.770	# 534.600	490.000
Period average[3]										
Moyenne sur période[3]	346.310	300.540	297.850	319.010	272.260	282.110	264.690	283.160	# 555.200	499.150
Costa Rica: Costa Rican colón Costa Rica : colón costa-ricien										
End of period										
Fin de période	58.875	69.250	79.500	84.350	103.550	135.425	137.430	151.440	165.070	194.900
Period average										
Moyenne sur période	55.986	62.776	75.805	81.504	91.579	122.432	134.506	142.172	157.067	179.729
Côte d'Ivoire: CFA franc Côte d'Ivoire : franc CFA										
End of period[3]										
Fin de période[3]	322.750	267.000	302.950	289.400	256.450	259.000	275.320	294.770	# 534.600	490.000
Period average[3]										
Moyenne sur période[3]	346.310	300.540	297.850	319.010	272.260	282.110	264.690	283.160	# 555.200	499.150
Croatia: kuna Croatie : kuna										
End of period										
Fin de période	...	...	...	...	...	...	0.798	6.562	5.629	5.316
Period average										
Moyenne sur période	...	...	...	...	...	...	...	3.577	5.996	5.230
Cuba: Cuban peso Cuba : peso cubain										
End of period										
Fin de période	0.793	0.773	0.776	0.791	0.700	0.700	0.700	0.700	...	1.000
Cyprus: Cyprus pound Chypre : livre chypriote										
End of period										
Fin de période	0.512	0.439	0.466	0.479	0.435	0.439	0.483	0.520	0.476	0.457
Period average										
Moyenne sur période	0.518	0.481	0.467	0.495	0.458	0.464	0.450	0.497	0.492	0.452
former Czechoslovakia†: koruna anc. Tchécoslovaquie† : couronne										
End of period										
Fin de période	9.710	9.400	9.400	10.000	23.600	28.900	27.300	...	...	...
Czech Republic: Czech koruna République tchèque : couronne tchèque										
End of period										
Fin de période	...	...	...	...	...	...	...	29.955	28.049	26.602
Period average										
Moyenne sur période	...	...	...	...	...	...	...	29.153	28.785	26.541
Denmark: Danish krone Danemark : couronne danoise										
End of period										
Fin de période	7.342	6.096	6.874	6.607	5.776	5.913	6.255	6.772	6.083	5.546
Period average										
Moyenne sur période	8.091	6.840	6.731	7.310	6.189	6.396	6.036	6.484	6.361	5.602
Djibouti: Djibouti franc Djibouti : franc de Djibouti										
End of period										
Fin de période	177.721	177.721	177.721	177.721	177.721	177.721	177.721	177.721	177.721	177.721
Dominica: EC dollar Dominique : dollar des Caraïbes orientales										
End of period										
Fin de période	2.700	2.700	2.700	2.700	2.700	2.700	2.700	2.700	2.700	2.700
Dominican Republic: Dominican peso Rép. dominicaine : peso dominicain										
End of period										
Fin de période	3.077	4.960	6.340	6.340	11.350	12.660	12.575	12.767	13.064	13.465

80
Exchange rates
National currency per US dollar [*cont.*]
Cours des changes
Valeur du dollar des Etats-Unis en monnaie nationale [*suite*]

Country (monetary unit) Pays (unité monétaire)	1986	1987	1988	1989	1990	1991	1992	1993	1994	1995
Period average Moyenne sur période	2.904	3.845	6.112	6.340	8.525	12.692	12.774	12.676	13.160	13.597
Ecuador: sucre Equateur : sucre										
End of period[1] Fin de période[1]	146.500	221.500	432.510	648.420	878.200	1 270.580	1 844.250	2 043.780	2 269.000	2 923.500
Period average[1] Moyenne sur période[1]	122.780	170.460	301.610	526.350	767.750	1 046.250	1 533.960	1 919.100	2 196.730	2 564.490
Egypt: Egyptian pound Egypte : livre égyptienne										
End of period Fin de période	0.700	0.700	0.700	1.100	2.000	3.332	3.339	3.372	3.391	3.390
El Salvador: El Salvador colón El Salvador : cólon salvadorien										
End of period[1] Fin de période[1]	5.000	5.000	5.000	5.000	8.030	8.080	9.170	8.670	8.750	8.755
Equatorial Guinea: CFA franc Guinée équatoriale : franc CFA										
End of period[3] Fin de période[3]	322.750	267.000	302.950	289.400	256.450	259.000	275.320	294.770	# 534.600	490.000
Period average[3] Moyenne sur période[3]	346.310	300.540	297.850	319.010	272.260	282.110	264.690	283.160	# 555.200	499.150
Estonia: Estonian kroon Estonie : couronne estonienne										
End of period Fin de période	...	...	...	...	...	...	12.912	13.878	12.390	11.462
Period average Moyenne sur période	...	...	...	...	...	...	...	13.223	12.991	11.465
Ethiopia: Ethiopian birr Ethiopie : birr éthiopien										
End of period Fin de période	2.070	2.070	2.070	2.070	2.070	2.070	5.000	5.000	5.950	6.320
Fiji: Fiji dollar Fidji : dollar des Fidji										
End of period Fin de période	1.145	1.441	1.405	1.494	1.459	1.473	1.564	1.541	1.409	1.429
Period average Moyenne sur période	1.133	1.244	1.430	1.483	1.481	1.476	1.503	1.542	1.464	1.406
Finland: Finnish markka Finlande : markka finlandais										
End of period Fin de période	4.794	3.946	4.169	4.059	3.634	4.133	5.245	5.784	4.743	4.359
Period average Moyenne sur période	5.069	4.396	4.183	4.291	3.823	4.044	4.479	5.712	5.223	4.367
France: French franc France : franc français										
End of period Fin de période	6.455	5.340	6.059	5.788	5.129	5.180	5.506	5.895	5.346	4.900
Period average Moyenne sur période	6.926	6.011	5.957	6.380	5.445	5.642	5.294	5.663	5.552	4.991
Gabon: CFA franc Gabon : franc CFA										
End of period[3] Fin de période[3]	322.750	267.000	302.950	289.400	256.450	259.000	275.320	294.770	# 534.600	490.000
Period average[3] Moyenne sur période[3]	346.310	300.540	297.850	319.010	272.260	282.110	264.690	283.160	# 555.200	499.150
Gambia: dalasi Gambie : dalasi										
End of period Fin de période	7.426	6.439	6.659	8.315	7.495	8.957	9.217	9.535	9.579	9.640
Period average Moyenne sur période	6.938	7.074	6.709	7.585	7.883	8.803	8.887	9.129	9.576	9.546
Germany †: deutsche mark Allemagne† : deutsche mark										
End of period Fin de période	...	...	...	...	...	1.516	1.614	1.726	1.549	1.433
Period average Moyenne sur période	...	...	...	...	...	1.660	1.562	1.653	1.623	1.433

80
Exchange rates
National currency per US dollar [*cont.*]
Cours des changes
Valeur du dollar des Etats-Unis en monnaie nationale [*suite*]

Country (monetary unit) Pays (unité monétaire)	1986	1987	1988	1989	1990	1991	1992	1993	1994	1995
F. R. Germany: deutsche mark R. f. Allemagne : deutsche mark										
End of period[6]										
Fin de période[6]	1.941	1.581	1.780	1.698	1.494	...	...	...	...	...
Period average[6]										
Moyenne sur période[6]	2.171	1.797	1.756	1.880	1.616	...	...	...	...	...
Ghana: cedi Ghana : cedi										
End of period										
Fin de période	90.009	176.056	229.885	303.030	344.828	390.625	520.833	819.672	1 052.630	1 449.280
Period average										
Moyenne sur période	89.204	153.733	202.346	270.000	326.332	367.831	437.087	649.061	956.711	1 200.430
Greece: drachma Grèce : drachme										
End of period										
Fin de période	138.760	125.925	148.100	157.790	157.625	175.280	214.580	249.220	240.100	237.040
Period average										
Moyenne sur période	139.981	135.429	141.860	162.417	158.514	182.266	190.624	229.250	242.603	231.663
Grenada: EC dollar Grenade : dollar des Caraïbes orientales										
End of period										
Fin de période	2.700	2.700	2.700	2.700	2.700	2.700	2.700	2.700	2.700	2.700
Guatemala: quetzal Guatemala : quetzal										
End of period										
Fin de période	2.500	2.500	2.705	3.400	5.015	5.043	5.274	5.815	5.649	6.042
Period average										
Moyenne sur période	1.875	2.500	2.620	2.816	4.486	5.029	5.171	5.635	5.751	5.810
Guinea: Guinean franc Guinée : franc guinéen										
End of period										
Fin de période	235.630	440.000	550.000	620.000	680.000	802.950	922.410	972.414	981.024	997.984
Period average										
Moyenne sur période	333.452	428.402	474.396	591.646	660.167	753.858	902.001	955.490	976.636	991.411
Guinea-Bissau: Guinea-Bissau peso Guinée-Bissau : peso de Guinée-Bissau										
End of period										
Fin de période	238.650	851.320	1 362.760	1 987.200	2 508.620	4 959.150	8 655.560	11 464.000	15 369.000	21 929.000
Period average										
Moyenne sur période	203.630	559.010	1 109.710	1 810.140	2 185.460	3 658.610	6 933.910	10 082.000	12 892.000	18 073.000
Guyana: Guyana dollar Guyana : dollar guyanien										
End of period										
Fin de période	4.400	10.000	10.000	33.000	45.000	122.000	126.000	130.750	142.500	140.500
Period average										
Moyenne sur période	4.272	9.756	10.000	27.159	39.533	111.811	125.002	126.730	138.290	141.989
Haiti: gourde Haïti : gourde										
End of period										
Fin de période	4.999	4.999	4.999	4.999	4.999	# 8.240	10.953	12.805	12.947	16.160
Honduras: lempira Honduras : lempira										
End of period										
Fin de période	2.000	2.000	2.000	2.000	2.000	5.400	5.830	7.260	9.400	10.343
Hong Kong: Hong Kong dollar Hong-kong : dollar de Hong Kong										
End of period										
Fin de période	7.795	7.760	7.808	7.807	7.801	7.781	7.743	7.726	7.738	7.732
Period average										
Moyenne sur période	7.803	7.798	7.806	7.800	7.790	7.771	7.741	7.736	7.728	7.736
Hungary: forint Hongrie : forint										
End of period										
Fin de période	45.927	46.387	52.537	62.543	61.449	75.620	83.970	100.700	110.690	139.470
Period average										
Moyenne sur période	45.832	46.971	50.413	59.066	63.206	74.735	78.988	91.933	105.160	125.681

80
Exchange rates
National currency per US dollar [cont.]
Cours des changes
Valeur du dollar des Etats-Unis en monnaie nationale [suite]

Country (monetary unit) Pays (unité monétaire)	1986	1987	1988	1989	1990	1991	1992	1993	1994	1995
Iceland: Icelandic króna Islande : couronne islandaise										
End of period										
Fin de période	40.240	35.660	46.220	61.170	55.390	55.620	63.920	72.730	68.300	65.230
Period average										
Moyenne sur période	41.104	38.677	43.014	57.042	58.284	58.996	57.546	67.603	69.944	64.692
India: Indian rupee Inde : roupie indienne										
End of period										
Fin de période	13.122	12.877	14.949	17.035	18.073	25.834	26.200	31.380	31.380	35.180
Period average										
Moyenne sur période	12.611	12.961	13.917	16.225	17.503	22.742	25.918	30.493	31.374	32.427
Indonesia: Indonesian rupiah Indonésie : rupiah indonésien										
End of period										
Fin de période	1 641.000	1 650.000	1 731.000	1 797.000	1 901.000	1 992.000	2 062.000	2 110.000	2 200.000	2 308.000
Period average										
Moyenne sur période	1 282.560	1 643.850	1 685.700	1 770.060	1 842.810	1 950.320	2 029.920	2 087.100	2 160.750	2 248.610
Iran, Islamic Rep. of: Iranian rial Iran, Rép. islamique d' : rial iranien										
End of period										
Fin de période	75.644	65.622	68.589	70.235	65.307	64.591	67.039	1 758.560	1 735.970	1 747.500
Period average										
Moyenne sur période	78.760	71.460	68.683	72.015	68.096	67.505	65.552	1 267.770	1 748.750	1 747.930
Iraq: Iraqi dinar Iraq : dinar iraquien										
End of period[1]										
Fin de période[1]	0.311	0.311	0.311	0.311	0.311	0.311	0.311	0.311	0.311	0.311
Ireland: Irish pound Irlande : livre irlandaise										
End of period										
Fin de période	0.715	0.597	0.663	0.643	0.563	0.571	0.614	0.709	0.646	0.623
Period average										
Moyenne sur période	0.743	0.673	0.656	0.706	0.605	0.621	0.588	0.677	0.669	0.624
Israel: new sheqel Israël : nouveau sheqel										
End of period										
Fin de période	1.486	1.539	1.685	1.963	2.048	2.283	2.764	2.986	3.018	3.135
Period average										
Moyenne sur période	1.488	1.595	1.599	1.916	2.016	2.279	2.459	2.830	3.011	3.011
Italy: Italian lira Italie : lire italienne										
End of period										
Fin de période	1 358.130	1 169.250	1 305.770	1 270.500	1 130.150	1 151.060	1 470.860	1 703.970	1 629.740	1 584.720
Period average										
Moyenne sur période	1 490.810	1 296.070	1 301.630	1 372.090	1 198.100	1 240.610	1 232.410	1 573.670	1 612.440	1 629.620
Jamaica: Jamaican dollar Jamaïque : dollar jamaïquain										
End of period										
Fin de période	5.480	5.500	5.480	6.480	8.038	21.492	22.185	32.474	33.201	39.616
Period average										
Moyenne sur période	5.478	5.487	5.489	5.745	7.184	12.116	22.960	24.948	33.086	35.142
Japan: yen Japon : yen										
End of period										
Fin de période	159.100	123.500	125.850	143.450	134.400	125.200	124.750	111.850	99.740	102.830
Period average										
Moyenne sur période	168.520	144.640	128.150	137.960	144.790	134.710	126.650	111.200	102.210	94.060
Jordan: Jordanian dinar Jordanie : dinar jordanien										
End of period										
Fin de période	0.344	0.329	0.477	0.648	0.665	0.675	0.691	0.704	0.701	0.709
Period average										
Moyenne sur période	0.350	0.338	0.374	0.575	0.664	0.681	0.680	0.693	0.699	0.700
Kenya: Kenya shilling Kenya : shilling kényen										
End of period[1]										
Fin de période[1]	16.042	16.515	18.599	21.601	24.084	28.074	36.216	68.163	44.839	55.850

80
Exchange rates
National currency per US dollar [cont.]
Cours des changes
Valeur du dollar des Etats-Unis en monnaie nationale [suite]

Country (monetary unit) Pays (unité monétaire)	1986	1987	1988	1989	1990	1991	1992	1993	1994	1995
Period average[1] Moyenne sur période[1]	16.226	16.454	17.747	20.572	22.915	27.508	32.217	58.001	56.051	51.430
Kiribati: Australian dollar										
End of period Fin de période	1.504	1.384	1.169	1.261	1.293	1.316	1.452	1.477	1.287	1.342
Period average Moyenne sur période	1.496	1.428	1.280	1.265	1.281	1.284	1.362	1.471	1.368	1.349
Korea, Republic of: won of the Rep. of Korea										
End of period Fin de période	861.400	792.300	684.100	679.600	716.400	760.800	788.400	808.100	788.700	774.700
Period average Moyenne sur période	881.450	822.570	731.470	671.460	707.760	733.350	780.650	802.670	803.450	771.270
Kuwait: Kuwaiti dinar										
End of period Fin de période	0.292	0.270	0.283	0.292	...	0.284	0.303	0.298	0.300	0.299
Period average Moyenne sur période	0.291	0.279	0.279	0.294	...	...	0.293	0.302	0.297	0.298
Kyrgyzstan: Kyrgyz som										
End of period Fin de période	...	...	...	...	...	...	...	9.400	...	11.000
Lao People's Dem. Rep.: kip										
End of period Fin de période	95.000	387.500	452.500	713.500	695.500	711.500	717.000	718.000	719.000	# 923.000
Period average Moyenne sur période	107.319	211.815	452.295	591.500	707.750	702.080	716.080	716.250	717.670	# 804.690
Latvia: lats										
End of period Fin de période	...	...	...	...	...	...	0.835	0.595	0.548	0.537
Period average Moyenne sur période	...	...	...	...	...	...	0.736	0.675	0.560	0.528
Lebanon: Lebanese pound										
End of period Fin de période	87.000	455.000	530.000	505.000	842.000	879.000	1 838.000	1 711.000	1 647.000	1 596.000
Period average Moyenne sur période	38.370	224.600	409.230	496.690	695.090	928.230	1 712.790	1 741.360	1 680.070	1 621.410
Lesotho: loti										
End of period[1] Fin de période[1]	2.183	1.930	2.378	2.536	2.563	2.743	3.053	3.397	3.543	3.647
Period average[1] Moyenne sur période[1]	2.285	2.036	2.273	2.623	2.587	2.761	2.852	3.268	3.551	3.627
Liberia: Liberian dollar										
End of period Fin de période	1.000	1.000	1.000	1.000	1.000	1.000	1.000	1.000	1.000	1.000
Libyan Arab Jamah.: Libyan dinar										
End of period Fin de période	0.314	0.271	0.285	0.292	0.270	0.268	0.301	0.325	0.360	0.353
Lithuania: litas										
End of period Fin de période	...	...	...	...	...	...	3.790	3.900	4.000	4.000
Period average Moyenne sur période	...	...	...	...	...	...	1.773	4.344	3.978	4.000
Luxembourg: Luxembourg franc										
End of period Fin de période	40.410	33.153	37.345	35.760	30.982	31.270	33.180	36.110	31.837	29.415

80
Exchange rates
National currency per US dollar [*cont.*]
Cours des changes
Valeur du dollar des Etats-Unis en monnaie nationale [*suite*]

Country (monetary unit) Pays (unité monétaire)	1986	1987	1988	1989	1990	1991	1992	1993	1994	1995
Period average Moyenne sur période	44.672	37.334	36.768	39.404	33.418	34.148	32.149	34.596	33.456	29.480
Madagascar: Malagasy franc Madagascar : franc malgache										
End of period Fin de période	769.810	1 234.270	1 526.430	1 532.540	1 465.830	1 832.660	1 910.170	1 962.670	3 871.080	3 422.970
Period average Moyenne sur période	676.340	1 069.210	1 407.110	1 603.440	1 494.150	1 835.360	1 863.970	1 913.780	3 067.340	4 265.630
Malawi: Malawi kwacha Malawi : kwacha malawien										
End of period Fin de période	1.952	2.054	2.535	2.679	2.647	2.664	4.396	4.494	15.299	15.303
Period average Moyenne sur période	1.861	2.209	2.561	2.760	2.729	2.803	3.603	4.403	8.736	15.284
Malaysia: ringgit Malaisie : ringgit										
End of period Fin de période	2.603	2.493	2.715	2.703	2.701	2.724	2.612	2.701	2.560	2.542
Period average Moyenne sur période	2.581	2.520	2.619	2.709	2.705	2.750	2.547	2.574	2.624	2.504
Maldives: rufiyaa Maldives : rufiyaa										
End of period Fin de période	7.244	9.395	8.525	9.205	9.620	10.320	10.535	11.105	11.770	11.770
Period average Moyenne sur période	7.151	9.223	8.785	9.041	9.552	10.253	10.569	10.957	11.586	11.770
Mali: CFA franc Mali : franc CFA										
End of period [3] Fin de période [3]	322.750	267.000	302.950	289.400	256.450	259.000	275.320	294.770	# 534.600	490.000
Period average [3] Moyenne sur période [3]	346.310	300.540	297.850	319.010	272.260	282.110	264.690	283.160	# 555.200	499.150
Malta: Maltese lira Malte : lire maltaise										
End of period Fin de période	0.369	0.312	0.332	0.337	0.301	0.306	0.374	0.395	0.368	0.352
Period average Moyenne sur période	0.393	0.345	0.331	0.348	0.318	0.323	0.319	0.382	0.378	0.353
Mauritania: ouguiya Mauritanie : ouguiya										
End of period Fin de période	74.080	71.600	75.730	83.550	77.840	77.820	115.100	124.160	128.370	137.110
Period average Moyenne sur période	74.375	73.878	75.261	83.051	80.609	81.946	87.027	120.806	123.575	129.768
Mauritius: Mauritian rupee Maurice : roupie mauricienne										
End of period Fin de période	13.137	12.175	13.834	14.996	14.322	14.794	16.998	18.656	17.863	17.664
Period average Moyenne sur période	13.466	12.878	13.438	15.250	14.863	15.652	15.563	17.648	17.960	17.386
Mexico: Mexican new peso Mexique : peso nouveau mexicain										
End of period Fin de période	0.924	2.210	2.281	2.641	2.945	3.071	3.115	3.106	5.325	7.643
Period average Moyenne sur période	0.612	1.378	2.273	2.461	2.813	3.018	3.095	3.116	3.375	6.419
Mongolia: tugrik Mongolie : tugrik										
End of period Fin de période	...	...	...	...	14.000	39.400	105.070	# 396.510	414.090	473.620
Period average Moyenne sur période	...	...	...	...	...	9.520	42.560	...	# 412.720	448.610
Morocco: Moroccan dirham Maroc : dirham marocain										
End of period Fin de période	8.712	7.800	8.211	8.122	8.043	8.150	9.049	9.651	8.960	8.469
Period average Moyenne sur période	9.104	8.359	8.209	8.488	8.242	8.706	8.538	9.299	9.203	8.540

80
Exchange rates
National currency per US dollar [cont.]
Cours des changes
Valeur du dollar des Etats-Unis en monnaie nationale [suite]

Country (monetary unit) Pays (unité monétaire)	1986	1987	1988	1989	1990	1991	1992	1993	1994	1995
Mozambique: metical Mozambique : metical										
End of period										
Fin de période	39.300	404.000	626.200	819.700	1 038.100	1 845.400	# 2 951.400	5 343.200	6 651.000	10 890.000
Period average										
Moyenne sur période	40.400	290.700	524.600	744.900	929.100	1 434.500	2 516.500	3 874.200	6 038.600	9 024.300
Myanmar: kyat Myanmar : kyat										
End of period										
Fin de période	7.039	6.110	6.410	6.494	6.080	6.014	6.241	6.246	5.903	5.781
Period average										
Moyenne sur période	7.330	6.653	6.395	6.705	6.339	6.284	6.105	6.157	5.975	5.667
Namibia: rand Namibie : rand										
End of period										
Fin de période	2.183	1.930	2.378	2.536	2.562	2.743	3.053	3.397	3.543	3.647
Period average										
Moyenne sur période	2.285	2.036	2.273	2.623	2.587	2.761	2.852	3.268	3.551	3.627
Nepal: Nepalese rupee Népal : roupie népalaise										
End of period										
Fin de période	22.000	21.600	25.200	28.600	30.400	42.700	43.200	49.240	49.880	56.000
Period average										
Moyenne sur période	21.230	21.819	23.289	27.189	29.369	37.255	42.717	48.607	49.397	51.890
Netherlands: Netherlands guilder Pays-Bas : florin néerlandais										
End of period										
Fin de période	2.192	1.777	1.999	1.915	1.690	1.710	1.814	1.941	1.735	1.604
Period average										
Moyenne sur période	2.450	2.026	1.977	2.121	1.821	1.870	1.758	1.857	1.820	1.606
Netherlands Antilles: Netherlands Antillean guilder Antilles néerlandaises : florin des Antilles néerlandaises										
End of period										
Fin de période	1.800	1.800	1.800	1.790	1.790	1.790	1.790	1.790	1.790	1.790
New Zealand: New Zealand dollar Nouvelle-Zélande : dollar néo-zélandais										
End of period										
Fin de période	1.910	1.521	1.592	1.674	1.701	1.848	1.944	1.790	1.556	1.531
Period average										
Moyenne sur période	1.913	1.695	1.526	1.672	1.676	1.734	1.862	1.851	1.687	1.524
Nicaragua: córdoba Nicaragua : córdoba										
End of period[17]										
Fin de période[17]	14.000	14.000	# 184.000	# 7.630	600.000	# 5.000	5.000	6.350	7.112	7.965
Period average[17]										
Moyenne sur période[17]	19.500	20.530	# 53.950	# 3.120	140.920	# 4.271	5.000	5.620	6.723	7.546
Niger: CFA franc Niger : franc CFA										
End of period[3]										
Fin de période[3]	322.750	267.000	302.950	289.400	256.450	259.000	275.320	294.770	# 534.600	490.000
Period average[3]										
Moyenne sur période[3]	346.310	300.540	297.850	319.010	272.260	282.110	264.690	283.160	# 555.200	499.150
Nigeria: naira Nigéria : naira										
End of period[1]										
Fin de période[1]	3.317	4.141	5.353	7.651	9.001	9.862	19.646	21.882	21.997	21.887
Period average[1]										
Moyenne sur période[1]	1.754	4.016	4.537	7.365	8.038	9.909	17.298	22.065	21.996	21.895
Norway: Norwegian krone Norvège : couronne norvégienne										
End of period										
Fin de période	7.400	6.232	6.570	6.615	5.907	5.973	6.924	7.518	6.762	6.319
Period average										
Moyenne sur période	7.395	6.737	6.517	6.904	6.260	6.483	6.214	7.094	7.058	6.335
Oman: rial Omani Oman : rial omani										
End of period										
Fin de période	0.384	0.384	0.384	0.384	0.384	0.384	0.384	0.384	0.384	0.384

80
Exchange rates
National currency per US dollar [*cont.*]
   Cours des changes
   Valeur du dollar des Etats-Unis en monnaie nationale [*suite*]

Country (monetary unit) Pays (unité monétaire)	1986	1987	1988	1989	1990	1991	1992	1993	1994	1995
Pakistan: Pakistan rupee Pakistan : roupie pakistanaise										
End of period										
Fin de période	17.250	17.450	18.650	21.420	21.900	24.720	25.700	30.120	30.800	34.250
Period average										
Moyenne sur période	16.647	17.399	18.003	20.541	21.707	23.801	25.083	28.107	30.567	31.643
Panama: balboa Panama : balboa										
End of period										
Fin de période	1.000	1.000	1.000	1.000	1.000	1.000	1.000	1.000	1.000	1.000
Papua New Guinea: kina Papouasie-Nvl-Guinée : kina										
End of period										
Fin de période	0.961	0.878	0.826	0.860	0.953	0.953	0.987	0.981	1.179	1.335
Period average										
Moyenne sur période	0.971	0.908	0.867	0.859	0.955	0.952	0.965	0.978	1.005	1.276
Paraguay: guaraní Paraguay : guaraní										
End of period										
Fin de période	550.000	550.000	550.000	1 218.000	1 258.000	1 380.000	1 630.000	1 880.000	1 940.000	1 995.000
Period average										
Moyenne sur période	339.170	550.000	550.000	1 056.220	1 229.810	1 325.180	1 500.260	1 744.350	1 911.540	1 970.400
Peru: nuevo sol Pérou : nouveau sol										
End of period[8]										
Fin de période[8]	13 950.000	33 000.000	# 500.000	5 261.000	# 517.000	960.000	1 630.000	2 160.000	2 180.000	2 310.000
Period average[8]										
Moyenne sur période[8]	13 948.000	16 835.800	# 128.800	2 666.200	# 188.000	773.000	1 246.000	1 988.000	2 195.000	2 253.000
Philippines: Philippine peso Philippines : peso philippin										
End of period										
Fin de période	20.530	20.800	21.335	22.440	28.000	26.650	25.096	27.699	24.418	26.214
Period average										
Moyenne sur période	20.386	20.568	21.095	21.737	24.310	27.479	25.512	27.120	26.417	25.714
Poland: zloty Pologne : zloty										
End of period										
Fin de période	0.020	0.032	0.050	0.650	0.950	1.096	1.577	2.134	2.437	2.468
Period average										
Moyenne sur période	0.018	0.027	0.043	0.144	0.950	1.058	1.363	1.811	2.272	2.425
Portugal: Portuguese escudo Portugal : escudo portugais										
End of period										
Fin de période	146.117	129.865	146.371	149.841	133.600	134.184	146.758	176.812	159.093	149.413
Period average										
Moyenne sur période	149.587	140.882	143.954	157.458	142.555	144.482	134.998	160.800	165.993	151.110
Qatar: Qatar riyal Qatar : riyal qatarien										
End of period										
Fin de période	3.640	3.640	3.640	3.640	3.640	3.640	3.640	3.640	3.640	3.640
Period average										
Moyenne sur période	3.640	3.640	3.640	3.640	3.640	3.640	3.640	3.640	3.640	3.640
Republic of Moldova: Moldovan leu République de Moldova : leu moldove										
End of period										
Fin de période	...	...	...	...	...	0.002	0.415	3.640	4.270	4.499
Period average										
Moyenne sur période	...	...	...	...	...	...	...	...	...	4.496
Romania: Romanian leu Roumanie : leu roumain										
End of period										
Fin de période	15.280	13.740	14.370	14.440	34.710	# 189.000	460.000	1 276.000	1 767.000	2 578.000
Period average										
Moyenne sur période	16.153	14.557	14.277	14.922	22.432	76.387	# 307.953	760.051	1 655.090	2 033.280
Russian Federation: rouble Fédération de Russie : rouble										
End of period										
Fin de période	...	...	...	...	...	...	415.000	1 247.000	3 550.000	4 640.000

80
Exchange rates
National currency per US dollar [*cont.*]
    Cours des changes
    Valeur du dollar des Etats-Unis en monnaie nationale [*suite*]

Country (monetary unit) Pays (unité monétaire)	1986	1987	1988	1989	1990	1991	1992	1993	1994	1995
Period average Moyenne sur période	...	...	...	...	...	...	...	992.000	2 191.000	4 559.000
Rwanda: Rwanda franc Rwanda : franc rwandais										
End of period Fin de période	84.180	73.020	76.710	77.620	121.120	119.790	146.270	201.300	138.330	299.811
Period average Moyenne sur période	87.640	79.672	76.445	79.977	82.597	125.140	133.350	168.197	...	...
Saint Kitts and Nevis: EC dollar Saint-Kitts-et-Nevis : dollar des Caraïbes orientales										
End of period Fin de période	2.700	2.700	2.700	2.700	2.700	2.700	2.700	2.700	2.700	2.700
Saint Lucia: EC dollar Sainte-Lucie : dollar des Caraïbes orientales										
End of period Fin de période	2.700	2.700	2.700	2.700	2.700	2.700	2.700	2.700	2.700	2.700
Samoa: tala Samoa : tala										
End of period Fin de période	2.198	2.011	2.148	2.290	2.333	2.449	2.558	2.608	2.452	2.527
Period average Moyenne sur période	2.235	2.120	2.079	2.269	3.309	2.398	2.465	2.568	2.535	2.552
St. Vincent-Grenadines: EC dollar St. Vincent-Grenadines : dollar des Caraïbes orientales										
End of period Fin de période	2.700	2.700	2.700	2.700	2.700	2.700	2.700	2.700	2.700	2.700
Sao Tome and Principe: dobra Sao Tomé-et-Principe : dobra										
End of period Fin de période	36.993	72.827	98.176	140.366	140.982	280.021	375.540	516.700	...	...
Period average Moyenne sur période	38.589	54.211	86.343	124.672	143.331	201.816	321.337	429.854	732.628	...
Saudi Arabia: Saudi Arabian riyal Arabie saoudite : riyal saoudien										
End of period Fin de période	3.745	3.745	3.745	3.745	3.745	3.745	3.745	3.745	3.745	3.745
Period average Moyenne sur période	3.703	3.745	3.745	3.745	3.745	3.745	3.745	3.745	3.745	3.745
Senegal: CFA franc Sénégal : franc CFA										
End of period[3] Fin de période[3]	322.750	267.000	302.950	289.400	256.450	259.000	275.320	294.770	# 534.600	490.000
Period average[3] Moyenne sur période[3]	346.310	300.540	297.850	319.010	272.260	282.110	264.690	283.160	# 555.200	499.150
Seychelles: Seychelles rupee Seychelles : roupie des Seychelles										
End of period Fin de période	5.929	5.143	5.397	5.467	5.119	5.063	5.254	5.258	4.969	4.864
Period average Moyenne sur période	6.177	5.600	5.384	5.646	5.337	5.289	5.122	5.182	5.056	4.762
Sierra Leone: leone Sierra Leone : leone										
End of period Fin de période	35.587	23.041	39.063	65.359	188.679	434.783	526.316	577.634	613.008	943.396
Period average Moyenne sur période	16.092	34.043	32.514	59.813	151.446	295.344	499.442	567.459	586.740	755.216
Singapore: Singapore dollar Singapour : dollar de Singapour										
End of period Fin de période	2.175	1.998	1.946	1.894	1.744	1.630	1.645	1.608	1.461	1.414
Period average Moyenne sur période	2.177	2.106	2.012	1.950	1.813	1.728	1.629	1.616	1.527	1.417
Slovakia: Slovak koruna Slovaquie : couronne slovaque										
End of period Fin de période	...	...	...	...	...	...	...	33.202	31.277	29.569
Period average Moyenne sur période	...	...	...	...	...	...	...	30.770	32.045	29.713

80
Exchange rates
National currency per US dollar [*cont.*]
Cours des changes
Valeur du dollar des Etats-Unis en monnaie nationale [*suite*]

Country (monetary unit) Pays (unité monétaire)	1986	1987	1988	1989	1990	1991	1992	1993	1994	1995
Slovenia: tolar Slovénie : tolar										
End of period										
Fin de période	...	...	...	...	...	56.690	98.700	131.840	126.460	125.990
Period average										
Moyenne sur période	...	...	...	...	...	27.570	81.290	113.240	128.810	118.520
Solomon Islands: Solomon Islands dollar Iles Salomon : dollar des Iles Salomon										
End of period										
Fin de période	1.986	1.974	2.118	2.397	2.614	2.795	3.100	3.248	3.329	3.476
Period average										
Moyenne sur période	1.741	2.003	2.083	2.293	2.529	2.715	2.928	3.188	3.291	3.406
Somalia: Somali shilling Somalie : shilling somali										
End of period[1]										
Fin de période[1]	90.500	100.000	270.000	929.500	...	...	...	...	...	...
Period average[1]										
Moyenne sur période[1]	72.000	105.177	170.453	490.675	...	...	...	...	...	...
South Africa: rand Afrique du Sud : rand										
End of period[1]										
Fin de période[1]	2.183	1.930	2.378	2.536	2.563	2.743	3.053	3.397	3.543	3.647
Period average[1]										
Moyenne sur période[1]	2.285	2.036	2.273	2.623	2.587	2.761	2.852	3.268	3.551	3.627
Spain: peseta Espagne : peseta										
End of period										
Fin de période	132.395	109.000	113.450	109.720	96.909	96.688	114.623	142.214	131.739	121.409
Period average										
Moyenne sur période	140.048	123.478	116.487	118.378	101.934	103.912	102.379	127.260	133.958	124.689
Sri Lanka: Sri Lanka rupee Sri Lanka : roupie sri-lankaise										
End of period										
Fin de période	28.520	30.763	33.033	40.000	40.240	42.580	46.000	49.561	49.980	54.047
Period average										
Moyenne sur période	28.017	29.445	31.807	36.047	40.063	41.371	43.830	48.322	49.415	51.252
Sudan: Sudanese pound Soudan : livre soudanaise										
End of period										
Fin de période	2.500	4.500	4.500	4.500	4.500	14.993	135.135	217.391	400.000	...
Period average										
Moyenne sur période	2.500	3.000	4.500	4.500	4.500	6.956	97.432	159.314	289.609	...
Suriname: Suriname guilder Suriname : florin du Suriname										
End of period										
Fin de période	1.785	1.785	1.785	1.785	1.785	1.785	1.785	1.785	# 409.500	407.000
Period average										
Moyenne sur période	1.785	1.785	1.785	1.785	1.785	1.785	1.785	1.785	134.120	442.230
Swaziland: lilangeni Swaziland : lilangeni										
End of period										
Fin de période	2.183	1.930	2.378	2.536	2.563	2.743	3.053	3.397	3.543	3.647
Period average										
Moyenne sur période	2.285	2.036	2.273	2.623	2.587	2.761	2.852	3.268	3.551	3.627
Sweden: Swedish krona Suède : couronne suédoise										
End of period										
Fin de période	6.819	5.848	6.157	6.227	5.698	5.529	7.043	8.303	7.461	6.658
Period average										
Moyenne sur période	7.124	6.340	6.127	6.447	5.919	6.047	5.824	7.783	7.716	7.133
Switzerland: Swiss franc Suisse : franc suisse										
End of period										
Fin de période	1.623	1.278	1.504	1.546	1.295	1.355	1.456	1.479	1.311	1.150
Period average										
Moyenne sur période	1.799	1.491	1.463	1.636	1.389	1.434	1.406	1.478	1.368	1.182

80
Exchange rates
National currency per US dollar [*cont.*]
Cours des changes
Valeur du dollar des Etats-Unis en monnaie nationale [*suite*]

Country (monetary unit) Pays (unité monétaire)	1986	1987	1988	1989	1990	1991	1992	1993	1994	1995
Syrian Arab Republic: Syrian pound Rép. arabe syrienne : livre syrienne										
End of period[1]										
Fin de période[1]	3.925	3.925	11.225	11.225	11.225	11.225	11.225	11.225	11.225	11.225
Tajikistan: Tajik rouble Tadjikistan : rouble tadjik										
Period average										
Moyenne sur période	...	...	...	...	...	...	222.200	932.200	2 204.300	...
Thailand: baht Thaïlande : baht										
End of period										
Fin de période	26.130	25.070	25.240	25.690	25.290	25.280	25.520	25.540	25.090	...
Period average										
Moyenne sur période	26.299	25.723	25.294	25.702	25.585	25.517	25.400	25.319	25.150	...
Togo: CFA franc Togo : franc CFA										
End of period[3]										
Fin de période[3]	322.750	267.000	302.950	289.400	256.450	259.000	275.320	294.770	# 534.600	490.000
Period average[3]										
Moyenne sur période[3]	346.310	300.540	297.850	319.010	272.260	282.110	264.690	283.160	# 555.200	499.150
Tonga: pa'anga Tonga : pa'anga										
End of period										
Fin de période	1.504	1.384	1.170	1.258	1.296	1.332	1.390	1.379	1.258	1.270
Period average										
Moyenne sur période	1.496	1.428	1.275	1.261	1.280	1.296	1.347	1.384	1.320	1.271
Trinidad and Tobago: Trinidad and Tobago dollar Trinité-et-Tobago : dollar de la Trinité-et-Tobago										
End of period										
Fin de période	3.600	3.600	4.250	4.250	4.250	4.250	4.250	5.814	5.933	5.997
Period average										
Moyenne sur période	3.600	3.600	3.844	4.250	4.250	4.250	4.250	5.351	5.925	5.948
Tunisia: Tunisian dinar Tunisie : dinar tunisien										
End of period										
Fin de période	0.840	0.778	0.898	0.905	0.837	0.864	0.951	1.047	0.991	0.951
Period average										
Moyenne sur période	0.794	0.829	0.858	0.949	0.878	0.925	0.884	1.004	1.012	0.946
Turkey: Turkish lira Turquie : livre turque										
End of period										
Fin de période	757.800	1 020.900	1 814.800	2 313.700	2 930.100	5 079.900	8 564.400	14 472.500	38 726.000	59 650.000
Period average										
Moyenne sur période	674.500	857.200	1 422.300	2 121.700	2 608.600	4 171.800	6 872.400	10 984.600	29 608.700	45 845.100
Turkmenistan: Turkmen manat Turkménistan : manat turkmene										
End of period										
Fin de période	...	...	...	...	...	...	...	...	...	1 450.000
Uganda: Uganda shilling Ouganda : shilling ougandais										
End of period[1]										
Fin de période[1]	14.000	60.000	165.000	370.000	540.000	915.000	1 217.150	1 130.150	926.770	1 009.500
Period average[1]										
Moyenne sur période[1]	14.000	42.840	106.140	223.090	428.850	734.010	1 133.830	1 195.020	979.450	968.900
Ukraine: karbovanets Ukraine : karbovanets										
End of period										
Fin de période	...	...	...	...	...	...	637.700	12 610.000	104 200.000	179 400.000
Period average										
Moyenne sur période	...	...	...	...	...	...	...	4 532.000	32 751.000	147 308.000
former USSR†: rouble ancienne URSS† : rouble										
End of period										
Fin de période	0.684	0.602	0.612	0.633	1.600	...	...	...	...	...
United Arab Emirates: UAE dirham Emirats arabes unis : dirham des EAU										
End of period										
Fin de période	3.671	3.671	3.671	3.671	3.671	3.671	3.671	3.671	3.671	3.671

80
Exchange rates
National currency per US dollar [*cont.*]
        Cours des changes
        Valeur du dollar des Etats-Unis en monnaie nationale [*suite*]

Country (monetary unit) Pays (unité monétaire)	1986	1987	1988	1989	1990	1991	1992	1993	1994	1995
Period average										
Moyenne sur période	3.671	3.671	3.671	3.671	3.671	3.671	3.671	3.671	3.671	3.671
United Kingdom: pound sterling Royaume-Uni : livre sterling										
End of period										
Fin de période	0.678	0.534	0.553	0.623	0.519	0.535	0.661	0.675	0.640	0.645
Period average										
Moyenne sur période	0.682	0.612	0.562	0.611	0.563	0.567	0.570	0.667	0.653	0.634
United Rep.Tanzania: Tanzanian shilling Rép. Unie de Tanzanie : shilling tanzanien										
End of period										
Fin de période	51.719	83.717	125.000	192.300	196.600	233.900	335.000	479.871	523.453	550.360
Period average										
Moyenne sur période	32.698	64.260	99.292	143.377	195.056	219.157	297.708	405.274	509.631	574.762
United States: US dollar Etats-Unis : dollar des Etats-Unis										
End of period										
Fin de période	1.000	1.000	1.000	1.000	1.000	1.000	1.000	1.000	1.000	1.000
Period average										
Moyenne sur période	1.000	1.000	1.000	1.000	1.000	1.000	1.000	1.000	1.000	1.000
Uruguay: Uruguayan peso Uruguay : peso uruguayen										
End of period										
Fin de période	0.181	0.281	0.451	0.805	1.594	2.490	3.481	# 4.418	5.615	7.113
Period average										
Moyenne sur période	0.152	0.227	0.359	0.605	1.171	2.019	3.027	# 3.948	5.053	6.349
Vanuatu: vatu Vanuatu : vatu										
End of period										
Fin de période	116.240	100.560	105.050	110.700	109.250	110.790	119.000	120.800	112.080	113.740
Period average										
Moyenne sur période	106.076	109.849	104.426	116.042	117.061	111.675	113.392	121.581	116.405	112.112
Venezuela: bolívar Venezuela : bolívar										
End of period										
Fin de période	14.500	14.500	14.500	43.079	50.380	61.554	79.450	105.640	# 170.000	290.000
Period average										
Moyenne sur période	8.083	14.500	14.500	34.681	46.900	56.816	68.376	90.826	148.503	# 176.843
Viet Nam: dong Viet Nam : dong										
End of period										
Fin de période	22.500	281.250	1 125.000	5 375.000	8 125.000	...	...	...	...	...
Period average										
Moyenne sur période	22.740	78.290	606.520	4 463.950	6 482.800	...	...	...	...	...
Yemen: Yemeni rial Yémen : rial yéménite										
End of period [1]										
Fin de période [1]	...	...	...	...	12.010	12.010	12.010	12.010	12.010	# 50.040
Period average [1]										
Moyenne sur période [1]	...	...	...	...	...	12.010	12.010	12.010	12.010	40.839
Zaire: new zaire Zaïre : nouveau zaïre										
End of period [9]										
Fin de période [9]	18.598	23.700	43.833	152.000	667.000	# 21.000	663.000	# 35.000	3 250.000	14 831.000
Period average [9]										
Moyenne sur période [9]	16.621	19.871	37.460	127.000	239.000	# 5.000	215.000	# 2.514	# 1 194.000	7 024.000
Zambia: Zambian kwacha Zambie : kwacha zambien										
End of period [1]										
Fin de période [1]	12.710	8.000	10.004	21.650	42.753	88.968	359.712	500.000	666.677	1 000.000
Period average [1]										
Moyenne sur période [1]	7.788	9.519	8.266	13.814	30.289	64.640	172.214	452.763	769.231	833.333
Zimbabwe: Zimbabwe dollar Zimbabwe : dollar zimbabwéen										
End of period										
Fin de période	1.678	1.663	1.943	2.270	2.636	5.051	5.482	6.935	8.387	9.311
Period average										
Moyenne sur période	1.667	1.662	1.806	2.119	2.452	3.621	5.098	6.483	8.152	8.665

80
Exchange rates
National currency per US dollar [*cont.*]
Cours des changes
Valeur du dollar des Etats-Unis en monnaie nationale [*suite*]

Source:
International Monetary Fund (Washington, DC).

† For detailed descriptions of data pertaining to
former Czechoslovakia, Germany, SFR Yugoslavia and former
USSR, see Annex I - Country or area nomenclature, regional
and other groupings.

1 Principal rate.
2 Peso per thousand US dollar.
3 The official rate is pegged to the French franc. Beginning
January 12, 1994, the CFA franc was devalued to CFAF 100 per
French franc from CFAF 50 at which it has been fixed since
1948.
4 Reais per billion US dollar through 1988, per million US
dollar through 1990, per thousand US dollar for 1991-1992
and per US dollar thereafter.

5 The official rate is pegged to the French franc. Beginning
January 12, 1994, the CFA franc was devalued to CFAF 75 per
French franc from CFAF 50 at which it has been fixed since
1948.
6 Data cover the former Federal Republic of Germany and the
former German Democratic Republic beginning July 1990.

7 Gold córdoba per billion US dollar through 1987, per million
US dollar for 1988, per thousand US dollar for 1989-1990 and
per US dollar thereafter.
8 New soles per billion US dollar through 1987, per million US
dollar for 1988-1989, and per thousand US dollar thereafter.
9 New Zaires per million US dollar through 1990, per thousand
US dollar for 1991-1992, and per US dollar thereafter.

Source:
Fonds monétaire international (Washington, DC).

† Pour les descriptions en détails des données
relatives à l'ancienne Tchécoslovaquie, l'Allemagne, la Rfs
Yougoslavie et l'ancienne URSS, voir l'Annexe I -
Nomenclature des pays ou zones, groupements régionaux et
autres groupements.

1 Taux principal.
2 Peso par millier de dollars des États-Unis.
3 Le taux de change officiel est raccroché au taux de change
du franc français. Le 12 janvier 1994, le franc CFA a été
dévalué de 50 par franc français, valeur qu'il avait
conservée depuis 1948, à 100 par franc français.
4 Reais par millard de dollars des États-Unis jusqu'en 1988,
par million de dollars des États-Unis jusqu'en 1990, par
millier de dollars des États-Unis en 1991 et 1992 et par
dollar des État-Unis après cette date.
5 Le taux de change officiel est raccroché au taux de change
du franc français. Le 12 janvier 1994, le CFA a été dévalué
de 50 par franc français, valeur qu'il avait conservée
depuis 1948, à 75 par franc français.
6 Les données se rapportent à l'ancienne République Fédéral
Allemagne et à l'ancienne République Démocratique Allemande
à partir de juillet 1990.
7 Cordobas or par milliard de dollars des États-Unis jusqu'en
1987, par million de dollars en 1988, par millier de dollars
des États-Unis en 1989-1990 et par dollar après cette date.
8 Nouveaux soles par milliard de dollars des États-Unis
jusqu'en 1987, par million de dollars après cette date.
9 Nouveaux zaïres par million dollar des États-Unis jusqu'en
1990, par millier de dollars des États-Unis en 1991 et 1992,
et par dollar des États-Unis après cette date.

81
Total external and public/publicly guaranteed long-term debt of developing countries

Total de la dette extérieure et dette publique extérieure à long terme garantie par l'Etat des pays en développement

Million US dollars
Millions de dollars E-U

A. Total external debt • Total de la dette extérieure

Country or area[1]	1987	1988	1989	1990	1991	1992	1993	1994	Pays ou zone[1]
Total long−term debt (LDOD)	1100148	1091601	1133938	1206118	1265151	1305097	1391083	1522570	**Total de la dette à long terme (LDOD)**
Public/publicly guaranteed	1025746	1029905	1079191	1140943	1188514	1209099	1275872	1382183	Dette publique ou garantie par l'Etat
Official creditors	482982	495667	544097	607202	653905	673754	725568	790751	Créanciers publics
Multilateral	175600	176258	184557	212057	229999	236698	254611	280607	Multilatéraux
IBRD	88329	83638	84407	95573	100104	97945	102861	110274	BIRD
IDA	33365	36178	39363	45103	49755	53607	58314	66505	IDA
Bilateral	307383	319409	359541	395144	423906	437056	470957	510144	Bilatéraux
Private creditors	542764	534238	535093	533742	534609	535345	550304	591432	Créanciers privés
Bonds	44317	48768	54564	115527	126409	140280	181934	256072	Obligations
Commercial banks	356305	352358	347198	271916	264106	251790	226172	180274	Banques commerciales
Other private	142142	133111	133330	146299	144095	143275	142198	155086	Autres institutions privées
Private non−guaranteed	74402	61696	54748	65175	76637	95998	115211	140387	**Dette privé non garantie**
Undisbursed debt	202040	196242	201681	216928	235853	240230	251454	246573	**Dette (montants non verses)**
Official creditors	143659	144207	153106	166843	183757	187592	193140	196160	Créanciers publics
Private creditors	58381	52034	48576	50085	52096	52638	58314	50414	Créanciers privés
Commitments	110386	112568	112143	122197	132144	133836	138434	108474	**Engagements**
Official creditors	52966	53393	60358	64142	75146	66827	62086	55811	Créanciers publics
Private creditors	57420	59175	51785	58056	56997	67009	76348	52663	Créanciers privés
Disbursements	117584	119623	116472	131307	132317	156052	171451	167894	**Versements**
Public/publicly guaranteed	109368	111222	103495	112656	113419	121310	128381	118125	Dette publique ou garantie par l'Etat
Official creditors	48507	46119	44679	54366	55399	51888	53608	50676	Créanciers publics
Multilateral	24354	23745	22681	27805	29211	28157	30876	29218	Multilatéraux
IBRD	11216	12092	10785	13587	12034	10429	13142	11621	BIRD
IDA	3915	3836	3591	4378	4604	5143	4862	6067	IDA
Bilateral	24153	22375	21998	26561	26188	23731	22732	21458	Bilatéraux
Private creditors	60861	65102	58816	58290	58020	69422	74773	67449	Créanciers privés
Bonds	3501	8556	8021	8317	12831	13861	30999	23395	Obligations
Commercial banks	34536	34861	24502	18048	16516	22349	17867	20705	Banques commerciales
Other private	22823	21685	26293	31925	28672	33212	25907	23350	Autres institutions privées
Private non−guaranteed	8215	8401	12978	18651	18898	34742	43071	49769	**Dette privé non garantie**
Principal repayments	80211	84165	82739	87519	85342	93354	107399	107976	**Remboursements du principal**
Public/publicly guaranteed	69575	72621	70285	78168	75024	79036	81698	83003	Dette publique ou garantie par l'Etat
Official creditors	22109	24510	23732	25844	27409	28798	29964	34533	Créanciers publics
Multilateral	9697	12601	11389	12781	14377	15869	16612	19132	Multilatéraux
IBRD	6464	9162	7672	8488	9429	10314	10390	11923	BIRD
IDA	151	173	209	250	308	346	393	458	IDA
Bilateral	12412	11910	12343	13063	13032	12929	13353	15400	Bilatéraux
Private creditors	47466	48111	46553	52324	47615	50239	51734	48470	Créanciers privés
Bonds	3222	6471	3683	6058	2851	9246	12224	8659	Obligations
Commercial banks	28148	22863	24200	24926	19768	20455	20536	18905	Banques commerciales
Other private	16095	18777	18669	21341	24996	20539	18974	20906	Autres institutions privées
Private non−guaranteed	10636	11544	12454	9351	10318	14317	25701	24973	**Dette privé non garantie**

81

Total external and public/publicly guaranteed long–term debt of developing countries
Million US dollars [*cont.*]

Total de la dette extérieure et dette publique extérieure à long terme garantie par l'Etat des pays en développement
Millions de dollars E–U [*suite*]

A. Total external debt · Total de la dette extérieure

Country or area	1987	1988	1989	1990	1991	1992	1993	1994	Pays ou zone
Net flows	37373	35457	33733	43788	46975	62699	64052	59918	**Apports nets**
Public/publicly									**Dette publique ou**
guaranteed	39794	38600	33210	34488	38395	42274	46682	35122	**garantie par l'Etat**
Official creditors	26398	21609	20947	28523	27990	23090	23644	16144	Créanciers publics
Multilateral	14657	11144	11292	15025	14835	12288	14264	10086	Multilatéraux
IBRD	4752	2930	3113	5099	2606	115	2753	−302	BIRD
IDA	3765	3664	3381	4128	4297	4798	4469	5609	IDA
Bilateral	11741	10465	9655	13498	13156	10802	9379	6058	Bilatéraux
Private creditors	13395	16992	12263	5965	10405	19183	23039	18979	Créanciers privés
Bonds	279	2085	4337	2259	9980	4615	18775	14735	Obligations
Commercial banks	6388	11999	302	−6878	−3251	1895	−2670	1799	Banques commerciales
Other private	6728	2908	7624	10584	3676	12673	6933	2444	Autres institutions privées
Private non–guaranteed	−2421	−3143	524	9300	8580	20425	17370	24796	**Dette privé non garantie**
Interest payments (LINT)	55890	63322	58535	57671	57582	55293	54135	61530	**Paiements d'intérêts (LINT)**
Public/publicly									**Dette publique ou**
guaranteed	49033	56769	53259	52739	52031	49370	47701	54208	**garantie par l'Etat**
Official creditors	15643	17483	17658	20446	21879	22629	23875	26132	Créanciers publics
Multilateral	9249	10201	9788	11217	12741	12834	13360	13729	Multilatéraux
IBRD	6195	6925	6339	7131	7943	7782	8018	8019	BIRD
IDA	277	296	268	303	349	372	393	433	IDA
Bilateral	6394	7282	7870	9230	9138	9795	10515	12403	Bilatéraux
Private creditors	33391	39285	35601	32292	30152	26741	23825	28076	Créanciers privés
Bonds	2716	3015	3406	5075	8331	8113	9109	12098	Obligations
Commercial banks	23681	28712	24704	19869	14151	12201	8978	9250	Banques commerciales
Other private	6994	7558	7492	7349	7669	6427	5738	6728	Autres institutions privées
Private non–guaranteed	6856	6553	5276	4933	5551	5923	6435	7322	**Dette privé non garantie**
Net transfers	−18517	−27864	−24802	−13883	−10608	7406	9917	−1612	**Transferts nets**
Public/publicly									**Dette publique ou**
guaranteed	−9240	−18168	−20050	−18251	−13636	−7097	−1018	−19086	**garantie par l'Etat**
Official creditors	10756	4125	3288	8076	6111	461	−232	−9988	Créanciers publics
Multilateral	5409	943	1504	3808	2093	−546	904	−3643	Multilatéraux
IBRD	−1443	−3995	−3226	−2031	−5337	−7667	−5266	−8321	BIRD
IDA	3488	3368	3113	3825	3948	4425	4076	5176	IDA
Bilateral	5347	3183	1784	4268	4018	1007	−1136	−6345	Bilatéraux
Private creditors	−19996	−22294	−23338	−26327	−19747	−7558	−787	−9098	Créanciers privés
Bonds	−2437	−931	932	−2816	1649	−3498	9666	2637	Obligations
Commercial banks	−17293	−16713	−24402	−26746	−17402	−10306	−11648	−7451	Banques commerciales
Other private	−266	−4650	132	3235	−3994	6246	1195	−4284	Autres institutions privées
Private non–guaranteed	−9277	−9696	−4752	4368	3028	14502	10935	17474	**Dette privé non garantie**
Total debt service									**Total du service de la**
(LTDS)	136100	147487	141274	145190	142924	148646	161535	169506	**dette (LTDS)**
Public/publicly									**Dette publique ou**
guaranteed	118608	129390	123544	130907	127055	128407	129399	137211	**garantie par l'Etat**
Official creditors	37752	41994	41391	46290	49288	51427	53840	60664	Créanciers publics
Multilateral	18945	22802	21177	23997	27118	28703	29972	32861	Multilatéraux
IBRD	12659	16087	14011	15619	17371	18096	18408	19941	BIRD
IDA	427	468	477	554	656	718	786	891	IDA
Bilateral	18806	19192	20214	22293	22170	22724	23868	27803	Bilatéraux
Private creditors	80856	87396	82154	84617	77767	76980	75560	76547	Créanciers privés
Bonds	5938	9486	7089	11133	11183	17359	21333	20757	Obligations
Commercial banks	51829	51574	48904	44794	33918	32655	29514	28156	Banques commerciales
Other private	23089	26335	26161	28690	32666	26966	24712	27634	Autres institutions privées
Private non–guaranteed	17492	18097	17730	14283	15870	20240	32136	32295	**Dette privé non garantie**

81
Total external and public/publicly guaranteed long–term debt of developing countries
Million US dollars [*cont.*]
Total de la dette extérieure et dette publique extérieure à long terme garantie par l'Etat des pays en développement
Millions de dollars E–U [*suite*]

B. Public and publicly guaranteed long–term debt • Dette publique extérieure à long terme garantie par l'Etat

Country or area Pays ou zone	1985	1986	1987	1988	1989	1990	1991	1992	1993	1994
Albania Albanie	...	...	...	...	...	35.7	86.2	126.8	180.1	229.9
Algeria Algérie	16397.9	19498.9	23095.1	24420.8	24628.9	26431.9	25979.1	25494.6	24881.3	28102.9
Angola Angola	2326.0	3399.9	5023.8	5901.7	6591.6	7490.3	7617.2	7999.8	8152.4	8450.1
Argentina Argentine	37327.2	40958.1	49221.0	47546.3	51832.3	46905.4	47567.8	47604.8	52023.9	55785.2
Armenia Arménie	...	...	...	...	...	...	...	2.9	133.9	188.7
Azerbaijan Azerbaïdjan	...	...	...	...	...	...	...	...	35.5	103.2
Bangladesh Bangladesh	6623.1	8059.2	9669.3	10219.4	10718.3	12288.6	12867.1	13203.2	14106.4	15713.4
Barbados Barbade	354.9	426.3	447.8	529.0	480.0	504.2	482.7	400.7	346.5	330.4
Belarus Bélarus	...	...	...	...	...	...	...	188.7	865.1	1099.7
Belize Belize	94.8	97.3	110.9	118.5	127.9	135.0	149.6	155.2	162.2	159.5
Benin Bénin	662.3	769.4	932.2	913.9	1107.8	1156.6	1263.9	1338.3	1379.7	1508.3
Bhutan Bhoutan	8.8	21.0	40.2	67.0	71.9	80.3	84.9	82.7	83.2	86.7
Bolivia Bolivie	3511.4	4070.3	4621.3	4139.8	3428.8	3690.4	3534.3	3674.0	3695.1	4113.2
Botswana Botswana	349.1	409.2	545.5	534.7	551.3	557.5	612.9	605.4	649.2	680.9
Brazil Brésil	74000.9	82420.1	90524.2	93982.6	89426.4	89186.9	86364.8	91988.0	92968.4	94512.1
Bulgaria Bulgarie	3801.5	5806.0	7914.6	8314.9	9283.0	9834.1	10070.5	10033.8	9819.3	9013.4
Burkina Faso Burkina Faso	456.2	576.7	744.0	767.4	648.2	749.9	882.6	978.9	1064.6	1037.0
Burundi Burundi	409.0	524.3	711.7	755.6	832.2	851.4	901.2	947.1	997.9	1064.2
Cambodia Cambodge	1.2	1.2	1.2	1.2	1578.3	1720.9	1721.4	1712.6	1718.3	1773.7
Cameroon Cameroun	2005.1	2432.5	2826.7	2905.9	3767.9	4709.4	4917.9	5595.0	5602.2	5970.2
Cape Verde Cap–Vert	96.3	108.5	121.3	122.1	125.3	130.6	130.4	136.2	141.7	158.9
Central African Rep. Rép. centrafricaine	290.5	393.1	538.2	583.6	630.6	635.6	728.5	741.3	782.3	807.4
Chad Tchad	159.6	200.2	266.9	308.6	325.3	445.6	541.5	658.8	705.0	743.8
Chile Chili	12896.8	14689.4	15541.7	13696.3	10865.5	10426.1	10070.7	9577.7	8867.7	8946.7
China Chine	9936.9	16571.5	25963.2	32620.3	37118.0	45515.1	49479.2	58462.4	70076.1	84553.8
Colombia Colombie	9573.1	12180.6	13827.7	13846.0	13988.9	14670.7	14468.8	13238.5	12865.2	13603.7
Comoros Comores	129.6	158.8	188.1	187.8	161.0	172.6	166.1	175.0	169.2	175.6
Congo Congo	2362.2	2799.3	3392.7	3486.8	3504.2	4207.9	4043.2	3877.5	4117.3	4666.7

81
Total external and public/publicly guaranteed long-term debt of developing countries
Million US dollars [*cont.*]

Total de la dette extérieure et dette publique extérieure à long terme garantie par l'Etat des pays en développement
Millions de dollars E-U [*suite*]

B. Public and publicly guaranteed long-term debt · Dette publique extérieure à long terme garantie par l'Etat

Country or area Pays ou zone	1985	1986	1987	1988	1989	1990	1991	1992	1993	1994
Costa Rica Costa Rica	3533.4	3625.3	3708.6	3546.7	3545.2	3063.0	3296.9	3180.0	3118.0	3154.9
Côte d'Ivoire Côte d'Ivoire	5787.9	6636.8	8199.0	7769.8	8239.3	9849.0	10508.8	10528.1	10429.7	11270.9
Croatia Croatie	...	...	...	...	...	...	...	...	869.8	902.2
Czech Republic République tchèque	1911.9	2113.4	2607.4	2764.6	3181.7	3971.1	4152.1	3909.8	5210.4	7421.7
Djibouti Djibouti	96.0	119.2	154.3	158.3	131.3	156.1	170.9	176.8	192.7	206.9
Dominica Dominique	42.2	45.4	57.2	59.3	66.5	77.5	84.9	84.9	84.7	86.5
Dominican Republic Rép. dominicaine	2690.9	2929.7	3220.2	3289.6	3341.6	3441.9	3751.1	3724.5	3762.9	3680.7
Ecuador Equateur	7198.7	8259.5	8991.1	9027.8	9427.0	9866.8	9951.0	9831.3	9935.2	10383.9
Egypt Egypte	28972.0	31640.1	35124.0	35967.7	34554.9	26976.3	28949.5	28253.8	28403.7	30537.8
El Salvador El Salvador	1555.3	1586.0	1675.3	1684.9	1825.7	1912.0	2056.9	2147.4	1897.0	1994.2
Equatorial Guinea Guinée équatoriale	112.8	139.5	173.2	184.5	205.3	209.2	215.5	214.3	217.7	222.5
Estonia Estonie	...	...	...	...	...	...	...	33.8	84.8	108.5
Ethiopia Ethiopie	1864.6	2220.8	2736.0	3070.6	3329.2	3633.9	3985.9	4187.7	4502.7	4815.4
Fiji Fidji	302.3	311.8	336.4	335.7	301.6	305.9	270.7	226.8	199.3	195.2
Gabon Gabon	943.8	1427.9	2146.3	2287.6	2596.2	3135.0	3180.0	3001.9	2891.1	3482.8
Gambia Gambie	176.6	212.1	265.4	276.9	289.2	308.6	322.4	346.0	347.9	364.4
Georgia Géorgie	...	...	...	...	...	...	...	79.3	577.7	683.3
Ghana Ghana	1312.1	1741.6	2280.5	2225.4	2392.5	2756.4	3088.9	3288.5	3584.1	4074.6
Grenada Grenade	46.7	51.8	65.6	69.9	72.1	91.1	101.2	97.8	96.4	96.6
Guatemala Guatemala	2169.0	2293.9	2338.0	2142.0	2120.3	2241.3	2235.0	2108.5	2237.4	2368.2
Guinea Guinée	1291.9	1620.6	1883.3	2030.9	1958.1	2243.7	2391.9	2457.1	2654.3	2881.3
Guinea−Bissau Guinée−Bissau	267.6	343.5	448.0	473.3	519.7	609.5	652.6	663.3	686.5	735.7
Guyana Guyana	786.3	867.6	967.6	994.7	1261.3	1757.3	1760.1	1673.1	1731.6	1787.7
Haiti Haïti	522.3	575.7	673.5	683.3	684.4	745.6	609.5	625.9	617.6	627.3
Honduras Honduras	2138.0	2378.9	2700.7	2756.6	2866.1	3424.4	3094.5	3231.9	3650.0	3883.8
Hungary Hongrie	9966.9	12383.8	15673.5	15612.2	16633.9	18006.4	18931.2	17843.1	19777.4	22090.4
India Inde	30283.6	37175.7	44379.2	48039.3	62770.7	69328.3	71880.9	77478.9	81667.6	87880.0
Indonesia Indonésie	26777.4	32625.9	40852.9	41200.2	44254.6	48065.5	52121.7	53958.3	57461.2	63847.6
Iran, Islamic Rep. of Iran, Rép. islamique d'	2389.9	2412.9	2279.9	2055.1	1861.6	1796.9	2064.5	1729.7	5758.6	15612.9
Jamaica Jamaïque	3153.9	3290.4	3750.0	3723.5	3743.5	3933.9	3709.2	3567.3	3459.7	3439.5
Jordan Jordanie	3267.3	4065.8	4917.0	5379.8	6260.6	7049.7	7460.9	6923.9	6770.1	6847.1
Kazakstan Kazakstan	...	...	...	...	...	...	...	25.8	1567.2	2200.8

81
Total external and public/publicly guaranteed long–term debt of developing countries
Million US dollars [cont.]
Total de la dette extérieure et dette publique extérieure à long terme garantie par l'Etat des pays en développement
Millions de dollars E-U [suite]

B. Public and publicly guaranteed long-term debt · Dette publique extérieure à long terme garantie par l'Etat

Country or area Pays ou zone	1985	1986	1987	1988	1989	1990	1991	1992	1993	1994
Kenya Kenya	2666.7	3294.8	4169.2	4143.6	4166.4	4759.6	5266.9	5157.4	5254.1	5650.8
Korea, Republic of Corée, République de	28279.1	29350.9	23889.6	20024.5	17038.1	18786.7	22481.4	24050.6	24566.5	27102.6
Kyrgyzstan Kirghizistan	...	...	...	...	...	...	...	0.6	248.8	350.9
Lao People's Dem. Rep. Rép. dém. pop. lao	606.3	857.1	1151.6	1322.7	1463.2	1757.5	1849.5	1886.7	1948.1	2022.0
Latvia Lettonie	...	...	...	...	...	...	...	26.0	119.7	197.6
Lebanon Liban	399.9	400.2	402.5	371.8	354.4	358.1	336.5	301.2	369.9	621.5
Lesotho Lesotho	167.3	190.5	252.2	275.5	313.3	375.4	414.5	447.5	465.1	516.1
Liberia Libéria	884.9	987.6	1114.5	1076.8	1064.2	1116.1	1106.3	1081.2	1101.9	1137.1
Lithuania Lituanie	...	...	...	...	...	...	...	9.5	163.5	212.7
Madagascar Madagascar	2219.8	2636.4	3302.8	3330.9	3168.6	3360.3	3542.5	3496.2	3357.2	3565.0
Malawi Malawi	791.7	947.5	1160.9	1201.7	1265.8	1399.1	1521.7	1556.5	1718.0	1889.2
Malaysia Malaisie	14506.0	16276.7	17884.1	14632.0	12627.7	12684.2	14013.8	13468.5	13828.4	13750.6
Maldives Maldives	49.0	58.7	61.9	59.3	54.4	64.0	78.0	92.7	111.7	125.7
Mali Mali	1301.2	1578.6	1905.9	1910.5	2043.9	2345.3	2452.3	2474.2	2499.1	2623.3
Malta Malte	99.4	95.2	95.6	84.8	78.5	124.6	146.4	129.4	127.9	157.6
Mauritania Mauritanie	1332.9	1584.2	1851.1	1831.1	1763.8	1827.4	1858.3	1866.7	1939.2	2081.3
Mauritius Maurice	398.1	449.3	582.5	656.5	640.1	751.9	807.2	731.0	709.0	817.5
Mexico Mexique	72703.1	75826.2	84357.6	80598.2	76114.1	75981.2	77821.7	71067.5	74891.9	79097.0
Mongolia Mongolie	...	...	...	...	...	...	...	272.2	328.3	382.4
Morocco Maroc	13822.1	15840.6	18610.0	19498.8	20310.6	22142.6	20300.7	20510.5	20311.0	21559.7
Mozambique Mozambique	2510.2	3004.3	3591.4	3583.9	3765.1	3996.0	4073.1	4470.9	4593.5	5033.1
Myanmar Myanmar	2896.6	3617.8	4245.1	4220.2	4044.9	4444.1	4556.7	4974.0	5366.7	6098.6
Nepal Népal	545.1	709.7	936.3	1099.7	1294.9	1571.8	1707.5	1752.8	1933.9	2202.2
Nicaragua Nicaragua	4970.7	5806.7	6447.3	7020.0	7660.4	8244.9	8770.4	8999.1	8770.1	9006.2
Niger Niger	832.5	995.1	1244.0	1286.2	1113.3	1294.0	1208.5	1226.8	1276.5	1310.7
Nigeria Nigéria	12232.8	17930.8	26901.9	27537.4	29251.3	31545.6	32325.0	26477.8	26420.7	28167.5
Oman Oman	1907.5	2461.4	2442.6	2480.4	2620.4	2400.3	2473.4	2340.3	2314.8	2607.5
Pakistan Pakistan	10580.2	11781.5	13449.6	13907.4	14504.7	16502.7	17730.1	18551.2	20428.7	22993.4
Panama Panama	3323.2	3494.7	4026.5	4005.3	3935.4	3988.1	3918.2	3771.2	3799.4	3922.5
Papua New Guinea Papouasie–Nvl–Guinée	1069.3	1232.9	1429.7	1252.9	1314.2	1500.6	1590.5	1543.2	1571.5	1622.2
Paraguay Paraguay	1533.8	1825.7	2223.8	2092.9	2095.3	1713.6	1685.4	1365.3	1282.8	1352.4
Peru Pérou	9815.8	10999.8	12635.0	12337.2	12616.8	13634.4	15443.9	15580.5	16383.6	17889.8

81
Total external and public/publicly guaranteed long-term debt of developing countries
Million US dollars [*cont.*]
Total de la dette extérieure et dette publique extérieure à long terme garantie par l'Etat des pays en développement
Millions de dollars E-U [*suite*]

B. Public and publicly guaranteed long-term debt · Dette publique extérieure à long terme garantie par l'Etat

Country or area Pays ou zone	1985	1986	1987	1988	1989	1990	1991	1992	1993	1994
Philippines Philippines	13714.1	19264.6	22895.5	22441.9	22403.1	24075.8	25065.2	25607.0	27472.2	29576.9
Poland Pologne	29734.1	31903.5	36038.4	33627.0	34499.8	39058.7	45031.4	42895.6	41447.1	39110.3
Republic of Moldova Moldova, Rép. de	...	...	...	...	...	...	...	38.5	201.6	318.8
Romania Roumanie	5805.1	5652.5	5342.7	2116.5	198.8	263.4	355.5	1334.5	2079.8	2941.6
Russian Federation Fédération de Russie	21396.4	23328.2	29735.5	30988.2	35742.1	48017.0	54972.5	64890.8	73107.9	80053.9
Rwanda Rwanda	329.8	416.5	559.9	609.2	598.9	687.9	768.9	804.6	840.1	905.0
Saint Kitts and Nevis Saint-Kitts-et-Nevis	12.8	16.9	21.0	26.7	32.0	36.5	39.6	39.3	39.6	43.0
Saint Lucia Sainte-Lucie	23.0	28.4	41.9	52.5	61.2	72.1	75.4	89.4	96.8	104.7
St. Vincent and the Grenadines St. Vincent-Grenadines	24.8	28.3	38.7	45.4	51.3	57.3	60.2	61.0	62.2	64.2
Samoa Samoa	63.7	64.6	71.4	71.1	71.9	91.0	113.3	117.8	140.9	154.7
Sao Tome and Principe Sao Tomé-et-Principe	62.0	76.7	91.0	100.8	114.8	135.6	180.4	195.6	208.5	229.0
Senegal Sénégal	2058.6	2623.3	3321.8	3253.4	2659.4	2938.6	2862.8	2960.9	3009.0	3069.6
Seychelles Seychelles	74.0	108.2	138.7	131.3	130.8	149.1	151.0	146.5	137.8	147.0
Sierra Leone Sierra Leone	387.5	465.8	543.8	537.7	529.7	604.4	657.0	680.3	698.7	736.7
Slovakia Slovaquie	783.6	776.2	998.5	1146.9	1212.1	1488.6	1747.8	1792.9	2203.3	2658.7
Slovenia Slovénie	...	...	...	...	...	...	...	...	1255.6	1357.6
Solomon Islands Iles Salomon	53.9	71.1	94.9	101.5	99.4	104.3	99.4	93.4	94.9	99.6
Somalia Somalie	1412.0	1554.3	1743.3	1779.2	1813.3	1925.8	1945.2	1897.9	1897.0	1934.9
Sri Lanka Sri Lanka	2838.6	3452.4	4081.5	4150.7	4277.5	4934.2	5651.1	5625.0	5945.7	6597.4
Sudan Soudan	6601.7	7121.6	8043.1	8002.7	8469.0	9155.2	9220.1	8983.6	8993.7	9372.0
Swaziland Swaziland	214.0	250.1	283.7	254.3	247.5	257.0	256.5	231.4	216.0	227.5
Syrian Arab Republic Rép. arabe syrienne	9508.8	11387.5	14347.2	15094.8	15693.4	14917.1	16353.2	15913.1	16235.0	16538.7
TFYR Macedonia L'ex-R.y. Macédoine	...	...	...	...	...	...	...	...	528.3	529.1
Tajikistan Tadjikistan	...	...	...	...	...	...	...	9.7	382.1	570.4
Thailand Thaïlande	9860.2	11487.9	13831.9	13195.4	12427.8	12569.9	13358.2	13426.6	14553.2	16671.9
Togo Togo	791.6	890.5	1052.3	1062.8	945.1	1085.0	1142.1	1133.5	1123.4	1228.4
Tonga Tonga	23.8	28.4	35.6	37.0	38.1	44.4	44.2	42.6	43.7	63.4
Trinidad and Tobago Trinité-et-Tobago	1299.3	1581.9	1636.2	1816.5	1785.3	1778.9	1737.3	1708.1	1698.8	1682.3
Tunisia Tunisie	4454.4	5281.0	6065.7	5953.0	6102.7	6662.2	7109.1	7201.8	7424.1	7913.8
Turkey Turquie	19553.6	24912.7	31541.1	33562.9	34859.3	38683.9	39702.6	40360.3	44259.1	48519.4
Turkmenistan Turkménistan	...	...	...	...	...	...	...	46.5	276.5	333.4
Uganda Ouganda	899.9	1116.8	1611.6	1643.0	1929.8	2235.7	2354.1	2516.7	2685.7	2955.1

81
Total external and public/publicly guaranteed long-term debt of developing countries
Million US dollars [*cont.*]
Total de la dette extérieure et dette publique extérieure à long terme garantie par l'Etat des pays en développement
Millions de dollars E-U [*suite*]

B. Public and publicly guaranteed long-term debt · Dette publique extérieure à long terme garantie par l'Etat

Country or area Pays ou zone	1985	1986	1987	1988	1989	1990	1991	1992	1993	1994
Ukraine Ukraine	...	...	...	...	...	...	...	456.5	3565.1	4603.0
United Rep. Tanzania Rép. Unie de Tanzanie	3331.7	4302.4	5041.0	5347.6	5359.7	5822.1	5859.8	5884.1	5896.5	6231.9
Uruguay Uruguay	2695.0	2895.3	3126.4	2950.6	3007.8	3044.9	2897.2	3139.3	3368.6	3774.0
Uzbekistan Ouzbékistan	...	...	...	...	...	...	...	8.1	889.7	865.5
Vanuatu Vanuatu	6.9	8.1	13.7	15.3	20.8	30.7	38.1	39.6	39.4	41.5
Venezuela Venezuela	17737.7	25329.1	25008.4	25180.9	25166.2	24508.7	24938.6	25829.5	26855.3	28038.9
Viet Nam Viet Nam	...	...	...	...	18443.5	20753.2	20763.1	21417.7	21824.6	22226.2
Yemen Yémen	2966.6	3439.0	4058.9	4393.8	4643.2	5153.9	5255.5	5253.3	5341.0	5306.2
Yugoslavia, SFR † Yougoslavie, Rfs †	11149.3	12236.1	14272.9	14053.0	14109.5	12986.3	11640.5	11116.9	8655.6	8962.8
Zaire Zaïre	4957.8	5917.4	7207.5	6941.3	7965.8	9006.1	9271.1	8947.7	8769.1	9280.7
Zambia Zambie	3100.0	3835.6	4463.7	4433.8	4229.3	4852.2	4999.0	4743.6	4668.4	4858.0
Zimbabwe Zimbabwe	1777.5	2046.8	2375.6	2227.5	2275.4	2464.1	2611.0	2787.5	3011.9	3252.8

Source:
World Debt Tables 1996 (volumes 1 and 2), The World Bank
(Washington, DC).

Source:
"World Debt Tables 1996 (volumes 1 and 2)", La Banque mondiale
(Washington, DC).

† For detailed descriptions of data pertaining to former
Czechoslovakia, Germany, SFR Yugoslavia and former USSR,
see Annex I – Country or area nomenclature, regional and
other groupings.

† Pour les descriptions en détails des données relatives à l'ancienne
Tchécoslovaquie, l'Allemagne, la Rfs Yougoslavie et l'ancienne URSS,
voir l'Annexe I – Nomenclature des pays ou zones, groupements
régionaux et autres groupements.

1 The following abbreviations have been used in the table:
LDOD: Long-term debt outstanding and disbursed
IBRD: International Bank for Reconstruction and Development
IDA: International Development Association
LINT: Loan interest
LTDS: Long-term debt service

1 Les abbréviations ci-après ont été utilisées dans le tableau:
LDOD : Dette à long terme
BIRD : Banque internationale pour la réconstruction et
le développement
IDA : Association internationale de développement
LINT : Paiement des intérêts
LTDS : Service de la dette

Technical notes, tables 80 and 81

Table 80:Foreign exchange rates are shown in units of national currency per US dollar. The exchange rates are classified into three broad categories, reflecting both the role of the authorities in the determination of the exchange and/or the multiciplicity of exchange rates in a country. The *market rate* is used to describe exchange rates determined largely by market forces; the *official rate* is an exchange rate determined by the authorities, sometimes in a flexible manner. For countries maintaining multiple exchange arrangements, the rates are labeled *principal rate*, *secondary rate*, and *tertiary rate*. Unless otherwise stated, the table refers to end of period and period averages of market exchange rates or official exchange rates. For further information see *International Financial Statistics*.[13]

Table 81: Data are extracted from *World Debt Tables 1996, External Debt for Developing Countries*, published by the World Bank.[30]

Long term external debt is defined as debt that has an original or extended maturity of more than one year and is owed to non-residents and repayable in foreign currency, goods, or services. A distinction is made between:

— Public debt which is an external obligation of a public debtor, which could be a national government, a political sub-division, an agency of either of the above or, in fact, any autonomous public body;

— Publicly guaranteed debt, which is an external obligation of a private debtor that is guaranteed for repayment by a public entity;

— Private non-guaranteed external debt, which is an external obligation of a private debtor that is not guaranteed for repayment by a public entity.

The data referring to public and publicly guaranteed debt do not include data for (a) transactions with International Monetary Fund, (b) debt repayable in local currency, (c) direct investment and (d) short-term debt (that is, debt with an original maturity of less than a year).

The data referring to private non-guaranteed debt also exclude the above items but include contractual obligations on loans to direct-investment enterprises by foreign parent companies or their affiliates.

Data are aggregated by type of creditor. The breakdown is as follows:

Official creditors:

(a) Loans from international organizations (multilateral loans), excluding loans from funds administered by an international organization on behalf of a single donor government. The latter are classified as loans from governments;

Notes techniques, tableaux 80 et 81

Tableau 80 : Les taux des changes sont exprimés par nombre d'unités de monnaie nationale pour un dollar des Etats-Unis. Les taux de change sont classés en trois catégories, qui dénotent le rôle des autorités dans l'établissement des taux de change et/ou la multiplicité des taux de change dans un pays. Par *taux du marché*, on entend les taux de change déterminés essentiellement par les forces du marché; le *taux officiel* est un taux de change établi par les autorités, parfois selon des dispositions souples. Pour les pays qui continuent de mettre en oeuvre des régimes de taux de change multiples, les taux sont désignés par les appellations suivantes : "taux principal", "taux secondaire" et "taux tertiaire". Sauf indication contraire, le tableau indique des taux de fin de période et les moyennes sur la période, des taux de change du marché ou des taux de change officiels. Pour plus de renseignements, voir *Satistiques financières internationales* [13].

Tableau 81 : les données sont extraites des *Tableaux de la dette internationale 1996, Dette extérieure des pays pour développement*, publiés par la Banque mondiale [30].

La dette extérieure à long terme désigne la dette dont l'échéance initiale ou reportée est de plus d'un an, due à des non-résidents et remboursable en devises, biens ou services. On établit les distinctions suivantes :

— La dette publique, qui est une obligation extérieure d'un débiteur public, pouvant être un gouvernement, un organe politique, une institution de l'un ou l'autre ou, en fait, tout organisme public autonome.

— La dette garantie par l'Etat, qui est une obligation extérieure d'un débiteur privé, dont le remboursement est garanti par un organisme public.

— La dette extérieure privée non garantie, qui est une obligation extérieure d'un débiteur privé, dont le remboursement n'est pas garanti par un organisme public.

Les statistiques relatives à la dette publique ou à la dette garantie par l'Etat ne comprennent pas les données concernant : (a) les transactions avec le Fonds monétaire international; (b) la dette remboursable en monnaie nationale; (c) les investissements directs; et (d) la dette à court terme (c'est-à-dire la dette dont l'échéance initiale est inférieure à un an).

Les statistiques relatives à la dette privée non garantie ne comprennent pas non plus les éléments précités, mais comprennent les obligations contractuelles au titre des prêts consentis par des sociétés mères étrangères ou leurs filiales à des entreprises créées dans le cadre d'investissements directs.

Les données sont groupées par type de créancier, comme suit :

(b) Loans from governments (bilateral loans) and from autonomous public bodies;

Private creditors:

(a) Suppliers: Credits from manufacturers, exporters, or other suppliers of goods;

(b) Financial markets: Loans from private banks and other private financial institutions as well as publicly issued and privately placed bonds;

(c) Other: External liabilities on account of nationalized properties and unclassified debts to private creditors.

A distinction is made between the following categories of external public debt:

— Debt outstanding (including undisbursed) is the sum of disbursed and undisbursed debt and represents the total outstanding external obligations of the borrower at year-end;

— Debt outstanding (disbursed only) is total outstanding debt drawn by the borrower at year end;

— Commitments are the total of loans for which contracts are signed in the year specified;

— Disbursements are drawings on outstanding loan commitments during the year specified;

— Service payments are actual repayments of principal amortization and interest payments made in foreign currencies, goods or services in the year specified;

— Net flows (or net lending) are disbursements minus principal repayments;

— Net transfers are net flows minus interest payments or disbursements minus total debt-service payments.

The countries included in the table are those for which data are sufficiently reliable to provide a meaningful presentation of debt outstanding and future service payments.

Créanciers publics :

(a) Les prêts obtenus auprès d'organisations internationales (prêts multilatéraux), à l'exclusion des prêts au titre de fonds administrés par une organisation internationale pour le compte d'un gouvernement donateur précis, qui sont classés comme prêts consentis par des gouvernements.

(b) Les prêts consentis par des gouvernements (prêts bilatéraux) et par des organisations publiques autonomes.

Créanciers privés :

(a) Fournisseurs : Crédits consentis par des fabricants exportateurs et autre fournisseurs de biens;

(b) Marchés financiers : prêts consentis par des banques privées et autres institutions financières privées, et émissions publiques d'obligations placées auprès d'investisseurs privés;

(c) Autres créanciers : engagements vis-à-vis de l'extérieur au titre des biens nationalisés et dettes diverses à l'égard de créanciers privés.

On fait une distinction entre les catégories suivantes de dette publique extérieure :

— L'encours de la dette (y compris les fonds non décaissés) est la somme des fonds décaissés et non décaissés et représente le total des obligations extérieures en cours de l'emprunteur à la fin de l'année;

— L'encours de la dette (fonds décaissés seulement) est le montant total des tirages effectués par l'emprunteur sur sa dette en cours à la fin de l'année;

— Les engagements représentent le total des prêts dont les contrats ont été signés au cours de l'année considérée;

— Les décaissements sont les sommes tirées sur l'encours des prêts pendant l'année considérée;

— Les paiements au titre du service de la dette sont les remboursements effectifs du principal et les paiements d'intérêts effectués en devises, biens ou services pendant l'année considérée;

— Les flux nets (ou prêts nets) sont les décaissements moins les remboursements de principal;

— Les transferts nets désignent les flux nets moins les paiements d'intérêts, ou les décaissements moins le total des paiements au titre du service de la dette.

Les pays figurant sur ce tableau sont ceux pour lesquels les données sont suffisamment fiables pour permettre une présentation significative de l'encours de la dette et des paiements futurs au titre du service de la dette.

82
Disbursements to individual recipients of bilateral and multilateral official development assistance
Paiements aux destinataires d'aide publique au développement, bilatérale et multilatérale

Region, country or area Région, pays ou zone	Year Année	Disbursements ($US) Paiements ($E–U)			
		Bilateral Bilatérale (millions)	Multilateral[1] Multilatérale[1] (millions)	Total (millions)	Per capita[2] Par habitant[2]
Total	**1992**	**43134.3**	**21292.6**	**64426.9**	...
	1993	**39330.4**	**23521.9**	**62852.3**	...
	1994	**41139.9**	**22709.1**	**63849.0**	...
Africa	**1992**	**16345.0**	**9727.7**	**26072.7**	**39.0**
Afrique	**1993**	**13569.3**	**8403.2**	**21972.5**	**31.9**
	1994	**14511.4**	**9010.7**	**23522.1**	**33.3**
Algeria	1992	375.5	265.3	640.8	24.5
Algérie	1993	265.1	129.7	394.8	14.8
	1994	373.5	179.9	553.4	20.3
Angola	1992	194.6	166.4	361.0	36.5
Angola	1993	155.5	139.8	295.3	28.7
	1994	224.4	227.0	451.4	42.3
Benin	1992	171.2	97.6	268.8	54.5
Bénin	1993	147.7	140.4	288.1	56.6
	1994	141.9	110.5	252.4	48.1
Botswana	1992	93.4	35.4	128.8	94.8
Botswana	1993	80.1	35.7	115.8	82.7
	1994	56.7	−1.7	55.0	38.1
Burkina Faso	1992	267.6	167.3	434.9	45.8
Burkina Faso	1993	254.7	210.8	465.5	47.6
	1994	263.9	167.1	431.0	42.9
Burundi	1992	148.8	160.9	309.7	53.0
Burundi	1993	125.7	92.2	217.9	36.2
	1994	105.7	203.4	309.1	49.8
Cameroon	1992	579.0	228.3	807.3	66.3
Cameroun	1993	528.0	−13.0	515.0	41.1
	1994	397.0	283.3	680.3	52.9
Cape Verde	1992	82.0	42.1	124.1	344.7
Cap–Vert	1993	83.0	34.9	117.9	318.6
	1994	78.4	38.3	116.7	306.3
Central African Rep.	1992	106.7	75.6	182.3	59.2
Rép. centrafricaine	1993	116.8	56.5	173.3	54.9
	1994	94.2	71.8	166.0	51.3
Chad	1992	148.4	92.4	240.8	41.2
Tchad	1993	145.7	79.3	225.0	37.4
	1994	103.5	110.2	213.7	34.6
Comoros	1992	23.1	24.4	47.5	81.2
Comores	1993	28.8	21.2	50.0	82.4
	1994	17.5	22.2	39.7	63.0
Congo	1992	101.7	10.5	112.2	47.3
Congo	1993	116.3	4.2	120.5	49.3
	1994	252.9	147.8	400.7	159.3
Côte d'Ivoire	1992	527.4	311.1	838.5	65.2
Côte d'Ivoire	1993	708.5	−22.7	685.8	51.5
	1994	820.1	653.5	1473.6	106.9
Djibouti	1992	92.0	22.0	114.0	208.8
Djibouti	1993	94.0	30.3	124.3	223.2
	1994	92.2	23.3	115.5	204.1
Egypt	1992	2996.2	348.9	3345.1	56.7
Egypte	1993	1823.8	368.2	2192.0	36.3
	1994	2310.6	322.5	2633.1	42.7
Equatorial Guinea	1992	35.9	24.5	60.4	163.7
Guinée équatoriale	1993	27.7	25.4	53.1	140.1
	1994	16.5	13.8	30.3	77.9
Eritrea	1992	..	..		..
Erythrée	1993	48.1	19.3	67.4	20.1
	1994	95.7	50.4	146.1	42.5
Ethiopia	1992	457.0	734.8	1191.8	23.7
Ethiopie	1993	417.1	684.9	1102.0	21.2
	1994	562.9	511.3	1074.2	20.1

82
Disbursements to individual recipients of bilateral and multilateral
official development assistance [*cont.*]
Paiements aux destinataires d'aide publique au développement,
bilatérale et multilatérale [*suite*]

Region, country or area Région, pays ou zone	Year Année	Disbursements ($US) Paiements ($E-U)			
		Bilateral Bilatérale (millions)	Multilateral[1] Multilatérale[1] (millions)	Total (millions)	Per capita[2] Par habitant[2]
Gabon Gabon	1992	64.8	16.9	81.7	67.4
	1993	97.5	16.3	113.8	91.2
	1994	161.2	105.5	266.7	207.9
Gambia Gambie	1992	50.4	61.2	111.6	111.4
	1993	49.9	37.1	87.0	83.5
	1994	36.9	33.4	70.3	65.0
Ghana Ghana	1992	332.7	300.9	633.6	39.7
	1993	312.4	390.6	703.0	42.7
	1994	331.8	203.1	534.9	31.6
Guinea Guinée	1992	233.5	233.1	466.6	76.3
	1993	184.6	261.5	446.1	70.7
	1994	186.3	204.4	390.7	60.1
Guinea-Bissau Guinée-Bissau	1992	59.2	45.0	104.2	103.6
	1993	58.3	38.0	96.3	93.7
	1994	125.3	51.6	176.9	168.5
Kenya Kenya	1992	519.7	299.6	819.3	32.2
	1993	426.5	376.1	802.6	30.4
	1994	400.5	175.6	576.1	21.1
Lesotho Lesotho	1992	69.0	75.0	144.0	76.2
	1993	73.8	91.0	164.8	84.8
	1994	45.5	87.9	133.4	66.8
Liberia Libéria	1992	26.1	92.7	118.8	43.2
	1993	24.6	97.5	122.1	42.9
	1994	35.5	27.7	63.2	21.5
Libyan Arab Jamah. Jamah. arabe libyenne	1992	1.5	-6.8	-5.3	-1.1
	1993	2.0	-28.9	-26.9	-5.3
	1994	1.8	-5.1	-3.3	-0.6
Madagascar Madagascar	1992	215.5	138.4	353.9	26.4
	1993	227.8	136.1	363.9	26.3
	1994	189.9	92.4	282.3	19.7
Malawi Malawi	1992	207.9	347.7	555.6	54.7
	1993	158.6	325.0	483.6	46.0
	1994	251.0	207.9	458.9	42.3
Mali Mali	1992	239.1	191.0	430.1	43.8
	1993	221.0	165.3	386.3	38.1
	1994	242.7	212.7	455.4	43.5
Mauritania Mauritanie	1992	116.4	111.1	227.5	108.0
	1993	196.0	132.8	328.8	152.2
	1994	128.1	138.9	267.0	120.4
Mauritius Maurice	1992	34.7	-4.9	29.8	27.6
	1993	26.8	-12.2	14.6	13.4
	1994	7.0	-9.3	-2.3	-2.1
Mayotte Mayotte	1992	73.2	1.5	74.7	...
	1993	82.1	1.2	83.3	...
	1994	96.4	8.3	104.7	...
Morocco Maroc	1992	733.7	605.0	1338.7	52.7
	1993	422.0	489.8	911.8	35.1
	1994	317.9	393.6	711.5	26.9
Mozambique Mozambique	1992	1010.1	457.5	1467.6	99.6
	1993	817.3	369.1	1186.4	78.6
	1994	732.3	487.6	1219.9	78.6
Namibia Namibie	1992	97.9	45.5	143.4	100.8
	1993	122.8	31.9	154.7	105.9
	1994	112.3	31.9	144.2	96.1
Niger Niger	1992	262.0	109.6	371.6	45.0
	1993	254.0	85.8	339.8	39.7
	1994	259.6	109.7	369.3	41.7
Nigeria Nigéria	1992	137.7	400.0	537.7	5.3
	1993	71.0	407.9	478.9	4.5
	1994	47.2	232.7	279.9	2.6
Rwanda Rwanda	1992	187.5	165.2	352.7	47.9
	1993	201.3	154.5	355.8	47.1
	1994	485.8	226.3	712.1	91.9

82
Disbursements to individual recipients of bilateral and multilateral
official development assistance [cont.]
Paiements aux destinataires d'aide publique au développement,
bilatérale et multilatérale [suite]

Region, country or area Région, pays ou zone	Year Année	Disbursements ($US) Paiements ($E–U)			
		Bilateral Bilatérale (millions)	Multilateral[1] Multilatérale[1] (millions)	Total (millions)	Per capita[2] Par habitant[2]
Saint Helena	1992	15.2	0.6	15.8	2633.3
Sainte–Hélène	1993	14.1	0.6	14.7	2450.0
	1994	13.1	1.0	14.1	2350.0
Sao Tome and Principe	1992	27.0	30.7	57.7	465.3
Sao Tomé–et–Principe	1993	28.8	18.7	47.5	374.0
	1994	27.1	23.3	50.4	387.7
Senegal	1992	454.0	252.7	706.7	91.7
Sénégal	1993	363.8	184.3	548.1	69.4
	1994	474.6	176.8	651.4	80.4
Seychelles	1992	15.4	8.0	23.4	329.6
Seychelles	1993	6.8	15.9	22.7	315.3
	1994	7.3	10.1	17.4	238.4
Sierra Leone	1992	74.1	62.5	136.6	32.6
Sierra Leone	1993	105.7	105.5	211.2	49.2
	1994	53.8	222.3	276.1	62.7
Somalia	1992	497.3	145.1	642.4	72.5
Somalie	1993	687.9	193.2	881.1	98.4
	1994	437.5	99.9	537.4	59.2
South Africa	1992	0.0	0.0	0.0	0.0
Afrique du Sud	1993	183.3	92.1	275.4	6.9
	1994	213.3	80.5	293.8	7.2
Sudan	1992	187.5	348.2	535.7	20.7
Soudan	1993	164.1	285.5	449.6	16.9
	1994	173.9	240.3	414.2	15.1
Swaziland	1992	26.7	20.6	47.3	60.1
Swaziland	1993	33.4	18.3	51.7	63.9
	1994	27.5	18.6	46.1	55.4
Togo	1992	134.9	89.2	224.1	59.6
Togo	1993	77.2	18.9	96.1	24.7
	1994	63.3	59.9	123.2	30.7
Tunisia	1992	298.2	248.3	546.5	65.0
Tunisie	1993	126.8	419.1	545.9	63.7
	1994	70.9	212.1	283.0	32.4
Uganda	1992	254.8	444.3	699.1	36.3
Ouganda	1993	347.8	245.3	593.1	29.7
	1994	344.4	383.6	728.0	35.3
United Rep. Tanzania	1992	816.2	496.4	1312.6	48.3
Rép. Unie de Tanzanie	1993	650.1	266.1	916.2	32.7
	1994	570.2	355.8	926.0	32.1
Zaire	1992	162.7	96.4	259.1	6.5
Zaïre	1993	99.1	77.7	176.8	4.3
	1994	97.0	146.7	243.7	5.7
Zambia	1992	699.0	310.9	1009.9	116.4
Zambie	1993	510.6	303.3	813.9	91.1
	1994	434.0	210.4	644.4	70.1
Zimbabwe	1992	535.8	425.3	961.1	91.8
Zimbabwe	1993	310.1	351.3	661.4	61.6
	1994	280.1	235.3	515.4	46.8
Other and unallocated	1992	1073.1	256.3	1329.4	...
Autres et non–ventilés	1993	663.2	203.9	867.1	...
	1994	1020.9	382.4	1403.3	...
Americas	**1992**	**4293.7**	**1278.7**	**5572.4**	**12.3**
Amériques	**1993**	**4270.5**	**4195.7**	**8466.2**	**18.4**
	1994	**4541.0**	**3319.7**	**7860.7**	**16.8**
Anguilla	1992	3.5	1.6	5.1	637.5
Anguilla	1993	3.6	1.2	4.8	600.0
	1994	5.2	1.1	6.3	787.5
Antigua and Barbuda	1992	4.0	0.6	4.6	70.8
Antigua–et–Barbuda	1993	2.4	0.7	3.1	47.7
	1994	1.6	2.4	4.0	61.5
Argentina	1992	254.7	−162.3	92.4	2.8
Argentine	1993	229.2	2297.9	2527.1	74.8
	1994	145.1	971.5	1116.6	32.7

82
Disbursements to individual recipients of bilateral and multilateral
official development assistance [*cont.*]
Paiements aux destinataires d'aide publique au développement,
bilatérale et multilatérale [*suite*]

Region, country or area Région, pays ou zone	Year Année	Disbursements ($US) Paiements ($E–U)			
		Bilateral Bilatérale (millions)	Multilateral[1] Multilatérale[1] (millions)	Total (millions)	Per capita[2] Par habitant[2]
Aruba	1992	29.9	0.6	30.5	448.5
Aruba	1993	23.0	2.3	25.3	366.7
	1994	15.9	4.2	20.1	291.3
Bahamas	1992	0.4	33.4	33.8	128.0
Bahamas	1993	0.4	14.5	14.9	55.6
	1994	0.2	11.9	12.1	44.5
Barbados	1992	0.8	−3.3	−2.5	−9.7
Barbade	1993	0.4	−3.1	−2.7	−10.4
	1994	0.1	−4.5	−4.4	−16.9
Belize	1992	13.9	12.2	26.1	131.2
Belize	1993	15.2	15.7	30.9	151.5
	1994	15.2	30.2	45.4	216.2
Bermuda	1992	−5.1	0.1	−5.0	−80.6
Bermudes	1993	−4.8	0.0	−4.8	−76.2
	1994	−12.5	0.0	−12.5	−198.4
Bolivia	1992	502.0	296.2	798.2	115.8
Bolivie	1993	431.4	204.3	635.7	90.0
	1994	385.1	273.4	658.5	91.0
Brazil	1992	−278.7	−695.6	−974.3	−6.3
Brésil	1993	148.6	−566.2	−417.6	−2.7
	1994	201.4	−246.3	−44.9	−0.3
British Virgin Islands	1992	2.1	9.0	11.1	652.9
Iles Vierges britanniques	1993	2.2	2.0	4.2	233.3
	1994	10.8	−0.4	10.4	577.8
Cayman Islands	1992	−1.4	7.6	6.2	221.4
Iles Caïmanes	1993	−1.1	0.8	−0.3	−10.3
	1994	−1.2	−2.7	−3.9	−130.0
Chile	1992	117.7	98.9	216.6	15.9
Chili	1993	159.1	−42.1	117.0	8.5
	1994	131.3	44.9	176.2	12.5
Colombia	1992	220.9	−65.4	155.5	4.7
Colombie	1993	84.9	−257.2	−172.3	−5.1
	1994	65.0	−315.4	−250.4	−7.2
Costa Rica	1992	134.0	31.2	165.2	51.8
Costa Rica	1993	92.9	38.9	131.8	40.3
	1994	71.2	72.6	143.8	43.0
Cuba	1992	11.8	12.7	24.5	2.3
Cuba	1993	14.4	29.5	43.9	4.0
	1994	18.7	28.8	47.5	4.3
Dominica	1992	8.3	5.1	13.4	188.7
Dominique	1993	6.2	2.6	8.8	123.9
	1994	9.3	7.2	16.5	232.4
Dominican Republic	1992	52.0	19.5	71.5	9.7
Rép. dominicaine	1993	−23.0	52.0	29.0	3.8
	1994	35.8	88.6	124.4	16.2
Ecuador	1992	204.5	59.4	263.9	24.6
Equateur	1993	168.4	76.6	245.0	22.3
	1994	172.9	179.0	351.9	31.4
El Salvador	1992	315.1	76.6	391.7	72.6
El Salvador	1993	279.1	184.9	464.0	84.1
	1994	235.2	172.6	407.8	72.3
Falkland Islands	1992	0.1	0.3	0.4	200.0
Iles Falkland	1993	0.4	5.9	6.3	3150.0
	1994	0.0	0.1	0.1	50.0
Grenada	1992	5.6	8.7	14.3	157.1
Grenade	1993	3.9	4.2	8.1	88.0
	1994	5.9	10.2	16.1	175.0
Guatemala	1992	177.1	−51.4	125.7	12.9
Guatemala	1993	179.7	76.5	256.2	25.5
	1994	157.3	122.7	280.0	27.1
Guyana	1992	26.0	54.6	80.6	99.8
Guyana	1993	27.3	67.5	94.8	116.2
	1994	28.1	43.3	71.4	86.5

82
Disbursements to individual recipients of bilateral and multilateral
official development assistance [cont.]
Paiements aux destinataires d'aide publique au développement,
bilatérale et multilatérale [suite]

Region, country or area Région, pays ou zone	Year Année	Disbursements ($US) Paiements ($E–U)			
		Bilateral Bilatérale (millions)	Multilateral[1] Multilatérale[1] (millions)	Total (millions)	Per capita[2] Par habitant[2]
Haiti Haïti	1992 1993 1994	76.9 96.6 596.8	24.7 27.1 4.2	101.6 123.7 601.0	15.0 17.9 85.4
Honduras Honduras	1992 1993 1994	206.9 201.6 178.2	121.1 168.0 143.1	328.0 369.6 321.3	63.3 69.3 58.5
Jamaica Jamaïque	1992 1993 1994	112.7 98.1 74.3	−24.6 62.1 8.8	88.1 160.2 83.1	36.8 66.4 34.2
Mexico Mexique	1992 1993 1994	300.7 396.9 396.7	468.8 313.3 335.6	769.5 710.2 732.3	8.7 7.9 8.0
Montserrat Montserrat	1992 1993 1994	4.7 5.8 11.3	2.5 6.0 0.7	7.2 11.8 12.0	654.5 1072.7 1090.9
Netherlands Antilles Antilles néerlandaises	1992 1993 1994	88.9 77.7 30.2	7.2 0.8 6.6	96.1 78.5 36.8	497.9 402.6 186.8
Nicaragua Nicaragua	1992 1993 1994	472.9 275.0 415.8	195.8 50.7 200.1	668.7 325.7 615.9	169.1 79.2 144.1
Panama Panama	1992 1993 1994	193.7 74.0 31.2	−232.6 −60.0 −43.3	−38.9 14.0 −12.1	−15.6 5.5 −4.7
Paraguay Paraguay	1992 1993 1994	65.5 93.9 84.3	−5.2 15.0 29.5	60.3 108.9 113.8	13.2 23.2 23.6
Peru Pérou	1992 1993 1994	377.8 513.5 292.9	−54.4 680.0 451.3	323.4 1193.5 744.2	14.4 52.1 31.9
Saint Kitts and Nevis Saint–Kitts–et–Nevis	1992 1993 1994	3.8 1.5 4.0	4.4 9.4 0.7	8.2 10.9 4.7	195.2 259.5 114.6
Saint Lucia Sainte–Lucie	1992 1993 1994	15.0 18.7 20.8	19.5 10.7 6.0	34.5 29.4 26.8	251.8 211.5 190.1
St. Vincent and Grenadines St. Vincent–et–Grenadines	1992 1993 1994	6.5 7.0 6.6	9.1 4.8 −0.1	15.6 11.8 6.5	143.1 107.3 58.6
Suriname Suriname	1992 1993 1994	73.0 74.8 57.5	8.1 5.7 3.3	81.1 80.5 60.8	198.3 194.4 145.5
Trinidad and Tobago Trinité–et–Tobago	1992 1993 1994	−3.3 −1.6 −0.9	71.5 67.9 115.8	68.2 66.3 114.9	53.9 51.9 88.9
Turks and Caicos Islands Iles Turques et Caiques	1992 1993 1994	14.1 10.1 15.0	0.9 1.0 0.4	15.0 11.1 15.4	1153.8 853.8 1100.0
Uruguay Uruguay	1992 1993 1994	59.9 108.1 67.7	149.4 132.6 124.8	209.3 240.7 192.5	66.9 76.4 60.8
Venezuela Venezuela	1992 1993 1994	30.7 34.9 21.8	574.4 257.3 190.0	605.1 292.2 211.8	29.6 14.0 9.9
Other and unallocated Autres et non–ventilés	1992 1993 1994	394.5 340.7 539.4	187.8 234.0 247.1	582.3 574.7 786.5	... ...
Asia **Asie**	**1992** **1993** **1994**	**13602.8** **12175.7** **13892.0**	**8430.9** **8837.0** **9180.6**	**22033.7** **21012.7** **23072.6**	**7.1** **6.6** **7.2**
Afghanistan Afghanistan	1992 1993 1994	126.7 107.3 132.9	74.2 192.2 88.8	200.9 299.5 221.7	12.1 16.9 11.7

82
Disbursements to individual recipients of bilateral and multilateral
official development assistance [*cont.*]
Paiements aux destinataires d'aide publique au développement,
bilatérale et multilatérale [*suite*]

Region, country or area Région, pays ou zone	Year Année	Disbursements ($US) Paiements ($E–U)			
		Bilateral Bilatérale (millions)	Multilateral[1] Multilatérale[1] (millions)	Total (millions)	Per capita[2] Par habitant[2]
Armenia	1992	17.3	5.2	22.5	6.5
Arménie	1993	69.9	24.0	93.9	26.9
	1994	100.1	54.4	154.5	43.5
Azerbaijan	1992	1.0	4.6	5.6	0.8
Azerbaïdjan	1993	4.6	15.4	20.0	2.7
	1994	25.9	43.6	69.5	9.3
Bahrain	1992	1.2	15.8	17.0	32.7
Bahreïn	1993	1.9	19.8	21.7	40.6
	1994	1.7	17.3	19.0	34.6
Bangladesh	1992	852.8	948.7	1801.5	16.0
Bangladesh	1993	690.4	683.9	1374.3	11.9
	1994	843.3	907.2	1750.5	14.9
Bhutan	1992	34.2	23.6	57.8	36.5
Bhoutan	1993	43.5	22.3	65.8	41.2
	1994	57.3	19.2	76.5	47.4
Brunei Darussalam	1992	5.3	0.1	5.4	20.1
Brunéi Darussalam	1993	5.0	0.1	5.1	18.6
	1994	5.2	0.0	5.2	18.6
Cambodia	1992	95.4	111.4	206.8	22.0
Cambodge	1993	196.6	120.2	316.8	32.7
	1994	178.9	155.6	334.5	33.6
China	1992	2077.3	1479.2	3556.5	3.0
Chine	1993	2239.8	2167.3	4407.1	3.7
	1994	2387.1	2386.0	4773.1	3.9
East Timor	1992	0.1	0.0	0.1	0.1
Timor oriental	1993	0.4	0.0	0.4	0.5
	1994	0.2	0.0	0.2	0.3
Georgia	1992	0.8	19.5	20.3	3.7
Géorgie	1993	94.1	11.1	105.2	19.3
	1994	67.4	37.7	105.1	19.3
Hong Kong	1992	−62.3	23.3	−39.0	−6.8
Hong−kong	1993	12.1	18.1	30.2	5.2
	1994	9.8	17.0	26.8	4.6
India	1992	1198.1	1943.4	3141.5	3.6
Inde	1993	811.7	1422.3	2234.0	2.5
	1994	1376.6	1446.9	2823.5	3.1
Indonesia	1992	1971.4	965.0	2936.4	15.6
Indonésie	1993	1924.5	1133.2	3057.7	16.0
	1994	1556.9	79.1	1636.0	8.4
Iran, Islamic Rep. of	1992	63.8	125.9	189.7	3.0
Iran, Rép. islamique d'	1993	90.6	109.9	200.5	3.1
	1994	87.1	98.8	185.9	2.8
Iraq	1992	66.0	74.1	140.1	7.4
Iraq	1993	70.2	112.0	182.2	9.4
	1994	187.3	72.0	259.3	13.0
Israel	1992	2058.6	7.2	2065.8	410.2
Israël	1993	1266.0	1.6	1267.6	241.3
	1994	1218.0	29.2	1247.2	228.5
Jordan	1992	313.0	174.0	487.0	104.2
Jordanie	1993	181.2	152.6	333.8	67.6
	1994	229.3	178.2	407.5	78.4
Kazakstan	1992	9.5	0.0	9.5	0.6
Kazakstan	1993	12.2	1.9	14.1	0.8
	1994	29.7	201.3	231.0	13.6
Korea, Dem. P. R.	1992	4.7	7.5	12.2	0.5
Corée, R. p. dém. de	1993	7.3	7.1	14.4	0.6
	1994	0.9	5.0	5.9	0.3
Korea, Republic of	1992	2.8	−149.7	−146.9	−3.4
Corée, République de	1993	−34.7	−219.9	−254.6	−5.8
	1994	−107.0	−333.2	−440.2	−9.9
Kuwait	1992	1.6	0.8	2.4	1.2
Koweït	1993	1.6	1.0	2.6	1.5
	1994	1.7	4.1	5.8	3.6

82
Disbursements to individual recipients of bilateral and multilateral
official development assistance [*cont.*]
Paiements aux destinataires d'aide publique au développement,
bilatérale et multilatérale [*suite*]

Region, country or area Région, pays ou zone	Year Année	Disbursements ($US) Paiements ($E–U) Bilateral Bilatérale (millions)	Multilateral[1] Multilatérale[1] (millions)	Total (millions)	Per capita[2] Par habitant[2]
Kyrgyzstan	1992	3.4	0.1	3.5	0.8
Kirghizistan	1993	69.4	24.2	93.6	20.4
	1994	86.8	67.6	154.4	33.1
Lao People's Dem. Rep.	1992	76.9	88.0	164.9	36.9
Rép. dém. pop. lao	1993	92.2	114.2	206.4	44.8
	1994	123.1	94.7	217.8	45.9
Lebanon	1992	68.7	54.9	123.6	45.8
Liban	1993	62.1	104.3	166.4	59.3
	1994	79.8	153.6	233.4	80.1
Macau	1992	0.1	0.0	0.1	0.3
Macao	1993	0.2	0.0	0.2	0.5
	1994	0.3	0.0	0.3	0.8
Malaysia	1992	195.0	2.8	197.8	10.5
Malaisie	1993	88.4	−185.3	−96.9	−5.0
	1994	64.7	−29.7	35.0	1.8
Maldives	1992	15.0	22.3	37.3	161.5
Maldives	1993	19.8	10.6	30.4	127.7
	1994	18.8	12.9	31.7	128.9
Mongolia	1992	67.5	55.4	122.9	54.1
Mongolie	1993	81.9	44.1	126.0	54.4
	1994	108.1	76.0	184.1	77.9
Myanmar	1992	82.7	32.0	114.7	2.6
Myanmar	1993	77.3	23.7	101.0	2.3
	1994	142.8	18.1	160.9	3.5
Nepal	1992	275.7	161.7	437.4	21.6
Népal	1993	245.6	122.3	367.9	17.7
	1994	267.5	182.8	450.3	21.1
Oman	1992	19.2	28.3	47.5	24.9
Oman	1993	26.6	−2.4	24.2	12.1
	1994	79.3	−10.5	68.8	33.1
Pakistan	1992	469.4	1072.2	1541.6	11.9
Pakistan	1993	490.3	951.7	1442.0	10.8
	1994	508.5	1530.0	2038.5	14.9
Philippines	1992	1538.7	530.7	2069.4	32.6
Philippines	1993	1330.1	598.2	1928.3	29.8
	1994	942.0	304.0	1246.0	18.8
Qatar	1992	1.3	0.8	2.1	4.1
Qatar	1993	1.1	2.7	3.8	7.2
	1994	1.7	2.4	4.1	7.6
Saudi Arabia	1992	48.1	7.2	55.3	3.3
Arabie saoudite	1993	21.5	8.1	29.6	1.7
	1994	14.0	6.7	20.7	1.2
Singapore	1992	18.6	−11.7	6.9	2.5
Singapour	1993	22.3	−1.1	21.2	7.6
	1994	14.9	1.9	16.8	6.0
Sri Lanka	1992	248.8	387.2	636.0	36.0
Sri Lanka	1993	316.4	337.6	654.0	36.5
	1994	334.0	249.5	583.5	32.2
Syrian Arab Republic	1992	50.4	63.3	113.7	8.6
Rép. arabe syrienne	1993	113.3	−2.2	111.1	8.1
	1994	361.4	40.4	401.8	28.4
Tajikistan	1992	11.5	8.9	20.4	3.6
Tadjikistan	1993	21.5	7.2	28.7	5.0
	1994	28.1	20.7	48.8	8.2
Thailand	1992	696.0	−406.7	289.3	5.1
Thaïlande	1993	566.2	141.2	707.4	12.3
	1994	543.2	26.8	570.0	9.8
Turkmenistan	1992	5.4	0.0	5.4	1.4
Turkménistan	1993	24.1	0.5	24.6	6.3
	1994	13.5	5.6	19.1	4.8
United Arab Emirates	1992	−10.4	2.1	−8.3	−4.7
Emirats arabes unis	1993	−10.6	1.9	−8.7	−4.8
	1994	−9.2	2.8	−6.4	−3.4

82
Disbursements to individual recipients of bilateral and multilateral
official development assistance [*cont.*]
Paiements aux destinataires d'aide publique au développement,
bilatérale et multilatérale [*suite*]

Region, country or area Région, pays ou zone	Year Année	Disbursements ($US) Paiements ($E-U)			
		Bilateral Bilatérale (millions)	Multilateral[1] Multilatérale[1] (millions)	Total (millions)	Per capita[2] Par habitant[2]
Uzbekistan	1992	1.4	0.0	1.4	0.1
Ouzbékistan	1993	3.8	1.9	5.7	0.3
	1994	10.9	68.4	79.3	3.5
Viet Nam	1992	474.0	109.3	583.3	8.4
Viet Nam	1993	224.0	33.7	257.7	3.6
	1994	585.8	315.9	901.7	12.4
Yemen	1992	149.0	89.1	238.1	19.0
Yémen	1993	184.9	105.7	290.6	22.0
	1994	106.0	64.4	170.4	12.3
Other and unallocated	1992	257.3	279.2	536.5	...
Autres et non-ventilés	1993	307.5	397.8	705.3	...
	1994	1076.1	467.0	1543.1	...
Europe	**1992**	**6667.9**	**3511.6**	**10179.5**	**25.2**
Europe	**1993**	**7075.3**	**4342.6**	**11417.9**	**28.2**
	1994	**6565.0**	**4307.1**	**10872.1**	**26.8**
Albania	1992	193.8	376.5	570.3	169.5
Albanie	1993	102.9	116.0	218.9	64.6
	1994	69.0	106.5	175.5	51.4
Belarus	1992	272.5	26.3	298.8	29.3
Bélarus	1993	185.1	100.1	285.2	28.0
	1994	111.4	56.4	167.8	16.5
Bulgaria	1992	72.1	167.6	239.7	26.9
Bulgarie	1993	66.5	55.0	121.5	13.7
	1994	51.3	480.2	531.5	60.3
Cyprus	1992	10.6	−36.0	−25.4	−35.4
Chypre	1993	17.0	22.8	39.8	54.8
	1994	26.6	−56.3	−29.7	−40.5
Czech Republic	1992	99.7	321.9	421.6	40.9
République tchèque	1993	80.0	200.8	280.8	27.3
	1994	54.4	283.2	337.6	32.8
Estonia	1992	90.3	17.1	107.4	68.7
Estonie	1993	35.4	75.2	110.6	71.3
	1994	30.7	10.5	41.2	26.7
Gibraltar	1992	3.1	0.0	3.1	110.7
Gibraltar	1993	0.0	0.0	0.0	0.0
	1994	0.6	0.0	0.6	21.4
Hungary	1992	127.4	438.6	566.0	55.2
Hongrie	1993	115.9	465.3	581.2	56.9
	1994	67.6	246.4	314.0	30.9
Latvia	1992	58.2	25.9	84.1	31.9
Lettonie	1993	23.2	80.0	103.2	39.5
	1994	34.0	60.1	94.1	36.4
Lithuania	1992	72.8	21.0	93.8	25.2
Lituanie	1993	50.5	115.0	165.5	44.6
	1994	48.8	30.7	79.5	21.5
Malta	1992	6.0	0.8	6.8	18.9
Malte	1993	29.0	21.7	50.7	140.4
	1994	43.4	5.9	49.3	135.4
Poland	1992	1359.8	554.9	1914.7	50.0
Pologne	1993	919.8	573.8	1493.6	39.0
	1994	1522.2	1156.2	2678.4	69.9
Republic of Moldova	1992	9.7	9.1	18.8	4.3
République de Moldova	1993	28.0	29.0	57.0	12.9
	1994	22.4	131.3	153.7	34.8
Romania	1992	134.3	823.9	958.2	41.4
Roumanie	1993	123.4	378.4	501.8	21.8
	1994	62.5	445.7	508.2	22.2
Russian Federation	1992	1709.2	230.2	1939.4	13.1
Fédération de Russie	1993	2409.3	910.8	3320.1	22.5
	1994	1735.1	484.7	2219.8	15.1
Slovakia	1992	47.9	152.5	200.4	37.8
Slovaquie	1993	40.7	77.8	118.5	22.3
	1994	30.7	270.8	301.5	56.5

82
Disbursements to individual recipients of bilateral and multilateral
official development assistance [*cont.*]
Paiements aux destinataires d'aide publique au développement,
bilatérale et multilatérale [*suite*]

Region, country or area Région, pays ou zone	Year Année	Disbursements ($US) Paiements ($E-U)			
		Bilateral Bilatérale (millions)	Multilateral[1] Multilatérale[1] (millions)	Total (millions)	Per capita[2] Par habitant[2]
Turkey	1992	133.1	−223.6	−90.5	−1.5
Turquie	1993	272.0	−291.4	−19.4	−0.3
	1994	41.8	−742.2	−700.4	−11.5
Ukraine	1992	557.4	63.3	620.7	12.0
Ukraine	1993	322.5	93.9	416.4	8.1
	1994	262.2	101.5	363.7	7.1
Yugoslavia, SFR †	1992	1039.8	319.3	1359.1	59.2
Yugoslavie, Rfs †	1993	1284.5	941.1	2225.6	97.2
	1994	955.4	675.7	1631.1	71.3
Other and unallocated	1992	670.2	222.6	892.8	...
Autres et non−ventilés	1993	969.6	377.3	1346.9	...
	1994	1394.9	559.8	1954.7	...
Oceania	**1992**	**1315.1**	**195.6**	**1510.7**	**241.3**
Océanie	**1993**	**1444.6**	**95.3**	**1539.9**	**240.7**
	1994	**1664.7**	**94.0**	**1758.7**	**269.0**
Cook Islands	1992	11.8	5.4	17.2	905.3
Iles Cook	1993	10.2	2.6	12.8	673.7
	1994	10.5	3.8	14.3	752.6
Fiji	1992	54.1	9.0	63.1	84.6
Fidji	1993	50.2	−3.4	46.8	61.7
	1994	34.9	−15.4	19.5	25.3
French Polynesia	1992	323.9	5.8	329.7	1600.5
Polynésie française	1993	333.9	−0.8	333.1	1578.7
	1994	364.2	2.0	366.2	1703.3
Kiribati	1992	22.0	4.8	26.8	357.3
Kiribati	1993	11.2	4.7	15.9	209.2
	1994	12.5	2.9	15.4	200.0
Marshall Islands	1992	5.3	2.4	7.7	157.1
Iles Marshall	1993	29.8	2.6	32.4	648.0
	1994	45.5	3.9	49.4	950.0
Micronesia	1992	12.5	1.4	13.9	121.9
Micronésie	1993	61.2	3.1	64.3	544.9
	1994	101.4	2.8	104.2	861.2
Nauru	1992	0.2	0.0	0.2	20.0
Nauru	1993	0.2	0.0	0.2	20.0
	1994	2.4	0.0	2.4	218.2
New Caledonia	1992	354.5	3.6	358.1	2069.9
Nouvelle−Calédonie	1993	392.6	1.5	394.1	2252.0
	1994	403.2	4.3	407.5	2289.3
Niue	1992	4.5	0.3	4.8	2400.0
Nioué	1993	4.5	0.1	4.6	2300.0
	1994	6.9	0.1	7.0	3500.0
Northern Mariana Islands	1992	7.2	0.2	7.4	157.4
Iles Mariannes du Nord	1993	88.5	0.5	89.0	1893.6
	1994	2.3	0.0	2.3	48.9
Palau	1992	0.0	0.0	0.0	0.0
Palau	1993	0.0	0.0	0.0	0.0
	1994	201.6	0.0	201.6	11858.8
Papua New Guinea	1992	348.9	103.2	452.1	112.5
Papouasie−Nvl−Guinée	1993	265.7	30.7	296.4	72.1
	1994	275.9	41.5	317.4	75.5
Samoa	1992	29.5	24.3	53.8	326.1
Samoa	1993	30.0	22.8	52.8	316.2
	1994	38.4	10.6	49.0	289.9
Solomon Islands	1992	27.3	17.5	44.8	130.6
Iles Salomon	1993	46.5	9.5	56.0	158.2
	1994	39.5	7.9	47.4	129.5
Tokelau	1992	4.0	0.3	4.3	2150.0
Tokélaou	1993	2.5	0.4	2.9	1450.0
	1994	2.8	0.2	3.0	1500.0
Tonga	1992	19.7	4.5	24.2	249.5
Tonga	1993	24.2	7.1	31.3	319.4
	1994	21.9	13.3	35.2	359.2

82
Disbursements to individual recipients of bilateral and multilateral
official development assistance [*cont.*]
Paiements aux destinataires d'aide publique au développement,
bilatérale et multilatérale [*suite*]

Region, country or area Région, pays ou zone	Year Année	Disbursements ($US) Paiements ($E–U)			
		Bilateral Bilatérale (millions)	Multilateral[1] Multilatérale[1] (millions)	Total (millions)	Per capita[2] Par habitant[2]
Tuvalu	1992	7.5	0.9	8.4	933.3
Tuvalu	1993	3.3	0.9	4.2	466.7
	1994	5.3	2.1	7.4	822.2
Vanuatu	1992	32.4	8.2	40.6	258.6
Vanuatu	1993	28.2	7.1	35.3	219.3
	1994	38.6	3.2	41.8	253.3
Wallis and Futuna Islands	1992	0.3	0.5	0.8	57.1
Iles Wallis et Futuna	1993	0.0	0.0	0.0	0.0
	1994	0.1	0.0	0.1	7.1
Other and unallocated	1992	49.6	3.3	52.9	...
Autres et non–ventilés	1993	61.9	5.8	67.7	...
	1994	56.8	10.7	67.5	...
Unspecified	**1992**	**6109.8**	**1149.8**	**7259.6**	...
Non–specifiés	**1993**	**6118.3**	**1116.6**	**7234.9**	...
	1994	**5381.0**	**969.8**	**6350.8**	...

Source:
Organization for Economic Co–operation and Development (Paris).

1   As reported by OECD/DAC, IDA, agencies of the United Nations
    family and the European Development Fund. Excluding
    non–concessional flows (i.e., less than 25% grant element).
2   Population based on estimates of midyear population.

Source:
Organisation de coopération et de développement économiques (Paris).

1   Chiffre communiqués par le Comité d'aide au développement de
    l'OCDE, l'IDA, les agences des Nations Unies et le Fonds Européen
    de Développement. Non compris les apports non libéraux
    (c'est–à–dire) dont l'élément de libéralité est intérieur à 25 p.100).
2   Population d'après des estimations de la population au milieu
    de l'année.

83
Net official development assistance from DAC countries to developing countries and multilateral organizations
Aide publique au développement nette de pays du CAD aux pays en développement et aux organisations multilatérales

Net disbursements: million US dollars and as % of GNP
Versements nets: millions de dollars E–U et en % de PNB

Country or area Pays ou zone	1989 Million US $ Millions E–U $	1989 As % of GNP En % de PNB	1990 [1] Million US $ Millions E–U $	1990 [1] As % of GNP En % de PNB	1991 [1] Million US $ Millions E–U $	1991 [1] As % of GNP En % de PNB	1992 [1] Million US $ Millions E–U $	1992 [1] As % of GNP En % de PNB	1993 Million US $ Millions E–U $	1993 As % of GNP En % de PNB	1994 Million US $ Millions E–U $	1994 As % of GNP En % de PNB
Total	**45737**	**0.32**	**54495**	**0.33**	**58561**	**0.33**	**62720**	**0.33**	**56472**	**0.31**	**59152**	**0.30**
Australia Australie	1020	0.38	955	0.34	1050	0.38	1015	0.37	954	0.35	1088	0.35
Austria Autriche	283	0.23	394	0.25	547	0.34	556	0.30	544	0.30	655	0.33
Belgium Belgique	703	0.46	889	0.46	831	0.41	870	0.39	810	0.39	726	0.32
Canada Canada	2320	0.44	2470	0.44	2604	0.45	2515	0.46	2373	0.45	2250	0.43
Denmark Danemark	937	0.93	1171	0.94	1200	0.96	1392	1.02	1340	1.03	1446	1.03
Finland Finlande	706	0.64	846	0.65	930	0.80	644	0.64	355	0.45	290	0.31
France France	5802	0.61	7164	0.60	7386	0.62	8270	0.63	7915	0.63	8466	0.64
Germany † Allemagne †	4948	0.41	6320	0.42	6890	0.40	7583	0.38	6954	0.36	6818	0.34
Ireland Irlande	49	0.17	57	0.16	72	0.19	70	0.16	81	0.20	109	0.25
Italy Italie	3613	0.42	3395	0.31	3347	0.30	4122	0.34	3043	0.31	2705	0.27
Japan Japon	8965	0.31	9069	0.31	10952	0.32	11151	0.30	11259	0.27	13239	0.29
Luxembourg Luxembourg	18	0.19	25	0.21	42	0.33	38	0.26	50	0.35	60	0.40
Netherlands Pays–Bas	2094	0.94	2538	0.92	2517	0.88	2753	0.86	2525	0.82	2517	0.76
New Zealand Nouvelle–Zélande	87	0.22	95	0.23	100	0.25	97	0.26	98	0.25	110	0.24
Norway Norvège	918	1.05	1205	1.17	1178	1.13	1273	1.16	1014	1.01	1137	1.05
Portugal Portugal	113	0.25	148	0.25	213	0.31	302	0.36	248	0.29	308	0.35
Spain Espagne	541	0.14	965	0.20	1262	0.24	1518	0.27	1304	0.28	1305	0.28
Sweden Suède	1799	0.96	2007	0.91	2116	0.90	2460	1.03	1769	0.99	1819	0.96
Switzerland Suisse	558	0.30	750	0.32	863	0.36	1139	0.45	793	0.33	982	0.36
United Kingdom Royaume–Uni	2587	0.31	2638	0.27	3201	0.32	3243	0.31	2920	0.31	3197	0.31
United States Etats–Unis	7677	0.15	11394	0.21	11262	0.20	11709	0.20	10123	0.16	9927	0.15

Source:
Organization for Economic Co–operation and Development (Paris).

† For detailed descriptions of data pertaining to former Czechoslovakia, Germany, SFR Yugoslavia and former USSR, see Annex I – Country or area nomenclature, regional and other groupings.

1 Except for total including debt forgiveness of non–official development assistance claims.

Source:
Organisation de coopération et de développement économiques (Paris).

† Pour les descriptions en détails des données relatives à l'ancienne Tchécoslovaquie, l'Allemagne, la Rfs Yougoslavie et l'ancienne URSS, voir l'Annexe I – Nomenclature des pays ou zones, groupements régionaux et autres groupements.

1 Sauf pour le total, ces chiffres incluent l'annulation des créances au titre de l'assistance autre que l'aide publique au développement.

84
Socio–economic development assistance through the United Nations system
Assistance en matière de développement socio–économique fournie par le système des Nations Unies

Thousand US dollars
Milliers de dollars E–U

A. Development grant expenditures [1] · Aide au développement [1]

Country or area / Pays ou zone	Year / Année	UNDP / PNUD — UNDP programme / Programme de PNUD	UNDP / PNUD — Special funds / Fonds gérés	UNFPA / FNUAP	UNICEF / FISE	WFP / PAM	Other UN system / Autres organis. –ONU — Regular budget / Budget ordinaire	Other UN system / Autres organis. –ONU — Extra-budgetary / Extra-budgétaire	Total	Gov't self-supporting / Auto-assistance gouverne-mentale
Total	1993	1031000	173393	134321	803701	1487716	345810	891889	4867830	73090
Total	1994	1036479	209774	201431	800625	1395132	280332	688385	4612158	76209
Regional programmes	1993	70882	44453	29715	117158	0	90254	477706	830168	4313
Totaux régionaux	1994	113908	50277	40096	86092	0	84067	375705	750145	10926
Africa	1993	0	10873	3932	1781	0	21451	89828	127865	1191
Afrique	1994	0	9820	5472	384	0	20867	72453	108996	920
Asia	1993	0	2786	3292	2391	0	13961	43702	66132	15
Asie	1994	0	3333	4363	880	0	14883	39775	63234	15
Latin America	1993	0	2593	1802	8013	0	17293	30973	60674	77
Amérique latine	1994	0	5513	3493	8313	0	18158	28055	63532	284
Middle East	1993	0	457	844	5	0	7741	4372	13419	223
Moyen orient	1994	0	583	646	23	0	7161	11202	19615	7148
Interregional	1993	41775	19746	19845	0	0	28133	271225	380724	472
Interrégional	1994	96267	19994	26122	0	0	22312	189117	353812	2405
Global	1993	29107	7998	0	104968	0	1675	37606	181354	2335
Global	1994	17641	11034	0	76492	0	686	35103	140956	154
Country programmes	1993	859068	122131	103484	684456	1462427	240474	309980	3782020	66248
Programmes, pays	1994	899840	135838	159066	710315	1372147	170762	278400	3726388	61502
Afghanistan	1993	18298	756	185	11201	39532	2781	3805	76558	1158
Afghanistan	1994	17254	246	6	8410	24593	1787	4878	57174	1522
Albania	1993	1446	0	262	922	0	711	1297	4638	24
Albanie	1994	1447	0	646	869	0	90	1736	4788	20
Algeria	1993	1793	0	592	1406	5168	1365	788	11112	244
Algérie	1994	593	0	1205	683	7059	906	560	11006	269
Angola	1993	3746	115	858	14357	57362	1544	906	78888	0
Angola	1994	1866	146	916	18435	106861	1369	1588	131181	0
Anguilla	1993	318	18	0	0	0	0	0	336	0
Anguilla	1994	169	9	0	0	0	0	0	178	0
Antigua and Barbuda	1993	107	5	1	0	38	16	42	209	0
Antigua–et–Barbuda	1994	115	6	37	0	0	152	4	314	0
Argentina	1993	59429	736	6	1559	0	1497	1920	65147	1417
Argentine	1994	78660	690	44	2046	0	2570	5008	89018	4223
Armenia										
Arménie	1993	0	0	0	779	844	71	0	1694	0
Aruba	1993	485	0	0	0	0	21	2	508	0
Aruba	1994	308	0	0	0	0	35	20	363	0
Azerbaijan										
Azerbaïdjan	1994	14	0	527	1856	8583	70	84	11134	0
Bahamas	1993	−17	0	0	0	0	529	288	800	6
Bahamas	1994	50	0	0	0	0	359	337	746	106
Bahrain	1993	63	0	−7	0	0	260	26	342	0
Bahreïn	1994	122	0	0	0	0	186	120	428	0
Bangladesh	1993	21450	8923	3157	31618	25004	6594	3408	100154	38
Bangladesh	1994	19164	4181	6111	37050	66999	3617	9525	146647	9
Barbados	1993	9	7	2	0	0	180	458	656	0
Barbade	1994	256	10	19	0	0	125	205	615	0
Belize	1993	387	159	43	821	0	589	504	2503	109
Belize	1994	407	411	123	817	0	533	257	2548	48
Benin	1993	6601	1527	605	3377	7290	1423	933	21756	331
Bénin	1994	3719	1216	825	2757	2454	1061	500	12532	14
Bermuda	1993	0	0	0	0	0	3	0	3	0
Bermudes	1994	0	0	0	0	0	0	0	0	0
Bhutan	1993	4576	1087	184	2601	2425	1011	1293	13177	0
Bhoutan	1994	3084	2934	736	2042	1020	893	807	11516	378
Bolivia	1993	13284	3329	1162	4648	10622	1704	5375	40124	0
Bolivie	1994	11572	1273	2107	6438	2124	1309	7519	32342	−6

84

Socio-economic development assistance through the United Nations system
Thousand US dollars [cont.]

Assistance en matière de développement socio-économique fournie par le système des Nations Unies
Milliers de dollars E-U [suite]

A. Development grant expenditures [1] · Aide au développement [1]

Country or area Pays ou zone	Year Année	UNDP PNUD UNDP programme Programme de PNUD	Special funds Fonds gérés	UNFPA FNUAP	UNICEF FISE	WFP PAM	Other UN system Autres organis. -ONU Regular budget Budget ordinaire	Extra- budgetary Extra- budgétaire	Total	Gov't self- supporting Auto- assistance gouverne- mentale
Botswana	1993	3654	701	476	1427	4708	1227	916	13109	38
Botswana	1994	3603	810	939	1247	3283	827	508	11217	52
Brazil	1993	37836	2813	938	9023	9208	3021	3689	66528	2219
Brésil	1994	81041	3507	2913	12197	7150	2193	3946	112947	2393
British Virgin Islands	1993	54	0	1	0	0	1	21	77	0
Iles Vierges britanniques	1994	50	0	6	0	0	1	0	57	0
Brunei Darussalam	1993	0	0	0	0	0	35	34	69	26
Brunéi Darussalam	1994	0	0	0	0	0	9	1	10	0
Bulgaria	1993	420	0	66	0	0	721	429	1636	5
Bulgarie	1994	1090	0	0	0	0	499	893	2482	74
Burkina Faso	1993	7979	3011	779	4358	7409	2175	985	26696	0
Burkina Faso	1994	6452	3220	1865	4514	2998	1194	981	21224	76
Burundi	1993	5885	643	826	2914	4968	1726	2104	19066	573
Burundi	1994	1937	764	938	4971	64189	1592	1449	75840	418
Cambodia	1993	24215	4548	20	15101	20094	1664	5405	71047	35
Cambodge	1994	21951	8082	586	10919	10031	1176	13274	66019	2
Cameroon	1993	1612	642	685	1603	1872	2133	1757	10304	540
Cameroun	1994	1502	380	1004	1883	2422	1094	790	9075	318
Cape Verde	1993	1226	337	363	1709	5606	1624	2553	13418	36
Cap-Vert	1994	803	293	419	1539	4646	1135	2216	11051	248
Cayman Islands	1993	11	0	0	0	0	0	15	26	0
Iles Caïmanes	1994	58	0	0	0	0	0	0	58	0
Central African Rep.	1993	2891	2767	853	1717	5744	1466	1325	16763	0
Rép. centrafricaine	1994	1671	1122	954	1551	3122	1091	582	10093	0
Chad	1993	8180	1907	954	2597	5485	1719	1478	22320	202
Tchad	1994	5716	1723	844	2777	4942	1387	882	18271	98
Chile	1993	8283	110	116	1081	0	1588	2106	13284	146
Chili	1994	9585	79	125	1112	−2	1523	1321	13743	54
China	1993	38410	6360	10319	17647	23782	6746	8411	111675	35
Chine	1994	32834	5518	7120	22491	24855	3190	7747	103755	240
Colombia	1993	24348	601	576	1566	1348	1887	2063	32389	162
Colombie	1994	54839	1443	466	1361	4949	1570	3807	68435	453
Comoros	1993	2611	1348	384	695	1649	1430	274	8391	7
Comores	1994	1871	1234	469	804	−25	1009	148	5510	2
Congo	1993	784	11	213	866	1083	1554	1344	5855	356
Congo	1994	741	4	354	875	445	904	374	3697	42
Cook Islands	1993	495	21	104	0	0	271	103	994	0
Iles Cook	1994	784	28	92	0	0	203	7	1114	0
Costa Rica	1993	2871	435	268	741	1015	1439	5355	12124	45
Costa Rica	1994	2053	1748	549	776	1079	1081	3764	11050	223
Côte d'Ivoire	1993	2504	1	833	1306	6335	1818	1386	14183	50
Côte d'Ivoire	1994	1954	105	886	2379	4463	1376	845	12008	42
Cuba	1993	2183	28	1040	1314	9300	1993	1339	17197	971
Cuba	1994	2013	430	705	1751	3571	1867	519	10856	155
Cyprus	1993	637	0	27	0	0	435	168	1267	3
Chypre	1994	434	80	9	0	0	414	158	1095	2
Czech Republic	1993	270	0	0	0	0	484	785	1539	1
République tchèque	1994	473	0	0	0	0	159	208	840	1
Djibouti	1993	1427	717	61	1037	2839	1132	472	7685	0
Djibouti	1994	883	447	90	843	3284	939	242	6728	0
Dominica	1993	207	13	6	0	223	98	130	677	0
Dominique	1994	198	15	15	0	0	237	36	501	0
Dominican Republic	1993	9753	13	288	1023	244	1359	588	13268	0
Rép. dominicaine	1994	8984	212	2026	1068	523	902	343	14058	0
Ecuador	1993	5838	94	662	1956	835	2422	2994	14801	215
Equateur	1994	6408	154	1038	3283	464	1591	3411	16349	309
Egypt	1993	13692	2517	576	5444	10461	3144	8038	43872	3375
Egypte	1994	11169	557	2706	5622	14004	2197	7669	43924	3728

84

Socio-economic development assistance through the United Nations system
Thousand US dollars [*cont.*]

Assistance en matière de développement socio-économique fournie par le système des Nations Unies
Milliers de dollars E-U [*suite*]

A. Development grant expenditures [1] · Aide au développement [1]

Country or area / Pays ou zone	Year / Année	UNDP PNUD — UNDP programme Programme de PNUD	Special funds Fonds gérés	UNFPA FNUAP	UNICEF FISE	WFP PAM	Other UN system Autres organis. -ONU — Regular budget Budget ordinaire	Extra-budgetary Extra-budgétaire	Total	Gov't self-supporting Auto-assistance gouverne-mentale
El Salvador	1993	11368	3532	668	1403	5831	1361	602	24765	32
El Salvador	1994	11326	4130	1054	1541	1316	1111	534	21012	5
Equatorial Guinea	1993	1638	280	273	1010	2832	1000	207	7240	-7
Guinée équatoriale	1994	1021	511	595	1010	-33	742	85	3931	0
Eritrea	1993	1645	1389	180	448	15243	326	83	19314	0
Erythrée	1994	3031	1061	134	6834	30738	502	3326	45626	0
Ethiopia	1993	14614	2394	2753	20069	101280	2752	8511	152373	414
Ethiopia	1994	9735	3436	4152	20982	26289	2560	8835	75989	181
Fiji	1993	877	337	253	0	0	1602	538	3607	329
Fidji	1994	322	330	337	0	0	911	405	2305	50
French Guiana	1993	0	0	0	0	0	39	0	39	0
Guyane française	1994	0	0	0	0	0	10	0	10	0
French Polynesia	1993	0	0	0	0	0	85	84	169	0
Polynésie française	1994	0	0	0	0	0	0	0	0	0
Gabon	1993	1149	0	258	313	0	1137	723	3580	281
Gabon	1994	854	12	58	559	0	784	446	2713	113
Gambia	1993	4176	1381	354	735	2640	1351	1176	11813	0
Gambie	1994	2159	1117	625	1189	2972	1290	852	10204	6
Ghana	1993	6851	538	1036	4431	15011	1515	3069	32451	914
Ghana	1994	4342	434	2339	1589	9257	1613	2231	21805	228
Greece	1993	0	0	0	0	0	265	167	432	3
Grèce	1994	0	0	0	0	0	360	589	949	421
Grenada	1993	264	3	3	0	270	83	92	715	0
Grenade	1994	119	62	60	4326	0	191	21	4779	0
Guam	1993	0	0	0	0	0	19	30	49	0
Guam	1994	0	0	0	0	0	11	0	11	0
Guatemala	1993	5129	19	504	2438	7379	1139	791	17399	0
Guatemala	1994	8515	16	246	1736	5173	559	944	17189	72
Guinea	1993	4780	1374	677	3654	3466	2066	1951	17968	501
Guinée	1994	3509	981	834	3447	2273	1423	1263	13730	432
Guinea-Bissau	1993	5075	4117	22	1989	4229	1479	1396	18307	727
Guinée-Bissau	1994	3905	3289	531	1571	2220	1259	600	13375	186
Guyana	1993	4169	280	23	721	1190	791	495	7669	0
Guyana	1994	2471	742	138	767	1414	643	375	6550	0
Haiti	1993	4154	711	713	4390	3676	784	2474	16902	0
Haïti	1994	2094	182	1369	4744	2046	497	1767	12699	0
Honduras	1993	9360	137	886	1266	4368	731	2856	19604	912
Honduras	1994	5519	209	1170	1045	5599	649	3963	18154	1370
Hong Kong	1993	39	0	0	0	0	133	18	190	18
Hong-kong	1994	30	0	0	0	0	9	0	39	0
Hungary	1993	55	0	-10	0	0	418	1732	2195	146
Hongrie	1994	129	0	46	0	0	854	1636	2665	2
India	1993	34000	93	7006	57322	26281	9203	15364	149269	4536
Inde	1994	27237	362	11901	68106	28284	2169	8822	146881	1637
Indonesia	1993	15277	535	2132	13778	3562	8652	5722	49658	1939
Indonésie	1994	14330	801	5256	11747	5603	6041	2978	46756	1230
Iran, Islamic Rep. of	1993	2867	10	1961	1791	12388	2446	1176	22639	804
Iran, Rép. islamique d'	1994	2090	'-	1822	1322	2945	2177	1130	11486	463
Iraq	1993	-12	327	1	55855	26631	1703	13343	97848	2
Iraq	1994	930	88	3	29191	14690	763	5693	51358	5
Jamaica	1993	3556	104	215	1900	5098	1335	471	12679	9
Jamaïque	1994	5387	22	507	2100	1307	866	274	10463	7
Jordan	1993	1535	543	465	1909	4503	1713	809	11477	9
Jordanie	1994	889	1474	1005	976	3675	1015	396	9430	26
Kazakstan										
Kazakstan	1994	134	5	597	886	0	168	121	1911	0
Kenya	1993	10669	583	829	18041	88918	2326	3560	124926	46
Kenya	1994	10320	513	4931	16549	48706	1457	2393	84869	12

84

Socio-economic development assistance through the United Nations system
Thousand US dollars [*cont.*]

Assistance en matière de développement socio-économique fournie par le système des Nations Unies
Milliers de dollars E-U [*suite*]

A. Development grant expenditures [1] · Aide au développement [1]

Country or area Pays ou zone	Year Année	UNDP PNUD UNDP programme Programme de PNUD	Special funds Fonds gérés	UNFPA FNUAP	UNICEF FISE	WFP PAM	Other UN system Autres organis. -ONU Regular budget Budget ordinaire	Extra- budgetary Extra- budgétaire	Total	Gov't self- supporting Auto- assistance gouverne- mentale
Kiribati	1993	303	140	110	0	0	465	117	1135	0
Kiribati	1994	292	71	22	0	0	257	68	710	0
Korea, Dem. P. R.	1993	3445	39	955	545	0	1763	534	7281	136
Corée, R. p. dém. de	1994	2878	23	357	620	0	962	273	5113	127
Korea, Republic of	1993	596	0	63	744	0	1872	300	3575	152
Corée, République de	1994	1562	28	474	20	0	933	305	3322	297
Kuwait	1993	1566	0	0	23	0	227	141	1957	82
Koweït	1994	3912	0	0	0	0	165	33	4110	26
Kyrgyzstan Kirghizistan	1994	1169	8	427	1370	1835	49	86	4944	0
Lao People's Dem. Rep.	1993	6512	3695	152	2642	926	1858	1830	17615	0
Rép. dém. pop. lao	1994	4858	2080	1142	3634	3162	1406	1739	18021	0
Lebanon	1993	3060	0	7	1902	1885	1283	2150	10287	125
Liban	1994	3230	0	593	2480	1124	1020	1789	10236	8
Lesotho	1993	2738	436	779	1907	7100	1545	2275	16780	1029
Lesotho	1994	2060	662	476	1745	5667	1140	1892	13642	1087
Liberia	1993	1953	151	17	9107	65976	1951	203	79358	0
Libéria	1994	1720	94	51	5880	65004	1212	732	74693	0
Libyan Arab Jamahiriya	1993	2336	23	7	0	0	790	11207	14363	10460
Jamah. arabe libyenne	1994	2819	11	11	0	0	557	10874	14272	10598
Macau Macao	1994	0	0	0	0	0	16	0	16	0
Madagscar	1993	11801	287	934	6673	2881	1950	1941	26467	309
Madagascar	1994	6952	177	1122	8013	1410	1286	2105	21065	922
Malawi	1993	10985	1740	1135	5910	68909	1606	1327	91612	0
Malawi	1994	9933	1930	1480	4337	45478	1307	669	65134	27
Malaysia	1993	2122	759	60	546	0	1638	381	5506	71
Malaisie	1994	2247	1041	306	662	0	1158	92	5506	0
Maldives	1993	1593	393	274	1111	0	1088	456	4915	18
Maldives	1994	1240	129	146	991	0	841	199	3546	13
Mali	1993	8344	2993	855	6788	3156	2550	2302	26988	0
Mali	1994	5706	1530	862	7106	1772	1550	1161	19687	0
Malta	1993	100	1	0	0	0	118	130	349	146
Malte	1994	10	0	0	0	0	153	222	385	163
Marshall Islands	1993	124	70	168	0	0	74	43	479	0
Iles Marshall	1994	411	70	310	0	0	65	5	861	0
Mauritania	1993	3397	2565	642	1882	21131	2329	480	32426	0
Mauritanie	1994	2075	1883	1188	2026	7259	2179	519	17129	55
Mauritius	1993	255	0	196	654	1457	735	215	3512	28
Maurice	1994	485	0	565	669	58	695	188	2660	10
Mexico	1993	2915	114	2505	3132	9858	2456	3147	24127	1174
Mexique	1994	6841	100	4226	3530	8443	1587	4340	29067	3512
Micronesia, Fed. States of Micronésie, Etats féd. de	1994	882	63	348	0	0	97	126	1516	0
Mongolia	1993	1470	655	813	719	1583	2490	2949	10679	0
Mongolie	1994	2024	921	1542	1141	700	1813	1133	9274	0
Montserrat	1993	149	50	0	0	0	1	0	200	0
Montserrat	1994	107	−9	3	0	0	1	0	102	0
Morocco	1993	2985	15	2706	2888	23149	2367	968	35078	110
Maroc	1994	3132	25	3832	1840	8939	1914	2404	22086	558
Mozambique	1993	12256	3766	1437	26570	58820	2034	3583	108466	35
Mozambique	1994	19917	29069	1884	19721	47702	1358	1926	121577	733
Myanmar	1993	8622	0	484	7453	0	4330	2742	23631	1252
Myanmar	1994	10894	3	61	6455	0	2427	960	20800	323
Namibia	1993	3698	757	339	4438	3991	1437	1689	16349	87
Namibie	1994	2908	673	734	4012	−36	1437	1014	10742	36
Nepal	1993	9844	965	2251	8319	9970	4269	4154	39772	344
Népal	1994	7899	1864	3856	9750	7728	2776	3368	37241	558

84

Socio-economic development assistance through the United Nations system
Thousand US dollars [*cont.*]

Assistance en matière de développement socio-économique fournie par le système des Nations Unies
Milliers de dollars E-U [*suite*]

A. Development grant expenditures [1] · Aide au développement [1]

Country or area Pays ou zone	Year Année	UNDP PNUD UNDP programme Programme de PNUD	Special funds Fonds gérés	UNFPA FNUAP	UNICEF FISE	WFP PAM	Other UN system Autres organis. -ONU Regular budget Budget ordinaire	Extra-budgetary Extra-budgétaire	Total	Gov't self-supporting Auto-assistance gouverne-mentale
Netherlands Antilles	1993	209	0	0	0	0	85	66	360	14
Antilles néerlandaises	1994	289	0	0	0	0	40	33	362	6
New Caledonia										
Nouvelle-Calédonie	1994	0	0	0	0	0	0	20	20	0
Nicaragua	1993	10520	1614	563	1973	2931	1396	5001	23998	38
Nicaragua	1994	11393	525	1517	3397	7568	1184	3788	29372	226
Niger	1993	9911	3411	1095	3487	6087	1958	5506	31455	0
Niger	1994	6161	615	966	4584	7120	1438	4529	25413	0
Nigeria	1993	9452	3	870	20273	0	2979	5261	38838	3900
Nigéria	1994	7338	4	4173	14846	0	2341	1163	29865	687
Niue	1993	96	15	0	0	0	10	0	121	0
Nioué	1994	74	23	5	0	0	7	0	109	0
Oman	1993	1187	37	184	751	0	1051	1702	4912	1231
Oman	1994	50	7	72	796	0	573	931	2429	900
Pakistan	1993	16018	259	854	12603	13035	4497	4208	51474	525
Pakistan	1994	12276	364	3389	15626	35229	3149	2985	73018	620
Palau										
Palaos	1994	0	0	0	0	0	23	0	23	0
Panama	1993	11620	14	314	743	697	1080	333	14801	8
Panama	1994	9278	110	471	830	-34	998	189	11842	15
Papua New Guinea	1993	5009	489	172	989	0	2318	1584	10561	327
Papouasie-Nvl-Guinée	1994	3583	1094	415	1131	0	1103	632	7958	0
Paraguay	1993	12670	24	208	1308	3842	841	-621	18272	-962
Paraguay	1994	9076	64	843	1641	163	753	109	12649	0
Peru	1993	23634	496	1587	2899	11321	2318	4445	46700	1813
Pérou	1994	74092	352	2183	6696	6117	1694	3218	94352	261
Philippines	1993	4237	467	6570	7689	785	2087	4952	26787	585
Philippines	1994	3700	288	4120	8820	1008	1499	5411	24846	2060
Poland	1993	500	15	6	0	0	528	1831	2880	451
Pologne	1994	455	-7	83	0	0	1052	2044	3627	747
Portugal	1993	403	0	43	0	0	281	146	873	28
Portugal	1994	138	0	40	0	0	330	3	511	0
Qatar	1993	1723	6	0	0	0	154	28	1911	22
Qatar	1994	1220	6	0	0	0	63	0	1289	0
Réunion	1993	0	0	0	0	0	44	0	44	0
Réunion	1994	0	0	0	0	0	10	0	10	0
Romania	1993	1141	0	199	876	0	759	1101	4076	91
Roumanie	1994	1306	0	100	886	0	1080	858	4230	1
Rwanda	1993	5110	1556	717	4638	53939	2242	2137	70339	0
Rwanda	1994	3096	542	565	32284	47738	1666	4780	90671	2
Saint Kitts and Nevis	1993	311	10	-1	0	153	124	77	674	0
Saint-Kitts-et-Nevis	1994	546	6	0	0	0	79	5	636	0
Saint Lucia	1993	345	24	19	0	0	143	112	643	0
Sainte-Lucie	1994	274	27	82	0	0	165	10	558	0
Saint Vincent/Grenadines	1993	302	50	22	0	315	121	77	887	0
Saint Vincent/Grenadines	1994	291	21	62	0	0	79	5	458	0
Samoa										
Samoa	1994	1027	165	128	0	0	875	111	2306	13
Sao Tome and Principe	1993	782	228	60	640	2608	885	298	5501	129
Sao Tomé-et-Principe	1994	889	67	256	609	1387	918	314	4440	181
Saudi Arabia	1993	6699	4	0	0	0	981	11357	19041	10935
Arabie saoudite	1994	5854	5		7695	0	503	4117	18174	3899
Senegal	1993	5402	3444	1234	3584	8582	2130	7806	32182	102
Sénégal	1994	2972	4966	1619	0	3021	1702	4827	19107	128
Seychelles	1993	222	11	177	0	125	842	165	1542	0
Seychelles	1994	237	0	138	0	-2	660	138	1171	0
Sierra Leone	1993	5044	823	342	3795	4764	1494	1473	17735	58
Sierra Leone	1994	5951	904	294	3245	883	1320	2993	15590	1176

84
Socio-economic development assistance through the United Nations system
Thousand US dollars [cont.]

Assistance en matière de développement socio-économique fournie par le système des Nations Unies
Milliers de dollars E-U [suite]

A. Development grant expenditures [1] · Aide au développement [1]

Country or area Pays ou zone	Year Année	UNDP PNUD — UNDP programme Programme de PNUD	Special funds Fonds gérés	UNFPA FNUAP	UNICEF FISE	WFP PAM	Other UN system Autres organis. -ONU — Regular budget Budget ordinaire	Extra-budgetary Extra-budgétaire	Total	Gov't self-supporting Auto-assistance gouverne-mentale
Singapore	1993	0	0	0	0	0	395	0	395	0
Singapour	1994	0	0	0	0	0	211	0	211	0
Solomon Islands	1993	694	4	191	0	0	667	309	1865	44
Iles Salomon	1994	474	18	366	0	0	400	403	1661	365
Somalia	1993	8511	753	19	31786	76451	2264	2628	122412	0
Somalie	1994	11791	640	8	18216	25975	1202	2214	60046	0
South Africa Afrique du Sud	1994	0	0	163	2394	0	245	2107	4909	0
Sri Lanka	1993	7298	781	701	3177	3301	3508	1912	20678	27
Sri Lanka	1994	6060	132	1202	3223	5614	1905	898	19034	81
Sudan	1993	11594	4314	2215	32414	90853	4242	6989	152621	597
Soudan	1994	7669	2347	1009	40147	110696	1821	4639	168328	99
Suriname	1993	119	4	12	0	0	434	395	964	12
Suriname	1994	73	4	77	0	0	300	272	726	12
Swaziland	1993	1459	94	249	905	5993	1254	498	10452	0
Swaziland	1994	1195	75	336	1199	2244	1377	182	6608	0
Syrian Arab Republic	1993	1655	24	1626	815	14328	2214	613	21275	162
Rép. arabe syrienne	1994	1756	411	2295	869	14070	2028	890	22319	188
Tajikistan Tajikistan	1994	27	1	363	2650	6046	159	178	9424	0
Thailand	1993	2372	806	186	4572	4969	4392	2766	20063	0
Thaïlande	1994	2822	395	931	3606	1487	1886	1871	12998	15
TFYR Macedonia	1993	0	0	0	0	187271	0	0	187271	0
L'ex-R.y. Macédoine	1994	0	0	0	20588	151009	7	0	171604	0
Togo	1993	2904	847	119	1994	416	987	1010	8277	0
Togo	1994	1728	638	327	1383	1652	1080	663	7471	0
Tokelau	1993	302	0	34	0	0	39	2	377	0
Tokélaou	1994	129	14	15	0	0	8	8	174	0
Tonga	1993	429	22	146	0	0	828	120	1545	0
Tonga	1994	205	21	144	0	0	651	95	1116	0
Trinidad and Tobago	1993	573	51	0	0	0	828	497	1949	37
Trinité-et-Tobago	1994	391	68	3	0	0	851	331	1644	33
Tunisia	1993	2016	0	1111	970	3722	1960	1377	11156	58
Tunisie	1994	1223	0	1508	1184	3652	1294	722	9583	428
Turkey	1993	3326	17	577	3277	1031	1579	3150	12957	2205
Turquie	1994	1749	44	762	1767	353	1096	2671	8442	1456
Turkmenistan Turkménistan	1994	0	0	376	994	0	6	69	1445	1
Turks and Caicos Islands	1993	169	0	-2	0	0	0	62	229	0
Iles Turques et Caiques	1994	258	0	3	0	0	0	52	313	0
Tuvalu	1993	294	48	43	0	0	99	12	496	0
Tuvalu	1994	197	37	27	0	0	122	0	383	0
Uganda	1993	12224	2344	2115	17209	16981	2149	1401	54423	486
Ouganda	1994	10087	1695	4480	16344	18417	1835	1776	54634	585
United Arab Emirates	1993	1580	6	0	0	0	299	69	1954	55
Emirats arabes unis	1994	2127	2	0	0	0	306	205	2640	205
United Rep. Tanzania	1993	17916	3418	2964	11934	7681	2252	8180	54345	2901
Rép. Unie de Tanzanie	1994	4656	3131	2242	11629	43587	3135	8154	76534	2380
Uruguay	1993	8973	433	58	728	0	812	1623	12627	70
Uruguay	1994	11816	1014	85	888	0	865	1692	16360	89
Uzbekistan Ouzbékistan	1994	809	8	1008	1564	0	69	49	3507	0
Vanuatu	1993	147	153	105	0	0	992	168	1565	0
Vanuatu	1994	312	44	117	0	0	373	23	869	0
Venezuela	1993	8758	111	32	1097	0	1160	628	11786	40
Venezuela	1994	4741	204	214	1075	0	1178	806	8218	6
Viet Nam	1993	12967	6195	3750	16596	15891	4375	1239	61013	-951
Viet Nam	1994	9493	5597	8903	15053	15046	2315	3338	59745	1428

84
Socio-economic development assistance through the United Nations system
Thousand US dollars [*cont.*]

Assistance en matière de développement socio-économique fournie par le système des Nations Unies
Milliers de dollars E-U [*suite*]

A. Development grant expenditures [1] · Aide au développement [1]

Country or area / Pays ou zone	Year / Année	UNDP programme / Programme de PNUD	Special funds / Fonds gérés	UNFPA FNUAP	UNICEF FISE	WFP PAM	Regular budget / Budget ordinaire	Extra-budgetary / Extra-budgétaire	Total	Gov't self-supporting / Auto-assistance gouverne-mentale
Yemen	1993	2859	2177	761	2834	10684	3880	3007	26202	753
Yémen	1994	1912	2412	1006	3983	2226	1657	2644	15840	781
Yugoslavia, SFR †	1993	243	7	15	19773	0	12	67	20117	2
Yougoslavie, Rfs †	1994	419	0	−11	23	0	0	0	431	0
Zaire	1993	6471	1	12	9026	5918	1955	716	24099	29
Zaïre	1994	7330	0	51	7656	53758	1206	872	70873	12
Zambia	1993	3645	212	587	6435	9042	2383	4913	27217	52
Zambie	1994	4202	115	541	7170	6013	1845	3616	23502	537
Zimbabwe	1993	5524	1530	1532	6506	5210	1847	2812	24961	0
Zimbabwe	1994	3563	1309	2849	5157	4409	1467	1623	20377	146
Other countries	1993	14844	178	2516	10330	5420	6029	13756	53073	834
Autre pays	1994	10622	14	−3	4882	14890	5141	14954	50500	721
Not elsewhere classified	1993	101050	6809	1122	2087	25289	15082	104203	255642	2529
Non-classé ailleurs	1994	22711	23659	2269	4218	22985	25503	34280	135625	3781

84
Socio-economic development assistance through the United Nations system
Thousand US dollars [*cont.*]

Assistance en matière de développement socio-économique fournie par le système des Nations Unies
Milliers de dollars E-U [*suite*]

B. Development loan, relief and other expenditures [1] · Prêts au développement, secours et autres dépenses [1]

Country or area Pays ou zone	Year Année	Loans Prêts IFAD FIDA	IDA IDA	IBRD BIRD	IFC SFI	Total develop. grants Aide totale au dévelop- pement	Grand total Total général	IBRD/IDA technical assistance BIRD/IDA assistance technique	Relief and related grants Secours et aide connexe
Total	1993	160777	4319000	−4317000	1910290	4867830	6940897	1447443	1347689
Total	1994	188496	4690000	−7010000	2199130	4612158	4679784	1503344	1198149
Regional programmes	1993	0	0	0	0	830168	830168	0	34435
Totaux régionaux	1994	22463	0	0	0	750145	772608	0	7662
Africa	1993	0	0	0	0	127865	127865	0	4359
Afrique	1994	22463	0	0	0	108996	131459	0	380
Asia	1993	0	0	0	0	66132	66132	0	12723
Asie	1994	0	0	0	0	63234	63234	0	1500
Latin America	1993	0	0	0	0	60674	60674	0	1474
Amérique latine	1994	0	0	0	0	63532	63532	0	2865
Middle East	1993	0	0	0	0	13419	13419	0	15721
Moyen orient	1994	0	0	0	0	19615	19615	0	2917
Interregional	1993	0	0	0	0	380724	380724	0	158
Interrégional	1994	0	0	0	0	353812	353812	0	0
Global	1993	0	0	0	0	181354	181354	0	0
Global	1994	0	0	0	0	140956	140956	0	0
Country programmes	1993	160777	4318000	−4313000	1910290	3782020	5858087	1447308	1175346
Programmes, pays	1994	165955	4689000	−7007000	2183580	3726388	3757923	1502945	962203
Afghanistan	1993	0	0	0	0	76558	76558	0	16623
Afghanistan	1994	0	0	−9000	0	57174	48174	0	10920
Albania	1993	0	26000	0	0	4638	30638	1360	23
Albanie	1994	0	39000	0	0	4788	43788	3365	207
Algeria	1993	1611	0	−107000	4460	11112	−89817	15592	5567
Algérie	1994	1000	0	−105000	4000	11006	−88994	14256	7801
Angola	1993	0	10000	0	0	78888	88888	6750	4333
Angola	1994	38	17000	0	0	131181	148219	13183	7902
Anguilla	1993	0	0	0	0	336	336	0	0
Anguilla	1994	0	0	0	0	178	178	0	0
Antigua and Barbuda	1993	0	0	0	0	209	209	0	0
Antigua−et−Barbuda	1994	0	0	0	0	314	314	0	0
Argentina	1993	2541	0	940000	261020	65147	1268708	89111	1482
Argentine	1994	2997	0	−325000	482400	89018	249415	51064	1728
Armenia									
Arménie	1993	0	0	1000	0	1694	2694	5	6865
Aruba	1993	0	0	0	0	508	508	0	0
Aruba	1994	0	0	0	0	363	363	0	0
Azerbaijan									
Azerbaïdjan	1994	0	0	0	0	11134	11134	0	6484
Bahamas	1993	0	0	0	0	800	800	72	0
Bahamas	1994	0	0	0	0	746	746	320	0
Bahrain	1993	0	0	0	0	342	342	0	0
Bahreïn	1994	0	0	0	0	428	428	0	0
Bangladesh	1993	5565	241000	0	500	100154	347219	26111	18964
Bangladesh	1994	5755	294000	0	0	146647	446402	24468	18002
Barbados	1993	0	0	−8000	0	656	−7344	179	0
Barbade	1994	0	0	−9000	0	615	−8385	894	0
Belize	1993	375	0	−1000	430	2503	2308	582	2557
Belize	1994	434	0	2000	12500	2548	17482	1545	2667
Benin	1993	1772	25000	0	0	21756	48528	5876	3535
Bénin	1994	2178	8000	0	0	12532	22710	6475	4151
Bermuda									
Bermudes	1993	0	0	0	0	3	3	0	
Bhutan	1993	1432	1000	0	0	13177	15609	0	0
Bhoutan	1994	1080	2000	0	0	11516	14596	0	0
Bolivia	1993	4348	60000	0	15080	40124	119552	11454	167
Bolivie	1994	3460	65000	0	800	32342	101602	14456	166
Botswana	1993	1381	0	0	0	13109	14490	3546	712
Botswana	1994	0	0	0	0	11217	11217	580	632

84
Socio-economic development assistance through the United Nations system
Thousand US dollars [*cont.*]

Assistance en matière de développement socio-économique fournie par le système des Nations Unies
Milliers de dollars E–U [*suite*]

B. Development loan, relief and expenditures [1] · Prêts au développement, secours et dépenses [1]

Country or area Pays ou zone	Year Année	Loans Prêts IFAD FIDA	IDA IDA	IBRD BIRD	IFC SFI	Total develop. grants Aide totale au dévelop- pement	Grand total Total général	IBRD/IDA technical assistance BIRD/IDA assistance technique	Relief and related grants Secours et aide connexe
Brazil	1993	0	0	−1387000	186370	66528	−1134102	56899	945
Brésil	1994	0	0	−1399000	97250	112947	−1188803	66111	1693
British Virgin Islands	1993	0	0	0	0	77	77	0	0
Iles Vierges britanniques	1994	0	0	0	0	57	57	0	0
Brunei Darussalam	1993	0	0	0	0	69	69	0	0
Brunéi Darussalam	1994	0	0	0	0	10	10	0	0
Bulgaria	1993	0	0	−9000	0	1636	−7364	735	64
Bulgarie	1994	0	0	66000	0	2482	68482	669	321
Burkina Faso	1993	0	58000	0	0	26696	84696	6747	717
Burkina Faso	1994	−214	60000	0	0	21224	81010	5595	1570
Burundi	1993	776	32000	0	0	19066	51842	9168	3435
Burundi	1994	855	24000	0	0	75840	100695	9684	21729
Cambodia	1993	0	0	0	0	71047	71047	0	31396
Cambodge	1994	0	29000	0	0	66019	95019	0	2768
Cameroon	1993	0	0	0	10000	10304	20304	14391	966
Cameroun	1994	0	95000	0	1110	9075	105185	6566	671
Cape Verde	1993	1257	3000	0	0	13418	17675	1116	0
Cap–Vert	1994	2709	6000	0	1000	11051	20760	3834	0
Cayman Islands	1993	0	0	0	0	26	26	0	0
Iles Caïmanes	1994	0	0	0	0	58	58	0	0
Central African Rep.	1993	2667	21000	0	0	16763	40430	9596	1947
Rép. centrafricaine	1994	2211	35000	0	0	10093	47304	6921	2564
Chad	1993	0	22000	0	0	22320	44320	8923	78
Tchad	1994	0	25000	0	0	18271	43271	9476	110
Chile	1993	0	0	−208000	22000	13284	−172716	23092	313
Chili	1994	0	0	−240000	48200	13743	−178057	15141	462
China	1993	18501	831000	433000	4000	111675	1398176	50116	3330
Chine	1994	14411	826000	453000	45730	103755	1442896	61447	3286
Colombia	1993	0	0	−395000	19720	32389	−342891	16522	40
Colombie	1994	0	0	−838000	55100	68435	−714465	17739	141
Comoros	1993	155	5000	0	0	8391	13546	1634	0
Comores	1994	135	3000	0	0	5510	8645	1309	0
Congo	1993	0	0	0	0	5855	5855	0	1152
Congo	1994	−48	96000	0	0	3697	99649	0	794
Cook Islands	1993	0	0	0	0	994	994	0	0
Iles Cook	1994	0	0	0	0	1114	1114	0	0
Costa Rica	1993	525	0	−65000	7900	12124	−44451	341	3966
Costa Rica	1994	773	0	−72000	7000	11050	−53177	2211	2032
Côte d'Ivoire	1993	398	2000	−314000	4860	14183	−292559	6219	9502
Côte d'Ivoire	1994	1096	290000	0	3200	12008	306304	6953	7436
Cuba	1993	0	0	0	0	17197	17197	0	812
Cuba	1994	0	0	0	0	10856	10856	0	396
Cyprus	1993	0	0	0	0	1267	1267	3936	9985
Chypre	1994	0	0	0	0	1095	1095	1900	12760
Czech Republic	1993	0	0	0	32160	1539	33699	0	218
République tchèque	1994	0	0	−9000	45570	840	38410	752	1768
Djibouti	1993	120	3000	0	0	7685	10805	949	5293
Djibouti	1994	10	2000	0	0	6728	8738	1255	3197
Dominica	1993	144	0	0	0	677	821	56	1223
Dominique	1994	0	0	0	0	501	501	377	0
Dominican Republic	1993	1932	0	−19000	7340	13268	3540	2502	16
Rép. dominicaine	1994	1360	0	−24000	32250	14058	23668	5918	950
Ecuador	1993	275	0	−108000	10000	14801	−82924	11723	112
Equateur	1994	1127	0	−56000	0	16349	−38524	14578	135
Egypt	1993	7783	1000	−160000	9500	43872	−97845	3436	2016
Egypte	1994	3237	10000	−146000	15510	43924	−73329	6699	2188
El Salvador	1993	800	0	19000	0	24765	44565	5471	2192
El Salvador	1994	2903	0	24000	3800	21012	51715	6012	1565

84
Socio-economic development assistance through the United Nations system
Thousand US dollars [*cont.*]
Assistance en matière de développement socio-économique fournie par le système des Nations Unies
Milliers de dollars E–U [*suite*]

B. Development loan, relief and expenditures [1] · Prêts au développement, secours et dépenses [1]

Country or area Pays ou zone	Year Année	Loans Prêts IFAD FIDA	IDA IDA	IBRD BIRD	IFC SFI	Total develop. grants Aide totale au développement pement	Grand total Total général	IBRD/IDA technical assistance BIRD/IDA assistance technique	Relief and related grants Secours et aide connexe
Equatorial Guinea	1993	1326	4000	0	0	7240	12566	1486	0
Guinée équatoriale	1994	257	0	0	0	3931	4188	1147	0
Eritrea	1993	0	0	0	0	19314	19314	0	131
Erythrée	1994	0	0	0	0	45626	45626	0	3771
Ethiopia	1993	0	218000	0	0	152373	370373	7647	34221
Ethiopie	1994	478	245000	0	0	75989	321467	10053	15672
Fiji	1993	0	0	−15000	4200	3607	−7193	355	0
Fidji	1994	0	0	−12000	0	2305	−9695	153	0
French Guiana	1993	0	0	0	0	39	39	0	22
Guyane française	1994	0	0	0	0	10	10	0	0
French Polynesia Polynésie française	1993	0	0	0	0	169	169	0	0
Gabon	1993	0	0	−1000	0	3580	2580	4152	170
Gabon	1994	1271	0	0	0	2713	3984	658	160
Gambia	1993	326	6000	0	840	11813	18979	1823	0
Gambie	1994	291	7000	0	570	10204	18065	1625	280
Ghana	1993	3191	189000	0	113960	32451	338602	27516	3940
Ghana	1994	2796	168000	0	4500	21805	197101	27420	3500
Greece	1993	0	0	0	0	432	432	0	1661
Grèce	1994	0	0	0	0	949	949	0	1679
Grenada	1993	0	0	0	0	715	715	0	0
Grenade	1994	0	0	0	0	4779	4779	0	0
Guam	1993	0	0	0	0	49	49	0	0
Guam	1994	0	0	0	0	11	11	0	0
Guatemala	1993	1660	0	−55000	81000	17399	45059	119	4686
Guatemala	1994	2873	0	−30000	4000	17189	−5938	536	6662
Guinea	1993	2060	128000	0	0	17968	148028	30388	16405
Guinée	1994	3837	72000	0	1500	13730	91067	24152	16039
Guinea−Bissau	1993	353	12000	0	0	18307	30660	4434	1150
Guinée−Bissau	1994	78	9000	0	0	13375	22453	3308	542
Guyana	1993	784	28000	0	0	7669	36453	3652	0
Guyana	1994	1023	25000	−9000	0	6550	23573	3163	0
Haiti	1993	0	0	0	0	16902	16902	0	256
Haïti	1994	0	0	0	0	12699	12699	0	944
Honduras	1993	412	53000	0	0	19604	73016	1001	496
Honduras	1994	726	54000	0	22890	18154	95770	4263	120
Hong Kong	1993	0	0	0	0	190	190	0	17195
Hong−kong	1994	0	0	0	0	39	39	0	14654
Hungary	1993	0	0	−62000	28150	2195	−31655	8699	4515
Hongrie	1994	0	0	−119000	7290	2665	−109045	16062	3082
India	1993	2589	661000	−293000	134090	149269	653948	60934	5209
Inde	1994	8348	337000	−422000	146090	146881	216319	47354	4557
Indonesia	1993	7143	0	−425000	155040	49658	−213159	267221	3150
Indonésie	1994	6177	0	−521000	70700	46756	−397367	290717	2178
Iran, Islamic Rep. of	1993	0	0	48000	0	22639	70639	1922	23767
Iran, Rép. islamique d'	1994	0	0	25000	0	11486	36486	2322	16201
Iraq	1993	0	0	0	0	97848	97848	0	2186
Iraq	1994	0	0	0	0	51358	51358	0	3910
Jamaica	1993	338	0	−45000	5000	12679	−26983	5527	0
Jamaïque	1994	298	0	−75000	3000	10463	−61239	4406	0
Jordan	1993	80	0	−31000	5000	11477	−14443	513	566
Jordanie	1994	619	0	−20000	0	9430	−9951	436	1003
Kazakstan Kazakstan	1994	0	0	116000	0	1911	117911	2166	0
Kenya	1993	646	208000	0	500	124926	334072	15089	59099
Kenya	1994	435	148000	0	5590	84869	238894	18551	41685
Kiribati	1993	0	0	0	0	1135	1135	0	0
Kiribati	1994	0	0	0	0	710	710	0	0

84
Socio-economic development assistance through the United Nations system
Thousand US dollars [*cont.*]
Assistance en matière de développement socio-économique fournie par le système des Nations Unies
Milliers de dollars E-U [*suite*]

B. Development loan, relief and expenditures [1] · Prêts au développement, secours et dépenses [1]

Country or area Pays ou zone	Year Année	Loans · Prêts IFAD FIDA	IDA IDA	IBRD BIRD	IFC SFI	Total develop. grants Aide totale au dévelop- pement	Grand total Total général	IBRD/IDA technical assistance BIRD/IDA assistance technique	Relief and related grants Secours et aide connexe
Korea, Dem. P. R.	1993	0	0	0	0	7281	7281	0	0
Corée, R. p. dém. de	1994	0	0	0	0	5113	5113	0	0
Korea, Republic of	1993	0	0	−378000	0	3575	−374425	6956	40
Corée, République de	1994	0	0	−478000	0	3322	−474678	5018	0
Kuwait	1993	0	0	0	0	1957	1957	0	0
Koweït	1994	0	0	0	0	4110	4110	0	0
Kyrgyzstan Kirghizistan	1994	0	39000	0	0	4944	43944	145	171
Lao People's Dem. Rep.	1993	0	36000	0	0	17615	53615	5943	3230
Rép. dém. pop. lao	1994	3046	43000	0	0	18021	64067	4334	4426
Lebanon	1993	0	0	15000	8650	10287	33937	0	1339
Liban	1994	0	0	16000	26800	10236	53036	2076	650
Lesotho	1993	431	5000	0	0	16780	22211	25653	256
Lesotho	1994	330	3000	9000	0	13642	25972	18524	101
Liberia	1993	0	0	0	0	79358	79358	0	4865
Libéria	1994	0	0	0	0	74693	74693	0	4675
Libyan Arab Jamahiriya	1993	0	0	0	0	14363	14363	0	1055
Jamah. arabe libyenne	1994	627	0	0	0	14272	14899	0	1068
Macau Macao	1994	0	0	0	0	16	16	0	0
Madagascar	1993	2002	35000	0	2850	26467	66319	14437	366
Madagascar	1994	2118	38000	0	950	21065	62133	17603	49
Malawi	1993	1950	134000	0	0	91612	227562	14133	28082
Malawi	1994	1609	72000	0	0	65134	138743	15109	18978
Malaysia	1993	0	0	−92000	0	5506	−86494	10159	3677
Malaisie	1994	0	0	−139000	0	5506	−133494	10387	3260
Maldives	1993	482	3000	0	0	4915	8397	2087	0
Maldives	1994	827	5000	0	0	3546	9373	1808	0
Mali	1993	1707	38000	0	16720	26988	83415	8133	1102
Mali	1994	474	75000	0	4670	19687	99831	8887	1525
Malta	1993	0	0	0	0	349	349	0	142
Malte	1994	0	0	0	0	385	385	0	520
Marshall Islands	1993	0	0	0	0	479	479	0	37
Iles Marshall	1994	0	0	0	0	861	861	0	0
Mauritania	1993	880	25000	0	0	32426	58306	4209	5843
Mauritanie	1994	0	29000	0	0	17129	46129	5596	6735
Mauritius	1993	0	0	−16000	0	3512	−12488	1976	0
Maurice	1994	0	0	−17000	0	2660	−14340	1201	0
Mexico	1993	3818	0	−800000	55950	24127	−716105	80307	10882
Mexique	1994	5659	0	−917000	254150	29067	−628124	98255	11349
Micronesia, Fed. States of Micronésie, Etats féd. de	1994	0	0	0	0	1516	1516	0	0
Mongolia	1993	0	3000	0	0	10679	13679	1161	179
Mongolie	1994	0	15000	0	0	9274	24274	1154	0
Montserrat	1993	0	0	0	0	200	200	0	0
Montserrat	1994	0	0	0	0	102	102	0	0
Morocco	1993	6243	0	−175000	42090	35078	−91589	17962	290
Maroc	1994	2673	0	−243000	21020	22086	−197221	18980	260
Mozambique	1993	0	90000	0	3500	108466	201966	15938	43048
Mozambique	1994	0	103000	0	0	121577	224577	30524	61069
Myanmar	1993	0	0	0	0	23631	23631	1071	259
Myanmar	1994	0	0	0	0	20800	20800	0	8252
Namibia	1993	0	0	0	0	16349	16349	0	784
Namibie	1994	0	0	0	6500	10742	17242	0	638
Nepal	1993	1039	60000	0	750	39772	101561	10105	7983
Népal	1994	808	59000	0	0	37241	97049	12155	6611
Netherlands Antilles	1993	0	0	0	0	360	360	0	0
Antilles néerlandaises	1994	0	0	0	0	362	362	0	0

84
Socio-economic development assistance through the United Nations system
Thousand US dollars [cont.]
Assistance en matière de développement socio-économique fournie par le système des Nations Unies
Milliers de dollars E-U [suite]

B. Development loan, relief and expenditures [1] · Prêts au développement, secours et dépenses [1]

Country or area Pays ou zone	Year Année	Loans Prêts IFAD FIDA	IDA IDA	IBRD BIRD	IFC SFI	Total develop. grants Aide totale au dévelop- pement	Grand total Total général	IBRD/IDA technical assistance BIRD/IDA assistance technique	Relief and related grants Secours et aide connexe
New Caledonia Nouvelle-Calédonie	1994	0	0	0	0	20	20	0	0
Nicaragua	1993	1803	13000	-30000	0	23998	8801	22	704
Nicaragua	1994	1202	19000	0	0	29372	49574	1266	95
Niger	1993	1710	16000	0	0	31455	49165	4425	172
Niger	1994	943	28000	0	0	25413	54356	3403	426
Nigeria	1993	2550	36000	-310000	72380	38838	-160232	46249	674
Nigéria	1994	5345	54000	0	200	29865	89410	53194	1233
Niue	1993	0	0	0	0	121	121	0	0
Nioué	1994	0	0	0	0	109	109	0	0
Oman	1993	0	0	0	0	4912	4912	1009	0
Oman	1994	0	0	0	0	2429	2429	65	0
Pakistan	1993	5060	203000	7000	19000	51474	285534	28884	26683
Pakistan	1994	4934	224000	-94000	104520	73018	312472	44394	22141
Palau Palaos	1994	0	0	0	0	23	23	0	0
Panama	1993	0	0	-75000	970	14801	-59229	278	202
Panama	1994	0	0	-75000	0	11842	-63158	50	162
Papua New Guinea	1993	69	0	-23000	0	10561	-12370	6533	987
Papouasie-Nvl-Guinée	1994	345	0	-21000	0	7958	-12697	6897	967
Paraguay	1993	1175	0	-53000	0	18272	-33553	3400	13
Paraguay	1994	1358	0	-52000	0	12649	-37993	-86	13
Peru	1993	4140	0	-69000	26340	46700	8180	0	155
Pérou	1994	3939	0	-189000	20340	94352	-70369	10734	173
Philippines	1993	2081	0	2000	31310	26787	62178	45375	8109
Philippines	1994	2822	0	-208000	167020	24846	-13312	40704	6703
Poland	1993	0	0	253000	11140	2880	267020	16095	315
Pologne	1994	0	0	234000	69400	3627	307027	12473	431
Portugal	1993	0	0	0	0	873	873	499	629
Portugal	1994	0	0	0	0	511	511	913	466
Qatar	1993	0	0	0	0	1911	1911	0	0
Qatar	1994	0	0	0	0	1289	1289	0	0
Réunion	1993	0	0	0	0	44	44	0	0
Réunion	1994	0	0	0	0	10	10	0	0
Romania	1993	0	0	170000	1870	4076	175946	3510	198
Roumanie	1994	0	0	140000	0	4230	144230	5558	427
Rwanda	1993	2869	34000	0	0	70339	107208	8326	4695
Rwanda	1994	200	23000	0	140	90671	114011	3628	31450
Saint Kitts and Nevis	1993	0	0	0	0	674	674	852	0
Saint-Kitts-et-Nevis	1994	0	0	0	0	636	636	658	0
Saint Lucia	1993	104	0	0	0	643	747	581	0
Sainte-Lucie	1994	0	0	0	0	558	558	535	63
Saint Vincent/Grenadines	1993	277	0	0	0	887	1164	115	0
St. Vincent/Grenadines	1994	152	0	0	0	458	610	27	0
Samoa Samoa	1994	856	6000	0	0	2306	9162	391	0
Sao Tome and Principe	1993	820	5000	0	0	5501	11321	1487	0
Sao Tomé-et-Principe	1994	221	7000	0	0	4440	11661	1052	0
Saudi Arabia	1993	0	0	0	0	19041	19041	0	0
Arabie saoudite	1994	0	0	0	0	18174	18174	0	0
Senegal	1993	0	36000	0	190	32182	68372	12192	3977
Sénégal	1994	528	49000	0	0	19107	68635	6866	3016
Seychelles	1993	215	0	-1000	2300	1542	3057	35	0
Seychelles	1994	638	0	0	0	1171	1809	0	0
Sierra Leone	1993	1152	34000	0	3000	17735	55887	4432	1554
Sierra Leone	1994	1898	44000	0	0	15590	61488	10965	1483
Singapore	1993	0	0	0	0	395	395	0	442
Singapour	1994	0	0	0	0	211	211	0	585

84
Socio-economic development assistance through the United Nations system
Thousand US dollars [*cont.*]
Assistance en matière de développement socio-économique fournie par le système des Nations Unies
Milliers de dollars E-U [*suite*]

B. Development loan, relief and expenditures [1] · Prêts au développement, secours et dépenses [1]

Country or area Pays ou zone	Year Année	Loans Prêts IFAD FIDA	IDA IDA	IBRD BIRD	IFC SFI	Total develop. grants Aide totale au dévelop- pement	Grand total Total général	IBRD/IDA technical assistance BIRD/IDA assistance technique	Relief and related grants Secours et aide connexe
Solomon Islands	1993	181	1000	0	0	1865	3046	0	28
Iles Salomon	1994	0	2000	0	0	1661	3661	120	0
Somalia	1993	0	0	0	0	122412	122412	0	29169
Somalie	1994	0	0	0	0	60046	60046	0	4902
South Africa									
Afrique du Sud	1994	0	0	0	0	4909	4909	0	5946
Sri Lanka	1993	2783	114000	0	0	20678	137461	13848	4739
Sri Lanka	1994	2739	61000	0	0	19034	82773	14281	5235
Sudan	1993	2473	0	0	0	152621	155094	12513	15963
Soudan	1994	4512	0	0	0	168328	172840	1957	14985
Suriname	1993	0	0	0	0	964	964	0	605
Suriname	1994	0	0	0	0	726	726	0	0
Swaziland	1993	593	0	−6000	1570	10452	6615	0	3143
Swaziland	1994	275	0	−6000	0	6608	883	0	1446
Syrian Arab Republic	1993	585	0	0	0	21275	21860	0	1080
Rép. arabe syrienne	1994	792	0	0	0	22319	23111	0	1160
Tajikistan									
Tajikistan	1994	0	0	0	0	9424	9424	0	2387
Thailand	1993	2542	0	−172000	46020	20063	−103375	15429	18221
Thaïlande	1994	1954	0	−451000	200090	12998	−235958	8216	13343
TFYR Macedonia	1993	0	0	0	0	187271	187271	0	533206
L'ex−R.y. Macédoine	1994	0	40000	−93000	0	171604	118604	0	3302
Togo	1993	606	3000	0	0	8277	11883	1900	144
Togo	1994	219	4000	0	0	7471	11690	2606	736
Tokelau	1993	0	0	0	0	377	377	0	0
Tokélaou	1994	0	0	0	0	174	174	0	0
Tonga	1993	0	0	0	0	1545	1545	0	0
Tonga	1994	1154	0	0	0	1116	2270	0	0
Trinidad and Tobago	1993	0	0	17000	0	1949	18949	975	0
Trinité−et−Tobago	1994	0	0	−5000	0	1644	−3356	907	0
Tunisia	1993	3020	0	−16000	11000	11156	9176	7396	103
Tunisie	1994	4245	0	−104000	3000	9583	−87172	4862	112
Turkey	1993	5151	0	−830000	210470	12957	−601422	44694	5383
Turquie	1994	4376	0	−782000	112010	8442	−657172	38936	3785
Turkmenistan									
Turkménistan	1994	0	0	0	0	1445	1445	0	0
Turks and Caicos Islands	1993	0	0	0	0	229	229	0	0
Iles Turques et Caiques	1994	0	0	0	0	313	313	0	0
Tuvalu	1993	0	0	0	0	496	496	0	0
Tuvalu	1994	0	0	0	0	383	383	0	0
Uganda	1993	3213	127000	0	300	54423	184936	30275	7584
Ouganda	1994	2486	150000	0	1100	54634	208220	37021	17100
United Arab Emirates	1993	0	0	0	0	1954	1954	0	0
Emirats arabes unis	1994	0	0	0	0	2640	2640	0	0
United Rep. Tanzania	1993	3757	123000	0	300	54345	181402	24568	3896
Rép. Unie de Tanzanie	1994	4881	193000	0	1940	76534	276355	44735	52915
Uruguay	1993	1072	0	−48000	2800	12627	−31501	5608	100
Uruguay	1994	463	0	−51000	1920	16360	−32257	8216	89
Uzbekistan									
Ouzbékistan	1994	0	0	0	0	3507	3507	171	0
Vanuatu	1993	0	0	0	0	1565	1565	12	0
Vanuatu	1994	0	0	0	0	869	869	361	0
Venezuela	1993	1581	0	−91000	129690	11786	52057	4027	822
Venezuela	1994	568	0	−73000	42310	8218	−21904	2991	922
Viet Nam	1993	951	−1000	0	0	61013	60964	0	15025
Viet Nam	1994	1255	−1000	0	4780	59745	64780	0	12075
Yemen	1993	8183	36000	0	0	26202	70385	7948	3484
Yémen	1994	4275	34000	0	0	15840	54115	11108	4335

84

Socio-economic development assistance through the United Nations system
Thousand US dollars [*cont.*]

Assistance en matière de développement socio-économique fournie par le système des Nations Unies
Milliers de dollars E–U [*suite*]

B. Development loan, relief and expenditures [1] · Prêts au développement, secours et dépenses [1]

Country or area / Pays ou zone	Year / Année	IFAD / FIDA	IDA / IDA	IBRD / BIRD	IFC / SFI	Total develop. grants Aide totale au développement	Grand total Total général	IBRD/IDA technical assistance BIRD/IDA assistance technique	Relief and related grants Secours et aide connexe
Yugoslavia, SFR † / Yougoslavie, Rfs †	1993	0	0	0	0	20117	20117	12	25
	1994	0	0	0	0	431	431	0	62262
Zaire / Zaïre	1993	57	0	0	0	24099	24156	14424	6275
	1994	−1	0	0	0	70873	70872	47	67203
Zambia / Zambie	1993	3673	168000	0	0	27217	198890	15649	3271
	1994	6216	179000	0	530	23502	209248	12553	4951
Zimbabwe / Zimbabwe	1993	2512	61000	39000	26010	24961	153483	4099	7174
	1994	4983	98000	−29000	15550	20377	109910	6495	10357
Other countries / Autres pays	1993	0	32000	636000	2714	60000	53073	781073	33567
	1994	0	3000	375000	2090	50500	430590	11674	206649
Not elsewhere classified / Non–classé ailleurs	1993	0	1000	−4000	0	255642	252642	135	137908
	1994	77	1000	−3000	15550	135625	149252	399	228284

Source:
Comprehensive statistical data on operational activities for development for the years 1993 (A/50/202/Add.2) and 1994 (A/50/202/Add.1, E/1995/76/Add.1).

Source:
Information statistique détail conçernant les activités opérationelles du développement, 1993 (A/50/202/Add.2) et 1994 (A/50/202/Add.1, E/1995/76/Add.1).

† For detailed descriptions of data pertaining to former Czechoslovakia, Germany, SFR Yugoslavia and former USSR, see Annex I – Country or area nomenclature, regional and other groupings.

† Pour les descriptions en détails des données relatives à l'ancienne Tchécoslovaquie, l'Allemagne, la Rfs Yougoslavie et l'ancienne URSS, voir l'Annexe I – Nomenclature des pays ou zones, groupements et régionaux autres groupements.

1 The following abbreviations have been used in the table:
UNDP: United Nations Development Programme
UNFPA: United Nations Population Fund
UNICEF: United Nations Children's Fund
WFP: World Food Programme
IDA: International Development Association
IFAD: International Fund for Agricultural Development
IBRD: International Bank for Reconstruction and Development
IFC: International Finance Corporation

1 Les abbréviations ci–après ont été utilisées dans le tableau:
PNUD : Programme des Nations Unies pour le développement
FNUAP : Fonds des Nations Unies pour la population
FISE : Fonds des Nations Unies pour l'enfance
PAM : Programme alimentaire mondiale
IDA : Association internationale de développement
FIDA : Fonds international de développement agricole
BIRD : Banque internationale pour la réconstruction et le développement
SFI : Société financière internationale

Technical notes, tables 82-84

Table 82 presents estimates of flows of financial resources to individual recipients either directly (bilaterally) or through multilateral institutions (multilaterally).

The multilateral institutions include the World Bank Group, regional banks, financial institutions of the European Community and a number of United Nations institutions, programmes and trust funds.

The main source of data is the Development Assistance Committee of OECD to which member countries reported data on their flow of resources to developing countries and multilateral institutions. Data in the *Statistical Yearbook* do not include the less developed countries in Europe as recipients.

Additional information on definitions, methods and sources can be found in OECD's *Geographical Distribution of Financial Flows to Developing Countries*.[18]

Table 83 presents the development assistance expenditures of donor countries. This table includes donors contributions to multilateral agencies, so the overall totals differ from those in table 82, which include disbursements by multilateral agencies.

Table 84: includes data on expenditures on operational activities for development undertaken by the organizations of the United Nations system. Operational activities encompass, in general, those activities of a development cooperation character that seek to mobilize or increase the potential and capacity of countries to promote economic and social development and welfare, including the transfer of resources to developing countries or regions in a tangible or intangible form. The table also covers, as a memo item, expenditures on activities of an emergency character, the purpose of which is immediate relief in crisis situations, such as assistance to refugees, humanitarian work and activities in respect of disasters.

Expenditures on operational activities for development are financed from contributions from governments and other official and non-official sources to a variety of funding channels in the United Nations system. These include United Nations funds and programmes such as contributions to the United Nations Development Programme; contributions to funds administered by United Nations Development Programme; regular (assessed) and other extrabudgetary contributions to specialized agencies, International Atomic Energy Agency, and other organizations for the purposes of operational activities; contributions to the International Development Association (IDA) and to the International Fund for Agricultural Development (IFAD).

Data are taken from the 1994 reports of the Secretary-General to the assembly on operational activities for development [20].

Notes techniques, tableaux 82 à 84

Le *Tableau 82* présente les estimations des flux de ressources financières mises à la disposition des pays soit directement (aide bilatérale) soit par l'intermédiaire d'institutions multilatérales (aide multilatérale).

Les institutions multilatérales comprennent le Groupe de la Banque mondiale, les banques régionales, les institutions financières de la Communauté européenne et un certain nombre d'institutions, de programmes et de fonds d'affectation spéciale des Nations Unies.

La principale source de données est le Comité d'aide au développement de l'OCDE, auquel les pays membres ont communiqué des données sur les flux de ressources qu'ils mettent à la disposition des pays en développement et des institutions multilatérales. Les données présentées dans l'*Annuaire statistique* ne comprennent pas l'aide fournie aux pays moins développés d'Europe.

Pour plus de renseignements sur les définitions, méthodes et sources, se reporter à la *Répartition géographique des ressources financières de l'OCDE* [18].

Le *Tableau 83* présente les dépenses que les pays donateurs consacrent à l'aide publique au développement (APD). Ces chiffres incluent les contributions des donateurs à des agences multilatérales, de sorte que les totaux diffèrent de ceux du tableau 82, qui incluent les dépenses des agences multilatérales.

Le *Tableau 84* présente des données sur les dépenses consacrées à des activités opérationnelles pour le développement par les organisations du système des Nations Unies. Par "activités opérationnelles", on entend en général les activités ayant trait à la coopération au développement, qui visent à mobiliser ou à accroître les potentialités et aptitudes que présentent les pays pour promouvoir le développement et le bien-être économiques et sociaux, y compris les transferts de ressources vers les pays ou régions en développement sous forme tangible ou non. Ce tableau indique également, pour mémoire, les dépenses liées à des activités revêtant un caractère d'urgence, qui ont pour but d'apporter un secours immédiat dans les situations de crise, telles que l'aide aux réfugiés, l'assistance humanitaire et les secours en cas de catastrophe.

Les dépenses consacrées aux activités opérationnelles pour le développement sont financées au moyen de contributions que les gouvernements et d'autres sources officielles et non officielles apportent à divers organes de financement, tels que fonds et programmes, du système des Nations Unies. On peut citer notamment les contributions au Programme des Nations Unies pour le développement; les contributions aux fonds gérés par le Programme des Nations Unies pour le développement; les contributions régulières (budgétaires) et les contributions extrabudgétaires aux institutions spécialisées, à l'Agence internationale de l'énergie atomique et à d'autres organismes aux fins d'activités opérationnelles; les contributions à l'Association internationale de développement (IDA) et au Fonds international de développement agricole (FIDA).

Les données sont extraites des rapports annuels de 1994 du Secrétaire général à la session de l'Assemblée générale sur les activités opérationnelles pour le développement [20].

Annex I

Country and area nomenclature, regional and other groupings

A. *Changes in country or area names*

In the periods covered by the statistics in the present issue of the *Statistical Yearbook* (in general, 1984-1993, 1985-1994), and as indicated at the end of each table, the following major changes in designation have taken place:

Former *Czechoslovakia*: Since 1 January 1993, data for the Czech Republic and Slovakia, where available, are shown separately under the appropriate country name. For periods prior to 1 January 1993, where no separate data are available for the Czech Republic and Slovakia, unless otherwise indicated, data for the former Czechoslovakia are shown under the country name "former Czechoslovakia".

Germany: Through the accession of the German Democratic Republic to the Federal Republic of Germany with effect from 3 October 1990, the two German States have united to form one sovereign State. As from the date of unification, the Federal Republic of Germany acts in the United Nations under the designation "Germany". All data shown which pertain to Germany prior to 3 October 1990 are indicated separately for the Federal Republic of Germany and the former German Democratic Republic based on their respective territories at the time indicated;

SFR Yugoslavia: Data provided for Yugoslavia prior to 1 January 1992 refer to the Socialist Federal Republic of Yugoslavia which was composed of six republics. Data provided for Yugoslavia after that date refer to the Federal Republic of Yugoslavia which is composed of two republics (Serbia and Montenegro);

Former *USSR*: In 1991, the Union of Soviet Socialist Republics formally dissolved into fifteen independent countries (Armenia, Azerbaijan, Belarus, Estonia, Georgia, Kazakstan, Kyrgyzstan, Latvia, Lithuania, Republic of Moldova, Russian Federation, Tajikistan, Turkmenistan, Ukraine and Uzbekistan). Whenever possible, data are shown for the individual countries. Otherwise, data are shown for the former USSR.

Other changes in designation during the periods are listed below:

Brunei Darussalam was formerly listed as Brunei;

Burkina Faso was formerly listed as Upper Volta;

Cambodia was formerly listed as Democratic Kampuchea;

Cameroon was formerly listed as United Republic of Cameroon;

Côte d'Ivoire was formerly listed as Ivory Coast;

Myanmar was formerly listed as Burma;

Annexe I

Nomenclature des pays ou zones, groupements régionaux et autres groupements

A. *Changements dans le nom des pays ou zones*

Au cours des périodes sur lesquelles portent les statistiques, dans cette édition de l'*Annuaire Statistique* (1984-1993 et 1985-1994, en générale), et comme indiqués à la fin de chaque tableau les changements principaux de désignation suivants ont eu lieu :

L'ancienne *Tchécoslovaquie*: Depuis le 1er janvier 1993, les données relatives à la République tchèque, et à la Slovaquie, lorsqu'elles sont disponibles, sont présentées séparément sous le nom de chacun des pays. En ce qui concerne la période précédant le 1er janvier 1993, pour laquelle on ne possède pas de données séparées pour les deux Républiques, les données relatives à l'ancienne Tchécoslovaquie sont, sauf indication contraire, présentées sous le titre "ancienne Tchécoslovaquie".

Allemagne: En vertu de l'adhésion de la République démocratique allemande à la République fédérale d'Allemagne, prenant effet le 3 octobre 1990, les deux Etats allemands se sont unis pour former un seul Etat souverain. A compter de la date de l'unification, la République fédérale d'Allemagne est désigné à l'ONU sous le nom d'"Allemagne". Toutes les données se rapportant à l'Allemagne avant le 3 octobre figurent dans deux rubriques séparées basées sur les territoires respectifs de la République fédérale d'Allemagne et l'ancienne République démocratique allemande selon la période indiquée;

Rfs Yougoslavie : Les données fournies pour la Yougoslavie avant le 1er janvier 1992 se rapportent à la République fédérative socialiste de Yougoslavie, qui était composée de six républiques. Les données fournies pour la Yougoslavie après cette date se rapportent à la République fédérative de Yougoslavie, qui est composée de deux républiques (Serbie et Monténégro);

Ancienne *URSS* : En 1991, l'Union des républiques socialistes soviétiques s'est séparé en 15 pays distincts (Arménie, Azerbaïdjan, Bélarus, Estonie, Géorgie, Kazakstan, Kirghizistan, Lettonie, Lituanie, la République de Moldova, Fédération de Russie, Tadjikistan, Turkménistan, Ukraine, Ouzbékistan). Les données sont présentées pour ces pays pris séparément quand cela est possible. Autrement, les données sont présentées pour l'ancienne URSS.

Les autres changements de désignation couvrant les périodes mentionnées sont énumérés ci-dessous :

Le *Brunéi Darussalam* apparaissait antérieurement sous le nom de Brunéi;

Le *Burkino Faso* apparaissait antérieurement sous le nom de la Haute-Volta;

Le *Cambodge* apparaissait antérieurement sous le nom de la Kampuchea démocratique;

Le *Cameroun* apparaissait antérieurement sous le nom de République-Unie du Cameroun;

Myanmar apparaissait antérieurement sous le nom de Birmanie;

Palau was formerly listed as Pacific Islands and includes data for Federated States of Micronesia, Marshall Islands and Northern Mariana Islands;

Saint Kitts and Nevis was formerly listed as Saint Christopher and Nevis;

Yemen comprises the former Republic of Yemen and the former Democratic Yemen;

Data relating to the People's Republic of China generally include those for Taiwan Province in the field of statistics relating to population, area, natural resources, natural conditions such as climate. In other fields of statistics, they do not include Taiwan Province unless otherwise stated.

B. *Regional groupings*

The scheme of regional groupings given below presents seven regions based mainly on continents. Five of the seven continental regions are further subdivided into 21 regions that are so drawn as to obtain greater homogeneity in sizes of population, demographic circumstances and accuracy of demographic statistics.[21, 57] This nomenclature is widely used in international statistics and is followed to the greatest extent possible in the present *Yearbook* in order to promote consistency and facilitate comparability and analysis. However, it is by no means universal in international statistical compilation, even at the level of continental regions, and variations in international statistical sources and methods dictate many unavoidable differences in particular fields in the present *Yearbook*. General differences are indicated in the footnotes to the classification presented below. More detailed differences are given in the footnotes and technical notes to individual tables.

Neither is there international standardization in the use of the terms "developed" and "developing" countries, areas or regions. These terms are used in the present publication to refer to regional groupings generally considered as "developed": these are Europe and former USSR, the United States of America and Canada in northern America, and Australia, Japan and New Zealand in Asia and Oceania. These designations are intended for statistical convenience and do not necessarily express a judgement about the stage reached by a particular country or area in the development process. Differences from this usage are indicated in the notes to individual tables.

Palaos apparaissait antétieurement sous le nom de Iles du Pacifique y compris les données pour les Etats fédérés de Micronésie, les îles Marshall et îles Mariannes du Nord;

Saint-Kitts-et-Nevis apparaissait antérieurement sous le nom de Saint-Christophe-et-Nevis;

Le *Yémen* comprend l'ancienne République de Yémen et l'ancien Yémen démocratique;

Les données relatives à la République populaire de Chine comprennent en général les données relatives à la province de Taïwan lorqu'il s'agit de statistiques concernant la population, la superficie, les ressources naturelles, les conditions naturelles telles que le climat, etc. Dans les statistiques relatives à d'autres domaines, la province de Taïwan n'est pas comprise, sauf indication contraire.

B. *Groupements régionaux*

Le système de groupements régionaux présenté ce-dessous comporte sept régions basés principalement sur les continents. Cinq des sept régions continentales sont elles-mêmes subdivisées, formant ainsi 21 régions délimitées de manière à obtenir une homogénéité accrue dans les effectifs de population, les situations démographiques et la précision des statistiques démographiques [21, 57]. Cette nomenclature est couramment utilisée aux fins des statistiques internationales et a été appliquée autant qu'il a été possible dans le présent *Annuaire* en vue de renforcer la cohérence et de faciliter la comparaison et l'analyse. Son utilisation pour l'établissement des statistiques internationales n'est cependant rien moins qu'universelle, même au niveau des régions continentales, et les variations que présentent les sources et méthodes statistiques internationales entraînent inévitablement de nombreuses différences dans certains domaines de cet *Annuaire*. Les différences d'ordre général sont indiquées dans les notes figurant au bas de la classification présentée ci-dessous. Les différences plus spécifiques sont mentionnées dans les notes techiques et notes infrapaginales accompagnant les divers tableaux.

L'application des expressions "développés" et "en développement" aux pays, zones ou régions n'est pas non plus normalisée à l'échelle internationale. Ces expressions sont utilisées dans la présente publication en référence aux groupements régionaux généralement considérés comme "développés", à savoir l'Europe et l'ancienne URSS, les Etats-Unis d'Amérique et le Canada en Amérique du Nord, et l'Australie, le Japon et la Nouvelle-Zélande dans la région de l'Asie et du Pacifique. Ces appellations sont employées pour des raisons de commodité statistique et n'expriment pas nécessairement un jugement sur le stade de développement atteint par tel ou tel pays ou zone. Les cas différant de cet usage sont signalés dans les notes accompagnant les tableaux concernés.

Africa	**Afrique**
Eastern Africa	*Afrique orientale*
Burundi	Burundi
Comoros	Comores
Djibouti	Djibouti
Eritrea	Erythrée
Ethiopia	Ethiopie
Kenya	Kenya
Madagascar	Madagascar
Malawi	Malawi
Mauritius	Maurice
Mozambique	Mozambique
Réunion	Réunion
Rwanda	Rwanda
Seychelles	Seychelles
Somalia	Somalie
Uganda	Ouganda
United Republic of Tanzania	République-Unie de Tanzanie
Zambia	Zambie
Zimbabwe	Zimbabwe
Middle Africa	*Afrique centrale*
Angola	Angola
Cameroon	Cameroun
Central African Republic	République centrafricaine
Chad	Tchad
Congo	Congo
Equatorial Guinea	Guinée équatoriale
Gabon	Gabon
Sao Tome and Principe	Sao Tomé-et-Principe
Zaire	Zaïre
Northern Africa	*Afrique septentrionale*
Algeria	Algérie
Egypt	Egypte
Libyan Arab Jamahiriya	Jam. arabe libyenne
Morocco	Maroc
Sudan	Soudan
Tunisia	Tunisie
Western Sahara	Sahara occidental
Southern Africa	*Afrique méridionale*
Botswana	Botswana
Lesotho	Lesotho
Namibia	Namibie
South Africa	Afrique du Sud
Swaziland	Swaziland
Western Africa	*Afrique occidentale*
Benin	Bénin
Burkina Faso	Burkina Faso
Cape Verde	Cap-Vert
Côte d'Ivoire	Côte d'Ivoire
Gambia	Gambie

Ghana	Ghana
Guinea	Guinée
Guinea-Bissau	Guinée-Bissau
Liberia	Libéria
Mali	Mali
Mauritania	Mauritanie
Niger	Niger
Nigeria	Nigéria
St. Helena	Sainte-Hélène
Senegal	Sénégal
Sierra Leone	Sierra Leone
Togo	Togo

Americas
Latin America and the Caribbean
Caribbean

Amérique
Amérique latine et les Caraïbes
Caraïbes

Anguilla	Anguilla
Antigua and Barbuda	Antigua-et-Barbuda
Aruba	Aruba
Bahamas	Bahamas
Barbados	Barbade
British Virgin Islands	Iles Vierges britanniques
Cayman Islands	Iles Caïmanes
Cuba	Cuba
Dominica	Dominique
Dominican Republic	République dominicaine
Grenada	Grenade
Guadeloupe	Guadeloupe
Haiti	Haïti
Jamaica	Jamaïque
Martinique	Martinique
Montserrat	Montserrat
Netherlands Antilles	Antilles néerlandaises
Puerto Rico	Porto Rico
St. Kitts and Nevis	St. Christophe/Nevis
St. Lucia	Sainte-Lucie
St. Vincent/Grenadines	St. Vincent/Grenadines
Trinidad and Tobago	Trinité-et-Tobago
Turks and Caicos Islands	Iles Turques et Caiques
US Virgin Islands	Iles Vierges américaines

Central America

Amérique centrale

Belize	Belize
Costa Rica	Costa Rica
El Salvador	El Salvador
Guatemala	Guatemala
Honduras	Honduras
Mexico	Mexique
Nicaragua	Nicaragua
Panama	Panama

South America

Amérique du Sud

Argentina	Argentine
Bolivia	Bolivie
Brazil	Brésil
Chile	Chili
Colombia	Colombie

Ecuador	Equateur
Falkland Islands (Malvinas)	Iles Falkland (Malvinas)
French Guiana	Guyane française
Guyana	Guyana
Paraguay	Paraguay
Peru	Pérou
Suriname	Suriname
Uruguay	Uruguay
Venezuela	Venezuela

Northern America | **Amérique septentrionale**
Bermuda | Bermudes
Canada | Canada
Greenland | Groenland
St. Pierre and Miquelon | Saint-Pierre-et-Miquelon
United States of America | Etats-Unis d'Amérique

Asia | **Asie**
Eastern Asia | *Asie orientale*
China | Chine
Hong Kong | Hong-kong
Japan | Japon
Korea, Democratic People's Republic | Corée, république populaire démocratique de
Korea, Republic of | Corée, République de
Macau | Macao
Mongolia | Mongolie

South-central Asia | *Asie méridionale centrale*
Afghanistan | Afghanistan
Bangladesh | Bangladesh
Bhutan | Bhoutan
India | Inde
Iran (Islamic Republic of) | Iran, République islamique d'
Kazakstan | Kazakstan
Kyrgyzstan | Kirghizistan
Maldives | Maldives
Nepal | Népal
Pakistan | Pakistan
Sri Lanka | Sri Lanka
Tajikistan | Tadjikistan
Turkmenistan | Turkménistan
Uzbekistan | Ouzbékistan

South-eastern Asia | *Asie méridionale orientale*
Brunei Darussalam | Brunéi Darussalam
Cambodia | Cambodge
East Timor | Timor oriental
Indonesia | Indonésie
Lao People's Democratic Republic | République démocratique populaire Lao
Malaysia | Malaisie
Myanmar | Myanmar
Philippines | Philippines
Singapore | Singapour
Thailand | Thaïlande
Viet Nam | Viet Nam

Western Asia	*Asie occidentale*
Armenia	Arménie
Azerbaijan	Azerbaïjan
Bahrain	Bahreïn
Cyprus	Chypre
Gaza Strip	Zone de Gaza
Georgia	Géorgie
Iraq	Iraq
Israel	Israël
Jordan	Jordanie
Kuwait	Koweït
Lebanon	Liban
Oman	Oman
Qatar	Qatar
Saudi Arabia	Arabie saoudite
Syrian Arab Republic	République arabe syrienne
Turkey	Turquie
United Arab Emirates	Emirats arabes unis
Yemen	Yémen

Europe	**Europe**
Eastern Europe	*Europe orientale*
Belarus	Bélarus
Bulgaria	Bulgarie
Czech Republic	République tchèque
Germany:[a]	Allemagne:[a]
former German Democratic Republic	ancienne République démocratique allemande
Hungary	Hongrie
Poland	Pologne
Republic of Maldova	République de Maldova
Romania	Roumanie
Russian Federation	Fédération de Russie
Slovakia	Slovaquie
Ukraine	Ukraine

Northern Europe	*Europe septentrionale*
Channel Islands	Iles Anglo-Normandes
Denmark	Danemark
Estonia	Estonie
Faeroe Islands	Iles Féroé
Finland	Finlande
Iceland	Islande
Ireland	Irlande
Isle of Man	Iles de Man
Latvia	Lettonie
Lithuania	Lithuanie
Norway	Norvège
Svalbard and Jan Mayen Islands	Svalbard et îles Jan Mayen
Sweden	Suède
United Kingdom	Royaume-Uni

Southern Europe
Albania
Andorra
Bosnia and Herzegovina
Croatia
Gibraltar
Greece
Holy See
Italy
Malta
Portugal
San Marino
Slovenia
Spain
The Former Yougoslav Rep. of Macedonia
Yugoslavia

Western Europe [b]
Austria
Belgium
France
Germany: [a]
    Federal Republic of Germany
Liechtenstein
Luxembourg
Monaco
Netherlands
Switzerland

Oceania
Australia and New Zealand
Australia
Christmas Islands
Cocos (Keeling) Islands
New Zealand
Norfolk Island

Melanesia
Fiji
New Caledonia
Papua New Guinea
Solomon Islands
Vanuatu

Micronesia-Polynesia
    Micronesia
Guam
Kiribati
Marshall Islands
Micronesia, Federated States of
Nauru
Northern Marianna Islands
Palau
Wake Island

Europe méridionale
Albanie
Andorre
Bosnie-Herzégovine
Croatie
Gibraltar
Grèce
Saint-Siège
Italie
Malte
Portugal
Saint-Marin
Slovénie
Espagne
L'ex-République yougoslave de Macédoine
Yougoslavie

Europe occidentale [b]
Autriche
Belgique
France
Allemagne: [a]
    République fédérale d'Allemagne
Liechtenstein
Luxembourg
Monaco
Pays-Bas
Suisse

Océanie
Australie et Nouvelle Zélande
Australie
Iles Christmas
Iles des Cocos (Keeling)
Nouvelle-Zélande
Ile Norfolk

Melenésie
Fidji
Nouvelle-Calédonie
Papouasie-Nouv.-Guinée
Iles Salomon
Vanuatu

Micronésie-Polynésie
    Micronésie
Guam
Kiribati
Iles Marshall
Micronésie, Etats fédératives de
Nauru
Iles Mariannes du Nord
Palaos
Ile de Wake

Polynesia	*Polynésie*
American Samoa	Samoa américaine
Cook Islands	Iles Cook
French Polynesia	Polynésie française
Johnston Island	Ile Johnston
Midway Islands	Iles Midway
Niue	Nioué
Pitcairn	Pitcairn
Samoa	Samoa
Tokelau	Tokélau
Tonga	Tonga
Tuvalu	Tuvalu
Wallis and Futuna Islands	Iles Wallis et Futuna

former **Union of Soviet Socialist Republics**
former USSR

ancienne **Union des républiques Socialistes Soviétiques**
ancienne URSS

---

a Through the accession of the German Democratic Republic to the Federal Republic of Germany with effect from 3 October 1990, the two German States have united to form one sovereign State. As from the date of unification, the Federal Republic of Germany acts in the United Nations under the designation of "Germany". All data shown which pertain to Germany prior to 3 October 1990 are indicated separately for the Federal Republic of Germany and the former German Democratic Republic based on their respective territories at the time indicated.

b Where the term "western Europe" is used in the present publication in distinction to "eastern Europe", it refers to all regions of Europe except eastern Europe (that is, it is comprised of northern and southern as well as western Europe).

---

a En vertu de l'adhésion de la République démocratique allemande à la République fédérale d'Allemagne, prenant effet le 3 octobre 1990, les deux Etats allemands se sont unis pour former un seul Etat souverain. A compter de la date de l'unification, la République fédérale d'Allemagne est désigné à l'ONU sous le nom d'Allemagne'. Toutes les données se rapportant à l'Allemagne avant le 3 octobre figurent dans deux rubriques séparées basées sur les territoires respectifs de la République fédérale d'Allemagne et l'ancienne République démocratique allemande selon la période indiquée.

b Lorsque l'expression "Europe occidentale" est utilisée dans la présente publication par opposition à l'expression "Europe orientale", elle s'applique à toutes les régions de l'Europe à l'exception de l'Europe orientale (c'est-à-dire qu'elle englobe l'Europe septentrionale et l'Europe méridionale aussi bien que l'Europe occidentale proprement dite).

C. *Other groupings*

Following is a list of other groupings and their compositions presented in the *Yearbook*. These groupings are organized mainly around economic and trade interests in regional associations.

Central American Common Market (CACM)
Costa Rica
El Salvador
Guatemala
Honduras
Nicaragua

Central African Customs and Economic Union (CACEU)
Cameroon
Central African Republic
Chad
Congo
Equatorial Guinea
Gabon

Economic Community of West African States (ECOWAS)
Benin
Burkina Faso
Cape Verde
Côte d'Ivoire
Gambia
Ghana
Guinea
Guinea-Bissau
Liberia
Mali
Mauritania
Niger
Nigeria
Senegal
Sierra Leone
Togo

European Community (EC) [a]
Belgium
Denmark
France
Germany
Greece
Ireland
Italy
Luxembourg
Netherlands
Portugal
Spain
United Kingdom

C. *Autres groupements*

On trouvera ci-après une liste des autres groupements et de leur composition, présentée dans l'*Annuaire*. Ces groupements correspondent essentiellement à des intérêts économiques, et commerciaux d'après les associations régionales.

Marché commun de l'Amérique centrale (MCAC)
Costa Rica
El Salvador
Guatemala
Honduras
Nicaragua

Union douanière et économique de l'Afrique centrale (UDEAC)
Cameroun
République centrafricaine
Tchad
Congo
Guinée équatoriale
Gabon

Communauté économique des états de l'Afrique de l'Ouest (CEDEAO)
Bénin
Burkina Faso
Cap-Vert
Côte d'Ivoire
Gambie
Ghana
Guinée
Guinée-Bissau
Libéria
Mali
Mauritanie
Niger
Nigéria
Sénégal
Sierra Leone
Togo

Communauté européenne (CE) [a]
Belgique
Danemark
France
Allemagne
Grèce
Irlande
Italie
Luxembourg
Pays-Bas
Portugal
Espagne
Poyaume-Uni

European Free Trade Association (EFTA) [b]
Austria
Finland
Iceland
Liechtenstein
Norway
Sweden
Switzerland

Latin American Integration Association (LAIA)
Argentina
Bolivia
Brazil
Chile
Colombia
Ecuador
Mexico
Paraguay
Peru
Uruguay
Venezuela

Least developed countries (LDC) [c]
Afghanistan
Angola
Bangladesh
Benin
Bhutan
Burkina Faso
Burundi
Cambodia
Cape Verde
Central African Republic
Chad
Comoros
Djibouti
Equatorial Guinea
Eritrea
Ethiopia
Gambia
Guinea
Guinea-Bissau
Haiti
Kiribati
Lao People's Democratic Republic
Lesotho
Liberia
Madagascar
Malawi
Maldives
Mali
Mauritania
Mozambique

Association européenne de libre échange (AELE) [b]
Autriche
Finlande
Islande
Liechtenstein
Norvège
Suède
Suisse

Association Latino-américaine d'intégration (LAIA)
Argentine
Bolivie
Brésil
Chili
Colombie
Equateur
Mexique
Paraguay
Pérou
Uruguay
Venezuela

Les pays moins avancés (PMA) [c]
Afghanistan
Angola
Bangladesh
Bénin
Bhoutan
Burkina Faso
Burundi
Cambodge
Cap-Vert
République centrafricaine
Tchad
Comores
Djibouti
Guinée équatoriale
Erythrée
Ethiopie
Gambie
Guinée
Guinée-Bissau
Haïti
Kiribati
République démocratique populaire lao
Lesotho
Libéria
Madagascar
Malawi
Maldives
Mali
Mauritanie
Mozambique

Myanmar
Nepal
Niger
Rwanda
Samoa
Sao Tomé and Principe
Sierra Leone
Solomon Islands
Somalia
Sudan
Togo
Tuvalu
Uganda
United Republic of Tanzania
Vanuatu
Yemen
Zaire
Zambia

Organization of Petroleum Exporting Countries (OPEC)
Algeria
Ecuador
Gabon
Indonesia
Iran, Islamic Republic of
Iraq
Kuwait
Libyan Arab Jamahiriya
Nigeria
Qatar
Saudi Arabia
United Arab Emirates
Venezuela

Myanmar
Népal
Niger
Rwanda
Samoa
Sao Tomé-et-Principe
Sierra Leone
Iles Salomon
Somalie
Soudan
Togo
Tuvalu
Ouganda
République-Unie de Tanzanie
Vanuatu
Yémen
Zaïre
Zambie

Organisation des pays exportateurs de pétrole (OPEP)
Algérie
Equateur
Gabon
Indonésie
Iran, République islamique d'
Iraq
Koweït
Jamahiriya arabe libyenne
Nigéria
Qatar
Arabie saoudite
Emirats arabes unis
Venezuela

---

a   Beginning January 1995, includes Austria, Finland and Sweden.
b   Beginning January 1995, excludes Austria, Finland and Sweden.
c   As determined by the General Assembly in its resolution 49/133.

a   A partir de janvier 1995, y compris Autriche, Finlande et Suède.
b   A partir de janvier 1995, non compris Autriche, Finlande et Suède.
c   Comme déterminés par l'Assemblée générale dans sa résolution 49/133.

Annex II

Conversion coefficients and factors

The metric system of weights and measures is employed in the *Statistical Yearbook*. In this system, the relationship between units of volume and capacity is: 1 litre = 1 cubic decimetre exactly (as decided by the 12th International Conference of Weights and Measures, New Delhi, November 1964).

Section A shows the equivalents of the basic metric, British imperial and United States units of measurements. According to an agreement between the national standards institutions of English-speaking nations, the British and United States units of length, area and volume are now identical, and based on the yard = 0.9144 metre exactly. The weight measures in both systems are based on the pound = 0.45359237 kilogram exactly (Weights and Measures Act 1963 (London), and *Federal Register* announcement of 1 July 1959: *Refinement of Values for the Yard and Pound* (Washington D.C.)).

Section B shows various derived or conventional conversion coefficients and equivalents.

Section C shows other conversion coefficients or factors which have been utilized in the compilation of certain tables in the *Statistical Yearbook*. Some of these are only of an approximate character and have been employed solely to obtain a reasonable measure of international comparability in the tables.

For a comprehensive survey of international and national systems of weights and measures and of units weights for a large number of commodities in different countries, see *World Weights and Measures* (United Nations publication, Sales No. E.66.XVII.3).

Annexe II

Coefficients et facteurs de conversion

L'Annuaire statistique utilise le système métrique pour les poids et mesures. La relation entre unités métriques de volume et de capacité est: 1 litre = 1 décimètre cube (dm³) exactement (comme fut décidé à la Conférence internationale des poids et mesures, New Delhi, novembre 1964).

La section A fournit les équivalents principaux des systèmes de mesure métrique, britannique et américain. Suivant un accord entre les institutions de normalisation nationales des pays de langue anglaise, les mesures britanniques et américaines de longueur, superficie et volume sont désormais identiques, et sont basées sur le yard = 0:9144 mètre exactement. Les mesures de poids se rapportent, dans les deux systèmes, à la livre (pound) = 0.45359237 kilogramme exactement ("Weights and Measures Act 1963" (Londres), et *"Federal Register Announcement of 1 July 1959: Refinement of Values for the Yard and Pound"* (Washington, D.C.)).

La section B fournit divers coefficients et facteurs de conversion conventionnels ou dérivés.

La section C fournit d'autres coefficients ou facteurs de conversion utilisés dans l'élaboration de certains tableaux de *l'Annuaire statistique*. D'aucuns ne sont que des approximations et n'ont été utilisés que pour obtenir un degré raisonnable de comparabilité sur le plan international.

Pour une étude d'ensemble des systèmes internationaux et nationaux de poids et mesures, et d'unités de poids pour un grand nombre de produits dans différents pays, voir *"World Weights and Measures"* (publication des Nations Unies, No de vente E.66.XVII.3).

A. Equivalents of metric, British imperial and United States units of measure

A. Equivalents des unités métriques, britanniques et des Etats-Unis

Metric units Unités métriques	British imperial and US equivalents Equivalents en mesures britanniques et des Etats-Unis	British imperial and US units Unités britannniques et des Etats-Unis	Metric equivalents Equivalents en mesures métriques	
Length–Longeur				
1 centimetre–centimètre (cm) . .	0.3937008 inch	1 inch.	2.540	cm
1 metre–mètre (m)	(3.280840 feet (1.093613 yard	1 foot . . . . 1 yard	30.480 0.9144	cm m
1 kilometre – kilomètre (km) . . .	(0.6213712 mile (0.5399568 int. naut. mile	1 mile . . . . 1 international nautical mile	1609.344 1852.000	m m
Area – Superficie				
1 square centimetre – cm². . . .	0.1550003 square inch	1 square inch	6.45160	cm²
1 square metre – m²	(10.763910 square feet (1.195990 square yards	1 square foot . . . . 1 square yard	9.290304 0.83612736	dm² m²
1 hectare – ha	2.471054 acres	1 acre	0.4046856	ha
1 square kilometre – km²	0.3861022 square mile	1 square mile	2.589988	km²
Volume				
1 cubic centimetre – cm³	0.06102374 cubic inch	1 cubic inch	16.38706	cm³
1 cubic metre – m³	(35.31467 cubic feet (1.307951 cubic yards	1 cubic foot . . . . 1 cubic yard	28.316847 0.76455486	dm³ m³
Capacity – Capacité				
1 litre (l)	(0.8798766 imp. quart (1.056688 U.S. liq. quart (0.908083 U.S. dry quart	1 British imperial quart . . . . 1 U.S. liquid quart . . . . 1 U.S. dry quart	1.136523 0.9463529 1.1012208	l l l
1 hectolitre (hl)	(21.99692 imp. gallons (26.417200 U.S. gallons (2.749614 imp. bushels (2.837760 U.S. bushels	1 imperial gallon . . . . 1 U.S. gallon . . . . 1 imperial bushel . . . . 1 U.S. bushel	4.546092 3.785412 36.368735 35.239067	l l l l
Weight or mass – Poids				
1 kilogram (kg)	(35.27396 av. ounces (32.15075 troy ounces (2.204623 av. pounds	1 av. ounce . . . . 1 troy ounce . . . . 1 av. pound . . . . 1 cental (100 lb.) . . . . 1 hundredweight (112 lb.)	28.349523 31.10348 453.59237 45.359237 50.802345	g g g kg kg
1 ton – tonne (t)	(1.1023113 short tons (0.9842065 long tons	1 short ton (2 000 lb.) . . . . 1 long ton (2 240 lb.)	0.9071847 1.0160469	t t

B. Various conventional or derived coefficients

Railway and air transport

1 passenger-mile = 1.609344 voyageur (passager) - kilomètre
1 short ton-mile = 1.459972 tonne-kilomètre
1 long ton-mile = 1.635169 tonne kilomètre

Tonnage de navire

$$1 \text{ cubic metre} - m^3 = \begin{cases} 0.353 \text{ register ton} - \text{tonne de jauge} \\ 0.841 \text{ British shipping ton} \\ 0.885 \text{ US shipping ton} \end{cases}$$

1 metric ton – tonne métrique – 0.984 dwt ton

Electric energy

$$1 \text{ Kilowatt (kW)} = \begin{cases} 1.34102 \text{ British horsepower (hp)} \\ 1.35962 \text{ cheval vapeur (cv)} \end{cases}$$

C. Other coefficients or conversion factors employed in *Statistical Yearbook* tables

Roundwood

Equivalent in solid volume without bark.

Sugar

1 metric ton raw sugar = 0.9 metric ton refined sugar.
For the United States and its possessions:
1 metric ton refined sugar = 1.07 metric tons raw sugar

B. Divers coefficients conventionnels ou dérivés

Transport ferroviaire et aérien

1 voyageur (passager) - kilomètre = 0.621371) passenger-mile

$$1 \text{ tonne-kilomètre} = \begin{cases} 0.684945 \text{ short ton-mile} \\ 0.611558 \text{ long ton-mile} \end{cases}$$ **Ship tonnage**

1 register ton (100 cubic feet) – tonne de jauge = 2.83m³
1 British shipping ton (42 cubic feet) = 1.19m³
1 U.S. shipping ton (40 cubic feet) = 1.13m³
1 deadweight ton (dwt ton = long ton) = 1.016047 metric ton – tonne métrique

Energie électrique

1 British horsepower (hp) = 0.7457 kW
1 cheval vapeur (cv) = 0.735499 kW

C. Autres coefficients ou facteurs de conversion utilisés dans les tableaux de l'*Annuaire statistique*

Bois rond

Equivalences en volume solide sans écorce.

Sucre

1 tonne métrique de sucre brut = 0.9 tonne métrique de sucre raffiné.
Pour les Etats-Unis et leurs possessions:
1 tonne métrique de sucre raffiné = 1.07 t.m. de sucre brut.

D. Selected energy conversion factors

Crude petroleum

1 barrel = 42 U.S. gallons = 34.97 imperial gallons = 158.99 litres = 0.15899 cubic metres.
1 cubic metre = 6.2898 barrels.

The equivalent of barrels in metric tons depends on the specific gravity of the petroleum which varies from country to country. The average specific gravity for each producing country is indicated in the table on the production of crude petroleum in the *Energy Statistics Yearbook*.

Coal equivalent[1] (metric tons unless otherwise indicated):

Coal, anthracite and bituminous	1.0
Coal briquettes	1.0
Cokes of coal	0.9
Lignite	0.385
Cokes of brown coal or lignite	0.67
Lignite briquettes	0.67
Peat for fuel	0.325
Peat briquettes	0.5
Crude petroleum	1.429
Natural gas liquids (weighted average)	1.542
Liquefied petroleum gases	1.554
Natural gas (terajoules[2])	34.121

Coal equivalent (metric tons of hydro, nuclear and geothermal electricity:
1000 kWh = 0.123

---

[1] It should be noted that the base used for coal equivalency comprises 7000 calories/gramme.

[2] Under standard conditions of 15°C, 1013.25 mbar, dry.

D. Facteurs de conversion pour certains produits en matière d'énergie

Pétrole brut

1 baril = 42 gallons E.U. = 34.97 gallons britanniques = 158.99 litres = 0.15899 m³.
1 m³ = 6.2898 barils.

L'équivalent du baril en tonnes métriques dépend du poids spécifique du pétrole qui varie d'un pays à l'autre. Le poids spécifique moyen utilisé pour chaque pays producteur se trouve dans l'Annuaire des statistiques de l'énergie dans le tableau relatif à la production de pétrole brut.

Equivalent en houille[1] (tonnes métriques sauf indication contraire):

Charbon, anthracite et la houille bitumineuse . . .	1.0
Briquettes de charbon	1.0
Cokes de charbon	0.9
Lignite	0.385
Cokes de charbon brun ou de lignite	0.67
Briquettes de lignite	0.67
Tourbe pour combustible	0.325
Briquettes de tourbe	0.5
Pétrole brut	1.429
Condensats provenant du gaz naturel	
(moyenne pondérée)	1.542
Gaz de pétrole liquéfié	1.554
Gaz naturel (terajoules[2])	34.121

Equivalent en houille (tonnes métriques) d'électricité, hydraulique, nucléaire et géothermique:
1000 kWh = 0.123

---

[1] Veuillez noter que l'équivalence en houille est faite sur la base de 7000 calories/gramme.

[2] En volume standard (à 15°C, 1013.25 mbar, gaz sec).

Annex III

Tables added and omitted

A. *Tables added*

In the present issue of the *Statistical Yearbook* (1994), the following table has been added:

Table 23: Relationships between the principal national accounting aggregates.

B. The following tables in the *1993* edition are not presented in the present issue because of insufficient new data:

Table 9: Population in urban and rural areas, rates of growth and largest city population;

Table 14: Book production: number of titles by UDC classes;

Table 15: Book production: number of titles by language of publication;

Table 22 (in *Yearbook*, 38th issue): Food supply;

Table 68: Number of scientists, engineers and technicians in research and experimental development;

Table 69: Expenditure for research and experimental development;

Table 84 (in *Yearbook*, 39th issue): Concentration of suspended particulate matter at selected sites;

Table 85 (in *Yearbook*, 39th issue): Global water quality in selected rivers;

Table 86 (in *Yearbook*, 39th issue): Surface and land area and land use.

These tables will be updated in future issues of the *Yearbook* when new data become available.

Annexe III

Tableaux ajoutés et supprimés

A. *Tableaux ajoutés*

Dans ce numéro de l'*Annuire statistique* (1994), le tableau suivant a été ajouté :

Tableau 23: Relations entre les principaux agrégats de comptabilité nationale.

B. Les tableaux suivants dans l'édition précédente *1993* de l'*Annuaire statistique* mais qui n'ont pas été repris dans la présente édition fautes de données nouvelles suffisantes :

Tableau 9: Population urbaine, population rurale, taux d'accroissement et population de la ville la plus peuplée;

Tableau 14: Production de livres: nombre de titres classé d'après la CDU;

Tableau 14: Production de livres: nombre de titres classé par langue de publication;

Tableau 22 (dans l'*Annuaire*, 38ème édition): Disponibilités alimentaires;

Tableau 68: Nombre de scientifiques, d'ingénieurs et de techniciens employés à des travaux de recherche et de développement expérimental;

Tableau 69: Dépenses consacrées à la recherche et au développement expérimental;

Tableau 84 (dans l'*Annuaire*, 39ème édition): Concentration de particules en suspension en divers lieux;

Tableau 85 (dans l'*Annuaire*, 39ème édition): Qualité générale de l'eau de certains cours d'eau;

Tableau 86 (dans l'*Annuaire*, 39ème édition): Superficie totale, superficie des terres et utilisation des terres.

Ces tableaux seront actualisés dans les futures livraisons de l'*Annuaire* à mesure que des données nouvelles deviendront disponibles.

Statistical sources and references

A.   *Statistical sources**
1.   AAMA Motor Vehicle, *Facts and Figures 1995*
(Detroit, USA) and previous issues.
2.   Auto and Truck International, *1995-96 World
Automotive Market Report* (Illinois, USA) and previous
issues.
3.   Carbon Dioxide Information Analysis Center,
*Estimates of Global, Regional, and National Annual CO,
emissions from Fossil-Fuel Burning, Hydraulic Cement
Production, and Gas Flaring: 1950-1992* (Oak Ridge,
Tennessee).
4.   Food and Agriculture Organization of the United
Nations, *FAO Yearbook: Fertilizer 1994* (Rome).
5.   _____, *FAO Yearbook: Fishery Statistics,
Catches and Landings 1993* (Rome).
6.   _____, *FAO Yearbook: Forest Products
1993* (Rome).
7.   _____, *Forest resources assessment 1990: Global
synthesis* (Rome).
8.   _____, *FAO Yearbook: Production 1994* (Rome).
9.   International Civil Aviation Organization, *Cvil
Aviation Statistics of the World 1994* (Montreal).
10.   _____, Digest of statistics, Traffic (Montreal).
11.   International Labour Office, *Year Book of Labour
Statistics 1995* (Geneva).
12.   International Monetary Fund, *Balance of Payments
Yearbook 1995* (Washington, DC).
13.   _____, *International Financial Statistics*
(Washington, DC, monthly).
14.   International Sugar Organization, *Sugar Yearbook
1994* (London) and previous issues.
15.   International Telecommunications Union, *Yearbook
of Telecommunication Statistics* (Geneva).
16.   Lloyd's Register of Shipping, *Annual Summary of
Merchant Ships Completed 1994* (London) and previous
issues.
17.   Organisation for Economic Cooperation and
Development, *Development Cooperation: Efforts and
Policies of the Members of the Development Assistance
Committee 1995* (Paris).
18.   _____,*Geographic Distribution of Financial
Flows to AID Recipients, 1990-1994* (Paris).
19.   United Nations, *Commodity Trade Statistics*,
Series D (United Nations serial publication).
20.   _____, "Comprehensive statistical data on
operational activities for development for the year 1994"
(A/50/202/add.1 and E/1995/76/Add.1).

_____
*   The following United Nations organization also provided data
for the present issue of the *Statistical Yearbook*: World Health
Organization, table 13.

Sources statistiques et références

A.   *Sources statistiques**
1.   "AAMA Motor Vehicle, *Facts and Figures 1995*"
(Detroit, USA) et les éditions précédentes.
2.   "Auto and Truck International, *1995-1996 World
Automotive Market Report*" (Illinois) et les éditions
précédentes.
3.   "Carbon Dioxide Information Analysis Center, *Estimates
of Global, Regional, and National Annual CO, emissions from
Fossil-Fuel Burning, Hydraulic Cement Production, and Gas
Flaring: 1950-1992*" (Oak Ridge, Tennessee).
4.   Organisation des Nations Unies pour l'alimentation et
l'agriculture, *FAO Annuaire: Engrais 1994* (Rome).
5.   _____, *FAO Annuaire: Statistiques des pêches,
captures et quantités débarquées 1993* (Rome).
6.   _____, *FAO Annuaire des produits forestiers 1993*
(Rome).
7.   _____, "*Forest resources assessment 1990: Global
synthesis*" (Rome).
8.   _____, *FAO Annuaire: Production 1994* (Rome).
9.   Organisation de l'aviation civile internationale,
Statistiques mondiales de l'aviation civile 1994 (Montréal).
10.   _____, "Digest of statistics, Traffic" (Montréal).
11.   Bureau international du Travail, *Annuaire des
statistiques du Travail 1995* (Genève).
12.   Fonds monétaire international, "*Balance of Payments
Yearbook 1995*", (Washington DC).
13.   _____, *Statistiques financières internationales*
(Washington, DC, mensuel).
14.   "International Sugar Organization, Sugar Yearbook
1994" (Londres) et éditions précédentes.
15.   Union international des télécommunications, *Annuaire
statistique des télécommunications* (Genève).
16.   "Lloyd's Register of Shipping, *Annual Summary of
Merchant Ships Completed 1994*" (Londres) et éditions
précédentes.
17.   Organisation de Coopération de Développement
Economiques, *Coopération pour le développement : Efforts et
politiques des membres du comité d'aide au développement
1995* (Paris).
18.   _____, *Répartition géographique des Ressources
Financières allouées aux pays bénéficiaires de l'AIDE, 1990-
1994* (Paris).
19.   Organisation des Nations Unies, "*Commodity Trade
Statistics*", (publication des Nations Unies, Série D).
20.   _____, *Données statistiques détaillées sur les
activités opérationnelles de développement pour l' année 1994*
(A/50/202/add.1 et E/1995/76/Add.1).

_____
*   L'organisation des Nations Unies suivante a envoyé aussi des
données pour ce numéro de l'Annuaire statistique: Organisation mondiale
de la santé, tableau 13.

21. _____, *Demographic Yearbook 1994* (United Nations publication, Sales No. E/F.96.XIII.1) and previous issues.

22. _____, *Energy Statistics Yearbook 1994* (United Nations publication, Sales No. E/F.96.XVII.8).

23. _____, *Industrial Commodity Statistics Yearbook 1993* (United Nations publications, Sales No. E/F.95.XVII.10).

24. _____, *International Trade Statistics Yearbook 1994*, vols. I and II (United Nations publication, Sales No. E/F.96.XVII.2).

25. _____, *Monthly Bulletin of Statistics*, various issues up to March 1996 (United Nations publication, Series Q).

26. _____, *National Accounts Statistics: Main Aggregates and Detailed Tables, 1993,* Parts I and II (United Nations publication, Sales No. E.96.XVII.5).

27. _____, *World Population Prospects: The 1994 Revision* (United Nations publications, Sales No. E.95.XIII.16).

28. _____, *World Urbanization Prospects 1994* (United Nations publication, Sales No. E.95.XIII.12).

29. United Nations Educational, Scientific and Cultural Organization, *Statistical Yearbook 1995* (Paris).

30. World Bank, *World Debt Tables, Vol. I and II, 1996* (Washington, DC).

31. World Conservation Monitoring Center, *Biodiversity Data Sourcebook* (Cambridge, UK).

32 World Energy Council, *1995 Survey of Energy Resources*, 17th Edition (Oxford, UK).

33. World Health Organization, "Revised 1990 Estimates of Maternal Mortality, A New Approach by WHO and UNICEF" (April 1996).

34. World Intellectual Property Organization, *Industrial Property Statistics 1993, Part I* (Geneva).

35. _____, *Yearbook of Tourism Statistics 1994* (Madrid).

B.   *References*

36. Food and Agriculture Organization of the United Nations, *The Fifth World Food Survey 1985* (Rome 1985).

37. International Labour Office, *International Standard Classification of Occupations, Revised Edition 1968* (Geneva, 1969); revised edition, 1988, ... *ISCO-88* (Geneva, 1990).

38. International Monetary Fund, *Balance of Payments Manual, Fifth Edition* (Washington, DC, 1993).

39. Stanton, C.et al (1996) *Modelling maternal mortality in the developing world* (forthcoming).

40. United Nations, *Basic Methodological Principles Governing the Compilation of the System of Statistical Balances of the National Economy*, Studies in Methods, Series F, No. 17, Rev. 1, vols. 1 and 2 (United Nations publications, Sales No. E.89.XVII.5 and E.89.XVII.3).

21. _____, *Annuaire démographique 1994* (publication des Nations Unies, No de vente 96.XIII.1) et les éditions précédentes.

22. _____, *Annuaire des statistiques de l'énergie 1994* (publication des Nations Unies, No de vente E/F.96.XVII.8).

23. _____, *Annuaire des statistiques industrielles par produit 1993* (publications des Nations Unies, No de vente E/F.95.XVII.10).

24. _____, *Annuaire statistique du Commerce international 1994*, Vols. I et II (publication des Nations Unies, No de vente E/F.96.XVII.2).

25. _____, *Bulletin mensuel de statistique*, différentes éditions, jusqu'en mars 1996 (publication des Nations Unies, Série Q).

26. _____, "*National Accounts Statistics: Main Aggregates and Detailed Tables 1993,* Parties I et II" (publication des Nations Unies, No de vente E.96.XVII.5).

27. _____, "*World Population Prospects: The 1994 Revision*", (publications des Nations Unies, No de vente E.95.XIII.16).

28. _____, "*World Urbanization Prospects 1994*" (publication des Nations Unies, No de vente E.95.XIII.12).

29. Organisation des Nations Unies pour l'éducation, la science et la culture, *Annuaire statistique 1995* (Paris).

30. Banque mondiale, "*World Debt Tables, Vol. I et II 1996*" (Washington, DC).

31. Centre mondial mixte de surveillance pour la conservation "*Biodiversity Data Sourcebook*"(Cambridge, Royaume Uni).

32. Conseil mondial de l'énergie, "*1995 Survey of Energy Resources*, 17th Edition" (Oxford, Royaume Uni).

33. Organisation mondiale de la santé, "Revised 1990 Estimates of Maternal Mortality, A New Approach by WHO and UNICEF" (avril 1996).

34. Organisation mondiale de la propriété intellectuelle, *Statistiques de propriété industrielle 1993. Partie I* (Genève).

35. _____, *Annuaire des statistiques du tourisme 1994* (Madrid).

B.   *Références*

36. Organisation des Nations Unies pour l'alimentation et l'agriculture, *Cinquième enquête mondiale sur l'alimentation 1985* (Rome, 1985).

37. Organisation internationale du Travail, *Classification internationale type des professions, édition révisée* 1968 (Genève, 1969); édition révisée 1988...*CITP-88* (Genève, 1990).

38. Fonds monétaire international, *Manuel de la balance des paiements, cinquième édition* (Washington, DC, 1993).

39. "Stanton, C.et al (1996) *Modelling maternal mortality in the developing world*" (à paraître).

40. Organisation des Nations Unies, *Principes méthodologiques de base régissant l'établissement des balances statistiques de l'économie nationale*, Série F, No 17, Rev.1 Vol. 1 et Vol. 2 (publication des Nations Unies, No de vente F.89.XVII.5 et F.89.XVII.3).

41. _____, *Energy Statistics: Definitions, Units of Measure and Conversion Factors*, Series F, No. 44 (United Nations publication, Sales No. E.86.XVII.21).

42. _____, *Energy Statistics—A Manual for Developing Countries*, Series F, No. 56 (United Nations publication, Sales No. E.91.XVII.10).

43. _____, *Handbook of Vital Statistics Systems and Methods*, vol. I, *Legal, Organization and Technical Aspects*, Series F, No. 35, vol. I (United Nations publication, Sales No. E.91.XVII.5).

44. _____, *Handbook on Social Indicators*, Studies in Methods, Series F, No. 49 (United Nations publication, Sales No. E.89.XVII.6).

45. _____, *International Recommendations for Industrial Statistics*, Series M, No. 48, Rev. 1 (United Nations publication, Sales No. E.83.XVII.8).

46. _____, *International Standard Industrial Classification of All Economic Activities*, Statistical Papers, Series M, No. 4, Rev. 2 (United Nations publication, Sales No. E.68.XVII.8); Rev. 3 (United Nations publication, Sales No. E.90.XVII.11).

47. _____, *International Trade Statistics: Concepts and Definitions*, Series M, No. 52, Rev. 1 (United Nations publication, Sales No. E.82.XVII.14).

48. _____, *Methods Used in Compiling the United Nations Price Indexes for External Trade*, volume 1, Statistical Papers, Series M, No. 82 (United Nations Publication, Sales No. E.87.XVII.4).

49. _____, *1977 Supplement to the Statistical Yearbook and the Monthly Bulletin of Statistics*, Series S and Series Q, Supplement 2 (United Nations publication, Sales No. E.78.XVII.10).

50. _____, *Principles and Recommendations for Population and Housing Censuses*, Statistical Papers, Series M, No. 67 (United Nations publication, Sales No. E.80.XVII.8).

51. _____, *Provisional Guidelines on Statistics of International Tourism*, Statistical Papers, Series M, No. 62 (United Nations publication, Sales No. E.78.XVII.6).

52. _____, *Standard International Trade Classification, Revision 3*, Statistical Papers, Series M, No. 34, Rev. 3 (United Nations publication, Sales No. E.86.XVII.12), *Revision 2*, Series M, No. 34, Rev. 2 (United Nations publication), *Revision*, Series M, No. 34, Revision (United Nations publication, Sales No. E.61.XVII.6).

53. _____, *A System of National Accounts, Studies in Methods*, Series F, No. 2, Rev. 3 (United Nations publication, Sales No. E.69.XVII.3).

54. _____, *A System of National Accounts 1993*, Studies in Methods, Series F, No. 2, Rev. 4 (United Nations publication, Sales No. E.94.XVII.4).

41. _____, *Statistiques de l'énergie: définitions, unités de mesures et facteurs de conversion*, Série F, No 44 (publication des Nations Unies, No de vente F.86.XVII.21).

42. _____, *Statistiques de l'énergie - Manuel pour les pays en développement*, Série F, No 56 (publication des Nations Unies, No de vente F.91.XVII.10).

43. _____, "*Handbook of Vital Statistics System and Methods*, Vol. 1, *Legal, Organization and Technical Aspects*", Série F, No 35, Vol. 1 (publication des Nations Unies, No de vente E.91.XVII.5).

44. _____, *Manuel des Indicateurs sociaux*, Série F, No 49 (publication des Nations Unies, No de vente F.89.XVII.6).

45. _____, *Recommandations internationales concernant les statistiques industrielles*, Série M, No 48, Rev. 1 (publication des Nations Unies, No de vente F.83.XVII.8).

46. _____, *Classification Internationale type, par Industrie, de toutes les branches d'activité économique*, Série M, No 4, Rev. 2 (publication des Nations Unies, No de vente F.68.XVII.8); Rev. 3 (publication des Nations Unies, No de vente F.90.XVII.11).

47. _____, *Statistiques du commerce International: Concepts et définitions*, Série M, No 52, Rev. 1 (publication des Nations Unies, No de vente F.82.XVII.14).

48. _____, *Méthodes utilisées par les Nations Unies pour établir les indices des prix des produits de base entrant dans le commerce international*, Série M, No 82, Vol. 1 (publication des Nations Unies, No de vente F.87.XVII.4).

49. _____, *1977 Supplément à l'Annuaire statistique et au bulletin mensuel de statistique*, Série S et Série Q, supplément 2 (publication des Nations Unies, No de vente F.78.XVII.10).

50. _____, *Principes et recommandations concernant les recensements de la population et de l'habitation*, Série M, No 67 (publication des Nations Unies, No de vente F.80.XVII.8).

51. _____, *Directives provisoires pour l'établissement des statistiques du tourisme International*, Série M, No 62 (publication des Nations Unies, No de vente 78.XVII.6).

52. _____, *Classification type pour le commerce International (troisième version révisée)*, Série M, No 34, Rev. 3 (publication des Nations Unies, No de vente F.86.XVII.12), *Révision 2*, Série M, No 34, Rev. 2 (publication des Nations Unies), *Révision*, Série M, No. 34, Révision (publication des Nations Unies, No de vente F.61.XVII.6).

53. _____, *Système de comptabilité nationale*, Série F, No 2, Rev. 3 (publication des Nations Unies, No de vente F.69.XVII.3).

54. _____, *Système de comptabilité nationale 1993*, Série F, No 2, Rev. 4 (publication des Nations Unies, No de vente F.94.XVII.4).

55.   _____, and World Tourism Organizations *Recommendations on Tourism Statistics*, Statistical Papers, Series M, No. 83 (United Nations publication, Sales No. E.94.XVII.6).

56.   _____, *Towards a System of Social and Demographic Statistics, Studies in Methods*, Series F, No. 18 (United Nations publication, Sales No. E.74.XVII.8).

57.   World Health Organization, *Manual of the International Statistical Classification of Diseases, Injuries and Causes of Death*, vol. 1 (Geneva, 1977). See also *Demographic Yearbook*.[19]

58.   World Tourism Organization, *Methodological Supplement to World Travel and Tourism Statistics* (Madrid, 1985).

55.   _____, et l'Organisation mondiale du tourisme "*Recommendations on Tourism Statistics*, Statistical Papers", Série M, No. 83 (publication des Nations Unies, No. de vente E.94.XVII.6).

56.   _____, *Vers un système de statistiques démographiques et sociales, Etudes méthodologiques*, Série F, No 18 (publication des Nations Unies, No. de vente F.74.XVII.8).

57.   Organisation mondiale de la santé, *Manuel de la classification statistique internationale des maladies, traumatismes et causes de décès*, Vol. 1 (Genève, 1977). Voir aussi *Annuaire démographique* [19].

58.   Organisation mondiale du tourisme, *Supplément méthodologique aux statistiques des voyages et du tourisme mondiaux* (Madrid, 1985).

Index

Note: References to tables are indicated by **boldface** type. For citations of organizations, see Index of organizations.

aggregates, national account (e.g., GDP), relationships between, **187–194**, 227
agricultural production, **14**, **305–311**
  method of calculating series, 29–30, 386–387
  per capita, **15**
agricultural products:
  defined, 386
  exports, **10**
  prices, **10**, **278–286**
agriculture, hunting, forestry, fishing:
  employment, **242–251**
  production, **9**, **177–186**, **305–388**
AIDS:
  cumulative cases, **90**
  deaths, **90**
  reported cases, by year, **90–97**
airline traffic. *See* civil aviation
aluminium:
  defined, 520
  production, **10**, **491–495**
animals, threatened. *See* threatened species
apparel, leather, footwear industries, production, **16–22**
asses, number raised, **328–346**
automobiles. *See* motor vehicles, passenger
aviation. *See* civil aviation

balance of payments, **775–806**
  definition of terms, 805–806
Balance of Payments Manual (IMF), 805
Balance of Payments Yearbook (IMF), 774
beef and veal, production, **400–425**
beer:
  defined, 518
  production, **426–431**
beverages, alcoholic. *See* beer
Biodiversity Data Sourcebook, 659, 660
birth, live, rate of, **12–13**
briquettes:
  defined, 633
  production, **618–631**
brown coal. *See* lignite and brown coal
Bulletin of Labour Statistics (ILO), 302

call money rates. *See* money market, rates
capital goods, prices, **278–286**
carbon dioxide emissions, method of calculating series, 661
cars. *See* motor vehicles, passenger
cattle, number raised, **328–346**
cellular telephones:

defined, 146
  subscribers, **128–134**
cellulosic and non-cellulosic fibres, fabric production, **444–446**
cement:
  defined, 519
  production, **10**, **468–474**
cereals (grain):
  defined, 386
  production, **9**, **312–319**
chemical products, production, **16–22**, **465–484**
child mortality, **83–89**
  defined, 98
cigarettes, production, **432–437**
cinemas:
  definition of terms, 145–146
  number, attendance, and receipts, **124–127**
civil aviation:
  definition of terms, 591
  passengers and freight carried, **575–589**
clothing and footwear:
  expenditures, as percentage of GDP, **200–203**
  See also apparel, leather, footwear industries
coal:
  defined, 632
  production, **9**, **618–631**, **635–643**
coal industry, production, **16–22**
coke:
  defined, 633
  production, **618–631**
commodities:
  classification of, 729, 730
  exports of, **10**, **692–705**
commodities, primary. *See* primary commodities
Commodity Trade Statistics (UN), 728
communications, **101–146**
community, social and personal service industries, employment, **242–251**
"Comprehensive Statistical Data . . . 1994" (UN), 857
construction industry:
  employment, **242–251**
  production, **177–186**
consumer prices, **278–286**, **287–301**
consumption. *See* final consumption expenditures
consumption of fixed capital, as percentage of GDP, **187–194**
conversion factors, currency, 226
conversion tables:
  for selected commodities, 872–873
  for units of measure and weight, 871–872
cotton, production, **9**
cotton fabrics, production, **438–441**
countries and areas:
  changes in designation, 860–861

economic and regional associations, 868–870
  regional groupings for statistical purposes, 3, 861–867
  surface area, **35–48**, 728
  See also developed countries or areas; developing
    countries or areas
crops:
  production, **9**
  See also agricultural production
crude oil. *See* petroleum, crude
cultural indicators, **101–146**
  sources of information, 145–146
currency:
  conversion factors, 226
  exchange rates, **807–822**
  method of calculating series, 729, 731

death, rate of, **12–13**, **83–89**
defence, national, expenditures, as percentage
    of GDP, **195–199**
Demographic Yearbook (UN), 47, 89
developed countries or areas:
  defined, 3, 861
  development assistance from, **833–842**, **843**
developing countries or areas:
  defined, 3, 861
  development assistance to, **833–842**, **843**
  external debt of, **823–829**
development assistance, **833–859**
  bilateral and multilateral, **833–842**, **843**
  grant expenditures, **844–850**
  loan and relief expenditures, **851–857**
  United Nations system, **844–857**, 858–859
Development Assistance Committee (DAC) countries:
  defined, 858
  development assistance from, **843**
discount rates, **229–233**
  defined, 241
domestic production, prices, **278–286**
domestic supply, prices, **278–286**
drilling and boring machines, production, **10**, **508–509**

earnings:
  defined, 302
  in manufacturing, **269–277**
economic associations, country lists, 868–870
economic relations, international. *See* international
    economic relations
economic services, expenditures, as percentage of
    GDP, **195–199**
economic statistics, **147–669**
education, **49–81**
  definition of terms, 80
  expenditures on, **62–73**, **195–199**
  first, second and third levels, number of students, **49–61**

governmental expenditures, as percentage of
    GDP, **195–199**
  literacy rate, **74–79**
  sources of information, 80
  See also recreation, entertainment and education
electricity:
  consumption, **24–25**
  defined, 634
  production, **10**, **24–25**, **204–225**, **592–617**, **618–631**
electricity, gas, water utilities:
  employment, **242–251**
  production, **16–22**, **177–186**
employment:
  defined, 267
  by industry, **242–251**
endangered species. *See* threatened species
energy:
  by category, production and consumption, **24–25**, **618–631**
  consumption, **24–25**, **592–617**
  conversion factors, 873
  definition of terms, 632–634
  international trade in, **24–25**, **592–617**
  method of calculating series, 632, 660
  production, **24–25**, **592–634**, **635–643**
energy reserves:
  defined, 660
  energy production as percentage of, **635–643**
Energy Statistics Yearbook (UN), 632, 660
entertainment. *See* recreation, entertainment and education
environment, **635–661**
environmental protection, indicators of, **644–650**
*Estimates of Global, Regional, and National Annual CO2
    Emissions . . .*, 661
European Patent Convention, 669
exchange rates, **807–822**
  method of calculating series, 830
exports:
  by commodity classes, **10**, **692–705**
  index numbers, **706–720**, **722–727**
  as percentage of GDP, **167–176**
  prices, **278–286**
  purchasing power of, **717–721**
  region-to-region, **692–705**
  value of, **10**, **26–27**, **672–691**, **711–715**
  volume of, **26**, **592–617**, **707–711**
external debt:
  definition of terms, 830–831
  of developing countries or areas, **823–829**
external trade. *See* international trade
extinct species, **635–643**
  defined, 659

fabrics:
  defined, 519

production, **9**, **204–225**, **438–447**
See also fibres
FAO Yearbook: Fishery Statistics, Catches and Landings, 386
FAO Yearbook: Production, 386
ferro-alloys, production, **9**
fertility rate, total, **83–89**
  defined, 98
fertilizer:
  consumption, **363–385**
  production, **10**, **363–385**
  types of, defined, 387–388
fibres:
  production, **9**, **204–225**
  See also fabrics
final consumption expenditures, as percentage of GDP, **167–176**, **187–194**
finance, insurance, real estate, business service industries, employment, **242–251**
finance, international. *See* international finance
financial statistics, **229–241**
finished goods, prices, **278–286**
fish:
  catches, **9**, **354–362**
  defined, 387
fixed capital. *See* gross fixed capital formation
food:
  defined, 386
  exports, **10**
  prices, **10**, **287–301**
  production, **9**, **14**, **305–311**
  production per capita, **15**
food, beverages, tobacco industries, production, **16–22**
food, beverages, tobacco products:
  expenditures, as percentage of GDP, **200–203**
  production, **204–225**, **389–437**
food and raw materials, exports, **696–699**
footwear, leather:
  defined, 519
  production, **9**, **448–452**
foreign exchange reserves, **11**
Forest Resources Assessment, 659
forests:
  area, **635–643**
  defined, 659
freight traffic:
  air, **575–589**
  rail, **523–533**
furniture and household equipment, expenditures, as percentage of GDP, **200–203**

gas. *See* liquified petroleum gas; natural gas; natural gas liquids; refinery gas
Geographical Distribution of Financial Flows to

Developing Countries (OECD), 858
government final consumption:
  expenditure by function, **195–199**
  as percentage of GDP, **167–176**
government finance, **11**, **229–241**
  sources of information, 241
grain. *See* cereals
grant expenditures, for development assistance, **844–850**
gross domestic product:
  distribution by economic activity, **177–186**
  distribution by expenditure (government final consumption, private final consumption, increase in stocks, gross fixed capital formation, exports, imports), **167–176**
  method of calculating series, 226–227
  related to other national accounting aggregates, **187–194**
  total and per capita, **149–166**
gross fixed capital formation, as percentage of GDP, **167–176**
gross national product, as percentage of GDP, **187–194**

Harare Protocol, 669
Havana Agreement, 669
health expenditures. *See* medical expenditures
health services, governmental, expenditures, as percentage of GDP, **195–199**
health statistics, **83–99**
heavy industry, production, **16–22**
heavy petroleum products:
  defined, 633
  production, **618–631**
HIV infection:
  cumulative, **90**
  See also AIDS
horses, number raised, **328–346**

illiteracy, **74–79**
  defined, 81
imports:
  index numbers, **706–720**
  as percentage of GDP, **167–176**
  prices, **278–286**
  value of, **10**, **27–28**, **672–691**, **710–714**
  volume of, **27**, **592–617**, **706–710**
Industrial Commodity Statistics Yearbook (UN), 518, 520
industrial production, **9–10**
  indexes of, **204–225**
  method of calculating series, 30–31
  by region, **16–22**
industrial products, prices, **278–286**
industry, employment by, **242–251**
infant mortality, **83–89**
  defined, 98
intellectual property, **663–669**

interest rates. *See* rates
intermediate products, prices, **278–286**
international economic relations, **671–859**
international finance, **807–831**
   sources of information, 830
International Financial Statistics (IMF), 226, 241, 830
international reserves minus gold, **11**
*International Standard Industrial Classification of
     All Economic Activities - Rev. 3* (UN), 30, 227,
     268, 518
international trade, **672–731**
   method of calculating series, 632, 729–730
   as percentage of GDP, **167–176**
   region to region, **692–705**
   sources of information, 728
   systems for recording of, 728–729
   value of, **10, 672–691**
   volume of, **10**
   See also exports; imports
*International Trade Statistics: Concepts and
     Definitions - Rev. 1* (UN), 728
International Trade Statistics Yearbook (UN), 728
internet, statistics available on the, iii
inventory. *See* stocks
iron. *See* pig iron

labour force, **242–268**
   sources of information, 267–268
   wages, **269–277**
lathes, production, **10, 509–510**
leather footwear. *See* footwear, leather
life expectancy, **83–89**
   defined, 98
light industry, production, **16–22**
light petroleum products:
   defined, 633
   production, **618–631**
lignite and brown coal:
   defined, 632
   production, **9, 618–631**
liquified petroleum gas (LPG):
   defined, 633
   production, **618–631**
literacy, **74–79**
   defined, 81
livestock:
   defined, 387
   production, **9, 328–346**
loan and relief expenditures, **851–857**
lorries (trucks):
   defined, 521
   production, **10, 514–517**

machine tools:
   defined, 520
   production, **10, 508–513**
manufactured goods, exports, **10, 700–703, 722–727**
manufacturing:
   earnings, **269–277**
   employment, **242–251**
   production, **9, 16–22, 177–186, 204–225, 389–521**
   sources of information, 518
maritime transport, international:
   definition of terms, 590
   vessels entered and cleared, **568–574**
maternal mortality, **83–89**
   defined, 98–99
meat:
   defined, 518
   production, **9, 400–425**
medical expenditures, private, as percentage of
     GDP, **200–203**
merchant vessels:
   defined, 590
   tonnage registered, **550–567**
metal mining, production, **16–22**
metal products industries, production, **16–22, 496–521**
metals, basic:
   defined, 520
   production, **16–22, 485–495**
   sources of information, 520
metal-working presses, production, **512–513**
*Methodological Supplement to World Travel and
     Tourism Statistics* (World Tourism Organization), 774
milling machines, production, **510–512**
mineral products, non-metallic, production, **16–22, 204–225**
minerals:
   exports, **10**
   prices, **10**
mining and quarrying:
   employment, **242–251**
   production, **9, 16–22, 177–186, 204–225**
money market rates, **234–240**
   defined, 241
Monthly Bulletin of Statistics (MBS) (UN), iii, 241,
     302, 303, 728
   internet subscription to, iii
mortality, **12–13, 83–89**
motor vehicles, commercial:
   defined, 590
   number in use, **10, 534–549**
   production, **10, 514–517**
motor vehicles, passenger:
   defined, 520, 590
   number in use, **10, 534–549**

production, **10, 500–501**
mules, number raised, **328–346**
multilateral institutions:
 defined, 858
 development assistance by, **833–842**
 development contributions to, **843**
mutton and lamb, production, **400–425**

national accounts, **149–228**
 definition of terms, 226–228
 relationships between principal aggregates of, **187–194**, 227
 sources of information, 226
National Accounts Statistics: Main Aggregates and Detailed Tables (UN), 226
national disposable income, as percentage of GDP, **187–194**
national income, as percentage of GDP, **187–194**
natural gas:
 defined, 634
 production, **9, 618–631, 635–643**
natural gas liquids (NGL):
 defined, 633
 production, **618–631**
natural resources, selected indicators of, **635–643**
net current transfers from the rest of the world, as percentage of GDP, **187–194**
net factor income from the rest of the world, **187–194**
net savings, as percentage of GDP, **187–194**
newspapers:
 daily, numbers and circulation, **101–107**
 non-daily, numbers and circulation, **108–115**
 types of, defined, 145

oil crops:
 defined, 386–387
 production, **9, 320–327**
oil tankers, tonnage registered, **558–563**
ore and bulk carriers, tonnage registered, **563–567**

paper, printing, publishing industries, production, **16–22**
paper and paperboard:
 defined, 519
 production, **460–464**
passenger traffic:
 air, **575–589**
 rail, **523–533**
Patent Cooperation Treaty (PCT), 669
patents:
 applied for, granted, and in force, **663–668**
 sources of information, 669
peat:
 defined, 633
 production, **618–631**

periodicals, numbers and circulation, **108–115**
petroleum, crude:
 defined, 633
 production, **9, 618–631, 635–643**
petroleum, gas industries, production, **16–22**
petroleum products:
 defined, 633–634
 production, **204–225, 618–631**
pig iron:
 defined, 520
 production, **9, 485–487**
pigs, number raised, **328–346**
population, **35–48**
 definition of terms, 29
 density, **12–13, 35–48**
 method of calculating series, 29, 47
 numbers, **9, 12–13, 35–48**
 rate of increase, **12–13, 35–48**
 by sex, **35–48**
 sources of information, 29, 47–48
pork, production, **400–425**
prices:
 consumer, **278–286, 287–301**
 indexes of, **10, 287–301**
 method of calculating series, 30, 302–303
 producer and wholesale, **278–286**
 types of, defined, 302
primary commodities (raw materials):
 price indexes, **10**
 prices, **278–286**
private final consumption:
 expenditure by type and purpose, **200–203**
 as percentage of GDP, **167–176**
producer prices, **278–286**
protected lands:
 defined, 660
 percentage of, **644–650**
public administration, expenditures, as percentage of GDP, **195–199**
public safety, expenditures, as percentage of GDP, **195–199**
purchasing power, of exports, **717–721**

radio receivers:
 number in use, **116–123**
 production, **496–499**
railway traffic:
 definition of terms, 590
 passengers and freight carried, **523–533**
rates:
 call money, **234–240**, 241
 defined, 241
 discount, **229–233**
 money market, **234–240**, 241

treasury bills, **234–240**

raw materials. *See* food and raw materials;
    primary commodities

receivers, radio and television:
    defined, 145
    number in use, **116–123**
    production, **496–499**

recreation, entertainment and education, expenditures,
    as percentage of GDP, **200–203**

Red List of Threatened Animals (IUCN), 659

refinery gas:
    defined, 633
    production, **618–631**

refrigerators, household:
    defined, 520
    production, **9, 502–504**

regional associations, country lists, 868–870

regions, statistical:
    countries included, 3, 861–867
    international trade between, **692–705**
    purpose of, 29
    surface area, **12–13**

relief. *See* loan and relief expenditures

rents, fuel and power, expenditures, as percentage of
    GDP, **200–203**

reserve positions in IMF, **11**

rest of the world, transfer and factor income from, **187–194**

retail trade. *See* trade, restaurants, hotel industries

Revised 1990 Estimates of Maternal Mortality, 98

roundwood, production, **9, 347–353**

sanitation services:
    access to, **644–650**
    defined, 660

savings, as percentage of GDP, **187–194**

sawnwood:
    defined, 519
    production, **10, 453–459**

sheep, number raised, **328–346**

shipping. *See* maritime transport, international

short term rates, **234–240**
    defined, 241

soap and detergent:
    defined, 519
    production, **9, 479–484**

social services, expenditures, as percentage of
    GDP, **195–199**

social statistics, **33–146**

special drawing rights (SDRs), **11**

species, endangered. *See* threatened species

Standard International Trade Classification (SITC)
    (UN), 729–731

Statbase Locator on Disk, iv

Statistical Yearbook (UN):

CD-ROM version, iv
    explanation of use, xiv
    purpose and organization of, iii–vi, 1–6
    tables added and omitted in present edition, 874

Statistical Yearbook (UNESCO), 80, 145

statistics:
    comparability of, 4–5
    on the internet, iii
    sources of, iv
    timeliness of, 5–6

Statistics Division, UN. *See* United Nations,
    Statistics Division

steel, crude:
    defined, 520
    production, **487–490**

stocks, increase in, as percentage of GDP, **167–176**

sugar:
    consumption, **389–399**
    defined, 518
    production, **10, 389–399**

sulphuric acid:
    defined, 519
    production, **9, 475–478**

*Supplement to the Statistical Yearbook and Monthly
    Bulletin of Statistics, 1977* (UN), 228, 303, 728

Survey of Energy Resources, 660

System of National Accounts (UN), 226, 805

telefax stations:
    defined, 146
    number in use, **128–134**

telephones:
    definition of terms, 146
    number in use and per capita, **135–144**
    See also cellular telephones

television receivers:
    number in use, **116–123**
    production, **496–499**

terms of trade, **28, 716–720**

textile industry, production, **16–22**

textiles. *See* fabrics; fibres

threatened species, **635–643**
    defined, 659
    sources of information, 659

tires:
    defined, 519
    production, **465–467**

ton of coal equivalent, defined, 632

tourism, international, **733–774**
    definition of terms, 773–774
    method of calculating series, 773–774
    sources of information, 773–774

tourists:
    expenditures of, **765–772**
    number of, **756–764**

origin and destination of, 733–755
receipts from, **756–764**
trade. *See* international trade
trade, restaurants, hotel industries:
  employment, **242–251**
  production, **177–186**
transport, storage and communication industries:
  employment, **242–251**
  production, **177–186**
transportation, **523–591**
transportation and communication, expenditures,
  as percentage of GDP, **200–203**
transportation equipment:
  production, **10**
  See also motor vehicles, commercial; motor vehicles,
    passenger
treasury bills:
  defined, 241
  rates, **234–240**
trucks. *See* lorries; motor vehicles, commercial

unemployment:
  defined, 267
  numbers and percentages, **252–266**
units of measure, conversion tables, 871–872
university education, **57–61**

visitors, international, defined, 773

wages, **269–277**

washing machines, household:
  defined, 520
  production, **9**, **505–507**
water, safe drinking:
  access to, **644–650**
  defined, 660
wholesale prices, **278–286**
wholesale trade. *See* trade, restaurants, hotel industries
wildlife species, threatened and extinct, **635–643**, 659
wood and wood products:
  production, **453–464**
  See also roundwood; sawnwood
wooded lands:
  area, **635–643**
  defined, 659
wood products, furniture industries, production, **16–22**
woodpulp, production, **10**
wool, production, **9**
wool fabrics, production, **441–444**
World Debt Tables (World Bank), 829, 830
World Population Prospects (UN), 29, 89
world statistics:
  selected, **9–11**
  summary, **7–31**
World Wide Web, statistics on the, iii

Year Book of Labour Statistics (ILO), 267, 302
Yearbook of Tourism Statistics (World Tourism
  Organization), 773–774

Index of Organizations

African Intellectual Property Organization (OAPI), 669
African Regional Industrial Property Organization (ARIPO), 669

Carbon Dioxide Information Analysis Center, 658, 661

Development Assistance Committee (DAC), 858

Food and Agriculture Organization (FAO), 11, 14, 15, 30, 311, 319, 327, 346, 353, 362, 384, 386, 425, 459, 464, 643, 659

Instituto Latin-Americano del Ferro y el Acero, 520
International Atomic Energy Agency (IAEA), 858
International Civil Aviation Organisation (ICAO), 589
International Development Association (IDA), 858
International Fund for Agricultural Development (IFAD), 858
International Labour Office (ILO), 250, 265, 267, 276, 300, 302
International Monetary Fund (IMF), 11, 226, 233, 240, 774, 804, 822, 830
International Sugar Organisation (ISO), 398
International Telecommunications Union (ITU), 134, 144
International Union for Conservation of Nature and Natural Resources (IUCN), 660

Lloyd's Register of Shipping, 567

Motor Vehicle Manufacturers' Association, 11

Organisation for Economic Cooperation and Development (OECD), 842, 843, 858

UNAIDS, 97, 99
United Nations (UN), 1, 29, 47–48, 518
    development assistance programs, **844–857**, 858–859
    Statistics Division, iii, 1, 11, 13, 22, 24, 28, 43, 165, 175, 185, 194, 198, 203, 224, 226–227, 285, 431, 437, 446, 452, 467, 474, 477, 483, 490, 495, 499, 501, 504, 507, 513, 517, 532, 548, 574, 616, 631, 643, 660, 689, 704, 720, 727, 728, 731
United Nations Children's Fund (UNICEF), 89
United Nations Development Programme (UNDP), 858
United Nations Economic Commission for Europe (ECE), 520
United Nations Educational, Scientific, and Cultural Organization (UNESCO), 60, 73, 78, 80, 107, 115, 123, 127, 145
United States of America, Bureau of Mines, 520

World Bank, 81, 829, 830
World Conservation Monitoring Center (WCMC), 643, 650, 659, 660
World Energy Council (WEC), 660
World Health Organisation (WHO), 89, 97, 99, 650, 660
World Intellectual Property Organisation (WIPO), 668, 669
World Tourism Organization (WTO), 754, 764, 771, 773–774

Litho in United Nations, New York
93319—October 1996—6,865
ISBN 92-1-061167-5
ISSN 0082-8459

United Nations publication
Sales No. E/F.96.XVII.1
ST/ESA/STAT/SER.S/17